P9-DNP-241

# The Merriam-Webster Thesaurus

# The Merriam-Webster Thesaurus

Merriam-Webster, Incorporated
Springfield, Massachusetts

## A GENUINE MERRIAM-WEBSTER

The name *Webster* alone is no guarantee of excellence. It is used by a number of publishers and may serve mainly to mislead an unwary buyer.

*Merriam-Webster*™ is the name you should look for when you consider the purchase of dictionaries or other fine reference books. It carries the reputation of a company that has been publishing since 1831 and is your assurance of quality and authority.

Copyright © 2005 by Merriam-Webster, Incorporated

ISBN-13: 978-0-87779-850-7
ISBN-10: 0-87779-850-8

All rights reserved. No part of this work covered by the copyrights hereon may be reproduced or copied in any form or by any means—graphic, electronic, or mechanical, including photocopying, recording, taping, or information storage and retrieval systems—without written permission of the publisher.

Made in the United States of America

2345DFC:QWB080706

*A powerful agent is the right word: it lights the reader's way and makes it plain; a close approximation to it will answer, and much traveling is done in a well-enough fashion by its help, but we do not welcome it and applaud it and rejoice in it as we do when the right one blazes out on us. Whenever we come upon one of those intensely right words in a book or a newspaper the resulting effect is physical as well as spiritual, and electrically prompt: it tingles exquisitely around through the walls of the mouth and tastes as tart and crisp and good as the autumn-butter that creams the sumac-berry.*

—Mark Twain

# PREFACE

This thesaurus is specially designed for those who want to enlarge their vocabularies and learn more about the rich variety of the English language. We hope and expect that users will readily turn to a dictionary whenever they need a better understanding of the meaning of any word used in the thesaurus.

In creating this thesaurus, the editors have drawn on years of experience with a thesaurus format that is at once easy to use, broad in its scope, and especially helpful to the user in the selection of the right word. We also believe that this thesaurus will prove to be highly useful as a vocabulary builder. We have parted ways with the more traditional approach of presenting long, undifferentiated lists of words that are tied to some topic or intellectual concept. Instead, we present a strictly alphabetical ordering of entries. These entries consist of lists of words that are centered on a specific—and specified—meaning. Main entries consist of lists of synonyms and related words, as well as antonyms and near antonyms whenever applicable. Phrases and idioms that function as synonyms are occasionally offered as well.

The purpose of the differentiated lists is to accommodate the various purposes for which a thesaurus is used. People use a thesaurus generally because they are dissatisfied with the word they already have in mind. They want a different word. The question is: how different?

If users of this thesaurus are trying to avoid a boring repetition of the same word, or are seeking to vary and enrich their vocabulary, then they will wish to select from the list of synonyms a word that shares the same basic meaning as the one they already have but differs from it in suggestion and tone. If they are seeking a word that is different from but still related to what they already have, then they will want to scan the lists of related words for a rewarding journey through the variety of possibilities that English offers.

If users are seeking a word that is to some degree opposite in meaning to what they have, then they will want to consult the lists of antonyms or near antonyms. By specifying the meaning under consideration, and by making distinctions between words that are truly synonymous and those that are only somewhat synonymous, we hope that we have given users the guidance they desire. We believe that this system minimizes the need to guess and to grope.

What makes this thesaurus unique is the content of the separate entries for each and every word appearing in the lists of synonyms. Since a user's search for the right word may start anywhere, the thesaurus is arranged so that any member of a synonym group can serve as the starting point. An entry for a listed synonym consists of a restatement of the meaning common to all the members of the group. A user who happens to use a particular synonym as a starting point should follow the cross-reference to the main entry for the complete listing of synonyms, related words, and any antonyms or near antonyms.

The thesaurus format is intended to encourage and facilitate users in finding the right word, which results in writing of greater precision and clarity. The word *thesaurus* literally means "treasury" in Latin, and we hope that the treasure trove of words contained in these pages will enhance the user's interest in and appreciation of the English language. We urge all users to read carefully the following sections entitled Introduction and Using Your Thesaurus in order to make the most of what the book has to offer. The Introduction contains an informative discussion of what distinguishes a synonym from a related word, an antonym from a near antonym. The section Using Your Thesaurus explains in detail the organization of the thesaurus and discusses the differences between the two basic types of entries. Study of this section is especially important.

The editor has been ably assisted in its composition by the editors Rose Martino Bigelow, Daniel B. Brandon, Adam Groff, Kory L. Stamper, and Deanna Stathis. The entire project was supervised by Madeline L. Novak, and Robert D. Copeland served as editor in charge of production. Stephen J. Perrault devised ways to facilitate the creation of the manuscript electronically. The difficult task of cross-referencing the text was accomplished by Christopher Chapin Connor and Allison S. Crawford. Credit for proofreading the text goes to Ilya A. Davidovich, Donna L. Rickerby, Maria Sansalone, Adrienne M. Scholz, Peter A. Sokolowski, Emily A. Vezina, and Judy Yeh. Michael D. Roundy acted as a consultant on miscellaneous scientific questions. Finally, John M. Morse, Merriam-Webster's President and Publisher, must be acknowledged and thanked for his unfailing support for this thesaurus.

Michael G. Belanger,
Editor

# INTRODUCTION

## Synonyms

The English language contains a wealth of words, and perhaps no other language has as many synonyms as English. Synonyms give color, precision, and variety to a person's writing, breaking up the dullness that can come from too many overused words.

So, just what are synonyms? Put simply, synonyms are words that mean the same thing. Words that are only somewhat similar in meaning—but do not mean the same thing—are not true synonyms. They are merely related words, and they belong in a different category. In this thesaurus a word is classified as a synonym if and only if it shares with another word at least one basic meaning.

Here's an example of how we arrived at a basic meaning shared by one group of words. The word *freight* can be defined as "goods or cargo carried by ship, train, truck, or airplane." We can break up the definition like this:

| | | |
|---|---|---|
| goods<br>cargo | carried by | ship<br>train<br>truck<br>airplane |

Since a person using *freight* as the starting point in his or her search for the right word is probably dissatisfied with that term, the word that he or she is seeking will most likely come under a broader or more basic meaning. We can phrase that more basic meaning as: "a mass or quantity of something taken up and carried, conveyed, or transported." The list of synonyms for *freight—burden, cargo, draft, haul, lading, load, loading, payload, weight*—can all be said to share this basic meaning.

If a word is more limited in scope than the basic meaning given at a main entry, then it cannot be regarded as a synonym. Hence, *truckload*, which refers specifically to the load carried by a truck, cannot be a synonym of *freight* and the other members of *freight's* synonym group. Likewise, the words *mass* and *quantity* cannot themselves be regarded as synonyms because the notion of being carried, conveyed, or transported is not an essential part of their meaning.

## Related Words

Oftentimes thesaurus users are not looking for something that means exactly the same as the word they already have. To help in this situation, this thesaurus includes lists of related words, which are words whose meanings are close enough to the synonymy group to be of interest to the user. These related words do not qualify as synonyms because they have meanings that differ from the basic meaning shared by the synonymy group in some significant way.

For example, the word *funny* has the meaning of "causing or intended to cause laughter." A person who is making "funny faces" is causing, or at least trying to cause, others to laugh. *Witty*, which is certainly closely related to *funny*, has a slightly different meaning: "given to or marked by mature intelligent humor." A witty person is someone who has a habit of making clever remarks that display a grown-up sense of humor. Thus, *funny* and *witty* are related, but the words are not synonymous. Because of the close relationship between two words like *funny* and *witty*, all of the words listed as synonyms at *witty* are given as related words at *funny*.

The lists of related words at a main entry in the thesaurus may be likened to the hyperlinks that connect one Web site to another on the Internet. Following the links between Web sites often takes one to new and unexpected places. Thesaurus users are encouraged to go from one related entry to another in their search for just the right word.

Some words are not true synonyms of anything, but because they are so fundamentally useful, they have been included in this thesaurus among the lists of related words and in places where they are likely to be most helpful. For example, the word *ballast*, which refers to any type of "heavy material used to make a ship steady," is too narrow in meaning to have any synonyms of its own. It is related to the more general term *load*, however, and so, fittingly, it is included as a related word at the entry for *load*.

## Antonyms

An antonym is a word whose meaning is directly opposite to another word's meaning. In this thesaurus, an antonym is a word that has a meaning that completely cancels out another word's meaning. *Short* and *tall* are complete opposites. Something cannot be both short and tall at the same time, and both words suggest about the same degree of difference from the norm or average in height. *Good* and *evil* are another pair of exact opposites. Logically, something cannot be both *good* and *evil* in the same way and at the same time.

Words that are only opposite in some aspect of their meaning cannot be said to be true antonyms. For example, *sad*, which means "causing unhappiness," is not a true antonym of *funny*, which means "causing or intended to cause laughter." The opposite of unhappiness is happiness, and so the opposite of sad is happy. There are things, like a frowning clown, that can be both funny and sad, so these words can't be antonyms. Pairs of words like *sad* and *funny* are better regarded as near antonyms.

## Near Antonyms

Near antonyms are words that do not qualify as antonyms under the strict definition used for this thesaurus but that clearly have meanings in marked contrast with the members of a synonym group. For example, *afraid* is not so exactly opposite to *courageous* as *cowardly* is, but *afraid* and *courageous* certainly have markedly contrasting meanings and so are considered near antonyms. And just as a user may not be seeking a word that is exactly synonymous with another, he or she may likewise not be seeking a word that is exactly opposite. The user may simply want a word that lies somewhere on the opposite side of the range of meaning.

## Phrases

This thesaurus also includes phrases that, taken as a whole, are synonymous with individual words. Within this category are some words that are commonly used in combination with one another but are not necessarily included as entry words in most dictionaries. Some of these fixed phrases represent virtually the only way in which the word is used in contemporary English. For example, *in jeopardy* appears as a synonymous phrase at *liable* because a person exposed to something dangerous or undesirable is a person in jeopardy. The word *jeopardy* is generally only used in the phrase *in jeopardy*.

Idioms constitute the other major class of word combinations that are entered under the heading of Phrases. Idioms are phrases that have a special meaning that is different from the literal meaning that a person would get if adding together the individual meanings of the components of the phrase. For example, the phrase *make good* is virtually meaningless if one attempts to piece together the literal meanings of *make* and *good*. As a fixed phrase, however, *make good* means "to reach a desired level of accomplishment" and is a synonym of *succeed*.

What this thesaurus does not enter are phrases that are simple restatements of the basic meaning shared by the members of the synonym group. The verb *remark*, for example, might be defined as "to express as an opinion." Such rewordings of a basic definition have no place in a thesaurus because they contribute nothing useful to the user's vocabulary.

## Choosing the Right Word—Using Your Dictionary

Even after you have mastered all of these categories, deciding which word in a thesaurus entry is best for your purposes is not always easy. The basic meaning shared by the members of a synonym group cannot tell you everything you need to know in order to choose the word that best suits your needs.

Something that is "very pleasing to look at" can be described as *attractive, beauteous, beautiful, bonny, comely, cute, fair, gorgeous, handsome, knockout, lovely, pretty, ravishing, sightly, stunning*, or *taking*, but which word is best for describing a sunset? A city? Should you use *knockout* to describe a cathedral or *ravishing* for a sports car?

If after reviewing the synonyms, you decide that you still have not found the right word, then you have the list of related words to consider:

***related words*** alluring, appealing, charming, delightful, eye-catching, glamorous (*also* glamourous), prepossessing; elegant, exquisite, glorious, resplendent, splendid, statuesque, sublime, superb; flawless, perfect, radiant; dainty, delicate; personable, presentable

Now you have 38 words that mean the same thing or nearly the same thing as *beautiful*. Here's where you need a good dictionary. You can consult the dictionary to get a precise definition of any word in the lists, and perhaps an example of its use. You should always use this thesaurus along with a good dictionary.

# EXPLANATORY NOTES

Every user of this thesaurus should read this section of the book carefully in order to use it effectively.

A thesaurus consists mostly of lists of words, and it is often difficult to know which word is best for a particular purpose. Because the English language has so many different ways of combining words with different shades of meaning, you should always use this thesaurus along with a reliable dictionary.

## ENTRY ORDER

The first word of a thesaurus entry is called a **headword**. Headwords are printed in boldface type and are in alphabetical order. Alphabetization is by first letter, then second letter, and so on, regardless of any spaces or hyphens that may appear in them:

**make** *vb*
**make–believe** *adj*
**make out** *vb*

**make over** *vb*
**Maker** *n*
**makeshift** *adj*

When a headword contains a numeral, the numeral is alphabetized as though it were a spelled-out word:

**anywise** *adv*
**A1** *adj*
**apace** *adv*

**Homographs** are words that are spelled the same, but each is a different part of speech or has a different etymology (word origin). Homographs that are different parts of speech are separate headwords:

**hail** *n* **1** a heavy fall of objects
**hail** *vb* **1** to declare enthusiastic approval of

Homographs that have a different etymology, even when they are the same part of speech, are entered as separate headwords. Those that are the same part of speech are grouped together and numbered in sequence:

[1]**list** *n* a record of a series of items (as names or titles) usually arranged according to some system
[2]**list** *n* the act of positioning or an instance of being positioned at an angle
[3]**list** *n* a long narrow piece of material
[1]**list** *vb* **1** to make a list of
[2]**list** *vb* to set or cause to be at an angle

Verbs that are used in combination with a preposition or an adverb are entered with the verb in boldface type followed by the preposition or adverb in parentheses in lightface type. Such combinations immediately follow the base verb in alphabetical order:

**go** *vb*
**go** (for) *vb*
**go** (on) *vb*
**go** (to) *vb*

When main entries are compound words, a closed form is entered before a hyphenated form and a hyphenated form is entered before a form that contains spaces:

**nosedive** *n*
**nose–dive** *vb*

**open–air** *adj*
**open air** *n*

## PLURAL NOUNS

Some nouns are always pluralized when they are used a certain way. When there are no thesaurus entries which include the singular form of a such a noun, the plural form is given as the headword:

**leavings** *n pl* a remaining group or portion — see REMAINDER 1

When a noun is usually, but not always, used in plural form in a certain sense, the singular form is the headword, and the plural follows the label *usually*:

**habiliment** *n usually* **habiliments** *pl* covering for the human body — see CLOTHING

Such nouns are followed by *s* in parentheses in the synonym list:

**clothing** *n* covering for the human body

***synonyms*** apparel, attire, clothes, dress, duds, habiliment(s), rags, raiment, togs, wear

When a noun is used in the singular form in one sense and in the plural form in another, the singular form is given as the headword. The plural form is indicated at the individual sense or senses:

**provision** *n* **1** something upon which the carrying out of an agreement or offer depends — see CONDITION 2 **2 provisions** *pl* substances intended to be eaten — see FOOD

## VARIANTS

An alternate spelling or form of a headword is called a **variant**. Variants are shown in boldface after the headword and are preceded by *or* or *also*. The label *or* means that the variant is as common or nearly as common as the headword. The headword is usually the form that comes first alphabetically:

**egotistic** *or* **egotistical** *adj*
**lighted** *or* **lit** *adj*
**OK** *or* **okay** *vb*

However, if one of the spellings or forms is used slightly more frequently, the more common one is entered first even though it may not fall first alphabetically:

**gizmo** *or* **gismo** *n*

A variant that is preceded by the label *also* is not as common as the headword:

**among** *also* **amongst** *prep*
**facade** *also* **façade** *n*
**naught** *also* **nought** *n*

When two variants are separated from the headword by *also* but from each other by *or*, it means that they are both less common than the headword:

**bogey** *also* **bogy** *or* **bogie** *n*

Variants are also given in the word lists:

**zero** *n* the numerical symbol 0 or the absence of number or quantity represented by it ⟨anything multiplied by *zero* comes out to zero⟩

***synonyms*** aught, cipher, goose egg, naught (*or* nought), nil, nothing, oh, zilch, zip

## PARTS OF SPEECH

Every headword is followed by a part-of-speech label. The abbreviations for the parts of speech are *adj* (adjective), *adv* (adverb), *conj* (conjunction), *interj* (interjection), *n* (noun), *prep* (preposition), *pron* (pronoun), and *vb* (verb).

## KINDS OF ENTRIES

There are two kinds of entries: main entries and secondary entries. Every headword with its part-of-speech label is followed by either one or more main entries, one or more secondary entries, or a combination of the two. If there is more than one entry, each one begins on a new line introduced by a boldface sense number. Main entries come first. A **main entry** consists of the meaning shared by the members of the synonym group, a verbal illustration, and lists of synonyms as well as any related words, phrases, near antonyms, and antonyms:

**eagerness** *n* urgent desire or interest
***synonyms*** appetite, ardor, avidity, desirousness, enthusiasm, excitement, hunger, impatience, keenness, thirst
***related words*** alacrity, quickness; ambition, gusto, zest
***near antonyms*** unconcern; aloofness, detachment; impassivity, languor
***antonyms*** apathy, indifference

A **secondary entry** has the same shared meaning that is shown at the main entry. The secondary entry does not contain lists of synonyms, antonyms, related words, phrases, or near antonyms. Instead, at the end of the entry, there is a direction to "see" the appropriate main entry at another headword. Secondary entries follow any main entries at a headword:

**gain** *vb* **1** to increase in
***synonyms*** build (up), gather, grow (in), pick up . . .
**2** to receive as return for effort — see EARN **1**
**3** to become healthy and strong again after illness or weakness — see CONVALESCE

**fade** *vb* **1** to cease to be visible — see DISAPPEAR
**2** to make white or whiter by removing color — see WHITEN

## CROSS-REFERENCES

The direction at the end of every secondary entry to see another entry is called a **cross-reference**. The cross-reference tells you where the main entry for a word's synonym group is located. No matter which member of a synonym group you used to begin your search, you can always find your way to the entry that has the lists of all the synonyms and any related words, phrases, near antonyms, or antonyms. If there is more than one sense at the headword referred to in the cross-reference, the cross-reference will also include a sense number. If the headword has more than one numbered homograph, the cross-reference will send you to the right homograph number as well:

**pain** *vb* to feel or cause physical pain — see HURT 1

**ranking** *n* 1 a scheme of rank or order — see ³SCALE 1

If a headword appears as more than one part of speech, the cross-reference is sending you to the same part of speech as the word you looked up. The cross-reference in the **ranking** example above tells you that the main entry where you will find *ranking* as a member of the synonym group with the shared meaning "a scheme of rank or order" is at sense 1 of the noun entry **³scale**:

**³scale** *n* 1 a scheme of rank or order ⟨how would you rate your experience on a *scale* of one to ten?⟩
***synonyms*** graduation, ladder, ordering, ranking

## SPECIAL USAGE LABELS

You will find special usage labels in italics after a headword whenever they apply. The labels are *chiefly British, British, chiefly Scottish, Scottish, Australian, chiefly dialect, chiefly Southern & Midland*, and *slang*.

These labels are placed directly after the part-of-speech label when the word has only one sense or when the label applies to all the senses:

**afore** *prep, chiefly dialect* 1
**bairn** *n, chiefly Scottish*
**bobby** *n, British*
**dis** *vb, slang* 1

The label comes after the sense number when the word has more than one sense and the label applies only to that sense:

**jack** *n* 1 *slang* something (as pieces of stamped metal or printed paper) customarily and legally used as a medium of exchange, a measure of value, or a means of payment — see MONEY

Special usage labels also appear in the word lists:

**before** *prep* 1 earlier than ⟨since I'm a faster runner, I got there *before* him⟩
***synonyms*** afore [*chiefly dialect*], ahead of, ere, of, previous to, prior to, to

## SHARED MEANING

The shared meaning follows the sense number when there is more than one sense and the part-of-speech label when there is only one sense. It is a meaning shared equally by the headword and the other members of the synonym group. This shared meaning is the "thing" that is referred to when we say that two or more words "mean the same thing" and thus are synonyms.

Sometimes there are words in parentheses within a shared meaning:

**district** *n* an area (as of a city) set apart for some purpose or having some special feature ⟨Independence Hall in Philadelphia's historic *district*⟩

***synonyms*** neighborhood, quarter, section
***related words*** belt, zone; department, . . .

In the shared meaning at **district**, the words in parentheses indicate that *district, neighborhood, quarter*, and *section* are synonyms when they refer to an area of a city or something like that, and that the words in the related words list also refer specifically to this type of area.

For information regarding the use and purpose of parentheses around certain words in entries for verbs, read below.

## SOME NOTES ABOUT VERBS

A boldface verb headword followed by a lightface word in parentheses tells you to use the parenthetical word with the verb:

**comply** (with) *vb* **1** to act according to the commands of
**hold off** (on) *vb* to assign to a later time
**knock** (about) *vb* to move about from place to place aimlessly

If there are two words inside the parentheses and they are separated by *or*, then either word can be used with the verb:

**fit** (in *or* into) *vb* to put among or between others

These verbs appear in the synonym lists followed by their customary adverb or preposition in parentheses. These entries are treated this way in the thesaurus because such verb combinations are not the usual form of dictionary entries, but it is only when the verb is used with the adverb or preposition that it matches the shared meaning of its synonym group.

When the meaning of a verb requires a direct object, all of the words in the synonym list take a direct object. If a verb does not take an object, none of the synonyms will take an object.

## VERBAL ILLUSTRATIONS

Every main entry in this thesaurus shows an example of typical use. The **verbal illustration**, as it is called, follows the shared meaning, is enclosed in angle brackets, and italicizes the synonym:

**fight** *vb* **1** to oppose (someone) in physical conflict ⟨a proud people who have fiercely *fought* all invaders of their homeland⟩
**rich** *adj* **1** having goods, property, or money in abundance ⟨Tanya's dad works as a chauffeur for the *richest* man in town, a big oil baron⟩

Words in parentheses after a boldface headword are italicized in the verbal illustration:

**stick** (to *or* with) *vb* to give steadfast support to ⟨thanks for *sticking with* me when all my other so-called friends have turned their backs⟩

Some verbal illustrations in the thesaurus are complete sentences and others are only sentence fragments. Though it may look a little odd, for the sake of consistency, all verbal illustrations in this thesaurus begin with a lowercase letter unless the initial word is normally capitalized. Question marks and exclamation points are used when appropriate at the end of a verbal illustration, but otherwise no ending punctuation is used.

## A WORD ABOUT SYNONYMS

If a word is used as the defining term in a shared meaning, it will not be listed as one of the synonyms. Since words can only be defined in terms of other words, the result of this restriction is that some terms that might be rightly regarded as synonyms do not appear in the synonym lists. Here is an example:

**go** *vb* . . . **2** to leave a place often for another
***synonyms*** begone, clear out, depart, exit, get, get off, move, pull (out), quit, sally (forth), shove (off), take off, walk out

*Leave*, used as the defining term, could be considered another synonym, but it is not entered as such in this thesaurus because it has been used as a defining term.

## RELATED WORDS

You will see that in most cases there are more related words than synonyms. That is because there is much more flexibility in choosing words for these lists. They do not have to match the shared meaning: they only need to relate to some aspect of it. Related words are often divided into subgroups separated by a semicolon. Words within each subgroup are generally closer in meaning to each other than to the members of the following subgroups. The subgroups tend to be presented in order of most relevant to least relevant.

**object** *n* **1** something material that can be perceived by the senses
***synonyms*** thing
***related words*** article, item, piece; being, entity, substance; commodity, good, ware; accessory, accompaniment; bauble, curio, knickknack, spangle, token, trinket

## PHRASES

Listed in alphabetical order after the heading **phrases** at some of the main entries are expressions that are synonymous with the headword and the other members of the synonym group. Although they have essentially the same meaning as the synonyms, these phrases tend to be used only in certain ways, and you should be careful about substituting one of them for a word in the synonym list. Since phrases are not entered as headwords in the thesaurus, they do not come with verbal illustrations. It's a good idea to look them up in a dictionary before considering them.

## NEAR ANTONYMS

Just as related words are not exact synonyms, near antonyms are not exact antonyms. Not every synonym group has near antonyms. As is the case with related words, when there are near antonyms, they are often divided into subgroups separated by a semicolon, with the members of each subgroup listed alphabetically.

**have** *vb* **1** to keep, control, or experience as one's own
***synonyms*** command, enjoy, hold, occupy, own, possess, retain
***related words*** keep, reserve, withhold; bear, carry; boast, show off, sport
***near antonyms*** abandon, cede, disclaim, disown, hand over, relinquish, renounce, surrender, yield; discard, dump; decline, reject, repudiate, spurn; need, require
***antonyms*** lack, want

## ANTONYMS

The words in the antonym lists are the exact opposites of the headword and the words in the synonym lists. Not every synonym group has antonyms, and antonym lists tend to be shorter than near antonym lists. Antonyms are listed alphabetically, just as synonyms are. They appear as boldface headwords at their own alphabetical places in the thesaurus only if they are part of a synonym group elsewhere.

Ordinarily, all the words in an antonym list are synonyms of each other. Sometimes, however, a semicolon in an antonym list divides words which, while they are exact opposites of the words in the synonym group, are not synonyms of each other.

Here is an example:

**present** *adj* **1** existing or in progress right now
***synonyms*** current, extant, ongoing, present-day
***antonyms*** ago, past; future

The opposite of "existing or in progress right now" is "*not* existing or in progress right now." All three of the words in the antonyms list fit that meaning. *Ago* and *past*, separated by a comma, are synonyms of each other; they both can mean "earlier than the present time." But *ago* and *past* are not synonyms of *future*, which means, of course, "occurring at a later time."

## A NOTE ABOUT THE LISTS: WORD DUPLICATION

No word appears in more than one list at any single main entry. Some words have slight variations in meaning. If they are used one way, they are synonymous with a headword; if they are used another way, they are merely closely related. To avoid confusion, such words have been entered in a main entry's synonym list only. For example, *nice* is in the synonym list at *pleasant* where the shared meaning is "giving pleasure or contentment to the mind or senses." *Nice* is also in the synonym list at *amiable*, where the shared meaning is "having an easygoing and pleasing manner especially in social situations." If you go back to *pleasant*, you will find *amiable* among the related words. So it would stand to reason that *nice*, having the same meaning as *amiable*, would also be entered in the related word list at *pleasant*. Since it's already in the synonym list, however, it was left out of the related words.

Some words can have two meanings that are opposite of each other—or nearly so. *Nervy* can mean both "fearless" and "fearful, timid." Thus, at the thesaurus entry for *bold*, where the shared meaning is "inclined or willing to take risks," *nervy* might qualify as both a synonym and an antonym (or near antonym). And, indeed, *nervy* appears as a synonym, along with *adventuresome, adventurous, audacious, daring, dashing, emboldened, enterprising, gutsy, hardy, nerved, venturesome*, and *venturous*. Although the near antonym list contains *fearful* and *timid* as expected, *nervy* is left off the list. Again, this is to avoid confusion.

## GUIDE WORDS

The two boldface words separated by a dot at the top of each page are **guide words**, and they show the alphabetical range of entries on the page. You can use them to find a word more quickly. The first guide word is the headword of the first entry beginning on that page, and the second guide is the headword of the last entry on the page.

# The Merriam-Webster Thesaurus

# A

**aback** *adv* without warning — see UNAWARES

**abaft** *adv* near, toward, or in the stern of a ship or the tail of an aircraft — see AFT

**abaft** *prep* at, to, or toward the rear of — see BEHIND 1

**abandon** *n* carefree freedom from constraint ⟨added spices to the stew with complete *abandon*⟩
***syn*** abandonment, ease, lightheartedness, naturalness, spontaneity, unrestraint
***rel*** ardor, enthusiasm, exuberance, fervor, spirit, warmth, zeal; carelessness, heedlessness, impulsiveness, indiscretion, insouciance, recklessness, thoughtlessness; excess, excessiveness, immoderacy, incontinence, indulgence, intemperance, licentiousness, permissiveness, wantonness, wildness
***near ant*** embarrassment, reserve, reticence, self-consciousness, uneasiness; inhibition, repression, self-restraint, suppression; carefulness, discreteness, discretion, heedfulness; discipline, self-control, self-discipline, willpower
***ant*** constraint, restraint

**abandon** *vb* to cause to remain behind — see LEAVE 1

**abandoned** *adj* left unoccupied or unused ⟨Marlene avoided walking past the *abandoned* house, with its broken windows and sagging porch⟩
***syn*** derelict, deserted, disused, forgotten, forsaken, rejected, vacated
***rel*** ignored, neglected, unattended, untended; castaway, cast-off, discarded, jettisoned, junked; desolate, godforsaken, miserable, shabby, wretched; empty, idle, vacant
***near ant*** reclaimed, recovered, redeemed, rescued, retrieved, salvaged, saved; reconditioned, rehabilitated, restored; repeopled

**abandonment** *n* **1** carefree freedom from constraint — see ABANDON
**2** the act of abandoning — see DERELICTION 1

**abase** *vb* **1** to lower in character or dignity — see DEBASE 1
**2** to reduce to a lower standing in one's own eyes or in others' eyes — see HUMBLE

**abash** *vb* to throw into a state of self-conscious distress — see EMBARRASS 1

**abashment** *n* the emotional state of being made self-consciously uncomfortable — see EMBARRASSMENT 1

**abate** *vb* **1** to grow less in scope or intensity especially gradually — see DECREASE 2
**2** to make smaller in amount, volume, or extent — see DECREASE 1

**abatement** *n* **1** something that is or may be subtracted — see DEDUCTION 1
**2** the amount by which something is lessened — see DECREASE

**abbey** *n* a residence for men under religious vows — see MONASTERY

**abbreviate** *vb* to make less in extent or duration — see SHORTEN

**abbreviation** *n* a shortened version of a written work — see ABRIDGMENT

**abdicate** *vb* to give up (as a position of authority) formally ⟨the revolutionary government forced Nicholas II to *abdicate* the Russian throne⟩
***syn*** abnegate, cede, relinquish, renounce, resign, step down (from), surrender
***rel*** abjure, deny, disavow, disclaim, disown, waive; forsake, give up, hand over, yield; abandon, desert, quit, vacate
***near ant*** appropriate, arrogate, assume, claim, confiscate; seize, take over, usurp, wrest; defend, guard, protect, safeguard, secure

**abdomen** *n* the part of the body between the chest and the pelvis — see STOMACH

**abduct** *vb* to carry a person away by unlawful force or against his or her will — see KIDNAP

**aberrant** *adj* **1** being out of the ordinary — see EXCEPTIONAL
**2** departing from some accepted standard of what is normal — see DEVIANT

**aberration** *n* a serious mental disorder that prevents one from living a safe and normal life — see INSANITY 1

**abet** *vb* **1** to cause or encourage the development of — see INCITE 1
**2** to provide (someone) with what is useful or necessary to achieve an end — see HELP 1

**abettor** *also* **abetter** *n* **1** one associated with another in wrongdoing — see ACCOMPLICE
**2** someone associated with another to give assistance or moral support — see ALLY

**abeyance** *n* a state of temporary inactivity ⟨our weekend plans were held in *abeyance* until we could get a weather forecast⟩
***syn*** doldrums, dormancy, latency, quiescence, suspense, suspension
***rel*** inaction, inertia, inertness, motionlessness; impasse, standstill; coma, hibernation, hypnosis, repose, rest, sleep, slumber, torpor; recession, remission; idleness
***near ant*** recommencement, renewal, resumption, resuscitation
***ant*** continuance, continuation

**abhor** *vb* to dislike strongly — see HATE

**abhorrence** *n* something or someone that is hated — see HATE 2
**2** a very strong dislike — see HATE 1

**abhorrent** *adj* causing intense displeasure, disgust, or resentment — see OFFENSIVE 1

**abide** *vb* **1** to continue to be in a place for a significant amount of time — see STAY 1
**2** to have a home — see LIVE 1
**3** to put up with (something painful or difficult) — see BEAR 2
**4** to remain indefinitely in existence or in the same state — see CONTINUE 1

**ability** *n* the physical or mental power to do something ⟨as a result of the accident he lost the *ability* to walk⟩
***syn*** capability, capacity, competence, competency, faculty
***rel*** aptitude, aptness, endowment, facility, gift, knack, talent; adroitness, deftness, dexterity, prowess, skill; gray matter, instinct, intelligence, reason, understanding; potency, staying power, stuff; adequacy, effectiveness, effectualness, fitness, form, influence, resourcefulness, usefulness; means, resources, wherewithal
***near ant*** helplessness, impotence, paralysis, powerlessness, weakness; defectiveness, deficiency, inadequacy, ineffectiveness, ineffectualness, uselessness; debilitation, disablement, impairment, incapacitation
***ant*** disability, inability, incapability, incapacity, incompetence, incompetency, ineptitude, ineptness

**abjure** *vb* to solemnly or formally reject or go back on (as something formerly adhered to) ⟨*abjured* some long-held beliefs when she converted to another religion⟩
***syn*** recant, renounce, retract, take back, unsay, withdraw
***rel*** contradict, deny, disavow, disclaim, disown, gainsay, negate, negative, repudiate; abandon, abnegate, forsake, give up, relinquish, spurn, surrender; controvert, disagree (with), disprove, dispute, rebut, refute; back down, back off, backtrack; disallow, recall, renege, revoke
***near ant*** acknowledge, admit, affirm, assert, avow, claim, contend, declare, maintain, proclaim, profess, state; back, confirm, defend, endorse (*also* indorse), espouse, maintain, support, uphold; accept, adopt, embrace
***ant*** adhere (to)

**ablaze** *adj* **1** being on fire ⟨the entire block was *ablaze* by the time fire fighters arrived⟩
***syn*** afire, aflame, blazing, burning, combusting, fiery, flaming, ignited, inflamed, kindled, lighted (*or* lit)
***rel*** aglow, alight, flaring, flickering, glowing, live, smoldering; broiling, hot, piping hot, red-hot, roasting, scalding, scorching, searing, sizzling; burnt, charred, incinerated, scorched, seared, singed
***near ant*** choked, damped, dead, doused, extinguished, quenched, smothered, snuffed (out), stamped (out), suffocated
**2** filled with much light — see BRIGHT 2

**able** *adj* having the required skills for an acceptable level of performance — see COMPETENT

**able–bodied** *adj* enjoying health and vigor — see HEALTHY 1

**ably** *adv* in a skillful or expert manner — see WELL 3

**abnegate** *vb* to give up (as a position of authority) formally — see ABDICATE

**abnegation** *n* the act or practice of giving up or rejecting something once enjoyed or desired — see RENUNCIATION

**abnormal** *adj* **1** being out of the ordinary — see EXCEPTIONAL
**2** departing from some accepted standard of what is normal — see DEVIANT

**abnormality** *n* a person, thing, or event that is not normal — see FREAK 1

**abode** *n* the place where one lives — see HOME 1

**abolish** *vb* to put an end to by formal action ⟨the U.S. *abolished* slavery by constitutional amendment on December 6, 1865⟩
***syn*** abrogate, annul, cancel, dissolve, invalidate, negate, nullify, quash, repeal, rescind, void
***rel*** countermand, override, overrule, overturn, veto; retract, reverse, revoke, suspend, withdraw; ban, enjoin, forbid, outlaw, prohibit; disallow, dismiss, reject; eliminate, eradicate, erase, liquidate, remove, throw out, write off
***phrases*** do away with
***near ant*** establish, found, institute; formalize, legalize, legitimate, legitimize, validate; pass, ratify; allow, approve, authorize, clear, endorse (*also* indorse), permit, sanction, warrant; command, decree, mandate, prescribe, order

**abominable** *adj* causing intense displeasure, disgust, or resentment — see OFFENSIVE 1

**abominate** *vb* to dislike strongly — see HATE

**abomination** *n* something or someone that is hated — see HATE 2
**2** a very strong dislike — see HATE 1

**aboriginal** *adj* belonging to a particular place by birth or origin — see NATIVE 1

**abort** *vb* to put an end to (something planned or previously agreed to) — see CANCEL 1

**abortion** *n* the act of putting an end to something planned or previously agreed to — see CANCELLATION

**abortive** *adj* producing no results — see FUTILE

**abounding** *adj* possessing or covered with great numbers or amounts of something specified — see RIFE

**about** *adv* **1** on all sides or in every direction — see AROUND 1
**2** toward the opposite direction — see AROUND 2
**3** very close to but not completely — see ALMOST

**about** *prep* **1** having to do with ⟨a story *about* a young man who goes off to war⟩

---

***syn*** synonym(s) ***rel*** related words
***ant*** antonym(s) ***near ant*** near antonym(s)

*syn* apropos of, concerning, of, on, regarding, respecting, toward (*or* towards)
*rel* as to, over
*phrases* as regards
2 close to — see AROUND 1
3 in random positions within the boundaries of — see AROUND 2

**above** *prep* higher than ⟨one minute our kite was *above* the telephone wires; the next minute it was tangled in them⟩
*syn* over
*rel* atop
*near ant* underneath
*ant* below, beneath, under

**above** *adv* to or in a higher place ⟨we eventually got used to the planes constantly flying *above*⟩
*syn* aloft, over, overhead, skyward
*near ant* underneath
*ant* below, beneath, under

**abrade** *vb* 1 to damage or diminish by continued friction ⟨ropes *abraæd* by the rocks were a huge danger to the climbers⟩
*syn* chafe, erode, fray, fret, gall, rub, wear
*rel* file, gnaw, grate, graze, grind, nibble, rasp, sandblast, sandpaper, scour, scrape, scuff, shave; erase, reduce, rub out, wear out, wipe (away); bite, break down, break up, chew, corrode, decompose, disintegrate, dissolve, eat; hone, sharpen, whet
2 to make sore by continued rubbing — see CHAFE 1
3 to damage by rubbing against a sharp or rough surface — see SCRAPE 2

**abreast** *adj* having information especially as a result of study or experience — see FAMILIAR 2

**abridge** *vb* to make less in extent or duration — see SHORTEN

**abridgment** *or* **abridgement** *n* a shortened version of a written work ⟨this Italian-English pocket dictionary is an *abridgment* of the hardback edition⟩
*syn* abbreviation, condensation, digest
*rel* abstract, brief, outline, overview, précis, recap, recapitulation, résumé (*or* resume *also* resumé), review, sketch, sum, summarization, summary, summation, survey, syllabus, synopsis, wrap-up
*near ant* amplification, elaboration, enlargement, expansion

**abrogate** *vb* to put an end to by formal action — see ABOLISH

**abrupt** *adj* 1 being or characterized by direct, brief, and potentially rude speech or manner — see BLUNT 1
2 having an incline approaching the perpendicular — see STEEP 1

**abruptly** *adv* with great suddenness — see SHORT

**abscond** *vb* to get free from a dangerous or confining situation — see ESCAPE 1

**absence** *n* 1 a state of being without something necessary, desirable, or useful — see NEED 1
2 the fact or state of being absent — see LACK 1

**absent** *adj* 1 not at a certain place ⟨three students were *absent* because of the flu⟩
*syn* away, missing, out
*rel* AWOL, truant; departed, gone, retired; abroad, vacationing
*near ant* accompanying, attending, participating
*ant* here, present
2 not present or in evidence ⟨the usual stir of activity was *absent* in the city due to the report of an escaped lion from the zoo⟩
*syn* lacking, missing, nonexistent, wanting
*rel* dead, departed, extinct, lost, perished, vanished; defunct, done, expired, finished, lapsed, obsolete, over, passé; inadequate, insufficient, rare, scarce, sparse, uncommon
*near ant* active, alive, animate, living, thriving; current, going, prevailing, uncanceled; common, prevalent; apparent, conspicuous, evident, obvious, plain
*ant* existent, present
3 lost in thought and unaware of one's surroundings or actions — see ABSENT-MINDED 1

**absentminded** *adj* 1 lost in thought and unaware of one's surroundings or actions ⟨the grieving woman was so *absentminded* that she left her key in the lock after opening the door⟩
*syn* absent, abstracted, preoccupied
*rel* absorbed, daydreaming, distracted, dreaming, dreamy, engrossed, faraway, intent, pensive, rapt; heedless, inattentive, insensible, oblivious, unaware, unconscious, unheeding, unknowing, unmindful, unobservant, unobserving, unperceiving, unperceptive, unseeing, unthinking, unwary, unwitting, vacant; befogged, befuddled, bemused, bewildered, confused, dazed, flighty, foggy, forgetful, forgetting, hazy, muddled, scatterbrained, unfocused
*near ant* alive, attentive, aware, conscious, heedful, mindful, observant, observing, open-eyed, sharp, vigilant, wary, watchful, wide-awake; clearheaded, unconfused
*ant* alert
2 inclined to forget what one has learned or to do what one should — see FORGETFUL

**absolute** *adj* 1 exercising power or authority without interference by others ⟨the *absolute* monarchy of Russia ended when Czar Nicholas II promised to share power with a legislative body⟩
*syn* autocratic, despotic, dictatorial, tyrannical (*also* tyrannic), tyrannous
*rel* authoritarian, totalitarian; arbitrary, high-handed, magisterial; domineering, imperious, masterful; all-powerful, almighty, omnipotent; autonomous, self-governing, sovereign; unconditional, unlimited
*near ant* circumscribed, restrained, restricted; constitutional, lawful
*ant* limited

**2** having no exceptions or restrictions ⟨ironing is an *absolute* bore⟩ ⟨I want the *absolute* truth⟩
***syn*** all-out, arrant, categorical (*also* categoric), complete, consummate, dead, downright, flat, out-and-out, outright, perfect, profound, pure, regular, sheer, simple, stark, thorough, thoroughgoing, total, unadulterated, unalloyed, unconditional, unequivocal, unmitigated, unqualified, utter
***rel*** authentic, classic, genuine, real, veritable; constant, endless, eternal, perpetual, undying, unremitting; extreme, rank, unrestricted; confirmed, habitual, hopeless, inveterate; deadly, extraordinary, frightful, horrible, huge, main, superlative, supreme, surpassing, terrible, terrific
***near ant*** doubtful, dubious, equivocal, qualified, questionable, restricted, uncertain
**3** being entirely without fault or flaw — see PERFECT 1
**4** free from added matter — see PURE 1
**5** serving to put an end to all debate or questioning — see CONCLUSIVE 1

**absolution** *n* release from the guilt or penalty of an offense — see PARDON

**absolve** *vb* to free from a charge of wrongdoing — see EXCULPATE

**absorb** *vb* **1** to take in (something liquid) through small openings ⟨most of the spilled water was *absorbed* by the tablecloth⟩
***syn*** drink, imbibe, soak (up), sponge, suck (up)
***rel*** gulp, guzzle, quaff, sip, slurp, swallow, swig, swill
**2** to hold the attention of — see ENGAGE 1

**absorbed** *adj* having the mind fixed on something — see ATTENTIVE

**absorbing** *adj* holding the attention or provoking interest — see INTERESTING

**absorption** *n* a focusing of the mind on something — see ATTENTION 1

**abstain** (from) *vb* to resist the temptation of — see FORBEAR

**abstract** *adj* **1** dealing with or expressing a quality or idea ⟨the book deals with *abstract* matters such as honesty and integrity on the job as well as practical subjects such as asking for a raise⟩
***syn*** conceptual, theoretical (*also* theoretic)
***rel*** conjectural, hypothetical, speculative; intellectual, mental, spiritual; ethereal, immaterial, incorporeal, insubstantial, metaphysical, nonmaterial, nonphysical, unsubstantial; impalpable, imperceptible, insensible, intangible, invisible; impractical, romantic, transcendent, transcendental, unreal, utopian, visionary
***near ant*** material, physical; appreciable, detectable, discernable, noticeable, observable, palpable, perceptible, sensible, substantial, tangible, visible; defined, definite, distinct; actual, factual, real
***ant*** concrete
**2** using elements of form (as color, line, or texture) with little or no attempt at creating a realistic picture ⟨Cubism is a style of *abstract* art in which natural forms are broken up into geometric shapes⟩
***syn*** nonrealistic
***rel*** impressionist, impressionistic; symbolist, symbolistic
***near ant*** lifelike, natural
***ant*** realistic, representational

**abstract** *n* a short statement of the main points — see SUMMARY

**abstract** *vb* to make into a short statement of the main points (as of a report) — see SUMMARIZE

**abstracted** *adj* lost in thought and unaware of one's surroundings or actions — see ABSENTMINDED 1

**abstruse** *adj* difficult for one of ordinary knowledge or intelligence to understand — see PROFOUND 1

**absurd** *adj* **1** conceived or made without regard for reason or reality — see FANTASTIC 1
**2** showing or marked by a lack of good sense or judgment — see FOOLISH 1
**3** so foolish or pointless as to be worthy of scornful laughter — see RIDICULOUS 1

**absurdity** *n* **1** a foolish act or idea — see FOLLY 1
**2** lack of good sense or judgment — see FOOLISHNESS 1

**abundance** *n* **1** a considerable amount — see LOT 2
**2** an amount or supply more than sufficient to meet one's needs — see PLENTY 1

**abundant** *adj* being more than enough without being excessive — see PLENTIFUL

**abuse** *n* **1** harsh insulting language ⟨spectators hurled *abuse* at the visiting team⟩
***syn*** fulmination, invective, vitriol, vituperation
***rel*** blasphemy, curse, execration, imprecation, maledicition, profanity; epithet, insult, put-down, slur; expletive, swearword; aspersion, bad-mouthing, belittlement, disparagement, revilement, vilification; castigation, chastisement, criticism, excoriation, opprobrium, rebuke, reprimand, reproof; broadside, diatribe, harangue, polemic, tirade
***near ant*** acclaim, applause, commendation, praise; compliments, congratulations, endearments, felicitations; adulation, blarney, flattery, overpraise, soft soap
**2** incorrect or improper use — see MISUSE

**abuse** *vb* **1** to inflict physical or emotional harm upon ⟨if you *abuse* your pet, he will always have an ugly disposition⟩
***syn*** ill-treat, ill-use, maltreat, manhandle, mishandle, mistreat, misuse

*rel* molest, outrage, violate; harass, harm, hurt, injure, oppress, persecute, torment, torture, victimize, wrong
*near ant* care (for), cherish, foster, nurture; baby, cater (to), coddle, favor, gratify, humor, indulge, mollycoddle, pamper, spoil
**2** to criticize harshly and usually publicly — see ATTACK 2
**3** to put to a bad or improper use — see MISAPPLY
**4** to take unfair advantage of — see EXPLOIT 1

**abut** *vb* to be adjacent to — see ADJOIN 1

**abutting** *adj* having a border in common — see ADJACENT

**abysmal** *adj* extending far downward or inward — see DEEP 1

**abyss** *n* an immeasurable depth or space ⟨looking down at the dark ocean from the ship's rail, Malcolm felt as though he was staring into an *abyss*⟩
*syn* chasm, gulf
*rel* cleft, crevasse, crevice, fissure; cavern, hole, hollow, pit; breadth, expanse, extent, reach, spread, stretch; emptiness, nothingness, vacuity, vacuum, void

**academic** *adj* of or relating to schooling or learning especially at an advanced level ⟨"If you spent more time in *academic* pursuits and less time in social ones, you could easily make good grades," the dean told Valerie⟩
*syn* educational, scholarly, scholastic
*rel* bookish, pedantic, professorial; curricular; educative, instructive; collegiate, graduate, postgraduate
*near ant* extracurricular; noncollegiate
*ant* nonacademic, unacademic

**academy** *n* a place or establishment for teaching and learning — see SCHOOL

**accelerate** *vb* to cause to move or proceed fast or faster — see HURRY 1

**accent** *n* a special notice or importance given to something — see EMPHASIS 1

**accent** *vb* to indicate the importance of by giving prominent display — see EMPHASIZE

**accentuate** *vb* to indicate the importance of by giving prominent display — see EMPHASIZE

**accentuation** *n* a special notice or importance given to something — see EMPHASIS 1

**accept** *vb* **1** to agree to receive whether willingly or reluctantly — see TAKE 2
**2** to have a favorable opinion of — see APPROVE (OF)
**3** to regard as right or true — see BELIEVE 1
**4** to take to or upon oneself — see ASSUME 1

**acceptability** *n* the quality or state of meeting one's needs adequately — see SUFFICIENCY

**acceptable** *adj* of a level of quality that meets one's needs or standards — see ADEQUATE

**acceptably** *adv* in a satisfactory way — see WELL 1

**accepting** *adj* showing or expressing acceptance or approval — see POSITIVE

**access** *n* the means or right of entering or participating in — see ENTRANCE 1

**access** *vb* to go or come in or into — see ENTER 1

**accessible** *adj* **1** possible to get — see AVAILABLE 1
**2** situated within easy reach — see CONVENIENT

**accessory** *adj* available to supply something extra when needed — see AUXILIARY

**accessory** *n* **1** something that is not necessary in itself but adds to the convenience or performance of the main piece of equipment ⟨bought a new car with lots of high-tech *accessories*⟩
*syn* accoutrement (*or* accouterment), adjunct, appendage, attachment
*rel* accompaniment, additive, complement, supplement; auxiliary, subsidiary; amenity, extra, filler, frill, incidental, luxury, nonessential, nonnecessity; equipment, furnishings, paraphernalia, trappings; adornment, decoration, embellishment, enhancement, garnish, ornament, trim
*near ant* essential, necessity, requirement, requisite
**2** one associated with another in wrongdoing — see ACCOMPLICE

**accident** *n* **1** a chance and usually sudden event bringing loss or injury ⟨was involved in an *accident* on her way home from work⟩
*syn* casualty, mischance, mishap
*rel* calamity, cataclysm, catastrophe, cropper, deathblow, disaster, tragedy; bummer, knock, misadventure, misfortune; collision, crack-up, crash, smashup, wreck
*near ant* boon, break, fluke, godsend, miracle, strike, windfall; fortune, luck, serendipity
**2** the uncertain course of events — see CHANCE 1

**accidental** *adj* happening by chance ⟨finding the gold was all the more remarkable because its discovery was entirely *accidental*⟩
*syn* casual, chance, fluky, fortuitous, inadvertent, incidental, unintended, unintentional, unplanned, unpremeditated, unwitting
*rel* coincidental; freak, odd; aimless, arbitrary, desultory, haphazard, random; uncertain, unexpected, unforeseeable, unforeseen; coerced, forced, involuntary; unconscious, unexpected, unprompted
*near ant* certain, destined, expected, fixed, foreordained, foreseeable, foreseen, inevitable, predestined, predetermined, predictable, preordained, prescribed, sure; conscious, freewill, knowing, unforced, voluntary, volunteer, willful (*or* wilful)
*ant* deliberate, intended, intentional, planned, premeditated

**acclaim** *n* public acknowledgment or admiration for an achievement — see GLORY 1

**acclaim** *vb* to declare enthusiastic approval of ⟨she was *acclaimed* by the critics for her realistic acting⟩

*syn* applaud, cheer, crack up, hail, laud, praise, salute, tout

*rel* ballyhoo; approve, commend, endorse (*also* indorse), favor, recommend, support; celebrate, emblazon, eulogize, extol (*also* extoll), glorify, sing; adulate, flatter, overpraise; deify, idolize

*near ant* belittle, disparage, put down; blame, censure, reprehend, reprobate; admonish, chide, criticize, rebuke, reprimand, reproach, reprove; castigate, excoriate, lambaste

*ant* knock, pan, slam

**acclamation** *n* enthusiastic and usually public expression of approval — see APPLAUSE

**acclimate** *vb* to change (something) so as to make it suitable for a new use or situation — see ADAPT

**acclimatize** *vb* to change (something) so as to make it suitable for a new use or situation — see ADAPT

**accolade** *n* **1** a formal expression of praise — see ENCOMIUM

**2** public acknowledgment or admiration for an achievement — see GLORY 1

**accommodate** *vb* **1** to make or have room for ⟨the back seat *accommodates* three people comfortably⟩

*syn* fit, hold, take

*rel* carry, contain, seat; enclose (*also* inclose), encompass; harbor, house

**2** to bring to a state free of conflicts, inconsistencies, or differences — see HARMONIZE 2

**3** to change (something) so as to make it suitable for a new use or situation — see ADAPT

**4** to do a service or favor for — see OBLIGE 1

**5** to provide with living quarters or shelter — see HOUSE 1

**accommodation** *n* the act or practice of each side giving up something in order to reach an agreement — see CONCESSION 1

**accompaniment** *n* something that is found along with something else ⟨the sound of crickets was the perfect *accompaniment* to our summer evenings on the porch⟩

*syn* companion, concomitant

*rel* accessory, adjunct, appendage; complement, supplement; counterpart, fellow, mate; consequence, corollary, follow-up; fixings, trimmings

**accompany** *vb* to go along with in order to provide assistance, protection, or companionship ⟨children must be *accompanied* by a parent at all times⟩

*syn* attend, chaperone (*or* chaperon), convoy, escort, squire

*rel* associate, consort, pal (around), team (up); defend, guard, protect; bring, conduct, guide, lead, pilot, see, steer, usher; follow, shadow, tag, tag along, tail; hang (around), hover (over)

*near ant* abandon, desert, ditch, dump, forsake

**accompanying** *adj* present at the same time and place — see COINCIDENT

**accomplice** *n* one associated with another in wrongdoing ⟨the thief and his *accomplices* were eventually caught and brought to justice⟩

*syn* abettor (*also* abetter), accessory, cohort, confederate

*rel* collaborator, collaborationist, informant, informer; companion, comrade, crony, henchman, partner; conspirator, plotter, traitor; gangster, mobster, racketeer

**accomplish** *vb* to carry through (as a process) to completion — see PERFORM 1

**accomplished** *adj* having or showing exceptional knowledge, experience, or skill in a field of endeavor — see PROFICIENT

**accomplishment** *n* **1** a successful result brought about by hard work ⟨Jared's biggest *accomplishment* this week was finishing his art project⟩

*syn* achievement, attainment, coup, success, triumph

*rel* blockbuster, hit, jackpot, megahit, smash, winner; conquest, gain, victory, win; acquirement, skill; deed, feat, performance; completion, consummation, culmination, execution, fruition, fulfillment, implementation, realization

*phrases* a feather in one's cap

*near ant* botch, mess, muddle, shambles; bummer, bust, catastrophe, debacle (*also* débâcle), dud, failure, fiasco, fizzle, flop, washout; disappointment, letdown, loss, setback

**2** the doing of an action — see COMMISSION 2

**3** the state of being actual or complete — see FRUITION

**accord** *n* **1** a formal agreement between two or more nations or peoples — see TREATY

**2** a state of consistency — see CONFORMITY 1

**3** an arrangement about action to be taken — see AGREEMENT 2

**4** the act or fact of being of one opinion about something — see AGREEMENT 1

**5** the act or power of making one's own choices or decisions — see FREE WILL

**accord** *vb* **1** to be in agreement on every point — see CHECK 1

**2** to give the ownership or benefit of (something) formally or publicly — see CONFER 1

**accordance** *n* a state of consistency — see CONFORMITY 1

**accordingly** *adv* for this or that reason — see THEREFORE

**account** *n* **1** a relating of events usually in the order in which they happened ⟨news-

*syn* synonym(s) *rel* related words
*ant* antonym(s) *near ant* near antonym(s)

paper reporters must strive to provide an accurate *account* of what happened〉
*syn* chronicle, history, narrative, record, report, story
*rel* version; deposition, documentation, testament, testimonial, testimony, witness; annals, diary, journal, log, logbook, memoir; anecdote, tale, yarn; epic, saga; recital, recitation
**2** a record of goods sold or services performed together with the cost due — see [1]BILL 1
**3** a sum of money set aside for a particular purpose — see FUND 1
**4** the capacity for being useful for some purpose — see USE 2
**5** the relative usefulness or importance of something as judged by specific qualities — see WORTH 1

**account** *vb* to think of in a particular way — see CONSIDER 1

**account** (for) *vb* to give the reason for or cause of — see EXPLAIN 2

**accountable** *adj* being the one who must meet an obligation or suffer the consequences for failing to do so — see RESPONSIBLE 1

**accoutre** *or* **accouter** *vb* to provide (someone) with what is needed for a task or activity — see FURNISH 1

**accoutrement** *or* **accouterment** *n* **1** something that is not necessary in itself but adds to the convenience or performance of the main piece of equipment — see ACCESSORY 1
**2 accoutrements** *or* **accouterments** *pl* items needed for the performance of a task or activity — see EQUIPMENT

**accredit** *vb* **1** to explain (something) as being the result of something else — see CREDIT 1
**2** to give official or legal power to — see AUTHORIZE 1

**accreditation** *n* the granting of power to perform various acts or duties — see COMMISSION 1

**accretion** *n* something added (as by growth) — see INCREASE 1

**accrual** *n* something added (as by growth) — see INCREASE 1

**accumulate** *vb* **1** to become greater in extent, volume, amount, or number — see INCREASE 2
**2** to bring together in one body or place — see GATHER 1
**3** to gradually form into a layer, pile, or mass — see COLLECT 2

**accumulating** *n* the act or process of becoming greater in number — see MULTIPLICATION

**accumulation** *n* **1** a mass or quantity that has piled up or that has been gathered 〈a vast *accumulation* of evidence about the dangers of smoking〉
*syn* assemblage, collection, gathering
*rel* agglomerate, assortment, conglomerate, conglomeration, hodgepodge, hotchpotch, jumble, medley, mélange, mishmash, mix, mixture, motley, potpourri; agglomeration, clutter, hash, heap, litter, mass, pile; aggregate, aggregation, sum, totality; cache, fund, hoard, inventory, nest egg, reserve, stock, stockpile, store, supply
**2** the act or process of becoming greater in number — see MULTIPLICATION

**accuracy** *n* the quality or state of being very accurate — see PRECISION

**accurate** *adj* **1** being in agreement with the truth or a fact or a standard — see CORRECT 1
**2** following an original exactly — see FAITHFUL 2
**3** meeting the highest standard of accuracy — see PRECISE 1

**accuse** *vb* to make a claim of wrongdoing against 〈she was *accused* of cheating on the test〉
*syn* charge, impeach, incriminate, indict
*rel* blame, castigate, censure, condemn, criticize, damn, denounce, fault, impugn, reproach, reprobate; chide, rebuke, reprove, tax; arraign, book, cite, summon; prosecute, sue, try; frame, implicate, inform (against), report; recriminate, retaliate
*near ant* advocate, champion, defend; excuse, forgive, justify, pardon, remit, shrive
*ant* absolve, acquit, clear, exculpate, exonerate, vindicate

**accustomed** *adj* being in the habit or custom 〈Josh felt uncomfortably full, as he was not *accustomed* to eating so much〉
*syn* given, habituated, used, wont
*rel* apt, inclined, liable, prone; hardened, inured; experienced, practiced (*or* practised), seasoned, veteran; addicted, hooked
*near ant* averse, disinclined, opposed; inexperienced, new, unseasoned
*ant* unaccustomed, unused

**ace** *adj* having or showing exceptional knowledge, experience, or skill in a field of endeavor — see PROFICIENT 1

**ace** *n* **1** a person with a high level of knowledge or skill in a field — see EXPERT
**2** a very small amount — see PARTICLE 1
**3** a very small distance or degree — see HAIR 1

**ache** *n* a sharp unpleasant sensation usually felt in some specific part of the body — see PAIN 1

**ache** *vb* to feel or cause physical pain — see HURT 1

**ache** (for) *vb* to have an earnest wish to own or enjoy — see DESIRE

**achievable** *adj* capable of being done or carried out — see POSSIBLE 1

**achieve** *vb* **1** to obtain (as a goal) through effort 〈finally *achieved* stardom〉
*syn* attain, hit, make, score, win
*rel* acquire, capture, carry, draw, garner, get, land, make, obtain, procure, realize, secure; amount (to), approach, equal, match, measure up (to), meet, rival, tie, touch; beat, excel, outdo, surpass, top
*near ant* fall short (of); fail (at); lose

2 to carry through (as a process) to completion — see PERFORM 1

**achievement** *n* 1 a successful result brought about by hard work — see ACCOMPLISHMENT 1
2 the doing of an action — see COMMISSION 2
3 the state of being actual or complete — see FRUITION

**aching** *adj* causing or feeling bodily pain — see PAINFUL 1

**acid** *adj* causing or characterized by the one of the four basic taste sensations that is produced chiefly by acids — see SOUR 1

**acidic** *adj* causing or characterized by the one of the four basic taste sensations that is produced chiefly by acids — see SOUR 1

**acidity** *n* 1 a harsh or sharp quality — see EDGE 1
2 biting sharpness of feeling or expression — see ACRIMONY 1

**acidness** *n* biting sharpness of feeling or expression — see ACRIMONY 1

**acknowledge** *vb* to accept the truth or existence of (something) usually reluctantly — see ADMIT

**acknowledgment** *also* **acknowledgement** *n* 1 a formal recognition of an achievement or praiseworthy deed — see COMMENDATION 1
2 an open declaration of something (as a fault or the commission of an offense) about oneself — see CONFESSION

**acme** *n* the highest part or point — see HEIGHT 1

**acoustic** *or* **acoustical** *adj* of, relating to, or experienced through the sense of hearing — see AUDITORY

**acquaint** *vb* 1 to impart knowledge of a new thing or situation to ⟨Mr. King spent the first week of class *acquainting* everyone with the new computers⟩
***syn*** familiarize, initiate, introduce, orient, orientate
***rel*** apprise, brief, clue (in), fill in, inform; educate, enlighten, ground, instruct, school, train; expose, present, subject; advise, tell, tip off, warn, wise up
2 to give information to — see ENLIGHTEN 1
3 to make (one person) known (to another) socially — see INTRODUCE 1

**acquaintance** *n* knowledge gained by personal experience ⟨Tiffany's *acquaintance* with cows is limited to a visit to a petting zoo when she was three⟩
***syn*** cognizance, familiarity
***rel*** association, experience, exposure, intimacy, involvement; initiation, introduction; awareness, comprehension, conception, inkling, notion, understanding; education, enlightenment, grounding, information, instruction, learning, schooling, training
***near ant*** callowness, greenness, ignorance, inexperience
***ant*** unfamiliarity

***syn*** synonym(s) ***rel*** related words
***ant*** antonym(s) ***near ant*** near antonym(s)

**acquainted** *adj* having information especially as a result of study or experience — see FAMILIAR 2

**acquiescent** *adj* receiving or enduring without offering resistance — see PASSIVE

**acquirable** *adj* possible to get — see AVAILABLE 1

**acquire** *vb* 1 to come to have gradually — see DEVELOP 2
2 to receive as return for effort — see EARN 1

**acquisitive** *adj* having or marked by an eager and often selfish desire especially for material possessions — see GREEDY 1

**acquisitiveness** *n* an intense selfish desire for wealth or possessions — see GREED

**acquit** *vb* 1 to free from a charge of wrongdoing — see EXCULPATE
2 to manage the actions of (oneself) in a particular way — see BEHAVE

**acrid** *adj* 1 having or showing deep-seated resentment — see BITTER 1
2 marked by the use of wit that is intended to cause hurt feelings — see SARCASTIC

**acridness** *n* 1 a harsh or sharp quality — see EDGE 1
2 biting sharpness of feeling or expression — see ACRIMONY 1

**acrimonious** *adj* having or showing deep-seated resentment — see BITTER 1

**acrimoniousness** *n* a harsh or sharp quality — see EDGE 1

**acrimony** *n* 1 biting sharpness of feeling or expression ⟨she responded with such *acrimony* that he never brought the subject up again⟩
***syn*** acidity, acidness, acridness, asperity, bitterness, cattiness, tartness, virulence, vitriol
***rel*** gruffness, harshness, hostility, relentlessness, severity, sternness, vehemence; coldness, crossness, discourteousness, iciness, impoliteness, incivility, nastiness, rudeness, sourness, surliness, ungraciousness; anger, animosity, bile, jaundice, malevolence, malice, rancor, scorn, spite, spleen, venom; jealousy, pique, resentment
***near ant*** civility, cordiality, courtesy, diplomacy, geniality, graciousness, politeness, tactfulness; compassion, softness, sweetness, sympathy, tenderness, warmth; oiliness, smoothness, suaveness, unctuousness, urbanity
2 a harsh or sharp quality — see EDGE 1

**across** *adv* from one side to the other of an intervening space — see OVER 1

**across** *prep* to the opposite side of ⟨we swam *across* the lake and visited the other summer camp⟩
***syn*** athwart, over, through
***rel*** around, round; beyond, past

**act** *n* 1 a display of emotion or behavior that is insincere or intended to deceive — see MASQUERADE
2 a rule of conduct or action laid down by a governing authority and especially a legislator — see LAW 1

3 something done by someone — see ACTION 1

**act** *vb* 1 to present a portrayal or performance of ⟨a very talented student *acted* the part of Tiny Tim in our production of *A Christmas Carol*⟩

*syn* impersonate, perform, play, portray

*rel* depict, dramatize, enact, pantomime, render, represent, role-play, take on; overact, underplay; ape, clown, ham, imitate, masquerade, mime, mimic, pose (as); star (in)

2 to produce a desired effect ⟨the painkiller *acted* quickly⟩

*syn* operate, perform, take, work

*rel* behave, react, respond; affect, influence, sway; pan out, redound, result

*phrases* take effect

*near ant* backfire; fizzle

3 to give the impression of being — see SEEM

4 to have a certain purpose — see FUNCTION

**act** (toward) *vb* to behave toward in a stated way — see TREAT 1

**action** *n* 1 something done by someone ⟨judge people by their *actions*, not by their words⟩

*syn* act, deed, doing, exploit, feat, thing

*rel* accomplishment, achievement, attainment; adventure, experience; enterprise, initiative, undertaking; handiwork, performance, work; stunt, trick; activity, dealing; maneuver, measure, move, operation, procedure, proceeding, step, tactic

2 a court case for enforcing a right or claim — see LAWSUIT

3 active fighting during the course of a war — see COMBAT 1

4 **actions** *pl* the way or manner in which one conducts oneself — see BEHAVIOR

**activate** *vb* to cause to function ⟨the thermostat is set to *activate* the heating system only when the temperature drops below 65 degrees⟩

*syn* actuate, crank (up), drive, move, propel, run, set off, spark, start, touch off, trigger, turn on

*rel* charge, electrify, energize, fire, fuel, generate, power, push; discharge, launch, release, switch, trip; reactivate, recharge; arouse, excite, stimulate, vitalize; incite, instigate, provoke, quicken, stir up; accelerate, catalyze, speed up, step up

*near ant* arrest, brake, chock, cut off, draw up, halt, jam, stall, stick, stop; decelerate, repress, slow, stunt, suppress

*ant* cut, deactivate, kill, shut off, turn off

**active** *adj* 1 being in effective operation ⟨the abandoned factory had not been *active* for years⟩

*syn* alive, functional, functioning, going, living, on, operating, operational, operative, running, working

*rel* effective, effectual; employable, operable, usable, viable, workable; performing, producing, productive, serving, useful, yielding; astir, bustling, busy, dynamic, flourishing, humming, roaring, thriving

*phrases* in commission

*near ant* deactivated, decommissioned; ineffective, ineffectual, useless; inoperable, unusable, unworkable; arrested, asleep, dormant, fallow, idle, inert, latent, lifeless, nonproductive, quiescent, sleepy, stagnating, unproductive, vegetating

*ant* broken, dead, inactive, inoperative, nonfunctional, nonfunctioning, nonoperating

2 having much high-spirited energy and movement — see LIVELY 1

3 involved in often constant activity — see BUSY 1

**activity** *n* energetic movement of the body for the sake of physical fitness — see EXERCISE 1

**actor** *n* one who acts professionally (as in a play, movie, or television show) ⟨my sister went to drama school to become an *actor*⟩

*syn* impersonator, mummer, player, trouper

*rel* barnstormer, entertainer, performer; actress, starlet; lead, leading lady, leading man, star; monologuist (*or* monologist); prima donna, scene-stealer, understudy; comedian, tragedian; ape, aper, ham, imitator, impressionist, masquerader, mime, mimic, pantomime, pantomimist, poser; buffoon, clown, harlequin, stooge, zany

**actual** *adj* existing in fact and not merely as a possibility ⟨the *actual* outcome of the election was quite different from what everybody expected⟩

*syn* concrete, existent, factual, real, true, very

*rel* attested, authenticated, confirmed, demonstrated, established, proven, substantiated, validated, verified; incontestable, incontrovertible, indisputable, indubitable, inescapable, irrefutable, undeniable, unquestionable; believable, convincing, literal, realistic, unmistakable, verifiable; authentic, bona fide, genuine, real-life; absolute, certain, final, hard, palpable, positive, substantial, tangible; authoritative, certifiable, certified

*near ant* alleged, assumed, reputed, supposed; conceived, envisaged, imagined, pictured, visualized; chimerical, fabled, fanciful, fictional, fictitious, legendary, illusory; fabricated, fake, imaginary, invented, made-up, make-believe, pretend, romantic; abstract, unreal

*ant* conjectural, hypothetical, ideal, nonexistent, possible, potential, theoretical (*also* theoretic)

**actuality** *n* 1 the fact of being or of being real — see EXISTENCE

2 the quality of being actual — see FACT 1

3 the state of being actual or complete — see FRUITION

**actually** *adv* 1 to tell the truth ⟨*actually*, I'd rather spend the evening at home⟩

*syn* forsooth, frankly, honestly, really, truly, truthfully, verily

*rel* absolutely, certainly, indisputably, indubitably, positively, realistically, undoubtedly, unquestionably, veritably
*phrases* in point of fact, in reality, in truth
**2** in actual fact — see VERY 2

**actuate** *vb* **1** to cause to function — see ACTIVATE
**2** to set or keep in motion — see MOVE 2

**act up** *vb* **1** to behave badly — see MISBEHAVE
**2** to engage in attention-getting playful or boisterous behavior — see CUT UP

**acute** *adj* **1** able to sense slight impressions or differences ⟨dogs, with their *acute* sense of smell, are used for finding toxic substances undetectable by humans⟩
*syn* delicate, keen, perceptive, sensitive, sharp
*rel* accurate, clear, discerning, fine, good, piercing, precise, quick, receptive, sensible, subtle; hypersensitive, oversensitive, supersensitive
*near ant* bad, deadened, dimmed, dull, dulled, fading; dead, imperceptive, insensible, insensitive, numb; imprecise, inaccurate
**2** needing immediate attention ⟨famine caused by an *acute* shortage of grain⟩
*syn* critical, crying, dire, imperative, imperious, instant, pressing, urgent
*rel* compelling, demanding, extreme, immediate, insistent, intense, overriding; crucial, desperate, grave, life-and-death, serious, severe, vital; dangerous, explosive, hazardous, perilous, precarious, unstable
*near ant* incidental, low-pressure, minor, negligible, trivial, unimportant; nonthreatening, safe, stable
*ant* noncritical, nonurgent
**3** causing intense mental or physical distress — see SHARP 2
**4** having a high musical pitch or range — see SHRILL

**acuteness** *n* a harsh or sharp quality — see EDGE 1

**ad** *n* a published statement informing the public of a matter of general interest — see ANNOUNCEMENT

**adage** *n* an often stated observation regarding something from common experience — see SAYING

**adamant** *adj* sticking to an opinion, purpose, or course of action in spite of reason, arguments, or persuasion — see OBSTINATE

**adamantine** *adj* sticking to an opinion, purpose, or course of action in spite of reason, arguments, or persuasion — see OBSTINATE

**adapt** *vb* to change (something) so as to make it suitable for a new use or situation ⟨it always takes freshmen a little while to *adapt* themselves to high school⟩
*syn* acclimate, acclimatize, accommodate, adjust, condition, conform, fit, shape
*rel* readapt, readjust; customize, tailor; attune, harmonize, reconcile, suit, tune; establish, root, settle; acquaint, familiarize, orient, orientate; equip, prepare, prime, rehearse; harden, inure, season, toughen; alter, convert, make over, modify, redo, refashion, refit, remake, remodel, revamp, revise, rework, transform

**adaptable** *adj* **1** able to do many different kinds of things — see VERSATILE
**2** capable of being readily changed — see FLEXIBLE 1

**add** *vb* **1** to join (something) to a mass, quantity, or number so as to bring about an overall increase ⟨the band recently *added* a saxophonist and a keyboard player to its ranks⟩ ⟨*add* another cup of flour to the mixture⟩
*syn* adjoin, annex, append, tack (on)
*rel* affix, attach, fasten, fix, graft, hitch, tie; infuse, inject, insert, introduce
*near ant* detach, disconnect, disjoin, separate, unfasten; amputate, cut, excise, lop off, sever
*ant* deduct, remove, subtract, take
**2** to combine (numbers) into a single sum ⟨when she *added* all the phone charges she discovered an error in her bill⟩
*syn* foot (up), sum, total
*rel* calculate, cast, cipher, compute, figure, reckon, tally; count, enumerate, number

**add** (to) *vb* to make greater in size, amount, or number — see INCREASE 1

**added** *adj* resulting in an increase in amount or number — see ADDITIONAL

**addendum** *n* something added (as by growth) — see INCREASE 1

**addict** *n* **1** a person who regularly uses drugs especially illegally — see DOPER
**2** a person with a strong and habitual liking for something — see FAN

**addition** *n* **1** a smaller structure added to a main building — see ANNEX
**2** something added (as by growth) — see INCREASE 1
**3** the act or process of becoming greater in number — see MULTIPLICATION

**additional** *adj* resulting in an increase in amount or number ⟨there turned out to be *additional* reasons for her absence besides those she had given⟩
*syn* added, another, else, farther, further, more, other
*rel* accessory, collateral, extraneous, side, supplemental, supplementary; fresh, new; extra, plus, spare, surplus
*near ant* fewer, less

**additionally** *adv* in addition to what has been said — see MORE 1

**additive** *adj* produced by a series of additions of identical or similar things — see CUMULATIVE

**addle** *vb* to throw into a state of mental uncertainty — see CONFUSE 1

**addled** *adj* having undergone organic breakdown — see ROTTEN 1

---

*syn* synonym(s) *rel* related words
*ant* antonym(s) *near ant* near antonym(s)

**address** *n* a usually formal discourse delivered to an audience — see SPEECH 1
**address** *vb* to occupy (oneself) diligently or with close attention — see APPLY 2
**adduce** *vb* to give as an example — see QUOTE 1
**add up** (to) *vb* **1** to be the same in meaning or effect — see AMOUNT (TO) 2
**2** to have a total of — see AMOUNT (TO) 1
**adept** *adj* having or showing exceptional knowledge, experience, or skill in a field of endeavor — see PROFICIENT
**adept** *n* a person with a high level of knowledge or skill in a field — see EXPERT
**adeptly** *adv* in a skillful or expert manner — see WELL 3
**adeptness** *n* subtle or imaginative ability in inventing, devising, or executing something — see SKILL 1
**adequacy** *n* the quality or state of meeting one's needs adequately — see SUFFICIENCY
**adequate** *adj* of a level of quality that meets one's needs or standards ⟨this old computer is probably *adequate* if you just want to type a book report⟩
***syn*** acceptable, all right, decent, fine, OK (*or* okay), passable, respectable, satisfactory, tolerable
***rel*** agreeable, bearable, endurable, sufferable; average, fair, mediocre, middling, minimal, unexceptional; appropriate, correct, due, fitting, good, meet, proper, right, seemly, suitable, useful, worthy; gratifying, satisfying
***near ant*** disreputable, improper, indecent, objectionable, unfit, unsuitable, unworthy, useless; bad, defective, faulty, imperfect, incomplete, lamentable, pitiful; dissatisfying, unsatisfying; insufficient, meager, mean, miserly, niggardly, poor, scanty, shabby, short, skimpy, spare, stingy; insufferable, intolerable, unbearable, unendurable; exceptional, exquisite, extreme, first-class, matchless, maximized, maximum, optimal, optimum, peerless, preeminent, superior, supreme, unmatched, unparalleled, unsurpassed
***ant*** deficient, inadequate, lacking, unacceptable, unsatisfactory, wanting
**adequately** *adv* **1** in a satisfactory way — see WELL 1
**2** in or to a degree or quantity that meets one's requirements or satisfaction — see ENOUGH 1
**adhere** *vb* to hold to something firmly as if by adhesion — see STICK 1
**adhere** (to) *vb* to give steadfast support to ⟨our coach *adheres to* the belief that we can win this game if we just have a positive attitude⟩
***syn*** cling (to), hew (to), keep (to), stick (to *or* with)
***rel*** cleave (to), hang on (to); back, confirm, defend, endorse (*also* indorse), espouse, support, uphold; accept, adopt, cherish, cultivate, embrace, follow, foster, heed
***phrases*** abide by, live up to, stand by
***near ant*** abandon, desert, forsake, give up, relinquish, spurn, surrender; abjure, disavow, disclaim, disown, recall, recant, reconsider, renege, renounce, retract, revoke, take back, unsay, withdraw
***ant*** defect (from)
**adherence** *n* a physical sticking to as if by glue — see ADHESION
**adherent** *n* one who follows the opinions or teachings of another — see FOLLOWER
**adhesion** *n* a physical sticking to as if by glue ⟨mom prefers photo albums that keep the pictures in place by *adhesion* to the pages⟩
***syn*** adherence, bonding
***rel*** agglutination, clumping, cohesion; adhesiveness, attachment, cohesiveness, tenacity; cementing, glueing
**adhesive** *adj* being of such a thick consistency as to readily cling to objects upon contact — see STICKY 1
**adhesive** *n* a substance used to stick things together — see GLUE
**adieu** *n* an expression of good wishes at parting — see GOOD-BYE
**adipose** *adj* containing animal fat especially in unusual amounts — see FATTY
**adiposity** *n* the condition of having an excess of body fat — see CORPULENCE
**adjacent** *adj* having a border in common ⟨Crystal's house is *adjacent* to a wooded park⟩
***syn*** abutting, adjoining, bordering, contiguous, flanking, fringing, joining, juxtaposed, skirting, touching, verging
***rel*** close, closest, immediate, near, nearest, nearby, neighboring, next, next-door, nigh; attached, communicating, connecting, interconnecting, linked; bounding, embracing, encircling, enclosing, fencing, rimming, surrounding; marginal, peripheral, tangent, tangential
***near ant*** apart, detached, free-standing, removed, separate, unattached, unconnected, unlinked; away, distant, far, far-off, farthest, remote; discontinuous, noncontinuous
***ant*** nonadjacent
**adjoin** *vb* **1** to be adjacent to ⟨Colleen, whose bedroom *adjoins* her little brother's room, sometimes hears him talking in his sleep⟩
***syn*** abut, border (on), flank, fringe, join, skirt, touch, verge (on)
***rel*** attach (to), communicate (with), connect (with), link (with), bound, embrace, encircle, enclose (*also* inclose), fence, line, rim, surround; contact, converge, meet, neighbor
**2** to join (something) to a mass, quantity, or number so as to bring about an overall increase — see ADD 1
**adjoining** *adj* having a border in common — see ADJACENT
**adjourn** *vb* to bring to a formal close for a period of time ⟨the meeting was *adjourned* by the chairperson until further notice⟩
***syn*** recess, suspend

***rel*** break off, discontinue, intermit, interrupt; defer, hold off, postpone, put off, reserve, shelve, table; abort, call off, cancel, dissolve, terminate; break up, close, conclude, wind up, wrap up
***near ant*** inaugurate, launch, open; carry on, continue, draw out, extend, proceed, prolong; renew, reopen, resume; convene, convoke

**adjudge** *vb* to give an opinion about (something at issue or in dispute) — see JUDGE 1

**adjudicate** *vb* to give an opinion about (something at issue or in dispute) — see JUDGE 1

**adjunct** *n* something that is not necessary in itself but adds to the convenience or performance of the main piece of equipment — see ACCESSORY 1

**adjure** *vb* to issue orders to (someone) by right of authority — see COMMAND 1

**adjust** *vb* to change (something) so as to make it suitable for a new use or situation — see ADAPT

**adjustable** *adj* capable of being readily changed — see FLEXIBLE 1

**adjutant** *n* a person who helps a more skilled person — see HELPER

**ad–lib** *adj* made or done without previous thought or preparation — see EXTEMPORANEOUS

**ad–lib** *vb* to perform, make, or do without preparation — see IMPROVISE

**administer** *vb* **1** to give out (something) in appropriate amounts or to appropriate individuals ⟨the principal *administers* discipline fairly when students break the rules⟩
***syn*** allocate, apportion, deal (out), dispense, distribute, dole (out), mete (out), parcel (out), portion, prorate
***rel*** allot, allow, appropriate, assign, dish (out), divide, measure (out), ration, redistribute, split; bestow, disburse, furnish, issue, provide, share, supply; circulate, disperse, disseminate, scatter, spread; chip in, contribute, donate, pledge
***near ant*** begrudge, deny, deprive (of), pinch, refuse, skimp, stint, withhold
**2** to carry out effectively — see ENFORCE
**3** to look after and make decisions about — see CONDUCT 1

**administration** *n* **1** lawful control over the affairs of a political unit (as a nation) — see RULE 2
**2** the act or activity of looking after and making decisions about something — see CONDUCT 1

**administrative** *adj* suited for or relating to the directing of things — see EXECUTIVE

**administrator** *n* a person who manages or directs — see EXECUTIVE

**admirable** *adj* deserving of high regard or great approval ⟨it's *admirable* the way Kory helps her grandmother with chores and errands every Saturday⟩
***syn*** commendable, creditable, laudable, meritorious, praiseworthy
***rel*** awesome, distinctive, distinguished, excellent, honorable, noteworthy, noticeable, outstanding, reputable, worthy; invaluable, precious, priceless, valuable; delightful, enjoyable, pleasing, satisfying
***near ant*** contemptible, deplorable, infamous, notorious, sorry, unlikable, unworthy, worthless; disgraceful, dishonorable, disreputable, low, mean, scandalous, seamy, shady, shameful, shocking, sordid, unsavory
***ant*** censurable, discreditable, reprehensible

**admiration** *n* **1** a feeling of great approval and liking ⟨my *admiration* for Yoko increased when I discovered she had learned English only since coming to the U.S.⟩
***syn*** appreciation, esteem, estimation, favor, regard, respect
***rel*** acclamation, adoration, approbation, deference, homage, honor, praise, reverence, veneration, worship; delight, enjoyment, fancy; amazement, awe, wonder, wonderment
***near ant*** condemnation, disapproval, disdain, opprobrium, scorn; disappointment, discontent, disenchantment, disgruntlement, disillusionment, displeasure, indignation, unhappiness; aversion, contempt, disgust, dislike, disregard, distaste
***ant*** disfavor
**2** the rapt attention and deep emotion caused by the sight of something extraordinary — see WONDER 2

**admire** *vb* to think very highly or favorably of ⟨I *admire* the way you handled such a touchy situation⟩
***syn*** appreciate, esteem, regard, respect
***rel*** acclaim, accredit, applaud, approve, commend, compliment, credit, praise; delight (in), drink (in), enjoy, relish, revel (in), savor; dig, fancy, favor, groove (on), like, love; adore, deify, idolize, revere, reverence, venerate, worship; cherish, prize, treasure, value
***phrases*** set store by (*or* on)
***near ant*** condemn, decry, deplore, disapprove, discount, discountenance, disdain, disfavor, dislike, dismiss, disregard, frown (on), scorn

**admiring** *adj* expressing approval — see FAVORABLE 1

**admissible** *adj* that may be permitted — see PERMISSIBLE

**admission** *n* **1** an open declaration of something (as a fault or the commission of an offense) about oneself — see CONFESSION
**2** the means or right of entering or participating in — see ENTRANCE 1

**admit** *vb* to accept the truth or existence of (something) usually reluctantly ⟨Eliza readily *admitted* she hadn't read the assignment⟩ ⟨you can't bring yourself to *admit* your mistakes⟩

---

***syn*** synonym(s) ***rel*** related words
***ant*** antonym(s) ***near ant*** near antonym(s)

*syn* acknowledge, agree, allow, concede, confess, grant, own (up)
*rel* disburden, unburden, unload; affirm, avow, confirm, profess; accept, recognize, yield; announce, break, broadcast, communicate, declare, disclose, divulge, impart, publish, reveal, spill, tell, unveil; betray, blab, expose, give away, inform, leak, rat, squeal, talk, tattle, tip off; warn, wise up; breathe, whisper
*near ant* disallow, disavow, disclaim, disown; contradict, dispute, gainsay, negate, negative; rebut, refute, reject, repudiate; conceal, cover (up), hide, obscure, veil
*ant* deny

**admittance** *n* the means or right of entering or participating in — see ENTRANCE 1

**admixture** *n* a distinct entity formed by the combining of two or more different things — see BLEND

**admonish** *vb* to criticize (someone) usually gently so as to correct a fault — see REBUKE 1

**admonishing** *adj* serving as or offering a warning — see CAUTIONARY

**admonition** *n* the act or an instance of telling beforehand of danger or risk — see WARNING 1

**admonitory** *adj* serving as or offering a warning — see CAUTIONARY

**adolescent** *adj* **1** being in the early stage of life, growth, or development — see YOUNG
**2** having or showing the annoying qualities (as silliness) associated with children — see CHILDISH
**3** lacking in adult experience or maturity — see CALLOW

**adopt** *vb* to take for one's own use (something originated by another) ⟨the family *adopted* the American tradition of having turkey for Thanksgiving after they moved to the U.S.⟩
*syn* borrow, embrace, take up
*rel* domesticate, naturalize; appropriate, arrogate, take over, usurp; absorb, assimilate, incorporate; cherish, prize, treasure; cultivate, follow, heed, honor; use, utilize; bring up, foster, nurture, raise, rear; affect, assume, copy, imitate, pretend, put on, simulate
*near ant* abandon, forsake, give up, relinquish, surrender; abjure, abnegate, disown; reject, renounce, repudiate, spurn; discard, jettison, junk, throw away, throw out

**adorable** *adj* having qualities that tend to make one loved — see LOVABLE

**adore** *vb* **1** to feel passion, devotion, or tenderness for — see LOVE 2
**2** to love or admire too much — see IDOLIZE
**3** to offer honor or respect to (someone) as a divine power — see WORSHIP 1
**4** to take pleasure in — see ENJOY 1

**adoring** *adj* **1** feeling or showing love — see LOVING
**2** reflecting great admiration or devotion — see WORSHIPFUL

**adorn** *vb* to make more attractive by adding something that is beautiful or becoming — see DECORATE

**adorning** *adj* serving to add beauty — see DECORATIVE

**adornment** *n* something that decorates or beautifies — see DECORATION 1

**adroit** *adj* accomplished with trained ability — see SKILLFUL

**adroitness** *n* **1** mental skill or quickness — see DEXTERITY 1
**2** subtle or imaginative ability in inventing, devising, or executing something — see SKILL 1

**adulate** *vb* **1** to love or admire too much — see IDOLIZE
**2** to praise too much — see FLATTER 1

**adulation** *n* **1** excessive admiration of or devotion to a person — see WORSHIP
**2** excessive praise — see FLATTERY

**adulatory** *adj* **1** overly or insincerely flattering — see FULSOME
**2** reflecting great admiration or devotion — see WORSHIPFUL

**adult** *adj* fully grown or developed — see MATURE 1

**adult** *n* a fully grown person ⟨at the beach, the *adults* sat under broad umbrellas while the children splashed in the water⟩
*syn* grown-up
*rel* ancient, elder, graybeard, oldster, old-timer, senior, senior citizen
*near ant* kid, moppet, tad, toddler, tot, tyke; baby, infant; adolescent, juvenile, minor, youngster, youth; preteen, teenager, teenybopper
*ant* child

**adulterant** *n* something that is or that makes impure — see IMPURITY

**adulterate** *vb* to alter (something) for the worse with the addition of foreign or lower-grade substances ⟨the company was fined for *adulterating* its "all beef" frankfurters with cereal⟩
*syn* dilute, thin, water (down), weaken
*rel* befoul, contaminate, corrupt, defile, dirty, foul, infect, poison, pollute, soil, spoil, sully, taint; cheapen, debase, degrade; manipulate, misrepresent, tamper (with); counterfeit, fake, falsify, fudge; doctor, spike
*near ant* fertilize, lard; augment, supplement; clarify, clean, cleanse, distill, filter, flush, leach, pasteurize, purge, purify, refine; better, enhance, improve
*ant* enrich, fortify, richen, strengthen

**adulterated** *adj* containing foreign or lower-grade substances — see IMPURE

**adulthood** *n* the state of being fully grown or developed — see MATURITY

**advance** *n* **1** forward movement in time or place ⟨during her long convalescence, Penny was barely aware of the *advance* of the seasons⟩
*syn* advancement, furtherance, going, headway, march, onrush, passage, process, procession, progress, progression
*rel* current, drift, flow, flux, stream, way; advent, approach, arrival, coming, near-

ing; bound, jump, leap, step, stride; impetus, momentum
*near ant* backwash, ebb, reflux; retraction, retreat, return, reversal, reverse; about-face, turnabout, turnaround
*ant* recession, regression, retrogression
**2** an instance of notable progress in the development of knowledge, technology, or skill ⟨with her new violin teacher, Nadia has made noticeable *advances* in her technique in just a few weeks⟩
*syn* advancement, breakthrough, enhancement, improvement, refinement
*rel* amelioration, boost, heightening, increase, melioration, strengthening, upgrade, uplift, upswing, uptrend, upturn; betterment, evolution, maturation, perfection, ripening; civilization, edification, education, enlightenment; renaissance, renascence, revival; discovery, find, windfall; innovation, invention
*near ant* breakdown, collapse, crash; hindrance, impediment, stumbling block; decline, decrease, deterioration, diminishment, failing, flagging, languishment, lapse, lessening, reduction, sinking, slowing, weakening, worsening; detriment, disablement, drawback, glitch, impairment, shortcoming
*ant* setback

**advance** *vb* **1** to give to another for temporary use with the understanding that it or a like thing will be returned — see LEND
**2** to help the growth or development of — see FOSTER 1
**3** to move forward along a course — see GO 1
**4** to move higher in rank or position — see PROMOTE 1
**5** to set before the mind for consideration — see PROPOSE 1
**6** to move closer to — see COME 1

**advanced** *adj* **1** being far along in development ⟨an *advanced* civilization, among the first anywhere to use the plow, developed on the banks of the Nile River thousands of years ago⟩
*syn* developed, evolved, high, higher, improved, progressive, refined
*rel* full-blown, full-fledged, full-grown, full-scale; aged, grown, mature, matured, perfected, ripe, ripened; civilized, educated, enhanced, enlightened; contemporary, latest, modern, newest, newfangled, new-fashioned, novel, recent, up-to-date; early, precocious
*near ant* green, immature, underdeveloped, undersized, underweight, unripe, unripened; uncivilized, uneducated; early, primeval, primordial; antediluvian, antiquated, Neanderthal, oldfangled, old-fashioned
*ant* backward, low, lower, nonprogressive, primitive, retarded, rudimentary, undeveloped
**2** being at a higher level than average — see HIGH 2

**advancement** *n* **1** a raising or a state of being raised to a higher rank or position ⟨Paul's rapid *advancement* in the company came as no surprise to those who knew he was the president's nephew⟩
*syn* ascent, elevation, preferment, promotion, rise, upgrade
*rel* aggrandizement, ennoblement, exaltation, glorification
*near ant* deposition, dethronement, dismissal, expulsion, impeachment, ouster, overthrow, removal, suspension, unmaking, unseating; downfall, fall
*ant* abasement, demotion, downgrade, reduction
**2** an instance of notable progress in the development of knowledge, technology, or skill — see ADVANCE 2
**3** forward movement in time or place — see ADVANCE 1

**advantage** *n* **1** the more favorable condition or position in a competition ⟨your experience volunteering at the hospital will put you at an *advantage* when you're applying for a job there⟩
*syn* better, drop, edge, jump, upper hand, vantage
*rel* allowance, head start, lead, margin, odds, start; ascendancy, command, dominance, mastery, predominance, superiority, supremacy, transcendence; favoritism, nepotism, precedence, preference, privilege, seniority; break, foothold, opportunity
*near ant* detriment, drawback, penalty, stranglehold; disparity, imbalance, inequality, unevenness; disability, impairment, shortcoming
*ant* disadvantage, handicap, liability
**2** a thing that helps — see HELP 2

**advantageous** *adj* conferring benefits; promoting or contributing to personal or social well-being — see BENEFICIAL

**advent** *n* the act of coming upon a scene — see ARRIVAL

**adventitious** *adj* not being a vital part of or belonging to something — see EXTRINSIC

**adventure** *n* an exciting or noteworthy event that one experiences firsthand ⟨our quiet hike turned into quite an *adventure* when we encountered a bear and her cub⟩
*syn* experience, happening, time
*rel* escapade, lark; act, action, deed, doing, exploit; episode, occasion; baptism, ordeal, test, trial, tribulation; enterprise, risk, venture; expedition, exploration, feat, mission, performance, quest, stunt
*near ant* bore, bummer, bust, drag

**adventure** *vb* to place in danger — see ENDANGER

**adventuresome** *adj* inclined or willing to take risks — see BOLD 1

**adventurous** *adj* inclined or willing to take risks — see BOLD 1

---

*syn* synonym(s) *rel* related words
*ant* antonym(s) *near ant* near antonym(s)

**adversary** *n* **1** one that is hostile toward another — see ENEMY
**2** one that takes a position opposite another in a competition or conflict — see OPPONENT 1

**adverse** *adj* **1** opposed to one's interests ⟨all the *adverse* publicity really caused the movie star's popularity to suffer⟩
*syn* counter, disadvantageous, hostile, inimical, negative, prejudicial, unfavorable, unfriendly, unsympathetic
*rel* bad, baleful, baneful, evil; damaging, deleterious, destructive, detrimental, fatal, harmful, hurtful, injurious, lethal, murderous, poisonous, ruinous, threatening, troublesome, unhealthy, wounding; dangerous, hazardous, imperiling, endangering, perilous, perilous, risky, unsafe; defamatory, detractive, offensive, scathing, slanderous; antagonistic, antipathetic, inhospitable, intolerant, uncongenial, uncooperative; competing, conflicting, counteracting, countering, opposing, resistant, resisting
*near ant* beneficial, good, helpful, propitious, useful; harmless, innocent, innocuous, inoffensive, nondestructive, nonfatal, nonlethal, nonthreatening; unresisting, unresistant; tolerant, understanding; agreeable, affable, amiable, amicable, benign, benignant, congenial, cordial, complying, friendly, hospitable
*ant* advantageous, favorable, friendly, positive, supportive, sympathetic, well-disposed
**2** causing or capable of causing harm — see HARMFUL

**adversity** *n* **1** bad luck or an example of this — see MISFORTUNE
**2** something that is a cause for suffering or special effort especially in the attainment of a goal — see DIFFICULTY 1

**advert** (to) *vb* to make reference to or speak about briefly but specifically — see MENTION 1

**advertise** *vb* to make known openly or publicly — see ANNOUNCE

**advertisement** *n* a published statement informing the public of a matter of general interest — see ANNOUNCEMENT

**advice** *n* an opinion suggesting a wise or proper course of action ⟨Stephanie got some good *advice* from the vet about dealing with her dog's habit of chasing cars⟩
*syn* counsel, guidance
*rel* recommendation, suggestion; hint, pointer, tip; data, feedback, information, answer, solution; advisement, consideration, thought; admonishment, admonition, caution, cautioning, expostulation, remonstration, urging, warning; judgment (*or* judgement), observation, verdict; assistance, briefing, coaching, direction, instruction, mentoring, priming, prompting, teaching, tutoring; interference, kibitzing, meddling; moralizing, pontificating, preaching; exhortation, lecture, lesson, sermon, speech

**advisable** *adj* suitable for bringing about a desired result under the circumstances — see EXPEDIENT

**advise** *vb* **1** to give advice to ⟨a popular guidance counselor who has been *advising* students about their college plans for two decades⟩
*syn* counsel
*rel* admonish, caution, warn; brief, clue (in), fill in, inform, wise (up); coach, direct, lead, guide, instruct, mentor, teach, tutor; acquaint, apprise, familiarize; convince, encourage, induce, persuade, talk (into); beg, exhort, implore, prevail (upon), urge; propose, recommend, suggest
**2** to put forward as one's choice for a wise or proper course of action ⟨she *advised* calling ahead for a reservation at the new restaurant⟩
*syn* counsel, recommend, suggest
*rel* advocate, back, favor, support; exhort, urge; advance, propose, submit
**3** to exchange viewpoints or seek advice for the purpose of finding a solution to a problem — see CONFER 2
**4** to give information to — see ENLIGHTEN 1

**advised** *adj* decided on as a result of careful thought — see DELIBERATE 1

**adviser** *or* **advisor** *n* a person who gives advice especially professionally — see CONSULTANT

**advocate** *n* **1** a person who actively supports or favors a cause — see EXPONENT
**2** a person whose profession is to conduct lawsuits for clients or to advise about legal rights and obligations — see LAWYER

**advocate** *vb* to promote the interests or cause of — see SUPPORT 1

**aegis** *n* means or method of defending — see DEFENSE 1

**aeon** *or* **eon** *n* a long or seemingly long period of time — see AGE 2

**aerodrome** *n*, *British* a place from which aircraft operate that usually has paved runways and a terminal — see AIRPORT

**affability** *n* the state or quality of having a pleasant or agreeable manner in socializing with others — see AMIABILITY 1

**affable** *adj* **1** having a relaxed, casual manner — see EASYGOING 1
**2** having an easygoing and pleasing manner especially in social situations — see AMIABLE
**3** showing a natural kindness and courtesy especially in social situations — see GRACIOUS 1

**affair** *n* **1** a brief romantic relationship ⟨an *affair* between two teenagers spending the summer at the same beach resort⟩
*syn* love affair, romance
*rel* amour, intrigue; attachment, infatuation; entanglement, fling, flirtation; liaison, passion
**2** a social gathering — see PARTY 1
**3** something produced by physical or intellectual effort — see PRODUCT 1
**4** something that happens — see EVENT 1

**5** something to be dealt with — see MATTER 2

[1]**affect** *vb* **1** to act upon (a person or a person's feelings) so as to cause a response ⟨Gary claims that scary movies don't *affect* him in the least⟩
***syn*** impact, impress, influence, move, strike, sway, tell (on), touch
***rel*** bias, color; inspire, stir; carry, engage, interest, involve, penetrate, pierce; afflict, agitate, bother, discomfort, discompose, disquiet, distress, disturb, fluster, harass, harry, perturb, pester, plague, smite, strain, stress, trouble, try, upset, worry, wring; allure, attract, bewitch, captivate, charm, dazzle, enchant
***phrases*** get to
***near ant*** bore, jade, pall, tire, weary
**2** to be the business or affair of — see CONCERN 2

[2]**affect** *vb* to present a false appearance of — see FEIGN

**affectation** *n* the quality or state of appearing or trying to appear more important or more valuable than is the case — see PRETENSE 1

**affected** *adj* **1** lacking in natural or spontaneous quality — see ARTIFICIAL 1
**2** self-consciously trying to present an appearance of grandeur or importance — see PRETENTIOUS 1

**affectedness** *n* the quality or state of appearing or trying to appear more important or more valuable than is the case — see PRETENSE 1

**affecting** *adj* having the power to affect the feelings or sympathies — see MOVING

[1]**affection** *n* a feeling of strong or constant regard for and dedication to someone — see LOVE 1

[2]**affection** *n* an abnormal state that disrupts a plant's or animal's normal bodily functioning — see DISEASE

**affectionate** *adj* feeling or showing love — see LOVING

**affianced** *adj* pledged in marriage — see ENGAGED

**affiliate** *n* a local unit of an organization — see CHAPTER

**affiliated** *adj* having a close connection like that between family members — see RELATED

**affiliation** *n* the state of having shared interests or efforts (as in social or business matters) — see ASSOCIATION 1

**affirm** *vb* **1** to state as a fact usually forcefully — see CLAIM 1
**2** to state clearly and strongly — see ASSERT 1

**affirmation** *n* a solemn and often public declaration of the truth or existence of something — see PROTESTATION

**affirmative** *adj* showing or expressing acceptance or approval — see POSITIVE

**affix** *vb* to cause (something) to hold to another — see FASTEN 1

---

***syn*** synonym(s) ***rel*** related words
***ant*** antonym(s) ***near ant*** near antonym(s)

**afflict** *vb* to cause persistent suffering to ⟨the South was *afflicted* by a severe drought⟩ ⟨he's been *afflicted* by nightmares ever since the accident⟩
***syn*** agonize, bedevil, curse, harrow, martyr, persecute, plague, rack, torment, torture
***rel*** assail, attack, beset, set upon; badger, dog, hound, ride; agitate, annoy, bother, distress, disturb, harass, harry, irk, molest, pester; discomfort, discompose, disquiet, fluster, perturb, strain, stress, trouble, try, upset, vex, worry; crush, oppress, overpower, overwhelm, smite, strike, tyrannize; pain, prick, stab, sting, wring
***near ant*** abet, aid, assist, help; deliver, release, relieve, reprieve; comfort, console, solace, soothe, succor

**afflicting** *adj* hard to accept or bear especially emotionally — see BITTER 2

**affliction** *n* **1** a state of great suffering of body or mind — see DISTRESS 1
**2** deep sadness especially for the loss of someone or something loved — see SORROW

**affluent** *adj* having goods, property, or money in abundance — see RICH 1

**affray** *n* a rough and often noisy fight usually involving several people — see BRAWL 1

**affright** *vb* to strike with fear — see FRIGHTEN

**affrighted** *adj* filled with fear or dread — see AFRAID 1

**affront** *n* an act or expression showing scorn and usually intended to hurt another's feelings — see INSULT

**affront** *vb* to cause hurt feelings or deep resentment in — see INSULT

**aficionado** *n* a person with a strong and habitual liking for something — see FAN

**afield** *adv* off the desired or intended path or course — see WRONG 1

**afire** *adj* being on fire — see ABLAZE 1

**aflame** *adj* being on fire — see ABLAZE 1

**aflutter** *adj* feeling or showing uncomfortable feelings of uncertainty — see NERVOUS 1

**afoot** *adj* being in progress or development — see ONGOING 1

**afore** *adv, chiefly dialect* so as to precede something in order of time — see AHEAD 1

**afore** *prep, chiefly dialect* **1** earlier than — see BEFORE 1
**2** preceding in space — see BEFORE 2

**afraid** *adj* **1** filled with fear or dread ⟨Melissa is *afraid* of flying, so she takes a train from Boston to visit her brother in Chicago⟩
***syn*** affrighted, aghast, alarmed, fearful, frightened, horrified, scared, spooked, terrified, terrorized
***rel*** fainthearted, fearsome, shrinking, shy, timid, timorous, tremulous; agitated, anxious, apprehensive, disconcerted, disquieted, disturbed, jittery, jumpy, nervous, panicky, perturbed, skittish, uneasy, upset, worried; appalled, dismayed, shocked, startled; cowed, daunted, intim-

idated, unnerved; coward, cowardly, craven, gutless, lily-livered, pusillanimous; careful, cautious, heedful, prudent, unadventurous, wary
*near ant* adventuresome, adventurous, audacious, bold, daredevil, daring, dashing, gutsy, plucky, spirited, spunky, venturesome, venturous; brave, courageous, gallant, hardy, heroic, intrepid, lionhearted, manful, stalwart, stout, stouthearted, valiant, valorous; assured, collected, composed, confident, cool, sanguine, sure, unperturbed; dauntless, resolute, undaunted
*ant* fearless, unafraid
2 having doubts about the wisdom of doing something — see HESITANT

**afresh** *adv* yet another time — see AGAIN 1

**aft** *adv* near, toward, or in the stern of a ship or the tail of an aircraft ⟨after transferring the controls to the copilot, the captain went *aft* to see what the disturbance was⟩
*syn* abaft, astern
*rel* after, back, backward, behind, posteriorly, rearward (*also* rearwards), rearwardly
*near ant* anteriorly; ahead, before
*ant* fore, forward

**after** *adj* being, occurring, or carried out at a time after something else — see SUBSEQUENT

**after** *adv* following in time or place ⟨upon seeing *The Nutcracker* for the first time, and for a long time *after*, Irma wanted to play the part of the Mouse King⟩
*syn* afterward (*or* afterwards), later, subsequently, thereafter
*rel* next; by and by, hereafter, presently, since, soon, then, thereupon
*near ant* antecedently, formerly; heretofore, theretofore
*ant* afore [*chiefly dialect*], before, beforehand, earlier, previously

**after** *prep* subsequent to in time or order ⟨the high school band came right *after* the mayor in the parade⟩
*syn* behind, following
*rel* next; since
*near ant* of, to, toward (*or* towards)
*ant* afore [*chiefly dialect*], ahead of, before, ere, previous to, prior to

**aftereffect** *n* a condition or occurrence traceable to a cause — see EFFECT 1

**afterlife** *n* unending existence after death — see ETERNITY 2

**aftermath** *n* a condition or occurrence traceable to a cause — see EFFECT 1

**afterward** *or* **afterwards** *adv* following in time or place — see AFTER

**again** *adv* 1 yet another time ⟨now I have to mop the floor *again* because you didn't wipe your feet⟩
*syn* afresh, anew, over
*rel* always, constantly, continuously, endlessly, ever, evermore, perpetually; frequently, often; recurrently, repeatedly; freshly, newly
*near ant* ne'er, never
*ant* nevermore
2 in addition to what has been said — see MORE 1
3 just the opposite being true — see CONTRARIWISE

**against** *prep* in or into contact with ⟨he leaned *against* the fence and it collapsed⟩ ⟨unwittingly rubbed his leg *against* some poison ivy⟩
*syn* on, upon
*rel* alongside, next, next to

**agape** *adj* having or showing signs of eagerly awaiting something — see EXPECTANT 1

**age** *n* 1 an extent of time associated with a particular person or thing ⟨the Bronze *Age* marks the beginning of the use of metal by ancient peoples⟩
*syn* day, epoch, era, period, time
*rel* cycle, generation, year; span, spell, stretch, while
2 a long or seemingly long period of time ⟨it took *ages* for the clerk to ring up three items⟩
*syn* aeon (*or* eon), cycle, eternity
*rel* infinity; lifetime
*near ant* flash, instant, jiffy, minute, moment, second, trice, twinkle, twinkling, wink; microsecond, nanosecond

**age** *vb* to become mature — see MATURE

**aged** *adj* 1 being of advanced years and especially past middle age — see ELDERLY
2 dating or surviving from the distant past — see ANCIENT 1

**agency** *n* something used to achieve an end — see AGENT 1

**agenda** *n* a listing of things to be presented or considered (as at a concert or play) — see PROGRAM 1

**agent** *n* 1 something used to achieve an end ⟨the whitening *agent* in the detergent is chlorine bleach⟩ ⟨the Church has been the traditional *agent* for social justice in impoverished countries⟩
*syn* agency, instrument, instrumentality, machinery, means, medium, organ, vehicle
*rel* determinant, expedient, factor, influence, ingredient, mechanism, tool; activator, catalyst, driver, energizer, executor, generator, instigator, launcher, mover, power, stimulus, trigger
2 a person who acts or does business for another ⟨the sports *agent* negotiated a record-breaking contract for the baseball player⟩
*syn* attorney, commissary, delegate, deputy, envoy, factor, procurator, proxy, representative
*rel* ambassador, emissary, foreign minister, legate, minister; alternate, backup, pinch hitter, relief, replacement, stand-in, sub, substitute, surrogate, understudy; informer, operative, spy; broker, distributor, manager; arbiter, arbitrator, go-between, intercessor, intermediary, interposer, liaison, mediator, middleman; mouthpiece, spokesperson

**age-old** *adj* dating or surviving from the distant past — see ANCIENT 1

**agglomerate** *vb* to form into a round compact mass — see WAD

**aggrandize** *vb* **1** to enhance the status of — see EXALT
**2** to make greater in size, amount, or number — see INCREASE 1

**aggravate** *vb* to disturb the peace of mind of (someone) especially by repeated disagreeable acts — see IRRITATE 1

**aggravating** *adj* **1** causing annoyance — see ANNOYING

**aggravation** *n* **1** something that is a source of irritation — see ANNOYANCE 3
**2** the act of making unwelcome intrusions upon another — see ANNOYANCE 1
**3** the feeling of impatience or anger caused by another's repeated disagreeable acts — see ANNOYANCE 2

**aggregate** *n* a complete amount of something — see WHOLE

**aggression** *n* **1** an inclination to fight or quarrel — see BELLIGERENCE
**2** the act or action of setting upon with force or violence — see ATTACK 1

**aggressive** *adj* **1** having or showing a bold forcefulness in the pursuit of a goal ⟨if you don't take a more *aggressive* approach to this yard pretty soon, the weeds are going to take over completely⟩
***syn*** ambitious, assertive, enterprising, fierce, go-getting, high-pressure, in-your-face, militant, self-assertive
***rel*** dynamic, energetic, gung ho, hustling, scrappy, strenuous, vigorous; emphatic, obtrusive; adventuresome, adventurous, venturesome, venturous; audacious, bold, brash, brassy, cheeky, cocksure, cocky, confident, determined, forward, impudent, insolent, overconfident, presumptuous, unapologetic, unsubdued, unyielding; dominating, domineering, imperious, lordly, magisterial, overbearing
***near ant*** easygoing, laid-back, relaxed; acquiescent, compliant, deferential, resigned, submissive, yielding; cowering, cringing, groveling (*or* grovelling), shrinking; bashful, diffident, meek, mousy (*or* mousey), overmodest, passive, quiet, reserved, retiring, shy, subdued, timid, unobtrusive
***ant*** low-pressure, unaggressive, unambitious, unassertive, unenterprising
**2** feeling or displaying eagerness to fight — see BELLIGERENT
**3** marked by or uttered with forcefulness — see EMPHATIC 1

**aggressiveness** *n* **1** readiness to engage in daring or difficult activity — see ENTERPRISE 2
**2** the quality or state of being forceful (as in expression) — see VEHEMENCE 1
**3** an inclination to fight or quarrel — see BELLIGERENCE

**aggressor** *n* one that starts armed conflict against another especially without reasonable cause ⟨the countries formed an alliance to deter potential *aggressors*⟩
***syn*** invader, raider
***rel*** initiator, instigator; ambuscader, assailant, attacker, pillager, plunderer; hawk, militarist, warmonger; belligerent, combatant
***near ant*** defender; dove, pacifist, peacemaker; nonbelligerent

**aggrieved** *adj* having a feeling that one has been wronged or thwarted in one's ambitions — see DISCONTENTED

**aghast** *adj* filled with fear or dread — see AFRAID 1

**agile** *adj* moving easily — see GRACEFUL 1

**agility** *n* ease and grace in physical activity — see DEXTERITY 2

**aging** *adj* being of advanced years and especially past middle age — see ELDERLY

**agitate** *vb* **1** to cause (as a liquid) to move about in a circle especially repeatedly — see STIR 1
**2** to trouble the mind of; to make uneasy — see DISTURB 1
**3** to make a series of small irregular or violent movements — see SHAKE 1

**agitated** *adj* **1** being in a state of increased activity or agitation — see FEVERISH 1
**2** feeling overwhelming fear or worry — see FRANTIC 1

**agitating** *adj* marked by or causing agitation or uncomfortable feelings — see NERVOUS 2

**agitation** *n* **1** a state of wildly excited activity or emotion — see FRENZY
**2** an uneasy state of mind usually over the possibility of an anticipated misfortune or trouble — see ANXIETY 1

**agitator** *n* a person who stirs up public feelings especially of discontent ⟨a political *agitator* who led an unsuccessful revolt against the government⟩
***syn*** demagogue (*also* demagog), exciter, firebrand, fomenter, incendiary, inciter, instigator, rabble-rouser
***rel*** demonstrator, marcher, objector, picketer, protester (*or* protestor); advocate, champion, exponent, persuader, promoter, proponent, reformer, supporter; alarmist, extremist, insurgent, insurrectionist, radical, rebel, revolter, revolutionary, revolutionist, subversive, troublemaker

**aglow** *adj* having or being an outward sign of good feelings (as of love, confidence, or happiness) — see RADIANT 1

**agog** *adj* **1** having or showing signs of eagerly awaiting something — see EXPECTANT 1
**2** showing urgent desire or interest — see EAGER

**agonize** *vb* **1** to cause persistent suffering to — see AFFLICT
**2** to feel deep sadness or mental pain — see GRIEVE

**agonizing** *adj* **1** hard to accept or bear especially emotionally — see BITTER 2
**2** intensely or unbearably painful — see EXCRUCIATING 1
**3** causing intense mental or physical distress — see SHARP 2

**agonizingly** *adv* with feelings of bitterness or grief — see HARD 2

**agony** *n* **1** a situation or state that causes great suffering and unhappiness — see HELL 2
**2** a state of great suffering of body or mind — see DISTRESS 1
**3** a sudden intense expression of strong feeling — see OUTBURST 1

**agrarian** *adj* engaged in or concerned with agriculture — see AGRICULTURAL

**agree** *vb* **1** to have or come to the same opinion or point of view ⟨since we couldn't *agree*, we tossed a coin to decide the matter⟩
*syn* coincide, concur
*rel* accede (to), accept, acquiesce, assent (to), comply (with), consent (to), go (by), subscribe; affiliate, ally, associate, unite; collaborate, cooperate, get along
*phrases* see eye to eye
*near ant* clash, collide, conflict; bicker, counter, dispute, dissent, diverge, fall out, object, oppose, protest, quarrel, resist, rival; dissociate, separate, split
*ant* differ, disagree
**2** to accept the truth or existence of (something) usually reluctantly — see ADMIT
**3** to be in agreement on every point — see CHECK 1
**4** to form a pleasing relationship — see HARMONIZE 1

**agreeable** *adj* **1** being to one's liking — see SATISFACTORY 1
**2** giving pleasure or contentment to the mind or senses — see PLEASANT
**3** having an easygoing and pleasing manner especially in social situations — see AMIABLE
**4** having or marked by agreement in feeling or action — see HARMONIOUS 3

**agreeableness** *n* the state or quality of having a pleasant or agreeable manner in socializing with others — see AMIABILITY 1

**agreeably** *adv* in a pleasing way — see WELL 5

**agreement** *n* **1** the act or fact of being of one opinion about something ⟨I only had the energy to nod in *agreement* when Cheryl said we'd never worked so hard in all our lives⟩
*syn* accord, concurrence, consensus, unanimity, unison
*rel* accession, assent, consent; acceptance, acquiescence, compliance, concession, conformity; approbation, approval, favor; alliance, collaboration, collusion, complicity, conspiracy; concord, consonance, harmony, oneness, solidarity, understanding, union; empathy, rapport, sympathy
*near ant* conflict, discord, dissension; opposition, resistance; disapprobation, disapproval, disfavor
*ant* disagreement, dissent
**2** an arrangement about action to be taken ⟨we finally reached an *agreement* regarding a fair division of the housework⟩
*syn* accord, bargain, compact, contract, convention, covenant, deal, pact, settlement, understanding
*rel* charter, treaty; pledge, promise; alliance, association, league, partnership; acceptance, approval, assent, concurrence, consent, OK (*or* okay)
**3** a state of consistency — see CONFORMITY 1

**agricultural** *adj* engaged in or concerned with agriculture ⟨he grew up in an *agricultural* community⟩
*syn* agrarian, farming
*rel* pastoral, rural
*near ant* metropolitan, urban; industrial, industrialized
*ant* nonagricultural

**agriculture** *n* the science or occupation of cultivating the soil, producing crops, and raising livestock ⟨the forest was cut down, and the land given over to *agriculture*⟩
*syn* farming, husbandry
*rel* agronomy; animal husbandry

**agriculturist** *or* **agriculturalist** *n* a person who cultivates the land and grows crops on it — see FARMER

**agronomist** *n* a person who cultivates the land and grows crops on it — see FARMER

**aground** *adj* resting on the shore or bottom of a body of water ⟨the villagers came to stare at the foreign ship that was *aground* on their beach and at the strangely dressed sailors on board⟩
*syn* beached, grounded, stranded
*rel* landed; alongshore
*near ant* offshore
*ant* afloat

**ah** *interj* how surprising, doubtful, or unbelievable — see NO

**aha** *interj* how surprising, doubtful, or unbelievable — see NO

**ahead** *adv* **1** so as to precede something in order of time ⟨we were cautioned not to fill out any of the test answers *ahead* of time⟩ ⟨call *ahead* for reservations⟩
*syn* afore [*chiefly dialect*], antecedently, anteriorly, before, beforehand, previously
*rel* formerly
*phrases* in advance
*near ant* behind, by and by, next, presently, subsequently
*ant* after, afterward (*or* afterwards), later
**2** toward a point ahead in space or time — see ONWARD 1
**3** toward or at a point lying in advance in space or time — see ALONG

**ahead of** *prep* **1** earlier than — see BEFORE 1
**2** preceding in space — see BEFORE 2

**aid** *n* **1** a person who helps a more skilled person — see HELPER
**2** a thing that helps — see HELP 2
**3** an act or instance of helping — see HELP 1

**aid** *vb* to provide (someone) with what is useful or necessary to achieve an end — see HELP 1

**aide** *n* a person who helps a more skilled person — see HELPER

**ailing** *adj* **1** chronically or repeatedly suffering from poor health — see SICKLY 1
**2** temporarily suffering from a disorder of the body — see SICK 1

**ailment** *n* an abnormal state that disrupts a plant's or animal's normal bodily functioning — see DISEASE

**aim** *n* something that one hopes or intends to accomplish — see GOAL

**aim** *vb* **1** to point or turn (something) toward a target or goal ⟨the anti-drug campaign was *aimed* primarily at preteens⟩
***syn*** bend, cast, direct, head, level, set, train
***rel*** bear, face; concentrate, focus; incline, orient, steer
***near ant*** avert, curve, deflect, detour, divert, rechannel, shunt, sidetrack
**2** to have in mind as a purpose or goal — see INTEND

**aimless** *adj* lacking a definite plan, purpose, or pattern — see RANDOM

**aimlessly** *adv* without definite aim, direction, rule, or method — see HIT OR MISS

**air** *n* **1** a rhythmic series of musical tones arranged to give a pleasing effect — see MELODY
**2** a slight or gentle movement of air — see BREEZE 1
**3** a special quality or impression associated with something — see AURA
**4 airs** *pl* a display of emotion or behavior that is insincere or intended to deceive — see MASQUERADE

**air** *vb* to make known (as an idea, emotion, or opinion) — see EXPRESS 1

**airdrome** *n* a place from which aircraft operate that usually has paved runways and a terminal — see AIRPORT

**airfield** *n* a place from which aircraft operate that usually has paved runways and a terminal — see AIRPORT

**airman** *n* one who flies or is qualified to fly an aircraft or spacecraft — see PILOT

**airport** *n* a place from which aircraft operate that usually has paved runways and a terminal ⟨the *airport* nearest us has plane service on only one major airline⟩
***syn*** aerodrome [*British*], airdrome, airfield
***rel*** air base, heliport; airstrip, landing field, landing strip, runway; launchpad, pad

**airy** *adj* **1** resembling air in lightness ⟨Aunt Helen's lemon pies are famous for their *airy* meringues⟩
***syn*** ethereal, fluffy, gossamer, gossamery, light
***rel*** dainty, delicate, downy, feathery, flimsy, insubstantial, tender, wispy; buoyant, lighter-than-air, lightweight, rarefied, unsubstantial, weightless
***near ant*** firm, solid, substantial; bulky, burdensome, cumbersome, hefty, hulking, lumpish, ponderous, unwieldy, weighty
***ant*** heavy, leaden
**2** having little weight — see [1]LIGHT 1
**3** located at a greater height than average or usual — see HIGH 3

**akin** *adj* **1** having a close connection like that between family members — see RELATED
**2** having qualities in common — see ALIKE

**alacritous** *adj* having or showing the ability to respond without delay or hesitation — see QUICK 1

**alacrity** *n* cheerful readiness to do something ⟨having just acquired his driver's license that morning, Sam agreed with *alacrity* to drive his cousin to the airport⟩
***syn*** amenability, gameness, goodwill, willingness
***rel*** celebrity, quickness, rapidity, speed, speediness, swiftness; dispatch, promptitude, promptness; ardor, avidity, eagerness, enthusiasm, exuberance, fervor, gusto, keenness, relish, zeal, zest; agreeableness, geniality, good-naturedness, heartiness, warmth; open-mindedness, receptivity, responsiveness
***near ant*** leisureliness, pokiness, slowness, sluggishness; apathy, disinterestedness, halfheartedness, indifference, lukewarmness, perfunctoriness; delay, dilatoriness, doubt, equivocation, hesitance, hesitancy, hesitation, reluctance, reservation, uncertainty, vacillation; disinclination, indisposition, recalcitrance, resistance, unwillingness; antipathy, averseness, aversion

**à la mode** *also* **a la mode** *adj* being in the latest or current fashion — see STYLISH

**alarm** *n* **1** suspicion or fear of future harm or misfortune — see APPREHENSION 1
**2** the act or an instance of telling beforehand of danger or risk — see WARNING 1
**3** the emotion experienced in the presence or threat of danger — see FEAR

**alarm** *vb* to strike with fear — see FRIGHTEN

**alarmed** *adj* filled with fear or dread — see AFRAID 1

**alarming** *adj* causing fear — see FEARFUL 1

**albeit** *conj* in spite of the fact that — see ALTHOUGH

**album** *n* a collection of writings — see ANTHOLOGY

**alcohol** *n* a fermented or distilled beverage that can make a person drunk ⟨once he joined the swim team, Sergei never again touched *alcohol*⟩
***syn*** booze, drink, grog, intoxicant, liquor, moonshine, spirits
***rel*** ale, beer, mead, sake (*or* saki), table wine, wine; brandy, gin, mescal, rum, tequila, vodka, whiskey (*or* whisky)

**alcove** *n* a hollowed-out space in a wall — see NICHE 1

---

***syn*** synonym(s) ***rel*** related words
***ant*** antonym(s) ***near ant*** near antonym(s)

**alert** *adj* **1** paying close attention usually for the purpose of anticipating approaching danger or opportunity ⟨Susan needed to stay *alert* throughout the train ride so as not to miss her stop⟩
***syn*** attentive, awake, open-eyed, vigilant, watchful, wide-awake
***rel*** alive, aware, conscious; sensitive; heedful, mindful, observant, observing, sharp, sharp-eyed; sleepless, wakeful; careful, cautious, chary, wary; prepared, ready
***phrases*** on guard, on the alert
***near ant*** absent, absentminded; absorbed, abstracted, daydreaming, dazed, distracted, dreaming, dreamy, engrossed, faraway, insensible, oblivious, preoccupied; asleep, sleeping, unaware, unconscious, unknowing, unperceiving, unseeing, unwitting; careless, heedless, inattentive, unheeding, unmindful, unobservant, unobserving, unthinking, unwary; unprepared, unready
**2** having or showing a close attentiveness to avoiding danger or trouble — see CAREFUL 1
**3** having or showing quickness of mind — see INTELLIGENT 1
**4** having or showing the ability to respond without delay or hesitation — see QUICK 1

**alert** *n* the act or an instance of telling beforehand of danger or risk — see WARNING 1

**alert** *vb* to give notice to beforehand especially of danger or risk — see WARN

**alertness** *n* **1** a close attentiveness to avoiding danger — see CAUTION 1
**2** the act or state of being constantly attentive and responsive to signs of opportunity, activity, or danger — see VIGILANCE

**alias** *n* **1** a descriptive or familiar name given instead of or in addition to the one belonging to an individual — see NICKNAME
**2** a fictitious or assumed name — see PSEUDONYM

**alibi** *n* an explanation that frees one from fault or blame — see EXCUSE

**alien** *adj* **1** being, relating to, or characteristic of a country other than one's own — see FOREIGN 1
**2** not being a vital part of or belonging to something — see EXTRINSIC

**alienate** *vb* **1** to cause to change from friendly or loving to unfriendly or unearing — see ESTRANGE
**2** to give over the legal possession or ownership of — see TRANSFER 1

**alienation** *n* the loss of friendship or affection — see ESTRANGEMENT

**alight** *adj* filled with much light — see BRIGHT 2

**alight** *vb* to come to rest after descending from the air ⟨a flock of eight swans circled above, then *alighted* on the pond⟩
***syn*** land, light, perch, roost, settle, touch down
***rel*** belly-land, crash-land
***near ant*** arise, ascend, climb, rise; float, fly, glide, plane, soar, wing; hang, hover
***ant*** take off

**alike** *adj* having qualities in common ⟨all the houses in the neighborhood are *alike* in that they all have a one-car garage and a fenced-in backyard⟩
***syn*** akin, analogous, comparable, correspondent, corresponding, like, matching, parallel, resembling, similar, such, suchlike
***rel*** commensurate, proportionate; tantamount, virtual; allied, kindred, related; approaching, approximating, close, coextensive, coincident, conformable, conforming, consistent, consonant, equal, equivalent, identical, indistinguishable, interchangeable, same, selfsame, synonymous, twin; homogeneous, unchanging, uniform, unvaried, unvarying
***phrases*** on the order of
***near ant*** disparate, distinct, distinguishable; variable, varied, varying; imprecise, inaccurate, inexact; unallied, unconnected, unrelated
***ant*** different, dissimilar, diverse, unlike

**alike** *adv* in like manner — see ALSO 1

**alikeness** *n* the quality or state of having many qualities in common — see SIMILARITY 1

**alive** *adj* **1** having or showing life ⟨after crashing into the plate glass window the little bird was not only still *alive*, it seemed merely dazed⟩
***syn*** animate, breathing, live, living
***rel*** active, animated, dynamic, lively, thriving, vibrant, vital, vivacious; current, existent, existing, extant, going, prevailing, surviving
***near ant*** dying, fading, moribund; stillborn; absent, extinct, fallen, finished, gone, lapsed, lost, nonexistent, perished, terminated, vanished, wiped out; barren, desert
***ant*** breathless, dead, deceased, defunct, departed, expired, inanimate, lifeless, nonliving
**2** marked by much life, movement, or activity ⟨the mall was *alive* with holiday shoppers⟩
***syn*** animated, astir, bustling, busy, buzzing, flourishing, humming, lively, thriving, vibrant
***rel*** abounding, crowded, overflowing, populous, swarming, teeming, thronging
***ant*** asleep, dead, inactive, lifeless, sleepy
**3** being in effective operation — see ACTIVE 1
**4** having being at the present time — see EXTANT 1
**5** having specified facts or feelings actively impressed on the mind — see CONSCIOUS

**all** *adj* not divided or scattered among several areas of interest or concern — see WHOLE 1

**all** *adv* **1** to a full extent or degree — see FULLY 1
**2** for each one — see APIECE

**all** *pron* every person — see EVERYBODY

**Allah** *n* the being worshipped as the creator and ruler of the universe — see DEITY 2

**all–around** *also* **all-round** *adj* **1** not limited or specialized in application or purpose — see GENERAL 4
**2** relating to the main elements and not to specific details — see GENERAL 2
**3** able to do many different kinds of things — see VERSATILE

**allay** *vb* **1** to free from distress or disturbance — see CALM 1
**2** to make more bearable or less severe — see HELP 2

**allege** *vb* to state as a fact usually forcefully — see CLAIM 1

**allegiance** *n* adherence to something to which one is bound by a pledge or duty — see FIDELITY

**allegory** *n* a story intended to teach a basic truth or moral about life ⟨Dr. Seuss's story "The Sneetches" is an *allegory* about tolerance for people's differences⟩
***syn*** fable, parable
***rel*** morality play; legend, myth, narrative, tale

**allergic** *adj* having a natural dislike for something — see ANTIPATHETIC

**allergy** *n* a strong feeling of not liking or approving — see DISLIKE 1

**alleviate** *vb* to make more bearable or less severe — see HELP 2

**alleviation** *n* reduction of or freedom from pain — see EASE 1

**alliance** *n* **1** a formal agreement between two or more nations or peoples — see TREATY
**2** an association of persons, parties, or states for mutual assistance and protection — see CONFEDERACY
**3** the state of having shared interests or efforts (as in social or business matters) — see ASSOCIATION 1

**allied** *adj* having a close connection like that between family members — see RELATED

**all–important** *adj* impossible to do without — see ESSENTIAL 1

**allocate** *vb* **1** to give as a share or portion — see ALLOT
**2** to give out (something) in appropriate amounts or to appropriate individuals — see ADMINISTER 1
**3** to keep or intend for a special purpose — see DEVOTE 1

**allocation** *n* **1** a sum of money allotted for a specific use by official or formal action — see APPROPRIATION
**2** the act or process of giving out something to each member of a group — see DISTRIBUTION 1

**allot** *vb* to give as a share or portion ⟨each speaker was *allotted* five minutes to present his or her opinion in the debate⟩
***syn*** allocate, allow, apportion, assign, ration
***rel*** deal, dispense, distribute, divide, dole (out), measure, mete (out), parcel (out), portion, prorate, reserve; accord, award, grant; chip in, contribute, donate
***near ant*** begrudge, deny, deprive (of); keep, retain, stint, withhold; appropriate, arrogate, confiscate

**allotment** *n* **1** a sum of money allotted for a specific use by official or formal action — see APPROPRIATION
**2** something belonging to, due to, or contributed by an individual member of a group — see SHARE 1

**all–out** *adj* **1** having no exceptions or restrictions — see ABSOLUTE 2
**2** trying all possibilities — see EXHAUSTIVE

**all out** *adv* with all power or resources being used — see FULL BLAST

**all over** *adv* in every place or in all places — see EVERYWHERE

**allow** *vb* **1** to give permission for or to approve of ⟨flash photography is not *allowed* inside the church⟩
***syn*** have, permit, suffer
***rel*** authorize, commission, license (*also* licence); accede (to), acquiesce, agree (to), assent (to), consent (to), OK (*or* okay), warrant; accord, concede, grant, sanction, vouchsafe; admit, brook, condone, countenance, endure, support, tolerate
***near ant*** hinder, impede, obstruct; censure, disallow, disapprove, deny, interdict, refuse, reject, revoke, suppress, withhold; deplore, discountenance, dislike, disfavor, frown (at *or* on); check, curb, repress, restrain
***ant*** ban, enjoin, forbid, prohibit, proscribe, veto
**2** to give permission to ⟨Cindy's parents sometimes *allow* her to take the bus by herself downtown⟩
***syn*** let, permit, suffer
***rel*** authorize, commission, empower, license (*also* licence); approve, endorse (*also* indorse), sanction; free, liberate, release; cater (to), give in (to), humor, indulge
***near ant*** deter, discourage; bar, block, constrain, curb, frustrate, hold back, impede, inhibit, obstruct, prevent
***ant*** enjoin, forbid, prohibit
**3** to accept the truth or existence of (something) usually reluctantly — see ADMIT
**4** to give as a share or portion — see ALLOT
**5** to make able or possible — see ENABLE 1

**allowable** *adj* that may be permitted — see PERMISSIBLE

**allowance** *n* **1** something belonging to, due to, or contributed by an individual member of a group — see SHARE 1
**2** the approval by someone in authority for the doing of something — see PERMISSION

**alloyed** *adj* containing foreign or lower-grade substances — see IMPURE

---

***syn*** synonym(s) ***rel*** related words
***ant*** antonym(s) ***near ant*** near antonym(s)

**all–powerful** *adj* having unlimited power or authority — see OMNIPOTENT

**all–purpose** *adj* not limited or specialized in application or purpose — see GENERAL 4

**all right** *adj* **1** being to one's liking — see SATISFACTORY 1
**2** not exposed to the threat of loss or injury — see SAFE 1
**3** of a level of quality that meets one's needs or standards — see ADEQUATE

**all right** *adv* **1** in a satisfactory way — see WELL 1
**2** used to express agreement — see YES

**allude** *vb* to convey an idea indirectly — see HINT

**allure** *n* the power of irresistible attraction — see CHARM 2

**allure** *vb* **1** to attract or delight as if by magic — see CHARM 1
**2** to lead away from a usual or proper course by offering some pleasure or advantage — see LURE

**allurement** *n* **1** something that persuades one to perform an action for pleasure or gain — see LURE 1
**2** the act or pressure of giving in to a desire especially when ill-advised — see TEMPTATION 1

**alluring** *adj* having an often mysterious or magical power to attract — see FASCINATING 1

**ally** *n* someone associated with another to give assistance or moral support ⟨in trying to convince his parents to send him to soccer camp, Toby had a real *ally* in his coach⟩
*syn* abettor (*also* abetter), backer, confederate, supporter, sympathizer
*rel* well-wisher; accessory, accomplice, collaborationist, collaborator; adjunct, assistant, coadjutor, helper; associate, cohort, colleague, fellow, partner; buddy, chum, companion, comrade, confidant, crony, familiar, friend, intimate, mate, pal
*near ant* belittler, detractor; adversary, enemy, foe, opponent

**ally** *vb* to form or enter into an association that furthers the interests of its members ⟨the area's small grape growers have *allied* and formed a cooperative that will help them get the best prices⟩
*syn* associate, band, club, confederate, conjoin, cooperate, federate, league, unite
*rel* collaborate, gang (up), team (up); incorporate, organize, unionize; affiliate; amalgamate, combine, conglomerate, consolidate, converge, group, join, merge; knot, link, tie, wed
*near ant* detach, disengage, dissolve, disunite, divorce, part, segregate, separate, sever, split, sunder; alienate, estrange, fall out
*ant* break up, disband

**almighty** *adj* having unlimited power or authority — see OMNIPOTENT

**Almighty** *n* the being worshipped as the creator and ruler of the universe — see DEITY 2

**almost** *adv* very close to but not completely ⟨we were *almost* finished with dinner when Uncle Richard showed up⟩ ⟨there were *almost* enough seats for everybody on the bus⟩
*syn* about, more or less, most, much, near, nearly, next to, nigh, practically, some, virtually, well-nigh
*rel* appreciably, by and large, chiefly, largely, mainly, mostly; partially, partly, somewhat
*phrases* as good as
*near ant* absolutely, altogether, completely, entirely, fully, plumb [*chiefly dialect*], quite, thoroughly; totally, utterly, wholly; barely, hardly, scarcely

**alms** *n* a gift of money or its equivalent to a charity, humanitarian cause, or public institution — see CONTRIBUTION

**almsgiving** *n* the giving of necessities and especially money to the needy — see CHARITY 1

**aloft** *adv* to or in a higher place — see ABOVE

**alone** *adj* **1** not being in the company of others ⟨no one realized Jeff was *alone* in his room so they all left for the movies without him⟩
*syn* lone, lonely, lonesome, solitary, solo, unaccompanied
*rel* unattended, unchaperoned; forlorn, friendless; cloistered, insulated, isolated, remote, retired, secluded, withdrawn; quarantined, segregated, separated, sequestered; separate, unattached, unconnected, unlinked; detached, disconnected, disjointed, dissociated, disunited, divided, fractionated; abandoned, adrift, deserted, desolate, forgotten, forsaken, lorn, neglected
*near ant* attended, chaperoned, escorted; adjacent, adjoining, communicating, contiguous, neighboring, next-door; attached, connected, coupled, linked
*ant* accompanied
**2** being the one or ones of a class with no other members — see ONLY 2

**alone** *adv* **1** without aid or support ⟨Rebecca managed to find her way home *alone*⟩
*syn* independently, single-handedly, singly, solely, unaided, unassisted
*rel* individually, separately
*phrases* by oneself
*near ant* collectively, conjointly, cooperatively, jointly, mutually, together; en masse
**2** for nothing other than — see SOLELY 1

**along** *adv* toward or at a point lying in advance in space or time ⟨traffic was inching *along* at a snail's pace⟩ ⟨work on the project is moving right *along*⟩
*syn* ahead, forth, forward, on, onward (*also* onwards)
*rel* before
*near ant* back, backward (*or* backwards), behind, rearward (*or* rearwards)

**aloof** *adj* having or showing a lack of friendliness or interest in others — see COOL 1

**aloud** *adv* with one's normal voice speaking the words ⟨Mr. Gripp likes to call on the sleepiest-looking students to read *aloud* from the textbook⟩
***syn*** audibly, out, out loud
***rel*** clearly, discernibly, distinctly, distinguishably, perceptibly, plainly; blatantly, boisterously, clamorously, loudly, lustily, mightily, noisily, resoundingly, stridently, thunderously, uproariously, vociferously
***near ant*** faintly, feebly, low, noiselessly, quietly, softly
***ant*** inaudibly, silently, soundlessly

**alp** *n* an elevation of land higher than a hill — see MOUNTAIN 1

**alpha** *n* the point at which something begins — see BEGINNING

**alright** *adj* **1** being to one's liking — see SATISFACTORY 1
**2** not exposed to the threat of loss or injury — see SAFE 1

**alright** *adv* used to express agreement — see YES

**also** *adv* **1** in like manner ⟨we stayed at an historic London hotel, the same establishment that had *also* welcomed our grandparents many years ago⟩
***syn*** alike, correspondingly, likewise, similarly, so
***rel*** equally, equivalently, identically
***near ant*** contrarily, conversely, inversely, oppositely, vice versa; diversely, unequally, variously
***ant*** differently, dissimilarly, otherwise
**2** in addition to what has been said — see MORE 1

**alter** *vb* **1** to make different in some way — see CHANGE 1
**2** to remove the sex organs of — see NEUTER

**alterable** *adj* capable of being readily changed — see FLEXIBLE 1

**alteration** *n* the act, process, or result of making different — see CHANGE

**altercation** *n* an often noisy or angry expression of differing opinions — see ARGUMENT 1

**alternative** *n* the power, right, or opportunity to choose — see CHOICE 1

**although** *also* **altho** *conj* in spite of the fact that ⟨*although* I've been to his house several times, I still can't remember how to get there⟩
***syn*** albeit, howbeit, though, when, while, whilst [*chiefly British*]
***rel*** but, whereas

**altitude** *n* **1** the distance of something or someone from bottom to top — see HEIGHT 3
**2** the most extreme or advanced point — see HEIGHT 2
**3** *usually* **altitudes** *pl* an area of high ground — see HEIGHT 4

**altogether** *adv* **1** for the most part — see CHIEFLY
**2** to a full extent or degree — see FULLY 1

**altruistic** *adj* having or showing a concern for the welfare of others — see CHARITABLE 1

**always** *adv* **1** on every relevant occasion ⟨Aunt Trina *always* insists we stay for dinner⟩
***syn*** consistently, constantly, continually, ever, forever, incessantly, invariably, perpetually, unfailingly
***rel*** commonly, frequently, oft, often, oftentimes (*or* ofttimes), recurrently, repeatedly; continuously, steadily, uninterruptedly; dependably, normally, ordinarily, regularly, routinely, typically, usually; inevitably; eternally, everlastingly
***near ant*** intermittently, occasionally, periodically, sometimes, sporadically; infrequently, rarely, seldom, unusually
***ant*** ne'er, never
**2** for all time — see EVER 1

**amalgam** *n* a distinct entity formed by the combining of two or more different things — see BLEND

**amalgamate** *vb* **1** to mix thoroughly so that the things mixed cannot be recognized — see BLEND 1
**2** to turn into a single mass that is more or less the same throughout — see BLEND 1

**amalgamated** *adj* made from the joining of two or more parts or elements — see COMPOSITE

**amalgamation** *n* a distinct entity formed by the combining of two or more different things — see BLEND

**amass** *vb* to bring together in one body or place — see GATHER 1

**amateur** *adj* lacking or showing a lack of expert skill — see AMATEURISH

**amateur** *n* a person who regularly or occasionally engages in an activity without being or becoming an expert at it ⟨a homemade doghouse that looked like it was built by an *amateur* who hadn't mastered basic carpentry⟩
***syn*** dabbler, dilettante, potterer, putterer
***rel*** apprentice, trainee; beginner, freshman, greenhorn, learner, neophyte, newcomer, novice, rookie, tenderfoot, tyro; hobbyist, tinkerer, trifler; layman, nonprofessional
***near ant*** authority, pro, professional; maestro, virtuoso, whiz, wizard; artisan, artist, craftsman, workman; initiate, journeyman; specialist, technician; old hand, old-timer, vet, veteran
***ant*** ace, adept, crackerjack, expert, master, past master

**amateurish** *adj* lacking or showing a lack of expert skill ⟨that's an *amateurish* wallpapering job—the pattern doesn't match at the seams⟩
***syn*** amateur, dilettante, inexperienced, inexpert, nonprofessional, unprofessional, unskilled, unskillful
***rel*** primitive, self-taught, uninitiated, unprepared, unqualified, unschooled, untaught, untrained, untutored; clumsy, crude, defective, faulty, flawed, unfin-

ished, unpolished; beginning, green, new, raw, unpracticed, unseasoned, untested, untried; incapable, incompetent, unable, unfit, ungifted, untalented
***near ant*** able, accomplished, capable, competent, dexterous (*also* dextrous), gifted, proficient, skilled, skillful, talented; experienced, practiced (*or* practised), seasoned, veteran; educated, fitted, initiated, knowledgeable, prepared, qualified, schooled, taught, trained, tutored, versed; all-around (*also* all-round), versatile, well-rounded; finished, polished
***ant*** ace, adept, consummate, crackerjack, expert, master, masterful, masterly, professional, virtuoso

**amatory** *adj* of, relating to, or expressing sexual attraction — see EROTIC

**amaze** *vb* to make a strong impression on (someone) with something unexpected — see SURPRISE 1

**amazed** *adj* **1** affected with sudden and great wonder or surprise — see THUNDERSTRUCK
**2** filled with amazement or wonder — see OPENMOUTHED

**amazement** *n* **1** the rapt attention and deep emotion caused by the sight of something extraordinary — see WONDER 2
**2** the state of being strongly impressed by something unexpected or unusual — see SURPRISE 2

**amazing** *adj* **1** causing a strong emotional reaction because unexpected — see SURPRISING 1
**2** causing wonder or astonishment — see MARVELOUS 1

**ambassador** *n* a person sent on a mission to represent another ⟨a beloved entertainer who has often been sent abroad by the president as his country's goodwill *ambassador*⟩
***syn*** delegate, emissary, envoy, minister, legate, representative
***rel*** agent, attaché, consul, deputy, diplomat, foreign minister, nuncio, procurator, proxy; apostle, evangelist, missionary; deputation, detachment, legation; courier, messenger; mouthpiece, spokesperson

**ambiguity** *n* the quality or state of having a veiled or uncertain meaning — see OBSCURITY 1

**ambiguous** *adj* having an often intentionally veiled or uncertain meaning — see OBSCURE 1

**ambiguousness** *n* the quality or state of having a veiled or uncertain meaning — see OBSCURITY 1

**ambition** *n* **1** eager desire for personal advancement ⟨"Talent without *ambition* will not make you a star," McKenzie's dance instructor liked to remind her⟩
***syn*** aspiration, go-getting
***rel*** determination, diligence, drive, energy, enterprise, go, hustle, industry, initiative, motivation, push; opportunism; aggression, assertiveness, daring, spirit; ardor, avidity, eagerness, keenness, passion; avarice, greed
***near ant*** apathy, indifference, unconcern; idleness, indolence, inertia, laziness, lethargy, shiftlessness, sloth
**2** readiness to engage in daring or difficult activity — see ENTERPRISE 2
**3** something that one hopes or intends to accomplish — see GOAL

**ambitious** *adj* **1** having a strong desire for personal advancement ⟨an *ambitious* child actor and his even more ambitious mother, who will do anything to get him in commercials⟩
***syn*** aspiring, go-getting, self-seeking
***rel*** determined, diligent, driving, dynamic, enterprising, gung ho, hustling, industrious, motivated, scrappy, venturesome, venturous; animated, lively, spirited; ardent, avid, eager, energetic, impassioned, keen, raring, vigorous; aggressive, assertive, opportunistic, pushy, self-assertive
***near ant*** apathetic, disinterested, indifferent, uneager, unenthusiastic, unexcited, uninterested; casual, easygoing, laid-adaisical; halfhearted, lukewarm, tepid; lazy, lethargic, listless, shiftless, sluggish, spiritless; unaggressive, unassertive
**2** having or showing a bold forcefulness in the pursuit of a goal — see AGGRESSIVE 1

**ambrosial** *adj* **1** having a pleasant smell — see FRAGRANT
**2** very pleasing to the sense of taste — see DELICIOUS 1

**ambuscade** *n* a scheme in which hidden persons wait to attack by surprise — see AMBUSH 1

**ambush** *n* **1** a scheme in which hidden persons wait to attack by surprise ⟨revolutionaries laid an *ambush* for the king along the route his carriage would travel⟩
***syn*** ambuscade, surprise, trap
***rel*** assault, attack, charge, sally; capture, entrapment, snare; hunting, stalking
**2** a device or scheme for capturing another by surprise — see TRAP 1

**ambush** *vb* to lie in wait for and attack by surprise ⟨the king's enemies planned to *ambush* the royal coach on the way to Paris and capture the king⟩
***syn*** surprise, waylay
***rel*** assail, assault, attack, storm, strike; jump, pounce (on), tackle; charge, sally; capture, ensnare, entrap, net, snare, trap; hunt, prey (on *or* upon), stalk
***phrases*** lay for

**ameliorate** *vb* to make better — see IMPROVE

**amenability** *n* **1** a desire or disposition to please — see COMPLAISANCE
**2** cheerful readiness to do something — see ALACRITY

**amenable** *adj* **1** having a desire or inclination (as for a specified course of action) — see WILLING 1
**2** readily giving in to the command or authority of another — see OBEDIENT

**amend** *vb* **1** to make better — see IMPROVE
**2** to remove errors, defects, deficiencies, or deviations from — see CORRECT 1
**amendment** *n* a change designed to correct or improve a written work — see CORRECTION 1
**amenity** *n* **1** an act or utterance that is a customary show of good manners — see CIVILITY 1
**2** something adding to pleasure or comfort but not absolutely necessary — see LUXURY 1
**3** something that adds to one's ease — see COMFORT 2
**4** the state or quality of having a pleasant or agreeable manner in socializing with others — see AMIABILITY 1
**American Indian** *n* a member of any of the native peoples of the western hemisphere usually not including the Eskimos ⟨Jeremy's great-grandfather was an *American Indian*, a member of the Shoshones⟩
***syn*** Amerindian (*also* Amerind), Indian, Native American
***rel*** mestizo
**Amerindian** *also* **Amerind** *n* a member of any of the native peoples of the western hemisphere usually not including the Eskimos — see AMERICAN INDIAN
**amiability** *n* **1** the state or quality of having a pleasant or agreeable manner in socializing with others ⟨the waitress's *amiability* is what makes eating at the diner so much fun⟩
***syn*** affability, agreeableness, amenity, amiableness, geniality, good-naturedness, good-temperedness, graciousness, niceness, pleasantness, sweetness
***rel*** amenability, complaisance; amicability, amity, cordiality, friendliness; benignity, gentleness, kindness; cheerfulness, cheeriness, sunniness; civility, comity, considerateness, consideration, courteousness, courtesy, politeness, thoughtfulness; attractiveness, delightfulness, enjoyableness
***near ant*** boorishness, discourtesy, impoliteness, incivility, rudeness, ungraciousness; biliousness, cantankerousness, churlishness, crankiness, fussiness, grouchiness, grumpiness, irascibility, irritability, peevishness, petulance, testiness; contentiousness, contrariness, orneriness, querulousness; hostility, unfriendliness
***ant*** disagreeableness, unpleasantness
**2** a desire or disposition to please — see COMPLAISANCE
**amiable** *adj* having an easygoing and pleasing manner especially in social situations ⟨the owner of the inn is an *amiable*, talkative widow who treats guests like family⟩
***syn*** affable, agreeable, genial, good-natured, good-tempered, gracious, nice, sweet, well-disposed
***rel*** amicable, cordial, friendly, neighborly; benign, gentle, kind; cheerful, cheery, sunny; companionable, sociable; civil, considerate, courteous, polite, thoughtful; accommodating, amenable, obliging; attractive, delightful, enjoyable
***near ant*** boorish, discourteous, ill-mannered, impolite, inconsiderate, rude, surly, uncivil, unmannerly; bearish, bilious, cantankerous, choleric, churlish, crabby, cranky, dyspeptic, fussy, grouchy, grumpy, ill-humored, irascible, irritable, peevish, petulant, quick-tempered, snappish, testy, touchy; argumentative, contentious, contrary, ornery, querulous; unappealing, unattractive
***ant*** disagreeable, ill-natured, ill-tempered, ungracious, unpleasant
**amiableness** *n* the state or quality of having a pleasant or agreeable manner in socializing with others — see AMIABILITY 1
**amicable** *adj* **1** having or marked by agreement in feeling or action — see HARMONIOUS 3
**2** having or showing kindly feeling and sincere interest — see FRIENDLY 1
**amid** *or* **amidst** *prep* in or into the middle of — see AMONG
**amiss** *adv* **1** in a mistaken or inappropriate way — see WRONGLY
**2** off the desired or intended path or course — see WRONG 1
**amity** *n* kindly concern, interest, or support — see GOODWILL 1
**ammunition** *n* means or method of defending — see DEFENSE 1
**amnesty** *n* release from the guilt or penalty of an offense — see PARDON
**amok** *or* **amuck** *adv* in a confused and reckless manner — see HELTER-SKELTER 1
**among** *also* **amongst** *prep* in or into the middle of ⟨a gull landed *among* the burgers-and-fries eaters at the outdoor snack bar, clearly looking for handouts⟩
***syn*** amid (*or* amidst), mid, midst, through
***rel*** between, betwixt
***phrases*** in the thick of
***near ant*** from, out of
**amorous** *adj* of, relating to, or expressing sexual attraction — see EROTIC
**amorphous** *adj* having no definite or recognizable form — see FORMLESS
**amount** *n* a given or particular mass or aggregate of matter ⟨is this small *amount* of food supposed to feed the whole hockey team?⟩
***syn*** measure, quantity, volume
***rel*** body, portion; many, number
**amount** (to) *vb* **1** to have a total of ⟨the expenses of the trip *amounted to* nearly double what we'd budgeted for⟩
***syn*** add up (to), come (to), number, sum (to *or* into), total
***rel*** average, equal, measure, reach; aggregate, comprise
**2** to be the same in meaning or effect ⟨it makes no difference whether you're going to the game or to the movies, for it

*amounts to* your unavailability for babysitting⟩
***syn*** add up (to), come (to), correspond (to), equal
***rel*** approach, match, measure (up), meet, rival, touch; connote, denote, express, import, mean, signify, smack (of), spell, suggest

**ample** *adj* **1** being more than enough without being excessive — see PLENTIFUL
**2** more than adequate or average in capacity — see SPACIOUS

**amplify** *vb* **1** to express more fully and in greater detail — see EXPAND 1
**2** to make greater in size, amount, or number — see INCREASE 1
**3** to make markedly greater in measure or degree — see INTENSIFY

**amplitude** *n* an area over which activity, capacity, or influence extends — see RANGE 2

**amulet** *n* something worn or kept to bring good luck or keep away evil — see CHARM 1

**amuse** *vb* to cause (someone) to pass the time agreeably occupied ⟨Christie *amused* her four-year-old sister at the family reunion by showing her off to all the relatives⟩
***syn*** disport, divert, entertain, regale
***rel*** absorb, busy, distract, engage, engross, immerse, interest, involve, occupy; beguile, bewitch, captivate, charm, delight, enchant, enthrall (*or* enthral), fascinate; grip, hypnotize, intrigue, mesmerize; coddle, gratify, humor, indulge, mollycoddle, pamper, please, pleasure, spoil; appease, comfort, conciliate, console, content, mollify, oblige, pacify, placate, propitiate, soothe
***near ant*** bore, jade; drain, enervate, exhaust, fatigue, tire, wear, wear out, weary; aggravate, annoy, bother, bug, chafe, disturb, exasperate, fret, gall, grate, harass, harry, irk, nettle, peeve, perturb, pester, pique, upset, vex

**amusement** *n* the act or activity of providing pleasure or amusement especially for the public — see ENTERTAINMENT 1

**amusing** *adj* providing amusement or enjoyment — see FUN

**analgesic** *n* something (as a drug) that relieves pain — see PAINKILLER

**analogous** *adj* having qualities in common — see ALIKE

**analysis** *n* **1** the separation and identification of the parts of a whole ⟨investigators took the mysterious powder to the lab for *analysis*⟩
***syn*** anatomizing, assay, breakdown, dissection
***rel*** assessment, evaluation, examination, inspection, investigation, scrutiny; arrangement, assortment, cataloging (*or* cataloguing), categorization, classification, codification, indexing; enumeration, inventory, itemization, tabulation; division, reduction, segmentation, separation, subdivision
***near ant*** agglomeration, aggregation, amalgamation, assimilation, coalescence, conglomeration, consolidation, integration, synthesis, unification
**2** a series of explanations or observations on something (as an event) — see COMMENTARY

**analytic** *or* **analytical** *adj* according to the rules of logic — see LOGICAL 1

**analyze** *vb* to identify and examine the basic elements or parts of (something) especially for discovering interrelationships ⟨*analyze* the park's ecosystem before deciding whether hunting should be allowed⟩
***syn*** anatomize, assay, break down, dissect
***rel*** assess, evaluate, examine, inspect, investigate, scrutinize; arrange, assort, catalog (*or* catalogue), categorize, classify, codify, diagram, index, order, schematize, sort, tabulate; divide, reduce, segment, separate, subdivide
***near ant*** agglomerate, aggregate, amalgamate, assimilate, coalesce, conglomerate, consolidate, integrate, synthesize, unify

**anarchic** *adj* not restrained by or under the control of legal authority — see LAWLESS

**anarchy** *n* a state in which there is widespread wrongdoing and disregard for rules and authority ⟨the *anarchy* that the country experienced after the dictator drained the treasury and fled the country⟩
***syn*** lawlessness, misrule
***rel*** commotion, tumult, uproar; chaos, confusion, disarray, disorder, disorderliness, disorganization; disruption, disturbance, havoc, riot, strife, turbulence, turmoil, unrest, upheaval; mutiny, rebellion, revolution, uprising; criminality, outlawry
***near ant*** law, lawfulness, legality, legitimacy, rule; calmness, harmony, order, orderliness, peace, peacefulness, quiet, tranquillity (*or* tranquility)

**anathema** *n* **1** a prayer that harm will come to someone — see CURSE 1
**2** something or someone that is hated — see HATE 2

**anatomize** *vb* to identify and examine the basic elements or parts of (something) especially for discovering interrelationships — see ANALYZE

**anatomizing** *n* the separation and identification of the parts of a whole — see ANALYSIS 1

**ancestor** *n* **1** a person who is several generations earlier in an individual's line of descent ⟨Bridie's Irish *ancestors* immigrated to the United States in the 19th century during the Great Potato Famine⟩
***syn*** father, forebear (*also* forbear), forefather, grandfather
***rel*** grandmother, matriarch, patriarch; ancestry, antecedents
***near ant*** children, issue, offspring, posterity, progeny, seed; heir, inheritor, son, successor

*ant* descendant (*or* descendent)
**2** something belonging to an earlier time from which something else was later developed ⟨pinball machines—the *ancestors* of today's video games—go back to the 19th century⟩
*syn* antecedent, foregoer, forerunner, precursor, predecessor
*rel* archetype, model, original, prototype; father, mother
*near ant* by-product, derivative, offshoot, outgrowth, spin-off; daughter, son
*ant* descendant (*or* descendent)

**ancestry** *n* the line of ancestors from whom a person is descended ⟨a Cambodian immigrant who can trace her Khmer *ancestry* as far back as the 16th century⟩
*syn* birth, blood, bloodline, breeding, descent, extraction, family tree, genealogy, line, lineage, origin, parentage, pedigree, stock, strain
*rel* heredity, succession; family, house; kin, kindred, relations, relatives; race
*near ant* offspring; child, heir, inheritor, son, successor
*ant* issue, posterity, progeny, seed

**anchor** *n* one who reads and introduces news reports on a news program — see ANCHORPERSON

**anchor** *vb* **1** to put securely in place or in a desired position — see FASTEN 2
**2** to stop at or near a place along the shore — see LAND 1

**anchorage** *n* a part of a body of water protected and deep enough to be a place of safety for ships — see HARBOR 1

**anchorite** *n* a person who lives away from others — see RECLUSE

**anchorperson** *n* one who reads and introduces news reports on a news program ⟨the new *anchorperson* did an admirable job of dealing with the late-breaking news story⟩
*syn* anchor
*rel* anchorman, anchorwoman; broadcaster, newscaster, telecaster; correspondent, interviewer, reporter; journalist, newsman

**ancient** *adj* **1** dating or surviving from the distant past ⟨Rome's *ancient* ruins are carefully preserved in the midst of the bustle of the modern city⟩
*syn* aged, age-old, antediluvian, antique, dateless, hoar, hoary, old, venerable
*rel* aging, mature; antiquated, obsolete, outmoded, out-of-date, passé; old-fashioned, old-time, old-world; durable, enduring, lasting, long-lived, permanent; ageless, hallowed, time-honored, timeless, time-tested, traditional, tried, tried-and-true; classic, classical; prehistoric, primeval, primordial
*near ant* fresh, young, youthful; contemporary, current, latest, mod, novel, present-day, ultramodern; untested, untried; brand-new, unused, unworn
*ant* modern, new, recent
**2** being of advanced years and especially past middle age — see ELDERLY
**3** relating to or occurring near the beginning of a process, series, or time period — see EARLY 1

**ancient** *n* a person of advanced years — see SENIOR CITIZEN

**anecdote** *n* a brief account of something interesting that happened especially to one personally — see STORY 2

**anesthetic** *n* something (as a drug) that relieves pain — see PAINKILLER

**anew** *adv* yet another time — see AGAIN 1

**angel** *n* **1** an innocent or gentle person — see LAMB
**2** one that announces or indicates the later arrival of another — see FORERUNNER 1

**anger** *n* an intense emotional state of displeasure with someone or something ⟨Dave stifled his *anger* when the kids on the bus made fun of him⟩
*syn* angriness, furor, fury, indignation, irateness, ire, outrage, rage, spleen, wrath, wrathfulness
*rel* aggravation, annoyance, exasperation, irritation, vexation; animosity, antagonism, antipathy, bile, bitterness, contempt, enmity, grudge, hostility, rancor; envy, jaundice, jealousy, pique, resentment; malevolence, malice, spite, venom, virulence, vitriol; belligerence, contentiousness, contrariness, disputatiousness, orneriness, pugnacity, querulousness; blowup, flare-up, outburst; dander, dudgeon, huff, pet, rise, ruffle, temper; delirium, heat, passion, warmth
*near ant* calmness, forbearance, patience
*ant* delight, pleasure

**anger** *vb* to make angry ⟨it's virtually impossible to *anger* Mrs. Peterson—she's the most easygoing person I've ever known⟩
*syn* antagonize, enrage, incense, inflame, infuriate, madden, outrage, rankle, rile, roil
*rel* affront, aggravate, annoy, cross, exasperate, get, irritate, nettle, offend, peeve, pique, provoke, put out, ruffle, vex; embitter, envenom
*phrases* get one's goat, rub the wrong way
*near ant* allay, assuage, relieve; comfort, console, soothe; appease, conciliate, mollify, pacify, placate; calm, lull, quiet, settle; beguile, bewitch, captivate, charm, disarm, enchant
*ant* delight, gratify, please

**angered** *adj* feeling or showing anger — see ANGRY

**angle** *n* **1** a certain way in which something appears or may be regarded — see ASPECT 1
**2** a way of looking at or thinking about something — see POINT OF VIEW
**3** something that curves or is curved — see BEND 1

**angle** *vb* to set or cause to be at an angle — see LEAN 1

---

*syn* synonym(s) *rel* related words
*ant* antonym(s) *near ant* near antonym(s)

**angling** *n* the act of positioning or an instance of being positioned at an angle — see TILT

**angriness** *n* an intense emotional state of displeasure with someone or something — see ANGER

**angry** *adj* feeling or showing anger ⟨my sister gets really *angry* and practically throws a tantrum if her soccer team loses⟩

***syn*** angered, apoplectic, enraged, foaming, fuming, furious, incensed, indignant, inflamed, infuriated, irate, ireful, mad, outraged, rabid, riled, roiled, shirty [*chiefly British*], sore, steaming, wrathful, wroth

***rel*** ranting, raving, stormy; bristling, burning, cross, huffy, livid, seething, smoldering, worked up, wrought (up); acrid, acrimonious, antagonistic, antipathetic, bitter, embittered, inimical, malevolent, piqued, rancorous, resentful, spiteful, vindictive, virulent; antisocial, cold, cool, disagreeable, disapproving, distant, frigid, icy, ill-tempered, sulky, unfriendly, unpleasant; aggravated, annoyed, bearish, bilious, cantankerous, choleric, churlish, crabby, cranky, dyspeptic, exasperated, fretful, fussy, grouchy, grumpy, ill-humored, irascible, irritable, peevish, perturbed, petulant, put out, quick-tempered, snappish, testy, touchy; argumentative, belligerent, contentious, contrary, disputatious, ornery, pugnacious, quarrelsome, querulous

***near ant*** accepting, accommodating, obliging; agreeable, amenable, complaisant; amicable, cordial, friendly; content, happy, satisfied; empathetic, sympathetic, tolerant, understanding; calm, pacific, peaceable, placid, serene, tranquil; affable, amiable, easygoing, genial, good-natured, good-tempered, kind, pleasant, sweet

***ant*** delighted, pleased

**anguish** *n* **1** a state of great suffering of body or mind — see DISTRESS 1
**2** deep sadness especially for the loss of someone or something loved — see SORROW

**anguished** *adj* expressing or suggesting mourning — see MOURNFUL 1

**animal** *adj* of or relating to the human body — see PHYSICAL 1

**animal** *n* one of the lower animals as distinguished from human beings ⟨we saw a lot of *animals* at the wildlife refuge—cranes, alligators, deer, a fox, even an armadillo⟩

***syn*** beast, brute, creature, critter

***rel*** varmint, vermin; biped, quadruped; carnivore, herbivore, insectivore; invertebrate, vertebrate

**animate** *adj* **1** having much high-spirited energy and movement — see LIVELY 1
**2** having or showing life — see ALIVE 1

**animate** *vb* to give life, vigor, or spirit to ⟨Mr. Clark *animates* history for his sixth graders by frequently showing up for class dressed like some famous historical figure⟩

***syn*** brace, energize, enliven, fire, invigorate, jazz (up), liven (up), pep (up), quicken, stimulate, vitalize, vivify

***rel*** arouse, awake, awaken, raise, rouse, stir, wake (up); activate, actuate, drive, impel, motivate, move, propel; charge, electrify, galvanize; excite, ferment, foment, incite, inflame, instigate, kindle, provoke, set off, spark, trigger, turn on, whip (up); abet, boost, buoy, cheer, embolden, fortify, hearten, inspire, lift, rally, steel, strengthen; reactivate, reanimate, reawake, reawaken, recharge, recreate, reenergize, refresh, regenerate, rejuvenate, rekindle, renew, resurrect, resuscitate, revitalize, revive

***near ant*** burn out, debilitate, do in, drain, enervate, enfeeble, exhaust, fag, fatigue, sap, tucker (out), undermine, weaken, wear, wear out; check, curb, inhibit, jade, quell, quench, repress, restrain, slow, still, stunt, suppress; daunt, demoralize, discourage, dishearten, dispirit

***ant*** damp, dampen, deaden, dull

**animated** *adj* **1** having much high-spirited energy and movement — see LIVELY 1
**2** marked by much life, movement, or activity — see ALIVE 2

**animatedly** *adv* in a quick and spirited manner — see GAILY 2

**animately** *adv* in a quick and spirited manner — see GAILY 2

**animation** *n* the quality or state of having abundant or intense activity — see VITALITY 1

**animosity** *n* a deep-seated ill will — see ENMITY

**annalist** *n* a student or writer of history — see HISTORIAN

**annals** *n pl* an account of important events in the order in which they happened — see HISTORY 1

**annex** *n* a smaller structure added to a main building ⟨a new *annex* that will serve as the permanent home for the school library⟩

***syn*** addition, extension, penthouse

***rel*** arm, ell, wing

**annex** *vb* to join (something) to a mass, quantity, or number so as to bring about an overall increase — see ADD 1

**annihilate** *vb* **1** to destroy all traces of ⟨the family's attempts to *annihilate* the roach population in their apartment had met with little success⟩

***syn*** blot out, efface, eradicate, expunge, exterminate, extirpate, liquidate, obliterate, root (out), rub out, snuff (out), stamp (out), wipe out

***rel*** decimate, demolish, destroy, devastate; dismantle, flatten, mow (down), raze, tear down; ruin, total, waste, wreck; blast, blow up, dash, dynamite, smash; atomize, consume, devour, dissolve, fragment, powder, pulverize, shatter, splinter; doom, finish, kill, terminate, zap; cancel, cut, discard, ditch, eject, excise, expel, jettison, oust, throw out

***near ant*** conserve, preserve, protect, save; build, construct, create, fabricate, fashion, forge, form, frame, make, manufacture, shape; fix, mend, patch, rebuild, recondition, reconstruct, renew, renovate, repair, restore, revamp

**2** to bring to a complete end the physical soundness, existence, or usefulness of — see DESTROY 1

**annihilation** *n* the state or fact of being rendered nonexistent, physically unsound, or useless — see DESTRUCTION

**announce** *vb* to make known openly or publicly ⟨Jeannie *announced* to everyone within hearing distance that she didn't care if she failed the test⟩

***syn*** advertise, blaze, broadcast, declare, enunciate, placard, post, proclaim, promulgate, publicize, publish, sound

***rel*** advise, apprise, inform, notify; communicate, impart, intimate; disclose, divulge, report, reveal; disseminate, spread

***near ant*** conceal, hush (up), silence, suppress, withhold; recall, recant, retract, revoke

**announcement** *n* a published statement informing the public of a matter of general interest ⟨an *announcement* was in today's paper regarding the merger of the two banks⟩

***syn*** ad, advertisement, bulletin, notice, notification, posting, release

***rel*** broadside, circular, flier (*or* flyer), handbill, handout; bill, billboard, placard, poster, sign; broadcast, newscast, telecast; advertising, commercial, message, spot, word; communication, dispatch, report; ballyhoo, boost, buildup, campaign, plug, promotion, propaganda, publicity

**annoy** *vb* to disturb the peace of mind of (someone) especially by repeated disagreeable acts — see IRRITATE 1

**annoyance** *n* **1** the act of making unwelcome intrusions upon another ⟨they have an unlisted number in the hopes that it will reduce the constant *annoyance* by telephone salespeople⟩

***syn*** aggravation, bedevilment, bothering, bugging, disturbance, harassment, harrying, pestering, teasing, vexation

***rel*** molestation, offense (*or* offence), persecution, provocation, torment, torture

**2** the feeling of impatience or anger caused by another's repeated disagreeable acts ⟨Carlene made known her *annoyance* at having to pick up her sister's dirty clothes⟩

***syn*** aggravation, bother, exasperation, frustration, irritation, vexation

***rel*** agitation, anger, angriness, discomfort, displeasure, distress, disturbance, indignation, irateness, ire, outrage, perturbation, resentment; dander, dudgeon, huff, peeve, pet, pique, umbrage, upset

***near ant*** delight, pleasure

**3** something that is a source of irritation ⟨flashing ads, visual clutter, and other *annoyances* that are the price for free information on the Internet⟩

***syn*** aggravation, bother, exasperation, frustration, hassle, headache, inconvenience, irritant, nuisance, peeve, pest, problem, thorn

***rel*** affront, insult, offense; upset, worry; affliction, cross, curse, menace, plague; plight, predicament, trial, tribulation; annoyer, disturber, offender

***near ant*** delight, joy, pleasure

**4** one who is obnoxiously annoying — see NUISANCE 1

**annoyer** *n* one who is obnoxiously annoying — see NUISANCE 1

**annoying** *adj* causing annoyance ⟨Sheldon has the *annoying* habit of eating all the pickles and leaving a jar full of pickle juice in the refrigerator⟩

***syn*** aggravating, bothersome, disturbing, exasperating, frustrating, galling, irksome, irritating, maddening, nettling, peeving, pesty, rankling, riling, vexatious, vexing

***rel*** burdensome, discomforting, displeasing, disquieting, distressing, importunate, inconveniencing; angering, enraging, infuriating; mischievous, offensive, pesky, troublesome, upsetting; stressful, tiresome, troubling, trying, worrisome

***near ant*** delightful, pleasing

**annuity** *n* a sum of money allotted for a specific use by official or formal action — see APPROPRIATION

**annul** *vb* **1** to balance with an equal force so as to make ineffective — see OFFSET

**2** to put an end to by formal action — see ABOLISH

**anoint** *vb* to rub an oily or sticky substance over — see SMEAR 1

**anomalous** *adj* departing from some accepted standard of what is normal — see DEVIANT

**anomaly** *n* a person, thing, or event that is not normal — see FREAK 1

**anon** *adv* at or within a short time — see SHORTLY 2

**anonymity** *n* the quality or state of being mostly or completely unknown — see OBSCURITY 2

**anonymous** *adj* **1** known but not named — see CERTAIN 1

**2** not named or identified by a name — see NAMELESS 1

**3** not widely known — see OBSCURE 2

**another** *adj* resulting in an increase in amount or number — see ADDITIONAL

**answer** *n* **1** something spoken or written in reaction especially to a question ⟨the standard *answer* of "Nothing" when asked, "What did you do in school today?"⟩

***syn*** comeback, rejoinder, reply, response, retort, return

***rel*** banter, persiflage, repartee; acknowledgment (*also* acknowledgement), comment, communication, correspondence, feedback, observation, reaction, remark;

defense, explanation, justification, rebuttal, refutation
*near ant* challenge, cross-examination, grilling, interrogation, quiz; poll, questionnaire, survey
*ant* inquiry, query, question
**2** something attained by mental effort and especially by computation ⟨the *answers* to the odd-numbered problems are at the back of the book⟩
*syn* result, solution
*rel* conclusion, determination, explanation, finding; clue, key

**answer** *vb* **1** to speak or write in reaction to a question or to another reaction ⟨Ryan didn't *answer* right away when Mrs. Jacobs asked him where he'd been for the last three hours⟩
*syn* rejoin, reply, respond, return
*rel* acknowledge, comment, communicate, correspond, react, remark; explain, rebut, refute
*near ant* challenge, cross-examine, examine, grill, interrogate, pump, quiz; poll, query, survey
*ant* inquire, question
**2** to be in agreement on every point — see CHECK 1
**3** to do what is required by the terms of — see FULFILL 1
**4** to find an answer for through reasoning — see SOLVE

**answerable** *adj* **1** being the one who must meet an obligation or suffer the consequences for failing to do so — see RESPONSIBLE 1
**2** capable of having the reason for or cause of determined — see SOLVABLE

**antagonism** *n* a deep-seated ill will — see ENMITY

**antagonist** *n* **1** one that is hostile toward another — see ENEMY
**2** one that takes a position opposite another in a competition or conflict — see OPPONENT 1

**antagonistic** *adj* marked by opposition or ill will — see HOSTILE 1

**antagonize** *vb* **1** to implant bitter feelings in — see EMBITTER
**2** to make angry — see ANGER

**antecedent** *adj* going before another in time or order — see PREVIOUS

**antecedent** *n* **1** someone or something responsible for a result — see CAUSE
**2** something belonging to an earlier time from which something else was later developed — see ANCESTOR 2

**antecedently** *adv* so as to precede something in order of time — see AHEAD 1

**antedate** *vb* to go or come before in time — see PRECEDE

**antediluvian** *adj* dating or surviving from the distant past — see ANCIENT 1

**antediluvian** *n* a person with old-fashioned ideas — see FOGY

**anterior** *adj* going before another in time or order — see PREVIOUS

**anteriorly** *adv* so as to precede something in order of time — see AHEAD 1

**anthem** *n* a religious song — see HYMN

**anthology** *n* a collection of writings ⟨an *anthology* of American short stories⟩
*syn* album, compilation, miscellany
*rel* archives; digest

**antic** *adj* **1** causing or intended to cause laughter — see FUNNY 1
**2** given to good-natured joking or teasing — see PLAYFUL

**antic** *n* a playful or mischievous act intended as a joke — see PRANK

**anticipate** *vb* **1** to believe in the future occurrence of (something) — see EXPECT
**2** to realize or know about beforehand — see FORESEE

**anticipated** *adj* being in accordance with the prescribed, normal, or logical course of events — see DUE 2

**anticipatory** *adj* having or showing signs of eagerly awaiting something — see EXPECTANT 1

**antipathetic** *adj* having a natural dislike for something ⟨a series of adventure books that turned boys who had been *antipathetic* to reading into avid readers⟩
*syn* allergic, averse
*rel* disinclined, loath (*or* loth), reluctant, unwilling; adverse, antagonistic, hostile, intolerant, negative, opposed, opposing, resistant, resisting, uncongenial, unfriendly, unsympathetic; disgusted, nauseated, repelled, repulsed, revolted, shocked, squeamish, turned off
*near ant* friendly, sympathetic, tolerant, understanding; admiring, appreciative, charmed, delighted, fond, pleased, tickled

**antipathy** *n* **1** a deep-seated ill will — see ENMITY
**2** something or someone that is hated — see HATE 2

**antipodal** *adj* being as different as possible — see OPPOSITE

**antipode** *n* something that is as different as possible from something else — see OPPOSITE

**antipodean** *adj* being as different as possible — see OPPOSITE

**antiquated** *adj* having passed its time of use or usefulness — see OBSOLETE

**antique** *adj* **1** dating or surviving from the distant past — see ANCIENT 1
**2** pleasantly reminiscent of an earlier time — see OLD-FASHIONED 1

**antique** *n* something belonging to or surviving from an earlier period ⟨Shamika's house is filled with *antiques*, including a collection of 19th-century African masks⟩
*syn* relic
*rel* artifact, fossil; antiquities, ruins; remains, remnant, trace, vestige

**antisocial** *adj* having or showing a lack of friendliness or interest in others — see COOL 1

**antithesis** *n* something that is as different as possible from something else — see OPPOSITE

**antithetical** *adj* being as different as possible — see OPPOSITE

**anxiety** *n* **1** an uneasy state of mind usually over the possibility of an anticipated

misfortune or trouble ⟨Dorothy's *anxiety* about her brother's operation kept her awake all night⟩
***syn*** agitation, anxiousness, apprehension, apprehensiveness, care, concern, disquiet, nervousness, perturbation, solicitude, uneasiness, worry
***rel*** strain, stress, tension; alarm, anguish, consternation, desperation, desperateness, discomfort, discomposure, dismay, distraction, distress, disturbance, edginess, jitters, jumpiness; fear, fearfulness, torment, upset, vexation; doubt, dread, foreboding, incertitude, misgiving, presentiment, suspense, uncertainty
***near ant*** calm, calmness, content, contentment, ease, peace, placidity, quiet, quietude, serenity, tranquillity (*or* tranquility); comfort, consolation, relief, solace
**2** the emotion experienced in the presence or threat of danger — see FEAR

**anxious** *adj* **1** feeling or showing uncomfortable feelings of uncertainty — see NERVOUS 1
**2** marked by or causing agitation or uncomfortable feelings — see NERVOUS 2
**3** showing urgent desire or interest — see EAGER

**anxiousness** *n* an uneasy state of mind usually over the possibility of an anticipated misfortune or trouble — see ANXIETY 1

**any** *adj* being one of a group — see EACH

**anyhow** *adv* **1** in spite of everything — see REGARDLESS
**2** without definite aim, direction, rule, or method — see HIT OR MISS

**anymore** *adv* at the present time — see NOW 1

**anyway** *adv* **1** in spite of everything — see REGARDLESS
**2** without definite aim, direction, rule, or method — see HIT OR MISS

**anywise** *adv* **1** in any way or respect — see AT ALL
**2** without definite aim, direction, rule, or method — see HIT OR MISS

**A1** *adj* of the very best kind — see EXCELLENT

**apace** *adv* with great speed — see FAST 1

**apart** *adv* into parts or to pieces ⟨the fancy new adjustable rake came *apart* the first time Chad tried to use it⟩
***syn*** asunder, piecemeal
***ant*** together

**apartment** *n* **1** a room or set of rooms in a private house or a block used as a separate dwelling place ⟨a spacious six-room *apartment* that occupies the entire upper floor of a two-family house⟩
***syn*** flat, lodgings, suite, tenement
***rel*** condominium, duplex, penthouse, salon, studio, triplex; apartment house, tenement house, walk-up
**2** an area within a building that has been set apart from surrounding space by a wall — see ROOM 2

**apathetic** *adj* **1** having or showing a lack of interest or concern — see INDIFFERENT 1
**2** not feeling or showing emotion — see IMPASSIVE 1

**apathy** *n* **1** a lack of emotion or emotional expressiveness ⟨the *apathy* of the people of that war-torn country comes from their having seen too many horrors⟩
***syn*** impassivity, insensibility, numbness, phlegm
***rel*** callousness, coldness, coolness, hardheartedness, hardness, heartlessness, insensitivity, obduracy; blankness, deadness, emptiness, vacancy; aloofness, detachment, indifference, unconcern; stiffness, woodenness
***near ant*** compassion, empathy, pity, sympathy; responsiveness, sensitivity; solicitude, tenderness, understanding, warmth; histrionics, hysteria, hysterics, melodrama
***ant*** emotion, feeling, sensibility
**2** lack of interest or concern — see INDIFFERENCE

**ape** *vb* to use (someone or something) as the model for one's speech, mannerisms, or behavior — see IMITATE 1

**aper** *n* a person who adopts the appearance or behavior of another especially in an obvious way — see COPYCAT

**aperture** *n* a place in a surface allowing passage into or through a thing — see HOLE 1

**apex** *n* **1** the highest part or point — see HEIGHT 1
**2** the last and usually sharp or tapering part of something long and narrow — see POINT 2

**aphorism** *n* **1** an idea or statement about all of the members of a group or all the instances of a situation — see GENERALIZATION
**2** an often stated observation regarding something from common experience — see SAYING

**aphoristic** *adj* marked by the use of few words to convey much information or meaning — see CONCISE

**apiece** *adv* for each one ⟨when you figure that it comes to six dollars *apiece*, it's too much to pay for used CDs⟩
***syn*** all, each, per capita
***rel*** apart, independently, individually, respectively, separately, singly
***near ant*** altogether, collectively, together

**apish** *adj* using or marked by the use of something else as a basis or model — see IMITATIVE

**aplomb** *n* **1** evenness of emotions or temper — see EQUANIMITY
**2** great faith in oneself or one's abilities — see CONFIDENCE 1

**apologetic** *adj* feeling sorrow for a wrong that one has done — see CONTRITE 1

**apoplectic** *adj* feeling or showing anger — see ANGRY

**apostate** *n* one who betrays a trust or an allegiance — see TRAITOR

**apostle** *n* a person who actively supports or favors a cause — see EXPONENT

**apothecary** *n* a person who prepares drugs according to a doctor's prescription — see DRUGGIST

**appall** *vb* to cause an often unpleasant surprise for — see SHOCK 1

**appalling** *adj* **1** causing intense displeasure, disgust, or resentment — see OFFENSIVE 1

**2** extremely disturbing or repellent — see HORRIBLE 1

**appanage** *n* **1** something granted as a special favor — see PRIVILEGE

**2** something to which one has a just claim — see RIGHT 1

**apparatus** *n* items needed for the performance of a task or activity — see EQUIPMENT

**apparel** *n* covering for the human body — see CLOTHING

**apparel** *vb* to outfit with clothes and especially fine or special clothes — see CLOTHE 1

**apparent** *adj* **1** appearing to be true on the basis of evidence that may or may not be confirmed ⟨at the start of the investigation, the *apparent* cause of the plane crash was mechanical failure⟩

***syn*** assumed, evident, ostensible, presumed, reputed, seeming, supposed

***rel*** external, outward, visible; conceivable, plausible; likely, probable; clear, distinct, manifest, obvious, plain; deceptive, delusive, delusory, illusive, illusory, imaginary; misleading, specious; fake, faked, feigned, phony (*also* phoney), pretended, pseudo, put-on; alleged, professed, purported, so-called

***near ant*** authenticated, confirmed, corroborated, established, real, substantiated, valid, validated, verified

**2** capable of being seen — see VISIBLE

**3** not subject to misinterpretation or more than one interpretation — see CLEAR 2

**apparently** *adv* to all outward appearances ⟨*apparently*, Phil didn't know the cake was for the raffle, since he helped himself to a piece⟩

***syn*** evidently, ostensibly, presumably, seemingly, supposedly

***rel*** externally, outwardly, visibly; believably, credibly; maybe, mayhap, perchance, perhaps, possibly, professedly; allegedly, reputedly; clearly, distinctly, obviously, plainly; assuredly, positively, surely

***near ant*** implausibly, impossibly, improbably, incredibly

**apparition** *n* the soul of a dead person thought of especially as appearing to living people — see GHOST

**appeal** *n* **1** an earnest request — see PLEA 1

**2** the power of irresistible attraction — see CHARM 2

**appeal** (to) *vb* to make a request to (someone) in an earnest or urgent manner — see BEG

**appealing** *adj* having an often mysterious or magical power to attract — see FASCINATING 1

**appear** *vb* **1** to come into view ⟨a police car *appeared* just as Michael ran a red light⟩

***syn*** come out, materialize, show up, turn up

***rel*** reappear, resurface; bulk, loom; arrive, come; dawn, debut; arise, break, break out, emanate, erupt, issue, rise, spring (up), surface; happen, occur

***near ant*** depart, leave, retire, withdraw

***ant*** clear, disappear, dissolve, evanesce, evaporate, fade, go (away), melt (away), vanish

**2** to give the impression of being — see SEEM

**appearance** *n* **1** the outward form of someone or something especially as indicative of a quality ⟨the dignified *appearance* of this church leader⟩ ⟨the country club's manicured lawns and well-groomed *appearance* in general⟩

***syn*** aspect, look, mien, presence

***rel*** air, attitude, bearing, behavior, comportment, demeanor, deportment, manner, poise, pose; carriage, posture, stance; color, complexion; countenance, face, features, physiognomy, visage

**2** outward and often deceptive indication ⟨can't you at least give the *appearance* of listening to what I say?⟩

***syn*** face, guise, name, semblance, show

***rel*** affectation, display, fiction, imposture, make-believe, pose, pretense (*or* pretence), simulation; cloak, disguise, exterior, facade (*also* façade), front, mask, masquerade, shell, surface

**3** the act of coming upon a scene — see ARRIVAL

**appease** *vb* to lessen the anger or agitation of — see PACIFY

**appeasing** *adj* tending to lessen or avoid conflict or hostility — see PACIFIC 1

**appellation** *n* a word or combination of words by which a person or thing is regularly known — see NAME 1

**append** *vb* to join (something) to a mass, quantity, or number so as to bring about an overall increase — see ADD 1

**appendage** *n* something that is not necessary in itself but adds to the convenience or performance of the main piece of equipment — see ACCESSORY 1

**appertain** *vb* **1** to be the property of a person or group of persons — see BELONG 2

**2** to have a relation or connection — see APPLY 1

**appetite** *n* **1** a need or desire for food — see HUNGER 1

**2** a strong wish for something — see DESIRE

**3** positive regard for something — see LIKING

**4** urgent desire or interest — see EAGERNESS

**appetizing** *adj* very pleasing to the sense of taste — see DELICIOUS 1

**applaud** *vb* to declare enthusiastic approval of — see ACCLAIM

**applauding** *adj* expressing approval — see FAVORABLE 1

**applause** *n* enthusiastic and usually public expression of approval ⟨a design for a memorial for the victims of the attack that has received nothing but *applause* from officials, commentators, and the general public⟩
*syn* acclamation, cheering, cheers, ovation, plaudit(s), rave(s)
*rel* clapping; bravo, hallelujah, hosanna; acclaim, accolade, citation, commendation, compliment, encomium, eulogy, homage, paean, panegyric, salutation, tribute
*near ant* boo, hiss, hoot, jeer, raspberry, smirk, sneer, snicker, snigger, snort, whistle; gibe (*or* jibe), put-down, taunt
*ant* booing, hissing

**appliance** *n* an interesting and often novel device with a practical use — see GADGET

**applicability** *n* the fact or state of being pertinent — see PERTINENCE

**applicable** *adj* **1** capable of being put to use or account — see PRACTICAL 1
**2** having to do with the matter at hand — see PERTINENT
**3** meeting the requirements of a purpose or situation — see FIT 1

**applicant** *n* one who seeks an office, honor, position, or award — see CANDIDATE

**application** *n* the act or practice of employing something for a particular purpose — see USE 1

**apply** *vb* **1** to have a relation or connection ⟨does your rule about calling home *apply* to me as well?⟩
*syn* appertain, bear, pertain, refer, relate
*rel* affect, concern, interest, involve, touch; associate, connect, couple, interrelate, link, tie in; deal (with), treat
*phrases* have to do with
**2** to occupy (oneself) diligently or with close attention ⟨Sam *applied* himself to writing thank-you letters to everyone who'd helped sponsor him for the jamboree⟩
*syn* address, bend, buckle, devote, give
*rel* readdress, reapply; knuckle down, set (to), settle (down); busy, commit, concern, engage, involve; exert, exhaust, put out, spend, strain, stress, tax, trouble, wear out; carry on, pitch in, plunge (in); grind, hump, hustle, peg (away), plod, plow, plug (away), work
*near ant* dally, dawdle, dillydally, fiddle, fool (around), idle, mess (around), monkey (around), play, potter, putter, trifle
**3** to put a layer of on a surface — see SPREAD 2
**4** to put into action or service — see USE 1
**5** to bring to bear especially forcefully or effectively — see EXERT
**6** to carry out effectively — see ENFORCE

**appoint** *vb* **1** to decide upon (the time or date for an event) usually from a position of authority ⟨at the *appointed* hour we were in our places⟩
*syn* designate, fix, name, set
*rel* adopt, assign, choose, determine, establish, opt (for), pick, pin down, prefer, select, settle, single (out), specify; arrange, coordinate, orchestrate; advertise, announce, declare, publish
**2** to pick (someone) by one's authority for a specific position or duty ⟨Igor was *appointed* hall monitor for May⟩
*syn* assign, attach, commission, constitute, designate, detail, name
*rel* authorize, delegate, depute, deputize; inaugurate, induct, install, instate, ordain, invest; crown, enthrone, throne; choose, elect, handpick, nominate, select, single (out), vote (in)
*near ant* depose, dethrone, displace, eject, oust, overthrow, remove, throw out, uncrown, unmake
*ant* discharge, dismiss, expel, fire

**appointment** *n* **1** the state or fact of being chosen for a position or duty ⟨the *appointment* of the mayor's husband to the Board of Health came as a surprise⟩
*syn* assignment, commission, designation
*rel* billet, job, office, place, position, situation, spot, station; authorization, delegation, deputation, placement, ranking; induction, installation, installment (*or* instalment), instating, investiture, investment, ordination; choosing, election, nomination, picking, selection, singling out
*near ant* deposition, dethronement, ejection, ouster, overthrow, rejection, removal
*ant* discharge, dismissal, expulsion, firing
**2** an agreement to be present at a specified time and place — see ENGAGEMENT 2
**3** an assignment at which one regularly works for pay — see JOB 1
**4 appointments** *pl* the movable articles in a room — see FURNITURE

**apportion** *vb* **1** to give as a share or portion — see ALLOT
**2** to give out (something) in appropriate amounts or to appropriate individuals — see ADMINISTER 1

**apportionment** *n* the act or process of giving out something to each member of a group — see DISTRIBUTION 1

**apposite** *adj* having to do with the matter at hand — see PERTINENT

**appraisal** *n* **1** an opinion on the nature, character, or quality of something — see ESTIMATION 1
**2** the act of placing a value on the nature, character, or quality of something — see ESTIMATE 1

---

*syn* synonym(s) *rel* related words
*ant* antonym(s) *near ant* near antonym(s)

**appraise** *vb* to make an approximate or tentative judgment regarding — see ESTIMATE 1

**appraisement** *n* **1** an opinion on the nature, character, or quality of something — see ESTIMATION 1
**2** the act of placing a value on the nature, character, or quality of something — see ESTIMATE 1

**appreciable** *adj* able to be perceived by a sense or by the mind — see PERCEPTIBLE

**appreciate** *vb* **1** to become greater in extent, volume, amount, or number — see INCREASE 2
**2** to hold dear — see LOVE 1
**3** to recognize the meaning of — see COMPREHEND 1
**4** to think very highly or favorably of — see ADMIRE

**appreciation** *n* **1** a feeling of great approval and liking — see ADMIRATION 1
**2** acknowledgment of having received something good from another — see THANKS
**3** the knowledge gained from the process of coming to know or understand something — see COMPREHENSION

**appreciative** *adj* **1** expressing approval — see FAVORABLE 1
**2** feeling or expressing gratitude — see GRATEFUL 1

**appreciativeness** *n* acknowledgment of having received something good from another — see THANKS

**apprehend** *vb* **1** to recognize the meaning of — see COMPREHEND 1
**2** to take or keep under one's control by authority of law — see ARREST 1

**apprehended** *adj* taken and held prisoner — see CAPTIVE

**apprehension** *n* **1** suspicion or fear of future harm or misfortune ⟨Erica entered the dark cave with a great deal of *apprehension*⟩
***syn*** alarm, apprehensiveness, dread, foreboding, misgiving
***rel*** agitation, anxiousness, concern, disquiet, distress, disturbance, fearfulness, perturbation, solicitude, uneasiness; scruple, worry; doubt, incertitude, suspense, uncertainty, wariness; defeatism, pessimism; foreknowledge, premonition, presage, presentiment
***near ant*** anticipation, excitement, hope, hopefulness; confidence, optimism, sanguinity
**2** the act of taking or holding under one's control by authority of law — see ARREST
**3** the emotion experienced in the presence or threat of danger — see FEAR
**4** an uneasy state of mind usually over the possibility of an anticipated misfortune or trouble — see ANXIETY 1
**5** the knowledge gained from the process of coming to know or understand something — see COMPREHENSION

**apprehensiveness** *n* **1** an uneasy state of mind usually over the possibility of an anticipated misfortune or trouble — see ANXIETY 1
**2** suspicion or fear of future harm or misfortune — see APPREHENSION 1

**apprentice** *n* a person who helps a more skilled person — see HELPER

**apprise** *vb* to give information to — see ENLIGHTEN 1

**approach** *n* **1** an established course for traveling from one place to another — see PASSAGE 1
**2** the means or procedure for doing something — see METHOD

**approach** *vb* **1** to come near or nearer ⟨The parade's *approaching* ! I can hear the band playing!⟩
***syn*** close, draw on, near
***rel*** arrive, attain, come, gain, hit, land, make, reach, show up, turn up; adjoin, border, touch, verge
***near ant*** clear out, depart, exit, go, leave, light out, pull (out), quit, remove, run away, shove (off), take off, walk out
***ant*** back (up *or* away), recede, retire, retreat, withdraw
**2** to move closer to — see COME 1
**3** to come near or nearer to in character or quality — see APPROXIMATE

**approaching** *adj* being soon to appear or take place — see FORTHCOMING

**approbation** *n* an acceptance of something as satisfactory — see APPROVAL 1

**appropriate** *adj* meeting the requirements of a purpose or situation — see FIT 1

**appropriate** *vb* **1** to take or make use of without authority or right ⟨archaeologists once *appropriated* artifacts excavated at ancient African sites for their museums in Europe⟩
***syn*** arrogate, commandeer, preempt, usurp
***rel*** annex, claim, confiscate, expropriate, preoccupy, sequester; grab, grasp, seize, snatch, steal, take over, wrench, wrest; encroach, infringe, invade, trespass
**2** to take (something) without right and with an intent to keep — see STEAL 1

**appropriately** *adv* in a manner suitable for the occasion or purpose — see PROPERLY

**appropriateness** *n* the quality or state of being especially suitable or fitting ⟨Mrs. Bryce-Jones remarked on the *appropriateness* of window boxes on the cottage, noting they gave it a quaint, cheerful look⟩
***syn*** aptness, felicitousness, fitness, fittingness, rightness, seemliness, suitability, suitableness
***rel*** agreeableness, compatibility, congruity, harmoniousness; applicability, bearing, connection, materiality, pertinence, relevance; acceptability, adequacy, adequateness, satisfactoriness, serviceableness, usefulness
***near ant*** inapplicability, irrelevance; meaninglessness, pointlessness; incompatibility, incongruity
***ant*** inappropriateness, inaptness, infelicity, unfitness

**appropriation** *n* a sum of money allotted for a specific use by official or formal action ⟨the National Park Service received an increased *appropriation* for wildlife management⟩
***syn*** allocation, allotment, annuity, grant, subsidy
***rel*** advance, allowance, benefit, endowment, fund, stipend, trust

**approval** *n* an acceptance of something as satisfactory ⟨Does this dress I bought for the wedding meet with your *approval* ?⟩
***syn*** approbation, blessing, favor, imprimatur, OK (*or* okay)
***rel*** backing, endorsement, sanction, support; benediction, goodwill; agreement, assent, concurrence, consent; countenance, liking, satisfaction
***near ant*** refusal, rejection, repudiation; dislike, dissatisfaction; censure, condemnation, criticism, denunciation, deprecation, depreciation, disparagement, opprobrium, reprehension, reproach, reprobation
***ant*** disapprobation, disapproval, disfavor

**approve** *vb* to give official acceptance of something as satisfactory ⟨as soon as the pond project was *approved*, the bulldozers were at the site⟩
***syn*** authorize, clear, OK (*or* okay), ratify, sanction, warrant
***rel*** accept, acknowledge, affirm, confirm; accredit, certify, endorse (*also* indorse), validate; initial, sign; allow, license (*or* licence), permit; reapprove
***near ant*** ban, enjoin, forbid, interdict, prohibit; disregard, ignore, neglect, overlook; rebuff, rebut, refuse, spurn
***ant*** decline, deny, disallow, disapprove, negative, reject, turn down

**approve** (of) *vb* to have a favorable opinion of ⟨Mrs. Pinkerton doesn't *approve of* people who stand in the "12 items or less" lane with 13 items⟩
***syn*** accept, care (for), countenance, favor, OK (*or* okay), subscribe (to)
***rel*** acclaim, applaud, laud, praise, salute; back (up), stand by, support, sustain, uphold; bear, endure, tolerate; assent (to), concur (with), consent (to); commend, recommend; enjoy, like
***phrases*** go for, hold with
***near ant*** censure, condemn, criticize, damn, denounce, deprecate, depreciate, disparage, reprehend, reprobate; detest, dislike, hate, loathe; object (to), oppose
***ant*** disapprove (of), discountenance, disfavor, frown (on *or* upon)

**approving** *adj* **1** expressing approval — see FAVORABLE 1
**2** showing or expressing acceptance or approval — see POSITIVE

**approximate** *adj* being such only when compared to something else — see COMPARATIVE

**approximate** *vb* to come near or nearer to in character or quality ⟨Rob's violin performance last night didn't even *approximate* what he's really capable of when he's not feeling sick⟩
***syn*** approach, compare (with), measure up (to), stack up (against *or* with)
***rel*** add up (to), amount (to), come (to); duplicate, equal, match; mirror, parallel, reflect; border (on), touch (on), verge (on)

**apropos** *adj* having to do with the matter at hand — see PERTINENT

**apropos of** *prep* having to do with — see ABOUT 1

**apt** *adj* **1** having a tendency to be or act in a certain way — see PRONE 1
**2** meeting the requirements of a purpose or situation — see FIT 1

**aptitude** *n* a special and usually inborn ability — see TALENT

**aptness** *n* **1** an established pattern of behavior — see TENDENCY 1
**2** the quality or state of being especially suitable or fitting — see APPROPRIATENESS

**aquatic** *adj* living, lying, or occurring below the surface of the water — see UNDERWATER

**aqueduct** *n* an open man-made passageway for water — see CHANNEL 1

**arbiter** *n* one who works with opposing sides in order to bring about an agreement — see MEDIATOR

**arbitrary** *adj* **1** having or showing a tendency to force one's will on others without any regard to fairness or necessity ⟨an *arbitrary* piano teacher who makes all her students do the same exercises over and over again⟩
***syn*** dictatorial, high-handed, imperious, peremptory, willful (*or* wilful)
***rel*** arrogant, commanding, demanding, dominant, domineering, haughty, imperative, lordly, masterful, overbearing, presumptuous; authoritarian, autocratic, despotic, totalitarian, tyrannical (*also* tyrannic), tyrannous; capricious, changeable, erratic, mercurial, whimsical; biased, inequitable, partisan, prejudiced, unequal, unfair, unjust, unreasonable; unconscionable, unethical, unprincipled, unscrupulous
***near ant*** balanced, disinterested, dispassionate, equal, equitable, evenhanded, fair, impartial, just, nonpartisan, objective; rational, reasonable, understanding; unbiased, unprejudiced; ethical, honorable, irreproachable, law-abiding, moral, principled, unimpeachable
**2** lacking a definite plan, purpose, or pattern — see RANDOM

**arbitrate** *vb* to give an opinion about (something at issue or in dispute) — see JUDGE 1

**arbitrator** *n* one who works with opposing sides in order to bring about an agreement — see MEDIATOR

**arc** *n* something that curves or is curved — see BEND 1

**arc** *vb* to turn away from a straight line or course — see CURVE 1

**arch** *adj* 1 coming before all others in importance — see FOREMOST 1
2 displaying or marked by rude boldness — see NERVY 1
**arch** *n* something that curves or is curved — see BEND 1
**arch** *vb* 1 to cause to turn away from a straight line — see BEND 1
2 to turn away from a straight line or course — see CURVE 1
**archaic** *adj* having passed its time of use or usefulness — see OBSOLETE
**archetypal** *adj* 1 constituting, serving as, or worthy of being a pattern to be imitated — see MODEL
2 having or showing the qualities associated with the members of a particular group or kind — see TYPICAL 1
**archetype** *n* something from which copies are made — see ORIGINAL
**archive** *n* a place where books, periodicals, and records are kept for use but not for sale — see LIBRARY
**arctic** *adj* having a low or subnormal temperature — see COLD 1
**ardent** *adj* 1 having or expressing great depth of feeling — see FERVENT
2 showing urgent desire or interest — see EAGER
**ardor** *n* 1 depth of feeling ⟨candidates for citizenship reciting the oath of allegiance to the United States with all the *ardor* that they could muster⟩
***syn*** emotion, fervency, fervidness, fervor, heat, intensity, passion, vehemence, warmth
***rel*** histrionics, mawkishness, melodrama, sappiness, sentimentality; eagerness, earnestness, enthusiasm, excitement, gusto, zest; fanaticism, fever, fire, hot-bloodedness, infatuation, mania, obsession, zeal; compassion, responsiveness, sympathy, tenderness
***near ant*** aloofness, calmness, coldness, collectedness, composure, coolness, detachedness, dryness, phlegm, reserve, reservedness, reticence, taciturnity apathy, indifference, unconcern; stiffness, woodenness
***ant*** impassivity
2 urgent desire or interest — see EAGERNESS
**arduous** *adj* 1 requiring considerable physical or mental effort — see HARD 2
2 requiring much time, effort, or careful attention — see DEMANDING 1
**arduously** *adv* with great effort or determination — see HARD 1
**area** *n* 1 a part or portion having no fixed boundaries — see REGION 1
2 a region of activity, knowledge, or influence — see FIELD 2
**arena** *n* 1 a large room or building for enclosed public gatherings — see HALL 3
2 a region of activity, knowledge, or influence — see FIELD 2
**argot** *n* the special terms or expressions of a particular group or field — see TERMINOLOGY
**argue** *vb* 1 to state (something) as a reason in support of or against something under consideration ⟨Luis *argued* that a bake sale would make a lot less money than a car wash⟩
***syn*** assert, contend, maintain, plead, reason
***rel*** claim, insist; affirm, aver, avouch, avow; advance, offer, propose, submit; advise, counsel, recommend, suggest, urge; convince, persuade; advocate, champion, espouse, support; explain, justify, rationalize; consider, debate, discuss; counter, disprove, rebut, refute
2 to express different opinions about something often angrily ⟨Francesca didn't *argue* with her little brother the whole time they were at Walt Disney World⟩
***syn*** bicker, brawl, dispute, fall out, fight, hassle, quarrel, row, scrap, spat, squabble, wrangle
***rel*** challenge, dare, defy; clash, contend, contest; cavil, fuss, nitpick, quibble; consider, debate, discuss; kick, object, protest
***phrases*** bandy words, fall foul
***near ant*** coexist, get along; accept, agree, assent, concur, consent
3 to cause (someone) to agree with a belief or course of action by using arguments or earnest requests — see PERSUADE
4 to talk about (an issue) usually from various points of view and for the purpose of arriving at a decision or opinion — see DISCUSS
**arguer** *n* a person who takes part in a dispute — see DISPUTANT
**argument** *n* 1 an often noisy or angry expression of differing opinions ⟨the couple's *arguments* were often loud enough to be heard all over the neighborhood⟩
***syn*** altercation, bicker, brawl, cross fire, disagreement, dispute, falling-out, fight, hassle, misunderstanding, quarrel, row, scrap, spat, squabble, tiff, wrangle
***rel*** clash, run-in, skirmish, tussle; feud, vendetta; attack, contention, dissension; controversy, debate; fuss, objection, protest, protestation; affray, feud, fisticuffs, fracas, fray free-for-all, melee
2 a statement given to explain a belief or act — see REASON 1
3 an exchange of views for the purpose of exploring a subject or deciding an issue — see DISCUSSION 1
4 an idea or opinion that is put forth in a discussion or debate — see CONTENTION
**argumentative** *adj* 1 given to arguing ⟨Ryan's *argumentative* nature is such that he's always insisting he didn't make the fouls that the referee calls⟩
***syn*** contentious, disputatious, quarrelsome, scrappy
***rel*** bellicose, belligerent, combative, pugnacious, truculent; balky, contrary, ornery, perverse, restive, wayward; disobedient, froward, insubordinate, intractable, recalcitrant, refractory; hardheaded, headstrong, mulish, obdurate,

obstinate, pigheaded, resistant, self-willed, stubborn, unbending, uncompromising, uncooperative, unreasonable, unyielding, willful (*or* wilful)
***near ant*** acquiescent, agreeable, amenable, complaisant, compliant, complying, conciliatory, cooperative, obliging; docile, obedient, submissive, tractable
**2** feeling or displaying eagerness to fight — see BELLIGERENT

**arid** *adj* marked by little or no precipitation or humidity — see DRY 1

**arise** *vb* **1** to leave one's bed ⟨the travelers *arose* before dawn and were on their way as the sun came up⟩
***syn*** get up, rise, uprise
***rel*** arouse, awake, awaken, bestir, stir, wake
***near ant*** doze, drop (off), nap, nod, sleep, slumber; bunk, perch, roost, settle; couch, lie (down), recline
***ant*** bed (down), retire, turn in
**2** to come to one's attention especially gradually or unexpectedly ⟨note in your report any problems that *arise* while you are conducting the experiment⟩
***syn*** crop (up), emerge, materialize, spring (up), surface
***rel*** appear, come out, show up, turn up; chance, come, come about, fall out, go (on), go off, hap, happen, occur, pass, transpire; interfere, interpose, intervene, intrude
**3** to come into existence — see BEGIN 2
**4** to move or extend upward — see ASCEND

**aristocracy** *n* the highest class in a society ⟨at one time in China only the *aristocracy* could own land⟩
***syn*** gentry, upper class, upper crust
***rel*** elect, elite, establishment, gentlefolk, jet set, nobility, quality, royalty, society
***near ant*** commoners, (the) crowd, (the) masses, peasantry, peonage, (the) people, plebeians, (the) populace, (the) public, rank and file; bourgeoisie, middle class, working class; dregs, (the) herd, (the) mob, rabble, riffraff, scum, trash
***ant*** proletarians, proletariat

**aristocrat** *n* a man of high birth or social position — see GENTLEMAN 1

**aristocratic** *adj* of high birth, rank, or station — see NOBLE 1

**arithmetic** *n* the act or process of performing mathematical operations to find a value — see CALCULATION

**[1]arm** *n* a portable weapon from which a shot is discharged by gunpowder — see GUN 1

**[2]arm** *n* **1** an area of land that juts out into a body of water — see [2]CAPE
**2** the right or means to command or control others — see POWER 1

**armada** *n* a group of vehicles traveling together or under one management — see FLEET

**armed forces** *n pl* the combined army, air force, and navy of a nation ⟨our nation's *armed forces* are stationed throughout the world⟩
***syn*** military, service, troops
***rel*** GI's (*or* GIs), men-at-arms, rank and file, servicemen, servicewomen, soldiers, soldiery; militia, reserves; armor, defense
***near ant*** civilians, noncombatants

**armistice** *n* a temporary stopping of fighting — see TRUCE

**armor** *n* **1** means or method of defending — see DEFENSE 1
**2** something that encloses another thing especially to protect it — see [1]CASE

**armory** *n* a place where military arms are stored ⟨the soldier was sent to the *armory* to get a replacement weapon for the one that had been stolen⟩
***syn*** arsenal, depot, dump, magazine
***rel*** fort, fortress, stronghold; repository, storehouse, warehouse

**army** *n* **1** a large body of men and women organized for land warfare ⟨In 218 B.C., Hannibal marched into Italy with an *army* of 26,000, and even a few elephants, after crossing the Alps⟩
***syn*** battalion, host, legion
***rel*** infantry, ranks, regulars, soldiers, troops, troopers
**2** a great number of persons or things gathered together — see CROWD 1

**aroma** *n* a sweet or pleasant smell — see FRAGRANCE

**aromatic** *adj* having a pleasant smell — see FRAGRANT

**around** *adv* **1** on all sides or in every direction ⟨he looked *around*⟩ ⟨butterflies were flying all *around*⟩
***syn*** about, round
***rel*** all over, everyplace, everywhere; abroad, afloat, hereabouts (*or* hereabout)
**2** toward the opposite direction ⟨she turned *around* and saw him⟩
***syn*** about, back, round
***rel*** backward (*or* backwards), behind, down, downward, rearward (*or* rearwards); across, athwart, counter, counterclockwise
**3** at, within, or to a short distance or time — see NEAR 1
**4** from beginning to end — see THROUGH 1

**around** *prep* **1** close to ⟨I wouldn't stand *around* those rocks—there could be snakes under them⟩
***syn*** about, by, near, next to
***rel*** alongside, beside; across, along, at; circa
**2** in random positions within the boundaries of ⟨huge, strangely shaped rocks were scattered *around* the canyon floor⟩
***syn*** about, over, round, through, throughout
***rel*** on

**arouse** *vb* **1** to cause to stop sleeping — see WAKE 1
**2** to cease to be asleep — see WAKE 2
**3** to rouse to strong feeling or action — see PROVOKE 1

**arrange** *vb* **1** to come to an agreement or decision concerning the details of ⟨*arrange* a time for the meeting⟩ ⟨*arrange* money matters for your trip⟩
***syn*** decide, fix, set, settle
***rel*** agree, contract, pledge, promise; draft, frame, hammer (out), intrigue, lay out, maneuver, map (out), plan, program, schematize, scheme, shape, square away, work out; affirm, approve, authorize, clear, confirm, OK (*or* okay), sanction, warrant; close, complete, conclude, end, finalize, finish, round (off *or* out), wind up, wrap up; bargain, chaffer, deal, dicker, haggle, horse-trade, negotiate
***phrases*** dispose of
**2** to put into a particular arrangement — see ORDER 1
**3** to bring about through discussion and compromise — see NEGOTIATE 1
**4** to work out the details of (something) in advance — see PLAN 1

**arrangement** *n* **1** a method worked out in advance for achieving some objective — see PLAN 1
**2** the way in which something is sized, arranged, or organized — see FORMAT 1
**3** the way in which the elements of something (as a work of art) are arranged — see COMPOSITION 3
**4** the way objects in space or events in time are arranged or follow one another — see ORDER 1

**arrant** *adj* having no exceptions or restrictions — see ABSOLUTE 2

**array** *n* **1** a number of things considered as a unit — see GROUP 1
**2** a usually small number of persons considered as a unit — see GROUP 2
**3** dressy clothing — see FINERY
**4** the way objects in space or events in time are arranged or follow one another — see ORDER 1

**array** *vb* **1** to make more attractive by adding something that is beautiful or becoming — see DECORATE
**2** to outfit with clothes and especially fine or special clothes — see CLOTHE 1
**3** to put into a particular arrangement — see ORDER 1

**arrest** *n* the act of taking or holding under one's control by authority of law ⟨there have been only two *arrests* for driving while intoxicated in the county in the last six months⟩
***syn*** apprehension, pinch
***rel*** bust [*slang*], raid; capture, entrapment, seizure; captivity, confinement, detention, enchainment, immurement, imprisonment, incarceration, restraint
***near ant*** emancipation, liberation, release
***ant*** discharge

**arrest** *vb* **1** to take or keep under one's control by authority of law ⟨the inept robber was promptly *arrested* by the off-duty policeman he had tried to hold up⟩
***syn*** apprehend, bust [*slang*], nab, pick up, pinch, restrain, seize
***rel*** bag, capture, catch, collar, get, grab, grapple, hook, land, nail, snare, snatch, trap; confine, detain, hold, immure, imprison, incarcerate, intern, jail, lock (up); bind, enchain, fetter, handcuff, manacle, shackle, trammel
***near ant*** emancipate, free, liberate, loose, loosen, release, spring; unbind, unchain
***ant*** discharge
**2** to bring (something) to a standstill — see [1]HALT 1
**3** to hold the attention of as if by a spell — see ENTHRALL 1

**arrested** *adj* taken and held prisoner — see CAPTIVE

**arresting** *adj* **1** holding the attention or provoking interest — see INTERESTING
**2** likely to attract attention — see NOTICEABLE

**arrival** *n* the act of coming upon a scene ⟨spring's late *arrival* meant we were still skiing in mid-April⟩ ⟨the groom blamed his belated *arrival* for the wedding on a huge traffic snarl⟩
***syn*** advent, appearance
***rel*** approach, entrance, ingress; beginning, birth, commencement, dawn, dawning, debut, genesis, inception, morning, onset, start
***near ant*** dissipation, dissolution, evaporation, fading, melting, passing, vanishing; clearing out, egress, exit, exiting, leaving, retirement, withdrawal
***ant*** departing, departure, disappearance, going

**arrive** *vb* to get to a destination — see COME 2

**arrogance** *n* an exaggerated sense of one's importance that shows itself in the making of excessive or unjustified claims ⟨in his *arrogance* the president of the club made all the arrangements for the annual banquet without consulting the members⟩
***syn*** haughtiness, imperiousness, loftiness, lordliness, masterfulness, peremptoriness, pompousness, presumptuousness, pretense (*or* pretence), pretension, pretentiousness, self-importance, superciliousness, superiority
***rel*** authoritativeness, bossiness, dominance, high-handedness; condescension, disdain, scorn; snobbery, snobbishness, snobbism, snootiness; cheek, cheekiness, impertinence, impudence, sauciness; boastfulness, bombast, braggadocio, swagger, vainglorious ness, vainglory; cockiness, complacence, conceit, egoism, egotism, pride, pridefulness, self-centeredness, self-conceit, self-satisfaction, smugness, vanity
***near ant*** bashfulness, demureness, retiringness, shyness; diffidence, self-doubt, timidity; meekness, passiveness, passivity, submissiveness; quietness, reserve, reservedness
***ant*** humility, modesty

**arrogant** *adj* having a feeling of superiority that shows itself in an overbearing attitude ⟨the *arrogant* young lawyer elbowed his way to the head of the line of custom-

ers, declaring that he was too busy to wait like everybody else〉
*syn* cavalier, haughty, highfalutin, high-handed, high-hat, imperious, important, lofty, lordly, masterful, overweening, peremptory, pompous, presumptuous, pretentious, supercilious, superior, uppish, uppity
*rel* authoritarian, bossy, dominant, dominating, domineering, magisterial, pontificating; condescending, disdainful, patronizing; impertinent, impudent, saucy; snobbish, snobby, snooty; boastful, bombastic, braggart, bragging, cocky, swaggering, vain, vainglorious; complacent, conceited, egocentric, egoistic, egotistic (*or* egotistical), prideful, proud, self-centered, self-conceited, self-satisfied, smug, stuck-up
*near ant* bashful, cowering, cringing, demure, diffident, mousy (*or* mousey), overmodest, self-doubting, shrinking, shy, subdued, timid; acquiescent, compliant, deferential, meek, passive, submissive, unaggressive, unassertive, unassuming, unobtrusive, yielding; quiet, reserved, retiring
*ant* humble, modest

**arrogate** *vb* to take or make use of without authority or right — see APPROPRIATE 1

**arsenal** *n* a place where military arms are stored — see ARMORY

**arsonist** *n* a person who deliberately and unlawfully sets fire to a building or other property 〈they finally caught the *arsonist*, but only after he'd set fire to four barns〉
*syn* firebug, incendiary
*rel* igniter (*or* ignitor)

**art** *n* subtle or imaginative ability in inventing, devising, or executing something — see SKILL 1

**artery** *n* a passage cleared for public vehicular travel — see WAY 1

**artful** *adj* **1** clever at attaining one's ends by indirect and often deceptive means 〈the lawyer, by her *artful* questioning, got the witness to admit he had been lying〉
*syn* beguiling, cagey (*also* cagy), crafty, cunning, devious, foxy, guileful, slick, sly, subtle, wily
*rel* astute, cute, facile, glib, sharp, shrewd; crooked, deceitful, deceptive, dishonest, insidious, insinuating, Machiavellian, shady, shifty, slippery, sneaky, treacherous, tricky, underhand, underhanded, unscrupulous; backhanded, double-dealing, hypocritical, insincere, mealymouthed, smooth-tongued, two-faced; circuitous, circular, roundabout; clandestine, concealed, covert, furtive, hugger-mugger, secret, stealthy, surreptitious, undercover; calculating, designing, scheming, plotting
*near ant* obvious, open, patent, plain, public, unconcealed; aboveboard, candid, direct, forthright, frank, honest, natural, outspoken, plainspoken, real, simple, sincere, straightforward, unaffected, unpretending
*ant* artless, guileless, ingenuous
**2** showing a use of the imagination and creativity especially in inventing — see CLEVER 1
**3** accomplished with trained ability — see SKILLFUL

**artfulness** *n* **1** skill in achieving one's ends through indirect, subtle, or underhanded means — see CUNNING 1
**2** subtle or imaginative ability in inventing, devising, or executing something — see SKILL 1

**article** *n* a short piece of writing typically expressing a point of view — see ESSAY 1

**articulate** *adj* able to express oneself clearly and well 〈the television crew covering the science fair were looking for photogenic and *articulate* students to explain their projects on the air〉
*syn* eloquent, fluent, well-spoken
*rel* facile, glib, smooth-tongued, voluble; expressive, outspoken, verbal, vocal; blabby, chatty, garrulous, loquacious, talkative, verbose; unfaltering, unhesitating
*near ant* faltering, halting, hesitant, maundering, mumbling, muttering, sputtering, stammering, stumbling, stuttering; mute, speechless, tongue-tied, voiceless
*ant* inarticulate

**articulate** *vb* **1** to utter clearly and distinctly 〈uses a very measured tone and *articulates* every syllable when issuing scoldings〉
*syn* enunciate
*rel* express, pronounce, say, verbalize, vocalize, voice; speak out, speak up
*near ant* falter, grunt, halt, hesitate, maunder, sputter, stammer, stumble, stutter; mouth, mumble, murmur, mutter, whisper
**2** to convey in appropriate or telling terms — see PHRASE
**3** to express (a thought or emotion) in words — see SAY 1

**articulateness** *n* the art or power of speaking or writing in a forceful and convincing way — see ELOQUENCE

**articulation** *n* **1** an act, process, or means of putting something into words — see EXPRESSION 1
**2** the clear and accurate pronunciation of words especially in public speaking — see DICTION 1

**artifice** *n* **1** a clever often underhanded means to achieve an end — see TRICK 1
**2** skill in achieving one's ends through indirect, subtle, or underhanded means — see CUNNING 1
**3** subtle or imaginative ability in inventing, devising, or executing something — see SKILL 1
**4** the inclination or practice of misleading others through lies or trickery — see DECEIT
**5** the use of clever underhanded actions to achieve an end — see TRICKERY

**artificer** *n* a person whose occupation requires skill with the hands — see ARTISAN

**artificial** *adj* **1** lacking in natural or spontaneous quality ⟨the beauty-pageant contestants' *artificial* smiles looked like they were glued on their faces⟩
*syn* affected, assumed, bogus, contrived, factitious, fake, false, feigned, forced, mechanical, mock, phony (*also* phoney), pretended, pseudo, put-on, sham, simulated, spurious, strained, unnatural
*rel* automatic, canned, concocted, fabricated, labored, manufactured, unauthentic, unreal, unrealistic; empty, facile, hollow, hypocritical, insincere, left-handed; exaggerated, histrionic, melodramatic, overacted, overdone, theatrical; cute, cutesy, goody-goody, mincing, overrefined, simpering; conventional, formal, impersonal, inflexible, rigid, stiff, stylized, wooden; artful, calculated, conscious, cultivated, deliberate, premeditated, studied
*near ant* authentic, bona fide, real, realistic, true; honest, ingenuous, sincere, unpretending; easy, effortless, smooth; extemporaneous, impromptu, impulsive, instinctive, unconscious, unprompted, unrehearsed
*ant* artless, genuine, natural, spontaneous, unaffected, unfeigned, unforced
**2** not being or expressing what one appears to be or express — see INSINCERE
**3** being such in appearance only and made with or manufactured from usually cheaper materials — see IMITATION

**artillery** *n* large firearms (as cannon or rockets) ⟨during the *artillery* attack families hid in their cellars⟩
*syn* guns, ordnance
*rel* ammunition, armament, arms, munitions, weaponry, weapons

**artisan** *n* a person whose occupation requires skill with the hands ⟨we visited a re-created 19th-century New England village that features an array of *artisans* —a cooper, a carpenter, a blacksmith, a potter, a glassblower⟩
*syn* artificer, craftsman, handicrafter, tradesman
*rel* artist, maker; journeyman, master; mechanic, smith, technician, wright; handyman

**artist** *n* a person with a high level of knowledge or skill in a field — see EXPERT

**artistic** *adj* of or relating to the fine arts — see CULTURAL

**artistry** *n* subtle or imaginative ability in inventing, devising, or executing something — see SKILL 1

**artless** *adj* **1** free from any intent to deceive or impress others — see GUILELESS
**2** hastily or roughly constructed — see RUDE 1

**artlessly** *adv* without any attempt to impress by deception or exaggeration — see NATURALLY 3

**artlessness** *n* the quality or state of being simple and sincere — see NAÏVETÉ 1

**as** *conj* for the reason that — see SINCE

**ascend** *vb* to move or extend upward ⟨the path *ascended* so steeply at one point that we had to scramble up on our hands and knees⟩
*syn* arise, climb, lift, mount, rise, soar, up, uprise, upsweep, upturn
*rel* boost, elevate, raise, uplift, upraise; take off, zoom; crest, scale, surmount, top
*near ant* dive, nose-dive, plummet, plunge, sink, slide
*ant* decline, descend, dip, drop, fall (off)

**ascendancy** *n* controlling power or influence over others — see SUPREMACY 1

**ascension** *n* the act or an instance of rising or climbing up — see ASCENT 1

**ascent** *n* **1** the act or an instance of rising or climbing up ⟨our plane broke through some heavy low clouds during its *ascent* and leveled off once we were above them⟩
*syn* ascension, climb, rise, rising, soar
*rel* boost, hike, increase, raise; elevation, levitation, lift-off, raising, takeoff; heave, upheaval, uplifting, upraising, upsurge, upsweep, upswing, uptrend, upturn, upwelling
*near ant* dive, nosedive, plop, plummeting, plunge, sinking; decline, decrease
*ant* descent, dip, drop, fall
**2** an upward slope ⟨we'd reached the final *ascent* of the trail to the summit⟩
*syn* rise, upgrade
*rel* grade, incline; climb, hump, mound, ridge, swell
*near ant* basin, depression, hollow
*ant* declension, decline, declivity, descent, downgrade
**3** a raising or a state of being raised to a higher rank or position — see ADVANCEMENT 1

**ascertain** *vb* **1** to come to an awareness — see DISCOVER 1
**2** to come upon after searching, study, or effort — see FIND 1

**ascribe** *vb* to explain (something) as being the result of something else — see CREDIT 1

**aseptic** *adj* free from filth, infection, or dangers to health — see SANITARY

**ashamed** *adj* suffering from or expressive of a feeling of responsibility for wrongdoing — see GUILTY 2

**ashen** *adj* lacking a healthy skin color — see PALE 2

**ashes** *n pl* the portion or bits of something left over or behind after it has been destroyed — see REMAINS 1

**ashy** *adj* lacking a healthy skin color — see PALE 2

**aside from** *prep* not including — see EXCEPT

**as if** *conj* the way it would be or one would do if ⟨she looked *as if* she wanted to ask one more question before we left⟩
*syn* as though, like

**asinine** *adj* showing or marked by a lack of good sense or judgment — see FOOLISH 1

**asininity** *n* **1** a foolish act or idea — see FOLLY 1
**2** lack of good sense or judgment — see FOOLISHNESS 1

**ask** *vb* **1** to put a question or questions to ⟨my grandfather *asked* me all about my trip⟩
***syn*** inquire (of), interrogate, query, question, quiz
***rel*** cross-examine, examine, grill, pump; poll, survey
***near ant*** rejoin, retort; comment, observe, remark
***ant*** answer, reply, respond
**2** to make a request of ⟨*ask* the sales clerk for assistance⟩
***syn*** request, solicit
***rel*** appeal (to), beg, beseech, entreat, implore, importune, invoke, petition, pray, supplicate; demand, enjoin, exact, press, require
***phrases*** call on (*or* upon)
**3** to set or receive as a price — see CHARGE 1

**ask** (for) *vb* **1** to make a request for ⟨don't be afraid to *ask for* help if you need it⟩
***syn*** call (for), plead (for), quest, request, seek, solicit, sue (for)
***rel*** apply (for), beg (for), clamor (for), urge; demand, enjoin, exact, insist (on), require, requisition
**2** to act so as to make (something) more likely — see COURT 1
**3** to give a request or demand for — see ORDER 2

**askance** *adv* with distrust ⟨we looked *askance* at the dealer's assertion that the car had never been in an accident⟩
***syn*** distrustfully, doubtfully, doubtingly, dubiously, mistrustfully, skeptically, suspiciously
***rel*** hesitantly, hesitatingly, incredulously, questioningly, quizzically, unbelievingly; charily, guardedly, warily; captiously, critically, cynically, deprecatingly, disapprovingly, disparagingly, negatively, reproachfully, unfavorably; anxiously, apprehensively, uncomfortably, uneasily
***phrases*** with a grain of salt
***near ant*** approvingly, favorably, positively; confidently, sanguinely; credulously, uncritically
***ant*** trustfully, trustingly

**askew** *adj* inclined or twisted to one side — see AWRY

**aslant** *adj* inclined or twisted to one side — see AWRY

**asleep** *adj* **1** being in a state of suspended consciousness ⟨Paul was *asleep* when the earthquake struck⟩
***syn*** dormant, dozing, napping, resting, sleeping, slumbering
***rel*** drowsy, nodding, sleepy, slumberous (*or* slumbrous), somnolent; dreaming, reposing; hypnotized, mesmerized, semiconscious
***near ant*** aware, conscious; sleepless; aroused, astir, up
***ant*** awake, wakeful, wide-awake
**2** lacking in sensation or feeling — see NUMB

**aspect** *n* **1** a certain way in which something appears or may be regarded ⟨depending on what *aspect* of college life you consider most important, there are several colleges which might be good for you⟩
***syn*** angle, facet, hand, phase, side
***rel*** air, appearance, character, color, complexion, condition, face, look, semblance, shape, state, visage; period, stage, step; point of view, position, posture, stance, standpoint, view, viewpoint; interpretation, reading, rendering, translation, version; article, case, component, count, detail, element, factor, instance, item, matter, part, particular, point, regard, respect
**2** the outward form of someone or something especially as indicative of a quality — see APPEARANCE 1

**asperity** *n* **1** a harsh or sharp quality — see EDGE 1
**2** biting sharpness of feeling or expression — see ACRIMONY 1
**3** something that is a cause for suffering or special effort especially in the attainment of a goal — see DIFFICULTY 1

**asperse** *vb* to make untrue and harmful statements about — see SLANDER

**aspersing** *n* the making of false statements that damage another's reputation — see SLANDER

**aspirant** *n* one who seeks an office, honor, position, or award — see CANDIDATE

**aspiration** *n* **1** eager desire for personal advancement — see AMBITION 1
**2** something that one hopes or intends to accomplish — see GOAL

**aspire** *vb* to have in mind as a purpose or goal — see INTEND

**aspiring** *adj* having a strong desire for personal advancement — see AMBITIOUS 1

**ass** *n* a sturdy and patient domestic mammal that is used especially to carry things — see DONKEY 1

**assail** *vb* **1** to criticize harshly and usually publicly — see ATTACK 2
**2** to take sudden, violent action against — see ATTACK 1

**assassin** *n* a person who kills another person ⟨shot down by an unknown *assassin*⟩
***syn*** killer, murderer
***rel*** butcher, executioner, slaughterer, slayer

**assault** *n* the act or action of setting upon with force or violence — see ATTACK 1

**assault** *vb* to take sudden, violent action against — see ATTACK 1

**assay** *n* the separation and identification of the parts of a whole — see ANALYSIS 1

**assay** *vb* **1** to identify and examine the basic elements or parts of (something) es-

---

***syn*** synonym(s) ***rel*** related words
***ant*** antonym(s) ***near ant*** near antonym(s)

pecially for discovering interrelationships — see ANALYZE
2 to make an effort to do — see ATTEMPT

**assemblage** *n* 1 a body of people come together in one place — see GATHERING 1
2 a mass or quantity that has piled up or that has been gathered — see ACCUMULATION 1
3 a number of things considered as a unit — see GROUP 1
4 an organized group of objects acquired and maintained for study, exhibition, or personal pleasure — see COLLECTION 1

**assemble** *vb* 1 to come together into one body or place ⟨the graduates were told to *assemble* in the cafeteria an hour before the ceremony⟩
***syn*** cluster, collect, concentrate, conglomerate, congregate, convene, converge, forgather (*or* foregather), gather, meet, rendezvous
***rel*** affiliate, ally, associate, band (together), club, collaborate, confederate, conjoin, consolidate, consort, cooperate, couple, federate, gang (up), join, merge, unite
***near ant*** depart, leave, take off; disjoin, dissociate, disunite
***ant*** break up, disband, disperse, split up
2 to form by putting together parts or materials — see BUILD
3 to bring together in assembly by or as if by command — see CONVOKE
4 to bring together in one body or place — see GATHER 1

**assembly** *n* 1 a body of people come together in one place — see GATHERING 1
2 a body of persons gathered for religious worship — see CONGREGATION 1
3 a coming together of a number of persons for a specified purpose — see MEETING 1

**assert** *vb* 1 to state clearly and strongly ⟨Mrs. Cartwright is never afraid to *assert* her allegiance to flag and country⟩
***syn*** affirm, aver, avouch, avow, declare, lay down, profess
***rel*** advance, advertise, boost, plug, promote, publicize; announce, blare, call, proclaim, pronounce, say; accent, accentuate, emphasize, stress, underline, underscore; advocate, champion, defend, espouse, support, uphold; assure, convince, persuade; explain, justify, rationalize
***near ant*** minimize, understate; disregard, ignore, neglect, overlook
2 to state (something) as a reason in support of or against something under consideration — see ARGUE 1
3 to state as a fact usually forcefully — see CLAIM 1

**assertion** *n* 1 a solemn and often public declaration of the truth or existence of something — see PROTESTATION
2 an idea or opinion that is put forth in a discussion or debate — see CONTENTION

**assertive** *adj* 1 having or showing a bold forcefulness in the pursuit of a goal — see AGGRESSIVE 1
2 marked by or uttered with forcefulness — see EMPHATIC 1

**assertiveness** *n* the quality or state of being forceful (as in expression) — see VEHEMENCE 1

**assess** *vb* 1 to establish or apply as a charge or penalty — see IMPOSE
2 to make an approximate or tentative judgment regarding — see ESTIMATE 1

**assessment** *n* 1 a charge usually of money collected by the government from people or businesses for public use — see TAX
2 an opinion on the nature, character, or quality of something — see ESTIMATION 1
3 the act of placing a value on the nature, character, or quality of something — see ESTIMATE 1

**assets** *n pl* the total of one's money and property — see WEALTH 1

**assiduity** *n* attentive and persistent effort — see DILIGENCE

**assiduous** *adj* involved in often constant activity — see BUSY 1

**assiduously** *adv* with great effort or determination — see HARD 1

**assiduousness** *n* attentive and persistent effort — see DILIGENCE

**assign** *vb* 1 to give a task, duty, or responsibility to — see ENTRUST 1
2 to give as a share or portion — see ALLOT
3 to give over the legal possession or ownership of — see TRANSFER 1
4 to pick (someone) by one's authority for a specific position or duty — see APPOINT 2

**assignment** *n* 1 a piece of work that needs to be done regularly — see CHORE 1
2 a specific task with which a person or group is charged — see MISSION
3 something assigned to be read or studied — see LESSON
4 the state or fact of being chosen for a position or duty — see APPOINTMENT 1

**assimilate** *vb* to make a part of a body or system — see EMBODY 1

**assist** *n* an act or instance of helping — see HELP 1

**assist** *vb* to provide (someone) with what is useful or necessary to achieve an end — see HELP 1

**assistance** *n* an act or instance of helping — see HELP 1

**assistant** *n* a person who helps a more skilled person — see HELPER

**associate** *n* 1 a person frequently seen in the company of another ⟨after he took up skateboarding, Michael gained a whole new set of *associates*⟩
***syn*** cohort, companion, comrade, crony, fellow, hobnobber, mate
***rel*** colleague, coworker, equal, peer, workmate; accomplice, affiliate, ally, collaborator, confederate, partner; buddy, chum, confidant, familiar, friend, hearty, intimate, pal; compatriot, countryman; classmate, housemate, messmate, playmate, roommate, schoolmate, shipmate,

teammate; attendant, escort; hanger-on, leech, parasite
2 a fellow worker — see COLLEAGUE

**associate** *vb* 1 to come or be together as friends ⟨a boy who would *associate* only with other hard-core basketball fans⟩
***syn*** chum, consort, fraternize, hang around, hobnob, pal (around)
***rel*** affiliate, ally, attach, band, bond, club, collaborate, collude, confederate, conjoin, connect, cooperate, couple, gang, get along, group, hook, interrelate, join, knot, league, link, mingle, mix, rally, relate, side, socialize, team, tie, wed
***phrases*** rub elbows (with), rub shoulders (with), take up with
***near ant*** avoid, cold-shoulder, shun, snub; alienate, estrange; break up, disband, disperse, split up; disjoin, dissociate, disunite, divorce, sever, split, sunder
2 to think of (something) in combination ⟨Kelly *associates* getting shots with ice cream cones, her treat every time she goes to the doctor⟩
***syn*** connect, correlate, identify, link, relate
***rel*** compare, equate, liken; group, join, lump (together), tie (together)
***near ant*** contrast, differentiate, discriminate, distinguish, separate, set off
3 to come together to form a single unit — see UNITE 1
4 to form or enter into an association that furthers the interests of its members — see ALLY
5 to take part in social activities — see SOCIALIZE

**association** *n* 1 the state of having shared interests or efforts (as in social or business matters) ⟨Rita was honored for her long *association* with the Montgomery Benevolent Society⟩
***syn*** affiliation, alliance, collaboration, confederation, connection, cooperation, hookup, liaison, linkup, partnership, relation, relationship, tie-up, union
***rel*** business, dealings, interaction; exchange, interconnection, interrelation, mutualism, reciprocity, symbiosis; incorporation, integration, merger, unification; affinity, attachment, closeness, intimacy, rapport, sympathy; kinship, oneness, solidarity, togetherness, unity; companionship, company, fellowship
***near ant*** breakup, dissolution, disunion; division, parting, separation, severance, split; alienation, divorce, estrangement
***ant*** dissociation
2 a group of persons formally joined together for some common interest ⟨all *associations* meeting on school property must be registered with and approved by the principal's office⟩
***syn*** brotherhood, club, college, congress, council, fellowship, fraternity, guild (*also* gild), institute, institution, junto, league, order, organization, society, sodality
***rel*** collective, commune, community, cooperative; alliance, bloc, coalition, partnership; body, group; circle, clan, clique, coterie, lot, set; crew, outfit, party, squad, team; branch, chapter, local; faithful, fold, membership; sisterhood, sorority; cabal, confederacy, conspiracy; band, gang, ring; cartel, combine, syndicate
3 the fact or state of having something in common — see CONNECTION 1

**assort** *vb* to arrange or assign according to type — see CLASSIFY 1

**assorted** *adj* consisting of many things of different sorts — see MISCELLANEOUS

**assortment** *n* 1 an unorganized collection or mixture of various things — see MISCELLANY 1
2 the quality or state of being composed of many different elements or types — see VARIETY 1

**assuage** *vb* 1 to make more bearable or less severe — see HELP 2
2 to put a complete end to (a physical need or desire) — see SATISFY 1

**assume** *vb* 1 to take to or upon oneself ⟨Josh promised to *assume* responsibility for any damage to the flower beds caused by the volleyball game in the backyard⟩
***syn*** accept, bear, shoulder, take over, undertake
***rel*** adopt, embrace; back, endorse (*also* indorse), espouse, stand by, support, uphold; accede, acquiesce, agree, assent, consent
***near ant*** abjure, recant, renounce, retract, take back; decline, refuse, reject, spurn, turn down; abstain, forbear, refrain; avoid, bypass, detour
***ant*** disavow, disclaim, disown, repudiate
2 to take as true or as a fact without actual proof ⟨everyone *assumed*, wrongly, that someone else was bringing dessert⟩
***syn*** postulate, premise, presume, presuppose, suppose
***rel*** accept, believe, credit, swallow; conclude, deduce, gather, judge, infer, take; conjecture, figure, guess, reckon [*chiefly dialect*], surmise, suspect, think; conceive, dream, fancy, imagine, perceive, preconceive; hypothesize, speculate, theorize; affirm, allege, assert, aver, avouch, avow, claim, contend, declare, insist, maintain, profess
***phrases*** take for granted
***near ant*** challenge, disbelieve, discount, discredit, dispute, distrust, doubt, mistrust, question, suspect, wonder (about); deny, disavow, disclaim, disown, reject, repudiate; confute, disprove, rebut, refute
3 to form an opinion from little or no evidence — see GUESS 1
4 to present a false appearance of — see FEIGN

**assumed** *adj* 1 appearing to be true on the basis of evidence that may or may not be confirmed — see APPARENT 1
2 lacking in natural or spontaneous quality — see ARTIFICIAL 1

---

***syn*** synonym(s) ***rel*** related words
***ant*** antonym(s) ***near ant*** near antonym(s)

**assumption** *n* something taken as being true or factual and used as a starting point for a course of action or reasoning ⟨the widespread *assumption* that violent entertainment leads to violent behavior in children⟩ ⟨your argument is faulty because it's based on erroneous *assumptions*⟩
***syn*** postulate, premise, presumption, presupposition, supposition
***rel*** hypothesis, proposition, theory, thesis; axiom, truism, verity; belief, canon, doctrine, dogma, gospel, law; precept, principle, rule, standard, tenet; basis, foundation, ground; conclusion, deduction, inference; affirmation, assertion, avouchment, declaration
**assurance** *n* **1** a state of mind in which one is free from doubt — see CONFIDENCE 2
**2** great faith in oneself or one's abilities — see CONFIDENCE 1
**assure** *vb* **1** to ease the grief or distress of — see COMFORT 1
**2** to make sure, certain, or safe — see ENSURE
**assured** *adj* **1** having or showing a mind free from doubt — see CERTAIN 2
**2** having or showing great faith in oneself or one's abilities — see CONFIDENT 1
**assuredly** *adv* without any question — see INDEED 1
**assuredness** *n* a state of mind in which one is free from doubt — see CONFIDENCE 2
**astern** *adv* near, toward, or in the stern of a ship or the tail of an aircraft — see AFT
**as though** *conj* the way it would be or one would do if — see AS IF
**astir** *adj* marked by much life, movement, or activity — see ALIVE 2
**astonish** *vb* to make a strong impression on (someone) with something unexpected — see SURPRISE 1
**astonished** *adj* **1** affected with sudden and great wonder or surprise — see THUNDERSTRUCK
**2** filled with amazement or wonder — see OPENMOUTHED
**astonishing** *adj* **1** causing a strong emotional reaction because unexpected — see SURPRISING 1
**2** causing wonder or astonishment — see MARVELOUS 1
**astonishment** *n* **1** the rapt attention and deep emotion caused by the sight of something extraordinary — see WONDER 2
**2** the state of being strongly impressed by something unexpected or unusual — see SURPRISE 2
**astound** *vb* to make a strong impression on (someone) with something unexpected — see SURPRISE 1
**astounded** *adj* **1** affected with sudden and great wonder or surprise — see THUNDERSTRUCK
**2** filled with amazement or wonder — see OPENMOUTHED
**astounding** *adj* **1** causing a strong emotional reaction because unexpected — see SURPRISING 1
**2** causing wonder or astonishment — see MARVELOUS 1
**astral** *adj* of or relating to the stars — see STELLAR 1
**astray** *adv* off the desired or intended path or course — see WRONG 1
**astronomical** *also* **astronomic** *adj* unusually large — see HUGE
**astronomically** *adv* to a large extent or degree — see GREATLY 2
**astute** *adj* having or showing a practical cleverness or judgment — see SHREWD
**asunder** *adv* into parts or to pieces — see APART
**as well as** *prep* in addition to — see BESIDES 1
**asylum** *n* **1** a place where insane people are cared for — see MADHOUSE 1
**2** something (as a building) that offers cover from the weather or protection from danger — see SHELTER
**at all** *adv* in any way or respect ⟨Ted wasn't *at all* pleased with the way his mother's birthday cake came out⟩
***syn*** anywise, ever, half
***rel*** somehow, someway; remotely
***phrases*** by any means
**athirst** *adj* showing urgent desire or interest — see EAGER
**athwart** *adv* in a line or direction running from corner to corner — see CROSSWISE
**athwart** *prep* to the opposite side of — see ACROSS
**atmosphere** *n* **1** a special quality or impression associated with something — see AURA
**2** the circumstances, conditions, or objects by which one is surrounded — see ENVIRONMENT
**atom** *n* a very small piece — see BIT 1
**atomic** *adj* very small in size — see TINY
**atomize** *vb* to reduce to fine particles — see POWDER
**atone** (for) *vb* to make up for (an offense) — see EXPIATE
**atrocious** *adj* **1** extremely disturbing or repellent — see HORRIBLE 1
**2** extremely unsatisfactory — see WRETCHED 1
**atrociousness** *n* **1** the quality of inspiring intense dread or dismay — see HORROR 1
**2** the state or quality of being utterly evil — see ENORMITY 1
**atrocity** *n* **1** the quality of inspiring intense dread or dismay — see HORROR 1
**2** the state or quality of being utterly evil — see ENORMITY 1
**attach** *vb* **1** to cause (something) to hold to another — see FASTEN 1
**2** to pick (someone) by one's authority for a specific position or duty — see APPOINT 2
**attached** *adj* having a liking or affection — see FOND 1
**attachment** *n* **1** a feeling of strong or constant regard for and dedication to someone — see LOVE 1

2 something that is not necessary in itself but adds to the convenience or performance of the main piece of equipment — see ACCESSORY 1

**attack** *n* 1 the act or action of setting upon with force or violence ⟨The USS Constitution was nicknamed "Old Ironsides" after its oaken hull successfully withstood a British *attack*⟩
***syn*** aggression, assault, blitzkrieg, charge, descent, offense (*or* offence), offensive, onset, onslaught, raid, rush, strike
***rel*** ambuscade, ambush; counterattack, counteroffensive, sally, sortie; foray, incursion, invasion; pillage, ravage, sack; air raid, blitz, bombardment; siege, storm
***near ant*** defense, defensive, guard, shield; opposition, resistance; protection, security, shelter
2 a sudden experiencing of a physical or mental disorder ⟨malaria is characterized by periodic *attacks* of chills and fever⟩
***syn*** bout, case, fit, seizure, siege, spell
***rel*** recurrence, relapse; brainstorm, convulsion, pang, paroxysm, spasm, throe; breakdown, collapse, prostration
***near ant*** arrest, relief, remission

**attack** *vb* 1 to take sudden, violent action against ⟨my dog unexpectedly *attacked* the mailman, sinking his teeth into the startled man's leg⟩
***syn*** assail, assault, beset, charge, descend (on *or* upon), jump (on), pounce (on *or* upon), raid, rush, storm, strike
***rel*** gang (up on), mob, swarm; mug, rob; ambuscade, ambush, surprise, waylay; blitz, bomb, bombard; beleaguer, besiege; harry, loot, pillage, plunder, ravage, sack; foray, invade, overrun
***phrases*** fly at, give it to, go at, set upon
***near ant*** cover, defend, guard, protect, secure, shield
2 to criticize harshly and usually publicly ⟨the mayor and all his aides were *attacked* mercilessly in the press when the scandal erupted⟩
***syn*** abuse, assail, belabor, blast, castigate, excoriate, jump (on), lambaste (*or* lambast), scathe, slam, vituperate
***rel*** berate, harangue, harass, harry, revile, scold; blaspheme, curse, execrate, imprecate, profane; affront, insult, slur; asperse, bad-mouth, belittle, disparage, put down; libel, slander, traduce; chastise, chide, criticize, rebuke, reprimand, reproof; fulminate, lash (out)
***near ant*** acclaim, commend, compliment, laud, praise
3 to start work on energetically ⟨Courtney *attacked* the huge mess in her room with determination and enthusiasm⟩
***syn*** tackle, wade (into)
***rel*** address, approach, face; buckle (down to), concentrate (on), focus (on), knuckle down (to), zero in (on); fall (to), pitch in, plunge (in), settle (down); pursue, take up, undertake
***phrases*** go at, have at, sail into
***near ant*** avoid, evade, shun; dally, dawdle, dillydally, fiddle, fool, idle, lag, mess, monkey, play, poke, potter, putter, trifle

**attain** *vb* 1 to obtain (as a goal) through effort — see ACHIEVE 1
2 to receive as return for effort — see EARN 1

**attainable** *adj* 1 capable of being done or carried out — see POSSIBLE 1
2 possible to get — see AVAILABLE 1

**attainment** *n* 1 a successful result brought about by hard work — see ACCOMPLISHMENT 1
2 the state of being actual or complete — see FRUITION

**attempt** *n* an effort to do or accomplish something ⟨it took several *attempts* before we made good ice cream with an old-fashioned hand-cranked ice cream freezer⟩
***syn*** crack, endeavor, essay, fling, go, pass, shot, stab, trial, try, whack
***rel*** bid, striving, struggle, throes, undertaking; trial and error

**attempt** *vb* to make an effort to do ⟨after *attempting*— and failing—to start the lawn mower on my own, I finally succeeded with Dad's help⟩ ⟨don't even *attempt* walking on your broken foot⟩
***syn*** assay, endeavor, essay, seek, strive, try
***rel*** fight, strain, struggle, toil, trouble, work; aim, aspire, hope; assume, take up, undertake
***phrases*** have a go at
***near ant*** drop, give up, quit

**attend** *vb* 1 to go along with in order to provide assistance, protection, or companionship — see ACCOMPANY
2 to pay attention especially through the act of hearing — see LISTEN
3 to take charge of especially on behalf of another — see ²TEND 1

**attendant** *adj* 1 coming as a result — see RESULTANT
2 present at the same time and place — see COINCIDENT

**attendant** *n* one that accompanies another for protection, guidance, or as a courtesy — see ESCORT

**attending** *adj* 1 being within the confines of a specified place — see PRESENT 2
2 present at the same time and place — see COINCIDENT

**attention** *n* 1 a focusing of the mind on something ⟨I need your full *attention* right now⟩
***syn*** absorption, concentration, engrossment, enthrallment, immersion
***rel*** fixation, obsession, preoccupation; alertness, application, awareness, consciousness, consideration, heedfulness, intentness, raptness
***near ant*** absence, absentmindedness, abstractedness, abstraction, detachment, distraction, obliviousness, remoteness, unawareness, unconsciousness, with-

drawal; disinterest, indifference, mindlessness, unconcern; befuddlement, bemusement, bewilderment, confusion
***ant*** inattention
**2** a state of being aware ⟨several mothers brought to the committee's *attention* the deplorable condition of the playground⟩
***syn*** awareness, cognizance, ear, eye, heed, notice, observance, observation
***rel*** advisement, care, concern, consideration, regard, watch; apprehension, discernment, grasp, mind, perception, recognition, thought, understanding
***near ant*** disregard, neglect, oblivousness, unawareness

**attentive** *adj* **1** having the mind fixed on something ⟨Susan became particularly *attentive* when the sportscaster turned to field hockey, her favorite sport⟩
***syn*** absorbed, engrossed, enthralled, focused (*also* focussed), immersed, intent, observant, rapt
***rel*** interested, intrigued, involved; hypnotized, mesmerized; alert, alive, conscious, open-eyed, watchful, wide-awake
***near ant*** daydreaming, dreamy, faraway, foggy, hazy, oblivious, preoccupied, remote; apathetic, disinterested, uninterested
***ant*** absent, absentminded, abstracted, distracted, inattentive, unabsorbed, unfocused (*also* unfocussed), unobservant
**2** given to or made with heedful anticipation of the needs and happiness of others — see THOUGHTFUL 1
**3** paying close attention usually for the purpose of anticipating approaching danger or opportunity — see ALERT 1

**attentiveness** *n* the act or state of being constantly attentive and responsive to signs of opportunity, activity, or danger — see VIGILANCE

**attest** *vb* **1** to declare (something) to be true or genuine — see CERTIFY 1
**2** to make a solemn declaration under oath for the purpose of establishing a fact — see TESTIFY

**attestation** *n* something presented in support of the truth or accuracy of a claim — see PROOF

**attire** *n* covering for the human body — see CLOTHING

**attire** *vb* to outfit with clothes and especially fine or special clothes — see CLOTHE 1

**attorney** *n* **1** a person who acts or does business for another — see AGENT 2
**2** a person whose profession is to conduct lawsuits for clients or to advise about legal rights and obligations — see LAWYER

**attraction** *n* something that attracts interest — see MAGNET

**attractive** *adj* **1** having an often mysterious or magical power to attract — see FASCINATING 1
**2** very pleasing to look at — see BEAUTIFUL

**attractiveness** *n* **1** the power of irresistible attraction — see CHARM 2
**2** the qualities in a person or thing that as a whole give pleasure to the senses — see BEAUTY 1

**attribute** *n* something that sets apart an individual from others of the same kind — see CHARACTERISTIC

**attribute** *vb* to explain (something) as being the result of something else — see CREDIT 1

**attrition** *n* a gradual weakening, loss, or destruction — see CORROSION

**atypical** *adj* **1** being out of the ordinary — see EXCEPTIONAL
**2** departing from some accepted standard of what is normal — see DEVIANT

**audacious** *adj* inclined or willing to take risks — see BOLD 1

**audacity** *n* shameless boldness — see EFFRONTERY

**audibly** *adv* with one's normal voice speaking the words — see ALOUD

**audit** *n* a close look at or over someone or something in order to judge condition — see INSPECTION

**audit** *vb* to look over closely (as for judging quality or condition) — see INSPECT

**auditorium** *n* a large room or building for enclosed public gatherings — see HALL 3

**auditory** *adj* of, relating to, or experienced through the sense of hearing ⟨I have a bad *auditory* memory—unless I see a word in writing, and not just hear it, I forget it easily⟩
***syn*** acoustic (*or* acoustical), aural, auricular
***rel*** audible, clear, discernible, distinct, distinguishable, heard, perceptible
***near ant*** faint, feeble, imperceptible, inaudible, indistinguishable, indistinct; low, noiseless, quiet, silent, soft, soundless

**aught** *n* the numerical symbol 0 or the absence of number or quantity represented by it — see ZERO 1

**augment** *vb* to make greater in size, amount, or number — see INCREASE 1

**augmentation** *n* something added (as by growth) — see INCREASE 1

**augur** *n* one who predicts future events or developments — see PROPHET

**augur** *vb* **1** to show signs of a favorable or successful outcome — see BODE
**2** to tell of or describe beforehand — see FORETELL

**auguring** *n* a declaration that something will happen in the future — see PREDICTION

**augury** *n* something believed to be a sign or warning of a future event — see OMEN

**august** *adj* **1** having or showing a serious and reserved manner — see DIGNIFIED
**2** large and impressive in size, grandeur, extent, or conception — see GRAND 1

**augustness** *n* **1** a dignified bearing or appearance befitting royalty — see MAJESTY 1
**2** impressiveness of beauty on a large scale — see MAGNIFICENCE

**auld lang syne** *n* the events or experience of former times — see PAST

**aura** *n* a special quality or impression associated with something ⟨the monastery perched high on a mountaintop had an *aura* of unreality and mystery about it⟩
***syn*** air, atmosphere, climate, flavor, mood, note, temper
***rel*** feel, feeling, sensation, sense, spirit; attribute, character, characteristic, image, mark, notion, peculiarity, picture, property, trait; color, illusion, overtone, semblance, suggestion, tone

**aural** *adj* of, relating to, or experienced through the sense of hearing — see AUDITORY

**au revoir** *n* an expression of good wishes at parting — see GOOD-BYE

**auricular** *adj* of, relating to, or experienced through the sense of hearing — see AUDITORY

**aurora** *n* the first appearance of light in the morning or the time of its appearance — see DAWN 1

**auspice** *n* something believed to be a sign or warning of a future event — see OMEN

**auspicious** *adj* **1** having qualities which inspire hope — see HOPEFUL 1
**2** pointing toward a happy outcome — see FAVORABLE 2

**austere** *adj* **1** given to exacting standards of discipline and self-restraint — see SEVERE 1
**2** harsh and threatening in manner or appearance — see GRIM 1

**authentic** *adj* **1** being exactly as appears or as claimed ⟨found an *authentic* Native American arrowhead⟩
***syn*** bona fide, genuine, real, right, true
***rel*** actual, historical, original; lawful, legal, legitimate; identifiable, recognizable, verifiable; proven, substantiated, validated, verified; incontestable, incontrovertible, indisputable, indubitable, irrefutable, undeniable, undoubted, unmistakable, unquestionable; veritable, very; accurate, correct, proper; pure, unadulterated, unalloyed
***near ant*** artificial, factitious, imitation, man-made, simulated, synthetic, unnatural; concocted, fabricated, manufactured; deceptive, delusive, delusory, misleading; unauthenticated, unverified
***ant*** bogus, counterfeit, fake, false, mock, phony (*also* phoney), pseudo, sham, spurious, unauthentic, unreal
**2** following an original exactly — see FAITHFUL 2

**authentically** *adv* in actual fact — see VERY 2

**authenticate** *vb* to declare (something) to be true or genuine — see CERTIFY 1

**author** *n* **1** a person who creates a written work ⟨a brilliant novel by a first-time *author*⟩
***syn*** penman, writer
***rel*** coauthor, ghostwriter, hack, scribbler; autobiographer, biographer; novelist; essayist, pamphleteer; dramatist, playwright, scenarist, screenwriter, scriptwriter; bard, poet, rhymer (*or* rimer); columnist, journalist, newspaperman, reporter, sportswriter
**2** a person who establishes a whole new field of endeavor — see FATHER 2

**author** *vb* to compose and set down on paper the words of — see WRITE 1

**authoritarian** *adj* **1** fond of ordering people around — see BOSSY
**2** given to exacting standards of discipline and self-restraint — see SEVERE 1

**authoritative** *adj* **1** being the most accurate and apparently thorough — see DEFINITIVE 1
**2** having power over the minds or behavior of others — see INFLUENTIAL 1

**authority** *n* **1** a person with a high level of knowledge or skill in a field — see EXPERT
**2** lawful control over the affairs of a political unit (as a nation) — see RULE 2
**3** the power to direct the thinking or behavior of others usually indirectly — see INFLUENCE 1
**4** the right or means to command or control others — see POWER 1

**authorization** *n* **1** the approval by someone in authority for the doing of something — see PERMISSION
**2** the granting of power to perform various acts or duties — see COMMISSION 1
**3** the right to act or move freely — see FREEDOM 2

**authorize** *vb* **1** to give official or legal power to ⟨only the school nurse is *authorized* to give any necessary shots⟩
***syn*** accredit, certify, commission, empower, enable, invest, license (*or* licence), qualify
***rel*** approve, clear, endorse (*also* indorse), OK (*or* okay), sanction; affirm, confirm, validate; inaugurate, induct, initiate, install, instate, swear in; allow, let, permit; enfranchise, entitle, privilege
***near ant*** ban, bar, block, constrain, deny, disallow, disbar, discourage, disenfranchise, disfranchise, disqualify, exclude, hinder, hold back, impede, inhibit, obstruct, prevent, shut out, stop; enjoin, forbid, interdict, outlaw, prohibit, proscribe, veto
**2** to give a right to — see ENTITLE 1
**3** to give official acceptance of something as satisfactory — see APPROVE

**authorized** *adj* ordered or allowed by those in authority — see OFFICIAL

**auto** *n* a self-propelled passenger vehicle on wheels — see CAR

**autocracy** *n* a system of government in which the ruler has unlimited power — see DESPOTISM

**autocrat** *n* **1** a person who uses power or authority in a cruel, unjust, or harmful way — see DESPOT
**2** one who rules over a people with a sole, supreme, and usually hereditary authority — see MONARCH

---

***syn*** synonym(s) ***rel*** related words
***ant*** antonym(s) ***near ant*** near antonym(s)

**autocratic** *adj* **1** exercising power or authority without interference by others — see ABSOLUTE 1
**2** fond of ordering people around — see BOSSY
**autograph** *vb* to write one's name on (as a document) — see SIGN
**automated** *adj* designed to replace or decrease human labor and especially physical labor — see LABORSAVING
**automatic** *adj* **1** done instantly and without conscious thought or decision ⟨Carl's *automatic* use of the brakes prevented a serious accident⟩
***syn*** instinctive, instinctual, involuntary, mechanical, spontaneous
***rel*** conditioned, natural, reactive, reflex, simple, subliminal, unconscious, unforced; blind, inadvertent, unintended, unintentional, unwilling, unwitting; abrupt, quick, ready, sudden; ad-lib, extemporaneous, extempore, impromptu, improvised, offhand, offhanded, snap, spur-of-the-moment, unconsidered, unplanned, unpremeditated, unprepared, unprompted, unreasoned, unrehearsed, unstudied; casual, chance, chancy, haphazard, hasty, hit-or-miss, impetuous, impulsive, perfunctory, random, rash
***near ant*** calculated, conscious, cultivated, deliberate, designed, intended, intentional, predetermined, prepared, projected, refined, rehearsed, volitional, voluntary, willed, willful (*or* wilful); advised, aforethought, careful, considered, foresighted, forethoughtful, measured, meticulous, reasoned, studied, thoughtful
**2** designed to replace or decrease human labor and especially physical labor — see LABORSAVING
**automobile** *n* a self-propelled passenger vehicle on wheels — see CAR
**automobile** *vb* to travel by a motorized vehicle — see DRIVE 2
**automobilist** *n* a person who travels by automobile — see MOTORIST
**autonomous** *adj* not being under the rule or control of another — see FREE 1
**autonomy** *n* the state of being free from the control or power of another — see FREEDOM 1
**autopsy** *n* examination of a dead body especially to find out the cause of death ⟨the *autopsy* revealed an advanced stage of cancer⟩
***syn*** postmortem, postmortem examination
***rel*** dissection
***near ant*** biopsy, vivisection
**auxiliary** *adj* available to supply something extra when needed ⟨the auditorium has an *auxiliary* cooling system used only on particularly sweltering days⟩
***syn*** accessory, peripheral, supplemental, supplementary
***rel*** backup, makeshift, substitute; added, additional, another, further; complementary, contributory; assistant, assisting, helping, supportive, tributary; secondary, subordinate, subservient, subsidiary; dispensable, excess, nonessential, superfluous, surplus, unessential
***near ant*** basic, fundamental, primary, prime; all-important, essential, imperative, indispensable, integral, necessary, needed, needful, required, requisite, vital
***ant*** chief, main, principal
**avail** *n* the capacity for being useful for some purpose — see USE 2
**avail** *vb* to provide with something useful or desirable — see BENEFIT
**available** *adj* **1** possible to get ⟨the nursery's orchids are *available* by mail order only⟩ ⟨fare information is readily *available* by using the toll-free number⟩
***syn*** accessible, acquirable, attainable, obtainable, procurable
***rel*** purchasable, rentable; furnished, provided, supplied; common, omnipresent, prevalent, ubiquitous, universal, widespread; free, free-for-all, open, public, unrestricted
***phrases*** on hand
***near ant*** limited, off-limits, restricted; deficient, lacking, missing, rare, scarce, uncommon
***ant*** inaccessible, unattainable, unavailable, unobtainable
**2** capable of or suitable for being used for a particular purpose — see USABLE 1
**avarice** *n* an intense selfish desire for wealth or possessions — see GREED
**avaricious** *adj* having or marked by an eager and often selfish desire especially for material possessions — see GREEDY 1
**avariciousness** *n* an intense selfish desire for wealth or possessions — see GREED
**avenge** *vb* to punish in kind the wrongdoer responsible for ⟨a play about a prince who struggles to *avenge* his father's death⟩
***syn*** requite, retaliate, revenge
***rel*** castigate, fix, get, penalize, punish, scourge; chasten, chastise, correct, discipline; redress, right; compensate, pay (back), recompense, repay
***phrases*** get even (for)
***near ant*** absolve, condone, excuse, forgive, pardon, remit
**avenger** *n* one who inflicts punishment in return for an injury or offense — see NEMESIS 1
**avenue** *n* **1** a passage cleared for public vehicular travel — see WAY 1
**2** an established course for traveling from one place to another — see PASSAGE 1
**aver** *vb* **1** to state as a fact usually forcefully — see CLAIM 1
**2** to state clearly and strongly — see ASSERT 1
**average** *adj* **1** being about midway between extremes of amount or size — see MIDDLE 2
**2** being of the type that is encountered in the normal course of events — see ORDINARY 1
**3** having or showing the qualities associated with the members of a particular group or kind — see TYPICAL 1

**average** *n* what is typical of a group, class, or series ⟨my cat's a cut above the *average* when it comes to being a finicky eater⟩
***syn*** norm, normal, par, standard
***rel*** golden mean, mean, median, middle; commonplace, ordinary, rule, run, status quo, usual; exemplar, representative
***near ant*** abnormality, anomaly, deviation, exception, rarity
**averse** *adj* having a natural dislike for something — see ANTIPATHETIC
**averseness** *n* a strong feeling of not liking or approving — see DISLIKE 1
**aversion** *n* **1** a dislike so strong as to cause stomach upset or queasiness — see DISGUST
**2** a strong feeling of not liking or approving — see DISLIKE 1
**3** something or someone that is hated — see HATE 2
**avert** *vb* to keep from happening by taking action in advance — see PREVENT
**averting** *n* the act or practice of keeping something from happening — see PREVENTION
**aviator** *n* one who flies or is qualified to fly an aircraft or spacecraft — see PILOT
**avid** *adj* **1** having or marked by an eager and often selfish desire especially for material possessions — see GREEDY 1
**2** showing urgent desire or interest — see EAGER
**avidity** *n* **1** an intense selfish desire for wealth or possessions — see GREED
**2** urgent desire or interest — see EAGERNESS
**avoid** *vb* to get or keep away from (as a responsibility) through cleverness or trickery — see ESCAPE 2
**avoidance** *n* the act or a means of getting or keeping away from something undesirable — see ESCAPE 2
**avoirdupois** *n* the state or quality of being heavy — see WEIGHTINESS 1
**avouch** *vb* **1** to declare (something) to be true or genuine — see CERTIFY 1
**2** to state as a fact usually forcefully — see CLAIM 1
**3** to state clearly and strongly — see ASSERT 1
**avouchment** *n* a solemn and often public declaration of the truth or existence of something — see PROTESTATION
**avow** *vb* **1** to state as a fact usually forcefully — see CLAIM 1
**2** to state clearly and strongly — see ASSERT 1
**avowal** *n* **1** a solemn and often public declaration of the truth or existence of something — see PROTESTATION
**2** an open declaration of something (as a fault or the commission of an offense) about oneself — see CONFESSION
**await** *vb* **1** to believe in the future occurrence of (something) — see EXPECT
**2** to remain in place in readiness or expectation of something — see WAIT
**awaited** *adj* being in accordance with the prescribed, normal, or logical course of events — see DUE 2
**awake** *adj* **1** not sleeping or able to sleep — see WAKEFUL
**2** paying close attention usually for the purpose of anticipating approaching danger or opportunity — see ALERT 1
**awake** *vb* **1** to cause to stop sleeping — see WAKE 1
**2** to cease to be asleep — see WAKE 2
**awaken** *vb* **1** to cause to stop sleeping — see WAKE 1
**2** to cease to be asleep — see WAKE 2
**award** *n* something given in recognition of achievement ⟨Faye received the highest *award* in the 16 and under category for her poem⟩
***syn*** decoration, distinction, honor, plume, premium, prize
***rel*** badge, crown, cup, laurel, medal, order, ribbon, trophy; accolade, applause, bravo, encomium, eulogy, hallelujah, homage, paean, panegyric, plaudit, tribute; citation, commendation, compliment
**award** *vb* **1** to give something as a token of gratitude or admiration for a service or achievement — see REWARD
**2** to give the ownership or benefit of (something) formally or publicly — see CONFER 1
**aware** *adj* having specified facts or feelings actively impressed on the mind — see CONSCIOUS
**awareness** *n* a state of being aware — see ATTENTION 2
**awash** *adj* containing, covered with, or thoroughly penetrated by water — see WET
**away** *adj* **1** not close in time or space — see DISTANT 1
**2** not at a certain place — see ABSENT 1
**away** *adv* from this or that place ⟨don't walk *away* while I'm still talking to you⟩
***syn*** hence, off
***rel*** apart, aside, elsewhere; abroad, afar, afield, astray
**awe** *n* the rapt attention and deep emotion caused by the sight of something extraordinary — see WONDER 2
**awed** *adj* filled with amazement or wonder — see OPENMOUTHED
**awesome** *adj* causing wonder or astonishment — see MARVELOUS 1
**awestruck** *adj* **1** affected with sudden and great wonder or surprise — see THUNDERSTRUCK
**2** filled with amazement or wonder — see OPENMOUTHED
**awful** *adj* **1** causing intense displeasure, disgust, or resentment — see OFFENSIVE 1
**2** causing wonder or astonishment — see MARVELOUS 1
**3** extremely disturbing or repellent — see HORRIBLE 1
**4** extremely unsatisfactory — see WRETCHED 1

**awful** *adv* to a great degree — see VERY 1
**awfully** *adv* to a great degree — see VERY 1
**awfulness** *n* the quality of inspiring intense dread or dismay — see HORROR 1
**awkward** *adj* **1** lacking social grace and assurance ⟨preteens feeling *awkward* at their first formal dance⟩
*syn* clumsy, gauche, graceless, inelegant, roughhewn, stiff, stilted, uncomfortable, uneasy, ungraceful, wooden
*rel* gawky, lubberly, ungainly; boorish, clownish, uncouth; abashed, discomfited, discomforted, discomposed, disconcerted, discountenanced, embarrassed; agitated, bothered, chagrined, dismayed, disquieted, distressed, disturbed, fazed, flustered, jittery, jumpy, mortified, nervous, nonplussed (*also* nonplused), perturbed, rattled, unhinged, unsettled, upset; diffident, insecure, meek, modest, self-doubting, timid, unassertive, unassuming, unpretentious
*near ant* assured, calm, collected, composed, confident, cool, placid, poised, serene, secure, self-assured, self-confident, self-possessed, tranquil, undisturbed, unperturbed
*ant* graceful, suave, urbane
**2** showing or marked by a lack of skill and tact (as in dealing with a situation) ⟨her *awkward* handling of the seating arrangements at the wedding reception resulted in many hurt feelings⟩
*syn* botched, bungling, clumsy, fumbled, inept, inexpert, maladroit
*rel* amateur, amateurish, crude, green, incompetent, ineffectual, inefficient, inexperienced, unpolished, unprofessional, unskilled, unskillful; careless, sloppy, tacky, tactless, undiplomatic; ill-advised, ineffective, ineffectual, misdirected, misguided
*near ant* able, accomplished, adept, capable, clever, competent, consummate, crackerjack, expert, masterful, masterly, polished, professional, proficient, skilled, skillful, talented; diplomatic, easy, effortless, gracious, smooth, tactful
*ant* adroit, deft, dexterous (*also* dextrous), facile
**3** causing embarrassment ⟨the *awkward* situation of having to listen in as your teacher talks about you to your parents⟩
*syn* discomfiting, disconcerting, disturbing, embarrassing, flustering, uncomfortable
*rel* confusing, difficult, disagreeable, impossible, inconvenient, intolerable, troublesome, unpleasant, unwieldy; debasing, degrading, demeaning, humbling, humiliating, mortifying
*near ant* agreeable, comfortable, convenient, pleasing
**4** causing difficulty, discomfort, or annoyance — see INCONVENIENT 1
**5** difficult to use or operate especially because of size, weight, or design — see CUMBERSOME
**6** lacking in physical ease and grace in movement or in the use of the hands — see CLUMSY 1
**awning** *n* a raised covering over something for decoration or protection — see CANOPY
**awry** *adj* inclined or twisted to one side ⟨the shutters that still remained on the run-down old house were all *awry*⟩
*syn* askew, aslant, cockeyed, crooked, listing, lopsided, oblique, skewed, slanted, slanting, slantwise, tilted, tipping, uneven
*rel* asymmetrical (*or* asymmetric), unbalanced, unsymmetrical; contorted, disordered, distorted, irregular
*near ant* ordered, orderly, regular, uniform; balanced, symmetrical (*or* symmetric)
*ant* even, level, straight
**awry** *adv* off the desired or intended path or course — see WRONG 1
[1]**aye** *also* **ay** *adv* for all time — see EVER 1
[2]**aye** *also* **ay** *adv* used to express agreement — see YES

# B

**babble** *n* unintelligible or meaningless talk — see GIBBERISH
**babble** *vb* **1** to speak rapidly, inarticulately, and usually unintelligibly ⟨in such a rush to tell us the news that she just *babbled*⟩
*syn* chatter, drivel, gabble, gibber, jabber, prattle, sputter
*rel* gab, jaw, patter, prate, rattle, run on; maunder, mouth, mumble, murmur, mutter; stammer, stutter; chat, converse; palaver, rap, visit; discourse; screech, shout, shriek
*near ant* articulate, enunciate, pronounce
**2** to engage in casual or rambling conversation — see CHAT
**babbler** *n* a person who talks constantly — see CHATTERBOX
**babe** *n* a recently born person — see BABY
**babel** *n* a place of uproar or confusion — see MADHOUSE 2
**babushka** *n* a scarf worn on the head — see BANDANNA
**baby** *n* a recently born person ⟨the *baby* is just learning to sit up, so be careful⟩
*syn* babe, child, infant, newborn
*rel* cherub; foundling, nursling, suckling; papoose; kid, moppet, toddler, tot, tyke;

boy, nipper, tad; juvenile, minor, youngster, youth; brat, imp, squirt, urchin, whippersnapper; girl, hoyden, tomboy
***phrases*** babe in arms
***near ant*** adult, grown-up; elder, graybeard, oldster, old-timer, senior citizen

**baby** *vb* to treat with great or excessive care ⟨he *babied* his car, faithfully washing it every week⟩
***syn*** coddle, dandle, mollycoddle, nurse, pamper, spoil
***rel*** cater (to), humor, indulge; gratify, mother, oblige, please, satisfy
***near ant*** control, discipline, restrain; oppress; neglect, overlook, slight
***ant*** abuse, ill-treat, ill-use, maltreat, mishandle, mistreat, misuse

**babyish** *adj* having or showing the annoying qualities (as silliness) associated with children — see CHILDISH

**babysitter** *n* a girl or woman employed to care for a young child or children — see NURSE

**back** *adj* being at or in the part of something opposite the front part ⟨she carried all the presents in the *back* door, as the children were playing in the front yard⟩
***syn*** hind, hindmost, posterior, rear, rearward
***ant*** anterior, fore, forward, front

**back** *adv* toward the opposite direction — see AROUND 2

**back** *vb* **1** to promote the interests or cause of — see SUPPORT 1
**2** to provide (someone) with what is useful or necessary to achieve an end — see HELP 1

**back away** *vb* to move back or away (as from something difficult, dangerous, or disagreeable) — see RETREAT 1

**backbone** *n* **1** a column of bones supporting the trunk of a vertebrate animal — see SPINE
**2** the strength of mind that enables a person to endure pain or hardship — see FORTITUDE

**back down** *vb* to break a promise or agreement — see RENEGE

**backdrop** *n* the physical conditions or features that form the setting against which something is viewed — see BACKGROUND 1

**backer** *n* **1** a person who actively supports or favors a cause — see EXPONENT
**2** a person who takes the responsibility for some other person or thing — see SPONSOR
**3** someone associated with another to give assistance or moral support — see ALLY

**background** *n* **1** the physical conditions or features that form the setting against which something is viewed ⟨they got married on a mountain top with the sunset as *background*⟩
***syn*** backdrop, ground
***rel*** scene, scenery, set, stage; environment, milieu, setting, surroundings
***near ant*** foreground; center, focal point, focus, heart
**2** the place and time in which the action for a portion of a dramatic work (as a movie) is set — see SCENE 1

**backhanded** *adj* not being or expressing what one appears to be or express — see INSINCERE

**backing** *n* an act or instance of helping — see HELP 1

**back of** *prep* at, to, or toward the rear of — see BEHIND 1

**back off** *vb* to break a promise or agreement — see RENEGE

**backpack** *n* a soft-sided case designed for carrying belongings especially on the back — see PACK 1

**backside** *n* the part of the body upon which someone sits — see BUTTOCKS

**backslider** *n* a person who has sunk below the normal moral standard — see DEGENERATE

**backstage** *adj or adv* off or away from the part of the stage visible to the audience — see OFFSTAGE

**back talk** *n* disrespectful or argumentative talk given in response to a command or request ⟨his mother sent him to his room because of his constant *back talk*⟩
***syn*** cheek, impertinence, impudence, insolence, sass, sauce
***rel*** comeback, rejoinder, retort, riposte, wisecrack; discourtesy, disrespect, impoliteness, rudeness, tactlessness; audaciousness, audacity, boldness, brazenness; coarseness, crassness, crudity, vulgarity; abruptness, bluffness, bluntness, brusqueness, crossness, curtness, gruffness, surliness
***near ant*** civility, cordiality, courtesy, diplomacy, politeness, tactfulness; consideration, gallantry, gentility, graciousness, smoothness, suaveness; deference, respect; affability

**backup** *adj* taking the place of one that came before — see NEW 1

**backup** *n* a person or thing that takes the place of another — see SUBSTITUTE

**backward** *adj* directed, turned, or done toward the back ⟨a *backward* turn on ice skates is hard to learn, because you can't see where you're going⟩
***syn*** rearward, retrograde
***rel*** reversed; hind, posterior, rear
***near ant*** forward

**backwater** *n* a rural region that forms the edge of the settled or developed part of a country — see FRONTIER 2

**backwoods** *n* a rural region that forms the edge of the settled or developed part of a country — see FRONTIER 2

**bad** *adj* **1** falling short of a standard ⟨a *bad* first attempt at making meat loaf resulted in a soggy inedible mess⟩
***syn*** deficient, inferior, lousy, off, poor, punk, rotten, substandard, unacceptable, ungodly, unsatisfactory, wanting, wretched, wrong

***rel*** defective, faulty, flawed; execrable, lesser, low-grade, mediocre, reprehensible, second-rate, unspeakable; bum, useless, valueless, worthless; inadequate, insufficient, lacking; astray; scurrilous, villainous
***phrases*** below (*or* under) par
***near ant*** choice, excellent, exceptional, first-class, first-rate, premium, prime, superior; adequate, sufficient
***ant*** acceptable, satisfactory
**2** not conforming to a high moral standard; morally unacceptable ⟨stealing is just plain *bad*⟩
***syn*** black, evil, immoral, iniquitous, nefarious, rotten, sinful, unethical, unrighteous, unsavory, vicious, vile, villainous, wicked, wrong
***rel*** base, contemptible, despicable, dirty, disreputable, evil-minded, ignoble, ill, infernal, low, mean; atrocious, cruel, nasty; blamable, blameworthy, censurable, reprehensible; corrupt, debased, debauched, degenerate, depraved, dissolute, libertine, loose, perverted, reprobate; banned, barred, condemned, discouraged, forbidden, interdicted, outlawed, prohibited, proscribed, unauthorized, unclean, disallowed; execrable, lousy, miserable, wretched; erring, fallen, unprincipled, unscrupulous; improper, incorrect, indecent, indecorous, unbecoming
***near ant*** high-minded, honest, honorable, law-abiding, legitimate, principled, reputable, right-minded, scrupulous, straight, upright; allowed, authorized, legal, licensed, permissible, permitted; approved, endorsed, sanctioned; abetted, encouraged, promoted, supported; clean, correct, decent, decorous, exemplary, proper, seemly; blameless, commendable, creditable, guiltless; chaste, immaculate, innocent, irreproachable, lily-white, perfect, pure, spotless
***ant*** good, ethical, moral, right, righteous, virtuous
**3** causing or capable of causing harm — see HARMFUL
**4** engaging in or marked by childish misbehavior — see NAUGHTY
**5** feeling unhappiness — see SAD 1
**6** having a fault — see FAULTY
**7** having undergone organic breakdown — see ROTTEN 1
**8** not giving pleasure to the mind or senses — see UNPLEASANT
**9** of low quality — see CHEAP 2
**10** temporarily suffering from a disorder of the body — see SICK 1

**bad** *n* that which is morally unacceptable — see EVIL

**badly** *adv* in an unsatisfactory way ⟨I'm afraid you performed quite *badly* in our last rehearsal⟩
***syn*** inadequately, poorly, unacceptably, unsatisfactorily
***rel*** rottenly; intolerably, unbearably; inappropriately, incorrectly, indecently, rakishly, unsuitably; naughtily
***near ant*** appropriately, congruously, correctly, decently, decorously, felicitously, fittingly, genteelly, rightly, seemly, suitably
***ant*** acceptably, adequately, all right, fine, good, palatably, passably, so-so, tolerably

**bad–mouth** *vb* to express scornfully one's low opinion of — see DECRY 1

**badness** *n* the state or quality of being utterly evil — see ENORMITY 1

**baffle** *vb* **1** to prevent from achieving a goal — see FRUSTRATE
**2** to throw into a state of mental uncertainty — see CONFUSE 1

**bafflement** *n* a state of mental uncertainty — see CONFUSION 1

**bag** *n* **1** a container made of a flexible material (as paper or plastic) ⟨she carries her towel and other supplies to the beach in a bright, colorful *bag* slung over her arm⟩
***syn*** poke [*chiefly Southern & Midland*], pouch, sack
***rel*** carryall, portmanteau, traveling bag; bundle, pack, package, packet, parcel; backpack, duffel bag, haversack, knapsack, rucksack; handbag, pocketbook, purse, tote bag
**2** a container for carrying money and small personal items — see PURSE

**bag** *vb* **1** to extend outward beyond a usual point — see BULGE
**2** to take physical control or possession of (something) suddenly or forcibly — see CATCH 1

**bail out** *vb* to remove from danger or harm — see SAVE 2

**bairn** *n*, *chiefly Scottish* a young person who is between infancy and adulthood — see CHILD 1

**bait** *n* **1** something used to attract animals to a hook or into a trap ⟨cheese is the traditional *bait* for trapping mice⟩
***syn*** decoy, lure
***rel*** ambush, trap; hook, snare, troll; appeal, attraction, call, draw, incentive, pull; enticement, seduction, temptation
***near ant*** repellent
**2** something that persuades one to perform an action for pleasure or gain — see LURE 1

**bait** *vb* to attack repeatedly with mean putdowns or insults — see TEASE 2

**baiter** *n* **1** a person who causes repeated emotional pain, distress, or annoyance to another — see TORMENTOR
**2** one that tries to get a person to give in to a desire — see TEMPTER

**balance** *n* **1** a condition in which opposing forces are equal to one another ⟨in order to determine the weight of that beaker, you need to get the two pans of the scale in perfect *balance*⟩
***syn*** equilibrium, equipoise, poise
***rel*** counterbalance, counterpoise; firmness, fixedness, security, stability, steadiness
***near ant*** changeability, fluctuation, inconstancy, insecurity, instability, mutability, precariousness, shakiness, unsteadiness, volatility

*ant* imbalance
**2** a balanced, pleasing, or suitable arrangement of parts — see HARMONY 1
**3** a device for measuring weight — see [1]SCALE
**4** a force or influence that makes an opposing force ineffective or less effective — see COUNTERBALANCE
**5** a remaining group or portion — see REMAINDER 1

**balance** *vb* to make equal in amount, degree, or status — see EQUALIZE

**balanced** *adj* **1** having full use of one's mind and control over one's actions — see SANE
**2** having the parts agreeably related — see HARMONIOUS 2

**bald** *adj* **1** lacking a usual or natural covering — see NAKED 2
**2** free from all additions or embellishment — see PLAIN 1

**baleful** *adj* **1** being or showing a sign of evil or calamity to come — see OMINOUS
**2** causing or capable of causing harm — see HARMFUL
**3** likely to cause or capable of causing death — see DEADLY

**balk** *vb* to prevent from achieving a goal — see FRUSTRATE

**balky** *adj* given to resisting authority or another's control — see DISOBEDIENT

[1]**ball** *n* **1** a more or less round body or mass ⟨the little rubber *ball* used in racquetball⟩ ⟨a *ball* of string⟩
*syn* globe, orb, sphere
*rel* egg, oval; circle, ring, round; chunk, clump, gob, hunk, lump, nugget, wad
*near ant* block, cube, rectangle, square
**2** a usually round or cone-shaped little piece of lead made to be fired from a firearm — see BULLET

[2]**ball** *n* a social gathering for dancing — see DANCE

**ball** *vb* to form into a round compact mass — see WAD

**ballad** *n* a short musical composition for the human voice often with instrumental accompaniment — see SONG 1

**balloon** *vb* **1** to become greater in extent, volume, amount, or number — see INCREASE 2
**2** to extend outward beyond a usual point — see BULGE

**ballot** *n* a piece of paper indicating a person's preferences in an election ⟨we collected all of the *ballots* from the students voting for class president⟩
*syn* vote
*rel* aye (*also* ay), nay, no, yea; blackball; referendum; ticket

**ballyhoo** *n* newsworthy information released to the media that is designed to gain public attention or support for a person, business, or cause — see PUBLICITY

**ballyhoo** *vb* **1** to praise or publicize lavishly and often excessively — see TOUT 1
**2** to provide publicity for — see PUBLICIZE 1

**balminess** *n* lack of good sense or judgment — see FOOLISHNESS 1

**balmy** *adj* **1** having or showing a very abnormal or sick state of mind — see INSANE 1
**2** marked by temperatures that are neither too high nor too low — see CLEMENT
**3** not harsh or stern especially in manner, nature, or effect — see GENTLE 1
**4** showing or marked by a lack of good sense or judgment — see FOOLISH 1

**balustrade** *n* a protective barrier consisting of a horizontal bar and its supports — see RAILING

**ban** *n* an order that something not be done or used — see PROHIBITION 2

**ban** *vb* **1** to order not to do or use or to be done or used — see FORBID
**2** to prevent the participation or inclusion of — see EXCLUDE

**banal** *adj* **1** lacking in qualities that make for spirit and character — see WISHY-WASHY 1
**2** used or heard so often as to be dull — see STALE

**banality** *n* an idea or expression that has been used by many people — see COMMONPLACE

**bananas** *adj* having or showing a very abnormal or sick state of mind — see INSANE 1

[1]**band** *n* **1** a circular strip — see RING 2
**2** something that physically prevents free movement — see BOND 1
**3** a line or long narrow section differing in color from the background — see STRIPE

[2]**band** *n* **1** a usually large group of musicians playing together ⟨that traveling *band* needs to find a new singer⟩
*syn* orchestra, philharmonic, symphony, symphony orchestra
*rel* brass band; brasses, strings, woodwinds; combo, ensemble, group; company, troupe; duo, octet, quartet (*also* quartette), quintet, septet (*also* septette), sextet, trio
**2** a group of people working together on a task — see GANG 1

**band** *vb* **1** to encircle or bind with or as if with a belt — see GIRD 1
**2** to form or enter into an association that furthers the interests of its members — see ALLY
**3** to gather into a tight mass by means of a line or cord — see TIE 1
**4** to make stripes on — see STRIPE

**bandage** *vb* to cover with a bandage ⟨her mother always *bandages* her scraped knees very carefully⟩
*syn* bind, dress
*rel* care (for), doctor, medicate, minister (to), nurse, treat; mend, heal

**bandanna** *or* **bandana** *n* a scarf worn on the head ⟨she uses her colorful print *bandanna* to keep the hair out of her eyes⟩

*syn* babushka, handkerchief, kerchief, mantilla
*rel* shawl

**bandwagon** *n* a series of activities undertaken to achieve a goal — see CAMPAIGN

**bandy** *vb* to talk about (an issue) usually from various points of view and for the purpose of arriving at a decision or opinion — see DISCUSS

**bane** *n* a substance that by chemical action can kill or injure a living thing — see POISON

**baneful** *adj* causing or capable of causing harm — see HARMFUL

**bang** *n* **1** a hard strike with a part of the body or an instrument — see [1]BLOW
**2** a loud explosive sound — see CLAP 1
**3** a pleasurably intense stimulation of the feelings — see THRILL

**bang** *vb* **1** to come into usually forceful contact with something — see HIT 2
**2** to deliver a blow to (someone or something) usually in a strong vigorous manner — see HIT 1
**3** to shove into a closed position with force and noise — see SLAM 1

**bangle** *n* an ornament worn on a chain around the neck or wrist — see PENDANT

**bang–up** *adj* of the very best kind — see EXCELLENT

**banish** *vb* **1** to force to leave a country ⟨in the old days, criminals were sometimes *banished*⟩
*syn* deport, displace, exile, expatriate, transport
*rel* dismiss, eject, eliminate, evict, exclude, expel, oust, throw out; excommunicate, ostracize, reject, repudiate, spurn; dispossess
*near ant* naturalize, repatriate; accept, admit, receive, take in; entertain, harbor, house, shelter
**2** to drive or force out — see EJECT 1

**banishment** *n* the forced removal from a homeland — see EXILE 1

**banister** *n* a protective barrier consisting of a horizontal bar and its supports — see RAILING

**[1]bank** *n* **1** a number of things considered as a unit — see GROUP 1
**2** a series of people or things arranged side by side — see ROW 1

**[2]bank** *n* a pile or ridge of granular matter (as sand or snow) ⟨he likes to play on the *bank* of dirt the construction workers left⟩
*syn* bar, drift, mound
*rel* snowbank, snowdrift; embankment, sandbar; heap, hill, mass, mountain, stack

**bank** *vb* **1** to form into a pile or ridge of earth — see MOUND 1
**2** to put in an account — see DEPOSIT 1

**bank note** *n* a piece of printed paper used as money — see [1]BILL 2

**bankroll** *n* available money — see FUND 2

**bankrupt** *vb* to cause to lose one's fortune and become unable to pay one's debts — see RUIN 1

**banned** *adj* that may not be permitted — see IMPERMISSIBLE

**banner** *adj* of the very best kind — see EXCELLENT

**banner** *n* a piece of cloth with a special design that is used as an emblem or for signaling — see FLAG 1

**banning** *n* the act of ordering that something not be done or used — see PROHIBITION 1

**banquet** *n* a large fancy meal often accompanied by ceremony or entertainment — see FEAST

**banquet** *vb* to entertain with a fancy meal — see FEAST

**bantam** *adj* of a size that is less than average — see SMALL 1

**banter** *n* good-natured teasing or exchanging of clever remarks ⟨those particular students are known for their brilliant and witty *banter* at lunchtime⟩
*syn* chaff, give-and-take, jesting, joshing, persiflage, raillery, repartee
*rel* barb, crack, dig, gag, jest, joke, quip, sally, wisecrack, witticism; facetiousness, humorousness; fooling, kidding, mocking, razzing, ribbing, ridiculing; humor, wit, wordplay; chatter, chitchat, gossip, small talk

**banter** *vb* to make jokes — see JOKE

**bantering** *adj* marked by or expressive of mild or good-natured teasing — see QUIZZICAL

**baptism** *n* the process or an instance of being formally placed in an office or organization — see INSTALLATION 1

**baptize** *vb* **1** to give a name to — see NAME 1
**2** to put into an office or welcome into an organization with special ceremonies — see INSTALL 1

**bar** *n* **1** a straight piece (as of wood or metal) that is longer than it is wide ⟨all of the prison's windows are partially covered with steel *bars*⟩
*syn* billet, rod
*rel* beam, board; band, strip; ingot, slab, stick
**2** a line or long narrow section differing in color from the background — see STRIPE
**3** a pile or ridge of granular matter (as sand or snow) — see [2]BANK
**4** a place of business where alcoholic beverages are sold to be consumed on the premises — see BARROOM
**5** an assembly of persons for the administration of justice — see COURT 3
**6** something that makes movement or progress more difficult — see ENCUMBRANCE

**bar** *prep* not including — see EXCEPT

**bar** *vb* **1** to make stripes on — see STRIPE
**2** to order not to do or use or to be done or used — see FORBID
**3** to prevent the participation or inclusion of — see EXCLUDE

**barb** *n* an act or expression showing scorn and usually intended to hurt another's feelings — see INSULT

**barbarian** *n* an uncivilized person — see HEATHEN 2

**barbaric** *adj* having or showing the desire to inflict severe pain and suffering on others — see CRUEL 1
**barbarity** *n* the willful infliction of pain and suffering on others — see CRUELTY
**barbarous** *adj* **1** having or showing the desire to inflict severe pain and suffering on others — see CRUEL 1
**2** not civilized — see SAVAGE 1
**bard** *n* a person who writes poetry — see POET
**bare** *adj* **1** being this and no more — see MERE
**2** free from all additions or embellishment — see PLAIN 1
**3** lacking a usual or natural covering — see NAKED 2
**4** lacking or shed of clothing — see NAKED 1
**5** lacking contents that could or should be present — see EMPTY 1
**bare** *vb* to make known (as information previously kept secret) — see REVEAL 1
**barely** *adv* by a very small margin — see JUST 2
**bareness** *n* the quality or state of being empty — see VACANCY 2
**bargain** *n* **1** something bought or offered for sale at a desirable price ⟨those shoes were a *bargain* because the store was going out of business⟩
***syn*** buy, steal
***rel*** markdown; bonus, freebie, gift, giveaway, premium, present; sale; boon, windfall
***near ant*** overcharge, rip-off; markup; extravagance, luxury
**2** an arrangement about action to be taken — see AGREEMENT 2
**bargain** *vb* to talk over or dispute the terms of a purchase ⟨they *bargained* with the car salesman for half an hour before settling on a price⟩
***syn*** chaffer, deal, dicker, haggle, horsetrade, negotiate, palter
***rel*** argue, bicker, clash, quibble, squabble, wrangle; comparison shop, shop (around); barter, exchange, trade; hawk, peddle; buy, purchase
**barge** *vb* to move heavily or clumsily — see LUMBER 1
**bark** *n* a boat equipped with one or more sails — see SAILBOAT
[1]**bark** *vb* to remove the natural covering of — see PEEL
[2]**bark** *vb* to speak sharply or irritably — see SNAP 1
**baron** *n* a person of rank, power, or influence in a particular field — see MAGNATE
**baronial** *adj* large and impressive in size, grandeur, extent, or conception — see GRAND 1
**barrage** *n* a rapid or overwhelming outpouring of many things at once ⟨the teacher's rapid-fire *barrage* of homework assignments went by too fast for me to write them all down⟩
***syn*** bombardment, cannonade, fusillade, hail, salvo, shower, storm, volley
***rel*** broadside, burst, deluge, flood, flood tide, flush, gush, inundation, outburst, outflow, outpouring, overflow, spate, surge, torrent; current, river, stream, tide; excess, glut, overabundance, overage, overkill, overmuch, oversupply, superabundance, superfluity, surfeit, surplus
***near ant*** dribble, drip, trickle
**barred** *adj* **1** having stripes — see STRIPED
**2** that may not be permitted — see IMPERMISSIBLE
**barrel** *n* **1** a considerable amount — see LOT 2
**2** a metal container in the shape of a cylinder — see CAN
**3** an enclosed wooden vessel for holding beverages — see CASK
**barrel** *vb* to proceed or move quickly — see HURRY 2
**barren** *adj* **1** producing inferior or only a small amount of vegetation ⟨if tobacco fields aren't allowed to lie idle once every few years, they will become *barren*⟩
***syn*** impoverished, infertile, poor, stark, unproductive, waste
***rel*** bleak, dead, desolate, inhospitable, lifeless; bankrupted, consumed, debilitated, depleted, diminished, drained, dried up, enfeebled, exhausted, expended, lessened, reduced, spent, used up; arid, desert, dry
***near ant*** arable, tillable; green, verdant
***ant*** fertile, fruitful, lush, luxuriant, productive, rich
**2** not able to produce fruit or offspring — see STERILE 1
**barren** *n* land that is uninhabited or not fit for crops — see WASTELAND
**barricade** *n* a physical object that blocks the way — see BARRIER
**barrier** *n* a physical object that blocks the way ⟨there was a big *barrier* plastered with signs saying "Keep Out" around the trash compactor⟩
***syn*** barricade, fence, hedge, wall
***rel*** bar, encumbrance, handicap, hindrance, hurdle, impediment, obstacle, obstruction, roadblock, stop; fetter, hobble, manacle, shackle; constraint, curb, restraint, snag
***near ant*** door, doorway, entrance, entry, entryway, gate, portal
**barring** *n* the act of ordering that something not be done or used — see PROHIBITION 1
**barring** *prep* not including — see EXCEPT
**barroom** *n* a place of business where alcoholic beverages are sold to be consumed on the premises ⟨her mother didn't like her even to walk past the *barroom* because she was worried that there might be drunk people inside⟩
***syn*** bar, café (*also* cafe), groggery, grogshop, pub, public house [*chiefly British*], saloon, tavern
***rel*** cabaret, dive, joint, nightclub, roadhouse, speakeasy; package store

**barter** *n* a giving or taking of one thing of value in return for another — see EXCHANGE 1

**base** *adj* not following or in accordance with standards of honor and decency — see IGNOBLE 2

**base** *n* **1** an immaterial thing upon which something else rests ⟨the firm belief that complete trust between husband and wife is the *base* of any successful marriage⟩
*syn* basis, bedrock, cornerstone, footing, foundation, ground, groundwork, keystone, underpinning
*rel* buttress, framework, prop, substructure, support; assumption, justification, premise, presumption, presupposition, theory, thesis, warrant; center, core, eye, focus, heart, hub, nucleus, seat; essence, quintessence, soul
**2** a place from which an advance (as for military operations) is made ⟨the Army's *base* of attack was kept top secret until the battle began⟩
*syn* bridgehead, foothold
*rel* beachhead, center, front, headquarters; bastion, fastness, fortress, stronghold
**3** a thing or place that is of greatest importance to an activity or interest — see CENTER 1
**4** the lowest part, place, or point — see BOTTOM 3
**5** the place from which a commander runs operations — see COMMAND 3

**base** *vb* to find a basis ⟨she *based* her argument against the death penalty on careful research⟩
*syn* ground, predicate, rest
*rel* establish, found; assume, postulate, premise, presume, presuppose, suppose

**baseborn** *adj* **1** belonging to the class of people of low social or economic rank — see IGNOBLE 1
**2** born to a father and mother who are not married — see ILLEGITIMATE 1

**basement** *n* a room or set of rooms below the surface of the ground — see CELLAR

**bash** *vb* **1** to come into usually forceful contact with something — see HIT 2
**2** to deliver a blow to (someone or something) usually in a strong vigorous manner — see HIT 1
**3** to strike repeatedly — see BEAT 1

**bashful** *adj* not comfortable around people — see SHY 2

**basic** *adj* of or relating to the simplest facts or theories of a subject — see ELEMENTARY

**basically** *adv* for the most part — see CHIEFLY

**basics** *n pl* general or basic truths on which other truths or theories can be based — see PRINCIPLES 1

**basis** *n* an immaterial thing upon which something else rests — see BASE 1

**bask** *vb* to refrain from labor or exertion — see REST 1

**bass** *adj* having a low musical pitch or range — see DEEP 2

**bastard** *adj* born to a father and mother who are not married — see ILLEGITIMATE 1

**bastion** *n* a structure or place from which one can resist attack — see FORT

**bat** *n* **1** a hard strike with a part of the body or an instrument — see [1]BLOW
**2** a heavy rigid stick used as a weapon or for punishment — see CLUB 1

**bat** *vb* **1** to deliver a blow to (someone or something) usually in a strong vigorous manner — see HIT 1
**2** to strike repeatedly — see BEAT 1

**batch** *n* **1** a number of things considered as a unit — see GROUP 1
**2** a usually small number of persons considered as a unit — see GROUP 2

**bath** *n* a room furnished with a fixture for flushing body waste — see TOILET

**bathe** *vb* to make wet — see WET

**bathed** *adj* containing, covered with, or thoroughly penetrated by water — see WET

**bathroom** *n* a room furnished with a fixture for flushing body waste — see TOILET

**battalion** *n* a large body of men and women organized for land warfare — see ARMY 1

**batter** *vb* to strike repeatedly — see BEAT 1

**battery** *n* **1** a number of things considered as a unit — see GROUP 1
**2** a usually small number of persons considered as a unit — see GROUP 2

**battle** *n* **1** a forceful effort to reach a goal or objective — see STRUGGLE 1
**2** a physical dispute between opposing individuals or groups — see FIGHT 1
**3** active fighting during the course of a war — see COMBAT 1
**4** an earnest effort for superiority or victory over another — see CONTEST 1

**battle** *vb* **1** to engage in a contest — see COMPETE
**2** to enter into contest or conflict with — see ENGAGE 2
**3** to oppose (someone) in physical conflict — see FIGHT 1
**4** to strive to reduce or eliminate — see FIGHT 2

**batty** *adj* having or showing a very abnormal or sick state of mind — see INSANE 1

**bauble** *n* a small object displayed for its attractiveness or interest — see KNICK-KNACK

**bawdiness** *n* the quality or state of being obscene — see OBSCENITY 1

**bawdy** *adj* **1** depicting or referring to sexual matters in a way that is unacceptable in polite society — see OBSCENE 1
**2** hinting at or intended to call to mind matters regarded as indecent — see SUGGESTIVE 1

**bawl** *vb* **1** to shed tears often while making meaningless sounds as a sign of pain or distress — see CRY 1
**2** to speak so as to be heard at a distance — see CALL 1

**bay** *n* **1** a part of a body of water that extends beyond the general shoreline — see GULF 1
**2** one of the parts into which an enclosed space is divided — see COMPARTMENT
**bay** *vb* to make a long loud mournful sound — see HOWL 1
**bazaar** *n* an establishment where goods are sold to consumers — see SHOP 1
**be** *vb* **1** to have life ⟨stories that begin with the familiar line "once upon a time there *was* a beautiful maiden"⟩
*syn* breathe, exist, live, subsist
*rel* abide, continue, endure, last, lead, persist, survive; move; flourish, prosper, thrive
*near ant* disappear, evaporate, vanish; cease, end, stop
*ant* depart, die, expire, pass away, perish, succumb
**2** to occupy a place or location — see STAND 1
**3** to take or have a certain position within a group arranged in vertical classes — see RANK 1
**4** to take place — see HAPPEN
**be** (to) *vb* to behave toward in a stated way — see TREAT 1
**beach** *n* the usually sandy or gravelly land bordering a body of water ⟨she loves walking along the *beach*, looking for shells that the waves cast up⟩
*syn* shore, strand
*rel* seaboard, seacoast, seashore, seaside; coast, coastline, shoreline; waterfront; bank, riverbank, riverside; esplanade; littoral
**beached** *adj* resting on the shore or bottom of a body of water — see AGROUND
**beacon** *n* something that provides illumination — see LIGHT 2
**beak** *n* the jaws of a bird together with their hornlike covering ⟨the bird cracked the walnut shell with its *beak* and ate its nut⟩
*syn* bill, nib
*rel* mouth; muzzle; mandible, maw, maxilla
**beam** *n* a narrow sharply defined line of light radiating from an object — see SHAFT 1
**beam** *vb* **1** to emit rays of light — see SHINE 1
**2** to express an emotion (as amusement) by curving the lips upward — see SMILE 1
**beaming** *adj* **1** giving off or reflecting much light — see BRIGHT 1
**2** having or being an outward sign of good feelings (as of love, confidence, or happiness) — see RADIANT 1
**bear** *n* an irritable and complaining person — see GROUCH
**bear** *vb* **1** to bring forth from the womb ⟨luckily, she turned out to be able to *bear* children after all⟩
*syn* drop, have, produce
*rel* deliver; create; breed, multiply, propagate, reproduce, spawn; beget, father, generate, get, mother, sire
*phrases* to give birth to
*near ant* abort, lose, miscarry
**2** to put up with (something painful or difficult) ⟨I can't *bear* having to eat my vegetables in order to have ice cream⟩
*syn* abide, brook, countenance, endure, meet, stand, stick out, stomach, support, sustain, take, tolerate
*rel* accept, allow, permit, suffer, swallow; acquiesce, agree (with *or* to), assent (to), capitulate, consent (to), respect, submit (to), yield (to)
*near ant* decline, dismiss, refuse, reject, repudiate, spurn, turn down; combat, contest, fight, oppose, resist; avoid, bypass, circumvent, dodge, elude, escape, evade, miss; abstain, forbear, refrain
**3** to have a relation or connection — see APPLY 1
**4** to go on a specified course or in a certain direction — see HEAD 1
**5** to hold up or serve as a foundation for — see SUPPORT 3
**6** to keep in one's mind or heart — see HARBOR 1
**7** to manage the actions of (oneself) in a particular way — see BEHAVE
**8** to support and take from one place to another — see CARRY 1
**9** to take to or upon oneself — see ASSUME 1
**10** to wear or have on one's person — see CARRY 2
**bearable** *adj* capable of being endured ⟨the pain from a sprained ankle is annoying but *bearable*⟩
*syn* endurable, sufferable, supportable, sustainable, tolerable
*rel* livable (*also* liveable); acceptable, allowable, reasonable
*near ant* agonizing, appalling, awful, bad, cruel, dire, dreadful, excruciating, ghastly, harrowing, harsh, horrible, nasty, painful, rotten, terrible, tormenting, torturous, unfortunate, vicious, vile, wretched; unacceptable; acute, extreme, intense, piercing
*ant* insufferable, insupportable, intolerable, unbearable, unendurable, unsupportable
**beard** *vb* to oppose (something hostile or dangerous) with firmness or courage — see FACE 2
**bear down on** *vb* to push steadily against with some force — see PRESS 1
**bearing** *n* **1** the fact or state of being pertinent — see PERTINENCE
**2** the fact or state of having something in common — see CONNECTION 1
**3** the way or manner in which one conducts oneself — see BEHAVIOR
**bearish** *adj* having or showing a habitually bad temper — see ILL-TEMPERED
**bear out** *vb* to give evidence or testimony to the truth or factualness of — see CONFIRM

**beast** *n* **1** a mean, evil, or unprincipled person — see VILLAIN
**2** a person whose behavior is offensive to others — see JERK 1
**3** one of the lower animals as distinguished from human beings — see ANIMAL

**beastly** *adv* to a great degree — see VERY 1

**beat** *adj* depleted in strength, energy, or freshness — see WEARY 1

**beat** *n* **1** a hard strike with a part of the body or an instrument — see [1]BLOW
**2** a rhythmic expanding and contracting — see PULSATION
**3** the recurrent pattern formed by a series of sounds having a regular rise and fall in intensity — see RHYTHM

**beat** *vb* **1** to strike repeatedly ⟨they attacked and *beat* him, but fortunately he'll be fine⟩
***syn*** bash, bat, batter, belt, bludgeon, buffet, bung (up), club, drub, flog, hammer, hide, lace, lambaste (*or* lambast), lick, maul, pelt, pommel, pound, pummel, thrash, thump, wallop, whale, whip
***rel*** assail, attack, box, bust, cane, chop, clobber, clout, crack, cudgel, cuff, hit, horsewhip, knock, lam, lash, lay on, paste, punch, slap, smack, smash, sock, spank, swat, swipe, thwack, whack; gore, lacerate, wound; maim, mangle, mutilate
**2** to achieve a victory over ⟨she always *beats* everyone at checkers, but she's not as good at chess⟩
***syn*** best, clobber, conquer, crush, defeat, drub, lick, master, overbear, overcome, overmatch, prevail (over), rout, skunk, subdue, surmount, thrash, trim, triumph (over), trounce, wallop whip, win (against), worst
***rel*** nose out; excel, flourish, score, succeed; overpower, overthrow, subjugate, vanquish; exceed, outdo, surpass
***phrases*** get around, get the better of
***near ant*** fail
***ant*** lose (to)
**3** to be greater, better, or stronger than — see SURPASS 1
**4** to expand and contract in a rhythmic manner — see PULSATE
**5** to move or cause to move with a striking motion — see FLAP
**6** to prevent from achieving a goal — see FRUSTRATE
**7** to shape with a hammer — see HAMMER 1
**8** to shine with a bright harsh light — see GLARE 1
**9** to strike or cause to strike lightly and usually rhythmically — see [1]TAP

**beater** *n* one that defeats an enemy or opponent — see VICTOR 1

**beating** *n* failure to win a contest — see DEFEAT 1

**beau** *n* a male romantic companion — see BOYFRIEND

**beau ideal** *n* **1** someone of such unequaled perfection as to deserve imitation — see IDEAL 1
**2** the most perfect type or example — see QUINTESSENCE 1

**beauteous** *adj* very pleasing to look at — see BEAUTIFUL

**beauteousness** *n* the qualities in a person or thing that as a whole give pleasure to the senses — see BEAUTY 1

**beautiful** *adj* very pleasing to look at ⟨a strikingly *beautiful* child who is being eagerly pursued by all the modeling agencies⟩
***syn*** attractive, beauteous, bonny [*chiefly British*], comely, cute, fair, gorgeous, handsome, knockout, lovely, pretty, ravishing, sightly, stunning, taking
***rel*** alluring, appealing, charming, delightful, eye-catching, glamorous (*also* glamourous), prepossessing; elegant, exquisite, glorious, resplendent, splendid, statuesque, sublime, superb; flawless, perfect, radiant; dainty, delicate; personable, presentable
***near ant*** abhorrent, abominable, bad, disagreeable, disgusting, dreadful, foul, frightful, ghastly, hideous, horrible, loathsome, nasty, nauseating, objectionable, offensive, repellent, repugnant, repulsive, revolting, shocking, sickening, terrible; unappealing, unappetizing, unpleasant, unpleasing, unprepossessing
***ant*** homely, ill-favored, plain, ugly, unattractive, unbeautiful, unhandsome, unlovely, unpretty, unsightly

**beautify** *vb* to make more attractive by adding something that is beautiful or becoming — see DECORATE

**beautifying** *adj* serving to add beauty — see DECORATIVE

**beauty** *n* **1** the qualities in a person or thing that as a whole give pleasure to the senses ⟨her *beauty* was enough to take your breath away⟩
***syn*** attractiveness, beauteousness, comeliness, cuteness, fairness, gorgeousness, handsomeness, looks, loveliness, prettiness
***rel*** allure, appeal, attraction, glamour (*also* glamor); charm, elegance, exquisiteness, flawlessness, gloriousness, perfection, radiance, resplendence; desirability, desirableness
***near ant*** dreadfulness, foulness, ghastliness, grotesqueness, hideousness, loathsomeness, nastiness, offensiveness, repellency, repulsiveness, unattractiveness; blemish, flaw, imperfection
***ant*** homeliness, plainness, ugliness, unsightliness
**2** a lovely woman ⟨she was quite a *beauty* in her younger days⟩
***syn*** eyeful, goddess, knockout, stunner
***rel*** belle, charmer, honey
***near ant*** hag, horror, witch
**3** something very good of its kind — see JIM-DANDY

**because** *conj* for the reason that — see SINCE

**because of** *prep* as the result of ⟨I was late for school *because of* the snowstorm, which made driving very hazardous⟩
***syn*** due to, owing to, through, with

**beckon** *vb* to direct or notify by a movement or gesture — see MOTION

**becloud** *vb* **1** to make (something) unclear to the understanding — see CONFUSE 2
**2** to make dark, dim, or indistinct — see CLOUD 1

**beclouded** *adj* **1** covered over by clouds — see OVERCAST
**2** filled with or dimmed by fine particles (as of dust or water) in suspension — see HAZY 1

**become** *vb* to eventually have as a state or quality ⟨many people *became* sick with the flu⟩ ⟨with autumn the days *become* crisper and breezier⟩
***syn*** come, get, go, grow, run, turn, wax
***rel*** alter, change, metamorphose, modify, mutate, transfigure, transform, transmute
***near ant*** abide, be, continue, linger, remain, stay

**becoming** *adj* meeting the requirements of a purpose or situation — see FIT 1

**bed** *n* **1** a place set aside for sleeping ⟨the sofa in the living room will be your *bed* for the night⟩
***syn*** bunk, pad, sack
***rel*** bedstead, mattress, pallet; cot, couch, daybed, feather bed, four-poster, hammock, sofa, sofa bed, studio couch, trundle bed, water bed; bassinet, cradle, crib
**2** the surface upon which a body of water lies — see BOTTOM 2

**bed** *vb* to go to one's bed in order to sleep ⟨the campers all *bedded* down for the night around 9 pm⟩
***syn*** retire, turn in
***rel*** bunk, perch, roost, settle; doze, drop (off), nap, nod, sleep, slumber, snooze; couch, lie (down), recline
***near ant*** arouse, awake, awaken, rouse, wake, waken; bestir, stir, wake; reawake, reawaken; shift, stir
***ant*** arise, get up, rise, uprise

**bedaub** *vb* to rub an oily or sticky substance over — see SMEAR 1

**bedazzle** *vb* to overpower with light — see DAZZLE

**bedazzling** *adj* giving off or reflecting much light — see BRIGHT 1

**bedeck** *vb* to make more attractive by adding something that is beautiful or becoming — see DECORATE

**bedevil** *vb* to cause persistent suffering to — see AFFLICT

**bedevilment** *n* the act of making unwelcome intrusions upon another — see ANNOYANCE 1

**bedim** *vb* to make dark, dim, or indistinct — see CLOUD 1

**bedizen** *vb* to make more attractive by adding something that is beautiful or becoming — see DECORATE

**bedizened** *adj* elaborately and often excessively decorated — see ORNATE

**bedlam** *n* a place of uproar or confusion — see MADHOUSE 2

**bedrock** *n* an immaterial thing upon which something else rests — see BASE 1

**bedspread** *n* a decorative cloth used as a top covering for a bed — see COUNTERPANE

**beef** *n* an expression of dissatisfaction, pain, or resentment — see COMPLAINT 1

**beef** *vb* to express dissatisfaction, pain, or resentment usually tiresomely — see COMPLAIN

**beef** (up) *vb* **1** to increase the ability of (as a muscle) to exert physical force — see STRENGTHEN 1
**2** to make markedly greater in measure or degree — see INTENSIFY

**beefy** *adj* strongly and heavily built — see [1]HUSKY

**beetle** *vb* to extend outward beyond a usual point — see BULGE

**befall** *vb* to take place — see HAPPEN

**befit** *vb* to be fitting or proper — see DO 1

**befitting** *adj* meeting the requirements of a purpose or situation — see FIT 1

**befog** *vb* **1** to make (something) unclear to the understanding — see CONFUSE 2
**2** to make dark, dim, or indistinct — see CLOUD 1
**3** to throw into a state of mental uncertainty — see CONFUSE 1

**befogged** *adj* filled with or dimmed by fine particles (as of dust or water) in suspension — see HAZY 1

**before** *adv* so as to precede something in order of time — see AHEAD 1

**before** *prep* **1** earlier than ⟨since I'm a faster runner, I got there *before* him⟩
***syn*** afore [*chiefly dialect*], ahead of, ere, of, previous to, prior to, to
***rel*** till, until, up to
***phrases*** in advance of
***near ant*** next, next to, since
***ant*** after, following
**2** preceding in space ⟨the children always insisted on running *before* their parents⟩
***syn*** afore [*chiefly dialect*], ahead of
***rel*** against
***phrases*** in advance of, in front of
***ant*** after, following

**beforehand** *adv* **1** before the usual or expected time — see EARLY
**2** so as to precede something in order of time — see AHEAD 1

**befoul** *vb* **1** to make dirty — see DIRTY
**2** to make unfit for use by the addition of something harmful or undesirable — see CONTAMINATE

**befuddle** *vb* to throw into a state of mental uncertainty — see CONFUSE 1

**befuddled** *adj* suffering from mental confusion — see DIZZY 2

**befuddlement** *n* a state of mental uncertainty — see CONFUSION 1

**beg** *vb* to make a request to (someone) in an earnest or urgent manner ⟨she *begged* her mother to let her go on the Girl Scout camporee⟩
***syn*** appeal (to), beseech, conjure, entreat, implore, importune, petition, plead (to), pray, solicit, supplicate

---

***syn*** synonym(s) ***rel*** related words
***ant*** antonym(s) ***near ant*** near antonym(s)

*rel* mooch, sponge; ask, desire, invoke, request, sue; claim, coerce, command, compel, demand, force, insist, require
*phrases* call on (*or* call upon)
*near ant* hint, imply, intimate, suggest; appease, conciliate, gratify, mollify, oblige, pacify, placate, please, satisfy; comfort, console, content, quiet

**beget** *vb* to become the father of — see FATHER

**begetter** *n* a person who establishes a whole new field of endeavor — see FATHER 2

**beggar** *n* a person who lives by public begging ⟨the poor *beggars* that are such a common sight in underdeveloped countries⟩
*syn* mendicant, panhandler
*rel* bum, drifter, hobo, tramp, vagabond, vagrant; pauper; hanger-on, leech, moocher, parasite, sponge, sponger; dependent; deadbeat, derelict, idler, ne'er-do-well

**beggared** *adj* lacking money or material possessions — see POOR 1

**beggary** *n* the state of lacking sufficient money or material possessions — see POVERTY 1

**begin** *vb* **1** to take the first step in (a process or course of action) ⟨she *began* walking to school⟩
*syn* commence, embark (on *or* upon), enter (into *or* upon), get off, kick off, launch, open, start, strike (into)
*rel* create, generate, inaugurate, initiate, innovate, invent, originate; adopt, embrace, take on, take up; establish, father, found, institute, organize, pioneer, set up, spawn
*phrases* get to, set about
*near ant* cease, desist, discontinue, halt, lay off, quit, stop; close, complete; abandon, forsake, leave; abolish, demolish, destroy, exterminate, extinguish, phase out
*ant* conclude, end, finish, terminate
**2** to come into existence ⟨the storm *began* late in the day and lasted all night⟩
*syn* arise, commence, dawn, form, materialize, originate, set in, spring, start
*rel* be, breathe, exist, live, subsist; appear, arrive, emerge; continue, endure, last, persist, survive
*near ant* conclude, desist, discontinue, finish, halt, quit, terminate; disappear, dissolve, evaporate, vanish; depart, die, expire, pass away, perish
*ant* cease, end, stop

**beginner** *n* a person who is just starting out in a field of activity ⟨although he is only a *beginner* at swimming, he is making excellent progress⟩
*syn* colt, fledgling, freshman, greenhorn, neophyte, newcomer, novice, recruit, rookie, tenderfoot, tyro
*rel* apprentice, cub; boot, novitiate; amateur, dilettante; learner, student, trainee; candidate, entrant, probationer
*near ant* expert, master, pro, professional
*ant* old hand, old-timer, vet, veteran

**beginning** *n* the point at which something begins ⟨the actual *beginning* of the universe is still under debate, with some scientists believing in the big bang theory⟩
*syn* alpha, birth, commencement, dawn, genesis, inception, incipiency, launch, morning, onset, outset, start, threshold
*rel* creation, inauguration, initiation, institution, origination; cradle, fountainhead, origin, root, source, spring, well, wellspring; dawning, opening; appearance, arrival, emergence; infancy
*near ant* cessation, closing, closure, completion, finale, finish, period, stop, termination, windup
*ant* close, conclusion, end, ending

**begone** *vb* to leave a place often for another — see GO 2

**begrime** *vb* to make dirty — see DIRTY

**beguile** *vb* **1** to attract or delight as if by magic — see CHARM 1
**2** to cause to believe what is untrue — see DECEIVE
**3** to lead away from a usual or proper course by offering some pleasure or advantage — see LURE

**beguiling** *adj* **1** clever at attaining one's ends by indirect and often deceptive means — see ARTFUL 1
**2** tending or having power to deceive — see DECEPTIVE 1

**behave** *vb* to manage the actions of (oneself) in a particular way ⟨if she *behaves* herself properly and sits quietly during church, she will get ice cream afterward⟩
*syn* acquit, bear, comport, conduct, demean, deport, quit
*rel* check, collect, compose, constrain, contain, control, curb, handle, inhibit, quiet, repress, restrain; moderate, modulate, temper; act, impersonate, play
*near ant* act up, carry on, cut up, misbehave, misconduct

**behavior** *n* the way or manner in which one conducts oneself ⟨he promised to be on his best *behavior* for the party⟩
*syn* actions, bearing, comportment, conduct, demeanor, deportment
*rel* etiquette, form, manners, mores, proprieties; amenity, civility, courtesy, decorum, politeness; air, attitude, carriage, poise, pose, posture, presence; aspect, look, mien; formality; protocol, rules; custom, habit, pattern, practice (*also* practise), trick, wont; convention, fashion, form, mode, style; affectation, attribute, characteristic, mark, trait; distinctiveness, oddity, peculiarity, singularity, strangeness, uniqueness, weirdness

**behead** *vb* to cut off the head of — see DECAPITATE

**behemoth** *n* something that is unusually large and powerful — see GIANT

**behest** *n* a statement of what to do that must be obeyed by those concerned — see COMMAND 1

**behind** *adj* not arriving, occurring, or settled at the due, usual, or proper time — see LATE 1

**behind** *prep* **1** at, to, or toward the rear of ⟨she preferred to be *behind* the lead hikers, who were always too much in a rush to enjoy the scenery⟩
***syn*** abaft, back of
***near ant*** ahead of
***ant*** before, in front of
**2** subsequent to in time or order — see AFTER

**behindhand** *adj* not arriving, occurring, or settled at the due, usual, or proper time — see LATE 1

**behold** *vb* to make note of (something) through the use of one's eyes — see SEE 1

**being** *n* **1** a member of the human race — see HUMAN
**2** one that has a real and independent existence — see ENTITY

**belabor** *vb* to criticize harshly and usually publicly — see ATTACK 2

**belated** *adj* not arriving, occurring, or settled at the due, usual, or proper time — see LATE 1

**belatedness** *n* the quality or state of being late — see LATENESS

**belch** *vb* to throw out or off (something from within) often violently — see ERUPT 1

**beldam** *or* **beldame** *n* a mean or ugly old woman — see CRONE

**beleaguer** *vb* to surround (as a fortified place) with armed forces for the purpose of capturing or preventing commerce and communication — see BESIEGE

**belie** *vb* **1** to give a false idea of ⟨his bright smile *belied* his actual mood, which was really one of great sadness⟩
***syn*** misrepresent
***rel*** contradict; camouflage, cloak, conceal, counterfeit, disguise, hide, mask, obscure; color, deceive, distort, falsify, garble, mislead, twist; dissemble, feign, pretend
***near ant*** bare, demonstrate, disclose, discover, exhibit, expose, evince, reveal; flaunt, parade, show off
***ant*** betray, represent
**2** to prove to be false — see DISPROVE

**belief** *n* **1** mental conviction of the truth of some statement or the reality of some being or phenomenon ⟨a *belief* in unicorns led him to look for them every time he walked through the woods⟩
***syn*** credence, credit, faith
***rel*** axiom, law, precept, principle, tenet; assurance, certainty, certitude, conviction, positiveness, sureness; confidence, dependance, reliance, trust; hope; doctrine, dogma, philosophy; dogmatism, fanaticism, insistence
***near ant*** distrust, mistrust, skepticism, suspicion, uncertainty
***ant*** disbelief, discredit, doubt, unbelief
**2** an idea that is believed to be true or valid without positive knowledge — see OPINION 1

***syn*** synonym(s) ***rel*** related words
***ant*** antonym(s) ***near ant*** near antonym(s)

**believable** *adj* worthy of being accepted as true or reasonable ⟨she had a *believable* story for why her homework was late, so she didn't receive any punishment⟩
***syn*** credible, likely, plausible, probable
***rel*** acceptable, conceivable, imaginable, possible, practical, reasonable; dependable, reliable, trustworthy
***near ant*** absurd, doubtful, dubious, fantastic, flimsy, outlandish, preposterous, questionable, ridiculous; impossible, inconceivable, unimaginable, unthinkable; skeptical, suspect, suspicious, uncertain, unsure; hopeless, unworkable, useless
***ant*** far-fetched, implausible, improbable, incredible, unbelievable, unlikely

**believe** *vb* **1** to regard as right or true ⟨the teacher *believed* the student's explanation that the assignment was late because she was sick, even though she didn't bring in a note from the doctor⟩
***syn*** accept, credit, swallow, trust
***rel*** account, accredit, understand; assume, presume, suppose; conclude, deduce, infer
***phrases*** set store by (*or* on)
***near ant*** distrust, doubt, mistrust, question, suspect; challenge, dispute
***ant*** disbelieve, discredit, reject
**2** to have as an opinion ⟨he *believed* that his favorite tennis player was the best in the world⟩
***syn*** consider, deem, feel, figure, guess, hold, imagine, reckon [*chiefly dialect*], suppose, think
***rel*** esteem, regard, view; accept, conceive, perceive; depend, rely, trust; assume, presume, presuppose; conclude, deduce, infer
***near ant*** distrust, doubt, mistrust, question, suspect; disbelieve, discredit, reject

**belittle** *vb* to express scornfully one's low opinion of — see DECRY 1

**belittlement** *n* the act of making a person or a thing seem little or unimportant — see DEPRECIATION

**belittling** *adj* intended to make a person or thing seem of little importance or value — see DEROGATORY

**bellicose** *adj* feeling or displaying eagerness to fight — see BELLIGERENT

**bellicosity** *n* an inclination to fight or quarrel — see BELLIGERENCE

**belligerence** *n* an inclination to fight or quarrel ⟨among the Native American tribes of the Colonial period, the Iroquois were known for their *belligerence*⟩
***syn*** aggression, aggressiveness, bellicosity, combativeness, contentiousness, disputatiousness, fight, militancy, pugnacity, scrappiness, truculence
***rel*** antagonism, fierceness, hostility, unfriendliness; acidity, biliousness, crabbiness, crankiness, crossness, disagreeableness, fretfulness, grouchiness, grumpiness, huffiness, irascibility, irritability, irritableness, orneriness, peevishness, pettishness, petulance, querulousness, rudeness, surliness, testiness, waspishness

*phrases* chip on one's shoulder
*near ant* affability, amiability, amicability, benevolence, complaisance, cordiality, friendliness, geniality, graciousness, pleasantness, sociability; gentleness, kindliness, mildness
*ant* pacifism

**belligerent** *adj* feeling or displaying eagerness to fight ⟨the coach became quite *belligerent* and spit on an umpire after being thrown out of the game⟩
*syn* aggressive, argumentative, bellicose, combative, contentious, discordant, disputatious, gladiatorial, militant, pugnacious, quarrelsome, scrappy, truculent, warlike
*rel* antagonistic, fierce, hostile, hot-tempered; acidic, bearish, bilious, choleric, crabby, cranky, cross, disagreeable, dyspeptic, fretful, grouchy, grumpy, huffy, ill-humored, ill-natured, ill-tempered, irascible, irritable, ornery, peevish, pettish, petulant, querulous, rude, snappish, snappy, surly, testy, touchy, ugly, waspish; battling, fighting, warring
*phrases* on the warpath
*near ant* affable, amiable, amicable, benevolent, complaisant, conciliatory, cordial, easygoing, friendly, genial, good-natured, good-tempered, gracious, ingratiating, obliging, pleasant, sociable; calm, quiet, relaxed, serene, tranquil; benign, gentle, kindly, mild
*ant* nonbelligerent, pacific, peaceable, peaceful

**bellow** *vb* to make a long loud deep noise or cry — see ROAR

**belly** *n* the part of the body between the chest and the pelvis — see STOMACH

**belly** *vb* to extend outward beyond a usual point — see BULGE

**bellyache** *n* abdominal pain especially when focused in the digestive organs — see STOMACHACHE

**bellyache** *vb* to express dissatisfaction, pain, or resentment usually tiresomely — see COMPLAIN

**belong** *vb* **1** to have or be in a usual or proper place ⟨your shoes *belong* in the closet, not out on the floor where people will trip on them⟩
*syn* go
*rel* place, stay; fit (in)
**2** to be the property of a person or group of persons ⟨those textbooks *belong* to the school system, and you have to give them back at the end of the year⟩
*syn* appertain, pertain
*rel* have, hold, own, possess

**belongings** *n pl* transportable items that one owns — see POSSESSION 2

**beloved** *adj* granted special treatment or attention — see DARLING 1

**beloved** *n* a person with whom one is in love — see SWEETHEART

**below** *adv* **1** in or to a lower place ⟨he climbed *below* to fix the engine⟩
*syn* beneath, under, underneath
*rel* beside, near, nearby
*near ant* aloft, overhead
*ant* up
**2** toward or in a lower position — see DOWN

**below** *prep* in a lower position than ⟨she sat *below* everyone else, on the floor⟩
*syn* beneath, under
*rel* underneath
*ant* above, over

**[1]belt** *n* a hard strike with a part of the body or an instrument — see [1]BLOW

**[2]belt** *n* a strip of flexible material (as leather) worn around the waist ⟨he loves his fancily decorated *belt*, but only gets to wear it on special occasions⟩
*syn* cincture, cummerbund, girdle, sash
*rel* band, waistband; circle, loop, ribbon, ring; baldric, bandolier (*or* bandoleer)
**2** a broad geographical area — see REGION 2

**belt** *vb* **1** to deliver a blow to (someone or something) usually in a strong vigorous manner — see HIT 1
**2** to encircle or bind with or as if with a belt — see GIRD 1
**3** to strike repeatedly — see BEAT 1

**bemoan** *vb* **1** to feel or express sorrow for — see LAMENT 1
**2** to feel sorry or dissatisfied about — see REGRET

**bemoaning** *adj* expressing or suggesting mourning — see MOURNFUL 1

**bemuse** *vb* to throw into a state of mental uncertainty — see CONFUSE 1

**bench** *n* a public official having authority to decide questions of law — see JUDGE 1

**benchmark** *n* something set up as an example against which others of the same type are compared — see STANDARD 1

**bend** *n* **1** something that curves or is curved ⟨it's hard to see around that *bend* in the road, so be careful⟩
*syn* angle, arc, arch, bow, crook, curvature, curve, turn, wind
*rel* kink, warp; circle, ring, ringlet, round; coil, curl, curlicue (*also* curlycue), flexure, fold, loop, spiral, swirl, twist; decline, inclination, incline, slope; corner, turnoff
*ant* straight line
**2** the act of positioning or an instance of being positioned at an angle — see TILT

**bend** *vb* **1** to cause to turn away from a straight line ⟨she *bent* the knife when she got it stuck in the drawer⟩
*syn* arch, crook, curve, hook, swerve
*rel* arc, bow, round; deflect, divert; entwine, kink, swirl, turn, twine, twist, veer, warp; coil, curl, loop, spiral; dent, dimple; meander, weave, wind; decline, incline, slope
*ant* straighten, unbend, uncurl
**2** to occupy (oneself) diligently or with close attention — see APPLY 2
**3** to point or turn (something) toward a target or goal — see AIM 1
**4** to turn away from a straight line or course — see CURVE 1

**bending** *adj* marked by a long series of irregular curves — see CROOKED 1

**beneath** *adv* in or to a lower place — see BELOW 1

**beneath** *prep* in a lower position than — see BELOW

**benediction** *n* a prayer calling for divine care, protection, or favor — see BLESSING 1

**benefaction** *n* a gift of money or its equivalent to a charity, humanitarian cause, or public institution — see CONTRIBUTION

**benefactor** *n* one that helps another with gifts or money ⟨an anonymous *benefactor* gave our school a dozen new computers⟩
***syn*** donator, donor, patron
***rel*** almsgiver, philanthropist; contributor, giver; subscriber, supporter, helper

**beneficence** *n* a gift of money or its equivalent to a charity, humanitarian cause, or public institution — see CONTRIBUTION

**beneficent** *adj* **1** having or marked by sympathy and consideration for others — see HUMANE 1
**2** having or showing a concern for the welfare of others — see CHARITABLE 1

**beneficial** *adj* conferring benefits; promoting or contributing to personal or social well-being ⟨tutoring can often be as *beneficial* and rewarding for the tutor as for the student receiving the help⟩
***syn*** advantageous, favorable, helpful, profitable, salutary
***rel*** gratifying, rewarding, satisfying; promising, propitious; advisable, desirable, healthful, healthy, salubrious, wholesome
***near ant*** bad, damaging, deleterious, harmful, injurious, unfavorable, unhelpful
***ant*** disadvantageous, unfavorable, unhelpful

**benefit** *n* **1** a thing that helps — see HELP 2
**2** something that provides happiness or does good for a person or thing — see BLESSING 2

**benefit** *vb* to provide with something useful or desirable ⟨his summer job *benefited* him in two ways: by giving him spending money and by offering some work experience⟩
***syn*** avail, profit, serve
***rel*** succeed, work (for); aid, assist, help, improve; content, delight, gladden, gratify, please, satisfy; bless
***near ant*** hinder, impede; damage, harm, hurt, impair, injure; afflict, distress, upset

**benevolence** *n* kindly concern, interest, or support — see GOODWILL 1

**benevolent** *adj* **1** having or marked by sympathy and consideration for others — see HUMANE 1
**2** having or showing a concern for the welfare of others — see CHARITABLE 1

**benighted** *adj* lacking in education or the knowledge gained from books — see IGNORANT 1

**benign** *adj* not harsh or stern especially in manner, nature, or effect — see GENTLE 1

**benignant** *adj* having or marked by sympathy and consideration for others — see HUMANE 1

**benison** *n* a prayer calling for divine care, protection, or favor — see BLESSING 1

**bent** *n* a habitual attraction to some activity or thing — see INCLINATION 1

**bent** (on *or* upon) *adj* fully committed to achieving a goal — see DETERMINED

**benumb** *vb* to reduce or weaken in strength or feeling — see DULL 1

**benumbed** *adj* lacking in sensation or feeling — see NUMB

**bequeath** *vb* to give by means of a will — see LEAVE 2

**bequest** *n* something that is or may be inherited — see INHERITANCE

**berate** *vb* to criticize (someone) severely or angrily especially for personal failings — see SCOLD

**bereaved** *adj* suffering the death of a loved one ⟨the *bereaved* parents cried often in the first year⟩
***syn*** bereft
***rel*** orphaned, widowed; distressed, grieving, melancholy, miserable, mournful, mourning, sad, sorrowing, suffering, unhappy, upset; bemoaning, crying, lamenting, wailing, weeping

**bereft** *adj* **1** suffering the death of a loved one — see BEREAVED
**2** utterly lacking in something needed, wanted, or expected — see DEVOID 1

**berserk** *adv* in a confused and reckless manner — see HELTER-SKELTER 1

**berth** *n* an assignment at which one regularly works for pay — see JOB 1

**beseech** *vb* to make a request to (someone) in an earnest or urgent manner — see BEG

**beseeching** *adj* asking humbly — see SUPPLIANT

**beset** *vb* to take sudden, violent action against — see ATTACK 1

**beside** *prep* **1** in addition to — see BESIDES 1
**2** not including — see EXCEPT

**besides** *adv* in addition to what has been said — see MORE 1

**besides** *prep* **1** in addition to ⟨*besides* me, there are five people working on this project⟩
***syn*** as well as, beside, over and above
***rel*** plus; including
***phrases*** along with, together with
***near ant*** except (*also* excepting); less, minus
**2** not including — see EXCEPT

**besiege** *vb* to surround (as a fortified place) with armed forces for the purpose of capturing or preventing commerce and communication ⟨the army *besieged* the fort for six months before it finally surrendered⟩
***syn*** beleaguer, blockade, invest
***rel*** barricade, block, cut off, dam, encircle; assail, assault, attack, beset; confine, insulate, isolate, quarantine
***phrases*** lay siege to

*near ant* emancipate, free, liberate, release, rescue

**besmear** *vb* to rub an oily or sticky substance over — see SMEAR 1

**besmirch** *vb* to make dirty — see DIRTY

**besmirched** *adj* not clean — see DIRTY 1

**bespatter** *vb* to wet or soil by striking with something liquid or mushy — see SPLASH 2

**bespeak** *vb* **1** to arrange to have something (as a hotel room) held for one's future use — see RESERVE 1
**2** to make known (something abstract) through outward signs — see SHOW 2

**best** *n* **1** dressy clothing — see FINERY
**2** individuals carefully selected as being the best of a class — see ELITE

**best** *vb* to achieve a victory over — see BEAT 2

**bestow** *vb* to make a present of — see GIVE 1

**bestowal** *n* something given to someone without expectation of a return — see GIFT 1

**bestrew** *vb* to cover by or as if by scattering something over or on — see SCATTER 2

**bet** *n* the money or thing risked on the outcome of an uncertain event ⟨she offered the *bet* of a free lunch if her team won the World Series⟩
*syn* stake, wager
*rel* collateral; jackpot, kitty, pot

**bet** *vb* to risk (something) on the outcome of an uncertain event ⟨he *bet* a month's allowance on the World Series⟩
*syn* gamble, go, lay, stake, wager
*rel* bid, offer; adventure, chance, hazard, speculate, venture; endanger, imperil, jeopardize

**bête noire** *n* **1** something or someone that causes fear or dread especially without reason — see BOGEY 1
**2** something or someone that is hated — see HATE 2

**betide** *vb* to take place — see HAPPEN

**betray** *vb* **1** to be unfaithful or disloyal to ⟨childhood friends of movie stars often *betray* them by telling their secrets to the supermarket tabloids⟩
*syn* cross, double-cross, sell (out)
*rel* give away; inform (on), rat (on), snitch (on), split (on) [*British*], tell (on)
*phrases* go back on
*near ant* defend, guard, protect, safeguard, save, shield
**2** to make known (something abstract) through outward signs — see SHOW 2

**betrayal** *n* the act or fact of violating the trust or confidence of another ⟨the terrible *betrayal* of having her best friend reveal her confidences to others⟩
*syn* disloyalty, double cross, faithlessness, falseness, falsity, infidelity, perfidy, sellout, treachery, treason, unfaithfulness
*rel* abandonment, desertion; deceit, deception, double-dealing, duplicity, guile; fraud, informing, lying, snitching, talebearing, trickery
*near ant* dependability, reliability, trustworthiness; allegiance, devotion, faithfulness, fealty, fidelity, loyalty, staunchness, steadfastness; defense, protection, safeguard, shield

**betrayer** *n* **1** a person who provides secret information about another's wrongdoing — see INFORMER
**2** one who betrays a trust or an allegiance — see TRAITOR

**betrothal** *n* the act or state of being engaged to be married — see ENGAGEMENT 1

**betrothed** *adj* pledged in marriage — see ENGAGED

**betrothed** *n* the person to whom one is engaged to be married ⟨he gazed lovingly at his *betrothed* throughout dinner⟩
*syn* fiancé, fiancée, intended
*rel* admirer, beau, beloved, boyfriend, darling, dear, favorite, fellow, flame, girlfriend, honey, love, lover, steady, swain, sweet, sweetheart, valentine; bride, groom

**better** *adv* to a greater or higher extent — see MORE 2

**better** *n* **1** one who is above another in rank, station, or office — see SUPERIOR
**2** the more favorable condition or position in a competition — see ADVANTAGE 1

**better** *vb* **1** to be greater, better, or stronger than — see SURPASS 1
**2** to make better — see IMPROVE

**bettor** *or* **better** *n* one that bets (as on the outcome of a contest or sports event) ⟨*bettors* on the horse race have to place their bets at least 20 minutes before the start of the race⟩
*syn* gambler, wagerer
*rel* dicer; speculator

**beverage** *n* a liquid suitable for drinking — see DRINK 1

**bewail** *vb* to feel or express sorrow for — see LAMENT 1

**bewailing** *adj* expressing or suggesting mourning — see MOURNFUL 1

**beware** (of) *vb* to be cautious of or on guard against ⟨*beware of* that parrot because it bites⟩
*syn* guard (against), mind, watch out (for)
*rel* attend, heed, mark, note, notice; behold, discern, observe, perceive, see, watch
*phrases* be on the lookout for, look out for
*near ant* discount, disregard, ignore, miss, overlook

**bewilder** *vb* to throw into a state of mental uncertainty — see CONFUSE 1

**bewildered** *adj* suffering from mental confusion — see DIZZY 2

**bewilderment** *n* a state of mental uncertainty — see CONFUSION 1

**bewitch** *vb* **1** to cast a spell on ⟨a wicked fairy *bewitched* Sleeping Beauty so that she would sleep for a hundred years⟩
*syn* charm, enchant, hex, spell

*rel* curse, jinx, possess; attract, beguile, captivate, fascinate, mesmerize, spellbind; entice, lure, seduce, tempt
*near ant* bless
**2** to attract or delight as if by magic — see CHARM 1

**bewitched** *adj* being or appearing to be under a magic spell — see ENCHANTED

**bewitching** *adj* having an often mysterious or magical power to attract — see FASCINATING 1

**bewitchment** *n* **1** a spoken word or set of words believed to have magic power — see SPELL 1
**2** the power to control natural forces through supernatural means — see MAGIC 1

**beyond** *adv* at or to a greater distance or more advanced point — see FARTHER

**beyond** *prep* **1** on or to the farther side of ⟨the arrow flew *beyond* the fence and in the woods⟩
*syn* over, past
*rel* outside
*near ant* inside
**2** out of the reach or sphere of ⟨although the school can keep you from screaming during school hours, making someone be quiet after school is *beyond* their authority⟩
*syn* outside, outside of, without
*rel* except (*also* excepting)
*near ant* inside
*ant* within

**bias** *n* an attitude that always favors one way of feeling or acting especially without considering any other possibilities ⟨he had a powerful *bias* towards doing all math problems by the same method, regardless of the problem⟩
*syn* favor, one-sidedness, partiality, partisanship, prejudice
*rel* favoritism, nepotism; bent, inclination, leaning, penchant, predilection, predisposition, proclivity, propensity, tendency; preconception, prejudgment
*near ant* calm, detachment, dispassion, indifference; aversion, dislike, distaste
*ant* impartiality, neutrality, objectivity, open-mindedness

**bias** *vb* to cause to have often negative opinions formed without sufficient knowledge — see PREJUDICE

**biased** *adj* inclined to favor one side over another — see PARTIAL 1

**Bible** *n* a book made up of the writings accepted by Christians as coming from God ⟨she received a lovely *Bible* as a First Communion gift⟩
*syn* Book, Good Book, Holy Writ, Scripture

**bicker** *n* an often noisy or angry expression of differing opinions — see ARGUMENT 1

**bicker** *vb* to express different opinions about something often angrily — see ARGUE 2

---

*syn* synonym(s) *rel* related words
*ant* antonym(s) *near ant* near antonym(s)

**bid** *vb* to issue orders to (someone) by right of authority — see COMMAND 1

**bide** *vb* to remain in place in readiness or expectation of something — see WAIT

**big** *adj* **1** having great meaning or lasting effect — see IMPORTANT 1
**2** of a size greater than average of its kind — see LARGE

**bight** *n* a part of a body of water that extends beyond the general shoreline — see GULF 1

**bigness** *n* the quality or state of being large in size — see LARGENESS

**bigoted** *adj* unwilling to grant other people social rights or to accept other viewpoints — see INTOLERANT 2

**bilious** *adj* having or showing a habitually bad temper — see ILL-TEMPERED

**biliousness** *n* readiness to show annoyance or impatience — see PETULANCE

**[1]bill** *n* **1** a record of goods sold or services performed together with the costs due ⟨luckily, the amount due on our electric *bill* wasn't too high this month, because we finally convinced everyone to stop wasting electricity⟩
*syn* account, check, invoice, statement, tab
*rel* receipt, reckoning; document, record; charge, cost, expense, fee, price, rate, toll; score, tally
**2** a piece of printed paper used as money ⟨the United States twenty-dollar *bill* has a picture of Andrew Jackson on the front⟩
*syn* bank note, greenback, note
*rel* paper money, scrip; buck, dollar; cash, chips, currency, dough, legal tender, lucre, money, pelf; check, draft, money order
**3** a sheet bearing an announcement for posting in a public place — see POSTER
**4** the amount owed at a bar or restaurant or the slip of paper stating the amount — see CHECK 1

**[2]bill** *n* **1** the jaws of a bird together with their hornlike covering — see BEAK
**2** the projecting front part of a hat or cap — see VISOR

**[1]billet** *n* a straight piece (as of wood or metal) that is longer than it is wide — see BAR 1

**[2]billet** *n* an assignment at which one regularly works for pay — see JOB 1

**billet** *vb* to provide with living quarters or shelter — see HOUSE 1

**bill of fare** *n* a list of foods served at or available for a meal — see MENU 1

**billow** *n* a moving ridge on the surface of water — see WAVE

**billow** *vb* to extend outward beyond a usual point — see BULGE

**billy** *n* a heavy rigid stick used as a weapon or for punishment — see CLUB 1

**binary** *adj* consisting of two members or parts that are usually joined — see DOUBLE 1

**bind** *vb* **1** to confine or restrain with or as if with chains ⟨prisons tend to *bind* convicted criminals for transport⟩ ⟨Angie

feels *bound* to her boyfriend by love and loyalty〉
***syn*** chain, enchain, fetter, handcuff, manacle, shackle, trammel
***rel*** lash, pinion, secure, tie, truss; attach, fasten, join, link; confine, constrain, curb, hamper, hinder, limit, restrict; entangle, tangle
***near ant*** emancipate, free, liberate, loose, release, rescue; undo, unfasten, untangle, untie; detach, disengage
***ant*** unbind, unfetter
**2** to cover with a bandage — see BANDAGE
**3** to gather into a tight mass by means of a line or cord — see TIE 1

**binge** *n* a time or instance of carefree fun — see FLING 1

**biography** *n* a history of a person's life 〈an unauthorized *biography* of the actor made him very unhappy〉
***syn*** life, memoir
***rel*** autobiography; chronicle, history, past, story; obituary; character sketch

**bipartite** *adj* consisting of two members or parts that are usually joined — see DOUBLE 1

**birch** *vb* to strike repeatedly with something long and thin or flexible — see WHIP 1

**bird** *n* a member of the human race — see HUMAN

**birdman** *n* one who flies or is qualified to fly an aircraft or spacecraft — see PILOT

**bird's–eye** *adj* relating to the main elements and not to specific details — see GENERAL 2

**birth** *n* **1** the act or instance of being born 〈biology class will be showing a movie of the *birth* of kittens〉
***syn*** nativity
***rel*** creation, genesis, origination, rise; bearing, childbearing, labor, parturition; begetting, breeding, fathering, generation, mothering, reproduction, siring, spawning; fatherhood, maternity, motherhood, parenthood, paternity
***near ant*** abortion, miscarriage
**2** the line of ancestors from whom a person is descended — see ANCESTRY
**3** the point at which something begins — see BEGINNING

**birthright** *n* **1** something that is or may be inherited — see INHERITANCE
**2** something to which one has a just claim — see RIGHT 1

**bisect** *vb* to divide by passing through or across — see INTERSECT

**bit** *n* **1** a very small piece 〈she left only a *bit* of the broccoli on her plate, so she was allowed to have dessert〉
***syn*** atom, crumb, fleck, flyspeck, grain, granule, molecule, morsel, mote, nubbin, particle, patch, scrap, scruple, snippet, speck, tittle
***rel*** ace, dab, glimmer, hint, hoot, iota, jot, lick, little, mite, modicum, ounce, peanuts, pinch, ray, shade, shred, smidgen (*also* smidgeon *or* smidgin), spot, strain, streak, suspicion, taste, touch, trace, whisper, whit; dash, driblet, drop; fragment, part, portion, section; bite, mouthful, nibble; handful, scattering, smattering, sprinkling; dose, shot; damn, darn; chip, flake, shard, shiver, sliver, splinter; clipping, paring, shaving; smithereens
***near ant*** chunk, gob, lump, hunk, slab; abundance, barrel, bucket, bushel, deal, heaps, loads, mass, mountain, much, peck, pile, plenty, pot, profusion, quantity, raft, scads, stack, volume, wad, wealth
**2** a broken or irregular part of something that often remains incomplete — see FRAGMENT
**3** a very small amount — see PARTICLE 1
**4** an indefinite but usually short period of time — see WHILE 1

**bite** *n* **1** a harsh or sharp quality — see EDGE 1
**2** a small piece or quantity of food — see MORSEL 1
**3** an uncomfortable degree of coolness — see CHILL

**bite** (at) *vb* to consume or wear away gradually — see EAT 2

**bite** (on) *vb* to crush or grind with the teeth 〈she likes to *bite on* her pencils when she thinks hard〉
***syn*** champ, chew, chomp (on), crunch (on), gnaw (on), masticate, nibble
***rel*** lap, lick, munch; consume, ingest, eat, swallow; bolt, devour, gobble (up *or* down), gorge, gulp, scarf, scoff, snack, wolf; peck (at), pick (at)

**biting** *adj* **1** causing intense discomfort to one's skin — see CUTTING 1
**2** causing intense mental or physical distress — see SHARP 2
**3** marked by the use of wit that is intended to cause hurt feelings — see SARCASTIC

**bitter** *adj* **1** having or showing deep-seated resentment 〈a *bitter* attitude about always having to work on Saturday〉 〈she's still *bitter* about the way her boyfriend broke up with her〉
***syn*** acrid, acrimonious, embittered, hard, rancorous, resentful, sore
***rel*** disaffected, discontented, disgruntled, malcontent; contemptuous, cynical, disdainful, scornful; angry, cruel, harsh, irritated, mad, rough, savage, vicious; acid, caustic, cutting, mordant, sarcastic, trenchant
***near ant*** caring, forgiving, gentle, kind, loving, sweet, sympathetic, tender, warm, warmhearted
**2** hard to accept or bear especially emotionally 〈discovering that he had been cut from the team was a *bitter* disappointment〉
***syn*** afflicting, agonizing, cruel, excruciating, galling, grievous, harrowing, harsh, heartrending, hurtful, painful, tormenting, tortuous
***rel*** insufferable, insupportable, intolerable, unacceptable, unbearable, unendurable, unsupportable; appalling, awful, bad, dire, dreadful, ghastly, horrible, miserable, nasty, rotten, terrible, vile,

wretched; acute, extreme, intense, piercing
*near ant* bearable, endurable, supportable, sustainable, tolerable; livable (*also* liveable), sufferable, survivable; acceptable, allowable, reasonable
*ant* gratifying, pleasing, sweet
**3** causing intense discomfort to one's skin — see CUTTING 1
**4** difficult to endure — see HARSH 1
**5** having a low or subnormal temperature — see COLD 1
**6** uncomfortably cool — see CHILLY 1

**bitterly** *adv* with feelings of bitterness or grief — see HARD 2

**bitterness** *n* **1** a deep-seated ill will — see ENMITY
**2** a harsh or sharp quality — see EDGE 1
**3** an uncomfortable degree of coolness — see CHILL
**4** biting sharpness of feeling or expression — see ACRIMONY 1

**bitty** *adj* very small in size — see TINY

**bivouac** *n* a place where a group of people live for a short time in tents or cabins — see CAMP 1

**bivouac** *vb* to live in a camp or the outdoors — see CAMP

**bizarre** *adj* **1** conceived or made without regard for reason or reality — see FANTASTIC 1
**2** different from the ordinary in a way that causes curiosity or suspicion — see ODD 2

**blab** *vb* **1** to engage in casual or rambling conversation — see CHAT
**2** to relate sometimes questionable or secret information of a personal nature — see GOSSIP

**blabber** *n* **1** a person who talks constantly — see CHATTERBOX
**2** unintelligible or meaningless talk — see GIBBERISH

**black** *adj* **1** having the color of soot or coal ⟨a little *black* dress blends into the night very well⟩
*syn* ebony, pitch-black, pitch-dark, pitchy, raven, sable
*rel* dark, dusky, inky; blackish, brunet (*or* brunette)
*near ant* bright, brilliant, light, pale
*ant* white
**2** causing or marked by an atmosphere lacking in cheer — see GLOOMY 1
**3** not conforming to a high moral standard; morally unacceptable — see BAD 2

**black art** *n* the power to control natural forces through supernatural means — see MAGIC 1

**blackball** *vb* to reject by or as if by a vote — see NEGATIVE 1

**blacken** *vb* **1** to make dirty — see DIRTY
**2** to make untrue and harmful statements about — see SLANDER
**3** to make dark, dim, or indistinct — see CLOUD 1

**blackened** *adj* not clean — see DIRTY 1

**blackening** *n* the making of false statements that damage another's reputation — see SLANDER

**black magic** *n* the power to control natural forces through supernatural means — see MAGIC 1

**blackmailer** *n* a person who gets money from another by using force or threats — see RACKETEER

**blackness** *n* a time or place of little or no light — see DARK 1

**blackout** *n* a temporary or permanent state of unconsciousness — see FAINT

**black out** *vb* to lose consciousness — see FAINT

**blade** *n* **1** a hand weapon with a length of metal sharpened on one or both sides and usually tapered to a sharp point — see SWORD
**2** an instrument with a sharp edge for cutting — see KNIFE

**blamable** *adj* **1** deserving reproach or blame — see BLAMEWORTHY
**2** responsible for a wrong — see GUILTY 1

**blame** *n* **1** responsibility for wrongdoing or failure ⟨willingly accepted the *blame* for not seeing that the kitchen was properly cleaned⟩
*syn* culpability, fault, guilt, rap
*rel* regret, remorse, self-reproach, shame; accountability, liability; complicity; blameworthiness, reprehensibleness, sinfulness; censure, condemnation, denunciation
*near ant* acclaim, plaudits, praise; achievement, success
*ant* blamelessness, faultlessness, guiltlessness, innocence
**2** the state of being held as the cause of something that needs to be set right — see RESPONSIBILITY 1

**blame** *vb* to express one's unfavorable opinion of the worth or quality of — see CRITICIZE

**blameless** *adj* free from guilt or blame — see INNOCENT 2

**blamelessness** *n* the quality or state of being free from guilt or blame — see INNOCENCE 1

**blameworthy** *adj* deserving reproach or blame ⟨copying another student's work was certainly a *blameworthy* act⟩
*syn* blamable, censurable, culpable, reprehensible, reproachable
*rel* bad, guilty, sinful, wicked; foolish, irresponsible, reckless; chargeable, impeachable, indictable, punishable; criminal, illegal, illicit, unlawful; illegitimate, improper, wrongful
*phrases* at fault
*near ant* flawless, perfect, pure; guiltless, innocent
*ant* blameless, faultless, impeccable, irreproachable

**blanch** *vb* to make white or whiter by removing color — see WHITEN

**blanched** *adj* lacking a healthy skin color — see PALE 2

**bland** *adj* not harsh or stern especially in manner, nature, or effect — see GENTLE 1

---

*syn* synonym(s) *rel* related words
*ant* antonym(s) *near ant* near antonym(s)

**blandish** *vb* to get (someone) to do something by gentle urging, special attention, or flattery — see COAX

**blank** *adj* **1** not expressing any emotion ⟨the teacher knew no one was paying attention when she looked out and saw all those *blank* faces⟩
*syn* deadpan, expressionless, impassive, inexpressive, stolid, vacant
*rel* dull, empty, vacuous, vapid; enigmatic (*also* enigmatical), impenetrable, inscrutable, mysterious; dead, inactive, quiescent, sleepy, sluggish; indolent, languorous, lazy, lethargic, listless; motionless, static, still, wooden; reserved, restrained, reticent, taciturn; aloof, apathetic, detached, indifferent, phlegmatic; cold, cool
*near ant* active, alive, animated, bright, busy, dynamic, effervescent, energetic, expansive, exuberant, lively, vigorous, vital, vivacious; eloquent, revealing, revelatory, significant, vivid; emotional, melodramatic, theatrical, unreserved, unrestrained
*ant* demonstrative, expressive
**2** lacking contents that could or should be present — see EMPTY 1

**blank** *n* **1** a piece of paper with information written or to be written on it — see FORM 2
**2** empty space — see VACANCY 1

**blanket** *adj* belonging or relating to the whole — see GENERAL 1

**blanket** *vb* **1** to form a layer over — see COVER 2
**2** to keep secret or shut off from view — see [1]HIDE 2

**blankness** *n* empty space — see VACANCY 1

**blaring** *adj* marked by a high volume of sound — see LOUD 1

**blarney** *n* excessive praise — see FLATTERY

**blarney** *vb* **1** to get (someone) to do something by gentle urging, special attention, or flattery — see COAX
**2** to praise too much — see FLATTER 1

**blaspheme** *vb* to use offensive or indecent language — see SWEAR 1

**blasphemous** *adj* not showing proper reverence for the holy or sacred — see IRREVERENT

**blasphemy** *n* an act of great disrespect shown to God or to sacred ideas, people, or things ⟨in the 17th century the Quakers were persecuted for beliefs and practices that older churches regarded as *blasphemies*⟩
*syn* defilement, desecration, impiety, irreverence, sacrilege
*rel* cursing, profanity, swearing; affront, insult; violation; contamination, corruption, debasement, pollution; sin, trespass
*near ant* consecration, purification, sanctification; reverence, veneration
*ant* adoration, glorification, worship

**blast** *n* **1** a loud explosive sound — see CLAP 1
**2** a sudden brief rush of wind — see GUST 1
**3** the act or an instance of exploding — see EXPLOSION 1

**blast** *vb* **1** to cause to break open or into pieces by or as if by an explosive ⟨the highway engineers will have to *blast* that hill in order to put a road through it⟩
*syn* blow up, burst, demolish, explode, pop, shatter, smash
*rel* dynamite; annihilate, decimate, destroy; ruin, wreck; detonate, discharge; fragment, splinter
*near ant* collapse, implode
**2** to cause (a projectile) to be driven forward with force — see SHOOT 1
**3** to cause a weapon to release a missile with great force — see SHOOT 2
**4** to criticize harshly and usually publicly — see ATTACK 2

**blasting** *adj* marked by a high volume of sound — see LOUD 1

**blasting** *n* a directed propelling of a missile by a firearm or artillery piece — see SHOT

**blatant** *adj* **1** engaging in or marked by loud and insistent cries especially of protest — see VOCIFEROUS
**2** very noticeable especially for being incorrect or bad — see EGREGIOUS

**blaze** *n* the steady giving off of the form of radiation that makes vision possible — see LIGHT 1

**blaze** *vb* **1** to be on fire especially brightly — see BURN 1
**2** to make known openly or publicly — see ANNOUNCE
**3** to shine with a bright harsh light — see GLARE 1

**blazing** *adj* **1** being on fire — see ABLAZE 1
**2** having or expressing great depth of feeling — see FERVENT

**bleach** *vb* to make white or whiter by removing color — see WHITEN

**bleak** *adj* **1** causing or marked by an atmosphere lacking in cheer — see GLOOMY 1
**2** marked by wet and windy conditions — see FOUL 1
**3** uncomfortably cool — see CHILLY 1

**bleakness** *n* an uncomfortable degree of coolness — see CHILL

**bleary** *adj* not seen or understood clearly — see FAINT 1

**bleed** *vb* **1** to feel deep sadness or mental pain — see GRIEVE
**2** to flow forth slowly through small openings — see EXUDE
**3** to remove (liquid) gradually or completely — see DRAIN 1
**4** to rob by the use of trickery or threats — see FLEECE

**bleed** (for) *vb* to have sympathy for — see PITY

**blemish** *n* something that spoils the appearance or completeness of a thing ⟨a slight *blemish* on the mirror was the only break in the gleaming surface⟩

*syn* defect, deformity, disfigurement, fault, flaw, imperfection, mark, pockmark, scar
*rel* abnormality, distortion, irregularity, malformation; bug, glitch, kink; blot, blotch, spot, stain; failing, vice, weakness
*near ant* adornment, decoration, embellishment, enhancement, ornament

**blemish** *vb* **1** to affect slightly with something morally bad or undesirable — see TAINT 1
**2** to reduce the soundness, effectiveness, or perfection of — see DAMAGE 1

[1]**blench** *vb* to draw back in fear, pain, or disgust — see FLINCH

[2]**blench** *vb* to make white or whiter by removing color — see WHITEN

**blend** *n* a distinct entity formed by the combining of two or more different things ⟨that fabric is a cotton and polyester *blend*, so it shouldn't shrink as much as pure cotton⟩
*syn* admixture, amalgam, amalgamation, combination, composite, compound, fusion, intermixture, mix, mixture
*rel* coalescence, concoction, incorporation, intermingling, mingling; assortment, hash, hodgepodge, hotchpotch, jumble, medley, mélange, mishmash, motley, patchwork, potpourri, variety; accumulation, aggregation, conglomeration
*near ant* component, constituent, element, ingredient

**blend** *vb* **1** to turn into a single mass that is more or less the same throughout ⟨she *blended* the ingredients for the brownies very thoroughly to eliminate lumps in the batter⟩
*syn* amalgamate, combine, commingle, fuse, incorporate, integrate, intermingle, intermix, merge, mingle, mix
*rel* fold, mix, stir, toss; coalesce, combine, compound, conjoin, join, link, unite
*near ant* cleave, disjoin, disunite, divide, divorce, part, rupture, sever, sunder; disperse, dissolve, scatter; detach, disengage, split
*ant* break down, break up, separate
**2** to form a pleasing relationship — see HARMONIZE 1

**bless** *vb* **1** to make holy through prayers or ritual ⟨the priest *blessed* the water, thus allowing it to be used as holy water for various rites⟩
*syn* consecrate, hallow, sanctify
*rel* cleanse, purify; commit, dedicate, devote; reconsecrate
*near ant* defile, desecrate, profane; dirty, foul, pollute, soil, taint; curse, damn, execrate; cast out, condemn, damn, punish
**2** to proclaim the glory of — see PRAISE 1

**blessed** *adj* **1** of, relating to, or being God — see HOLY 3
**2** set apart or worthy of veneration by association with God — see HOLY 2

*syn* synonym(s) *rel* related words
*ant* antonym(s) *near ant* near antonym(s)

**blessedness** *n* **1** a feeling or state of well-being and contentment — see HAPPINESS 1
**2** the quality or state of being spiritually pure or virtuous — see HOLINESS

**blessing** *n* **1** a prayer calling for divine care, protection, or favor ⟨that rabbi also always ends the service with a short *blessing*⟩
*syn* benediction, benison
*rel* Godspeed; appeal, entreaty, grace, invocation, orison, petition, plea, prayer, supplication; sanctification
*ant* anathema, curse, execration, imprecation, malediction
**2** something that provides happiness or does good for a person or thing ⟨finding money on the sidewalk just when he needed to buy new sneakers was an unexpected *blessing*⟩
*syn* benefit, boon, felicity, godsend, good, manna, windfall
*rel* bonus, extra, lagniappe; advantage, aid, assistance, gift, help, relief, support; comfort, consolation, solace; delight, joy, pleasure
*near ant* hex, hoodoo, jinx; bother, irritant, nuisance, pest
*ant* affliction, bane, curse, evil, plague, scourge
**3** an acceptance of something as satisfactory — see APPROVAL 1
**4** the act of making something holy through religious ritual — see CONSECRATION

**blind** *adj* lacking the power of sight ⟨our old *blind* cat kept walking into walls and furniture⟩
*syn* eyeless, sightless, stone blind
*rel* unobservant, unobserving; blinded, purblind
*near ant* observant, observing
*ant* sighted

**blind** *vb* to overpower with light — see DAZZLE

**blink** *vb* **1** to shine with light at regular intervals ⟨she loves to sit in the dark and watch the lights on the Christmas tree *blink* in ever-changing patterns⟩
*syn* flash, twinkle, wink
*rel* flicker, glance, glimmer, glint, glisten, glister, glitter, scintillate, shimmer, sparkle; beam, gleam, irradiate, radiate
**2** to rapidly open and close one's eyes — see WINK 1

**bliss** *n* a feeling or state of well-being and contentment — see HAPPINESS 1

**blissful** *adj* experiencing pleasure, satisfaction, or delight — see GLAD 1

**blissfulness** *n* a feeling or state of well-being and contentment — see HAPPINESS 1

**blithe** *adj* **1** having or showing a good mood or disposition — see CHEERFUL 1
**2** indicative of or marked by high spirits or good humor — see MERRY

**blithesome** *adj* **1** having or showing a good mood or disposition — see CHEERFUL 1

2 indicative of or marked by high spirits or good humor — see MERRY

**blitz** *vb* to use bombs or artillery against — see BOMBARD

**blitzkrieg** *n* the act or action of setting upon with force or violence — see ATTACK 1

**blob** *n* 1 a small uneven mass — see LUMP 1
2 the quantity of fluid that falls naturally in one rounded mass — see DROP 1

**bloc** *n* 1 a group of people acting together within a larger group — see FACTION
2 an association of persons, parties, or states for mutual assistance and protection — see CONFEDERACY

**block** *n* 1 a number of things considered as a unit — see GROUP 1
2 something that makes movement or progress more difficult — see ENCUMBRANCE

**block** *vb* 1 to close up so that no empty spaces remain — see FILL 2
2 to prevent passage through — see CLOG 1

**blockade** *n* the cutting off of an area by military means to stop the flow of people or supplies ⟨it was the *blockade* of all the enemy's major ports that finally won the war⟩
***syn*** investment, siege
***rel*** encompassment, encirclement; confinement, insulation, isolation, quarantine, seclusion, segregation, sequestration; incarceration, internment
***near ant*** emancipation, freedom, liberation, release, rescue

**blockade** *vb* to surround (as a fortified place) with armed forces for the purpose of capturing or preventing commerce and communication — see BESIEGE

**blockbuster** *n* 1 a person or thing that is successful — see HIT 1
2 something that is unusually large and powerful — see GIANT

**blockhead** *n* a stupid person — see IDIOT

**bloke** *n, chiefly British* an adult male human being — see MAN 1

**blond** *or* **blonde** *adj* of a pale yellow or yellowish brown color ⟨the little boy's *blond* hair darkened to brown as he grew older⟩
***syn*** fair, flaxen, golden, sandy, straw, tawny
***rel*** gold, light, white
***near ant*** brunet (*or* brunette), dark, swarthy; black, ebony, raven
***ant*** dark

**blood** *n* 1 a group of persons who come from the same ancestor — see FAMILY 1
2 the line of ancestors from whom a person is descended — see ANCESTRY

**bloodline** *n* the line of ancestors from whom a person is descended — see ANCESTRY

**bloodstained** *adj* containing, smeared, or stained with blood — see BLOODY 1

**bloodthirsty** *adj* eager for or marked by the shedding of blood, extreme violence, or killing ⟨the Goths were a wild and *bloodthirsty* people⟩
***syn*** bloody, homicidal, murdering, murderous, sanguinary, sanguine
***rel*** barbaric, barbarous, cruel, heartless, inhumane, sadistic, savage, vicious, wanton; antagonistic, fierce, gladiatorial, hostile; aggressive, assertive, bellicose, belligerent, combative, contentious, discordant, pugnacious, quarrelsome, scrappy, truculent, violent; merciless, pitiless, ruthless; fell, ferocious, grim; despiteful, hateful, malevolent, malicious, malign, malignant, mean, nasty, spiteful; destructive, devastating, ruinous
***near ant*** appeasing, conciliatory, disarming, dovish, mollifying, pacific, pacifying, peaceable, peaceful, peacemaking, placating, propitiatory; unaggressive, unassertive; benign, benignant, compassionate, good-hearted, humane, kind, kindhearted, sympathetic, tenderhearted; tender, warm, warmhearted; clement, lenient, merciful; affable, amiable, amicable, benevolent, gentle, kindly; submissive, surrendering, yielding

**bloody** *adj* 1 containing, smeared, or stained with blood ⟨after the fight, her shirt was all *bloody*⟩
***syn*** bloodstained, gory
***rel*** carmine, crimson, red, ruby, sanguine; bloodthirsty, sanguinary
2 eager for or marked by the shedding of blood, extreme violence, or killing — see BLOODTHIRSTY

**bloom** *n* 1 a state or time of great activity, thriving, or achievement ⟨a handsome young man in the full *bloom* of youth⟩
***syn*** blossom, flower, flush, heyday, prime
***rel*** acme, apex, climax, meridian, peak, pinnacle, summit, zenith; glory, grandeur, splendor; haleness, heartiness; energy, force, potency, power, vigor
***near ant*** decline, bottom, nadir; feebleness, fragility, frailty, weakness; illness, infirmity, sickness; shriveling, wilting, withering
2 a rosy appearance of the cheeks ⟨after a snowball fight, she came inside with a *bloom*⟩
***syn*** blush, flush
***rel*** brightness, brilliance, glow; pinkness, rosiness
3 the usually showy plant part that produces seeds — see FLOWER 1

**bloom** *vb* 1 to produce flowers ⟨forsythias only *bloom* at the beginning of spring⟩
***syn*** blossom, blow, burgeon, flower, unfold
***rel*** leaf, leave; bud; open
***near ant*** dry (up), fade, shrivel, wilt, wither; die, drop, expire, perish
2 to develop a rosy facial color (as from excitement or embarrassment) — see BLUSH

**blooming** *adj* having a healthy reddish skin tone — see RUDDY

**blossom** *n* 1 a state or time of great activity, thriving, or achievement — see BLOOM 1

**2** the usually showy plant part that produces seeds — see FLOWER 1

**blossom** *vb* to produce flowers — see BLOOM

**blot** *n* a mark of guilt or disgrace — see STAIN 1

**blotch** *n* a small area that is different (as in color) from the main part — see SPOT 1

**blotch** *vb* **1** to mark with blotches especially of different colors or shades — see MOTTLE 1

**2** to mark with small spots especially unevenly — see SPOT

**blotched** *adj* having blotches of two or more colors — see PIED

**blot out** *vb* **1** to destroy all traces of — see ANNIHILATE 1

**2** to keep secret or shut off from view — see [1]HIDE 2

[1]**blow** *n* a hard strike with a part of the body or an instrument ⟨he was dizzy for the rest of the day after the *blow* to his head⟩

***syn*** bang, bat, beat, belt, bop, box, buffet, bust, chop, clap, clip, clout, crack, cuff, hit, hook, knock, lick, pound, punch, rap, slam, slap, slug, smack, smash, sock, spank, stroke, swat, swipe, thud, thump, thwack, wallop, whack

***rel*** flick, jab, poke, roundhouse, stab; beating, battering, bludgeoning, clobbering, drubbing, hammering, lambasting, licking, pasting, pounding, pummeling, thrashing; flogging, walloping, whipping

[2]**blow** *n* a sudden brief rush of wind — see GUST 1

[1]**blow** *vb* **1** to breathe hard, quickly, or with difficulty — see GASP

**2** to use up carelessly — see WASTE 1

[2]**blow** *vb* to produce flowers — see BLOOM

**blow** (out) *vb* to let or force out of the lungs — see EXHALE 1

**blowout** *n* a social gathering — see PARTY 1

**blowup** *n* an outburst or display of excited anger — see TANTRUM

**blow up** *vb* **1** to become very angry ⟨she *blew up* at everybody after a very long and very bad day⟩

***syn*** flare (up), flip

***rel*** fulminate, rant, vituperate; bristle, burn, foam, fume, rage, seethe; burst, explode; enrage, incense, inflame, infuriate, madden; aggravate, anger, annoy, bother, bug, displease, distress, exasperate, gall, get, irk, irritate, nettle, peeve, pique, provoke, put out, rile, vex; agitate, disturb, perturb, upset

***phrases*** fly into a rage, fly off the handle, forget oneself, lose one's temper

***near ant*** appease, conciliate, mollify, pacify, placate; comfort, console, quiet, soothe

***ant*** calm (down)

**2** to break open or into pieces usually because of internal pressure — see EXPLODE 1

**3** to cause to break open or into pieces by or as if by an explosive — see BLAST 1

**blowy** *adj* marked by strong wind or more wind than usual — see WINDY 1

**blubber** *vb* to shed tears often while making meaningless sounds as a sign of pain or distress — see CRY 1

**bludgeon** *n* a heavy rigid stick used as a weapon or for punishment — see CLUB 1

**bludgeon** *vb* **1** to deliver a blow to (someone or something) usually in a strong vigorous manner — see HIT 1

**2** to strike repeatedly — see BEAT 1

**blue** *adj* feeling unhappiness — see SAD 1

**blue** *n* **1** the expanse of air surrounding the earth — see SKY

**2** the whole body of salt water that covers nearly three-fourths of the earth — see OCEAN

**blueprint** *n* a method worked out in advance for achieving some objective — see PLAN 1

**blueprint** *vb* to work out the details of (something) in advance — see PLAN 1

**blues** *n pl* a state or spell of low spirits — see SADNESS

**bluff** *adj* being or characterized by direct, brief, and potentially rude speech or manner — see BLUNT 1

**bluff** *n* a steep wall of rock, earth, or ice — see CLIFF

**bluff** *vb* to cause to believe what is untrue — see DECEIVE

**blunder** *n* an unintentional departure from truth or accuracy — see ERROR 1

**blunt** *adj* **1** being or characterized by direct, brief, and potentially rude speech or manner ⟨he values honesty and is quite *blunt* about telling people their flaws⟩

***syn*** abrupt, bluff, brusque, crusty, curt, downright, snippy

***rel*** gruff, rough, short; hearty, honest, sincere; candid, direct, forthright, foursquare, frank, free-spoken, open, outspoken, plain, plainspoken, straightforward; discourteous, disrespectful, impertinent, impolite, inconsiderate, rude, tactless, undiplomatic; closemouthed, laconic, reserved, reticent, terse, tight-lipped; artless, earnest, sincere; coarse, crass, crude, low, uncouth, vulgar

***near ant*** civil, considerate, courteous, diplomatic, gracious, polite, politic, smooth, suave, tactful; loquacious, talkative, voluble; long-winded, prolix, verbose; courtly, cultivated, gallant, genteel, polished, refined

***ant*** circuitous, mealymouthed

**2** lacking sharpness of edge or point — see DULL 1

**blunt** *vb* to reduce or weaken in strength or feeling — see DULL 1

**blunted** *adj* lacking sharpness of edge or point — see DULL 1

**blur** *vb* **1** to make (something) unclear to the understanding — see CONFUSE 2

**2** to make dark, dim, or indistinct — see CLOUD 1

**blurt** (out) *vb* to utter with a sudden burst of strong feeling — see EXCLAIM

---

***syn*** synonym(s) ***rel*** related words
***ant*** antonym(s) ***near ant*** near antonym(s)

**blush** *n* a rosy appearance of the cheeks — see BLOOM 2

**blush** *vb* to develop a rosy facial color (as from excitement or embarrassment) ⟨she *blushed* when she realized she had walked into the boys' bathroom by mistake⟩
*syn* bloom, color, crimson, flush, glow, redden
*rel* rouge; abash, chagrin, discomfit, disconcert, embarrass, faze, humiliate, mortify

**bluster** *n* **1** boastful speech or writing — see BOMBAST 1
**2** loud, confused, and usually unharmonious sound — see NOISE 1

**bluster** *vb* to talk loudly and wildly — see RANT

**blustery** *adj* marked by strong wind or more wind than usual — see WINDY 1

**board** *n* a leg-mounted piece of furniture with a broad flat top designed for the serving of food — see TABLE 1

**board** *vb* **1** to provide food or meals for — see FEED 1
**2** to provide with living quarters or shelter — see HOUSE 1

**boarder** *n* one who rents a room or apartment in another's house — see TENANT

**boast** *n* an asset that brings praise or renown — see GLORY 2

**boast** *vb* to praise or express pride in one's own possessions, qualities, or accomplishments often to excess ⟨he *boasted* that he was the best hockey goalie in the whole school⟩
*syn* brag, crow, swagger
*rel* puff (up); pride; gush; exult, glory, rejoice; brandish, display, exhibit, expose, flaunt, parade, show off; magnify, maximize
*near ant* bad-mouth, belittle, decry, deprecate, depreciate, diminish, discount, disparage, minimize; bemoan, lament, mourn, regret

**boat** *n* **1** a small buoyant structure for travel on water ⟨paddling the little *boat* across the lake is great exercise, but tiring⟩
*syn* bottom, craft, vessel, watercraft
*rel* canoe, catamaran, catboat, cockleshell, coracle, dinghy, dory, dugout, flatboat, float, gig, gondola, houseboat, ironclad, kayak, launch, life boat, longboat, motorboat, outrigger, pirogue, pontoon, punt, raft, rowboat, sail, sampan, scow, scull, shallop, shell, sloop, tender, umiak; bark, brig, brigantine, caravel, clipper, galleon, galley, junk, ketch, pinnace, sailboat, schooner, ship, square-rigger, windjammer, xebec, yacht; corvette, cutter, destroyer, fireship, flagship, gunboat, landing craft, privateer, torpedo boat, warship; argosy, barge, coaster, collier, containership, ferryboat, icebreaker, lighter, lightship, liner, merchantman, merchant ship, packet, revenuer, riverboat, showboat, steamboat, steamer, supertanker, taxi, towboat, trader, tugboat; sealer, shrimper, trawler, whaler; derelict, hulk, tub; air-cushion vehicle, hovercraft; hydrofoil, hydroplane
**2** a large craft for travel by water — see SHIP

**boat** *vb* to travel on water in a vessel — see SAIL 1

**[1]bob** *vb* to make (as hair) shorter with or as if with the use of shears — see CLIP

**[2]bob** *vb* to make short up-and-down movements — see NOD

**bobble** *vb* **1** to make or do (something) in a clumsy or unskillful way — see BOTCH
**2** to make short up-and-down movements — see NOD

**bobby** *n, British* a member of a force charged with law enforcement at the local level — see OFFICER 1

**bobby–soxer** *n* a young usually unmarried woman — see GIRL 1

**bode** *vb* to show signs of a favorable or successful outcome ⟨her natural gift for reading *boded* well for her future in school⟩
*syn* augur, forebode (*also* forbode), promise
*rel* forecast, foretell, predict, presage, prognosticate, prophesy; forewarn, warn; anticipate, divine, foreknow, foresee; foreshadow, portend, prefigure; allude, connote, hint, imply, insinuate, intimate, suggest
*phrases* bid fair, give promise of

**bodiless** *adj* not composed of matter — see IMMATERIAL 1

**bodily** *adj* of or relating to the human body — see PHYSICAL 1

**boding** *n* something believed to be a sign or warning of a future event — see OMEN

**body** *n* **1** the main or greater part of something as distinguished from its appendages ⟨the *body* of the novel was quite good, even if the beginning was a bit slow⟩
*syn* bulk, core, generality, main, mass, staple, weight
*rel* majority; aggregate, amount, entirety, sum, sum total, total, totality, whole; bottom, essence, essentiality, marrow, nature, quintessence, soul, stuff, substance; center, heart, hub, middle, nucleus, seat; affair, argument, burden, crux, focus, gist, kernel, nub, pitch, point, purport; matter, motif, subject, text, theme, topic
*near ant* accessory, adjunct, appendage, extension, offshoot; component, constituent, element, ingredient; division, part, piece, section, segment; angle, aspect, facet, feature, quality, side
**2** a distinct and separate portion of matter ⟨the Atlantic is a gigantic *body* of water⟩
*syn* mass
*rel* aggregate, amount, bulk, quantity, volume; item, object, thing; material, stuff, substance; entirety, totality, whole
**3** a group of people acting together within a larger group — see FACTION
**4** a group of people sharing a common interest and relating together socially — see GANG 2

**5** a member of the human race — see HUMAN
**6** a usually small number of persons considered as a unit — see GROUP 2

**bog** *n* spongy land saturated or partially covered with water — see SWAMP

**bog** (down) *vb* to place in conflict or difficulties — see EMBROIL

**bogey** *also* **bogy** *or* **bogie** *n* **1** something or someone that causes fear or dread especially without reason ⟨math and math tests have long been *bogeys* for many students⟩
***syn*** bête noire, bugaboo, bugbear, hobgoblin, ogre
***rel*** apparition, ghost, phantasm, phantom, poltergeist, shade, specter (*or* spectre), spirit, spook, wraith; banshee, bogeyman, demon, devil, fiend, imp, incubus; fright, horror, monster, monstrosity, terror; bane, curse, plague, scourge, torment; abomination, anathema
**2** the soul of a dead person thought of especially as appearing to living people — see GHOST

**bogus** *adj* **1** being such in appearance only and made with or manufactured from usually cheaper materials — see IMITATION
**2** being such in appearance only and made or manufactured with the intention of committing fraud — see COUNTERFEIT
**3** lacking in natural or spontaneous quality — see ARTIFICIAL 1

**bohemian** *n* a person who does not conform to generally accepted standards or customs — see NONCONFORMIST 1

**boil** *vb* **1** to be excited or emotionally stirred up with anger ⟨she was *boiling* at the thought of her so-called best friend trying to steal her boyfriend⟩
***syn*** burn, fume, rage, seethe, steam
***rel*** fulminate, rant, rave; smolder; bristle, flare (up); chafe, fret, stew; agitate, convulse, shake; disturb, perturb, upset
**2** to cook in a liquid heated to the point that it gives off steam ⟨*boil* the potatoes very well before you try to mash them⟩
***syn*** coddle, parboil, poach, simmer, stew
***rel*** scald; braise, fricassee, pressure-cook, steam; reboil
**3** to be in a state of violent rolling motion — see SEETHE 1

**boisterous** *adj* being rough or noisy in a high-spirited way ⟨the fans at the baseball game became particularly *boisterous* after the home run⟩
***syn*** knockabout, rambunctious, raucous, rowdy
***rel*** rampageous, riotous, stormy, tempestuous, turbulent, violent; disorderly, raffish, ruffianly; headstrong, intractable, obstreperous, recalcitrant, uncontrollable, uncontrolled, undisciplined, ungovernable, uninhibited, unmanageable, unruly, wild, willful (*or* wilful); bubbly, buoyant, effervescent, exuberant, high-spirited, impassioned, lively, passionate, sprightly, vivacious; clamorous, loudmouthed, noisy, strident, vociferous; howling, screaming, yelling
***near ant*** sedate, sober, solemn, somber (*or* sombre), staid; decorous, dignified, proper, seemly; calm, hushed, noiseless, peaceful, placid, quiet, restrained, serene, silent, soundless, tranquil; collected, composed, constrained, controlled, imperturbable, inhibited, repressed, self-controlled, unflappable, unruffled; moderate, reasonable, subdued, temperate; impassive, phlegmatic, stoic (*or* stoical), stolid; depressed; aloof, detached, indifferent
***ant*** orderly

**bold** *adj* **1** inclined or willing to take risks ⟨our youngest brother was the *boldest* one in the family, instantly taking to everything from skiing to skateboarding⟩
***syn*** adventuresome, adventurous, audacious, daring, dashing, emboldened, enterprising, gutsy, hardy, nerved, nervy, venturesome, venturous
***rel*** brash, daredevil, foolhardy, heedless, hotheaded, impetuous, imprudent, impulsive, incautious, madcap, overbold, overconfident, rash, reckless, spirited, thoughtless, wild; brave, courageous, dauntless, fearless, gallant, greathearted, heroic, intrepid, lionhearted, stalwart, stout, stouthearted, unafraid, undaunted, valiant, valorous; gritty, plucky, spirited, spunky; hasty, headlong, precipitate; absurd, asinine, balmy, brainless, crazy, foolish, half-witted, harebrained, insane, lunatic, mad, nutty, scatterbrained, silly, wacky, witless; unnecessary; dumb, idiotic, moronic, stupid; irrational, unreasonable
***near ant*** chickenhearted, coward, cowardly, craven, lily-livered, pusillanimous, shy, timid, timorous; careful, cautious, heedful, prudent, wary; overcareful, overcautious; affrighted, afraid, alarmed, fainthearted, fearful, frightened, horrified, scared, shocked, spooked, startled, terrified, terrorized; unnerved; calm, cool, levelheaded, rational, reasonable, sage, sane, sensible, sound, wise; appalled, concerned, dismayed, upset, worried
***ant*** unadventurous, unenterprising
**2** displaying or marked by rude boldness — see NERVY 1
**3** likely to attract attention — see NOTICEABLE
**4** showing a lack of proper social reserve or modesty — see PRESUMPTUOUS 1
**5** having an incline approaching the perpendicular — see STEEP 1

**bold-faced** *adj* displaying or marked by rude boldness — see NERVY 1

**bolster** *vb* to hold up or serve as a foundation for — see SUPPORT 3

**bolt** *n* something that makes a strong impression because it is so unexpected — see SURPRISE 1

**bolt** *vb* **1** to move suddenly and sharply (as in surprise) — see START 1
**2** to proceed or move quickly — see HURRY 2
**3** to hasten away from something dangerous or frightening — see RUN 2
**4** to utter with a sudden burst of strong feeling — see EXCLAIM

**bomb** *vb* to use bombs or artillery against — see BOMBARD

**bombard** *vb* to use bombs or artillery against ⟨the Allies *bombarded* Germany for a great many months during World War II⟩
*syn* blitz, bomb, shell
*rel* rake, strafe; assail, assault, attack, devastate, hit, pound, ravage, strike

**bombardment** *n* a rapid or overwhelming outpouring of many things at once — see BARRAGE

**bombast** *n* **1** boastful speech or writing ⟨filling a speech with *bombast* about one's unique qualifications for student council is usually a bad idea⟩
*syn* bluster, brag, braggadocio, gas, grandiloquence, hot air, rant
*rel* rhapsody, rhetoric; babble, blab, chatter, drivel, gabble, gibber, jabber, prattle; jawing, patter, prating, yammering; egotism, self-conceit, self-importance
**2** language that is impressive-sounding but not meaningful or sincere — see RHETORIC 1

**bombastic** *adj* marked by the use of impressive-sounding but mostly meaningless words and phrases — see RHETORICAL

**bombshell** *n* something that makes a strong impression because it is so unexpected — see SURPRISE 1

**bona fide** *adj* being exactly as appears or as claimed — see AUTHENTIC 1

**bond** *n* **1** something that physically prevents free movement ⟨before they could release the captive, they had to undo a number of *bonds*⟩
*syn* band, bracelet, chain, fetter, handcuff(s), irons, ligature, manacle, shackle
*rel* confinement, constraint, curb, hamper, hindrance, restraint, restriction; entanglement, net, trammel, trap; collar, straitjacket (*also* straightjacket); hobble, tie
**2** a uniting or binding force or influence ⟨the *bond* of love between them was so strong that even death could not break it⟩
*syn* cement, knot, ligature, link, tie
*rel* attachment, connection, entanglement, fastening, joint, linkage; affection, fondness, sympathy; fetter, handcuff, manacle, shackle, trammel; constraint, curb, hampering, limit, limitation, restraint, restriction
*near ant* detaching, disengaging, parting, separation; unbinding, unfastening, unfettering, untying; emancipation, freedom, liberation, release
**3** a formal agreement to fulfill an obligation — see GUARANTEE 1

**bondage** *n* the state of being a slave — see SLAVERY 1

**bonding** *n* a physical sticking to as if by glue — see ADHESION

**bondman** *n* a person who is considered the property of another person — see SLAVE 1

**bondsman** *n* a person who is considered the property of another person — see SLAVE 1

**bone** *n, usually* **bones** *pl* a small cube marked on each side with one to six spots and usually played in pairs in various games — see DIE

**bone** (up) *vb* to use the mind to acquire knowledge — see STUDY 1

**bonny** *adj, chiefly British* very pleasing to look at — see BEAUTIFUL

**bonus** *n* something given in addition to what is ordinarily expected or owed ⟨this job offers a nice Christmas *bonus* in addition to the salary⟩
*syn* dividend, extra, gratuity, gravy, lagniappe, perquisite, tip
*rel* fillip; bestowal, presentation; benefaction, benevolence, bounty, charity, generosity, largess (*or* largesse), philanthropy; contribution, donation, gift, offering, present; grant, subsidy; boon, manna, windfall; favor, freebie (*or* freebee), giveaway, premium; award, prize, reward; fringe benefit

**bon voyage** *n* an expression of good wishes at parting — see GOOD-BYE

**boo** *n* a vocal sound made to express scorn or disapproval — see CATCALL

**booby** *n* a person who lacks good sense or judgment — see FOOL 1

**boobytrap** *vb* to place hidden explosive devices in or under — see MINE

**booby trap** *n* **1** a usually concealed explosive device designed to go off when disturbed ⟨luckily, the bomb squad didn't find any *booby traps*⟩
*syn* mine
*rel* bomb, explosive; pitfall, snare, trap; ambush
**2** a danger or difficulty that is hidden or not easily recognized — see PITFALL 1

**book** *n* **1** a set of printed sheets of paper bound together between covers and forming a work of fiction or nonfiction ⟨I bought another new *book* yesterday, and I can't wait to read it⟩
*syn* tome, volume
*rel* hardback, paperback, pocket book; folio, quarto; guidebook, handbook, manual; catalog (*or* catalogue), dictionary, encyclopedia; booklet, brochure, circular, flier (*or* flyer), folder, leaflet, magazine, pamphlet, program; textbook, tract, treatise; novel, novelette, pulp
**2** *cap* a book made up of the writings accepted by Christians as coming from God — see BIBLE

**book** *vb* to arrange to have something (as a hotel room) held for one's future use — see RESERVE 1

**bookish** *adj* suggestive of the vocabulary used in books ⟨*fealty* is a *bookish* synonym for *loyalty*⟩
***syn*** erudite, learned, literary
***rel*** academic, pedantic, scholastic; highbrow, intellectual; educated, schooled; formal
***near ant*** chatty, conversational; familiar, informal; slangy
***ant*** colloquial, nonliterary

**booklet** *n* a short printed publication with no cover or with a paper cover — see PAMPHLET

**bookworm** *n* a person slavishly devoted to intellectual or academic pursuits — see NERD

**boom** *n* a loud explosive sound — see CLAP 1

**boom** *vb* to make a long loud deep noise or cry — see ROAR

**booming** *adj* **1** marked by a high volume of sound — see LOUD 1
**2** marked by vigorous growth and well-being especially economically — see PROSPEROUS 1

**boon** *adj* likely to seek or enjoy the company of others — see CONVIVIAL

**boon** *n* **1** a thing that helps — see HELP 2
**2** an act of kind assistance — see FAVOR 1
**3** something granted as a special favor — see PRIVILEGE
**4** something that provides happiness or does good for a person or thing — see BLESSING 2

**boor** *n* a person whose behavior is offensive to others — see JERK 1

**boorish** *adj* having or showing crudely insensitive or impolite manners — see CLOWNISH

**boost** *n* **1** an act or instance of helping — see HELP 1
**2** something added (as by growth) — see INCREASE 1
**3** something that arouses action or activity — see IMPULSE

**boost** *vb* **1** to lift with effort — see HEAVE 1
**2** to make greater in size, amount, or number — see INCREASE 1
**3** to make markedly greater in measure or degree — see INTENSIFY
**4** to move from a lower to a higher place or position — see RAISE 1
**5** to provide publicity for — see PUBLICIZE 1

**booster** *n* a person who actively supports or favors a cause — see EXPONENT

**boot** (out) *vb* to drive or force out — see EJECT 1

**bootleg** *n* illegally produced liquor — see MOONSHINE 1

**bootless** *adj* producing no results — see FUTILE

**booty** *n* valuables stolen or taken by force — see LOOT

**booze** *n* a fermented or distilled beverage that can make a person drunk — see ALCOHOL

**bop** *n* a hard strike with a part of the body or an instrument — see [1]BLOW

**bop** *vb* to deliver a blow to (someone or something) usually in a strong vigorous manner — see HIT 1

**border** *n* **1** the line or relatively narrow space that marks the outer limit of something ⟨a rug with a fancily embroidered *border*⟩
***syn*** bound, boundary, brim, circumference, compass, confines, edge, end, fringe, margin, perimeter, periphery, rim, skirt, verge
***rel*** crest, hem, lip; ceiling, maximum; demarcation, extent, limitation, measure, restriction, termination; borderland, frontier, march, pale
***near ant*** center; inner, inside, interior
**2** a region along the dividing line between two countries — see FRONTIER 1

**border** *vb* to serve as a border for ⟨that velvet *bordered* the sleeves on this shirt, until it fell off⟩
***syn*** bound, fringe, margin, rim, skirt
***rel*** edge, hem, trim; circumscribe, define, delineate, demarcate, frame, outline; circle, compass, encircle, girdle, girth, loop, ring, round, surround; check, confine, control, curb, limit, restrain, restrict

**border** (on) *vb* **1** to come very close to being ⟨that comment *borders on* insubordination, and you should be more careful in the future⟩
***syn*** verge (on)
***rel*** approach, near; appear, look, resemble, seem, suggest
**2** to be adjacent to — see ADJOIN 1

**bordering** *adj* having a border in common — see ADJACENT

**borderland** *n* a region along the dividing line between two countries — see FRONTIER 1

**bore** *n* someone or something boring — see DRAG 1

[1]**bore** *vb* to make a hole or series of holes in — see PERFORATE

[2]**bore** *vb* to make weary and restless by being dull or monotonous ⟨the teacher's lifeless and unimaginative teaching style *bored* the students to death⟩
***syn*** jade, tire, weary
***rel*** pall; drain, enervate, exhaust, fatigue, wear, wear out; debilitate, disable, enfeeble; deject, demoralize, discourage, dishearten, dispirit
***phrases*** put to sleep
***near ant*** animate, energize, enliven, excite, galvanize, invigorate, stimulate, vitalize; amuse, entertain; allure, attract, beguile, bewitch, captivate, charm, enchant, enthrall (*or* enthral), fascinate, hypnotize, mesmerize; monopolize, preoccupy; busy, immerse, involve, occupy; rally, rouse, stir
***ant*** absorb, engage, engross, grip, interest, intrigue

**bored** *adj* having one's patience, interest, or pleasure exhausted — see WEARY 2

**boredom** *n* the state of being bored ⟨she spends that whole class in a state of complete *boredom*, waiting for lunch⟩

***syn*** doldrums, ennui, listlessness, restlessness, tedium, tiredness, weariness

***rel*** cheerlessness, dispiritedness, joylessness, melancholy; languor, lassitude, lethargy, lifelessness, torpor; dullness (*also* dulness), monotonousness, monotony, sameness; apathy, indifference, unconcern

***near ant*** beguilement, bewitchment, captivation, enchantment, fascination; absorption, engagement, engrossment, immersion, involvement; animation, enlivenment, excitement, invigoration, stimulation; amusement, entertainment

**boring** *adj* causing weariness, restlessness, or lack of interest ⟨I wish this book weren't so *boring;* I keep falling asleep whenever I try to read it⟩

***syn*** drab, dreary, dry, dull, flat, heavy, humdrum, jading, leaden, monotonous, pedestrian, ponderous, stodgy, stuffy, stupid, tame, tedious, tiresome, tiring, unanimated, uninteresting, wearisome, weary, wearying

***rel*** undramatic, unentertaining, uneventful, unexciting, uninspiring, unnewsworthy, unrewarding, unsatisfying, unsensational, unspectacular; annoying, bothersome, irksome, irritating; drudging, palling; draining, enervating, exhausting, fatiguing, wearing; debilitating, enfeebling; demoralizing, discouraging, disheartening, dispiriting; common, commonplace, ordinary, stale, unexceptional; lumbering, plodding, slow

***near ant*** amazing, astonishing, astounding, awesome, eye-opening, fabulous, marvelous (*or* marvellous), sensational, spectacular, surprising, wonderful, wondrous; animating, energizing, enlivening, exciting, galvanizing, invigorating, stimulating; amusing, diverting, entertaining; alluring, attracting, attractive, beguiling, bewitching, captivating, charming, enchanting, enthralling, entrancing, fascinating; mesmerizing

***ant*** absorbing, engaging, engrossing, gripping, interesting, intriguing, involving

**born** *adj* **1** being such from birth or by nature — see NATURAL 1

**2** belonging to a particular place by birth or origin — see NATIVE 1

**borrow** *vb* to take for one's own use (something originated by another) — see ADOPT

**bosom** *adj* closely acquainted — see FAMILIAR 1

**boss** *adj, slang* of the very best kind — see EXCELLENT

**boss** *n* the person (as an employer or supervisor) who tells people and especially workers what to do ⟨every morning the *boss* hands out a list of top-priority tasks⟩

***syn*** captain, chief, foreman, head, headman, helmsman, kingpin, leader, master, taskmaster

***rel*** administrator, commander, director, executive, general, manager, overseer, principal, standard-bearer, straw boss, superintendent, superior, supervisor; dominator, lord, overlord, potentate, ruler; figurehead; slave driver; baron, czar (*also* tsar *or* tzar), king, magnate, mogul, president, prince

***near ant*** dependent, inferior, secondary, subject, subordinate, underling

**boss** *vb* **1** to be in charge of ⟨she *bossed* that project for years, until she was promoted again⟩

***syn*** captain, head, oversee, superintend, supervise

***rel*** command, control, direct, guide, manage, order, run, shepherd, show, steer; quarterback; administer; monitor; govern, reign, rule

**2** to exercise authority or power over — see GOVERN 1

**3** to serve as leader of — see LEAD 2

**boss** (around) *vb* to issue orders to (someone) by right of authority — see COMMAND 1

**bossy** *adj* fond of ordering people around ⟨I don't want to work with him because he's so *bossy* and always runs roughshod over me⟩

***syn*** authoritarian, autocratic, despotic, dictatorial, domineering, imperious, masterful, overbearing, peremptory, tyrannical (*also* tyrannic), tyrannous

***rel*** arrogant, disdainful, haughty, lofty, lordly, proud, supercilious, superior; commanding, dictating; arbitrary, high-handed, imperial; authoritative, directorial, magisterial; aggressive, assertive, self-assertive; conceited, narcissistic, pompous, vain; all-powerful, almighty, omnipotent; firm, stern

***near ant*** humble, meek, modest, unassuming; amenable, docile, obedient, tractable; indecisive, irresolute; acquiescent, compliant, passive, resigned, submissive, yielding

**botch** *vb* to make or do (something) in a clumsy or unskillful way ⟨the first time we tried to make a cake, we *botched* the job completely⟩

***syn*** bobble, bungle, butcher, flub, foozle, foul up, fumble, louse up, mangle, mess (up), muff, murder

***rel*** blunder, goof (up), gum (up); blemish, blight, damage, flaw, harm, hurt, impair, injure, mar, mutilate, ruin, spoil, vitiate; destroy, wreck; mishandle, mismanage

***near ant*** ameliorate, better, enhance, help, improve, meliorate, rectify, refine, reform, remedy

**botched** *adj* showing or marked by a lack of skill and tact (as in dealing with a situation) — see AWKWARD 2

**bother** *n* **1** a state of noisy, confused activity — see COMMOTION

**2** one who is obnoxiously annoying — see NUISANCE 1

3 something that is a source of irritation — see ANNOYANCE 3
4 the feeling of impatience or anger caused by another's repeated disagreeable acts — see ANNOYANCE 2

**bother** *vb* 1 to thrust oneself upon (another) without invitation ⟨I am never going to get this work done if people don't stop wandering into the room and *bothering* me⟩
*syn* bug, chivy, disturb, intrude (upon), pester
*rel* inconvenience, trouble; aggravate, anger, annoy, bedevil, devil, exasperate, fret, gall, get, gnaw, hassle, irritate, nettle, peeve, pique, put out, rile, torment, vex, worry; beleaguer, beset, besiege; distress, plague; afflict, harass, torment; grate, inflame, provoke; enrage, incense, inflame, infuriate, madden; agitate, perturb
*near ant* ignore, leave; appease, conciliate, mollify, oblige, placate; delight, gladden, gratify, please, satisfy; comfort, console, content
2 to disturb the peace of mind of (someone) especially by repeated disagreeable acts — see IRRITATE 1
3 to experience concern or anxiety — see WORRY 1
4 to trouble the mind of; to make uneasy — see DISTURB 1

**bothering** *n* the act of making unwelcome intrusions upon another — see ANNOYANCE 1

**bothersome** *adj* causing annoyance — see ANNOYING

**bottom** *n* 1 the side or part facing downward from something ⟨that side of the shelf is supposed to be the *bottom*, so turn it over before you assemble the bookcase⟩
*syn* underbelly, underbody, underside, undersurface
*rel* belly, sole; base, floor, foot, ground, seat, underpinning
*near ant* acme, apex, crest, crown, height, peak, pinnacle, roof, summit; cusp, head, point, tip
*ant* face, top
2 the surface upon which a body of water lies ⟨my missing fishing pole is probably lying on the *bottom* of the lake⟩
*syn* bed, floor
*rel* riverbed; base, basement, foundation, ground
*near ant* surface
3 the lowest part, place, or point ⟨sliding all the way to the *bottom* of the snow-covered slope⟩
*syn* base, foot, rock bottom
*rel* basis, bed, bedrock, foundation, ground, groundwork, keystone, seat, underpinning
*near ant* acme, apex, climax, crest, face, height, peak, pinnacle, summit, tip-top, zenith
*ant* head, top
4 the part of the body upon which someone sits — see BUTTOCKS
5 a small buoyant structure for travel on water — see BOAT 1

**bottomless** *adj* extending far downward or inward — see DEEP 1

**bough** *n* a major outgrowth from the main stem of a woody plant — see BRANCH 1

**boulevard** *n* a passage cleared for public vehicular travel — see WAY 1

**bounce** *n* active strength of body or mind — see VIGOR 1

**bounce** *vb* 1 to drive or force out — see EJECT 1
2 to strike and fly off at an angle — see GLANCE 1

**bouncing** *adj* 1 enjoying health and vigor — see HEALTHY 1
2 having much high-spirited energy and movement — see LIVELY 1

**bound** *adj* fully committed to achieving a goal — see DETERMINED 1

**[1]bound** *n* 1 a real or imaginary point beyond which a person or thing cannot go — see LIMIT
2 the line or relatively narrow space that marks the outer limit of something — see BORDER 1

**[2]bound** *n* an act of leaping into the air — see JUMP 1

**[1]bound** *vb* 1 to mark the limits of — see LIMIT 2
2 to serve as a border for — see BORDER

**[2]bound** *vb* 1 to move with a light bouncing step — see SKIP 1
2 to propel oneself upward or forward into the air — see JUMP 1

**boundary** *n* 1 a real or imaginary point beyond which a person or thing cannot go — see LIMIT
2 the line or relatively narrow space that marks the outer limit of something — see BORDER 1

**bounded** *adj* having distinct or certain limits — see LIMITED 1

**boundless** *adj* being or seeming to be without limits — see INFINITE

**bounteous** *adj* giving or sharing in abundance and without hesitation — see GENEROUS 1

**bountiful** *adj* 1 being more than enough without being excessive — see PLENTIFUL
2 giving or sharing in abundance and without hesitation — see GENEROUS 1

**bountifully** *adv* in a generous manner — see WELL 2

**bountifulness** *n* the quality or state of being generous — see LIBERALITY

**bounty** *n* 1 something offered or given in return for a service performed — see REWARD
2 the quality or state of being generous — see LIBERALITY

**bouquet** *n* 1 a bunch of flowers ⟨I bought my mother a nice *bouquet* for her birthday⟩
*syn* nosegay, posy
*rel* boutonniere, corsage; arrangement; garland, lei

---

*syn* synonym(s) *rel* related words
*ant* antonym(s) *near ant* near antonym(s)

2 a sweet or pleasant smell — see FRAGRANCE

**bout** *n* 1 a competitive encounter between individuals or groups carried on for amusement, exercise, or in pursuit of a prize — see GAME 1
2 a sudden experiencing of a physical or mental disorder — see ATTACK 2

**bow** *n* something that curves or is curved — see BEND 1

[1]**bow** *vb* 1 to cease resistance (as to another's arguments, demands, or control) — see YIELD 3
2 to give up and cease resistance (as to a liking, temptation, or habit) — see YIELD 1

[2]**bow** *vb* to turn away from a straight line or course — see CURVE 1

**bowed** *adj* bending downward or forward — see NODDING

**bowing** *adj* bending downward or forward — see NODDING

**bowl** *n* a large usually roofless building for sporting events with tiers of seats for spectators — see STADIUM

**bowl** *vb* 1 to move or proceed smoothly and readily — see FLOW 2
2 to proceed or move quickly — see HURRY 2

**bowl** (down *or* over) *vb* to strike (someone) so forcefully as to cause a fall — see FELL 1

**bowl** (over) *vb* 1 to cause an often unpleasant surprise for — see SHOCK 1
2 to make a strong impression on (someone) with something unexpected — see SURPRISE 1

**bowled over** *adj* affected with sudden and great wonder or surprise — see THUNDERSTRUCK

[1]**box** *n* a covered rectangular container for storing or transporting things — see CHEST

[2]**box** *n* a hard strike with a part of the body or an instrument — see [1]BLOW

**boxer** *n* one that engages in the sport of fighting with the fists ⟨that *boxer* is quite famous for being the youngest heavyweight champion ever⟩
*syn* fighter, prizefighter, pugilist
*rel* bantamweight, featherweight, flyweight, heavyweight, light heavyweight, lightweight, middleweight, welterweight

**boy** *n* a male person who has not yet reached adulthood ⟨a giggling little *boy* ran by⟩
*syn* lad, laddie, nipper, shaver, sonny, stripling, tad, youth
*rel* adolescent, juvenile, kid, minor, moppet, teenager, youngster; brat, garain, hobbledehoy, imp, squirt, urchin, whippersnapper; schoolboy

**boyfriend** *n* a male romantic companion ⟨her *boyfriend* always brings her flowers for Valentine's Day⟩
*syn* beau, fellow, man, swain
*rel* admirer, crush, steady; gallant, suitor, wooer; beloved, darling, dear, favorite, flame, honey, love, lover, sweet, sweetheart, valentine; date, escort; groom, husband; fiancé, intended

**brace** *n* 1 something that holds up or serves as a foundation for something else — see SUPPORT 1
2 two things of the same or similar kind that match or are considered together — see PAIR

**brace** *vb* 1 to give life, vigor, or spirit to — see ANIMATE
2 to hold up or serve as a foundation for — see SUPPORT 3
3 to prepare (oneself) mentally or emotionally — see FORTIFY 1

**bracelet** *n* something that physically prevents free movement — see BOND 1

**bracing** *adj* having a renewing effect on the state of the body or mind — see TONIC

**bracket** *n* one of the units into which a whole is divided on the basis of a common characteristic — see CLASS 2

**bracket** *vb* to describe as similar — see COMPARE 1

**brag** *n* boastful speech or writing — see BOMBAST 1

**brag** *vb* to praise or express pride in one's own possessions, qualities, or accomplishments often to excess — see BOAST

**braggadocio** *n* boastful speech or writing — see BOMBAST 1

**braid** *n* a length of something formed of three or more strands woven together ⟨until she was fifteen, she had a *braid* that reached to her knees⟩
*syn* lace, lacing, plait
*rel* rickrack (*or* ricrac), stripe; pigtail

**braid** *vb* to form into a braid ⟨they taught each other how to *braid* yarn into bracelets⟩
*syn* plait, pleat
*rel* interlace, interweave, weave

**brain** *n* 1 a very smart person — see GENIUS 1
2 *often* **brains** *pl* the ability to learn and understand or to deal with problems — see INTELLIGENCE 1

**brainless** *adj* 1 not having or showing an ability to absorb ideas readily — see STUPID 1
2 showing or marked by a lack of good sense or judgment — see FOOLISH 1

**brainlessness** *n* 1 lack of good sense or judgment — see FOOLISHNESS 1
2 the quality or state of lacking intelligence or quickness of mind — see STUPIDITY 1

**brainstorm** *vb* to engage in an exchange of information or ideas — see COMMUNICATE 2

**brainy** *adj* having or showing quickness of mind — see INTELLIGENT 1

**brake** *n* a thick patch of shrubbery, small trees, or underbrush — see THICKET

**brake** *vb* to cause to move or proceed at a less rapid pace — see SLOW 1

**braking** *n* a usually gradual decrease in the pace or level of activity of something — see SLOWDOWN

**brambly** *adj* likely to cause a scratch — see SCRATCHY 1

**branch** *n* **1** a major outgrowth from the main stem of a woody plant ⟨I loved climbing among the *branches* of that old tree⟩
***syn*** bough, limb
***rel*** offshoot, outgrowth, shoot; spray, sprig, twig
**2** a local unit of an organization — see CHAPTER

**branch** *vb* to extend outwards from or as if from a central point — see RADIATE 1

**branch** (out) *vb* to go or move in different directions from a central point — see SEPARATE 2

**brand** *n* **1** a device (as a word) identifying the maker of a piece of merchandise and legally reserved for the exclusive use of that person or company — see TRADEMARK 1
**2** a mark of guilt or disgrace — see STAIN 1

**brand–new** *adj* **1** being in an original and unused or unspoiled state — see FRESH 1
**2** recently made and never used before — see NEW 3

**brash** *adj* **1** displaying or marked by rude boldness — see NERVY 1
**2** foolishly adventurous or bold — see FOOLHARDY 1

**brashness** *n* shameless boldness — see EFFRONTERY

**brass** *n* shameless boldness — see EFFRONTERY

**brassiness** *n* shameless boldness — see EFFRONTERY

**brassy** *adj* displaying or marked by rude boldness — see NERVY 1

**brave** *adj* feeling or displaying no fear by temperament ⟨the *brave* little boy sat still for the flu shot⟩
***syn*** courageous, dauntless, doughty, fearless, gallant, greathearted, heroic, intrepid, lionhearted, manful, stalwart, stout, stouthearted, undaunted, valiant, valorous
***rel*** determined, firm, game, plucky, resolute, undeterred, undismayed, unflinching, unswerving; mettlesome, spirited, spunky; adventuresome, adventurous, audacious, bold, daring, dashing, gutsy, hardy, venturesome, venturous; crazy, foolish, half-witted, insane, lunatic, mad, nutty; brash, brazen, daredevil, foolhardy, heedless, hotheaded, impetuous, imprudent, impulsive, incautious, madcap, overbold, overconfident, rash, reckless, thoughtless, wild; hasty, headlong, precipitate; comforted, emboldened, encouraged, heartened, reassured, unafraid
***near ant*** mousy (*or* mousey), scary, shy, skittish, timid, timorous; anxious, apprehensive, nervous; careful, cautious, heedful, prudent, unadventurous; afraid, agitated, disconcerted, disquieted, disturbed, frightened, horrified, panicked, perturbed, scared, shocked, spooked, startled, terrified, terrorized, unnerved, upset; appalled, concerned, dismayed, worried
***ant*** chicken, chickenhearted, coward, cowardly, craven, fainthearted, fearful, lily-livered, pusillanimous, timorous

**brave** *vb* to oppose (something hostile or dangerous) with firmness or courage — see FACE 2

**bravery** *n* **1** dressy clothing — see FINERY
**2** strength of mind to carry on in spite of danger — see COURAGE

**brawl** *n* **1** a rough and often noisy fight usually involving several people ⟨they were thrown out of the party after starting a *brawl*⟩
***syn*** affray, fracas, fray, free-for-all, melee, row, ruckus, ruction
***rel*** battle, clash, combat, conflict, contest, fight, fisticuffs, scrap, scrimmage, scuffle, struggle, tussle; horseplay, roughhousing; altercation, argument, dispute, quarrel, spat, squabble, tiff, wrangle
**2** an often noisy or angry expression of differing opinions — see ARGUMENT 1

**brawl** *vb* to express different opinions about something often angrily — see ARGUE 2

**brawn** *n* muscular strength — see MUSCLE 1

**brawny** *adj* **1** having muscles capable of exerting great physical force — see STRONG 1
**2** marked by a well-developed musculature — see MUSCULAR 1
**3** strongly and heavily built — see [1]HUSKY

**brazen** *adj* displaying or marked by rude boldness — see NERVY 1

**brazen** *vb* to oppose (something hostile or dangerous) with firmness or courage — see FACE 2

**brazenness** *n* shameless boldness — see EFFRONTERY

**breach** *n* **1** a failure to uphold the requirements of law, duty, or obligation ⟨the president's deliberate misstatements were widely seen as a *breach* of the public trust⟩
***syn*** infraction, infringement, transgression, trespass, violation
***rel*** offense, sin, wrong; disregard, forgetting, ignoring, nonobservance, overlooking; delinquency, dereliction, neglect; intrusion, invasion
***near ant*** respecting, upholding
***ant*** nonviolation, observance
**2** a breaking of a moral or legal code — see OFFENSE 1
**3** an open space in a barrier (as a wall or hedge) — see GAP 1

**breach** *vb* to fail to keep — see VIOLATE 1

**bread** *n* **1** *slang* something (as pieces of stamped metal or printed paper) customarily and legally used as a medium of exchange, a measure of value, or a means of payment — see MONEY
**2** substances intended to be eaten — see FOOD

**breadbasket** *n, slang* the part of the body between the chest and the pelvis — see STOMACH

**breadth** *n* **1** a wide space or area — see EXPANSE
**2** an area over which activity, capacity, or influence extends — see RANGE 2

**break** *n* **1** a momentary halt in an activity — see PAUSE
**2** a period during which the usual routine of school or work is suspended — see VACATION
**3** an open space in a barrier (as a wall or hedge) — see GAP 1

**break** *vb* **1** to cause to separate into pieces usually suddenly or forcibly ⟨I hated admitting to Mom that I had *broken* her favorite glass vase⟩
***syn*** bust, fracture, fragment
***rel*** blast, blow up, burst, detonate, explode; pop, shatter, shiver, smash; sliver, splinter, split; collapse, implode; demolish, destroy, ruin, wreck
***near ant*** fix, heal, mend, patch, rebuild, reconstruct, repair
**2** to bring (as an action or operation) to an immediate end — see STOP 1
**3** to bring to a lower grade or rank — see DEMOTE
**4** to change (as a secret message) from code into ordinary language — see DECODE
**5** to come to a temporary halt in one's activity — see PAUSE
**6** to cut into and turn over the sod of (a piece of land) using a bladed implement — see PLOW 1
**7** to fail to keep — see VIOLATE 1
**8** to find an answer for through reasoning — see SOLVE
**9** to reduce the soundness, effectiveness, or perfection of — see DAMAGE 1
**10** to stop functioning — see FAIL 1
**11** to hasten away from something dangerous or frightening — see RUN 2

**breakable** *adj* easily broken — see FRAGILE 1

**breakdown** *n* **1** the process by which dead organic matter separates into simpler substances — see CORRUPTION 1
**2** the separation and identification of the parts of a whole — see ANALYSIS 1

**break down** *vb* **1** to arrange or assign according to type — see CLASSIFY 1
**2** to go through decomposition — see DECAY 1
**3** to identify and examine the basic elements or parts of (something) especially for discovering interrelationships — see ANALYZE
**4** to stop functioning — see FAIL 1
**5** to yield to mental or emotional stress — see CRACK 2

**break in** *vb* **1** to enter a house or building by force usually with illegal intent ⟨the burglars *broke in* by smashing a window⟩
***syn*** burglarize
***rel*** invade, trespass; hold up, loot, plunder, rip off, rob, stick up; ransack, rifle; despoil, devastate, maraud, pillage, ravage, sack
**2** to cause a disruption in a conversation or discussion — see INTERRUPT

**breakneck** *adj* moving, proceeding, or acting with great speed — see FAST 1

**break off** *vb* **1** to bring (as an action or operation) to an immediate end — see STOP 1
**2** to come to an end — see CEASE 1

**break out** *vb* to develop suddenly and violently — see ERUPT 2

**breakthrough** *n* an instance of notable progress in the development of knowledge, technology, or skill — see ADVANCE 2

**breakup** *n* the act or process of a whole separating into two or more parts or pieces — see SEPARATION 1

**break up** *vb* **1** to cease to exist or cause to cease to exist as a group or organization — see DISBAND 1
**2** to come to an end — see CEASE 1
**3** to set or force apart — see SEPARATE 1

**breast** *n* the seat of one's deepest thoughts and emotions — see CORE 1

**breast** *vb* to oppose (something hostile or dangerous) with firmness or courage — see FACE 2

**breath** *n* **1** a momentary halt in an activity — see PAUSE
**2** a slight or gentle movement of air — see BREEZE 1

**breathe** *vb* **1** to inhale and exhale air ⟨sometimes it gets so hot in here that it's hard to even *breathe*⟩
***syn*** respire
***rel*** expire, inspire; gasp, huff, pant, puff, wheeze; sniff, snore, snort, snuffle; yawn
***near ant*** asphyxiate, choke, gag, smother, suffocate; garrotte (*or* garotte), stifle, strangle, throttle
**2** to have life — see BE 1

**breathe** (out) *vb* to let or force out of the lungs — see EXHALE 1

**breather** *n* a momentary halt in an activity — see PAUSE

**breathing** *adj* having or showing life — see ALIVE 1

**breathless** *adj* **1** lacking fresh air — see STUFFY 1
**2** moving, proceeding, or acting with great speed — see FAST 1
**3** no longer living — see DEAD 1

**breathtaking** *adj* causing great emotional or mental stimulation — see EXCITING 1

**breech** *n* **1** the part of the body upon which someone sits — see BUTTOCKS
**2 breeches** *pl* an outer garment covering each leg separately from waist to ankle — see PANTS

**breed** *n* a number of persons or things that are grouped together because they have something in common — see SORT 1

**breed** *vb* **1** to bring forth offspring — see PROCREATE
**2** to bring to maturity through care and education — see BRING UP 1

**breeding** *n* the line of ancestors from whom a person is descended — see ANCESTRY

**breeze** *n* **1** a slight or gentle movement of air ⟨a warm spring *breeze* ruffled our hair⟩
*syn* air, breath, puff, waft, zephyr
*rel* draft, whiff; land breeze, sea breeze; blast, blow, flurry, gale, northeaster, norther, northwester, southeaster, southwester, westerly, wind; squall, tempest, tornado, windstorm; airflow
*near ant* calm
**2** something that is easy to do — see CINCH

**breeze** *vb* **1** to move or proceed smoothly and readily — see FLOW 2
**2** to proceed or move quickly — see HURRY 2

**breezy** *adj* **1** having a relaxed, casual manner — see EASYGOING 1
**2** marked by strong wind or more wind than usual — see WINDY 1

**brevity** *n* **1** the condition of being short ⟨the best quality a graduation speech can have is *brevity*⟩
*syn* briefness, conciseness, shortness
*rel* abbreviation, abridgment (*or* abridgement), compression, condensation, contraction, curtailment; decreasing, diminishing, lessening, reducing, shortening, shrinking; abruptness, brusqueness, curtness; pithiness, succinctness, terseness; littleness, minuteness, smallness, tininess
*near ant* extensiveness; elongating, elongation, extending, extension, prolongation, prolonging, protraction, stretching; expansion, growth, spread; diffuseness, prolixity, talkativeness, verboseness, volubility, wordiness; bigness, bulkiness, greatness, heftiness, largeness
*ant* lengthiness
**2** the quality or state of being marked by or using only few words to convey much meaning — see SUCCINCTNESS

**brew** *vb* to be about to happen — see LOOM

**bribable** *adj* open to improper influence and especially bribery — see VENAL

**bribe** *n* something given or promised in order to improperly influence a person's conduct or decision ⟨that judge refused a huge *bribe* to dismiss the charges against the wealthy defendant⟩
*syn* fix, sop
*rel* incentive, incitement, motivation, spur, stimulation, stimulus; boost, goad, inducement; allurement, bait, enticement, lure, temptation; flattery, persuasion; decoy, snare, trap

**bribe** *vb* to influence someone with a bribe ⟨meat inspectors were *bribed*, and the contaminated beef was sold to the public⟩
*syn* have, square
*rel* fix, tamper (with); corrupt, debase, defile, dishonor, taint; allure, bait, entice, lure, tempt; motivate, provoke, spur, stimulate; goad, induce; flatter, persuade; snare, trap

**bridal** *n* a ceremony in which two people are united in matrimony — see WEDDING

**bridgehead** *n* a place from which an advance (as for military operations) is made — see BASE 2

**bridle** *vb* to keep from exceeding a desirable degree or level (as of expression) — see CONTROL 1

**brief** *adj* **1** marked by the use of few words to convey much information or meaning — see CONCISE
**2** not lasting for a considerable time — see SHORT 2

**brief** *vb* to give information to — see ENLIGHTEN 1

**briefly** *adv* in a few words — see SHORTLY 1

**briefness** *n* **1** the condition of being short — see BREVITY 1
**2** the quality or state of being marked by or using only few words to convey much meaning — see SUCCINCTNESS

**brig** *n* a place of confinement for persons held in lawful custody — see JAIL

**bright** *adj* **1** giving off or reflecting much light ⟨in the desert the sun was so *bright* that it hurt my eyes⟩ ⟨the moon is *bright* tonight⟩
*syn* beaming, bedazzling, brilliant, dazzling, effulgent, glowing, incandescent, lambent, lucent, lucid, luminous, lustrous, radiant, refulgent, shining, shiny
*rel* blazing, burning, combusting, fiery, flaming; agleam, aglitter, blinding, flaring, flashing, flickering, glaring, gleaming, glimmering, glinting, glistening, glittering, scintillating, shimmering, sparkling, twinkling; burnished, polished; sunny
*near ant* blackened, dark, darkened, darkish, darkling, darksome, dimmed, dusky, gloomy, murky, obscure, obscured, pitch-black, pitch-dark, somber (*or* sombre), sunless; cloudy, shadowy, shady; gray (*also* grey), leaden, pale
*ant* dim, dull, lackluster
**2** filled with much light ⟨the display windows of department stores are especially *bright* at Christmastime⟩
*syn* ablaze, alight, brightened, illuminated, illumined, light, lighted (*or* lit)
*rel* floodlit (*or* floodlighted), highlighted, spotlighted (*or* spotlit); kindled, ignited
*near ant* gloomy, somber, sunless; cloudy, murky, obscured, shadowy; gray (*also* grey), leaden, pale
*ant* blackened, dark, darkened, darkish, darkling, dimmed, dusky, pitch-black, pitch-dark
**3** having or showing a good mood or disposition — see CHEERFUL 1
**4** having or showing quickness of mind — see INTELLIGENT 1
**5** having qualities which inspire hope — see HOPEFUL 1
**6** pointing toward a happy outcome — see FAVORABLE 2

---

*syn* synonym(s) *rel* related words
*ant* antonym(s) *near ant* near antonym(s)

7 serving to lift one's spirits — see CHEERFUL 2

**brighten** *vb* to become glad or hopeful — see CHEER (UP) 1

**brightened** *adj* filled with much light — see BRIGHT 2

**brightness** *n* the quality or state of having or giving off light — see BRILLIANCE 1

**brilliance** *n* 1 the quality or state of having or giving off light ⟨the *brilliance* of the flash from the camera was so intense that I was blinded for a moment afterwards⟩
*syn* brightness, brilliancy, dazzle, effulgence, illumination, lightness, lucidity, luminosity, radiance, refulgence, splendor
*rel* blaze, flare, flicker, light; fluorescence, incandescence, luminescence; burnish, gloss, luster, polish, sheen, shine; fire, flame, glare, glow; flash, gleam, glimmer, glint, glisten, glitter, scintillation, shimmer, sparkle, twinkle
*near ant* dimness, dullness (*also* dulness), gloominess, somberness; cloudiness, haziness, murkiness, obscurity; colorlessness, grayness, paleness
*ant* blackness, dark, darkness, duskiness
2 impressiveness of beauty on a large scale — see MAGNIFICENCE

**brilliancy** *n* the quality or state of having or giving off light — see BRILLIANCE 1

**brilliant** *adj* 1 giving off or reflecting much light — see BRIGHT 1
2 having or showing quickness of mind — see INTELLIGENT 1

**brilliant** *n* a usually valuable stone cut and polished for ornament — see GEM 1

**brim** *n* 1 the line or relatively narrow space that marks the outer limit of something — see BORDER 1
2 the projecting front part of a hat or cap — see VISOR

**brimful** *adj* containing or seeming to contain the greatest quantity or number possible — see FULL 1

**brimming** *adj* containing or seeming to contain the greatest quantity or number possible — see FULL 1

**brine** *n* the whole body of salt water that covers nearly three-fourths of the earth — see OCEAN

**bring** *vb* to have a price of — see COST

**bring about** *vb* to be the cause of (a situation, action, or state of mind) — see EFFECT

**bring up** *vb* 1 to bring to maturity through care and education ⟨it takes an immense commitment and a lot of love to *bring up* a child properly⟩
*syn* breed, foster, raise, rear
*rel* father, mother; attend, care (for), cultivate, mind, minister (to), nurse, nurture, watch; discipline, educate, instruct, mentor, school, teach, train, tutor; edify, enlighten, indoctrinate; feed, nourish, provide (for), supply; advance, forward, further, promote; prepare; direct, guide, lead, shepherd, show
*near ant* abuse, ill-treat, ill-use, maltreat, mishandle, mistreat; ignore, neglect; harm, hurt, injure
2 to present or bring forward for discussion — see INTRODUCE 2

**brininess** *n* the quality or state of being salty — see SALTINESS

**briny** *adj* of, relating to, or containing salt — see SALTY 1

**brisk** *adj* 1 having much high-spirited energy and movement — see LIVELY 1
2 moving, proceeding, or acting with great speed — see FAST 1

**briskly** *adv* with great speed — see FAST 1

**briskness** *n* the quality or state of having abundant or intense activity — see VITALITY 1

**bristle** *vb* to express one's anger usually violently — see RAGE 1

**bristly** *adj* covered with or as if with hair — see HAIRY 1

**brittle** *adj* having a texture that readily breaks into little pieces under pressure — see CRISP 1

**broach** *vb* 1 to penetrate the surface (as of water) from below ⟨the immense whales *broaching* was a magnificent sight⟩
*syn* surface
*rel* break, emerge, rise
*near ant* dive, drop, founder, plunge, sink, submerge, submerse
2 to present or bring forward for discussion — see INTRODUCE 2

**broad** *adj* 1 having a greater than usual measure across — see WIDE 1
2 having considerable extent — see EXTENSIVE
3 not subject to misinterpretation or more than one interpretation — see CLEAR 2
4 relating to the main elements and not to specific details — see GENERAL 2

**broadcast** *vb* 1 to cause to be known over a considerable area or by many people — see SPREAD 1
2 to make known openly or publicly — see ANNOUNCE

**broadly** *adv* to a large extent or degree — see GREATLY 2

**broad-minded** *adj* 1 not bound by traditional ways or beliefs — see LIBERAL 1
2 willing to consider new or different ideas — see OPEN-MINDED 1

**broadside** *adv* with one side faced forward — see SIDEWAYS

**brochure** *n* a short printed publication with no cover or with a paper cover — see PAMPHLET

**broiling** *adj* having a notably high temperature — see HOT 1

**broke** *adj* lacking money or material possessions — see POOR 1

**broken** *adj* 1 having an uneven edge or outline — see RAGGED 1
2 not having a level or smooth surface — see UNEVEN 1

**brokenhearted** *adj* feeling unhappiness — see SAD 1

**brood** *vb* to cover and warm eggs to hatch them — see SET 1

**brook** *n* a natural body of running water smaller than a river — see CREEK 1

**brook** *vb* to put up with (something painful or difficult) — see BEAR 2
**brooklet** *n* a natural body of running water smaller than a river — see CREEK 1
**brotherhood** *n* **1** a group of persons formally joined together for some common interest — see ASSOCIATION 2
**2** the body of people in a profession or field of activity — see CORPS
**brotherly** *adj* of, relating to, or befitting brothers — see FRATERNAL
**browbeat** *vb* to make timid or fearful by or as if by threats — see INTIMIDATE
**brownie** *n* an imaginary being usually having a small human form and magical powers — see FAIRY
**browse** *vb* **1** to feed on grass or herbs — see GRAZE
**2** to take a quick or hasty look — see [1]GLANCE 2
**bruise** *n* a bodily injury in which small blood vessels are broken but the overlying skin is not — see CONTUSION
**bruit** (about) *vb* to make (as a piece of information) the subject of common talk without any authority or confirmation of accuracy — see RUMOR
**brush** *n* a brief clash between enemies or rivals — see ENCOUNTER
**brush** *vb* to pass lightly across or touch gently especially in passing ⟨spiderwebs *brushed* her cheek as she walked through the basement⟩
*syn* graze, kiss, nudge, shave, skim
*rel* bump, contact, scrape, strike, sweep, swipe, touch; bounce, carom, glance, rebound, ricochet, sideswipe, skip; caress, cuddle, fondle, pet, stroke
*near ant* clash, collide, hit, knock, punch, slap, smack, smash, thwack, whack
**brush** (aside *or* off) *vb* to overlook or dismiss as of little importance — see EXCUSE 1
**brush–off** *n* treatment that is deliberately unfriendly — see COLD SHOULDER
**brushwood** *n* a thick patch of shrubbery, small trees, or underbrush — see THICKET
**brusque** *adj* being or characterized by direct, brief, and potentially rude speech or manner — see BLUNT 1
**brutal** *adj* **1** difficult to endure — see HARSH 1
**2** having or showing the desire to inflict severe pain and suffering on others — see CRUEL 1
**brutality** *n* the willful infliction of pain and suffering on others — see CRUELTY
**brute** *n* **1** one of the lower animals as distinguished from human beings — see ANIMAL
**2** a mean, evil, or unprincipled person — see VILLAIN
**bubble** *vb* to flow in a broken irregular stream — see GURGLE
**bubbly** *adj* joyously unrestrained — see EXUBERANT

*syn* synonym(s) *rel* related words
*ant* antonym(s) *near ant* near antonym(s)

**buccaneer** *n* someone who engages in robbery of ships at sea — see PIRATE
**buck** *n* **1** a man extremely interested in his clothing and personal appearance — see DANDY 1
**2** an adult male human being — see MAN 1
**buck** *vb* **1** to move or cause to move with a sharp quick motion — see JERK 1
**2** to refuse to give in to — see RESIST
**buckaroo** *n* a hired hand who tends cattle or horses at a ranch or on the range — see COWBOY
**bucket** *n* **1** a considerable amount — see LOT 2
**2** a round container that is open at the top and outfitted with a handle — see PAIL
**buckle** *vb* to occupy (oneself) diligently or with close attention — see APPLY 2
**bucolic** *adj* of, relating to, associated with, or typical of open areas with few buildings or people — see RURAL
**buddy** *n* a person who has a strong liking for and trust in another — see FRIEND 1
**budge** *vb* **1** to cease resistance (as to another's arguments, demands, or control) — see YIELD 3
**2** to change one's position — see MOVE 3
**3** to change the place or position of — see MOVE 1
**budget** *n* **1** a sum of money set aside for a particular purpose — see FUND 1
**2** the number of individuals or amount of something available at any given time — see SUPPLY
**buff** *n* a person with a strong and habitual liking for something —see FAN
**buff** *vb* **1** to make smooth by friction — see GRIND 1
**2** to make smooth or glossy usually by repeatedly applying surface pressure — see POLISH
**buffed** *adj* having a shiny surface or finish — see GLOSSY
**buffer** *n* something that serves as a protective barrier — see CUSHION
**buffer** *vb* to lessen the shock of — see CUSHION
[1]**buffet** *n* a hard strike with a part of the body or an instrument — see [1]BLOW
[2]**buffet** *n* a storage case typically having doors and shelves — see CABINET
**buffet** *vb* to strike repeatedly — see BEAT 1
**buffoon** *n* a comically dressed performer (as at a circus) who entertains with playful tricks and ridiculous behavior — see CLOWN 1
**bug** *n* **1** a person with a strong and habitual liking for something — see FAN
**2** an abnormal state that disrupts a plant's or animal's normal bodily functioning — see DISEASE
**bug** *vb* **1** to attack repeatedly with mean put-downs or insults — see TEASE 2
**2** to disturb the peace of mind of (someone) especially by repeated disagreeable acts — see IRRITATE 1
**3** to thrust oneself upon (another) without invitation — see BOTHER 1

**bugaboo** *n* something or someone that causes fear or dread especially without reason — see BOGEY 1

**bugbear** *n* something or someone that causes fear or dread especially without reason — see BOGEY 1

**bugging** *n* the act of making unwelcome intrusions upon another — see ANNOYANCE

**build** *n* the type of body that a person has — see PHYSIQUE

**build** *vb* to form by putting together parts or materials ⟨he spent hours *building* a model airplane from a kit⟩
*syn* assemble, construct, erect, fabricate, make, make up, piece, put up, raise, rear, set up
*rel* fashion, forge, frame, manufacture, mold, produce, shape; prefabricate; begin, coin, create, generate, inaugurate, initiate, innovate, invent, originate; constitute, establish, father, found, institute, organize; conceive, concoct, contrive, cook up, design, devise, imagine, think (up); rebuild; rig up
*phrases* put together
*near ant* dismember; demolish, destroy, devastate, flatten, pulverize, raze, ruin, shatter, smash, wreck; blow up, explode
*ant* disassemble, dismantle, take down

**build** (up) *vb* **1** to become greater in extent, volume, amount, or number — see INCREASE 2
**2** to increase in — see GAIN 1
**3** to produce or bring about especially by long or repeated effort — see HAMMER (OUT)

**building** *n* something built as a dwelling, shelter, or place for human activity ⟨English class will be in that big stone *building* over there⟩
*syn* edifice, structure
*rel* construction, erection; bungalow, cabin, chalet, cottage, house, lodge, summerhouse; hovel, hut, shack, shanty, shed; castle, château, estate, hall, manor, mansion, palace, villa; skyscraper, tower

**bulge** *n* a part that sticks out from the general mass of something ⟨several *bulges* in the old vinyl flooring in the dingy bathroom⟩
*syn* jut, overhang, projection, protrusion, protuberance
*rel* dome; blob, bump, knob, lump, nub, swelling; block, piece, portion, section; enlargement, escalation, expansion, increase
*near ant* cavity, crater, hole; basin, dip, valley
*ant* concavity, dent, depression, hollow, indentation, pit

**bulge** *vb* to extend outward beyond a usual point ⟨the sides of the returning camper's suitcase *bulged* with a month's worth of dirty laundry⟩
*syn* bag, balloon, beetle, belly, billow, jut, overhang, poke, project, protrude, stand out, start, stick out
*rel* dome; blow up, inflate; distend, expand, swell; mushroom, snowball; elongate, extend, lengthen, stretch
*near ant* compress, condense, constrict, contract, shrink

**bulk** *n* the main or greater part of something as distinguished from its appendages — see BODY 1

**bulkiness** *n* the quality or state of being large in size — see LARGENESS

**bulky** *adj* of a size greater than average of its kind — see LARGE

**bull** *n, slang* a member of a force charged with law enforcement at the local level — see OFFICER 1

**bulldoze** *vb* to force one's way — see PRESS 4

**bullet** *n* a usually round or cone-shaped little piece of lead made to be fired from a firearm ⟨it is possible to make your own *bullets*, but it takes a lot of patience and some extra money⟩
*syn* ball, pellet
*rel* ammunition, cannonball, cap, cartridge, charge, gunshot, lead, load, missile, pop, projectile, round, shell, shot, slug; twenty-two
*near ant* blank

**bulletin** *n* a published statement informing the public of a matter of general interest — see ANNOUNCEMENT

**bully** *n* **1** a person who teases, threatens, or hurts smaller or weaker persons ⟨the *bully* spent most of the afternoon in detention for pushing people down on the playground⟩
*syn* intimidator
*rel* antagonist, enemy; harrier, nuisance, persecutor, pest, tease, teaser; heckler; goon, hood, hoodlum, punk, rough, roughneck, rowdy, ruffian, thug, tough; cutthroat, felon, gangster, gunman, mobster, racketeer
**2** a violent, brutal person who is often a member of an organized gang — see HOODLUM

**bully** *vb* to make timid or fearful by or as if by threats — see INTIMIDATE

**bulwark** *n* something that holds up or serves as a foundation for something else — see SUPPORT 1

**bum** *adj* of low quality — see CHEAP 2

**bum** *n* a homeless wanderer who may beg or steal for a living — see TRAMP

**bummer** *n* **1** something (as a situation or event) that is depressing — see DOWNER
**2** something that disappoints — see DISAPPOINTMENT 2
**3** something that has failed — see FAILURE 3

**bump** *n* **1** a small rounded mass of swollen tissue ⟨that's a nasty *bump* on your arm where you hit the table⟩
*syn* knot, lump, node, nodule, swelling
*rel* growth, tumor, wart; hump, hunch; bruise, contusion; blob, chunk, clod, clump, gob, gobbet, hunk, knob, nub, nubble, nugget, wad
**2** a forceful coming together of two things — see IMPACT 1

**bump** *vb* to come into usually forceful contact with something — see HIT 2
**bumper** *adj* unusually large — see HUGE
**bumper** *n* something that serves as a protective barrier — see CUSHION
**bumpkin** *n* an awkward or simple person especially from a small town or the country — see HICK
**bumpy** *adj* **1** marked by a series of sharp quick motions — see JERKY 1
**2** not having a level or smooth surface — see UNEVEN 1
**bunch** *n* **1** a group of people sharing a common interest and relating together socially — see GANG 2
**2** a number of things considered as a unit — see GROUP 1
**3** a usually small number of persons considered as a unit — see GROUP 2
**bunch** *vb* to gather into a closely packed group — see PRESS 3
**bundle** *n* a wrapped or sealed case containing an item or set of items — see PACKAGE 1
**bung** *vb* to close up so that no empty spaces remain — see FILL 2
**bungle** *vb* to make or do (something) in a clumsy or unskillful way — see BOTCH
**bungling** *adj* showing or marked by a lack of skill and tact (as in dealing with a situation) — see AWKWARD 2
[1]**bunk** *n* a place set aside for sleeping — see BED 1
[2]**bunk** *n* **1** language, behavior, or ideas that are absurd and contrary to good sense — see NONSENSE 1
**2** unintelligible or meaningless talk — see GIBBERISH
**bunk** *vb* to provide with living quarters or shelter — see HOUSE 1
**buoy** (up) *vb* to fill with courage or strength of purpose — see ENCOURAGE 1
**buoyant** *adj* **1** having or showing a good mood or disposition — see CHEERFUL 1
**2** joyously unrestrained — see EXUBERANT
**burden** *n* **1** a mass or quantity of something taken up and carried, conveyed, or transported — see LOAD 1
**2** a part of a song or hymn that is repeated every so often — see CHORUS 2
**3** something one must do because of prior agreement — see OBLIGATION
**burden** *vb* **1** to place a weight or burden on — see LOAD 1
**2** to make sad — see DEPRESS 1
**burdensome** *adj* **1** difficult to endure — see HARSH 1
**2** requiring much time, effort, or careful attention — see DEMANDING 1
**bureau** *n* a large unit of a governmental, business, or educational organization — see DIVISION 2
**bureaucrat** *n* a worker in a government agency ⟨the *bureaucrats* at the town hall seem to think that we need a building permit to build a tree house⟩
***syn*** functionary, public servant
***rel*** clerk, officeholder, official; employee, underling, worker
**burg** *n* a thickly settled, highly populated area — see CITY
**burgeon** *vb* **1** to become greater in extent, volume, amount, or number — see INCREASE 2
**2** to grow vigorously — see THRIVE 1
**3** to produce flowers — see BLOOM
**burgher** *n* a person who lives in a town on a permanent basis ⟨many of the college students are regarded by the local *burghers* as obnoxious louts⟩
***syn*** citizen, townie, villager
***rel*** denizen, dweller, habitant, homeowner, inhabitant, national, native, occupant, resident, resider; town, townsfolk, townspeople; suburbanite, urbanite
***near ant*** foreigner, guest, tourist, transient, visitor
**burglarize** *vb* **1** to enter a house or building by force usually with illegal intent — see BREAK IN 1
**2** to remove valuables from (a place) unlawfully — see ROB
**burial** *n* the act or ceremony of putting a dead body in its final resting place ⟨the children wanted to give the dead bird a proper *burial* in the backyard⟩
***syn*** burying, entombing, entombment, interment, interring, sepulture
***rel*** embalmment, funeral
***near ant*** cremation
***ant*** disinterment, exhumation, unearthing
**burlesque** *n* a work that imitates and exaggerates another work for comic effect — see PARODY 1
**burlesque** *vb* to copy or exaggerate (someone or something) in order to make fun of — see MIMIC 1
**burly** *adj* strongly and heavily built — see [1]HUSKY
**burn** *vb* **1** to be on fire especially brightly ⟨all evening long we just sat there, contentedly watching the Yule log *burn*⟩
***syn*** blaze, combust, flame, glow
***rel*** fire, ignite, kindle; flare (up), light (up); flicker, gutter, waver; bake, broil, char, cook, melt, roast, scorch, swelter; smolder, spark, sputter; beam, brighten, radiate; beat (down), flash, glare, gleam, glimmer, glint, glisten, glitter, scintillate, shimmer, shine, sparkle, twinkle
**2** to set (something) on fire ⟨it is not a good idea to try to *burn* old papers in the sink⟩
***syn*** fire, ignite, inflame, kindle, light
***rel*** char, scorch; bake, cremate, incinerate, kiln; brighten, illumine, illuminate, irradiate, lighten, radiate; scald, scathe, sear; rekindle, relight
***near ant*** choke, smother, suffocate; stamp (out); blacken, darken, dim, dull, obscure
***ant*** douse, extinguish, put out, quench, snuff (out)
**3** to be excited or emotionally stirred up with anger — see BOIL 1

4 to shine with a bright harsh light — see GLARE 1

**burnable** *adj* capable of catching or being set on fire — see COMBUSTIBLE

**burned–out** *or* **burnt–out** *adj* depleted in strength, energy, or freshness — see WEARY 1

**burning** *adj* 1 being on fire — see ABLAZE 1
2 having a notably high temperature — see HOT 1
3 having or expressing great depth of feeling — see FERVENT

**burnish** *vb* to make smooth or glossy usually by repeatedly applying surface pressure — see POLISH

**burnished** *adj* having a shiny surface or finish — see GLOSSY

**burnout** *n* a complete depletion of energy or strength — see FATIGUE

**burn out** *vb* to use up all the physical energy of — see EXHAUST 1

**burro** *n* a sturdy and patient domestic mammal that is used especially to carry things — see DONKEY 1

**burrow** *n* the shelter or resting place of a wild animal — see DEN 1

**burst** *n* 1 a sudden and usually temporary growth of activity — see OUTBREAK
2 a sudden intense expression of strong feeling — see OUTBURST 1

**burst** *vb* 1 to break open or into pieces usually because of internal pressure — see EXPLODE 1
2 to cause to break open or into pieces by or as if by an explosive — see BLAST 1

**burst** (forth) *vb* to develop suddenly and violently — see ERUPT 2

**bursting** *adj* containing or seeming to contain the greatest quantity or number possible — see FULL 1

**bursting** *n* the act or an instance of exploding — see EXPLOSION 1

**bury** *vb* 1 to place (a dead body) in the earth, a tomb, or the sea ⟨he died on Tuesday and was *buried* on Friday⟩
*syn* entomb, inter
*rel* enshrine; conceal, cover, ensconce, hide; obscure, shade, shield; cloak, curtain, enshroud, shroud
*near ant* burn, cremate; bare, disclose, discover, display, exhibit, expose, reveal, show
*ant* disinter, exhume, unearth
2 to put into a hiding place — see [1]HIDE 1

**burying** *n* the act or ceremony of putting a dead body in its final resting place — see BURIAL

**bush** *n* a rural region that forms the edge of the settled or developed part of a country — see FRONTIER 2

**bushed** *adj* depleted in strength, energy, or freshness — see WEARY 1

**bushel** *n* a considerable amount — see LOT 2

**business** *n* 1 a commercial or industrial activity or organization — see ENTERPRISE 1
2 something to be dealt with — see MATTER 2
3 the buying and selling of goods especially on a large scale and between different places — see COMMERCE

**bust** *n* 1 a hard strike with a part of the body or an instrument — see [1]BLOW
2 something that has failed — see FAILURE 3

**bust** *vb* 1 to bring to a lower grade or rank — see DEMOTE
2 to cause to lose one's fortune and become unable to pay one's debts — see RUIN 1
3 to cause to separate into pieces usually suddenly or forcibly — see BREAK 1
4 to deliver a blow to (someone or something) usually in a strong vigorous manner — see HIT 1
5 *slang* to take or keep under one's control by authority of law — see ARREST 1

**bustle** *n* a state of noisy, confused activity — see COMMOTION

**bustling** *adj* marked by much life, movement, or activity — see ALIVE 2

**busy** *adj* 1 involved in often constant activity ⟨the deadline is in two days, so everyone at work has been extremely *busy*⟩
*syn* active, assiduous, diligent, employed, engaged, industrious, laborious, occupied, sedulous, working
*rel* absorbed, concentrating, engrossed, focused (*also* focussed), immersed, intent, preoccupied; alive, functional, functioning, going, living, operating, operational, operative, running; energetic, vigorous; indefatigable, tireless, untiring
*near ant* asleep, dormant, latent, quiescent, sleepy; inert, passive; dead, dull, slow; inoperative, nonoperating
*ant* idle, inactive, unemployed, unengaged, unoccupied
2 marked by much life, movement, or activity — see ALIVE 2

**busy** *vb* to hold the attention of — see ENGAGE 1

**busybody** *n* a person who meddles in the affairs of others ⟨that *busybody* across the street is always telling me how to tend to my own garden⟩
*syn* interferer, interloper, intruder, kibitzer, meddler
*rel* peeper, peeping Tom, snoop, snooper, spy; blabber, discloser, gossip, gossiper, prattler, revealer, teller; betrayer, talebearer, tattletale; snake, sneak; informer, snitcher, squealer, stool pigeon

**but** *adv* nothing more than — see JUST 3

**but** *conj* 1 if it were not for the fact that — see EXCEPT
2 in spite of that — see HOWEVER

**but** *prep* not including — see EXCEPT

**butcher** *vb* 1 to kill on a large scale — see MASSACRE
2 to make or do (something) in a clumsy or unskillful way — see BOTCH

**butchery** *n* the killing of a large number of people — see MASSACRE

[1]**butt** *n* the part of the body upon which someone sits — see BUTTOCKS

**[2]butt** *n* **1** a person or thing that is made fun of — see LAUGHINGSTOCK
**2** a person or thing that is the object of abuse, criticism, or ridicule — see TARGET 1
**butt in** *vb* to interest oneself in what is not one's concern — see INTERFERE
**buttocks** *n pl* the part of the body upon which someone sits ⟨she slipped in the mud puddle and hit the ground square on her *buttocks*⟩
***syn*** backside, bottom, breech, butt, fanny, hams, haunches, posterior, rear, rump, seat
**buttress** *n* **1** something or someone to which one looks for support — see DEPENDENCE 2
**2** something that holds up or serves as a foundation for something else — see SUPPORT 1
**buttress** *vb* to hold up or serve as a foundation for — see SUPPORT 3
**buy** *n* something bought or offered for sale at a desirable price — see BARGAIN 1
**buy** *vb* to get possession of (something) by giving money in exchange for ⟨I really want to *buy* that new book, but I don't have enough money right now⟩
***syn*** pick up, purchase, take
***rel*** acquire, get, obtain, procure, secure; finance, pay (for), spring (for); barter (for), deal (for), exchange (for), trade (for); bargain (with), chaffer (with), dicker (over), horse-trade (with), negotiate (about), palter (with); bid, offer; rebuy, repurchase
**buzz** *n* **1** a communication by telephone — see CALL 3
**2** a monotonous sound like that of an insect in motion — see HUM
**buzz** *vb* to fly, turn, or move rapidly with a fluttering or vibratory sound — see WHIRR
**buzzing** *adj* marked by much life, movement, or activity — see ALIVE 2
**by** *adv* at, within, or to a short distance or time — see NEAR 1
**by** *prep* **1** along the way of ⟨went *by* the woods to get to the summer cottage⟩
***syn*** through, via
***rel*** across, along, alongside, beyond, near, nearby, over; below, beneath, under, underneath; outside, past
***phrases*** by way of
**2** using the means or agency of ⟨try to convince them *by* reason alone, if possible⟩
***syn*** per, through, with
***phrases*** by means of, by (*or* in) virtue of, through the medium of
**3** close to — see AROUND 1
**by–and–by** *n* time that is to come — see FUTURE 1
**by and large** *adv* for the most part — see CHIEFLY
**bygone** *adj* no longer existing — see EXTINCT
**bylaw** *n* a statement spelling out the proper procedure or conduct for an activity — see RULE 1
**bypass** *vb* to avoid by going around — see DETOUR 1
**by–product** *n* something that naturally develops or is developed from something else — see DERIVATIVE
**byword** *n* an often stated observation regarding something from common experience — see SAYING

# C

**cab** *n* an automobile that carries passengers for a fare usually determined by the distance traveled — see TAXI
**cabal** *n* a group involved in secret or criminal activities — see RING 1
**cabaret** *n* a bar or restaurant offering special nighttime entertainment (as music, dancing, or comedy acts) — see NIGHTCLUB
**cabin** *n* **1** a small, simply constructed, and often temporary dwelling — see SHACK
**2** an often small house for recreational or seasonal use — see COTTAGE
**3** one of the parts into which an enclosed space is divided — see COMPARTMENT
**cabinet** *n* a storage case typically having doors and shelves ⟨the most precious knickknacks were kept in a *cabinet* with glass doors⟩
***syn*** buffet, closet, cupboard, hutch, locker, sideboard
***rel*** bookcase, secretary; shelving; console
**cabinetwork** *n* the movable articles in a room — see FURNITURE
**cable** *n* a length of braided, flexible material that is used for tying or connecting things — see CORD
**cache** *n* **1** a collection of things kept available for future use or need — see STORE 1
**2** a supply stored up and often hidden away — see HOARD 1
**cache** *vb* **1** to put (something of future use or value) in a safe or secret place — see HOARD
**2** to put into a hiding place — see [1]HIDE 1

**caching** *n* the placing of something out of sight — see CONCEALMENT 1

**cackle** *n* an explosive sound that is a sign of amusement — see LAUGH

**cackle** *vb* to engage in casual or rambling conversation — see CHAT

**cackler** *n* a person who talks constantly — see CHATTERBOX

**cacophony** *n* loud, confused, and usually unharmonious sound — see NOISE 1

**cad** *n* a person whose behavior is offensive to others — see JERK 1

**cadaver** *n* a dead body — see CORPSE

**cadaverous** *adj* **1** lacking a healthy skin color — see PALE 2
**2** suffering extreme weight loss as a result of hunger or disease — see EMACIATED

**caddy** *n* a covered rectangular container for storing or transporting things — see CHEST

**cadence** *n* the recurrent pattern formed by a series of sounds having a regular rise and fall in intensity — see RHYTHM

**cadenced** *adj* marked by or occurring with a noticeable regularity in the rise and fall of sound — see RHYTHMIC

**café** *also* **cafe** *n* **1** a bar or restaurant offering special nighttime entertainment (as music, dancing, or comedy acts) — see NIGHTCLUB
**2** a place of business where alcoholic beverages are sold to be consumed on the premises — see BARROOM
**3** a public establishment where meals are served to paying customers for consumption on the premises — see RESTAURANT

**cage** *n* an enclosure with an open framework for keeping animals ⟨the dogs and cats at the animal shelter looked so sad in their *cages*⟩
*syn* coop, corral, pen, pound
*rel* fence; cote, dovecote, fold; aquarium, terrarium

**cage** *vb* to close or shut in by or as if by barriers — see ENCLOSE 1

**cagey** *also* **cagy** *adj* clever at attaining one's ends by indirect and often deceptive means — see ARTFUL 1

**caginess** *n* skill in achieving one's ends through indirect, subtle, or underhanded means — see CUNNING 1

**cajole** *vb* to get (someone) to do something by gentle urging, special attention, or flattery — see COAX

**cake** *n* a small usually rounded mass of minced food that has been fried ⟨the rich, tender *cakes* of crabmeat had been lightly fried⟩
*syn* croquette, cutlet, fritter, patty (*also* pattie)
*rel* finger, stick

**cake** *vb* to cover with a hardened layer — see ENCRUST

**calamitous** *adj* **1** bringing about ruin or misfortune — see FATAL 1
**2** causing or tending to cause destruction — see DESTRUCTIVE 1

**calamity** *n* a sudden violent event that brings about great loss or destruction — see DISASTER

**calculate** *vb* **1** to determine (a value) by doing the necessary mathematical operations ⟨the family has been *calculating* what a week at the beach resort would end up costing⟩
*syn* compute, figure, reckon, work out
*rel* conjecture, estimate, guess, judge, suppose; add up, sum, tally, total; add, cipher, divide, multiply, subtract; calibrate, gauge (*also* gage), measure, scale; ascertain, discover, cope (out), figure out, find out; recompute, refigure
**2** to decide the size, amount, number, or distance of (something) without actual measurement — see ESTIMATE 2
**3** to work out the details of (something) in advance — see PLAN 1

**calculated** *adj* decided on as a result of careful thought — see DELIBERATE 1

**calculation** *n* the act or process of performing mathematical operations to find a value ⟨by my *calculation*, it should take me a month to save up for the sneakers⟩
*syn* arithmetic, ciphering, computation, figures, figuring, reckoning
*rel* mathematics; addition, division, multiplication, subtraction; appraisal, assessment, estimation, evaluation, judgment (*or* judgement)

**calendar** *n* a listing of things to be presented or considered (as at a concert or play) — see PROGRAM 1

**caliber** *or* **calibre** *n* degree of excellence — see QUALITY 1

**call** *n* **1** a natural vocal sound made by an animal ⟨a ranger who could immediately identify the *call* of every creature in the forest⟩
*syn* cry, note
*rel* bark, bay, bellow, bleat, bray, caterwaul, caw, cheep, chirp, grunt, hoot, howl, low, meow, moo, neigh, peep, roar, screech, squawk, squeak, squeal, twitter, whinny, yap, yelp, yip, yowl
**2** a coming to see another briefly for social or business reasons ⟨we paid a *call* on the new neighbors the day after they moved in⟩
*syn* visit, visitation
*rel* meeting, rendezvous, tryst; stopover
**3** a communication by telephone ⟨give me a *call* as soon as you arrive, so I'll know you got there safely⟩
*syn* buzz, ring
*rel* callback; toll call; message
**4** an act or instance of asking for information — see QUESTION 2
**5** an entitlement to something — see CLAIM 1

**call** *vb* **1** to speak so as to be heard at a distance ⟨we could hear someone *calling* for help from the other side of the wall⟩
*syn* bawl, cry, holler, shout, vociferate, yell
*rel* bellow, roar; whoop; scream, screech, shriek, shrill, squeak, squeal; caterwaul, howl, wail, yawp (*or* yaup), yowl
*near ant* breathe, mumble, murmur, mutter, whisper

2 to make a telephone call to ⟨use this cell phone to *call* me if there's an emergency⟩
*syn* dial, phone, ring (up) [*chiefly British*], telephone
*rel* beep, buzz
3 to make a brief visit ⟨the hospital posts the hours during which friends and relatives may *call*⟩
*syn* drop (by *or* in), pop (in), stop (by *or* in), visit
*rel* barge (in); look up, see; frequent, hang around (in), hang out (at), haunt, resort (to)
4 to put an end to (something planned or previously agreed to) — see CANCEL 1
5 to think of in a particular way — see CONSIDER 1
6 to utter one's distinctive animal sound — see CRY 2
7 to bring together in assembly by or as if by command — see CONVOKE
8 to decide the size, amount, number, or distance of (something) without actual measurement — see ESTIMATE 2
9 to demand or request the presence or service of — see SUMMON 1
10 to give a name to — see NAME 1

**call** (for) *vb* 1 to ask for (something) earnestly or with authority — see DEMAND 1
2 to make a request for — see ASK (FOR) 1

**call** (on *or* upon) *vb* to make a social call upon — see VISIT 1

**caller** *n* a person who visits another — see GUEST 1

**calligraphy** *n* writing done by hand — see HANDWRITING 2

**calling** *n* 1 the act of putting an end to something planned or previously agreed to — see CANCELLATION
2 the activity by which one regularly makes a living — see OCCUPATION

**calling off** *n* the act of putting an end to something planned or previously agreed to — see CANCELLATION

**call off** *vb* to put an end to (something planned or previously agreed to) — see CANCEL 1

**callous** *adj* having or showing a lack of sympathy or tender feelings — see HARD 1

**callow** *adj* lacking in adult experience or maturity ⟨a story about a *callow* youth who learns the value of hard work and self-reliance⟩
*syn* adolescent, green, immature, inexperienced, juvenile, puerile, raw, unfledged, unripe, unripened
*rel* babyish, childish, infantile; boyish, girlish, maidenly, virginal, youthful; ingenuous, innocent, naive (*or* naïve); unpracticed, unseasoned, untrained, untried
*near ant* advanced, precocious; knowing, sophisticated, worldly-wise
*ant* adult, experienced, grown-up, mature, ripe

**calm** *adj* 1 free from storms or physical disturbance ⟨after a stormy night of high winds and driving rains, the day dawned on a *calm* sea⟩
*syn* halcyon, hushed, peaceful, placid, quiet, serene, still, stilly, tranquil, untroubled
*rel* calming, pacific, restful, soothing; inactive, inert, quiescent, reposing, resting; smooth, unruffled; clear, cloudless, fair, rainless, sunny, sunshiny
*near ant* bleak, cloudy, dirty, foul, nasty, overcast, rainy, raw, rough, squally
*ant* agitated, angry, stormy, turbulent
2 free from emotional or mental agitation ⟨bystanders tried to help the injured person remain *calm* while they waited for the ambulance to arrive⟩
*syn* collected, composed, cool, coolheaded, placid, self-possessed, serene, tranquil, undisturbed, unperturbed, unshaken, untroubled, unworried
*rel* imperturbable, nerveless, unflappable, unshakable; disciplined, self-contained, self-controlled; affable, breezy, devil-may-care, easygoing, happy-go-lucky, laid-back, low-pressure; carefree, nonchalant, unconcerned; assured, confident, self-assured; aloof, detached, dispassionate, indifferent; impassive, phlegmatic, stolid
*near ant* anxious, bothered, distressed, worried; jittery, jumpy, nervous, skittish, tense; high-strung, uptight
*ant* agitated, discomposed, disturbed, flustered, perturbed, upset
3 free from disturbing noise or uproar — see QUIET 1

**calm** *n* a state of freedom from storm or disturbance ⟨vacationing city dwellers who are tired of the hustle and bustle enjoy the *calm* of the secluded mountain village⟩
*syn* calmness, hush, peace, peacefulness, placidity, quiet, quietness, quietude, repose, restfulness, sereneness, serenity, still, stillness, tranquillity (*or* tranquility)
*rel* lull, pause, respite; silence; comity, concord, harmony
*near ant* clamor, din, noise, racket
*ant* bustle, commotion, hubbub, hurly-burly, pandemonium, tumult, turmoil, uproar

**calm** *vb* 1 to free from distress or disturbance ⟨the president's reassuring words did much to *calm* the public during the national emergency⟩
*syn* allay, compose, quiet, settle, soothe, still, tranquilize (*also* tranquillize)
*rel* alleviate, assuage, ease, mitigate, relieve; appease, conciliate, mollify, pacify, placate; lull, relax, stupefy
*near ant* aggravate, heighten, intensify; arouse, excite, foment, incite, rouse, stir (up)
*ant* agitate, discompose, disquiet, disturb, perturb, upset
2 to gain emotional or mental control of — see COLLECT 1

**calm** (down) *vb* to become still and orderly — see QUIET 1

**calming** *adj* tending to calm the emotions and relieve stress — see SOOTHING 1

**calmness** *n* **1** a state of freedom from storm or disturbance — see CALM
**2** evenness of emotions or temper — see EQUANIMITY

**camaraderie** *n* the feeling of closeness and friendship that exists between companions — see COMPANIONSHIP

**camouflage** *n* clothing put on to hide one's true identity or imitate someone or something else — see DISGUISE

**camouflage** *vb* to change the dress or looks of so as to conceal true identity — see DISGUISE

**camp** *n* **1** a place where a group of people live for a short time in tents or cabins ⟨the war forced people to flee their homes and to live in crowded *camps* along the border⟩
***syn*** bivouac, campground, campsite, encampment
***rel*** barracks; colony, plantation, settlement; shantytown; concentration camp, prison camp
**2** a small, simply constructed, and often temporary dwelling — see SHACK
**3** an often small house for recreational or seasonal use — see COTTAGE

**camp** *vb* to live in a camp or the outdoors ⟨rather than stay in motels, my family usually *camps* when we're on vacation⟩
***syn*** bivouac, encamp
***rel*** tent; backpack
***phrases*** rough it

**campaign** *n* a series of activities undertaken to achieve a goal ⟨an all-out *campaign* to bring a minor league baseball team to the city⟩
***syn*** bandwagon, cause, crusade, drive, movement
***rel*** attack, march, offensive

**campaigner** *n* one who seeks an office, honor, position, or award — see CANDIDATE

**camper** *n* a motor vehicle that is specially equipped for living while traveling ⟨the family loaded up the *camper* and headed off for the tour of several national parks⟩
***syn*** caravan, mobile home, motor home, trailer
***rel*** van

**campground** *n* a place where a group of people live for a short time in tents or cabins — see CAMP 1

**campsite** *n* a place where a group of people live for a short time in tents or cabins — see CAMP 1

**can** *vb* **1** to bring (as an action or operation) to an immediate end — see STOP 1
**2** to let go from office, service, or employment — see DISMISS 1

**can** *n* a metal container in the shape of a cylinder ⟨the shelter stores huge *cans* of water for an emergency⟩
***syn*** barrel, drum
***rel*** tube; tin

**canal** *n* an open man-made passageway for water — see CHANNEL 1

**cancel** *vb* **1** to put an end to (something planned or previously agreed to) ⟨please call to *cancel* your appointment with the dentist if you can't make it⟩
***syn*** abort, call, call off, drop, recall, repeal, rescind, revoke
***rel*** abrogate, annul, invalidate, nullify, void, write off; recant, retract, take back, withdraw; countermand, reverse; end, halt, stop, terminate; give up, relinquish, surrender
***near ant*** engage, pledge, promise; begin, commence, initiate, start; take on, take up, undertake
***ant*** continue, keep
**2** to put an end to by formal action — see ABOLISH
**3** to show (something written) to be no longer valid by drawing a cross over or a line through it — see X (OUT)

**cancel** (out) *vb* to balance with an equal force so as to make ineffective — see OFFSET

**canceler** *or* **canceller** *n* a force or influence that makes an opposing force ineffective or less effective — see COUNTERBALANCE

**cancellation** *n* the act of putting an end to something planned or previously agreed to ⟨the misbehavior of a few bad apples at the end of the football game resulted in the *cancellation* of the victory party⟩
***syn*** abortion, calling, calling off, dropping, recall, repeal, rescission, revocation
***rel*** annulment, invalidation, neutralization, nullification; abolishment, abolition, ending, halting, stopping, termination; giving up, relinquishment, surrender
***near ant*** beginning, commencement, initiation; engagement, undertaking
***ant*** continuation

**candid** *adj* free in expressing one's true feelings and opinions — see FRANK

**candidate** *n* one who seeks an office, honor, position, or award ⟨each *candidate* for student council was allowed to speak at the school assembly⟩
***syn*** applicant, aspirant, campaigner, contender, hopeful, prospect, seeker
***rel*** competitor, contestant, entrant; also-ran, dark horse, favorite, finisher, has-been, runner-up; nominee; claimant, pretender
***near ant*** incumbent, officeholder; dropout

**candor** *n* the free expression of one's true feelings and opinions ⟨an interview in which the members of the rock band speak with *candor* about their recent squabbling⟩
***syn*** directness, forthrightness, frankness, openheartedness, openness, plainness, straightforwardness
***rel*** earnestness, sincerity, sobriety; artlessness, genuineness, naïveté (*also* naivete), simplicity, unsophistication; bluffness, bluntness, brusqueness; freedom, license (*or* licence), unrestraint

*near ant* inhibition, reserve, restraint; diplomacy, tact
*ant* dissembling, pretense (*or* pretence)

**cane** *n* a heavy rigid stick used as a weapon or for punishment — see CLUB 1

**canine** *n* a domestic mammal that is related to the wolves and foxes — see DOG

**canniness** *n* skill in achieving one's ends through indirect, subtle, or underhanded means — see CUNNING 1

**cannonade** *n* a rapid or overwhelming outpouring of many things at once — see BARRAGE

**canny** *adj* having or showing a practical cleverness or judgment — see SHREWD

**canon** *n* **1** a statement or body of statements concerning faith or morals proclaimed by a church — see DOCTRINE 1
**2** a record of a series of items (as names or titles) usually arranged according to some system — see [1]LIST

**canonize** *vb* **1** to declare to be a saint and worthy of public respect — see SAINT
**2** to love or admire too much — see IDOLIZE

**canopy** *n* a raised covering over something for decoration or protection ⟨trees line both sides of the garden path, with their foliage forming a leafy *canopy* for walkers⟩
*syn* awning, ceiling, roof, tent
*rel* screen, shade, shelter, shield, sunshade; canvas, fly

[1]**cant** *n* the degree to which something rises up from a position level with the horizon — see SLANT

[2]**cant** *n* **1** the pretending of having virtues, principles, or beliefs that one in fact does not have — see HYPOCRISY
**2** the special terms or expressions of a particular group or field — see TERMINOLOGY

**cant** *vb* to set or cause to be at an angle — see LEAN 1

**cantankerous** *adj* having or showing a habitually bad temper — see ILL-TEMPERED

**canted** *adj* running in a slanting direction — see DIAGONAL

**canticle** *n* a religious song — see HYMN

**canvas** *n* a picture created with usually oil paint — see PAINTING

**canvass** *vb* to go around and approach (people) with a request for opinions or information ⟨we *canvassed* people all over town, asking if they would be interested in participating in a recycling program⟩
*syn* poll, solicit, survey
*rel* interrogate, interview, question; feel (out), sound (out)
*near ant* report

**canyon** *also* **cañon** *n* a narrow opening between hillsides or mountains that can be used for passage ⟨as the scouts made their way through the *canyon*, they marveled at the sheer walls of rock on both sides⟩
*syn* defile, flume, gap, gorge, gulch, gulf, notch, pass, ravine
*rel* abyss, chasm, cirque, cleft, crevasse, crevice, fissure; dale, glen, hollow, vale, valley; basin, floodplain, plain; arroyo, coulee, gully, gutter, wash [*Western*]

**cap** *n* **1** a covering for the head usually having a shaped crown — see HAT
**2** a piece placed over an open container to hold in, protect, or conceal its contents — see COVER 1

**capability** *n* **1** a skill, an ability, or knowledge that makes a person able to do a particular job — see QUALIFICATION 1
**2** the physical or mental power to do something — see ABILITY

**capable** *adj* having the required skills for an acceptable level of performance — see COMPETENT

**capably** *adv* in a skillful or expert manner — see WELL 3

**capacious** *adj* more than adequate or average in capacity — see SPACIOUS

**capacity** *n* **1** the largest number or amount that something can hold ⟨the seating *capacity* of the school auditorium is 800 people⟩
*syn* complement, content
*rel* area, room, space, volume; fill, load, measure
**2** an assignment at which one regularly works for pay — see JOB 1
**3** the action for which a person or thing is specially fitted or used or for which a thing exists — see ROLE
**4** the physical or mental power to do something — see ABILITY

**caparison** *n* **1** dressy clothing — see FINERY
**2** something that decorates or beautifies — see DECORATION 1

**caparison** *vb* to outfit with clothes and especially fine or special clothes — see CLOTHE 1

[1]**cape** *n* a sleeveless garment worn so as to hang over the shoulders, arms, and back ⟨the mysterious figure wrapped his *cape* tightly around his shoulders⟩
*syn* cloak, mantle, roquelaure
*rel* frock, gown, robe; shawl, stole, wrap; poncho, serape (*or* sarape)

[2]**cape** *n* an area of land that juts out into a body of water ⟨residents fled the *cape* as the hurricane roared up the coast⟩
*syn* arm, headland, peninsula, point, promontory, spit
*rel* breakwater, jetty

**caper** *n* a playful or mischievous act intended as a joke — see PRANK

**caper** *vb* to play and run about happily — see FROLIC 1

**capital** *adj* of the very best kind — see EXCELLENT

**capital** *n* **1** a thing or place that is of greatest importance to an activity or interest — see CENTER 1
**2** the total of one's money and property — see WEALTH

**capitalize** *vb* to provide money for — see FINANCE 1

---

*syn* synonym(s) *rel* related words
*ant* antonym(s) *near ant* near antonym(s)

**capitalize** (on) *vb* to take unfair advantage of — see EXPLOIT 1

**capitol** *n* the building in which a state legislature meets ⟨the legislators were called to the *capitol* for an emergency session⟩
*syn* state house
*rel* meetinghouse; chamber, hall

**capitulate** *vb* **1** to cease resistance (as to another's arguments, demands, or control) — see YIELD 3
**2** to yield to the control or power of enemy forces — see FALL 2

**capitulating** *n* the usually forced yielding of one's person or possessions to the control of another — see SURRENDER

**capitulation** *n* the usually forced yielding of one's person or possessions to the control of another — see SURRENDER

**caprice** *n* a sudden impulsive and apparently unmotivated idea or action — see WHIM

**capricious** *adj* **1** likely to change frequently, suddenly, or unexpectedly — see FICKLE 1
**2** prone to sudden illogical changes of mind, ideas, or actions — see WHIMSICAL

**capriciousness** *n* an inclination to sudden illogical changes of mind, ideas, or actions — see WHIMSICALITY

**capsize** *vb* to turn on one's side or upside down ⟨a huge wave out of nowhere caused our little sailboat to *capsize*⟩
*syn* overturn, upset
*rel* invert, topple; keel over; heel, list, tilt; founder, sink, swamp
*phrases* turn turtle
*ant* right

**capsule** *n* **1** a small mass containing medicine to be taken orally — see PILL
**2** something that encloses another thing especially to protect it — see ¹CASE 1

**captain** *n* **1** a person in overall command of a ship ⟨the *captain* is responsible for everything that happens to his ship in the course of a voyage⟩
*syn* commander, skipper
*rel* master; commanding officer; admiral, commodore, vice admiral
**2** one in official command especially of a military force or base — see COMMANDER 1
**3** the person (as an employer or supervisor) who tells people and especially workers what to do — see BOSS

**captain** *vb* **1** to be in charge of — see BOSS 1
**2** to exercise authority or power over — see GOVERN 1
**3** to serve as leader of — see LEAD 2

**caption** *n* **1** an explanation or description accompanying a pictorial illustration ⟨for the school yearbook, funny *captions* were written for snapshots showing a typical day at school⟩
*syn* legend
*rel* key; subtitle, translation; motto, tag line
**2** a word or series of words often in larger letters placed at the beginning of a passage or at the top of a page in order to introduce or categorize — see HEADING

**captious** *adj* given to making or expressing unfavorable judgments about things — see CRITICAL 1

**captivate** *vb* to attract or delight as if by magic — see CHARM 1

**captivating** *adj* having an often mysterious or magical power to attract — see FASCINATING 1

**captivation** *n* the power of irresistible attraction — see CHARM 2

**captive** *adj* taken and held prisoner ⟨the *captive* soldiers were treated humanely by the guards⟩
*syn* apprehended, arrested, captured, caught, imprisoned, incarcerated, interned, jailed
*rel* bound, enslaved, indentured; subdued, subjugated
*near ant* emancipated, enfranchised, freed, liberated, released
*ant* free

**captive** *n* one that has been taken and held in confinement ⟨the *captives* in the concentration camp had devised a daring plan of escape⟩
*syn* capture, internee, prisoner
*rel* convict, jailbird; parolee
*near ant* custodian, guard, guardian, jailer (*or* jailor), keeper, warden
*ant* captor

**captivity** *n* the act of confining or the state of being confined — see INTERNMENT

**capture** *n* one that has been taken and held in confinement — see CAPTIVE

**capture** *vb* **1** to receive as return for effort — see EARN 1
**2** to take physical control or possession of (something) suddenly or forcibly — see CATCH 1

**captured** *adj* taken and held prisoner — see CAPTIVE

**car** *n* a self-propelled passenger vehicle on wheels ⟨every teenager's dream of getting a driver's license and a first *car*⟩
*syn* auto, automobile, machine, motor, motorcar, motor vehicle
*rel* bus, coach, minibus; beach buggy, brougham, compact, convertible, coupe, dune buggy, fastback, gas-guzzler, hardtop, hatchback, hot rod, jeep, limousine, roadster, sedan, sports car, station wagon, stock car, subcompact, van; flivver, jalopy

**caravan** *n* **1** a group of vehicles traveling together or under one management — see FLEET
**2** a motor vehicle that is specially equipped for living while traveling — see CAMPER

**caravansary** *or* **caravanserai** *n* a place that provides rooms and usually a public dining room for overnight guests — see HOTEL

**carbon copy** *n* **1** something or someone that strongly resembles another — see IMAGE 1
**2** something that is made to look exactly like something else — see COPY

**carcass** *n* a dead body — see CORPSE

**card** *n* a person (as a writer) noted for or specializing in humor — see HUMORIST

**cardinal** *adj* coming before all others in importance — see FOREMOST 1

**care** *n* **1** strict attentiveness to what one is doing ⟨that's an extremely valuable violin, so handle it with *care*⟩
*syn* carefulness, conscientiousness, heed, heedfulness, pains, scrupulousness
*rel* exactness, meticulousness, particularity, punctiliousness; dutifulness, responsibility; bother, effort, trouble; alertness, vigilance, watchfulness
*ant* carelessness, heedlessness
**2** a close attentiveness to avoiding danger — see CAUTION 1
**3** an uneasy state of mind usually over the possibility of an anticipated misfortune or trouble — see ANXIETY 1
**4** responsibility for the safety and well-being of someone or something — see CUSTODY
**5** the duty or function of watching or guarding for the sake of proper direction or control — see SUPERVISION 1

**care** *vb* to have an interest or concern for ⟨a teacher who *cares* what happens to her students long after they leave her classroom⟩
*syn* mind, watch
*rel* attend, heed, regard; note, notice, observe; empathize (with), feel (for), sympathize (with)
*phrases* look out for
*near ant* disregard, ignore, overlook

**care** (for) *vb* **1** to take charge of especially on behalf of another — see ²TEND 1
**2** to attend to the needs and comforts of — see NURSE 1
**3** to have a favorable opinion of — see APPROVE (OF)
**4** to wish to have — see LIKE 1

**careen** *vb* **1** to make a series of unsteady side-to-side motions — see ROCK 1
**2** to move forward while swaying from side to side — see STAGGER 1

**career** *vb* to proceed or move quickly — see HURRY 2

**carefree** *adj* having or showing a lack of concern or seriousness ⟨passengers on a luxury cruise ship enjoying a *carefree* vacation⟩ ⟨*carefree* college students on spring break⟩
*syn* careless, cavalier, devil-may-care, easygoing, gay, happy-go-lucky, insouciant, lighthearted, unconcerned
*rel* breezy, nonchalant; casual, informal, laid-back, low-pressure, relaxed; heedless, irresponsible, lackadaisical, negligent, reckless
*near ant* earnest, grave, serious, somber (*or* sombre); careful, cautious, heedful, wary; concerned, upset, worried; long-suffering, overburdened, sorrowful
*ant* careworn

**careful** *adj* **1** having or showing a close attentiveness to avoiding danger or trouble ⟨*careful* drivers slow down on slick or icy roadways⟩
*syn* alert, cautious, circumspect, considerate, gingerly, guarded, heedful, safe, wary
*rel* attentive, chary, observant, vigilant, watchful; foresighted, forethoughtful, provident; cagey (*also* cagy), noncommittal; calculating, scheming, shrewd; considerate, thoughtful; deliberate, slow
*near ant* bold, impetuous, rash, reckless; inattentive, unobservant; inconsiderate, thoughtless; lax, neglectful, negligent; imprudent, indiscreet, injudicious
*ant* careless, heedless, incautious, unguarded, unsafe, unwary
**2** taking great care and effort — see PAINSTAKING

**carefulness** *n* **1** a close attentiveness to avoiding danger — see CAUTION 1
**2** strict attentiveness to what one is doing — see CARE 1

**careless** *adj* **1** not paying or showing close attention especially for the purpose of avoiding trouble ⟨a *careless* reporter who often doesn't get his facts straight⟩ ⟨a *careless* mistake that caused the plane to crash⟩
*syn* heedless, incautious, mindless, unguarded, unsafe, unwary
*rel* bold, impetuous, rash, reckless; inattentive, unobservant; blithe, inconsiderate, thoughtless; absentminded, forgetful, unmindful; lax, neglectful, negligent, remiss; imprudent, indiscreet, injudicious; inadvertent, unintentional, unplanned
*near ant* attentive, chary, observant, vigilant, watchful; foresighted, forethoughtful, provident; calculating, scheming, shrewd; considerate, thoughtful
*ant* alert, cautious, circumspect, gingerly, guarded, heedful, safe, wary
**2** failing to give proper care and attention — see NEGLIGENT
**3** having or showing a lack of concern or seriousness — see CAREFREE

**carelessness** *n* failure to take the care that a cautious person usually takes — see NEGLIGENCE 1

**caress** *vb* to touch or handle in a tender or loving manner — see FONDLE

**caretaker** *n* a person who takes care of a property sometimes for an absent owner — see CUSTODIAN 1

**cargo** *n* a mass or quantity of something taken up and carried, conveyed, or transported — see LOAD 1

**caricature** *n* **1** a poor, insincere, or insulting imitation of something — see MOCKERY 1
**2** a work that imitates and exaggerates another work for comic effect — see PARODY 1
**3** the representation of something in terms that go beyond the facts — see EXAGGERATION

**caricature** *vb* to copy or exaggerate (someone or something) in order to make fun of — see MIMIC 1

**carnage** *n* the killing of a large number of people — see MASSACRE

**carnal** *adj* **1** having to do with life on earth especially as opposed to that in heaven — see EARTHLY
**2** of or relating to the human body — see PHYSICAL 1
**3** pleasing to the physical senses — see SENSUAL

**carnival** *n* a time or program of special events and entertainment in honor of something — see FESTIVAL

**carol** *n* a religious song — see HYMN

**carol** *vb* to produce musical sounds with the voice — see SING 1

**caroler** *or* **caroller** *n* one who sings — see SINGER

**carom** *vb* to strike and fly off at an angle — see GLANCE 1

**carousal** *n* a bout of drinking — see CAROUSE

**carouse** *n* a bout of drinking ⟨the Old West custom of heading to the saloon at night for a *carouse* and some poker playing⟩
***syn*** carousal, drunk, wassail
***rel*** binge, jag, spree; blowout, orgy

**carp** *vb* **1** to express dissatisfaction, pain, or resentment usually tiresomely — see COMPLAIN
**2** to make often peevish criticisms or objections about matters that are minor, unimportant, or irrelevant — see QUIBBLE

**carper** *n* a person given to harsh judgments and to finding faults — see CRITIC 1

**carpet** *vb* to form a layer over — see COVER 2

**carping** *adj* given to making or expressing unfavorable judgments about things — see CRITICAL 1

**carriage** *n* **1** a horse-drawn wheeled vehicle for carrying passengers ⟨a museum with a large collection of beautiful, old *carriages*⟩
***syn*** equipage, rig
***rel*** brougham, buckboard, cab, chaise, coach, hackney, hansom, surrey
**2** a general way of holding the body — see POSTURE 1

**carry** *vb* **1** to support and take from one place to another ⟨each camper must be able to *carry* his or her own backpack⟩
***syn*** bear, cart, convey, ferry, haul, lug, pack, tote, transport
***rel*** deliver, hand over, transfer; forward, send, ship, transmit; bring, fetch, take; move, remove, shift
**2** to wear or have on one's person ⟨I always *carry* a camera with me so as to never miss a great shot⟩
***syn*** bear, pack
***rel*** flaunt, show off, sport; display, exhibit, parade, show
**3** to bring before the public in performance or exhibition — see PRESENT 1
**4** to have as part of a whole — see INCLUDE
**5** to hold up or serve as a foundation for — see SUPPORT 3
**6** to receive as return for effort — see EARN 1

**carryall** *n* a bag carried by hand and designed to hold a traveler's clothing and personal articles — see TRAVELING BAG

**carry away** *vb* **1** to fill with overwhelming emotion (as wonder or delight) — see ENTRANCE
**2** to subject to incapacitating emotional or mental stress — see OVERWHELM 1

**carry on** *vb* **1** to behave badly — see MISBEHAVE
**2** to continue despite difficulties, opposition, or discouragement — see PERSEVERE
**3** to look after and make decisions about — see CONDUCT 1

**carry out** *vb* to carry through (as a process) to completion — see PERFORM 1

**cart** *n* a wheeled usually horse-drawn vehicle used for hauling ⟨an old *cart* piled up with hay⟩
***syn*** wagon, wain
***rel*** barrow, pushcart, wheelbarrow; oxcart

**cart** *vb* to support and take from one place to another — see CARRY 1

**cartel** *n* a number of businesses or enterprises united for commercial advantage ⟨a *cartel* of oil-producing nations that controls production and influences prices⟩
***syn*** combination, combine, syndicate, trust
***rel*** chain, conglomerate, multinational; association, organization, pool

**cartoon** *n* **1** a picture using lines to represent the chief features of an object or scene — see DRAWING
**2** a series of drawings that tell a story or part of a story — see COMIC STRIP

**carve** *vb* to create a three-dimensional representation of (something) using solid material — see SCULPT

**carve** (out) *vb* to produce or bring about especially by long or repeated effort — see HAMMER (OUT)

**cascade** *n* a fall of water usually from a great height — see WATERFALL

**[1]case** *n* **1** something that encloses another thing especially to protect it ⟨those binoculars come with their own *case*⟩
***syn*** armor, capsule, casing, cocoon, cover, covering, housing, husk, jacket, pod, sheath, shell
***rel*** bark, crust; mail, plate, plating, shield; hide, skin; envelope, wrapper; backing, coating, facing
**2** a covered rectangular container for storing or transporting things — see CHEST

**[2]case** *n* **1** an individual awaiting or under medical care and treatment — see PATIENT
**2** one of a group or collection that shows what the whole is like — see EXAMPLE
**3** something that actually exists — see FACT 2
**4** a statement given to explain a belief or act — see REASON 1

5 a sudden experiencing of a physical or mental disorder — see ATTACK 2
6 something that might happen — see EVENT 2
7 something that requires thought and skill for resolution — see PROBLEM 1

**cash** *n* something (as pieces of stamped metal or printed paper) customarily and legally used as a medium of exchange, a measure of value, or a means of payment — see MONEY

**cashier** *vb* to let go from office, service, or employment — see DISMISS 1

**cash in** (on) *vb* to take unfair advantage of — see EXPLOIT 1

**casing** *n* something that encloses another thing especially to protect it — see [1]CASE 1

**cask** *n* an enclosed wooden vessel for holding beverages ⟨*casks* of wine that had been in the castle for many years⟩
***syn*** barrel, firkin, hogshead, keg, pipe, puncheon
***rel*** tub, vat; can, drum

**casket** *n* 1 a box for holding a dead body — see COFFIN
2 a covered rectangular container for storing or transporting things — see CHEST

**cast** *n* 1 a declaration that something will happen in the future — see PREDICTION
2 a property that becomes apparent when light falls on an object and by which things that are identical in form can be distinguished — see COLOR 1
3 an instance of looking especially briefly — see LOOK 2
4 facial appearance regarded as an indication of mood or feeling — see LOOK 1
5 the outward appearance of something as distinguished from its substance — see FORM 1

**cast** *vb* 1 to get rid of as useless or unwanted — see DISCARD
2 to point or turn (something) toward a target or goal — see AIM 1
3 to put (something) into proper and usually carefully worked out written form — see COMPOSE 1
4 to send through the air especially with a quick forward motion of the arm — see THROW

**cast** (off) *vb* to throw or give off — see EMIT 1

**cast** (out) *vb* to drive or force out — see EJECT 1

**cast about** (for) *vb* to go in search of — see SEEK 1

**cast around** (for) *vb* to go in search of — see SEEK 1

**castaway** *n* one who is cast out or rejected by society — see OUTCAST

**caste** *n* one of the segments of society into which people are grouped — see CLASS 1

**castigate** *vb* 1 to criticize (someone) severely or angrily especially for personal failings — see SCOLD
2 to criticize harshly and usually publicly — see ATTACK 2
3 to inflict a penalty on for a fault or crime — see PUNISH

**castigating** *adj* inflicting, involving, or serving as punishment — see PUNITIVE

**castigation** *n* suffering, loss, or hardship imposed in response to a crime or offense — see PUNISHMENT

**castigator** *n* 1 a person given to harsh judgments and to finding faults — see CRITIC 1
2 one who inflicts punishment in return for an injury or offense — see NEMESIS 1

**castle** *n* a large impressive residence — see MANSION

**castoff** *n* one who is cast out or rejected by society — see OUTCAST

**casual** *adj* 1 not designed for special occasions ⟨a restaurant where people in *casual* clothes are always welcome⟩
***syn*** everyday, informal, workaday
***rel*** sporty; shabby, sloppy, slovenly, unkempt
***near ant*** best, Sunday; chic, elegant, fashionable, smart, stylish; neat, tidy, trim; semiformal
***ant*** dressy, formal
2 happening by chance — see ACCIDENTAL
3 having or showing a lack of interest or concern — see INDIFFERENT 1
4 lacking in steadiness or regularity of occurrence — see FITFUL

**casualness** *n* lack of interest or concern — see INDIFFERENCE

**casualty** *n* 1 a person or thing harmed, lost, or destroyed ⟨the real *casualties* in the war against drugs are millions of innocent children⟩
***syn*** fatality, loss, victim
***rel*** failure, loser
***near ant*** gainer, victor, winner
2 a chance and usually sudden event bringing loss or injury — see ACCIDENT 1

**cat** *n* 1 a small domestic animal known for catching mice ⟨the family's *cat* did a good job of keeping the house and yard free of all rodents⟩
***syn*** feline, house cat, kitty, puss, pussy
***rel*** mouser; kit, kitten; tabby, tomcat
2 *slang* an adult male human being — see MAN 1

**cataclysm** *n* 1 a great flow of water or of something that overwhelms — see FLOOD
2 a sudden violent event that brings about great loss or destruction — see DISASTER
3 a violent disturbance (as of the political or social order) — see CONVULSION

**cataclysmal** *or* **cataclysmic** *adj* 1 bringing about ruin or misfortune — see FATAL 1
2 causing or tending to cause destruction — see DESTRUCTIVE 1
3 marked by sudden or violent disturbance — see CONVULSIVE

**catacomb** *n, usually* **catacombs** *pl* an underground burial chamber — see CRYPT

---

***syn*** synonym(s) ***rel*** related words
***ant*** antonym(s) ***near ant*** near antonym(s)

**catalog** *or* **catalogue** *n* a record of a series of items (as names or titles) usually arranged according to some system — see [1]LIST

**catalog** *or* **catalogue** *vb* to put (someone or something) on a list — see [1]LIST 2

**catamount** *n* a large tawny cat of the wild — see COUGAR

**catapult** *vb* to send through the air especially with a quick forward motion of the arm — see THROW

**cataract** *n* **1** a fall of water usually from a great height — see WATERFALL
**2** a great flow of water or of something that overwhelms — see FLOOD

**catastrophe** *n* **1** a sudden violent event that brings about great loss or destruction — see DISASTER
**2** something that has failed — see FAILURE 3

**catastrophic** *adj* bringing about ruin or misfortune — see FATAL 1

**catcall** *n* a vocal sound made to express scorn or disapproval ⟨the band's sloppy playing produced only *catcalls* from the crowd⟩
***syn*** boo, hiss, hoot, jeer, raspberry, snort
***rel*** smirk, sneer, snicker, snigger; gibe (*or* jibe), put-down, taunt; whistle
***near ant*** applause, clapping
***ant*** cheer

**catch** *n* **1** a danger or difficulty that is hidden or not easily recognized — see PITFALL 1
**2** someone or something unusually desirable — see PRIZE 1
**3** the total amount collected or obtained especially at one time — see HAUL 1

**catch** *vb* **1** to take physical control or possession of (something) suddenly or forcibly ⟨we tried to *catch* the kitten before she could sneak out the door⟩
***syn*** bag, capture, collar, corral, get, grab, grapple, hook, land, nab, nail, seize, snap (up), snare, snatch, trap
***rel*** lasso, rope; apprehend, arrest, detain; clasp, clutch, grasp, grip, hold, secure; rend, wrest; ensnare, entangle, entrap; abduct, kidnap, spirit (away *or* off)
***phrases*** lay hold of
***near ant*** discharge, free, liberate, release; drop, loosen
***ant*** miss
**2** to become affected with (a disease or disorder) — see CONTRACT 1
**3** to bring (something) to a standstill — see [1]HALT 1
**4** to put securely in place or in a desired position — see FASTEN 2
**5** to recognize the meaning of — see COMPREHEND 1

**catching** *adj* **1** capable of being passed by physical contact from one person to another — see CONTAGIOUS 1
**2** exciting a similar feeling or reaction in others — see CONTAGIOUS 2

**catch on** *vb* to come to an awareness — see DISCOVER 1

**catch on** (to) *vb* to recognize the meaning of — see COMPREHEND 1

**catch up** (with) *vb* to move fast enough to get even with — see OVERTAKE

**catchy** *adj* **1** likely to attract attention — see NOTICEABLE
**2** requiring exceptional skill or caution in performance or handling — see TRICKY

**categorical** *also* **categoric** *adj* having no exceptions or restrictions — see ABSOLUTE 2

**categorize** *vb* to arrange or assign according to type — see CLASSIFY 1

**category** *n* one of the units into which a whole is divided on the basis of a common characteristic — see CLASS 2

**cater** *vb* to provide food or meals for — see FEED 1

**cater** (to) *vb* to give in to (a desire) — see INDULGE

**catnap** *n* a short sleep — see [1]NAP

**catnap** *vb* **1** be in a state of sleep — see SLEEP 1
**2** to sleep lightly or briefly — see NAP 1

**catnapping** *n* a natural periodic loss of consciousness during which the body restores itself — see SLEEP 1

**cattily** *adv* in a mean or spiteful manner — see NASTILY

**cattiness** *n* **1** biting sharpness of feeling or expression — see ACRIMONY 1
**2** the desire to cause pain for the satisfaction of doing harm — see MALICE

**catty** *adj* having or showing a desire to cause someone pain or suffering for the sheer enjoyment of it — see HATEFUL

**caught** *adj* taken and held prisoner — see CAPTIVE

**cause** *n* **1** someone or something responsible for a result ⟨the much-debated *causes* of the American Civil War⟩
***syn*** antecedent, occasion, reason
***rel*** consideration, determinant, factor; impetus, incentive, inspiration, instigation, stimulus; mother, origin, root, source, spring
***near ant*** ramification; denouement, repercussion; conclusion, end; by-product, side effect
***ant*** aftereffect, aftermath, consequence, corollary, development, effect, fate, fruit, issue, outcome, outgrowth, product, result, resultant, sequel, sequence, upshot
**2** a series of activities undertaken to achieve a goal — see CAMPAIGN

**cause** *vb* to be the cause of (a situation, action, or state of mind) — see EFFECT

**caustic** *adj* marked by the use of wit that is intended to cause hurt feelings — see SARCASTIC

**caution** *n* **1** a close attentiveness to avoiding danger ⟨the extreme *caution* with which the zookeeper handled the snake⟩
***syn*** alertness, care, carefulness, cautiousness, circumspection, heedfulness, wariness
***rel*** attentiveness, chariness, vigilance, watchfulness; foresight, foresightedness, providence; calculation, canniness, deliberateness, deliberation, shrewdness

*near ant* abruptness, hastiness, impetuousness, precipitousness, rashness, suddenness; inconsideration, thoughtlessness
*ant* brashness, carelessness, heedlessness, incautiousness, recklessness, unwariness
**2** something extraordinary or surprising — see WONDER 1
**3** something that tells of approaching danger or risk — see WARNING 2
**4** the act or an instance of telling beforehand of danger or risk — see WARNING 1

**caution** *vb* to give notice to beforehand especially of danger or risk — see WARN

**cautionary** *adj* serving as or offering a warning ⟨the story of King Midas is a *cautionary* tale about the perils of wishing for something—you just might get it⟩
*syn* admonishing, admonitory, cautioning, warning
*rel* didactic, moralistic, moralizing; advisory, counseling (*or* counselling); punishing, punitive

**cautioning** *adj* serving as or offering a warning — see CAUTIONARY

**cautious** *adj* having or showing a close attentiveness to avoiding danger or trouble — see CAREFUL 1

**cautiousness** *n* a close attentiveness to avoiding danger — see CAUTION 1

**cavalcade** *n* **1** a group of vehicles traveling together or under one management — see FLEET
**2** a staged presentation often with music that consists of a procession of narrated or enacted scenes — see PAGEANT

**cavalier** *adj* **1** having a feeling of superiority that shows itself in an overbearing attitude — see ARROGANT
**2** having or showing a lack of concern or seriousness — see CAREFREE

**cavalier** *n* an honorable and courteous man ⟨a novel about the dashing *cavaliers* and gracious ladies of the South before the Civil War⟩
*syn* gentleman
*rel* knight, prince; blade, buck, dandy, fop, gallant; charmer, smoothy (*or* smoothie); aristocrat, patrician

**cave** *n* a naturally formed underground chamber with an opening to the surface ⟨Kentucky's Mammoth *Cave* is actually a series of large chambers on five levels⟩
*syn* cavern, grot, grotto
*rel* abyss, chasm, gulf, hollow; subway, tunnel; excavation, mine, pit, shaft, well; bunker, dugout, foxhole; burrow, covert, den, hole, lair, lodge, shelter

**cave** (in) *vb* to fall down or in as a result of physical pressure — see COLLAPSE 1

**cavern** *n* a naturally formed underground chamber with an opening to the surface — see CAVE

**cavil** *vb* to make often peevish criticisms or objections about matters that are minor, unimportant, or irrelevant — see QUIBBLE

**caviler** *or* **caviller** *n* a person given to harsh judgments and to finding faults — see CRITIC 1

**caviling** *or* **cavilling** *adj* given to making or expressing unfavorable judgments about things — see CRITICAL 1

**cavity** *n* a sunken area forming a separate space — see HOLE 2

**cavort** *vb* to play and run about happily — see FROLIC 1

**cease** *vb* **1** to come to an end ⟨the rain finally *ceased*, and we were able to continue the baseball game⟩
*syn* break off, break up, close, conclude, die, discontinue, elapse, end, expire, finish, halt, lapse, leave off, let up, pass, quit, stop, terminate, wind up
*rel* desist (from), lay off (of), refrain (from); knock off; break down, conk (out), cut out, stall; pause, stay, suspend
*near ant* draw out, extend, prolong, protract
*ant* continue, hang on, persist
**2** to bring (as an action or operation) to an immediate end — see STOP 1

**cease–fire** *n* a temporary stopping of fighting — see TRUCE

**ceaseless** *adj* **1** going on and on without any interruptions — see CONTINUOUS
**2** lasting forever — see EVERLASTING

**cede** *vb* **1** to give (something) over to the control or possession of another usually under duress — see SURRENDER 1
**2** to give over the legal possession or ownership of — see TRANSFER 1
**3** to give up (as a position of authority) formally — see ABDICATE

**ceiling** *n* **1** a real or imaginary point beyond which a person or thing cannot go — see LIMIT
**2** a raised covering over something for decoration or protection — see CANOPY

**celebrant** *n* one who engages in merrymaking especially in honor of a special occasion ⟨all of the *celebrants* at the birthday party received a favor to take home⟩
*syn* celebrator, merrymaker, reveler (*or* reveller), roisterer
*rel* carouser, wassailer; cutup, skylarker
*ant* killjoy, party pooper

**celebrate** *vb* to act properly in relation to — see KEEP 1

**celebrated** *adj* widely known — see FAMOUS

**celebration** *n* a time or program of special events and entertainment in honor of something — see FESTIVAL

**celebrator** *n* one who engages in merrymaking especially in honor of a special occasion — see CELEBRANT

**celebrity** *n* **1** a person who is widely known and usually much talked about ⟨*celebrities* from sports and entertainment attended the opening ceremonies of the Olympic Games⟩
*syn* figure, light, luminary, notable, personage, personality, somebody, standout, star, superstar, VIP

---

*syn* synonym(s) *rel* related words
*ant* antonym(s) *near ant* near antonym(s)

*rel* favorite, hero, idol; demigod, dignitary, eminence, immortal, pillar, worthy; baron, big shot, bigwig, magnate, mogul, nabob
*near ant* lightweight, mediocrity; has-been
*ant* nobody
**2** the fact or state of being known to the public — see FAME

**celerity** *n* a high rate of movement or performance — see SPEED

**celestial** *adj* of, relating to, or suggesting heaven ⟨movie scenes depicting life after death are usually accompanied by *celestial* music⟩
*syn* Elysian, empyreal, empyrean, heavenly, supernal
*rel* ethereal, supernatural, transcendent, transcendental, unearthly, unworldly; angelic, beatific, blissful; Olympian, utopian; cosmic, stellar
*near ant* earthly, mundane, terrestrial, worldly
*ant* hellish, infernal

**cell** *n* **1** an area within a building that has been set apart from surrounding space by a wall — see ROOM 2
**2** one of the parts into which an enclosed space is divided — see COMPARTMENT

**cellar** *n* a room or set of rooms below the surface of the ground ⟨an amazing variety of interesting things were found in the *cellar* of the old house⟩
*syn* basement
*rel* bunker, crawlway, foundation, hold

**cement** *n* **1** a substance used to stick things together — see GLUE
**2** a uniting or binding force or influence — see BOND 2

**cemetery** *n* a piece of land used for burying the dead ⟨many of the soldiers who died in the battle are buried in a *cemetery* nearby⟩
*syn* graveyard, potter's field
*rel* catacombs, churchyard; crypt, grave, mausoleum, sepulcher (*or* sepulchre), sepulture, tomb, vault

**censor** *vb* to remove objectionable parts from ⟨the producers were told that they would have to *censor* their movie if they wanted a PG rating⟩
*syn* clean (up), expurgate
*rel* cleanse, purge, purify; abbreviate, edit, shorten; cut (out), delete, excise, expunge; repress, silence, suppress; censure, condemn, denounce; examine, review, screen, scrutinize
*near ant* approve, authorize, sanction

**censurable** *adj* **1** deserving reproach or blame — see BLAMEWORTHY
**2** provoking or likely to provoke protest — see OBJECTIONABLE

**censure** *n* an often public or formal expression of disapproval ⟨a rare *censure* of a senator by the full United States Senate for misconduct⟩
*syn* condemnation, denunciation, rebuke, reprimand, reproach, reproof, stricture
*rel* admonishment, admonition, castigation, chastisement, punishment; belittlement, criticism, deprecation, depreciation, disparagement
*near ant* acclamation, honor, tribute; encomium, eulogy, panegyric, plaudit(s), praise; approval, blessing, sanction
*ant* citation, commendation, endorsement

**censure** *vb* **1** to express public or formal disapproval of ⟨a vote to *censure* the President for conduct that was unbecoming to his office⟩
*syn* condemn, denounce, rebuke, reprimand, reproach, reprove
*rel* admonish, castigate, chastise, punish; belittle, criticize, deprecate, depreciate, disparage
*near ant* acclaim, applause, honor; eulogize, laud, praise; approve, bless, sanction
*ant* cite, commend, endorse (*also* indorse)
**2** to declare to be morally wrong or evil — see CONDEMN 1
**3** to express one's unfavorable opinion of the worth or quality of — see CRITICIZE

**censurer** *n* a person given to harsh judgments and to finding faults — see CRITIC 1

**center** *n* **1** a thing or place that is of greatest importance to an activity or interest ⟨a stretch of coastline that has long been the area's *center* of tourism⟩
*syn* base, capital, core, cynosure, eye, focus, heart, hub, mecca, nucleus, seat
*rel* focus, headquarters; kernel, nub, pith; deep, thick; essence, quintessence, soul; attraction, lodestone, magnet
**2** an area or point that is an equal distance from all points along an edge or outer surface ⟨the *center* of the earth⟩
*syn* core, middle, midpoint, midst
*rel* inside, interior
*ant* perimeter, periphery

**center** *vb* to bring (something) to a central point or under a single control — see CENTRALIZE

**central** *adj* coming before all others in importance — see FOREMOST 1

**centralize** *vb* to bring (something) to a central point or under a single control ⟨the company decided to *centralize* all of its operations at its Ohio plant⟩
*syn* center, compact, concentrate, consolidate, unify, unite
*rel* coordinate, harmonize, integrate, orchestrate; blend, coalesce, combine, fuse, incorporate, merge; conjoin, join, link; assemble, collect, gather; reunify, reunite
*near ant* segregate, separate
*ant* decentralize, spread (out)

**cerebral** *adj* **1** much given to learning and thinking — see INTELLECTUAL 1
**2** of or relating to the mind — see MENTAL 1

**cerebrum** *n* the part of a person that feels, thinks, perceives, wills, and especially reasons — see MIND 1

**ceremonial** *adj* following or agreeing with established form, custom, or rules — see FORMAL 1

**ceremonial** *n* an oft-repeated action or series of actions performed in accordance with tradition or a set of rules — see RITE

**ceremonious** *adj* **1** marked by or showing careful attention to set forms and details ⟨a century ago everyday life was much more *ceremonious* than in our anything-goes era⟩
*syn* correct, decorous, formal, proper, starchy
*rel* sober, solemn, stately; chivalrous, courtly, gallant; genteel, polished, refined; civil, courteous, polite, red-carpet
*near ant* improper, indecorous, unmannerly; discourteous, impolite, rude
*ant* casual, easygoing, informal, laid-back
**2** following or agreeing with established form, custom, or rules — see FORMAL 1

**ceremony** *n* an oft-repeated action or series of actions performed in accordance with tradition or a set of rules — see RITE

**certain** *adj* **1** known but not named ⟨a *certain* person told me that today is your birthday⟩
*syn* anonymous, one, some, unidentified, unnamed, unspecified
*rel* particular, specific
*near ant* known, named, specified
**2** having or showing a mind free from doubt ⟨I'm *certain* that they'll arrive on time⟩
*syn* assured, clear, cocksure, confident, doubtless, positive, sanguine, sure
*rel* self-assured, self-conceited, self-confident; decisive, resolute, unfaltering, unhesitating, unwavering
*near ant* hesitant, indecisive, wavering; diffident, unassuming
*ant* doubtful, dubious, uncertain, unsure
**3** having been established and usually not subject to change — see FIXED 1
**4** impossible to avoid or evade — see INEVITABLE
**5** not likely to fail — see INFALLIBLE 2

**certainly** *adv* without any question — see INDEED 1

**certainty** *n* a state of mind in which one is free from doubt — see CONFIDENCE 2

**certificate** *n* a written or printed paper giving information about or proof of something ⟨a *certificate* will be awarded to each person who completes the course in lifesaving⟩
*syn* document, instrument
*rel* credentials; diploma, parchment; warrant, writ; warranty; coupon, voucher

**certify** *vb* **1** to declare (something) to be true or genuine ⟨experts *certified* the letter as indeed having been written by Abraham Lincoln⟩
*syn* attest, authenticate, avouch, testify (to), vouch (for), witness
*rel* guarantee, warrant; affirm, assert, aver, avow, profess
**2** to give official or legal power to — see AUTHORIZE 1

**certitude** *n* a state of mind in which one is free from doubt — see CONFIDENCE 2

**cessation** *n* the stopping of a process or activity — see END 1

**chafe** *vb* **1** to make sore by continued rubbing ⟨ill-fitting boots that had badly *chafed* my heels⟩
*syn* abrade, gall, irritate
*rel* graze, scrape, scratch; burn, inflame; flay, peel, skin
**2** to damage or diminish by continued friction — see ABRADE 1
**3** to disturb the peace of mind of (someone) especially by repeated disagreeable acts — see IRRITATE 1

**chaff** *n* **1** discarded or useless material — see GARBAGE
**2** good-natured teasing or exchanging of clever remarks — see BANTER

**chaff** *vb* to make fun of in a good-natured way — see TEASE 1

**chaffer** *vb* to talk over or dispute the terms of a purchase — see BARGAIN

**chaffing** *adj* marked by or expressive of mild or good-natured teasing — see QUIZZICAL

**chaffy** *adj* having no usefulness — see WORTHLESS

**chain** *n* **1** a series of things linked together ⟨the *chain* of events that led the American colonies to seek independence from Great Britain⟩
*syn* concatenation, progression, sequence, string, train
*rel* chain reaction; belt, circle, cycle; continuum, gamut, scale, spectrum; flow, river, stream; file, line, queue, row, succession
**2** something that makes movement or progress more difficult — see ENCUMBRANCE
**3** something that physically prevents free movement — see BOND 1

**chain** *vb* **1** to confine or restrain with or as if with chains — see BIND 1
**2** to put or bring together so as to form a new and longer whole — see CONNECT 1

**chair** *n* **1** a person in charge of a meeting ⟨all questions and comments should be directed to the *chair*⟩
*syn* chairman, chairperson, moderator, president, speaker
*rel* chairwoman
**2** the place of leadership or command — see HEAD 2

**chairman** *n* a person in charge of a meeting — see CHAIR 1

**chairperson** *n* a person in charge of a meeting — see CHAIR 1

**chalet** *n* an often small house for recreational or seasonal use — see COTTAGE

**challenge** *n* a feeling or declaration of disapproval or dissent — see OBJECTION

**challenge** *vb* **1** to demand proof of the truth or rightness of ⟨don't hesitate to *challenge* any statement that generalizes about people⟩
*syn* contest, dispute, query, question
*rel* doubt, mistrust; kick (about), object (to), protest; combat, fight, oppose, resist

---

*syn* synonym(s) *rel* related words
*ant* antonym(s) *near ant* near antonym(s)

*near ant* back, defend, support advocate, champion, promote; abide, endure, stomach, tolerate
*ant* accept, believe, embrace, swallow
**2** to invite (someone) to take part in a contest or to perform a feat ⟨ *challenge* you to swim to the other side of the pond⟩
*syn* dare, defy, stump
*rel* beard, brave, brazen, breast confront, face, outbrave

**challenged** *adj* deprived of the power to perform one or more natural bodily activities — see DISABLED

**challenger** *n* one who strives for the same thing as another — see COMPETITOR

**challenging** *adj* requiring much time, effort, or careful attention — see DEMANDING 1

**chamber** *n* **1** an area within a building that has been set apart from surrounding space by a wall — see ROOM 2
**2** one of the parts into which an enclosed space is divided — see COMPARTMENT

**chamber** *vb* to provide with living quarters or shelter — see HOUSE 1

**champ** *n* the person who comes in first in a competition — see CHAMPION 1

**champ** *vb* to crush or grind with the teeth — see BITE (ON)

**champion** *n* **1** the person who comes in first in a competition ⟨the *champion* of the national spelling bee⟩
*syn* champ, victor, winner
*rel* finalist, semifinalist; medalist, prizewinner; star, superstar
*near ant* loser
**2** a person who actively supports or favors a cause — see EXPONENT

**champion** *vb* to promote the interests or cause of — see SUPPORT 1

**championship** *n* the position occupied by the one who comes in first in a competition — see CROWN 2

**chance** *adj* happening by chance — see ACCIDENTAL

**chance** *n* **1** the uncertain course of events ⟨rather than leave everything to *chance*, let's plan how we're going to spend our time in New York City⟩
*syn* accident, circumstance, happ hazard, luck
*rel* fortuitousness, randomness, uncertainty; fluke; destiny, doom, fate, fortune, lot; danger, peril, risk
*near ant* intent, intention, purpose; design, outline, plan, scheme
**2** a favorable combination of circumstances, time, and place — see OPPORTUNITY
**3** a measure of how often an event will occur instead of another — see PROBABILITY 2
**4** a risky undertaking — see GAMBLE

**chance** *vb* **1** to take a chance on — see RISK 1
**2** to take place — see HAPPEN

**chance** (upon) *vb* **1** to come upon face-to-face or as if face-to-face — see MEET
**2** to come upon unexpectedly or by chance — see HAPPEN (ON *OR* UPON)

**change** *n* the act, process, or result of making different ⟨the positive *change* in our students' attitude toward people who are somehow different was a long and gradual process⟩
*syn* alteration, difference, modification, redoing, refashioning, remaking, remodeling, revamping, revise, revision, reworking, variation
*rel* amendment, correction, rectification; conversion, deformation, distortion, metamorphosis, mutation, transfiguration, transformation; fluctuation, oscillation, shift; displacement, replacement, substitution; adjustment, modulation, regulation
*ant* fixation, stabilization

**change** *vb* **1** to make different in some way ⟨Mother has *changed* the look of our living room more times than we care to remember⟩
*syn* alter, make over, modify, recast, redo, refashion, remake, remodel, revamp, revise, rework, vary
*rel* deform, metamorphose, mutate; revolutionize, transfigure, transform, transmute; commute, convert, exchange
*ant* fix, freeze, set, stabilize
**2** to pass from one form, state, or level to another ⟨the weather in New England is constantly *changing*⟩
*syn* fluctuate, mutate, shift, vary
*rel* metamorphose, transmute; better, improve; deteriorate, worsen; seesaw, teeter, vacillate, waver
*ant* stabilize
**3** to give up (something) and take something else in return ⟨would you mind *changing* your seat so my friends can sit together?⟩
*syn* commute, exchange, shift, substitute, swap, switch, trade
*rel* interchange; displace, replace, supersede; cede, surrender, yield

**changeable** *adj* **1** capable of being readily changed — see FLEXIBLE 1
**2** likely to change frequently, suddenly, or unexpectedly — see FICKLE 1

**changeful** *adj* likely to change frequently, suddenly, or unexpectedly — see FICKLE 1

**changeless** *adj* not undergoing a change in condition — see CONSTANT 1

**changelessness** *n* the state of continuing without change — see CONSTANCY 1

**changeover** *n* a change in form, appearance, or use — see CONVERSION

**changing** *adj* not staying constant — see UNEVEN 2

**channel** *n* **1** an open man-made passageway for water ⟨water was drained from the swamp through a specially constructed *channel*⟩
*syn* aqueduct, canal, conduit, flume, raceway, watercourse, waterway
*rel* millrace, millstream; river, rivulet, stream

2 a narrow body of water between two land masses ⟨the world record for swimming the *channel* between France and Great Britain⟩
*syn* narrows, sound, strait
*rel* arm, bay, gulf, inlet; roads, roadstead; reach, stretch
3 a direct way of passing along information or supplies — see PIPELINE
4 a long hollow cylinder for carrying a substance (as a liquid or gas) — see PIPE 1

**channel** *vb* to cause to move to a central point or along a restricted pathway ⟨an athletic youth who *channeled* all of his energy into sports⟩
*syn* channelize, conduct, direct, funnel, pipe, siphon
*rel* carry, convey, transmit; concentrate, consolidate, focus

**channelize** *vb* to cause to move to a central point or along a restricted pathway — see CHANNEL

**chant** *vb* 1 to utter in musical or drawn out tones ⟨the frustrated crowd at the rock concert started to *chant*, "We want the show to start!"⟩
*syn* intone, sing
*rel* bellow, belt, roar; chime, chorus
2 to produce musical sounds with the voice — see SING 1

**chaos** *n* a state in which everything is out of order ⟨your room is in such *chaos* that it looks as though a tornado had struck⟩
*syn* confusion, disarrangement, disarray, disorder, disorganization, havoc, hell, jumble, mess, muddle, shambles
*rel* anarchy, lawlessness, misrule; knot, snarl, tangle; labyrinth, maze, web; maelstrom, storm; clutter, litter, mishmash, shuffle; hodgepodge, medley, miscellany, motley
*near ant* method, pattern, plan, system
*ant* order, orderliness

**chaotic** *adj* lacking in order, neatness, and often cleanliness — see MESSY

**chap** *n, chiefly British* an adult male human being — see MAN 1

**chaparral** *n* a thick patch of shrubbery, small trees, or underbrush — see THICKET

**chaperone** *or* **chaperon** *vb* to go along with in order to provide assistance, protection, or companionship — see ACCOMPANY

**chapter** *n* a local unit of an organization ⟨our *chapter* of the 4-H Club came in first in the competition⟩
*syn* affiliate, branch, local
*rel* arm, division, wing; offshoot; lodge, post

**char** *vb* to burn on the surface — see SCORCH

**character** *n* 1 a written or printed mark that is meant to convey information to the reader ⟨the pictorial *characters* of the ancient Egyptians were long a mystery⟩
*syn* sign, symbol
*rel* cipher, letter, numeral; hieroglyph, pictogram, pictograph; rune
2 a person of odd or whimsical habits — see ECCENTRIC
3 conduct that conforms to an accepted standard of right and wrong — see MORALITY 1
4 overall quality as seen or judged by people in general — see REPUTATION
5 something that sets apart an individual from others of the same kind — see CHARACTERISTIC
6 the set of qualities that make a person different from other people — see INDIVIDUALITY
7 the set of qualities that makes a person, a group of people, or a thing different from others — see NATURE 1

**characteristic** *adj* 1 serving to identify as belonging to an individual or group ⟨the *characteristic* taste of licorice⟩
*syn* classic, distinct, distinctive, distinguishing, identifying, individual, peculiar, proper, symptomatic, typical
*rel* idiosyncratic; identifiable, pronounced, unmistakable; general, generic; common, normal, regular, usual; particular, special, specific; archetypal, model, paradigmatic
*ant* atypical, nontypical
2 having or showing the qualities associated with the members of a particular group or kind — see TYPICAL 1

**characteristic** *n* something that sets apart an individual from others of the same kind ⟨the ability to fashion tools and other *characteristics* that distinguish human beings from other animals⟩
*syn* attribute, character, feature, mark, peculiarity, point, property, quality, trait
*rel* badge, indication, sign; emblem, symbol, token; excellence, merit, virtue; individuality, singularity, uniqueness

**characterize** *vb* 1 to point out the chief quality or qualities of an individual or group ⟨how would you *characterize* the mission of this environmental organization?⟩
*syn* define, depict, describe, portray, represent
*rel* categorize, classify, pigeonhole, type; identify, indicate, name, specify; distinguish, individualize, mark, particularize, stamp
2 to be an important feature of ⟨an unsightly rash *characterizes* chicken pox⟩
*syn* distinguish, mark
*rel* differentiate; customize, individualize, particularize

**characterless** *adj* lacking strength of will or character — see WEAK 2

**charade** *n* a display of emotion or behavior that is insincere or intended to deceive — see MASQUERADE

**charge** *n* 1 a formal claim of criminal wrongdoing against a person ⟨*charges* of burglary and armed robbery that have yet to be proved⟩
*syn* complaint, count, indictment, rap

---

*syn* synonym(s) *rel* related words
*ant* antonym(s) *near ant* near antonym(s)

*rel* accusation, allegation; arraignment, impeachment; implication, innuendo, insinuation; censure, condemnation, denunciation; incrimination
**2** a specific task with which a person or group is charged — see MISSION
**3** a statement of what to do that must be obeyed by those concerned — see COMMAND 1
**4** something one must do because of prior agreement — see OBLIGATION
**5** the act or action of setting upon with force or violence — see ATTACK 1
**6** the amount of money that is demanded as payment for something — see PRICE 1
**7** the duty or function of watching or guarding for the sake of proper direction or control — see SUPERVISION 1

**charge** *vb* **1** to set or receive as a price ⟨any shop would *charge* $100 to repair that thing⟩
*syn* ask, command, demand
*rel* overcharge, undercharge; bring, fetch, sell (for); discount, mark down, mark up; assess, price, value
**2** to establish or apply as a charge or penalty — see IMPOSE
**3** to give a task, duty, or responsibility to — see ENTRUST 1
**4** to issue orders to (someone) by right of authority — see COMMAND 1
**5** to make a claim of wrongdoing against — see ACCUSE
**6** to put into (something) as much as can be held or contained — see FILL 1
**7** to take sudden, violent action against — see ATTACK 1

**charged** *adj* having or expressing great depth of feeling — see FERVENT

**charisma** *n* the power of irresistible attraction — see CHARM 2

**charitable** *adj* **1** having or showing a concern for the welfare of others ⟨a *charitable* couple who have donated a sizable chunk of their fortune to the local university⟩
*syn* altruistic, beneficent, benevolent, humanitarian, philanthropic
*rel* selfless, self-sacrificing; bounteous, bountiful, free, freehanded, generous, greathearted, handsome, liberal, magnanimous, munificent, openhanded openhearted, unselfish, unsparing; compassionate, humane, kind
*near ant* self-indulgent, self-seeking; cheap, closefisted, miserly, niggardly, parsimonious, stingy, tight, tightfisted; hardhearted, pitiless, unfeeling
*ant* self-centered, selfish
**2** giving or sharing in abundance and without hesitation — see GENEROUS 1

**charity** *n* **1** the giving of necessities and especially money to the needy ⟨after amassing a fortune in the computer industry, they devoted themselves to *charity*⟩
*syn* almsgiving, philanthropy
*rel* altruism, humanitarianism; beneficence, benevolence, goodwill; alms, benefaction, contribution, donation; dole, relief, welfare; endowment, fund, grant, subsidy
**2** a gift of money or its equivalent to a charity, humanitarian cause, or public institution — see CONTRIBUTION
**3** kind, gentle, or compassionate treatment especially towards someone who is undeserving of it — see MERCY 1
**4** the capacity for feeling for another's unhappiness or misfortune — see HEART 1

**charlatan** *n* one who makes false claims of identity or expertise — see IMPOSTOR

**charley horse** *n* a painful sudden tightening of a muscle — see CRAMP

**charm** *n* **1** something worn or kept to bring good luck or keep away evil ⟨an old cap that I use as a *charm* for whenever I play softball⟩
*syn* amulet, fetish (*also* fetich), mascot, mojo, phylactery, talisman
*rel* emblem, symbol, token, totem
*near ant* curse, hex, spell
*ant* hoodoo, jinx
**2** the power of irresistible attraction ⟨a young singer with the kind of *charm* that turns a performer into a star⟩
*syn* allure, appeal, attractiveness, captivation, charisma, enchantment, fascination, glamour (*also* glamor), magic, magnetism, seductiveness, witchery
*rel* allurement, attraction, call, lure, seduction; agreeableness, delightfulness, desirableness, niceness, pleasantness, sweetness
*near ant* disagreeableness, distastefulness, obnoxiousness, offensiveness, unpleasantness
*ant* repulsion, repulsiveness
**3** a spoken word or set of words believed to have magic power — see SPELL 1
**4** an ornament worn on a chain around the neck or wrist — see PENDANT

**charm** *vb* **1** to attract or delight as if by magic ⟨a quaint seaside village that *charms* all who visit it⟩
*syn* allure, beguile, bewitch, captivate, enchant, fascinate, magnetize, wile
*rel* disarm, draw, entice, lure, pull, seduce, tempt; delight, gratify, please; arrest, enrapture, enthrall (*or* enthral), entrance; appeal (to), interest, intrigue; beckon, court, invite, solicit, woo
*near ant* disgust, offend, repel, revolt; annoy, displease, irk; bore, tire, weary
**2** to cast a spell on — see BEWITCH 1

**charmed** *adj* being or appearing to be under a magic spell — see ENCHANTED

**charmer** *n* a person skilled in using supernatural forces — see MAGICIAN 1

**charming** *adj* having an often mysterious or magical power to attract — see FASCINATING 1

**chart** *n* an illustration of certain features of a geographical area — see MAP

**chart** *vb* to work out the details of (something) in advance — see PLAN 1

**charter** *vb* to take or give the temporary use of (something) for a set sum — see HIRE 1

**charwoman** *n* a female domestic servant — see MAID 1

**chase** *n* **1** an animal that is hunted or killed — see PREY
**2** the act of going after or in the tracks of another — see PURSUIT
**chase** *vb* **1** to drive or force out — see EJECT 1
**2** to go after or on the track of — see FOLLOW 2
**3** to seek out (game) for food or sport — see HUNT 1
**chasing** *n* the act of going after or in the tracks of another — see PURSUIT
**chasm** *n* an immeasurable depth or space — see ABYSS
**chaste** *adj* free from any trace of the coarse or indecent ⟨as one would expect, the minister's small talk is always *chaste*, even though he likes a joke as much as the next person⟩
***syn*** clean, decent, immaculate, modest, pure
***rel*** spotless, stainless, unblemished, undefiled, unsoiled, unspotted, unstained, unsullied, untainted, untarnished; decorous, proper, seemly; cultivated, refined, tasteful; harmless, innocent, innocuous, inoffensive
***near ant*** blemished, defiled, soiled, spotted, stained, sullied, tainted, tarnished; improper, indecorous, ribald, unseemly; crude, tacky, tasteless, unrefined
***ant*** coarse, dirty, filthy, immodest, impure, indecent, obscene, smutty, unchaste, unclean, vulgar
**chastely** *adv* with purity of thought and deed — see PURELY
**chasten** *vb* to inflict a penalty on for a fault or crime — see PUNISH
**chasteness** *n* the quality or state of being morally pure — see CHASTITY
**chastening** *adj* inflicting, involving, or serving as punishment — see PUNITIVE
**chastise** *vb* to inflict a penalty on for a fault or crime — see PUNISH
**chastisement** *n* suffering, loss, or hardship imposed in response to a crime or offense — see PUNISHMENT
**chastiser** *n* one who inflicts punishment in return for an injury or offense — see NEMESIS 1
**chastising** *adj* inflicting, involving, or serving as punishment — see PUNITIVE
**chastity** *n* the quality or state of being morally pure ⟨a saint who is often held up as a model of *chastity*⟩
***syn*** chasteness, modesty, purity
***rel*** goodness, righteousness, virtuousness; morality, probity, rectitude; decency, decorum, propriety, seemliness
***near ant*** badness, evil, sinfulness, unrighteousness, wickedness; impropriety, indecency
***ant*** immodesty, impurity, unchastity
**chat** *n* friendly, informal conversation or an instance of this ⟨short *chats* between parents and teachers during the school's open house⟩
***syn*** chatter, chitchat, gabfest, gossip, palaver, rap, small talk, table talk, talk, tête-à-tête
***rel*** colloquy, conference, discourse, parley, powwow, symposium; debate, dialogue (*or* dialog), exchange, give-and-take
**chat** *vb* to engage in casual or rambling conversation ⟨the coffeehouse is a great place to meet friends and *chat* for hours⟩
***syn*** babble, blab, cackle, chatter, converse, gab, gabble, gas, jabber, jaw, palaver, patter, prate, prattle, rap, rattle, run on, talk, twitter, visit
***rel*** gossip, tattle; descant, discuss, expatiate
***phrases*** shoot the breeze
**chat** (with) *vb* to communicate with by means of spoken words — see TALK 1
**château** *n* a large impressive residence — see MANSION
**chattel** *n* **1** a person who is considered the property of another person — see SLAVE 1
**2 chattels** *pl* transportable items that one owns — see POSSESSION 2
**chatter** *n* friendly, informal conversation or an instance of this — see CHAT
**chatter** *vb* **1** to engage in casual or rambling conversation — see CHAT
**2** to speak rapidly, inarticulately, and usually unintelligibly — see BABBLE 1
**chatterbox** *n* a person who talks constantly ⟨my seat companion was a *chatterbox* who never once shut up during the whole trip⟩
***syn*** babbler, blabber, cackler, chatterer, conversationalist, gabbler, jabberer, magpie, prattler, talker
***rel*** blabbermouth, gossip, gossiper, talebearer, tattler, tattletale; converser
**chatterer** *n* a person who talks constantly — see CHATTERBOX
**chatty** *adj* **1** having the style and content of everyday conversation ⟨a time when campers were expected to write a *chatty* letter to their folks every week⟩
***syn*** colloquial, conversational, gossipy, newsy
***rel*** casual, familiar, informal, intimate; digressive, discursive, rambling; communicative, expansive, garrulous, talkative
***near ant*** ceremonious, dignified, elevated, formal, solemn, stately
***ant*** bookish, literary
**2** fond of talking or conversation — see TALKATIVE
**chauvinism** *n* excessive favoritism towards one's own country ⟨their *chauvinism* blinded them to their country's faults⟩
***syn*** jingoism, nationalism
***rel*** loyalty, patriotism; xenophobia
***near ant*** internationalism
**chauvinist** *n* one who shows excessive favoritism towards his or her country — see NATIONALIST
**cheap** *adj* **1** costing little ⟨e-mail is so popular because it's a *cheap* way to send messages⟩
***syn*** cut-rate, inexpensive, low, reasonable

***syn*** synonym(s) ***rel*** related words
***ant*** antonym(s) ***near ant*** near antonym(s)

*rel* moderate, popular; discounted, lowered, reduced; wholesale
*near ant* precious, priceless, valuable; increased, inflated
*ant* costly, dear, expensive, high, premium
**2** of low quality ⟨a *cheap* sweater that started to unravel almost as soon as I bought it⟩
*syn* bad, bum, cheesy, coarse, common, cut-rate, execrable, inferior, junky, lousy, low-grade, mediocre, miserable, poor, rotten, rubbishy, second-rate, shoddy, sleazy, terrible, trashy, trumpery, wretched
*rel* useless, valueless, worthless; flashy, garish, gaudy, meretricious, showy, tawdry; seedy, shabby, tacky; counterfeit, fake, phony (*also* phoney), sham
*near ant* elegant, handsome, tasteful; handcrafted, polished, refined
*ant* excellent, fine, first-class, first-rate, good, high-grade, superior, top-notch
**3** giving or sharing as little as possible — see STINGY 1

**cheapen** *vb* to lower the price or value of — see DEPRECIATE 1

**cheapness** *n* the quality of being overly sparing with money — see PARSIMONY

**cheapskate** *n* a mean grasping person who is usually stingy with money — see MISER

**cheat** *n* a dishonest person who uses clever means to cheat others out of something of value — see TRICKSTER 1

**cheat** *vb* **1** to use dishonest methods to achieve a goal ⟨students who *cheat* on tests end up never knowing anything⟩
*syn* fudge
*rel* distort, falsify, misrepresent, twist; doctor, fake, tamper (with); color, elaborate, embellish, embroider, exaggerate, magnify, pad, stretch; dodge, evade, hedge
**2** to fall short in satisfying the expectation or hope of — see DISAPPOINT
**3** to rob by the use of trickery or threats — see FLEECE

**cheater** *n* a dishonest person who uses clever means to cheat others out of something of value — see TRICKSTER

**check** *n* **1** the amount owed at a bar or restaurant or the slip of paper stating the amount ⟨diners at the fancy restaurant often look shocked when they receive the *check*⟩
*syn* bill, tab
*rel* invoice, receipt; account, record, statement; charge, fee; score, tally
**2** a close look at or over someone or something in order to judge condition — see INSPECTION
**3** a record of goods sold or services performed together with the costs due — see [1]BILL 1
**4** a small sheet of plastic, paper, or paperboard showing that the bearer has a claim to something (as admittance) — see TICKET 1
**5** something that limits one's freedom of action or choice — see RESTRICTION 1

**check** *vb* **1** to be in agreement on every point ⟨their story of what happened *checks* with the report of the eyewitness⟩
*syn* accord, agree, answer, cohere, coincide, comport, conform, correspond, dovetail, fit, go, harmonize, jibe, square, tally
*rel* equal, match, parallel
*near ant* contradict, dispute, gainsay; negate, nullify; clash, conflict, jar
*ant* differ (from), disagree (with)
**2** to bring (something) to a standstill — see [1]HALT 1
**3** to keep from exceeding a desirable degree or level (as of expression) — see CONTROL 1

**check** (out) *vb* to look over closely (as for judging quality or condition) — see INSPECT

**checklist** *n* a record of a series of items (as names or titles) usually arranged according to some system — see [1]LIST

**checkmate** *vb* to prevent from achieving a goal — see FRUSTRATE

**checkup** *n* a close look at or over someone or something in order to judge condition — see INSPECTION

**cheek** *n* **1** disrespectful or argumentative talk given in response to a command or request — see BACK TALK
**2** shameless boldness — see EFFRONTERY

**cheekiness** *n* shameless boldness — see EFFRONTERY

**cheeky** *adj* displaying or marked by rude boldness — see NERVY 1

**cheep** *vb* to make a short sharp sound like a small bird — see CHIRP

**cheer** *n* **1** a mood characterized by high spirits and amusement and often accompanied by laughter — see MIRTH
**2** a feeling of ease from grief or trouble — see COMFORT 1
**3** a state of mind dominated by a particular emotion — see MOOD 1
**4 cheers** *pl* enthusiastic and usually public expression of approval — see APPLAUSE

**cheer** *vb* **1** to declare enthusiastic approval of — see ACCLAIM
**2** to ease the grief or distress of — see COMFORT 1

**cheer** (up) *vb* **1** to become glad or hopeful ⟨*cheer up* —things are bound to get better⟩
*syn* brighten, perk (up)
*rel* rejoice; liven (up), revive; beam, glow, radiate, sparkle; encourage, gladden, hearten
*near ant* despair, despond; brood, fret, mope
*ant* darken, sadden
**2** to fill with courage or strength of purpose — see ENCOURAGE 1

**cheerful** *adj* **1** having or showing a good mood or disposition ⟨a *cheerful* person who is always fun to work with and a pleasure to be around⟩

*syn* blithe, blithesome, bright, buoyant, cheery, chipper, gay, gladsome, lightsome, sunny, upbeat
*rel* hopeful, optimistic, sanguine; jaunty, lively, perky, sprightly, vivacious; carefree, careless, cavalier, devil-may-care, easygoing, happy-go-lucky, insouciant, lighthearted, unconcerned; boon, jolly, jovial, merry, mirthful; glad, happy, pleased
*near ant* dull, lethargic, listless, sluggish, torpid; blue, dejected, depressed, heavy-hearted, melancholy, sorrowful; discontented, disgruntled, unhappy
*ant* dour, gloomy, glum, morose, saturnine, sulky, sullen
**2** serving to lift one's spirits ⟨a hospital with sunny, *cheerful* rooms that are designed to make a patient's stay as pleasant as possible⟩
*syn* bright, cheering, cheery, gay, glad
*rel* gladdening, heartening, heartwarming; gleaming, radiant, sparkling
*near ant* discouraging, disheartening; colorless, drab, dull, lackluster, lusterless
*ant* bleak, cheerless, dark, depressing, dismal, dreary, gloomy, gray (*also* grey)

**cheerfully** *adv* in a cheerful or happy manner — see GAILY 1

**cheerfulness** *n* a mood characterized by high spirits and amusement and often accompanied by laughter — see MIRTH

**cheeriness** *n* a mood characterized by high spirits and amusement and often accompanied by laughter — see MIRTH

**cheering** *adj* **1** making one feel good inside — see HEARTWARMING
**2** serving to lift one's spirits — see CHEERFUL 2

**cheering** *n* enthusiastic and usually public expression of approval — see APPLAUSE

**cheerless** *adj* causing or marked by an atmosphere lacking in cheer — see GLOOMY 1

**cheery** *adj* **1** having or showing a good mood or disposition — see CHEERFUL 1
**2** serving to lift one's spirits — see CHEERFUL 2

**cheesy** *adj* **1** marked by an obvious lack of style or good taste — see TACKY 1
**2** of low quality — see CHEAP 2

**chef** *n* a person who prepares food by some manner of heating — see COOK

**cherish** *vb* **1** to feel passion, devotion, or tenderness for — see LOVE 2
**2** to hold dear — see LOVE 1
**3** to keep in one's mind or heart — see HARBOR 1

**cherished** *adj* granted special treatment or attention — see DARLING 1

**chest** *n* a covered rectangular container for storing or transporting things ⟨a *chest* containing almost every tool that the home do-it-yourselfer is likely to need⟩
*syn* box, caddy, case, casket, locker, trunk
*rel* crate; footlocker; coffer, safe, safe-deposit box, strongbox; coffin; compartment, vault

**chesterfield** *n* a long upholstered piece of furniture designed for several sitters — see COUCH

**chew** *vb* to crush or grind with the teeth — see BITE (ON)

**chew out** *vb* to criticize (someone) severely or angrily especially for personal failings — see SCOLD

**chew over** *vb* **1** to give serious and careful thought to — see PONDER
**2** to talk about (an issue) usually from various points of view and for the purpose of arriving at a decision or opinion — see DISCUSS

**chewy** *adj* not easily chewed — see TOUGH 1

**chic** *adj* being in the latest or current fashion — see STYLISH

**chicanery** *n* the use of clever underhanded actions to achieve an end — see TRICKERY

**chick** *n, slang* a young usually unmarried woman — see GIRL 1

**chicken** *adj* having or showing a shameful lack of courage — see COWARDLY

**chicken** *n* a person who shows a shameful lack of courage in the face of danger — see COWARD

**chickenhearted** *adj* having or showing a shameful lack of courage — see COWARDLY

**chide** *vb* to criticize (someone) usually gently so as to correct a fault — see REBUKE 1

**chief** *adj* **1** coming before all others in importance — see FOREMOST 1
**2** highest in rank or authority — see HEAD

**chief** *n* the person (as an employer or supervisor) who tells people and especially workers what to do — see BOSS

**chiefly** *adv* for the most part ⟨our video collection consists *chiefly* of comedies, but we have a few horror movies⟩
*syn* altogether, basically, by and large, generally, largely, mainly, mostly, overall, predominantly, primarily, principally, substantially
*rel* nearly, practically, virtually; approximately, broadly, roughly; commonly, frequently, normally, ordinarily, usually; incompletely, partially, partly
*phrases* in general, on the whole
*near ant* completely, entirely, fully, totally, wholly; barely, hardly, marginally, minimally, scarcely

**child** *n* **1** a young person who is between infancy and adulthood ⟨an imaginative animated film that appeals to adults as well as to *children*⟩
*syn* bairn [*chiefly Scottish*], cub, juvenile, kid, youngster, youth
*rel* adolescent, minor; schoolboy, schoolchild, schoolgirl; moppet, nestling, toddler, tot, tyke; brat, imp, squirt, urchin, whippersnapper; cherub; preteen, subteen, teenager, teenybopper; lad, nipper,

shaver, stripling, tad; bobby-soxer, hoyden, tomboy
*near ant* golden-ager, oldster, senior citizen
*ant* adult, grown-up
2 a recently born person — see BABY

**childbearing** *n* the act or process of giving birth to children — see CHILDBIRTH

**childbirth** *n* the act or process of giving birth to children ⟨women who choose to undergo *childbirth* without the use of anesthetics and other drugs⟩
*syn* childbearing, delivery, labor, parturition
*rel* pains; pregnancy; abortion, miscarriage; cesarean section (*also* cesarian section)

**childhood** *n* the state or time of being a child ⟨enjoy your *childhood* — it won't last forever⟩
*syn* youth
*rel* boyhood, girlhood; adolescence, minority; immaturity, juvenility; babyhood, infancy
*near ant* majority
*ant* adulthood

**childish** *adj* having or showing the annoying qualities (as silliness) associated with children ⟨you almost spoiled the ceremony for everyone with your *childish* giggling⟩
*syn* adolescent, babyish, immature, infantile, juvenile, kiddish, puerile
*rel* boyish, girlish; childlike, innocent, naive (*or* naïve), simple, unsophisticated
*near ant* experienced, sophisticated, worldly-wise
*ant* adult, grown-up, mature

**child's play** *n* 1 something of little importance — see TRIFLE
2 something that is easy to do — see CINCH

**chill** *adj* 1 lacking in friendliness or warmth of feeling — see COLD 2
2 uncomfortably cool — see CHILLY 1

**chill** *n* an uncomfortable degree of coolness ⟨there's a *chill* in the air, so you'd better wear a sweater⟩
*syn* bite, bitterness, bleakness, chilliness, nip, rawness, sharpness
*rel* briskness, crispness; coldness, frigidity, frigidness, frostiness, iciness; cold, freeze, snap
*near ant* balminess, warmth

**chill** *vb* to cause to lose heat — see COOL 1

**chilliness** *n* an uncomfortable degree of coolness — see CHILL

**chilling** *adj* uncomfortably cool — see CHILLY 1

**chilly** *adj* 1 uncomfortably cool ⟨those *chilly* nights when a warm fire can be especially comforting⟩
*syn* bitter, bleak, chill, chilling, nippy, raw, sharp
*rel* brisk, crisp; arctic, cold, freezing, frigid, frosty, icy
*near ant* balmy, warm
2 lacking in friendliness or warmth of feeling — see COLD 2

**chime** *vb* to make the clear sound heard when metal vibrates — see RING 1

**chime** *n, usually* **chimes** *pl* a series of short high ringing sounds — see TINKLE

**chime in** *vb* to cause a disruption in a conversation or discussion — see INTERRUPT

**chimera** *n* a conception or image created by the imagination and having no objective reality — see FANTASY 1

**chimerical** *adj* not real and existing only in the imagination — see IMAGINARY

**chine** *n* a column of bones supporting the trunk of a vertebrate animal — see SPINE

**chink** *n* an irregular usually narrow break in a surface created by pressure — see CRACK 1

**chink** *vb* to make a repeated sharp light ringing sound — see JINGLE

**chip** *n* 1 a small flat piece separated from a whole ⟨wood *chips* were spread over the ground between the plants⟩
*syn* flake, sliver, splint, splinter
*rel* bit, disk (*or* disc), fragment, particle, scrap, shard; shiver, smithereens; shred, tatter; clipping, paring, shaving, snippet; leaf, sheet, slice; chunk, hunk, lump, slab
2 a V-shaped cut usually on an edge or a surface — see NOTCH 1
3 **chips** *pl* something (as pieces of stamped metal or printed paper) customarily and legally used as a medium of exchange, a measure of value, or a means of payment — see MONEY

**chip in** *vb* to make a donation as part of a group effort — see CONTRIBUTE 1

**chipper** *adj* 1 enjoying health and vigor — see HEALTHY 1
2 having or showing a good mood or disposition — see CHEERFUL 1

**chirp** *vb* to make a short sharp sound like a small bird ⟨the sparrows were *chirping* up a storm in the backyard⟩
*syn* cheep, chirrup, peep, pipe, tweet, twitter
*rel* cackle, chatter, jabber; sing, trill, warble

**chirr** *n* a monotonous sound like that of an insect in motion — see HUM

**chirrup** *vb* to make a short sharp sound like a small bird — see CHIRP

**chisel** *vb* to rob by the use of trickery or threats — see FLEECE

**chitchat** *n* friendly, informal conversation or an instance of this — see CHAT

**chivalrous** *adj* having, characterized by, or arising from a dignified and generous nature — see NOBLE 2

**chivy** *vb* to thrust oneself upon (another) without invitation — see BOTHER 1

**chock-full** *or* **chockful** *adj* containing or seeming to contain the greatest quantity or number possible — see FULL 1

**choice** *adj* having qualities that appeal to a refined taste ⟨*choice* chocolates for which chocolate lovers are willing to pay extra⟩
*syn* dainty, delicate, elegant, exquisite, rare, select
*rel* elite, exclusive; excellent, outstanding, premium, prime, superior

*near ant* coarse, gross, vulgar; commercial, mass-produced, popular; common, ordinary; average, mediocre, run-of-the-mill, second-rate

**choice** *n* **1** the power, right, or opportunity to choose ⟨you have no *choice* : you have to go to school⟩
*syn* alternative, discretion, option, pick, preference, way
*rel* say, voice, vote; inclination, liking, partiality, penchant, predilection, proclivity, propensity, tendency; discernment, judgment (*or* judgement), perspicacity
*near ant* coercion, duress, force; duty, obligation
**2** a person or thing that is chosen ⟨my *choice* for best song of all time⟩
*syn* pick, selection
*rel* favorite, like, liking, preference; elective, option; appointment, designation, nomination; appointee, candidate, nominee
**3** individuals carefully selected as being the best of a class — see ELITE
**4** the act or power of making one's own choices or decisions — see FREE WILL
**5** the act or process of selecting — see SELECTION 1

**choir** *n* an organized group of singers — see CHORUS 1

**choke** *vb* **1** to keep (someone) from breathing by exerting pressure on the windpipe ⟨let go of my throat—you're *choking* me!⟩
*syn* garrote (*or* garotte), strangle, throttle
*rel* asphyxiate, smother, suffocate
*near ant* restore, resuscitate, revive
**2** to experience complete or partial blockage of the windpipe ⟨the recommended procedure for helping someone who is *choking*⟩
*syn* gag
*rel* heave, retch, throw up, vomit; asphyxiate, smother, suffocate
*near ant* breathe, respire
**3** to be or cause to be killed by lack of breathable air — see SMOTHER 1
**4** to prevent passage through — see CLOG 1

**choke** (back) *vb* to refrain from openly showing or uttering — see SUPPRESS 2

**choker** *n* an ornamental chain or string (as of beads) worn around the neck — see NECKLACE

**choleric** *adj* easily irritated or annoyed — see IRRITABLE

**chomp** (on) *vb* to crush or grind with the teeth — see BITE (ON)

**choose** *vb* **1** to decide to accept (someone or something) from a group of possibilities ⟨*choose* a computer that best suits your needs⟩
*syn* cull, elect, handpick, name, opt (for), pick, prefer, select, single (out), take
*rel* appoint, designate, nominate, tab; accept, adopt, embrace, espouse
*near ant* discard, jettison, throw away, throw out
*ant* decline, refuse, reject, turn down
**2** to see fit ⟨you can wear whatever you *choose* to the party⟩
*syn* like, want, will, wish
*rel* crave, desire, fancy, hanker (for), hunger (for), long (for), yearn (for); decide, determine, resolve
**3** to come to a judgment after discussion or consideration — see DECIDE 1

**chooser** *n* someone with the right or responsibility for making a selection — see SELECTOR

**choosing** *n* the act or process of selecting — see SELECTION 1

**choosy** *or* **choosey** *adj* **1** hard to please — see FINICKY
**2** tending to select carefully — see SELECTIVE

**chop** *n* a hard strike with a part of the body or an instrument — see [1]BLOW

**chop** *vb* to cut into small pieces ⟨*chop* the onions before adding them to the pot⟩
*syn* dice, hash, mince
*rel* chip, grind, mash, puree, slice

**chop** (down) *vb* to bring down by cutting — see FELL 2

**choppy** *adj* lacking in steadiness or regularity of occurrence — see FITFUL

**chorale** *n* **1** a religious song — see HYMN
**2** an organized group of singers — see CHORUS 1

**chore** *n* **1** a piece of work that needs to be done regularly ⟨everyone in this household is expected to do weekly *chores*⟩
*syn* assignment, duty, job, stint, task
*rel* endeavor, enterprise, project, undertaking; care, charge, commission, responsibility; function, mission, office; errand; circuit, round, route
**2** a dull, unpleasant, or difficult piece of work ⟨cleaning everything out of the attic was a real *chore*⟩
*syn* headache, labor
*rel* drudgery, grind; effort, strain, sweat; burden, load, weight; bother, nuisance, trouble
*near ant* breeze, child's play, cinch, duck soup, snap

**chortle** *n* an explosive sound that is a sign of amusement — see LAUGH 1

**chorus** *n* **1** an organized group of singers ⟨the annual Christmas program presented by the school's *chorus*⟩
*syn* choir, chorale, glee club
*rel* ensemble; minstrelsy
**2** a part of a song or hymn that is repeated every so often ⟨the whole congregation will join in for the *chorus*⟩
*syn* burden, refrain
*rel* repeat

**chosen** *adj* singled out from a number or group as more to one's liking — see SELECT 1

**chow** *n* **1** food eaten or prepared for eating at one time — see MEAL
**2** substances intended to be eaten — see FOOD

---

*syn* synonym(s) *rel* related words
*ant* antonym(s) *near ant* near antonym(s)

**christen** *vb* to give a name to — see NAME 1
**Christian name** *n* a name that is placed before one's family name — see FORENAME
**Christmastime** *n* the season celebrating Christmas — see YULETIDE
**chronic** *adj* being such by habit and not likely to change — see HABITUAL 1
**chronicle** *n* **1** a relating of events usually in the order in which they happened — see ACCOUNT 1
**2** an account of important events in the order in which they happened — see HISTORY 1
**chronicler** *n* a student or writer of history — see HISTORIAN
**chronometer** *n* a device to measure time — see TIMEPIECE
**chubbiness** *n* the condition of having an excess of body fat — see CORPULENCE
**chubby** *adj* having an excess of body fat — see FAT 1
**chuck** *vb* to send through the air especially with a quick forward motion of the arm — see THROW
**chuckle** *n* an explosive sound that is a sign of amusement — see LAUGH 1
**chum** *n* a person who has a strong liking for and trust in another — see FRIEND 1
**chum** *vb* to come or be together as friends — see ASSOCIATE 1
**chumminess** *n* the state of being in a very personal or private relationship — see FAMILIARITY 1
**chummy** *adj* closely acquainted — see FAMILIAR 1
**chump** *n* one who is easily deceived or cheated — see DUPE
**chunk** *n* a small uneven mass — see LUMP 1
**chunky** *adj* **1** having small pieces or lumps spread throughout ⟨*chunky* peanut butter adds an interesting layer of texture when paired with jelly⟩
*syn* clumpy, curdy, lumpy, nubbly, nubby
*rel* ropy, thick, viscous; clabbered [*dialect*], clotted, coagulated, congealed, curdled, gelled, thickened
*ant* smooth
**2** being compact and broad in build and often short in stature — see STOCKY
**3** having or being of relatively great depth or extent from one surface to its opposite — see THICK 1
**church** *n* **1** a building for public worship and especially Christian worship ⟨a city that is noted for its many historic *churches*⟩
*syn* kirk [*chiefly Scottish*], tabernacle, temple
*rel* abbey, bethel, cathedral, chapel, oratory, sanctuary, shrine; meetinghouse; mosque, pagoda, synagogue (*or* synagog)
**2** a body of persons gathered for religious worship — see CONGREGATION 1
**churchly** *adj* of or relating to a church — see ECCLESIASTICAL
**churl** *n* a person whose behavior is offensive to others — see JERK 1
**churlish** *adj* having or showing crudely insensitive or impolite manners — see CLOWNISH
**churn** *vb* **1** to be in a state of violent rolling motion — see SEETHE 1
**2** to cause (as a liquid) to move about in a circle especially repeatedly — see STIR 1
**chutzpah** *also* **chutzpa** *or* **hutzpah** *or* **hutzpa** *n* shameless boldness — see EFFRONTERY
**cinch** *n* something that is easy to do ⟨the clear instructions made setting up the audiovisual system a *cinch*⟩
*syn* breeze, child's play, duck soup, picnic, pushover, snap
*rel* nothing; sitting duck
*phrases* piece of cake
*near ant* bother, nuisance, trouble
*ant* chore, headache, labor
**cinch** *vb* to make sure, certain, or safe — see ENSURE
**cincture** *n* a strip of flexible material (as leather) worn around the waist — see ²BELT
**cinema** *n* **1** the art or business of making a movie — see MOVIE 2
**2** a building or part of a building where movies are shown — see THEATER 1
**cipher** *n* the numerical symbol 0 or the absence of number or quantity represented by it — see ZERO 1
**ciphering** *n* the act or process of performing mathematical operations to find a value — see CALCULATION
**circle** *n* **1** something with a perfectly round circumference ⟨a *circle* of columns surrounds the memorial to the fallen heroes⟩
*syn* ring, round
*rel* circlet; ellipse, loop, oval; ball, globe, orb, sphere
**2** a circular strip — see RING 2
**3** a group of people sharing a common interest and relating together socially — see GANG 2
**4** a series of events or actions that repeat themselves regularly and in the same order — see CYCLE 1
**circle** *vb* **1** to form a circle around — see SURROUND
**2** to pass completely around — see ENCIRCLE 1
**circuitous** *adj* **1** not straightforward or direct — see INDIRECT
**2** using or containing more words than necessary to express an idea — see WORDY
**circular** *adj* not straightforward or direct — see INDIRECT
**circular** *n* a short printed publication with no cover or with a paper cover — see PAMPHLET
**circulate** *vb* **1** to cause to be known over a considerable area or by many people — see SPREAD 1
**2** to make (as a piece of information) the subject of common talk without any au-

thority or confirmation of accuracy — see RUMOR

**circumference** *n* **1** the distance around a round body ⟨the *circumference* of the earth at the equator⟩
***syn*** girth
***rel*** waistline; equator; diameter, perimeter
**2** the line or relatively narrow space that marks the outer limit of something — see BORDER 1

**circumlocution** *n* the use of too many words to express an idea — see VERBIAGE

**circumlocutory** *adj* using or containing more words than necessary to express an idea — see WORDY

**circumnavigate** *vb* to pass completely around — see ENCIRCLE 1

**circumscribe** *vb* **1** to set bounds or an upper limit for — see LIMIT 1
**2** to mark the limits of — see LIMIT 2

**circumscribed** *adj* having distinct or certain limits — see LIMITED 1

**circumspect** *adj* having or showing a close attentiveness to avoiding danger or trouble — see CAREFUL 1

**circumspection** *n* a close attentiveness to avoiding danger — see CAUTION 1

**circumstance** *n* **1** a state or end that seemingly has been decided beforehand — see FATE 1
**2** something that happens — see EVENT 1
**3** the uncertain course of events — see CHANCE 1

**circumstantial** *adj* including many small descriptive features — see DETAILED 1

**circumvent** *vb* **1** to avoid having to comply with (something) especially through cleverness ⟨students who try to *circumvent* the school's dress code⟩
***syn*** dodge, sidestep, skirt
***rel*** avoid, duck, elude, escape, eschew, evade, shake, shun; disobey, disregard, flout, ignore
***phrases*** get around
***near ant*** accede (to), acquiesce (to), assent (to)
***ant*** comply (with), follow, keep, obey, observe
**2** to avoid by going around — see DETOUR 1

**circus** *n* **1** a large usually roofless building for sporting events with tiers of seats for spectators — see STADIUM
**2** a place of uproar or confusion — see MADHOUSE 2

**citadel** *n* a structure or place from which one can resist attack — see FORT

**citation** *n* **1** a formal expression of praise — see ENCOMIUM
**2** a formal recognition of an achievement or praiseworthy deed — see COMMENDATION 1
**3** a passage referred to, repeated, or offered as an example — see QUOTATION

**cite** *vb* **1** to give as an example — see QUOTE 1
**2** to make reference to or speak about briefly but specifically — see MENTION 1

**citify** *vb* to accustom to the ways of the city ⟨we've become so *citified* that many people have no idea where their food comes from⟩
***syn*** urbanize
***rel*** civilize, cultivate

**citizen** *n* **1** a person who owes allegiance to a government and is protected by it ⟨conscientious *citizens* who regard voting as a duty as well as a right⟩
***syn*** national, subject
***rel*** compatriot, countryman; inhabitant, native, nonimmigrant, resident
***near ant*** foreigner, stranger; immigrant, nonnative
***ant*** alien, noncitizen
**2** a person who lives in a town on a permanent basis — see BURGHER

**city** *n* a thickly settled, highly populated area ⟨commuters who drive every day between their homes in the suburbs and their jobs in the *city*⟩
***syn*** burg, megalopolis, metropolis, municipality, town
***rel*** borough; conurbation; urban sprawl; suburbia

**civil** *adj* **1** of or relating to a nation — see NATIONAL
**2** showing consideration, courtesy, and good manners — see POLITE 1

**civility** *n* **1** an act or utterance that is a customary show of good manners ⟨after the usual *civilities*, the parents and the principal had a serious talk about the boy⟩
***syn*** amenity, courtesy, formality, gesture
***rel*** ceremony, observance, rite, ritual; etiquette, manners, proprieties; greetings, regards, respects; favor, grace, kindness
**2** speech or behavior that is a sign of good breeding — see POLITENESS

**civilization** *n* **1** the way people live at a particular time and place ⟨a study unit on the advanced *civilization* created by the Mayas over a thousand years ago⟩
***syn*** culture, life, lifestyle, society
***rel*** customs, manners, mores, values; folklore, heritage, tradition
**2** a high level of taste and enlightenment as a result of extensive intellectual training and exposure to the arts — see CULTURE 1

**civilized** *adj* having or showing a taste for the fine arts and gracious living — see CULTIVATED

**clack** *vb* to make a series of short sharp noises — see RATTLE 1

**claim** *n* **1** an entitlement to something ⟨I'm announcing my *claim* to that last slice of pizza⟩
***syn*** call, pretense (*or* pretence), pretension, right
***rel*** birthright, prerogative; favor, privilege; refusal
**2** a legal right to participation in the advantages, profits, and responsibility of something — see INTEREST 1

---

***syn*** synonym(s) ***rel*** related words
***ant*** antonym(s) ***near ant*** near antonym(s)

3 a solemn and often public declaration of the truth or existence of something — see PROTESTATION
4 something that someone insists upon having — see DEMAND 1

**claim** *vb* 1 to state as a fact usually forcefully ⟨people who *claim* that they have been kidnapped by aliens from other worlds⟩
*syn* affirm, allege, assert, aver, avouch, avow, contend, declare, insist, maintain, profess, protest, warrant
*rel* announce, broadcast, proclaim; argue, rationalize, reason; confirm, justify, vindicate; defend, support, uphold
*near ant* disavow, disclaim, disown; challenge, dispute, question; confute, disprove, rebut, refute; contradict
*ant* deny, gainsay
2 to ask for (something) earnestly or with authority — see DEMAND 1

**clairvoyance** *n* the power of seeing or knowing about things that are not present to the senses ⟨people who claim to have *clairvoyance* are sometimes asked to help locate missing persons⟩
*syn* extrasensory perception, sixth sense
*rel* foreknowledge, foresight, prescience; telepathy

**clamber** *vb* to move (as up or over something) often with the help of the hands in holding or pulling — see CLIMB 1

**clamor** *n* 1 a violent shouting ⟨a *clamor* arose from the crowd as the prisoner was brought forward⟩
*syn* howl, hubbub, hue and cry, hullabaloo, noise, outcry, roar, tumult, uproar
*rel* clangor, din, jangle, racket
*near ant* mumble, mumbling, murmur, murmuring, rumble, rumbling
2 loud, confused, and usually unharmonious sound — see NOISE 1

**clamor** (for) *vb* to ask for (something) earnestly or with authority — see DEMAND 1

**clamorous** *adj* 1 engaging in or marked by loud and insistent cries especially of protest — see VOCIFEROUS
2 full of or characterized by the presence of noise — see NOISY 2
3 marked by a high volume of sound — see LOUD 1

**clamp** *vb* to put securely in place or in a desired position — see FASTEN 2

**clamp down** (on) *vb* to put a stop to (something) by the use of force — see QUELL 1

**clam up** *vb* to stop talking — see SHUT UP

**clan** *n* 1 a group of people sharing a common interest and relating together socially — see GANG 2
2 a group of persons who come from the same ancestor — see FAMILY 1

**clandestine** *adj* undertaken or done so as to escape being observed or known by others — see SECRET 1

**clang** *n* the loud sound made when metal strikes metal ⟨the horseshoe hit the stake with a satisfying *clang*⟩
*syn* clangor, clank, clash
*rel* chime, dingdong, peal, ring; clink, jangle, jingle, tinkle; clap, clop, crack, crash

**clangor** *n* 1 loud, confused, and usually unharmonious sound — see NOISE 1
2 the loud sound made when metal strikes metal — see CLANG

**clangorous** *adj* 1 full of or characterized by the presence of noise — see NOISY 2
2 making loud, confused, and usually unharmonious sounds — see NOISY 1
3 marked by a high volume of sound — see LOUD 1

**clank** *n* the loud sound made when metal strikes metal — see CLANG

**clannish** *adj* bound together by feelings of very close association — see CLOSE-KNIT

**clap** *n* 1 a loud explosive sound ⟨a *clap* of thunder that woke the whole house up⟩
*syn* bang, blast, boom, crack, crash, pop, report, slam, smash, snap, thwack, whack
*rel* clang, clangor, clank, clash; knock, rap, tap; clamor, howl, hubbub, hue and cry, hullabaloo, outcry, roar, tumult, uproar
2 a hard strike with a part of the body or an instrument — see [1]BLOW

**clap** *vb* to deliver a blow to (someone or something) usually in a strong vigorous manner — see HIT 1

**claptrap** *n* 1 language, behavior, or ideas that are absurd and contrary to good sense — see NONSENSE 1
2 unintelligible or meaningless talk — see GIBBERISH

**clarification** *n* a statement that makes something clear — see EXPLANATION 1

**clarify** *vb* 1 to remove usually visible impurities from ⟨*clarify* the melted butter by skimming off the milky bits⟩
*syn* clear, distill, filter, purify
*rel* process, refine; clean, cleanse, purge; extract, leach; screen, sieve, sift
*near ant* cloud, dull, muddy; contaminate, dirty, soil
2 to make plain or understandable — see EXPLAIN 1

**clarity** *n* 1 the state or quality of being easily seen through ⟨mountain streams with water of incredible *clarity*⟩
*syn* clearness, limpidity, limpidness, transparency
*rel* lucidity, lucidness, translucency; brightness, brilliance, effulgence, luminosity, luminousness; definition, resolution, sharpness
*near ant* fogginess, haziness, murkiness
*ant* cloudiness, opacity, opaqueness
2 clearness of expression — see SIMPLICITY 2

**clash** *n* 1 a physical dispute between opposing individuals or groups — see FIGHT 1
2 the loud sound made when metal strikes metal — see CLANG

**clash** *vb* to be out of harmony or agreement usually noticeably ⟨the colors of your shirt and pants *clash*⟩ ⟨Mom's idea of proper dress often *clashes* with mine⟩
*syn* collide, conflict, jar

*rel* mismatch; battle, combat, fight, war (against); chafe, gall, grate, jangle; differ, disagree
*near ant* agree, coincide, correspond
*ant* blend, harmonize, match

**clash** (with) *vb* to oppose (someone) in physical conflict — see FIGHT 1

**clashing** *adj* not being in agreement or harmony — see INCONSISTENT

**clasp** *n* the act or manner of holding — see HOLD 1

**clasp** *vb* **1** to put one's arms around and press tightly — see EMBRACE 1
**2** to reach for and take hold of by embracing with the fingers or arms — see TAKE 1

**class** *n* **1** one of the segments of society into which people are grouped ⟨a politician who appeals to people of every *class*⟩
*syn* caste, estate, folk, order, stratum
*rel* bracket, echelon, grade, layer, level, tier; place, position, rank, standing, status; grouping, hierarchy, stratification; clan, family, people, race, tribe
**2** one of the units into which a whole is divided on the basis of a common characteristic ⟨a new *class* of wireless devices that could be used for Internet access as well as personal communication⟩
*syn* bracket, category, division, family, grade, group, kind, order, rank(s), set, species, type
*rel* description, feather, ilk, nature, sort; branch, section, subdivision, subgroup, variety; breed, race; classification, heading, label, rubric, title
**3** a number of persons or things that are grouped together because they have something in common — see SORT 1
**4** a series of lectures on a subject — see COURSE 2
**5** degree of excellence — see QUALITY 1
**6** dignified or restrained beauty of form, appearance, or style — see ELEGANCE
**7** high position within society — see RANK 2

**class** *vb* to arrange or assign according to type — see CLASSIFY 1

**classic** *adj* **1** constituting, serving as, or worthy of being a pattern to be imitated — see MODEL
**2** of the very best kind — see EXCELLENT
**3** serving to identify as belonging to an individual or group — see CHARACTERISTIC 1

**classic** *n* **1** someone of such unequaled perfection as to deserve imitation — see IDEAL 1
**2** something (as a work of art) that is a great achievement and often its creator's greatest achievement — see MASTERPIECE
**3** the most perfect type or example — see QUINTESSENCE 1

**classical** *adj* based on customs usually handed down from a previous generation — see TRADITIONAL 1

**classify** *vb* **1** to arrange or assign according to type ⟨*classify* the baseball cards in your collection on the basis of rarity⟩
*syn* assort, break down, categorize, class, grade, group, peg, place, range, rank, separate, sort
*rel* arrange, order, organize, systematize; alphabetize, catalog (*or* catalogue), codify, file, index, list; pigeonhole, shelve; distinguish, identify, recognize; cull, screen, sift, winnow
*near ant* confuse, disarrange, jumble, lump, mix (up), scramble
**2** to put into a particular arrangement — see ORDER 1

**clatter** *n* a state of noisy, confused activity — see COMMOTION

**clatter** *vb* to make a series of short sharp noises — see RATTLE 1

**clattering** *adj* full of or characterized by the presence of noise — see NOISY 2

**clattery** *adj* full of or characterized by the presence of noise — see NOISY 2

**clean** *adj* **1** free from dirt or stain ⟨although the soccer team always starts out with *clean* uniforms, they don't stay that way for long⟩
*syn* immaculate, spick-and-span (*or* spic-and-span), spotless, stainless, unsoiled, unsullied
*rel* pure, taintless, undefiled, unpolluted, untainted, wholesome; cleanly, hygienic, sanitary; bleached, cleansed, purified, whitened; milky, snowy, white; flawless, unblemished; bright, shiny, sparkling
*near ant* dingy, greasy, grimy, mucky, muddy; defiled, polluted, tainted; blackened, discolored
*ant* besmirched, dirty, filthy, foul, grubby, soiled, spotted, stained, sullied, unclean
**2** following or according to the rules — see FAIR 3
**3** free from any trace of the coarse or indecent — see CHASTE
**4** trying all possibilities — see EXHAUSTIVE

**clean** *adv* to a full extent or degree — see FULLY 1

**clean** *vb* **1** to make clean ⟨we *cleaned* the clothes before donating them to charity⟩
*syn* cleanse
*rel* decontaminate, purge, purify; disinfect, sanitize; brush, dry-clean, dust, launder, mop, rinse, scour, scrub, sweep, wash, wipe; brighten, deodorize, freshen, spruce (up), sweeten; pick up, straighten (up), tidy
*near ant* begrime, muddy; defile, pollute, taint; blacken, discolor
*ant* besmirch, dirty, foul, soil, spot, stain, sully
**2** to take the internal organs out of — see GUT

**clean** (out) *vb* to make complete use of — see DEPLETE

**clean** (up) *vb* to remove objectionable parts from — see CENSOR

**cleaner** *n* a substance used for cleaning ⟨a kitchen shelf loaded with household *cleaners*⟩
***syn*** cleanser, detergent, soap
***rel*** disinfectant, purifier, solvent
**cleanse** *vb* **1** to free from moral guilt or blemish especially ceremonially — see PURIFY 1
**2** to make clean — see CLEAN 1
**cleanser** *n* a substance used for cleaning — see CLEANER
**cleansing** *n* the act or fact of freeing from sin or moral guilt — see PURIFICATION
**clear** *adj* **1** easily seen through ⟨the *clear* glass walls of the aquarium's giant ocean tank⟩
***syn*** limpid, liquid, lucent, pellucid, transparent
***rel*** colorless, uncolored; lucid, translucent; crystal, crystalline, glassy, sparkling; bright, brilliant, effulgent, luminous
***near ant*** foggy, hazy, misty, murky, smoky (*also* smokey)
***ant*** cloudy, nontransparent, opaque
**2** not subject to misinterpretation or more than one interpretation ⟨the meaning of her broad smile was *clear* to the whole class⟩
***syn*** apparent, broad, clear-cut, decided, distinct, evident, lucid, manifest, obvious, open-and-shut, palpable, patent perspicuous, plain, transparent, unambiguous, unequivocal, unmistakable
***rel*** comprehendible, comprehensible, decipherable, fathomable, graspable, intelligible, knowable, understandable; self-evident, self-explanatory; simple, uncomplicated; overt, undisguised; appreciable, perceptible, recognizable, sensible, tangible; discernible, noticeable, observable, visible
***near ant*** incomprehensible, unfathomable, unintelligible, unknowable; imperceptible, inappreciable, insensible; delicate, subtle
***ant*** dark, enigmatic, indistinct, mysterious, obscure, unclear; ambiguous, equivocal
**3** having or showing a mind free from doubt — see CERTAIN 2
**4** not stormy or cloudy — see FAIR 1
**5** serving to put an end to all debate or questioning — see CONCLUSIVE 1
**6** allowing passage without obstruction — see OPEN 1
**7** free from guilt or blame — see INNOCENT 2
**clear** *vb* **1** to rid the surface of (as an area) from things in the way ⟨the early settlers worked hard to *clear* the land for crops⟩
***syn*** free, open, unblock
***rel*** ease, facilitate, loosen (up), smooth, unclog, unstop
***near ant*** clog, dam, obstruct, plug, stop
***ant*** block
**2** to set (a person or thing) free of something that encumbers — see RID
**3** to give what is owed for — see PAY 2
**4** to remove the contents of — see EMPTY
**5** to remove usually visible impurities from — see CLARIFY 1
**6** to set free from entanglement or difficulty — see EXTRICATE
**7** to arrange clear passage of (something) by removing obstructions — see OPEN 2
**8** to free from a charge of wrongdoing — see EXCULPATE
**9** to give official acceptance of something as satisfactory — see APPROVE
**10** to take away from a place or position — see REMOVE 2
**clear** (up) *vb* to make plain or understandable — see EXPLAIN 1
**clearance** *n* the approval by someone in authority for the doing of something — see PERMISSION
**clear–cut** *adj* **1** not subject to misinterpretation or more than one interpretation — see CLEAR 2
**2** so clearly expressed as to leave no doubt about the meaning — see EXPLICIT
**cleared** *adj* allowing passage without obstruction — see OPEN 1
**clearheaded** *adj* **1** having full use of one's mind and control over one's actions — see SANE
**2** not having one's mind affected by alcohol — see SOBER 1
**clearing** *n* a small area of usually open land — see FIELD 1
**clearness** *n* the state or quality of being easily seen through — see CLARITY 1
**clear out** *vb* **1** to cause (members of a group) to move widely apart — see SCATTER 1
**2** to get free from a dangerous or confining situation — see ESCAPE 1
**3** to leave a place often for another — see GO 2
**clear–sighted** *adj* **1** having or showing a practical cleverness or judgment — see SHREWD
**2** having unusually keen vision — see SHARP-EYED
**cleave** *vb* to hold to something firmly as if by adhesion — see STICK 1
**cleft** *n* an irregular usually narrow break in a surface created by pressure — see CRACK 1
**clemency** *n* kind, gentle, or compassionate treatment especially towards someone who is undeserving of it — see MERCY 1
**clement** *adj* marked by temperatures that are neither too high nor too low ⟨Hawaii is known for its delightfully *clement* climate⟩
***syn*** balmy, equable, gentle, mild, moderate, temperate
***rel*** clear, cloudless, fair, rainless, sunny, sunshiny; calm, halcyon, peaceful, placid, tranquil; delightful, fine, pleasant
***near ant*** blustering, blustery, breezy, gusty; foggy, hazy, misty; bleak, cloudy, dirty, foul, nasty, overcast, rainy, raw, rough, squally, stormy, sunless
***ant*** harsh, inclement, intemperate, severe
**clench** *vb* to have or keep in one's hands — see HOLD 1

**clergyman** *n* a person specially trained and authorized to conduct religious services in a Christian church ⟨a special memorial service that attracted *clergymen* from all over the city⟩
*syn* cleric, deacon, divine, dominie, ecclesiastic, father, minister, padre, parson, preacher, priest, reverend
*rel* evangelist, missionary; deaconess, priestess; dean, pastor, rector, vicar; chaplain, confessor; canon, curate; friar, mendicant, monastic, monk, religious
*ant* layman

**cleric** *n* a person specially trained and authorized to conduct religious services in a Christian church — see CLERGYMAN

**clerical** *adj* of, relating to, or characteristic of the clergy ⟨*clerical* duties such as providing spiritual counseling and leading classes in Bible study⟩
*syn* ministerial, pastoral, priestly, sacerdotal
*rel* evangelical, missionary; apostolic, canonical, episcopal, papal, patriarchal, pontifical; churchly, ecclesiastical (*or* ecclesiastic); divine, holy, religious, sacramental; rabbinic (*or* rabbinical)
*ant* lay, nonclerical

**clerk** *n* **1** a person whose job is to keep records ⟨you'll need to get a copy of your birth certificate from the office of the town *clerk*⟩
*syn* register, registrar, scribe
*rel* archivist, bookkeeper, recorder; annalist, chronicler
**2** a person employed to sell goods or services especially in a store — see SALESPERSON

**clever** *adj* **1** showing a use of the imagination and creativity especially in inventing ⟨an inventor who was constantly coming up with *clever* devices for doing everyday chores⟩
*syn* artful, creative, imaginative, ingenious
*rel* innovative, novel, original; convenient, handy, practical, useful; complex, sophisticated; adroit, deft, dexterous (*also* dextrous); brainy, intelligent, sharp, smart
*near ant* dull, pedestrian, stodgy
*ant* uncreative, unimaginative
**2** having or showing quickness of mind — see INTELLIGENT 1
**3** skillful with the hands — see DEXTEROUS 1
**4** given to or marked by mature intelligent humor — see WITTY

**cleverness** *n* **1** mental skill or quickness — see DEXTERITY 1
**2** subtle or imaginative ability in inventing, devising, or executing something — see SKILL 1

**cliché** *n* an idea or expression that has been used by many people — see COMMONPLACE

**click** *vb* **1** to form a close personal relationship — see COMMUNE
**2** to turn out as planned or desired — see SUCCEED 1

**client** *n* a person who buys a product or uses a service from a business — see CUSTOMER 1

**cliff** *n* a steep wall of rock, earth, or ice ⟨the *cliff* rises 200 feet from the island's south shore⟩
*syn* bluff, crag, escarpment, palisade, precipice, scarp
*rel* tor; bulwark, embankment

**climate** *n* **1** a special quality or impression associated with something — see AURA
**2** the circumstances, conditions, or objects by which one is surrounded — see ENVIRONMENT

**climax** *n* **1** a point in a chain of events at which an important change (as in one's fortunes) occurs — see TURNING POINT
**2** the highest part or point — see HEIGHT 1

**climax** *vb* to bring to a triumphant conclusion — see CROWN

**climb** *n* the act or an instance of rising or climbing up — see ASCENT 1

**climb** *vb* **1** to move (as up or over something) often with the help of the hands in holding or pulling ⟨visitors should use caution when *climbing* over the wet rocks along the shore⟩
*syn* clamber, scramble
*rel* shin, shinny; inch; mount, scale, surmount; claw, struggle
**2** to move or extend upward — see ASCEND

**clinch** *vb* to make final, definite, or beyond dispute ⟨the rain *clinched* the matter: we would have the party indoors⟩
*syn* decide, settle
*rel* demonstrate, determine, establish, prove, show; clarify, clear (up), illuminate; conclude, end, finish
*near ant* confuse, muddle, muddy

**clincher** *n* something (as a fact or argument) that is decisive or overwhelming ⟨the fact that the resort had tennis courts was the *clincher* in our deciding to stay there⟩
*syn* crusher, topper
*rel* deathblow, knockout; coup

**cling** *vb* to hold to something firmly as if by adhesion — see STICK 1

**cling** (to) *vb* **1** to give steadfast support to — see ADHERE
**2** to have or keep in one's hands — see HOLD 1

**clink** *vb* to make a repeated sharp light ringing sound — see JINGLE

**clip** *n* a hard strike with a part of the body or an instrument — see [1]BLOW

**clip** *vb* to make (as hair) shorter with or as if with the use of shears ⟨toddlers are often fearful the first time they get their hair *clipped*⟩
*syn* bob, crop, curtail, cut, cut back, dock, lop (off), nip, pare, prune, shave, shear, snip, trim

***rel*** manicure, mow; abbreviate, abridge, shorten
***near ant*** elongate, extend, lengthen

**clique** *n* a group of people sharing a common interest and relating together socially — see GANG 2

**cloak** *n* **1** something that covers or conceals like a piece of cloth ⟨the *cloak* of mystery that surrounds the royal family⟩
***syn*** curtain, hood, mantle, mask, shroud, veil
***rel*** cover, screen, shield; façade (*also* façade), face, veneer
**2** a sleeveless garment worn so as to hang over the shoulders, arms, and back — see [1]CAPE

**cloak** *vb* **1** to change the dress or looks of so as to conceal true identity — see DISGUISE
**2** to keep secret or shut off from view — see [1]HIDE 2

**clobber** *vb* **1** to deliver a blow to someone or something) usually in a strong vigorous manner — see HIT 1
**2** to defeat by a large margin — see WHIP 2
**3** to achieve a victory over — see BEAT 2

**clock** *n* a device to measure time — see TIMEPIECE

**clod** *n* **1** a big clumsy often slow-witted person — see OAF
**2** a small uneven mass — see LUMP 1

**cloddish** *adj* having or showing crudely insensitive or impolite manners — see CLOWNISH

**clodhopper** *n* an awkward or simple person especially from a small town or the country — see HICK

**clog** *n* something that makes movement or progress more difficult — see ENCUMBRANCE

**clog** *vb* **1** to prevent passage through ⟨the discovery that a ton of hair was *clogging* the drain in the tub⟩
***syn*** block, choke, close (off) congest, dam, jam, obstruct, plug (up), stop (up), stuff
***rel*** bung, fill, pack; flood, glut, inundate, overwhelm, swamp
***near ant*** excavate, hollow (out), scoop (out); empty, lighten
***ant*** clear, free, open (up), unclog
**2** to create difficulty for the work or activity of — see HAMPER

**cloister** *n* a residence for men under religious vows — see MONASTERY

**cloistered** *adj* hidden from view — see SECLUDED

**close** *adj* **1** having little space between items or parts ⟨the soldiers marched in *close* formation against the enemy⟩
***syn*** compact, crowded, dense, jam-packed, packed, serried, thick, tight
***rel*** airtight, snug; compacted, compressed, condensed; firm, hard, solid; impenetrable, impermeable, impervious
***near ant*** commodious, roomy, spacious
***ant*** loose, uncrowded
**2** not being distant in time, space, or significance ⟨my birthday is *close* to Christmas⟩ ⟨a shopping mall that is very *close* to the highway⟩ ⟨these words are *close* synonyms⟩
***syn*** immediate, near, nearby, neighboring, next-door, nigh
***rel*** abutting, adjacent, adjoining, bordering, contiguous; approaching, coming, forthcoming, oncoming, upcoming; accessible, convenient, handy
***phrases*** at hand
***near ant*** divorced, removed, separated
***ant*** away, distant, far, faraway, far-off, remote
**3** showing little difference in the standing of the competitors ⟨the election results were so *close* that the votes had to be recounted⟩
***syn*** narrow, nip and tuck, tight
***rel*** crowded
**4** closely acquainted — see FAMILIAR 1
**5** given to keeping one's activities hidden from public observation or knowledge — see SECRETIVE
**6** giving or sharing as little as possible — see STINGY 1
**7** lacking fresh air — see STUFFY 1
**8** meeting the highest standard of accuracy — see PRECISE 1

**close** *adv* at, within, or to a short distance or time — see NEAR 1

**[1]close** *n* an open space wholly or partly enclosed (as by buildings or walls) — see COURT 2

**[2]close** *n* **1** the stopping of a process or activity — see END 1
**2** the last part of a process or action — see FINALE

**close** *vb* **1** to position (something) so as to prevent passage through an opening ⟨be sure to *close* the gate when you leave⟩
***syn*** shut
***rel*** bar, batten (down), bolt, chain, fasten, latch, lock; plug, seal, stopper; secure; bang, clap, slam
***near ant*** unbar, unbolt, unchain, unfasten, unlatch, unlock, unseal
***ant*** open
**2** to stop the operations of ⟨the merchant will *close* the store if business doesn't improve⟩
***syn*** shut
***rel*** phase out, turn off; extinguish, quell, suppress; gag, muzzle, silence; fail, fold
***near ant*** build, expand
***ant*** open, start
**3** to bring (an event) to a natural or appropriate stopping point ⟨we'll *close* the assembly with the singing of our national anthem⟩
***syn*** conclude, end, finish, round (off *or* out), terminate, wind up, wrap up
***rel*** climax, crown; complete, consummate, perfect; halt, stop, suspend
***ant*** begin, commence, inaugurate, open, start
**4** to come to an end — see CEASE 1
**5** to come near or nearer — see APPROACH 1

**close** (off) *vb* to prevent passage through — see CLOG 1

**closefisted** *adj* giving or sharing as little as possible — see STINGY 1

**close–knit** *adj* bound together by feelings of very close association ⟨a *close-knit* family that constantly keeps in touch⟩
***syn*** clannish
***rel*** bosom, chummy, close, familiar, friendly, intimate, thick; exclusive, snobbish, snobby; forbidding, inhospitable, unfriendly

**closely** *adv* to a close degree — see NEAR 2

**closemouthed** *adj* **1** given to keeping one's activities hidden from public observation or knowledge — see SECRETIVE
**2** tending not to speak frequently (as by habit or inclination) — see SILENT 2

**closeness** *n* **1** the practice or habit of keeping secrets or keeping one's affairs secret — see SECRECY
**2** the quality of being overly sparing with money — see PARSIMONY
**3** the quality or state of being very accurate — see PRECISION
**4** the state of being in a very personal or private relationship — see FAMILIARITY 1
**5** the state or condition of being near — see PROXIMITY

**closer** *adj* being the less far of two — see NEAR 1

**closet** *n* **1** a storage case typically having doors and shelves — see CABINET
**2** an area within a building that has been set apart from surrounding space by a wall — see ROOM 2

**closet** *vb* to close or shut in by or as if by barriers — see ENCLOSE 1

**closing** *adj* following all others of the same kind in order or time — see LAST

**closing** *n* the last part of a process or action — see FINALE

**closure** *n* the stopping of a process or activity — see END 1

**clot** *vb* to turn from a liquid into a substance resembling jelly — see COAGULATE

**cloth** *n* a woven or knitted material (as of cotton or nylon) ⟨cotton canvas was the *cloth* traditionally used for a ship's sails⟩
***syn*** fabric, textile
***rel*** fiber, thread, yarn

**clothe** *vb* **1** to outfit with clothes and especially fine or special clothes ⟨they liked to *clothe* the twins in identical outfits just to confuse people⟩
***syn*** apparel, array, attire, caparison, costume, deck, dress, garb, garment, gown, invest, rig (out), robe, suit
***rel*** cloak, mantle; drape, swaddle, swathe; accoutre (*or* accouter), equip, furnish, outfit
***near ant*** divest, uncover, undrape, unveil
***ant*** disrobe, strip, unclothe, undress
**2** to convey in appropriate or telling terms — see PHRASE

**clothes** *n pl* covering for the human body — see CLOTHING

**clothing** *n* covering for the human body ⟨a store that sells both men's and women's *clothing*⟩
***syn*** apparel, attire, clothes, dress, duds, habiliment(s), rags, raiment, togs, wear
***rel*** garment, vestment; array, bravery, finery; tatters; costume, garb, getup, guise, outfit, rig, wardrobe; haberdashery

**cloud** *vb* **1** to make dark, dim, or indistinct ⟨unfortunately, smog *clouds* the view of the city from the hilltop⟩
***syn*** becloud, bedim, befog, blacken, blur, darken, dim, fog, haze, mist, obscure, overcast, overcloud, overshadow, shadow, shroud
***rel*** blot out, conceal, hide, screen, shade; camouflage, cloak, cover, curtain, disguise, mask, veil; distort, falsify, garble, misrepresent
***near ant*** expose, reveal, uncover, unveil; clarify, clear, purify; highlight, spotlight
***ant*** brighten, illuminate, illumine, light (up), lighten
**2** to make (something) unclear to the understanding — see CONFUSE 2

**cloudburst** *n* a steady falling of water from the sky in significant quantity — see RAIN 1

**clouded** *adj* **1** covered over by clouds — see OVERCAST
**2** filled with or dimmed by fine particles (as of dust or water) in suspension — see HAZY 1

**cloudless** *adj* not stormy or cloudy — see FAIR 1

**cloudy** *adj* **1** having visible particles in liquid suspension ⟨the water coming out of the faucet was unusually *cloudy*⟩
***syn*** muddy, roiled, turbid
***rel*** dingy, filmy, hazy, unfiltered; inky, murky; nontransparent, opaque
***near ant*** clarified, filtered, purified
***ant*** clear
**2** covered over by clouds — see OVERCAST
**3** filled with or dimmed by fine particles (as of dust or water) in suspension — see HAZY 1

**clout** *n* **1** a hard strike with a part of the body or an instrument — see [1]BLOW
**2** the power to direct the thinking or behavior of others usually indirectly — see INFLUENCE 1

**clout** *vb* to deliver a blow to (someone or something) usually in a strong vigorous manner — see HIT 1

**clown** *n* **1** a comically dressed performer (as at a circus) who entertains with playful tricks and ridiculous behavior ⟨a *clown* wearing big floppy shoes and a red wig⟩
***syn*** buffoon, harlequin, zany
***rel*** cutup, madcap; fool, jester, motley; mime, mummer; comedian, comedienne, comic, joker, jokester, wag
**2** a person whose behavior is offensive to others — see JERK 1

**clown** (around) *vb* to engage in attention-getting playful or boisterous behavior — see CUT UP

---

***syn*** synonym(s) ***rel*** related words
***ant*** antonym(s) ***near ant*** near antonym(s)

**clowning** *n* wildly playful or mischievous behavior — see HORSEPLAY

**clownish** *adj* having or showing crudely insensitive or impolite manners ⟨the *clownish* antics of some of the teenagers at the wedding reception⟩
*syn* boorish, churlish, cloddish, loutish, uncouth
*rel* coarse, ill-bred, uncultivated, unpolished, unrefined; tasteless, vulgar; beastly, bestial; doltish, oafish, stupid; discourteous, impolite, rude, uncivil
*ant* cultivated, polished, refined, well-bred; courtly, genteel, gentlemanly, ladylike; civil, courteous, polite

**club** *n* **1** a heavy rigid stick used as a weapon or for punishment ⟨he the prisoner with a *club* if he tries anything funny⟩
*syn* bat, billy, bludgeon, cane, cudgel, nightstick, rod, shillelagh, staff, truncheon
*rel* blackjack, mace; birch, switch; hammer, mallet, maul; walking stick
**2** the meeting place of an organization ⟨the Scouts gather at their *club* every Monday evening⟩
*syn* clubhouse, lodge
*rel* den, hangout, haunt, hideaway, hideout, lair; camp, headquarters meetinghouse
**3** a group of persons formally joined together for some common interest — see ASSOCIATION 2

**club** *vb* **1** to form or enter into an association that furthers the interests of its members — see ALLY
**2** to strike repeatedly — see BEAT 1

**clubhouse** *n* the meeting place of an organization — see CLUB 2

**clue** *n* a slight or indirect pointing to something (as a solution or explanation) — see HINT 1

**clue** *vb* to give information to — see ENLIGHTEN 1

**clump** *n* **1** a number of things considered as a unit — see GROUP 1
**2** a small uneven mass — see LUMP 1

**clump** *vb* to move heavily or clumsily — see LUMBER 1

**clumpy** *adj* having small pieces or lumps spread throughout — see CHUNKY 1

**clumsy** *adj* **1** lacking in physical ease and grace in movement or in the use of the hands ⟨diamond cutting is no job for a *clumsy* person⟩
*syn* awkward, gawky, graceless, heavy-handed, lubberly, lumbering, lumpish, ungainly, unhandy
*rel* butterfingered, uncoordinated; oafish; bungling, gauche, inept, inexpert, maladroit, unskilled, unskillful; cumbersome, unwieldy
*near ant* expert, masterly, skilled, skillful; lissome (*also* lissom), lithe, nimble; light, light-footed, surefooted
*ant* deft, dexterous (*also* dextrous), graceful, handy
**2** lacking social grace and assurance — see AWKWARD 1
**3** showing or marked by a lack of skill and tact (as in dealing with a situation) — see AWKWARD 2
**4** difficult to use or operate especially because of size, weight, or design — see CUMBERSOME
**5** hastily or roughly constructed — see RUDE 1

**cluster** *n* **1** a number of things considered as a unit — see GROUP 1
**2** a usually small number of persons considered as a unit — see GROUP 2

**cluster** *vb* **1** to come together into one body or place — see ASSEMBLE 1
**2** to gather into a closely packed group — see PRESS 3

**clutch** *n* **1** a time or state of affairs requiring prompt or decisive action — see EMERGENCY
**2** the right or means to command or control others — see POWER 1

**clutch** *vb* to have or keep in one's hands — see HOLD 1

**clutter** *n* an unorganized collection or mixture of various things — see MISCELLANY 1

**cluttered** *adj* lacking in order, neatness, and often cleanliness — see MESSY

**coach** *n* a person who trains performers or athletes ⟨a *coach* who is highly respected by all of the baseball players⟩
*syn* trainer
*rel* instructor, teacher; driller, drillmaster; adviser (*or* advisor), counselor (*or* counsellor), mentor

**coach** *vb* to give advice and instruction to (someone) regarding the course or process to be followed — see GUIDE 1

**coadjutor** *n* a person who helps a more skilled person — see HELPER

**coagulate** *vb* to turn from a liquid into a substance resembling jelly ⟨the blood *coagulated*, and a scab formed on the wound⟩
*syn* clot, congeal, gel, jell, jelly, set
*rel* concrete, firm (up), freeze, harden, solidify, stiffen; condense, thicken; curdle, lump (up)
*near ant* deliquesce, flux, fuse, liquefy, melt, thaw

**coalesce** *vb* to come together to form a single unit — see UNITE 1

**coalition** *n* **1** a group of people acting together within a larger group — see FACTION
**2** an association of persons, parties, or states for mutual assistance and protection — see CONFEDERACY

**coarse** *adj* **1** made up of large particles ⟨*coarse* rock salt was sprinkled on the icy walkway⟩
*syn* grainy, granular, granulated
*rel* rough; unfiltered, unrefined; gravelly, gritty, sandy; pebbly, rocky, stony (*also* stoney); lumpy, mealy
*near ant* smooth; filtered, pulverized, refined
*ant* dusty, fine, floury, powdery

**2** lacking in refinement or good taste ⟨the hockey player's *coarse* manners turned his date off completely⟩
***syn*** common, crass, crude, gross, ill-bred, low, lowbred, lowbrow, raffish, rough, roughhewn, rude, tasteless, uncouth, uncultivated, uncultured, unpolished, unrefined, vulgar
***rel*** boorish, churlish, cloddish, clownish, loutish, ungentlemanly; clumsy, lubberly, lumpish, oafish; inconsiderate, insensitive, thoughtless; countrified (*also* countryfied), provincial, rustic; graceless, inelegant, tacky
***near ant*** aristocratic, courtly, patrician; elegant, graceful, gracious; considerate, sensitive, thoughtful; citified, sophisticated, urbane
***ant*** cultivated, cultured, genteel, polished, refined, smooth, tasteful, well-bred
**3** depicting or referring to sexual matters in a way that is unacceptable in polite society — see OBSCENE 1
**4** harsh and dry in sound — see HOARSE
**5** not having a level or smooth surface — see UNEVEN 1
**6** of low quality — see CHEAP 2

**coarseness** *n* **1** the quality or state of being obscene — see OBSCENITY 1
**2** the quality or state of lacking refinement or good taste — see VULGARITY 1

**coast** *vb* to move or proceed smoothly and readily — see FLOW 2

**coat** *n* the hairy covering of a mammal especially when fine, soft, and thick — see FUR 1

**coat** *vb* to form a layer over — see COVER 2

**coax** *vb* to get (someone) to do something by gentle urging, special attention, or flattery ⟨trying to *coax* Dad into taking us on a ski trip, we mentioned what a great skier he is⟩
***syn*** blandish, blarney, cajole, soft-soap, wheedle
***rel*** adulate, flatter, overpraise; compliment, praise; beguile, charm, woo; beg, importune, urge; bug, nag, pester
***near ant*** browbeat, bulldoze, bully, cow, intimidate; coerce, compel, constrain, force, oblige

**cobble** (together) *vb* to make or assemble roughly or hastily ⟨the stranded hikers *cobbled together* a rickety shelter for the night⟩
***syn*** patch (together), throw up
***rel*** dash (off)
***phrases*** knock together
***near ant*** craft, handcraft; fashion, forge, hammer (out), pound (out)

[1]**cock** *n* a fixture for controlling the flow of a liquid — see FAUCET

[2]**cock** *n* a quantity of things thrown or stacked on one another — see [1]PILE 1

[3]**cock** *n* the act of positioning or an instance of being positioned at an angle — see TILT

**cock** *vb* to set or cause to be at an angle — see LEAN 1

**cockcrow** *n* the first appearance of light in the morning or the time of its appearance — see DAWN 1

**cockeyed** *adj* **1** inclined or twisted to one side — see AWRY
**2** showing or marked by a lack of good sense or judgment — see FOOLISH 1

**cocksure** *adj* having or showing a mind free from doubt — see CERTAIN 2

**cocky** *adj* displaying or marked by rude boldness — see NERVY 1

**cocoon** *n* something that encloses another thing especially to protect it — see [1]CASE 1

**coddle** *vb* **1** to cook in a liquid heated to the point that it gives off steam — see BOIL 2
**2** to treat with great or excessive care — see BABY

**code** *n* a collection or system of rules of conduct ⟨Hammurabi was an ancient king of Babylon with a famous *code* of laws⟩
***syn*** decalogue, law
***rel*** constitution

**codger** *n* a person of odd or whimsical habits — see ECCENTRIC

**codify** *vb* to put into a particular arrangement — see ORDER 1

**coequal** *adj* resembling another in every respect — see SAME 1

**coerce** *vb* to cause (a person) to give in to pressure — see FORCE

**coerced** *adj* not made or done willingly or by choice — see INVOLUNTARY 1

**coercion** *n* the use of power to impose one's will on another — see FORCE 2

**coeval** *adj* existing or occurring at the same period of time — see CONTEMPORARY 1

**coeval** *n* a person who lives at the same time or is about the same age as another — see CONTEMPORARY

**coexist** *vb* to occur or exist at the same time — see COINCIDE 1

**coexistence** *n* the occurrence or existence of several things at once — see CONCURRENCE 1

**coexistent** *adj* **1** existing or occurring at the same period of time — see CONTEMPORARY 1
**2** present at the same time and place — see COINCIDENT

**coexisting** *adj* **1** existing or occurring at the same period of time — see CONTEMPORARY 1
**2** present at the same time and place — see COINCIDENT

**coextensive** *adj* existing or occurring at the same period of time — see CONTEMPORARY 1

**coffer** *n* a specially reinforced container to keep valuables safe — see SAFE

**coffin** *n* a box for holding a dead body ⟨*coffins* are said to be the preferred sleeping places of vampires⟩
***syn*** casket

*rel* sarcophagus, vault; urn; sepulcher (*or* sepulchre), sepulture

**cogency** *n* **1** the capacity to persuade ⟨the *cogency* of Thomas Paine's case for American independence⟩
*syn* effectiveness, force, forcefulness, persuasiveness
*rel* impact, punch, strength; soundness, validity; pertinence, relevance
*near ant* invalidity, unsoundness; weakness
*ant* ineffectiveness
**2** the quality of an utterance that provokes interest and produces an effect — see [1]PUNCH 1

**cogent** *adj* having the power to persuade ⟨the results of the DNA fingerprinting were the most *cogent* evidence for acquittal⟩
*syn* compelling, conclusive, convincing, decisive, effective, forceful, persuasive, satisfying, strong, telling
*rel* sound, valid, well-founded; important, significant, weighty; material, pertinent, relevant
*near ant* groundless, invalid, unfounded, unsound; inconsequential, insignificant, unimportant; immaterial, irrelevant
*ant* inconclusive, indecisive, ineffective, unconvincing

**cogitate** *vb* to give serious and careful thought to — see PONDER

**cognizance** *n* **1** a state of being aware — see ATTENTION 2
**2** knowledge gained by personal experience — see ACQUAINTANCE

**cognizant** *adj* having specified facts or feelings actively impressed on the mind — see CONSCIOUS

**cognomen** *n* **1** a descriptive or familiar name given instead of or in addition to the one belonging to an individual — see NICKNAME
**2** a word or combination of words by which a person or thing is regularly known — see NAME 1

**cohere** *vb* to be in agreement on every point — see CHECK 1

**coherence** *n* a balanced, pleasing, or suitable arrangement of parts — see HARMONY 1

**coherent** *adj* according to the rules of logic — see LOGICAL 1

**cohort** *n* **1** a person frequently seen in the company of another — see ASSOCIATE 1
**2** one associated with another in wrongdoing — see ACCOMPLICE

**coil** *vb* to follow a circular or spiral course — see WIND

**coiling** *adj* turning around an axis like the thread of a screw — see SPIRAL

**coinage** *n* something (as a device) created for the first time through the use of the imagination — see INVENTION 1

**coincide** *vb* **1** to occur or exist at the same time ⟨the heaviest snowfall of the season *coincided* with the start of our week-long ski vacation⟩
*syn* coexist, concur
*rel* chance, happen, transpire
*near ant* antedate, precede, predate; follow, succeed
**2** to be in agreement on every point — see CHECK 1
**3** to have or come to the same opinion or point of view — see AGREE 1

**coincidence** *n* the occurrence or existence of several things at once — see CONCURRENCE 1

**coincident** *adj* present at the same time and place ⟨the hard economic times and the *coincident* increase in crime were a double strain on the city's social services⟩
*syn* accompanying, attendant, attending, coexistent, coexisting, coincidental, concomitant, concurrent
*rel* contemporaneous, contemporary, simultaneous, synchronous; associated, collateral, connected, linked, related; consequent, resultant, resulting; ensuing, following, subsequent; accidental, casual, chance, fluky, fortuitous, freak, incident, incidental
*near ant* unassociated, unconnected, unrelated

**coincidental** *adj* present at the same time and place — see COINCIDENT

**coincidentally** *adv* at one and the same time — see TOGETHER 1

**coincidently** *adv* at one and the same time — see TOGETHER 1

**coitus** *n* sexual union involving penetration of the vagina by the penis — see SEXUAL INTERCOURSE

**cold** *adj* **1** having a low or subnormal temperature ⟨the *cold* climate of the Yukon⟩ ⟨an unusually *cold* spring that was followed by a sweltering summer⟩
*syn* arctic, bitter, cool, coolish, freezing, frigid, frosty, glacial, ice-cold, icy, nipping, nippy, numbing, polar, shivery, snappy, wintry
*rel* subfreezing, subzero; cutting, keen, penetrating, piercing, sharp; bracing, brisk, crisp, invigorating, rigorous; chilled, cooled, frosted, frozen, iced, refrigerated, unheated
*near ant* lukewarm, tepid; heated, warmed
*ant* broiling, burning, fiery, hot, piping hot, red-hot, roasting, scalding, scorching, searing, sultry, summery, sweltering, torrid, tropical, warm, warming
**2** lacking in friendliness or warmth of feeling ⟨the prisoners got only a *cold* stare when they tried to befriend the guard⟩
*syn* chill, chilly, cold-blooded, cool, frigid, frosty, glacial, icy, unfriendly, unsympathetic, wintry
*rel* hardhearted, heartless, pitiless, uncaring, unfeeling; reserved, soulless, undemonstrative, unemotional, unresponsive; apathetic, indifferent, unenthusiastic, uninterested; aloof, detached, impersonal
*near ant* compassionate, kind, kindhearted; demonstrative, emotional, expressive; eager, enthusiastic, passionate

*ant* cordial, friendly, genial, hearty, sympathetic, warm, warm-blooded, warm-hearted
**3** having or showing a lack of friendliness or interest in others — see COOL 1
**4** having lost consciousness — see UNCONSCIOUS 1

**cold** *n* a weather condition marked by low temperatures ⟨the *cold* will stay with us for another day, then temperatures should rise⟩
*syn* freeze, snap
*rel* frost; glaciation, ice age; bite, chill, nip, wintriness
*near ant* heat wave; dog days

**cold–blooded** *adj* **1** having or showing a lack of sympathy or tender feelings — see HARD 1
**2** lacking in friendliness or warmth of feeling — see COLD 2
**3** not feeling or showing emotion — see IMPASSIVE 1

**cold–shoulder** *vb* to deliberately ignore or treat rudely — see SNUB 1

**cold shoulder** *n* treatment that is deliberately unfriendly ⟨at the party the two former friends gave each other the *cold shoulder*⟩
*syn* brush-off, rebuff, repulse, snub
*rel* dismissal, rejection; banishment, ostracism
*near ant* welcome

**coliseum** *n* a large usually roofless building for sporting events with tiers of seats for spectators — see STADIUM

**collaborate** *vb* to participate or assist in a joint effort to accomplish an end — see COOPERATE 1

**collaboration** *n* **1** the state of having shared interests or efforts (as in social or business matters) — see ASSOCIATION 1
**2** the work and activity of a number of persons who individually contribute toward the efficiency of the whole — see TEAMWORK

**collapse** *n* **1** a complete depletion of energy or strength — see FATIGUE
**2** a falling short of one's goals — see FAILURE 2

**collapse** *vb* **1** to fall down or in as a result of physical pressure ⟨the motel balcony *collapsed* under the weight of so many people⟩
*syn* cave (in), crumple, give, go, yield
*rel* deflate, flatten, melt; break, break down, conk (out), crash, die, fail, give out, stall; burst, shatter, smash; crack, pop, snap
*phrases* give way
*near ant* inflate, rise, swell
**2** to be unsuccessful — see FAIL 2

**collar** *vb* to take physical control or possession of (something) suddenly or forcibly — see CATCH 1

**colleague** *n* a fellow worker ⟨on her first day at work her *colleagues* went out of their way to make her feel welcome⟩
*syn* associate, coworker
*rel* equal, fellow, peer; accomplice, ally, cohort, collaborator, confederate, partner; buddy, chum, companion, comrade, crony, pal; compatriot, countryman

**collect** *vb* **1** to gain emotional or mental control of ⟨applicants should *collect* their thoughts while waiting to be interviewed⟩
*syn* calm, compose, contain, control, recollect, settle
*rel* allay, lull, quiet, soothe, still, tranquilize (*also* tranquillize)
*phrases* pull oneself together
**2** to gradually form into a layer, pile, or mass ⟨dust has been *collecting* under my bed for years⟩
*syn* accumulate, conglomerate, gather, heap, pile (up)
*rel* bank, drift, ridge
*near ant* disperse, dissipate, scatter
**3** to bring together from several sources into a single volume or list — see COMPILE
**4** to bring together in one body or place — see GATHER 1
**5** to come together into one body or place — see ASSEMBLE 1

**collected** *adj* free from emotional or mental agitation — see CALM 2

**collection** *n* **1** an organized group of objects acquired and maintained for study, exhibition, or personal pleasure ⟨his stamp *collection* has become quite valuable⟩
*syn* assemblage, library
*rel* cache, hoard, repertory, reserve, stock, stockpile, store, supply; accumulation, gathering, heap, pile; clutter, jumble, litter
**2** a mass or quantity that has piled up or that has been gathered — see ACCUMULATION 1
**3** a number of things considered as a unit — see GROUP 1

**collective** *adj* used or done by a number of people as a group ⟨the cleanup of the neighborhood park was a *collective* effort for which many people should be thanked⟩
*syn* combined, common, communal, concerted, conjoint, joint, mutual, public, shared, united
*rel* cooperative, reciprocal, symbiotic; mass, popular; general, generic, universal
*near ant* personal, private; independent, separate; particular, special, specialized
*ant* individual, single, sole

**college** *n* a group of persons formally joined together for some common interest — see ASSOCIATION 2

**collide** *vb* **1** to be out of harmony or agreement usually noticeably — see CLASH
**2** to come into usually forceful contact with something — see HIT 2

**collision** *n* **1** a forceful coming together of two things — see IMPACT 1
**2** the violent coming together of two bodies into destructive contact — see CRASH 1

---

*syn* synonym(s) *rel* related words
*ant* antonym(s) *near ant* near antonym(s)

**colloquial** *adj* **1** used in or suitable for speech and not formal writing ⟨the new kid's rudeness soon began—to use a *colloquial* expression—to rub me the wrong way⟩
*syn* conversational, informal, nonliterary, unliterary, vernacular, vulgar
*rel* dialectal, dialectical, nonstandard, substandard, uneducated; slang, slangy
*near ant* educated, standard; correct, genteel, grammatical, proper
*ant* bookish, formal, learned, literary
**2** having the style and content of everyday conversation — see CHATTY 1

**colloquy** *n* **1** a meeting featuring a group discussion — see FORUM
**2** an exchange of views for the purpose of exploring a subject or deciding an issue — see DISCUSSION 1
**3** talking or a talk between two or more people — see CONVERSATION

**collusion** *n* a secret agreement or cooperation between two parties for an illegal or dishonest purpose ⟨there was *collusion* between the two companies to fix prices⟩
*syn* complicity, connivance, conspiracy
*rel* chicanery, foul play, skulduggery (*or* skullduggery); double-dealing, duplicity; cover-up, frame-up; intrigue, plot, scheme

**colonist** *n* a person who settles in a new region — see FRONTIERSMAN

**colonizer** *n* a person who settles in a new region — see FRONTIERSMAN

**colony** *n* **1** a settlement in a new country or region ⟨the early history of New York City when it was a Dutch *colony*⟩
*syn* plantation
*rel* outpost; dependency, mandate, possession, protectorate, territory
**2** a group of people with a common interest living in one place — see COMMUNITY 2

**color** *n* **1** a property that becomes apparent when light falls on an object and by which things that are identical in form can be distinguished ⟨a shirt that is available in every *color* of the rainbow⟩
*syn* cast, hue, shade, tinge, tint, tone
*rel* complementary color, primary color, secondary color; brightness, saturation, value; coloration, coloring
**2** a substance used to color other materials — see PIGMENT
**3** the hue or appearance of the skin and especially of the face — see COMPLEXION 1
**4 colors** *pl* a piece of cloth with a special design that is used as an emblem or for signaling — see FLAG 1

**color** *vb* **1** to give color or a different color to ⟨she's *colored* her hair for so long and so often that no one knows what her natural color is⟩
*syn* dye, paint, stain, tinge, tint
*rel* brighten, lighten; darken, tone (down); daub
*near ant* blanch, bleach, whiten
*ant* decolorize
**2** to add to the interest of by including made-up details — see EMBROIDER
**3** to change so much as to create a wrong impression or alter the meaning of — see GARBLE
**4** to develop a rosy facial color (as from excitement or embarrassment) — see BLUSH

**colorful** *adj* marked by a variety of usually vivid colors ⟨the *colorful* robes and blankets of the Native Americans of the Southwest⟩
*syn* motley, multicolored, polychromatic, polychrome, varicolored, variegated
*rel* brave, bright, brilliant, gay; flashy, garish, gaudy, loud, showy, splashy; deep, rich, unbleached; checkered, dotted, plaid, striped; colored, pigmented; dappled, shaded; marbled, mottled, piebald, pied, pinto; flecked, spotted, streaked; specked, speckled; banded, barred, brindled (*or* brindle)
*near ant* achromatic; bleached, decolorized, faded, washed out; dull, faint, gray (*also* grey), neutral, pale, pallid
*ant* colorless; monochromatic, solid

**coloring** *n* **1** a substance used to color other materials — see PIGMENT
**2** the hue or appearance of the skin and especially of the face — see COMPLEXION 1
**3** the representation of something in terms that go beyond the facts — see EXAGGERATION

**colorless** *adj* lacking an addition of color ⟨since we can't decide what color to paint the doghouse, our latest home project remains *colorless* for the time being⟩
*syn* uncolored, undyed, unpainted, unstained, white
*rel* clear, limpid, liquid, lucent, pellucid, transparent; bleached, faded, washed; dull, faint, gray (*also* grey), neutral, pale, pallid
*near ant* colorful, multicolored, polychromatic, polychrome, varicolored, variegated
*ant* colored, dyed, painted, stained, tinged, tinted

**colossal** *adj* unusually large — see HUGE

**colossally** *adv* to a large extent or degree — see GREATLY 2

**colosseum** *n* a large usually roofless building for sporting events with tiers of seats for spectators — see STADIUM

**colossus** *n* something that is unusually large and powerful — see GIANT

**colt** *n* a person who is just starting out in a field of activity — see BEGINNER

**coltish** *adj* given to good-natured joking or teasing — see PLAYFUL

**column** *n* **1** a series of persons or things arranged one behind another — see LINE 1
**2** an upright shaft that supports an overhead structure — see PILLAR 1

**coma** *n* a temporary or permanent state of unconsciousness — see FAINT

**comb** *vb* to look through (as a place) carefully or thoroughly in an effort to find or discover something — see SEARCH 1

**combat** *n* **1** active fighting during the course of a war ⟨a soldier who served through the war without actually seeing *combat*⟩
*syn* action, battle
*rel* attack, fire; hostilities, operations, warfare; duty, service
**2** a physical dispute between opposing individuals or groups — see FIGHT 1
**3** an earnest effort for superiority or victory over another — see CONTEST 1
**combat** *vb* **1** to oppose (someone) in physical conflict — see FIGHT 1
**2** to strive to reduce or eliminate — see FIGHT 2
**combative** *adj* feeling or displaying eagerness to fight — see BELLIGERENT
**combativeness** *n* an inclination to fight or quarrel — see BELLIGERENCE
**combination** *n* **1** a distinct entity formed by the combining of two or more different things — see BLEND
**2** the act or an instance of joining two or more things into one — see UNION 1
**3** a number of businesses or enterprises united for commercial advantage — see CARTEL
**4** an association of persons, parties, or states for mutual assistance and protection — see CONFEDERACY
**combine** *n* **1** a number of businesses or enterprises united for commercial advantage — see CARTEL
**2** an association of persons, parties, or states for mutual assistance and protection — see CONFEDERACY
**combine** *vb* **1** to come together to form a single unit — see UNITE 1
**2** to turn into a single mass that is more or less the same throughout — see BLEND 1
**combined** *adj* used or done by a number of people as a group — see COLLECTIVE
**combining** *n* the act or an instance of joining two or more things into one — see UNION 1
**combust** *vb* to be on fire especially brightly — see BURN 1
**combustible** *adj* capable of catching or being set on fire ⟨don't store oily rags and other *combustible* materials in a hot attic⟩
*syn* burnable, flammable, ignitable, inflammable
*rel* explosive, incendiary
*near ant* nonexplosive
*ant* fireproof, incombustible, noncombustible, nonflammable, noninflammable
**combusting** *adj* being on fire — see ABLAZE 1
**come** *vb* **1** to move closer to ⟨*come* here and sit by the fire⟩
*syn* advance, approach, near
*rel* drop (in), enter, pop (in)
*near ant* depart, exit, leave
*ant* go, retreat, withdraw
**2** to get to a destination ⟨when do you think they'll *come* ?⟩
*syn* arrive, land, show up, turn up
*rel* hit, make, reach; pull (in), touch down; debark, disembark; barge (in), breeze (in), burst (in *or* into), waltz (in)
*ant* go
**3** to eventually have as a state or quality — see BECOME
**4** to take place — see HAPPEN
**come** (to) *vb* **1** to have a total of — see AMOUNT (TO) 1
**2** to be the same in meaning or effect — see AMOUNT (TO) 2
**come about** *vb* to take place — see HAPPEN
**come around** *vb* to gain consciousness again — see COME TO
**comeback** *n* **1** a quick witty response — see RETORT 1
**2** something spoken or written in reaction especially to a question — see ANSWER 1
**3** the process or period of gradually regaining one's health and strength — see CONVALESCENCE
**comedian** *n* a person (as a writer) noted for or specializing in humor — see HUMORIST
**comedown** *n* a loss of status ⟨after a rapid rise to stardom, the rock band's *comedown* was just as quick⟩
*syn* decline, descent, down, downfall, fall
*rel* breakdown, collapse, crash, meltdown, ruin, undoing; defeat, disappointment, reversal, setback; bottom, nadir
*near ant* advance, headway, progress; flower, heyday, prime
*ant* aggrandizement, ascent, exaltation, rise, up
**come down** (with) *vb* to become affected with (a disease or disorder) — see CONTRACT 1
**comedy** *n* humorous entertainment ⟨presented a night of *comedy* as part of the week-long celebrations⟩
*syn* farce, humor, slapstick
*rel* burlesque, parody, satire; banter, persiflage, wit; foolery, fun, horseplay, monkeyshines, shenanigans
**comeliness** *n* the qualities in a person or thing that as a whole give pleasure to the senses — see BEAUTY 1
**comely** *adj* very pleasing to look at — see BEAUTIFUL
**come out** *vb* **1** to come to be ⟨in the end everything *came out* OK⟩
*syn* pan out, prove, turn out
*rel* develop, emerge, evolve, play out, unfold, work out
**2** to come into view — see APPEAR 1
**3** to become known — see GET OUT 1
**come round** *vb* to gain consciousness again — see COME TO
**come to** *vb* to gain consciousness again ⟨after being in a coma for months, the patient suddenly *came to*⟩
*syn* come around, come round, revive
*rel* pull through, rally, recover; awake, awaken, wake up
*near ant* black out, faint, pass out

---

*syn* synonym(s) *rel* related words
*ant* antonym(s) *near ant* near antonym(s)

**comfort** *n* **1** a feeling of ease from grief or trouble ⟨the mourners found *comfort* in their pastor's words⟩
***syn*** cheer, consolation, relief, solace
***rel*** encouragement, inspiration uplift; assurance, reassurance; alleviation, assuagement, mitigation; contentment, gladness, happiness; commiseration, empathy, sympathy
***near ant*** anguish, distress, heartache, heartbreak, torment, torture
**2** something that adds to one's ease ⟨a family campground with all the *comforts* of home⟩
***syn*** amenity, convenience, luxury
***rel*** extra; benefit, help, service; delight, indulgence, joy, pleasure
***ant*** burden, millstone, weight
**3** reduction of or freedom from pain — see EASE 1
**4** something adding to pleasure or comfort but not absolutely necessary — see LUXURY 1

**comfort** *vb* **1** to ease the grief or distress of ⟨the minister did his best to *comfort* the victims of the terrible tornado⟩
***syn*** assure, cheer, console, reassure, solace, soothe
***rel*** commiserate, condole, empathize, sympathize; boost, buoy (up), elevate, lift, uplift; allay, alleviate, assuage, relieve; calm, quiet, relax, tranquilize (*also* tranquillize)
***near ant*** demoralize, discourage, dishearten; fret, upset, worry; aggravate, intensify, worsen; annoy, irk, irritate; harass, pester
***ant*** distress, torment, torture, trouble
**2** to fill with courage or strength of purpose — see ENCOURAGE 1

**comfortable** *adj* **1** providing physical comfort ⟨a large, overstuffed chair that is very *comfortable*⟩
***syn*** cozy, cushy, easy, snug, soft
***rel*** relaxing, reposeful, restful; genial, hospitable, inviting, pleasant; commodious, roomy, spacious; homelike, homely, homey
***near ant*** hard, harsh, severe; inhospitable, uninviting, unpleasant
***ant*** uncomfortable
**2** enjoying physical comfort ⟨make yourself *comfortable* in the living room while I fix us some snacks⟩
***syn*** cozy, relaxed, snug
***rel*** content, contented, pleased, satisfied; peaceful, resting; easygoing, laid-back; undisturbed, unperturbed, untroubled
***phrases*** at ease, at home
***near ant*** discontented, displeased, dissatisfied; agitated, disturbed, perturbed, troubled
***ant*** uncomfortable
**3** being more than enough without being excessive — see PLENTIFUL

**comforting** *adj* **1** making one feel good inside — see HEARTWARMING
**2** tending to calm the emotions and relieve stress — see SOOTHING 1

**comforting** *n* the giving of hope and strength in times of grief, distress, or suffering — see CONSOLATION 1

**comfortless** *adj* **1** causing discomfort — see UNCOMFORTABLE 1
**2** causing or marked by an atmosphere lacking in cheer — see GLOOMY 1

**comic** *adj* causing or intended to cause laughter — see FUNNY 1

**comic** *n* **1** a person (as a writer) noted for or specializing in humor — see HUMORIST
**2** a series of drawings that tell a story or part of a story — see COMIC STRIP

**comical** *adj* **1** causing or intended to cause laughter — see FUNNY 1
**2** so foolish or pointless as to be worthy of scornful laughter — see RIDICULOUS 1

**comic strip** *n* a series of drawings that tell a story or part of a story ⟨a *comic strip* that is beloved by both children and adults⟩
***syn*** cartoon, comic, funny
***rel*** comic book, funny paper(s); animated cartoon, animation; caricature

**coming** *adj* **1** being soon to appear or take place — see FORTHCOMING
**2** being the one that comes immediately after another — see NEXT
**3** of a time after the present — see FUTURE

**comity** *n* peaceful coexistence — see HARMONY 2

**command** *n* **1** a statement of what to do that must be obeyed by those concerned ⟨the captain's *commands* were followed without question⟩
***syn*** behest, charge, commandment, decree, dictate, direction, directive, edict, instruction, order, word
***rel*** demand, requirement; injunction, mandate; law, precept, rule; ordinance, regulation, statute
***near ant*** appeal, entreaty, petition, plea, urging; proposal, recommendation, suggestion
**2** a highly developed skill in or knowledge of something ⟨a *command* of French that is the result of a year spent in France as an exchange student⟩
***syn*** mastership, mastery, proficiency
***rel*** virtuosity; fluency, literacy; experience, expertise, know-how, practice (*also* practise), skill(s); acquaintance, familiarity, intimacy
***near ant*** incompetence, incompetency; ignorance, illiteracy, unfamiliarity
**3** the place from which a commander runs operations ⟨the general set up his *command* in the old port city⟩
***syn*** base, headquarters
***rel*** home, seat
**4** a place from which authority is exercised — see SEAT 1
**5** the right or means to command or control others — see POWER 1

**command** *vb* **1** to issue orders to (someone) by right of authority ⟨the general *commanded* the troops to advance⟩

*syn* adjure, bid, boss (around), charge, direct, enjoin, instruct, order, tell
*rel* ask, petition, request; beg, beseech, entreat; advise, counsel, warn; appoint, assign, authorize, commission; oversee, superintend, supervise; conduct, control, lead, manage; coerce, compel, constrain, force, oblige, require
*near ant* comply (with), follow, keep, observe
*ant* mind, obey
**2** to give an order ⟨the governor has *commanded* that all state flags be flown at half-mast⟩
*syn* decree, dictate, direct, ordain, order
*rel* ask, petition, request; demand, require
*phrases* call for
**3** to ask for (something) earnestly or with authority — see DEMAND 1
**4** to exercise authority or power over — see GOVERN 1
**5** to keep, control, or experience as one's own — see HAVE 1
**6** to look down on — see OVERLOOK 1
**7** to serve as leader of — see LEAD 2
**8** to set or receive as a price — see CHARGE 1

**commandant** *n* one in official command especially of a military force or base — see COMMANDER 1

**commandeer** *vb* **1** to take control of (a vehicle) by force ⟨an airliner *commandeered* by terrorists⟩
*syn* hijack (*also* highjack)
*rel* appropriate, confiscate, expropriate, seize
**2** to take or make use of without authority or right — see APPROPRIATE 1

**commander** *n* **1** one in official command especially of a military force or base ⟨a surrender of the fort by the *commander* without a single shot having been fired⟩
*syn* captain, commandant, commanding officer
*rel* commissioned officer
*phrases* commander in chief
**2** a person in overall command of a ship — see CAPTAIN 1

**commanding** *adj* highest in rank or authority — see HEAD

**commanding officer** *n* one in official command especially of a military force or base — see COMMANDER 1

**commandment** *n* a statement of what to do that must be obeyed by those concerned — see COMMAND 1

**commemorate** *vb* **1** to be a memorial of ⟨a stone obelisk *commemorates* the Battle of Bunker Hill⟩
*syn* memorialize
*rel* celebrate, keep, observe, remember; enshrine, exalt, glorify, honor; bless, consecrate, sanctify, solemnize
*near ant* disgrace, dishonor
**2** to act properly in relation to — see KEEP 1

**commemorating** *adj* serving to preserve the memory of a person, thing, or an event — see COMMEMORATIVE

**commemorative** *adj* serving to preserve the memory of a person, thing, or an event ⟨*commemorative* stamps for the stars of American popular music⟩
*syn* commemorating, memorial, memorializing
*rel* dedicatory, testimonial; enshrining, glorifying, honorary

**commemorative** *n* something that serves to keep alive the memory of a person or event — see MEMORIAL

**commence** *vb* **1** to take the first step in (a process or course of action) — see BEGIN 1
**2** to come into existence — see BEGIN 2

**commencement** *n* the point at which something begins — see BEGINNING

**commend** *vb* to put (something) into the possession or safekeeping of another — see GIVE 2

**commendable** *adj* deserving of high regard or great approval — see ADMIRABLE

**commendation** *n* **1** a formal recognition of an achievement or praiseworthy deed ⟨a firefighter who has been awarded several *commendations* for bravery⟩
*syn* acknowledgment (*also* acknowledgement), citation
*rel* decoration, medal, ribbon; accolade, award, prize, tribute; dedication
**2** a formal expression of praise — see ENCOMIUM

**commendatory** *adj* expressing approval — see FAVORABLE 1

**commensurate** *adj* corresponding in size, amount, extent, or degree — see PROPORTIONAL

**comment** *n* **1** a briefly expressed opinion — see REMARK
**2 comments** *pl* a series of explanations or observations on something (as an event) — see COMMENTARY

**comment** *vb* to make a statement of one's opinion — see REMARK 1

**commentary** *n* a series of explanations or obser-vations on something (as an event) ⟨the TV anchors provided a running *commentary* on the parade⟩
*syn* analysis, comment, exposition
*rel* annotation, explication; note, observation, remark; report, review, write-up

**commerce** *n* the buying and selling of goods especially on a large scale and between different places ⟨a government agency in charge of regulating interstate *commerce*⟩
*syn* business, marketplace, trade, traffic
*rel* free trade; dealings, horse-trading; merchandising, retailing, wholesaling; bartering

**commercial** *adj* fit or likely to be sold especially on a large scale ⟨the *commercial* fare produced by the Hollywood movie studios⟩
*syn* marketable, salable (*or* saleable)
*rel* mass-produced, wholesale

***ant*** noncommercial, nonsalable, uncommercial, unmarketable, unsalable

**commingle** *vb* to turn into a single mass that is more or less the same throughout — see BLEND 1

**commiserate** (with) *vb* to have sympathy for — see PITY

**commiseration** *n* **1** sorrow or the capacity to feel sorrow for another's suffering or misfortune — see SYMPATHY 1
**2** the capacity for feeling for another's unhappiness or misfortune — see HEART 1

**commissary** *n* a person who acts or does business for another — see AGENT 2

**commission** *n* **1** the granting of power to perform various acts or duties ⟨President Jefferson's *commission* to Lewis and Clark to explore the Louisiana Territory⟩
***syn*** accreditation, authorization, delegation, license (*or* licence), mandate
***rel*** commendation, consignment, entrustment; facilitation, fostering, promotion; commanding, directing, ordering
**2** the doing of an action ⟨a single burglar was responsible for the *commission* of all the break-ins⟩
***syn*** accomplishment, achievement, discharge, enactment, execution, fulfillment, implementation, performance, perpetration
***rel*** dispatch, expedition; administration, direction, handling, management; application, operation, practice (*also* practise)
***ant*** nonfulfillment, nonperformance
**3** a select group of persons assigned to consider or take action on some matter — see COMMITTEE
**4** the state or fact of being chosen for a position or duty — see APPOINTMENT 1

**commission** *vb* **1** to appoint as one's representative — see DELEGATE 1
**2** to give official or legal power to — see AUTHORIZE 1
**3** to give a task, duty, or responsibility to — see ENTRUST 1
**4** to pick (someone) by one's authority for a specific position or duty — see APPOINT 2

**commit** *vb* **1** to carry through (as a process) to completion — see PERFORM 1
**2** to obligate by prior agreement — see PLEDGE 1
**3** to put (something) into the possession or safekeeping of another — see GIVE 2
**4** to put in or as if in prison — see IMPRISON

**commitment** *n* something one must do because of prior agreement — see OBLIGATION

**committee** *n* a select group of persons assigned to consider or take action on some matter ⟨a *committee* in charge of planning the organization's annual Christmas party⟩
***syn*** commission, panel
***rel*** subcommittee; delegation, mission; assembly, body, congress, convocation, council, synod

**commodious** *adj* more than adequate or average in capacity — see SPACIOUS

**commodities** *n pl* products that are bought and sold in business — see MERCHANDISE

**common** *adj* **1** often observed or encountered ⟨horse ranches are a *common* sight in that part of the state⟩
***syn*** commonplace, everyday, familiar, frequent, garden, household, ordinary, routine, ubiquitous, usual
***rel*** normal, regular, standard; general, universal; ceaseless, constant, continual, continuous, incessant, unceasing; popular, prevailing, prevalent, rampant; perennial, recurrent, repeated
***near ant*** aberrant; abnormal, irregular, unnatural; intermittent, occasional, sporadic
***ant*** extraordinary, infrequent, rare, uncommon, unfamiliar, unusual
**2** being of the type that is encountered in the normal course of events — see ORDINARY 1
**3** belonging or relating to the whole — see GENERAL 1
**4** belonging to the class of people of low social or economic rank — see IGNOBLE 1
**5** held by or applicable to a majority of the people — see GENERAL 3
**6** used or done by a number of people as a group — see COLLECTIVE
**7** of average to below average quality — see MEDIOCRE 1
**8** of low quality — see CHEAP 2
**9** lacking in refinement or good taste — see COARSE 2

**commoners** *n pl* the body of the community as contrasted with the elite — see MASS 1

**commonly** *adv* according to the usual course of things — see NATURALLY 2

**commonness** *n* **1** the fact or state of happening often — see FREQUENCY
**2** the quality or state of lacking refinement or good taste — see VULGARITY 1

**commonplace** *adj* **1** being of the type that is encountered in the normal course of events — see ORDINARY 1
**2** often observed or encountered — see COMMON 1
**3** used or heard so often as to be dull — see STALE

**commonplace** *n* an idea or expression that has been used by many people ⟨the familiar summertime *commonplace* that "it's not the heat, it's the humidity"⟩
***syn*** banality, cliché, platitude, shibboleth, truism
***rel*** inanity; generality, generalization, simplification; adage, proverb, saw, saying; old wives' tale, stereotype
***near ant*** profundity

**commonsense** *adj* based on sound reasoning or information — see GOOD 1

**common sense** *n* the ability to make intelligent decisions especially in everyday matters ⟨*common sense* should tell you not to meet face-to-face with someone who is just an online acquaintance⟩

*syn* discreetness, discretion, horse sense, levelheadedness, prudence, sense, sensibleness, wisdom, wit
*rel* street smarts; farsightedness, foresight, foresightedness, judgment (*or* judgement); brains, gray matter, intelligence; logicalness, practicality, rationality; discernment, discrimination, insight, sagacity, sapience; acumen, astuteness, keenness, penetration, perspicacity, shrewdness; care, caution, circumspection, precaution, premeditation
*near ant* shortsightedness; brainlessness, foolishness, idiocy, senselessness, stupidity; carelessness, heedlessness
*ant* imprudence, indiscretion

**commonwealth** *n* a body of people composed of one or more nationalities usually with its own territory and government — see NATION

**commotion** *n* a state of noisy, confused activity ⟨the *commotion* created when the nation's top rock band arrived in town⟩
*syn* bother, bustle, clatter, disturbance, furor, furore, fuss, hubbub, hullabaloo, hurly-burly, pandemonium, pother, row, ruckus, ruction, rumpus, shindy, squall, stew, stir, storm, to-do, tumult, turmoil, uproar, welter, whirl
*rel* cacophony, clamor, din, howl, hue and cry, outcry, noise, racket, roar; disorder, unrest, upheaval; eruption, flare-up, flurry, outbreak, outburst; brawl, fracas, fray, hassle, melee, scuffle; dither, fever, fret, lather, tizzy
*near ant* calm, hush, peace, quiet, quietude, rest, stillness, tranquillity (*or* tranquility); order, orderliness

**communal** *adj* used or done by a number of people as a group — see COLLECTIVE

**commune** *vb* to form a close personal relationship ⟨after a week in the wilderness, the scouts were really starting to *commune* with nature⟩
*syn* click, relate
*rel* bond; befriend

**communicable** *adj* capable of being passed by physical contact from one person to another — see CONTAGIOUS 1

**communicate** *vb* **1** to cause (something) to pass from one to another ⟨the infected cook unknowingly *communicated* the disease to hundreds of people⟩
*syn* convey, impart, spread, transfer, transfuse, transmit
*rel* deliver, hand over, surrender, turn over; broadcast, diffuse, disseminate, propagate; contaminate, infect, poison
*near ant* catch, come down (with), contract
**2** to engage in an exchange of information or ideas ⟨for decades the two medical centers have been *communicating* about cancer research⟩
*syn* brainstorm, intercommunicate
*rel* correspond; converse, talk; bond, commune, relate; accost, approach, contact

**communicate** (with) *vb* to transmit information or requests to — see CONTACT

**communication** *n* a piece of conveyed information ⟨the latest *communication* from the crew of the space station⟩
*syn* dispatch, message
*rel* bulletin, communiqué, report; memo, memorandum, notice; epistle, letter, missive, note; electronic mail, e-mail; intelligence, news, tidings, word; command, directive, instruction, order

**communion** *n* a friendly relationship marked by ready communication and mutual understanding — see RAPPORT

**community** *n* **1** the people living in a particular area ⟨the whole *community* rallied to the aid of the family who had lost its home⟩
*syn* neighborhood
*rel* city, commune, town, village; denizens, dwellers, inhabitants, residents; citizenry, culture, people, populace, public, society
**2** a group of people with a common interest living in one place ⟨a picturesque seacoast village that is known for its sizable *community* of artists⟩
*syn* colony
*rel* circle, clique, coterie, set, society; band, company, troop; clan, family
**3** a group of people sharing a common interest and relating together socially — see GANG 2
**4** the body of people in a profession or field of activity — see CORPS
**5** the quality or state of having many qualities in common — see SIMILARITY 1

**commutation** *n* a giving or taking of one thing of value in return for another — see EXCHANGE 1

**commute** *vb* to give up (something) and take something else in return — see CHANGE 3

**compact** *adj* **1** having a consistency that does not easily yield to pressure — see FIRM 2
**2** having little space between items or parts — see CLOSE 1
**3** marked by the use of few words to convey much information or meaning — see CONCISE

**compact** *n* **1** a formal agreement between two or more nations or peoples — see TREATY
**2** an arrangement about action to be taken — see AGREEMENT 2

**compact** *vb* **1** to bring (something) to a central point or under a single control — see CENTRALIZE
**2** to reduce in size or volume by or as if by pressing parts or members together — see COMPRESS 1

**compacting** *n* the act or process of reducing the size or volume of something by or as if by pressing — see COMPRESSION

**compactly** *adv* in a few words — see SHORTLY 1

---

*syn* synonym(s) *rel* related words
*ant* antonym(s) *near ant* near antonym(s)

**compactness** *n* the quality or state of being marked by or using only few words to convey much meaning — see SUCCINCTNESS

**companion** *n* **1** a person frequently seen in the company of another — see ASSOCIATE 1
**2** one that accompanies another for protection, guidance, or as a courtesy — see ESCORT
**3** either of a pair matched in one or more qualities — see MATE 1
**4** something that is found along with something else — see ACCOMPANIMENT

**companionable** *adj* **1** having or showing kindly feeling and sincere interest — see FRIENDLY 1
**2** likely to seek or enjoy the company of others — see CONVIVIAL

**companionship** *n* the feeling of closeness and friendship that exists between companions ⟨the widow's pet cats provided her with her only *companionship*⟩
***syn*** camaraderie, company, comradeship, fellowship, society
***rel*** amity, benevolence, cordiality, friendliness, friendship, goodwill, kindliness; civility, comity, concord, harmony, rapport; charity, generosity; affinity, compassion, empathy, sympathy; chumminess, familiarity, inseparability, intimacy, nearness; affection, devotion, fondness, love
***near ant*** forlornness, loneliness, lonesomeness

**company** *n* **1** an organized group of stage performers ⟨a city that is fortunate enough to have two thriving opera *companies*⟩
***syn*** troop, troupe
***rel*** stock company; cast, dramatis personae, ensemble
**2** a group of people working together on a task — see GANG 1
**3** a commercial or industrial activity or organization — see ENTERPRISE 1
**4** the feeling of closeness and friendship that exists between companions — see COMPANIONSHIP

**comparable** *adj* having qualities in common — see ALIKE

**comparative** *adj* being such only when compared to something else ⟨if you consider the multimillionaire's yearly income, we're living in *comparative* poverty⟩
***syn*** approximate, near, relative
***rel*** alike, comparable, similar; equal, equivalent
***near ant*** genuine, real, true
***ant*** absolute, complete, downright, out-and-out, outright, perfect, pure, unqualified

**compare** *vb* **1** to describe as similar ⟨reviews that *compared* the adventure movie to a thrilling ride on a roller coaster⟩
***syn*** bracket, equate, liken
***rel*** associate, connect, couple, link; allude, refer, relate; equal, match, parallel
***ant*** contrast
**2** to regard or represent as equal or comparable — see EQUATE 1

**compare** (with) *vb* to come near or nearer to in character or quality — see APPROXIMATE

**compartment** *n* one of the parts into which an enclosed space is divided ⟨a backpack with many handy *compartments* for storing your camping gear⟩
***syn*** bay, cabin, cell, chamber, cubicle
***rel*** cubbyhole, pigeonhole, snuggery [*chiefly British*]; alcove, niche, nook, recess; cabinet, drawer; cavity, hole, hollow; booth, crib, stall; crypt, vault

**compass** *n* **1** an area over which activity, capacity, or influence extends — see RANGE 2
**2** the line or relatively narrow space that marks the outer limit of something — see BORDER 1

**compass** *vb* **1** to carry through (as a process) to completion — see PERFORM 1
**2** to pass completely around — see ENCIRCLE 1

**compassion** *n* **1** sorrow or the capacity to feel sorrow for another's suffering or misfortune — see SYMPATHY 1
**2** the capacity for feeling for another's unhappiness or misfortune — see HEART 1

**compassionate** *adj* **1** having or marked by sympathy and consideration for others — see HUMANE 1
**2** having or showing the capacity for sharing the feelings of another — see SYMPATHETIC 1

**compatibility** *n* peaceful coexistence — see HARMONY 2

**compatible** *adj* **1** having or marked by agreement in feeling or action — see HARMONIOUS 3
**2** not having or showing any apparent conflict — see CONSISTENT

**compatriot** *n* a person living in or originally from the same country as another ⟨an appeal to all of his *compatriots* to come to their country's aid in its hour of need⟩
***syn*** countryman
***rel*** nationalist; patriot; citizen, national, subject; aborigine, native; homeboy, resident
***near ant*** alien, foreigner, immigrant, outsider

**compel** *vb* to cause (a person) to give in to pressure — see FORCE

**compelling** *adj* having the power to persuade — see COGENT

**compendious** *adj* **1** covering everything or all important points — see ENCYCLOPEDIC
**2** marked by the use of few words to convey much information or meaning — see CONCISE

**compensate** *vb* **1** to provide (someone) with a just payment for loss or injury ⟨you'll have to *compensate* the neighbors for cutting down their tree⟩
***syn*** indemnify, recompense, recoup, remunerate, requite

*rel* refund, reimburse, repay; redress, remedy, repair; discharge, pay, quit
**2** to give (someone) the sum of money owed for goods or services received — see PAY 1

**compensate** (for) *vb* to balance with an equal force so as to make ineffective — see OFFSET

**compensation** *n* **1** payment to another for a loss or injury ⟨a warehouse worker who received a large *compensation* for his crippling injury while on the job⟩
*syn* damages, indemnification, indemnity, quittance, recompense, recoupment, redress, remuneration, reparation, requital, restitution, satisfaction
*rel* amends, atonement, expiation; refund, reimbursement, repayment; adjustment, settlement; punishment, reprisal, retaliation
**2** something (as money) that is given or received in return for goods or services — see PAYMENT 2
**3** the act of offering money in exchange for goods or services — see PAYMENT 1

**compete** *vb* to engage in a contest ⟨prizefighters *competing* for the world heavyweight championship⟩
*syn* battle, contend, fight, race, vie
*rel* challenge, engage, play; jockey, maneuver; go out, try out; train, work

**competence** *n* the physical or mental power to do something — see ABILITY

**competency** *n* the physical or mental power to do something — see ABILITY

**competent** *adj* having the required skills for an acceptable level of performance ⟨any *competent* mechanic should be able to fix that⟩
*syn* able, capable, fit, good, qualified, suitable
*rel* accomplished, ace, adept, experienced, expert, master, masterful, masterly, practiced (*or* practised), proficient, seasoned, skilled, skillful, veteran; prepared, schooled, trained
*near ant* inexperienced, inexpert, unseasoned, unskilled, unskillful; unprepared, unschooled, untrained; beginning, green, new, raw, untested, untried
*ant* incompetent, inept, poor, unfit, unqualified

**competently** *adv* in a skillful or expert manner — see WELL 3

**competition** *n* **1** a competitive encounter between individuals or groups carried on for amusement, exercise, or in pursuit of a prize — see GAME 1
**2** one who strives for the same thing as another — see COMPETITOR

**competitor** *n* one who strives for the same thing as another ⟨the *competitors* for the science award come from the best high schools in the country⟩
*syn* challenger, competition, contender, contestant, rival
*rel* finalist, semifinalist; entrant, player; adversary, antagonist, opponent

**compilation** *n* a collection of writings — see ANTHOLOGY

**compile** *vb* to bring together from several sources into a single volume or list ⟨*compiled* the best short stories ever written into one fat book⟩
*syn* collect
*rel* edit, redraft, revamp, revise, rework; accumulate, amass, assemble, gather, group

**complacence** *n* an often unjustified feeling of being pleased with oneself or with one's situation or achievements ⟨the *complacence* of some of the rich kids at the exclusive private school⟩
*syn* complacency, conceit, conceitedness, ego, egotism, pompousness, pride, pridefulness, self-admiration, self-conceit, self-esteem, self-importance, self-satisfaction, smugness, vaingloriousness, vainglory, vainness, vanity
*rel* assurance, confidence, self-assurance, self-confidence; self-righteousness; arrogance, disdainfulness, haughtiness, imperiousness, lordliness, self-assertion, snobbishness, superciliousness, superiority; overconfidence, presumption; pretense (*or* pretence), pretension, pretentiousness; egoism, self-centeredness, selfishness; self-respect
*near ant* diffidence, self-doubt; altruism, unselfishness; bashfulness, demureness, shyness, timidity, timidness; passiveness, passivity
*ant* humbleness, humility, modesty

**complacency** *n* an often unjustified feeling of being pleased with oneself or with one's situation or achievements — see COMPLACENCE

**complacent** *adj* having too high an opinion of oneself — see CONCEITED

**complain** *vb* to express dissatisfaction, pain, or resentment usually tiresomely ⟨the time-honored tradition of students *complaining* about the food in the cafeteria⟩
*syn* beef, bellyache, carp, crab, croak, fuss, gripe, grouse, growl, grumble, kick, moan, murmur, mutter, repine, squawk, wail, whine, yammer
*rel* object (to), protest, quarrel (with); cavil, quibble; fret, stew, worry; blubber, cry, sob; bemoan, bewail, deplore, lament
*near ant* accept, bear, countenance, endure, tolerate; applaud, cheer, commend
*ant* rejoice

**complainant** *n* the person in a legal proceeding who makes a charge of wrongdoing against another ⟨the *complainant* charged that the defendant had broken the ironclad contract that both had signed⟩
*syn* plaintiff, suer
*rel* accuser; litigant, party, suitor; appellant, petitioner, pleader
*near ant* accused
*ant* defendant

**complainer** *n* **1** a person who makes frequent complaints usually about little things — see CRYBABY
**2** an irritable and complaining person — see GROUCH

**complaint** *n* **1** an expression of dissatisfaction, pain, or resentment ⟨a warning that if there were any more *complaints*, we were turning around and not going to the beach after all⟩
***syn*** beef, fuss, grievance, gripe, grumble, murmur, plaint, squawk
***rel*** challenge, demur, expostulation, kick, objection, protest, quibble, remonstrance
***near ant*** commendation, compliment, plaudit; acclaim, applause, praise; approval, endorsement, sanction
**2** a feeling or declaration of disapproval or dissent — see OBJECTION
**3** a formal claim of criminal wrongdoing against a person — see CHARGE 1
**4** an abnormal state that disrupts a plant's or animal's normal bodily functioning — see DISEASE

**complaisance** *n* a desire or disposition to please ⟨the *complaisance* of his girlfriend is such that she goes along with everything he says⟩
***syn*** amenability, amiability, good-naturedness
***rel*** affability, amicability, congeniality, cordiality, friendliness, geniality, sociability; agreeableness, graciousness, pleasantness; kindheartedness, kindliness, warmheartedness; compliance, docility, passivity, submissiveness
***near ant*** disagreeableness, sullenness, surliness, ungraciousness; disobedience, intractability, recalcitrance

**complement** *n* **1** something that serves to complete or make up for a deficiency in something else ⟨with his practicality and her refreshing enthusiasm, they are perfect *complements* to each other⟩
***syn*** supplement
***rel*** addendum, addition, appendix; adjunct, annex, appendage, extension; accessory, appliance, attachment, additive, filler
**2** the largest number or amount that something can hold — see CAPACITY 1

**complement** *vb* to serve as a completing element to ⟨this cap *complements* your Boy Scout uniform⟩
***syn*** complete, round (off *or* out)
***rel*** finish (off), flesh (out); adorn, beautify, decorate, embellish; better, enhance, improve; constitute, form, make up

**complementary** *adj* related to each other in such a way that one completes the other ⟨the *complementary* contributions of the cooking and cleanup committees were essential to the success of the church barbecue⟩
***syn*** reciprocal, supplementary
***rel*** cooperative, mutual, symbiotic; collective, combined, common, communal, conjoint, joint, shared, united
***ant*** noncomplementary, nonreciprocal

**complete** *adj* **1** not lacking any part or member that properly belongs to it ⟨a *complete* deck of cards⟩
***syn*** comprehensive, entire, full, grand, intact, integral, perfect, plenary, total, whole
***rel*** unabridged, uncut, undiminished; all-out, exhaustive, extensive; full-blown, full-fledged, full-scale
***near ant*** abbreviated, abridged, cut, diminished, reduced
***ant*** imperfect, incomplete, partial
**2** brought or having come to an end ⟨your education is never *complete* — there's always something more to learn⟩
***syn*** completed, concluded, done, down, ended, finished, over, terminated, through, up
***rel*** accomplished, achieved, attained, compassed, realized; dead, defunct, extinct, obsolete; expired
***ant*** continuing, incomplete, ongoing, uncompleted, unfinished
**3** covering everything or all important points — see ENCYCLOPEDIC
**4** having no exceptions or restrictions — see ABSOLUTE 2
**5** trying all possibilities — see EXHAUSTIVE

**complete** *vb* **1** to bring (something) to a state where nothing remains to be done — see FINISH 1
**2** to serve as a completing element to — see COMPLEMENT

**completed** *adj* brought or having come to an end — see COMPLETE 2

**completely** *adv* **1** to a full extent or degree — see FULLY 1
**2** with attention to all aspects or details — see THOROUGHLY 1

**complex** *adj* **1** having many parts or aspects that are usually interrelated ⟨this camera is a *complex* instrument that requires careful handling⟩ ⟨*complex* issues regarding free speech and school discipline⟩
***syn*** complicated, convoluted, elaborate, intricate, involved, knotty, labyrinthine, sophisticated
***rel*** composite, compound, heterogeneous, mixed, multifarious, varied; challenging, difficult, tough; impenetrable, incomprehensible, inexplicable, unfathomable, unintelligible
***near ant*** oversimplified, simplified; homogeneous, uniform, unvaried
***ant*** plain, simple, uncomplicated
**2** made or done with great care or with much detail — see ELABORATE 1

**complex** *n* **1** a structure that is designed and built for a particular purpose — see FACILITY
**2** something made up of many interdependent or related parts — see SYSTEM 1

**complexion** *n* **1** the hue or appearance of the skin and especially of the face ⟨a sunscreen for people with very light *complexions*⟩
***syn*** color, coloring

*rel* shade, tint, tone; features, lineaments, looks; countenance, face, visage
**2** the set of qualities that makes a person, a group of people, or a thing different from others — see NATURE 1

**complexity** *n* **1** the state or quality of having many interrelated parts or aspects ⟨the *complexity* of the company's computer system is such that a full-time repairman is needed⟩
*syn* complicatedness, elaborateness, intricacy, involution, sophistication
*rel* diversity, heterogeneousness; impenetrability, incomprehensibility, inexplicability
*near ant* simplification; homogeneity, uniformity
*ant* plainness, simpleness, simplicity
**2** something that makes a situation more complicated or difficult — see COMPLICATION 1

**compliance** *n* **1** a readiness or willingness to yield to the wishes of others ⟨a strong-willed pop star who is not known for her *compliance*⟩
*syn* compliancy, deference, docility, obedience, submissiveness
*rel* amenability, amiability, complaisance, good-naturedness; servility, slavishness, subservience, subserviency; conformity; cooperativeness, receptiveness, receptivity; humoring, indulgence; acceptance, acquiescence, assent, consent; capitulation, submission, surrender; affability, amicability, congeniality, cordiality, friendliness, geniality, sociability
*near ant* animosity, antipathy, enmity, hostility, ill will
*ant* defiance, disobedience, intractability, recalcitrance
**2** a bending to the authority or control of another — see OBEDIENCE 1

**compliancy** *n* a readiness or willingness to yield to the wishes of others — see COMPLIANCE 1

**compliant** *adj* readily giving in to the command or authority of another — see OBEDIENT

**complicate** *vb* to make complex or difficult ⟨the need to go to both a soccer game and band practice really *complicates* tonight's schedule⟩
*syn* perplex, sophisticate
*rel* develop, elaborate, expand; intensify, magnify; confound, confuse, mess (up), mix (up), muddle; entangle, snarl, tangle
*near ant* abbreviate, cut, shorten; ease, facilitate; disentangle, straighten (out), untangle; oversimplify
*ant* simplify, streamline

**complicated** *adj* **1** having many parts or aspects that are usually interrelated — see COMPLEX 1
**2** made or done with great care or with much detail — see ELABORATE 1

*syn* synonym(s) *rel* related words
*ant* antonym(s) *near ant* near antonym(s)

**complicatedness** *n* the state or quality of having many interrelated parts or aspects — see COMPLEXITY 1

**complication** *n* **1** something that makes a situation more complicated or difficult ⟨the food allergies of the guests were just another *complication* for the couple trying to plan their wedding reception⟩
*syn* complexity, difficulty, intricacy
*rel* aftereffect, ramification, side effect; subtlety, technicality; annoyance, bother, headache, inconvenience, matter, trouble
*phrases* fly in the ointment
**2** an abnormal state that disrupts a plant's or animal's normal bodily functioning — see DISEASE

**complicity** *n* a secret agreement or cooperation between two parties for an illegal or dishonest purpose — see COLLUSION

**compliment** *vb* to express to (someone) admiration for his or her success or good fortune — see CONGRATULATE

**complimentary** *adj* **1** expressing approval — see FAVORABLE 1
**2** not costing or charging anything — see FREE 4

**compliments** *n pl* best wishes ⟨please extend our *compliments* to the chef for a great meal⟩
*syn* congratulations, felicitations, greetings, regards, respects
*rel* approval, blessing, endorsement; acknowledgment (*also* acknowledgement), citation, commendation; adulation, flattery, praise
*near ant* dig, gibe (*or* jibe), insult, put-down, taunt

**comply** (with) *vb* **1** to act according to the commands of — see OBEY
**2** to do what is required by the terms of — see FULFILL 1

**component** *n* one of the parts that make up a whole — see ELEMENT 1

**comport** *vb* **1** to be in agreement on every point — see CHECK 1
**2** to manage the actions of (oneself) in a particular way — see BEHAVE

**comportment** *n* the way or manner in which one conducts oneself — see BEHAVIOR

**compose** *vb* **1** to put (something) into proper and usually carefully worked out written form ⟨the whole class *composed* a request to the governor asking that the endangered species be adopted as the official state animal⟩
*syn* cast, craft, draft, draw (up), formulate, frame, prepare
*rel* fabricate, fashion, form, mold, sculpture, shape; couch, express, phrase, state, verbalize, word; author, pen, write; conceive, concoct, devise; build, construct, make; assemble, compound, piece (together)
*phrases* put together
**2** to be all the substance of — see CONSTITUTE 1
**3** to free from distress or disturbance — see CALM 1

4 to gain emotional or mental control of — see COLLECT 1

**composed** *adj* free from emotional or mental agitation — see CALM 2

**composer** *n* a person who writes musical compositions ⟨a versatile *composer* whose works include operas, symphonies, concertos, and sonatas⟩
*syn* musician, songwriter
*rel* arranger, scorer; librettist

**composite** *adj* made from the joining of two or more parts or elements ⟨the movie's special effects included the use of many *composite* photographs⟩
*syn* amalgamated, compound
*rel* blended, combined, commingled, mingled, mixed; fused, integrated; interlaced, intermixed, intertwined, interwoven
*near ant* uncombined, unmixed
*ant* simple

**composite** *n* a distinct entity formed by the combining of two or more different things — see BLEND

**composition** *n* 1 a literary, musical, or artistic production ⟨the *compositions* of Michelangelo include the dome of St. Peter's, the ceiling of the Sistine Chapel, and his monumental statue of David⟩
*syn* opus, piece, work
*rel* classic, magnum opus, masterpiece, pièce de résistance, showpiece; model, outline, sketch; étude
2 a short piece of writing done as a school exercise ⟨a teacher who is fond of having her class write *compositions*⟩
*syn* paper, theme
*rel* article, essay, story
3 the way in which the elements of something (as a work of art) are arranged ⟨student photographers learn the importance of *composition* in creating striking images⟩
*syn* arrangement, configuration, design, form, format, layout, makeup, pattern
*rel* motif, theme
4 a short piece of writing typically expressing a point of view — see ESSAY 1

**composure** *n* evenness of emotions or temper — see EQUANIMITY

**compound** *adj* made from the joining of two or more parts or elements — see COMPOSITE

**compound** *n* a distinct entity formed by the combining of two or more different things — see BLEND

**compound** *vb* 1 to make greater in size, amount, or number — see INCREASE 1
2 to put or bring together so as to form a new and longer whole — see CONNECT 1

**comprehend** *vb* 1 to recognize the meaning of ⟨the age at which children can *comprehend* the difference between right and wrong⟩
*syn* appreciate, apprehend, catch, catch on (to), dig [*slang*], get, grasp, make, make out, perceive, see, seize, tumble (to), understand
*rel* absorb, assimilate, digest, take in; know, realize, sense; fathom, penetrate
*near ant* misapprehend, misconstrue, misinterpret, misunderstand
*ant* miss
2 to have a practical understanding of — see KNOW 1
3 to have as part of a whole — see INCLUDE

**comprehension** *n* the knowledge gained from the process of coming to know or understand something ⟨the president's *comprehension* of the current situation in the Middle East⟩
*syn* appreciation, apprehension, grasp, grip, perception, understanding
*rel* absorption, assimilation, uptake; conception, visualization; awareness, consciousness, realization
*near ant* misapprehension, misinterpretation, misunderstanding

**comprehensive** *adj* 1 covering everything or all important points — see ENCYCLOPEDIC
2 not lacking any part or member that properly belongs to it — see COMPLETE 1
3 trying all possibilities — see EXHAUSTIVE

**comprehensively** *adv* with attention to all aspects or details — see THOROUGHLY 1

**compress** *vb* 1 to reduce in size or volume by or as if by pressing parts or members together ⟨a science textbook that *compresses* a lot of information about human reproduction into a few short chapters⟩
*syn* compact, condense, constrict, contract, squeeze
*rel* cram, crowd, jam, jam-pack, pack; abbreviate, abridge, curtail, shorten; downsize, shrink; concentrate, consolidate; simplify, streamline; decrease, diminish, lessen
*near ant* disperse, dissipate, scatter; distend, inflate, swell
*ant* expand, open, outspread, outstretch
2 to become smaller in size or volume through the drawing together of particles of matter — see CONTRACT 2

**compression** *n* the act or process of reducing the size or volume of something by or as if by pressing ⟨the *compression* of a long, complicated story into a two-hour movie is never easy⟩
*syn* compacting, condensation, constriction, contraction, squeezing
*rel* abbreviation, abridgment (*or* abridgement), curtailment, shortening; concentration, consolidation; simplification, streamlining; decreasing, diminishment, lessening
*near ant* dispersion, dissipation, scattering; distension (*or* distention), inflation, swelling
*ant* expansion

**comprise** *vb* 1 to be made up of ⟨the mall *comprises* three department stores and eighty smaller shops selling specialized goods⟩
*syn* consist (of), contain
*rel* embrace, encompass, entail, include, involve, take in; assimilate, embody, incorporate

2 to be all the substance of — see CONSTITUTE 1

**compromise** *n* the act or practice of each side giving up something in order to reach an agreement — see CONCESSION 1

**compromise** *vb* to place in danger — see ENDANGER

**compulsion** *n* the use of power to impose one's will on another — see FORCE 2

**compulsive** *adj* caused by or suggestive of an irresistible urge ⟨his *compulsive* clowning around can sometimes be annoying⟩
***syn*** impulsive, obsessive
***rel*** uncontrollable, irrepressible; automatic, instinctive, involuntary, reflex, spontaneous; conditioned, mechanical; unconscious, unthinking, unwitting
***near ant*** unforced, voluntary, willful (*or* wilful); controllable, manageable, resistible

**compulsory** *adj* forcing one's compliance or participation by or as if by law — see MANDATORY

**compunction** *n* an uneasy feeling about the rightness of what one is doing or going to do — see QUALM

**computation** *n* the act or process of performing mathematical operations to find a value — see CALCULATION

**compute** *vb* to determine (a value) by doing the necessary mathematical operations — see CALCULATE 1

**comrade** *n* 1 a person frequently seen in the company of another — see ASSOCIATE 1
2 a person who has a strong liking for and trust in another — see FRIEND 1

**comradely** *adj* having or showing kindly feeling and sincere interest — see FRIENDLY 1

**comradeship** *n* the feeling of closeness and friendship that exists between companions — see COMPANIONSHIP

**con** *vb* to commit to memory — see MEMORIZE

**concatenate** *vb* to put together into a series by means of or as if by means of a thread — see THREAD 2

**concatenation** *n* a series of things linked together — see CHAIN 1

**concave** *adj* curved inward — see HOLLOW

**concavity** *n* a sunken area forming a separate space — see HOLE 2

**conceal** *vb* 1 to put into a hiding place — see [1]HIDE 1
2 to keep secret or shut off from view — see [1]HIDE 2

**concealment** *n* 1 the placing of something out of sight ⟨your choice of the oven for the *concealment* of the money was unwise⟩
***syn*** caching, hiding, secretion, stashing
***rel*** burial, burying, entombment, interment, interring
***near ant*** disinterment, unearthing
***ant*** display, exhibition, exposure, parading, showing
2 a place where a person goes to hide — see HIDEOUT

**concede** *vb* 1 to accept the truth or existence of (something) usually reluctantly — see ADMIT
2 to cease resistance (as to another's arguments, demands, or control) — see YIELD 3

**conceit** *n* 1 an elaborate or fanciful way of expressing something ⟨the *conceit* that the crowd at the outdoor rock concert was a vast sea of people waving to the beat of the music⟩
***syn*** metaphor
***rel*** analogy, circumlocution, euphemism, simile
***phrases*** figure of speech
2 a conception or image created by the imagination and having no objective reality — see FANTASY 1
3 an often unjustified feeling of being pleased with oneself or with one's situation or achievements — see COMPLACENCE

**conceited** *adj* having too high an opinion of oneself ⟨a *conceited* basketball player who was always too busy even to sign autographs⟩
***syn*** complacent, egoistic, egotistic (*or* egotistical), important, overweening, pompous, prideful, proud, self-conceited, self-important, self-satisfied, smug, stuck-up, vain, vainglorious
***rel*** boastful, braggart, bragging; arrogant, cavalier, disdainful, haughty, lordly, self-assertive, snobbish, supercilious, superior, uppity; domineering, high-handed, imperious; highfalutin, pretentious; overconfident, presumptuous; confident, self-assured, self-confident; self-centered, selfish
***near ant*** diffident, self-doubting; meek, unassertive; down-to-earth, unassuming, unpretentious; bashful, retiring, shy
***ant*** humble, modest

**conceitedness** *n* an often unjustified feeling of being pleased with oneself or with one's situation or achievements — see COMPLACENCE

**conceivably** *adv* it is possible — see PERHAPS

**conceive** *vb* to form a mental picture of — see IMAGINE 1

**concentrate** *vb* 1 to increase the amount of (a substance in a mixture) by removing other substances ⟨prolonged boiling is required to *concentrate* the sap when making maple syrup⟩
***syn*** condense
***rel*** distill (*or* distil), purify, refine; compact, harden, solidify; deepen, enhance, heighten, intensify; evaporate, extract, remove
***near ant*** weaken
***ant*** dilute, water (down)
2 to fix (as one's attention) steadily toward a central objective ⟨a president who

---

***syn*** synonym(s) ***rel*** related words
***ant*** antonym(s) ***near ant*** near antonym(s)

will try to *concentrate* public attention on the problems of inner cities〉
***syn*** fasten, focus, rivet, train
***rel*** aim, direct, level, point, zero (in on); attend, heed, mind
**3** to bring (something) to a central point or under a single control — see CENTRALIZE
**4** to bring together in one body or place — see GATHER 1
**5** to come together into one body or place — see ASSEMBLE 1

**concentrated** *adj* **1** having an abundance of some characteristic quality (as flavor) — see FULL-BODIED
**2** not divided or scattered among several areas of interest or concern — see WHOLE 1

**concentration** *n* a focusing of the mind on something — see ATTENTION 1

**concept** *n* something imagined or pictured in the mind — see IDEA

**conception** *n* something imagined or pictured in the mind — see IDEA

**conceptual** *adj* dealing with or expressing a quality or idea — see ABSTRACT 1

**concern** *n* **1** a commercial or industrial activity or organization — see ENTERPRISE 1
**2** an uneasy state of mind usually over the possibility of an anticipated misfortune or trouble — see ANXIETY 1

**concern** *vb* **1** to have (something) as a subject matter 〈the book *concerns* the challenges faced by children growing up in single-parent households〉
***syn*** cover, deal (with), pertain (to), treat (of)
***rel*** appertain (to), bear (on *or* upon), refer (to), relate (to); allude (to); glance (upon), mention, touch (upon); offer, present; contain, embrace, encompass, entail, include, incorporate
***phrases*** have to do with
***near ant*** exclude, omit; disregard, ignore, neglect, overlook, pass over, slight
**2** to be the business or affair of 〈the problems of air and water pollution that *concern* all of us〉
***syn*** affect, involve, touch
***rel*** apply (to), relate (to); embroil, ensnare, entangle, implicate
**3** to trouble the mind of; to make uneasy — see DISTURB 1

**concerning** *prep* having to do with — see ABOUT 1

**concert** *n* an entertainment featuring singing or the playing of musical instruments 〈during the summer various groups give *concerts* on the town green〉
***syn*** musicale
***rel*** performance, presentation recital; hootenanny, jam session, sing, songfest; festival

**concert** *vb* **1** to bring about through discussion and compromise — see NEGOTIATE 1
**2** to participate or assist in a joint effort to accomplish an end — see COOPERATE 1

**concerted** *adj* used or done by a number of people as a group — see COLLECTIVE

**concession** *n* **1** the act or practice of each side giving up something in order to reach an agreement 〈when trying to get a raise in your allowance, it's good to know the art of *concession*〉
***syn*** accommodation, compromise, give-and-take, negotiation
***rel*** arrangement, bargain, deal, understanding; agreement, settlement
**2** an open declaration of something (as a fault or the commission of an offense) about oneself — see CONFESSION
**3** something granted as a special favor — see PRIVILEGE

**conciliate** *vb* **1** to bring to a state free of conflicts, inconsistencies, or differences — see HARMONIZE 2
**2** to lessen the anger or agitation of — see PACIFY

**conciliating** *adj* tending to lessen or avoid conflict or hostility — see PACIFIC 1

**conciliator** *n* one who works with opposing sides in order to bring about an agreement — see MEDIATOR

**conciliatory** *adj* tending to lessen or avoid conflict or hostility — see PACIFIC 1

**concise** *adj* marked by the use of few words to convey much information or meaning 〈a *concise* article on violence in the media that manages to say more than most books on the subject〉
***syn*** aphoristic, brief, compact, compendious, crisp, epigrammatic, laconic, pithy, succinct, summary, terse
***rel*** abrupt, blunt, brusque, curt, short, snippy; abbreviated, abridged, condensed, shortened; meaty, substantial; meaningful, significant
***near ant*** redundant, repetitious, tautological; enlarged, expanded, supplemented; embellished, embroidered, exaggerated
***ant*** diffuse, long-winded, prolix, rambling, verbose, wordy

**concisely** *adv* in a few words — see SHORTLY 1

**conciseness** *n* **1** the condition of being short — see BREVITY 1
**2** the quality or state of being marked by or using only few words to convey much meaning — see SUCCINCTNESS

**conclude** *vb* **1** to bring (an event) to a natural or appropriate stopping point — see CLOSE 3
**2** to come to an end — see CEASE 1
**3** to bring about through discussion and compromise — see NEGOTIATE 1
**4** to come to a judgment after discussion or consideration — see DECIDE 1
**5** to form an opinion through reasoning and information — see INFER 1

**concluded** *adj* brought or having come to an end — see COMPLETE 2

**concluding** *adj* following all others of the same kind in order or time — see LAST

**conclusion** *n* **1** an opinion arrived at through a process of reasoning 〈the detective's *conclusion* that the murderer had to be left-handed〉

*syn* deduction, determination, inference
*rel* decision, judgment (*or* judgement), ruling, verdict; conjecture, guess, surmise; assumption, presumption, supposition
**2** a position arrived at after consideration — see DECISION 1
**3** a condition or occurrence traceable to a cause — see EFFECT 1
**4** the last part of a process or action — see FINALE
**5** the stopping of a process or activity — see END 1

**conclusive** *adj* **1** serving to put an end to all debate or questioning ⟨the archeological discovery was *conclusive* proof that the Vikings had indeed settled in North America around 1000 A.D.⟩
*syn* absolute, clear, decisive, definitive
*rel* incontestable, incontrovertible, indisputable, indubitable, irrefutable, undeniable, unquestionable; unchallenged, uncontested, undisputed; unambiguous, unequivocal; certain, definite, positive, sure
*near ant* debatable, disputable, questionable, refutable; ambiguous, equivocal
*ant* inconclusive, indecisive, unclear
**2** having the power to persuade — see COGENT

**concoct** *vb* to create or think of by clever use of the imagination — see INVENT

**concoction** *n* something (as a device) created for the first time through the use of the imagination — see INVENTION 1

**concomitant** *n* something that is found along with something else — see ACCOMPANIMENT

**concomitant** *adj* present at the same time and place — see COINCIDENT

**concord** *n* peaceful coexistence — see HARMONY 2

**concourse** *n* a typically long narrow way connecting parts of a building — see HALL 2

**concrete** *adj* **1** existing in fact and not merely as a possibility — see ACTUAL
**2** relating to or composed of matter — see MATERIAL 1

**concrete** *vb* to become physically firm or solid — see HARDEN 1

**concur** *vb* **1** to have or come to the same opinion or point of view — see AGREE 1
**2** to occur or exist at the same time — see COINCIDE 1

**concurrence** *n* **1** the occurrence or existence of several things at once ⟨the *concurrence* of my birthday and the concert by my favorite rock band made my preference for a birthday present pretty obvious⟩
*syn* coexistence, coincidence
*rel* development, happening, occurrence
**2** the act or fact of being of one opinion about something — see AGREEMENT 1

*syn* synonym(s) *rel* related words
*ant* antonym(s) *near ant* near antonym(s)

**3** the approval by someone in authority for the doing of something — see PERMISSION

**concurrent** *adj* **1** existing or occurring at the same period of time — see CONTEMPORARY 1
**2** present at the same time and place — see COINCIDENT

**concurrently** *adv* at one and the same time — see TOGETHER 1

**concussion** *n* a forceful coming together of two things — see IMPACT 1

**condemn** *vb* **1** to declare to be morally wrong or evil ⟨it is a sign of human progress that slavery, which was once common, is now universally *condemned*⟩
*syn* censure, damn, decry, denounce, execrate, reprehend, reprobate
*rel* attack, blast, criticize, knock, pan, slam; belittle, deprecate, disparage; doom, sentence; convict; blacklist, excommunicate, ostracize; rebuke, reprimand, reproach; admonish, chide, reprove; berate, lambaste (*or* lambast), scold, upbraid; curse, imprecate; abhor, abominate, detest, hate, loathe, revile
*near ant* approve, endorse (*also* indorse), sanction; eulogize, exalt, extol (*also* extoll), glorify, laud, praise; acclaim, applaud, commend, hail; consecrate, hallow, sanctify; honor, revere, venerate
*ant* bless
**2** to express one's unfavorable opinion of the worth or quality of — see CRITICIZE
**3** to express public or formal disapproval of — see CENSURE 1
**4** to find or pronounce guilty — see CONVICT
**5** to impose a judicial punishment on — see SENTENCE

**condemnation** *n* an often public or formal expression of disapproval — see CENSURE

**condensation** *n* **1** a shortened version of a written work — see ABRIDGMENT
**2** the act or process of reducing the size or volume of something by or as if by pressing — see COMPRESSION

**condense** *vb* **1** to become smaller in size or volume through the drawing together of particles of matter — see CONTRACT 2
**2** to reduce in size or volume by or as if by pressing parts or members together — see COMPRESS 1
**3** to increase the amount of (a substance in a mixture) by removing other substances — see CONCENTRATE 1

**condensed** *adj* not lasting for a considerable time — see SHORT 2

**condescend** *vb* **1** to descend to a level that is beneath one's dignity ⟨I will not *condescend* to answer the sore loser's charge that I cheated in order to win the race⟩
*syn* deign, stoop
*rel* debase, degrade, demean, humble, humiliate, lower
*near ant* rise
**2** to assume or treat with an air of superiority ⟨wealthy people who tend to be

*condescending* toward their poor relations〉
***syn*** lord (it over), patronize
***rel*** cold-shoulder, cut, high-hat, snub

**condiment** *n* something used to enhance the flavor of cooked or prepared food 〈the cafeteria's self-serve table has a full array of *condiments*〉
***syn*** seasoning
***rel*** herb, savory, spice; relish, sauce; flavoring

**condition** *n* **1** a state of being or fitness 〈a car that was ten years old but in still good *condition*〉
***syn*** estate, fettle, form, kilter, order, repair, shape, trim
***rel*** practice (*also* practise); pass, phase, stage
***near ant*** disorder, disrepair
**2** something upon which the carrying out of an agreement or offer depends 〈you'll get a raise in your allowance with the *condition* that you'll do a better job of keeping your room clean〉
***syn*** provision, proviso, qualification, reservation, stipulation
***rel*** strings, terms; prerequisite, requirement, requisite; limitation, modification, restriction; exception, exemption; essential, must, necessity
**3** an abnormal state that disrupts a plant's or animal's normal bodily functioning — see DISEASE
**4** something necessary, indispensable, or unavoidable — see ESSENTIAL 1
**5** something that limits one's freedom of action or choice — see RESTRICTION 1

**condition** *vb* **1** to bring to a proper or desired state of fitness 〈the length of time that it takes for runners to *condition* their bodies for a marathon〉
***syn*** season, train
***rel*** fit, prepare, ready; acclimate, acclimatize, break in, orient, orientate; accustom, familiarize, habituate; harden, inure
**2** to change (something) so as to make it suitable for a new use or situation — see ADAPT

**conditional** *adj* determined by something else — see DEPENDENT 2

**conditioning** *n* energetic movement of the body for the sake of physical fitness — see EXERCISE 1

**condole** (with) *vb* to have sympathy for — see PITY

**condone** *vb* to overlook or dismiss as of little importance — see EXCUSE 1

**conduct** *n* **1** the act or activity of looking after and making decisions about something 〈the president was happy to leave the *conduct* of foreign affairs to his secretary of state〉
***syn*** administration, control, direction, governance, government, guidance, handling, management, operation, oversight, regulation, running, superintendence, supervision
***rel*** care, custody, guardianship, protection, tutelage; engineering, machination, manipulation
**2** the way or manner in which one conducts oneself — see BEHAVIOR

**conduct** *vb* **1** to look after and make decisions about 〈the company's president continues to *conduct* the everyday affairs of the software firm he founded many years ago〉
***syn*** administer, carry on, control, direct, govern, guide, handle, manage, operate, oversee, regulate, run, superintend, supervise
***rel*** care (for), keep, mind, tend, watch; lead, pilot, steer; guard, protect, safeguard
**2** to cause to move to a central point or along a restricted pathway — see CHANNEL
**3** to manage the actions of (oneself) in a particular way — see BEHAVE
**4** to point out the way for (someone) especially from a position in front — see LEAD 1

**conduit** *n* **1** a long hollow cylinder for carrying a substance (as a liquid or gas) — see PIPE 1
**2** an open man-made passageway for water — see CHANNEL 1

**confection** *n* a food having a high sugar content — see SWEET 1

**confederacy** *n* an association of persons, parties, or states for mutual assistance and protection 〈a *confederacy* of several small nations who had promised to come to one another's aid if any were attacked〉
***syn*** alliance, bloc, coalition, combination, combine, confederation, federation, league, union
***rel*** cabal, conspiracy, junto; cartel, syndicate, trust; faction, side, wing; association, group, organization; affiliation, cooperative, partnership

**confederate** *n* **1** one associated with another in wrongdoing — see ACCOMPLICE
**2** someone associated with another to give assistance or moral support — see ALLY

**confederate** *vb* to form or enter into an association that furthers the interests of its members — see ALLY

**confederation** *n* **1** an association of persons, parties, or states for mutual assistance and protection — see CONFEDERACY
**2** the state of having shared interests or efforts (as in social or business matters) — see ASSOCIATION 1

**confer** *vb* **1** to give the ownership or benefit of (something) formally or publicly 〈the British monarch continues to *confer* knighthood on those who are outstanding in their fields〉
***syn*** accord, award, grant
***rel*** bestow, contribute, donate, give, present; furnish, provide, supply; extend, offer, proffer; allocate, appropriate, assign
***near ant*** rescind, revoke
**2** to exchange viewpoints or seek advice for the purpose of finding a solution to a problem 〈my parents are going to *confer*

with a financial advisor about saving for my college education〉
*syn* advise, consult, counsel, parley, powwow, treat
*rel* debate, deliberate, discuss, hash (over); coach, guide, tutor; recommend, suggest; direct, refer (to)

**conference** *n* **1** a body of people come together in one place — see GATHERING 1
**2** a coming together of a number of persons for a specified purpose — see MEETING 1
**3** a meeting featuring a group discussion — see FORUM
**4** an exchange of views for the purpose of exploring a subject or deciding an issue — see DISCUSSION 1

**confess** *vb* to accept the truth or existence of (something) usually reluctantly — see ADMIT

**confession** *n* an open declaration of something (as a fault or the commission of an offense) about oneself 〈a *confession* that he had been lying all along〉
*syn* acknowledgment (*also* acknowledgement), admission, avowal, concession
*rel* allowance; betrayal, disclosure, divulgence, revelation; announcement, declaration, proclamation; contrition, regret, remorse, repentance

**confidant** *n* a person who has a strong liking for and trust in another — see FRIEND 1

**confidence** *n* **1** great faith in oneself or one's abilities 〈a lifelong *confidence* that enabled her to achieve great things despite powerful obstacles〉
*syn* aplomb, assurance, self-assurance, self-confidence, self-esteem
*rel* cockiness, complacence, complacency, conceit, conceitedness, ego, egotism, overconfidence, pompousness, pride, self-admiration, self-conceit, self-importance, self-satisfaction, smugness, vainglory, vanity; calmness, composure, coolness, equanimity; self-possession
*near ant* apprehension, doubt, misgiving
*ant* diffidence, self-doubt
**2** a state of mind in which one is free from doubt 〈the *confidence* with which the game show contestant answered every question〉
*syn* assurance, assuredness, certainty, certitude, conviction, positiveness, sureness
*rel* authoritarianism, dogmatism; decisiveness, firmness, resolution
*near ant* hesitancy, hesitation, indecisiveness, irresolution
*ant* doubt, incertitude, nonconfidence, uncertainty
**3** firm belief in the integrity, ability, effectiveness, or genuineness of someone or something — see TRUST 1
**4** information shared only with another or with a select few — see SECRET 1

**confidence game** *n* a scheme in which the victim is cheated out of his money after first gaining his trust 〈the old *confidence game* in which the victims are told that they must pay a fee in order to collect their prize money〉
*syn* hustle, racket, swindle
*rel* double cross, fix; gyp, rip-off; squeeze; ruse, subterfuge, trick

**confidence man** *n* a dishonest person who uses clever means to cheat others out of something of value — see TRICKSTER 1

**confident** *adj* **1** having or showing great faith in oneself or one's abilities 〈you'll need to be *confident* —even in the face of rejection—if you want to pursue a career in show business〉
*syn* assured, secure, self-assured, self-confident
*rel* hopeful, optimistic, rosy, sanguine, upbeat; complacent, conceited, egoistic, egotistic (*or* egotistical), important, overweening, pompous, prideful, proud, self-conceited, self-important, self-satisfied, smug, stuck-up, vain, vainglorious; calm, collected, composed, cool, placid, self-possessed, serene, tranquil, undisturbed, unperturbed
*near ant* meek, timid, unassertive; modest, unassuming, unpretentious; jittery, jumpy, nervous
*ant* diffident, insecure, self-doubting
**2** having or showing a mind free from doubt — see CERTAIN 2

**confidential** *adj* not known or meant to be known by the general populace — see PRIVATE 1

**confiding** *adj* having or showing trust in another — see TRUSTING 1

**configuration** *n* **1** the arrangement of parts that gives something its basic form — see FRAME 1
**2** the way in which something is sized, arranged, or organized — see FORMAT 1
**3** the way in which the elements of something (as a work of art) are arranged — see COMPOSITION 3
**4** the outward appearance of something as distinguished from its substance — see FORM 1

**confine** *vb* **1** to set bounds or an upper limit for — see LIMIT 1
**2** to put in or as if in prison — see IMPRISON

**confinement** *n* **1** the act of confining or the state of being confined — see INTERNMENT
**2** the act or practice of keeping something (as an activity) within certain boundaries — see RESTRICTION 2

**confines** *n pl* **1** a real or imaginary point beyond which a person or thing cannot go — see LIMIT
**2** the line or relatively narrow space that marks the outer limit of something — see BORDER 1

**confirm** *vb* to give evidence or testimony to the truth or factualness of 〈several

---

*syn* synonym(s) *rel* related words
*ant* antonym(s) *near ant* near antonym(s)

eyewitnesses who can *confirm* the youngster's account of what happened〉
***syn*** bear out, corroborate, substantiate, support, validate, verify, vindicate
***rel*** attest, authenticate, avouch, certify, testify (to), vouch (for), witness; guarantee, warrant; affirm, assert, aver, avow, profess
***near ant*** contradict, gainsay; deny, disavow, disclaim
***ant*** disprove, rebut, refute

**confirmable** *adj* capable of being proven as true or real — see VERIFIABLE

**confirmation** *n* something presented in support of the truth or accuracy of a claim — see PROOF

**confirmatory** *adj* serving to give support to the truth or factualness of something — see CORROBORATIVE

**confirmed** *adj* **1** being such by habit and not likely to change — see HABITUAL 1
**2** firmly established over time — see INVETERATE 1

**confirming** *adj* serving to give support to the truth or factualness of something — see CORROBORATIVE

**confiscate** *vb* to take ownership or control of (something) by right of one's authority 〈anything that might be used as a weapon will be *confiscated* by the security guards〉
***syn*** expropriate, sequester
***rel*** appropriate, arrogate, preempt, usurp; commandeer, seize, take over
***near ant*** release, relinquish, surrender, yield

**conflagration** *n* a destructive burning — see FIRE

**conflict** *n* **1** a lack of agreement or harmony — see DISCORD
**2** a physical dispute between opposing individuals or groups — see FIGHT 1
**3** a state of armed violent struggle between states, nations, or groups — see WAR 1
**4** an earnest effort for superiority or victory over another — see CONTEST 1

**conflict** *vb* to be out of harmony or agreement usually noticeably — see CLASH

**conflicting** *adj* not being in agreement or harmony — see INCONSISTENT

**confluence** *n* the coming together of two or more things to the same point — see CONVERGENCE

**conform** *vb* **1** to be in agreement on every point — see CHECK 1
**2** to form a pleasing relationship — see HARMONIZE 1
**3** to bring to a state free of conflicts, inconsistencies, or differences — see HARMONIZE 2
**4** to change (something) so as to make it suitable for a new use or situation — see ADAPT

**conform** (to) *vb* to act according to the commands of — see OBEY

**conformable** *adj* readily giving in to the command or authority of another — see OBEDIENT

**conformable** (to) *adj* not having or showing any apparent conflict — see CONSISTENT

**conformation** *n* **1** the outward appearance of something as distinguished from its substance — see FORM 1
**2** the way in which something is sized, arranged, or organized — see FORMAT 1

**conformity** *n* **1** a state of consistency 〈the simple lifestyle of the Amish is in *conformity* with their ascetic religious beliefs〉
***syn*** accord, accordance, agreement, congruity, consonance, harmony, tune
***rel*** assimilation, integration; oneness, solidarity, togetherness; affinity, empathy, sympathy
***near ant*** discrepancy, disparity, dissimilarity
***ant*** conflict, disagreement
**2** a bending to the authority or control of another — see OBEDIENCE 1

**confound** *vb* **1** to throw into a state of mental uncertainty — see CONFUSE 1
**2** to throw into a state of self-conscious distress — see EMBARRASS 1

**confront** *vb* to oppose (something hostile or dangerous) with firmness or courage — see FACE 2

**confrontation** *n* an earnest effort for superiority or victory over another — see CONTEST 1

**confuse** *vb* **1** to throw into a state of mental uncertainty 〈the similar-sounding words "censure" and "censor" often *confuse* people〉
***syn*** addle, baffle, befog, befuddle, bemuse, bewilder, confound, disorient, muddle, muddy, mystify, perplex, puzzle
***rel*** stick, stump; abash, discomfit, disconcert, discountenance, embarrass, faze, fluster, mortify, nonplus, rattle; agitate, bother, chagrin, discomfort, discompose, dismay, disquiet, distress, disturb, perturb, stun, unhinge, unsettle, upset; deceive, misguide, mislead
***near ant*** assure, reassure, satisfy; enlighten, inform
**2** to make (something) unclear to the understanding 〈stop *confusing* the issue with irrelevant facts〉
***syn*** becloud, befog, blur, cloud, fog, muddy
***rel*** complicate, perplex, sophisticate; entangle, snarl, tangle; disorder, jumble, mess (up), mix (up)
***near ant*** simplify, streamline; disentangle, straighten (out), untangle
***ant*** clarify
**3** to throw into a state of self-conscious distress — see EMBARRASS 1
**4** to undo the proper order or arrangement of — see DISORDER

**confused** *adj* **1** lacking in order, neatness, and often cleanliness — see MESSY
**2** suffering from mental confusion — see DIZZY 2

**confusion** *n* **1** a state of mental uncertainty 〈the farmer's driving directions to the fairground just left us in total *confusion*〉

*syn* bafflement, befuddlement, bewilderment, distraction, muddle, mystification, perplexity, puzzlement, whirl
*rel* abashment, discomfiture, embarrassment, fluster, mortification; agitation, chagrin, discomfort, dismay, disquiet, distress, disturbance, perturbation, upset
*near ant* assurance, certainty, certitude, confidence, conviction, positiveness, sureness
**2** a state in which everything is out of order — see CHAOS
**3** the emotional state of being made self-consciously uncomfortable — see EMBARRASSMENT 1

**confute** *vb* to prove to be false — see DISPROVE

**congeal** *vb* **1** to become physically firm or solid — see HARDEN 1
**2** to turn from a liquid into a substance resembling jelly — see COAGULATE

**congenial** *adj* **1** giving pleasure or contentment to the mind or senses — see PLEASANT
**2** having or marked by agreement in feeling or action — see HARMONIOUS 3

**congenital** *adj* being such from birth or by nature — see NATURAL 1

**congest** *vb* to prevent passage through — see CLOG 1

**conglomerate** *n* a group of businesses or enterprises under one control ⟨the huge media *conglomerate* owns TV and radio stations, a cable company, and a movie studio⟩
*syn* empire
*rel* multinational; cartel, combination, syndicate, trust; chain; association, corporation, organization, pool

**conglomerate** *vb* **1** to come together into one body or place — see ASSEMBLE 1
**2** to gradually form into a layer, pile, or mass — see COLLECT 2

**congratulate** *vb* to express to (someone) admiration for his or her success or good fortune ⟨let me be the first to *congratulate* you on winning the award⟩
*syn* compliment, felicitate
*rel* applaud, cheer, commend, hail; extol (*also* extoll), glorify, laud, praise
*near ant* bad-mouth, belittle, decry, disparage, put down; jeer, mock, ridicule, taunt, tease

**congratulations** *n pl* best wishes — see COMPLIMENTS

**congregate** *vb* to come together into one body or place — see ASSEMBLE 1

**congregation** *n* **1** a body of persons gathered for religious worship ⟨the whole *congregation* began to sing with great fervor⟩
*syn* assembly, church
*rel* laity, parish; communion, denomination, fold, sect
**2** a body of people come together in one place — see GATHERING 1

**congress** *n* **1** the highest lawmaking body of a political unit ⟨the national emergency required a special session of *congress*⟩
*syn* parliament
*rel* assembly, chamber, council, diet, house, legislature
**2** a coming together of a number of persons for a specified purpose — see MEETING 1
**3** a group of persons formally joined together for some common interest — see ASSOCIATION 2

**congruity** *n* a state of consistency — see CONFORMITY 1

**congruous** *adj* **1** having the parts agreeably related — see HARMONIOUS 2
**2** not having or showing any apparent conflict — see CONSISTENT

**congruously** *adv* in a manner suitable for the occasion or purpose — see PROPERLY

**conjectural** *adj* existing only as an assumption or speculation — see THEORETICAL 1

**conjecture** *n* an opinion or judgment based on little or no evidence ⟨the many *conjectures* about the true identity of Jack the Ripper⟩
*syn* guess, supposition, surmise
*rel* hypothesis, theory, thesis; guesswork, speculation; hunch, intuition; belief, faith

**conjecture** *vb* **1** to decide the size, amount, number, or distance of (something) without actual measurement — see ESTIMATE 2
**2** to form an opinion from little or no evidence — see GUESS 1

**conjoin** *vb* **1** to come together to form a single unit — see UNITE 1
**2** to form or enter into an association that furthers the interests of its members — see ALLY

**conjoint** *adj* used or done by a number of people as a group — see COLLECTIVE

**conjointly** *adv* in or by combined action or effort — see TOGETHER 2

**conjugal** *adj* of or relating to marriage — see MARITAL

**conjugate** *vb* **1** to come together to form a single unit — see UNITE 1
**2** to put or bring together so as to form a new and longer whole — see CONNECT 1

**conjunction** *n* the coming together of two or more things to the same point — see CONVERGENCE

**conjuration** *n* a spoken word or set of words believed to have magic power — see SPELL 1

**conjure** *vb* to make a request to (someone) in an earnest or urgent manner — see BEG

**conjure** (up) *vb* to call into being through the use of one's inner resources or powers — see SUMMON 2

**conjurer** *or* **conjuror** *n* **1** a person skilled in using supernatural forces — see MAGICIAN 1
**2** one who practices tricks and illusions for entertainment — see MAGICIAN 2

---

*syn* synonym(s) *rel* related words
*ant* antonym(s) *near ant* near antonym(s)

**conjuring** *n* **1** the power to control natural forces through supernatural means — see MAGIC 1
**2** the art or skill of performing tricks or illusions for entertainment — see MAGIC 2
**conk** (out) *vb* to stop functioning — see FAIL 1
**connect** *vb* **1** to put or bring together so as to form a new and longer whole ⟨*connect* all the sets of lights and attach them to the branches of the Christmas tree⟩
***syn*** chain, compound, conjugate, couple, hitch, hook, join, link, yoke
***rel*** dovetail; concatenate, string; cement, coalesce, combine, fuse, unite
***near ant*** divide, part, split
***ant*** disconnect, disjoin, separate, unchain, uncouple, unhitch, unlink, unyoke
**2** to come together to form a single unit — see UNITE 1
**3** to think of (something) in combination — see ASSOCIATE 2
**connecting** *n* the act or an instance of joining two or more things into one — see UNION 1
**connection** *n* **1** the fact or state of having something in common ⟨the endless debate about the *connection* between crime and poverty⟩
***syn*** association, bearing, kinship, liaison, linkage, relation, relationship
***rel*** correlation, interrelation; materiality, pertinence, relevance; bond, link, tie; affiliation, alliance, union; likeness, resemblance, similarity
**2** a place where two or more things are united — see JOINT 1
**3** an acquaintance who has influence especially in the business or political world — see CONTACT
**4** the act or an instance of joining two or more things into one — see UNION 1
**5** the fact or state of being pertinent — see PERTINENCE
**6** the state of having shared interests or efforts (as in social or business matters) — see ASSOCIATION 1
**connivance** *n* a secret agreement or cooperation between two parties for an illegal or dishonest purpose — see COLLUSION
**connive** *vb* to secretly sympathize with or pretend ignorance of something improper or unlawful ⟨the principal *connived* at all the school absences that were recorded on the day of the city's celebration of its Super Bowl victory⟩
***syn*** wink
***rel*** condone, disregard, excuse, ignore, overlook, tolerate
***near ant*** disapprove (of), frown (on *or* upon); deny, disallow, refuse
**connoisseur** *n* a person having a knowledgeable and fine appreciation of the arts ⟨a forthcoming exhibit at the art museum that is eagerly awaited by *connoisseurs* of ancient Greek pottery⟩
***syn*** dilettante
***rel*** adept, authority, expert, master; critic, reviewer; amateur, dabbler; collector
***near ant*** materialist, philistine
**connubial** *adj* of or relating to marriage — see MARITAL
**conquer** *vb* **1** to bring under one's control by force of arms ⟨before his final defeat, Napoleon had managed to *conquer* much of Europe⟩
***syn*** dominate, overpower, subdue, subject, subjugate, vanquish
***rel*** beat, crush, defeat, drub, lick, mow (down), rout, smash, thrash, trounce; enslave; break, put down, quell, suppress
***near ant*** emancipate, free, liberate, manumit, release
**2** to achieve a victory over — see BEAT 2
**3** to achieve victory (as in a contest) — see WIN 1
**conqueror** *n* one that defeats an enemy or opponent — see VICTOR 1
**conquest** *n* the act or process of bringing someone or something under one's control ⟨the *conquest* of much of North and South America by the Spanish during the 16th century⟩
***syn*** dominating, domination, overpowering, subduing, subjecting, subjection, subjugating, subjugation, vanquishing
***rel*** triumph, victory, winning; beating, defeat, drubbing, licking, trouncing; enslavement
***near ant*** emancipation, freeing, liberation, manumission, release
**conscientious** *adj* **1** guided by or in accordance with one's sense of right and wrong ⟨operated on the belief that most people are *conscientious*, the unattended farm stand has a price list and a money drawer for customers to leave payment for their purchases⟩
***syn*** ethical, honest, honorable, just, moral, principled, scrupulous
***rel*** good, righteous, upright, virtuous; dutiful, observant, respectful; overconscientious; reliable, trustworthy, trusty
***near ant*** unreliable, untrustworthy
***ant*** cutthroat, dishonest, dishonorable, immoral, unethical, unjust, unprincipled, unscrupulous
**2** taking great care and effort — see PAINSTAKING
**conscientiousness** *n* strict attentiveness to what one is doing — see CARE 1
**conscious** *adj* having specified facts or feelings actively impressed on the mind ⟨*conscious* of the fact that my hands were sweating the whole time that I was making my presentation⟩
***syn*** alive, aware, cognizant, mindful, sensible, sentient
***rel*** attentive, heedful, observant, regardful, vigilant, watchful
***near ant*** inattentive, unheeding, unobservant, unobserving
***ant*** insensible, unaware, unconscious, unmindful
**consciously** *adv* with full awareness of what one is doing — see INTENTIONALLY
**conscript** *n* a person forced or required to enroll in military service ⟨as the war continued, the body of enlisted soldiers was

supplemented by an increasing number of *conscripts*⟩
***syn*** draftee, inductee
***rel*** recruit, rookie

**conscript** *vb* to pick especially for required military service — see DRAFT 1

**consecrate** *vb* **1** to keep or intend for a special purpose — see DEVOTE 1
**2** to make holy through prayers or ritual — see BLESS 1

**consecrated** *adj* set apart or worthy of veneration by association with God — see HOLY 2

**consecration** *n* the act of making something holy through religious ritual ⟨the *consecration* of the Host during Communion⟩
***syn*** blessing, hallowing, sanctification
***rel*** dedication
***near ant*** defilement, desecration, profanation

**consecutive** *adj* following one after another without others coming in between ⟨the team's winning streak has lasted for seven *consecutive* games⟩
***syn*** sequential, succeeding, successional, successive
***rel*** serial; constant, continuous, uninterrupted; ensuing, following, later, next, subsequent

**consensus** *n* the act or fact of being of one opinion about something — see AGREEMENT 1

**consent** *n* the approval by someone in authority for the doing of something — see PERMISSION

**consequence** *n* **1** a condition or occurrence traceable to a cause — see EFFECT 1
**2** the quality or state of being important — see IMPORTANCE

**consequent** *adj* coming as a result — see RESULTANT

**consequential** *adj* **1** coming as a result — see RESULTANT
**2** having great meaning or lasting effect — see IMPORTANT 1

**consequently** *adv* for this or that reason — see THEREFORE

**conservation** *n* **1** the careful maintaining and protection of something valuable especially in its natural or original state ⟨everyone has a duty to aid in the *conservation* of our nation's wilderness areas⟩
***syn*** preservation
***rel*** care, maintenance, upkeep; salvation, saving; guardianship, protection, safeguarding, safekeeping; economy, husbandry, management
***near ant*** neglect, squandering, waste; destruction, ruin; damage, injury
**2** the act or activity of keeping something in an existing and usually satisfactory condition — see MAINTENANCE

**conservative** *adj* **1** tending to favor established ideas, conditions, or institutions ⟨*conservative* baseball fans consider the new ballpark too modern-looking and plain ugly⟩
***syn*** old-fashioned, orthodox, reactionary, traditional, unprogressive
***rel*** conventional; faithful, loyal, steadfast, true-blue
***near ant*** extremist, radical, revolutionary; nonconformist
***ant*** liberal, nonorthodox, nontraditional, progressive, unorthodox
**2** not excessively showy — see QUIET 2

**conservative** *n* a person whose political beliefs are centered on tradition and keeping things the way they are ⟨proposed legislation that was opposed by *conservatives* throughout the state⟩
***syn*** reactionary, rightist
***rel*** conformist
***near ant*** extremist, radical, revolutionary, revolutionist
***ant*** leftist, liberal, progressive

**conservatory** *n* a glass-enclosed building for growing plants ⟨the college's *conservatory* is entirely devoted to cultivating and displaying orchids⟩
***syn*** greenhouse, hothouse
***rel*** cold frame; nursery

**conserve** *vb* to keep in good condition — see MAINTAIN 1

**conserving** *n* the act or activity of keeping something in an existing and usually satisfactory condition — see MAINTENANCE

**consider** *vb* **1** to think of in a particular way ⟨I *consider* him a very good friend⟩
***syn*** account, call, count, esteem, hold, rate, reckon, regard, take (for)
***rel*** believe, feel, sense, think; conceive, fancy, imagine
***phrases*** look on (*or* upon)
**2** to give serious and careful thought to — see PONDER
**3** to have as an opinion — see BELIEVE 2

**considerable** *adj* **1** sufficiently large in size, amount, or number to merit attention ⟨the *considerable* number of auto accidents that resulted from the surprise snowstorm⟩
***syn*** good, goodly, good-sized, healthy, largish, respectable, significant, sizable (*or* sizeable), substantial, tidy
***rel*** big, colossal, enormous, gigantic, great, huge, immense, mammoth
***near ant*** piddling, puny, trivial, unimportant; marginal, meager, slight; little, small, tiny
***ant*** inconsiderable, insignificant, insubstantial
**2** of a size greater than average of its kind — see LARGE

**considerably** *adv* to a large extent or degree — see GREATLY 2

**considerate** *adj* **1** given to or made with heedful anticipation of the needs and happiness of others — see THOUGHTFUL 1
**2** having or showing a close attentiveness to avoiding danger or trouble — see CAREFUL 1

**considerately** *adv* with good reason or courtesy — see WELL 4

**consideration** *n* **1** a careful weighing of the reasons for or against something ⟨after much *consideration* we decided to make an offer on the house⟩
***syn*** debate, deliberation, thought
***rel*** cogitation, contemplation, meditation, pondering, rumination; introspection, reflection; agonizing, hesitation, indecision
**2** something (as money) that is given or received in return for goods or services — see PAYMENT 2
**considered** *adj* decided on as a result of careful thought — see DELIBERATE 1
**consign** *vb* **1** to cause to go or be taken from one place to another — see SEND
**2** to put (something) into the possession or safekeeping of another — see GIVE 2
**consist** (of) *vb* to be made up of — see COMPRISE 1
**consistency** *n* the degree to which a fluid can resist flowing ⟨beat the egg whites until they take on the *consistency* of whipped cream⟩
***syn*** density, thickness, viscosity
***rel*** compactness, firmness, solidity; ropiness, stickiness
**consistent** *adj* not having or showing any apparent conflict ⟨the clothes you wear to class must be *consistent* with the school's dress code⟩
***syn*** compatible, conformable (to), congruous, consonant, correspondent (with *or* to), harmonious, nonconflicting
***rel*** appropriate, fitting, meet, suitable
***phrases*** of a piece
***ant*** conflicting, incompatible, incongruous, inconsistent, inharmonious, unharmonious
**consistently** *adv* on every relevant occasion — see ALWAYS 1
**consolation** *n* **1** the giving of hope and strength in times of grief, distress, or suffering ⟨the *consolation* of the grieving family by their pastor⟩
***syn*** comforting, consoling, solace, solacing
***rel*** commiseration, condolence, sympathy; counseling (*or* counselling)
**2** a feeling of ease from grief or trouble — see COMFORT 1
**console** *vb* to ease the grief or distress of — see COMFORT 1
**consolidate** *vb* **1** to bring (something) to a central point or under a single control — see CENTRALIZE
**2** to make markedly greater in measure or degree — see INTENSIFY
**consolidation** *n* the act or an instance of joining two or more things into one — see UNION 1
**consoling** *n* the giving of hope and strength in times of grief, distress, or suffering — see CONSOLATION 1
**consonance** *n* **1** a balanced, pleasing, or suitable arrangement of parts — see HARMONY 1
**2** a state of consistency — see CONFORMITY 1
**consonant** *adj* **1** having the parts agreeably related — see HARMONIOUS 2
**2** not having or showing any apparent conflict — see CONSISTENT
**consort** *n* the person to whom another is married — see SPOUSE
**consort** *vb* to come or be together as friends — see ASSOCIATE 1
**conspicuous** *adj* **1** likely to attract attention — see NOTICEABLE
**2** very noticeable especially for being incorrect or bad — see EGREGIOUS
**conspiracy** *n* **1** a group involved in secret or criminal activities — see RING 1
**2** a secret agreement or cooperation between two parties for an illegal or dishonest purpose — see COLLUSION
**3** a secret plan for accomplishing evil or unlawful ends — see PLOT 1
**conspire** *vb* to engage in a secret plan to accomplish evil or unlawful ends — see PLOT
**constable** *n* a member of a force charged with law enforcement at the local level — see OFFICER 1
**constabulary** *n* a body of officers of the law — see POLICE 2
**constancy** *n* **1** the state of continuing without change ⟨the mistaken notion that there is *constancy* in language—words do indeed change their meanings over time⟩
***syn*** changelessness, fixedness, immutability, invariability, stability, steadiness, unchangeableness
***rel*** consistency, regularity, sameness, uniformity; durability, lastingness, permanence
***near ant*** inconsistency, irregularity, unevenness; evanescence, impermanence
***ant*** changeability, changeableness, instability, mutability, unsteadiness, variability
**2** adherence to something to which one is bound by a pledge or duty — see FIDELITY
**constant** *adj* **1** not undergoing a change in condition ⟨change is the only *constant* thing in the world of fashion⟩
***syn*** changeless, stable, stationary, steady, unchanging, unvarying
***rel*** fast, fixed, hard-and-fast, immutable, inflexible, invariable, unalterable, unchangeable; established, set, settled; durable, enduring, lasting, permanent
***near ant*** alterable, changeable, flexible, mutable, variable; ephemeral, evanescent, fleeting, momentary, transient, transitory
***ant*** changeful, changing, fluctuating, inconstant, unstable, unsteady, varying
**2** appearing or occurring repeatedly from time to time — see REGULAR 1
**3** firm in one's allegiance to someone or something — see FAITHFUL 1
**constantly** *adv* **1** many times — see OFTEN
**2** on every relevant occasion — see ALWAYS 1
**consternation** *n* the emotion experienced in the presence or threat of danger — see FEAR
**constituent** *n* one of the parts that make up a whole — see ELEMENT 1

**constitute** *vb* **1** to be all the substance of ⟨nine players *constitute* a baseball team⟩
***syn*** compose, comprise, form, make up
***rel*** embody, incorporate, integrate; complement, complete, supplement; fill out, flesh (out)
**2** to be responsible for the creation and early operation or use of — see FOUND
**3** to pick (someone) by one's authority for a specific position or duty — see APPOINT 2

**constitution** *n* **1** the set of qualities that makes a person, a group of people, or a thing different from others — see NATURE 1
**2** the type of body that a person has — see PHYSIQUE

**constitutional** *n* a relaxed journey on foot for exercise or pleasure — see WALK

**constitutionally** *adv* by natural character or ability — see NATURALLY 1

**constrain** *vb* **1** to cause (a person) to give in to pressure — see FORCE
**2** to keep from exceeding a desirable degree or level (as of expression) — see CONTROL 1

**constraint** *n* **1** the checking of one's true feelings and impulses when dealing with others ⟨in civilized society people do not just say or do whatever they feel like—they exercise some *constraint*⟩
***syn*** inhibition, repression, reserve, restraint, self-control, self-restraint, suppression
***rel*** control, discipline, self-denial, self-discipline; composure, self-possession; aloofness, detachedness, distance; bashfulness, modesty, shyness; reticence, silence, taciturnity
***near ant*** self-indulgence; bluntness, candor, frankness
**2** something that limits one's freedom of action or choice — see RESTRICTION 1
**3** the use of power to impose one's will on another — see FORCE 2

**constrict** *vb* **1** to become smaller in size or volume through the drawing together of particles of matter — see CONTRACT 2
**2** to reduce in size or volume by or as if by pressing parts or members together — see COMPRESS 1

**constriction** *n* the act or process of reducing the size or volume of something by or as if by pressing — see COMPRESSION

**construct** *vb* to form by putting together parts or materials — see BUILD

**construction** *n* **1** something put together by arranging or connecting an array of parts ⟨the swing set turned out to be a more complicated *construction* than the "some assembly required" warning suggested⟩
***syn*** erection, structure
***rel*** arrangement, assembly; frame, framework, skeleton
**2** a statement that makes something clear — see EXPLANATION 1

***syn*** synonym(s) ***rel*** related words
***ant*** antonym(s) ***near ant*** near antonym(s)

**constructive** *adj* having a role in deciding something's final form — see FORMATIVE

**construe** *vb* to make plain or understandable — see EXPLAIN 1

**consult** *vb* to exchange viewpoints or seek advice for the purpose of finding a solution to a problem — see CONFER 2

**consultant** *n* a person who gives advice especially professionally ⟨a *consultant* in public relations to a number of large corporations⟩
***syn*** adviser (*or* advisor), counselor (*or* counsellor)
***rel*** authority, expert, professional; confidant

**consume** *vb* **1** to destroy all trace of ⟨massive fires had *consumed* hundreds of square miles of forest⟩
***syn*** devour, eat (up)
***rel*** gut; deplete, exhaust, use up; raze, ruin, waste; annihilate, extinguish
**2** to make complete use of — see DEPLETE
**3** to take in as food — see EAT 1

**consummate** *adj* **1** having or showing exceptional knowledge, experience, or skill in a field of endeavor — see PROFICIENT
**2** having no exceptions or restrictions — see ABSOLUTE 2
**3** of the greatest or highest degree or quantity — see ULTIMATE 1

**consummate** *vb* to bring (something) to a state where nothing remains to be done — see FINISH 1

**consummation** *n* **1** the last part of a process or action — see FINALE
**2** the state of being actual or complete — see FRUITION

**contact** *n* an acquaintance who has influence especially in the business or political world ⟨an intern who got her summer job in the governor's office through *contacts*⟩
***syn*** connection
***rel*** big shot, bigwig, somebody, VIP; go-between, intermediary, mediator

**contact** *vb* to transmit information or requests to ⟨you can *contact* me at this number⟩
***syn*** communicate (with), reach
***rel*** apprise, fill in, inform, notify; buzz, call, phone, ring [*chiefly British*], telephone
***phrases*** get (*or* keep) in touch with

**contagious** *adj* **1** capable of being passed by physical contact from one person to another ⟨chicken pox, measles, German measles, and other *contagious* diseases⟩
***syn*** catching, communicable, transmittable
***rel*** infectious, infective
***near ant*** noninfectious
***ant*** noncommunicable
**2** exciting a similar feeling or reaction in others ⟨the enthusiasm of the new club members was *contagious*⟩
***syn*** catching, infectious, spreading
***rel*** palpable, perceptible, tangible; irresistible, overpowering, overwhelming; fetching, inviting, winning

**contain** *vb* **1** to have within ⟨the top drawer of the cabinet *contains* my stamp collection⟩
***syn*** hold
***rel*** accommodate, fit; encase, enclose (*also* inclose), encompass; harbor, house, lodge, shelter
**2** to have as part of a whole — see INCLUDE
**3** to be made up of — see COMPRISE 1
**4** to gain emotional or mental control of — see COLLECT 1
**5** to keep from exceeding a desirable degree or level (as of expression) — see CONTROL 1

**container** *n* something into which a liquid or smaller objects can be put for storage or transportation ⟨save the plastic *containers* from the deli for other uses⟩
***syn*** holder, receptacle, vessel
***rel*** cartridge; bin, box, carton, case, crate; bag, pocket, sack; cooler, warmer

**contaminant** *n* something that is or that makes impure — see IMPURITY

**contaminate** *vb* to make unfit for use by the addition of something harmful or undesirable ⟨a supply of drinking water that was *contaminated* by a toxic waste dump⟩
***syn*** befoul, defile, foul, poison, pollute, taint
***rel*** infect; besmirch, dirty, soil, sully; corrupt, rot, spoil; adulterate, doctor; dilute, water (down)
***near ant*** clean, cleanse, purge; filter; disinfect, sanitize
***ant*** decontaminate, purify

**contaminated** *adj* containing foreign or lower-grade substances — see IMPURE

**contemplate** *vb* **1** to give serious and careful thought to — see PONDER
**2** to have in mind as a purpose or goal — see INTEND

**contemplation** *n* long or deep thinking about spiritual matters ⟨the decision to enter a monastery and to spend one's life in prayer and *contemplation*⟩
***syn*** meditation
***rel*** introspection, reflection, retrospection; cogitation, deliberation, musing, pondering, rumination

**contemplative** *adj* given to or marked by long, quiet thinking ⟨a *contemplative* person who likes to go on solitary walks⟩ ⟨the *contemplative* life of the monks at the abbey⟩
***syn*** meditative, melancholy, pensive, reflective, ruminant, thoughtful
***rel*** introspective, retrospective; earnest, serious, sober, somber (*or* sombre); analytic (*or* analytical), logical, rational; deliberate, purposeful
***near ant*** flighty, flippant, frivolous; brainless, mindless, silly, thoughtless, unthinking
***ant*** unreflective

**contemporaneous** *adj* existing or occurring at the same period of time — see CONTEMPORARY 1

**contemporaneously** *adv* at one and the same time — see TOGETHER 1

**contemporary** *adj* **1** existing or occurring at the same period of time ⟨the absurd notion that early cave dwellers were *contemporary* with the dinosaurs⟩
***syn*** coeval, coexistent, coexisting, coextensive, concurrent, contemporaneous, simultaneous, synchronous
***rel*** accompanying, attendant, attending, coincident, concomitant
***ant*** noncontemporary
**2** being or involving the latest methods, concepts, information, or styles — see MODERN

**contemporary** *n* a person who lives at the same time or is about the same age as another ⟨Abraham Lincoln and Charles Darwin were exact *contemporaries*, actually being born on the same day in 1809⟩
***syn*** coeval
***rel*** accompaniment, companion, concomitant; equal, peer

**contempt** *n* open dislike for someone or something considered unworthy of one's concern or respect ⟨my undying *contempt* for people who abuse animals⟩
***syn*** despite, despitefulness, disdain, scorn
***rel*** abhorrence, abomination, execration, hate, hatred, loathing; cattiness, hatefulness, invidiousness, malevolence, malice, maliciousness, malignancy, malignity, meanness, spite, spitefulness; aversion, disgust, distaste, horror, odium, repugnance, repulsion, revulsion; animosity, antagonism, antipathy, bitterness, enmity, grudge, hostility, jealousy, pique, resentment; bile, jaundice, rancor, spleen, venom, virulence, vitriol
***near ant*** acceptance, tolerance; adoration, veneration, worship; affection, fondness, liking
***ant*** admiration, esteem, regard, respect

**contemptible** *adj* **1** arousing or deserving of one's loathing and disgust ⟨the *contemptible* thieves who stole the Christmas gifts intended for needy children⟩
***syn*** despicable, lousy, nasty, pitiable, pitiful, scabby, scummy, scurvy, sorry, wretched
***rel*** abhorrent, abominable, detestable, execrable, hateful, loathsome, odious; disgusting, repugnant, repulsive; disgraceful, dishonorable, shameful; base, ignoble, low, mean; shabby, sordid, squalid, vile; cowardly, craven, dastardly
***near ant*** high-minded, honorable, noble, principled; commendable, creditable, laudable, praiseworthy
***ant*** admirable
**2** deserving pitying scorn (as for inadequacy) — see PITIFUL 1
**3** not following or in accordance with standards of honor and decency — see IGNOBLE 2

**contemptuous** *adj* **1** feeling or showing open dislike for someone or something regarded as undeserving of respect or concern ⟨loutish tourists who are *con-*

*temptuous* of the ways and traditions of their host countries⟩
***syn*** disdainful, scornful
***rel*** discourteous; disrespectful, impudent, insolent; arrogant, cavalier, high-handed; haughty, lofty, lordly, prideful, sniffish, snobbish, supercilious; pompous, self-important, superior
***near ant*** deferential, respectful; accepting, tolerant; courteous, polite
***ant*** admiring, appreciative
**2** intended to make a person or thing seem of little importance or value — see DEROGATORY

**contend** *vb* **1** to engage in a contest — see COMPETE
**2** to state (something) as a reason in support of or against something under consideration — see ARGUE 1
**3** to state as a fact usually forcefully — see CLAIM 1

**contend** (with) *vb* **1** to deal with (something) usually skillfully or efficiently — see HANDLE 1
**2** to strive to reduce or eliminate — see FIGHT 2

**contender** *n* **1** one who seeks an office, honor, position, or award — see CANDIDATE
**2** one who strives for the same thing as another — see COMPETITOR

**content** *adj* feeling that one's needs or desires have been met ⟨are you *content* with your present allowance?⟩
***syn*** contented, gratified, happy, pleased, satisfied
***rel*** delighted, glad, joyful, joyous, jubilant; ecstatic, elated, enraptured, euphoric, overjoyed, rapturous, thrilled; appeased, mollified, pacified, placated
***near ant*** disaffected, disgruntled; discouraged, disheartened, dispirited
***ant*** discontent, discontented, displeased, dissatisfied, malcontent, unhappy

[1]**content** *n* **1** a major object of interest or concern (as in a discussion or artistic composition) — see MATTER 1
**2** the amount of something (as subject matter) included — see COVERAGE
**3** the largest number or amount that something can hold — see CAPACITY 1

[2]**content** *n* the feeling experienced when one's wishes are met — see PLEASURE 1

**content** *vb* to give satisfaction to — see PLEASE

**contented** *adj* feeling that one's needs or desires have been met — see CONTENT

**contentedness** *n* the feeling experienced when one's wishes are met — see PLEASURE 1

**contention** *n* an idea or opinion that is put forth in a discussion or debate ⟨my *contention* is that today's lower batting averages are the result of better pitching⟩
***syn*** argument, assertion, thesis
***rel*** hypothesis, theory; proposal, proposition; assumption, presupposition, supposition; position, stand

**contentious** *adj* **1** feeling or displaying eagerness to fight — see BELLIGERENT
**2** given to arguing — see ARGUMENTATIVE 1

**contentiousness** *n* an inclination to fight or quarrel — see BELLIGERENCE

**contentment** *n* the feeling experienced when one's wishes are met — see PLEASURE 1

**contest** *n* **1** an earnest effort for superiority or victory over another ⟨the eternal *contest* between the forces of good and the forces of evil⟩
***syn*** battle, combat, conflict, confrontation, duel, face-off, rivalry, struggle, tug-of-war, warfare
***rel*** showdown; contention, discord, friction, strife; controversy, debate, disagreement
***near ant*** concord, harmony, peace
**2** a competitive encounter between individuals or groups carried on for amusement, exercise, or in pursuit of a prize — see GAME 1
**3** a physical dispute between opposing individuals or groups — see FIGHT 1

**contest** *vb* to demand proof of the truth or rightness of — see CHALLENGE 1

**contestant** *n* one who strives for the same thing as another — see COMPETITOR

**contiguity** *n* the state or condition of being near — see PROXIMITY

**contiguous** *adj* having a border in common — see ADJACENT

**continent** *n* one of the great divisions of land on the globe or the main part of such a division — see MAINLAND

**contingency** *n* something that might happen — see EVENT 2

**contingent** *n* a body of persons chosen as representatives of a larger group ⟨our Scout troop sent a large *contingent* to the jamboree⟩
***syn*** delegation
***rel*** embassy, legation, mission; crew, detachment, gang, outfit, squad

**contingent** (on *or* upon) *adj* determined by something else — see DEPENDENT 2

**continual** *adj* **1** going on and on without any interruptions — see CONTINUOUS
**2** occurring or appearing at intervals — see INTERMITTENT 1

**continually** *adv* **1** many times — see OFTEN
**2** on every relevant occasion — see ALWAYS 1

**continuance** *n* **1** continuing existence — see PERSISTENCE 1
**2** uninterrupted or lasting existence — see CONTINUATION

**continuation** *n* uninterrupted or lasting existence ⟨the *continuation* of high unemployment has cost the government much support⟩
***syn*** continuance, duration, endurance, persistence, subsistence

---

***syn*** synonym(s) ***rel*** related words
***ant*** antonym(s) ***near ant*** near antonym(s)

***rel*** elongation, extension, lengthening, prolongation
***near ant*** abridgment (*or* abridgement), curtailment, shortening
***ant*** ending, termination

**continue** *vb* **1** to remain indefinitely in existence or in the same state ⟨the heavy snow *continued* throughout the night⟩
***syn*** abide, endure, hold (up), hold on, keep up, last, persist, run on
***rel*** linger, remain, stay, stick around, tarry
***near ant*** abate, die (down), ebb, let up, moderate, subside, wane
***ant*** cease, desist, discontinue, quit, stop
**2** to begin again or return to after an interruption — see RESUME

**continuous** *adj* going on and on without any interruptions ⟨a city that has been under *continuous* bombardment for three days⟩
***syn*** ceaseless, continual, incessant, unbroken, unceasing, uninterrupted, unremitting
***rel*** endless, eternal, everlasting, interminable, perpetual, unending; changeless, constant, stable, steady, unchanging, unvarying
***near ant*** intermittent, periodic, recurrent, recurring
***ant*** noncontinuous

**contort** *vb* to twist (something) out of a natural or normal shape or condition ⟨the acrobat is able to *contort* his body so that it almost looks like a pretzel⟩
***syn*** deform, distort, screw, squinch, warp
***rel*** deface, disfigure; wrench, wrest, wring; coil, curl, twine, wind, wreathe

**contortion** *n* the twisting of something out of its natural or normal shape or condition ⟨the comedian is renowned for his seemingly endless variety of facial *contortions*⟩
***syn*** deformation, distortion, screwing, squinching, warping
***rel*** defacement, disfigurement

**contour** *n* a line that traces the outer limits of an object or surface — see OUTLINE 1

**contract** *n* **1** a formal agreement to fulfill an obligation — see GUARANTEE 1
**2** an arrangement about action to be taken — see AGREEMENT 2

**contract** *vb* **1** to become affected with (a disease or disorder) ⟨before vaccines were invented, people lived in fear of *contracting* polio⟩
***syn*** catch, come down (with), get, sicken (with), take
***rel*** break out (with); die (from), succumb (to); fail, sink, weaken
***near ant*** recover (from), shake (off)
**2** to become smaller in size or volume through the drawing together of particles of matter ⟨metal *contracts* at low temperatures⟩
***syn*** compress, condense, constrict, shrink
***rel*** collapse, deflate; dry (up), shrivel, wither; decrease, diminish, dwindle, lessen; recede, retreat, withdraw
***near ant*** accumulate, grow, increase; balloon, inflate, puff (up)
***ant*** expand, swell
**3** to reduce in size or volume by or as if by pressing parts or members together — see COMPRESS 1

**contraction** *n* the act or process of reducing the size or volume of something by or as if by pressing — see COMPRESSION

**contradict** *vb* **1** to make an assertion that is contrary to one made by (another) ⟨no matter what I say, you always have to *contradict* me⟩
***syn*** disagree (with), gainsay
***rel*** challenge, contest, dispute, question; confute, rebut, refute; cross, fight, oppose, resist
***near ant*** concur (with); confirm, corroborate, substantiate, verify
***ant*** agree (with)
**2** to declare not to be true — see DENY 1

**contradiction** *n* **1** someone or something with qualities or features that seem to conflict with one another ⟨a loving father as well as a ruthless killer, the gangster is a living *contradiction*⟩
***syn*** incongruity, paradox
***rel*** conundrum, enigma, mystery, puzzle, riddle
**2** a refusal to confirm the truth of a statement — see DENIAL 2

**contradictory** *adj* being as different as possible — see OPPOSITE

**contraption** *n* an interesting and often novel device with a practical use — see GADGET

**contrariness** *n* refusal to obey — see DISOBEDIENCE

**contrariwise** *adv* just the opposite being true ⟨the rock singer is hardly a carouser; *contrariwise*, he totally abstains from alcohol⟩
***syn*** again, conversely
***phrases*** on the contrary
***near ant*** even, indeed, nay, truly, verily, yea

**contrary** *adj* **1** being as different as possible — see OPPOSITE
**2** engaging in or marked by childish misbehavior — see NAUGHTY
**3** given to resisting authority or another's control — see DISOBEDIENT

**contrary** *n* something that is as different as possible from something else — see OPPOSITE

**contrast** *n* the quality or state of being different — see DIFFERENCE 1

**contribute** *vb* **1** to make a donation as part of a group effort ⟨would you like to *contribute* to the Thanksgiving fund for needy families?⟩
***syn*** chip in, kick in, pitch in
***rel*** bestow, donate, give, present
**2** to make a present of — see GIVE 1

**contribution** *n* a gift of money or its equivalent to a charity, humanitarian cause, or public institution ⟨*contributions* for the victims of the earthquake began pouring in⟩

*syn* alms, benefaction, beneficence, charity, donation, philanthropy
*rel* offering, tithe; bequest, endowment, legacy; aid, assistance, relief, welfare; grant, subsidy

**contrite** *adj* **1** feeling sorrow for a wrong that one has done ⟨being *contrite* is not enough to spare you an arrest if you're caught shoplifting⟩
*syn* apologetic, penitent, regretful, remorseful, repentant, rueful, sorry
*rel* sad, grieving, mournful, sorrowful, woeful
*near ant* merciless, pitiless, ruthless
*ant* impenitent, remorseless, unapologetic, unrepentant
**2** suffering from or expressive of a feeling of responsibility for wrongdoing — see GUILTY 2

**contriteness** *n* a feeling of responsibility for wrongdoing — see GUILT 1

**contrition** *n* a feeling of responsibility for wrongdoing — see GUILT 1

**contrivance** *n* **1** an interesting and often novel device with a practical use — see GADGET
**2** something (as a device) created for the first time through the use of the imagination — see INVENTION 1

**contrive** *vb* **1** to create or think of by clever use of the imagination — see INVENT
**2** to engage in a secret plan to accomplish evil or unlawful ends — see PLOT
**3** to plan out usually with subtle skill or care — see ENGINEER

**contrived** *adj* lacking in natural or spontaneous quality — see ARTIFICIAL 1

**contriver** *n* one who creates or introduces something new — see INVENTOR

**control** *n* **1** a mechanism for adjusting the operation of a device, machine, or system ⟨the *controls* for the player are well marked⟩
*syn* regulator
*rel* button, dial, key, knob, lever, push button, switch
**2** the ability to direct the course of something ⟨after the tail fell off, the plane went out of the pilot's *control*⟩ ⟨firefighters keeping *control* of the blaze⟩
*syn* grasp, hand(s)
*rel* clutch, grip, hold, mastery; command, dominion, helm; authority, jurisdiction, might, power
**3** the act or activity of looking after and making decisions about something — see CONDUCT 1
**4** the fact or state of having (something) at one's disposal — see POSSESSION 1
**5** the right or means to command or control others — see POWER 1

**control** *vb* **1** to keep from exceeding a desirable degree or level (as of expression) ⟨you must learn to *control* your temper⟩
*syn* bridle, check, constrain, contain, curb, govern, hold in, inhibit, regulate, rein (in), restrain, tame
*rel* bottle (up), repress, suppress; arrest, interrupt, stop; block, hinder, impede, obstruct; gag, muzzle, silence
*near ant* liberate, loose, loosen, unleash; air, express, take out, vent
**2** to gain emotional or mental control of — see COLLECT 1
**3** to exercise authority or power over — see GOVERN 1
**4** to look after and make decisions about — see CONDUCT 1

**controversy** *n* variance of opinion on a matter — see DISAGREEMENT 1

**contusion** *n* a bodily injury in which small blood vessels are broken but the overlying skin is not ⟨*contusions* occurred as a result of a car accident⟩
*syn* bruise
*rel* black eye; discoloration

**conundrum** *n* something hard to understand or explain — see MYSTERY

**convalesce** *vb* to become healthy and strong again after illness or weakness ⟨the long months that the soldier spent in the hospital slowly *convalescing*⟩
*syn* gain, heal, mend, rally, recover, recuperate, snap back
*rel* come around, come round, come to, improve, pick up, revive; cheer (up), perk (up); pull through, survive; recruit
*near ant* ail, collapse, come down, sicken; decline, degenerate, deteriorate, fade, fail, languish, sink, waste (away), weaken, wilt, wither, worsen; relapse

**convalescence** *n* the process or period of gradually regaining one's health and strength ⟨her release from the hospital was followed by a long *convalescence* at home⟩
*syn* comeback, healing, mending, rally, recovery, recuperation, rehabilitation, snapback
*rel* resuscitation, revival; survival
*near ant* decline, deterioration, failing, languishing, sinking, wasting (away), weakening

**convene** *vb* **1** to bring together in assembly by or as if by command — see CONVOKE
**2** to come together into one body or place — see ASSEMBLE 1

**convenience** *n* something that adds to one's ease — see COMFORT 2

**convenient** *adj* situated within easy reach ⟨the shopping mall is *convenient* to all of the area's major highways⟩
*syn* accessible, handy, reachable
*rel* close, near, nigh; abutting, adjacent, adjoining
*near ant* distant, far, remote
*ant* inaccessible, inconvenient, unhandy, unreachable

**convention** *n* **1** a coming together of a number of persons for a specified purpose — see MEETING 1
**2** a formal agreement between two or more nations or peoples — see TREATY

3 an arrangement about action to be taken — see AGREEMENT 2
4 an inherited or established way of thinking, feeling, or doing — see TRADITION 1

**conventional** *adj* 1 accepted, used, or practiced by most people — see CURRENT 1
2 based on customs usually handed down from a previous generation — see TRADITIONAL 1
3 following or agreeing with established form, custom, or rules — see FORMAL 1

**converge** *vb* to come together into one body or place — see ASSEMBLE 1

**convergence** *n* the coming together of two or more things to the same point ⟨the *convergence* of the city's major arteries on a single rotary⟩
*syn* confluence, conjunction, meeting
*rel* joining, juncture, merging, union
*ant* divergence

**conversant** *adj* having information especially as a result of study or experience — see FAMILIAR 2

**conversation** *n* talking or a talk between two or more people ⟨Thomas Jefferson was celebrated for his brilliant, wide-ranging *conversations* with a host of friends and acquaintances⟩
*syn* colloquy, dialogue (*also* dialog), discourse, discussion, exchange
*rel* banter, cross fire, give-and-take, repartee; conference, parley, powwow; babble, chat, chatter, chitchat, gabfest, gossip, palaver, prate, prattle, rap, small talk, table talk; roundtable, symposium; debate, deliberation

**conversational** *adj* 1 fond of talking or conversation — see TALKATIVE
2 having the style and content of everyday conversation — see CHATTY 1
3 used in or suitable for speech and not formal writing — see COLLOQUIAL 1

**conversationalist** *n* a person who talks constantly — see CHATTERBOX

**converse** *vb* to engage in casual or rambling conversation — see CHAT

**converse** (with) *vb* to communicate with by means of spoken words — see TALK (TO)

**conversely** *adv* just the opposite being true — see CONTRARIWISE

**conversion** *n* a change in form, appearance, or use ⟨the *conversion* of the spare bedroom into a home office was easily accomplished⟩
*syn* changeover, metamorphosis, transfiguration, transformation
*rel* shift, transition; adjustment, alteration, modification; redoing, refashioning, remaking, remodeling, revamping, revision, reworking, variation; deformation, disfigurement, distortion, mutation, transmutation; displacement, replacement, substitution, supplantation

**convert** *n* 1 a person who has recently been persuaded to join a religious sect ⟨the *converts* were the most vocal and fervent worshippers in the church⟩
*syn* proselyte
*rel* newcomer, novice, recruit
2 one who follows the opinions or teachings of another — see FOLLOWER

**convert** *vb* 1 to persuade to change to one's religious faith ⟨young missionaries who go door-to-door trying to *convert* people⟩
*syn* proselytize
*rel* brainwash, influence, sway; propagate
*near ant* dissuade
2 to change in form, appearance, or use ⟨the old factory was *converted* into an apartment building⟩
*syn* make over, metamorphose, transfigure, transform
*rel* adjust, alter, modify; redo, refashion, remake, remodel, revamp, revise, rework, vary; deform, disfigure, distort, mutate, transmute; displace, replace, substitute, supplant

**convey** *vb* 1 to cause (something) to pass from one to another — see COMMUNICATE 1
2 to support and take from one place to another — see CARRY 1

**conveyance** *n* something used to carry goods or passengers ⟨the covered wagon was the major *conveyance* that transported settlers and their belongings across the frontier⟩
*syn* transport, transportation, vehicle
*rel* carrier, hauler, mover; transit

**convict** *n* a person convicted as a criminal and serving a prison sentence ⟨a warning that the three escaped *convicts* were armed and dangerous⟩
*syn* jailbird
*rel* captive, capture, inmate, internee, prisoner

**convict** *vb* to find or pronounce guilty ⟨an accused person is presumed innocent until *convicted* in a court of law⟩
*syn* condemn
*rel* censure, denounce, rebuke, reprimand, reproach, reprove; admonish, castigate, chastise; penalize, punish, sentence
*near ant* cite, commend, endorse (*also* indorse); approve, bless, sanction
*ant* absolve, acquit, clear, exonerate, vindicate

**conviction** *n* 1 a state of mind in which one is free from doubt — see CONFIDENCE 2
2 an idea that is believed to be true or valid without positive knowledge — see OPINION 1

**convince** *vb* to cause (someone) to agree with a belief or course of action by using arguments or earnest requests — see PERSUADE

**convincing** *adj* having the power to persuade — see COGENT

**convincing** *n* the act of reasoning or pleading with someone to accept a belief or course of action — see PERSUASION 1

**convivial** *adj* likely to seek or enjoy the company of others ⟨the hiking club at-

tracts a wide range of *convivial* people who share a love of the outdoors〉
***syn*** boon, companionable, extroverted (*also* extraverted), gregarious, outgoing, sociable, social
***rel*** cordial, friendly, hospitable; affable, genial, gracious; animated, lively, sprightly, vivacious; communicative, expansive, garrulous, talkative
***near ant*** misanthropic; aloof, reserved, standoffish; reticent, silent, taciturn
***ant*** antisocial, introverted, reclusive, unsociable

**conviviality** *n* **1** joyful or festive activity — see MERRYMAKING
**2** the quality or state of being social — see SOCIABILITY

**convocation** *n* **1** a body of people come together in one place — see GATHERING 1
**2** a coming together of a number of persons for a specified purpose — see MEETING 1

**convoke** *vb* to bring together in assembly by or as if by command 〈*convoked* the leading experts on juvenile delinquency to study the situation〉
***syn*** assemble, call, convene, muster, summon
***rel*** amass, collect, gather, group, round up
***near ant*** break up, dissolve

**convoluted** *adj* having many parts or aspects that are usually interrelated — see COMPLEX 1

**convoy** *vb* to go along with in order to provide assistance, protection, or companionship — see ACCOMPANY

**convulse** *vb* to make a series of small irregular or violent movements — see SHAKE 1

**convulsion** *n* a violent disturbance (as of the political or social order) 〈the Russian Revolution was one of the major *convulsions* of the 20th century〉
***syn*** cataclysm, paroxysm, storm, tempest, tumult, upheaval, uproar
***rel*** overthrow, overturn, revolution, subversion, upset; fit, seizure, spasm; eruption, flare-up, outbreak, outburst; commotion, furor, fuss, hubbub, hullabaloo, row, ruckus, stew, turmoil; quaking, rocking, shaking, trembling

**convulsive** *adj* marked by sudden or violent disturbance 〈the assassination of Martin Luther King was one of the most *convulsive* events of the 1960s〉
***syn*** cataclysmal (*or* cataclysmic), stormy, tempestuous, tumultuous
***rel*** fitful, spasmodic, sporadic
***near ant*** calm, peaceful, serene, tranquil

**cook** *n* a person who prepares food by some manner of heating 〈the hearty meals prepared by the *cook* at summer camp〉
***syn*** chef, cooker
***rel*** baker

**cook** (up) *vb* to create or think of by clever use of the imagination — see INVENT

**cooker** *n* **1** an appliance that prepares food for consumption by heating it 〈a portable gas-fired *cooker* that's perfect for camping trips〉
***syn*** cookstove, range
***rel*** broiler, fryer (*also* frier), microwave oven, oven, roaster, rotisserie, stove, toaster, toaster oven
**2** a person who prepares food by some manner of heating — see COOK

**cookery** *n* the art or style of preparing food (as in a specified region) 〈tacos represented my introduction to Mexican *cookery*〉
***syn*** cooking, cuisine

**cooking** *n* the art or style of preparing food (as in a specified region) — see COOKERY

**cookstove** *n* an appliance that prepares food for consumption by heating it — see COOKER 1

**cool** *adj* **1** having or showing a lack of friendliness or interest in others 〈the locals were *cool* towards outsiders〉 〈the schoolmaster's *cool* manner did not encourage chitchat〉
***syn*** aloof, antisocial, cold, detached, distant, frosty, remote, standoffish, unsociable
***rel*** introverted, reclusive, reserved, withdrawn; misanthropic; apathetic, indifferent, unconcerned; disinterested, incurious, uninterested; reticent, silent, taciturn; diffident, shy, timid
***near ant*** companionable, convivial, extroverted (*also* extraverted), gregarious, outgoing; communicative, expansive, garrulous, talkative
***ant*** cordial, friendly, sociable, warm
**2** free from emotional or mental agitation — see CALM 2
**3** having a low or subnormal temperature — see COLD 1
**4** lacking in friendliness or warmth of feeling — see COLD 2

**cool** *vb* **1** to cause to lose heat 〈*cool* your drinks in the icy mountain stream〉
***syn*** chill, refrigerate
***rel*** air-condition; freeze, ice, quick-freeze, supercool; air-cool, ventilate
***near ant*** bake, boil, broil, steam
***ant*** heat, warm
**2** to become still and orderly — see QUIET 1

**coolheaded** *adj* free from emotional or mental agitation — see CALM 2

**coolheadedness** *n* evenness of emotions or temper — see EQUANIMITY

**coolish** *adj* having a low or subnormal temperature — see COLD 1

**coolness** *n* evenness of emotions or temper — see EQUANIMITY

**coop** *n* an enclosure with an open framework for keeping animals — see CAGE

**coop** (up) *vb* to close or shut in by or as if by barriers — see ENCLOSE 1

**cooperate** *vb* **1** to participate or assist in a joint effort to accomplish an end 〈conser-

---

***syn*** synonym(s) ***rel*** related words
***ant*** antonym(s) ***near ant*** near antonym(s)

vation groups *cooperated* with state authorities to find a humane way to manage the area's overpopulation of deer〉
*syn* collaborate, concert, join, team (up)
*rel* connive, conspire; affiliate, ally, associate, band, combine, confederate, league, unite
*phrases* play ball
2 to form or enter into an association that furthers the interests of its members — see ALLY

**cooperation** *n* 1 the state of having shared interests or efforts (as in social or business matters) — see ASSOCIATION 1
2 the work and activity of a number of persons who individually contribute toward the efficiency of the whole — see TEAMWORK

**coordinate** *n* one that is equal to another in status, achievement, or value — see EQUAL

**coordinate** *vb* 1 to bring to a state free of conflicts, inconsistencies, or differences — see HARMONIZE 2
2 to form a pleasing relationship — see HARMONIZE 1

**coordination** *n* the work and activity of a number of persons who individually contribute toward the efficiency of the whole — see TEAMWORK

**cop** *n* a member of a force charged with law enforcement at the local level — see OFFICER 1

**copacetic** *also* **copasetic** *or* **copesetic** *adj* being to one's liking — see SATISFACTORY 1

**cope** *vb* to meet one's day-to-day needs — see GET ALONG 1

**cope** (with) *vb* to deal with (something) usually skillfully or efficiently — see HANDLE 1

**copious** *adj* pouring forth in great amounts — see PROFUSE

**cop–out** *n* the act or a means of getting or keeping away from something undesirable — see ESCAPE 2

**cop out** *vb* to break a promise or agreement — see RENEGE

**coppice** *n* a thick patch of shrubbery, small trees, or underbrush — see THICKET

**copse** *n* a thick patch of shrubbery, small trees, or underbrush — see THICKET

**copulate** *vb* to engage in sexual intercourse 〈the time of year when deer in the wild are likely to *copulate*〉
*syn* mate, sleep
*rel* fornicate

**copulating** *n* sexual union involving penetration of the vagina by the penis — see SEXUAL INTERCOURSE

**copulation** *n* sexual union involving penetration of the vagina by the penis — see SEXUAL INTERCOURSE

**copy** *n* something that is made to look exactly like something else 〈a *copy* of the famous painting "Washington Crossing the Delaware"〉
*syn* carbon copy, duplicate, duplication, facsimile, imitation, reduplication, replica, replication, reproduction
*rel* counterfeit, fake, forgery, phony (*also* phoney), sham; dummy, mock-up, simulation; reconstruction, re-creation; image, likeness, semblance, shadow; impression, imprint, print
*ant* original

**copy** *vb* 1 to make an exact likeness of 〈for the movie, set designers *copied* the Oval Office in the White House down to the smallest detail〉
*syn* duplicate, imitate, reduplicate, replicate, reproduce
*rel* counterfeit, fake, forge; simulate; reconstruct, re-create
*near ant* create, imagine, initiate, invent
*ant* originate
2 to use (someone or something) as the model for one's speech, mannerisms, or behavior — see IMITATE 1

**copycat** *n* a person who adopts the appearance or behavior of another especially in an obvious way 〈every rock singer who makes it big soon has a whole cluster of *copycats*〉
*syn* aper, copyist, imitator
*rel* parrot

**copyist** *n* a person who adopts the appearance or behavior of another especially in an obvious way — see COPYCAT

**coquettish** *adj* affecting shyness or modesty in order to attract masculine interest — see COY 1

**cord** *n* a length of braided, flexible material that is used for tying or connecting things 〈a vacuum cleaner with an extra long *cord*〉
*syn* cable, lace, lacing, line, rope, string, wire
*rel* guy, lanyard, stay

**cordial** *adj* 1 having or showing kindly feeling and sincere interest — see FRIENDLY 1
2 showing a natural kindness and courtesy especially in social situations — see GRACIOUS 1

**cordiality** *n* kindly concern, interest, or support — see GOODWILL 1

**core** *n* 1 the seat of one's deepest thoughts and emotions 〈in my very *core* I knew that an injustice was being committed〉
*syn* breast, heart, quick, soul
*rel* conscience, mind
*phrases* bottom of one's heart
2 a thing or place that is of greatest importance to an activity or interest — see CENTER 1
3 the central part or aspect of something under consideration — see CRUX
4 the main or greater part of something as distinguished from its appendages — see BODY 1
5 an area or point that is an equal distance from all points along an edge or outer surface — see CENTER 2

**corker** *n* something very good of its kind — see JIM-DANDY

**corkscrew** *adj* turning around an axis like the thread of a screw — see SPIRAL
**corn** *n* something (as a work of literature or music) that is too sentimental ⟨a story about a lost puppy that was pure *corn*⟩
*syn* mush, schmaltz (*also* schmalz)
*rel* claptrap, drivel, rubbish, slush
**corner** *n* **1** a difficult, puzzling, or embarrassing situation from which there is no easy escape — see PREDICAMENT
**2** a place where roads meet — see CROSSROAD 1
**cornerstone** *n* an immaterial thing upon which something else rests — see BASE 1
**cornet** *n* something shaped like a hollow cone and used as a container ⟨*cornets* of pastry dough that were baked and later filled with cream⟩
*syn* cornucopia, horn
*rel* funnel, tube
**cornucopia** *n* something shaped like a hollow cone and used as a container — see CORNET
**corny** *adj* appealing to the emotions in an obvious and tiresome way ⟨*corny* violin music during the movie's love scenes⟩
*syn* maudlin, mawkish, mushy, saccharine, sappy, schmaltzy, sentimental, sloppy, sugarcoated, sugary
*rel* dreamy, moonstruck, nostalgic; flat, insipid, tasteless, vapid, watery
*near ant* unadulterated, unvarnished; cynical, hard-boiled, hardheaded
*ant* unsentimental
**corollary** *n* a condition or occurrence traceable to a cause — see EFFECT 1
**coronet** *n* a decorative band or wreath worn about the head as a symbol of victory or honor — see CROWN 1
**corporal** *adj* of or relating to the human body — see PHYSICAL 1
**corporeal** *adj* of or relating to the human body — see PHYSICAL 1
**corps** *n* the body of people in a profession or field of activity ⟨a reporter who is widely respected throughout the press *corps*⟩
*syn* brotherhood, community, fellowship, fraternity
*rel* calling, profession; association, club, federation, guild (*also* gild), organization, society, sodality
**corpse** *n* a dead body ⟨the discovery of a *corpse* required a call to the police⟩
*syn* cadaver, carcass, remains
*rel* deceased, decedent
**corpulence** *n* the condition of having an excess of body fat ⟨the doctor warned that *corpulence* is unhealthy and not just unattractive⟩
*syn* adiposity, chubbiness, fatness, fleshiness, grossness, obesity, plumpness, portliness, pudginess, rotundity
*rel* bulkiness, heaviness; huskiness, stoutness; brawniness, burliness
*near ant* fitness, trimness; scrawniness, skinniness
*ant* leanness, slenderness, slimness, thinness
**corpulent** *adj* having an excess of body fat — see FAT 1
**corral** *n* an enclosure with an open framework for keeping animals — see CAGE
**corral** *vb* **1** to close or shut in by or as if by barriers — see ENCLOSE 1
**2** to take physical control or possession of (something) suddenly or forcibly — see CATCH
**correct** *adj* **1** being in agreement with the truth or a fact or a standard ⟨a real brainteaser with only one *correct* solution to it⟩
*syn* accurate, exact, precise, proper, right, so, true
*rel* legitimate, logical, valid; errorless, faultless, flawless, impeccable, letter-perfect, perfect; rigorous, strict, stringent
*near ant* defective, faulty, flawed, imperfect
*ant* false, improper, inaccurate, incorrect, inexact, untrue, wrong
**2** following the established traditions of refined society and good taste — see PROPER 1
**3** marked by or showing careful attention to set forms and details — see CEREMONIOUS 1
**correct** *vb* **1** to remove errors, defects, deficiencies, or deviations from ⟨students who never take the time to *correct* their own compositions before handing them in⟩
*syn* amend, debug, emend, rectify, reform, remedy
*rel* redraft, redraw, restyle, revise, rework, rewrite; redress, right; ameliorate, better, improve; perfect, polish, touch up; fix, mend, repair; adjust, modulate, regulate; alter, change, modify
*near ant* damage, harm, hurt, impair, injure, mar, spoil; aggravate, worsen
**2** to balance with an equal force so as to make ineffective — see OFFSET
**3** to inflict a penalty on for a fault or crime — see PUNISH
**correctable** *adj* capable of being corrected — see REMEDIABLE
**correcting** *adj* inflicting, involving, or serving as punishment — see PUNITIVE
**correction** *n* **1** a change designed to correct or improve a written work ⟨here's your theme back with the *corrections* marked in blue⟩
*syn* amendment, emendation
*rel* cut, deletion; addition, amplification, supplement; alteration, modification, revision; improvement, renovation; clarification, explanation, explication
**2** suffering, loss, or hardship imposed in response to a crime or offense — see PUNISHMENT
**correctional** *adj* inflicting, involving, or serving as punishment — see PUNITIVE
**corrective** *adj* **1** serving to raise or adjust something to some standard or proper condition ⟨eyeglasses are called *corrective*

*syn* synonym(s) *rel* related words
*ant* antonym(s) *near ant* near antonym(s)

lenses by the department of motor vehicles⟩
***syn*** rectifying, remedial, remedying, reformative, reformatory
***rel*** curative, medicinal, therapeutic; reparative, restorative; beneficial, helpful, salutary, wholesome
**2** inflicting, involving, or serving as punishment — see PUNITIVE

**corrective** *n* something that corrects or counteracts something undesirable — see CURE 1

**correctly** *adv* in a manner suitable for the occasion or purpose — see PROPERLY

**correlate** *vb* to think of (something) in combination — see ASSOCIATE 2

**correspond** *vb* **1** to engage in an exchange of written messages ⟨old friends who have been *corresponding* for years⟩
***syn*** write
***rel*** communicate, intercommunicate; airmail, e-mail, telegraph; mail, post; answer, reply
**2** to be in agreement on every point — see CHECK 1

**correspond** (to) *vb* **1** to be the exact counterpart of — see MATCH 1
**2** to be the same in meaning or effect — see AMOUNT (TO) 2

**correspondence** *n* **1** a point which two or more things share in common — see SIMILARITY 2
**2** the quality or state of having many qualities in common — see SIMILARITY 1

**correspondent** *n* a person employed by a newspaper, magazine, or radio or television station to gather, write, or report news — see REPORTER

**correspondent** *adj* having qualities in common — see ALIKE

**correspondent** (with *or* to) *adj* not having or showing any apparent conflict — see CONSISTENT

**corresponding** *adj* having qualities in common — see ALIKE

**correspondingly** *adv* in like manner — see ALSO 1

**corridor** *n* a typically long narrow way connecting parts of a building — see HALL 2

**corroborate** *vb* to give evidence or testimony to the truth or factualness of — see CONFIRM

**corroborating** *adj* serving to give support to the truth or factualness of something — see CORROBORATIVE

**corroboration** *n* something presented in support of the truth or accuracy of a claim — see PROOF

**corroborative** *adj* serving to give support to the truth or factualness of something ⟨the results of the DNA fingerprinting was all the *corroborative* evidence the jury needed to convict⟩
***syn*** confirmatory, confirming, corroborating, corroboratory, substantiating, supporting, supportive, verifying, vindicating
***rel*** auxiliary, supplementary, beneficial, helpful
***near ant*** contradictory, contrary, counter, opposing
***ant*** confuting, disproving, refuting

**corroboratory** *adj* serving to give support to the truth or factualness of something — see CORROBORATIVE

**corrode** *vb* to consume or wear away gradually — see EAT 2

**corrosion** *n* a gradual weakening, loss, or destruction ⟨the *corrosion* of family values that is often brought on by great wealth⟩
***syn*** attrition, erosion
***rel*** breakdown, decay, decomposition, disintegration, dissolution
***near ant*** gain, increase
***ant*** buildup

**corrupt** *adj* having or showing lowered moral character or standards ⟨*corrupt* businessmen who are out to fleece the public⟩ ⟨*corrupt* business practices that should be investigated⟩
***syn*** debased, debauched, decadent, degenerate, degraded, demoralized, depraved, dissipated, dissolute, perverse, perverted, reprobate, warped
***rel*** crooked, cutthroat, dishonest, unethical, unprincipled, unscrupulous; contaminated, spoiled, tainted; bad, evil, immoral, iniquitous, nefarious, sinful, vicious, wicked
***near ant*** incorruptible, uncorruptible; ethical, honest, principled; good, moral, righteous, virtuous
***ant*** uncorrupted

**corrupt** *vb* **1** to go through decomposition — see DECAY 1
**2** to lower in character or dignity — see DEBASE 1

**corrupted** *adj* having undergone organic breakdown — see ROTTEN 1

**corruptible** *adj* open to improper influence and especially bribery — see VENAL

**corruption** *n* **1** the process by which dead organic matter separates into simpler substances ⟨the ancient Egyptians used special preservatives to spare their dead from complete *corruption*⟩
***syn*** breakdown, decay, decomposition, putrefaction, rot, spoilage
***rel*** crumbling, disintegration, dissolution; curdling, fermentation, moldering, souring
***near ant*** growth, maturation, ripening
**2** a sinking to a state of low moral standards and behavior ⟨the *corruption* of the upper classes eventually led to the fall of the Roman empire⟩
***syn*** corruptness, debasement, debauchery, decadence, degeneracy, degeneration, degradation, demoralization, depravity, dissipatedness, dissipation, dissoluteness, perversion
***rel*** evil, immorality, nefariousness, sinfulness, wickedness
***near ant*** goodness, morality, righteousness, virtue
**3** immoral conduct or practices harmful or offensive to society — see VICE 1

**corruptness** *n* a sinking to a state of low moral standards and behavior — see CORRUPTION 2

**corsair** *n* someone who engages in robbery of ships at sea — see PIRATE

**cortege** *also* **cortège** *n* **1** a body of employees or servants who accompany and wait on a person ⟨the movie star's *cortege* included her hair stylist, makeup artist, personal assistant, and press agent⟩
*syn* following, retinue, suite, train
*rel* crew, personnel, staff; assistant, attendant, helper, retainer
**2** a body of individuals moving along in an orderly and often ceremonial way ⟨the funeral *cortege* of mourners stretched for three city blocks⟩
*syn* parade, procession
*rel* column, line, string, train

**cosmetics** *n pl* preparations intended to beautify the face or hair — see MAKEUP 1

**cosmic** *adj* unusually large — see HUGE

**cosmopolitan** *adj* having a wide and refined knowledge of the world especially from personal experience — see WORLDLY-WISE

**cosmopolitan** *n* a person with the outlook, experience, and manners thought to be typical of big city dwellers ⟨as someone who had lived in Paris for a year as an exchange student, she seemed very much the *cosmopolitan* to her old classmates⟩
*syn* metropolitan, sophisticate
*rel* urbanite; worldling
*ant* bumpkin, hick, provincial, rustic, yokel

**cosmos** *n* the whole body of things observed or assumed — see UNIVERSE

**cost** *n* **1** a payment made in the course of achieving a result — see EXPENSE
**2** the amount of money that is demanded as payment for something — see PRICE 1
**3** the loss or penalty involved in achieving a goal — see PRICE 2

**cost** *vb* to have a price of ⟨the raffle tickets *cost* a dollar each⟩
*syn* bring, fetch, go (for), sell (for)
*rel* amount (to), come (to), total; command, exact; ask, demand

**costly** *adj* commanding a large price ⟨running is one sport that does not require a lot of *costly* equipment⟩
*syn* dear, expensive, high, precious, premium, valuable
*rel* exorbitant, extravagant, overpriced, prohibitive, steep, stiff, unreasonable; invaluable, priceless
*near ant* moderate, reasonable; valueless, worthless; discounted
*ant* cheap, inexpensive

**costume** *n* **1** clothing chosen as appropriate for a specific situation — see OUTFIT 1
**2** clothing put on to hide one's true identity or imitate someone or something else — see DISGUISE

**costume** *vb* to outfit with clothes and especially fine or special clothes — see CLOTHE 1

**coterie** *n* a group of people sharing a common interest and relating together socially — see GANG 2

**cotillion** *n* a social gathering for dancing — see DANCE

**cottage** *n* an often small house for recreational or seasonal use ⟨for a month every summer we rent a *cottage* on the ocean⟩
*syn* cabin, camp, chalet, lodge
*rel* bungalow, cot; hut, shack, shanty

**cottony** *adj* smooth or delicate in appearance or feel — see SOFT 2

**couch** *n* a long upholstered piece of furniture designed for several sitters ⟨find yourself a place on the *couch* and make yourself at home⟩
*syn* chesterfield, davenport, divan, lounge, settee, sofa
*rel* love seat; day bed, sofa bed; bench

**couch** *vb* to convey in appropriate or telling terms — see PHRASE

**cougar** *n* a large tawny cat of the wild ⟨in many areas suburban developments have encroached upon the habitat of the *cougar*⟩
*syn* catamount, mountain lion, panther, puma

**council** *n* **1** a coming together of a number of persons for a specified purpose — see MEETING 1
**2** a group of persons formally joined together for some common interest — see ASSOCIATION 2
**3** a meeting featuring a group discussion — see FORUM

**counsel** *n* **1** a person whose profession is to conduct lawsuits for clients or to advise about legal rights and obligations — see LAWYER
**2** an opinion suggesting a wise or proper course of action — see ADVICE

**counsel** *vb* **1** to exchange viewpoints or seek advice for the purpose of finding a solution to a problem — see CONFER 2
**2** to give advice and instruction to (someone) regarding the course or process to be followed — see GUIDE 1
**3** to give advice to — see ADVISE 1
**4** to put forward as one's choice for a wise or proper course of action — see ADVISE 2

**counselor** *or* **counsellor** *n* **1** a person who gives advice especially professionally — see CONSULTANT
**2** a person whose profession is to conduct lawsuits for clients or to advise about legal rights and obligations — see LAWYER

**count** *n* **1** a total number obtained or recorded by noting each thing as it was being added ⟨my *count* for the number of bird species and subspecies that visited the sanctuary that weekend was 43⟩
*syn* tally
*rel* score; amount, gross, sum, total, whole
**2** a formal claim of criminal wrongdoing against a person — see CHARGE 1

**count** *vb* **1** to find the sum of (a collection of things) by noting each one as it is being added ⟨*count* the baseball gloves in the storage locker to see if there are enough to go around⟩
*syn* enumerate, number, tell
*rel* add (up), tally, total; calculate, compute, reckon, table, tabulate; check, mark, tick (off)
**2** to be of importance — see MATTER
**3** to place reliance or trust — see DEPEND 2
**4** to think of in a particular way — see CONSIDER 1

**countenance** *n* **1** facial appearance regarded as an indication of mood or feeling — see LOOK 1
**2** the front part of the head — see FACE 1

**countenance** *vb* **1** to have a favorable opinion of — see APPROVE (OF)
**2** to put up with (something painful or difficult) — see BEAR 2

**counter** *adj* opposed to one's interests — see ADVERSE 1

**counter** *vb* to strive to reduce or eliminate — see FIGHT 2

**counteract** *vb* to balance with an equal force so as to make ineffective — see OFFSET

**counteraction** *n* a force or influence that makes an opposing force ineffective or less effective — see COUNTERBALANCE

**counterattack** *n* an attack made to counter an enemy's attack ⟨suddenly the tide of battle turned, and the rebels, who had been falling back, made a furious *counterattack*⟩
*syn* counteroffensive
*rel* sally, sortie; blitzkrieg, charge; assault, attack, offensive, onslaught

**counterbalance** *n* a force or influence that makes an opposing force ineffective or less effective ⟨charitable giving is usually a good *counterbalance* to the self-indulgent commercialism of the Christmas season⟩
*syn* balance, canceler (*or* canceller), counteraction, counterpoise, counterweight, equipoise, neutralizer, offset
*rel* trade-off

**counterbalance** *vb* to balance with an equal force so as to make ineffective — see OFFSET

**counterfeit** *adj* being such in appearance only and made or manufactured with the intention of committing fraud ⟨*counterfeit* money that had been passed all over town⟩
*syn* bogus, fake, false, forged, inauthentic, phony (*also* phoney), sham, spurious, unauthentic
*rel* artificial, factitious, imitation, man-made, mimic, mock, simulated, substitute, synthetic; dummy, nonfunctioning, ornamental; cultured, fabricated, manufactured; deceptive, delusive, misleading
*near ant* natural; actual, true, valid
*ant* authentic, bona fide, genuine, real

**counterfeit** *n* an imitation that is passed off as genuine — see FAKE 1

**counterfeit** *vb* **1** to imitate or copy especially in order to deceive — see FAKE 1
**2** to present a false appearance of — see FEIGN

**counteroffensive** *n* an attack made to counter an enemy's attack — see COUNTERATTACK

**counterpane** *n* a decorative cloth used as a top covering for a bed ⟨a beautiful *counterpane* that was a family heirloom⟩
*syn* bedspread, coverlet, spread
*rel* comforter, puff, quilt; bedclothes, bedding

**counterpart** *n* **1** one that is equal to another in status, achievement, or value — see EQUAL
**2** something or someone that strongly resembles another — see IMAGE 1

**counterpoise** *n* a force or influence that makes an opposing force ineffective or less effective — see COUNTERBALANCE

**counterpoise** *vb* to balance with an equal force so as to make ineffective — see OFFSET

**countersign** *n* a word or phrase that must be spoken by a person in order to pass a guard — see PASSWORD

**counterweight** *n* a force or influence that makes an opposing force ineffective or less effective — see COUNTERBALANCE

**countless** *adj* too many to be counted ⟨I've told you *countless* times not to do that⟩
*syn* innumerable, numberless, uncountable, uncounted, unnumbered, untold
*rel* endless, infinite, unlimited, vast; many, multitudinous, numerous
*near ant* finite, limited
*ant* countable

**count out** *vb* to prevent the participation or inclusion of — see EXCLUDE

**country** *adj* of, relating to, associated with, or typical of open areas with few buildings or people — see RURAL

**country** *n* **1** the land of one's birth, residence, or citizenship ⟨a great love for my *country*⟩
*syn* fatherland, home, homeland, motherland, sod
*rel* old country; community, neighborhood
**2** the open rural area outside of big towns and cities ⟨out in the *country*, where the air is fresh and the rivers are clean⟩
*syn* countryside, sticks
*rel* exurbia; backwater, backwoods, bush, frontier, hinterland, up-country; wild, wilderness
*near ant* conurbation, megalopolis, urban sprawl
**3** a body of people composed of one or more nationalities usually with its own territory and government — see NATION

**countryman** *n* **1** a person living in or originally from the same country as another — see COMPATRIOT
**2** an awkward or simple person especially from a small town or the country — see HICK

**countryseat** *n* a large impressive residence — see MANSION

**countryside** *n* the open rural area outside of big towns and cities — see COUNTRY 2

**coup** *n* a successful result brought about by hard work — see ACCOMPLISHMENT 1

**couple** *n* two things of the same or similar kind that match or are considered together — see PAIR

**couple** *vb* **1** to come together to form a single unit — see UNITE 1
**2** to put or bring together so as to form a new and longer whole — see CONNECT 1

**coupling** *n* **1** a place where two or more things are united — see JOINT 1
**2** the act or an instance of joining two or more things into one — see UNION 1

**coupon** *n* a small sheet of plastic, paper, or paperboard showing that the bearer has a claim to something (as admittance) — see TICKET 1

**courage** *n* strength of mind to carry on in spite of danger ⟨the moral *courage* to speak out against injustice when no one else will⟩
***syn*** bravery, courageousness, daring, dauntlessness, doughtiness, fearlessness, gallantry, greatheartedness, guts, hardihood, heart, heroism, intrepidity, intrepidness, nerve, stoutness, valor
***rel*** backbone, fiber, fortitude, grit, gumption, mettle, pluck, spunk; determination, perseverance, resolution; endurance, stamina, tenacity; audacity, boldness, brazenness, cheek, effrontery, gall, temerity
***near ant*** faintheartedness, fearfulness, timidity, timorousness; feebleness, softness, weakness; impotence, ineffectualness; hesitation, indecision, indecisiveness, irresolution
***ant*** cowardice, cowardliness, cravenness, dastardliness, spinelessness, yellowness

**courageous** *adj* feeling or displaying no fear by temperament — see BRAVE

**courageousness** *n* strength of mind to carry on in spite of danger — see COURAGE

**courier** *n* one that carries a message or does an errand — see MESSENGER

**course** *n* **1** a way of acting or proceeding ⟨the president's usual *course* has been to obtain advice from several people and then make up his own mind⟩
***syn*** line, policy, procedure, program
***rel*** blueprint, design, plan, scheme, strategy; intent, intention, purpose; approach, direction, path, pathway, tack
**2** a series of lectures on a subject ⟨a *course* on American history from the colonial period to the present⟩
***syn*** class
***rel*** elective, refresher, seminar; core, curriculum
**3** a usually fixed or ordered series of actions or events leading to a result — see PROCESS 1
**4** the direction along which something or someone moves — see PATH 1

**course** *vb* to proceed or move quickly — see HURRY 2

**court** *n* **1** the residence of a ruler ⟨Hampton *Court* was the residence of King Henry VIII⟩
***syn*** palace
***rel*** castle, château, estate, mansion, villa
**2** an open space wholly or partly enclosed (as by buildings or walls) ⟨the art museum boasts a glass-sided *court* that is filled with an array of greenery and sculpture⟩
***syn*** close, courtyard, enclosure (*also* inclosure), patio, quadrangle, yard
***rel*** place, plaza, square; deck, terrace
**3** an assembly of persons for the administration of justice ⟨this *court* is now called to order⟩
***syn*** bar, tribunal
***rel*** judiciary; court-martial; inquisition, kangaroo court
**4** a public official having authority to decide questions of law — see JUDGE 1

**court** *vb* **1** to act so as to make (something) more likely ⟨you're *courting* disaster if you keep playing with matches⟩
***syn*** ask (for), invite, woo
***rel*** angle (for), fish (for); hunt, search, seek
***phrases*** look for
**2** to go on dates that may eventually lead to marriage ⟨they *courted* for a year before getting married⟩
***syn*** date
***rel*** romance, spark, woo; escort, see, take out
***phrases*** go steady, make love

**courteous** *adj* showing consideration, courtesy, and good manners — see POLITE 1

**courteously** *adv* with good reason or courtesy — see WELL 4

**courteousness** *n* speech or behavior that is a sign of good breeding — see POLITENESS

**courtesy** *n* **1** an act of kind assistance — see FAVOR 1
**2** an act or utterance that is a customary show of good manners — see CIVILITY 1
**3** speech or behavior that is a sign of good breeding — see POLITENESS

**courting** *n* the series of social engagements shared by a couple looking to get married — see COURTSHIP

**courtship** *n* the series of social engagements shared by a couple looking to get married ⟨a long-married couple who look back on their whirlwind *courtship* with fondness and laughter⟩
***syn*** courting, dating
***rel*** affair, love affair, romance; betrothal, engagement

**courtyard** *n* an open space wholly or partly enclosed (as by buildings or walls) — see COURT 2

**cove** *n* a part of a body of water that extends beyond the general shoreline — see GULF 1

---

*syn* synonym(s) *rel* related words
*ant* antonym(s) *near ant* near antonym(s)

**covenant** *n* **1** a formal agreement between two or more nations or peoples — see TREATY
**2** a formal agreement to fulfill an obligation — see GUARANTEE 1
**3** an arrangement about action to be taken — see AGREEMENT 2
**covenant** *vb* to make a solemn declaration of intent — see PROMISE 1
**cover** *n* **1** a piece placed over an open container to hold in, protect, or conceal its contents ⟨where's the *cover* for the cookie jar?⟩
***syn*** cap, lid, top
***rel*** dome, hood, roof; capsule, case, casing, covering, housing, jacket, sheath, shell
**2** means or method of defending — see DEFENSE 1
**3** something that encloses another thing especially to protect it — see [1]CASE 1
**cover** *vb* **1** to serve as a replacement usually for a time only ⟨a friend *covered* for me as a hospital volunteer while my family went on vacation⟩
***syn*** fill in, pinch-hit, stand in, sub, substitute, take over
***rel*** understudy; relieve, spell; double (as)
**2** to form a layer over ⟨by morning a foot of snow *covered* the ground⟩
***syn*** blanket, carpet, coat, overlay, overlie, overspread, sheet
***rel*** enclose (*also* inclose), enshroud, envelop, enwrap, mantle, shawl, shroud, swathe, wrap; cloak, clothe, curtain, veil; circle, encircle, encompass
**3** to place a protective layer over ⟨*cover* your skin with sunblock so you won't get sunburned⟩
***syn*** screen, shield
***rel*** cloak, clothe, veil; disguise, mask, obscure
***near ant*** bare, expose, uncover
**4** to have (something) as a subject matter — see CONCERN 1
**5** to keep secret or shut off from view — see [1]HIDE 2
**6** to make one's way through, across, or over — see TRAVERSE
**7** to pay continued close attention to (something) for a particular purpose — see MONITOR
**8** to drive danger or attack away from — see DEFEND 1
**cover** (up) *vb* to keep from being publicly known — see SUPPRESS 1
**coverage** *n* the amount of something (as subject matter) included ⟨the biographical dictionary's *coverage* is limited to people no longer living⟩
***syn*** content
***rel*** compass, gamut, range, scope, sweep; membership, participation
**covering** *n* something that encloses another thing especially to protect it — see [1]CASE 1
**coverlet** *n* a decorative cloth used as a top covering for a bed — see COUNTERPANE
**covert** *adj* **1** hidden from view — see SECLUDED
**2** undertaken or done so as to escape being observed or known by others — see SECRET 1
**covert** *n* **1** a place where a person goes to hide — see HIDEOUT
**2** a thick patch of shrubbery, small trees, or underbrush — see THICKET
**covet** *vb* to have an earnest wish to own or enjoy — see DESIRE
**coveting** *adj* having or marked by an eager and often selfish desire especially for material possessions — see GREEDY 1
**covetous** *adj* **1** having or marked by an eager and often selfish desire especially for material possessions — see GREEDY 1
**2** having or showing mean resentment of another's possessions or advantages — see ENVIOUS
**covetousness** *n* **1** a painful awareness of another's possessions or advantages and a desire to have them too — see ENVY
**2** an intense selfish desire for wealth or possessions — see GREED
**cow** *vb* to make timid or fearful by or as if by threats — see INTIMIDATE
**coward** *n* a person who shows a shameful lack of courage in the face of danger ⟨the soldiers who ran as soon as the first shots were fired were branded as *cowards*⟩
***syn*** chicken, craven, dastard, poltroon, recreant, sissy
***rel*** defeatist, quitter; pushover, weakling, wimp; snake, sneak
***near ant*** daredevil
***ant*** hero, stalwart, valiant
**cowardice** *n* a shameful lack of courage in the face of danger ⟨the *cowardice* shown by political leaders who were willing to give the Nazis whatever they wanted⟩
***syn*** cowardliness, cravenness, dastardliness, spinelessness, yellowness
***rel*** diffidence, faintheartedness, fearfulness, timidity, timorousness; carefulness, cautiousness, wariness; bashfulness, shyness; feebleness, softness, weakness
***near ant*** audacity, boldness, brazenness; backbone, fiber, fortitude, grit, gumption, mettle, pluck, spunk; determination, perseverance, resolution; endurance, stamina, tenacity
***ant*** bravery, courage, courageousness, daring, dauntlessness, doughtiness, fearlessness, gallantry, greatheartedness, guts, hardihood, heart, heroism, intrepidity, intrepidness, nerve, stoutness, valor
**cowardliness** *n* a shameful lack of courage in the face of danger — see COWARDICE
**cowardly** *adj* having or showing a shameful lack of courage ⟨a *cowardly* bully who picks on much smaller kids⟩ ⟨vile charges that were made in a *cowardly*, unsigned letter⟩
***syn*** chicken, chickenhearted, craven, dastardly, lily-livered, pusillanimous, recreant, spineless, unheroic, yellow
***rel*** diffident, fainthearted, fearful, timid, timorous; afraid, frightened, scared; careful, cautious, wary; bashful, coy, shy; feeble, soft, weak

***near ant*** audacious, bold, brazen, cheeky, nervy; plucky, spirited, spunky; determined, resolute
***ant*** brave, courageous, daring, dauntless, doughty, fearless, gallant, greathearted, gutsy, hardy, heroic, intrepid, lionhearted, stalwart, stout, stouthearted, valiant, valorous

**cowboy** *n* a hired hand who tends cattle or horses at a ranch or on the range ⟨*cowboys* were rounding up the cattle for branding⟩
***syn*** buckaroo, cowhand, cowman, cowpoke, cowpuncher
***rel*** cowgirl; gaucho, vaquero; horseman, horsewoman, wrangler; cattleman, rancher; herdsman

**cower** *vb* to draw back or crouch down in fearful submission ⟨the abused dog always *cowered* in the presence of its master⟩
***syn*** cringe, grovel, quail
***rel*** flinch, recoil, shrink, squinch; blanch, blench, whiten; fawn, kowtow, toady

**cowhand** *n* a hired hand who tends cattle or horses at a ranch or on the range — see COWBOY

**cowhide** *vb* to strike repeatedly with something long and thin or flexible — see WHIP 1

**cowman** *n* a hired hand who tends cattle or horses at a ranch or on the range — see COWBOY

**coworker** *n* a fellow worker — see COLLEAGUE

**cowpoke** *n* a hired hand who tends cattle or horses at a ranch or on the range — see COWBOY

**cowpuncher** *n* a hired hand who tends cattle or horses at a ranch or on the range — see COWBOY

**coy** *adj* **1** affecting shyness or modesty in order to attract masculine interest ⟨not wanting him to know that she was interested in him, she acted very *coy* at the dance⟩
***syn*** coquettish, demure, kittenish
***rel*** flirtatious; goody-goody, overmodest, priggish, prim, prudish
**2** not comfortable around people — see SHY 2

**cozen** *vb* **1** to cause to believe what is untrue — see DECEIVE
**2** to rob by the use of trickery or threats — see FLEECE

**cozener** *n* a dishonest person who uses clever means to cheat others out of something of value — see TRICKSTER 1

**cozy** *adj* **1** enjoying physical comfort — see COMFORTABLE 2
**2** providing physical comfort — see COMFORTABLE 1

**crab** *n* an irritable and complaining person — see GROUCH

**crab** *vb* to express dissatisfaction, pain, or resentment usually tiresomely — see COMPLAIN

**crabby** *adj* **1** easily irritated or annoyed — see IRRITABLE
**2** given to complaining a lot — see FUSSY 1

**crack** *adj* having or showing exceptional knowledge, experience, or skill in a field of endeavor — see PROFICIENT

**crack** *n* **1** an irregular usually narrow break in a surface created by pressure ⟨a pebble struck the car's windshield and left a *crack* in it⟩
***syn*** chink, cleft, cranny, crevice, fissure, rift, split
***rel*** craze, hairline; fracture, rupture; breach, gap, opening; cut, gash, incision, slit
**2** a hard strike with a part of the body or an instrument — see [1]BLOW
**3** a loud explosive sound — see CLAP 1
**4** an effort to do or accomplish something — see ATTEMPT
**5** something said or done to cause laughter — see JOKE 1

**crack** *vb* **1** to break suddenly with an explosive sound ⟨the tree branch unexpectedly *cracked* under our weight⟩
***syn*** pop, snap
***rel*** crackle, hiss, sizzle, sputter; burst, explode, shatter; clack, click, clatter
**2** to yield to mental or emotional stress ⟨after hours of tough questioning the suspect finally *cracked* and blurted out a confession⟩
***syn*** break (down), flip, freak (out)
***phrases*** go to pieces
**3** to change (as a secret message) from code into ordinary language — see DECODE
**4** to deliver a blow to (someone or something) usually in a strong vigorous manner — see HIT 1
**5** to find an answer for through reasoning — see SOLVE

**crackbrain** *n* **1** a person judged to be legally or medically insane — see LUNATIC 1
**2** a person of odd or whimsical habits — see ECCENTRIC

**crackbrained** *adj* having or showing a very abnormal or sick state of mind — see INSANE 1

**crack down** (on) *vb* to put a stop to (something) by the use of force — see QUELL 1

**cracked** *adj* having or showing a very abnormal or sick state of mind — see INSANE 1

**crackerjack** *adj* **1** having or showing exceptional knowledge, experience, or skill in a field of endeavor — see PROFICIENT
**2** of the very best kind — see EXCELLENT

**crackerjack** *n* **1** a person with a high level of knowledge or skill in a field — see EXPERT
**2** something very good of its kind — see JIM-DANDY

**crackpot** *n* a person of odd or whimsical habits — see ECCENTRIC

**crack–up** *n* the violent coming together of two bodies into destructive contact — see CRASH 1

---

***syn*** synonym(s) ***rel*** related words
***ant*** antonym(s) ***near ant*** near antonym(s)

**crack up** *vb* **1** to declare enthusiastic approval of — see ACCLAIM
**2** to praise or publicize lavishly and often excessively — see TOUT 1
**craft** *n* **1** an occupation requiring skillful use of the hands ⟨the *craft* of cabinetmaking was much admired in colonial times⟩
*syn* handcraft, handicraft, trade
*rel* art, skill; calling, occupation, profession, vocation
**2** a small buoyant structure for travel on water — see BOAT 1
**3** the inclination or practice of misleading others through lies or trickery — see DECEIT
**4** skill in achieving one's ends through indirect, subtle, or underhanded means — see CUNNING 1
**5** subtle or imaginative ability in inventing, devising, or executing something — see SKILL 1
**craft** *vb* to put (something) into proper and usually carefully worked out written form — see COMPOSE 1
**craftiness** *n* **1** skill in achieving one's ends through indirect, subtle, or underhanded means — see CUNNING 1
**2** the inclination or practice of misleading others through lies or trickery — see DECEIT
**craftsman** *n* a person whose occupation requires skill with the hands — see ARTISAN
**crafty** *adj* clever at attaining one's ends by indirect and often deceptive means — see ARTFUL 1
**crag** *n* a steep wall of rock, earth, or ice — see CLIFF
**craggy** *adj* having an uneven edge or outline — see RAGGED 1
**cram** *vb* **1** to fit (something) into a tight space — see CROWD 1
**2** to put into (something) as much as can be held or contained — see FILL 1
**crammed** *adj* containing or seeming to contain the greatest quantity or number possible — see FULL 1
**cramp** *n* a painful sudden tightening of a muscle ⟨I was suddenly awakened by a *cramp* in my leg⟩
*syn* charley horse, crick, spasm
*rel* contraction, jerk, stitch, twinge, twitch
**cramp** *vb* to create difficulty for the work or activity of — see HAMPER
**crane** *vb* to move from a lower to a higher place or position — see RAISE 1
**cranium** *n* the case of bone that encloses the brain and supports the jaws of vertebrates — see SKULL
**crank** *n* **1** a person of odd or whimsical habits — see ECCENTRIC
**2** an irritable and complaining person — see GROUCH
**crank** (up) *vb* to cause to function — see ACTIVATE
**crankiness** *n* readiness to show annoyance or impatience — see PETULANCE
**cranky** *adj* **1** difficult to use or operate especially because of size, weight, or design — see CUMBERSOME
**2** easily irritated or annoyed — see IRRITABLE
**3** given to complaining a lot — see FUSSY 1
**cranny** *n* an irregular usually narrow break in a surface created by pressure — see CRACK 1
**crash** *n* **1** the violent coming together of two bodies into destructive contact ⟨the fiery *crash* of two jumbo jet airplanes in midair⟩
*syn* collision, crack-up, smash, smashup, wreck
*rel* accident; demolishment, destruction, ruin
**2** a falling short of one's goals — see FAILURE 2
**3** a loud explosive sound — see CLAP 1
**4** a forceful coming together of two things — see IMPACT 1
**crash** *vb* **1** to cause to break with violence and much noise — see SMASH 1
**2** to come into usually forceful contact with something — see HIT 2
**3** to stop functioning — see FAIL 1
**crass** *adj* lacking in refinement or good taste — see COARSE 2
**crassness** *n* the quality or state of lacking refinement or good taste — see VULGARITY 1
**crave** *vb* to have an earnest wish to own or enjoy — see DESIRE
**craven** *adj* having or showing a shameful lack of courage — see COWARDLY
**craven** *n* a person who shows a shameful lack of courage in the face of danger — see COWARD
**cravenness** *n* a shameful lack of courage in the face of danger — see COWARDICE
**craving** *n* a strong wish for something — see DESIRE
**crawl** *vb* **1** to move slowly with the body close to the ground ⟨the time we had to *crawl* through a narrow passageway from one cave to another⟩
*syn* creep, grovel, slither, snake, worm, wriggle
*rel* crouch, squat; slide; edge, inch, nose; skulk, sneak, steal, tiptoe
**2** to move slowly ⟨the weekend traffic on the road to the beach just *crawled*⟩
*syn* creep, drag, inch, plod, poke
*rel* lumber, shamble, shuffle, tramp, trudge
*near ant* float, glide, sail; hurry, tear
*ant* fly, race, speed, whiz (*or* whizz), zip
**3** to move or act slowly — see DELAY 1
**crawler** *n* someone who moves slowly or more slowly than others — see SLOWPOKE
**crawling** *adj* moving or proceeding at less than the normal, desirable, or required speed — see SLOW 1
**craze** *n* a practice or interest that is very popular for a short time — see FAD
**craze** *vb* to cause to go insane or as if insane ⟨soldiers who had been *crazed* by

months of combat and chaos in the countryside⟩
*syn* derange, madden, unbalance, unhinge, unstring
*rel* agitate, bother, confuse, discompose, disquiet, distract, disturb, perturb, unsettle, upset; annoy, irritate, vex
*near ant* calm, quiet, relax, settle, soothe, tranquilize (*or* tranquillize)

**crazed** *adj* having or showing a very abnormal or sick state of mind — see INSANE 1

**craziness** *n* lack of good sense or judgment — see FOOLISHNESS 1

**crazy** *adj* **1** conceived or made without regard for reason or reality — see FANTASTIC 1
**2** having or showing a very abnormal or sick state of mind — see INSANE 1
**3** showing or marked by a lack of good sense or judgment — see FOOLISH 1
**4** showing urgent desire or interest — see EAGER

**crazy** (about *or* over) *adj* filled with an intense or excessive love for — see ENAMORED (OF)

**creak** *n* a harsh grating sound — see RASP

**creak** *vb* to make a short shrill noise — see SQUEAK

**cream** *n* individuals carefully selected as being the best of a class — see ELITE

**crease** *n* a small fold in a soft and otherwise smooth surface — see WRINKLE 1

**crease** *vb* to develop creases or folds — see WRINKLE 1

**create** *vb* to be the cause of (a situation, action, or state of mind) — see EFFECT

**creation** *n* **1** something (as a device) created for the first time through the use of the imagination — see INVENTION 1
**2** the whole body of things observed or assumed — see UNIVERSE

**creative** *adj* **1** having the skill and imagination to create new things ⟨Thomas Edison's status as perhaps America's greatest *creative* genius⟩
*syn* imaginative, ingenious, innovative, inventive, original
*rel* gifted, inspired, talented; resourceful; fecund, fertile, fruitful, productive, prolific
*near ant* imitative, uninspired; infertile, unproductive
*ant* uncreative, unimaginative, unoriginal
**2** showing a use of the imagination and creativity especially in inventing — see CLEVER 1

**creativeness** *n* the skill and imagination to create new things — see CREATIVITY 1

**creativity** *n* **1** the skill and imagination to create new things ⟨the arts and crafts fair showed the remarkable *creativity* of local artists and artisans⟩
*syn* creativeness, imaginativeness, ingeniousness, ingenuity, invention, inventiveness, originality
*rel* resourcefulness; fecundity, fertility, fruitfulness, productiveness, productivity; freshness, newness, novelty; genius, inspiration, talent
*near ant* dryness, dullness (*also* dulness)
**2** the ability to form mental images of things that either are not physically present or have never been conceived or created by others — see IMAGINATION

**creator** *n* **1** a person who establishes a whole new field of endeavor — see FATHER 2
**2** *cap* the being worshipped as the creator and ruler of the universe — see DEITY 2

**creature** *n* **1** a member of the human race — see HUMAN
**2** one of the lower animals as distinguished from human beings — see ANIMAL

**credence** *n* **1** firm belief in the integrity, ability, effectiveness, or genuineness of someone or something — see TRUST 1
**2** mental conviction of the truth of some statement or the reality of some being or phenomenon — see BELIEF 1

**credentials** *n pl* a skill, an ability, or knowledge that makes a person able to do a particular job — see QUALIFICATION 1

**credible** *adj* worthy of being accepted as true or reasonable — see BELIEVABLE

**credit** *n* **1** the right to take possession of goods before paying for them ⟨because of their reputation for not paying their bills, no store will extend the family *credit*⟩
*syn* trust
*rel* installment plan, layaway
**2** an asset that brings praise or renown — see GLORY 2
**3** mental conviction of the truth of some statement or the reality of some being or phenomenon — see BELIEF 1
**4** public acknowledgment or admiration for an achievement — see GLORY 1

**credit** *vb* **1** to explain (something) as being the result of something else ⟨has to *credit* his success in picking winning lottery numbers to pure luck⟩
*syn* accredit, ascribe, attribute, impute
*rel* blame, pin (on); associate, connect, link
**2** to regard as right or true — see BELIEVE 1

**creditable** *adj* deserving of high regard or great approval — see ADMIRABLE

**credo** *n* **1** a body of beliefs and practices regarding the supernatural and the worship of one or more deities — see RELIGION 1
**2** the basic beliefs or guiding principles of a person or group — see CREED 1

**credulity** *n* readiness to believe the claims of others without sufficient evidence ⟨the quack pushing the phony medicine was taking advantage of the *credulity* of people hoping for miracle cures⟩
*syn* credulousness, gullibility, naïveté (*also* naivete)
*rel* artlessness, simplicity, unsophistication; trust, unwariness

*near ant* sophistication, worldliness; distrust, mistrust, suspicion, wariness; doubt, uncertainty
*ant* incredulity, skepticism

**credulousness** *n* readiness to believe the claims of others without sufficient evidence — see CREDULITY

**creed** *n* **1** the basic beliefs or guiding principles of a person or group ⟨central to the *creed* of this organization of medical volunteers is the belief that health care is a basic human right⟩
*syn* credo, doctrine, gospel, ideology, philosophy
*rel* manifesto
**2** a body of beliefs and practices regarding the supernatural and the worship of one or more deities — see RELIGION 1

**creek** *n* **1** a natural body of running water smaller than a river ⟨the shallow *creek* that runs in back of our house⟩
*syn* brook, brooklet, rill, rivulet, run [*chiefly Midland*], streamlet
*rel* freshet, runoff; river, stream, watercourse, waterway; canal, millrace, millstream, race
**2** *chiefly British* a part of a body of water that extends beyond the general shoreline — see GULF 1

**creep** *n* a person whose behavior is offensive to others — see JERK 1

**creep** *vb* **1** to advance gradually beyond the usual or desirable limits — see ENCROACH
**2** to move or act slowly — see DELAY 1
**3** to move slowly with the body close to the ground — see CRAWL 1
**4** to move slowly — see CRAWL 2

**creeper** *n* someone who moves slowly or more slowly than others — see SLOWPOKE

**creeping** *adj* moving or proceeding at less than the normal, desirable, or required speed — see SLOW 1

**creepy** *adj* fearfully and mysteriously strange or fantastic — see EERIE

**crest** *n* the line formed when two sloping surfaces come together along their topmost edge — see RIDGE

**crestfallen** *adj* feeling unhappiness — see SAD 1

**cretin** *n* **1** a person whose behavior is offensive to others — see JERK 1
**2** a stupid person — see IDIOT

**crevice** *n* an irregular usually narrow break in a surface created by pressure — see CRACK 1

**crew** *n* a group of people working together on a task — see GANG 1

**crick** *n* a painful sudden tightening of a muscle — see CRAMP

**crime** *n* **1** activities that are in violation of the laws of the state ⟨a promise by the president to step up the war against *crime*⟩
*syn* criminality, lawbreaking, lawlessness
*rel* malfeasance, misconduct; wrongdoing; evil, immorality, sin, wickedness; corruption, depravity; malefaction, misdeed, misdoing, offense (*or* offence), transgression, trespass
**2** a regrettable or blameworthy act ⟨it's a *crime* to waste food, so give the rest of the pizza to me⟩
*syn* disgrace, pity, shame, sin
*rel* outrage, scandal
**3** a breaking of a moral or legal code — see OFFENSE 1
**4** a cause of shame — see DISGRACE 2

**criminal** *adj* contrary to or forbidden by law — see ILLEGAL 1

**criminal** *n* a person who has committed a crime ⟨car thieves, pickpockets, burglars, and other *criminals*⟩
*syn* crook, culprit; felon, lawbreaker, malefactor, offender
*rel* desperado, outlaw; convict, jailbird; perpetrator; evildoer, sinner, transgressor, trespasser, wrongdoer; gangster, gunman, hoodlum, mobster, racketeer, thug; backslider, relapser, repeater

**criminality** *n* activities that are in violation of the laws of the state — see CRIME 1

**crimp** *n* **1** a small fold in a soft and otherwise smooth surface — see WRINKLE 1
**2** something that makes movement or progress more difficult — see ENCUMBRANCE

**crimson** *vb* to develop a rosy facial color (as from excitement or embarrassment) — see BLUSH

**cringe** *vb* to draw back or crouch down in fearful submission — see COWER

**crinkle** *n* a small fold in a soft and otherwise smooth surface — see WRINKLE 1

**crinkle** *vb* **1** to create (as by crushing) an irregular mass of creases in — see CRUMPLE 1
**2** to develop creases or folds — see WRINKLE 1

**cripple** *vb* **1** to cause severe or permanent injury to — see MAIM
**2** to reduce the soundness, effectiveness, or perfection of — see DAMAGE 1
**3** to render powerless, ineffective, or unable to move — see PARALYZE

**crisis** *n* a time or state of affairs requiring prompt or decisive action — see EMERGENCY

**crisp** *adj* **1** having a texture that readily breaks into little pieces under pressure ⟨the bag of *crisp* cookies had a lot of crumbs on the bottom⟩
*syn* brittle, crispy, crumbly, flaky, friable, short
*rel* crunchy; breakable, delicate, fragile
*near ant* elastic, flexible, pliable, pliant, resilient; strong, sturdy, tough
**2** being clean and in good order — see NEAT 1
**3** marked by the use of few words to convey much information or meaning — see CONCISE

**crisply** *adv* in a few words — see SHORTLY 1

**crispness** *n* the quality or state of being marked by or using only few words to convey much meaning — see SUCCINCTNESS

**crispy** *adj* having a texture that readily breaks into little pieces under pressure — see CRISP 1

**crisscross** *vb* to make one's way through, across, or over — see TRAVERSE

**criterion** *n* something set up as an example against which others of the same type are compared — see STANDARD 1

**critic** *n* **1** a person given to harsh judgments and to finding faults ⟨the president's hard-core *critics* are going to criticize him no matter what he does⟩
*syn* carper, castigator, caviler (*or* caviller), censurer, faultfinder, nitpicker, railer, scold
*rel* belittler, derider, detractor; pettifogger, quibbler; complainer, crybaby, fussy, whiner
**2** a person who makes or expresses a judgment on the quality of offerings in some field of endeavor ⟨the restaurant *critic* said that the fries at that fast-food outlet were the worst that she had ever eaten⟩
*syn* reviewer
*rel* analyst, columnist, commentator; appraiser, evaluator, judge

**critical** *adj* **1** given to making or expressing unfavorable judgments about things ⟨adults tend to be *critical* of teenagers' taste in music and movies⟩
*syn* captious, carping, caviling (*or* cavilling), faultfinding, hypercritical, overcritical
*rel* discerning, discriminating, judicious; demanding, exacting, fastidious, finicky, fussy, particular
*near ant* undiscerning
*ant* uncritical
**2** needing immediate attention — see ACUTE 2
**3** of the greatest possible importance — see CRUCIAL

**criticism** *n* an essay evaluating or analyzing something ⟨every *criticism* of the movie has noted that there are major holes in its plot⟩
*syn* notice, review
*rel* rave; appraisal, assessment, evaluation; analysis, examination, study

**criticize** *vb* to express one's unfavorable opinion of the worth or quality of ⟨the students who feel the need to *criticize* every single idea by the principal for improving the school⟩
*syn* blame, censure, condemn, denounce, dis [*slang*], fault, knock, pan, reprehend
*rel* assail, attack, blast, slam, slash; beef, bellyache, carp, complain, crab, croak, fuss, gripe, grouse, growl, grumble, kick, moan, murmur, mutter, repine, squawk, wail, whine, yammer; admonish, chide, rebuke, reprimand, reproach, reprove; berate, castigate, crucify, excoriate, flay, lambaste (*or* lambast), lash, pillory, scold, upbraid; bad-mouth, belittle, disparage, put down
*phrases* find fault (with), take to task
*near ant* approve, endorse (*also* indorse), recommend, sanction
*ant* extol (*also* extoll), laud, praise

**critter** *n* one of the lower animals as distinguished from human beings — see ANIMAL

**croak** *vb* **1** to express dissatisfaction, pain, or resentment usually tiresomely — see COMPLAIN
**2** *slang* to stop living — see DIE 1
**3** *slang* to deprive of life — see KILL 1

**croaker** *n* an irritable and complaining person — see GROUCH

**croaking** *adj* harsh and dry in sound — see HOARSE

**crockery** *n* articles made of baked clay ⟨a display of beautifully hand-painted *crockery* on the kitchen countertop⟩
*syn* earthenware, pottery, stoneware
*rel* ceramics; china, porcelain

**crone** *n* a mean or ugly old woman ⟨a rundown house that was inhabited by a cantankerous *crone* who kept to herself⟩
*syn* beldam (*or* beldame), hag, witch
*rel* grandam (*or* grandame); harpy, shrew, virago

**crony** *n* **1** a person frequently seen in the company of another — see ASSOCIATE 1
**2** a person who has a strong liking for and trust in another — see FRIEND 1

**crook** *n* **1** a person who has committed a crime — see CRIMINAL
**2** something that curves or is curved — see BEND 1

**crook** *vb* **1** to cause to turn away from a straight line — see BEND 1
**2** to turn away from a straight line or course — see CURVE 1

**crooked** *adj* **1** marked by a long series of irregular curves ⟨a long, *crooked* line of people had formed in front of the ticket booth⟩
*syn* bending, curled, curling, curved, curving, devious, serpentine, sinuous, tortuous, twisted, twisting, winding
*rel* zigzag, zigzagging; circling, coiled, coiling, corkscrew, looping, spiral, spiraling (*or* spiralling), swirling; circuitous, indirect, roundabout; meandering, rambling, wandering
*near ant* direct, linear
*ant* straight, straightaway
**2** given to or marked by cheating and deception — see DISHONEST 2
**3** inclined or twisted to one side — see AWRY
**4** marked by, based on, or done by the use of dishonest methods to acquire something of value — see FRAUDULENT 1

**crookedness** *n* the inclination or practice of misleading others through lies or trickery — see DECEIT

**crop** *n* **1** the quantity of an animal or vegetable product gathered at the end of a season ⟨the wheat *crop* is going to be exceptionally large this year⟩
*syn* harvest
*rel* return, yield

---

*syn* synonym(s) *rel* related words
*ant* antonym(s) *near ant* near antonym(s)

**2** a usually small number of persons considered as a unit — see GROUP 2

**crop** *vb* **1** to look after or assist the growth of by labor and care — see GROW 1
**2** to make (as hair) shorter with or as if with the use of shears — see CLIP

**crop** (up) *vb* to come to one's attention especially gradually or unexpectedly — see ARISE 2

**cropper** *n* a falling short of one's goals — see FAILURE 2

**croquette** *n* a small usually rounded mass of minced food that has been fried — see CAKE

**cross** *adj* easily irritated or annoyed — see IRRITABLE

**cross** *n* **1** a test of faith, patience, or strength — see TRIAL 1
**2** an offspring of parents with different genes especially when of different races, breeds, species, or genera — see HYBRID

**cross** *vb* **1** to be unfaithful or disloyal to — see BETRAY 1
**2** to divide by passing through or across — see INTERSECT
**3** to make one's way through, across, or over — see TRAVERSE

**cross** (out) *vb* to show (something written) to be no longer valid by drawing a cross over or a line through it — see X (OUT)

**crossbred** *adj* being offspring produced by parents of different races, breeds, species, or genera — see MIXED

**crossbreed** *n* an offspring of parents with different genes especially when of different races, breeds, species, or genera — see HYBRID

**cross fire** *n* an often noisy or angry expression of differing opinions — see ARGUMENT 1

**crossing** *n* **1** a journey over water in a vessel — see SAIL
**2** a place where roads meet — see CROSSROAD 1

**crossness** *n* readiness to show annoyance or impatience — see PETULANCE

**crossroad** *n* **1** *usually* **crossroads** *pl* a place where roads meet ⟨the fast-food chain has a restaurant at practically every *crossroads*⟩
***syn*** corner, crossing, intersection
***rel*** overpass, underpass
**2** *usually* **crossroads** *pl* a time or state of affairs requiring prompt or decisive action — see EMERGENCY

**cross section** *n* a number of things selected from a group to stand for the whole — see SAMPLE 1

**crossways** *adv* in a line or direction running from corner to corner — see CROSSWISE

**crosswise** *adv* in a line or direction running from corner to corner ⟨first cut the sandwiches *crosswise* and then trim the crusts⟩
***syn*** athwart, crossways, obliquely, transversely

**crotchet** *n* an odd or peculiar habit — see IDIOSYNCRASY

**crotchetiness** *n* readiness to show annoyance or impatience — see PETULANCE

**crotchety** *adj* easily irritated or annoyed — see IRRITABLE

**crouch** *vb* to lie low with the limbs close to the body ⟨the cat *crouched* in the bushes, waiting for the right moment to pounce on the chipmunk⟩
***syn*** huddle, hunch, scrunch, squat, squinch
***rel*** curl up

**crow** *vb* **1** to feel or express joy or triumph — see EXULT
**2** to praise or express pride in one's own possessions, qualities, or accomplishments often to excess — see BOAST

**crowd** *n* **1** a great number of persons or things gathered together ⟨a huge *crowd* of fans was on hand to greet the returning Super Bowl champions⟩
***syn*** army, crush, drove, flock, horde, host, legion, mob, multitude, press, swarm, throng
***rel*** masses, rabble, riffraff; gaggle, herd; heap, mountain, pile
**2** a group of people sharing a common interest and relating together socially — see GANG 2

**crowd** *vb* **1** to fit (something) into a tight space ⟨*crowded* all the boats into the harbor before the storm struck⟩
***syn*** cram, jam, ram, sandwich, squeeze, stuff, wedge
***rel*** fill, heap, jam-pack, load, pack
**2** to move upon or fill (something) in great numbers ⟨cars *crowded* the roads over the long holiday weekend⟩
***syn*** flock, mob, swarm, throng
***rel*** beset, infest, invade, overrun; clog, dam, obstruct, plug (up)
**3** to gather into a closely packed group — see PRESS 3

**crowded** *adj* **1** containing or seeming to contain the greatest quantity or number possible — see FULL 1
**2** having little space between items or parts — see CLOSE 1

**crown** *n* **1** a decorative band or wreath worn about the head as a symbol of victory or honor ⟨the *crown* of laurel leaves that is traditionally placed on the winner of the marathon⟩
***syn*** coronet, diadem
***rel*** tiara; garland, laurel
**2** the position occupied by the one who comes in first in a competition ⟨his lifelong dream of someday winning the heavyweight boxing *crown*⟩
***syn*** championship, title
**3** the highest part or point — see HEIGHT 1

**crown** *vb* to bring to a triumphant conclusion ⟨the Olympic Games were *crowned* by spectacular closing ceremonies⟩
***syn*** climax, culminate
***rel*** complete, conclude, finish, round (off *or* out), terminate, wrap up

**crucial** *adj* of the greatest possible importance ⟨water is *crucial* to our survival⟩
***syn*** critical, key, pivotal, vital

*rel* decisive, life-and-death; basic, elementary, fundamental; essential, indispensable, necessary, requisite; pressing, urgent
*near ant* inconsequential, insignificant, trivial, unimportant

**crucible** *n* a test of faith, patience, or strength — see TRIAL 1

**crude** *adj* **1** being such as found in nature and not altered by processing or refining ⟨a spill of *crude* oil along a coastline is the worst kind of environmental disaster⟩
*syn* native, natural, raw, undressed, unprocessed, unrefined, untreated
*rel* undeveloped; roughhewn, unfinished, unpolished; unbaked, uncooked; impure, unfiltered, unpurified
*phrases* in the rough
*near ant* filtered, pure, purified
*ant* dressed, processed, refined, treated
**2** belonging to or characteristic of an early level of skill or development — see PRIMITIVE 1
**3** depicting or referring to sexual matters in a way that is unacceptable in polite society — see OBSCENE 1
**4** lacking in refinement or good taste — see COARSE 2
**5** hastily or roughly constructed — see RUDE 1

**crudeness** *n* **1** the quality or state of being obscene — see OBSCENITY 1
**2** the quality or state of lacking refinement or good taste — see VULGARITY 1

**cruel** *adj* **1** having or showing the desire to inflict severe pain and suffering on others ⟨a *cruel* dictator who tortured anyone who dared to speak out against him⟩ ⟨*cruel* and unusual punishments are forbidden by the U.S. Constitution⟩
*syn* barbaric, barbarous, brutal, heartless, inhumane, sadistic, savage, vicious, wanton
*rel* cutthroat, merciless, pitiless, ruthless; fell, ferocious, grim; bloodthirsty, murderous, sanguinary, sanguine; catty, despiteful, hateful, malevolent, malicious, malign, malignant, mean, nasty, spiteful
*near ant* tender, warm, warmhearted; charitable, clement, lenient, merciful, pitying; pacific, peaceable, peaceful
*ant* benign, benignant, compassionate, good-hearted, humane, kind, kindhearted, sympathetic, tenderhearted
**2** difficult to endure — see HARSH 1
**3** hard to accept or bear especially emotionally — see BITTER 2
**4** having or showing a desire to cause someone pain or suffering for the sheer enjoyment of it — see HATEFUL

**cruelness** *n* the willful infliction of pain and suffering on others — see CRUELTY

**cruelty** *n* the willful infliction of pain and suffering on others ⟨centuries after he ravaged Europe, Attila the Hun remains notorious for his *cruelty*⟩
*syn* barbarity, brutality, cruelness, heartlessness, inhumanity, sadism, savageness, savagery, viciousness, wantonness
*rel* mercilessness, ruthlessness; ferocity, fierceness; bloodthirstiness, sanguinity; cattiness, despitefulness, hatefulness, malevolence, maliciousness, malignity, meanness, nastiness, spitefulness
*near ant* tenderness, warmheartedness, warmth; clemency, leniency, mercifulness, mercy, pity
*ant* benignity, compassion, good-heartedness, humanity, kindheartedness, kindness, sympathy

**cruise** *n* a journey over water in a vessel — see SAIL

**cruise** *vb* to travel on water in a vessel — see SAIL 1

**crumb** *n* **1** a very small amount — see PARTICLE 1
**2** a very small piece — see BIT 1

**crumble** *vb* to become worse or of less value — see DETERIORATE

**crumbly** *adj* having a texture that readily breaks into little pieces under pressure — see CRISP 1

**crumple** *vb* **1** to create (as by crushing) an irregular mass of creases in ⟨*crumpled* the piece of paper and angrily threw it in the wastebasket⟩
*syn* crinkle, rumple, scrunch, wrinkle
*rel* corrugate, crease, crimp, fold, furrow, pleat; ripple, ruffle; disarrange, jumble, mess (up), muss (up)
*ant* iron out, smooth
**2** to fall down or in as a result of physical pressure — see COLLAPSE 1

**crunch** *n* a time or state of affairs requiring prompt or decisive action — see EMERGENCY

**crunch** *vb* to press or strike against or together so as to make a scraping sound — see GRIND 2

**crunch** (on) *vb* to crush or grind with the teeth — see BITE (ON)

**crusade** *n* a series of activities undertaken to achieve a goal — see CAMPAIGN

**crusader** *n* one who is intensely or excessively devoted to a cause — see ZEALOT

**crush** *n* **1** a strong but often short-lived liking for another person ⟨the *crush* that she had on a boy whom she had met over the summer⟩
*syn* infatuation, passion
*rel* fixation, obsession; affection, devotion, fondness, love; craze, fad, rage, vogue
**2** a great number of persons or things gathered together — see CROWD 1

**crush** *vb* **1** to cause to become a pulpy mass ⟨dark-colored grapes that will be *crushed* to make red wine⟩
*syn* mash, pulp, squash
*rel* press, squeeze; beat, pound, powder, pulverize
**2** to achieve a victory over — see BEAT 2
**3** to put a stop to (something) by the use of force — see QUELL 1
**4** to reduce to fine particles — see POWDER

---

*syn* synonym(s) *rel* related words
*ant* antonym(s) *near ant* near antonym(s)

**5** to subject to incapacitating emotional or mental stress — see OVERWHELM 1
**6** to apply external pressure or so as to force out the juice or contents of — see PRESS 2

**crusher** *n* something (as a fact or argument) that is decisive or overwhelming — see CLINCHER

**crusty** *adj* being or characterized by direct, brief, and potentially rude speech or manner — see BLUNT 1

**crux** *n* the central part or aspect of something under consideration ⟨the *crux* of the problem is that the school's current budget is totally inadequate⟩
*syn* core, gist, heart, nub, pith, pivot
*rel* course, direction, drift, tenor; body, essence, substance

**cry** *n* **1** a loud vocal expression of strong emotion — see SHOUT
**2** a natural vocal sound made by an animal — see CALL 1
**3** an attention-getting word or phrase used to publicize something (as a campaign or product) — see SLOGAN
**4** an earnest request — see PLEA 1

**cry** *vb* **1** to shed tears often while making meaningless sounds as a sign of pain or distress ⟨some kids started to *cry* even before the doctor had given them their shot⟩
*syn* bawl, blubber, sob, weep
*rel* grieve, keen, lament, mourn; howl, scream, squall, wail, yowl; pule, whimper, whine; sniffle, snivel; groan, moan, sigh
**2** to utter one's distinctive animal sound ⟨we knew that we were getting very close to the ocean when we could hear sea gulls *crying*⟩
*syn* call, sing
**3** to speak so as to be heard at a distance — see CALL 1

**cry** (out) *vb* to utter with a sudden burst of strong feeling — see EXCLAIM

**crybaby** *n* a person who makes frequent complaints usually about little things ⟨car trips that were often spoiled by a couple of *crybabies* in the back seat⟩
*syn* complainer, fusser, griper, growler, grumbler, whiner
*rel* malcontent; carper, critic, faultfinder, nitpicker, squawker; bawler, wailer, weeper

**cry down** *vb* to express scornfully one's low opinion of — see DECRY 1

**crying** *adj* needing immediate attention — see ACUTE 2

**crypt** *n* an underground burial chamber ⟨the old church's *crypt* is the final resting place for the president and his beloved wife⟩
*syn* catacomb(s), vault
*rel* mausoleum, sepulcher (*or* sepulchre), tomb

**cryptic** *adj* **1** being beyond one's powers to know, understand, or explain — see MYSTERIOUS 1
**2** having an often intentionally veiled or uncertain meaning — see OBSCURE 1

**crystallize** *vb* to take on a definite form — see FORM 1

**cub** *n* a young person who is between infancy and adulthood — see CHILD 1

**cubicle** *n* one of the parts into which an enclosed space is divided — see COMPARTMENT

**cuckoo** *adj* **1** having or showing a very abnormal or sick state of mind — see INSANE 1
**2** showing or marked by a lack of good sense or judgment — see FOOLISH 1

**cuddle** *vb* **1** to lie close — see NUZZLE
**2** to sit or recline comfortably or cozily — see SNUGGLE 1

**cudgel** *n* a heavy rigid stick used as a weapon or for punishment — see CLUB 1

**cue** *n* **1** a series of persons or things arranged one behind another — see LINE 1
**2** a slight or indirect pointing to something (as a solution or explanation) — see HINT 1

**cuff** *n* a hard strike with a part of the body or an instrument — see [1]BLOW

**cuisine** *n* the art or style of preparing food (as in a specified region) — see COOKERY

**cull** *n* something separated from a group or lot for not being as good as the others ⟨the unbruised apples will be packed in bags, and the *culls* will be used for cider⟩
*syn* discard, reject, rejection
*rel* second, throwaway

**cull** *vb* to decide to accept (someone or something) from a group of possibilities — see CHOOSE 1

**culminate** *vb* to bring to a triumphant conclusion — see CROWN

**culmination** *n* the highest part or point — see HEIGHT 1

**culpability** *n* responsibility for wrongdoing or failure — see BLAME 1

**culpable** *adj* **1** deserving reproach or blame — see BLAMEWORTHY
**2** responsible for a wrong — see GUILTY 1

**culprit** *n* a person who has committed a crime — see CRIMINAL

**cult** *n* **1** a group of people showing intense devotion to a cause, person, or work (as a film) ⟨long after it had gone off the air, the TV series continued to have a huge *cult*⟩
*syn* following
*rel* discipleship
**2** a body of beliefs and practices regarding the supernatural and the worship of one or more deities — see RELIGION 1

**cultivate** *vb* **1** to come to have gradually — see DEVELOP 2
**2** to help the growth or development of — see FOSTER 1
**3** to look after or assist the growth of by labor and care — see GROW 1
**4** to work by plowing, sowing, and raising crops on — see FARM

**cultivated** *adj* having or showing a taste for the fine arts and gracious living ⟨the museum's annual gala for charity usually attracts a *cultivated* crowd⟩
*syn* civilized, cultured, genteel, polished, refined

***rel*** cerebral, highbrow, intellectual; educated, erudite, knowledgeable, learned, literate, scholarly, well-read; civil, courteous, mannerly, polite, well-bred; cosmopolitan, sophisticated, urbane
***near ant*** ignorant, illiterate, uneducated, unlettered; lowbrow, unintelligent; coarse, ill-bred, ill-mannered; provincial, rustic, unsophisticated; boorish, churlish, cloddish, clownish, crude, uncouth, vulgar
***ant*** philistine, uncivilized, uncultured, unpolished, unrefined

**cultivation** *n* a high level of taste and enlightenment as a result of extensive intellectual training and exposure to the arts — see CULTURE 1

**cultivator** *n* a person who cultivates the land and grows crops on it — see FARMER

**cultural** *adj* of or relating to the fine arts ⟨with its many museums, theaters, and opera and ballet companies, the city is a *cultural* paradise⟩
***syn*** artistic
***rel*** aesthetic, tasteful

**culture** *n* **1** a high level of taste and enlightenment as a result of extensive intellectual training and exposure to the arts ⟨because of its wide reputation as a place of *culture*, Boston became known as "the Athens of America"⟩
***syn*** civilization, cultivation, polish, refinement
***rel*** education, erudition, learning, literacy, scholarship; sophistication, urbanity; breeding, gentility, manners; class, elegance, grace, taste; civility, courtesy, politeness
***near ant*** ignorance, illiteracy; parochialism, provincialism, unsophistication; boorishness, churlishness, clownishness, coarseness, crudeness, vulgarity
***ant*** philistinism
**2** the way people live at a particular time and place — see CIVILIZATION 1

**culture** *vb* to look after or assist the growth of by labor and care — see GROW 1

**cultured** *adj* having or showing a taste for the fine arts and gracious living — see CULTIVATED

**cumbersome** *adj* difficult to use or operate especially because of size, weight, or design ⟨a long-handled wrench that is too *cumbersome* for tight spots, like under the sink⟩
***syn*** awkward, clumsy, cranky, cumbrous, ungainly, unhandy, unwieldy
***rel*** uncontrollable, unmanageable; bulky, heavy, massive; impracticable, impractical
***near ant*** functional, practicable, practical, serviceable, useful
***ant*** handy

**cumbrous** *adj* difficult to use or operate especially because of size, weight, or design — see CUMBERSOME

**cummerbund** *n* a strip of flexible material (as leather) worn around the waist — see ²BELT

**cumulative** *adj* produced by a series of additions of identical or similar things ⟨a *cumulative* weight gain of 20 pounds over the course of a year⟩
***syn*** additive, incremental
***rel*** gradual, step-by-step

**cunning** *adj* **1** clever at attaining one's ends by indirect and often deceptive means — see ARTFUL 1
**2** skillful with the hands — see DEXTEROUS 1

**cunning** *n* **1** skill in achieving one's ends through indirect, subtle, or underhanded means ⟨the *cunning* with which Tom Sawyer was able to get others to whitewash the fence for him⟩
***syn*** artfulness, artifice, caginess, canniness, craft, craftiness, deviousness, foxiness, guile, slickness, slyness, sneakiness, subtleness, subtlety, wiliness
***rel*** calculation, care, design; savvy, sharpness, shrewdness; cleverness, ingeniousness, ingenuity, inventiveness; ease, facility, finesse; deceitfulness, duplicity, shiftiness
**2** subtle or imaginative ability in inventing, devising, or executing something — see SKILL 1
**3** the inclination or practice of misleading others through lies or trickery — see DECEIT

**cup** *n* a round vessel equipped with a handle and designed for drinking ⟨a large *cup* that can hold almost a pint of hot chocolate⟩
***syn*** mug
***rel*** stein, tankard; demitasse, noggin; teacup

**cupboard** *n* a storage case typically having doors and shelves — see CABINET

**cupidity** *n* an intense selfish desire for wealth or possessions — see GREED

**cur** *n* a person whose behavior is offensive to others — see JERK 1

**curb** *n* something that limits one's freedom of action or choice — see RESTRICTION 1

**curb** *vb* to keep from exceeding a desirable degree or level (as of expression) — see CONTROL 1

**curdy** *adj* having small pieces or lumps spread throughout — see CHUNKY 1

**cure** *n* **1** something that corrects or counteracts something undesirable ⟨a fun hobby is always a good *cure* for boredom⟩
***syn*** corrective, remedy
***rel*** cure-all, elixir, panacea; answer, solution; aid, help, relief, succor; balm, palliative
**2** a substance or preparation used to treat disease — see MEDICINE

**cure** *vb* **1** to bring about recovery from ⟨do you have anything that will *cure* my headache?⟩
***syn*** heal, remedy

*rel* allay, alleviate, assuage, relieve; palliate, salve, soothe; ease, lighten, moderate, temper; doctor, treat
*near ant* aggravate, worsen
**2** to restore to a healthy condition — see HEAL 1

**cure–all** *n* something that cures all ills or problems ⟨raising a young person's self-esteem is not the *cure-all* that some people think⟩
*syn* elixir, panacea
*rel* corrective, cure, remedy

**curio** *n* **1** a small object displayed for its attractiveness or interest — see KNICKKNACK
**2** something strange or unusual that is an object of interest — see CURIOSITY 2

**curiosity** *n* **1** an eager desire to find out about things that are often none of one's business ⟨the neighbors' *curiosity* about what we paid for our new car was really offensive⟩
*syn* curiousness, inquisitiveness, nosiness
*rel* attentiveness, concern, interest, regard; inquiry, interrogation, questioning; intrusiveness, obtrusiveness, officiousness; eavesdropping, rubbernecking
*near ant* apathy, disinterestedness, disregard, indifference, unconcern
**2** something strange or unusual that is an object of interest ⟨the museum's *curiosities* include items constructed entirely out of toothpicks⟩
*syn* curio, exotic, oddity, rarity
*rel* marvel, prodigy, wonder; abnormality, anomaly, freak, monster, monstrosity; malformation, mutant, mutation
**3** a small object displayed for its attractiveness or interest — see KNICKKNACK

**curious** *adj* **1** interested in what is not one's own business ⟨*curious* neighbors peered out of their windows as the new people moved in⟩
*syn* inquisitive, nosy (*or* nosey), prying, snoopy
*rel* interfering, intrusive, meddlesome, meddling, obtrusive, officious; inquisitional, inquisitorial; concerned, interested
*near ant* apathetic, disinterested, indifferent, unconcerned, uninterested
*ant* incurious, uncurious
**2** different from the ordinary in a way that causes curiosity or suspicion — see ODD 2
**3** noticeably different from what is generally found or experienced — see UNUSUAL 1

**curiousness** *n* an eager desire to find out about things that are often none of one's business — see CURIOSITY 1

**curl** *n* a length of hair that forms a loop or series of loops ⟨a young girl with beautiful golden *curls*⟩
*syn* ringlet
*rel* kink, wave; lock, tress

**curl** *vb* to follow a circular or spiral course — see WIND

**curled** *adj* **1** forming or styled into loops — see CURLY
**2** marked by a long series of irregular curves — see CROOKED 1

**curling** *adj* marked by a long series of irregular curves — see CROOKED 1

**curl up** *vb* to sit or recline comfortably or cozily — see SNUGGLE 1

**curly** *adj* forming or styled into loops ⟨the boy's naturally *curly* hair⟩
*syn* curled
*rel* frizzy, kinky, waved, wavy
*near ant* lank, limp
*ant* straight

**curmudgeon** *n* an irritable and complaining person — see GROUCH

**currency** *n* something (as pieces of stamped metal or printed paper) customarily and legally used as a medium of exchange, a measure of value, or a means of payment — see MONEY

**current** *adj* **1** accepted, used, or practiced by most people ⟨the *current* theories on parenting favor allowing children lots of self-expression⟩
*syn* conventional, customary, going, popular, prevailing, prevalent, standard, stock, usual
*rel* average, common, everyday, normal, ordinary; regular, routine; ubiquitous, universal, widespread; accustomed, wonted; fashionable, in, modish, stylish
*near ant* abnormal, exceptional, extraordinary, uncommon
*ant* nonstandard, unconventional, unpopular, unusual
**2** being or involving the latest methods, concepts, information, or styles — see MODERN
**3** existing or in progress right now — see PRESENT 1

**current** *n* **1** a prevailing or general movement or inclination — see TREND 1
**2** noticeable movement of air in a particular direction — see [1]WIND 1

**currently** *adv* at the present time — see NOW 1

**curse** *n* **1** a prayer that harm will come to someone ⟨the victim's *curse* that the man who robbed her never receive any pleasure from her money⟩
*syn* anathema, execration, imprecation, malediction
*rel* censure, condemnation, damnation, denunciation; hex, spell
*near ant* citation, commendation, endorsement
*ant* benediction, benison, blessing
**2** a disrespectful or indecent word or expression — see SWEARWORD

**curse** *vb* **1** to ask a divine power to send harm or evil upon ⟨I *curse* the guy who had the idea of having annoying salespeople call up innocent people to sell them things they don't want⟩
*syn* imprecate
*rel* condemn, damn, denounce, execrate, reprobate; hex, jinx; fulminate (against), rail (against), revile
*near ant* applaud, commend, congratulate
*ant* bless

2 to cause persistent suffering to — see AFFLICT
3 to use offensive or indecent language — see SWEAR 1

**cursorily** *adv* with excessive or careless speed — see HASTILY 1

**cursory** *adj* acting or done with excessive or careless speed — see HASTY 1

**curt** *adj* being or characterized by direct, brief, and potentially rude speech or manner — see BLUNT 1

**curtail** *vb* 1 to make (as hair) shorter with or as if with the use of shears — see CLIP
2 to make less in extent or duration — see SHORTEN

**curtain** *n* 1 something that covers or conceals like a piece of cloth — see CLOAK 1
2 **curtains** *pl* pieces of cloth hung to darken, decorate, or divide a room — see DRAPERY

**curtain** *vb* to keep secret or shut off from view — see [1]HIDE 2

**curvature** *n* something that curves or is curved — see BEND 1

**curve** *n* something that curves or is curved — see BEND 1

**curve** *vb* 1 to turn away from a straight line or course ⟨after following a straight path most of the way down the mountain, the ski trail abruptly *curves* to the right⟩
***syn*** arc, arch, bend, bow, crook, hook, round, sweep, swerve, wheel
***rel*** circle, coil, curl, loop, spiral; turn, twist, wind; deviate, veer
***ant*** straighten
2 to cause to turn away from a straight line — see BEND 1

**curved** *adj* marked by a long series of irregular curves — see CROOKED 1

**curving** *adj* marked by a long series of irregular curves — see CROOKED 1

**cushion** *n* something that serves as a protective barrier ⟨used a blanket as a *cushion* between the two tables in the moving van⟩
***syn*** buffer, bumper, fender, pad
***rel*** baffle, muffler; padding; safeguard, shield; barricade, cordon

**cushion** *vb* to lessen the shock of ⟨a substantial nest egg helped to *cushion* the sudden loss of her job⟩
***syn*** buffer, gentle, soften
***rel*** baffle, dampen, deaden, dull; moderate, modulate, temper; allay, alleviate, assuage, ease; lighten, mitigate, relieve
***near ant*** heighten, intensify, sharpen

**cushy** *adj* providing physical comfort — see COMFORTABLE 1

**cusp** *n* the last and usually sharp or tapering part of something long and narrow — see POINT 2

**cuss** *n* a disrespectful or indecent word or expression — see SWEARWORD

**cuss** *vb* to use offensive or indecent language — see SWEAR 1

**custodian** *n* 1 a person who takes care of a property sometimes for an absent owner ⟨the *custodian* made his usual rounds of the building to make sure that everything was OK⟩
***syn*** caretaker, guardian, janitor, keeper, warden, watchman
***rel*** curator; sexton; steward
2 a person or group that watches over someone or something — see GUARD 1
3 someone that protects — see PROTECTOR

**custody** *n* responsibility for the safety and well-being of someone or something ⟨the divorcing parents will share *custody* of the children⟩
***syn*** care, guardianship, keeping, safekeeping, trust, ward
***rel*** control, governorship, management, superintendence, supervision

**custom** *adj* made or fitted to the needs or preferences of a specific customer — see CUSTOM-MADE

**custom** *n* 1 a usual manner of behaving or doing — see HABIT
2 an inherited or established way of thinking, feeling, or doing — see TRADITION 1

**customary** *adj* 1 accepted, used, or practiced by most people — see CURRENT 1
2 based on customs usually handed down from a previous generation — see TRADITIONAL 1

**customer** *n* 1 a person who buys a product or uses a service from a business ⟨the store greatly values its regular *customers*⟩
***syn*** client, guest, patron
***rel*** consumer, end user, user; buyer, purchaser; browser, prospect, shopper, window-shopper
***near ant*** merchant, seller, vendor (*also* vender)
2 a member of the human race — see HUMAN

**customized** *adj* made or fitted to the needs or preferences of a specific customer — see CUSTOM-MADE

**custom–made** *adj* made or fitted to the needs or preferences of a specific customer ⟨an odd-sized window that will require the purchase of *custom-made* curtains⟩
***syn*** custom, customized, tailored, tailor-made
***rel*** particular, special, specialized; handcrafted, handmade
***ant*** mass-produced, ready-made

**cut** *n* 1 a piece that has been separated from the whole by cutting ⟨choose *cuts* of meat that have very little visible fat⟩
***syn*** cutting, slice
***rel*** chop, cutlet; chunk, hunk, lump; clipping, paring, shaving, snippet; sliver, splinter
2 an individual part of a process, series, or ranking — see DEGREE 1
3 something belonging to, due to, or contributed by an individual member of a group — see SHARE 1

**cut** *vb* 1 to penetrate with a sharp edge (as a knife) ⟨I *cut* my hand on a piece of broken glass⟩

***syn*** gash, incise, rip, slash, slice, slit
***rel*** saw, scissor; cleave, rive, split; pierce, stab; bruise, hack, lacerate, mangle; rend, tear; butcher, carve, dissect; chop, dice, mince; amputate, cut off, sever
**2** to fail to attend ⟨a warning that she had been *cutting* too many classes without valid excuses⟩
***syn*** miss, skip
***rel*** ignore, neglect, pass over
***phrases*** absent oneself, play hooky
***ant*** attend, show up (for)
**3** to deliberately ignore or treat rudely — see SNUB 1
**4** to make (as hair) shorter with or as if with the use of shears — see CLIP
**5** to shorten the standing leafy plant cover of — see MOW 1

**cut** (across) *vb* to make one's way through, across, or over — see TRAVERSE
**cut** (down) *vb* to bring down by cutting — see FELL 2
**cut** (out) *vb* to bring (as an action or operation) to an immediate end — see STOP 1
**cut back** *vb* **1** to make (as hair) shorter with or as if with the use of shears — see CLIP
**2** to make less in extent or duration — see SHORTEN
**cute** *adj* very pleasing to look at — see BEAUTIFUL
**cuteness** *n* the qualities in a person or thing that as a whole give pleasure to the senses — see BEAUTY 1
**cut in** *vb* to cause a disruption in a conversation or discussion — see INTERRUPT
**cutlet** *n* a small usually rounded mass of minced food that has been fried — see CAKE
**cut off** *vb* to set or keep apart from others — see ISOLATE
**cut out** *vb* to stop functioning — see FAIL 1
**cut–rate** *adj* **1** costing little — see CHEAP 1
**2** of low quality — see CHEAP 2
**cutter** *n* an instrument with a sharp edge for cutting — see KNIFE
**cutthroat** *adj* not guided by or showing a concern for what is right — see UNPRINCIPLED
**cutting** *adj* **1** causing intense discomfort to one's skin ⟨a frigid day with a *cutting* wind that made it seem even colder⟩
***syn*** biting, bitter, keen, penetrating, piercing, raw, sharp, smarting, stinging
***rel*** brisk, invigorating, nippy, snappy; needlelike, prickly, tingling; caustic, corrosive
***near ant*** balmy, gentle, mild, soothing
**2** having an edge thin enough to cut or pierce something — see SHARP 1
**3** marked by the use of wit that is intended to cause hurt feelings — see SARCASTIC
**cutting** *n* a piece that has been separated from the whole by cutting — see CUT 1
**cut up** *vb* to engage in attention-getting playful or boisterous behavior ⟨high-spirited cousins who *cut up* at every family gathering⟩
***syn*** act up, clown (around), fool (around), horse (around), monkey (around), show off, skylark
***rel*** carry on, misbehave; roughhouse; caper, cavort, disport, frisk, frolic, gambol, lark, rollick, romp; carouse, revel, wassail
**cycle** *n* **1** a series of events or actions that repeat themselves regularly and in the same order ⟨the *cycle* of birth, growth, decline, and death that is experienced by all life forms⟩
***syn*** circle, round
***rel*** pattern, syndrome; course, development, progression, run; circuit, loop, ring; rotation, revolution, turn; chain, sequence, series, string, succession, train
**2** a long or seemingly long period of time — see AGE 2
**cynic** *n* a person who distrusts other people and believes that everything is done for selfish reasons ⟨a *cynic* who believes that nobody does a good deed without expecting something in return⟩
***syn*** misanthrope, pessimist
***rel*** misogynist; doubter, skeptic; belittler, derider, detractor, sneeffer; malcontent; defeatist, quitter
***near ant*** optimist; idealist; sentimentalist
**cynical** *adj* having or showing a deep distrust of human beings and their motives ⟨so *cynical* that he can't understand why anyone would volunteer to help out at a homeless shelter⟩
***syn*** misanthropic, pessimistic
***rel*** distrustful, mistrustful, skeptical, suspicious; derisive, mocking, sardonic, scornful; defeatist, fatalistic, negative; ironic (*or* ironical), sarcastic; jaded, sophisticated, worldly-wise; hard-bitten, hard-boiled, unsentimental
***near ant*** trustful, trusting, unsuspicious; cheerful, optimistic, rose-colored; ingenuous, innocent, naive (*or* naïve), unsophisticated; idealistic, impractical, romantic; maudlin, mushy, saccharine, sappy, sentimental
**cynosure** *n* a thing or place that is of greatest importance to an activity or interest — see CENTER 1
**czar** *also* **tsar** *or* **tzar** *n* a person of rank, power, or influence in a particular field — see MAGNATE

# D

**[1]dab** *n* a quick thrust — see [1]POKE

**[2]dab** *n* a very small amount — see PARTICLE 1

**dabbler** *n* a person who regularly or occasionally engages in an activity without being or becoming an expert at it — see AMATEUR

**dad** *n* a male human parent — see FATHER 1

**daddy** *n* a male human parent — see FATHER 1

**daffy** *adj* **1** having or showing a very abnormal or sick state of mind — see INSANE 1
**2** showing or marked by a lack of good sense or judgment — see FOOLISH 1

**daft** *adj* **1** having or showing a very abnormal or sick state of mind — see INSANE 1
**2** showing or marked by a lack of good sense or judgment — see FOOLISH 1

**daftness** *n* lack of good sense or judgment — see FOOLISHNESS 1

**daily** *adj* occurring, done, produced, or appearing every day ⟨they made their *daily* stop at the coffee shop after work to relax before dinner⟩
***syn*** day-to-day, diurnal
***rel*** alternate, cyclical, intermittent, periodic, recurrent, recurring, regular; continuous, frequent, incessant
***near ant*** nightly, nocturnal; monthly, weekly, yearly; erratic, infrequent, irregular; occasional, spasmodic, sporadic; interrupted

**daintiness** *n* the state or quality of having a delicate structure — see DELICACY 2

**dainty** *adj* **1** hard to please — see FINICKY
**2** having qualities that appeal to a refined taste — see CHOICE
**3** satisfying or pleasing because of fineness or mildness — see DELICATE 1

**dainty** *n* something that is pleasing to eat because it is rare or a luxury — see DELICACY 1

**dais** *n* a level usually raised surface — see PLATFORM

**dale** *n* an area of lowland between hills or mountains — see VALLEY

**dalliance** *n* activity engaged in to amuse oneself — see PLAY 1

**dallier** *n* someone who moves slowly or more slowly than others — see SLOWPOKE

**dally** *vb* **1** to engage in activity for amusement — see PLAY 1
**2** to move or act slowly — see DELAY 1
**3** to show a liking for someone of the opposite sex just for fun — see FLIRT
**4** to spend time doing nothing — see IDLE

**dallying** *adj* moving or proceeding at less than the normal, desirable, or required speed — see SLOW 1

**dam** *n* a bank of earth constructed to control water ⟨the river backed up behind the *dam* until it formed a new lake⟩
***syn*** dike, embankment, levee
***rel*** breakwater, jetty, seawall; breastwork, bulwark, earthwork, rampart; canal, channel, ditch, gutter, trough; lock; barricade, barrier, block; floodgate, sluice

**dam** *vb* **1** to prevent passage through — see CLOG 1
**2** to close up so that no empty spaces remain — see FILL 2

**damage** *n* **1** something that causes loss or pain — see INJURY 1
**2 damages** *pl* a sum of money to be paid as a punishment — see FINE
**3 damages** *pl* payment to another for a loss or injury — see COMPENSATION 1

**damage** *vb* **1** to reduce the soundness, effectiveness, or perfection of ⟨the explosion in the sewers *damaged* the entire city's water supply⟩
***syn*** blemish, break, cripple, deface, disfigure, flaw, harm, hurt, impair, injure, mar, spoil, vitiate
***rel*** enfeeble, undermine, weaken; erode, scour, wash out, wear (away); blight, tarnish; dent, dint; botch, gum (up); lacerate, wound; maim, mangle, mutilate, torment, torture; annihilate, crush, dash, decimate, demolish, destroy, devastate, pulverize, raze, ruin, scourge, shatter, smash, tear down, waste, wipe out, wreck
***near ant*** cure, heal, help, rectify, remedy; edit, remodel, revise; ameliorate, better, enhance, improve, meliorate
***ant*** fix, mend, patch, rebuild, recondition, reconstruct, renovate, repair, revamp
**2** to cause bodily damage to — see INJURE 1

**damaging** *adj* causing or capable of causing harm — see HARMFUL

**dame** *n* **1** a dignified usually elderly woman of some rank or authority — see MATRIARCH
**2** a woman of high birth or social position — see GENTLEWOMAN

**damn** *vb* **1** to declare to be morally wrong or evil — see CONDEMN 1
**2** to impose a judicial punishment on — see SENTENCE

**damp** *adj* slightly or moderately wet — see MOIST

**damp** *vb* to reduce or weaken in strength or feeling — see DULL 1

---

***syn*** synonym(s) ***rel*** related words
***ant*** antonym(s) ***near ant*** near antonym(s)

**dampen** *vb* **1** to make or become slightly or moderately wet — see MOISTEN
**2** to reduce or weaken in strength or feeling — see DULL 1

**damper** *n* a device on a musical instrument that deadens or softens its tone — see MUTE

**dampness** *n* the amount of water suspended in the air in tiny droplets — see MOISTURE

**damsel** *n* a young usually unmarried woman — see GIRL 1

**dance** *n* a social gathering for dancing ⟨who are you taking to the *dance* Saturday night?⟩
*syn* ball, cotillion, formal, hop, prom
*rel* blowout, celebration, event, festival, festivity, fete (*or* fête), gala, masquerade, mixer, party, reception, shindig, soiree (*or* soirée)

**dance** *vb* **1** to perform a series of usually rhythmic bodily movements to music ⟨she liked to *dance* to her favorite rock bands⟩
*syn* foot (it), hoof (it), step
*rel* prance, strut, trip; gavotte, jig, jitterbug, jive, mambo, polka, tango, tap-dance, waltz; tread
**2** to make an irregular series of quick, sudden movements — see FLIT

**dandle** *vb* to treat with great or excessive care — see BABY

**dandy** *adj* of the very best kind — see EXCELLENT

**dandy** *n* **1** a man extremely interested in his clothing and personal appearance ⟨that *dandy* was willing to spend all day and hundreds of dollars just to get the perfect pair of shoes⟩
*syn* buck, dude, fop, gallant
*rel* coxcomb, popinjay; blade, cavalier; swell; clotheshorse
*near ant* slattern, slob, sloven, slut
**2** something very good of its kind — see JIM-DANDY

**danger** *n* **1** the state of not being protected from injury, harm, or evil ⟨he knew he was in *danger* when he received the threatening phone calls at home⟩
*syn* distress, endangerment, imperilment, jeopardy, peril, risk, trouble
*rel* exposure, liability, vulnerability; precariousness, threat
*near ant* preservation, salvation; defense, protection; exemption, immunity, impunity
*ant* safeness, safety, security
**2** something that may cause injury or harm ⟨she was willing to face the *dangers* of the construction site in order to get her Frisbee back⟩
*syn* hazard, menace, peril, pitfall, risk, threat, trouble
*rel* snare, trap
*near ant* guard, protection, safeguard, shield, ward

**dangerous** *adj* involving potential loss or injury ⟨the soldiers were commanded to go on a *dangerous* mission behind enemy lines⟩
*syn* grave, grievous, hazardous, jeopardizing, menacing, parlous, perilous, risky, serious, threatening, unhealthy, unsafe, venturesome
*rel* insecure, precarious, treacherous, uncertain; chance, haphazard, random; distressing, sickening, unpleasant; ugly, wicked; adverse, bad, baleful, baneful, deleterious, detrimental, evil, harmful, hurtful, ill, inimical, injurious, malignant, nasty, noxious, pernicious, pestilent; deadly, deathly, destructive, dire, fatal, fateful, fell, killer, lethal, mortal, murderous
*near ant* advantageous, beneficial, good
*ant* harmless, innocent, innocuous, safe

**dangle** *vb* to place on an elevated point without support from below — see HANG 1

**dangling** *adj* extending freely from a support from above — see DEPENDENT 1

**dank** *adj* slightly or moderately wet — see MOIST

**dapper** *adj* being strikingly neat and trim in style or appearance — see SMART 1

**dapple** *n* a small area that is different (as in color) from the main part — see SPOT 1

**dapple** *vb* to mark with small spots especially unevenly — see SPOT

**dappled** *also* **dapple** *adj* **1** marked with spots — see SPOTTED 1
**2** having blotches of two or more colors — see PIED

**dare** *vb* **1** to invite (someone) to take part in a contest or to perform a feat — see CHALLENGE 2
**2** to oppose (something hostile or dangerous) with firmness or courage — see FACE 2

**daredevil** *adj* **1** foolishly adventurous or bold — see FOOLHARDY 1
**2** having or showing a lack of concern for the consequences of one's actions — see RECKLESS 1

**daring** *adj* inclined or willing to take risks — see BOLD 1

**daring** *n* strength of mind to carry on in spite of danger — see COURAGE

**dark** *adj* **1** being without light or without much light ⟨a *dark* alley that most people wisely avoided⟩
*syn* darkened, darkish, darkling, darksome, dim, dimmed, dusky, gloomy, murky, obscure, obscured, pitch-black, pitch-dark, sombre (*or* sombre)
*rel* moonless, sunless; cloudy, dull, dulled, lackluster; shadowy, shady; gray (*also* grey), leaden, pale
*near ant* beaming, effulgent, glowing, lambent, radiant, shining; glossy, lustrous, shiny
*ant* bright, brightened, brilliant, illuminated, illumined, light, lighted (*or* lit), lucent, lucid, luminous
**2** causing or marked by an atmosphere lacking in cheer — see GLOOMY 1
**3** given to keeping one's activities hidden from public observation or knowledge — see SECRETIVE

4 having an often intentionally veiled or uncertain meaning — see OBSCURE 1
5 lacking in education or the knowledge gained from books — see IGNORANT 1

**dark** *n* 1 a time or place of little or no light ⟨I have a bad habit of running into tables in the *dark*⟩
*syn* blackness, darkness, dusk, gloaming, gloom, murk, night, semidarkness, shade, shadows, twilight, umbra
*rel* blackout, brownout; shadiness; dullness (*also* dulness), somberness; cloudiness, fogginess, haziness, mistiness, murkiness; dimness, faintness, gloominess, grayness, paleness
*near ant* moonlight, starlight, sunlight; effulgence, radiance, shine, sunshine; incandescence, luminescence, luminosity
*ant* blaze, brightness, brilliance, day, daylight, glare, glow, light, lightness
2 the time from sunset to sunrise when there is no visible sunlight — see NIGHT 1

**darken** *vb* 1 to take on a gloomy or forbidding look ⟨his face slowly *darkened* as we told him the sad news⟩
*syn* gloom, glower, lower (*also* lour)
*rel* frown, scowl; glare, stare; brood, mope, pout, sulk; anger, fume, rage, steam; intimidate, menace, threaten
*ant* brighten, cheer (up), lighten, perk (up)
2 to make dark, dim, or indistinct — see CLOUD 1

**darkened** *adj* being without light or without much light — see DARK 1

**darkening** *adj* causing or marked by an atmosphere lacking in cheer — see GLOOMY 1

**darkish** *adj* being without light or without much light — see DARK 1

**darkling** *adj* 1 being beyond one's powers to know, understand, or explain — see MYSTERIOUS 1
2 being without light or without much light — see DARK 1
3 having an often intentionally veiled or uncertain meaning — see OBSCURE 1

**darkness** *n* 1 a time or place of little or no light — see DARK 1
2 the quality or state of having a veiled or uncertain meaning — see OBSCURITY 1
3 the time from sunset to sunrise when there is no visible sunlight — see NIGHT 1

**darksome** *adj* being without light or without much light — see DARK 1

**darling** *adj* 1 granted special treatment or attention ⟨they poured gifts and affection on their *darling* child⟩
*syn* beloved, cherished, dear, favored, favorite, loved, pet, precious, special, sweet
*rel* admired, adored, appreciated, esteemed, relished, revered; prized, treasured; preferred
*near ant* despised, detested, disdained, disfavored, disliked, execrated, hated, loathed; abandoned, forgotten, ignored

*syn* synonym(s) *rel* related words
*ant* antonym(s) *near ant* near antonym(s)

2 having qualities that tend to make one loved — see LOVABLE
3 giving pleasure or contentment to the mind or senses — see PLEASANT

**darling** *n* 1 a person or thing that is preferred over others — see FAVORITE
2 a person with whom one is in love — see SWEETHEART

**darn** *vb* to close up with a series of interlacing stitches — see SEW

**dart** *n* an act or expression showing scorn and usually intended to hurt another's feelings — see INSULT

**dart** *vb* to make an irregular series of quick, sudden movements — see FLIT

**dash** *n* active strength of body or mind — see VIGOR 1

**dash** *vb* 1 to go at a pace faster than a walk — see RUN 1
2 to proceed or move quickly — see HURRY 2
3 to send through the air especially with a quick forward motion of the arm — see THROW
4 to wet or soil by striking with something liquid or mushy — see SPLASH 2

**dashing** *adj* inclined or willing to take risks — see BOLD 1

**dashingly** *adv* 1 in a bright and showy way — see GAILY 3
2 in a strikingly neat and trim manner — see SMARTLY

**dastard** *n* a person who shows a shameful lack of courage in the face of danger — see COWARD

**dastardliness** *n* a shameful lack of courage in the face of danger — see COWARDICE

**dastardly** *adj* having or showing a shameful lack of courage — see COWARDLY

**date** *n* 1 an agreement to be present at a specified time and place — see ENGAGEMENT 2
2 the period during which something exists, lasts, or is in progress — see DURATION 1

**date** *vb* 1 to go on a social engagement with ⟨I don't want to *date* him—I'd rather just be friends⟩
*syn* take out
*rel* accompany, escort, see; court, woo
2 to go on dates that may eventually lead to marriage — see COURT 2

**dated** *adj* having passed its time of use or usefulness — see OBSOLETE

**dateless** *adj* 1 dating or surviving from the distant past — see ANCIENT 1
2 lasting forever — see EVERLASTING

**dating** *n* the series of social engagements shared by a couple looking to get married — see COURTSHIP

**datum** *n* a single piece of information — see FACT 3

**daub** *vb* to rub an oily or sticky substance over — see SMEAR 1

**daunt** *vb* to lessen the courage or confidence of — see DISCOURAGE 1

**dauntless** *adj* feeling or displaying no fear by temperament — see BRAVE

**dauntlessness** *n* strength of mind to carry on in spite of danger — see COURAGE

**davenport** *n* a long upholstered piece of furniture designed for several sitters — see COUCH

**dawdle** *vb* **1** to move or act slowly — see DELAY 1
**2** to spend time doing nothing — see IDLE

**dawdler** *n* someone who moves slowly or more slowly than others — see SLOWPOKE

**dawdling** *adj* moving or proceeding at less than the normal, desirable, or required speed — see SLOW 1

**dawn** *n* **1** the first appearance of light in the morning or the time of its appearance ⟨we stayed up talking until *dawn*⟩
***syn*** aurora, cockcrow, dawning, daybreak, daylight, morn, morning, sunrise, sunup
***rel*** day, daytime, light; twilight; forenoon
***near ant*** dark, darkness, night, nighttime; afternoon, dusk, evening, gloaming
***ant*** nightfall, sundown, sunset
**2** the point at which something begins — see BEGINNING

**dawn** *vb* to come into existence — see BEGIN 2

**dawn** (on) *vb* to come into the mind of — see OCCUR (TO)

**dawning** *n* the first appearance of light in the morning or the time of its appearance — see DAWN 1

**day** *n* **1** the hours of light between one night and the next ⟨during the *day*, we like to go play ball in the park⟩
***syn*** daylight, daytime
***rel*** light, sunlight, sunshine; dawn, dawning, daybreak, morn, morning, sunrise, sunset; dusk, evening, gloaming, nightfall, sundown, twilight
***near ant*** dark, darkness
***ant*** night, nighttime
**2** an extent of time associated with a particular person or thing — see AGE 1

**daybreak** *n* the first appearance of light in the morning or the time of its appearance — see DAWN 1

**daydream** *n* a conception or image created by the imagination and having no objective reality — see FANTASY 1

**daydreaming** *n* the state of being lost in thought — see REVERIE

**daylight** *n* **1** the first appearance of light in the morning or the time of its appearance — see DAWN 1
**2** the hours of light between one night and the next — see DAY 1

**daytime** *n* the hours of light between one night and the next — see DAY 1

**day–to–day** *adj* occurring, done, produced, or appearing every day — see DAILY

**daze** *n* a state of mental confusion — see HAZE 2

**daze** *vb* **1** to make senseless or dizzy by a blow — see STUN 1
**2** to overpower with light — see DAZZLE

**dazed** *adj* suffering from mental confusion — see DIZZY 2

**dazzle** *n* the quality or state of having or giving off light — see BRILLIANCE 1

**dazzle** *vb* to overpower with light ⟨skiers were *dazzled* by the glare off of the slopes of freshly packed snow⟩
***syn*** bedazzle, blind, daze
***rel*** confuse, overpower, overwhelm, stun

**dazzling** *adj* giving off or reflecting much light — see BRIGHT 1

**deacon** *n* a person specially trained and authorized to conduct religious services in a Christian church — see CLERGYMAN

**dead** *adj* **1** no longer living ⟨I inherited this heirloom from my *dead* great-grandfather⟩
***syn*** breathless, deceased, defunct, departed, fallen, gone, late, lifeless
***rel*** extinct; dying, fading, moribund; stillborn; finished, lapsed, terminated; barren, desert; inanimate, insensate, nonliving, unanimated
***phrases*** bitten the dust, passed away, passed on
***near ant*** animate, animated; dynamic, lively, thriving, vibrant, vital, vivacious; active, functioning, operative, running
***ant*** alive, breathing, going, living
**2** depleted in strength, energy, or freshness — see WEARY 1
**3** having no exceptions or restrictions — see ABSOLUTE 2
**4** lacking in sensation or feeling — see NUMB
**5** no longer existing — see EXTINCT
**6** not being in a state of use, activity, or employment — see INACTIVE 2
**7** of, relating to, or suggestive of death — see DEATHLY 1

**dead** *adv* **1** in a direct line or course — see DIRECTLY 1
**2** to a full extent or degree — see FULLY 1

**deaden** *vb* to reduce or weaken in strength or feeling — see DULL 1

**dead heat** *n* a situation in which neither participant in a contest, competition, or struggle comes out ahead of the other — see TIE 1

**deadlock** *n* a point in a struggle where neither side is capable of winning or willing to give in — see IMPASSE

**deadly** *adj* likely to cause or capable of causing death ⟨the doctors were alarmed about the outbreak of the *deadly* new virus⟩
***syn*** baleful, deathly, fatal, fell, killer, lethal, mortal, murderous, pestilent, vital
***rel*** baneful, destructive, harmful, noxious, pernicious; poisonous, toxic, virulent; dangerous, grave, grievous, hazardous, jeopardizing, menacing, parlous, perilous, risky, serious, threatening, ugly, unhealthy, unsound; capital; bloody, internecine, sanguinary, sanguine
***near ant*** beneficial, restorative; nonpoisonous, nontoxic, safe
***ant*** healthful, healthy, nonfatal, nonlethal, wholesome

**deadly** *adv* to a great degree — see VERY 1
**deadness** *n* the state of being dead — see DEATH 2
**deadpan** *adj* not expressing any emotion — see BLANK 1
**deadwood** *n* discarded or useless material — see GARBAGE
**deafening** *adj* marked by a high volume of sound — see LOUD 1
[1]**deal** *n* a considerable amount — see LOT 2
[2]**deal** *n* 1 an arrangement about action to be taken — see AGREEMENT 2
2 the transfer of ownership of something from one person to another for a price — see SALE
**deal** *vb* 1 to carry on the business of buying and selling goods or other property — see TRADE 1
2 to talk over or dispute the terms of a purchase — see BARGAIN
**deal** (in) *vb* to offer for sale to the public — see MARKET
**deal** (out) *vb* to give out (something) in appropriate amounts or to appropriate individuals — see ADMINISTER 1
**deal** (with) *vb* 1 to behave toward in a stated way — see TREAT 1
2 to have (something) as a subject matter — see CONCERN 1
**dealer** *n* 1 a buyer and seller of goods for profit — see MERCHANT
2 the person in a business deal who hands over an item in exchange for money — see VENDOR
**dealings** *n pl* doings between individuals or groups — see RELATION 1
**dean** *n* the senior member of a group ⟨the *dean* of the Aspen ski instructors oversaw the training of the rescue team⟩
***syn*** elder, elder statesman, senior
***rel*** better, superior
***near ant*** inferior, subordinate, underling; beginner, freshman, newcomer, rookie
***ant*** baby
**dear** *adj* 1 commanding a large price — see COSTLY
2 granted special treatment or attention — see DARLING 1
3 having qualities that tend to make one loved — see LOVABLE
**dear** *n* a person with whom one is in love — see SWEETHEART
**dearth** *n* 1 a falling short of an essential or desirable amount or number — see DEFICIENCY
2 the fact or state of being absent — see LACK 1
**death** *n* 1 the permanent stopping of all the vital bodily activities ⟨we were all saddened by the *death* of our teacher⟩
***syn*** decease, demise, doom, end, passing, quietus
***rel*** casualty, fatality; martyrdom, self-destruction, suicide; annihilation, destruction, ending, expiration, extermination, ruin
***near ant*** existence, life; creation
***ant*** birth
2 the state of being dead ⟨*death* is one of the few constants in the universe⟩
***syn*** deadness, lifelessness, sleep
***ant*** existence, life
3 the act of ceasing to exist ⟨the *death* of the Soviet economic system in the wake of the breakup of the USSR⟩
***syn*** demise, expiration, termination
***rel*** dispersion, dissolution; shutdown; decease, doom, end, ending, passing, quietus; suicide; annihilation, destruction, ruin
***near ant*** existence
***ant*** beginning, creation, start
**deathless** *adj* lasting forever — see EVERLASTING
**deathlike** *adj* of, relating to, or suggestive of death — see DEATHLY 1
**deathly** *adj* 1 of, relating to, or suggestive of death ⟨his *deathly* pallor suggested that any attempt to find a pulse would be futile⟩
***syn*** dead, deathlike, mortal
***rel*** ghostly, phantom, spectral; inactive, inert, inoperative, lifeless, quiescent, still; macabre; baleful, fatal, fateful, fell, killer, lethal, murderous, pestilent
***near ant*** active, alive, living; animated, energetic, lively, vigorous, vivacious; hale, healthy, hearty, robust, sound
2 likely to cause or capable of causing death → see DEADLY
**debacle** *also* **débâcle** *n* 1 a sudden violent event that brings about great loss or destruction — see DISASTER
2 something that has failed — see FAILURE 3
**debar** *vb* to prevent the participation or inclusion of — see EXCLUDE
**debark** *vb* to go ashore from a ship — see DISEMBARK
**debase** *vb* 1 to lower in character or dignity ⟨we *debased* ourselves when we cheated on the test⟩
***syn*** abase, corrupt, debauch, degrade, demean, deprave, pervert, poison, profane, prostitute, subvert, warp
***rel*** contaminate, pollute, taint; descend; disgrace, humble, humiliate; blemish, damage, deface, destroy, flaw, harm, hurt, impair, mar, ruin, spoil, stain, tarnish, vitiate, wreck; depreciate, downgrade
***near ant*** dignify, exalt, honor; amend, improve; cleanse, purify, restore; respect
***ant*** elevate, ennoble, uplift
2 to reduce to a lower standing in one's own eyes or in others' eyes — see HUMBLE
**debased** *adj* having or showing lowered moral character or standards — see CORRUPT
**debasement** *n* a sinking to a state of low moral standards and behavior — see CORRUPTION 2
**debatable** *adj* 1 open to question or dispute ⟨it's always *debatable* which college football team is really number one, since there's more than one ranking system⟩

***syn*** synonym(s) ***rel*** related words
***ant*** antonym(s) ***near ant*** near antonym(s)

***syn*** disputable, doubtable, doubtful, moot, questionable
***rel*** refutable; controversial, debated, disputed; dubious, inconclusive, indecisive, problematic (*also* problematical), uncertain; academic, hypothetical, speculative, theoretical (*also* theoretic); ambiguous, equivocal
***near ant*** irrefutable; certain, definite, positive, sure; unambiguous, unequivocal; absolute, clear, conclusive, decisive; uncontested, undisputed
***ant*** incontestable, incontrovertible, indisputable, indubitable, undeniable, unquestionable
**2** giving good reason for being doubted, questioned, or challenged — see DOUBTFUL 2

**debate** *n* **1** a careful weighing of the reasons for or against something — see CONSIDERATION 1
**2** variance of opinion on a matter — see DISAGREEMENT 1

**debate** *vb* **1** to give serious and careful thought to — see PONDER
**2** to talk about (an issue) usually from various points of view and for the purpose of arriving at a decision or opinion — see DISCUSS

**debater** *n* a person who takes part in a dispute — see DISPUTANT

**debauch** *vb* to lower in character or dignity — see DEBASE 1

**debauched** *adj* having or showing lowered moral character or standards — see CORRUPT

**debaucher** *n* a person who has sunk below the normal moral standard — see DEGENERATE

**debauchery** *n* **1** immoral conduct or practices harmful or offensive to society — see VICE 1
**2** a sinking to a state of low moral standards and behavior — see CORRUPTION 2

**debilitate** *vb* to diminish the physical strength of — see WEAKEN 1

**debilitated** *adj* lacking bodily strength — see WEAK 1

**debilitation** *n* **1** a gradual sinking and wasting away of mind or body — see DECLINE 1
**2** the quality or state of lacking physical strength or vigor — see WEAKNESS 1

**debility** *n* the quality or state of lacking physical strength or vigor — see WEAKNESS 1

**debonair** *adj* having or showing very polished and worldly manners — see SUAVE

**debris** *n* the portion or bits of something left over or behind after it has been destroyed — see REMAINS 1

**debt** *n* a breaking of a moral or legal code — see OFFENSE 1

**debug** *vb* to remove errors, defects, deficiencies, or deviations from — see CORRECT 1

**debunk** *vb* to reveal the true nature of — see EXPOSE 1

**decadence** *n* **1** a change to a lower state or level — see DECLINE 2
**2** a sinking to a state of low moral standards and behavior — see CORRUPTION 2

**decadent** *adj* **1** having lost forcefulness, courage, or spirit — see EFFETE 1
**2** having or showing lowered moral character or standards — see CORRUPT

**decadent** *n* a person who has sunk below the normal moral standard — see DEGENERATE

**decalogue** *n* a collection or system of rules of conduct — see CODE

**decamping** *n* the act of leaving a place — see DEPARTURE

**decampment** *n* the act of leaving a place — see DEPARTURE

**decapitate** *vb* to cut off the head of ⟨he started *decapitating* wildflowers with his walking stick as they strolled through the park⟩
***syn*** behead, guillotine
***rel*** prune, shorten, trim; scalp

**decay** *n* **1** a gradual sinking and wasting away of mind or body — see DECLINE 1
**2** the process by which dead organic matter separates into simpler substances — see CORRUPTION 1

**decay** *vb* **1** to go through decomposition ⟨the logs *decayed* on the rain forest floor⟩ ⟨the atom of plutonium *decayed* in the test chamber⟩
***syn*** break down, corrupt, decompose, disintegrate, molder, putrefy, rot, spoil
***rel*** sour, turn; contaminate, defile, pollute, taint; curdle, ferment; crumble, degenerate, deteriorate
***phrases*** go to seed, run to seed
***near ant*** develop, grow, mature, ripen; refresh, renew, restore; cleanse, purify; assemble, compose, integrate
**2** to become worse or of less value — see DETERIORATE
**3** to lose bodily strength or vigor — see WEAKEN 2

**decayed** *adj* **1** having lost forcefulness, courage, or spirit — see EFFETE 1
**2** having undergone organic breakdown — see ROTTEN 1

**decaying** *n* a gradual sinking and wasting away of mind or body — see DECLINE 1

**decease** *n* the permanent stopping of all the vital bodily activities — see DEATH 1

**decease** *vb* to stop living — see DIE 1

**deceased** *adj* no longer living — see DEAD 1

**deceit** *n* the inclination or practice of misleading others through lies or trickery ⟨the evil queen in the story was full of *deceit*⟩
***syn*** artifice, craft, craftiness, crookedness, cunning, deceitfulness, dishonesty, dissembling, dissimulation, double-dealing, duplicity, fakery, foxiness, guile, wiliness
***rel*** equivocation, prevarication; chicanery, skulduggery (*or* skullduggery), subterfuge, trickery; hypocrisy, insincerity; deviousness, shrewdness; treacherousness, underhandedness, unscrupulousness; covertness, furtiveness, secrecy, shadiness, sneakiness, stealthiness; oili-

ness, shiftiness, slickness, slipperiness, slyness, smoothness
***near ant*** candidness, candor, directness, frankness, ingenuousness, openness, plainness; honesty, probity; reliability, trustworthiness
***ant*** artlessness, forthrightness, good faith, guilelessness, sincerity

**deceitful** *adj* **1** marked by, based on, or done by the use of dishonest methods to acquire something of value — see FRAUDULENT 1
**2** tending or having power to deceive — see DECEPTIVE 1

**deceitfulness** *n* **1** the inclination or practice of misleading others through lies or trickery — see DECEIT
**2** the tendency to tell lies — see DISHONESTY 1

**deceive** *vb* to cause to believe what is untrue ⟨he went to great lengths to *deceive* his younger brother about the nature of his new job at the mall⟩
***syn*** beguile, bluff, cozen, delude, dupe, fool, gull, have, hoax, hoodwink, humbug, misguide, misinform, mislead, snow, string along, take in, trick
***rel*** cheat, chisel, defraud, fleece, gyp, hustle, rook, swindle
***near ant*** debunk, expose, reveal, show up, uncloak, uncover, unmask; disclose, divulge, tell, unveil; disabuse, disenchant, disillusion; edify, enlighten
***ant*** undeceive

**deceiving** *adj* tending or having power to deceive — see DECEPTIVE 1

**decelerate** *vb* to cause to move or proceed at a less rapid pace — see SLOW 1

**deceleration** *n* a usually gradual decrease in the pace or level of activity of something — see SLOWDOWN

**decency** *n* **1** socially acceptable behavior ⟨the standards of basic *decency* demanded that they help the old lady with her groceries⟩
***syn*** decorum, form, propriety
***rel*** civility, courtesy, politeness; dignity, grace, refinement; discretion, prudence; correctness, decorousness, fitness, rightness, seemliness; attention, attentiveness, care, carefulness; goodness, high-mindedness, honesty, morality, probity, rectitude, righteousness, straightness, uprightness, virtue, virtuousness
***near ant*** coarseness, crudeness, gracelessness; discourtesy, impoliteness, incivility; imprudence, indiscretion; badness, evil, immorality, wickedness
***ant*** impropriety, indecency, indecorum
**2** conduct that conforms to an accepted standard of right and wrong — see MORALITY 1

**decent** *adj* **1** conforming to a high standard of morality or virtue — see GOOD 2
**2** following the accepted rules of moral conduct — see HONORABLE 1
**3** following the established traditions of refined society and good taste — see PROPER 1
**4** free from any trace of the coarse or indecent — see CHASTE
**5** of a level of quality that meets one's needs or standards — see ADEQUATE

**deceptive** *adj* **1** tending or having power to deceive ⟨in his *deceptive* answer about the vehicle's history, the salesman said that the used car had never been hit by another car⟩
***syn*** beguiling, deceitful, deceiving, deluding, delusive, delusory, fallacious, false, misleading, specious
***rel*** devious, guileful, shady, shifty, sly, sneaking, sneaky, trick, tricky, underhand, underhanded; inaccurate, incorrect, wrong; bewildering, confounding, distracting, perplexing, puzzling; crooked, dishonest, double-dealing, faithless, fast, fraudulent, knavish, lying, mendacious, untrustworthy, untruthful; insidious, perfidious, treacherous; artificial, backhanded, feigned, hypocritical, insincere, left-handed, two-faced
***near ant*** candid, frank, open, plain; clarifying, elucidative, explanatory, illuminating; revealing, revelatory; honest, trustworthy, truthful
***ant*** aboveboard, forthright, straightforward
**2** given to or marked by cheating and deception — see DISHONEST 2

**decide** *vb* **1** to come to a judgment after discussion or consideration ⟨they *decided* to go out for pizza after the movie was over⟩
***syn*** choose, conclude, determine, figure, opt, resolve
***rel*** decree, rule; cull, elect, handpick, pick, prefer, select, single (out), take
***phrases*** make up one's mind
***near ant*** abstain, decline, refuse, reject, turn down; delay, hesitate, stall, temporize; shilly-shally, vacillate, waver
**2** to give an opinion about (something at issue or in dispute) — see JUDGE 1
**3** to come to an agreement or decision concerning the details of — see ARRANGE 1
**4** to make final, definite, or beyond dispute — see CLINCH

**decided** *adj* not subject to misinterpretation or more than one interpretation — see CLEAR 2

**decidedness** *n* firm or unwavering adherence to one's purpose — see DETERMINATION 1

**decimate** *vb* to bring to a complete end the physical soundness, existence, or usefulness of — see DESTROY 1

**decimation** *n* the state or fact of being rendered nonexistent, physically unsound, or useless — see DESTRUCTION

**decipher** *vb* to change (as a secret message) from code into ordinary language — see DECODE

**decision** *n* **1** a position arrived at after consideration ⟨after much deliberation,

***syn*** synonym(s) ***rel*** related words
***ant*** antonym(s) ***near ant*** near antonym(s)

we made a *decision* about what to have on our pizza〉
***syn*** conclusion, deliverance, determination, diagnosis, judgment (*or* judgement), opinion, resolution, verdict
***rel*** decree, mandate, order; say-so; doom, finding, ruling, sentence; choice, option, selection
***near ant*** deadlock, draw, stalemate, standoff, tie
**2** firm or unwavering adherence to one's purpose — see DETERMINATION 1

**decisive** *adj* **1** fully committed to achieving a goal — see DETERMINED 1
**2** having the power to persuade — see COGENT
**3** serving to put an end to all debate or questioning — see CONCLUSIVE 1

**decisiveness** *n* firm or unwavering adherence to one's purpose — see DETERMINATION 1

**deck** *vb* **1** to make more attractive by adding something that is beautiful or becoming — see DECORATE
**2** to outfit with clothes and especially fine or special clothes — see CLOTHE 1

**declaim** *vb* **1** to give a formal often extended talk on a subject — see TALK 1
**2** to talk as if giving an important and formal speech — see ORATE 1

**declamation** *n* a usually formal discourse delivered to an audience — see SPEECH 1

**declaration** *n* a solemn and often public declaration of the truth or existence of something — see PROTESTATION

**declare** *vb* **1** to make known openly or publicly — see ANNOUNCE
**2** to state as a fact usually forcefully — see CLAIM 1
**3** to state clearly and strongly — see ASSERT 1

**declension** *n* **1** a gradual sinking and wasting away of mind or body — see DECLINE 1
**2** a change to a lower state or level — see DECLINE 2

**decline** *n* **1** a gradual sinking and wasting away of mind or body 〈her sad *decline* from a robust athlete to an old woman with arthritis〉
***syn*** debilitation, decay, decaying, declension, degeneration, descent, deterioration, ebbing, enfeeblement, weakening
***rel*** atrophy; exhaustion; drooping, flagging, limping; relapse, setback
***near ant*** invigoration, strengthening; progress
***ant*** improvement, recovery, revitalization
**2** a change to a lower state or level 〈the *decline* of the Roman Empire〉
***syn*** decadence, declension, degeneracy, degeneration, degradation, descent, deterioration, downfall, downgrade, fall
***rel*** decay, rotting, spoiling; breakup, crumbling, decomposition, disintegration, dissolution; abasement, debasement; depreciation, lessening; decimation, demolishment, demolition, desolation, destruction, havoc, ruin, ruination; abatement, decrease, decrement, de-escalation, deflation, diminishment, diminution, dip, drop, fall, loss, lowering, reduction, sag, shrinkage
***near ant*** advancement, development, evolution, growth; blossoming, flourishing, flowering; renewal, restoration, revitalization; heightening; accretion, accrual, addendum, addition, augmentation, boost, enhancement, gain, increase, increment, raise, supplement
***ant*** ascent, rise, upswing
**3** a loss of status — see COMEDOWN
**4** the amount by which something is lessened — see DECREASE

**decline** *vb* **1** to show unwillingness to accept, do, engage in, or agree to 〈he *declined* the invitation to the party〉 〈she *declined* to participate in the soccer game〉
***syn*** disapprove, negative, refuse, reject, repudiate, spurn, turn down
***rel*** overrule, veto; forbid, prohibit, proscribe; dismiss; abstain, forbear, refrain; deny, dispute, gainsay; balk, stick; abjure, renounce; avoid, bypass, detour
***near ant*** condone, countenance, swallow, tolerate; adopt, embrace, receive, take; accede, acquiesce, agree, assent, consent; choose, select; espouse, support
***ant*** accept, agree (to), approve
**2** to be unwilling to grant — see DENY 2
**3** to go to a lower level — see DROP 2
**4** to become worse or of less value — see DETERIORATE
**5** to grow less in scope or intensity especially gradually — see DECREASE 2
**6** to lead or extend downward — see DESCEND 1

**declined** *adj* bending downward or forward — see NODDING

**declining** *adj* bending downward or forward — see NODDING

**decode** *vb* to change (as a secret message) from code into ordinary language 〈the agents worked into the night to *decode* the transmission from the enemy spy〉
***syn*** break, crack, decipher
***rel*** render, translate; dope (out), figure out, puzzle (out), solve, unravel, work, work out
***ant*** cipher, code, encode

**decolorize** *vb* to make white or whiter by removing color — see WHITEN

**decompose** *vb* to go through decomposition — see DECAY 1

**decomposed** *adj* having undergone organic breakdown — see ROTTEN 1

**decomposition** *n* the process by which dead organic matter separates into simpler substances — see CORRUPTION 1

**decorate** *vb* to make more attractive by adding something that is beautiful or becoming 〈they *decorated* the hallway with paintings and tapestries〉
***syn*** adorn, array, beautify, bedeck, bedizen, deck, do, dress, embellish, enrich, garnish, grace, ornament, trim
***rel*** doll up, dress up, trick (out); brighten, freshen, smarten, spruce (up); boss, chase, emboss; embroider, figure,

flounce, fringe, garland, hang, lace, wreathe; gild, paint; redecorate, redo
***near ant*** simplify, streamline; bare, denude, dismantle, display, divest, expose, reveal, strip, uncover
***ant*** blemish, deface, disfigure, mar, scar, spoil

**decoration** *n* **1** something that decorates or beautifies ⟨they put lots of *decorations* on and around the Christmas tree⟩
***syn*** adornment, caparison, embellishment, frill, garnish, ornament, trim
***rel*** finery, frippery; flounce, flourish, furbelow, ruffle; enhancement, enrichment, improvement; embossment, embroidery, fancywork; gilt, glitter; design, figure, pattern; furnishings, regalia, trappings
***near ant*** blemish, defacement, disfigurement, scar; blot, spot, stain
**2** something given in recognition of achievement — see AWARD

**decorative** *adj* serving to add beauty ⟨they planted *decorative* flowers all along the path to the cottage⟩
***syn*** adorning, beautifying, embellishing, ornamental
***rel*** alluring, appealing, attractive, charming, delightful, glamorous (*also* glamourous), pleasing, prepossessing; beauteous, beautiful, bonny, comely, fair, gorgeous, handsome, lovely, pretty, stunning; detailed, elaborate, fancy, ornate
***ant*** functional, utilitarian

**decorous** *adj* **1** following the established traditions of refined society and good taste — see PROPER 1
**2** marked by or showing careful attention to set forms and details — see CEREMONIOUS 1

**decorum** *n* socially acceptable behavior — see DECENCY 1

**decoy** *n* something used to attract animals to a hook or into a trap — see BAIT 1

**decoy** *vb* to lead away from a usual or proper course by offering some pleasure or advantage — see LURE

**decrease** *n* the amount by which something is lessened ⟨the average *decrease* in the price of milk was five cents per gallon⟩
***syn*** abatement, decline, decrement, diminishment, diminution, drop, fall, loss, reduction, shrinkage
***rel*** deduction, dent, depression; slip, slump; curtailment, cut, cutback
***near ant*** accretion, accrual, accumulation, addition, supplement; continuation, extension; upswing, uptrend, upturn
***ant*** boost, enlargement, gain, increase, increment, raise, rise

**decrease** *vb* **1** to make smaller in amount, volume, or extent ⟨they *decreased* the amount of water flowing through the pipes in order to prevent an overflow⟩
***syn*** abate, de-escalate, diminish, downsize, dwindle, lessen, lower, reduce
***rel*** compress, condense, constrict, contract; abbreviate, abridge, clip, crop, curtail, cut, cut back, cut down, dock, pare, prune, retrench, shorten, slash, trim, truncate, whittle; deflate, shrink; moderate, modify, modulate, qualify
***near ant*** blow up, dilate, distend, inflate, swell; elongate, extend, lengthen, prolong, protract; add (to), complement, supplement; enhance, heighten, intensify
***ant*** aggrandize, amplify, augment, boost, enlarge, escalate, expand, increase, raise
**2** to grow less in scope or intensity especially gradually ⟨the force of the wind slowly *decreased* until the flowers were standing upright again⟩
***syn*** abate, decline, de-escalate, die (down), diminish, dwindle, ebb, fall, lessen, let up, lower, moderate, recede, relent, remit, shrink, subside, taper, taper off, wane
***rel*** compress, condense, constrict, contract; evaporate, fade (away), give out, melt (away), peter (out), vanish; slacken, slow (down); alleviate, ease, relax; flag, sink, weaken; cave (in), collapse, deflate, give out
***near ant*** appear, emerge, show up; blow up, distend, elongate, lengthen
***ant*** accumulate, balloon, build, burgeon, enlarge, escalate, expand, grow, increase, intensify, mount, mushroom, pick up, rise, snowball, soar, swell, wax

**decree** *n* **1** a statement of what to do that must be obeyed by those concerned — see COMMAND 1
**2** an order publicly issued by an authority — see EDICT 1

**decree** *vb* to give an order — see COMMAND 2

**decrement** *n* the amount by which something is lessened — see DECREASE

**decry** *vb* **1** to express scornfully one's low opinion of ⟨scientists were quick to *decry* the claims of the psychic⟩
***syn*** bad-mouth, belittle, cry down, deprecate, depreciate, diminish, discount, disparage, minimize, put down, write off
***rel*** abuse, scold; disapprove (of), dislike; censure, condemn, criticize, denounce, reprehend, reprobate; asperse, defame, malign, slander, traduce, vilify; discredit, disgrace
***near ant*** approve, countenance, endorse (*also* indorse), favor, recommend, sanction; commend, compliment, eulogize
***ant*** acclaim, applaud, exalt, extol (*also* extoll), glorify, laud, magnify, praise
**2** to declare to be morally wrong or evil — see CONDEMN 1

**decrying** *adj* intended to make a person or thing seem of little importance or value — see DEROGATORY

**dedicate** *vb* to keep or intend for a special purpose — see DEVOTE 1

**dedication** *n* adherence to something to which one is bound by a pledge or duty — see FIDELITY

**deduce** *vb* to form an opinion through reasoning and information — see INFER 1

**deducible** *adj* being or provable by reasoning in which the conclusion follows necessarily from given information — see DEDUCTIVE

**deduct** *vb* to take away (an amount or number) from a total — see SUBTRACT

**deduction** *n* **1** something that is or may be subtracted ⟨contestants get a *deduction* from their scores for every incorrect guess⟩
*syn* abatement, discount, reduction
*rel* kickback, rebate; dent, depreciation; decline, decrement, diminishment, diminution, drop, fall, loss; forfeit, forfeiture, penalty
*near ant* accretion, accrual, augmentation, boost, gain, increase, increment, raise, rise; appreciation
*ant* accession, addition
**2** the act or an instance of taking away from a total — see SUBTRACTION
**3** an opinion arrived at through a process of reasoning — see CONCLUSION 1

**deductive** *adj* being or provable by reasoning in which the conclusion follows necessarily from given information ⟨using *deductive* reasoning we must conclude that since everyone eventually dies, sooner or later it's going to be our turn⟩
*syn* deducible, derivable, inferable, reasoned
*rel* conjectural, hypothetical, purported, supposed, suppositional; academic, speculative, theoretical (*also* theoretic); logical, rational
*near ant* inducible, inductive; absolute, categorical (*also* categoric), definite, explicit, express; instinctive, intuitive; illogical, irrational

**deed** *n* **1** an act of notable skill, strength, or cleverness — see FEAT 1
**2** something done by someone — see ACTION 1

**deed** *vb* to give over the legal possession or ownership of — see TRANSFER 1

**deem** *vb* to have as an opinion — see BELIEVE 2

**deep** *adj* **1** extending far downward or inward ⟨they dropped their bucket down a *deep* well⟩ ⟨the knife made a *deep* cut into the wood⟩
*syn* abysmal, bottomless
*rel* abyssal, unfathomable; boundless, endless, immeasurable, inestimable, infinite, limitless, measureless, unlimited, vast
*near ant* depthless, two-dimensional; even, flat, flush, horizontal, level, plane, smooth; confined, finite, limited, measured, restricted
*ant* shallow, shoal, skin-deep, superficial, surface
**2** having a low musical pitch or range ⟨the tour guide had a very *deep* voice⟩
*syn* bass, low, throaty
*rel* gruff, hoarse, husky, rough
*near ant* squeaking, squeaky; squealing, thin; earsplitting, penetrating, piercing, strident; peeping, tinny
*ant* acute, high, high-pitched, piping, sharp, shrill, treble
**3** being beyond one's powers to know, understand, or explain — see MYSTERIOUS 1
**4** difficult for one of ordinary knowledge or intelligence to understand — see PROFOUND 1
**5** having an often intentionally veiled or uncertain meaning — see OBSCURE 1
**6** extreme in degree, power, or effect — see INTENSE

**deep** *n* **1** the most intense or characteristic phase of something — see THICK
**2** the whole body of salt water that covers nearly three-fourths of the earth — see OCEAN

**deepen** *vb* to make markedly greater in measure or degree — see INTENSIFY

**deep–rooted** *adj* firmly established over time — see INVETERATE 1

**deep–seated** *adj* firmly established over time — see INVETERATE 1

**de–escalate** *vb* **1** to make smaller in amount, volume, or extent — see DECREASE 1
**2** to grow less in scope or intensity especially gradually — see DECREASE 2

**deface** *vb* **1** to deliberately cause the damage or destruction of another's property — see VANDALIZE 1
**2** to reduce the soundness, effectiveness, or perfection of — see DAMAGE 1

**defacement** *n* deliberate damaging or destroying of another's property — see VANDALISM

**defacer** *n* a person who damages or destroys property on purpose — see VANDAL

**defamation** *n* the making of false statements that damage another's reputation — see SLANDER

**defamatory** *adj* causing or intended to cause unjust injury to a person's good name — see LIBELOUS

**defame** *vb* to make untrue and harmful statements about — see SLANDER

**defaming** *n* the making of false statements that damage another's reputation — see SLANDER

**default** *n* the nonperformance of an assigned or expected action — see FAILURE 1

**defeat** *n* **1** failure to win a contest ⟨sore losers griping about their *defeat* in the basketball game earlier that week⟩
*syn* beating, drubbing, licking, loss, overthrow, rout, shellacking, trimming, trouncing, whipping
*rel* collapse, debacle (*also* débâcle), failure, fizzle, flop, nonsuccess, setback, upset, washout; lurch, shutout
*near ant* accomplishment, achievement; landslide, sweep
*ant* success, triumph, victory, win
**2** a falling short of one's goals — see FAILURE 2

**defeat** *vb* to achieve a victory over — see BEAT 2

**defeatist** *adj* emphasizing or expecting the worst — see PESSIMISTIC 1

**defeatist** *n* one who emphasizes bad aspects or conditions and expects the worst — see PESSIMIST 1

**defect** *n* something that spoils the appearance or completeness of a thing — see BLEMISH

**defect** (from) *vb* to leave (a cause or party) often in order to take up another ⟨many soldiers *defected from* the rebel army as soon as they realized the uprising was hopeless⟩
*syn* desert, rat (on)
*rel* abandon, abdicate, abjure, cut off, disown, forsake, quit, reject, renounce, repudiate, spurn; renege; depart, go, leave, withdraw
*phrases* go back on, walk out on
*near ant* adhere (to), cling (to), stick (to *or* with); cherish, cultivate, foster

**defective** *adj* having a fault — see FAULTY

**defector** *n* a person who abandons a cause or organization usually without right — see RENEGADE

**defend** *vb* **1** to drive danger or attack away from ⟨a solemn oath to *defend* the country at any cost⟩
*syn* cover, guard, protect, safeguard, screen, secure, shield, ward
*rel* avert, prevent; fend (off), oppose, resist, withstand; battle, contend, fight, war; conserve, keep, preserve, save; buffer, palisade, picket, wall
*phrases* look out for, stand up for
*near ant* bombard, storm; beset, besiege, overrun; capitulate, cave, submit, yield
*ant* assail, assault, attack
**2** to continue to declare to be true or proper despite opposition or objections — see MAINTAIN 2

**defendable** *adj* capable of being defended with good reasoning against verbal attack — see TENABLE 2

**defender** *n* someone that protects — see PROTECTOR

**defense** *n* **1** means or method of defending ⟨thorns are a rose's *defense* against grazing animals⟩
*syn* aegis, ammunition, armor, cover, guard, protection, safeguard, screen, security, shield, wall, ward
*rel* arm, armament, munitions, weapon, weaponry; fastness, fort, fortress, palisade, stronghold
*near ant* aggression, assault, attack, offense (*or* offence), offensive
**2** an explanation that frees one from fault or blame — see EXCUSE

**defenseless** *adj* lacking protection from danger or resistance against attack — see HELPLESS 1

**defenselessness** *n* the quality or state of having little resistance to some outside agent — see SUSCEPTIBILITY

**defensible** *adj* capable of being defended with good reasoning against verbal attack — see TENABLE 1

**defensive** *adj* intended to resist or prevent attack or aggression ⟨a *defensive* alliance against the aggressors⟩
*syn* protective, self-protective
*rel* deterrent, preventive; safe, secure
*near ant* aggressive, bellicose, belligerent, combative, contentious, militant, pugnacious, quarrelsome, scrappy, truculent, warlike
*ant* offensive

**defensive** *n* a position or readiness to oppose actual or expected attack ⟨their harsh words put him on the *defensive*⟩
*syn* guard
*rel* alert, watch
*ant* offensive

**defer** *vb* to assign to a later time — see POSTPONE

**deference** *n* a readiness or willingness to yield to the wishes of others — see COMPLIANCE 1

**deferential** *adj* marked by or showing proper regard for another's higher status — see RESPECTFUL

**deferentially** *adv* in manner showing no signs of pride or self-assertion — see LOWLY

**defiance** *n* **1** refusal to obey — see DISOBEDIENCE
**2** the inclination to resist — see RESISTANCE 1

**defiant** *adj* given to resisting authority or another's control — see DISOBEDIENT

**deficiency** *n* a falling short of an essential or desirable amount or number ⟨there was a *deficiency* of fresh food in the house⟩
*syn* dearth, deficit, failure, famine, inadequacy, insufficiency, lack, paucity, poverty, scantiness, scarceness, scarcity, shortage, want
*rel* absence, omission; meagerness, poorness, skimpiness; necessity, need, privation
*near ant* bountifulness, copiousness; excess, overabundance, oversupply, surfeit, surplus
*ant* abundance, adequacy, amplitude, plenitude, plenty, sufficiency

**deficient** *adj* **1** lacking some necessary part — see INCOMPLETE
**2** falling short of a standard — see BAD 1
**3** not coming up to a usual standard or meeting a particular need — see SHORT 3

**deficit** *n* a falling short of an essential or desirable amount or number — see DEFICIENCY

**defile** *n* a narrow opening between hillsides or mountains that can be used for passage — see CANYON

**defile** *vb* **1** to make unfit for use by the addition of something harmful or undesirable — see CONTAMINATE
**2** to treat (a sacred place or object) shamefully or with great disrespect — see DESECRATE

**defilement** *n* 1 an act of great disrespect shown to God or to sacred ideas, people, or things — see BLASPHEMY
2 something that is or that makes impure — see IMPURITY
**define** *vb* 1 to draw or make apparent the outline of — see OUTLINE 1
2 to mark the limits of — see LIMIT 2
3 to point out the chief quality or qualities of an individual or group — see CHARACTERIZE 1
4 to give the rules about (something) clearly and exactly — see PRESCRIBE
**defined** *adj* having distinct or certain limits — see LIMITED 1
**definite** *adj* 1 having distinct or certain limits — see LIMITED 1
2 so clearly expressed as to leave no doubt about the meaning — see EXPLICIT
**definitely** *adv* without any question — see INDEED 1
**definitive** *adj* 1 being the most accurate and apparently thorough ⟨the *definitive* work on the attack on Pearl Harbor⟩
***syn*** authoritative
***rel*** conclusive, decisive; official; accurate, correct; complete, thorough
2 serving to put an end to all debate or questioning — see CONCLUSIVE
3 so clearly expressed as to leave no doubt about the meaning — see EXPLICIT
**deflect** *vb* to change the course or direction of (something) — see TURN 2
**deform** *vb* to twist (something) out of a natural or normal shape or condition — see CONTORT
**deformation** *n* the twisting of something out of its natural or normal shape or condition — see CONTORTION
**deformed** *adj* badly or imperfectly formed — see MALFORMED
**deformity** *n* something that spoils the appearance or completeness of a thing — see BLEMISH
**defraud** *vb* to rob by the use of trickery or threats — see FLEECE
**defrauder** *n* a dishonest person who uses clever means to cheat others out of something of value — see TRICKSTER 1
**defrauding** *adj* marked by, based on, or done by the use of dishonest methods to acquire something of value — see FRAUDULENT 1
**defrosted** *adj* freed from a frozen state by exposure to warmth — see THAWED
**deft** *adj* skillful with the hands — see DEXTEROUS 1
**deftness** *n* 1 ease and grace in physical activity — see DEXTERITY 2
2 subtle or imaginative ability in inventing, devising, or executing something — see SKILL 1
**defunct** *adj* 1 no longer existing — see EXTINCT
2 no longer living — see DEAD 1
**defy** *vb* 1 to go against the commands, prohibitions, or rules of — see DISOBEY
2 to invite (someone) to take part in a contest or to perform a feat — see CHALLENGE 2
3 to oppose (something hostile or dangerous) with firmness or courage — see FACE 2
4 to refuse to give in to — see RESIST
**degeneracy** *n* 1 a change to a lower state or level — see DECLINE 2
2 a sinking to a state of low moral standards and behavior — see CORRUPTION 2
**degenerate** *adj* 1 having lost forcefulness, courage, or spirit — see EFFETE 1
2 having or showing lowered moral character or standards — see CORRUPT
**degenerate** *n* a person who has sunk below the normal moral standard ⟨the *degenerate* would stop at nothing to get satisfaction⟩
***syn*** backslider, debaucher, decadent, libertine, pervert, profligate
***rel*** delinquent, derelict, incorrigible; blackguard, cad, heel, knave, rascal, miscreant, reprobate, rogue, scoundrel, villain; playboy, satyr
***near ant*** saint
**degenerate** *vb* to become worse or of less value — see DETERIORATE
**degeneration** *n* 1 a change to a lower state or level — see DECLINE 2
2 a gradual sinking and wasting away of mind or body — see DECLINE 1
3 a sinking to a state of low moral standards and behavior — see CORRUPTION 2
**degradation** *n* 1 a change to a lower state or level — see DECLINE 2
2 a sinking to a state of low moral standards and behavior — see CORRUPTION 2
**degrade** *vb* 1 to bring to a lower grade or rank — see DEMOTE
2 to lower in character or dignity — see DEBASE 1
3 to reduce to a lower standing in one's own eyes or in others' eyes — see HUMBLE
**degraded** *adj* having or showing lowered moral character or standards — see CORRUPT
**degrading** *adj* intended to make a person or thing seem of little importance or value — see DEROGATORY
**degree** *n* 1 an individual part of a process, series, or ranking ⟨they completed the project by *degrees*⟩
***syn*** cut, grade, inch, notch, peg, phase, point, stage, step
***rel*** amount, measure, plane; decrement, increment
2 the placement of someone or something in relation to others in a vertical arrangement — see RANK 1
**dehydrate** *vb* to make dry — see DRY 1
**deification** *n* excessive admiration of or devotion to a person — see WORSHIP
**deify** *vb* 1 to love or admire too much — see IDOLIZE
2 to offer honor or respect to (someone) as a divine power — see WORSHIP 1
**deifying** *adj* reflecting great admiration or devotion — see WORSHIPFUL
**deign** *vb* to descend to a level that is beneath one's dignity — see CONDESCEND 1

**deity** *n* **1** a being having superhuman powers and control over a particular part of life or the world ⟨to the ancient Greeks, Zeus was the *deity* who ruled over the sky and weather, and Poseidon was god of the sea⟩
*syn* divinity, god
*rel* angel, demigod, demon (*or* daemon), devil, spirit, supernatural
**2** *cap* the being worshipped as the creator and ruler of the universe ⟨we prayed to the *Deity* for salvation⟩
*syn* Allah, Almighty, Creator, Divinity, Father, God, Godhead, Jehovah, Lord, Maker, Providence, Supreme Being
**3** the quality or state of being divine — see DIVINITY

**dejected** *adj* feeling unhappiness — see SAD 1

**dejection** *n* a state or spell of low spirits — see SADNESS

**delay** *n* an instance or period of being prevented from going about one's business ⟨there was a *delay* for our boarding while the airplane unloaded incoming passengers⟩
*syn* detainment, holdup, wait
*rel* deferment, postponement; reprieve, respite; hesitation, lag, pause, setback, slowdown
*near ant* haste, rush; dispatch, promptness

**delay** *vb* **1** to move or act slowly ⟨she told them to stop *delaying* and get to bed⟩
*syn* crawl, creep, dally, dawdle, dillydally, drag, lag, linger, loiter, poke, tarry
*rel* hang around, hang out, idle, loaf, loll, lounge; amble, ease, inch, lumber, plod, saunter, shuffle, stagger, stroll; decelerate, slow (down *or* up); filibuster, procrastinate, stall, temporize
*phrases* mark time
*near ant* bowl, breeze, dart, hump, hurtle, hustle, scramble, stampede; gallop, jog, run, sprint, trot; accelerate, quicken, speed up; catch up, fast-forward, outpace, outrun, outstrip, overtake
*ant* barrel, bolt, career, course, dash, fly, hasten, hotfoot (it), hurry, race, rip, rocket, run, rush, scoot, scud, scurry, speed, tear, whirl, whisk, whiz (*or* whizz), zip
**2** to assign to a later time — see POSTPONE
**3** to create difficulty for the work or activity of — see HAMPER

**delectable** *adj* **1** giving pleasure or contentment to the mind or senses — see PLEASANT
**2** very pleasing to the sense of taste — see DELICIOUS 1

**delectably** *adv* in a pleasing way — see WELL 5

**delectation** *n* **1** a source of great satisfaction — see DELIGHT 1
**2** the feeling experienced when one's wishes are met — see PLEASURE 1

**delegate** *n* **1** a person sent on a mission to represent another — see AMBASSADOR
**2** a person who acts or does business for another — see AGENT 2

**delegate** *vb* **1** to appoint as one's representative ⟨he *delegated* his son to go pick up the tickets for him⟩
*syn* commission, depute, deputize
*rel* assign, charge; appoint, designate, name, nominate
*near ant* abrogate; abdicate
**2** to put (something) into the possession or safekeeping of another — see GIVE 2

**delegation** *n* **1** a body of persons chosen as representatives of a larger group — see CONTINGENT
**2** the granting of power to perform various acts or duties — see COMMISSION 1

**delete** *vb* to show (something written) to be no longer valid by drawing a cross over or a line through it — see X (OUT)

**deleterious** *adj* causing or capable of causing harm — see HARMFUL

**deletion** *n* something left out — see OMISSION

**deliberate** *adj* **1** decided on as a result of careful thought ⟨the judge made a *deliberate* decision to impose the maximum sentence⟩
*syn* advised, calculated, considered, measured, reasoned, studied, thoughtful, weighed
*rel* aforethought, premeditated; educated, informed; intentional, purposeful; designed, intended, planned, projected; careful, meticulous; foresighted, forethoughtful, provident, prudent
*near ant* ill-advised; chance, haphazard, hit-or-miss, random; aimless, desultory, purposeless; hasty, hurried, rushed; abrupt, impetuous, sudden; automatic, extemporaneous, impromptu, instinctive, spontaneous
*ant* casual
**2** made, given, or done with full awareness of what one is doing — see INTENTIONAL

**deliberate** *vb* to give serious and careful thought to — see PONDER

**deliberately** *adv* with full awareness of what one is doing — see INTENTIONALLY

**deliberation** *n* **1** a careful weighing of the reasons for or against something — see CONSIDERATION 1
**2** an exchange of views for the purpose of exploring a subject or deciding an issue — see DISCUSSION 1

**delicacy** *n* **1** something that is pleasing to eat because it is rare or a luxury ⟨they were given a plate of *delicacies* while they waited for the queen⟩
*syn* dainty, goody, tidbit (*also* titbit), treat
*rel* morsel; candy, dessert, junket, sweet, sweetmeat
**2** the state or quality of having a delicate structure ⟨they marvelled at the *delicacy* of a snowflake⟩
*syn* daintiness, delicateness, exquisiteness, fineness, fragility
*rel* flimsiness, insubstantiality, wispiness

---

*syn* synonym(s) *rel* related words
*ant* antonym(s) *near ant* near antonym(s)

*near ant* firmness, solidity; strength
*ant* coarseness, crudeness, crudity, roughness, rudeness
3 the tendency to be or state of being squeamish ⟨the urgent need for blood prompted many people to overcome their habitual *delicacy* and become first-time donors⟩
*syn* qualmishness, queasiness, squeamishness
*rel* daintiness, fastidiousness, finickiness, fussiness
*near ant* boldness
*ant* indelicacy
4 the quality or state of being very accurate — see PRECISION
5 the quality or state of lacking physical strength or vigor — see WEAKNESS 1
**delicate** *adj* 1 satisfying or pleasing because of fineness or mildness ⟨a heavy sauce would spoil the *delicate* flavor of this fish⟩
*syn* dainty, exquisite, refined, subtle
*rel* choice, elegant, extraordinary, incomparable, peerless, preeminent, prime, rare, select, superior, superlative, supreme, transcendent, unsurpassed; picked, selected; fine, fragile, frail
*near ant* coarse, crude, rough; common, ordinary; average, fair, indifferent, mediocre, medium, middling, run-of-the-mill, second-rate
*ant* robust, strong, sturdy
2 able to sense slight impressions or differences — see ACUTE 1
3 accomplished with trained ability — see SKILLFUL
4 easily broken — see FRAGILE 1
5 easily injured without careful handling — see TENDER 1
6 hard to please — see FINICKY
7 having qualities that appeal to a refined taste — see CHOICE
8 lacking bodily strength — see WEAK 1
9 made or done with extreme care and accuracy — see FINE 2
10 meeting the highest standard of accuracy — see PRECISE 1
11 not harsh or stern especially in manner, nature, or effect — see GENTLE 1
12 requiring exceptional skill or caution in performance or handling — see TRICKY
**delicateness** *n* 1 the quality or state of lacking physical strength or vigor — see WEAKNESS 1
2 the state or quality of having a delicate structure — see DELICACY 2
**delicious** *adj* 1 very pleasing to the sense of taste ⟨the family sat down to a *delicious* Thanksgiving dinner⟩
*syn* ambrosial, appetizing, delectable, flavorful, luscious, palatable, savory, scrumptious, tasty, toothsome, yummy
*rel* digestible, eatable, edible; delightful, heavenly, pleasing; agreeable, gratifying, pleasant; satisfying; choice, dainty, delicate, exquisite, rare
*near ant* banal, boring, commonplace, tedious; noisome, smelly, stinky; noxious, unwholesome; miserable, wretched; abhorrent, abominable, awful, detestable, disagreeable, disgusting, distasteful, foul, horrid, nauseating, offensive, repellent, repugnant, repulsive, sickening, unpleasant
*ant* flat, flavorless, insipid, stale, tasteless, unappetizing, unpalatable
2 giving pleasure or contentment to the mind or senses — see PLEASANT
**deliciously** *adv* in a pleasing way — see WELL 5
**deliciousness** *n* the quality of being delicious ⟨the fancy feast was *deliciousness* itself⟩
*syn* lusciousness, savor, savoriness, tastiness
**delight** *n* 1 a source of great satisfaction ⟨the school play was a *delight* for the parents⟩
*syn* delectation, gas [*slang*], joy, kick, manna, pleasure, treat
*rel* amusement, diversion, entertainment, fun, recreation; comfort, relief, solace; gratification, indulgence; ambrosia
2 someone or something that provides amusement or enjoyment — see FUN 1
3 the feeling experienced when one's wishes are met — see PLEASURE 1
**delight** *vb* 1 to feel or express joy or triumph — see EXULT
2 to give satisfaction to — see PLEASE
**delight** (in) *vb* to take pleasure in — see ENJOY 1
**delighted** *adj* experiencing pleasure, satisfaction, or delight — see GLAD 1
**delightful** *adj* 1 giving pleasure or contentment to the mind or senses — see PLEASANT
2 providing amusement or enjoyment — see FUN
**delightfully** *adv* in a pleasing way — see WELL 5
**delimit** *vb* to mark the limits of — see LIMIT 2
**delineate** *vb* 1 to draw or make apparent the outline of — see OUTLINE 1
2 to give a representation or account of in words — see DESCRIBE 1
**delineated** *adj* producing a mental picture through clear and impressive description — see GRAPHIC 1
**delineation** *n* 1 a picture using lines to represent the chief features of an object or scene — see DRAWING
2 a vivid representation in words of someone or something — see DESCRIPTION 1
**delinquency** *n* 1 the nonperformance of an assigned or expected action — see FAILURE 1
2 the quality or state of being late — see LATENESS
**delinquent** *adj* not arriving, occurring, or settled at the due, usual, or proper time — see LATE 1
**deliquesce** *vb* to go from a solid to a liquid state — see LIQUEFY
**delirious** *adj* 1 feeling overwhelming fear or worry — see FRANTIC 1

2 marked by great and often stressful excitement or activity — see FURIOUS 1

**delirium** *n* a state of wildly excited activity or emotion — see FRENZY

**deliver** *vb* 1 to free from the penalties or consequences of sin — see SAVE 1
2 to remove from danger or harm — see SAVE 2
3 to give (something) over to the control or possession of another usually under duress — see SURRENDER 1
4 to put (something) into the possession of someone for use or consumption — see FURNISH 2
5 to put (something) into the possession or safekeeping of another — see GIVE 2
6 to turn out as planned or desired — see SUCCEED 1

**deliverance** *n* 1 the saving from danger or evil — see SALVATION
2 a position arrived at after consideration — see DECISION 1

**deliverer** *n* 1 a person who delivers goods to customers usually over a regular local route — see DELIVERYMAN
2 one that saves from danger or destruction — see SAVIOR

**delivery** *n* 1 a freeing from an obligation or responsibility — see RELEASE 1
2 the act or process of giving birth to children — see CHILDBIRTH

**deliveryman** *n* a person who delivers goods to customers usually over a regular local route ⟨the *deliveryman* dropped off a package for us while we were at the store⟩
***syn*** deliverer
***rel*** bearer, carrier, courier, go-between, liaison, messenger

**delude** *vb* to cause to believe what is untrue — see DECEIVE

**deluding** *adj* tending or having power to deceive — see DECEPTIVE 1

**deluge** *n* 1 a great flow of water or of something that overwhelms — see FLOOD
2 a steady falling of water from the sky in significant quantity — see RAIN 1

**deluge** *vb* to cover or become filled with a flood — see FLOOD

**delusion** *n* a conception or image created by the imagination and having no objective reality — see FANTASY 1

**delusive** *adj* tending or having power to deceive — see DECEPTIVE 1

**delusory** *adj* tending or having power to deceive — see DECEPTIVE 1

**deluxe** *adj* showing obvious signs of wealth and comfort — see LUXURIOUS

**delve** (into) *vb* to search through or into — see EXPLORE 1

**delving** *n* a systematic search for the truth or facts about something — see INQUIRY 1

**demagogue** *also* **demagog** *n* a person who stirs up public feelings especially of discontent — see AGITATOR

**demand** *n* 1 something that someone insists upon having ⟨the terrorists presented their list of *demands*⟩
***syn*** claim, dun, requisition, ultimatum
***rel*** desire, request, want, wish; drive, need, requirement, stipulation; basic, essential, must; imposition; condition, provision
2 something necessary, indispensable, or unavoidable — see ESSENTIAL 1

**demand** *vb* 1 to ask for (something) earnestly or with authority ⟨the losing party *demanded* a recount of the votes cast in the election⟩
***syn*** call (for), claim, clamor (for), command, enjoin, exact, insist (on), press (for), quest, stipulate (for)
***rel*** ask, plead (for), request, want; cry (for), necessitate, need, require, take, warrant; requisition; impose; badger, dun, hound
***near ant*** give up, relinquish, surrender, yield
2 to have as a requirement — see NEED 1
3 to set or receive as a price — see CHARGE 1

**demanding** *adj* 1 requiring much time, effort, or careful attention ⟨the *demanding* assignment kept them working all night⟩
***syn*** arduous, burdensome, challenging, exacting, grueling (*or* gruelling), laborious, onerous, taxing, toilsome
***rel*** difficult, formidable, hard, herculean, rough, rugged, stiff, strenuous, tough; oppressive, trying; rigid, rigorous, severe, stern, strict, stringent
***near ant*** easy, effortless, facile, simple, smooth
***ant*** light, undemanding
2 hard to please — see FINICKY
3 requiring considerable physical or mental effort — see HARD 2

**demarcate** *vb* to mark the limits of — see LIMIT 2

**demarcation** *n* the state of being kept distinct — see SEPARATION 2

[1]**demean** *vb* 1 to lower in character or dignity — see DEBASE 1
2 to reduce to a lower standing in one's own eyes or in others' eyes — see HUMBLE

[2]**demean** *vb* to manage the actions of (oneself) in a particular way — see BEHAVE

**demeaning** *adj* intended to make a person or thing seem of little importance or value — see DEROGATORY

**demeanor** *n* the way or manner in which one conducts oneself — see BEHAVIOR

**demented** *adj* having or showing a very abnormal or sick state of mind — see INSANE 1

**dementia** *n* a serious mental disorder that prevents one from living a safe and normal life — see INSANITY 1

**demerit** *n* a defect in character — see FAULT 1

**demesne** *n* 1 a part or portion having no fixed boundaries — see REGION 1
2 a region of activity, knowledge, or influence — see FIELD 2

3 the area around and belonging to a building — see GROUND 1

**demilitarization** *n* the reduction or elimination of a country's armed forces or weapons — see DISARMAMENT

**demilitarize** *vb* to reduce the size and strength of the armed forces of — see DISARM 1

**demise** *n* 1 the permanent stopping of all the vital bodily activities — see DEATH 1
2 the act of ceasing to exist — see DEATH 3

**democracy** *n* government in which the supreme power is held by the people and used by them directly or indirectly through representation ⟨under our *democracy* the people have some control over their lives by being able to decide who their political leaders will be⟩
***syn*** republic, self-government, self-rule
***rel*** home rule, self-determination; autonomy, sovereignty
***near ant*** despotism, dictatorship, monarchy, totalitarianism, tyranny

**democratic** *adj* of, relating to, or favoring political democracy ⟨the *democratic* system ensured that every citizen's voice was heard⟩
***syn*** popular, republican, self-governing, self-ruling
***rel*** representative; libertarian
***near ant*** autocratic, despotic, dictatorial, monarchal (*or* monarchial), monarchical (*also* monarchic), tyrannical (*also* tyrannic)
***ant*** undemocratic

**demolish** *vb* 1 to destroy (as a building) completely by knocking down or breaking to pieces ⟨they *demolished* the old warehouse to make room for the new shopping mall⟩
***syn*** raze, tear down
***rel*** blow up, dynamite; abolish, annihilate, crack up, crush, dash, decimate, destroy, devastate, devour, dissolve, do in, eradicate, extirpate, finish, flatten, obliterate, overturn, pulverize, ravage, ruin, scourge, smash, total, unmake, waste, wipe out, wreck
***near ant*** build, construct, erect, put up, raise; rebuild, renew, renovate, restore; create, fabricate, fashion, forge, form, make, manufacture, shape
2 to bring to a complete end the physical soundness, existence, or usefulness of — see DESTROY 1
3 to cause to break open or into pieces by or as if by an explosive — see BLAST 1

**demolishment** *n* the state or fact of being rendered nonexistent, physically unsound, or useless — see DESTRUCTION

**demolition** *n* the state or fact of being rendered nonexistent, physically unsound, or useless — see DESTRUCTION

**demon** *or* **daemon** *n* an evil spirit ⟨only in rare cases is the ancient rite of exorcism performed to cast out a troublesome *demon*⟩
***syn*** devil, fiend, ghoul, imp, incubus
***rel*** apparition, bogey (*also* bogy *or* bogie), familiar, ghost, phantasm, phantom, poltergeist, shade, shadow, specter (*or* spectre), spirit, spook, vision, wraith; brownie, dwarf, elf, faerie (*also* faery), fairy, fay, gnome, goblin, gremlin, hobgoblin, leprechaun, pixie (*also* pixy), puck, sprite, troll; monster, ogre
***near ant*** angel

**demoniac** *also* **demoniacal** *adj* of, relating to, or worthy of an evil spirit — see FIENDISH

**demonic** *adj* of, relating to, or worthy of an evil spirit — see FIENDISH

**demonstrable** *adj* capable of being proven as true or real — see VERIFIABLE

**demonstrate** *vb* 1 to gain full recognition or acceptance of — see ESTABLISH 1
2 to show the existence or truth of by evidence — see PROVE 1
3 to make known (something abstract) through outward signs — see SHOW 2
4 to make plain or understandable — see EXPLAIN 1
5 to show or make clear by using examples — see ILLUSTRATE 1

**demonstration** *n* 1 a mass meeting for the purpose of displaying or arousing support for a cause or person — see RALLY 2
2 an outward and often exaggerated indication of something abstract (as a feeling) for effect — see SHOW 1

**demonstrative** *adj* showing feeling freely ⟨my grandmother was always very *demonstrative* when we visited, showering us with hugs and kisses⟩
***syn*** effusive, emotional, uninhibited, unreserved, unrestrained
***rel*** dramatic, histrionic, melodramatic, theatrical; gushing, maudlin, mawkish, mushy, schmaltzy, sentimental; communicative, expansive; extroverted (*also* extraverted), outgoing; affectionate, feeling, intense, loving, passionate, sensitive, soulful, warm; blunt, candid, frank, outspoken, plain
***near ant*** constrained; quiet, reticent, silent, taciturn; bashful, modest, retiring, shy; introverted, self-directed; aloof, detached, dispassionate, impassive, indifferent, phlegmatic, stolid, unconcerned, unfeeling; chilly, cold, frigid, glacial, hard-boiled, hardhearted, icy, unfriendly
***ant*** inhibited, reserved, restrained, undemonstrative, unemotional

**demoralization** *n* 1 a sinking to a state of low moral standards and behavior — see CORRUPTION 2
2 the state of being discouraged — see DISCOURAGEMENT

**demoralize** *vb* 1 to deprive of courage or confidence — see UNNERVE 1
2 to lessen the courage or confidence of — see DISCOURAGE 1

**demoralized** *adj* having or showing lowered moral character or standards — see CORRUPT

**demote** *vb* to bring to a lower grade or rank ⟨the court-martial's decision was to

*demote* the officer responsible for the failed mission⟩
***syn*** break, bust, degrade, downgrade, reduce
***rel*** can, dismiss, fire, lay off, sack; abase, debase, demean, humble, humiliate, lower
***near ant*** hire
***ant*** advance, elevate, promote, raise

**demount** *vb* to take apart — see DISASSEMBLE

**demur** *n* a feeling or declaration of disapproval or dissent — see OBJECTION

**demur** *vb* to present an opposing opinion or argument — see OBJECT

**demure** *adj* **1** affecting shyness or modesty in order to attract masculine interest — see COY 1
**2** not comfortable around people — see SHY 2
**3** not having or showing any feelings of superiority, self-assertiveness, or showiness — see HUMBLE 1

**demureness** *n* the absence of any feelings of being better than others — see HUMILITY

**den** *n* **1** the shelter or resting place of a wild animal ⟨the foxes hid in their *den* until the bear left the area⟩
***syn*** burrow, hole, lair, lodge
***rel*** nest
**2** a place where a person goes to hide — see HIDEOUT

**denial** *n* **1** an unwillingness to grant something asked for ⟨our principal's *denial* of our request to come to school on Halloween dressed in costumes⟩
***syn*** disallowance, nay, no, refusal, rejection
***rel*** decline, rebuff, repudiation; negative
***near ant*** acceptance, accession, consent, leave, permission, sufferance
***ant*** allowance, grant
**2** a refusal to confirm the truth of a statement ⟨the senator issued a flat *denial* of the accusation against her⟩
***syn*** contradiction, disallowance, disavowal, disclaimer, negation, rejection, repudiation
***rel*** disproof, rebuttal, refutation; negative
***near ant*** confession; affirmation, assertion, declaration
***ant*** acknowledgment (*also* acknowledgement), admission, avowal, confirmation

**denizen** *n* one who lives permanently in a place — see INHABITANT

**denominate** *vb* to give a name to — see NAME 1

**denomination** *n* a word or combination of words by which a person or thing is regularly known — see NAME 1

**denotation** *n* **1** a word or combination of words by which a person or thing is regularly known — see NAME 1
**2** the idea that is conveyed or intended to be conveyed to the mind by language, symbol, or action — see MEANING 1

***syn*** synonym(s) ***rel*** related words
***ant*** antonym(s) ***near ant*** near antonym(s)

**denotative** *adj* indicating something — see INDICATIVE

**denote** *vb* to communicate or convey (as an idea) to the mind — see MEAN 1

**denoting** *adj* indicating something — see INDICATIVE

**denounce** *vb* **1** to declare to be morally wrong or evil — see CONDEMN 1
**2** to express one's unfavorable opinion of the worth or quality of — see CRITICIZE
**3** to express public or formal disapproval of — see CENSURE 1

**dense** *adj* **1** having little space between items or parts — see CLOSE 1
**2** not having or showing an ability to absorb ideas readily — see STUPID 1

**denseness** *n* the quality or state of lacking intelligence or quickness of mind — see STUPIDITY 1

**density** *n* **1** the degree to which a fluid can resist flowing — see CONSISTENCY
**2** the quality or state of lacking intelligence or quickness of mind — see STUPIDITY 1

**dent** *n* a sunken area forming a separate space — see HOLE 2

**dented** *adj* curved inward — see HOLLOW

**denuded** *adj* lacking a usual or natural covering — see NAKED 2

**denunciation** *n* an often public or formal expression of disapproval — see CENSURE

**deny** *vb* **1** to declare not to be true ⟨the congressman *denied* all charges of wrongdoing⟩
***syn*** contradict, disallow, disavow, disclaim, gainsay, negate, negative, reject, repudiate
***rel*** disown, renounce; challenge, confute, disprove, rebut, refute; disagree (with), dispute
***near ant*** accept, adopt, embrace, espouse; affirm, announce, assert, aver, claim, declare, maintain, profess, submit; authenticate, corroborate, substantiate, validate, verify
***ant*** acknowledge, admit, allow, avow, concede, confirm, own
**2** to be unwilling to grant ⟨he *denied* access to the top secret files to the nosy reporters⟩
***syn*** decline, disallow, refuse, reject, withhold
***rel*** rebuff, repel, spurn; check, constrain, hold, keep, restrain, restrict
***near ant*** afford, furnish, give, provide, supply
***ant*** allow, concede, grant, let, permit

**depart** *vb* **1** to leave a place often for another — see GO 2
**2** to stop living — see DIE 1

**departed** *adj* **1** no longer existing — see EXTINCT
**2** no longer living — see DEAD 1

**departing** *n* the act of leaving a place — see DEPARTURE

**department** *n* **1** a large unit of a governmental, business, or educational organization — see DIVISION 2

2 a region of activity, knowledge, or influence — see FIELD 2

**departure** *n* the act of leaving a place ⟨his sudden *departure* left them wondering if they'd upset him⟩
*syn* decamping, decampment, departing, exit, exiting, farewell, going, leave-taking, lighting out, parting, quitting, walking out
*rel* flight, retirement, retreat, running away, withdrawal; emigration, evacuation, exodus; egress; abandonment, forsaking, relinquishment
*near ant* advent, coming; entrance, ingress
*ant* arrival

**depend** *vb* 1 to be determined by, based on, or subject (to) ⟨whether or not we play baseball will *depend* on how much rain we get⟩
*syn* hang, hinge
*rel* base, establish, found, rest, stay; ground
2 to place reliance or trust ⟨I know I can always *depend* on you for help when I really need it⟩
*syn* count, lean, reckon, rely
*rel* commit, confide, entrust, trust
*phrases* bank on, figure on
*near ant* distrust, mistrust

**dependability** *n* worthiness as the recipient of another's trust or confidence — see RELIABILITY

**dependable** *adj* worthy of one's trust ⟨Boy Scouts are supposed to be always *dependable*⟩
*syn* good, reliable, responsible, safe, solid, steady, sure, tried, tried-and-true, true, trustworthy, trusty
*rel* constant, devoted, faithful, fast, loyal, staunch (*or* stanch), steadfast; honest, sincere, single-minded; infallible, unerring; firm, sound, strong; effective, telling; attested, authenticated, confirmed, proven, valid, validated, verified; blameless, irreproachable, unimpeachable, unquestionable
*near ant* disloyal, faithless, false, unfaithful; deceitful, dishonest; doubtful, dubious, questionable, suspect, uncertain, unsound; hazardous, risky; unauthenticated, unconfirmed, untried, unverified
*ant* irresponsible, undependable, unreliable, untrustworthy

**dependence** *n* 1 the quality or state of needing something or someone ⟨a baby's total *dependence* upon his or her parents for every one of life's needs⟩
*syn* dependency, reliance
*rel* reciprocity, relativity; confidence, faith, stock, trust
*near ant* autonomy, sovereignty
*ant* independence, self-reliance
2 something or someone to which one looks for support ⟨ultimately rice became the chief *dependence* in that state⟩
*syn* buttress, mainstay, pillar, reliance, standby, support
*rel* backbone, spine; crutch, prop, stay

**dependency** *n* the quality or state of needing something or someone — see DEPENDENCE 1

**dependent** *adj* 1 extending freely from a support from above ⟨the *dependent* willow branches swayed in the gentle breeze⟩
*syn* dangling, hanging, pendent (*or* pendant), pendulous
2 determined by something else ⟨our going to the movies tonight is *dependent* on whether or not we have any money left after we eat out⟩
*syn* conditional, contingent (on *or* upon), subject (to), tentative
*rel* liable, open, susceptible; limited, modified, qualified, restricted; doubtful, iffy, problematic (*also* problematical), questionable, uncertain
*near ant* absolute, categorical (*also* categoric), ultimate; basal, basic, fundamental, primary
*ant* independent, unconditional

**depict** *vb* 1 to give a representation or account of in words — see DESCRIBE 1
2 to point out the chief quality or qualities of an individual or group — see CHARACTERIZE 1
3 to present a picture of — see PICTURE 1

**depiction** *n* a vivid representation in words of someone or something — see DESCRIPTION 1

**deplete** *vb* to make complete use of ⟨miners *depleted* the vein of copper ore after months of working⟩
*syn* clean (out), consume, drain, exhaust, expend, spend, use up
*rel* decrease, diminish, lessen, reduce; eat, use; bankrupt, impoverish; cripple, debilitate, disable, enfeeble, sap, undermine, weaken; dry up, empty; dissipate, squander, waste
*near ant* augment, enlarge, increase; bolster, fortify, reinforce, strengthen; rebuild, repair, restore, revive
*ant* renew, replace

**deplorable** *adj* of a kind to cause great distress — see REGRETTABLE

**deplore** *vb* 1 to feel or express sorrow for — see LAMENT 1
2 to feel sorry or dissatisfied about — see REGRET

**deploring** *adj* expressing or suggesting mourning — see MOURNFUL 1

**deport** *vb* 1 to force to leave a country — see BANISH 1
2 to manage the actions of (oneself) in a particular way — see BEHAVE

**deportation** *n* the forced removal from a homeland — see EXILE 1

**deportee** *n* a person forced to emigrate for political reasons — see ÉMIGRÉ 1

**deportment** *n* the way or manner in which one conducts oneself — see BEHAVIOR

**depose** *vb* 1 to remove from a position of prominence or power (as a throne) ⟨they *deposed* the dictator after he had bankrupted the country⟩
*syn* dethrone, oust, uncrown, unmake, unseat, unthrone

*rel* discharge, dismiss; overthrow, usurp, subvert, topple; eject, throw out
*near ant* inaugurate, induct, install, instate, invest; appoint, designate, elect
*ant* crown, enthrone, throne
2 to make a solemn declaration under oath for the purpose of establishing a fact — see TESTIFY

**deposit** *n* 1 matter that settles to the bottom of a body of liquid ⟨a *deposit* of silt on the river bed⟩
*syn* deposition, dregs, grounds, precipitate, sediment
*rel* lees; ooze, sludge; dross, slag, waste
2 a collection of things kept available for future use or need — see STORE 1
3 a sum of money set aside for a particular purpose — see FUND 1

**deposit** *vb* 1 to put in an account ⟨we *deposited* the check in a bank account⟩
*syn* bank
*rel* cache, hoard, lay away, reserve, salt away, save, squirrel (away), stash, store, stow; invest
*near ant* remove, take out; disburse, expend, lay out, spend
*ant* withdraw
2 to arrange something in a certain spot or position — see PLACE 1

**deposition** *n* matter that settles to the bottom of a body of liquid — see DEPOSIT 1

**depository** *n* a building for storing goods — see STOREHOUSE

**depot** *n* 1 a building for storing goods — see STOREHOUSE
2 a place where military arms are stored — see ARMORY

**deprave** *vb* to lower in character or dignity — see DEBASE 1

**depraved** *adj* having or showing lowered moral character or standards — see CORRUPT

**depravedness** *n* the state or quality of being utterly evil — see ENORMITY 1

**depravity** *n* 1 a sinking to a state of low moral standards and behavior — see CORRUPTION 2
2 immoral conduct or practices harmful or offensive to society — see VICE 1
3 the state or quality of being utterly evil — see ENORMITY 1

**deprecate** *vb* 1 to express scornfully one's low opinion of — see DECRY 1
2 to hold an unfavorable opinion of — see DISAPPROVE

**deprecation** *n* 1 refusal to accept as right or desirable — see DISAPPROVAL
2 the act of making a person or a thing seem little or unimportant — see DEPRECIATION

**depreciate** *vb* 1 to lower the price or value of ⟨a faded finish will really *depreciate* your car when you decide to trade it in⟩
*syn* cheapen, depress, mark down, write off
*rel* underrate, undervalue; abate, abridge, compress, contract, de-escalate, deflate, diminish, dwindle, lessen, lower, moderate, reduce, shrink
*near ant* bloat, blow up, inflate; add, aggrandize, amplify, augment, balloon, boost, dilate, enlarge, escalate, expand, extend, heighten, increase, maximize, raise, swell
*ant* appreciate, mark up
2 to express scornfully one's low opinion of — see DECRY 1

**depreciation** *n* the act of making a person or a thing seem little or unimportant ⟨the boys' *depreciation* of the girls' basketball victories only showed how jealous they were⟩
*syn* belittlement, deprecation, detraction, diminishment, disparagement, put-down
*rel* aspersion, backbiting, defamation, libel, slander, vilification; derision, mockery, ridicule; abuse, invective, vituperation; censure, condemnation, denunciation
*near ant* acclaim, praise; approbation, approval, commendation
*ant* aggrandizement, ennoblement, exaltation, glorification, magnification

**depreciative** *adj* intended to make a person or thing seem of little importance or value — see DEROGATORY

**depreciatory** *adj* intended to make a person or thing seem of little importance or value — see DEROGATORY

**depress** *vb* 1 to make sad ⟨the thought of failing the test *depressed* me⟩
*syn* burden, oppress, sadden
*rel* ail, distress, trouble; afflict, torment, torture; discourage, dishearten, dispirit; bother, disquiet, disturb, perturb, upset
*near ant* animate, enliven, invigorate; comfort, console, solace; excite, inspire, stimulate; elate, exhilarate; encourage, hearten; delight, gratify, please
*ant* brighten, buoy, cheer, gladden
2 to cause to fall intentionally or unintentionally — see DROP 1
3 to lower the price or value of — see DEPRECIATE 1
4 to push steadily against with some force — see PRESS 1

**depressed** *adj* 1 curved inward — see HOLLOW
2 feeling unhappiness — see SAD 1

**depressing** *adj* 1 causing or marked by an atmosphere lacking in cheer — see GLOOMY 1
2 causing unhappiness — see SAD 2

**depression** *n* 1 a period of decreased economic activity ⟨during the 1930s the U.S. suffered a great *depression*⟩
*syn* recession, slump
*rel* crash, panic; stagnation
*near ant* development, growth; advancement, progress
*ant* boom
2 a state or spell of low spirits — see SADNESS
3 a sunken area forming a separate space — see HOLE 2

---

*syn* synonym(s) *rel* related words
*ant* antonym(s) *near ant* near antonym(s)

**deprivation** *n* the state of being robbed of something normally enjoyed — see PRIVATION

**deprived** *adj* kept from having the necessities of life or a healthful environment ⟨*deprived* children growing up in the slums⟩
*syn* disadvantaged, underprivileged
*rel* impoverished, needy, poor; hapless, ill-fated, ill-starred, unfortunate, unlucky
*near ant* fortunate, lucky; affluent, rich, wealthy; coddled, indulged, pampered, spoiled
*ant* privileged

**depth** *n* 1 distance measured from the top to the bottom of something ⟨be sure to check the *depth* of the water before diving off the dock⟩
*syn* drop
*rel* lowness; draft, sounding
*near ant* shallowness; altitude, elevation, height
2 the quality of being great in extent (as of insight) ⟨the *depth* of the poet's understanding of human nature has given his works a timeless appeal⟩
*syn* profoundness, profundity
*rel* discernment, sense, wisdom; brain, intellect, intelligence; acuteness, keenness, penetration, sharpness
*near ant* shallowness, superficiality; smattering
3 the most intense or characteristic phase of something — see THICK

**depthless** *adj* lacking significant physical depth — see SHALLOW 1

**depute** *vb* to appoint as one's representative — see DELEGATE 1

**deputize** *vb* to appoint as one's representative — see DELEGATE 1

**deputy** *n* 1 a person who acts or does business for another — see AGENT 2
2 a person who helps a more skilled person — see HELPER

**derange** *vb* 1 to cause to go insane or as if insane — see CRAZE
2 to undo the proper order or arrangement of — see DISORDER

**deranged** *adj* having or showing a very abnormal or sick state of mind — see INSANE 1

**derangement** *n* 1 a serious mental disorder that prevents one from living a safe and normal life — see INSANITY 1
2 an act or instance of the order of things being disturbed — see UPSET

**derelict** *adj* 1 failing to give proper care and attention — see NEGLIGENT
2 left unoccupied or unused — see ABANDONED

**dereliction** *n* 1 the act of abandoning ⟨the family's shameful *dereliction* of their pets at the end of the summer season⟩
*syn* abandonment, desertion, forsaking
*rel* defection; discard, dumping, jettison
*near ant* retention
*ant* reclamation
2 failure to take the care that a cautious person usually takes — see NEGLIGENCE 1
3 the nonperformance of an assigned or expected action — see FAILURE 1

**deride** *vb* to make (someone or something) the object of unkind laughter — see RIDICULE

**derision** *n* the making of unkind jokes as a way of showing one's scorn for someone or something — see RIDICULE

**derisive** *adj* so foolish or pointless as to be worthy of scornful laughter — see RIDICULOUS 1

**derisory** *adj* so foolish or pointless as to be worthy of scornful laughter — see RIDICULOUS 1

**derivable** *adj* being or provable by reasoning in which the conclusion follows necessarily from given information — see DEDUCTIVE

**derivative** *adj* taken or created from something original or basic — see SECONDARY 1

**derivative** *n* something that naturally develops or is developed from something else ⟨the whole field of industrial robots is a *derivative* of technology developed for the space program⟩
*syn* by-product, offshoot, outgrowth, spin-off
*rel* descendant (*or* descendent); aftermath, consequence, result; aftereffect, side effect; copy, duplicate, facsimile, replica, reproduction
*near ant* archetype, original, prototype; antecedent, cause, determinant
*ant* origin, root, source

**derogatory** *adj* intended to make a person or thing seem of little importance or value ⟨fans made a steady stream of *derogatory* remarks about the players on the visiting team⟩
*syn* belittling, contemptuous, decrying, degrading, demeaning, depreciative, depreciatory, disdainful, disparaging, scornful, slighting, uncomplimentary
*rel* aspersing, defamatory, detractive, insulting, libelous, maligning, slandering, slanderous, vilifying; abusive, opprobrious, scurrilous; despiteful, malevolent, malicious, spiteful
*near ant* admiring, adulatory, laudatory; appreciative, respectful
*ant* commendatory, complimentary

**descant** *vb* 1 to give a formal often extended talk on a subject — see TALK 1
2 to produce musical sounds with the voice — see SING 1

**descend** *vb* 1 to lead or extend downward ⟨the pathway *descends* to the river bank⟩
*syn* decline, dip, drop, fall, plunge
*rel* cant, incline, lean, list, recline, slant, slope, tilt, tip
*near ant* even, flatten, level, straighten
*ant* ascend, climb, rise
2 to become worse or of less value — see DETERIORATE
3 to go to a lower level — see DROP 2

**descend** (on *or* upon) *vb* to take sudden, violent action against — see ATTACK 1

**descendant** *or* **descendent** *adj* bending downward or forward — see NODDING

**descending** *adj* bending downward or forward — see NODDING

**descent** *n* **1** the act or process of going to a lower level or altitude ⟨the airplane began its gradual *descent* to the landing field⟩
*syn* dip, dive, down, drop, fall, nosedive, plunge
*rel* comedown, downfall, downgrade; sinking
*near ant* advance, headway, progress, progression; betterment, improvement
*ant* ascent, climb, rise, upswing, upturn
**2** a gradual sinking and wasting away of mind or body — see DECLINE 1
**3** a change to a lower state or level — see DECLINE 2
**4** a loss of status — see COMEDOWN
**5** a sudden attack on and entrance into hostile territory — see RAID 1
**6** the act or action of setting upon with force or violence — see ATTACK 1
**7** the line of ancestors from whom a person is descended — see ANCESTRY

**describe** *vb* **1** to give a representation or account of in words ⟨he tried to *describe* the dream he had last night as accurately as he could⟩
*syn* delineate, depict, draw, image, paint, picture, portray, sketch
*rel* characterize, qualify, represent; demonstrate, illustrate; narrate, recite, recount, relate; display, exhibit, show; hint, suggest; draft, outline
*near ant* color, distort, falsify, garble, misrepresent, pervert, twist, warp
**2** to give an oral or written account of in some detail — see TELL 1
**3** to point out the chief quality or qualities of an individual or group — see CHARACTERIZE 1

**description** *n* **1** a vivid representation in words of someone or something ⟨we recognized his cousin from his *description*⟩
*syn* delineation, depiction, picture, portrait, portrayal, sketch
*rel* account, chronicle, narrative, report, story, tale; demonstration, exemplification, illustration
**2** a number of persons or things that are grouped together because they have something in common — see SORT 1

**descry** *vb* **1** to come upon after searching, study, or effort — see FIND 1
**2** to make note of (something) through the use of one's eyes — see SEE 1

**desecrate** *vb* to treat (a sacred place or object) shamefully or with great disrespect ⟨vandals *desecrated* the cemetery last night with graffiti⟩
*syn* defile, profane, violate
*rel* blaspheme, curse, swear; befoul, contaminate, foul, pollute; affront, insult, offend; crush, decimate, demolish, destroy, devastate, ravage, raze, ruin, waste, wreck; despoil, loot, pillage, plunder, raid, ransack, rob, sack, spoil, strip
*near ant* bless, consecrate, dedicate, hallow, sanctify; honor, respect; cleanse, purify

**desecration** *n* an act of great disrespect shown to God or to sacred ideas, people, or things — see BLASPHEMY

**[1]desert** *n* land that is uninhabited or not fit for crops — see WASTELAND

**[2]desert** *n* suffering, loss, or hardship imposed in response to a crime or offense — see PUNISHMENT

**desert** *vb* **1** to leave (a cause or party) often in order to take up another — see DEFECT
**2** to cause to remain behind — see LEAVE 1

**deserted** *adj* left unoccupied or unused — see ABANDONED

**deserter** *n* a person who abandons a cause or organization usually without right — see RENEGADE

**desertion** *n* the act of abandoning — see DERELICTION 1

**deserve** *vb* to be or make worthy of (as a reward or punishment) — see EARN 2

**deserved** *adj* being what is called for by accepted standards of right and wrong — see JUST 1

**deserving** *adj* having sufficient worth or merit to receive one's honor, esteem, or reward — see WORTHY

**desex** *vb* to remove the sex organs of — see NEUTER

**design** *n* **1** a method worked out in advance for achieving some objective — see PLAN 1
**2** a secret plan for accomplishing evil or unlawful ends — see PLOT 1
**3** something that one hopes or intends to accomplish — see GOAL
**4** a unit of decoration that is repeated all over something (as a fabric) — see PATTERN 1
**5** the way in which the elements of something (as a work of art) are arranged — see COMPOSITION 3

**design** *vb* **1** to have in mind as a purpose or goal — see INTEND
**2** to work out the details of (something) in advance — see PLAN 1

**designate** *vb* **1** to decide upon (the time or date for an event) usually from a position of authority — see APPOINT 1
**2** to pick (someone) by one's authority for a specific position or duty — see APPOINT 2
**3** to give a name to — see NAME 1

**designation** *n* **1** a word or combination of words by which a person or thing is regularly known — see NAME 1
**2** the state or fact of being chosen for a position or duty — see APPOINTMENT 1

**designedly** *adv* with full awareness of what one is doing — see INTENTIONALLY

**designer** *n* one who creates or introduces something new — see INVENTOR

**desirable** *adj* suitable for bringing about a desired result under the circumstances — see EXPEDIENT

---

*syn* synonym(s) *rel* related words
*ant* antonym(s) *near ant* near antonym(s)

**desire** *n* a strong wish for something ⟨a *desire* for adventure and excitement prompted him to travel to America⟩
*syn* appetite, craving, drive, hankering, hunger, itch, longing, lust, passion, pining, thirst, urge, yearning, yen
*rel* compulsion, impulse, urge, will, zeal; liking, love, taste; eagerness, impatience; wish, want; necessity, need, requirement; avarice, cupidity, greed, rapacity
*near ant* abhorrence, aversion, disfavor, disgust, dislike, distaste, hatred, repugnance, repulsion; apathy, indifference, unconcern

**desire** *vb* to have an earnest wish to own or enjoy ⟨he greatly *desired* a new mountain bike for his next birthday⟩
*syn* ache (for), covet, crave, die (for), hanker (for *or* after), hunger (for), itch (for), long (for), lust (for *or* after), pant (after), pine (for), repine (for), sigh (for), thirst (for), want, wish (for), yearn (for)
*rel* delight (in), enjoy, fancy, like, relish
*near ant* abhor, abominate, detest, hate, loathe; decline, refuse, reject, spurn

**desirous** *adj* showing urgent desire or interest — see EAGER

**desirousness** *n* urgent desire or interest — see EAGERNESS

**desist** (from) *vb* to bring (an action or operation) to an immediate end — see STOP 1

**desk** *n* a large unit of a governmental, business, or educational organization — see DIVISION 2

**desolate** *adj* **1** causing or marked by an atmosphere lacking in cheer — see GLOOMY 1
**2** sad from lack of companionship or separation from others — see LONESOME 1

**desolate** *vb* to bring to a complete end the physical soundness, existence, or usefulness of — see DESTROY 1

**desolation** *n* **1** a state or spell of low spirits — see SADNESS
**2** land that is uninhabited or not fit for crops — see WASTELAND
**3** the state of being unattended to or not cared for — see NEGLECT 1
**4** the state or fact of being rendered nonexistent, physically unsound, or useless — see DESTRUCTION

**despair** *n* **1** utter loss of hope ⟨the endless drought drove the farmers to *despair*⟩
*syn* desperation, despondency, forlornness, hopelessness
*rel* blues, depression, dejection, desolation, doldrums, dolor, downheartedness, dumps, gloom, melancholy, mopes, oppression, sadness, sorrow, unhappiness; cynicism, pessimism; acceptance, resignation
*near ant* cheer, cheerfulness, sunniness; optimism
*ant* hope, hopefulness
**2** the state of being discouraged — see DISCOURAGEMENT

**despair** *vb* to lose all hope or confidence ⟨we *despaired* when we saw how little time we had left to complete our project⟩
*syn* despond
*rel* give up, surrender, yield; darken, sadden; grieve, mourn, sorrow; discourage, dishearten, dispirit
*near ant* assure, encourage, hearten, reassure; hope
*ant* brighten, cheer (up), perk (up)

**despairing** *adj* emphasizing or expecting the worst — see PESSIMISTIC 1

**desperation** *n* utter loss of hope — see DESPAIR 1

**despicable** *adj* **1** arousing or deserving of one's loathing and disgust — see CONTEMPTIBLE 1
**2** not following or in accordance with standards of honor and decency — see IGNOBLE 2
**3** deserving pitying scorn (as for inadequacy) — see PITIFUL 1

**despise** *vb* **1** to dislike strongly — see HATE
**2** to ignore in a disrespectful manner — see SCORN 2

**despite** *n* **1** open dislike for someone or something considered unworthy of one's concern or respect — see CONTEMPT
**2** the desire to cause pain for the satisfaction of doing harm — see MALICE

**despite** *prep* without being prevented by ⟨we went to the party *despite* the bad weather outside⟩
*syn* notwithstanding, with
*phrases* in despite of, in spite of

**despiteful** *adj* having or showing a desire to cause someone pain or suffering for the sheer enjoyment of it — see HATEFUL

**despitefully** *adv* in a mean or spiteful manner — see NASTILY

**despitefulness** *n* open dislike for someone or something considered unworthy of one's concern or respect — see CONTEMPT

**despoil** *vb* to search through with the intent of committing robbery — see RANSACK 1

**despond** *vb* to lose all hope or confidence — see DESPAIR

**despondency** *n* **1** a state or spell of low spirits — see SADNESS
**2** the state of being discouraged — see DISCOURAGEMENT
**3** utter loss of hope — see DESPAIR 1

**despondent** *adj* feeling unhappiness — see SAD 1

**despot** *n* a person who uses power or authority in a cruel, unjust, or harmful way ⟨the *despot* threw anyone who dared to criticize his rule into jail⟩
*syn* autocrat, dictator, oppressor, potentate, tyrant
*rel* dominator, master, overlord, ruler; king, lord, monarch, prince, queen, sovereign; baron, czar (*also* tsar *or* tzar), magnate, mogul, tycoon; authoritarian, disciplinarian, discipliner, martinet

**despotic** *adj* **1** exercising power or authority without interference by others — see ABSOLUTE 1
**2** fond of ordering people around — see BOSSY

**despotism** *n* a system of government in which the ruler has unlimited power ⟨by the end of the 20th century many countries around the world had rejected *despotism* in favor of democracy⟩
***syn*** autocracy, dictatorship, totalitarianism, tyranny
***rel*** monarchy; authoritarianism, fascism; domination, oppression
***near ant*** democracy; freedom; anarchy

**destine** *vb* to determine the fate of in advance ⟨his extreme height seemed to *destine* him for a career in basketball⟩
***syn*** doom, fate, foredoom, foreordain, ordain, predestine, predetermine
***rel*** forecast, foretell, predict, prognosticate, prophesy; preconceive, prejudge; condemn, sentence

**destiny** *n* a state or end that seemingly has been decided beforehand — see FATE 1

**destitute** *adj* **1** lacking money or material possessions — see POOR 1
**2** utterly lacking in something needed, wanted, or expected — see DEVOID 1

**destitution** *n* the state of lacking sufficient money or material possessions — see POVERTY 1

**destroy** *vb* **1** to bring to a complete end the physical soundness, existence, or usefulness of ⟨they practically *destroyed* the safe in order to get at the money inside⟩ ⟨their poor scores on the final exam *destroyed* any chance they might have had to pass the course⟩
***syn*** annihilate, decimate, demolish, desolate, devastate, do in, extinguish, pulverize, raze, ruin, shatter, smash, tear down, waste, wreck
***rel*** gut; beat, best, clobber, conquer, crush, defeat, lick, master, overbear, overcome, prevail (over), scotch, subdue, surmount, thrash, triumph (over), win (against); blow up, break, damage, deface, disintegrate, dynamite, mangle, mar, mutilate, spoil, vitiate; erode, scour, wash out, wear (away); dismantle, undo, unmake; blot out, eradicate, exterminate, extirpate, obliterate, remove, rub out, stamp (out), wipe out; despoil, loot, pillage, plunder, ravage, sack, vandalize; assassinate, butcher, cut down, dispatch, execute, kill, massacre, murder, slaughter, slay, zap
***near ant*** create, invent; fabricate, fashion, forge, form, make, manufacture, shape; bring about; establish, found, institute, organize; conserve, preserve, protect, save; rebuild, reconstruct, remodel, renovate, restore
***ant*** build, construct, erect, put up, raise
**2** to bring destruction to (something) through violent action — see RAVAGE
**3** to deprive of life — see KILL 1

**destruction** *n* the state or fact of being rendered nonexistent, physically unsound, or useless ⟨the violent storm resulted in the *destruction* of their tree house⟩
***syn*** annihilation, decimation, demolishment, demolition, desolation, devastation, extermination, extinction, havoc, loss, obliteration, ruin, ruination, wastage, wreckage
***rel*** depredation, despoilment, despoliation; breakup, disintegration, dissolution; assassination, execution, killing, massacre, slaughter
***near ant*** conservation, preservation, protection; reconstruction, re-creation, remodeling, renovation, restoration
***ant*** building, construction, erection, raising

**destructive** *adj* **1** causing or tending to cause destruction ⟨the *destructive* storm blew down trees all over town, and blew the roof off our neighbor's house⟩
***syn*** calamitous, cataclysmal (*or* cataclysmic), devastating, disastrous, ruinous
***rel*** deadly, fatal, lethal, mortal, vital; deleterious, detrimental, harmful, pernicious
***near ant*** preservative, protective; creative, formative; harmless, innocuous, inoffensive, nondestructive; ameliorative, helpful, useful
***ant*** constructive
**2** bringing about ruin or misfortune — see FATAL 1

**desultorily** *adv* without definite aim, direction, rule, or method — see HIT OR MISS

**desultory** *adj* **1** lacking a definite plan, purpose, or pattern — see RANDOM
**2** passing from one topic to another — see DISCURSIVE

**detached** *adj* **1** having or showing a lack of friendliness or interest in others — see COOL 1
**2** not physically attached to another unit — see SEPARATE 2

**detachment** *n* **1** lack of favoritism toward one side or another ⟨the judge showed great *detachment* when deciding the controversial case⟩
***syn*** disinterestedness, impartiality, neutrality, objectivity
***rel*** equitableness, fairness; apathy, indifference, unconcern; broad-mindedness, open-mindedness, tolerance
***near ant*** chauvinism, nepotism; subjectivity; bent, inclination, leaning, penchant, predilection, predisposition, proclivity, propensity, tendency; preconception, prejudgment
***ant*** bias, favor, favoritism, one-sidedness, partiality, partisanship, prejudice
**2** a small military unit with a special task or function ⟨the general sent a *detachment* ahead to scout the enemy's position⟩
***syn*** detail
***rel*** commando, firing squad, paratroops, patrol, picket; battalion, command, company, corps, division, platoon, regiment, squad, troop, wing

**detail** *n* **1** a separate part in a list, account, or series — see ITEM 1

2 a single piece of information — see FACT 3
3 a small military unit with a special task or function — see DETACHMENT 2

**detail** *vb* 1 to assign to a place or position — see [2]POST
2 to pick (someone) by ones authority for a specific position or duty — see APPOINT 2
3 to specify one after another — see ENUMERATE 1

**detailed** *adj* 1 including many small descriptive features ⟨a *detailed* report on all the activities that their Scout troop had been involved in over the past year⟩
***syn*** circumstantial, elaborate, full, minute, particularized, thorough
***rel*** enumerated, inventoried, itemized, listed; delineated, specific, specified; abundant, copious; comprehensive, exhausting, exhaustive, thoroughgoing; accurate, exact, precise; complete, entire, replete; distinct, explicit, precise, sharp; inclusive, mapped (out); descriptive, graphic (*also* graphical), picturesque, vivid
***near ant*** concise, pithy, short, succinct; abbreviated, abridged, curtailed, cut, pruned, shortened, trimmed; indeterminate; nebulous, nondescript, sketchy, vague; bird's-eye, broad, general, nonspecific, overall, unspecified
***ant*** compendious, summary
2 made or done with great care or with much detail — see ELABORATE 1

**detailedly** *adv* with attention to all aspects or details — see THOROUGHLY 1

**detainment** *n* an instance or period of being prevented from going about one's business — see DELAY

**detect** *vb* to come upon after searching, study, or effort — see FIND 1

**detectable** *adj* able to be perceived by a sense or by the mind — see PERCEPTIBLE

**detection** *n* the act or process of sighting or learning the existence of something for the first time — see DISCOVERY 1

**detective** *n* a person whose business is solving crimes and catching criminals or gathering information that is not easy to get ⟨the *detective* tracked the criminals to an abandoned warehouse on the south side of town⟩
***syn*** investigator, operative, plainclothesman, shadow, sleuth, tail
***rel*** Federal, G-man, narc (*or* mark) [*slang*]

**detector** *n* a device that detects some physical quantity and responds usually with a transmitted signal — see SENSOR

**deter** *vb* to steer (a person) from an activity or course of action — see DISCOURAGE 2

**detergent** *n* a substance used for cleaning — see CLEANER

**deteriorate** *vb* to become worse or of less value ⟨the garden slowly *deteriorated* after months of neglect⟩
***syn*** crumble, decay, decline, degenerate, descend, ebb, rot, sink, worsen
***rel*** recede, wane; decompose, degrade, disintegrate; sour, spoil; lessen, lower, reduce; debilitate, undermine, weaken
***phrases*** go to pot
***near ant*** better, upgrade; enhance, enrich, fortify, heighten, intensify, strengthen; advance, develop, progress
***ant*** ameliorate, improve, meliorate

**deterioration** *n* 1 a gradual sinking and wasting away of mind or body — see DECLINE 1
2 a change to a lower state or level — see DECLINE 2

**determinate** *adj* 1 having been established and usually not subject to change — see FIXED 1
2 having distinct or certain limits — see LIMITED 1

**determination** *n* 1 firm or unwavering adherence to one's purpose ⟨the *determination* with which the pioneers settled the land despite many hardships and setbacks⟩
***syn*** decidedness, decision, decisiveness, firmness, granite, purposefulness, resoluteness, resolution, resolve
***rel*** doggedness, obstinacy, perseverance, persistence, stubbornness, tenaciousness, tenacity; backbone, fortitude, grit, pluck
***near ant*** uncertainty
***ant*** hesitation, indecision, irresolution, vacillation
2 a position arrived at after consideration — see DECISION 1
3 an opinion arrived at through a process of reasoning — see CONCLUSION 1

**determine** *vb* 1 to give an opinion about (something at issue or in dispute) — see JUDGE 1
2 to come to a judgment after discussion or consideration — see DECIDE 1
3 to come upon after searching, study, or effort — see FIND 1

**determined** *adj* 1 fully committed to achieving a goal ⟨his *determined* opponent would not be bluffed or shaken⟩
***syn*** bent (on *or* upon), bound, decisive, firm, intent, purposeful, resolute, resolved, set
***rel*** certain, cocksure, positive, sure; earnest, serious; steady, unfaltering, unhesitating, unswerving, unwavering
***near ant*** doubtful, dubious, uncertain, unsure
***ant*** faltering, hesitant, indecisive, irresolute, undetermined, unresolved, vacillating, wavering
2 showing no signs of slackening or yielding in one's purpose — see UNYIELDING 1

**determinedly** *adv* with great effort or determination — see HARD 1

**deterrent** *n* something that makes movement or progress more difficult — see ENCUMBRANCE

**detest** *vb* to dislike strongly — see HATE

**detestable** *adj* not following or in accordance with standards of honor and decency — see IGNOBLE 2

**dethrone** *vb* to remove from a position of prominence or power (as a throne) — see DEPOSE 1

**detonate** *vb* to break open or into pieces usually because of internal pressure — see EXPLODE 1

**detonation** *n* the act or an instance of exploding — see EXPLOSION 1

**detour** *vb* **1** to avoid by going around ⟨we had to *detour* the construction zone in order to get to the stadium⟩
***syn*** bypass, circumvent, skirt
***rel*** circumnavigate; avoid, dodge, duck, elude, escape, eschew, evade, shake, shun
***near ant*** confront, face, meet; accept, court, embrace, pursue, seek, welcome
**2** to change one's course or direction — see TURN 3

**detraction** *n* the act of making a person or a thing seem little or unimportant — see DEPRECIATION

**detriment** *n* something that causes loss or pain — see INJURY 1

**detrimental** *adj* causing or capable of causing harm — see HARMFUL

**devastate** *vb* **1** to bring destruction to (something) through violent action — see RAVAGE
**2** to bring to a complete end the physical soundness, existence, or usefulness of — see DESTROY 1
**3** to subject to incapacitating emotional or mental stress — see OVERWHELM 1

**devastating** *adj* causing or tending to cause destruction — see DESTRUCTIVE 1

**devastation** *n* the state or fact of being rendered nonexistent, physically unsound, or useless — see DESTRUCTION

**develop** *vb* **1** to gradually become clearer or more detailed ⟨as the story of the bombing *developed*, the scope of the tragedy became more apparent⟩
***syn*** evolve, unfold
***rel*** advance, proceed, progress; mature, ripen; materialize
**2** to come to have gradually ⟨they *developed* a taste for green olives⟩
***syn*** acquire, cultivate, form
***rel*** gain, get, obtain; achieve, attain, reach; foster, nourish, nurture, promote
***ant*** lose
**3** to become mature — see MATURE
**4** to express more fully and in greater detail — see EXPAND 1

**developed** *adj* being far along in development — see ADVANCED 1

**developer** *n* one who creates or introduces something new — see INVENTOR

**development** *n* **1** the act or process of going from the simple or basic to the complex or advanced ⟨the *development* of an idea into a marketable product⟩
***syn*** elaboration, evolution, expansion, growth, progress, progression
***rel*** advancement, betterment, improvement, perfection, refinement; maturation
***near ant*** decadence, decay, decaying, declension, decline, degeneration, descent, deterioration, downgrade, ebbing, weakening
***ant*** regression, retrogression
**2** a condition or occurrence traceable to a cause — see EFFECT 1
**3** the process of becoming mature — see MATURATION

**deviant** *adj* departing from some accepted standard of what is normal ⟨some studies show that many violent criminals begin exhibiting *deviant* behavior in early childhood⟩
***syn*** aberrant, abnormal, anomalous, atypical, irregular, unnatural
***rel*** extraordinary, preternatural; rare, uncommon, uncustomary, unusual, unwonted; odd, peculiar, strange, weird
***near ant*** common, familiar, ordinary; customary, usual, wonted
***ant*** natural, normal, regular, standard, typical

**deviant** *n* a person who does not conform to generally accepted standards or customs — see NONCONFORMIST 1

**deviate** *vb* to change one's course or direction — see TURN 3

**device** *n* **1** a clever often underhanded means to achieve an end — see TRICK 1
**2** an article intended for use in work — see IMPLEMENT
**3 devices** *pl* a habitual attraction to some activity or thing — see INCLINATION 1

**devil** *n* **1** *cap* the supreme personification of evil often represented as the ruler of Hell ⟨the *Devil* is traditionally seen as a being who relentlessly tempts people to commit evil⟩
***syn*** Lucifer, Satan
***rel*** deuce, dickens
***phrases*** Prince of Darkness
**2** an evil spirit — see DEMON
**3** a member of the human race — see HUMAN
**4** an appealingly mischievous person — see SCAMP 1
**5** a mean, evil, or unprincipled person — see VILLAIN

**devilfish** *n* any of several extremely large rays ⟨they saw a *devilfish* when they went scuba diving in the Caribbean, but it swam away quickly⟩
***syn*** devil ray, manta, manta ray, sea devil
***rel*** ray, skate

**devilish** *adj* **1** going beyond a normal or acceptable limit in degree or amount — see EXCESSIVE
**2** of, relating to, or worthy of an evil spirit — see FIENDISH
**3** tending to or exhibiting reckless playfulness — see MISCHIEVOUS 1

**devilishly** *adv* beyond a normal or acceptable limit — see TOO 1

**devilishness** *n* playful, reckless behavior that is not intended to cause serious harm — see MISCHIEF 1

**devil–may–care** *adj* **1** having a relaxed, casual manner — see EASYGOING 1

---

***syn*** synonym(s) ***rel*** related words
***ant*** antonym(s) ***near ant*** near antonym(s)

2 having or showing a lack of concern or seriousness — see CAREFREE
3 having or showing a lack of concern for the consequences of one's actions — see RECKLESS 1

**devilment** *n* playful, reckless behavior that is not intended to cause serious harm — see MISCHIEF 1

**devil ray** *n* any of several extremely large rays — see DEVILFISH

**devilry** *or* **deviltry** *n* playful, reckless behavior that is not intended to cause serious harm — see MISCHIEF 1

**devious** *adj* 1 clever at attaining one's ends by indirect and often deceptive means — see ARTFUL 1
2 marked by a long series of irregular curves — see CROOKED 1

**deviousness** *n* skill in achieving one's ends through indirect, subtle, or underhanded means — see CUNNING 1

**devise** *vb* to create or think of by clever use of the imagination — see INVENT

**deviser** *n* one who creates or introduces something new — see INVENTOR

**devoid** *adj* 1 utterly lacking in something needed, wanted, or expected ⟨the so-called comedy is totally *devoid* of intelligence, originality, and even laughs⟩
*syn* bereft, destitute, void
*rel* bare, barren, blank, empty, lacking, stark, vacant, wanting; deficient, fragmental, fragmentary, incomplete, partial; absent, missing
*near ant* filled, full; furnished, provided, supplied
*ant* replete
2 lacking contents that could or should be present — see EMPTY 1

**devote** *vb* 1 to keep or intend for a special purpose ⟨he *devoted* several hours every weekend to playing with his dog⟩
*syn* allocate, consecrate, dedicate, earmark, reserve, save
*rel* hallow, sanctify; commit, confide, consign, entrust
*phrases* set apart, set aside
2 to occupy (oneself) diligently or with close attention — see APPLY

**devoted** *adj* 1 feeling or showing love — see LOVING
2 firm in one's allegiance to someone or something — see FAITHFUL 1

**devotedness** *n* 1 a feeling of strong or constant regard for and dedication to someone — see LOVE 1
2 adherence to something to which one is bound by a pledge or duty — see FIDELITY

**devotee** *n* a person with a strong and habitual liking for something — see FAN

**devotion** *n* 1 a feeling of strong or constant regard for and dedication to someone — see LOVE 1
2 adherence to something to which one is bound by a pledge or duty — see FIDELITY
3 belief and trust in and loyalty to God — see FAITH 1

**devotional** *adj* of, relating to, or used in the practice or worship services of a religion — see RELIGIOUS 1

**devour** *vb* to destroy all trace of — see CONSUME 1

**devout** *adj* showing a devotion to God and to a life of virtue — see HOLY 1

**devoutness** *n* the quality or state of being spiritually pure or virtuous — see HOLINESS

**dexterity** *n* 1 mental skill or quickness ⟨the ambassador showed great *dexterity* in his handling of the touchy situation⟩
*syn* adroitness, cleverness, finesse, sleight
*rel* ability, prowess, talent; competence, efficiency, expertise, know-how, proficiency; ingeniousness, ingenuity, resourcefulness
*near ant* inadequacy, ineptitude, ineptness; slowness, stupidity
2 ease and grace in physical activity ⟨the juggler needed lots of *dexterity* in order to keep all five balls in the air at the same time⟩
*syn* agility, deftness, nimbleness, sleight, spryness
*rel* coordination
*ant* awkwardness, clumsiness, gawkiness

**dexterous** *also* **dextrous** *adj* 1 skillful with the hands ⟨the *dexterous* watchmaker was able to repair the tiny gears and parts in the antique watch⟩
*syn* clever, cunning, deft, handy
*rel* agile, flexible, graceful, limber, lissome (*also* lissom), lithe, nimble, spry; coordinated; adept, competent, expert, masterful, masterly, proficient, skilled, skillful; double-jointed, loose-jointed
*near ant* awkward, bungling, clumsy, fumbling, gawky; uncoordinated; incompetent, inept, maladroit
*ant* butterfingered, heavy-handed, unhandy
2 accomplished with trained ability — see SKILLFUL

**diabolical** *or* **diabolic** *adj* of, relating to, or worthy of an evil spirit — see FIENDISH

**diadem** *n* a decorative band or wreath worn about the head as a symbol of victory or honor — see CROWN 1

**diagnosis** *n* a position arrived at after consideration — see DECISION 1

**diagonal** *adj* running in a slanting direction ⟨the *diagonal* design ran up the wall all the way from the lower left to the upper right-hand corner⟩
*syn* canted, inclined, leaning, listing, oblique, pitched, slanted, slantwise, sloped, sloping, tilted, tilting
*near ant* horizontal, vertical; parallel, perpendicular

**diagonal** *n* the degree to which something rises up from a position level with the horizon — see SLANT

**diagram** *n* something that visually explains or decorates a text — see ILLUSTRATION 1

**dial** *vb* to make a telephone call to — see CALL 2

**dialect** *n* the special terms or expressions of a particular group or field — see TERMINOLOGY
**dialogue** *also* **dialog** *n* talking or a talk between two or more people — see CONVERSATION
**diametric** *or* **diametrical** *adj* being as different as possible — see OPPOSITE
**diatribe** *n* a long angry speech or scolding — see TIRADE
**dice** *n* a small cube marked on each side with one to six spots and usually played in pairs in various games — see DIE
**dice** *vb* to cut into small pieces — see CHOP
**dicker** *vb* to talk over or dispute the terms of a purchase — see BARGAIN
**dictate** *n* a statement of what to do that must be obeyed by those concerned — see COMMAND 1
**dictate** *vb* to give an order — see COMMAND 2
**dictator** *n* a person who uses power or authority in a cruel, unjust, or harmful way — see DESPOT
**dictatorial** *adj* **1** exercising power or authority without interference by others — see ABSOLUTE 1
**2** fond of ordering people around — see BOSSY
**3** having or showing a tendency to force one's will on others without any regard to fairness or necessity — see ARBITRARY 1
**dictatorship** *n* a system of government in which the ruler has unlimited power — see DESPOTISM
**diction** *n* **1** the clear and accurate pronunciation of words especially in public speaking ⟨the actors had very good *diction*, clearly speaking every single word of the Shakespearean play that they were performing⟩
***syn*** articulation, enunciation
***rel*** elocution; speech, wording
**2** the way in which something is put into words — see WORDING
**dictionary** *n* a reference book giving information about the meanings, pronunciations, uses, and origins of words listed in alphabetical order ⟨try to develop the habit of going to the *dictionary* whenever you encounter an unfamiliar word⟩
***syn*** lexicon, wordbook
***rel*** glossary, thesaurus, vocabulary
**die** *n* a small cube marked on each side with one to six spots and usually played in pairs in various games ⟨he rolled the *die*, hoping for a six⟩
***syn*** bone(s), dice
**die** *vb* **1** to stop living ⟨the king *died* of old age after ruling for many years⟩
***syn*** croak [*slang*], decease, depart, expire, pass (on), pass away, perish, succumb
***rel*** disappear, fade
***phrases*** bite the dust
***near ant*** be, exist, subsist; flourish, prosper, thrive
***ant*** breathe, live
**2** to come to an end — see CEASE 1
**3** to stop functioning — see FAIL 1
**die** (down) *vb* to grow less in scope or intensity especially gradually — see DECREASE 2
**die** (for) *vb* to have an earnest wish to own or enjoy — see DESIRE
**differ** *vb* **1** to be unlike; to not be the same ⟨my brother and I *differ* in looks⟩
***syn*** disagree, vary
***rel*** clash, conflict, jar; distinguish, divide, separate
***near ant*** blend, harmonize
***ant*** accord, agree, conform, correspond
**2** to have a different opinion — see DISAGREE 1
**difference** *n* **1** the quality or state of being different ⟨there's a great *difference* between claiming to care about the environment and living like you really do⟩
***syn*** contrast, disagreement, discrepancy, disparateness, disparity, dissimilarity, distinction, distinctiveness, distinctness, diverseness, diversity, unlikeness
***rel*** deviance, divergence; change, modification, variation; conflict, discord, discordance, dissension, dissent, dissidence, disunity, friction, strife; variability, variance; incompatibility, incongruity, incongruousness; disproportion
***near ant*** identicalness, identity; analogy, similitude; accordance, agreement, conformity, congruity, correspondence; equality, equivalence, equivalency; parallelism
***ant*** alikeness, community, likeness, resemblance, sameness, similarity
**2** variance of opinion on a matter — see DISAGREEMENT 1
**3** the act, process, or result of making different — see CHANGE
**different** *adj* **1** being not of the same kind ⟨apples are *different* from oranges⟩
***syn*** disparate, dissimilar, distinct, distinctive, distinguishable, diverse, other, unalike, unlike
***rel*** divers, miscellaneous, several, sundry, variant, varied, various; individual, particular, peculiar, single; unequal; disproportionate
***near ant*** identical, selfsame; equal, equivalent, tantamount; akin, analogous, comparable, related; homogeneous, uniform
***ant*** alike, indistinguishable, like, parallel, same, similar
**2** not the same or shared — see SEPARATE 1
**differential** *adj* favoring, applying, or being unequal treatment of different classes of people — see DISCRIMINATORY
**differentiate** *vb* to understand or point out the difference — see DISTINGUISH 1
**differently** *adv* in a different way — see OTHERWISE
**difficult** *adj* **1** requiring considerable physical or mental effort — see HARD 2
**2** requiring exceptional skill or caution in performance or handling — see TRICKY

**difficulty** *n* **1** something that is a cause for suffering or special effort especially in the attainment of a goal ⟨the many *difficulties* that he encountered on the road from poor orphan to head of a major corporation⟩
***syn*** adversity, asperity, hardness, hardship, rigor
***rel*** discomfort, inconvenience, nuisance; affliction, trial, tribulation; knock, misfortune, mishap, tragedy; bar, catch, check, clog, crimp, embarrassment, handicap, hindrance, hitch, hurdle, impediment, interference, let, manacle, obstacle, obstruction, rub, shackle, snag, stop, trammel; block, chain, deterrent, encumbrance, fetter, inhibition; hump
***near ant*** advantage, break, opportunity
**2** something that makes a situation more complicated or difficult — see COMPLICATION 1

**diffident** *adj* not comfortable around people — see SHY 2

**diffuse** *adj* using or containing more words than necessary to express an idea — see WORDY

**diffuseness** *n* the use of too many words to express an idea — see VERBIAGE

**dig** *n* **1** a quick thrust — see [1]POKE
**2** an act or expression showing scorn and usually intended to hurt another's feelings — see INSULT

**dig** *vb* **1** to hollow out or form (something) by removing earth ⟨a backhoe *dug* a hole in the backyard to make a swimming pool⟩
***syn*** excavate, shovel
***rel*** dredge; burrow, claw, grub; dig in; scoop, spade; delve; mine, quarry
***near ant*** fill (in); smooth (out *or* over)
**2** to take pleasure in — see ENJOY 1
**3** *slang* to recognize the meaning of — see COMPREHEND 1

**dig** (into) *vb* to search through or into — see EXPLORE 1

**dig** (through) *vb* to look through (as a place) carefully or thoroughly in an effort to find or discover something — see SEARCH 1

**dig** (up) *vb* to come upon after searching, study, or effort — see FIND 1

**digest** *n* **1** a short statement of the main points — see SUMMARY
**2** a shortened version of a written work — see ABRIDGMENT

**digest** *vb* to make into a short statement of the main points (as of a report) — see SUMMARIZE

**diggings** *n pl* the place where one lives — see HOME 1

**digit** *n* a character used to represent a mathematical value — see NUMBER

**dignified** *adj* having or showing a serious and reserved manner ⟨the chief justice of the U.S. Supreme Court is always very *dignified* when swearing in the new president⟩ ⟨*dignified* funeral services for the fallen firemen⟩
***syn*** august, imposing, solemn, stately
***rel*** decorous, formal, proper, seemly; grim, sober, somber (*or* sombre); aristocratic, lordly, majestic, noble
***near ant*** coarse, crass, crude, improper, indecent, uncouth, unseemly, vulgar
***ant*** flighty, frivolous, giddy, goofy, silly, undignified

**dignify** *vb* to enhance the status of — see EXALT

**dignity** *n* high position within society — see RANK 2

**digression** *n* a departure from the subject under consideration — see TANGENT

**digressive** *adj* passing from one topic to another — see DISCURSIVE

**dike** *n* **1** a bank of earth constructed to control water — see DAM
**2** a long narrow channel dug in the earth — see DITCH

**dilapidated** *adj* showing signs of advanced wear and tear and neglect — see SHABBY 1

**dilapidation** *n* the state of being unattended to or not cared for — see NEGLECT 1

**dilatory** *adj* moving or proceeding at less than the normal, desirable, or required speed — see SLOW 1

**dilemma** *n* a situation in which one has to choose between two or more equally unsatisfactory choices ⟨they were faced with a *dilemma* : either they could spend the night out in the cold or they could walk back into their house and face their father⟩
***syn*** quandary
***rel*** deadlock, halt, impasse, quagmire, stalemate, standoff; knot, problem; difficulty, fix, hole, jam, pickle, pinch, plight, predicament, spot
***near ant*** breeze, cinch, duck soup, snap

**dilettante** *adj* lacking or showing a lack of expert skill — see AMATEURISH

**dilettante** *n* **1** a person having a knowledgeable and fine appreciation of the arts — see CONNOISSEUR
**2** a person who regularly or occasionally engages in an activity without being or becoming an expert at it — see AMATEUR

**diligence** *n* attentive and persistent effort ⟨through the *diligence* and ingenuity of a single detective, the gang's ringleader was finally caught⟩
***syn*** assiduity, assiduousness, industriousness, industry
***rel*** application, concentration; doggedness, perseverance, persistence, tenacity, tirelessness
***near ant*** carelessness; idleness, indolence, laziness

**diligent** *adj* involved in often constant activity — see BUSY 1

**diligently** *adv* with great effort or determination — see HARD 1

**dillydally** *vb* **1** to move or act slowly — see DELAY 1
**2** to spend time doing nothing — see IDLE

**dillydallying** *adj* moving or proceeding at less than the normal, desirable, or required speed — see SLOW 1
**dilute** *adj* **1** not containing very much of some important element — see WEAK 3
**2** containing foreign or lower-grade substances — see IMPURE
**dilute** *vb* to alter (something) for the worse with the addition of foreign or lower-grade substances — see ADULTERATE
**diluted** *adj* **1** not containing very much of some important element — see WEAK 3
**2** containing foreign or lower-grade substances — see IMPURE
**dim** *adj* **1** being without light or without much light — see DARK 1
**2** lacking a surface luster or gloss — see MATTE
**3** not seen or understood clearly — see FAINT 1
**dim** *vb* to make dark, dim, or indistinct — see CLOUD 1
**dimension** *n* **1** the total amount of measurable space or surface occupied by something — see [1]SIZE
**2 dimensions** *pl* an area over which activity, capacity, or influence extends — see RANGE 2
**diminish** *vb* **1** to express scornfully one's low opinion of — see DECRY 1
**2** to make smaller in amount, volume, or extent — see DECREASE 1
**3** to grow less in scope or intensity especially gradually — see DECREASE 2
**diminishment** *n* **1** the act of making a person or a thing seem little or unimportant — see DEPRECIATION
**2** the amount by which something is lessened — see DECREASE
**diminution** *n* the amount by which something is lessened — see DECREASE
**diminutive** *adj* of a size that is less than average — see SMALL 1
**diminutive** *n* a living thing much smaller than others of its kind — see DWARF 1
**diminutiveness** *n* the quality or state of being little in size — see SMALLNESS
**dimmed** *adj* being without light or without much light — see DARK 1
**din** *n* loud, confused, and usually unharmonious sound — see NOISE 1
**din** *vb* to say or state again — see REPEAT 1
**dine** *vb* **1** to take a meal ⟨they *dined* elegantly at the city's finest restaurant before taking in an opera downtown⟩
***syn*** eat, fare, feed
***rel*** banquet, feast, fete (*or* fête); board, mess; breakfast, lunch, sup; picnic
**2** to entertain with a fancy meal — see FEAST
**diner** *n* a public establishment where meals are served to paying customers for consumption on the premises — see RESTAURANT
**dinghy** *n* a boat equipped with one or more sails — see SAILBOAT

***syn*** synonym(s) ***rel*** related words
***ant*** antonym(s) ***near ant*** near antonym(s)

**dinginess** *n* the state or quality of being dirty — see DIRTINESS 1
**dingy** *adj* not clean — see DIRTY 1
**dinky** *adj* of a size that is less than average — see SMALL 1
**dinner** *n* a large fancy meal often accompanied by ceremony or entertainment — see FEAST
**dinnerware** *n* dishes used for eating or serving food or drink — see TABLEWARE 2
**dinning** *adj* making loud, confused, and usually unharmonious sounds — see NOISY 1
**dint** *n* a sunken area forming a separate space — see HOLE 2
**dip** *n* the act or process of going to a lower level or altitude — see DESCENT 1
**dip** *vb* **1** to sink or push (something) briefly into or as if into a liquid ⟨he went to *dip* a paper towel in water and clean off the window⟩ ⟨she *dipped* a hand into her pocket and pulled out a piece of candy⟩
***syn*** douse, duck, dunk, immerse, souse, submerge, submerse
***rel*** drench, flood, soak, wet; plunge, thrust
**2** to lift out with something that holds liquid ⟨they *dipped* water from the bucket to pour into the kettle⟩
***syn*** lade, ladle, scoop, spoon
***rel*** bail; deplete, drain, eliminate, exhaust; bleed, draw (off); dish; draw, siphon
***near ant*** pour; fill
**3** to go to a lower level — see DROP 2
**4** to lead or extend downward — see DESCEND 1
**5** to take a quick or hasty look — see GLANCE 2
**diplomacy** *n* the ability to deal with others in touchy situations without offending them — see TACT
**diplomatic** *adj* having or showing tact — see TACTFUL
**dipper** *n* a utensil with a bowl and a handle that is used especially in cooking and serving food — see SPOON
**dire** *adj* **1** being or showing a sign of evil or calamity to come — see OMINOUS
**2** causing fear — see FEARFUL
**3** needing immediate attention — see ACUTE 2
**direct** *adj* **1** done or working without something else coming in between ⟨a zoologist whose works are based entirely on her *direct* observation of animals in the wild⟩ ⟨the virus was the *direct* cause of the disease⟩
***syn*** firsthand, immediate, primary
***rel*** clinical
***ant*** indirect, secondhand
**2** free in expressing one's true feelings and opinions — see FRANK
**3** going straight to the point clearly and firmly — see STRAIGHTFORWARD 1
**direct** *adv* in a direct line or course — see DIRECTLY 1

**direct** *vb* **1** to cause to move to a central point or along a restricted pathway — see CHANNEL
**2** to issue orders to (someone) by right of authority — see COMMAND 1
**3** to give an order — see COMMAND 2
**4** to look after and make decisions about — see CONDUCT 1
**5** to point or turn (something) toward a target or goal — see AIM 1
**6** to point out the way for (someone) especially from a position in front — see LEAD 1

**direction** *n* **1** a statement of what to do that must be obeyed by those concerned — see COMMAND 1
**2** the act or activity of looking after and making decisions about something — see CONDUCT 1

**directive** *n* **1** a statement of what to do that must be obeyed by those concerned — see COMMAND 1
**2** an order publicly issued by an authority — see EDICT 1
**3** a written communication giving information or directions — see MEMORANDUM 1

**directly** *adv* **1** in a direct line or course ⟨we went *directly* to the school without stopping⟩
***syn*** dead, direct, due, plumb, plump, right, straight
***phrases*** as the crow flies
***near ant*** circuitously, deviously
***ant*** indirectly
**2** in an honest and direct manner — see STRAIGHTFORWARD
**3** in the same words — see VERBATIM
**4** without delay — see IMMEDIATELY

**directness** *n* the free expression of one's true feelings and opinions — see CANDOR

**director** *n* a person who manages or directs — see EXECUTIVE

**directorial** *adj* suited for or relating to the directing of things — see EXECUTIVE

**direful** *adj* causing fear — see FEARFUL 1

**dirge** *n* a composition expressing one's grief over a loss — see LAMENT 2

**dirt** *n* **1** the loose surface material in which plants naturally grow ⟨dig into the *dirt* to a depth of about three inches⟩
***syn*** earth, ground, soil
***rel*** clay, duff, dust, gravel, humus, loam, loess, marl, mud, sand, silt, subsoil, topsoil
**2** the solid part of our planet's surface as distinguished from the sea and air — see EARTH 2
**3** foul matter that mars the purity or cleanliness of something — see FILTH 1
**4** the quality or state of being obscene — see OBSCENITY 1

**dirtiness** *n* **1** the state or quality of being dirty ⟨when the maid arrived, she exclaimed over the *dirtiness* of the china⟩
***syn*** dinginess, dustiness, filthiness, foulness, griminess, grubbiness, nastiness, squalidness, uncleanliness, uncleanness
***rel*** impurity; messiness, sloppiness, untidiness; shabbiness; squalor; smuttiness, sootiness
***near ant*** purity
***ant*** cleanliness, immaculateness, spotlessness
**2** the quality or state of being obscene — see OBSCENITY 1

**dirty** *adj* **1** not clean ⟨after playing in the mud all day, his clothes were very *dirty*⟩
***syn*** besmirched, blackened, dingy, dusty, filthy, foul, grimy, grubby, grungy, mucky, muddy, nasty, smutty, soiled, sordid, stained, sullied, unclean, uncleanly
***rel*** contaminated, defiled, impure, polluted, tainted; uncleaned, unsanitary, unsterile, unsterilized, unwashed; discolored; bedraggled, draggled; chaotic, cluttered, confused, disarranged, disarrayed, disheveled (*or* dishevelled), disordered, jumbled, littered, messed, messy, muddled, mussed, mussy, rumpled, scruffy, sloppy, slovenly, unkempt, untidy; shabby, sleazy, squalid; smutty, sooty
***near ant*** clear, limpid, pure; cleaned, cleansed, combed, groomed, neat, ordered, orderly, tidy; bleached, purified, whitened; bright, flawless, perfect, shiny, sparkling, unspotted, untouched; taintless, unblemished, undefiled, unpolluted, untainted, wholesome
***ant*** clean, cleanly, immaculate, spick-and-span (*or* spic-and-span), spotless, stainless, unsoiled, unstained, unsullied
**2** depicting or referring to sexual matters in a way that is unacceptable in polite society — see OBSCENE 1
**3** marked by wet and windy conditions — see FOUL 1
**4** not being in accordance with the rules or standards of what is fair in sport — see FOUL 2
**5** not following or in accordance with standards of honor and decency — see IGNOBLE 2

**dirty** *vb* to make dirty ⟨she *dirtied* her new shoes when she splashed in the puddle⟩
***syn*** befoul, begrime, besmirch, blacken, foul, grime, mire, muddy, smirch, smudge, soil, stain, sully
***rel*** contaminate, defile, pollute, taint; discolor; confuse, disarrange, disarray, dishevel, disorder, jumble, mess, muddle
***near ant*** decontaminate, purge, purify; disinfect, sanitize; brush, dry-clean, dust, launder, mop, rinse, scour, scrub, sweep, wash, wipe; brighten, deodorize, freshen, renew, spruce (up); straighten (up), tidy (up)
***ant*** clean, cleanse

**dis** *vb, slang* **1** to cause hurt feelings or deep resentment in — see INSULT
**2** to express one's unfavorable opinion of the worth or quality of — see CRITICIZE

**disable** *vb* **1** to cause severe or permanent injury to — see MAIM
**2** to render powerless, ineffective, or unable to move — see PARALYZE

**disabled** *adj* deprived of the power to perform one or more natural bodily activities ⟨the *disabled* man was unable to climb the stairs without help⟩
***syn*** challenged, incapacitated
***rel*** blind, deaf, mute; halt, lame, paralyzed, quadriplegic; immobile, immobilized; ailing, diseased, ill, sick, unfit, unhealthy, unsound, unwell
***near ant*** bouncing, chipper, fit, hale, healthy, hearty, robust, sound, well, whole, wholesome
***ant*** able-bodied, nondisabled

**disabuse** *vb* to free from mistaken beliefs or foolish hopes — see DISILLUSION

**disadvantage** *n* a feature of someone or something that creates difficulty for achieving success ⟨their lack of height was a *disadvantage* on the basketball court⟩
***syn*** drawback, handicap, liability, minus, penalty, strike
***rel*** stranglehold; detriment, disability, impairment; failing, shortcoming; bar, catch, check, clog, crimp, embarrassment, hindrance, hitch, hurdle, impediment, interference, let, manacle, obstacle, obstruction, rub, shackle, stop, trammel
***near ant*** vantage; head start, jump, lead, margin, start; ascendancy, better, command, control, drop, mastery, predominance, superiority, supremacy, transcendence, upper hand; prerogative, privilege; break, opportunity; aid, assistance, help
***ant*** advantage, asset, edge, plus

**disadvantaged** *adj* kept from having the necessities of life or a healthful environment — see DEPRIVED

**disadvantageous** *adj* opposed to one's interests — see ADVERSE 1

**disaffect** *vb* **1** to cause to change from friendly or loving to unfriendly or uncaring — see ESTRANGE
**2** to make discontented — see DISCONTENT

**disaffection** *n* the loss of friendship or affection — see ESTRANGEMENT

**disagree** *vb* **1** to have a different opinion ⟨she thought we were still headed north on the trail, but I *disagreed*⟩
***syn*** differ, dissent
***rel*** clash, collide, conflict, contrast; counter, debate, object, oppose, protest, resist; contest, dispute; argue, bicker, fall out, quarrel
***near ant*** accede, accept, acquiesce, comply, consent, subscribe; affiliate, ally, associate, collaborate, collude, compromise, cooperate, get along, side
***ant*** agree, assent, concur
**2** to be unlike; to not be the same — see DIFFER 1

**disagree** (with) *vb* to make an assertion that is contrary to one made by (another) — see CONTRADICT 1

***syn*** synonym(s) ***rel*** related words
***ant*** antonym(s) ***near ant*** near antonym(s)

**disagreeable** *adj* **1** having or showing a habitually bad temper — see ILL-TEMPERED
**2** not giving pleasure to the mind or senses — see UNPLEASANT

**disagreeing** *adj* not being in agreement or harmony — see INCONSISTENT

**disagreement** *n* **1** variance of opinion on a matter ⟨there was some *disagreement* about what the color of the missing sweater actually was⟩
***syn*** controversy, debate, difference, disputation, dispute, dissension
***rel*** clash, collision, conflict, contention, discord, strife; discussion; altercation, argument, bicker, falling-out, fight, quarrel
***near ant*** acceptance, compliance; concord, peace
***ant*** accord, agreement, consensus, harmony, unanimity
**2** an often noisy or angry expression of differing opinions — see ARGUMENT 1
**3** the quality or state of being different — see DIFFERENCE 1

**disallow** *vb* **1** to declare not to be true — see DENY 1
**2** to be unwilling to grant — see DENY 2

**disallowance** *n* **1** an unwillingness to grant something asked for — see DENIAL 1
**2** a refusal to confirm the truth of a statement — see DENIAL 2

**disappear** *vb* to cease to be visible ⟨the stranger *disappeared* into the mists, never to be seen again⟩
***syn*** dissolve, evanesce, evaporate, fade, flee, go (away), melt, vanish
***rel*** clear, dissipate
***near ant*** arrive, break out, come out, emerge, issue, loom, show up
***ant*** appear, materialize

**disappoint** *vb* to fall short in satisfying the expectation or hope of ⟨they were *disappointed* by the outcome of the big game⟩
***syn*** cheat, dissatisfy, fail, let down
***rel*** discontent, disgruntle, displease; disenchant, disillusion
***near ant*** gladden
***ant*** satisfy

**disappointment** *n* **1** the emotion felt when one's expectations are not met ⟨we felt *disappointment* after failing a test that we thought would be easy⟩
***syn*** dismay, dissatisfaction, frustration, letdown
***rel*** disenchantment, disillusionment; blues, dejection, depression, desolateness, desolation, despondency, disconsolateness, distress, doldrums, dolefulness, dolor, downheartedness, dreariness, dumps, gloom, gloominess, joylessness, melancholy, mopes, oppression, sadness, sorrow, unhappiness; alarm, concern, consternation; chagrin, discomfiture
***near ant*** bliss, felicity, gladness, happiness, joy
***ant*** contentment, gratification, satisfaction
**2** something that disappoints ⟨after all the publicity and high expectations, the se-

quel to the movie blockbuster was a *disappointment*⟩
***syn*** bummer, letdown
***rel*** anticlimax, failure, fiasco, fizzle; lemon, loser
***near ant*** success, winner; relief

**disapprobation** *n* refusal to accept as right or desirable — see DISAPPROVAL

**disapproval** *n* refusal to accept as right or desirable ⟨thus far, every one of her boyfriends has met with her parents' *disapproval*⟩
***syn*** deprecation, disapprobation, disfavor, dislike, displeasure
***rel*** blame, censure, criticism, condemnation, denunciation, dressing down, opprobrium, reproach, reprobation; antagonism, antipathy, hostility; belittlement, disparagement, opposition
***near ant*** acclaim, commendation, praise; endorsement, sanction; empathy, sympathy
***ant*** approbation, approval, favor

**disapprove** *vb* to show unwillingness to accept, do, engage in, or agree to — see DECLINE 1

**disapprove** (of) *vb* to hold an unfavorable opinion of ⟨my sister *disapproves of* smoking and refuses to date anyone who thinks it's cool⟩
***syn*** deprecate, discountenance, disfavor, dislike, frown (on), reprove
***rel*** blame, censure, condemn, criticize, denounce, reprehend, reprobate; chide, rebuke, reproach, scold
***near ant*** endorse (*also* indorse), sanction, support; adore, delight (in), dig, enjoy, fancy, groove (on), love, relish, revel (in)
***ant*** approve, favor, like

**disarm** *vb* **1** to reduce the size and strength of the armed forces of ⟨the defeated nation was *disarmed* so that it would never again be a threat to international order⟩
***syn*** demilitarize
***rel*** demobilize
***near ant*** equip, mobilize
***ant*** arm, militarize
**2** to lessen the anger or agitation of — see PACIFY

**disarmament** *n* the reduction or elimination of a country's armed forces or weapons ⟨the ambassador spoke at length about the possible unilateral *disarmament* of his country⟩
***syn*** demilitarization
***rel*** demobilization
***near ant*** mobilization
***ant*** militarization

**disarming** *adj* **1** having qualities that tend to make one loved — see LOVABLE
**2** likely to win one's affection — see INGRATIATING
**3** tending to lessen or avoid conflict or hostility — see PACIFIC 1

**disarrange** *vb* to undo the proper order or arrangement of — see DISORDER

**disarranged** *adj* lacking in order, neatness, and often cleanliness — see MESSY

**disarrangement** *n* a state in which everything is out of order — see CHAOS

**disarray** *n* a state in which everything is out of order — see CHAOS

**disarray** *vb* to undo the proper order or arrangement of — see DISORDER

**disarrayed** *adj* lacking in order, neatness, and often cleanliness — see MESSY

**disassemble** *vb* to take apart ⟨they had to *disassemble* the television set in order to replace the wiring⟩
***syn*** demount, dismantle, dismember, knock down, strike, take down
***rel*** detach, disengage; disconnect, disjoin, disunite, divide, separate
***near ant*** build, erect; combine, unite
***ant*** assemble, construct, put together

**disaster** *n* a sudden violent event that brings about great loss or destruction ⟨hurricanes are natural *disasters*⟩
***syn*** calamity, cataclysm, catastrophe, debacle (*also* débâcle), tragedy
***rel*** collapse, crash, meltdown; convulsion, paroxysm, upheaval; accident, casualty, fatality; misadventure, mischance, misfortune, mishap, woe; bummer, downer
***near ant*** godsend, manna, windfall

**disastrous** *adj* **1** bringing about ruin or misfortune — see FATAL 1
**2** causing or tending to cause destruction — see DESTRUCTIVE 1

**disavow** *vb* **1** to declare not to be true — see DENY 1
**2** to refuse to acknowledge as one's own or as one's responsibility — see DISCLAIM 1

**disavowal** *n* a refusal to confirm the truth of a statement — see DENIAL 2

**disband** *vb* **1** to cease to exist or cause to cease to exist as a group or organization ⟨they *disbanded* the committee after the report had been submitted⟩ ⟨the rock group *disbanded* upon finishing the tour⟩
***syn*** break up, disperse, dissolve
***near ant*** incorporate; consolidate
***ant*** band, join, unite
**2** to cause (members of a group) to move widely apart — see SCATTER 1

**disbandment** *n* an act or process in which something scatters or is scattered — see SCATTERING 1

**disbelief** *n* refusal to accept as true ⟨their story explaining their absence was met with frank *disbelief*⟩
***syn*** incredulity, unbelief
***rel*** distrust, doubt, mistrust, skepticism, suspicion, uncertainty; denial, rejection, repudiation
***near ant*** acceptance, faith; trust
***ant*** belief, credence, credit

**disbelieve** *vb* to think not to be true or real ⟨many *disbelieved* the medium's claims that she could communicate with the spirits of the dead⟩
***syn*** discredit, negate
***rel*** deny, reject, repudiate; distrust, doubt, mistrust, suspect; debunk, disprove; deride, pooh-pooh, scoff (at)
***near ant*** trust
***ant*** accept, believe, credit, swallow

**disbeliever** *n* a person who is always ready to doubt or question the truth or existence of something — see SKEPTIC
**disbelieving** *adj* inclined to doubt or question claims — see SKEPTICAL 1
**disburden** *vb* 1 to empty or rid of cargo — see UNLOAD 1
2 to set (a person or thing) free of something that encumbers — see RID
**disburse** *vb* to hand over or use up in payment — see SPEND 1
**disbursement** *n* 1 a payment made in the course of achieving a result — see EXPENSE
2 the act of offering money in exchange for goods or services — see PAYMENT 1
**discard** *n* something separated from a group or lot for not being as good as the others — see CULL
**discard** *vb* to get rid of as useless or unwanted ⟨*discard* an old, torn sweater⟩
*syn* cast, ditch, dump, fling (off *or* away), jettison, junk, lose, reject, scrap, shed, shuck (off), slough (*also* sluff), throw away, throw out, unload
*rel* abandon, desert, forsake; dismiss; abolish, annihilate, eliminate, eradicate, expunge, exterminate, extinguish, extirpate, liquidate, remove, root (out), stamp (out), wipe out
*phrases* dispose of, set aside
*near ant* adopt, embrace, take on; employ, use, utilize; hold, hold back, keep, retain
**discarding** *n* the getting rid of whatever is unwanted or useless — see DISPOSAL 1
**discern** *vb* 1 to make note of (something) through the use of one's eyes — see SEE 1
2 to understand or point out the difference — see DISTINGUISH 1
**discernible** *adj* able to be perceived by a sense or by the mind — see PERCEPTIBLE
**discerning** *adj* having or showing deep understanding and intelligent application of knowledge — see WISE 1
**discernment** *n* the ability to understand inner qualities or relationships — see WISDOM 1
**discharge** *n* 1 a directed propelling of a missile by a firearm or artillery piece — see SHOT
2 a freeing from an obligation or responsibility — see RELEASE 1
3 the termination of the employment of an employee or a work force often temporarily — see LAYOFF
4 the doing of an action — see COMMISSION 2
**discharge** *vb* 1 to cause (a projectile) to be driven forward with force — see SHOOT 1
2 to empty or rid of cargo — see UNLOAD 1
3 to give what is owed for — see PAY 2
4 to set free (as from slavery or confinement) — see FREE 1
5 to throw or give off — see EMIT 1
6 to cause a weapon to release a missile with great force — see SHOOT 2
**disciple** *n* one who follows the opinions or teachings of another — see FOLLOWER
**disciplinary** *adj* inflicting, involving, or serving as punishment — see PUNITIVE
**discipline** *n* 1 a region of activity, knowledge, or influence — see FIELD 2
2 suffering, loss, or hardship imposed in response to a crime or offense — see PUNISHMENT
**discipline** *vb* to inflict a penalty on for a fault or crime — see PUNISH
**disciplining** *adj* inflicting, involving, or serving as punishment — see PUNITIVE
**disclaim** *vb* 1 to refuse to acknowledge as one's own or as one's responsibility ⟨the prisoner *disclaimed* any part in the prank⟩
*syn* disavow, disown, repudiate
*rel* contradict, deny, disallow, gainsay, negate, negative, refuse, reject; challenge, confute, criticize, disprove, rebut, refute; dispute, question
*near ant* accept, adopt, embrace, espouse; admit, concede, confess, grant; affirm, announce, assert, aver, declare, maintain, profess, submit; authenticate, confirm, corroborate, substantiate, validate, verify
*ant* acknowledge, avow, claim, own, recognize
2 to declare not to be true — see DENY 1
**disclaimer** *n* a refusal to confirm the truth of a statement — see DENIAL 2
**disclose** *vb* to make known (as information previously kept secret) — see REVEAL 1
**disclosure** *n* the act or an instance of making known something previously unknown or concealed — see REVELATION
**disco** *n* a bar or restaurant offering special nighttime entertainment (as music, dancing, or comedy acts) — see NIGHTCLUB
**discomfit** *vb* to throw into a state of self-conscious distress — see EMBARRASS 1
**discomfiting** *adj* causing embarrassment — see AWKWARD 3
**discomfiture** *n* the emotional state of being made self-consciously uncomfortable — see EMBARRASSMENT 1
**discomfort** *vb* to trouble the mind of; to make uneasy — see DISTURB 1
**discomforting** *adj* 1 causing discomfort — see UNCOMFORTABLE 1
2 causing worry or anxiety — see TROUBLESOME
**discommode** *vb* to cause discomfort to or trouble for — see INCONVENIENCE
**discommoding** *adj* causing difficulty, discomfort, or annoyance — see INCONVENIENT 1
**discompose** *vb* 1 to trouble the mind of; to make uneasy — see DISTURB 1
2 to undo the proper order or arrangement of — see DISORDER
**discomposing** *adj* causing worry or anxiety — see TROUBLESOME
**disconcert** *vb* to throw into a state of self-conscious distress — see EMBARRASS 1

*syn* synonym(s) *rel* related words
*ant* antonym(s) *near ant* near antonym(s)

**disconcerting** *adj* causing embarrassment — see AWKWARD 3

**disconnect** *vb* to set or force apart — see SEPARATE 1

**disconnected** *adj* **1** not clearly or logically connected — see INCOHERENT 1
**2** not physically attached to another unit — see SEPARATE 2

**disconsolate** *adj* feeling unhappiness — see SAD 1

**disconsolateness** *n* a state or spell of low spirits — see SADNESS

**discontent** *adj* having a feeling that one has been wronged or thwarted in one's ambitions — see DISCONTENTED

**discontent** *n* the condition of being dissatisfied with one's life or situation ⟨the rebels tried to stir up *discontent* among the citizens⟩
***syn*** discontentedness, discontentment, disgruntlement, displeasure, dissatisfaction
***rel*** bitterness, resentment; disquiet, perturbation, uneasiness; blues, dejection, depression, desolateness, desolation, despondency, disconsolateness, doldrums, dolefulness, dolor, downheartedness, dreariness, dumps; misery, sadness, sorrow, unhappiness, wretchedness
***near ant*** bliss, felicity, gladness, happiness, joy, lightheartedness; elatedness, exultation, jubilation, triumph
***ant*** contentedness, contentment, pleasure, satisfaction

**discontent** *vb* to make discontented ⟨the ongoing lack of decent food *discontented* and demoralized the soldiers in the rebel army⟩
***syn*** disaffect, disgruntle, displease, dissatisfy
***rel*** alienate, estrange; agitate, discompose, disquiet, disturb, perturb, upset; annoy, irk, irritate, nettle, peeve; depress, sadden
***near ant*** delight, gladden, tickle; calm, soothe, tranquilize (*also* tranquillize)
***ant*** content, gratify, please, satisfy

**discontented** *adj* having a feeling that one has been wronged or thwarted in one's ambitions ⟨he was *discontented* with his small role in the school play⟩
***syn*** aggrieved, discontent, disgruntled, displeased, dissatisfied, malcontent
***rel*** disappointed, frustrated, unfulfilled; disquieted, disturbed, perturbed, upset; dejected, depressed, despairing, despondent, disconsolate, doleful, down, downcast, downhearted, forlorn, hangdog, inconsolable, joyless, low-spirited, miserable, mournful, sad, sorrowful, unhappy
***near ant*** blissful, delighted, glad, happy, joyful, joyous; elated, exultant, jubilant, triumphant
***ant*** content, contented, gratified, pleased, satisfied

**discontentedness** *n* the condition of being dissatisfied with one's life or situation — see DISCONTENT

**discontentment** *n* the condition of being dissatisfied with one's life or situation — see DISCONTENT

**discontinuance** *n* the stopping of a process or activity — see END 1

**discontinue** *vb* **1** to bring (as an action or operation) to an immediate end — see STOP 1
**2** to stop doing (something) permanently — see QUIT 2
**3** to come to an end — see CEASE 1

**discontinuity** *n* **1** an open space in a barrier (as a wall or hedge) — see GAP 1
**2** a break in continuity — see GAP 2

**discontinuous** *adj* lacking in steadiness or regularity of occurrence — see FITFUL

**discord** *n* a lack of agreement or harmony ⟨the *discord* between the two scout leaders threatened to tear our troop apart⟩
***syn*** conflict, discordance, dissension, dissent, dissidence, disunity, friction, schism, strife, variance, war, warfare
***rel*** clash, collision, competition, contention; altercation, argument, bicker, brawl, debate, disagreement, dispute, falling-out, fight, hassle, jar, quarrel, row, run-in, scrap, spat, squabble, tiff, wrangle; incompatibility, incongruity, inconsistency, inconsonance; animosity, antagonism, antipathy, enmity, hostility, ill will, rancor
***near ant*** concurrence, cooperation
***ant*** accord, agreement, concord, concordance, harmony, peace

**discordance** *n* **1** a lack of agreement or harmony — see DISCORD
**2** loud, confused, and usually unharmonious sound — see NOISE 1

**discordant** *adj* **1** marked by or producing a harsh combination of sounds — see DISSONANT
**2** making loud, confused, and usually unharmonious sounds — see NOISY 1
**3** feeling or displaying eagerness to fight — see BELLIGERENT
**4** not being in agreement or harmony — see INCONSISTENT

**discotheque** *n* a bar or restaurant offering special nighttime entertainment (as music, dancing, or comedy acts) — see NIGHTCLUB

**discount** *n* something that is or may be subtracted — see DEDUCTION 1

**discount** *vb* to express scornfully one's low opinion of — see DECRY 1

**discountenance** *vb* **1** to hold an unfavorable opinion of — see DISAPPROVE
**2** to throw into a state of self-conscious distress — see EMBARRASS 1

**discourage** *vb* **1** to lessen the courage or confidence of ⟨I didn't let losing *discourage* me from trying again⟩
***syn*** daunt, demoralize, dishearten, dismay, dispirit, unman, unnerve
***rel*** browbeat, bully, cow, intimidate; depress, sadden, weigh; afflict, try; damp, dampen, deaden; distress, trouble; bother, irk, vex, worry; debilitate, enfeeble, undermine, weaken; frighten, horrify, scare

***near ant*** buoy (up), cheer, gladden; animate, enliven, invigorate; fortify, reinforce, strengthen; assure, reassure; boost, energize, excite, galvanize, inspire, lift, provoke, quicken, rally, stimulate, stir
***ant*** embolden, encourage, hearten, nerve, steel
**2** to steer (a person) from an activity or course of action ⟨the higher fines may help *discourage* drivers from speeding on the highway⟩
***syn*** deter, dissuade, inhibit
***rel*** divert
***near ant*** egg (on), exhort, goad, prod, urge; impel, induce, prompt
***ant*** encourage, persuade

**discouragement** *n* the state of being discouraged ⟨we tried to avoid *discouragement* after failing the test twice⟩
***syn*** demoralization, despair, despondency, disheartenment, dismay, dispiritedness
***rel*** blues, dejection, depression, dumps, gloom, melancholy, mopes; defeatism, pessimism, resignation
***near ant*** optimism, sanguinity
***ant*** encouragement

**discourse** *n* **1** an exchange of views for the purpose of exploring a subject or deciding an issue — see DISCUSSION 1
**2** talking or a talk between two or more people — see CONVERSATION

**discourse** *vb* **1** to give a formal often extended talk on a subject — see TALK 1
**2** to talk as if giving an important and formal speech — see ORATE 1

**discourteous** *adj* showing a lack of manners or consideration for others — see IMPOLITE

**discourteousness** *n* rude behavior — see DISCOURTESY

**discourtesy** *n* rude behavior ⟨the courtiers shuddered at the *discourtesy* shown to the king⟩
***syn*** discourteousness, disrespect, impertinence, impoliteness, impudence, incivility, inconsideration, insolence, rudeness, ungraciousness
***rel*** audacity, boldness, brashness, brassiness, sauciness, shamelessness; boorishness, churlishness, clownishness, crudeness, loutishness, vulgarity; abruptness, bluntness, brusqueness, crustiness, curtness, gruffness, sharpness; crabbedness, crossness, disagreeableness, grumpiness, sullenness, surliness; impropriety, inappropriateness, incorrectness, indecency, unfitness, unsuitability; arrogance, conceit, conceitedness, presumption, pretense (*or* pretence), pretension, pretentiousness
***near ant*** humility, meekness, modesty; deference, dutifulness, respectfulness, submissiveness; acceptability, appropriateness, correctness, decency, decorousness, fitness, goodness, propriety, respectability, respectableness, rightness, seemliness, suitability, suitableness; affability, cordiality, friendliness, geniality, hospitality; felicitousness, grace, gracefulness
***ant*** civility, considerateness, consideration, courtesy, genteelness, gentility, graciousness, politeness, thoughtfulness

**discover** *vb* **1** to come to an awareness ⟨I was startled to *discover* that my keys were missing⟩
***syn*** ascertain, catch on, find out, hear, learn, realize, see
***rel*** hit (on *or* upon), tumble (to); descry, detect, encounter, espy, spot; dope (out), figure out, puzzle (out); discern, note, observe, perceive; divine
***near ant*** miss, overlook; disregard, ignore; forget, unlearn; blanket, blot out, cloak, conceal, cover, curtain, enshroud, hide, mask, occult, screen, shroud, veil
**2** to come upon after searching, study, or effort — see FIND 1
**3** to make known (as information previously kept secret) — see REVEAL 1

**discovery** *n* **1** the act or process of sighting or learning the existence of something for the first time ⟨the *discovery* of a new species of starfish⟩
***syn*** detection, finding, spotting, unearthing
***rel*** disclosure, exposure, revelation, uncovering, unveiling; creation, invention; exploration; rediscovery
***near ant*** concealment, hiding
**2** something discovered ⟨his many zoological *discoveries* included several species of birds⟩
***syn*** find
***rel*** pay dirt, strike, treasure trove; breakthrough

**discredit** *n* the state of having lost the esteem of others — see DISGRACE 1

**discredit** *vb* **1** to reduce to a lower standing in one's own eyes or in others' eyes — see HUMBLE
**2** to think not to be true or real — see DISBELIEVE

**discreditable** *adj* not respectable — see DISREPUTABLE

**discreet** *adj* having or showing good judgment and restraint especially in conduct or speech ⟨he was very *discreet*, only saying what was necessary⟩
***syn*** judicious, prudent
***rel*** cautious, chary, circumspect; foresighted, forethoughtful; discerning, discrim-inating, sage, sane, sapient, sensible, wise; canny, provident; astute, perspicacious, sagacious, shrewd
***near ant*** careless, heedless; improvident, shortsighted; foolish, unwise
***ant*** imprudent, indiscreet, injudicious

**discreetness** *n* the ability to make intelligent decisions especially in everyday matters — see COMMON SENSE

**discrepancy** *n* the quality or state of being different — see DIFFERENCE 1

**discrepant** *adj* not being in agreement or harmony — see INCONSISTENT

---

***syn*** synonym(s) ***rel*** related words
***ant*** antonym(s) ***near ant*** near antonym(s)

**discrete** *adj* not physically attached to another unit — see SEPARATE 2

**discreteness** *n* the state of being kept distinct — see SEPARATION 2

**discretion** *n* **1** the ability to make intelligent decisions especially in everyday matters — see COMMON SENSE
**2** the power, right, or opportunity to choose — see CHOICE 1

**discretionary** *adj* subject to one's freedom of choice — see OPTIONAL

**discriminate** *vb* to understand or point out the difference — see DISTINGUISH 1

**discriminating** *adj* favoring, applying, or being unequal treatment of different classes of people — see DISCRIMINATORY

**discrimination** *n* the state of being kept distinct — see SEPARATION 2

**discriminational** *adj* favoring, applying, or being unequal treatment of different classes of people — see DISCRIMINATORY

**discriminative** *adj* favoring, applying, or being unequal treatment of different classes of people — see DISCRIMINATORY

**discriminatory** *adj* favoring, applying, or being unequal treatment of different classes of people ⟨a company that was fined for its *discriminatory* practices in the hiring of women⟩
***syn*** differential, discriminating, discriminational, discriminative
***rel*** biased, inequitable, partial, partisan, prejudiced, prejudicial, unequal, unfair, unjust
***near ant*** equal, equitable, fair, just; impartial, neutral, objective, unbiased, uncolored, unprejudiced
***ant*** nondiscriminatory

**discursive** *adj* passing from one topic to another ⟨the speaker's *discursive* style made it difficult to understand his point⟩
***syn*** desultory, digressive, leaping, maundering, rambling
***rel*** circuitous, deviating, devious, roundabout
***near ant*** focused (*also* focussed)

**discuss** *vb* to talk about (an issue) usually from various points of view and for the purpose of arriving at a decision or opinion ⟨we *discussed* the new proposal for the school stadium⟩
***syn*** argue, bandy, chew over, debate, dispute, hash (over), moot, talk over
***rel*** descant (on), lecture (on *or* about), speak (about), talk (about); broach, introduce; forge, hammer (out), thrash (out); consider, deliberate, weigh; reason (with)

**discussion** *n* **1** an exchange of views for the purpose of exploring a subject or deciding an issue ⟨the *discussion* about the club budget went on for hours⟩
***syn*** argument, colloquy, conference, deliberation, discourse, give-and-take, parley, talk
***rel*** debate, dialogue (*also* dialog); forum, meeting, powwow, roundtable, seminar, symposium; chat, conversation, rap
**2** talking or a talk between two or more people — see CONVERSATION

**disdain** *n* open dislike for someone or something considered unworthy of one's concern or respect — see CONTEMPT

**disdain** *vb* to show contempt for — see SCORN 1

**disdainful** *adj* **1** feeling or showing open dislike for someone or something regarded as undeserving of respect or concern — see CONTEMPTUOUS 1
**2** having or displaying feelings of scorn for what is regarded as beneath oneself — see PROUD 1
**3** intended to make a person or thing seem of little importance or value — see DEROGATORY

**disease** *n* an abnormal state that disrupts a plant's or animal's normal bodily functioning ⟨they caught a rare *disease* while they were traveling in Africa and were sick for weeks⟩
***syn*** affection, ailment, bug, complaint, complication, condition, disorder, fever, ill, illness, infirmity, malady, sickness, trouble
***rel*** contagion, contagious disease; infection, infectious disease; deficiency disease; attack, bout, fit, spell; debility, decrepitude, feebleness, frailness, lameness, weakness; malaise, matter; pest, pestilence, plague
***near ant*** fitness, healthiness, heartiness, robustness, soundness, wholeness, wholesomeness
***ant*** health, wellness

**disembark** *vb* to go ashore from a ship ⟨the cruise passengers *disembarked* as soon as they got to the terminal in Miami⟩
***syn*** debark, land
***rel*** beach; anchor, dock, put in
***near ant*** board, get (on); weigh (anchor)
***ant*** embark

**disembowel** *vb* to take the internal organs out of — see GUT

**disenchant** *vb* to free from mistaken beliefs or foolish hopes — see DISILLUSION

**disencumber** *vb* **1** to empty or rid of cargo — see UNLOAD 1
**2** to set (a person or thing) free of something that encumbers — see RID

**disencumbered** *adj* no longer burdened with something unpleasant or painful — see FREE 2

**disengage** *vb* to set free from entanglement or difficulty — see EXTRICATE

**disentangle** *vb* **1** to separate the various strands of — see UNRAVEL 1
**2** to set free from entanglement or difficulty — see EXTRICATE

**disfavor** *n* **1** a strong feeling of not liking or approving — see DISLIKE 1
**2** refusal to accept as right or desirable — see DISAPPROVAL

**disfavor** *vb* **1** to feel dislike for — see DISLIKE 1
**2** to hold an unfavorable opinion of — see DISAPPROVE

**disfigure** *vb* to reduce the soundness, effectiveness, or perfection of — see DAMAGE 1

**disfigurement** *n* something that spoils the appearance or completeness of a thing — see BLEMISH

**disgorge** *vb* to throw out or off (something from within) often violently — see ERUPT 1

**disgrace** *n* **1** the state of having lost the esteem of others ⟨the players who threw the game were in *disgrace* with their schoolmates⟩
*syn* discredit, dishonor, disrepute, ignominy, infamy, odium, opprobrium, reproach, shame
*rel* contempt, disdain, scorn; deprecation, disapprobation, disapproval, disfavor; abasement, debasement, debasing, degradation, humbling, humiliation; blot, brand, slur, smirch, spot, stain, stigma
*near ant* admiration, regard; awe, fear, reverence; fame, glory, renown, repute
*ant* esteem, honor, respect
**2** a cause of shame ⟨the exposure of his criminal activities was a huge *disgrace* for the councilman⟩
*syn* crime, dishonor, reflection, reproach, scandal
*rel* brand, smirch, spot, stain, stigma
*ant* credit, honor
**3** a regrettable or blameworthy act — see CRIME 2

**disgrace** *vb* to reduce to a lower standing in one's own eyes or in others' eyes — see HUMBLE

**disgraceful** *adj* not respectable — see DISREPUTABLE

**disgruntle** *vb* **1** to cause to change from friendly or loving to unfriendly or uncaring — see ESTRANGE
**2** to make discontented — see DISCONTENT

**disgruntled** *adj* having a feeling that one has been wronged or thwarted in one's ambitions — see DISCONTENTED

**disgruntlement** *n* **1** the condition of being dissatisfied with one's life or situation — see DISCONTENT
**2** the loss of friendship or affection — see ESTRANGEMENT

**disguise** *n* clothing put on to hide one's true identity or imitate someone or something else ⟨Mardi Gras revelers dressed in a colorful array of outlandish *disguises*⟩
*syn* camouflage, costume, guise
*rel* domino, mask, veil, vizard; dress, getup, outfit, rig; coloring, cosmetic, makeup, paint

**disguise** *vb* to change the dress or looks of so as to conceal true identity ⟨the spies *disguised* themselves as harmless tourists⟩
*syn* camouflage, cloak, dress up, mask
*rel* blanket, blot out, conceal, cover, curtain, enshroud, hide, obscure, occult, screen, shroud, veil; affect, assume, counterfeit, dissemble, dissimulate, feign, pose, pretend, sham, simulate
*near ant* display, exhibit, expose, flaunt, parade, show, uncover, unmask; betray, disclose, discover, reveal

**disgust** *n* a dislike so strong as to cause stomach upset or queasiness ⟨we turned from the grisly scene with *disgust*⟩
*syn* aversion, distaste, loathing, nausea, repugnance, repulsion, revulsion
*rel* abhorrence, abomination, execration, hate, hatred; disapproval, disfavor, disinclination, dislike, disliking, displeasure
*near ant* appetite, bent, fondness, like, liking, partiality, penchant, predilection, preference, propensity, taste

**disgust** *vb* to cause to feel disgust ⟨the usual school lunch *disgusted* us, so we started bringing our lunches from home⟩
*syn* nauseate, repel, repulse, revolt, sicken, turn off
*rel* displease, distress; appall, horrify; affront, insult, offend, outrage, shock
*near ant* attract, charm, entice, tempt; delight, gratify, please, rejoice, tickle

**disgusted** *adj* filled with disgust — see SICK 2

**dish** *n* a usually circular utensil for holding something (as food) ⟨we threw all of the ingredients for the salsa into a *dish* and mixed them together⟩
*syn* vessel
*rel* bowl, casserole, charger, cup, plate, platter, salver, saucer, tray

**dishearten** *vb* to lessen the courage or confidence of — see DISCOURAGE 1

**disheartenment** *n* the state of being discouraged — see DISCOURAGEMENT

**dishevel** *vb* to undo the proper order or arrangement of — see DISORDER

**disheveled** *or* **dishevelled** *adj* lacking in order, neatness, and often cleanliness — see MESSY

**dishonest** *adj* **1** telling or containing lies ⟨*dishonest* kids who lie about their ages in order to get into R-rated movies⟩ ⟨*dishonest* statements about the fight in the locker room⟩
*syn* lying, mendacious, untruthful
*rel* erroneous, fallacious, false, misleading; double-dealing, hypocritical, two-faced
*near ant* candid, open, straightforward; earnest, sincere, true
*ant* honest, truthful, veracious
**2** given to or marked by cheating and deception ⟨*dishonest* car dealers who roll back mileage gauges⟩ ⟨*dishonest* business deals that landed him in jail⟩
*syn* crooked, deceptive, fast, fraudulent, shady, sharp, shifty, underhand, underhanded
*rel* unconscionable, unethical, unprincipled, unscrupulous; deceitful, deceiving, deluding, delusive, delusory; artful, cunning; devious, furtive, sneaking, sneaky, tricky; insidious, perfidious, treacherous
*near ant* conscientious, honorable, just, scrupulous, upright; forthright, straightforward
*ant* aboveboard, honest, straight

*syn* synonym(s) *rel* related words
*ant* antonym(s) *near ant* near antonym(s)

3 marked by, based on, or done by the use of dishonest methods to acquire something of value — see FRAUDULENT 1

**dishonesty** *n* 1 the tendency to tell lies ⟨if you gain a reputation for *dishonesty*, no one will believe you even when you're telling the truth⟩

***syn*** deceitfulness, mendacity, untruthfulness

***rel*** artifice, craft, craftiness, crookedness, cunning, deceit, dissembling, dissimulation, double-dealing, duplicity, fakery, foxiness, guile, wiliness; falseness; hypocrisy

***near ant*** honor, incorruptibility; candidness, candor, frankness, good faith, sincerity, straightforwardness; dependability, reliability, reliableness, trustworthiness; accuracy, objectivity; authenticity, correctness, genuineness; credibility

***ant*** honesty, integrity, probity, truthfulness, veracity, verity

2 the inclination or practice of misleading others through lies or trickery — see DECEIT

**dishonor** *n* 1 the state of having lost the esteem of others — see DISGRACE 1

2 a cause of shame — see DISGRACE 2

**dishonor** *vb* to reduce to a lower standing in one's own eyes or in others' eyes — see HUMBLE

**dishonorable** *adj* 1 not following or in accordance with standards of honor and decency — see IGNOBLE 2

2 not respectable — see DISREPUTABLE

**disillusion** *vb* to free from mistaken beliefs or foolish hopes ⟨we were *disillusioned* when we saw how the movie star acted in real life⟩

***syn*** disabuse, disenchant, undeceive

***rel*** debunk, expose, show up, uncloak, uncover, unmask; disclose, divulge, tell, unveil

***near ant*** beguile, bluff, cozen, delude, dupe, fool, gull, hoax, hoodwink, kid, misguide, misinform, mislead, misrepresent, snow, take in, trick

**disinclination** *n* 1 a lack of willingness or desire to do or accept something — see RELUCTANCE

2 a strong feeling of not liking or approving — see DISLIKE 1

**disinclined** *adj* having doubts about the wisdom of doing something — see HESITANT

**disintegrate** *vb* to go through decomposition — see DECAY 1

**disinter** *vb* to remove from place of burial — see EXHUME

**disinterested** *adj* 1 having or showing a lack of interest or concern — see INDIFFERENT 1

2 marked by justice, honesty, and freedom from bias — see FAIR 2

**disinterestedness** *n* 1 lack of favoritism toward one side or another — see DETACHMENT 1

2 lack of interest or concern — see INDIFFERENCE

**disjoin** *vb* to set or force apart — see SEPARATE 1

**disjoint** *vb* to set or force apart — see SEPARATE 1

**disjointed** *adj* not clearly or logically connected — see INCOHERENT 1

**dislike** *n* 1 a strong feeling of not liking or approving ⟨we have a strong *dislike* for olives and wouldn't eat them even if we were paid⟩

***syn*** allergy, averseness, aversion, disfavor, disinclination, disliking

***rel*** disgust, distaste, loathing, nausea, repugnance, repulsion, revulsion; abomination, antipathy, detestation, hate, hatred; deprecation, disapproval, displeasure, dissatisfaction; jaundice

***near ant*** affection, attachment, love; bent, leaning, penchant, predilection, propensity, tendency

***ant*** appetite, fondness, like, liking, partiality, preference, taste

2 refusal to accept as right or desirable — see DISAPPROVAL

**dislike** *vb* 1 to feel dislike for ⟨the two dogs *disliked* each other the first time they met, and never did become friends⟩

***syn*** disfavor

***rel*** abhor, abominate, detest, hate, loathe; condemn, despise, scorn; disapprove (of), frown (on *or* upon), object (to)

***near ant*** admire, appreciate, cherish, revere, venerate, worship; prize, treasure, value; drink (in), savor; dote (on), idolize; favor, prefer

***ant*** adore, cotton (to), delight (in), dig, enjoy, fancy, groove (on), like, love, relish, revel (in)

2 to hold an unfavorable opinion of — see DISAPPROVE

**disliking** *n* a strong feeling of not liking or approving — see DISLIKE 1

**dislocate** *vb* 1 to change the place or position of — see MOVE 1

2 to undo the proper order or arrangement of — see DISORDER

**dislocation** *n* an act or instance of the order of things being disturbed — see UPSET

**disloyal** *adj* not true in one's allegiance to someone or something — see FAITHLESS

**disloyalty** *n* 1 lack of faithfulness especially to one's husband or wife — see INFIDELITY 1

2 the act or fact of violating the trust or confidence of another — see BETRAYAL

**dismal** *adj* 1 causing or marked by an atmosphere lacking in cheer — see GLOOMY 1

2 causing unhappiness — see SAD 2

**dismantle** *vb* to take apart — see DISASSEMBLE

**dismay** *n* 1 the emotion felt when one's expectations are not met — see DISAPPOINTMENT 1

2 the state of being discouraged — see DISCOURAGEMENT

**dismay** *vb* to lessen the courage or confidence of — see DISCOURAGE 1

**dismember** *vb* to take apart — see DISASSEMBLE

**dismiss** *vb* **1** to let go from office, service, or employment ⟨the secretary was *dismissed* after it was discovered that she was stealing office supplies⟩
***syn*** can, cashier, fire, muster out, remove, retire, sack
***rel*** downsize, furlough, lay off; boot (out), bounce
***near ant*** contract, subcontract
***ant*** employ, hire
**2** to drive or force out — see EJECT 1

**dismissal** *n* the termination of the employment of an employee or a work force often temporarily — see LAYOFF

**disobedience** *n* refusal to obey ⟨they gave up on training the dog to fetch because of his constant *disobedience*⟩
***syn*** contrariness, defiance, frowardness, insubordination, intractability, rebelliousness, recalcitrance, refractoriness, unruliness, willfulness
***rel*** disrespect, impudence, insolence, rudeness; doggedness, hardheadedness, mulishness, obstinacy, pertinaciousness, pertinacity, perversity, stubbornness; mischievousness, naughtiness
***near ant*** agreeability, amiability; slavishness, submissiveness, subservience
***ant*** amenability, compliance, docility, obedience

**disobedient** *adj* given to resisting authority or another's control ⟨the *disobedient* child refused to eat his vegetables⟩
***syn*** balky, contrary, defiant, froward, insubordinate, intractable, rebellious, recalcitrant, refractory, restive, ungovernable, unruly, untoward, wayward, willful (*or* wilful)
***rel*** insurgent, mutinous; dogged, hardheaded, headstrong, mulish, obdurate, obstinate, peevish, pertinacious, pigheaded, self-willed, stubborn, unyielding; obstreperous, uncontrollable, unmanageable, wild; perverse, resistant, wrongheaded; bad, disorderly, errant, misbehaving, mischievous, monkeying, monkeyish, naughty; undisciplined; dissident, nonconformist; disrespectful, ill-mannered, ill-natured, impolite, impudent, insolent, ornery, rude, uncouth
***near ant*** acquiescent, agreeable, amiable, deferential, obliging; submissive, yielding; behaved, disciplined, well-bred; courteous, polite, respectful; servile, slavish, subservient; decorous, orderly, proper; controllable, governable, manageable
***ant*** amenable, compliant, docile, obedient, tractable

**disobey** *vb* to go against the commands, prohibitions, or rules of ⟨students who *disobey* their teachers and use cell phones in class⟩ ⟨drivers who consistently *disobey* traffic laws⟩
***syn*** defy, rebel (against)
***rel*** mutiny (against), revolt (against); disregard, ignore, tune out; dismiss, flout, pooh-pooh, reject, scoff (at), scorn, shrug off; break, transgress, violate; combat, contest, dispute, fight, oppose, resist, withstand
***near ant*** defer (to), serve, submit (to), surrender (to), yield (to); keep, observe; accede (to), acquiesce (to), agree (to), assent (to), comply (with), conform (to), oblige; attend, hear, heed, listen (to), mark, note, notice, regard, watch
***ant*** follow, mind, obey

**disoblige** *vb* to cause discomfort to or trouble for — see INCONVENIENCE

**disobliging** *adj* causing difficulty, discomfort, or annoyance — see INCONVENIENT 1

**disorder** *n* **1** a state in which everything is out of order — see CHAOS
**2** an abnormal state that disrupts a plant's or animal's normal bodily functioning — see DISEASE

**disorder** *vb* to undo the proper order or arrangement of ⟨be careful not to *disorder* the carefully arranged contents of the dresser⟩
***syn*** confuse, derange, disarrange, disarray, discompose, dishevel, dislocate, disorganize, disrupt, disturb, hash, jumble, mess (up), mix (up), muddle, muss, rumple, scramble, shuffle, tousle, tumble, upset
***rel*** embroil, entangle, snarl, tangle; agitate, stir (up), unsettle
***near ant*** align, line, line up; systematize; adjust, fix
***ant*** arrange, array, draw up, marshal, order, organize, range, regulate, straighten (up), tidy

**disordered** *adj* lacking in order, neatness, and often cleanliness — see MESSY

**disorderly** *adj* **1** not restrained by or under the control of legal authority — see LAWLESS
**2** lacking in order, neatness, and often cleanliness — see MESSY

**disorganization** *n* a state in which everything is out of order — see CHAOS

**disorganize** *vb* to undo the proper order or arrangement of — see DISORDER

**disorient** *vb* to throw into a state of mental uncertainty — see CONFUSE 1

**disown** *vb* to refuse to acknowledge as one's own or as one's responsibility — see DISCLAIM 1

**disparage** *vb* to express scornfully one's low opinion of — see DECRY 1

**disparagement** *n* the act of making a person or a thing seem little or unimportant — see DEPRECIATION

**disparaging** *adj* intended to make a person or thing seem of little importance or value — see DEROGATORY

**disparate** *adj* being not of the same kind — see DIFFERENT 1

**disparateness** *n* the quality or state of being different — see DIFFERENCE 1

**disparity** *n* the quality or state of being different — see DIFFERENCE 1

**dispassionate** *adj* marked by justice, honesty, and freedom from bias — see FAIR 2

**dispatch** *n* **1** a message on paper from one person or group to another — see LETTER
**2** a piece of conveyed information — see COMMUNICATION

**dispatch** *vb* **1** to cause to go or be taken from one place to another — see SEND
**2** to deprive of life — see KILL 1
**3** to put to death deliberately — see MURDER 1

**dispel** *vb* to cause (members of a group) to move widely apart — see SCATTER 1

**dispensable** *adj* not needed by the circumstances or to accomplish an end — see UNNECESSARY

**dispensation** *n* the act or process of giving out something to each member of a group — see DISTRIBUTION 1

**dispense** *vb* to give out (something) in appropriate amounts or to appropriate individuals — see ADMINISTER 1

**dispersal** *n* an act or process in which something scatters or is scattered — see SCATTERING 1

**disperse** *vb* **1** to cause (members of a group) to move widely apart — see SCATTER 1
**2** to cease to exist or cause to cease to exist as a group or organization — see DISBAND 1

**dispersion** *n* an act or process in which something scatters or is scattered — see SCATTERING 1

**dispirit** *vb* to lessen the courage or confidence of — see DISCOURAGE 1

**dispiritedness** *n* **1** a state or spell of low spirits — see SADNESS
**2** the state of being discouraged — see DISCOURAGEMENT

**displace** *vb* **1** to change the place or position of — see MOVE 1
**2** to force to leave a country — see BANISH 1
**3** to take the place of — see REPLACE 1

**displacement** *n* the forced removal from a homeland — see EXILE 1

**display** *n* **1** a public showing of objects of interest — see EXHIBITION 1
**2** an outward and often exaggerated indication of something abstract (as a feeling) for effect — see SHOW 1

**display** *vb* **1** to present so as to invite notice or attention — see SHOW 1
**2** to make known (something abstract) through outward signs — see SHOW 2

**displease** *vb* to make discontented — see DISCONTENT

**displeased** *adj* having a feeling that one has been wronged or thwarted in one's ambitions — see DISCONTENTED

**displeasing** *adj* not giving pleasure to the mind or senses — see UNPLEASANT

**displeasure** *n* **1** refusal to accept as right or desirable — see DISAPPROVAL
**2** the condition of being dissatisfied with one's life or situation — see DISCONTENT

**disport** *vb* **1** to cause (someone) to pass the time agreeably occupied — see AMUSE
**2** to engage in activity for amusement — see PLAY 1
**3** to play and run about happily — see FROLIC 1
**4** to present so as to invite notice or attention — see SHOW 1

**disposal** *n* **1** the getting rid of whatever is unwanted or useless ⟨trash *disposal* is on Wednesday in our neighborhood⟩
***syn*** discarding, disposition, dumping, jettison, junking, removal, riddance, scrapping, throwing away
***rel*** clearance, clearing; decimation, demolishment, demolition, destruction
***near ant*** accumulation, acquirement, acquisition, collection, deposit
**2** the way objects in space or events in time are arranged or follow one another — see ORDER 1

**dispose** *vb* **1** to arrange something in a certain spot or position — see PLACE 1
**2** to put into a particular arrangement — see ORDER 1

**disposed** *adj* having a desire or inclination (as for a specified course of action) — see WILLING 1

**disposition** *n* **1** one's characteristic attitude or mood ⟨he had a cheerful *disposition* and was very rarely depressed⟩
***syn*** grain, nature, temper, temperament
***rel*** cheer, frame, humor, mode, mood; attitude, outlook, perspective, point of view, standpoint, viewpoint; emotion, feeling, heart, passion, sentiment; strain; belief, conviction, mind, opinion, persuasion; expression, tone, vein; character, individuality, personality; responsiveness, sensibility, sensitiveness, sensitivity
**2** a habitual attraction to some activity or thing — see INCLINATION 1
**3** the getting rid of whatever is unwanted or useless — see DISPOSAL 1
**4** the way objects in space or events in time are arranged or follow one another — see ORDER 1

**disprove** *vb* to prove to be false ⟨Magellan's circumnavigation of the globe *disproved* any lingering notions that the earth is flat⟩
***syn*** belie, confute, rebut, refute
***rel*** overthrow, overturn
***phrases*** give the lie to
***near ant*** evidence, show; demonstrate, display, illustrate, manifest; argue, reason
***ant*** confirm, prove, verify

**disputable** *adj* **1** giving good reason for being doubted, questioned, or challenged — see DOUBTFUL
**2** open to question or dispute — see DEBATABLE 2

**disputant** *n* a person who takes part in a dispute ⟨there were only three *disputants* in the argument, but they made enough noise for a dozen⟩
***syn*** arguer, debater, disputer, quarreler (*or* quarreller), squabbler, wrangler

*rel* advocate, defendant, plaintiff, pleader; nitpicker, pettifogger, quibbler

**disputation** *n* variance of opinion on a matter — see DISAGREEMENT 1

**disputatious** *adj* 1 feeling or displaying eagerness to fight — see BELLIGERENT 2 given to arguing — see ARGUMENTATIVE 1

**disputatiousness** *n* an inclination to fight or quarrel — see BELLIGERENCE

**dispute** *n* 1 variance of opinion on a matter — see DISAGREEMENT 1
2 an often noisy or angry expression of differing opinions — see ARGUMENT 1

**dispute** *vb* 1 to demand proof of the truth or rightness of — see CHALLENGE 1
2 to express different opinions about something often angrily — see ARGUE 2
3 to talk about (an issue) usually from various points of view and for the purpose of arriving at a decision or opinion — see DISCUSS

**disputer** *n* a person who takes part in a dispute — see DISPUTANT

**disquiet** *n* 1 a disturbed or uneasy state — see UNREST
2 an uneasy state of mind usually over the possibility of an anticipated misfortune or trouble — see ANXIETY 1

**disquiet** *vb* to trouble the mind of; to make uneasy — see DISTURB 1

**disquieting** *adj* 1 causing worry or anxiety — see TROUBLESOME
2 marked by or causing agitation or uncomfortable feelings — see NERVOUS 2

**disregard** *n* lack of interest or concern — see INDIFFERENCE

**disregard** *vb* 1 to ignore in a disrespectful manner — see SCORN 2
2 to fail to give proper attention to — see NEGLECT 1
3 to overlook or dismiss as of little importance — see EXCUSE 1

**disrepair** *n* the state of being unattended to or not cared for — see NEGLECT 1

**disreputable** *adj* not respectable ⟨a *disreputable* Internet retailer that had a record of hundreds of complaints for shoddy merchandise and slow refunds⟩
*syn* discreditable, disgraceful, dishonorable, ignominious, infamous, notorious, shameful
*rel* bad, immoral, seamy, shady, sordid, unethical, unsavory, wicked; base, contemptible, despicable, detestable, dirty, low, mean, vile, wretched
*near ant* ethical, good, moral
*ant* honorable, reputable, respectable

**disrepute** *n* the state of having lost the esteem of others — see DISGRACE 1

**disrespect** *n* rude behavior — see DISCOURTESY

**disrobe** *vb* to remove clothing from — see UNDRESS

**disrobed** *adj* lacking or shed of clothing — see NAKED 1

**disrupt** *vb* to undo the proper order or arrangement of — see DISORDER

**disruption** *n* an act or instance of the order of things being disturbed — see UPSET

**dissatisfaction** *n* 1 the condition of being dissatisfied with one's life or situation — see DISCONTENT
2 the emotion felt when one's expectations are not met — see DISAPPOINTMENT 1

**dissatisfied** *adj* having a feeling that one has been wronged or thwarted in one's ambitions — see DISCONTENTED

**dissatisfy** *vb* 1 to fall short in satisfying the expectation or hope of — see DISAPPOINT
2 to make discontented — see DISCONTENT

**dissect** *vb* to identify and examine the basic elements or parts of (something) especially for discovering interrelationships — see ANALYZE

**dissection** *n* the separation and identification of the parts of a whole — see ANALYSIS 1

**dissemble** *vb* to take on a false or deceptive appearance — see PRETEND 1

**dissembling** *n* 1 the inclination or practice of misleading others through lies or trickery — see DECEIT
2 the pretending of having virtues, principles, or beliefs that one in fact does not have — see HYPOCRISY

**disseminate** *vb* to cause to be known over a considerable area or by many people — see SPREAD 1

**dissension** *n* 1 a lack of agreement or harmony — see DISCORD
2 variance of opinion on a matter — see DISAGREEMENT 1

**dissent** *n* 1 a lack of agreement or harmony — see DISCORD
2 departure from a generally accepted theory, opinion, or practice — see HERESY

**dissent** *vb* to have a different opinion — see DISAGREE 1

**dissenter** *n* a person who believes or teaches something opposed to accepted beliefs — see HERETIC

**dissentient** *adj* deviating from commonly accepted beliefs or practices — see HERETICAL

**dissenting** *adj* deviating from commonly accepted beliefs or practices — see HERETICAL

**disservice** *n* unfair or inadequate treatment of someone or something or an instance of this ⟨you do a great *disservice* to the professionals at the day-care center when you refer to them as "babysitters"⟩
*syn* injury, injustice, raw deal, wrong
*rel* insult, offense, outrage; complaint, grievance
*near ant* cricket
*ant* justice

**dissever** *vb* to set or force apart — see SEPARATE 1

**dissidence** *n* **1** a lack of agreement or harmony — see DISCORD
**2** departure from a generally accepted theory, opinion, or practice — see HERESY
**dissident** *adj* deviating from commonly accepted beliefs or practices — see HERETICAL
**dissident** *n* a person who believes or teaches something opposed to accepted beliefs — see HERETIC
**dissimilar** *adj* being not of the same kind — see DIFFERENT 1
**dissimilarity** *n* the quality or state of being different — see DIFFERENCE 1
**dissimulation** *n* **1** the inclination or practice of misleading others through lies or trickery — see DECEIT
**2** the pretending of having virtues, principles, or beliefs that one in fact does not have — see HYPOCRISY
**dissipate** *vb* **1** to cause (members of a group) to move widely apart — see SCATTER 1
**2** to use up carelessly — see WASTE 1
**dissipated** *adj* having or showing lowered moral character or standards — see CORRUPT
**dissipatedness** *n* a sinking to a state of low moral standards and behavior — see CORRUPTION 2
**dissipation** *n* **1** a sinking to a state of low moral standards and behavior — see CORRUPTION 2
**2** an act or process in which something scatters or is scattered — see SCATTERING 1
**dissociate** *vb* to set or force apart — see SEPARATE 1
**dissolute** *adj* having or showing lowered moral character or standards — see CORRUPT
**dissoluteness** *n* a sinking to a state of low moral standards and behavior — see CORRUPTION 2
**dissolution** *n* the act or process of a whole separating into two or more parts or pieces — see SEPARATION 1
**dissolve** *vb* **1** to cease to be visible — see DISAPPEAR
**2** to cease to exist or cause to cease to exist as a group or organization — see DISBAND 1
**3** to put an end to by formal action — see ABOLISH
**dissonant** *adj* marked by or producing a harsh combination of sounds ⟨a *dissonant* chorus of noises arose from the busy construction site⟩
***syn*** discordant, inharmonious, unmelodious, unmusical
***rel*** blaring, clanging, clashing, clattering, grating, harsh, jangling, jarring, metallic, raspy, raucous, scratching, screeching, shrill, squeaky, strident; disagreeable, unpleasant, unpleasing; atonal, off-key
***near ant*** dulcet, euphonious, mellifluous, mellow, melodic, sweet, tuneful; resonant, sonorous; quavering, trilling, warbling; agreeable, appealing, pleasant; cadenced, lilting, lyric, lyrical, rhythmic (*or* rhythmical); chordal, harmonic, homophonic, orchestral, polyphonic, symphonic, tonal
***ant*** harmonious, harmonizing, melodious, musical
**dissuade** *vb* to steer (a person) from an activity or course of action — see DISCOURAGE 2
**distance** *n* the space or amount of space between two points, lines, surfaces, or objects ⟨the *distance* between the earth and the sun is about 93 million miles⟩
***syn*** lead, length, remove, spacing, spread, stretch, way
***rel*** altitude, area, breadth, depth, height, rise, space, volume, width; extension, extent; cast, range, reach, scope, shot, sweep, throw; drop, fall, flight, haul; berth, clearance
***phrases*** a far cry
**distant** *adj* **1** not close in time or space ⟨the *distant* towers were barely visible in the fog⟩
***syn*** away, far, faraway, far-off, remote, removed
***rel*** apart, isolated, obscure, outlying, out-of-the-way, retired, secluded, secret, sequestered
***near ant*** adjacent, adjoining, contiguous
***ant*** close, near, nearby, nigh
**2** having or showing a lack of friendliness or interest in others — see COOL 1
**distaste** *n* a dislike so strong as to cause stomach upset or queasiness — see DISGUST
**distasteful** *adj* **1** disagreeable or disgusting to the sense of taste ⟨cod-liver oil is so *distasteful* that it's worse than anything it cures⟩
***syn*** unappetizing, unpalatable, unsavory
***rel*** abominable, awful, bad, filthy, foul, horrible, loathsome, nasty, nauseating, noisome, obnoxious, offensive, repellent, repugnant, repulsive, revolting, shocking, sickening; bland, flat, flavorless, insipid, savorless, tasteless
***near ant*** appealing, attractive, flavorful, piquant, rich
***ant*** appetizing, delectable, delicious, palatable, savory, tasty
**2** not giving pleasure to the mind or senses — see UNPLEASANT
**3** causing intense displeasure, disgust, or resentment — see OFFENSIVE 1
**distill** *vb* to remove usually visible impurities from — see CLARIFY 1
**distinct** *adj* **1** being not of the same kind — see DIFFERENT 1
**2** not subject to misinterpretation or more than one interpretation — see CLEAR 2
**3** of a particular or exact sort — see EXPRESS 1
**4** serving to identify as belonging to an individual or group — see CHARACTERISTIC 1
**distinction** *n* **1** exceptionally high quality — see EXCELLENCE 1

2 a quality that gives something special worth — see EXCELLENCE 2
3 public acknowledgment or admiration for an achievement — see GLORY 1
4 the fact or state of being above others in rank or importance — see EMINENCE 1
5 something given in recognition of achievement — see AWARD
6 the quality or state of being different — see DIFFERENCE 1
7 the state of being kept distinct — see SEPARATION 2

**distinctive** *adj* 1 being not of the same kind — see DIFFERENT 1
2 serving to identify as belonging to an individual or group — see CHARACTERISTIC 1

**distinctiveness** *n* the quality or state of being different — see DIFFERENCE 1

**distinctness** *n* the quality or state of being different — see DIFFERENCE 1

**distinguish** *vb* 1 to understand or point out the difference ⟨even at such a young age, he could *distinguish* between right and wrong⟩
*syn* differentiate, discern, discriminate, separate
*rel* comprehend, grasp, know, understand; divide, part, sever; demarcate, mark (off), set off
*near ant* confound, lump (together), mingle
*ant* confuse, mistake, mix (up)
2 to be an important feature of — see CHARACTERIZE 2
3 to find out or establish the identity of — see IDENTIFY 1
4 to make note of (something) through the use of one's eyes — see SEE 1

**distinguishable** *adj* 1 able to be perceived by a sense or by the mind — see PERCEPTIBLE
2 being not of the same kind — see DIFFERENT 1

**distinguished** *adj* standing above others in rank, importance, or achievement — see EMINENT

**distinguishing** *adj* serving to identify as belonging to an individual or group — see CHARACTERISTIC 1

**distort** *vb* 1 to change so much as to create a wrong impression or alter the meaning of — see GARBLE
2 to twist (something) out of a natural or normal shape or condition — see CONTORT

**distorted** *adj* badly or imperfectly formed — see MALFORMED

**distortion** *n* the twisting of something out of its natural or normal shape or condition — see CONTORTION

**distract** *vb* 1 to draw the attention or mind to something else ⟨we were *distracted* from our homework by the noise outside⟩
*syn* divert
*rel* amuse, entertain; stray, wander
*near ant* focus
2 to trouble the mind of; to make uneasy — see DISTURB 1

**distraction** *n* 1 a state of mental uncertainty — see CONFUSION 1
2 a state of wildly excited activity or emotion — see FRENZY
3 the act or activity of providing pleasure or amusement especially for the public — see ENTERTAINMENT 1

**distraught** *adj* feeling overwhelming fear or worry — see FRANTIC 1

**distress** *n* 1 a state of great suffering of body or mind ⟨the upcoming final exam is causing us considerable *distress*⟩ ⟨the survivors were in extreme *distress* after having been stranded on the island for a week with no food⟩
*syn* affliction, agony, anguish, misery, pain, strait(s), torment, torture, tribulation, woe
*rel* discomfort; cross, crucible, trial; heartbreak, joylessness, sadness, sorrow, unhappiness; emergency, pinch; asperity, difficulty, hardship, rigor; ache, hurt, pang, smarting, soreness, stitch, throe, twinge; danger, jeopardy, trouble
*near ant* comfort, consolation, solace; alleviation, assuagement, ease, relief; peace, security
2 the state of not being protected from injury, harm, or evil — see DANGER 1

**distress** *vb* to trouble the mind of; to make uneasy — see DISTURB 1

**distressful** *adj* 1 marked by or causing agitation or uncomfortable feelings — see NERVOUS 2
2 of a kind to cause great distress — see REGRETTABLE

**distressing** *adj* 1 causing worry or anxiety — see TROUBLESOME
2 of a kind to cause great distress — see REGRETTABLE
3 marked by or causing agitation or uncomfortable feelings — see NERVOUS 2

**distribute** *vb* to give out (something) in appropriate amounts or to appropriate individuals — see ADMINISTER 1

**distribution** *n* 1 the act or process of giving out something to each member of a group ⟨we oversaw the *distribution* of medicine to the natives⟩
*syn* allocation, apportionment, dispensation, division, issuance
*rel* disbursement; reapportionment, redistribution
2 the way objects in space or events in time are arranged or follow one another — see ORDER 1

**district** *n* an area (as of a city) set apart for some purpose or having some special feature ⟨Independence Hall in Philadelphia's historic *district*⟩
*syn* neighborhood, quarter, section
*rel* belt, zone; department, division, part; precinct, ward; area, locality, place, region; barrio, enclave, ghetto

**distrust** *n* a feeling or attitude that one does not know the truth, truthfulness, or trustworthiness of someone or something — see DOUBT

**distrust** *vb* to have no trust or confidence in ⟨we *distrusted* the stranger when he offered us free candy⟩
*syn* doubt, mistrust, question, suspect
*rel* disbelieve, discount, discredit, negate
*phrases* look askance at
*near ant* bank (on *or* upon), count (on *or* upon), depend (on *or* upon), rely (on *or* upon)
*ant* trust

**distrustful** *adj* **1** inclined to doubt or question claims — see SKEPTICAL 1
**2** not feeling sure about the truth, wisdom, or trustworthiness of someone or something — see DOUBTFUL 1

**distrustfully** *adv* with distrust — see ASKANCE

**distrustfulness** *n* a feeling or attitude that one does not know the truth, truthfulness, or trustworthiness of someone or something — see DOUBT

**disturb** *vb* **1** to trouble the mind of; to make uneasy ⟨all that talk of war *disturbed* us⟩
*syn* agitate, bother, concern, discomfort, discompose, disquiet, distract, distress, exercise, freak (out), perturb, undo, unhinge, unsettle, upset, worry
*rel* aggravate, anger, annoy, bug, chafe, chivy, exasperate, fret, gall, get, grate, harass, harry, irk, irritate, nettle, peeve, pester, pique, put out, rile, vex; bedevil, haunt, plague; abash, confound, confuse, discomfit, disconcert, discountenance, embarrass, faze, fluster, mortify, nonplus, rattle; daunt, demoralize, discourage, dishearten, dismay, dispirit
*near ant* allay, alleviate, assuage; appease, conciliate, mollify, pacify, placate, propitiate
*ant* calm, compose, quiet, settle, soothe, tranquilize (*also* tranquillize)
**2** to change the place or position of — see MOVE 1
**3** to undo the proper order or arrangement of — see DISORDER
**4** to thrust oneself upon (another) without invitation — see BOTHER 1
**5** to cause discomfort to or trouble for — see INCONVENIENCE

**disturbance** *n* **1** a state of noisy, confused activity — see COMMOTION
**2** an act or instance of the order of things being disturbed — see UPSET
**3** the act of making unwelcome intrusions upon another — see ANNOYANCE 1

**disturbing** *adj* **1** causing annoyance — see ANNOYING
**2** causing embarrassment — see AWKWARD 3
**3** causing worry or anxiety — see TROUBLESOME
**4** marked by or causing agitation or uncomfortable feelings — see NERVOUS 2

**disunion** *n* the act or process of a whole separating into two or more parts or pieces — see SEPARATION 1

**disunite** *vb* to set or force apart — see SEPARATE 1

**disunited** *adj* disagreeing with each other — see DIVIDED

**disunity** *n* a lack of agreement or harmony — see DISCORD

**disuse** *n* lack of use ⟨the old farmhouse showed signs of *disuse*⟩
*syn* idleness, inactivity
*rel* abandonment, desertion, neglect; dormancy, latency, quiescence
*ant* use

**disused** *adj* left unoccupied or unused — see ABANDONED

**ditch** *n* a long narrow channel dug in the earth ⟨after skidding on the ice, our car went right into the *ditch*⟩
*syn* dike, gutter, trench, trough
*rel* culvert, drain, draw, gully, ravine; drill, furrow

**ditch** *vb* to get rid of as useless or unwanted — see DISCARD

**dither** *n* **1** a state of nervous or irritated concern — see FRET
**2** a sense of panic or extreme nervousness — see JITTERS

**dithery** *adj* feeling or showing uncomfortable feelings of uncertainty — see NERVOUS 1

**ditty** *n* a short musical composition for the human voice often with instrumental accompaniment — see SONG 1

**diurnal** *adj* occurring, done, produced, or appearing every day — see DAILY

**divan** *n* a long upholstered piece of furniture designed for several sitters — see COUCH

**dive** *n* **1** an act or instance of diving ⟨the penguin took a *dive* off of the ice sheet⟩
*syn* pitch, plunge
*rel* dip, immersion, submersion; fall, slip, spill, stumble, tumble; descent, drop; belly flop, header, jackknife
*near ant* jump, leap
**2** the act or process of going to a lower level or altitude — see DESCENT 1

**dive** *vb* to cast oneself head first into deep water ⟨we watched her *dive* in after the drowning man⟩
*syn* pitch, plunge, sound
*rel* dip, immerse, submerge; belly flop
*near ant* surface

**diverge** *vb* **1** to extend outwards from or as if from a central point — see RADIATE 1
**2** to go or move in different directions from a central point — see SEPARATE 2

**divergence** *n* a movement in different directions away from a common point ⟨a growing *divergence* of opinion about that U.S. president's place in history⟩
*syn* separation
*rel* difference, disagreement, discrepancy, disparateness, disparity, dissidence, dissimilarity, distinction, distinctiveness, distinctness, diversity, unlikeness
*near ant* accord, agreement; likeness, similarity
*ant* convergence

**divers** *adj* being of many and various kinds — see MANIFOLD

**diverse** *adj* being not of the same kind — see DIFFERENT 1

**diverseness** *n* **1** the quality or state of being composed of many different elements or types — see VARIETY 1
**2** the quality or state of being different — see DIFFERENCE 1

**diversion** *n* **1** someone or something that provides amusement or enjoyment — see FUN 1
**2** the act or activity of providing pleasure or amusement especially for the public — see ENTERTAINMENT 1

**diversity** *n* **1** the quality or state of being composed of many different elements or types — see VARIETY 1
**2** the quality or state of being different — see DIFFERENCE 1

**divert** *vb* **1** to cause (someone) to pass the time agreeably occupied — see AMUSE
**2** to change the course or direction of (something) — see TURN 2
**3** to draw the attention or mind to something else — see DISTRACT 1

**diverting** *adj* providing amusement or enjoyment — see FUN

**divide** *vb* **1** to set or force apart — see SEPARATE 1
**2** to go or move in different directions from a central point — see SEPARATE 2

**divided** *adj* disagreeing with each other ⟨the club members were *divided* on the need for more fundraising⟩
***syn*** disunited, split
***phrases*** at loggerheads, at odds
***ant*** undivided, united

**dividend** *n* something given in addition to what is ordinarily expected or owed — see BONUS

**divider** *n* something that divides, separates, or marks off — see DIVISION 1

**divine** *adj* **1** of the very best kind — see EXCELLENT
**2** of, relating to, or being God — see HOLY 3

**divine** *n* a person specially trained and authorized to conduct religious services in a Christian church — see CLERGYMAN

**divine** *vb* to realize or know about beforehand — see FORESEE

**diviner** *n* one who predicts future events or developments — see PROPHET

**divinity** *n* **1** the quality or state of being divine ⟨Henry David Thoreau felt the presence of *divinity* in every part of nature⟩
***syn*** deity, godhead, godhood
**2** a being having superhuman powers and control over a particular part of life or the world — see DEITY 1
**3** *cap* the being worshipped as the creator and ruler of the universe — see DEITY 2

**divisible** *adj* capable of being split into two or more parts or pieces — see SEPARABLE

**division** *n* **1** something that divides, separates, or marks off ⟨we poked our heads over the *division* between the yards to see what the fuss was about⟩
***syn*** divider, partition
***rel*** barrier, fence, wall; border, boundary, limit
**2** a large unit of a governmental, business, or educational organization ⟨the complaints *division* handled all of the calls from the angry townsfolk⟩
***syn*** bureau, department, desk, office
**3** one of the units into which a whole is divided on the basis of a common characteristic — see CLASS 2
**4** the act or process of a whole separating into two or more parts or pieces — see SEPARATION 1
**5** the act or process of giving out something to each member of a group — see DISTRIBUTION 1

**divorce** *vb* to set or force apart — see SEPARATE 1

**divulge** *vb* to make known (as information previously kept secret) — see REVEAL 1

**divulgence** *n* the act or an instance of making known something previously unknown or concealed — see REVELATION

**dizzy** *adj* **1** having a feeling of being whirled about and in danger of falling down ⟨I felt very *dizzy* after I got off of the roller coaster⟩
***syn*** giddy, light-headed, reeling, whirling
***rel*** faint, weak; addled, befuddled, confused, dazed
***near ant*** clearheaded; stable, steady
**2** suffering from mental confusion ⟨he felt *dizzy* from trying to remember all of the dates and names that were sure to be asked on the test⟩
***syn*** befuddled, bewildered, confused, dazed, stunned, stupefied
***rel*** senseless, unconscious
***phrases*** at sea
***near ant*** alert, conscious
***ant*** clearheaded, unconfused
**3** moving, proceeding, or acting with great speed — see FAST 1

**do** *vb* **1** to be fitting or proper ⟨Oh, that outfit just won't *do* for the opera⟩
***syn*** befit, fit, go, serve, suit
***rel*** satisfy, suffice; function, work
**2** to be enough — see SERVE 2
**3** to carry through (as a process) to completion — see PERFORM 1
**4** to make more attractive by adding something that is beautiful or becoming — see DECORATE
**5** to meet one's day-to-day needs — see GET ALONG 1

**doable** *adj* capable of being done or carried out — see POSSIBLE 1

**docile** *adj* readily giving in to the command or authority of another — see OBEDIENT

**docility** *n* a readiness or willingness to yield to the wishes of others — see COMPLIANCE 1

**dock** *n* a structure used by boats and ships for taking on or landing cargo and passengers ⟨the boat remained tied up at the

*dock* for a week, waiting for the weather to clear⟩
*syn* float, jetty, landing, levee, pier, quay, wharf
*rel* berth, mooring, slip; dockyard, marina, shipyard

[1]**dock** *vb* to make (as hair) shorter with or as if with the use of shears — see CLIP

[2]**dock** *vb* to stop at or near a place along the shore — see LAND 1

**docket** *n* a listing of things to be presented or considered (as at a concert or play) — see PROGRAM 1

**dockworker** *n* one who loads and unloads ships at a port ⟨the *dockworker* spent all afternoon taking crates off of the ship⟩
*syn* longshoreman, stevedore

**doctor** *n* a person specially trained in healing human medical disorders ⟨we called a *doctor* as soon as we realized the baby was sick⟩
*syn* medic, physician
*rel* dermatologist, general practitioner, gynecologist, internist, neurologist, obstetrician, ophthalmologist, orthopedist, pediatrician, specialist, surgeon; intern, resident; nurse, paramedic

**doctor** *vb* **1** to give medical treatment to ⟨a pledge to *doctor* the burn victims until they were whole again⟩
*syn* treat
*rel* cure, heal, mend, rehabilitate, remedy; attend, care (for), dose, drug, minister (to), nurse
**2** to put into good shape or working order again — see MEND 1

**doctrine** *n* **1** a statement or body of statements concerning faith or morals proclaimed by a church ⟨the Catholic Church's *doctrine* on the Eucharist⟩
*syn* canon, dogma
*rel* belief, conviction, tenet; credo, creed, ideology, philosophy, theology; axiom, precept, principle
**2** the basic beliefs or guiding principles of a person or group — see CREED 1

**document** *n* **1** a piece of paper with information written or to be written on it — see FORM 2
**2** a written or printed paper giving information about or proof of something — see CERTIFICATE

**document** *vb* to show the existence or truth of by evidence — see PROVE 1

**documentary** *adj* restricted to or based on fact — see FACTUAL 1

**documentation** *n* something presented in support of the truth or accuracy of a claim — see PROOF

**dodder** *vb* to move forward while swaying from side to side — see STAGGER 1

**dodge** *n* a clever often underhanded means to achieve an end — see TRICK 1

**dodge** *vb* **1** to move suddenly aside or to and fro ⟨*dodging* through the crowd on his way to the exit⟩
*syn* duck, sidestep, zigzag
*rel* avoid, elude, escape, evade, parry, shirk, skirt; deflect, turn; slide, slip
**2** to avoid having to comply with (something) especially through cleverness — see CIRCUMVENT 1
**3** to get or keep away from (as a responsibility) through cleverness or trickery — see ESCAPE 2

**dodger** *n* a dishonest person who uses clever means to cheat others out of something of value — see TRICKSTER 1

**dodging** *n* the act or a means of getting or keeping away from something undesirable — see ESCAPE 2

**dodo** *n* **1** a person with old-fashioned ideas — see FOGY
**2** a stupid person — see IDIOT

**doff** *vb* to rid oneself of (a garment) — see REMOVE 1

**dog** *n* a domestic mammal that is related to the wolves and foxes ⟨we got a *dog* from the pound to keep as a pet⟩
*syn* canine, doggy (*or* doggie), hound, pooch
*rel* cur, mongrel, mutt; bitch; lapdog, pup, puppy, whelp; bird dog, hunter, police dog, sheepdog, sled dog, watchdog, wolf dog, wolfhound

**dog** *vb* to go after or on the track of — see FOLLOW 2

**dog–eared** *adj* showing signs of advanced wear and tear and neglect — see SHABBY 1

**dogged** *adj* **1** continuing despite difficulties, opposition, or discouragement — see PERSISTENT
**2** sticking to an opinion, purpose, or course of action in spite of reason, arguments, or persuasion — see OBSTINATE
**3** showing no signs of slackening or yielding in one's purpose — see UNYIELDING 1

**doggedness** *n* a steadfast adherence to an opinion, purpose, or course of action — see OBSTINACY

**dogging** *n* the act of going after or in the tracks of another — see PURSUIT

**doggy** *or* **doggie** *n* a domestic mammal that is related to the wolves and foxes — see DOG

**dogma** *n* a statement or body of statements concerning faith or morals proclaimed by a church — see DOCTRINE 1

**do in** *vb* **1** to bring to a complete end the physical soundness, existence, or usefulness of — see DESTROY 1
**2** to deprive of life — see KILL 1
**3** to put to death deliberately — see MURDER 1
**4** to use up all the physical energy of — see EXHAUST 1

**doing** *n* something done by someone — see ACTION 1

**doldrums** *n pl* **1** a state of temporary inactivity — see ABEYANCE
**2** a state or spell of low spirits — see SADNESS
**3** the state of being bored — see BOREDOM

**dole** (out) *vb* to give out (something) in appropriate amounts or to appropriate individuals — see ADMINISTER 1

**doleful** *adj* **1** expressing or suggesting mourning — see MOURNFUL 1
**2** feeling unhappiness — see SAD 1
**dolefulness** *n* deep sadness especially for the loss of someone or something loved — see SORROW
**doll** *n* **1** a small figure often of a human being used especially as a child's plaything ⟨there was a row of *dolls* along the shelf in the bedroom⟩
*syn* dolly, puppet
*rel* rag doll; figure, figurine; plaything, toy
**2** a young usually unmarried woman — see GIRL 1
**doll up** *vb* to put on one's best or formal clothes — see DRESS UP
**dolly** *n* a small figure often of a human being used especially as a child's plaything — see DOLL 1
**dolor** *n* deep sadness especially for the loss of someone or something loved — see SORROW
**dolorous** *adj* expressing or suggesting mourning — see MOURNFUL 1
**dolt** *n* a stupid person — see IDIOT
**doltish** *adj* not having or showing an ability to absorb ideas readily — see STUPID 1
**doltishness** *n* the quality or state of lacking intelligence or quickness of mind — see STUPIDITY 1
**domain** *n* a region of activity, knowledge, or influence — see FIELD 2
**domestic** *adj* **1** of or relating to a household or family ⟨the surest way to maintain *domestic* peace and harmony is to have everyone pitch in on chores⟩
*syn* familial, household
*rel* homelike, homely, homey; residential
**2** changed from the wild state so as to become useful and obedient to humans — see TAME 1
**domestic** *n* **1** a female domestic servant — see MAID 1
**2** a person hired to perform household or personal services — see SERVANT
**domesticated** *adj* changed from the wild state so as to become useful and obedient to humans — see TAME 1
**domicile** *n* the place where one lives — see HOME 1
**domicile** *vb* to provide with living quarters or shelter — see HOUSE 1
**dominance** *n* **1** controlling power or influence over others — see SUPREMACY 1
**2** the fact or state of being above others in rank or importance — see EMINENCE 1
**dominant** *adj* coming before all others in importance — see FOREMOST 1
**dominate** *vb* **1** to bring under one's control by force of arms — see CONQUER 1
**2** to look down on — see OVERLOOK 1
**3** to serve as leader of — see LEAD 2
**dominating** *n* the act or process of bringing someone or something under one's control — see CONQUEST
**domination** *n* the act or process of bringing someone or something under one's control — see CONQUEST
**domineering** *adj* fond of ordering people around — see BOSSY
**dominie** *n* a person specially trained and authorized to conduct religious services in a Christian church — see CLERGYMAN
**dominion** *n* **1** controlling power or influence over others — see SUPREMACY 1
**2** the right or means to command or control others — see POWER 1
**don** *vb* to place on one's person — see PUT ON 1
**donate** *vb* to make a present of — see GIVE 1
**donation** *n* **1** a gift of money or its equivalent to a charity, humanitarian cause, or public institution — see CONTRIBUTION
**2** something given to someone without expectation of a return — see GIFT 1
**donator** *n* one that helps another with gifts or money — see BENEFACTOR
**done** *adj* brought or having come to an end — see COMPLETE 2
**done in** *adj* depleted in strength, energy, or freshness — see WEARY 1
**donkey** *n* **1** a sturdy and patient domestic mammal that is used especially to carry things ⟨we put our bags on the *donkey* and headed down the canyon⟩
*syn* ass, burro, jackass
*rel* jack, jenny; hinny, mule; pack animal
**2** a stupid person — see IDIOT
**donor** *n* one that helps another with gifts or money — see BENEFACTOR
**doom** *n* **1** a decision made by a court or tribunal regarding a case it has heard — see SENTENCE
**2** a state or end that seemingly has been decided beforehand — see FATE 1
**3** the permanent stopping of all the vital bodily activities — see DEATH 1
**doom** *vb* **1** to determine the fate of in advance — see DESTINE
**2** to impose a judicial punishment on — see SENTENCE
**door** *n* **1** a barrier by which an entry is closed and opened ⟨we locked the *door* to the room so that no one could get in⟩
*syn* gate, hatch, portal
*rel* Dutch door, French door, lattice, portcullis, postern, trapdoor, wicket
**2** the opening through which one can enter or leave a structure ⟨a steady stream of visitors through the front *door*⟩
*syn* doorway, entrance, gate, gateway, way
*rel* hatch, hatchway
**doorkeeper** *n* a person who tends a door ⟨the *doorkeeper* held the door open for us so we didn't have to put down our packages⟩
*syn* doorman, gatekeeper, janitor, porter [*chiefly British*]
**doorman** *n* a person who tends a door — see DOORKEEPER
**doorway** *n* **1** the means or right of entering or participating in — see ENTRANCE 1

*syn* synonym(s) *rel* related words
*ant* antonym(s) *near ant* near antonym(s)

2 the opening through which one can enter or leave a structure — see DOOR 2

**dope** *n* 1 information not generally available to the public ⟨he gave us the *dope* on the deal taking place that night at the warehouse⟩
*syn* lowdown, scoop, tip
*rel* dirt, gossip, rumor, story; hint, pointer; information, intelligence, news, tidings, word
2 a stupid person — see IDIOT

**dope** (out) *vb* to find an answer for through reasoning — see SOLVE

**doper** *n* a person who regularly uses drugs especially illegally ⟨the *doper* had to go straight, since he couldn't keep a steady job while using drugs⟩
*syn* addict, fiend, junkie (*also* junky), substance abuser, user
*rel* pothead

**dopey** *adj* not having or showing an ability to absorb ideas readily — see STUPID 1

**dopiness** *n* the quality or state of lacking intelligence or quickness of mind — see STUPIDITY 1

**dork** *n, slang* a stupid person — see IDIOT

**dorky** *adj, slang* not having or showing an ability to absorb ideas readily — see STUPID 1

**dormancy** *n* 1 a state of temporary inactivity — see ABEYANCE
2 lack of action or activity — see INACTION

**dormant** *adj* 1 being in a state of suspended consciousness — see ASLEEP 1
2 not being in a state of use, activity, or employment — see INACTIVE 2

**dot** *n* a small area that is different (as in color) from the main part — see SPOT 1

**dot** *vb* 1 to cover by or as if by scattering something over or on — see SCATTER 2
2 to mark with small spots especially unevenly — see SPOT

**dote** (on) *vb* to love or admire too much — see IDOLIZE

**dotted** *adj* marked with spots — see SPOTTED 1

**dotty** *adj* showing or marked by a lack of good sense or judgment — see FOOLISH 1

**double** *adj* 1 consisting of two members or parts that are usually joined ⟨an egg with a *double* yolk⟩
*syn* binary, bipartite, dual, duplex, twin
*rel* mated, paired
*ant* single
2 being twice as great or as many ⟨after it was ranked the best in the country, the college had *double* the usual number of applicants⟩
*syn* twofold

**double** *adv* to two times the amount or degree — see DOUBLY

**double** *n* something or someone that strongly resembles another — see IMAGE 1

**double** *vb* 1 to make twice as great or as many ⟨we *doubled* our efforts to find a solution to the problem⟩
*syn* duplicate, redouble
*rel* compound, multiply; accumulate, balloon, build (up), burgeon, enlarge, escalate, expand, increase, mount, mushroom, proliferate, rise, snowball, swell, wax
2 to lay one part over or against another part of — see FOLD 1

**double–cross** *vb* to be unfaithful or disloyal to — see BETRAY 1

**double cross** *n* the act or fact of violating the trust or confidence of another — see BETRAYAL

**double–crosser** *n* one who betrays a trust or an allegiance — see TRAITOR

**double–dealing** *adj* 1 marked by, based on, or done by the use of dishonest methods to acquire something of value — see FRAUDULENT 1
2 not being or expressing what one appears to be or express — see INSINCERE

**double–dealing** *n* the inclination or practice of misleading others through lies or trickery — see DECEIT

**doubly** *adv* to two times the amount or degree ⟨we were *doubly* certain of her guilt after we read the article in the newspaper⟩
*syn* double, twice, twofold

**doubt** *n* a feeling or attitude that one does not know the truth, truthfulness, or trustworthiness of someone or something ⟨from the beginning I had my *doubts* about the new kid in school⟩
*syn* distrust, distrustfulness, incertitude, misgiving, mistrust, mistrustfulness, skepticism, suspicion, uncertainty
*rel* disbelief, incredulity, unbelief; anxiety, concern; compunction, qualm, scruple
*near ant* credence, faith
*ant* assurance, belief, certainty, certitude, confidence, conviction, sureness, surety, trust

**doubt** *vb* to have no trust or confidence in — see DISTRUST

**doubtable** *adj* 1 giving good reason for being doubted, questioned, or challenged — see DOUBTFUL 2
2 open to question or dispute — see DEBATABLE 1

**doubter** *n* a person who is always ready to doubt or question the truth or existence of something — see SKEPTIC

**doubtful** *adj* 1 not feeling sure about the truth, wisdom, or trustworthiness of someone or something ⟨he was *doubtful* about the decision to complete the project despite its mounting problems⟩
*syn* distrustful, dubious, mistrustful, skeptical, suspicious, uncertain, unconvinced, undecided, unsettled, unsure
*rel* diffident, insecure; hesitant, indecisive, irresolute, vacillating, wavering
*phrases* on the fence
*near ant* assured, confident, sanguine, self-assured; decisive, determined, resolute
*ant* certain, convinced, positive, sure
2 giving good reason for being doubted, questioned, or challenged ⟨the election

results were highly *doubtful*, so an investigation was begun〉
***syn*** debatable, disputable, doubtable, dubious, equivocal, fishy, problematic (*also* problematical), questionable, shady, shaky, suspect, suspicious
***rel*** moot; ambiguous, open, unclear; uncertain, undecided, undetermined; far-fetched, flimsy, improbable, unlikely
***near ant*** decisive, definitive; clear, obvious, open-and-shut, positive
***ant*** certain, incontestable, indisputable, indubitable, sure, undeniable, undoubted, unquestionable
**3** not likely to be true or to occur — see IMPROBABLE
**4** open to question or dispute — see DEBATABLE 1

**doubtfully** *adv* with distrust — see ASKANCE

**doubting** *adj* inclined to doubt or question claims — see SKEPTICAL 1

**doubtingly** *adv* with distrust — see ASKANCE

**doubtless** *adj* having or showing a mind free from doubt — see CERTAIN 2

**doubtless** *adv* **1** without any question — see INDEED 1
**2** without much doubt — see PROBABLY

**dough** *n* something (as pieces of stamped metal or printed paper) customarily and legally used as a medium of exchange, a measure of value, or a means of payment — see MONEY

**doughtiness** *n* strength of mind to carry on in spite of danger — see COURAGE

**doughty** *adj* feeling or displaying no fear by temperament — see BRAVE

**dour** *adj* harsh and threatening in manner or appearance — see GRIM 1

**douse** *vb* **1** to cause to cease burning — see EXTINGUISH 1
**2** to make wet — see WET
**3** to sink or push (something) briefly into or as if into a liquid — see DIP 1

**doused** *adj* containing, covered with, or thoroughly penetrated by water — see WET

**dove** *n* **1** a person who opposes war or warlike policies 〈the *doves* were in favor of using the money to improve the school system instead of the army〉
***syn*** pacifist
***rel*** peacemaker
***near ant*** militarist; chauvinist, nationalist
***ant*** hawk, jingo, warmonger
**2** an innocent or gentle person — see LAMB

**dovetail** *vb* to be in agreement on every point — see CHECK 1

**dowager** *n* a dignified usually elderly woman of some rank or authority — see MATRIARCH

**dowdily** *adv* in a careless or unfashionable manner — see SLOPPILY

**dowdy** *adj* **1** lacking neatness in dress or person — see SLOPPY 1
**2** marked by an obvious lack of style or good taste — see TACKY 1

**down** *adj* **1** brought or having come to an end — see COMPLETE 2
**2** directed down — see DOWNCAST 1
**3** feeling unhappiness — see SAD 1
**4** temporarily suffering from a disorder of the body — see SICK 1

**down** *adv* toward or in a lower position 〈the stairs went *down* to the basement〉
***syn*** below, downward, over
***rel*** facedown; low; downgrade, downhill, downstairs
***near ant*** aloft
***ant*** up, upward (*or* upwards), upwardly

**[1]down** *n* a soft airy substance or covering — see FUZZ

**[2]down** *n* **1** the act or process of going to a lower level or altitude — see DESCENT 1
**2** a loss of status — see COMEDOWN

**down** *vb* **1** to strike (someone) so forcefully as to cause a fall — see FELL 1
**2** to take into the stomach through the mouth and throat — see SWALLOW 1

**downcast** *adj* **1** directed down 〈her *downcast* gaze made us realize that she was shy〉
***syn*** down, downward, lowered
***near ant*** elevated, lifted, raised, uplifted, upward
**2** feeling unhappiness — see SAD 1

**downer** *n* something (as a situation or event) that is depressing 〈that math exam was a real *downer*〉
***syn*** bummer
***rel*** bore, drag; accident, fatality, mishap, woe; calamity, catastrophe, debacle (*also* débâcle), misfortune, tragedy
***near ant*** pick-me-up

**downfall** *n* **1** a change to a lower state or level — see DECLINE 2
**2** a loss of status — see COMEDOWN

**downgrade** *n* a change to a lower state or level — see DECLINE 2

**downgrade** *vb* to bring to a lower grade or rank — see DEMOTE

**downhearted** *adj* feeling unhappiness — see SAD 1

**downheartedness** *n* a state or spell of low spirits — see SADNESS

**downpour** *n* a steady falling of water from the sky in significant quantity — see RAIN 1

**downright** *adj* **1** being or characterized by direct, brief, and potentially rude speech or manner — see BLUNT 1
**2** having no exceptions or restrictions — see ABSOLUTE 2

**downs** *n pl* a broad area of level or rolling treeless country — see PLAIN

**downsize** *vb* to make smaller in amount, volume, or extent — see DECREASE 1

**down–to–earth** *adj* willing to see things as they really are and deal with them sensibly — see REALISTIC 1

**downward** *adv* toward or in a lower position — see DOWN

**downward** *adj* directed down — see DOWNCAST 1

**downwind** *adj* being in the direction that the wind is blowing ⟨we were *downwind* of the deer, so it couldn't smell us⟩
*syn* leeward
*ant* upwind, windward
**downy** *adj* smooth or delicate in appearance or feel — see SOFT 2
**doze** *n* a short sleep — see [1]NAP
**doze** *vb* 1 to be in a state of sleep — see SLEEP 1
2 to sleep lightly or briefly — see NAP 1
**dozer** *n* one who sleeps — see SLEEPER
**dozing** *adj* being in a state of suspended consciousness — see ASLEEP 1
**dozing** *n* a natural periodic loss of consciousness during which the body restores itself — see SLEEP 1
**drab** *adj* causing weariness, restlessness, or lack of interest — see BORING
**draft** *n* 1 a mass or quantity of something taken up and carried, conveyed, or transported — see LOAD 1
2 the portion of a serving of a beverage that is swallowed at one time — see DRINK 2
3 noticeable movement of air in a particular direction — see [1]WIND 1
**draft** *vb* 1 to pick especially for required military service ⟨my grandfather was *drafted* to fight in the war, even though he didn't want to go⟩
*syn* conscript
*rel* impress, press; enlist, enroll (*also* enrol); sign up, volunteer
*near ant* discharge
2 to put (something) into proper and usually carefully worked out written form — see COMPOSE 1
**draftee** *n* a person forced or required to enroll in military service — see CONSCRIPT
**drag** *n* 1 someone or something boring ⟨that lecture was such a *drag* that half of the audience fell asleep⟩
*syn* bore
*rel* bummer, downer; pill
*near ant* gas [*slang*]
2 a passage cleared for public vehicular travel — see WAY 1
3 something that makes movement or progress more difficult — see ENCUMBRANCE
4 the portion of a serving of a beverage that is swallowed at one time — see DRINK 2
**drag** *vb* 1 to cause to follow by applying steady force on — see PULL 1
2 to move or act slowly — see DELAY 1
3 to move slowly — see CRAWL 2
**dragger** *n* someone who moves slowly or more slowly than others — see SLOWPOKE
**dragging** *adj* moving or proceeding at less than the normal, desirable, or required speed — see SLOW 1
**drain** *vb* 1 to remove (liquid) gradually or completely ⟨we *drained* the water from the tank before cleaning it⟩
*syn* bleed, draw (off), pump, siphon, tap
*rel* milk; suck; clear, empty, evacuate, exhaust, vacate, void
*ant* fill
2 to make complete use of — see DEPLETE
3 to use up all the physical energy of — see EXHAUST 1
**drained** *adj* depleted in strength, energy, or freshness — see WEARY 1
**drainpipe** *n* a pipe or channel for carrying off water from a roof — see GUTTER 1
**drama** *n* 1 the public performance of plays ⟨he has been interested in *drama* from the first time he ever saw a play⟩
*syn* dramatics, stage, theater (*or* theatre), theatricals
*rel* boards; acting, footlights; entertainment, show business
2 a written work in which the story is told through speech and action that is intended to be acted out on stage — see PLAY 2
**dramatic** *adj* 1 having the general quality or effect of a stage performance ⟨the basketball player's *dramatic* announcement of his sudden retirement held everybody spellbound⟩
*syn* histrionic, melodramatic, theatrical
*rel* affected, emotional, sensational
*near ant* matter-of-fact, monotonous
*ant* undramatic, untheatrical
2 given to or marked by attention-getting behavior suggestive of stage acting — see THEATRICAL 1
3 likely to attract attention — see NOTICEABLE
**dramatics** *n pl* the public performance of plays — see DRAMA 1
**dramatization** *n* a written work in which the story is told through speech and action that is intended to be acted out on stage — see PLAY 2
**drapery** *n* pieces of cloth hung to darken, decorate, or divide a room ⟨the *drapery* for the picture window matched the color of the furniture in the center of the room⟩
*syn* curtains, drapes
*rel* hanging(s), tapestry, window shade
**drapes** *n pl* pieces of cloth hung to darken, decorate, or divide a room — see DRAPERY
**draw** *n* 1 a situation in which neither participant in a contest, competition, or struggle comes out ahead of the other — see TIE 1
2 something that attracts interest — see MAGNET
3 the act or an instance of applying force on something so that it moves in the direction of the force — see PULL 1
**draw** *vb* 1 to cause to follow by applying steady force on — see PULL 1
2 to give a representation or account of in words — see DESCRIBE 1
3 to receive as return for effort — see EARN 1
4 to take away from a place or position — see REMOVE 2
5 to take the internal organs out of — see GUT

**draw** (off) *vb* to remove (liquid) gradually or completely — see DRAIN 1

**draw** (up) *vb* to put (something) into proper and usually carefully worked out written form — see COMPOSE 1

**drawback** *n* a feature of someone or something that creates difficulty for achieving success — see DISADVANTAGE

**drawing** *n* a picture using lines to represent the chief features of an object or scene ⟨he made a *drawing* of the tree in his sketchpad while he was waiting for the bus⟩
*syn* cartoon, delineation, sketch
*rel* outline, silhouette; caricature, doodle, illustration; depiction, image, likeness, portrait, representation; engraving, etching; blueprint

**drawing out** *n* the act of making longer — see EXTENSION 1

**drawn** *adj* stretched with little or no give — see TAUT

**draw on** *vb* to come near or nearer — see APPROACH 1

**draw out** *vb* to make longer — see EXTEND 1

**draw up** *vb* **1** to bring (something) to a standstill — see [1]HALT 1
**2** to put into a particular arrangement — see ORDER 1

**dread** *n* **1** suspicion or fear of future harm or misfortune — see APPREHENSION 1
**2** the emotion experienced in the presence or threat of danger — see FEAR

**dreadful** *adj* **1** causing fear — see FEARFUL 1
**2** causing intense displeasure, disgust, or resentment — see OFFENSIVE 1
**3** extremely disturbing or repellent — see HORRIBLE 1

**dreadfulness** *n* the quality of inspiring intense dread or dismay — see HORROR 1

**dream** *n* **1** a series of often striking pictures created by the imagination during sleep ⟨I had a *dream* last night about flying without any support⟩
*syn* nightmare, vision
*rel* daydream, pipe dream, reverie (*also* revery); chimera, delusion, fancy, fantasy (*also* phantasy), figment, hallucination, illusion, mirage, phantasm
**2** a conception or image created by the imagination and having no objective reality — see FANTASY 1
**3** something that one hopes or intends to accomplish — see GOAL

**dream** *vb* to form a mental picture of — see IMAGINE 1

**dreamer** *n* one whose conduct is guided more by the image of perfection than by the real world — see IDEALIST

**dreamily** *adv* in a pleasing way — see WELL 5

**dreamy** *adj* **1** giving pleasure or contentment to the mind or senses — see PLEASANT
**2** tending to calm the emotions and relieve stress — see SOOTHING 1

**drear** *adj* **1** causing or marked by an atmosphere lacking in cheer — see GLOOMY 1
**2** causing unhappiness — see SAD 2

**dreariness** *n* a state or spell of low spirits — see SADNESS

**dreary** *adj* **1** causing or marked by an atmosphere lacking in cheer — see GLOOMY 1
**2** causing unhappiness — see SAD 2
**3** causing weariness, restlessness, or lack of interest — see BORING

**dredge** *vb* to look through (as a place) carefully or thoroughly in an effort to find or discover something — see SEARCH 1

**dregs** *n pl* matter that settles to the bottom of a body of liquid — see DEPOSIT 1

**drench** *vb* **1** to make wet — see WET
**2** to wet thoroughly with liquid — see SOAK 1

**drenched** *adj* containing, covered with, or thoroughly penetrated by water — see WET

**dress** *adj* relating to or suitable for wearing to an event requiring elegant dress and manners ⟨the naval commander wore his *dress* uniform to the ball⟩
*syn* dressy, formal
*rel* costume; chic, dapper, fashionable, modish, natty, sharp, smart, stylish; custom-made, fitted, tailored; state
*near ant* street; dowdy, unfashionable, unstylish
*ant* casual, informal, sporty

**dress** *n* **1** a garment with a joined blouse and skirt for a woman or girl ⟨what a lovely *dress* you're wearing today!⟩
*syn* frock, gown
*rel* chemise, granny, housedress, jumper, Mother Hubbard, muumuu (*or* mumu), overdress
**2** clothing chosen as appropriate for a specific situation — see OUTFIT 1
**3** covering for the human body — see CLOTHING

**dress** *vb* **1** to cover with a bandage — see BANDAGE
**2** to make more attractive by adding something that is beautiful or becoming — see DECORATE
**3** to make smooth or glossy usually by repeatedly applying surface pressure — see POLISH
**4** to outfit with clothes and especially fine or special clothes — see CLOTHE 1
**5** to put on one's best or formal clothes — see DRESS UP

**dress down** *vb* to criticize (someone) severely or angrily especially for personal failings — see SCOLD

**dressing** *n* **1** a medicated covering used to heal an injury ⟨nurses put a *dressing* over his cuts so they wouldn't get infected⟩
*syn* plaster, poultice
*rel* balm, cream, liniment, lotion, ointment, salve, unguent

2 a savory fluid food used as a topping or accompaniment to a main dish — see SAUCE 1

**dress up** *vb* 1 to put on one's best or formal clothes ⟨we always like to *dress up* when going to parties⟩
*syn* doll up, dress
*rel* apparel, array, attire, bedeck, bedizen, caparison, clothe, costume, deck, garb, garment, invest, rig (out), robe
2 to change the dress or looks of so as to conceal true identity — see DISGUISE

**dressy** *adj* relating to or suitable for wearing to an event requiring elegant dress and manners — see DRESS

**dribble** *vb* 1 to fall or let fall in or as if in drops — see DRIP
2 to flow in a broken irregular stream — see GURGLE
3 to let saliva or some other substance flow from the mouth — see DROOL

**driblet** *n* 1 a very small amount — see PARTICLE 1
2 the quantity of fluid that falls naturally in one rounded mass — see DROP 1

**drift** *n* 1 a pile or ridge of granular matter (as sand or snow) — see [2]BANK
2 a prevailing or general movement or inclination — see TREND 1
3 the idea that is conveyed or intended to be conveyed to the mind by language, symbol, or action — see MEANING 1

**drift** *vb* 1 to move or proceed smoothly and readily — see FLOW 2
2 to rest or move along the surface of a liquid or in the air — see FLOAT

**drifter** *n* a person who roams about without a fixed route or destination — see NOMAD

**drill** *n* something done over and over in order to develop skill — see EXERCISE 2

[1]**drill** *vb* 1 to make a hole or series of holes in — see PERFORATE
2 to strike with a missile from a gun — see SHOOT 3

[2]**drill** *vb* to put or set into the ground to grow — see PLANT

**drink** *n* 1 a liquid suitable for drinking ⟨we went inside to have a *drink* after mowing the lawn⟩
*syn* beverage, libation, quencher
*rel* potion; pop, soda, soda pop, soft drink; alcohol, brew, intoxicant, liquor, spirits
2 the portion of a serving of a beverage that is swallowed at one time ⟨the thirsty scout took a long *drink* from his canteen⟩
*syn* draft, drag, gulp, nip, quaff, shot, sip, slug, snort, sup, swallow, swig, swill
3 a fermented or distilled beverage that can make a person drunk — see ALCOHOL

**drink** *vb* 1 to swallow in liquid form ⟨the doctor wants her to *drink* lots of water before the examination⟩
*syn* gulp, guzzle, imbibe, quaff, sip, slurp, sup, swig, swill, toss (down *or* off)
*rel* lap, lick; consume, down, mouth (down); tipple; toast, wine
2 to take in (something liquid) through small openings — see ABSORB 1

**drinkable** *adj* suitable for drinking — see POTABLE

**drip** *n* the quantity of fluid that falls naturally in one rounded mass — see DROP 1

**drip** *vb* to fall or let fall in or as if in drops ⟨water from the leaky roof was *dripping* all over the floor⟩ ⟨the cracked bottle *dripped* wine⟩
*syn* dribble, trickle
*rel* bleed, exude, ooze, seep, weep; discharge

**dripping** *adj* containing, covered with, or thoroughly penetrated by water — see WET

**drive** *n* 1 a passage cleared for public vehicular travel — see WAY 1
2 a series of activities undertaken to achieve a goal — see CAMPAIGN
3 a strong wish for something — see DESIRE
4 active strength of body or mind — see VIGOR 1
5 readiness to engage in daring or difficult activity — see ENTERPRISE 2

**drive** *vb* 1 to urge, push, or force onward ⟨cowboys *drove* the herd of cattle from San Antonio to San Francisco⟩
*syn* herd, punch, run
*rel* shepherd; wrangle; egg, exhort, goad, prick, prod, spur, urge
2 to travel by a motorized vehicle ⟨I'm going to *drive* across the country—want to come?⟩
*syn* automobile, motor
*rel* roll, wheel; chauffeur, taxi; ride; drag, race
3 to apply force to (someone or something) so that it moves in front of one — see PUSH 1
4 to cause (a person) to give in to pressure — see FORCE
5 to cause to function — see ACTIVATE
6 to set or keep in motion — see MOVE 2

**drivel** *n* 1 language, behavior, or ideas that are absurd and contrary to good sense — see NONSENSE 1
2 unintelligible or meaningless talk — see GIBBERISH

**drivel** *vb* 1 to let saliva or some other substance flow from the mouth — see DROOL
2 to speak rapidly, inarticulately, and usually unintelligibly — see BABBLE 1

**driver** *n* a person who travels by automobile — see MOTORIST

**drizzle** *n* a light or fine rain ⟨the intermittent *drizzle* was just heavy enough to spoil all of our outdoor activities⟩
*syn* mist, sprinkle
*rel* precipitation, rainfall, shower
*near ant* cloudburst, deluge, downpour, storm; rainstorm, thunderstorm; monsoon

**droll** *adj* causing or intended to cause laughter — see FUNNY 1

**drollness** *n* the amusing quality or element in something — see HUMOR 1

[1]**drone** *n* a lazy person — see LAZYBONES

**²drone** *n* a monotonous sound like that of an insect in motion — see HUM

**drone** *vb* to fly, turn, or move rapidly with a fluttering or vibratory sound — see WHIRR

**drool** *vb* to let saliva or some other substance flow from the mouth ⟨the dog *drooled* when we put the steak down on the floor⟩
*syn* dribble, drivel, salivate, slaver, slobber
*rel* water; expectorate, spit; foam, froth; sputter

**droop** *n* the extent to which something hangs or dips below a straight line — see SAG

**droop** *vb* **1** to be limp from lack of water or vigor ⟨the flowers *drooped* on their stalks in the blazing sun⟩
*syn* flag, hang, loll, sag, wilt
*rel* slouch, slump; collapse, drop, fall, sink, subside
*near ant* distend, stiffen; rise, straighten
**2** to lose bodily strength or vigor — see WEAKEN 2

**drooping** *adj* bending downward or forward — see NODDING

**droopy** *adj* **1** bending downward or forward — see NODDING
**2** not stiff in structure — see LIMP 1
**3** feeling unhappiness — see SAD 1

**drop** *n* **1** the quantity of fluid that falls naturally in one rounded mass ⟨a *drop* of water fell from the leaky faucet every few seconds⟩
*syn* blob, driblet, drip, droplet, glob, globule
*rel* dewdrop, raindrop, tear; spatter; dribble, trickle
**2** distance measured from the top to the bottom of something — see DEPTH 1
**3** the act or process of going to a lower level or altitude — see DESCENT 1
**4** the amount by which something is lessened — see DECREASE
**5** the more favorable condition or position in a competition — see ADVANTAGE 1

**drop** *vb* **1** to cause to fall intentionally or unintentionally ⟨I *dropped* the fly ball⟩ ⟨*drop* the anchor⟩
*syn* depress, lower
*rel* flatten, floor, level; bobble, bungle, foozle, fumble; immerse, sink, submerge
*ant* lift, pick up, raise
**2** to go to a lower level ⟨although they start out high, prices for home electronics eventually *drop*⟩
*syn* decline, descend, dip, fall, lower, nose-dive, plummet, plunge, sink, tumble
*rel* decrease, diminish, lessen; recede, retreat
*ant* arise, lift, rise, soar
**3** to bring (as an action or operation) to an immediate end — see STOP 1
**4** to stop doing (something) permanently — see QUIT 2
**5** to lead or extend downward — see DESCEND 1
**6** to put an end to (something planned or previously agreed to) — see CANCEL 1
**7** to bring forth from the womb — see BEAR 1
**8** to strike (someone) so forcefully as to cause a fall — see FELL 1

**drop** (by *or* in) *vb* to make a brief visit — see CALL 3

**droplet** *n* the quantity of fluid that falls naturally in one rounded mass — see DROP 1

**dropping** *n* **1 droppings** *pl* solid matter discharged from an animal's alimentary canal ⟨the only bad part about owning a rabbit was cleaning the *droppings* out of the cage every night⟩
*syn* dung, excrement, excreta, feces, slops, waste
*rel* stool; dunghill, guano, manure, muck; spoor; sewage
**2** the act of putting an end to something planned or previously agreed to — see CANCELLATION

**dross** *n* discarded or useless material — see GARBAGE

**droughty** *adj* marked by little or no precipitation or humidity — see DRY 1

**drove** *n* **1** a great number of persons or things gathered together — see CROWD 1
**2** a group of domestic animals assembled or herded together — see HERD

**drown** *vb* **1** to cover or become filled with a flood — see FLOOD
**2** to wet thoroughly with liquid — see SOAK 1

**drowse** *n* a short sleep — see ¹NAP

**drowse** *vb* to sleep lightly or briefly — see NAP 1

**drowsiness** *n* the quality or state of desiring or needing sleep — see SLEEPINESS

**drowsy** *adj* **1** desiring or needing sleep — see SLEEPY 1
**2** tending to cause sleep — see HYPNOTIC

**drub** *vb* **1** to strike repeatedly — see BEAT 1
**2** to achieve a victory over — see BEAT 2
**3** to defeat by a large margin — see WHIP 2

**drubbing** *n* failure to win a contest — see DEFEAT 1

**drudge** *n* a person who does very hard or dull work — see SLAVE 2

**drudge** *vb* to devote serious and sustained effort — see LABOR

**drudger** *n* a person who does very hard or dull work — see SLAVE 2

**drudgery** *n* very hard or unpleasant work — see TOIL

**drug** *n* a substance or preparation used to treat disease — see MEDICINE

**druggist** *n* a person who prepares drugs according to a doctor's prescription ⟨she got her prescription for antibiotics filled by the *druggist*⟩
*syn* apothecary, pharmacist
*rel* pharmacologist

**drugstore** *n* a retail store where medicines and miscellaneous articles are sold

⟨we picked up her medicine and some toothpaste at the *drugstore*⟩
***syn*** pharmacy
***rel*** dispensary

**drum** *n* a metal container in the shape of a cylinder — see CAN

**drum** *vb* to strike or cause to strike lightly and usually rhythmically — see [1]TAP

**drum** (out) *vb* to drive or force out — see EJECT 1

**drunk** *adj* being under the influence of alcohol ⟨several wedding guests who got a little *drunk*⟩
***syn*** drunken, high, inebriate, inebriated, intoxicated, loaded [*slang*], soused, tipsy
***rel*** maudlin; befuddled, stupefied; debauched, dissipated, dissolute
***near ant*** abstemious, abstinent, temperate; clearheaded, cool, level, steady
***ant*** sober

**drunk** *n* **1** a person who makes a habit of getting drunk ⟨you can't trust anything that old *drunk* says⟩
***syn*** drunkard, inebriate, soak, sot, souse, tippler
***rel*** alcoholic, substance abuser; drinker
***near ant*** abstainer
**2** a bout of drinking — see CAROUSE

**drunkard** *n* a person who makes a habit of getting drunk — see DRUNK

**drunken** *adj* being under the influence of alcohol — see DRUNK

**dry** *adj* **1** marked by little or no precipitation or humidity ⟨the *dry* climate of the American Southwest⟩
***syn*** arid, droughty, sere, thirsty, waterless
***rel*** baked, dehydrated, parched, sun-baked; rainless
***near ant*** drenched, dripping, saturated, soaked, soaking, sodden, sopping, soppy, soused
***ant*** damp, dank, humid, moist, wet
**2** causing weariness, restlessness, or lack of interest — see BORING

**dry** *vb* **1** to make dry ⟨they *dried* the grapes to make raisins⟩
***syn*** dehydrate, parch, sear
***rel*** dehumidify; evaporate; shrivel, wither
***near ant*** deluge, douse, drench, saturate, soak, sop, souse; damp, dampen, moisten; rehydrate
***ant*** hydrate, wet
**2** to lose liveliness, force, or freshness — see WITHER

**dryad** *n* a mythical goddess represented as a young girl and said to live outdoors — see NYMPH 1

**dry run** *n* a private performance or session in preparation for a public appearance — see REHEARSAL

**dual** *adj* consisting of two members or parts that are usually joined — see DOUBLE 1

**dub** *vb* to give a name to — see NAME 1

**dubious** *adj* **1** giving good reason for being doubted, questioned, or challenged — see DOUBTFUL 2
**2** having doubts about the wisdom of doing something — see HESITANT
**3** not likely to be true or to occur — see IMPROBABLE
**4** not feeling sure about the truth, wisdom, or trustworthiness of someone or something — see DOUBTFUL 1

**dubiously** *adv* with distrust — see ASKANCE

**duck** *vb* **1** to get or keep away from (as a responsibility) through cleverness or trickery — see ESCAPE 2
**2** to move suddenly aside or to and fro — see DODGE 1
**3** to sink or push (something) briefly into or as if into a liquid — see DIP 1

**ducking** *n* the act or a means of getting or keep-ing away from something undesirable — see ESCAPE 2

**duck soup** *n* something that is easy to do — see CINCH

**duct** *n* a long hollow cylinder for carrying a substance (as a liquid or gas) — see PIPE 1

**dud** *n* **1** something that has failed — see FAILURE 3
**2 duds** *pl* covering for the human body — see CLOTHING

**dude** *n* **1** a man extremely interested in his clothing and personal appearance — see DANDY 1
**2** an adult male human being — see MAN 1

**dudgeon** *n* the feeling of being offended or resentful after a slight or indignity — see PIQUE

**due** *adj* **1** having reached the date at which payment is required ⟨the loan is *due* next April⟩
***syn*** mature
***rel*** delinquent, outstanding, overdue, owed, owing, receivable, unpaid, unsettled; payable
**2** being in accordance with the prescribed, normal or logical course of events ⟨their train is *due* to arrive in half an hour⟩
***syn*** anticipated, awaited, expected, scheduled, slated
***near ant*** belated, delinquent, dilatory, latish, overdue, tardy
**3** being what is called for by accepted standards of right and wrong — see JUST 1

**due** *adv* in a direct line or course — see DIRECTLY 1

**due** (to) *adj* coming as a result — see RESULTANT

**duel** *n* an earnest effort for superiority or victory over another — see CONTEST 1

**due to** *prep* as the result of — see BECAUSE OF

**dull** *adj* **1** lacking sharpness of edge or point ⟨the *dull* knife just bounced off the skin of the tomato without cutting it⟩
***syn*** blunt, blunted, dulled, obtuse
***rel*** rounded
***near ant*** cutting, edged, edgy, ground, honed, stropped; jagged, needlelike, prickly, spiked, spiky, spiny
***ant*** keen, pointed, sharp, sharpened, whetted

**2** causing weariness, restlessness, or lack of interest — see BORING
**3** covered over by clouds — see OVERCAST
**4** lacking a surface luster or gloss — see MATTE
**5** lacking intensity of color — see PALE 1
**6** not having or showing an ability to absorb ideas readily — see STUPID 1
**7** not loud in pitch or volume — see SOFT 1
**8** slow to move or act — see INACTIVE 1

**dull** *vb* **1** to reduce or weaken in strength or feeling ⟨the aspirin *dulled* his headache and he was soon feeling better⟩
***syn*** benumb, blunt, damp, dampen, deaden, numb
***rel*** muffle, mute, tone (down); decrease, diminish, lessen, let up (on), reduce, subdue; debilitate, enfeeble, weaken; dwindle, recede, subside, taper (off), wane; alleviate, ease, lighten; abate, moderate
***near ant*** amplify, beef (up), boost, consolidate, deepen, enhance, heighten, intensify, magnify, redouble, step up, strengthen; animate, arouse, stimulate
***ant*** sharpen; whet
**2** to make white or lighter by removing color — see WHITEN

**dulled** *adj* **1** lacking a surface luster or gloss — see MATTE
**2** lacking intensity of color — see PALE 1
**3** lacking sharpness of edge or point — see DULL 1

**dullness** *also* **dulness** *n* the quality or state of lacking intelligence or quickness of mind — see STUPIDITY 1

**dumb** *adj* **1** deliberately refraining from speech — see SILENT 1
**2** not having or showing an ability to absorb ideas readily — see STUPID 1

**dumbbell** *n* a stupid person — see IDIOT

**dumbfound** *also* **dumfound** *vb* to make a strong impression on (someone) with something unexpected — see SURPRISE 1

**dumbfounded** *or* **dumfounded** *adj* **1** affected with sudden and great wonder or surprise — see THUNDERSTRUCK
**2** filled with amazement or wonder — see OPENMOUTHED

**dumbfounding** *or* **dumfounding** *adj* causing a strong emotional reaction because unexpected — see SURPRISING 1

**dumbness** *n* **1** incapacity for or restraint from speaking — see SILENCE 1
**2** the quality or state of lacking intelligence or quickness of mind — see STUPIDITY 1

**dummy** *n* **1** a stupid person — see IDIOT
**2** a three-dimensional representation of the human body used especially for displaying clothes — see MANNEQUIN 1

**dump** *n* **1** a place where discarded materials (as trash) are dumped ⟨all of the used packaging eventually ends up in the *dump*⟩
***syn*** landfill, sanitary landfill
***rel*** pigpen, pigsty
**2** a place where military arms are stored — see ARMORY

**dump** *vb* to get rid of as useless or unwanted — see DISCARD

**dumping** *n* the getting rid of whatever is unwanted or useless — see DISPOSAL 1

**dumps** *n pl* a state or spell of low spirits — see SADNESS

**dumpy** *adj* being compact and broad in build and often short in stature — see STOCKY

**dun** *n* something that someone insists upon having — see DEMAND 1

**dunce** *n* a stupid person — see IDIOT

**dung** *n* solid matter discharged from an animal's alimentary canal — see DROPPING 1

**dunk** *vb* to sink or push (something) briefly into or as if into a liquid — see DIP 1

**duo** *n* two things of the same or similar kind that match or are considered together — see PAIR

**dupe** *n* one who is easily deceived or cheated ⟨the swindler was able to escape with all of the *dupe's* money⟩
***syn*** chump, gull, pigeon, sap, sucker, tool
***rel*** victim; schlemiel; butt, derision, laughingstock, mark, mock, mockery; booby, dodo, fool, goose, half-wit, jackass, lunatic, monkey, nincompoop, ninny, nitwit, simpleton, turkey; pushover; loser
***near ant*** confidence man, shark, sharper, swindler, trickster

**dupe** *vb* to cause to believe what is untrue — see DECEIVE

**duplex** *adj* consisting of two members or parts that are usually joined — see DOUBLE 1

**duplicate** *adj* resembling another in every respect — see SAME 1

**duplicate** *n* **1** something or someone that strongly resembles another — see IMAGE 1
**2** something that is made to look exactly like something else — see COPY 1

**duplicate** *vb* **1** to make an exact likeness of — see COPY 1
**2** to make or do again — see REPEAT 4
**3** to make twice as great or as many — see DOUBLE 1

**duplication** *n* **1** something or someone that strongly resembles another — see IMAGE 1
**2** something that is made to look exactly like something else — see COPY
**3** the act of saying or doing over again — see REPEAT

**duplicity** *n* the inclination or practice of misleading others through lies or trickery — see DECEIT

**durability** *n* continuing existence — see PERSISTENCE 1

**duration** *n* **1** the period during which something exists, lasts, or is in progress ⟨for the whole *duration* of the speech the bored audience fidgeted⟩
***syn*** date, life, life span, lifetime, run, standing, time

---

***syn*** synonym(s) ***rel*** related words
***ant*** antonym(s) ***near ant*** near antonym(s)

*rel* spell, stretch; span, tenure, term; hitch, tour, turn
**2** uninterrupted or lasting existence — see CONTINUATION

**duress** *n* the use of power to impose one's will on another — see FORCE 2

**during** *prep* in the course of ‹we wrote notes *during* the boring lecture›
*syn* over, through, throughout

**dusk** *n* **1** the time from when the sun begins to set to the onset of total darkness ‹we stopped playing at *dusk*, since it was getting too dark to see the ball›
*syn* evening, eventide, gloaming, nightfall, sundown, sunset, twilight
*rel* dark, darkness, night, nighttime
*near ant* day, daytime, light
*ant* aurora, cockcrow, dawn, dawning, daybreak, daylight, morn, morning, sunrise, sunup
**2** a time or place of little or no light — see DARK 1

**dusky** *adj* being without light or without much light — see DARK 1

**dust** *n* **1** discarded or useless material — see GARBAGE
**2** the solid part of our planet's surface as distinguished from the sea and air — see EARTH 2

**dustiness** *n* the state or quality of being dirty — see DIRTINESS 1

**dusty** *adj* **1** consisting of very small particles — see FINE 1
**2** not clean — see DIRTY 1

**dutiful** *adj* marked by or showing proper regard for another's higher status — see RESPECTFUL

**duty** *n* **1** a charge usually of money collected by the government from people or businesses for public use — see TAX
**2** a piece of work that needs to be done regularly — see CHORE 1
**3** something one must do because of prior agreement — see OBLIGATION

**dwarf** *adj* of a size that is less than average — see SMALL 1

**dwarf** *n* **1** a living thing much smaller than others of its kind ‹Shetland ponies are the *dwarfs* of the horse world›
*syn* diminutive, midget, mite, peewee, pygmy, runt, scrub, shrimp
*rel* mini, miniature
*near ant* whale
*ant* behemoth, colossus, giant, jumbo, leviathan, mammoth, monster, titan
**2** an imaginary being usually having a small human form and magical powers — see FAIRY

**dwarf** *vb* to hold back the normal growth of — see STUNT

**dwarfish** *adj* of a size that is less than average — see SMALL 1

**dwell** *vb* **1** to continue to be in a place for a significant amount of time — see STAY 1
**2** to have a home — see LIVE 1

**dweller** *n* one who lives permanently in a place — see INHABITANT

**dwelling** *n* the place where one lives — see HOME 1

**dwindle** *vb* **1** to make smaller in amount, volume, or extent — see DECREASE 1
**2** to grow less in scope or intensity especially gradually — see DECREASE 2

**dye** *n* a substance used to color other materials — see PIGMENT

**dye** *vb* to give color or a different color to — see COLOR 1

**dyestuff** *n* a substance used to color other materials — see PIGMENT

**dying** *adj* nearly dead — see MORIBUND

**dynamic** *adj* **1** having active strength of body or mind — see VIGOROUS 1
**2** marked by or uttered with forcefulness — see EMPHATIC 1

**dyspeptic** *adj* having or showing a habitually bad temper — see ILL-TEMPERED

# E

**each** *adj* being one of a group ‹*each* park visitor receives a free souvenir›
*syn* any, every
*rel* all; several, various; particular; respective, specific
*phrases* each and every

**each** *adv* for each one — see APIECE

**eager** *adj* showing urgent desire or interest ‹Tom was *eager* to try out his new pair of skis›
*syn* agog, anxious, ardent, athirst, avid, crazy, desirous, enthusiastic, excited, gung ho, hot, hungry, impatient, keen, nuts, raring, solicitous, thirsty, voracious
*rel* engaged, interested; hung up, obsessed; ambitious, covetous, craving, hankering, longing, pining; restive, restless; disposed, inclined, ready, unreluctant, willing
*phrases* champing at the bit
*near ant* incurious, unconcerned, uninterested; aloof, detached, disinterested; impassive, stolid; halfhearted, lackadaisical, languid, languorous, spiritless; averse, disinclined, hesitant, loath (*or* loth), reluctant, unwilling
*ant* apathetic, indifferent, uneager

**eagerness** *n* urgent desire or interest ‹students with an *eagerness* to learn›
*syn* appetite, ardor, avidity, desirousness, enthusiasm, excitement, hunger, impatience, keenness, thirst
*rel* alacrity, quickness; ambition, gusto, zest

*near ant* unconcern; aloofness, detachment; impassivity, languor
*ant* apathy, indifference

**ear** *n* a state of being aware — see ATTENTION 2

**earliest** *adj* coming before all others in time or order — see FIRST 1

**early** *adj* 1 relating to or occurring near the beginning of a process, series, or time period ⟨*early* birds of the Jurassic period⟩
*syn* ancient, primal, primeval, primitive, primordial
*rel* aged, antediluvian, antiquated, antique, hoary
*near ant* advanced, complex
*ant* late
2 occurring before the usual or expected time ⟨we had an *early* dinner so as not to miss the concert⟩
*syn* inopportune, precocious, premature, unseasonable, untimely
*rel* unanticipated, unexpected; abrupt, sudden
*near ant* slow, tardy; anticipated, expected
*ant* late

**early** *adv* before the usual or expected time ⟨that year spring arrived *early*⟩
*syn* beforehand, inopportunely, precociously, prematurely, unseasonably
*rel* immediately, promptly, punctually; betimes, seasonably
*near ant* belatedly, tardily
*ant* late

**earmark** *vb* to keep or intend for a special purpose — see DEVOTE 1

**earn** *vb* 1 to receive as return for effort ⟨for years I've *earned* pocket money by mowing lawns⟩
*syn* acquire, attain, capture, carry, draw, gain, garner, get, land, make, obtain, procure, realize, secure, win
*rel* clear, net; accomplish, achieve, notch (up), score; accumulate, draw, rack up; catch, pick up; occupy, take over; reacquire, recapture, regain, remake
*phrases* come by
*near ant* give up, hand over, part (with), relinquish, surrender, yield
*ant* forfeit, lose
2 to be or make worthy of (as a reward or punishment) ⟨you've *earned* the afternoon off after all that hard work⟩
*syn* deserve, merit, rate
*rel* entitle, qualify

**earnest** *adj* not joking or playful in mood or manner — see SERIOUS 1

**earnestness** *n* a mental state free of jesting or trifling ⟨practiced the art of acting with great *earnestness*⟩
*syn* gravity, intentness, seriousness, soberness, sobriety, solemnity
*rel* deliberation, determination, firmness, purposefulness, resolve; absorption, attentiveness, concentration, engrossment
*near ant* lightness, shallowness, superficiality; dalliance, dilettantism
*ant* frivolity, levity, lightheartedness

**earnings** *n pl* 1 an increase usually measured in money that comes from labor, business, or property — see INCOME
2 the amount of money left when expenses are subtracted from the total amount received — see PROFIT 1

**earshot** *n* range of hearing ⟨babysitters should remain within *earshot* of young children⟩
*syn* hearing, sound
*rel* volume; distance, sight

**earsplitting** *adj* marked by a high volume of sound — see LOUD 1

**earth** *n* 1 the celestial body on which we live ⟨environmentalists who are committed to preserving the *earth*⟩
*syn* globe, planet, world
*rel* cosmos, creation, universe; orb, sphere; macrocosm, microcosm
2 the solid part of our planet's surface as distinguished from the sea and air ⟨after nearly drowning, I was glad to feel the *earth* under my feet⟩
*syn* dirt, dust, ground, land, soil
*rel* continent, landmass; island, isthmus, mainland, peninsula
3 the loose surface material in which plants naturally grow — see DIRT 1

**earthenware** *n* articles made of baked clay — see CROCKERY

**earthlike** *adj* consisting or suggestive of earth — see EARTHY 1

**earthly** *adj* having to do with life on earth especially as opposed to that in heaven ⟨a sermon against our obsession with *earthly* pursuits⟩
*syn* carnal, fleshly, material, mundane, temporal, terrestrial, worldly
*rel* bodily, corporal, corporeal, physical; daily, diurnal; unspiritual
*near ant* celestial, empyreal, empyrean; divine, spiritual, utopian; extraterrestrial
*ant* heavenly, nontemporal

**earthquake** *n* a shaking of the earth ⟨the San Andreas Fault is notorious for its *earthquakes*⟩
*syn* quake, tremor
*rel* shock; cataclysm, convulsion, upheaval

**earthy** *adj* 1 consisting or suggestive of earth ⟨the unmistakably *earthy* aroma of a greenhouse⟩
*syn* earthlike, loamy
*rel* clayey, dusty, muddy, sandy
2 willing to see things as they really are and deal with them sensibly — see REALISTIC 1

**ease** *n* 1 reduction of or freedom from pain ⟨the sunburn medication brought me instant *ease*⟩
*syn* alleviation, comfort, relief
*rel* appeasement, assuagement, decrease, diminishment, moderation, mollification; calming, salving, soothing
*near ant* discomfort, unrest; agony, anguish, pain
2 carefree freedom from constraint — see ABANDON
3 freedom from activity or labor — see [1]REST 1

---

*syn* synonym(s) *rel* related words
*ant* antonym(s) *near ant* near antonym(s)

**ease** *vb* **1** to free from obstruction or difficulty ⟨measures intended to *ease* the flow of traffic during rush hour⟩
*syn* facilitate, loosen (up), smooth, unclog
*rel* accelerate, expedite, hasten, speed; advance, further, promote; aid, assist, help, improve
*phrases* pave the way (for)
*near ant* hinder, impede; retard
*ant* complicate
**2** to make less taut — see SLACKEN
**3** to make more bearable or less severe — see HELP 2

**easily** *adv* without difficulty ⟨a skater who *easily* executes even the most difficult jumps⟩
*syn* effortlessly, facilely, fluently, freely, handily, lightly, painlessly, readily, smoothly
*rel* ably, adeptly, adroitly, competently, dexterously, efficiently, expertly, proficiently, skillfully; instinctively, intuitively, naturally, spontaneously
*near ant* awkwardly, clumsily, gracelessly, ineptly, maladroitly; painfully, painstakingly
*ant* arduously, laboriously

**easy** *adj* **1** involving minimal difficulty or effort ⟨a minor problem with an *easy* solution⟩
*syn* effortless, facile, fluent, fluid, light, painless, ready, simple, smooth, snap, soft
*rel* apparent, clear, distinct, evident, manifest, obvious, plain; clear-cut, straightforward, uncomplicated
*near ant* painful, troublesome; abstruse, complex, complicated, intricate, knotty
*ant* arduous, difficult, hard, labored
**2** readily taken advantage of ⟨senior citizens who are *easy* prey for scam artists⟩
*syn* exploitable, gullible, naive (*or* naïve), susceptible, trusting
*rel* credulous, trustful, uncritical, unsuspecting, unsuspicious; artless, simple, unsophisticated
*near ant* critical, cynical, mistrustful, skeptical, suspicious; sophisticated
**3** providing physical comfort — see COMFORTABLE 1

**easygoing** *adj* **1** having a relaxed, casual manner ⟨counselors at the summer camp are pretty *easygoing*⟩
*syn* affable, breezy, devil-may-care, happy-go-lucky, laid-back, low-pressure
*rel* carefree, lackadaisical, nonchalant, unaffected, unconcerned; familiar, homey, informal; lax, lenient, permissive, soft
*near ant* ceremonious, decorous; formal, rigid, strict
*ant* uptight
**2** not bound by rigid standards ⟨boys are pretty *easygoing* about housekeeping⟩
*syn* flexible, lax, loose, relaxed, slack, unrestrained, unrestricted
*rel* careless, heedless, negligent, slipshod, sloppy, slovenly, unfussy
*near ant* constrained, restrained, restricted, rigid, strict, tight; exact, fussy, meticulous, scrupulous
*ant* rigorous
**3** having or showing a lack of concern or seriousness — see CAREFREE

**eat** *vb* **1** to take in as food ⟨having gone all day without food, we greedily *ate* the hamburgers⟩
*syn* consume, ingest
*rel* digest, down, mouth (down), swallow; bolt, devour, gobble (up *or* down), gorge, gulp, wolf; chew, gnaw (at *or* on), lap, lick, nibble (on); relish, savor, taste; banquet, dine, feast, gormandize, pig out; dispatch, polish off; breakfast, lunch, sup; munch, snack
**2** to consume or wear away gradually ⟨the pot's protective coating was *eaten* away by the acid⟩
*syn* bite (at), corrode, erode, fret
*rel* break down, break up, decompose, disintegrate, dissolve; destroy, ruin, wreck
**3** to take a meal — see DINE 1

**eat (up)** *vb* to destroy all trace of — see CONSUME 1

**eatable** *adj* suitable for use as food — see EDIBLE

**eatables** *n pl* substances intended to be eaten — see FOOD

**eavesdrop (on)** *vb* to listen to (another in private conversation) ⟨a nosy traveler who likes to *eavesdrop on* his fellow airline passengers⟩
*syn* listen in (on), overhear
*rel* bug, tap, wiretap; monitor, snoop, spy; hear, hearken

**eaves trough** *n* a pipe or channel for carrying off water from a roof — see GUTTER 1

**ebb** *vb* **1** to become worse or of less value — see DETERIORATE
**2** to grow less in scope or intensity especially gradually — see DECREASE 2

**ebbing** *n* a gradual sinking and wasting away of mind or body — see DECLINE 1

**ebony** *adj* having the color of soot or coal — see BLACK 1

**eccentric** *n* a person of odd or whimsical habits ⟨an *eccentric* who designed his house to look like a Scottish castle⟩
*syn* character, codger, crackbrain, crackpot, crank, kook, nut, oddball, screwball, weirdo
*rel* bohemian, maverick, nonconformist; coot, rarity; freak
*near ant* conformer, conformist, follower, sheep

**eccentricity** *n* an odd or peculiar habit — see IDIOSYNCRASY

**ecclesiastic** *n* a person specially trained and authorized to conduct religious services in a Christian church — see CLERGYMAN

**ecclesiastical** *or* **ecclesiastic** *adj* of or relating to a church ⟨*ecclesiastical* laws that have been in existence for centuries⟩
*syn* churchly
*rel* divine, holy, religious, sacramental; apostolic, canonical, clerical, episcopal, evangelical, ministerial, papal, pastoral,

patriarchal, pontifical, priestly, rabbinical, sacerdotal
*near ant* lay, profane, secular, temporal

**echo** *vb* **1** to continue or be repeated in a series of reflected sound waves — see REVERBERATE
**2** to say after another — see REPEAT 3

**eclipse** *vb* to be greater, better, or stronger than — see SURPASS 1

**economical** *adj* careful in the management of money or resources — see FRUGAL

**economize** *vb* to avoid unnecessary waste or expense ⟨in tough times people learn how to *economize*⟩
*syn* save, scrimp, skimp
*rel* conserve, husband, manage; scrape; cut back, cut down, retrench
*near ant* dissipate, fritter (away), squander, throw away
*ant* waste

**economizing** *adj* careful in the management of money or resources — see FRUGAL

**economy** *n* careful management of material resources ⟨people on fixed incomes are used to practicing *economy*⟩
*syn* frugality, husbandry, providence, scrimping, skimping, thrift
*rel* conservation, saving; miserliness, stinginess; discretion, prudence
*near ant* extravagance, improvidence, lavishness, prodigality, squandering
*ant* wastefulness

**ecstasy** *n* a state of overwhelming usually pleasurable emotion ⟨actors are typically in *ecstasy* upon winning an Oscar⟩
*syn* elation, euphoria, exhilaration, heaven, intoxication, paradise, rapture, rhapsody, transport
*rel* exaltation; bliss, blissfulness, delight, enchantment, gladness, happiness, joy, joyfulness, pleasure; reverie, trance; inspiration; fervor, frenzy, madness, passion
*near ant* blues, dejection, despondency, doldrums, downheartedness, dumps, melancholy, mopes
*ant* depression

**ecstatic** *adj* experiencing or marked by overwhelming usually pleasurable emotion ⟨a football player who was *ecstatic* upon receiving a full athletic scholarship to the college of his choice⟩
*syn* elated, enraptured, entranced, euphoric, exhilarated, intoxicated, rapturous, rhapsodic (*also* rhapsodical)
*rel* exultant, jubilant, triumphant; enthusiastic, excited, gung ho, thrilled; blissful, delighted, glad, gratified, happy, joyful, joyous, pleased, satisfied, tickled
*near ant* blue, dejected, despondent, disconsolate, disheartened, downhearted, melancholy
*ant* depressed

**Eden** *n* a place or state of great happiness — see PARADISE 1

**edge** *n* **1** a harsh or sharp quality ⟨the teacher's voice had a sarcastic *edge* as she welcomed the tardy student to class⟩
*syn* acidity, acridness, acrimoniousness, acrimony, acuteness, asperity, bite, bitterness, harshness, keenness, poignancy, pungency, roughness, sharpness, tartness
*rel* ginger, punch, spice, tang; severity, shrillness, virulence; pointedness, thorniness
**2** the line or relatively narrow space that marks the outer limit of something — see BORDER 1
**3** the more favorable condition or position in a competition — see ADVANTAGE 1

**edge** *vb* to make sharp or sharper — see SHARPEN

**edged** *adj* having an edge thin enough to cut or pierce something — see SHARP 1

**edgewise** *adv* with one side faced forward — see SIDEWAYS

**edginess** *n* a state of nervousness marked by sudden jerky movements — see JUMPINESS

**edgy** *adj* **1** feeling or showing uncomfortable feelings of uncertainty — see NERVOUS 1
**2** having an edge thin enough to cut or pierce something — see SHARP 1

**edible** *adj* suitable for use as food ⟨*edible* plant products⟩
*syn* eatable, esculent
*rel* absorbable, chewable, digestible; nourishing, nutritious, nutritive; appetizing, delicious, flavorful, palatable, savory, succulent, tasty, toothsome
*near ant* indigestible, nondigestible
*ant* inedible

**edibles** *n pl* substances intended to be eaten — see FOOD

**edict** *n* **1** an order publicly issued by an authority ⟨the school board's *edict* put a new student dress code into effect⟩
*syn* decree, directive, fiat, ruling
*rel* call, decision, judgment (*or* judgement); announcement, declaration, dictum, manifesto, proclamation, pronouncement; canon, encyclical
**2** a statement of what to do that must be obeyed by those concerned — see COMMAND 1

**edifice** *n* **1** a large, magnificent, or massive building ⟨the U.S. Capitol is one of our nation's most impressive *edifices*⟩
*syn* hall, palace, tower
*rel* construction, erection, structure; castle, château, estate, manor, mansion, villa; mausoleum, memorial, monument
**2** something built as a dwelling, shelter, or place for human activity — see BUILDING

**edify** *vb* to provide (someone) with moral or spiritual understanding — see ENLIGHTEN 2

**edit** *vb* to prepare for publication by correcting, rewriting, or updating ⟨the publisher *edited* a new version of its best-selling school dictionary⟩
*syn* redraft, revamp, revise, rework

*rel* amend, correct, emend, rectify; collect, compile; issue, print, publish

**educate** *vb* **1** to cause to acquire knowledge or skill in some field — see TEACH **2** to provide (someone) with moral or spiritual understanding — see ENLIGHTEN 2

**educated** *adj* having or displaying advanced knowledge or education ⟨*educated* people are often more aware and tolerant of cultural and ethnic diversity⟩
*syn* erudite, knowledgeable, learned, literate, scholarly, well-read
*rel* civilized, cultivated, cultured; cerebral, highbrow, intellectual; polished, refined, well-bred; academic, bookish, didactic, pedantic, professorial; instructed, schooled, skilled, trained; homeschooled, self-educated, self-taught; briefed, enlightened, informed, versed
*near ant* uncivilized, uncultivated, uncultured; lowbrow, unintelligent ill-bred, unpolished, unrefined; uninformed
*ant* ignorant, illiterate, uneducated

**education** *n* **1** the act or process of imparting knowledge or skills to another ⟨a teacher who devoted herself to the *education* of children with special needs⟩
*syn* instruction, schooling, teaching, training, tutelage, tutoring
*rel* coaching, conditioning, cultivation, preparation, readying; development, direction, guidance, nurturance, nurturing; edification, enlightenment, improvement **2** the understanding and information gained from being educated ⟨a person whose extensive *education* was obvious to all who met him⟩
*syn* erudition, knowledge, learnedness, learning, scholarship, science
*rel* culture, edification, enlightenment; literacy, reading; bookishness, pedantry
*near ant* ignorance, illiteracy

**educational** *adj* **1** providing useful information or knowledge — see INFORMATIVE **2** of or relating to schooling or learning especially at an advanced level — see ACADEMIC

**educative** *adj* providing useful information or knowledge — see INFORMATIVE

**educator** *n* a person whose occupation is to give formal instruction in a school — see TEACHER

**educe** *vb* to draw out (something hidden, latent, or reserved) ⟨the gift of a puppy finally *educed* a response from the shy boy⟩
*syn* elicit, evoke, raise
*rel* drag, dredge (up), extort, pull, wangle, wrest, wring; gain, get, obtain procure, secure; expose, reveal, uncover
*near ant* miss, overlook, pass over

**eerie** *adj* fearfully and mysteriously strange or fantastic ⟨*eerie* noises would occasionally come from locked rooms in the castle⟩
*syn* creepy, haunting, spooky, uncanny, unearthly, weird
*rel* ghostly, spectral; odd, strange, uncommon, unusual; preternatural, supernatural; enigmatic (*also* enigmatical), inscrutable, mysterious, puzzling; dreadful, fearsome, horrible horrifying, terrible, terrifying
*near ant* common, commonplace, everyday, normal, ordinary usual

**efface** *vb* to destroy all traces of — see ANNIHILATE 1

**effect** *n* **1** a condition or occurrence traceable to a cause ⟨better health is always one of the *effects* of improved hygiene⟩
*syn* aftereffect, aftermath, conclusion, consequence, corollary, development, fate, fruit, issue, outcome, outgrowth, product, result, resultant, sequel, sequence, upshot
*rel* ramification; denouement, repercussion; conclusion, end; by-product, side effect
*phrases* matter of course
*near ant* consideration, determinant, factor; base, basis, foundation, ground, groundwork
*ant* antecedent, cause, occasion, reason **2** the power to bring about a result on another ⟨religion has a profound *effect* on our lives⟩
*syn* impact, influence, mark, repercussion, sway
*rel* authority, clout, prestige, weight; command, domination, dominion; consequence, importance, significance
**3 effects** *pl* transportable items that one owns — see POSSESSION 2

**effect** *vb* to be the cause of (a situation, action, or state of mind) ⟨classroom discussions designed to *effect* a change in racial attitudes⟩
*syn* bring about, cause, create, effectuate, engender, generate, induce, make, produce, prompt, result (in), spawn, work, yield
*rel* decide, determine; begin, establish, father, found, inaugurate, initiate, institute, introduce, set, set up; advance, encourage, forward, foster, promote; enact, render, turn out
*phrases* bring forth, give rise to
*near ant* impede, limit, restrict; dampen, repress, smother, stifle, suppress; arrest, check, curb, restrain, retard; can, kill, snuff (out), still; abolish, demolish, destroy, extinguish, liquidate, quash, quell, quench

**effective** *adj* **1** producing or capable of producing a desired result ⟨an *effective* treatment of the once-dreaded disease⟩
*syn* effectual, efficacious, efficient, fruitful, potent, productive
*rel* adequate, capable, competent; adept, expert, masterly, proficient, skilled, skillful; cogent, convincing, killer, sound, striking, telling, valid; active, dynamic; operative, useful, working; feasible, practical, realizable, workable
*near ant* incapable, incompetent, inexpert, unqualified; abortive, bootless, fu-

tile, vain; empty, hollow, idle, pointless; inoperative, useless, worthless
*ant* fruitless, ineffective, ineffectual, inefficient, unproductive
**2** having the power to persuade — see COGENT

**effectiveness** *n* **1** the capacity to persuade — see COGENCY 1
**2** the power to produce a desired result — see EFFICACY
**3** the quality of an utterance that provokes interest and produces an effect — see [1]PUNCH 1

**effectual** *adj* producing or capable of producing a desired result — see EFFECTIVE 1

**effectualness** *n* the power to produce a desired result — see EFFICACY

**effectuate** *vb* to be the cause of (a situation, action, or state of mind) — see EFFECT

**effeminate** *adj* having or displaying qualities more suitable for women than for men ⟨a comedian deliberately affecting *effeminate* mannerisms⟩
*syn* feminine, girlish, sissy, unmanly, womanish, womanlike, womanly
*rel* old-maidish, overnice, spinsterish; dandyish, foppish, sappy
*ant* manlike, manly, mannish, masculine

**effervescent** *adj* joyously unrestrained — see EXUBERANT

**effete** *adj* **1** having lost forcefulness, courage, or spirit ⟨the soft, *effete* society that marked the final years of the Roman empire⟩
*syn* decadent, decayed, degenerate, overripe, washed-up
*rel* decaying, declining, dying, failing, waning; soft, weak; dissolute, immoral
**2** depleted in strength, energy, or freshness — see WEARY 1
**3** lacking bodily strength — see WEAK 1
**4** lacking strength of will or character — see WEAK 2

**efficacious** *adj* producing or capable of producing a desired result — see EFFECTIVE 1

**efficaciousness** *n* the power to produce a desired result — see EFFICACY

**efficacy** *n* the power to produce a desired result ⟨questioned the *efficacy* of the alarms in actually preventing auto theft⟩
*syn* effectiveness, effectualness, efficaciousness, efficiency, productiveness
*rel* ability, capability, capacity; potency, strength
*near ant* inability, inadequacy, incompetence
*ant* ineffectiveness, ineffectualness, inefficiency

**efficiency** *n* the power to produce a desired result — see EFFICACY

**efficient** *adj* producing or capable of producing a desired result — see EFFECTIVE 1

**effort** *n* the active use of energy in producing a result ⟨the finished parade float was well worth the *effort*⟩
*syn* elbow grease, exertion, expenditure, labor, pains, sweat, trouble, while, work
*rel* drudgery, grind, toil, travail; dint, energy; force, might, muscle, power, puissance; attempt, endeavor, essay
*near ant* adroitness, ease, facility, fluency, smoothness; idleness, inaction, inactivity, indolence, inertia, languor, laziness

**effortless** *adj* involving minimal difficulty or effort — see EASY 1

**effortlessly** *adv* without difficulty — see EASILY

**effrontery** *n* shameless boldness ⟨the little squirt had the *effrontery* to deny eating any cookies, even with the crumbs still on his lips⟩
*syn* audacity, brashness, brass, brassiness, brazenness, cheek, cheekiness, chutzpah (*also* chutzpa *or* hutzpah *or* hutzpa), gall, nerve, nerviness, pertness, presumption, presumptuousness, sauce, sauciness, temerity
*rel* arrogance, assurance, cockiness, confidence, overconfidence, sanguinity, self-assurance, self-confidence; impertinence, impudence, insolence, rudeness
*near ant* bashfulness, diffidence, hesitancy, modesty, shyness, timidity

**effulgence** *n* the quality or state of having or giving off light — see BRILLIANCE 1

**effulgent** *adj* giving off or reflecting much light — see BRIGHT 1

**effusive** *adj* showing feeling freely — see DEMONSTRATIVE

**egg** (on) *vb* to try to persuade (someone) through earnest appeals to follow a course of action — see URGE

**ego** *n* **1** a reasonable or justifiable sense of one's worth or importance — see PRIDE 1
**2** an often unjustified feeling of being pleased with oneself or with one's situation or achievements — see COMPLACENCE

**egocentric** *adj* overly concerned with one's own desires, needs, or interests ⟨the cult attracts *egocentric* people who are preoccupied with reaching their potential as individuals⟩
*syn* egoistic, egotistic (*or* egotistical), self-centered, selfish, self-seeking
*rel* complacent, conceited, self-conceited, self-directed, self-important, self-indulgent, self-satisfied, smug, vain
*near ant* altruistic, generous, greatheart-ed, magnanimous, self-sacrificing
*ant* selfless

**egoism** *n* excessive interest in oneself ⟨because of her *egoism*, she never gave a thought to asking how the others felt⟩
*syn* egotism, self-centeredness, self-interest, selfishness, self-regard
*rel* conceit, self-admiration, self-conceit, self-esteem, self-importance, self-indulgence, self-respect, self-satisfaction, self-sufficiency

---

*syn* synonym(s) *rel* related words
*ant* antonym(s) *near ant* near antonym(s)

*near ant* altruism, generosity, magnanimity, self-sacrifice
*ant* selflessness

**egoistic** *adj* **1** having too high an opinion of oneself — see CONCEITED
**2** overly concerned with one's own desires, needs, or interests — see EGOCENTRIC

**egotism** *n* **1** an often unjustified feeling of being pleased with oneself or with one's situation or achievements — see COMPLACENCE
**2** excessive interest in oneself — see EGOISM

**egotistic** *or* **egotistical** *adj* **1** having too high an opinion of oneself — see CONCEITED
**2** overly concerned with one's own desires, needs, or interests — see EGOCENTRIC

**egregious** *adj* very noticeable especially for being incorrect or bad ⟨the student's theme was marred by a number of *egregious* errors in spelling⟩
*syn* blatant, conspicuous, flagrant, glaring, gross, obvious, patent, pronounced, rank, striking
*rel* clear, distinct, evident, notable, outstanding, plain, salient; absolute, arrant, downright, out-and-out, outright sheer, stark, utter; abominable, atrocious, awful, deplorable, execrable, heinous, monstrous, outrageous, preposterous, shameful, shocking
*near ant* imperceptible, inconspicuous; insignificant, slight, trifling, trivial; concealed, hidden, invisible

**egress** *n* a place or means of going out — see EXIT 1

**ejaculate** *vb* to utter with a sudden burst of strong feeling — see EXCLAIM

**eject** *vb* **1** to drive or force out ⟨we quickly *ejected* the unwanted guest from our party⟩
*syn* banish, boot (out), bounce, cast (out), chase, dismiss, drum (out) expel, extrude, oust, rout, run off, throw out
*rel* deport, displace, dispossess evict, exile, expatriate, ostracize, shut out; discharge, fire, sack
*phrases* send packing
*near ant* accept, admit, receive, take in; welcome; entertain, harbor, house lodge, shelter
**2** to throw out or off (something from within) often violently — see ERUPT 1

**eke out** *vb* to get with great difficulty ⟨*eked out* a living from the family's small farm⟩
*syn* scrape, scrounge, squeeze, wrest, wring
*rel* acquire, earn, gain, obtain, procure, secure

**elaborate** *adj* **1** made or done with great care or with much detail ⟨*elaborate* festivities for the 200th anniversary of the town's founding⟩
*syn* complex, complicated, detailed, fancy, intricate, involved, sophisticated
*rel* elegant, grand, ornate, magnificent, splendid; extravagant, flamboyant, frilly, grandiose, ostentatious, overwrought; labyrinthine
*near ant* modest, plain, uncomplicated, unsophisticated
*ant* simple
**2** including many small descriptive features — see DETAILED 1
**3** having many parts or aspects that are usually interrelated — see COMPLEX 1

**elaborate** (on) *vb* **1** to add to the interest of by including made-up details — see EMBROIDER
**2** to express more fully and in greater detail — see EXPAND 1

**elaborateness** *n* the state or quality of having many interrelated parts or aspects — see COMPLEXITY 1

**elaboration** *n* **1** the act or process of going from the simple or basic to the complex or advanced — see DEVELOPMENT 1
**2** the representation of something in terms that go beyond the facts — see EXAGGERATION

**elapse** *vb* to come to an end — see CEASE 1

**elastic** *adj* **1** able to revert to original size and shape after being stretched, squeezed, or twisted ⟨*elastic* rubber bands⟩
*syn* flexible, resilient, rubberlike, rubbery, springy, stretch, stretchable, supple
*rel* adaptable, ductile, malleable, moldable, plastic, pliable, pliant; limber, lissome (*also* lissom), lithe
*near ant* firm, hard, solid; brittle, crisp, friable
*ant* inelastic, inflexible, nonelastic, rigid, stiff
**2** capable of being readily changed — see FLEXIBLE 1

**elate** *vb* to fill with great joy ⟨the winning of the state basketball championship *elated* the whole student body⟩
*syn* elevate, enrapture, exhilarate, overjoy, transport
*rel* excite, inspire, stimulate, uplift; delight, gladden, gratify, please
*near ant* demoralize, discourage, dishearten, dispirit; distress, oppress, sadden
*ant* depress

**elated** *adj* experiencing or marked by overwhelming usually pleasurable emotion — see ECSTATIC

**elation** *n* a state of overwhelming usually pleasurable emotion — see ECSTASY

**elbow** *vb* to force one's way — see PRESS 4

**elbow grease** *n* the active use of energy in producing a result — see EFFORT

**elbowroom** *n* an extent or area available for or used up by some activity or thing — see ROOM 1

**elder** *n* **1** a person of advanced years — see SENIOR CITIZEN
**2** one who is above another in rank, station, or office — see SUPERIOR
**3** one who is older than another — see SENIOR 1

4 the senior member of a group — see DEAN

**elderly** *adj* being of advanced years and especially past middle age ⟨*elderly* people who stay active are usually the healthiest and the happiest⟩
*syn* aged, aging, ancient, geriatric, long-lived, old, older, senior
*rel* adult, grown-up, mature, middle-aged; pensioned, retired, superannuated; matriarchal, patriarchal, venerable; doddering, senile, tottery
*near ant* youngish; adolescent, immature, juvenile, puerile
*ant* young, youthful

**elder statesman** *n* the senior member of a group — see DEAN

**elect** *adj* singled out from a number or group as more to one's liking — see SELECT 1

**elect** *n* individuals carefully selected as being the best of a class — see ELITE

**elect** *vb* to decide to accept (someone or something) from a group of possibilities — see CHOOSE 1

**election** *n* the act or process of selecting — see SELECTION 1

**elective** *adj* subject to one's freedom of choice — see OPTIONAL

**electric** *adj* causing great emotional or mental stimulation — see EXCITING 1

**electrify** *vb* to cause a pleasurable stimulation of the feelings — see THRILL

**electrifying** *adj* causing great emotional or mental stimulation — see EXCITING 1

**elegance** *n* dignified or restrained beauty of form, appearance, or style ⟨the *elegance* of the hotel's French furnishings⟩
*syn* class, elegancy, grace, gracefulness, handsomeness, majesty, refinement, stateliness
*rel* grandeur, lavishness, luxuriousness, magnificence, ornateness, richness, splendor; artfulness, chic, polish, sophistication, taste, tastefulness; choiceness, classicism, dignity, exquisiteness, restraint, simplicity; affectedness, grandiosity, pretentiousness
*near ant* coarseness, crudeness, flashiness, garishness, gaudiness, gracelessness, grotesqueness, tastelessness, tawdriness

**elegancy** *n* dignified or restrained beauty of form, appearance, or style — see ELEGANCE

**elegant** *adj* 1 having or showing elegance ⟨the most *elegant* First Lady in the nation's history⟩ ⟨the bride's *elegant* gown received nothing but praise⟩
*syn* graceful, handsome, majestic, refined, stately, tasteful
*rel* grand, lavish, luxurious, magnificent, ornate, rich, splendid; artful, genteel, polished, sophisticated; classic, exquisite, restrained, simple; chic, fashionable, posh, smart, stylish; affected, grandiose, pretentious
*near ant* coarse, crude, flashy, garish, gaudy, grotesque, tacky, tawdry
*ant* graceless, inelegant, tasteless, unhandsome
2 having qualities that appeal to a refined taste — see CHOICE

**elegiac** *adj* causing or marked by an atmosphere lacking in cheer — see GLOOMY 1

**elegy** *n* a composition expressing one's grief over a loss — see LAMENT 2

**element** *n* 1 one of the parts that make up a whole ⟨a free press is an essential *element* of a democracy⟩
*syn* component, constituent, factor, ingredient, member
*rel* detail, item, particular, point; aspect, characteristic, facet, feature, trait; division, fragment, particle, piece, portion, section, sector, segment
*near ant* aggregate, composite, compound; sum, total, totality
*ant* whole
2 **elements** *pl* general or basic truths on which other truths or theories can be based — see PRINCIPLES 1

**elemental** *adj* of or relating to the simplest facts or theories of a subject — see ELEMENTARY

**elementary** *adj* of or relating to the simplest facts or theories of a subject ⟨students who do not have even an *elementary* knowledge of geography⟩
*syn* basic, elemental, essential, fundamental, rudimentary, underlying
*rel* primal, primary, prime; primitive; beginning, introductory, preliminary
*near ant* complex, sophisticated; detailed, extensive, intricate
*ant* advanced

**elephantine** *adj* unusually large — see HUGE

**elevate** *vb* 1 to fill with great joy — see ELATE
2 to move from a lower to a higher place or position — see RAISE 1
3 to move higher in rank or position — see PROMOTE 1

**elevated** *adj* 1 being positioned above a surface ⟨an *elevated* monorail that transports visitors all over the theme park⟩
*syn* lifted, raised, uplifted, upraised
*rel* aerial, suspended; erect, upright
*near ant* low-lying
*ant* sunken
2 very dignified in form, tone, or style ⟨the *elevated* language of Lincoln's Gettysburg Address⟩
*syn* eloquent, formal, high-flown, lofty, majestic, stately, towering
*rel* bombastic, declamatory, florid, flowery, grandiloquent, highfalutin, pompous, stilted
*near ant* casual, colloquial, conversational, informal, slangy; coarse, crude, indecent, vulgar
*ant* low, undignified
3 being at a higher level than average — see HIGH 2

---

*syn* synonym(s) *rel* related words
*ant* antonym(s) *near ant* near antonym(s)

4 having, characterized by, or arising from a dignified and generous nature — see NOBLE 2
5 located at a greater height than average or usual — see HIGH 3

**elevation** *n* 1 a raising or a state of being raised to a higher rank or position — see ADVANCEMENT 1
2 an area of high ground — see HEIGHT 4
3 the distance of something or someone from bottom to top — see HEIGHT 3
4 the most extreme or advanced point — see HEIGHT 2

**elf** *n* an imaginary being usually having a small human form and magical powers — see FAIRY

**elfin** *adj* having an often mysterious or magical power to attract — see FASCINATING 1

**elfish** *adj* given to good-natured joking or teasing — see PLAYFUL

**elicit** *vb* to draw out (something hidden, latent, or reserved) — see EDUCE

**eliminate** *vb* to prevent the participation or inclusion of — see EXCLUDE

**elite** *n* individuals carefully selected as being the best of a class ⟨the winners of this science award represent the *elite* of our high schools⟩
***syn*** best, choice, cream, elect, fat, flower, pick, prime, upper crust
***rel*** aristocracy, (the) establishment, gentry, nobility, society, (the) top, upper class
***phrases*** cream of the crop
***near ant*** commoners, masses, rank and file

**elixir** *n* something that cures all ills or problems — see CURE-ALL

**elliptic** *or* **elliptical** *adj* having the shape of an egg — see OVAL

**elocution** *n* the art of speaking in public eloquently and effectively — see ORATORY 1

**elongate** *vb* to make longer — see EXTEND 1

**elongated** *adj* of great extent from end to end — see LONG 1

**elongation** *n* the act of making longer — see EXTENSION 1

**eloquence** *n* the art or power of speaking or writing in a forceful and convincing way ⟨the *eloquence* of Martin Luther King's "I Have a Dream" speech⟩
***syn*** articulateness, poetry, rhetoric
***rel*** expression, expressiveness; declamation, elocution, oratory; forcefulness, meaningfulness, persuasiveness; ardor, fervor, passion, power

**eloquent** *adj* 1 able to express oneself clearly and well — see ARTICULATE
2 clearly conveying a special meaning (as one's mood) — see EXPRESSIVE
3 very dignified in form, tone, or style — see ELEVATED 2

**else** *adj* resulting in an increase in amount or number — see ADDITIONAL

**else** *adv* in a different way — see OTHERWISE

**elucidate** *vb* to make plain or understandable — see EXPLAIN 1

**elucidation** *n* a statement that makes something clear — see EXPLANATION 1

**elucidative** *adj* serving to explain — see EXPLANATORY

**elude** *vb* to get or keep away from (as a responsibility) through cleverness or trickery — see ESCAPE 2

**eluding** *n* the act or a means of getting or keeping away from something undesirable — see ESCAPE 2

**elusive** *adj* hard to find, capture, or isolate ⟨the giant squid is one of the ocean's most *elusive* inhabitants⟩
***syn*** evasive, fugitive, slippery
***rel*** cagey (*also* cagy), shifty; ephemeral, evanescent, fleeting, momentary, passing, short-lived, transitory; unavailable, unobtainable
***near ant*** accessible, approachable, attainable, available, obtainable

**elvish** *adj* tending to or exhibiting reckless playfulness — see MISCHIEVOUS 1

**Elysian** *adj* of, relating to, or suggesting heaven — see CELESTIAL

**Elysium** *n* 1 a dwelling place of perfect bliss for the soul after death — see HEAVEN 1
2 a place or state of great happiness — see PARADISE 1

**emaciated** *adj* suffering extreme weight loss as a result of hunger or disease ⟨the *emaciated* bodies of the survivors of the concentration camps⟩
***syn*** cadaverous, gaunt, haggard, skeletal, wasted
***rel*** bony, rawboned, scrawny, skinny, thin; starved, underfed, undernourished; shriveled, withered
***near ant*** beefy, brawny, burly, fit, hale, healthy, hearty, husky; chubby, corpulent, fat, fleshy, heavyset, plump, portly, stocky, thickset

**emancipate** *vb* to set free (as from slavery or confinement) — see FREE 1

**emancipation** *n* the act of setting free from slavery — see LIBERATION

**emasculate** *vb* to deprive of courage or confidence — see UNNERVE 1

**embankment** *n* a bank of earth constructed to control water — see DAM

**embargo** *n* an order that something not be done or used — see PROHIBITION 2

**embark** (on *or* upon) *vb* to take the first step in (a process or course of action) — see BEGIN 1

**embarrass** *vb* 1 to throw into a state of self-conscious distress ⟨the young soldier was *embarrassed* by the public praise for his heroism⟩
***syn*** abash, confound, confuse, discomfit, disconcert, discountenance, faze, fluster, mortify, nonplus, rattle
***rel*** agitate, bother, chagrin, discomfort, discompose, dismay, disquiet, distress, disturb, perturb, unhinge, unsettle, upset; debase, degrade, demean, humble, humiliate
***near ant*** calm, comfort, console, relieve, soothe; buoy, cheer, embolden, encourage, hearten; assure, reassure

2 to create difficulty for the work or activity of — see HAMPER

**embarrassing** *adj* causing embarrassment — see AWKWARD 3

**embarrassment** *n* 1 the emotional state of being made self-consciously uncomfortable ⟨experienced the great *embarrassment* of tripping while on stage⟩
*syn* abashment, confusion, discomfiture, fluster, mortification
*rel* agitation, bother, chagrin, discomfort, discomposure, dismay, disquiet, distress, disturbance, perturbation, uneasiness, upset; debasement, degradation, humiliation
*near ant* aplomb, assurance, composure, confidence, coolness, equanimity, poise, self-assurance, self-confidence, self-possession
2 something that makes movement or progress more difficult — see ENCUMBRANCE

**embed** *also* **imbed** *vb* to set solidly in or as if in surrounding matter — see ENTRENCH

**embellish** *vb* 1 to add to the interest of by including made-up details — see EMBROIDER
2 to make more attractive by adding something that is beautiful or becoming — see DECORATE

**embellishing** *adj* serving to add beauty — see DECORATIVE

**embellishment** *n* 1 something that decorates or beautifies — see DECORATION 1
2 the representation of something in terms that go beyond the facts — see EXAGGERATION

**embitter** *vb* to implant bitter feelings in ⟨the family refused to allow their collision with a drunk driver *embitter* them⟩
*syn* antagonize, envenom
*rel* aggravate, anger, enrage, incense, infuriate, madden; alienate, disaffect, disgruntle, estrange; sour
*near ant* endear, ingratiate; appease, assuage, mollify, pacify, placate, propitiate; sweeten

**embittered** *adj* having or showing deep-seated resentment — see BITTER 1

**emblem** *n* a device, design, or figure used as an identifying mark ⟨the oil company uses a scallop shell as its *emblem*⟩
*syn* hallmark, logo, symbol, trademark
*rel* icon, pictograph; badge, coat of arms, crest, insignia; monogram, stamp, token

**emblematic** *also* **emblematical** *adj* having the function or meaning of a symbol — see SYMBOLIC

**embodiment** *n* a visible representation of something abstract (as a quality) ⟨Mother Theresa was often regarded as the *embodiment* of selfless devotion to others⟩
*syn* epitome, incarnation, manifestation, personification
*rel* exemplification, incorporation, substantiation; essence, quintessence; archetype, exemplar, model, paradigm, pattern; acme, apex, culmination, peak, pinnacle, summit, zenith

**embody** *vb* 1 to make a part of a body or system ⟨concepts of moral behavior that we should *embody* into our daily life⟩
*syn* assimilate, incorporate, integrate
*rel* amalgamate, blend, combine, commingle, fuse, intermingle, merge, mingle
2 to represent in visible form ⟨George Washington *embodied* so many of the virtues that Americans hold dear⟩
*syn* epitomize, incarnate, manifest, materialize, personalize, personify, substantiate
*rel* actualize, realize; symbolize; exemplify, illustrate

**embolden** *vb* to fill with courage or strength of purpose — see ENCOURAGE 1

**emboldened** *adj* inclined or willing to take risks — see BOLD 1

**embosom** *vb* to surround or cover closely — see ENFOLD 1

**embower** *vb* to surround or cover closely — see ENFOLD 1

**embrace** *vb* 1 to put one's arms around and press tightly ⟨upon being finally reunited, the overjoyed father *embraced* his son⟩
*syn* clasp, enfold, grasp, hug
*rel* cling, cradle, grab, grip, hold; embosom, encircle, entwine, envelop; fold, lock, twine, wrap; cuddle, fondle, nestle, nuzzle, pat, pet, snuggle, stroke
2 to surround or cover closely — see ENFOLD 1
3 to take for one's own use (something originated by another) — see ADOPT
4 receive or accept gladly or readily — see WELCOME
5 to have as part of a whole — see INCLUDE

**embroider** *vb* to add to the interest of by including made-up details ⟨Dad likes to *embroider* his fishing stories⟩
*syn* color, elaborate (on), embellish, exaggerate, magnify, pad, stretch
*rel* amplify, enhance, enlarge (upon), expand, flesh (out); fudge, hedge; overdo, overdraw, overemphasize, overplay, overstate; caricature; satirize
*near ant* belittle, minimize, play (down), understate

**embroidering** *n* the representation of something in terms that go beyond the facts — see EXAGGERATION

**embroidery** *n* decorative stitching done on cloth with the use of a needle — see NEEDLEWORK

**embroil** *vb* to place in conflict or difficulties ⟨the town has been *embroiled* in controversy over the building of the huge shopping mall⟩
*syn* bog (down), mire
*rel* enmesh, ensnare, entangle, entrap, snare, tangle, trap
*near ant* emancipate, free, liberate, release

---

*syn* synonym(s) *rel* related words
*ant* antonym(s) *near ant* near antonym(s)

**emend** *vb* to remove errors, defects, deficiencies, or deviations from — see CORRECT 1

**emendation** *n* a change designed to correct or improve a written work — see CORRECTION 1

**emerge** *vb* to come to one's attention especially gradually or unexpectedly — see ARISE 2

**emergency** *n* a time or state of affairs requiring prompt or decisive action ⟨an alert, quick-thinking girl who is good to have around in an *emergency*⟩
*syn* clutch, crisis, crossroad(s), crunch, exigency, head, juncture, zero hour
*rel* contingency, possibility; climax, landmark, milestone, turning point; condition, pass, situation, strait; deadlock, impasse, stalemate; corner, fix, hole, hot water, jam, pinch, predicament, scrape, spot

**emigrant** *n* one that leaves one place to settle in another ⟨a city teeming with *emigrants* from many lands⟩
*syn* émigré (*also* emigré), immigrant, migrant, settler
*rel* defector, deportee, evacuee, exile, expatriate, refugee; alien, foreigner, noncitizen, nonnative; colonist, newcomer, squatter
*near ant* aborigine, native; citizen, inhabitant, national, resident
*ant* nonimmigrant

**émigré** *also* **emigré** *n* **1** a person forced to emigrate for political reasons ⟨the revolution resulted in a flood of *émigrés* into neighboring countries⟩
*syn* deportee, evacuee, exile, expatriate, refugee
*rel* alien, fugitive; castoff, outcast, pariah; loyalist, patriot
**2** one that leaves one place to settle in another — see EMIGRANT

**eminence** *n* **1** the fact or state of being above others in rank or importance ⟨the *eminence* of the Nobel Prize in the field of awards and prizes⟩
*syn* distinction, dominance, noteworthiness, preeminence, superiority
*rel* celebrity, fame, famousness, glory, honor, renown, reputation, repute; authority, greatness, influence, power, weight
*near ant* insignificance, unimportance; inferiority, mediocrity; obscurity
**2** an area of high ground — see HEIGHT 4

**eminent** *adj* standing above others in rank, importance, or achievement ⟨many *eminent* surgeons are on the hospital's staff⟩
*syn* distinguished, illustrious, noble, notable, noteworthy, outstanding, preeminent, prestigious, signal, star, superior
*rel* celebrated, famed, famous, glorious, honored, renowned, reputable; infamous, notorious; dominant, paramount, predominant
*near ant* insignificant, minor, unimportant; average, inferior, mediocre; obscure, uncelebrated, unsung

**emissary** *n* a person sent on a mission to represent another — see AMBASSADOR

**emit** *vb* **1** to throw or give off ⟨the cabin's chimney *emitted* smoke⟩
*syn* cast (off), discharge, exhale, expel, issue, release, shoot, vent
*rel* eliminate, evacuate, excrete, exude, ooze, secrete; gush, pour, spew
*near ant* absorb, inhale
**2** to send forth using the vocal chords — see UTTER 1

**emolument** *n* the money paid regularly to a person for labor or services — see WAGE

**emotion** *n* **1** a subjective response to a person, thing, or situation — see FEELING 1
**2** depth of feeling — see ARDOR 1

**emotional** *adj* **1** having or expressing great depth of feeling — see FERVENT
**2** having the power to affect the feelings or sympathies — see MOVING
**3** showing feeling freely — see DEMONSTRATIVE

**emphasis** *n* **1** a special notice or importance given to something ⟨a prep school with a long-established *emphasis* on sports⟩
*syn* accent, accentuation, stress, weight
*rel* attention, concentration, consideration, heed, note, regard; value, worth; consequence, import, moment, significance; precedence, primacy, priority
*near ant* apathy, disregard, indifference
**2** the quality or state of being forceful (as in expression) — see VEHEMENCE 1

**emphasize** *vb* to indicate the importance of by giving prominent display ⟨supermarket tabloids that *emphasize* sensational news stories⟩
*syn* accent, accentuate, feature, highlight, play (up), point (up), stress, underline, underscore
*rel* focus, identify, pinpoint, spotlight; advertise, boost, plug, promote, publicize
*near ant* tone (down), understate; belittle, discount, disparage, minimize
*ant* play (down)

**emphatic** *adj* **1** marked by or uttered with forcefulness ⟨the governor issued an *emphatic* denial of all charges⟩
*syn* aggressive, assertive, dynamic, energetic, forceful, resounding, strenuous, vehement, vigorous
*rel* decided, insistent, marked, pointed; arresting, compelling, conspicuous, noticeable, striking; absolute, categorical (*also* categoric), clear, plain, unambiguous, unequivocal
*near ant* guarded, mild, weak, wishy-washy; ambiguous, equivocal; understated
*ant* unemphatic
**2** likely to attract attention — see NOTICEABLE

**empire** *n* a group of businesses or enterprises under one control — see CONGLOMERATE

**empirical** *adj* based on observation or experience ⟨guidelines for raising children that are based on *empirical* evidence⟩

***syn*** experimental, objective, observational
***rel*** actual, factual, genuine, hard, real; accepted, established, tried, tried-and-true; indisputable, undeniable; demonstrable, provable, verifiable
***near ant*** conjectural, hypothetical, speculative; unproven, unsubstantiated, unverified
***ant*** nonempirical, theoretical (*also* theoretic)

**employ** *n* the state of being provided with a paying job — see HIRE 1

**employ** *vb* **1** to provide with a paying job ⟨a new factory that will *employ* 500 people⟩
***syn*** engage, hire, retain, take on
***rel*** recruit, sign on; keep
***near ant*** furlough, lay off
***ant*** can, discharge, dismiss, fire, sack
**2** to put into action or service — see USE 1

**employable** *adj* capable of or suitable for being used for a particular purpose — see USABLE 1

**employed** *adj* involved in often constant activity — see BUSY 1

**employee** *n* one who works for another for wages or a salary ⟨an employer who was loved and admired by generations of *employees*⟩
***syn*** hand, hireling, jobholder, worker
***rel*** assistant, cog, flunky (*also* flunkey), subordinate, underling, yes-man; drudge, grub, laborer, navvy [*chiefly British*], toiler, workingman, workman; associate, colleague, coworker
***near ant*** boss, superior, supervisor
***ant*** employer

**employment** *n* **1** the act or practice of employing something for a particular purpose — see USE 1
**2** the activity by which one regularly makes a living — see OCCUPATION
**3** the state of being provided with a paying job — see HIRE 1

**emporium** *n* an establishment where goods are sold to consumers — see SHOP 1

**empower** *vb* to give official or legal power to — see AUTHORIZE 1

**emptiness** *n* **1** a need or desire for food — see HUNGER 1
**2** empty space — see VACANCY 1
**3** the quality or state of being empty — see VACANCY 2

**empty** *adj* **1** lacking contents that could or should be present ⟨the refrigerator is *empty*, so we'll have to eat out⟩
***syn*** bare, blank, devoid, stark, vacant, void
***rel*** barren, hollow; available, clear, free, open; unfilled, unfurnished; unattended, uninhabited, unoccupied; abandoned, deserted, emptied, forsaken, vacated; depleted, drained, dry, exhausted
***near ant*** complete; replete; furnished, provided, supplied; filled, occupied; flush, overflowing, packed, teeming
***ant*** full
**2** feeling a desire or need for food — see HUNGRY 1
**3** having no meaning — see MEANINGLESS
**4** having no usefulness — see WORTHLESS
**5** producing no results — see FUTILE

**empty** *vb* to remove the contents of ⟨*empty* the room before starting to paint the ceiling⟩
***syn*** clear, evacuate, vacate, void
***rel*** deplete, drain, eliminate, exhaust; bleed, draw (off); clean, flush, purge, scour, sweep
***ant*** fill, load

**empyreal** *adj* of, relating to, or suggesting heaven — see CELESTIAL

**empyrean** *adj* of, relating to, or suggesting heaven — see CELESTIAL

**emulate** *vb* to use (someone or something) as the model for one's speech, mannerisms, or behavior — see IMITATE 1

**emulative** *adj* using or marked by the use of something else as a basis or model — see IMITATIVE

**enable** *vb* **1** to make able or possible ⟨my new glasses *enable* me to read⟩
***syn*** allow, let, permit
***rel*** fit, prepare, qualify, ready; approve, endorse (*also* indorse), sanction; condition, equip
***near ant*** inhibit, preclude; disallow, enjoin, forbid, prohibit
***ant*** prevent
**2** to give official or legal power to — see AUTHORIZE 1

**enact** *vb* to put into effect through legislative or authoritative action ⟨Congress *enacts* all laws relating to foreign trade and immigration⟩
***syn*** lay down, legislate, make, pass
***rel*** bring about, effect; allow, authorize, permit, sanction; decree, dictate, proclaim; administer, execute; approve, confirm, ratify
***near ant*** abolish, abrogate, annul, cancel, invalidate, nullify; overturn, reverse
***ant*** repeal, rescind, revoke

**enactment** *n* **1** a rule of conduct or action laid down by a governing authority and especially a legislator — see LAW 1
**2** the doing of an action — see COMMISSION 2

**enamored** (of) *adj* filled with an intense or excessive love for ⟨many teenage girls became *enamored of* the movie idol for his boyish good looks⟩
***syn*** crazy (about *or* over), enraptured (by), infatuated (with), mad (about), nuts (about)
***rel*** hung up, obsessed; foolish, silly, wild; bewitched, captivated, charmed, enchanted, entranced, fascinated
***phrases*** sweet on
***near ant*** cool, detached, unimpressed; disenchanted, disillusioned

---

***syn*** synonym(s) ***rel*** related words
***ant*** antonym(s) ***near ant*** near antonym(s)

**encamp** *vb* **1** to live in a camp or the outdoors — see CAMP
**2** to provide with living quarters or shelter — see HOUSE 1

**encampment** *n* a place where a group of people live for a short time in tents or cabins — see CAMP 1

**encapsulate** *vb* to make into a short statement of the main points (as of a report) — see SUMMARIZE

**encapsulation** *n* a short statement of the main points — see SUMMARY

**encase** *vb* to close or shut in by or as if by barriers — see ENCLOSE 1

**enchain** *vb* to confine or restrain with or as if with chains — see BIND 1

**enchant** *vb* **1** to attract or delight as if by magic — see CHARM 1
**2** to cast a spell on — see BEWITCH 1
**3** to hold the attention of as if by a spell — see ENTHRALL 1

**enchanted** *adj* being or appearing to be under a magic spell ⟨an *enchanted* isle of the South Pacific⟩
***syn*** bewitched, charmed, enchanted, magic, magical, spellbound
***rel*** dreamy, fairy, fairylike; fantastic, miraculous, utopian, wondrous; hypnotized, mesmerized; captivated, fascinated

**enchanter** *n* a person skilled in using supernatural forces — see MAGICIAN 1

**enchanting** *adj* having an often mysterious or magical power to attract — see FASCINATING 1

**enchantment** *n* **1** a spoken word or set of words believed to have magic power — see SPELL 1
**2** the power of irresistible attraction — see CHARM 2
**3** the power to control natural forces through supernatural means — see MAGIC 1

**enchantress** *n* **1** a woman believed to have often harmful supernatural powers — see WITCH 1
**2** a woman whom men find irresistibly attractive — see SIREN

**encircle** *vb* **1** to pass completely around ⟨communication satellites *encircling* the earth⟩
***syn*** circle, circumnavigate, compass, girdle, girth, loop, orbit, ring, round
***rel*** cross, perambulate, traverse
**2** to form a circle around — see SURROUND

**enclose** *also* **inclose** *vb* **1** to close or shut in by or as if by barriers ⟨dogs who spend the day *enclosed* in small cages⟩
***syn*** cage, closet, coop (up), corral, encase, envelop, fence (in), hedge, hem, house, immure, pen, wall (in)
***rel*** bound, circumscribe, confine, contain, limit, restrict; encircle, encompass, ring, surround
**2** to form a circle around — see SURROUND
**3** to surround or cover closely — see ENFOLD 1

**enclosure** *also* **inclosure** *n* an open space wholly or partly enclosed (as by buildings or walls) — see COURT 2

**encomium** *n* a formal expression of praise ⟨the *encomiums* bestowed on a teacher at her retirement ceremonies⟩
***syn*** accolade, citation, commendation, eulogy, homage, paean, panegyric, salutation, tribute
***rel*** award, decoration, honor, prize; acclaim, acclamation approval, compliment, recommendation; applause, plaudits; bravo, hallelujah
***near ant*** censure, condemnation, denunciation, indictment, rebuke, reprimand, reproof; admonition, correction, lecture, sermon

**encompass** *vb* **1** to form a circle around — see SURROUND
**2** to have as part of a whole — see INCLUDE
**3** to surround or cover closely — see ENFOLD 1

**encounter** *n* a brief clash between enemies or rivals ⟨survived an *encounter* with the school bully at the local park⟩
***syn*** brush, hassle, run-in, scrape, skirmish
***rel*** argument, fight, quarrel, row, spat, squabble, tiff; battle, brawl, fray, wrangle

**encounter** *vb* **1** to come upon face-to-face or as if face-to-face — see MEET 1
**2** to come upon unexpectedly or by chance — see HAPPEN (ON *OR* UPON)
**3** to enter into contest or conflict with — see ENGAGE 2

**encourage** *vb* **1** to fill with courage or strength of purpose ⟨a pep talk that *encouraged* the team to get out there and win⟩
***syn*** buoy (up), cheer (up), comfort, embolden, hearten, inspire, steel
***rel*** animate, enliven invigorate; fortify, reinforce, strengthen; assure, reassure; boost, energize, excite, galvanize, provoke, quicken, rally, stimulate, stir
***near ant*** demoralize, depress, sadden; debilitate, enfeeble, undermine, weaken
***ant*** daunt, discourage, dishearten, dispirit
**2** to help the growth or development of — see FOSTER 1
**3** to rouse to strong feeling or action — see PROVOKE 1
**4** to try to persuade (someone) through earnest appeals to follow a course of action — see URGE

**encouragement** *n* something that arouses action or activity — see IMPULSE

**encouraging** *adj* **1** having qualities which inspire hope — see HOPEFUL 1
**2** making one feel good inside — see HEARTWARMING
**3** pointing toward a happy outcome — see FAVORABLE 2

**encroach** *vb* to advance gradually beyond the usual or desirable limits ⟨each year the sea continues to *encroach* upon the island's beaches⟩
***syn*** creep, inch, worm

*rel* snake, sneak; entrench (*also* intrench), impinge, infringe, intrude, invade; overpass, overreach, overrun, overshoot, overstep

**encrust** *also* **incrust** *vb* to cover with a hardened layer ⟨refrigerator shelves that were *encrusted* with the residue of many spills⟩
*syn* cake, rime
*rel* besmear, coat, smear, spread; cover, daub; coagulate, congeal, harden

**encumber** *vb* **1** to create difficulty for the work or activity of — see HAMPER
**2** to place a weight or burden on — see LOAD 1

**encumbrance** *n* something that makes movement or progress more difficult ⟨without the *encumbrance* of a heavy backpack, I could sprint along the trail⟩
*syn* bar, block, chain, clog, crimp, deterrent, drag, embarrassment, fetter, handicap, hindrance, hurdle, impediment, inhibition, interference, let, manacle, obstacle, obstruction, shackles, stop, stumbling block, trammel
*rel* catch, hitch, rub, snag; hobble; arrest, check, constraint, curb, rein, restraint, stop; delay, holdup; burden, load; danger, hazard, peril; adversity, difficulty, disadvantage, hardship
*near ant* catalyst, goad, impetus, incentive, spur, stimulant, stimulus; advantage, edge; break
*ant* aid, assistance, benefit, help

**encyclopedic** *also* **encyclopaedic** *adj* covering everything or all important points ⟨a tour guide with an *encyclopedic* knowledge of New York City and its people⟩
*syn* compendious, complete, comprehensive, full, global, inclusive, in-depth, omnibus, panoramic, universal
*rel* broad, catholic, extensive, far-reaching, general, overall, sweeping, vast, wide; blanket, indiscriminate, unrestricted
*near ant* circumscribed, limited, narrow, restricted, specialized; exact, precise; individual, singular, specific

**end** *n* **1** the stopping of a process or activity ⟨the *end* of hostilities brought general rejoicing⟩
*syn* cessation, close, closure, conclusion, discontinuance, ending, expiration, finish, halt, lapse, shutdown, shutoff, stop, stoppage, surcease, termination
*rel* abeyance, interruption, moratorium, suspension
*near ant* extension, persistence, prolongation
*ant* continuation
**2** a real or imaginary point beyond which a person or thing cannot go — see LIMIT
**3** an unused or unwanted piece or item typically of small size or value — see [1]SCRAP 1
**4** something that one hopes or intends to accomplish — see GOAL
**5** the last and usually sharp or tapering part of something long and narrow — see POINT 2
**6** the last part of a process or action — see FINALE
**7** the line or relatively narrow space that marks the outer limit of something — see BORDER 1
**8** the permanent stopping of all the vital bodily activities — see DEATH 1

**end** *vb* **1** to bring (an event) to a natural or appropriate stopping point — see CLOSE 3
**2** to bring (as an action or operation) to an immediate end — see STOP 1
**3** to come to an end — see CEASE 1

**endanger** *vb* to place in danger ⟨a reckless use of fireworks that *endangered* the lives of many people⟩
*syn* adventure, compromise, gamble (with), hazard, imperil, jeopardize, menace, risk, venture
*rel* intimidate, threaten; expose; subject; chance, wager
*near ant* guard, protect, shelter, shield; preserve, resume, save

**endangered** *adj* being in a situation where one is likely to meet with harm — see LIABLE 1

**endangerment** *n* the state of not being protected from injury, harm, or evil — see DANGER 1

**endearing** *adj* **1** having qualities that tend to make one loved — see LOVABLE
**2** likely to win one's affection — see INGRATIATING

**endeavor** *n* an effort to do or accomplish something — see ATTEMPT

**endeavor** *vb* **1** to devote serious and sustained effort — see LABOR
**2** to make an effort to do — see ATTEMPT

**ended** *adj* brought or having come to an end — see COMPLETE 2

**endemic** *adj* belonging to a particular place by birth or origin — see NATIVE 1

**ending** *n* **1** the last part of a process or action — see FINALE
**2** the stopping of a process or activity — see END 1

**endless** *adj* **1** being or seeming to be without limits — see INFINITE
**2** lasting forever — see EVERLASTING

**endorse** *also* **indorse** *vb* to promote the interests or cause of — see SUPPORT 1

**endow** *vb* **1** to furnish with something freely or naturally ⟨a young performer *endowed* with a great singing voice⟩
*syn* endue, invest
*rel* equip, provide, supply; bestow, confer; accord, award, grant; empower, enable, enhance, enrich, heighten; bless, favor, grace; bequeath, will
*near ant* dispossess, divest, strip; deplete, drain, exhaust; skimp, stint
**2** to furnish (as an institution) with a regular source of income ⟨a wealthy businessman who *endowed* several museums⟩
*syn* finance, fund, subsidize

*rel* establish, found, organize; bequeath, contribute, donate, subscribe, support; award, grant; back, promote, sponsor
*near ant* draw, receive; subsist
3 to provide money for — see FINANCE 1

**endowment** *n* a special and usually inborn ability — see TALENT

**endue** *vb* to furnish with something freely or naturally — see ENDOW 1

**endurable** *adj* capable of being endured — see BEARABLE

**endurance** *n* 1 continuing existence — see PERSISTENCE 1
2 uninterrupted or lasting existence — see CONTINUATION

**endure** *vb* 1 to come to a knowledge of (something) by living through it — see EXPERIENCE
2 to put up with (something painful or difficult) — see BEAR 2
3 to remain indefinitely in existence or in the same state — see CONTINUE 1

**enemy** *n* one that is hostile toward another ⟨a beloved minister with no known *enemies*⟩
*syn* adversary, antagonist, foe, opponent
*rel* archenemy; (the) opposition; nemesis; bane, bête noire; assailant, attacker, combatant, invader; competitor, emulator, rival
*near ant* ally, collaborator, colleague, confederate, friendly, partner; adherent, disciple, follower; backer, benefactor, supporter
*ant* friend

**energetic** *adj* 1 having active strength of body or mind — see VIGOROUS 1
2 having much high-spirited energy and movement — see LIVELY 1
3 marked by or uttered with forcefulness — see EMPHATIC 1

**energetically** *adv* in a vigorous and forceful manner — see HARD 3

**energize** *vb* to give life, vigor, or spirit to — see ANIMATE

**energized** *adj* made or become fresh in spirits or vigor — see NEW 4

**energy** *n* 1 active strength of body or mind — see VIGOR 1
2 something with a usable capacity for doing work — see FUEL
3 the ability to exert effort for the accomplishment of a task — see POWER 2

**enervate** *vb* to diminish the physical strength of — see WEAKEN 1

**enervated** *adj* 1 lacking bodily energy or motivation — see LISTLESS
2 lacking bodily strength — see WEAK 1

**enfeeble** *vb* to diminish the physical strength of — see WEAKEN 1

**enfeebled** *adj* lacking bodily strength — see WEAK 1

**enfeeblement** *n* 1 a gradual sinking and wasting away of mind or body — see DECLINE 1
2 the quality or state of lacking physical strength or vigor — see WEAKNESS 1

**enfold** *vb* 1 to surround or cover closely ⟨darkness began to *enfold* the lonely house on the hill⟩
*syn* embosom, embower, embrace, enclose (*also* inclose), encompass, enshroud, envelop, enwrap, invest, lap, mantle, shroud, swathe, veil, wrap
*rel* curtain, drape; encase; swaddle; blanket, overlay, overspread; camouflage, cloak, disguise, mask; circle, encircle, encompass
*near ant* bare, denude, expose, strip
2 to put one's arms around and press tightly — see EMBRACE 1

**enforce** *vb* to carry out effectively ⟨the duty of the police is to *enforce* the law⟩
*syn* administer, apply, execute, implement
*rel* effect, effectuate; discharge, fulfill (*or* fulfil), render; cite, invoke; enact, legislate; honor, observe; prosecute; promulgate
*near ant* disregard, ignore, neglect

**enfranchise** *vb* to set free (as from slavery or confinement) — see FREE 1

**enfranchisement** *n* 1 the act of setting free from slavery — see LIBERATION
2 the right to formally express one's position or will in an election — see VOTE 1

**engage** *vb* 1 to hold the attention of ⟨the challenging jigsaw puzzle *engaged* us all evening⟩
*syn* absorb, busy, engross, enthrall (*or* enthral), fascinate, grip, immerse, interest, intrigue, involve, occupy
*rel* allure, attract, bewitch, captivate, charm, enchant; hypnotize, mesmerize; monopolize, preoccupy
*near ant* bore, jade, pall, tire, weary
2 to enter into contest or conflict with ⟨the daring young captain was eager to *engage* the enemy⟩
*syn* battle, encounter, face, meet, take on
*rel* emulate, rival; contend, fight, oppose
*near ant* elude, escape, evade; retreat
3 to obligate by prior agreement — see PLEDGE 1
4 to provide with a paying job — see EMPLOY 1
5 to take or get the temporary use of (something) for a set sum — see HIRE 1

**engaged** *adj* 1 involved in often constant activity — see BUSY 1
2 pledged in marriage ⟨the *engaged* couple make a charming pair⟩
*syn* affianced, betrothed
*rel* committed
*ant* unengaged

**engagement** *n* 1 the act or state of being engaged to be married ⟨the fun couple recently announced their *engagement*⟩
*syn* betrothal, espousal, troth
*ant* disengagement
2 an agreement to be present at a specified time and place ⟨a lifelong practice of marking all of my *engagements* on a weekly calendar⟩
*syn* appointment, date, rendezvous, tryst
*rel* arrangement; invitation; interview; get-together, meeting; call, visit; schedule
3 the state of being provided with a paying job — see HIRE 1

**engaging** *adj* **1** having an often mysterious or magical power to attract — see FASCINATING 1
**2** holding the attention or provoking interest — see INTERESTING
**engender** *vb* to be the cause of (a situation, action, or state of mind) — see EFFECT
**engine** *n* a device that changes energy into mechanical motion ⟨a car with a 200-horsepower *engine*⟩
***syn*** machine, motor
***rel*** converter, transformer; appliance, mechanism; equipment; mill
**engineer** *vb* to plan out usually with subtle skill or care ⟨the mayor *engineered* an agreement to have a major league team play in our city⟩
***syn*** contrive, finagle, finesse, frame, machinate, maneuver, manipulate, mastermind, negotiate, wangle
***rel*** intrigue, plot, scheme; connive; concoct, cook (up), hatch; captain, command, conduct, direct, handle, manage, quarterback, run; gerrymander
***near ant*** blow, bobble, botch, bungle, butcher, flub, fumble, gum (up), louse up, mangle, mess (up), mishandle, muff
**engrave** *vb* **1** to cut (as letters or designs) on a hard surface ⟨*engraved* the birth and death dates on the tombstone⟩
***syn*** etch, grave, incise, inscribe
***rel*** carve, chisel, sculpt, sculpture; chase; score
**2** to produce a vivid impression of ⟨a scar that forever *engraved* the killer's face in the witness's mind⟩
***syn*** etch, impress, imprint, ingrain
***rel*** imbue, implant, inculcate, infuse, instill
**engross** *vb* to hold the attention of — see ENGAGE 1
**engrossed** *adj* having the mind fixed on something — see ATTENTIVE
**engrossing** *adj* holding the attention or provoking interest — see INTERESTING
**engrossment** *n* a focusing of the mind on something — see ATTENTION 1
**engulf** *vb* to cover or become filled with a flood — see FLOOD
**enhance** *vb* **1** to make better — see IMPROVE
**2** to make markedly greater in measure or degree — see INTENSIFY
**enhancement** *n* an instance of notable progress in the development of knowledge, technology, or skill — see ADVANCE 2
**enigma** *n* something hard to understand or explain — see MYSTERY
**enigmatic** *also* **enigmatical** *adj* **1** being beyond one's powers to know, understand, or explain — see MYSTERIOUS 1
**2** having an often intentionally veiled or uncertain meaning — see OBSCURE 1
**enjoin** *vb* **1** to ask for (something) earnestly or with authority — see DEMAND 1
**2** to issue orders to (someone) by right of authority — see COMMAND 1
**3** to order not to do or use or to be done or used — see FORBID
**enjoining** *n* the act of ordering that something not be done or used — see PROHIBITION 1
**enjoy** *vb* **1** to take pleasure in ⟨TV and videos are OK, but we still *enjoy* seeing movies on the big screen⟩
***syn*** adore, delight (in), dig, fancy, groove (on), like, love, relish, revel (in)
***rel*** admire, appreciate, cherish, revere, venerate, worship; prize, treasure, value; devour, drink (in), savor; dote (on), idolize; cotton (to), favor, prefer
***phrases*** be partial to, get a kick (*or* charge) out of, go for, have a soft spot for, take to
***near ant*** abhor, abominate, detest, dislike, hate, loathe; condemn, despise, scorn
**2** to keep, control, or experience as one's own — see HAVE 1
**enjoyable** *adj* **1** giving pleasure or contentment to the mind or senses — see PLEASANT
**2** providing amusement or enjoyment — see FUN
**enjoyment** *n* the feeling experienced when one's wishes are met — see PLEASURE 1
**enlarge** *vb* **1** to become greater in extent, volume, amount, or number — see INCREASE 2
**2** to make greater in size, amount, or number — see INCREASE 1
**enlarge** (on) *vb* to express more fully and in greater detail — see EXPAND 1
**enlighten** *vb* **1** to give information to ⟨the lecturer at the planetarium *enlightened* us about the latest astronomical discoveries⟩
***syn*** acquaint, advise, apprise, brief, clue, familiarize, fill in, inform, instruct, tell, wise (up)
***rel*** clarify, clear (up), construe, elucidate, explain, explicate, expound, illuminate, illustrate, interpret, spell out; announce, disclose, report; disabuse, disenchant, disillusion
***near ant*** misinform, mislead
**2** to provide (someone) with moral or spiritual understanding ⟨many people around the world have been *enlightened* by the teachings of Gautama Buddha⟩
***syn*** edify, educate, nurture
***rel*** elevate, ennoble, lift, uplift; better, improve, transform; exalt, glorify, transfigure
***near ant*** confuse, perplex, puzzle; becloud, cloud, darken, obscure
**enlist** (in) *vb* to become a member of — see ENTER 2
**enliven** *vb* to give life, vigor, or spirit to — see ANIMATE
**enmesh** *vb* to catch or hold as if in a net — see ENTANGLE 2
**enmity** *n* a deep-seated ill will ⟨*enmity* had existed between the two families for generations⟩

*syn* animosity, antagonism, antipathy, bitterness, gall, grudge, hostility, jaundice, rancor
*rel* hate, hatred, loathing; vindictiveness, virulence, vitriol; alienation, disaffection, estrangement; abhorrence, aversion, repugnance, repulsion; disgust, horror; conflict, coolness, friction, strain, tension; discord, unfriendliness; malice, malignancy, malignity, spite, spitefulness, venom
*near ant* amiability, amicability, civility, cordiality, friendliness, hospitality, neighborliness; comity, empathy, friendship, goodwill, sympathy, understanding
*ant* amity

**ennoble** *vb* to enhance the status of — see EXALT

**ennui** *n* the state of being bored — see BOREDOM

**enormity** *n* **1** the state or quality of being utterly evil ⟨the *enormity* of the crimes committed by the Nazis⟩
*syn* atrociousness, atrocity, badness, depravedness, depravity, evilness, heinousness, monstrosity, nefariousness, sinfulness, vileness, wickedness
*rel* accursedness, baseness, devilishness, execrableness, fiendishness, hellishness; corruption, decadence, degeneracy; immorality; infamy, notoriety
*near ant* morality; chasteness, innocence, purity
*ant* goodness, righteousness, virtuousness
**2** the quality or state of being very large — see IMMENSITY

**enormous** *adj* unusually large — see HUGE

**enormously** *adv* to a large extent or degree — see GREATLY 2

**enormousness** *n* the quality or state of being very large — see IMMENSITY

**enough** *adv* **1** in or to a degree or quantity that meets one's requirements or satisfaction ⟨the elevator is big *enough* to hold everyone⟩
*syn* adequately, satisfactorily, sufficiently
*rel* acceptably, decently, fairly, moderately, passably, tolerably; abundantly, amply; commensurately, proportionately
*ant* inadequately, insufficiently, unsatisfactorily
**2** to some degree or extent — see FAIRLY

**enrage** *vb* to make angry — see ANGER

**enraged** *adj* feeling or showing anger — see ANGRY

**enrapture** *vb* **1** to fill with great joy — see ELATE
**2** to fill with overwhelming emotion (as wonder or delight) — see ENTRANCE

**enraptured** *adj* experiencing or marked by overwhelming usually pleasurable emotion — see ECSTATIC

**enraptured** (by) *adj* filled with an intense or excessive love for — see ENAMORED (OF)

**enrich** *vb* **1** to make better — see IMPROVE
**2** to make more attractive by adding something that is beautiful or becoming — see DECORATE

**enroll** *also* **enrol** *vb* **1** to enter in a list or roll ⟨the school *enrolls* about 800 students⟩
*syn* inscribe, list, matriculate, register
*rel* catalog (*or* catalogue), itemize, tabulate, tally; file, index; book, log, post; program, schedule; check in
*near ant* cancel, delete, exclude, expel, expunge, reject; omit, overlook
**2** to put (someone or something) on a list — see [1]LIST 2

**enroll** (in) *vb* to become a member of — see ENTER 2

**enrollment** *n* the number of individuals registered — see REGISTRATION

**ensconce** *vb* **1** to establish or place comfortably or snugly ⟨the kids had contentedly *ensconced* themselves on the couch before the TV⟩
*syn* install, lodge, perch, roost, settle
*rel* curl up; park, plant; anchor, bivouac, camp; burrow; locate, situate
**2** to put into a hiding place — see [1]HIDE 1

**enshrine** *vb* to enhance the status of — see EXALT

**enshroud** *vb* **1** to keep secret or shut off from view — see [1]HIDE 2
**2** to surround or cover closely — see ENFOLD 1

**ensign** *n* a piece of cloth with a special design that is used as an emblem or for signaling — see FLAG 1

**enslavement** *n* the state of being a slave — see SLAVERY 1

**ensnare** *vb* to catch or hold as if in a net — see ENTANGLE 2

**ensuing** *adj* **1** being the one that comes immediately after another — see NEXT
**2** being, occurring, or carried out at a time after something else — see SUBSEQUENT

**ensure** *vb* to make sure, certain, or safe ⟨regulations that *ensure* the wholesomeness of our food⟩
*syn* assure, cinch, guarantee, guaranty, insure, secure
*rel* attest, certify, vouch, warrant, witness; pledge, promise, swear
*near ant* enfeeble, undermine, weaken

**entail** *vb* to have as part of a whole — see INCLUDE

**entangle** *vb* **1** to twist together into a usually confused mass ⟨in the process of taking down the Christmas tree, we managed to *entangle* the string of lights into a hopeless mess of wires⟩
*syn* interlace, intertwine, interweave, knot, snarl, tangle
*rel* weave, wind, wreathe; braid, plait
*ant* disentangle
**2** to catch or hold as if in a net ⟨the young runaway gradually became *entangled* in a web of lies⟩
*syn* enmesh, ensnare, entrap, mesh, snare, tangle, trap
*rel* bag, capture, collar; embroil, implicate, involve, mire
*near ant* extricate, untangle; detach, disengage; clear, free, liberate
*ant* disentangle

**entanglement** *n* something that catches and holds — see WEB 1

**enter** *vb* **1** to go or come in or into ⟨the hikers *entered* the cave with considerable caution⟩
*syn* access, penetrate, pierce
*rel* barge (in), breeze (in), burst (in *or* into), waltz (in); drop (in), pop (in)
*phrases* set foot in, step in
*ant* depart, exit, leave
**2** to become a member of ⟨patriotic young men and women *entering* the armed services⟩
*syn* enlist (in), enroll (in), join, sign on (for), sign up (for)
*rel* reenlist, reenroll, reenter
**3** to put (someone or something) on a list — see [1]LIST 2

**enter** (into *or* upon) *vb* to take the first step in (a process or course of action) — see BEGIN 1

**enterprise** *n* **1** a commercial or industrial activity or organization ⟨the booming economy witnessed the launch of many small *enterprises*⟩
*syn* business, company, concern, establishment, firm, house, outfit
*rel* conglomerate, corporation, multinational; association, cartel, chain, combine, syndicate, trust; agency, dealer, outlet
**2** readiness to engage in daring or difficult activity ⟨the *enterprise* shown by the early developers and promoters of personal computers⟩
*syn* aggressiveness, ambition, drive, go, hustle, initiative
*rel* gumption, pluck, snap, spirit, spunk, starch; assertiveness, self-reliance; energy, hardihood, pep, vigor, vitality
*near ant* inactivity, inertia, passivity; diffidence, faintheartedness, timidity; hesitation, reluctance; indolence, laziness, lethargy
**3** a risky undertaking — see GAMBLE

**enterprising** *adj* **1** having or showing a bold forcefulness in the pursuit of a goal — see AGGRESSIVE 1
**2** inclined or willing to take risks — see BOLD 1

**entertain** *vb* **1** to cause (someone) to pass the time agreeably occupied — see AMUSE
**2** to give serious and careful thought to — see PONDER
**3** to keep in one's mind or heart — see HARBOR 1

**entertaining** *adj* providing amusement or enjoyment — see FUN

**entertainment** *n* **1** the act or activity of providing pleasure or amusement especially for the public ⟨a variety show was staged as *entertainment* for the scouts at the jamboree⟩
*syn* amusement, distraction, diversion, recreation
*rel* show business; delectation, delight, enjoyment, joy, mirth; gratification, relaxation, relief, satisfaction; exhibition, performance, presentation, production, show, spectacle; escapism
**2** someone or something that provides amusement or enjoyment — see FUN 1

**enthrall** *or* **enthral** *vb* **1** to hold the attention of as if by a spell ⟨*enthralled* by the flickering fire in the hearth, we lost all track of time⟩
*syn* arrest, enchant, fascinate, grip, hypnotize, mesmerize, spellbind
*rel* enrapture, entrance, thrill; beguile, bewitch, charm; absorb, engage, engross, involve
*phrases* cast a spell on
**2** to fill with overwhelming emotion (as wonder or delight) — see ENTRANCE
**3** to hold the attention of — see ENGAGE 1

**enthralled** *adj* having the mind fixed on something — see ATTENTIVE

**enthralling** *adj* holding the attention or provoking interest — see INTERESTING

**enthrallment** *n* a focusing of the mind on something — see ATTENTION 1

**enthuse** *vb* to make an exaggerated display of affection or enthusiasm — see GUSH 2

**enthusiasm** *n* **1** a practice or interest that is very popular for a short time — see FAD
**2** urgent desire or interest — see EAGERNESS

**enthusiast** *n* a person with a strong and habitual liking for something — see FAN

**enthusiastic** *adj* showing urgent desire or interest — see EAGER

**enthusiastically** *adv* in an enthusiastic manner — see SKY-HIGH

**entice** *vb* to lead away from a usual or proper course by offering some pleasure or advantage — see LURE

**enticement** *n* **1** something that persuades one to perform an action for pleasure or gain — see LURE 1
**2** the act or pressure of giving in to a desire especially when ill-advised — see TEMPTATION 1

**entire** *adj* **1** not divided or scattered among several areas of interest or concern — see WHOLE 1
**2** not lacking any part or member that properly belongs to it — see COMPLETE 1

**entirely** *adv* to a full extent or degree — see FULLY 1

**entitle** *vb* **1** to give a right to ⟨the card *entitles* my grandmother to the discount for senior citizens⟩
*syn* authorize, qualify
*rel* empower, enable, license (*also* licence); approve, endorse (*also* indorse); allow, let, permit; certify, ratify, sanction, validate
*ant* disqualify
**2** to give a name to — see NAME 1

**entity** *n* one that has a real and independent existence ⟨the question of whether

---

*syn* synonym(s) *rel* related words
*ant* antonym(s) *near ant* near antonym(s)

extrasensory perception will ever be a scientifically recognized *entity*〉
***syn*** being, individual, object, something, substance, thing
***rel*** body; material, matter, stuff

**entomb** *vb* to place (a dead body) in the earth, a tomb, or the sea — see BURY 1

**entombing** *n* the act or ceremony of putting a dead body in its final resting place — see BURIAL

**entombment** *n* the act or ceremony of putting a dead body in its final resting place — see BURIAL

**entrails** *n pl* the internal organs of the body — see GUT 1

**entrance** *n* **1** the means or right of entering or participating in 〈*entrance* to the club is by invitation only〉
***syn*** access, admission, admittance, doorway, entrée (*or* entree), entry, gateway
***rel*** approval, certification, qualification
**2** the opening through which one can enter or leave a structure — see DOOR 2

**entrance** *vb* to fill with overwhelming emotion (as wonder or delight) 〈a production of *The Nutcracker* ballet that will *entrance* audiences〉
***syn*** carry away, enrapture, enthrall (*or* enthral), overjoy, ravish, transport
***rel*** delight, gladden, gratify, please, satisfy; bewitch, captivate, charm, enchant, fascinate; elate, excite, exhilarate, stir

**entranced** *adj* **1** being or appearing to be under a magic spell — see ENCHANTED
**2** experiencing or marked by overwhelming usually pleasurable emotion — see ECSTATIC

**entrancing** *adj* having an often mysterious or magical power to attract — see FASCINATING 1

**entrap** *vb* to catch or hold as if in a net — see ENTANGLE 2

**entreat** *vb* to make a request to (someone) in an earnest or urgent manner — see BEG

**entreating** *adj* asking humbly — see SUPPLIANT

**entreaty** *n* an earnest request — see PLEA 1

**entrée** *or* **entree** *n* the means or right of entering or participating in — see ENTRANCE 1

**entrench** *also* **intrench** *vb* to set solidly in or as if in surrounding matter 〈a father who *entrenched* in our minds the belief that hard work pays off〉
***syn*** embed (*also* imbed), fix, implant, ingrain, lodge, root
***rel*** imbue, infuse, instill; establish, place, put, settle, stick
***near ant*** eliminate, eradicate; eject, expel; detach, disconnect, disengage, remove
***ant*** dislodge, root (out), uproot

**entrenched** *also* **intrenched** *adj* firmly established over time — see INVETERATE 1

**entrust** *vb* **1** to give a task, duty, or responsibility to 〈we *entrusted* our financial adviser with the investment of all of our savings〉
***syn*** assign, charge, commission, trust
***rel*** confer, impose; commit, consign, delegate, relegate; allocate, allot; authorize, empower, invest
**2** to put (something) into the possession or safekeeping of another — see GIVE 2

**entry** *n* **1** the entrance room of a building — see HALL 1
**2** the means or right of entering or participating in — see ENTRANCE 1

**entryway** *n* the entrance room of a building — see HALL 1

**entwine** *vb* to follow a circular or spiral course — see WIND

**enumerate** *vb* **1** to specify one after another 〈I proceeded to *enumerate* the reasons why my allowance needed raising〉
***syn*** detail, itemize, list, numerate, rehearse, tick (off)
***rel*** outline; tabulate, tally; catalog (*or* catalogue), inventory; chart, diagram, graph; calculate, compute, estimate, figure, reckon; cite, mention, name
**2** to find the sum of (a collection of things) by noting each one as it is being added — see COUNT 1
**3** to make a list of — see [1]LIST 1

**enunciate** *vb* **1** to utter clearly and distinctly — see ARTICULATE 1
**2** to make known openly or publicly — see ANNOUNCE

**enunciation** *n* the clear and accurate pronunciation of words especially in public speaking — see DICTION 1

**envelop** *vb* **1** to close or shut in by or as if by barriers — see ENCLOSE 1
**2** to surround or cover closely — see ENFOLD 1

**envenom** *vb* to implant bitter feelings in — see EMBITTER

**envenomed** *adj* containing or contaminated with a substance capable of injuring or killing a living thing — see POISONOUS

**envious** *adj* having or showing mean resentment of another's possessions or advantages 〈a family that is *envious* of their neighbors' big house〉
***syn*** covetous, invidious, jaundiced, jealous, resentful
***rel*** begrudging, grudging; avaricious, grasping, greedy; distrustful, suspicious; malicious, petty, spiteful
***phrases*** green with envy
***near ant*** generous, kind, kindhearted; altruistic, benevolent, charitable; well-meaning

**enviousness** *n* a painful awareness of another's possessions or advantages and a desire to have them too — see ENVY

**environment** *n* the circumstances, conditions, or objects by which one is surrounded 〈the joys of growing up in the *environment* that a small town offers〉
***syn*** atmosphere, climate, environs, medium, milieu, setting, surroundings
***rel*** backdrop, background, context; element; situation, status; habitat

**environs** *n pl* **1** the area around a city 〈the city and its *environs* total about a million in population〉

*syn* exurbia, outskirts, purlieu, suburbia
*rel* backwater, backwoods, hinterland
**2** the circumstances, conditions, or objects by which one is surrounded — see ENVIRONMENT

**envisage** *vb* to form a mental picture of — see IMAGINE 1

**envoy** *n* **1** a person sent on a mission to represent another — see AMBASSADOR
**2** a person who acts or does business for another — see AGENT 2

**envy** *n* a painful awareness of another's possessions or advantages and a desire to have them too ⟨her *envy* of her neighbor's fancy clothes wrecked their friendship⟩
*syn* covetousness, enviousness, invidiousness, jealousy, resentment
*rel* animosity, enmity, hatred, ill will; malice, maliciousness, spitefulness
*near ant* benevolence, goodwill, kindness, sympathy

**enwrap** *vb* to surround or cover closely — see ENFOLD 1

**ephemeral** *adj* lasting only for a short time — see MOMENTARY

**epicure** *n* a person with refined tastes in food and wine ⟨Thomas Jefferson was one of America's first great *epicures*⟩
*syn* gourmand, gourmet
*rel* connoisseur, dilettante; savorer
*near ant* glutton, gorger, hog, trencherman

**epigram** *n* an often stated observation regarding something from common experience — see SAYING

**epigrammatic** *adj* marked by the use of few words to convey much information or meaning — see CONCISE

**episode** *n* something that happens — see EVENT 1

**episodic** *adj* appearing in parts or numbers that follow regularly — see SERIAL

**epistle** *n* a message on paper from one person or group to another — see LETTER

**epithet** *n* **1** a descriptive or familiar name given instead of or in addition to the one belonging to an individual — see NICKNAME
**2** an act or expression showing scorn and usually intended to hurt another's feelings — see INSULT

**epitome** *n* **1** a short statement of the main points — see SUMMARY
**2** a visible representation of something abstract (as a quality) — see EMBODIMENT
**3** the most perfect type or example — see QUINTESSENCE 1

**epitomize** *vb* **1** to make into a short statement of the main points (as of a report) — see SUMMARIZE
**2** to represent in visible form — see EMBODY 2

**epoch** *n* an extent of time associated with a particular person or thing — see AGE 1

**equable** *adj* marked by temperatures that are neither too high nor too low — see CLEMENT

**equal** *vb* **1** to produce something equal to (as in quality or value) ⟨no one has *equaled* Shakespeare's plays⟩
*syn* match, meet, tie
*rel* beat, excel, outdo, surpass, top; amount (to), approach, touch; measure (up), rival
**2** to be the same in meaning or effect — see AMOUNT (TO) 2
**3** to be the exact counterpart of — see MATCH 1

**equal** *adj* **1** marked by justice, honesty, and freedom from bias — see FAIR 2
**2** resembling another in every respect — see SAME 1

**equal** *n* one that is equal to another in status, achievement, or value ⟨a basketball player who truly has no *equal* in his sport⟩
*syn* coordinate, counterpart, equivalent, fellow, like, match, parallel, peer, rival
*rel* analogue (*or* analog); double, mate, twin; associate, colleague, companion, partner; competitor

**equality** *n* the state or fact of being exactly the same in number, amount, status, or quality — see EQUIVALENCE

**equalize** *vb* to make equal in amount, degree, or status ⟨a plan to *equalize* educational opportunities for all the state's children, rich and poor alike⟩
*syn* balance, equate, even, level
*rel* accommodate, adjust, compensate, fit; homogenize, normalize, regularize, standardize; democratize

**equanimity** *n* evenness of emotions or temper ⟨an Olympic diver who always displays remarkable *equanimity* on the platform⟩
*syn* aplomb, calmness, composure, coolheadedness, coolness, imperturbability, placidity, self-possession, serenity, tranquillity (*or* tranquility)
*rel* assurance, confidence, poise, self-assurance, self-confidence; apathy, detachment, indifference, phlegm
*near ant* alarm, anxiety, apprehension, disquiet; excitability, nervousness; disturbance
*ant* agitation, discomposure, perturbation

**equate** *vb* **1** to regard or represent as equal or comparable ⟨a value system that *equates* money with success⟩
*syn* compare, liken
*rel* associate, connect, join, link, match; group, lump (together)
*near ant* differentiate, discriminate, distinguish
**2** to describe as similar — see COMPARE 1
**3** to make equal in amount, degree, or status — see EQUALIZE

**equatorial** *adj* being near the equator — see LOW 1

**equilibrium** *n* a condition in which opposing forces are equal to one another — see BALANCE 1

---

*syn* synonym(s) *rel* related words
*ant* antonym(s) *near ant* near antonym(s)

**equine** *n* a large hoofed domestic animal that is used for carrying or drawing loads and for riding — see HORSE

**equip** *vb* **1** to make competent (as by training, skill, or ability) for a particular office or function — see QUALIFY 2
**2** to provide (someone) with what is needed for a task or activity — see FURNISH 1

**equipage** *n* a horse-drawn wheeled vehicle for carrying passengers — see CARRIAGE 1

**equipment** *n* items needed for the performance of a task or activity ⟨the *equipment* for the polar expedition included ships, instruments, sleds, dogs, and provisions⟩
*syn* accoutrements (*or* accouterments), apparatus, gear, material(s), matériel (*or* materiel), outfit, paraphernalia, tackle
*rel* accessories, attachments, fittings; baggage, belongings, impedimenta; appliances, facilities, instruments, machinery, tools; apparel, attire, habiliments, raiment, trappings; battery

**equipoise** *n* **1** a condition in which opposing forces are equal to one another — see BALANCE 1
**2** a force or influence that makes an opposing force ineffective or less effective — see COUNTERBALANCE

**equitable** *adj* marked by justice, honesty, and freedom from bias — see FAIR 2

**equity** *n* the act or practice of giving to others what is their due — see JUSTICE 1

**equivalence** *n* the state or fact of being exactly the same in number, amount, status, or quality ⟨moviegoers who mistakenly believe that there is an *equivalence* between the personality of an actor and that of his character⟩
*syn* equality, equivalency, par, parity, sameness
*rel* compatibility, correlation, correspondence; likeness, similarity; exchangeability, interchangeability
*near ant* difference, discrepancy, disparity, divergence; incompatibility; dissimilarity, unlikeness
*ant* inequality

**equivalency** *n* the state or fact of being exactly the same in number, amount, status, or quality — see EQUIVALENCE

**equivalent** *n* one that is equal to another in status, achievement, or value — see EQUAL

**equivocal** *adj* **1** giving good reason for being doubted, questioned, or challenged — see DOUBTFUL 2
**2** having an often intentionally veiled or uncertain meaning — see OBSCURE 1

**equivocalness** *n* the quality or state of having a veiled or uncertain meaning — see OBSCURITY 1

**equivocate** *vb* to avoid giving a definite answer or position ⟨the candidate *equivocated* as long as he could on controversial issues⟩
*syn* fudge, hedge, pussyfoot
*rel* dodge, duck, evade, sidestep, skirt; bypass, circumvent; cavil, quibble
*phrases* beat around (*or* about) the bush, dance around, hem and haw

**equivocation** *n* the quality or state of having a veiled or uncertain meaning — see OBSCURITY 1

**era** *n* an extent of time associated with a particular person or thing — see AGE 1

**eradicate** *vb* to destroy all traces of — see ANNIHILATE 1

**ere** *prep* earlier than — see BEFORE 1

**erect** *adj* rising straight up ⟨a lone tree remained *erect* after the terrible tornado had passed⟩
*syn* perpendicular, plumb, raised, standing, upright, upstanding, vertical
*rel* elevated, lifted, upended, upraised; freestanding
*near ant* prostrate, supine; hanging, sagging, slanted, slanting
*ant* flat, recumbent

**erect** *vb* **1** to fix in an upright position ⟨the tribes of the Pacific Northwest *erected* totem poles in front of their dwellings⟩
*syn* pitch, put up, raise, rear, set up, upend, upraise
*rel* brace, buttress, prop (up), shore (up), support; elevate, hoist, lift
*near ant* demolish, flatten, knock down, level, raze, tear down
**2** to form by putting together parts or materials — see BUILD

**erection** *n* something put together by arranging or connecting an array of parts — see CONSTRUCTION 1

**ergo** *adv* for this or that reason — see THEREFORE

**erode** *vb* **1** to consume or wear away gradually — see EAT 2
**2** to damage or diminish by continued friction — see ABRADE 1

**erosion** *n* a gradual weakening, loss, or destruction — see CORROSION

**erotic** *adj* of, relating to, or expressing sexual attraction ⟨the *erotic* aspects of the story of Beauty and the Beast⟩
*syn* amatory, amorous, sexy
*rel* carnal, sensual, sensuous; bawdy, lascivious, lewd, lustful, obscene, prurient, spicy

**err** *vb* to commit an offense — see OFFEND 1

**errant** *adj* **1** engaging in or marked by childish misbehavior — see NAUGHTY
**2** traveling from place to place — see ITINERANT

**erratic** *adj* **1** lacking a definite plan, purpose, or pattern — see RANDOM
**2** lacking in steadiness or regularity of occurrence — see FITFUL
**3** not staying constant — see UNEVEN 2

**erratically** *adv* without definite aim, direction, rule, or method — see HIT OR MISS

**erroneous** *adj* not being in agreement with what is true — see FALSE 1

**erroneously** *adv* in a mistaken or inappropriate way — see WRONGLY

**erroneousness** *n* the quality or state of being false — see FALLACY 2

**error** *n* **1** an unintentional departure from truth or accuracy ⟨a report on the earthquake contained several unfortunate *errors*⟩
*syn* blunder, fault, flub, fumble, goof, inaccuracy, lapse, miscue, misstep, mistake, oversight, slip, slipup, stumble
*rel* boner, howler; foul-up, muff; misapprehension, miscalculation, misconception, misjudgment, misstatement, misunderstanding
*near ant* accuracy, correctness, precision
**2** a breaking of a moral or legal code — see OFFENSE 1
**3** a false idea or belief — see FALLACY 1
**erstwhile** *adj* having been such at some previous time — see FORMER
**erudite** *adj* **1** having or displaying advanced knowledge or education — see EDUCATED
**2** suggestive of the vocabulary used in books — see BOOKISH
**erudition** *n* the understanding and information gained from being educated — see EDUCATION 2
**erupt** *vb* **1** to throw out or off (something from within) often violently ⟨the volcano *erupted* clouds of poisonous gas and tons of hot ash⟩
*syn* belch, disgorge, eject, expel, jet, spew, spout, spurt
*rel* gush, pour, stream, surge; emanate, issue, spring; discharge, emit, fire; cast, fling, heave, hurl, launch, pitch, toss
*near ant* bottle (up), contain, restrain, shut (in *or* up)
**2** to develop suddenly and violently ⟨a fire *erupted*, and flames soon engulfed the room⟩
*syn* break out, burst (forth), explode, flame, flare (up)
*rel* burgeon, mushroom, snowball; blow up, detonate, touch off
**eruption** *n* **1** a sudden intense expression of strong feeling — see OUTBURST 1
**2** the act or an instance of exploding — see EXPLOSION 1
**escalate** *vb* **1** to become greater in extent, volume, amount, or number — see INCREASE 2
**2** to make greater in size, amount, or number — see INCREASE 1
**escalated** *adj* being at a higher level than average — see HIGH 2
**escapade** *n* a playful or mischievous act intended as a joke — see PRANK
**escape** *n* **1** the act or an instance of getting free from danger or confinement ⟨a daring prison *escape*⟩
*syn* flight, getaway, lam, slip
*rel* deliverance, liberation, redemption, release, rescue, salvation
*near ant* imprisonment, incarceration; custody, detention, hold, holding, retention; danger, hazard, jeopardy, peril, risk
**2** the act or a means of getting or keeping away from something undesirable ⟨the reading of science fiction novels as an *escape* from boring reality⟩
*syn* avoidance, cop-out, dodging, ducking, eluding, eschewing, evasion, out, shaking, shunning
*rel* bypassing, circumvention; averting, deflection, prevention
*near ant* abidance, endurance, submission, toleration
**escape** *vb* **1** to get free from a dangerous or confining situation ⟨everyone managed to *escape* from the burning building in time⟩
*syn* abscond, clear out, flee, fly, get away, get out, lam, run away, run off
*rel* avoid, elude, evade, lose, shun; decamp, depart, exit, leave; disentangle, extricate; emancipate, free, liberate, redeem, release
*phrases* fly the coop, free oneself
*near ant* abide, linger, remain, stay, tarry; come back, return
**2** to get or keep away from (as a responsibility) through cleverness or trickery ⟨a judge who is very determined not to let criminals *escape* punishment⟩
*syn* avoid, dodge, duck, elude, eschew, evade, shake, shirk, shun
*rel* miss; avert, deflect, divert, obviate, parry, prevent, ward (off); debar, exclude, preclude; bypass, circumvent, skirt; foil, frustrate, outwit, thwart
*phrases* get around, have nothing to do with, shy away from, steer clear of
*near ant* accept, court, embrace, pursue, seek, welcome; catch, contract, incur
**escarpment** *n* a steep wall of rock, earth, or ice — see CLIFF
**eschew** *vb* to get or keep away from (as a responsibility) through cleverness or trickery — see ESCAPE 2
**eschewing** *n* the act or a means of getting or keeping away from something undesirable — see ESCAPE 2
**escort** *n* one that accompanies another for protection, guidance, or as a courtesy ⟨the mayor served as the First Lady's *escort* for her tour of the city⟩
*syn* attendant, companion, guard, guide
*rel* chaperone (*or* chaperon), squire; shadow, sidekick; conductor, leader, pilot
**escort** *vb* to go along with in order to provide assistance, protection, or companionship — see ACCOMPANY
**esculent** *adj* suitable for use as food — see EDIBLE
**esoteric** *adj* difficult for one of ordinary knowledge or intelligence to understand — see PROFOUND 1
**especial** *adj* of a particular or exact sort — see EXPRESS 1
**especially** *adv* to a great degree — see VERY 1
**espionage** *n* the secret gathering of information on others ⟨the acts of *espionage* on behalf of the Confederacy carried on by Belle Boyd and Rose Greenhow⟩
*syn* spying
*rel* dope, goods, lowdown; counterintelligence, intelligence; observation, recon-

*syn* synonym(s) *rel* related words
*ant* antonym(s) *near ant* near antonym(s)

naissance, surveillance; bugging, eavesdropping, wiretapping

**espousal** *n* **1** a ceremony in which two people are united in matrimony — see WEDDING
**2** the act or state of being engaged to be married — see ENGAGEMENT 1

**espouse** *vb* **1** to give in marriage — see MARRY 2
**2** to take as a spouse — see MARRY 3

**esprit** *n* active strength of body or mind — see VIGOR 1

**espy** *vb* to make note of (something) through the use of one's eyes — see SEE 1

**essay** *n* **1** a short piece of writing typically expressing a point of view ⟨school *essays* on what it means to be a patriot⟩
***syn*** article, composition, paper, theme
***rel*** column, commentary, editorial, feature, report, review, write-up; dissertation, thesis; tract, treatise; discourse, discussion, exposition, study
**2** an effort to do or accomplish something — see ATTEMPT

**essay** *vb* to make an effort to do — see ATTEMPT

**essence** *n* the quality or qualities that make a thing what it is ⟨the belief that power ultimately rests with the people is the very *essence* of democracy⟩
***syn*** essentiality, nature, quintessence, soul, stuff, substance
***rel*** heart, spirit; center, core, keynote, marrow, pith, seat; embodiment, epitome, incarnation, manifestation, personification; aspect, attribute, feature, property; gist, kernel, nub

**essential** *adj* **1** impossible to do without ⟨a well-stocked public library is *essential* for the well-being of a community⟩
***syn*** all-important, imperative, indispensable, integral, necessary, needed, needful, required, requisite, vital
***rel*** prerequisite; compulsory, mandatory, obligatory; important, momentous, significant; basic, central, fundamental, key, organic; insistent, persistent, pressing, urgent
***near ant*** undesired, unwanted; inconsequential, insignificant, unimportant; excess, extra, superfluous, surplus
***ant*** dispensable, needless, nonessential, unnecessary, unneeded
**2** of or relating to the simplest facts or theories of a subject — see ELEMENTARY
**3** being a part of the innermost nature of a person or thing — see INHERENT

**essential** *n* **1** something necessary, indispensable, or unavoidable ⟨the *essentials* for success include a willingness to work and the right attitude⟩
***syn*** condition, demand, must, necessity, need, requirement, requisite
***rel*** precondition, prerequisite; advantage, edge, plus
***near ant*** extra, extravagance, frill, luxury, superfluity
***ant*** nonessential, nonnecessity
**2 essentials** *pl* general or basic truths on which other truths or theories can be based — see PRINCIPLES 1

**essentiality** *n* the quality or qualities that make a thing what it is — see ESSENCE

**establish** *vb* **1** to gain full recognition or acceptance of ⟨the teenagers accused of shoplifting were able to *establish* their innocence⟩
***syn*** demonstrate, prove, show, substantiate
***rel*** attest, authenticate, bear out, document, evidence, support, sustain, uphold; confirm, corroborate, justify, validate, verify
***phrases*** prove beyond a reasonable doubt
***near ant*** confute, discredit, invalidate, rebut, refute
***ant*** disprove
**2** to show the existence or truth of by evidence — see PROVE 1
**3** to be responsible for the creation and early operation or use of — see FOUND

**establisher** *n* a person who establishes a whole new field of endeavor — see FATHER 2

**establishment** *n* **1** a building, room, or suite of rooms occupied by a service business — see PLACE 2
**2** a commercial or industrial activity or organization — see ENTERPRISE 1
**3** a public organization with a particular purpose or function — see INSTITUTION 1
**4** a structure that is designed and built for a particular purpose — see FACILITY

**estate** *n* **1** a large impressive residence — see MANSION
**2** a state of being or fitness — see CONDITION 1
**3** one of the segments of society into which people are grouped — see CLASS 1

**esteem** *n* a feeling of great approval and liking — see ADMIRATION 1

**esteem** *vb* **1** to think of in a particular way — see CONSIDER 1
**2** to think very highly or favorably of — see ADMIRE

**esteemed** *adj* having a good reputation especially in a field of knowledge — see RESPECTABLE 1

**estimate** *n* **1** the act of placing a value on the nature, character, or quality of something ⟨what we owe our war veterans is beyond *estimate*⟩
***syn*** appraisal, appraisement, assessment, estimation, evaluation, reckoning, valuation
***rel*** calculation, computation, measurement
**2** an opinion on the nature, character, or quality of something — see ESTIMATION 1

**estimate** *vb* **1** to make an approximate or tentative judgment regarding ⟨experts *estimated* the value of the painting at a million dollars⟩
***syn*** appraise, assess, evaluate, rate, set, value
***rel*** adjudge, deem, judge; ascertain, determine, discover, learn; price, prize; decide,

settle; analyze, assay, survey, test; reappraise, reassess, reevaluate, revalue
**2** to decide the size, amount, number, or distance of (something) without actual measurement ⟨we *estimated* the snowfall to be about a foot⟩
***syn*** calculate, call, conjecture, figure, gauge (*also* gage), guess, judge, make, place, put, reckon, suppose
***near ant*** calibrate, measure, scale; compute

**estimation** *n* **1** an opinion on the nature, character, or quality of something ⟨the teacher's *estimation* of her student's scientific aptitude proved to be well-founded when he won a national science award⟩
***syn*** appraisal, appraisement, assessment, estimate, evaluation, judgment (*or* judgement)
***rel*** impression, notion, perception; confidence, faith, stock, trust
**2** the act of placing a value on the nature, character, or quality of something — see ESTIMATE 1
**3** a feeling of great approval and liking — see ADMIRATION 1

**estrange** *vb* to cause to change from friendly or loving to unfriendly or uncaring ⟨Carrie's tendency to tattle *estranged* her classmates⟩
***syn*** alienate, disaffect, disgruntle, sour
***rel*** antagonize, embitter, envenom; aggravate, anger, enrage, incense, infuriate, madden; disunite, divide, separate, sever, sunder; disappoint, disenchant, disillusion
***near ant*** endear, ingratiate; appease, conciliate, mollify, pacify, propitiate
***ant*** reconcile

**estrangement** *n* the loss of friendship or affection ⟨a silly quarrel that eventually resulted in a complete and lasting *estrangement* between the onetime friends⟩
***syn*** alienation, disaffection, disgruntlement, souring
***rel*** antagonism, embitterment, envenoming; aggravation, incensing, infuriation; disunion, division, divorce, schism, separation; disenchantment, disillusionment
***near ant*** endearment, ingratiation; appeasement, conciliation, mollification, pacification, propitiation
***ant*** reconciliation

**estuary** *n* a part of a body of water that extends beyond the general shoreline — see GULF 1

**etch** *vb* **1** to cut (as letters or designs) on a hard surface — see ENGRAVE 1
**2** to produce a vivid impression of — see ENGRAVE 2

**eternal** *adj* lasting forever — see EVERLASTING

**eternally** *adv* for all time — see EVER 1

**eternity** *n* **1** endless time ⟨the question whether the universe will end someday or continue to exist in *eternity*⟩
***syn*** infinity, perpetuity
***rel*** boundlessness, endlessness, interminableness, permanence, timelessness
**2** unending existence after death ⟨a firm belief in the *eternity* of the soul⟩
***syn*** afterlife, hereafter, immortality
***rel*** otherworld
***phrases*** life after death
**3** a long or seemingly long period of time — see AGE 2

**ethereal** *adj* resembling air in lightness — see AIRY 1

**ethical** *adj* **1** conforming to a high standard of morality or virtue — see GOOD 2
**2** following the accepted rules of moral conduct — see HONORABLE 1
**3** guided by or in accordance with one's sense of right and wrong — see CONSCIENTIOUS 1

**ethics** *n pl* the code of good conduct for an individual or group ⟨the *ethics* of scouting require scouts to be loyal, clean, and reverent⟩
***syn*** morality, morals, principles, standards
***rel*** customs, etiquette, manners, mores; beliefs, dogma, faith, tenets

**ethnic** *adj* of, relating to, or reflecting the traits exhibited by a group of people with a common ancestry and culture — see RACIAL

**etiquette** *n* personal conduct or behavior as evaluated by an accepted standard of appropriateness for a social or professional setting — see MANNER 1

**eulogy** *n* a formal expression of praise — see ENCOMIUM

**euphonious** *adj* **1** having a pleasantly flowing quality suggestive of music — see LYRIC 1
**2** having a pleasing mixture of notes — see HARMONIOUS 1

**euphoria** *n* a state of overwhelming usually pleasurable emotion — see ECSTASY

**euphoric** *adj* experiencing or marked by overwhelming usually pleasurable emotion — see ECSTATIC

**evacuate** *vb* to remove the contents of — see EMPTY

**evacuee** *n* a person forced to emigrate for political reasons — see ÉMIGRÉ 1

**evade** *vb* to get or keep away from (as a responsibility) through cleverness or trickery — see ESCAPE 2

**evaluate** *vb* to make an approximate or tentative judgment regarding — see ESTIMATE 1

**evaluation** *n* **1** an opinion on the nature, character, or quality of something — see ESTIMATION 1
**2** the act of placing a value on the nature, character, or quality of something — see ESTIMATE 1

**evanesce** *vb* to cease to be visible — see DISAPPEAR

**evanescent** *adj* lasting only for a short time — see MOMENTARY

**evaporate** *vb* to cease to be visible — see DISAPPEAR

**evasion** *n* the act or a means of getting or keep-ing away from something undesirable — see ESCAPE 2
**evasive** *adj* hard to find, capture, or isolate — see ELUSIVE
**even** *adj* 1 being neither more nor less than a certain amount, number, or extent ⟨the distance to town is an *even* mile⟩
*syn* exact, flat, precise, round
*near ant* approximate, comparative, relative
2 having a surface without bends, breaks, or irregularities — see LEVEL
3 resembling another in every respect — see SAME 1
**even** *adv* not merely this but also ⟨the blue whale is a huge, *even* awesome animal by any measure⟩
*syn* indeed, nay, truly, verily, yea
*rel* assuredly, certainly, decidedly, definitely, positively, really, surely undeniably, unquestionably
*phrases* in fact, in reality, in truth
**even** *vb* 1 to make free from breaks, curves, or bumps ⟨*even* the filling before adding the top layer of the cake⟩
*syn* flatten, level, plane, smooth
*rel* clip, crop, pare, prune, shave, trim; lay, spread; card, comb, rake
*near ant* coarsen, rumple, wrinkle
*ant* rough, roughen
2 to make equal in amount, degree, or status — see EQUALIZE
**evening** *n* the time from when the sun begins to set to the onset of total darkness — see DUSK 1
**event** *n* 1 something that happens ⟨dinner-time was devoted to talking over the day's *events*, not to watching television⟩
*syn* affair, circumstance, episode, hap, happening, incident, occasion, occurrence, thing
*rel* coincidence, fluke, freak; landmark, milestone, page, phenomenon turning point; adventure, experience; accident, crisis, emergency, juncture; achievement, deed, exploit, feat; news, tidings
2 something that might happen ⟨in the *event* of rain, graduation ceremonies will be held indoors⟩
*syn* case, contingency, eventuality, possibility
*rel* probability; chance, risk
3 a competitive encounter between individuals or groups carried on for amusement, exercise, or in pursuit of a prize — see GAME 1
4 a social gathering — see PARTY 1
**eventful** *adj* having great meaning or lasting effect — see IMPORTANT 1
**eventide** *n* the time from when the sun begins to set to the onset of total darkness — see DUSK 1
**eventuality** *n* 1 something that can develop or become actual — see POTENTIAL
2 something that might happen — see EVENT 2
**eventually** *adv* at a later time — see YET 1
**ever** *adv* 1 for all time ⟨the name of Benedict Arnold will *ever* be linked with treason⟩
*syn* always, aye (*also* ay), eternally, everlastingly, evermore, forever, forevermore, permanently, perpetually
*rel* enduringly, long, perennially
*phrases* forever and a day, forever and ever, for good, to (*or* until) the end of time
*ant* never, nevermore
2 in any way or respect — see AT ALL
3 on every relevant occasion — see ALWAYS 1
**everlasting** *adj* lasting forever ⟨valentines typically express the giver's *everlasting* love and devotion⟩
*syn* ceaseless, dateless, deathless, endless, eternal, immortal, permanent, perpetual, undying, unending
*rel* durable, enduring, lasting, persistent; imperishable, indestructible; timeless; abiding, steadfast, steady, unfailing, unfaltering
*near ant* ephemeral, evanescent, fleeting, momentary, passing, short-lived, transitory
*ant* impermanent, mortal, temporary
**everlastingly** *adv* for all time — see EVER 1
**evermore** *adv* for all time — see EVER 1
**every** *adj* being one of a group — see EACH
**everybody** *pron* every person ⟨*everybody* must do what his or her conscience dictates⟩
*syn* all, everyone
*phrases* each and everyone, one and all
*ant* nobody
**everyday** *adj* 1 being of the type that is encountered in the normal course of events — see ORDINARY 1
2 having to do with the practical details of regular life — see MUNDANE 1
3 not designed for special occasions — see CASUAL 1
4 often observed or encountered — see COMMON 1
**everyone** *pron* every person — see EVERYBODY
**everyplace** *adv* in every place or in all places — see EVERYWHERE
**everywhere** *adv* in every place or in all places ⟨freedom and happiness are the goals of people *everywhere*⟩
*syn* all over, everyplace, throughout
*phrases* all over the place (*or* map), far and near, far and wide, high and low, in every corner (*or* quarter)
*ant* nowhere
**evidence** *n* something presented in support of the truth or accuracy of a claim — see PROOF
**evident** *adj* 1 appearing to be true on the basis of evidence that may or may not be confirmed — see APPARENT 1
2 not subject to misinterpretation or more than one interpretation — see CLEAR 2

**evidently** *adv* to all outward appearances — see APPARENTLY

**evil** *adj* **1** causing or capable of causing harm — see HARMFUL
**2** not conforming to a high moral standard; morally unacceptable — see BAD 2

**evil** *n* that which is morally unacceptable ⟨our free will allows us to choose between good and *evil*⟩
***syn*** bad, evildoing, ill, immorality, iniquity, sin, villainy, wrong
***rel*** atrociousness, badness, evilness, heinousness, nefariousness, sinfulness, vileness, wickedness; devilry (*or* deviltry), fiendishness; cancer, decay, rot, squalor; corruption, debauchery, degeneracy, depravity, indecency, perversion; abomination, anathema, taboo (*also* tabu)
***near ant*** integrity, probity, rectitude, uprightness; goodness, righteousness, virtuousness
***ant*** good, morality, right, virtue

**evildoer** *n* **1** a person who commits moral wrongs ⟨if good people stand by and do nothing, *evildoers* will triumph⟩
***syn*** malefactor, sinner, wrongdoer
***rel*** criminal, crook, felon, lawbreaker, miscreant, reprobate, transgressor, villain
***near ant*** angel, saint
**2** a mean, evil, or unprincipled person — see VILLAIN

**evildoing** *n* that which is morally unacceptable — see EVIL

**evilness** *n* the state or quality of being utterly evil — see ENORMITY 1

**evince** *vb* to make known (something abstract) through outward signs — see SHOW 2

**eviscerate** *vb* to take the internal organs out of — see GUT

**evocative** *adj* provoking a memory or mental association — see SUGGESTIVE 2

**evoke** *vb* to draw out (something hidden, latent, or reserved) — see EDUCE

**evolution** *n* the act or process of going from the simple or basic to the complex or advanced — see DEVELOPMENT 1

**evolve** *vb* to gradually become clearer or more detailed — see DEVELOP 1

**evolved** *adj* being far along in development — see ADVANCED 1

**exact** *adj* **1** being in agreement with the truth or a fact or a standard — see CORRECT 1
**2** being neither more nor less than a certain amount, number, or extent — see EVEN 1
**3** following an original exactly — see FAITHFUL 2
**4** made or done with extreme care and accuracy — see FINE 2
**5** meeting the highest standard of accuracy — see PRECISE 1

**exact** *vb* **1** to ask for (something) earnestly or with authority — see DEMAND 1
**2** to establish or apply as a charge or penalty — see IMPOSE
**3** to get (as money) by the use of force or threats — see EXTORT

**exacting** *adj* **1** hard to please — see FINICKY
**2** not allowing for any exceptions or loosening of standards — see RIGID 1
**3** requiring considerable physical or mental effort — see HARD 2
**4** requiring much time, effort, or careful attention — see DEMANDING 1

**exactitude** *n* the quality or state of being very accurate — see PRECISION

**exactly** *adv* **1** as stated or indicated without the slightest difference ⟨we will meet at *exactly* six o'clock⟩
***syn*** just, precisely, right, sharp, smackdab, squarely
**2** in a like manner — see JUST 1
**3** in the same words — see VERBATIM
**4** without any relaxation of standards or precision — see STRICTLY

**exactness** *n* the quality or state of being very accurate — see PRECISION

**exaggerate** *vb* **1** to add to the interest of by including made-up details — see EMBROIDER
**2** to describe or express in too strong terms — see OVERSTATE

**exaggeration** *n* the representation of something in terms that go beyond the facts ⟨their *exaggeration* was such that a rainstorm became a hurricane⟩
***syn*** caricature, coloring, elaboration, embellishment, embroidering, hyperbole, magnification, overstatement, padding, stretching
***rel*** amplification, enhancement; fabrication, misrepresentation; fudging, hedging
***near ant*** belittlement, disparagement, minimizing
***ant*** understatement

**exalt** *vb* to enhance the status of ⟨popular support and media hype have *exalted* Super Bowl Sunday to the level of a national holiday⟩
***syn*** aggrandize, dignify, ennoble, enshrine, glorify, magnify
***rel*** boost, elevate, lift, promote, raise, upgrade, uplift; heighten, intensify; idealize, romanticize, sanitize, sugarcoat; canonize, deify; acclaim, extol (*also* extoll), honor, laud, praise
***near ant*** belittle, decry, depreciate, detract, disparage, minimize
***ant*** abase, degrade, demean, humble, humiliate

**exam** *n* a set of questions or problems designed to assess knowledge, skills, or intelligence — see EXAMINATION 1

**examination** *n* **1** a set of questions or problems designed to assess knowledge, skills, or intelligence ⟨applicants to the prep school are required to take an *examination*⟩
***syn*** exam, quiz, test
***rel*** catechism; audition; final; checkup, inspection, review; inquiry, interrogation, investigation, probe, research
**2** a systematic search for the truth or facts about something — see INQUIRY 1

**3** a close look at or over someone or something in order to judge condition — see INSPECTION

**examine** *vb* **1** to put a series of questions to ⟨the defense attorney was eager to *examine* her star witness⟩
***syn*** grill, interrogate, pump, query, question, quiz
***rel*** debrief; cross-examine, catechize; annoy, harass, hound, pester
***phrases*** give the third degree to
**2** to look over closely (as for judging quality or condition) — see INSPECT

**example** *n* one of a group or collection that shows what the whole is like ⟨a war bonnet that is a fine *example* of Native American handicraft⟩
***syn*** case, exemplar, illustration, instance, representative, sample, specimen
***rel*** cross section; evidence, indication, manifestation, sign
***phrases*** case in point

**exasperate** *vb* to disturb the peace of mind of (someone) especially by repeated disagreeable acts — see IRRITATE 1

**exasperating** *adj* causing annoyance — see ANNOYING

**exasperation** *n* **1** something that is a source of irritation — see ANNOYANCE 3
**2** the feeling of impatience or anger caused by another's repeated disagreeable acts — see ANNOYANCE 2

**excavate** *vb* to hollow out or form (something) by removing earth — see DIG 1

**exceed** *vb* to go beyond the limit of ⟨by resorting to corporal punishment, the teacher had *exceeded* his authority⟩
***syn*** overreach, overrun, overshoot, overstep, surpass
***rel*** encroach, entrench (*also* intrench), infringe, invade, trespass; overdo, overuse, overwork

**exceedingly** *also* **exceeding** *adv* to a great degree — see VERY 1

**excel** *vb* to be greater, better, or stronger than — see SURPASS 1

**excellence** *n* **1** exceptionally high quality ⟨the annual awards honor *excellence* in children's literature⟩
***syn*** distinction, excellency, greatness, preeminence, superbness, superiority, supremacy
***rel*** faultlessness, flawlessness, impeccability, perfection; goodness, value, worth; consequence, importance, notability
***near ant*** averageness, badness, inferiority, mediocrity, ordinariness, worthlessness
**2** a quality that gives something special worth ⟨the particular *excellence* of down in clothing and sleeping bags is its lightness⟩
***syn*** distinction, excellency, merit, value, virtue
***rel*** advantage, edge, superiority
***near ant*** blemish, defect, failing, fault, flaw
***ant*** deficiency

**excellency** *n* **1** a quality that gives something special worth — see EXCELLENCE 2
**2** exceptionally high quality — see EXCELLENCE 1

**excellent** *adj* of the very best kind ⟨fast-food fans rate this chain's fries as *excellent*⟩
***syn*** A1, bang-up, banner, boss [*slang*], capital, classic, crackerjack, dandy, divine, fabulous, fine, first-class, first-rate, grand, great, groovy, heavenly, jim-dandy, keen, marvelous (*or* marvellous), mean, neat, nifty, noble, par excellence, prime, sensational, splendid, stellar, sterling, superb, superior, superlative, supernal, swell, terrific, tip-top, top, top-notch, unsurpassed, wonderful
***rel*** acceptable, adequate, all right, decent, good, OK, passable, satisfactory, tolerable; better, exceptional, fancy, high-grade, premium, special
***phrases*** out of sight
***near ant*** bad, inferior, low-grade, substandard, unsatisfactory; mediocre, second-class, second-rate; atrocious, execrable, vile, wretched
***ant*** poor

**except** *also* **excepting** *conj* if it were not for the fact that ⟨I'd go, *except* it's too far⟩
***syn*** but, only, saving, yet

**except** *also* **excepting** *prep* not including ⟨the store is open daily *except* Sundays⟩
***syn*** aside from, bar, barring, beside, besides, but, except for, excluding, outside, outside of, save, saving

**except** *vb* to prevent the participation or inclusion of — see EXCLUDE

**except for** *prep* not including — see EXCEPT

**exceptionable** *adj* provoking or likely to provoke protest — see OBJECTIONABLE

**exceptional** *adj* being out of the ordinary ⟨an *exceptional* amount of snow fell in March⟩
***syn*** aberrant, abnormal, atypical, extraordinary, freak, odd, peculiar, phenomenal, rare, singular, uncommon, uncustomary, unique, unusual, unwonted
***rel*** conspicuous, notable, noticeable, outstanding, prominent, remarkable, salient, striking; bizarre, deviant, eccentric, outlandish, quaint, strange, weird; incomprehensible, inconceivable, incredible, unimaginable, unthinkable
***near ant*** everyday, familiar, frequent
***ant*** common, customary, normal, ordinary, typical, unexceptional, usual

**excerpt** *n* a part taken from a longer work ⟨we'll read an *excerpt* from the novel⟩
***syn*** extract, passage
***rel*** snippet; citation, quotation; context; selection

**excess** *adj* being over what is needed — see SPARE 1

**excess** *n* the state or an instance of going beyond what is usual, proper, or needed ⟨a new television season with an *excess* of wisecracking teenagers⟩
***syn*** fat, overabundance, overage, overflow, overkill, overmuch, oversupply, su-

perabundance, superfluity, surfeit, surplus
*rel* abundance, bounty, plentitude, plenty, profusion, sufficiency; overproduction, overstock
*near ant* dearth, lack, scarcity
*ant* deficiency, deficit, insufficiency

**excessive** *adj* going beyond a normal or acceptable limit in degree or amount ⟨nerdy hackers who spend an *excessive* amount of time sitting in front of their computers⟩
*syn* devilish, exorbitant, extravagant, extreme, immoderate, inordinate, lavish, overmuch, overweening, steep, stiff, towering, unconscionable, undue
*rel* boundless, endless, immeasurable, infinite, limitless; intolerable, unbearable, unjustifiable, unwarranted; improper, inappropriate, thick, unseemly
*near ant* deficient, inadequate, insufficient; minimal, minimum
*ant* moderate, modest, reasonable, temperate

**excessively** *adv* beyond a normal or acceptable limit — see TOO 1

**exchange** *n* **1** a giving or taking of one thing of value in return for another ⟨*exchanges* of commemorative pins are common among Olympic athletes⟩
*syn* barter, commutation, swap, trade, truck
*rel* replacement, substitution; reciprocation, recompense, requital; bargain, deal, horse trade, negotiation, transaction; bargaining, dealing, dickering, haggling, horse trading; logrolling
**2** talking or a talk between two or more people — see CONVERSATION

**exchange** *vb* to give up (something) and take something else in return — see CHANGE 3

**excitable** *adj* easily excited by nature ⟨an *excitable* child who needed a stable home life⟩
*syn* flighty, fluttery, high-strung, jittery, jumpy, nervous, skittish, spooky
*rel* hot-blooded, mercurial, temperamental, unstable, volatile, volcanic; anxious, edgy, jumpy, nervy, tense, uptight; emotional, hypersensitive, intense, sensitive, soulful; dramatic, histrionic, melodramatic; irascible, irritable, prickly, testy, touchy
*near ant* calm, collected, cool, serene, tranquil; easy, easygoing, laid-back, relaxed
*ant* unflappable

**excite** *vb* **1** to cause a pleasurable stimulation of the feelings — see THRILL
**2** to rouse to strong feeling or action — see PROVOKE 1

**excited** *adj* **1** being in a state of increased activity or agitation — see FEVERISH 1
**2** showing urgent desire or interest — see EAGER

**excitement** *n* **1** something that arouses a strong response from another — see PROVOCATION 1
**2** urgent desire or interest — see EAGERNESS

**exciter** *n* a person who stirs up public feelings especially of discontent — see AGITATOR

**exciting** *adj* **1** causing great emotional or mental stimulation ⟨an *exciting*, come-from-behind victory for the underdogs in the last game of the World Series⟩
*syn* breathtaking, electric, electrifying, exhilarating, galvanizing, inspiring, rip-roaring, rousing, stimulating, stirring, thrilling
*rel* arresting, interesting, intriguing, provocative, tantalizing; absorbing, engrossing, gripping, riveting; moving, poignant, touching; enchanting, enthralling, fascinating, spellbinding
*near ant* boring, tedious, tiresome; dreary, dull, humdrum, monotonous, uninteresting
*ant* unexciting
**2** serving or likely to arouse a strong reaction — see PROVOCATIVE

**exclaim** *vb* to utter with a sudden burst of strong feeling ⟨the whole team *exclaimed* with one voice, "We won!"⟩
*syn* blurt (out), bolt, cry (out), ejaculate
*rel* blunder, leak; bellow, bleat, crow, holler, hoot, howl, roar, shout, whoop, yowl; interject

**exclude** *vb* to prevent the participation or inclusion of ⟨troublemakers were *excluded* from the club⟩
*syn* ban, bar, count out, debar, eliminate, except, rule out
*rel* blackball, blacklist, ostracize; banish, deport, exile, expel, oust, throw out; block, hinder, impede, obstruct; cease, discontinue, halt, suspend; deter, stave off, ward (off)
*near ant* accept, entertain, receive, welcome
*ant* admit, include

**excluding** *prep* not including — see EXCEPT

**exclusive** *adj* **1** belonging only to the one person, unit, or group named — see SOLE 1
**2** not divided or scattered among several areas of interest or concern — see WHOLE 1

**exclusively** *adv* for nothing other than — see SOLELY 1

**excoriate** *vb* to criticize harshly and usually publicly — see ATTACK 2

**excrement** *n* solid matter discharged from an animal's alimentary canal — see DROPPING 1

**excrescence** *n* an abnormal mass of tissue — see GROWTH 1

**excreta** *n pl* solid matter discharged from an animal's alimentary canal — see DROPPING 1

**excruciating** *adj* **1** intensely or unbearably painful ⟨those who publicly dis-

---

*syn* synonym(s) *rel* related words
*ant* antonym(s) *near ant* near antonym(s)

agreed with the government were subjected to *excruciating* torture⟩
***syn*** agonizing, harrowing, racking, tormenting, torturing, torturous
***rel*** acute, exquisite, extreme, fierce, intense, vehement, violent; piercing, sharp, shooting, stabbing, stinging, tearing, tingling
**2** causing intense mental or physical distress — see SHARP 2
**3** difficult to endure — see HARSH 1
**4** hard to accept or bear especially emotionally — see BITTER 2

**exculpate** *vb* to free from a charge of wrongdoing ⟨I will present evidence that will *exculpate* my client⟩
***syn*** absolve, acquit, clear, exonerate, vindicate
***rel*** atone (for), expiate; discharge, liberate, redeem, release, unburden; condone, excuse, forgive, pardon, remit; avenge, redress, revenge
***near ant*** accuse, arraign, charge, impeach, indict; convict
***ant*** incriminate

**excursion** *n* **1** a short trip for pleasure ⟨our weekend *excursions* have been to all parts of our home state⟩
***syn*** jaunt, junket, outing, sally
***rel*** journey, travel(s); circuit, tour; expedition, odyssey, safari; detour; hike, peregrination, trek, walk; pilgrimage
**2** a departure from the subject under consideration — see TANGENT

**excursionist** *n* a person who travels for pleasure — see TOURIST

**excusable** *adj* worthy of forgiveness — see VENIAL

**excuse** *n* an explanation that frees one from fault or blame ⟨a whole evening of must-see TV is no *excuse* for not having your homework done⟩
***syn*** alibi, defense, justification, plea, reason
***rel*** guise, pretense (*or* pretence), pretext, rationale, rationalization; cop-out, out; acknowledgment (*also* acknowledgement), apology, atonement, confession

**excuse** *vb* **1** to overlook or dismiss as of little importance ⟨the student's theme is so good that I'm willing to *excuse* the spelling errors⟩
***syn*** brush (aside *or* off), condone, disregard, forgive, gloss (over), gloze (over), ignore, pardon, pass over, remit, shrug off, wink (at)
***rel*** explain, justify, rationalize, whitewash; absolve, acquit, clear, exculpate, exonerate, vindicate
***phrases*** forgive and forget
***near ant*** heed, mark, mind, note, object (to)
**2** to be an acceptable reason for — see JUSTIFY 1
**3** to make (something) seem less bad by offering excuses — see PALLIATE 1

**execrable** *adj* **1** extremely unsatisfactory — see WRETCHED 1
**2** of low quality — see CHEAP 2

**execrate** *vb* **1** to declare to be morally wrong or evil — see CONDEMN 1
**2** to dislike strongly — see HATE

**execration** *n* **1** a prayer that harm will come to someone — see CURSE 1
**2** a very strong dislike — see HATE 1

**execute** *vb* **1** to carry out effectively — see ENFORCE
**2** to carry through (as a process) to completion — see PERFORM 1
**3** to put to death deliberately — see MURDER 1

**execution** *n* the doing of an action — see COMMISSION 2

**executive** *adj* suited for or relating to the directing of things ⟨the *executive* skills needed to manage a large business office⟩
***syn*** administrative, directorial, managerial, supervisory
***rel*** bureaucratic, governmental, ministerial, official, parliamentary; regulatory; authoritarian, despotic, dictatorial

**executive** *n* a person who manages or directs ⟨a program that teaches company *executives* how to better manage their staffs⟩
***syn*** administrator, director, manager, superintendent, supervisor
***rel*** officer, official; commissioner, minister; boss, chief, head, leader, president

**exemplar** *n* **1** one of a group or collection that shows what the whole is like — see EXAMPLE
**2** someone of such unequaled perfection as to deserve imitation — see IDEAL 1
**3** the most perfect type or example — see QUINTESSENCE 1

**exemplary** *adj* constituting, serving as, or worthy of being a pattern to be imitated — see MODEL

**exemplify** *vb* to show or make clear by using examples — see ILLUSTRATE 1

**exemption** *n* freedom from punishment, harm, or loss — see IMPUNITY

**exercise** *n* **1** energetic movement of the body for the sake of physical fitness ⟨the doctor ordered plenty of fresh air and *exercise*⟩
***syn*** activity, conditioning, exertion
***rel*** training, warm-up, workout; toning, trimming; aerobics, bodybuilding, calisthenics, isometrics, weight lifting; physical therapy
**2** something done over and over in order to develop skill ⟨a young piano student dutifully going through the standard finger *exercises*⟩
***syn*** drill, practice (*also* practise), routine, training, workout
***rel*** assignment, homework, lesson
**3** the act or practice of employing something for a particular purpose — see USE 1

**exercise** *vb* **1** to bring to bear especially forcefully or effectively — see EXERT
**2** to do over and over so as to become skilled — see PRACTICE
**3** to put into action or service — see USE 1

4 to trouble the mind of; to make uneasy — see DISTURB 1

**exert** *vb* to bring to bear especially forcefully or effectively ⟨parental involvement has been shown to *exert* the most influence over a child's success in school⟩
***syn*** apply, exercise, ply, put out, wield
***rel*** employ, use, utilize

**exertion** *n* **1** energetic movement of the body for the sake of physical fitness — see EXERCISE 1
**2** the active use of energy in producing a result — see EFFORT

**exfoliate** *vb* to cast (a natural bodily covering or appendage) aside — see SHED 1

**exhale** *vb* **1** to let or force out of the lungs ⟨before answering, the suspect *exhaled* a cloud of cigarette smoke⟩
***syn*** blow (out), breathe (out), expire
***rel*** expectorate
***ant*** inhale, inspire
**2** to throw or give off — see EMIT 1

**exhaust** *vb* **1** to use up all the physical energy of ⟨the long day at the county fair had *exhausted* everyone⟩
***syn*** burn out, do in, drain, fag, fatigue, tire, tucker (out), wash out, wear, wear out, weary
***rel*** debilitate, enervate, enfeeble, sap, waste, weaken
***phrases*** wear to a frazzle
***near ant*** activate, energize, invigorate, strengthen, vitalize; relax, rest, unwind
**2** to make complete use of — see DEPLETE

**exhausted** *adj* depleted in strength, energy, or freshness — see WEARY 1

**exhaustion** *n* a complete depletion of energy or strength — see FATIGUE

**exhaustive** *adj* trying all possibilities ⟨after an *exhaustive* search of our house, we still hadn't found the cat⟩
***syn*** all-out, clean, complete, comprehensive, full-scale, out-and-out, thorough, thoroughgoing, total
***rel*** broad, extensive, far-reaching, in-depth, wide; general, global, inclusive
***near ant*** aimless, desultory, haphazard, hit-or-miss, random; cursory, shallow, slipshod, superficial; limited, narrow, restricted

**exhaustively** *adv* with attention to all aspects or details — see THOROUGHLY 1

**exhibit** *n* a public showing of objects of interest — see EXHIBITION 1

**exhibit** *vb* to present so as to invite notice or attention — see SHOW 1

**exhibition** *n* **1** a public showing of objects of interest ⟨an *exhibition* of valuable and fascinating artifacts from a recovered pirate ship⟩
***syn*** display, exhibit, exposition, fair, show
***rel*** demonstration, performance, presentation, production; extravaganza, pageant, spectacle; auction, offering, sale
**2** an outward and often exaggerated indication of something abstract (as a feeling) for effect — see SHOW 1

**exhilarate** *vb* **1** to cause a pleasurable stimulation of the feelings — see THRILL
**2** to fill with great joy — see ELATE

**exhilarated** *adj* experiencing or marked by overwhelming usually pleasurable emotion — see ECSTATIC

**exhilarating** *adj* causing great emotional or mental stimulation — see EXCITING 1

**exhilaration** *n* **1** a pleasurably intense stimulation of the feelings — see THRILL
**2** a state of overwhelming usually pleasurable emotion — see ECSTASY

**exhort** *vb* to try to persuade (someone) through earnest appeals to follow a course of action — see URGE

**exhume** *vb* to remove from place of burial ⟨the remains of John Paul Jones were *exhumed* in Paris and transported with great ceremony to the U.S. Naval Academy⟩
***syn*** disinter, unearth
***ant*** bury, entomb, inter

**exigency** *n* a time or state of affairs requiring prompt or decisive action — see EMERGENCY

**exile** *n* **1** the forced removal from a homeland ⟨the *exile* of French settlers from Nova Scotia resulted in the birth of the Cajun community in the U.S.⟩
***syn*** banishment, deportation, displacement, expatriation, expulsion
***rel*** ostracism; extradition; dispersion, scattering; emigration, migration; evacuation
***near ant*** repatriation, return; immigration
**2** a person forced to emigrate for political reasons — see ÉMIGRÉ 1

**exile** *vb* to force to leave a country — see BANISH 1

**exist** *vb* to have life — see BE 1

**existence** *n* the fact of being or of being real ⟨the *existence* of UFOs is something that people continue to argue about⟩
***syn*** actuality, reality, subsistence
***rel*** genuineness, realness; activity, animation, life; currency, presence, prevalence
***near ant*** absence, dearth, lack, want
***ant*** nonexistence

**existent** *adj* **1** existing in fact and not merely as a possibility — see ACTUAL
**2** having being at the present time — see EXTANT 1

**existing** *adj* having being at the present time — see EXTANT 1

**exit** *n* **1** a place or means of going out ⟨all of the building's *exits* were being watched by security guards⟩
***syn*** egress, issue, outlet
***rel*** escape, release; opening, passage, vent
***near ant*** access, entrée (*or* entree)
***ant*** entrance, entry, entryway, ingress
**2** the act of leaving a place — see DEPARTURE

**exit** *vb* to leave a place often for another — see GO 2

---

***syn*** synonym(s) ***rel*** related words
***ant*** antonym(s) ***near ant*** near antonym(s)

**exiting** *n* the act of leaving a place — see DEPARTURE

**exodus** *n* a flowing or going out — see OUTFLOW

**exonerate** *vb* to free from a charge of wrongdoing — see EXCULPATE

**exorbitant** *adj* going beyond a normal or acceptable limit in degree or amount — see EXCESSIVE

**exorbitantly** *adv* beyond a normal or acceptable limit — see TOO 1

**exotic** *adj* excitingly or mysteriously unusual ⟨the dream of someday traveling to *exotic* lands⟩
*syn* fantastic, glamorous (*also* glamourous), marvelous (*or* marvellous), outlandish, romantic, strange
*rel* colorful, picturesque, quaint; alien, foreign; distant, faraway, remote; alluring, captivating, enchanting, fascinating

**exotic** *n* something strange or unusual that is an object of interest — see CURIOSITY 2

**expand** *vb* **1** to express more fully and in greater detail ⟨an article on the First Ladies that the author later *expanded* into a book⟩
*syn* amplify, develop, elaborate (on), enlarge (on)
*rel* add (to), complement, supplement; discourse, expatiate, ramble, run on
*near ant* compress, contract; outline, summarize, sum up
*ant* abbreviate, abridge, condense, shorten
**2** to make greater in size, amount, or number — see INCREASE 1
**3** to arrange the parts of (something) over a wider area — see OPEN 3
**4** to become greater in extent, volume, amount, or number — see INCREASE 2

**expanse** *n* a wide space or area ⟨the great explorers who crossed the vast *expanse* of the ocean in small ships⟩
*syn* breadth, extent, reach, spread, stretch
*rel* domain, field, sphere, territory; compass, range, scope, sweep; gamut, scale, spectrum; depth, emptiness, void; distance, extension, latitude, length, span; amplitude, immensity, magnitude

**expansion** *n* **1** something added (as by growth) — see INCREASE 1
**2** the act or process of going from the simple or basic to the complex or advanced — see DEVELOPMENT 1

**expansive** *adj* having considerable extent — see EXTENSIVE

**expatiate** *vb* to give a formal often extended talk on a subject — see TALK 1

**expatriate** *n* a person forced to emigrate for political reasons — see ÉMIGRÉ 1

**expatriate** *vb* to force to leave a country — see BANISH 1

**expatriation** *n* the forced removal from a homeland — see EXILE 1

**expect** *vb* to believe in the future occurrence of (something) ⟨we *expect* their arrival late this afternoon⟩
*syn* anticipate, await, hope (for), watch (for)
*rel* bank on, count (on *or* upon), depend (on *or* upon), rely (on *or* upon); envisage, foresee; foretell, predict, prophesy; assume, presume, presuppose; contemplate, eye, view
*phrases* look for, look forward to
*near ant* doubt, question

**expectant** *adj* **1** having or showing signs of eagerly awaiting something ⟨*expectant* crowds gathered at the spot where the President was scheduled to make an appearance⟩
*syn* agape, agog, anticipatory
*rel* open-eyed, openmouthed; alert, vigilant, watchful; anxious, breathless, eager, enthusiastic, raring; impatient, restive, restless
*near ant* apathetic, indifferent, unconcerned, unimpressed, uninterested, unmoved
**2** containing unborn young within the body — see PREGNANT 1

**expected** *adj* being in accordance with the prescribed, normal, or logical course of events — see DUE 2

**expedient** *adj* suitable for bringing about a desired result under the circumstances ⟨made the *expedient* decision to sell the land to whomever offered the most money⟩
*syn* advisable, desirable, judicious, politic, prudent, tactical, wise
*rel* advantageous, beneficial, profitable; useful, utilitarian; feasible, possible, practicable, practical; opportune, seasonable, timely; opportunistic, self-seeking
*near ant* impractical, unfeasible, unprofitable; inopportune, unseasonable, untimely
*ant* imprudent, inadvisable, inexpedient, injudicious, unwise

**expedient** *n* **1** a temporary replacement — see MAKESHIFT
**2** an action planned or taken to achieve a desired result — see MEASURE 1
**3** something that one uses to accomplish an end especially when the usual means is not available — see RESOURCE 1

**expedition** *n* a going from one place to another usually of some distance — see JOURNEY

**expeditious** *adj* having or showing the ability to respond without delay or hesitation — see QUICK 1

**expel** *vb* **1** to drive or force out — see EJECT 1
**2** to throw or give off — see EMIT 1
**3** to throw out or off (something from within) often violently — see ERUPT 1

**expend** *vb* **1** to hand over or use up in payment — see SPEND 1
**2** to make complete use of — see DEPLETE

**expenditure** *n* **1** a payment made in the course of achieving a result — see EXPENSE
**2** the active use of energy in producing a result — see EFFORT

**expense** *n* a payment made in the course of achieving a result ⟨they spared no *expense* in building the house of their dreams⟩
***syn*** cost, disbursement, expenditure, outgo, outlay
***rel*** overhead; outflow; spending money; charge, price, rate, tab, tariff, toll
**expensive** *adj* commanding a large price — see COSTLY
**expensively** *adv* in a luxurious manner — see HIGH
**experience** *n* **1** knowledge gained by actually doing or living through something ⟨the hospital is looking for nurses with operating-room *experience*⟩
***syn*** expertise, know-how, proficiency, savvy, skills
***rel*** background; command, mastery; acquaintance, familiarity, intimacy
***near ant*** ignorance, unawareness, unfamiliarity
***ant*** inexperience
**2** an exciting or noteworthy event that one experiences firsthand — see ADVENTURE
**experience** *vb* to come to a knowledge of (something) by living through it ⟨eventually we all have to *experience* the loss of a loved one⟩
***syn*** endure, feel, have, know, see, suffer, sustain, taste, undergo
***rel*** encounter, meet; accept, receive
***phrases*** go through
**experienced** *adj* having or showing exceptional knowledge, experience, or skill in a field of endeavor — see PROFICIENT
**experiment** *n* a procedure or operation carried out to resolve an uncertainty ⟨Benjamin Franklin's famous *experiment* in which he flew a kite in a thunderstorm to see if lightning and electricity were identical⟩
***syn*** experimentation, test, trial
***rel*** trial and error; dry run, shakedown; exercise, practice (*also* practise), rehearsal, tryout, workout; crucible, ordeal; attempt, effort, try
**experimental** *adj* **1** made or done as an experiment ⟨an *experimental* procedure for patients suffering from leukemia⟩
***syn*** pilot, trial
***rel*** developmental, investigative, preparatory; preliminary, provisional, temporary, tentative; conjectural, hypothetical, speculative, theoretical (*also* theoretic); untested, untried; unproved, unproven
***near ant*** accepted, established, standard; tested, tried; advanced, developed; proved, proven; conclusive, decisive, definitive, final, permanent
**2** based on observation or experience — see EMPIRICAL
**experimentation** *n* a procedure or operation carried out to resolve an uncertainty — see EXPERIMENT

***syn*** synonym(s) ***rel*** related words
***ant*** antonym(s) ***near ant*** near antonym(s)

**expert** *adj* **1** accomplished with trained ability — see SKILLFUL
**2** having or showing exceptional knowledge, experience, or skill in a field of endeavor — see PROFICIENT
**expert** *n* a person with a high level of knowledge or skill in a field ⟨*experts* at the crime lab were able to tell the sex, race, and approximate age of the murderer⟩
***syn*** ace, adept, artist, authority, crackerjack, maestro, master, past master, scholar, shark, virtuoso, whiz, wizard
***rel*** pro, professional; specialist; addict, aficionado, buff, devotee, enthusiast, fan; craftsman, journeyman; jack-of-all-trades
***near ant*** apprentice, beginner, neophyte, novice; dabbler, dilettante; layman, nonprofessional
***ant*** amateur
**expertise** *n* knowledge gained by actually doing or living through something — see EXPERIENCE 1
**expertly** *adv* in a skillful or expert manner — see WELL 3
**expiate** *vb* to make up for (an offense) ⟨Yom Kippur is the holy day on which Jews are expected to *expiate* sins committed during the past year⟩
***syn*** atone (for)
***rel*** compensate, recompense, reimburse, remunerate, repay; amend, correct, rectify, redress; propitiate
***phrases*** make amends for, make good for
**expiration** *n* **1** the act of ceasing to exist — see DEATH 3
**2** the stopping of a process or activity — see END 1
**expire** *vb* **1** to come to an end — see CEASE 1
**2** to let or force out of the lungs — see EXHALE 1
**3** to stop living — see DIE 1
**expired** *adj* no longer existing — see EXTINCT
**explain** *vb* **1** to make plain or understandable ⟨write an essay that *explains* the meaning of the poem⟩
***syn*** clarify, clear (up), construe, demonstrate, elucidate, explicate, expound, illuminate, illustrate, interpret, spell out
***rel*** decipher, decode; analyze, break down; disentangle, undo, unravel, unscramble, untangle; resolve, solve; define, specify
***phrases*** get across
***near ant*** befog, cloud; confound, confuse
***ant*** obscure
**2** to give the reason for or cause of ⟨can you *explain* your very odd behavior at the wedding reception?⟩
***syn*** account (for), explain away, rationalize
***rel*** condone, excuse, forgive, justify; absolve, acquit, exculpate, exonerate, vindicate
**explainable** *adj* capable of having the reason for or cause of determined — see SOLVABLE

**explain away** *vb* to give the reason for or cause of — see EXPLAIN 2

**explanation** *n* **1** a statement that makes something clear ⟨an *explanation* of photosynthesis that the whole class was able to understand⟩
***syn*** clarification, construction, elucidation, explication, exposition, illumination, illustration, interpretation
***rel*** paraphrase, restatement, translation; deciphering, decoding; disentanglement, unscrambling; analysis; definition, meaning; demonstration, enactment; justification, rationale, rationalization, reasoning
**2** a statement given to explain a belief or act — see REASON 1

**explanatory** *adj* serving to explain ⟨the *explanatory* section has as its heading "Using Your Dictionary"⟩
***syn*** elucidative, expository, illuminative, illustrative, interpretive
***rel*** analytic (*also* analytical), demonstrative, discursive; exculpatory

**expletive** *n* a disrespectful or indecent word or expression — see SWEARWORD

**explicable** *adj* capable of having the reason for or cause of determined — see SOLVABLE

**explicate** *vb* to make plain or understandable — see EXPLAIN 1

**explication** *n* a statement that makes something clear — see EXPLANATION 1

**explicit** *adj* so clearly expressed as to leave no doubt about the meaning ⟨*explicit* instructions about what to do in an emergency⟩
***syn*** clear-cut, definite, definitive, express, specific, unambiguous, unequivocal
***rel*** avowed, declared, stated; categorical (*also* categoric), complete, comprehensive, exhaustive, full; certain, sure, unmistakable; clear, distinct, lucid; exact, precise; direct, literal, plain, simple, straightforward; comprehensible, intelligible, understandable
***near ant*** cryptic, dark, enigmatic (*also* enigmatical), obscure, unclear; imprecise, inaccurate, incorrect, inexact; incomprehensible, unintelligible
***ant*** implicit, implied, inferred; ambiguous, circuitous; equivocal, indefinite

**explicitness** *n* **1** careful thoroughness of detail — see PARTICULARITY 1
**2** clearness of expression — see SIMPLICITY 2

**explode** *vb* **1** to break open or into pieces usually because of internal pressure ⟨the building was wrecked when a powerful bomb *exploded*⟩
***syn*** blow up, burst, detonate, go off, pop
***rel*** fragment, shatter, smash, splinter; discharge, fire, shoot; balloon, burgeon, mushroom
***near ant*** collapse, fizzle
***ant*** implode
**2** to cause to break open or into pieces by or as if by an explosive — see BLAST 1
**3** to develop suddenly and violently — see ERUPT 2

**exploit** *n* **1** an act of notable skill, strength, or cleverness — see FEAT 1
**2** something done by someone — see ACTION 1

**exploit** *vb* **1** to take unfair advantage of ⟨a student who *exploits* his friend's good nature by always sponging off him⟩
***syn*** abuse, capitalize (on), cash in (on), impose (on *or* upon), play (on *or* upon), use
***rel*** manipulate, mistreat; bleed, cheat, fleece, overcharge, skin, soak, stick; commercialize
**2** to control or take advantage of by artful, unfair, or insidious means — see MANIPULATE 1
**3** to put into action or service — see USE 1

**exploitable** *adj* **1** capable of or suitable for being used for a particular purpose — see USABLE 1
**2** readily taken advantage of — see EASY 2

**exploration** *n* a systematic search for the truth or facts about something — see INQUIRY 1

**explore** *vb* **1** to search through or into ⟨let's *explore* new ways of raising money for the school band⟩
***syn*** delve (into), dig (into), inquire (into), investigate, look (into), probe, research
***rel*** examine, inspect, sift, study, view; browse, peruse, scan, skim (through), thumb (through)
**2** to go into or range over for purposes of discovery ⟨we must continue to *explore* the depths of the ocean⟩
***syn*** hunt, probe, prospect, search
***rel*** reconnoiter (*or* reconnoitre), scout; disclose, discover, reveal, unearth; fathom, plumb, sound

**explosion** *n* **1** the act or an instance of exploding ⟨the *explosion* of the first atomic bomb at Hiroshima⟩
***syn*** blast, bursting, detonation, eruption
***rel*** discharge, firing, shooting; blowout, flare-up; bang, boom, pop
***ant*** implosion
**2** a sudden intense expression of strong feeling — see OUTBURST 1
**3** an outburst or display of excited anger — see TANTRUM

**explosive** *adj* **1** extreme in degree, power, or effect — see INTENSE
**2** marked by bursts of destructive force or intense activity — see VIOLENT 1

**exponent** *n* a person who actively supports or favors a cause ⟨*exponents* of space exploration called for more missions to the outer reaches of the solar system⟩
***syn*** advocate, apostle, backer, booster, champion, friend, promoter, proponent, supporter
***rel*** loyalist, partisan, stalwart; adherent, cohort, disciple, follower; expounder, interpreter; cheerleader
***near ant*** enemy, foe, rival; belittler, critic, faultfinder
***ant*** adversary, antagonist, opponent

**expose** *vb* **1** to reveal the true nature of ⟨a well-researched article that *exposes* the UFO story as a hoax⟩
***syn*** debunk, show up, uncloak, uncover, unmask
***rel*** discredit, disprove; disclose, divulge, tell, unveil
***near ant*** conceal, hide, secrete
***ant*** camouflage, cloak, disguise, mask
**2** to make known (as information previously kept secret) — see REVEAL 1
**3** to make known (something abstract) through outward signs — see SHOW 2
**4** to present so as to invite notice or attention — see SHOW 1

**exposed** *adj* **1** being in a situation where one is likely to meet with harm — see LIABLE 1
**2** lacking a usual or natural covering — see NAKED 2
**3** lacking protection from danger or resistance against attack — see HELPLESS 1

**exposition** *n* **1** a public showing of objects of interest — see EXHIBITION 1
**2** a series of explanations or observations on something (as an event) — see COMMENTARY
**3** a statement that makes something clear — see EXPLANATION 1

**expository** *adj* serving to explain — see EXPLANATORY

**expostulate** (with) *vb* to present an opposing opinion or argument — see OBJECT

**expostulation** *n* a feeling or declaration of disapproval or dissent — see OBJECTION

**exposure** *n* **1** the state of being left without shelter or protection against something harmful ⟨some people avoid situations in which there is a high level of *exposure* to germs⟩
***syn*** liability, openness, vulnerability
***rel*** susceptibility; defenselessness, helplessness, weakness; danger, jeopardy, peril, risk
***near ant*** protection, safeguarding, sheltering, shielding
**2** the act or an instance of making known something previously unknown or concealed — see REVELATION

**expound** *vb* to make plain or understandable — see EXPLAIN 1

**express** *adj* **1** of a particular or exact sort ⟨a trip to the supermarket with the *express* purpose of buying milk⟩
***syn*** distinct, especial, precise, set, special, specific
***rel*** lone, only, separate, single, sole, solitary; distinctive, exclusive, individual, peculiar, unique; limited, restricted; specified
***near ant*** general, generic, nonexclusive, universal
***ant*** nonspecific
**2** so clearly expressed as to leave no doubt about the meaning — see EXPLICIT

***syn*** synonym(s) ***rel*** related words
***ant*** antonym(s) ***near ant*** near antonym(s)

**express** *vb* **1** to make known (as an idea, emotion, or opinion) ⟨in a true democracy, a person can freely *express* his or her views⟩
***syn*** air, give, look, sound, state, vent, ventilate, voice
***rel*** advertise, announce, declare, enunciate, proclaim; broadcast, circulate, disseminate, publish; describe, write, write up; sound off, speak out, speak up; chime in; communicate, convey, put across, put over; offer, submit
***phrases*** put forth
***near ant*** censor, restrain, restrict
***ant*** stifle, suppress
**2** to apply external pressure on so as to force out the juice or contents of — see PRESS 2
**3** to communicate or convey (as an idea) to the mind — see MEAN 1
**4** to convey in appropriate or telling terms — see PHRASE

**expression** *n* **1** an act, process, or means of putting something into words ⟨the poem is his *expression* of his grief upon the loss of his beloved dog⟩
***syn*** articulation, formulation, statement, utterance, voice
***rel*** outlet, vent; observation, reflection, remark, thought; speech, tongue
**2** facial appearance regarded as an indication of mood or feeling — see LOOK 1
**3** a pronounceable series of letters having a distinct meaning especially in a particular field — see WORD 1
**4** a sequence of words having a specific meaning — see PHRASE

**expressionless** *adj* not expressing any emotion — see BLANK 1

**expressive** *adj* clearly conveying a special meaning (as one's mood) ⟨the teacher's *expressive* sigh showed that she had heard that excuse many times before⟩
***syn*** eloquent, meaning, meaningful, pregnant, revealing, significant, suggestive
***rel*** graphic (*also* graphical), pictorial, vivid; evocative, redolent, reminiscent; sententious, weighty; flavorful, rich

**expressway** *n* a passage cleared for public vehicular travel — see WAY 1

**expropriate** *vb* to take ownership or control of (something) by right of one's authority — see CONFISCATE

**expulsion** *n* the forced removal from a homeland — see EXILE 1

**expunge** *vb* to destroy all traces of — see ANNIHILATE 1

**expurgate** *vb* to remove objectionable parts from — see CENSOR

**exquisite** *adj* **1** extreme in degree, power, or effect — see INTENSE
**2** having qualities that appeal to a refined taste — see CHOICE
**3** satisfying or pleasing because of fineness or mildness — see DELICATE 1

**exquisiteness** *n* the state or quality of having a delicate structure — see DELICACY 2

**extant** *adj* **1** having being at the present time ⟨a celebrated author who is general-

ly regarded as America's greatest novelist *extant*〉
***syn*** alive, existent, existing, living
***rel*** active, busy, flourishing, functioning, operating, working
***near ant*** defunct, destroyed, exterminated; departed, gone, lost; nonexistent; idle, inactive, inert
***ant*** dead, extinct
**2** existing or in progress right now — see PRESENT 1

**extemporaneous** *adj* made or done without previous thought or preparation 〈caught by surprise, I had to make an *extemporaneous* speech at the awards banquet〉
***syn*** ad-lib, extempore, impromptu, improvised, offhand, offhanded, snap, spur-of-the-moment, unconsidered, unplanned, unpremeditated, unprepared, unrehearsed
***rel*** automatic, impulsive, instinctive, involuntary, spontaneous; casual, informal, unauthorized
***near ant*** deliberate, intended, intentional
***ant*** considered, planned, premeditated, prepared, rehearsed

**extempore** *adj* made or done without previous thought or preparation — see EXTEMPORANEOUS

**extemporize** *vb* to perform, make, or do without preparation — see IMPROVISE

**extend** *vb* **1** to make longer 〈our guests from out of town *extended* their visit by a week〉
***syn*** draw out, elongate, lengthen, prolong, protract, stretch
***rel*** amplify, enlarge, expand, increase; attenuate, thin
***near ant*** decrease, diminish, lessen, reduce; thicken
***ant*** abbreviate, abridge, curtail, cut, cut back, shorten
**2** to put before another for acceptance or consideration — see OFFER 1
**3** to arrange the parts of (something) over a wider area — see OPEN 3
**4** to be positioned along a certain course or in a certain direction — see RUN 3
**5** to make greater in size, amount, or number — see INCREASE 1

**extended** *adj* **1** expressing one thing in terms normally used for another — see FIGURATIVE
**2** having considerable extent — see EXTENSIVE
**3** lasting for a considerable time — see LONG 2
**4** of great extent from end to end — see LONG 1

**extended family** *n* those who live as a family in one house — see HOUSEHOLD

**extension** *n* **1** the act of making longer 〈the board's *extension* of the school year drew howls of protest〉
***syn*** drawing out, elongation, lengthening, prolongation, prolonging, stretching
***ant*** abbreviation, abridgment (*or* abridgement), curtailment, cutback, shortening
**2** a smaller structure added to a main building — see ANNEX

**extensive** *adj* having considerable extent 〈a rock hound whose *extensive* reading enables him to identify just about any rock or mineral〉
***syn*** broad, expansive, extended, far-flung, far-reaching, wide, widespread
***rel*** comprehensive, general, global, inclusive; boundless, endless, limitless, unlimited; capacious, commodious, roomy, spacious
***near ant*** circumscribed, limited, restricted
***ant*** narrow

**extensively** *adv* to a large extent or degree — see GREATLY 2

**extent** *n* **1** a real or imaginary point beyond which a person or thing cannot go — see LIMIT
**2** a wide space or area — see EXPANSE
**3** an area over which activity, capacity, or influence extends — see RANGE 2
**4** the total amount of measurable space or surface occupied by something — see [1]SIZE

**extenuate** *vb* to make (something) seem less bad by offering excuses — see PALLIATE 1

**exterior** *adj* situated on the outside or farther out — see OUTER

**exterior** *n* an outer part or layer 〈the *exterior* of the tooth consists of very hard enamel〉
***syn*** face, outside, skin, surface, veneer
***rel*** facade (*also* façade), front, top; cover, covering, facing; appearance, disguise, guise, mask, semblance, show
***ant*** inside, interior

**exterminate** *vb* to destroy all traces of — see ANNIHILATE 1

**extermination** *n* the state or fact of being rendered nonexistent, physically unsound, or useless — see DESTRUCTION

**external** *adj* situated on the outside or farther out — see OUTER

**extinct** *adj* no longer existing 〈a few overgrown ruins are all that remain of that once mighty but now *extinct* civilization〉
***syn*** bygone, dead, defunct, departed, expired, gone, vanished
***rel*** nonexistent; dying, faded, moribund; collapsed, fallen, overthrown; antiquated, dated, obsolete, passé; finished, lapsed, terminated; lost, missing
***near ant*** active, dynamic, thriving, vibrant
***ant*** alive, existent, existing, extant, living

**extinction** *n* the state or fact of being rendered nonexistent, physically unsound, or useless — see DESTRUCTION

**extinguish** *vb* **1** to cause to cease burning 〈the fire in the skillet was quickly *extinguished* by slamming the lid on〉
***syn*** douse, put out, quench, snuff (out)
***rel*** choke, smother, suffocate; stamp (out)
***ant*** fire, ignite, inflame, kindle
**2** to bring to a complete end the physical soundness, existence, or usefulness of — see DESTROY 1

**extirpate** *vb* to destroy all traces of — see ANNIHILATE 1
**extol** *also* **extoll** *vb* to proclaim the glory of — see PRAISE 1
**extort** *vb* to get (as money) by the use of force or threats ⟨a school bully who was used to *extorting* lunch money from weaker kids⟩
*syn* exact, wrest, wring
*rel* bleed, fleece, gouge, milk, skin, squeeze; cheat, gyp, racketeer, swindle; coerce, compel, force
**extortioner** *n* a person who gets money from another by using force or threats — see RACKETEER
**extortionist** *n* a person who gets money from another by using force or threats — see RACKETEER
**extra** *adj* being over what is needed — see SPARE 1
**extra** *adv* to a great degree — see VERY 1
**extra** *n* 1 an interchangeable part or piece of equipment that is kept on hand for replacement of an original — see SPARE
2 something adding to pleasure or comfort but not absolutely necessary — see LUXURY 1
3 something given in addition to what is ordinarily expected or owed — see BONUS
**extract** *n* a part taken from a longer work — see EXCERPT
**extract** *vb* to draw out by force or with effort ⟨*extracted* a splinter from my hand⟩
*syn* prize, pry, pull, root (out), tear (out), uproot, wrest, yank
*rel* remove, take (out), withdraw
*near ant* implant, insert, install, instill; cram, jam, ram, stuff, wedge
**extraction** *n* the line of ancestors from whom a person is descended — see ANCESTRY
**extraneous** *adj* 1 not being a vital part of or belonging to something — see EXTRINSIC
2 not having anything to do with the matter at hand — see IRRELEVANT
**extraneousness** *n* the quality or state of not having anything to do with the matter at hand — see IRRELEVANCE
**extraordinary** *adj* 1 being out of the ordinary — see EXCEPTIONAL
2 noticeably different from what is generally found or experienced — see UNUSUAL 1
**extrapolate** *vb* to form an opinion through reasoning and information — see INFER 1
**extrasensory perception** *n* the power of seeing or knowing about things that are not present to the senses — see CLAIRVOYANCE
**extravagance** *n* 1 the quality or fact of being free or wasteful in the expenditure of money ⟨Hollywood stars are famous for the *extravagance* of their parties⟩
*syn* lavishness, prodigality, wastefulness
*rel* bountifulness, generosity, liberality; improvidence, squandering; indulgence, overindulgence, self-indulgence; excess, immoderacy, overkill
*near ant* austerity, moderation, restraint, temperance
*ant* economy, frugality
2 an instance of spending money or resources without care or restraint — see WASTE 1
**extravagant** *adj* 1 given to spending money freely or foolishly — see PRODIGAL
2 going beyond a normal or acceptable limit in degree or amount — see EXCESSIVE
**extravagantly** *adv* in a luxurious manner — see HIGH
**extreme** *adj* 1 most distant from a center ⟨spacecraft that is specially designed to explore the *extreme* edge of our solar system⟩
*syn* farthermost, farthest, furthermost, furthest, outermost, outmost, remotest, ultimate, utmost
*near ant* intermediate, medial, median, mid, middle, middlemost, midmost
*ant* inmost, innermost, nearest
2 being very far from the center of public opinion ⟨their *extreme* political views attracted only a small band of followers⟩
*syn* extremist, fanatic (*or* fanatical), rabid, radical, revolutionary, revolutionist, ultra
*rel* subversive, violent, wild; reactionary
*near ant* conservative, moderate, temperate; conventional, orthodox, traditional; liberal, progressive
*ant* middle-of-the-road
3 going beyond a normal or acceptable limit in degree or amount — see EXCESSIVE
**extremely** *adv* to a great degree — see VERY 1
**extremist** *adj* being very far from the center of public opinion — see EXTREME 2
**extremist** *n* a person who favors rapid and sweeping changes especially in laws and methods of government — see RADICAL
**extricate** *vb* to set free from entanglement or difficulty ⟨you've woven such a web of lies that it's hard to see how you can *extricate* yourself now⟩
*syn* clear, disengage, disentangle, free, liberate, release, untangle
*rel* deliver, redeem, rescue, save; disburden, disencumber, unburden; unravel, unsnarl, untie, untwine
*near ant* block, hamper, hinder, impede, obstruct; burden, encumber, load, weigh
*ant* embroil, entangle
**extrinsic** *adj* not being a vital part of or belonging to something ⟨the fact that the ring belonged to your grandmother is *extrinsic* to its value to a jeweler⟩
*syn* adventitious, alien, extraneous, foreign

*rel* exterior, external, outside; immaterial, inapplicable, insignificant, irrelevant; nonessential, unessential, unnecessary
*near ant* congenital, deep-seated, inborn, inbred; inside, interior, internal; basic, essential, necessary
*ant* inherent, innate, intrinsic

**extroverted** *also* **extraverted** *adj* likely to seek or enjoy the company of others — see CONVIVIAL

**extrude** *vb* to drive or force out — see EJECT 1

**exuberance** *n* the quality or state of having abundant or intense activity — see VITALITY 1

**exuberant** *adj* joyously unrestrained ⟨*exuberant* crowds rushed to greet the returning national champions in collegiate basketball⟩
*syn* bubbly, buoyant, effervescent, frolicsome, high-spirited, vivacious
*rel* extroverted (*also* extraverted), outgoing, uninhibited; carefree, insouciant, joyful, lighthearted, lively, sprightly; boisterous, raucous, rollicking, rowdy; giddy, light-headed, silly; ecstatic, euphoric, rapturous; audacious, bold, brash, brazen, impertinent, impudent, insolent, saucy
*near ant* constrained, inhibited, repressed, restrained, subdued; impassive, phlegmatic, stoic (*or* stoical), stolid; depressed, dour, glum, morose, surly
*ant* low-spirited, noneffervescent, sullen

**exuberantly** *adv* **1** in a quick and spirited manner — see GAILY 2
**2** in an enthusiastic manner — see SKY-HIGH

**exude** *vb* to flow forth slowly through small openings ⟨a sticky resin *exudes* from the bark of the tree⟩
*syn* bleed, ooze, percolate, seep, strain, sweat, weep
*rel* dribble, drip, trickle; discharge, emit, give off, vent; emanate, flow, spring
*near ant* flood, gush, pour, stream, surge

**exult** *vb* to feel or express joy or triumph ⟨the winners of the Super Bowl spent the next week *exulting* in their victory⟩
*syn* crow, delight, glory, joy, rejoice, triumph
*rel* gloat; boast, brag; flaunt, parade, show off, strut, swagger
*near ant* bemoan, bewail, grieve, lament, weep

**exultant** *adj* having or expressing feelings of joy or triumph ⟨the *exultant* winner of the award for best country artist of the year⟩
*syn* exulting, glorying, jubilant, rejoicing, triumphant
*rel* ecstatic, elated, euphoric; arrogant, boastful, cocky; conquering, victorious, winning
*near ant* crestfallen, defeated, dejected, depressed, disconsolate, dispirited, downcast

**exulting** *adj* having or expressing feelings of joy or triumph — see EXULTANT

**exurbia** *n* the area around a city — see ENVIRONS 1

**eye** *n* **1** a circular strip — see RING 2
**2** a state of being aware — see ATTENTION 2
**3** a thing or place that is of greatest importance to an activity or interest — see CENTER 1
**4** an idea that is believed to be true or valid without positive knowledge — see OPINION 1
**5** an instance of looking especially briefly — see LOOK 2
**6** the ability to see — see EYESIGHT

**eye** *vb* **1** to keep one's eyes on — see WATCH 1
**2** to make note of (something) through the use of one's eyes — see SEE 1

**eye–catching** *adj* likely to attract attention — see NOTICEABLE

**eyeful** *n* a lovely woman — see BEAUTY 2

**eyeglasses** *n pl* a pair of lenses set in a frame that is held in place with ear supports and which are usually worn to correct vision — see GLASSES 1

**eyeless** *adj* lacking the power of sight — see BLIND

**eye–opening** *adj* **1** causing a strong emotional reaction because unexpected — see SURPRISING 1
**2** causing wonder or astonishment — see MARVELOUS 1

**eyesight** *n* the ability to see ⟨the keen *eyesight* of a bird of prey⟩
*syn* eye, sight, vision
*rel* myopia, nearsightedness; farsightedness; astigmatism

**eyesore** *n* something unpleasant to look at ⟨the old abandoned house was a neighborhood *eyesore*⟩
*syn* fright, horror, mess, monstrosity, sight
*rel* blot, smear, smudge, spot, stain

**eyespot** *n* a small area that is different (as in color) from the main part — see SPOT 1

# F

**fable** *n* **1** a story intended to teach a basic truth or moral about life — see ALLEGORY
**2** a traditional but unfounded story that gives the reason for a current custom, belief, or fact of nature — see MYTH 1
**3** something that is the product of the imagination — see FICTION

**fabled** *adj* based on, described in, or being a myth — see MYTHICAL 1

**fabric** *n* a woven or knitted material (as of cotton or nylon) — see CLOTH

**fabricate** *vb* **1** to bring into being by combining, shaping, or transforming materials — see MAKE 1
**2** to create or think of by clever use of the imagination — see INVENT
**3** to form by putting together parts or materials — see BUILD
**4** to make a statement one knows to be untrue — see LIE 1

**fabrication** *n* **1** a statement known by its maker to be untrue and made in order to deceive — see LIE
**2** something that is the product of the imagination — see FICTION

**fabricator** *n* a person who tells lies — see LIAR

**fabulous** *adj* **1** based on, described in, or being a myth — see MYTHICAL 1
**2** causing wonder or astonishment — see MARVELOUS 1
**3** not real and existing only in the imagination — see IMAGINARY
**4** of the very best kind — see EXCELLENT

**facade** *also* **façade** *n* **1** a forward part or surface — see FRONT 1
**2** a display of emotion or behavior that is insincere or intended to deceive — see MASQUERADE

**face** *n* **1** the front part of the head ⟨the criminal hid his *face* from the news cameras as he slumped into the patrol car⟩
***syn*** countenance, kisser [*slang*], mug, puss [*slang*], visage
***rel*** appearance, features, lineaments, looks; expression, physiognomy
**2** a forward part or surface — see FRONT 1
**3** a twisting of the facial features in disgust or disapproval — see GRIMACE
**4** an outer part or layer — see EXTERIOR
**5** facial appearance regarded as an indication of mood or feeling — see LOOK 1
**6** outward and often deceptive indication — see APPEARANCE 2

**face** *vb* **1** to stand or sit with the face or front toward ⟨the house *faces* the sparkling blue waters of the Pacific Ocean⟩
***syn*** front, look (toward), point (toward)
***rel*** abut, adjoin, border, meet, neighbor, touch; command, dominate, overlook
**2** to oppose (something hostile or dangerous) with firmness or courage ⟨movie superheroes who are ever ready to *face* danger without blinking an eye⟩
***syn*** beard, brave, brazen, breast, confront, dare, defy, outbrave
***rel*** encounter, meet; accost, approach; repel, resist, withstand; battle, combat, contend (with), fight, oppose, square (off)
***phrases*** stand up to
***near ant*** avoid, eschew, shun; elude, escape, evade
***ant*** dodge, duck, shirk, sidestep
**3** to cover with something that protects — see SHEATHE
**4** to enter into contest or conflict with — see ENGAGE 2

**face–off** *n* an earnest effort for superiority or victory over another — see CONTEST 1

**facet** *n* a certain way in which something appears or may be regarded — see ASPECT 1

**facetious** *adj* **1** given to or marked by mature intelligent humor — see WITTY
**2** making light of something usually regarded as serious or sacred — see FLIPPANT

**facetiousness** *n* a lack of seriousness often at an improper time — see FRIVOLITY 1

**face–to–face** *adv* in person and usually privately — see TÊTE-À-TÊTE

**facile** *adj* **1** having or showing a lack of depth of understanding or character — see SUPERFICIAL 2
**2** involving minimal difficulty or effort — see EASY 1

**facilely** *adv* without difficulty — see EASILY

**facilitate** *vb* to free from obstruction or difficulty — see EASE 1

**facility** *n* a structure that is designed and built for a particular purpose ⟨the city is known for its outstanding medical *facilities*⟩
***syn*** complex, establishment, installation
***rel*** building, edifice; institute, institution; business, company, concern, outfit

**facsimile** *n* **1** something or someone that strongly resembles another — see IMAGE 1
**2** something that is made to look exactly like something else — see COPY

**fact** *n* **1** the quality of being actual ⟨scientists deal in the realm of *fact*, not speculation⟩
***syn*** actuality, factuality, materiality, reality
***rel*** authenticity, genuineness, truth

***near ant*** fancy, fantasy (*also* phantasy), fiction; fictitiousness
***ant*** unreality
**2** something that actually exists ⟨once considered a wild fantasy, the Internet is now a *fact* of everyday life⟩
***syn*** case, materiality, reality
***rel*** certainty, inevitability; circumstance, event, occurrence, phenomenon; element, item, particular, thing
***near ant*** eventuality, possibility, potentiality, probability
***ant*** fantasy (*also* phantasy), fiction, illusion
**3** a single piece of information ⟨a book of little-known *facts* about famous people⟩
***syn*** datum, detail, nicety, particular, particularity, point
***rel*** article, item; element, ingredient, part; aspect, facet, factor; evidence, exhibit; database, information, knowledge
***near ant*** error, fallacy, falsehood, misconception, myth

**faction** *n* a group of people acting together within a larger group ⟨several *factions* within the environmental movement have joined forces⟩
***syn*** bloc, body, coalition, party, sect, set, side, wing
***rel*** crew, gang, pack, team; denomination, persuasion, schism

**factitious** *adj* **1** being such in appearance only and made with or manufactured from usually cheaper materials — see IMITATION
**2** lacking in natural or spontaneous quality — see ARTIFICIAL 1

**factor** *n* **1** a person who acts or does business for another — see AGENT 2
**2** one of the parts that make up a whole — see ELEMENT 1

**factory** *n* a building or set of buildings for the manufacturing of goods ⟨the new *factory* will create hundreds of much-needed jobs⟩
***syn*** manufactory, mill, plant, shop, works, workshop
***rel*** sweatshop; workroom; yard

**factual** *adj* **1** restricted to or based on fact ⟨a *factual* biography of George Washington that scoffs at the story about the cherry tree⟩
***syn*** documentary, hard, historical, literal, matter-of-fact, nonfictional, objective, true
***rel*** actual, authentic, genuine, real; documented, established; reliable, verifiable; demonstrable, provable; incontestable, incontrovertible, indisputable, irrefutable, undeniable, unquestionable; plain, simple, unexaggerated; certain, undoubted
***near ant*** hypothetical, speculative, theoretical (*also* theoretic); fabulous, fanciful, imaginary, legendary, mythical (*or* mythic); embroidered, exaggerated
***ant*** fictional, fictionalized, fictitious, nondocumentary, nonhistorical
**2** existing in fact and not merely as a possibility — see ACTUAL

**factuality** *n* **1** agreement with fact or reality — see TRUTH
**2** the quality of being actual — see FACT 1

**faculty** *n* **1** a natural ability of the mind or body — see POWER 3
**2** a special and usually inborn ability — see TALENT
**3** the physical or mental power to do something — see ABILITY

**fad** *n* a practice or interest that is very popular for a short time ⟨the *fad* for that kind of music had long passed⟩
***syn*** craze, enthusiasm, fashion, go, last word, mode, rage, sensation, style, trend, vogue
***rel*** crush, infatuation; fervor, passion; furor, fuss, hullabaloo, to-do, uproar; bandwagon, crusade, cult, movement; novelty, wrinkle; caprice, fancy, whim
***near ant*** classic, standard

**fade** *vb* **1** to cease to be visible — see DISAPPEAR
**2** to make white or whiter by removing color — see WHITEN

**faded** *adj* lacking intensity of color — see PALE 1

**faerie** *also* **faery** *n* an imaginary being usually having a small human form and magical powers — see FAIRY

**fag** *n* a person who does very hard or dull work — see SLAVE 2

**fag** *vb* **1** to devote serious and sustained effort — see LABOR
**2** to use up all the physical energy of — see EXHAUST 1

**fag end** *n* an unused or unwanted piece or item typically of small size or value — see [1]SCRAP 1

**fail** *vb* **1** to stop functioning ⟨my video camera *failed* just as I was about to shoot the big mo-ment⟩
***syn*** break, break down, conk (out), crash, cut out, die, give out, stall
***rel*** fizzle, sputter, wheeze; malfunction
***ant*** start (up)
**2** to be unsuccessful ⟨despite all the publicity, the movie *failed* miserably at the box office⟩
***syn*** collapse, flop, flunk, fold, wash out
***rel*** flounder, struggle; decline, slip, slump, wane
***phrases*** fall flat
***near ant*** flourish, prosper, thrive
***ant*** succeed
**3** to fall short in satisfying the expectation or hope of — see DISAPPOINT
**4** to lose bodily strength or vigor — see WEAKEN 2
**5** to miss the opportunity or obligation — see NEGLECT 3

**failing** *n* a defect in character — see FAULT 1

**failure** *n* **1** the nonperformance of an assigned or expected action ⟨your *failure* to check the batteries in the smoke detector could have tragic results⟩
***syn*** default, delinquency, dereliction, neglect, negligence, oversight
***rel*** carelessness, heedlessness, laxity

*near ant* compliance, discharge, fulfillment
**2** a falling short of one's goals ⟨the *failure* of the school's fund-raising drive was a big disappointment to all⟩
*syn* collapse, crash, cropper, defeat, fizzle, nonsuccess
*rel* futility, uselessness; ineffectiveness, ineffectualness; deficiency, inadequacy, insufficiency; disappointment, letdown, setback
*ant* accomplishment, achievement, success
**3** something that has failed ⟨the students' first attempt to build a homemade rocket was a disappointing *failure*⟩
*syn* bummer, bust, catastrophe, debacle (*also* débâcle), dud, fiasco, fizzle, flop, lemon, loser, turkey, washout
*rel* also-ran, disappointment, has-been; botch, hash, mess, muddle, shambles
*near ant* corker, crackerjack, dandy, jim-dandy, phenomenon
*ant* blockbuster, hit, smash, success, winner
**4** a falling short of an essential or desirable amount or number — see DEFICIENCY

**faint** *adj* **1** not seen or understood clearly ⟨after wandering in the woods for hours, we had only a *faint* idea of where we were⟩
*syn* bleary, dim, foggy, fuzzy, hazy, indefinite, indistinct, indistinguishable, murky, nebulous, obscure, opaque, shadowy, unclear, undefined, undetermined, vague
*rel* dark, dusky, gloomy; impalpable, inappreciable, intangible, invisible; incomprehensible, inexplicable, mysterious, puzzling
*near ant* bright, distinct, evident, obvious; certain, firm, strong, sure
*ant* clear, definite
**2** lacking bodily strength — see WEAK 1

**faint** *n* a temporary or permanent state of unconsciousness ⟨shocking news can cause a person to fall into a *faint*⟩
*syn* blackout, coma, insensibility, knockout, swoon
*rel* daze, stupor, trance; drowsiness, narcosis, sleep, somnolence

**faint** *vb* to lose consciousness ⟨the kind of person who *faints* at the sight of blood⟩
*syn* black out, pass out, swoon
*rel* break down, collapse
*ant* come around, come round, come to, revive

**fainthearted** *adj* easily frightened — see SHY 1

**faintheartedness** *n* lack of willingness to assert oneself and take risks — see TIMIDITY

**faintness** *n* the quality or state of lacking physical strength or vigor — see WEAKNESS 1

---

*syn* synonym(s) *rel* related words
*ant* antonym(s) *near ant* near antonym(s)

**fair** *adj* **1** not stormy or cloudy ⟨we prayed that there would be *fair* weather during our vacation at the beach⟩
*syn* clear, cloudless, sunny, sunshiny, unclouded
*rel* balmy, clement, gentle, mild, temperate; calm, halcyon, peaceful, placid, tranquil; fine, pleasant
*near ant* harsh, inclement, severe; blustering, blustery, breezy, gusty; foggy, hazy, misty
*ant* bleak, cloudy, dirty, foul, nasty, overcast, rainy, raw, rough, squally, stormy, sunless
**2** marked by justice, honesty, and freedom from bias ⟨a commanding officer who enjoyed the respect of his soldiers because his decisions were always *fair*⟩
*syn* disinterested, dispassionate, equal, equitable, impartial, just, nonpartisan, objective, square, unbiased, unprejudiced
*rel* candid, frank, forthright, open, straightforward; balanced, rational, reasonable
*near ant* deceitful, deceptive, dishonest; arbitrary, unconscionable, unreasonable
*ant* biased, inequitable, partisan, prejudiced, unequal, unjust
**3** following or according to the rules ⟨a hockey player who is respected for his *fair* play⟩
*syn* clean, legal, sportsmanlike, sportsmanly
*rel* just, law-abiding; ethical, moral, principled; honorable, irreproachable, unimpeachable
*near ant* immoral, unethical, unprincipled, unscrupulous
*ant* dirty, foul, nasty, unfair, unsportsmanlike
**4** of light complexion ⟨*fair* people tend to sunburn easily⟩
*syn* light
*rel* ashen, pale, pallid, pasty, peaked, sallow, wan, white
*ant* black, brunet (*or* brunette), dark, swarthy
**5** having qualities which inspire hope — see HOPEFUL 1
**6** of a pale yellow or yellowish brown color — see BLOND
**7** of average to below average quality — see MEDIOCRE 1
**8** very pleasing to look at — see BEAUTIFUL

**fair** *n* a public showing of objects of interest — see EXHIBITION 1

**fairly** *adv* to some degree or extent ⟨for someone without professional training, she sings *fairly* well⟩
*syn* enough, kind of, like, moderately, more or less, pretty, quite, rather, relatively, something, somewhat, sort of
*rel* acceptably, decently, passably, tolerably
*near ant* awfully, exceedingly (*also* exceeding), exceptionally, extremely, greatly, surpassingly, very

**fairness** *n* the qualities in a person or thing that as a whole give pleasure to the senses — see BEAUTY 1

**fairy** *n* an imaginary being usually having a small human form and magical powers ⟨*fairies* are part of the folklore of many countries and cultures⟩
*syn* brownie, dwarf, elf, faerie (*also* fairy), fay, gnome, goblin, gremlin, hobgoblin, leprechaun, pixie (*also* pixy), puck, sprite, troll
*rel* changeling; imp; banshee, ghoul, ogre

**fairy tale** *n* a statement known by its maker to be untrue and made in order to deceive — see LIE

**faith** *n* 1 belief and trust in and loyalty to God ⟨a people who are known for their strong and steadfast *faith*⟩
*syn* devotion, piety, religion
*rel* devoutness, piousness, religiousness; adoration, reverence, veneration, worship
*near ant* disbelief, doubt, unbelief
*ant* atheism, godlessness
2 a body of beliefs and practices regarding the supernatural and the worship of one or more deities — see RELIGION 1
3 adherence to something to which one is bound by a pledge or duty — see FIDELITY
4 firm belief in the integrity, ability, effectiveness, or genuineness of someone or something — see TRUST 1
5 mental conviction of the truth of some statement or the reality of some being or phenomenon — see BELIEF 1

**faithful** *adj* 1 firm in one's allegiance to someone or something ⟨fans of the Chicago Cubs are famously *faithful*⟩
*syn* constant, devoted, fast, good, loyal, pious, staunch (*or* stanch), steadfast, steady, true, true-blue
*rel* dependable, dutiful, reliable, tried, trustworthy; unfaltering, unhesitating, unwavering; determined, intent, resolute; confirmed, dyed-in-the-wool, inveterate, sworn; ardent, fervent, fervid, impassioned, passionate
*near ant* undependable, unreliable, untrustworthy; faltering, hesitant, vacillating, wavering; dubious, irresolute, uncertain; apathetic, dispassionate, uninterested
*ant* disloyal, faithless, false, fickle, inconstant, perfidious, recreant, traitorous, treacherous, unfaithful, untrue
2 following an original exactly ⟨a *faithful* filming of Robert Louis Stevenson's novel *Treasure Island*⟩
*syn* accurate, authentic, exact, precise, right, strict, true, veracious
*rel* lifelike, realistic; careful, conscientious, meticulous, punctilious, scrupulous; authoritative; bona fide, genuine, real
*near ant* careless, slack, slipshod, slovenly
*ant* false, imprecise, inaccurate, inauthentic, inexact, loose, unfaithful

**faithfulness** *n* adherence to something to which one is bound by a pledge or duty — see FIDELITY

**faithless** *adj* not true in one's allegiance to someone or something ⟨*faithless* friends who deserted him in his time of need⟩
*syn* disloyal, false, fickle, inconstant, perfidious, recreant, traitorous, treacherous, unfaithful, untrue
*rel* undependable, unreliable, untrustworthy; faltering, hesitant, vacillating, wavering; dubious, irresolute, uncertain; apathetic, dispassionate, uninterested
*near ant* dependable, reliable, tried, trustworthy; unfaltering, unhesitating, unwavering; determined, intent, resolute; confirmed, dyed-in-the-wool, inveterate, sworn; ardent, fervent, fervid, impassioned, passionate
*ant* constant, devoted, faithful, fast, loyal, staunch (*or* stanch), steadfast, steady, true

**faithlessness** *n* 1 lack of faithfulness especially to one's husband or wife — see INFIDELITY 1
2 the act or fact of violating the trust or confidence of another — see BETRAYAL

**fake** *adj* 1 being such in appearance only and made with or manufactured from usually cheaper materials — see IMITATION
2 being such in appearance only and made or manufactured with the intention of committing fraud — see COUNTERFEIT
3 lacking in natural or spontaneous quality — see ARTIFICIAL 1

**fake** *n* 1 an imitation that is passed off as genuine ⟨experts declared that one of the museum's prized paintings was actually a *fake*⟩
*syn* counterfeit, forgery, hoax, humbug, phony (*also* phoney), sham
*rel* copy, reproduction; dummy; fraud, imposture, swindle; simulation, synthetic
*near ant* original
2 one who makes false claims of identity or expertise — see IMPOSTOR

**fake** *vb* 1 to imitate or copy especially in order to deceive ⟨pranksters *faked* giant footprints and then claimed that they had seen Bigfoot⟩
*syn* counterfeit, forge
*rel* simulate; crib, plagiarize; adulterate, doctor, fudge, juggle, manipulate, tamper (with); concoct, cook (up), fabricate, invent
2 to present a false appearance of — see FEIGN

**faker** *n* one who makes false claims of identity or expertise — see IMPOSTOR

**fakery** *n* the inclination or practice of misleading others through lies or trickery — see DECEIT

**fall** *n* 1 the act of going down from an upright position suddenly and involuntarily ⟨a bad *fall* that resulted in several broken bones⟩
*syn* slip, spill, stumble, tumble
*rel* header, pratfall; trip; descent, dive, plunge, slide; free-fall

2 a change to a lower state or level — see DECLINE 2
3 a loss of status — see COMEDOWN
4 the act or process of going to a lower level or altitude — see DESCENT 1
5 the amount by which something is lessened — see DECREASE
6 *usually* **falls** *pl* a fall of water usually from a great height — see WATERFALL

**fall** *vb* 1 to go down from an upright position suddenly and involuntarily ⟨better sand that walkway before somebody *falls* on the ice⟩
*syn* slip, stumble, topple, trip, tumble
*rel* collapse, crumple, drop, keel over, slump (over); nose-dive, plunge, precipitate
*ant* get up, rise, stand (up), uprise
2 to yield to the control or power of enemy forces ⟨the city *fell* after weeks of merciless bombardment⟩
*syn* capitulate, give up, knuckle under, submit, succumb, surrender
*rel* bow, buckle, cave (in), collapse; hand over, relinquish, yield; lose; fail, fold
*near ant* fight, oppose, resist, withstand; beat, overcome, win; prevail, triumph
*ant* stand
3 to go to a lower level — see DROP 2
4 to grow less in scope or intensity especially gradually — see DECREASE 2
5 to lead or extend downward — see DESCEND 1

**fallacious** *adj* 1 not using or following good reasoning — see ILLOGICAL
2 tending or having power to deceive — see DECEPTIVE 1

**fallaciousness** *n* the quality or state of being false — see FALLACY 2

**fallacy** *n* 1 a false idea or belief ⟨the once-common *fallacy* that girls just weren't any good at math⟩
*syn* error, falsehood, falsity, illusion, misconception, myth, old wives' tale, untruth
*rel* superstition; distortion, inaccuracy, misinterpretation, misrepresentation, misstatement, misunderstanding; sophism, sophistry; fib, lie, story, tale
*ant* truth, verity
2 the quality or state of being false ⟨the *fallacy* of the notion of spontaneous generation was demonstrated by the Dutch naturalist Leeuwenhoek⟩
*syn* erroneousness, fallaciousness, falseness, falsity, untruth
*rel* speciousness, spuriousness; deception, deceptiveness, delusion
*near ant* accuracy, correctness, factualness, genuineness
*ant* truth

**fall back** *vb* to move back or away (as from something difficult, dangerous, or disagreeable) — see RETREAT 1

**fallen** *adj* no longer living — see DEAD 1

**fall guy** *n* a person or thing taking the blame for others — see SCAPEGOAT

**falling-out** *n* an often noisy or angry expression of differing opinions — see ARGUMENT 1

**fall out** *vb* to express different opinions about something often angrily — see ARGUE 2

**fallow** *adj* not being in a state of use, activity, or employment — see INACTIVE 2

**false** *adj* 1 not being in agreement with what is true ⟨early reports about the explosion contained much *false* information⟩
*syn* erroneous, inaccurate, incorrect, inexact, invalid, off, unsound, untrue, untruthful, wrong
*rel* specious, spurious; deceptive, delusive, delusory, distorted, fallacious, misleading; amiss, askew, awry; deceitful, dishonest, fraudulent, lying, mendacious, untruthful; unconfirmed, unproven, untested; fabricated, invented, made-up, trumped-up
*near ant* confirmed, demonstrated, established, proven, tested
*ant* accurate, correct, errorless, factual, right, sound, true, valid
2 being such in appearance only and made with or manufactured from usually cheaper materials — see IMITATION
3 being such in appearance only and made or manufactured with the intention of committing fraud — see COUNTERFEIT
4 lacking in natural or spontaneous quality — see ARTIFICIAL 1
5 marked by, based on, or done by the use of dishonest methods to acquire something of value — see FRAUDULENT 1
6 not true in one's allegiance to someone or something — see FAITHLESS
7 tending or having power to deceive — see DECEPTIVE 1

**falsehood** *n* 1 a false idea or belief — see FALLACY 1
2 a statement known by its maker to be untrue and made in order to deceive — see LIE

**falseness** *n* 1 lack of faithfulness especially to one's husband or wife — see INFIDELITY 1
2 the act or fact of violating the trust or confidence of another — see BETRAYAL
3 the quality or state of being false — see FALLACY 2

**falsify** *vb* to change so much as to create a wrong impression or alter the meaning of — see GARBLE

**falsity** *n* 1 a false idea or belief — see FALLACY 1
2 a statement known by its maker to be untrue and made in order to deceive — see LIE
3 lack of faithfulness especially to one's husband or wife — see INFIDELITY 1
4 the act or fact of violating the trust or confidence of another — see BETRAYAL
5 the quality or state of being false — see FALLACY 2

**falter** *vb* 1 to show uncertainty about the right course of action — see HESITATE

---

*syn* synonym(s) *rel* related words
*ant* antonym(s) *near ant* near antonym(s)

2 to swing unsteadily back and forth or from side to side — see TEETER 1

**faltering** *n* the act or an instance of pausing because of uncertainty about the right course of action — see HESITATION

**fame** *n* the fact or state of being known to the public ⟨many go to Hollywood in search of *fame* and fortune⟩
*syn* celebrity, notoriety, renown
*rel* infamy; name, report, reputation, repute; cachet, position, prestige, rank, standing, stature; distinction, eminence, glory, greatness, honor, illustriousness, note, preeminence, prominence; acclaim, acknowledgment (*also* acknowledgement), praise, recognition; adoration, idolization
*near ant* disgrace, dishonor, disrepute, ignominy, odium, opprobrium, shame; unimportance
*ant* anonymity, obscurity

**famed** *adj* widely known — see FAMOUS

**familial** *adj* of or relating to a household or family — see DOMESTIC 1

**familiar** *adj* 1 closely acquainted ⟨the little inside jokes that people who have long been *familiar* like to share⟩
*syn* bosom, chummy, close, friendly, intimate, thick
*rel* affable, boon, companionable, convivial, cordial, genial, gracious, hearty; gregarious, sociable, social; comfortable, cozy, easy, snug; amicable, neighborly; confidential, secretive; affectionate, dear, devoted, fond, loving, warm
*near ant* aloof, cold, cool, reserved, standoffish, unfriendly, unsociable, withdrawn
*ant* distant
2 having information especially as a result of study or experience ⟨book editors who are *familiar* with what is being taught in the schools⟩
*syn* abreast, acquainted, conversant, informed, knowledgeable, up, up-to-date, versed
*rel* aware, cognizant, conscious, heedful, mindful
*phrases* in the know
*near ant* unaware, unconscious, unmindful; blind, oblivious, unknowing, unwitting
*ant* ignorant, unacquainted, unfamiliar, uninformed
3 often observed or encountered — see COMMON 1
4 showing a lack of proper social reserve or modesty — see PRESUMPTUOUS 1

**familiar** *n* a person who has a strong liking for and trust in another — see FRIEND 1

**familiarity** *n* 1 the state of being in a very personal or private relationship ⟨the elderly couple enjoys a *familiarity* that is the result of many years of happy marriage⟩
*syn* chumminess, closeness, inseparability, intimacy, nearness
*rel* immediacy; affinity, kinship; commitment, devotion; affection, fondness, love; constancy, faithfulness, fidelity, amity, fellowship, friendship, goodwill; affability, conviviality, cordiality, geniality
*near ant* aloofness, coldness, coolness, reserve
*ant* distance
2 a socially improper or unsuitable act or remark — see IMPROPRIETY 2
3 knowledge gained by personal experience — see ACQUAINTANCE

**familiarize** *vb* 1 to give information to — see ENLIGHTEN 1
2 to impart knowledge of a new thing or situation to — see ACQUAINT 1

**family** *n* 1 a group of persons who come from the same ancestor ⟨the Adams *family* made remarkable contributions to American life for more than two centuries⟩
*syn* blood, clan, folks, house, kin, kindred, kinfolk, kinsfolk, line, lineage, people, race, stock, tribe
*rel* nuclear family; extended family, kith; brood; descendant (*or* descendent), issue, offspring, progeny, scion, seed; clansman, kinsman, kinswoman, relative; dynasty
*near ant* ancestry, birth, descent, extraction, origin, pedigree
2 one of the units into which a whole is divided on the basis of a common characteristic — see CLASS 2

**family tree** *n* the line of ancestors from whom a person is descended — see ANCESTRY

**famine** *n* a falling short of an essential or desirable amount or number — see DEFICIENCY

**famished** *adj* feeling a desire or need for food — see HUNGRY 1

**famishment** *n* a need or desire for food — see HUNGER 1

**famous** *adj* widely known ⟨a book about some of the most *famous* people of the last century⟩
*syn* celebrated, famed, noted, notorious, prominent, renowned, star, well-known
*rel* fabled, fabulous, legendary; infamous; distinguished, eminent, exceptional, great, illustrious, leading, notable, outstanding, prestigious, remarkable; important, significant; favorite, popular, preferred; estimable, honorable, reputable, respectable; formidable, redoubtable
*near ant* insignificant, unimportant; inconspicuous; undistinguished, unexceptional; unpopular
*ant* anonymous, obscure, unknown

**fan** *n* a person with a strong and habitual liking for something ⟨life-long *fans* of country and western music⟩
*syn* addict, aficionado, buff, bug, devotee, enthusiast, fanatic, fancier, fiend, freak, lover, maniac, nut
*rel* groupie; admirer, collector, connoisseur, dilettante; authority, expert; cultist, disciple, follower, votary; backer, patron, promoter, supporter; partisan, zealot; booster, rooter, well-wisher; faddist
*near ant* belittler, carper, critic, detractor

**fan** (out) *vb* 1 to arrange the parts of (something) over a wider area — see OPEN 3

2 to extend outwards from or as if from a central point — see RADIATE 1

**fanatic** *n* 1 a person with a strong and habitual liking for something — see FAN
2 one who is intensely or excessively devoted to a cause — see ZEALOT

**fanatic** *or* **fanatical** *adj* being very far from the center of public opinion — see EXTREME 2

**fancier** *n* a person with a strong and habitual liking for something — see FAN

**fanciful** *adj* 1 conceived or made without regard for reason or reality — see FANTASTIC 1
2 not real and existing only in the imagination — see IMAGINARY

**fancy** *adj* made or done with great care or with much detail — see ELABORATE 1

**fancy** *n* 1 a conception or image created by the imagination and having no objective reality — see FANTASY 1
2 a sudden impulsive and apparently unmotivated idea or action — see WHIM
3 positive regard for something — see LIKING
4 the ability to form mental images of things that either are not physically present or have never been conceived or created by others — see IMAGINATION

**fancy** *vb* 1 to form a mental picture of — see IMAGINE 1
2 to take pleasure in — see ENJOY 1

**fanny** *n* the part of the body upon which someone sits — see BUTTOCKS

**fantastic** *adj* 1 conceived or made without regard for reason or reality ⟨a *fantastic* scheme for getting rich quick⟩
*syn* absurd, bizarre, crazy, fanciful, foolish, insane, nonsensical, preposterous, unreal, wild
*rel* inconceivable, incredible, unbelievable; extravagant, grotesque; eccentric, odd, peculiar, strange, weird; farcical, laughable, ludicrous, ridiculous
*ant* realistic, reasonable
2 excitingly or mysteriously unusual — see EXOTIC
3 not real and existing only in the imagination — see IMAGINARY
4 too extraordinary or improbable to believe — see INCREDIBLE

**fantasy** *also* **phantasy** *n* 1 a conception or image created by the imagination and having no objective reality ⟨a constant daydreamer who started to believe his own *fantasies*⟩
*syn* chimera, conceit, daydream, delusion, dream, fancy, figment, hallucination, illusion, phantasm, pipe dream, unreality, vision
*rel* mirage; brainchild, idea; concoction, fabrication, fiction, invention; envisaging, imaging, visualization
*near ant* actuality, fact, reality
2 the ability to form mental images of things that either are not physically present or have never been conceived or created by others — see IMAGINATION
3 something that is the product of the imagination — see FICTION

**far** *adj* 1 lasting for a considerable time — see LONG 2
2 not close in time or space — see DISTANT 1

**far** *adv* to a great degree — see VERY 1

**faraway** *adj* not close in time or space — see DISTANT 1

**farce** *n* 1 a poor, insincere, or insulting imitation of something — see MOCKERY 1
2 humorous entertainment — see COMEDY

**farcical** *adj* 1 causing or intended to cause laughter — see FUNNY 1
2 so foolish or pointless as to be worthy of scornful laughter — see RIDICULOUS 1

**fare** *n* substances intended to be eaten — see FOOD

**fare** *vb* 1 to meet one's day-to-day needs — see GET ALONG 1
2 to move forward along a course — see GO 1
3 to take a meal — see DINE 1

**farewell** *adj* given, taken, or performed at parting — see PARTING 1

**farewell** *n* 1 an expression of good wishes at parting — see GOOD-BYE
2 the act of leaving a place — see DEPARTURE
3 the act or process of two or more persons going off in different directions — see PARTING

**far–fetched** *adj* not likely to be true or to occur — see IMPROBABLE

**far–flung** *adj* having considerable extent — see EXTENSIVE

**farm** *n* a piece of land and its buildings used to grow crops or raise livestock ⟨a *farm* that has been in the same family for five generations⟩
*syn* farmstead, grange, ranch
*rel* cropland, farmland, farmyard; farmhouse, homestead, manor, plantation; croft [*chiefly British*], station; garden, orchard

**farm** *vb* to work by plowing, sowing, and raising crops on ⟨we're planning on *farming* 50 acres the first year⟩
*syn* cultivate, tend, till
*rel* crop, plant; harvest, reap; harrow, hoe

**farmer** *n* a person who cultivates the land and grows crops on it ⟨a young *farmer* whose family has been growing wheat for many generations⟩
*syn* agriculturist (*or* agriculturalist), agronomist, cultivator, grower, planter, tiller
*rel* farmhand, gleaner, harvester, reaper; crofter [*chiefly British*], cropper, sharecropper; homesteader, nester [*West*]; granger; rancher, ranchero, ranchman

**farming** *adj* engaged in or concerned with agriculture — see AGRICULTURAL

**farming** *n* the science or occupation of cultivating the soil, producing crops, and raising livestock — see AGRICULTURE

---

*syn* synonym(s) *rel* related words
*ant* antonym(s) *near ant* near antonym(s)

**farmstead** *n* a piece of land and its buildings used to grow crops or raise livestock — see FARM
**far–off** *adj* not close in time or space — see DISTANT 1
**far–out** *adj* different from the ordinary in a way that causes curiosity or suspicion — see ODD 2
**far–reaching** *adj* having considerable extent — see EXTENSIVE
**farsighted** *adj* having or showing awareness of and preparation for the future — see FORESIGHTED
**farsightedness** *n* concern or preparation for the future — see FORESIGHT 2
**farther** *adj* resulting in an increase in amount or number — see ADDITIONAL
**farther** *adv* at or to a greater distance or more advanced point ⟨they had traveled *farther* down the Colorado River than any previous explorers⟩
*syn* beyond, further, yon, yonder
**farthermost** *adj* most distant from a center — see EXTREME 1
**farthest** *adj* most distant from a center — see EXTREME 1
**fascinate** *vb* 1 to attract or delight as if by magic — see CHARM 1
2 to hold the attention of as if by a spell — see ENTHRALL 1
3 to hold the attention of — see ENGAGE 1
**fascinating** *adj* 1 having an often mysterious or magical power to attract ⟨the *fascinating* cities and peoples of central Asia have been intriguing travelers at least since the time of Marco Polo⟩
*syn* alluring, appealing, attractive, bewitching, captivating, charming, elfin, enchanting, engaging, entrancing, fetching, glamorous (*also* glamourous), luring, magnetic, seductive
*rel* enthralling, gripping, hypnotizing, mesmerizing, riveting, spellbinding; enticing, tantalizing, tempting; exciting, haunting, interesting, intriguing, titillating; beckoning, inviting, winning; darling, delightful, pleasing
*near ant* boring, irksome, tedious, tiresome; abhorrent, distasteful, invidious, loathsome, obnoxious, offensive
*ant* repellant, repelling, repugnant, repulsive, revolting
2 holding the attention or provoking interest — see INTERESTING
**fascination** *n* the power of irresistible attraction — see CHARM 2
**fashion** *n* 1 a practice or interest that is very popular for a short time — see FAD
2 a distinctive way of putting ideas into words — see STYLE 1
3 a usual manner of behaving or doing — see HABIT
4 the means or procedure for doing something — see METHOD
**fashion** *vb* to bring into being by combining, shaping, or transforming materials — see MAKE 1
**fashionable** *adj* 1 being in the latest or current fashion — see STYLISH
2 enjoying widespread favor or approval — see POPULAR 1
**fashionableness** *n* the state of enjoying widespread approval — see POPULARITY
**fast** *adj* 1 moving, proceeding, or acting with great speed ⟨the *fast* pace of construction resulted in our new house being done ahead of schedule⟩
*syn* breakneck, breathless, brisk, dizzy, fleet, fleet-footed, flying, hasty, lightning, nippy, quick, rapid, rapid-fire, rattling, snappy, speedy, swift, whirlwind
*rel* expeditious, prompt, ready; hurried, quickened; breathtaking; energetic, strenuous, strong, vigorous
*near ant* crawling, dawdling, laggard, lingering, plodding, poky (*or* pokey), slowish, sluggish, unhurried; deliberate, leisurely, measured; dilatory, late
*ant* slow
2 firm in one's allegiance to someone or something — see FAITHFUL 1
3 firmly positioned in place and difficult to dislodge — see TIGHT 2
4 given to or marked by cheating and deception — see DISHONEST 2
5 marked by the ability to withstand stress without structural damage or distortion — see STABLE 1
**fast** *adv* 1 with great speed ⟨run as *fast* as you can to get help⟩
*syn* apace, briskly, fleetly, full tilt, hastily, posthaste, presto, pronto, quick, quickly, rapidly, snappily, soon, speedily, swift, swiftly
*rel* immediately, promptly, readily; impetuously, impulsively, rashly, recklessly; abruptly, suddenly; energetically, vigorously
*phrases* at full tilt, by leaps and bounds, in short order
*near ant* laggardly, lingeringly, ploddingly, sluggishly; deliberately, leisurely
*ant* slow, slowly
2 to a full extent or degree — see FULLY 1
**fasten** *vb* 1 to cause (something) to hold to another ⟨use this paperclip to *fasten* your picture to the application form⟩
*syn* affix, attach, fix
*rel* adhere, bolt, clamp, clasp, clinch, clip, glue, hang, harness, lace, lash, latch, nail, paste, pin, rivet, screw, staple, stick, strap, tack, tie, yoke; connect, join, link, unite; reattach, refasten, refix
*near ant* part, separate, sever; loose, loosen
*ant* detach, undo, unfasten
2 to put securely in place or in a desired position ⟨don't forget to *fasten* all the lines on your tent⟩
*syn* anchor, catch, clamp, fix, hitch, moor, secure, set
*rel* embed (*also* imbed), entrench (*also* intrench), implant, ingrain, lodge, wedge
*near ant* extract, pry, yank
*ant* loose, loosen, unfasten, unloose, unloosen
3 to fix (as one's attention) steadily toward a central objective — see CONCENTRATE 2

**fastidious** *adj* hard to please — see FINICKY

**fastness** *n* **1** a high rate of movement or performance — see SPEED
**2** a structure or place from which one can resist attack — see FORT
**3** adherence to something to which one is bound by a pledge or duty — see FIDELITY

**fat** *adj* **1** having an excess of body fat ⟨the popular image of Santa Claus as a *fat* man in a red suit⟩
***syn*** chubby, corpulent, fleshy, full, gross, obese, overweight, plump, portly, pudgy, roly-poly, rotund, round, tubby
***rel*** beefy, bulky, chunky, heavy, heavyset, stocky, stout, thick, thickset, weighty; brawny, burly, husky; dumpy, squat, stubby; paunchy, potbellied; flabby, soft; buxom
***near ant*** angular, bony, gaunt, lank, lanky, rawboned, sinewy, skinny; cadaverous, haggard, skeletal, wasted; puny, scraggy, scrawny, slight; reedy, twiggy, willowy
***ant*** lean, slender, slim, spare, thin
**2** containing or seeming to contain the greatest quantity or number possible — see FULL 1
**3** having a greater than usual measure across — see WIDE 1
**4** having or being of relatively great depth or extent from one surface to its opposite — see THICK 1
**5** producing abundantly — see FERTILE
**6** yielding a profit — see PROFITABLE 1

**fat** *n* **1** individuals carefully selected as being the best of a class — see ELITE
**2** the state or an instance of going beyond what is usual, proper, or needed — see EXCESS

**fatal** *adj* **1** bringing about ruin or misfortune ⟨I made the *fatal* mistake of sharing my secret with the school's biggest blabbermouth⟩
***syn*** calamitous, cataclysmal (*or* cataclysmic), catastrophic, destructive, disastrous, fateful, ruinous, unfortunate
***rel*** hapless, ill-fated, ill-starred, luckless
***near ant*** fluky, fortuitous, fortunate, happy, lucky, providential; auspicious, bright, encouraging, golden, heartening, hopeful, promising, propitious
**2** likely to cause or capable of causing death — see DEADLY

**fatality** *n* a person or thing harmed, lost, or destroyed — see CASUALTY 1

**fate** *n* **1** a state or end that seemingly has been decided beforehand ⟨the belief that it was this country's *fate* to extend from sea to sea⟩
***syn*** circumstance, destiny, doom, fortune, lot, portion
***rel*** accident, chance, hazard, luck; predestination; consequence, effect, issue, outcome, result, upshot
**2** a condition or occurrence traceable to a cause — see EFFECT 1

**fate** *vb* to determine the fate of in advance — see DESTINE

**fateful** *adj* bringing about ruin or misfortune — see FATAL 1

**fathead** *n* a stupid person — see IDIOT

**father** *n* **1** a male human parent ⟨the special relationship that exists between *fathers* and sons⟩
***syn*** dad, daddy, old man, pa, papa, pop
***rel*** patriarch
**2** a person who establishes a whole new field of endeavor ⟨Sir Isaac Newton is regarded by many as the *father* of modern science⟩
***syn*** author, begetter, creator, establisher, founder, generator, inaugurator, initiator, instituter (*or* institutor), originator
***rel*** conceiver, contriver, designer, formulator, innovator, inventor, spawner; builder, maker, producer; developer, pioneer, researcher; organizer, promoter; encourager, inspiration, inspirer
***near ant*** disciple, follower, supporter
**3** a person specially trained and authorized to conduct religious services in a Christian church — see CLERGYMAN
**4** a person who is several generations earlier in an individual's line of descent — see ANCESTOR 1
**5** *cap* the being worshipped as the creator and ruler of the universe — see DEITY 2

**father** *vb* to become the father of ⟨Paul Revere somehow found room in his small house for the large family he had *fathered*⟩
***syn*** beget, get, sire
***rel*** breed, multiply, procreate, propagate, reproduce, spawn; bear, engender, generate, produce

**fatherland** *n* the land of one's birth, residence, or citizenship — see COUNTRY 1

**fathom** *vb* to measure the depth of (as a body of water) typically with a weighted line — see ²SOUND 1

**fatigue** *n* a complete depletion of energy or strength ⟨the day-long battle against the blaze left firefighters in a state of utter *fatigue*⟩
***syn*** burnout, collapse, exhaustion, lassitude, prostration, tiredness, weariness
***rel*** debilitation, enervation, faintness, feebleness, weakness; languor, lethargy, listlessness; sluggishness, slumber, stupor, torpor; apathy, inertia, passivity
***near ant*** energy, go, liveliness, pep, vigor, vitality; might, potency, strength
***ant*** refreshment, rejuvenation, revitalization

**fatigue** *vb* to use up all the physical energy of — see EXHAUST 1

**fatigued** *adj* depleted in strength, energy, or freshness — see WEARY 1

**fatness** *n* the condition of having an excess of body fat — see CORPULENCE

**fatty** *adj* containing animal fat especially in unusual amounts ⟨*fatty* ground beef that was the cheapest available⟩
***syn*** adipose

---

***syn*** synonym(s) ***rel*** related words
***ant*** antonym(s) ***near ant*** near antonym(s)

*rel* greasy, oily
*near ant* fibrous, gristly, stringy, tough; nonfat
*ant* lean

**fatuity** *n* **1** a foolish act or idea — see FOLLY 1
**2** lack of good sense or judgment — see FOOLISHNESS 1
**3** the quality or state of lacking intelligence or quickness of mind — see STUPIDITY 1

**fatuous** *adj* **1** not having or showing an ability to absorb ideas readily — see STUPID 1
**2** showing or marked by a lack of good sense or judgment — see FOOLISH 1

**faucet** *n* a fixture for controlling the flow of a liquid ⟨don't forget to turn off the *faucet*⟩
*syn* cock, gate, spigot, stopcock, tap, valve
*rel* hydrant, spout

**fault** *n* **1** a defect in character ⟨the common *fault* of being quick to judge others⟩
*syn* demerit, failing, foible, frailty, shortcoming, vice, weakness
*rel* blot, spot, stain; blemish, deficiency, flaw; Achilles' heel; corruption, depravity, evil, immorality, sinfulness, wickedness
*near ant* excellence, perfection; goodness, integrity, morality, probity, rectitude, righteousness
*ant* merit, virtue
**2** an unintentional departure from truth or accuracy — see ERROR 1
**3** responsibility for wrongdoing or failure — see BLAME 1
**4** something that spoils the appearance or completeness of a thing — see BLEMISH
**5** the state of being held as the cause of something that needs to be set right — see RESPONSIBILITY 1

**fault** *vb* to express one's unfavorable opinion of the worth or quality of — see CRITICIZE

**faultfinder** *n* a person given to harsh judgments and to finding faults — see CRITIC 1

**faultfinding** *adj* given to making or expressing unfavorable judgments about things — see CRITICAL 1

**faultily** *adv* in a mistaken or inappropriate way — see WRONGLY

**faultless** *adj* **1** being entirely without fault or flaw — see PERFECT 1
**2** free from guilt or blame — see INNOCENT 2

**faultlessly** *adv* without any flaws or errors — see PERFECTLY 1

**faultlessness** *n* the quality or state of being free from guilt or blame — see INNOCENCE 1

**faulty** *adj* having a fault ⟨the cause of the plane crash was traced to *faulty* wiring⟩
*syn* bad, defective, flawed, imperfect
*rel* fallible; blemished, broken, damaged, defaced, disfigured, impaired, injured, marred, spoiled; deficient, inadequate, incomplete, insufficient, wanting
*near ant* complete, entire, intact, whole; undamaged, unimpaired, unspoiled
*ant* faultless, flawless, impeccable, perfect

**favor** *n* **1** an act of kind assistance ⟨a good and generous friend who is always doing *favors* for others⟩
*syn* boon, courtesy, grace, indulgence, kindness, mercy, service, turn
*rel* dispensation, waiver; advantage, benefit, blessing, godsend, manna; liberty, license (*or* licence), privilege
*near ant* hindrance, impediment, obstacle
**2** a feeling of great approval and liking — see ADMIRATION 1
**3** an acceptance of something as satisfactory — see APPROVAL 1
**4** an attitude that always favors one way of feeling or acting especially without considering any other possibilities — see BIAS
**5** positive regard for something — see LIKING
**6** the state of enjoying widespread approval — see POPULARITY

**favor** *vb* **1** to do a service or favor for — see OBLIGE 1
**2** to have a favorable opinion of — see APPROVE (OF)
**3** to show partiality toward — see PREFER 1

**favorable** *adj* **1** expressing approval ⟨*favorable* reviews for the movie were few⟩
*syn* admiring, applauding, appreciative, approving, commendatory, complimentary, friendly, good, positive
*rel* eulogistic, laudatory, praiseful; respectful, supportive; adulatory, worshipful
*near ant* captious, carping, caviling (*or* cavilling), censuring, hypercritical, overcritical
*ant* adverse, disapproving, negative, unappreciative, uncomplimentary, unfavorable, unfriendly
**2** pointing toward a happy outcome ⟨*favorable* conditions for opening a new business⟩
*syn* auspicious, bright, encouraging, golden, heartening, hopeful, promising, propitious
*rel* fortunate, happy, lucky, providential; advantageous, beneficial, profitable
*near ant* unfortunate, unhappy, unlucky; calamitous, catastrophic, disastrous, fatal, ruinous
*ant* discouraging, disheartening, futureless, hopeless, inauspicious, unfavorable, unpromising
**3** conferring benefits; promoting or contributing to personal or social well-being — see BENEFICIAL
**4** showing or expressing acceptance or approval — see POSITIVE

**favorably** *adv* in a pleasing way — see WELL 5

**favored** *adj* **1** granted special treatment or attention — see DARLING 1
**2** singled out from a number or group as more to one's liking — see SELECT 1

**favorite** *adj* granted special treatment or attention — see DARLING 1

**favorite** *n* a person or thing that is preferred over others ⟨the youngest child was always Mother's *favorite*⟩
*syn* darling, minion, pet, preference
*rel* beloved, dear; jewel, prize, treasure
*near ant* abomination, anathema, bête noire, bugbear

**fawn** *vb* to use flattery or the doing of favors in order to win approval especially from a superior ⟨a student who could not wait to *fawn* over the new teacher⟩
*syn* fuss, kowtow, toady
*rel* drool, gush, slaver, slobber; endear, ingratiate; court, woo; adulate, idolize, worship; blandish, cajole, coax, flatter, soft-soap; cower, cringe, grovel; abase, debase, demean; defer, submit, yield
*phrases* curry favor
*near ant* despise, disdain, scorn; gibe (*or* jibe), jeer, scoff; brave, challenge, defy

**fawner** *n* a person who flatters another in order to get ahead — see SYCOPHANT

**fay** *adj* given to good-natured joking or teasing — see PLAYFUL

**fay** *n* an imaginary being usually having a small human form and magical powers — see FAIRY

**faze** *vb* to throw into a state of self-conscious distress — see EMBARRASS 1

**fealty** *n* adherence to something to which one is bound by a pledge or duty — see FIDELITY

**fear** *n* the emotion experienced in the presence or threat of danger ⟨the sight of the headless horseman filled the schoolmaster with *fear*⟩
*syn* alarm, anxiety, apprehension, consternation, dread, fearfulness, fright, horror, panic, terror, trepidation
*rel* phobia; creeps, jitters, nervousness, willies; pang, qualm, twinge; agitation, discomposure, disquiet, perturbation; concern, dismay, worry; cowardice, faintheartedness, timidity, timorousness
*near ant* aplomb, assurance, boldness, confidence, self-assurance, self-confidence; courage, dauntlessness, fearlessness, fortitude

**fear** *vb* to experience concern or anxiety — see WORRY 1

**fearful** *adj* **1** causing fear ⟨the *fearful* roar of a lion⟩
*syn* alarming, dire, direful, dreadful, fearsome, forbidding, formidable, frightening, frightful, hair-raising, horrendous, horrible, horrifying, intimidating, redoubtable, scary, shocking, terrible, terrifying
*rel* daunting, disconcerting, discouraging, dismaying, disquieting, distressing, disturbing, perturbing, startling, threatening, troubling, trying; creepy, eerie (*also* eery), weird; ghastly, gruesome, nightmarish
*near ant* comforting, consoling, inviting, reassuring, soothing; nonthreatening
**2** easily frightened — see SHY 1
**3** extreme in degree, power, or effect — see INTENSE
**4** filled with fear or dread — see AFRAID 1

**fearfulness** *n* the emotion experienced in the presence or threat of danger — see FEAR

**fearless** *adj* feeling or displaying no fear by temperament — see BRAVE

**fearlessness** *n* strength of mind to carry on in spite of danger — see COURAGE

**fearsome** *adj* causing fear — see FEARFUL 1

**feasible** *adj* capable of being done or carried out — see POSSIBLE 1

**feast** *n* a large fancy meal often accompanied by ceremony or entertainment ⟨some 90 Native Americans showed up for the *feast* put on by the Pilgrims at Plymouth⟩
*syn* banquet, dinner, feed, spread
*rel* chow, repast; blowout, festival, fete (*or* fête), gala, party, shindig; festivity; barbecue, clambake, cookout, fry, luau, roast

**feast** *vb* to entertain with a fancy meal ⟨the returning war heroes were *feasted* all over the country⟩
*syn* banquet, dine, junket, regale
*rel* cater, feed; fete (*or* fête), honor

**feat** *n* **1** an act of notable skill, strength, or cleverness ⟨Washington's legendary *feat* of tossing a silver dollar across the Rappahannock River⟩
*syn* deed, exploit, stunt, trick
*rel* accomplishment, achievement, coup; adventure; performance
**2** something done by someone — see ACTION 1

**feather** *n* **1** a number of persons or things that are grouped together because they have something in common — see SORT 1
**2** dressy clothing — see FINERY

**featherbrained** *adj* lacking in seriousness or maturity — see GIDDY 1

**feathery** *adj* having little weight — see [1]LIGHT 1

**feature** *n* something that sets apart an individual from others of the same kind — see CHARACTERISTIC

**feature** *vb* to indicate the importance of by giving prominent display — see EMPHASIZE

**feces** *n pl* solid matter discharged from an animal's alimentary canal — see DROPPING 1

**fecund** *adj* producing abundantly — see FERTILE

**fed up** *adj* having one's patience, interest, or pleasure exhausted — see WEARY 2

**federate** *vb* to form or enter into an association that furthers the interests of its members — see ALLY

**federation** *n* an association of persons, parties, or states for mutual assistance and protection — see CONFEDERACY

**fee** *n* the amount of money that is demanded as payment for something — see PRICE 1

*syn* synonym(s) *rel* related words
*ant* antonym(s) *near ant* near antonym(s)

**feeble** *adj* lacking bodily strength — see WEAK 1

**feebleness** *n* the quality or state of lacking physical strength or vigor — see WEAKNESS 1

**feed** *n* **1** a large fancy meal often accompanied by ceremony or entertainment — see FEAST
**2** food eaten or prepared for eating at one time — see MEAL

**feed** *vb* **1** to provide food or means for ⟨a charity dedicated to *feeding* the hungry⟩
*syn* board, cater, provision
*rel* serve, wait; nourish, nurture; banquet, dine, feast, regale; mess
**2** to put (something) into the possession of someone for use or consumption — see FURNISH 2
**3** to take a meal — see DINE 1

**feed (on)** *vb* to seize and eat (something) as prey — see PREY

**feel** *n* an indefinite physical response to a stimulus — see SENSATION 1

**feel** *vb* **1** to have a vague awareness of ⟨I *feel* trouble brewing in the town⟩
*syn* perceive, scent, see, sense, smell, taste
*rel* behold, discern, observe, view; ascertain, discover, learn; anticipate, expect, foresee
**2** to come into bodily contact with (something) so as to perceive a slight pressure on the skin — see TOUCH 1
**3** to come to a knowledge of (something) by living through it — see EXPERIENCE
**4** to have as an opinion — see BELIEVE 2
**5** to search for something blindly or uncertainly — see GROPE

**feel (for)** *vb* to have sympathy for — see PITY

**feeling** *n* **1** a subjective response to a person, thing, or situation ⟨an overall *feeling* of happiness about their new home⟩
*syn* emotion, passion, sentiment
*rel* impression, perception, sense; attitude, outlook, perspective, viewpoint; belief, opinion, view; responsiveness, sensibility, sensitiveness, sensitivity
**2 feelings** *pl* general emotional condition ⟨a remark that thoughtlessly hurt her *feelings*⟩
*syn* heartstrings, passions, sensibilities
*rel* cheer, frame, humor, mode, mood, temper
**3** an idea that is believed to be true or valid without positive knowledge — see OPINION 1
**4** an indefinite physical response to a stimulus — see SENSATION 1
**5** sorrow or the capacity to feel sorrow for another's suffering or misfortune — see SYMPATHY 1
**6** the capacity for feeling for another's unhappiness or misfortune — see HEART 1

**feign** *vb* to present a false appearance of ⟨I would never *feign* illness just to get out of a test⟩
*syn* affect, assume, counterfeit, fake, pretend, profess, put on, sham, simulate
*rel* act, dissemble, impersonate, masquerade; forge, imitate; camouflage, conceal, disguise, mask; bluff, feint; malinger

**feigned** *adj* **1** lacking in natural or spontaneous quality — see ARTIFICIAL 1
**2** not being or expressing what one appears to be or express — see INSINCERE

**felicitate** *vb* to express to (someone) admiration for his or her success or good fortune — see CONGRATULATE

**felicitations** *n pl* best wishes — see COMPLIMENTS

**felicitous** *adj* **1** giving pleasure or contentment to the mind or senses — see PLEASANT
**2** meeting the requirements of a purpose or situation — see FIT 1

**felicitously** *adv* in a pleasing way — see WELL 5

**felicitousness** *n* the quality or state of being especially suitable or fitting — see APPROPRIATENESS

**felicity** *n* **1** a feeling or state of well-being and contentment — see HAPPINESS 1
**2** something that provides happiness or does good for a person or thing — see BLESSING 2

**feline** *n* a small domestic animal known for catching mice — see CAT 1

**fell** *adj* **1** likely to cause or capable of causing death — see DEADLY
**2** violently unfriendly or aggressive in disposition — see FIERCE 1

**fell** *vb* **1** to strike (someone) so forcefully as to cause a fall ⟨a boxer who was often *felled* in the first round⟩
*syn* bowl (down *or* over), down, drop, floor, knock (down *or* over), level
*rel* hit, jab, poke, punch, smite, sock, strike, whack
**2** to bring down by cutting ⟨the settlers began the daunting task of *felling* the mighty trees that blanketed the island⟩
*syn* chop (down), cut (down), hew, mow
*rel* bulldoze, flatten, level, raze, tear down
**3** to deprive of life — see KILL 1

**fellow** *n* **1** a male romantic companion — see BOYFRIEND
**2** a person frequently seen in the company of another — see ASSOCIATE 1
**3** an adult male human being — see MAN 1
**4** either of a pair matched in one or more qualities — see MATE 1
**5** one that is equal to another in status, achievement, or value — see EQUAL

**fellowship** *n* **1** a friendly relationship marked by ready communication and mutual understanding — see RAPPORT
**2** a group of persons formally joined together for some common interest — see ASSOCIATION 2
**3** kindly concern, interest, or support — see GOODWILL 1
**4** the body of people in a profession or field of activity — see CORPS
**5** the feeling of closeness and friendship that exists between companions — see COMPANIONSHIP

**female** *adj* of, relating to, or marked by qualities traditionally associated with women — see FEMININE 1

**female** *n* an adult female human being — see WOMAN

**feminine** *adj* **1** of, relating to, or marked by qualities traditionally associated with women ⟨the *feminine* furnishings suggested that the bedroom was intended for a girl⟩
*syn* female, womanish, womanlike, womanly
*rel* effeminate, girlish, sissy, unmanly; ladylike; distaff, petticoat
*near ant* boyish, hoydenish, tomboyish; gentlemanly
*ant* male, manlike, manly, mannish, masculine
**2** having or displaying qualities more suitable for women than for men — see EFFEMINATE

**fen** *n* spongy land saturated or partially covered with water — see SWAMP

**fence** *n* a physical object that blocks the way — see BARRIER

**fence** (in) *vb* to close or shut in by or as if by barriers — see ENCLOSE 1

**fend** (off) *vb* to drive back — see REPEL 1

**fender** *n* something that serves as a protective barrier — see CUSHION

**feral** *adj* living outdoors without taming or domestication by humans — see WILD 1

**ferment** *n* a disturbed or uneasy state — see UNREST

**ferment** *vb* to cause or encourage the development of — see INCITE 1

**ferocious** *adj* **1** extreme in degree, power, or effect — see INTENSE
**2** marked by bursts of destructive force or intense activity — see VIOLENT 1
**3** violently unfriendly or aggressive in disposition — see FIERCE 1

**ferry** *vb* to support and take from one place to another — see CARRY 1

**fertile** *adj* producing abundantly ⟨the *fertile* mind of Leonardo da Vinci explored art, architecture, engineering, mathematics, and many other fields⟩
*syn* fat, fecund, fruitful, luxuriant, productive, prolific, rich
*rel* bearing, producing, yielding; abounding, abundant, bountiful; copious, plenteous, plentiful; blooming, bursting, flourishing, swarming, teeming, thriving; creative, inventive, original
*near ant* meager (*or* meagre), scant, scanty, skimpy, spare, sparse
*ant* barren, infertile, sterile, unfruitful, unproductive

**fervency** *n* depth of feeling — see ARDOR 1

**fervent** *adj* having or expressing great depth of feeling ⟨a *fervent* speech that called for tolerance and compassion for those who are different⟩
*syn* ardent, blazing, burning, charged, emotional, fervid, feverish, fiery, flaming, glowing, hot-blooded, impassioned, passionate, red-hot, vehement, warm, warm-blooded
*rel* gushing, maudlin, mawkish, mushy, sentimental; histrionic, melodramatic; enthusiastic, gung ho, zealous; enamored, infatuated, obsessed
*phrases* on fire
*near ant* detached, dry, impersonal, objective; reserved, undemonstrative
*ant* cold, cool, dispassionate, impassive, unemotional

**fervid** *adj* having or expressing great depth of feeling — see FERVENT

**fervidness** *n* depth of feeling — see ARDOR 1

**fervor** *n* depth of feeling — see ARDOR 1

**festival** *n* a time or program of special events and entertainment in honor of something ⟨tourists flock to the town for its annual strawberry *festival*⟩
*syn* carnival, celebration, festivity, fete (*or* fête), fiesta, gala, jubilee
*rel* jamboree, jollification, merrymaking, revel, revelry; exhibit, exhibition, exposition, fair, show; exercises, honors

**festive** *adj* indicative of or marked by high spirits or good humor — see MERRY

**festivity** *n* **1** a mood characterized by high spirits and amusement and often accompanied by laughter — see MIRTH
**2** a time or program of special events and entertainment in honor of something — see FESTIVAL
**3** joyful or festive activity — see MERRYMAKING

**fetch** *vb* to have a price of — see COST

**fetching** *adj* having an often mysterious or magical power to attract — see FASCINATING 1

**fetch up** *vb* to bring (something) to a standstill — see [1]HALT 1

**fete** *or* **fête** *vb* to show appreciation, respect, or affection for (someone) with a public celebration — see HONOR

**fete** *or* **fête** *n* **1** a social gathering — see PARTY 1
**2** a time or program of special events and entertainment in honor of something — see FESTIVAL

**fetid** *adj* having an unpleasant smell — see MALODOROUS

**fetish** *also* **fetich** *n* **1** something about which one is constantly thinking or concerned — see FIXATION
**2** something worn or kept to bring good luck or keep away evil — see CHARM 1

**fetter** *n* **1** something that limits one's freedom of action or choice — see RESTRICTION 1
**2** something that makes movement or progress more difficult — see ENCUMBRANCE
**3** something that physically prevents free movement — see BOND 1

**fetter** *vb* **1** to confine or restrain with or as if with chains — see BIND 1
**2** to create difficulty for the work or activity of — see HAMPER

---

*syn* synonym(s) *rel* related words
*ant* antonym(s) *near ant* near antonym(s)

**fettle** *n* a state of being or fitness — see CONDITION 1

**fever** *n* an abnormal state that disrupts a plant's or animal's normal bodily functioning — see DISEASE

**feverish** *adj* 1 being in a state of increased activity or agitation ⟨scary stories that were the product of a *feverish* imagination⟩
*syn* agitated, excited, frenzied, heated, hectic, overactive, overwrought
*rel* ardent, burning, fervent, fiery; impassioned; high-strung, jittery, jumpy, nervous
*phrases* keyed up
*near ant* calm, composed, cool, serene, tranquil
2 having or expressing great depth of feeling — see FERVENT
3 marked by great and often stressful excitement or activity — see FURIOUS 1

**few** *n* a small number ⟨a *few* of the songs on the album are good, but most are forgettable⟩
*syn* handful, scattering, smattering, sprinkle, sprinkling
*rel* minority
*near ant* majority, most; abundance, excess, plenty, surplus
*ant* army, crowd, flock, horde, host, legion, many, mountain, multitude

**fiancé** *n* the person to whom one is engaged to be married — see BETROTHED

**fiancée** *n* the person to whom one is engaged to be married — see BETROTHED

**fiasco** *n* something that has failed — see FAILURE 3

**fiat** *n* an order publicly issued by an authority — see EDICT 1

**fib** *n* a statement known by its maker to be untrue and made in order to deceive — see LIE

**fib** *vb* to make a statement one knows to be untrue — see LIE 1

**fibber** *n* a person who tells lies — see LIAR

**fiber** *n* the strength of mind that enables a person to endure pain or hardship — see FORTITUDE

**fibrous** *adj* resembling or having the texture of a mass of strings — see STRINGY

**fickle** *adj* 1 likely to change frequently, suddenly, or unexpectedly ⟨a *fickle* friendship that was on and off over the years⟩
*syn* capricious, changeable, changeful, flickery, fluctuating, fluid, inconstant, mercurial, mutable, temperamental, uncertain, unpredictable, unsettled, unstable, unsteady, variable, volatile
*rel* aimless, erratic, haphazard, irregular, random; hesitating, shilly-shallying, vacillating, wavering; undependable, unreliable, untrustworthy; adaptable, mobile, protean, versatile
*near ant* equable, even, uniform; abiding, durable, lasting, permanent, persistent; dependable, reliable, trustworthy
*ant* certain, changeless, constant, immutable, invariable, settled, stable, steady, unchangeable
2 not true in one's allegiance to someone or something — see FAITHLESS

**fiction** *n* something that is the product of the imagination ⟨most stories about famous outlaws of the Old West are *fictions* that have little or nothing to do with fact⟩
*syn* fable, fabrication, fantasy (*also* phantasy), figment, invention
*rel* anecdote, narrative, novel, story, tale, yarn; falsehood, fib, lie, misrepresentation, untruth
*near ant* actuality, reality
*ant* fact

**fictional** *adj* not real and existing only in the imagination — see IMAGINARY

**fictitious** *adj* not real and existing only in the imagination — see IMAGINARY

**fiddle** *vb* to make jerky or restless movements — see FIDGET

**fiddle** (around) *vb* to spend time in aimless activity ⟨we spent the snow day just *fiddling around*⟩
*syn* fool (around), mess (around), monkey (around), play, potter (around), putter (around), trifle
*rel* dally, dawdle, dillydally, hang around, hang out, idle, loaf, loll, lounge; clown (around), horse (around); tinker
*near ant* buckle (down)

**fiddle** (with) *vb* to handle thoughtlessly, ignorantly, or mischievously — see TAMPER

**fiddlesticks** *n pl* language, behavior, or ideas that are absurd and contrary to good sense — see NONSENSE 1

**fidelity** *n* adherence to something to which one is bound by a pledge or duty ⟨they have never wavered in their *fidelity* to the cause of freedom⟩
*syn* allegiance, constancy, dedication, devotedness, devotion, faith, faithfulness, fastness, fealty, loyalty, steadfastness
*rel* affection, attachment, fondness; determination, firmness, resolution; dependability, reliability, trustworthiness
*near ant* alienation, disaffection, estrangement, separation
*ant* disloyalty, faithlessness, falseness, inconstancy, infidelity, perfidiousness, perfidy, treachery

**fidget** *vb* to make jerky or restless movements ⟨small children are likely to *fidget* in church⟩
*syn* fiddle, jerk, squirm, toss, twitch, wiggle, wriggle, writhe
*rel* flit, flutter, twitter; quake, quiver, shake, shiver, tremble; pace
*near ant* relax, rest, unwind

**fidgets** *n pl* a state of nervousness marked by sudden jerky movements — see JUMPINESS

**fie** *interj* how surprising, doubtful, or unbelievable — see NO

**field** *n* 1 a small area of usually open land ⟨a *field* that is the frequent site of neighborhood softball games⟩
*syn* clearing, ground, lot, parcel, plat, plot, tract

*rel* common(s); grass, green, greensward, lawn; glade, grassland, heath, lea, meadow, moor, pasture
**2** a region of activity, knowledge, or influence ⟨the first woman to enter the *field* of medicine⟩
*syn* area, arena, demesne, department, discipline, domain, line, province, realm, specialty, sphere
*rel* study, subject; territory, turf; business, occupation, profession, pursuit, racket, vocation
**3** a part or portion having no fixed boundaries — see REGION 1

**fiend** *n* **1** a mean, evil, or unprincipled person — see VILLAIN
**2** a person who regularly uses drugs especially illegally — see DOPER
**3** a person with a strong and habitual liking for something — see FAN
**4** an evil spirit — see DEMON

**fiendish** *adj* of, relating to, or worthy of an evil spirit ⟨a *fiendish* delight in playing cruel tricks⟩
*syn* demoniac (*also* demoniacal), demonic, devilish, diabolical (*or* diabolic), satanic
*rel* hellish, infernal; baleful, evil, sinister; malevolent, malicious, malignant; heinous, monstrous; barbarous, cruel, ferocious, inhuman, savage, vicious
*near ant* celestial, heavenly; beneficent, benevolent, benign, benignant; godly, holy, saintly
*ant* angelic

**fierce** *adj* **1** violently unfriendly or aggressive in disposition ⟨the Vikings had a well-earned reputation for being *fierce* warriors⟩
*syn* fell, ferocious, grim, savage, vicious
*rel* bellicose, belligerent, pugnacious, warlike; contentious, quarrelsome, truculent; menacing, threatening; bestial, brute, inhuman, inhumane; barbaric, uncivilized, wild; heartless, implacable, merciless, pitiless, relentless, ruthless, unrelenting, wanton; bloodthirsty, bloody, murderous; rapacious, ravenous, voracious
*near ant* amicable, congenial, friendly; compliant, submissive, tame, unaggressive; compassionate, kind, merciful; pacific, peaceable, peaceful; amiable, complaisant, obliging; human, humane; civilized, cultured
*ant* gentle, mild
**2** extreme in degree, power, or effect — see INTENSE
**3** harsh and threatening in manner or appearance — see GRIM 1
**4** having or showing a bold forcefulness in the pursuit of a goal — see AGGRESSIVE 1
**5** marked by bursts of destructive force or intense activity — see VIOLENT 1
**6** marked by great and often stressful excitement or activity — see FURIOUS 1

**fierceness** *n* the quality or state of being forceful (as in expression) — see VEHEMENCE 1

**fiery** *adj* **1** being on fire — see ABLAZE 1
**2** having a notably high temperature — see HOT 1
**3** having or expressing great depth of feeling — see FERVENT
**4** marked by a lively display of strong feeling — see SPIRITED 1

**fiesta** *n* a time or program of special events and entertainment in honor of something — see FESTIVAL

**fight** *n* **1** a physical dispute between opposing individuals or groups ⟨a troubled youth who got into one *fight* after another⟩
*syn* battle, clash, combat, conflict, contest, fracas, fray, hassle, scrap, scrimmage, scuffle, skirmish, struggle, tussle
*rel* pitched battle; brawl, free-for-all, melee; fisticuffs; confrontation, duel, face-off; altercation, argument, disagreement, quarrel, row, wrangle
**2** a forceful effort to reach a goal or objective — see STRUGGLE 1
**3** an inclination to fight or quarrel — see BELLIGERENCE
**4** an often noisy or angry expression of differing opinions — see ARGUMENT 1

**fight** *vb* **1** to oppose (someone) in physical conflict ⟨a proud people who have fiercely *fought* all invaders of their homeland⟩
*syn* battle, clash (with), combat, scrimmage (with), skirmish (with), war (against)
*rel* duel; bash, batter, beat, buffet, hit, punch, slug, strike; box, spar; brawl; grapple, scuffle, tussle, wrestle; bump, collide
*phrases* fall foul (of)
*near ant* give up, submit, surrender
**2** to strive to reduce or eliminate ⟨a civil rights leader who dedicated his life to *fighting* prejudice⟩
*syn* battle, combat, contend (with), counter, oppose
*rel* baffle, foil, frustrate, resist, thwart, withstand; confront, defy, face, meet
*near ant* abide, bear, endure, suffer; advocate, back, support, uphold
*ant* advance, encourage, foster, further, promote
**3** to engage in a contest — see COMPETE
**4** to express different opinions about something often angrily — see ARGUE 2
**5** to refuse to give in to — see RESIST

**fighter** *n* **1** a person engaged in military service — see SOLDIER
**2** one that engages in the sport of fighting with the fists — see BOXER

**figment** *n* **1** a conception or image created by the imagination and having no objective reality — see FANTASY 1
**2** something that is the product of the imagination — see FICTION

**figurative** *adj* expressing one thing in terms normally used for another ⟨the *figurative* meaning of "allergy" is "a feeling of dislike"⟩

*syn* extended, metaphorical
*rel* allegorical, emblematic (*also* emblematical), symbolic (*also* symbolical); euphemistic
*near ant* nonsymbolic
*ant* literal, nonfigurative

**figure** *n* **1** a character used to represent a mathematical value — see NUMBER
**2** a line that traces the outer limits of an object or surface — see OUTLINE 1
**3** a person who is widely known and usually much talked about — see CELEBRITY 1
**4** a small statue — see FIGURINE
**5** a three-dimensional representation of the human body used especially for displaying clothes — see MANNEQUIN 1
**6** a unit of decoration that is repeated all over something (as a fabric) — see PATTERN 1
**7** something that visually explains or decorates a text — see ILLUSTRATION 1
**8** the amount of money that is demanded as payment for something — see PRICE 1
**9** the outward appearance of something as distinguished from its substance — see FORM 1
**10** the type of body that a person has — see PHYSIQUE
**11 figures** *pl* the act or process of performing mathematical operations to find a value — see CALCULATION

**figure** *vb* **1** to come to a judgment after discussion or consideration — see DECIDE 1
**2** to decide the size, amount, number, or distance of (something) without actual measurement — see ESTIMATE 2
**3** to determine (a value) by doing the necessary mathematical operations — see CALCULATE 1
**4** to have as an opinion — see BELIEVE 2

**figure out** *vb* to find an answer for through reasoning — see SOLVE

**figurine** *n* a small statue ⟨his collection of *figurines* includes toy soldiers from every war that America has fought⟩
*syn* figure, statuette
*rel* doll, marionette, puppet; bust, figurehead; carving, model, sculpture; dummy, form, mannequin
*ant* colossus

**figuring** *n* the act or process of performing mathematical operations to find a value — see CALCULATION

**filch** *vb* to take (something) without right and with an intent to keep — see STEAL 1

**file** *n* a series of persons or things arranged one behind another — see LINE

[1]**file** *vb* to make smooth by friction — see GRIND 1

[2]**file** *vb* to move along with a steady regular step especially in a group — see MARCH 1

**fill** *n* soft material that is used to fill the hollow parts of something — see FILLING

**fill** *vb* **1** to put into (something) as much as can be held or contained ⟨*fill* the basket with apples⟩
*syn* charge, cram, heap, jam, jam-pack, load, pack, stuff
*rel* flood, glut, swamp; crowd, crush, press, ram, shove, squash, squeeze; refill, reload, repack
*near ant* lighten
*ant* empty
**2** to close up so that no empty spaces remain ⟨before starting to paint, *fill* all the cracks with putty⟩
*syn* block, bung, dam, pack, plug, stop, stuff
*rel* choke, clog, obstruct; caulk, chink
*near ant* excavate, hollow (out), scoop (out)
**3** to do what is required by the terms of — see FULFILL 1

**filled** *adj* containing or seeming to contain the greatest quantity or number possible — see FULL 1

**filler** *n* soft material that is used to fill the hollow parts of something — see FILLING

**fill in** *vb* **1** to give information to — see ENLIGHTEN 1
**2** to serve as a replacement usually for a time only — see COVER 1

**filling** *n* soft material that is used to fill the hollow parts of something ⟨the *filling* for the parka is goose down⟩
*syn* fill, filler, padding, stuffing
*rel* interlining, lining, wadding; cushion

**film** *n* **1** a story told by means of a series of continuously projected pictures and a sound track — see MOVIE 1
**2** the art or business of making a movie — see MOVIE 2

**filmy** *adj* **1** being of a material lacking in sturdiness or substance — see FLIMSY 1
**2** very thin and easy to see through — see SHEER 1

**filter** *vb* **1** to pass through a filter — see STRAIN 2
**2** to remove usually visible impurities from — see CLARIFY 1

**filth** *n* **1** foul matter that mars the purity or cleanliness of something ⟨the *filth* in the restaurant's kitchen was unbelievable⟩
*syn* dirt, grime, muck, smut, soil
*rel* scum, sewage, slime, sludge, swill; garbage, refuse, trash; soot; dirtiness, filthiness, foulness, griminess, grubbiness, nastiness, squalidness, uncleanliness, uncleanness
*near ant* cleanliness, cleanness
**2** the quality or state of being obscene — see OBSCENITY 1

**filthiness** *n* **1** the quality or state of being obscene — see OBSCENITY 1
**2** the state or quality of being dirty — see DIRTINESS 1

**filthy** *adj* **1** depicting or referring to sexual matters in a way that is unacceptable in polite society — see OBSCENE 1
**2** not clean — see DIRTY 1

**finagle** *vb* to plan out usually with subtle skill or care — see ENGINEER

**final** *adj* **1** following all others of the same kind in order or time — see LAST
**2** having been established and usually not subject to change — see FIXED 1

**finale** *n* the last part of a process or action ⟨the *finale* to the festivities was a grand display of fireworks⟩
***syn*** close, closing, conclusion, consummation, end, ending, finis, finish, windup
***rel*** apex, climax, crescendo, culmination, peak, summit, zenith; aftermath, anticlimax, coda, epilogue, postscript; tag end, tail end
***near ant*** introduction, overture, prelude, prologue
***ant*** beginning, dawn, opening, start
**finalize** *vb* to bring (something) to a state where nothing remains to be done — see FINISH 1
**finally** *adv* at a later time — see YET 1
**finance** *vb* **1** to provide money for ⟨a local business kindly *financed* the high school band's trip to New York City⟩
***syn*** capitalize, endow, fund, stake, subsidize, underwrite
***rel*** grubstake; aid, back, patronize, sponsor, support
**2** to furnish (as an institution) with a regular source of income — see ENDOW 2
**finances** *n pl* available money — see FUND 2
**financial** *adj* of or relating to money, banking, or investments ⟨the *financial* world was watching the stock market closely⟩
***syn*** fiscal, monetary, pecuniary
***rel*** capitalist (*or* capitalistic), commercial, economic
**find** *n* something discovered — see DISCOVERY 2
**find** *vb* **1** to come upon after searching, study, or effort ⟨we finally *found* the information after searching dozens of Internet sites⟩
***syn*** ascertain, descry, detect, determine, dig (up), discover, find out, get, hit (on *or* upon), hunt (down *or* up), learn, locate, run down, scare up, scout (up), track (down)
***rel*** espy, sight, spot; look for, search (for *or* out), seek
***near ant*** lose, mislay, misplace
***ant*** miss, overlook, pass over
**2** to come upon unexpectedly or by chance — see HAPPEN (ON *OR* UPON)
**finding** *n* **1** a decision made by a court or tribunal regarding a case it has heard — see SENTENCE
**2** the act or process of sighting or learning the existence of something for the first time — see DISCOVERY 1
**find out** *vb* **1** to come to an awareness — see DISCOVER 1
**2** to come upon after searching, study, or effort — see FIND 1
**fine** *adj* **1** consisting of very small particles ⟨the *fine* sand found on the island's beaches⟩
***syn*** dusty, floury, powdery
***rel*** smooth; filtered, pulverized, refined
***near ant*** rough; unfiltered, unrefined; gravelly, gritty, sandy; pebbly, rocky, stony (*also* stoney); lumpy, mealy
***ant*** coarse, grainy, granular, granulated
**2** made or done with extreme care and accuracy ⟨the *fine* distinction between bravery and recklessness⟩
***syn*** delicate, exact, hairline, hairsplitting, minute, nice, refined, subtle
***rel*** nitpicking, quibbling; petty, piddling, trifling, trivial; fastidious, finicky, fussy, particular
***near ant*** apparent, clear, obvious; broad, indefinite; careless, slapdash, slipshod, sloppy
***ant*** coarse, inexact, rough
**3** being of less than usual width — see NARROW 1
**4** being to one's liking — see SATISFACTORY 1
**5** free from added matter — see PURE 1
**6** meeting the highest standard of accuracy — see PRECISE 1
**7** of a level of quality that meets one's needs or standards — see ADEQUATE
**8** of a size that is less than average — see SMALL 1
**9** of the very best kind — see EXCELLENT
**fine** *adv* in a satisfactory way — see WELL 1
**fine** *n* a sum of money to be paid as a punishment ⟨a $50 *fine* for speeding⟩
***syn*** damages, forfeit, forfeiture, mulct, penalty
***rel*** reparations; award, compensation; indemnity
**fine** *vb* to establish or apply as a charge or penalty — see IMPOSE
**fineness** *n* **1** the quality or state of being little in size — see SMALLNESS
**2** the quality or state of being very accurate — see PRECISION
**3** the state or quality of having a delicate structure — see DELICACY 2
**finery** *n* dressy clothing ⟨the guests arrived at the wedding in all their *finery*⟩
***syn*** array, best, bravery, caparison, feather, frippery, full dress, gaiety (*also* gayety), regalia
***rel*** apparel, attire, costume, duds, raiment
***near ant*** rags, tatters
**finesse** *n* mental skill or quickness — see DEXTERITY 1
**finesse** *vb* to plan out usually with subtle skill or care — see ENGINEER
**finicky** *adj* hard to please ⟨cats have a reputation for being *finicky* eaters⟩
***syn*** choosy (*or* choosey), dainty, delicate, demanding, exacting, fastidious, fussy, nice, old-maidish, particular, picky
***rel*** discerning, discriminating, insightful, knowledgeable; carping, critical; careful, meticulous, punctilious, scrupulous; queasy (*also* queazy), squeamish; peevish, petulant, prickly, touchy
***near ant*** affable, breezy, devil-may-care, happy-go-lucky, laid-back; flexible, lax, loose; lenient, permissive; uncritical
***ant*** undemanding, unfussy
**finis** *n* the last part of a process or action — see FINALE

**finish** *n* 1 the last part of a process or action — see FINALE
2 the stopping of a process or activity — see END 1

**finish** *vb* 1 to bring (something) to a state where nothing remains to be done ⟨we should *finish* the painting of the house by tomorrow⟩
*syn* complete, consummate, finalize, perfect
*rel* follow through, see out, stick out; accomplish, achieve, effect; discharge, execute, fulfill (*or* fulfil), perform; machine, polish, refine, round (off *or* out), shine, touch up
*near ant* abandon, desert, drop, forsake, quit
2 to bring (an event) to a natural or appropriate stopping point — see CLOSE 3
3 to come to an end — see CEASE 1

**finished** *adj* brought or having come to an end — see COMPLETE 2

**finite** *adj* 1 having a limit ⟨our nation's natural resources are abundant, but they are also *finite*⟩
*syn* limited
*rel* confined, restricted; definable, defined, definite, determinate; decided, established, fixed, set; exact, precise, specific
*near ant* unconfined, unrestricted; indefinite, indeterminate, undefinable, undefined
*ant* boundless, infinite, unbounded, unlimited
2 having distinct or certain limits — see LIMITED 1

**fire** *n* a destructive burning ⟨a number of suspicious *fires* in the neighborhood recently⟩
*syn* conflagration, holocaust, inferno
*rel* blaze, flare-up; backfire, bonfire, forest fire, wildfire; arson

**fire** *vb* 1 to cause (a projectile) to be driven forward with force — see SHOOT 1
2 to cause a weapon to release a missile with great force — see SHOOT 2
3 to give life, vigor, or spirit to — see ANIMATE
4 to let go from office, service, or employment — see DISMISS 1
5 to send through the air especially with a quick forward motion of the arm — see THROW
6 to set (something) on fire — see BURN 2

**fire** (up) *vb* to rouse to strong feeling or action — see PROVOKE 1

**firearm** *n* a portable weapon from which a shot is discharged by gunpowder — see GUN 1

**firebrand** *n* a person who stirs up public feelings especially of discontent — see AGITATOR

**firebug** *n* a person who deliberately and unlawfully sets fire to a building or other property — see ARSONIST

**fireproof** *adj* incapable of being burned — see INCOMBUSTIBLE

**fireside** *n* the place where one lives — see HOME 1

**fireworks** *n pl* an outburst or display of excited anger — see TANTRUM

**firing** *n* a directed propelling of a missile by a firearm or artillery piece — see SHOT

**firkin** *n* an enclosed wooden vessel for holding beverages — see CASK

**firm** *adj* 1 not showing weakness or uncertainty ⟨a friendly fellow with a ready smile and a *firm* handshake⟩
*syn* forceful, hearty, iron, lusty, robust, solid, stout, strong, sturdy, vigorous
*rel* mighty, powerful, tough, unyielding; animated, energetic, lively, spirited; certain, confident, sanguine, sure
*near ant* feeble, fragile, frail; limp, listless, spiritless
*ant* uncertain, weak
2 having a consistency that does not easily yield to pressure ⟨cold butter that was too *firm* to spread⟩
*syn* compact, hard, rigid, solid, stiff, unyielding
*rel* case-hardened, compacted, compressed, hardened, indurated, stiffened, tempered; close, dense, heavy, thick, thickset; inelastic, inflexible, ramrod, unbending; compressed, condensed; sturdy, substantial; impenetrable, impermeable, nonporous
*near ant* loose, scattered, thin; bendable, elastic, flexible, malleable, pliable; flaccid, floppy, limp, slack; airy, light; permeable, porous
*ant* flabby, soft, spongy, squashy, squishy
3 firmly positioned in place and difficult to dislodge — see TIGHT 2
4 fully committed to achieving a goal — see DETERMINED 1
5 having been established and usually not subject to change — see FIXED 1
6 marked by the ability to withstand stress without structural damage or distortion — see STABLE 1

**firm** *n* a commercial or industrial activity or organization — see ENTERPRISE 1

**firm** (up) *vb* to become physically firm or solid — see HARDEN 1

**firmament** *n* the expanse of air surrounding the earth — see SKY

**firmly** *adv* in a vigorous and forceful manner — see HARD 3

**firmness** *n* 1 firm or unwavering adherence to one's purpose — see DETERMINATION 1
2 the ability to withstand force or stress without being distorted, dislodged, or damaged — see STABILITY 1

**first** *adj* 1 coming before all others in time or order ⟨the much-studied *first*—and last—voyage of the *Titanic*⟩
*syn* earliest, inaugural, initial, maiden, original, pioneer, premier
*rel* ancient, early, primal, primary, primeval, primitive, primordial; antecedent, preceding, previous
*near ant* advanced, late; ensuing, following, subsequent, succeeding
*ant* final, last, terminal, ultimate
2 coming before all others in importance — see FOREMOST 1

3 highest in rank or authority — see HEAD

**first** *adv* 1 as a substitute — see INSTEAD 2 by choice or preference — see RATHER 1

**first-class** *adj* of the very best kind — see EXCELLENT

**firsthand** *adj* done or working without something else coming in between — see DIRECT 1

**firstly** *adv* in the beginning — see ORIGINALLY

**first-rate** *adj* of the very best kind — see EXCELLENT

**firth** *n* a part of a body of water that extends beyond the general shoreline — see GULF 1

**fiscal** *adj* of or relating to money, banking, or investments — see FINANCIAL

**fish** *vb* to search for something blindly or uncertainly — see GROPE

**fishy** *adj* giving good reason for being doubted, questioned, or challenged — see DOUBTFUL 2

**fissure** *n* an irregular usually narrow break in a surface created by pressure — see CRACK 1

**fit** *adj* 1 meeting the requirements of a purpose or situation ⟨clothing that is *fit* for horseback riding⟩

*syn* applicable, appropriate, apt, becoming, befitting, felicitous, fitting, good, happy, meet, proper, right, suitable

*rel* just, justified, right; needed, required, requisite; able, capable, competent, qualified, trained; acceptable, adequate, decent, satisfactory, tolerable; correct, decorous, respectable, seemly

*near ant* incompetent, unqualified, untrained; inadequate, intolerable, unacceptable, unsatisfactory; incorrect, indecorous, unseemly

*ant* improper, inapplicable, inappropriate, inapt, infelicitous, unhappy, unsuitable, wrong

2 being in a state of fitness for some experience or action — see READY 1

3 capable of or suitable for being used for a particular purpose — see USABLE 1

4 enjoying health and vigor — see HEALTHY 1

5 having the required skills for an acceptable level of performance — see COMPETENT

**fit** *n* 1 a sudden experiencing of a physical or mental disorder — see ATTACK 2

2 a sudden intense expression of strong feeling — see OUTBURST 1

3 an outburst or display of excited anger — see TANTRUM

**fit** *vb* 1 to be fitting or proper — see DO 1

2 to be in agreement on every point — see CHECK 1

3 to change (something) so as to make it suitable for a new use or situation — see ADAPT

4 to make competent (as by training, skill, or ability) for a particular office or function — see QUALIFY 2

5 to make or have room for — see ACCOMMODATE 1

6 to make ready in advance — see PREPARE 1

**fit** (in *or* into) *vb* to put among or between others — see INSERT

**fit** (out) *vb* to provide (someone) with what is needed for a task or activity — see FURNISH 1

**fitful** *adj* lacking in steadiness or regularity of occurrence ⟨a night of *fitful* sleep did not leave me feeling well rested the next morning⟩

*syn* casual, choppy, discontinuous, erratic, intermittent, irregular, occasional, spasmodic, sporadic, spotty, unsteady

*rel* convulsive, sudden, violent; broken, disconnected, fragmentary, interrupted; desultory, haphazard, hit-or-miss, random; changing, fluctuating, unstable, varying, wavering; changeable, fickle, variable

*near ant* equable, even, stable, uniform; unchanging, unvarying, unwavering; methodical, orderly, systematic

*ant* constant, continuous, regular, steady

**fitness** *n* 1 the condition of being sound in body — see HEALTH

2 the quality or state of being especially suitable or fitting — see APPROPRIATENESS

**fitting** *adj* meeting the requirements of a purpose or situation — see FIT 1

**fittingly** *adv* in a manner suitable for the occasion or purpose — see PROPERLY

**fittingness** *n* the quality or state of being especially suitable or fitting — see APPROPRIATENESS

**fix** *n* 1 a difficult, puzzling, or embarrassing situation from which there is no easy escape — see PREDICAMENT

2 something given or promised in order to improperly influence a person's conduct or decision — see BRIBE

**fix** *vb* 1 to arrange something in a certain spot or position — see PLACE 1

2 to cause (something) to hold to another — see FASTEN 1

3 to come to an agreement or decision concerning the details of — see ARRANGE 1

4 to decide upon (the time or date for an event) usually from a position of authority — see APPOINT 1

5 to make ready in advance — see PREPARE 1

6 to put into good shape or working order again — see MEND 1

7 to put securely in place or in a desired position — see FASTEN 2

8 to set solidly in or as if in surrounding matter — see ENTRENCH

**fixable** *adj* capable of being corrected — see REMEDIABLE

**fixation** *n* something about which one is constantly thinking or concerned ⟨their

---

*syn* synonym(s) *rel* related words
*ant* antonym(s) *near ant* near antonym(s)

weight is an unfortunate *fixation* for many teenagers⟩
***syn*** fetish (*also* fetich), idée fixe, mania, obsession, preoccupation, preposession
***rel*** complex, hang-up, problem; compulsion, craving, enthusiasm, fascination, infatuation, passion; idiosyncrasy, quirk; penchant, predilection, proclivity
***near ant*** apathy, indifference, unconcern

**fixed** *adj* **1** having been established and usually not subject to change ⟨the baseball card dealer's prices were *fixed*, so bargaining was not an option⟩
***syn*** certain, determinate, final, firm, flat, frozen, hard, hard-and-fast, set, settled, stable
***rel*** nonadjustable, nonnegotiable, unchangeable; constant, steady, unchanging, uniform, unwavering; definite, exact, explicit, specific; stated, stipulated
***near ant*** adjustable, changeable, negotiable; indefinite, unspecified
**2** not capable of changing or being changed — see INFLEXIBLE 1

**fixedness** *n* the state of continuing without change — see CONSTANCY 1

**fizz** *n* a sound similar to the speech sound \s\ stretched out — see HISS 1

**fizz** *vb* to make a sound like that of stretching out the speech sound \s\ — see HISS

**fizzle** *n* **1** a falling short of one's goals — see FAILURE 2
**2** something that has failed — see FAILURE 3

**fjord** *or* **fiord** *n* a part of a body of water that extends beyond the general shoreline — see GULF 1

**flabbergast** *vb* to make a strong impression on (someone) with something unexpected — see SURPRISE 1

**flabbergasted** *adj* **1** affected with sudden and great wonder or surprise — see THUNDERSTRUCK
**2** filled with amazement or wonder — see OPENMOUTHED

**flabbergasting** *adj* causing a strong emotional reaction because unexpected — see SURPRISING 1

**flabby** *adj* giving easily to the touch — see SOFT 3

**flaccid** *adj* not stiff in structure — see LIMP 1

**flag** *n* **1** a piece of cloth with a special design that is used as an emblem or for signaling ⟨the *flags* of both countries were prominently displayed at the treaty signing⟩
***syn*** banner, colors, ensign, guidon, jack, pennant, pennon, standard, streamer
***rel*** bunting; black flag, Jolly Roger, union jack, white flag; semaphore, signaler; badge, coat of arms, crest, insignia
**2** an object intended to give public notice or warning — see SIGNAL 1

[1]**flag** *vb* **1** to be limp from lack of water or vigor — see DROOP
**2** to lose bodily strength or vigor — see WEAKEN 2

[2]**flag** *vb* to direct or notify by a movement or gesture — see MOTION

**flagellate** *vb* to strike repeatedly with something long and thin or flexible — see WHIP 1

**flagon** *n* a handled container for holding and pouring liquids that usually has a lip or a spout — see PITCHER

**flagrant** *adj* very noticeable especially for being incorrect or bad — see EGREGIOUS

**flail** *vb* **1** to move or cause to move with a striking motion — see FLAP
**2** to strike repeatedly with something long and thin or flexible — see WHIP 1

**flair** *n* a special and usually inborn ability — see TALENT

**flake** *n* a small flat piece separated from a whole — see CHIP 1

**flaky** *adj* having a texture that readily breaks into little pieces under pressure — see CRISP 1

**flamboyance** *n* excessive or unnecessary display — see OSTENTATION

**flamboyant** *adj* **1** likely to attract attention — see NOTICEABLE
**2** excessively showy — see GAUDY

**flamboyantly** *adv* in a bright and showy way — see GAILY 3

**flame** *n* a person with whom one is in love — see SWEETHEART

**flame** *vb* **1** to be on fire especially brightly — see BURN 1
**2** to develop suddenly and violently — see ERUPT 2
**3** to shine with a bright harsh light — see GLARE 1
**4** to shoot forth bursts of light — see FLASH 1

**flaming** *adj* **1** being on fire — see ABLAZE 1
**2** having or expressing great depth of feeling — see FERVENT

**flammable** *adj* capable of catching or being set on fire — see COMBUSTIBLE

**flank** *n* a place, space, or direction away from or beyond a central point or line — see SIDE 1

**flank** *vb* to be adjacent to — see ADJOIN 1

**flanking** *adj* having a border in common — see ADJACENT

**flap** *vb* to move or cause to move with a striking motion ⟨the stirring sight of a huge flock of geese *flapping* their wings⟩
***syn*** beat, flail, flop, flutter, whip
***rel*** bang, batter, buffet, knock, pound, smack, spank, thump; flick, flicker, flit; oscillate, sway, swing; undulate, wave; palpitate, pulse, throb

**flapjack** *n* a flat cake made from thin batter and cooked on both sides (as on a griddle) — see PANCAKE

**flare** *n* **1** a sudden and usually temporary growth of activity — see OUTBREAK
**2** a sudden intense expression of strong feeling — see OUTBURST 1
**3** the steady giving off of the form of radiation that makes vision possible — see LIGHT 1

**flare** *vb* to shine with a bright harsh light — see GLARE 1

**flare** (out) *vb* to arrange the parts of (something) over a wider area — see OPEN 3

**flare** (up) *vb* **1** to become very angry — see BLOW UP
**2** to develop suddenly and violently — see ERUPT 2

**flare–up** *n* **1** a sudden and usually temporary growth of activity — see OUTBREAK
**2** a sudden intense expression of strong feeling — see OUTBURST 1

**flash** *adj* lasting only for a short time — see MOMENTARY

**flash** *n* **1** a sudden and usually temporary growth of activity — see OUTBREAK
**2** a sudden intense expression of strong feeling — see OUTBURST 1
**3** a very small space of time — see INSTANT
**4** something extraordinary or surprising — see WONDER 1

**flash** *vb* **1** to shoot forth bursts of light ⟨the actress's diamond necklace *flashed* as she hurried on stage to accept the award⟩
***syn*** flame, glance, gleam, glimmer, glint, glisten, glister, glitter, scintillate, shimmer, sparkle, twinkle, wink
***rel*** beam, radiate, shine; bedazzle, blind, daze, dazzle; blaze, burn, flare, glare, glow
**2** to present so as to invite notice or attention — see SHOW 1
**3** to shine with light at regular intervals — see BLINK 1

**flashily** *adv* in a bright and showy way — see GAILY 3

**flashiness** *n* excessive or unnecessary display — see OSTENTATION

**flashy** *adj* **1** attractively eye-catching in style — see JAZZY 1
**2** excessively showy — see GAUDY

**flat** *adj* **1** being neither more nor less than a certain amount, number, or extent — see EVEN 1
**2** causing weariness, restlessness, or lack of interest — see BORING
**3** having a surface without bends, breaks, or irregularities — see LEVEL
**4** having been established and usually not subject to change — see FIXED 1
**5** having no exceptions or restrictions — see ABSOLUTE 2
**6** lacking a surface luster or gloss — see MATTE
**7** lacking in qualities that make for spirit and character — see WISHY-WASHY 1
**8** lacking in taste or flavor — see INSIPID 1

**flat** *adv* to a full extent or degree — see FULLY 1

**flat** *n, chiefly British* a room or set of rooms in a private house or a block used as a separate dwelling place — see APARTMENT 1

**flatten** *vb* to make free from breaks, curves, or bumps — see EVEN 1

**flatter** *vb* **1** to praise too much ⟨the billionaire had an army of assistants who *flattered* him at every opportunity⟩
***syn*** adulate, blarney, overpraise, soft-soap
***rel*** blandish, cajole, coax, wheedle; fawn, kowtow, toady; idolize, worship; eulogize, extol (*also* extoll), laud, praise; applaud, commend, compliment; congratulate, felicitate; drool, gush, slaver, slobber; endear, ingratiate; court, woo
***near ant*** bad-mouth, belittle, decry, depreciate, disparage, put down
**2** to think highly of (oneself) — see PRIDE

**flattery** *n* excessive praise ⟨a talk show host who is known for charming her guests with *flattery*⟩
***syn*** adulation, blarney, overpraise, soft soap
***rel*** allurements, blandishments, endearments; compliments, congratulations, felicitations, greetings, regards, respects; adoration, idolatry, worship; cajolery, endearment, ingratiation; acclaim, applause, commendation, praise
***near ant*** bad-mouthing, belittlement, depreciation, detraction, disparagement, put-down

**flatware** *n* eating and serving utensils — see TABLEWARE 1

**flaunt** *vb* to present so as to invite notice or attention — see SHOW 1

**flaunting** *n* an outward and often exaggerated indication of something abstract (as a feeling) for effect — see SHOW 1

**flavor** *n* **1** a special quality or impression associated with something — see AURA
**2** something (as a spice or herb) that adds an agreeable or interesting taste to food — see SEASONING 1
**3** the property of a substance that can be identified by the sense of taste — see TASTE 1

**flavor** *vb* to make more pleasant to the taste by adding something intensely flavored — see SEASON 1

**flavorful** *adj* very pleasing to the sense of taste — see DELICIOUS 1

**flavoring** *n* something (as a spice or herb) that adds an agreeable or interesting taste to food — see SEASONING 1

**flavorless** *adj* lacking in taste or flavor — see INSIPID 1

**flaw** *n* something that spoils the appearance or completeness of a thing — see BLEMISH

**flaw** *vb* to reduce the soundness, effectiveness, or perfection of — see DAMAGE 1

**flawed** *adj* having a fault — see FAULTY

**flawless** *adj* being entirely without fault or flaw — see PERFECT 1

**flawlessly** *adv* without any flaws or errors — see PERFECTLY 1

**flaxen** *adj* of a pale yellow or yellowish brown color — see BLOND

**flay** *vb* **1** to criticize (someone) severely or angrily especially for personal failings — see SCOLD

2 to remove the natural covering of — see PEEL

**fleck** *n* 1 a small area that is different (as in color) from the main part — see SPOT 1
2 a very small piece — see BIT 1

**fleck** *vb* to mark with small spots especially unevenly — see SPOT

**flecked** *adj* marked with spots — see SPOTTED 1

**fledgling** *n* a person who is just starting out in a field of activity — see BEGINNER

**flee** *vb* 1 to cease to be visible — see DISAPPEAR
2 to get free from a dangerous or confining situation — see ESCAPE 1
3 to hasten away from something dangerous or frightening — see RUN 2

**fleece** *n* the hairy covering of a mammal especially when fine, soft, and thick — see FUR 1

**fleece** *vb* to rob by the use of trickery or threats ⟨swindlers who use the telephone to *fleece* senior citizens out of their savings⟩
*syn* bleed, cheat, chisel, cozen, defraud, gyp, hustle, mulct, rook, shortchange, skin, squeeze, stick, sting, swindle, victimize
*rel* extort, wrench, wrest, wring; gouge, overcharge, soak; exploit, milk; deceive, dupe, fool, gull, trick; rope (in); betray, double-cross

**fleecy** *adj* covered with or as if with hair — see HAIRY 1

**fleet** *adj* moving, proceeding, or acting with great speed — see FAST 1

**fleet** *n* a group of vehicles traveling together or under one management ⟨a *fleet* of buses rolling down the highway⟩
*syn* armada, caravan, cavalcade, line, motorcade, train
*rel* convoy, flotilla, navy; column, cortege (*also* cortège), parade, procession

**fleet–footed** *adj* moving, proceeding, or acting with great speed — see FAST 1

**fleeting** *adj* lasting only for a short time — see MOMENTARY

**fleetly** *adv* with great speed — see FAST 1

**fleetness** *n* a high rate of movement or performance — see SPEED

**flesh** *n* animal and especially mammal tissue used as food — see MEAT 1

**fleshiness** *n* 1 the condition of having an excess of body fat — see CORPULENCE
2 the quality or state of being full of juice — see SUCCULENCE

**fleshly** *adj* 1 having to do with life on earth especially as opposed to that in heaven — see EARTHLY
2 of or relating to the human body — see PHYSICAL 1
3 pleasing to the physical senses — see SENSUAL

**fleshy** *adj* 1 full of juice — see JUICY
2 having an excess of body fat — see FAT 1

**flexible** *adj* 1 capable of being readily changed ⟨fortunately, Mom has a very *flexible* schedule for her office job⟩
*syn* adaptable, adjustable, alterable, changeable, elastic, fluid, malleable, modifiable, variable
*rel* changing, fluctuating, inconstant, unstable, unsteady; varying
*near ant* constant, stable, steady, unchanging, uniform, unvarying
*ant* established, fixed, immutable, inelastic, inflexible, invariable, nonmalleable, ramrod, set, unalterable, unchangeable
2 not bound by rigid standards — see EASYGOING 2
3 able to bend easily without breaking — see WILLOWY
4 able to revert to original size and shape after being stretched, squeezed, or twisted — see ELASTIC 1

**flick** *vb* to make an irregular series of quick, sudden movements — see FLIT

**flicker** *n* a sudden and usually temporary growth of activity — see OUTBREAK

**flicker** *vb* to make an irregular series of quick, sudden movements — see FLIT

**flickery** *adj* likely to change frequently, suddenly, or unexpectedly — see FICKLE 1

**flier** *or* **flyer** *n* 1 a risky undertaking — see GAMBLE
2 one who flies or is qualified to fly an aircraft or spacecraft — see PILOT
3 a short printed publication with no cover or with a paper cover — see PAMPHLET

**[1]flight** *n* the act or an instance of getting free from danger or confinement — see ESCAPE 1

**[2]flight** *n* travel through the air by the use of wings ⟨for centuries people had been fascinated by the *flight* of birds⟩
*syn* flying
*rel* aviation; aeronautics; ballooning, gliding, skydiving, soaring

**flightiness** *n* 1 a lack of seriousness often at an improper time — see FRIVOLITY 1
2 a state of nervousness marked by sudden jerky movements — see JUMPINESS

**flighty** *adj* 1 easily excited by nature — see EXCITABLE
2 lacking in seriousness or maturity — see GIDDY 1

**flimsy** *adj* 1 being of a material lacking in sturdiness or substance ⟨a *flimsy* scarf that was more for decoration than for warmth⟩
*syn* filmy, gauzy, gossamer, gossamery, insubstantial, unsubstantial
*rel* dainty, delicate, fine; feeble, fragile, frail; sheer, transparent
*near ant* durable, lasting, tough; coarse, heavy, rough, rude
*ant* sturdy, substantial
2 not likely to be true or to occur — see IMPROBABLE

**flinch** *vb* to draw back in fear, pain, or disgust ⟨there are some patients who *flinch* at the mere sight of a needle⟩
*syn* blench, quail, recoil, shrink, wince
*rel* blanch, pale, whiten; quake, quiver, shake, shudder, tremble; crouch, squinch;

jerk, start, twitch; recede, retire, retreat, withdraw; falter, hesitate, reel, waver
***near ant*** advance, approach, near; confront, challenge, defy, face

**fling** *n* **1** a time or instance of carefree fun ⟨most families spend Labor Day weekend having one last summer *fling*⟩
***syn*** binge, frolic, gambol, lark, revel, rollick, romp, spree
***rel*** caper, escapade, prank; antic, monkeyshine(s), shenanigans; field day; festivity, merriment, merrymaking; enjoyment, indulgence, pleasure, self-indulgence; amusement, diversion, entertainment, recreation
**2** an effort to do or accomplish something — see ATTEMPT

**fling** *vb* to send through the air especially with a quick forward motion of the arm — see THROW

**fling** (off *or* away) *vb* to get rid of as useless or unwanted — see DISCARD

**flinty** *adj* **1** given to exacting standards of discipline and self-restraint — see SEVERE 1
**2** harsh and threatening in manner or appearance — see GRIM 1

**flip** *adj* making light of something usually regarded as serious or sacred — see FLIPPANT

**flip** *vb* **1** to become very angry — see BLOW UP
**2** to change the position of (an object) so that the opposite side or end is showing — see REVERSE 2
**3** to yield to mental or emotional stress — see CRACK 2

**flippancy** *n* a lack of seriousness often at an improper time — see FRIVOLITY 1

**flippant** *adj* making light of something usually regarded as serious or sacred ⟨his *flippant* comment that the poor save on taxes offended many people⟩
***syn*** facetious, flip, pert, smart, smart-alecky (*or* smart-aleck)
***rel*** flighty, frivolous; cheeky, cocky, cute, fresh, impertinent, impish, impudent, mischievous, playful, roguish, sassy, saucy, waggish; disrespectful, rude; breezy, casual, glib, inappropriate, thoughtless
***near ant*** grave, serious, sober, solemn, somber (*or* sombre)
***ant*** earnest, sincere

**flirt** *vb* to show a liking for someone of the opposite sex just for fun ⟨the servers at that restaurant *flirt* with all the customers⟩
***syn*** dally, frivol, trifle
***rel*** josh, kid, put on, razz, rib, tease; fool, lead on, string along; play (with), toy (with)

**flit** *vb* to make an irregular series of quick, sudden movements ⟨bargain hunters at the flea market *flitted* from table to table like hummingbirds in a garden⟩
***syn*** dance, dart, flick, flicker, flutter, zip
***rel*** dash, fly, sail, shoot, speed, sprint, zoom; scamper, scud, scurry, scuttle, skip, skitter; meander, ramble, roam, wander
***near ant*** float, hang, hover

**float** *n* a structure used by boats and ships for taking on or landing cargo and passengers — see DOCK

**float** *vb* to rest or move along the surface of a liquid or in the air ⟨a canoe *floating* down the river⟩ ⟨particles of dust *floating* in the air⟩
***syn*** drift, glide, hang, hover, poise, ride, sail, waft
***rel*** bob, dangle, suspend; buoy; balloon, raft
***near ant*** dive, lunge, plunge; dip, immerse, submerge, submerse
***ant*** settle, sink

**flock** *n* **1** a great number of persons or things gathered together — see CROWD 1
**2** a group of domestic animals assembled or herded together — see HERD

**flock** *vb* to move upon or fill (something) in great numbers — see CROWD 2

**flog** *vb* **1** to strike repeatedly with something long and thin or flexible — see WHIP 1
**2** to strike repeatedly — see BEAT 1

**flogger** *n* a long thin or flexible tool for striking — see WHIP

**flood** *n* a great flow of water or of something that overwhelms ⟨a *flood* nearly wiped out the town⟩ ⟨a *flood* of messages on my computer⟩
***syn*** cataclysm, cataract, deluge, flood tide, inundation, overflow, spate, torrent
***rel*** current, river, stream, tide; discharge, flush, gush, outflow, outpouring; flux, inflow, influx; engulfment, washout; avalanche; cascade, waterfall; excess, glut, overabundance, overage, overkill, overmuch, oversupply, superabundance, superfluity, surfeit, surplus
***near ant*** dribble, drip, trickle
***ant*** drought

**flood** *vb* to cover or become filled with a flood ⟨the lowlands were completely *flooded*⟩ ⟨angry calls *flooded* the radio station⟩
***syn*** deluge, drown, engulf, inundate, overflow, overwhelm, submerge, submerse, swamp
***rel*** overcome, overrun; flow, flush, gush, pour, sluice, spout, spurt, stream; douse, drench, soak, wet
***near ant*** dehydrate, dry, parch
***ant*** drain

**flood tide** *n* a great flow of water or of something that overwhelms — see FLOOD

**floor** *n* the surface upon which a body of water lies — see BOTTOM 2

**floor** *vb* **1** to cause an often unpleasant surprise for — see SHOCK 1
**2** to make a strong impression on (someone) with something unexpected — see SURPRISE 1
**3** to strike (someone) so forcefully as to cause a fall — see FELL 1

4 to subject to incapacitating emotional or mental stress — see OVERWHELM 1

**flop** *n* something that has failed — see FAILURE 3

**flop** *vb* 1 to throw or set down clumsily or casually ⟨they *flopped* themselves onto the couch to watch the game⟩ ⟨*flopped* the bag of groceries onto the counter⟩
*syn* plop, plump, plunk
*rel* fling, heave, sling, toss; ensconce, install, plant, settle
2 to be unsuccessful — see FAIL 2
3 to move or cause to move with a striking motion — see FLAP

**floppy** *adj* not stiff in structure — see LIMP 1

**flora** *n* green leaves or plants — see GREENERY 1

**floral** *adj* of or relating to flowers ⟨wallpaper with a *floral* pattern for the bedroom⟩
*syn* flowered, flowery
*rel* florid; abloom

**florid** *adj* 1 elaborately and often excessively decorated — see ORNATE
2 full of fine words and fancy expressions — see FLOWERY 1
3 having a healthy reddish skin tone — see RUDDY

**floss** *n* a soft airy substance or covering — see FUZZ

**flounce** *n* a strip of fabric gathered or pleated on one edge and used as trimming — see RUFFLE

**flounder** *vb* 1 to make progress in a clumsy, struggling manner ⟨unprepared choristers who *floundered* helplessly through the musical number⟩
*syn* limp, lumber, plod, stumble, trudge
*rel* shamble, shuffle; wallow, welter; falter, lurch, reel, stagger, sway, teeter, totter; blunder, fumble, muddle
*near ant* coast, fly, glide, sail, zip, zoom
2 to move heavily or clumsily — see LUMBER 1

**flourish** *vb* 1 to grow vigorously — see THRIVE 1
2 to reach a desired level of accomplishment — see SUCCEED 2

**flourishing** *adj* 1 having attained a desired end or state of good fortune — see SUCCESSFUL 1
2 marked by much life, movement, or activity — see ALIVE 2
3 marked by vigorous growth and well-being especially economically — see PROSPEROUS 1

**floury** *adj* consisting of very small particles — see FINE 1

**flout** *vb* to ignore in a disrespectful manner — see SCORN 2

**flow** *vb* 1 to move in a stream ⟨water was *flowing* over the dam at a tremendous rate⟩
*syn* pour, roll, run, stream
*rel* arise, emanate, issue, spring; course, race, rush; gush, spout, spurt; deluge, engulf, flood, inundate, overflow; swamp; cascade, dribble, drip, gutter, riffle, ripple, trickle; flush, wash out
*near ant* clot, coagulate, congeal, gel, harden, set
*ant* back up
2 to move or proceed smoothly and readily ⟨as everyone relaxed, the conversation really started to *flow*⟩
*syn* bowl, breeze, coast, drift, glide, roll, sail, skim, slide, slip, stream, sweep, whisk
*rel* fly, race, rush, speed
*near ant* limp, lumber, plod, stumble, trudge; shamble, shuffle; stamp, stomp, stump, tramp; labor, toil
*ant* flounder, struggle

**flower** *n* 1 the usually showy plant part that produces seeds ⟨*flowers* are always a thoughtful gift⟩
*syn* bloom, blossom
*rel* bud, floret; bouquet, nosegay, posy; arrangement, boutonniere, corsage, garland, lei, spray, wreath
2 a state or time of great activity, thriving, or achievement — see BLOOM 1
3 individuals carefully selected as being the best of a class — see ELITE

**flower** *vb* to produce flowers — see BLOOM

**flowered** *adj* of or relating to flowers — see FLORAL

**flowery** *adj* 1 full of fine words and fancy expressions ⟨the *flowery* verses that always appear on valentines⟩
*syn* florid, grandiloquent, highfalutin, high-flown, high-sounding
*rel* affected, grandiose, inflated, pompous, pretentious, stilted; excessive, flattering, fulsome; boastful, bombastic; elevated, eloquent, lofty
*near ant* prosaic, unpoetic; bald, direct, matter-of-fact, plain, plainspoken, simple, stark, straightforward, unadorned; natural, unaffected, unpretentious
2 of or relating to flowers — see FLORAL

**flowing** *adj* capable of moving like a liquid — see FLUID 1

**flub** *n* an unintentional departure from truth or accuracy — see ERROR 1

**flub** *vb* to make or do (something) in a clumsy or unskillful way — see BOTCH

**fluctuate** *vb* to pass from one form, state, or level to another — see CHANGE 2

**fluctuating** *adj* 1 likely to change frequently, suddenly, or unexpectedly — see FICKLE 1
2 not staying constant — see UNEVEN 2

**fluent** *adj* 1 able to express oneself clearly and well — see ARTICULATE
2 capable of moving like a liquid — see FLUID 1
3 involving minimal difficulty or effort — see EASY 1

**fluently** *adv* without difficulty — see EASILY

**fluff** *n* a soft airy substance or covering — see FUZZ

**fluffy** *adj* resembling air in lightness — see AIRY 1

**fluid** *adj* 1 capable of moving like a liquid ⟨warm the jam until it is *fluid*, then spread it over the cake⟩

*syn* flowing, fluent, liquid
*rel* diluted, thin, watery, weak
*near ant* clotted, coagulated, gelatinous, gelled, jelled, jellied, thick; gluey, glutinous, gooey, gummy, viscous
*ant* hard, solid
**2** capable of being readily changed — see FLEXIBLE 1
**3** involving minimal difficulty or effort — see EASY 1
**4** likely to change frequently, suddenly, or unexpectedly — see FICKLE 1

**fluky** *adj* **1** coming or happening by good luck especially unexpectedly — see FORTUNATE 1
**2** happening by chance — see ACCIDENTAL

**flume** *n* **1** a narrow opening between hillsides or mountains that can be used for passage — see CANYON
**2** an open man-made passageway for water — see CHANNEL 1

**flunk** *vb* to be unsuccessful — see FAIL 2

**flunky** *also* **flunkey** *n* **1** a person hired to perform household or personal services — see SERVANT
**2** a person who flatters another in order to get ahead — see SYCOPHANT

**fluorescence** *n* the steady giving off of the form of radiation that makes vision possible — see LIGHT 1

**flurry** *n* **1** a sudden and usually temporary growth of activity — see OUTBREAK
**2** a sudden brief rush of wind — see GUST 1

**flush** *adj* **1** having a healthy reddish skin tone — see RUDDY
**2** having a surface without bends, breaks, or irregularities — see LEVEL
**3** having active strength of body or mind — see VIGOROUS 1
**4** having goods, property, or money in abundance — see RICH 1
**5** possessing or covered with great numbers or amounts of something specified — see RIFE

**flush** *n* **1** a rosy appearance of the cheeks — see BLOOM 2
**2** a state or time of great activity, thriving, or achievement — see BLOOM 1
**3** a sudden intense expression of strong feeling — see OUTBURST 1

**flush** *vb* **1** to pour liquid over or through in order to cleanse ⟨use this cleaner to *flush* the drain in the sink⟩
*syn* irrigate, rinse, sluice, wash
*rel* deluge, engulf, flood, inundate, swamp; flow, gush, rush, stream; douche, hose; drench, saturate, soak; douse, slosh, splash
**2** to develop a rosy facial color (as from excitement or embarrassment) — see BLUSH

**fluster** *n* **1** a state of nervous or irritated concern — see FRET
**2** the emotional state of being made self-consciously uncomfortable — see EMBARRASSMENT 1

**fluster** *vb* to throw into a state of self-conscious distress — see EMBARRASS 1

**flustering** *adj* causing embarrassment — see AWKWARD 3

**flutter** *n* a sudden and usually temporary growth of activity — see OUTBREAK

**flutter** *vb* **1** to make an irregular series of quick, sudden movements — see FLIT
**2** to move or cause to move with a striking motion — see FLAP

**fluttery** *adj* easily excited by nature — see EXCITABLE

**flux** *n* a flowing or coming in — see INFLUX

**flux** *vb* to go from a solid to a liquid state — see LIQUEFY

**fly** *vb* **1** to move through the air with or as if with outstretched wings ⟨the Wright brothers realized mankind's age-old wish to *fly*⟩
*syn* glide, plane, soar, wing
*rel* drift, float, hang, hover, waft; coast, cruise, sail, sweep; dart, flit, flutter; catapult, jet, orbit, rocket
**2** to get free from a dangerous or confining situation — see ESCAPE 1
**3** to proceed or move quickly — see HURRY 2
**4** to hasten away from something dangerous or frightening — see RUN 2

**flying** *adj* **1** acting or done with excessive or careless speed — see HASTY 1
**2** moving, proceeding, or acting with great speed — see FAST 1

**flying** *n* travel through the air by the use of wings — see [1]FLIGHT

**flyspeck** *n* a very small piece — see BIT 1

**foam** *n* a light mass of fine bubbles formed in or on a liquid ⟨a steaming cup of hot cocoa with a sprinkling of marshmallows drifting through the *foam*⟩
*syn* froth, head, lather, spume, suds, surf
*rel* mousse; mist, spindrift, spray; scum

**foaming** *adj* feeling or showing anger — see ANGRY

**foamy** *adj* covered with, consisting of, or resembling foam ⟨*foamy* milk shakes⟩
*syn* frothy, lathery, sudsy
*rel* bubbly, effervescent, fizzy, sparkling; soapy

**focus** *n* a thing or place that is of greatest importance to an activity or interest — see CENTER 1

**focus** *vb* to fix (as one's attention) steadily toward a central objective — see CONCENTRATE 2

**focused** *also* **focussed** *adj* **1** having the mind fixed on something — see ATTENTIVE
**2** not divided or scattered among several areas of interest or concern — see WHOLE 1

**foe** *n* one that is hostile toward another — see ENEMY

**fog** *n* **1** a state of mental confusion — see HAZE 2

---

*syn* synonym(s) *rel* related words
*ant* antonym(s) *near ant* near antonym(s)

**2** an atmospheric condition in which suspended particles in the air rob it of its transparency — see HAZE 1

**fog** *vb* **1** to make (something) unclear to the understanding — see CONFUSE 2
**2** to make dark, dim, or indistinct — see CLOUD 1

**foggy** *adj* **1** filled with or dimmed by fine particles (as of dust or water) in suspension — see HAZY 1
**2** not seen or understood clearly — see FAINT 1

**fogy** *also* **fogey** *n* a person with old-fashioned ideas ⟨old *fogies* who said that rap music would never last⟩
***syn*** antediluvian, dodo, fossil, fuddy-duddy, reactionary, stick-in-the-mud
***rel*** conservative, rightist, tory; old hand, old-timer, veteran; old maid
***near ant*** liberal, progressive, radical
***ant*** modern

**foible** *n* a defect in character — see FAULT 1

**foil** *vb* to prevent from achieving a goal — see FRUSTRATE

**foist** *vb* to offer (something fake, useless, or inferior) as genuine, useful, or valuable ⟨shopkeepers who *foist* shoddy souvenirs on unsuspecting tourists⟩
***syn*** palm off, pass off
***rel*** force, impose, inflict; counterfeit, fake, forge; distort, falsify, misrepresent

**fold** *n* a group of people sharing a common interest and relating together socially — see GANG 2

**fold** *vb* **1** to lay one part over or against another part of ⟨*fold* the blanket so that it will fit inside the trunk⟩
***syn*** double
***rel*** overlap, overlay, overlie; collapse, telescope; close, shut
***ant*** extend, open, spread, unfold
**2** to be unsuccessful — see FAIL 2

**folder** *n* a short printed publication with no cover or with a paper cover — see PAMPHLET

**foliage** *n* green leaves or plants — see GREENERY 1

**folk** *n* **1 folks** *pl* a group of persons who come from the same ancestor — see FAMILY 1
**2** one of the segments of society into which people are grouped — see CLASS 1
**3 folks** *pl* human beings in general — see PEOPLE 1

**folklore** *n* the body of customs, beliefs, stories, and sayings associated with a people, thing, or place ⟨the Scottish Highlands are rich in *folklore*⟩
***syn*** legend, lore, myth, mythology, tradition
***rel*** information, knowledge, wisdom; anecdote, fable, folktale, old wives' tale, tale, yarn

**follow** *vb* **1** to come after in time ⟨a wrap-up always *follows* the Super Bowl broadcast⟩
***syn*** postdate, succeed, supervene
***rel*** displace, replace, supersede; supplant; ensue
***ant*** antedate, precede, predate
**2** to go after or on the track of ⟨let's *follow* the boys to their hiding place⟩
***syn*** chase, dog, hound, pursue, shadow, tag, tail, trace, track, trail
***rel*** accompany, chaperone (*or* chaperon), escort; hunt, search (for), seek; eye, observe, watch
***near ant*** head
***ant*** guide, lead, pilot
**3** to act according to the commands of — see OBEY
**4** to make one's way through, across, or over — see TRAVERSE
**5** to take notice of and be guided by — see HEED 1

**follower** *n* one who follows the opinions or teachings of another ⟨the *followers* of Gandhi have spread his philosophy of nonviolence all over the world⟩
***syn*** adherent, convert, disciple, partisan, pupil, votary
***rel*** apostle; faithful, loyalist; advocate, backer, champion, supporter; scholar, student; ideologist, sectarian; admirer, cultist, devotee, enthusiast, fan, idolater (*or* idolator), worshipper (*or* worshiper), zealot; flunky (*also* flunkey), hanger-on, henchman, lackey, satellite, stooge, sycophant, toady, yes-man
***near ant*** apostate, defector, renegade, traitor, turncoat
***ant*** leader

**following** *prep* subsequent to in time or order — see AFTER

**following** *adj* being the one that comes immediately after another — see NEXT

**following** *n* **1** a body of employees or servants who accompany and wait on a person — see CORTEGE 1
**2** a group of people showing intense devotion to a cause, person, or work (as a film) — see CULT 1
**3** the act of going after or in the tracks of another — see PURSUIT

**follow through** *vb* to carry through (as a process) to completion — see PERFORM 1

**folly** *n* **1** a foolish act or idea ⟨the American purchase of Alaska was originally considered a grand *folly*⟩
***syn*** absurdity, asininity, fatuity, foolery, idiocy, imbecility, inanity, insanity, lunacy, stupidity
***rel*** absurdness, craziness, foolishness, madness, senselessness, witlessness; monkeyshine(s), shenanigans, tomfoolery; drivel, humbug, nonsense, twaddle; blunder, bungle, flub, goof, howler
***near ant*** discretion, forethought, prudence, sagacity, wisdom; brainstorm, inspiration
**2** lack of good sense or judgment — see FOOLISHNESS 1
**3** language, behavior, or ideas that are absurd and contrary to good sense — see NONSENSE 1

**foment** *vb* to cause or encourage the development of — see INCITE 1

**fomenter** *n* a person who stirs up public feelings especially of discontent — see AGITATOR

**fond** *adj* **1** having a liking or affection ⟨even lots of city people are *fond* of country music⟩
*syn* attached, inclined, partial
*rel* crazy (about *or* over), enamored, enraptured, gone (on), infatuated, mad (about), nuts (about); desirous, eager, enthusiastic, excited, gung ho, keen
*near ant* apathetic, cool, indifferent, uninterested; contemptuous, disdainful, scornful; antagonistic, antipathetic, hostile; alienated, disaffected, disenchanted, estranged
*ant* allergic, averse, disinclined
**2** feeling or showing love — see LOVING

**fondle** *vb* to touch or handle in a tender or loving manner ⟨a cat who enjoys being *fondled* by his loving owners⟩
*syn* caress, love, pat, pet, stroke
*rel* cuddle, nestle, nose, nuzzle, snuggle; cradle, embrace, enfold, hug; bounce, dandle; knead, massage; baby, coddle, indulge, mollycoddle, pamper, spoil

**fondness** *n* **1** a feeling of strong or constant regard for and dedication to someone — see LOVE 1
**2** positive regard for something — see LIKING

**food** *n* substances intended to be eaten ⟨a simple, little restaurant with excellent *food*⟩
*syn* bread, chow, eatables, edibles, fare, foodstuffs, grub, meat, provender, provisions, table, viands, victuals, vittles
*rel* rations; aliment, nutriment; diet, nurture, sustenance; mess, pap; feed, fodder, forage, slop, swill; feast, meal, refreshments, repast, spread; board; dish, plate, serving
*near ant* poison

**foodstuffs** *n pl* substances intended to be eaten — see FOOD

**fool** *n* **1** a person who lacks good sense or judgment ⟨only a *fool* would attempt to climb that mountain unprepared⟩
*syn* booby, goose, half-wit, jackass, lunatic, nincompoop, ninny, nitwit, nut, simpleton, turkey, yo-yo
*rel* daredevil; madman, madwoman; blockhead, cretin, dodo, dolt, dope, dumbbell, dummy, dunce, idiot, imbecile, moron; featherbrain, scatterbrain; butt, dupe, laughingstock, mockery, monkey; chump, loser, schlemiel
*near ant* sage, thinker; brain, genius
**2** a person formerly kept in a royal or noble household to amuse with jests and pranks ⟨a king's *fool* could get away with saying things that others in the palace couldn't⟩
*syn* jester, motley
*rel* buffoon, clown, comedian, comedienne, comic, cutup, harlequin, zany

*syn* synonym(s) *rel* related words
*ant* antonym(s) *near ant* near antonym(s)

**fool** *vb* **1** to cause to believe what is untrue — see DECEIVE
**2** to make jokes — see JOKE

**fool** (around) *vb* **1** to engage in attention-getting playful or boisterous behavior — see CUT UP
**2** to spend time in aimless activity — see FIDDLE (AROUND)

**fool** (with) *vb* to handle thoughtlessly, ignorantly, or mischievously — see TAMPER

**foolery** *n* **1** a foolish act or idea — see FOLLY 1
**2** wildly playful or mischievous behavior — see HORSEPLAY

**foolhardy** *adj* **1** foolishly adventurous or bold ⟨hikers who were *foolhardy* enough to remain on the summit during a thunderstorm⟩
*syn* brash, daredevil, madcap, overbold, overconfident, reckless
*rel* adventuresome, adventurous, audacious, bold, daring, venturesome, venturous; brave, courageous, dauntless, fearless, intrepid, lionhearted, stouthearted, undaunted, valiant; hotheaded; impetuous, impulsive, rash; brainless, foolish, harebrained, scatterbrained; careless, heedless, thoughtless; hasty, headlong, precipitate
*near ant* unadventurous, unambitious; fainthearted, timid, timorous; calm, cool, levelheaded, sensible; alert, intelligent, quick-witted, sharp
*ant* careful, cautious, heedful, prudent
**2** having or showing a lack of concern for the consequences of one's actions — see RECKLESS 1

**fooling** *adj* marked by or expressive of mild or good-natured teasing — see QUIZZICAL

**foolish** *adj* **1** showing or marked by a lack of good sense or judgment ⟨*foolish* people who thought that the world would end in the year 2000⟩ ⟨a *foolish* scheme that was supposed to make us all rich⟩
*syn* absurd, asinine, balmy, brainless, cockeyed, crazy, cuckoo, daffy, daft, dotty, fatuous, harebrained, half-witted, insane, jerky, kooky, loony (*also* looney), lunatic, mad, nonsensical, nutty, preposterous, sappy, screwball, senseless, silly, simpleminded, stupid, unwise, wacky, weak-minded, witless, zany
*rel* dumb, idiotic, imbecilic, moronic; fallacious, illogical, invalid, irrational, unreasonable; farcical, laughable, ludicrous, ridiculous
*near ant* brainy, bright, clever, intelligent, smart; logical, rational, reasonable, valid
*ant* judicious, prudent, sage, sane, sapient, sensible, sound, wise
**2** conceived or made without regard for reason or reality — see FANTASTIC 1

**foolishness** *n* **1** lack of good sense or judgment ⟨the *foolishness* of going off to search for the fountain of youth⟩
*syn* absurdity, asininity, balminess, brainlessness, craziness, daftness, fatuity, folly, inanity, insanity, lunacy, madness, non-

sensicalness, nuttiness, preposterousness, senselessness, silliness, simplicity, wackiness, witlessness, zaniness
*rel* idiocy, imbecility, stupidity; fallacy, irrationality, unreasonableness; laughableness, ludicrousness, ridiculousness
*near ant* logicalness, rationality, reasonableness, validity
*ant* prudence, sageness, sanity, sapience, sensibleness, soundness, wisdom
**2** language, behavior, or ideas that are absurd and contrary to good sense — see NONSENSE 1
**3** the quality or state of lacking intelligence or quickness of mind — see STUPIDITY 1

**foot** *n* the lowest part, place, or point — see BOTTOM 3

**foot** *vb* to give what is owed for — see PAY 2

**foot** (it) *vb* **1** to go on foot — see WALK
**2** to perform a series of usually rhythmic bodily movements to music — see DANCE 1

**foot** (up) *vb* to combine (numbers) into a single sum — see ADD 2

**foothold** *n* a place from which an advance (as for military operations) is made — see BASE 2

**footing** *n* **1** an immaterial thing upon which something else rests — see BASE 1
**2** position with regard to conditions and circumstances — see SITUATION 1
**3** the placement of someone or something in relation to others in a vertical arrangement — see RANK 1

**footloose** *adj* **1** not bound, confined, or detained by force — see FREE 3
**2** not held back by rules, duties, or worries — see FREEWHEELING

**footpath** *n* a rough course or way formed by or as if by repeated footsteps — see TRAIL 1

**footprint** *n* the mark or impression made by a foot ⟨mysterious *footprints* along the beach⟩
*syn* footstep, step
*rel* hoofprint; spoor, track; sign, trace, vestige

**footstep** *n* the mark or impression made by a foot — see FOOTPRINT

**foozle** *vb* to make or do (something) in a clumsy or unskillful way — see BOTCH

**fop** *n* a man extremely interested in his clothing and personal appearance — see DANDY 1

**for** *conj* for the reason that — see SINCE

**forage** *vb* to feed on grass or herbs — see [1]GRAZE

**forage** (for) *vb* to go in search of — see SEEK 1

**foray** *n* a sudden attack on and entrance into hostile territory — see RAID 1

**foray** (into) *vb* to enter for conquest or plunder — see INVADE

**forbear** *vb* to resist the temptation of ⟨she's old enough to make her own decisions, so we must *forbear* criticizing her taste in clothes⟩
*syn* abstain (from), forgo (*also* forego), keep (from), refrain (from)
*rel* avoid, eschew, shun; check, constrain, curb, inhibit; deny, refuse, withhold; buck, combat, fight
*near ant* capitulate, knuckle under, submit, surrender
*ant* give in (to), succumb (to), yield (to)

**forbearance** *n* the capacity to endure what is difficult or disagreeable without complaining — see PATIENCE

**forbearing** *adj* accepting pains or hardships calmly or without complaint — see PATIENT 1

**forbid** *vb* to order not to do or use or to be done or used ⟨smoking is *forbidden* throughout the building⟩ ⟨we *forbid* you to see him⟩
*syn* ban, bar, enjoin, interdict, outlaw, prohibit, proscribe
*rel* deter, discourage, dissuade; repress, suppress; halt, preclude, prevent, stop; embargo, exclude, rule out, shut out; debar, deprive, disallow, reject, veto; check, curb, inhibit, restrain; block, hinder, impede, obstruct
*near ant* approve, endorse (*also* indorse), sanction; authorize, license (*also* licence); abet, encourage, promote, support; bid, command, order; abide, bear, endure, tolerate
*ant* allow, let, permit, suffer

**forbidden** *adj* that may not be permitted — see IMPERMISSIBLE

**forbidding** *adj* **1** causing fear — see FEARFUL 1
**2** harsh and threatening in manner or appearance — see GRIM 1

**forbidding** *n* the act of ordering that something not be done or used — see PROHIBITION 1

**force** *n* **1** a body of persons at work or available for work ⟨the nation's labor *force*⟩
*syn* help, manpower, personnel, pool, staff
*rel* labor, proletariat, rank and file; hand, company, crew, gang, outfit, party, team; employee, helper, hireling, worker
**2** the use of power to impose one's will on another ⟨a cruel tyrant who disbanded the parliament and ruled by *force*⟩
*syn* coercion, compulsion, constraint, duress, pressure
*rel* browbeating, bulldozing, bullying; fear, intimidation, menace, sword, terror, terrorism, threat, violence; might, muscle, strength; hardheadedness, self-will, willfulness; strain, stress
*near ant* agreement, approval, consent, permission; persuasion, reason
**3** the ability to exert effort for the accomplishment of a task — see POWER 2
**4** the capacity to persuade — see COGENCY 1
**5** the quality of an utterance that provokes interest and produces an effect — see [1]PUNCH 1
**6** the use of brute strength to cause harm to a person or property — see VIOLENCE

**force** *vb* to cause (a person) to give in to pressure ⟨*forced* the natives to sell their land⟩ ⟨hunger *forced* the refugees to steal⟩
***syn*** coerce, compel, constrain, drive, make, muscle, obligate, oblige, press, pressure
***rel*** browbeat, bulldoze, bully; high-pressure, intimidate, menace, terrorize, threaten
***near ant*** allow, let, permit; convince, induce, persuade

**forced** *adj* **1** forcing one's compliance or participation by or as if by law — see MANDATORY
**2** lacking in natural or spontaneous quality — see ARTIFICIAL 1
**3** not made or done willingly or by choice — see INVOLUNTARY 1

**forceful** *adj* **1** having the power to persuade — see COGENT
**2** marked by or uttered with forcefulness — see EMPHATIC 1
**3** not showing weakness or uncertainty — see FIRM 1
**4** having power over the minds or behavior of others — see INFLUENTIAL 1

**forcefully** *adv* in a vigorous and forceful manner — see HARD 3

**forcefulness** *n* **1** the capacity to persuade — see COGENCY 1
**2** the quality of an utterance that provokes interest and produces an effect — see [1]PUNCH 1
**3** the quality or state of being forceful (as in expression) — see VEHEMENCE 1

**forcibly** *adv* in a vigorous and forceful manner — see HARD 3

**ford** *n* a place where a body of water (as a sea or river) is shallow — see SHOAL

**forearm** *vb* to prepare (oneself) mentally or emotionally — see FORTIFY 1

**forebear** *also* **forbear** *n* a person who is several generations earlier in an individual's line of descent — see ANCESTOR 1

**forebode** *also* **forbode** *vb* to show signs of a favorable or successful outcome — see BODE

**foreboding** *adj* being or showing a sign of evil or calamity to come — see OMINOUS

**foreboding** *n* **1** a feeling that something bad will happen — see PREMONITION
**2** something believed to be a sign or warning of a future event — see OMEN
**3** suspicion or fear of future harm or misfortune — see APPREHENSION 1

**forecast** *n* a declaration that something will happen in the future — see PREDICTION

**forecast** *vb* to tell of or describe beforehand — see FORETELL

**forecaster** *n* one who predicts future events or developments — see PROPHET

**forecasting** *n* a declaration that something will happen in the future — see PREDICTION

**foredoom** *vb* to determine the fate of in advance — see DESTINE

**forefather** *n* a person who is several generations earlier in an individual's line of descent — see ANCESTOR 1

**forefront** *n* the leading or most important part of a movement ⟨a politician who was in the *forefront* of women's rights⟩
***syn*** vanguard
***rel*** spearhead
***near ant*** rank and file

**forego** *vb* to go or come before in time — see PRECEDE

**foregoer** *n* **1** one that announces or indicates the later arrival of another — see FORERUNNER 1
**2** something belonging to an earlier time from which something else was later developed — see ANCESTOR 2

**foregoing** *adj* going before another in time or order — see PREVIOUS

**forehanded** *adj* having or showing awareness of and preparation for the future — see FORESIGHTED

**foreign** *adj* **1** being, relating to, or characteristic of a country other than one's own ⟨more Americans should take an interest in *foreign* languages⟩
***syn*** alien, nonnative
***rel*** imported, introduced, naturalized, transplanted; international, multicultural, multinational; distant, far-off, overseas, remote; bizarre, exotic, outlandish, strange
***near ant*** endemic, local; aboriginal, indigenous
***ant*** domestic, native
**2** not being a vital part of or belonging to something — see EXTRINSIC

**foreigner** *n* a person who is not native to or known to a community — see STRANGER

**foreknow** *vb* to realize or know about beforehand — see FORESEE

**foreknowledge** *n* the special ability to see or know about events before they actually occur — see FORESIGHT 1

**foreman** *n* the person (as an employer or supervisor) who tells people and especially workers what to do — see BOSS

**foremost** *adj* **1** coming before all others in importance ⟨Albert Einstein is regarded by many as the *foremost* figure of the 20th century⟩
***syn*** arch, cardinal, central, chief, dominant, first, grand, greatest, highest, key, leading, main, paramount, predominant, preeminent, premier, primary, principal, sovereign, supreme
***rel*** distinguished, eminent, notable, noteworthy, illustrious, outstanding, prestigious, stellar, superior; important, major, momentous, significant; incomparable, matchless, unequaled (*or* unequalled), unparalleled, unsurpassed
***near ant*** inconsequential, insignificant, minor, trivial, unimportant; collateral, inferior, secondary, subordinate, subsidiary
***ant*** last, least

2 highest in rank or authority — see HEAD

**forename** *n* a name that is placed before one's family name ⟨a long string of *forenames* was given to the latest addition to the royal family⟩
*syn* Christian name, given name
*rel* appellation, denomination, designation; epithet, handle, nickname, sobriquet (*also* soubriquet); alias, nom de plume, pen name, pseudonym

**forenoon** *n* the time from sunrise until noon — see MORNING 1

**foreordain** *vb* to determine the fate of in advance — see DESTINE

**forepart** *n* a forward part or surface — see FRONT 1

**forerunner** *n* 1 one that announces or indicates the later arrival of another ⟨the return of the swallows is traditionally regarded as a *forerunner* of spring⟩
*syn* angel, foregoer, harbinger, herald, precursor
*rel* foreboder, foreshadower, foretaste, forewarning; advertiser, announcer, crier, proclaimer; courier, messenger, runner; augury, omen, portent, presage; mark, sign, symptom; bellwether
2 something belonging to an earlier time from which something else was later developed — see ANCESTOR 2

**foresee** *vb* to realize or know about beforehand ⟨a freak accident that no one could possibly have *foreseen*⟩
*syn* anticipate, divine, foreknow
*rel* augur, forecast, foretell, presage, prognosticate, prophesy; envisage, foreshadow, prefigure, visualize; forewarn; preview; descry, discern, perceive; apprehend, dread, fear

**foreseeing** *adj* having or showing awareness of and preparation for the future — see FORESIGHTED

**foreseer** *n* one who predicts future events or developments — see PROPHET

**foreshadow** *vb* to give a slight indication of beforehand ⟨a series of small tremors that *foreshadowed* the massive earthquake the next day⟩
*syn* prefigure
*rel* anticipate, foreknow, foresee; forecast, foretell, predict, prognosticate, prophesy; forewarn; augur, bode, forebode (*also* forbode), portend, presage, promise; connote, hint, imply, insinuate, intimate, suggest

**foreshadowing** *n* something believed to be a sign or warning of a future event — see OMEN

**foresight** *n* 1 the special ability to see or know about events before they actually occur ⟨a mysterious woman who claims to have the gift of *foresight*⟩
*syn* foreknowledge, prescience
*rel* premonition, presentiment; clairvoyance, extrasensory perception, sixth sense; omniscience; divination
2 concern or preparation for the future ⟨had the *foresight* to realize the global importance of the Internet⟩
*syn* farsightedness, foresightedness, forethought, prescience, providence
*rel* precaution, premeditation; discretion, insight, prudence, sagacity, wisdom
*near ant* hindsight
*ant* improvidence, shortsightedness

**foresighted** *adj* having or showing awareness of and preparation for the future ⟨the *foresighted* conservationists who worked to create the national park system⟩
*syn* farsighted, forehanded, foreseeing, forethoughtful, prescient, provident
*rel* careful, cautious; insightful, perceptive, prudent, sage, wise
*near ant* careless, heedless, incautious
*ant* improvident, shortsighted

**foresightedness** *n* concern or preparation for the future — see FORESIGHT 2

**forest** *n* a dense growth of trees and shrubs covering a large area ⟨the endless *forest* that the first European settlers encountered⟩
*syn* timber, timberland, wood(s), woodland
*rel* coppice, copse, grove, scrubland, stand, thicket; greenwood, wildwood; woodlot

**forestall** *vb* to keep from happening by taking action in advance — see PREVENT

**forestallment** *n* the act or practice of keeping something from happening — see PREVENTION

**foretell** *vb* to tell of or describe beforehand ⟨a 16th century astrologer who, some claim, accurately *foretold* 20th century events⟩
*syn* augur, forecast, predict, presage, prognosticate, prophesy
*rel* forewarn; bode, forebode (*also* forbode), portend; anticipate, divine, foreknow, foresee; announce, declare, proclaim
*near ant* recount, relate, report

**foreteller** *n* one who predicts future events or developments — see PROPHET

**foretelling** *n* a declaration that something will happen in the future — see PREDICTION

**forethought** *n* concern or preparation for the future — see FORESIGHT 2

**forethoughtful** *adj* having or showing awareness of and preparation for the future — see FORESIGHTED

**forever** *adv* 1 for all time — see EVER 1
2 on every relevant occasion — see ALWAYS 1

**forevermore** *adv* for all time — see EVER 1

**forewarn** *vb* to give notice to beforehand especially of danger or risk — see WARN

**forewarning** *n* the act or an instance of telling beforehand of danger or risk — see WARNING 1

**foreword** *n* a short section (as of a book) that leads to or explains the main part — see INTRODUCTION

**forfeit** *n* a sum of money to be paid as a punishment — see FINE

**forfeiture** *n* a sum of money to be paid as a punishment — see FINE

**forgather** *or* **foregather** *vb* to come together into one body or place — see ASSEMBLE 1

[1]**forge** *vb* **1** to imitate or copy especially in order to deceive — see FAKE 1
**2** to produce or bring about especially by long or repeated effort — see HAMMER (OUT)
**3** to shape with a hammer — see HAMMER 1

[2]**forge** *vb* to move forward along a course — see GO 1

**forged** *adj* being such in appearance only and made or manufactured with the intention of committing fraud — see COUNTERFEIT

**forgery** *n* an imitation that is passed off as genuine — see FAKE 1

**forget** *vb* **1** to be unable to recall or think of ⟨I *forget* exactly on which street that the house is⟩
***syn*** unlearn
***rel*** lose, miss; blank; disregard, ignore, neglect, overlook
***near ant*** reminisce; remind
***ant*** mind [*chiefly dialect*], recall, recollect, remember
**2** to fail to give proper attention to — see NEGLECT 1
**3** to leave undone or unattended to especially through carelessness — see NEGLECT 2
**4** to miss the opportunity or obligation — see NEGLECT 3

**forgetful** *adj* inclined to forget what one has learned or to do what one should ⟨we become more *forgetful* as we get older⟩
***syn*** absentminded
***rel*** absent, abstracted, lost, oblivious, preoccupied, unmindful; amnesiac, senile; lax, neglectful, negligent, remiss, slack; careless, heedless, inconsiderate, thoughtless
***near ant*** alert, keen, sharp; careful, conscientious, heedful, thoughtful
***ant*** retentive

**forgetfulness** *n* a state of being disregardful or unconscious of one's surroundings, concerns, or obligations — see OBLIVION

**forgivable** *adj* worthy of forgiveness — see VENIAL

**forgive** *vb* **1** to cease to have feelings of anger or bitterness toward ⟨it is not easy to *forgive* those who have hurt us⟩
***syn*** pardon
***rel*** absolve, acquit, clear, exculpate, exonerate, vindicate; remit, shrive; condone, disregard, excuse, ignore, pass over, shrug off
***near ant*** smart; despise, detest, dislike, hate, loathe; avenge, redress, revenge
***ant*** resent
**2** to overlook or dismiss as of little importance — see EXCUSE 1

**forgiveness** *n* release from the guilt or penalty of an offense — see PARDON

***syn*** synonym(s) ***rel*** related words
***ant*** antonym(s) ***near ant*** near antonym(s)

**forgo** *also* **forego** *vb* to resist the temptation of — see FORBEAR

**forgotten** *adj* left unoccupied or unused — see ABANDONED

**fork** *vb* to go or move in different directions from a central point — see SEPARATE 2

**forlorn** *adj* **1** feeling unhappiness — see SAD 1
**2** sad from lack of companionship or separation from others — see LONESOME 1

**forlornness** *n* **1** a state or spell of low spirits — see SADNESS
**2** utter loss of hope — see DESPAIR 1

**form** *n* **1** the outward appearance of something as distinguished from its substance ⟨carved the block of wood into the *form* of a duck⟩
***syn*** cast, configuration, conformation, figure, geometry, shape
***rel*** contour, outline, profile, silhouette; framework, skeleton, situation; arrangement, layout, organization, pattern, plan, setup
***near ant*** composition, material, matter, stuff, substance
**2** a piece of paper with information written or to be written on it ⟨I filled out all the *forms* for applying to the school⟩
***syn*** blank, document, paper
***rel*** instrument, writ
**3** personal conduct or behavior as evaluated by an accepted standard of appropriateness for a social or professional setting — see MANNER 1
**4** a state of being or fitness — see CONDITION 1
**5** a three-dimensional representation of the human body used especially for displaying clothes — see MANNEQUIN 1
**6** an oft-repeated action or series of actions performed in accordance with tradition or a set of rules — see RITE
**7** socially acceptable behavior — see DECENCY 1
**8** the means or procedure for doing something — see METHOD
**9** the type of body that a person has — see PHYSIQUE
**10** the way in which the elements of something (as a work of art) are arranged — see COMPOSITION 3

**form** *vb* **1** to take on a definite form ⟨my ideas on the subject are just starting to *form*⟩
***syn*** crystallize, jell, shape (up), solidify
***rel*** coalesce, cohere, fuse; combine, connect, join, unite
***near ant*** break down, decompose, disintegrate
**2** to be all the substance of — see CONSTITUTE 1
**3** to bring into being by combining, shaping, or transforming materials — see MAKE 1
**4** to come into existence — see BEGIN 2
**5** to come to have gradually — see DEVELOP 2

**formal** *adj* **1** following or agreeing with established form, custom, or rules ⟨a *formal*

meeting of the school board⟩ ⟨a *formal* contract that was legally binding⟩
***syn*** ceremonial, ceremonious, conventional, orthodox, regular, routine
***rel*** authorized, certified, official; accepted, correct, decorous, proper; formalistic, ritual, ritualistic; methodical, orderly, systematic
***near ant*** unauthorized, unofficial; improper, incorrect, indecorous
***ant*** informal, irregular, unceremonious, unconventional, unorthodox
**2** being something in name or form only — see NOMINAL 1
**3** marked by or showing careful attention to set forms and details — see CEREMONIOUS 1
**4** relating to or suitable for wearing to an event requiring elegant dress and manners — see DRESS
**5** very dignified in form, tone, or style — see ELEVATED 2

**formal** *n* a social gathering for dancing — see DANCE

**formality** *n* **1** an act or utterance that is a customary show of good manners — see CIVILITY 1
**2** an oft-repeated action or series of actions performed in accordance with tradition or a set of rules — see RITE

**formalize** *vb* to make agree with a single established standard or model — see STANDARDIZE

**format** *n* **1** the way in which something is sized, arranged, or organized ⟨the book's *format* is very user-friendly⟩
***syn*** arrangement, configuration, conformation, formation, layout, setup
***rel*** design, plan, scheme; composition, constitution, makeup; build, construction, structure
**2** the way in which the elements of something (as a work of art) are arranged — see COMPOSITION 3

**formation** *n* the way in which something is sized, arranged, or organized — see FORMAT 1

**formative** *adj* having a role in deciding something's final form ⟨a teacher who was a *formative* influence on generations of students⟩
***syn*** constructive, productive
***rel*** causal, creative; consequential, influential
***ant*** nonconstructive, nonproductive, unproductive

**former** *adj* having been such at some previous time ⟨the coach is a *former* professional baseball player⟩
***syn*** erstwhile, late, old, onetime, past, sometime, whilom
***rel*** bygone, dead, extinct
***near ant*** contemporary, current, present; future, prospective

**formidable** *adj* **1** causing fear — see FEARFUL 1
**2** requiring considerable physical or mental effort — see HARD 2

**formless** *adj* having no definite or recognizable form ⟨a *formless* mass of clay that the potter transformed into an attractive bowl⟩
***syn*** amorphous, shapeless, unformed, unshaped, unstructured
***rel*** characterless, featureless, nondescript; chaotic, disorganized, incoherent, unordered, unorganized; fuzzy, hazy, indeterminate, indistinct, obscure, unclear, vague
***near ant*** coherent, ordered, organized; clear, definite, distinct
***ant*** formed, shaped, structured

**formulaic** *adj* using or marked by the use of something else as a basis or model — see IMITATIVE

**formulate** *vb* **1** to convey in appropriate or telling terms — see PHRASE
**2** to put (something) into proper and usually carefully worked out written form — see COMPOSE 1

**formulation** *n* an act, process, or means of putting something into words — see EXPRESSION 1

**formulator** *n* one who creates or introduces something new — see INVENTOR

**forsake** *vb* to cause to remain behind — see LEAVE 1

**forsaken** *adj* left unoccupied or unused — see ABANDONED

**forsaking** *n* the act of abandoning — see DERELICTION 1

**forsooth** *adv* **1** to tell the truth — see ACTUALLY 1
**2** without any question — see INDEED 1

**fort** *n* a structure or place from which one can resist attack ⟨a series of *forts* along the frontier⟩
***syn*** bastion, citadel, fastness, fortification, fortress, hold, stronghold
***rel*** breastwork, bulwark, parapet, rampart; bunker, dugout

**forte** *n* something for which a person shows a special talent ⟨doing funny impressions of people has always been my *forte*⟩
***syn*** speciality, specialty
***rel*** area, demesne, department, discipline, domain, field, line, province, realm, sphere; element; aptness, bent, faculty, flair, genius, gift, knack, talent

**forth** *adv* **1** toward a point ahead in space or time — see ONWARD 1
**2** toward or at a point lying in advance in space or time — see ALONG

**forthcoming** *adj* being soon to appear or take place ⟨everyone's excited about the *forthcoming* school vacation⟩
***syn*** approaching, coming, imminent, impending, nearing, oncoming, pending, upcoming
***rel*** future; anticipated, awaited, expected, foreseen, predicted
***near ant*** bygone, former, past
***ant*** late, recent

**forthright** *adj* **1** free in expressing one's true feelings and opinions — see FRANK
**2** going straight to the point clearly and firmly — see STRAIGHTFORWARD 1

**forthrightly** *adv* in an honest and direct manner — see STRAIGHTFORWARD

**forthrightness** *n* the free expression of one's true feelings and opinions — see CANDOR

**forthwith** *adv* without delay — see IMMEDIATELY

**fortification** *n* a structure or place from which one can resist attack — see FORT

**fortify** *vb* **1** to prepare (oneself) mentally or emotionally ⟨Kelly *fortified* herself for the basketball tournament with a series of confidence-boosting exercises⟩
*syn* brace, forearm, nerve, ready, steel, strengthen
*rel* harden, inure, season, toughen; bolster, boost, buoy (up), buttress, prop (up), reinforce, support, sustain; embolden, encourage, hearten; rally, rouse, stir
*near ant* demoralize, discourage, dishearten, unnerve; debilitate, enfeeble, undermine, weaken
**2** to increase the ability of (as a muscle) to exert physical force — see STRENGTHEN 1
**3** to make able to withstand physical hardship, strain, or exposure — see HARDEN 2

**fortitude** *n* the strength of mind that enables a person to endure pain or hardship ⟨it was only with the greatest *fortitude* that the Pilgrims were able to survive their first winter in Plymouth⟩
*syn* backbone, fiber, grit, guts, pluck, spunk
*rel* determination, purposefulness, resoluteness, resolution; bravery, courage, fearlessness, intrepidity; endurance, stamina, tolerance; heart, mettle, spirit; audacity, boldness, brass, cheek, chutzpah (*also* chutzpa *or* hutzpah *or* hutzpa), effrontery, hardihood, nerve, temerity
*near ant* indecisiveness, irresoluteness, irresolution, vacillation; cowardliness, cravenness, faintheartedness, timidity, timorousness
*ant* spinelessness

**fortress** *n* a structure or place from which one can resist attack — see FORT

**fortuitous** *adj* **1** coming or happening by good luck especially unexpectedly — see FORTUNATE 1
**2** happening by chance — see ACCIDENTAL

**fortunate** *adj* **1** coming or happening by good luck especially unexpectedly ⟨in a *fortunate* turn of events, the motel had one last vacancy⟩
*syn* fluky, fortuitous, happy, lucky, providential
*rel* convenient, opportune, seasonable, timely; unexpected, unforeseen, unlooked-for; accidental, chance, coincidental; auspicious, bright, fair, promising, propitious; benign, favorable, golden, good; advantageous, beneficial, profitable
*near ant* inconvenient, inopportune, unseasonable, untimely; anticipated, expected, foreseen; deliberate, intentional, planned; inauspicious, unpromising
*ant* luckless, unfortunate, unhappy, unlucky
**2** having good luck — see LUCKY 1

**fortunateness** *n* success that is partly the result of chance — see LUCK 1

**fortune** *n* **1** what is going to happen to someone in the time ahead ⟨the telephone psychic proceeded to tell me my *fortune*—at great length⟩
*syn* future
*rel* circumstance, destiny, doom, lot, portion; futurities, outlook, prospect
*near ant* present
*ant* past
**2** a very large amount of money ⟨the billionaire's huge mansion must have cost a *fortune*⟩
*syn* king's ransom, mint, wad
*rel* heap, pile, pot; bonanza, mine, treasure trove; assets, property, riches, wealth
*ant* mite, pittance
**3** a state or end that seemingly has been decided beforehand — see FATE 1
**4** success that is partly the result of chance — see LUCK 1
**5** the total of one's money and property — see WEALTH 1

**fortune–teller** *n* one who predicts future events or developments — see PROPHET

**forty winks** *n pl* a short sleep — see [1]NAP

**forum** *n* a meeting featuring a group discussion ⟨a public *forum* called to find out how residents felt about a large high school being built in their neighborhood⟩
*syn* colloquy, conference, council, panel, parley, powwow, roundtable, seminar, symposium
*rel* caucus, town meeting; assembly, conclave, congregation, congress, convention, convocation, synod; debate, deliberation; brainstorming

**forward** *adv* **1** toward or at a point lying in advance in space or time — see ALONG
**2** toward a point ahead in space or time — see ONWARD 1

**forward** *adj* showing a lack of proper social reserve or modesty — see PRESUMPTUOUS 1

**forward** *vb* to help the growth or development of — see FOSTER 1

**fossil** *n* a person with old-fashioned ideas — see FOGY

**foster** *vb* **1** to help the growth or development of ⟨the head librarian firmly declared that it is indeed the duty of local government to *foster* learning and a love of reading⟩
*syn* advance, cultivate, encourage, forward, further, nourish, nurture, promote
*rel* back, champion, support, uphold; endow, finance, fund, patronize, subsidize; abet, aid, assist; advertise, boost, plug, publicize, tout; agitate (for), campaign (for), work (for)
*near ant* forbid, prevent, prohibit; battle, combat, counter, fight, oppose; repress, stifle, suppress; arrest, check, halt, retard
*ant* discourage, frustrate, hinder, inhibit

---

*syn* synonym(s) *rel* related words
*ant* antonym(s) *near ant* near antonym(s)

2 to bring to maturity through care and education — see BRING UP 1

**foul** *adj* 1 marked by wet and windy conditions ⟨the *foul* weather brought out the windbreakers and rain slickers as everyone braced for a day of rough sailing⟩
*syn* bleak, dirty, inclement, nasty, raw, rough, squally, stormy, tempestuous, turbulent
*rel* blustering, blustery, breezy, gusty, windblown, windswept; cloudy, overcast, sunless; rainy, snowy; foggy, hazy, misty
*near ant* clear, cloudless, rainless, sunny; balmy, calm, halcyon, peaceful, placid
*ant* clement, fair
2 not being in accordance with the rules or standards of what is fair in sport ⟨an aggressive hockey player who is known for his *foul* play and readiness for a fight⟩
*syn* dirty, illegal, unfair, unsportsmanlike
*rel* dishonorable, shabby, shameful; ignoble, low, mean, ungentlemanly; immoral, unethical, unjust, unprincipled, unrighteous, unscrupulous
*near ant* just, law-abiding; ethical, moral, principled, righteous; honorable, irreproachable, unimpeachable
*ant* clean, fair, legal, sportsmanlike, sportsmanly
3 causing intense displeasure, disgust, or resentment — see OFFENSIVE 1
4 depicting or referring to sexual matters in a way that is unacceptable in polite society — see OBSCENE 1
5 having an unpleasant smell — see MALODOROUS
6 not clean — see DIRTY 1

**foul** *vb* 1 to make dirty — see DIRTY
2 to make unfit for use by the addition of something harmful or undesirable — see CONTAMINATE

**foulness** *n* 1 the quality or state of being obscene — see OBSCENITY 1
2 the state or quality of being dirty — see DIRTINESS 1

**foul play** *n* 1 the intentional and unlawful taking of another person's life — see HOMICIDE
2 the use of brute strength to cause harm to a person or property — see VIOLENCE

**foul–up** *n* an instance of confusion ⟨there was a *foul-up* with our mail order and not one item arrived as ordered⟩
*syn* mix-up
*rel* bobble, botch, bungle, fumble; blunder, error, flub, goof, mistake, slipup; chaos, confusion, disarrangement, disarray, disorder, hash, jumble, mess, muddle, shambles

**foul up** *vb* to make or do (something) in a clumsy or unskillful way — see BOTCH

**found** *vb* to be responsible for the creation and early operation or use of ⟨John Harvard did not actually *found* the university that now bears his name⟩
*syn* constitute, establish, inaugurate, initiate, innovate, institute, introduce, launch, pioneer, set up, start
*rel* author, father, originate; create, invent, produce; construct, erect, put up; develop, enlarge, expand; endow, finance, fund, subsidize; arrange, organize, systematize
*near ant* abolish, annihilate, annul, nullify; end, finish, stop, terminate
*ant* close (down), phase out, shut (up)

**foundation** *n* 1 a public organization with a particular purpose or function — see INSTITUTION 1
2 an immaterial thing upon which something else rests — see BASE 1

**founder** *n* a person who establishes a whole new field of endeavor — see FATHER 2

**foursquare** *adj* 1 free in expressing one's true feelings and opinions — see FRANK
2 going straight to the point clearly and firmly — see STRAIGHTFORWARD 1

**foursquare** *adv* in an honest and direct manner — see STRAIGHTFORWARD

**fox** *vb* to get the better of through cleverness — see OUTWIT

**foxiness** *n* 1 skill in achieving one's ends through indirect, subtle, or underhanded means — see CUNNING 1
2 the inclination or practice of misleading others through lies or trickery — see DECEIT

**foxy** *adj* clever at attaining one's ends by indirect and often deceptive means — see ARTFUL 1

**foyer** *n* 1 a centrally located room in a building that serves as a gathering or waiting area or as a passageway into the interior ⟨theatergoers crowded the *foyer* during the play's intermission⟩
*syn* hall, lobby
*rel* entry, entryway, hallway, vestibule; concourse, corridor, gallery, passageway; antechamber, anteroom, waiting room
2 the entrance room of a building — see HALL 1

**fracas** *n* 1 a physical dispute between opposing individuals or groups — see FIGHT 1
2 a rough and often noisy fight usually involving several people — see BRAWL 1

**fractionation** *n* the act or process of a whole separating into two or more parts or pieces — see SEPARATION 1

**fracture** *vb* to cause to separate into pieces usually suddenly or forcibly — see BREAK 1

**fragile** *adj* 1 easily broken ⟨attaching the beautiful but *fragile* ornaments to the Christmas tree is always a touchy operation⟩
*syn* breakable, delicate, frail
*rel* dainty, fine, gossamer; flimsy, slight, tenuous; brittle, crisp, crumbly, flaky, friable, short; feeble, infirm, weak; inelastic, inflexible, stiff
*near ant* firm, solid, substantial; elastic, flexible, resilient
*ant* nonbreakable, strong, sturdy, tough, unbreakable
2 easily injured without careful handling — see TENDER 1

**fragility** *n* the state or quality of having a delicate structure — see DELICACY 2

**fragment** *n* a broken or irregular part of something that often remains incomplete ⟨charred *fragments* of the exploded rocket were scattered over a huge area of ground⟩
*syn* bit, piece, scrap
*rel* shred, tatter; end, leftover, remainder, remnant; part, portion, section, segment
**fragment** *vb* to cause to separate into pieces usually suddenly or forcibly — see BREAK 1
**fragmental** *adj* lacking some necessary part — see INCOMPLETE
**fragmentary** *adj* lacking some necessary part — see INCOMPLETE
**fragrance** *n* a sweet or pleasant smell ⟨the *fragrance* of lilac trees in full bloom⟩
*syn* aroma, bouquet, incense, perfume, redolence, scent, spice
*rel* odor
*ant* reek, stench, stink
**fragrant** *adj* having a pleasant smell ⟨the balsam fir is a favorite as a Christmas tree because it is so *fragrant*⟩
*syn* ambrosial, aromatic, perfumed, redolent, savory, scented, sweet
*rel* flowery, fruity, pungent, spicy; odoriferous, odorous; clean, fresh, pure
*near ant* odorless, unscented; fusty, musty, stale; gamy (*or* gamey)
*ant* fetid, foul, malodorous, noisome, putrid, rancid, rank, reeking, reeky, smelly, stinking, stinky, strong
**frail** *adj* 1 easily broken — see FRAGILE 1
2 easily injured without careful handling — see TENDER 1
3 lacking bodily strength — see WEAK 1
4 lacking strength of will or character — see WEAK 2
**frailness** *n* 1 the quality or state of lacking physical strength or vigor — see WEAKNESS 1
2 the quality or state of lacking strength of will or character — see WEAKNESS 2
**frailty** *n* 1 a defect in character — see FAULT 1
2 the quality or state of lacking physical strength or vigor — see WEAKNESS 1
3 the quality or state of lacking strength of will or character — see WEAKNESS 2
**frame** *n* 1 the arrangement of parts that gives something its basic form ⟨now that the *frame* has been built, we have a better idea of the size of our new house⟩
*syn* configuration, framework, shell, skeleton, structure
*rel* lattice, network; contour, figure, outline, profile, shape, silhouette; chassis
2 a state of mind dominated by a particular emotion — see MOOD 1
3 the type of body that a person has — see PHYSIQUE
**frame** *vb* 1 to bring into being by combining, shaping, or transforming materials — see MAKE 1
2 to plan out usually with subtle skill or care — see ENGINEER
3 to put (something) into proper and usually carefully worked out written form — see COMPOSE 1
4 to work out the details of (something) in advance — see PLAN 1
**framework** *n* the arrangement of parts that gives something its basic form — see FRAME 1
**franchise** *n* the right to formally express one's position or will in an election — see VOTE 1
**frank** *adj* free in expressing one's true feelings and opinions ⟨our ballet teacher is very *frank* about telling her students whether she thinks they have the talent for a career in dance⟩
*syn* candid, direct, forthright, foursquare, free-spoken, honest, open, openhearted, outspoken, plain, plainspoken, straight, straightforward, unguarded, unreserved
*rel* artless, earnest, sincere; outgoing, uninhibited, unrestrained; vocal, vociferous; abrupt, bluff, blunt, brusque, curt, gruff, sharp; impolite, inconsiderate, rude, tactless, undiplomatic, unsubtle
*near ant* inhibited, reserved, restrained; close-mouthed, reticent, tight-lipped; ambiguous, circuitous, equivocal, evasive; diplomatic, politic, tactful; civil, considerate, courteous, polite
*ant* dissembling
**frankly** *adv* to tell the truth — see ACTUALLY 1
**frankness** *n* the free expression of one's true feelings and opinions — see CANDOR
**frantic** *adj* 1 feeling overwhelming fear or worry ⟨the *frantic* parents were searching all over the fairgrounds for their lost child⟩
*syn* agitated, delirious, distraught, frenzied, hysterical
*rel* alarmed, anxious, disquieted, disturbed, troubled, upset, worried, wrought (up); berserk, crazed, demented, deranged, mad, maniacal (*also* maniac); raging, ranting, raving
*near ant* calm, peaceful, serene, tranquil; cool, coolheaded, undisturbed, unperturbed, untroubled
*ant* collected, composed, self-possessed
2 marked by great and often stressful excitement or activity — see FURIOUS 1
**frantically** *adv* in a confused and reckless manner — see HELTER-SKELTER 1
**fraternal** *adj* of, relating to, or befitting brothers ⟨there was a *fraternal* bond between the two boys all throughout their school years⟩
*syn* brotherly
*rel* familial, sisterly; chummy, friendly, neighborly
**fraternity** *n* 1 a group of persons formally joined together for some common interest — see ASSOCIATION 2
2 the body of people in a profession or field of activity — see CORPS
**fraternize** *vb* 1 to come or be together as friends — see ASSOCIATE 1

2 to take part in social activities — see SOCIALIZE

**fraud** *n* one who makes false claims of identity or expertise — see IMPOSTOR

**fraudulent** *adj* 1 marked by, based on, or done by the use of dishonest methods to acquire something of value ⟨hoping to get millions from the insurance company, the man made the *fraudulent* claim that he had been seriously injured in the accident⟩
*syn* crooked, deceitful, defrauding, dishonest, double-dealing, false
*rel* deceptive, misleading, specious
*near ant* legitimate, true, valid
*ant* aboveboard, honest, truthful
2 given to or marked by cheating and deception — see DISHONEST 2

**fraught** *adj* possessing or covered with great numbers or amounts of something specified — see RIFE

**fray** *n* 1 a forceful effort to reach a goal or objective — see STRUGGLE 1
2 a physical dispute between opposing individuals or groups — see FIGHT
3 a rough and often noisy fight usually involving several people — see BRAWL 1

**fray** *vb* to damage or diminish by continued friction — see ABRADE 1

**frayed** *adj* worn or torn into or as if into rags — see RAGGED 2

**freak** *adj* being out of the ordinary — see EXCEPTIONAL

**freak** *n* 1 a person, thing, or event that is not normal ⟨that snowstorm in April was a *freak*, since our weather is usually much balmier by then⟩
*syn* abnormality, anomaly, monster, monstrosity
*rel* malformation, mutant, mutation; character, crackbrain, crackpot, eccentric, kook, oddball, screwball, weirdo; deviant; maverick, nonconformist
*near ant* sample, specimen; standard
*ant* average, norm
2 a person with a strong and habitual liking for something — see FAN
3 a sudden impulsive and apparently unmotivated idea or action — see WHIM

**freak** (out) *vb* 1 to trouble the mind of; to make uneasy — see DISTURB 1
2 to yield to mental or emotional stress — see CRACK 2

**freakish** *adj* prone to sudden illogical changes of mind, ideas, or actions — see WHIMSICAL

**freakishness** *n* an inclination to sudden illogical changes of mind, ideas, or actions — see WHIMSICALITY

**freckle** *vb* to mark with small spots especially unevenly — see SPOT

**freckled** *adj* marked with spots — see SPOTTED 1

**free** *adj* 1 not being under the rule or control of another ⟨the 20th century saw many African countries become *free* after many years of European rule⟩
*syn* autonomous, independent, self-governing, separate, sovereign
*rel* freeborn; delivered, emancipated, freed, liberated, manumitted, redeemed, released; unconquered, ungoverned, unruled, unsupervised; empowered, enfranchised; democratic, republican
*near ant* captive, conquered, enslaved, subdued, subjugated; inferior, subordinate, subservient
*ant* dependent, subject, unfree
2 no longer burdened with something unpleasant or painful ⟨after our son arrived home safely, we were grateful to be *free* from worry⟩
*syn* disencumbered, quit, unburdened
*rel* delivered, freed, liberated, released; unhampered, unimpeded
3 not bound, confined, or detained by force ⟨all of the animals in the game preserve are *free* to roam all over its vast area⟩
*syn* footloose, loose, unbound, unconfined, unrestrained
*rel* escaped; uncaged, unchained, unfettered, unleashed; uncaught; unanchored, unbolted, undone, unfastened, untied; clear, disengaged, unengaged
*phrases* at large, at liberty
*near ant* caught; caged, chained, leashed; anchored, bolted, fastened, shackled, tied
*ant* bound, confined, restrained, unfree
4 not costing or charging anything ⟨although the museum normally charges admission, on Wednesdays it is *free* to all⟩
*syn* complimentary, gratis, gratuitous
*rel* nominal; discretionary, freewill, optional, voluntary; honorary, uncompensated, unpaid
*near ant* paid
5 allowing passage without obstruction — see OPEN 1
6 giving or sharing in abundance and without hesitation — see GENEROUS 1
7 not being in a state of use, activity, or employment — see INACTIVE 2
8 showing a lack of proper social reserve or modesty — see PRESUMPTUOUS 1

**free** *vb* 1 to set free (as from slavery or confinement) ⟨a global crusade to *free* Nelson Mandela from a South African prison had emerged⟩
*syn* discharge, emancipate, enfranchise, liberate, loose, loosen, manumit, release, spring, unbind, uncage, unchain, unfetter
*rel* bail (out), deliver, parole, ransom, redeem, rescue; disengage, disentangle, extricate
*near ant* manacle, shackle, trammel; immure, imprison, incarcerate, intern, jail; conquer, enslave, subdue, subjugate
*ant* bind, confine, enchain, fetter, restrain
2 to arrange clear passage of (something) by removing obstructions — see OPEN 2
3 to rid the surface of (as an area) from things in the way — see CLEAR 1
4 to set (a person or thing) free of something that encumbers — see RID
5 to set free from entanglement or difficulty — see EXTRICATE

**freebie** *or* **freebee** *n* something given to someone without expectation of a return — see GIFT 1

**freebooter** *n* someone who engages in robbery of ships at sea — see PIRATE

**freedom** *n* **1** the state of being free from the control or power of another ⟨we owe our *freedom* to the untold numbers of soldiers who have fought in our nation's wars since its founding⟩
*syn* autonomy, independence, liberty, self-government, sovereignty
*rel* emancipation, enfranchisement, liberation, manumission, release
*near ant* captivity, enchainment, enslavement, imprisonment, incarceration, subjugation
*ant* dependence, subjection
**2** the right to act or move freely ⟨as special guests of the owners, the youngsters had full *freedom* of the resort and its private beach⟩
*syn* authorization, free hand, latitude, license (*or* licence), run
*rel* authority, mandate, power; range, room, space

**free–for–all** *adj* freely available for use or participation by all — see OPEN 2

**free–for–all** *n* a rough and often noisy fight usually involving several people — see BRAWL 1

**free hand** *n* the right to act or move freely — see FREEDOM 2

**freehanded** *adj* giving or sharing in abundance and without hesitation — see GENEROUS 1

**freeing** *n* the act of setting free from slavery — see LIBERATION

**freely** *adv* **1** of one's own free will — see VOLUNTARILY
**2** without difficulty — see EASILY

**free–spoken** *adj* free in expressing one's true feelings and opinions — see FRANK

**freestanding** *adj* not physically attached to another unit — see SEPARATE 2

**freeway** *n* a passage cleared for public vehicular travel — see WAY 1

**freewheeling** *adj* not held back by rules, duties, or worries ⟨James Bond has long been the model of the *freewheeling* hero who encounters danger and excitement in every corner of the globe⟩
*syn* footloose
*rel* easygoing, nonchalant, relaxed; unattached, uncommitted; unbridled, ungoverned, unrestrained; uninhibited, unsuppressed; self-assured, self-confident, self-reliant
*near ant* attached, committed
*ant* tied

**freewill** *adj* **1** made, given, or done with one's own free will — see INTENTIONAL 1
**2** done, made, or given with one's own free will — see VOLUNTARY 1

**free will** *n* the act or power of making one's own choices or decisions ⟨all of the workers at the homeless shelter are unpaid and are there of their own *free will*⟩
*syn* accord, choice, option, self-determination, volition, will
*rel* election, preference; inclination, penchant, predilection, predisposition
*near ant* coercion, compulsion, constraint, duress, force

**freeze** *n* a weather condition marked by low temperatures — see COLD

**freeze** *vb* to become physically firm or solid — see HARDEN 1

**freezing** *adj* having a low or subnormal temperature — see COLD 1

**freight** *n* a mass or quantity of something taken up and carried, conveyed, or transported — see LOAD 1

**frenetic** *adj* marked by great and often stressful excitement or activity — see FURIOUS 1

**frenzied** *adj* **1** being in a state of increased activity or agitation — see FEVERISH 1
**2** feeling overwhelming fear or worry — see FRANTIC 1
**3** marked by great and often stressful excitement or activity — see FURIOUS 1

**frenziedly** *adv* in a confused and reckless manner — see HELTER-SKELTER 1

**frenzy** *n* a state of wildly excited activity or emotion ⟨in its *frenzy* to flee the danger the crowd became uncontrollable, and a number of people were trampled to death⟩
*syn* agitation, delirium, distraction, furor, furore, fury, hysteria, rage, rampage, uproar
*rel* chaos, confusion, disorder, turmoil; clamor, commotion, hubbub, hurly-burly, tumult
*near ant* calm, peacefulness, serenity, tranquillity (*or* tranquility)

**frequency** *n* the fact or state of happening often ⟨the *frequency* of twins in that family is remarkable⟩
*syn* commonness, prevalence
*rel* constancy, continualness, regularity; appearance, incidence, occurrence
*ant* infrequency, uncommonness, unusualness

**frequent** *adj* **1** appearing or occurring repeatedly from time to time — see REGULAR 1
**2** often observed or encountered — see COMMON 1

**frequent** *vb* to go to or spend time in often ⟨like their counterparts elsewhere, the town's teenagers like to *frequent* the local malls⟩
*syn* hang around (in), hang out (at), haunt, resort (to), visit
*rel* attend, take in; infest, invade, swarm, overrun; drop (in *or* by), pop (in), run (in), stop (in *or* by); sojourn (at), stay (at), stop (over), tarry (in)
*near ant* elude, escape, evade
*ant* avoid, shun

**frequenter** *n* a person who visits another — see GUEST 1

**frequently** *adv* many times — see OFTEN

**fresh** *adj* **1** being in an original and unused or unspoiled state ⟨the restaurant uses only really *fresh* ingredients in all of its dishes⟩
***syn*** brand-new, pristine, virgin
***rel*** unaltered, unblemished, unbruised, uncontaminated, undamaged, undefiled, unharmed, unhurt, unimpaired, uninjured, unpolluted, unsoiled, unspoiled, unsullied, untainted, untouched, unused, unworn
***near ant*** blemished, bruised, damaged, defiled, harmed, hurt, impaired, injured, soiled, sullied, tainted; faded, shopworn, used, worn; contaminated, polluted, spoiled
***ant*** stale
**2** displaying or marked by rude boldness — see NERVY 1
**3** not known or experienced before — see NEW 2
**freshen** *vb* to bring back to a former condition or vigor — see RENEW 1
**freshened** *adj* made or become fresh in spirits or vigor — see NEW 4
**freshly** *adv* not long ago — see NEWLY
**freshman** *n* a person who is just starting out in a field of activity — see BEGINNER
**freshness** *n* the quality or appeal of being new — see NOVELTY 1
**fret** *n* a state of nervous or irritated concern ⟨one of my customers always gets into a *fret* if I'm so much as 15 minutes late delivering his newspaper⟩
***syn*** dither, fluster, fuss, huff, lather, pother, stew, tizzy, twitter
***rel*** dudgeon, pique; alarm, panic; ado, agitation, delirium, distraction, furor, hysteria, uproar; nervous breakdown
**fret** *vb* **1** to consume or wear away gradually — see EAT 2
**2** to damage or diminish by continued friction — see ABRADE 1
**3** to experience concern or anxiety — see WORRY 1
**friable** *adj* having a texture that readily breaks into little pieces under pressure — see CRISP 1
**friary** *n* a residence for men under religious vows — see MONASTERY
**friction** *n* a lack of agreement or harmony — see DISCORD
**frictionless** *adj* having or marked by agreement in feeling or action — see HARMONIOUS 3
**friend** *n* **1** a person who has a strong liking for and trust in another ⟨really close *friends* who like to do everything together and are always sharing secrets⟩
***syn*** buddy, chum, comrade, confidant, crony, familiar, intimate, pal
***rel*** acquaintance; associate, cohort, colleague, companion, fellow, hearty, hobnobber, mate, partner, peer; brother, sister; accomplice, ally, collaborator, confederate; benefactor, supporter, sympathizer, well-wisher; friendly
***near ant*** adversary, antagonist, opponent, rival; archenemy, nemesis
***ant*** enemy, foe
**2** a person who actively supports or favors a cause — see EXPONENT
**friendliness** *n* kindly concern, interest, or support — see GOODWILL 1
**friendly** *adj* **1** having or showing kindly feeling and sincere interest ⟨all of the kids at Stacy's new school seemed *friendly*⟩ ⟨as a *friendly* gesture, we presented our new neighbors with a plate of homemade cookies⟩
***syn*** amicable, companionable, comradely, cordial, genial, hearty, neighborly, warm, warmhearted
***rel*** affable, approachable, gracious; convivial, gregarious, hospitable, sociable, social; jolly, jovial, merry; extroverted (*also* extraverted), outgoing; brotherly, fraternal, sisterly; close, familiar, intimate; affectionate, devoted, loving
***near ant*** cold, cool, frigid; bellicose, belligerent, contentious, quarrelsome
***ant*** antagonistic, hostile, unfriendly
**2** closely acquainted — see FAMILIAR 1
**3** expressing approval — see FAVORABLE 1
**friendship** *n* kindly concern, interest, or support — see GOODWILL 1
**fright** *n* **1** something unpleasant to look at — see EYESORE
**2** the emotion experienced in the presence or threat of danger — see FEAR
**frighten** *vb* to strike with fear ⟨around the campfire the campers tried to *frighten* one another with ghostly legends and grisly tales⟩
***syn*** affright, alarm, horrify, panic, scare, shock, spook, startle, terrify, terrorize
***rel*** appall, dismay; amaze, astound, awe; chill, daunt, demoralize, dispirit, unman, unnerve; discompose, disconcert, disquiet, disturb, perturb, upset
***near ant*** cheer, comfort, console, solace, soothe; embolden, encourage, hearten
***ant*** reassure
**frightened** *adj* filled with fear or dread — see AFRAID 1
**frightening** *adj* causing fear — see FEARFUL 1
**frightful** *adj* **1** causing fear — see FEARFUL 1
**2** extremely disturbing or repellent — see HORRIBLE 1
**frightfully** *adv* to a great degree — see VERY 1
**frightfulness** *n* the quality of inspiring intense dread or dismay — see HORROR 1
**frigid** *adj* **1** having a low or subnormal temperature — see COLD 1
**2** lacking in friendliness or warmth of feeling — see COLD 2
**frill** *n* **1** a strip of fabric gathered or pleated on one edge and used as trimming — see RUFFLE
**2** something adding to pleasure or comfort but not absolutely necessary — see LUXURY 1
**3** something that decorates or beautifies — see DECORATION 1

**fringe** *n* the line or relatively narrow space that marks the outer limit of something — see BORDER 1
**fringe** *vb* 1 to be adjacent to — see ADJOIN 1
2 to serve as a border for — see BORDER
**fringing** *adj* having a border in common — see ADJACENT
**frippery** *n* 1 dressy clothing — see FINERY
2 something of little importance — see TRIFLE
**frisk** *vb* to play and run about happily — see FROLIC 1
**friskiness** *n* a natural disposition for playful behavior — see PLAYFULNESS
**frisky** *adj* 1 given to good-natured joking or teasing — see PLAYFUL
2 having much high-spirited energy and movement — see LIVELY 1
**fritter** *n* a small usually rounded mass of minced food that has been fried — see CAKE
**fritter** (away) *vb* to use up carelessly — see WASTE 1
**frivol** *vb* to show a liking for someone of the opposite sex just for fun — see FLIRT
**frivolity** *n* a lack of seriousness often at an improper time ⟨the boys were scolded for joking during the funeral service, which was hardly the time for *frivolity*⟩
*syn* facetiousness, flightiness, flippancy, frivolousness, levity, light-headedness, lightness
*rel* cheerfulness, gaiety (*also* gayety), glee, high-spiritedness, lightheartedness, merriment, mirth
*near ant* gloom, melancholy, moroseness, sadness, sullenness
*syn* gravity, intentness, seriousness, soberness, sobriety
**frivolous** *adj* 1 lacking importance — see UNIMPORTANT
2 lacking in seriousness or maturity — see GIDDY 1
**frivolousness** *n* a lack of seriousness often at an improper time — see FRIVOLITY 1
**frock** *n* a garment with a joined blouse and skirt for a woman or girl — see DRESS 1
**frolic** *n* 1 a playful or mischievous act intended as a joke — see PRANK
2 a time or instance of carefree fun — see FLING 1
3 activity engaged in to amuse oneself — see PLAY 1
**frolic** *vb* 1 to play and run about happily ⟨scores of swimmers were *frolicking* in the ocean surf along the beach⟩
*syn* caper, cavort, disport, frisk, gambol, lark, rollick, romp, sport
*rel* bound, leap, skip, spring, tumble; curvet, dance, prance; carouse, revel, roister; carry on, fool (around), horse (around); clown, cut up; joyride, rough-house, skylark
*phrases* kick up one's heels
*near ant* mope, stew, sulk
2 to engage in activity for amusement — see PLAY 1
**frolicking** *n* activity engaged in to amuse oneself — see PLAY 1
**frolicsome** *adj* 1 given to good-natured joking or teasing — see PLAYFUL
2 joyously unrestrained — see EXUBERANT
**front** *n* 1 a forward part or surface ⟨the *front* of the church features a magnificent stained-glass window⟩
*syn* exterior, facade (*also* façade), face, forepart, outside, skin, surface, veneer
*near ant* innards, inside, interior
*ant* back, rear, reverse
2 a display of emotion or behavior that is insincere or intended to deceive — see MASQUERADE
**front** *vb* to stand or sit with the face or front toward — see FACE 1
**frontier** *n* 1 a region along the dividing line between two countries ⟨the Apaches were once feared on both sides of the U.S.-Mexico *frontier*⟩
*syn* border, borderland, march
*rel* no-man's-land
2 a rural region that forms the edge of the settled or developed part of a country ⟨Alaska has been called America's last *frontier*⟩
*syn* backwater, backwoods, bush, hinterland, up-country
*rel* country, countryside, sticks
**frontiersman** *n* a person who settles in a new region ⟨the *frontiersmen* were willing to brave harsh living conditions in order to achieve a better life⟩
*syn* colonist, colonizer, homesteader, pioneer, settler
*rel* explorer, pathfinder, trailblazer
**frost** *n* a covering of tiny ice crystals on a cold surface ⟨the wintertime routine of scraping the *frost* off the car's windshield every morning⟩
*syn* hoar, hoarfrost, rime
*rel* frostwork
**frosty** *adj* 1 having a low or subnormal temperature — see COLD 1
2 having or showing a lack of friendliness or interest in others — see COOL 1
3 lacking in friendliness or warmth of feeling — see COLD 2
**froth** *n* a light mass of fine bubbles formed in or on a liquid — see FOAM
**frothy** *adj* covered with, consisting of, or resembling foam — see FOAMY
**froward** *adj* 1 engaging in or marked by childish misbehavior — see NAUGHTY
2 given to resisting authority or another's control — see DISOBEDIENT
3 given to resisting control or discipline by others — see UNCONTROLLABLE
**frowardness** *n* refusal to obey — see DISOBEDIENCE
**frown** *n* a twisting of the facial features in disgust or disapproval — see GRIMACE
**frown** *vb* to look with anger or disapproval ⟨the principal just stood there and *frowned* at the student who, once again, was in trouble⟩

***syn*** glare, gloom, glower, lower (*also* lour), scowl
***rel*** gape, gaze, ogle, stare; grimace, pout; growl, snarl, sneer
***phrases*** look daggers
***ant*** beam, smile

**frown** (on) *vb* to hold an unfavorable opinion of — see DISAPPROVE

**frowsy** *or* **frowzy** *adj* lacking neatness in dress or person — see SLOPPY 1

**frozen** *adj* **1** firmly positioned in place and difficult to dislodge — see TIGHT 2
**2** having been established and usually not subject to change — see FIXED 1

**frugal** *adj* careful in the management of money or resources ⟨by being *frugal*, the family is able to stretch its monthly budget⟩
***syn*** economical, economizing, provident, scrimping, sparing, thrifty
***rel*** conserving, preserving, saving; forehanded, foresighted, prudent; pennywise; cheap, close, closefisted, miserly, niggardly, parsimonious, stingy, stinting, tight, tightfisted
***near ant*** improvident, shortsighted; freehanded, generous, liberal, openhanded, unsparing; extravagant, indulgent, lavish
***ant*** prodigal, wasteful

**frugality** *n* careful management of material resources — see ECONOMY

**fruit** *n* **1** a condition or occurrence traceable to a cause — see EFFECT 1
**2** something produced by physical or intellectual effort — see PRODUCT 1

**fruitful** *adj* **1** producing abundantly — see FERTILE
**2** producing or capable of producing a desired result — see EFFECTIVE 1

**fruition** *n* the state of being actual or complete ⟨when she landed the lead in a Broadway play, a lifelong dream was brought to *fruition*⟩
***syn*** accomplishment, achievement, actuality, attainment, consummation, fulfillment, realization
***ant*** naught (*also* nought), nonfulfillment

**fruitless** *adj* producing no results — see FUTILE

**frustrate** *vb* to prevent from achieving a goal ⟨a multitude of conflicting opinions *frustrated* me in my attempt to find a computer that best suits my needs⟩
***syn*** baffle, balk, beat, checkmate, foil, thwart
***rel*** bar, block, hinder, impede, obstruct; arrest, check, halt, stop; forestall, obviate, preclude; negate, neutralize, nullify; counteract, offset; conquer, defeat, overcome
***near ant*** abet, aid, assist; ease, facilitate, smooth;
***ant*** advance, cultivate, encourage, forward, foster, further, nurture, promote

**frustrating** *adj* causing annoyance — see ANNOYING

**frustration** *n* **1** something that is a source of irritation — see ANNOYANCE 3
**2** the emotion felt when one's expectations are not met — see DISAPPOINTMENT 1
**3** the feeling of impatience or anger caused by another's repeated disagreeable acts — see ANNOYANCE 2

**fuddy–duddy** *n* a person with old-fashioned ideas — see FOGY

**fudge** *n* **1** language, behavior, or ideas that are absurd and contrary to good sense — see NONSENSE 1
**2** unintelligible or meaningless talk — see GIBBERISH

**fudge** *vb* **1** to avoid giving a definite answer or position — see EQUIVOCATE
**2** to use dishonest methods to achieve a goal — see CHEAT 1

**fuel** *n* something with a usable capacity for doing work ⟨such fossil *fuels* as coal, petroleum, and natural gas⟩
***syn*** energy, power
***rel*** kindling, propellant

**fugitive** *adj* **1** hard to find, capture, or isolate — see ELUSIVE
**2** lasting only for a short time — see MOMENTARY

**fulfill** *or* **fulfil** *vb* **1** to do what is required by the terms of ⟨the football player must remain with the team one more year to *fulfill* his contract⟩
***syn*** answer, comply (with), fill, keep, meet, redeem, satisfy
***rel*** complete, conclude, finalize, finish; accomplish, achieve, bring about, bring off, effect; discharge, execute, perform
***phrases*** abide by, make good
***near ant*** disregard, ignore, neglect, overlook, slight
***ant*** breach, break, violate
**2** to carry through (as a process) to completion — see PERFORM 1

**fulfilling** *adj* making one feel good inside — see HEARTWARMING

**fulfillment** *n* **1** the doing of an action — see COMMISSION 2
**2** the state of being actual or complete — see FRUITION

**full** *adj* **1** containing or seeming to contain the greatest quantity or number possible ⟨at the start of the game everyone was *full* of energy and hope⟩ ⟨the boy's bedroom is *full* of sports trophies and medals⟩
***syn*** brimful, brimming, bursting, chockfull (*or* chockful), crammed, crowded, fat, filled, jammed, jam-packed, loaded, packed, stuffed
***rel*** overcrowded, overfilled, overflowing, overfull, overloaded, overstuffed; abounding, fraught, replete, rife, swarming, teeming
***near ant*** deficient, incomplete, insufficient, short; depleted, drained, exhausted
***ant*** bare, blank, devoid, empty, stark, vacant, void
**2** of the highest degree ⟨even at the age of eighteen he hadn't reached his *full* height⟩ ⟨a boat going at *full* speed⟩
***syn*** greatest, maximum, top, topmost, utmost
***rel*** high

***near ant*** low
***ant*** least, lowest, minimal, minimum
**3** having one's appetite completely satisfied ⟨even the heartiest eaters are sure to be *full* when they leave that restaurant⟩
***syn*** sated, satiate, satiated, stuffed, surfeited
***rel*** glutted, gorged, overfed, overfull, overstuffed
***near ant*** underfed, undernourished
***ant*** empty, hungry, starving
**4** covering everything or all important points — see ENCYCLOPEDIC
**5** having an abundance of some characteristic quality (as flavor) — see FULL-BODIED
**6** having an excess of body fat — see FAT 1
**7** including many small descriptive features — see DETAILED 1
**8** not lacking any part or member that properly belongs to it — see COMPLETE 1

**full** *adv* **1** to a full extent or degree — see FULLY 1
**2** to a great degree — see VERY 1

**full** *n* a complete amount of something — see WHOLE

**full blast** *adv* with all power or resources being used ⟨Mom and Dad arrived home to find the stereo going *full blast* and the kitchen a mess⟩
***syn*** all out, full steam ahead, full tilt, tooth and nail
***rel*** completely, fully, totally; extremely, utterly
***phrases*** in full career, to the hilt

**full–blooded** *adj* of unmixed ancestry — see PUREBRED

**full–blown** *adj* fully grown or developed — see MATURE 1

**full–bodied** *adj* having an abundance of some characteristic quality (as flavor) ⟨after that huge Sunday brunch, Mom and Dad needed a *full-bodied* coffee⟩
***syn*** concentrated, full, potent, rich, robust, strong
***rel*** heavy; straight, undiluted, unmixed
***near ant*** diluted, watered (down), watery
***ant*** light, mild, thin, weak

**full dress** *n* dressy clothing — see FINERY

**full–fledged** *adj* fully grown or developed — see MATURE 1

**full–grown** *adj* fully grown or developed — see MATURE 1

**full–scale** *adj* trying all possibilities — see EXHAUSTIVE

**full steam ahead** *adv* with all power or resources being used — see FULL BLAST

**full tilt** *adv* **1** with all power or resources being used — see FULL BLAST
**2** with great speed — see FAST 1

**fully** *adv* **1** to a full extent or degree ⟨only with daybreak did we *fully* realize the extent of the damage from the storm⟩
***syn*** all, altogether, clean, completely, dead, entirely, fast, flat, full, perfectly, plumb [*chiefly dialect*], quite, thoroughly, totally, utterly, well, wholly
***rel*** absolutely, categorically, unqualifiedly; by and large, chiefly, generally, largely, mainly, more or less, mostly, predominately, primarily, principally
***phrases*** at length, to pieces, to the hilt
***near ant*** barely, hardly, just, scarcely
***ant*** partially, partly
**2** with attention to all aspects or details — see THOROUGHLY 1

**fulminate** *vb* to talk loudly and wildly — see RANT

**fulmination** *n* harsh insulting language — see ABUSE 1

**fulsome** *adj* overly or insincerely flattering ⟨the player's *fulsome* praise for the coach showed just how hard he was trying to be named captain of the team⟩
***syn*** adulatory, gushing, unctuous
***rel*** drooling, slavering, slobbering; cloying, sickening; demonstrative, effusive, mushy; hypocritical, insincere, sanctimonious; endearing, ingratiating; extravagant, lavish, unrestrained; abundant, copious, profuse
***near ant*** earnest, genuine, heartfelt, sincere, unfeigned

**fumble** *n* an unintentional departure from truth or accuracy — see ERROR 1

**fumble** *vb* **1** to make or do (something) in a clumsy or unskillful way — see BOTCH
**2** to search for something blindly or uncertainly — see GROPE

**fumbled** *adj* showing or marked by a lack of skill and tact (as in dealing with a situation) — see AWKWARD 2

**fume** *vb* **1** to be excited or emotionally stirred up with anger — see BOIL 1
**2** to express one's anger usually violently — see RAGE 1

**fuming** *adj* feeling or showing anger — see ANGRY

**fun** *adj* providing amusement or enjoyment ⟨there were so many *fun* things to do at summer camp that I really hated to leave⟩
***syn*** amusing, delightful, diverting, enjoyable, entertaining, pleasurable
***rel*** agreeable, beguiling, pleasant; funny, hilarious, humorous; gay, happy, jolly, merry; exciting, stimulating, thrilling
***near ant*** disagreeable, unpleasant
***ant*** boring, dull

**fun** *n* **1** someone or something that provides amusement or enjoyment ⟨theme parks with their rides, shows, and games are great *fun* for the whole family⟩
***syn*** delight, diversion, entertainment, pleasure, recreation
***rel*** binge, fling, frolic, gambol, lark, revel, rollick, romp, spree; carousing, festivity, gaiety (*also* gayety), hilarity, merrymaking, revelry; picnic; laugh, riot, scream
***ant*** bore, bummer, downer, drag
**2** an attitude or manner not to be taken seriously ⟨when I said that playing the piano like that could get you arrested, I only said it in *fun*⟩
***syn*** game, jest, play, sport

***rel*** facetiousness, flippancy, levity
***near ant*** earnestness, gravity, seriousness
***ant*** earnest
**3** activity engaged in to amuse oneself — see PLAY 1

**fun** *vb* to make jokes — see JOKE

**function** *n* **1** a social gathering — see PARTY 1
**2** an assignment at which one regularly works for pay — see JOB 1
**3** the action for which a person or thing is specially fitted or used or for which a thing exists — see ROLE

**function** *vb* to have a certain purpose ⟨the heart *functions* as a pump for the blood⟩
***syn*** act, perform, serve, work
***rel*** operate, run; control, direct, manage

**functional** *adj* **1** being in effective operation — see ACTIVE 1
**2** capable of being put to use or account — see PRACTICAL 1
**3** capable of or suitable for being used for a particular purpose — see USABLE 1

**functionary** *n* **1** a person who holds a public office — see OFFICIAL
**2** a worker in a government agency — see BUREAUCRAT

**functioning** *adj* being in effective operation — see ACTIVE 1

**fund** *n* **1** a sum of money set aside for a particular purpose ⟨our club has a *fund* for parties—which we like to have as often as possible⟩
***syn*** account, budget, deposit, kitty, nest egg, pool
***rel*** chest, coffer(s); assets, savings, savings account; bankroll, cache, collection, hoard, reserve, treasure; petty cash, pin money, pocket money, spending money
**2 funds** *pl* available money ⟨my *funds* were a little low, so I asked my favorite lending institution—Dad—for a small advance on my allowance⟩
***syn*** bankroll, finances, pocket, resources, wherewithal
***rel*** cash, money; assets, capital, means, wealth; purse, treasury
**3** the number of individuals or amount of something available at any given time — see SUPPLY

**fund** *vb* **1** to furnish (as an institution) with a regular source of income — see ENDOW 2
**2** to provide money for — see FINANCE 1

**fundamental** *adj* of or relating to the simplest facts or theories of a subject — see ELEMENTARY

**fundamentals** *n pl* general or basic truths on which other truths or theories can be based — see PRINCIPLES 1

**funeral** *adj* expressing or suggesting mourning — see MOURNFUL 1

**funeral director** *n* a person who manages funerals and prepares the dead for burial or cremation ⟨the *funeral director* instructed the pallbearers on how to proceed⟩
***syn*** mortician, undertaker
***rel*** embalmer

**funereal** *adj* causing or marked by an atmosphere lacking in cheer — see GLOOMY 1

**funnel** *vb* to cause to move to a central point or along a restricted pathway — see CHANNEL

**funniness** *n* the amusing quality or element in something — see HUMOR 1

**funning** *adj* marked by or expressive of mild or good-natured teasing — see QUIZZICAL

**funny** *adj* **1** causing or intended to cause laughter ⟨a very *funny* movie that had audiences rolling in the aisles⟩
***syn*** antic, comic, comical, droll, farcical, hilarious, humorous, hysterical, laughable, ludicrous, ridiculous, riotous, risible, screaming, side-splitting, uproarious
***rel*** amusing, diverting, entertaining; clownish, slapstick, zany; facetious, flip, flippant, pert, smart, smart-alecky (*or* smart-aleck); jocular, playful, waggish; priceless, rich, whimsical, witty; gleeful, merry, mirthful
***near ant*** grave, serious, sober, solemn, somber (*or* sombre); affecting, moving, poignant, touching, tragic; lachrymose, mournful, sad, tearful
***ant*** humorless, lame, uncomic, unfunny
**2** different from the ordinary in a way that causes curiosity or suspicion — see ODD 2
**3** noticeably different from what is generally found or experienced — see UNUSUAL 1

**funny** *n* a series of drawings that tell a story or part of a story — see COMIC STRIP

**fur** *n* **1** the hairy covering of a mammal especially when fine, soft, and thick ⟨the chinchilla is known for its exceptionally soft *fur*⟩
***syn*** coat, fleece, hair, pelage, pile, wool
***rel*** hide, pelt, skin
**2** a soft airy substance or covering — see FUZZ
**3** the outer covering of an animal removed for its commercial value — see HIDE 1

**furbelow** *n* a strip of fabric gathered or pleated on one edge and used as trimming — see RUFFLE

**furious** *adj* **1** marked by great and often stressful excitement or activity ⟨everyone worked at a *furious* pace in order to get the float ready for the parade⟩
***syn*** delirious, feverish, fierce, frantic, frenetic, frenzied, mad, rabid, violent, wild
***rel*** concentrated, high-pressured, intense, vehement; excessive, extreme, inordinate; crazy, demented, insane, irrational
***near ant*** calm, peaceful, quiet, subdued, tranquil; moderate, reasonable, temperate; casual, easygoing, low-pressure
***ant*** relaxed
**2** extreme in degree, power, or effect — see INTENSE
**3** feeling or showing anger — see ANGRY
**4** marked by bursts of destructive force or intense activity — see VIOLENT 1

**furlough** *n* the termination of the employment of an employee or a work force often temporarily — see LAYOFF

**furnish** *vb* **1** to provide (someone) with what is needed for a task or activity ⟨the students were *furnished* with brushes, crayons, pencils, and various other art supplies⟩
*syn* accoutre (*or* accouter), equip, fit (out), outfit, rig, supply
*rel* stock, store; bestow, donate, give, present; deal, dispense, distribute, dole (out); allocate, allot, assign
*near ant* deprive, dispossess, divest, strip
**2** to put (something) into the possession of someone for use or consumption ⟨we'll gladly *furnish* the food for any out-of-town guests⟩
*syn* deliver, feed, give, hand, hand over, provide, supply
*rel* administer, dispense, distribute, dole (out), mete (out), parcel (out); cede, deed, transfer
*near ant* conserve, preserve, save
*ant* hold (back), keep (back), reserve, retain, withhold

**furnishings** *n pl* the movable articles in a room — see FURNITURE

**furniture** *n* the movable articles in a room ⟨we bought all new *furniture* for our new house⟩
*syn* appointments, cabinetwork, furnishings, movables (*or* moveables)
*rel* effects, goods, possessions
*near ant* fixtures

**furor** *n* **1** a state of noisy, confused activity — see COMMOTION
**2** a state of wildly excited activity or emotion — see FRENZY
**3** an intense emotional state of displeasure with someone or something — see ANGER

**furore** *n* **1** a state of noisy, confused activity — see COMMOTION
**2** a state of wildly excited activity or emotion — see FRENZY

**furrow** *n* a small fold in a soft and otherwise smooth surface — see WRINKLE 1

**furrow** *vb* **1** to cut into and turn over the sod of (a piece of land) using a bladed implement — see PLOW 1
**2** to develop creases or folds — see WRINKLE 1

**furry** *adj* **1** covered with or as if with hair — see HAIRY 1
**2** made of or resembling hair — see HAIRY 2

**further** *adj* resulting in an increase in amount or number — see ADDITIONAL

**further** *adv* **1** at or to a greater distance or more advanced point — see FARTHER
**2** in addition to what has been said — see MORE 1

**further** *vb* to help the growth or development of — see FOSTER 1

**furtherance** *n* forward movement in time or place — see ADVANCE 1

**furthermore** *adv* in addition to what has been said — see MORE 1

**furthermost** *adj* most distant from a center — see EXTREME 1

**furthest** *adj* most distant from a center — see EXTREME 1

**furtive** *adj* **1** given to acting in secret and to concealing one's intentions — see SNEAKY 1
**2** undertaken or done so as to escape being observed or known by others — see SECRET 1

**fury** *n* **1** a bad-tempered scolding woman — see SHREW
**2** a state of wildly excited activity or emotion — see FRENZY
**3** an intense emotional state of displeasure with someone or something — see ANGER

**fuse** *vb* **1** to come together to form a single unit — see UNITE 1
**2** to go from a solid to a liquid state — see LIQUEFY
**3** to turn into a single mass that is more or less the same throughout — see BLEND 1

**fusillade** *n* a rapid or overwhelming outpouring of many things at once — see BARRAGE

**fusion** *n* a distinct entity formed by the combining of two or more different things — see BLEND

**fuss** *n* **1** a feeling or declaration of disapproval or dissent — see OBJECTION
**2** a state of nervous or irritated concern — see FRET
**3** a state of noisy, confused activity — see COMMOTION
**4** an expression of dissatisfaction, pain, or resentment — see COMPLAINT 1

**fuss** *vb* **1** to express dissatisfaction, pain, or resentment usually tiresomely — see COMPLAIN
**2** to make an exaggerated display of affection or enthusiasm — see GUSH 2
**3** to make often peevish criticisms or objections about matters that are minor, unimportant, or irrelevant — see QUIBBLE
**4** to use flattery or the doing of favors in order to win approval especially from a superior — see FAWN

**fusser** *n* **1** a person who makes frequent complaints usually about little things — see CRY-BABY
**2** an irritable and complaining person — see GROUCH

**fussy** *adj* **1** given to complaining a lot ⟨the kids riding in the back were *fussy* passengers, always asking "Are we there yet?"⟩
*syn* crabby, cranky, grouchy, grumpy, querulous
*rel* fidgety, restive, restless, squirmy, uneasy; discontented, disgruntled, displeased, dissatisfied; fretful, nervous, worrisome; cantankerous, crotchety, irascible, irritable, ornery
*near ant* amiable, genial, good-humored, good-natured, good-tempered; accommodating, complaisant, obliging; easygoing, laid-back, relaxed

---

*syn* synonym(s) *rel* related words
*ant* antonym(s) *near ant* near antonym(s)

*ant* uncomplaining
**2** hard to please — see FINICKY
**3** taking great care and effort — see PAINSTAKING

**fusty** *adj* having an unpleasant smell — see MALODOROUS

**futile** *adj* producing no results ⟨the prison is so well guarded that all attempts to escape have been *futile*⟩
*syn* abortive, bootless, empty, fruitless, ineffective, ineffectual, unavailing, unproductive, unprofitable, unsuccessful, useless, vain
*rel* hollow, idle, meaningless, pointless, worthless; hopeless, impossible; inadequate, insufficient
*phrases* in vain, of no avail
*near ant* meaningful, worthwhile; adequate, sufficient
*ant* effective, effectual, efficacious, efficient, fruitful, productive, profitable, successful

**future** *adj* of a time after the present ⟨we must preserve our national parks in all their glory so that *future* generations can experience the majesty of nature⟩
*syn* coming, unborn
*rel* approaching, forthcoming, imminent, impending, nearing, oncoming, pending, upcoming; later, posterior, subsequent; anticipated, awaited, expected, planned, predicted, projected; eventual, final, last, ultimate
*near ant* ancient, olden
*ant* bygone, past

**future** *n* **1** time that is to come ⟨in the *future*, there may be medical discoveries that are beyond our fondest dreams⟩
*syn* by-and-by, futurity, hereafter, offing
*rel* eventuality, finality; posterity
*near ant* yesterday, yesteryear; antiquity, old, yore
*ant* past
**2** what is going to happen to someone in the time ahead — see FORTUNE 1

**futurist** *n* one who predicts future events or developments — see PROPHET

**futurity** *n* time that is to come — see FUTURE 1

**fuzz** *n* a soft airy substance or covering ⟨a comfortable old sweater with clumps of *fuzz* all over it⟩
*syn* down, floss, fluff, fur, lint, nap, pile
*rel* batting

**fuzzy** *adj* **1** made of or resembling hair — see HAIRY 2
**2** not clearly expressed — see VAGUE 1
**3** not seen or understood clearly — see FAINT 1

# G

**gab** *vb* to engage in casual or rambling conversation — see CHAT

**gabble** *n* unintelligible or meaningless talk — see GIBBERISH

**gabble** *vb* **1** to engage in casual or rambling conversation — see CHAT
**2** to speak rapidly, inarticulately, and usually unintelligibly — see BABBLE 1

**gabbler** *n* a person who talks constantly — see CHATTERBOX

**gabby** *adj* fond of talking or conversation — see TALKATIVE

**gabfest** *n* friendly, informal conversation or an instance of this — see CHAT

**gad** (about) *vb* to move about from place to place aimlessly — see WANDER

**gadabout** *n* a person who roams about without a fixed route or destination — see NOMAD

**gadfly** *n* one who is obnoxiously annoying — see NUISANCE 1

**gadget** *n* an interesting and often novel device with a practical use ⟨she tried out a new *gadget* for weeding the garden⟩
*syn* appliance, contraption, contrivance, gimmick, gizmo (*or* gismo), jigger
*rel* implement, instrument, tool, utensil; ingenuity, innovation, invention; accessory, adjunct; mechanism, trick

**gaffe** *n* a socially improper or unsuitable act or remark — see IMPROPRIETY 2

**gag** *n* something said or done to cause laughter — see JOKE 1

**gag** *vb* **1** to discharge the contents of the stomach through the mouth — see VOMIT
**2** to experience complete or partial blockage of the windpipe — see CHOKE 2

**gage** *n* something given or held to assure that the giver will keep a promise — see PLEDGE 1

**gaiety** *also* **gayety** *n* **1** dressy clothing — see FINERY
**2** joyful or festive activity — see MERRYMAKING

**gaily** *also* **gayly** *adv* **1** in a cheerful or happy manner ⟨we sat around the table, *gaily* teasing each other and laughing about the good old days⟩
*syn* cheerfully, happily, heartily, jocosely, jovially, merrily, mirthfully
*rel* blithely, blithesomely, breezily, brightly, buoyantly; cheerily, gladly, gladsomely, sanguinely, sunnily; good-humoredly, good-naturedly
*near ant* abjectly, dejectedly, despondently, disconsolately, dispiritedly, wretchedly; dolefully, dolorously, forlornly, mournfully, plaintively, sorrowfully; dourly, glumly, sternly, sulkily, sullenly; dismally, drearily, gloomily

*ant* bleakly, cheerlessly, darkly, heavily, miserably, morosely, unhappily
**2** in a quick and spirited manner ⟨children *gaily* running to the buses on the last day of school⟩
*syn* animatedly, animately, exuberantly, high-spiritedly, jauntily, pertly, sprightly, trippingly
*rel* friskily, playfully, skittishly, sportively; briskly, crisply, snappily, springily; breezily, cockishly; allegro
*near ant* idly, indolently, lazily, slothfully; heavily, inactively, listlessly
*ant* dully, inanimately, sluggishly, tardily
**3** in a bright and showy way ⟨the Mexican dancers were *gaily* dressed in lavish, bright costumes⟩
*syn* dashingly, flamboyantly, flashily, jauntily, rakishly, swankily
*rel* garishly, gaudily, loud, loudly, ostentatiously; fancily, gallantly, ornately; nattily, neatly, smartly; conspicuously, luridly, spectacularly, strikingly; gorgeously, splendidly
*near ant* inconspicuously, unobtrusively, unpretentiously; chastely, demurely, homely, modestly; plainly, simply; colorlessly, dirtily, drably, dully; bleakly, severely, somberly
*ant* conservatively, plain, quietly

**gain** *n* **1** something added (as by growth) — see INCREASE 1
**2** the amount of money left when expenses are subtracted from the total amount received — see PROFIT 1
**3 gains** *pl* an increase usually measured in money that comes from labor, business, or property — see INCOME

**gain** *vb* **1** to increase in ⟨as the car coasted downhill, it gradually *gained* speed and momentum⟩
*syn* build (up), gather, grow (in), pick up
*rel* accrue, accumulate, amass; excite, stimulate; enhance, enrich, maximize; boost, jack (up), mount, step up
*near ant* abate, diminish (in), dip, dwindle, fall (in), lessen, taper, taper off
*ant* decrease (in), lose
**2** to receive as return for effort — see EARN 1
**3** to become healthy and strong again after illness or weakness — see CONVALESCE

**gainful** *adj* yielding a profit — see PROFITABLE 1

**gainsay** *vb* **1** to declare not to be true — see DENY 1
**2** to make an assertion that is contrary to one made by (another) — see CONTRADICT 1

**gal** *n* **1** a woman with whom one is in love — see GIRLFRIEND
**2** a young usually unmarried woman — see GIRL 1

**gala** *n* a time or program of special events and entertainment in honor of something — see FESTIVAL

**gale** *n* a sudden intense expression of strong feeling — see OUTBURST 1

**gall** *n* **1** a deep-seated ill will — see ENMITY
**2** shameless boldness — see EFFRONTERY

**gall** *vb* **1** to damage or diminish by continued friction — see ABRADE 1
**2** to disturb the peace of mind of (someone) especially by repeated disagreeable acts — see IRRITATE 1
**3** to make sore by continued rubbing — see CHAFE 1

**gallant** *adj* **1** feeling or displaying no fear by temperament — see BRAVE
**2** having, characterized by, or arising from a dignified and generous nature — see NOBLE 2
**3** large and impressive in size, grandeur, extent, or conception — see GRAND 1

**gallant** *n* **1** a man extremely interested in his clothing and personal appearance — see DANDY 1
**2** a man who courts a woman usually with the goal of marrying her — see SUITOR 1

**gallantly** *adv* in a manner befitting a person of the highest character and ideals — see GREATLY 1

**gallantry** *n* strength of mind to carry on in spite of danger — see COURAGE

**gallery** *n* **1** a building or part of a building in which objects of interest are displayed — see MUSEUM
**2** a typically long narrow way connecting parts of a building — see HALL 2

**galling** *adj* **1** causing annoyance — see ANNOYING
**2** hard to accept or bear especially emotionally — see BITTER 2

**gallivant** *also* **galavant** *vb* to move about from place to place aimlessly — see WANDER

**gallivanting** *also* **galavanting** *adj* traveling from place to place — see ITINERANT

**gallop** *vb* to go at a pace faster than a walk — see RUN 1

**galore** *adj* pouring forth in great amounts — see PROFUSE

**galvanize** *vb* to cause a pleasurable stimulation of the feelings — see THRILL

**galvanizing** *adj* causing great emotional or mental stimulation — see EXCITING 1

**gamble** *n* a risky undertaking ⟨would never take a *gamble* on such a poorly researched business deal⟩
*syn* chance, enterprise, flier (*or* flyer), speculation, venture
*rel* bet, hazard, stake, wager; liberty; dark horse, long shot, play

**gamble** *vb* to risk (something) on the outcome of an uncertain event — see BET

**gamble** (on) *vb* to take a chance on — see RISK 1

**gamble** (with) *vb* to place in danger — see ENDANGER

**gambler** *n* one that bets (as on the outcome of a contest or sports event) — see BETTOR

**gambol** *n* a time or instance of carefree fun — see FLING 1

---

*syn* synonym(s) *rel* related words
*ant* antonym(s) *near ant* near antonym(s)

**gambol** *vb* to play and run about happily — see FROLIC 1

**game** *adj* having a desire or inclination (as for a specified course of action) — see WILLING 1

**game** *n* **1** a competitive encounter between individuals or groups carried on for amusement, exercise, or in pursuit of a prize ⟨decided he would indulge in a friendly basketball *game* with his friends before dinner⟩
*syn* bout, competition, contest, event, match, meet, sweepstakes, tournament, tourney
*rel* athletics, sport; battle, conflict, scrimmage, skirmish, struggle, tug-of-war, tussle; championship, final, nightcap, playoff, semifinal; derby, field day, open; marathon, race; heat, round, run, set; rally, volley; rubber, runoff sudden death; dead heat, photo finish, seesaw; classic
**2** a method worked out in advance for achieving some objective — see PLAN 1
**3** an attitude or manner not to be taken seriously — see FUN 2

**gameness** *n* cheerful readiness to do something — see ALACRITY

**gamut** *n* the distance or extent between possible extremes — see RANGE 3

**gander** *n* an instance of looking especially briefly — see LOOK 2

**gang** *n* **1** a group of people working together on a task ⟨a *gang* of neighborhood residents spent the weekend cleaning up the park⟩
*syn* band, company, crew, outfit, party, squad, team
*rel* army, battalion, brigade, corps, troop; force, host, posse, stable, troupe; administration, department, help, personnel, staff
**2** a group of people sharing a common interest and relating together socially ⟨the whole *gang* went out for pizza⟩ ⟨the school's computer hackers had their own little *gang*⟩
*syn* body, bunch, circle, clan, clique, community, coterie, crowd, fold, lot, ring, set
*rel* bevy, covey, flock, herd, horde, mob, swarm, throng; club, college, fellowship, guild (*also* gild), league, organization, society; cohort, pack; camp, faction, sect, side, tribe; mess, squad; brotherhood, fraternity, order, sisterhood, sodality, sorority; commune; alliance, bloc, coalition, confederation, congress, council, federation, union
*near ant* loner; individualist
**3** a group involved in secret or criminal activities — see RING 1

**gangling** *adj* being tall, thin and usually loose-jointed — see LANKY

**gangly** *adj* being tall, thin and usually loose-jointed — see LANKY

**gangster** *n* a violent, brutal person who is often a member of an organized gang — see HOODLUM

**gaol** *n, chiefly British* a place of confinement for persons held in lawful custody — see JAIL

**gap** *n* **1** an open space in a barrier (as a wall or hedge) ⟨there were several visible *gaps* in the wall where the drywall had pulled away from the wall framing⟩
*syn* breach, break, discontinuity, gulf, hole, interval, opening, rent, rift, separation
*rel* chink, cleft, crack, cranny, crevice, fissure; notch, slit, slot, split; interspace, pore, space; abyss, aperture, cavity, chasm, gape, orifice; fracture, rupture, severance, sundering
**2** a break in continuity ⟨there was a 15-minute *gap* between the two televised sporting events⟩
*syn* discontinuity, hiatus, interim, interlude, intermission, interruption, interval
*rel* caesura, pause, space; lapse, suspension; lull, recess, respite, rest
*near ant* continuum, run, stretch; procession, progression
*ant* continuation, continuity
**3** a narrow opening between hillsides or mountains that can be used for passage — see CANYON

**gape** *vb* to look long and hard in wonder or surprise ⟨she *gaped* openmouthed at the young man in the mall with purple and green hair⟩
*syn* gawk, gaze, goggle, peer, rubberneck, stare
*rel* glare, gloat, glower; eye, observe, watch; leer, ogle
*near ant* glance, glimpse, peek, peep; browse, dip (into), scan; blink, wink

**garb** *n* clothing chosen as appropriate for a specific situation — see OUTFIT 1

**garb** *vb* to outfit with clothes and especially fine or special clothes — see CLOTHE 1

**garbage** *n* discarded or useless material ⟨the stray dogs were looking for leftover food in the family's *garbage*⟩
*syn* chaff, deadwood, dross, dust, junk, litter, refuse, riffraff, rubbish, scrap, trash, waste
*rel* offal, sewage, slop, swill, wash; debris, detritus, rubble, ruins; lumber, odds and ends; flotsam, jetsam; castoff, cull, discard, reject, throwaway; nothing, straw, two bits
*near ant* catch, treasure, treasure trove
*ant* find, prize

**garble** *vb* to change so much as to create a wrong impression or alter the meaning of ⟨the candidate complained that his views had been deliberately *garbled* by his opponent⟩
*syn* color, distort, falsify, misinterpret, misrepresent, misstate, pervert, twist, warp
*rel* belie, camouflage, disguise, mask, veil; complicate, confound, confuse, mix up; mystify, obscure, puzzle; equivocate, fib, lie, palter, prevaricate
*near ant* clarify, clear (up), explain, illuminate, illustrate, interpret, spell out; decipher

**garden** *adj* **1** being of the type that is encountered in the normal course of events — see ORDINARY 1
**2** often observed or encountered — see COMMON 1

**garish** *adj* excessively showy — see GAUDY

**garishness** *n* excessive or unnecessary display — see OSTENTATION

**garment** *vb* to outfit with clothes and especially fine or special clothes — see CLOTHE 1

**garner** *vb* **1** to bring together in one body or place — see GATHER 1
**2** to receive as return for effort — see EARN 1

**garnish** *n* something that decorates or beautifies — see DECORATION 1

**garnish** *vb* to make more attractive by adding something that is beautiful or becoming — see DECORATE

**garrote** *or* **garotte** *vb* to keep (someone) from breathing by exerting pressure on the windpipe — see CHOKE 1

**garrulous** *adj* fond of talking or conversation — see TALKATIVE

**gas** *n* **1** boastful speech or writing — see BOMBAST 1
**2** language that is impressive-sounding but not meaningful or sincere — see RHETORIC 1
**3** *slang* a source of great satisfaction — see DELIGHT 1

**gas** *vb* to engage in casual or rambling conversation — see CHAT

**gaseous** *adj* marked by the use of impressive-sounding but mostly meaningless words and phrases — see RHETORICAL

**gash** *n* a long deep cut ⟨got a *gash* in his knee that required four stitches⟩
***syn*** incision, laceration, rent, rip, slash, slit, tear
***rel*** abrasion, score, scrape, scratch; injury, wound

**gash** *vb* to penetrate with a sharp edge (as a knife) — see CUT 1

**gasp** *vb* to breathe hard, quickly, or with difficulty ⟨the runner was *gasping* by the end of the marathon⟩
***syn*** blow, hyperventilate, pant, puff, wheeze
***rel*** choke, gulp, huff; exhale, expire
***phrases*** to be out of breath

**gassy** *adj* marked by the use of impressive-sounding but mostly meaningless words and phrases — see RHETORICAL

**gate** *n* **1** a barrier by which an entry is closed and opened — see DOOR 1
**2** the opening through which one can enter or leave a structure — see DOOR 2
**3** a fixture for controlling the flow of a liquid — see FAUCET

**gatekeeper** *n* a person who tends a door — see DOORKEEPER

**gateway** *n* **1** something that allows someone to achieve a desired goal — see PASSPORT
**2** the means or right of entering or participating in — see ENTRANCE 1
**3** the opening through which one can enter or leave a structure — see DOOR 2

**gather** *vb* **1** to bring together in one body or place ⟨he *gathered* the leftovers from the table and gave them to the dog⟩ ⟨let's *gather* the students and have them line up on the playground before going in from recess⟩
***syn*** accumulate, amass, assemble, collect, concentrate, garner, group, lump, pick up, round up, scrape (together)
***rel*** agglomerate, aggregate, ball, bunch, cluster, huddle; heap, pile, stack; muster, raise, rally; flock, herd, hive, pack, press, swarm, throng, troop; congregate, forgather (*or* foregather), meet, rendezvous; affiliate, ally, combine, connect, join, link, merge, unite; arrange, organize, systematize; regather, regroup
***phrases*** get together
***near ant*** break up, disband, disintegrate, dissolve, separate, sever, split (up); dismiss, send
***ant*** dispel, disperse, dissipate, scatter
**2** to catch or collect (a crop or natural resource) for human use — see HARVEST
**3** to come together into one body or place — see ASSEMBLE 1
**4** to form an opinion through reasoning and information — see INFER 1
**5** to gradually form into a layer, pile, or mass — see COLLECT 2
**6** to increase in — see GAIN 1

**gather** (up) *vb* to call into being through the use of one's inner resources or powers — see SUMMON 2

**gathering** *n* **1** a body of people come together in one place ⟨the President spoke before the *gathering* of student leaders⟩
***syn*** assemblage, assembly, conference, congregation, convocation, meeting, muster
***rel*** aggregation, collection, conglomeration; company, coterie, gang, pack; caucus, forum, market, panel, rally, symposium, synod; crowd, flock, horde, legion, multitude, press, swarm, throng; crush, mob, rabble
**2** a coming together of a number of persons for a specified purpose — see MEETING 1
**3** a mass or quantity that has piled up or that has been gathered — see ACCUMULATION 1

**gauche** *adj* lacking social grace and assurance — see AWKWARD 1

**gaud** *n* a small object displayed for its attractiveness or interest — see KNICKKNACK

**gaudiness** *n* excessive or unnecessary display — see OSTENTATION

**gaudy** *adj* excessively showy ⟨the bright purple sequined miniskirt she wore to the wedding was *gaudy*⟩
***syn*** flamboyant, flashy, garish, glitzy, loud, ostentatious, splashy, swank (*or* swanky), tawdry

---

***syn*** synonym(s) ***rel*** related words
***ant*** antonym(s) ***near ant*** near antonym(s)

*rel* meretricious, pretentious; graceless, inelegant, tacky, tasteless, vulgar; bedizened, extravagant, fancy, florid, glittery, spectacular; lurid, ornate, overdone, overwrought
*near ant* appropriate, fitting, proper; inconspicuous, muted, restrained, subdued, toned (down), unobtrusive; elegant, graceful, tasteful; modest, plain, simple, unpretentious
*ant* conservative, quiet, understated

**gauge** *also* **gage** *vb* **1** to decide the size, amount, number, or distance of (something) without actual measurement — see ESTIMATE 2
**2** to find out the size, extent, or amount of — see MEASURE

**gaunt** *adj* suffering extreme weight loss as a result of hunger or disease — see EMACIATED

**gauntlet** *also* **gantlet** *n* a test of faith, patience, or strength — see TRIAL

**gauzy** *adj* **1** being of a material lacking in sturdiness or substance — see FLIMSY 1
**2** very thin and easy to see through — see SHEER 1

**gawk** *n* a big clumsy often slow-witted person — see OAF

**gawk** *vb* to look long and hard in wonder or surprise — see GAPE

**gawky** *adj* lacking in physical ease and grace in movement or in the use of the hands — see CLUMSY 1

**gay** *adj* **1** having much high-spirited energy and movement — see LIVELY 1
**2** having or showing a lack of concern or seriousness — see CAREFREE
**3** indicative of or marked by high spirits or good humor — see MERRY
**4** having or showing a good mood or disposition — see CHEERFUL 1
**5** serving to lift one's spirits — see CHEERFUL 2

**gaze** *vb* to look long and hard in wonder or surprise — see GAPE

**gazette** *n* a publication that appears at regular intervals — see JOURNAL

**gear** *n* items needed for the performance of a task or activity — see EQUIPMENT

**gel** *vb* to turn from a liquid into a substance resembling jelly — see COAGULATE

**gelatinous** *adj* being of such a thick consistency as to readily cling to objects upon contact — see STICKY 1

**gem** *n* **1** a usually valuable stone cut and polished for ornament ⟨a ring set with diamonds and other precious *gems*⟩
*syn* brilliant, gemstone, jewel
*rel* birthstone; baguette, cameo, scarab, solitaire, teardrop; paste, rhinestone, zircon
*near ant* rough
**2** someone or something unusually desirable — see PRIZE 1

**gemstone** *n* a usually valuable stone cut and polished for ornament — see GEM 1

**genealogy** *n* the line of ancestors from whom a person is descended — see ANCESTRY

**general** *adj* **1** belonging or relating to the whole ⟨a *general* increase in postage rates⟩ ⟨there's been a *general* improvement in the economy⟩
*syn* blanket, common, generic, global, overall, universal
*rel* broad, collective, comprehensive, extensive, pervasive, sweeping, ubiquitous, wholesale, wide, widespread; complete, full, plenary; planetary, worldwide
*near ant* component, constituent; cross-sectional, divisional, fragmentary, partial; local, localized, regional, sectional
*ant* individual, particular
**2** relating to the main elements and not to specific details ⟨gave the *general* impression of being kindhearted⟩ ⟨a *general* course of study in American history⟩
*syn* all-around (*also* all-round), bird's-eye, broad, nonspecific, overall
*rel* comprehensive, inclusive; absolute, boundless, expansive, extensive, infinite, panoramic, sweeping, vast, wide; indeterminate, nebulous, nondescript, vague; nonspecific, unlimited, unrestricted, unspecified
*near ant* limited, restricted, specified; distinct, explicit, precise, sharp; comprehensive, elaborate, full, mapped (out), thorough; enumerated, inventoried, itemized, listed; individual, singular; particular, peculiar
*ant* delineated, detailed, particularized, specific
**3** held by or applicable to a majority of the people ⟨it was the *general* opinion that the politician was a liar⟩ ⟨the *general* mood of the nation was one of hope and optimism⟩
*syn* common, public, popular, prevailing, vulgar
*rel* unanimous, universal; pop; everyday, familiar, household, usual, well-known; contemporary, current, present; dominant, predominant, preponderant; characteristic, typical; pandemic, pervasive, prevalent, rife, widespread; communal, shared
*near ant* rare, strange, unknown, unusual; distinctive, especial, idiosyncratic, peculiar, special, unique; individual, separate, singular; nonpublic, personal, private
*ant* uncommon, unpopular
**4** not limited or specialized in application or purpose ⟨a new kitchen tool of *general* usefulness⟩
*syn* all-around (*also* all-round), all-purpose, unlimited, unqualified, unrestricted, unspecialized
*rel* broad, wide; nonspecific, unspecified, vague
*near ant* bounded, circumscribed, confined, definite, demarcated, determinate, finite, qualified
*ant* limited, restricted, specialized, technical

**generality** *n* **1** an idea or statement about all of the members of a group or all the

instances of a situation — see GENERALIZATION
2 the main or greater part of something as distinguished from its appendages — see BODY 1

**generalization** *n* an idea or statement about all of the members of a group or all the instances of a situation ⟨the *generalization* that children who like violent entertainment grow up to be violent criminals⟩
***syn*** aphorism, generality, maxim, stereotype
***rel*** concept, conception, notion; precept, rule, rule of thumb; adage, proverb, saw, saying; cliché, commonplace, platitude, truism; hypothesis, proposition, theory

**generally** *adv* 1 according to the usual course of things — see NATURALLY 2
2 for the most part — see CHIEFLY

**generate** *vb* to be the cause of (a situation, action, or state of mind) — see EFFECT

**generator** *n* a person who establishes a whole new field of endeavor — see FATHER 2

**generic** *adj* belonging or relating to the whole — see GENERAL 1

**generosity** *n* the quality or state of being generous — see LIBERALITY

**generous** *adj* 1 giving or sharing in abundance and without hesitation ⟨a civic leader who is very *generous* with his money and time⟩
***syn*** bounteous, bountiful, charitable, free, freehanded, liberal, munificent, openhanded, unselfish, unsparing
***rel*** extravagant, handsome, lavish, profuse, unstinting; altruistic, beneficent, benevolent, hospitable, humanitarian, philanthropic; compassionate, goodhearted, greathearted, kindly, magnanimous, openhearted
***near ant*** mean, petty, small; frugal, spare, sparing, thrifty; chary, stinting; acquisitive, avaricious, avid, coveting, covetous, desirous, grasping, hoggish, itchy, mercenary, rapacious; begrudging, envious, grudging, resentful
***ant*** cheap, close, closefisted, miserly, niggardly, parsimonious, penurious, selfish, stingy, tight, tightfisted, uncharitable
2 being more than enough without being excessive — see PLENTIFUL

**generously** *adv* in a generous manner — see WELL 2

**genesis** *n* the point at which something begins — see BEGINNING

**genetic** *also* **genetical** *adj* genetically passed or capable of being passed from parent to offspring — see HEREDITARY

**genial** *adj* 1 having an easygoing and pleasing manner especially in social situations — see AMIABLE
2 having or showing kindly feeling and sincere interest — see FRIENDLY 1
3 showing a natural kindness and courtesy especially in social situations — see GRACIOUS 1

**geniality** *n* the state or quality of having a pleasant or agreeable manner in socializing with others — see AMIABILITY 1

**genius** *n* 1 a very smart person ⟨the 16-year-old college graduate was considered to be a *genius*⟩
***syn*** brain, intellect, thinker, whiz, wizard
***rel*** egghead, highbrow, intellectual; master, virtuoso; ace, crackerjack, natural; sage, savant
***near ant*** ignoramus, illiterate, knownothing; ass, donkey, fool, jackass; beast, boor, cad, churl, clown, creep, cretin, cur, heel, jerk, louse, lout, skunk, snake, stinker
***ant*** blockhead, dodo, dolt, dope, dumbbell, dummy, dunce, fathead, goon, halfwit, idiot, imbecile, knothead, moron, nitwit, numskull (*or* numbskull), pinhead
2 a special and usually inborn ability — see TALENT
3 a habitual attraction to some activity or thing — see INCLINATION 1
4 the set of qualities that makes a person, a group of people, or a thing different from others — see NATURE 1

**gent** *n* an adult male human being — see MAN 1

**genteel** *adj* 1 following the established traditions of refined society and good taste — see PROPER 1
2 having or showing a taste for the fine arts and gracious living — see CULTIVATED
3 of high birth, rank, or station — see NOBLE 1
4 showing consideration, courtesy, and good manners — see POLITE 1

**gentile** *n* a person who does not worship the God of the Bible — see HEATHEN 1

**gentility** *n* speech or behavior that is a sign of good breeding — see POLITENESS

**gentle** *adj* 1 not harsh or stern especially in manner, nature, or effect ⟨use a *gentle* detergent on that delicate silk blouse⟩ ⟨the pastor had a *gentle* disposition that calmed everyone he met⟩
***syn*** balmy, benign, bland, delicate, light, mellow, mild, soft, soothing, tender
***rel*** sleek, slick, smooth; calm, pacific, peaceful, placid, quiet, serene, tranquil; clement, compassionate, easy, lenient, merciful; buffering, cushioning, softening
***near ant*** exquisite, fierce, intense, powerful, severe; forceful, forcible, savage, violent; roughened, rugged, strong; abrading, irritating, roughening; grim, gruff, rude, stiff; heavy-handed, oppressive, tyrannical (*also* tyrannic)
***ant*** abrasive, caustic, coarse, hard, harsh, rough, scathing, stern, ungentle
2 marked by temperatures that are neither too high nor too low — see CLEMENT
3 of high birth, rank, or station — see NOBLE 1

---

***syn*** synonym(s) ***rel*** related words
***ant*** antonym(s) ***near ant*** near antonym(s)

**gentle** *vb* to lessen the shock of — see CUSHION

**gentleman** *n* **1** a man of high birth or social position ⟨many of the signers of the Declaration of Independence were *gentlemen* who were risking everything⟩
*syn* aristocrat, grandee, noble, nobleman, patrician
*rel* squire; cavalier, knight; don, nawab, seigneur, seignior, sheikh (*or* sheik); baron, baronet, count, duke, earl, esquire, lord, marquess, marquis, prince, thane, viscount; czar (*also* tsar *or* tzar), magnate, mogul, nabob; socialite, swell
*near ant* boor, churl, cotter (*or* cottar), fellah, peasant, peon; commoner, plebeian; proletarian; toiler
**2** an adult male human being — see MAN 1
**3** an honorable and courteous man — see CAVALIER

**gentlewoman** *n* a woman of high birth or social position ⟨in the 19th century a number of American *gentlewomen* used their wealth and influence to further abolitionism, women's rights, and other worthy causes⟩
*syn* dame, lady, noblewoman
*rel* ladyship, madam; baroness, countess, duchess, marchioness; czarina (*also* tsarina *or* tzarina), empress, queen; dowager, matriarch, matron, mistress

**gentry** *n* the highest class in a society — see ARISTOCRACY

**genuine** *adj* **1** being exactly as appears or as claimed — see AUTHENTIC 1
**2** free from any intent to deceive or impress others — see GUILELESS

**genuinely** *adv* in actual fact — see VERY 2

**geometry** *n* the outward appearance of something as distinguished from its substance — see FORM 1

**geriatric** *adj* being of advanced years and especially past middle age — see ELDERLY

**germane** *adj* having to do with the matter at hand — see PERTINENT

**germfree** *adj* free from filth, infection, or dangers to health — see SANITARY

**gestation** *n* the state of containing unborn young within the body — see PREGNANCY

**gesticulation** *n* a movement of the body or limbs that expresses or emphasizes an idea or feeling — see GESTURE

**gesture** *n* **1** a movement of the body or limbs that expresses or emphasizes an idea or feeling ⟨a teenager who often shrugs her shoulders in a *gesture* of indifference⟩
*syn* gesticulation, pantomime, sign, signal
*rel* beck, flourish, shrug, wave; body language, posture; indication, motion
**2** an act or utterance that is a customary show of good manners — see CIVILITY 1

**gesture** *vb* to direct or notify by a movement or gesture — see MOTION

**get** *vb* **1** to acquire complete knowledge, understanding, or skill in — see LEARN 1
**2** to become affected with (a disease or disorder) — see CONTRACT 1
**3** to become the father of — see FATHER
**4** to cause (someone) to agree with a belief or course of action by using arguments or earnest requests — see PERSUADE
**5** to come upon after searching, study, or effort — see FIND 1
**6** to disturb the peace of mind of (someone) especially by repeated disagreeable acts — see IRRITATE 1
**7** to eventually have as a state or quality — see BECOME
**8** to receive as return for effort — see EARN 1
**9** to recognize the meaning of — see COMPREHEND 1
**10** to take physical control or possession of (something) suddenly or forcibly — see CATCH 1
**11** to leave a place often for another — see GO 2

**get along** *vb* **1** to meet one's day-to-day needs ⟨most college students can *get along* with just a few hours of sleep at night⟩
*syn* cope, do, fare, get by, get on, make out, manage, shift
*rel* carry on, contrive, fend, handle, scrape (by *or* through), survive; eke out, scrape (out), scrounge, squeeze, wrest, wring; afford, swing
*phrases* make shift
*near ant* collapse, fail, fall short, fizzle, flounder; decline, peter (out), slump, wane; give up
**2** to move forward along a course — see GO 1

**getaway** *n* the act or an instance of getting free from danger or confinement — see ESCAPE 1

**get by** *vb* to meet one's day-to-day needs — see GET ALONG 1

**get off** *vb* **1** to leave a place often for another — see GO 2
**2** to take the first step in (a process or course of action) — see BEGIN 1

**get on** *vb* to meet one's day-to-day needs — see GET ALONG 1

**get out** *vb* **1** to become known ⟨news of the rock star's secret wedding *got out* to the news media⟩
*syn* come out, leak (out), out, spread
*rel* break, develop, transpire, unfold; circulate, disclose, reveal, spill, tell
*near ant* hush (up), suppress; conceal, disguise, hide, mask; secrete
**2** to get free from a dangerous or confining situation — see ESCAPE 1
**3** to produce and release for distribution in printed form — see PUBLISH 1

**get–together** *n* **1** a coming together of a number of persons for a specified purpose — see MEETING 1
**2** a social gathering — see PARTY 1

**getup** *n* clothing chosen as appropriate for a specific situation — see OUTFIT 1

**get up** *vb* to leave one's bed — see ARISE 1

**gewgaw** *n* a small object displayed for its attractiveness or interest — see KNICK-KNACK

**ghastliness** *n* the quality of inspiring intense dread or dismay — see HORROR 1

**ghastly** *adj* extremely disturbing or repellent — see HORRIBLE 1

**ghost** *n* the soul of a dead person thought of especially as appearing to living people ⟨looked for *ghosts* in the graveyard on Halloween⟩
*syn* apparition, bogey (*also* bogy *or* bogie), phantasm, phantom, poltergeist, shade, shadow, specter (*or* spectre), spirit, spook, vision, wraith
*rel* banshee, demon (*or* daemon), familiar (*or* familiar spirit), genie, imp, incubus, puck; vampire, zombie

**ghoul** *n* an evil spirit — see DEMON

**giant** *adj* unusually large — see HUGE

**giant** *n* something that is unusually large and powerful ⟨the Great Pyramids of Egypt are *giants*⟩
*syn* behemoth, blockbuster, colossus, jumbo, leviathan, mammoth, monster, titan, whale, whopper
*rel* amazon; bulk, hulk; heavyweight
*near ant* lightweight, weakling, wimp, wisp; nonentity, twerp, whippersnapper
*ant* dwarf, midget, mini, miniature, peewee, pygmy, runt, shrimp

**gibber** *vb* to speak rapidly, inarticulately, and usually unintelligibly — see BABBLE 1

**gibberish** *n* unintelligible or meaningless talk ⟨was so excited he could only talk *gibberish*⟩
*syn* babble, blabber, bunk, claptrap, drivel, fudge, gabble, gobbledygook (*also* gobbledegook), hogwash, jabber, jabberwocky, jazz, moonshine, mumbo jumbo, nonsense, piffle, prattle, rigmarole, rot
*rel* abracadabra; chatter, clatter, gab, gibber, prate, tattle, twaddle; double-talk, hocus-pocus, jive; gas, hot air, wind

**gibe** *or* **jibe** *vb* to make (someone or something) the object of unkind laughter — see RIDICULE

**giddy** *adj* **1** lacking in seriousness or maturity ⟨the *giddy* youngsters continued to laugh, joke, and make faces during the ceremonies⟩
*syn* featherbrained, flighty, frivolous, goofy, harebrained, light-headed, puerile, scatterbrained, silly
*rel* fatuous, foolish, inane, nonsensical, thoughtless, witless; crazy, daffy, daft, exuberant, flippant, fluttery, light, light-hearted, playful; sappy, shallow, superficial
*near ant* grave, melancholy, somber (*or* sombre), thoughtful; dignified, heavy, nonnonsense, sedate, severe, solemn, staid
*ant* earnest, serious, serious-minded, sober
**2** having a feeling of being whirled about and in danger of falling down — see DIZZY 1

**gift** *n* **1** something given to someone without expectation of a return ⟨gave him a *gift* for his birthday⟩
*syn* bestowal, donation, freebie (*or* freebee), giveaway, lagniappe, largess (*or* largesse), present, presentation
*rel* alms, benefaction, beneficence, benevolence, charity, contribution, dole, generosity, offering, philanthropy; grant, subsidy; remembrance, tribute; bonus, boon, windfall; favor, valentine; gratuity, tip; award, prize, reward; bequest, legacy; sacrifice
*near ant* advance, loan; bribe, sop
**2** a special and usually inborn ability — see TALENT

**gigantic** *adj* unusually large — see HUGE

**giggle** *n* an explosive sound that is a sign of amusement — see LAUGH 1

**gimmick** *n* **1** a clever often underhanded means to achieve an end — see TRICK 1
**2** an interesting and often novel device with a practical use — see GADGET

**ginger** *n* active strength of body or mind — see VIGOR 1

**gingerbread** *adj* elaborately and often excessively decorated — see ORNATE

**gingerly** *adj* having or showing a close attentiveness to avoiding danger or trouble — see CAREFUL 1

**gingery** *adj* **1** having active strength of body or mind — see VIGOROUS 1
**2** marked by a lively display of strong feeling — see SPIRITED 1

**gird** *vb* **1** to encircle or bind with or as if with a belt ⟨for the celebration of the heroes' return, well-wishers *girded* hundreds of trees with yellow ribbons⟩ ⟨she *girded* her waist with a delicate sash⟩
*syn* band, belt, girdle, girt, girth, wrap
*rel* tie up, truss; circle, loop, wind, wreathe; bandage, swathe; chain, cord, enchain, lash, rope, shackle, tape, wire
*near ant* loose, loosen, unbind, unchain, undo, unfasten, unlash, untie, unwind
*ant* unwrap
**2** to gather into a tight mass by means of a line or cord — see TIE 1

**girdle** *n* a strip of flexible material (as leather) worn around the waist — see [2]BELT

**girdle** *vb* **1** to encircle or bind with or as if with a belt — see GIRD 1
**2** to pass completely around — see ENCIRCLE 1

**girl** *n* **1** a young usually unmarried woman ⟨a book that discusses the special challenges that *girls* face as they enter their teenage years⟩
*syn* bobby-soxer, chick [*slang*], damsel, doll, gal, lass, lassie, mademoiselle, maid, maiden, miss
*rel* gamine; hoyden, tomboy; hussy; ingenue; belle, deb, debutante, sylph; schoolgirl; teenybopper; senorita (*or* señorita)
**2** a woman with whom one is in love — see GIRLFRIEND

---

*syn* synonym(s) *rel* related words
*ant* antonym(s) *near ant* near antonym(s)

**girlfriend** *n* a woman with whom one is in love ⟨he proposed to his *girlfriend* of seven years⟩
*syn* gal, girl, ladylove
*rel* mistress; beloved, darling, dear, favorite, flame, honey, love, lover, sweet, sweetheart, valentine
**girlish** *adj* having or displaying qualities more suitable for women than for men — see EFFEMINATE
**girt** *vb* to encircle or bind with or as if with a belt — see GIRD 1
**girth** *n* the distance around a round body — see CIRCUMFERENCE 1
**girth** *vb* **1** to encircle or bind with or as if with a belt — see GIRD 1
**2** to pass completely around — see ENCIRCLE 1
**gist** *n* the central part or aspect of something under consideration — see CRUX
**give** *vb* **1** to make a present of ⟨tutors *gave* their time to help students after school⟩
*syn* bestow, contribute, donate, present
*rel* chip in, kick in, pitch in; award, confer, dole (out), endow; afford, furnish, provide; lavish, regale; aid, assist, benefit, help; administer, dispense, impart, issue, render; extend, offer, pay, proffer, tender; sacrifice
*near ant* hold, keep, pocket, retain, withhold; preserve, save; advance, lend, loan; sell
**2** to put (something) into the possession or safekeeping of another ⟨*gave* my camera to my father to hold while I went swimming⟩
*syn* commend, commit, consign, delegate, deliver, entrust, hand over, leave, pass, transfer, transmit, trust, turn over, vest
*rel* confer, grant; assign, deal (out), dispense, disperse, distribute, divide; release, relinquish, submit, surrender, turn in, yield; bequeath, hand down, will; advance, lend, loan; furnish, supply
*near ant* detain, hold back, reserve, withhold; own, possess; accept, receive, take in; occupy, take, take over
*ant* hold, keep, retain
**3** to bring before the public in performance or exhibition — see PRESENT 1
**4** to fall down or in as a result of physical pressure — see COLLAPSE 1
**5** to hand over or use up in payment — see SPEND 1
**6** to make known (as an idea, emotion, or opinion) — see EXPRESS 1
**7** to occupy (oneself) diligently or with close attention — see APPLY 2
**8** to produce as revenue — see YIELD 2
**9** to put (something) into the possession of someone for use or consumption — see FURNISH 2
**10** to put before another for acceptance or consideration — see OFFER 1
**give–and–take** *n* **1** an exchange of views for the purpose of exploring a subject or deciding an issue — see DISCUSSION 1
**2** the act or practice of each side giving up something in order to reach an agreement — see CONCESSION 1
**3** good-natured teasing or exchanging of clever remarks — see BANTER
**giveaway** *n* something given to someone without expectation of a return — see GIFT 1
**give away** *vb* to make known (something abstract) through outward signs — see SHOW 2
**give in** *vb* **1** to give up and cease resistance (as to a liking, temptation, or habit) — see YIELD 1
**2** to cease resistance (as to another's arguments, demands, or control) — see YIELD 3
**given** *adj* **1** being in the habit or custom — see ACCUSTOMED
**2** having a tendency to be or act in a certain way — see PRONE 1
**given name** *n* a name that is placed before one's family name — see FORENAME
**give out** *vb* to stop functioning — see FAIL 1
**give up** *vb* **1** to give (something) over to the control or possession of another usually under duress — see SURRENDER 1
**2** to stop doing (something) permanently — see QUIT 2
**3** to yield to the control or power of enemy forces — see FALL 2
**giving** *n* the act of offering money in exchange for goods or services — see PAYMENT 1
**gizmo** *or* **gismo** *n* an interesting and often novel device with a practical use — see GADGET
**glacial** *adj* **1** having a low or subnormal temperature — see COLD 1
**2** lacking in friendliness or warmth of feeling — see COLD 2
**glad** *adj* **1** experiencing pleasure, satisfaction, or delight ⟨the husband was *glad* to see his wife again, after so long an absence⟩
*syn* blissful, delighted, gratified, happy, joyful, joyous, pleased, satisfied, tickled
*rel* beaming, blithe, blithesome, buoyant, cheerful, cheery, gay, gladsome, lighthearted, sunny, upbeat; gleeful, jocund, jolly, jovial, laughing, merry, mirthful, smiling; carried away, ecstatic, elated, enraptured, entranced, euphoric, exhilarated, intoxicated, rapturous, rhapsodic; exuberant, exultant, jubilant, rapt, rejoicing, thrilled; hopeful, optimistic, rosy, sanguine
*near ant* abject, aggrieved, anguished, blue, brokenhearted, dejected, depressed, despondent, disconsolate, disheartened, downcast, downhearted, forlorn, melancholy; doleful, dolorous, lachrymose, mournful, plaintive, sorrowful, sorry, woeful; black, dark, desolate, dispirited, gloomy, glum, gray (*also* grey), grieved, heartbroken, heartsick, miserable, woebegone, wretched
*ant* displeased, joyless, sad, unhappy, unsatisfied

2 having a desire or inclination (as for a specified course of action) — see WILLING 1
3 serving to lift one's spirits — see CHEERFUL 2

**gladden** *vb* to give satisfaction to — see PLEASE

**gladdening** *adj* making one feel good inside — see HEARTWARMING

**gladiatorial** *adj* feeling or displaying eagerness to fight — see BELLIGERENT

**gladness** *n* 1 a feeling or state of well-being and contentment — see HAPPINESS 1
2 the feeling experienced when one's wishes are met — see PLEASURE 1

**gladsome** *adj* having or showing a good mood or disposition — see CHEERFUL 1

**glamorize** *also* **glamourize** *vb* to represent or think of as better than reality — see IDEALIZE

**glamorous** *also* **glamourous** *adj* 1 excitingly or mysteriously unusual — see EXOTIC
2 having an often mysterious or magical power to attract — see FASCINATING 1

**glamour** *also* **glamor** *n* the power of irresistible attraction — see CHARM 2

**glance** *n* an instance of looking especially briefly — see LOOK 2

**glance** *vb* 1 to strike and fly off at an angle ⟨the basketball *glanced* off the rim⟩ ⟨her wild pitch *glanced* off my shoulder and landed in the dugout⟩
*syn* bounce, carom, rebound, ricochet, skim, skip
*rel* brush, graze, nudge, shave, sweep; bump, contact, hit, kiss, touch; sideswipe; reflect
2 to take a quick or hasty look ⟨just *glanced* at the instructions before assembling the bike⟩ ⟨*glanced* over his shoulder to see if she was still there⟩
*syn* browse, dip, glimpse, peek, skim
*rel* peep; blink, squint; look over, scan
*near ant* examine, overlook, oversee, question, survey; study, view; peer, pry; gawk, goggle, rubberneck; leer, ogle
*ant* gaze, stare
3 to shoot forth bursts of light — see FLASH 1

**glare** *n* the steady giving off of the form of radiation that makes vision possible — see LIGHT 1

**glare** *vb* 1 to shine with a bright harsh light ⟨the spotlight *glared* down on the suspect as the police questioned him relentlessly⟩
*syn* beat, blaze, burn, flame, flare
*rel* beam, glow, radiate; flash, glance, gleam, glimmer, glint, glisten, glister, glitter, scintillate, shimmer, sparkle, twinkle; bedazzle, blind, daze, dazzle
2 to look with anger or disapproval — see FROWN

**glaring** *adj* very noticeable especially for being incorrect or bad — see EGREGIOUS

**glasses** *n pl* a pair of lenses set in a frame that is held in place with ear supports and which are usually worn to correct vision ⟨I'm a little nearsighted, so I'm going to need *glasses*⟩
*syn* eyeglasses, specs, spectacles
*rel* bifocals; monocle, pince-nez; sunglasses; goggles; contact lens

**gleam** *n* the steady giving off of the form of radiation that makes vision possible — see LIGHT 1

**gleam** *vb* to shoot forth bursts of light — see FLASH 1

**glee** *n* a mood characterized by high spirits and amusement and often accompanied by laughter — see MIRTH

**glee club** *n* an organized group of singers — see CHORUS 1

**gleeful** *adj* indicative of or marked by high spirits or good humor — see MERRY

**gleefulness** *n* a mood characterized by high spirits and amusement and often accompanied by laughter — see MIRTH

**glide** *vb* 1 to move or proceed smoothly and readily — see FLOW 2
2 to move through the air with or as if with outstretched wings — see FLY 1
3 to rest or move along the surface of a liquid or in the air — see FLOAT

**glimmer** *n* a very small amount — see PARTICLE 1

**glimmer** *vb* to shoot forth bursts of light — see FLASH 1

**glimpse** *n* an instance of looking especially briefly — see LOOK 2

**glimpse** *vb* to take a quick or hasty look — see GLANCE 2

**glint** *vb* to shoot forth bursts of light — see FLASH 1

**glisten** *vb* to shoot forth bursts of light — see FLASH 1

**glistening** *adj* having a shiny surface or finish — see GLOSSY

**glister** *vb* to shoot forth bursts of light — see FLASH 1

**glitter** *vb* to shoot forth bursts of light — see FLASH 1

**glitz** *n* excessive or unnecessary display — see OSTENTATION

**glitzy** *adj* excessively showy — see GAUDY

**gloaming** *n* 1 a time or place of little or no light — see DARK 1
2 the time from when the sun begins to set to the onset of total darkness — see DUSK 1

**glob** *n* 1 a small uneven mass — see LUMP 1
2 the quantity of fluid that falls naturally in one rounded mass — see DROP 1

**global** *adj* 1 belonging or relating to the whole — see GENERAL 1
2 covering everything or all important points — see ENCYCLOPEDIC
3 having every part of the surface the same distance from the center — see ROUND 1

**globe** *n* 1 a more or less round body or mass — see [1]BALL 1
2 the celestial body on which we live — see EARTH 1

---

*syn* synonym(s) *rel* related words
*ant* antonym(s) *near ant* near antonym(s)

**globule** *n* the quantity of fluid that falls naturally in one rounded mass — see DROP 1

**gloom** *n* **1** a state or spell of low spirits — see SADNESS
**2** a time or place of little or no light — see DARK 1

**gloom** *vb* **1** to look with anger or disapproval — see FROWN
**2** to take on a gloomy or forbidding look — see DARKEN 1

**gloominess** *n* a state or spell of low spirits — see SADNESS

**gloomy** *adj* **1** causing or marked by an atmosphere lacking in cheer ⟨the cold rain made for a *gloomy* day⟩
***syn*** black, bleak, cheerless, comfortless, dark, darkening, depressing, desolate, dismal, drear, dreary, elegiac, funereal, glum, gray (*also* grey), miserable, morbid, morose, murky, saturnine, sepulchral, somber (*or* sombre), sullen, wretched
***rel*** dejected, depressed, despondent, disconsolate, droopy, inconsolable, low, melancholy, sad, unhappy, woebegone, woeful; discomfiting, discouraging, disheartening, dismaying, dispiriting, distressful, distressing, upsetting; desperate, hopeless, pessimistic; lamentable, lugubrious, mournful, sorrowful; cloudy, colorless, drab, dull; dour, grim, lowering (*also* louring), menacing, negative, oppressive, threatening
***near ant*** blithe, blithesome, buoyant, gay, jocund, jolly, joyful, joyous, merry, mirthful; encouraging, hopeful, optimistic; lighthearted, lightsome
***ant*** bright, cheerful, cheering, cheery, comforting, cordial, gay, festive, friendly, heartwarming, sunshiny
**2** feeling unhappiness — see SAD 1
**3** being without light or without much light — see DARK 1

**glorify** *vb* **1** to enhance the status of — see EXALT
**2** to offer honor or respect to (someone) as a divine power — see WORSHIP 1
**3** to praise or publicize lavishly and often excessively — see TOUT 1
**4** to proclaim the glory of — see PRAISE 1
**5** to represent or think of as better than reality — see IDEALIZE

**glorious** *adj* large and impressive in size, grandeur, extent, or conception — see GRAND 1

**gloriously** *adv* in a pleasing way — see WELL 5

**gloriousness** *n* impressiveness of beauty on a large scale — see MAGNIFICENCE

**glory** *n* **1** public acknowledgment or admiration for an achievement ⟨the drama teacher gave the stage crew all the *glory* for the successful production⟩
***syn*** acclaim, accolade, credit, distinction, homage, honor, laurels
***rel*** celebrity, fame, renown, repute; compliment, encomium, eulogy, panegyric, toast, tribute; acclamation, ovation, plaudit, praise, rave, rhapsody; citation, commendation, note, recommendation; elevation, exaltation, glorification
**2** an asset that brings praise or renown ⟨the new computer lab was the *glory* of the middle school⟩
***syn*** boast, credit, honor, jewel, pride, treasure
***rel*** pièce de résistance, showpiece; attraction, feature, highlight; distinction, excellence, merit, value, virtue
***phrases*** a feather in one's cap
***near ant*** disgrace, dishonor; blemish, blot, defect, shame, slur, smirch, smudge, stain, stigma; eyesore, fright, horror, mess
**3** impressiveness of beauty on a large scale — see MAGNIFICENCE

**glory** *vb* to feel or express joy or triumph — see EXULT

**glorying** *adj* having or expressing feelings of joy or triumph — see EXULTANT

**gloss** *n* brightness created by light reflected from a surface — see SHINE 1

**gloss** *vb* to make smooth or glossy usually by repeatedly applying surface pressure — see POLISH

**gloss** (over) *vb* **1** to make (something) seem less bad by offering excuses — see PALLIATE 1
**2** to overlook or dismiss as of little importance — see EXCUSE 1

**glossy** *adj* having a shiny surface or finish ⟨the *glossy* finish on the gym floor⟩ ⟨a sports car with an interior upholstered with *glossy* leather⟩
***syn*** buffed, burnished, glistening, lustrous, polished, rubbed, satin, satiny, sleek
***rel*** silken, silky, slick, slippery; glassy, glazed, lacquered, shellacked, varnished; gleaming, glittering, reflective, shining
***near ant*** lackluster
***ant*** dim, dull, flat, lusterless, matte (*also* mat *or* matt)

**glow** *n* the steady giving off of the form of radiation that makes vision possible — see LIGHT 1

**glow** *vb* **1** to be on fire especially brightly — see BURN 1
**2** to develop a rosy facial color (as from excitement or embarrassment) — see BLUSH

**glower** *vb* **1** to look with anger or disapproval — see FROWN
**2** to take on a gloomy or forbidding look — see DARKEN 1

**glowing** *adj* **1** giving off or reflecting much light — see BRIGHT 1
**2** having a healthy reddish skin tone — see RUDDY
**3** having or being an outward sign of good feelings (as of love, confidence, or happiness) — see RADIANT 1
**4** having or expressing great depth of feeling — see FERVENT

**gloze** (over) *vb* **1** to make (something) seem less bad by offering excuses — see PALLIATE 1
**2** to overlook or dismiss as of little importance — see EXCUSE 1

**glue** *n* a substance used to stick things together ⟨used *glue* to stick the photo in the album⟩
*syn* adhesive, cement, size
*rel* epoxy, epoxy resin, library paste, mucilage, superglue; dope, goo, gum
**gluey** *adj* being of such a thick consistency as to readily cling to objects upon contact — see STICKY 1
**glum** *adj* 1 causing or marked by an atmosphere lacking in cheer — see GLOOMY 1
2 feeling unhappiness — see SAD 1
3 given to or displaying a resentful silence and often irritability — see SULKY
**glut** *vb* to fill with food to capacity — see GORGE 1
**glutinous** *adj* being of such a thick consistency as to readily cling to objects upon contact — see STICKY 1
**glutton** *n* one who eats greedily or too much ⟨he's such a *glutton* that he ate the whole cake⟩
*syn* gorger, gormandizer, gourmand, hog, overeater, stuffer, swiller
*rel* feaster, trencherman; muncher; guzzler
*near ant* dieter, nibbler, picker
**gluttonous** *adj* having a huge appetite — see VORACIOUS 1
**gnash** *vb* to press or strike against or together so as to make a scraping sound — see GRIND 2
**gnaw** (on) *vb* to crush or grind with the teeth — see BITE (ON)
**gnawer** *n* one who is obnoxiously annoying — see NUISANCE 1
**gnome** *n* an imaginary being usually having a small human form and magical powers — see FAIRY
**go** *adj* being in a state of fitness for some experience or action — see READY 1
**go** *n* 1 a practice or interest that is very popular for a short time — see FAD
2 active strength of body or mind — see VIGOR 1
3 an effort to do or accomplish something — see ATTEMPT
4 readiness to engage in daring or difficult activity — see ENTERPRISE 2
**go** *vb* 1 to move forward along a course ⟨everything is *going* according to our plans⟩
*syn* advance, fare, forge, get along, march, proceed, progress
*rel* accelerate, fast-forward, speed; approach, near; journey, pass, repair, run, travel, wend; actuate, drive, impel, propel, push; do, go off, take out
*phrases* gain ground
*near ant* arrest, balk, block, check, detain, halt, hinder, hold back, impede, nip, obstruct, slow (down *or* up), stem; repress, retard, stunt, suppress; delay, interrupt, stall; cramp, hamper, inhibit; cease, let up, pause; regress
*ant* remain, stand, stay, stop
2 to leave a place often for another ⟨will *go* on vacation at the end of the year⟩ ⟨decided it would be better to *go* before she got any angrier⟩
*syn* begone, clear out, depart, exit, get, get off, move, pull (out), quit, sally (forth), shove (off), take off, walk out
*rel* set out, start, strike out; abscond, decamp, escape, evacuate, flee, fly, get out, run away, scat, scram, skip; go out, light out, step out; abandon, desert, forsake, vacate; emigrate; remove, retire, retreat, withdraw
*phrases* beat it
*near ant* abide, dwell, lodge, remain, settle, stay, tarry; approach, close, near; hit, land, reach
*ant* arrive, come, show up, turn up
3 to be fitting or proper — see DO 1
4 to be in agreement on every point — see CHECK 1
5 to be positioned along a certain course or in a certain direction — see RUN 3
6 to eventually have as a state or quality — see BECOME
7 to fall down or in as a result of physical pressure — see COLLAPSE 1
8 to have or be in a usual or proper place — see BELONG 1
9 to lose bodily strength or vigor — see WEAKEN 2
10 to make one's way through, across, or over — see TRAVERSE
11 to occur within a continuous range of variation — see RUN 4
12 to risk (something) on the outcome of an uncertain event — see BET
**go** (for) *vb* to have a price of — see COST
**go** (on) *vb* to take place — see HAPPEN
**go** (to) *vb* to use or seek out as a source of aid, relief, or advantage — see RESORT (TO) 1
**goad** *n* something that arouses action or activity — see IMPULSE
**goad** *vb* 1 to try to persuade (someone) through earnest appeals to follow a course of action — see URGE
2 to urge or push forward with or as if with a pointed object — see PROD 1
**goal** *n* something that one hopes or intends to accomplish ⟨graduating from high school with honors is one of my main *goals*⟩
*syn* aim, ambition, aspiration, design, dream, end, intent, intention, mark, meaning, object, objective, plan, pretension, purpose, target, thing
*rel* plot, project, scheme; desire, hope, wish; destination, terminus
*near ant* means, method, way
**goat** *n* a person or thing taking the blame for others — see SCAPEGOAT
**[1]gob** *n* 1 a small uneven mass — see LUMP 1
2 **gobs** *pl* a considerable amount — see LOT 2
**[2]gob** *n* one who operates or navigates a seagoing vessel — see SAILOR
**gobbet** *n* a small uneven mass — see LUMP 1

*syn* synonym(s) *rel* related words
*ant* antonym(s) *near ant* near antonym(s)

**gobbledygook** *also* **gobbledegook** *n* unintelligible or meaningless talk — see GIBBERISH

**go–between** *n* **1** one that carries a message or does an errand — see MESSENGER
**2** one who works with opposing sides in order to bring about an agreement — see MEDIATOR

**goblin** *n* an imaginary being usually having a small human form and magical powers — see FAIRY

**god** *n* **1** a being having superhuman powers and control over a particular part of life or the world — see DEITY 1
**2** *cap* the being worshipped as the creator and ruler of the universe — see DEITY 2

**goddess** *n* a lovely woman — see BEAUTY 2

**godhead** *n* **1** the quality or state of being divine — see DIVINITY
**2** *cap* the being worshipped as the creator and ruler of the universe — see DEITY 2

**godhood** *n* the quality or state of being divine — see DIVINITY

**godless** *adj* lacking religious emotions, principles, or practices — see IRRELIGIOUS

**godlike** *adj* of, relating to, or being God — see HOLY 3

**godliness** *n* the quality or state of being spiritually pure or virtuous — see HOLINESS

**godly** *adj* showing a devotion to God and to a life of virtue — see HOLY 1

**godsend** *n* something that provides happiness or does good for a person or thing — see BLESSING 2

**Godspeed** *n* an expression of good wishes at parting — see GOOD-BYE

**go–getter** *n* an ambitious person who eagerly goes after what is desired ⟨a *go-getter* with his sights set on the presidency⟩
***syn*** hummer, hustler, live wire, powerhouse, rustler, self-starter
***rel*** dasher; doer, enterpriser; he-man
***near ant*** dawdler, idler, loafer, lounger, putterer, trifler; goldbrick; malingerer, procrastinator, shirker, slacker; drone, lazybones, sluggard; dallier, laggard, lingerer, loiterer, slowpoke, stick-in-the-mud; ignorer, ne'er-do-well, neglecter; daydreamer, dreamer; dropout, quitter

**go–getting** *adj* **1** having a strong desire for personal advancement — see AMBITIOUS 1
**2** having or showing a bold forcefulness in the pursuit of a goal — see AGGRESSIVE 1

**go–getting** *n* eager desire for personal advancement — see AMBITION 1

**goggle** *vb* to look long and hard in wonder or surprise — see GAPE

**going** *adj* **1** accepted, used, or practiced by most people — see CURRENT 1
**2** being in effective operation — see ACTIVE 1
**3** having attained a desired end or state of good fortune — see SUCCESSFUL 1

**going** *n* **1** forward movement in time or place — see ADVANCE 1
**2** the act of leaving a place — see DEPARTURE

**gold** *n* something (as pieces of stamped metal or printed paper) customarily and legally used as a medium of exchange, a measure of value, or a means of payment — see MONEY

**goldbrick** *n* one who deliberately avoids work or duty — see SLACKER

**golden** *adj* **1** having qualities which inspire hope — see HOPEFUL 1
**2** marked by conspicuously full and rich sounds or tones — see RESONANT
**3** marked by vigorous growth and well-being especially economically — see PROSPEROUS 1
**4** of a pale yellow or yellowish brown color — see BLOND
**5** pointing toward a happy outcome — see FAVORABLE 2

**golden–ager** *n* a person of advanced years — see SENIOR CITIZEN

**golden mean** *n* a middle point between extremes — see MEAN 1

**gone** *adj* **1** no longer existing — see EXTINCT
**2** no longer living — see DEAD 1
**3** no longer possessed — see LOST

**good** *adj* **1** based on sound reasoning or information ⟨had enough information to make a *good* assessment of the situation⟩
***syn*** commonsense, hard, informed, just, justified, levelheaded, logical, rational, reasonable, reasoned, sensible, sober, solid, valid, well-founded
***rel*** actual, real, true; certain, sure; certified, validated, verified; confirmed, corroborated, substantiated; cogent, convincing, credible
***near ant*** unsubstantiated, unsupported, unwarranted; flimsy, implausible, unconvincing, weak; fallacious, false, misled
***ant*** groundless, illogical, invalid, irrational, nonrational, nonsensical, nonvalid, unfounded, ungrounded, uninformed, unjustified, unreasonable, unsound
**2** conforming to a high standard of morality or virtue ⟨a *good* person who seldom did wrong⟩ ⟨*good* behavior will earn you the respect of others⟩
***syn*** decent, ethical, honest, honorable, just, moral, right, righteous, right-minded, straight, upright, virtuous
***rel*** correct, decorous, proper, seemly; high-minded, noble, principled; commendable, creditable, exemplary, legitimate; esteemed, law-abiding, reputable, respected, upstanding, worthy; blameless, clean, guiltless, immaculate, incorruptible, innocent, inoffensive, irreproachable, unobjectionable; lily-white, pure, scrupulous, spotless, uncorrupted, unerring; goody-goody, moralistic, sanctimonious, self-righteous
***near ant*** improper, incorrect, indecorous, naughty, unbecoming, unseemly; corrupt, debased, debauched, degenerate,

depraved, dissolute, perverted, reprobate; unprincipled, unscrupulous; atrocious, infamous, villainous; base, low, mean, vicious, vile; blameworthy, objectionable, offensive; iniquitous, nefarious; errant, erring, fallen
***ant*** bad, black, dishonest, dishonorable, evil, evil-minded, immoral, indecent, sinful, unethical, unrighteous, wicked, wrong
**3** according to the rules of logic — see LOGICAL 1
**4** being to one's liking — see SATISFACTORY 1
**5** expressing approval — see FAVORABLE 1
**6** firm in one's allegiance to someone or something — see FAITHFUL 1
**7** giving pleasure or contentment to the mind or senses — see PLEASANT
**8** having or showing exceptional knowledge, experience, or skill in a field of endeavor — see PROFICIENT
**9** having sufficient worth or merit to receive one's honor, esteem, or reward — see WORTHY
**10** having the required skills for an acceptable level of performance — see COMPETENT
**11** meeting the requirements of a purpose or situation — see FIT 1
**12** showing or expressing acceptance or approval — see POSITIVE
**13** sufficiently large in size, amount, or number to merit attention — see CONSIDERABLE 1
**14** worthy of one's trust — see DEPENDABLE

**good** *adv* in a satisfactory way — see WELL 1

**good** *n* **1** something that provides happiness or does good for a person or thing — see BLESSING 2
**2** the state of doing well especially in relation to one's happiness or success — see WELFARE
**3 goods** *pl* products that are bought and sold in business — see MERCHANDISE

**Good Book** *n* a book made up of the writings accepted by Christians as coming from God — see BIBLE

**good–bye** *or* **good-by** *n* an expression of good wishes at parting ⟨said our *goodbyes* and headed for home⟩
***syn*** adieu, au revoir, bon voyage, farewell, Godspeed
***rel*** leave-taking, send-off
***near ant*** greeting(s), salutation, salute; welcome
***ant*** hello

**good–hearted** *adj* having or marked by sympathy and consideration for others — see HUMANE 1

**goodly** *adj* **1** of a size greater than average of its kind — see LARGE
**2** sufficiently large in size, amount, or number to merit attention — see CONSIDERABLE 1

**good–natured** *adj* having an easygoing and pleasing manner especially in social situations — see AMIABLE

**good–naturedness** *n* **1** a desire or disposition to please — see COMPLAISANCE
**2** the state or quality of having a pleasant or agreeable manner in socializing with others — see AMIABILITY 1

**goodness** *n* conduct that conforms to an accepted standard of right and wrong — see MORALITY 1

**good–sized** *adj* **1** of a size greater than average of its kind — see LARGE
**2** sufficiently large in size, amount, or number to merit attention — see CONSIDERABLE 1

**good–tempered** *adj* having an easygoing and pleasing manner especially in social situations — see AMIABLE

**good–temperedness** *n* the state or quality of having a pleasant or agreeable manner in socializing with others — see AMIABILITY 1

**goodwill** *n* **1** kindly concern, interest, or support ⟨the long tradition of *goodwill* that exists between the United States and Canada⟩
***syn*** amity, benevolence, cordiality, fellowship, friendliness, friendship, kindliness
***rel*** camaraderie, community, companionship, comradeship; civility, comity, concord, harmony, rapport; charity, generosity, neighborliness; affinity, communion, empathy, sympathy, tolerance; altruism, philanthropy, selflessness
***near ant*** disfavor, intolerance; animosity, antagonism, antipathy, enmity, hate, hatred, hostility, incivility, malice, rancor
***ant*** ill will, malevolence
**2** cheerful readiness to do something — see ALACRITY

**goody** *n* something that is pleasing to eat because it is rare or a luxury — see DELICACY 1

**gooey** *adj* being of such a thick consistency as to readily cling to objects upon contact — see STICKY 1

**goof** *n* an unintentional departure from truth or accuracy — see ERROR 1

**go off** *vb* to break open or into pieces usually because of internal pressure — see EXPLODE 1

**goofy** *adj* lacking in seriousness or maturity — see GIDDY 1

**goon** *n* **1** a stupid person — see IDIOT
**2** a violent, brutal person who is often a member of an organized gang — see HOODLUM

**goose** *n* a person who lacks good sense or judgment — see FOOL 1

**goose egg** *n* the numerical symbol 0 or the absence of number or quantity represented by it — see ZERO 1

**go over** *vb* to turn out as planned or desired — see SUCCEED 1

**gore** *vb* to penetrate or hold (something) with a pointed object — see IMPALE

**gorge** *n* a narrow opening between hillsides or mountains that can be used for passage — see CANYON

**gorge** *vb* **1** to fill with food to capacity ⟨they *gorged* themselves on the four pies Aunt Martha brought for Thanksgiving⟩
*syn* glut, sate, stuff, surfeit
*rel* gobble, gormandize, pig out; gulp, guzzle; cloy, fill; banquet, feast, regale
*near ant* diet, fast
**2** to eat greedily or to excess ⟨the kids *gorged* on Halloween candy when they got home from trick-or-treating⟩
*syn* gormandize, overeat, pig out, swill
*rel* devour, glut, sate, stuff, surfeit, wolf; banquet, feast, regale; bolt, cram, gulp, guzzle
*near ant* nibble, peck, pick, taste

**gorgeous** *adj* very pleasing to look at — see BEAUTIFUL

**gorgeousness** *n* the qualities in a person or thing that as a whole give pleasure to the senses — see BEAUTY 1

**gorger** *n* one who eats greedily or too much — see GLUTTON

**gormandize** *vb* to eat greedily or to excess — see GORGE 2

**gormandizer** *n* one who eats greedily or too much — see GLUTTON

**gory** *adj* containing, smeared, or stained with blood — see BLOODY 1

**gospel** *n* the basic beliefs or guiding principles of a person or group — see CREED 1

**gossamer** *adj* **1** being of a material lacking in sturdiness or substance — see FLIMSY 1
**2** resembling air in lightness — see AIRY 1
**3** very thin and easy to see through — see SHEER 1

**gossamery** *adj* **1** being of a material lacking in sturdiness or substance — see FLIMSY 1
**2** resembling air in lightness — see AIRY 1
**3** very thin and easy to see through — see SHEER 1

**gossip** *n* friendly, informal conversation or an instance of this — see CHAT

**gossip** *vb* to relate sometimes questionable or secret information of a personal nature ⟨likes to *gossip* with others about our neighbors' arguments⟩
*syn* blab, talk, tattle
*rel* bandy (about), circulate, noise (about), rumor; disclose, divulge, reveal, tell; hint, imply, insinuate, intimate, let on, suggest; inform, report, snitch, squeal, tip (off); babble, spill; confide
*phrases* spill the beans
*near ant* clam up, shut up

**gossipy** *adj* having the style and content of everyday conversation — see CHATTY 1

**gouge** *vb* to charge (someone) too much for goods or services — see OVERCHARGE 1

**gourmand** *n* **1** a person with refined tastes in food and wine — see EPICURE
**2** one who eats greedily or too much — see GLUTTON

**gourmet** *n* a person with refined tastes in food and wine — see EPICURE

**govern** *vb* **1** to exercise authority or power over ⟨the president is elected in order to *govern* the country⟩
*syn* boss, captain, command, control, preside (over), rule
*rel* conduct, direct, head, lead; administer, manage, oversee, regulate, superintend, supervise; dictate, dominate, domineer, lord (it over), master, oppress, reign (over), tyrannize; conquer, subdue, subjugate
**2** to keep from exceeding a desirable degree or level (as of expression) — see CONTROL 1
**3** to look after and make decisions about — see CONDUCT 1

**governance** *n* **1** lawful control over the affairs of a political unit (as a nation) — see RULE 2
**2** the act or activity of looking after and making decisions about something — see CONDUCT 1

**government** *n* **1** lawful control over the affairs of a political unit (as a nation) — see RULE 2
**2** the act or activity of looking after and making decisions about something — see CONDUCT 1

**gown** *n* a garment with a joined blouse and skirt for a woman or girl — see DRESS 1

**gown** *vb* to outfit with clothes and especially fine or special clothes — see CLOTHE 1

**grab** *n* an instance of theft — see THEFT 2

**grab** *vb* to take physical control or possession of (something) suddenly or forcibly — see CATCH 1

**grace** *n* **1** an act of kind assistance — see FAVOR 1
**2** dignified or restrained beauty of form, appearance, or style — see ELEGANCE

**grace** *vb* to make more attractive by adding something that is beautiful or becoming — see DECORATE

**graceful** *adj* **1** moving easily ⟨the *graceful* ballerina effortlessly leapt across the dance floor⟩
*syn* agile, light, light-footed, lissome (*also* lissom), lithe, lithesome, nimble, spry
*rel* flexible, limber, loose-jointed, pliable, pliant, supple; adroit, deft, dexterous (*also* dextrous); fleet-footed, surefooted
*near ant* inflexible, rigid, stiff; bungling, inept, maladroit
*ant* awkward, clumsy, gawky, graceless, lumbering, ungainly, ungraceful
**2** having or showing elegance — see ELEGANT 1

**gracefulness** *n* dignified or restrained beauty of form, appearance, or style — see ELEGANCE

**graceless** *adj* **1** lacking in physical ease and grace in movement or in the use of the hands — see CLUMSY 1

**2** lacking social grace and assurance — see AWKWARD 1
**3** not appropriate for a particular occasion or situation — see INAPPROPRIATE

**gracious** *adj* **1** showing a natural kindness and courtesy especially in social situations ⟨a *gracious* teacher who made the new student feel welcome⟩
***syn*** affable, cordial, genial, hospitable, sociable
***rel*** agreeable, amiable, benignant, congenial, convivial, friendly, kind, kindly, neighborly; accommodating, obliging; considerate, courteous, polite, thoughtful; sophisticated, urbane; approachable, attentive, outgoing
***near ant*** boorish, churlish; abrupt, blunt, brusque, curt, gruff, sharp, snippy; antisocial, disagreeable, discourteous, ill-mannered, impolite, rude, sullen, surly, uncivil, unfriendly, unkind, unmannerly; crabbed, crabby, cross, crusty, grumpy
***ant*** inhospitable, ungracious, unsociable
**2** having an easygoing and pleasing manner especially in social situations — see AMIABLE
**3** showing consideration, courtesy, and good manners — see POLITE 1

**graciousness** *n* **1** speech or behavior that is a sign of good breeding — see POLITENESS
**2** the state or quality of having a pleasant or agreeable manner in socializing with others — see AMIABILITY 1

**gradational** *adj* proceeding or changing by steps or degrees — see GRADUAL

**gradationally** *adv* by small steps or amounts — see GRADUALLY

**grade** *n* **1** an individual part of a process, series, or ranking — see DEGREE 1
**2** degree of excellence — see QUALITY 1
**3** one of the units into which a whole is divided on the basis of a common characteristic — see CLASS 2
**4** something set up as an example against which others of the same type are compared — see STANDARD 1
**5** the degree to which something rises up from a position level with the horizon — see SLANT

**grade** *vb* **1** to arrange or assign according to type — see CLASSIFY 1
**2** to take or have a certain position within a group arranged in vertical classes — see RANK 1

**gradient** *n* the degree to which something rises up from a position level with the horizon — see SLANT

**gradual** *adj* proceeding or changing by steps or degrees ⟨a *gradual* drop in gas prices will take place over the next several months⟩
***syn*** gradational, incremental, phased, piecemeal, step-by-step
***rel*** progressive, stepped, tapered; imperceptible, inching
***near ant*** abrupt, acute, sharp; changeable, dynamic, volatile
***ant*** sudden

**gradually** *adv* by small steps or amounts ⟨*gradually* worked his way down the class roster⟩ ⟨add the sugar to the beaten egg whites *gradually* to make the meringue⟩
***syn*** gradationally, little by little, piece by piece, piecemeal
***rel*** hierarchically, increasingly, progressively; fractionally, imperceptibly; slowly
***near ant*** acutely, sharply, steeply, unprogressively; hastily, precipitously
***ant*** abruptly, suddenly

**graduation** *n* a scheme of rank or order — see ³SCALE 1

**grain** *n* **1** a very small piece — see BIT 1
**2** one's characteristic attitude or mood — see DISPOSITION 1

**grainy** *adj* made up of large particles — see COARSE 1

**grand** *adj* **1** large and impressive in size, grandeur, extent, or conception ⟨the *grand* ceremonies that typically mark the opening of the Olympic Games⟩
***syn*** august, baronial, gallant, glorious, grandiose, heroic, imposing, magnificent, majestic, monumental, noble, proud, regal, royal, splendid, stately
***rel*** colossal, monstrous, prodigious, stupendous, tremendous; kingly, lordly, princely, queenly; awesome, awful, cosmic, sublime, wondrous; formidable, impressive, prepossessing, redoubtable; marvelous (*or* marvellous), superb, terrific, wonderful; extravagant, lavish, luxurious, opulent, sumptuous; gorgeous, resplendent, splendiferous; extraordinary, killer, remarkable, sensational, striking; celestial, divine, heavenly
***near ant*** lowly, modest, unprepossessing; average, common, mediocre, ordinary, run-of-the-mill, second-rate; abject, mean, meretricious, shabby, sordid; insignificant, measly, paltry, petty, puny, trifling, trivial
***ant*** humble, unheroic, unimposing, unimpressive
**2** coming before all others in importance — see FOREMOST 1
**3** not lacking any part or member that properly belongs to it — see COMPLETE 1
**4** of a size greater than average of its kind — see LARGE
**5** of high birth, rank, or station — see NOBLE 1
**6** of the very best kind — see EXCELLENT
**7** unusually large — see HUGE

**grandee** *n* a man of high birth or social position — see GENTLEMAN 1

**grandeur** *n* impressiveness of beauty on a large scale — see MAGNIFICENCE

**grandfather** *n* a person who is several generations earlier in an individual's line of descent — see ANCESTOR 1

**grandiloquence** *n* **1** boastful speech or writing — see BOMBAST 1
**2** language that is impressive-sounding but not meaningful or sincere — see RHETORIC 1

**grandiloquent** *adj* **1** full of fine words and fancy expressions — see FLOWERY 1
**2** marked by the use of impressive-sounding but mostly meaningless words and phrases — see RHETORICAL

**grandiose** *adj* **1** large and impressive in size, grandeur, extent, or conception — see GRAND 1
**2** self-consciously trying to present an appearance of grandeur or importance — see PRETENTIOUS 1

**grandiosity** *n* the quality or state of appearing or trying to appear more important or more valuable than is the case — see PRETENSE 1

**grandly** *adv* **1** in a luxurious manner — see HIGH
**2** in a manner befitting a person of the highest character and ideals — see GREATLY 1

**grandness** *n* **1** impressiveness of beauty on a large scale — see MAGNIFICENCE
**2** the quality or state of being large in size — see LARGENESS

**grange** *n* a piece of land and its buildings used to grow crops or raise livestock — see FARM

**granite** *n* firm or unwavering adherence to one's purpose — see DETERMINATION 1

**grant** *n* a sum of money allotted for a specific use by official or formal action — see APPROPRIATION

**grant** *vb* **1** to accept the truth or existence of (something) usually reluctantly — see ADMIT
**2** to give the ownership or benefit of (something) formally or publicly — see CONFER 1

**granting** *n* the approval by someone in authority for the doing of something — see PERMISSION

**granular** *adj* made up of large particles — see COARSE 1

**granulated** *adj* made up of large particles — see COARSE 1

**granule** *n* a very small piece — see BIT 1

**graphic** *also* **graphical** *adj* **1** producing a mental picture through clear and impressive description ⟨the report offered many *graphic* details about the huge earthquake that rocked the area⟩
***syn*** delineated, pictorial, picturesque, vivid
***rel*** depicted, descriptive, expressive; concrete, explicit, specific; faithful, lifelike, natural, realistic; fresh, incisive, sharp
***near ant*** indeterminate, nebulous, obscure, sketchy, unclear, vague; blurry, dark, dim, muddy, murky, shadowy
**2** consisting of or relating to pictures — see PICTORIAL 1

**graphic** *n* something that visually explains or decorates a text — see ILLUSTRATION 1

**grapple** *n* the act or manner of holding — see HOLD 1

**grapple** *vb* **1** to seize and attempt to unbalance one another for the purpose of achieving physical mastery — see WRESTLE
**2** to take physical control or possession of (something) suddenly or forcibly — see CATCH 1

**grapple** (with) *vb* to deal with (something) usually skillfully or efficiently — see HANDLE 1

**grasp** *n* **1** the ability to direct the course of something — see CONTROL 2
**2** the act or manner of holding — see HOLD 1
**3** the knowledge gained from the process of coming to know or understand something — see COMPREHENSION

**grasp** *vb* **1** to have a practical understanding of — see KNOW 1
**2** to put one's arms around and press tightly — see EMBRACE 1
**3** to reach for and take hold of by embracing with the fingers or arms — see TAKE 1
**4** to recognize the meaning of — see COMPREHEND 1

**grasping** *adj* having or marked by an eager and often selfish desire especially for material possessions — see GREEDY 1

**grassland** *n* a broad area of level or rolling treeless country — see PLAIN

**grate** *vb* **1** to disturb the peace of mind of (someone) especially by repeated disagreeable acts — see IRRITATE 1
**2** to pass roughly and noisily over or against a surface — see SCRAPE 1
**3** to press or strike against or together so as to make a scraping sound — see GRIND 2

**grateful** *adj* **1** feeling or expressing gratitude ⟨was *grateful* for her neighbor's help after she broke her foot⟩
***syn*** appreciative, obliged, thankful
***rel*** beholden, indebted; gratified, pleased; thanking
***ant*** thankless, unappreciative, ungrateful, unthankful
**2** giving pleasure or contentment to the mind or senses — see PLEASANT

**gratefulness** *n* acknowledgment of having received something good from another — see THANKS

**gratification** *n* the feeling experienced when one's wishes are met — see PLEASURE 1

**gratified** *adj* **1** experiencing pleasure, satisfaction, or delight — see GLAD 1
**2** feeling that one's needs or desires have been met — see CONTENT

**gratify** *vb* **1** to give in to (a desire) — see INDULGE
**2** to give satisfaction to — see PLEASE

**gratifying** *adj* **1** giving pleasure or contentment to the mind or senses — see PLEASANT
**2** making one feel good inside — see HEARTWARMING

**grating** *adj* **1** disagreeable to one's aesthetic or artistic sense — see HARSH 2
**2** harsh and dry in sound — see HOARSE

**gratis** *adj* not costing or charging anything — see FREE 4

**gratitude** *n* acknowledgment of having received something good from another — see THANKS

**gratuitous** *adj* **1** not costing or charging anything — see FREE 4
**2** not needed by the circumstances or to accomplish an end — see UNNECESSARY

**gratuity** *n* **1** a small sum of money given for a service over and above what is due — see [2]TIP 1
**2** something given in addition to what is ordinarily expected or owed — see BONUS

**grave** *adj* **1** having a matter of importance as its topic — see SERIOUS 2
**2** involving potential loss or injury — see DANGEROUS
**3** not joking or playful in mood or manner — see SERIOUS 1

**grave** *n* a final resting place for a dead person ⟨put flowers on his mother's *grave*⟩
***syn*** sepulcher (*or* sepulchre), sepulture, tomb
***rel*** catacomb, charnel, crypt, mausoleum, vault; cemetery, churchyard, graveyard, potter's field; barrow, mound, tumulus

**grave** *vb* to cut (as letters or designs) on a hard surface — see ENGRAVE 1

**gravel** *adj* harsh and dry in sound — see HOARSE

**gravelly** *adj* harsh and dry in sound — see HOARSE

**gravestone** *n* a shaped stone laid over or erected near a grave and usually bearing an inscription to identify and preserve the memory of the deceased — see TOMBSTONE

**graveyard** *n* a piece of land used for burying the dead — see CEMETERY

**gravid** *adj* containing unborn young within the body — see PREGNANT 1

**gravity** *n* a mental state free of jesting or trifling — see EARNESTNESS

**gravy** *n* **1** a savory fluid food used as a topping or accompaniment to a main dish — see SAUCE 1
**2** something given in addition to what is ordinarily expected or owed — see BONUS

**gray** *also* **grey** *adj* **1** of the color gray ⟨the *gray* elephant and the gaudily dressed circus performer created a striking contrast⟩
***syn*** grayish, leaden, pewter, silver, silvery, slate, slaty, steely
***rel*** achromatic, neutral; dirty, dull, faded, washed-out; ashen, ashy, chalky, livid, mousy (*or* mousey), pale, white, whitish; chocolate, dun, sandy, sepia; brindled, grizzled, hoar, hoary
***near ant*** ablaze, bright, deep, gay, rich; chromatic, colored
**2** causing or marked by an atmosphere lacking in cheer — see GLOOMY 1

**grayish** *adj* of the color gray — see GRAY 1

**gray matter** *n* the ability to learn and understand or to deal with problems — see INTELLIGENCE 1

[1]**graze** *vb* to feed on grass or herbs ⟨cows *grazing* in the meadow⟩
***syn*** browse, forage, pasture
***rel*** eat, feed, nibble

[2]**graze** *vb* **1** to damage by rubbing against a sharp or rough surface — see SCRAPE 2
**2** to pass lightly across or touch gently especially in passing — see BRUSH

**grease** *vb* to coat (something) with a slippery substance in order to reduce friction — see LUBRICATE

**greased** *adj* having or being a surface so smooth as to make sliding or falling likely — see SLICK 1

**greasy** *adj* having or being a surface so smooth as to make sliding or falling likely — see SLICK 1

**great** *adj* **1** having or showing exceptional knowledge, experience, or skill in a field of endeavor — see PROFICIENT
**2** having, characterized by, or arising from a dignified and generous nature — see NOBLE 2
**3** lasting for a considerable time — see LONG 2
**4** of a size greater than average of its kind — see LARGE
**5** of the very best kind — see EXCELLENT

**greatcoat** *n* a warm outdoor coat — see OVERCOAT

**greatest** *adj* **1** coming before all others in importance — see FOREMOST 1
**2** of the highest degree — see FULL 2

**greathearted** *adj* **1** feeling or displaying no fear by temperament — see BRAVE
**2** having, characterized by, or arising from a dignified and generous nature — see NOBLE 2

**greatheartedness** *n* strength of mind to carry on in spite of danger — see COURAGE

**greatly** *adv* **1** in a manner befitting a person of the highest character and ideals ⟨as commander of the Union army's first black regiment, Robert Gould Shaw died as *greatly* as he had lived⟩
***syn*** gallantly, grandly, heroically, highmindedly, honorably, magnanimously, nobly
***rel*** loftily, venerably; magnificently, majestically
***near ant*** abominably, contemptibly, despicably, detestably, hatefully; degenerately
***ant*** basely, dishonorably, ignobly
**2** to a large extent or degree ⟨Todd has *greatly* increased the scope of his theme on civic responsibility⟩
***syn*** astronomically, broadly, colossally, considerably, enormously, extensively, hugely, largely, massively, monstrously, much, sizably, stupendously, tremendously, utterly, vastly
***rel*** appreciably, noticeably, significantly; abundantly, amply, copiously, healthily, plentifully

*near ant* modestly; fractionally; imperceptibly, infinitesimally, insignificantly, invisibly, microscopically, minutely, negligibly; barely, hardly, just, scarcely
*ant* little, slightly
**3** to a great degree — see VERY 1

**greatness** *n* **1** exceptionally high quality — see EXCELLENCE 1
**2** the quality of state of being large in size — see LARGENESS

**greed** *n* an intense selfish desire for wealth or possessions ⟨don't let *greed* for riches control you⟩
*syn* acquisitiveness, avarice, avariciousness, avidity, covetousness, cupidity, greediness, rapaciousness, rapacity
*rel* materialism, possessiveness; appetite, craving, hankering, hunger, itch, longing, lust, passion, ravenousness, thirst, voracity, yearning, yen
*near ant* contentment, fulfillment, satisfaction; bounteousness, bounty, charity, generosity, generousness, liberality, openhandedness, openheartedness, unselfishness

**greediness** *n* an intense selfish desire for wealth or possessions — see GREED

**greedy** *adj* **1** having or marked by an eager and often selfish desire especially for material possessions ⟨a young rocker who was *greedy* for fame and riches⟩ ⟨the *greedy* exploitation of the land by developers⟩
*syn* acquisitive, avaricious, avid, coveting, covetous, grasping, mercenary, rapacious
*rel* materialistic, philistine; desirous, eager, itchy, miserly; hoggish, piggish, swinish; devouring, gluttonous, gobbling, insatiable, ravenous, unquenchable, voracious; discontent, discontented, malcontent, unquenched, unsatisfied; begrudging, grudging, resentful
*near ant* bounteous, bountiful, charitable, freehanded, generous, greathearted, handsome, liberal, munificent, openhanded, openhearted, unselfish, unsparing; controlled, moderate, restrained, temperate; content, sated, satisfied
**2** having a huge appetite — see VORACIOUS 1

**green** *adj* **1** covered with a thick, healthy natural growth — see LUSH 1
**2** lacking in adult experience or maturity — see CALLOW
**3** lacking in worldly wisdom or informed judgment — see NAIVE 1
**4** lacking the warm skin color indicative of or associated with good health — see SICKLY 2

**green** *n* green leaves or plants — see GREENERY 1

**greenback** *n* a piece of printed paper used as money — see [1]BILL 2

**greenery** *n* green leaves or plants ⟨Scottish highlands covered with lush *greenery*⟩
*syn* flora, foliage, green, herbage, leafage, vegetation, verdure
*rel* grassland, prairie; underbrush, undergrowth

**greenhorn** *n* a person who is just starting out in a field of activity — see BEGINNER

**greenhouse** *n* a glass-enclosed building for growing plants — see CONSERVATORY

**greenness** *n* the quality or state of being simple and sincere — see NAÏVETÉ 1

**greeting** *n* **1** an expression of goodwill upon meeting — see HELLO
**2 greetings** *pl* best wishes — see COMPLIMENT

**gregarious** *adj* likely to seek or enjoy the company of others — see CONVIVIAL

**gregariousness** *n* the quality or state of being social — see SOCIABILITY

**gremlin** *n* an imaginary being usually having a small human form and magical powers — see FAIRY

**griddle cake** *n* a flat cake made from thin batter and cooked on both sides (as on a griddle) — see PANCAKE

**grief** *n* deep sadness especially for the loss of someone or something loved — see SORROW

**grievance** *n* **1** a lingering ill will towards a person for a real or imagined wrong — see GRUDGE 1
**2** an expression of dissatisfaction, pain, or resentment — see COMPLAINT 1

**grieve** *vb* to feel deep sadness or mental pain ⟨*grieved* over the lost cat⟩
*syn* agonize, bleed, hurt, mourn, sorrow, suffer
*rel* ache, long (for), pine (away); rack, torment, torture; bemoan, bewail, deplore, lament, rue; bawl, cry, groan, howl, keen, moan, take on, wail, weep, yammer
*near ant* beam, cheer, exult, joy, laugh, overjoy, ravish, rejoice; comfort, console

**grieve** (for) *vb* to feel or express sorrow for — see LAMENT 1

**grieving** *adj* expressing or suggesting mourning — see MOURNFUL 1

**grievous** *adj* **1** difficult to endure — see HARSH 1
**2** hard to accept or bear especially emotionally — see BITTER 2
**3** involving potential loss or injury — see DANGEROUS
**4** of a kind to cause great distress — see REGRETTABLE

**grievously** *adv* with feelings of bitterness or grief — see HARD 2

**grill** *n* a public establishment where meals are served to paying customers for consumption on the premises — see RESTAURANT

**grill** *vb* to put a series of questions to — see EXAMINE 1

**grim** *adj* **1** harsh and threatening in manner or appearance ⟨a *grim* and desolate landscape⟩ ⟨a *grim* and short-tempered shopkeeper who didn't exactly invite friendly conversation⟩
*syn* austere, dour, fierce, flinty, forbidding, gruff, intimidating, lowering (*also* louring), rough, rugged, severe, stark, steely, stern, ungentle

*rel* bleak, cold, hostile, unfriendly; adamant, determined, firm, resolute, steadfast, unflinching; fixed, hard, immovable, implacable, inflexible, obdurate, rigid, set, stiff, unbending, uncompromising, unyielding; immutable, unchangeable; black, cheerless, dark, gloomy, glum, joyless, moody, morose, sulky, sullen, surly; brooding, grave, melancholy, serious, sober, solemn, somber (*or* sombre), unsmiling, weighty
*near ant* bland, meek, mellow, soft; easy, quiet, tranquil; agreeable, bright, cheerful, inviting, pleasant, pleasing, sweet; glad, happy, lighthearted, merry, mirthful, sunny; featherbrained, flighty, frivolous, giddy, goofy, light-headed, playful
*ant* benign, benignant, gentle, mild, tender
**2** difficult to endure — see HARSH 1
**3** showing no signs of slackening or yielding in one's purpose — see UNYIELDING 1
**4** violently unfriendly or aggressive in disposition — see FIERCE 1

**grimace** *n* a twisting of the facial features in disgust or disapproval ⟨made a *grimace* when he tasted the medicine⟩
*syn* face, frown, lower (*also* lour), mouth, pout, scowl
*rel* flinch, squinch, wince; growl, snarl; simper, smirk; scoff, sneer; glare, glower, look, stare
*near ant* grin, smile

**grimace** *vb* to distort one's face — see MUG 1

**grime** *n* foul matter that mars the purity or cleanliness of something — see FILTH 1

**grime** *vb* to make dirty — see DIRTY

**griminess** *n* the state or quality of being dirty — see DIRTINESS 1

**grimy** *adj* not clean — see DIRTY 1

**grin** *vb* to express an emotion (as amusement) by curving the lips upward — see SMILE 1

**grind** *n* **1** a harsh grating sound — see RASP
**2** a person slavishly devoted to intellectual or academic pursuits — see NERD
**3** very hard or unpleasant work — see TOIL

**grind** *vb* **1** to make smooth by friction ⟨after they are *ground* and polished, these stones can be used for jewelry⟩
*syn* buff, file, hone, rasp, rub, sand
*rel* plane, scrape; sandblast, scour; burnish, polish; sharpen, whet; regrind
*near ant* coarsen, roughen
**2** to press or strike against or together so as to make a scraping sound ⟨everyone in the car winced when the driver *ground* the gears trying to shift into second⟩
*syn* crunch, gnash, grate, grit, scrape, scrunch
*rel* creak, groan, rasp, scratch; clash, jangle, jar
**3** to make sharp or sharper — see SHARPEN
**4** to make smooth or glossy usually by repeatedly applying surface pressure — see POLISH
**5** to pass roughly and noisily over or against a surface — see SCRAPE 1
**6** to reduce to fine particles — see POWDER

**grind** (out) *vb* to produce or bring about especially by long or repeated effort — see HAMMER (OUT)

**grinder** *n* a large sandwich on a long split roll — see SUBMARINE

**grip** *n* **1** a bag carried by hand and designed to hold a traveler's clothing and personal articles — see TRAVELING BAG
**2** the act or manner of holding — see HOLD 1
**3** the knowledge gained from the process of coming to know or understand something — see COMPREHENSION
**4** the right or means to command or control others — see POWER 1

**grip** *vb* **1** to have or keep in one's hands — see HOLD 1
**2** to hold the attention of as if by a spell — see ENTHRALL 1
**3** to hold the attention of — see ENGAGE 1
**4** to reach for and take hold of by embracing with the fingers or arms — see TAKE 1

**gripe** *n* an expression of dissatisfaction, pain, or resentment — see COMPLAINT 1

**gripe** *vb* to express dissatisfaction, pain, or resentment usually tiresomely — see COMPLAIN

**griper** *n* **1** a person who makes frequent complaints usually about little things — see CRYBABY
**2** an irritable and complaining person — see GROUCH

**gripping** *adj* holding the attention or provoking interest — see INTERESTING

**grisliness** *n* the quality of inspiring intense dread or dismay — see HORROR 1

**grisly** *adj* extremely disturbing or repellent — see HORRIBLE 1

**grit** *n* the strength of mind that enables a person to endure pain or hardship — see FORTITUDE

**grit** *vb* to press or strike against or together so as to make a scraping sound — see GRIND 2

**groan** *n* **1** a crying out in grief — see LAMENT 1
**2** a long low sound indicating pain or grief — see MOAN 1

**groan** *vb* to utter a moan — see MOAN 1

**grog** *n* a fermented or distilled beverage that can make a person drunk — see ALCOHOL

**groggery** *n* a place of business where alcoholic beverages are sold to be consumed on the premises — see BARROOM

**grogshop** *n* a place of business where alcoholic beverages are sold to be consumed on the premises — see BARROOM

**groomed** *adj* being clean and in good order — see NEAT 1

**groove** *n* an established and often automatic or monotonous series of actions followed when engaging in some activity — see ROUTINE 1
**groove** *vb* to mark with or as if with a line or groove — see SCORE 1
**groove** (on) *vb* to take pleasure in — see ENJOY 1
**groovy** *adj* of the very best kind — see EXCELLENT
**grope** *vb* to search for something blindly or uncertainly ⟨*groped* for her car keys⟩ ⟨*groping* for the right answer⟩
*syn* feel, fish, fumble
*rel* cast about, hunt, look, reach, seek (out); clutch, grab, scrabble, snatch
**gross** *adj* 1 depicting or referring to sexual matters in a way that is unacceptable in polite society — see OBSCENE 1
2 having an excess of body fat — see FAT 1
3 lacking in refinement or good taste — see COARSE 2
4 very noticeable especially for being incorrect or bad — see EGREGIOUS
**grossness** *n* 1 the condition of having an excess of body fat — see CORPULENCE
2 the quality or state of being obscene — see OBSCENITY 1
3 the quality or state of lacking refinement or good taste — see VULGARITY 1
**grot** *n* a naturally formed underground chamber with an opening to the surface — see CAVE
**grotesque** *adj* 1 disagreeable to one's aesthetic or artistic sense — see HARSH 2
2 unpleasant to look at — see UGLY 1
**grotto** *n* a naturally formed underground chamber with an opening to the surface — see CAVE
**grouch** *n* an irritable and complaining person ⟨an uncle who is a real *grouch* when he's sick⟩
*syn* bear, complainer, crab, crank, croaker, curmudgeon, fusser, griper, grouser, growler, grumbler, grump, murmurer, mutterer, whiner
*rel* fulminator, malcontent, sorehead; killjoy, party pooper, spoilsport; defeatist, pessimist; faultfinder, kicker, nagger, nitpicker, quibbler
*near ant* optimist; rejoicer
**grouchiness** *n* readiness to show annoyance or impatience — see PETULANCE
**grouchy** *adj* 1 easily irritated or annoyed — see IRRITABLE
2 given to complaining a lot — see FUSSY 1
**ground** *adj* having an edge thin enough to cut or pierce something — see SHARP 1
**ground** *n* 1 **grounds** *pl* the area around and belonging to a building ⟨an escorted tour of the White House and its surrounding *grounds*⟩
*syn* demesne, park, premises, yard
*rel* acres, estate, land, lot, parcel, plot, property, real estate, realty; campus; backyard, churchyard, dooryard, schoolyard
2 **grounds** *pl* matter that settles to the bottom of a body of liquid — see DEPOSIT 1
3 **grounds** *pl* something (as a belief) that serves as the basis for another thing — see REASON 2
4 a small area of usually open land — see FIELD 1
5 an immaterial thing upon which something else rests — see BASE 1
6 the loose surface material in which plants naturally grow — see DIRT 1
7 the physical conditions or features that form the setting against which something is viewed — see BACKGROUND 1
8 the solid part of our planet's surface as distinguished from the sea and air — see EARTH 2
**ground** *vb* to find a basis — see BASE
**grounded** *adj* resting on the shore or bottom of a body of water — see AGROUND
**groundless** *adj* having no basis in reason or fact ⟨please stop making *groundless* accusations against the teachers you dislike⟩ ⟨fears of a strike proved *groundless*⟩
*syn* invalid, nonvalid, unfounded, ungrounded, unreasonable, unsubstantiated, unsupported, unwarranted
*rel* illogical, irrational, nonlogical, unconscionable, unsound; fallacious, false, misled, wrong; gratuitous, uncalled-for, unnecessary; flimsy, implausible, misleading, specious, unconvincing, unsatisfying, untenable, weak; ill-advised, unreasoned; inconsistent; absurd, asinine, foolish, meaningless, nonsensical, preposterous, senseless, silly; insane, nutty, mad, wacky
*near ant* certified, validated, verified; confirmed, corroborated; informed, logical, rational; commonsense, sane, sensible, sober, wise; actual, genuine, real, true; certain, sure; clear, cogent, compelling, convincing, credible, persuasive, plausible, satisfying, solid
*ant* good, hard, just, justified, reasonable, reasoned, substantiated, valid, well-founded
**ground plan** *n* a method worked out in advance for achieving some objective — see PLAN 1
**ground rule** *n* a statement spelling out the proper procedure or conduct for an activity — see RULE 1
**groundwork** *n* an immaterial thing upon which something else rests — see BASE 1
**group** *n* 1 a number of things considered as a unit ⟨car buffs stood around admiring a *group* of classic cars in the parking lot⟩
*syn* array, assemblage, bank, batch, battery, block, bunch, clump, cluster, collection, grouping, huddle, knot, lot, package, parcel, passel, set, suite
*rel* accumulation, aggregate, aggregation, conglomeration; agglomeration, assortment, hodgepodge, jumble, miscellany, mixture, odds and ends, sundries, variety; series, suit
*phrases* the whole kit and caboodle

***near ant*** entity, item, single, unit
**2** a usually small number of persons considered as a unit ⟨the next *group* of guests were being seated for dinner⟩
***syn*** array, batch, battery, body, bunch, cluster, crop, grouping, huddle, knot, lot, parcel, party, passel
***rel*** assembly, congregation, gathering, organization; circle, clan, clique, coterie, fellowship, gang, ring, set; faction, guild (*also* gild), order, school, sect; brigade, crew, outfit, platoon, posse; alliance, bloc, coalition, confederacy, confederation, federation, league, union; bevy, covey
***phrases*** the whole kit and caboodle
***near ant*** individual, single
**3** one of the units into which a whole is divided on the basis of a common characteristic — see CLASS 2

**group** *vb* **1** to arrange or assign according to type — see CLASSIFY 1
**2** to bring together in one body or place — see GATHER 1

**grouping** *n* **1** a number of things considered as a unit — see GROUP 1
**2** a usually small number of persons considered as a unit — see GROUP 2

**grouse** *vb* to express dissatisfaction, pain, or resentment usually tiresomely — see COMPLAIN

**grouser** *n* an irritable and complaining person — see GROUCH

**grovel** *vb* **1** to draw back or crouch down in fearful submission — see COWER
**2** to move slowly with the body close to the ground — see CRAWL 1

**grow** *vb* **1** to look after or assist the growth of by labor and care ⟨a dedicated home gardener who *grows* tomatoes in her small garden every summer⟩
***syn*** crop, cultivate, culture, promote, raise, rear, tend
***rel*** breed, produce, propagate; plant, sow; gather, glean, harvest, reap; germinate, quicken, root, sprout
***near ant*** kill; dig, extirpate, pick, pluck, pull (up), uproot; cut, hay, mow
**2** to become mature — see MATURE
**3** to eventually have as a state or quality — see BECOME

**grow** (in) *vb* to increase in — see GAIN 1

**grower** *n* a person who cultivates the land and grows crops on it — see FARMER

**growl** *vb* **1** to express dissatisfaction, pain, or resentment usually tiresomely — see COMPLAIN
**2** to make a long loud deep noise or cry — see ROAR
**3** to make a low heavy rolling sound — see RUMBLE

**growler** *n* **1** a person who makes frequent complaints usually about little things — see CRYBABY
**2** an irritable and complaining person — see GROUCH

**grown–up** *n* a fully grown person — see ADULT

**growth** *n* **1** an abnormal mass of tissue ⟨found a *growth* on the dog's neck under her collar⟩
***syn*** excrescence, lump, neoplasm, tumor
***rel*** outgrowth; cancer, carcinoma, lymphoma, malignancy, melanoma; cyst, tubercle, wart
**2** the act or process of going from the simple or basic to the complex or advanced — see DEVELOPMENT 1
**3** the process of becoming mature — see MATURATION

**grow up** *vb* to become mature — see MATURE

**grub** *n* substances intended to be eaten — see FOOD

**grub** *vb* to devote serious and sustained effort — see LABOR

**grubber** *n* a person who does very hard or dull work — see SLAVE 2

**grubbiness** *n* the state or quality of being dirty — see DIRTINESS 1

**grubby** *adj* not clean — see DIRTY 1

**grudge** *n* **1** a lingering ill will towards a person for a real or imagined wrong ⟨he's had a *grudge* against her ever since she snubbed him at the dance⟩
***syn*** grievance, resentment, score
***rel*** condemnation; offense (*or* offence), umbrage; complaint; peeve, pique
**2** a deep-seated ill will — see ENMITY

**grueling** *or* **gruelling** *adj* **1** requiring considerable physical or mental effort — see HARD 2
**2** requiring much time, effort, or careful attention — see DEMANDING 1

**gruesome** *adj* extremely disturbing or repellent — see HORRIBLE 1

**gruesomeness** *n* the quality of inspiring intense dread or dismay — see HORROR 1

**gruff** *adj* **1** harsh and dry in sound — see HOARSE
**2** harsh and threatening in manner or appearance — see GRIM 1

**grumble** *n* an expression of dissatisfaction, pain, or resentment — see COMPLAINT 1

**grumble** *vb* **1** to express dissatisfaction, pain, or resentment usually tiresomely — see COMPLAIN
**2** to make a low heavy rolling sound — see RUMBLE

**grumbler** *n* **1** a person who makes frequent complaints usually about little things — see CRY-BABY
**2** an irritable and complaining person — see GROUCH

**grump** *n* an irritable and complaining person — see GROUCH

**grumpiness** *n* readiness to show annoyance or impatience — see PETULANCE

**grumpy** *adj* **1** easily irritated or annoyed — see IRRITABLE
**2** given to complaining a lot — see FUSSY 1

**grungy** *adj* **1** not clean — see DIRTY 1
**2** showing signs of advanced wear and tear and neglect — see SHABBY 1

---

***syn*** synonym(s) ***rel*** related words
***ant*** antonym(s) ***near ant*** near antonym(s)

**grunt** *n* speech that is not clear enough to be understood — see MUMBLE

**grunt** *vb* to speak softly and unclearly — see MUMBLE

**grunting** *n* speech that is not clear enough to be understood — see MUMBLE

**guarantee** *n* **1** a formal agreement to fulfill an obligation ⟨the contractors gave us a written *guarantee* that the work on the house would be done by Christmas⟩
*syn* bond, contract, covenant, guaranty, surety, warranty
*rel* oath, pledge, vow, word; bargain, compact, pact, treaty; assurance, insurance; bail, deposit, pawn, security
**2** something given or held to assure that the giver will keep a promise — see PLEDGE 1

**guarantee** *vb* **1** to assume responsibility for the satisfactory quality or performance of — see WARRANT 1
**2** to make sure, certain, or safe — see ENSURE

**guarantor** *n* a person who takes the responsibility for some other person or thing — see SPONSOR

**guaranty** *n* **1** a formal agreement to fulfill an obligation — see GUARANTEE 1
**2** something given or held to assure that the giver will keep a promise — see PLEDGE 1

**guaranty** *vb* to make sure, certain, or safe — see ENSURE

**guard** *n* **1** a person or group that watches over someone or something ⟨checked in with the security *guard* at the gate⟩
*syn* custodian, guardian, keeper, lookout, picket, sentinel, sentry, warden, warder, watch, watchman
*rel* observer, patrol, spotter, watchdog; bodyguard, convoy, defender, escort, honor guard
**2** a position or readiness to oppose actual or expected attack — see DEFENSIVE
**3** a protective device (as on a weapon) to prevent accidental operation — see SAFETY 2
**4** means or method of defending — see DEFENSE 1
**5** one that accompanies another for protection, guidance, or as a courtesy — see ESCORT
**6** someone that protects — see PROTECTOR

**guard** *vb* to drive danger or attack away from — see DEFEND 1

**guard** (against) *vb* to be cautious of or on guard against — see BEWARE (OF)

**guarded** *adj* having or showing a close attentiveness to avoiding danger or trouble — see CAREFUL 1

**guardian** *n* **1** a person or group that watches over someone or something — see GUARD 1
**2** a person who takes care of a property sometimes for an absent owner — see CUSTODIAN 1

**guardianship** *n* responsibility for the safety and well-being of someone or something — see CUSTODY

**guardrail** *n* a protective barrier consisting of a horizontal bar and its supports — see RAILING

**guardroom** *n* a place of confinement for persons held in lawful custody — see JAIL

**guess** *n* an opinion or judgment based on little or no evidence — see CONJECTURE

**guess** *vb* **1** to form an opinion from little or no evidence ⟨though she does not speak with an accent, I would still *guess* that she is a foreigner⟩
*syn* assume, conjecture, presume, speculate, suppose, surmise, suspect, suspicion [*chiefly dialect*]
*rel* conclude, deduce, gather, infer; hypothesize, theorize; believe, conceive, expect, imagine, reckon [*chiefly dialect*], take, think
*near ant* demonstrate, establish, prove; ascertain, determine, find out
**2** to decide the size, amount, number, or distance of (something) without actual measurement — see ESTIMATE 2
**3** to have as an opinion — see BELIEVE 2

**guest** *n* **1** a person who visits another ⟨invited the afternoon *guests* to stay for dinner⟩
*syn* caller, frequenter, visitant, visitor
*rel* company; crasher, hanger-on
*near ant* denizen, dweller, habitant, inhabitant, occupant, resident, resider
**2** a person who buys a product or uses a service from a business — see CUSTOMER 1

**guffaw** *n* an explosive sound that is a sign of amusement — see LAUGH 1

**guidance** *n* **1** an opinion suggesting a wise or proper course of action — see ADVICE
**2** the act or activity of looking after and making decisions about something — see CONDUCT 1
**3** the duty or function of watching or guarding for the sake of proper direction or control — see SUPERVISION 1

**guide** *n* one that accompanies another for protection, guidance, or as a courtesy — see ESCORT

**guide** *vb* **1** to give advice and instruction to (someone) regarding the course or process to be followed ⟨the famous chef *guided* her through the creation of the wedding cake, showing her how to ice the layers, fashion the elaborate decorations, and assemble the whole shebang⟩
*syn* coach, counsel, lead, mentor, pilot, shepherd, show, tutor
*rel* direct, steer; accompany, escort, see; oversee, superintend, supervise; drill, train; brief, enlighten, inform; instruct, school, teach; inculcate, indoctrinate; cultivate, foster, nurture
**2** to look after and make decisions about — see CONDUCT 1
**3** to point out the way for (someone) especially from a position in front — see LEAD 1

**guidon** *n* a piece of cloth with a special design that is used as an emblem or for signaling — see FLAG 1

**guild** *also* **gild** *n* a group of persons formally joined together for some common interest — see ASSOCIATION 2

**guile** *n* **1** skill in achieving one's ends through indirect, subtle, or underhanded means — see CUNNING 1
**2** the inclination or practice of misleading others through lies or trickery — see DECEIT

**guileful** *adj* clever at attaining one's ends by indirect and often deceptive means — see ARTFUL 1

**guileless** *adj* free from any intent to deceive or impress others ⟨she was an easy-going, *guileless* young woman who was comfortable just being herself⟩
***syn*** artless, genuine, honest, ingenuous, innocent, naive (*or* naïve), natural, real, simple, sincere, true, unaffected, unpretending, unpretentious
***rel*** childlike, impressionable, inexperienced, malleable, persuadable, simple-minded, unsophisticated, unworldly; unforced, unstudied; candid, frank, free, openhearted, plain, plainspoken, single-minded; trustful, trusting
***phrases*** on the level
***near ant*** sophisticated, worldly, worldly-wise; crooked, deceitful, deceptive, devious, double-dealing, hypocritical, two-faced; arch, calculating, canny, crafty, cunning, designing, scheming, sharp, shifty, shrewd, slick, slippery, sly, tricky, underhanded, wily; flattering, mealy-mouthed, smooth, sycophantic, unctuous; feigned, forced, strained
***ant*** affected, artful, artificial, assuming, dishonest, dissembling, dissimulating, fake, false, guileful, insincere, phony (*also* phoney), pretentious

**guilelessly** *adv* without any attempt to impress by deception or exaggeration — see NATURALLY 3

**guilelessness** *n* the quality or state of being simple and sincere — see NAÏVETÉ 1

**guillotine** *vb* to cut off the head of — see DECAPITATE

**guilt** *n* **1** a feeling of responsibility for wrongdoing ⟨he was wracked with *guilt* after he accidentally broke his sister's antique grandfather clock⟩
***syn*** contriteness, contrition, penitence, regret, remorse, remorsefulness, repentance, rue, self-reproach, shame
***rel*** compunction, misgiving, qualm, scruple; blame, fault, responsibility; chagrin, embarrassment; anguish, distress, grief, sadness, sorrow
***ant*** impenitence, remorselessness
**2** responsibility for wrongdoing or failure — see BLAME 1

**guiltless** *adj* free from guilt or blame — see INNOCENT 2

**guiltlessness** *n* the quality or state of being free from guilt or blame — see INNOCENCE 1

**guilty** *adj* **1** responsible for a wrong ⟨he was found *guilty* on all charges brought against him⟩
***syn*** blamable, culpable
***rel*** blameworthy, censurable, impeachable, indictable, punishable, reprehensible, reproachable; accused, arraigned, impeached, implicated, indicted; accountable, answerable; condemned, convicted
***phrases*** at fault
***near ant*** absolved, acquitted, exonerated, vindicated; faultless, impeccable, irreproachable, unimpeachable
***ant*** blameless, guiltless, innocent
**2** suffering from or expressive of a feeling of responsibility for wrongdoing ⟨she was burdened with a *guilty* conscience after stealing the newspaper from the newsstand⟩
***syn*** ashamed, contrite, hangdog, penitent, remorseful, repentant, shamed, shamefaced
***rel*** apologetic, sorry; regretful, rueful; penitential; blushing, chagrined, embarrassed, sheepish
***near ant*** unapologetic; brazen, cheeky, impudent
***ant*** impenitent, remorseless, shameless, unashamed, unrepentant

**guise** *n* **1** a display of emotion or behavior that is insincere or intended to deceive — see MASQUERADE
**2** clothing chosen as appropriate for a specific situation — see OUTFIT 1
**3** clothing put on to hide one's true identity or imitate someone or something else — see DISGUISE
**4** outward and often deceptive indication — see APPEARANCE 2

**gulch** *n* a narrow opening between hillsides or mountains that can be used for passage — see CANYON

**gulf** *n* **1** a part of a body of water that extends beyond the general shoreline ⟨dipped our feet in the warm waters of the *gulf*⟩
***syn*** bay, bight, cove, creek [*chiefly British*], estuary, firth, fjord (*or* fiord), inlet, loch [*Scottish*]
***rel*** harbor, port, road(s), roadstead; narrow, sound, strait; bayou
**2** an immeasurable depth or space — see ABYSS
**3** a narrow opening between hillsides or mountains that can be used for passage — see CANYON
**4** an open space in a barrier (as a wall or hedge) — see GAP 1

**gull** *n* one who is easily deceived or cheated — see DUPE

**gull** *vb* to cause to believe what is untrue — see DECEIVE

**gullibility** *n* readiness to believe the claims of others without sufficient evidence — see CREDULITY

**gullible** *adj* readily taken advantage of — see EASY 2

---

***syn*** synonym(s) ***rel*** related words
***ant*** antonym(s) ***near ant*** near antonym(s)

**gulp** *n* the portion of a serving of a beverage that is swallowed at one time — see DRINK 2

**gulp** *vb* to swallow in liquid form — see DRINK 1

**gummy** *adj* being of such a thick consistency as to readily cling to objects upon contact — see STICKY 1

**gun** *n* **1** a portable weapon from which a shot is discharged by gunpowder ⟨while her father preferred hunting with a crossbow, she preferred a *gun*⟩
***syn*** arm, firearm, piece, small arm
***rel*** forty-five (*or* .45), gat [*slang*], handgun, pistol, revolver, rod [*slang*], six-gun, six-shooter, zip gun; blunderbuss, flintlock, harquebus (*or* arquebus), matchlock, musket, muzzleloader, rifle, shotgun; automatic, machine gun, repeater, submachine gun, tommy gun; speargun
**2 guns** *pl* large firearms (as cannon or rockets) — see ARTILLERY

**gun** *vb* to strike with a missile from a gun — see SHOOT 3

**gung ho** *adj* showing urgent desire or interest — see EAGER

**gurgle** *vb* to flow in a broken irregular stream ⟨the tiny stream *gurgled* down the rocky slope and joined the larger river at the bottom of the hill⟩
***syn*** bubble, dribble, lap, plash, ripple, splash, trickle, wash
***rel*** eddy, purl, swirl; swash, swish, whish; drip, drop; gush, jet, rush, spout, spurt, squirt
***near ant*** run
***ant*** pour, roll, stream

**gush** *n* **1** a flowing or going out — see OUTFLOW
**2** a sudden intense expression of strong feeling — see OUTBURST 1

**gush** *vb* **1** to flow out in great quantities or with force ⟨the dam cracked and water *gushed* from the break⟩
***syn*** jet, pour, rush, spew, spout, spurt, squirt
***rel*** cascade, issue, roll, run, stream; plash, slosh, splash; surge, swell; flush, sluice; deluge, engulf, flood, inundate, overflow, overwhelm, submerge, swamp
***near ant*** spatter, sprinkle; exude, leak, ooze, seep, weep
***ant*** dribble, drip, drop, trickle
**2** to make an exaggerated display of affection or enthusiasm ⟨he *gushed* about his favorite basketball player, calling him "the best there ever was"⟩
***syn*** enthuse, fuss, rave, rhapsodize, slobber
***rel*** dote (on), fawn; emote

**gushing** *adj* **1** overly or insincerely flattering — see FULSOME
**2** pouring forth in great amounts — see PROFUSE

**gust** *n* **1** a sudden brief rush of wind ⟨a *gust* tore her umbrella from her grip and blew it down the street⟩
***syn*** blast, blow, flurry, williwaw
***rel*** breeze, zephyr; air, breath, waft; puff, whiff; gale, hurricane, squall, tempest, tornado, windstorm; northeaster, norther, northerly, northwester, southeaster, southwester, westerly
**2** a sudden intense expression of strong feeling — see OUTBURST 1

**gusty** *adj* marked by strong wind or more wind than usual — see WINDY 1

**gut** *n* **1 guts** *pl* the internal organs of the body ⟨dissected the frog and looked at its *guts*⟩
***syn*** entrails, innards, inside(s), viscera, vitals
***rel*** bowel(s), intestine(s); giblet(s), variety meat
**2 guts** *pl* strength of mind to carry on in spite of danger — see COURAGE
**3 guts** *pl* the strength of mind that enables a person to endure pain or hardship — see FORTITUDE
**4** the part of the body between the chest and the pelvis — see STOMACH

**gut** *vb* to take the internal organs out of ⟨you'll need to *gut* the fish and wash it out before you can cook it⟩
***syn*** clean, disembowel, draw, eviscerate
***rel*** bone, dress; cut, excise, extract, remove, withdraw; transplant

**gutsy** *adj* inclined or willing to take risks — see BOLD 1

**gutter** *n* **1** a pipe or channel for carrying off water from a roof ⟨one of his chores is to clean leaves and sticks out of the *gutters* before winter sets in⟩
***syn*** drainpipe, eaves trough, spout, trough, waterspout
***rel*** drain, flume, sluice; conduit, duct
**2** a long narrow channel dug in the earth — see DITCH

**guy** *n* **1** a member of the human race — see HUMAN
**2** an adult male human being — see MAN 1

**guzzle** *vb* to swallow in liquid form — see DRINK 1

**gym** *n* a building or room used for sports activities and exercising ⟨decided to get up early and go to the *gym* to lift weights⟩
***syn*** gymnasium, spa
***rel*** arena, bowl, coliseum, colosseum, stadium

**gymnasium** *n* a building or room used for sports activities and exercising — see GYM

**gyp** *vb* to rob by the use of trickery or threats — see FLEECE

**gyrate** *vb* to move in circles around an axis or center — see SPIN 1

**gyration** *n* a rapid turning about on an axis or central point — see SPIN 1

# H

**habiliment** *n, usually* **habiliments** *pl* covering for the human body — see CLOTHING

**habit** *n* a usual manner of behaving or doing ⟨it was his *habit* to rise early⟩
*syn* custom, fashion, pattern, practice (*also* practise), trick, way, wont
*rel* addiction; disposition; bent, inclination, proclivity, tendency, turn; convention, form, mode, style; usage; manners, mores; groove, rote, routine, rut; affectation, airs, pose; attribute, characteristic, mark, trait; oddity, peculiarity, quirk, singularity, tic; strangeness, weirdness

**habitable** *adj* suitable for living in — see LIVABLE

**habitant** *n* one who lives permanently in a place — see INHABITANT

**habitat** *n* the place where a plant or animal is usually or naturally found — see HOME 2

**habitation** *n* the place where one lives — see HOME 1

**habitual** *adj* **1** being such by habit and not likely to change ⟨Sarah admits she's an *habitual* procrastinator, but she still manages to complete her assignments on time⟩
*syn* chronic, confirmed, inveterate
*rel* incorrigible, unregenerate; born, natural; persistent, regular, steady, unfailing; addicted; accustomed, habituated, used; deep-rooted, entrenched (*also* intrenched), inbred, inherent, innate
*near ant* unaccustomed, unused; occasional
**2** appearing or occurring repeatedly from time to time — see REGULAR 1

**habituated** *adj* being in the habit or custom — see ACCUSTOMED

**hacienda** *n* a large impressive residence — see MANSION

[1]**hack** *n* a V-shaped cut usually on an edge or a surface — see NOTCH 1

[2]**hack** *n* an automobile that carries passengers for a fare usually determined by the distance traveled — see TAXI

**hackney** *adj* used or heard so often as to be dull — see STALE

**hackneyed** *adj* used or heard so often as to be dull — see STALE

**hag** *n* **1** a mean or ugly old woman — see CRONE
**2** a woman believed to have often harmful supernatural powers — see WITCH 1

**haggard** *adj* suffering extreme weight loss as a result of hunger or disease — see EMACIATED

**haggle** *vb* to talk over or dispute the terms of a purchase — see BARGAIN

**hail** *n* **1** a heavy fall of objects — see RAIN 2
**2** a rapid or overwhelming outpouring of many things at once — see BARRAGE

**hail** *vb* **1** to declare enthusiastic approval of — see ACCLAIM
**2** to demand or request the presence or service of — see SUMMON 1

**hair** *n* **1** a very small distance or degree ⟨a race that was won by a *hair*⟩
*syn* ace, hairbreadth (*or* hairsbreadth), inch
*rel* bit, crumb, jot, mite, particle, smidgen, trace, trifle
**2** the hairy covering of a mammal especially when fine, soft, and thick — see FUR 1

**hairbreadth** *or* **hairsbreadth** *n* a very small distance or degree — see HAIR 1

**hairline** *adj* **1** being of less than usual width — see NARROW 1
**2** made or done with extreme care and accuracy — see FINE 2
**3** meeting the highest standard of accuracy — see PRECISE 1

**hair–raising** *adj* causing fear — see FEARFUL 1

**hairsplitting** *adj* made or done with extreme care and accuracy — see FINE 2

**hairy** *adj* **1** covered with or as if with hair ⟨a *hairy* spider⟩
*syn* bristly, fleecy, furry, hirsute, rough, shaggy, unshorn, woolly (*also* wooly)
*rel* bearded, mustachioed, whiskered; downy, fluffy, fuzzy, nappy
*near ant* beardless, shaved, shaven
*ant* bald, furless, hairless, shorn, smooth
**2** made of or resembling hair ⟨enough *hairy* clumps around the house to make another cat⟩ ⟨a *hairy* mass of fiberglass insulation⟩
*syn* furry, fuzzy, rough, shaggy, woolly (*also* wooly)
*rel* downy, fluffy, nappy

**halcyon** *adj* free from storms or physical disturbance — see CALM 1

**hale** *adj* enjoying health and vigor — see HEALTHY 1

**hale** *vb* to cause to follow by applying steady force on — see PULL 1

**half** *adv* in any way or respect — see AT ALL

**half** *n* **1** one of two equal or nearly equal parts ⟨to be fair, we each get *half* the pie⟩
*syn* moiety
*rel* hemisphere, meridian, semicircle; component, division, fraction, part, piece, portion, section, segment
*near ant* aggregate, whole

---

*syn* synonym(s) *rel* related words
*ant* antonym(s) *near ant* near antonym(s)

2 either of a pair matched in one or more qualities — see MATE 1

**halfhearted** *adj* showing little or no interest or enthusiasm — see TEPID 1

**halfway** *adj* 1 lacking some necessary part — see INCOMPLETE

2 occupying a position equally distant from the ends or extremes — see MIDDLE 1

**half–wit** *n* 1 a person who lacks good sense or judgment — see FOOL 1

2 a stupid person — see IDIOT

**half–witted** *adj* 1 not having or showing an ability to absorb ideas readily — see STUPID 1

2 showing or marked by a lack of good sense or judgment — see FOOLISH 1

**hall** *n* 1 the entrance room of a building ⟨the guests hung their coats in the *hall*⟩

*syn* entry, entryway, foyer, lobby, vestibule

*rel* antechamber, anteroom, waiting room; doorway, entrance, threshold

2 a typically long narrow way connecting parts of a building ⟨the bedroom is at the end of the *hall*⟩

*syn* concourse, corridor, gallery, hallway, passage, passageway

*rel* arcade, breezeway, cloister

3 a large room or building for enclosed public gatherings ⟨the concert *hall* was full⟩

*syn* arena, auditorium, theater (*or* theatre)

*rel* amphitheater, hippodrome, house, playhouse; ballroom; lyceum; chamber, senate

4 a centrally located room in a building that serves as a gathering or waiting area or as a passageway into the interior — see FOYER 1

5 a large impressive residence — see MANSION

6 a large, magnificent, or massive building — see EDIFICE 1

**hallmark** *n* a device, design, or figure used as an identifying mark — see EMBLEM

**hallow** *vb* to make holy through prayers or ritual — see BLESS 1

**hallowed** *adj* 1 deserving honor and respect especially by reason of age — see VENERABLE 1

2 set apart or worthy of veneration by association with God — see HOLY 2

**hallowing** *n* the act of making something holy through religious ritual — see CONSECRATION

**hallucination** *n* a conception or image created by the imagination and having no objective reality — see FANTASY 1

**hallway** *n* a typically long narrow way connecting parts of a building — see HALL 2

**halt** *n* 1 a point in a struggle where neither side is capable of winning or willing to give in — see IMPASSE

2 the stopping of a process or activity — see END 1

[1]**halt** *vb* 1 to bring (something) to a standstill ⟨traffic was *halted* by the parade⟩

*syn* arrest, catch, check, draw up, fetch up, hold up, stall, stay, still, stop

*rel* balk, block, blockade, dam, detain, hinder, hold, hold back, impede, obstruct, stem; conclude, end, terminate; call, discontinue, suspend; clamp down, rein (in), squash, squelch, stamp, stanch (*also* staunch), stunt, suppress, turn back

*near ant* carry on, continue, follow through, keep on, keep up, run on; advance, fare, move, proceed, progress, wend; actuate, budge, drive, impel, propel, push, stir

2 to bring (as an action or operation) to an immediate end — see STOP 1

3 to come to an end — see CEASE 1

[2]**halt** *vb* to walk while favoring one leg — see LIMP 1

**hammer** *vb* 1 to shape with a hammer ⟨medieval artisans *hammered* brass into bowls and trays which they embossed with elaborate designs⟩

*syn* beat, forge, pound

*rel* chase, fashion, form, knead, model, mold, work; coin, mint, stamp; carve, chisel, hew, sculpt, sculpture

2 to deliver a blow to (someone or something) usually in a strong vigorous manner — see HIT 1

3 to strike repeatedly — see BEAT 1

**hammer** (out) *vb* to produce or bring about especially by long or repeated effort ⟨the school committee *hammered out* a new sports-participation policy with input from students, parents, and administrators⟩

*syn* build (up), carve (out), forge, grind (out), work out

*rel* cobble (together *or* up), create, construct, fabricate, fashion, form, frame, manufacture, model, shape, tailor; conceive, concoct, contrive, cook (up), devise, hatch, invent, originate; bring forth, effect; accomplish, achieve, bring off

*near ant* demolish, destroy, dismantle, raze, tear down; ruin, undo, unmake, wreck

**hamper** *vb* to create difficulty for the work or activity of ⟨fallen branches *hampered* the hikers as they made their way along the narrow path⟩

*syn* clog, cramp, delay, embarrass, encumber, fetter, handicap, hinder, hobble, hold back, hold up, impede, inhibit, interfere (with), manacle, obstruct, shackle, tie up, trammel

*rel* arrest, brake, check, constrain, curb, rein, restrain, snag; bind, chain, handcuff, leash, muzzle, strap, tether, tie; barricade, block, blockade, dam, head (off), plug; balk, choke, hurt, repress, retard, stifle, straiten, strangle, stunt; baffle, foil, frustrate, interrupt, sabotage, thwart; bog (down), confine, hedge (in), hem (in), limit, tie (down)

*phrases* cramp one's style, give a hard time

*near ant* clear, make way, open, unclog, unplug, unstop; free, liberate, release, untie; loosen, smooth; further, promote
*ant* aid, assist, facilitate, help

**hams** *n pl* the part of the body upon which someone sits — see BUTTOCKS

**hamstring** *vb* to render powerless, ineffective, or unable to move — see PARALYZE

**hand** *n* **1** a certain way in which something appears or may be regarded — see ASPECT 1
**2** a place, space, or direction away from or beyond a central point or line — see SIDE 1
**3** an arrow-shaped piece on a dial or scale for registering information — see POINTER 1
**4** one who works for another for wages or a salary — see EMPLOYEE
**5** the form or style of a particular person's writing — see HANDWRITING 1
**6** *usually* **hands** *pl* the ability to direct the course of something — see CONTROL 2
**7 hands** *pl* the fact or state of having (something) at one's disposal — see POSSESSION 1

**hand** *vb* **1** to put (something) into the possession of someone for use or consumption — see FURNISH 2
**2** to shift possession of (something) from one person to another — see PASS 1

**handbag** *n* **1** a bag carried by hand and designed to hold a traveler's clothing and personal articles — see TRAVELING BAG
**2** a container for carrying money and small personal items — see PURSE

**handbook** *n* a book used for instruction in a subject — see TEXTBOOK

**handcraft** *n* an occupation requiring skillful use of the hands — see CRAFT 1

**handcuff** *vb* to confine or restrain with or as if with chains — see BIND 1

**handcuff** *n usually* **handcuffs** *pl* something that physically prevents free movement — see BOND 1

**handful** *n* a small number — see FEW

**handicap** *n* **1** a feature of someone or something that creates difficulty for achieving success — see DISADVANTAGE
**2** something that makes movement or progress more difficult — see ENCUMBRANCE

**handicap** *vb* to create difficulty for the work or activity of — see HAMPER

**handicraft** *n* an occupation requiring skillful use of the hands — see CRAFT 1

**handicrafter** *n* a person whose occupation requires skill with the hands — see ARTISAN

**handily** *adv* without difficulty — see EASILY

**handiwork** *n* something produced by physical or intellectual effort — see PRODUCT 1

**handkerchief** *n* a scarf worn on the head — see BANDANNA

**handle** *n* a word or combination of words by which a person or thing is regularly known — see NAME 1

**handle** *vb* **1** to deal with (something) usually skillfully or efficiently ⟨as host of a live TV talk show, she must *handle* any situation that comes up⟩
*syn* contend (with), cope (with), grapple (with), manage, maneuver, manipulate, negotiate, swing, treat
*rel* bring off, carry out, pull, swing; command, direct, guide, steer; control, regulate, run
*phrases* have a grip on
*near ant* botch, bungle, goof (up), louse up, mess (up)
*ant* fumble, muddle (through)
**2** to behave toward in a stated way — see TREAT 1
**3** to control the mechanical operation of — see OPERATE 1
**4** to look after and make decisions about — see CONDUCT 1

**handling** *n* the act or activity of looking after and making decisions about something — see CONDUCT 1

**hand over** *vb* **1** to give (something) over to the control or possession of another usually under duress — see SURRENDER 1
**2** to put (something) into the possession of someone for use or consumption — see FURNISH 2
**3** to put (something) into the possession or safekeeping of another — see GIVE 2
**4** to shift possession of (something) from one person to another — see PASS 1

**handpick** *vb* to decide to accept (someone or something) from a group of possibilities — see CHOOSE 1

**handsome** *adj* **1** having or showing elegance — see ELEGANT 1
**2** of a size greater than average of its kind — see LARGE
**3** very pleasing to look at — see BEAUTIFUL

**handsomely** *adv* in a generous manner — see WELL 2

**handsomeness** *n* **1** dignified or restrained beauty of form, appearance, or style — see ELEGANCE
**2** the qualities in a person or thing that as a whole give pleasure to the senses — see BEAUTY 1

**hand–to–mouth** *adj* less plentiful than what is normal, necessary, or desirable — see MEAGER

**handwriting** *n* **1** the form or style of a particular person's writing ⟨she immediately recognized the *handwriting* on the envelope as that of her old college roommate⟩
*syn* hand, penmanship, script
*rel* scratch, scrawl, scribble; backhand, print; autograph, signature
**2** writing done by hand ⟨most students are taught the value of good *handwriting*⟩
*syn* calligraphy, longhand, manuscript, penmanship, script
*rel* lettering; shorthand
*ant* print, type

---

*syn* synonym(s) *rel* related words
*ant* antonym(s) *near ant* near antonym(s)

**handy** *adj* **1** situated within easy reach — see CONVENIENT
**2** skillful with the hands — see DEXTEROUS 1
**hang** *vb* **1** to place on an elevated point without support from below ⟨*hang* your coats on the coat rack in the hall⟩
*syn* dangle, sling, suspend, swing
*rel* hook, pin, tack; drape, festoon, garland, string; extend (out), jut, project, stick out; overhang, protrude; cascade, depend, fall
**2** to be determined by, based on, or subject (to) — see DEPEND 1
**3** to be limp from lack of water or vigor — see DROOP 1
**4** to rest or move along the surface of a liquid or in the air — see FLOAT
**hang** (over) *vb* to remain poised to inflict harm, danger, or distress on — see THREATEN
**hang around** *vb* **1** to come or be together as friends — see ASSOCIATE 1
**2** to continue to be in a place for a significant amount of time — see STAY 1
**3** to spend time doing nothing — see IDLE
**hang around** (in) *vb* to go to or spend time in often — see FREQUENT
**hang back** *vb* to show uncertainty about the right course of action — see HESITATE
**hangdog** *adj* suffering from or expressive of a feeling of responsibility for wrongdoing — see GUILTY 2
**hanger–on** *n* a person who is supported or seeks support from another without making an adequate return — see LEECH
**hanging** *adj* **1** bending downward or forward — see NODDING
**2** extending freely from a support from above — see DEPENDENT 1
**hang on** (to) *vb* **1** to continue to have in one's possession or power — see KEEP 2
**2** to have or keep in one's hands — see HOLD 1
**hangout** *n* a place for spending time or for socializing ⟨Jake's favorite *hangout* is the local community center⟩
*syn* haunt, rendezvous, resort
*rel* camp, canteen, club, clubhouse, den, harbor, haven, nest, refuge, retreat
**hang out** *vb* to spend time doing nothing — see IDLE
**hang out** (at) *vb* to go to or spend time in often — see FREQUENT
**hanker** (for *or* after) *vb* to have an earnest wish to own or enjoy — see DESIRE
**hankering** *n* a strong wish for something — see DESIRE
**hanky–panky** *n* the use of clever underhanded actions to achieve an end — see TRICKERY
**hap** *n* **1** something that happens — see EVENT 1
**2** the uncertain course of events — see CHANCE 1
**hap** *vb* to take place — see HAPPEN
**haphazard** *adj* lacking a definite plan, purpose, or pattern — see RANDOM
**haphazard** *adv* without definite aim, direction, rule, or method — see HIT OR MISS
**haphazardly** *adv* without definite aim, direction, rule, or method — see HIT OR MISS
**hapless** *adj* having, prone to, or marked by bad luck — see UNLUCKY
**happen** *vb* to take place ⟨did anything exciting *happen* over the summer?⟩
*syn* be, befall, betide, chance, come, come about, go (on), hap, occur, pass, transpire
*rel* arise, crop (up), develop, materialize, spring (up); intervene; fall out, go off, proceed, turn out
*phrases* come to pass
**happen** (on *or* upon) *vb* to come upon unexpectedly or by chance ⟨*happened on* the filming of a movie⟩
*syn* chance (upon), encounter, find, hit (upon), meet, stumble (on *or* onto)
*rel* confront, face; discover, turn up
*phrases* bump into, come across, run across, run into
**happen** (upon) *vb* to come upon face-to-face or as if face-to-face — see MEET 1
**happening** *n* **1** an exciting or noteworthy event that one experiences firsthand — see ADVENTURE
**2** something that happens — see EVENT 1
**happily** *adv* **1** in a cheerful or happy manner — see GAILY 1
**2** in a manner suitable for the occasion or purpose — see PROPERLY
**happiness** *n* **1** a feeling or state of well-being and contentment ⟨Marta's *happiness* was complete when she got her very own horse⟩
*syn* blessedness, bliss, blissfulness, felicity, gladness, joy
*rel* elatedness, elation, exhilaration, exultation, intoxication; ecstasy, euphoria, heaven, rapture, rapturousness; delectation, delight, enjoyment, pleasure; cheer, cheerfulness, exuberance, gaiety (*also* gayety), gladsomeness, glee, gleefulness, jollity, joyfulness, joyousness, jubilation, lightheartedness; content, contentedness, gratification, satisfaction
*near ant* anguish, desolation, joylessness, sorrow, woe, woefulness; blues, dejection, depression, despondency, disheartenment, dispiritedness, doldrums, downheartedness, gloom, gloominess, melancholy, mournfulness
*ant* misery, sadness, unhappiness, wretchedness
**2** the feeling experienced when one's wishes are met — see PLEASURE 1
**happy** *adj* **1** coming or happening by good luck especially unexpectedly — see FORTUNATE 1
**2** experiencing pleasure, satisfaction, or delight — see GLAD 1
**3** feeling that one's needs or desires have been met — see CONTENT
**4** having good luck — see LUCKY 1
**5** meeting the requirements of a purpose or situation — see FIT 1

**happy–go–lucky** *adj* **1** having a relaxed, casual manner — see EASYGOING 1
**2** having or showing a lack of concern or seriousness — see CAREFREE

**harangue** *n* **1** a long angry speech or scolding — see TIRADE
**2** a usually formal discourse delivered to an audience — see SPEECH 1

**harangue** *vb* **1** to give a formal often extended talk on a subject — see TALK 1
**2** to talk as if giving an important and formal speech — see ORATE 1

**harassment** *n* the act of making unwelcome intrusions upon another — see ANNOYANCE 1

**harbinger** *n* one that announces or indicates the later arrival of another — see FORERUNNER 1

**harbor** *n* **1** a part of a body of water protected and deep enough to be a place of safety for ships ⟨the tanker stayed in Boston *harbor* three days to undergo repairs⟩
***syn*** anchorage, harborage, haven, port
***rel*** seaport; arm, bay, bight, cove, creek [*chiefly British*], estuary, firth, fjord (*or* fiord), gulf, inlet, loch [*Scottish*], narrow, roads, roadstead; canal, channel, sound, strait
**2** something (as a building) that offers cover from the weather or protection from danger — see SHELTER

**harbor** *vb* **1** to keep in one's mind or heart ⟨Grandpa *harbored* a grudge against his first boss for nearly 50 years⟩
***syn*** bear, cherish, entertain, have, hold, nurse
***rel*** cultivate, foster, nurture, sustain, support; carry, keep, maintain, preserve, remember, retain, treasure; cleave (to), cling (to), hang on (to), stick (to)
***near ant*** disregard, drop, forget, ignore, neglect, overlook; abjure, decline, deny, disdain, refuse, reject, repudiate, scorn; abandon, desert, discard, forsake, give up, quit, renounce, throw out
**2** to provide with living quarters or shelter — see HOUSE 1
**3** to be or provide a shelter for — see SHELTER 1

**harborage** *n* **1** a part of a body of water protected and deep enough to be a place of safety for ships — see HARBOR 1
**2** something (as a building) that offers cover from the weather or protection from danger — see SHELTER

**hard** *adj* **1** having or showing a lack of sympathy or tender feelings ⟨a *hard* man, who never had a kind word for anyone⟩
***syn*** callous, cold-blooded, hard-boiled, hardhearted, heartless, inhuman, inhumane, insensate, insensitive, merciless, obdurate, pitiless, ruthless, soulless, stony (*also* stoney), uncharitable, unfeeling, unmerciful, unsparing, unsympathetic
***rel*** inconsiderate, thoughtless, uncaring, unfriendly, unloving, unthinking; grim, hard-bitten, harsh, heavy-handed, oppressive, rough, severe, stern, tough, ungentle; abusive, acrimonious, disagreeable, hateful, ill-natured, ill-tempered, malevolent, malicious, mean, rancorous, spiteful, surly, virulent; barbarous, bestial, brutal, brutish, cruel, evil-minded, savage, vicious
***near ant*** benevolent, benignant, gentle, kind; clement, lenient, mild; cordial, friendly, good-natured, good-tempered, gracious; tolerant, understanding; affectionate, loving
***ant*** charitable, compassionate, humane, merciful, sensitive, softhearted, sympathetic, tender, tenderhearted, warm, warmhearted
**2** requiring considerable physical or mental effort ⟨clearing land is *hard* work⟩ ⟨a *hard* Spanish test⟩
***syn*** arduous, demanding, difficult, exacting, formidable, grueling (*or* gruelling), herculean, killer, laborious, murderous, rough, severe, stiff, strenuous, tall, toilsome, tough
***rel*** abstract, abstruse, complex, complicated, insoluble, intricate, involved, knotty, problematic (*also* problematical), recondite, serious, spiny, thorny, ticklish, tricky, stubborn; burdensome, exhausting, labored, onerous, oppressive, problem, sore, stressful, taxing, tight, trying, uphill; annoying, bothersome, distressing, irksome, troublesome, vexatious; grievous, grim, heavy, strict, stringent; brutal, cruel, inhuman, painful
***near ant*** achievable, clear, doable, elementary, manageable, uncomplicated; comforting, gentle, painless, relaxed, smooth, soothing
***ant*** easy, effortless, facile, simple, soft, undemanding
**3** able to withstand hardship, strain, or exposure — see HARDY 1
**4** based on sound reasoning or information — see GOOD 1
**5** difficult to endure — see HARSH 1
**6** extreme in degree, power, or effect — see INTENSE
**7** given to exacting standards of discipline and self-restraint — see SEVERE 1
**8** having a consistency that does not easily yield to pressure — see FIRM 2
**9** having been established and usually not subject to change — see FIXED 1
**10** having or showing deep-seated resentment — see BITTER 1
**11** sticking to an opinion, purpose, or course of action in spite of reason, arguments, or persuasion — see OBSTINATE
**12** restricted to or based on fact — see FACTUAL 1

**hard** *adv* **1** with great effort or determination ⟨we took a much-needed break after working *hard* all week⟩ ⟨a *hard* -won victory⟩
***syn*** arduously, assiduously, determinedly, diligently, hardly, indefatigably, industriously, intensely, intensively, intently, la-

boriously, mightily, sedulously, slavishly, strenuously, tirelessly
***rel*** actively, animatedly, briskly, busily, dynamically, energetically, feverishly, spiritedly, vehemently, vigorously, zealously; continuously, ploddingly, steadily, unabatedly, unrelentingly, unremittingly; ardently, attentively, conscientiously, earnestly, exhaustively, meticulously, painstakingly, seriously, thoroughly
***near ant*** casually, desultorily, indolently, lackadaisically, languidly, lazily, listlessly, shiftlessly, sluggishly, spiritlessly, tiredly, wearily
**2** with feelings of bitterness or grief ⟨took the news of their grandfather's death *hard*⟩
***syn*** agonizingly, bitterly, grievously, hardly, mournfully, painfully, regretfully, resentfully, ruefully, sadly, sorely, sorrowfully, unhappily, woefully, wretchedly
***rel*** abjectly, dejectedly, despondently, dispiritedly; blackly, darkly, distressfully, distressingly, forlornly, gloomily, miserably; acutely, harshly, keenly, poignantly, severely, sharply; cruelly, hurtfully, ill, rancorously
***near ant*** cheerfully, cheerily, delightedly, gaily (*also* gayly), gleefully, good-naturedly, lightheartedly, merrily; blithely, calmly, casually, dispassionately, easily, indifferently, lightly, nonchalantly, unconcernedly; favorably, well
***ant*** gladly, happily, joyfully, joyously
**3** in a vigorous and forceful manner ⟨Terry hit the ball *hard* and it soared out of bounds⟩ ⟨the wind blew *hard* all day⟩
***syn*** energetically, firmly, forcefully, forcibly, mightily, powerfully, stiffly, stoutly, strenuously, strongly, sturdily, vigorously
***rel*** robustly, sharply, vehemently, violently; animatedly, briskly, crisply, dynamically, heartily, lustily, snappily, spiritedly, vivaciously; decidedly, determinedly, directly, emphatically, fast, fixedly, intensively, intently, resolutely, rigidly, smartly, solidly, soundly, squarely, steadfastly, steadily, surely; aggressively, assertively, manfully, potently
***phrases*** with might and main
***near ant*** delicately, faintly, frailly, shakily; indirectly, languidly, listlessly, spiritlessly; impotently, ineffectively, ineffectually, nervelessly, spinelessly, uncertainly
***ant*** feebly, gently, softly, weakly
**4** at, within, or to a short distance or time — see NEAR 1
**5** in a manner so as to cause loss or suffering — see HARDLY 1

**hard–and–fast** *adj* **1** having been established and usually not subject to change — see FIXED 1
**2** not capable of changing or being changed — see INFLEXIBLE 1

**hard–bitten** *adj* able to withstand hardship, strain, or exposure — see HARDY 1

**hard–boiled** *adj* having or showing a lack of sympathy or tender feelings — see HARD 1

**hard–core** *adj* firmly established over time — see INVETERATE 1

**harden** *vb* **1** to become physically firm or solid ⟨waited for the bubbly caramel-and-nut sauce to cool and *harden* into peanut brittle⟩
***syn*** concrete, congeal, firm (up), freeze, set, solidify
***rel*** cake, callus, encrust (*also* incrust); coagulate, clot, gel, jell, jelly, stiffen, thicken; calcify, crystallize, ossify, petrify; anneal, case harden, temper
***near ant*** deliquesce, dissolve, flux, fuse, liquefy, melt, smelt, thaw
***ant*** soften
**2** to make able to withstand physical hardship, strain, or exposure ⟨pioneer women who had been *hardened* by years of living on the plains⟩
***syn*** fortify, inure, season, steel, strengthen, toughen
***rel*** acclimate, acclimatize, adapt, adjust; anneal, temper; invigorate, vitalize; immunize; bolster, boost, brace, buttress, forearm, prop (up), reinforce, support; break in, limber (up), train; accustom, condition, habituate, naturalize
***near ant*** emasculate, enervate, enfeeble, exhaust, sap, weaken; cripple, debilitate, incapacitate; sensitize
***ant*** soften
**3** to increase the ability of (as a muscle) to exert physical force — see STRENGTHEN 1

**hardened** *adj* **1** able to withstand hardship, strain, or exposure — see HARDY 1
**2** sticking to an opinion, purpose, or course of action in spite of reason, arguments, or persuasion — see OBSTINATE

**hardheaded** *adj* **1** having or showing a practical cleverness or judgment — see SHREWD
**2** sticking to an opinion, purpose, or course of action in spite of reason, arguments, or persuasion — see OBSTINATE
**3** willing to see things as they really are and deal with them sensibly — see REALISTIC 1

**hardheadedness** *n* a steadfast adherence to an opinion, purpose, or course of action — see OBSTINACY

**hardhearted** *adj* **1** having or showing a lack of sympathy or tender feelings — see HARD 1
**2** sticking to an opinion, purpose, or course of action in spite of reason, arguments, or persuasion — see OBSTINATE

**hardihood** *n* **1** active strength of body or mind — see VIGOR 1
**2** strength of mind to carry on in spite of danger — see COURAGE

**hardly** *adv* **1** in a manner so as to cause loss or suffering ⟨the new judge vowed to deal *hardly* with repeat offenders⟩
***syn*** hard, harshly, ill, oppressively, roughly, severely, sternly, stiffly
***rel*** callously, cold-bloodedly, hardheartedly, heartlessly, inhumanely, inhumanly, insensately, insensitively, mercilessly, obdurately, pitilessly, ruthlessly, tyranni-

cally, uncharitably, unfeelingly, unmercifully, unsparingly; abusively, brutally, brutishly, savagely, viciously; aggressively, assertively, decidedly, determinedly, firmly, grimly, gruffly, resolutely, strongly, toughly
***near ant*** benevolently, benignantly, considerately, cordially, graciously, kindly, lovingly, tenderly; charitably, compassionately, humanely, mercifully, softheartedly, sympathetically, tolerantly, understandingly
***ant*** clemently, gently, leniently, lightly, mildly, softly
**2** certainly not ⟨it's *hardly* surprising that our team won, considering how weak the opponents were⟩
***syn*** no, none, no way, scarcely
***rel*** near, never, nothing, nowhere, nowise
***phrases*** by no means, nothing doing, on no account
***near ant*** awful, awfully, enormously, exceedingly (*also* exceeding), extremely, greatly, highly, hugely, immensely, mighty, most, quite, terribly, very; assuredly, clearly, perfectly, plainly, positively, really, truly, unequivocally, unquestionably, utterly; doubtless, more or less, mostly, rather, slightly, somewhat
***ant*** absolutely, certainly, completely, definitely, positively, surely
**3** by a very small margin — see JUST 2
**4** with feelings of bitterness or grief — see HARD 2
**5** with great effort or determination — see HARD 1

**hardness** *n* **1** something that is a cause for suffering or special effort especially in the attainment of a goal — see DIFFICULTY 1
**2** the quality or state of being demanding or unyielding (as in discipline or criticism) — see SEVERITY

**hardship** *n* something that is a cause for suffering or special effort especially in the attainment of a goal — see DIFFICULTY 1

**hardy** *adj* **1** able to withstand hardship, strain, or exposure ⟨chrysanthemums are *hardy* enough to survive a light frost⟩ ⟨the men and women who settled the West were a *hardy* lot⟩
***syn*** hard, hard-bitten, hardened, inured, rugged, stout, strong, sturdy, tough, toughened, vigorous
***rel*** flinty, leathery, resilient, stalwart; durable, enduring, everlasting, immortal, imperishable, lasting, permanent, stable, staunch (*or* stanch), staying, tenacious, unyielding; flourishing, prospering, thriving; able-bodied, brawny, muscular; fit, fortified, hale, healthy, husky, lusty, redblooded, robust, sound, strapping, virile; annealed, seasoned, tempered
***near ant*** emasculated, enervated, enfeebled, exhausted, run-down, sapped, wasted, weakened, worn, worn out; crippled, debilitated, diseased, incapacitated, infirm, unsound; fragile, frail, puny; resistless, sensitive, susceptible, unresistant, vulnerable, yielding; mortal, perishable, temporary, transient
***ant*** delicate, nonhardy, soft, tender, weak
**2** inclined or willing to take risks — see BOLD 1

**harebrained** *adj* **1** lacking in seriousness or maturity — see GIDDY 1
**2** showing or marked by a lack of good sense or judgment — see FOOLISH 1

**hark** *vb* to pay attention especially through the act of hearing — see LISTEN

**hark back** (to) *vb* to bring back to mind — see REMEMBER

**harlequin** *n* a comically dressed performer (as at a circus) who entertains with playful tricks and ridiculous behavior — see CLOWN 1

**harlot** *n* a woman who engages in sexual activities for money — see PROSTITUTE

**harlotry** *n* the practice of engaging in sexual activities for money — see PROSTITUTION

**harm** *n* something that causes loss or pain — see INJURY 1

**harm** *vb* **1** to cause bodily damage to — see INJURE 1
**2** to reduce the soundness, effectiveness, or perfection of — see DAMAGE 1

**harmful** *adj* causing or capable of causing harm ⟨DDT has been proven extremely *harmful* to the environment⟩
***syn*** adverse, bad, baleful, baneful, damaging, deleterious, detrimental, evil, hurtful, ill, injurious, mischievous, noxious, pernicious, prejudicial
***rel*** hostile, inimical, unfriendly; contagious, deadly, infectious, pestilent, pestilential, poisonous, venomous; insidious, menacing, ominous, sinister, threatening; dangerous, hazardous, imperiling, jeopardizing, parlous, perilous, risky, unsafe, unsound; nasty, noisome, unhealthful, unhealthy, unwholesome; destructive, fatal, lethal, malignant, ruinous
***near ant*** advantageous, beneficial, useful; favorable, good, propitious; curative, healthful, healthy, helpful, palliative, remedial, salubrious, salutary, wholesome; secure, sound; benign, benignant; noncorrosive, nondestructive, nonfatal, noninfectious, nonlethal, nonpoisonous, nonpolluting, nontoxic, nonvenomous
***ant*** harmless, innocent, innocuous, inoffensive, safe

**harmless** *adj* not causing injury or hurt ⟨a perfectly *harmless* little spider⟩
***syn*** innocent, innocuous, inoffensive, safe, white
***rel*** healthful, healthy, salubrious, wholesome; benign, benignant; sound, trustworthy; gentle, gracious, mild; nonthreatening, painless, unobjectionable; noncorrosive, nondestructive, nonfatal, noninfectious, nonlethal, nonpoisonous, nonpolluting, nontoxic, nonvenomous
***near ant*** poisonous, venomous; menacing, ominous, sinister, threatening; dangerous, hazardous, imperiling, jeopardizing, parlous, perilous, risky, unsafe,

unsound; nasty, noisome, unhealthful, unhealthy, unwholesome; offensive, painful, scathing, wounding; deadly, fatal, lethal, ruinous; contaminated, corrosive, malignant, noxious, pestilent, polluted, tainted
***ant*** adverse, bad, baleful, baneful, damaging, deleterious, detrimental, evil, harmful, hurtful, ill, injurious, mischievous, noxious, pernicious, prejudicial

**harmonious** *adj* **1** having a pleasing mixture of notes ⟨the naturally *harmonious* sounds of a forest glen in springtime⟩
***syn*** euphonious, harmonizing, melodious, musical, symphonic, tuneful
***rel*** blending, chiming, flowing, mellifluous; dulcet, mellow, melodic, sweet; echoing, resonant, sonorous; quavering, trilling, warbling; agreeable, appealing, pleasant; cadenced, lilting, lyric, lyrical, rhythmic (*or* rhythmical); chordal, harmonic, homophonic, orchestral, polyphonic, tonal
***near ant*** blaring, clanging, clashing, clattering, grating, harsh, jangling, jarring, metallic, raspy, raucous, scratching, screeching, shrill, squeaky, strident; disagreeable, unpleasant, unpleasing; atonal, off-key
***ant*** discordant, dissonant, inharmonious, unharmonious, unmelodious, unmusical
**2** having the parts agreeably related ⟨a *harmonious* arrangement of archways and doorways in the palace courtyard⟩
***syn*** balanced, congruous, consonant
***rel*** even, proportioned, regular, symmetrical (*or* symmetric); aesthetic (*or* esthetic), artistic, becoming, elegant, graceful, tasteful; agreeable, felicitous, pleasant, pleasing, satisfying; compatible, coordinated, correspondent, matched, matching
***near ant*** asymmetrical, disordered, irregular, skewed, unequal, uneven, unsymmetrical; distasteful, graceless, inartistic, inelegant, tasteless, unaesthetic, unbecoming, ungraceful, unlovely; disagreeable, displeasing, dissatisfying, infelicitous, unfortunate, unpleasant, unsightly; clashing, conflicting, disunited, incompatible, uncoordinated
***ant*** incongruous, inharmonious, unbalanced
**3** having or marked by agreement in feeling or action ⟨an unusually *harmonious* meeting among the leaders resulted in a quick peace agreement⟩
***syn*** agreeable, amicable, compatible, congenial, frictionless, kindred, unanimous, united
***rel*** pacific, peaceable, peaceful; collaborating, cooperative, symbiotic; noncompetitive, nonconflicting, uncompetitive; sympathetic, tolerant, understanding; affable, amiable, cordial, friendly, genial, neighborly; collaborating
***near ant*** antagonistic, antipathetic, clashing, conflicting, hostile, inimical, unfriendly; belligerent, contentious, quarrelsome; contradicting, contradictory, contrary, opposing, opposite; competing, competitive, rivaling (*or* rivalling)
***ant*** disagreeable, disunited, incompatible, inharmonious, uncongenial
**4** not having or showing any apparent conflict — see CONSISTENT

**harmonize** *vb* **1** to form a pleasing relationship ⟨the color of the walls *harmonized* nicely with the blue tones in the carpet⟩
***syn*** agree, blend, conform, coordinate
***rel*** balance, correlate, correspond, dovetail, match; meet, parallel; bond, coalesce, cohere, conjoin, fuse, merge, square, tally
***near ant*** contradict, contrast, counter, differ, diverge, jar; cancel (out), counteract, negate, offset
***ant*** clash, collide, conflict
**2** to bring to a state free of conflicts, inconsistencies, or differences ⟨an attempt to *harmonize* the New Testament version of events with the accounts of the ancient Romans⟩
***syn*** accommodate, conciliate, conform, coordinate, key, reconcile
***rel*** adapt, attune, tune; blend, combine, connect, correlate, dovetail, fit, fuse, integrate, join, match, merge, orchestrate, pair, square, suit, synchronize, synthesize, unify, unite; align, arrange, array, balance, equalize, even, order, proportion, regularize, standardize
***near ant*** confuse, disarray, disorder, disorganize, disrupt, disturb, skew, upset
***ant*** alienate, disjoin
**3** to be in agreement on every point — see CHECK 1

**harmonizing** *adj* having a pleasing mixture of notes — see HARMONIOUS 1

**harmony** *n* **1** a balanced, pleasing, or suitable arrangement of parts ⟨her face had an angelic *harmony* that fascinated the leading painters of her day⟩
***syn*** balance, coherence, consonance, proportion, symmetry, symphony, unity
***rel*** coordination, correlation, correspondence, equalization, equilibrium, evenness, order, orderliness, regularity, uniformity
***near ant*** confusion, disorganization, dissonance, disturbance, tension; disconnectedness, disjointedness, incompatibility; irregularity, unevenness
***ant*** asymmetry, discordance, disproportion, disunity, imbalance, incoherence
**2** peaceful coexistence ⟨Mary Beth was determined to live in *harmony* with her new stepsister⟩
***syn*** comity, compatibility, concord, peace
***rel*** amity, congeniality, fellowship, fraternization, friendship; collaboration, reciprocity, symbiosis; consensus, unanimity, unity; affinity, connection, empathy, kinship, oneness, rapport, solidarity, sympathy, understanding; peacefulness, serenity, tranquillity (*or* tranquility)
***near ant*** antagonism, antipathy, enmity, hatred, hostility, unfriendliness; alienation, breach, divorce, estrangement,

rupture, schism, severance; dissent, dissidence; disturbance, strife, turmoil
*ant* conflict, discord, dissension
**3** a state of consistency — see CONFORMITY 1

**harness** *vb* to put into action or service — see USE 1

**harpoon** *vb* to penetrate or hold (something) with a pointed object — see IMPALE

**harpy** *n* a bad-tempered scolding woman — see SHREW

**harrow** *vb* to cause persistent suffering to — see AFFLICT

**harrowing** *adj* **1** hard to accept or bear especially emotionally — see BITTER 2
**2** intensely or unbearably painful — see EXCRUCIATING 1

**harrying** *n* the act of making unwelcome intrusions upon another — see ANNOYANCE 1

**harsh** *adj* **1** difficult to endure ⟨*harsh* conditions in the refugee camp⟩
*syn* bitter, brutal, burdensome, cruel, excruciating, grievous, grim, hard, heavy, inhuman, murderous, onerous, oppressive, rough, rugged, severe, stiff, tough, trying
*rel* austere, bleak, comfortless, discomforting, forbidding, hostile, inhospitable, Spartan, uncomfortable; biting, inclement, intemperate; rigorous, strict, stringent; agonizing, heartbreaking, heartrending, painful, wretched; crushing, grinding, overwhelming, wearing; insufferable, insupportable, intolerable, unbearable, unendurable; harrowing, tortuous; bad, disagreeable, hostile, unfriendly, unpleasant
*near ant* comfortable, cozy, luxurious, snug; agreeable, friendly, genial, hospitable, pleasant; peaceful, relaxing, reposeful, restful; bearable, endurable, painless, tolerable; balmy, calm, clement, gentle, mild, moderate, temperate
*ant* easy, light, soft
**2** disagreeable to one's aesthetic or artistic sense ⟨the *harsh* lighting in the cafeteria makes the food look slightly off-color⟩
*syn* grating, grotesque, jarring, unaesthetic
*rel* flashy, garish, gaudy, loud, tawdry; tacky, tasteless, vulgar; inartistic, unartistic; artless, clumsy, crude, graceless, inelegant, rude; uncouth, uncultured, unrefined; disgusting, gross, obscene, repugnant, repulsive, ugly; disagreeable, jolting, unpleasant, unpleasing; blaring, clashing, discordant, dissonant, inharmonious, off-key, jangling, raspy, raucous, unharmonious, unmelodious, unmusical; bizarre, kinky, odd, outlandish, shocking
*near ant* artful, artistic; attractive, beautiful, becoming, comely; agreeable, appealing, felicitous, good, harmonious, harmonizing, pleasing, seemly; calming, comforting, soothing; softened, subdued; cultured, elegant, graceful, gracious, polished, refined, tasteful
*ant* aesthetic (*or* esthetic)
**3** causing discomfort — see UNCOMFORTABLE 1
**4** given to exacting standards of discipline and self-restraint — see SEVERE 1
**5** hard to accept or bear especially emotionally — see BITTER 2

**harshly** *adv* in a manner so as to cause loss or suffering — see HARDLY 1

**harshness** *n* **1** a harsh or sharp quality — see EDGE 1
**2** the quality or state of being demanding or unyielding (as in discipline or criticism) — see SEVERITY

**harum-scarum** *adv* in a confused and reckless manner — see HELTER-SKELTER 1

**harvest** *n* the quantity of an animal or vegetable product gathered at the end of a season — see CROP 1

**harvest** *vb* to catch or collect (a crop or natural resource) for human use ⟨*harvest* salmon from nearby rivers⟩ ⟨every year we *harvest* corn from our own garden⟩
*syn* gather, pick, reap
*rel* clam, fish, seal, shrimp, whale; accumulate, garner; glean; cut, hay, mow; bag, capture, hunt, net, snare, trap; crop, grow, raise
*near ant* plant, seed, sow

**hash** *n* an unorganized collection or mixture of various things — see MISCELLANY 1

**hash** *vb* **1** to cut into small pieces — see CHOP
**2** to undo the proper order or arrangement of — see DISORDER

**hash** (over) *vb* to talk about (an issue) usually from various points of view and for the purpose of arriving at a decision or opinion — see DISCUSS

**hassle** *n* **1** a brief clash between enemies or rivals — see ENCOUNTER
**2** a physical dispute between opposing individuals or groups — see FIGHT 1
**3** an often noisy or angry expression of differing opinions — see ARGUMENT 1
**4** something that is a source of irritation — see ANNOYANCE 3

**hassle** *vb* **1** to attack repeatedly with mean put-downs or insults — see TEASE 2
**2** to express different opinions about something often angrily — see ARGUE 2

**haste** *n* **1** a high rate of movement or performance — see SPEED
**2** excited and often showy or disorderly speed — see HURRY 1

**hasten** *vb* **1** to cause to move or proceed fast or faster — see HURRY 1
**2** to proceed or move quickly — see HURRY 2

**hastily** *adv* **1** with excessive or careless speed ⟨the *hastily* put together report contained a lot of errors⟩
*syn* cursorily, headlong, hotfoot, hurriedly, pell-mell, precipitately, precipitously, rashly

***rel*** headily, hotheadedly, impatiently, impetuously, impulsively, recklessly, thoughtlessly; automatically, glancingly, haphazardly; impromptu, spontaneously; abruptly, suddenly; offhand, offhandedly
***phrases*** on the spur of the moment
***near ant*** calculatingly, circumspectly, designedly; falteringly, hesitantly, hesitatingly, tentatively; leisurely, slowly
***ant*** deliberately, studiedly
**2** with great speed — see FAST 1

**hastiness** *n* excited and often showy or disorderly speed — see HURRY 1

**hasty** *adj* **1** acting or done with excessive or careless speed ⟨Anna later regretted her *hasty* decision to sell her car⟩
***syn*** cursory, flying, headlong, hurried, pell-mell, precipitate, precipitous, rash, rushed
***rel*** breakneck, breathtaking; headstrong, heady, hotheaded, impatient, impetuous, impulsive, madcap, reckless, unadvised; quick, rapid, speedy, swift; impromptu, makeshift, offhand, offhanded, slap-dash, snap, spontaneous, spur-of-the-moment; abrupt, sudden
***near ant*** calculated, calculating, measured; circumspect, foresighted, forethoughtful; drawn-out, extended, long-term, prolonged; faltering, hesitant, hesitating, tentative; dallying, dawdling, laggard, leisurely, poky (*or* pokey); shilly-shallying, slow
***ant*** deliberate, unhurried
**2** moving, proceeding, or acting with great speed — see FAST 1

**hat** *n* a covering for the head usually having a shaped crown ⟨Paul brought back warm fur *hats* for everyone from Russia⟩
***syn*** cap, headdress, headgear, headpiece, lid [*slang*]
***rel*** beret, biretta, boater, bonnet, bowler, derby, fedora, fez, hard hat, helm, helmet, homburg, hood, leghorn, miter, nightcap, panama, pillbox, poke bonnet, shako, skullcap, sombrero, sou'wester, Stetson, stocking cap, stovepipe, sunbonnet, tam-o'-shanter, top hat, topper, toque, turban; war bonnet; coronet, crown, diadem, headband, tiara; babushka, coif, kerchief, mantilla, scarf, shawl, tallith, veil, wimple

**hatch** *n* a barrier by which an entry is closed and opened — see DOOR 1

**hatch** *vb* to cover and warm eggs to hatch them — see SET 1

**hate** *n* **1** a very strong dislike ⟨*hate* can sometimes be replaced with tolerance when people meet face to face⟩
***syn*** abhorrence, abomination, execration, hatred, loathing
***rel*** cattiness, despite, despitefulness, hatefulness, invidiousness, malevolence, malice, maliciousness, malignancy, malignity, meanness, spite, spitefulness; aversion, disgust, distaste; horror, odium, repugnance, repulsion, revulsion; animosity, antagonism, antipathy, bitterness, contempt, disdain, enmity, grudge, hostility, jealousy, pique, resentment, scorn; bile, jaundice, rancor, spleen, venom, virulence, vitriol
***near ant*** appetite, inclination, liking; adoration, veneration, worship; acceptance, tolerance; passion, relish, taste
***ant*** affection, devotion, fondness, love
**2** something or someone that is hated ⟨the Alaska pipeline is a pet *hate* of environmentalists⟩
***syn*** abhorrence, abomination, anathema, antipathy, aversion, bête noire
***rel*** dread, hang-up, horror, phobia; bogey (*also* bogy *or* bogie), bugaboo, bugbear; adversary, enemy; annoyance, grievance, hassle, nuisance, peeve
***near ant*** beloved, darling, dear, honey; delight, enjoyment, felicity, joy, pleasure; favorite, like, preference; treasure
***ant*** love

**hate** *vb* to dislike strongly ⟨Pete *hated* the farm and dreamed of working in the city⟩
***syn*** abhor, abominate, despise, detest, execrate, loathe
***rel*** deplore, deprecate, disapprove (of), discountenance, disdain, disfavor, scorn
***phrases*** have it in for
***near ant*** fancy, favor, like, prefer; enjoy, relish; adore, esteem, idolize, revere, venerate, worship; cherish, prize, treasure
***ant*** love

**hateful** *adj* having or showing a desire to cause someone pain or suffering for the sheer enjoyment of it ⟨a *hateful* bully who loved to pick on little kids⟩ ⟨Janet's *hateful* remarks drove Penny to tears⟩
***syn*** catty, cruel, despiteful, malevolent, malicious, malign, malignant, mean, nasty, spiteful, virulent
***rel*** devious, scoundrelly, scurvy, snake-like; acrimonious, bitter, envious, jaundiced, jealous, rancorous, resentful; contemptuous, deprecating, disdainful, obnoxious, opprobrious, scornful, snide, unkind, unkindly, unloving; baleful, baneful, evil; harsh, hostile, inimical; acrid, caustic, scathing, venomous
***near ant*** compassionate, good, good-hearted, kind, kindhearted, kindly, sympathetic, warm, warmhearted; affable, agreeable, amiable, cordial, friendly, genial, gracious, nice, pleasant; affectionate, amorous, sweet, tender, tenderhearted; altruistic, high-minded, humanitarian, magnanimous, noble, philanthropic
***ant*** benevolent, benign, benignant, loving, unmalicious

**hatefully** *adv* in a mean or spiteful manner — see NASTILY

**hatefulness** *n* the desire to cause pain for the satisfaction of doing harm — see MALICE

**hatred** *n* a very strong dislike — see HATE 1

**haughtiness** *n* an exaggerated sense of one's importance that shows itself in the making of excessive or unjustified claims — see ARROGANCE

**haughty** *adj* **1** having a feeling of superiority that shows itself in an overbearing attitude — see ARROGANT
**2** having or displaying feelings of scorn for what is regarded as beneath oneself — see PROUD 1

**haul** *n* **1** the total amount collected or obtained especially at one time ⟨the trick-or-treaters showed off their *haul*⟩
***syn*** catch, take, yield
***rel*** bag; earnings, gain, gross, income, net, payoff, proceeds, profit, receipts, return, revenue, winnings; booty, loot, plunder, spoils, swag; appropriation, collection
***near ant*** deduction, loss, subtraction
**2** a mass or quantity of something taken up and carried, conveyed, or transported — see LOAD 1
**3** the act or an instance of applying force on something so that it moves in the direction of the force — see PULL 1

**haul** *vb* **1** to cause to follow by applying steady force on — see PULL 1
**2** to support and take from one place to another — see CARRY 1

**haunches** *n pl* the part of the body upon which someone sits — see BUTTOCKS

**haunt** *n* a place for spending time or for socializing — see HANGOUT

**haunt** *vb* to go to or spend time in often — see FREQUENT

**haunting** *adj* fearfully and mysteriously strange or fantastic — see EERIE

**have** *vb* **1** to keep, control, or experience as one's own ⟨Aunt Chloe *has* 31 pairs of red shoes⟩
***syn*** command, enjoy, hold, occupy, own, possess, retain
***rel*** keep, reserve, withhold; bear, carry; boast, show off, sport
***near ant*** abandon, cede, disclaim, disown, hand over, relinquish, renounce, surrender, yield; discard, dump; decline, reject, repudiate, spurn; need, require
***ant*** lack, want
**2** to agree to receive whether willingly or reluctantly — see TAKE 2
**3** to bring forth from the womb — see BEAR 1
**4** to cause to believe what is untrue — see DECEIVE
**5** to come to a knowledge of (something) by living through it — see EXPERIENCE
**6** to give permission for or to approve of — see ALLOW 1
**7** to influence someone with a bribe — see BRIBE
**8** to keep in one's mind or heart — see HARBOR 1

**have** (to) *vb* to be under necessity or obligation to — see NEED 2

**haven** *n* **1** a part of a body of water protected and deep enough to be a place of safety for ships — see HARBOR 1
**2** something (as a building) that offers cover from the weather or protection from danger — see SHELTER

***syn*** synonym(s) ***rel*** related words
***ant*** antonym(s) ***near ant*** near antonym(s)

**havoc** *n* **1** a state in which everything is out of order — see CHAOS
**2** the state or fact of being rendered nonexistent, physically unsound, or useless — see DESTRUCTION

**hawk** *n* one who urges or attempts to cause a war — see WARMONGER

**hawk** *vb* to sell from place to place usually in small quantities — see PEDDLE

**hawker** *n* one who sells things outdoors — see PEDDLER

**hazard** *n* **1** something that may cause injury or harm — see DANGER 2
**2** the uncertain course of events — see CHANCE 1

**hazard** *vb* **1** to place in danger — see ENDANGER
**2** to take a chance on — see RISK 1

**hazardous** *adj* involving potential loss or injury — see DANGEROUS

**haze** *n* **1** an atmospheric condition in which suspended particles in the air rob it of its transparency ⟨Jim could barely make out the tall buildings through the *haze*⟩
***syn*** fog, mist, murk, reek, smog, soup
***rel*** cloud, fume, miasma, smoke, steam
**2** a state of mental confusion ⟨people wandered around in a *haze* in the days following the earthquake⟩
***syn*** daze, fog, muddle, spin
***rel*** reverie, stupor, trance; befuddlement, bewilderment, perplexity, puzzlement; delirium, malaise, paralysis; cloudiness, fogginess
***near ant*** alertness, levelheadedness

**haze** *vb* to make dark, dim, or indistinct — see CLOUD 1

**hazed** *adj* covered over by clouds — see OVERCAST

**hazy** *adj* **1** filled with or dimmed by fine particles (as of dust or water) in suspension ⟨*hazy* skies made it dangerous to fly⟩ ⟨the *hazy* sunshine so common in August⟩
***syn*** beclouded, befogged, clouded, cloudy, foggy, misty, murky, smoggy, soupy
***rel*** overcast, rainy, stormy, thick; dirty, miry, mucky, muddy, slimy, slushy, turbid; smoky (*also* smokey), sooty; filmy, milky, opaque
***near ant*** bright, clean; fair, rainless, sunny, sunshiny; translucent, transparent
***ant*** clear, cloudless, limpid, pellucid, unclouded
**2** covered over by clouds — see OVERCAST
**3** not seen or understood clearly — see FAINT 1

**head** *adj* highest in rank or authority ⟨Mr. Pendergast, *head* editor at the TV station for 17 years, has hired and fired innumerable staff members⟩
***syn*** chief, commanding, first, foremost, high, lead, leading, managing, preeminent, premier, presiding, primary, prime, principal, supreme
***rel*** high-level, senior; controlling, directing, officiating, overseeing, reigning, rul-

ing, supervisory; main, major, paramount, predominant; dominant, grand, superior, topmost, upmost, upper, uppermost
*phrases* in charge
*near ant* inferior, last, lesser, lower, lowly, second, secondary, subordinate; assistant, assisting, coadjutor, deputy, junior, under

**head** *n* **1** the upper or front part of the body that contains the brain, the major sense organs, and the mouth ⟨I hit my *head* as I went through the low doorway⟩
*syn* noddle, noggin, pate, poll
*rel* cranium, crown, scalp, skull
**2** the place of leadership or command ⟨every year a different parent is placed at the *head* of the troop's cookie drive⟩
*syn* chair, headship, helm, rein
*rel* chieftainship, commandership, directorship; forefront, lead, preferment; chairmanship, deanship, dictatorship, governorship, kingship, mastership, mastery, presidency, superintendency; dominance, dominion, jurisdiction, sovereignty, sway, upper hand; eminence, height, pedestal, pinnacle, seat, throne, top
*near ant* ranks
**3** a light mass of fine bubbles formed in or on a liquid — see FOAM
**4** a member of the human race — see HUMAN
**5** a time or state of affairs requiring prompt or decisive action — see EMERGENCY
**6** the beginning part of a stream — see HEADWATER
**7** the highest part or point — see HEIGHT 1
**8** the normal or healthy condition of the mental abilities — see MIND 2
**9** the part of a person that feels, thinks, perceives, wills, and especially reasons — see MIND 1
**10** the person (as an employer or supervisor) who tells people and especially workers what to do — see BOSS

**head** *vb* **1** to go on a specified course or in a certain direction ⟨the migrant workers were *heading* for California for the grape harvest⟩
*syn* bear, make
*rel* aim, bend, direct, point, turn; put, put out, set forth, set off, set out, strike, take off; face, orient, steer; about-face, back, come about, come round, cue, incline, put about, reverse, swerve, tack, veer, yaw, wheel
**2** to be at the front of — see LEAD 3
**3** to be in charge of — see BOSS 1
**4** to be positioned along a certain course or in a certain direction — see RUN 3
**5** to point or turn (something) toward a target or goal — see AIM
**6** to serve as leader of — see LEAD 2

**headache** *n* **1** a dull, unpleasant, or difficult piece of work — see CHORE 2
**2** something that is a source of irritation — see ANNOYANCE 3

**headdress** *n* a covering for the head usually having a shaped crown — see HAT

**headgear** *n* a covering for the head usually having a shaped crown — see HAT

**heading** *n* a word or series of words often in larger letters placed at the beginning of a passage or at the top of a page in order to introduce or categorize ⟨Fran found the recipe for turkey gumbo under the *heading* "stews" rather than under "soups"⟩
*syn* caption, headline, rubric, title
*rel* guide word, legend; greeting, salutation; superscript, superscription; subhead, subheading, subtitle

**headland** *n* **1** an area of high ground jutting out into a body of water beyond the line of the coast ⟨the lighthouse, situated on a narrow, rocky *headland,* commands an expansive view of the coast⟩
*syn* point, promontory
*rel* cape, peninsula; breakwater, jetty, levee; spit
**2** an area of land that juts out into a body of water — see [2]CAPE

**headline** *n* a word or series of words often in larger letters placed at the beginning of a passage or at the top of a page in order to introduce or categorize — see HEADING

**headlong** *adj* acting or done with excessive or careless speed — see HASTY 1

**headlong** *adv* with excessive or careless speed — see HASTILY 1

**headman** *n* the person (as an employer or supervisor) who tells people and especially workers what to do — see BOSS

**headpiece** *n* a covering for the head usually having a shaped crown — see HAT

**headquarters** *n pl* **1** a place from which authority is exercised — see SEAT 1
**2** the place from which a commander runs operations — see COMMAND 3

**headship** *n* **1** the duty or function of watching or guarding for the sake of proper direction or control — see SUPERVISION 1
**2** the place of leadership or command — see HEAD 2

**headstone** *n* a shaped stone laid over or erected near a grave and usually bearing an inscription to identify and preserve the memory of the deceased — see TOMBSTONE

**headstrong** *adj* **1** given to resisting control or discipline by others — see UNCONTROLLABLE
**2** sticking to an opinion, purpose, or course of action in spite of reason, arguments, or persuasion — see OBSTINATE

**headwater** *n usually* **headwaters** *pl* the beginning part of a stream ⟨the first exploration of the Missouri River from its mouth to its *headwaters* was made by Meriwether Lewis and William Clark in the early 1800s⟩
*syn* head, source
*rel* fountain, fountainhead, geyser, hot spring, spring, thermal spring, wellspring

**headway** *n* forward movement in time or place — see ADVANCE 1

**heal** *vb* **1** to restore to a healthy condition ⟨a low-fat vegetarian diet, moderate exercise, and stress management help *heal* a diseased heart⟩ ⟨*heal* the sick⟩
***syn*** cure, mend, rehabilitate
***rel*** attend (to), care (for), doctor, minister (to), nurse, treat; fortify, rejuvenate, renew, resuscitate, revive; alleviate, fix, relieve, remedy, repair
***phrases*** take care of
***near ant*** damage, disable, harm, hurt, impair, injure, lacerate, lame, maim, mangle, mutilate, wound; afflict, ail, debilitate, enervate, enfeeble, lay up, sap, sicken, waste, weaken
**2** to become healthy and strong again after illness or weakness — see CONVALESCE
**3** to bring about recovery from — see CURE 1

**healing** *n* the process or period of gradually regaining one's health and strength — see CONVALESCENCE

**health** *n* the condition of being sound in body ⟨Sam gradually regained his *health* after a long bout with cholera⟩
***syn*** fitness, healthiness, heartiness, robustness, soundness, wellness, wholeness, wholesomeness
***rel*** fettle, shape; cleanliness, hygiene; hardiness, lustiness, ruggedness, stamina, strength, toughness, vigor, vigorousness, vitality; bloom, flush, flushness; activeness, agility, liveliness, spryness; weal, welfare, well-being
***near ant*** debility, decrepitude, feebleness, frailness, infirmity, lameness, weakness; ailment, condition, disease, disorder, malady, trouble
***ant*** illness, sickness, unhealthiness, unsoundness

**healthful** *adj* good for the health ⟨one of the most *healthful* forms of exercise is a brisk walk⟩
***syn*** healthy, restorative, salubrious, salutary, wholesome
***rel*** alleviative, corrective, curative, remedial, tonic; advantageous, beneficial, useful; antiseptic, clean, hygienic, sanitary; nonfattening, nonpoisonous, nontoxic
***near ant*** deleterious, injurious, pernicious; infectious, poisonous, toxic; insanitary, unhygienic, unsanitary
***ant*** insalubrious, noxious, unhealthful, unhealthy, unwholesome

**healthiness** *n* the condition of being sound in body — see HEALTH

**healthy** *adj* **1** enjoying health and vigor ⟨always a hard worker, Grandma has remained *healthy* into her eighties⟩
***syn*** able-bodied, bouncing, chipper, fit, hale, hearty, robust, sound, well, whole, wholesome
***rel*** hardy, lusty, rugged, stalwart, strong, sturdy, tough; nondisabled, nonhandicapped, uncrippled; active, agile, lively, sprightly, spry, vigorous, vital; blooming, clean-cut, flourishing, flush, thriving; all right, good, right
***phrases*** in fine fettle
***near ant*** decrepit, enfeebled, feeble, infirm, run-down, sickened, sickly, weak, weakened, weakly, worn-out; challenged, crippled, debilitated, disabled, incapacitated, lame; delicate, fragile, frail; undernourished; afflicted, troubled; bad, poorly
***ant*** ailing, diseased, ill, sick, unfit, unhealthy, unsound, unwell
**2** good for the health — see HEALTHFUL
**3** sufficiently large in size, amount, or number to merit attention — see CONSIDERABLE 1

**heap** *n* **1** a considerable amount — see LOT 2
**2** a quantity of things thrown or stacked on one another — see [1]PILE 1

**heap** *vb* **1** to give readily and in large quantities — see RAIN 2
**2** to gradually form into a layer, pile, or mass — see COLLECT 2
**3** to lay or throw on top of one another — see PILE
**4** to put into (something) as much as can be held or contained — see FILL 1

**hear** *vb* **1** to come to an awareness — see DISCOVER 1
**2** to pay attention especially through the act of hearing — see LISTEN

**hearing** *n* range of hearing — see EARSHOT

**hearken** *vb* to pay attention especially through the act of hearing — see LISTEN

**heart** *n* **1** the capacity for feeling for another's unhappiness or misfortune ⟨when her parents refused her request for a puppy, Jessica asked, "Have you no *heart*?"⟩
***syn*** charity, commiseration, compassion, feeling, humanity, kindheartedness, kindliness, kindness, mercy, pity, softheartedness, sympathy
***rel*** responsiveness, sensitivity; affection, love, regard; affinity, empathy, rapport; altruism, benevolence, benignity, generosity, goodwill, humanitarianism, philanthropy
***near ant*** callousness, coldness, indifference, unconcern; cruelty, harshness; animosity, antipathy, dislike, hatred, hostility
***ant*** hardheartedness, inhumanity, mercilessness
**2** the body of knowledge that has been retained in one's mind or the use of it ⟨Dan can recite the entire Declaration of Independence by *heart*⟩
***syn*** memory, rote
***rel*** association, conning, memorization
**3** a thing or place that is of greatest importance to an activity or interest — see CENTER 1
**4** strength of mind to carry on in spite of danger — see COURAGE
**5** the central part or aspect of something under consideration — see CRUX
**6** the seat of one's deepest thoughts and emotions — see CORE 1

**heartache** *n* deep sadness especially for the loss of someone or something loved — see SORROW
**heartbreak** *n* deep sadness especially for the loss of someone or something loved — see SORROW
**heartbreaking** *adj* **1** causing unhappiness — see SAD 2
**2** of a kind to cause great distress — see REGRETTABLE
**3** deserving of one's pity — see PATHETIC 1
**heartbroken** *adj* **1** feeling unhappiness — see SAD 1
**2** expressing or suggesting mourning — see MOURNFUL 1
**hearten** *vb* to fill with courage or strength of purpose — see ENCOURAGE 1
**heartening** *adj* **1** having qualities which inspire hope — see HOPEFUL 1
**2** making one feel good inside — see HEARTWARMING
**3** pointing toward a happy outcome — see FAVORABLE 2
**hearth** *n* the place where one lives — see HOME 1
**hearthstone** *n* the place where one lives — see HOME 1
**heartily** *adv* in a cheerful or happy manner — see GAILY 1
**heartiness** *n* the condition of being sound in body — see HEALTH
**heartless** *adj* **1** having or showing a lack of sympathy or tender feelings — see HARD 1
**2** having or showing the desire to inflict severe pain and suffering on others — see CRUEL 1
**heartlessness** *n* the willful infliction of pain and suffering on others — see CRUELTY
**heartrending** *adj* **1** causing unhappiness — see SAD 2
**2** hard to accept or bear especially emotionally — see BITTER 2
**3** of a kind to cause great distress — see REGRETTABLE
**4** deserving of one's pity — see PATHETIC 1
**heartsick** *adj* feeling unhappiness — see SAD 1
**heartsickness** *n* a state or spell of low spirits — see SADNESS
**heartsore** *adj* feeling unhappiness — see SAD 1
**heartstrings** *n pl* general emotional condition — see FEELING 2
**heartwarming** *adj* making one feel good inside ⟨Sarah appreciated the *heartwarming* welcome she received from her relatives in Israel⟩
***syn*** cheering, comforting, encouraging, fulfilling, gladdening, gratifying, heartening, rewarding, satisfying
***rel*** affecting, inspiring, moving, poignant, stirring, touching; edifying, elevating, uplifting; sympathetic, tender; kind, kindly, loving, warm; exciting, exhilarating, rousing, stimulating, thrilling; pleasing, welcoming
***near ant*** cheerless, depressing, disappointing, discouraging, disgruntling, disheartening, displeasing, dissatisfying, saddening; cold, unfeeling, unfriendly, unkind, unloving, unpleasant
***ant*** depressing, discouraging, disheartening, dispiriting
**hearty** *adj* **1** characterized by unqualified enthusiasm ⟨Frank expressed *hearty* approval of his aunt's suggestion to rendezvous in Tokyo⟩
***syn*** wholehearted
***rel*** single-minded; ardent, avid, eager, enthusiastic, excited, exuberant, gung ho, impassioned, keen, raring, vehement, warm, zealous; alacritous, immediate, prompt, ready, willing, unhesitating; animated, energetic, lively, spirited, vigorous; absolute, bona fide, genuine, unaffected, undisguised, unequivocal, unrestrained
***near ant*** apathetic, disinterested, indifferent, uninterested; lackadaisical, listless, perfunctory, spiritless, uneager, unenthusiastic, unexcited; equivocal, hesitant, qualified, tentative, uncertain; delayed, dilatory, doubtful, hedging, hesitating; forced, reluctant, resistant, unwilling
***ant*** grudging, halfhearted, lukewarm, tepid
**2** enjoying health and vigor — see HEALTHY 1
**3** having or showing kindly feeling and sincere interest — see FRIENDLY 1
**4** not showing weakness or uncertainty — see FIRM 1
**heat** *n* depth of feeling — see ARDOR 1
**heat** *vb* to cause to have or give off heat to a moderate degree — see WARM 1
**heated** *adj* **1** being in a state of increased activity or agitation — see FEVERISH 1
**2** having or giving off heat to a moderate degree — see WARM 1
**heathen** *adj* not civilized — see SAVAGE 1
**heathen** *n* **1** a person who does not worship the God of the Bible ⟨a missionary sent to distant lands to convert the *heathens*⟩
***syn*** gentile, idolater (*or* idolator), pagan
***rel*** atheist, infidel, nonbeliever, non-Christian, unbeliever; polytheist, theist
***near ant*** Christian, Jew, Muslim
**2** an uncivilized person ⟨European colonizers, who considered the New World peoples to be *heathens*, forced them to conform to European ways⟩
***syn*** barbarian, savage
***rel*** Neanderthal, primitive
**heathenish** *adj* not civilized — see SAVAGE 1
**heave** *vb* **1** to lift with effort ⟨I *heaved* my duffel bag into the bus's overhead compartment⟩
***syn*** boost, heft, hoist, jack (up)
***rel*** elevate, hike, raise, rear, up, uplift, upraise
***near ant*** drop, lower; sink, submerge, submerse
**2** to discharge the contents of the stomach through the mouth — see VOMIT

3 to move from a lower to a higher place or position — see RAISE 1
4 to send through the air especially with a quick forward motion of the arm — see THROW

**heaven** *n* 1 a dwelling place of perfect bliss for the soul after death ⟨prayed that the souls of the deceased would go to *heaven*⟩
***syn*** Elysium, kingdom come, paradise
***rel*** empyrean; glory; otherworld
***phrases*** on high
***near ant*** inferno; limbo, purgatory; hades, netherworld, underworld
***ant*** hell, perdition
2 a place or state of great happiness — see PARADISE 1
3 a state of overwhelming usually pleasurable emotion — see ECSTASY
4 *usually* **heavens** *pl* the expanse of air surrounding the earth — see SKY

**heavenly** *adj* 1 of the very best kind — see EXCELLENT
2 of, relating to, or being God — see HOLY 3
3 of, relating to, or suggesting heaven — see CELESTIAL
4 giving pleasure or contentment to the mind or senses — see PLEASANT

**heavily** *adv* to a great degree — see VERY 1

**heaviness** *n* 1 the amount that something weighs — see WEIGHT 1
2 the state or quality of being heavy — see WEIGHTINESS 1

**heavy** *adj* 1 having great weight ⟨this trunk full of books is much too *heavy* for one person to lift⟩
***syn*** hefty, massive, ponderous, weighty
***rel*** burdensome, leaden, lumpish; bulky, elephantine, outsize; overweight, top-heavy; solid, substantial
***near ant*** airy, ethereal, feathery, gossamer, gossamery; flimsy, fluffy, insubstantial
***ant*** light, lightweight, weightless
2 causing weariness, restlessness, or lack of interest — see BORING
3 containing much seasoning, fat, or sugar — see RICH 2
4 covered over by clouds — see OVERCAST
5 difficult to endure — see HARSH 1
6 extreme in degree, power, or effect — see INTENSE
7 having a matter of importance as its topic — see SERIOUS 2

**heavy** *n* a mean, evil, or unprincipled person — see VILLAIN

**heavy–handed** *adj* 1 given to exacting standards of discipline and self-restraint — see SEVERE 1
2 lacking in physical ease and grace in movement or in the use of the hands — see CLUMSY 1

**heavyset** *adj* being compact and broad in build and often short in stature — see STOCKY

**heckle** *vb* to attack repeatedly with mean put-downs or insults — see TEASE 2

**heckler** *n* a person who causes repeated emotional pain, distress, or annoyance to another — see TORMENTOR

**hectic** *adj* being in a state of increased activity or agitation — see FEVERISH 1

**hectically** *adv* in a confused and reckless manner — see HELTER-SKELTER 1

**hector** *vb* to make timid or fearful by or as if by threats — see INTIMIDATE

**hedge** *n* a physical object that blocks the way — see BARRIER

**hedge** *vb* 1 to avoid giving a definite answer or position — see EQUIVOCATE
2 to close or shut in by or as if by barriers — see ENCLOSE 1

**heed** *n* 1 a state of being aware — see ATTENTION 2
2 strict attentiveness to what one is doing — see CARE 1

**heed** *vb* 1 to take notice of and be guided by ⟨if Paul had *heeded* his brother's advice, he might not have gotten lost⟩
***syn*** follow, listen (to), mind, note, observe, regard, watch
***rel*** consider, contemplate, mull, ponder, weigh; comply (with), keep, obey, respect; hark (to), hear, hearken (to); mark, notice, see
***near ant*** brush (off), dismiss, pooh-pooh, scorn, shrug off; defy, flout; slight, snub
***ant*** disregard, ignore, tune out
2 to pay attention especially through the act of hearing — see LISTEN

**heedful** *adj* having or showing a close attentiveness to avoiding danger or trouble — see CAREFUL 1

**heedfulness** *n* 1 a close attentiveness to avoiding danger — see CAUTION 1
2 strict attentiveness to what one is doing — see CARE 1

**heedless** *adj* not paying or showing close attention especially for the purpose of avoiding trouble — see CARELESS 1

**heedlessness** *n* failure to take the care that a cautious person usually takes — see NEGLIGENCE 1

**heel** *n* a person whose behavior is offensive to others — see JERK 1

**heel** *vb* to set or cause to be at an angle — see LEAN 1

**heft** *n* the amount that something weighs — see WEIGHT 1

**heft** *vb* 1 to lift with effort — see HEAVE 1
2 to move from a lower to a higher place or position — see RAISE 1

**heftiness** *n* 1 the quality or state of being large in size — see LARGENESS
2 the state or quality of being heavy — see WEIGHTINESS 1

**hefty** *adj* 1 having great weight — see HEAVY 1
2 of a size greater than average of its kind — see LARGE

**height** *n* **1** the highest part or point ⟨many regard the painting of the Sistine Chapel as the *height* of Michelangelo's career⟩
***syn*** acme, apex, climax, crown, culmination, head, high-water mark, meridian, peak, pinnacle, summit, tip-top, top, zenith
***rel*** bloom, flood tide, flower, glory, heyday; high; cap, ceiling, crest, roof; crescendo, extremity, maximum, tip, vertex
***near ant*** abyss, base, foot; minimum
***ant*** bottom, nadir
**2** the most extreme or advanced point ⟨the student's defiant use of a cell phone during class was regarded by the teacher as the *height* of insolence⟩
***syn*** depth, extremity, limit
***rel*** consummation, epitome, quintessence, ultimate
**3** the distance of something or someone from bottom to top ⟨the average *height* of the players on the volleyball team is well over six feet⟩
***syn*** altitude, elevation, stature
***rel*** rise; highness, loftiness, tallness
**4** an area of high ground ⟨Gulliver, standing on a *height* near the shore, saw an island suspended above the sea⟩
***syn*** altitude(s), elevation, eminence, highland, hill, mound, prominence, rise, upland
***rel*** alp, mount, mountain, peak; butte, mesa, plateau, table, tableland; cliff, crag, precipice, tor; ridge, sierra; dome, sugarloaf; foothill, hillock, knob, knoll; down
***near ant*** dale, dell, dingle, glen, hollow, vale, valley; basin, bottom, bottomland, fen, flat, floodplain, plain, tidewater
***ant*** lowland
**5** the most intense or characteristic phase of something — see THICK

**heighten** *vb* **1** to make markedly greater in measure or degree — see INTENSIFY
**2** to move from a lower to a higher place or position — see RAISE 1

**heightened** *adj* being at a higher level than average — see HIGH 2

**heinousness** *n* the state or quality of being utterly evil — see ENORMITY 1

**heir** *n* a person who has the right to inherit property ⟨upon his death, Mr. Parkworth's property was divided evenly among his *heirs*, four sons and three daughters⟩
***syn*** inheritor, legatee
***rel*** claimant; heir apparent, successor; heiress; assignee, beneficiary, grantee; descendant (*or* descendent), scion (*also* cion)

**helical** *adj* turning around an axis like the thread of a screw — see SPIRAL

**hell** *n* **1** the place of punishment for the wicked after death ⟨condemned to *hell* for their sins⟩
***syn*** perdition
***rel*** inferno; purgatory; hades, netherworld, underworld
***near ant*** empyrean; glory
***ant*** Elysium, heaven, kingdom come, paradise
**2** a situation or state that causes great suffering and unhappiness ⟨picking cotton under the hot summer sun was *hell*⟩
***syn*** agony, horror, misery, murder, nightmare, torment, torture
***rel*** cross, ordeal, trial, tribulation; gall, thorn; bummer, downer, drag
***near ant*** delight, diversion, entertainment, fun, pleasure, recreation; lark, picnic, riot
***ant*** heaven, paradise
**3** a place of uproar or confusion — see MADHOUSE 2
**4** a state in which everything is out of order — see CHAOS

**hellion** *n* an appealingly mischievous person — see SCAMP 1

**hello** *n* an expression of goodwill upon meeting ⟨we said our *hellos* and got right down to business⟩
***syn*** greeting, salutation, salute, welcome
***rel*** amenities, civilities, pleasantries; regards, respects, wishes
***ant*** adieu, bon voyage, farewell, Godspeed, good-bye (*or* good-by)

**helm** *n* the place of leadership or command — see HEAD 2

**helmsman** *n* the person (as an employer or supervisor) who tells people and especially workers what to do — see BOSS

**help** *n* **1** an act or instance of helping ⟨Andrew didn't get any *help* with his homework⟩
***syn*** aid, assist, assistance, backing, boost, lift, support
***rel*** advancement, encouragement, facilitation, forwarding, furtherance, furthering, nurturance; benefaction, patronage, promotion, sponsorship; advice, care, counsel, guidance, mentoring; attendance, attention, service; beneficence, charity, favor, kindness, philanthropy; relief, succor
***near ant*** constraint, frustration, inhibition, interference, obstruction, repression, restraint; deterrence, discouragement
***ant*** hindrance
**2** a thing that helps ⟨the computer is a great *help* for writing reports⟩
***syn*** advantage, aid, benefit, boon
***rel*** lift, pick-me-up; support, sustenance; blessing, godsend, windfall; recourse, resort, resource; asset
***near ant*** constraint, inhibitor, liability, obstacle, obstruction, restraint, stranglehold
***ant*** disadvantage, drawback, hindrance, impediment
**3** a body of persons at work or available for work — see FORCE 1

**help** *vb* **1** to provide (someone) with what is useful or necessary to achieve an end ⟨Mary Beth flew to Chicago to *help* her dad when he moved into an apartment⟩
***syn*** abet, aid, assist, back, prop (up), support

*rel* advance, facilitate, forward, foster, further; champion, endorse (*also* indorse), patronize, promote, sponsor; attend, care (for), comfort, minister (to), succor; bolster, boost, buttress, reinforce; advise, counsel, guide, mentor, nurture; bail out, deliver, rescue, save; embolden, encourage, hearten; benefit, favor, profit, serve
*phrases* to stand one in good stead
*near ant* balk, bar, block, constrain, hamper, hold back, impede, inhibit, obstruct, restrain, strangle; baffle, foil, frustrate, interfere, oppose, sabotage, thwart; desert, disappoint, fail, let down; discourage, dishearten; repress, retard, stifle, straiten, stunt; damage, harm, hurt, injure
*ant* hinder
2 to make more bearable or less severe ⟨the new ointment didn't *help* Josh's sunburn one bit⟩
*syn* allay, alleviate, assuage, ease, mitigate, mollify, palliate, relieve, soothe
*rel* abate, lighten, moderate, soften, temper; cure, heal, remedy; amend, correct, emend, fix, mend, rectify, reform, repair; ameliorate, better, enhance, enrich, improve, meliorate, perfect, refine
*near ant* harm, hurt, impair, injure; heighten, intensify, sharpen
*ant* aggravate
3 to keep from happening by taking action in advance — see PREVENT

**helper** *n* a person who helps a more skilled person ⟨over the summer Chris worked as a carpenter's *helper*⟩
*syn* adjutant, aid, aide, apprentice, assistant, coadjutor, deputy, helpmate, helpmeet, mate, sidekick
*rel* attendant, handmaiden (*also* handmaid), maid, maidservant, scullion, servant; auxiliary, subordinate, underling; employee, hand, help, hireling, laborer, worker

**helpful** *adj* conferring benefits; promoting or contributing to personal or social well-being — see BENEFICIAL

**helpless** *adj* 1 lacking protection from danger or resistance against attack ⟨after the storm we found a *helpless* baby bird that had fallen out of its nest⟩
*syn* defenseless, exposed, susceptible, undefended, unguarded, unprotected, unresistant, unshielded, vulnerable
*rel* indefensible, untenable; uncovered, unsafe, unsheltered; overcome, preyed (on *or* upon); disarmed, passive, resistless, unarmed; feeble, frail, weak; abandoned, marooned
*phrases* in the lurch
*near ant* defensible; covered, fortified, safe, secure, screened, sheltered; armed, armored; immune, impenetrable, impregnable, invincible, strong, unassailable, unbeatable, unconquerable
*ant* guarded, invulnerable, protected, resistant, shielded
2 unable to act or achieve one's purpose — see POWERLESS

**helpmate** *n* 1 a person who helps a more skilled person — see HELPER
2 the female partner in a marriage — see WIFE

**helpmeet** *n* 1 a person who helps a more skilled person — see HELPER
2 the female partner in a marriage — see WIFE

**helter–skelter** *adv* 1 in a confused and reckless manner ⟨the sheep ran *helter-skelter* inside their pen when the coyote appeared in their midst⟩
*syn* amok (*or* amuck), berserk, frantically, frenziedly, harum-scarum, hectically, madly, pell-mell, wild, wildly
*rel* agitatedly, confusedly, crazily, desperately, feverishly, skittishly, uncontrollably; heedlessly, hotheadedly, recklessly, wantonly; chaotically, riotously, tumultuously, turbulently; aimlessly, haphazardly, hit-or-miss
*near ant* calmly, collectedly, composedly, coolly, imperturbably, peacefully, placidly, serenely, unconcernedly; meekly, mildly, passively, tamely; methodically, orderly, systematically
2 without definite aim, direction, rule, or method — see HIT OR MISS

**hem** *vb* to close or shut in by or as if by barriers — see ENCLOSE 1

**hence** *adv* 1 for this or that reason — see THEREFORE
2 from this or that place — see AWAY

**henceforth** *adv* from this point on ⟨*henceforth*, there will be no more prolonged coffee breaks⟩
*syn* henceforward, hereafter

**henceforward** *adv* from this point on — see HENCEFORTH

**henpeck** *vb* to subject (someone) to constant scoldings and sharp reminders — see NAG

**herald** *n* one that announces or indicates the later arrival of another — see FORERUNNER 1

**herbage** *n* green leaves or plants — see GREENERY 1

**herculean** *adj* 1 requiring considerable physical or mental effort — see HARD 2
2 unusually large — see HUGE

**herd** *n* 1 a group of domestic animals assembled or herded together ⟨the great *herds* of cattle that cowboys once drove across the plains⟩
*syn* drove, flock
*rel* colony, covey, gaggle, pack, school, swarm
2 the body of the community as contrasted with the elite — see MASS 1

**herd** *vb* to urge, push, or force onward — see DRIVE 1

**herder** *n* a tender of livestock ⟨the nomadic reindeer *herders* of Siberia live in reindeer-skin tents⟩
*syn* herdsman
*rel* buckaroo, cowboy, cowgirl, cowhand, cowherd, cowman, cowpoke, cowpuncher, gaucho, ranchero, vaquero; shepherd,

sheepherder, shepherdess; gatherd; wrangler; drover

**herdsman** *n* a tender of livestock — see HERDER

**hereafter** *adv* from this point on — see HENCEFORTH

**hereafter** *n* **1** time that is to come — see FUTURE 1
**2** unending existence after death — see ETERNITY 2

**hereditary** *adj* genetically passed or capable of being passed from parent to offspring ⟨eye and hair color are *hereditary*⟩
***syn*** genetic (*also* genetical), heritable, inborn, inheritable, inherited
***rel*** congenital, inbred, inherent, innate, native, natural
***near ant*** acquired

**heresy** *n* departure from a generally accepted theory, opinion, or practice ⟨the *heresy* of asserting that Shakespeare was not a great writer⟩
***syn*** dissent, dissidence, heterodoxy, nonconformity
***rel*** error, fallacy, falsehood, misbelief, misconception, myth; apostasy, defection, schism, sectarianism, separatism; deviance, deviation, unconventionality; disagreement, discord, dissension
***near ant*** agreement, conformation, conventionality
***ant*** conformity, orthodoxy

**heretic** *n* a person who believes or teaches something opposed to accepted beliefs ⟨Galileo was condemned as a *heretic* for supporting Copernicus's thesis that the earth revolves around the sun and not vice versa⟩
***syn*** dissenter, dissident, nonconformist
***rel*** apostate, defector, renegade; schismatic, sectarian, separatist; disbeliever, infidel, unbeliever; bohemian, individualist
***near ant*** believer
***ant*** conformer, conformist

**heretical** *adj* deviating from commonly accepted beliefs or practices ⟨the belief that women should be allowed to have careers outside the home was once considered *heretical*⟩
***syn*** dissentient, dissenting, dissident, heterodox nonconformist, nonorthodox, unconventional, unorthodox
***rel*** nontraditional; apostate, defecting, renegade; schismatic, sectarian, separatist
***ant*** conforming, conformist, conventional, orthodox

**heretofore** *adv* up to this or that time — see HITHERTO

**heritable** *adj* genetically passed or capable of being passed from parent to offspring — see HEREDITARY

**heritage** *n* something that is or may be inherited — see INHERITANCE

**hermit** *n* a person who lives away from others — see RECLUSE

**hero** *n* a large sandwich on a long split roll — see SUBMARINE

**heroic** *adj* **1** feeling or displaying no fear by temperament — see BRAVE
**2** large and impressive in size, grandeur, extent, or conception — see GRAND 1
**3** unusually large — see HUGE

**heroically** *adv* in a manner befitting a person of the highest character and ideals — see GREATLY 1

**heroism** *n* strength of mind to carry on in spite of danger — see COURAGE

**hesitance** *n* **1** a lack of willingness or desire to do or accept something — see RELUCTANCE
**2** the act or an instance of pausing because of uncertainty about the right course of action — see HESITATION

**hesitancy** *n* **1** a lack of willingness or desire to do or accept something — see RELUCTANCE
**2** the act or an instance of pausing because of uncertainty about the right course of action — see HESITATION

**hesitant** *adj* having doubts about the wisdom of doing something ⟨Ivan was *hesitant* about lending CDs to his friends after he'd lost several of them that way⟩
***syn*** afraid, disinclined, dubious, indisposed, loath (*or* loth), reluctant
***rel*** uneager, unenthusiastic; averse, unwilling; doubtful, faltering, irresolute, questioning, uncertain, undecided, unsure, vacillating, wobbly; fainthearted, shy, timid
***near ant*** eager, enthusiastic, glad, happy, keen; ready, willing; certain, decided, resolute, sure, unquestioning
***ant*** disposed, inclined

**hesitate** *vb* to show uncertainty about the right course of action ⟨Keri didn't *hesitate* before answering the question⟩
***syn*** falter, hang back, shilly-shally, stagger, teeter, vacillate, waver, wobble
***rel*** haw, hem; dally, dawdle, delay, linger, procrastinate, pause, wait; back down, chicken (out); consider, debate, deliberate, ponder, weigh; oscillate; equivocate, hedge, pussyfoot
***near ant*** budge, stir; advance, continue
***ant*** dive (in), plunge (in)

**hesitation** *n* the act or an instance of pausing because of uncertainty about the right course of action ⟨one moment's *hesitation* on my part, and the elusive butterfly was lost to me forever⟩
***syn*** faltering, hesitance, hesitancy, indecision, irresolution, shilly-shallying, vacillation, wavering, wobbling
***rel*** delay, hawing, procrastination, waiting; consideration, debate, deliberation, doubt, incertitude, indetermination, uncertainty; avoidance, equivocation; aversion, disinclination, indisposition, reluctance, unwillingness; fainthearted ness, shyness, timidness
***near ant*** certainty, certitude, confidence, decisiveness, determination, firmness, resoluteness, resolution, sureness; alacrity, eagerness, readiness

**heterodox** *adj* deviating from commonly accepted beliefs or practices — see HERETICAL

**heterodoxy** *n* departure from a generally accepted theory, opinion, or practice — see HERESY

**heterogeneous** *adj* consisting of many things of different sorts — see MISCELLANEOUS

**het up** *adj* feeling or showing uncomfortable feelings of uncertainty — see NERVOUS 1

**hew** *vb* 1 to bring down by cutting — see FELL 2
2 to hold to something firmly as if by adhesion — see STICK 1

**hew** (to) *vb* to give steadfast support to — see ADHERE

**hex** *n* 1 a woman believed to have often harmful supernatural powers — see WITCH 1
2 something that brings bad luck — see JINX

**hex** *vb* to cast a spell on — see BEWITCH 1

**heyday** *n* a state or time of great activity, thriving, or achievement — see BLOOM 1

**hiatus** *n* a break in continuity — see GAP 2

**hick** *n* an awkward or simple person especially from a small town or the country ⟨city dwellers who looked down on their cousins from northern Maine as *hicks*⟩
*syn* bumpkin, clodhopper, countryman, hillbilly, provincial, rustic, yokel
*rel* boor, clod, gawk, lout, oaf; greenhorn, tenderfoot; peasant, peon; mountaineer
*near ant* slicker, smoothy (*or* smoothie); suburbanite, urbanite
*ant* cosmopolitan, sophisticate

**hide** *n* 1 the outer covering of an animal removed for its commercial value ⟨seal *hides* are used by Eskimos to make footwear, boats, shelters, bags, and clothing⟩
*syn* fur, leather, pelt, skin
*rel* badger, beaver, chamois, chinchilla, ermine, fisher, fox, mink, muskrat, otter, Persian lamb, rabbit, raccoon (*also* racoon), sable, seal, silver fox; bearskin, buckskin, calfskin, coonskin, cowhide, deerskin, doeskin, goatskin, horsehide, kidskin, lambskin, pigskin, rawhide, sealskin, sharkskin, sheepskin, snakeskin; fleece, mouton; alligator; cordovan, morocco, patent leather, suede
2 the hairless natural covering of an animal prepared for use — see LEATHER 1

[1]**hide** *vb* 1 to put into a hiding place ⟨the thief *hid* the stolen jewelry under the floorboards⟩
*syn* bury, cache, conceal, ensconce, secrete
*rel* hoard, squirrel (away), stash; entomb, inter
*near ant* bare, expose, reveal, show, uncover, unmask, unveil, unwrap; flaunt, parade, show off; disinter, unearth
*ant* display, exhibit
2 to keep secret or shut off from view ⟨he tried to *hide* his criminal past⟩ ⟨she *hid* the cat's litter box behind a screen⟩
*syn* blanket, blot out, cloak, conceal, cover, curtain, enshroud, mask, obscure, occult, screen, shroud, veil
*rel* camouflage, cover (up), disguise, smother; gild, gloss (over), varnish, whitewash; becloud, bedim, befog, cloud, darken, eclipse, overcast, overshadow, shade
*near ant* bring out, present; clarify, illuminate; advertise, air, broadcast, proclaim, publicize
*ant* bare, disclose, display, divulge, expose, reveal, show, uncloak, uncover, unmask, unveil
3 to strike repeatedly with something long and thin or flexible — see WHIP 1

[2]**hide** *vb* to strike repeatedly — see BEAT 1

**hideaway** *n* a place where a person goes to hide — see HIDEOUT

**hideous** *adj* 1 causing intense displeasure, disgust, or resentment — see OFFENSIVE 1
2 extremely disturbing or repellent — see HORRIBLE 1
3 unpleasant to look at — see UGLY 1

**hideousness** *n* the quality of inspiring intense dread or dismay — see HORROR 1

**hideout** *n* a place where a person goes to hide ⟨they found the stolen jewels under the floorboards in the thief's *hideout*, a cabin deep in the woods⟩
*syn* concealment, covert, den, hideaway, lair, nest
*rel* blind, cover, nook, recess; hangout, harbor, haunt, haven, refuge, retreat, shelter

**hiding** *n* the placing of something out of sight — see CONCEALMENT 1

**higgledy–piggledy** *adj* lacking in order, neatness, and often cleanliness — see MESSY

**high** *adj* 1 extending to a great distance upward ⟨Mt. Everest is the *highest* mountain in the world⟩
*syn* lofty, tall, towering
*rel* dominant, dominating, eminent, prominent; elevated, lifted, raised, uplifted, upswept; high-rise, statuesque
*near ant* flat, stubby, stumpy
*ant* low, low-lying, short, squat
2 being at a higher level than average ⟨gasoline prices are *high* right now⟩ ⟨a *high* fever⟩ ⟨people with *high* incomes⟩
*syn* advanced, elevated, escalated, heightened, increased, jacked (up), raised, up
*rel* extreme, full, maximized, maximum, peaked, sky-high, utmost; inflated, over, overfilled, overflowing, overfull, overlarge, overloaded, oversize (*or* oversized)
*near ant* decreased, depressed, dropped, receded, under
*ant* down, low
3 located at a greater height than average or usual ⟨an eagle's nest *high* on the cliff⟩ ⟨an old house with *high* ceilings⟩
*syn* airy, elevated
*rel* aerial, ascendant, ascending, soaring; overhead, overlooking, raised, upheld, uplifted, upraised; topmost, upmost, upper, uppermost, upward

***near ant*** depressed, descendant (*or* descendent), descending, down, dropped, fallen, grounded, lowered, sunken; lowermost, nethermost, undermost; abreast, even, level
***ant*** low, low-lying
**4** being far along in development — see ADVANCED 1
**5** being under the influence of alcohol — see DRUNK
**6** commanding a large price — see COSTLY
**7** having, characterized by, or arising from a dignified and generous nature — see NOBLE 2
**8** highest in rank or authority — see HEAD

**high** *n* the expanse of air surrounding the earth — see SKY

**high** *adv* in a luxurious manner ⟨after he won the lottery Philip lived *high* until all the money was gone⟩
***syn*** expensively, extravagantly, grandly, lavishly, luxuriously, opulently, richly, sumptuously
***rel*** imposingly, impressively, magnificently, splendidly; grandiosely, ostentatiously, pretentiously; affluently, comfortably, fine; immoderately, indulgently, intemperately, prodigally, wantonly, wastefully
***near ant*** unassumingly, unpretentiously; cheaply, economically, frugally, inexpensively, meagerly, poorly, skimpily, sparely, sparingly, thriftily; conservatively, moderately, prudently, reasonably, restrainedly, sensibly, temperately
***ant*** austerely, humbly, modestly, plainly, simply

**highborn** *adj* of high birth, rank, or station — see NOBLE 1

**highbrow** *adj* much given to learning and thinking — see INTELLECTUAL 1

**higher** *adj* being far along in development — see ADVANCED 1

**highest** *adj* **1** being at a point or level higher than all others — see TOP 1
**2** coming before all others in importance — see FOREMOST 1

**highfalutin** *adj* **1** full of fine words and fancy expressions — see FLOWERY 1
**2** having a feeling of superiority that shows itself in an overbearing attitude — see ARROGANT
**3** having or displaying feelings of scorn for what is regarded as beneath oneself — see PROUD 1
**4** self-consciously trying to present an appearance of grandeur or importance — see PRETENTIOUS 1

**high-flown** *adj* **1** full of fine words and fancy expressions — see FLOWERY 1
**2** very dignified in form, tone, or style — see ELEVATED 2

**high-handed** *adj* **1** having a feeling of superiority that shows itself in an overbearing attitude — see ARROGANT
**2** having or showing a tendency to force one's will on others without any regard to fairness or necessity — see ARBITRARY 1

**high-hat** *adj* having a feeling of superiority that shows itself in an overbearing attitude — see ARROGANT

**high-hat** *vb* to show contempt for — see SCORN 1

**high jinks** *n pl* wildly playful or mischievous behavior — see HORSEPLAY

**highland** *n* an area of high ground — see HEIGHT 4

**highlight** *vb* to indicate the importance of by giving prominent display — see EMPHASIZE

**highly** *adv* to a great degree — see VERY 1

**high-minded** *adj* having, characterized by, or arising from a dignified and generous nature — see NOBLE 2

**high-mindedly** *adv* in a manner befitting a person of the highest character and ideals — see GREATLY 1

**high noon** *n* the middle of the day — see NOON

**high-pitched** *adj* having a high musical pitch or range — see SHRILL

**high-pressure** *adj* having or showing a bold forcefulness in the pursuit of a goal — see AGGRESSIVE 1

**highroad** *n* a passage cleared for public vehicular travel — see WAY 1

**high-sounding** *adj* full of fine words and fancy expressions — see FLOWERY 1

**high-spirited** *adj* **1** joyously unrestrained — see EXUBERANT
**2** marked by a lively display of strong feeling — see SPIRITED 1

**high-spiritedly** *adv* in a quick and spirited manner — see GAILY 2

**high-strung** *adj* easily excited by nature — see EXCITABLE

**high-water mark** *n* the highest part or point — see HEIGHT 1

**highway** *n* a passage cleared for public vehicular travel — see WAY 1

**hijack** *also* **highjack** *vb* to take control of (a vehicle) by force — see COMMANDEER 1

**hike** *vb* to move from a lower to a higher place or position — see RAISE 1

**hilarious** *adj* causing or intended to cause laughter — see FUNNY 1

**hilariousness** *n* the amusing quality or element in something — see HUMOR 1

**hilarity** *n* a mood characterized by high spirits and amusement and often accompanied by laughter — see MIRTH

**hill** *n* **1** a quantity of things thrown or stacked on one another — see [1]PILE 1
**2** an area of high ground — see HEIGHT 4

**hill** *vb* to form into a pile or ridge of earth — see MOUND 1

**hillbilly** *n* an awkward or simple person especially from a small town or the country — see HICK

**hind** *adj* being at or in the part of something opposite the front part — see BACK

**hinder** *vb* to create difficulty for the work or activity of — see HAMPER

**hindmost** *adj* **1** being at or in the part of something opposite the front part — see BACK
**2** following all others of the same kind in order or time — see LAST

**hindrance** *n* **1** something that makes movement or progress more difficult — see ENCUMBRANCE
**2** something that stands in the way of one's progress or achievement — see OBSTACLE 1
**hinge** *vb* to be determined by, based on, or subject (to) — see DEPEND 1
**hint** *n* **1** a slight or indirect pointing to something (as a solution or explanation) ⟨can't you give me some *hint* as to where you're taking me?⟩
*syn* clue, cue, indication, inkling, intimation, lead, suggestion
*rel* breath, flicker, glimmer, glimpse, mention, scent, whiff, wind; hunch, idea, inspiration, notion; allusion, implication, inference, innuendo, insinuation; evidence, mark, overtone, pointer, sign, signal, telltale, token; assistance, nod, prompt, tip, tip-off, wink; feeling, foreboding, intuition, premonition, presentiment, suspicion; augury, foreshadower, foretaste, omen, portent, prefigurement, symptom
*near ant* answer, solution
**2** a piece of advice or useful information especially from an expert — see [1]TIP 1
**3** a very small amount — see PARTICLE 1
**hint** *vb* to convey an idea indirectly ⟨Cecilia kept *hinting* that she wanted an invitation to Patty's party⟩
*syn* allude, imply, indicate, infer, insinuate, intimate, suggest
*rel* advert, mention, point, refer, signal, signify; smack (of), smell (of)
*near ant* announce, declare, proclaim; elucidate, explain, spell out
**hinterland** *n* a rural region that forms the edge of the settled or developed part of a country — see FRONTIER 2
**hip** *adj* having inside information — see WISE 2
**hire** *n* **1** the state of being provided with a paying job ⟨college graduates seeking *hire* by big corporations⟩
*syn* employ, employment, engagement
*rel* appointment, assignment, conscription, enlistment, recruitment; incumbency, tenure; occupation, place, position, post, situation, work
*near ant* boot, discharge, dismissal, firing, removal, sack; demotion, suspension; furlough, layoff, leave, liberty, retirement
*ant* joblessness, unemployment
**2** the money paid regularly to a person for labor or services — see WAGE
**hire** *vb* **1** to take or get the temporary use of (something) for a set sum ⟨the Young's *hired* a limousine for their daughter's wedding⟩
*syn* charter, engage, lease, rent
*rel* sublease, sublet; check out; arrange (for), bespeak, book, contract (for), order, reserve, sign up (for)
**2** to provide with a paying job — see EMPLOY 1

*syn* synonym(s) *rel* related words
*ant* antonym(s) *near ant* near antonym(s)

**hireling** *n* one who works for another for wages or a salary — see EMPLOYEE
**hirsute** *adj* covered with or as if with hair — see HAIRY 1
**hiss** *n* **1** a sound similar to the speech sound \s\ stretched out ⟨the *hiss* of air escaping from a balloon⟩
*syn* fizz, sizzle, swish, whish, whiz (*or* whizz)
*rel* wheeze, whistle, whoosh, zip; sibilant
**2** a vocal sound made to express scorn or disapproval — see CATCALL
**hiss** *vb* to make a sound like that of stretching out the speech sound \s\ ⟨the frightened kitten *hissed* at us when we tried to pick it up⟩
*syn* fizz, sizzle, swish, whish, whiz (*or* whizz)
*rel* wheeze, whistle, whoosh, zip; bubble, effervesce; buzz, drone, hum
**historian** *n* a student or writer of history ⟨*historians* are still trying to sort out fact from fiction in the story of Kateri Tekakwitha, the Lily of the Mohawks⟩
*syn* annalist, chronicler
*rel* autobiographer, biographer; archivist, chronologist, genealogist
**historical** *adj* restricted to or based on fact — see FACTUAL 1
**history** *n* **1** an account of important events in the order in which they happened ⟨a *history* of the American civil rights movement during the 1960s⟩
*syn* annals, chronicle, record
*rel* autobiography, diary, journal, memoir, reminiscence(s); biography, life; epic, legend, narrative, saga, story, tale; archives, documentation, log, register, report; chronology, genealogy
**2** a relating of events usually in the order in which they happened — see ACCOUNT 1
**3** the events or experience of former times — see PAST
**histrionic** *adj* **1** given to or marked by attention-getting behavior suggestive of stage acting — see THEATRICAL 1
**2** having the general quality or effect of a stage performance — see DRAMATIC 1
**hit** *n* **1** a person or thing that is successful ⟨the new babysitter turned out to be a great *hit* with the kids⟩
*syn* blockbuster, megahit, smash, success, winner
*rel* corker, crackerjack, dandy, jim-dandy, pip, prizewinner; gem, jewel, treasure; marvel, phenomenon, sensation, wonder; coup, triumph, victory
*near ant* disappointment, fizzle, lemon, loser
*ant* bummer, bust, catastrophe, debacle (*also* débâcle), dud, failure, fiasco, flop, turkey, washout
**2** a hard strike with a part of the body or an instrument — see [1]BLOW
**hit** *vb* **1** to deliver a blow to (someone or something) usually in a strong vigorous manner ⟨a good carpenter *hits* a nail just two or three times to drive it in⟩

*syn* bang, bash, bat, belt, bludgeon, bop, bust, clap, clobber, clout, crack, hammer, knock, paste, pound, punch, rap, slam, slap, slog, slug, smack, smite, sock, strike, swat, swipe, thump, thwack, wallop, whack, whale, zap
*rel* batter, beat, buffet, bung, chop, drub, lace, lambaste (*or* lambast), lick, mangle, maul, pelt, pepper, pummel, rough; bunt, flick, stroke, tap; bump, butt, jab, jostle, kick, knee, poke, prod, push, shove, stamp; bowl (over), knock (down); cane, club, cudgel, flail, flog, lash, slash, spear, stab, switch, thrash, whip; brain
2 to come into usually forceful contact with something ⟨when she fell on the ice, she *hit* hard and badly bruised her elbow⟩
*syn* bang, bash, bump, collide, crash, impact, impinge, knock, ram, slam, smash, strike, swipe, thud
*rel* bounce, carom, glance, rebound, ricochet, skim, skip; contact, land, touch; brush, graze, kiss, nudge, scrape, shave, sweep; bulldoze, jostle, muscle, press, push
*near ant* miss, skirt
3 to obtain (as a goal) through effort — see ACHIEVE 1

**hit** (on *or* upon) *vb* to come upon after searching, study, or effort — see FIND 1

**hit** (upon) *vb* to come upon unexpectedly or by chance — see HAPPEN (ON *or* UPON)

**hitch** *n* a fixed period of time during which a person holds a job or position — see TERM 1

**hitch** *vb* 1 to move or cause to move with a sharp quick motion — see JERK 1
2 to put or bring together so as to form a new and longer whole — see CONNECT 1
3 to put securely in place or in a desired position — see FASTEN 2
4 to travel by securing free rides — see HITCHHIKE

**hitcher** *n* one who hitchhikes — see HITCHHIKER

**hitchhike** *vb* to travel by securing free rides ⟨Andrew *hitchhiked* from Baltimore to attend his sister's wedding in New Jersey⟩
*syn* hitch, thumb
*rel* bum; stow away; hijack (*also* highjack)

**hitchhiker** *n* one who hitchhikes ⟨on the highway out of town we picked up a *hitchhiker* who was trying to get to his sister's wedding⟩
*syn* hitcher
*rel* stowaway; hijacker

**hither** *adj* being the less far of two — see NEAR 1

**hitherto** *adv* up to this or that time ⟨at the talent show Kyle revealed his *hitherto* unknown gift for doing impressions⟩
*syn* heretofore, theretofore, thus far, yet
*rel* before, formerly, previously
*near ant* afterward (*or* afterwards), later, subsequently; hereupon, thereupon
*ant* henceforth, henceforward, hereafter, thenceforth, thenceforward (*also* thenceforwards), thereafter

**hit–or–miss** *adj* lacking a definite plan, purpose, or pattern — see RANDOM

**hit or miss** *adv* without definite aim, direction, rule, or method ⟨Angelo was learning Spanish *hit or miss*, mostly just by hearing his friends speak it⟩
*syn* aimlessly, anyhow, anyway, anywise, desultorily, erratically, haphazard, haphazardly, helter-skelter, irregularly, randomly
*rel* capriciously, carelessly, casually, indiscriminately, informally, offhand, offhandedly, promiscuously, whimsically; accidentally, fortuitously, inadvertently, unconsciously, unintentionally, unwittingly; disconnectedly, disjointedly, fitfully, intermittently, spottily, unpredictably; higgledy-piggledy, topsy-turvy
*phrases* at random
*near ant* carefully, formally, meticulously, orderly, punctiliously; deliberately, intentionally, purposefully, purposely
*ant* methodically, systematically

**hoagie** *n* a large sandwich on a long split roll — see SUBMARINE

**hoar** *adj* dating or surviving from the distant past — see ANCIENT 1

**hoar** *n* a covering of tiny ice crystals on a cold surface — see FROST

**hoard** *n* 1 a supply stored up and often hidden away ⟨Dad was upset when Mom put his entire *hoard* of empty yogurt containers in the recycling bin⟩
*syn* cache, stash, stockpile, store
*rel* coffers, deposit, funds, nest egg, savings, sinking fund, treasure; inventory, reserve, reservoir, stock; provisions, resources; accumulation, collection; repertory
2 a collection of things kept available for future use or need — see STORE 1

**hoard** *vb* to put (something of future use or value) in a safe or secret place ⟨Dad's been *hoarding* empty yogurt containers all winter, with the intention of using them to start seedlings in the spring⟩
*syn* cache, lay away, lay up, put by, salt away, squirrel (away), stash, stockpile, store, stow
*rel* accumulate, acquire, amass, assemble, collect, concentrate, garner, gather, round up, scrape (together); heap, pile, stack; conserve, husband, preserve; bank, deposit, hold, keep, reserve, retain, save, stock, withhold; conceal, ensconce, secrete
*phrases* set aside
*near ant* discard, dump, throw away, throw out; consume, squander, use up, waste; hand over, relinquish, surrender; blow, dissipate, fritter (away), lavish, misspend, run through, spend; deplete, exhaust, expend; dispel, disperse, dissipate, scatter

**hoarfrost** *n* a covering of tiny ice crystals on a cold surface — see FROST

**hoarse** *adj* harsh and dry in sound ⟨the dying man spoke in a *hoarse* whisper⟩
*syn* coarse, croaking, grating, gravel, gravelly, gruff, husky, rasping, raspy, scratchy, throaty
*rel* guttural; abrasive, cacophonous, discordant, grinding, jarring, rough, scraping, scratching; cawing, raucous, squawking, strident; choked, cracked, strained, strangled
*near ant* gentle, gliding, golden, liquid, mellifluous, mellow, sweet, tender; satiny, silken, smooth, soft, velvety

**hoary** *adj* dating or surviving from the distant past — see ANCIENT 1

**hoax** *n* an imitation that is passed off as genuine — see FAKE 1

**hoax** *vb* to cause to believe what is untrue — see DECEIVE

**hoaxer** *n* **1** a dishonest person who uses clever means to cheat others out of something of value — see TRICKSTER 1
**2** one who makes false claims of identity or expertise — see IMPOSTOR

**hob** *n* playful, reckless behavior that is not intended to cause serious harm — see MISCHIEF 1

**hobble** *vb* **1** to create difficulty for the work or activity of — see HAMPER
**2** to walk while favoring one leg — see LIMP 1

**hobgoblin** *n* **1** an imaginary being usually having a small human form and magical powers — see FAIRY
**2** something or someone that causes fear or dread especially without reason — see BOGEY 1

**hobnob** *vb* **1** to come or be together as friends — see ASSOCIATE 1
**2** to take part in social activities — see SOCIALIZE

**hobnobber** *n* a person frequently seen in the company of another — see ASSOCIATE 1

**hobo** *n* a homeless wanderer who may beg or steal for a living — see TRAMP

**hock** *vb* to leave as a guarantee of repayment of a loan — see PAWN

**hodgepodge** *n* an unorganized collection or mixture of various things — see MISCELLANY 1

**hog** *n* one who eats greedily or too much — see GLUTTON

**hoggish** *adj* having a huge appetite — see VORACIOUS 1

**hogshead** *n* an enclosed wooden vessel for holding beverages — see CASK

**hogwash** *n* **1** language, behavior, or ideas that are absurd and contrary to good sense — see NONSENSE 1
**2** unintelligible or meaningless talk — see GIBBERISH

**hoist** *vb* **1** to lift with effort — see HEAVE 1
**2** to move from a lower to a higher place or position — see RAISE 1

**hold** *n* **1** the act or manner of holding ⟨make sure you have a firm *hold* on the chain saw before you turn it on⟩
*syn* clasp, grapple, grasp, grip
*rel* anchorage, leverage, purchase; grab, seizure; foothold, footing, toehold; embrace, hug
*near ant* release, relinquishment
**2** a structure or place from which one can resist attack — see FORT
**3** the right or means to command or control others — see POWER 1

**hold** *vb* **1** to have or keep in one's hands ⟨this casserole dish is too hot to *hold,* so grab a potholder⟩
*syn* clench, cling (to), clutch, grip, hang on (to), hold on (to)
*rel* bear, carry; catch, grapple, nab, seize, snatch, take; feel, finger, handle, paw; clasp, embrace, grasp, hug
*near ant* drop, give, hand, unclasp, unhand; release, relinquish
**2** to continue to have in one's possession or power — see KEEP 2
**3** to have as an opinion — see BELIEVE 2
**4** to have within — see CONTAIN 1
**5** to keep in one's mind or heart — see HARBOR 1
**6** to keep, control, or experience as one's own — see HAVE 1
**7** to make or have room for — see ACCOMMODATE 1
**8** to reach for and take hold of by embracing with the fingers or arms — see TAKE 1
**9** to think of in a particular way — see CONSIDER 1

**hold** (up) *vb* **1** to continue to operate or to meet one's needs — see HOLD OUT
**2** to remain indefinitely in existence or in the same state — see CONTINUE 1

**hold back** *vb* to create difficulty for the work or activity of — see HAMPER

**holder** *n* **1** one who has a legal or rightful claim to ownership — see PROPRIETOR
**2** something into which a liquid or smaller objects can be put for storage or transportation — see CONTAINER

**hold in** *vb* to keep from exceeding a desirable degree or level (as of expression) — see CONTROL 1

**holding** *n* **1** a decision made by a court or tribunal regarding a case it has heard — see SENTENCE
**2** *usually* **holdings** *pl* transportable items that one owns — see POSSESSION 2

**hold off** (on) *vb* to assign to a later time — see POSTPONE

**hold on** *vb* **1** to remain indefinitely in existence or in the same state — see CONTINUE 1
**2** to remain in place in readiness or expectation of something — see WAIT

**hold on** (to) *vb* to have or keep in one's hands — see HOLD 1

**hold out** *vb* to continue to operate or to meet one's needs ⟨we hoped our supply of firewood would *hold out* until power was restored⟩ ⟨luckily, the old outboard motor *held out* till we made it to shore⟩

---

*syn* synonym(s) *rel* related words
*ant* antonym(s) *near ant* near antonym(s)

*syn* hold (up), last, keep up, prevail, survive
*rel* bear up, carry on, cope, endure, go, hang in, persevere; continue, draw out, hang on, linger, persist, remain, stretch
*near ant* break down, collapse, conk (out), crash, die, expire, stall, stop; run down, wane
*ant* fail, fizzle, give out, go out, peter (out), run out

**holdup** *n* an instance or period of being prevented from going about one's business — see DELAY

**hold up** *vb* **1** to assign to a later time — see POSTPONE
**2** to bring (something) to a standstill — see [1]HALT 1
**3** to create difficulty for the work or activity of — see HAMPER

**hole** *n* **1** a place in a surface allowing passage into or through a thing ⟨Mark was beside himself after seeing that his little sister had punched *holes* in his homework⟩
*syn* aperture, opening, orifice perforation
*rel* chink, cleft, crack, cranny, crevice, cut, breach, break, fissure, gash, notch, rent, rift, rupture, slash, slit, split; gap, slot, space; exit, mouth, outlet, pore, vent; entrance, inlet, intake; pinprick, punch, puncture; armhole, buttonhole, knothole, peephole, pinhole, wormhole
*near ant* fill, filler, filling, patch, plug, seal, stopper; barrier, blockage obstacle, obstruction
**2** a sunken area forming a separate space ⟨Ann dug a *hole* big enough to plant the tree⟩
*syn* cavity, concavity, dent, depression, dint, hollow, indentation, pit, recess
*rel* burrow, cave, cavern, ditch, excavation, furrow, groove, trench, trough; basin, bowl, valley; alcove, cleft, niche, nook, opening, recess, socket alveolus, dimple, gouge, notch, impression, pocket; chuckhole, crater, posthole, pothole, sinkhole, wallow, waterhole, well; abyss, chasm, gulf, vacuity, vacuum, void
*near ant* hill, mound, projection, rise; bump, lump, pimple, swell, swelling, tumor
*ant* bulge, convexity, protrusion, protuberance
**3** a difficult, puzzling, or embarrassing situation from which there is no easy escape — see PREDICAMENT
**4** a dirty or messy place — see PIGPEN
**5** an open space in a barrier (as a wall or hedge) — see GAP 1
**6** the shelter or resting place of a wild animal — see DEN 1

**hole** *vb* to make a hole or series of holes in — see PERFORATE

**holiday** *n, chiefly British* a period during which the usual routine of school or work is suspended — see VACATION

**holiday** *vb* to take or spend a vacation — see VACATION

**holiness** *n* the quality or state of being spiritually pure or virtuous ⟨known throughout the world for his *holiness*, the prophet was visited daily by hundreds of pilgrims⟩
*syn* blessedness, devoutness, godliness, piety, piousness, sainthood, saintliness, saintship, sanctity
*rel* asceticism, devotion, morality, prayerfulness, religiousness, spirituality; righteousness, virtuousness
*near ant* blasphemousness, irreverence, sacrilegiousness; depravity, sinfulness, wickedness
*ant* godlessness, impiety, ungodliness, unholiness

**holler** *n* a loud vocal expression of strong emotion — see SHOUT

**holler** *vb* to speak so as to be heard at a distance — see CALL 1

**hollow** *adj* curved inward ⟨there's a *hollow* spot in the mattress where Jim sleeps⟩
*syn* concave, dented, depressed, indented, recessed sunken
*rel* alveolar, cavernous, cuplike, cupped; dimpled, pockmarked; compressed, condensed, contracted, diminished, reduced
*near ant* ballooning, bloated, blown up, bulbous, distended, enlarged, expanded, extended, inflated, jutting, projecting, puffed (up), puffy, risen, swollen; domed, globular, rounded, spherical
*ant* bulging, convex, protruding, protuberant

**hollow** *n* **1** a sunken area forming a separate space — see HOLE 2
**2** an area of lowland between hills or mountains — see VALLEY

**holocaust** *n* a destructive burning — see FIRE

**holy** *adj* **1** showing a devotion to God and to a life of virtue ⟨the *holy* monk spent many hours on his knees in prayer⟩
*syn* devout, godly, pious, religious, sainted, saintly
*rel* ascetic, prayerful, reverent, reverential, spiritual, worshipful; beatified, blessed, canonized, venerable; angelic (*or* angelical), cherubic; chaste, pure, righteous, virtuous
*near ant* blasphemous, desecrating, irreverent, profane, sacrilegious, unspiritual; backsliding, unfaithful; sinful, sinning, wicked
*ant* faithless, godless, impious, irreligious, ungodly, unholy
**2** set apart or worthy of veneration by association with God ⟨the Torah contains the *holy* writings of Judaism⟩
*syn* blessed, consecrated, hallowed, sacred, sacrosanct, sanctified
*rel* adored, enshrined, glorified, revered, venerated, worshipped (*also* worshiped); ceremonial, liturgical, priestly, religious, ritual, spiritual; biblical, scriptural
*near ant* nonreligious, unspiritual; earthly, mundane, secular, temporal, worldly
*ant* unconsecrated, unhallowed, unsanctified

3 of, relating to, or being God ⟨the *Holy* Trinity⟩
*syn* blessed, divine, godlike, heavenly, sacred, supernatural
*rel* eternal, everlasting, immortal; almighty, omnipotent, omniscient, supreme
*near ant* human, mortal
4 not to be violated, criticized, or tampered with — see SACRED 1

**Holy Writ** *n* a book made up of the writings accepted by Christians as coming from God — see BIBLE

**homage** *n* 1 a formal expression of praise — see ENCOMIUM
2 public acknowledgment or admiration for an achievement — see GLORY 1

**hombre** *n* an adult male human being — see MAN 1

**home** *n* 1 the place where one lives ⟨as we entered his 34-room mansion, Ernest said, "Welcome to my humble *home* !"⟩
*syn* abode, diggings, domicile, dwelling, fireside, habitation, hearth, hearthstone, house, lodging, pad, place, quarters, residence, roof
*rel* accommodations, housing, nest, residency, shelter; bungalow, cabin, chalet, cottage; duplex, ranch, split level, town house, tract house, triplex; apartment, apartment house, condominium, flat, tenement, tenement house, walk-up; penthouse, salon, suite; barracks, boardinghouse, dorm, dormitory, lodgment (*or* lodgement), lodging house, room(s), rooming house; castle, château, country seat, estate, manor, manor house, mansion, palace, villa; farmhouse, grange, hacienda, homestead, ranch house; houseboat, mobile home, motor home, trailer; hermitage, manse, parsonage, vicarage; hovel, hut, shack
2 the place where a plant or animal is usually or naturally found ⟨the American south, the *home* of the armadillo⟩
*syn* habitat, niche, range, territory
*rel* element, environment, environs, haunt, locality, milieu, neighborhood, setting, surroundings
3 the land of one's birth, residence, or citizenship — see COUNTRY 1

**homeboy** *n* a violent, brutal person who is often a member of an organized gang — see HOODLUM

**homeland** *n* the land of one's birth, residence, or citizenship — see COUNTRY 1

**homely** *adj* unpleasant to look at — see UGLY 1

**homesteader** *n* a person who settles in a new region — see FRONTIERSMAN

**homicidal** *adj* eager for or marked by the shedding of blood, extreme violence, or killing — see BLOODTHIRSTY

**homicide** *n* the intentional and unlawful taking of another person's life ⟨the missing man was thought to be the victim of a *homicide,* but his body was never found⟩
*syn* foul play, murder, slaying
*rel* killing, manslaughter; bloodshed, butchery, carnage, decimation, destruction, massacre, slaughter; assassination, execution; euthanasia, mercy killing

**homily** *n* a public speech usually by a member of the clergy for the purpose of giving moral guidance or uplift — see SERMON

**homogenize** *vb* to make agree with a single established standard or model — see STANDARDIZE

**Homo sapiens** *n* the human race — see MANKIND

**hone** *vb* 1 to make sharp or sharper — see SHARPEN
2 to make smooth by friction — see GRIND 1

**honed** *adj* having an edge thin enough to cut or pierce something — see SHARP 1

**honest** *adj* 1 being in the habit of telling the truth — see TRUTHFUL
2 conforming to a high standard of morality or virtue — see GOOD 2
3 following the accepted rules of moral conduct — see HONORABLE 1
4 free from any intent to deceive or impress others — see GUILELESS
5 free in expressing one's true feelings and opinions — see FRANK
6 guided by or in accordance with one's sense of right and wrong — see CONSCIENTIOUS 1

**honestly** *adv* to tell the truth — see ACTUALLY 1

**honesty** *n* 1 devotion to telling the truth ⟨George Washington has gone down in history for his *honesty*⟩
*syn* integrity, probity, truthfulness, veracity, verity
*rel* honor, incorruptibility; candidness, candor, frankness, good faith, sincerity, straightforwardness; dependability, reliability, reliableness, trustworthiness; accuracy, objectivity; authenticity, correctness, genuineness; credibility
*near ant* deception, dissembling, dissimulation, duplicity, fakery, falseness, falsity, fraudulentness, hypocrisy, insincerity; beguilement, craftiness, cunning, furtiveness, guile, insidiousness, oiliness, slickness, slipperiness, slyness, smoothness, trickery, underhandedness, wiliness; equivocation, prevarication; exaggeration, inaccuracy
*ant* deceit, deceitfulness, dishonesty, lying, mendacity, untruthfulness
2 conduct that conforms to an accepted standard of right and wrong — see MORALITY 1
3 faithfulness to high moral standards — see HONOR 1

**honey** *n* a person with whom one is in love — see SWEETHEART

**honor** *n* 1 faithfulness to high moral standards ⟨the mayor, a man of *honor,* never broke a promise to the voters⟩
*syn* honesty, integrity, probity, rectitude, righteousness, uprightness
*rel* blamelessness, character, conscientiousness, decency, fairness, high-mind-

edness, incorruptibility, justice, morality, nobility, reputability, respectability, scrupulousness, virtue, virtuousness
***near ant*** corruptibility, corruption, corruptness, debasement, decadence, degeneracy, depravity, disgracefulness, disreputableness, dissipation, dissoluteness, looseness, perversion, profligacy, shamelessness, venality; blameworthiness, criminality, crookedness, dishonesty, immorality, unrighteousness, unscrupulousness; knavery, rascality, roguishness; meanness, reprehensibleness, rottenness, sinfulness, vileness, villainy, wretchedness
***ant*** baseness, lowness
**2** an asset that brings praise or renown — see GLORY 2
**3** public acknowledgment or admiration for an achievement — see GLORY 1
**4** something given in recognition of achievement — see AWARD
**5** something granted as a special favor — see PRIVILEGE

**honor** *vb* to show appreciation, respect, or affection for (someone) with a public celebration ⟨the newlyweds were *honored* with a dinner given by the bride's grandmother⟩
***syn*** fete (*or* fête), recognize
***rel*** acknowledge, cite, commend, compliment, credit, thank; extol (*also* extoll), glorify, laud, praise; acclaim, applaud, cheer, hail, salute; celebrate, commemorate, memorialize, observe; congratulate, felicitate
***near ant*** bad-mouth, defame, libel, malign, slander; boo, hiss, hoot, jeer; censure, condemn, damn, denounce, reprobate; mock, put down, ridicule, slight

**honorable** *adj* **1** following the accepted rules of moral conduct ⟨the only *honorable* thing to do is to admit that you were wrong and apologize⟩
***syn*** decent, ethical, honest, just, noble, principled, respectable, righteous, upright, upstanding
***rel*** decorous, proper, seemly; blameless, guiltless, irreproachable, unassailable, unimpeachable; chivalrous, high-minded, right-minded; conscientious, fair, good, incorruptible, moral, reputable, respected, scrupulous, uncorrupted, virtuous
***near ant*** bad, blackguardly, corrupt, criminal, crooked, immoral, iniquitous, knavish, mean, rascally, reprehensible, roguish, rotten, scoundrelly, sinful; unfair, unscrupulous, vile, villainous, wicked, wretched; blamable, blameworthy, censurable; debased, debauched, decadent, degenerate, depraved, disgraceful, disreputable, dissipated, dissolute, libertine, loose, perverted, profligate, reprobate, shameful, unscrupulous, venal
***ant*** base, dishonest, ignoble, low, unethical, unjust, unprincipled, unrighteous
**2** conforming to a high standard of morality or virtue — see GOOD 2
**3** guided by or in accordance with one's sense of right and wrong — see CONSCIENTIOUS 1

**honorably** *adv* in a manner befitting a person of the highest character and ideals — see GREATLY 1

**[1]hood** *n* a violent, brutal person who is often a member of an organized gang — see HOODLUM

**[2]hood** *n* something that covers or conceals like a piece of cloth — see CLOAK 1

**hoodlum** *n* a violent, brutal person who is often a member of an organized gang ⟨a couple of *hoodlums* held up the convenience store⟩
***syn*** bully, gangster, goon, homeboy, hood, mobster, mug, punk, roughneck, rowdy, ruffian, thug, tough, toughie
***rel*** cutthroat, scoundrel, villain; assassin, bandit, bravo, brigand, criminal, crook, desperado, felon, gunman, highwayman, lawbreaker, mafioso, outlaw, perpetrator, pickpocket, racketeer, robber, swindler, thief

**hoodoo** *n* something that brings bad luck — see JINX

**hoodwink** *vb* to cause to believe what is untrue — see DECEIVE

**hoof** (it) *vb* **1** to go on foot — see WALK
**2** to perform a series of usually rhythmic bodily movements to music — see DANCE 1

**hook** *n* a hard strike with a part of the body or an instrument — see [1]BLOW

**hook** *vb* **1** to cause to turn away from a straight line — see BEND 1
**2** to put or bring together so as to form a new and longer whole — see CONNECT 1
**3** to take (something) without right and with an intent to keep — see STEAL 1
**4** to take physical control or possession of (something) suddenly or forcibly — see CATCH 1
**5** to turn away from a straight line or course — see CURVE 1

**hookup** *n* the state of having shared interests or efforts (as in social or business matters) — see ASSOCIATION 1

**hoop** *n* a circular strip — see RING 2

**hoosegow** *n* a place of confinement for persons held in lawful custody — see JAIL

**hoot** *n* **1** a loud vocal expression of strong emotion — see SHOUT
**2** a vocal sound made to express scorn or disapproval — see CATCALL
**3** the smallest amount or part imaginable — see JOT

**hop** *n* **1** a social gathering for dancing — see DANCE
**2** an act of leaping into the air — see JUMP 1

**hop** *vb* **1** to move with a light bouncing step — see SKIP 1
**2** to propel oneself upward or forward into the air — see JUMP 1

**hope** (for) *vb* to believe in the future occurrence of (something) — see EXPECT

**hopeful** *adj* **1** having qualities which inspire hope ⟨economists are offering a

*hopeful* forecast for a healthy economy in the coming year〉
***syn*** auspicious, bright, encouraging, fair, golden, heartening, likely, optimistic, promising, propitious, rose-colored, rosy, upbeat
***rel*** cheering, comforting, reassuring; assured, confident, decisive, doubtless, positive, sure, unhesitating; bullish, favorable, good
***near ant*** cheerless, comfortless; doubtful, dubious, uncertain; bearish, grim, negative, unfavorable
***ant*** bleak, dark, desperate, discouraging, disheartening, dismal, dreary, gloomy, hopeless, inauspicious, pessimistic, unlikely, unpromising
**2** pointing toward a happy outcome — see FAVORABLE 2

**hopeful** *n* one who seeks an office, honor, position, or award — see CANDIDATE

**hopeless** *adj* **1** not capable of being cured or reformed 〈a *hopeless* optimist who looked for the good in everyone and everything〉 〈a *hopeless* criminal who spent most of his life in jail〉
***syn*** incorrigible, incurable, irrecoverable, irredeemable, irremediable, irretrievable, unrecoverable, unredeemable
***rel*** irreparable, irreversible; unpromising; impenitent, unreformed, unregenerate, unrepentant
***near ant*** reversible; promising; penitent, repentant; repairable, reparable, salvageable
***ant*** correctable, curable, reclaimable, recoverable, redeemable, reformable, remediable, retrievable
**2** emphasizing or expecting the worst — see PESSIMISTIC 1
**3** incapable of being solved or accomplished — see IMPOSSIBLE

**hopelessness** *n* utter loss of hope — see DESPAIR 1

**horde** *n* a great number of persons or things gathered together — see CROWD 1

**horn** *n* something shaped like a hollow cone and used as a container — see CORNET

**horrendous** *adj* **1** causing fear — see FEARFUL 1
**2** causing intense displeasure, disgust, or resentment — see OFFENSIVE 1
**3** extremely disturbing or repellent — see HORRIBLE 1

**horrible** *adj* **1** extremely disturbing or repellent 〈a *horrible* car accident that left eyewitnesses in a state of shock〉
***syn*** appalling, atrocious, awful, dreadful, frightful, ghastly, grisly, gruesome, hideous, horrendous, horrid, horrifying, lurid, macabre, monstrous, nightmarish, shocking, terrible
***rel*** bloodcurdling, dire, direful, fearful, fearsome, forbidding, formidable, frightening, hair-raising, terrifying; abhorrent, deplorable, disagreeable, disgusting, distasteful, loathsome, nauseating, obnoxious, offensive, repugnant, repulsive, revolting, sickening; abominable, evil, foul, heinous, noxious, odious, unspeakable, vile
***near ant*** agreeable, appealing, attractive, enticing, inviting; cheering, comforting, soothing
**2** causing fear — see FEARFUL 1
**3** causing intense displeasure, disgust, or resentment — see OFFENSIVE 1

**horrid** *adj* **1** causing intense displeasure, disgust, or resentment — see OFFENSIVE 1
**2** extremely disturbing or repellent — see HORRIBLE 1

**horridness** *n* the quality of inspiring intense dread or dismay — see HORROR 1

**horrified** *adj* filled with fear or dread — see AFRAID 1

**horrify** *vb* to strike with fear — see FRIGHTEN

**horrifying** *adj* **1** causing fear — see FEARFUL 1
**2** extremely disturbing or repellent — see HORRIBLE 1

**horror** *n* **1** the quality of inspiring intense dread or dismay 〈it's difficult to even begin to comprehend the *horror* of the Holocaust〉
***syn*** atrociousness, atrocity, awfulness, dreadfulness, frightfulness, ghastliness, grisliness, gruesomeness, hideousness, horridness, monstrosity, repulsiveness
***rel*** badness, baseness, diabolicalness, evil, foulness, heinousness, immorality, iniquity, invidiousness, nefariousness, ungodliness, viciousness, vileness, wickedness; accursedness, cursedness, deplorableness, despicableness, detestableness, execrableness, hatefulness, loathsomeness, reprehensibleness; creepiness, eeriness, fearfulness, fearsomeness, ghostliness, scariness; agony, hellishness, misery, torment, torture
***near ant*** agreeableness, delightfulness, pleasantness; allurement, appeal, attraction, attractiveness, desirability, desirableness
**2** a situation or state that causes great suffering and unhappiness — see HELL 2
**3** something unpleasant to look at — see EYESORE
**4** the emotion experienced in the presence or threat of danger — see FEAR

**horse** *n* a large hoofed domestic animal that is used for carrying or drawing loads and for riding 〈the mounted police stable their *horses* in the city park〉
***syn*** equine, nag, steed
***rel*** colt, filly, foal, gelding, mare, stallion; bronco, mustang, pony; charger, courser, cow pony, mount, palfrey, prancer, quarter horse, racehorse, saddle horse, trotter, war-horse, workhorse; bay, black, buckskin, chestnut, dun, palomino, pinto, roan, sorrel; cob, jade, plug

**horse** (around) *vb* to engage in attention-getting playful or boisterous behavior — see CUT UP

**horseplay** *n* wildly playful or mischievous behavior ⟨when he saw us spraying each other with the hose instead of washing the car, Dad yelled, "Cut out the *horseplay*!"⟩
*syn* clowning, foolery, high jinks horsing (around), monkeying, monkeyshines, roughhouse, roughhousing, shenanigans, skylarking, tomfoolery
*rel* buffoonery, clownishness, foolishness, funning, jesting, joking, nonsense, waggery; boisterousness, rowdiness devilry (*or* deviltry), impishness, mischief, mischievousness, prankishness, roguishness, trickery; cavorting, frivolity, frolicking, gamboling (*or* gambolling), merrymaking, playfulness, revelry, roistering, romping, sporting, sportiveness
**horse sense** *n* the ability to make intelligent decisions especially in everyday matters — see COMMON SENSE
**horse–trade** *vb* to talk over or dispute the terms of a purchase — see BARGAIN
**horsewhip** *vb* to strike repeatedly with something long and thin or flexible — see WHIP 1
**horsing** (around) *n* wildly playful or mischievous behavior — see HORSEPLAY
**hose** *n* a close-fitting covering for the foot and leg — see STOCKING
**hospice** *n* a place that provides rooms and usually a public dining room for overnight guests — see HOTEL
**hospitable** *adj* showing a natural kindness and courtesy especially in social situations — see GRACIOUS 1
**host** *n* **1** a great number of persons or things gathered together — see CROWD 1
**2** a large body of men and women organized for land warfare — see ARMY 1
**hostel** *n* a place that provides rooms and usually a public dining room for overnight guests — see HOTEL
**hostelry** *n* a place that provides rooms and usually a public dining room for overnight guests — see HOTEL
**hostile** *adj* **1** marked by opposition or ill will ⟨our landlord has a *hostile* attitude toward foreigners and refuses to rent to them⟩
*syn* antagonistic, inhospitable, inimical, jaundiced, negative, unfriendly, unsympathetic
*rel* adverse, bellicose, belligerent, clashing, conflicting, contentious, contrary, opposed, pugnacious, quarrelsome, resisting; antisocial, cold, cool, disagreeable, disapproving, distant, frigid, icy, biased, prejudiced; discourteous, impolite, rude, surly, uncivil, unfavorable, unkind, unpleasant, unsociable; acrimonious, antipathetic, bitter, hateful, malevolent, opprobrious, rancorous, spiteful, unloving, vindictive, virulent
*near ant* affable, amiable, amicable, companionable, convivial, cordial, civil, genial, gracious, gregarious, neighborly, pleasant, sociable, social, warm; affectionate, devoted, kind, loving, nice, sweet; accepting, agreeable approving, benign, empathetic, favorable, understanding, warmhearted, welcoming
*ant* friendly, hospitable, sympathetic
**2** opposed to one's interests — see ADVERSE 1
**hostility** *n* **1** a deep-seated ill will — see ENMITY
**2 hostilities** *pl* a state of armed violent struggle between states, nations, or groups — see WAR 1
**hot** *adj* **1** having a notably high temperature ⟨the casserole, just out of the oven, was too *hot* to eat⟩
*syn* broiling, burning, fiery, piping hot, red-hot, roasting, scalding, scorching, searing, sultry, superheated, sweltering, torrid
*rel* blazing, glowing, molten, sizzling; heated, overheated, reheated, warmed; snug, toasty, warm; feverish, flushed, inflamed; muggy, steamy, summery, tropical
*near ant* chilly, cool, frosty, nippy, snowy, subzero, wintry; cooled, refrigerated, unheated, unthawed; benumbed, numb, shivering; lukewarm, temperate, tepid
*ant* arctic, chill, chilled, cold, freezing, frigid, frozen, glacial, ice-cold, iced, icy
**2** being or involving the latest methods, concepts, information, or styles — see MODERN
**3** enjoying widespread favor or approval — see POPULAR 1
**4** marked by bursts of destructive force or intense activity — see VIOLENT 1
**5** showing urgent desire or interest — see EAGER
**hot air** *n* **1** boastful speech or writing — see BOMBAST 1
**2** language that is impressive-sounding but not meaningful or sincere — see RHETORIC 1
**hot–blooded** *adj* having or expressing great depth of feeling — see FERVENT
**hotcake** *n* a flat cake made from thin batter and cooked on both sides (as on a griddle) — see PANCAKE
**hotchpotch** *n* an unorganized collection or mixture of various things — see MISCELLANY 1
**hotel** *n* a place that provides rooms and usually a public dining room for overnight guests ⟨for their 50th anniversary they stayed at one of the finest *hotels* in San Francisco⟩
*syn* caravansary (*or* caravanserai), hospice, hostel, hostelry, inn, lodge, public house, tavern
*rel* bed-and-breakfast; accommodations, lodgings, rest; motel, motor court, resort, spa, youth hostel; camp, campground; bunkhouse, dorm, dormitory; boardinghouse, lodging house, rooming house
**hotfoot** *adv* with excessive or careless speed — see HASTILY 1
**hotfoot** (it) *vb* to proceed or move quickly — see HURRY 2
**hothouse** *n* a glass-enclosed building for growing plants — see CONSERVATORY

**hotness** *n* the state of enjoying widespread approval — see POPULARITY

**hot war** *n* a state of armed violent struggle between states, nations, or groups — see WAR 1

**hound** *n* a domestic mammal that is related to the wolves and foxes — see DOG

**hound** *vb* **1** to go after or on the track of — see FOLLOW 2
**2** to subject (someone) to constant scoldings and sharp reminders — see NAG

**hounding** *n* the act of going after or in the tracks of another — see PURSUIT

**house** *n* **1** a commercial or industrial activity or organization — see ENTERPRISE 1
**2** a group of persons who come from the same ancestor — see FAMILY 1
**3** the place where one lives — see HOME 1
**4** those who live as a family in one house — see HOUSEHOLD

**house** *vb* **1** to provide with living quarters or shelter ⟨some of the freshmen were temporarily *housed* in the gym while the new dorm was being finished⟩
***syn*** accommodate, billet, board, bunk, chamber, domicile, encamp, harbor, lodge, put up, quarter, roof, shelter, take in
***rel*** ensconce, home, roost, secure, stable, tent
***near ant*** eject, evict
**2** to close or shut in by or as if by barriers — see ENCLOSE 1

**house cat** *n* a small domestic animal known for catching mice — see CAT 1

**household** *adj* **1** of or relating to a household or family — see DOMESTIC 1
**2** often observed or encountered — see COMMON 1

**household** *n* those who live as a family in one house ⟨a *household* that consists of a single mom, her two kids, and her widowed mother⟩
***syn*** extended family, house, ménage
***rel*** folks, kin, kindred, kinfolk, kinsfolk, kith; brood; nuclear family; clan, community

**housekeeper** *n* a female domestic servant — see MAID 1

**housemaid** *n* a female domestic servant — see MAID 1

**housing** *n* something that encloses another thing especially to protect it — see [1]CASE 1

**hovel** *n* a small, simply constructed, and often temporary dwelling — see SHACK

**hover** *vb* to rest or move along the surface of a liquid or in the air — see FLOAT

**hover** (over) *vb* to remain poised to inflict harm, danger, or distress on — see THREATEN

**howbeit** *adv* in spite of that — see HOWEVER

**howbeit** *conj* in spite of the fact that — see ALTHOUGH

**however** *adv* in spite of that ⟨I'm all out of eggs; *however,* I can still make us a nice breakfast⟩
***syn*** howbeit, nevertheless, nonetheless, notwithstanding, still, though, withal, yet
***rel*** after all, anyhow, regardless

**howl** *n* **1** a crying out in grief — see LAMENT 1
**2** a loud vocal expression of strong emotion — see SHOUT
**3** a violent shouting — see CLAMOR 1

**howl** *vb* **1** to make a long loud mournful sound ⟨several coyotes began *howling* close by as the sun went down⟩ ⟨the wind *howled* on the open plain⟩
***syn*** bay, keen, wail, yowl
***rel*** bawl, caterwaul, squall, yawp (*or* yaup), yell, yelp
**2** to cry out loudly and emotionally — see SCREAM

**hoydenish** *adj* having qualities or traits that are traditionally considered inappropriate for a girl or woman — see UNFEMININE

**hub** *n* a thing or place that is of greatest importance to an activity or interest — see CENTER 1

**hubbub** *n* **1** a state of noisy, confused activity — see COMMOTION
**2** a violent shouting — see CLAMOR 1

**huckster** *n* one who sells things outdoors — see PEDDLER

**huddle** *n* **1** a coming together of a number of persons for a specified purpose — see MEETING 1
**2** a number of things considered as a unit — see GROUP 1
**3** a usually small number of persons considered as a unit — see GROUP 2

**huddle** *vb* **1** to gather into a closely packed group — see PRESS 3
**2** to lie low with the limbs close to the body — see CROUCH

**hue** *n* a property that becomes apparent when light falls on an object and by which things that are identical in form can be distinguished — see COLOR 1

**hue and cry** *n* a violent shouting — see CLAMOR 1

**huff** *n* **1** a state of nervous or irritated concern — see FRET
**2** an outburst or display of excited anger — see TANTRUM
**3** the feeling of being offended or resentful after a slight or indignity — see PIQUE

**huffiness** *n* readiness to show annoyance or impatience — see PETULANCE

**hug** *vb* to put one's arms around and press tightly — see EMBRACE 1

**huge** *adj* unusually large ⟨the old stadium was replaced by a *huge* new one that seats 100,000 spectators⟩
***syn*** astronomical (*also* astronomic), bumper, colossal, cosmic, elephantine, enormous, giant, gigantic, grand, herculean, heroic, immense, jumbo, king-size (*or* king-sized), mammoth, massive, monster, monstrous, monumental, mountainous, prodigious, super, titanic,

---

***syn*** synonym(s) ***rel*** related words
***ant*** antonym(s) ***near ant*** near antonym(s)

tremendous, vast, vasty, whacking, whopping
***rel*** big, bulky, considerable, extensive, good, goodly, good-sized, great, gross, handsome, hefty, hulking, largish, major, sizable (*or* sizeable), substantial, voluminous; august, formidable, grandiose, imposing, lofty, majestic; cavernous, monolithic, overwhelming, staggering, stupendous, towering; boundless, cosmic, immeasurable, infinite
***near ant*** little, petite, pint-size (*or* pint-sized), puny, small, smallish, undersized
***ant*** bitty, diminutive, microscopic (*or* microscopical), midget, miniature, minute, pocket, pygmy, teeny, teeny-weeny, tiny, wee

**hugely** *adv* **1** to a great degree — see VERY 1
**2** to a large extent or degree — see GREATLY 2

**hugeness** *n* the quality or state of being very large — see IMMENSITY

**hugger–mugger** *adj* **1** lacking in order, neatness, and often cleanliness — see MESSY
**2** undertaken or done so as to escape being observed or known by others — see SECRET 1

**hulk** *n* a big clumsy often slow-witted person — see OAF

**hulking** *adj* **1** of a size greater than average of its kind — see LARGE
**2** strongly and heavily built — see [1]HUSKY

**hull** *vb* to remove the natural covering of — see PEEL

**hullabaloo** *n* **1** a state of noisy, confused activity — see COMMOTION
**2** a violent shouting — see CLAMOR 1

**hum** *n* a monotonous sound like that of an insect in motion ⟨we heard the *hum* of an outboard motor and a few minutes later the small craft came into sight⟩
***syn*** buzz, chirr, drone, purr, thrum, whir (*also* whirr), whiz (*or* whizz), zoom
***rel*** babble, coo, gurgle, hiss, moan, murmur, rustle, sigh, whisper; whish, zing, zip
***near ant*** bawl, howl, roar, scream, screech, shriek

**hum** *vb* to fly, turn, or move rapidly with a fluttering or vibratory sound — see WHIRR

**human** *adj* relating to or characteristic of human beings ⟨it's *human* nature to care about what people think of us⟩
***syn*** mortal, natural
***rel*** anthropoid, hominid, humanlike, humanoid
***near ant*** angelic (*or* angelical), divine, godlike, superhuman, supernatural; immortal, omnipotent, omniscient; animal, beastly, bestial, brute; inhuman, robotic
***ant*** nonhuman

**human** *n* a member of the human race ⟨*humans* are the only mammals not endowed with a natural defense against the elements, such as fur or a thick hide⟩
***syn*** being, bird, body, creature, customer, devil, guy, head, individual, life, man, mortal, party, person, scout, sort, soul, specimen, thing, wight
***rel*** hominid, homo, humanoid; brother, fellow, fellowman, neighbor; celebrity, personage, personality, self, somebody
***near ant*** animal, beast, brute

**humane** *adj* **1** having or marked by sympathy and consideration for others ⟨*humane* guards who treated the prisoners decently⟩ ⟨the Geneva conventions spelled out standards for *humane* treatment of prisoners of war⟩
***syn*** beneficent, benevolent, benignant, compassionate, good-hearted, kind, kind-hearted, kindly, softhearted, sympathetic, tender, tenderhearted, warmhearted
***rel*** attentive, considerate, thoughtful; affable, benign, cordial, friendly, gentle, good, good-natured, good-tempered, gracious, mild, nice, pleasant; clement, forbearing, forgiving, lenient, merciful, soft; patient, pitying, tolerant, understanding; altruistic, brotherly, charitable, generous, greathearted, humanitarian, magnanimous, noble, openhearted, philanthropic, unselfish, unsparing
***near ant*** merciless, pitiless, ruthless; inconsiderate, insensitive, thoughtless, uncaring, unthinking; grim, hard-boiled, harsh, heavy-handed, severe, stern, tough, unsentimental; hateful, malevolent, malicious, mean, spiteful, virulent
***ant*** barbarous, bestial, brutal, brutish, callous, cold-blooded, cruel, hardhearted, heartless, inhuman, inhumane, insensate, savage, unfeeling, unkind, unkindly, unsympathetic
**2** having or showing the capacity for sharing the feelings of another — see SYMPATHETIC 1

**humanitarian** *adj* having or showing a concern for the welfare of others — see CHARITABLE 1

**humanity** *n* **1** human beings in general — see PEOPLE 1
**2** the capacity for feeling for another's unhappiness or misfortune — see HEART 1
**3** the human race — see MANKIND

**humankind** *n* **1** human beings in general — see PEOPLE 1
**2** the human race — see MANKIND

**humble** *adj* **1** not having or showing any feelings of superiority, self-assertiveness, or showiness ⟨a medical scientist who remained remarkably *humble* even after winning the Nobel Prize⟩ ⟨even though she'd been twice proven wrong, Janet's attitude was still far from *humble*⟩
***syn*** demure, lowly, meek, modest, retiring, unassuming, unpretentious
***rel*** acquiescent, compliant, deferential, resigned, submissive, unaggressive, unassertive, yielding; cowering, cringing, shrinking; ingenuous, naive (*or* naïve), plain, simple, unaffected; bashful, diffident, mousy (*or* mousey), overmodest, passive, quiet, reserved, shy, subdued, timid, unobtrusive
***near ant*** aggressive, assertive, audacious, bold, brash, brassy, cheeky, forward;

cocksure, cocky, confident, overconfident, self-confident; egocentric, egoistic, self-centered, self-satisfied; boastful, bombastic, vain, vainglorious; condescending, disdainful, dominant, dominating, domineering, imperious, lofty, lordly, magisterial, masterful, overbearing, patronizing, pontificating; flamboyant, flaunting, highfalutin, parading, ostentatious, showy
***ant*** arrogant, conceited, egotistic (*or* egotistical), haughty, high-hat, pompous, presumptuous, pretentious, prideful, proud, self-assertive, self-conceited, self-important, stuck-up, supercilious, superior
**2** belonging to the class of people of low social or economic rank — see IGNOBLE 1

**humble** *vb* to reduce to a lower standing in one's own eyes or in others' eyes ⟨Philip was utterly *humbled* by a crushing defeat in the first round of the state chess tournament⟩
***syn*** abase, debase, degrade, demean, discredit, disgrace, dishonor, humiliate, lower, shame, smirch, take down
***rel*** abash, discomfit, discountenance, embarrass, fluster, mortify; belittle, castigate, criticize, decry, depreciate, detract, disparage, minimize, put down, ridicule; bad-mouth, defame, defile, libel, malign, slander; affront, insult; censure, condemn, damn, denounce, reprobate
***near ant*** acclaim, applaud, boast, celebrate, cite, commend, compliment, congratulate, decorate, eulogize, extol (*also* extoll), fete (*or* fête), hail, honor, laud, praise, salute, tout; acknowledge, recognize; highlight, play up, spotlight; dignify, ennoble, enshrine, glorify, magnify; lift, promote, raise, upgrade, uplift
***ant*** aggrandize, elevate, exalt

**humbleness** *n* the absence of any feelings of being better than others — see HUMILITY

**humbly** *adv* in manner showing no signs of pride or self-assertion — see LOWLY

**humbug** *n* **1** an imitation that is passed off as genuine — see FAKE 1
**2** language, behavior, or ideas that are absurd and contrary to good sense — see NONSENSE 1
**3** one who makes false claims of identity or expertise — see IMPOSTOR

**humbug** *vb* to cause to believe what is untrue — see DECEIVE

**humbuggery** *n* language, behavior, or ideas that are absurd and contrary to good sense — see NONSENSE 1

**humdrum** *adj* causing weariness, restlessness, or lack of interest — see BORING

**humid** *adj* containing or characterized by an uncomfortable amount of moisture ⟨the air was so *humid* that our beach towels hanging on the line never really got dry⟩
***syn*** muggy, sticky, sultry
***rel*** summery, sweltering, torrid; semitropical (*also* semitropic), subtropical (*also* subtropic), tropic, tropical; close, heavy, oppressive, smothering, stifling, stuffy, suffocating; clammy, damp, dank, moist; drenched, dripping, soaked, sodden, soggy, sopping, soppy, waterlogged, wet
***near ant*** bracing, cool, crisp, fresh, invigorating, refreshing; arid, baked, burned, burnt, dehydrated, desert, droughty, dusty, parched, scorched, seared, semiarid, sere, thirsty
***ant*** dry

**humidity** *n* the amount of water suspended in the air in tiny droplets — see MOISTURE

**humiliate** *vb* to reduce to a lower standing in one's own eyes or in others' eyes — see HUMBLE

**humility** *n* the absence of any feelings of being better than others ⟨displaying genuine *humility,* the peace activist accepted the Nobel Prize on behalf of all who have worked to end the violence⟩
***syn*** demureness, humbleness, lowliness, meekness, modesty, retiringness
***rel*** acquiescence, compliance, deference, resignedness, submission, submissiveness; ingenuousness, naïveté (*also* naivete); directness, plainness, simpleness; bashfulness, diffidence, passiveness, passivity, quietness, reserve, reservedness, shyness, timidity, timidness
***near ant*** aggressiveness, assertiveness; audaciousness, boldness, brashness, brassiness, cheek, cheekiness, cockiness, forwardness, overconfidence, presumptuousness, temerity; impudence, insolence, nerve; boastfulness, self-centeredness, self-satisfaction; vanity, vainglorious; condescension, disdain, imperiousness, lordliness, masterfulness; flamboyance, ostentation, ostentatiousness, showiness
***ant*** arrogance, conceit, egoism, egotism, haughtiness, pompousness, pretense (*or* pretence), pretension, pretentiousness, pride, pridefulness, superciliousness, superiority

**hummer** *n* an ambitious person who eagerly goes after what is desired — see GO-GETTER

**humming** *adj* marked by much life, movement, or activity — see ALIVE 2

**humor** *n* **1** the amusing quality or element in something ⟨Sarah failed to see any *humor* in being chased by the dog, but Tom thought it was quite funny⟩
***syn*** drollness, funniness, hilariousness, humorousness, richness
***rel*** amusement, enjoyment, fun, pleasure; absurdity, irony, laughableness, ludicrousness, ridiculousness; burlesque, caricature, comedy, farce, jest, lampoon, parody, satire, slapstick
***near ant*** agony, anguish, heartache, misery, sorrow, woe
***ant*** pathos
**2** humorous entertainment — see COMEDY

**3** a state of mind dominated by a particular emotion — see MOOD 1

**humor** *vb* to give in to (a desire) — see INDULGE

**humorist** *n* a person (as a writer) noted for or specializing in humor ⟨Mark Twain is perhaps America's most beloved *humorist*⟩
*syn* card, comedian, comic, jester, joker, jokester, wag, wit
*rel* comedienne, entertainer; banterer, cut up, kidder, practical joker, prankster, teaser, wisecracker; buffoon, clown, fool, harlequin, zany; caricaturist, lampooner, parodist, satirist

**humorless** *adj* not joking or playful in mood or manner — see SERIOUS 1

**humorous** *adj* **1** causing or intended to cause laughter — see FUNNY 1
**2** given to or marked by mature intelligent humor — see WITTY

**humorousness** *n* the amusing quality or element in something — see HUMOR 1

**hump** *vb* **1** to devote serious and sustained effort — see LABOR
**2** to proceed or move quickly — see HURRY 2

**hunch** *vb* to lie low with the limbs close to the body — see CROUCH

**hung** *also* **hanged** *adj* bending downward or forward — see NODDING

**hunger** *n* **1** a need or desire for food ⟨no amount of *hunger* would induce me to eat octopus⟩
*syn* appetite, emptiness, famishment
*rel* rapaciousness, ravenousness, voracity; malnutrition, starvation, undernourishment; craving, sweet tooth; stomach; famine, fast, hunger strike; gluttony, gourmandism, greed, hoggishness
*near ant* fill, fullness, glut, repletion, satiation, satiety, satisfaction
**2** a strong wish for something — see DESIRE
**3** urgent desire or interest — see EAGERNESS

**hunger** (for) *vb* to have an earnest wish to own or enjoy — see DESIRE

**hungry** *adj* **1** feeling a desire or need for food ⟨John was still *hungry* after eating only a muffin for breakfast⟩
*syn* empty, famished, starved, starving
*rel* rapacious, ravenous, voracious, wolfish; malnourished, underfed, undernourished; gluttonous, gormandizing, greedy, hoggish, insatiable, piggish
*near ant* engorged, glutted, gorged, overfed, overfull, replete, sated, satiated, stuffed, surfeited
*ant* full, satisfied
**2** showing urgent desire or interest — see EAGER

**hung up** *adj* **1** having extreme or relentless concern ⟨Stephanie's parents are already *hung up* about her getting into a good college, and she's only six years old⟩
*syn* obsessed
*rel* absorbed, anxious, concerned, distracted, engaged, engrossed, full, involved, occupied, prepossessed, preoccupied, worried; ardent, crazy, fervent, fervid, foolish, impassioned, nuts, passionate, silly
*near ant* apathetic, cool, detached, dispassionate, unconcerned, unenthusiastic, uninterested, uninvolved
**2** feeling or showing uncomfortable feelings of uncertainty — see NERVOUS 1

**hunk** *n* a small uneven mass — see LUMP 1

**hunt** *n* an act or process of looking carefully or thoroughly for someone or something — see SEARCH

**hunt** *vb* **1** to seek out (game) for food or sport ⟨Indians of the plains *hunted* buffalo for food, clothing, and shelter⟩
*syn* chase, stalk
*rel* capture, drag, net, snare, trap; ferret, dog, hawk, hound; pursue, run down, track, trail; gun (for), harpoon, kill, shoot; poach
**2** to go in search of — see SEEK 1
**3** to go into or range over for purposes of discovery — see EXPLORE 2

**hunt** (down *or* up) *vb* to come upon after searching, study, or effort — see FIND 1

**hunt** (through) *vb* to look through (as a place) carefully or thoroughly in an effort to find or discover something — see SEARCH 1

**hunter** *n* a person who hunts game ⟨*hunters* must have a license to shoot deer⟩
*syn* huntsman
*rel* huntress, sportsman, sportswoman; archer, gunner; falconer, hawker; hunter-gatherer, trapper; poacher

**huntsman** *n* a person who hunts game — see HUNTER

**hurdle** *n* something that makes movement or progress more difficult — see ENCUMBRANCE

**hurl** *vb* to send through the air especially with a quick forward motion of the arm — see THROW

**hurly-burly** *n* a state of noisy, confused activity — see COMMOTION

**hurried** *adj* acting or done with excessive or careless speed — see HASTY 1

**hurriedly** *adv* with excessive or careless speed — see HASTILY 1

**hurry** *n* **1** excited and often showy or disorderly speed ⟨after all her *hurry* to get her history report done on time, Elizabeth learned that it wasn't due till the following week⟩
*syn* haste, hastiness, hustle, precipitation, precipitousness, rush
*rel* bustle, flurry, flutter, scurry, scuttle, stir, whirl; beeline, dash, scramble, stampede; hotheadedness, impetuosity, impetuousness, impulsiveness, rashness; fleetness, quickness, rapidity, rapidness, speed, speediness, swiftness; celerity, dispatch, expeditiousness, promptness
*near ant* dilatoriness, lateness, pokiness, procrastination, slowness; languor, leisureliness, lethargy, sluggishness, torpor; inaction, inactivity, inertia, inertness, quiescence
*ant* deliberateness, deliberation

2 a high rate of movement or performance — see SPEED

**hurry** *vb* 1 to cause to move or proceed fast or faster ⟨the new nursing staff was *hurried* through the orientation because they were so desperately needed on the ward⟩
*syn* accelerate, hasten, quicken, rush, speed (up), whisk
*rel* drive, goad, prod, propel, push, race, spur, stir, urge; advance, aid, dispatch, ease, encourage, expedite, facilitate, forward, further
*near ant* delay, hamper, hinder, restrain; brake, check, stay
*ant* decelerate, retard, slow (down)
2 to proceed or move quickly ⟨if we *hurry,* we'll make the four o'clock train⟩
*syn* barrel, bolt, bowl, breeze, career, course, dash, fly, hasten, hotfoot (it), hump, hurtle, hustle, pelt, race, rip, rocket, run, rush, rustle, scoot, scurry, scuttle, shoot, speed, step (along), tear, trot, whirl, whisk, zip, zoom
*rel* dart, flit, scamper, scud, scuffle; stampede, streak, whiz (*or* whizz); gallop, jog, sprint; accelerate, quicken; catch up, fastforward, outpace, outrun, outstrip, overtake
*phrases* shake a leg
*near ant* dally, dawdle, drag, lag, linger, loiter, tarry; amble, lumber, plod, saunter, shuffle, stroll; decelerate, slow (down *or* up)
*ant* crawl, creep, poke

**hurt** *n* something that causes loss or pain — see INJURY 1

**hurt** *vb* 1 to feel or cause physical pain ⟨my head *hurts*⟩ ⟨a bad sprain that really *hurts*⟩ ⟨I *hurt* all over⟩
*syn* ache, pain, smart
*rel* bleed, bite, burn, chafe, cramp, fester, itch, nag, pinch, pound, rack, sting, swell, throb, tingle, twinge; agonize, suffer
2 to reduce the soundness, effectiveness, or perfection of — see DAMAGE 1
3 to cause bodily damage to — see INJURE 1
4 to feel deep sadness or mental pain — see GRIEVE

**hurtful** *adj* 1 causing or capable of causing harm — see HARMFUL
2 hard to accept or bear especially emotionally — see BITTER 2

**hurting** *adj* causing or feeling bodily pain — see PAINFUL 1

**hurtle** *vb* 1 to proceed or move quickly — see HURRY 2
2 to send through the air especially with a quick forward motion of the arm — see THROW

**husband** *n* the male partner in a marriage ⟨she and her *husband* just celebrated their 50th wedding anniversary⟩
*syn* man, old man
*rel* consort, mate, partner, spouse; bridegroom, groom; widower

**husbandry** *n* 1 careful management of material resources — see ECONOMY
2 the science or occupation of cultivating the soil, producing crops, and raising livestock — see AGRICULTURE

**hush** *n* 1 a state of freedom from storm or disturbance — see CALM
2 the near or complete absence of sound — see SILENCE 2

**hush** *vb* 1 to become still and orderly — see QUIET 1
2 to stop talking — see SHUT UP
3 to stop the noise or speech of — see SILENCE 1

**hush** (up) *vb* to keep from being publicly known — see SUPPRESS 1

**hushed** *adj* 1 free from disturbing noise or uproar — see QUIET 1
2 free from storms or physical disturbance — see CALM 1
3 mostly or entirely without sound — see SILENT 3
4 not known or meant to be known by the general populace — see PRIVATE 1

**husk** *n* something that encloses another thing especially to protect it — see [1]CASE 1

**husk** *vb* to remove the natural covering of — see PEEL

[1]**husky** *adj* strongly and heavily built ⟨a *husky* weight lifter⟩
*syn* beefy, brawny, burly, hulking
*rel* able-bodied, athletic, heavy, hefty, herculean, mighty, muscle-bound, muscular, powerful, robust, rugged, stalwart, strapping, strong, sturdy; chunky, compact, heavyset, solid, squat, squatty, stocky, thickset; dumpy, lumpish, portly, pudgy, stout
*near ant* lean, light, lightweight, slender, slight, slim, svelte, sylphlike, thin, willowy; bony, gangling, gangly, gaunt, gawky, lanky, scrawny, skinny, spare, twiggy; sinewy, spidery, wiry; delicate, emaciated, fragile, frail, puny, weakly

[2]**husky** *adj* harsh and dry in sound — see HOARSE

**hustle** *n* 1 a scheme in which the victim is cheated out of his money after first gaining his trust — see CONFIDENCE GAME
2 excited and often showy or disorderly speed — see HURRY 1
3 readiness to engage in daring or difficult activity — see ENTERPRISE 2

**hustle** *vb* 1 to devote serious and sustained effort — see LABOR
2 to proceed or move quickly — see HURRY 2
3 to rob by the use of trickery or threats — see FLEECE

**hustler** *n* an ambitious person who eagerly goes after what is desired — see GO-GETTER

**hut** *n* a small, simply constructed, and often temporary dwelling — see SHACK

**hutch** *n* 1 a small, simply constructed, and often temporary dwelling — see SHACK
2 a storage case typically having doors and shelves — see CABINET

**hybrid** *adj* being offspring produced by parents of different races, breeds, species, or genera — see MIXED 1

**hybrid** *n* an offspring of parents with different genes especially when of different races, breeds, species, or genera ⟨a tangelo is a *hybrid* of the tangerine and the grapefruit⟩
*syn* cross, crossbreed, mongrel
*rel* mulatto
*near ant* purebred, thoroughbred

**hygienic** *adj* free from filth, infection, or dangers to health — see SANITARY

**hymn** *n* a religious song ⟨our Sunday church services always open with a *hymn*⟩
*syn* anthem, canticle, carol, chorale, psalm, spiritual
*rel* dirge, lament, requiem, threnody; Gloria Patri, hallelujah, paean; mass, oratorio; processional, recessional

**hymnal** *n* a book of hymns ⟨*hymnals* are distributed among the congregation before the church service so everyone can join in the singing⟩
*syn* hymnbook, psalmody
*rel* breviary, missal, Psalter, songster

**hymnbook** *n* a book of hymns — see HYMNAL

**hyperbole** *n* the representation of something in terms that go beyond the facts — see EXAGGERATION

**hypercritical** *adj* given to making or expressing unfavorable judgments about things — see CRITICAL 1

**hyperventilate** *vb* to breathe hard, quickly, or with difficulty — see GASP

**hypnosis** *n* the art or act of inducing in a person a sleep-like state during which he or she readily follows suggestions ⟨with *hypnosis* there's some question as to just how involuntary the actions of the hypnotized person really are⟩
*syn* hypnotism, mesmerism
*rel* bewitchment, enchantment, spellbinding

**hypnotic** *adj* tending to cause sleep ⟨her eyes soon grew heavy from the *hypnotic* rhythm of the train's wheels⟩
*syn* drowsy, narcotic, opiate, slumberous (*or* slumbrous)
*rel* depressant, relaxant, sedative, tranquilizing (*also* tranquillizing); calming, lulling, quieting, relaxing, restful, settling, soothing; analgesic, anesthetic, anesthetizing, benumbing, deadening, dulling, numbing; hypnotizing, mesmerizing, stupefying
*near ant* arousing, awakening, energizing, invigorating, rousing, stimulating, wakening, waking
*ant* stimulant

**hypnotism** *n* the art or act of inducing in a person a sleep-like state during which he or she readily follows suggestions — see HYPNOSIS

**hypnotize** *vb* to hold the attention of as if by a spell — see ENTHRALL 1

**hypocrisy** *n* the pretending of having virtues, principles, or beliefs that one in fact does not have ⟨the *hypocrisy* of people who claim to care about the environment but ride around in gas-guzzlers⟩
*syn* cant, dissembling, dissimulation, insincerity, piousness, sanctimoniousness
*rel* deception, deceptiveness, dishonesty, falsity, pretense, pretension, pretentiousness, self-righteousness, self-satisfaction; duplicity, fakery, falseness, fraudulentness, shamming; artificiality, glibness, oiliness, smoothness, unctuousness
*near ant* candor, honesty, openness, probity, straightforwardness, truthfulness; artlessness, guilelessness, naturalness, unaffectedness
*ant* genuineness, sincerity

**hypocritical** *adj* not being or expressing what one appears to be or express — see INSINCERE

**hypodermic** *n* a slender hollow instrument by which material is put into or taken from the body through the skin — see NEEDLE 1

**hypodermic needle** *n* a slender hollow instrument by which material is put into or taken from the body through the skin — see NEEDLE 1

**hypodermic syringe** *n* a slender hollow instrument by which material is put into or taken from the body through the skin — see NEEDLE 1

**hypothesis** *n* an idea that is the starting point for making a case or conducting an investigation — see THEORY

**hypothetical** *adj* existing only as an assumption or speculation — see THEORETICAL 1

**hysteria** *n* a state of wildly excited activity or emotion — see FRENZY

**hysterical** *adj* **1** causing or intended to cause laughter — see FUNNY 1
**2** feeling overwhelming fear or worry — see FRANTIC 1

# I

**ice–cold** *adj* having a low or subnormal temperature — see COLD 1

**icy** *adj* **1** having a low or subnormal temperature — see COLD 1

**2** lacking in friendliness or warmth of feeling — see COLD 2

**idea** *n* something imagined or pictured in the mind ⟨my *idea* of the perfect vacation spot is an unspoiled beach⟩

***syn*** concept, conception, image, impression, notion, picture, thought

***rel*** apprehension, premonition, presentiment; chimera, illusion, phantasm; caprice, conceit, fancy, freak, notion, vagary, whim; observation, perception, reflection; assumption, belief, conclusion, conviction; conjecture, guess, hunch, hypothesis, speculation, supposition, surmise, theory; brainstorm, inspiration

***near ant*** actuality, fact, reality

**ideal** *adj* being entirely without fault or flaw — see PERFECT 1

**ideal** *n* **1** someone of such unequaled perfection as to deserve imitation ⟨she's our *ideal* of the concerned, caring physician⟩

***syn*** beau ideal, classic, exemplar, model, nonpareil, paragon

***rel*** role model; embodiment, epitome, incarnation, manifestation, personification; archetype, example, paradigm, pattern; guideline, principle, rule; gauge (*also* gage), standard, touchstone; essence, quintessence; acme, apex, culmination, peak, pinnacle, summit, zenith

**2** the most perfect type or example — see QUINTESSENCE 1

**idealist** *n* one whose conduct is guided more by the image of perfection than by the real world ⟨an *idealist* sees the best in everyone, regardless of how they behave⟩

***syn*** dreamer, romantic, romanticist, utopian, visionary

***rel*** sentimentalist; daydreamer, optimist, theorist; perfectionist; thinker

***near ant*** cynic, defeatist, pessimist

***ant*** pragmatist, realist

**idealize** *vb* to represent or think of as better than reality ⟨he had a tendency to *idealize* his heroes and believe they could do no wrong⟩

***syn*** glamorize (*also* glamourize), glorify, romanticize

***rel*** daydream, imagine, romance, theorize, vision; better, perfect

***near ant*** blame, condemn, criticize, denounce; worsen

**ideally** *adv* without any flaws or errors — see PERFECTLY 1

***syn*** synonym(s) ***rel*** related words
***ant*** antonym(s) ***near ant*** near antonym(s)

**idée fixe** *n* something about which one is constantly thinking or concerned — see FIXATION

**identical** *adj* **1** being one and not another — see SAME 2

**2** resembling another in every respect — see SAME 1

**identicalness** *n* the state of being exactly alike — see IDENTITY 1

**identify** *vb* **1** to find out or establish the identity of ⟨with a quick look at everyone's tongue, Mom was able to *identify* the person who had sneaked a piece of blueberry pie⟩

***syn*** distinguish, pinpoint, single (out)

***rel*** diagnose; determine, find; locate, pick out, place, recognize, spot; check, examine, inspect, investigate, notice, observe, scrutinize; betray, disclose, discover, reveal

***near ant*** camouflage, conceal, disguise, hide; counterfeit, feign, sham, simulate

**2** to think of (something) in combination — see ASSOCIATE 2

**identifying** *adj* serving to identify as belonging to an individual or group — see CHARACTERISTIC 1

**identity** *n* **1** the state of being exactly alike ⟨although the covers of the two paperback editions of the novel are different, there's a complete *identity* in the texts⟩

***syn*** identicalness, sameness

***rel*** oneness; homogeneity, homology; equality, equivalence; accordance, agreement, conformity, congruity, correspondence, likeness, resemblance, similarity

***near ant*** alteration, change, modification, variation; distinction, distinctiveness, distinctness, exoticness, individuality, separateness, separation, uniqueness, unusualness; deviance, divergence; variance; incompatibility, incongruity, incongruousness; contrast

***ant*** difference, disagreement, discrepancy, disparateness, disparity, dissimilarity, unlikeness

**2** the set of qualities that make a person different from other people — see INDIVIDUALITY

**ideology** *n* the basic beliefs or guiding principles of a person or group — see CREED 1

**idiocy** *n* a foolish act or idea — see FOLLY 1

**idiom** *n* a sequence of words having a specific meaning — see PHRASE

**idiosyncrasy** *n* an odd or peculiar habit ⟨his only *idiosyncrasy* was collecting pencil erasers and making little dolls out of them⟩

*syn* crotchet, eccentricity, mannerism, oddity, peculiarity, quirk, singularity, trick
*rel* affectation, airs; attribute, characteristic, mark, property, trait; custom, habit, pattern, practice (*also* practise), way, wont; addiction; abnormality, perversion; disposition, genius, leaning, partiality; bent, inclination, penchant, predilection, predisposition, proclivity, propensity, tendency, turn; attitude, character, humor, identity, individuality, nature, personality, temperament
*near ant* conformity, sameness

**idiot** *n* a stupid person ⟨only an *idiot* would jump off a bridge just because their friends told them to⟩
*syn* blockhead, cretin, dodo, dolt, donkey, dope, dork [*slang*], dumbbell, dummy, dunce, fathead, goon, half-wit, ignoramus, imbecile, jackass, knothead, moron, nincompoop, ninny, nitwit, numskull (*or* numbskull), pinhead, simpleton, stock, turkey
*rel* booby, fool, goose, loony (*also* looney), lunatic, madman, nut, zany; loser; gawk; featherbrain, scatterbrain; beast, boor, cad, churl, clown, creep, cur, heel, jerk, skunk, snake, stinker, villain
*near ant* egghead, intellectual, sage, thinker
*ant* brain, genius

**idle** *vb* to spend time doing nothing ⟨she likes to *idle* during the summer even though her parents always tell her to get out and do something⟩
*syn* dally, dawdle, dillydally, hang around, hang out, loaf, loll, lounge
*rel* fiddle, fool, mess, monkey, play, potter, putter, trifle; estivate, hibernate; lag, linger, loiter, poke, relax, rest, tarry; amble, mosey, saunter, stroll; bum, furlough, goldbrick, malinger
*phrases* kill time, lie around, mark time, waste time
*near ant* drudge, grind, grub, hump, hustle, labor, moil, peg, plod, plow, plug, slave, sweat, toil, travail, work; apply, buckle (down); exert, put out

**idle** *adj* **1** not being in a state of use, activity, or employment — see INACTIVE 2
**2** not easily aroused to action or work — see LAZY

**idleness** *n* **1** an inclination not to do work or engage in activities — see LAZINESS
**2** lack of action or activity — see INACTION
**3** lack of use — see DISUSE

**idler** *n* a lazy person — see LAZYBONES

**idolater** *or* **idolator** *n* a person who does not worship the God of the Bible — see HEATHEN 1

**idolatry** *n* excessive admiration of or devotion to a person — see WORSHIP

**idolization** *n* excessive admiration of or devotion to a person — see WORSHIP

**idolize** *vb* to love or admire too much ⟨she *idolized* her big sister⟩
*syn* adore, adulate, canonize, deify, dote (on), worship
*rel* appreciate, cherish, esteem, prize, treasure, value; fancy, favor, like, prefer; regard; respect, revere, venerate; approve, endorse (*also* indorse), support
*near ant* abhor, abominate, despise, detest, disdain, dislike, hate, loathe; belittle, deprecate, disparage, put down

**idolizing** *adj* reflecting great admiration or devotion — see WORSHIPFUL

**ignitable** *adj* capable of catching or being set on fire — see COMBUSTIBLE

**ignite** *vb* to set (something) on fire — see BURN 2

**ignited** *adj* being on fire — see ABLAZE 1

**ignoble** *adj* **1** belonging to the class of people of low social or economic rank ⟨an *ignoble* child cannot grow up to be king⟩
*syn* baseborn, common, humble, inferior, low, lower-class, lowly, mean, plebeian, proletarian, vulgar
*rel* bourgeois, middle-class; peasant, plain, poor, simple, working-class
*near ant* eminent, illustrious, notable, prominent
*ant* aristocratic, high, highborn, lofty, noble, wellborn
**2** not following or in accordance with standards of honor and decency ⟨cheating on a test is an *ignoble* act and can get you expelled⟩
*syn* base, contemptible, despicable, detestable, dirty, dishonorable, low, mean, snide, sordid, vile, wretched
*rel* bad, black, evil, foul, immoral, iniquitous, wicked, wrong; cruel, nasty, vicious; blamable, blameworthy, censurable, reprehensible; corrupt, debased, debauched, degenerate, depraved, dissolute, perverted; atrocious, villainous; unethical, unprincipled, unscrupulous; discreditable, disgraceful, disreputable, ignominious, shameful
*near ant* ethical, honest, just, principled, righteous, right-minded, scrupulous; commendable, excellent, exemplary, good, moral, right; decent, proper, reputable, respectable, seemly; blameless, guiltless; incorruptible, irreproachable; uncorrupted, unerring
*ant* high, high-minded, honorable, lofty, noble, straight, upright, venerable, virtuous

**ignominious** *adj* not respectable — see DISREPUTABLE

**ignominy** *n* the state of having lost the esteem of others — see DISGRACE 1

**ignoramus** *n* a stupid person — see IDIOT

**ignorance** *n* **1** the state of being unaware or uninformed ⟨*ignorance* of the law is no excuse⟩
*syn* obliviousness, unawareness, unfamiliarity
*rel* callowness, greenness, inexperience, innocence, naïveté (*also* naivete), rawness, simpleness, unsophistication
*near ant* experience, know-how; sophistication
*ant* acquaintance, awareness, familiarity

2 the state of being unlearned ⟨with such vast sums spent on education, the level of *ignorance* among graduating seniors is a national disgrace⟩
***syn*** illiteracy
***rel*** brainlessness, dumbness, idiocy, imbecility, stupidity; philistinism; foolishness, mindlessness, senselessness, witlessness
***near ant*** education, instruction, training; enlightenment, knowledge; erudition, scholarship
***ant*** learning, literacy

**ignorant** *adj* **1** lacking in education or the knowledge gained from books ⟨the teacher was committed to educating the children of those poor, *ignorant* farmers⟩
***syn*** benighted, dark, illiterate, nonliterate, simple, uneducated, uninstructed, unlearned, unlettered, unread, unschooled, untaught, untutored
***rel*** lowbrow, uncultivated, uncultured; callow, green, inexperienced, innocent, naive (*or* naïve); unsophisticated; raw, untrained; brainless, dumb, idiotic, imbecilic, moronic, stupid, witless; foolish, senseless, silly
***near ant*** brilliant, intelligent, smart; experienced, expert, trained; erudite, learned, scholarly; cultivated, cultured, highbrow, intellectual; sophisticated; acquainted, aware, familiar
***ant*** educated, knowledgeable, literate, schooled
**2** not informed about or aware of something ⟨he was *ignorant* of their plans⟩
***syn*** oblivious, unacquainted, unaware, unconscious, ungrounded, uninformed, unknowing, unmindful, unwitting
***rel*** uneducated, unschooled, untaught; absent, absentminded, abstracted, heedless, inattentive
***near ant*** conversant, educated, knowledgeable, schooled, taught; heedful, observant; sensitive, sentient
***ant*** acquainted, aware, cognizant, conscious, conversant, grounded, informed, knowing, mindful, witting

**ignore** *vb* **1** to fail to give proper attention to — see NEGLECT 1
**2** to overlook or dismiss as of little importance — see EXCUSE 1

**ilk** *n* a number of persons or things that are grouped together because they have something in common — see SORT 1

**ill** *adj* **1** affected with nausea — see NAUSEOUS
**2** causing or capable of causing harm — see HARMFUL
**3** temporarily suffering from a disorder of the body — see SICK 1

**ill** *adv* in a manner so as to cause loss or suffering — see HARDLY 1

**ill** *n* **1** an abnormal state that disrupts a plant's or animal's normal bodily functioning — see DISEASE
**2** that which is morally unacceptable — see EVIL

***syn*** synonym(s) ***rel*** related words
***ant*** antonym(s) ***near ant*** near antonym(s)

**ill–advised** *adj* showing poor judgment especially in personal relationships or social situations — see INDISCREET

**ill–bred** *adj* **1** lacking in refinement or good taste — see COARSE 2
**2** showing a lack of manners or consideration for others — see IMPOLITE

**illegal** *adj* **1** contrary to or forbidden by law ⟨it is *illegal* to steal⟩
***syn*** criminal, illegitimate, illicit, unlawful, wrongful
***rel*** bad, evil, immoral, shameful, sinful, unethical, wicked, wrong; blamable, blameworthy, censurable, reprehensible; banned, barred, disallowed, discouraged, forbidden, interdicted, outlawed, prohibited, proscribed; unauthorized, unlicensed, unsanctioned; corrupt, unprincipled, unscrupulous, villainous
***near ant*** ethical, good, just, principled, right, righteous, virtuous; allowed, permitted; authorized, licensed (*also* licenced); approved, endorsed, sanctioned; abetted, encouraged, promoted, suggested, supported; correct, decent, decorous, proper, seemly
***ant*** lawful, legal, legitimate
**2** not being in accordance with the rules or standards of what is fair in sport — see FOUL 2

**illegitimate** *adj* **1** born to a father and mother who are not married ⟨despite being *illegitimate*, Alexander Hamilton rose to greatness⟩
***syn*** baseborn, bastard, misbegotten
***rel*** fatherless, motherless; adopted, orphaned
***ant*** legitimate
**2** contrary to or forbidden by law — see ILLEGAL 1

**ill–fated** *adj* having, prone to, or marked by bad luck — see UNLUCKY

**ill–favored** *adj* unpleasant to look at — see UGLY 1

**ill–humored** *adj* having or showing a habitually bad temper — see ILL-TEMPERED

**illicit** *adj* contrary to or forbidden by law — see ILLEGAL 1

**illimitable** *adj* being or seeming to be without limits — see INFINITE

**illiteracy** *n* the state of being unlearned — see IGNORANCE 2

**illiterate** *adj* lacking in education or the knowledge gained from books — see IGNORANT 1

**ill–mannered** *adj* showing a lack of manners or consideration for others — see IMPOLITE

**ill–natured** *adj* having or showing a habitually bad temper — see ILL-TEMPERED

**illness** *n* **1** an abnormal state that disrupts a plant's or animal's normal bodily functioning — see DISEASE
**2** the condition of not being in good health — see SICKNESS 1

**illogical** *adj* not using or following good reasoning ⟨the *illogical* claim that playing basketball makes people taller because one sees so many tall players⟩ ⟨*illogical*

people are likely to believe every sensational claim on TV⟩
*syn* fallacious, invalid, irrational, nonrational, unreasonable, unreasoning, unsound, weak
*rel* misleading, specious; ill-advised, unconsidered, unreasoned; inconsistent; absurd, asinine, foolish, meaningless, nonsensical, preposterous, senseless, silly; odd, peculiar, strange, unusual, weird; insane, mad, nutty, wacky; disordered, disorganized, rambling, random; unconvincing, unsatisfying; inexplicable, unaccountable, unexplainable
*near ant* commonsense, sane, sensible, sober, wise; enlightened, informed, just, justified, reasoned; ordered, organized; clear, cogent, compelling, convincing, credible, persuasive, plausible, satisfying, solid; certain, sure, true; confirmed, corroborated, demonstrated, established, substantiated, validated, well-founded
*ant* logical, rational, reasonable sound, valid

**ill–starred** *adj* having, prone to, or marked by bad luck — see UNLUCKY

**ill–tempered** *adj* having or showing a habitually bad temper ⟨an *ill-tempered* cat will scratch⟩
*syn* bearish, bilious, cantankerous, disagreeable, dyspeptic, ill-humored, ill-natured, ornery, splenetic, surly
*rel* choleric, crabby, cranky, crotchety, fussy, grouchy, grumpy, querulous; irascible, irritable, peevish, petulant, quick-tempered, snappish, testy, touchy; argumentative, contentious, contrary; angry, exasperated, indignant, irate, mad, upset, uptight; depressed, dour, glum, morose, sullen
*near ant* agreeable, amicable, congenial, friendly, pleasant; benign, gentle, kind, nice, sweet; bubbly, cheerful, cheery, effervescent, exuberant, high-spirited, lighthearted, lively, joyful, vivacious; content, glad, happy; calm, placid, serene; long-suffering, patient, tolerant
*ant* amiable, good-natured, good-tempered

**ill–treat** *vb* to inflict physical or emotional harm upon — see ABUSE 1

**illuminate** *vb* **1** to supply with light ⟨a floor lamp *illuminates* a living room rather nicely⟩
*syn* illumine, irradiate, light, lighten
*rel* brighten; beam, beat (down), radiate, shine; floodlight; highlight, spotlight; blaze, burn, fire, flame, glare, glow, ignite, incinerate, kindle; bedazzle, blind, daze, dazzle; gleam, glisten, glitter
*near ant* dim, dull, obscure; cover, shroud, veil; douse, extinguish, put out, quench, snuff (out)
*ant* blacken, darken
**2** to make plain or understandable — see EXPLAIN 1

**illuminated** *adj* filled with much light — see BRIGHT 2

**illumination** *n* **1** a statement that makes something clear — see EXPLANATION 1
**2** the quality or state of having or giving off light — see BRILLIANCE 1
**3** the steady giving off of the form of radiation that makes vision possible — see LIGHT 1

**illuminative** *adj* serving to explain — see EXPLANATORY

**illumine** *vb* to supply with light — see ILLUMINATE 1

**illumined** *adj* filled with much light — see BRIGHT 2

**ill–use** *vb* to inflict physical or emotional harm upon — see ABUSE 1

**illusion** *n* **1** a conception or image created by the imagination and having no objective reality — see FANTASY 1
**2** a false idea or belief — see FALLACY 1

**illustrate** *vb* **1** to show or make clear by using examples ⟨she *illustrated* her point with a story about her last experiment and the results it provided⟩
*syn* demonstrate, exemplify, instance
*rel* cite, mention, quote; name, specify; analyze, break down; clarify, clear (up), explain, explicate, expound; edify, elucidate, enlighten; illuminate; construe, interpret; simplify, spell out; detail, enumerate, list
*near ant* becloud, blur, cloud, darken, fog, muddy, obscure; confuse, perplex, puzzle
**2** to make plain or understandable — see EXPLAIN 1

**illustration** *n* **1** something that visually explains or decorates a text ⟨the book on birds had gorgeous *illustrations*⟩
*syn* diagram, figure, graphic, plate
*rel* drawing, illumination, image, pictogram, pictograph, picture; caption, key, legend; depiction, portrait, portrayal, representation; clarification, elucidation, explanation, explication, exposition
**2** a statement that makes something clear — see EXPLANATION 1
**3** a two-dimensional design intended to look like a person or thing — see PICTURE 1
**4** one of a group or collection that shows what the whole is like — see EXAMPLE

**illustrative** *adj* serving to explain — see EXPLANATORY

**illustrious** *adj* standing above others in rank, importance, or achievement — see EMINENT

**image** *n* **1** something or someone that strongly resembles another ⟨the girl is growing up to be the perfect *image* of her mother⟩
*syn* carbon copy, counterpart, double, duplicate, duplication, facsimile, likeness, match, picture, replica, ringer, spit
*rel* effigy, portrait, portrayal; companion, counterpart, fellow, mate; equal, equivalent, identical twin; analogue (*or* analog), parallel
*near ant* antithesis, converse, opposite, reverse
**2** a two-dimensional design intended to look like a person or thing — see PICTURE 1

3 something imagined or pictured in the mind — see IDEA

**image** *vb* **1** to present a picture of — see PICTURE 1
**2** to give a representation or account of in words — see DESCRIBE 1
**3** to reproduce or show (an exact likeness) as a mirror would — see REFLECT

**imaginary** *adj* not real and existing only in the imagination ⟨his *imaginary* friend had purple hair⟩
***syn*** chimerical, fabulous, fanciful, fantastic, fictional, fictitious, imagined, invented, made-up, make-believe, mythical (*or* mythic), phantasmal, phantom, pretend, unreal
***rel*** fabled, legendary, romantic; abstract, hypothetical, theoretical (*also* theoretic); unbelievable, unconvincing, unlikely; conceived, envisaged, pictured, visualized; deceptive, delusional, delusive, hallucinatory, illusory; concocted, fabricated
***near ant*** authentic, genuine, true; factual, verifiable, verified; believable, convincing, realistic; corporeal, material, physical, solid, substantial; palpable, tangible
***ant*** actual, existent, existing, real

**imagination** *n* the ability to form mental images of things that either are not physically present or have never been conceived or created by others ⟨a cartoonist needs a good *imagination* in order to think up and draw interesting cartoons⟩
***syn*** creativity, fancy, fantasy (*also* phantasy), imaginativeness, invention, inventiveness
***rel*** brainstorm, brainstorming, inspiration; fecundity, fertility; ingenuity, originality; versatility; chimera, daydream, delusion, dream, figment, hallucination, illusion, mirage, phantasm, pipe dream; envisaging, visualization
***near ant*** literalness

**imaginative** *adj* **1** having the skill and imagination to create new things — see CREATIVE 1
**2** showing a use of the imagination and creativity especially in inventing — see CLEVER 1

**imaginativeness** *n* **1** the ability to form mental images of things that either are not physically present or have never been conceived or created by others — see IMAGINATION
**2** the skill and imagination to create new things — see CREATIVITY 1

**imagine** *vb* **1** to form a mental picture of ⟨she *imagined* meeting the members of her favorite rock band face-to-face⟩
***syn*** conceive, dream, envisage, fancy, picture, vision, visualize
***rel*** daydream, stargaze; hallucinate; reflect, relive, reminisce; contemplate, meditate, muse, ponder, ruminate; concoct, fabricate, invent, make up, manufacture, plan, project
**2** to have as an opinion — see BELIEVE 2

***syn*** synonym(s) ***rel*** related words
***ant*** antonym(s) ***near ant*** near antonym(s)

**imagined** *adj* not real and existing only in the imagination — see IMAGINARY

**imbecile** *n* a stupid person — see IDIOT

**imbecility** *n* a foolish act or idea — see FOLLY 1

**imbibe** *vb* **1** to swallow in liquid form — see DRINK 1
**2** to take in (something liquid) through small openings — see ABSORB 1

**imbue** *vb* to cause (as a person) to become filled or saturated with a certain quality or principle — see INFUSE

**imitate** *vb* **1** to use (someone or something) as the model for one's speech, mannerisms, or behavior ⟨teenage boys who *imitate* whichever rock stars are hot⟩
***syn*** ape, copy, emulate, mime, mimic
***rel*** burlesque, caricature, lampoon, mock, parody, travesty; impersonate, perform, play; pantomime
**2** to copy or exaggerate (someone or something) in order to make fun of — see MIMIC 1
**3** to make an exact likeness of — see COPY 1

**imitation** *adj* being such in appearance only and made with or manufactured from usually cheaper materials ⟨you have to be careful not to buy an *imitation* diamond passed off as the real thing⟩
***syn*** artificial, factitious, bogus, fake, false, man-made, mimic, mock, sham, simulated, substitute, synthetic
***rel*** dummy, phony (*also* phoney); cultured, manufactured; unauthentic; adulterated, doctored, fudged, juggled, manipulated, tampered (with); concocted, fabricated; counterfeit, deceptive, forged, fraudulent, misleading; affected, feigned, pseudo, spurious
***near ant*** authentic, bona fide, legitimate, true; premium, quality, valuable; pure, unadulterated
***ant*** genuine, natural, real

**imitation** *n* something that is made to look exactly like something else — see COPY

**imitative** *adj* using or marked by the use of something else as a basis or model ⟨your writing style tends to be *imitative* of whichever author you've recently read⟩
***syn*** apish, emulative, formulaic, mimetic, mimic, slavish, unoriginal
***rel*** copied, cribbed, plagiarized; artificial, bogus, factitious, fake, false, imitation, man-made, mock, sham, simulated, substitute, synthetic; duplicated, photocopied, reduplicated, reproduced, transcribed; backup; counterfeit, deceptive, forged, fraudulent, misleading; uninspired
***near ant*** authentic, bona fide, legitimate, true; genuine, natural, real; classic, ideal, model
***ant*** archetypal, original

**imitator** *n* **1** a person who adopts the appearance or behavior of another especially in an obvious way — see COPYCAT

**2** a person who imitates another's voice and mannerisms for comic effect — see MIMIC

**immaculate** *adj* **1** free from any trace of the coarse or indecent — see CHASTE
**2** free from dirt or stain — see CLEAN 1

**immaterial** *adj* **1** not composed of matter ⟨it is only possible to study *immaterial* forces like gravity by observing their effects on the physical world⟩
***syn*** bodiless, incorporeal, insubstantial, nonmaterial, nonphysical, spiritual, unsubstantial
***rel*** metaphysical, supernatural; impalpable, insensible, intangible, invisible; airy, diaphanous, ethereal, tenuous, thin, vaporous
***near ant*** animal, carnal, fleshly; detectable, discernable, noticeable, observable, palpable, sensible, tangible, visible; bulky, heavy, massive, solid
***ant*** bodily, corporeal, material, physical, substantial
**2** not having anything to do with the matter at hand — see IRRELEVANT

**immature** *adj* **1** being in the early stage of life, growth, or development — see YOUNG
**2** having or showing the annoying qualities (as silliness) associated with children — see CHILDISH
**3** lacking in adult experience or maturity — see CALLOW

**immeasurable** *adj* being or seeming to be without limits — see INFINITE

**immediacy** *n* the state or condition of being near — see PROXIMITY

**immediate** *adj* **1** done or occurring without any noticeable lapse in time — see INSTANTANEOUS
**2** done or working without something else coming in between — see DIRECT 1
**3** done, carried out, or given without delay — see PROMPT 1
**4** not being distant in time, space, or significance — see CLOSE 2

**immediately** *adv* without delay ⟨if you don't leave *immediately*, you'll be late for school and probably get in trouble⟩
***syn*** directly, forthwith, instantly, now, promptly, pronto, right away, right now, straightaway, straightway
***rel*** away, freely; anon, momentarily, shortly, soon; apace, briskly, fast, fleetly, full-tilt, posthaste, quick, quickly, rapidly, readily, snappily, speedily, swift, swiftly; abruptly, presto, suddenly, unexpectedly; hastily, impetuously, impulsively, rashly, recklessly; exactly, opportunely, punctually, seasonably
***phrases*** at once, on the line, on the spot
***near ant*** slowly; late, tardily

**immense** *adj* unusually large — see HUGE

**immenseness** *n* the quality or state of being very large — see IMMENSITY

**immensity** *n* the quality or state of being very large ⟨the *immensity* of the mountain was awe-inspiring, especially up close⟩
***syn*** enormity, enormousness, hugeness, immenseness, magnitude, massiveness, vastness
***rel*** bigness, extensiveness, greatness, largeness, voluminousness, weightiness; awesomeness, grandness, stupendousness; excessiveness, extravagance, extremeness, immoderacy
***near ant*** littleness, puniness, smallness; triviality, unimportance
***ant*** diminutiveness, minuteness, tininess

**immerse** *vb* **1** to hold the attention of — see ENGAGE 1
**2** to sink or push (something) briefly into or as if into a liquid — see DIP 1

**immersed** *adj* having the mind fixed on something — see ATTENTIVE

**immersing** *adj* holding the attention or provoking interest — see INTERESTING

**immersion** *n* a focusing of the mind on something — see ATTENTION 1

**immigrant** *n* one that leaves one place to settle in another — see EMIGRANT

**imminent** *adj* **1** giving signs of immediate occurrence ⟨a storm is *imminent*, so you should seek shelter now⟩
***syn*** impending, pending, threatening
***rel*** approaching, coming, forthcoming, future, near, nearing, oncoming, upcoming; brewing, gathering; likely, possible, probable; inevitable, unavoidable; menacing, ominous, portentous; anticipated, awaited, expected, foreseen, predicted
***near ant*** distant, far-off, remote; eventual, ultimate; bygone, former, past; late, recent
**2** being soon to appear or take place — see FORTHCOMING

**immobile** *adj* **1** fixed in a place or position — see STATIONARY 1
**2** incapable of moving or being moved — see IMMOVABLE 1

**immobilize** *vb* to render powerless, ineffective, or unable to move — see PARALYZE

**immoderate** *adj* going beyond a normal or acceptable limit in degree or amount — see EXCESSIVE

**immodest** *adj* showing a lack of proper social reserve or modesty — see PRESUMPTUOUS 1

**immolate** *vb* to give up as an offering to a god — see SACRIFICE

**immolation** *n* something offered to a god — see SACRIFICE

**immoral** *adj* **1** not conforming to a high moral standard; morally unacceptable — see BAD 2
**2** not guided by or showing a concern for what is right — see UNPRINCIPLED

**immorality** *n* **1** immoral conduct or practices harmful or offensive to society — see VICE 1
**2** that which is morally unacceptable — see EVIL

**immortal** *adj* lasting forever — see EVERLASTING

**immortality** *n* unending existence after death — see ETERNITY 2

**immortalize** *vb* to give eternal or lasting existence to — see PERPETUATE

**immovable** *adj* **1** incapable of moving or being moved ⟨that boulder is *immovable,* even with a bulldozer⟩
*syn* immobile, irremovable, nonmotile, nonmoving, unbudging, unmovable
*rel* motionless, moveless, static, stationary, still, unmoving; fast, fixed, rooted, steadfast, stuck, wedged
*near ant* portable, removable, transferable, transportable
*ant* mobile, motile, movable (*or* moveable), moving
**2** sticking to an opinion, purpose, or course of action in spite of reason, arguments, or persuasion — see OBSTINATE

**immunity** *n* freedom from punishment, harm, or loss — see IMPUNITY

**immure** *vb* **1** to close or shut in by or as if by barriers — see ENCLOSE 1
**2** to put in or as if in prison — see IMPRISON

**immurement** *n* the act of confining or the state of being confined — see INTERNMENT

**immutability** *n* the state of continuing without change — see CONSTANCY 1

**immutable** *adj* not capable of changing or being changed — see INFLEXIBLE 1

**imp** *n* **1** an appealingly mischievous person — see SCAMP 1
**2** an evil spirit — see DEMON

**impact** *n* **1** a forceful coming together of two things ⟨the glass shattered on *impact* with the floor⟩
*syn* bump, collision, concussion, crash, jar, jolt, shock, smash, strike, wallop
*rel* blow, buffet, hit, knock, punch, rap, slap, thump; bashing, battering, bludgeoning, clobbering, hammering, lambasting, licking, pounding, pummelling, thrashing; contact, encounter, meeting, touch
**2** the power to bring about a result on another — see EFFECT 2
**3** the quality of an utterance that provokes interest and produces an effect — see [1]PUNCH 1

**impact** *vb* **1** to act upon (a person or a person's feelings) so as to cause a response — see [1]AFFECT 1
**2** to come into usually forceful contact with something — see HIT 2

**impair** *vb* to reduce the soundness, effectiveness, or perfection of — see DAMAGE 1

**impale** *vb* to penetrate or hold (something) with a pointed object ⟨*impale* a marshmallow or two on that stick and let's start toasting⟩
*syn* gore, harpoon, lance, pierce, puncture, skewer, spear, spike, stab, stick, transfix
*rel* spindle; perforate; jab, poke, prick, punch, thrust; cut, knife, slice

*syn* synonym(s) *rel* related words
*ant* antonym(s) *near ant* near antonym(s)

**impalpable** *adj* **1** not capable of being perceived by the sense of touch — see INTANGIBLE
**2** not perceptible by a sense or by the mind — see IMPERCEPTIBLE

**impart** *vb* to cause (something) to pass from one to another — see COMMUNICATE 1

**impartial** *adj* marked by justice, honesty, and freedom from bias — see FAIR 2

**impartiality** *n* lack of favoritism toward one side or another — see DETACHMENT 1

**impassable** *adj* impossible to get through or into — see IMPENETRABLE 1

**impasse** *n* a point in a struggle where neither side is capable of winning or willing to give in ⟨if we cannot ever agree on which movie to see tonight, we are at an *impasse*⟩
*syn* deadlock, halt, stalemate, standstill
*rel* dead end; bottleneck, corner, dilemma, fix, hole, jam, pickle, pinch, plight, predicament, quagmire, quandary, spot; difficulty; problem

**impassioned** *adj* having or expressing great depth of feeling — see FERVENT

**impassive** *adj* **1** not feeling or showing emotion ⟨she remained *impassive* as they told her the bad news⟩
*syn* apathetic, cold-blooded, phlegmatic, stoic (*or* stoical), stolid, undemonstrative, unemotional
*rel* cold, cool, dispassionate, unmoved; calm, collected, composed; imperturable, unflappable; reserved, reticent, taciturn; blank, deadpan, dry, empty, expressionless, inexpressive, vacant, wooden; enigmatic (*also* enigmatical), impenetrable, inscrutable; aloof, detached, unconcerned, unsentimental; impersonal, objective, unresponsive; hardhearted, pitiless, unfeeling; inconsiderate, thoughtless
*near ant* blazing, burning, fiery, flaming, glowing, red-hot; ardent, enthusiastic, gung ho, zealous; gushing, maudlin, mawkish, mushy, sentimental; dramatic, histrionic, melodramatic; compassionate, responsive, sympathetic; reactive, sensitive
*ant* demonstrative, emotional, fervent, fervid, hot-blooded, impassioned, passionate
**2** not expressing any emotion — see BLANK 1

**impassivity** *n* a lack of emotion or emotional expressiveness — see APATHY 1

**impatience** *n* urgent desire or interest — see EAGERNESS

**impatient** *adj* **1** showing urgent desire or interest — see EAGER
**2** unable or unwilling to endure — see INTOLERANT 1

**impeach** *vb* to make a claim of wrongdoing against — see ACCUSE

**impeccability** *n* the quality or state of being free from guilt or blame — see INNOCENCE 1

**impeccable** *adj* **1** being entirely without fault or flaw — see PERFECT 1

2 free from guilt or blame — see INNOCENT 2

**impeccably** *adv* without any flaws or errors — see PERFECTLY 1

**impecunious** *adj* lacking money or material possessions — see POOR 1

**impecuniousness** *n* the state of lacking sufficient money or material possessions — see POVERTY 1

**impede** *vb* to create difficulty for the work or activity of — see HAMPER

**impediment** *n* something that makes movement or progress more difficult — see ENCUMBRANCE

**impel** *vb* to set or keep in motion — see MOVE 2

**impend** *vb* to be about to happen — see LOOM

**impend** (over) *vb* to remain poised to inflict harm, danger, or distress on — see THREATEN

**impending** *adj* 1 being soon to appear or take place — see FORTHCOMING
2 giving signs of immediate occurrence — see IMMINENT 1

**impenetrable** *adj* 1 impossible to get through or into ⟨the ancient temple was surrounded by vast stretches of *impenetrable* jungle⟩
***syn*** impassable, impermeable, impervious
***rel*** close, compact, dense, thick; compressed, condensed; sturdy, substantial, tough; firm, frozen, hard, solid, stiff; inflexible, rigid, unbending, unyielding
***near ant*** soft, squishy; bendable, elastic, flexible, giving, malleable, pliable, yielding; absorbent, porous
***ant*** negotiable, passable, penetrable, permeable
2 being beyond one's powers to know, understand, or explain — see MYSTERIOUS 1
3 impossible to understand — see INCOMPREHENSIBLE
4 not allowing penetration (as by gas, liquid, or light) — see TIGHT 1

**impenitent** *adj* not sorry for having done wrong — see REMORSELESS

**imperative** *adj* 1 forcing one's compliance or participation by or as if by law — see MANDATORY
2 impossible to do without — see ESSENTIAL 1
3 needing immediate attention — see ACUTE 2

**imperceptible** *adj* not perceptible by a sense or by the mind ⟨a slight difference in hue between the two glasses that's *imperceptible* unless they're placed side by side⟩
***syn*** impalpable, inappreciable, indistinguishable, insensible
***rel*** inaudible, intangible, invisible; inconspicuous, indistinct, unnoticeable, unseeable, unseen; faint, insignificant, slight, trivial; buried, concealed, covert, disguised, hidden, obscure, shrouded, unapparent, vague
***near ant*** audible, observable, tangible, visible; clear, conspicuous, evident, eye-catching, manifest, noticeable, obvious, plain, prominent, striking; apparent, distinct, significant, straightforward
***ant*** appreciable, discernible, palpable, perceptible, sensible

**imperfect** *adj* having a fault — see FAULTY

**imperfection** *n* something that spoils the appearance or completeness of a thing — see BLEMISH

**imperil** *vb* to place in danger — see ENDANGER

**imperilment** *n* the state of not being protected from injury, harm, or evil — see DANGER 1

**imperious** *adj* 1 fond of ordering people around — see BOSSY
2 having a feeling of superiority that shows itself in an overbearing attitude — see ARROGANT
3 having or showing a tendency to force one's will on others without any regard to fairness or necessity — see ARBITRARY 1
4 needing immediate attention — see ACUTE 2

**imperiousness** *n* an exaggerated sense of one's importance that shows itself in the making of excessive or unjustified claims — see ARROGANCE

**imperishable** *adj* impossible to destroy — see INDESTRUCTIBLE

**impermanent** *adj* 1 intended to last, continue, or serve for a limited time — see TEMPORARY 1
2 lasting only for a short time — see MOMENTARY

**impermeable** *adj* 1 impossible to get through or into — see IMPENETRABLE 1
2 not allowing penetration (as by gas, liquid, or light) — see TIGHT 1

**impermissible** *adj* that may not be permitted ⟨chewing gum is an *impermissible* activity in school⟩
***syn*** banned, barred, forbidden, interdicted, outlawed, prohibited, proscribed, taboo (*also* tabu)
***rel*** intolerable, unacceptable, unbearable, unendurable; illegal, illegitimate, illicit, improper, inappropriate, unadvisable, unauthorized, unlawful, unlicensed, unmentionable; unseemly, unsuitable; objectionable; disallowed, disapproved, discouraged; refused, rejected, revoked, unsanctioned, vetoed; repressed, suppressed; precluded, prevented, stopped; excluded, ruled out, shut out; blocked, hindered, impeded, obstructed
***near ant*** acceptable, bearable, endurable, tolerable; accepted, accredited, allowed, appropriate, approved, authorized, certified, endorsed, lawful, legal, legitimate, licensed (*also* licenced), OK (*or* okay), permitted, warranted; accorded, granted, sanctioned, vouchsafed; brooked, condoned, countenanced; encouraged, promoted, supported; commanded, mandatory, ordered, required; proper, seemly, suitable, tolerated, unobjectionable

*ant* allowable, licensable, permissible, permissive, sufferable

**impersonate** *vb* **1** to pretend to be (what one is not) in appearance or behavior ⟨a school intruder was caught trying to *impersonate* a teacher⟩
*syn* masquerade (as), play, pose (as)
*rel* ape, copy, imitate, mime, mimic, mock, parody, travesty; act, perform, portray
**2** to present a portrayal or performance of — see ACT 1

**impersonator** *n* **1** a person who imitates another's voice and mannerisms for comic effect — see MIMIC
**2** one who acts professionally (as in a play, movie, or television show) — see ACTOR

**impertinence** *n* **1** disrespectful or argumentative talk given in response to a command or request — see BACK TALK
**2** rude behavior — see DISCOURTESY

**impertinent** *adj* **1** displaying or marked by rude boldness — see NERVY 1
**2** showing a lack of manners or consideration for others — see IMPOLITE

**imperturbability** *n* evenness of emotions or temper — see EQUANIMITY

**imperturbable** *adj* not easily panicked or upset — see UNFLAPPABLE

**impervious** *adj* **1** not allowing penetration (as by gas, liquid, or light) — see TIGHT 1
**2** impossible to get through or into — see IMPENETRABLE 1

**impetus** *n* something that arouses action or activity — see IMPULSE

**impiety** *n* an act of great disrespect shown to God or to sacred ideas, people, or things — see BLASPHEMY

**impinge** *vb* to come into usually forceful contact with something — see HIT 2

**impious** *adj* not showing proper reverence for the holy or sacred — see IRREVERENT

**impish** *adj* tending to or exhibiting reckless playfulness — see MISCHIEVOUS 1

**impishness** *n* **1** a natural disposition for playful behavior — see PLAYFULNESS
**2** playful, reckless behavior that is not intended to cause serious harm — see MISCHIEF 1

**implacable** *adj* **1** sticking to an opinion, purpose, or course of action in spite of reason, arguments, or persuasion — see OBSTINATE
**2** showing no signs of slackening or yielding in one's purpose — see UNYIELDING 1

**implant** *vb* to set solidly in or as if in surrounding matter — see ENTRENCH

**implausible** *adj* too extraordinary or improbable to believe — see INCREDIBLE

**implement** *n* an article intended for use in work ⟨gardening *implements* such as hoes, spades, and pruners⟩
*syn* device, instrument, tool, utensil
*rel* apparatus, appliance, mechanism; contraption, contrivance, gadget, gizmo (*or* gismo), jigger

**implement** *vb* to carry out effectively — see ENFORCE

**implementation** *n* the doing of an action — see COMMISSION 2

**implicit** *adj* understood although not put into words ⟨the *implicit* agreement in the outing club is that every member pays his or her own way on all trips⟩
*syn* implied, tacit, unexpressed, unspoken, unvoiced, wordless
*rel* inferred; unannounced, undeclared, unsaid, untold; hinted, intimated, suggested
*near ant* apparent, blatant, evident, obvious, plain, straightforward; unambiguous, unequivocal, unmistakable
*ant* explicit, express, expressed, spoken, stated

**implied** *adj* understood although not put into words — see IMPLICIT

**implore** *vb* to make a request to (someone) in an earnest or urgent manner — see BEG

**imploring** *adj* asking humbly — see SUPPLIANT

**imply** *vb* to convey an idea indirectly — see HINT

**impolite** *adj* showing a lack of manners or consideration for others ⟨the librarian was shocked that anyone could be so *impolite* as to continue talking despite repeated warnings to be quiet⟩
*syn* discourteous, ill-bred, ill-mannered, impertinent, inconsiderate, rude, thoughtless, uncalled-for, uncivil, ungracious, unmannerly
*rel* audacious, bold, bold-faced, brash, brassy, disrespectful, impudent, insolent, saucy, shameless; boorish, churlish, clownish, loutish, uncouth, vulgar; undiplomatic, unsportsmanlike; abrupt, blunt, brusque, crusty, curt, gruff, sharp, snippy; antisocial, crabbed, cross, disagreeable, grumpy, sullen, surly; improper, inappropriate, incorrect, indecent, indecorous, unseemly; arrogant, conceited, presumptuous, pretentious
*near ant* humble, meek, modest, unassertive; deferential, dutiful, respectful, submissive, yielding; acceptable, appropriate, becoming, befitting, correct, decent, decorous, fit, fitting, good, meet, proper, respectable, right, seemly, suitable; affable, cordial, friendly, genial, hospitable, sociable; felicitous, graceful
*ant* civil, considerate, courteous, genteel, gracious, mannerly, polite, thoughtful, well-bred

**impoliteness** *n* rude behavior — see DISCOURTESY

**import** *n* **1** the quality or state of being important — see IMPORTANCE
**2** the idea that is conveyed or intended to be conveyed to the mind by language, symbol, or action — see MEANING 1

**import** *vb* **1** to be of importance — see MATTER

---

*syn* synonym(s) *rel* related words
*ant* antonym(s) *near ant* near antonym(s)

2 to communicate or convey (as an idea) to the mind — see MEAN 1

**importance** *n* the quality or state of being important ⟨a final exam has great *importance*⟩
*syn* consequence, import, magnitude, moment, significance, weight, weightiness
*rel* celebrity, distinction, eminence, fame, note, noteworthiness, notoriety, preeminence, prominence, renown; store, substance, value, worth, worthiness; gravity, seriousness; authority, potency, power; mark, name, report, reputation, repute; cachet, position, prestige, rank, standing, stature; glory, greatness, honor, illustriousness
*near ant* paltriness, pettiness, worthlessness; disgrace, dishonor, disrepute, ignominy, odium, opprobrium, shame; anonymity; obscurity
*ant* insignificance, littleness, slightness, smallness, triviality, unimportance

**important** *adj* 1 having great meaning or lasting effect ⟨the discovery of penicillin was a very *important* event in the history of medicine⟩
*syn* big, consequential, eventful, major, material, meaningful, momentous, significant, substantial, weighty
*rel* decisive, fatal, fateful, strategic; earnest, grave, serious, sincere; distinctive, exceptional, impressive, outstanding, prominent, remarkable; valuable, worthwhile, worthy; distinguished, eminent, great, illustrious, preeminent, prestigious; famous, notorious, renowned; all-important, critical, crucial
*near ant* inconsiderable, minor, paltry, petty, worthless; anonymous, nameless, obscure, uncelebrated, unknown
*ant* insignificant, little, minor, slight, small, trivial, unimportant
2 having great power or influence ⟨Rachel Carson was an *important* figure in the environmental movement⟩
*syn* influential, mighty, potent, powerful, puissant, significant, strong
*rel* high-level, senior, top; able, capable, competent, effective, efficient; authoritarian, autocratic, despotic, dictatorial, magisterial, tyrannical (*also* tyrannic); distinguished, dominant, eminent, famous, great, illustrious, notorious, preeminent, prestigious, renowned; dynamic, energetic, forceful, robust, sturdy, tough, vigorous
*near ant* feeble, flimsy, frail, infirm; anonymous, obscure; incapable, incompetent, ineffective, inept, unfit, useless
*ant* impotent, insignificant, little, powerless, unimportant, weak
3 having a feeling of superiority that shows itself in an overbearing attitude — see ARROGANT
4 having too high an opinion of oneself — see CONCEITED

**importune** *vb* to make a request to (someone) in an earnest or urgent manner — see BEG

**impose** *vb* to establish or apply as a charge or penalty ⟨every town *imposes* a fine for speeding⟩
*syn* assess, charge, exact, fine, lay, levy, put
*rel* dock, mulct, penalize, tax; extort, shake down, wrest, wring; bleed, fleece, gouge, milk, skin, squeeze; coerce, compel, force; inflict, wreak; set; reapply, reimpose, relay
*near ant* abate, diminish, lessen; forgive, release
*ant* remit

**impose** (on *or* upon) *vb* to take unfair advantage of — see EXPLOIT 1

**imposing** *adj* 1 having or showing a serious and reserved manner — see DIGNIFIED
2 large and impressive in size, grandeur, extent, or conception — see GRAND 1

**imposition** *n* a charge usually of money collected by the government from people or businesses for public use — see TAX

**impossible** *adj* incapable of being solved or accomplished ⟨the seemingly *impossible* problem of world hunger⟩ ⟨fitting everything in my backpack seemed an *impossible* task⟩
*syn* hopeless, unachievable, unattainable, unsolvable
*rel* impracticable, impractical; doubtful, dubious, far-fetched, improbable, unlikely; implausible, inconceivable, incredible, unbelievable, unthinkable; futile, useless; absurd, fantastic, outlandish, preposterous, ridiculous
*near ant* practicable, practical, reasonable; likely, probable; acceptable, believable, conceivable, credible, plausible
*ant* achievable, attainable, doable, feasible, possible, realizable, workable

**impost** *n* a charge usually of money collected by the government from people or businesses for public use — see TAX

**impostor** *or* **imposter** *n* one who makes false claims of identity or expertise ⟨the man who claimed to be a prince turned out to be an *impostor*⟩
*syn* charlatan, fake, faker, fraud, hoaxer, humbug, mountebank, phony (*also* phoney), pretender, quack
*rel* imitator, impersonator, mimic; actor, bluffer, counterfeiter, deceiver, dissembler, duper, feigner, misleader, trickster; poseur
*near ant* adept, expert, master, professional, virtuoso, whiz, wizard

**impotence** *n* the lack of sufficient ability, power, or means — see INABILITY

**impotent** *adj* 1 not able to produce fruit or offspring — see STERILE 1
2 unable to act or achieve one's purpose — see POWERLESS

**impoverished** *adj* 1 lacking money or material possessions — see POOR 1
2 producing inferior or only a small amount of vegetation — see BARREN 1

**impoverishment** *n* the state of lacking sufficient money or material possessions — see POVERTY 1

**impracticable** *adj* not capable of being put to use or account — see IMPRACTICAL

**impractical** *adj* not capable of being put to use or account ⟨the flimsy little toy shovel was cute, but completely *impractical* for digging up tree stumps⟩
*syn* impracticable, inoperable, nonpractical, unusable, unworkable, useless
*rel* unsuitable; inaccessible, unattainable, unavailable, unobtainable, unreachable; dead, dormant, fallow, free, idle, inactive, inert, inoperative, latent; arrested, interrupted, suspended; unrealistic
*near ant* accessible, available, obtainable, reachable; all-around (*also* all-round), handy; active, alive, busy, employed, functioning, operating, operative, running, working
*ant* applicable, feasible, functional, operable, operational, practicable, practical, usable, useful, workable

**imprecate** *vb* to ask a divine power to send harm or evil upon — see CURSE 1

**imprecation** *n* a prayer that harm will come to someone — see CURSE 1

**imprecise** *adj* not precisely correct — see INEXACT 1

**impregnable** *adj* incapable of being defeated, overcome, or subdued — see INVINCIBLE

**impregnate** *vb* to wet thoroughly with liquid — see SOAK 1

**impress** *n* a perceptible trace left by pressure — see PRINT 1

**impress** *vb* **1** to act upon (a person or a person's feelings) so as to cause a response — see ¹AFFECT 1
**2** to produce a vivid impression of — see ENGRAVE 2

**impression** *n* **1** a perceptible trace left by pressure — see PRINT 1
**2** something imagined or pictured in the mind — see IDEA

**impressionist** *n* a person who imitates another's voice and mannerisms for comic effect — see MIMIC

**impressive** *adj* having the power to affect the feelings or sympathies — see MOVING

**imprimatur** *n* an acceptance of something as satisfactory — see APPROVAL 1

**imprint** *n* **1** a mark or series of marks left on a surface by something that has passed along it — see TRACK 1
**2** a perceptible trace left by pressure — see PRINT 1

**imprint** *vb* to produce a vivid impression of — see ENGRAVE 2

**imprison** *vb* to put in or as if in prison ⟨in this society, we try to *imprison* criminals so that they can't do any more harm⟩
*syn* commit, confine, immure, incarcerate, intern, jail, jug, lock (up)
*rel* constrain, limit, restrain, restrict, shut; apprehend, arrest, capture, catch, detain; impress, shanghai; hold, keep; enslave, subjugate
*near ant* emancipate, manumit
*ant* discharge, free, liberate, release

**imprisoned** *adj* taken and held prisoner — see CAPTIVE

**imprisonment** *n* the act of confining or the state of being confined — see INTERNMENT

**improbable** *adj* not likely to be true or to occur ⟨it is *improbable* that we will be allowed to stay out all night⟩
*syn* doubtful, dubious, far-fetched, flimsy, questionable, unapt, unlikely
*rel* implausible, impossible, inconceivable, incredible, last, unbelievable, unthinkable; absurd, outlandish, preposterous, ridiculous; outside, remote, slight
*near ant* believable, conceivable, credible, plausible; possible; liable
*ant* likely, probable

**impromptu** *adj* made or done without previous thought or preparation — see EXTEMPORANEOUS

**improper** *adj* not appropriate for a particular occasion or situation — see INAPPROPRIATE

**improperly** *adv* in a mistaken or inappropriate way — see WRONGLY

**impropriety** *n* **1** the quality or state of not being socially proper ⟨the *impropriety* of the song that the campers sang for the visitors was embarrassing⟩
*syn* inappropriateness, incorrectness, indecency, unfitness
*rel* coarseness, crudeness; imprudence, indiscretion
*near ant* discretion, prudence; etiquette
*ant* appropriateness, correctness, decency, decorousness, fitness, propriety, rightness, seemliness, suitability
**2** a socially improper or unsuitable act or remark ⟨such *improprieties* as asking people how much money they make⟩
*syn* familiarity, gaffe, indiscretion, solecism
*rel* blunder, error, flub, fumble, goof, lapse, miscue, misstep, mistake, slip, slipup, stumble; discourtesy, incivility, offense (*or* offence); boner, howler, screamer; foul-up, muff; misapprehension, miscalculation, misconception, misjudgment, misstatement, misunderstanding
*near ant* manners, proprieties
*ant* amenity, civility, courtesy, formality, gesture

**improve** *vb* to make better ⟨a little salt would *improve* this bland food⟩
*syn* ameliorate, amend, better, enhance, enrich, meliorate, perfect, refine
*rel* correct, emend, rectify, reform, remedy; help; edit, revise; upgrade; fortify, intensify, strengthen; retouch, touch up
*near ant* damage, harm, hurt, impair, injure, spoil, tarnish; blemish, blight, deface, disfigure, flaw, mar; diminish, lessen, lower, reduce
*ant* worsen

**improved** *adj* being far along in development — see ADVANCED 1

**improvement** *n* an instance of notable progress in the development of knowledge, technology, or skill — see ADVANCE 2

**improvident** *adj* not thinking about and providing for the future ⟨the *improvident* view that the wearing away of the ozone layer need not concern us⟩
*syn* myopic, shortsighted
*rel* careless, heedless, imprudent incautious, injudicious, unwise; extravagant, prodigal, profligate, spendthrift, thriftless, unthrifty; indulgent, lavish, reckless, wasteful
*near ant* careful, judicious, prudent, sensible, wise; economical, economizing, frugal, scrimping, sparing, thrifty; conserving, preserving, saving
*ant* farsighted, forehanded, foreseeing, foresighted, forethoughtful, provident

**improvise** *vb* to perform, make or do without preparation ⟨since the award was a complete surprise, I *improvised* an acceptance speech⟩
*syn* ad-lib, extemporize
*rel* concoct, contrive, cook (up) devise, hatch, invent, make up, think up cobble (together *or* up), dash (off)
*near ant* arrange, prepare, ready; consider, contemplate, ponder, study think; practice (*or* practise), rehearse

**improvised** *adj* made or done without previous thought or preparation — see EXTEMPORANEOUS

**imprudent** *adj* showing poor judgment especially in personal relationships or social situations — see INDISCREET

**impudence** *n* **1** disrespectful or argumentative talk given in response to a command or request — see BACK TALK
**2** rude behavior — see DISCOURTESY

**impudent** *adj* displaying or marked by rude boldness — see NERVY 1

**impulse** *n* something that arouses action or activity ⟨the new auto factory was just the *impulse* that the local economy needed⟩
*syn* boost, encouragement, goad, impetus, incentive, incitement, instigation, momentum, motivation, provocation, spur, stimulant, stimulus, yeast
*rel* inducement, invitation; cause consideration, motive, reason

**impulsive** *adj* **1** caused by or suggestive of an irresistible urge — see COMPULSIVE
**2** prone to sudden illogical changes of mind, ideas, or actions — see WHIMSICAL

**impulsiveness** *n* an inclination to sudden illogical changes of mind, ideas, or actions — see WHIMSICALITY

**impunity** *n* freedom from punishment, harm, or loss ⟨she mistakenly believed that she could insult people with *impunity*⟩
*syn* exemption, immunity
*rel* armor, defense, guard, protection, safeguard, safety, security, shield; buffer, bumper, screen; absolution, absolving, dispensation, forgiveness
*near ant* exposure, liability, susceptibility, vulnerability

**impure** *adj* containing foreign or lower-grade substances ⟨be careful, because *impure* motor oil can damage your car's engine⟩
*syn* adulterated, alloyed, contaminated, dilute, diluted, polluted, tainted, thinned, weakened
*rel* befouled, besmirched, corrupted, debased, defiled, dirtied, fouled, soiled, spoiled, sullied; blended, commingled, incorporated, intermingled, intermixed, merged, mingled, mixed; coalesced, combined, compounded; cheapened, doctored
*near ant* clarified, filtered, purified, refined; neat, plain, straight; concentrated, strong; uncombined; pasteurized
*ant* pure, unadulterated, unalloyed, uncontaminated, undiluted, unpolluted, untainted

**impurity** *n* something that is or that makes impure ⟨*impurities* in the water made it cloudy⟩
*syn* adulterant, contaminant, defilement, pollutant
*rel* blot, blotch, spot, stain, taint; dirt, filth, grime; blemish, defect, disfigurement, fault, flaw; abnormality, imperfection, irregularity
*near ant* clarifier, filter, purifier, refiner; cleanliness, immaculateness, purity

**impute** *vb* to explain (something) as being the result of something else — see CREDIT 1

**in** *adj* **1** being in the latest or current fashion — see STYLISH
**2** enjoying widespread favor or approval — see POPULAR 1

**in** *adv* at, within, or to a short distance or time — see NEAR 1

**inability** *n* the lack of sufficient ability, power, or means ⟨the apparent *inability* of young children to sit still⟩
*syn* impotence, inadequacy, incapability, incapacity, incompetence, ineptitude, powerlessness
*rel* inaptitude; ineffectiveness, ineffectualness, inefficiency
*near ant* aptitude, bent, flair, talent; effectiveness, effectualness, efficaciousness, efficiency; fitness, suitability; power, strength
*ant* ability, adequacy, capability, capacity, competence, potency

**inaccessible** *adj* hard or impossible to get to or get at ⟨my pen is *inaccessible* now that it's fallen down the crack behind my desk⟩
*syn* inconvenient, unapproachable, unattainable, unavailable, unobtainable, unreachable, untouchable
*rel* distant, far, faraway, far-off, remote, removed; apart, hidden, isolated, out-of-the-way, secluded
*near ant* close, near, nearby

*ant* accessible, approachable, attainable, convenient, obtainable, reachable

**inaccuracy** *n* an unintentional departure from truth or accuracy — see ERROR 1

**inaccurate** *adj* **1** not being in agreement with what is true — see FALSE 1
**2** not precisely correct — see INEXACT 1

**inaccurately** *adv* in a mistaken or inappropriate way — see WRONGLY

**inaction** *n* lack of action or activity ⟨as a result of the park department's *inaction*, the city's pools are not ready to open for the summer⟩
*syn* dormancy, idleness, inactivity, inertness, nonaction, quiescence
*rel* indolence, languor, lassitude, laziness, lethargy, listlessness, sleepiness, sloth, sluggishness
*near ant* animateness, briskness, liveliness, sprightliness; business, diligence, employment, industriousness, occupation
*ant* action, activeness, activity

**inactive** *adj* **1** slow to move or act ⟨it's easiest to catch snakes early in the morning, while they're still cold and *inactive*⟩
*syn* dull, inert, lethargic, quiescent, sleepy, sluggish, torpid
*rel* apathetic, indolent, languorous, lazy, lazyish, listless, slothful; dormant, inanimate, motionless, sedentary, static, still; dead; dopey, drugged
*near ant* busy, engaged, occupied, working; animated, dynamic, energetic, lively, sprightly, vigorous; assiduous, diligent, hardworking, industrious
*ant* active
**2** not being in a state of use, activity, or employment ⟨an *inactive* oil well⟩
*syn* dead, dormant, fallow, free, idle, inert, inoperative, latent, off, vacant
*rel* arrested, interrupted, suspended; asleep, lifeless, quiescent, sleepy; inoperable, unusable, unworkable, useless; dead, dull, slow
*phrases* out of commission
*near ant* functional, operable, operational, workable; assiduous, industrious; energetic, vigorous; feasible, practical, usable, useful, viable
*ant* active, alive, busy, employed, functioning, on, operating, operative, running, working

**inactivity** *n* **1** lack of action or activity — see INACTION
**2** lack of use — see DISUSE

**inadequacy** *n* **1** a falling short of an essential or desirable amount or number — see DEFICIENCY
**2** the lack of sufficient ability, power, or means — see INABILITY

**inadequate** *adj* not coming up to a usual standard or meeting a particular need — see SHORT 3

**inadequately** *adv* in an unsatisfactory way — see BADLY

**inadvertent** *adj* happening by chance — see ACCIDENTAL

---

*syn* synonym(s) *rel* related words
*ant* antonym(s) *near ant* near antonym(s)

**inadvisable** *adj* showing poor judgment especially in personal relationships or social situations — see INDISCREET

**inane** *adj* having no meaning — see MEANINGLESS

**inanity** *n* **1** a foolish act or idea — see FOLLY 1
**2** lack of good sense or judgment — see FOOLISHNESS 1

**inapplicability** *n* the quality or state of not having anything to do with the matter at hand — see IRRELEVANCE

**inapplicable** *adj* not having anything to do with the matter at hand — see IRRELEVANT

**inappreciable** *adj* not perceptible by a sense or by the mind — see IMPERCEPTIBLE

**inappropriate** *adj* not appropriate for a particular occasion or situation ⟨a bathing suit is *inappropriate* dress for strolling the streets of this seaside village⟩
*syn* graceless, improper, inapt, incongruous, incorrect, indecorous, inept, infelicitous, unapt, unbecoming, unfit, unhappy, unseemly, unsuitable, wrong
*rel* inopportune, unfortunate, unseasonable, untimely; immaterial, irrelevant; incompatible, uncongenial, unharmonious; bad, naughty, sinful; blamable, blameworthy, censurable; banned, barred, disallowed; forbidden, interdicted, outlawed, prohibited, proscribed; awkward, gauche, ungraceful; unacceptable, unsatisfactory
*near ant* fortunate, opportune, seasonable, timely; apt, material, relevant; compatible, congenial, harmonious; allowed, authorized, permitted; approved, endorsed, licensed (*also* licenced), sanctioned; abetted, encouraged, promoted, supported; acceptable, adequate, satisfactory; commendable, creditable, exemplary; blameless, irreproachable
*ant* appropriate, becoming, befitting, correct, decorous, felicitous, fit, fitting, genteel, happy, meet, proper, right, seemly, suitable

**inappropriately** *adv* in a mistaken or inappropriate way — see WRONGLY

**inappropriateness** *n* **1** the quality or state of being unsuitable or unfitting ⟨I cannot even begin to describe the *inappropriateness* of such language for the dinner table⟩
*syn* inaptness, incorrectness, infelicity, unfitness, wrongness
*rel* inadmissibility, inapplicability, extraneousness, inadequacy, irrelevance, meaninglessness, pointlessness, senselessness; inauspiciousness, intolerability, undesirability, undesirableness, unsatisfactorability, uselessness
*near ant* admissibility, applicability, bearing, connection, materiality, pertinence, pointedness, relevance
*ant* appropriateness, aptness, correctness, felicitousness, felicity, fitness, fittingness, rightness, seemliness, suitability, suitableness

2 the quality or state of not being socially proper — see IMPROPRIETY 1

**inapt** *adj* not appropriate for a particular occasion or situation — see INAPPROPRIATE

**inaptly** *adv* in a mistaken or inappropriate way — see WRONGLY

**inaptness** *n* the quality or state of being unsuitable or unfitting — see INAPPROPRIATENESS 1

**inarticulate** *adj* unable to speak — see INAPPROMUTE 1

**inasmuch as** *conj* for the reason that — see SINCE

**inaugural** *adj* coming first in time or order — see FIRST 1

**inaugural** *n* the process or ceremony of being formally placed in an office or organization — see INSTALLATION 1

**inaugurate** *vb* 1 to be responsible for the creation or establishment of — see FOUND 1
2 to put into operation or use of — see INSTALL 1
2 to welcome into an office or organization with special ceremonies — see INSTALL 1

**inauguration** *n* the process or an instance of being formally placed in an office or organization — see INSTALLATION 1

**inaugurator** *n* a person who establishes a new field of endeavor — see FAIR 2

**inauspicious** *adj* being or showing a sign of evil or calamity to come — see OMINOUS

**inauthentic** *adj* being such in appearance only and made or manufactured with the intention of committing fraud — see INTERFEIT

**inborn** *adj* 1 being a part of the innermost nature of a person or thing — see INHERENT
2 genetically passed or capable of being passed from parent to offspring — see HEREDITARY

**inbred** *adj* being a part of the innermost nature of a person or thing — see INHERENT

**incandescence** *n* the steady giving off of the form of radiation that makes vision possible — see LIGHT 1

**incandescent** *adj* giving off or reflecting much light — see BRIGHT 1

**incantation** *n* a spoken word or set of words believed to have magic power — see SPELL 1

**incapability** *n* the lack of sufficient ability, power, or means — see INABILITY

**incapable** *adj* lacking qualities (as knowledge, skill, or ability) required to do a job — see INCOMPETENT

**incapacitate** *vb* to render powerless, ineffective, or unable to move — see PARALYZE

**incapacitated** *adj* deprived of the power to perform one or more natural bodily activities — see DISABLED

**incapacity** *n* the lack of sufficient ability, power, or means — see INABILITY

**incarcerate** *vb* to put in or as if in prison — see IMPRISON

**incarcerated** *adj* taken and held prisoner — see CAPTIVE

**incarceration** *n* the act of confining or the state of being confined — see INTERNMENT

**incarnate** *vb* to represent in visible form — see EMBODY 2

**incarnation** *n* a visible representation of something abstract (as a quality) — see EMBODIMENT

**incautious** *adj* not paying or showing close attention especially for the purpose of avoiding trouble — see CARELESS 1

**incautiousness** *n* failure to take the care that a cautious person usually takes — see NEGLIGENCE 1

**incendiary** *n* 1 a person who deliberately and unlawfully sets fire to a building or other property — see ARSONIST
2 a person who stirs up public feelings especially of discontent — see AGITATOR

**incense** *n* a sweet or pleasant smell — see FRAGRANCE

**incense** *vb* to make angry — see ANGER

**incensed** *adj* feeling or showing anger — see ANGRY

**incentive** *n* something that arouses action or activity — see IMPULSE

**inception** *n* the point at which something begins — see BEGINNING

**incertitude** *n* a feeling or attitude that one does not know the truth, truthfulness, or trustworthiness of someone or something — see DOUBT

**incessant** *adj* going on and on without any interruptions — see CONTINUOUS

**incessantly** *adv* on every relevant occasion — see ALWAYS 1

**inch** *n* 1 a very small distance or degree — see HAIR 1
2 an individual part of a process, series, or ranking — see DEGREE 1

**inch** *vb* 1 to advance gradually beyond the usual or desirable limits — see ENCROACH
2 to move slowly — see CRAWL 2

**incident** *n* something that happens — see EVENT 1

**incidental** *adj* happening by chance — see ACCIDENTAL

**incipiency** *n* the point at which something begins — see BEGINNING

**incise** *vb* 1 to cut (as letters or designs) on a hard surface — see ENGRAVE 1
2 to penetrate with a sharp edge (as a knife) — see CUT 1

**incision** *n* a long deep cut — see GASH

**incite** *vb* 1 to cause or encourage the development of ⟨the rock band's failure to show up *incited* a riot, as the crowd had waited for hours⟩
***syn*** abet, ferment, foment, instigate, provoke, raise, stir (up), whip (up)
***rel*** forward, foster, further, promote, sow, stimulate; set off, trigger; excite, galvanize, inflame, inspire, motivate, rouse; activate, energize, quicken, vitalize
***near ant*** check, curb, discourage, inhibit, restrain; calm, soothe, subdue, tranquilize (*also* tranquillize)

2 to rouse to stro[illegible]ing or a[illegible] see PROVOKE 1

**incitement** *n* 1 someth[illegible] at arous[illegible] strong response from [illegible] — see PROVOCATION 1

2 something that arouses action or activity — see IMPULSE

**inciter** *n* a person who stirs up public [illegible] ings especially of discontent — see [illegible] TATOR

**inciting** *adj* serving or likely to arouse [illegible] strong reaction — see PROVOCATIVE

**incivility** *n* rude behavior — see DISCOURTESY

**inclement** *adj* marked by wet and windy conditions — see FOUL 1

**inclination** *n* 1 a habitual attraction to some activity or thing ⟨her natural *inclination* to help people in need⟩

***syn*** bent, devices, disposition, genius, leaning, partiality, penchant, predilection, predisposition, proclivity, propensity, tendency, turn

***rel*** bias, prejudice; aptitude, faculty, flair, gift, knack, talent; addiction, fondness, liking; forte, speciality, specialty; convention, custom, habit, pattern, practice (*also* practise), routine, trick, way, wont; oddity, peculiarity, quirk, singularity

***near ant*** aversion, dislike, distaste; impartiality, neutrality, objectivity; apathy, disinterestedness, indifference

2 the act of positioning or an instance of being positioned at an angle — see TILT

3 the degree to which something rises up from a position level with the horizon — see SLANT

**incline** *n* the degree to which something rises up from a position level with the horizon — see SLANT

**incline** *vb* 1 to set or cause to be at an angle — see LEAN 1

2 to show a liking or p[illegible] something) — see LEAN 2

**inclined** *adj* 1 having a de[illegible] tion (as for a specified cou[illegible] of action) — see WILLING 1

2 having a liking or affection — see FOND 1

3 having a tendency to be or act in a certain way — see PRONE 1

4 running in a slanting direction — see DIAGONAL

**inclining** *adj* bending downward or forward — see NODDING

**include** *vb* to have as part of a whole ⟨the test *included* some hard essay questions⟩

***syn*** carry, comprehend, contain, embrace, encompass, entail, involve, number, take in

***rel*** comprise, consist (of); have, hold, own, possess; admit, receive; compose, constitute, form, make; assimilate, embody, incorporate, integrate

***near ant*** bar, debar, preclude, prevent, prohibit; deny, refuse, reject; eliminate, except, rule out; lose, mislay, misplace

***ant*** exclude, omit

**[illegible]usive** *adj* covering everything or all [illegible]ant points — see ENCYCLOPEDIC

**in[illegible]** *adj* not named or identified by a [illegible] — see NAMELESS 1

**incog[illegible]** *adj* 1 not clearly or logically [illegible] thriller's *incoherent* plot [illegible]nces wondering who did [illegible]

**[illegible]coh[illegible]erent** [illegible] disjointed, unconnected [illegible]

***rel*** bewil[illegible]ng, confounding, disordered, disorderly, [illegible] perplexing, confusing, [illegible] frustrating; fallacious, illogical, incoherent, [illegible] strange, unsound; absurd, [illegible]; meaningless, nonsensical, nutty, [illegible] ridiculous, senseless, silly; unconvincing, unsatisfying; inexplicable, [illegible] able, unexplainable

***near ant*** ordered, orderly, organized; [illegible] ical, rational, reasonable, sensible, so[illegible] sound, valid; cogent, compelling, [illegible] vincing, persuasive, plausible, satisfy[illegible] clear, lucid, perspicuous

***ant*** coherent, connected

2 consisting of particles that do n[illegible] together — see LOOSE 2

**incombustible** *adj* incapable of being burned ⟨we keep our important papers in an *incombustible* safe in the basement⟩

***syn*** fireproof, noncombustible, nonflammable, noninflammable, uninflammable

***rel*** nonexplosive

***near ant*** ablaze, afire, blazing, burning, fiery; consumable; explosive, incendiary, volcanic

***ant*** burnable, combustible, flammable, ignitable, inflammable

**income** *n* an increase usually measured in money that comes from labor, business, or property ⟨her summer job gave her some extra *income*⟩

***syn*** earnings, gain(s), proceeds, profit, return, revenue, yield

***rel*** killing, windfall; salary, tips, wages; capital, finances, funds, money

***near ant*** cost, expenditures, expenses, outgo, outlay

**incommode** *vb* to cause discomfort to or trouble for — see INCONVENIENCE

**incommoding** *adj* causing difficulty, discomfort, or annoyance — see INCONVENIENT 1

**incommunicable** *adj* beyond the power to describe — see INDESCRIBABLE

**incomparable** *adj* having no equal or rival for excellence or desirability — see ONLY 1

**incompatible** *adj* not being in agreement or harmony — see INCONSISTENT

**incompetence** *n* the lack of sufficient ability, power, or means — see INABILITY

---

***syn*** synonym(s) ***rel*** related words
***ant*** antonym(s) ***near ant*** near antonym(s)

**incompetent** *adj* lacking qualities (as knowledge, skill, or ability) required to do a job ⟨an *incompetent* carpenter had built the deck, and the railings were loose already⟩
*syn* incapable, inept, inexpert, unfit, unqualified, unskilled, unskillful
*rel* ineffective, ineffectual, inefficient; callow, green, inexperienced, raw; unequipped, unprepared, untrained; useless, worthless; ineligible; wanting
*near ant* prepared, ready, trained; experienced, practiced (*or* practised), seasoned, veteran
*ant* able, capable, competent, expert, fit, qualified, skilled, skillful

**incomplete** *adj* lacking some necessary part ⟨an *incomplete* puzzle that has several pieces missing⟩
*syn* deficient, fragmental, fragmentary, halfway, partial
*rel* broken, damaged, flawed, impaired, imperfect, injured, marred, spoiled; sketchy, uncompleted, unfinished
*near ant* flawless, perfect, unbroken, undamaged, unimpaired, uninjured, unmarred; completed, finished
*ant* complete, entire, full, intact, whole

**incompletely** *adv* in some measure or degree — see PARTLY

**incomprehensible** *adj* impossible to understand ⟨rocket science is *incomprehensible* to most people⟩
*syn* impenetrable, unfathomable, unintelligible
*rel* abstruse, enigmatic (*also* enigmatical), esoteric, inscrutable, recondite, cryptic, mysterious, obscure; unanswerable, unknowable; baffling, bewildering, confounding, confusing, mystifying, perplexing, puzzling
*near ant* basic, elementary, rudimentary; easy, simple; coherent, connected, ordered, orderly, organized; clear, cogent, compelling, convincing, lucid, perspicuous, plain, straightforward
*ant* fathomable, intelligible, understandable

**inconceivable** *adj* too extraordinary or improbable to believe — see INCREDIBLE

**incongruity** *n* someone or something with qualities or features that seem to conflict with one another — see CONTRADICTION 1

**incongruous** *adj* **1** not appropriate for a particular occasion or situation — see INAPPROPRIATE
**2** not being in agreement or harmony — see INCONSISTENT

**inconsequential** *adj* **1** lacking importance — see UNIMPORTANT
**2** so small or unimportant as to warrant little or no attention — see NEGLIGIBLE

**inconsiderable** *adj* **1** lacking importance — see UNIMPORTANT
**2** so small or unimportant as to warrant little or no attention — see NEGLIGIBLE 1

**inconsiderate** *adj* showing a lack of manners or consideration for others — see IMPOLITE

**inconsideration** *n* rude behavior — see DISCOURTESY

**inconsistent** *adj* not being in agreement or harmony ⟨*inconsistent* theories make it difficult to settle on one explanation⟩
*syn* clashing, conflicting, disagreeing, discordant, discrepant, incompatible, incongruous, inharmonious
*rel* irreconcilable; antagonistic, antithetical, contradictory, contrary, opposing, opposite
*near ant* akin, like, similar
*ant* agreeing, compatible, congruous, consistent, consonant, harmonious, nonconflicting

**inconsolable** *adj* feeling unhappiness — see SAD 1

**inconspicuous** *adj* not readily seen or noticed — see UNOBTRUSIVE

**inconstancy** *n* lack of faithfulness especially to one's husband or wife — see INFIDELITY 1

**inconstant** *adj* **1** likely to change frequently, suddenly, or unexpectedly — see FICKLE 1
**2** not true in one's allegiance to someone or something — see FAITHLESS

**incontestable** *adj* not capable of being challenged or proved wrong — see IREFUTABLE

**incontestably** *adv* without any question — see INDEED 1

**incontrovertible** *adj* not capable of being challenged or proved wrong — see IREFUTABLE

**incontrovertibly** *adv* without any question — see INDEED 1

**inconvenience** *n* something that is a source of irritation — see ANNOYANCE 3

**inconvenience** *vb* to cause discomfort to or trouble for ⟨he *inconvenienced* his sister by moving into her tiny apartment⟩
*syn* discommode, disoblige, disturb, incommode, trouble
*rel* burden, encumber, saddle, weigh; hamper, hamstring, hinder, hobble, impede; aggravate, anger, annoy, bother, bug, exasperate, gall, get, nettle, peeve, pique, put out, rile, vex; grate, inflame, provoke; agitate, perturb, upset
*near ant* aid, assist, help; ease, facilitate; appease, conciliate, mollify, pacify, placate; delight, gladden, gratify, please; comfort, console, content
*ant* accommodate, oblige

**inconvenient** *adj* **1** causing difficulty, discomfort, or annoyance ⟨the unexpected visitors showed up at an *inconvenient* time⟩
*syn* awkward, discommoding, disobliging, incommoding
*rel* bothersome, burdensome, onerous, troublesome; annoying, exasperating, irritating
*near ant* acceptable, bearable, tolerable; advantageous, desirable, good, helpful
*ant* convenient
**2** hard or impossible to get to or get at — see INACCESSIBLE

**incorporate** *vb* **1** to make a part of a body or system — see EMBODY 1
**2** to turn into a single mass that is more or less the same throughout — see BLEND 1
**incorporeal** *adj* not composed of matter — see IMMATERIAL 1
**incorrect** *adj* **1** having an opinion that does not agree with truth or the facts ⟨you're *incorrect* about the date of the final exam—it's next Tuesday, not Wednesday⟩
***syn*** mistaken, wrong
***rel*** confused, misguided, misled; erroneous, false; deceived, deluded, tricked
***phrases*** all wet, full of it
***near ant*** informed; accurate, exact, precise
***ant*** correct, right
**2** not appropriate for a particular occasion or situation — see INAPPROPRIATE
**3** not being in agreement with what is true — see FALSE 1
**incorrectly** *adv* in a mistaken or inappropriate way — see WRONGLY
**incorrectness** *n* **1** the quality or state of being unsuitable or unfitting — see INAPPROPRIATENESS 1
**2** the quality or state of not being socially proper — see IMPROPRIETY 1
**incorrigible** *adj* not capable of being cured or reformed — see HOPELESS 1
**increase** *n* **1** something added (as by growth) ⟨shortly after he turned 12, he had a sudden height *increase*⟩
***syn*** accretion, accrual, addendum, addition, augmentation, boost, expansion, gain, increment, plus, proliferation, raise, rise, supplement
***rel*** accumulation; complement; appendix, continuation, extension, uptrend, upturn; jump
***near ant*** deduction
***ant*** abatement, decrease, diminishment, lessening, lowering, reduction
**2** the act or process of becoming greater in number — see MULTIPLICATION
**increase** *vb* **1** to make greater in size, amount, or number ⟨if you *increase* the number by two, how much do you have now?⟩
***syn*** add (to), aggrandize, amplify, augment, boost, compound, enlarge, escalate, expand, extend, multiply, raise, swell, up
***rel*** skyrocket; blow up, dilate, distend, inflate; elongate, lengthen, prolong, protract; enhance, heighten, intensify, magnify; complement, supplement; beef (up), reinforce, strengthen; maximize; accumulate, amass, collect; follow up, parlay
***near ant*** abbreviate, abridge, curtail, shorten; compress, condense, constrict, cut back, retrench
***ant*** abate, contract, decrease, diminish, lessen, lower, reduce, subtract (from)
**2** to become greater in extent, volume, amount, or number ⟨the number of Internet users *increased* rapidly during the 1990s⟩
***syn*** accumulate, appreciate, balloon, build (up), burgeon, enlarge, escalate, expand, mount, multiply, mushroom, proliferate, rise, snowball, swell, wax
***rel*** rocket, skyrocket; heighten, intensify; blow up, distend, inflate; crest, peak, surge
***ant*** contract, decrease, diminish, lessen, wane
**increased** *adj* being at a higher level than average — see HIGH 2
**incredible** *adj* too extraordinary or improbable to believe ⟨she came in on Monday with an *incredible* story about monsters eating her homework⟩
***syn*** fantastic, implausible, inconceivable, unbelievable, unconvincing, unimaginable, unthinkable
***rel*** doubtful, dubious, far-fetched, fishy, flimsy, questionable, suspect, unlikely, unreasonable; hopeless, impossible; absurd, outlandish, preposterous, ridiculous; indefensible, insupportable, untenable
***near ant*** likely, possible, probable; reasonable
***ant*** believable, conceivable, convincing, credible, imaginable, plausible
**incredulity** *n* refusal to accept as true — see DISBELIEF
**incredulous** *adj* inclined to doubt or question claims — see SKEPTICAL 1
**increment** *n* something added (as by growth) — see INCREASE 1
**incremental** *adj* **1** proceeding or changing by steps or degrees — see GRADUAL
**2** produced by a series of additions of identical or similar things — see CUMULATIVE
**incriminate** *vb* to make a claim of wrongdoing against — see ACCUSE
**incubate** *vb* to cover and warm eggs to hatch them — see SET 1
**incubus** *n* an evil spirit — see DEMON
**inculcate** *vb* to cause (as a person) to become filled or saturated with a certain quality or principle — see INFUSE
**incumbent** *adj* forcing one's compliance or participation by or as if by law — see MANDATORY
**incurable** *adj* not capable of being cured or reformed — see HOPELESS 1
**incurious** *adj* having or showing a lack of interest or concern — see INDIFFERENT 1
**incursion** *n* a sudden attack on and entrance into hostile territory — see RAID 1
**indecency** *n* **1** the quality or state of being obscene — see OBSCENITY 1
**2** the quality or state of not being socially proper — see IMPROPRIETY 1
**indecent** *adj* depicting or referring to sexual matters in a way that is unacceptable in polite society — see OBSCENE 1
**indecision** *n* the act or an instance of pausing because of uncertainty about the right course of action — see HESITATION

**indecorous** *adj* not appropriate for a particular occasion or situation — see INAPPROPRIATE

**indeed** *interj* how surprising, doubtful, or unbelievable — see NO

**indeed** *adv* **1** without any question ⟨I know that you can *indeed* do better than that⟩
*syn* assuredly, certainly, definitely, doubtless, forsooth, incontestably, incontrovertibly, indisputably, really, surely, truly, undeniably, undoubtedly, unquestionably
*rel* conceivably, likely, perhaps, possibly, probably; clearly, obviously, unmistakably
*phrases* by all means, for sure
**2** not merely this but also — see EVEN

**indefatigable** *adj* showing no signs of weariness even after long hard effort — see TIRELESS

**indefatigably** *adv* with great effort or determination — see HARD 1

**indefensible** *adj* too bad to be excused or justified — see INEXCUSABLE

**indefinable** *adj* beyond the power to describe — see INDESCRIBABLE

**indefinite** *adj* **1** being or seeming to be without limits — see INFINITE
**2** not clearly expressed — see VAGUE 1
**3** not seen or understood clearly — see FAINT 1

**indelicacy** *n* the quality or state of lacking refinement or good taste — see VULGARITY 1

**indelicateness** *n* the quality or state of lacking refinement or good taste — see VULGARITY 1

**indemnification** *n* payment to another for a loss or injury — see COMPENSATION 1

**indemnify** *vb* to provide (someone) with a just payment for loss or injury — see COMPENSATE 1

**indemnity** *n* payment to another for a loss or injury — see COMPENSATION 1

**indentation** *n* **1** a sunken area forming a separate space — see HOLE 2
**2** a V-shaped cut usually on an edge or a surface — see NOTCH 1

**indented** *adj* curved inward — see HOLLOW

**independence** *n* **1** the ability to care for one's self — see SELF-SUFFICIENCY
**2** the state of being free from the control or power of another — see FREEDOM 1

**independent** *adj* **1** able to take care of oneself without outside help — see SELF-SUFFICIENT
**2** not being under the rule or control of another — see FREE 1

**independently** *adv* without aid or support — see ALONE 1

**in–depth** *adj* covering everything or all important points — see ENCYCLOPEDIC

**indescribable** *adj* beyond the power to describe ⟨the *indescribable* immensity of Mount Everest⟩
*syn* incommunicable, indefinable, ineffable, inexpressible, nameless, unspeakable, unutterable
*rel* inconceivable, incredible, unbelievable, unimaginable, unthinkable; characterless, featureless, nondescript
*near ant* conceivable, imaginable, thinkable
*ant* communicable, definable, expressible, speakable

**indestructible** *adj* impossible to destroy ⟨diamonds are widely considered to be *indestructible,* because they are one of the hardest known substances⟩
*syn* imperishable, inextinguishable
*rel* incorruptible; deathless, immortal, perpetual, undying; indelible; durable, enduring, lasting, permanent, unbreakable; strong, sturdy, tough
*near ant* mortal; impermanent, transient, transitory; breakable, delicate, flimsy, fragile, frail
*ant* destructible, extinguishable, perishable

**index** *n* an arrow-shaped piece on a dial or scale for registering information — see POINTER 1

**index** *vb* to put (someone or something) on a list — see [1]LIST 2

**Indian** *n* a member of any of the native peoples of the western hemisphere usually not including the Eskimos — see AMERICAN INDIAN

**indicate** *vb* to convey an idea indirectly — see HINT

**indication** *n* a slight or indirect pointing to something (as a solution or explanation) — see HINT 1

**indicative** *adj* indicating something ⟨a wide-eyed look that is *indicative* of his constant curiosity⟩
*syn* denotative, denoting, significant, signifying, telltale
*rel* alluding, allusive, referring; characteristic, symptomatic; demonstrative, exhibiting, expressive; symbolic (*also* symbolical); connoting, hinting, implying, insinuating, suggestive

**indicator** *n* an arrow-shaped piece on a dial or scale for registering information — see POINTER

**indict** *vb* to make a claim of wrongdoing against — see ACCUSE

**indictment** *n* a formal claim of criminal wrongdoing against a person — see CHARGE 1

**indifference** *n* lack of interest or concern ⟨he felt only *indifference* towards his schoolwork⟩
*syn* apathy, casualness, disinterestedness, disregard, insouciance, nonchalance, unconcern
*rel* halfheartedness, lukewarmness; carelessness, heedlessness, recklessness, unawareness; lethargy, listlessness; calmness, detachment, dispassion; callousness, hardheartedness, hardness, insensitivity; impassivity, phlegm; aloofness, coldness
*near ant* attentiveness, awareness, conscientiousness, heedfulness; sensitivity,

warmheartedness; bias, partiality, prejudice; ardor, fervency, passion, warmth, zeal
***ant*** concern, interest, regard

**indifferent** *adj* **1** having or showing a lack of interest or concern ⟨*indifferent* about the result of the football game⟩
***syn*** apathetic, casual, disinterested, incurious, insouciant, nonchalant, perfunctory, unconcerned, uncurious, uninterested
***rel*** halfhearted, lukewarm; aloof, cold, numb, remote, unemotional; calm, detached, dispassionate; careless, heedless, mindless; impassive, phlegmatic, stoic (*or* stoical), stolid; lethargic, listless; unawed, undazzled, unimpressed
***near ant*** attentive, aware, conscientious, heedful, mindful; caring, sensitive, warmhearted; ardent, fervent, passionate, warm, zealous
***ant*** concerned, interested
**2** of average to below average quality — see MEDIOCRE 1

**indigence** *n* the state of lacking sufficient money or material possessions — see POVERTY 1

**indigenous** *adj* belonging to a particular place by birth or origin — see NATIVE 1

**indigent** *adj* lacking money or material possessions — see POOR 1

**indignant** *adj* feeling or showing anger — see ANGRY

**indignation** *n* an intense emotional state of displeasure with someone or something — see ANGER

**indignity** *n* an act or expression showing scorn and usually intended to hurt another's feelings — see INSULT

**indirect** *adj* not straightforward or direct ⟨the cab driver took a very *indirect* route to the hotel⟩ ⟨a long-winded, *indirect* answer to a very simple question⟩
***syn*** circuitous, circular, roundabout
***rel*** crooked, serpentine, sinuous, tortuous, twisting, winding; meandering, rambling, wandering; circumlocutory, long-winded, prolix, verbose; deceitful, deceptive, devious, dishonest, duplicitous, insidious, misleading, sneaky, underhand, underhanded; calculating, crafty, cunning, subtle, tricky
***near ant*** candid, forthright, frank, honest, open, plain, unconcealed, undisguised
***ant*** direct, straight, straightforward

**indiscreet** *adj* showing poor judgment especially in personal relationships or social situations ⟨telling a friend's secrets is *indiscreet,* and unkind as well⟩
***syn*** ill-advised, imprudent, inadvisable, injudicious, tactless, unadvisable, unwise
***rel*** dumb, idiotic, moronic, stupid; inconsiderate, thoughtless; ill-mannered, improper, inappropriate, indecorous, unbecoming, uncivil, unseemly; foolish, harebrained, nonsensical, preposterous, senseless, silly
***near ant*** intelligent, logical, rational, sensible, smart, sound; appropriate, becoming, civil, decorous, proper, seemly; sage, sane, sapient
***ant*** advisable, discreet, judicious, prudent, tactful, wise

**indiscretion** *n* a socially improper or unsuitable act or remark — see IMPROPRIETY 2

**indispensable** *adj* impossible to do without — see ESSENTIAL 1

**indisposed** *adj* **1** having doubts about the wisdom of doing something — see HESITANT
**2** temporarily suffering from a disorder of the body — see SICK 1

**indisposition** *n* the condition of not being in good health — see SICKNESS 1

**indisputable** *adj* not capable of being challenged or proved wrong — see IRREFUTABLE

**indisputably** *adv* without any question — see INDEED 1

**indistinct** *adj* not seen or understood clearly — see FAINT 1

**indistinguishable** *adj* **1** not perceptible by a sense or by the mind — see IMPERCEPTIBLE
**2** not seen or understood clearly — see FAINT 1
**3** resembling another in every respect — see SAME 1

**individual** *adj* **1** of, relating to, or belonging to a single person ⟨everyone has his or her own *individual* opinion about the subject, but you will have to work together⟩
***syn*** individualized, particular, peculiar, personal, personalized, private, privy, separate, singular, unique
***rel*** characteristic, distinctive, intimate; identifying, idiosyncratic; special, specific; independent, nonconformist, self-directed, self-sufficient; custom, customized, specialized
***near ant*** broad, prevailing, prevalent, widespread; common, normal, regular, typical
***ant*** general, generic, popular, public, shared, universal
**2** not the same or shared — see SEPARATE 1
**3** serving to identify as belonging to an individual or group — see CHARACTERISTIC 1

**individual** *n* **1** a member of the human race — see HUMAN
**2** one that has a real and independent existence — see ENTITY

**individualist** *n* a person who does not conform to generally accepted standards or customs — see NONCONFORMIST 1

**individuality** *n* the set of qualities that make a person different from other people ⟨her *individuality* showed through in everything she did⟩
***syn*** character, identity, personality, selfhood, self-identity
***rel*** distinctiveness, oneness, peculiarity, separateness, singleness, singularity,

---

***syn*** synonym(s) ***rel*** related words
***ant*** antonym(s) ***near ant*** near antonym(s)

uniqueness; disposition, humor, nature, temper, temperament; independence
*near ant* conformity, conventionality

**individualized** *adj* of, relating to or belonging to a single person — see INDIVIDUAL 1

**indoctrinate** *vb* to cause to acquire knowledge or skill in some field — see TEACH

**indolence** *n* an inclination not to do work or engage in activities — see LAZINESS

**indolent** *adj* not easily aroused to action or work — see LAZY

**indomitable** *adj* incapable of being defeated, overcome, or subdued — see INVINCIBLE

**indubitable** *adj* not capable of being challenged or proved wrong — see IREFUTABLE

**induce** *vb* **1** to be the cause of (a situation, action, or state of mind) — see EFFECT
**2** to cause (someone) to agree with a belief or course of action by using arguments or earnest requests — see PERSUADE

**inducement** *n* the act of reasoning or pleading with someone to accept a belief or course of action — see PERSUASION 1

**inducing** *n* the act of reasoning or pleading with someone to accept a belief or course of action — see PERSUASION 1

**induct** *vb* to put into an office or welcome into an organization with special ceremonies — see INSTALL 1

**inductee** *n* a person forced or required to enroll in military service — see CONSCRIPT

**induction** *n* the process or an instance of being formally placed in an office or organization — see INSTALLATION 1

**indulge** *vb* to give in to (a desire) ⟨the grandparents generally *indulged* the child's wishes⟩
*syn* cater (to), gratify, humor
*rel* bask, luxuriate, revel, wallow; coddle, mollycoddle, pamper, spoil; delight, please, pleasure; sate, satiate, satisfy
*near ant* bridle, check, constrain, curb, inhibit, restrain, stifle

**indulgence** *n* **1** an act of kind assistance — see FAVOR 1
**2** something adding to pleasure or comfort but not absolutely necessary — see LUXURY 1

**industrious** *adj* involved in often constant activity — see BUSY 1

**industriously** *adv* with great effort or determination — see HARD 1

**industriousness** *n* attentive and persistent effort — see DILIGENCE

**industry** *n* attentive and persistent effort — see DILIGENCE

**inebriate** *adj* being under the influence of alcohol — see DRUNK 1

**inebriate** *n* a person who makes a habit of getting drunk — see DRUNK

**inebriated** *adj* being under the influence of alcohol — see DRUNK

**ineffable** *adj* beyond the power to describe — see INDESCRIBABLE

**ineffective** *adj* **1** not producing the desired result ⟨an *ineffective* effort to move the bookcase⟩
*syn* ineffectual, inefficient, inexpedient
*rel* abortive, bootless, fruitless, futile, nonproductive, pointless, unavailing, unproductive, unprofitable, unsuccessful, useless, worthless
*near ant* availing, beneficial, helpful, productive, profitable, successful, useful, worthwhile
*ant* effective, effectual, efficacious, efficient, expedient
**2** producing no results — see FUTILE

**ineffectual** *adj* **1** not producing the desired result — see INEFFECTIVE 1
**2** producing no results — see FUTILE

**inefficient** *adj* not producing the desired result — see INEFFECTIVE 1

**inelegant** *adj* **1** lacking social grace and assurance — see AWKWARD 1
**2** marked by an obvious lack of style or good taste — see TACKY 1

**inept** *adj* **1** lacking qualities (as knowledge, skill, or ability) required to do a job — see INCOMPETENT
**2** not appropriate for a particular occasion or situation — see INAPPROPRIATE
**3** showing or marked by a lack of skill and tact (as in dealing with a situation) — see AWKWARD 2

**ineptitude** *n* the lack of sufficient ability, power, or means — see INABILITY

**inequity** *n* the state of being unfair or unjust — see INJUSTICE 1

**inert** *adj* **1** not being in a state of use, activity, or employment — see INACTIVE 2
**2** slow to move or act — see INACTIVE 1

**inertia** *n* an inclination not to do work or engage in activities — see LAZINESS

**inertness** *n* lack of action or activity — see INACTION

**inescapable** *adj* impossible to avoid or evade — see INEVITABLE

**inescapably** *adv* because of necessity — see NEEDS

**inevitable** *adj* impossible to avoid or evade ⟨getting wet is *inevitable* if you are going to try to give your dog a bath⟩
*syn* certain, inescapable, necessary, sure, unavoidable
*rel* decided, definite, settled; likely, possible, probable; destined, fated, foreordained, predestined, predetermined, preordained; inexorable, relentless, unremitting
*phrases* in the bag
*near ant* preventable (*also* preventible); doubtful, dubious, questionable, shaky, unclear; undecided, unsettled; undependable, unreliable; improbable, unlikely
*ant* avoidable, escapable, uncertain, unsure

**inevitably** *adv* because of necessity — see NEEDS

**inexact** *adj* **1** not precisely correct ⟨a thousand is an *inexact* figure for the number of islands in the St. Lawrence River⟩
*syn* imprecise, inaccurate, loose

*rel* approximate; erroneous, false, incorrect, off, wrong; general, indefinable, indefinite, indeterminate, indistinct, undefined, undetermined, unsettled, vague; faulty, flawed, mistaken; specious; distorted, fallacious, misleading; doubtful, dubious, questionable, uncertain; inconclusive, indecisive; debatable, disputable; invalidated, unconfirmed, unsubstantiated, unsupported
*near ant* certain, incontestable, indubitable, positive, sure, undeniable, unquestionable; correct, errorless, factual, right, sound, true, valid; clear-cut, decisive, definable, defined, definite; incontrovertible, indisputable, irrefutable; absolute, unqualified; confirmed, corroborated, determined, established, substantiated, supported, validated
*ant* accurate, dead, exact, precise
**2** not being in agreement with what is true — see FALSE 1

**inexcusable** *adj* too bad to be excused or justified ⟨spitting at a teacher is *inexcusable* behavior and will be severely punished⟩
*syn* indefensible, unforgivable, unjustifiable, unpardonable, unwarrantable
*rel* insufferable, insupportable, intolerable, unbearable, unendurable; abominable, atrocious, heinous, monstrous, outrageous, scandalous, shocking; egregious, flagrant, glaring, gross, rank; unacceptable, untenable; black, evil, iniquitous, vicious, wicked; base, contemptible, deplorable, despicable, dirty, execrable, ignoble, reprobate, vile, wretched; cruel, nasty; blamable, blameworthy, censurable, reprehensible; banned, barred, condemned, disallowed, forbidden, interdicted, outlawed, prohibited, proscribed
*near ant* acceptable, tolerable; authorized, legal, permissible; allowed, permitted, tolerated; approved, endorsed, sanctioned; abetted, encouraged, promoted, supported; ethical, good, moral, virtuous
*ant* defensible, excusable, forgivable, justifiable, pardonable

**inexhaustible** *adj* showing no signs of weariness even after long hard effort — see TIRELESS

**inexpedient** *adj* not producing the desired result — see INEFFECTIVE 1

**inexpensive** *adj* costing little — see CHEAP 1

**inexperienced** *adj* **1** lacking in adult experience or maturity — see CALLOW
**2** lacking or showing a lack of expert skill — see AMATEURISH

**inexpert** *adj* **1** lacking or showing a lack of expert skill — see AMATEURISH
**2** lacking qualities (as knowledge, skill, or ability) required to do a job — see INCOMPETENT
**3** showing or marked by a lack of skill and tact (as in dealing with a situation) — see AWKWARD 2

**inexplicable** *adj* impossible to explain ⟨an *inexplicable* desire for ice cream at two in the morning⟩
*syn* unaccountable, unexplainable
*rel* indefinable, indescribable, inexpressible; enigmatic (*also* enigmatical), impenetrable, incomprehensible, inscrutable, mysterious, unfathomable, unknowable; irrational, unreasonable, unsound; foolish, mindless, senseless; absurd, odd, peculiar, strange, unusual, weird
*near ant* logical, rational, reasonable, understandable; sane, sensible, wise; compelling, convincing, persuasive, plausible, satisfying; confirmed, corroborated, determined, established, explained, substantiated, validated
*ant* accountable, explainable, explicable

**inexpressible** *adj* beyond the power to describe — see INDESCRIBABLE

**inexpressive** *adj* not expressing any emotion — see BLANK 1

**inextinguishable** *adj* impossible to destroy — see INDESTRUCTIBLE

**infallible** *adj* **1** not being or likely to be wrong ⟨a teacher with an *infallible* memory for names⟩
*syn* unerring, unfailing
*rel* errorless, faultless, flawless, impeccable; certain, foolproof, perfect, sure; dependable, reliable
*near ant* defective, faulty, flawed, imperfect; undependable, unreliable
*ant* fallible
**2** not likely to fail ⟨an *infallible* cure for hiccups⟩
*syn* certain, sure, unfailing
*rel* dependable, reliable, surefire; deadly, unerring
*near ant* doubtful, questionable, uncertain
*ant* fallible

**infamous** *adj* not respectable — see DISREPUTABLE

**infamy** *n* the state of having lost the esteem of others — see DISGRACE 1

**infant** *n* a recently born person — see BABY

**infantile** *adj* having or showing the annoying qualities (as silliness) associated with children — see CHILDISH

**infatuated** (with) *adj* filled with an intense or excessive love for — see ENAMORED (OF)

**infatuation** *n* a strong but often short-lived liking for another person — see CRUSH 1

**infectious** *adj* exciting a similar feeling or reaction in others — see CONTAGIOUS 2

**infelicitous** *adj* not appropriate for a particular occasion or situation — see INAPPROPRIATE

**infelicity** *n* the quality or state of being unsuitable or unfitting — see INAPPROPRIATENESS 1

**infer** *vb* **1** to form an opinion through reasoning and information ⟨he *inferred* that she had left because her coat was gone⟩
*syn* conclude, deduce, extrapolate, gather, judge, reason, understand

*rel* conjecture, guess, speculate, surmise; construe, interpret; contemplate, rationalize, think; ascertain, dope (out), find out
*phrases* draw a conclusion
**2** to convey an idea indirectly — see HINT

**inferable** *adj* being or provable by reasoning in which the conclusion follows necessarily from given information — see DEDUCTIVE

**inference** *n* an opinion arrived at through a process of reasoning — see CONCLUSION 1

**inferior** *adj* **1** situated lower down ⟨creatures that inhabit the dark, *inferior* depths of the ocean⟩
*syn* lower, nether
*rel* lowest, nethermost; underlying
*near ant* highest, uppermost; overhanging, overhead
*ant* higher, superior, upper
**2** of little or less value or merit ⟨a girl who has always felt *inferior* to her older sister⟩
*syn* mean, minor, secondary, second-class, second-rate
*rel* junior, lesser, lower, petty, smaller, subordinate, under; average, common, fair, middling, ordinary; amiss, bad, defective, unsatisfactory, wrong; deficient, inadequate, insufficient, unacceptable; littler, slighter, smaller; jerkwater, one-horse, two-bit
*near ant* major, more, primary, senior; choice, exceptional, first-class, first-rate, high-grade, premium, prime; acceptable, adequate, sufficient
*ant* greater, higher, superior
**3** belonging to the class of people of low social or economic rank — see IGNOBLE 1
**4** falling short of a standard — see BAD 1
**5** having not so great importance or rank as another — see LESSER
**6** of low quality — see CHEAP 2

**inferior** *n* one who is of lower rank and typically under the authority of another — see UNDERLING

**inferno** *n* a destructive burning — see FIRE

**infertile** *adj* **1** not able to produce fruit or offspring — see STERILE
**2** producing inferior or only a small amount of vegetation — see BARREN 1

**infest** *vb* to spread or swarm over in a troublesome manner ⟨called in an exterminator because the house was *infested* with ants⟩
*syn* overrun
*rel* beset, overspread, overwhelm; abound, crawl, teem; annoy, pester, plague; contaminate, infect

**infidelity** *n* **1** lack of faithfulness especially to one's husband or wife ⟨*infidelity* can lead to divorce⟩
*syn* disloyalty, faithlessness, falseness, falsity, inconstancy, perfidiousness, perfidy, unfaithfulness
*rel* adultery; betrayal, double-cross, double-dealing, duplicity, sellout, treachery, treason; deceit, deception, lying
*near ant* staunchness, steadfastness; dependability, reliability; honesty, trustworthiness
*ant* allegiance, constancy, devotedness, devotion, faith, faithfulness, fealty, fidelity, loyalty
**2** the act or fact of violating the trust or confidence of another — see BETRAYAL

**infiltrate** *vb* to introduce in a gradual, secret, or clever way — see INSINUATE

**infinite** *adj* being or seeming to be without limits ⟨the *infinite* expanse of outer space⟩
*syn* boundless, endless, illimitable, immeasurable, indefinite, limitless, measureless, unbounded, unfathomable, unlimited
*rel* abysmal, bottomless; countless, incalculable, inestimable, innumerable, unmeasured; inexhaustible; far-flung, immense, vast
*near ant* fathomable, measurable; depthless, shallow, superficial
*ant* bounded, circumscribed, confined, definite, finite, limited, restricted

**infinitesimal** *adj* very small in size — see TINY

**infinity** *n* endless time — see ETERNITY 1

**infirm** *adj* lacking bodily strength — see WEAK 1

**infirmity** *n* **1** an abnormal state that disrupts a plant's or animal's normal bodily functioning — see DISEASE
**2** the quality or state of lacking physical strength or vigor — see WEAKNESS 1

**inflame** *vb* **1** to make angry — see ANGER
**2** to set (something) on fire — see BURN 2

**inflamed** *adj* **1** being on fire — see ABLAZE 1
**2** feeling or showing anger — see ANGRY

**inflammable** *adj* capable of catching or being set on fire — see COMBUSTIBLE

**inflexibility** *n* the quality or state of being demanding or unyielding (as in discipline or criticism) — see SEVERITY

**inflexible** *adj* **1** not capable of changing or being changed ⟨the *inflexible* law of gravity⟩
*syn* fixed, hard-and-fast, immutable, invariable, unalterable, unchangeable
*rel* changeless, constant, determinate, established, set, settled, stable, steadfast, steady, unaltered, unchanging, unvarying; immovable, unmovable
*near ant* adaptable, adjustable; fickle, fluctuating, inconstant, uncertain, unstable, varying
*ant* alterable, changeable, flexible, mutable, variable
**2** incapable of or highly resistant to bending — see STIFF 1
**3** not allowing for any exceptions or loosening of standards — see RIGID 1
**4** sticking to an opinion, purpose, or course of action in spite of reason, arguments, or persuasion — see OBSTINATE

**inflow** *n* a flowing or coming in — see INFLUX

**influence** *n* **1** the power to direct the thinking or behavior of others usually in-

directly ⟨a mayor who doesn't hesitate to use her *influence* to get business leaders behind civic improvements⟩
***syn*** authority, clout, pull, sway, weight
***rel*** command, dominance, dominion, mastery, predominance, scepter, sovereignty, supremacy; consequence, eminence, importance, moment; impact, impression, mark
***near ant*** helplessness, impotence, powerlessness, weakness
**2** the power to bring about a result on another — see EFFECT 2

**influence** *vb* to act upon (a person or a person's feelings) so as to cause a response — see [1]AFFECT 1

**influential** *adj* **1** having power over the minds or behavior of others ⟨in light of the effect that they have had, religious leaders such as Jesus and Muḥammad must be regarded as among the most *influential* people ever⟩
***syn*** authoritative, forceful, weighty
***rel*** controlling, dominating, masterful; dominant, predominant, sovereign, supreme; eminent, important, momentous
***near ant*** helpless, impotent, powerless, weak; incapable, unable
**2** having great power or influence — see IMPORTANT 2

**influx** *n* a flowing or coming in ⟨a sudden *influx* of people⟩
***syn*** flux, inflow, inrush
***rel*** deluge, flood, flow, inundation, overflow, spate, torrent; rush, stampede; flow, river, stream, tide
***near ant*** emigration, exodus, flight
***ant*** outflow, outpouring

**inform** *vb* **1** to give information (as to the authorities) about another's improper or unlawful activities — see SQUEAL 1
**2** to give information to — see ENLIGHTEN 1

**informal** *adj* **1** not rigidly following established form, custom, or rules ⟨an *informal* meeting allowed everyone to get acquainted⟩
***syn*** irregular, unceremonious, unconventional, unorthodox
***rel*** unauthorized, unofficial; casual, easygoing, lax, loose, relaxed
***near ant*** correct, decorous, proper; constrained, inhibited, restrained, rigid, stiff, stuffy, uptight
***ant*** ceremonial, ceremonious, conventional, formal, orthodox, regular, routine
**2** not designed for special occasions — see CASUAL 1
**3** used in or suitable for speech and not formal writing — see COLLOQUIAL 1

**informant** *n* a person who provides secret information about another's wrongdoing — see INFORMER

**information** *n* a report of recent events or facts not previously known — see NEWS

**informational** *adj* providing useful information or knowledge — see INFORMATIVE

**informative** *adj* providing useful information or knowledge ⟨some Web sites for family vacation resorts are very *informative* and some are practically useless⟩
***syn*** educational, educative, informational, instructional, instructive
***rel*** comprehensive, detailed, full; edifying, elucidative, enlightening, explanatory, illuminating; chatty, gossipy, newsy; availing, beneficial, constructive, helpful, profitable; practical, serviceable, usable, useful, worthwhile
***near ant*** impractical, unhelpful, unusable, useless
***ant*** uninstructive

**informed** *adj* **1** based on sound reasoning or information — see GOOD 1
**2** having information especially as a result of study or experience — see FAMILIAR 2

**informer** *n* a person who provides secret information about another's wrongdoing ⟨the *informer* who told the police about that conspiracy angered a lot of dangerous people⟩
***syn*** betrayer, informant, snitcher, squealer, stool pigeon, talebearer, tattler, tattletale, telltale
***rel*** collaborator; blabbermouth, gossip, gossiper; snoop, snooper, spy; notifier

**infraction** *n* a failure to uphold the requirements of law, duty, or obligation — see BREACH 1

**infrequent** *adj* not often occurring or repeated ⟨a shut-in who made *infrequent* trips to the store⟩
***syn*** occasional, rare, sporadic
***rel*** scarce, scattered, uncommon, unique, unusual; choppy, discontinuous, erratic, fitful, intermittent, irregular, spasmodic, spotty, unsteady
***near ant*** common, ordinary, routine
***ant*** frequent

**infrequently** *adv* not often — see SELDOM

**infringe** *vb* to fail to keep — see VIOLATE 1

**infringement** *n* a failure to uphold the requirements of law, duty, or obligation — see BREACH 1

**infuriate** *vb* to make angry — see ANGER

**infuriated** *adj* feeling or showing anger — see ANGRY

**infuse** *vb* to cause (as a person) to become filled or saturated with a certain quality or principle ⟨parents who *infuse* their children with strong moral values⟩
***syn*** imbue, inculcate, ingrain, inoculate, invest, steep, suffuse
***rel*** animate, enliven, invigorate; implant, instill, plant; impregnate, permeate, pervade, saturate; deluge, drown, fill, flood, inundate, overwhelm, submerge
***near ant*** deprive, divest, strip; clear, empty; eliminate, remove, take away

**ingenious** *adj* **1** having the skill and imagination to create new things — see CREATIVE 1

2 showing a use of the imagination and creativity especially in inventing — see CLEVER 1

**ingeniousness** *n* the skill and imagination to create new things — see CREATIVITY 1

**ingenuity** *n* the skill and imagination to create new things — see CREATIVITY 1

**ingenuous** *adj* 1 free from any intent to deceive or impress others — see GUILELESS
2 lacking in worldly wisdom or informed judgment — see NAIVE 1

**ingenuously** *adv* without any attempt to impress by deception or exaggeration — see NATURALLY 3

**ingenuousness** *n* the quality or state of being simple and sincere — see NAIVETÉ 1

**ingest** *vb* 1 to take in as food — see EAT 1
2 to take into the stomach through the mouth and throat — see SWALLOW 1

**ingrain** *vb* 1 to cause (as a person) to become filled or saturated with a certain quality or principle — see INFUSE
2 to produce a vivid impression of — see ENGRAVE 2
3 to set solidly in or as if in surrounding matter — see ENTRENCH

**ingrained** *adj* being a part of the innermost nature of a person or thing — see INHERENT

**ingratiating** *adj* likely to win one's affection ⟨one of the orphans had a most *ingratiating* smile⟩
***syn*** disarming, endearing, winning, winsome
***rel*** adorable, charming, likable, lovable; affecting, poignant, touching; adulatory, deferential, groveling (*or* grovelling), kowtowing, obsequious, servile, sycophantic; drooling, slavering, slobbering; soapy, sugary, unctuous
***near ant*** alienating, disaffecting, displeasing; repugnant, repulsive; arrogant, disdainful, haughty, insolent, proud, scornful

**ingredient** *n* one of the parts that make up a whole — see ELEMENT 1

**inhabitable** *adj* suitable for living in — see LIVABLE

**inhabitant** *n* one who lives permanently in a place ⟨the *inhabitants* of the town don't like the tourists⟩
***syn*** denizen, dweller, habitant, occupant, resident, resider
***rel*** aborigine, native; citizen, national, subject; colonist, émigré (*also* emigré), migrant, newcomer, settler; burgher, townie, villager
***near ant*** alien, foreigner; guest, tourist, visitor; defector, escaper, evacuee, exile, expatriate, refugee
***ant*** transient

**inharmonious** *adj* 1 not being in agreement or harmony — see INCONSISTENT
2 marked by or producing a harsh combination of sounds — see DISSONANT

**inherent** *adj* being a part of the innermost nature of a person or thing ⟨an *inherent* concept of justice⟩
***syn*** essential, inborn, inbred, ingrained, innate, integral, intrinsic, natural
***rel*** basic, constitutional, elemental, fundamental; congenital, hereditary, inherited, inmost, inner, interior; internal; characteristic, distinctive, peculiar; normal, regular, typical
***near ant*** alien, foreign; accidental, coincidental, incidental; acquired; superficial, surface; exterior, external
***ant*** adventitious, extraneous, extrinsic

**inherently** *adv* by natural character or ability — see NATURALLY 1

**inheritable** *adj* genetically passed or capable of being passed from parent to offspring — see HEREDITARY

**inheritance** *n* something that is or may be inherited ⟨a sense of humor was her *inheritance* from her mother⟩
***syn*** bequest, birthright, heritage, legacy, patrimony
***rel*** heirloom; bestowal, gift, offering, present

**inherited** *adj* genetically passed or capable of being passed from parent to offspring — see HEREDITARY

**inheritor** *n* a person who has the right to inherit property — see HEIR

**inhibit** *vb* 1 to create difficulty for the work or activity of — see HAMPER
2 to keep from exceeding a desirable degree or level (as of expression) — see CONTROL 1
3 to steer (a person) from an activity or course of action — see DISCOURAGE 2

**inhibition** *n* 1 the checking of one's true feelings and impulses when dealing with others — see CONSTRAINT 1
2 something that makes movement or progress more difficult — see ENCUMBRANCE

**inhospitable** *adj* marked by opposition or ill will — see HOSTILE 1

**inhuman** *adj* 1 difficult to endure — see HARSH 1
2 having or showing a lack of sympathy or tender feelings — see HARD 1

**inhumane** *adj* 1 having or showing a lack of sympathy or tender feelings — see HARD 1
2 having or showing the desire to inflict severe pain and suffering on others — see CRUEL 1

**inhumanity** *n* the willful infliction of pain and suffering on others — see CRUELTY

**inimical** *adj* 1 marked by opposition or ill will — see HOSTILE 1
2 opposed to one's interests — see ADVERSE 1

**inimitable** *adj* having no equal or rival for excellence or desirability — see ONLY 1

**iniquitous** *adj* not conforming to a high moral standard; morally unacceptable — see BAD 2

**iniquity** *n* 1 immoral conduct or practices harmful or offensive to society — see VICE 1
2 that which is morally unacceptable — see EVIL

**initial** *adj* coming before all others in time or order — see FIRST 1

**initially** *adv* in the beginning — see ORIGINALLY

**initiate** *vb* **1** to be responsible for the creation and early operation or use of — see FOUND

**2** to impart knowledge of a new thing or situation to — see ACQUAINT 1

**3** to put into an office or welcome into an organization with special ceremonies — see INSTALL 1

**initiation** *n* the process or an instance of being formally placed in an office or organization — see INSTALLATION 1

**initiative** *n* readiness to engage in daring or difficult activity — see ENTERPRISE 2

**initiator** *n* a person who establishes a whole new field of endeavor — see FATHER 2

**inject** *vb* to put among or between others — see INSERT

**injudicious** *adj* showing poor judgment especially in personal relationships or social situations — see INDISCREET

**injure** *vb* **1** to cause bodily damage to ⟨*injured* himself while skiing⟩

***syn*** damage, harm, hurt, wound

***rel*** batter, bruise, contuse, gash, gore, lacerate, scald, scar, scathe, tear; cripple, lame, maim, mangle, mutilate; afflict, torment, torture; lay up; blemish, impair, mar, scrape, spoil

***near ant*** cure, fix, heal, mend, remedy

**2** to reduce the soundness, effectiveness, or perfection of — see DAMAGE 1

**injurious** *adj* causing or capable of causing harm — see HARMFUL

**injury** *n* **1** something that causes loss or pain ⟨the harsh words were the worst *injury*⟩

***syn*** damage, detriment, harm, hurt

***rel*** disservice, injustice, outrage, wrong; affront, dart, indignity, insult, offense (*or* offence); crippling, mayhem, mutilation; defacement, disablement, disability, disfigurement; abrasion, bruise, bump, contusion, scald, scar, scathe, scrape, scratch, sear

***near ant*** healing, recovery; cure, fix, remedy

**2** unfair or inadequate treatment of someone or something or an instance of this — see DISSERVICE

**injustice** *n* **1** the state of being unfair or unjust ⟨the *injustice* of the coach's accusation that I'd been lazy frustrated and angered me⟩

***syn*** inequity, unfairness, unjustness

***rel*** dirtiness, foulness

***ant*** equity, fairness, justice

**2** unfair or inadequate treatment of someone or something or an instance of this — see DISSERVICE

**inkling** *n* a slight or indirect pointing to something (as a solution or explanation) — see HINT 1

**inlet** *n* a part of a body of water that extends beyond the general shoreline — see GULF 1

**inn** *n* a place that provides rooms and usually a public dining room for overnight guests — see HOTEL

**innards** *n pl* the internal organs of the body — see GUT 1

**innate** *adj* being a part of the innermost nature of a person or thing — see INHERENT

**innately** *adv* by natural character or ability — see NATURALLY 1

**inner** *adj* **1** situated farther in ⟨an *inner* area of the national park that is some distance from the nearest road⟩

***syn*** inside, interior, internal, inward

***rel*** inmost, innermost; central, mid, middle

***near ant*** outermost, outmost

***ant*** exterior, external, outer, outside, outward

**2** of or relating to the mind — see MENTAL 1

**innocence** *n* **1** the quality or state of being free from guilt or blame ⟨the accused criminal eventually proved her *innocence* and was released⟩

***syn*** blamelessness, faultlessness, guiltlessness, impeccability

***rel*** decency, goodness, honesty, incorruptibility, integrity, righteousness, uprightness, virtuousness; morality, virtue; chastity, purity; harmlessness, inoffensiveness

***near ant*** blame, fault, responsibility; corruption, criminality, depravity, evil, immorality, reprehensibleness, sinfulness, wickedness; harmfulness, offensiveness

***ant*** blameworthiness, culpability, guilt, guiltiness

**2** the quality or state of being simple and sincere — see NAÏVETÉ 1

**innocent** *adj* **1** free from sin ⟨an *innocent* baby⟩

***syn*** pure

***rel*** chaste, moral, virtuous; immaculate, spotless, unblemished, unstained, unsullied; decent, ethical, good, honest, honorable, righteous, upright, virtuous; blameless, guiltless

***near ant*** lascivious, lewd, lustful, unchaste; evil, immoral, iniquitous, reprobate, unrighteous, wicked; corrupt, debased, debauched, degenerate, depraved, dissolute, erring, fallen, lost, perverted; condemned, damned

***ant*** impure, sinful

**2** free from guilt or blame ⟨the robbery suspect was found to be *innocent*⟩

***syn*** blameless, clear, faultless, guiltless, impeccable, irreproachable

***rel*** absolved, acquitted, cleared, exonerated, vindicated; ethical, law-abiding, moral, righteous, upright, virtuous

***phrases*** in the clear

***near ant*** blamable, blameworthy, censurable, culpable, impeachable, indictable, punishable; accused, impeached, in-

dicted; condemned, convicted; hangdog, shamed, shamefaced
*ant* guilty
**3** free from any intent to deceive or impress others — see GUILELESS
**4** lacking in worldly wisdom or informed judgment — see NAIVE 1
**5** not causing injury or hurt — see HARMLESS

**innocent** *n* an innocent or gentle person — see LAMB

**innocently** *adv* **1** without any attempt to impress by deception or exaggeration — see NATURALLY 3
**2** with purity of thought and deed — see PURELY

**innocuous** *adj* not causing injury or hurt — see HARMLESS

**innovate** *vb* to be responsible for the creation and early operation or use of — see FOUND

**innovation** *n* something (as a device) created for the first time through the use of the imagination — see INVENTION 1

**innovative** *adj* having the skill and imagination to create new things — see CREATIVE 1

**innovator** *n* one who creates or introduces something new — see INVENTOR

**innumerable** *adj* too many to be counted — see COUNTLESS

**inoculate** *vb* to cause (as a person) to become filled or saturated with a certain quality or principle — see INFUSE

**inoffensive** *adj* not causing injury or hurt — see HARMLESS

**inoperable** *adj* **1** not being in working order ⟨we have several *inoperable* cars on the property⟩
*syn* inoperative, malfunctioning, nonfunctional, nonfunctioning, nonoperating
*rel* broken; off; deactivated, deadlocked, ineffective, ineffectual, nonproductive, unproductive, unusable, unworkable, useless
*phrases* on the blink, out of commission
*near ant* effective, effectual, employable, performing, producing, productive, serving, usable, useful, viable, workable
*ant* functional, functioning, operable, operating, operational, operative, running, working
**2** not capable of being put to use or account — see IMPRACTICAL

**inoperative** *adj* **1** not being in a state of use, activity, or employment — see INACTIVE 2
**2** not being in working order — see INOPERABLE 1

**inopportune** *adj* occurring before the usual or expected time — see EARLY 2

**inopportunely** *adv* before the usual or expected time — see EARLY

**inordinate** *adj* going beyond a normal or acceptable limit in degree or amount — see EXCESSIVE

**inordinately** *adv* beyond a normal or acceptable limit — see TOO 1

**inquest** *n* a systematic search for the truth or facts about something — see INQUIRY 1

**inquire** (into) *vb* to search through or into — see EXPLORE 1

**inquire** (of) *vb* to put a question or questions to — see ASK 1

**inquiry** *n* **1** a systematic search for the truth or facts about something ⟨an *inquiry* into the origins of the universe⟩
*syn* delving, examination, exploration, inquest, inquisition, investigation, probe, probing, research, study
*rel* quest; audit, check; checkup, diagnosis, inspection; hearing, interrogation, trial; feeler, query, question; poll, questionnaire; challenge, cross-examination, grilling, quiz
**2** an act or instance of asking for information — see QUESTION 2

**inquisition** *n* a systematic search for the truth or facts about something — see INQUIRY 1

**inquisitive** *adj* interested in what is not one's own business — see CURIOUS 1

**inquisitiveness** *n* an eager desire to find out about things that are often none of one's business — see CURIOSITY 1

**inroad** *n* a sudden attack on and entrance into hostile territory — see RAID 1

**inrush** *n* a flowing or coming in — see INFLUX

**insane** *adj* **1** having or showing a very abnormal or sick state of mind ⟨only an *insane* person would jump off a skyscraper⟩
*syn* balmy, bananas, batty, crackbrained, cracked, crazed, crazy, cuckoo, daffy, daft, demented, deranged, loco, loony (*also* looney), lunatic, mad, maniacal (*also* maniac), mental, moonstruck, nuts, nutty, screwy, unbalanced, unsound, wacky
*rel* dotty, off; aberrant, delusional, disordered; eccentric, odd, queer, strange; foolish, senseless, witless; irrational, unreasonable; berserk, delirious; depressed; distraught, frantic, frenzied, hysterical
*phrases* around the bend, off one's rocker, out of one's head (*or* mind)
*near ant* clear, lucid, rational, reasonable; judicious, sensible, wise; healthy, normal
*ant* balanced, sane, sound
**2** conceived or made without regard for reason or reality — see FANTASTIC 1
**3** showing or marked by a lack of good sense or judgment — see FOOLISH 1

**insanity** *n* **1** a serious mental disorder that prevents one from living a safe and normal life ⟨his *insanity* requires that he spend the rest of his life in a mental hospital⟩
*syn* aberration, dementia, derangement, lunacy, madness, mania
*rel* irrationality, unreasonableness; delirium, frenzy, hysteria; neurosis, psychosis, schizophrenia; delusion, hallucination, obsession, phobia; abnormality, unsoundness

***near ant*** lucidity, rationality, reasonableness; normality, soundness
***ant*** mind, saneness, sanity
**2** a foolish act or idea — see FOLLY 1
**3** lack of good sense or judgment — see FOOLISHNESS 1

**inscribe** *vb* **1** to cut (as letters or designs) on a hard surface — see ENGRAVE 1
**2** to enter in a list or roll — see ENROLL 1
**3** to put (someone or something) on a list — see [1]LIST 2

**inscrutable** *adj* **1** being beyond one's powers to know, understand, or explain — see MYSTERIOUS 1
**2** having an often intentionally veiled or uncertain meaning — see OBSCURE 1

**insecure** *adj* not tightly fastened, tied, or stretched — see LOOSE 1

**insecurity** *n* the quality or state of not being firmly fixed in position — see INSTABILITY

**insensate** *adj* having or showing a lack of sympathy or tender feelings — see HARD 1

**insensibility** *n* **1** a lack of emotion or emotional expressiveness — see APATHY 1
**2** a temporary or permanent state of unconsciousness — see FAINT

**insensible** *adj* **1** having lost consciousness — see UNCONSCIOUS 1
**2** not perceptible by a sense or by the mind — see IMPERCEPTIBLE

**insensitive** *adj* **1** having or showing a lack of sympathy or tender feelings — see HARD 1
**2** lacking in sensation or feeling — see NUMB

**inseparability** *n* the state of being in a very personal or private relationship — see FAMILIARITY 1

**insert** *vb* to put among or between others ⟨*inserted* a book in its proper place on the shelf⟩
***syn*** fit (in *or* into), inject, insinuate, interject, interpolate, interpose, introduce
***rel*** inlay, inset, install, weave, work (in); cram, sandwich, shove, thrust, wedge; add, append, attach
***near ant*** eject, eliminate, exclude, expel, extract, withdraw; deduct, detach, subtract; reject

**inside** *adj* **1** not known or meant to be known by the general populace — see PRIVATE 1
**2** situated farther in — see INNER 1

**inside** *n* **1** an interior or internal part ⟨the *inside* of the clock features an amazingly complex mechanism⟩
***syn*** interior, within
***rel*** bowels, guts, innards; stuffing; recesses; center, core, heart
***near ant*** border, boundary, brim, brink, edge, end, extremity, fringe, limit, lip, margin, perimeter, periphery, rim
***ant*** exterior, outside
**2** *usually* **insides** *pl* the internal organs of the body — see GUT 1

**insight** *n* the ability to understand inner qualities or relationships — see WISDOM 1

**insightful** *adj* having or showing deep understanding and intelligent application of knowledge — see WISE 1

**insignificant** *adj* **1** lacking importance — see UNIMPORTANT
**2** so small or unimportant as to warrant little or no attention — see NEGLIGIBLE 1

**insincere** *adj* not being or expressing what one appears to be or express ⟨the *insincere* compliments of a spiteful gossip⟩
***syn*** artificial, backhanded, double-dealing, feigned, hypocritical, left-handed, mealy, mealymouthed, two-faced, unctuous
***rel*** empty, hollow, meaningless; deceitful, devious, dishonest, untruthful; facile, glib, superficial; bogus, counterfeit, fake, false, phony (*also* phoney), sham; facetious, jocular
***near ant*** candid, direct, forthright, frank, open, plain, straightforward
***ant*** genuine, heartfelt, honest, sincere, unfeigned

**insincerity** *n* the pretending of having virtues, principles, or beliefs that one in fact does not have — see HYPOCRISY

**insinuate** *vb* **1** to introduce in a gradual, secret, or clever way ⟨the spy *insinuated* himself into the terrorist organization⟩
***syn*** infiltrate, slip, sneak, work (in), worm
***rel*** creep, edge, wiggle; insert, interpolate, interpose, introduce
**2** to convey an idea indirectly — see HINT
**3** to put among or between others — see INSERT

**insipid** *adj* **1** lacking in taste or flavor ⟨an apple pie with a mushy, *insipid* filling that strongly resembled soggy cardboard⟩
***syn*** flat, flavorless, savorless, tasteless
***rel*** bland, dilute, thin, watery, weak; plain, unflavored
***near ant*** disgusting, distasteful, loathsome, sickening, unappetizing, unpalatable; appetizing, delectable, delicious, palatable, toothsome; piquant, seasoned, spicy; flavored; heavy, rich
***ant*** flavorful, savory, tasty
**2** lacking in qualities that make for spirit and character — see WISHY-WASHY 1

**insist** *vb* to state as a fact usually forcefully — see CLAIM 1

**insist** (on) *vb* to ask for (something) earnestly or with authority — see DEMAND 1

**insistence** *n* a solemn and often public declaration of the truth or existence of something — see PROTESTATION

**insistent** *adj* continuing despite difficulties, opposition, or discouragement — see PERSISTENT

**insolence** *n* **1** disrespectful or argumentative talk given in response to a command or request — see BACK TALK
**2** rude behavior — see DISCOURTESY

**insolent** *adj* displaying or marked by rude boldness — see NERVY 1

---

***syn*** synonym(s) ***rel*** related words
***ant*** antonym(s) ***near ant*** near antonym(s)

**insouciance** *n* lack of interest or concern — see INDIFFERENCE

**insouciant** *adj* **1** having or showing a lack of concern or seriousness — see CAREFREE
**2** having or showing a lack of interest or concern — see INDIFFERENT 1

**inspect** *vb* to look over closely (as for judging quality or condition) ⟨*inspected* the animal before the show⟩
***syn*** audit, check (out), examine, review, scan, scrutinize, survey
***rel*** notice, observe, watch; peruse, pore (over); analyze, dissect; delve (into), explore, investigate, probe, research, study; categorize, classify
***phrases*** go over
***near ant*** skim; glance (at *or* over); miss, overlook

**inspection** *n* a close look at or over someone or something in order to judge condition ⟨a room *inspection* should include looking under the bed⟩
***syn*** audit, check, checkup, examination, review, scan, scrutiny, survey
***rel*** analysis, dissection; exploration, investigation, probe, research, study; inquisition, interrogation; perusal, observation, surveillance, watch

**inspire** *vb* to fill with courage or strength of purpose — see ENCOURAGE 1

**inspiring** *adj* causing great emotional or mental stimulation — see EXCITING 1

**instability** *n* the quality or state of not being firmly fixed in position ⟨the *instability* of the bridge became apparent when it suddenly collapsed⟩
***syn*** insecurity, precariousness, shakiness, unsteadiness
***rel*** insubstantiality, unsoundness; changeability, inconstancy, mutability
***near ant*** firmness, soundness, substantiality
***ant*** fixedness, security, stability, steadiness

**install** *vb* **1** to put into an office or welcome into an organization with special ceremonies ⟨*installed* her as the new principal⟩
***syn*** baptize, inaugurate, induct, initiate, instate, invest
***rel*** swear in; accept, admit, receive, take in; enlist, enroll (*also* enrol)
***near ant*** can, discharge, fire, terminate; muster out
**2** to establish or place comfortably or snugly — see ENSCONCE 1

**installation** *n* **1** the process or an instance of being formally placed in an office or organization ⟨the *installation* of a new president takes place once every four years⟩
***syn*** baptism, inaugural, inauguration, induction, initiation, installment, investiture
***rel*** enlistment, enrollment; promotion
***near ant*** discharge, removal
**2** a structure that is designed and built for a particular purpose — see FACILITY

**installment** *n* the process or an instance of being formally placed in an office or organization — see INSTALLATION 1

**instance** *n* one of a group or collection that shows what the whole is like — see EXAMPLE

**instance** *vb* **1** to give as an example — see QUOTE 1
**2** to make reference to or speak about briefly but specifically — see MENTION 1
**3** to show or make clear by using examples — see ILLUSTRATE 1

**instant** *adj* **1** done or occurring without any noticeable lapse in time — see INSTANTANEOUS
**2** needing immediate attention — see ACUTE 2

**instant** *n* a very small space of time ⟨it all happened in an *instant*⟩
***syn*** flash, jiffy, minute, moment, second, shake, split second, trice, twinkle, twinkling, wink
***rel*** microsecond, nanosecond; snatch, spurt
***near ant*** aeon (*or* eon), age, eternity; infinity, lifetime

**instantaneous** *adj* done or occurring without any noticeable lapse in time ⟨the thunder following the lightning was nearly *instantaneous*⟩
***syn*** immediate, instant, straightaway
***rel*** summary; fast, hit-and-run, prompt, quick, rapid, speedy, swift
***near ant*** dilatory, tardy; slow, sluggish; prolonged, protracted; deferred, delayed

**instantly** *adv* without delay — see IMMEDIATELY

**instate** *vb* to put into an office or welcome into an organization with special ceremonies — see INSTALL 1

**instead** *adv* as a substitute ⟨I was offered a ride, but I chose to walk *instead*⟩
***syn*** first, rather
***rel*** alternately, alternatively

**instigate** *vb* **1** to cause or encourage the development of — see INCITE 1
**2** to rouse to strong feeling or action — see PROVOKE 1

**instigating** *adj* serving or likely to arouse a strong reaction — see PROVOCATIVE

**instigation** *n* **1** something that arouses a strong response from another — see PROVOCATION 1
**2** something that arouses action or activity — see IMPULSE

**instigator** *n* a person who stirs up public feelings especially of discontent — see AGITATOR

**instinctive** *adj* done instantly and without conscious thought or decision — see AUTOMATIC 1

**instinctual** *adj* done instantly and without conscious thought or decision — see AUTOMATIC 1

**institute** *n* **1** a group of persons formally joined together for some common interest — see ASSOCIATION 2
**2** a public organization with a particular purpose or function — see INSTITUTION 1

**institute** *vb* to be responsible for the creation and early operation or use of — see FOUND

**instituter** *or* **institutor** *n* a person who establishes a whole new field of endeavor — see FATHER 2

**institution** *n* **1** a public organization with a particular purpose or function ⟨a charitable *institution* devoted to raising funds to feed the hungry⟩
***syn*** establishment, foundation, institute
***rel*** body, collective, group; corporation, enterprise; charity, philanthropy; think tank
**2** a group of persons formally joined together for some common interest — see ASSOCIATION 2

**instruct** *vb* **1** to cause to acquire knowledge or skill in some field — see TEACH
**2** to give information to — see ENLIGHTEN 1
**3** to issue orders to (someone) by right of authority — see COMMAND 1

**instruction** *n* **1** a statement of what to do that must be obeyed by those concerned — see COMMAND 1
**2** the act or process of imparting knowledge or skills to another — see EDUCATION 1

**instructional** *adj* providing useful information or knowledge — see INFORMATIVE

**instructive** *adj* providing useful information or knowledge — see INFORMATIVE

**instructor** *n* a person whose occupation is to give formal instruction in a school — see TEACHER

**instrument** *n* **1** a written or printed paper giving information about or proof of something — see CERTIFICATE
**2** an article intended for use in work — see IMPLEMENT
**3** something used to achieve an end — see AGENT 1

**instrumentalist** *n* a person who plays a musical instrument — see MUSICIAN 1

**instrumentality** *n* something used to achieve an end — see AGENT 1

**insubordinate** *adj* given to resisting authority or another's control — see DISOBEDIENT

**insubordination** *n* refusal to obey — see DISOBEDIENCE

**insubstantial** *adj* **1** being of a material lacking in sturdiness or substance — see FLIMSY 1
**2** not composed of matter — see IMMATERIAL 1

**insufferable** *adj* more than can be put up with — see UNBEARABLE

**insufficiency** *n* a falling short of an essential or desirable amount or number — see DEFICIENCY

**insufficient** *adj* not coming up to a usual standard or meeting a particular need — see SHORT 3

**insular** *adj* not broad or open in views or opinions — see NARROW 2

**insulate** *vb* to set or keep apart from others — see ISOLATE

**insulation** *n* the state of being alone or kept apart from others — see ISOLATION

**insult** *n* an act or expression showing scorn and usually intended to hurt another's feelings ⟨yelling an *insult* at the bully was not a very smart thing to do⟩
***syn*** affront, barb, dart, dig, epithet, indignity, name, offense (*or* offence), outrage, put-down, sarcasm, slight, slur
***rel*** gibe (*or* jibe), jeer, sneer, taunt; abuse, invective, vituperation; disapproval, opprobrium; disgrace, dishonor, shame; attack, criticism, slam; torment, torture
***near ant*** accolade, commendation, compliment; acclaim, applause, praise; adulation, flattery

**insult** *vb* to cause hurt feelings or deep resentment in ⟨*insulted* the people by saying their home was ugly⟩
***syn*** affront, dis [*slang*], offend, outrage, slight, wound
***rel*** cut, snub; displease, distress, disturb, hurt, pain, trouble, upset; jeer, mock, ridicule, sneer (at), taunt; defame, disparage, libel, malign, revile, slander, slur, smear; oppress, persecute, torment, torture
***near ant*** acclaim, applaud, approve, hail; commend, compliment, eulogize, praise; adulate, flatter; exalt, glorify, honor; delight, gratify, please, satisfy

**insupportable** *adj* more than can be put up with — see UNBEARABLE

**insure** *vb* to make sure, certain, or safe — see ENSURE

**insurgency** *n* open fighting against authority (as one's own government) — see REBELLION

**insurgent** *adj* taking part in a rebellion — see REBELLIOUS 1

**insurgent** *n* a person who rises up against authority — see REBEL

**insurmountable** *adj* incapable of being defeated, overcome, or subdued — see INVINCIBLE

**insurrection** *n* open fighting against authority (as one's own government) — see REBELLION

**insurrectionary** *adj* taking part in a rebellion — see REBELLIOUS 1

**insurrectionary** *n* a person who rises up against authority — see REBEL

**insurrectionist** *n* a person who rises up against authority — see REBEL

**intact** *adj* not lacking any part or member that properly belongs to it — see COMPLETE 1

**intangible** *adj* not capable of being perceived by the sense of touch ⟨electrical energy is completely *intangible*⟩
***syn*** impalpable
***rel*** bodiless, immaterial, incorporeal, insubstantial, unsubstantial; ethereal, spiritual, unreal

---

***syn*** synonym(s) ***rel*** related words
***ant*** antonym(s) ***near ant*** near antonym(s)

***near ant*** tactile; corporeal, physical; embodied, material, real, solid, substantial
***ant*** palpable, tangible, touchable

**integer** *n* a character used to represent a mathematical value — see NUMBER

**integral** *adj* **1** being a part of the innermost nature of a person or thing — see INHERENT
**2** impossible to do without — see ESSENTIAL 1
**3** not lacking any part or member that properly belongs to it — see COMPLETE 1

**integrate** *vb* **1** to make a part of a body or system — see EMBODY 1
**2** to turn into a single mass that is more or less the same throughout — see BLEND 1

**integrity** *n* **1** conduct that conforms to an accepted standard of right and wrong — see MORALITY 1
**2** devotion to telling the truth — see HONESTY 1
**3** faithfulness to high moral standards — see HONOR 1

**intellect** *n* **1** a very smart person — see GENIUS 1
**2** the ability to learn and understand or to deal with problems — see INTELLIGENCE 1

**intellectual** *adj* **1** much given to learning and thinking ⟨as the daughter of college professors, she's used to being around *intellectual* people⟩
***syn*** cerebral, highbrow
***rel*** cultivated, cultured; erudite, learned, literate, scholarly, well-read; academic, bookish, professorial; didactic, pedantic; high-hat, snobbish, snobby, snooty; educated, schooled; brainy, bright, brilliant, clever, intelligent, quick-witted, smart
***near ant*** uncultivated, uncultured; ignorant, illiterate, uneducated, unlettered, unread; dumb, foolish, idiotic, moronic, slow, stupid, unintelligent
***ant*** lowbrow, nonintellectual
**2** of or relating to the mind — see MENTAL 1

**intelligence** *n* **1** the ability to learn and understand or to deal with problems ⟨high scores on this test supposedly demonstrate great *intelligence*⟩
***syn*** brain(s), gray matter, intellect, reason, sense
***rel*** acumen, alertness, astuteness, discernment, insight, judgment (*or* judgement), mentality, perception, perspicacity; sagacity, sapience, wisdom, wit; head, mind, skull
***near ant*** denseness, density, doltishness, dopiness, dullness (*also* dulness), dumbness, fatuity, feeblemindedness, foolishness, idiocy, imbecility, senselessness, simpleness, slowness, stupidity
**2** a report of recent events or facts not previously known — see NEWS

**intelligent** *adj* **1** having or showing quickness of mind ⟨the dolphin is considered one of the most *intelligent* animals⟩ ⟨running for help was an *intelligent* response to the emergency⟩
***syn*** alert, brainy, bright, brilliant, clever, keen, nimble, quick, quick-witted, sharp, sharp-witted, smart
***rel*** apt, ingenious, resourceful; acute, astute, discerning, insightful, knowing, perceptive, perspicacious, sagacious, sapient, savvy, wise; cerebral, erudite, highbrow, knowledgeable, learned, literate, scholarly, well-read; educated, informed, schooled, skilled, trained; creative, inventive, judicious, prudent, sage, sane, sapient, sensible, sound, wise; crafty, cunning, foxy, shrewd, wily; logical, rational, reasonable
***near ant*** retarded; foolish, idiotic, imbecile, imbecilic, moronic, silly, witless; ignorant, illiterate, lowbrow, nonintellectual, unacademic, uneducated, uninformed
***ant*** brainless, dense, doltish, dorky, dull, dumb, mindless, obtuse, simple, slow, stupid, thick, unintelligent
**2** having the ability to reason — see RATIONAL 1

**intemperate** *adj* showing no signs of being under control — see RAMPANT 1

**intend** *vb* to have in mind as a purpose or goal ⟨he *intends* to be the president of a large corporation someday⟩
***syn*** aim, aspire, contemplate, design, mean, meditate, plan, propose
***rel*** dream, hope, wish; consider, debate, mull (over), ponder; attempt, endeavor, strive, struggle, try; plot, scheme; accomplish, achieve, effect, execute, perform
***phrases*** figure on

**intended** *n* the person to whom one is engaged to be married — see BETROTHED

**intense** *adj* extreme in degree, power, or effect ⟨the *intense* cold of the polar regions⟩
***syn*** deep, explosive, exquisite, fearful, ferocious, fierce, furious, hard, heavy, intensive, profound, terrible, vehement, vicious, violent
***rel*** accentuated, aggravated, concentrated, deepened; emphasized, enhanced, heightened, intensified, magnified; stressed; exhaustive, thorough; harsh, rigorous, severe
***near ant*** feeble, weak; shallow, superficial; moderated, qualified; alleviated, eased, lightened, toned (down); abated, decreased, diminished, lessened, reduced, subdued
***ant*** light, moderate, soft

**intensely** *adv* with great effort or determination — see HARD 1

**intensify** *vb* to make markedly greater in measure or degree ⟨*intensified* her efforts to move that bookcase by herself⟩
***syn*** amplify, beef (up), boost, consolidate, deepen, enhance, heighten, magnify, redouble, step up, strengthen
***rel*** broaden, enlarge, expand, extend, lengthen; accelerate, hasten, quicken; accentuate, emphasize, stress; augment, reinforce, supplement; maximize; enliven, jazz (up); aggravate, exacerbate

*near ant* decrease, diminish, lessen, let up (on), reduce, subdue, tone (down), weaken; dwindle, recede, subside, taper (off), wane; alleviate, ease, lighten
*ant* abate, moderate

**intensity** *n* **1** depth of feeling — see ARDOR 1
**2** the quality or state of being forceful (as in expression) — see VEHEMENCE 1

**intensive** *adj* extreme in degree, power, or effect — see INTENSE

**intensively** *adv* with great effort or determination — see HARD 1

**intent** *adj* **1** fully committed to achieving a goal — see DETERMINED 1
**2** having the mind fixed on something — see ATTENTIVE

**intent** *n* **1** something that one hopes or intends to accomplish — see GOAL
**2** the idea that is conveyed or intended to be conveyed to the mind by language, symbol, or action — see MEANING 1

**intention** *n* something that one hopes or intends to accomplish — see GOAL

**intentional** *adj* made, given, or done with full awareness of what one is doing ⟨I'm fairly sure that your "accidental" attack on your sister with a water balloon was really *intentional*⟩
*syn* deliberate, purposeful, willful (*or* wilful)
*rel* knowing, witting; designed, intended, planned; conscious; advised, calculated, considered, measured, reasoned, studied, thoughtful, weighed; premeditated; discretionary, elective, optional, volunteer
*near ant* inadvertent, unwitting; accidental, chance, haphazard, hit-or-miss, incidental, random; aimless, desultory, purposeless; abrupt, impetuous, sudden; coerced, forced, involuntary; compulsory, mandatory, necessary, nonelective, obligatory, ordered, required; casual; extemporaneous, impromptu, impulsive, instinctive, spontaneous, unforced, unpremeditated
*ant* unintentional

**intentionally** *adv* with full awareness of what one is doing ⟨the witness *intentionally* gave misleading answers to the questions⟩
*syn* consciously, deliberately, designedly, knowingly, purposefully, purposely, willfully, wittingly
*rel* calculatingly, studiedly; voluntarily, willingly
*phrases* on purpose
*near ant* accidentally, incidentally, randomly; involuntarily, unwillingly; impulsively, instinctively, spontaneously
*ant* inadvertently, unconsciously, unintentionally, unknowingly, unwittingly

**intently** *adv* with great effort or determination — see HARD 1

**intentness** *n* a mental state free of jesting or trifling — see EARNESTNESS

**inter** *vb* to place (a dead body) in the earth, a tomb, or the sea — see BURY 1

**interaction** *n* doings between individuals or groups — see RELATION 1

**intercede** *vb* to act as a go-between for opposing sides — see INTERVENE

**intercessor** *n* one who works with opposing sides in order to bring about an agreement — see MEDIATOR

**intercommunicate** *vb* to engage in an exchange of information or ideas — see COMMUNICATE 2

**intercourse** *n* **1** doings between individuals or groups — see RELATION 1
**2** sexual union involving penetration of the vagina by the penis — see SEXUAL INTERCOURSE

**interdict** *n* an order that something not be done or used — see PROHIBITION 2

**interdict** *vb* to order not to do or use or to be done or used — see FORBID

**interdicted** *adj* that may not be permitted — see IMPERMISSIBLE

**interdicting** *n* the act of ordering that something not be done or used — see PROHIBITION 1

**interdiction** *n* **1** an order that something not be done or used — see PROHIBITION 2
**2** the act of ordering that something not be done or used — see PROHIBITION 1

**interest** *n* **1** a legal right to participation in the advantages, profits, and responsibility of something ⟨all of the workers at the food cooperative have an *interest* in it⟩
*syn* claim, share, stake
*rel* ownership, part, partnership, possession, title
**2** the state of doing well especially in relation to one's happiness or success — see WELFARE

**interest** *vb* to hold the attention of — see ENGAGE 1

**interesting** *adj* holding the attention or provoking interest ⟨the history lecture was so *interesting* that I didn't fall asleep after all⟩
*syn* absorbing, arresting, engaging, engrossing, enthralling, fascinating, gripping, immersing, intriguing, involving, riveting
*rel* breathtaking, electric, electrifying, exciting, exhilarating, galvanizing, inspiring, rousing, stimulating, stirring, thrilling; provocative, tantalizing; emphatic, showy, splashy, striking; alluring, attractive, bewitching, captivating, charming, enchanting, spellbinding; hypnotizing, mesmerizing; curious, odd, unusual, weird; amazing, astonishing, astounding, eye-opening, fabulous, marvelous (*or* marvellous), surprising, wonderful, wondrous; amusing, entertaining
*near ant* tiresome, tiring, wearisome, wearying; unexciting; dreary, humdrum, pedestrian; demoralizing, discouraging, disheartening, dispiriting
*ant* boring, drab, dry, dull, heavy, monotonous, tedious, uninteresting

**interfere** *vb* to interest oneself in what is not one's concern ⟨a strong resentment

---

*syn* synonym(s) *rel* related words
*ant* antonym(s) *near ant* near antonym(s)

of outsiders who *interfered* with their traditional ways of doing things⟩
***syn*** butt in, intrude, meddle, mess, nose, obtrude, poke, pry, snoop
***rel*** intercede, interpose, intervene; encroach, infringe, invade, trespass; fiddle, fool, monkey, play, tamper
***near ant*** avoid, eschew, shun; disregard, ignore, neglect, overlook

**interfere** (with) *vb* to create difficulty for the work or activity of — see HAMPER

**interference** *n* something that makes movement or progress more difficult — see ENCUMBRANCE

**interferer** *n* a person who meddles in the affairs of others — see BUSYBODY

**interfering** *adj* thrusting oneself where one is not welcome or invited — see INTRUSIVE

**interim** *adj* intended to last, continue, or serve for a limited time — see TEMPORARY 1

**interim** *n* a break in continuity — see GAP 2

**interior** *adj* situated farther in — see INNER 1

**interior** *n* an interior or internal part — see INSIDE 1

**interject** *vb* to put among or between others — see INSERT

**interlace** *vb* **1** to cause to twine about one another — see INTERTWINE 1
**2** to scatter or set here and there among other things — see THREAD 1
**3** to twist together into a usually confused mass — see ENTANGLE 1

**interloper** *n* a person who meddles in the affairs of others — see BUSYBODY

**interlude** *n* a break in continuity — see GAP 2

**intermediary** *adj* occupying a position equally distant from the ends or extremes — see MIDDLE 1

**intermediary** *n* one who works with opposing sides in order to bring about an agreement — see MEDIATOR

**intermediate** *adj* **1** being about midway between extremes of amount or size — see MIDDLE 2
**2** occupying a position equally distant from the ends or extremes — see MIDDLE 1

**interment** *n* the act or ceremony of putting a dead body in its final resting place — see BURIAL

**intermingle** *vb* to turn into a single mass that is more or less the same throughout — see BLEND 1

**intermission** *n* a break in continuity — see GAP 2

**intermittent** *adj* **1** occurring or appearing at intervals ⟨*intermittent* showers had me opening and closing my umbrella all day long⟩
***syn*** continual, periodic, periodical, recurrent, recurring
***rel*** alternate, alternating, cyclic (*or* cyclical), rhythmic (*or* rhythmical), seasonal, serial; erratic, fitful, irregular, occasional, spasmodic, sporadic, spotty, unsteady
***near ant*** eternal, everlasting, interminable, perpetual
***ant*** constant, continuous, incessant, unceasing
**2** lacking in steadiness or regularity of occurrence — see FITFUL

**intermix** *vb* to turn into a single mass that is more or less the same throughout — see BLEND 1

**intermixture** *n* a distinct entity formed by the combining of two or more different things — see BLEND

**intern** *vb* to put in or as if in prison — see IMPRISON

**internal** *adj* situated farther in — see INNER 1

**interned** *adj* taken and held prisoner — see CAPTIVE

**internee** *n* one that has been taken and held in confinement — see CAPTIVE

**internment** *n* the act of confining or the state of being confined ⟨the *internment* of Americans of Japanese descent during World War II is one of the more shameful chapters in United States history⟩
***syn*** captivity, confinement, immurement, imprisonment, incarceration
***rel*** bondage, enslavement, servitude; restraint, restriction; arrest, capture, entrapment; custody, detainment, detention
***near ant*** emancipation, liberation, manumission, redemption, release; freedom, independence, liberty

**interpenetrate** *vb* to spread throughout — see PERMEATE

**interpolate** *vb* to put among or between others — see INSERT

**interpose** *vb* **1** to act as a go-between for opposing sides — see INTERVENE
**2** to cause a disruption in a conversation or discussion — see INTERRUPT
**3** to put among or between others — see INSERT

**interposer** *n* one who works with opposing sides in order to bring about an agreement — see MEDIATOR

**interpret** *vb* to make plain or understandable — see EXPLAIN 1

**interpretation** *n* a statement that makes something clear — see EXPLANATION 1

**interpretive** *adj* serving to explain — see EXPLANATORY

**interring** *n* the act or ceremony of putting a dead body in its final resting place — see BURIAL

**interrogate** *vb* **1** to put a question or questions to — see ASK 1
**2** to put a series of questions to — see EXAMINE 1

**interrupt** *vb* to cause a disruption in a conversation or discussion ⟨it's rude to *interrupt* when someone is making an important point⟩
***syn*** break (in), chime in, cut in, interpose, intrude
***rel*** barge (in), bother; add, chip in, contribute, put in

**interruption** *n* **1** a break in continuity — see GAP 2

2 a momentary halt in an activity — see PAUSE

**intersect** *vb* to divide by passing through or across ⟨the highway *intersects* that road⟩
*syn* bisect, cross
*rel* crisscross

**intersection** *n* a place where roads meet — see CROSSROAD 1

**intersperse** *vb* to scatter or set here and there among other things — see THREAD 1

**intertwine** *vb* 1 to cause to twine about one another ⟨*intertwined* two different colors of yarn⟩
*syn* interlace, interweave, lace
*rel* blend, fuse, join, link, mix
*near ant* disentangle, uncoil, untangle, untwine, unwind
2 to twist together into a usually confused mass — see ENTANGLE

**interval** *n* 1 a break in continuity — see GAP 2
2 an open space in a barrier (as a wall or hedge) — see GAP 1

**intervene** *vb* to act as a go-between for opposing sides ⟨*intervened* in the argument before any real harm was done⟩
*syn* intercede, interpose, mediate
*rel* butt in, interfere, intrude, meddle, obtrude, pry, snoop; arbitrate, moderate, negotiate; barge (in), bother; break (in), chime in, cut in; infringe, invade, trespass
*near ant* stand by; avoid, eschew, shun; disregard, ignore, overlook

**interweave** *vb* 1 to cause to twine about one another — see INTERTWINE 1
2 to scatter or set here and there among other things — see THREAD 1
3 to twist together into a usually confused mass — see ENTANGLE 1

**intimacy** *n* the state of being in a very personal or private relationship — see FAMILIARITY 1

**intimate** *adj* 1 closely acquainted — see FAMILIAR 1
2 not known or meant to be known by the general populace — see PRIVATE 1

**intimate** *n* a person who has a strong liking for and trust in another — see FRIEND 1

**intimate** *vb* to convey an idea indirectly — see HINT

**intimation** *n* a slight or indirect pointing to something (as a solution or explanation) — see HINT 1

**intimidate** *vb* to make timid or fearful by or as if by threats ⟨refusing to be *intimidated* by the manager's harsh stare, I demanded my money back⟩
*syn* browbeat, bully, cow, hector
*rel* affright, alarm, frighten, horrify, scare, shock, spook, startle, terrify; menace, terrorize, threaten; badger, harass, hound; bulldoze, coerce, compel, constrain, dragoon, force, make, oblige, press, pressure; demoralize, unman, unnerve; discompose, disconcert, disquiet, distress, disturb, perturb, upset
*near ant* cheer, comfort, console, reassure, solace, soothe; embolden, encourage, hearten, steel; convince, persuade

**intimidating** *adj* 1 causing fear — see FEARFUL 1
2 harsh and threatening in manner or appearance — see GRIM 1

**intimidator** *n* a person who teases, threatens, or hurts smaller or weaker persons — see BULLY 1

**intolerable** *adj* more than can be put up with — see UNBEARABLE

**intolerant** *adj* 1 unable or unwilling to endure ⟨*intolerant* of pain⟩
*syn* impatient
*rel* uncompromising, unforgiving, unyielding; complaining, fussing, griping, grumbling, protesting, squawking, whining
*near ant* accepting, forgiving, long-suffering, resigned, uncomplaining, willing; indulgent
*ant* abiding, enduring, forbearing, patient, tolerant
2 unwilling to grant other people social rights or to accept other viewpoints ⟨*intolerant* people supported racism⟩
*syn* bigoted, narrow, narrow-minded, prejudiced, small-minded
*rel* conservative, hidebound, old-fashioned, reactionary; insular, parochial, provincial; biased, one-sided, partial, partisan
*near ant* extreme, progressive, radical; impartial, objective, unbiased
*ant* broad-minded, liberal, open-minded, tolerant, unprejudiced

**intone** *vb* to utter in musical or drawn out tones — see CHANT 1

**intoxicant** *n* a fermented or distilled beverage that can make a person drunk — see ALCOHOL

**intoxicate** *vb* to cause a pleasurable stimulation of the feelings — see THRILL

**intoxicated** *adj* 1 being under the influence of alcohol — see DRUNK
2 experiencing or marked by overwhelming usually pleasurable emotion — see ECSTATIC

**intoxication** *n* a state of overwhelming usually pleasurable emotion — see ECSTASY

**intractability** *n* refusal to obey — see DISOBEDIENCE

**intractable** *adj* 1 given to resisting authority or another's control — see DISOBEDIENT
2 given to resisting control or discipline by others — see UNCONTROLLABLE

**intrepid** *adj* feeling or displaying no fear by temperament — see BRAVE

**intrepidity** *n* strength of mind to carry on in spite of danger — see COURAGE

**intrepidness** *n* strength of mind to carry on in spite of danger — see COURAGE

**intricacy** *n* 1 something that makes a situation more complicated or difficult — see COMPLICATION 1

---

*syn* synonym(s) *rel* related words
*ant* antonym(s) *near ant* near antonym(s)

2 the state or quality of having many interrelated parts or aspects — see COMPLEXITY 1

**intricate** *adj* 1 having many parts or aspects that are usually interrelated — see COMPLEX 1
2 made or done with great care or with much detail — see ELABORATE 1

**intrigue** *n* a secret plan for accomplishing evil or unlawful ends — see PLOT 1

**intrigue** *vb* 1 to engage in a secret plan to accomplish evil or unlawful ends — see PLOT
2 to hold the attention of — see ENGAGE 1

**intriguing** *adj* holding the attention or provoking interest — see INTERESTING

**intrinsic** *adj* being a part of the innermost nature of a person or thing — see INHERENT

**intrinsically** *adv* by natural character or ability — see NATURALLY 1

**introduce** *vb* 1 to make (one person) known (to another) socially ⟨a friend *introduced* him to the woman who later became his wife⟩
***syn*** acquaint, present
***rel*** address, greet, hail, meet
2 to present or bring forward for discussion ⟨the moderator *introduced* a new topic for the debate⟩
***syn*** bring up, broach, moot, raise
***rel*** allude (to), cite, mention, name, refer (to); offer, propose, suggest; air express, speak (of), talk (about), vent, ventilate; interject, interrupt; debate, discuss, thrash (out *or* over)
***near ant*** censor, hush (up), quiet, silence, suppress
3 to be responsible for the creation and early operation or use of — see FOUND
4 to impart knowledge of a new thing or situation to — see ACQUAINT 1
5 to put among or between others — see INSERT

**introducer** *n* one who creates or introduces something new — see INVENTOR

**introduction** *n* a short section (as of a book) that leads to or explains the main part ⟨a famous person wrote the *introduction* to that new textbook⟩
***syn*** foreword, preamble, preface, prelude, prologue
***rel*** beginning, commencement, initiation, opening, origin, origination, outset, start
***near ant*** postscript; aftermath, cessation, close, closing, conclusion, end, finale, finish, stop, termination
***ant*** epilogue

**introductory** *adj* coming before the main part or item usually to introduce or prepare for what follows — see PRELIMINARY

**introverted** *adj* not comfortable around people — see SHY 2

**intrude** *vb* 1 to cause a disruption in a conversation or discussion — see INTERRUPT
2 to interest oneself in what is not one's concern — see INTERFERE

**intrude** (upon) *vb* to thrust oneself upon (another) without invitation — see BOTHER 1

**intruder** *n* a person who meddles in the affairs of others — see BUSYBODY

**intruding** *adj* thrusting oneself where one is not welcome or invited — see INTRUSIVE

**intrusive** *adj* thrusting oneself where one is not welcome or invited ⟨that *intrusive* neighbor never knocks before coming in⟩
***syn*** interfering, intruding, meddlesome, meddling, nosy (*or* nosey), obtrusive, officious, presumptuous, prying, snoopy
***rel*** bold, brazen, impertinent, impudent, insolent, rude; invading, trespassing; curious, inquisitive; annoying, harassing, pestiferous
***near ant*** quiet, reserved, reticent, retiring, silent, taciturn, withdrawn; inhibited, restrained, subdued
***ant*** unobtrusive

**inundate** *vb* to cover or become filled with a flood — see FLOOD

**inundation** *n* a great flow of water or of something that overwhelms — see FLOOD

**inure** *vb* to make able to withstand physical hardship, strain, or exposure — see HARDEN 2

**inured** *adj* able to withstand hardship, strain, or exposure — see HARDY 1

**invade** *vb* to enter for conquest or plunder ⟨a superpower that had a tendency to *invade* and take over smaller and weaker countries⟩
***syn*** foray (into), overrun, raid
***rel*** despoil, loot, marauid, pillage, plunder, ravage, sack; conquer, crush, overcome, overpower, overwhelm, subdue, subjugate; assail, assault, attack; battle, combat, fight, war (with); encroach, infringe, trespass; besiege, blockade; occupy
***near ant*** defend, guard, protect, shield; oppose, resist, withstand; capitulate (to), cede (to), submit (to), succumb (to), surrender (to), yield (to)

**invader** *n* one that starts armed conflict against another especially without reasonable cause — see AGGRESSOR

[1]**invalid** *adj* chronically or repeatedly suffering from poor health — see SICKLY 1

[2]**invalid** *adj* 1 having no legal or binding force — see NULL 1
2 not being in agreement with what is true — see FALSE 1
3 not using or following good reasoning — see ILLOGICAL
4 having no basis in reason or fact — see GROUNDLESS

**invalidate** *vb* to put an end to by formal action — see ABOLISH

**invariability** *n* the state of continuing without change — see CONSTANCY 1

**invariable** *adj* not capable of changing or being changed — see INFLEXIBLE 1

**invariably** *adv* on every relevant occasion — see ALWAYS 1

**invariant** *adj* not varying — see UNIFORM

**invasion** *n* a sudden attack on and entrance into hostile territory — see RAID 1

**invective** *n* harsh insulting language — see ABUSE 1

**invent** *vb* to create or think of by clever use of the imagination ⟨they *invented* an explanation for the broken vase that would satisfy their grandmother⟩
***syn*** concoct, contrive, cook (up), devise, fabricate, make up, manufacture, think (up)
***rel*** coin, contrive, create, design, hatch, produce; daydream, dream, fantasize; conceive, envisage, imagine, picture, visualize
***near ant*** copy, duplicate, imitate, mimic, replicate

**invented** *adj* not real and existing only in the imagination — see IMAGINARY

**invention** *n* **1** something (as a device) created for the first time through the use of the imagination ⟨his clever *invention* made people's lives easier⟩
***syn*** coinage, concoction, contrivance, creation, innovation, wrinkle
***rel*** contraption, device, gadget, gizmo (*or* gismo), novelty; design, product, work; dream, fantasy (*also* phantasy), picture, vision; conception, imagining, origination
***near ant*** copy, duplicate, imitation
**2** something that is the product of the imagination — see FICTION
**3** the ability to form mental images of things that either are not physically present or have never been conceived or created by others — see IMAGINATION
**4** the skill and imagination to create new things — see CREATIVITY 1

**inventive** *adj* having the skill and imagination to create new things — see CREATIVE 1

**inventiveness** *n* **1** the ability to form mental images of things that either are not physically present or have never been conceived or created by others — see IMAGINATION
**2** the skill and imagination to create new things — see CREATIVITY 1

**inventor** *n* one who creates or introduces something new ⟨the *inventor* of the electric light bulb⟩
***syn*** contriver, designer, developer, deviser, formulator, innovator, introducer, originator
***rel*** author, creator, establisher, father, founder, inaugurator, originator; pioneer, researcher; builder, maker, producer; dreamer
***near ant*** copier, duplicator, imitator

**inventory** *vb* to make a list of — see [1]LIST 1

**invert** *vb* to change the position of (an object) so that the opposite side or end is showing — see REVERSE 2

**invertebrate** *adj* lacking strength of will or character — see WEAK 2

**invest** *vb* **1** to cause (as a person) to become filled or saturated with a certain quality or principle — see INFUSE
**2** to furnish with something freely or naturally — see ENDOW 1
**3** to give official or legal power to — see AUTHORIZE 1
**4** to outfit with clothes and especially fine or special clothes — see CLOTHE 1
**5** to put into an office or welcome into an organization with special ceremonies — see INSTALL 1
**6** to surround (as a fortified place) with armed forces for the purpose of capturing or preventing commerce and communication — see BESIEGE
**7** to surround or cover closely — see ENFOLD 1

**investigate** *vb* to search through or into — see EXPLORE 1

**investigation** *n* a systematic search for the truth or facts about something — see INQUIRY 1

**investigator** *n* a person whose business is solving crimes and catching criminals or gathering information that is not easy to get — see DETECTIVE

**investiture** *n* the process or an instance of being formally placed in an office or organization — see INSTALLATION 1

**investment** *n* the cutting off of an area by military means to stop the flow of people or supplies — see BLOCKADE

**inveterate** *adj* **1** firmly established over time ⟨he has an *inveterate* tendency to tell tall tales that began when he was just a little boy⟩
***syn*** confirmed, deep-rooted, deep-seated, entrenched (*also* intrenched), hard-core, rooted, settled
***rel*** fixed, immutable, set; implanted, inculcated, instilled; inborn, inbred, inherent, innate, natural; accustomed, chronic, customary, habitual, regular, typical, usual; abiding, enduring, lifelong, persistent, persisting
***near ant*** brief, ephemeral, fleeting, impermanent, momentary, short-lived, temporary, transient
**2** being such by habit and not likely to change — see HABITUAL 1

**invidious** *adj* having or showing mean resentment of another's possessions or advantages — see ENVIOUS

**invidiousness** *n* a painful awareness of another's possessions or advantages and a desire to have them too — see ENVY

**invigorate** *vb* to give life, vigor, or spirit to — see ANIMATE

**invigorated** *adj* made or become fresh in spirits or vigor — see NEW 4

**invigorating** *adj* having a renewing effect on the state of the body or mind — see TONIC

**invincible** *adj* incapable of being defeated, overcome, or subdued ⟨an *invincible* wrestler who has never lost a match⟩
***syn*** impregnable, indomitable, insurmountable, invulnerable, unbeatable, unconquerable
***rel*** inviolable, unassailable, untouchable; armored, defended, guarded, protected, safe, safeguarded, secure, shielded; un-

beaten, unconquered, undefeated, unsubdued
*near ant* exposed, imperiled, insecure, liable, open, susceptible, unguarded, unprotected, unsafe, unshielded; defenseless, helpless, powerless, weak
*ant* surmountable, vulnerable

**inviolable** *adj* not to be violated, criticized, or tampered with — see SACRED 1

**invite** *vb* to act so as to make (something) more likely — see COURT 1

**invoice** *n* a record of goods sold or services performed together with the costs due — see [1]BILL 1

**involuntary** *adj* 1 not made or done willingly or by choice ⟨my long stays on the sidelines during our football games were strictly *involuntary*⟩
*syn* coerced, forced, unintended, unintentional, unwilling
*rel* accidental, unplanned, unpremeditated; automatic, impulsive, instinctive, spontaneous, unprompted; inadvertent, unconscious, unknowing, unwitting
*near ant* advised, conscious, considered, knowing, planned, premeditated, purposeful; volitional
*ant* deliberate, intentional, unforced, voluntary, willful (*or* wilful), willing
2 done instantly and without conscious thought or decision — see AUTOMATIC 1
3 forcing one's compliance or participation by or as if by law — see MANDATORY

**involution** *n* the state or quality of having many interrelated parts or aspects — see COMPLEXITY 1

**involve** *vb* 1 to be the business or affair of — see CONCERN 2
2 to have as part of a whole — see INCLUDE
3 to hold the attention of — see ENGAGE 1

**involved** *adj* 1 having many parts or aspects that are usually interrelated — see COMPLEX 1
2 made or done with great care or with much detail — see ELABORATE 1

**involving** *adj* holding the attention or provoking interest — see INTERESTING

**invulnerable** *adj* incapable of being defeated, overcome, or subdued — see INVINCIBLE

**inward** *adj* situated farther in — see INNER 1

**in-your-face** *adj* having or showing a bold forcefulness in the pursuit of a goal — see AGGRESSIVE 1

**iota** *n* the smallest amount or part imaginable — see JOT

**irascibility** *n* readiness to show annoyance or impatience — see PETULANCE

**irascible** *adj* easily irritated or annoyed — see IRRITABLE

**irate** *adj* feeling or showing anger — see ANGRY

**irateness** *n* an intense emotional state of displeasure with someone or something — see ANGER

**ire** *n* an intense emotional state of displeasure with someone or something — see ANGER

**ireful** *adj* feeling or showing anger — see ANGRY

**irk** *vb* to disturb the peace of mind of (someone) especially by repeated disagreeable acts — see IRRITATE 1

**irksome** *adj* causing annoyance — see ANNOYING

**iron** *adj* not showing weakness or uncertainty — see FIRM 1

**irons** *n pl* something that physically prevents free movement — see BOND 1

**irradiate** *vb* to supply with light — see ILLUMINATE 1

**irrational** *adj* not using or following good reasoning — see ILLOGICAL

**irrecoverable** *adj* 1 not capable of being cured or reformed — see HOPELESS 1
2 not capable of being repaired, regained, or undone — see IRREPARABLE

**irredeemable** *adj* 1 not capable of being cured or reformed — see HOPELESS 1
2 not capable of being repaired, regained, or undone — see IRREPARABLE

**irrefutable** *adj* not capable of being challenged or proved wrong ⟨the *irrefutable* reply of "Because I like it!"⟩
*syn* incontestable, incontrovertible, indisputable, indubitable, unanswerable, undeniable, unquestionable
*rel* certain, definite, positive, sure; unambiguous, unequivocal; absolute, clear, conclusive, decisive; uncontested, undisputed
*near ant* controversial, debated, disputed; doubtful, dubious, inconclusive, indecisive, uncertain; ambiguous, equivocal
*ant* answerable, debatable, disputable, questionable

**irregular** *adj* 1 departing from some accepted standard of what is normal — see DEVIANT
2 lacking in steadiness or regularity of occurrence — see FITFUL
3 not having a level or smooth surface — see UNEVEN 1
4 not rigidly following established form, custom, or rules — see INFORMAL 1
5 not staying constant — see UNEVEN 2

**irregularly** *adv* without definite aim, direction, rule, or method — see HIT OR MISS

**irrelevance** *n* the quality or state of not having anything to do with the matter at hand ⟨the *irrelevance* of the comment brought conversation to a standstill⟩
*syn* extraneousness, inapplicability
*rel* inappropriateness, inaptness, unfitness, unsuitability; insignificance, unimportance; pointlessness, uselessness
*near ant* bearing, connection; appropriateness, aptness, fitness, suitability; importance, significance; usefulness
*ant* applicability, materiality, pertinence, relevance

**irrelevant** *adj* not having anything to do with the matter at hand ⟨*irrelevant* ques-

tions that merely disrupted the classroom lesson〉
***syn*** extraneous, immaterial, inapplicable
***rel*** inconsequential, insignificant, unimportant; meaningless, pointless, senseless, useless; inappropriate, inapt, unsuitable
***phrases*** beside the point
***near ant*** important, meaningful, significant; sensible, useful; appropriate, apt, fit, suitable
***ant*** applicable, apposite, apropos, germane, material, pertinent, relevant

**irreligious** *adj* lacking religious emotions, principles, or practices 〈raised in an *irreligious* family where the subject of God was never even discussed〉
***syn*** godless, nonreligious
***rel*** ungodly, unholy; blasphemous, impious, irreverent, sacrilegious; agnostic, atheistic; unconsecrated, unhallowed; profane, secular, worldly
***near ant*** devout, godly, holy, pious, prayerful, reverent, worshipful, worshipping (*also* worshiping); sanctimonious
***ant*** religious

**irremediable** *adj* **1** not capable of being cured or reformed — see HOPELESS 1
**2** not capable of being repaired, regained, or undone — see IRREPARABLE

**irremovable** *adj* incapable of moving or being moved — see IMMOVABLE 1

**irreparable** *adj* not capable of being repaired, regained, or undone 〈*irreparable* damage to the car〉
***syn*** irrecoverable, irredeemable, irremediable, irretrievable, irreversible, unrecoverable, unredeemable
***rel*** irreplaceable, irrevocable; unredeemed, unrepaired
***near ant*** corrected, fixed, recovered, remedied, repaired
***ant*** fixable, redeemable, remediable, retrievable

**irreproachable** *adj* **1** free from guilt or blame — see INNOCENT 2
**2** being entirely without fault — see PERFECT 1

**irresolution** *n* the act or an instance of pausing because of uncertainty about the right course of action — see HESITATION

**irresponsible** *adj* having or showing a lack of concern for the consequences of one's actions — see RECKLESS 1

**irretrievable** *adj* **1** not capable of being cured or reformed — see HOPELESS 1
**2** not capable of being repaired, regained, or undone — see IRREPARABLE

**irreverence** *n* an act of great disrespect shown to God or to sacred ideas, people, or things — see BLASPHEMY

**irreverent** *adj* not showing proper reverence for the holy or sacred 〈*irreverent* behavior during church services〉
***syn*** blasphemous, impious, profane, sacrilegious
***rel*** agnostic, atheistic; godless, irreligious, nonreligious, secular; ungodly, unholy; unconsecrated, unhallowed, unsanctified
***near ant*** devout, godly, holy, prayerful, religious, worshipful, worshipping (*also* worshiping); consecrated, hallowed, sanctified
***ant*** pious, reverent

**irreversible** *adj* not capable of being repaired, regained, or undone — see IRREPARABLE

**irrigate** *vb* to pour liquid over or through in order to cleanse — see FLUSH 1

**irritability** *n* readiness to show annoyance or impatience — see PETULANCE

**irritable** *adj* easily irritated or annoyed 〈that *irritable* old man always yells at people to stay off of his lawn〉
***syn*** choleric, crabby, cranky, cross, crotchety, grouchy, grumpy, irascible, peevish, perverse, pettish, petulant, quick-tempered, short-tempered, snappish, snappy, snippy, testy, waspish
***rel*** bearish, bilious, cantankerous, disagreeable, dyspeptic, ill-humored, ill-natured, ill-tempered, ornery, surly; sensitive, sulky, thin-skinned, touchy; hot-blooded, passionate
***phrases*** out of sorts
***near ant*** affable, cordial, friendly, genial, sociable; amiable, good-natured, good-tempered, well-disposed; carefree, easy-going, relaxed; obliging, patient, tolerant, uncomplaining, understanding

**irritableness** *n* readiness to show annoyance or impatience — see PETULANCE

**irritant** *n* something that is a source of irritation — see ANNOYANCE 3

**irritate** *vb* **1** to disturb the peace of mind of (someone) especially by repeated disagreeable acts 〈constant chatter *irritated* the student, who was trying to concentrate on a hard assignment〉
***syn*** aggravate, annoy, bother, bug, chafe, exasperate, gall, get, grate, irk, nettle, peeve, persecute, pique, put out, rasp, rile, vex
***rel*** hassle, heckle; nag; inflame, provoke, rouse; bait, harass, harry, pester; anger, enrage, incense, infuriate, madden; agitate, disturb, fret, perturb, upset; affront, insult, offend, outrage
***phrases*** rub the wrong way
***near ant*** appease, conciliate, mollify, oblige, pacify, placate, propitiate; delight, gladden, gratify, please, satisfy; comfort, console, content, quiet, soothe
**2** to make sore by continued rubbing — see CHAFE 1

**irritating** *adj* causing annoyance — see ANNOYING

**irritation** *n* the feeling of impatience or anger caused by another's repeated disagreeable acts — see ANNOYANCE 2

**irruption** *n* a sudden attack on and entrance into hostile territory — see RAID 1

**island** *n* a fairly small area of land completely surrounded by water 〈they're taking a trip to an *island* in Hawaii for vacation〉

*syn* isle, islet
*rel* barrier reef, cay, coral reef, key; archipelago, atoll; cape, headland, peninsula, promontory
*near ant* continent, main, mainland

**isle** *n* a fairly small area of land completely surrounded by water — see ISLAND

**islet** *n* a fairly small area of land completely surrounded by water — see ISLAND

**isolate** *vb* to set or keep apart from others ⟨*isolated* her in a corner for a five-minute punishment after she threw a book at her friend⟩
*syn* cut off, insulate, seclude, segregate, separate, sequester
*rel* quarantine; confine, immure, incarcerate, intern, jail, lock (up), restrain, restrict; detach, disengage, remove; detain, hold, keep
*near ant* associate, connect, join, link, unite; discharge, free, liberate, loose, release
*ant* desegregate, integrate

**isolated** *adj* hidden from view — see SECLUDED

**isolation** *n* the state of being alone or kept apart from others ⟨*isolation* always made the sociable child lonely⟩
*syn* insulation, secludedness, seclusion, segregation, separateness, sequestration, solitariness, solitude
*rel* loneliness, lonesomeness; confinement, incarceration, internment, quarantine; retirement, withdrawal
*near ant* companionship, company

**issuance** *n* the act or process of giving out something to each member of a group — see DISTRIBUTION 1

**issue** *n* **1** a condition or occurrence traceable to a cause — see EFFECT 1
**2** a place or means of going out — see EXIT 1
**3** the descendants of a person, animal, or plant — see OFFSPRING

**issue** *vb* **1** to produce and release for distribution in printed form — see PUBLISH 1
**2** to throw or give off — see EMIT 1

**Italian sandwich** *n* a large sandwich on a long split roll — see SUBMARINE

**itch** *n* a strong wish for something — see DESIRE

**itch** (for) *vb* to have an earnest wish to own or enjoy — see DESIRE

**item** *n* **1** a separate part in a list, account, or series ⟨she got all the *items* on her grocery list except cereal⟩
*syn* detail, particular, point
*rel* article, belonging, object, stuff, thing; characteristic, constituent, element, feature; ingredient; division, particle, piece, portion, section, segment
*near ant* aggregate, composite, compound, conglomerate; entirety, sum, total, totality, whole
**2** a report of recent events or facts not previously known — see NEWS

**itemize** *vb* **1** to make a list of — see [1]LIST 1
**2** to specify one after another — see ENUMERATE 1

**itinerant** *adj* traveling from place to place ⟨an *itinerant* musician can see a lot of the world⟩
*syn* errant, gallivanting (*also* galavanting), nomad (*or* nomadic), peripatetic, ranging, roaming, roving, vagabond, vagrant, wandering, wayfaring
*rel* drifting, footloose, meandering, rambling; sauntering, strolling, traipsing, walking
*near ant* immobile, settled, stationary

# J

**jab** *n* a quick thrust — see [1]POKE

**jabber** *n* unintelligible or meaningless talk — see GIBBERISH

**jabber** *vb* **1** to engage in casual or rambling conversation — see CHAT
**2** to speak rapidly, inarticulately, and usually unintelligibly — see BABBLE 1

**jabberer** *n* a person who talks constantly — see CHATTERBOX

**jabberwocky** *n* unintelligible or meaningless talk — see GIBBERISH

**jack** *n* **1** *slang* something (as pieces of stamped metal or printed paper) customarily and legally used as a medium of exchange, a measure of value, or a means of payment — see MONEY
**2** a piece of cloth with a special design that is used as an emblem or for signaling — see FLAG 1
**3** an adult male human being — see MAN 1
**4** one who operates or navigates a seagoing vessel — see SAILOR

**jack** (up) *vb* **1** to lift with effort — see HEAVE 1
**2** to move from a lower to a higher place or position — see RAISE 1

**jackass** *n* **1** a person who lacks good sense or judgment — see FOOL 1
**2** a stupid person — see IDIOT
**3** a sturdy and patient domestic mammal that is used especially to carry things — see DONKEY 1

**jacked** (up) *adj* being at a higher level than average — see HIGH 2

**jacket** *n* something that encloses another thing especially to protect it — see [1]CASE 1

**jackpot** *n* the total of the bets at stake at one time — see POT 1

**jack–tar** *n* one who operates or navigates a seagoing vessel — see SAILOR

**jade** *vb* to make weary and restless by being dull or monotonous — see ²BORE

**jaded** *adj* **1** depleted in strength, energy, or freshness — see WEARY 1
**2** having one's patience, interest, or pleasure exhausted — see WEARY 2

**jading** *adj* causing weariness, restlessness, or lack of interest — see BORING

**jagged** *adj* **1** having an uneven edge or outline — see RAGGED 1
**2** not having a level or smooth surface — see UNEVEN 1

**jail** *n* a place of confinement for persons held in lawful custody ⟨sentenced to three years in *jail* for his crime⟩
***syn*** brig, gaol [*chiefly British*], guardroom, hoosegow, jug, lockup, pen, penitentiary, prison, stockade
***rel*** bull pen; concentration camp, prison camp; dungeon, keep; reformatory, reform school
***near ant*** freedom

**jail** *vb* to put in or as if in prison — see IMPRISON

**jailbird** *n* a person convicted as a criminal and serving a prison sentence — see CONVICT

**jailed** *adj* taken and held prisoner — see CAPTIVE

**jam** *n* a difficult, puzzling, or embarrassing situation from which there is no easy escape — see PREDICAMENT

**jam** *vb* **1** to fit (something) into a tight space — see CROWD 1
**2** to prevent passage through — see CLOG 1
**3** to put into (something) as much as can be held or contained — see FILL 1

**jammed** *adj* **1** containing or seeming to contain the greatest quantity or number possible — see FULL 1
**2** firmly positioned in place and difficult to dislodge — see TIGHT 2

**jam–pack** *vb* to put into (something) as much as can be held or contained — see FILL 1

**jam–packed** *adj* **1** containing or seeming to contain the greatest quantity or number possible — see FULL 1
**2** having little space between items or parts — see CLOSE 1

**janitor** *n* **1** a person who takes care of a property sometimes for an absent owner — see CUSTODIAN 1
**2** a person who tends a door — see DOOR KEEPER

**jar** *n* **1** a forceful coming together of two things — see IMPACT 1
**2** something that makes a strong impression because it is so unexpected — see SURPRISE 1

**jar** *vb* to be out of harmony or agreement usually noticeably — see CLASH

**jargon** *n* the special terms or expressions of a particular group or field — see TERMINOLOGY

**jarring** *adj* disagreeable to one's aesthetic or artistic sense — see HARSH 2

**jaundice** *n* a deep-seated ill will — see ENMITY

**jaundiced** *adj* **1** having or showing mean resentment of another's possessions or advantages — see ENVIOUS
**2** marked by opposition or ill will — see HOSTILE 1

**jaunt** *n* a short trip for pleasure — see EXCURSION 1

**jauntily** *adv* **1** in a bright and showy way — see GAILY 3
**2** in a quick and spirited manner — see GAILY 2

**jaunty** *adj* having much high-spirited energy and movement — see LIVELY 1

**javelin** *n* a weapon with a long straight handle and sharp head or blade — see SPEAR

**jaw** *vb* **1** to criticize (someone) severely or angrily especially for personal failings — see SCOLD
**2** to engage in casual or rambling conversation — see CHAT

**jazz** *n* unintelligible or meaningless talk — see GIBBERISH

**jazz** (up) *vb* to give life, vigor, or spirit to — see ANIMATE

**jazziness** *n* the quality or state of having abundant or intense activity — see VITALITY 1

**jazzy** *adj* **1** attractively eye-catching in style ⟨that's a *jazzy* bathing suit, with all those spangles⟩
***syn*** flashy, snazzy, splashy
***rel*** cool, hip, neat; à la mode (*also* a la mode), chic, dashing; faddish, fashionable, in, modish, posh, ritzy, sharp, smart, snappy, spruce, stylish; custom, designer; garish, gaudy, loud, rakish, wild
***near ant*** classic, elegant, genteel, polished, refined, sophisticated, stately, swank; plain, quiet, restrained, simple, understated
**2** having much high-spirited energy and movement — see LIVELY 1

**jealous** *adj* **1** intolerant of rivalry or unfaithfulness ⟨became *jealous* whenever she paid attention to anyone but him⟩
***syn*** possessive
***rel*** controlling, demanding, grasping; covetous, envious, invidious, jaundiced; distrustful, mistrustful, suspicious
***phrases*** green with envy
***near ant*** undemanding; tolerant, trustful, trusting, understanding
**2** having or showing mean resentment of another's possessions or advantages — see ENVIOUS

**jealousy** *n* a painful awareness of another's possessions or advantages and a desire to have them too — see ENVY

**jeer** *n* a vocal sound made to express scorn or disapproval — see CATCALL

---

***syn*** synonym(s) ***rel*** related words
***ant*** antonym(s) ***near ant*** near antonym(s)

**jeer** *vb* to make (someone or something) the object of unkind laughter — see RIDICULE

**Jehovah** *n* the being worshipped as the creator and ruler of the universe — see DEITY 2

**jell** *vb* **1** to take on a definite form — see FORM 1
**2** to turn from a liquid into a substance resembling jelly — see COAGULATE

**jelly** *vb* to turn from a liquid into a substance resembling jelly — see COAGULATE

**jeopardize** *vb* to place in danger — see ENDANGER

**jeopardizing** *adj* involving potential loss or injury — see DANGEROUS

**jeopardy** *n* the state of not being protected from injury, harm, or evil — see DANGER 1

**jerk** *n* **1** a person whose behavior is offensive to others ⟨his constant rudeness and insensitivity made everyone think he was a real *jerk*⟩
***syn*** beast, boor, cad, churl, clown, creep, cretin, cur, heel, joker, louse, lout, skunk, slob, snake, stinker
***rel*** brute, Neanderthal, savage; rascal, rogue, scamp, villain; fool, jackass, nincompoop, nitwit; blockhead, dolt, goon, idiot
***near ant*** hero, idol, role model
**2** the act or an instance of applying force on something so that it moves in the direction of the force — see PULL 1

**jerk** *vb* **1** to move or cause to move with a sharp quick motion ⟨I *jerked* to one side to avoid getting hit⟩ ⟨*jerked* the leash to get the dog's attention⟩
***syn*** buck, hitch, jolt, twitch, yank
***rel*** bump, jounce, lurch, stagger; jiggle, shake; lug, pull, tug; pluck, tweak; grab, snap, snatch, wrench, wrest, wring
**2** to make jerky or restless movements — see FIDGET

**jerky** *adj* **1** marked by a series of sharp quick motions ⟨made *jerky* progress walking with the new crutches⟩
***syn*** bumpy, rough
***rel*** choppy, erratic, fitful, irregular, spasmodic, spastic, unsteady
***near ant*** calm, placid, smooth, steady, still
**2** showing or marked by a lack of good sense or judgment — see FOOLISH 1

**jest** *n* **1** an attitude or manner not to be taken seriously — see FUN 2
**2** something said or done to cause laughter — see JOKE 1

**jest** *vb* to make jokes — see JOKE

**jester** *n* **1** a person (as a writer) noted for or specializing in humor — see HUMORIST
**2** a person formerly kept in a royal or noble household to amuse with jests and pranks — see FOOL 2

**jesting** *adj* marked by or expressive of mild or good-natured teasing — see QUIZZICAL

**jesting** *n* good-natured teasing or exchanging of clever remarks — see BANTER

**jet** *vb* **1** to flow out in great quantities or with force — see GUSH 1
**2** to throw out or off (something from within) often violently — see ERUPT 1

**jettison** *n* the getting rid of whatever is unwanted or useless — see DISPOSAL 1

**jettison** *vb* to get rid of as useless or unwanted — see DISCARD

**jetty** *n* a structure used by boats and ships for taking on or landing cargo and passengers — see DOCK

**jewel** *n* **1** a usually valuable stone cut and polished for ornament — see GEM 1
**2** an asset that brings praise or renown — see GLORY 2
**3** someone or something unusually desirable — see PRIZE 1

**jibe** *vb* to be in agreement on every point — see CHECK 1

**jiffy** *n* a very small space of time — see INSTANT

**jig** *n* a clever often underhanded means to achieve an end — see TRICK 1

**jigger** *n* an interesting and often novel device with a practical use — see GADGET

**jiggling** *n* a series of slight movements by a body back and forth or from side to side — see VIBRATION

**jim–dandy** *adj* of the very best kind — see EXCELLENT

**jim–dandy** *n* something very good of its kind ⟨the brand new car was a *jim-dandy*⟩
***syn*** beauty, corker, crackerjack, dandy, knockout, nifty, pip
***rel*** marvel, wonder; gem, jewel, treasure
***near ant*** disappointment, failure, lemon, loser

**jimmy** *vb* to raise, move, or pull apart with or as if with a lever — see [1]PRY 1

**jingle** *n* **1** a series of short high ringing sounds — see TINKLE
**2** a short musical composition for the human voice often with instrumental accompaniment — see SONG 1

**jingle** *vb* to make a repeated sharp light ringing sound ⟨the bell on the kitten's collar *jingled* as she walked⟩
***syn*** chink, clink, tinkle
***rel*** clack, clang, clank; clatter, rattle; ding, jangle, ping, ring

**jingo** *n* **1** one who shows excessive favoritism towards his or her country — see NATIONALIST
**2** one who urges or attempts to cause a war — see WARMONGER

**jingoism** *n* excessive favoritism towards one's own country — see CHAUVINISM

**jinx** *n* something that brings bad luck ⟨believed the broken mirror was a *jinx*⟩
***syn*** hex, hoodoo
***rel*** curse, evil eye, spell; augury, omen, portent
***near ant*** amulet, charm, talisman

**jitters** *n pl* a sense of panic or extreme nervousness ⟨always got the *jitters* right before a test⟩

*syn* dither, nerves, shakes, shivers, willies
*rel* cold sweat, creeps; anxiety, fear, hysteria; frazzle, nervous breakdown
*near ant* aplomb, composure, coolheadedness, equanimity, imperturbability, self-possession

**jittery** *adj* **1** easily excited by nature — see EXCITABLE
**2** feeling or showing uncomfortable feelings of uncertainty — see NERVOUS 1

**jive** *vb* **1** to make fun of in a good-natured way — see TEASE 1
**2** to make jokes — see JOKE

**job** *n* **1** an assignment at which one regularly works for pay ⟨a high-paying *job* as a banker⟩
*syn* appointment, berth, billet, capacity, function, place, position, post, situation
*rel* business, employment, occupation, profession; work; office, spot; calling, pursuit, vocation; line, racket; engagement; livelihood, living; assignment, mission, task
*near ant* avocation; joblessness, unemployment
**2** a piece of work that needs to be done regularly — see CHORE 1
**3** a specific task with which a person or group is charged — see MISSION
**4** the action for which a person or thing is specially fitted or used or for which a thing exists — see ROLE

**jobholder** *n* one who works for another for wages or a salary — see EMPLOYEE

**jocose** *adj* indicative of or marked by high spirits or good humor — see MERRY

**jocosely** *adv* in a cheerful or happy manner — see GAILY 1

**jocular** *adj* given to or marked by mature intelligent humor — see WITTY

**jocund** *adj* indicative of or marked by high spirits or good humor — see MERRY

**jog** *vb* **1** to go at a pace faster than a walk — see RUN 1
**2** to make short up-and-down movements — see NOD

**joggle** *vb* to make a series of small irregular or violent movements — see SHAKE 1

**join** *vb* **1** to be adjacent to — see ADJOIN 1
**2** to become a member of — see ENTER 2
**3** to come together to form a single unit — see UNITE 1
**4** to participate or assist in a joint effort to accomplish an end — see COOPERATE 1
**5** to put or bring together so as to form a new and longer whole — see CONNECT 1

**joining** *adj* having a border in common — see ADJACENT

**joint** *adj* used or done by a number of people as a group — see COLLECTIVE

**joint** *n* **1** a place where two or more things are united ⟨the leak was found at a *joint* in the pipe⟩
*syn* connection, coupling, junction, juncture
*rel* crux, link, tie; interconnection, intersection; abutment, articulation; seam, suture; concourse, confluence, meeting; union
*near ant* crack, separation
**2** a building, room, or suite of rooms occupied by a service business — see PLACE 2

**jointly** *adv* in or by combined action or effort — see TOGETHER 2

**joke** *n* **1** something said or done to cause laughter ⟨he was known for his hilarious *jokes*⟩
*syn* crack, gag, jest, laugh, pleasantry, quip, sally, waggery, wisecrack, witticism
*rel* funning, joking, wisecracking; antic, buffoonery, caper, monkeyshine(s), prank; caricature, lampoon, parody, put-on; banter, persiflage, raillery, repartee; facetiousness, funniness, hilariousness, humorousness; barb, humor, wit, wordplay
**2** a poor, insincere, or insulting imitation of something — see MOCKERY 1

**joke** *vb* to make jokes ⟨he was known for his ability to *joke*⟩
*syn* banter, fool, fun, jest, jive, josh, kid, quip, wisecrack
*rel* chaff, mock, rally, razz, rib, ridicule, tease; caricature, lampoon, parody, satirize; amuse, divert, entertain

**joker** *n* **1** a person (as a writer) noted for or specializing in humor — see HUMORIST
**2** a person whose behavior is offensive to others — see JERK 1
**3** an adult male human being — see MAN 1

**jokester** *n* a person (as a writer) noted for or specializing in humor — see HUMORIST

**joking** *adj* marked by or expressive of mild or good-natured teasing — see QUIZZICAL

**jollification** *n* joyful or festive activity — see MERRYMAKING

**jollity** *n* joyful or festive activity — see MERRYMAKING

**jolly** *adj* indicative of or marked by high spirits or good humor — see MERRY

**jolly** *adv* to a great degree — see VERY 1

**jolt** *n* **1** a forceful coming together of two things — see IMPACT 1
**2** something that makes a strong impression because it is so unexpected — see SURPRISE 1

**jolt** *vb* **1** to make a series of small irregular or violent movements — see SHAKE 1
**2** to move or cause to move with a sharp quick motion — see JERK 1
**3** to cause an often unpleasant surprise for — see SHOCK 1

**josh** *vb* **1** to make fun of in a good-natured way — see TEASE 1
**2** to make jokes — see JOKE

**joshing** *adj* marked by or expressive of mild or good-natured teasing — see QUIZZICAL

**joshing** *n* good-natured teasing or exchanging of clever remarks — see BANTER

**jot** *n* the smallest amount or part imaginable ⟨it's obvious that he doesn't have a *jot* of interest in history⟩
***syn*** hoot, iota, lick, modicum, rap, tittle, whit
***rel*** ace, bit, crumb, dab, driblet, grimmer, hint, little, mite, nip, ounce, peanuts, ray, scruple, shade, shadow, shred, smidgen, snap, speck, spot, sprinkling, strain, streak, suspicion, touch, trace
**jot** (down) *vb* to make a written note of — see RECORD 1
**jounce** *vb* **1** to make a series of small irregular or violent movements — see SHAKE 1
**2** to make short up-and-down movements — see NOD
**journal** *n* a publication that appears at regular intervals ⟨a monthly scientific *journal*⟩
***syn*** gazette, magazine, newspaper, organ, paper, periodical, review
***rel*** annual, bimonthly, biweekly, daily, monthly, quarterly, semimonthly, semiweekly, weekly, yearbook; broadside, extra, sheet, tabloid
**journalist** *n* a person employed by a newspaper, magazine, or radio or television station to gather, write, or report news — see REPORTER
**journey** *n* a going from one place to another usually of some distance ⟨they were hungry and tired after their long *journey*⟩
***syn*** expedition, passage, peregrination, travel(s), trek, trip
***rel*** errand, excursion, flight, hop, jaunt, junket, outing, sally, tour; cruise, sail, voyage; drive, ride, spin; odyssey, pilgrimage, progress, quest, safari
**journey** *vb* to take a trip especially of some distance — see TRAVEL 1
**jovial** *adj* indicative of or marked by high spirits or good humor — see MERRY
**joviality** *n* a mood characterized by high spirits and amusement and often accompanied by laughter — see MIRTH
**jovially** *adv* in a cheerful or happy manner — see GAILY 1
**joy** *n* **1** a feeling or state of well-being and contentment — see HAPPINESS 1
**2** a source of great satisfaction — see DELIGHT 1
**joy** *vb* to feel or express joy or triumph — see EXULT
**joyful** *adj* experiencing pleasure, satisfaction, or delight — see GLAD 1
**joyless** *adj* feeling unhappiness — see SAD 1
**joylessness** *n* a state or spell of low spirits — see SADNESS
**joyous** *adj* experiencing pleasure, satisfaction, or delight — see GLAD 1
**jubilant** *adj* having or expressing feelings of joy or triumph — see EXULTANT
**jubilee** *n* a time or program of special events and entertainment in honor of something — see FESTIVAL
**judge** *n* **1** a person who impartially decides or resolves a dispute or controversy ⟨their father always played the role of *judge* when there was a disagreement⟩
***syn*** arbiter, arbitrator, referee, umpire
***rel*** justice, magistrate; intermediary, mediator, negotiator; conciliator, go-between, peacemaker, reconciler; decider
**2** a public official having authority to decide questions of law ⟨the *judge* gave the defendant a suspended sentence⟩
***syn*** bench, court, justice, magistrate
***rel*** justice of the peace
***near ant*** claimant, plaintiff; defendant
**judge** *vb* **1** to give an opinion about (something at issue or in dispute) ⟨the committee will *judge* the case based on the evidence⟩
***syn*** adjudge, adjudicate, arbitrate, decide, determine, referee, rule (on), settle, umpire
***rel*** consider, hear, ponder, weigh; size (up); mediate, moderate, negotiate; prosecute, try; find (for *or* against)
***near ant*** equivocate, skirt
**2** to decide the size, amount, number, or distance of (something) without actual measurement — see ESTIMATE 2
**3** to form an opinion through reasoning and information — see INFER 1
**judgment** *or* **judgement** *n* **1** a decision made by a court or tribunal regarding a case it has heard — see SENTENCE
**2** a position arrived at after consideration — see DECISION 1
**3** an idea that is believed to be true or valid without positive knowledge — see OPINION 1
**4** an opinion on the nature, character, or quality of something — see ESTIMATION 1
**judicious** *adj* **1** having or showing good judgment and restraint especially in conduct or speech — see DISCREET
**2** suitable for bringing about a desired result under the circumstances — see EXPEDIENT
**jug** *n* **1** a place of confinement for persons held in lawful custody — see JAIL
**2** a handled container for holding and pouring liquids that usually has a lip or a spout — see PITCHER
**jug** *vb* to put in or as if in prison — see IMPRISON
**jugglery** *n* the use of clever underhanded actions to achieve an end — see TRICKERY
**juiciness** *n* the quality or state of being full of juice — see SUCCULENCE
**juicy** *adj* full of juice ⟨she bit into the *juicy* orange⟩
***syn*** fleshy, pulpy, succulent
***rel*** sappy, watery
***near ant*** dehydrated, dry, withered
**jumble** *n* **1** a state in which everything is out of order — see CHAOS
**2** an unorganized collection or mixture of various things — see MISCELLANY 1
**jumble** *vb* to undo the proper order or arrangement of — see DISORDER
**jumbled** *adj* lacking in order, neatness, and often cleanliness — see MESSY
**jumbo** *adj* unusually large — see HUGE

**jumbo** *n* something that is unusually large and powerful — see GIANT

**jump** *n* **1** an act of leaping into the air ⟨her first *jump* from an airplane at the age of 12⟩
*syn* bound, hop, leap, spring, vault
*rel* bounce, lope, skip; caper, gambol; attack, pounce; dive, pitch, plunge
**2** the more favorable condition or position in a competition — see ADVANTAGE 1

**jump** *vb* **1** to propel oneself upward or forward into the air ⟨*jumped* across the ditch⟩
*syn* bound, hop, leap, spring, vault
*rel* bounce, hurdle, lope, skip; buck; caper, cavort, frolic, gambol, romp; attack, pounce; shoot, skyrocket
**2** to move suddenly and sharply (as in surprise) — see START 1

**jump** (on) *vb* **1** to take sudden, violent action against — see ATTACK 1
**2** to criticize harshly and usually publicly — see ATTACK 2

**jumpiness** *n* a state of nervousness marked by sudden jerky movements ⟨the police detective interpreted the suspect's *jumpiness* as a sign of guilt⟩
*syn* edginess, fidgets, flightiness, restiveness, skittishness
*rel* agitation, anxiety, anxiousness, apprehension, apprehensiveness, disquiet, feverishness, nervousness, perturbation, uneasiness, upset, worry; nerves, tenseness, tension; dither, jitters, shakes, shivers, willies
*near ant* confidence, self-assurance, self-confidence, sureness; control, self-control; aplomb, calm, calmness, collectedness, composure, coolheadedness, coolness, ease, easiness, equanimity, imperturbability, self-possession

**jumpy** *adj* **1** easily excited by nature — see EXCITABLE
**2** feeling or showing uncomfortable feelings of uncertainty — see NERVOUS 1

**junction** *n* **1** a place where two or more things are united — see JOINT 1
**2** the act or an instance of joining two or more things into one — see UNION 1

**juncture** *n* **1** a particular and often important moment in time — see POINT 1
**2** a place where two or more things are united — see JOINT 1
**3** a time or state of affairs requiring prompt or decisive action — see EMERGENCY

**junior** *adj* having not so great importance or rank as another — see LESSER

**junior** *n* one who is of lower rank and typically under the authority of another — see UNDERLING

**junk** *n* discarded or useless material — see GARBAGE

**junk** *vb* to get rid of as useless or unwanted — see DISCARD

**junket** *n* a short trip for pleasure — see EXCURSION 1

**junket** *vb* to entertain with a fancy meal — see FEAST

**junkie** *also* **junky** *n* a person who regularly uses drugs especially illegally — see DOPER

**junking** *n* the getting rid of whatever is unwanted or useless — see DISPOSAL 1

**junky** *adj* **1** having no usefulness — see WORTHLESS
**2** of low quality — see CHEAP 2

**junto** *n* a group of persons formally joined together for some common interest — see ASSOCIATION 2

**jurisdiction** *n* lawful control over the affairs of a political unit (as a nation) — see RULE 2

**just** *adj* **1** being what is called for by accepted standards of right and wrong ⟨a *just* punishment should fit the crime⟩
*syn* deserved, due, merited, right, rightful, warranted
*rel* applicable, appropriate, apt, fit, fitting, meet, proper, requisite, suitable; lawful, legal; accurate, correct
*near ant* incoherent, irrelevant; improper, inapplicable, inappropriate, inapt, inequitable; arbitrary, despotic
*ant* undeserved, undue, unjust, unwarranted
**2** based on sound reasoning or information — see GOOD 1
**3** conforming to a high standard of morality or virtue — see GOOD 2
**4** following the accepted rules of moral conduct — see HONORABLE 1
**5** guided by or in accordance with one's sense of right and wrong — see CONSCIENTIOUS 1
**6** marked by justice, honesty, and freedom from bias — see FAIR 2

**just** *adv* **1** in a like manner ⟨you can do it *just* the way they do⟩
*syn* exactly, precisely
*rel* as well, dead, even, expressly, perfectly
*phrases* to a T
*near ant* slightly, somewhat, vaguely
**2** by a very small margin ⟨I was *just* over the minimum height requirement for admittance to the amusement park ride⟩
*syn* barely, hardly, marginally, scarcely, slightly
*rel* minimally, minutely; approximately, more or less, roughly, somewhat
*near ant* definitely, easily, plainly, positively, quite, unquestionably; abundantly, completely, copiously, generously, greatly
*ant* considerably, significantly, substantially, well
**3** nothing more than ⟨I was *just* kidding⟩
*syn* but, merely, only, simply
**4** as stated or indicated without the slightest difference — see EXACTLY 1
**5** for nothing other than — see SOLELY 1
**6** not long ago — see NEWLY

**justice** *n* **1** the act or practice of giving to others what is their due ⟨they felt that *justice* had been done in the case⟩

*syn* equity, right
*rel* fairness, impartiality; goodness, virtue; honor; decorum
*near ant* bias, partiality, prejudice; corruption, foul play; crime
*ant* inequity, injustice, wrong
**2** a public official having authority to decide questions of law — see JUDGE 1

**justifiable** *adj* capable of being defended with good reasoning against verbal attack — see TENABLE 1

**justification** *n* an explanation that frees one from fault or blame — see EXCUSE

**justified** *adj* based on sound reasoning or information — see GOOD 1

**justify** *vb* **1** to be an acceptable reason for ⟨you seem to think that losing a basketball game *justifies* a temper tantrum⟩
*syn* excuse
*rel* account (for), explain, rationalize; brush (aside *or* off), condone, disregard, forgive, gloss (over), ignore, pardon, pass over, remit, shrug off, wink (at)
**2** to continue to declare to be true or proper despite opposition or objections — see MAINTAIN 2

**jut** *n* a part that sticks out from the general mass of something — see BULGE

**jut** *vb* to extend outward beyond a usual point — see BULGE

**juvenile** *adj* **1** being in the early stage of life, growth, or development — see YOUNG
**2** having or showing the annoying qualities (as silliness) associated with children — see CHILDISH
**3** lacking in adult experience or maturity — see CALLOW

**juvenile** *n* a young person who is between infancy and adulthood — see CHILD 1

**juxtaposed** *adj* having a border in common — see ADJACENT

# K

**keelhaul** *vb* to criticize (someone) severely or angrily especially for personal failings — see SCOLD

**keen** *adj* **1** able to sense slight impressions or differences — see ²ACUTE 1
**2** causing intense discomfort to one's skin — see CUTTING 1
**3** having an edge thin enough to cut or pierce something — see SHARP 1
**4** having or showing quickness of mind — see INTELLIGENT 1
**5** of the very best kind — see EXCELLENT
**6** showing urgent desire or interest — see EAGER

**keen** *n* a crying out in grief — see LAMENT 1

**keen** *vb* to make a long loud mournful sound — see HOWL 1

**keenness** *n* **1** a harsh or sharp quality — see EDGE 1
**2** urgent desire or interest — see EAGERNESS

**keep** *vb* **1** to act properly in relation to ⟨*keep* the Sabbath by not working⟩
*syn* celebrate, commemorate, observe
*rel* bless, consecrate, sanctify, solemnize; honor, laud, praise; obey, respect, revere, reverence, venerate; remember
*phrases* live up to
*near ant* disregard, forget ignore, neglect, overlook
*ant* break, transgress, violate
**2** to continue to have in one's possession or power ⟨the money is yours to *keep*⟩ ⟨*keep* my secret and don't tell it to anyone⟩
*syn* hang on (to), hold, reserve, retain, withhold
*rel* conserve, preserve, save; enjoy, have, own, possess; conduct, control, detain, direct; bear, harbor
*near ant* abandon, cede, yield; contribute, donate, give; discard, dump; decline, reject, repudiate, spurn
*ant* hand over, relinquish, surrender
**3** to do what is required by the terms of — see FULFILL 1
**4** to place somewhere for safekeeping or ready availability — see STORE 1

**keep** (from) *vb* to resist the temptation of — see FORBEAR

**keep** (to) *vb* to give steadfast support to — see ADHERE

**keeper** *n* **1** a person or group that watches over someone or something — see GUARD 1
**2** a person who takes care of a property sometimes for an absent owner — see CUSTODIAN 1

**keeping** *n* **1** responsibility for the safety and well-being of someone or something — see CUSTODY
**2** the fact or state of having (something) at one's disposal — see POSSESSION 1

**keepsake** *n* something that serves to keep alive the memory of a person or event — see MEMORIAL

**keep up** *vb* **1** to continue to operate or to meet one's needs — see HOLD OUT
**2** to keep in good condition — see MAINTAIN 1
**3** to remain indefinitely in existence or in the same state — see CONTINUE 1

**keg** *n* an enclosed wooden vessel for holding beverages — see CASK

**kerchief** *n* a scarf worn on the head — see BANDANNA

**kerf** *n* a V-shaped cut usually on an edge or a surface — see NOTCH 1

**key** *adj* **1** coming before all others in importance — see FOREMOST 1
**2** of the greatest possible importance — see CRUCIAL

**key** *n* **1** an explanatory list of the symbols on a map or chart — see LEGEND 1
**2** something that allows someone to achieve a desired goal — see PASSPORT

**key** *vb* to bring to a state free of conflicts, inconsistencies, or differences — see HARMONIZE 2

**keystone** *n* an immaterial thing upon which something else rests — see BASE 1

**kibitzer** *n* a person who meddles in the affairs of others — see BUSYBODY

**kick** *n* **1** a pleasurably intense stimulation of the feelings — see THRILL
**2** a source of great satisfaction — see DELIGHT 1
**3** a feeling or declaration of disapproval or dissent — see OBJECTION

**kick** *vb* **1** to express dissatisfaction, pain, or resentment usually tiresomely — see COMPLAIN
**2** to present an opposing opinion or argument — see OBJECT

**kick in** *vb* to make a donation as part of a group effort — see CONTRIBUTE 1

**kick off** *vb* to take the first step in (a process or course of action) — see BEGIN 1

**kid** *n* a young person who is between infancy and adulthood — see CHILD 1

**kid** *vb* **1** to make fun of in a good-natured way — see TEASE 1
**2** to make jokes — see JOKE

**kidding** *adj* marked by or expressive of mild or good-natured teasing — see QUIZZICAL

**kiddish** *adj* having or showing the annoying qualities (as silliness) associated with children — see CHILDISH

**kidnap** *vb* to carry a person away by unlawful force or against his or her will ⟨the child was *kidnapped* and held for ransom⟩
***syn*** abduct
***rel*** impress, shanghai, waylay; snatch, spirit
***phrases*** make away with
***near ant*** deliver, ransom, redeem, rescue; restore, return

**kill** *vb* **1** to deprive of life ⟨the soldier was *killed* in battle⟩
***syn*** croak [*slang*], destroy, dispatch, do in, fell, slay
***rel*** annihilate, blot out, butcher, decimate, massacre, slaughter, wipe out; cut down, finish, nip, snuff; assassinate, execute, murder, smite
***phrases*** do away with
***near ant*** restore, resurrect, resuscitate, revive; nurture
***ant*** animate
**2** to reject by or as if by a vote — see NEGATIVE 1
**3** to show (something written) to be no longer valid by drawing a cross over or a line through it — see X (OUT)

**killer** *adj* **1** likely to cause or capable of causing death — see DEADLY
**2** requiring considerable physical or mental effort — see HARD 2

**killer** *n* a person who kills another person — see ASSASSIN

**killjoy** *n* a person who spoils the pleasure of others ⟨his constant negative attitude made him a real *killjoy* when others were trying to have fun⟩
***syn*** party pooper, spoilsport
***rel*** fuddy-duddy, goody-goody, old maid, stick-in-the-mud; defeatist, pessimist; complainer, grouch, sorehead, whiner
***near ant*** cutup, live wire; carouser, celebrant, celebrator, merrymaker, reveler (*or* reveller), roisterer; libertine, playboy, rake

**kilter** *n* a state of being or fitness — see CONDITION 1

**kin** *n* **1** a group of persons who come from the same ancestor — see FAMILY 1
**2** a person connected with another by blood or marriage — see RELATIVE

**kind** *adj* **1** given to or made with heedful anticipation of the needs and happiness of others — see THOUGHTFUL 1
**2** having or marked by sympathy and consideration for others — see HUMANE 1

**kind** *n* **1** a number of persons or things that are grouped together because they have something in common — see SORT 1
**2** one of the units into which a whole is divided on the basis of a common characteristic — see CLASS 2

**kindhearted** *adj* having or marked by sympathy and consideration for others — see HUMANE 1

**kindheartedness** *n* the capacity for feeling for another's unhappiness or misfortune — see HEART 1

**kindle** *vb* to set (something) on fire — see BURN 2

**kindled** *adj* being on fire — see ABLAZE 1

**kindliness** *n* **1** kindly concern, interest, or support — see GOODWILL 1
**2** the capacity for feeling for another's unhappiness or misfortune — see HEART 1

**kindly** *adj* having or marked by sympathy and consideration for others — see HUMANE 1

**kindly** *adv* with good reason or courtesy — see WELL 4

**kindness** *n* **1** an act of kind assistance — see FAVOR 1
**2** the capacity for feeling for another's unhappiness or misfortune — see HEART 1

**kind of** *adv* to some degree or extent — see FAIRLY

**kindred** *adj* **1** having a close connection like that between family members — see RELATED
**2** having or marked by agreement in feeling or action — see HARMONIOUS 3

**kindred** *n* a group of persons who come from the same ancestor — see FAMILY 1

**kinfolk** *n pl* a group of persons who come from the same ancestor — see FAMILY 1
**king** *n* a person of rank, power, or influence in a particular field — see MAGNATE
**kingdom come** *n* a dwelling place of perfect bliss for the soul after death — see HEAVEN 1
**kingly** *adj* fit for or worthy of a royal ruler — see MONARCHICAL
**kingpin** *n* the person (as an employer or supervisor) who tells people and especially workers what to do — see BOSS
**king–size** *or* **king–sized** *adj* **1** unusually large — see HUGE
**2** of great extent from end to end — see LONG 1
**king's ransom** *n* a very large amount of money — see FORTUNE 2
**kinky** *adj* different from the ordinary in a way that causes curiosity or suspicion — see ODD 2
**kinsfolk** *n pl* a group of persons who come from the same ancestor — see FAMILY 1
**kinship** *n* the fact or state of having something in common — see CONNECTION 1
**kinsman** *n* a person connected with another by blood or marriage — see RELATIVE
**kirk** *n, chiefly Scottish* a building for public worship and especially Christian worship — see CHURCH 1
**kiss** *vb* **1** to touch one another with the lips as a sign of love ⟨it's traditional for couples to *kiss* under the mistletoe at Christmastime⟩
***syn*** make out, pet, smooch
***rel*** smack; caress, fondle, hug; bill, cuddle, nestle, snuggle
**2** to pass lightly across or touch gently especially in passing — see BRUSH
**kisser** *n, slang* **1** the front part of the head — see FACE 1
**2** the opening through which food passes into the body of an animal — see MOUTH 1
**kittenish** *adj* affecting shyness or modesty in order to attract masculine interest — see COY 1
**[1]kitty** *n* a small domestic animal known for catching mice — see CAT 1
**[2]kitty** *n* a sum of money set aside for a particular purpose — see FUND 1
**knack** *n* a special and usually inborn ability — see TALENT
**knapsack** *n* a soft-sided case designed for carrying belongings especially on the back — see PACK 1
**knave** *n* a mean, evil, or unprincipled person — see VILLAIN
**knavery** *n* playful, reckless behavior that is not intended to cause serious harm — see MISCHIEF 1
**knavish** *adj* tending to or exhibiting reckless playfulness — see MISCHIEVOUS 1
**knell** *vb* to make the clear sound heard when metal vibrates — see RING 1
**knickknack** *n* a small object displayed for its attractiveness or interest ⟨a variety of pretty porcelain *knickknacks* adorned the mantel⟩
***syn*** bauble, curio, curiosity, gaud, gewgaw, novelty, ornamental, trinket
***rel*** bric-a-brac, trumpery; trifle; figurine, objet d'art, ornament; souvenir
**knife** *n* an instrument with a sharp edge for cutting ⟨be careful in using the *knife* to split open the cardboard box⟩
***syn*** blade, cutter
***rel*** bayonet, bolo, bowie knife, dagger, dirk, machete, pocketknife, poniard, stiletto, switchblade; saber, steel, sword; scalpel
**knob** *n* a small uneven mass — see LUMP 1
**knock** *n* **1** a hard strike with a part of the body or an instrument — see [1]BLOW
**2** bad luck or an example of this — see MISFORTUNE
**knock** *vb* **1** to come into usually forceful contact with something — see HIT 2
**2** to deliver a blow to (someone or something) usually in a strong vigorous manner — see HIT 1
**3** to express one's unfavorable opinion of the worth or quality of — see CRITICIZE
**knock** (about) *vb* to move about from place to place aimlessly — see WANDER
**knock** (down *or* over) *vb* to strike (someone) so forcefully as to cause a fall — see FELL 1
**knockabout** *adj* being rough or noisy in a high-spirited way — see BOISTEROUS
**knock down** *vb* to take apart — see DISASSEMBLE
**knock off** *vb* **1** to bring (as an action or operation) to an immediate end — see STOP 1
**2** to stop doing (something) permanently — see QUIT 2
**knockout** *adj* very pleasing to look at — see BEAUTIFUL
**knockout** *n* **1** a lovely woman — see BEAUTY 2
**2** a temporary or permanent state of unconsciousness — see FAINT
**3** something very good of its kind — see JIM-DANDY
**knot** *n* **1** a number of things considered as a unit — see GROUP 1
**2** a small rounded mass of swollen tissue — see BUMP 1
**3** a uniting or binding force or influence — see BOND 2
**4** a usually small number of persons considered as a unit — see GROUP 2
**5** something that requires thought and skill for resolution — see PROBLEM 1
**knot** *vb* to twist together into a usually confused mass — see ENTANGLE 1
**knothead** *n* a stupid person — see IDIOT
**knotty** *adj* **1** having many parts or aspects that are usually interrelated — see COMPLEX 1
**2** requiring exceptional skill or caution in performance or handling — see TRICKY
**know** *vb* **1** to have a practical understanding of ⟨he *knows* several languages⟩
***syn*** comprehend, grasp, understand
***rel*** appreciate, apprehend, fathom, perceive; have, possess

***near ant*** misapprehend, misconceive, misinterpret, misunderstand

**2** to come to a knowledge of (something) by living through it — see EXPERIENCE

**know–how** *n* knowledge gained by actually doing or living through something — see EXPERIENCE 1

**knowing** *adj* **1** having inside information — see WISE 2

**2** having or showing a practical cleverness or judgment — see SHREWD

**knowingly** *adv* with full awareness of what one is doing — see INTENTIONALLY

**knowledge** *n* **1** a body of facts learned by study or experience ⟨the forest ranger shared some of his vast *knowledge* of the woods with us⟩

***syn*** lore, science, wisdom

***rel*** information, intelligence, lowdown, news; data, evidence, facts; acquaintance, awareness, familiarity, literacy

***near ant*** ignorance, inexperience, unfamiliarity

**2** the understanding and information gained from being educated — see EDUCATION 2

**knowledgeable** *adj* **1** having information especially as a result of study or experience — see FAMILIAR 2

**2** having or displaying advanced knowledge or education — see EDUCATED

**knuckle under** *vb* **1** to cease resistance (as to another's arguments, demands, or control) — see YIELD 3

**2** to yield to the control or power of enemy forces — see FALL 2

**kook** *n* a person of odd or whimsical habits — see ECCENTRIC

**kooky** *adj* showing or marked by a lack of good sense or judgment — see FOOLISH 1

**kowtow** *vb* to use flattery or the doing of favors in order to win approval especially from a superior — see FAWN

# L

**label** *n* a slip (as of paper or cloth) that is attached to something to identify or describe it ⟨on its frame the painting had a *label* with its title and the name of the artist⟩

***syn*** marker, tag, ticket

***rel*** caption, legend; brand, emblem, logo, mark, symbol; badge, decal, plaque, seal, stamp, sticker

**label** *vb* **1** to attach an identifying slip to ⟨he *labeled* all of the poisonous materials with the familiar skull and crossbones⟩

***syn*** mark, tag, ticket

***rel*** caption, earmark, stamp; call, designate, identify, name, tab; brand, stigmatize

**2** to give a name to — see NAME 1

**labor** *n* **1** a dull, unpleasant, or difficult piece of work — see CHORE 2

**2** the active use of energy in producing a result — see EFFORT

**3** very hard or unpleasant work — see TOIL

**4** the act or process of giving birth to children — see CHILDBIRTH

**labor** *vb* to devote serious and sustained effort ⟨he *labored* most of the evening over the difficult homework assignment⟩

***syn*** drudge, endeavor, fag, grub, hump, hustle, moil, peg (away), plod, plow, plug, slave, slog, strain, strive, struggle, sweat, toil, travail, work

***rel*** apply (oneself), attempt, buckle (down), hammer (away), pitch in; attack, drive; essay, try; exercise, exert, overexert, overwork; eke out, grind (out), put out, scratch; trudge, wade; employ, ply, use, utilize, wield

***near ant*** break, ease (up), let up, slacken; bum, goldbrick, idle, loaf, lounge, shirk, slack (off); dawdle, poke, tarry; relax, rest; disport, frolic, gambol, play, recreate, rollick, romp, sport

***ant*** dabble, fiddle (around), fool (around), mess (around), putter (around)

**laborer** *n* a person who does very hard or dull work — see SLAVE 2

**laborious** *adj* **1** involved in often constant activity — see BUSY 1

**2** requiring considerable physical or mental effort — see HARD 2

**3** requiring much time, effort, or careful attention — see DEMANDING 1

**laboriously** *adv* with great effort or determination — see HARD 1

**laborsaving** *adj* designed to replace or decrease human labor and especially physical labor ⟨a new *laborsaving* device let us clean the house in half the time⟩

***syn*** automated, automatic, robotic, self-acting

***rel*** mechanical, motorized; computerized; aiding, helping; easing, relieving; timesaving

**labyrinth** *n* a confusing and complicated arrangement of passages — see MAZE

**labyrinthine** *adj* having many parts or aspects that are usually interrelated — see COMPLEX 1

**lace** *n* **1** a length of braided, flexible material that is used for tying or connecting things — see CORD

**2** a length of something formed of three or more strands woven together — see BRAID

**lace** *vb* **1** to cause to twine about one another — see INTERTWINE 1
**2** to scatter or set here and there among other things — see THREAD 1
**3** to strike repeatedly — see BEAT 1

**laceration** *n* a long deep cut — see GASH

**lachrymose** *adj* given to expressing strong emotion (as sorrow) by readily shedding tears — see TEARFUL

**lacing** *n* **1** a length of braided flexible material that is used for tying or connecting things — see CORD
**2** a length of something formed of three or more strands woven together — see BRAID

**lack** *n* **1** the fact or state of being absent ⟨the *lack* of news about the fate of the soldiers was frustrating⟩
***syn*** absence, dearth, want
***rel*** deficiency, deficit, inadequacy, insufficiency, meagerness, paucity, poverty, scantiness, scarceness, scarcity shortage, skimpiness; deprivation, loss, necessity, need, needfulness, omission; privation; vacuum, void
***near ant*** abundance, amplitude, bounty, plenitude, plenty, wealth; adequacy, sufficiency; excess, overabundance, oversupply, surfeit, surplus; deluge, flood; heap, mountain, peck, pile, pot, quantity, raft, stack, volume, wad; fund, pool, stock, supply; hoard, stockpile
***ant*** presence
**2** a falling short of an essential or desirable amount or number — see DEFICIENCY
**3** a state of being without something necessary, desirable, or useful — see NEED 1

**lackadaisical** *adj* lacking bodily energy or motivation — see LISTLESS

**lackey** *n* a person hired to perform household or personal services — see SERVANT

**lacking** *adj* **1** not coming up to a usual standard or meeting a particular need — see SHORT 3
**2** not present or in evidence — see ABSENT 2

**laconic** *adj* **1** marked by the use of few words to convey much information or meaning — see CONCISE
**2** tending not to speak frequently (as by habit or inclination) — see SILENT 2

**laconically** *adv* in a few words — see SHORTLY 1

**lad** *n* **1** a male person who has not yet reached adulthood — see BOY
**2** an adult male human being — see MAN 1

**ladder** *n* a scheme of rank or order — see [3]SCALE 1

**laddie** *n* a male person who has not yet reached adulthood — see BOY

**lade** *vb* **1** to lift out with something that holds liquid — see DIP 2
**2** to place a weight or burden on — see LOAD 1

**lading** *n* a mass or quantity of something taken up and carried, conveyed, or transported — see LOAD 1

**ladle** *n* a utensil with a bowl and a handle that is used especially in cooking and serving food — see SPOON

**ladle** *vb* to lift out with something that holds liquid — see DIP 2

**lady** *n* **1** an adult female human being — see WOMAN
**2** the female partner in a marriage — see WIFE
**3** a woman of high birth or social position — see GENTLEWOMAN

**ladylove** *n* a woman with whom one is in love — see GIRLFRIEND

**lag** *vb* **1** to lose bodily strength or vigor — see WEAKEN 2
**2** to move or act slowly — see DELAY 1

**laggard** *adj* moving or proceeding at less than the normal, desirable, or required speed — see SLOW 1

**laggard** *n* someone who moves slowly or more slowly than others — see SLOWPOKE

**laggardly** *adv* at a pace that is less than usual, desirable, or expected — see SLOW

**lagger** *n* someone who moves slowly or more slowly than others — see SLOWPOKE

**lagging** *adj* moving or proceeding at less than the normal, desirable, or required speed — see SLOW

**lagniappe** *n* **1** something given in addition to what is ordinarily expected or owed — see BONUS
**2** something given to someone without expectation of a return — see GIFT 1

**laid–back** *adj* having a relaxed, casual manner — see EASYGOING 1

**lair** *n* **1** a place where a person goes to hide — see HIDEOUT
**2** the shelter or resting place of a wild animal — see DEN 1

**lam** *n* the act or an instance of getting free from danger or confinement — see ESCAPE 1

**lam** *vb* to get free from a dangerous or confining situation — see ESCAPE 1

**lamb** *n* an innocent or gentle person ⟨the new guys at football camp were *lambs* who hardly knew what awaited them⟩
***syn*** angel, dove, innocent, sheep
***rel*** fledgling, greenhorn, ingenue (*or* ingénue); cherub, saint; mollycoddle, sissy, softy (*or* softie), weakling, wimp; dupe, pigeon, sap, sucker
***near ant*** bully, roughneck, rowdy, tough; beast, boor, cad, churl, clown, creep, cretin, cur, heel, jerk; shark, skunk, snake, stinker; rascal, rogue, scamp, villain
***ant*** wolf

**lambaste** *or* **lambast** *vb* **1** to criticize (someone) severely or angrily especially for personal failings — see SCOLD
**2** to criticize harshly and usually publicly — see ATTACK 2
**3** to strike repeatedly — see BEAT 1

**lambent** *adj* giving off or reflecting much light — see BRIGHT 1

**lame** *vb* to cause severe or permanent injury to — see MAIM

**lamella** *n* a small thin piece of material that resembles an animal scale — see ²SCALE

**lament** *n* **1** a crying out in grief ⟨the national *lament* that was heard when President Kennedy was assassinated⟩
*syn* groan, howl, keen, lamentation, moan, plaint, wail
*rel* grieving, mourning, weeping; regret; complaint, outcry, protest
*near ant* cheering, laughing, smiling
*ant* exultation, rejoicing
**2** a composition expressing one's grief over a loss ⟨a poem that is her *lament* for her late grandmother⟩
*syn* dirge, elegy, requiem, threnody
*rel* taps
*near ant* encomium, eulogy, paean, panegyric

**lament** *vb* **1** to feel or express sorrow for ⟨she *lamented* the loss of her beloved pet⟩
*syn* bemoan, bewail, deplore, grieve (for), mourn, wail (for)
*rel* elegize; complain (about), cry (for), groan (about), keen, moan, weep; regret, rue; deprecate, disapprove (of)
*near ant* beam, cheer, laugh, smile; boast, brag, crow
*ant* exult (in), glory (in), rejoice (in)
**2** to feel sorry or dissatisfied about — see REGRET

**lamentable** *adj* **1** expressing or suggesting mourning — see MOURNFUL 1
**2** of a kind to cause great distress — see REGRETTABLE

**lamentation** *n* a crying out in grief — see LAMENT 1

**lamina** *n* a small thin piece of material that resembles an animal scale — see ²SCALE

**lamp** *n* something that provides illumination — see LIGHT 2

**lampoon** *n* a creative work that uses sharp humor to point up the foolishness of a person, institution, or human nature in general — see SATIRE

**lance** *n* a weapon with a long straight handle and sharp head or blade — see SPEAR

**lance** *vb* to penetrate or hold (something) with a pointed object — see IMPALE

**land** *n* **1** a body of people composed of one or more nationalities usually with its own territory and government — see NATION
**2** a broad geographical area — see REGION 2
**3** the solid part of our planet's surface as distinguished from the sea and air — see EARTH 2

**land** *vb* **1** to stop at or near a place along the shore ⟨the Pilgrims *landed* at Plymouth after exploring Cape Cod Bay⟩
*syn* anchor, dock
*rel* moor, tie up; beach, ground; harbor; arrive, reach; debark, disembark
*phrases* drop anchor, make port
*near ant* embark, launch, sail
**2** to get to a destination — see COME 2
**3** to go ashore from a ship — see DISEMBARK
**4** to come to rest after descending from the air — see ALIGHT
**5** to receive as return for effort — see EARN 1
**6** to take physical control or possession of (something) suddenly or forcibly — see CATCH 1

**landfill** *n* a place where discarded materials (as trash) are dumped — see DUMP 1

**landing** *n* a structure used by boats and ships for taking on or landing cargo and passengers — see DOCK

**landlord** *n* the owner of land or housing that is rented to another ⟨agreed to pay the *landlord* the rent on the first Monday of each month⟩
*syn* lessor, renter
*rel* landlady; laird, landholder, landowner; host, proprietor; slumlord
*ant* lessee, lodger, tenant

**landmark** *n* a point in a chain of events at which an important change (as in one's fortunes) occurs — see TURNING POINT

**language** *n* **1** the stock of words, pronunciation, and grammar used by a people as their basic means of communication ⟨Great Britain, the United States, Australia, and other countries where English is the dominant *language*⟩
*syn* lingo, mother tongue, speech, tongue, vocabulary
*rel* argot, cant, dialect, idiom, jargon, parlance, patois, patter, pidgin, slang, vernacular; colloquialism, localism, regionalism; terminology
**2** the special terms or expressions of a particular group or field — see TERMINOLOGY
**3** the way in which something is put into words — see WORDING

**languid** *adj* **1** lacking bodily energy or motivation — see LISTLESS
**2** lacking bodily strength — see WEAK 1
**3** moving or proceeding at less than the normal, desirable, or required speed — see SLOW 1

**languish** *vb* to lose bodily strength or vigor — see WEAKEN 2

**languishing** *adj* lacking bodily energy or motivation — see LISTLESS

**languor** *n* the quality or state of lacking physical strength or vigor — see WEAKNESS 1

**languorous** *adj* lacking bodily energy or motivation — see LISTLESS

**lank** *adj* not stiff in structure — see LIMP 1

**lanky** *adj* being tall, thin and usually loose-jointed ⟨the *lanky* basketball star was great at slam-dunking⟩
*syn* gangling, gangly, rangy, spindling, spindly
*rel* angular, bony, gaunt, lank, rawboned, scrawny, skinny; lean, slender, slim, spare, thin; racy, reedy, spidery, stringy, twiggy, wiry; spindle-shanked
*near ant* chubby, chunky, heavyset, pudgy, squat, stocky, stout, stubby,

---

*syn* synonym(s) *rel* related words
*ant* antonym(s) *near ant* near antonym(s)

stumpy, sturdy, thick-bodied, thickset; muscle-bound

**lap** *n* a portion of a trip — see LEG 2

[1]**lap** *vb* **1** to flow along or against — see WASH 1
**2** to flow in a broken irregular stream — see GURGLE
**3** to move with a splashing motion — see SLOSH

[2]**lap** *vb* **1** to lie over parts of one another — see OVERLAP
**2** to surround or cover closely — see ENFOLD 1

**lapping** *n* a partial covering of one thing by an adjoining thing — see OVERLAP

**lapse** *n* **1** a change in status for the worse usually temporarily — see REVERSE 1
**2** an unintentional departure from truth or accuracy — see ERROR 1
**3** the stopping of a process or activity — see END 1

**lapse** *vb* to come to an end — see CEASE 1

**larceny** *n* the unlawful taking and carrying away of property without the consent of its owner — see THEFT 1

**large** *adj* of a size greater than average of its kind ⟨he was hungry, so he ordered the *large* pizza⟩
***syn*** big, bulky, considerable, goodly, good-sized, grand, great, handsome, hefty, hulking, largish, outsize (*also* outsized), oversize (*or* oversized), sizable (*or* sizeable), substantial, tidy, voluminous
***rel*** astronomical (*also* astronomic), bumper, cavernous, colossal, enormous, gigantic, gross, heroic, huge, immense, jumbo, king-size (*or* king-sized), major, mammoth, massive, monolithic, monstrous, monumental, prodigious, staggering, stupendous, super, tremendous, vast, vasty, whacking, whopping; excessive, exorbitant, extravagant, extreme, immoderate, inordinate; abundant, ample, appreciable, copious, plentiful; fat, thick; capacious, commodious, roomy, spacious
***near ant*** diminutive, microscopic (*or* microscopical), midget, miniature, minute, pint-size (*or* pint-sized), pocket-size (*also* pocket-sized), pygmy, smallish, teeny, teeny-weeny, tiny, wee; petite, slender, slight, slim, thin
***ant*** little, puny, small, undersized

**largely** *adv* **1** for the most part — see CHIEFLY
**2** to a large extent or degree — see GREATLY 2

**largeness** *n* the quality or state of being large in size ⟨I was impressed by the *largeness* of the portions at the new restaurant⟩
***syn*** bigness, bulkiness, grandness, greatness, heftiness, substantiality, voluminousness
***rel*** enormity, enormousness, extensiveness, grossness, healthiness, hugeness, immenseness, immensity, magnitude, massiveness, stupendousness, vastness; excessiveness, extravagance, extremeness, immoderacy; abundance, ampleness, bountifulness, copiousness, liberality; adequacy, sufficiency; weightiness
***near ant*** diminutiveness, minuteness, tininess; slightness; meagerness, poorness, scantiness, scarceness, scarcity, skimpiness, slenderness, slimness, spareness, sparseness, stinginess; deficiency, inadequacy
***ant*** fineness, littleness, puniness, smallness

**largess** *or* **largesse** *n* **1** something given to someone without expectation of a return — see GIFT 1
**2** the quality or state of being generous — see LIBERALITY

**largish** *adj* **1** of a size greater than average of its kind — see LARGE
**2** sufficiently large in size, amount, or number to merit attention — see CONSIDERABLE 1

**lariat** *n* a rope or long leather thong with a noose used especially for catching livestock — see LASSO

**lark** *n* a time or instance of carefree fun — see FLING 1

**lark** *vb* to play and run about happily — see FROLIC 1

**larva** *n* a young wingless often wormlike form (as a grub or caterpillar) that hatches from the egg of many insects ⟨the *larva* looked ugly, but it was destined to hatch into a beautiful butterfly⟩
***syn*** naiad, nymph

**lascivious** *adj* **1** depicting or referring to sexual matters in a way that is unacceptable in polite society — see OBSCENE 1
**2** having a strong sexual desire — see LUSTFUL

**lasciviousness** *n* the quality or state of being obscene — see OBSCENITY 1

**lash** *n* a long thin or flexible tool for striking — see WHIP

**lash** *vb* to strike repeatedly with something long and thin or flexible — see WHIP 1

**lass** *n* a young usually unmarried woman — see GIRL 1

**lassie** *n* a young usually unmarried woman — see GIRL 1

**lassitude** *n* a complete depletion of energy or strength — see FATIGUE

**lasso** *n* a rope or long leather thong with a noose used especially for catching livestock ⟨the cowpuncher skillfully tossed the *lasso* around the calf's neck⟩
***syn*** lariat, reata, riata

**last** *adj* following all others of the same kind in order or time ⟨*last* one in the pool is a rotten egg⟩
***syn*** closing, concluding, final, hindmost, latest, latter, rearmost, terminal, terminating, ultimate
***rel*** consequent, ensuing, eventual, following, succeeding; conclusive, crowning, decisive, definitive; farthest, furthest, remotest; lowermost, lowest, nethermost; endmost, extreme, outermost, outmost; penultimate
***near ant*** eminent, premier, superior

*ant* beginning, earliest, first, inaugural, initial, maiden, opening, original, primary, starting

**last** *vb* **1** to continue to operate or to meet one's needs — see HOLD OUT
**2** to remain indefinitely in existence or in the same state — see CONTINUE 1

**last word** *n* a practice or interest that is very popular for a short time — see FAD

**late** *adj* **1** not arriving, occurring, or settled at the due, usual, or proper time ⟨I ran as fast as I could, but was still *late* for class⟩
*syn* behind, behindhand, belated, delinquent, latish, overdue, tardy
*rel* delayed, detained, postponed; dilatory, laggard, slow, sluggish
*near ant* opportune, seasonable, timely; prompt, punctual
*ant* early, premature
**2** having been such at some previous time — see FORMER
**3** no longer living — see DEAD 1

**late** *adv* not long ago — see NEWLY

**lately** *adv* not long ago — see NEWLY

**latency** *n* a state of temporary inactivity — see ABEYANCE

**lateness** *n* the quality or state of being late ⟨we were unable to get into the movie due to our *lateness* in arriving⟩
*syn* belatedness, delinquency, tardiness
*rel* dilatoriness, sluggishness
*near ant* promptness, punctuality
*ant* earliness

**latent** *adj* not being in a state of use, activity, or employment — see INACTIVE 2

**later** *adj* being, occurring, or carried out at a time after something else — see SUBSEQUENT

**later** *adv* following in time or place — see AFTER

**lateral** *adj* of, relating to, or located on one side — see SIDE

**latest** *adj* following all others of the same kind in order or time — see LAST

**lather** *n* **1** a light mass of fine bubbles formed in or on a liquid — see FOAM
**2** a state of nervous or irritated concern — see FRET

**lathery** *adj* covered with, consisting of, or resembling foam — see FOAMY

**latish** *adj* not arriving, occurring, or settled at the due, usual, or proper time — see LATE 1

**latitude** *n* the right to act or move freely — see FREEDOM 2

**latrine** *n* a room furnished with a fixture for flushing body waste — see TOILET

**latter** *adj* following all others of the same kind in order or time — see LAST

**laud** *vb* **1** to declare enthusiastic approval of — see ACCLAIM
**2** to proclaim the glory of — see PRAISE 1

**laudable** *adj* deserving of high regard or great approval — see ADMIRABLE

---

*syn* synonym(s) *rel* related words
*ant* antonym(s) *near ant* near antonym(s)

**laugh** *n* **1** an explosive sound that is a sign of amusement ⟨the child's frown turned into a *laugh* when he saw the clown⟩
*syn* cackle, chortle, chuckle, giggle, guffaw, laughter, snicker, snigger, titter
*rel* crow, whoop; grin, simper, smile, smirk
*near ant* cry, groan, moan, sob, wail
**2** someone or something that is very funny — see SCREAM
**3** something said or done to cause laughter — see JOKE 1

**laugh** *vb* to express scornful amusement by means of facial contortions — see SNEER

**laugh** (at) *vb* to make (someone or something) the object of unkind laughter — see RIDICULE

**laughable** *adj* **1** causing or intended to cause laughter — see FUNNY 1
**2** so foolish or pointless as to be worthy of scornful laughter — see RIDICULOUS 1

**laughing** *adj* indicative of or marked by high spirits or good humor — see MERRY

**laughingstock** *n* a person or thing that is made fun of ⟨his nerdy clothes made him the *laughingstock* of the schoolyard⟩
*syn* butt, mark, mock, mockery, target
*rel* chump, dupe, fall guy, fool, gull, monkey, pigeon, sap, sucker, victim
*near ant* favorite, darling, pet

**laughter** *n* an explosive sound that is a sign of amusement — see LAUGH 1

**launch** *n* **1** a rising from a surface at the start of a flight (as of a rocket) — see LIFT-OFF
**2** the point at which something begins — see BEGINNING

**launch** *vb* **1** to be responsible for the creation and early operation or use of — see FOUND
**2** to take the first step in (a process or course of action) — see BEGIN 1
**3** to send through the air especially with a quick forward motion of the arm — see THROW

**laurels** *n pl* public acknowledgment or admiration for an achievement — see GLORY 1

**lavaliere** *also* **lavalliere** *n* an ornament worn on a chain around the neck or wrist — see PENDANT

**lavatory** *n* a room furnished with a fixture for flushing body waste — see TOILET

**lave** *vb* to flow along or against — see WASH 1

**lavish** *adj* **1** going beyond a normal or acceptable limit in degree or amount — see EXCESSIVE
**2** pouring forth in great amounts — see PROFUSE
**3** showing obvious signs of wealth and comfort — see LUXURIOUS

**lavish** *vb* **1** to give readily and in large quantities — see RAIN 2
**2** to use up carelessly — see WASTE 1

**lavishly** *adv* in a luxurious manner — see HIGH

**lavishness** *n* the quality or fact of being free or wasteful in the expenditure of money — see EXTRAVAGANCE 1

**law** *n* **1** a rule of conduct or action laid down by a governing authority and especially a legislator ⟨a record number of *laws* were passed in that legislative session⟩
*syn* act, enactment, ordinance, statute
*rel* decree, directive, edict, fiat, ruling; bylaw, regulation, rule; amendment, bill, legislation; common law, martial law; prohibition, restriction; canon, encyclical
**2** a collection or system of rules of conduct — see CODE
**3** the department of government that keeps order, fights crime, and enforces statutes — see POLICE 1

**law-abiding** *adj* readily giving in to the command or authority of another — see OBEDIENT

**lawbreaker** *n* a person who has committed a crime — see CRIMINAL

**lawbreaking** *adj* not restrained by or under the control of legal authority — see LAWLESS

**lawbreaking** *n* **1** a breaking of a moral or legal code — see OFFENSE 1
**2** activities that are in violation of the laws of the state — see CRIME 1

**lawful** *adj* permitted by law — see LEGAL 1

**lawfulness** *n* the quality or state of being legal — see LEGALITY

**lawgiver** *n* a member of an organized body of persons having the authority to make laws — see LEGISLATOR

**lawless** *adj* not restrained by or under the control of legal authority ⟨the *lawless* rioters were destroying everything in sight⟩
*syn* anarchic, disorderly, lawbreaking, unruly
*rel* defiant, insubordinate, mutinous, rebellious, refractory, riotous; undisciplined; criminal, illegal, illegitimate, illicit, unlawful, wrongful
*near ant* lawful, legal, legalized, legitimate
*ant* law-abiding, orderly

**lawlessness** *n* **1** a state in which there is widespread wrongdoing and disregard for rules and authority — see ANARCHY
**2** activities that are in violation of the laws of the state — see CRIME 1

**lawmaker** *n* a member of an organized body of persons having the authority to make laws — see LEGISLATOR

**lawsuit** *n* a court case for enforcing a right or claim ⟨she filed a *lawsuit* against the moving company that was responsible for breaking her furniture⟩
*syn* action, proceeding, suit
*rel* litigation; case, cause, complaint

**lawyer** *n* a person whose profession is to conduct lawsuits for clients or to advise about legal rights and obligations ⟨their *lawyers* told them that they couldn't use the park for the concert without permission from the city⟩
*syn* advocate, attorney, counsel, counselor (*or* counsellor)
*rel* pettifogger, shyster; district attorney, prosecutor; solicitor; jurist; lawgiver, lawmaker, legislator, solon

**lax** *adj* **1** failing to give proper care and attention — see NEGLIGENT
**2** not bound by rigid standards — see EASYGOING 2
**3** not tightly fastened, tied, or stretched — see LOOSE 1

**laxness** *n* failure to take the care that a cautious person usually takes — see NEGLIGENCE 1

**lay** *n* **1** a rhythmic series of musical tones arranged to give a pleasing effect — see MELODY
**2** a short musical composition for the human voice often with instrumental accompaniment — see SONG 1

**lay** *vb* **1** to arrange something in a certain spot or position — see PLACE 1
**2** to cause to come to rest at the bottom (as of a liquid) — see SETTLE 1
**3** to establish or apply as a charge or penalty — see IMPOSE
**4** to make ready in advance — see PREPARE 1
**5** to put a layer of on a surface — see SPREAD 2
**6** to risk (something) on the outcome of an uncertain event — see BET

**lay away** *vb* to put (something of future use or value) in a safe or secret place — see HOARD

**lay down** *vb* **1** to put into effect through legislative or authoritative action — see ENACT
**2** to state clearly and strongly — see ASSERT 1
**3** to give the rules about (something) clearly and exactly — see PRESCRIBE

**layoff** *n* the termination of the employment of an employee or a work force often temporarily ⟨many people lost their jobs in the *layoff*⟩
*syn* discharge, dismissal, furlough
*rel* closing, shutdown; downsizing

**lay off** *vb* to bring (as an action or operation) to an immediate end — see STOP 1

**lay off** (of) *vb* to stop doing (something) permanently — see QUIT 2

**layout** *n* **1** the way in which something is sized, arranged, or organized — see FORMAT 1
**2** the way in which the elements of something (as a work of art) are arranged — see COMPOSITION 3

**lay out** *vb* **1** to hand over or use up in payment — see SPEND 1
**2** to work out the details of (something) in advance — see PLAN 1

**layover** *n* a brief halt in a journey — see STOP 1

**lay up** *vb* to put (something of future use or value) in a safe or secret place — see HOARD

**laziness** *n* an inclination not to do work or engage in activities ⟨although she often talks about ambitious household projects, nothing even gets started because of her *laziness*⟩

*syn* idleness, indolence, inertia, shiftlessness, sloth
*rel* apathy, languor, lassitude, lethargy, listlessness, sluggishness; goldbricking, loafing
*near ant* enterprise, initiative; assiduity, diligence, perseverance; energy, pep, vigor, vim, vitality
*ant* drive, industriousness, industry

**lazy** *adj* not easily aroused to action or work ⟨the *lazy* dog just wanted to lie on the couch all day and sleep⟩
*syn* idle, indolent, shiftless, slothful
*rel* apathetic, languorous, lazyish, lethargic, listless, sluggish, torpid
*near ant* ambitious, diligent, enterprising, zealous; dynamic, energetic, exuberant, lively, vigorous
*ant* industrious

**lazybones** *n pl* a lazy person ⟨he's a *lazybones* who is never willing to do any work⟩
*syn* drone, idler, loafer, slouch, slug, sluggard
*rel* bum, ne'er-do-well; sleepyhead; dawdler, laggard, putterer, slowpoke, stick-in-the-mud, trifler; goldbrick, malingerer, shirker, slacker; dallier, lingerer, loiterer, lounger, saunterer; delayer, procrastinator; dropout, quitter
*near ant* live wire, powerhouse
*ant* doer, go-getter, hummer, hustler, rustler, self-starter

**lea** *n* open land over which livestock may roam and feed — see RANGE 1

**lead** *adj* highest in rank or authority — see HEAD

**lead** *n* **1** the person who has the most important role in a play, movie, or TV show — see STAR 2
**2** the space or amount of space between two points, lines, surfaces, or objects — see DISTANCE
**3** a piece of advice or useful information especially from an expert — see ¹TIP 1
**4** a slight or indirect pointing to something (as a solution or explanation) — see HINT 1

**lead** *vb* **1** to point out the way for (someone) especially from a position in front ⟨the tour guide *led* the group through the museum⟩
*syn* conduct, direct, guide, marshal, pilot, route, show, steer, usher
*rel* precede; accompany, attend, chaperone (*or* chaperon), convoy, escort, see; control, manage
*near ant* dog, hound, shadow, tail, tailgate
*ant* follow, trail
**2** to serve as leader of ⟨the honor of *leading* the soccer squad⟩
*syn* boss, captain, command, dominate, head, spearhead
*rel* control, direct, govern, handle, manage, oversee, regulate, superintend, supervise
*near ant* bow (to), comply (with), defer (to), follow, obey, serve, submit (to), yield (to)
**3** to be at the front of ⟨the marching band *led* the parade⟩
*syn* head
*rel* precede; announce, herald; accompany, attend, escort, usher
*near ant* conclude, end, finish, stop, terminate; tail, tailgate; dog, follow, trail
**4** to be positioned along a certain course or in a certain direction — see RUN 3
**5** to give advice and instruction to (someone) regarding the course or process to be followed — see GUIDE 1

**leaden** *adj* **1** causing weariness, restlessness, or lack of interest — see BORING
**2** of the color gray — see GRAY 1

**leader** *n* **1** a long hollow cylinder for carrying a substance (as a liquid or gas) — see PIPE 1
**2** the person (as an employer or supervisor) who tells people and especially workers what to do — see BOSS

**leading** *adj* **1** coming before all others in importance — see FOREMOST 1
**2** highest in rank or authority — see HEAD

**lead on** *vb* to lead away from a usual or proper course by offering some pleasure or advantage — see LURE

**leafage** *n* green leaves or plants — see GREENERY 1

**leaflet** *n* a short printed publication with no cover or with a paper cover — see PAMPHLET

**leafy** *adj* covered with a thick, healthy natural growth — see LUSH 1

**league** *n* **1** a group of persons formally joined together for some common interest — see ASSOCIATION 2
**2** an association of persons, parties, or states for mutual assistance and protection — see CONFEDERACY

**league** *vb* to form or enter into an association that furthers the interests of its members — see ALLY

**leak** (out) *vb* to become known — see GET OUT 1

**lean** *adj* having a noticeably small amount of body fat — see THIN 1

**lean** *n* the degree to which something rises up from a position level with the horizon — see SLANT

**lean** *vb* **1** to set or cause to be at an angle ⟨just *lean* the ladder against the tree and climb up it⟩
*syn* angle, cant, cock, heel, incline, list, slant, slope, tilt, tip
*rel* bank; bend, deviate, swerve, veer; decline, descend, recline, retreat
*near ant* even, flatten, level, straighten
**2** to show a liking or proneness (for something) ⟨his diet *leans* toward greasy food⟩
*syn* incline, run, tend, trend
*rel* go, gravitate; indicate, point, suggest
*near ant* avoid, shun, shy (from *or* away from)

---

*syn* synonym(s) *rel* related words
*ant* antonym(s) *near ant* near antonym(s)

3 to place reliance or trust — see DEPEND 2

**lean** (toward) *vb* to show partiality toward — see PREFER 1

**leaning** *adj* running in a slanting direction — see DIAGONAL

**leaning** *n* 1 a prevailing or general movement or inclination — see TREND 1
2 a habitual attraction to some activity or thing — see INCLINATION 1

**leap** *n* an act of leaping into the air — see JUMP 1

**leap** *vb* to propel oneself upward or forward into the air — see JUMP 1

**leaping** *adj* passing from one topic to another — see DISCURSIVE

**learn** *vb* 1 to acquire complete knowledge, understanding, or skill in ⟨after months of trying, he finally *learned* the dance steps⟩
*syn* get, master, pick up
*rel* apprehend, comprehend, grasp, know, understand; absorb, assimilate, digest, imbibe; ascertain, descry, detect, determine, dig up, discern, discover, examine, find out, hear, hit (on *or* upon), run down, scare up, search (for), see, track (down), tumble (to), unearth; major (in), study; memorize
*phrases* get the hang (*or* knack) of
*near ant* forget, misunderstand; miss, overlook; disregard, ignore, neglect
*ant* unlearn
2 to come to an awareness — see DISCOVER 1
3 to come upon after searching, study, or effort — see FIND 1
4 to commit to memory — see MEMORIZE

**learned** *adj* 1 having or displaying advanced knowledge or education — see EDUCATED
2 suggestive of the vocabulary used in books — see BOOKISH

**learnedness** *n* the understanding and information gained from being educated — see EDUCATION 2

**learning** *n* the understanding and information gained from being educated — see EDUCATION 2

**lease** *vb* 1 to give the possession and use of (something) in return for periodic payment — see RENT 1
2 to take or get the temporary use of (something) for a set sum — see HIRE 1

**least** *adj* being the least in amount, number, or size possible — see MINIMAL

**leather** *n* 1 the hairless natural covering of an animal prepared for use ⟨the company claims to use only the finest *leathers* for its shoes and handbags⟩
*syn* hide, skin
*rel* coat, fleece, fur, pelt; alligator, buckskin, calfskin, chamois, cordovan, cowhide, deerskin, doeskin, goatskin, horsehide, kid, kidskin, lambskin, morocco, pigskin, seal, sharkskin, sheepskin, snakeskin, suede
2 the outer covering of an animal removed for its commercial value — see HIDE 1

**leathery** *adj* not easily chewed — see TOUGH 1

**leave** *n* 1 a period during which the usual routine of school or work is suspended — see VACATION
2 the approval by someone in authority for the doing of something — see PERMISSION

**leave** *vb* 1 to cause to remain behind ⟨you can *leave* your lunch in the refrigerator while we're outside⟩ ⟨lovers who promise never to *leave* one another⟩
*syn* abandon, desert, forsake, maroon, quit
*rel* discard, ditch, dump, fling, jettison, junk, scrap, shed, shuck (off), throw away, throw out; deliver, give up, hand over, relinquish, surrender, yield; retreat (from), take off (from), vacate, withdraw (from); abjure, cut off, disown, reject, renounce, repudiate, separate (from); sacrifice; distance; disregard, forget, ignore, neglect
*phrases* walk out on
*near ant* harbor, have, hold, keep, own, possess, reserve, retain, withhold; redeem, rescue, save
*ant* reclaim
2 to give by means of a will ⟨I'm going to *leave* all of my possessions to my children⟩
*syn* bequeath, will
*rel* deed; hand down, pass (down); devise
3 to give up (a job or office) — see QUIT 1
4 to put (something) into the possession or safekeeping of another — see GIVE 2

**leave off** *vb* 1 to bring (as an action or operation) to an immediate end — see STOP 1
2 to come to an end — see CEASE 1

**leave–taking** *n* 1 the act of leaving a place — see DEPARTURE
2 the act or process of two or more persons going off in different directions — see PARTING 1

**leavings** *n pl* a remaining group or portion — see REMAINDER 1

**lecture** *vb* 1 to criticize (someone) severely or angrily especially for personal failings — see SCOLD
2 to give a formal often extended talk on a subject — see TALK 1

**leech** *n* a person who is supported or seeks support from another without making an adequate return ⟨whenever the gang went out for pizza, the *leech* in the group always had an excuse for not paying his fair share⟩
*syn* hanger-on, parasite, sponge, sponger
*rel* dependent; deadbeat, idler; flunky (*also* flunkey), henchman, lackey, satellite, stooge, sycophant, toady, yesman; cheapskate, miser, niggard, piker, scrooge, skinflint, tightwad
*near ant* benefactor, philanthropist, supporter

**leer** (at) *vb* to look at in a flirtatious or desiring way — see OGLE

**leery** *adj* inclined to doubt or question claims — see SKEPTICAL 1

**leeward** *adj* being in the direction that the wind is blowing — see DOWNWIND

**left** *n* a political belief stressing progress, the essential goodness of humankind, and individual freedom — see LIBERALISM

**left–handed** *adj* not being or expressing what one appears to be or express — see INSINCERE

**leftover** *n* an unused or unwanted piece of item typically of small size or value — see [1]SCRAP 1

**leftovers** *n* a remaining group or portion — see REMAINDER 1

**leg** *n* **1** a lower limb of an animal ⟨he broke his *leg* when he accidentally stepped in that gopher hole⟩
*syn* pin
*rel* member; foreleg, forelimb; calf, drumstick, shank, shin, thigh
**2** a portion of a trip ⟨on the first *leg* of the cruise they went south to the Caribbean⟩
*syn* lap, stage
*rel* layover, stopover

**leg** (it) *vb* to go on foot — see WALK

**legacy** *n* something that is or may be inherited — see INHERITANCE

**legal** *adj* **1** permitted by law ⟨drinking is only *legal* if you are 21 years old⟩
*syn* lawful, legitimate
*rel* allowable, authorized, noncriminal, permissible; justifiable, warrantable; regulation, statutory; good, innocent, proper, right
*near ant* bad, corrupt, evil, immoral, iniquitous, reprobate, sinful, wicked, wrong; banned, criminal, forbidden, guilty, outlawed, prohibited, unauthorized, unjust; nonconstitutional, unconstitutional
*ant* illegal, illegitimate, illicit, unlawful, wrongful
**2** following or according to the rules — see FAIR 3

**legality** *n* the quality or state of being legal ⟨the senator questioned the *legality* of the proposed program⟩
*syn* lawfulness, legitimacy
*rel* rightfulness, rightness; permissibility, permissibleness
*near ant* badness, immorality, iniquity, sinfulness, unjustness, wickedness, wrongness; criminality, unconstitutionality
*ant* illegality, illegitimacy, unlawfulness, wrongfulness

**legal tender** *n* something (as pieces of stamped metal or printed paper) customarily and legally used as a medium of exchange, a measure of value, or a means of payment — see MONEY

**legate** *n* a person sent on a mission to represent another — see AMBASSADOR

**legatee** *n* a person who has the right to inherit property — see HEIR

**legend** *n* **1** an explanatory list of the symbols on a map or chart ⟨the *legend* indicated that a large circle represented each city, while a small circle stood for a small town⟩
*syn* key
*rel* scale; caption; guide, table
**2** an explanation or description accompanying a pictorial illustration — see CAPTION 1
**3** a traditional but unfounded story that gives the reason for a current custom, belief, or fact of nature — see MYTH 1
**4** the body of customs, beliefs, stories, and sayings associated with a people, thing, or place — see FOLKLORE

**legendary** *adj* based on, described in, or being a myth — see MYTHICAL 1

**legerdemain** *n* **1** the art or skill of performing tricks or illusions for entertainment — see MAGIC 2
**2** the use of clever underhanded actions to achieve an end — see TRICKERY

**legion** *n* **1** a large body of men and women organized for land warfare — see ARMY 1
**2** a great number of persons or things gathered together — see CROWD 1

**legionary** *n* a person engaged in military service — see SOLDIER

**legionnaire** *n* a person engaged in military service — see SOLDIER

**legislate** *vb* to put into effect through legislative or authoritative action — see ENACT

**legislator** *n* a member of an organized body of persons having the authority to make laws ⟨the *legislators* met in an all-night session to hammer out the details of the bill⟩
*syn* lawgiver, lawmaker, solon
*rel* assemblyman, assemblywoman; congressman, congresswoman; senator

**legitimacy** *n* the quality or state of being legal — see LEGALITY

**legitimate** *adj* permitted by law — see LEGAL 1

**lei** *n* an ornamental chain or string (as of beads) worn around the neck — see NECKLACE

**leisure** *n* freedom from activity or labor — see [1]REST 1

**leisurely** *adj* moving or proceeding at less than the normal, desirable, or required speed — see SLOW 1

**leisurely** *adv* at a pace that is less than usual, desirable, or expected — see SLOW

**lemon** *n* something that has failed — see FAILURE 3

**lend** *vb* to give to another for temporary use with the understanding that it or a like thing will be returned ⟨I can *lend* you my copy of the textbook until the weekend⟩ ⟨can you *lend* me five dollars?⟩
*syn* advance, loan
*rel* furnish, give, grant; lease, let [*chiefly British*], rent
*near ant* receive, take
*ant* borrow

**length** *n* the space or amount of space between two points, lines, surfaces, or objects — see DISTANCE
**lengthen** *vb* to make longer — see EXTEND 1
**lengthening** *n* the act of making longer — see EXTENSION 1
**lengthy** *adj* 1 of great extent from end to end — see LONG 1
2 lasting for a considerable time — see LONG 2
**lenience** *n* kind, gentle, or compassionate treatment especially towards someone who is undeserving of it — see MERCY 1
**leniency** *n* kind, gentle, or compassionate treatment especially towards someone who is undeserving of it — see MERCY 1
**lenity** *n* kind, gentle, or compassionate treatment especially towards someone who is undeserving of it — see MERCY 1
**leprechaun** *n* an imaginary being usually having a small human form and magical powers — see FAIRY
**less** *adj* having not so great importance or rank as another — see LESSER
**lessen** *vb* 1 to make smaller in amount, volume, or extent — see DECREASE 1
2 to grow less in scope or intensity especially gradually — see DECREASE 2
**lesser** *adj* having not so great importance or rank as another ⟨it was the *lesser* evil of the two choices⟩
*syn* inferior, junior, less, lower, minor, smaller, subordinate, under
*rel* little, mean, small; minute, petty; jerkwater, one-horse, second-class, second-rate, two-bit; secondary, subsidiary
*near ant* exceptional, first-class, first-rate
*ant* greater, higher, major, more, primary, prime, senior, superior
**lesson** *n* something assigned to be read or studied ⟨your *lesson* for tonight will be the chapter on chemical reactions⟩
*syn* assignment, reading
*rel* homework, schoolwork; lecture; drill, exercise, practice (*also* practise); etude, study
**lessor** *n* the owner of land or housing that is rented to another — see LANDLORD
**let** *n* something that makes movement or progress more difficult — see ENCUMBRANCE
**let** *vb* 1 to give permission to — see ALLOW
2 *chiefly British* to give the possession and use of (something) in return for periodic payment — see RENT 1
3 to make able or possible — see ENABLE 1
**letdown** *n* 1 the emotion felt when one's expectations are not met — see DISAPPOINTMENT 1
2 something that disappoints — see DISAPPOINTMENT 2
**let down** *vb* to fall short in satisfying the expectation or hope of — see DISAPPOINT
**lethal** *adj* likely to cause or capable of causing death — see DEADLY
**lethargic** *adj* slow to move or act — see INACTIVE 1
**let on** *vb* to take on a false or deceptive appearance — see PRETEND 1
**letter** *n* a message on paper from one person or group to another ⟨he wrote her a *letter* every week she was away⟩
*syn* dispatch, epistle, memo, memorandum, missive, note
*rel* airmail, card, electronic mail, e-mail, junk mail, mail, postal card, postcard; communication, report; encyclical
**letter carrier** *n* a person who delivers mail — see POSTMAN
**letter–perfect** *adj* being entirely without fault or flaw — see PERFECT 1
**letup** *n* a usually gradual decrease in the pace or level of activity of something — see SLOWDOWN
**let up** *vb* 1 to come to an end — see CEASE 1
2 to grow less in scope or intensity especially gradually — see DECREASE 2
**levee** *n* 1 a bank of earth constructed to control water — see DAM
2 a structure used by boats and ships for taking on or landing cargo and passengers — see DOCK
**level** *adj* having a surface without bends, breaks, or irregularities ⟨looked for a *level* place to land the plane⟩
*syn* even, flat, flush, plane, smooth
*rel* exact, uniform; aligned, regular, true; horizontal, tabular; plumb, straight, vertical
*near ant* inexact, irregular, unaligned; undulating, wavy
*ant* bumpy, coarse, lumpy, rough, uneven
**level** *n* the placement of someone or something in relation to others in a vertical arrangement — see RANK 1
**level** *vb* 1 to make equal in amount, degree, or status — see EQUALIZE
2 to make free from breaks, curves, or bumps — see EVEN 1
3 to point or turn (something) toward a target or goal — see AIM 1
4 to strike (someone) so forcefully as to cause a fall — see FELL 1
**levelheaded** *adj* based on sound reasoning or information — see GOOD 1
**levelheadedness** *n* the ability to make intelligent decisions especially in everyday matters — see COMMON SENSE
**lever** *vb* to raise, move, or pull apart with or as if with a lever — see [1]PRY 1
**leviathan** *n* something that is unusually large and powerful — see GIANT
**levity** *n* a lack of seriousness often at an improper time — see FRIVOLITY 1
**levy** *n* a charge usually of money collected by the government from people or businesses for public use — see TAX
**levy** *vb* to establish or apply as a charge or penalty — see IMPOSE
**lewd** *adj* 1 depicting or referring to sexual matters in a way that is unacceptable in polite society — see OBSCENE 1
2 having a strong sexual desire — see LUSTFUL

3 hinting at or intended to call to mind matters regarded as indecent — see SUGGESTIVE 1

**lewdness** *n* the quality or state of being obscene — see OBSCENITY 1

**lexical** *adj* of or relating to words or language — see VERBAL 1

**lexicon** *n* a reference book giving information about the meanings, pronunciations, uses, and origins of words listed in alphabetical order — see DICTIONARY

**liability** *n* 1 a feature of someone or something that creates difficulty for achieving success — see DISADVANTAGE

2 the state of being held as the cause of something that needs to be set right — see RESPONSIBILITY 1

3 the state of being left without shelter or protection against something harmful — see EXPOSURE 1

**liable** *adj* 1 being in a situation where one is likely to meet with harm ⟨because of his frail constitution, he's *liable* to diseases⟩

***syn*** endangered, exposed, open, sensitive, subject (to), susceptible, vulnerable

***rel*** likely, prone; uncovered, undefended, unguarded, unprotected, unscreened, unsecured, unsheltered, unshielded

***phrases*** in jeopardy

***near ant*** covered, guarded, protected, safeguarded, screened, secured, sheltered, shielded, warded

***ant*** invulnerable, unexposed

2 being the one who must meet an obligation or suffer the consequences for failing to do so — see RESPONSIBLE 1

**liaison** *n* 1 the fact or state of having something in common — see CONNECTION 1

2 the state of having shared interests or efforts (as in social or business matters) — see ASSOCIATION 1

**liar** *n* a person who tells lies ⟨she knew he was a *liar* when he started claiming that he was an astronaut⟩

***syn*** fabricator, fibber, prevaricator, storyteller

***rel*** defamer, libeler (*or* libeller), slanderer; perjurer; distorter, falsifier; equivocator, palterer; gossip, gossiper, talebearer; charlatan, cheat, cheater, confidence man, counterfeiter, cozener, deceiver, defrauder, dissembler, dissimulator, double-dealer, fraud, hustler, mountebank, pretender

***near ant*** square shooter

**libation** *n* a liquid suitable for drinking — see DRINK 1

**libel** *n* the making of false statements that damage another's reputation — see SLANDER

**libel** *vb* to make untrue and harmful statements about — see SLANDER

**libeling** *n* the making of false statements that damage another's reputation — see SLANDER

**libelous** *or* **libellous** *adj* causing or intended to cause unjust injury to a person's good name ⟨*libelous* statements about a celebrity for which the tabloid was sued⟩

***syn*** defamatory, scandalous, slanderous

***rel*** erroneous, false, inaccurate, incorrect, inexact, invalid, off, unsound, untrue, wrong; depreciative, depreciatory, derogatory, detractive, disparaging, uncomplimentary, unfavorable; invidious, objectionable; maligning, traducing, vilifying; hateful, malevolent, malicious, spiteful

***near ant*** appreciative, complimentary, favorable; adulatory, commendatory, eulogistic, laudatory; accurate, correct, errorless, factual, right, sound, true, valid

**liberal** *adj* 1 not bound by traditional ways or beliefs ⟨parents who take a very *liberal* attitude toward letting their children stay out late⟩

***syn*** broad-minded, nonconventional, nonorthodox, nontraditional, open-minded, progressive, radical, unconventional, unorthodox

***rel*** advanced, contemporary, modern; forbearing, indulgent, lenient, permissive, tolerant; extreme; impartial, objective, unbiased

***near ant*** hard, rigid, strict; doctrinal, dogmatic; bigoted, intolerant, narrow-minded; reactionary

***ant*** conservative, conventional, nonprogressive, old-fashioned, orthodox, traditional

2 being more than enough without being excessive — see PLENTIFUL

3 giving or sharing in abundance and without hesitation — see GENEROUS 1

**liberalism** *n* a political belief stressing progress, the essential goodness of humankind, and individual freedom ⟨*liberalism* had always claimed to stand for the greatest social good⟩

***syn*** left

***rel*** radicalism, socialism

***ant*** conservatism, right

**liberality** *n* the quality or state of being generous ⟨already known for his *liberality*, the billionaire continued to give away record amounts of money⟩

***syn*** bountifulness, bounty, generosity, largess (*or* largesse), openhandedness, openheartedness, philanthropy, unselfishness

***rel*** beneficence, charity; kindness; gift, gratuity, lagniappe; tribute; extravagance, improvidence, lavishness, prodigality, wastefulness; spendthrift; dissipating, squandering

***near ant*** conserving, economizing, economy, frugality, husbandry, providence, scrimping, skimping, thrift; conservation, saving; husbanding, managing; scraping; cutting back

***ant*** cheapness, closeness, meanness, miserliness, parsimony, penuriousness, pinching, stinginess, tightness

**liberally** *adv* in a generous manner — see WELL 2

**liberate** *vb* **1** to set free (as from slavery or confinement) — see FREE 1

**2** to set free from entanglement or difficulty — see EXTRICATE

**liberation** *n* the act of setting free from slavery ⟨the *liberation* of the slaves was one of the key results of the Civil War⟩

***syn*** emancipation, enfranchisement, freeing, manumission

***rel*** deliverance, redemption, salvation; autonomy, freedom, independence, liberty, self-government, sovereignty

***near ant*** bondage, serfdom, servitude, thralldom (*or* thraldom), yoke; captivity, enchainment, imprisonment, incarceration; conquest, subjugation

***ant*** enslavement

**libertine** *n* a person who has sunk below the normal moral standard — see DEGENERATE

**liberty** *n* the state of being free from the control or power of another — see FREEDOM 1

**library** *n* **1** a place where books, periodicals, and records are kept for use but not for sale ⟨I went to the *library* to do some research for my report⟩

***syn*** archive

***rel*** stacks

**2** an organized group of objects acquired and maintained for study, exhibition, or personal pleasure — see COLLECTION 1

**licensable** *adj* that may be permitted — see PERMISSIBLE

**license** *also* **licence** *vb* to give official or legal power to — see AUTHORIZE 1

**license** *or* **licence** *n* **1** the approval by someone in authority for the doing of something — see PERMISSION

**2** the granting of power to perform various acts or duties — see COMMISSION 1

**3** the right to act or move freely — see FREEDOM 2

**licentious** *adj* having a strong sexual desire — see LUSTFUL

**licentiousness** *n* immoral conduct or practices harmful or offensive to society — see VICE 1

**lick** *n* **1** a hard strike with a part of the body or an instrument — see [1]BLOW

**2** a very small amount — see PARTICLE 1

**3** the smallest amount or part imaginable — see JOT

**lick** *vb* **1** to strike repeatedly — see BEAT 1

**2** to achieve a victory over — see BEAT 2

**licking** *n* failure to win a contest — see DEFEAT 1

**lid** *n* **1** a piece placed over an open container to hold in, protect, or conceal its contents — see COVER 1

**2** *slang* a covering for the head usually having a shaped crown — see HAT

**lie** *n* a statement known by its maker to be untrue and made in order to deceive ⟨he wanted to deny the accusation, but he couldn't tell a *lie*⟩

***syn*** fabrication, fairy tale, falsehood, falsity, fib, mendacity, prevarication, story, tale, untruth, whopper

***rel*** distortion, exaggeration, half-truth; ambiguity, equivocation; defamation, libel, slander; perjury; bluff, pose, pretense (*or* pretence); humbug, jive, nonsense; fallacy, misconception, myth; misinformation, misrepresentation, misstatement; deceit, deceitfulness, dishonesty, duplicity, fraudulence

***near ant*** fact, truism, verity; honesty, truthfulness, veracity; authentication, confirmation, substantiation, validation, verification

***ant*** truth

**lie** *vb* **1** to make a statement one knows to be untrue ⟨would I *lie* to you about that?⟩

***syn*** fabricate, fib, prevaricate

***rel*** forswear, perjure; equivocate, fudge, palter; beguile, cozen, deceive, delude, dupe, fool, gull, hoax, hoodwink, kid, snow, take in, trick; defame, libel, slander, traduce; falsify, misrepresent, misstate; distort, garble; dissemble, dissimulate; misguide, misinform, mislead

***phrases*** tell stories (*or* tales)

***near ant*** assert, swear, testify; authenticate, confirm, substantiate, validate, verify

**2** to be positioned along a certain course or in a certain direction — see RUN 3

**3** to occupy a place or location — see STAND 1

**lie detector** *n* an instrument for detecting physical signs of the tension that goes with lying ⟨hooked the suspect up to a *lie detector* before interrogating him about the robbery⟩

***syn*** polygraph

**life** *n* **1** a history of a person's life — see BIOGRAPHY

**2** a member of the human race — see HUMAN

**3** active strength of body or mind — see VIGOR 1

**4** the period during which something exists, lasts, or is in progress — see DURATION 1

**5** the way people live at a particular time and place — see CIVILIZATION 1

**lifeless** *adj* no longer living — see DEAD 1

**lifelessness** *n* the state of being dead — see DEATH 2

**lifelike** *adj* closely resembling the object imitated — see NATURAL 2

**life span** *n* the period during which something exists, lasts, or is in progress — see DURATION 1

**lifestyle** *n* the way people live at a particular time and place — see CIVILIZATION 1

**lifetime** *n* the period during which something exists, lasts, or is in progress — see DURATION 1

**lift** *n* **1** an act or instance of helping — see HELP 1

**2** a means of getting to a destination in a vehicle driven by another — see RIDE

**lift** *vb* **1** to move from a lower to a higher place or position — see RAISE 1
**2** to move or extend upward — see ASCEND
**lifted** *adj* being positioned above a surface — see ELEVATED 1
**lift–off** *n* a rising from a surface at the start of a flight (as of a rocket) ⟨everyone was quiet in the control room as they waited for *lift-off*⟩
*syn* launch, takeoff
*near ant* crash; splashdown
*ant* landing
**ligature** *n* **1** something that physically prevents free movement — see BOND 1
**2** a uniting or binding force or influence — see BOND 2
[1]**light** *adj* **1** having little weight ⟨the suitcase was as *light* as a feather after all the clothes fell out⟩
*syn* airy, feathery, lightweight, underweight, weightless
*rel* bantam, diminutive, little, minute, small, smallish, puny, tiny, undersized, wee; flimsy, fragile, insubstantial; petite, slender, slight, slim, thin
*near ant* big, considerable, extensive, goodly, good-sized, great, handsome, huge, hulking, jumbo, king-size (*or* king-sized), large, largish, massive, oversize (*or* oversized), sizable (*or* sizeable), substantial, super, voluminous, whacking; bulky, cumbersome, unwieldy
*ant* heavy, hefty, leaden, overweight, ponderous, weighty
**2** involving minimal difficulty or effort — see EASY 1
**3** less plentiful than what is normal, necessary, or desirable — see MEAGER
**4** moving easily — see GRACEFUL 1
**5** not harsh or stern especially in manner, nature, or effect — see GENTLE 1
**6** resembling air in lightness — see AIRY 1
[2]**light** *adj* **1** filled with much light — see BRIGHT 2
**2** lacking intensity of color — see PALE 1
**3** of light complexion — see FAIR 4
**light** *n* **1** the steady giving off of the form of radiation that makes vision possible ⟨he read poetry by the *light* of the moon⟩
*syn* blaze, flare, fluorescence, glare, gleam, glow, illumination, incandescence, luminescence, radiance, shine
*rel* flash, glimmer, glint, glitter, scintillation, shimmer, sparkle, twinkle; daylight, moonlight, sunlight; afterglow, aureole, aurora, beam, ray, shaft, streak, stream; glisten, gloss, luster (*or* lustre), polish, reflection, sheen
*near ant* blackness, dark, darkness, dimness, dusk, duskiness, gloom, night, shadow
**2** something that provides illumination ⟨turn off the *light* when you go to bed⟩
*syn* beacon, lamp
*rel* arc lamp (*also* arc light), candelabra, candelabrum, candle, chandelier, dark lantern, electric, flare, flash, flashbulb, flashcube, flashlight, floodlight, fluorescent lamp, gaslight, headlight, incandescent lamp, klieg light (*or* kleig light), lantern, light bulb, lighthouse, lighting, sconce, spotlight, streetlight
**3** a person who is widely known and usually much talked about — see CELEBRITY 1
[1]**light** *vb* to come to rest after descending from the air — see ALIGHT
[2]**light** *vb* **1** to set (something) on fire — see BURN 2
**2** to supply with light — see ILLUMINATE 1
**lighted** *or* **lit** *adj* **1** filled with much light — see BRIGHT 2
**2** being on fire — see ABLAZE 1
**lighten** *vb* to supply with light — see ILLUMINATE 1
**light–footed** *adj* moving easily — see GRACEFUL 1
**light–headed** *adj* **1** having a feeling of being whirled about and in danger of falling down — see DIZZY 1
**2** lacking in seriousness or maturity — see GIDDY 1
**light–headedness** *n* a lack of seriousness often at an improper time — see FRIVOLITY 1
**lighthearted** *adj* having or showing a lack of concern or seriousness — see CAREFREE
**lightheartedness** *n* carefree freedom from constraint — see ABANDON
**lighting out** *n* the act of leaving a place — see DEPARTURE
**lightly** *adv* without difficulty — see EASILY
[1]**lightness** *n* **1** the state or quality of having little weight ⟨the first thing I noticed about the little bird was its *lightness*; I could hardly tell I was holding it in my hand⟩
*syn* slightness, weightlessness
*rel* airiness, delicacy, etherealness; flimsiness, fluffiness, insubstantiality
*near ant* solidity, solidness, substantiality
*ant* heaviness, heftiness, massiveness, ponderousness, weightiness
**2** a lack of seriousness often at an improper time — see FRIVOLITY 1
[2]**lightness** *n* the quality or state of having or giving off light — see BRILLIANCE 1
**lightning** *adj* moving, proceeding, or acting with great speed — see FAST 1
**lightsome** *adj* having or showing a good mood or disposition — see CHEERFUL 1
**lightweight** *adj* having little weight — see [1]LIGHT 1
**lightweight** *n* a person of no importance or influence — see NOBODY
**like** *adj* having qualities in common — see ALIKE
**like** *adv* to some degree or extent — see FAIRLY
**like** *conj* the way it would be or one would do if — see AS IF
[1]**like** *n* **1** a number of persons or things that are grouped together because they have something in common — see SORT 1

*syn* synonym(s) *rel* related words
*ant* antonym(s) *near ant* near antonym(s)

2 one that is equal to another in status, achievement, or value — see EQUAL

²**like** *n* positive regard for something — see LIKING

**like** *vb* 1 to wish to have ⟨I'd *like* another slice of pizza, but I've already eaten more than I should have⟩
*syn* care (for), want
*rel* adore, delight (in), dig, enjoy, fancy, groove (on), like, love, relish, revel (in); covet, crave, die (for), wish (for), yearn (for)
2 to show partiality toward — see PREFER 1
3 to take pleasure in — see ENJOY 1
4 to see fit — see CHOOSE 2

**likelihood** *n* the quality or state of being likely to occur — see PROBABILITY 1

**likeliness** *n* the quality or state of being likely to occur — see PROBABILITY 1

**likely** *adj* 1 having a high chance of occurring ⟨if you don't do well in school, your *likely* fate is a low-paying job⟩
*syn* probable
*rel* conceivable, earthly, imaginable, possible, potential; apt, bound, certain, doubtless, inescapable, inevitable, necessary, sure, unavoidable
*near ant* impossible, inconceivable, unimaginable
*ant* doubtful, dubious, improbable, questionable, unlikely
2 having qualities which inspire hope — see HOPEFUL 1
3 worthy of being accepted as true or reasonable — see BELIEVABLE

**likely** *adv* without much doubt — see PROBABLY

**liken** *vb* 1 to describe as similar — see COMPARE 1
2 to regard or represent as equal or comparable — see EQUATE 1

**likeness** *n* 1 a two-dimensional design intended to look like a person or thing — see PICTURE 1
2 something or someone that strongly resembles another — see IMAGE 1
3 the quality or state of having many qualities in common — see SIMILARITY 1

**likewise** *adv* 1 in addition to what has been said — see MORE 1
2 in like manner — see ALSO 1

**liking** *n* positive regard for something ⟨I have a *liking* for dark chocolate⟩
*syn* appetite, fancy, favor, fondness, like, love, partiality, preference, relish, shine, taste, use
*rel* craving, desire, longing, thirst, yen; enthusiasm, interest, passion; bias, prejudice; bent, inclination, leaning, propensity, tendency; weakness
*near ant* apathy, disinclination; indifference, unconcern
*ant* aversion, disfavor, dislike, distaste, hatred, loathing

**lily-livered** *adj* having or showing a shameful lack of courage — see COWARDLY

**limb** *n* a major outgrowth from the main stem of a woody plant — see BRANCH 1

**limber** *adj* able to bend easily without breaking — see WILLOWY

**limit** *n* a real or imaginary point beyond which a person or thing cannot go ⟨there was no *limit* to the number of challenges they faced⟩
*syn* bound, boundary, ceiling, confines, end, extent, limitation, line, termination
*rel* extremity, fag end; border, brim, edge, margin, rim, verge; outside; bar, barrier, fence, hedge, restraint, stop, wall

**limit** *vb* 1 to set bounds or an upper limit for ⟨*limit* the note to a few words⟩
*syn* circumscribe, confine, restrict
*rel* bar, block, hinder, impede, obstruct; constrict, contract, lessen, narrow, pinch, squeeze, tighten; quell, repress, suppress; number; modify, qualify
*near ant* broaden, expand, widen; overextend, overreach
*ant* exceed
2 to mark the limits of ⟨adjectives *limit* the meanings of nouns⟩
*syn* bound, circumscribe, define, delimit, demarcate, mark (out), terminate
*rel* control, determine, govern; delineate, describe

**limitation** *n* 1 a real or imaginary point beyond which a person or thing cannot go — see LIMIT
2 something that limits one's freedom of action or choice — see RESTRICTION 1
3 the act or practice of keeping something (as an activity) within certain boundaries — see RESTRICTION 2

**limited** *adj* 1 having distinct or certain limits ⟨to avoid overcrowding, the number of tickets to the outdoor concerts is *limited*⟩
*syn* bounded, circumscribed, defined, definite, determinate, finite, measured, narrow, restricted
*rel* modified, qualified; detailed, exact, precise, specific; confined, constricted, moderate, modest; minute, puny, small, tiny; determined, fixed, settled
*near ant* bottomless, countless, incalculable, inestimable, inexhaustible, innumerable, unfathomable; general, indeterminate, nebulous, vague; enlarged, escalated, expanded; considerable, copious, plentiful; big, bulky, bumper, extensive, goodly, good-sized, great, handsome, hefty, hulking, jumbo, king-size (*or* king-sized), large, largish, oversize (*or* oversized), respectable, sizable (*or* sizeable), substantial, super, vast, voluminous, whacking; epic, grandiose, major; ample, broad, comprehensive, cosmopolitan, expansive, global, inclusive, universal, whole
*ant* boundless, dimensionless, endless, illimitable, immeasurable, indefinite, infinite, limitless, measureless, unbounded, undefined, unlimited, unmeasured
2 having a limit — see FINITE 1

**limitless** *adj* being or seeming to be without limits — see INFINITE

**limp** *adj* **1** not stiff in structure ⟨his broken arm was *limp* as he held it against his side⟩
***syn*** droopy, flaccid, floppy, lank, yielding
***rel*** flabby, mushy, semisoft, soft, squashy, squishy; delicate, flimsy, insubstantial; elastic, flexible, lax, loose, pliant, relaxed, resilient, springy, stretchy, supple
***near ant*** firm, hard, indurated, solid, sound, strong; brittle, crisp; compact, dense, substantial
***ant*** inflexible, resilient, rigid, stiff, sturdy, tense; firm, hard, indurated, solid, sound, strong
**2** depleted in strength, energy, or freshness — see WEARY 1
**3** lacking bodily energy or motivation — see LISTLESS

**limp** *vb* **1** to walk while favoring one leg ⟨she *limped* all day after stubbing her toe on the lawn sprinkler⟩
***syn*** halt, hobble
***rel*** hitch; blunder, falter, lurch, shuffle, stagger, stumble, teeter, totter, waver, wobble; dodder
***near ant*** breeze, glide, sail
***ant*** stride
**2** to make progress in a clumsy, struggling manner — see FLOUNDER 1

**limpid** *adj* easily seen through — see CLEAR 1

**limpidity** *n* the state or quality of being easily seen through — see CLARITY 1

**limpidness** *n* the state or quality of being easily seen through — see CLARITY 1

**line** *n* **1** a series of persons or things arranged one behind another ⟨we waited in the *line* for lunch for what seemed like hours⟩
***syn*** column, cue, file, queue, range, string, train
***rel*** echelon, rank, row, tier; progression, sequence, succession; array
**2** a way of acting or proceeding — see COURSE 1
**3** the activity by which one regularly makes a living — see OCCUPATION
**4** a region of activity, knowledge, or influence — see FIELD 2
**5** a real or imaginary point beyond which a person or thing cannot go — see LIMIT
**6** a long hollow cylinder for carrying a substance (as a liquid or gas) — see PIPE 1
**7** a length of braided, flexible material that is used for tying or connecting things — see CORD
**8** a group of vehicles traveling together or under one management — see FLEET
**9** the direction along which something or someone moves — see PATH 1
**10** a group of persons who come from the same ancestor — see FAMILY 1
**11** the line of ancestors from whom a person is descended — see ANCESTRY

**lineage** *n* **1** the line of ancestors from whom a person is descended — see ANCESTRY
**2** a group of persons who come from the same ancestor — see FAMILY 1

**linear** *adj* free from irregularities (as curves, bends, or angles) in course — see STRAIGHT 1

**linger** *vb* to move or act slowly — see DELAY 1

**lingerer** *n* someone who moves slowly or more slowly than others — see SLOWPOKE

**lingo** *n* **1** the stock of words, pronunciation, and grammar used by a people as their basic means of communication — see LANGUAGE 1
**2** the special terms or expressions of a particular group or field — see TERMINOLOGY

**linguistic** *adj* of or relating to words or language — see VERBAL 1

**link** *n* **1** a rod-shaped portion of seasoned ground meat in a casing — see SAUSAGE
**2** a uniting or binding force or influence — see BOND 2

**link** *vb* **1** to put or bring together so as to form a new and longer whole — see CONNECT 1
**2** to think of (something) in combination — see ASSOCIATE 2

**link** (up) *vb* to come together to form a single unit — see UNITE 1

**linkage** *n* the fact or state of having something in common — see CONNECTION 1

**linking** *n* the act or an instance of joining two or more things into one — see UNION 1

**linkup** *n* the state of having shared interests or efforts (as in social or business matters) — see ASSOCIATION 1

**lint** *n* a soft airy substance or covering — see FUZZ

**lionhearted** *adj* feeling or displaying no fear by temperament — see BRAVE

**liquefy** *vb* to go from a solid to a liquid state ⟨the steel *liquefied* in the intense heat of the forge⟩
***syn*** deliquesce, flux, fuse, melt, run, thaw
***rel*** found, gutter, smelt, try; dissolve, render; soften, thin
***near ant*** clot, coagulate, congeal, gel, jell, jelly, thicken
***ant*** harden, set, solidify

**liquid** *adj* **1** capable of moving like a liquid — see FLUID 1
**2** easily seen through — see CLEAR 1

**liquidate** *vb* **1** to destroy all traces of — see ANNIHILATE 1
**2** to put to death deliberately — see MURDER 1
**3** to give what is owed for — see PAY 2

**liquor** *n* a fermented or distilled beverage that can make a person drunk — see ALCOHOL

**lissome** *also* **lissom** *adj* **1** moving easily — see GRACEFUL 1
**2** able to bend easily without breaking — see WILLOWY

[1]**list** *n* a record of a series of items (as names or titles) usually arranged according to some system ⟨we put eggs, sour

---

***syn*** synonym(s) ***rel*** related words
***ant*** antonym(s) ***near ant*** near antonym(s)

cream, tomatoes, roast beef, and cheddar cheese on the shopping *list*⟩
***syn*** canon, catalog (*or* catalogue), checklist, listing, menu, register, registry, roll, roster, schedule, table
***rel*** agenda, bibliography, compilation, directory, docket, glossary, index, inventory, manifest, payroll; calendar, chronology, timetable

**[2]list** *n* the act of positioning or an instance of being positioned at an angle — see TILT

**[3]list** *n* a long narrow piece of material — see STRIP

**[1]list** *vb* **1** to make a list of ⟨he *listed* the people on the team⟩
***syn*** enumerate, inventory, itemize, numerate
***rel*** count, mark, number; check (off), tick (off)
**2** to put (someone or something) on a list ⟨her number isn't *listed* in the phone book⟩
***syn*** catalog (*or* catalogue), enroll (*also* enrol), enter, index, inscribe, put down, record, register, schedule, slate
***rel*** book, file, note; classify, compile, tabulate; reschedule
***near ant*** delete
**3** to enter in a list or roll — see ENROLL 1
**4** to specify one after another — see ENUMERATE 1

**[2]list** *vb* to set or cause to be at an angle — see LEAN 1

**listen** *vb* to pay attention especially through the act of hearing ⟨would you *listen* to what I have to say?⟩
***syn*** attend, hark, hear, hearken, heed, mind
***phrases*** prick up one's ears
***near ant*** discount, disregard
***ant*** ignore, tune out

**listen** (to) *vb* to take notice of and be guided by — see HEED 1

**listen in** (on) *vb* to listen to (another in private conversation) — see EAVESDROP (ON)

**listing** *adj* **1** inclined or twisted to one side — see AWRY
**2** running in a slanting direction — see DIAGONAL

**listing** *n* a record of a series of items (as names or titles) usually arranged according to some system — see [1]LIST

**listless** *adj* lacking bodily energy or motivation ⟨when I had the flu, I felt *listless* and worn-out⟩
***syn*** enervated, lackadaisical, languid, languishing, languorous, limp, spiritless
***rel*** indolent, lazy, slothful; lethargic, logy, sleepy, sluggish, torpid; exhausted, tired, weary; feeble, frail, weak; apathetic, impassive, phlegmatic, stolid; careless, heedless, thoughtless, unwary; inactive, inert
***near ant*** active, dynamic, industrious; avid, eager, enthusiastic, keen, lively, vivacious; cheerful, chipper, perky, up; agog, alert, awake, dapper, open-eyed, sleepless, vigilant, watchful, wide-awake
***ant*** ambitious, animated, energetic, enterprising, motivated

**listlessness** *n* the state of being bored — see BOREDOM

**literal** *adj* restricted to or based on fact — see FACTUAL 1

**literary** *adj* suggestive of the vocabulary used in books — see BOOKISH

**literate** *adj* having or displaying advanced knowledge or education — see EDUCATED

**lithe** *adj* **1** able to bend easily without breaking — see WILLOWY
**2** moving easily — see GRACEFUL 1

**lithesome** *adj* moving easily — see GRACEFUL 1

**litter** *n* **1** an unorganized collection or mixture of various things — see MISCELLANY 1
**2** discarded or useless material — see GARBAGE

**littered** *adj* lacking in order, neatness, and often cleanliness — see MESSY

**little** *adj* **1** having relatively little height — see SHORT 1
**2** lacking importance — see UNIMPORTANT
**3** not broad or open in views or opinions — see NARROW 2
**4** not lasting for a considerable time — see SHORT 2
**5** of a size that is less than average — see SMALL 1

**little** *adv* **1** in a very small quantity or degree ⟨we had *little* more than we needed to survive in the wilderness⟩
***syn*** negligibly, nominally, slightly
***rel*** meagerly, scantily; barely, hardly, just, marginally, minimally, scarcely
***phrases*** a bit
***near ant*** completely, entirely, purely, thoroughly, totally, utterly; eminently, exceptionally; appreciably, discernibly, noticeably, palpably; abundantly, plentifully; generously, handsomely, liberally; astronomically, grandly, hugely, monstrously, monumentally
***ant*** awful, awfully, beastly, considerably, deadly, especially, exceedingly (*also* exceeding), extensively, extra, extremely, far, frightfully, full, greatly, heavily, highly, jolly, mightily, mighty, mortally, most, much, particularly, rattling, real, right, significantly, so, something, substantially, super, terribly, too, very, whacking
**2** not often — see SELDOM

**little** *n* a very small amount — see PARTICLE 1

**little by little** *adv* by small steps or amounts — see GRADUALLY

**littleness** *n* the quality or state of being little in size — see SMALLNESS

**littlest** *adj* being the least in amount, number, or size possible — see MINIMAL

**livable** *also* **liveable** *adj* suitable for living in ⟨after adding some furniture and painting the walls, the apartment was *livable*⟩
***syn*** habitable, inhabitable

*rel* comfortable, cozy, homelike, homey, intimate, snug; deluxe, lavish, luxuriant, luxurious, plush, sumptuous; opulent, palatial, rich; acceptable, bearable, endurable, sufferable, supportable, sustainable, tolerable
*near ant* uncomfortable; humble, Spartan; economical, frugal, spare, thrifty; intolerable, unacceptable, unbearable, unendurable, insupportable
*ant* uninhabitable, unlivable

**live** *adj* having or showing life — see ALIVE 1

**live** *vb* **1** to have a home ⟨he *lived* next door to the hospital⟩
*syn* abide, dwell, reside
*rel* lodge, settle, stay; frequent, hang out (at), haunt; inhabit, occupy; people, populate; lease, rent, sublet, tenant
**2** to have life — see BE 1

**liveliness** *n* the quality or state of having abundant or intense activity — see VITALITY 1

**lively** *adj* **1** having much high-spirited energy and movement ⟨the *lively* puppy was racing around the dining room floor chasing after people's shoelaces⟩
*syn* active, animate, animated, bouncing, brisk, energetic, frisky, gay, jaunty, jazzy, peppy, perky, pert, racy, snappy, spanking, sparky, spirited, sprightly, springy, vital, vivacious, zippy
*rel* dapper, dashing, spiffy; agog, alert, awake, open-eyed, up, wide-awake; agile, nimble, spry; bright, buoyant, cheerful, chipper, effervescent, upbeat; eager, enthusiastic, keen; frolicsome, impish, playful; bubbly, exuberant, high-spirited; high-strung, nervous, skittish
*phrases* on the go
*near ant* indolent, lazy, unambitious; inert, lethargic, sleepy, sluggish, tired, torpid, weary; apathetic, impassive, phlegmatic, stolid; boring, dull, irksome, tedious
*ant* dead, inactive, inanimate, lackadaisical, languid, languishing, languorous, lifeless, limp, listless, spiritless, unanimated
**2** marked by much life, movement, or activity — see ALIVE 2

**liven** (up) *vb* to give life, vigor, or spirit to — see ANIMATE

**livery** *n* the distinctive clothing worn by members of a particular group — see UNIFORM

**live wire** *n* an ambitious person who eagerly goes after what is desired — see GO-GETTER

**livid** *adj* lacking a healthy skin color — see PALE 2

**living** *adj* **1** being in effective operation — see ACTIVE 1
**2** having being at the present time — see EXTANT 1
**3** having or showing life — see ALIVE 1

*syn* synonym(s) *rel* related words
*ant* antonym(s) *near ant* near antonym(s)

**load** *n* **1** a mass or quantity of something taken up and carried, conveyed, or transported ⟨they placed a *load* of grain on the truck going to Florida⟩
*syn* burden, cargo, draft, freight, haul, lading, loading, payload, weight
*rel* consignment, boatload, carload, shipload, truckload; ballast, deadweight; overload, surcharge; bale, bundle, pack, package, packet, parcel, shipment; manifest; body, bulk, mass
**2 loads** *pl* a considerable amount — see LOT 2

**load** *vb* **1** to place a weight or burden on ⟨students complaining that their teachers were *loading* them with work⟩
*syn* burden, encumber, lade, lumber, saddle, weight
*rel* clog, clutter, fill, heap; press, weigh; strain, tax; overburden, overload, overtax, surcharge; handicap; afflict, oppress
*near ant* alleviate, ease, lighten, relieve
*ant* disencumber, unburden, unload
**2** to put into (something) as much as can be held or contained — see FILL 1

**loaded** *adj* **1** containing or seeming to contain the greatest quantity or number possible — see FULL 1
**2** having goods, property, or money in abundance — see RICH 1
**3** *slang* being under the influence of alcohol — see DRUNK

**loading** *n* a mass or quantity of something taken up and carried, conveyed, or transported — see LOAD 1

**loaf** *vb* to spend time doing nothing — see IDLE

**loafer** *n* a lazy person — see LAZYBONES

**loamy** *adj* consisting or suggestive of earth — see EARTHY 1

**loan** *vb* to give to another for temporary use with the understanding that it or a like thing will be returned — see LEND

**loath** *or* **loth** *adj* having doubts about the wisdom of doing something — see HESITANT

**loathe** *vb* to dislike strongly — see HATE

**loathing** *n* **1** a dislike so strong as to cause stomach upset or queasiness — see DISGUST
**2** a very strong dislike — see HATE 1

**loathsome** *adj* causing intense displeasure, disgust, or resentment — see OFFENSIVE 1

**lob** *vb* to send through the air especially with a quick forward motion of the arm — see THROW

**lobby** *n* **1** a centrally located room in a building that serves as a gathering or waiting area or as a passageway into the interior — see FOYER 1
**2** the entrance room of a building — see HALL 1

**local** *n* a local unit of an organization — see CHAPTER

**locale** *n* the area or space occupied by or intended for something — see PLACE 1

**locality** *n* the area or space occupied by or intended for something — see PLACE 1

**locate** *vb* to come upon after searching, study, or effort — see FIND 1
**location** *n* the area or space occupied by or intended for something — see PLACE 1
**loch** *n, Scottish* a part of a body of water that extends beyond the general shoreline — see GULF 1
**lock** (up) *vb* to put in or as if in prison — see IMPRISON
**locker** *n* 1 a covered rectangular container for storing or transporting things — see CHEST
2 a storage case typically having doors and shelves — see CABINET
**lockup** *n* a place of confinement for persons held in lawful custody — see JAIL
**loco** *adj* having or showing a very abnormal or sick state of mind — see INSANE 1
**locus** *n* the area or space occupied by or intended for something — see PLACE 1
**locution** *n* a distinctive way of putting ideas into words — see STYLE 1
**lodestone** *n* something that attracts interest — see MAGNET
**lodge** *n* 1 a place that provides rooms and usually a public dining room for overnight guests — see HOTEL
2 an often small house for recreational or seasonal use — see COTTAGE
3 the meeting place of an organization — see CLUB 2
4 the shelter or resting place of a wild animal — see DEN 1
**lodge** *vb* to provide with living quarters or shelter — see HOUSE 1
2 to establish or place comfortably or snugly — see ENSCONCE 1
3 to set solidly in or as if in surrounding matter — see ENTRENCH
**lodged** *adj* firmly positioned in place and difficult to dislodge — see TIGHT 2
**lodger** *n* one who rents a room or apartment in another's house — see TENANT
**lodging** *n* 1 the place where one lives — see HOME 1
2 **lodgings** *pl* a room or set of rooms in a private house or a block used as a separate dwelling place — see APARTMENT 1
**loft** *vb* to send through the air especially with a quick forward motion of the arm — see THROW
**loftiest** *adj* being at a point or level higher than all others — see TOP 1
**loftiness** *n* an exaggerated sense of one's importance that shows itself in the making of excessive or unjustified claims — see ARROGANCE
**lofty** *adj* 1 extending to a great distance upward — see HIGH 1
2 having a feeling of superiority that shows itself in an overbearing attitude — see ARROGANT
3 having or displaying feelings of scorn for what is regarded as beneath oneself — see PROUD 1
4 having, characterized by, or arising from a dignified and generous nature — see NOBLE 2
5 very dignified in form, tone, or style — see ELEVATED 2
**log** *vb* to make a written note of — see RECORD 1
**logger** *n* a person whose job is to cut down trees — see LUMBERJACK
**logic** *n* the thought processes that have been established as leading to valid solutions to problems ⟨I tried to use *logic* to figure out the solution to the puzzle⟩
***syn*** reason, reasoning, sense
***rel*** cogency, coherence, rationality, thought; analysis, deduction, induction
***near ant*** incoherence, insanity, irrationality
**logical** *adj* 1 according to the rules of logic ⟨the lawyer won the case with a *logical* argument about the motives of the suspect⟩
***syn*** analytic (*or* analytical), coherent, good, rational, reasonable, sensible, sound, valid
***rel*** sane; thoughtful; scientific
***near ant*** specious; crazy, insane; senseless, thoughtless
***ant*** illogical, incoherent, invalid, irrational, unreasonable, unsound
2 based on sound reasoning or information — see GOOD 1
**logo** *n* a device, design, or figure used as an identifying mark — see EMBLEM
**logy** *adj* depleted in strength, energy, or freshness — see WEARY 1
**loiter** *vb* to move or act slowly — see DELAY 1
**loiterer** *n* someone who moves slowly or more slowly than others — see SLOWPOKE
**loll** *vb* 1 to be limp from lack of water or vigor — see DROOP 1
2 to refrain from labor or exertion — see REST 1
3 to spend time doing nothing — see IDLE
**lone** *adj* 1 being the one or ones of a class with no other members — see ONLY 2
2 not being in the company of others — see ALONE 1
**lonely** *adj* 1 not being in the company of others — see ALONE 1
2 sad from lack of companionship or separation from others — see LONESOME 1
**loner** *n* a person who does not conform to generally accepted standards or customs — see NONCONFORMIST 1
**lonesome** *adj* 1 sad from lack of companionship or separation from others ⟨a *lonesome* kitten left at the pound by its owners⟩
***syn*** desolate, forlorn, lonely, lorn
***rel*** friendless; abandoned, deserted, forgotten, forsaken, neglected; alone, lone, solitary; only, sole
***near ant*** accompanied, attended, escorted
2 not being in the company of others — see ALONE 1
**lone wolf** *n* a person who does not conform to generally accepted standards or customs — see NONCONFORMIST 1
**long** *adj* 1 of great extent from end to end ⟨giraffes have *long* necks to help them reach leaves on tall trees⟩

*syn* elongated, extended, king-size (*or* king-sized), lengthy
*rel* extensive, far-reaching, longish, outstretched; oblong, rectangular; big, considerable, good-sized, hefty, hulking, jumbo, large, largish, oversize (*or* oversized), sizable (*or* sizeable), substantial, super
*near ant* abbreviated, abridged, curtailed, diminished, shortened; diminutive, little, minute, puny, small, smallish, tiny, undersized, wee
*ant* brief, short
**2** lasting for a considerable time ⟨summer vacation seemed *long*, but we had to go back to school soon enough⟩
*syn* extended, far, great, lengthy, long-lived, long-range, long-term, marathon
*rel* endless, everlasting, interminable, persistent; longish, overlong, prolonged, protracted; permanent
*near ant* abrupt, sudden; abbreviated, condensed, curtailed; ephemeral, fleeting, momentary, transient, transitory; impermanent
*ant* brief, short, short-lived, short-range, short-term

**long** (for) *vb* to have an earnest wish to own or enjoy — see DESIRE

**longhand** *n* writing done by hand — see HANDWRITING 2

**longing** *n* a strong wish for something — see DESIRE

**long–lived** *adj* **1** being of advanced years and especially past middle age — see ELDERLY
**2** lasting for a considerable time — see LONG 2

**long–range** *adj* lasting for a considerable time — see LONG 2

**longshoreman** *n* one who loads and unloads ships at a port — see DOCKWORKER

**long–suffering** *adj* accepting pains or hardships calmly or without complaint — see PATIENT 1

**long–suffering** *n* the capacity to endure what is difficult or disagreeable without complaining — see PATIENCE

**long–term** *adj* lasting for a considerable time — see LONG 2

**long–winded** *adj* using or containing more words than necessary to express an idea — see WORDY

**long–windedness** *n* the use of too many words to express an idea — see VERBIAGE

**look** *n* **1** facial appearance regarded as an indication of mood or feeling ⟨you should have seen the *look* on your face when we yelled "Surprise!"⟩
*syn* cast, countenance, expression, face, visage
*rel* frown, grimace, mouth, scowl; air, appearance, aspect, bearing, demeanor, manner, mien
**2** an instance of looking especially briefly ⟨she gave the junk mail a quick *look* before throwing it in the garbage pail⟩
*syn* cast, eye, gander, glance, glimpse, peek, peep, regard, sight, view
*rel* gape, gaze, glare, leer, ogle, stare; squint
**3** the outward form of someone or something especially as indicative of a quality — see APPEARANCE 1
**4 looks** *pl* the qualities in a person or thing that as a whole give pleasure to the senses — see BEAUTY 1

**look** *vb* **1** to give the impression of being — see SEEM
**2** to make known (as an idea, emotion, or opinion) — see EXPRESS 1

**look** (at) *vb* to make note of (something) through the use of one's eyes — see SEE 1

**look** (into) *vb* to search through or into — see EXPLORE 1

**look** (toward) *vb* to stand or sit with the face or front toward — see FACE 1

**looking glass** *n* a smooth or polished surface (as of glass) that forms images by reflection — see MIRROR

**lookout** *n* **1** a high place or structure from which a wide view is possible ⟨we went up to the *lookout* on the top of the hill to watch the fireworks⟩
*syn* observatory, outlook
*rel* aerie, crow's nest, tower, watchtower
**2** all that can be seen from a certain point — see VIEW 1
**3** the act or state of being constantly attentive and responsive to signs of opportunity, activity, or danger — see VIGILANCE
**4** a person or group that watches over someone or something — see GUARD 1

**look up** *vb* to go in search of — see SEEK 1

**loom** *vb* to be about to happen ⟨he could tell that trouble was *looming* when the bullies swaggered into the park⟩
*syn* brew, impend
*rel* advance, approach, close in, draw on, gather, near; lower (*also* lour), menace, threaten
*near ant* die down, diminish, disappear, dwindle, fade, vanish, wane; fall back, pass, recede, retreat, withdraw

**loony** *n* a person judged to be legally or medically insane — see LUNATIC 1

**loony** *also* **looney** *adj* **1** showing or marked by a lack of good sense or judgment — see FOOLISH 1
**2** having or showing a very abnormal or sick state of mind — see INSANE 1

**loop** *n* a circular strip — see RING 2

**loop** *vb* to pass completely around — see ENCIRCLE 1

**loose** *adj* **1** not tightly fastened, tied, or stretched ⟨secure your neckerchief with a *loose* knot⟩
*syn* insecure, lax, loosened, relaxed, slack, slackened, unsecured
*rel* detached, free, unattached, unbound, undone, unfastened, untied; baggy; nonrestrictive
*near ant* constrained, restrained; attached, bound, fastened, tied
*ant* taut, tense, tight

---

*syn* synonym(s) *rel* related words
*ant* antonym(s) *near ant* near antonym(s)

2 consisting of particles that do not stick together ⟨the car wheels slipped on the *loose* gravel in the driveway⟩
*syn* incoherent, unconsolidated
*rel* nonadhesive; disconnected, disjointed, separate, unconnected; coarse, granular, rough
*near ant* connected, solid; compacted, compressed; adhesive, gluey, sticky
*ant* coherent, compact, dense, packed
3 not bound by rigid standards — see EASYGOING 2
4 not bound, confined, or detained by force — see FREE 3
5 not precisely correct — see INEXACT 1

**loose** *vb* 1 to cause (a projectile) to be driven forward with force — see SHOOT 1
2 to find emotional release for — see TAKE OUT 1
3 to set free (as from slavery or confinement) — see FREE 1
4 to set free (from a state of being held in check) — see RELEASE 1

**loosen** *vb* 1 to make less taut — see SLACKEN
2 to set free (as from slavery or confinement) — see FREE 1
3 to set free (from a state of being held in check) — see RELEASE 1

**loosen** (up) *vb* to free from obstruction or difficulty — see EASE 1

**loosened** *adj* not tightly fastened, tied, or stretched — see LOOSE 1

**loot** *n* valuables stolen or taken by force ⟨the burglar was caught when he stopped to examine the *loot* from the robbery⟩
*syn* booty, plunder, spoil, swag
*rel* prize; catch, haul, take; pilferage; windfall

**loot** *vb* to search through with the intent of committing robbery — see RANSACK 1

**lop** (off) *vb* to make (as hair) shorter with or as if with the use of shears — see CLIP

**lope** *vb* to move with a light bouncing step — see SKIP 1

**lopsided** *adj* inclined or twisted to one side — see AWRY

**loquacious** *adj* fond of talking or conversation — see TALKATIVE

**Lord** *n* the being worshipped as the creator and ruler of the universe — see DEITY 2

**lord** (it over) *vb* to assume or treat with an air of superiority — see CONDESCEND 2

**lordliness** *n* an exaggerated sense of one's importance that shows itself in the making of excessive or unjustified claims — see ARROGANCE

**lordly** *adj* 1 having a feeling of superiority that shows itself in an overbearing attitude — see ARROGANT
2 having or displaying feelings of scorn for what is regarded as beneath oneself — see PROUD 1
3 having, characterized by, or arising from a dignified and generous nature — see NOBLE 2

**lore** *n* 1 a body of facts learned by study or experience — see KNOWLEDGE 1
2 the body of customs, beliefs, stories, and sayings associated with a people, thing, or place — see FOLKLORE

**lorn** *adj* sad from lack of companionship or separation from others — see LONESOME 1

**lose** *vb* 1 to be unable to find or have at hand ⟨I always *lose* my keys⟩
*syn* mislay, misplace
*near ant* have
*ant* find, locate
2 to get rid of as useless or unwanted — see DISCARD

**loser** *n* something that has failed — see FAILURE 3

**loss** *n* 1 the act or an instance of not having or being able to find ⟨he was upset over the *loss* of his bike⟩
*syn* mislaying, misplacement
*rel* deprivation, dispossession; forfeit, forfeiture, penalty; sacrifice; bereavement
*ant* acquisition, gain
2 a person or thing harmed, lost, or destroyed — see CASUALTY 1
3 failure to win a contest — see DEFEAT 1
4 the amount by which something is lessened — see DECREASE
5 the state of being robbed of something normally enjoyed — see PRIVATION
6 the state or fact of being rendered nonexistent, physically unsound, or useless — see DESTRUCTION

**lost** *adj* no longer possessed ⟨they searched all over the house for the *lost* keys⟩
*syn* gone, mislaid, misplaced, missing
*rel* absent, castaway; irrecoverable, irretrievable; forgotten, unknown
*near ant* cherished, protected, treasured
*ant* owned, possessed, retained

**lot** *n* 1 a small piece of land that is developed or available for development ⟨we often played in the vacant *lot* down at the end of the street⟩
*syn* parcel, plat, plot, property, tract
*rel* patch; frontage; lease; development; real estate
2 a considerable amount ⟨they needed to do a *lot* of studying for the test⟩
*syn* abundance, barrel, bucket, bushel, deal, gobs, heap, loads, mass, mountain, much, oodles, peck, pile, plenitude, plenty, pot, profusion, quantity, raft, reams, scads, stack, volume, wad, wealth
*rel* embarrassment, excess, overabundance, overage, overkill, overmuch, oversupply, superabundance, superfluity, surfeit, surplus; deluge, flood, overflow
*near ant* atom, crumb, fragment, grain, iota, jot, modicum, molecule, particle, scrap, shred, tittle, whit; scattering, smattering; drop, morsel, shot; piece, portion, section; absence, dearth, lack, paucity, poverty, scarceness, scarcity, shortage, want; deficiency, deficit, inadequacy, insufficiency, meagerness, scantiness, skimpiness
*ant* ace, bit, dab, driblet, glimmer, hint, lick, little, mite, mouthful, ounce, peanuts, pinch, scruple, smidgen, speck,

spot, sprinkling, suspicion, taste, touch, trace
**3** a small area of usually open land — see FIELD 1
**4** a number of things considered as a unit — see GROUP 1
**5** a state or end that seemingly has been decided beforehand — see FATE 1
**6** a group of people sharing a common interest and relating together socially — see GANG 2
**7** a usually small number of persons considered as a unit — see GROUP 2

**loud** *adj* **1** marked by a high volume of sound ⟨*loud* music that could be heard all over the neighborhood⟩
***syn*** blaring, blasting, booming, clamorous, clangorous, deafening, earsplitting, piercing, resounding, ringing, roaring, sonorous, stentorian, thunderous
***rel*** brazen, dinning, discordant, noisy, obstreperous, raucous, rip-roaring, vociferous; grating, harsh, shrill, strident
***near ant*** dead, quiet, silent, still; dreamy, peaceful, restful, soothing, tranquil; softened, toned (down)
***ant*** gentle, low, soft
**2** excessively showy — see GAUDY

**lounge** *n* a long upholstered piece of furniture designed for several sitters — see COUCH

**lounge** *vb* **1** to refrain from labor or exertion — see REST 1
**2** to spend time doing nothing — see IDLE

**louse** *n* a person whose behavior is offensive to others — see JERK 1

**louse up** *vb* to make or do (something) in a clumsy or unskillful way — see BOTCH

**lousy** *adj* **1** arousing or deserving of one's loathing and disgust — see CONTEMPTIBLE 1
**2** falling short of a standard — see BAD 1
**3** extremely unsatisfactory — see WRETCHED 1
**4** of low quality — see CHEAP 2

**lout** *n* **1** a big clumsy often slow-witted person — see OAF
**2** a person whose behavior is offensive to others — see JERK 1

**loutish** *adj* having or showing crudely insensitive or impolite manners — see CLOWNISH

**lovable** *adj* having qualities that tend to make one loved ⟨she was a *lovable* child, always helpful and kind⟩
***syn*** adorable, darling, dear, disarming, endearing, precious, sweet, winning
***rel*** embraceable, kissable; beloved, cherished, treasured; attractive, beautiful, desirable, lovely; captivating, charming, fascinating; admirable, likable (*or* likeable), reputable, respectable; affable, agreeable, cheerful, cordial, friendly, genial, gracious, kind, pleasant; delightful, pleasing
***near ant*** unloved; contemptible, disagreeable, disgusting, distasteful, heinous, horrible, offensive, unlikable, unpleasant; frightful, grotesque, hideous, ill-favored, monstrous, ogreish, repellent (*also* repellant), repugnant, repulsive; ugly, unattractive, unsightly, vile
***ant*** abhorrent, abominable, detestable, hateful, odious, unlovable

**love** *n* **1** a feeling of strong or constant regard for and dedication to someone ⟨her *love* for her children was truly selfless⟩
***syn*** affection, attachment, devotedness, devotion, fondness, passion
***rel*** appetite, favor, like, liking, partiality, preference, taste; craving, crush, desire, infatuation, longing, lust, yearning; ardor, eagerness, enthusiasm, fervor, zeal; esteem, regard, respect; adoration, idolatry, worship; allegiance, fealty, fidelity, loyalty
***near ant*** allergy, animosity, antipathy, aversion, disfavor, dislike; abhorrence, disgust, repugnance, repulsion, revulsion; misanthropy
***ant*** abomination, hate, hatred, loathing, rancor
**2** a person with whom one is in love — see SWEETHEART
**3** positive regard for something — see LIKING

**love** *vb* **1** to hold dear ⟨patriots who *loved* their country well enough to die for it⟩
***syn*** appreciate, cherish, prize, treasure, value
***rel*** delight (in), dig, enjoy, fancy, groove (on), like, relish, revel (in); admire, esteem, regard, respect, revere, reverence, venerate; enshrine, memorialize; adore, dote (on), idolize, worship
***phrases*** set store (by *or* on)
***near ant*** undervalue; abhor, abominate, despise, detest, execrate, hate, loathe; disdain, scorn, scout; belittle, decry, deprecate, depreciate, disparage; abandon, forget, neglect
**2** to feel passion, devotion, or tenderness for ⟨a husband who *loves* his wife more than anything⟩
***syn*** adore, cherish, worship
***rel*** idealize, idolize; revere, reverence, venerate; delight (in), dote (on)
***phrases*** fall for, lose one's heart (to)
***near ant*** antagonize, displease; disapprove (of), disfavor, dislike; disgust, repulse, turn off
***ant*** abhor, abominate, despise, detest, execrate, hate, loathe
**3** to take pleasure in — see ENJOY 1
**4** to touch or handle in a tender or loving manner — see FONDLE

**love affair** *n* a brief romantic relationship — see AFFAIR 1

**loved** *adj* granted special treatment or attention — see DARLING 1

**loveliness** *n* the qualities in a person or thing that as a whole give pleasure to the senses — see BEAUTY 1

**lovely** *adj* very pleasing to look at — see BEAUTIFUL

**lover** *n* a person with a strong and habitual liking for something — see FAN

---

***syn*** synonym(s) ***rel*** related words
***ant*** antonym(s) ***near ant*** near antonym(s)

**loving** *adj* feeling or showing love ⟨they were a *loving* family, supporting each other when times were bad⟩
*syn* adoring, affectionate, devoted, fond, tender, tenderhearted
*rel* caring, compassionate, considerate, cordial, doting, forgiving, friendly, kind, warmhearted; ardent, fervent, impassioned, passionate, warm; amatory, amorous, erotic; enamored, infatuated, lovesick; mushy, romantic, sentimental; brotherly, fatherly, motherly, sisterly
*near ant* aloof, detached, hardhearted, indifferent, pitiless, reserved, uncaring, unfeeling; disaffected, unconcerned, uninvolved; cold, frigid, unfriendly; hardboiled, unromantic, unsentimental
*ant* unloving

**low** *adj* **1** being near the equator ⟨we took a cruise to the *low* northern latitudes⟩
*syn* equatorial, tropical
*near ant* temperate
*ant* polar
**2** belonging to or characteristic of an early level of skill or development — see PRIMITIVE 1
**3** belonging to the class of people of low social or economic rank — see IGNOBLE 1
**4** feeling unhappiness — see SAD 1
**5** having a low musical pitch or range — see DEEP 2
**6** having relatively little height — see SHORT 1
**7** lacking bodily strength — see WEAK 1
**8** lacking in refinement or good taste — see COARSE 2
**9** not following or in accordance with standards of honor and decency — see IGNOBLE 2
**10** not loud in pitch or volume — see SOFT 1
**11** costing little — see CHEAP 1

**lowbred** *adj* lacking in refinement or good taste — see COARSE 2

**lowbrow** *adj* lacking in refinement or good taste — see COARSE 2

**lowbrow** *n* a person who is chiefly interested in material comfort and is hostile or indifferent to art and culture — see PHILISTINE

**lowdown** *n* information not generally available to the public — see DOPE 1

**lower** *adj* **1** having not so great importance or rank as another — see LESSER
**2** situated lower down — see INFERIOR 1

[1]**lower** *vb* **1** to cause to fall intentionally or unintentionally — see DROP 1
**2** to go to a lower level — see DROP 2
**3** to make smaller in amount, volume, or extent — see DECREASE 1
**4** to grow less in scope or intensity especially gradually — see DECREASE 2
**5** to reduce to a lower standing in one's own eyes or in others' eyes — see HUMBLE

[2]**lower** *also* **lour** *vb* **1** to take on a gloomy or forbidding look — see DARKEN 1
**2** to look with anger or disapproval — see FROWN

**lower** *also* **lour** *n* a twisting of the facial features in disgust or disapproval — see GRIMACE

**lower–class** *adj* belonging to the class of people of low social or economic rank — see IGNOBLE 1

**lowered** *adj* directed down — see DOWNCAST 1

**lowering** *also* **louring** *adj* **1** covered over by clouds — see OVERCAST
**2** harsh and threatening in manner or appearance — see GRIM 1

**lowest** *adj* being the least in amount, number, or size possible — see MINIMAL

**low–grade** *adj* of low quality — see CHEAP 2

**lowliness** *n* the absence of any feelings of being better than others — see HUMILITY

**lowly** *adj* **1** belonging to the class of people of low social or economic rank — see IGNOBLE 1
**2** not having or showing any feelings of superiority, self-assertiveness, or showiness — see HUMBLE 1

**lowly** *adv* in manner showing no signs of pride or self-assertion ⟨the courtier bowed *lowly* before his king during the ceremony⟩
*syn* deferentially, humbly, meekly, modestly, sheepishly, submissively
*rel* fearfully, timidly; bashfully, diffidently, shyly; civilly, courteously, politely, respectfully
*near ant* fearlessly; discourteously, disdainfully, disrespectfully, impertinently, rashly, recklessly, saucily; impolitely, impudently, rudely, ungraciously
*ant* arrogantly, audaciously, boldly, brashly, brazenly, contemptuously, haughtily, pridefully, proudly, scornfully, swaggeringly

**low–lying** *adj* having relatively little height — see SHORT 1

**lowness** *n* **1** the quality or state of lacking refinement or good taste — see VULGARITY 1
**2** the quality or state of lacking physical strength or vigor — see WEAKNESS 1

**low–pressure** *adj* having a relaxed, casual manner — see EASYGOING 1

**low–spirited** *adj* feeling unhappiness — see SAD 1

**loyal** *adj* firm in one's allegiance to someone or something — see FAITHFUL 1

**loyalist** *n* a person who loves his or her country and supports its interests and policies — see PATRIOT

**loyalty** *n* adherence to something to which one is bound by a pledge or duty — see FIDELITY

**lozenge** *n* a small mass containing medicine to be taken orally — see PILL

**lubber** *n* a big clumsy often slow-witted person — see OAF

**lubberly** *adj* lacking in physical ease and grace in movement or in the use of the hands — see CLUMSY 1

**lubricate** *vb* to coat (something) with a slippery substance in order to reduce fric-

tion ⟨it's not a good idea to use olive oil to *lubricate* the gears in an appliance⟩
***syn*** grease, oil, slick, wax
***near ant*** coarsen, rough, roughen

**lubricated** *adj* having or being a surface so smooth as to make sliding or falling likely — see SLICK 1

**lucent** *adj* **1** easily seen through — see CLEAR 1
**2** giving off or reflecting much light — see BRIGHT 1

**lucid** *adj* **1** giving off or reflecting much light — see BRIGHT 1
**2** having full use of one's mind and control over one's actions — see SANE
**3** not subject to misinterpretation or more than one interpretation — see CLEAR 2

**lucidity** *n* **1** clearness of expression — see SIMPLICITY 2
**2** the quality or state of having or giving off light — see BRILLIANCE 1

**lucidness** *n* clearness of expression — see SIMPLICITY 2

**Lucifer** *n* the supreme personification of evil often represented as the ruler of Hell — see DEVIL 1

**luck** *n* **1** success that is partly the result of chance ⟨some people have all the *luck*⟩
***syn*** fortunateness, fortune, luckiness
***rel*** break, fluke, godsend, hit, serendipity, strike, windfall; chance, opportunity; coup, stroke
***near ant*** knock, misadventure, mishap; adversity, curse, sorrow, tragedy, trouble; calamity, cataclysm, catastrophe, disaster; defeat, failure, fizzle, nonsuccess; accident, casualty; disappointment, letdown, setback; circumstance, destiny, doom, fate, lot, portion
***ant*** mischance, misfortune, unluckiness
**2** the uncertain course of events — see CHANCE 1

**luckiness** *n* success that is partly the result of chance — see LUCK 1

**luckless** *adj* having, prone to, or marked by bad luck — see UNLUCKY

**lucky** *adj* **1** having good luck ⟨the *lucky* gambler walked out of the casino with $10,000⟩
***syn*** fortunate, happy
***rel*** blessed, favored, gifted, privileged; fair, golden, promising
***near ant*** cursed, disadvantaged
***ant*** hapless, ill-fated, ill-starred, luckless, star-crossed, unfortunate, unhappy, unlucky
**2** coming or happening by good luck especially unexpectedly — see FORTUNATE 1

**lucrative** *adj* yielding a profit — see PROFITABLE 1

**lucre** *n* **1** something (as pieces of stamped metal or printed paper) customarily and legally used as a medium of exchange, a measure of value, or a means of payment — see MONEY
**2** the amount of money left when expenses are subtracted from the total amount received — see PROFIT 1

**ludicrous** *adj* **1** causing or intended to cause laughter — see FUNNY 1
**2** so foolish or pointless as to be worthy of scornful laughter — see RIDICULOUS 1

**lug** *n* a big clumsy often slow-witted person — see OAF

**lug** *vb* **1** to cause to follow by applying steady force on — see PULL 1
**2** to support and take from one place to another — see CARRY 1

**lugubrious** *adj* expressing or suggesting mourning — see MOURNFUL 1

**lukewarm** *adj* **1** having or giving off heat to a moderate degree — see WARM 1
**2** showing little or no interest or enthusiasm — see TEPID 1

**lukewarmness** *n* the quality or state of being moderate in temperature — see WARMTH 1

**lull** *n* a momentary halt in an activity — see PAUSE

**lulling** *adj* tending to calm the emotions and relieve stress — see SOOTHING 1

**lumber** *n* tree logs as prepared for human use — see WOOD

**lumber** *vb* **1** to move heavily or clumsily ⟨the elephant *lumbered* through the jungle⟩
***syn*** barge, clump, flounder, lump, pound, scuff, scuffle, shamble, shuffle, stamp, stomp, stumble, stump, tramp, tromp
***rel*** drag, flop, haul; labor, plod, trudge; careen, lurch, stagger, sway, teeter, totter, waddle, weave, wobble
***near ant*** float, hover, waft
***ant*** breeze, coast, glide, slide, waltz, whisk
**2** to make progress in a clumsy, struggling manner — see FLOUNDER 1
**3** to make a low heavy rolling sound — see RUMBLE
**4** to place a weight or burden on — see LOAD 1

**lumbering** *adj* lacking in physical ease and grace in movement or in the use of the hands — see CLUMSY 1

**lumberjack** *n* a person whose job is to cut down trees ⟨the sawmill gets most of its business from the *lumberjacks* up north⟩
***syn*** logger
***rel*** sawyer; forester

**luminary** *n* **1** a ball-shaped gaseous celestial body that shines by its own light — see STAR 1
**2** a person who is widely known and usually much talked about — see CELEBRITY 1

**luminescence** *n* the steady giving off of the form of radiation that makes vision possible — see LIGHT 1

**luminosity** *n* the quality or state of having or giving off light — see BRILLIANCE 1

**luminous** *adj* giving off or reflecting much light — see BRIGHT 1

**lump** *n* **1** a small uneven mass ⟨she dumped a *lump* of clay on the table and started to sculpt⟩

---

***syn*** synonym(s) ***rel*** related words
***ant*** antonym(s) ***near ant*** near antonym(s)

*syn* blob, chunk, clod, clump, glob, gob, gobbet, hunk, knob, nub, nubble, nugget, wad
*rel* bead, drop, globule; block, body, bulk; particle, piece, portion; bit, chip, crumb, morsel, scrap
**2** a small rounded mass of swollen tissue — see BUMP 1
**3** an abnormal mass of tissue — see GROWTH 1

**lump** *vb* **1** to bring together in one body or place — see GATHER 1
**2** to move heavily or clumsily — see LUMBER 1

**lumpish** *adj* lacking in physical ease and grace in movement or in the use of the hands — see CLUMSY 1

**lumpy** *adj* **1** having small pieces or lumps spread throughout — see CHUNKY 1
**2** not having a level or smooth surface — see UNEVEN 1

**lunacy** *n* **1** a foolish act or idea — see FOLLY 1
**2** a serious mental disorder that prevents one from living a safe and normal life — see INSANITY 1
**3** lack of good sense or judgment — see FOOLISHNESS 1

**lunatic** *adj* **1** having or showing a very abnormal or sick state of mind — see INSANE 1
**2** showing or marked by a lack of good sense or judgment — see FOOLISH 1

**lunatic** *n* **1** a person judged to be legally or medically insane ⟨the *lunatic* was committed to an institution after running naked through the department store⟩
*syn* crackbrain, loony (*also* looney), maniac, neurotic, nut, psychopath, psychotic
*rel* madman, madwoman; deviant; paranoid, schizophrenic; character, crackpot, crank, eccentric, kook, oddball, screwball; case, patient
**2** a person who lacks good sense or judgment — see FOOL 1

**lurch** *vb* **1** to make a series of unsteady side-to-side motions — see ROCK 1
**2** to move forward while swaying from side to side — see STAGGER 1

**lure** *n* **1** something that persuades one to perform an action for pleasure or gain ⟨the promise of easy money is always the *lure* for some people to take up a life of crime⟩
*syn* allurement, bait, enticement, temptation, turn-on
*rel* appeal, call; attraction, goad, incentive, inducement, persuasion, seduction, spur; decoy, snare, trap
*near ant* caution, warning
**2** something used to attract animals to a hook or into a trap — see BAIT 1
**3** the act or pressure of giving in to a desire especially when ill-advised — see TEMPTATION 1

**lure** *vb* to lead away from a usual or proper course by offering some pleasure or advantage ⟨the hunter *lured* the lion into the open with the antelope carcass⟩
*syn* allure, beguile, decoy, entice, lead on, seduce, tempt
*rel* inveigle, persuade, rope (in), snow; catch, ensnare, entrap, snare; captivate, charm, enchant
*near ant* caution, ward (off), warn; drive (away *or* off), repulse, turn away

**lurid** *adj* **1** extremely disturbing or repellent — see HORRIBLE 1
**2** lacking a healthy skin color — see PALE 2
**3** arousing a strong and usually superficial interest or emotional reaction — see SENSATIONAL 1

**luring** *adj* having an often mysterious or magical power to attract — see FASCINATING 1

**lurk** *vb* to move about in a sly or secret manner — see SNEAK 1

**lurker** *n* someone who acts in a sly and secret manner — see SNEAK

**luscious** *adj* **1** very pleasing to the sense of taste — see DELICIOUS 1
**2** pleasing to the physical senses — see SENSUAL
**3** giving pleasure or contentment to the mind or senses — see PLEASANT

**lusciousness** *n* the quality of being delicious — see DELICIOUSNESS

**lush** *adj* **1** covered with a thick healthy natural growth ⟨they loved to go for picnics in the *lush* woodlands⟩
*syn* green, leafy, luxuriant, overgrown, verdant
*rel* fat, fecund, fertile, fruitful, productive, rich; dense, tangled
*near ant* bleak, depleted, infertile, poor, unproductive; arid, dead, desert, dry, parched
*ant* barren, leafless
**2** growing thickly and vigorously — see RANK 1

**lust** (for *or* after) *vb* to have an earnest wish to own or enjoy — see DESIRE

**lust** *n* a strong wish for something — see DESIRE

**luster** *or* **lustre** *n* brightness created by light reflected from a surface — see SHINE 1

**lusterless** *adj* lacking a surface luster or gloss — see MATTE

**lustful** *adj* having a strong sexual desire ⟨the *lustful* student was always chasing after girls⟩
*syn* lascivious, lewd, licentious, passionate, wanton
*rel* prurient; dissipated, dissolute, libertine; corrupt, debauched, depraved, immoral, indecent
*near ant* celibate, chaste, decent, modest, moral, pure, virtuous; monastic, monkish; maidenly, virginal; innocent, lily-white

**lustiness** *n* the quality or state of having abundant or intense activity — see VITALITY 1

**lustrous** *adj* **1** giving off or reflecting much light — see BRIGHT 1
**2** having a shiny surface or finish — see GLOSSY

**lusty** *adj* **1** having active strength of body or mind — see VIGOROUS 1
**2** not showing weakness or uncertainty — see FIRM 1
**luxuriant** *adj* **1** covered with a thick, healthy natural growth — see LUSH 1
**2** growing thickly and vigorously — see RANK 1
**3** producing abundantly — see FERTILE
**4** showing obvious signs of wealth and comfort — see LUXURIOUS
**luxurious** *adj* showing obvious signs of wealth and comfort ⟨the *luxurious* apartment was filled with the latest electronic gadgets and fine works of art⟩
***syn*** deluxe, lavish, luxuriant, opulent, palatial, plush, sumptuous
***rel*** costly, expensive; rich; extravagant, grandiose, ostentatious, pretentious, showy; awesome, awful, beautiful, gorgeous, grand, imposing, impressive, magnificent, majestic, splendid, stately; comfortable, cozy, homelike, homey, snug
***near ant*** economical, frugal, meager (*or* meagre), spare, thrifty
***ant*** ascetic, austere, humble, Spartan
**luxuriously** *adv* in a luxurious manner — see HIGH
**luxury** *n* something adding to pleasure or comfort but not absolutely necessary ⟨a private yacht is a *luxury*⟩
***syn*** amenity, comfort, extra, frill, indulgence, superfluity
***rel*** extravagance; dainty, delicacy, treat; accessory, option
***ant*** basic, essential, fundamental, necessity, requirement
**2** something that adds to one's ease — see COMFORT 2
**lying** *adj* telling or containing lies — see DISHONEST 1
**lynx-eyed** *adj* having unusually keen vision — see SHARP-EYED
**lyric** *adj* **1** having a pleasantly flowing quality suggestive of music ⟨they performed a slow, *lyric* dance for the audience⟩
***syn*** euphonious, lyrical, mellifluous, mellow, melodic, melodious, musical
***rel*** dulcet, golden, sweet
***near ant*** disconnected, staccato; discordant, grating, harsh, jarring, strident
**2** having qualities suggestive of poetry — see POETIC
**lyric** *n* **1** a composition using rhythm and often rhyme to create a lyrical effect — see POEM
**2** a short musical composition for the human voice often with instrumental accompaniment — see SONG 1
**lyrical** *adj* **1** having a pleasantly flowing quality suggestive of music — see LYRIC 1
**2** having qualities suggestive of poetry — see POETIC

# M

**ma** *n* a female human parent — see MOTHER
**macabre** *adj* extremely disturbing or repellent — see HORRIBLE 1
**Machiavellian** *adj* not guided by or showing a concern for what is right — see UNPRINCIPLED
**machinate** *vb* **1** to engage in a secret plan to accomplish evil or unlawful ends — see PLOT
**2** to plan out usually with subtle skill or care — see ENGINEER
**machination** *n* a secret plan for accomplishing evil or unlawful ends — see PLOT 1
**machine** *n* **1** a device that changes energy into mechanical motion — see ENGINE
**2** a self-propelled passenger vehicle on wheels — see CAR
**machinery** *n* something used to achieve an end — see AGENT 1
**mackintosh** *or* **macintosh** *n chiefly British* a coat made of water-resistant material — see RAINCOAT
**macrocosm** *n* the whole body of things observed or assumed — see UNIVERSE
**mad** *adj* **1** feeling or showing anger — see ANGRY
**2** having or showing a very abnormal or sick state of mind — see INSANE 1
**3** marked by great and often stressful excitement or activity — see FURIOUS 1
**4** showing or marked by a lack of good sense or judgment — see FOOLISH 1
**mad** (about) *adj* filled with an intense or excessive love for — see ENAMORED (OF)
**madcap** *adj* foolishly adventurous or bold — see FOOLHARDY 1
**madden** *vb* **1** to cause to go insane or as if insane — see CRAZE
**2** to make angry — see ANGER
**maddening** *adj* causing annoyance — see ANNOYING
**mademoiselle** *n* a young usually unmarried woman — see GIRL 1
**made-up** *adj* not real and existing only in the imagination — see IMAGINARY
**madhouse** *n* **1** a place where insane people are cared for ⟨it was hard to believe that this place with the bright cheery walls was really a *madhouse*⟩
***syn*** asylum

*rel* institution; hospice, hospital, sanatorium, sanitarium; home
**2** a place of uproar or confusion ⟨our house is always a *madhouse* on school mornings, with five kids and two dogs running around⟩
*syn* babel, bedlam, circus, hell
*rel* commotion, havoc, pandemonium, racket, ruckus, tumult, turmoil; clamor, clatter, din, hubbub, noise; chaos confusion, disarrangement, disarray, disorder, maelstrom, mess, muss
*near ant* heaven, paradise, utopia; order, orderliness, organization; calm, peace; hush, quiet, silence, soundlessness, stillness

**madly** *adv* **1** in a confused and reckless manner — see HELTER-SKELTER 1
**2** in an enthusiastic manner — see SKY-HIGH

**madness** *n* **1** a serious mental disorder that prevents one from living a safe and normal life — see INSANITY 1
**2** lack of good sense or judgment — see FOOLISHNESS 1

**maelstrom** *n* water moving rapidly in a circle with a hollow in the center — see WHIRLPOOL

**maestro** *n* a person with a high level of knowledge or skill in a field — see EXPERT

**Mafia** *n* a group involved in secret or criminal activities — see RING 1

**magazine** *n* **1** a building for storing goods — see STOREHOUSE
**2** a place where military arms are stored — see ARMORY
**3** a publication that appears at regular intervals — see JOURNAL

**magic** *adj* **1** being or appearing to be under a magic spell — see ENCHANTED
**2** having seemingly supernatural qualities or powers — see MYSTIC 1

**magic** *n* **1** the power to control natural forces through supernatural means ⟨he claimed that he could summon a storm through *magic*⟩
*syn* bewitchment, black art, black magic, conjuring, enchantment, mojo, necromancy, sorcery, voodooism, witchcraft, witchery, wizardry
*rel* abracadabra, amulet, charm, fetish (*also* fetich), mascot, phylactery, talisman; curse, hex, incantation, jinx, spell; augury, divining, forecasting, foreknowing, foreseeing, foretelling, fortune-telling, predicting, presaging, prognosticating, prophesying, soothsaying; hoodoo, occultism, spiritualism; augur, omen; exorcism; alchemy
*near ant* science
**2** the art or skill of performing tricks or illusions for entertainment ⟨they hired someone to do *magic* for their child's tenth birthday party⟩
*syn* conjuring, legerdemain
*rel* deception, trickery
*phrases* sleight of hand
**3** the power of irresistible attraction — see CHARM 2

**magical** *adj* **1** being or appearing to be under a magic spell — see ENCHANTED
**2** being so extraordinary or abnormal as to suggest powers which violate the laws of nature — see SUPERNATURAL 2
**3** having seemingly supernatural qualities or powers — see MYSTIC 1

**magician** *n* **1** a person skilled in using supernatural forces ⟨the *magician* was able to turn birds purple with a simple spell⟩
*syn* charmer, conjurer (*or* conjuror), enchanter, necromancer, sorcerer, voodoo, witch, wizard
*rel* enchantress, hag, hex, sorceress, warlock; medicine man; foreseer, fortune-teller, prognosticator, prophesier, prophet, soothsayer; medium; exorcist
**2** one who practices tricks and illusions for entertainment ⟨the famous *magician's* best trick was always pulling a rabbit out of a hat⟩
*syn* conjurer (*or* conjuror), prestidigitator, trickster
*rel* charmer, enchanter, enchantress

**magistrate** *n* a public official having authority to decide questions of law — see JUDGE 1

**magnanimous** *adj* having, characterized by, or arising from a dignified and generous nature — see NOBLE 2

**magnanimously** *adv* in a manner befitting a person of the highest character and ideals — see GREATLY 1

**magnate** *n* a person of rank, power, or influence in a particular field ⟨the film studio *magnate* had movie stars at his beck and call⟩
*syn* baron, czar (*also* tsar *or* tzar), king, mogul, prince, tycoon
*rel* big shot, bigwig, figure, nabob, notable, personage, VIP; celebrity, personality, star; moneybags, plutocrat

**magnet** *n* something that attracts interest ⟨the giant theme park is a *magnet* for tourists to the area⟩
*syn* attraction, draw, lodestone
*rel* capital, cynosure, mecca; allure, allurement, bait, enticement, fascination, lure, temptation, turn-on; appeal, call; incentive, inducement, persuasion, spur

**magnetic** *adj* having an often mysterious or magical power to attract — see FASCINATING 1

**magnetism** *n* the power of irresistible attraction — see CHARM 2

**magnetize** *vb* to attract or delight as if by magic — see CHARM 1

**magnification** *n* the representation of something in terms that go beyond the facts — see EXAGGERATION

**magnificence** *n* impressiveness of beauty on a large scale ⟨the *magnificence* of the great castle hallway is beyond description⟩
*syn* augustness, brilliance, gloriousness, glory, grandeur, grandness, majesty, nobility, nobleness, resplendence, splendor, stateliness, stupendousness, sublimeness, superbness

*rel* awesomeness, marvelousness, wondrousness; lavishness, luxuriance, luxury, opulence, sumptuousness; grandiosity, ostentation, pretentiousness; flashiness, gaudiness, ornateness, showiness; extraordinariness, remarkableness

**magnificent** *adj* large and impressive in size, grandeur, extent, or conception — see GRAND 1

**magnify** *vb* **1** to add to the interest of by including made-up details — see EMBROIDER
**2** to enhance the status of — see EXALT
**3** to make markedly greater in measure or degree — see INTENSIFY
**4** to proclaim the glory of — see PRAISE 1

**magnitude** *n* **1** the quality or state of being important — see IMPORTANCE
**2** the quality or state of being very large — see IMMENSITY
**3** the total amount of measurable space or surface occupied by something — see [1]SIZE

**magnum opus** *n* something (as a work of art) that is a great achievement and often its creator's greatest achievement — see MASTERPIECE

**magpie** *n* a person who talks constantly — see CHATTERBOX

**maid** *n* **1** a female domestic servant ⟨they hired a *maid* to do the housework after the baby was born⟩
*syn* charwoman, domestic, housekeeper, housemaid, maidservant
*rel* attendant, chambermaid, handmaiden (*also* handmaid), lady-in-waiting; nursemaid
**2** a young usually unmarried woman — see GIRL 1

**maiden** *adj* **1** coming before all others in time or order — see FIRST 1
**2** never having had sexual relations — see VIRGIN 1

**maiden** *n* a young usually unmarried woman — see GIRL 1

**maidservant** *n* a female domestic servant — see MAID 1

**mail** *n* communications or parcels sent or carried through the postal system ⟨whenever they were separated, the lovers always sent each other lots of *mail*⟩
*syn* matter, parcel post, post [*chiefly British*]
*rel* electronic mail, e-mail; dispatch, epistle, message, missive, note, postcard; airmail, rural free delivery, special delivery; junk mail

**mail** *vb* to send through the postal system ⟨if you don't *mail* that letter soon, it's going to arrive late⟩
*syn* post
*rel* airmail; address, consign; direct, dispatch, forward, remit, route, ship, transmit, transport; register
*near ant* receive

**mail carrier** *n* a person who delivers mail — see POSTMAN

**mailman** *n* a person who delivers mail — see POSTMAN

**maim** *vb* to cause severe or permanent injury to ⟨on-the-job accidents *maim* far too many workers every year⟩
*syn* cripple, disable, lame, mutilate
*rel* dismember, hamstring, hobble; batter, bruise, bung (up), mangle, maul, rough (up); gore, lacerate, wound; disfigure, scar; break, damage, harm, hurt, impair, injure; bash, beat, belt, bludgeon, buffet, drub, hammer, lace, lambaste (*or* lambast), lick, paste, pelt, pound, pummel, thump; bang, box, hit, punch, slap, smack, smash, sock, spank, swat, swipe, thrash, thwack, whack; flog, lash, wallop, whip; kill, murder; torment, torture
*near ant* cure, heal, remedy; doctor, fix, mend, patch; rebuild, recondition, reconstruct, rejuvenate, renew, renovate, repair, restore

**main** *adj* coming before all others in importance — see FOREMOST 1

**main** *n* **1** muscular strength — see MUSCLE 1
**2** one of the great divisions of land on the globe or the main part of such a division — see MAINLAND
**3** the main or greater part of something as distinguished from its appendages — see BODY 1

**mainland** *n* one of the great divisions of land on the globe or the main part of such a division ⟨the boat back to the *mainland* leaves once every two days⟩
*syn* continent, main
*rel* subcontinent, supercontinent
*near ant* island, isle, islet; atoll, barrier reef, cay, coral reef, key; cape, headland, peninsula, promontory

**mainly** *adv* for the most part — see CHIEFLY

**mainstay** *n* something or someone to which one looks for support — see DEPENDENCE 2

**maintain** *vb* **1** to keep in good condition ⟨he repairs and *maintains* antique cars as a hobby⟩
*syn* conserve, keep up, preserve, save
*rel* support, sustain; care (for), husband, manage; defend, guard, protect, safeguard, screen, shield; cure, fix, heal, remedy; mend, patch, rebuild, reconstruct
*near ant* disregard, ignore, neglect; break, damage, destroy, harm, hurt, impair, injure, ruin, wreck
**2** to continue to declare to be true or proper despite opposition or objections ⟨part of debating is learning to *maintain* your position in the face of harsh challenges⟩
*syn* defend, justify, support, uphold
*rel* advocate, champion, espouse; confirm, vindicate, warrant; affirm, assert, avow, claim, contend, declare, insist, proclaim, profess, state; argue, debate, discuss; emphasize, stress, underline, underscore

***near ant*** abandon, forsake, recant, retract, take back, withdraw; controvert, disprove, rebut, refute
**3** to pay the living expenses of — see SUPPORT 2
**4** to state (something) as a reason in support of or against something under consideration — see ARGUE 1
**5** to state as a fact usually forcefully — see CLAIM 1

**maintainable** *adj* capable of being defended with good reasoning against verbal attack — see TENABLE 1

**maintenance** *n* the act or activity of keeping something in an existing and usually satisfactory condition ⟨I was hired to perform basic *maintenance* until the property could be sold⟩
***syn*** conservation, conserving, preservation, preserving, upkeep
***rel*** support, sustaining; care, guardianship; defense, guarding, protection, safeguarding, safekeeping
***near ant*** dereliction, ignoring, neglect; damage, destruction, harm, hurt, injury, ruin

**majestic** *adj* **1** having or showing elegance — see ELEGANT 1
**2** large and impressive in size, grandeur, extent, or conception — see GRAND 1
**3** very dignified in form, tone, or style — see ELEVATED 2

**majesty** *n* **1** a dignified bearing or appearance befitting royalty ⟨even as a child, the princess possessed a certain *majesty* that would later serve her well⟩
***syn*** augustness, stateliness
***rel*** high-mindedness, magnanimity, nobility; haughtiness, lordliness, pompousness; dignity, poise; grandeur, grandness, greatness, impressiveness, magnificence, resplendence, splendor
**2** dignified or restrained beauty of form, appearance, or style — see ELEGANCE
**3** impressiveness of beauty on a large scale — see MAGNIFICENCE

**major** *adj* having great meaning or lasting effect — see IMPORTANT 1

**majority** *n* the state of being fully grown or developed — see MATURITY

**make** *vb* **1** to bring into being by combining, shaping, or transforming materials ⟨will you help me *make* the dough for the cookies?⟩
***syn*** fabricate, fashion, form, frame, manufacture, produce
***rel*** assemble, build, construct, erect, make up, put up, raise, rear, structure, throw up; craft, handcraft; forge, mold, shape; prefabricate; create, invent, originate; establish, father, institute, organize; concoct, contrive, cook up, design, devise, imagine, think (up); conceive, envisage, picture, visualize; refashion, remake, remanufacture
***phrases*** put together
***near ant*** disassemble, dismantle, take apart; break up, dismember; abolish, annihilate, demolish, destroy, devastate, eradicate, exterminate, extinguish, flatten, pulverize, raze, ruin, shatter, smash, wreck; break, damage, harm, hurt, impair; blow up, explode
**2** to obtain (as a goal) through effort — see ACHIEVE 1
**3** to be the cause of (a situation, action, or state of mind) — see EFFECT
**4** to carry through (as a process) to completion — see PERFORM 1
**5** to cause (a person) to give in to pressure — see FORCE
**6** to decide the size, amount, number, or distance of (something) without actual measurement — see ESTIMATE 2
**7** to form by putting together parts or materials — see BUILD
**8** to give the impression of being — see SEEM
**9** to go on a specified course or in a certain direction — see HEAD 1
**10** to put into effect through legislative or authoritative action — see ENACT
**11** to receive as return for effort — see EARN 1
**12** to recognize the meaning of — see COMPREHEND 1

**make–believe** *adj* not real and existing only in the imagination — see IMAGINARY

**make out** *vb* **1** to meet one's day-to-day needs — see GET ALONG 1
**2** to recognize the meaning of — see COMPREHEND 1
**3** to touch one another with the lips as a sign of love — see KISS 1

**make over** *vb* **1** to change in form, appearance, or use — see CONVERT 2
**2** to give over the legal possession or ownership of — see TRANSFER 1
**3** to make different in some way — see CHANGE 1

**Maker** *n* the being worshipped as the creator and ruler of the universe — see DEITY 2

**makeshift** *adj* taking the place of one that came before — see NEW 1

**makeshift** *n* a temporary replacement ⟨when his belt broke, he used string as a *makeshift* until he could get home to replace it⟩
***syn*** expedient, stopgap
***rel*** recourse, refuge, resort; alternate, backup, standby, stand-in, substitute, understudy
***near ant*** archetype, original, prototype

**makeup** *n* **1** preparations intended to beautify the face or hair ⟨she never left the house without applying her *makeup* and arranging her jewelry⟩
***syn*** cosmetics, paint
***rel*** greasepaint; camouflage; cold cream, cream, eye shadow, kohl, lipstick, lotion, mascara, oil, powder, rouge, vanishing cream
**2** the way in which the elements of something (as a work of art) are arranged — see COMPOSITION 3

**make up** *vb* **1** to be all the substance of — see CONSTITUTE 1

**2** to create or think of by clever use of the imagination — see INVENT
**3** to form by putting together parts or materials — see BUILD

**make up** (for) *vb* to balance with an equal force so as to make ineffective — see OFFSET

**making** *n* the basic elements from which something can be developed ⟨she had all the *makings* of an excellent leader, but she needed some experience first⟩
***syn*** material, raw material, stuff, substance
***rel*** possibility, potential, potentiality; matter

**maladroit** *adj* showing or marked by a lack of skill and tact (as in dealing with a situation) — see AWKWARD 2

**malady** *n* an abnormal state that disrupts a plant's or animal's normal bodily functioning — see DISEASE

**malcontent** *adj* having a feeling that one has been wronged or thwarted in one's ambitions — see DISCONTENTED

**male** *adj* considered characteristic of or appropriate for men — see MASCULINE

**male** *n* an adult male human being — see MAN 1

**malediction** *n* a prayer that harm will come to someone — see CURSE 1

**malefaction** *n* a breaking of a moral or legal code — see OFFENSE 1

**malefactor** *n* **1** a person who commits moral wrongs — see EVILDOER 1
**2** a person who has committed a crime — see CRIMINAL

**malevolence** *n* the desire to cause pain for the satisfaction of doing harm — see MALICE

**malevolent** *adj* having or showing a desire to cause someone pain or suffering for the sheer enjoyment of it — see HATEFUL

**malevolently** *adv* in a mean or spiteful manner — see NASTILY

**malfeasance** *n* improper or illegal behavior — see MISCONDUCT

**malformed** *adj* badly or imperfectly formed ⟨a clay sculpture of an eagle that was so *malformed* that it looked more like a feathered football⟩
***syn*** deformed, distorted, misshapen, monstrous, shapeless
***rel*** defaced, disfigured; aberrant, abnormal, freakish, mutant; asymmetrical (*or* asymmetric), crooked, disproportionate, irregular, lopsided, nonsymmetrical, overbalanced, unbalanced, unequal; horrible, horrific, terrible; ugly, unattractive
***near ant*** flawless, perfect
***ant*** shapely

**malfunctioning** *adj* not being in working order — see INOPERABLE 1

**malice** *n* the desire to cause pain for the satisfaction of doing harm ⟨there was no reason other than pure *malice* to spread such disgusting lies all over school⟩
***syn*** cattiness, despite, hatefulness, malevolence, maliciousness, malignancy, malignity, meanness, nastiness, spite, spitefulness, spleen, venom, viciousness
***rel*** abusiveness, cruelty; abhorrence, abomination, execration, hate, hatred, loathing; animosity, antagonism, antipathy, bitterness, enmity, grudge, hostility, ill will, jaundice, rancor, resentment; despicableness, invidiousness; vengefulness, vindictiveness; aversion, disgust, distaste, horror, repugnance, repulsion, revulsion; contempt, disdain; jealousy, pique, resentment, scorn; bile, rancor, virulence, vitriol
***near ant*** devotion, love, passion; amiability, amicability, amity, civility, cordiality, friendliness, hospitality; adoration, ardor, infatuation, veneration, worship; affection, charity, kindliness; comity, empathy, friendship, goodwill, sympathy, understanding

**malicious** *adj* having or showing a desire to cause someone pain or suffering for the sheer enjoyment of it — see HATEFUL

**maliciously** *adv* in a mean or spiteful manner — see NASTILY

**maliciousness** *n* the desire to cause pain for the satisfaction of doing harm — see MALICE

**malign** *adj* having or showing a desire to cause someone pain or suffering for the sheer enjoyment of it — see HATEFUL

**malign** *vb* to make untrue and harmful statements about — see SLANDER

**malignancy** *n* the desire to cause pain for the satisfaction of doing harm — see MALICE

**malignant** *adj* having or showing a desire to cause someone pain or suffering for the sheer enjoyment of it — see HATEFUL

**malignantly** *adv* in a mean or spiteful manner — see NASTILY

**maligning** *n* the making of false statements that damage another's reputation — see SLANDER

**malignity** *n* the desire to cause pain for the satisfaction of doing harm — see MALICE

**malleability** *n* the quality or state of being easily molded — see PLASTICITY

**malleable** *adj* **1** capable of being easily molded or modeled — see PLASTIC
**2** capable of being readily changed — see FLEXIBLE 1

**malodorous** *adj* having an unpleasant smell ⟨the garbage became quite *malodorous* after it sat there for two weeks⟩
***syn*** fetid, foul, fusty, musty, noisome, rank, reeking, reeky, smelly, stinking, stinky, strong
***rel*** putrid, rancid, stale; bad, disgusting, offensive, repulsive, revolting, vile; decayed, decaying, decomposed, decomposing, rotted, rotten, rotting, spoiled, spoiling; dirty, filthy, nasty, noxious; odoriferous, odorous
***near ant*** flowery, fruity, spicy, woodsy
***ant*** ambrosial, aromatic, fragrant, perfumed, redolent, savory, scented, sweet

**maltreat** *vb* **1** to inflict physical or emotional harm upon — see ABUSE 1
**2** to abuse physically — see MANHANDLE 1
**mama** *n* a female human parent — see MOTHER
**mammoth** *adj* unusually large — see HUGE
**mammoth** *n* something that is unusually large and powerful — see GIANT
**mammy** *n* a female human parent — see MOTHER
**man** *n* **1** an adult male human being ⟨the children always feel better when there's a *man* or a woman around⟩
***syn*** bloke [*chiefly British*], buck, cat [*slang*], chap [*chiefly British*], dude, fellow, gent, gentleman, guy, hombre, jack, joker, lad, male
***rel*** master, mister, sir
**2** a male romantic companion — see BOYFRIEND
**3** a member of the human race — see HUMAN
**4** the human race — see MANKIND
**5** the male partner in a marriage — see HUSBAND
**manacle** *n* **1** something that physically prevents free movement — see BOND 1
**2** something that makes movement or progress more difficult — see ENCUMBRANCE
**manacle** *vb* **1** to confine or restrain with or as if with chains — see BIND 1
**2** to create difficulty for the work or activity of — see HAMPER
**manage** *vb* **1** to deal with (something) usually skillfully or efficiently — see HANDLE 1
**2** to look after and make decisions about — see CONDUCT 1
**3** to meet one's day-to-day needs — see GET ALONG 1
**management** *n* the act or activity of looking after and making decisions about something — see CONDUCT 1
**manager** *n* a person who manages or directs — see EXECUTIVE
**managerial** *adj* suited for or relating to the directing of things — see EXECUTIVE
**managing** *adj* highest in rank or authority — see HEAD
**man–at–arms** *n* a person engaged in military service — see SOLDIER
**mandate** *n* the granting of power to perform various acts or duties — see COMMISSION 1
**mandatory** *adj* forcing one's compliance or participation by or as if by law ⟨the tests are *mandatory* for all students wishing to graduate⟩
***syn*** compulsory, forced, imperative, incumbent, involuntary, necessary, nonelective, obligatory, peremptory, required
***rel*** all-important, essential, indispensable, needed, requisite; insistent, persistent, pressing, urgent; demanded, enforced; coercive
***near ant*** chosen, discretionary, dispensable, unnecessary, unneeded, unwanted; inconsequential, insignificant, nonessential, unimportant
***ant*** elective, optional, voluntary
**maneuver** *vb* **1** to deal with (something) usually skillfully or efficiently — see HANDLE 1
**2** to plan out usually with subtle skill or care — see ENGINEER
**manful** *adj* feeling or displaying no fear by temperament — see BRAVE
**mangle** *vb* to make or do (something) in a clumsy or unskillful way — see BOTCH
**mangy** *adj* showing signs of advanced wear and tear and neglect — see SHABBY 1
**manhandle** *vb* **1** to abuse physically ⟨charges that the police *manhandled* peaceful protesters⟩
***syn*** maltreat, maul, mishandle, rough (up)
***rel*** abuse, ill-treat, ill-use, mistreat, misuse; roughhouse, wrestle; bash, batter, beat, buffet, drub, lambaste (*or* lambast), lick, pound, pummel, slap, thrash; harm, hurt, injure, wound; oppress, persecute, wrong; ambush, assail, attack; clobber, fight, gang up (on), hit, jump, knock; torment, torture
***near ant*** caress, fondle, pet; coddle, mollycoddle, pamper; care (for), foster, nurture
**2** to inflict physical or emotional harm upon — see ABUSE 1
**manhood** *n* the set of qualities considered appropriate for or characteristic of men — see VIRILITY
**mania** *n* **1** a serious mental disorder that prevents one from living a safe and normal life — see INSANITY 1
**2** something about which one is constantly thinking or concerned — see FIXATION
**maniac** *n* **1** a person judged to be legally or medically insane — see LUNATIC 1
**2** a person with a strong and habitual liking for something — see FAN
**maniacal** *also* **maniac** *adj* having or showing a very abnormal or sick state of mind — see INSANE 1
**manifest** *adj* not subject to misinterpretation or more than one interpretation — see CLEAR 2
**manifest** *vb* **1** to make known (something abstract) through outward signs — see SHOW 2
**2** to represent in visible form — see EMBODY 2
**manifestation** *n* a visible representation of something abstract (as a quality) — see EMBODIMENT
**manifold** *adj* being of many and various kinds ⟨the *manifold* attractions of that state make it an ideal destination for a family vacation⟩
***syn*** divers, multifarious, myriad
***rel*** multiform, multiple, multiplex, multitudinous; heterogeneous, miscellaneous, mixed, sundry, various; different, diverse, unlike, varied
***near ant*** homogeneous, monolithic, unmixed, unvaried; alike, identical, same;

distinct, distinctive, individual, separate; alone, lone, only, sole, solitary; singular, unique

**manikin** *or* **mannikin** *n* **1** a three-dimensional representation of the human body used especially for displaying clothes — see MANNEQUIN 1
**2** a person who poses with or wears merchandise (as clothes) often for pictorial advertising — see MODEL 2

**manipulate** *vb* **1** to control or take advantage of by artful, unfair, or insidious means ⟨*manipulated* their parents into agreeing to let them stay out later by telling their mother that their father agreed, and vice versa⟩
***syn*** exploit, play (upon)
***rel*** engineer, finagle, jockey, maneuver; beguile, bluff, cozen, deceive, delude, dupe, fool, gull, hoax, hoodwink, kid, snow, take in, trick; intrigue, machinate, plot, scheme; arrange, contrive, devise, finesse, mastermind; cheat, chisel, defraud, fleece, gyp, hustle, swindle
**2** to deal with (something) usually skillfully or efficiently — see HANDLE 1
**3** to plan out usually with subtle skill or care — see ENGINEER

**mankind** *n* the human race ⟨all of *mankind* stands to gain if world peace is finally achieved⟩
***syn*** Homo sapiens, humanity, humankind, man
***rel*** being, body, creature, fellowman, human, individual, mortal, party, person

**manlike** *adj* **1** considered characteristic of or appropriate for men — see MASCULINE
**2** having qualities or traits that are traditionally considered inappropriate for a girl or woman — see UNFEMININE

**manliness** *n* the set of qualities considered appropriate for or characteristic of men — see VIRILITY

**manly** *adj* considered characteristic of or appropriate for men — see MASCULINE

**man–made** *adj* being such in appearance only and made with or manufactured from usually cheaper materials — see IMITATION

**manna** *n* **1** a source of great satisfaction — see DELIGHT 1
**2** something that provides happiness or does good for a person or thing — see BLESSING 2

**mannequin** *n* **1** a three-dimensional representation of the human body used especially for displaying clothes ⟨the *mannequin* over there looks so real⟩
***syn*** dummy, figure, form, manikin (*or* mannikin)
***rel*** doll
**2** a person who poses with or wears merchandise (as clothes) often for pictorial advertising — see MODEL 2

**manner** *n* **1** **manners** *pl* personal conduct or behavior as evaluated by an accepted standard of appropriateness for a social or professional setting ⟨her table *manners* were so impeccable that she even knew how to use all five forks⟩
***syn*** etiquette, form, mores, proprieties
***rel*** amenities, civilities, pleasantries; bearing, demeanor, deportment; courtesy, decorum, mannerliness, politeness; formalities, protocol, rules; air, attitude, carriage, poise, polish, pose, posture, presence; custom, habit, pattern, practice (*also* practise), trick, way, wont; convention, fashion, mode, style
**2** a distinctive way of putting ideas into words — see STYLE 1
**3** a number of persons or things that are grouped together because they have something in common — see SORT 1
**4** the means or procedure for doing something — see METHOD

**mannerism** *n* an odd or peculiar habit — see IDIOSYNCRASY

**mannerliness** *n* speech or behavior that is a sign of good breeding — see POLITENESS

**mannerly** *adj* showing consideration, courtesy, and good manners — see POLITE 1

**mannish** *adj* **1** considered characteristic of or appropriate for men — see MASCULINE
**2** having qualities or traits that are traditionally considered inappropriate for a girl or woman — see UNFEMININE

**manor** *n* a large impressive residence — see MANSION

**manor house** *n* a large impressive residence — see MANSION

**manpower** *n* a body of persons at work or available for work — see FORCE 1

**mansion** *n* a large impressive residence ⟨if I ever win the lottery, I'm going to buy a *mansion* in the mountains⟩
***syn*** castle, château, countryseat, estate, hacienda, hall, manor, manor house, palace, villa
***rel*** showplace; abode, domicile, dwelling, habitation, hearth, home, house, lodging(s), pad, place; housing, nest, quarter(s), residency, roof; aerie, penthouse; salon, suite, townhouse

**man–size** *or* **man–sized** *adj* considered characteristic of or appropriate for men — see MASCULINE

**manta** *n* any of several extremely large rays — see DEVILFISH

**manta ray** *n* any of several extremely large rays — see DEVILFISH

**mantilla** *n* a scarf worn on the head — see BANDANNA

**mantle** *n* **1** a sleeveless garment worn so as to hang over the shoulders, arms, and back — see [1]CAPE
**2** something that covers or conceals like a piece of cloth — see CLOAK 1

**mantle** *vb* to surround or cover closely — see ENFOLD 1

**manual** *n* a book used for instruction in a subject — see TEXTBOOK

**manufactory** *n* a building or set of buildings for the manufacturing of goods — see FACTORY

**manufacture** *vb* **1** to bring into being by combining, shaping, or transforming materials — see MAKE 1
**2** to create or think of by clever use of the imagination — see INVENT

**manumission** *n* the act of setting free from slavery — see LIBERATION

**manumit** *vb* to set free (as from slavery or confinement) — see FREE 1

**manuscript** *n* writing done by hand — see HANDWRITING 2

**many** *adj* being of a large but indefinite number ⟨a journey of *many* miles begins with a single step⟩
***syn*** multiple, multiplex, multitudinous, numerous
***rel*** countless, innumerable, numberless, uncountable, unnumbered, untold; several, some; miscellaneous, mixed, sundry, various; divers, manifold, multifarious, myriad
***near ant*** countable, limited
***ant*** few

**map** *n* an illustration of certain features of a geographical area ⟨there is a *map* of the United States on the wall over there⟩
***syn*** chart
***rel*** graph, graphic; relief map

**map** (out) *vb* to work out the details of (something) in advance — see PLAN 1

**mar** *vb* **1** to affect slightly with something morally bad or undesirable — see TAINT 1
**2** to reduce the soundness, effectiveness, or perfection of — see DAMAGE 1

**marathon** *adj* lasting for a considerable time — see LONG 2

**maraud** *vb* to search through with the intent of committing robbery — see RANSACK 1

**marble** *vb* to mark with small spots especially unevenly — see SPOT 1

**marbled** *adj* having blotches of two or more colors — see PIED

**march** *n* **1** a region along the dividing line between two countries — see FRONTIER 1
**2** forward movement in time or place — see ADVANCE 1

**march** *vb* **1** to move along with a steady regular step especially in a group ⟨the band had to practice for hours to be able to *march* in perfect step⟩
***syn*** file, pace, parade, stride
***rel*** goose-step; perambulate, step, traipse, tread; hike, tramp; lumber, plod, stamp, stomp, stride, trudge
***near ant*** amble, meander, ramble, stroll, wander
**2** to move forward along a course — see GO 1

**margin** *n* the line or relatively narrow space that marks the outer limit of something — see BORDER 1

**margin** *vb* to serve as a border for — see BORDER

**marginally** *adv* by a very small margin — see JUST 2

**marine** *adj* **1** of or relating to the sea ⟨he loves collecting little *marine* creatures while at the beach⟩
***syn*** maritime, oceanic, pelagic
***rel*** abyssal, deep-sea, deepwater, saltwater; admiralty, nautical, naval; undersea, underwater; hydrographic, oceanographic
**2** of or relating to navigation of the sea ⟨a collection of *marine* instruments, including a sextant⟩
***syn*** maritime, nautical, navigational
***rel*** admiralty, naval; oceangoing, seafaring, seagoing; hydrographic, oceanographic

**mariner** *n* one who operates or navigates a seagoing vessel — see SAILOR

**marital** *adj* of or relating to marriage ⟨neither of them ever forgot their *marital* vows, no matter how hard things sometimes were⟩
***syn*** conjugal, connubial, married, matrimonial, nuptial, wedded
***rel*** espoused, matched, mated; bridal; wifely; affianced, betrothed, committed, engaged, pledged, promised

**maritime** *adj* **1** of or relating to navigation of the sea — see MARINE 2
**2** of or relating to the sea — see MARINE 1

**mark** *n* **1** a person or thing that is made fun of — see LAUGHINGSTOCK
**2** a person or thing that is the object of abuse, criticism, or ridicule — see TARGET 1
**3** overall quality as seen or judged by people in general — see REPUTATION
**4** something set up as an example against which others of the same type are compared — see STANDARD 1
**5** something that one hopes or intends to accomplish — see GOAL
**6** something that sets apart an individual from others of the same kind — see CHARACTERISTIC
**7** something that spoils the appearance or completeness of a thing — see BLEMISH
**8** the power to bring about a result on another — see EFFECT 2

**mark** *vb* **1** to attach an identifying slip to — see LABEL 1
**2** to be an important feature of — see CHARACTERIZE 2
**3** to make a written note of — see RECORD 1

**mark** (out) *vb* to mark the limits of — see LIMIT 2

**mark down** *vb* to lower the price or value of — see DEPRECIATE 1

**marked** *adj* likely to attract attention — see NOTICEABLE

**marker** *n* a slip (as of paper or cloth) that is attached to something to identify or describe it — see LABEL

**market** *vb* to offer for sale to the public ⟨local farmers *market* their garden-fresh produce in roadside stands all over the valley⟩
***syn*** deal (in), merchandise, put up, retail, sell, vend

*rel* wholesale; hawk, peddle; barter, distribute, exchange, export, handle, trade, traffic (in); advertise, ballyhoo, boost, plug, promote, tout; bargain, chaffer, dicker, haggle, horse-trade, palter; auction; provide, supply; keep, stock
*ant* buy, purchase

**marketable** *adj* **1** fit to be offered for sale ⟨you'll need to clean that car up a bit before it's *marketable*⟩
*syn* salable (*or* saleable)
*rel* commercial, profitable; costly, fancy, fine, high-grade, precious, premium, prime, valuable; dear, expensive, extravagant
*near ant* damaged, shopworn; cheap, useless, worthless; bad, inferior, low-grade, substandard, unsatisfactory
*ant* nonsalable, unmarketable, unsalable
**2** fit or likely to be sold especially on a large scale — see COMMERCIAL

**marketplace** *n* the buying and selling of goods especially on a large scale and between different places — see COMMERCE

**market value** *n* the amount of money for which something will find a buyer — see VALUE 1

**marksman** *n* a person skilled in shooting at a target ⟨only the best *marksmen* can hit the bull's-eye at 500 feet⟩
*syn* sharpshooter, shooter, shot
*rel* rifleman, trapshooter; gunman, gunner, sniper

**maroon** *vb* to cause to remain behind — see LEAVE 1

**marriage** *n* **1** a union representing a special kind of social and legal partnership between two people ⟨some religions consider *marriage* a sacrament⟩
*syn* match, matrimony, wedlock
*rel* bigamy, monogamy, polygamy; intermarriage, miscegenation, remarriage; attachment, commitment, relationship; betrothal, engagement, espousal, hand, pledge, promise, proposal, troth
*near ant* annulment, divorce, separation
**2** a ceremony in which two people are united in matrimony — see WEDDING

**married** *adj* of or relating to marriage — see MARITAL

**marry** *vb* **1** to perform the ceremony of marriage for ⟨they chose a very nice priest to *marry* them⟩
*syn* wed
*rel* match, mate; conjoin, connect, unite; affiance
**2** to give in marriage ⟨they worried about the cost of *marrying* off five daughters⟩
*syn* espouse, match, wed
*rel* commit, engage; affiance, betroth, pledge, promise
**3** to take as a spouse ⟨he *married* his girlfriend three years ago, and they've been happy ever since⟩
*syn* espouse, wed
*rel* affiance, betroth, commit, engage, pledge, promise, propose; remarry
*near ant* separate (from)
*ant* divorce
**4** to take a spouse ⟨she had always believed she would never *marry*, but fate proved her wrong⟩
*syn* wed
*rel* couple, mate; pair off, remarry
*phrases* tie the knot
*near ant* divorce, separate
**5** to come together to form a single unit — see UNITE 1

**marsh** *n* spongy land saturated or partially covered with water — see SWAMP

**marshal** *vb* **1** to assemble and make ready for action — see MOBILIZE
**2** to point out the way for (someone) especially from a position in front — see LEAD 1
**3** to put into a particular arrangement — see ORDER 1

**marshaling** *or* **marshalling** *n* an act of gathering forces together to renew or attempt an effort — see RALLY 1

**marshland** *n* spongy land saturated or partially covered with water — see SWAMP

**martial** *adj* **1** of, relating to, or suitable for war or a warrior ⟨the young recruit looked all grown up in his new *martial* uniform⟩
*syn* military, soldierly
*rel* aggressive, bellicose, combative, contentious, guerrilla, pugnacious, quarrelsome, scrappy, truculent, warlike; belligerent, militant, warring; antagonistic, argumentative, fierce, gladiatorial, hot-tempered; mercenary
*near ant* civil, civilian, nonmilitary; conciliatory, nonviolent, pacific, peaceable, peaceful; affable, amiable, amicable, benevolent, complaisant, cordial, easygoing, friendly, genial, good-natured, gracious, ingratiating, obliging
*ant* unsoldierly
**2** of or relating to the armed services — see MILITARY 1

**martyr** *vb* to cause persistent suffering to — see AFFLICT

**marvel** *n* something extraordinary or surprising — see WONDER 1

**marveling** *or* **marvelling** *adj* filled with amazement or wonder — see OPEN-MOUTHED

**marvelous** *or* **marvellous** *adj* **1** causing wonder or astonishment ⟨the sheer immensity of the ancient ruin known as Stonehenge is *marvelous* to behold⟩
*syn* amazing, astonishing, astounding, awesome, awful, eye-opening, fabulous, miraculous, portentous, prodigious, staggering, stunning, stupendous, sublime, surprising, wonderful, wondrous
*rel* incomprehensible, inconceivable, incredible, unbelievable, unimaginable, unthinkable; extraordinary, phenomenal, rare, sensational, spectacular; singular, uncommon, unique, unusual, unwonted; conspicuous, notable, noticeable, outstanding, remarkable; impressive, striking; animating, energizing, enlightening,

enlivening, exciting, galvanizing, invigorating, stimulating; alluring, attracting, attractive, beguiling, bewitching, captivating, charming, enchanting, entertaining, enthralling, fascinating, interesting
***near ant*** unimpressive, uninspiring, unremarkable; boring, dull, jading, monotonous, tedious, tiring, uninspired, uninteresting, wearisome, weary, wearying; common, customary, mundane, normal, ordinary, typical, unexceptional, usual; draining, enervating, exhausting, fatiguing, wearing; debilitating, enfeebling; demoralizing, discouraging, disheartening, dispiriting
**2** excitingly or mysteriously unusual — see EXOTIC
**3** of the very best kind — see EXCELLENT

**mascot** *n* something worn or kept to bring good luck or keep away evil — see CHARM 1

**masculine** *adj* considered characteristic of or appropriate for men ⟨some people consider chest hair to be a particularly appealing *masculine* trait⟩
***syn*** male, manlike, manly, mannish, mansize (*or* man-sized), virile
***rel*** boyish, tomboyish
***near ant*** girlish, sissy; feminine, womanish, womanlike, womanly; emasculated, impotent, weakened
***ant*** effeminate, unmanly, unmasculine

**masculinity** *n* the set of qualities considered appropriate for or characteristic of men — see VIRILITY

**mash** *vb* **1** to apply external pressure on so as to force out the juice or contents of — see PRESS 2
**2** to cause to become a pulpy mass — see CRUSH 1

**mask** *n* **1** a cover or partial cover for the face used to disguise oneself ⟨he loved his gorilla *mask* so much that he even tried to sleep with it on⟩
***syn*** vizard
***rel*** camouflage, disguise; bill, cloak, domino, hood, veil, visor (*also* vizor)
**2** something that covers or conceals like a piece of cloth — see CLOAK 1

**mask** *vb* **1** to change the dress or looks of so as to conceal true identity — see DISGUISE
**2** to keep secret or shut off from view — see [1]HIDE 2

**masquerade** *n* a display of emotion or behavior that is insincere or intended to deceive ⟨although she was deeply bored, she maintained a *masquerade* of polite interest as her guest droned on⟩
***syn*** act, airs, charade, facade (*also* façade), front, guise, pose, pretense (*or* pretence), put-on, semblance, show
***rel*** appearance, color, gloss; camouflage, cloak, disguise; affectation, deceit, deception, double-dealing, duplicity, fraud, guile; betrayal, double cross, faithlessness, falseness, falsity, infidelity, perfidy, treachery, treason, unfaithfulness; excuse, pretext
***near ant*** candor, frankness, openheartedness, sincerity

**masquerade** (as) *vb* to pretend to be (what one is not) in appearance or behavior — see IMPERSONATE 1

**mass** *n* **1 masses** *pl* the body of the community as contrasted with the elite ⟨the *masses* demanded the elimination of tax breaks for the rich⟩
***syn*** commoners, herd, mob, people, plebeians, populace, rank and file
***rel*** proletariat, rabble, riffraff, scum, trash; bourgeoisie, middle class; public
***near ant*** aristocracy, gentry, nobility, upper class, upper crust
***ant*** elite
**2** a considerable amount — see LOT 2
**3** a distinct and separate portion of matter — see BODY 2
**4** the main or greater part of something as distinguished from its appendages — see BODY 1

**massacre** *n* the killing of a large number of people ⟨the infamous *massacre* of more than 200 Sioux at Wounded Knee, South Dakota⟩
***syn*** butchery, carnage, slaughter
***rel*** bloodshed, foul play, homicide, killing, manslaughter, murder, slaying; mortality; annihilation, decimation, demolishing, destruction, devastation, eradication, extermination; genocide; assassination, execution

**massacre** *vb* to kill on a large scale ⟨the country's rival ethnic groups began *massacring* one another⟩
***syn*** butcher, mow (down), slaughter
***rel*** assassinate, execute, murder, slay; annihilate, decimate, demolish, destroy, devastate, eradicate, exterminate, waste, wipe out

**massive** *adj* **1** having great weight — see HEAVY 1
**2** unusually large — see HUGE

**massively** *adv* to a large extent or degree — see GREATLY 2

**massiveness** *n* **1** the quality or state of being very large — see IMMENSITY
**2** the state or quality of being heavy — see WEIGHTINESS 1

**mass-produced** *adj* made beforehand in large numbers — see READY-MADE

**master** *adj* having or showing exceptional knowledge, experience, or skill in a field of endeavor — see PROFICIENT

**master** *n* **1** a person with a high level of knowledge or skill in a field — see EXPERT
**2** one that defeats an enemy or opponent — see VICTOR 1
**3** the person (as an employer or supervisor) who tells people and especially workers what to do — see BOSS

**master** *vb* **1** to achieve a victory over — see BEAT 2
**2** to acquire complete knowledge, understanding, or skill in — see LEARN 1

**masterful** *adj* **1** accomplished with trained ability — see SKILLFUL 1

2 fond of ordering people around — see BOSSY
3 having a feeling of superiority that shows itself in an overbearing attitude — see ARROGANT
4 having or showing exceptional knowledge, experience, or skill in a field of endeavor — see PROFICIENT

**masterfully** *adv* in a skillful or expert manner — see WELL 3

**masterfulness** *n* 1 subtle or imaginative ability in inventing, devising, or executing something — see SKILL 1
2 an exaggerated sense of one's importance that shows itself in the making of excessive or unjustified claims — see ARROGANCE

**masterly** *adj* 1 accomplished with trained ability — see SKILLFUL 1
2 having or showing exceptional knowledge, experience, or skill in a field of endeavor — see PROFICIENT

**mastermind** *vb* to plan out usually with subtle skill or care — see ENGINEER

**masterpiece** *n* something (as a work of art) that is a great achievement and often its creator's greatest achievement ⟨Michelangelo's frescoes in the Sistine Chapel are often considered to be his *masterpieces*⟩
***syn*** classic, magnum opus
***rel*** pièce de résistance, showpiece; blockbuster, success; gem, jewel, prize, treasure
***near ant*** debacle (*also* débâcle), disaster, failure, fiasco, fizzle, turkey

**mastership** *n* a highly developed skill in or knowledge of something — see COMMAND 2

**mastery** *n* 1 a highly developed skill in or knowledge of something — see COMMAND 2
2 the right or means to command or control others — see POWER 1

**masticate** *vb* to crush or grind with the teeth — see BITE (ON)

**match** *n* 1 a competitive encounter between individuals or groups carried on for amusement, exercise, or in pursuit of a prize — see GAME 1
2 a union representing a special kind of social and legal partnership between two people — see MARRIAGE 1
3 either of a pair matched in one or more qualities — see MATE 1
4 one that is equal to another in status, achievement, or value — see EQUAL
5 something or someone that strongly resembles another — see IMAGE 1

**match** *vb* 1 to be the exact counterpart of ⟨does this handbag's shade of blue *match* my navy blue pants?⟩ ⟨the rare blood type that exactly *matched* that of the transplant recipient⟩
***syn*** correspond (to), equal, parallel
***rel*** blend (with), coordinate (with), go (with), harmonize (with); complement, supplement; counterbalance, counterpoise; echo, mirror, repeat; amount (to), approach, near; measure (up), partake (of), rival, suggest
2 to give in marriage — see MARRY 2
3 to produce something equal to (as in quality or value) — see EQUAL 1

**matching** *adj* having qualities in common — see ALIKE

**matchless** *adj* having no equal or rival for excellence or desirability — see ONLY 1

**mate** *n* 1 either of a pair matched in one or more qualities ⟨have you seen the *mate* to this glove anywhere?⟩
***syn*** companion, fellow, half, match, twin
***rel*** coordinate; counterpart, equal, equivalent, like, parallel, peer, rival; carbon copy, double, duplicate, identical twin, ringer; analogue (*or* analog), similarity
***near ant*** antithesis, converse, opposite, reverse
2 a person frequently seen in the company of another — see ASSOCIATE 1
3 *chiefly British* a person who helps a more skilled person — see HELPER
4 the person to whom another is married — see SPOUSE

**mate** *vb* to engage in sexual intercourse — see COPULATE

**material** *adj* 1 relating to or composed of matter ⟨there's no *material* evidence, such as a dead body, that a murder has been committed⟩
***syn*** concrete, physical, substantial
***rel*** bodily, carnal, corporal, corporeal, fleshly; appreciable, detectable, discernible, noticeable, observable, palpable, perceptible, sensible, tangible; objective, phenomenal; bulky, heavy, massive, solid, weighty
***near ant*** bodiless, disembodied, incorporeal; ethereal, insubstantial, unsubstantial; impalpable, imperceptible, insensible, intangible, invisible, unnoticeable; airy, diaphanous, tenuous, thin, vaporous; metaphysical, spiritual
***ant*** immaterial, nonmaterial, nonphysical
2 having great meaning or lasting effect — see IMPORTANT 1
3 having to do with life on earth especially as opposed to that in heaven — see EARTHLY
4 having to do with the matter at hand — see PERTINENT
5 of or relating to the human body — see PHYSICAL 1

**material** *n* 1 the basic elements from which something can be developed — see MAKING
2 *usually* **materials** *pl* items needed for the performance of a task or activity — see EQUIPMENT

**materialist** *n* a person who is chiefly interested in material comfort and is hostile or indifferent to art and culture — see PHILISTINE

**materiality** *n* 1 something that actually exists — see FACT 2

---

***syn*** synonym(s) ***rel*** related words
***ant*** antonym(s) ***near ant*** near antonym(s)

**2** the fact or state of being pertinent — see PERTINENCE
**3** the quality of being actual — see FACT 1

**materialize** *vb* **1** to come into existence — see BEGIN 2
**2** to come into view — see APPEAR 1
**3** to come to one's attention especially gradually or unexpectedly — see ARISE 2
**4** to represent in visible form — see EMBODY 2

**matériel** *or* **materiel** *n* items needed for the performance of a task or activity — see EQUIPMENT

**maternal** *adj* of, relating to, or characteristic of a mother — see MOTHERLY

**maternity** *n* motherly character or qualities ⟨she had such *maternity* at such a young age that all her classmates went to her for comfort⟩
***syn*** motherliness
***rel*** nurturance; fertility, fruitfulness, productivity, richness

**mathematical** *adj* meeting the highest standard of accuracy — see PRECISE 1

**mating** *n* sexual union involving penetration of the vagina by the penis — see SEXUAL INTERCOURSE

**matriarch** *n* a dignified usually elderly woman of some rank or authority ⟨even though she was 87, the *matriarch* of the family knew everything that was going on⟩
***syn*** dame, dowager, matron
***rel*** grandam (*or* grandame); headmistress, mistress; ma, mama, mammy, mom, momma

**matriculate** *vb* to enter in a list or roll — see ENROLL 1

**matrimonial** *adj* of or relating to marriage — see MARITAL

**matrimony** *n* a union representing a special kind of social and legal partnership between two people — see MARRIAGE 1

**matron** *n* a dignified usually elderly woman of some rank or authority — see MATRIARCH

**matte** *also* **mat** *or* **matt** *adj* lacking a surface luster or gloss ⟨I chose a paint with a *matte* finish so the walls wouldn't be too shiny⟩
***syn*** dim, dull, dulled, flat, lusterless
***rel*** tarnished, unpolished; cloudy, dingy, dirty, drab, mousy (*or* mousey), muddy; gray (*also* grey), leaden, pale; dark, darkened, dimmed, dusky, gloomy, murky, obscure, obscured, somber (*or* sombre)
***near ant*** buffed, burnished, glazed, lacquered, polished, shellacked, varnished; satin, satiny; silken, silky; slick, slippery; gleaming, glimmering, gliding, glistening, glittering, scintillating, shimmering, shining, sparkling, twinkling; beaming, bedazzling, bright, brightened, brilliant, dazzling, effulgent, lucent, lucid, luminous, radiant, shining
***ant*** glossy, lustrous, shiny, sleek

**matter** *n* **1** a major object of interest or concern (as in a discussion or artistic composition) ⟨that is not relevant to the *matter* under discussion⟩
***syn*** content, motif, motive, question, subject, theme, topic
***rel*** idea, point, purpose; issue, problem; body, bulk, burden, core, crux, fundamental, generality, gist, heart, kernel, keynote, main, marrow, mass, nub, nucleus, pith, purport, quick, staple, substance, sum; basis; bottom, essential, essentiality; affair, argument, debate
***near ant*** aside, digression, interjection, parenthesis, tangent
**2** something to be dealt with ⟨we must take care of this *matter* before it becomes a real problem⟩
***syn*** affair, business, thing
***rel*** problem; crisis, crossroad, emergency, exigency, juncture, strait, zero hour; concern, trouble, worry; care, lookout, responsibility; deadlock, impasse, stalemate; corner, fix, hole, hot water, pinch, predicament, scrape, spot
**3** communications or parcels sent or carried through the postal system — see MAIL
**4** something that requires thought and skill for resolution — see PROBLEM 1

**matter** *vb* to be of importance ⟨she believes that doing well in school really does *matter*⟩
***syn*** count, import, mean, signify, weigh
***rel*** affect, influence, sway; add up (to), amount (to)
***phrases*** carry weight, cut ice

**matter–of–fact** *adj* **1** restricted to or based on fact — see FACTUAL 1
**2** willing to see things as they really are and deal with them sensibly — see REALISTIC 1

**maturation** *n* the process of becoming mature ⟨a flower's *maturation* from bud to full bloom can take weeks⟩
***syn*** development, growth, maturing, ripening
***rel*** blossoming, flourishing, flowering; mellowing, softening
***near ant*** decadence, decline, declining, deterioration; fading, shriveling, waning, wilting, withering; death, dying, expiring, perishing; regression, retrogression, reversion

**mature** *adj* **1** fully grown or developed ⟨I like pears when they're still hard, before they're *mature*⟩
***syn*** adult, full-blown, full-fledged, full-grown, matured, ripe, ripened
***rel*** aged, aging (*or* ageing), old; golden, mellow
***near ant*** blooming, blossoming, burgeoning, flourishing, flowering; undeveloped, unfinished, unformed
***ant*** green, immature, juvenile, unripened, young, youthful
**2** having reached the date at which payment is required — see DUE 1

**mature** *vb* to become mature ⟨a young figure skater whose talent is still *maturing*⟩
***syn*** age, develop, grow, grow up, progress, ripen

*rel* mellow, soften; bloom, blossom, burgeon, flourish, flower; open, unfold; advance, evolve
*near ant* decline, deteriorate; dry, fade, shrivel, wane, wilt, wither; regress, retrogress, revert; backslide, lapse, return

**matured** *adj* fully grown or developed — see MATURE 1

**maturing** *n* the process of becoming mature — see MATURATION

**maturity** *n* the state of being fully grown or developed ⟨people are legally considered to have reached *maturity* at eighteen years old in the United States⟩
*syn* adulthood, majority
*rel* manhood, womanhood; bloom, flush, heyday, prime; middle age, seniority

**maudlin** *adj* appealing to the emotions in an obvious and tiresome way — see CORNY

**maul** *vb* **1** to abuse physically — see MANHANDLE 1
**2** to strike repeatedly — see BEAT 1

**maunder** *vb* **1** to move about from place to place aimlessly — see WANDER
**2** to talk at length without sticking to a topic or getting to a point — see RAMBLE 1

**maundering** *adj* passing from one topic to another — see DISCURSIVE

**maverick** *n* a person who does not conform to generally accepted standards or customs — see NONCONFORMIST 1

**mawkish** *adj* appealing to the emotions in an obvious and tiresome way — see CORNY

**mawkishness** *n* the state or quality of having an excess of tender feelings (as of love, nostalgia, or compassion) — see SENTIMENTALITY

**maxim** *n* **1** an idea or statement about all of the members of a group or all the instances of a situation — see GENERALIZATION
**2** an often stated observation regarding something from common experience — see SAYING

**maximum** *adj* **1** of the greatest or highest degree or quantity — see ULTIMATE 1
**2** of the highest degree — see FULL 2

**maximum** *n* the greatest amount, number, or part — see MOST

**maybe** *adv* it is possible — see PERHAPS

**mayhap** *adv* it is possible — see PERHAPS

**maze** *n* a confusing and complicated arrangement of passages ⟨the mansion had a beautifully landscaped *maze* constructed of tall cypresses⟩
*syn* labyrinth
*rel* meander; jungle, quagmire; knot, snarl, tangle, web; entanglement, entrapment, snare, trap

**meager** *or* **meagre** *adj* less plentiful than what is normal, necessary, or desirable ⟨ever since he started the diet, his dinners have been more *meager* than he would like⟩
*syn* hand-to-mouth, light, niggardly, poor, scant, scanty, scarce, skimpy, slender, slim, spare, sparse, stingy
*rel* deficient, inadequate, insufficient, lacking, wanting; bare, mere, minimum; slight, small; barren, infertile, sterile, unfruitful, unproductive
*near ant* adequate, enough, sufficient; fat, fecund, fertile, fruitful, prolific, rich; lavish, luxuriant; blooming, bursting, flourishing, swarming, teeming, thriving
*ant* abundant, ample, bountiful, copious, generous, liberal, plenteous, plentiful

**meal** *n* food eaten or prepared for eating at one time ⟨all she wants to do is sit quietly after the large Thanksgiving *meal*⟩
*syn* chow, feed, mess, repast, table
*rel* board; breakfast, buffet, dinner, lunch, luncheon, refreshments, smorgasbord, snack, supper, tea; bite, gulp, morsel, serving, taste; banquet, feast, spread; bake, barbecue, clambake, cookout, fry, luau, picnic, potluck, roast

**mealy** *adj* not being or expressing what one appears to be or express — see INSINCERE

**mealymouthed** *adj* not being or expressing what one appears to be or express — see INSINCERE

**mean** *adj* **1** belonging to the class of people of low social or economic rank — see IGNOBLE 1
**2** giving or sharing as little as possible — see STINGY 1
**3** having or showing a desire to cause someone pain or suffering for the sheer enjoyment of it — see HATEFUL
**4** not following or in accordance with standards of honor and decency — see IGNOBLE 2
**5** of little or less value or merit — see INFERIOR 2
**6** of the very best kind — see EXCELLENT
**7** showing signs of advanced wear and tear and neglect — see SHABBY 1

**mean** *n* **1** a middle point between extremes ⟨that candidate's moderate views were seen as the *mean* that voters were looking for⟩
*syn* golden mean, medium, middle, midpoint
*rel* arithmetic mean, average; median, norm, par, standard
*near ant* maximum, minimum
**2 means** *pl* an action planned or taken to achieve a desired result — see MEASURE 1
**3 means** *pl* something used to achieve an end — see AGENT 1
**4 means** *pl* the total of one's money and property — see WEALTH 1

**mean** *vb* **1** to communicate or convey (as an idea) to the mind ⟨the national anthem *means* various things to various people⟩
*syn* denote, express, import, signify, spell
*rel* connote, imply, suggest; add up (to), amount (to); hint, insinuate, intimate; embody, epitomize, personify, represent, symbolize; advert, allude (to), mention,

refer (to); indicate, point (to), signal; announce, declare; elucidate, explain
2 to be of importance — see MATTER
3 to have in mind as a purpose or goal — see INTEND

**meander** *vb* to move about from place to place aimlessly — see WANDER

**meaning** *adj* clearly conveying a special meaning (as one's mood) — see EXPRESSIVE

**meaning** *n* 1 the idea that is conveyed or intended to be conveyed to the mind by language, symbol, or action ‹the unmistakable *meaning* of the skier's upraised arms as he finished his spectacular run›
*syn* denotation, drift, import, intent, purport, sense, significance, signification
*rel* connotation; hint, implication, intimation, suggestion; message, tenor, theme; bottom, essence, essentiality, nature, soul, stuff; acceptance, definition; burden, crux, gist; core, heart, kernel, marrow, nub, nucleus, pith, point, quick; matter, motif, motive, subject, topic
2 something that one hopes or intends to accomplish — see GOAL

**meaningful** *adj* 1 clearly conveying a special meaning (as one's mood) — see EXPRESSIVE
2 having great meaning or lasting effect — see IMPORTANT 1

**meaningless** *adj* having no meaning ‹this is an utterly *meaningless* bit of nonsense›
*syn* empty, inane, pointless, senseless
*rel* insignificant, trivial, unimportant; absurd, asinine, balmy, brainless, crazy, daffy, daft, dotty, fatuous, foolish, half-witted, harebrained, insane, jerky, kooky, loony (*also* looney), lunatic, mad, mindless, nonsensical, nutty, preposterous, sappy, silly, unintelligent, unwise, wacky, weak-minded, witless, zany; irrational, unreasonable; aimless, haphazard, purposeless
*near ant* eloquent, expressive, pregnant, revealing, suggestive, telling; logical, rational, reasonable, valid
*ant* meaningful

**meanly** *adv* in a mean or spiteful manner — see NASTILY

**meanness** *n* the desire to cause pain for the satisfaction of doing harm — see MALICE

**measly** *adj* so small or unimportant as to warrant little or no attention — see NEGLIGIBLE 1

**measure** *n* 1 an action planned or taken to achieve a desired result ‹such new security *measures* as metal detectors at all the entrances›
*syn* expedient, means, move, shift, step
*rel* act, deed, doing, feat, thing; procedure, proceeding, process; accomplishment, achievement, exploit; activity, affair, business, dealing, enterprise, event; attempt, endeavor, essay, initiative, operation, undertaking; effort, exertion, labor, pains, trouble, work; project, proposal, proposition; makeshift, resort, resource, stopgap
2 a given or particular mass or aggregate of matter — see AMOUNT
3 something set up as an example against which others of the same type are compared — see STANDARD 1
4 the recurrent pattern formed by a series of sounds having a regular rise and fall in intensity — see RHYTHM
5 the total amount of measurable space or surface occupied by something — see [1]SIZE

**measure** *vb* to find out the size, extent, or amount of ‹for this experiment, you need to carefully *measure* all the chemicals before you mix them together›
*syn* gauge (*also* gage), scale, span
*rel* weigh; calibrate; lay off, mark (off); calculate, compute, figure, reckon, work out; conjecture, estimate, guess, judge, suppose; add up, sum, tally, total; ascertain, discover, dope (out), figure out, find out

**measured** *adj* 1 decided on as a result of careful thought — see DELIBERATE 1
2 having distinct or certain limits — see LIMITED 1
3 marked by or occurring with a noticeable regularity in the rise and fall of sound — see RHYTHMIC

**measureless** *adj* being or seeming to be without limits — see INFINITE

**measurement** *n* the total amount of measurable space or surface occupied by something — see [1]SIZE

**measure up** (to) *vb* to come near or nearer to in character or quality — see APPROXIMATE

**meat** *n* 1 animal and especially mammal tissue used as food ‹we need to go shopping; there's only enough *meat* in the freezer for one more dinner›
*syn* flesh
*rel* game, poultry, variety meat
2 substances intended to be eaten — see FOOD

**mecca** *n* a thing or place that is of greatest importance to an activity or interest — see CENTER 1

**mechanical** *adj* 1 done instantly and without conscious thought or decision — see AUTOMATIC 1
2 lacking in natural or spontaneous quality — see ARTIFICIAL 1

**medal** *n* a piece of metal given in honor of a special event, a person, or an achievement ‹the display case held an impressive array of military *medals* from World War II›
*syn* medallion, order
*rel* decoration, honor; crown, insignia, laurel, ribbon, title; badge, button, chevron, cockade, color, ensign, rosette; distinction; award, prize, trophy; citation, commendation

**medallion** *n* a piece of metal given in honor of a special event, a person, or an achievement — see MEDAL

**meddle** *vb* to interest oneself in what is not one's concern — see INTERFERE

**meddler** *n* a person who meddles in the affairs of others — see BUSYBODY

**meddlesome** *adj* thrusting oneself where one is not welcome or invited — see INTRUSIVE

**meddling** *adj* thrusting oneself where one is not welcome or invited — see INTRUSIVE

**medial** *adj* occupying a position equally distant from the ends or extremes — see MIDDLE 1

**median** *adj* **1** being about midway between extremes of amount or size — see MIDDLE 2
**2** occupying a position equally distant from the ends or extremes — see MIDDLE 1

**mediate** *vb* to act as a go-between for opposing sides — see INTERVENE

**mediator** *n* one who works with opposing sides in order to bring about an agreement ⟨if you two cannot resolve this argument on your own, we'll have to bring in a *mediator*⟩
***syn*** arbiter, arbitrator, conciliator, go-between, intercessor, intermediary, interposer, middleman, peacemaker
***rel*** moderator; bargainer, negotiator; appeaser, pacifier, reconciler; broker; agent, attorney, deputy, factor, procurator, proxy; liaison; ambassador, emissary, envoy, messenger; delegate, representative; busybody, interferer, meddler; judge, referee, umpire; adviser (*or* advisor), counselor

**medic** *n* a person specially trained in healing human medical disorders — see DOCTOR

**medication** *n* a substance or preparation used to treat disease — see MEDICINE

**medicine** *n* a substance or preparation used to treat disease ⟨if you don't take all the doses of your *medicine*, you might get sick again⟩
***syn*** cure, drug, medication, pharmaceutical, physic, remedy, specific
***rel*** botanical, patent medicine, prescription; cordial, tonic; miracle drug, wonder drug; capsule, pill, tablet; injection, shot; liniment, lotion, ointment, potion, poultice, salve; syrup, tincture; antibiotic, antiseptic, serum

**mediocre** *adj* **1** of average to below average quality ⟨your grades are *mediocre* and barely acceptable⟩
***syn*** common, fair, indifferent, medium, middling, ordinary, passable, run-of-the-mill, second-rate, so-so
***rel*** acceptable, adequate, all right, alright, decent, OK (*or* okay), reasonable, satisfactory, sufficient, sufficing, tolerable; moderate, modest; presentable, respectable; minimal, unexceptional; fine, good, nice
***near ant*** distinguished, excellent, exceptional, exquisite, first-class, first-rate, matchless, maximum, optimal, optimum, outstanding, peerless, preeminent, special, superior, supreme, top-notch; unmatched, unparalleled, unsurpassed; deficient, inadequate, insufficient, lacking, unacceptable, unsatisfactory, wanting
**2** of low quality — see CHEAP 2

**meditate** *vb* **1** to give serious and careful thought to — see PONDER
**2** to have in mind as a purpose or goal — see INTEND

**meditation** *n* long or deep thinking about spiritual matters — see CONTEMPLATION

**meditative** *adj* given to or marked by long, quiet thinking — see CONTEMPLATIVE

**medium** *adj* **1** being about midway between extremes of amount or size — see MIDDLE 2
**2** occupying a position equally distant from the ends or extremes — see MIDDLE 1
**3** of average to below average quality — see MEDIOCRE 1

**medium** *n* **1** a middle point between extremes — see MEAN 1
**2** something used to achieve an end — see AGENT 1
**3** the circumstances, conditions, or objects by which one is surrounded — see ENVIRONMENT

**medley** *n* an unorganized collection or mixture of various things — see MISCELLANY 1

**meek** *adj* not having or showing any feelings of superiority, self-assertiveness, or showiness — see HUMBLE 1

**meekly** *adv* in manner showing no signs of pride or self-assertion — see LOWLY

**meekness** *n* the absence of any feelings of being better than others — see HUMILITY

**meet** *adj* meeting the requirements of a purpose or situation — see FIT 1

**meet** *n* a competitive encounter between individuals or groups carried on for amusement, exercise, or in pursuit of a prize — see GAME 1

**meet** *vb* **1** to come upon face-to-face or as if face-to-face ⟨we never once *met* another car on that lonely country road⟩
***syn*** chance (upon), encounter, happen (upon), stumble (upon)
***rel*** accost, confront; face, greet, salute; collide (with), crash (into); crisscross, cross, pass; hit (upon), light (upon), tumble (to)
***phrases*** bump into
***near ant*** avoid, elude, escape, evade, shun
**2** to come together into one body or place — see ASSEMBLE 1
**3** to come upon unexpectedly or by chance — see HAPPEN (ON *OR* UPON)
**4** to do what is required by the terms of — see FULFILL 1
**5** to enter into contest or conflict with — see ENGAGE 2
**6** to produce something equal to (as in quality or value) — see EQUAL 1
**7** to put up with (something painful or difficult) — see BEAR 2

**meeting** *n* **1** a coming together of a number of persons for a specified purpose ⟨there will be another committee *meeting* next week to discuss the parish fair⟩
***syn*** assembly, conference, congress, convention, convocation, council, gathering, get-together, huddle, powwow, roundtable, seminar
***rel*** caucus, conclave, synod; demonstration, rally; conversation, dialogue (*also* dialog), discourse, discussion, palaver, talk; negotiation, parley; audience, interview, session
**2** a body of people come together in one place — see GATHERING 1
**3** the coming together of two or more things to the same point — see CONVERGENCE

**meetly** *adv* in a manner suitable for the occasion or purpose — see PROPERLY

**megahit** *n* a person or thing that is successful — see HIT 1

**megalopolis** *n* a thickly settled, highly populated area — see CITY

**melancholy** *adj* **1** causing unhappiness — see SAD 2
**2** feeling unhappiness — see SAD 1
**3** given to or marked by long, quiet thinking — see CONTEMPLATIVE

**melancholy** *n* a state or spell of low spirits — see SADNESS

**mélange** *n* an unorganized collection or mixture of various things — see MISCELLANY 1

**melee** *n* a rough and often noisy fight usually involving several people — see BRAWL 1

**meliorate** *vb* to make better — see IMPROVE

**mellifluous** *adj* having a pleasantly flowing quality suggestive of music — see LYRIC 1

**mellow** *adj* **1** having a pleasantly flowing quality suggestive of music — see LYRIC 1
**2** not harsh or stern especially in manner, nature, or effect — see GENTLE 1

**melodic** *adj* having a pleasantly flowing quality suggestive of music — see LYRIC 1

**melodious** *adj* **1** having a pleasantly flowing quality suggestive of music — see LYRIC 1
**2** having a pleasing mixture of notes — see HARMONIOUS 1

**melodramatic** *adj* **1** given to or marked by attention-getting behavior suggestive of stage acting — see THEATRICAL 1
**2** having the general quality or effect of a stage performance — see DRAMATIC 1

**melody** *n* a rhythmic series of musical tones arranged to give a pleasing effect ⟨this week, we'll learn to play a more complicated *melody* on the saxophone⟩
***syn*** air, lay, song, strain, tune, warble
***rel*** descant; cadence, measure, meter, rhythm; ballad, ditty, hymn, lyric, madrigal

**melt** *vb* **1** to cease to be visible — see DISAPPEAR
**2** to go from a solid to a liquid state — see LIQUEFY

**member** *n* **1** one of the parts that make up a whole — see ELEMENT 1
**2** one of the pieces from which something is designed to be assembled — see PART 1

**memento** *n* something that serves to keep alive the memory of a person or event — see MEMORIAL

**memo** *n* **1** a message on paper from one person or group to another — see LETTER
**2** a usually brief written reminder — see NOTE 1
**3** a written communication giving information or directions — see MEMORANDUM 1

**memoir** *n* a history of a person's life — see BIOGRAPHY

**memorandum** *n* **1** a written communication giving information or directions ⟨I'm waiting for the *memorandum* that will explain the new vacation policy⟩
***syn*** directive, memo, notice
***rel*** announcement, declaration, proclamation, pronouncement; charge, command, dictate; directions, instructions, orders, word; encyclical, epistle, letter, mail, message, missive, note
**2** a message on paper from one person or group to another — see LETTER
**3** a usually brief written reminder — see NOTE 1

**memorial** *adj* serving to preserve the memory of a person, thing, or an event — see COMMEMORATIVE

**memorial** *n* something that serves to keep alive the memory of a person or event ⟨the Vietnam War *Memorial* is a starkly beautiful testimonial to the bravery of the soldiers who served in Vietnam⟩
***syn*** commemorative, keepsake, memento, monument, remembrance, reminder, souvenir, token
***rel*** memorabilia; relic, vestige; cairn, landmark, marker; testimonial, tribute

**memorialize** *vb* to be a memorial of — see COMMEMORATE 1

**memorializing** *adj* serving to preserve the memory of a person, thing, or an event — see COMMEMORATIVE

**memorize** *vb* to commit to memory ⟨everyone has to *memorize* a poem for next week⟩
***syn*** con, learn, study
***rel*** recall, recollect, relive, remember, reminisce, retain; accept, apprehend, comprehend, get, grasp, understand; absorb, digest
***near ant*** forget; ignore, neglect, overlook
***ant*** unlearn

**memory** *n* **1** the power or process of recalling what has been previously learned or experienced ⟨a photographic *memory* makes taking tests entirely too easy⟩
***syn*** mind, recollection, remembrance, reminiscence
***rel*** contemplation, musing, reflection, retrospection, thinking; awareness, cognizance, consciousness; apprehension, comprehension, understanding
***near ant*** forgetfulness

**2** a particular act or instance of recalling or the thing remembered ⟨I have only the vaguest *memory* of the family vacation we took the year I turned three⟩
***syn*** recall, recollection, remembrance, reminiscence
***rel*** flashback; memento, memorial, reminder, souvenir, token; association
**3** the body of knowledge that has been retained in one's mind or the use of it — see HEART 2

**menace** *n* something that may cause injury or harm — see DANGER 2

**menace** *vb* **1** to place in danger — see ENDANGER
**2** to remain poised to inflict harm, danger, or distress on — see THREATEN

**menacing** *adj* **1** being or showing a sign of evil or calamity to come — see OMINOUS
**2** involving potential loss or injury — see DANGEROUS

**ménage** *n* those who live as a family in one house — see HOUSEHOLD

**mend** *vb* **1** to put into good shape or working order again ⟨that shirt will be as good as new when I'm finished *mending* it⟩
***syn*** doctor, fix, patch, recondition, renovate, repair, revamp
***rel*** overhaul, rebuild, reconstruct, refurbish; aid, cure, heal, help; condition, prepare, ready; care (for), maintain, service; rejuvenate, renew, restore; adjust, correct, modify, rectify, redress, reform, right; ameliorate, better, improve, meliorate
***near ant*** break, damage, harm, hurt, impair, injure, mar, ruin, spoil, wreck; cripple, disable
**2** to become healthy and strong again after illness or weakness — see CONVALESCE
**3** to restore to a healthy condition — see HEAL 1

**mendacious** *adj* telling or containing lies — see DISHONEST 1

**mendacity** *n* **1** a statement known by its maker to be untrue and made in order to deceive — see LIE
**2** the tendency to tell lies — see DISHONESTY 1

**mendicant** *n* a person who lives by public begging — see BEGGAR

**mending** *n* the process or period of gradually regaining one's health and strength — see CONVALESCENCE

**menial** *n* a person hired to perform household or personal services — see SERVANT

**menstruation** *n* an occurrence of menstruating — see PERIOD 1

**mental** *adj* **1** of or relating to the mind ⟨a funny *mental* image made him laugh out loud⟩
***syn*** cerebral, inner, intellectual, psychological (*also* psychologic)
***rel*** cognitive, conscious; psychic (*also* psychical), telepathic; spiritual; alert, brainy, bright, clever, intelligent, quick-witted, rational, reasoning, smart, thinking
***near ant*** bodily, carnal, corporal, corporeal, fleshly, physical, somatic
**2** having or showing a very abnormal or sick state of mind — see INSANE 1

**mention** *vb* **1** to make reference to or speak about briefly but specifically ⟨you only *mentioned* in passing some of your accomplishments⟩
***syn*** advert (to), cite, instance, name, note, notice, quote, refer (to), specify, touch (on *or* upon)
***rel*** allude (to), hint (at), imply, infer, intimate, suggest; point (out), signal, signify; denominate, designate; indicate; bring up, broach, interject, interpolate, interpose, introduce; infiltrate, insinuate, worm; announce, declare, pronounce; elucidate, explain
***near ant*** disregard, ignore, neglect, overlook, pass over, slight
**2** to give as an example — see QUOTE 1

**mentor** *vb* to give advice and instruction to (someone) regarding the course or process to be followed — see GUIDE 1

**menu** *n* **1** a list of foods served at or available for a meal ⟨the *menu* at the fancy restaurant listed many dishes that I had never heard of⟩
***syn*** bill of fare
***rel*** chow, cuisine, fare, grub
**2** a record of a series of items (as names or titles) usually arranged according to some system — see [1]LIST

**mercenary** *adj* having or marked by an eager and often selfish desire especially for material possessions — see GREEDY 1

**merchandise** *n* products that are bought and sold in business ⟨we stock only the finest-quality *merchandise* in this store⟩
***syn*** commodities, goods, wares
***rel*** line; export, import; inventory, staples, stock, stuff

**merchandise** *vb* to offer for sale to the public — see MARKET

**merchandiser** *n* **1** a buyer and seller of goods for profit — see MERCHANT
**2** the person in a business deal who hands over an item in exchange for money — see VENDOR

**merchant** *n* a buyer and seller of goods for profit ⟨free trade agreements that are favored by *merchants* on both sides of the border⟩
***syn*** dealer, merchandiser, trader, tradesman, trafficker
***rel*** businessman; buyer, purchaser; hawker, peddler (*also* pedlar); retailer, seller, shopkeeper, storekeeper, vendor (*also* vender); jobber, middleman, wholesaler; distributor, provider, supplier

**mercifulness** *n* kind, gentle, or compassionate treatment especially towards someone who is undeserving of it — see MERCY 1

**merciless** *adj* having or showing a lack of sympathy or tender feelings — see HARD 1

**mercurial** *adj* likely to change frequently, suddenly, or unexpectedly — see FICKLE 1

**mercy** *n* **1** kind, gentle, or compassionate treatment especially towards someone who is undeserving of it ⟨always show your enemies *mercy*, because it makes you a better person⟩
***syn*** charity, clemency, lenience, leniency, lenity, mercifulness, quarter
***rel*** humanitarianism, philanthropy; empathy, pity, sympathy, understanding; commiseration, favor, grace; benevolence, care, compassion, gentleness, goodness, goodwill, kindliness, kindness, meekness, mildness, niceness, softness, tenderness; altruism, generosity, magnanimity, nobility; affection, devotion, love, worship
***near ant*** reprisal, retaliation, retribution, revenge, vengeance; venom, vindictiveness, virulence, vitriol; brutality, cruelty, savagery, violence; castigation, chastisement, punishment, scolding; abhorrence, abomination, execration, hate, hatred, loathing; cattiness, malevolence, malice, malignity, meanness, spite, spitefulness, spleen; animosity, antagonism, antipathy, bitterness, enmity, grudge, hostility, jealousy, pique, resentment; bile, jaundice, rancor; hatefulness, invidiousness; coarseness, grimness, hardness, harshness, roughness
**2** an act of kind assistance — see FAVOR 1
**3** the capacity for feeling for another's unhappiness or misfortune — see HEART 1

**mere** *n, chiefly British* a small often deep body of water — see [1]POOL

**mere** *adj* being this and no more ⟨the *mere* idea of your traveling alone to Europe is ridiculous⟩
***syn*** bare, very
***rel*** absolute, sheer, simple, stark, utter; alone, only, singular, sole, solitary, solo, unique

**merely** *adv* nothing more than — see JUST 3

**merge** *vb* to turn into a single mass that is more or less the same throughout — see BLEND 1

**merging** *n* the act or an instance of joining two or more things into one — see UNION 1

**meridian** *n* the highest part or point — see HEIGHT 1

**merit** *n* **1** a quality that gives something special worth — see EXCELLENCE 2
**2** the relative usefulness or importance of something as judged by specific qualities — see WORTH 1

**merit** *vb* to be or make worthy of (as a reward or punishment) — see EARN 2

**merited** *adj* being what is called for by accepted standards of right and wrong — see JUST 1

**meritorious** *adj* **1** deserving of high regard or great approval — see ADMIRABLE
**2** having sufficient worth or merit to receive one's honor, esteem, or reward — see WORTHY

**merrily** *adv* in a cheerful or happy manner — see GAILY 1

**merriment** *n* **1** a mood characterized by high spirits and amusement and often accompanied by laughter — see MIRTH
**2** joyful or festive activity — see MERRYMAKING

**merriness** *n* a mood characterized by high spirits and amusement and often accompanied by laughter — see MIRTH

**merry** *adj* indicative of or marked by high spirits or good humor ⟨Santa Claus has *merry*, twinkling blue eyes⟩
***syn*** blithesome, festive, gay, gleeful, jocose, jocund, jolly, jovial, laughing, mirthful, sunny
***rel*** amused, beaming, chuckling, giggling, smiling; bright, buoyant, carefree, cheerful, cheery, chipper, lighthearted, lightsome, upbeat; animated, jaunty, lively, perky, sprightly, vivacious; blessed, blissful, delighted, ecstatic, elated, enraptured, entranced, euphoric, exhilarated, exuberant, exultant, gladsome, happy, high, joyful, joyous, jubilant, overjoyed, radiant, rapturous, ravished, thrilled; amusing, facetious, flippant, funny, hilarious, jesting, joking, joshing, playful, witty; careless, cavalier, devil-may-care, easygoing, happy-go-lucky, insouciant, unconcerned; hopeful, optimistic, rosy, sanguine
***near ant*** abject, aggrieved, anguished, blue, brokenhearted, dejected, depressed, despondent, disconsolate, disheartened, dispirited, downcast, downhearted, forlorn, heartbroken, heartsick, melancholy, sad, sorrowful, unhappy; crying, groaning, moaning, sobbing, wailing; discontented, disgruntled, moody; doleful, dolorous, joyless, lachrymose, mournful, plaintive, sorry, woeful; black, dark, desolate, gloomy, glum, gray (*also* grey); miserable, woebegone, wretched; dull, lethargic, listless, sluggish, torpid

**merrymaker** *n* one who engages in merrymaking especially in honor of a special occasion — see CELEBRANT

**merrymaking** *n* joyful or festive activity ⟨Christmas Eve is always an occasion of much *merrymaking* at our home⟩
***syn*** conviviality, festivity, gaiety (*also* gayety), jollification, jollity, merriment, reveling, revelry
***rel*** carousal, carouse; delight, diversion, entertainment, fun, pleasure, recreation, riot; glee, gleefulness, joviality, merriness, mirth, mirthfulness; carnival, celebration, party, revel; frolicking, gamboling, rollicking, romping; enjoyment, happiness, joy; binge, fling, frolic, gambol, lark, rollick, romp, spree; buffoonery, clownishness, flippancy, frivolity, funning, jesting, jocularity, joking, joshing, levity, lightheartedness, playfulness; zaniness
***near ant*** blackness, darkness, gloominess, glumness, grief, grieving, heartbreak, miserableness, misery, mournfulness, mourning, wretchedness; anguish, dejec-

tion, depression, despondence, forlornness, melancholy, sorrow, unhappiness

**mesa** *n* a broad flat area of elevated land — see PLATEAU

**mesh** *n* a fabric made of strands loosely twisted, knotted, or woven together at regular intervals — see [1]NET 1

**mesh** *vb* to catch or hold as if in a net — see ENTANGLE 2

**mesmerism** *n* the art or act of inducing in a person a sleep-like state during which he or she readily follows suggestions — see HYPNOSIS

**mesmerize** *vb* to hold the attention of as if by a spell — see ENTHRALL 1

**mess** *n* **1** a state in which everything is out of order — see CHAOS
**2** food eaten or prepared for eating at one time — see MEAL
**3** something unpleasant to look at — see EYESORE

**mess** *vb* to interest oneself in what is not one's concern — see INTERFERE

**mess** (around) *vb* to spend time in aimless activity — see FIDDLE (AROUND)

**mess** (up) *vb* **1** to make or do (something) in a clumsy or unskillful way — see BOTCH
**2** to undo the proper order or arrangement of — see DISORDER

**mess** (with) *vb* to handle thoughtlessly, ignorantly, or mischievously — see TAMPER

**message** *n* a piece of conveyed information — see COMMUNICATION

**messed** *adj* lacking in order, neatness, and often cleanliness — see MESSY

**messenger** *n* one that carries a message or does an errand ⟨the *messenger* comes by twice a day to pick up packages⟩
***syn*** courier, go-between, page, runner
***rel*** forerunner, harbinger, herald; agent, ambassador, delegate, deputy, emissary, envoy, representative; bearer, carrier, deliveryman, letter carrier, mail carrier, mailman

**messy** *adj* lacking in order, neatness, and often cleanliness ⟨you cannot go out to play until you clean up this *messy* room and put away all your toys⟩
***syn*** chaotic, cluttered, confused, disarranged, disarrayed, disheveled (*or* dishevelled), disordered, disorderly, higgledy-piggledy, hugger-mugger, jumbled, littered, messed, muddled, mussed, mussy, pell-mell, rumpled, sloppy, topsy-turvy, tousled, tumbled, unkempt, untidy, upside-down
***rel*** besmirched, blackened, dingy, dirty, filthy, foul, grimy, grubby, grungy, mucky, nasty, soiled, spotted, squalid, stained, sullied, unclean, uncleanly; dowdy, frowsy (*or* frowzy), slatternly, slovenly, uncombed; wrinkled; contaminated, defiled, polluted, tainted; knotted, snarled, tangled; seedy, shabby, sleazy, sordid; neglected, neglectful, negligent
***phrases*** at sixes and sevens
***near ant*** clean, cleaned, cleanly, hygienic, immaculate, sparkling, spick-and-span (*or* spic-and-span), spotless, stainless, unsoiled, unsullied; methodical, systematic; careful, fastidious, fussy, meticulous; combed, groomed, manicured; taintless, undefiled, unpolluted, untainted, wholesome
***ant*** neat, ordered, orderly, organized, shipshape, snug, tidied, tidy, trim

**metamorphose** *vb* to change in form, appearance, or use — see CONVERT 2

**metamorphosis** *n* a change in form, appearance, or use — see CONVERSION

**metaphor** *n* an elaborate or fanciful way of expressing something — see CONCEIT 1

**metaphorical** *adj* expressing one thing in terms normally used for another — see FIGURATIVE

**metaphysical** *adj* of, relating to, or being part of a reality beyond the observable physical universe — see SUPERNATURAL 1

**mete** (out) *vb* to give out (something) in appropriate amounts or to appropriate individuals — see ADMINISTER 1

**meter** *n* the recurrent pattern formed by a series of sounds having a regular rise and fall in intensity — see RHYTHM

**method** *n* the means or procedure for doing something ⟨all experiments must be conducted using the proper scientific *method*⟩
***syn*** approach, fashion, form, manner, strategy, style, system, tack, tactics, technique, way
***rel*** mode; blueprint, design, game, ground plan, intrigue, layout, line, plan, plot, program, route, scheme; expedient, move, shift, step; practice (*also* practise), process, routine; project, proposal, proposition; policy

**methodical** *adj* following a set method, arrangement, or pattern ⟨a *methodical* study plan that included lists of points to memorize⟩
***syn*** orderly, organized, regular, systematic, systematized
***rel*** regularized, standardized; accurate, correct, exact, precise; detailed, specific; businesslike
***near ant*** chaotic, disordered, disorderly, unordered
***ant*** disorganized, haphazard, irregular, unsystematic

**meticulous** *adj* taking great care and effort — see PAINSTAKING

**metric** *adj* marked by or occurring with a noticeable regularity in the rise and fall of sound — see RHYTHMIC

**metrical** *adj* marked by or occurring with a noticeable regularity in the rise and fall of sound — see RHYTHMIC

**metropolis** *n* a thickly settled, highly populated area — see CITY

**metropolitan** *n* a person with the outlook, experience, and manners thought to be typical of big city dwellers — see COSMOPOLITAN

**mettlesome** *adj* marked by a lively display of strong feeling — see SPIRITED 1
**mewl** *vb* to utter feeble plaintive cries — see WHIMPER
**microminiature** *adj* very small in size — see TINY
**microscopic** *also* **microscopical** *adj* very small in size — see TINY
**mid** *adj* occupying a position equally distant from the ends or extremes — see MIDDLE 1
**mid** *prep* in or into the middle of — see AMONG
**midday** *n* the middle of the day — see NOON
**middle** *adj* **1** occupying a position equally distant from the ends or extremes ⟨you must mark the exact *middle* point of each of these lines in order to solve the problem⟩
*syn* halfway, intermediary, intermediate, medial, median, medium, mid, middlemost, midmost, midway
*rel* equidistant; central, inmost, inner, innermost, nearest
*near ant* outer, peripheral
*ant* extreme, farthest, farthermost, furthermost, furthest, outermost, outmost, remotest, utmost
**2** being about midway between extremes of amount or size ⟨a house that is *middle* -sized for that neighborhood⟩ ⟨a man of *middle* height⟩
*syn* average, intermediate, median, medium, moderate, modest
*rel* reasonable; common, commonplace, conventional, normal, popular, regular, routine, standard, typical, usual; passable, tolerable
*near ant* excessive, extreme; rare, strange, uncommon, unusual; distinctive, idiosyncratic, special, unique; individual, peculiar, private
**middle** *n* **1** a middle point between extremes — see MEAN 1
**2** an area or point that is an equal distance from all points along an edge or outer surface — see CENTER 2
**3** the middle region of the human body — see MIDRIFF
**4** the most intense or characteristic phase of something — see THICK
**middleman** *n* one who works with opposing sides in order to bring about an agreement — see MEDIATOR
**middlemost** *adj* occupying a position equally distant from the ends or extremes — see MIDDLE 1
**middle-of-the-road** *adj* avoiding major social change or extreme political ideas — see MODERATE 2
**middling** *adj* of average to below average quality — see MEDIOCRE 1
**midget** *n* a living thing much smaller than others of its kind — see DWARF 1
**midmost** *adj* occupying a position equally distant from the ends or extremes — see MIDDLE 1
**midpoint** *n* **1** a middle point between extremes — see MEAN 1
**2** an area or point that is an equal distance from all points along an edge or outer surface — see CENTER 2
**midriff** *n* the middle region of the human body ⟨*midriff* -baring tops are popular this summer⟩
*syn* middle, waist, waistline
*rel* abdomen, torso, trunk
**midst** *n* **1** an area or point that is an equal distance from all points along an edge or outer surface — see CENTER 2
**2** the most intense or characteristic phase of something — see THICK
**midst** *prep* in or into the middle of — see AMONG
**midway** *adj* occupying a position equally distant from the ends or extremes — see MIDDLE 1
**mien** *n* the outward form of someone or something especially as indicative of a quality — see APPEARANCE 1
**might** *n* the ability to exert effort for the accomplishment of a task — see POWER 2
**mightily** *adv* **1** to a great degree — see VERY 1
**2** with great effort or determination — see HARD 1
**3** in a vigorous and forceful manner — see HARD 3
**mighty** *adj* having great power or influence — see IMPORTANT 2
**mighty** *adv* to a great degree — see VERY 1
**migrant** *adj* having a way of life that involves moving from one region to another typically on a seasonal basis — see MIGRATORY
**migrant** *n* one that leaves one place to settle in another — see EMIGRANT
**migratory** *adj* having a way of life that involves moving from one region to another typically on a seasonal basis ⟨most of the apple crop is picked by *migratory* workers⟩ ⟨*migratory* birds heading south for the winter⟩
*syn* migrant, mobile
*rel* errant, itinerant, nomadic, peripatetic, ranging, roaming, roving, traveling (*or* travelling), vagabond, vagrant, wandering, wayfaring; ambulatory, drifting, footloose, gallivanting (*also* galavanting), lingering, meandering, rambling, sauntering, strolling, traipsing, walking
*near ant* immobile, stationary; established, fast, fixed, rooted, set, settled
*ant* nonmigratory, resident
**mild** *adj* **1** marked by temperatures that are neither too high nor too low — see CLEMENT
**2** not harsh or stern especially in manner, nature, or effect — see GENTLE 1
**milestone** *n* a point in a chain of events at which an important change (as in one's fortunes) occurs — see TURNING POINT
**milieu** *n* the circumstances, conditions, or objects by which one is surrounded — see ENVIRONMENT
**militancy** *n* an inclination to fight or quarrel — see BELLIGERENCE

**militant** *adj* **1** feeling or displaying eagerness to fight — see BELLIGERENT
**2** having or showing a bold forcefulness in the pursuit of a goal — see AGGRESSIVE 1

**militant** *n* one who is intensely or excessively devoted to a cause — see ZEALOT

**militarist** *n* one who urges or attempts to cause a war — see WARMONGER

**military** *adj* **1** of or relating to the armed services ⟨the colonel testified that revealing any more information would have required giving away *military* secrets⟩
***syn*** martial, service
***rel*** naval; GI, gladiatorial, mercenary, soldierly; aggressive, bellicose, combative, contentious, militant, militaristic, pugnacious, quarrelsome, scrappy, truculent, warlike
***near ant*** civilian
***ant*** nonmilitary
**2** of, relating to, or suitable for war or a warrior — see MARTIAL 1

**military** *n* the combined army, air force, and navy of a nation — see ARMED FORCES

**mill** *n* a building or set of buildings for the manufacturing of goods — see FACTORY

**mime** *n* an actor in a story performed silently and entirely by body movements ⟨that annoying *mime* on the sidewalk is pretending to be in an invisible box again⟩
***syn*** mimic, mummer, pantomime, pantomimist
***rel*** entertainer, performer, player, trouper; imitator, impersonator, impressionist

**mime** *vb* to use (someone or something) as the model for one's speech, mannerisms, or behavior — see IMITATE 1

**mimetic** *adj* using or marked by the use of something else as a basis or model — see IMITATIVE

**mimic** *adj* **1** being such in appearance only and made with or manufactured from usually cheaper materials — see IMITATION
**2** using or marked by the use of something else as a basis or model — see IMITATIVE

**mimic** *n* **1** a person who imitates another's voice and mannerisms for comic effect ⟨a gifted *mimic* who can do a terrific imitation of anyone's voice⟩
***syn*** imitator, impersonator, impressionist
***rel*** caricaturist, lampooner, mocker, parodist, satirist; mime, mummer, pantomimist; entertainer, performer, player, trouper; parrot
**2** an actor in a story performed silently and entirely by body movements — see MIME

**mimic** *vb* **1** to copy or exaggerate (someone or something) in order to make fun of ⟨the comedian was famous for *mimicking* the President's distinctive lisp⟩
***syn*** burlesque, caricature, imitate, mock, parody, take off (on), travesty
***rel*** lampoon, satirize; deride, ridicule; ape, parrot; duplicate, emulate, replicate, reproduce; act, counterfeit, dissemble, fake, feign, pretend, sham, simulate; elaborate, embellish, embroider, exaggerate, magnify, pad, stretch; amplify, enhance, enlarge (upon), expand, flesh (out), overdraw, overstate; mime, pantomime; impersonate, perform, play
**2** to use (someone or something) as the model for one's speech, mannerisms, or behavior — see IMITATE 1

**mince** *vb* to cut into small pieces — see CHOP

**mind** *vb* **1** to pay attention especially through the act of hearing — see LISTEN
**2** *chiefly dialect* to bring back to mind — see REMEMBER
**3** to act according to the commands of — see OBEY
**4** to be cautious of or on guard against — see BEWARE (OF)
**5** to have an interest or concern for — see CARE
**6** to take charge of especially on behalf of another — see ²TEND 1
**7** to take notice of and be guided by — see HEED 1

**mind** *n* **1** the part of a person that feels, thinks, perceives, wills, and especially reasons ⟨scientists still disagree about exactly where the *mind* is located⟩
***syn*** cerebrum, head
***rel*** brain, gray matter, intellect, intelligence, reason; acumen, alertness, astuteness, brilliance, insight, judgment (*or* judgement), mentality, perception, perspicacity, sagacity, sapience, wisdom, wit; awareness, cognizance, consciousness, self-awareness, self-consciousness
**2** the normal or healthy condition of the mental abilities ⟨everyone used to tease him and tell him he was out of his *mind* when he swore he'd seen a flying saucer⟩
***syn*** head, reason, saneness, sanity, wit
***rel*** rationality, reasonableness, sense; health, healthfulness, healthiness, wholesomeness; lucidity, lucidness, normality, soundness; wisdom
***near ant*** delusion, hallucination; delirium, frenzy, hysteria
***ant*** derangement, insanity, lunacy, madness, mania
**3** an idea that is believed to be true or valid without positive knowledge — see OPINION 1
**4** the power or process of recalling what has been previously learned or experienced — see MEMORY 1

**mindful** *adj* having specified facts or feelings actively impressed on the mind — see CONSCIOUS

**mindless** *adj* **1** not having or showing an ability to absorb ideas readily — see STUPID 1
**2** not paying or showing close attention especially for the purpose of avoiding trouble — see CARELESS 1

**mindlessness** *n* the quality or state of lacking intelligence or quickness of mind — see STUPIDITY 1

**mine** *n* a usually concealed explosive device designed to go off when disturbed — see BOOBY TRAP 1

**mine** *vb* to place hidden explosive devices in or under ⟨the troops *mined* the field before they gave it up to the enemy⟩
***syn*** boobytrap
***rel*** blow up, bomb; ambush, snare, trap; attack

**mingle** *vb* **1** to turn into a single mass that is more or less the same throughout — see BLEND 1
**2** to take part in social activities — see SOCIALIZE

**miniature** *adj* very small in size — see TINY

**miniature** *n* an exact representation of something in greatly reduced size — see MODEL 1

**minimal** *adj* being the least in amount, number, or size possible ⟨the beached whales were returned to the sea with only *minimal* loss of life⟩
***syn*** least, littlest, lowest, minimum, slightest
***rel*** fewer, lesser, low, slight, small, smaller
***near ant*** highest
***ant*** full, greatest, largest, maximum, top, topmost, utmost

**minimize** *vb* to express scornfully one's low opinion of — see DECRY 1

**minimum** *adj* being the least in amount, number, or size possible — see MINIMAL

**minion** *n* a person or thing that is preferred over others — see FAVORITE

**minister** *n* **1** a person sent on a mission to represent another — see AMBASSADOR
**2** a person specially trained and authorized to conduct religious services in a Christian church — see CLERGYMAN

**minister** (to) *vb* to attend to the needs and comforts of — see NURSE 1

**ministerial** *adj* of, relating to, or characteristic of the clergy — see CLERICAL

**minor** *adj* **1** having not so great importance or rank as another — see LESSER
**2** of little or less value or merit — see INFERIOR 2
**3** lacking importance — see UNIMPORTANT

**minstrel** *n* a person who writes poetry — see POET

**minstrelsy** *n* writing that uses rhythm, vivid language, and often rhyme to provoke an emotional response — see POETRY 1

**mint** *n* a very large amount of money — see FORTUNE 2

**minus** *n* a feature of someone or something that creates difficulty or achieving success — see DISADVANTAGE

**minus** *prep* not having — see WITHOUT 1

**minute** *adj* **1** including many small descriptive features — see DETAILED 1
**2** lacking importance — see UNIMPORTANT
**3** so small or unimportant as to warrant little or no attention — see NEGLIGIBLE 1
**4** made or done with extreme care and accuracy — see FINE 2
**5** very small in size — see TINY

**minute** *n* a very small space of time — see INSTANT

**minutely** *adv* with attention to all aspects or details — see THOROUGHLY 1

**miracle** *n* something extraordinary or surprising — see WONDER 1

**miraculous** *adj* **1** being so extraordinary or abnormal as to suggest powers which violate the laws of nature — see SUPERNATURAL 2
**2** causing wonder or astonishment — see MARVELOUS 1

**mire** *n* **1** soft wet earth — see MUD
**2** spongy land saturated or partially covered with water — see SWAMP

**mire** *vb* **1** to make dirty — see DIRTY
**2** to place in conflict or difficulties — see EMBROIL

**mirror** *n* a smooth or polished surface (as of glass) that forms images by reflection ⟨breaking a *mirror* is supposed to bring seven years of bad luck⟩
***syn*** looking glass
***rel*** pier glass; reflector

**mirror** *vb* to reproduce or show (an exact likeness) as a mirror would — see REFLECT

**mirth** *n* a mood characterized by high spirits and amusement and often accompanied by laughter ⟨as charming as your mutual *mirth* is, could you refrain from nudging each other and giggling during class?⟩
***syn*** cheer, cheerfulness, cheeriness, festivity, glee, gleefulness, hilarity, joviality, merriment, merriness, mirthfulness
***rel*** frivolity, levity; carnival, gaiety (*also* gayety), jollification, jollity, reveling, revelry; brightness, buoyancy, good-humoredness, good-naturedness, humor, sunniness; insouciance, lightheartedness, playfulness; buffoonery, clownishness, flippancy, funning, jesting, jocularity, joking, joshing; animation, jauntiness, liveliness, perkiness, vivacity; joyfulness, joyousness, jubilance, rejoicing; frolicking, gamboling (*or* gambolling), rollicking, romping
***near ant*** blues, dejection, depression, despondence, forlornness, sadness, sorrow, unhappiness; bile, gloom, melancholy, sourness, spleen; earnestness, graveness, gravity, grimness, seriousness, soberness, solemnity; discontent, disgruntlement, moodiness; dolefulness, dolorousness, joylessness, mournfulness, plaintiveness, woe, woefulness; blackness, darkness, gloominess, gumness; desolateness, desolation; heartbreak, miserableness, misery, mourning, wretchedness

**mirthful** *adj* indicative of or marked by high spirits or good humor — see MERRY

**mirthfully** *adv* in a cheerful or happy manner — see GAILY 1

**mirthfulness** *n* a mood characterized by high spirits and amusement and often accompanied by laughter — see MIRTH

**miry** *adj* full of or covered with soft wet earth — see MUDDY 1

**misadventure** *n* bad luck or an example of this — see MISFORTUNE

**misanthrope** *n* a person who distrusts other people and believes that everything is done for selfish reasons — see CYNIC

**misanthropic** *adj* having or showing a deep distrust of human beings and their motives — see CYNICAL

**misapplication** *n* incorrect or improper use — see MISUSE

**misapply** *vb* to put to a bad or improper use ⟨you've *misapplied* the theorem to certain problems that require a different formula⟩ ⟨kids who *misapply* their boundless energy and get into trouble⟩
***syn*** abuse, misuse, pervert, profane, prostitute
***rel*** degrade, twist; mismanage; corrupt, debase, desecrate
***near ant*** apply, employ, use, utilize; respect

**misapprehend** *vb* to fail to understand the true or actual meaning of — see MISUNDERSTAND

**misapprehension** *n* **1** a failure to understand correctly — see MISUNDERSTANDING 1
**2** a wrong judgment — see MISTAKE 1

**misappropriate** *vb* to take (something) without right and with an intent to keep — see STEAL 1

**misbegotten** *adj* born to a father and mother who are not married — see ILLEGITIMATE 1

**misbehave** *vb* to behave badly ⟨if the two of you *misbehave* in public like that again, you'll have to go to bed early for a week⟩
***syn*** act up, carry on
***rel*** misconduct; disobey; clown (around), cut up, fool (around), horse (around); show off; roughhouse
***phrases*** raise Cain, run riot
***near ant*** obey; acquit, act, bear, comport, demean, deport, quit; comply, conform; check, collect, compose, constrain, contain, control, curb, handle, inhibit, move, quiet, repress, restrain

**misbehaving** *adj* engaging in or marked by childish misbehavior — see NAUGHTY

**misbehavior** *n* improper or illegal behavior — see MISCONDUCT

**miscalculate** *vb* to make an incorrect judgment regarding ⟨they *miscalculated* how difficult the long trip would be⟩
***syn*** misconceive, misjudge, mistake
***rel*** misconstrue, misinterpret, misunderstand; overestimate, overrate, overvalue; underestimate, underrate, undervalue; miscount

**miscarry** *vb* to go wrong ⟨the scheme to save the dolphins *miscarried*, and all were lost⟩
***syn*** misfire
***rel*** miss; break down, conk (out), crash, die, fail, stall; fizzle, flop, flunk, fold, wash out; flounder, struggle; decline, slip, slump, wane
***phrases*** fall flat, fall short
***near ant*** prevail, succeed; flourish, prosper, thrive

**miscellaneous** *adj* consisting of many things of different sorts ⟨the bottom of the drawer was always a *miscellaneous* accumulation of odds and ends⟩
***syn*** assorted, heterogeneous, mixed, motley, patchwork, promiscuous, varied
***rel*** manifold, multifarious; multiple, multiplex, myriad; disparate, divergent, diverse, sundry, various; chaotic, cluttered, confused, disarranged, disarrayed, disheveled (*or* dishevelled), disordered, jumbled, littered, messed, messy, muddled; amalgamated, blended, combined, conglomerated, fused, incorporated, intermingled, intermixed, merged, mingled; unclassified, unsorted
***near ant*** monolithic, uniform; alike, identical, like, same; distinct, distinctive, individual, separate
***ant*** homogeneous

**miscellaneousness** *n* the quality or state of being composed of many different elements or types — see VARIETY 1

**miscellany** *n* **1** an unorganized collection or mixture of various things ⟨the box from the attic contained a *miscellany* of old records, family photo albums, and long-forgotten love letters⟩
***syn*** assortment, clutter, hash, hodgepodge, hotchpotch, jumble, litter, medley, mélange, mishmash, motley, muddle, potpourri, rummage, scramble, shuffle, tumble, variety, welter
***rel*** notions, odds and ends, sundries; accumulation, aggregation, conglomeration; catchall, patchwork; admixture, amalgam, blend, combination, composite, compound, fusion, intermixture, mix, mixture; chaos, confusion, disarrangement, disarray, disorder, mess, muddle, shambles; knot, snarl, tangle
***phrases*** odds and ends
**2** a collection of writings — see ANTHOLOGY

**mischance** *n* **1** a chance and usually sudden event bringing loss or injury — see ACCIDENT 1
**2** bad luck or an example of this — see MISFORTUNE

**mischief** *n* **1** playful, reckless behavior that is not intended to cause serious harm ⟨the children claimed that setting off a firecracker was harmless *mischief*, but they got a lecture anyway⟩
***syn*** devilishness, devilment, devilry (*or* deviltry), hob, impishness, knavery, mischievousness, rascality, roguishness, shenanigans, waggery, wickedness

---

***syn*** synonym(s) ***rel*** related words
***ant*** antonym(s) ***near ant*** near antonym(s)

*rel* diabolicalness, naughtiness; friskiness, playfulness, sportiveness; chicanery, hanky-panky, trickery; high jinks, monkeyshines, skylarking, tomfoolery; antic, caper, practical joke; aggravation, annoyance, exasperation, irritation
*near ant* gravity, seriousness, solemnity
2 a natural disposition for playful behavior — see PLAYFULNESS
3 an appealingly mischievous person — see SCAMP 1

**mischievous** *adj* 1 tending to or exhibiting reckless playfulness ⟨the children had been so *mischievous* that we had to pay the babysitter extra and then clean up the mess⟩
*syn* devilish, elvish, impish, knavish, pixieish, prankish, rascally, roguish, sly, waggish, wicked
*rel* antic, coltish, frisky, kittenish, playful, sportive; gay, happy, lighthearted, whimsical; energetic, lively, spirited, sprightly; artful, cunning, tricky; misbehaving, naughty; pestering, riling, teasing
*near ant* grave, grim, sober, solemn, stern
2 engaging in or marked by childish misbehavior — see NAUGHTY
3 causing or capable of causing harm — see HARMFUL

**mischievousness** *n* 1 a natural disposition for playful behavior — see PLAYFULNESS
2 playful, reckless behavior that is not intended to cause serious harm — see MISCHIEF 1

**misconceive** *vb* to make an incorrect judgment regarding — see MISCALCULATE

**misconception** *n* a false idea or belief — see FALLACY 1

**misconduct** *n* improper or illegal behavior ⟨some rough play got the hockey player fined for *misconduct* on the ice⟩
*syn* malfeasance, misbehavior, misdoing, wrongdoing
*rel* crime, malefaction, misdeed, sin, wrong; malpractice; familiarity, gaffe, impropriety, indiscretion; blunder, error, fault, flub, fumble, goof, lapse, miscue, misstep, mistake, slip, slipup, stumble

**misconduct** *vb* to manage badly — see MISMANAGE

**misconstruction** *n* a failure to understand correctly — see MISUNDERSTANDING 1

**misconstrue** *vb* to fail to understand the true or actual meaning of — see MISUNDERSTAND

**misconstruing** *n* a failure to understand correctly — see MISUNDERSTANDING 1

**miscreant** *n* a mean, evil, or unprincipled person — see VILLAIN

**miscue** *n* an unintentional departure from truth or accuracy — see ERROR 1

**misdeed** *n* a breaking of a moral or legal code — see OFFENSE 1

**misdoing** *n* 1 a breaking of a moral or legal code — see OFFENSE 1
2 improper or illegal behavior — see MISCONDUCT

**miser** *n* a mean grasping person who is usually stingy with money ⟨the *miser* liked to sit and play with his money⟩
*syn* cheapskate, niggard, piker, scrooge, skinflint, tightwad
*rel* hoarder, saver
*near ant* prodigal, profligate, spender, spendthrift, squanderer, waster, wastrel

**miserable** *adj* 1 causing or marked by an atmosphere lacking in cheer — see GLOOMY 1
2 feeling unhappiness — see SAD 1
3 of low quality — see CHEAP 2
4 showing signs of advanced wear and tear and neglect — see SHABBY 1
5 deserving of one's pity — see PATHETIC 1

**miserliness** *n* the quality of being overly sparing with money — see PARSIMONY

**misery** *n* 1 a situation or state that causes great suffering and unhappiness — see HELL 2
2 a state of great suffering of body or mind — see DISTRESS 1

**misfire** *vb* to go wrong — see MISCARRY

**misfortune** *n* bad luck or an example of this ⟨through sheer *misfortune* our car got a flat tire and we were late⟩ ⟨our *misfortunes* of the last year included the loss of a beloved pet⟩
*syn* adversity, knock, misadventure, mischance, mishap
*rel* calamity, cataclysm, catastrophe, disaster; tragedy; affliction, hardship, trial, tribulation; distress, misery, suffering, unhappiness; defeat, failure, fizzle, nonsuccess; curse, sorrow, trouble; accident, casualty; disappointment, letdown, setback; circumstance, destiny, doom, fate, lot, portion
*near ant* break, chance, fluke, godsend, hit, opportunity, stroke, windfall; accomplishment, achievement, success
*ant* fortune, luck

**misgiving** *n* 1 a feeling or attitude that one does not know the truth, truthfulness, or trustworthiness of someone or something — see DOUBT
2 an uneasy feeling about the rightness of what one is doing or going to do — see QUALM
3 suspicion or fear of future harm or misfortune — see APPREHENSION 1

**misgovern** *vb* to manage badly — see MISMANAGE

**misguide** *vb* to cause to believe what is untrue — see DECEIVE

**mishandle** *vb* 1 to inflict physical or emotional harm upon — see ABUSE 1
2 to abuse physically — see MANHANDLE 1
3 to manage badly — see MISMANAGE

**mishap** *n* 1 a chance and usually sudden event bringing loss or injury — see ACCIDENT 1
2 bad luck or an example of this — see MISFORTUNE

**mishmash** *n* an unorganized collection or mixture of various things — see MISCELLANY 1

**misinform** *vb* to cause to believe what is untrue — see DECEIVE
**misinterpret** *vb* **1** to change so much as to create a wrong impression or alter the meaning of — see GARBLE
**2** to fail to understand the true or actual meaning of — see MISUNDERSTAND
**misinterpretation** *n* a failure to understand correctly — see MISUNDERSTANDING 1
**misjudge** *vb* to make an incorrect judgment regarding — see MISCALCULATE
**misjudging** *n* a wrong judgment — see MISTAKE 1
**misjudgment** *n* a wrong judgment — see MISTAKE 1
**mislaid** *adj* no longer possessed — see LOST
**mislay** *vb* to be unable to find or have at hand — see LOSE 1
**mislaying** *n* the act or an instance of not having or being able to find — see LOSS 1
**mislead** *vb* to cause to believe what is untrue — see DECEIVE
**misleading** *adj* tending or having power to deceive — see DECEPTIVE 1
**mismanage** *vb* to manage badly ⟨the business was *mismanaged* so seriously that it had to declare bankruptcy⟩
***syn*** misconduct, misgovern, mishandle, misrule
***rel*** abuse, ill-treat, ill-use, maltreat, mistreat, misuse; damage, harm, hurt, violate
***near ant*** govern, handle, manage, rule; care (for), nurture; aid, help, protect, rescue
**misplace** *vb* to be unable to find or have at hand — see LOSE 1
**misplaced** *adj* no longer possessed — see LOST
**misplacement** *n* the act or an instance of not having or being able to find — see LOSS 1
**misread** *vb* to fail to understand the true or actual meaning of — see MISUNDERSTAND
**misreading** *n* a failure to understand correctly — see MISUNDERSTANDING 1
**misrepresent** *vb* **1** to change so much as to create a wrong impression or alter the meaning of — see GARBLE
**2** to give a false idea of — see BELIE 1
**misrule** *n* a state in which there is widespread wrongdoing and disregard for rules and authority — see ANARCHY
**misrule** *vb* to manage badly — see MISMANAGE
**miss** *n* a young usually unmarried woman — see GIRL 1
**miss** *vb* **1** to fail to attend — see CUT 2
**2** to fail to understand the true or actual meaning of — see MISUNDERSTAND
**misshapen** *adj* badly or imperfectly formed — see MALFORMED
**missing** *adj* **1** no longer possessed — see LOST
**2** not present or in evidence — see ABSENT 2
**3** not at a certain place — see ABSENT 1
**mission** *n* a specific task with which a person or group is charged ⟨your *mission* is to clean up the house before company arrives⟩
***syn*** assignment, charge, job, operation, post
***rel*** burden, chore, duty, need, obligation, requirement, responsibility; labor, work; commitment, pledge, promise; appointment, designation, nomination; compulsion, constraint, restraint
**missive** *n* a message on paper from one person or group to another — see LETTER
**misspend** *vb* to use up carelessly — see WASTE 1
**misstate** *vb* to change so much as to create a wrong impression or alter the meaning of — see GARBLE
**misstep** *n* an unintentional departure from truth or accuracy — see ERROR 1
**mist** *n* **1** a light or fine rain — see DRIZZLE
**2** an atmospheric condition in which suspended particles in the air rob it of its transparency — see HAZE 1
**mist** *vb* to make dark, dim, or indistinct — see CLOUD 1
**mistake** *n* **1** a wrong judgment ⟨I made a *mistake* when I assumed that you were the one who broke the window⟩
***syn*** misapprehension, misjudging, misjudgment
***rel*** blunder, error, fault, flub, fumble, goof, inaccuracy, lapse, miscue, misstep, slipup, stumble; foul-up, muff; miscalculation, misstatement; misconception, misconstruction, misconstruing, misinterpretation
**2** an unintentional departure from truth or accuracy — see ERROR 1
**mistake** *vb* **1** to fail to understand the true or actual meaning of — see MISUNDERSTAND
**2** to make an incorrect judgment regarding — see MISCALCULATE
**mistaken** *adj* having an opinion that does not agree with truth or the facts — see INCORRECT 1
**mistakenly** *adv* in a mistaken or inappropriate way — see WRONGLY
**mistreat** *vb* to inflict physical or emotional harm upon — see ABUSE 1
**mistrust** *n* a feeling or attitude that one does not know the truth, truthfulness, or trustworthiness of someone or something — see DOUBT
**mistrust** *vb* to have no trust or confidence in — see DISTRUST
**mistrustful** *adj* **1** inclined to doubt or question claims — see SKEPTICAL 1
**2** not feeling sure about the truth, wisdom, or trustworthiness of someone or something — see DOUBTFUL 1
**mistrustfully** *adv* with distrust — see ASKANCE
**mistrustfulness** *n* a feeling or attitude that one does not know the truth, truth-

fulness, or trustworthiness of someone or something — see DOUBT

**misty** *adj* filled with or dimmed by fine particles (as of dust or water) in suspension — see HAZY 1

**misunderstand** *vb* to fail to understand the true or actual meaning of ⟨you *misunderstood* that poem because you didn't look up the words you didn't know⟩
*syn* misapprehend, misconstrue, misinterpret, misread, miss, mistake
*rel* misconceive
*ant* apprehend, catch, comprehend, conceive, fathom, grasp, know, make out, penetrate, perceive, savvy, see, seize, take in, understand

**misunderstanding** *n* **1** a failure to understand correctly ⟨people once thought that there were canals on Mars because of a common *misunderstanding* of a report by an Italian astronomer⟩
*syn* misapprehension, misconstruction, misconstruing, misinterpretation, misreading
*rel* misconception, mistake
*near ant* appreciation, apprehension, comprehension, conception, grasp, knowledge, perception, understanding; awareness, consciousness, realization
**2** an often noisy or angry expression of differing opinions — see ARGUMENT 1

**misusage** *n* incorrect or improper use — see MISUSE

**misuse** *n* incorrect or improper use ⟨the warranty for this dryer is null and void if you subject the product to deliberate *misuse*⟩
*syn* abuse, misapplication, misusage, perversion
*rel* mishandling, mismanagement, mismanaging; maltreatment, mistreatment; damage, destruction, ruin, spoiling, wrecking; corruption, debasement, desecration, profanation, prostitution
*near ant* application, employment, use, utilization

**misuse** *vb* **1** to put to a bad or improper use — see MISAPPLY
**2** to inflict physical or emotional harm upon — see ABUSE 1

**mite** *n* **1** a very small sum of money ⟨I have only a *mite* left to buy lunch for the rest of the week⟩
*syn* peanuts, pittance, shoestring, song
*rel* petty cash, pin money, pocket money, spending money
*near ant* capital, means, wherewithal; opulence, riches, treasure, wealth; heap, pile, pot; bonanza, mine, treasure trove, treasury
*ant* fortune, king's ransom, mint, wad
**2** a living thing much smaller than others of its kind — see DWARF 1
**3** a very small amount — see PARTICLE 1

**mitigate** *vb* to make more bearable or less severe — see HELP 2

**mix** *n* a distinct entity formed by the combining of two or more different things — see BLEND

**mix** *vb* **1** to turn into a single mass that is more or less the same throughout — see BLEND 1
**2** to take part in social activities — see SOCIALIZE

**mix (up)** *vb* to undo the proper order or arrangement of — see DISORDER

**mixed** *adj* **1** being offspring produced by parents of different races, breeds, species, or genera ⟨our *mixed* dog has a greyhound's body but the features of a collie⟩
*syn* crossbred, hybrid, mongrel
*rel* dihybrid, trihybrid; crossbred, crossed, hybridized, interbred, outcrossed
*near ant* pedigreed; inbred
*ant* full-blooded, purebred, thoroughbred
**2** consisting of many things of different sorts — see MISCELLANEOUS

**mixture** *n* a distinct entity formed by the combining of two or more different things — see BLEND

**mix-up** *n* an instance of confusion — see FOUL-UP

**moan** *n* **1** a long low sound indicating pain or grief ⟨she uttered an agonized *moan* and clutched her stomach⟩
*syn* groan, wail
*rel* blubbering, crying, sniveling, sobbing, weeping, whimpering, whining, yammering; keen, lament; bawl, cry, howl, shriek, squall, whimper, whine, yelp, yowl
*near ant* cackle, chuckle, chortle, giggle, guffaw, laugh, snicker, titter
**2** a crying out in grief — see LAMENT 1

**moan** *vb* **1** to utter a moan ⟨he *moaned* and cried for days after his dog died⟩
*syn* groan, wail
*rel* cry, blubber, sob, weep; sniff, snivel, whimper, whine; bemoan, bewail, deplore, keen, lament, rue; bleed, grieve, mourn, sorrow, suffer; bawl, howl, shriek, squall, yammer, yelp, yowl
*near ant* cackle, chuckle, chortle, giggle, guffaw, laugh, snicker, titter
**2** to express dissatisfaction, pain, or resentment usually tiresomely — see COMPLAIN

**mob** *n* **1** a great number of persons or things gathered together — see CROWD 1
**2** a group involved in secret or criminal activities — see RING 1
**3** the body of the community as contrasted with the elite — see MASS 1

**mob** *vb* to move upon or fill (something) in great numbers — see CROWD 2

**mobile** *adj* **1** capable of being moved especially with ease — see MOVABLE
**2** having a way of life that involves moving from one region to another typically on a seasonal basis — see MIGRATORY

**mobile home** *n* a motor vehicle that is specially equipped for living while traveling — see CAMPER

**mobilization** *n* an act of gathering forces together to renew or attempt an effort — see RALLY 1

**mobilize** *vb* to assemble and make ready for action ⟨we are prepared to *mobilize* the troops on very short notice⟩

*syn* marshal, muster, rally
*rel* arrange, line up, order, organize; call (up), convene, summon; activate
*near ant* disarrange, disorder, disorganize; deactivate, dismiss
*ant* demobilize

**mobster** *n* a violent, brutal person who is often a member of an organized gang — see HOODLUM

**mock** *adj* **1** being such in appearance only and made with or manufactured from usually cheaper materials — see IMITATION
**2** lacking in natural or spontaneous quality — see ARTIFICIAL 1

**mock** *n* a person or thing that is made fun of — see LAUGHINGSTOCK

**mock** *vb* **1** to copy or exaggerate (someone or something) in order to make fun of — see MIMIC 1
**2** to make (someone or something) the object of unkind laughter — see RIDICULE

**mocker** *n* a person who causes repeated emotional pain, distress, or annoyance to another — see TORMENTOR

**mockery** *n* **1** a poor, insincere, or insulting imitation of something ⟨the resort's Old West show for tourists is a *mockery* of Native American culture⟩
*syn* caricature, farce, joke, parody, sham, travesty
*rel* burlesque, comedy; lampoon, takeoff; counterfeit, fake, feigning, pretense (*or* pretence), simulation
*near ant* homage, tribute
**2** a person or thing that is made fun of — see LAUGHINGSTOCK
**3** the making of unkind jokes as a way of showing one's scorn for someone or something — see RIDICULE

**mod** *adj* being or involving the latest methods, concepts, information, or styles — see MODERN

[1]**mode** *n* **1** a distinctive way of putting ideas into words — see STYLE 1
**2** a state of mind dominated by a particular emotion — see MOOD 1

[2]**mode** *n* a practice or interest that is very popular for a short time — see FAD

**model** *adj* constituting, serving as, or worthy of being a pattern to be imitated ⟨why can't you be like your sister, who is such a well-behaved *model* child?⟩
*syn* archetypal, classic, exemplary, paradigmatic, quintessential
*rel* ideal, nonpareil, special, unique; absolute, flawless, impeccable, perfect; bang-up, banner, capital, dandy, fine, first-class, first-rate, grand, great, groovy, jim-dandy, par excellence, prime, superb, superior, superlative, terrific, tip-top, top, top-notch, unsurpassed, wonderful; exceptional, fancy, high-grade
*near ant* bad, poor, substandard, unsatisfactory; atrocious, execrable, wretched; deficient, disappointing, failed, inadequate, inferior, poor; average, normal, ordinary, representative, typical; mediocre, second-class, second-rate

**model** *n* **1** an exact representation of something in greatly reduced size ⟨the dollhouse was a tiny, perfect *model* of the family's actual house⟩
*syn* miniature
*rel* copy, duplicate, duplication, imitation, replica, replication, reproduction; dwarf, midget, mini, pygmy
*near ant* archetype, original, prototype; blowup, enlargement
**2** a person who poses with or wears merchandise (as clothes) often for pictorial advertising ⟨the most famous *models* can earn thousands of dollars an hour⟩
*syn* manikin, mannequin
*rel* figure, form; doll, dummy
**3** someone of such unequaled perfection as to deserve imitation — see IDEAL 1

**moderate** *adj* **1** avoiding extremes in behavior or expression ⟨he was only a *moderate* drinker, stopping after a couple of glasses of wine⟩
*syn* temperate
*rel* controlled, curbed, disciplined, restrained, self-controlled; calculated, deliberate, measured; rational, reasonable; average, medio-cre, medium, modest, ordinary, run-of-the-mill, so-so; normal, ordinary, regular, routine, typical, usual
*near ant* excessive, extreme, inordinate, radical; irrational, unreasonable; extremist, fanatic (*or* fanatical), rabid, radical
*ant* immoderate, intemperate
**2** avoiding major social change of extreme political ideas ⟨the principal's *moderate* position on cell phones is that students can use them at school but only for emergencies⟩
*syn* middle-of-the-road
*rel* conventional, orthodox, traditional, rational, reasonable; neutral
*near ant* excessive; conservative, reactionary, rightist; leftist, liberal, progressive; fanatic (*or* fanatical), revolutionary, revolutionist, subversive, violent; agitating, fomenting, incendiary, inciting, instigating, provocative, provoking; rabble-rousing; dissenting
*ant* extremist, radical
**3** being about midway between extremes of amount or size — see MIDDLE 2
**4** marked by temperatures that are neither too high nor too low — see CLEMENT

**moderate** *vb* to grow less in scope or intensity especially gradually — see DECREASE 2

**moderately** *adv* to some degree or extent — see FAIRLY

**moderateness** *n* an avoidance of extremes in one's actions, beliefs, or habits — see TEMPERANCE

**moderation** *n* an avoidance of extremes in one's actions, beliefs, or habits — see TEMPERANCE

**moderator** *n* a person in charge of a meeting — see CHAIR 1

---

*syn* synonym(s) *rel* related words
*ant* antonym(s) *near ant* near antonym(s)

**modern** *adj* being or involving the latest methods, concepts, information, or styles ⟨this hairstyle is absolutely the most *modern* fashion out there⟩
*syn* contemporary, current, hot, mod, modernistic, new, newfangled, new-fashioned, present-day, red-hot, space-age, ultramodern, up-to-date
*rel* fashionable, in, modish, stylish; last, latest; modernized, updated; futuristic, nontraditional
*near ant* anachronistic; aged, age-old, ancient, antediluvian, hoary, old, venerable; bygone, former, late, olden, past; antique, historic, historical; obsolete, outmoded, outworn; old-world; discarded, disused, moth-eaten; forgotten, remote; ageless, dateless, timeless
*ant* antiquated, archaic, dated, fusty, musty, noncontemporary, old-fangled, old-fashioned, old-time, out-of-date, passé
**modern** *n* a person with very modern ideas ⟨the leaders of the American suffragists were originally regarded by many people as uppity *moderns* who should have stayed in their place⟩
*syn* ultramodernist
*rel* leftist, liberal, progressive; extremist, radical; bohemian
*near ant* conservative, rightist, Tory; old hand, old-timer, veteran
*ant* antediluvian, dodo, fogy (*also* fogey), fossil, fuddy-duddy, reactionary, stick-in-the-mud
**modernistic** *adj* being or involving the latest methods, concepts, information, or styles — see MODERN
**modest** *adj* **1** being about midway between extremes of amount or size — see MIDDLE 2
**2** free from any trace of the coarse or indecent — see CHASTE
**3** not comfortable around people — see SHY 2
**4** not having or showing any feelings of superiority, self-assertiveness, or showiness — see HUMBLE 1
**modestly** *adv* **1** in manner showing no signs of pride or self-assertion — see LOWLY
**2** with purity of thought and deed — see PURELY
**modesty** *n* **1** the absence of any feelings of being better than others — see HUMILITY
**2** the quality or state of being morally pure — see CHASTITY
**modicum** *n* the smallest amount or part imaginable — see JOT
**modifiable** *adj* capable of being readily changed — see FLEXIBLE 1
**modification** *n* the act, process, or result of making different — see CHANGE
**modify** *vb* **1** to limit the meaning of (as a noun) — see QUALIFY 1
**2** to make different in some way — see CHANGE 1
**modish** *adj* **1** being in the latest or current fashion — see STYLISH
**2** enjoying widespread favor or approval — see POPULAR 1
**modishness** *n* the state of enjoying widespread approval — see POPULARITY
**mogul** *n* a person of rank, power, or influence in a particular field — see MAGNATE
**moiety** *n* one of two equal or nearly equal parts — see HALF 1
**moil** *vb* to devote serious and sustained effort — see LABOR
**moist** *adj* slightly or moderately wet ⟨luckily, my new suede shoes are only a bit *moist* after I accidentally wore them in the rain⟩
*syn* damp, dank
*rel* dewy; clammy; humid, muggy, sticky; sultry, summery, sweltering, torrid, tropical; dripping, drenched, saturated, soaked, soaking, sodden, soggy, sopping, soppy, steeped, water-logged
*near ant* arid, dry, waterless; baked, burned, burnt, dehydrated, desert, droughty, dusty, parched, scorched, seared, sere
**moisten** *vb* to make or become slightly or moderately wet ⟨*moisten* the cloth before cleaning with it⟩
*syn* dampen
*rel* drench, saturate, soak, steep; humidify; dip, immerge, immerse
*near ant* dehumidify, dehydrate, parch, scorch, sear
*ant* dry
**moisture** *n* the amount of water suspended in the air in tiny droplets ⟨dew is really just *moisture* from the air that condenses and collects when the temperature drops at night⟩
*syn* dampness, humidity
*rel* mugginess, stickiness, stuffiness; sultriness; clamminess, dankness, sogginess, wetness
*near ant* aridity, dehydration, dryness
**mojo** *n* **1** something worn or kept to bring good luck or keep away evil — see CHARM 1
**2** the power to control natural forces through supernatural means — see MAGIC 1
**molder** *vb* to go through decomposition — see DECAY 1
**molecule** *n* a very small piece — see BIT 1
**mollify** *vb* **1** to lessen the anger or agitation of — see PACIFY
**2** to make more bearable or less severe — see HELP 2
**mollifying** *adj* tending to lessen or avoid conflict or hostility — see PACIFIC 1
**mollycoddle** *n* a person without strength of character — see WEAKLING 2
**mollycoddle** *vb* to treat with great or excessive care — see BABY
**molt** *vb* to cast (a natural bodily covering or appendage) aside — see SHED 1
**mom** *n* a female human parent — see MOTHER
**moment** *n* **1** a particular point at which an event takes place — see OCCASION 1
**2** the quality or state of being important — see IMPORTANCE

**3** a very small space of time — see INSTANT
**4** the time currently existing or in progress — see PRESENT 1

**momentarily** *adv* at or within a short time — see SHORTLY 2

**momentary** *adj* lasting only for a short time ⟨the pain of the flu shot was only *momentary*⟩
***syn*** ephemeral, evanescent, flash, fleeting, fugitive, impermanent, passing, short-lived, temporary, transient, transitory
***rel*** brief, short; acting, interim
***near ant*** lifelong
***ant*** enduring, eternal, everlasting, lasting, long-lived, permanent, perpetual

**momentous** *adj* having great meaning or lasting effect — see IMPORTANT 1

**momentum** *n* something that arouses action or activity — see IMPULSE

**momma** *n* a female human parent — see MOTHER

**monarch** *n* one who rules over a people with a sole, supreme, and usually hereditary authority ⟨the ruling *monarch* of Britain at that time was Queen Elizabeth I⟩
***syn*** autocrat, ruler, sovereign
***rel*** czar (*also* tsar *or* tzar), emperor, empress, kaiser, king, lord, mogul, prince, queen, satrap, sultan; authoritarian, despot, dictator, overlord, potentate, tyrant; royalty

**monarchal** *or* **monarchial** *adj* fit for or worthy of a royal ruler — see MONARCHICAL

**monarchical** *also* **monarchic** *adj* fit for or worthy of a royal ruler ⟨guests who stay in the hotel's most expensive suite live in *monarchical* splendor⟩
***syn*** kingly, monarchal (*or* monarchial), princely, queenly, regal, royal
***rel*** aristocratic, baronial, imperial, lordly, noble, patrician

**monastery** *n* a residence for men under religious vows ⟨Gregory Mendel worked out his concepts of genetics by doing breeding experiments using pea plants in the *monastery's* garden⟩
***syn*** abbey, cloister, friary, priory
***rel*** house; convent, nunnery; lamasery

**monetary** *adj* of or relating to money, banking, or investments — see FINANCIAL

**money** *n* something (as pieces of stamped metal or printed paper) customarily and legally used as a medium of exchange, a measure of value, or a means of payment ⟨are you sure you have enough *money* to buy all that?⟩
***syn*** bread [*slang*], cash, chips, currency, dough, gold, jack [*slang*], legal tender, lucre, pelf, tender, wampum [*slang*]
***rel*** change, coinage, specie; paper money, scrip; banknote, cashier's check, check, draft, money order, note; bill, buck, dollar, greenback; bankroll, capital, finances, funds; mite, pittance; bundle, fortune, king's ransom, mint, wad; abundance, means, opulence, riches, treasure, wealth; resources, wherewithal; pin money, pocket money, spending money

**moneyed** *or* **monied** *adj* having goods, property, or money in abundance — see RICH 1

**mongrel** *adj* being offspring produced by parents of different races, breeds, species, or genera — see MIXED 1

**mongrel** *n* an offspring of parents with different genes especially when of different races, breeds, species, or genera — see HYBRID

**monitor** *vb* to pay continued close attention to (something) for a particular purpose ⟨police regularly *monitor* that road to record traffic density and catch speeders⟩
***syn*** cover, watch
***rel*** eye; behold, look; regard, see; gape, gawk, gaze, glare, goggle, peer, stare; glance, glimpse, peek, peep
***phrases*** keep an eye on

**monkey** *n* an appealingly mischievous person — see SCAMP 1

**monkey** (around) *vb* **1** to engage in attention-getting playful or boisterous behavior — see CUT UP
**2** to spend time in aimless activity — see FIDDLE (AROUND)

**monkey** (with) *vb* to handle thoughtlessly, ignorantly, or mischievously — see TAMPER

**monkeying** *n* wildly playful or mischievous behavior — see HORSEPLAY

**monkeyshines** *n pl* wildly playful or mischievous behavior — see HORSEPLAY

**monochromatic** *adj* having or consisting of a single color ⟨although marble and bronze sculptures are *monochromatic*, they can be amazingly lifelike⟩
***syn*** solid
***rel*** colored, colorful, pigmented; chromatic
***near ant*** dappled (*also* dapple), marbled, shaded; mottled, piebald, pied, pinto; barred, brindled (*or* brindle); checkered, patterned, plaid, striped
***ant*** motley, multicolored, polychromatic, varicolored, variegated

**monopolize** *vb* to have complete control over ⟨it is illegal in the United States to *monopolize* an entire industry or product⟩ ⟨you shouldn't *monopolize* that toy while your friends are waiting to play with it⟩
***syn*** sew up
***rel*** corner, hog; absorb, consume, engross; have, hold, own, possess; control, direct, govern, manage, reign (over), rule

**monotonous** *adj* causing weariness, restlessness, or lack of interest — see BORING

**monotonousness** *n* a tedious lack of variety — see MONOTONY

**monotony** *n* a tedious lack of variety ⟨the *monotony* of the cafeteria's selections was almost as bad as the quality⟩

*syn* monotonousness, sameness
*rel* uniformity; boredom, dullness (*also* dulness), ennui, restlessness, tediousness, tedium, tiresomeness, weariness, wearisomeness
*near ant* diversity, multiplicity, variety; variability, variation; absorption, engagement, engrossment, enthrallment, fascination, grip, interest, intrigue; animation, excitement, invigoration, stimulation

**monster** *adj* unusually large — see HUGE

**monster** *n* **1** a strange or horrible and often frightening creature ⟨both children insisted that their parents check under the bed for *monsters* every night⟩
*syn* monstrosity, ogre
*rel* ogre; bête noire, bogey (*also* bogy *or* bogie), bugaboo, bugbear; banshee, bogeyman, demon (*or* daemon), devil fiend, fright, imp, incubus; horror, terror; abomination, anathema; abnormality, freak; mutant, mutation
**2** a person, thing, or event that is not normal — see FREAK 1
**3** a mean, evil, or unprincipled person — see VILLAIN 1
**4** something that is unusually large and powerful — see GIANT

**monstrosity** *n* **1** a person, thing, or event that is not normal — see FREAK 1
**2** a strange or horrible and often frightening creature — see MONSTER 1
**3** something unpleasant to look at — see EYESORE
**4** the quality of inspiring intense dread or dismay — see HORROR 1
**5** the state or quality of being utterly evil — see ENORMITY 1

**monstrous** *adj* **1** badly or imperfectly formed — see MALFORMED
**2** extremely disturbing or repellent — see HORRIBLE 1
**3** unusually large — see HUGE

**monstrously** *adv* **1** beyond a normal or acceptable limit — see TOO 1
**2** to a large extent or degree — see GREATLY 2

**monthlies** *n pl* an occurrence of menstruating — see PERIOD 1

**monument** *n* **1** a shaped stone laid over or erected near a grave and usually bearing an inscription to identify and preserve the memory of the deceased — see TOMBSTONE
**2** something that serves to keep alive the memory of a person or event — see MEMORIAL

**monumental** *adj* **1** large and impressive in size, grandeur, extent, or conception — see GRAND 1
**2** unusually large — see HUGE

**mooch** *vb* to move about from place to place aimlessly — see WANDER

**mood** *n* **1** a state of mind dominated by a particular emotion ⟨losing my favorite sweater left me in a bad *mood* for the rest of the day⟩
*syn* cheer, frame, humor, mood, spirit, temper
*rel* attitude, outlook, perspective, standpoint, viewpoint; emotion, feeling, heart, passion, sentiment; strain; belief, conviction, mind, opinion; expression, tone, vein; character, disposition, individuality, personality, temperament; responsiveness, sensibility, sensitiveness, sensitivity
**2** a special quality or impression associated with something — see AURA

**moody** *adj* frequently influenced by moods and especially bad moods ⟨teenagers are often both *moody* and changeable⟩
*syn* temperamental
*rel* capricious, changeable, changeful, fickle, fluctuating, fluid, inconstant, mercurial, mutable, uncertain, unsettled, unstable, unsteady, variable, volatile, whimsical
*near ant* equable, even; changeless, constant, settled, stable, steady, unchanging

**moonshine** *n* **1** illegally produced liquor ⟨during Prohibition, *moonshine* and "bathtub gin" were made secretly⟩
*syn* bootleg
*rel* alcohol, booze, drink, grog, spirits
**2** a fermented or distilled beverage that can make a person drunk — see ALCOHOL
**3** unintelligible or meaningless talk — see GIBBERISH

**moonstruck** *adj* having or showing a very abnormal or sick state of mind — see INSANE 1

**moor** *vb* to put securely in place or in a desired position — see FASTEN 2

**moot** *adj* open to question or dispute — see DEBATABLE 1

**moot** *vb* **1** to present or bring forward for discussion — see INTRODUCE 2
**2** to talk about (an issue) usually from various points of view and for the purpose of arriving at a decision or opinion — see DISCUSS

**mope** *vb* **1** to move about from place to place aimlessly — see WANDER
**2** to silently go about in a bad mood — see SULK

**mopes** *n pl* a state or spell of low spirits — see SADNESS

**moral** *adj* **1** conforming to a high standard of morality or virtue — see GOOD 2
**2** guided by or in accordance with one's sense of right and wrong — see CONSCIENTIOUS 1

**moralist** *n* a person who is greatly concerned with seemly behavior and morality especially regarding sexual matters — see PRUDE

**morality** *n* **1** conduct that conforms to an accepted standard of right and wrong ⟨the candidate claimed to be the best choice because of his unswerving *morality*⟩
*syn* character, decency, goodness, honesty, integrity, probity, rectitude, righteousness, uprightness, virtue, virtuousness
*rel* high-mindedness, honor, incorruptibility; appropriateness, correctness, dec-

orousness, decorum, etiquette, fitness, propriety, seemliness; ethics, morals
*near ant* impropriety, indecency, indiscretion; debauchery, degeneracy, degradation, depravity, perversion; crookedness, dishonesty, underhandedness, unscrupulousness; lowness, meanness, viciousness, vileness; corruption, sin
*ant* badness, evil, immorality, wickedness
**2** the code of good conduct for an individual or group — see ETHICS

**morally** *adv* with purity of thought and deed — see PURELY

**morals** *n pl* the code of good conduct for an individual or group — see ETHICS

**morass** *n* spongy land saturated or partially covered with water — see SWAMP

**morbid** *adj* causing or marked by an atmosphere lacking in cheer — see GLOOMY 1

**mordant** *adj* marked by the use of wit that is intended to cause hurt feelings — see SARCASTIC

**more** *adj* resulting in an increase in amount or number — see ADDITIONAL

**more** *adv* **1** in addition to what has been said ⟨the sci-fi movie was totally unbelievable and, what's *more*, it was boring⟩
*syn* additionally, again, also, besides, further, furthermore, likewise, moreover, then, too, withal, yet
*phrases* as well, in addition to, to boot
**2** to a greater or higher extent ⟨the boxers for this bout are *more* evenly matched than the last two were⟩
*syn* better

**more or less** *adv* **1** very close to but not completely — see ALMOST
**2** to some degree or extent — see FAIRLY

**moreover** *adv* in addition to what has been said — see MORE 1

**mores** *n pl* personal conduct or behavior as evaluated by an accepted standard of appropriateness for a social or professional setting — see MANNER 1

**moribund** *adj* nearly dead ⟨with its rundown look and empty aisles, the business appeared *moribund*⟩
*syn* dying
*rel* expiring, fading, passing away, sinking; decadent, declining, deteriorating; dead, deceased, defunct, departed, gone, passed away; terminal
*near ant* alive, animate, living; being, breathing, existing, subsisting, surviving; flourishing, prospering, thriving

**morn** *n* **1** the first appearance of light in the morning or the time of its appearance — see DAWN 1
**2** the time from sunrise until noon — see MORNING 1

**morning** *n* **1** the time from sunrise until noon ⟨I hate getting up in the *morning* to go to school⟩
*syn* forenoon, morn
*rel* aurora, dawn, dawning, daybreak, daylight; cockcrow, sunrise, sunup; day, daytime, light
*near ant* dark, darkness, night, nighttime, twilight; dusk, evening, nightfall, sundown, sunset; afternoon
**2** the first appearance of light in the morning or the time of its appearance — see DAWN 1
**3** the point at which something begins — see BEGINNING

**moron** *n* a stupid person — see IDIOT

**morose** *adj* causing or marked by an atmosphere lacking in cheer — see GLOOMY 1

**morsel** *n* **1** a small piece or quantity of food ⟨I suppose you can have dessert, since you only left a couple *morsels* on your plate⟩
*syn* bite, mouthful, nibble, taste, tidbit (*also* titbit)
*rel* snack; appetizer, hors d'oeuvre; bit, chew, crumb, dab, driblet, hint, lick, nubbin, nugget, pinch, scrap, shred, smidgen (*also* smidgeon *or* smidgin), speck, spot, sprinkling, suspicion, touch, trace; dash, drop; gulp, swallow, swig
**2** a very small piece — see BIT 1

**mortal** *adj* **1** likely to cause or capable of causing death — see DEADLY
**2** of, relating to, or suggestive of death — see DEATHLY 1
**3** relating to or characteristic of human beings — see HUMAN

**mortal** *n* a member of the human race — see HUMAN

**mortally** *adv* to a great degree — see VERY 1

**mortician** *n* a person who manages funerals and prepares the dead for burial or cremation — see FUNERAL DIRECTOR

**mortification** *n* the emotional state of being made self-consciously uncomfortable — see EMBARRASSMENT 1

**mortify** *vb* to throw into a state of self-conscious distress — see EMBARRASS 1

**[1]most** *adv* to a great degree — see VERY 1

**[2]most** *adv* very close to but not completely — see ALMOST

**most** *adj* of the greatest or highest degree or quantity — see ULTIMATE 1

**most** *n* the greatest amount, number, or part ⟨this room will accommodate 50 people at the *most*⟩
*syn* maximum, outside
*rel* best, utmost
*ant* least, minimum

**mostly** *adv* for the most part — see CHIEFLY

**mote** *n* a very small piece — see BIT 1

**moth–eaten** *adj* **1** having passed its time of use or usefulness — see OBSOLETE
**2** showing signs of advanced wear and tear and neglect — see SHABBY 1
**3** used or heard so often as to be dull — see STALE

**mother** *n* a female human parent ⟨he dreaded telling his *mother* that her favorite figurine had gotten broken⟩

*syn* ma, mama, mammy, mom, momma, mum [*chiefly British*]
*rel* matriarch, matron
**mother** *vb* to attend to the needs and comforts of — see NURSE 1
**motherland** *n* the land of one's birth, residence, or citizenship — see COUNTRY 1
**motherliness** *n* motherly character or qualities — see MATERNITY
**motherly** *adj* of, relating to, or characteristic of a mother ⟨she showed a sweet *motherly* tenderness toward the tiny kitten she was taking care of⟩
*syn* maternal
*rel* parental; female, feminine, womanish, womanlike, womanly; matriarchal, matronly; caring, giving, nurturing
**mother tongue** *n* the stock of words, pronunciation, and grammar used by a people as their basic means of communication — see LANGUAGE 1
**motif** *n* **1** a major object of interest or concern (as in a discussion or artistic composition) — see MATTER 1
**2** a unit of decoration that is repeated all over something (as a fabric) — see PATTERN 1
**motion** *n* the act or an instance of changing position — see MOVEMENT 1
**motion** *vb* to direct or notify by a movement or gesture ⟨the referee *motioned* the team captains to confer with him on the sideline⟩
*syn* beckon, flag, gesture, signal, wave
*rel* gesticulate, pantomime, sign; signalize; acquaint, advise, inform, relate, tell; flourish, shrug
**motionlessly** *adv* without motion — see STILL 1
**motion picture** *n* **1** a story told by means of a series of continuously projected pictures and a sound track — see MOVIE 1
**2 motion pictures** *pl* the art or business of making a movie — see MOVIE 2
**motivation** *n* something that arouses action or activity — see IMPULSE
**motive** *n* **1** a major object of interest or concern (as in a discussion or artistic composition) — see MATTER 1
**2** a unit of decoration that is repeated all over something (as a fabric) — see PATTERN 1
**3** something (as a belief) that serves as the basis for another thing — see REASON 2
**motley** *adj* **1** consisting of many things of different sorts — see MISCELLANEOUS
**2** marked by a variety of usually vivid colors — see COLORFUL
**motley** *n* **1** a person formerly kept in a royal or noble household to amuse with jests and pranks — see FOOL 2
**2** an unorganized collection or mixture of various things — see MISCELLANY 1
**motor** *n* **1** a device that changes energy into mechanical motion — see ENGINE
**2** a self-propelled passenger vehicle on wheels — see CAR
**motor** *vb* to travel by a motorized vehicle — see DRIVE 2
**motorboat** *n* a boat equipped with a motor ⟨*motorboats* are banned on the lake because they are a hazard to swimmers⟩
*syn* powerboat, speedboat
*rel* cabin cruiser, cruiser, runabout
**motorcade** *n* a group of vehicles traveling together or under one management — see FLEET
**motorcar** *n* a self-propelled passenger vehicle on wheels — see CAR
**motor home** *n* a motor vehicle that is specially equipped for living while traveling — see CAMPER
**motorist** *n* a person who travels by automobile ⟨environmental organizations suggest that *motorists* get together and carpool to avoid using several cars and adding to pollution⟩
*syn* automobilist, driver
*rel* operator; chauffeur; carpooler
**motor vehicle** *n* a self-propelled passenger vehicle on wheels — see CAR
**mottle** *n* a small area that is different (as in color) from the main part — see SPOT 1
**mottle** *vb* to mark with small spots especially unevenly — see SPOT
**mottled** *adj* **1** having blotches of two or more colors — see PIED
**2** marked with spots — see SPOTTED 1
**mound** *n* **1** a pile or ridge of granular matter (as sand or snow) — see [2]BANK
**2** a quantity of things thrown or stacked on one another — see [1]PILE 1
**3** an area of high ground — see HEIGHT 4
**mound** *vb* **1** to form into a pile or ridge of earth ⟨he likes to sit on the beach and *mound* sand into sand castles⟩
*syn* bank, hill
*rel* heap, pile, pyramid, stack; embank; bunch, bundle, clump, lump, mass, wad; accumulate, amass, assemble, collect, gather, group
**2** to lay or throw on top of one another — see PILE
**[1]mount** *n* an elevation of land higher than a hill — see MOUNTAIN 1
**[2]mount** *n* something that holds up or serves as a foundation for something else — see SUPPORT 1
**mount** *vb* **1** to become greater in extent, volume, amount, or number — see INCREASE 2
**2** to bring before the public in performance or exhibition — see PRESENT 1
**3** to move or extend upward — see ASCEND
**mountain** *n* **1** an elevation of land higher than a hill ⟨my cousin likes to climb *mountains* just because she can⟩
*syn* alp, mount, peak
*rel* mountain range, seamount; mountaintop, pinnacle, precipice, summit
*near ant* basin, bowl, depression, hollow, vale, valley
**2** a considerable amount — see LOT 2
**3** a quantity of things thrown or stacked on one another — see [1]PILE 1
**mountain lion** *n* a large tawny cat of the wild — see COUGAR

**mountainous** *adj* unusually large — see HUGE

**mountebank** *n* one who makes false claims of identity or expertise — see IMPOSTOR

**mounting** *n* something that holds up or serves as a foundation for something else — see SUPPORT 1

**mourn** *vb* **1** to feel deep sadness or mental pain — see GRIEVE
**2** to feel or express sorrow for — see LAMENT 1

**mournful** *adj* **1** expressing or suggesting mourning ⟨she had such a *mournful* expression that someone teasingly asked if her dog had died⟩
***syn*** anguished, bemoaning, bewailing, deploring, doleful, dolorous, funeral, grieving, heartbroken, lamentable, lugubrious, plaintive, regretful, rueful, sorrowful, sorry, wailing, weeping, woeful
***rel*** elegiac, melancholy; dejected, depressed, despondent, disconsolate, dispirited, downcast, downhearted, heartsick, inconsolable; careworn, sad, unhappy, woebegone; bawling, crying, groaning, howling, keening, moaning, yammering; bleeding, suffering; black, bleak, cheerless, comfortless, dark, darkening, desolate, dismal, dreary, funereal, gloomy, glum, gray (*also* grey), joyless, low, miserable, moody, morbid, morose, pathetic, pessimistic, piteous, saturnine, somber (*or* sombre), sullen, wretched
***near ant*** delighted, exulting, glorying, happy, joyful, rejoicing, triumphant; bright, cheerful, cheering, cheery; laughing, smiling; blithe, blithesome, buoyant, gay, jocund, jolly, joyous, lighthearted, merry, mirthful; encouraging, hopeful, optimistic
**2** feeling unhappiness — see SAD 1

**mournfully** *adv* with feelings of bitterness or grief — see HARD 2

**mouse** *vb* to move about in a sly or secret manner — see SNEAK 1

**mousy** *or* **mousey** *adj* easily frightened — see SHY 1

**mouth** *n* **1** the opening through which food passes into the body of an animal ⟨the baby chicks opened their *mouths* very wide and chirped piteously when their mother came back with worms⟩
***syn*** kisser [*slang*], mug
***rel*** countenance, face, puss [*slang*], visage; muzzle; jaws, mandible, maxilla; gullet, maw
**2** a twisting of the facial features in disgust or disapproval — see GRIMACE

**mouth** *vb* to speak softly and unclearly — see MUMBLE

**mouth** (off) *vb* to talk as if giving an important and formal speech — see ORATE 1

**mouthful** *n* a small piece or quantity of food — see MORSEL 1

**mouthpiece** *n* a person who speaks for another or for a group — see SPOKESPERSON

**movable** *or* **moveable** *adj* capable of being moved especially with ease ⟨any furniture that is not *movable* will be covered with protective cloths by the painters⟩
***syn*** mobile, portable
***rel*** adjustable, flexible, modular; removable, transferable, transportable; motile, moving; unsteady, unstable; manageable
***near ant*** motionless, moveless, static, stationary, still, stuck, unmoving, wedged; fast, fixed, rooted, steadfast
***ant*** immobile, immovable, irremovable, unmovable

**movables** *or* **moveables** *n pl* **1** the movable articles in a room — see FURNITURE
**2** transportable items that one owns — see POSSESSION 2

**move** *n* **1** an action planned or taken to achieve a desired result — see MEASURE 1
**2** the act or an instance of changing position — see MOVEMENT 1

**move** *vb* **1** to change the place or position of ⟨I need you to *move* all your books off the chair before company gets here⟩
***syn*** budge, dislocate, displace, disturb, remove, shift, transfer, transpose
***rel*** bear, carry, convey, drive, haul, transmit, transport; transplant; replace, supersede, supplant; alter, make over, modify, redo, refashion, remake, remodel, revamp, revise, rework, vary
***near ant*** fix, freeze, set, stabilize
**2** to set or keep in motion ⟨the hands of the wall clock are *moved* by battery⟩
***syn*** actuate, drive, impel, propel, work
***rel*** activate, motivate, provoke; abet, ferment, foment, incite, raise, stir (up), whip (up); set off, trigger; excite, galvanize, inflame, inspire, motivate, rouse
***near ant*** check, curb, inhibit, restrain
**3** to change one's position ⟨don't *move* while I'm trying to draw your portrait⟩
***syn*** budge, shift, stir
***rel*** fidget, jiggle, squirm, twitch, wiggle, writhe; rouse
***near ant*** remain, stay; stabilize
***ant*** freeze
**4** to act upon (a person or a person's feelings) so as to cause a response — see [1]AFFECT 1
**5** to rouse to strong feeling or action — see PROVOKE 1
**6** to cause (someone) to agree with a belief or course of action by using arguments or earnest requests — see PERSUADE
**7** to cause to function — see ACTIVATE
**8** to leave a place often for another — see GO 2

**movement** *n* **1** the act or an instance of changing position ⟨a sudden *movement* in the far corner of the room made her turn in that direction⟩
***syn*** motion, move, shift, shifting, stir, stirring

*rel* dislocation, migration, relocation; locomotion, mobility, motility; fiddling, fidgeting, squirming, twitching, wriggling, writhing; flailing, flapping, waving
*near ant* immobility; inertia, inertness, stillness; ending, finish, halt, pause, stop, termination
*ant* motionlessness
**2** a series of activities undertaken to achieve a goal — see CAMPAIGN

**movie** *n* **1** a story told by means of a series of continuously projected pictures and a sound track ⟨there was much excitement when it was announced that the popular children's book would be turned into a *movie*⟩
*syn* film, motion picture, moving picture, picture
*rel* animated cartoon, cartoon, docudrama, documentary, feature
**2 movies** *pl* the art or business of making a movie ⟨many a small-town girl has gone to Hollywood, dreaming of making it big in the *movies*⟩
*syn* cinema, film, motion pictures, pictures, screen
*rel* show business

**moving** *adj* having the power to affect the feelings or sympathies ⟨he gave a truly *moving* graduation speech that had some graduates in tears⟩
*syn* affecting, emotional, impressive, poignant, stirring, touching
*rel* eloquent, expressive, meaningful, significant; demonstrative, excitable, feeling, passionate, responsive, sensitive; exciting, provoking, rousing, stimulating; dramatic, histrionic, melodramatic, theatrical
*near ant* cold, cool, detached, dispassionate; deadpan
*ant* unemotional, unimpressive

**moving picture** *n* a story told by means of a series of continuously projected pictures and a sound track — see MOVIE 1

**mow** *vb* **1** to shorten the standing leafy plant cover of ⟨you really should *mow* the lawn before it gets much higher⟩
*syn* cut
*rel* clip, crop, dock, lop, manicure, pare, prune, trim; shave, shear
**2** to bring down by cutting — see FELL 2

**mow** (down) *vb* to kill on a large scale — see MASSACRE

**much** *adv* **1** to a great degree — see VERY 1
**2** to a large extent or degree — see GREATLY 2
**3** very close to but not completely — see ALMOST

**much** *n* a considerable amount — see LOT 2

**muck** *n* **1** foul matter that mars the purity or cleanliness of something — see FILTH 1
**2** soft wet earth — see MUD

**mucky** *adj* **1** full of or covered with soft wet earth — see MUDDY 1
**2** not clean — see DIRTY 1

**mud** *n* soft wet earth ⟨we cannot play softball today because the field turned to *mud* after last night's heavy rain⟩
*syn* mire, muck, ooze, slime, slop, sludge, slush
*rel* gumbo, silt; clay, dirt, gravel, humus, loam, sand, soil

**muddle** *n* **1** a state in which everything is out of order — see CHAOS
**2** a state of mental confusion — see HAZE 2
**3** a state of mental uncertainty — see CONFUSION 1
**4** an unorganized collection or mixture of various things — see MISCELLANY 1

**muddle** *vb* **1** to throw into a state of mental uncertainty — see CONFUSE 1
**2** to undo the proper order or arrangement of — see DISORDER

**muddled** *adj* lacking in order, neatness, and often cleanliness — see MESSY

**muddy** *adj* **1** full of or covered with soft wet earth ⟨please do not walk in the house with *muddy* boots on, as you will get the carpet dirty⟩
*syn* miry, mucky, oozy, slimy, sludgy, slushy
*rel* clayey, loamy, silty; bedraggled; dirty, filthy, foul, grimy, grubby, grungy, impure, squalid, unclean, uncleanly
*near ant* clean, cleanly, immaculate, spotless, unsoiled, unsullied
**2** having visible particles in liquid suspension — see CLOUDY 1
**3** not clean — see DIRTY 1

**muddy** *vb* **1** to throw into a state of mental uncertainty — see CONFUSE 1
**2** to make (something) unclear to the understanding — see CONFUSE 2
**3** to make dirty — see DIRTY

**muff** *vb* to make or do (something) in a clumsy or unskillful way — see BOTCH

**muffle** *vb* to deaden the sound of ⟨the walls *muffled* their conversation so that only a low murmur was heard⟩
*syn* mute
*rel* insulate, soundproof; dampen, mellow, soften, subdue, tone (down); baffle; smother
*near ant* amplify, enhance, heighten, increase, magnify, strengthen

**mug** *n* **1** a round vessel equipped with a handle and designed for drinking — see CUP
**2** a violent, brutal person who is often a member of an organized gang — see HOODLUM
**3** the front part of the head — see FACE 1
**4** the opening through which food passes into the body of an animal — see MOUTH 1

**mug** *vb* **1** to distort one's face ⟨every time their picture was snapped, both children *mugged* by sticking out their tongues or scrunching up their faces⟩
*syn* grimace
*rel* pout; contort, deform, twist, warp; frown, glare, gloom, glower, lower (*also* lour), scowl; gape, gaze, ogle, stare; growl, snarl, sneer; simper, smirk

***phrases*** make faces
***near ant*** beam, grin, smile
**2** to take a photograph of — see PHOTOGRAPH

**muggy** *adj* containing or characterized by an uncomfortable amount of moisture — see HUMID

**mulct** *n* a sum of money to be paid as a punishment — see FINE

**mulct** *vb* to rob by the use of trickery or threats — see FLEECE

**mulish** *adj* sticking to an opinion, purpose, or course of action in spite of reason, arguments, or persuasion — see OBSTINATE

**mulishness** *n* a steadfast adherence to an opinion, purpose, or course of action — see OBSTINACY

**mull** (over) *vb* to give serious and careful thought to — see PONDER

**multicolored** *adj* marked by a variety of usually vivid colors — see COLORFUL

**multifarious** *adj* being of many and various kinds — see MANIFOLD

**multiple** *adj* being of a large but indefinite number — see MANY

**multiplex** *adj* being of a large but indefinite number — see MANY

**multiplication** *n* the act or process of becoming greater in number ⟨there's been a steady *multiplication* in our attic of old video equipment since the revolution in consumer electronics⟩
***syn*** accumulating, accumulation, addition, increase, proliferation
***rel*** doubling, quadrupling, tripling; growth, rise, spread; enlargement, escalation, expansion; amplification, distention, inflation; accretion, accrual, augmentation; extension, lengthening
***near ant*** compressing, compression, condensation, condensing, constricting, constriction, contracting, contraction, diminishing, diminishment, lessening, lowering, shrinking; retrenching, retrenchment, shortening
***ant*** decrease

**multiply** *vb* **1** to bring forth offspring — see PROCREATE
**2** to make greater in size, amount, or number — see INCREASE 1
**3** to become greater in extent, volume, amount, or number — see INCREASE 2

**multitude** *n* a great number of persons or things gathered together — see CROWD 1

**multitudinous** *adj* being of a large but indefinite number — see MANY

**mum** *n, chiefly British* a female human parent — see MOTHER

**mum** *adj* deliberately refraining from speech — see SILENT 1

**mumble** *n* speech that is not clear enough to be understood ⟨please answer the question without your usual *mumble* and try to use complete sentences⟩
***syn*** grunt, grunting, murmur, murmuring, mutter, muttering
***rel*** undertone, whisper; babble, babbling, blab, blabbing, chatter, chattering, drivel, driveling (*or* drivelling), gabble, gabbling, jabber, jabbering, maundering, prattle, prattling, rambling

**mumble** *vb* to speak softly and unclearly ⟨I can't understand you if you *mumble*⟩
***syn*** grunt, mouth, murmur, mutter
***rel*** babble, blab, chatter, drivel, gabble, gibber, jabber, maunder, prattle, ramble; breathe, gasp, pant, whisper
***near ant*** articulate, enunciate
***ant*** speak out, speak up

**mumbo jumbo** *n* unintelligible or meaningless talk — see GIBBERISH

**mummer** *n* **1** an actor in a story performed silently and entirely by body movements — see MIME
**2** one who acts professionally (as in a play, movie, or television show) — see ACTOR

**mundane** *adj* **1** having to do with the practical details of regular life ⟨they didn't want to be bothered with *mundane* concerns like doing the dishes while on vacation⟩
***syn*** everyday, prosaic, workaday
***rel*** earthly, temporal, worldly; average, common, commonplace, customary, familiar, garden, normal, ordinary, plain, popular, routine, run-of-the-mill, typical, unexceptional, unremarkable, usual; frequent, habitual, regular; expected, predictable
***near ant*** high-minded, lofty, noble, sublime; aberrant, abnormal, atypical; exceptional, extraordinary, odd, peculiar, phenomenal, rare, singular, special, uncommon, uncustomary, unique, unusual, unwonted; bizarre, curious, funny, odd, outlandish, quaint, remarkable, strange, weird
**2** having to do with life on earth especially as opposed to that in heaven — see EARTHLY

**municipality** *n* a thickly settled, highly populated area — see CITY

**munificent** *adj* giving or sharing in abundance and without hesitation — see GENEROUS 1

**munificently** *adv* in a generous manner — see WELL 2

**murder** *n* **1** a situation or state that causes great suffering and unhappiness — see HELL 2
**2** the intentional and unlawful taking of another person's life — see HOMICIDE

**murder** *vb* **1** to put to death deliberately ⟨those people made me so mad I felt like I wanted to *murder* them⟩
***syn*** dispatch, do in, execute, liquidate, slay
***rel*** blot out, destroy, fell, kill, smite, zap; assassinate; butcher, massacre, mow (down), slaughter; annihilate, eliminate, eradicate, exterminate, wipe out
***phrases*** do away with
**2** to make or do (something) in a clumsy or unskillful way — see BOTCH

**murderer** *n* a person who kills another person — see ASSASSIN

**murdering** *adj* eager for or marked by the shedding of blood, extreme violence, or killing — see BLOODTHIRSTY
**murderous** *adj* 1 difficult to endure — see HARSH 1
2 requiring considerable physical or mental effort — see HARD 2
3 likely to cause or capable of causing death — see DEADLY
4 eager for or marked by the shedding of blood, extreme violence, or killing — see BLOODTHIRSTY
**murk** *n* 1 a time or place of little or no light — see DARK 1
2 an atmospheric condition in which suspended particles in the air rob it of its transparency — see HAZE 1
**murkiness** *n* the quality or state of having a veiled or uncertain meaning — see OBSCURITY 1
**murky** *adj* 1 being without light or without much light — see DARK 1
2 causing or marked by an atmosphere lacking in cheer — see GLOOMY 1
3 filled with or dimmed by fine particles (as of dust or water) in suspension — see HAZY 1
4 having an often intentionally veiled or uncertain meaning — see OBSCURE 1
5 not seen or understood clearly — see FAINT 1
**murmur** *n* 1 an expression of dissatisfaction, pain, or resentment — see COMPLAINT 1
2 speech that is not clear enough to be understood — see MUMBLE
**murmur** *vb* 1 to express dissatisfaction, pain, or resentment usually tiresomely — see COMPLAIN
2 to speak softly and unclearly — see MUMBLE
**murmurer** *n* an irritable and complaining person — see GROUCH
**murmuring** *n* speech that is not clear enough to be understood — see MUMBLE
**muscle** *n* 1 muscular strength ⟨I'm going to need someone with real *muscle* to help me move all this furniture⟩
***syn*** brawn, main
***rel*** force, might, potency, power, puissance, sinew
***near ant*** impotence, weakness
2 the ability to exert effort for the accomplishment of a task — see POWER 2
**muscle** *vb* 1 to cause (a person) to give in to pressure — see FORCE
2 to force one's way — see PRESS 4
**muscular** *adj* 1 marked by a well-developed musculature ⟨Olympic runners tend to have very *muscular* legs⟩
***syn*** brawny, sinewy
***rel*** wiry; powerful, strong; beefy, burly, hefty, hulking, husky; able-bodied, athletic, herculean, mighty, robust, rugged, stalwart, strapping, sturdy
***near ant*** nonathletic; delicate, feeble, fragile, frail, weak, weakly, wimpy; light, lightweight, slight; lean, slender, slim, svelte, sylphlike, thin, willowy; emaciated, gaunt, lank, rawboned, spare
***ant*** scrawny, skinny
2 having muscles capable of exerting great physical force — see STRONG 1
**museum** *n* a building or part of a building in which objects of interest are displayed ⟨we're taking a trip to the *Museum* of Natural History as a special treat for science class⟩
***syn*** gallery, salon
***rel*** archives, collection, library; display, exhibition; studio
**mush** *n* 1 something (as a work of literature or music) that is too sentimental — see CORN
2 the state or quality of having an excess of tender feelings (as of love, nostalgia, or compassion) — see SENTIMENTALITY
**mushroom** *vb* to become greater in extent, volume, amount, or number — see INCREASE 2
**mushy** *adj* 1 appealing to the emotions in an obvious and tiresome way — see CORNY
2 giving easily to the touch — see SOFT 3
**musical** *adj* 1 having a pleasantly flowing quality suggestive of music — see LYRIC 1
2 having a pleasing mixture of notes — see HARMONIOUS 1
**musicale** *n* an entertainment featuring singing or the playing of musical instruments — see CONCERT
**musician** *n* 1 a person who plays a musical instrument ⟨the violinist was a famous and exquisitely talented *musician*⟩
***syn*** instrumentalist, player
***rel*** artist, performer; maestro, virtuoso; accompanist, recitalist, soloist; accordionist, bassoonist, clarinetist (*or* clarinettist), cornetist (*or* cornettist), drummer, fiddler, flautist, flutist, guitarist, harpist, oboist, organ-grinder, organist, percussionist, pianist, piper, saxophonist, trombonist, trumpeter, violinist
2 a person who writes musical compositions — see COMPOSER
**muskeg** *n* spongy land saturated or partially covered with water — see SWAMP
**muss** *vb* to undo the proper order or arrangement of — see DISORDER
**mussed** *adj* lacking in order, neatness, and often cleanliness — see MESSY
**mussy** *adj* lacking in order, neatness, and often cleanliness — see MESSY
**must** *n* something necessary, indispensable, or unavoidable — see ESSENTIAL 1
**must** *vb* to be under necessity or obligation to — see NEED 2
**muster** *n* a body of people come together in one place — see GATHERING 1
**muster** *vb* 1 to assemble and make ready for action — see MOBILIZE
2 to bring together in assembly by or as if by command — see CONVOKE
**muster out** *vb* to let go from office, service, or employment — see DISMISS 1
**musty** *adj* 1 having an unpleasant smell — see MALODOROUS
2 used or heard so often as to be dull — see STALE

**mutable** *adj* likely to change frequently, suddenly, or unexpectedly — see FICKLE 1

**mutate** *vb* to pass from one form, state, or level to another — see CHANGE 2

**mute** *adj* **1** unable to speak ⟨the child is both deaf and *mute* because her hearing was lost at birth⟩
*syn* inarticulate, speechless, voiceless
*rel* tongue-tied; incoherent, incomprehensible; closemouthed, laconic, taciturn, tight-lipped, uncommunicative; mum, nonspeaking, quiet, silent, wordless
*near ant* communicative, gabby, garrulous, loquacious, talkative, talky, vocal; expatiating, speaking out, speaking up; articulating, speaking, talking; articulate, eloquent, fluent, voluble
**2** deliberately refraining from speech — see SILENT 1

**mute** *n* a device on a musical instrument that deadens or softens its tone ⟨I got in trouble for practicing my trumpet at three in the morning when the *mute* fell out, and I woke everyone up⟩
*syn* damper
*rel* muffler, quieter, softener

**mute** *vb* **1** to stop the noise or speech of — see SILENCE 1
**2** to deaden the sound of — see MUFFLE

**muted** *adj* **1** mostly or entirely without sound — see SILENT 3
**2** not excessively showy — see QUIET 2

**muteness** *n* incapacity for or restraint from speaking — see SILENCE 1

**mutilate** *vb* to cause severe or permanent injury to — see MAIM

**mutineer** *n* a person who rises up against authority — see REBEL

**mutinous** *adj* taking part in a rebellion — see REBELLIOUS 1

**mutiny** *n* open fighting against authority (as one's own government) — see REBELLION

**mutiny** *vb* to rise up against established authority — see REBEL

**mutter** *n* speech that is not clear enough to be understood — see MUMBLE

**mutter** *vb* **1** to express dissatisfaction, pain, or resentment usually tiresomely — see COMPLAIN
**2** to speak softly and unclearly — see MUMBLE

**mutterer** *n* an irritable and complaining person — see GROUCH

**muttering** *n* speech that is not clear enough to be understood — see MUMBLE

**mutual** *adj* used or done by a number of people as a group — see COLLECTIVE

**myopic** *adj* **1** able to see near things more clearly than distant ones — see NEARSIGHTED
**2** not thinking about and providing for the future — see IMPROVIDENT

**myriad** *adj* being of many and various kinds — see MANIFOLD

---

*syn* synonym(s) *rel* related words
*ant* antonym(s) *near ant* near antonym(s)

**mysterious** *adj* **1** being beyond one's powers to know, understand, or explain ⟨the huge stone statues on Easter Island are ancient, *mysterious*, and haunting⟩
*syn* cryptic, darkling, deep, enigmatic (*also* enigmatical), impenetrable, inscrutable, mystic, occult, uncanny
*rel* dark, murky, obscure, shadowy, vague; ambiguous, equivocal; incomprehensible, unfathomable, unintelligible; inexplicable, unaccountable, unexplainable; unanswerable, unknowable; metaphysical, mystical, supernatural; abstruse, esoteric, recondite; baffling, bewildering, confounding, confusing, mystifying, perplexing, puzzling
*near ant* fathomable, intelligible, understandable; clear, obvious, open-and-shut, plain, straightforward, transparent
**2** having an often intentionally veiled or uncertain meaning — see OBSCURE 1

**mystery** *n* something hard to understand or explain ⟨why my sister dyed her hair bright blue is still a *mystery* to my parents⟩
*syn* conundrum, enigma, mystification, puzzle, puzzlement, riddle, secret
*rel* brainteaser, challenge, perplexity, poser, problem, stumper

**mystic** *adj* **1** having seemingly supernatural qualities or powers ⟨the notion that a cat has nine lives is based upon the belief that nine is a *mystic* number⟩
*syn* magic, magical, occult, weird
*rel* bewitched, enchanted, spellbound; bewitching, charming, conjuring, enchanting, wiling; awesome, extraordinary, marvelous (*or* marvellous), wondrous; divining, forecasting, foreknowing, fore-seeing, foretelling, fortune-telling, pre-dicting, presaging, prognosticating, prophesying, soothsaying
*near ant* commonplace, ordinary, unremarkable
**2** being beyond one's powers to know, understand, or explain — see MYSTERIOUS 1
**3** having an often intentionally veiled or uncertain meaning — see OBSCURE 1

**mystification** *n* **1** a state of mental uncertainty — see CONFUSION 1
**2** something hard to understand or explain — see MYSTERY

**mystify** *vb* to throw into a state of mental uncertainty — see CONFUSE 1

**myth** *n* **1** a traditional but unfounded story that gives the reason for a current custom, belief, or fact of nature ⟨according to an ancient Greek *myth*, humans acquired fire from a giant who had stolen it from heaven⟩
*syn* fable, legend
*rel* allegory, parable; fabrication, fantasy (*also* phantasy), fiction, figment, invention; narrative, saga, story, tale, yarn
**2** the body of customs, beliefs, stories, and sayings associated with a people, thing, or place — see FOLKLORE
**3** a false idea or belief — see FALLACY 1

**mythical** *or* **mythic** *adj* **1** based on, described in, or being a myth ⟨for years the

Spanish conquistadors searched for the *mythical* El Dorado, a place of unimaginable riches〉
***syn*** fabled, fabulous, legendary
***rel*** famed, romanticized, storied; fabricated, fantastic, fantastical, fictional, fictitious; fanciful; allegorical, mythological
***near ant*** actual, real; historical; factual, true
**2** not real and existing only in the imagination — see IMAGINARY
**mythology** *n* the body of customs, beliefs, stories, and sayings associated with a people, thing, or place — see FOLKLORE

# N

**nab** *vb* **1** to take or keep under one's control by authority of law — see ARREST 1
**2** to take physical control or possession of (something) suddenly or forcibly — see CATCH 1
**nag** *n* a large hoofed domestic animal that is used for carrying or drawing loads and for riding — see HORSE
**nag** *vb* to subject (someone) to constant scoldings and sharp reminders 〈she kept *nagging* him to fix the furnace before the weather got any colder〉
***syn*** henpeck, hound, needle
***rel*** carp (at), fuss (about *or* over), nitpick; annoy, badger, bait, bother, bug, chivy, harass, harry, hassle, irk, pester, plague, ride, vex, yap (at); egg, goad, incite, prod, prompt, spur, urge; exhort, insist, press, pressure, push; blandish, cajole, coax, wheedle; beg, importune, plead
***near ant*** compliment; commend, laud, praise, recommend, tout; acclaim, applaud, eulogize, extol (*also* extoll)
**naiad** *n* **1** a mythical goddess represented as a young girl and said to live outdoors — see NYMPH 1
**2** a young wingless often wormlike form (as a grub or caterpillar) that hatches from the egg of many insects — see LARVA
**nail** *vb* to take physical control or possession of (something) suddenly or forcibly — see CATCH 1
**naive** *or* **naïve** *adj* **1** lacking in worldly wisdom or informed judgment 〈a first-time buyer who was so *naive* that he believed the salesman and paid good money for the rusty and broken-down car〉
***syn*** green, ingenuous, innocent, simple, simpleminded, uncritical, unknowing, unsophisticated, unsuspecting, unsuspicious, unwary, unworldly, wide-eyed
***rel*** callow, dewy, inexperienced, raw; childlike, idealistic, impractical; believing, credulous, gullible, susceptible, trustful, trusting, unguarded; beguiled, duped, gulled, tricked; careless, heedless
***near ant*** critical, doubting, incredulous, skeptical, suspecting, suspicious, unconvinced; careful, cautious, guarded, leery, wary, watchful; down-to-earth, hardheaded, pragmatic (*also* pragmatical), realistic, sober
***ant*** cynical, experienced, knowing, sophisticated, worldly, worldly-wise
**2** free from any intent to deceive or impress others — see GUILELESS
**3** readily taken advantage of — see EASY 2
**naively** *adv* without any attempt to impress by deception or exaggeration — see NATURALLY 3
**naïveté** *also* **naïvete** *n* **1** the quality or state of being simple and sincere 〈her *naïveté* led her to leave her new bike outside the mall unchained while she shopped〉
***syn*** artlessness, greenness, guilelessness, ingenuousness, innocence, naturalness, simpleness, simplicity, unsophistication, unworldliness
***rel*** candor, frankness, genuineness, honesty, openness, sincerity, straightforwardness; callowness, childishness, inexperience, rawness; carelessness, heedlessness; ignorance, obliviousness, unawareness; credulity, credulousness, gullibility; idealism, impracticality, optimism
***near ant*** affectedness, artificiality, pretentiousness; deviousness, dishonesty, insincerity; disbelief, doubtfulness, incredulity, suspiciousness; carefulness, caution, wariness; pessimism, skepticism; maturity
***ant*** artfulness, cynicism, sophistication, worldliness
**2** readiness to believe the claims of others without sufficient evidence — see CREDULITY
**naked** *adj* **1** lacking or shed of clothing 〈had recurrent nightmares about being *naked* in public〉
***syn*** bare, disrobed, nude, stripped, unclad, unclothed, undressed
***rel*** denuded, peeled; raw, stark; unveiled
***near ant*** covered, veiled; arrayed, caparisoned, decked (out), rigged (out), tricked (out); vested; decent
***ant*** appareled (*or* apparelled), attired, clad, clothed, dressed, garbed, invested, robed, suited
**2** lacking a usual or natural covering 〈the winter trees were *naked* without their colorful fall leaves〉
***syn*** bald, bare, denuded, exposed, open, peeled, stripped, uncovered

*rel* displayed, revealed; hairless, shaven; disrobed, unclad, unclothed, undressed; skinned; divested; unprotected, unsheltered
*near ant* mantled; overgrown, overrun, overspread; bearded, hairy
*ant* covered
**3** free from all additions or embellishment — see PLAIN 1

**name** *adj* having a good reputation especially in a field of knowledge — see RESPECTABLE 1

**name** *n* **1** a word or combination of words by which a person or thing is regularly known ⟨introduced himself and then asked what my *name* was⟩
*syn* appellation, cognomen, denomination, denotation, designation, handle, title
*rel* christian name, forename, given name; family name, maiden name, surname; epithet, nickname, sobriquet (*also* soubriquet); alias, nom de plume, pen name, pseudonym; binomial, vernacular; misnomer; label, trademark
**2** an act or expression showing scorn and usually intended to hurt another's feelings — see INSULT
**3** outward and often deceptive indication — see APPEARANCE 2
**4** overall quality as seen or judged by people in general — see REPUTATION

**name** *vb* **1** to give a name to ⟨decided to *name* her new puppy "Bubbles"⟩
*syn* baptize, call, christen, denominate, designate, dub, entitle, label, style, term, title
*rel* denote, specify; miscall, misname; nickname; rename
**2** to make reference to or speak about briefly but specifically — see MENTION 1
**3** to pick (someone) by one's authority for a specific position or duty — see APPOINT 2
**4** to decide to accept (someone or something) from a group of possibilities — see CHOOSE 1
**5** to decide upon (the time or date for an event) usually from a position of authority — see APPOINT 1

**nameless** *adj* **1** not named or identified by a name ⟨the victim of the crime will remain *nameless* to protect his privacy⟩ ⟨*nameless* editors who write TV listings in the newspaper⟩
*syn* anonymous, incognito, unbaptized, unchristened, unidentified, unnamed, untitled
*rel* unspecified; obscure, uncelebrated, unheard-of, unknown, unnoted, unremarkable
*near ant* denominated, designated, specified; labeled (*or* labelled), tabbed, titled; celebrated, famed, famous, known, notable, noted, noteworthy, remarkable, renowned, well-known
*ant* baptized, christened, dubbed, named, termed
**2** beyond the power to describe — see INDESCRIBABLE
**3** not widely known — see OBSCURE 2

**namer** *n* someone with the right or responsibility for making a selection — see SELECTOR

**[1]nap** *n* a short sleep ⟨so tired that she needed to take a refreshing *nap* before soccer practice⟩
*syn* catnap, doze, drowse, forty winks, siesta, snooze, wink
*rel* repose, rest; slumber; bed

**[2]nap** *n* a soft airy substance or covering — see FUZZ

**nap** *vb* **1** to sleep lightly or briefly ⟨decided to let the kids *nap* for a few more minutes before waking them⟩
*syn* catnap, doze, drowse, slumber, snooze
*rel* relax, repose, rest; couch, lay, lie, roost; lull
*near ant* arise, arouse, awake, awaken, get up, rise, rouse, uprise, wake (up), waken
**2** be in a state of sleep — see SLEEP 1

**napping** *adj* being in a state of suspended consciousness — see ASLEEP 1

**napping** *n* a natural periodic loss of consciousness during which the body restores itself — see SLEEP 1

**narcotic** *adj* **1** tending to calm the emotions and relieve stress — see SOOTHING 1
**2** tending to cause sleep — see HYPNOTIC

**narrate** *vb* to give an oral or written account of in some detail — see TELL 1

**narrative** *n* **1** a relating of events usually in the order in which they happened — see ACCOUNT 1
**2** a work with imaginary characters and events that is shorter and usually less complex than a novel — see STORY 1

**narrow** *adj* **1** being of less than usual width ⟨found a *narrow* opening in the fence that he was able to squeeze through⟩
*syn* fine, hairline, needlelike, skinny, slender, slim, thin
*rel* attenuated, elongated, linear; close, compressed, condensed, constricted, contracted, squeezed, tight, tightened; reedy, stalky, stringy, twiggy, wispy; spare
*near ant* chunky, squat, stocky, stumpy, thick, thickset; bulky, massive
*ant* broad, fat, wide
**2** not broad or open in views or opinions ⟨a *narrow* person who thought that anyone who owned a television was morally corrupt⟩
*syn* insular, little, parochial, petty, provincial, sectarian, small, small-minded
*rel* inflexible, obdurate, obstinate, rigid, set, stubborn, unyielding, wrongheaded; bigoted, intolerant, narrow-minded; biased, discriminating, discriminatory, jaundiced, one-sided, partial, partisan, prejudiced; old-fashioned, reactionary, stodgy, straitlaced (*or* straightlaced); dogmatic, opinionated; limited
*near ant* impartial, nonpartisan, objective, unbiased, unprejudiced

---

*syn* synonym(s) *rel* related words
*ant* antonym(s) *near ant* near antonym(s)

***ant*** broad-minded, catholic, cosmopolitan, liberal, open, open-minded, receptive, tolerant

**3** having distinct or certain limits — see LIMITED 1

**4** showing little difference in the standing of the competitors — see CLOSE 3

**5** unwilling to grant other people social rights or to accept other viewpoints — see INTOLERANT 2

**narrow-minded** *adj* unwilling to grant other people social rights or to accept other viewpoints — see INTOLERANT 2

**narrows** *n pl* a narrow body of water between two land masses — see CHANNEL 2

**nastily** *adv* in a mean or spiteful manner ⟨he *nastily* stuck his foot out and tripped the front runner because he couldn't stand to see her win⟩

***syn*** cattily, despitefully, hatefully, malevolently, maliciously, malignantly, meanly, spitefully, viciously, villainously, virulently, wickedly

***rel*** contemptuously, deprecatingly, disdainfully, scornfully; acrimoniously, antagonistically, caustically, hostilely, invidiously, obnoxiously, rancorously, venomously; bitterly, enviously, jealously, resentfully; balefully, callously, cruelly, hardheartedly, heartlessly, inhumanely, mercilessly, pitilessly, ruthlessly, soullessly, unfeelingly; disagreeably, ill, ungraciously, unkindly; ill-naturedly, inconsiderately, insensitively, thoughtlessly; diabolically, fiendishly; misanthropically

***near ant*** affably, agreeably, amiably, cordially, genially, good-humoredly, good-naturedly, graciously, nicely, pleasantly; altruistically, humanely; considerately, feelingly, lovingly, mercifully, sensitively, softheartedly, solicitously, soulfully, thoughtfully; compassionately, sympathetically; angelically, divinely, sweetly, tenderly

***ant*** benevolently, benignantly, goodheartedly, kindheartedly, kindly

**nastiness** *n* **1** the desire to cause pain for the satisfaction of doing harm — see MALICE

**2** the quality or state of being obscene — see OBSCENITY 1

**3** the state or quality of being dirty — see DIRTINESS 1

**nasty** *adj* **1** arousing or deserving of one's loathing and disgust — see CONTEMPTIBLE 1

**2** causing intense displeasure, disgust, or resentment — see OFFENSIVE 1

**3** causing or feeling bodily pain — see PAINFUL 1

**4** depicting or referring to sexual matters in a way that is unacceptable in polite society — see OBSCENE 1

**5** having or showing a desire to cause someone pain or suffering for the sheer enjoyment of it — see HATEFUL

**6** marked by wet and windy conditions — see FOUL 1

**7** not clean — see DIRTY 1

**8** not giving pleasure to the mind or senses — see UNPLEASANT

**nation** *n* a body of people composed of one or more nationalities usually with its own territory and government ⟨the American people became one *nation* when they adopted the Constitution in 1789⟩

***syn*** commonwealth, country, land, sovereignty, state

***rel*** city-state; domain, dominion, empire, kingdom, realm, republic; duchy, dukedom, principality, seigniory (*or* seignory), sultanate; democracy, dictatorship, monarchy, oligarchy, sovereign, theocracy; colony, dependency, province, settlement, soil; fatherland, homeland, motherland; power, superpower

**national** *adj* of or relating to a nation ⟨played the home team's *national* anthem before the start of the soccer game⟩

***syn*** civil, public, state

***rel*** civic, federal, municipal; government, governmental; domestic, internal; democratic, republican; nationwide

***near ant*** global, international; alien, external, foreign

***ant*** nonnational

**national** *n* a person who owes allegiance to a government and is protected by it — see CITIZEN 1

**nationalism** *n* **1** excessive favoritism towards one's own country — see CHAUVINISM

**2** love and support for one's country — see PATRIOTISM

**nationalist** *adj* having or showing love and support for one's country — see PATRIOTIC

**nationalist** *n* one who shows excessive favoritism towards his or her country ⟨a staunch *nationalist* who favored any policy that would give the country more power in the international arena⟩

***syn*** chauvinist, jingo

***rel*** loyalist, patriot; hawk, warmonger

***near ant*** internationalist; neutralist

**nationalistic** *adj* having or showing love and support for one's country — see PATRIOTIC

**native** *adj* **1** belonging to a particular place by birth or origin ⟨though she now lived in the Northeast, she was a *native* Midwesterner⟩

***syn*** aboriginal, born, endemic, indigenous

***rel*** domestic, local; original

***near ant*** imported, introduced, transplanted; alien, exotic, foreign, strange; expatriate, immigrant

***ant*** nonnative

**2** being such as found in nature and not altered by processing or refining — see CRUDE 1

**Native American** *n* a member of any of the native peoples of the western hemisphere usually not including the Eskimos — see AMERICAN INDIAN

**nativity** *n* the act or instance of being born — see BIRTH 1

**nattily** *adv* in a strikingly neat and trim manner — see SMARTLY

**natty** *adj* being strikingly neat and trim in style or appearance — see SMART 1

**natural** *adj* **1** being such from birth or by nature ⟨from his first visits to the wading pool, we could tell he loved water and was a *natural* swimmer⟩
*syn* born, congenital
*rel* chronic, confirmed, habitual, ingrained, inveterate, proper, regular; constitutional, consummate; elemental, elementary, essential, hereditary, inborn, inherent, innate, intimate, intrinsic, native; instinctual, intuitive
*near ant* cultivated, developed, trained; alien, foreign, unnatural
*ant* nonnatural
**2** closely resembling the object imitated ⟨the display of stuffed birds and plastic plants actually looked very *natural*⟩
*syn* lifelike, near, realistic
*rel* alike, like, living, matching; akin, analogous, approximate, comparable, resembling; accurate, close, faithful, true; convincing
*near ant* dissimilar, off, unalike, unlike; incomparable, unmatched; contrasted, contrasting, different, disparate; fake, mock, phony (*also* phoney), sham
*ant* nonnatural, nonrealistic, unrealistic
**3** being a part of the innermost nature of a person or thing — see INHERENT
**4** being such as found in nature and not altered by processing or refining — see CRUDE 1
**5** existing without human habitation or cultivation — see WILD 2
**6** free from any intent to deceive or impress others — see GUILELESS
**7** relating to or characteristic of human beings — see HUMAN

**naturally** *adv* **1** by natural character or ability ⟨tour guides who are *naturally* outgoing and can easily approach and converse with strangers⟩
*syn* constitutionally, inherently, innately, intrinsically
*rel* elementally, essentially, fundamentally; instinctively, intuitively; intimately
*near ant* artificially, unnaturally
**2** according to the usual course of things ⟨we *naturally* like to be as comfortable as possible⟩
*syn* commonly, generally, normally, ordinarily, typically, usually
*rel* customarily, habitually, regularly, routinely; familiarly; conventionally, traditionally
*phrases* of course
*near ant* oddly, peculiarly, queerly, strangely; anomalously, irregularly; radically
*ant* abnormally, atypically, extraordinarily, uncommonly, unusually
**3** without any attempt to impress by deception or exaggeration ⟨he tried to act *naturally* around the girl he had a crush on⟩
*syn* artlessly, guilelessly, ingenuously, innocently, naively, sincerely, unaffectedly, unfeignedly, unpretentiously
*rel* genuinely, honestly, simply, truly; freely, openheartedly, openly; candidly, frankly, matter-of-factly; informally, relaxedly, unceremoniously
*near ant* artfully, cannily, deceitfully, deceptively, deviously, dishonestly, falsely; archly, calculatingly, craftily, cunningly, furtively, insidiously, sharply, shiftily, slickly, slyly, underhand, underhanded, underhandedly; flatteringly, sycophantically, unctuously
*ant* affectedly, artificially, hypocritically, insincerely, pretentiously, unnaturally

**naturalness** *n* **1** carefree freedom from constraint — see ABANDON
**2** the quality or state of being simple and sincere — see NAÏVETÉ 1

**nature** *n* **1** the set of qualities that makes a person, a group of people, or a thing different from others ⟨it was the violent *nature* of his stories that got them banned from school libraries⟩ ⟨her *nature* was such that lying was never an option for her⟩ ⟨the stoic *nature* of these people enables them to endure one calamity after another⟩
*syn* character, complexion, constitution, genius, personality, tone
*rel* distinctiveness, distinctness, individuality, singularity, uniqueness; attribute, characteristic, earmark, feature, flavor, hallmark, mark, point, property, savor, stamp, trait; disposition, grain, sort, temper, temperament; composition, makeup; essence, essentiality, soul, spirit, stuff, substance; habit, way
**2** that part of the physical world that is removed from human habitation ⟨needed to get out of the office and be out in *nature* to clear his head⟩
*syn* open, open air, outdoors, out-of-doors, wild, wilderness
*rel* backwoods, bush, country, frontier, hinterland, sticks, up-country; outside, without; badland, barren, desert, waste, wasteland
**3** a number of persons or things that are grouped together because they have something in common — see SORT 1
**4** one's characteristic attitude or mood — see DISPOSITION 1
**5** the quality or qualities that make a thing what it is — see ESSENCE
**6** the whole body of things observed or assumed — see UNIVERSE

**naught** *also* **nought** *n* the numerical symbol 0 or the absence of number or quantity represented by it — see ZERO 1

**naughty** *adj* engaging in or marked by childish misbehavior ⟨told her to act her age and stop throwing temper tantrums like a *naughty* little girl⟩
*syn* bad, contrary, errant, froward, misbehaving, mischievous

---

*syn* synonym(s) *rel* related words
*ant* antonym(s) *near ant* near antonym(s)

***rel*** defiant, disrespectful, ill-mannered, ill-natured, impolite, improper, impudent, indecorous, insolent, rude, uncouth, unmannerly; disobedient, headstrong, intractable, obstreperous, recalcitrant, refractory, transgressing, unruly, untoward, willful (*or* wilful); balky, restive, uncontrollable, ungovernable, wayward, wild; arch, elfish, impish, monkeying, monkeyish, ornery, pixieish, prankish, rascally, roguish, waggish; dissolute, perverse, wrongheaded; disorderly, rowdy, ruffianly; corrupt, evil, wicked; insurgent, mutinous, rebellious; disobliging, inconsiderate, selfish, thoughtless, unkind, unkindly; babyish, childish, immature, infantile, puerile

***near ant*** acquiescent, compliant, complying, dutiful, obedient, submissive; clean, correct, decent, decorous, moral, proper, respectable; considerate, courteous, kindly, mannerly, polite, thoughtful; angelic, divine, heavenly; amenable, docile, governable, tractable; amiable, complaisant, good-natured, obliging, pleasant; discreet, modest; grown-up, mature

***ant*** behaved, behaving, nice, orderly

**nausea** *n* **1** a disturbed condition of the stomach in which one feels like vomiting ⟨symptoms include fever accompanied by a loss of appetite and *nausea*⟩

***syn*** qualmishness, queasiness, queerness, sickness, squeamishness

***rel*** qualm; airsickness, morning sickness, motion sickness, seasickness

**2** a dislike so strong as to cause stomach upset or queasiness — see DISGUST

**nauseate** *vb* to cause to feel disgust — see DISGUST

**nauseated** *adj* **1** affected with nausea — see NAUSEOUS

**2** filled with disgust — see SICK 2

**nauseating** *adj* causing intense displeasure, disgust, or resentment — see OFFENSIVE 1

**nauseous** *adj* affected with nausea ⟨after eating the last four pieces of the two-week-old pizza, he was feeling a little *nauseous*⟩

***syn*** ill, nauseated, qualmish, queasy (*also* queazy), queer, queerish, sick, sickish, squeamish

***rel*** green, peaked, sickly; unsettled, upset, woozy

***near ant*** settled; healthy, well

**nautical** *adj* of or relating to navigation of the sea — see MARINE 2

**navigable** *adj* capable of being traveled on — see PASSABLE 1

**navigate** *vb* to travel on water in a vessel — see SAIL 1

**navigational** *adj* of or relating to navigation of the sea — see MARINE 2

**navigator** *n* one who operates or navigates a seagoing vessel — see SAILOR

**nay** *adv* not merely this but also — see EVEN

**nay** *n* **1** a vote or decision against something — see NO 1

**2** an unwillingness to grant something asked for — see DENIAL 1

**Neanderthal** *adj* not civilized — see SAVAGE 1

**near** *adj* **1** being the less far of two ⟨grab the comforter from the *near* side of the bed⟩

***syn*** closer, hither, nigher, this

***rel*** fore, forward, front, inside

***near ant*** distant, remote, remoter; back, outside

***ant*** far, farther, further, opposite, other, that

**2** being such only when compared to something else — see COMPARATIVE

**3** closely resembling the object imitated — see NATURAL 2

**4** not being distant in time, space, or significance — see CLOSE 2

**near** *adv* **1** at, within, or to a short distance or time ⟨the campers were cold, so they moved *nearer* to the campfire⟩ ⟨as summer draws *near*, we usually start planning our annual vacation⟩

***syn*** around, by, close, hard, in, nearby, nigh

***rel*** hereabouts (*or* hereabout), thereabouts (*or* thereabout); along, alongside

***phrases*** at close quarters, at hand

**2** to a close degree ⟨copy the artist's drawing into your own sketchbook as *near* as you can⟩

***syn*** closely, nearly

***near ant*** distantly, remotely

**3** very close to but not completely — see ALMOST

**near** *prep* close to — see AROUND 1

**near** *vb* **1** to come near or nearer — see APPROACH 1

**2** to move closer to — see COME 1

**nearby** *adj* not being distant in time, space, or significance — see CLOSE 2

**nearby** *adv* at, within, or to a short distance or time — see NEAR 1

**nearing** *adj* being soon to appear or take place — see FORTHCOMING

**nearly** *adv* **1** to a close degree — see NEAR 2

**2** very close to but not completely — see ALMOST

**nearness** *n* **1** the state of being in a very personal or private relationship — see FAMILIARITY 1

**2** the state or condition of being near — see PROXIMITY

**nearsighted** *adj* able to see near things more clearly than distant ones ⟨I am a little *nearsighted* and need to wear glasses to drive⟩

***syn*** myopic, shortsighted

***rel*** astigmatic

***ant*** farsighted

**neat** *adj* **1** being clean and in good order ⟨keep the kitchen *neat* so the cook doesn't have to work around piles of dirty dishes⟩

***syn*** crisp, groomed, orderly, picked up, shipshape, snug, tidied, tidy, trim, uncluttered

*rel* dapper, natty, prim, saucy, smart, spiffy, spruce; immaculate, spick-and-span (*or* spic-and-span), spotless; rakish, sleek, streamlined, taut; organized, straight, systematic
*near ant* seedy, shabby, slipshod, sloppy; dirty, filthy, foul, nasty, sordid, squalid; frowzy, rumpled, tousled, tumbled; disorganized, unsystematic
*ant* disheveled (*or* dishevelled), disordered, disorderly, messy, mussed, mussy, slovenly, unkempt, untidy
**2** free from added matter — see PURE 1
**3** of the very best kind — see EXCELLENT

**nebulous** *adj* **1** having an often intentionally veiled or uncertain meaning — see OBSCURE 1
**2** not seen or understood clearly — see FAINT 1

**nebulousness** *n* the quality or state of having a veiled or uncertain meaning — see OBSCURITY 1

**necessarily** *adv* because of necessity — see NEEDS

**necessary** *adj* **1** forcing one's compliance or participation by or as if by law — see MANDATORY
**2** impossible to avoid or evade — see INEVITABLE
**3** impossible to do without — see ESSENTIAL 1

**necessitate** *vb* to have as a requirement — see NEED 1

**necessity** *n* something necessary, indispensable, or unavoidable — see ESSENTIAL 1

**necklace** *n* an ornamental chain or string (as of beads) worn around the neck ⟨found a lovely *necklace* to match the bracelet and ring her mother had given her⟩
*syn* choker, lei
*rel* rope, strand; bangle, lavaliere (*also* lavalliere), locket, pendant (*also* pendent)

**necromancer** *n* a person skilled in using supernatural forces — see MAGICIAN 1

**necromancy** *n* the power to control natural forces through supernatural means — see MAGIC 1

**need** *n* **1** a state of being without something necessary, desirable, or useful ⟨when it came time to wrap the presents, he found he was in *need* of adhesive tape⟩
*syn* absence, lack, needfulness, want
*rel* deficiency, deficit, inadequacy, insufficiency; dearth, meagerness, paucity, poverty, scantiness, scarceness, scarcity, shortage, skimpiness; defect, minus; deprivation, famishment, privation; demand, essential, necessity, requirement, requisite
*near ant* adequacy, enough, sufficiency; fund, pool, stock, supply; excess, fill, overabundance, oversupply, plenty, surfeit, surplus; hoard, stockpile
**2** something necessary, indispensable, or unavoidable — see ESSENTIAL 1
**3** something one must do because of prior agreement — see OBLIGATION
**4** the state of lacking sufficient money or material possessions — see POVERTY 1

**need** *vb* **1** to have as a requirement ⟨a national crisis that *needs* a strong leader to solve it⟩
*syn* demand, necessitate, require, take, want, warrant
*rel* entail, involve; ask, beg, claim, clamor (for), cry (for); lack; command, enjoin, exact, insist, press, quest, stipulate
*phrases* call for
*near ant* own, possess
*ant* have, hold
**2** to be under necessity or obligation to ⟨you *need* not stand when she enters the room⟩
*syn* have (to), must, ought (to), shall, should
*rel* will

**needed** *adj* impossible to do without — see ESSENTIAL 1

**needful** *adj* impossible to do without — see ESSENTIAL 1

**needfulness** *n* a state of being without something necessary, desirable, or useful — see NEED 1

**neediness** *n* the state of lacking sufficient money or material possessions — see POVERTY 1

**needle** *n* **1** a slender hollow instrument by which material is put into or taken from the body through the skin ⟨the nurse inserted the *needle* into his vein and collected some blood for testing⟩
*syn* hypodermic, hypodermic needle, hypodermic syringe, syringe
**2** an arrow-shaped piece on a dial or scale for registering information — see POINTER 1

**needle** *vb* **1** to attack repeatedly with mean put-downs or insults — see TEASE 2
**2** to subject (someone) to constant scoldings and sharp reminders — see NAG

**needlelike** *adj* being of less than usual width — see NARROW 1

**needler** *n* a person who causes repeated emotional pain, distress, or annoyance to another — see TORMENTOR

**needless** *adj* not needed by the circumstances or to accomplish an end — see UNNECESSARY

**needlework** *n* decorative stitching done on cloth with the use of a needle ⟨a school outing to the museum to see an exhibition of 18th century *needlework*⟩
*syn* embroidery
*rel* crewel, cross-stitch, needlepoint; hemstitch, fagoting (*or* faggoting), smocking; fancywork

**needs** *adv* because of necessity ⟨the dangers of global warming must *needs* be recognized—and recognized soon—by the industrialized nations of the world⟩
*syn* inescapably, inevitably, necessarily, perforce, unavoidably
*rel* involuntarily
*ant* unnecessarily

**needy** *adj* lacking money or material possessions — see POOR 1
**ne'er** *adv* at no time — see NEVER 1
**nefarious** *adj* not conforming to a high moral standard; morally unacceptable — see BAD 2
**nefariousness** *n* the state or quality of being utterly evil — see ENORMITY 1
**negate** *vb* 1 to declare not to be true — see DENY 1
2 to put an end to by formal action — see ABOLISH
3 to think not to be true or real — see DISBELIEVE
**negation** *n* a refusal to confirm the truth of a statement — see DENIAL 2
**negative** *adj* 1 marked by opposition or ill will — see HOSTILE 1
2 opposed to one's interests — see ADVERSE 1
**negative** *n* 1 a vote or decision against something — see NO 1
2 something that is as different as possible from something else — see OPPOSITE
**negative** *vb* 1 to reject by or as if by a vote ⟨though the rebuttal was very eloquent, he *negatived* it in favor of the first argument⟩ ⟨she *negatived* pizza for dinner, noting that they had already had it for three nights that week⟩
*syn* blackball, kill, veto
*rel* decline, disallow, disapprove, dismiss, refuse; blacklist
*near ant* admit, allow, approve, assent (to), pass, sanction; elect, support
*ant* confirm, ratify
2 to declare not to be true — see DENY 1
3 to show unwillingness to accept, do, engage in, or agree to — see DECLINE 1
**neglect** *n* 1 the state of being unattended to or not cared for ⟨the barn sat in *neglect* until it finally fell down⟩
*syn* desolation, dilapidation, disrepair, seediness
*rel* inattention, negligence; abandonment, desertion; decay, decrepitude, dereliction, deterioration, disintegration, ruin, ruination
*near ant* conservation, preservation
*ant* repair
2 the nonperformance of an assigned or expected action — see FAILURE 1
**neglect** *vb* 1 to fail to give proper attention to ⟨the news media *neglected* the real issues of the campaign and focused on personalities⟩
*syn* disregard, forget, ignore, overlook, overpass, pass over, slight, slur (over)
*rel* fail; miss, omit; brush (aside *or* off), reject, shrug off, slough (off); disdain, poohpooh, scorn; scant, skimp
*near ant* appreciate, cherish, prize, treasure, value; cultivate, foster, nurse, nurture; pamper; remember; listen (to), watch; follow, mark, note, notice, observe, remark
*ant* attend (to), heed, mind, regard, tend (to)
2 to leave undone or unattended to especially through carelessness ⟨she plays too much and *neglects* her homework⟩ ⟨I've *neglected* my garden, and now it's overgrown with weeds⟩
*syn* forget, shirk
*rel* slack (off)
*near ant* carry out, do, execute, perform; accomplish, achieve
*ant* attend (to), remember
3 to miss the opportunity or obligation ⟨the job applicant *neglected* to mention his criminal record⟩
*syn* fail, forget, omit
*rel* disregard, ignore, overlook, overpass, pass over, slight; slide, slip; default; skip
*near ant* heed, mind, remember; keep, observe; carry out, do, execute, perform, practice (*or* practise); discharge, fulfill (*or* fulfil), meet, satisfy; comply (with)
**neglected** *adj* showing signs of advanced wear and tear and neglect — see SHABBY 1
**neglectful** *adj* failing to give proper care and attention — see NEGLIGENT
**neglecting** *adj* failing to give proper care and attention — see NEGLIGENT
**negligence** *n* 1 failure to take the care that a cautious person usually takes ⟨exhibiting his usual *negligence*, he failed to set the emergency brake, and the car rolled down the steep hill and crashed into the telephone pole⟩
*syn* carelessness, dereliction, heedlessness, incautiousness, laxness, remissness, slackness
*rel* foolhardiness, rashness, recklessness, wildness; neglect, omission; delinquency, irresponsibility, malfeasance, malpractice, misconduct; misdirection, mishandling, mismanagement; forgetfulness, inattention, inattentiveness, obliviousness, shortsightedness, unwariness
*near ant* alertness, attention, attentiveness, awareness; circumspection, observance, vigilance, watchfulness; responsibility, responsibleness
*ant* care, carefulness, caution, cautiousness, heedfulness
2 the nonperformance of an assigned or expected action — see FAILURE 1
**negligent** *adj* failing to give proper care and attention ⟨has been *negligent* in taking care of the neighbor's dog, repeatedly forgetting to feed the poor animal⟩
*syn* careless, derelict, lax, neglectful, neglecting, remiss, slack
*rel* heedless, incautious, irresponsible, reckless, wild; unguarded, unwary; forgetful; disregardful, disregarding, inattentive, oblivious, thoughtless, unheeding, unmindful, unthinking; apathetic, disinterested, indifferent, unconcerned, uninterested; delinquent; loose
*near ant* meticulous, painstaking, punctilious; cautious, chary, circumspect, gingerly, guarded; alert, heedful, heeding, mindful, observant, regardful, regarding, vigilant, wary, watchful; foresighted, forethoughtful, provident, responsible; thinking, thoughtful; concerned, interested
*ant* attentive, careful, conscientious

**negligible** *adj* **1** so small or unimportant as to warrant little or no attention ⟨the two cents in change was such a *negligible* sum that she left the store without collecting the pennies from the cashier⟩
***syn*** inconsequential, inconsiderable, insignificant, measly, minute, nominal, paltry, petty, picayune, piddling, slight, trifling, trivial
***rel*** inferior, mean; imperceptible, inappreciable; little, puny, tiny; hairsplitting, nitpicking, pettifogging; one-horse, small-fry, two-bit
***near ant*** serious, substantial, weighty; eventful, momentous; conspicuous, noteworthy, prominent, outstanding, remarkable, striking; appreciable, discernible, measurable
***ant*** big, consequential, considerable, important, material, significant
**2** lacking importance — see UNIMPORTANT
**3** small in degree — see REMOTE 1

**negligibly** *adv* in a very small quantity or degree — see LITTLE 1

**negotiable** *adj* capable of being traveled on — see PASSABLE 1

**negotiate** *vb* **1** to bring about through discussion and compromise ⟨wanted to *negotiate* a higher salary before she accepted the job offer⟩
***syn*** arrange, concert, conclude
***rel*** settle (on *or* upon); bargain, chaffer, deal, dicker, haggle, horse-trade, palter; agree; contract, covenant; argue, debate, discuss, hammer (out), hash (over), reason, talk, talk over, work out
**2** to deal with (something) usually skillfully or efficiently — see HANDLE 1
**3** to plan out usually with subtle skill or care — see ENGINEER
**4** to talk over or dispute the terms of a purchase — see BARGAIN

**negotiation** *n* the act or practice of each side giving up something in order to reach an agreement — see CONCESSION 1

**neigh** *vb* to make the cry typical of a horse ⟨the horses *neighed* when the rider came into the barn⟩
***syn*** nicker, whinny

**neighborhood** *n* **1** an area (as of a city) set apart for some purpose or having some special feature — see DISTRICT
**2** the people living in a particular area — see COMMUNITY 1

**neighboring** *adj* not being distant in time, space, or significance — see CLOSE 2

**neighborly** *adj* having or showing kindly feeling and sincere interest — see FRIENDLY 1

**nemesis** *n* **1** one who inflicts punishment in return for an injury or offense ⟨Batman is the Joker's main *nemesis* and always foils his wicked plots⟩
***syn*** avenger, castigator, chastiser, punisher, scourge, vigilante
***rel*** revenger; redresser, righter; requiter
***near ant*** ransomer, redeemer, vindicator
**2** suffering, loss, or hardship imposed in response to a crime or offense — see PUNISHMENT

**neophyte** *n* a person who is just starting out in a field of activity — see BEGINNER

**neoplasm** *n* an abnormal mass of tissue — see GROWTH 1

**nerd** *n* a person slavishly devoted to intellectual or academic pursuits ⟨was such a *nerd* she stayed home from the party to study for the exam on Monday⟩
***syn*** bookworm, grind
***rel*** egghead, highbrow, intellectual; brain, genius; scholar
***near ant*** slacker, underachiever; lowbrow

**nerve** *n* **1** shameless boldness — see EFFRONTERY
**2** strength of mind to carry on in spite of danger — see COURAGE
**3 nerves** *pl* a sense of panic or extreme nervousness — see JITTERS

**nerve** *vb* to prepare (oneself) mentally or emotionally — see FORTIFY 1

**nerved** *adj* inclined or willing to take risks — see BOLD 1

**nerveless** *adj* **1** lacking strength of will or character — see WEAK 2
**2** not easily panicked or upset — see UNFLAPPABLE

**nerviness** *n* shameless boldness — see EFFRONTERY

**nervous** *adj* **1** feeling or showing uncomfortable feelings of uncertainty ⟨he was *nervous* about how he would do at the varsity basketball tryouts⟩
***syn*** aflutter, anxious, dithery, edgy, het up, hung up, jittery, jumpy, nervy, perturbed, tense, troubled, uneasy, unquiet, upset, uptight, worried
***rel*** aggrieved, bothered, concerned, disquieted, distraught, distressed, disturbed; apprehensive, foreboding, hesitant, misgiving; fretful, fretting, stewing, vexed; qualmish, qualmy; flustered, twittered, undone, unnerved, unstrung; obsessed, preoccupied, restless; fidgety, flighty, fluttery, high-strung, skittish, spooky
***phrases*** keyed up, on edge, on pins and needles
***near ant*** confident, self-assured, self-confident, sure; controlled, self-controlled
***ant*** calm, collected, cool, easy, nerveless, relaxed
**2** marked by or causing agitation or uncomfortable feelings ⟨a *nervous* silence filled the room as the teacher handed out the graded exams⟩
***syn*** agitating, anxious, disquieting, distressful, distressing, disturbing, restless, tense, unnerving, unsettling, worrisome
***rel*** bothersome, troublesome; foreboding, misgiving; discouraging, disheartening, strained; restive, restless, unrestful; awkward, embarrassing
***near ant*** restful; pacific
***ant*** calming, comfortable, easy, peaceful, quiet, quieting, tranquil
**3** easily excited by nature — see EXCITABLE

**nervousness** *n* an uneasy state of mind usually over the possibility of an anticipated misfortune or trouble — see ANXIETY 1

**nervy** *adj* **1** displaying or marked by rude boldness ⟨the *nervy* waiter held up the small tip and called out to the departing customers, "Hope it doesn't break the bank!"⟩
*syn* arch, bold, bold-faced, brash, brassy, brazen, cheeky, cocky, fresh, impertinent, impudent, insolent, sassy, saucy
*rel* assertive, forward, obtrusive; audacious, defiant, disrespectful; shameless, unabashed, unblushing; bluff, blunt, curt; facetious, flip, flippant, pert, smart, smart-alecky (*or* smart-aleck)
*near ant* demure, humble, modest; courteous, genteel, mannerly, polite, proper; deferential, respectful; abashed, ashamed, blushing, embarrassed; gentle, mild; inconspicuous, unobtrusive
*ant* meek, mousy (*or* mousey) retiring, shy, timid
**2** feeling or showing uncomfortable feelings of uncertainty — see NERVOUS 1
**3** inclined or willing to take risks — see BOLD 1

**nest** *n* a place where a person goes to hide — see HIDEOUT

**nest egg** *n* a sum of money set aside for a particular purpose — see FUND 1

**nestle** *vb* **1** to lie close — see NUZZLE
**2** to sit or recline comfortably or cozily — see SNUGGLE 1

**[1]net** *n* **1** a fabric made of strands loosely twisted, knotted, or woven together at regular intervals ⟨the basketball didn't go into the basket, it just hit the *net*⟩
*syn* mesh, netting, network
*rel* web, webbing; grille (*also* grill), lattice, screen, screening; filigree, lace
**2** a device or scheme for capturing another by surprise — see TRAP 1
**3** something that catches and holds — see WEB 1

**[2]net** *n* the amount of money left when expenses are subtracted from the total amount received — see PROFIT 1

**nether** *adj* situated lower down — see INFERIOR 1

**netting** *n* a fabric made of strands loosely twisted, knotted, or woven together at regular intervals — see [1]NET 1

**nettle** *vb* to disturb the peace of mind of (someone) especially by repeated disagreeable acts — see IRRITATE 1

**nettling** *adj* causing annoyance — see ANNOYING

**network** *n* **1** a fabric made of strands loosely twisted, knotted, or woven together at regular intervals — see [1]NET 1
**2** something made up of many interdependent or related parts — see SYSTEM 1

**neurotic** *n* a person judged to be legally or medically insane — see LUNATIC 1

**neuter** *vb* to remove the sex organs of ⟨Dad agreed to buy us the dog on the condition that we have her *neutered* so she couldn't have puppies⟩
*syn* alter, desex
*rel* castrate, emasculate, geld; spay; sterilize

**neutral** *adj* not favoring or joined to either side in a quarrel, contest, or war ⟨Sweden remained *neutral* during World War II, refusing to join either side of the conflict⟩
*syn* nonpartisan, unallied
*rel* autonomous, independent, sovereign, unaffiliated; nonbelligerent; individualistic; disinterested, evenhanded, fair, impartial, unbiased, uninfluenced, unprejudiced; bipartisan
*near ant* biased, partial, partisan, prejudiced, unfair; affiliated, associated, federated; belligerent
*ant* allied, confederate

**neutrality** *n* lack of favoritism toward one side or another — see DETACHMENT 1

**neutralize** *vb* to balance with an equal force so as to make ineffective — see OFFSET

**neutralizer** *n* a force or influence that makes an opposing force ineffective or less effective — see COUNTERBALANCE

**never** *adv* **1** at no time ⟨I have *never* been out of the country⟩
*syn* ne'er
*rel* nevermore; not; infrequently, little, rarely, seldom
*near ant* eternally, everlastingly, evermore, invariably; frequently, often, recurrently, repeatedly
*ant* always, constantly, continuously, endlessly, ever, forever, perpetually
**2** not in any degree, way, or under any condition ⟨though she turned down his offer of marriage twice, he was *never* convinced that she did not love him⟩
*syn* no, none, nothing, noway (*or* noways), nowise
*rel* nowhere near
*phrases* by no means, in no wise, nothing doing, on no account
*near ant* completely, extremely, full, fully, par excellence, right, very; altogether, exactly; somehow, someway (*also* someways); out
*ant* anyhow, anyway, anywise, at all, ever, half, however

**nevertheless** *adv* in spite of that — see HOWEVER

**new** *adj* **1** taking the place of one that came before ⟨after my bike was stolen, my scooter became my *new* mode of transportation⟩
*syn* backup, makeshift, substitute
*rel* alternate, alternative; different, other, separate; extra, spare; another, second; utility; successive; equivalent
*near ant* first, former; equal, identical, same; lasting, permanent
*ant* original
**2** not known or experienced before ⟨Spanish was a *new* course of study for her⟩ ⟨the Americas were *new* lands for the European explorers⟩
*syn* fresh, novel, original, strange, unaccustomed, unfamiliar, unheard-of, unknown, unprecedented

*rel* innovative, unique; nontraditional, unconventional, untried, unused, unworn
*near ant* conventional, established, traditional, tried, tried-and-true; derivative, imitative
*ant* familiar, old, time-honored, tired
**3** recently made and never used before ⟨that unique scent that is the telltale sign of a *new* car⟩
*syn* brand-new, spick-and-span (*or* spic-and-span), unused
*rel* clean, fresh, pristine, unspoiled; untouched; newfangled, new-fashioned; natural, raw, virgin, unprocessed, untreated, unworked
*near ant* dirty, soiled, spoiled, stale; aged, beat-up, old, worn
*ant* hand-me-down, second hand, used
**4** made or become fresh in spirits or vigor ⟨a little rest made him a *new* man after the exhausting basketball game⟩
*syn* energized, freshened, invigorated, reanimated, recreated, reenergized, refreshed, regenerated, renewed, resuscitated, revived
*rel* animated, enlivened, exhilarated, jazzed (up); resurrected; rested, untired, unwearied
*near ant* tired, weary; dampened, deadened; emasculated, unmanned; demoralized, disheartened, dispirited
*ant* drained, enervated, exhausted, weakened
**5** being or involving the latest methods, concepts, information, or styles — see MODERN

**new** *adv* not long ago — see NEWLY

**newborn** *n* a recently born person — see BABY

**newcomer** *n* a person who is just starting out in a field of activity — see BEGINNER

**newfangled** *adj* being or involving the latest methods, concepts, information, or styles — see MODERN

**new–fashioned** *adj* being or involving the latest methods, concepts, information, or styles — see MODERN

**newly** *adv* not long ago ⟨as soon as he left the room, his dog jumped on the *newly* made bed and rumpled it again⟩
*syn* freshly, just, late, lately, new, now, only, recently
*rel* latterly
*phrases* of late
*near ant* ago, before, earlier, early, erstwhile, formerly, previously; heretofore, hitherto
*ant* anciently

**newness** *n* the quality or appeal of being new — see NOVELTY 1

**news** *n pl* a report of recent events or facts not previously known ⟨dropped by to give me the latest *news* about her daughter⟩
*syn* information, intelligence, item, story, tidings, word
*rel* announcement, communication, message; dope, lowdown, scoop, tidbit (*also* titbit), tip; gossip, rumor, tale, tattle; feedback

**newspaper** *n* a publication that appears at regular intervals — see JOURNAL

**newsy** *adj* having the style and content of everyday conversation — see CHATTY 1

**next** *adj* being the one that comes immediately after another ⟨my house is the *next* one⟩ ⟨turn at the *next* street, not this one⟩ ⟨she was *next* in line for concert tickets⟩
*syn* coming, ensuing, following, succeeding
*rel* consecutive, sequential, successive; posterior, subsequent; immediate; second
*phrases* on deck
*near ant* anterior, former; past; last
*ant* antecedent, foregoing, precedent, preceding, previous, prior

**next–door** *adj* not being distant in time, space, or significance — see CLOSE 2

**next to** *adv* very close to but not completely — see ALMOST

**next to** *prep* close to — see AROUND 1

**nib** *n* the jaws of a bird together with their hornlike covering — see BEAK

**nibble** *n* a small piece or quantity of food — see MORSEL 1

**nibble** *vb* to crush or grind with the teeth — see BITE (ON)

**nice** *adj* **1** following the established traditions of refined society and good taste — see PROPER 1
**2** giving pleasure or contentment to the mind or senses — see PLEASANT
**3** hard to please — see FINICKY
**4** having an easygoing and pleasing manner especially in social situations — see AMIABLE
**5** made or done with extreme care and accuracy — see FINE 2

**nicely** *adv* **1** in a pleasing way — see WELL 5
**2** in a satisfactory way — see WELL 1
**3** with good reason or courtesy — see WELL 4

**niceness** *n* the state or quality of having a pleasant or agreeable manner in socializing with others — see AMIABILITY 1

**nicety** *n* a single piece of information — see FACT 3

**niche** *n* **1** a hollowed-out space in a wall ⟨statues of various saints occupy the *niches* lining the abbey's many corridors⟩
*syn* alcove, nook, recess
*rel* corner, cranny, cubbyhole; cubicle; dent, indentation
**2** the place where a plant or animal is usually or naturally found — see HOME 2

**nick** *n* a V-shaped cut usually on an edge or a surface — see NOTCH 1

**nicker** *vb* to make the cry typical of a horse — see NEIGH

**nickname** *n* a descriptive or familiar name given instead of or in addition to the one belonging to an individual ⟨his wavy hair earned him the *nickname* "Curly" early in life⟩

*syn* alias, cognomen, epithet, sobriquet (*also* soubriquet)
*rel* appellation, denomination, denotation, designation, handle, label, title; nom de plume, pen name, pseudonym
**nifty** *adj* of the very best kind — see EXCELLENT
**nifty** *n* something very good of its kind — see JIM-DANDY
**niggard** *adj* giving or sharing as little as possible — see STINGY 1
**niggard** *n* a mean grasping person who is usually stingy with money — see MISER
**niggardly** *adj* 1 giving or sharing as little as possible — see STINGY 1
2 less plentiful than what is normal, necessary, or desirable — see MEAGER
**nigh** *adj* not being distant in time, space, or significance — see CLOSE 2
**nigh** *adv* 1 at, within, or to a short distance or time — see NEAR 1
2 very close to but not completely — see ALMOST
**nigher** *adj* being the less far of two — see NEAR 1
**night** *adj* of, relating to, or occurring in the night — see NOCTURNAL
**night** *n* 1 the time from sunset to sunrise when there is no visible sunlight ⟨loved to sit outside at *night* and watch the stars⟩
*syn* dark, darkness, nighttime
*rel* dusk, evening, gloaming, nightfall, twilight; midnight
*near ant* dawn, daybreak, forenoon, morning; high noon, midday, noon, noonday, noontide, noontime; afternoon
*ant* day, daytime
2 a time or place of little or no light — see DARK 1
**nightclub** *n* a bar or restaurant offering special nighttime entertainment (as music, dancing, or comedy acts) ⟨decided to go dancing at a local *nightclub* after the long dinner and movie⟩
*syn* cabaret, café (*also* cafe), disco, discotheque, roadhouse
*rel* barroom, pub [*chiefly British*], public house [*chiefly British*], saloon, tavern; dive, speakeasy; canteen
**nightdress** *n* a loose pullover garment worn in bed — see NIGHTGOWN
**nightfall** *n* the time from when the sun begins to set to the onset of total darkness — see DUSK 1
**nightgown** *n* a loose pullover garment worn in bed ⟨decided to buy a flannel *nightgown* instead of pajamas⟩
*syn* nightdress, nightshirt
*rel* nightclothes; pajamas, pjs, pyjamas [*chiefly British*]; nightcap; lingerie
**nightly** *adj* of, relating to, or occurring in the night — see NOCTURNAL
**nightmare** *n* 1 a series of often striking pictures created by the imagination during sleep — see DREAM 1
2 a situation or state that causes great suffering and unhappiness — see HELL 2
**nightmarish** *adj* extremely disturbing or repellent — see HORRIBLE 1
**nightshirt** *n* a loose pullover garment worn in bed — see NIGHTGOWN
**nightstick** *n* a heavy rigid stick used as a weapon or for punishment — see CLUB 1
**nighttime** *adj* of, relating to, or occurring in the night — see NOCTURNAL
**nighttime** *n* the time from sunset to sunrise when there is no visible sunlight — see NIGHT 1
**nil** *n* the numerical symbol 0 or the absence of number or quantity represented by it — see ZERO 1
**nimble** *adj* 1 having or showing quickness of mind — see INTELLIGENT 1
2 moving easily — see GRACEFUL 1
**nimbleness** *n* ease and grace in physical activity — see DEXTERITY 2
**nincompoop** *n* 1 a person who lacks good sense or judgment — see FOOL 1
2 a stupid person — see IDIOT
**ninny** *n* 1 a person who lacks good sense or judgment — see FOOL 1
2 a stupid person — see IDIOT
[1]**nip** *n* 1 a very small amount — see PARTICLE 1
2 an uncomfortable degree of coolness — see CHILL
[2]**nip** *n* the portion of a serving of a beverage that is swallowed at one time — see DRINK 2
**nip** *vb* 1 to make (as hair) shorter with or as if with the use of shears — see CLIP
2 to squeeze tightly between two surfaces, edges, or points — see PINCH 1
3 to take (something) without right and with an intent to keep — see STEAL 1
**nip and tuck** *adj* showing little difference in the standing of the competitors — see CLOSE 3
**nipper** *n* a male person who has not yet reached adulthood — see BOY
**nipping** *adj* having a low or subnormal temperature — see COLD 1
**nippy** *adj* 1 having a low or subnormal temperature — see COLD 1
2 having a powerfully stimulating odor or flavor — see SHARP 3
3 moving, proceeding, or acting with great speed — see FAST 1
4 uncomfortably cool — see CHILLY 1
**nitpick** *vb* to make often peevish criticisms or objections about matters that are minor, unimportant, or irrelevant — see QUIBBLE
**nitpicker** *n* a person given to harsh judgments and to finding faults — see CRITIC 1
**nitwit** *n* 1 a person who lacks good sense or judgment — see FOOL 1
2 a stupid person — see IDIOT
**no** *interj* how surprising, doubtful, or unbelievable ⟨*no*—you can't possibly mean that I failed that test! I studied for days!⟩
*syn* ah, aha, fie, indeed, pshaw, well, what, why
*rel* gee, ha, hello, hey, lo, oh; fiddlesticks, phooey, pooh; there; oops, ugh; egad, gad, the deuce, the devil, the dickens, zounds

**no** *adv* **1** not in any degree, way, or under any condition — see NEVER 2
**2** certainly not — see HARDLY 2

**no** *n* **1** a vote or decision against something ⟨though I wanted spaghetti for dinner, the consensus was a decisive *no*⟩
*syn* nay, negative
*rel* con; blackball, veto; denial, negation, refusal
*near ant* pro; acceptance, approval, grace
*ant* positive, yea, yes
**2** an unwillingness to grant something asked for — see DENIAL 1

**nobility** *n* impressiveness of beauty on a large scale — see MAGNIFICENCE

**noble** *adj* **1** of high birth, rank, or station ⟨despite his *noble* background, the prince is known for his unpretentious way with common people⟩
*syn* aristocratic, genteel, gentle, grand, highborn, patrician, upper-class, well-born
*rel* high, lofty, superior; elevated, ennobled, exalted; gentlemanly, kingly, knightly, ladylike, lordly, princely, queenly, regal, royal; high-level, senior
*near ant* inferior, knavish; bastard, illegitimate; ordinary, plain; abased, degraded; junior, subordinate
*ant* baseborn, common, humble, ignoble, low, lower-class, lowly, mean, plebeian
**2** having, characterized by, or arising from a dignified and generous nature ⟨the factory owner had a kind, *noble* disposition that showed in his unstinting generosity toward the poor⟩ ⟨our country was founded on the *noble* ideas that are put forth in the founding fathers' writings⟩
*syn* chivalrous, elevated, gallant, great, greathearted, high, high-minded, lofty, lordly, magnanimous, sublime
*rel* ennobled, exalted, glorified; heroic, honorable, venerable, worthy; knightly, princely, regal; moving, inspiring, uplifting; august, magnificent, majestic
*near ant* sordid, squalid, vile, wretched; abominable, contemptible, despicable, detestable, hateful, offensive, repulsive, ugly; dastardly, dirty, lousy, sorry; little, mean, narrow, small-minded; degrading, discreditable, humiliating, ignominious; coarse, crude, vulgar
*ant* base, debased, degenerate, degraded, ignoble, low
**3** following the accepted rules of moral conduct — see HONORABLE 1
**4** large and impressive in size, grandeur, extent, or conception — see GRAND 1
**5** of the very best kind — see EXCELLENT
**6** standing above others in rank, importance, or achievement — see EMINENT

**noble** *n* a man of high birth or social position — see GENTLEMAN 1

**nobleman** *n* a man of high birth or social position — see GENTLEMAN 1

**nobleness** *n* impressiveness of beauty on a large scale — see MAGNIFICENCE

**noblewoman** *n* a woman of high birth or social position — see GENTLEWOMAN

**nobly** *adv* in a manner befitting a person of the highest character and ideals — see GREATLY 1

**nobody** *n* a person of no importance or influence ⟨she felt like a *nobody* until she won the National Spelling Bee⟩
*syn* lightweight, nonentity, nothing, shrimp, twerp, whippersnapper, zero, zilch
*rel* least; inferior, mediocrity, obscurity; figurehead, puppet
*near ant* chief, head, lead, leader; celebrity, luminary, notable, personality, star, superstar; authority, superior; great power, party, power
*ant* big shot, bigwig, eminence, figure, magnate, nabob, personage, somebody, VIP

**nobody** *pron* no person ⟨there is *nobody* home⟩ ⟨*nobody* wants to clean up that mess⟩
*syn* none, no one
*near ant* anybody, anyone; somebody, someone
*ant* everybody, everyone

**nocturnal** *adj* of, relating to, or occurring in the night ⟨he bought a new telescope so he could pursue his favorite *nocturnal* hobby of astronomy⟩
*syn* night, nightly, nighttime
*rel* late; midnight, overnight
*near ant* noon
*ant* daily, diurnal

**nod** *vb* to make short up-and-down movements ⟨though she couldn't see the rain, she knew it had started because she could see the flowers *nod* as raindrops hit them⟩
*syn* bob, bobble, jog, jounce, pump, seesaw
*rel* jerk, jiggle, shake, wiggle, wobble; oscillate, rock, sway, swing, undulate; drop, duck

**nodding** *adj* bending downward or forward ⟨some students, with *nodding* heads, were falling asleep during the boring lecture⟩
*syn* bowed, bowing, declined, declining, descendant (*or* descendent), descending, drooping, droopy, hanging, hung (*also* hanged), inclining, pendulous, sagging, stooping
*rel* floppy, limp; dangling, falling, pendent (*or* pendant), suspended; dipping, sinking, slumping
*near ant* erect, inflexible, rigid, stiff; elevated, raised, upraised
*ant* unbending, upright

**noddle** *n* the upper or front part of the body that contains the brain, the major sense organs, and the mouth — see HEAD 1

**node** *n* a small rounded mass of swollen tissue — see BUMP 1

**nodule** *n* a small rounded mass of swollen tissue — see BUMP 1

**Noel** *n* the season celebrating Christmas — see YULETIDE

**noggin** *n* the upper or front part of the body that contains the brain, the major sense organs, and the mouth — see HEAD 1

**no–good** *adj* having no usefulness — see WORTHLESS

**no–good** *n* a mean, evil, or unprincipled person — see VILLAIN

**noise** *n* **1** loud, confused, and usually unharmonious sound ⟨the blaring *noise* of traffic on Fifth Avenue made casual conversation impossible⟩
*syn* bluster, cacophony, clamor, clangor, din, discordance, racket, roar
*rel* discord, dissonance; commotion, furor, hubbub, hullabaloo, hurly-burly, rumpus, tumult, uproar; babel; clatter, jangle; bang, blast, boom, clap, crack, crash
*near ant* calm, hush, lull; quietude, serenity, tranquillity (*or* tranquility)
*ant* quiet, silence, still, stillness
**2** a violent shouting — see CLAMOR 1

**noise** (about) *vb* to make (as a piece of information) the subject of common talk without any authority or confirmation of accuracy — see RUMOR

**noiseless** *adj* mostly or entirely without sound — see SILENT 3

**noisome** *adj* **1** bad for the well-being of the body — see UNHEALTHY 1
**2** causing intense displeasure, disgust, or resentment — see OFFENSIVE 1
**3** having an unpleasant smell — see MALODOROUS

**noisy** *adj* **1** making loud, confused, and usually unharmonious sounds ⟨the *noisy* crowd moved up the street, shouting louder as they went along⟩
*syn* clangorous, dinning, discordant
*rel* cacophonous, dissonant; resounding, sonorous; clamorous, uproarious; blatant, obstreperous, strident, vociferous; blaring, booming, brassy, brazen, clanging, earsplitting
*near ant* calm, hushed
*ant* noiseless, quiet, silent, soundless, still
**2** full of or characterized by the presence of noise ⟨the crowded auditorium was *noisy*, packed with excited theatergoers eager for the show to start⟩ ⟨the manufacturing company was a *noisy* place, so we wore ear protection while we toured⟩
*syn* clamorous, clangorous, clattering, clattery, resounding
*rel* resonant, sonorous; buzzing, humming, murmuring; blustery, boisterous, raucous, rip-roaring, roaring, roistering, romping, rowdy; tumultuous, uproarious, woolly (*also* wooly); obstreperous, vociferous
*near ant* calm, peaceful, serene, tranquil
*ant* hushed, noiseless, quiet, silent, soundless, stilled, stilly

**nomad** *or* **nomadic** *adj* traveling from place to place — see ITINERANT

**nomad** *n* a person who roams about without a fixed route or destination ⟨after college she became quite the *nomad*, backpacking through Europe with no particular destination⟩
*syn* drifter, gadabout, rambler, roamer, rover, stroller, vagabond, wanderer, wayfarer
*rel* laggard, straggler; lingerer, loiterer, sojourner; bum, hobo, tramp; sightseer, traveler (*or* traveller); transient, vagrant; ambler, saunterer
*near ant* homebody; denizen, dweller, habitant, inhabitant, resident, settler

**nominal** *adj* **1** being something in name or form only ⟨he was the *nominal* head of state—everyone knew the country was actually run by one of his advisers⟩
*syn* formal, paper, titular
*rel* so-called; phantom, virtual
*near ant* actual, real, true
**2** so small or unimportant as to warrant little or no attention — see NEGLIGIBLE 1

**nominally** *adv* in a very small quantity or degree — see LITTLE 1

**nonaction** *n* lack of action or activity — see INACTION

**nonbinding** *adj* having no legal or binding force — see NULL 1

**nonchalance** *n* lack of interest or concern — see INDIFFERENCE

**nonchalant** *adj* having or showing a lack of interest or concern — see INDIFFERENT 1

**noncombustible** *adj* incapable of being burned — see INCOMBUSTIBLE

**nonconflicting** *adj* not having or showing any apparent conflict — see CONSISTENT

**nonconformist** *adj* deviating from commonly accepted beliefs or practices — see HERETICAL

**nonconformist** *n* **1** a person who does not conform to generally accepted standards or customs ⟨always the *nonconformist*, she insisted on wearing red on St. Patrick's Day and not green like everyone else⟩
*syn* bohemian, deviant, individualist, loner, lone wolf, maverick
*rel* character, codger, crackbrain, crackpot, crank, eccentric, freak, kook, nut, oddball, screwball, weirdo; misfit, outsider; anomaly
*near ant* adherent, follower, supporter; sheep
*ant* conformer, conformist
**2** a person who believes or teaches something opposed to accepted beliefs — see HERETIC

**nonconformity** *n* departure from a generally accepted theory, opinion, or practice — see HERESY

**nonconventional** *adj* not bound by traditional ways or beliefs — see LIBERAL 1

**none** *adv* **1** certainly not — see HARDLY 2
**2** not in any degree, way, or under any condition — see NEVER 2

**none** *pron* no person — see NOBODY

**nonelective** *adj* forcing one's compliance or participation by or as if by law — see MANDATORY

**nonentity** *n* a person of no importance or influence — see NOBODY
**nonessential** *adj* not needed by the circumstances or to accomplish an end — see UNNECESSARY
**nonetheless** *adv* in spite of that — see HOWEVER
**nonexistent** *adj* not present or in evidence — see ABSENT 2
**nonfictional** *adj* restricted to or based on fact — see FACTUAL 1
**nonflammable** *adj* incapable of being burned — see INCOMBUSTIBLE
**nonfunctional** *adj* not being in working order — see INOPERABLE 1
**nonfunctioning** *adj* not being in working order — see INOPERABLE 1
**noninflammable** *adj* incapable of being burned — see INCOMBUSTIBLE
**nonliterary** *adj* used in or suitable for speech and not formal writing — see COLLOQUIAL 1
**nonliterate** *adj* lacking in education or the knowledge gained from books — see IGNORANT 1
**nonmaterial** *adj* not composed of matter — see IMMATERIAL 1
**nonmotile** *adj* incapable of moving or being moved — see IMMOVABLE 1
**nonmoving** *adj* **1** fixed in a place or position — see STATIONARY 1
**2** incapable of moving or being moved — see IMMOVABLE 1
**nonnative** *adj* being, relating to, or characteristic of a country other than one's own — see FOREIGN 1
**nonnative** *n* a person who is not native to or known to a community — see STRANGER
**no–nonsense** *adj* not joking or playful in mood or manner — see SERIOUS 1
**nonoperating** *adj* not being in working order — see INOPERABLE 1
**nonorthodox** *adj* **1** deviating from commonly accepted beliefs or practices — see HERETICAL
**2** not bound by traditional ways or beliefs — see LIBERAL 1
**nonpareil** *adj* having no equal or rival for excellence or desirability — see ONLY 1
**nonpareil** *n* someone of such unequaled perfection as to deserve imitation — see IDEAL 1
**nonpartisan** *adj* **1** marked by justice, honesty, and freedom from bias — see FAIR 2
**2** not favoring or joined to either side in a quarrel, contest, or war — see NEUTRAL
**nonphysical** *adj* not composed of matter — see IMMATERIAL 1
**nonplus** *vb* to throw into a state of self-conscious distress — see EMBARRASS 1
**nonpractical** *adj* not capable of being put to use or account — see IMPRACTICAL
**nonprofessional** *adj* lacking or showing a lack of expert skill — see AMATEURISH
**nonpublic** *adj* not known or meant to be known by the general populace — see PRIVATE 1
**nonrational** *adj* not using or following good reasoning — see ILLOGICAL
**nonrealistic** *adj* using elements of form (as color, line, or texture) with little or no attempt at creating a realistic picture — see ABSTRACT 2
**nonreligious** *adj* **1** lacking religious emotions, principles, or practices — see IRRELIGIOUS
**2** not involving religion or religious matters — see PROFANE 1
**nonresistant** *adj* receiving or enduring without offering resistance — see PASSIVE
**nonsense** *n* **1** language, behavior, or ideas that are absurd and contrary to good sense ⟨told him to stop his mischievous *nonsense* and start behaving properly⟩ ⟨the discussion about building a time machine was complete *nonsense*⟩ ⟨a hundred years ago, the idea that man could walk on the moon was regarded as impractical *nonsense*⟩
***syn*** bunk, claptrap, drivel, fiddlesticks, folly, foolishness, fudge, hogwash, humbug, humbuggery, piffle, rot, senselessness, silliness, slush, stupidity, trash
***rel*** absurdity, asininity, fatuity, foolery, idiocy, imbecility, inanity, insanity, lunacy; absurdness, craziness, foolishness, madness, senselessness, witlessness; monkeyshines, shenanigans, tomfoolery; gas, hot air, jazz, moonshine, rigmarole, twaddle; double-talk
***near ant*** levelheadedness, rationality, reasonability, reasonableness, sensibleness; common sense, horse sense, sense; discernment, judgment (*or* judgement), wisdom
**2** unintelligible or meaningless talk — see GIBBERISH
**nonsensical** *adj* **1** conceived or made without regard for reason or reality — see FANTASTIC 1
**2** showing or marked by a lack of good sense or judgment — see FOOLISH 1
**nonsensicalness** *n* lack of good sense or judgment — see FOOLISHNESS 1
**nonspecific** *adj* relating to the main elements and not to specific details — see GENERAL 2
**nonsuccess** *n* a falling short of one's goals — see FAILURE 2
**nontraditional** *adj* not bound by traditional ways or beliefs — see LIBERAL 1
**nonvalid** *adj* **1** having no legal or binding force — see NULL 1
**2** having no basis in reason or fact — see GROUNDLESS
**nonviolent** *adj* not involving violence or force — see PEACEFUL 2
**nook** *n* a hollowed-out space in a wall — see NICHE 1
**noon** *n* the middle of the day ⟨we eat a big lunch around *noon* then have dinner in the evening⟩
***syn*** high noon, midday, noonday, noontide, noontime

***syn*** synonym(s) ***rel*** related words
***ant*** antonym(s) ***near ant*** near antonym(s)

*rel* forenoon, morning; afternoon, evening
**noonday** *n* the middle of the day — see NOON
**no one** *pron* no person — see NOBODY
**noontide** *n* the middle of the day — see NOON
**noontime** *n* the middle of the day — see NOON
**norm** *n* what is typical of a group, class, or series — see AVERAGE
**normal** *adj* **1** being of the type that is encountered in the normal course of events — see ORDINARY 1
**2** having full use of one's mind and control over one's actions — see SANE
**3** having or showing the qualities associated with the members of a particular group or kind — see TYPICAL 1
**normal** *n* what is typical of a group, class, or series — see AVERAGE
**normalcy** *n* the state or fact of being the way things usually are — see NORMALITY
**normality** *n* the state or fact of being the way things usually are ⟨the county slowly has returned to *normality* after a week of flash flooding⟩
*syn* normalcy, status quo
*rel* groove, routine, rut; currency, prevalence; conventionality; orderliness, peace
*near ant* irregularity, uncommonness, unusualness; disorderliness, disruptiveness; disruption, disturbance; anomalousness, deviance; exceptionalness, extraordinariness, noteworthiness, remarkableness; unconventionality
*ant* abnormality
**normalize** *vb* to make agree with a single established standard or model — see STANDARDIZE
**normally** *adv* according to the usual course of things — see NATURALLY 2
**nose** *vb* **1** to become aware of by means of the sense organs in the nose — see SMELL 1
**2** to interest oneself in what is not one's concern — see INTERFERE
**nosedive** *n* the act or process of going to a lower level or altitude — see DESCENT 1
**nose–dive** *vb* to go to a lower level — see DROP 2
**nosegay** *n* a bunch of flowers — see BOUQUET 1
**nosiness** *n* an eager desire to find out about things that are often none of one's business — see CURIOSITY 1
**nosy** *or* **nosey** *adj* **1** interested in what is not one's own business — see CURIOUS 1
**2** thrusting oneself where one is not welcome or invited — see INTRUSIVE
**notable** *adj* standing above others in rank, importance, or achievement — see EMINENT
**notable** *n* a person who is widely known and usually much talked about — see CELEBRITY 1
**notation** *n* a usually brief written reminder — see NOTE 1
**notch** *n* **1** a V-shaped cut usually on an edge or a surface ⟨lifted up the fence rail and put it in the *notch* cut into the post⟩
*syn* chip, hack, indentation, kerf, nick
*rel* punch; groove, score; slit, slot
**2** a narrow opening between hillsides or mountains that can be used for passage — see CANYON
**3** an individual part of a process, series, or ranking — see DEGREE 1
**note** *n* **1** a usually brief written reminder ⟨I'll make a *note* to myself so I don't forget to pick up some milk on the way home⟩
*syn* memo, memorandum, notation
*rel* memoir, minutes, report; line; document, writing
**2** a message on paper from one person or group to another — see LETTER
**3** a natural vocal sound made by an animal — see CALL 1
**4** a piece of printed paper used as money — see [1]BILL 2
**5** a special quality or impression associated with something — see AURA
**6** overall quality as seen or judged by people in general — see REPUTATION
**7** a briefly expressed opinion — see REMARK
**note** *vb* **1** to make a statement of one's opinion — see REMARK 1
**2** to make a written note of — see RECORD 1
**3** to make note of (something) through the use of one's eyes — see SEE 1
**4** to make reference to or speak about briefly but specifically — see MENTION 1
**5** to take notice of and be guided by — see HEED 1
**noted** *adj* widely known — see FAMOUS
**notepad** *n* a number of sheets of writing paper glued together at one edge — see PAD 1
**noteworthiness** *n* the fact or state of being above others in rank or importance — see EMINENCE 1
**noteworthy** *adj* standing above others in rank, importance, or achievement — see EMINENT
**nothing** *adv* not in any degree, way, or under any condition — see NEVER 2
**nothing** *n* **1** a person of no importance or influence — see NOBODY
**2** something of little importance — see TRIFLE
**3** the numerical symbol 0 or the absence of number or quantity represented by it — see ZERO 1
**notice** *n* **1** a published statement informing the public of a matter of general interest — see ANNOUNCEMENT
**2** a state of being aware — see ATTENTION 2
**3** a written communication giving information or directions — see MEMORANDUM 1
**4** an essay evaluating or analyzing something — see CRITICISM
**5** the act or an instance of telling beforehand of danger or risk — see WARNING 1

**notice** *vb* **1** to make note of (something) through the use of one's eyes — see SEE 1
**2** to make reference to or speak about briefly but specifically — see MENTION 1

**noticeable** *adj* likely to attract attention ⟨the stain on the new carpet was quite *noticeable,* and nothing we did made it any lighter⟩
***syn*** arresting, bold, catchy, conspicuous, dramatic, emphatic, eye-catching, flamboyant, marked, prominent, pronounced, remarkable, showy, splashy, striking
***rel*** detectable, discernible, observable, perceptible, visible; outstanding, salient; distinguished, eminent, impressive, notable, noteworthy; highlighted, spotlighted; flagrant, glaring, screaming; flashy, garish, gaudy, glitzy, jazzy, loud, meretricious, swank (*or* swanky), tawdry; high-falutin, ostentatious, pretentious; extravagant, fancy, florid, glittery, spectacular; opulent, ornate, overdone, overwrought; absorbing, engrossing, enthralling, fascinating, interesting, riveting
***near ant*** subtle; concealed, hidden, shrouded; dim, faint, obscure; insignificant, undistinguished, unimportant; modest, unaffected, unassuming, unpretentious; conservative, plain, quiet, simple, unaffected, understated; muted, restrained, subdued, subtle, toned-down
***ant*** inconspicuous, unemphatic, unnoticeable, unobtrusive, unremarkable

**notification** *n* a published statement informing the public of a matter of general interest — see ANNOUNCEMENT

**notion** *n* **1 notions** *pl* small useful items ⟨the fabric store had a wide variety of thread, pins, buttons, and other *notions*⟩
***syn*** novelties, odds and ends, sundries
***rel*** bauble(s), bric-a-brac, gewgaw(s), knickknack(s), trinket(s); hodgepodge, miscellany, variety
**2** a sudden impulsive and apparently unmotivated idea or action — see WHIM
**3** an idea that is believed to be true or valid without positive knowledge — see OPINION 1
**4** something imagined or pictured in the mind — see IDEA

**notoriety** *n* the fact or state of being known to the public — see FAME

**notorious** *adj* **1** not respectable — see DISREPUTABLE
**2** widely known — see FAMOUS

**notwithstanding** *adv* in spite of that — see HOWEVER

**notwithstanding** *prep* without being prevented by — see DESPITE

**nourish** *vb* **1** to help the growth or development of — see FOSTER 1
**2** to supply with nourishment — see SUSTAIN 1

**nourishing** *adj* providing the substances necessary for health and bodily growth — see NUTRITIOUS

***syn*** synonym(s) ***rel*** related words
***ant*** antonym(s) ***near ant*** near antonym(s)

**novel** *adj* not known or experienced before — see NEW 2

**novelette** *n* a work with imaginary characters and events that is shorter and usually less complex than a novel — see STORY 1

**novella** *n* a work with imaginary characters and events that is shorter and usually less complex than a novel — see STORY 1

**novelty** *n* **1** the quality or appeal of being new ⟨the *novelty* of having a cat quickly wore off⟩
***syn*** freshness, newness, originality
***rel*** strangeness, unfamiliarity, unusualness; progressiveness; up-to-dateness; departure, divergence, innovation, offshoot, shoot
***near ant*** banality, commonness, familiarity, staleness
**2 novelties** *pl* small useful items — see NOTION 1
**3** a small object displayed for its attractiveness or interest — see KNICKKNACK

**novice** *n* a person who is just starting out in a field of activity — see BEGINNER

**now** *adv* **1** at the present time ⟨that company doesn't make those toys *now* because they are unsafe⟩
***syn*** anymore, currently, nowadays, presently, right now, today
***rel*** here
***near ant*** away, far, farthest, remotest; heretofore, hitherto, since; ago, previously
***ant*** before, formerly, long, once, then
**2** not long ago — see NEWLY
**3** on some occasions — see SOMETIMES
**4** without delay — see IMMEDIATELY

**now** *conj* for the reason that — see SINCE

**now** *n* the time currently existing or in progress — see PRESENT 1

**nowadays** *adv* at the present time — see NOW 1

**noway** *or* **noways** *adv* not in any degree, way, or under any condition — see NEVER 2

**no way** *adv* certainly not — see HARDLY 2

**nowise** *adv* not in any degree, way, or under any condition — see NEVER 2

**noxious** *adj* **1** bad for the well-being of the body — see UNHEALTHY 1
**2** causing or capable of causing harm — see HARMFUL

**nth** *adj* of the greatest or highest degree or quantity — see ULTIMATE 1

**nub** *n* **1** a small uneven mass — see LUMP 1
**2** the central part or aspect of something under consideration — see CRUX

**nubbin** *n* a very small piece — see BIT 1

**nubble** *n* a small uneven mass — see LUMP 1

**nubbly** *adj* having small pieces or lumps spread throughout — see CHUNKY 1

**nubby** *adj* having small pieces or lumps spread throughout — see CHUNKY 1

**nucleus** *n* a thing or place that is of greatest importance to an activity or interest — see CENTER 1

**nude** *adj* lacking or shed of clothing — see NAKED 1

**nudge** *vb* to pass lightly across or touch gently especially in passing — see BRUSH

**nugget** *n* a small uneven mass — see LUMP 1

**nuisance** *n* **1** one who is obnoxiously annoying ⟨my little brother was being a *nuisance* by poking and prodding me throughout the long car trip⟩
*syn* annoyance, annoyer, bother, gadfly, gnawer, persecutor, pest, tease, teaser
*rel* headache; harrier, heckler; hassle, plague; molester, tormentor, torturer
*near ant* charmer, smoothy (or smoothie)
**2** something that is a source of irritation — see ANNOYANCE 3

**null** *adj* **1** having no legal or binding force ⟨the contract was *null* because the other person forgot to sign it⟩
*syn* invalid, nonbinding, nonvalid, null and void, void
*rel* illegal; useless, worthless; ineffective, ineffectual
*near ant* legal; working
*ant* binding, good, valid
**2** having no usefulness — see WORTHLESS

**null and void** *adj* having no legal or binding force — see NULL 1

**nullify** *vb* to put an end to by formal action — see ABOLISH

**numb** *adj* lacking in sensation or feeling ⟨I sat in one position too long and now my feet are *numb*⟩
*syn* asleep, benumbed, dead, insensitive, numbed, unfeeling
*rel* chilled, nipped; anesthetized, deadened, drugged, stupefied; insensible, senseless, unconscious; inanimate, insensate
*near ant* awake
*ant* feeling, sensitive

**numb** *vb* to reduce or weaken in strength or feeling — see DULL 1

**numbed** *adj* lacking in sensation or feeling — see NUMB

**number** *n* a character used to represent a mathematical value ⟨asked him to write out the equation in *numbers*, not letters⟩
*syn* digit, figure, integer, numeral, whole number
*rel* decimal, fraction; cipher; symbol

**number** *vb* **1** to find the sum of (a collection of things) by noting each one as it is being added — see COUNT 1
**2** to have a total of — see AMOUNT (TO) 1
**3** to have as part of a whole — see INCLUDE

**numberless** *adj* too many to be counted — see COUNTLESS

**numbing** *adj* having a low or subnormal temperature — see COLD 1

**numbness** *n* a lack of emotion or emotional expressiveness — see APATHY 1

**numeral** *n* a character used to represent a mathematical value — see NUMBER

**numerate** *vb* **1** to make a list of — see [1]LIST 1
**2** to specify one after another — see ENUMERATE 1

**numerous** *adj* being of a large but indefinite number — see MANY

**numskull** *or* **numbskull** *n* a stupid person — see IDIOT

**nuptial** *adj* of or relating to marriage — see MARITAL

**nuptial** *n, usually* **nuptials** *pl* a ceremony in which two people are united in matrimony — see WEDDING

**nurse** *n* a girl or woman employed to care for a young child or children ⟨sent his little son back to his *nurse* so that he could return to his study to work⟩
*syn* babysitter, nursemaid, nurser, sitter
*rel* mammy; governess

**nurse** *vb* **1** to attend to the needs and comforts of ⟨took some time to *nurse* his grandmother, helping her get from one room to the other and making sure she was warm⟩
*syn* care (for), minister (to), mother
*rel* cure, heal, remedy; doctor, treat; aid, conserve, preserve, provide (for), support; baby, coddle, mollycoddle, pamper, spoil; cater (to), humor; indulge
*phrases* look after, look out for, look to, see to, take care of
*near ant* brush (aside *or* off), forget, ignore, neglect, overlook, slight
**2** to keep in one's mind or heart — see HARBOR 1
**3** to treat with great or excessive care — see BABY

**nursemaid** *n* a girl or woman employed to care for a young child or children — see NURSE

**nurser** *n* a girl or woman employed to care for a young child or children — see NURSE

**nurture** *vb* **1** to help the growth or development of — see FOSTER 1
**2** to provide (someone) with moral or spiritual understanding — see ENLIGHTEN 2
**3** to supply with nourishment — see SUSTAIN 1

**nut** *n* **1** a person of odd or whimsical habits — see ECCENTRIC
**2** a person who lacks good sense or judgment — see FOOL 1
**3** a person with a strong and habitual liking for something — see FAN
**4** a person judged to be legally or medically insane — see LUNATIC 1

**nutrient** *adj* providing the substances necessary for health and bodily growth — see NUTRITIOUS

**nutritional** *adj* providing the substances necessary for health and bodily growth — see NUTRITIOUS

**nutritious** *adj* providing the substances necessary for health and bodily growth ⟨opted for a *nutritious* snack and bought an apple instead of a candy bar⟩
*syn* nourishing, nutrient, nutritional, nutritive
*rel* dietary, dietetic; beneficial, healthful, healthy, restorative, salubrious, salutary, wholesome
*near ant* insalubrious, unhealthful, unhealthy, unwholesome
*ant* nonnutritious

**nutritive** *adj* providing the substances necessary for health and bodily growth — see NUTRITIOUS

**nuts** *adj* **1** having or showing a very abnormal or sick state of mind — see INSANE 1
**2** showing urgent desire or interest — see EAGER

**nuts** (about) *adj* filled with an intense or excessive love for — see ENAMORED (OF)

**nuttiness** *n* lack of good sense or judgment — see FOOLISHNESS 1

**nutty** *adj* **1** having or showing a very abnormal or sick state of mind — see INSANE 1
**2** showing or marked by a lack of good sense or judgment — see FOOLISH 1

**nuzzle** *vb* to lie close ⟨newborn puppies *nuzzling* against their mother to stay warm⟩
***syn*** cuddle, nestle, snuggle
***rel*** curl up; crouch, huddle
***near ant*** blench, flinch, quail, recoil, shrink, shy, start, wince

**nymph** *n* **1** a mythical goddess represented as a young girl and said to live outdoors ⟨she bought the book of fairy tales for the beautiful engravings of *nymphs* and fairies featured between the stories⟩
***syn*** dryad, naiad, oread
***rel*** mermaid, siren
**2** a young wingless often wormlike form (as a grub or caterpillar) that hatches from the egg of many insects — see LARVA

# O

**oaf** *n* a big clumsy often slow-witted person ⟨it is not polite to call your brother a stupid *oaf*⟩
***syn*** clod, gawk, hulk, lout, lubber, lug
***rel*** chump, loser, schlemiel, turkey; ass, blockhead, dolt, donkey, dope, dumbbell, dummy, goon, half-wit, idiot, ignoramus, imbecile, jackass, moron, nincompoop, ninny, nitwit, simpleton; beast, boor, brute, cad, churl, clown, creep, cretin, cur, heel, louse, skunk, snake, stinker, villain; booby, fool, goose, loony (*also* looney), lunatic, madman, nut; featherbrain, scatterbrain; rascal, rogue, scamp
***near ant*** brain, genius; egghead, intellectual, sage, thinker

**oafish** *adj* not having or showing an ability to absorb ideas readily — see STUPID 1

**oafishness** *n* the quality or state of lacking intelligence or quickness of mind — see STUPIDITY 1

**oar** *vb* to move a boat by means of oars — see [1]ROW

**oarsman** *n* a person who drives a boat forward by means of oars ⟨the only *oarsman* in a rowboat designed for two⟩
***syn*** rower, sculler
***rel*** coxswain, crewman; puller, sailor

**oath** *n* a person's solemn declaration that he or she will do or not do something — see PROMISE

**obduracy** *n* a steadfast adherence to an opinion, purpose, or course of action — see OBSTINACY

**obdurate** *adj* **1** having or showing a lack of sympathy or tender feelings — see HARD 1
**2** sticking to an opinion, purpose, or course of action in spite of reason, arguments, or persuasion — see OBSTINATE

**obedience** *n* **1** a bending to the authority or control of another ⟨the drill sergeant demanded complete and unquestioning *obedience* from the recruits⟩
***syn*** compliance, conformity, observance, submission, subordination
***rel*** acquiescence, agreeability, amenability; docility, submissiveness; capitulation, surrender, yielding; servility, slavishness, subservience; inhibition, repression, restraint, suppression; control, discipline, order
***near ant*** contrariness, frowardness, intractability, rebelliousness, recalcitrance, refractoriness; disrespect, impudence, insolence, rudeness; insurgency, insurrection, mutiny, revolt; hardheadedness, mulishness, obstinacy, perversity, stubbornness, willfulness; misbehavior, mischievousness, naughtiness; dissent, dissidence
***ant*** disobedience, insubordination, noncompliance, rebelling, rebellion
**2** a readiness or willingness to yield to the wishes of others — see COMPLIANCE 1

**obedient** *adj* readily giving in to the command or authority of another ⟨that boy is so *obedient* that he does everything the first time he is asked⟩
***syn*** amenable, compliant, conformable, docile, law-abiding, submissive, tractable
***rel*** acquiescent, agreeable, amiable, obliging; surrendering, yielding; obsequious, servile, slavish, subservient; decorous, disciplined, mannerly, orderly; constrained, curbed, inhibited, repressed, restrained; controllable, governable, manageable; gentle, meek, mild
***near ant*** insurgent, mutinous; dogged, hardheaded, headstrong, mulish, obdurate, obstinate, peevish, pigheaded, self-

willed, stubborn, unyielding, willful (*or* wilful); obstreperous, restive, uncontrollable, ungovernable, unmanageable, wild; balky, defiant, perverse, resistant, wayward; bad, disorderly, errant, misbehaving, mischievous, naughty; ill-bred, undisciplined; dissident, nonconformist; disrespectful, ill-mannered, impolite, impudent, insolent, rude

***ant*** contrary, disobedient, froward, insubordinate, intractable, rebellious, recalcitrant, refractory, unruly

**obese** *adj* having an excess of body fat — see FAT 1

**obesity** *n* the condition of having an excess of body fat — see CORPULENCE

**obey** *vb* to act according to the commands of ⟨it is important to *obey* your teachers immediately in the case of an emergency⟩ ⟨most people *obey* the law and wear their seat belts⟩

***syn*** comply (with), conform (to), follow, mind, observe

***rel*** defer (to), submit (to), surrender (to), yield (to); accede (to), acquiesce (to), agree (to), assent (to); attend, hear, heed, listen (to), mark, note, notice, regard, watch

***phrases*** abide by

***near ant*** challenge, dare; rebel (against); defy; direct, lead; brush off, disregard, ignore, overlook, overpass, pass over, tune out, wink (at); dismiss, pooh-pooh, shrug off; break, transgress, violate; deride, flout, scorn

***ant*** disobey

**object** *n* **1** something material that can be perceived by the senses ⟨I kept tripping over countless little *objects* scattered about the darkened room⟩

***syn*** thing

***rel*** article, item, piece; being, entity, substance; commodity, good, ware; accessory, accompaniment, bauble, curio; knickknack, spangle, token, trinke

**2** one that has a real and independent existence — see ENTITY

**3** something that one hopes or intends to accomplish — see GOAL

**object** *vb* to present an opposing opinion or argument ⟨they *objected* to the conductor's insistence that their train tickets were not valid⟩

***syn*** demur, expostulate (with), kick, protest, remonstrate (with)

***rel*** cavil, quibble; challenge, dare, defy; conflict (with), debate, dispute, hassle, quarrel, squabble, wrangle; complain, inveigh (against); balk (at), stick (at); censure, criticize, denounce; disobey, rebel (against); demonstrate (against)

***phrases*** take exception

***near ant*** approve, sanction; accept; accede (to), acquiesce (to), agree (with), assent (to); comply (with), obey; advocate, champion, defend, maintain, support, sustain, uphold

**objection** *n* a feeling or declaration of disapproval or dissent ⟨pardon me, but I have an *objection* to any plan that requires staying out all night⟩

***syn*** challenge, complaint, demur, expostulation, fuss, protest, question, remonstrance

***rel*** compunction, doubt, misgiving, qualm, scruple; difficulty, misunderstanding; cavil, quibble; argument, conflict, debate, dispute, dissent, hassle, quarrel, squabble; censure, criticism; defiance, disobedience, rebellion

***near ant*** willingness; approval, sanction; acceptance, acquiescence, agreement, assent; compliance, obedience

**objectionable** *adj* provoking or likely to provoke protest ⟨that T-shirt displays *objectionable* images which are not appropriate for school⟩

***syn*** censurable, exceptionable, obnoxious, offensive, reprehensible

***rel*** bawdy, coarse, crude, dirty, filthy, foul, gross, indecent, lewd, nasty, obscene, smutty, vulgar; blamable, blameworthy, lascivious, pornographic, ribald, scurrilous; debasing, perverted, profane; racy, salty, suggestive; unacceptable, undesirable, unwanted, unwelcome; abhorrent, disgusting, loathsome, repellent (*also* repellant), repugnant, repulsive, revolting; disagreeable, displeasing, distasteful, unpleasant; bad, execrable, lousy, miserable; atrocious, infamous; indecent, indecorous, unbecoming; earthy, unprintable; naughty, wicked

***near ant*** acceptable, agreeable, pleasant, pleasing, welcome; good; approved, endorsed, sanctioned; abetted, encouraged, promoted, supported; becoming, correct, decent, decorous, exemplary, seemly; blameless, commendable, creditable; immaculate, perfect, pure, spotless

***ant*** inoffensive, unobjectionable

**objective** *adj* **1** based on observation or experience — see EMPIRICAL

**2** marked by justice, honesty, and freedom from bias — see FAIR 2

**3** restricted to or based on fact — see FACTUAL 1

**objective** *n* something that one hopes or intends to accomplish — see GOAL

**objectivity** *n* lack of favoritism toward one side or another — see DETACHMENT 1

**obligate** *vb* to cause (a person) to give in to pressure — see FORCE

**obligation** *n* something one must do because of prior agreement ⟨their financial *obligations* keep them from giving to charities as much as they would like⟩

***syn*** burden, charge, commitment, duty, need, responsibility

***rel*** pledge, promise; arrangement, prearrangement, setup; compact, contract, covenant, pact; payment, tribute; compulsion, constraint, restraint; must, requirement; coercion, duress, force; appointment, engagement, reservation

***near ant*** grace, postponement, stay; discharge, exemption, release, waiver; alternative, choice, option, pick, preference, selection

**obligatory** *adj* forcing one's compliance or participation by or as if by law — see MANDATORY

**oblige** *vb* **1** to do a service or favor for ⟨I would appreciate it greatly if you could *oblige* me by bringing a dessert to the party⟩
***syn*** accommodate, favor
***rel*** humor, indulge; coddle, mollycoddle, pamper; appease, conciliate, mollify, pacify, placate; delight, gladden, gratify, please, satisfy; abet, aid, assist, help, support; attend, care (for), minister (to), relieve, succor
***near ant*** bother, discommode, disturb, incommode, inconvenience, trouble; burden, encumber, saddle, weigh; desert, disappoint, fail, let down; constrain, hamper, hamstring, hinder, hobble, hold back, impede, obstruct, restrain; frustrate, oppose, sabotage, thwart
***ant*** disoblige
**2** to cause (a person) to give in to pressure — see FORCE

**obliged** *adj* feeling or expressing gratitude — see GRATEFUL 1

**oblique** *adj* **1** inclined or twisted to one side — see AWRY
**2** running in a slanting direction — see DIAGONAL

**obliquely** *adv* in a line or direction running from corner to corner — see CROSSWISE

**obliterate** *vb* to destroy all traces of — see ANNIHILATE 1

**obliteration** *n* the state or fact of being rendered nonexistent, physically unsound, or useless — see DESTRUCTION

**oblivion** *n* a state of being disregardful or unconscious of one's surroundings, concerns, or obligations ⟨for two weeks each year the stressed-out couple enjoy the blissful *oblivion* that comes with a vacation at the beach⟩
***syn*** forgetfulness, obliviousness
***rel*** ignorance, unawareness, unconsciousness, unfamiliarity
***near ant*** memory, recall, recollection, remembrance; alertness, awareness, cognizance, consciousness

**oblivious** *adj* not informed about or aware of something — see IGNORANT 2

**obliviousness** *n* **1** a state of being disregardful or unconscious of one's surroundings, concerns, or obligations — see OBLIVION
**2** the state of being unaware or uninformed — see IGNORANCE 1

**obnoxious** *adj* **1** causing intense displeasure, disgust, or resentment — see OFFENSIVE 1
**2** provoking or likely to provoke protest — see OBJECTIONABLE

**obscene** *adj* **1** depicting or referring to sexual matters in a way that is unacceptable in polite society ⟨*obscene* language and artwork is forbidden in this school⟩
***syn*** bawdy, coarse, crude, dirty, filthy, foul, gross, indecent, lascivious, lewd, nasty, pornographic, ribald, smutty, unprintable, vulgar, wanton
***rel*** earthy, racy, salty, suggestive; indecorous, unbecoming; debasing, perverted, profane; naughty, wicked; exceptionable, objectionable, unacceptable, undesirable, unwanted, unwelcome; abhorrent, disgusting, loathsome, offensive, repellent (*also* repellant), repugnant, repulsive, revolting; distasteful, obnoxious, unpleasant; blamable, blameworthy, censurable, reprehensible; atrocious, infamous; abusive, scurrilous
***near ant*** priggish, prim, prudish, puritanical, straitlaced (*or* straightlaced), Victorian; correct, decorous, genteel, polite, proper, seemly; innocuous, inoffensive; acceptable, agreeable, desirable, pleasant, pleasing, welcome; appropriate, becoming, fit, meet, suitable; immaculate, perfect, pure, spotless; approved, endorsed, sanctioned
***ant*** clean, decent
**2** causing intense displeasure, disgust, or resentment — see OFFENSIVE 1

**obscenity** *n* **1** the quality or state of being obscene ⟨the issue of whether *obscenity* is a fundamental part of rap music⟩
***syn*** bawdiness, coarseness, crudeness, dirt, dirtiness, filth, filthiness, foulness, grossness, indecency, lasciviousness, lewdness, nastiness, ribaldry, smuttiness, vulgarity
***rel*** raciness, saltiness, suggestiveness; perversion, profanity; naughtiness, wickedness; loathsomeness, offensiveness, repulsiveness; distastefulness, obnoxiousness, unpleasantness
***near ant*** priggishness, primness, prudery, prudishness, puritanism; correctness, decency, decorousness, decorum, seemliness; appropriateness, fitness, suitability, suitableness; immaculateness, perfection, purity, spotlessness
**2** a disrespectful or indecent word or expression — see SWEARWORD

**obscure** *adj* **1** having an often intentionally veiled or uncertain meaning ⟨a fantasy writer who likes to put lots of *obscure* references and images in her tales of wizards and warlocks⟩
***syn*** ambiguous, cryptic, dark, darkling, deep, enigmatic (*also* enigmatical), equivocal, inscrutable, murky, mysterious, mystic, nebulous, occult
***rel*** abstruse, esoteric, recondite; bleary, cloudy, dim, faint, foggy, fuzzy, hazy, indefinite, indistinct, indistinguishable, shadowy, unclear, uncertain, undefined, undetermined, vague; impenetrable, incomprehensible; inexplicable; eerie, uncanny, weird; impalpable, inappreciable, intangible, invisible; unanswerable, unknowable; baffling, bewildering, confounding, confusing, mystifying, perplex-

---

***syn*** synonym(s) ***rel*** related words
***ant*** antonym(s) ***near ant*** near antonym(s)

ing, puzzling, unfathomable; difficult, complex, complicated, obtuse
***near ant*** comprehensible, fathomable, intelligible, knowable, understandable; bright, distinct, evident; certain, firm, strong, sure; defined, determined; direct, straightforward; definite, exact, explicit; appreciable, palpable, tangible, visible; blatant, patent, unmistakable
***ant*** clear, obvious, plain, unambiguous, unequivocal
**2** not widely known ⟨he's an *obscure* artist now, but he's sure to be famous someday⟩
***syn*** anonymous, nameless, uncelebrated, unknown, unnoted, unsung
***rel*** insignificant, minor, unimportant; undistinguished, unexceptional; unpopular; faceless
***near ant*** fabled, fabulous, legendary; infamous; distinguished, eminent, exceptional, great, illustrious, leading, notable, outstanding, prestigious, remarkable; important, significant; favorite, popular, preferred; estimable, honorable, reputable, respectable; influential, major
***ant*** celebrated, famed, famous, noted, notorious, prominent, renowned, well-known
**3** being without light or without much light — see DARK 1
**4** not seen or understood clearly — see FAINT 1

**obscure** *vb* **1** to keep secret or shut off from view — see [1]HIDE 2
**2** to make dark, dim, or indistinct — see CLOUD 1

**obscured** *adj* being without light or without much light — see DARK 1

**obscurity** *n* **1** the quality or state of having a veiled or uncertain meaning ⟨the 16th-century astrologer's predictions are so filled with *obscurity* that people can interpret them any way they want⟩
***syn*** ambiguity, ambiguousness, darkness, equivocalness, equivocation, murkiness, nebulousness, opacity
***rel*** cloudiness, dimness, faintness, fogginess, fuzziness, haziness, indefiniteness, indistinctness, uncertainty, vagueness; impenetrability, incomprehensibility; deepness, profoundness; intangibility, invisibility; abstruseness; complexity, complication, difficulty, obtuseness
***near ant*** comprehensibility, intelligibility; brightness, distinctness; certainty, surety; definiteness, exactness, explicitness; directness, straightforwardness; palpability, tangibility, visibility
***ant*** clarity, clearness, obviousness, plainness
**2** the quality or state of being mostly or completely unknown ⟨the singer languished in relative *obscurity* for years before becoming famous⟩
***syn*** anonymity
***rel*** oblivion; inconspicuousness, invisibility; insignificance, unimportance; unpopularity
***near ant*** name, report, reputation, repute; popularity; importance, significance; distinction, eminence, glory, greatness, honor, illustriousness, note, preeminence, prominence; cachet, position, prestige, rank, standing, stature; acclaim, acknowledgment (*also* acknowledgement), praise, recognition; adoration, idolization
***ant*** celebrity, fame, notoriety, renown

**observable** *adj* capable of being seen — see VISIBLE

**observance** *n* **1** an act of following a custom, rule, or law ⟨the *observance* of this family tradition would make your grandmother very happy⟩
***syn*** observation
***rel*** attention, heed, notice; respecting, upholding
***near ant*** infraction, offense (*or* offence), sin, trespass, wrong; disregard, forgetting, ignoring, neglect, overlooking; delinquency, dereliction
***ant*** breach, infringement, nonobservance, transgression, violation
**2** an oft-repeated action or series of actions performed in accordance with tradition or a set of rules — see RITE
**3** a bending to the authority or control of another — see OBEDIENCE 1
**4** a state of being aware — see ATTENTION 2

**observation** *n* **1** a state of being aware — see ATTENTION 2
**2** an act of following a custom, rule, or law — see OBSERVANCE 1

**observational** *adj* based on observation or experience — see EMPIRICAL

**observatory** *n* a high place or structure from which a wide view is possible — see LOOKOUT 1

**observe** *vb* **1** to act according to the commands of — see OBEY
**2** to act properly in relation to — see KEEP 1
**3** to keep one's eyes on — see WATCH 1
**4** to make a statement of one's opinion — see REMARK 1
**5** to make note of (something) through the use of one's eyes — see SEE 1
**6** to take notice of and be guided by — see HEED 1

**obsessed** *adj* having extreme or relentless concern — see HUNG UP 1

**obsession** *n* something about which one is constantly thinking or concerned — see FIXATION

**obsessive** *adj* caused by or suggestive of an irresistible urge — see COMPULSIVE

**obsolete** *adj* having passed its time of use or usefulness ⟨the abacus was considered *obsolete* once the electronic calculator was invented⟩
***syn*** antiquated, archaic, dated, moth-eaten, outdated, outmoded, out-of-date, outworn, passé
***rel*** aging, obsolescent; discarded, disused, superannuated, worn-out; inoperable, unusable, unworkable, useless; dead, defunct, extinct; dormant, fallow, free, idle, inactive, inert, inoperative, latent; an-

cient, antediluvian, antique, fusty, musty, old, oldfangled, old-fashioned, old-time, old-world; aged, age-old, hoary, venerable; bygone, erstwhile, former, late, past; historic, historical
***near ant*** contemporary, current, mod, modern, new, newfangled, new-fashioned, present-day, recent, ultramodern, up-to-date; fresh; modernized, refurbished, remodeled, renewed; functional, operable, operational, workable; active, alive, busy, employed, functioning, operating, operative

**obstacle** *n* something that makes movement or progress more difficult — see ENCUMBRANCE

**obstinacy** *n* a steadfast adherence to an opinion, purpose, or course of action ⟨the mindless *obstinacy* of those people who continue to insist that the earth is flat⟩
***syn*** doggedness, hardheadedness, mulishness, obduracy, peevishness, persistence, pertinaciousness, pertinacity, self-will, stubbornness, tenaciousness, tenacity, willfulness
***rel*** perverseness, perversity, resistance, waywardness, wrongheadedness; hardness, inflexibility, relentlessness, sternness, strictness; certainty, determination, firmness; inexorability, resolve, rigidity, rigidness, steadfastness; contrariness, defiance, disobedience, insubordination, recalcitrance
***near ant*** broad-mindedness, open-mindedness, reasonableness, receptivity; acceptance, acquiescence, flexibility, pliability; compliance, docility, obedience; submission, surrender, willingness, yielding; slavishness, subservience

**obstinate** *adj* sticking to an opinion, purpose, or course of action in spite of reason, arguments, or persuasion ⟨the child was *obstinate* about wanting that specific toy, despite being offered several others⟩
***syn*** adamant, adamantine, dogged, hard, hardened, hardheaded, hardhearted, headstrong, immovable, implacable, inflexible, mulish, obdurate, opinionated, ossified, pat, peevish, pertinacious, perverse, pigheaded, rigid, self-willed, stubborn, unbending, uncompromising, unrelenting, unyielding, willful (*or* wilful)
***rel*** hidebound, narrow-minded; resistant, wayward, wrongheaded; persistent, tenacious; iron, relentless; grim, severe, stern, strict; determined, firm, inexorable, resolved, single-minded, steadfast, sure, unflinching; contrary, disobedient, froward, insubordinate, intractable, recalcitrant, refractory, uncooperative, ungovernable, unmanageable, unruly; defiant, insurgent, mutinous; indomitable, invincible, unconquerable; confirmed, inveterate, unregenerate; demanding, exacting
***near ant*** docile, law-abiding, obedient, submissive, tractable; accepting, receptive, responsive, willing; governable, manageable, reasonable, temperate; slavish, subservient
***ant*** acquiescent, agreeable, amenable, compliant, complying, flexible, pliable, pliant, relenting, yielding

**obstreperous** *adj* engaging in or marked by loud and insistent cries especially of protest — see VOCIFEROUS

**obstruct** *vb* **1** to create difficulty for the work or activity of — see HAMPER
**2** to prevent passage through — see CLOG 1

**obstruction** *n* something that makes movement or progress more difficult — see ENCUMBRANCE

**obtain** *vb* to receive as return for effort — see EARN 1

**obtainable** *adj* possible to get — see AVAILABLE 1

**obtrude** *vb* to interest oneself in what is not one's concern — see INTERFERE

**obtrusive** *adj* thrusting oneself where one is not welcome or invited — see INTRUSIVE

**obtuse** *adj* **1** lacking sharpness of edge or point — see DULL 1
**2** not having or showing an ability to absorb ideas readily — see STUPID 1

**obtuseness** *n* the quality or state of lacking intelligence or quickness of mind — see STUPIDITY 1

**obviate** *vb* to keep from happening by taking action in advance — see PREVENT

**obviating** *n* the act or practice of keeping something from happening — see PREVENTION

**obvious** *adj* **1** not subject to misinterpretation or more than one interpretation — see CLEAR 2
**2** very noticeable especially for being incorrect or bad — see EGREGIOUS

**occasion** *n* **1** a particular point at which an event takes place ⟨the *occasion* of our last meeting with our old friend was several years ago, unfortunately⟩
***syn*** moment, time
***rel*** flash, instant, jiffy, minute, second, shake, split second, trice, twinkle, wink; while
**2** a favorable combination of circumstances, time, and place — see OPPORTUNITY
**3** someone or something responsible for a result — see CAUSE 1
**4** something that happens — see EVENT 1

**occasional** *adj* **1** lacking in steadiness or regularity of occurrence — see FITFUL
**2** not often occurring or repeated — see INFREQUENT

**occasionally** *adv* on some occasions — see SOMETIMES

**occult** *adj* **1** being beyond one's powers to know, understand, or explain — see MYSTERIOUS 1
**2** having an often intentionally veiled or uncertain meaning — see OBSCURE 1
**3** having seemingly supernatural qualities or powers — see MYSTIC 1

**occult** *vb* to keep secret or shut off from view — see [1]HIDE 2

**occupant** *n* one who lives permanently in a place — see INHABITANT

**occupation** *n* the activity by which one regularly makes a living ⟨my primary *occupation* is as a stockbroker, but I'm a drummer in a rock band on the weekends⟩
*syn* calling, employment, line, profession, trade, vocation, work
*rel* racket; art, craft, handicraft; appointment, assignment, berth, billet, duty, function, job, office, place, position, post, situation; business, engagement, livelihood, living
*near ant* avocation, hobby, pursuit

**occupied** *adj* involved in often constant activity — see BUSY 1

**occupy** *vb* **1** to hold the attention of — see ENGAGE 1
**2** to keep, control, or experience as one's own — see HAVE 1

**occur** *vb* to take place — see HAPPEN

**occur** (to) *vb* to come into the mind of ⟨it didn't *occur to* me to ask until much later⟩
*syn* dawn (on), strike
*rel* appear, arrive, come, emerge, materialize; con, learn, memorize; recall, recollect, remember, reminisce
*near ant* forget, unlearn; disregard, neglect, overlook

**occurrence** *n* something that happens — see EVENT 1

**ocean** *n* the whole body of salt water that covers nearly three-fourths of the earth ⟨the Vikings explored the *ocean* in small open boats, beginning in the eighth century⟩
*syn* blue, brine, deep, sea, seven seas
*rel* high seas, main, waters; basin; Davy Jones's locker

**oceanic** *adj* of or relating to the sea — see MARINE 1

**ocular** *adj* of, relating to, or used in vision — see VISUAL 1

**odd** *adj* **1** being one of a pair or set without a corresponding mate ⟨somehow, there's always at least one *odd* sock that comes out of the dryer⟩
*syn* unmatched, unpaired
*rel* alone, lone, only, single, singular, sole, solitary
*ant* matched, paired
**2** different from the ordinary in a way that causes curiosity or suspicion ⟨one girl dyed her hair purple with pink polka dots, which was a rather *odd* effect⟩
*syn* bizarre, curious, far-out, funny, kinky, outlandish, out-of-the-way, outré, peculiar, quaint, queer, queerish, quirky, remarkable, screwy, strange, wacky, way-out, weird, wild
*rel* aberrant, abnormal, atypical, extraordinary, fantastic, flaky, freak, freakish, idiosyncratic, phenomenal, singular, unique, unusual, unwonted; conspicuous, notable, noticeable, outstanding, prominent, salient, striking; atrocious, outrageous, shocking; nonconformist, unconventional, unorthodox; eccentric, idiosyncratic; rare, uncommon, uncustomary; baffling, bewildering, confounding, mystifying, perplexing, puzzling
*near ant* average, commonplace, everyday, garden, ordinary, prosaic, routine, run-of-the-mill, typical, unexceptional, unremarkable, usual, workaday; conformist, conservative, conventional; expected, familiar, predictable; common, customary, frequent, habitual, regular, wonted
**3** being out of the ordinary — see EXCEPTIONAL
**4** noticeably different from what is generally found or experienced — see UNUSUAL 1

**oddball** *n* a person of odd or whimsical habits — see ECCENTRIC

**oddity** *n* **1** an odd or peculiar habit — see IDIOSYNCRASY
**2** something strange or unusual that is an object of interest — see CURIOSITY 2

**oddment** *n* an unused or unwanted piece or item typically of small size or value — see [1]SCRAP 1

**odds** *n pl* a measure of how often an event will occur instead of another — see PROBABILITY 2

**odds and ends** *n pl* **1** small useful items — see NOTION 1
**2** a remaining group or portion — see REMAINDER 1

**odious** *adj* causing intense displeasure, disgust, or resentment — see OFFENSIVE 1

**odium** *n* the state of having lost the esteem of others — see DISGRACE 1

**odor** *n* the quality of a thing that makes it perceptible to the sense organs in the nose — see SMELL

**of** *prep* **1** earlier than — see BEFORE 1
**2** having to do with — see ABOUT 1

**off** *adv* from this or that place — see AWAY

**off** *adj* **1** falling short of a standard — see BAD 1
**2** not being in a state of use, activity, or employment — see INACTIVE 2
**3** not being in agreement with what is true — see FALSE 1
**4** small in degree — see REMOTE 1

**offbeat** *adj* noticeably different from what is generally found or experienced — see UNUSUAL 1

**offend** *vb* **1** to commit an offense ⟨since this is the first time you've *offended,* we'll let you off lightly⟩
*syn* err, sin, transgress, trespass
*rel* breach, break, infringe, violate; backslide, lapse
*phrases* break the law, fall from grace
*near ant* forgive, justify; repent
**2** to cause hurt feelings or deep resentment in — see INSULT

**offender** *n* a person who has committed a crime — see CRIMINAL

**offense** *or* **offence** *n* **1** a breaking of a moral or legal code ⟨wartime *offenses* that are crimes against all of humanity⟩

*syn* breach, crime, debt, error, lawbreaking, malefaction, misdeed, misdoing, sin, transgression, trespass, violation, wrongdoing
*rel* felony, misdemeanor; fault, foible, peccadillo; break, infringement; immorality, iniquity, sinfulness, vice, wickedness; criminality, illegality, lawlessness, unlawfulness
*near ant* blamelessness, faultlessness, guiltlessness, innocence; goodness, morality, righteousness, virtue, virtuousness
**2** the act or action of setting upon with force or violence — see ATTACK 1
**3** an act or expression showing scorn and usually intended to hurt another's feelings — see INSULT
**4** the feeling of being offended or resentful after a slight or indignity — see PIQUE

**offensive** *adj* **1** causing intense displeasure, disgust, or resentment ⟨I find your disrespectful attitude toward religion very *offensive*⟩ ⟨the smell of rotting food is quite *offensive*⟩
*syn* abhorrent, abominable, appalling, awful, distasteful, dreadful, foul, hideous, horrendous, horrible, horrid, loathsome, nasty, nauseating, noisome, obnoxious, obscene, odious, repellent (*also* repellant), repugnant, repulsive, revolting, scandalous, shocking, sickening, ugly
*rel* exceptionable, objectionable; disagreeable, unpleasant; contemptible, despicable, detestable, hateful; unhealthy, unwholesome; execrable, lousy, miserable; atrocious, heinous, unspeakable; barbarous, unchristian, uncivilized, ungodly, unholy
*near ant* acceptable, agreeable, attractive, delectable, delightful, desirable, likable (*or* likeable), pleasant, pleasing, welcome; unobjectionable; healthy, wholesome
*ant* inoffensive
**2** provoking or likely to provoke protest — see OBJECTIONABLE

**offensive** *n* the act or action of setting upon with force or violence — see ATTACK 1

**offer** *n* something which is presented for consideration — see PROPOSAL

**offer** *vb* **1** to put before another for acceptance or consideration ⟨I *offered* my boss an alternative to the plan that required me to work overtime⟩
*syn* extend, give, proffer, tender
*rel* pose, propose
*near ant* accept, receive, take; decline, refuse, reject; retract, withdraw; consider, contemplate, mull (over), ponder, study, think (over)
**2** to set before the mind for consideration — see PROPOSE 1
**3** to bring before the public in performance or exhibition — see PRESENT 1
**4** to give up as an offering to a god — see SACRIFICE

**offering** *n* something offered to a god — see SACRIFICE

**offhand** *adj* made or done without previous thought or preparation — see EXTEMPORANEOUS

**offhanded** *adj* made or done without previous thought or preparation — see EXTEMPORANEOUS

**office** *n* a large unit of a governmental, business, or educational organization — see DIVISION 2

**officeholder** *n* a person who holds a public office — see OFFICIAL

**officer** *n* **1** a member of a force charged with law enforcement at the local level ⟨if you are ever lost, find the nearest *officer* and ask for help⟩
*syn* bobby [*British*], bull [*slang*], constable, cop, policeman, police officer
*rel* patrolman, policewoman; detective, inspector, plainclothesman; marshal, sheriff, trooper; captain, lieutenant, sergeant
**2** a person who holds a public office — see OFFICIAL

**official** *adj* ordered or allowed by those in authority ⟨the *official* languages for those Olympic Games were French and English⟩
*syn* authorized, sanctioned
*rel* legal, permissible; approved, endorsed; abetted, encouraged, promoted, suggested, supported; certified, licensed (*also* licenced); authoritative, canonical, ex officio; semiofficial
*near ant* illegal, illicit, unlawful; unapproved, unendorsed, unlicensed
*ant* unauthorized, unofficial, unsanctioned

**official** *n* a person who holds a public office ⟨some of our best public *officials* do their jobs quietly and are never in the news⟩
*syn* functionary, officeholder, officer, public servant
*rel* bureaucrat; administrator, commissioner, director, executive, manager, superintendent, supervisor; chair, chairman

**officious** *adj* thrusting oneself where one is not welcome or invited — see INTRUSIVE

**offing** *n* time that is to come — see FUTURE 1

**offset** *n* a force or influence that makes an opposing force ineffective or less effective — see COUNTERBALANCE

**offset** *vb* to balance with an equal force so as to make ineffective ⟨if you get a high grade on this quiz, it will *offset* the D from your last one⟩
*syn* annul, cancel (out), compensate (for), correct, counteract, counterbalance, counterpoise, make up (for), neutralize
*rel* invalidate, negate, nullify; atone (for); outweigh, redeem; redress, relieve, remedy; override, overrule

**offshoot** *n* **1** a branch of a main stem especially of a plant ⟨we knew the rose bush had survived the winter when it be-

*syn* synonym(s) *rel* related words
*ant* antonym(s) *near ant* near antonym(s)

gan producing *offshoots* and turning green again⟩
*syn* outgrowth, shoot
*rel* excrescence, growth; bough, limb, twig; bud, floret; spray, sprig
**2** something that naturally develops or is developed from something else — see DERIVATIVE

**offspring** *n* the descendants of a person, animal, or plant ⟨the racehorse's *offspring* all proved to be very good racers as well⟩ ⟨the couple celebrated their 50th wedding anniversary surrounded by three generations of *offspring*⟩
*syn* issue, posterity, progeny, seed, spawn
*rel* brood, hatch, litter, young; child, scion (*also* cion)
*near ant* ancestor, antecedent, forebear (*also* forbear), forefather, parent

**offstage** *adj or adv* off or away from the part of the stage visible to the audience ⟨please wait until you are *offstage* to start changing costumes⟩
*syn* backstage
*rel* upstage
*phrases* behind the scenes

**oft** *adv* many times — see OFTEN

**often** *adv* many times ⟨I seem to stumble *often* when I try to walk in high heels⟩
*syn* constantly, continually, frequently, oft, oftentimes (*or* ofttimes), repeatedly
*rel* always, consistently, continuously, perpetually; afresh, again, anew; commonly, ordinarily, regularly, routinely; intermittently, periodically, recurrently; generally, usually
*phrases* again and again, over and over, time after time, time and again
*near ant* occasionally, sometimes, sporadically, never; once
*ant* infrequently, rarely, seldom

**oftentimes** *or* **ofttimes** *adv* many times — see OFTEN

**ogle** *vb* to look at in a flirtatious or desiring way ⟨I do wish you two would stop *ogling* each other during class⟩
*syn* leer (at)
*rel* eye, gape, gawk, gaze, glare, goggle, peer, rubberneck, stare

**ogre** *n* **1** a strange or horrible and often frightening creature — see MONSTER 1
**2** something or someone that causes fear or dread especially without reason — see BOGEY 1

**oh** *n* the numerical symbol 0 or the absence of number or quantity represented by it — see ZERO 1

**oil** *n* a picture created with usually oil paint — see PAINTING

**oil** *vb* to coat (something) with a slippery substance in order to reduce friction — see LUBRICATE

**oiled** *adj* having or being a surface so smooth as to make sliding or falling likely — see SLICK 1

**oil painting** *n* a picture created with usually oil paint — see PAINTING

**oilskin** *n* a coat made of water-resistant material — see RAINCOAT

**OK** *or* **okay** *adj* **1** being to one's liking — see SATISFACTORY 1
**2** of a level of quality that meets one's needs or standards — see ADEQUATE

**OK** *or* **okay** *adv* **1** in a satisfactory way — see WELL 1
**2** used to express agreement — see YES

**OK** *or* **okay** *n* an acceptance of something as satisfactory — see APPROVAL 1

**OK** *or* **okay** *vb* **1** to give official acceptance of something as satisfactory — see APPROVE
**2** to have a favorable opinion of — see APPROVE (OF)

**old** *adj* **1** being of advanced years and especially past middle age — see ELDERLY
**2** dating or surviving from the distant past — see ANCIENT 1
**3** having been such at some previous time — see FORMER

**older** *adj* being of advanced years and especially past middle age — see ELDERLY

**oldfangled** *adj* pleasantly reminiscent of an earlier time — see OLD-FASHIONED 1

**old-fashioned** *adj* **1** pleasantly reminiscent of an earlier time ⟨an elegant, *old-fashioned* bun that was held in place with pearl hairpins⟩
*syn* antique, oldfangled, old-time, old-world, quaint
*rel* antiquated, obsolete; historic, historical, olden, traditional; outdated, outmoded, out-of-date, outworn, passé; dated, fusty, moth-eaten, musty; aged, age-old, ancient, antediluvian, fossilized, hoary, venerable; bygone, erstwhile, former, late, past; forgotten, remote; ageless, dateless; timeless
*near ant* fresh, new, up-to-date; chic, fashionable, smart, stylish; modernized, refurbished, remodeled, renewed
*ant* contemporary, hot, mod, modern, newfangled, new-fashioned, ultramodern
**2** tending to favor established ideas, conditions, or institutions — see CONSERVATIVE 1

**old hand** *n* a person with long experience in a specified area — see VETERAN

**old-maidish** *adj* hard to please — see FINICKY

**old man** *n* **1** a male human parent — see FATHER 1
**2** the male partner in a marriage — see HUSBAND

**oldster** *n* a person of advanced years — see SENIOR CITIZEN

**old-time** *adj* pleasantly reminiscent of an earlier time — see OLD-FASHIONED 1

**old-timer** *n* **1** a person of advanced years — see SENIOR CITIZEN
**2** a person with long experience in a specified area — see VETERAN

**old wives' tale** *n* a false idea or belief — see FALLACY 1

**old-world** *adj* pleasantly reminiscent of an earlier time — see OLD-FASHIONED 1

**omen** *n* something believed to be a sign or warning of a future event ⟨some people believe that a black cat crossing your

path is an *omen* that something bad is about to happen to you〉
*syn* augury, auspice, boding, foreboding, foreshadowing, portent, prefiguring, presage
*rel* forerunner, harbinger, herald, precursor; foretaste, hint, inkling, intimation, suggestion; forewarning; forecast, foretelling, prediction, prognostication, prophecy; badge, mark, note, token

**ominous** *adj* being or showing a sign of evil or calamity to come 〈that comment about downsizing from the company president sounded *ominous*〉
*syn* baleful, dire, foreboding, inauspicious, menacing, portentous, sinister, threatening
*rel* black, dark, gloomy; unfavorable, unpromising; ill-fated, ill-starred, star-crossed, unfortunate, unlucky; evil, malign, malignant
*near ant* auspicious, benign, favorable, promising, propitious

**omission** *n* something left out 〈the disk contains a selection of deleted scenes, and a couple of the *omissions* greatly add to the intelligibility of the movie's plot〉
*syn* deletion
*rel* elimination; blank, skip; lapse, slip; deduction, reduction, subtraction
*near ant* inclusion; accretion, accrual, addendum, addition, augmentation, boost, gain, increase, increment, raise, rise, supplement

**omit** *vb* to miss the opportunity or obligation — see NEGLECT 3

**omnibus** *adj* covering everything or all important points — see ENCYCLOPEDIC

**omnipotent** *adj* having unlimited power or authority 〈the nearly universal religious belief that God is *omnipotent* and can do anything〉
*syn* all-powerful, almighty
*rel* great, sovereign, supreme, towering, transcendent; authoritative, chief, majestic, masterful; mighty, potent, powerful, strong; divine, godlike
*near ant* helpless, impotent, powerless; limited, restricted

**omnipresent** *adj* present in all places and at all times 〈seeking some much-needed relief from the *omnipresent* noise of the big city〉
*syn* ubiquitous, universal
*rel* boundless, endless, illimitable, immeasurable, indefinite, infinite, limitless, measureless, unbounded, unfathomable, unlimited
*near ant* bounded, circumscribed, confined, finite, limited, restricted

**on** *adj* being in effective operation — see ACTIVE 1

**on** *adv* **1** toward a point ahead in space or time — see ONWARD 1
**2** toward or at a point lying in advance in space or time — see ALONG

**on** *prep* **1** having to do with — see ABOUT 1
**2** in or into contact with — see AGAINST

**oncoming** *adj* being soon to appear or take place — see FORTHCOMING

**one** *adj* known but not named — see CERTAIN 1

**one–dimensional** *adj* having or showing a lack of depth of understanding or character — see SUPERFICIAL 2

**onerous** *adj* **1** difficult to endure — see HARSH 1
**2** requiring much time, effort, or careful attention — see DEMANDING 1

**one–sided** *adj* inclined to favor one side over another — see PARTIAL 1

**one–sidedness** *n* an attitude that always favors one way of feeling or acting especially without considering any other possibilities — see BIAS

**onetime** *adj* having been such at some previous time — see FORMER

**ongoing** *adj* **1** being in progress or development 〈we do seem to be making some headway on that *ongoing* project〉 〈the ever *ongoing* quest for knowledge by men and women of science〉
*syn* afoot, proceeding, under way
*rel* functioning, happening, operating, working; afloat, alive, going; advancing, gaining
*near ant* receding, regressing, retrogressing
*ant* arrested, halted, stalled, stopped
**2** existing or in progress right now — see PRESENT 1

**only** *adj* **1** having no equal or rival for excellence or desirability 〈the *only* way to really appreciate the beauty of the forest is to walk through it〉
*syn* incomparable, inimitable, matchless, nonpareil, peerless, unequaled (*or* unequalled), unexampled, unmatched, unparalleled, unrivaled (*or* unrivalled), unsurpassable, unsurpassed
*rel* singular, unique; exceptional, extraordinary, rare, uncommon, unusual; A1, bang-up, banner, boss [*slang*], capital, classic, dandy, excellent, fabulous, fine, first-class, first-rate, grand, great, groovy, jim-dandy, keen, marvelous (*or* marvellous), mean, neat, par excellence, prime, superb, superior, superlative, terrific, tip-top, top-notch; better, preferred; exceptional, fancy, high-grade, special
*near ant* common, everyday, normal, ordinary, usual; inferior, lesser, worse, worst; bad, low, lower; low-grade, substandard, unsatisfactory; mediocre, second-class, second-rate; atrocious, execrable, wretched
**2** being the one or ones of a class with no other members 〈that is the *only* possible right answer〉 〈we were the *only* passengers on the tour bus〉
*syn* alone, lone, singular, sole, solitary, special, unique
*rel* solo, unaccompanied, unattended; incomparable, inimitable, matchless, peerless, unequaled (*or* unequalled), un-

matched, unparalleled, unrivaled (*or* unrivalled), unsurpassable, unsurpassed; distinct, distinctive, individual, separate
***near ant*** manifold, multifarious, myriad; assorted, heterogenous, miscellaneous, mixed, motley

**only** *adv* **1** for nothing other than — see SOLELY 1
**2** not long ago — see NEWLY
**3** nothing more than — see JUST 3

**only** *conj* if it were not for the fact that — see EXCEPT

**onrush** *n* forward movement in time or place — see ADVANCE 1

**onset** *n* **1** the act or action of setting upon with force or violence — see ATTACK 1
**2** the point at which something begins — see BEGINNING

**onslaught** *n* the act or action of setting upon with force or violence — see ATTACK 1

**onward** *also* **onwards** *adv* **1** toward a point ahead in space or time ⟨we must continue to move *onward,* or we will die in this desert⟩
***syn*** ahead, forth, forward, on
***near ant*** backward
**2** toward or at a point lying in advance in space or time — see ALONG

**oodles** *n* a considerable amount — see LOT 2

**ooze** *n* soft wet earth — see MUD

**ooze** *vb* to flow forth slowly through small openings — see EXUDE 1

**oozy** *adj* full of or covered with soft wet earth — see MUDDY 1

**opacity** *n* the quality or state of having a veiled or uncertain meaning — see OBSCURITY 1

**opaque** *adj* not seen or understood clearly — see FAINT 1

**open** *adj* **1** allowing passage without obstruction ⟨thank you for clearing out the hallway so that it's *open* again⟩
***syn*** clear, cleared, free, unclogged, unclosed, unobstructed, unstopped
***rel*** emptied, unoccupied, vacant; exposed, revealed; gaping, wide, yawning; unbarred, unbolted, unclasped, unfastened, unlatched, unlocked, unsealed; unbuttoned, unclenched, unfolded, unfurled, unzipped
***near ant*** constricted, cramped, encumbered; hampered, hindered, impeded, interfered (with), trammeled; barricaded, blockaded, dammed
***ant*** blocked, clogged, closed, jammed, obstructed, plugged, shut, stopped, stuffed, uncleared
**2** freely available for use or participation by all ⟨the beach's *open* sand castle-building contest that every year attracts competitors of all ages and abilities⟩
***syn*** free-for-all, public, unrestricted
***rel*** collective, common, communal, shared; accessible, available, free; unregulated
***near ant*** limited; inaccessible, unavailable
***ant*** closed, exclusive, off-limits, private, restricted
**3** being in a situation where one is likely to meet with harm — see LIABLE 1
**4** free in expressing one's true feelings and opinions — see FRANK
**5** lacking a usual or natural covering — see NAKED 2
**6** not known by only a select few — see PUBLIC 1
**7** not yet settled or decided — see PENDING 1
**8** willing to consider new or different ideas — see OPEN-MINDED 1

**open** *n* that part of the physical world that is removed from human habitation — see NATURE 2

**open** *vb* **1** to change from a closed to an open position ⟨please *open* the door to let the cat out⟩
***syn*** unclose
***rel*** unbar, unbolt, unclasp, unfasten, unlatch, unlock; unbutton, unclench, unfold, unfurl, unzip; disengage, release, slip
***near ant*** bar, bolt, clasp, fasten, latch, lock; button (up), zip (up)
***ant*** close, shut
**2** to arrange clear passage of (something) by removing obstructions ⟨we need to *open* this drain that's clogged with hair⟩
***syn*** clear, free, unclog, unstop
***rel*** ease, facilitate, loosen (up), smooth
***near ant*** constrict, encumber, hamper, hinder, impede, interfere (with), obstruct, trammel; barricade, blockade
***ant*** block, clog (up), close, dam (up), plug (up), stop
**3** to arrange the parts of (something) over a wider area ⟨when we got too close, the cardinal *opened* its wings and flew to a higher branch⟩
***syn*** expand, extend, fan (out), flare (out), spread (out), stretch (out), outspread, outstretch, unfold
***rel*** overspread
***near ant*** compact, compress, condense, reduce
***ant*** close, contract, fold
**4** to rid the surface of (as an area) from things in the way — see CLEAR 1
**5** to take the first step in (a process or course of action) — see BEGIN 1

**open–air** *adj* of, relating to, or held in the open air — see OUTDOORS

**open air** *n* that part of the physical world that is removed from human habitation — see NATURE 2

**open–and–shut** *adj* not subject to misinterpretation or more than one interpretation — see CLEAR 2

**open–eyed** *adj* paying close attention usually for the purpose of anticipating approaching danger or opportunity — see ALERT 1

**openhanded** *adj* giving or sharing in abundance and without hesitation — see GENEROUS 1

**openhandedness** *n* the quality or state of being generous — see LIBERALITY

**openhearted** *adj* free in expressing one's true feelings and opinions — see FRANK

**openheartedness** *n* **1** the free expression of one's true feelings and opinions — see CANDOR
**2** the quality or state of being generous — see LIBERALITY

**opening** *n* **1** a favorable combination of circumstances, time, and place — see OPPORTUNITY
**2** a place in a surface allowing passage into or through a thing — see HOLE 1
**3** an open space in a barrier (as a wall or hedge) — see GAP 1

**open–minded** *adj* **1** willing to consider new or different ideas ⟨all I ask is that you try to be *open-minded* when we present our suggestions⟩
***syn*** broad-minded, open, receptive
***rel*** impartial, neutral, objective, unbiased, unprejudiced; easygoing, tolerant; calm, detached, dispassionate; amenable, compliant; impressionable, suggestible, susceptible; persuadable, persuasible
***near ant*** biased, one-sided, partial, partisan, prejudiced; bigoted, intolerant
***ant*** narrow-minded
**2** not bound by traditional ways or beliefs — see LIBERAL 1

**openmouthed** *adj* filled with amazement or wonder ⟨I was *openmouthed* at the stunning view from the mountaintop⟩
***syn*** amazed, astonished, astounded, awed, awestruck, dumbfounded (*or* dumfounded), flabbergasted, marveling (*or* marvelling), wondering
***rel*** startled, surprised; bemused, bewildered, puzzled; overwhelmed, staggered, stunned, stupefied
***near ant*** unimpressed; disinterested, incurious, indifferent, unconcerned, uninterested; dispassionate, emotionless, impassive, unemotional; bored, jaded

**openness** *n* **1** the free expression of one's true feelings and opinions — see CANDOR
**2** the state of being left without shelter or protection against something harmful — see EXPOSURE 1

**open sesame** *n* something that allows someone to achieve a desired goal — see PASSPORT

**operable** *adj* capable of or suitable for being used for a particular purpose — see USABLE 1

**operate** *vb* **1** to control the mechanical operation of ⟨do not *operate* heavy machinery, including cars, after taking this medication⟩
***syn*** handle, run, work
***rel*** use; maneuver, manipulate, ply, wield; command, control, direct, drive, guide, pilot, steer
**2** to look after and make decisions about — see CONDUCT 1
**3** to produce a desired effect — see ACT 2
**4** to put into action or service — see USE 1

**operating** *adj* being in effective operation — see ACTIVE 1

**operation** *n* **1** a specific task with which a person or group is charged — see MISSION
**2** a usually fixed or ordered series of actions or events leading to a result — see PROCESS 1
**3** the act or activity of looking after and making decisions about something — see CONDUCT 1
**4** the act or practice of employing something for a particular purpose — see USE 1

**operational** *adj* being in effective operation — see ACTIVE 1

**operative** *adj* being in effective operation — see ACTIVE 1

**operative** *n* **1** a person who tries secretly to obtain information for one country in the territory of another usually unfriendly country — see SPY
**2** a person whose business is solving crimes and catching criminals or gathering information that is not easy to get — see DETECTIVE

**opiate** *adj* tending to cause sleep — see HYPNOTIC

**opine** *vb* to make a statement of one's opinion — see REMARK 1

**opinion** *n* **1** an idea that is believed to be true or valid without positive knowledge ⟨my *opinion* is that such interference was unnecessary⟩
***syn*** belief, conviction, eye, feeling, judgment (*or* judgement), mind, notion, persuasion, sentiment, verdict, view
***rel*** say; impression, perception, take; attitude; assumption, presumption, presupposition; conclusion, decision, determination; deliverance, esteem, estimate, estimation; credence, credit, faith; concept, conception, idea, thought; position, stand; comment, observation, reflection, remark; conjecture, guess, hunch, hypothesis, surmise, theory; advice, recommendation, suggestion; angle, outlook, perspective, point of view, shoes, slant, standpoint, viewpoint
***near ant*** fact, truth
**2** a position arrived at after consideration — see DECISION 1

**opinionated** *adj* sticking to an opinion, purpose, or course of action in spite of reason, arguments, or persuasion — see OBSTINATE

**opponent** *n* **1** one that takes a position opposite another in a competition or conflict ⟨in martial arts, before the match begins, always bow to your *opponent*⟩
***syn*** adversary, antagonist, rival
***rel*** equal, match; enemy, foe; archenemy, nemesis; competitor, contestant; bane, bête noire, curse; assailant, attacker, combatant, invader
***near ant*** accomplice, ally, confederate, partner; advocate, champion, exponent, proponent, supporter
**2** one that is hostile toward another — see ENEMY

**opportune** *adj* especially suitable for a certain time — see TIMELY 1

**opportunist** *n* one who does things only for his own benefit and with little regard for right and wrong — see SELF-SEEKER
**opportunity** *n* a favorable combination of circumstances, time, and place ⟨his art school could be a wonderful *opportunity* for you to finally develop your talent for painting⟩
*syn* chance, occasion, opening, room
*rel* break; play, way; juncture, pass
**oppose** *vb* **1** to refuse to give in to — see RESIST
**2** to strive to reduce or eliminate — see FIGHT 2
**opposite** *adj* being as different as possible ⟨your suggestion that we hold the meeting at night is precisely *opposite* to our original plan for a nice breakfast⟩
*syn* antipodal, antipodean, antithetical, contradictory, contrary, diametric (*or* diametrical), polar
*rel* adverse, negative, unfavorable; antagonistic, antipathetic, counter, hostile; converse, inverse, reverse; disparate, dissimilar, divergent, unalike, unlike
*near ant* alike, analogous, like, similar; equivalent, identical, same; synonymous
*ant* noncontradictory
**opposite** *n* something that is as different as possible from something else ⟨no matter what I say, you insist on the *opposite*⟩
*syn* antipode, antithesis, contrary, negative, reverse
*rel* negation; antonym; converse, inverse
*near ant* synonym; analogue, counterpart; carbon copy, copy, duplicate, replica
**opposition** *n* the inclination to resist — see RESISTANCE 1
**oppress** *vb* **1** to make sad — see DEPRESS 1
**2** to subject to incapacitating emotional or mental stress — see OVERWHELM 1
**oppression** *n* a state or spell of low spirits — see SADNESS
**oppressive** *adj* difficult to endure — see HARSH 1
**oppressively** *adv* in a manner so as to cause loss or suffering — see HARDLY 1
**oppressor** *n* **1** a person who causes repeated emotional pain, distress, or annoyance to another — see TORMENTOR
**2** a person who uses power or authority in a cruel, unjust, or harmful way — see DESPOT
**opprobrium** *n* the state of having lost the esteem of others — see DISGRACE 1
**opt** *vb* to come to a judgment after discussion or consideration — see DECIDE 1
**opt** (for) *vb* to decide to accept (someone or something) from a group of possibilities — see CHOOSE 1
**optic** *adj* of, relating to, or used in vision — see VISUAL 1
**optical** *adj* of, relating to, or used in vision — see VISUAL 1
**optimism** *n* an inclination to believe in the most favorable outcome ⟨your perpetual *optimism* even when things look bleak⟩
*syn* sanguinity
*rel* brightness, cheerfulness, perkiness, sunniness; hope, hopefulness, rosiness; idealism
*near ant* pessimism, skepticism; cynicism; desperation, discouragement, disheartenment, hopelessness; bleakness, cheerlessness, dreariness, gloom, gloominess; pragmatism, realism
**optimistic** *adj* having qualities which inspire hope — see HOPEFUL 1
**option** *n* **1** the act or power of making one's own choices or decisions — see FREE WILL
**2** the power, right, or opportunity to choose — see CHOICE 1
**optional** *adj* subject to one's freedom of choice ⟨certain activities are *optional*, and you may choose not to participate if you wish⟩
*syn* discretionary, elective, voluntary
*rel* alternative, chosen; dispensable, unnecessary, unneeded, unwanted
*near ant* essential, indispensable, necessary, requisite
*ant* compulsory, mandatory, nonelective, obligatory, required
**opulence** *n* the total of one's money and property — see WEALTH 1
**opulent** *adj* **1** having goods, property, or money in abundance — see RICH 1
**2** showing obvious signs of wealth and comfort — see LUXURIOUS
**opulently** *adv* in a luxurious manner — see HIGH
**opus** *n* a literary, musical, or artistic production — see COMPOSITION 1
**oral** *adj* **1** created by the body's organs of sound — see VOCAL
**2** made or carried on through speaking rather than in writing — see VERBAL 2
**orate** *vb* **1** to talk as if giving an important and formal speech ⟨politicians will *orate* lengthily at any opportunity⟩
*syn* declaim, discourse, harangue, mouth (off)
*rel* rant, rave; lecture, preach; advertise, announce, broadcast, declare, proclaim, pronounce; speak, talk
**2** to give a formal often extended talk on a subject — see TALK 1
**oration** *n* a usually formal discourse delivered to an audience — see SPEECH 1
**oratorical** *adj* marked by the use of impressive-sounding but mostly meaningless words and phrases — see RHETORICAL
**oratory** *n* **1** the art of speaking in public eloquently and effectively ⟨this debate class will teach you all to be skilled at *oratory*⟩
*syn* elocution
*rel* bombast, grandiloquence; rhetoric; discourse, speech, talk
**2** language that is impressive-sounding but not meaningful or sincere — see RHETORIC 1
**orb** *n* a more or less round body or mass — see [1]BALL 1
**orbit** *vb* to pass completely around — see ENCIRCLE 1

**orchestra** *n* a usually large group of musicians playing together — see ²BAND 1

**ordain** *vb* **1** to determine the fate of in advance — see DESTINE
**2** to give an order — see COMMAND 2

**ordeal** *n* a test of faith, patience, or strength — see TRIAL 1

**order** *n* **1** the way objects in space or events in time are arranged or follow one another ⟨you always keep your books in perfect alphabetical *order*⟩ ⟨we haven't found out the *order* of the speeches yet⟩
***syn*** arrangement, array, disposal, disposition, distribution, ordering, sequence, setup
***rel*** continuity; precedence, priority; chain, progression, succession; series; aligning, alignment, lining up; design, layout, pattern, structure, system
***near ant*** confusion, disorder, disorganization, disruption, upset; disconnection, disjointedness
**2** a group of persons formally joined together for some common interest — see ASSOCIATION 2
**3** a number of persons or things that are grouped together because they have something in common — see SORT 1
**4** a piece of metal given in honor of a special event, a person, or an achievement — see MEDAL
**5** a state of being or fitness — see CONDITION 1
**6** a statement of what to do that must be obeyed by those concerned — see COMMAND 1
**7** one of the segments of society into which people are grouped — see CLASS 1
**8** one of the units into which a whole is divided on the basis of a common characteristic — see CLASS 2

**order** *vb* **1** to put into a particular arrangement ⟨I've *ordered* all of my CDs according to type of music⟩ ⟨he likes to *order* his life so that there are few surprises⟩
***syn*** arrange, array, classify, codify, dispose, draw up, marshal, organize, range, systematize
***rel*** groom, make up, spruce (up), straighten (up), tidy (up); unscramble; align, line, line up, queue; alphabetize, file; emplace, place, set; display, lay out, map (out)
***ant*** derange, disarrange, disarray, disorder, mess (up), muss (up), rumple, upset
**2** to give a request or demand for ⟨they *ordered* hamburgers for lunch⟩
***syn*** ask (for), request, requisition
***rel*** commission, solicit; charter, hire, license (*also* licence)
***phrases*** call for
**3** to give an order — see COMMAND 2
**4** to issue orders to (someone) by right of authority — see COMMAND 1

**ordering** *n* **1** a scheme of rank or order — see ³SCALE 1
**2** the way objects in space or events in time are arranged or follow one another — see ORDER 1

**orderly** *adj* **1** being clean and in good order — see NEAT 1
**2** following a set method, arrangement, or pattern — see METHODICAL

**ordinance** *n* a rule of conduct or action laid down by a governing authority and especially a legislator — see LAW 1

**ordinarily** *adv* according to the usual course of things — see NATURALLY 2

**ordinary** *adj* **1** being of the type that is encountered in the normal course of events ⟨it was a perfectly *ordinary* and undistinguished shirt⟩
***syn*** average, common, commonplace, everyday, garden, normal, prosaic, routine, run-of-the-mill, standard, unexceptional, unremarkable, usual, workaday
***rel*** regular, typical; familiar, homely, plain, popular, vulgar; natural; customary, wonted; insignificant, trivial, unimportant; customary, frequent, habitual; expected, predictable
***near ant*** curious, funny, peculiar, quaint, queer; aberrant, atypical, irregular; rare, scarce; fantastic, phenomenal; bizarre, far-out, outrageous, outré, weird, wild; eccentric, idiosyncratic, nonconformist, unconventional, unorthodox; freak, freakish; conspicuous, notable, outstanding, prominent, salient, signal, striking; singular, unique
***ant*** abnormal, exceptional, extraordinary, odd, out-of-the-way, strange, unusual
**2** of average to below average quality — see MEDIOCRE 1
**3** often observed or encountered — see COMMON 1

**ordnance** *n* large firearms (as cannon or rockets) — see ARTILLERY

**oread** *n* a mythical goddess represented as a young girl and said to live outdoors — see NYMPH 1

**organ** *n* **1** a publication that appears at regular intervals — see JOURNAL
**2** something used to achieve an end — see AGENT 1

**organization** *n* a group of persons formally joined together for some common interest — see ASSOCIATION 2

**organize** *vb* to put into a particular arrangement — see ORDER 1

**organized** *adj* following a set method, arrangement, or pattern — see METHODICAL

**orient** *vb* to impart knowledge of a new thing or situation to — see ACQUAINT 1

**orientate** *vb* to impart knowledge of a new thing or situation to — see ACQUAINT 1

**orifice** *n* a place in a surface allowing passage into or through a thing — see HOLE 1

**origin** *n* the line of ancestors from whom a person is descended — see ANCESTRY

**original** *adj* **1** coming before all others in time or order — see FIRST 1
**2** having the skill and imagination to create new things — see CREATIVE 1

---

***syn*** synonym(s) ***rel*** related words
***ant*** antonym(s) ***near ant*** near antonym(s)

3 not known or experienced before — see NEW 2

**original** *n* something from which copies are made ⟨please make copies to hand out, but keep the *original*⟩
*syn* archetype, prototype
*rel* example, paradigm, pattern; beau ideal, exemplar, classic, ideal, model, nonpareil, paragon; blueprint, draft
*near ant* copy, imitation, replica, reproduction; counterfeit, fake, forgery, sham

**originality** *n* 1 the quality or appeal of being new — see NOVELTY 1
2 the skill and imagination to create new things — see CREATIVITY 1

**originally** *adv* in the beginning ⟨we *originally* planned to go out tonight, but we changed our minds⟩
*syn* firstly, initially, primarily
*rel* incipiently; primitively
*phrases* at first
*near ant* finally, lastly, ultimately

**originate** *vb* to come into existence — see BEGIN 2

**originator** *n* 1 one who creates or introduces something new — see INVENTOR
2 a person who establishes a whole new field of endeavor — see FATHER 2

**orison** *n* an address to God or a deity — see PRAYER 1

**ornament** *n* something that decorates or beautifies — see DECORATION 1

**ornament** *vb* to make more attractive by adding something that is beautiful or becoming — see DECORATE

**ornamental** *adj* serving to add beauty — see DECORATIVE

**ornamental** *n* a small object displayed for its attractiveness or interest — see KNICKKNACK

**ornate** *adj* elaborately and often excessively decorated ⟨an *ornate* gambling casino that is designed to look like an Italian palace⟩
*syn* bedizened, florid, gingerbread, overdecorated, overwrought
*rel* arabesque, baroque, rococo; extravagant, flamboyant, spectacular; splashy; flashy, garish, gaudy, glitzy, loud; ostentatious, pretentious, showy, swank, tawdry; elaborate, extreme; adorned, arrayed, beautified, bedecked, decked, decorated, dressed, embellished, enriched, garnished, ornamented, trimmed; flowery, frilly, lacy; enhanced, heightened, intensified; bossed, chased, emblazoned, embossed, embroidered, flounced, fringed, garlanded, gilded, laced, wreathed
*near ant* bare, denuded, exposed, naked, stripped, uncovered; modest, simple, unassuming, unpretentious; conservative, muted, quiet, restrained, subdued, tasteful, toned-down, understated, unobtrusive
*ant* austere, plain, severe, stark, unadorned

**ornery** *adj* having or showing a habitually bad temper — see ILL-TEMPERED

**orthodox** *adj* 1 following or agreeing with established form, custom, or rules — see FORMAL 1
2 tending to favor established ideas, conditions, or institutions — see CONSERVATIVE 1

**oscillation** *n* a series of slight movements by a body back and forth or from side to side — see VIBRATION

**ossified** *adj* sticking to an opinion, purpose, or course of action in spite of reason, arguments, or persuasion — see OBSTINATE

**ostensible** *adj* appearing to be true on the basis of evidence that may or may not be confirmed — see APPARENT 1

**ostensibly** *adv* to all outward appearances — see APPARENTLY

**ostentation** *n* excessive or unnecessary display ⟨the sheer *ostentation* of the rock star's mansion was overwhelming⟩
*syn* flamboyance, flashiness, garishness, gaudiness, glitz, ostentatiousness, pretentiousness, showiness, swank
*rel* extravaganza, pageant, parade, show; dazzle, pageantry, spectacle; adornment, decoration, dressing, embellishment, garnishment, ornamentation, trimming; extravagance, fanciness, luxuriousness, opulence, richness, sumptuousness; loudness, luridness; meretriciousness, tawdriness, vulgarity
*near ant* conservativeness, moderation, modesty, restraint, simplicity, understatement; elegance, gracefulness, tastefulness
*ant* austerity, plainness, severity

**ostentatious** *adj* 1 excessively showy — see GAUDY
2 self-consciously trying to present an appearance of grandeur or importance — see PRETENTIOUS 1

**ostentatiousness** *n* excessive or unnecessary display — see OSTENTATION

**other** *adj* 1 being not of the same kind — see DIFFERENT 1
2 resulting in an increase in amount or number — see ADDITIONAL

**other** *adv* in a different way — see OTHERWISE

**otherwise** *adv* in a different way ⟨a serious student who always does his best, for his conscience will not let him do *otherwise*⟩
*syn* differently, else, other
*rel* diversely, variously
*near ant* similarly
*ant* likewise

**ought** (to) *vb* to be under necessity or obligation to — see NEED 2

**ounce** *n* a very small amount — see PARTICLE 1

**oust** *vb* 1 to drive or force out — see EJECT 1
2 to remove from a position of prominence or power (as a throne) — see DEPOSE 1

**out** *adv* 1 in or into the open air — see OUTDOORS
2 with one's normal voice speaking the words — see ALOUD

**out** *adj* not at a certain place — see ABSENT 1

**out** *n* the act or a means of getting or keeping away from something undesirable — see ESCAPE 2

**out** *vb* to become known — see GET OUT 1

**out–and–out** *adj* **1** having no exceptions or restrictions — see ABSOLUTE 2
**2** trying all possibilities — see EXHAUSTIVE

**outbrave** *vb* to oppose (something hostile or dangerous) with firmness or courage — see FACE 2

**outbreak** *n* a sudden and usually temporary growth of activity ⟨there was an immediate *outbreak* of paper shuffling and a pretense of work when the teacher re-entered the room⟩
***syn*** burst, flare, flare-up, flash, flicker, flurry, flutter, outburst, spurt
***rel*** binge, jag, spree; boost, increase, pick-up, upswing, upturn; epidemic, eruption, explosion, paroxysm; deluge, flood, rush, spate, surge; commotion, furor, uproar
***near ant*** calm, doldrums, slump

**outburst** *n* **1** a sudden intense expression of strong feeling ⟨when the coach suddenly started crying hysterically, everyone was shocked by the unexpected *outburst*⟩
***syn*** agony, burst, eruption, explosion, fit, flare, flare-up, flash, flush, gale, gush, gust, paroxysm, spasm, storm
***rel*** blowup, grouch, rage, tantrum; ecstasy, rapture, transport; delirium, frenzy, furor
**2** a sudden and usually temporary growth of activity — see OUTBREAK

**outcast** *n* one who is cast out or rejected by society ⟨they were convinced that they would become total *outcasts* if they didn't buy the newest fashions⟩
***syn*** castaway, castoff, pariah, reject
***rel*** untouchable; outsider; deportee, exile
***near ant*** insider

**outcome** *n* a condition or occurrence traceable to a cause — see EFFECT 1

**outcry** *n* a violent shouting — see CLAMOR 1

**outdated** *adj* having passed its time of use or usefulness — see OBSOLETE

**outdistance** *vb* to be greater, better, or stronger than — see SURPASS 1

**outdo** *vb* to be greater, better, or stronger than — see SURPASS 1

**outdoor** *also* **outdoors** *adj* of, relating to, or held in the open air ⟨an *outdoor* picnic is always at the mercy of the weather, of course⟩
***syn*** open-air, out-of-door (*or* out-of-doors)
***rel*** airy; exterior, external, outer, outside, outward; outermost, outmost
***near ant*** inner, inside, interior, internal, inward; inmost, innermost
***ant*** indoor

**outdoors** *adv* in or into the open air ⟨please wait until you're *outdoors* to run around and scream⟩
***syn*** out, outside
***rel*** without
***near ant*** in, inside, within
***ant*** indoors

**outdoors** *n* that part of the physical world that is removed from human habitation — see NATURE 2

**outer** *adj* situated on the outside or farther out ⟨the *outer* edge of the blade of your figure skate always wears out faster than the inner because you use it more⟩
***syn*** exterior, external, outside, outward
***rel*** outermost, outlying, outmost; superficial, surface
***near ant*** inmost, innermost
***ant*** inner, inside, interior, internal, inward

**outermost** *adj* most distant from a center — see EXTREME 1

**outfit** *n* **1** clothing chosen as appropriate for a specific situation ⟨you'll need a special *outfit* for the scout troop⟩ ⟨do you want to buy a new *outfit* for the Halloween party?⟩
***syn*** costume, dress, garb, getup, guise, togs
***rel*** apparel, attire, clothes, duds, raiment; fashion, mode, style; array, caparison, vestments
**2** a commercial or industrial activity or organization — see ENTERPRISE 1
**3** a group of people working together on a task — see GANG 1
**4** items needed for the performance of a task or activity — see EQUIPMENT
**5** the distinctive clothing worn by members of a particular group — see UNIFORM

**outfit** *vb* to provide (someone) with what is needed for a task or activity — see FURNISH 1

**outflow** *n* a flowing or going out ⟨there was an immediate *outflow* of students from the door when the bell rang⟩
***syn*** exodus, gush, outpouring
***rel*** drain, flow; ebb, reflux; rush, stampede; emigration, flight; discharge, emanation, emission
***near ant*** deluge, flood, inundation, overflow, spate, torrent; flow, river, stream, tide
***ant*** flux, inflow, influx, inrush

**outfox** *vb* to get the better of through cleverness — see OUTWIT

**outgo** *n* a payment made in the course of achieving a result — see EXPENSE

**outgoing** *adj* likely to seek or enjoy the company of others — see CONVIVIAL

**outgrowth** *n* **1** a branch of a main stem especially of a plant — see OFFSHOOT 1
**2** a condition or occurrence traceable to a cause — see EFFECT 1
**3** something that naturally develops or is developed from something else — see DERIVATIVE

**outing** *n* a short trip for pleasure — see EXCURSION 1

---

***syn*** synonym(s) ***rel*** related words
***ant*** antonym(s) ***near ant*** near antonym(s)

**outlander** *n* a person who is not native to or known to a community — see STRANGER

**outlandish** *adj* **1** different from the ordinary in a way that causes curiosity or suspicion — see ODD 2
**2** excitingly or mysteriously unusual — see EXOTIC

**outlast** *vb* to last longer than ⟨I truly hope this car will *outlast* our previous one⟩ ⟨your work will probably *outlast* you⟩
***syn*** outlive, outwear
***rel*** survive; outstay; abide (beyond), endure (past), hold (past), hold out (past), last (beyond), persist (beyond); draw out, perpetuate; succeed

**outlaw** *vb* to order not to do or use or to be done or used — see FORBID

**outlawed** *adj* that may not be permitted — see IMPERMISSIBLE

**outlawing** *n* the act of ordering that something not be done or used — see PROHIBITION 1

**outlay** *n* a payment made in the course of achieving a result — see EXPENSE

**outlet** *n* a place or means of going out — see EXIT 1

**outline** *n* **1** a line that traces the outer limits of an object or surface ⟨place your hand on the paper and draw an *outline* around it⟩
***syn*** contour, figure, silhouette
***rel*** delineation, sketch; profile, skyline; form, cast, configuration, conformation, geometry, shape; framework, skeleton
**2** a short statement of the main points — see SUMMARY

**outline** *vb* **1** to draw or make apparent the outline of ⟨she carefully *outlined* the tree before she started drawing in the leaves⟩
***syn*** define, delineate, silhouette, sketch, trace
***rel*** line; bound, fringe, margin, skirt; edge, hem, rim, trim; frame; circle, compass, encircle, girdle, girth, loop, ring, round, surround; chart, diagram, draw, map (out)
**2** to make into a short statement of the main points (as of a report) — see SUMMARIZE

**outlive** *vb* to last longer than — see OUTLAST

**outlook** *n* **1** a high place or structure from which a wide view is possible — see LOOKOUT 1
**2** a way of looking at or thinking about something — see POINT OF VIEW
**3** all that can be seen from a certain point — see VIEW 1

**out loud** *adv* with one's normal voice speaking the words — see ALOUD

**outmaneuver** *vb* to get the better of through cleverness — see OUTWIT

**outmoded** *adj* having passed its time of use or usefulness — see OBSOLETE

**outmost** *adj* most distant from a center — see EXTREME 1

**out–of–date** *adj* having passed its time of use or usefulness — see OBSOLETE

**out–of–door** *or* **out–of–doors** *adj* of, relating to, or held in the open air — see OUTDOORS

**out–of–doors** *n* that part of the physical world that is removed from human habitation — see NATURE 2

**out–of–the–way** *adj* different from the ordinary in a way that causes curiosity or suspicion — see ODD 2

**outpouring** *n* a flowing or going out — see OUTFLOW

**output** *n* something produced by physical or intellectual effort — see PRODUCT 1

**outrage** *n* **1** an act or expression showing scorn and usually intended to hurt another's feelings — see INSULT
**2** an intense emotional state of displeasure with someone or something — see ANGER

**outrage** *vb* **1** to cause hurt feelings or deep resentment in — see INSULT
**2** to make angry — see ANGER

**outraged** *adj* feeling or showing anger — see ANGRY

**outrank** *vb* to be greater in importance than — see OUTWEIGH

**outré** *adj* different from the ordinary in a way that causes curiosity or suspicion — see ODD 2

**outright** *adj* having no exceptions or restrictions — see ABSOLUTE 2

**outset** *n* the point at which something begins — see BEGINNING

**outshine** *vb* to be greater, better, or stronger than — see SURPASS 1

**outside** *adj* **1** situated on the outside or farther out — see OUTER
**2** small in degree — see REMOTE 1

**outside** *adv* in or into the open air — see OUTDOORS

**outside** *n* **1** an outer part or layer — see EXTERIOR
**2** the greatest amount, number, or part — see MOST

**outside** *prep* **1** not including — see EXCEPT
**2** out of the reach or sphere of — see BEYOND 2

**outside of** *prep* **1** not including — see EXCEPT
**2** out of the reach or sphere of — see BEYOND 2

**outsider** *n* a person who is not native to or known to a community — see STRANGER

**outsize** *also* **outsized** *adj* **1** unusually large — see HUGE
**2** of a size greater than average of its kind — see LARGE

**outskirts** *n pl* the area around a city — see ENVIRONS 1

**outsmart** *vb* to get the better of through cleverness — see OUTWIT

**outspoken** *adj* free in expressing one's true feelings and opinions — see FRANK

**outspread** *vb* to arrange the parts of (something) over a wider area — see OPEN 3

**outstanding** *adj* **1** not yet paid ⟨there are several *outstanding* bills left, but at least we paid the rest⟩

*syn* overdue, owed, owing, payable, unpaid, unsettled
*rel* due, mature
*near ant* prepaid
*ant* cleared, liquidated, paid (off *or* up), repaid, settled
2 standing above others in rank, importance, or achievement — see EMINENT

**outstretch** *vb* to arrange the parts of (something) over a wider area — see OPEN 3

**outstrip** *vb* to be greater, better, or stronger than — see SURPASS 1

**outward** *adj* situated on the outside or farther out — see OUTER

**outwear** *vb* to last longer than — see OUTLAST

**outweigh** *vb* to be greater in importance than ⟨the need to finish your homework *outweighs* your desire to see your favorite TV show⟩
*syn* outrank, overbalance, overshadow, overweigh
*rel* count, import, matter, mean, signify, weigh; dwarf; exceed, outstrip, surpass, transcend

**outwit** *vb* to get the better of through cleverness ⟨a plan to *outwit* their opponents at their own game⟩
*syn* fox, outfox, outsmart, outmaneuver, overreach
*rel* outguess, second-guess; baffle, balk, circumvent, foil, frustrate, thwart; cozen, deceive, dupe, fool, gull, trick; conquer, defeat, lick, overcome; bar, block, hinder, impede, obstruct

**outworn** *adj* having passed its time of use or usefulness — see OBSOLETE

**oval** *adj* having the shape of an egg ⟨the *Oval* Office in the White House⟩
*syn* elliptic (*or* elliptical), ovate, ovoid

**ovate** *adj* having the shape of an egg — see OVAL

**ovation** *n* enthusiastic and usually public expression of approval — see APPLAUSE

**over** *adj* brought or having come to an end — see COMPLETE 2

**over** *adv* 1 from one side to the other of an intervening space ⟨let's swim *over* to that island⟩
*syn* across, through
*rel* clear
2 yet another time — see AGAIN 1
3 to or in a higher place — see ABOVE
4 from beginning to end — see THROUGH 1
5 toward or in a lower position — see DOWN

**over** *prep* 1 higher than — see ABOVE
2 in the course of — see DURING
3 on or to the farther side of — see BEYOND 1
4 to the opposite side of — see ACROSS
5 in random positions within the boundaries of — see AROUND 2

---

*syn* synonym(s) *rel* related words
*ant* antonym(s) *near ant* near antonym(s)

**overabundance** *n* the state or an instance of going beyond what is usual, proper, or needed — see EXCESS

**overactive** *adj* being in a state of increased activity or agitation — see FEVERISH 1

**overage** *n* the state or an instance of going beyond what is usual, proper, or needed — see EXCESS

**overall** *adj* 1 belonging or relating to the whole — see GENERAL 1
2 relating to the main elements and not to specific details — see GENERAL 2

**overall** *adv* for the most part — see CHIEFLY

**over and above** *prep* in addition to — see BESIDES 1

**overbalance** *vb* to be greater in importance than — see OUTWEIGH

**overbear** *vb* to achieve a victory over — see BEAT 2

**overbearing** *adj* fond of ordering people around — see BOSSY

**overbold** *adj* foolishly adventurous or bold — see FOOLHARDY 1

**overburden** *vb* to fill or load to excess — see OVERLOAD

**overcast** *adj* covered over by clouds ⟨the dark, *overcast* sky made the whole day seem depressing⟩
*syn* beclouded, clouded, cloudy, dull, hazed, hazy, heavy, lowering (*also* louring), overclouded
*rel* bedimmed, befogged, blackened, darkened, darksome, dim, dimmed, dulled, dusky, misty, murky, obscure, obscured, overshadowed; sunless; black, bleak, cheerless, dark, desolate, dismal, drear, dreary, funereal, gloomy, glum, gray (*also* grey), somber (*or* sombre), sullen
*near ant* sunny, sunshiny; brightened, brilliant, dazzling, illuminated, illumined, lighted (*or* lit), lightened, radiant, shiny
*ant* clear, cloudless

**overcast** *vb* to make dark, dim, or indistinct — see CLOUD 1

**overcharge** *vb* 1 to charge (someone) too much for goods or services ⟨I think that store may have *overcharged* us for the shoes, which were supposed to be on sale⟩
*syn* gouge, soak, sting, surcharge
*rel* cheat, defraud, stick; clip, fleece, skin
*ant* undercharge
2 to fill or load to excess — see OVERLOAD

**overcloud** *vb* to make dark, dim, or indistinct — see CLOUD 1

**overclouded** *adj* covered over by clouds — see OVERCAST

**overcoat** *n* a warm outdoor coat ⟨put your *overcoat* on—it's freezing out there!⟩
*syn* greatcoat, surcoat, topcoat
*rel* chesterfield, frock coat, mackinaw, ulster; jacket, parka; oilskin, raincoat, sou'wester; wrap
*near ant* undercoat

**overcome** *vb* 1 to achieve a victory over — see BEAT 2

2 to subject to incapacitating emotional or mental stress — see OVERWHELM 1

**overconfident** *adj* foolishly adventurous or bold — see FOOLHARDY 1

**overcritical** *adj* given to making or expressing unfavorable judgments about things — see CRITICAL 1

**overdecorated** *adj* elaborately and often excessively decorated — see ORNATE

**overdo** *vb* to describe or express in too strong terms — see OVERSTATE

**overdraw** *vb* to describe or express in too strong terms — see OVERSTATE

**overdue** *adj* 1 not arriving, or occurring, or settled at the due, usual, or proper time — see LATE 1
2 not yet paid — see OUTSTANDING 1

**overeat** *vb* to eat greedily or to excess — see GORGE 2

**overeater** *n* one who eats greedily or too much — see GLUTTON

**overestimate** *vb* to place too high a value on ⟨they *overestimated* their ability to do the work on such short notice⟩
*syn* overrate, overvalue
*rel* appreciate, cherish, prize, treasure, value; admire, esteem, regard, respect; adore, idolize, revere, reverence, venerate, worship
*near ant* belittle, decry, depreciate, disparage; despise, disdain, scorn; abhor, abominate, detest, loathe
*ant* underestimate, underrate, undervalue

**overfamiliar** *adj* showing a lack of proper social reserve or modesty — see PRESUMPTUOUS 1

**overfill** *vb* 1 to fill or load to excess — see OVERLOAD
2 to flow over the brim or top of — see OVERFLOW 1

**overflow** *n* 1 a great flow of water or of something that overwhelms — see FLOOD
2 the state or an instance of going beyond what is usual, proper, or needed — see EXCESS

**overflow** *vb* 1 to flow over the brim or top of ⟨the tea in the cup *overflowed* onto the saucer⟩
*syn* overfill, run over
*rel* boil over, spill, well (up); flow, flush, gush, pour, sluice, spout, spurt, stream; deluge, drown, engulf, flood, inundate, overwhelm, submerge, submerge, swamp; wash (over); brim, cascade, sloo, slosh
*near ant* recede
2 to cover or become filled with a flood — see FLOOD

**overgrown** *adj* covered with a thick, healthy natural growth — see LUSH 1

**overhang** *n* a part that sticks out from the general mass of something — see BULGE

**overhang** *vb* 1 to extend outward beyond a usual point — see BULGE
2 to remain poised to inflict harm, danger, or distress on — see THREATEN

**overhaul** *vb* to move fast enough to get even with — see OVERTAKE

**overhead** *adv* to or in a higher place — see ABOVE

**overhear** *vb* to listen to (another in private conversation) — see EAVESDROP (ON)

**overjoy** *vb* 1 to fill with overwhelming emotion (as wonder or delight) — see ENTRANCE
2 to fill with great joy — see ELATE

**overkill** *n* the state or an instance of going beyond what is usual, proper, or needed — see EXCESS

**overlap** *n* a partial covering of one thing by an adjoining thing ⟨the orthodontist will try to fix that *overlap* of two of your upper incisors⟩
*syn* lapping, overlaying, overlying, overspreading
*rel* shingling

**overlap** *vb* to lie over parts of one another ⟨there were so many papers on the desk that many of them *overlapped*⟩
*syn* lap, overlay, overlie, overspread
*rel* shingle

**overlay** *vb* 1 to form a layer over — see COVER 2
2 to lie over parts of one another — see OVERLAP

**overlaying** *n* a partial covering of one thing by an adjoining thing — see OVERLAP

**overlie** *vb* 1 to lie over parts of one another — see OVERLAP
2 to form a layer over — see COVER 2

**overload** *vb* to fill or load to excess ⟨try not to *overload* your backpack, or you could end up with back problems⟩
*syn* overburden, overcharge, overfill
*rel* stuff; burden, charge, encumber, lade, load, lumber, saddle, weight
*near ant* lighten, unburden, unload

**overlook** *vb* 1 to look down on ⟨the fortress *overlooks* the city⟩
*syn* command, dominate
*rel* face, front
2 to fail to give proper attention to — see NEGLECT 1

**overly** *adv* beyond a normal or acceptable limit — see TOO 1

**overlying** *n* a partial covering of one thing by an adjoining thing — see OVERLAP

**overmaster** *vb* to subject to incapacitating emotional or mental stress — see OVERWHELM 1

**overmatch** *vb* to achieve a victory over — see BEAT 2

**overmuch** *adj* going beyond a normal or acceptable limit in degree or amount — see EXCESSIVE

**overmuch** *adv* beyond a normal or acceptable limit — see TOO 1

**overmuch** *n* the state or an instance of going beyond what is usual, proper, or needed — see EXCESS

**overpass** *vb* to fail to give proper attention to — see NEGLECT 1

**overpower** *vb* 1 to bring under one's control by force of arms — see CONQUER 1
2 to subject to incapacitating emotional or mental stress — see OVERWHELM 1

**overpowering** *n* the act or process of bringing someone or something under one's control — see CONQUEST

**overpraise** *n* excessive praise — see FLATTERY

**overpraise** *vb* to praise too much — see FLATTER 1

**overrate** *vb* to place too high a value on — see OVERESTIMATE

**overreach** *vb* **1** to get the better of through cleverness — see OUTWIT
**2** to go beyond the limit of — see EXCEED

**overripe** *adj* having lost forcefulness, courage, or spirit — see EFFETE 1

**overrun** *vb* **1** to enter for conquest or plunder — see INVADE
**2** to go beyond the limit of — see EXCEED
**3** to spread or swarm over in a troublesome manner — see INFEST

**oversee** *vb* **1** to look after and make decisions about — see CONDUCT 1
**2** to be in charge of — see BOSS 1
**3** to take charge of especially on behalf of another — see ²TEND 1

**overshadow** *vb* **1** to make dark, dim, or indistinct — see CLOUD 1
**2** to be greater in importance than — see OUTWEIGH

**overshoot** *vb* to go beyond the limit of — see EXCEED

**oversight** *n* **1** the act or activity of looking after and making decisions about something — see CONDUCT 1
**2** an unintentional departure from truth or accuracy — see ERROR 1
**3** the duty or function of watching or guarding for the sake of proper direction or control — see SUPERVISION 1
**4** the nonperformance of an assigned or expected action — see FAILURE 1

**oversize** *or* **oversized** *adj* **1** unusually large — see HUGE
**2** of a size greater than average of its kind — see LARGE

**overspread** *vb* **1** to form a layer over — see COVER 2
**2** to lie over parts of one another — see OVERLAP

**overspreading** *n* a partial covering of one thing by an adjoining thing — see OVERLAP

**overstate** *vb* to describe or express in too strong terms ⟨it appears you've somewhat *overstated* your computer skills, if you can't find the "on" button!⟩
***syn*** exaggerate, overdo, overdraw, put on
***rel*** color, elaborate, embellish, embroider, magnify, pad, stretch; fudge, hedge; overemphasize, overplay
***near ant*** belittle, minimize, play down
***ant*** understate

**overstatement** *n* the representation of something in terms that go beyond the facts — see EXAGGERATION

**overstep** *vb* to go beyond the limit of — see EXCEED

**oversupply** *n* the state or an instance of going beyond what is usual, proper, or needed — see EXCESS

**overtake** *vb* to move fast enough to get even with ⟨she had to hurry to *overtake* her friends, who had forgotten their umbrellas⟩ ⟨the thunderstorm *overtook* them suddenly⟩
***syn*** catch up (with), overhaul
***rel*** chase, pursue; gain, reach; pass, surpass
***near ant*** fall short

**overthrow** *n* failure to win a contest — see DEFEAT 1

**overtop** *vb* to be greater, better, or stronger than — see SURPASS 1

**overturn** *vb* to turn on one's side or upside down — see CAPSIZE

**overvalue** *vb* to place too high a value on — see OVERESTIMATE

**overweening** *adj* **1** having too high an opinion of oneself — see CONCEITED
**2** going beyond a normal or acceptable limit in degree or amount — see EXCESSIVE
**3** having a feeling of superiority that shows itself in an overbearing attitude — see ARROGANT

**overweigh** *vb* to be greater in importance than — see OUTWEIGH

**overweight** *adj* having an excess of body fat — see FAT 1

**overwhelm** *vb* **1** to subject to incapacitating emotional or mental stress ⟨just the thought of how much work there is to do *overwhelms* me⟩
***syn*** carry away, crush, devastate, floor, oppress, overcome, overmaster, overpower, prostrate, snow under, swamp, whelm
***rel*** deluge, drown; confute, defeat, refute; demoralize, distress, disturb, rock, shatter, stagger, unman, unnerve, upset
**2** to cover or become filled with a flood — see FLOOD

**overwrought** *adj* **1** being in a state of increased activity or agitation — see FEVERISH 1
**2** elaborately and often excessively decorated — see ORNATE

**ovoid** *adj* having the shape of an egg — see OVAL

**owed** *adj* not yet paid — see OUTSTANDING 1

**owing** *adj* not yet paid — see OUTSTANDING 1

**owing to** *prep* as the result of — see BECAUSE OF

**own** *vb* to keep, control, or experience as one's own — see HAVE 1

**own** (up) *vb* to accept the truth or existence of (something) usually reluctantly — see ADMIT

**owner** *n* one who has a legal or rightful claim to ownership — see PROPRIETOR

# P

**pa** *n* a male human parent — see FATHER 1

**pace** *vb* to move along with a steady regular step especially in a group — see MARCH 1

**pacific** *adj* 1 tending to lessen or avoid conflict or hostility ⟨as a *pacific* gesture, we invited our feuding neighbors to our backyard barbecue⟩
*syn* appeasing, conciliating, conciliatory, disarming, mollifying, pacifying, peacemaking, placating, propitiatory
*rel* endearing, ingratiating; peaceable, peaceful; nonbelligerent, unaggressive, unassertive; calming, comforting, quieting, soothing; obliging, satisfying affable, amiable, amicable, benevolent gentle, kind, kindly; submissive, surrendering, yielding
*near ant* aggravating, annoying, exasperating, inflammatory, irritating, nettling, offensive, provocative, provoking, vexing; engaging, incensing, infuriating, maddening; antagonistic, hostile; aggressive, assertive, bellicose, belligerent, combative, contentious, pugnacious, quarrelsome, scrappy, truculent; martial, militant, military, warlike
*ant* antagonizing
2 inclined to live in peace and to avoid war — see PEACEFUL 1

**pacifist** *n* a person who opposes war or warlike policies — see DOVE 1

**pacify** *vb* to lessen the anger or agitation of ⟨the only thing that would *pacify* the child and end the tantrum was a new toy⟩
*syn* appease, conciliate, disarm, mollify, placate, propitiate
*rel* calm, comfort, console, content, quiet, soothe; endear (to), ingratiate; delight, gladden, gratify, please; blarney, flatter, overpraise, soft-soap; assuage, quench, sate, satiate, satisfy; cater (to), humor, indulge; blandish, cajole, coax, wheedle; coddle, mollycoddle, pamper, spoil
*near ant* aggravate, annoy, bother, bug, chafe, cross, exasperate, gall, get, grate, irk, irritate, nettle, peeve, pique, put out, rankle, rile, roil, ruffle, vex; provoke, rouse; harass, harry, pester; agitate, distress, disturb, fret, perturb, upset; affront, insult, offend
*ant* anger, enrage, incense, infuriate, madden, outrage

**pacifying** *adj* 1 tending to calm the emotions and relieve stress — see SOOTHING 1
2 tending to lessen or avoid conflict or hostility — see PACIFIC 1

**pack** *n* 1 a soft-sided case designed for carrying belongings especially on the back ⟨part of basic training is becoming accustomed to taking very long hikes with an eighty-pound *pack*⟩
*syn* backpack, knapsack, rucksack
*rel* haversack; grip, luggage, suitcase, traveling bag
2 a wrapped or sealed case containing an item or set of items — see PACKAGE 1

**pack** *vb* 1 to close up so that no empty spaces remain — see FILL 2
2 to put into (something) as much as can be held or contained — see FILL 1
3 to support and take from one place to another — see CARRY 1
4 to wear or have on one's person — see CARRY 2

**pack** (off) *vb* to cause to go or be taken from one place to another — see SEND

**package** *n* 1 a wrapped or sealed case containing an item or set of items ⟨Mom needed our help carrying all the *packages* and bags home from the store⟩
*syn* bundle, pack, packet, parcel
*rel* bag, poke [*chiefly Southern and Midland*], pouch, sack; box, container, crate
2 a number of things considered as a unit — see GROUP 1

**packed** *adj* 1 containing or seeming to contain the greatest quantity or number possible — see FULL 1
2 having little space between items or parts — see CLOSE 1

**packet** *n* a wrapped or sealed case containing an item or set of items — see PACKAGE 1

**pact** *n* 1 a formal agreement between two or more nations or peoples — see TREATY
2 an arrangement about action to be taken — see AGREEMENT 2

**pad** *n* 1 a number of sheets of writing paper glued together at one edge ⟨we'll need to buy a new *pad* for telephone messages soon⟩
*syn* notepad, tablet
*rel* album, notebook, scrapbook; booklet, pamphlet
2 a place set aside for sleeping — see BED 1
3 something that serves as a protective barrier — see CUSHION
4 the place where one lives — see HOME 1

**pad** *vb* 1 to add to the interest of by including made-up details — see EMBROIDER
2 to go on foot — see WALK

**padding** *n* 1 soft material that is used to fill the hollow parts of something — see FILLING
2 the representation of something in terms that go beyond the facts — see EXAGGERATION

**paddle** *vb* to move a boat by means of oars — see [1]ROW

**padre** *n* a person specially trained and authorized to conduct religious services in a Christian church — see CLERGYMAN

**paean** *n* a formal expression of praise — see ENCOMIUM

**pagan** *n* a person who does not worship the God of the Bible — see HEATHEN 1

**page** *n* one that carries a message or does an errand — see MESSENGER

**pageant** *n* a staged presentation often with music that consists of a procession of narrated or enacted scenes ⟨we always put on a Christmas *pageant* every year⟩
*syn* cavalcade
*rel* tableau; kaleidoscope, montage, panorama; drama, play; demonstration, performance, presentation, production; exhibition, extravaganza, show, spectacle; parade

**pail** *n* a round container that is open at the top and outfitted with a handle ⟨fetch me a *pail* full of water, please⟩
*syn* bucket
*rel* cauldron, kettle, pot; canteen, flagon, jar, jug, pitcher; bail, hod; tank, tub, vat

**pain** *n* **1** a sharp unpleasant sensation usually felt in some specific part of the body ⟨the child was crying because of a *pain* in her knee⟩
*syn* ache, pang, prick, smart, sting, stitch, throe, tingle, twinge
*rel* discomfort, distress, soreness, tenderness; agony, anguish, misery, suffering, torment, torture; inflammation, swelling; damage, harm, hurt, injury; backache, bellyache, charley horse, colic, earache, gripe, headache, stomachache, toothache
*near ant* comfort, ease
**2** a state of great suffering of body or mind — see DISTRESS 1
**3 pains** *pl* strict attentiveness to what one is doing — see CARE 1
**4 pains** *pl* the active use of energy in producing a result — see EFFORT

**pain** *vb* to feel or cause physical pain — see HURT 1

**painful** *adj* **1** causing or feeling bodily pain ⟨her broken arm was too *painful* for her to go on the trip⟩
*syn* aching, hurting, nasty, sore
*rel* damaging, harmful, hurtful, injurious; raw, tender; bleeding, burning, chafing, cramping, festering; itching, nagging, pinching, pricking, prickling, smarting, stinging; inflamed, swollen; threatening, wounding
*near ant* curative, healing, helping, remedial
*ant* painless
**2** hard to accept or bear especially emotionally — see BITTER 2

**painfully** *adv* with feelings of bitterness or grief — see HARD 2

**painkiller** *n* something (as a drug) that relieves pain ⟨a lot of *painkillers* have turned out to be addictive substances for patients⟩
*syn* analgesic, anesthetic
*rel* sedative, tranquilizer (*also* tranquillizer); narcotic, opiate

**painless** *adj* involving minimal difficulty or effort — see EASY 1

**painlessly** *adv* without difficulty — see EASILY

**painstaking** *adj* taking great care and effort ⟨she was always *painstaking* about her homework⟩
*syn* careful, conscientious, fussy, meticulous
*rel* assiduous, diligent, indefatigable, persevering, sedulous; exhaustive, thorough, thoroughgoing; attentive, observant, vigilant, watchful; accurate, precise; critical, demanding, discriminating, exacting, finicky, particular; cautious, chary, circumspect, gingerly, guarded, heedful, wary; deliberate, plodding, slow; studied, thoughtful; all-out, determined, dogged, intensive, tenacious, tireless, zealous
*near ant* cursory; heedless, inattentive, incautious, mindless, unguarded, unsafe, unwary; lax, neglectful, negligent, slipshod, sloppy, slovenly; imprecise; inaccurate, uncritical, undemanding, undiscriminating; bold, impetuous, rash, reckless; apathetic, indifferent, lackadaisical, lazy
*ant* careless

**paint** *n* preparations intended to beautify the face or hair — see MAKEUP 1

**paint** *vb* **1** to give a representation or account of in words — see DESCRIBE 1
**2** to give color or a different color to — see COLOR 1

**painting** *n* a picture created with usually oil paint ⟨the Mona Lisa is a beautiful *painting* of a woman with a most mysterious smile⟩
*syn* canvas, oil, oil painting
*rel* fresco, mural, panorama; cartoon, drawing, etching, pastel, sketch, watercolor, work; masterpiece; pièce de résistance, showpiece
*phrases* work of art

**pair** *n* two things of the same or similar kind that match or are considered together ⟨a *pair* of blue socks⟩ ⟨the cheerleader and the computer nerd make quite a *pair* together⟩
*syn* brace, couple, duo, twain, twosome
*rel* span, yoke; partnership, team; companion, complement, doublet, fellow, half, match, mate, twin; counterpart, equal, equivalent, like, parallel, peer

**pal** *n* a person who has a strong liking for and trust in another — see FRIEND 1

**pal** (around) *vb* to come or be together as friends — see ASSOCIATE 1

**palace** *n* **1** a large impressive residence — see MANSION
**2** a large, magnificent, or massive building — see EDIFICE 1
**3** the residence of a ruler — see COURT 1

**palatable** *adj* **1** being to one's liking — see SATISFACTORY 1
**2** giving pleasure or contentment to the mind or senses — see PLEASANT

3 very pleasing to the sense of taste — see DELICIOUS 1

**palatial** *adj* showing obvious signs of wealth and comfort — see LUXURIOUS

**palaver** *n* friendly, informal conversation or an instance of this — see CHAT

**palaver** *vb* to engage in casual or rambling conversation — see CHAT

**pale** *adj* 1 lacking intensity of color ⟨we chose a very *pale* pink for the walls of the room⟩
*syn* dull, dulled, faded, light, pastel, washed-out
*rel* flat, lackluster, lusterless, matte (*also* mat *or* matt); dim, faint; dirty, muddy; achromatic, colorless, uncolored, undyed, unpainted, unstained; blanched, bleached, washed, white, whitened; gray (*also* grey), indistinct, neutral
*near ant* bright, brilliant, vibrant, vivid; chromatic, colored, dyed, painted, stained, tinged, tinted; colorful, multicolored, polychromatic, polychrome, varicolored, variegated; flashy, garish, gaudy, loud, showy, splashy
*ant* dark, deep, gay, rich
2 lacking a healthy skin color ⟨after a week with the flu, she was deathly *pale* and noticeably thinner⟩
*syn* ashen, ashy, blanched, cadaverous, livid, lurid, paled, pallid, pasty, peaked, wan
*rel* sallow, sick, sickly, waxen, waxy; white, whitened; deathlike; anemic, bloodless; untanned
*near ant* blooming, blushing, flushed, glowing, pink
*ant* florid, flush, rubicund, ruddy, sanguine

**pale** *vb* to make white or whiter by removing color — see WHITEN

**paled** *adj* lacking a healthy skin color — see PALE 2

**palisade** *n* a steep wall of rock, earth, or ice — see CLIFF

**palliate** *vb* 1 to make (something) seem less bad by offering excuses ⟨don't try to *palliate* your constant lying by claiming that everybody lies⟩
*syn* excuse, extenuate, gloss (over), gloze (over), whitewash
*rel* sugarcoat, varnish; apologize, atone, confess; explain, justify, rationalize; alleviate, lessen, lighten, mitigate, moderate, soften, temper; absolve, acquit, clear, exculpate, exonerate, vindicate
2 to make more bearable or less severe — see HELP 2

**pallid** *adj* lacking a healthy skin color — see PALE 2

**palm off** *vb* to offer (something fake, useless, or inferior) as genuine, useful, or valuable — see FOIST

**palmy** *adj* 1 having attained a desired end or state of good fortune — see SUCCESSFUL 1
2 marked by vigorous growth and well-being especially economically — see PROSPEROUS 1

**palpable** *adj* 1 able to be perceived by a sense or by the mind — see PERCEPTIBLE
2 capable of being perceived by the sense of touch — see TANGIBLE
3 not subject to misinterpretation or more than one interpretation — see CLEAR 2

**palpitate** *vb* to expand and contract in a rhythmic manner — see PULSATE

**palpitation** *n* a rhythmic expanding and contracting — see PULSATION

**palsy** *n* complete or partial loss of physical function (as motion or sensation) in a part of the body — see PARALYSIS

**palter** *vb* to talk over or dispute the terms of a purchase — see BARGAIN

**paltry** *adj* so small or unimportant as to warrant little or no attention — see NEGLIGIBLE 1

**pamper** *vb* to treat with great or excessive care — see BABY

**pamphlet** *n* a short printed publication with no cover or with a paper cover ⟨*pamphlets* about common safety precautions that we all can put into use⟩
*syn* booklet, brochure, circular, flier (*or* flyer), folder, leaflet
*rel* advertisement, catalog (*or* catalogue); tract; paperback, pocket book; guidebook, handbook, instructions, manual

**pan** *vb* to express one's unfavorable opinion of the worth or quality of — see CRITICIZE

**panacea** *n* something that cures all ills or problems — see CURE-ALL

**pancake** *n* a flat cake made from thin batter and cooked on both sides (as on a griddle) ⟨every Sunday morning, we have *pancakes* and bacon for breakfast⟩
*syn* flapjack, griddle cake, hotcake, slapjack
*rel* crepe (*or* crêpe); waffle

**pandemonium** *n* a state of noisy, confused activity — see COMMOTION

**panegyric** *n* a formal expression of praise — see ENCOMIUM

**panel** *n* 1 a meeting featuring a group discussion — see FORUM
2 a select group of persons assigned to consider or take action on some matter — see COMMITTEE

**pang** *n* a sharp unpleasant sensation usually felt in some specific part of the body — see PAIN 1

**panhandler** *n* a person who lives by public begging — see BEGGAR

**panic** *n* the emotion experienced in the presence or threat of danger — see FEAR

**panic** *vb* to strike with fear — see FRIGHTEN

**panorama** *n* all that can be seen from a certain point — see VIEW 1

**panoramic** *adj* covering everything or all important points — see ENCYCLOPEDIC

**pan out** *vb* 1 to come to be — see COME OUT 1
2 to turn out as planned or desired — see SUCCEED 1

**pant** *vb* to breathe hard, quickly, or with difficulty — see GASP

**pant** (after) *vb* to have an earnest wish to own or enjoy — see DESIRE

**pantaloons** *n pl* an outer garment covering each leg separately from waist to ankle — see PANTS

**panther** *n* a large tawny cat of the wild — see COUGAR

**pantomime** *n* **1** a movement of the body or limbs that expresses or emphasizes an idea or feeling — see GESTURE 1
**2** an actor in a story performed silently and entirely by body movements — see MIME

**pantomimist** *n* an actor in a story performed silently and entirely by body movements — see MIME

**pants** *n pl* an outer garment covering each leg separately from waist to ankle ⟨you'll need a nice pair of *pants* for the job interview⟩
***syn*** breeches, pantaloons, slacks, trousers
***rel*** corduroys, denims, jeans; hose, legging (*or* leggin), pantsuit

**papa** *n* a male human parent — see FATHER 1

**paper** *adj* being something in name or form only — see NOMINAL 1

**paper** *n* **1** a piece of paper with information written or to be written on it — see FORM 2
**2** a publication that appears at regular intervals — see JOURNAL
**3** a short piece of writing done as a school exercise — see COMPOSITION 2
**4** a short piece of writing typically expressing a point of view — see ESSAY 1

**par** *n* **1** something set up as an example against which others of the same type are compared — see STANDARD 1
**2** the state or fact of being exactly the same in number, amount, status, or quality — see EQUIVALENCE
**3** what is typical of a group, class, or series — see AVERAGE

**parable** *n* a story intended to teach a basic truth or moral about life — see ALLEGORY

**parade** *n* a body of individuals moving along in an orderly and often ceremonial way — see CORTEGE 2

**parade** *vb* **1** to move along with a steady regular step especially in a group — see MARCH 1
**2** to present so as to invite notice or attention — see SHOW 1

**paradigmatic** *adj* constituting, serving as, or worthy of being a pattern to be imitated — see MODEL

**paradise** *n* **1** a place or state of great happiness ⟨Susan's idea of *paradise* was a world where no one had to go to work⟩
***syn*** Eden, Elysium, heaven, utopia
***rel*** dreamland, fairyland, promised land, wonderland; bliss, euphoria, gladness, joy
***ant*** hell
**2** a dwelling place of perfect bliss for the soul after death — see HEAVEN 1
**3** a state of overwhelming usually pleasurable emotion — see ECSTASY

**paradox** *n* someone or something with qualities or features that seem to conflict with one another — see CONTRADICTION 1

**paragon** *n* someone of such unequaled perfection as to deserve imitation — see IDEAL 1

**parallel** *adj* having qualities in common — see ALIKE

**parallel** *n* **1** a point which two or more things share in common — see SIMILARITY 2
**2** one that is equal to another in status, achievement, or value — see EQUAL

**parallel** *vb* to be the exact counterpart of — see MATCH 1

**parallelism** *n* the quality or state of having many qualities in common — see SIMILARITY 1

**paralysis** *n* complete or partial loss of physical function (as motion or sensation) in a part of the body ⟨the car accident left one athlete with *paralysis* from the waist down⟩
***syn*** palsy
***rel*** cerebral palsy, multiple sclerosis, poliomyelitis; debilitation, debility, decrepitude, enfeeblement, feebleness, frailness, weakness; infirmity, lameness; disability, impairment
***near ant*** mobility, motility, sensation

**paralytic** *adj* affected with paralysis ⟨at first, he would not accept that he was now *paralytic* and needed help⟩
***syn*** paralyzed
***rel*** challenged, crippled, disabled, handicapped, maimed, mutilated; hobbled, lame, lamed; impaired, incapacitated; hamstrung; debilitated, decrepit, enfeebled, feeble, infirm, weak, weakened
***near ant*** able-bodied

**paralyze** *vb* to render powerless, ineffective, or unable to move ⟨a blizzard *paralyzed* the city for two days⟩
***syn*** cripple, disable, hamstring, immobilize, incapacitate, prostrate
***rel*** attenuate, debilitate, enfeeble, sap, undermine, weaken; hobble, lame; maim, mutilate
***near ant*** energize, galvanize, vitalize; fortify, strengthen; empower; refresh, rejuvenate, restore

**paralyzed** *adj* affected with paralysis — see PARALYTIC

**paramount** *adj* **1** coming before all others in importance — see FOREMOST 1
**2** of the greatest or highest degree or quantity — see ULTIMATE 1

**paraphernalia** *n* **1** items needed for the performance of a task or activity — see EQUIPMENT
**2** transportable items that one owns — see POSSESSION 2

**paraphrase** *n* an instance of expressing something in different words ⟨your essays on human rights should have some original thought and not be simply a *paraphrase* of what's in the textbook⟩

---

***syn*** synonym(s) ***rel*** related words
***ant*** antonym(s) ***near ant*** near antonym(s)

*syn* rephrasing, restatement, restating, rewording, translating, translation
*rel* rehash; summary
*near ant* copy, transcript, transcription
*ant* quotation, quote

**paraphrase** *vb* to express something (as a text or statement) in different words ⟨could you *paraphrase* your diagnosis of my medical condition, using simpler language?⟩
*syn* rephrase, restate, reword, translate
*rel* summarize
*near ant* repeat; copy, reproduce, transcribe
*ant* quote

**parasite** *n* a person who is supported or seeks support from another without making an adequate return — see LEECH

**parboil** *vb* to cook in a liquid heated to the point that it gives off steam — see BOIL 2

**parcel** *n* **1** a number of things considered as a unit — see GROUP 1
**2** a small area of usually open land — see FIELD 1
**3** a small piece of land that is developed or available for development — see LOT 1
**4** a usually small number of persons considered as a unit — see GROUP 2
**5** a wrapped or sealed case containing an item or set of items — see PACKAGE 1

**parcel** (out) *vb* to give out (something) in appropriate amounts or to appropriate individuals — see ADMINISTER 1

**parcel post** *n* communications or parcels sent or carried through the postal system — see MAIL

**parch** *vb* to make dry — see DRY 1

**pardon** *n* release from the guilt or penalty of an offense ⟨the criminal is hoping for a Presidential *pardon*⟩
*syn* absolution, amnesty, forgiveness, remission, remittal
*rel* parole; acquittal, exculpation, exoneration, vindication; exemption, immunity, impunity, indemnity; commutation, commuting, reprieve
*near ant* conviction, sentence; assessment, charge, fine, imposition, levying; castigation, chastening, chastisement, condemnation
*ant* penalty, punishment, retribution

**pardon** *vb* **1** to cease to have feelings of anger or bitterness toward — see FORGIVE 1
**2** to overlook or dismiss as of little importance — see EXCUSE 1

**pardonable** *adj* worthy of forgiveness — see VENIAL

**pare** *vb* to make (as hair) shorter with or as if with the use of shears — see CLIP

**parentage** *n* the line of ancestors from whom a person is descended — see ANCESTRY

**parenthood** *n* the caring for a child by its parents — see PARENTING

**parenting** *n* the caring for a child by its parents ⟨as the big day approaches, the expectant couple are starting to get worried about their fitness for *parenting*⟩
*syn* parenthood
*rel* raising, rearing, upbringing; fatherhood, fathering, paternity; maternity, motherhood, mothering

**par excellence** *adj* of the very best kind — see EXCELLENT

**pariah** *n* one who is cast out or rejected by society — see OUTCAST

**parity** *n* the state or fact of being exactly the same in number, amount, status, or quality — see EQUIVALENCE

**park** *n* the area around and belonging to a building — see GROUND 1

**parley** *n* **1** a meeting featuring a group discussion — see FORUM
**2** an exchange of views for the purpose of exploring a subject or deciding an issue — see DISCUSSION 1

**parley** *vb* to exchange viewpoints or seek advice for the purpose of finding a solution to a problem — see CONFER 2

**parliament** *n* the highest lawmaking body of a political unit — see CONGRESS 1

**parlor** *n* a building, room, or suite of rooms occupied by a service business — see PLACE 2

**parlous** *adj* involving potential loss or injury — see DANGEROUS

**parochial** *adj* not broad or open in views or opinions — see NARROW 2

**parody** *n* **1** a work that imitates and exaggerates another work for comic effect ⟨the musical was a *parody* of *Romeo and Juliet*, with silly songs during the sad scenes⟩
*syn* burlesque, caricature, spoof, takeoff
*rel* lampoon, mockery, satire, travesty; comedy, farce, sketch, slapstick, squib; distortion, exaggeration; imitation, impersonation, mimicking
*near ant* archetype, original, prototype
**2** a poor, insincere, or insulting imitation of something — see MOCKERY 1

**parody** *vb* to copy or exaggerate (someone or something) in order to make fun of — see MIMIC 1

**paroxysm** *n* **1** a sudden intense expression of strong feeling — see OUTBURST 1
**2** a violent disturbance (as of the political or social order) — see CONVULSION

**parrot** *vb* to say after another — see REPEAT 3

**parsimonious** *adj* giving or sharing as little as possible — see STINGY 1

**parsimony** *n* the quality of being overly sparing with money ⟨her *parsimony* was so extreme that she'd walk five miles to the store to save a few cents on gas⟩
*syn* cheapness, closeness, miserliness, penuriousness, pinching, stinginess, tightness
*rel* conserving, economizing, economy, frugality, husbandry, providence, scrimping, skimping, thrift; conservation, saving; husbanding, managing
*near ant* extravagance, lavishness; dissipation, improvidence, prodigality, squandering, wastefulness
*ant* generosity, liberality, openhandedness, openheartedness, philanthropy

**parson** *n* a person specially trained and authorized to conduct religious services in a Christian church — see CLERGYMAN
**part** *adv* in some measure or degree — see PARTLY
**part** *n* **1** one of the pieces from which something is designed to be assembled ⟨the model car came in several small *parts* that had to be assembled⟩
***syn*** member, partition, portion, section, segment
***rel*** component, constituent, element, factor, ingredient, moiety, parcel; cut, length; bit, fragment, particle, scrap
***near ant*** whole; aggregate, composite, compound, sum, total, totality
**2** something belonging to, due to, or contributed by an individual member of a group — see SHARE 1
**3** the action for which a person or thing is specially fitted or used or for which a thing exists — see ROLE
**4** *usually* **parts** *pl* a broad geographical area — see REGION 2
**part** *vb* to set or force apart — see SEPARATE 1
**partake** *vb* to take a share or part ⟨we should all *partake* of this fine meal together⟩
***syn*** participate, share
***rel*** endure, experience, feel, see, taste, undergo; encounter, meet; accept, receive
**partaker** *n* one who takes part in something — see PARTICIPANT
**partial** *adj* **1** inclined to favor one side over another ⟨that judge is always *partial* to the defense, so be careful⟩
***syn*** biased, one-sided, partisan, prejudiced
***rel*** jaundiced, unfriendly, unsympathetic; colored, distorted, misrepresented, warped; convinced, influenced, persuaded, predisposed, prepossessed, swayed; affected, concerned, interested
***near ant*** open, open-minded, persuasible, receptive; fair, honest, just, reasonable; bipartisan; autonomous, independent, unallied; aloof, detached, dispassionate, hardheaded, impersonal, objective, unemotional; apathetic, indifferent, unenthusiastic, uninterested
***ant*** evenhanded, impartial, neutral, nonpartisan, unbiased, unprejudiced
**2** having a liking or affection — see FOND 1
**3** lacking some necessary part — see INCOMPLETE
**partiality** *n* **1** an attitude that always favors one way of feeling or acting especially without considering any other possibilities — see BIAS
**2** a habitual attraction to some activity or thing — see INCLINATION 1
**3** positive regard for something — see LIKING
**partially** *adv* in some measure or degree — see PARTLY

***syn*** synonym(s) ***rel*** related words
***ant*** antonym(s) ***near ant*** near antonym(s)

**participant** *n* one who takes part in something ⟨he seemed to be a willing *participant* in the prank⟩
***syn*** partaker, participator, party, sharer
***rel*** actor; accessory, aide, assistant, helper; colleague, partner
***near ant*** bystander, looker-on, observer, onlooker, spectator, watcher
***ant*** nonparticipant
**participate** *vb* to take a share or part — see PARTAKE
**participator** *n* one who takes part in something — see PARTICIPANT
**particle** *n* **1** a very small amount ⟨I did all but a *particle* of my work⟩
***syn*** ace, bit, crumb, dab, driblet, glimmer, hint, lick, little, mite, nip, ounce, peanuts, ray, scruple, shade, shadow, shred, smidgen (*also* smidgeon *or* smidgin), snap, spark, speck, spot, sprinkling, strain, streak, suspicion, touch, trace
***rel*** iota, jot, modicum, tittle, whit; atom, dot, fleck, flyspeck, grain, granule, molecule, morsel, mote, nubbin, patch, scrap; dash, drop, pinch; part, portion, section; bite, nibble, taste; handful, scattering, smattering; dose, shot; chip, flake, fragment, shard, shiver, sliver, smithereens, splinter; shred, tatter; clipping, paring, shaving
***near ant*** abundance, barrel, bucket, bushel, deal, gobs, heaps, loads, mass, mountain, much, peck, pile, plenty, profusion, quantity, raft, scads, stack, wad, wealth; volume; embarrassment, excess, overabundance, overage, overflow, overkill, overmuch, oversupply, superabundance, superfluity, surfeit, surplus; chunk, hunk, lump, slab
**2** a very small piece — see BIT 1
**particular** *adj* **1** hard to please — see FINICKY
**2** of, relating to, or belonging to a single person — see INDIVIDUAL 1
**3** tending to select carefully — see SELECTIVE
**particular** *n* **1** a separate part in a list, account, or series — see ITEM 1
**2** a single piece of information — see FACT 3
**particularity** *n* **1** careful thoroughness of detail ⟨with great *particularity* she described the qualities she's looking for in a boyfriend⟩
***syn*** explicitness, specificity
***rel*** attentiveness, care, carefulness, conscientiousness, finickiness, fussiness, meticulousness; alertness, cautiousness, circumspection, heedfulness, safeness; discrimination; accuracy, exactitude, exactness, precision
***near ant*** imprecision, inaccuracy, inexactness; indistinctness, vagueness
***ant*** generality
**2** a single piece of information — see FACT 3
**particularized** *adj* including many small descriptive features — see DETAILED 1
**particularly** *adv* to a great degree — see VERY 1

**parting** *adj* given, taken, or performed at parting ⟨she gave him a *parting* gift to remember her by⟩
*syn* farewell, valedictory
*rel* final, last, ultimate; departing, leaving

**parting** *n* **1** the act or process of two or more persons going off in different directions ⟨although their *parting* was sad, they knew they would see each other again⟩
*syn* farewell, leave-taking, separation
*rel* departure, egress, exit, exiting, exodus, going, leaving, quitting, running away; decampment, flight, withdrawal; abandonment, desertion, forsaking
*near ant* reunion; arrival, greeting, welcome; gathering, joining, meeting
**2** the act of leaving a place — see DEPARTURE

**partisan** *adj* inclined to favor one side over another — see PARTIAL 1

**partisan** *n* **1** one who follows the opinions or teachings of another — see FOLLOWER
**2** one who is intensely or excessively devoted to a cause — see ZEALOT

**partisanship** *n* an attitude that always favors one way of feeling or acting especially without considering any other possibilities — see BIAS

**partition** *n* **1** one of the pieces from which something is designed to be assembled — see PART 1
**2** something that divides, separates, or marks off — see DIVISION 1
**3** the act or process of a whole separating into two or more parts or pieces — see SEPARATION 1

**partly** *adv* in some measure or degree ⟨you're only *partly* right⟩
*syn* incompletely, part, partially
*rel* in part
*near ant* absolutely, dead, downright, plain, plumb, utterly
*ant* completely, entirely, totally, wholly

**partner** *n* the person to whom another is married — see SPOUSE

**partnership** *n* the state of having shared interests or efforts (as in social or business matters) — see ASSOCIATION 1

**parturition** *n* the act or process of giving birth to children — see CHILDBIRTH

**party** *n* **1** a social gathering ⟨we're all invited to the big *party* to celebrate the end of the term⟩
*syn* affair, blowout, event, fete (*or* fête), function, get-together, reception, shindig
*rel* ball, formal, prom; celebration, gala, occasion; orgy, saturnalia; benefit, clambake, hen party, housewarming, masquerade, mixer, shower, salon, soiree (*or* soirée), stag, tea
**2** a group of people acting together within a larger group — see FACTION
**3** a group of people working together on a task — see GANG 1
**4** a member of the human race — see HUMAN
**5** a usually small number of persons considered as a unit — see GROUP 2
**6** one who takes part in something — see PARTICIPANT

**party pooper** *n* a person who spoils the pleasure of others — see KILLJOY

**pass** *n* **1** a narrow opening between hillsides or mountains that can be used for passage — see CANYON
**2** a passage cleared for public vehicular travel — see WAY 1
**3** a small sheet of plastic, paper, or paperboard showing that the bearer has a claim to something (as admittance) — see TICKET 1
**4** an effort to do or accomplish something — see ATTEMPT

**pass** *vb* **1** to shift possession of (something) from one person to another ⟨could you please *pass* me the phone?⟩
*syn* hand, hand over, reach, transfer
*rel* relay; bear, carry; finger, handle, paw; cede, give, give up, release, relinquish, surrender
**2** to come to an end — see CEASE 1
**3** to put (something) into the possession or safekeeping of another — see GIVE 2
**4** to put into effect through legislative or authoritative action — see ENACT
**5** to take place — see HAPPEN

**pass** (on) *vb* to stop living — see DIE 1

**pass** (over) *vb* to make one's way through, across, or over — see TRAVERSE

**passable** *adj* **1** capable of being traveled on ⟨after the snowstorm, the roads might not be *passable* for the morning ride to school⟩
*syn* navigable, negotiable
*rel* clear, cleared, open, unclogged, unobstructed
*near ant* blocked, choked, clogged, closed, congested, dammed, jammed, obstructed; barricaded, blockaded
*ant* impassable
**2** capable of being passed into or through — see PENETRABLE
**3** of a level of quality that meets one's needs or standards — see ADEQUATE
**4** of average to below average quality — see MEDIOCRE 1

**passably** *adv* in a satisfactory way — see WELL 1

**passage** *n* **1** an established course for traveling from one place to another ⟨the long *passage* down the Atlantic seaboard, around Cape Horn, and up the Pacific Coast to California⟩
*syn* approach, avenue, path, route, way
*rel* bypath, byway, lane; bypass, drive, freeway, highway, road, street, thoroughfare; trace, track, trail; airway; channel, watercourse, waterway; door, doorway, gate, gateway, portal
**2** a going from one place to another usually of some distance — see JOURNEY
**3** a journey over water in a vessel — see SAIL
**4** a part taken from a longer work — see EXCERPT
**5** forward movement in time or place — see ADVANCE 1

**passageway** *n* **1** a passage cleared for public vehicular travel — see WAY 1
**2** a typically long narrow way connecting parts of a building — see HALL 2
**pass away** *vb* to stop living — see DIE 1
**passé** *adj* having passed its time of use or usefulness — see OBSOLETE
**passel** *n* **1** a number of things considered as a unit — see GROUP 1
**2** a usually small number of persons considered as a unit — see GROUP 2
**passing** *adj* lasting only for a short time — see MOMENTARY
**passing** *n* the permanent stopping of all the vital bodily activities — see DEATH 1
**passion** *n* **1** a feeling of strong or constant regard for and dedication to someone — see LOVE 1
**2** a strong but often short-lived liking for another person — see CRUSH 1
**3** a strong wish for something — see DESIRE
**4** a subjective response to a person, thing, or situation — see FEELING 1
**5** depth of feeling — see ARDOR 1
**6 passions** *pl* general emotional condition — see FEELING 2
**passionate** *adj* **1** having a strong sexual desire — see LUSTFUL
**2** having or expressing great depth of feeling — see FERVENT
**passive** *adj* receiving or enduring without offering resistance ⟨the student body was surprisingly *passive* about having recess shortened⟩
***syn*** acquiescent, nonresistant, resigned, tolerant, tolerating, unresistant, unresisting, yielding
***rel*** forbearing, long-suffering, patient, uncomplaining; agreeable, amenable, compliant, complying, conformist, docile, guidable, law-abiding, obedient, subordinate, tractable, willing; submissive, surrendering; amiable, obliging; slavish, subservient; disciplined, governable, manageable; apathetic, uncaring, unresponsive
***near ant*** defiant; contrary, disobedient, insubordinate, insurgent, intractable, mutinous, rebellious, recalcitrant, refractory, uncontrollable, ungovernable, unruly; balky, perverse, wayward, wrongheaded; headstrong, willful (*or* wilful); indomitable; undisciplined, unmanageable; dissident, nonconformist
***ant*** protesting, resistant, resisting, unyielding
**pass off** *vb* to offer (something fake, useless, or inferior) as genuine, useful, or valuable — see FOIST
**pass out** *vb* to lose consciousness — see FAINT
**pass over** *vb* **1** to fail to give proper attention to — see NEGLECT 1
**2** to overlook or dismiss as of little importance — see EXCUSE 1

***syn*** synonym(s) ***rel*** related words
***ant*** antonym(s) ***near ant*** near antonym(s)

**passport** *n* something that allows someone to achieve a desired goal ⟨meeting that movie director could be your *passport* to a big acting career⟩
***syn*** gateway, key, open sesame
***rel*** password; accomplishment, achievement, success; manner, means, method, system, technique, way; blueprint, design, plan, scheme, strategy
**password** *n* a word or phrase that must be spoken by a person in order to pass a guard ⟨the *password* for the dance party will be changed next week⟩
***syn*** countersign, watchword
***rel*** shibboleth, sign; signal; hint, indication
**past** *adj* having been such at some previous time — see FORMER
**past** *n* the events or experience of former times ⟨we spent a pleasant evening recalling the *past* together⟩
***syn*** auld lang syne, history, yesterday, yesteryear, yore
***rel*** bygone; flashback; annals, chronicle, record; memoir; antiquity
***near ant*** future, tomorrow; present
**past** *prep* on or to the farther side of — see BEYOND 1
**paste** *vb* to deliver a blow to (someone or something) usually in a strong vigorous manner — see HIT 1
**pastel** *adj* lacking intensity of color — see PALE 1
**past master** *n* a person with a high level of knowledge or skill in a field — see EXPERT
**pastoral** *adj* **1** of, relating to, associated with, or typical of open areas with few buildings or people — see RURAL
**2** of, relating to, or characteristic of the clergy — see CLERICAL
**pasturage** *n* open land over which livestock may roam and feed — see RANGE 1
**pasture** *n* open land over which livestock may roam and feed — see RANGE 1
**pasture** *vb* to feed on grass or herbs — see [1]GRAZE
**pasty** *adj* lacking a healthy skin color — see PALE 2
**pat** *adj* sticking to an opinion, purpose, or course of action in spite of reason, arguments, or persuasion — see OBSTINATE
**pat** *vb* to touch or handle in a tender or loving manner — see FONDLE
**patch** *n* **1** a small area that is different (as in color) from the main part — see SPOT 1
**2** a very small piece — see BIT 1
**patch** *vb* to put into good shape or working order again — see MEND 1
**patch** (together) *vb* to make or assemble roughly or hastily — see COBBLE (TOGETHER)
**patchwork** *adj* consisting of many things of different sorts — see MISCELLANEOUS
**pate** *n* the upper or front part of the body that contains the brain, the major sense organs, and the mouth — see HEAD 1
**patent** *adj* **1** not subject to misinterpretation or more than one interpretation — see CLEAR 2

2 very noticeable especially for being incorrect or bad — see EGREGIOUS

**path** *n* 1 the direction along which something or someone moves ⟨try to stay out of the *path* of the golf balls while playing⟩ ⟨I tripped over a rock directly in my *path*⟩
*syn* course, line, pathway, route, steps, track, way
*rel* circle, circuit, loop, orbit; flight path, trajectory; ascent, descent
2 a rough course or way formed by or as if by repeated footsteps — see TRAIL 1
3 an established course for traveling from one place to another — see PASSAGE 1

**pathetic** *adj* 1 deserving of one's pity ⟨the plight of the homeless family was quite *pathetic*⟩
*syn* heartbreaking, heartrending, miserable, piteous, pitiable, pitiful, poor, rueful, sorry, wretched
*rel* deplorable, lamentable, regrettable; emotional, impressive, inspiring; affecting, moving, poignant, stirring, touching; awful, horrible, terrible; distressing, disturbing, upsetting; grievous, sad, sorrowful, woeful
*near ant* unimpressive, uninspiring
2 causing unhappiness — see SAD 2

**pathway** *n* 1 a rough course or way formed by or as if by repeated footsteps — see TRAIL 1
2 the direction along which something or someone moves — see PATH 1

**patience** *n* the capacity to endure what is difficult or disagreeable without complaining ⟨my mother is endowed with nearly endless *patience*⟩
*syn* forbearance, long-suffering, sufferance, tolerance
*rel* acquiescence, resignation; passiveness, passivity; amenability, compliance, conformism, docility, obedience, subordination, tractability, willingness; discipline, self-control; submission, submissiveness
*near ant* defiance; contrariness, disobedience, insubordination, intractability, recalcitrance, resistance, willfulness
*ant* impatience

**patient** *adj* 1 accepting pains or hardships calmly or without complaint ⟨you were very *patient* about having to wait for me for so long⟩
*syn* forbearing, long-suffering, stoic (*or* stoical), tolerant, uncomplaining
*rel* lenient; acquiescent, passive, resigned, unresistant, unresisting, yielding; agreeable, amenable, compliant, complying, conformist, docile, law-abiding, obedient, submissive, subordinate, tractable, willing; slavish, subservient; amiable, obliging; collected, composed; constrained, contained, curbed, inhibited, repressed, restrained; disciplined, self-contained, self-controlled; apathetic, uncaring, unresponsive
*near ant* bored, tired, weary; defiant, resistant; contrary, disobedient, insubordinate, intractable, rebellious, recalcitrant, refractory, ungovernable, unmanageable, unruly
*ant* complaining, fed up, impatient, protesting
2 continuing despite difficulties, opposition, or discouragement — see PERSISTENT

**patient** *n* an individual awaiting or under medical care and treatment ⟨the nurse asked the *patient* to change into a paper gown⟩
*syn* case
*rel* inpatient, outpatient; sufferer, victim; convalescent, nursling

**patio** *n* an open space wholly or partly enclosed (as by buildings or walls) — see COURT 2

**patois** *n* the special terms or expressions of a particular group or field — see TERMINOLOGY

**patrician** *adj* of high birth, rank, or station — see NOBLE 1

**patrician** *n* a man of high birth or social position — see GENTLEMAN 1

**patrimony** *n* something that is or may be inherited — see INHERITANCE

**patriot** *n* a person who loves his or her country and supports its interests and policies ⟨the contention that true *patriots* would be willing to do anything for their country⟩
*syn* loyalist
*rel* chauvinist; jingoist, nationalist; compatriot, countryman
*near ant* collaborator, quisling, spy, traitor; betrayer, deserter, recreant; renegade

**patriotic** *adj* having or showing love and support for one's country ⟨hanging a flag outside is a *patriotic* gesture⟩
*syn* nationalist, nationalistic
*rel* chauvinist; jingoistic; constant, devoted, faithful, loyal, staunch (*or* stanch), steadfast, steady, true; ardent, fervent, fervid, impassioned, passionate
*near ant* traitorous, treasonous; disaffected, disloyal, faithless, false, fickle, inconstant, perfidious, recreant, treacherous, unfaithful
*ant* unpatriotic

**patriotism** *n* love and support for one's country ⟨her *patriotism* was so great that she quit her job to work for the war effort⟩
*syn* nationalism
*rel* chauvinism; jingoism; allegiance, constancy, devotion, faithfulness, fealty, loyalty, staunchness, steadfastness; fervency, fervidness, passion
*near ant* desertion, treason; disaffection, disloyalty, faithlessness, falseness, fickleness, inconstancy, perfidiousness, treachery, unfaithfulness

**patron** *n* 1 a person who buys a product or uses a service from a business — see CUSTOMER 1
2 a person who takes the responsibility for some other person or thing — see SPONSOR
3 one that helps another with gifts or money — see BENEFACTOR

**patronize** *vb* **1** to assume or treat with an air of superiority — see CONDESCEND 2
**2** to promote the interests or cause of — see SUPPORT 1

**patter** *vb* to engage in casual or rambling conversation — see CHAT

**patter** *n* the special terms or expressions of a particular group or field — see TERMINOLOGY

**pattern** *n* **1** a unit of decoration that is repeated all over something (as a fabric) ⟨a quilt with tiny pink roses as the *pattern*⟩
*syn* design, figure, motif, motive
*rel* device; adornment, caparison, decoration, embellishment, frill, garnish, ornament, trim
**2** a usual manner of behaving or doing — see HABIT
**3** an established and often automatic or monotonous series of actions followed when engaging in some activity — see ROUTINE 1
**4** the way in which the elements of something (as a work of art) are arranged — see COMPOSITION 3

**patty** *also* **pattie** *n* a small usually rounded mass of minced food that has been fried — see CAKE

**paucity** *n* a falling short of an essential or desirable amount or number — see DEFICIENCY

**paunch** *n* an enlarged or bulging abdomen — see POTBELLY

**pauperism** *n* the state of lacking sufficient money or material possessions — see POVERTY 1

**pause** *n* a momentary halt in an activity ⟨there was a brief *pause* for applause in her speech⟩
*syn* break, breath, breather, interruption, lull, recess
*rel* time-out; interim, interlude, intermission, interval, respite, rest; cessation, discontinuance, ending, expiration, finishing, lapse, stopping, termination; abeyance, moratorium, surcease, suspension; discontinuity, gap, hiatus
*near ant* continuation, endurance, persistence, progress, progression; extension, prolongation

**pause** *vb* to come to a temporary halt in one's activity ⟨he *paused* for a moment to tie his shoe⟩
*syn* break
*rel* break in, interrupt; cease, discontinue, end, finish, stop, terminate; knock off, lay off, quit; lapse, let up
*near ant* continue, persist; advance, progress; extend, prolong, stretch

**pawn** *n* **1** one that is or can be used to further the purposes of another ⟨she disliked being a *pawn* in her friends' power games⟩
*syn* puppet, tool
*rel* chump, dupe, foil, gull, sucker, victim; minion, stooge; yes-man

---

*syn* synonym(s) *rel* related words
*ant* antonym(s) *near ant* near antonym(s)

**2** something given or held to assure that the giver will keep a promise — see PLEDGE 1

**pawn** *vb* to leave as a guarantee of repayment of a loan ⟨he *pawned* his watch in order to pay off his gambling debt⟩
*syn* hock, pledge
*rel* deposit, mortgage; bond
*near ant* buy (back), redeem, win (back)

**pay** *n* **1** the money paid regularly to a person for labor or services — see WAGE
**2** something (as money) that is given or received in return for goods or services — see PAYMENT 2

**pay** *vb* **1** to give (someone) the sum of money owed for goods or services received ⟨we need to *pay* the cashier and then we can leave⟩
*syn* compensate, recompense, remunerate
*rel* reimburse, repay, requite; pay off, pay up, prepay
**2** to give what is owed for ⟨you ought to *pay* that bill before it's overdue⟩
*syn* clear, discharge, foot, liquidate, pay off, pay up, quit, recompense, settle, spring (for), stand
*ant* repudiate
**3** to hand over or use up in payment — see SPEND 1
**4** to produce as revenue — see YIELD 2

**payable** *adj* not yet paid — see OUTSTANDING 1

**paying** *adj* yielding a profit — see PROFITABLE 1

**paying** *n* the act of offering money in exchange for goods or services — see PAYMENT 1

**payload** *n* a mass or quantity of something taken up and carried, conveyed, or transported — see LOAD 1

**payment** *n* **1** the act of offering money in exchange for goods or services ⟨they are very prompt in the *payment* of their credit card bills⟩
*syn* compensation, disbursement, giving, paying, remitment, remittance, remuneration
*rel* rendering, tendering; reimbursement, repayment; paying off, paying up, prepayment; overpayment
*near ant* underpayment
*ant* nonpayment, repudiation
**2** something (as money) that is given or received in return for goods or services ⟨their *payment* for mowing the lawn was $20⟩ ⟨we finally mailed our last car *payment* last week⟩
*syn* compensation, consideration, pay, recompense, remittance, remuneration, requital
*rel* salary, stipend, wage(s); disbursement, expenditure, outlay; rebate, refund; indemnity, recoupment, redress, reparation, restitution; adjustment, settlement; deposit; reimbursement, repayment; prepayment; overpayment; rent, rental
**3** the money paid regularly to a person for labor or services — see WAGE

**payoff** *n* the amount of money left when expenses are subtracted from the total amount received — see PROFIT 1

**pay off** *vb* to give what is owed for — see PAY 2

**pay up** *vb* to give what is owed for — see PAY 2

**peace** *n* **1** a state without war ⟨after a long and bitter war, the troubled region finally achieved *peace*⟩
*syn* peacefulness
*rel* accord, amity, concord, harmony; calm, quiet, serenity, tranquillity (*or* tranquility); order, stability; pacification
*near ant* conflict, contention, discord, dissidence, strife, trouble; tumult, turmoil, unrest, upheaval; fighting, warfare; action, battle, combat
*ant* war
**2** a state of freedom from storm or disturbance — see CALM
**3** peaceful coexistence — see HARMONY 2

**peaceable** *adj* **1** inclined to live in peace and to avoid war — see PEACEFUL 1
**2** not involving violence or force — see PEACEFUL 2

**peaceful** *adj* **1** inclined to live in peace and to avoid war ⟨a *peaceful* tribe that had quietly inhabited these shores for centuries before the arrival of the Europeans⟩
*syn* pacific, peaceable
*rel* calm, mild, neutral, quiet, relaxed, serene, tranquil; affable, amiable, amicable, benevolent, gentle, kind, kindly; nonbelligerent, unaggressive; submissive, yielding
*near ant* militaristic; aggressive, bellicose, belligerent, combative, contentious, discordant, pugnacious, quarrelsome, scrappy, truculent; antagonistic, argumentative, fierce, gladiatorial, hostile, hot-tempered
*ant* warlike
**2** not involving violence or force ⟨UN officials struggled to find a *peaceful* solution to the troublesome conflict⟩
*syn* nonviolent, peaceable
*rel* conciliatory, pacific, peacemaking; nonbelligerent, unaggressive, unassertive; appeasing, conciliating, mollifying, pacifying, placating; calming, quieting, soothing
*near ant* armed, martial, militant, military, warlike; aggressive, assertive, bellicose, belligerent, combative, contentious, quarrelsome; antagonistic, argumentative, fierce, gladiatorial, hostile; tempestuous, volcanic
*ant* forced, violent
**3** free from disturbing noise or uproar — see QUIET 1
**4** free from storms or physical disturbance — see CALM 1

**peacefulness** *n* **1** a state of freedom from storm or disturbance — see CALM
**2** a state without war — see PEACE 1

**peacemaker** *n* one who works with opposing sides in order to bring about an agreement — see MEDIATOR

**peacemaking** *adj* tending to lessen or avoid conflict or hostility — see PACIFIC 1

**peak** *n* **1** an elevation of land higher than a hill — see MOUNTAIN 1
**2** the highest part or point — see HEIGHT 1
**3** the projecting front part of a hat or cap — see VISOR

**peaked** *adj* **1** lacking a healthy skin color — see PALE 2
**2** tapering to a thin tip — see POINTED 1
**3** temporarily suffering from a disorder of the body — see SICK 1

**peal** *vb* to make the clear sound heard when metal vibrates — see RING 1

**peanuts** *n pl* **1** a very small amount — see PARTICLE 1
**2** a very small sum of money — see MITE 1

**pearl** *n* someone or something unusually desirable — see PRIZE 1

**pebbly** *adj* not having a level or smooth surface — see UNEVEN 1

**peck** *n* a considerable amount — see LOT 2

**peculiar** *adj* **1** being out of the ordinary — see EXCEPTIONAL
**2** different from the ordinary in a way that causes curiosity or suspicion — see ODD 2
**3** noticeably different from what is generally found or experienced — see UNUSUAL 1
**4** of, relating to, or belonging to a single person — see INDIVIDUAL 1
**5** serving to identify as belonging to an individual or group — see CHARACTERISTIC 1

**peculiarity** *n* **1** an odd or peculiar habit — see IDIOSYNCRASY
**2** something that sets apart an individual from others of the same kind — see CHARACTERISTIC

**pecuniary** *adj* of or relating to money, banking, or investments — see FINANCIAL

**pedagogue** *n* a person whose occupation is to give formal instruction in a school — see TEACHER

**peddle** *vb* to sell from place to place usually in small quantities ⟨he traveled around the country *peddling* Bibles⟩
*syn* hawk
*rel* retail, wholesale; deal (in), distribute, high-pressure, hustle, market, merchandise, trade (in), vend

**peddler** *also* **pedlar** *n* one who sells things outdoors ⟨the *peddler* on the street corner selling baseball caps⟩
*syn* hawker, huckster
*rel* dealer, merchandiser, seller, vendor (*also* vender); concessionaire; black marketer, bootlegger, fence, fencer, hustler, smuggler, trader
*near ant* buyer, purchaser; consumer, end user, user

**pedestrian** *adj* causing weariness, restlessness, or lack of interest — see BORING

**pedigree** *n* the line of ancestors from whom a person is descended — see ANCESTRY

**pedigreed** *adj* of unmixed ancestry — see PUREBRED
**peek** *n* an instance of looking especially briefly — see LOOK 2
**peek** *vb* to take a quick or hasty look — see GLANCE 2
**peel** *vb* to remove the natural covering of ⟨she *peeled* an apple with great care⟩
***syn*** bark, flay, hull, husk, shell, shuck, skin
***rel*** bare, denude, expose, scale, strip; pare
**peel** (off) *vb* to rid oneself of (a garment) — see REMOVE 1
**peeled** *adj* lacking a usual or natural covering — see NAKED 2
**peep** *n* an instance of looking especially briefly — see LOOK 2
**peep** *vb* to make a short sharp sound like a small bird — see CHIRP
**peer** *n* one that is equal to another in status, achievement, or value — see EQUAL
**peer** *vb* to look long and hard in wonder or surprise — see GAPE
**peerless** *adj* having no equal or rival for excellence or desirability — see ONLY 1
**peeve** *n* **1** something that is a source of irritation — see ANNOYANCE 3
**2** the feeling of being offended or resentful after a slight or indignity — see PIQUE
**peeve** *vb* to disturb the peace of mind of (someone) especially by repeated disagreeable acts — see IRRITATE 1
**peeving** *adj* causing annoyance — see ANNOYING
**peevish** *adj* **1** easily irritated or annoyed — see IRRITABLE
**2** sticking to an opinion, purpose, or course of action in spite of reason, arguments, or persuasion — see OBSTINATE
**peevishness** *n* **1** a steadfast adherence to an opinion, purpose, or course of action — see OBSTINACY
**2** readiness to show annoyance or impatience — see PETULANCE
**peewee** *n* a living thing much smaller than others of its kind — see DWARF 1
**peg** *n* an individual part of a process, series, or ranking — see DEGREE 1
**peg** *vb* **1** to arrange or assign according to type — see CLASSIFY 1
**2** to send through the air especially with a quick forward motion of the arm — see THROW
**peg** (away) *vb* to devote serious and sustained effort — see LABOR
**pelage** *n* the hairy covering of a mammal especially when fine, soft, and thick — see FUR 1
**pelagic** *adj* of or relating to the sea — see MARINE 1
**pelf** *n* something (as pieces of stamped metal or printed paper) customarily and legally used as a medium of exchange, a measure of value, or a means of payment — see MONEY

***syn*** synonym(s) ***rel*** related words
***ant*** antonym(s) ***near ant*** near antonym(s)

**pellet** *n* a usually round or cone-shaped little piece of lead made to be fired from a firearm — see BULLET
**pell–mell** *adj* **1** acting or done with excessive or careless speed — see HASTY 1
**2** lacking in order, neatness, and often cleanliness — see MESSY
**pell–mell** *adv* **1** in a confused and reckless manner — see HELTER-SKELTER 1
**2** with excessive or careless speed — see HASTILY 1
**pellucid** *adj* easily seen through — see CLEAR 1
**pelt** *n* the outer covering of an animal removed for its commercial value — see HIDE 1
**pelt** *vb* **1** to proceed or move quickly — see HURRY 2
**2** to send through the air especially with a quick forward motion of the arm — see THROW
**3** to strike repeatedly — see BEAT 1
**pen** *n* **1** a place of confinement for persons held in lawful custody — see JAIL
**2** an enclosure with an open framework for keeping animals — see CAGE
**pen** *vb* **1** to close or shut in by or as if by barriers — see ENCLOSE 1
**2** to compose and set down on paper the words of — see WRITE 1
**penal** *adj* inflicting, involving, or serving as punishment — see PUNITIVE
**penalize** *vb* to inflict a penalty on for a fault or crime — see PUNISH
**penalizing** *adj* inflicting, involving, or serving as punishment — see PUNITIVE
**penalty** *n* **1** a feature of someone or something that creates difficulty for achieving success — see DISADVANTAGE
**2** a sum of money to be paid as a punishment — see FINE
**3** suffering, loss, or hardship imposed in response to a crime or offense — see PUNISHMENT
**penchant** *n* a habitual attraction to some activity or thing — see INCLINATION 1
**pencil** (in) *vb* to compose and set down on paper the words of — see WRITE 1
**pendant** *also* **pendent** *n* an ornament worn on a chain around the neck or wrist ⟨Navajo necklaces with *pendants* finely crafted in genuine sky-blue turquoise⟩
***syn*** bangle, charm, lavalier (*also* lavalliere)
***rel*** locket, teardrop
**pendent** *or* **pendant** *adj* extending freely from a support from above — see DEPENDENT 1
**pending** *adj* **1** not yet settled or decided ⟨a decision is *pending* about whether to buy computers or sports equipment with this money⟩
***syn*** open, undecided, undetermined, unresolved, unsettled
***rel*** hanging; arguable, debatable, disputable, moot, uncertain, unsure
***near ant*** confirmed, established; certain, sure
***ant*** decided, determined, resolved, settled

2 being soon to appear or take place — see FORTHCOMING
3 giving signs of immediate occurrence — see IMMINENT 1

**pendulous** *adj* 1 bending downward or forward — see NODDING
2 extending freely from a support from above — see DEPENDENT 1

**penetrable** *adj* capable of being passed into or through ⟨unfortunately, our netting proved to be a rather *penetrable* barrier that allowed in our cabin a steady stream of mosquitoes⟩
*syn* passable, permeable, porous
*rel* absorbent
*near ant* airtight, watertight; close, compact, dense, thick
*ant* impassable, impenetrable, impermeable, impervious, nonporous

**penetrate** *vb* to go or come in or into — see ENTER 1

**penetrating** *adj* causing intense discomfort to one's skin — see CUTTING 1

**peninsula** *n* an area of land that juts out into a body of water — see ²CAPE

**penitence** *n* a feeling of responsibility for wrongdoing — see GUILT 1

**penitent** *adj* 1 feeling sorrow for a wrong that one has done — see CONTRITE 1
2 suffering from or expressive of a feeling of responsibility for wrongdoing — see GUILTY 2

**penitentiary** *n* a place of confinement for persons held in lawful custody — see JAIL

**penman** *n* a person who creates a written work — see AUTHOR 1

**penmanship** *n* 1 the form or style of a particular person's writing — see HANDWRITING 1
2 writing done by hand — see HANDWRITING 2

**pennant** *n* a piece of cloth with a special design that is used as an emblem or for signaling — see FLAG 1

**penniless** *adj* lacking money or material possessions — see POOR 1

**pennon** *n* a piece of cloth with a special design that is used as an emblem or for signaling — see FLAG 1

**pensive** *adj* given to or marked by long, quiet thinking — see CONTEMPLATIVE

**penstock** *n* a long hollow cylinder for carrying a substance (as a liquid or gas) — see PIPE 1

**penthouse** *n* a smaller structure added to a main building — see ANNEX

**penumbra** *n* partial darkness due to the obstruction of light rays — see SHADE 1

**penurious** *adj* 1 giving or sharing as little as possible — see STINGY 1
2 lacking money or material possessions — see POOR 1

**penuriousness** *n* 1 the quality of being overly sparing with money — see PARSIMONY
2 the state of lacking sufficient money or material possessions — see POVERTY 1

**penury** *n* the state of lacking sufficient money or material possessions — see POVERTY 1

**peon** *n* a person who does very hard or dull work — see SLAVE 2

**people** *n pl* 1 human beings in general ⟨despite the horrors she witnessed, Anne Frank never lost her faith in *people*⟩
*syn* folks, humanity, humankind, public, society, world
*rel* crowd, masses, mob, populace, proletariat, rabble, riffraff
2 the body of the community as contrasted with the elite — see MASS 1
3 a group of persons who come from the same ancestor — see FAMILY 1

**pep** *n* active strength of body or mind — see VIGOR 1

**pep** (up) *vb* to give life, vigor, or spirit to — see ANIMATE

**pepper** *vb* 1 to cover by or as if by scattering something over or on — see SCATTER 2
2 to mark with small spots especially unevenly — see SPOT

**peppery** *adj* marked by a lively display of strong feeling — see SPIRITED 1

**peppiness** *n* the quality or state of having abundant or intense activity — see VITALITY 1

**peppy** *adj* 1 having active strength of body or mind — see VIGOROUS 1
2 having much high-spirited energy and movement — see LIVELY 1

**per** *prep* using the means or agency of — see BY 2

**perambulation** *n* a relaxed journey on foot for exercise or pleasure — see WALK

**per capita** *adv* for each one — see APIECE

**perceive** *vb* 1 to have a vague awareness of — see FEEL 1
2 to make note of (something) through the use of one's eyes — see SEE 1
3 to recognize the meaning of — see COMPREHEND 1

**percentage** *n* a measure of how often an event will occur instead of another — see PROBABILITY 2

**perceptible** *adj* able to be perceived by a sense or by the mind ⟨you should note a *perceptible* temperature change when you add the second element⟩
*syn* appreciable, detectable, discernible, distinguishable, palpable, sensible
*rel* audible, observable, tangible, visible; clear, conspicuous, evident, eye-catching, manifest, noticeable, obvious, plain, prominent, striking; apparent, distinct, significant, straightforward
*near ant* inaudible, intangible, invisible; inconspicuous, indistinct, unnoticeable; faint, insignificant, slight, trivial; buried, concealed, covert, disguised, hidden, obscure, shrouded, vague
*ant* impalpable, imperceptible, inappreciable, indistinguishable, insensible

**perception** *n* 1 the ability to understand inner qualities or relationships — see WISDOM 1
2 the knowledge gained from the process of coming to know or understand something — see COMPREHENSION

**perceptive** *adj* **1** able to sense slight impressions or differences — see ACUTE 1
**2** having or showing deep understanding and intelligent application of knowledge — see WISE 1
**perceptiveness** *n* the ability to understand inner qualities or relationships — see WISDOM 1
**perch** *vb* **1** to come to rest after descending from the air — see ALIGHT
**2** to establish or place comfortably or snugly — see ENSCONCE 1
**perchance** *adv* it is possible — see PERHAPS
**percolate** *vb* to flow forth slowly through small openings — see EXUDE
**percolate** (into) *vb* to spread throughout — see PERMEATE
**perdition** *n* the place of punishment for the wicked after death — see HELL 1
**peregrinate** *vb* to take a trip especially of some distance — see TRAVEL 1
**peregrination** *n* a going from one place to another usually of some distance — see JOURNEY
**peremptoriness** *n* an exaggerated sense of one's importance that shows itself in the making of excessive or unjustified claims — see ARROGANCE
**peremptory** *adj* **1** fond of ordering people around — see BOSSY
**2** forcing one's compliance or participation by or as if by law — see MANDATORY
**3** having a feeling of superiority that shows itself in an overbearing attitude — see ARROGANT
**4** having or showing a tendency to force one's will on others without any regard to fairness or necessity — see ARBITRARY 1
**perfect** *adj* **1** being entirely without fault or flaw ⟨a stunningly *perfect* performance—not the slightest mistake—won her the gold medal in women's figure skating⟩
***syn*** absolute, faultless, flawless, ideal, impeccable, irreproachable, letter-perfect, unblemished
***rel*** consummate, expert, masterly; classic, dandy, excellent, fabulous, fine, first-class, first-rate, grand, great, marvelous (*or* marvellous), prime, superb, superior, superlative, terrific, top, top-notch, unsurpassed; completed, finished, perfected, polished; complete, entire, intact, whole; immaculate, unbruised, undamaged, unimpaired, uninjured, unmarred, unspoiled; exceptional, fancy, high-grade, special; accurate, correct, exact, precise; infallible, unerring, unfailing
***near ant*** deficient, inadequate, incomplete, insufficient, wanting; unfinished, unpolished; fallible; blemished, blighted, broken, damaged, defaced, disfigured, impaired, injured, marred, spoiled, vitiated; atrocious, execrable, wretched; imprecise, inaccurate, incorrect, inexact, wrong
***ant*** bad, censurable, defective, faulty, flawed, imperfect, reproachable
**2** having no exceptions or restrictions — see ABSOLUTE 2
**3** not lacking any part or member that properly belongs to it — see COMPLETE 1
**perfect** *vb* **1** to bring (something) to a state where nothing remains to be done — see FINISH 1
**2** to make better — see IMPROVE
**perfection** *n* the most perfect type or example — see QUINTESSENCE 1
**perfectly** *adv* **1** without any flaws or errors ⟨you did that handspring *perfectly* on your first try⟩
***syn*** faultlessly, flawlessly, ideally, impeccably
***rel*** excellently, fabulously, finely, grandly, greatly, marvelously, superbly, superiorly, superlatively, terrifically; exceptionally, fancily, specially
***phrases*** to a nicety, to a T, to a turn
***near ant*** deficiently, inadequately, incompletely, insufficiently; fallibly; atrociously, execrably, wretchedly
***ant*** badly, defectively, faultily, imperfectly
**2** to a full extent or degree — see FULLY 1
**perfidious** *adj* not true in one's allegiance to someone or something — see FAITHLESS
**perfidiousness** *n* lack of faithfulness especially to one's husband or wife — see INFIDELITY 1
**perfidy** *n* **1** lack of faithfulness especially to one's husband or wife — see INFIDELITY 1
**2** the act or fact of violating the trust or confidence of another — see BETRAYAL
**perforate** *vb* to make a hole or series of holes in ⟨he *perforated* the sheet with his pencil and put it in his binder⟩
***syn*** bore, drill, hole, pierce, punch, puncture
***rel*** broach, tap; poke, prick; penetrate; burrow (into), excavate, gouge, groove, hollow; break, cut, gash, notch, rend, rupture, slash, slit, split
***near ant*** fill, patch, plug, seal
**perforation** *n* **1** a mark or small hole made by a pointed instrument — see PRICK 1
**2** a place in a surface allowing passage into or through a thing — see HOLE 1
**perforce** *adv* because of necessity — see NEEDS
**perform** *vb* **1** to carry through (as a process) to completion ⟨she *performed* the task quickly and expertly⟩
***syn*** accomplish, achieve, carry out, commit, compass, do, execute, follow through, fulfill (*or* fulfil), make
***rel*** bring about, effect, effectuate, implement; engage (in), practice (*or* practise); work (at); reduplicate, reenact, repeat; actualize, attain, realize; complete, end, finish, wind up
***phrases*** go through
***near ant*** fail; skimp, slight, slur

***syn*** synonym(s) ***rel*** related words
***ant*** antonym(s) ***near ant*** near antonym(s)

2 to have a certain purpose — see FUNCTION
3 to present a portrayal or performance of — see ACT 1
4 to produce a desired effect — see ACT 2

**performance** *n* the doing of an action — see COMMISSION 2

**perfume** *n* a sweet or pleasant smell — see FRAGRANCE

**perfume** *vb* to fill or infuse with a pleasant odor or odor-releasing substance — see SCENT 1

**perfumed** *adj* having a pleasant smell — see FRAGRANT

**perfunctory** *adj* having or showing a lack of interest or concern — see INDIFFERENT 1

**perhaps** *adv* it is possible ⟨*perhaps* we will not have to take this exam, but I doubt it⟩
***syn*** conceivably, maybe, mayhap, perchance, possibly
***rel*** likely, probably; certainly, doubtless, surely, undoubtedly; presumably

**peril** *n* 1 something that may cause injury or harm — see DANGER 2
2 the state of not being protected from injury, harm, or evil — see DANGER 1

**perilous** *adj* involving potential loss or injury — see DANGEROUS

**perimeter** *n* the line or relatively narrow space that marks the outer limit of something — see BORDER 1

**period** *n* 1 an occurrence of menstruating ⟨girls having their *period* will be excused from gym class⟩
***syn*** menstruation, monthlies
***rel*** menses
2 an extent of time associated with a particular person or thing — see AGE 1

**periodic** *adj* 1 appearing in parts or numbers that follow regularly — see SERIAL
2 appearing or occurring repeatedly from time to time — see REGULAR 1
3 occurring or appearing at intervals — see INTERMITTENT 1

**periodical** *adj* 1 appearing in parts or numbers that follow regularly — see SERIAL
2 occurring or appearing at intervals — see INTERMITTENT 1

**periodical** *n* a publication that appears at regular intervals — see JOURNAL

**peripatetic** *adj* traveling from place to place — see ITINERANT

**peripheral** *adj* available to supply something extra when needed — see AUXILIARY

**periphery** *n* the line or relatively narrow space that marks the outer limit of something — see BORDER 1

**perish** *vb* to stop living — see DIE 1

**perk** (up) *vb* 1 to become glad or hopeful — see CHEER (UP) 1
2 to move from a lower to a higher place or position — see RAISE 1

**perky** *adj* having much high-spirited energy and movement — see LIVELY 1

**permanent** *adj* lasting forever — see EVERLASTING

**permanently** *adv* for all time — see EVER 1

**permeable** *adj* capable of being passed into or through — see PENETRABLE

**permeate** *vb* to spread throughout ⟨the smell of freshly baked bread *permeated* the house⟩
***syn*** interpenetrate, percolate (into), pervade, suffuse, transfuse
***rel*** diffuse (through), impregnate, pass (into), penetrate; fill (up); drench, infuse, saturate, soak, steep; flood, glut

**permissible** *adj* that may be permitted ⟨fortunately, that is a *permissible* shortcut to the answer⟩
***syn*** admissible, allowable, licensable
***rel*** acceptable, bearable, endurable, tolerable; accredited, allowed, authorized, certified, endorsed, licensed (*also* licenced), OK (*or* okay), permitted, sanctioned, warranted; mandatory, ordered, required
***near ant*** intolerable, unacceptable, unbearable, unendurable; objectionable; denied, disallowed, refused, rejected, vetoed; repressed, suppressed; outlawed
***ant*** banned, barred, forbidden, impermissible, inadmissible, interdicted, prohibited, proscribed

**permission** *n* the approval by someone in authority for the doing of something ⟨she asked for *permission* to have a piece of candy⟩ ⟨the President granted *permission* for the foreign diplomats to have special quarters⟩
***syn*** allowance, authorization, clearance, concurrence, consent, granting, leave, license (*or* licence), sanction, sufferance
***rel*** imprimatur, seal, signature, stamp; accreditation, certification; liberty, pass; concession, patent, permit; acceptance, acquiescence, agreement, assent, OK (*or* okay); accord, grant
***near ant*** denial, refusal, rejection, revocation; taboo; injunction, veto; deterrence, discouragement, repression, suppression; ban, embargo, exclusion
***ant*** interdiction, prohibition, proscription

**permit** *vb* 1 to give permission for or to approve of — see ALLOW 1
2 to give permission to — see ALLOW 2
3 to make able or possible — see ENABLE 1

**pernicious** *adj* causing or capable of causing harm — see HARMFUL

**perpendicular** *adj* rising straight up — see ERECT

**perpetration** *n* the doing of an action — see COMMISSION 2

**perpetual** *adj* lasting forever — see EVERLASTING

**perpetually** *adv* 1 for all time — see EVER 1
2 on every relevant occasion — see ALWAYS 1

**perpetuate** *vb* to give eternal or lasting existence to ⟨we hope to *perpetuate* this holiday tradition⟩
***syn*** immortalize

***rel*** commemorate, memorialize; celebrate, enshrine, honor; conserve, keep up, maintain, preserve, support, sustain; defend, guard, protect, safeguard
***near ant*** extinguish, put out, snuff (out); annihilate, crush, decimate, demolish, destroy, devastate; eradicate, erase, expunge, extirpate, obliterate, wipe out

**perpetuity** *n* endless time — see ETERNITY 1

**perplex** *vb* **1** to make complex or difficult — see COMPLICATE
**2** to throw into a state of mental uncertainty — see CONFUSE 1

**perplexity** *n* a state of mental uncertainty — see CONFUSION 1

**perquisite** *n* **1** a small sum of money given for a service over and above what is due — see ²TIP 1
**2** something given in addition to what is ordinarily expected or owed — see BONUS

**persecute** *vb* **1** to cause persistent suffering to — see AFFLICT
**2** to disturb the peace of mind of (someone) especially by repeated disagreeable acts — see IRRITATE 1

**persecutor** *n* **1** a person who causes repeated emotional pain, distress, or annoyance to another — see TORMENTOR
**2** one who is obnoxiously annoying — see NUISANCE 1

**persevere** *vb* to continue despite difficulties, opposition, or discouragement ⟨although he was frustrated by the lack of financial resources and support, he *persevered* in his scientific research⟩
***syn*** carry on, persist
***rel*** hang on; follow through; knuckle down
***phrases*** hang in there
***near ant*** give up, quit, surrender, yield; falter, hesitate, vacillate, waver

**persevering** *adj* continuing despite difficulties, opposition, or discouragement — see PERSISTENT

**persiflage** *n* good-natured teasing or exchanging of clever remarks — see BANTER

**persist** *vb* **1** to continue despite difficulties, opposition, or discouragement — see PERSEVERE
**2** to remain indefinitely in existence or in the same state — see CONTINUE 1

**persistence** *n* **1** continuing existence ⟨the *persistence* of the child's fever made us start to worry⟩
***syn*** continuance, durability, endurance
***rel*** longevity, staying power, tenacity; permanence; survival; continuation
***near ant*** discontinuance; cessation, desisting, ending, finish, quitting, stop
**2** uninterrupted or lasting existence — see CONTINUATION
**3** a steadfast adherence to an opinion, purpose, or course of action — see OBSTINACY

***syn*** synonym(s) ***rel*** related words
***ant*** antonym(s) ***near ant*** near antonym(s)

**persistent** *adj* continuing despite difficulties, opposition, or discouragement ⟨although his first attempts were unsuccessful, he was *persistent* in his pursuit of a career in rock music⟩
***syn*** dogged, insistent, patient, persevering, pertinacious, tenacious
***rel*** assured, certain, dedicated, determined, firm, intent, positive, resolute, resolved, single-minded, sure; hardheaded, headstrong, mulish, obdurate, obstinate, opinionated, peevish, perverse, pigheaded, self-willed, stubborn, unyielding; unfaltering, unhesitating, unwavering; resistant, wayward, wrongheaded; constant, devoted, faithful, good, loyal, staunch (*or* stanch), steadfast, steady, true; indomitable, unconquerable; hard, inflexible, relentless, stern, unbending, unrelenting, unyielding
***near ant*** quitting, surrendering, yielding; faltering, hesitant, hesitating, irresolute, vacillating, wavering; disloyal, faithless, false, fickle, inconstant, perfidious, traitorous, treacherous

**person** *n* a member of the human race — see HUMAN

**personage** *n* a person who is widely known and usually much talked about — see CELEBRITY 1

**personal** *adj* of, relating to, or belonging to a single person — see INDIVIDUAL 1

**personality** *n* **1** a person who is widely known and usually much talked about — see CELEBRITY 1
**2** the set of qualities that make a person different from other people — see INDIVIDUALITY
**3** the set of qualities that makes a person, a group of people, or a thing different from others — see NATURE 1

**personalize** *vb* to represent in visible form — see EMBODY 2

**personalized** *adj* of, relating to, or belonging to a single person — see INDIVIDUAL 1

**personally** *adv* in person and usually privately — see TÊTE-À-TÊTE

**personalty** *n* transportable items that one owns — see POSSESSION 2

**personification** *n* a visible representation of something abstract (as a quality) — see EMBODIMENT

**personify** *vb* to represent in visible form — see EMBODY 2

**personnel** *n* a body of persons at work or available for work — see FORCE 1

**perspective** *n* a way of looking at or thinking about something — see POINT OF VIEW

**perspicuity** *n* clearness of expression — see SIMPLICITY 2

**perspicuous** *adj* not subject to misinterpretation or more than one interpretation — see CLEAR 2

**perspicuousness** *n* clearness of expression — see SIMPLICITY 2

**persuade** *vb* to cause (someone) to agree with a belief or course of action by using arguments or earnest request ⟨she *per-*

*suaded* us that she can indeed communicate with the dead⟩ ⟨he *persuaded* his teachers to grant an extension⟩
***syn*** argue, convince, get, induce, move, prevail (on *or* upon), satisfy, talk (into), win (over)
***rel*** cajole, coax, exhort, urge; lead on, seduce, snow, tempt; incline, influence, move, prompt, sell, sway; attract, bring, draw, entice, interest; chew over, converse, debate, discuss, dispute, hash (over), moot; reason (with)
***near ant*** dissuade

**persuading** *n* the act of reasoning or pleading with someone to accept a belief or course of action — see PERSUASION 1

**persuasion** *n* **1** the act of reasoning or pleading with someone to accept a belief or course of action ⟨the suffragists' gradual *persuasion* of the American people that voting rights had to be extended to women⟩
***syn*** convincing, inducement, inducing, persuading, suasion
***rel*** cajolery, coaxing, exhortation, urging; seduction, tempting; influencing, prompting, swaying; lobbying, pressuring
**2** a body of beliefs and practices regarding the supernatural and the worship of one or more deities — see RELIGION 1
**3** an idea that is believed to be true or valid without positive knowledge — see OPINION 1

**persuasive** *adj* having the power to persuade — see COGENT

**persuasiveness** *n* the capacity to persuade — see COGENCY 1

**pert** *adj* **1** having much high-spirited energy and movement — see LIVELY 1
**2** making light of something usually regarded as serious or sacred — see FLIPPANT

**pertain** *vb* **1** to be the property of a person or group of persons — see BELONG 2
**2** to have a relation or connection — see APPLY 1

**pertain** (to) *vb* to have (something) as a subject matter — see CONCERN 1

**pertinacious** *adj* **1** continuing despite difficulties, opposition, or discouragement — see PERSISTENT
**2** sticking to an opinion, purpose, or course of action in spite of reason, arguments, or persuasion — see OBSTINATE

**pertinaciousness** *n* a steadfast adherence to an opinion, purpose, or course of action — see OBSTINACY

**pertinacity** *n* a steadfast adherence to an opinion, purpose, or course of action — see OBSTINACY

**pertinence** *n* the fact or state of being pertinent ⟨job applicants should question the *pertinence* of any questions about their personal lives⟩
***syn*** applicability, bearing, connection, materiality, relevance, relevancy
***rel*** appropriateness, aptness, fitness, suitability; importance, significance; usefulness
***near ant*** inappropriateness, inaptness, unfitness, unsuitability; insignificance, unimportance; pointlessness, uselessness
***ant*** extraneousness, inapplicability, irrelevance

**pertinent** *adj* having to do with the matter at hand ⟨he impressed the jury with his concise, *pertinent* answers to the attorney's questions⟩
***syn*** applicable, apposite, apropos, germane, material, pointed, relative, relevant
***rel*** appropriate, apt, fit, fitting, suitable; important, meaningful, significant; sensible, useful; admissible, allowable
***phrases*** in point, to the point
***near ant*** inconsequential, insignificant, unimportant; meaningless, purposeless, senseless, useless; inappropriate, inapt, unsuitable; inadmissible
***ant*** extraneous, immaterial, inapplicable, irrelevant, pointless

**pertly** *adv* in a quick and spirited manner — see GAILY 2

**pertness** *n* shameless boldness — see EFFRONTERY

**perturb** *vb* to trouble the mind of; to make uneasy — see DISTURB 1

**perturbation** *n* an uneasy state of mind usually over the possibility of an anticipated misfortune or trouble — see ANXIETY 1

**perturbed** *adj* feeling or showing uncomfortable feelings of uncertainty — see NERVOUS 1

**perturbing** *adj* causing worry or anxiety — see TROUBLESOME

**peruse** *vb* to go over and mentally take in the content of — see READ

**pervade** *vb* to spread throughout — see PERMEATE

**perverse** *adj* **1** easily irritated or annoyed — see IRRITABLE
**2** having or showing lowered moral character or standards — see CORRUPT
**3** sticking to an opinion, purpose, or course of action in spite of reason, arguments, or persuasion — see OBSTINATE

**perverseness** *n* readiness to show annoyance or impatience — see PETULANCE

**perversion** *n* **1** a sinking to a state of low moral standards and behavior — see CORRUPTION 2
**2** incorrect or improper use — see MISUSE

**perversity** *n* readiness to show annoyance or impatience — see PETULANCE

**pervert** *n* a person who has sunk below the normal moral standard — see DEGENERATE

**pervert** *vb* **1** to change so much as to create a wrong impression or alter the meaning of — see GARBLE
**2** to lower in character or dignity — see DEBASE 1
**3** to put to a bad or improper use — see MISAPPLY

**perverted** *adj* having or showing lowered moral character or standards — see CORRUPT

**pessimist** *n* **1** one who emphasizes bad aspects or conditions and expects the worst ⟨she's such a *pessimist* that she's convinced she'll fail every test⟩
***syn*** defeatist
***rel*** cynic, fatalist; pragmatist, realist
***near ant*** dreamer, idealist, romantic, utopian, visionary; sentimentalist
***ant*** optimist
**2** a person who distrusts other people and believes that everything is done for selfish reasons — see CYNIC

**pessimistic** *adj* **1** emphasizing or expecting the worst ⟨with that *pessimistic* attitude, it's no wonder you're depressed⟩
***syn*** defeatist, despairing, hopeless
***rel*** cynical, fatalistic; desperate, discouraging, disheartening, inauspicious, unlikely, unpromising; bleak, cheerless, comfortless, dismal, dreary, gloomy; grim; contrary, hostile, negative
***near ant*** auspicious, encouraging, fair, heartening, likely, promising, propitious; cheering, comforting, reassuring; favorable, good, positive; idealist, romantic, utopian, visionary
***ant*** hopeful, optimistic, rose-colored, rosy, upbeat
**2** having or showing a deep distrust of human beings and their motives — see CYNICAL

**pest** *n* **1** a widespread disease resulting in a high rate of death — see PLAGUE
**2** one who is obnoxiously annoying — see NUISANCE 1
**3** something that is a source of irritation — see ANNOYANCE 3

**pester** *vb* to thrust oneself upon (another) without invitation — see BOTHER 1

**pestering** *n* the act of making unwelcome intrusions upon another — see ANNOYANCE 1

**pestilence** *n* a widespread disease resulting in a high rate of death — see PLAGUE

**pestilent** *adj* likely to cause or capable of causing death — see DEADLY

**pesty** *adj* causing annoyance — see ANNOYING

**pet** *adj* granted special treatment or attention — see DARLING 1

**pet** *n* **1** a person or thing that is preferred over others — see FAVORITE
**2** a state of resentful silence or irritability — see SULK

**pet** *vb* **1** to touch or handle in a tender or loving manner — see FONDLE
**2** to touch one another with the lips as a sign of love — see KISS 1

**petition** *n* an earnest request — see PLEA 1

**petition** *vb* to make a request to (someone) in an earnest or urgent manner — see BEG

**petitioner** *n* one who asks earnestly for a favor or gift — see SUPPLICANT

**pettish** *adj* easily irritated or annoyed — see IRRITABLE

**pettishness** *n* readiness to show annoyance or impatience — see PETULANCE

**petty** *adj* **1** not broad or open in views or opinions — see NARROW 2
**2** so small or unimportant as to warrant little or no attention — see NEGLIGIBLE 1

**petulance** *n* readiness to show annoyance or impatience ⟨I do not appreciate your *petulance* and eagerness to argue⟩
***syn*** biliousness, crankiness, crossness, crotchetiness, grouchiness, grumpiness, huffiness, irascibility, irritability, irritableness, peevishness, perverseness, perversity, pettishness, testiness, waspishness
***rel*** cantankerousness, disagreeableness, dyspepsia, fretfulness, orneriness, sulkiness, surliness; aggression, aggressiveness, bellicosity, belligerence, combativeness, contentiousness, contrariness, disputatiousness, fight, pugnacity, scrappiness, truculence; fussiness, querulousness, rudeness; oversensitiveness, sensitivity; antagonism, fierceness, hostility, unfriendliness; anger, exasperation, rage, wrath; hot-bloodedness, passion
***near ant*** forbearance, patience, tolerance, understanding; affability, amicability, cordiality, friendliness, sociability; amiability, good-humoredness, good-naturedness, good-temperedness; coolness, serenity, tranquility; easygoingness, gentleness, kindliness, mildness

**petulant** *adj* easily irritated or annoyed — see IRRITABLE

**pewter** *adj* of the color gray — see GRAY 1

**phantasm** *n* **1** a conception or image created by the imagination and having no objective reality — see FANTASY 1
**2** the soul of a dead person thought of especially as appearing to living people — see GHOST

**phantasmal** *adj* not real and existing only in the imagination — see IMAGINARY

**phantom** *adj* not real and existing only in the imagination — see IMAGINARY

**phantom** *n* the soul of a dead person thought of especially as appearing to living people — see GHOST

**pharmaceutical** *n* a substance or preparation used to treat disease — see MEDICINE

**pharmacist** *n* a person who prepares drugs according to a doctor's prescription — see DRUGGIST

**pharmacy** *n* a retail store where medicines and miscellaneous articles are sold — see DRUGSTORE

**phase** *n* **1** a certain way in which something appears or may be regarded — see ASPECT 1
**2** an individual part of a process, series, or ranking — see DEGREE 1

**phased** *adj* proceeding or changing by steps or degrees — see GRADUAL

**phenomenal** *adj* **1** being out of the ordinary — see EXCEPTIONAL
**2** being so extraordinary or abnormal as to suggest powers which violate the laws of nature — see SUPERNATURAL 2

---

***syn*** synonym(s) ***rel*** related words
***ant*** antonym(s) ***near ant*** near antonym(s)

**phenomenon** *n* something extraordinary or surprising — see WONDER 1

**philanthropic** *adj* having or showing a concern for the welfare of others — see CHARITABLE 1

**philanthropy** *n* **1** a gift of money or its equivalent to a charity, humanitarian cause, or public institution — see CONTRIBUTION
**2** the giving of necessities and especially money to the needy — see CHARITY 1
**3** the quality or state of being generous — see LIBERALITY

**philharmonic** *n* a usually large group of musicians playing together — see ²BAND 1

**philistine** *n* a person who is chiefly interested in material comfort and is hostile or indifferent to art and culture ⟨the town's *philistines* who think that spending on the arts is a waste of taxpayers' money⟩
***syn*** lowbrow, materialist
***rel*** capitalist, plutocrat; boor, cad, churl, clown, creep, cur, jerk, lout
***near ant*** highbrow; egghead, intellectual, sage, thinker; brain, genius

**philosophy** *n* the basic beliefs or guiding principles of a person or group — see CREED 1

**phlegm** *n* a lack of emotion or emotional expressiveness — see APATHY 1

**phlegmatic** *adj* not feeling or showing emotion — see IMPASSIVE 1

**phone** *vb* to make a telephone call to — see CALL 2

**phony** *also* **phoney** *adj* **1** being such in appearance only and made or manufactured with the intention of committing fraud — see COUNTERFEIT
**2** lacking in natural or spontaneous quality — see ARTIFICIAL 1

**phony** *also* **phoney** *n* **1** an imitation that is passed off as genuine — see FAKE 1
**2** one who makes false claims of identity or expertise — see IMPOSTOR

**photo** *n* a picture created from an image recorded on a light-sensitive surface by a camera — see PHOTOGRAPH

**photo** *vb* to take a photograph of — see PHOTOGRAPH

**photograph** *n* a picture created from an image recorded on a light-sensitive surface by a camera ⟨the old *photograph* was faded but still clear enough to make out⟩
***syn*** photo, print, shot, snap, snapshot
***rel*** blowup, close-up, enlargement, still; daguerreotype, monochrome, tintype

**photograph** *vb* to take a photograph of ⟨we *photographed* the baby birds frequently⟩
***syn*** mug, photo, shoot, snap
***rel*** image, picture, retake; film, videotape
***phrases*** capture on film

**photographer** *n* one who takes photographs ⟨we'll need to choose a *photographer* for the wedding⟩
***syn*** shooter, shutterbug
***rel*** cinematographer

**phrase** *n* a sequence of words having a specific meaning ⟨draw a literal representation of the *phrase* "to rain cats and dogs"⟩
***syn*** expression, idiom
***rel*** cliché; location, term; epithet, expletive, name; byword, cry, motto, shibboleth, slogan, watchword; archaism, colloquialism, euphemism, modernism, neologism, provincialism, vulgarism
***phrases*** figure of speech

**phrase** *vb* to convey in appropriate or telling terms ⟨he had trouble thinking of how to *phrase* his question for the visiting dignitary⟩
***syn*** articulate, clothe, couch, express, formulate, put, say, state, word
***rel*** craft, frame; hint, imply, insinuate, intimate, suggest; paraphrase, rephrase, restate, reword, summarize, translate; communicate, disclose, speak, tell; describe, render, write up

**phraseology** *n* **1** a distinctive way of putting ideas into words — see STYLE 1
**2** the way in which something is put into words — see WORDING

**phrasing** *n* the way in which something is put into words — see WORDING

**phylactery** *n* something worn or kept to bring good luck or keep away evil — see CHARM 1

**physic** *n* a substance or preparation used to treat disease — see MEDICINE

**physical** *adj* **1** of or relating to the human body ⟨*physical* sensations such as heat and pain⟩
***syn*** animal, bodily, carnal, corporal, corporeal, fleshly, material, somatic
***rel*** anatomic (*or* anatomical), physiological; sensual, sensuous; hand-to-hand
***near ant*** intellectual, mental, psychological (*also* psychologic); bodiless, immaterial, incorporeal, spiritual; ethereal, metaphysical, psychic (*also* psychical)
***ant*** nonmaterial, nonphysical
**2** relating to or composed of matter — see MATERIAL 1

**physician** *n* a person specially trained in healing human medical disorders — see DOCTOR

**physique** *n* the type of body that a person has ⟨she had a well-toned *physique*⟩
***syn*** build, constitution, figure, form, frame, shape
***rel*** anatomy, structure

**picayune** *adj* so small or unimportant as to warrant little or no attention — see NEGLIGIBLE 1

**pick** *n* **1** a person or thing that is chosen — see CHOICE 2
**2** individuals carefully selected as being the best of a class — see ELITE
**3** the power, right, or opportunity to choose — see CHOICE 1

**pick** *vb* **1** to catch or collect (a crop or natural resource) for human use — see HARVEST
**2** to decide to accept (someone or something) from a group of possibilities — see CHOOSE 1

**picked** *adj* singled out from a number or group as more to one's liking — see SELECT 1

**picked up** *adj* being clean and in good order — see NEAT 1

**picker** *n* someone with the right or responsibility for making a selection — see SELECTOR

**picket** *n* a person or group that watches over someone or something — see GUARD 1

**picking** *n* the act or process of selecting — see SELECTION 1

**pickle** *n* a difficult, puzzling, or embarrassing situation from which there is no easy escape — see PREDICAMENT

**pick up** *vb* **1** to acquire complete knowledge, understanding, or skill in — see LEARN 1
**2** to bring together in one body or place — see GATHER 1
**3** to get possession of (something) by giving money in exchange for — see BUY
**4** to increase in — see GAIN 1
**5** to move from a lower to a higher place or position — see RAISE 1
**6** to take or keep under one's control by authority of law — see ARREST 1

**picky** *adj* **1** hard to please — see FINICKY
**2** tending to select carefully — see SELECTIVE

**picnic** *n* something that is easy to do — see CINCH

**pictorial** *adj* **1** consisting of or relating to pictures ⟨he's planning to do a primarily *pictorial* report on Africa⟩
***syn*** graphic (*also* graphical), visual
***rel*** photographic, video; drawn, painted, represented; illustrative; pictographic
**2** producing a mental picture through clear and impressive description — see GRAPHIC 1

**picture** *n* **1** a two-dimensional design intended to look like a person or thing ⟨she produced a beautiful *picture* of her mother using watercolors⟩
***syn*** illustration, image, likeness
***rel*** delineation, depiction, representation; portrait; drawing, finger painting; etching, silhouette, sketch, watercolor; caricature, cartoon, doodle; collage, montage, photograph; hieroglyphic, ideogram; pictograph
**2** a story told by means of a series of continuously projected pictures and a sound track — see MOVIE 1
**3** a vivid representation in words of someone or something — see DESCRIPTION 1
**4** position with regard to conditions and circumstances — see SITUATION 1
**5** something or someone that strongly resembles another — see IMAGE 1
**6** something imagined or pictured in the mind — see IDEA
**7 pictures** *pl* the art or business of making a movie — see MOVIE 2

**picture** *vb* **1** to present a picture of ⟨the famous painting that *pictures* the Founding Fathers signing the Declaration of Independence⟩
***syn*** depict, image, portray, represent
***rel*** delineate, describe, render; outline, sketch; illustrate, show; caricature
**2** to form a mental picture of — see IMAGINE 1
**3** to give a representation or account of in words — see DESCRIBE 1

**picturesque** *adj* producing a mental picture through clear and impressive description — see GRAPHIC 1

**piddling** *adj* so small or unimportant as to warrant little or no attention — see NEGLIGIBLE 1

**piebald** *adj* having blotches of two or more colors — see PIED

**piece** *n* **1** a broken or irregular part of something that often remains incomplete — see FRAGMENT
**2** a literary, musical, or artistic production — see COMPOSITION 1
**3** a portable weapon from which a shot is discharged by gunpowder — see GUN 1

**piece** *vb* to form by putting together parts or materials — see BUILD

**piece by piece** *adv* by small steps or amounts — see GRADUALLY

**piecemeal** *adj* proceeding or changing by steps or degrees — see GRADUAL

**piecemeal** *adv* **1** by small steps or amounts — see GRADUALLY
**2** into parts or to pieces — see APART

**pied** *adj* having blotches of two or more colors ⟨although the mother's was pure black, the foal's coat was *pied*⟩
***syn*** blotched, dappled (*also* dapple), marbled, mottled, piebald, pinto, splotched, spotted
***rel*** shaded; checkered, motley, multicolored, polychromatic, polychrome, varicolored, variegated; blotted, brindled (*or* brindle), specked, speckled, streaked; colored, colorful, pigmented; dotted, peppered, sprinkled; stippled; discolored, dyed, marked, stained; flecked, streaked; bespattered, spattered
***near ant*** monochromatic, solid

**pier** *n* **1** a structure used by boats and ships for taking on or landing cargo and passengers — see DOCK
**2** an upright shaft that supports an overhead structure — see PILLAR 1

**pierce** *vb* **1** to go or come in or into — see ENTER 1
**2** to make a hole or series of holes in — see PERFORATE
**3** to penetrate or hold (something) with a pointed object — see IMPALE

**piercing** *adj* **1** causing intense discomfort to one's skin — see CUTTING 1
**2** marked by a high volume of sound — see LOUD 1

**piety** *n* **1** belief and trust in and loyalty to God — see FAITH 1
**2** the quality or state of being spiritually pure or virtuous — see HOLINESS

---

***syn*** synonym(s) ***rel*** related words
***ant*** antonym(s) ***near ant*** near antonym(s)

**piffle** *n* **1** language, behavior, or ideas that are absurd and contrary to good sense — see NONSENSE 1
**2** unintelligible or meaningless talk — see GIBBERISH

**pigeon** *n* one who is easily deceived or cheated — see DUPE

**piggish** *adj* having a huge appetite — see VORACIOUS 1

**pigheaded** *adj* sticking to an opinion, purpose, or course of action in spite of reason, arguments, or persuasion — see OBSTINATE

**pigment** *n* a substance used to color other materials ⟨I'm running out of the black *pigment*⟩
***syn*** color, coloring, dye, dyestuff stain, tincture
***rel*** cast, hue, shade, tinge, tint, tone

**pig out** *vb* to eat greedily or to excess — see GORGE 2

**pigpen** *n* a dirty or messy place ⟨your room is a *pigpen* —so clean it up!⟩
***syn*** hole, pigsty, shambles
***rel*** chaos, confusion, disarrangement, disarray, disorder, jumble, mess, muddle; dump; clutter, litter, mishmash

**pigsty** *n* a dirty or messy place — see PIGPEN

**[1]pike** *n* a passage cleared for public vehicular travel — see WAY 1

**[2]pike** *n* a weapon with a long straight handle and sharp head or blade — see SPEAR

**[3]pike** *n* the last and usually sharp or tapering part of something long and narrow — see POINT 2

**piker** *n* a mean grasping person who is usually stingy with money — see MISER

**pikestaff** *n* a weapon with a long straight handle and sharp head or blade — see SPEAR

**pilaster** *n* an upright shaft that supports an overhead structure — see PILLAR 1

**[1]pile** *n* **1** a quantity of things thrown or stacked on one another ⟨a large *pile* of newspapers that needed to be disposed of⟩
***syn*** cock, heap, hill, mound, mountain, rick, stack
***rel*** bank, bar, drift, embankment; pyramid; barrow, cairn, pyre; accumulation, aggregate, assemblage, collection, conglomeration, gathering, grouping, hoard, jumble
**2** a considerable amount — see LOT 2

**[2]pile** *n* **1** a soft airy substance or covering — see FUZZ
**2** the hairy covering of a mammal especially when fine, soft, and thick — see FUR 1

**pile** *vb* to lay or throw on top of one another ⟨*piled* all the clothes on the chair before putting them away⟩
***syn*** heap, mound, stack
***rel*** bank; layer, pyramid; accumulate, amass, assemble, collect, gather, group, mass; bunch, clump, lump
***ant*** unpile

**pile** (up) *vb* to gradually form into a layer, pile, or mass — see COLLECT 2

**pilfer** *vb* to take (something) without right and with an intent to keep — see STEAL 1

**pilgrimage** *vb* to take a trip especially of some distance — see TRAVEL 1

**pill** *n* a small mass containing medicine to be taken orally ⟨you'll have to take one of these *pills* every six hours for your flu⟩
***syn*** capsule, lozenge, tablet
***rel*** drug, medication, pharmaceutical, specific; miracle drug, wonder drug; potion, preparation; dosage, dose, drop, sleeping pill, tranquilizer (*also* tranquillizer)

**pillage** *vb* to search through with the intent of committing robbery — see RANSACK 1

**pillar** *n* **1** an upright shaft that supports an overhead structure ⟨the ancient Greek temple boasted graceful marble *pillars* with richly ornamented tops⟩
***syn*** column, pier, pilaster, post, stanchion
***rel*** caryatid, pedestal; buttress, flying buttress; needle, obelisk
**2** something or someone to which one looks for support — see DEPENDENCE 2

**pilot** *adj* made or done as an experiment — see EXPERIMENTAL 1

**pilot** *n* one who flies or is qualified to fly an aircraft or spacecraft ⟨the airline is seeking experienced *pilots* to fly the new airplane⟩
***syn*** airman, aviator, birdman, flier (*or* flyer)
***rel*** ace, bush pilot, copilot, test pilot

**pilot** *vb* **1** to give advice and instruction to (someone) regarding the course or process to be followed — see GUIDE 1
**2** to point out the way for (someone) especially from a position in front — see LEAD 1

**pin** *n* a lower limb of an animal — see LEG 1

**pinch** *n* an instance of theft — see THEFT 2
**2** the act of taking or holding under one's control by authority of law — see ARREST

**pinch** *vb* **1** to squeeze tightly between two surfaces, edges, or points ⟨the zipper on those jeans always *pinches* me⟩
***syn*** nip
***rel*** clasp, clutch, grasp, grip
***near ant*** drop, free, loose, loosen, release
**2** to take (something) without right and with an intent to keep — see STEAL 1
**3** to take or keep under one's control by authority of law — see ARREST 1

**pincher** *n* one who steals — see THIEF

**pinch-hit** *vb* to serve as a replacement usually for a time only — see COVER 1

**pinch hitter** *n* a person or thing that takes the place of another — see SUBSTITUTE

**pinching** *adj* giving or sharing as little as possible — see STINGY 1

**pinching** *n* the quality of being overly sparing with money — see PARSIMONY

**pine** (for) *vb* to have an earnest wish to own or enjoy — see DESIRE

**pinhead** *n* a stupid person — see IDIOT

**pinhole** *n* a mark or small hole made by a pointed instrument — see PRICK 1

**pining** *n* a strong wish for something — see DESIRE

**pinnacle** *n* the highest part or point — see HEIGHT 1

**pinpoint** *adj* meeting the highest standard of accuracy — see PRECISE 1

**pinpoint** *vb* to find out or establish the identity of — see IDENTIFY 1

**pinprick** *n* a mark or small hole made by a pointed instrument — see PRICK 1

**pinto** *adj* having blotches of two or more colors — see PIED

**pint-size** *or* **pint-sized** *adj* of a size that is less than average — see SMALL 1

**pioneer** *adj* coming before all others in time or order — see FIRST 1

**pioneer** *n* a person who settles in a new region — see FRONTIERSMAN

**pioneer** *vb* to be responsible for the creation and early operation or use of — see FOUND

**pious** *adj* **1** firm in one's allegiance to someone or something — see FAITHFUL 1
**2** showing a devotion to God and to a life of virtue — see HOLY 1

**piousness** *n* **1** the pretending of having virtues, principles, or beliefs that one in fact does not have — see HYPOCRISY
**2** the quality or state of being spiritually pure or virtuous — see HOLINESS

**pip** *n* something very good of its kind — see JIM-DANDY

**pipe** *n* **1** a long hollow cylinder for carrying a substance (as a liquid or gas) ⟨the plumber came and fixed the water *pipe* that was leaking⟩
***syn*** channel, conduit, duct, leader, line, penstock, trough, tube
***rel*** drain, drainpipe, funnel, hydrant, main, smokestack, spout, stovepipe, tile, waterspout; pipeline, piping
**2** an enclosed wooden vessel for holding beverages — see CASK

**pipe** *vb* **1** to cause to move to a central point or along a restricted pathway — see CHANNEL
**2** to make a short sharp sound like a small bird — see CHIRP

**pipe dream** *n* a conception or image created by the imagination and having no objective reality — see FANTASY 1

**pipeline** *n* a direct way of passing along information or supplies ⟨an equipment hauler serves as the columnist's *pipeline* for gossip about the rock band⟩ ⟨the battle was ultimately lost because the enemy had destroyed our *pipeline* for resupply⟩
***syn*** channel
***rel*** conduit; grapevine, outlet; fountainhead, origin, source, wellspring; supplier; connection, contact

**piping** *adj* having a high musical pitch or range — see SHRILL

**piping hot** *adj* having a notably high temperature — see HOT 1

**piquancy** *n* the quality or state of being stimulating to the mind or senses ⟨a talk show host known for the quickness and *piquancy* of his wit⟩ ⟨I appreciated the *piquancy* of the peppers in the sauce⟩
***syn*** pungency, zest
***rel*** raciness, spiciness; fieriness, hotness; acuteness, keenness, sharpness; provocativeness; excitement, invigoration, stimulation, thrill; flavor, savor, tastiness
***near ant*** flatness, tastelessness; dullness (*also* dulness), monotonousness, predictability, tediousness; blandness, thinness, weakness
***ant*** insipidity

**piquant** *adj* sharp and pleasantly stimulating to the mind or senses ⟨a *piquant* tidbit of information about the new neighbors⟩ ⟨the *piquant* cuisine of India boasts some highly spiced dishes⟩
***syn*** pungent, zesty
***rel*** racy, spicy; fiery, hot; acute, keen; biting, bitter, cutting, mordant, trenchant; animating, energizing, enlightening, exciting, galvanizing, invigorating, provocative; appetizing, delectable, delicious, palatable, toothsome; flavorful, savory, tasty; absorbing, engaging, engrossing, enthralling, fascinating, gripping, interesting, intriguing
***near ant*** flat, flavorless, savorless, tasteless; banal, boring, dull, monotonous, pedestrian, predictable, tedious, tiring, uninteresting, wearisome, wearying; bland, dilute, thin, watery, weak
***ant*** insipid

**pique** *n* the feeling of being offended or resentful after a slight or indignity ⟨she's still in a *pique* over being snubbed by a so-called friend at the party⟩
***syn*** dudgeon, huff, offense (*or* offence), peeve, resentment, umbrage
***rel*** aggravation, anger, annoyance, bother, discomfort, exasperation, frustration, irritation, vexation; agitation, angriness, displeasure, distress, disturbance, indignation, irateness, ire, outrage, perturbation, upset; dander, temper; fit, pet, sulk(s), tantrum, tizzy; affront, insult
***near ant*** satisfaction; appeasement, mollification, pacification; delight, pleasure

**pique** *vb* **1** to disturb the peace of mind of (someone) especially by repeated disagreeable acts — see IRRITATE 1
**2** to rouse to strong feeling or action — see PROVOKE 1

**piquing** *adj* serving or likely to arouse a strong reaction — see PROVOCATIVE

**piracy** *n* the act or pursuit of robbing ships at sea ⟨many countries have harsh penalties for *piracy* now⟩
***syn*** pirating
***rel*** depredation, despoilment, despoliation, looting, marauding, pillaging, plunder, plundering, raiding, robbery; privateering; burglary, housebreaking, stealing, thieving; hijacking (*also* highjacking), rustling

**pirate** *n* someone who engages in robbery of ships at sea ⟨Sir Francis Drake was a British *pirate* who preyed on Spanish

---

***syn*** synonym(s) ***rel*** related words
***ant*** antonym(s) ***near ant*** near antonym(s)

ships with the permission of the British queen〉
*syn* buccaneer, corsair, freebooter, rover
*rel* looter, marauder, pillager, plunderer, raider, robber; privateer; burglar, housebreaker, stealer, thief; hijacker, rustler
**pirating** *n* the act or pursuit of robbing ships at sea — see PIRACY
**pirouette** *n* a rapid turning about on an axis or central point — see SPIN 1
**pirouette** *vb* to move in circles around an axis or center — see SPIN 1
**pit** *n* a sunken area forming a separate space — see HOLE 2
**pit–a–pat** *vb* to expand and contract in a rhythmic manner — see PULSATE
**pitch** *n* **1** an act or instance of diving — see DIVE 1
**2** the degree to which something rises up from a position level with the horizon — see SLANT
**pitch** *vb* **1** to fix in an upright position — see ERECT 1
**2** to cast oneself head first into deep water — see DIVE
**3** to make a series of unsteady side-to-side motions — see ROCK 1
**4** to send through the air especially with a quick forward motion of the arm — see THROW
**pitch–black** *adj* **1** being without light or without much light — see DARK 1
**2** having the color of soot or coal — see BLACK 1
**pitch–dark** *adj* **1** being without light or without much light — see DARK 1
**2** having the color of soot or coal — see BLACK 1
**pitched** *adj* running in a slanting direction — see DIAGONAL
**pitcher** *n* a handled container for holding and pouring liquids that usually has a lip or a spout 〈please bring me the *pitcher* full of lemonade from the table〉
*syn* flagon, jug
*rel* carafe, decanter; bucket, pail, pot; canteen, cup, flask, mug, stein; barrel, cask, hogshead, pipe, puncheon
**pitch in** *vb* to make a donation as part of a group effort — see CONTRIBUTE 1
**pitchy** *adj* having the color of soot or coal — see BLACK 1
**piteous** *adj* deserving of one's pity — see PATHETIC 1
**pitfall** *n* **1** a danger or difficulty that is hidden or not easily recognized 〈buying a house can be full of *pitfalls* for the unwary〉
*syn* booby trap, catch, snag
*rel* snare, trap, web; hazard, peril, risk; bombshell, surprise; bait, lure
**2** something that may cause injury or harm — see DANGER 2
**pith** *n* the central part or aspect of something under consideration — see CRUX
**pithily** *adv* in a few words — see SHORTLY 1
**pithiness** *n* the quality or state of being marked by or using only few words to convey much meaning — see SUCCINCTNESS
**pithy** *adj* marked by the use of few words to convey much information or meaning — see CONCISE
**pitiable** *adj* **1** arousing or deserving of one's loathing and disgust — see CONTEMPTIBLE 1
**2** deserving pitying scorn (as for inadequacy) — see PITIFUL 1
**3** deserving of one's pity — see PATHETIC 1
**pitiful** *adj* **1** deserving pitying scorn (as for inadequacy) 〈that is a *pitiful* attempt at an essay on patriotism; you'll have to do it over〉
*syn* contemptible, despicable, pitiable, sorry
*rel* deplorable, discreditable, disgraceful, disreputable, infamous, notorious; abhorrent, abominable, detestable, hateful, odious; bad, inferior, poor; disgusting, dishonorable, shameful; unworthy, worthless; scandalous, shocking, sordid, unsavory
*near ant* admirable, creditable, laudable, meritorious, praiseworthy; notable, noteworthy, noticeable, outstanding, reputable, worthy; excellent; flawless, perfect; honorable, noble; honest, straight
*ant* decent, presentable, respectable
**2** arousing or deserving of one's loathing and disgust — see CONTEMPTIBLE 1
**3** deserving of one's pity — see PATHETIC 1
**pitiless** *adj* having or showing a lack of sympathy or tender feelings — see HARD 1
**pittance** *n* a very small sum of money — see MITE 1
**pitter–patter** *vb* to expand and contract in a rhythmic manner — see PULSATE
**pity** *n* **1** a regrettable or blameworthy act — see CRIME 2
**2** the capacity for feeling for another's unhappiness or misfortune — see HEART 1
**pity** *vb* to have sympathy for 〈I always *pity* the people who have to work in this freezing weather〉
*syn* bleed (for), commiserate (with), condole (with), feel (for), sympathize (with)
*rel* care (for); grieve (for), sorrow (for); love; tolerate, understand
*near ant* disregard, ignore, neglect, overlook; dislike, hate, scorn
**pivot** *n* the central part or aspect of something under consideration — see CRUX
**pivot** *vb* to move (something) in a curved or circular path on or as if on an axis — see TURN 1
**pivotal** *adj* of the greatest possible importance — see CRUCIAL
**pixie** *also* **pixy** *n* an imaginary being usually having a small human form and magical powers — see FAIRY
**pixieish** *adj* tending to or exhibiting reckless playfulness — see MISCHIEVOUS 1
**placard** *n* a sheet bearing an announcement for posting in a public place — see POSTER

**placard** *vb* **1** to affix (as a notice) to or on a suitable place — see [1]POST 1
**2** to make known openly or publicly — see ANNOUNCE
**placate** *vb* to lessen the anger or agitation of — see PACIFY
**placating** *adj* tending to lessen or avoid conflict or hostility — see PACIFIC 1
**place** *n* **1** the area or space occupied by or intended for something ⟨the *place* chosen for the picnic⟩ ⟨there's the *place* where I left my umbrella⟩
***syn*** locale, locality, location, locus, point, position, site, spot
***rel*** scene; region, section, sector
**2** a building, room, or suite of rooms occupied by a service business ⟨we're going to our favorite *place* to eat⟩
***syn*** establishment, joint, parlor, salon
***rel*** spot, station; facility, installation; studio; den, dive, hole
**3** an assignment at which one regularly works for pay — see JOB 1
**4** an extent or area available for or used up by some activity or thing — see ROOM 1
**5** the action for which a person or thing is specially fitted or used or for which a thing exists — see ROLE
**6** the place where one lives — see HOME 1
**7** the placement of someone or something in relation to others in a vertical arrangement — see RANK 1
**place** *vb* **1** to arrange something in a certain spot or position ⟨he carefully *placed* the flowers in a vase⟩
***syn*** deposit, dispose, fix, lay, position, put, set, set up, situate, stick
***rel*** rearrange, reorder; orient; establish, locate, settle; assemble, collect; carry; berth, park; affix, anchor, wedge; lay out, line up, queue, rank; set down
***near ant*** relocate, remove, take; banish; displace, replace, supplant
**2** to arrange or assign according to type — see CLASSIFY 1
**3** to decide the size, amount, number, or distance of (something) without actual measurement — see ESTIMATE 2
**4** to take or have a certain position within a group arranged in vertical classes — see RANK 1
**placid** *adj* **1** free from emotional or mental agitation — see CALM 2
**2** free from storms or physical disturbance — see CALM 1
**placidity** *n* **1** a state of freedom from storm or disturbance — see CALM
**2** evenness of emotions or temper — see EQUANIMITY
**plague** *n* a widespread disease resulting in a high rate of death ⟨the Black Death was a *plague* that killed about one third of Europe's population in the Middle Ages⟩
***syn*** pest, pestilence
***rel*** epidemic, pandemic; affection, affliction, contagion, contagious disease, infection, infectious disease, infirmity, malady; curse, scourge
**plague** *vb* to cause persistent suffering to — see AFFLICT
**plain** *adj* **1** free from all additions or embellishment ⟨I like my hamburgers *plain*, with no ketchup or relish⟩ ⟨just give us the *plain* facts and none of your snide comments⟩
***syn*** bald, bare, naked, simple, unadorned, undecorated, unvarnished
***rel*** chaste, modest; unexaggerated, unsophisticated; denuded, divested, stripped; dry, laconic, terse; unpretentious; austere, bleak, severe, spartan, stark; inconspicuous, muted, restrained, subdued, toned (down), unobtrusive; conservative, quiet, understated
***near ant*** flamboyant, flashy, garish, gaudy, glittery, glitzy, loud, ostentatious, showy, splashy, swank (*or* swanky), tawdry; bedizened, florid, lurid, ornate; exaggerated, overdecorated, overdone, overwrought; baroque, extravagant, rococo; arrayed, bedecked, decked-out, dressed, garnished, trimmed
***ant*** adorned, decorated, embellished, fancy, ornamented
**2** free from added matter — see PURE 1
**3** free in expressing one's true feelings and opinions — see FRANK
**4** going straight to the point clearly and firmly — see STRAIGHTFORWARD 1
**5** not subject to misinterpretation or more than one interpretation — see CLEAR 2
**plain** *adv* in an honest and direct manner — see STRAIGHTFORWARD
**plain** *n* a broad area of level or rolling treeless country ⟨the first settlers in that area lived on the vast *plains* in lonely log cabins⟩
***syn*** down, grassland, prairie, savanna (*also* savannah), steppe, tundra, veld (*or* veldt)
***rel*** pampas; floodplain; bottom, bottomland, flat, lowland; plateau, table, tableland, upland
**plainclothesman** *n* a person whose business is solving crimes and catching criminals or gathering information that is not easy to get — see DETECTIVE
**plainly** *adv* in an honest and direct manner — see STRAIGHTFORWARD
**plainness** *n* **1** the free expression of one's true feelings and opinions — see CANDOR
**2** the quality or state of having a form or structure of few parts or elements — see SIMPLICITY 1
**plainspoken** *adj* free in expressing one's true feelings and opinions — see FRANK
**plaint** *n* **1** a crying out in grief — see LAMENT 1
**2** an expression of dissatisfaction, pain, or resentment — see COMPLAINT 1
**plaintiff** *n* the person in a legal proceeding who makes a charge of wrongdoing against another — see COMPLAINANT
**plaintive** *adj* expressing or suggesting mourning — see MOURNFUL 1

**plait** *n* a length of something formed of three or more strands woven together — see BRAID

**plait** *vb* to form into a braid — see BRAID

**plan** *n* **1** a method worked out in advance for achieving some objective ⟨there is a contingency *plan* in the office for handling almost any emergency⟩
*syn* arrangement, blueprint, design, game, ground plan, program, project, scheme, strategy, system
*rel* collusion, conspiracy, plot; maneuver, ruse, stratagem, subterfuge, trick; means, method, tactic, technique, way; conception, idea, proposal; aim, intention, purpose; diagram, formula, layout, map, policy, recipe, setup
**2** something that one hopes or intends to accomplish — see GOAL

**plan** *vb* **1** to work out the details of (something) in advance ⟨we *planned* the school dance down to the smallest detail⟩
*syn* arrange, blueprint, calculate, chart, design, frame, lay out, map (out), project, schematize, scheme (out)
*rel* conspire, intrigue, machinate; draft, outline, sketch; aim, figure, intend, mean; contemplate, meditate, premeditate
**2** to have in mind as a purpose or goal — see INTEND

**plane** *adj* having a surface without bends, breaks, or irregularities — see LEVEL

**plane** *vb* **1** to make free from breaks, curves, or bumps — see EVEN 1
**2** to move through the air with or as if with outstretched wings — see FLY 1

**planet** *n* the celestial body on which we live — see EARTH 1

**plant** *n* a building or set of buildings for the manufacturing of goods — see FACTORY

**plant** *vb* to put or set into the ground to grow ⟨I'll *plant* the marigold seeds in the spring⟩
*syn* drill, put in, seed, sow
*rel* bed; replant, transplant; scatter; pot
*near ant* gather, harvest, reap

**plantation** *n* a settlement in a new country or region — see COLONY 1

**planter** *n* a person who cultivates the land and grows crops on it — see FARMER

**plash** *vb* **1** to flow in a broken irregular stream — see GURGLE
**2** to move with a splashing motion — see SLOSH
**3** to wet or soil by striking with something liquid or mushy — see SPLASH 2

**plaster** *n* a medicated covering used to heal an injury — see DRESSING 1

**plastic** *adj* capable of being easily molded or modeled ⟨Silly Putty is famous for being very *plastic*⟩
*syn* malleable
*rel* adaptable; ductile, pliable, pliant, supple, willowy; elastic, flexible, resilient, workable; bending, giving, tractable, yielding
*near ant* inflexible, rigid, stiff

**plasticity** *n* the quality or state of being easily molded ⟨we chose that type of clay for its greater *plasticity*⟩
*syn* malleability
*rel* adaptability; pliability, suppleness; elasticity, flexibility, resilience
*near ant* inflexibility, rigidity, stiffness

**plat** *n* **1** a small area of usually open land — see FIELD 1
**2** a small piece of land that is developed or available for development — see LOT 1

**plate** *n* **1** a small thin piece of material that resembles an animal scale — see ²SCALE
**2** something that visually explains or decorates a text — see ILLUSTRATION 1

**plateau** *n* a broad flat area of elevated land ⟨Native Americans have inhabited the *plateau* for centuries⟩
*syn* mesa, table, tableland
*rel* butte, dome, height, highland, upland

**platform** *n* a level usually raised surface ⟨you'll have to stand up there on the *platform* for your speech⟩
*syn* dais, podium, rostrum, stage, stand
*rel* altar, pulpit; balcony

**platitude** *n* an idea or expression that has been used by many people — see COMMONPLACE

**plaudit** *n usually* **plaudits** *pl* enthusiastic and usually public expression of approval — see APPLAUSE

**plausible** *adj* worthy of being accepted as true or reasonable — see BELIEVABLE

**play** *n* **1** activity engaged in to amuse oneself ⟨it's such a delight to watch the children in their *play*⟩
*syn* dalliance, frolic, frolicking, fun, recreation, relaxation, rollicking, sport
*rel* gamboling, romping; amusement, diversion, entertainment; delight, enjoyment, pleasure; friskiness, playfulness, sportiveness, wantonness; devilment, devilry (*or* deviltry), hob, impishness, mischief, mischievousness, rascality, roguishness, waggery; binge, fling, lark, revel, spree; hilarity, merrymaking, revelry; buffoonery, horseplay, tomfoolery
*near ant* drudgery, labor, work; duty, obligation, responsibility
**2** a written work in which the story is told through speech and action that is intended to be acted out on stage ⟨we'll be putting on a school *play* using that stage⟩
*syn* drama, dramatization
*rel* comedy, melodrama, musical, musical comedy, tragedy, tragicomedy; magnum opus, opus, work; adaptation
**3** an attitude or manner not to be taken seriously — see FUN 2
**4** the act or practice of employing something for a particular purpose — see USE 1

**play** *vb* **1** to engage in activity for amusement ⟨you need some time to run and *play* in the yard after that hard work⟩
*syn* dally, disport, frolic, recreate, rollick, sport
*rel* gambol, romp; dabble, trifle; amuse, divert, entertain; delight, please; dabble, mess (around), putter; bum (around),

dawdle, goldbrick, idle, loaf, lounge (around *or* about), relax, rest, slack (off); jest, joke, tease

***near ant*** drudge, labor, plod, plug (away), slave, strain, strive, struggle, sweat, toil, work

**2** to present a portrayal or performance of — see ACT 1

**3** to pretend to be (what one is not) in appearance or behavior — see IMPERSONATE 1

**4** to spend time in aimless activity — see FIDDLE (AROUND)

**play** (on *or* upon) *vb* to take unfair advantage of — see EXPLOIT 1

**play** (up) *vb* to indicate the importance of by giving prominent display — see EMPHASIZE

**play** (upon) *vb* to control or take advantage of by artful, unfair, or insidious means — see MANIPULATE 1

**play** (with) *vb* to handle thoughtlessly, ignorantly, or mischievously — see TAMPER

**played out** *adj* depleted in strength, energy, or freshness — see WEARY 1

**player** *n* **1** a person who plays a musical instrument — see MUSICIAN 1

**2** one who acts professionally (as in a play, movie, or television show) — see ACTOR

**playful** *adj* given to good-natured joking or teasing ⟨the little girl was lighthearted and *playful*⟩

***syn*** antic, coltish, elfish, fay, frisky, frolicsome, rollicking, sportive

***rel*** kittenish; gay, happy, lighthearted, whimsical; energetic, lively, spirited, sprightly; devilish, knavish, rascally; amusing, diverting, enjoyable, entertaining, fun, pleasurable; dabbling, frivolous, trifling; delightful, pleasant, pleasing; jesting, joking, teasing

***near ant*** dutiful, responsible; grave, grim, serious, solemn, somber (*or* sombre), stern, stolid; no-nonsense, priggish, starchy, stuffy; decorous, formal, proper, sedate, staid; guarded, inhibited, restrained

***ant*** earnest, serious-minded, sober

**playfulness** *n* a natural disposition for playful behavior ⟨the *playfulness* of the kitten can be quite amusing⟩

***syn*** friskiness, impishness, mischief, mischievousness, prankishness, sportiveness

***rel*** devilment, devilry (*or* deviltry), hob, rascality, waggery; devilishness, diabolicalness, knavery; frivolousness; energy, liveliness, sprightliness; gaiety (*also* gayety), lightheartedness, whimsicality

***near ant*** graveness, grimness, seriousness, solemnity, sternness; priggishness, starchiness, stuffiness; constraint, restraint, self-control

***ant*** earnestness, soberness

---

***syn*** synonym(s) ***rel*** related words
***ant*** antonym(s) ***near ant*** near antonym(s)

**playhouse** *n* a building or part of a building where movies are shown — see THEATER 1

**plea** *n* **1** an earnest request ⟨the student made an impassioned *plea* for more time to finish the test⟩

***syn*** appeal, cry, entreaty, petition, prayer, solicitation, suit, supplication

***rel*** application; call, demand, insistence

**2** an explanation that frees one from fault or blame — see EXCUSE

**plead** *vb* to state (something) as a reason in support of or against something under consideration — see ARGUE 1

**plead** (for) *vb* to make a request for — see ASK (FOR) 1

**plead** (to) *vb* to make a request to (someone) in an earnest or urgent manner — see BEG

**pleader** *n* one who asks earnestly for a favor or gift — see SUPPLICANT

**pleading** *adj* asking humbly — see SUPPLIANT

**pleasant** *adj* giving pleasure or contentment to the mind or senses ⟨the massage was extremely *pleasant* and relaxing⟩

***syn*** agreeable, congenial, darling, delectable, delicious, delightful, dreamy, enjoyable, felicitous, good, grateful, gratifying, heavenly, luscious, nice, palatable, pleasing, pleasurable, satisfying, welcome

***rel*** alluring, attractive, desirable, inviting, tempting; charming, enchanting, fascinating; calming, comforting, soothing; affable, amiable, amusing, cheerful, cheery, genial, goodly, good-natured, gracious, hospitable, kindly, personable; blissful, glad, happy, joyous; elating, exhilarating, intoxicating; ecstatic, euphoric, rapturous

***near ant*** abominable, horrid, miserable, wretched; disgusting, distasteful, obnoxious, offensive, repellent (*also* repellant), repugnant, repulsive; abhorrent, detestable, hateful, odious; boring, commonplace, dull, flat, insipid, irksome, stale, tedious; displeasing, dissatisfying; depressing, disheartening, dismal, dreary, gloomy; black, blue, dejected, depressed, despondent, disconsolate, down, downcast, downhearted, forlorn, hangdog, heartbreaking, heartrending, heartsick, heartsore, inconsolable, joyless, lachrymose, low-spirited, sad, unhappy; bemoaning, bewailing, deploring, doleful, dolorous, grieving, lugubrious, mournful, plaintive, regretful, rueful, sorrowful, wailing, weeping; aggravating, annoying, exasperating, irritating, peeving, perturbing, vexing; forbidding; hostile, intimidating; angering, enraging, incensing, inflaming, infuriating, maddening, outraging, rankling, riling; distressing, disturbing, upsetting

***ant*** disagreeable, unpalatable, unpleasant, unwelcome

**pleasantly** *adv* in a pleasing way — see WELL 5

**pleasantness** *n* the state or quality of having a pleasant or agreeable manner in socializing with others — see AMIABILITY 1

**pleasantry** *n* something said or done to cause laughter — see JOKE 1

**please** *vb* to give satisfaction to ⟨fresh flowers *please* me greatly⟩
*syn* content, delight, gladden, gratify, rejoice, satisfy, suit, warm
*rel* appease, mollify, pacify, placate, soothe; assuage, quench, sate, satiate; excite, tickle, titillate; overjoy, thrill; calm, comfort; cater (to), humor, indulge; coddle, mollycoddle, pamper, spoil
*near ant* aggravate, annoy, bother, bug, chafe, cross, exasperate, gall, get, grate, irk, irritate, nettle, peeve, perturb, pique, put out, ruffle, vex; anger, enrage, incense, inflame, infuriate, maiden, outrage, rankle, rile, roil; provoke rouse; agitate, distress, disturb, fret, upset; harass, harry, pester; affront, insult, offend
*ant* displease

**pleased** *adj* **1** experiencing pleasure, satisfaction, or delight — see GLAD 1
**2** feeling that one's needs or desires have been met — see CONTENT

**pleasing** *adj* giving pleasure or contentment to the mind or senses — see PLEASANT

**pleasingly** *adv* in a pleasing way — see WELL 5

**pleasurable** *adj* **1** giving pleasure or contentment to the mind or senses — see PLEASANT
**2** providing amusement or enjoyment — see FUN

**pleasure** *n* **1** the feeling experienced when one's wishes are met ⟨nothing gives me more *pleasure* than a hot meal after a long day⟩
*syn* content, contentedness, contentment, delectation, delight, enjoyment, gladness, gratification, happiness, relish, satisfaction
*rel* bliss, felicity, glee, gleefulness, joy; amusement, diversion, entertainment; elatedness, elation, exhilaration, exultation, intoxication; ecstasy, euphoria, heaven, rapture; cheer, cheerfulness, exuberance, gaiety (*also* gayety), jollity, joyfulness, jubilation; comfort, ease, restfulness
*near ant* misery, sadness, unhappiness, wretchedness; anguish, desolation, joylessness, sorrow, woe; dejection, depression, despondency, dispiritedness, gloom, melancholy; aggravation, annoyance, exasperation, irritation, pique, vexation; anger, fury, rage; agitation, distress, disturbance, upset; discomfort, restlessness, uneasiness
*ant* discontent, discontentedness, discontentment, displeasure, dissatisfaction, unhappiness
**2** a source of great satisfaction — see DELIGHT 1
**3** someone or something that provides amusement or enjoyment — see FUN 1

**pleat** *vb* to form into a braid — see BRAID

**plebeian** *adj* belonging to the class of people of low social or economic rank — see IGNOBLE 1

**plebeians** *n pl* the body of the community as contrasted with the elite — see MASS 1

**pledge** *n* **1** something given or held to assure that the giver will keep a promise ⟨I was required to leave my keys as a *pledge* that I would bring the car back⟩
*syn* gage, guarantee, guaranty, pawn, security
*rel* bail, bond; deposit, down payment; surety, warranty; oath, promise, word; commitment, compact, contract, covenant; recognizance
**2** a person's solemn declaration that he or she will do or not do something — see PROMISE

**pledge** *vb* **1** to obligate by prior agreement ⟨I would love to go to dinner with you, but I've *pledged* myself to a play with my parents that night⟩
*syn* commit, engage, troth
*rel* affiance, betroth, plight, promise, swear, vow; contract, enlist, enroll (*also* enrol), sign on, sign up
*near ant* renege
**2** to leave as a guarantee of repayment of a loan — see PAWN
**3** to make a solemn declaration of intent — see PROMISE 1

**plenary** *adj* not lacking any part or member that properly belongs to it — see COMPLETE 1

**plenitude** *n* **1** a considerable amount — see LOT 2
**2** an amount or supply more than sufficient to meet one's needs — see PLENTY 1

**plenteous** *adj* being more than enough without being excessive — see PLENTIFUL

**plentiful** *adj* being more than enough without being excessive ⟨a *plentiful* amount of strawberries that will be more than enough for a couple of pies⟩
*syn* abundant, ample, bountiful, comfortable, generous, liberal, plenteous
*rel* abounding, overflowing, replete, rich, rife, teeming, wealthy; adequate, enough, sufficient; fat, fecund, fertile, fruitful, prolific; copious, galore, lavish, profuse; luxuriant
*near ant* deficient, inadequate, insufficient, lacking, wanting; meager (*or* meagre), niggardly, stingy; skimpy; least, minimum; light, slight, small; barren, infertile, sterile, unfruitful, unproductive
*ant* bare, minimal, scant

**plentitude** *n* an amount or supply more than sufficient to meet one's needs — see PLENTY 1

**plenty** *n* **1** an amount or supply more than sufficient to meet one's needs ⟨you'll have *plenty* of time to do your science project⟩
*syn* abundance, plenitude, plentitude, superabundance, wealth
*rel* adequacy, competence, competency, enough, sufficiency; amplitude, liberality; excess, overflow, overkill, oversupply, su-

perfluity, surfeit, surplus; fecundity, fertility, fruitfulness, richness; lavishness, luxuriance
*near ant* paucity, poverty, scarcity; barrenness, infertility, sterility
*ant* deficiency, inadequacy, insufficiency
**2** a considerable amount — see LOT 2

**pliable** *adj* able to bend easily without breaking — see WILLOWY

**pliant** *adj* able to bend easily without breaking — see WILLOWY

**plod** *vb* **1** to devote serious and sustained effort — see LABOR
**2** to make progress in a clumsy, struggling manner — see FLOUNDER 1
**3** to move slowly — see CRAWL 2

**plop** *vb* to throw or set down clumsily or casually — see FLOP 1

**plot** *n* **1** a secret plan for accomplishing evil or unlawful ends ⟨they uncovered a *plot* to assassinate the President just in time⟩
*syn* conspiracy, design, intrigue, machination, scheme
*rel* frame-up; manipulation, subterfuge, trickery; artifice, contrivance, maneuver, stratagem, trick; cabal, confederacy, ring; game, gimmick, racket; ground plan, program, strategy, system; collusion, complicity, connivance, conniving
**2** a small area of usually open land — see FIELD 1
**3** a small piece of land that is developed or available for development — see LOT 1

**plot** *vb* to engage in a secret plan to accomplish evil or unlawful ends ⟨mobsters were caught *plotting* to take over the company⟩
*syn* conspire, contrive, intrigue, machinate, scheme
*rel* brew, concoct, cook (up), hatch; connive; engineer, jockey, maneuver, manipulate; design, frame, lay out, map, plan, shape

**plow** *vb* **1** to cut into and turn over the sod of (a piece of land) using a bladed implement ⟨we'll have to get out there and *plow* and plant both fields before it rains⟩
*syn* break, furrow
*rel* cultivate, till; fallow; harrow, hoe, rake
**2** to devote serious and sustained effort — see LABOR

**ploy** *n* a clever often underhanded means to achieve an end — see TRICK 1

**pluck** *n* **1** the act or an instance of applying force on something so that it moves in the direction of the force — see PULL 1
**2** the strength of mind that enables a person to endure pain or hardship — see FORTITUDE

**plug** *vb* **1** to close up so that no empty spaces remain — see FILL 2
**2** to devote serious and sustained effort — see LABOR
**3** to provide publicity for — see PUBLICIZE 1
**4** to strike with a missile from a gun — see SHOOT 3

**plug** (up) *vb* to prevent passage through — see CLOG 1

**plugger** *n* a person who does very hard or dull work — see SLAVE 2

**plum** *n* someone or something unusually desirable — see PRIZE 1

**plumb** *adj* rising straight up — see ERECT

**plumb** *adv* **1** in a direct line or course — see DIRECTLY 1
**2** *chiefly dialect* to a full extent or degree — see FULLY 1

**plumb** *vb* to measure the depth of (as a body of water) typically with a weighted line — see ²SOUND 1

**plume** *n* something given in recognition of achievement — see AWARD

**plume** *vb* to think highly of (oneself) — see PRIDE

**plummet** *vb* to go to a lower level — see DROP 2

**plump** *adj* having an excess of body fat — see FAT 1

**plump** *adv* in a direct line or course — see DIRECTLY 1

**plump** *vb* to throw or set down clumsily or casually — see FLOP 1

**plumpness** *n* the condition of having an excess of body fat — see CORPULENCE

**plunder** *n* valuables stolen or taken by force — see LOOT

**plunder** *vb* to search through with the intent of committing robbery — see RANSACK 1

**plunge** *n* **1** an act or instance of diving — see DIVE 1
**2** the act or process of going to a lower level or altitude — see DESCENT 1

**plunge** *vb* **1** to cast oneself head first into deep water — see DIVE
**2** to go to a lower level — see DROP 2
**3** to lead or extend downward — see DESCEND 1

**plunk** *vb* to throw or set down clumsily or casually — see FLOP 1

**plus** *n* something added (as by growth) — see INCREASE 1

**plush** *adj* showing obvious signs of wealth and comfort — see LUXURIOUS

**ply** *vb* to bring to bear especially forcefully or effectively — see EXERT

**poach** *vb* to cook in a liquid heated to the point that it gives off steam — see BOIL 2

**po'boy** *also* **poor boy** *n* a large sandwich on a long split roll — see SUBMARINE

**pocket** *adj* of a size that is less than average — see SMALL 1

**pocket** *n* available money — see FUND 2

**pocket** *vb* **1** to refrain from openly showing or uttering — see SUPPRESS 2
**2** to take (something) without right and with an intent to keep — see STEAL 1

**pocketbook** *n* a container for carrying money and small personal items — see PURSE

**pocket–size** *also* **pocket–sized** *adj* of a size that is less than average — see SMALL 1

---

*syn* synonym(s) *rel* related words
*ant* antonym(s) *near ant* near antonym(s)

**pockmark** *n* something that spoils the appearance or completeness of a thing — see BLEMISH

**pod** *n* something that encloses another thing especially to protect it — see [1]CASE 1

**podium** *n* a level usually raised surface — see PLATFORM

**poem** *n* a composition using rhythm and often rhyme to create a lyrical effect ⟨your assignment is to write two *poems* about springtime⟩
*syn* lyric, song, verse
*rel* rhyme (*also* rime); ballad, lay; elegy, English sonnet, epic, epigram, haiku, jingle, lament, limerick, ode, psalm, sonnet; blank verse, free verse, minstrelsy, poesy, poetry

**poesy** *n* writing that uses rhythm, vivid language, and often rhyme to provoke an emotional response — see POETRY 1

**poet** *n* a person who writes poetry ⟨Emily Dickinson is famous as the *poet* who rarely left the house but often journeyed to the depths of the human heart⟩
*syn* bard, minstrel, versifier
*rel* poetess; poet laureate; troubadour; epigrammatist, rhymer, sonneteer

**poetic** *adj* having qualities suggestive of poetry ⟨your description of the sun setting over the Grand Canyon was a particularly *poetic* piece of writing⟩
*syn* lyric, lyrical, poetical
*rel* metric, metrical, rhyming, rhythmic (*or* rhythmical); rhapsodic (*also* rhapsodical); florid, flowery, grandiloquent, high-falutin, high-flown, ornate; figurative, metaphorical, symbolic (*also* symbolical)
*near ant* factual, literal, matter-of-fact
*ant* prosaic, prose, unpoetic

**poetical** *adj* having qualities suggestive of poetry — see POETIC

**poetry** *n* **1** writing that uses rhythm, vivid language, and often rhyme to provoke an emotional response ⟨not all *poetry* has to rhyme⟩
*syn* minstrelsy, poesy, song, verse
*rel* rhyme (*also* rime); blank verse, free verse
*ant* prose
**2** the art or power of speaking or writing in a forceful and convincing way — see ELOQUENCE

**poignancy** *n* a harsh or sharp quality — see EDGE 1

**poignant** *adj* having the power to affect the feelings or sympathies — see MOVING

**point** *n* **1** a particular and often important moment in time ⟨it was at that *point* that I had to stop and check on the experiment⟩
*syn* juncture
*rel* flash, instant, jiffy, minute, moment, second, shake, split second, trice, twinkle, wink; bit, spell, stretch, while; brink, threshold, verge
**2** the last and usually sharp or tapering part of something long and narrow ⟨be careful with the *point* on that umbrella, or you could hurt someone⟩
*syn* apex, cusp, end, pike, tip
*rel* prong, tine; barb, jag, prickle, snag, spike, sticker
**3** a separate part in a list, account, or series — see ITEM 1
**4** a single piece of information — see FACT 3
**5** a small area that is different (as in color) from the main part — see SPOT 1
**6** an area of high ground jutting out into a body of water beyond the line of the coast — see HEADLAND 1
**7** an area of land that juts out into a body of water — see [2]CAPE
**8** an individual part of a process, series, or ranking — see DEGREE 1
**9** something that sets apart an individual from others of the same kind — see CHARACTERISTIC
**10** the area or space occupied by or intended for something — see PLACE 1
**11** the quality of an utterance that provokes interest and produces an effect — see [1]PUNCH 1

**point** (toward) *vb* to stand or sit with the face or front toward — see FACE 1

**point** (up) *vb* to indicate the importance of by giving prominent display — see EMPHASIZE

**pointed** *adj* **1** tapering to a thin tip ⟨the snake plant's long *pointed* leaves make it an easily recognized houseplant⟩
*syn* peaked, sharp, tipped
*rel* barbed, jagged, pronged, spiky
*near ant* dull, rounded
*ant* blunt
**2** having to do with the matter at hand — see PERTINENT

**pointer** *n* **1** an arrow-shaped piece on a dial or scale for registering information ⟨the *pointer* on my bathroom scale must be stuck—I know I lost weight⟩
*syn* hand, index, indicator, needle
*rel* dial, face, gauge (*also* gage)
**2** a piece of advice or useful information especially from an expert — see [1]TIP 1

**pointless** *adj* having no meaning — see MEANINGLESS

**point of view** *n* a way of looking at or thinking about something ⟨who actually has the right to possession of that wilderness area depends on your *point of view*⟩
*syn* angle, outlook, perspective, shoes, slant, standpoint, viewpoint
*rel* interpretation, spin; belief, conviction, eye, feeling, judgment (*or* judgement), mind, notion, opinion, perception, persuasion, sentiment, verdict, view; impression, take; wavelength; side; attitude, position, posture, stand

**poise** *n* a condition in which opposing forces are equal to one another — see BALANCE 1

**poise** *vb* to rest or move along the surface of a liquid or in the air — see FLOAT

**poison** *adj* containing or contaminated with a substance capable of injuring or killing a living thing — see POISONOUS

**poison** *n* a substance that by chemical action can kill or injure a living thing ⟨the

only way to get rid of rats is to leave out *poison*⟩
***syn*** bane, toxin, venom
***rel*** cancer, contagion, disease, virus; fungicide, germicide, herbicide, insecticide
***near ant*** antidote, antivenin; cure; cure-all, elixir, panacea

**poison** *vb* **1** to affect slightly with something morally bad or undesirable — see TAINT 1
**2** to make unfit for use by the addition of something harmful or undesirable — see CONTAMINATE
**3** to lower in character or dignity — see DEBASE 1

**poisoned** *adj* containing or contaminated with a substance capable of injuring or killing a living thing — see POISONOUS

**poisonous** *adj* containing or contaminated with a substance capable of injuring or killing a living thing ⟨some evil person was leaving out *poisonous* meat for neighborhood dogs to eat⟩
***syn*** envenomed, poison, poisoned, toxic, venomous
***rel*** contagious, infectious; deleterious, harmful, hurtful, injurious, malignant, noxious, virulent; unhealthful, unhealthy, unwholesome; calamitous, deadly, fatal, lethal, murderous
***near ant*** beneficial, curative, healthful, healthy, helpful, palliative, remedial, salubrious, salutary, wholesome; benign, harmless, innocuous, inoffensive; nonfatal, nonlethal
***ant*** nonpoisonous, nontoxic, nonvenomous

[1]**poke** *n* a quick thrust ⟨please stop giving the cat *pokes* while it's trying to sleep⟩
***syn*** dab, dig, jab
***rel*** punch; stab, stick; push, shove; jam, jerk, jog, nudge

[2]**poke** *n chiefly Southern & Midland* a container made of a flexible material (as paper or plastic) — see BAG 1

**poke** *vb* **1** to extend outward beyond a usual point — see BULGE
**2** to interest oneself in what is not one's concern — see INTERFERE
**3** to move or act slowly — see DELAY 1
**4** to move slowly — see CRAWL 2

**poking** *adj* moving or proceeding at less than the normal, desirable, or required speed — see SLOW 1

**poky** *or* **pokey** *adj* moving or proceeding at less than the normal, desirable, or required speed — see SLOW 1

**polar** *adj* **1** being as different as possible — see OPPOSITE
**2** having a low or subnormal temperature — see COLD 1

**police** *n* **1** the department of government that keeps order, fights crime, and enforces statutes ⟨the appearance of a ransom note meant that the teenager's disappearance was now a matter for the *police*⟩
***syn*** law
***rel*** judiciary, jurisprudence, justice
**2** a body of officers of the law ⟨the National Guard will serve as backup for the metropolitan *police* in the event of violent protests⟩
***syn*** constabulary, police force
***rel*** constable, cop, gendarme, officer, policeman, police officer, policewoman, trooper

**police force** *n* a body of officers of the law — see POLICE 2

**policeman** *n* a member of a force charged with law enforcement at the local level — see OFFICER 1

**police officer** *n* a member of a force charged with law enforcement at the local level — see OFFICER 1

**policy** *n* a way of acting or proceeding — see COURSE 1

**polish** *n* **1** a high level of taste and enlightenment as a result of extensive intellectual training and exposure to the arts — see CULTURE 1
**2** brightness created by light reflected from a surface — see SHINE 1

**polish** *vb* to make smooth or glossy usually by repeatedly applying surface pressure ⟨you'll need to *polish* your shoes with a clean rag before the performance⟩
***syn*** buff, burnish, dress, gloss, grind, rub, shine, smooth
***rel*** sleek, slick; coat, glaze; finish, veneer; brighten; rasp, sand, sandblast, sandpaper, scour, scrape, scrub
***near ant*** rough (up), roughen, scuff (up)

**polished** *adj* **1** having a shiny surface or finish — see GLOSSY
**2** having or showing a taste for the fine arts and gracious living — see CULTIVATED

**polite** *adj* **1** showing consideration, courtesy, and good manners ⟨it's only *polite* to hold the door for the person behind you⟩
***syn*** civil, courteous, genteel, gracious, mannerly, well-bred
***rel*** attentive, considerate, thoughtful; chivalrous, courtly, gallant; ceremonial, ceremonious; formal, suave, unctuous, urbane; elegant, refined; deferential, dutiful, respectful, submissive, yielding; acceptable, appropriate, becoming, befitting, correct, decent, decorous, fit, fitting, good, meet, proper, respectable, right, seemly, suitable; affable, cordial, friendly, genial, hospitable, sociable; felicitous, graceful; humble, meek, modest, unassertive
***near ant*** heedless, inconsiderate, thoughtless; audacious, bold, bold-faced, brash, brassy, disrespectful, impertinent, impudent, insolent, saucy, shameless; boorish, churlish, clownish, loutish, uncouth, vulgar; casual, informal, unceremonious; improper, inappropriate, incorrect, indecent, indecorous, uncalled-for, unrespectable, unseemly; arrogant, conceited, presumptuous, pretentious

---

***syn*** synonym(s) ***rel*** related words
***ant*** antonym(s) ***near ant*** near antonym(s)

*ant* discourteous, ill-bred, ill-mannered, impolite, inconsiderate, rude, thoughtless, uncivil, ungracious, unmannerly
**2** following the established traditions of refined society and good taste — see PROPER 1

**politeness** *n* speech or behavior that is a sign of good breeding ⟨the little girl's *politeness* greatly impressed her teacher⟩
*syn* civility, courteousness, courtesy, gentility, graciousness, mannerliness
*rel* attentiveness, consideration, thoughtfulness; ceremonialness, ceremoniousness, ceremony, formality; chivalrousness, chivalry, courtliness, gallantry; breeding, manners; suaveness, unctuousness, urbanity; elegance, refinement; deference, respect; decency, decorousness, decorum, propriety, respectability, seemliness; affability, cordiality, friendliness, geniality, hospitality, sociability; felicitousness, gracefulness; humility, meekness, modesty, shyness
*near ant* audaciousness, audacity, boldness, brashness, brassiness disrespect, impertinence, impudence, insolence, sauciness, shamelessness; boorishness, churlishness, clownishness, loutishness, vulgarity; casualness, informality; impropriety, inappropriateness, incorrectness, indecency; inconsideration, thoughtlessness; arrogance, conceit, presumption, pretentiousness
*ant* discourteousness, discourtesy, impoliteness, incivility, rudeness, ungraciousness

**politic** *adj* suitable for bringing about a desired result under the circumstances — see EXPEDIENT

**poll** *n* the upper or front part of the body that contains the brain, the major sense organs, and the mouth — see HEAD 1

**poll** *vb* to go around and approach (people) with a request for opinions or information — see CANVASS

**pollutant** *n* something that is or that makes impure — see IMPURITY

**pollute** *vb* to make unfit for use by the addition of something harmful or undesirable — see CONTAMINATE

**polluted** *adj* containing foreign or lower-grade substances — see IMPURE

**poltergeist** *n* the soul of a dead person thought of especially as appearing to living people — see GHOST

**poltroon** *n* a person who shows a shameful lack of courage in the face of danger — see COWARD

**polychromatic** *adj* marked by a variety of usually vivid colors — see COLORFUL

**polychrome** *adj* marked by a variety of usually vivid colors — see COLORFUL

**polygraph** *n* an instrument for detecting physical signs of the tension that goes with lying — see LIE DETECTOR

**pommel** *vb* to strike repeatedly — see BEAT 1

**pompous** *adj* **1** having a feeling of superiority that shows itself in an overbearing attitude — see ARROGANT
**2** having too high an opinion of oneself — see CONCEITED
**3** self-consciously trying to present an appearance of grandeur or importance — see PRETENTIOUS 1

**pompousness** *n* **1** an exaggerated sense of one's importance that shows itself in the making of excessive or unjustified claims — see ARROGANCE
**2** an often unjustified feeling of being pleased with oneself or with one's situation or achievements — see COMPLACENCE

**ponder** *vb* to give serious and careful thought to ⟨I'm *pondering* whether or not I should join another club⟩
*syn* chew over, cogitate, consider, contemplate, debate, deliberate, entertain, meditate, mull (over), question, ruminate, study, think (about *or* over), weigh
*rel* muse (upon), reflect (on *or* upon), reminisce; conclude, reason; second-guess, speculate; brood (about *or* over), fret (about *or* over), obsess (about *or* over); believe, conceive, opine; absorb, assimilate, digest, drink (in)
*phrases* cudgel one's brains
*near ant* disregard, ignore, overlook, slight; dismiss, pooh-pooh (*also* pooh), reject

**ponderous** *adj* **1** causing weariness, restlessness, or lack of interest — see BORING
**2** having great weight — see HEAVY 1

**ponderousness** *n* the state or quality of being heavy — see WEIGHTINESS 1

**pooch** *n* a domestic mammal that is related to the wolves and foxes — see DOG

**[1]pool** *n* a small often deep body of water ⟨when it rains, that small *pool* grows to almost the size of a lake⟩
*syn* mere [*chiefly British*], puddle
*rel* basin, hole, sinkhole; swimming pool; lake

**[2]pool** *n* **1** a body of persons at work or available for work — see FORCE 1
**2** the number of individuals or amount of something available at any given time — see SUPPLY
**3** a sum of money set aside for a particular purpose — see FUND 1
**4** the total of the bets at stake at one time — see POT 1

**poor** *adj* **1** lacking money or material possessions ⟨every year, we make up a basket of food at Thanksgiving for a *poor* family in the neighborhood⟩
*syn* beggared, broke, destitute, impecunious, impoverished, indigent, needy, penniless, penurious, poverty-stricken, stone-broke
*rel* deprived, disadvantaged, underprivileged; bankrupt, bankrupted, insolvent; depressed, pinched, reduced, straitened; low, short
*phrases* hard up
*near ant* comfortable, prosperous
*ant* affluent, flush, moneyed (*or* monied), opulent, rich, wealthy, well-heeled, well-off, well-to-do

2 producing inferior or only a small amount of vegetation — see BARREN 1
3 less plentiful than what is normal, necessary, or desirable — see MEAGER
4 falling short of a standard — see BAD 1
5 of low quality — see CHEAP 2
6 deserving of one's pity — see PATHETIC 1

**poorly** *adj* temporarily suffering from a disorder of the body — see SICK 1

**poorly** *adv* in an unsatisfactory way — see BADLY

**poorness** *n* the state of lacking sufficient money or material possessions — see POVERTY 1

**[1]pop** *n* a loud explosive sound — see CLAP 1

**[2]pop** *n* a male human parent — see FATHER 1

**pop** *vb* 1 to break open or into pieces usually because of internal pressure — see EXPLODE 1
2 to break suddenly with an explosive sound — see CRACK 1
3 to cause to break open or into pieces by or as if by an explosive — see BLAST 1
4 to strike with a missile from a gun — see SHOOT 3

**pop** (in) *vb* to make a brief visit — see CALL 3

**populace** *n* the body of the community as contrasted with the elite — see MASS 1

**popular** *adj* 1 enjoying widespread favor or approval ⟨bell-bottom jeans were *popular* in the seventies⟩
*syn* fashionable, hot, in, modish, popularized, vogue
*rel* favorite, preferred; desirable, liked, wanted; celebrated, famed, famous, noted, notorious, prominent, renowned, well-known; fabled, fabulous, legendary; leading, notable, outstanding, remarkable; important, significant
*near ant* washed-up; despised, detested, disliked, hated, rejected; insignificant, unimportant; indistinguished, unexceptional; anonymous, nameless, obscure, unknown; inconspicuous
*ant* out, unpopular
2 accepted, used, or practiced by most people — see CURRENT 1
3 held by or applicable to a majority of the people — see GENERAL 3
4 of, relating to, or favoring political democracy — see DEMOCRATIC

**popularity** *n* the state of enjoying widespread approval ⟨the sudden *popularity* of low-cut blouses horrified my mother⟩
*syn* fashionableness, favor, hotness, modishness, vogue
*rel* craze, fad, mode, rage, style, trend; bandwagon; fame, notoriety, prominence, renown; enthusiasm; fervor, passion
*near ant* oblivion, obscurity
*ant* disfavor, unpopularity

**popularized** *adj* enjoying widespread favor or approval — see POPULAR 1

---

*syn* synonym(s) *rel* related words
*ant* antonym(s) *near ant* near antonym(s)

**pore** (over) *vb* to go over and mentally take in the content of — see READ

**pornographic** *adj* depicting or referring to sexual matters in a way that is unacceptable in polite society — see OBSCENE 1

**porous** *adj* capable of being passed into or through — see PENETRABLE

**port** *n* a part of a body of water protected and deep enough to be a place of safety for ships — see HARBOR 1

**portable** *adj* capable of being moved especially with ease — see MOVABLE

**portal** *n* a barrier by which an entry is closed and opened — see DOOR 1

**portent** *n* 1 something believed to be a sign or warning of a future event — see OMEN
2 something extraordinary or surprising — see WONDER 1

**portentous** *adj* 1 being or showing a sign of evil or calamity to come — see OMINOUS
2 causing wonder or astonishment — see MARVELOUS 1

**porter** *n chiefly British* a person who tends a door — see DOORKEEPER

**portion** *n* 1 a state or end that seemingly has been decided beforehand — see FATE 1
2 one of the pieces from which something is designed to be assembled — see PART 1
3 something belonging to, due to, or contributed by an individual member of a group — see SHARE 1

**portion** *vb* to give out (something) in appropriate amounts or to appropriate individuals — see ADMINISTER 1

**portliness** *n* the condition of having an excess of body fat — see CORPULENCE

**portly** *adj* having an excess of body fat — see FAT 1

**portmanteau** *n* a bag carried by hand and designed to hold a traveler's clothing and personal articles — see TRAVELING BAG

**portrait** *n* a vivid representation in words of someone or something — see DESCRIPTION 1

**portray** *vb* 1 to give a representation or account of in words — see DESCRIBE 1
2 to point out the chief quality or qualities of an individual or group — see CHARACTERIZE 1
3 to present a picture of — see PICTURE 1
4 to present a portrayal or performance of — see ACT 1

**portrayal** *n* a vivid representation in words of someone or something — see DESCRIPTION 1

**pose** *n* a display of emotion or behavior that is insincere or intended to deceive — see MASQUERADE

**pose** *vb* to set before the mind for consideration — see PROPOSE 1

**pose** (as) *vb* to pretend to be (what one is not) in appearance or behavior — see IMPERSONATE 1

**position** *n* 1 an assignment at which one regularly works for pay — see JOB 1

2 the action for which a person or thing is specially fitted or used or for which a thing exists — see ROLE
3 the area or space occupied by or intended for something — see PLACE 1
4 the place where someone is assigned to stand or remain — see STATION 1
5 the placement of someone or something in relation to others in a vertical arrangement — see RANK 1

**position** *vb* to arrange something in a certain spot or position — see PLACE 1

**positive** *adj* 1 expressing approval — see FAVORABLE 1
2 having or showing a mind free from doubt — see CERTAIN 2

**positiveness** *n* a state of mind in which one is free from doubt — see CONFIDENCE 2

**possess** *vb* to keep, control, or experience as one's own — see HAVE 1

**possession** *n* 1 the fact or state of having (something) at one's disposal ‹a student who was found to have several overdue library books in his *possession*›
*syn* control, hands, keeping
*rel* ownership, proprietorship; authority, command, dominion, mastery, power; enjoyment, repossession, retention; claiming, collaring, commandeering confiscation, procurement
*near ant* dispossession, relinquishment, surrendering, transferal
*ant* nonpossession
2 **possessions** *pl* transportable items that one owns ‹we packed up all of our *possessions* and moved to a new house›
*syn* belongings, chattels, effects, holdings, movables (*or* moveables), paraphernalia, personalty, things
*rel* treasures, valuables; junk, stuff; appointments, fixtures, furnishings; property, tangibles; collateral
*near ant* real estate

**possessive** *adj* intolerant of rivalry or unfaithfulness — see JEALOUS 1

**possessor** *n* one who has a legal or rightful claim to ownership — see PROPRIETOR

**possibility** *n* 1 something that can develop or become actual — see POTENTIAL
2 something that might happen — see EVENT 2

**possible** *adj* 1 capable of being done or carried out ‹I think that building the entire set in two days is *possible*, if difficult›
*syn* achievable, attainable, doable, feasible, practicable, realizable, viable, workable
*rel* practical, reasonable, sensible; likely, probable; acceptable, believable, conceivable, creditable, plausible; available, usable
*near ant* impractical, unrealistic; doubtful, dubious, far-fetched, improbable, unlikely; implausible, inconceivable, incredible, unbelievable; futile, useless, vain; absurd, fantastic, outlandish, preposterous, ridiculous; unthinkable
*ant* hopeless, impossible, impracticable, unachievable, unattainable, unworkable
2 existing only as a possibility and not in fact — see POTENTIAL

**possibly** *adv* it is possible — see PERHAPS

[1]**post** *n* *chiefly British* communications or parcels sent or carried through the postal system — see MAIL

[2]**post** *n* 1 a specific task with which a person or group is charged — see MISSION
2 the place where someone is assigned to stand or remain — see STATION 1
3 an assignment at which one regularly works for pay — see JOB 1

[3]**post** *n* an upright shaft that supports an overhead structure — see PILLAR 1

[1]**post** *vb* 1 to affix (as a notice) to or on a suitable place ‹the student organizations always *post* their announcements on the cafeteria walls›
*syn* placard
*rel* nail, plaster, tack (up); advertise, announce, blaze, broadcast, call, declare, proclaim, promulgate, publicize, publish
*near ant* remove, take down
2 to make known openly or publicly — see ANNOUNCE

[2]**post** *vb* to assign to a place or position ‹the police are planning to *post* an officer outside the hospital room of the witness›
*syn* detail, station
*rel* set; appoint; place, position

[3]**post** *vb* to send through the postal system — see MAIL

**postdate** *vb* to come after in time — see FOLLOW 1

**poster** *n* a sheet bearing an announcement for posting in a public place ‹we put up a hundred *posters* announcing the concert›
*syn* bill, placard
*rel* billboard, sign, signboard; broadside, flier (*or* flyer), handbill, handout, playbill; ad, advertisement, announcement, bulletin, dispatch, release

**posterior** *adj* 1 being at or in the part of something opposite the front part — see BACK
2 being, occurring, or carried out at a time after something else — see SUBSEQUENT

**posterior** *n* the part of the body upon which someone sits — see BUTTOCKS

**posterity** *n* the descendants of a person, animal, or plant — see OFFSPRING

**posthaste** *adv* with great speed — see FAST 1

**posthumous** *adj* occurring after one's death ‹the soldier was awarded a *posthumous* medal for valor›
*syn* postmortem
*rel* belated, delayed, late

**posting** *n* a published statement informing the public of a matter of general interest — see ANNOUNCEMENT

**postman** *n* a person who delivers mail ‹the *postman* comes at around nine every morning›
*syn* letter carrier, mail carrier, mailman
*rel* messenger; postmaster

**postmortem** *adj* occurring after one's death — see POSTHUMOUS

**postmortem** *n* examination of a dead body especially to find out the cause of death — see AUTOPSY

**postmortem examination** *n* examination of a dead body especially to find out the cause of death — see AUTOPSY

**postpone** *vb* to assign to a later time ⟨we'll have to *postpone* the decision until we have all the information⟩
*syn* defer, delay, hold off (on), hold up, put off, shelve
*rel* suspend; hesitate, pause, stay; detain, retard, slow; extend, lengthen, prolong, protract, stretch (out); wait
*near ant* act, deal (with), decide (upon), do, work (on)

**postulate** *n* something taken as being true or factual and used as a starting point for a course of action or reasoning — see ASSUMPTION

**postulate** *vb* to take as true or as a fact without actual proof — see ASSUME 2

**posture** *n* **1** a general way of holding the body ⟨a good upright *posture* will prevent backaches⟩
*syn* carriage, stance
*rel* attention; body language; pose, seat; bearing, behavior, conduct, demeanor, deportment; air, poise, presence; aspect, look, mien
**2** position with regard to conditions and circumstances — see SITUATION 1

**posy** *n* a bunch of flowers — see BOUQUET 1

**pot** *n* **1** the total of the bets at stake at one time ⟨everyone got a bit nervous when the *pot* was more than a hundred dollars⟩
*syn* jackpot, pool
*rel* fund, kitty; bet, stake, wager
**2** a considerable amount — see LOT 2

**potable** *adj* suitable for drinking ⟨around here, the only *potable* water comes from wells⟩
*syn* drinkable
*rel* clean, fresh, pure, uncontaminated, unpolluted; nonpoisonous
*near ant* contaminated, dirty, foul, polluted; poison, poisonous, toxic; unhealthful, unhealthy, unwholesome
*ant* undrinkable

**potbelly** *n* an enlarged or bulging abdomen ⟨he began exercising to get rid of his growing *potbelly* and tighten up his stomach⟩
*syn* paunch
*rel* belly, breadbasket [*slang*], gut, stomach, tummy; chubbiness, corpulence, fat, fatness, fleshiness, obesity, overweight, paunchiness, plumpness, portliness, pudginess; chunkiness, heaviness, stoutness

**potency** *n* the ability to exert effort for the accomplishment of a task — see POWER 2

**potent** *adj* **1** having an abundance of some characteristic quality (as flavor) — see FULL-BODIED
**2** having great power or influence — see IMPORTANT 2
**3** producing or capable of producing a desired result — see EFFECTIVE 1

**potentate** *n* a person who uses power or authority in a cruel, unjust, or harmful way — see DESPOT

**potential** *adj* existing only as a possibility and not in fact ⟨I can see a few *potential* problems with getting a puppy, but we'll wait and see if they come up⟩
*syn* possible
*rel* conceivable, imaginable, plausible, thinkable; likely, probable; conjectural, hypothetical, suppositional, theoretical (*also* theoretic); alleged, assumed, purported, reputed, supposed; achievable, attainable, doable, feasible, practicable, viable, workable
*near ant* authenticated, confirmed, demonstrated, established, proven, substantiated; authentic, bona fide, genuine, true
*ant* actual, existent, factual, real

**potential** *n* something that can develop or become actual ⟨a time when cloning was merely a *potential* and the stuff of science fiction⟩
*syn* eventuality, possibility, potentiality
*rel* likelihood, probability; latency
*near ant* actuality, reality; certainty

**potentiality** *n* something that can develop or become actual — see POTENTIAL

**pother** *n* **1** a state of nervous or irritated concern — see FRET
**2** a state of noisy, confused activity — see COMMOTION

**potpourri** *n* an unorganized collection or mixture of various things — see MISCELLANY 1

**potter** (around) *vb* to spend time in aimless activity — see FIDDLE (AROUND)

**potterer** *n* a person who regularly or occasionally engages in an activity without being or becoming an expert at it — see AMATEUR

**potter's field** *n* a piece of land used for burying the dead — see CEMETERY

**pottery** *n* articles made of baked clay — see CROCKERY

**pouch** *n* a container made of a flexible material (as paper or plastic) — see BAG 1

**poultice** *n* a medicated covering used to heal an injury — see DRESSING 1

**pounce** (on *or* upon) *vb* to take sudden, violent action against — see ATTACK 1

**pound** *n* **1** a hard strike with a part of the body or an instrument — see [1]BLOW
**2** an enclosure with an open framework for keeping animals — see CAGE

**pound** *vb* **1** to move heavily or clumsily — see LUMBER 1
**2** to deliver a blow to (someone or something) usually in a strong vigorous manner — see HIT 1
**3** to strike repeatedly — see BEAT 1
**4** to shape with a hammer — see HAMMER 1

---

*syn* synonym(s) *rel* related words
*ant* antonym(s) *near ant* near antonym(s)

**pour** *vb* **1** to cause to flow in a stream ⟨she lifted the teakettle and *poured* some hot water through the spout⟩
*syn* stream
*rel* ladle, spoon; cascade, trickle; deluge, flood, inundate, overflow
**2** to move in a stream — see FLOW 1
**3** to flow out in great quantities or with force — see GUSH 1
**4** to fall as water in a continuous stream of drops from the clouds — see RAIN 1
**5** to give readily and in large quantities — see RAIN 2

**pouring** *adj* marked by or abounding with rain — see RAINY

**pout** *n* **1** a twisting of the facial features in disgust or disapproval — see GRIMACE
**2 pouts** *pl* a state of resentful silence or irritability — see SULK

**pout** *vb* to silently go about in a bad mood — see SULK

**pouting** *adj* given to or displaying a resentful silence and often irritability — see SULKY

**poverty** *n* **1** the state of lacking sufficient money or material possessions ⟨he dreamed of finding a good job and working his way out of *poverty* and debt⟩
*syn* beggary, destitution, impecuniousness, impoverishment, indigence, need, neediness, pauperism, penuriousness, penury, poorness, want
*rel* misery, woe, wretchedness; exigency, necessity; austerity, deprivation, privation; bankruptcy, insolvency; belt-tightening, pinching, straitening
*near ant* luxury, prosperity
*ant* affluence, opulence, richness, wealthiness
**2** a falling short of an essential or desirable amount or number — see DEFICIENCY

**poverty–stricken** *adj* lacking money or material possessions — see POOR 1

**powder** *vb* to reduce to fine particles ⟨you have to *powder* the antibiotic tablet and mix it with food⟩
*syn* atomize, crush, grind, pulverize
*rel* grate; crumble, crunch; break, bust, dash, fracture; fragment; shatter, smash, splinter; mill

**powdery** *adj* consisting of very small particles — see FINE 1

**power** *n* **1** the right or means to command or control others ⟨the principal has nearly complete *power* over this school⟩
*syn* arm, authority, clutch, command, control, dominion, grip, hold, mastery, sway
*rel* clout, influence, pull, weight; jurisdiction; direction, management; dominance, predominance, sovereignty, supremacy; prerogative, privilege, right; eminence, importance, moment
*near ant* helplessness, weakness
*ant* impotence, powerlessness
**2** the ability to exert effort for the accomplishment of a task ⟨the corporation has the *power* to accomplish almost anything⟩ ⟨you'll need to build a bit more *power* in order to be a star pitcher⟩
*syn* energy, force, might, muscle, potency, puissance, sinew, strength, vigor
*rel* aptitude, capability, capacity, competence, competency; adequacy, effectiveness, effectualness, usefulness
*near ant* disability, inability, inaptitude, incapability, incapacity, incompetence, incompetency; ineffectiveness, ineffectualness, uselessness; helplessness, paralysis
*ant* impotence, powerlessness, weakness
**3** a natural ability of the mind or body ⟨dogs have a very highly developed *power* of smell⟩
*syn* faculty
*rel* function; capability, capacity; aptitude, endowment, flair, genius, gift, instinct, knack, talent
*near ant* inability, incapability, incapacity; inaptitude, inaptness, ineptness
**4** something with a usable capacity for doing work — see FUEL

**powerboat** *n* a boat equipped with a motor — see MOTORBOAT

**powerful** *adj* having great power or influence — see IMPORTANT 2

**powerfully** *adv* in a vigorous and forceful manner — see HARD 3

**powerhouse** *n* an ambitious person who eagerly goes after what is desired — see GO-GETTER

**powerless** *adj* unable to act or achieve one's purpose ⟨I wish I could help you, but I am *powerless* in this situation⟩
*syn* helpless, impotent, weak
*rel* incapable, incompetent, ineffective, ineffectual, inept, unfit, useless; feeble, frail, infirm, passive, spineless, supine, unaggressive
*near ant* able, capable, competent, effective, efficient; authoritarian, autocratic, despotic, dictatorial, magisterial, tyrannical (*also* tyrranic); dominant, dynamic, energetic, forceful, robust, sturdy, tough, vigorous; important, major, significant; high-level, senior, top
*ant* mighty, potent, powerful, puissant, strong

**powerlessness** *n* the lack of sufficient ability, power, or means — see INABILITY

**powwow** *n* **1** a coming together of a number of persons for a specified purpose — see MEETING 1
**2** a meeting featuring a group discussion — see FORUM

**powwow** *vb* to exchange viewpoints or seek advice for the purpose of finding a solution to a problem — see CONFER 2

**practicable** *adj* **1** capable of being done or carried out — see POSSIBLE 1
**2** capable of being put to use or account — see PRACTICAL 1
**3** capable of or suitable for being used for a particular purpose — see USABLE 1

**practical** *adj* **1** capable of being put to use or account ⟨a *practical* and simple solution for the town's waste disposal⟩ ⟨she has some *practical* information on sightseeing in San Francisco⟩

*syn* applicable, functional, practicable, serviceable, usable, useful, workable, working
*rel* down-to-earth, pragmatic (*also* pragmatical), utilitarian; accessible, available, obtainable, reachable; all-around (*also* all-round), handy; active, alive, busy, employed, functioning, operating, operative
*near ant* abstract, academic, theoretical (*also* theoretic); inaccessible, unattainable, unavailable, unobtainable, unreachable; unsuitable
*ant* impracticable, impractical, unusable, unworkable, useless
**2** willing to see things as they really are and deal with them sensibly — see REALISTIC 1

**practical joke** *n* a playful or mischievous act intended as a joke — see PRANK

**practically** *adv* very close to but not completely — see ALMOST

**practice** *also* **practise** *n* **1** a private performance or session in preparation for a public appearance — see REHEARSAL
**2** a usual manner of behaving or doing — see HABIT
**3** something done over and over in order to develop skill — see EXERCISE 2

**practice** *or* **practise** *vb* to do over and over so as to become skilled ⟨in order to play the guitar well, you need to *practice* fingering every single day⟩
*syn* exercise, rehearse
*rel* prepare (for), train (with); drill, repeat; work (at *or* on); review, study

**practiced** *or* **practised** *adj* **1** having or showing exceptional knowledge, experience, or skill in a field of endeavor — see PROFICIENT
**2** accomplished with trained ability — see SKILLFUL

**pragmatic** *also* **pragmatical** *adj* willing to see things as they really are and deal with them sensibly — see REALISTIC 1

**prairie** *n* a broad area of level or rolling treeless country — see PLAIN

**praise** *vb* **1** to proclaim the glory of ⟨hymns that *praise* God⟩
*syn* bless, extol (*also* extoll), glorify, laud, magnify
*rel* adore, deify, idolize, worship; acclaim, applaud, commend, compliment, hail, salute; celebrate, cheer, eulogize, rhapsodize; cite; flatter; crack up, recommend, tout
*near ant* blame, censure, reprehend, reprobate; criticize, reprove; admonish, chide, rebuke, reprimand, reproach; castigate, lambaste (*or* lambast)
**2** to declare enthusiastic approval of — see ACCLAIM

**praiseworthy** *adj* deserving of high regard or great approval — see ADMIRABLE

**prance** *vb* to walk with exaggerated arm and leg movements — see STRUT 1

**prank** *n* a playful or mischievous act intended as a joke ⟨as a *prank*, several students managed to change all the classroom clocks to different times⟩
*syn* antic, caper, escapade, frolic, practical joke, trick
*rel* skylarking; adventure, experience, game, lark, time; high jinks, horseplay, play, roughhousing, rowdiness; shenanigans, tomfoolery; joking, kidding, teasing; gambit, hoax, maneuver, ploy; deed, feat, mission, performance, stunt; caprice, conceit, fancy, vagary, whim, whimsy; deceit, deception, delusion, fooling, fraud, hoodwinking, ruse, sham, stratagem, subterfuge, trickery, wile

**prankish** *adj* tending to or exhibiting reckless playfulness — see MISCHIEVOUS 1

**prankishness** *n* a natural disposition for playful behavior — see PLAYFULNESS

**prate** *vb* to engage in casual or rambling conversation — see CHAT

**prattle** *n* unintelligible or meaningless talk — see GIBBERISH

**prattle** *vb* **1** to engage in casual or rambling conversation — see CHAT
**2** to speak rapidly, inarticulately, and usually unintelligibly — see BABBLE 1

**prattler** *n* a person who talks constantly — see CHATTERBOX

**pray** *vb* to make a request to (someone) in an earnest or urgent manner — see BEG

**prayer** *n* **1** an address to God or a deity ⟨he always directed a bedside *prayer* to God before going to sleep⟩
*syn* orison
*rel* collect, grace, invocation, litany, thanksgiving; evensong, matins, vespers; appeal, begging, beseeching, entreaty, imploring, petition, pleading, request, soliciting, suit, supplication
**2** an earnest request — see PLEA 1

**prayerful** *adj* asking humbly — see SUPPLIANT

**preacher** *n* a person specially trained and authorized to conduct religious services in a Christian church — see CLERGYMAN

**preamble** *n* a short section (as of a book) that leads to or explains the main part — see INTRODUCTION

**precariousness** *n* the quality or state of not being firmly fixed in position — see INSTABILITY

**precautionary** *adj* concerned with or serving to keep something from happening — see PREVENTIVE

**precede** *vb* to go or come before in time ⟨there are two speeches which will *precede* yours⟩
*syn* antedate, forego, predate
*ant* follow, succeed

**precedence** *n* the right to one's attention before other things considered less important — see PRIORITY

**precedent** *adj* going before another in time or order — see PREVIOUS

**preceding** *adj* going before another in time or order — see PREVIOUS

**preceptor** *n* a person whose occupation is to give formal instruction in a school — see TEACHER

*syn* synonym(s) *rel* related words
*ant* antonym(s) *near ant* near antonym(s)

**precious** *adj* **1** commanding a large price — see COSTLY
**2** granted special treatment or attention — see DARLING 1
**3** having qualities that tend to make one loved — see LOVABLE
**precipice** *n* a steep wall of rock, earth, or ice — see CLIFF
**precipitate** *adj* acting or done with excessive or careless speed — see HASTY 1
**precipitate** *n* matter that settles to the bottom of a body of liquid — see DEPOSIT 1
**precipitate** *vb* to fall as water in a continuous stream of drops from the clouds — see RAIN 1
**precipitately** *adv* with excessive or careless speed — see HASTILY 1
**precipitating** *adj* marked by or abounding with rain — see RAINY
**precipitation** *n* excited and often showy or disorderly speed — see HURRY 1
**precipitous** *adj* **1** acting or done with excessive or careless speed — see HASTY 1
**2** having an incline approaching the perpendicular — see STEEP 1
**precipitously** *adv* with excessive or careless speed — see HASTILY 1
**precipitousness** *n* excited and often showy or disorderly speed — see HURRY 1
**précis** *n* a short statement of the main points — see SUMMARY
**precise** *adj* **1** meeting the highest standard of accuracy ⟨a machine which takes very *precise* measurements⟩
***syn*** accurate, close, delicate, exact, fine, hairline, mathematical, pinpoint, rigorous
***rel*** correct, right, strict, true; definite, definitive; nice, subtle; careful, fastidious, finicky
***near ant*** approximate, round; false, incorrect, untrue, wrong; careless, loose; indefinite, unclear, vague; doubtful, dubious, questionable, unreliable, untrustworthy
***ant*** coarse, imprecise, inaccurate, inexact, rough
**2** being in agreement with the truth or a fact or a standard — see CORRECT 1
**3** being neither more nor less than a certain amount, number, or extent — see EVEN 1
**4** following an original exactly — see FAITHFUL 2
**5** of a particular or exact sort — see EXPRESS 1
**precisely** *adv* **1** as stated or indicated without the slightest difference — see EXACTLY 1
**2** in a like manner — see JUST 1
**3** without any relaxation of standards or precision — see STRICTLY
**preciseness** *n* the quality or state of being very accurate — see PRECISION
**precision** *n* the quality or state of being very accurate ⟨the company that measures TV ratings prides itself on the *precision* of its calculations⟩
***syn*** accuracy, closeness, delicacy, exactitude, exactness, fineness, preciseness, rigorousness, veracity
***rel*** correctness, rightness, strictness, truth; definiteness, definitiveness; nicety, subtlety; care, carefulness, fastidiousness
***near ant*** approximation, roundness; falseness, falsity, incorrectness, wrongness; carelessness, guesswork, looseness; indefiniteness, unclearness, vagueness
***ant*** coarseness, impreciseness, imprecision, inaccuracy, inexactness, roughness
**preclude** *vb* to keep from happening by taking action in advance — see PREVENT
**precluding** *n* the act or practice of keeping something from happening — see PREVENTION
**precocious** *adj* occurring before the usual or expected time — see EARLY 2
**precociously** *adv* before the usual or expected time — see EARLY
**preconception** *n* an attitude, belief, or impression formed in advance of actual experience of something — see PREPOSSESSION 1
**precursor** *n* **1** one that announces or indicates the later arrival of another — see FORERUNNER 1
**2** something belonging to an earlier time from which something else was later developed — see ANCESTOR 2
**predaceous** *or* **predacious** *adj* living by killing and eating other animals — see PREDATORY
**predate** *vb* to go or come before in time — see PRECEDE
**predatory** *adj* living by killing and eating other animals ⟨hawks are *predatory* and pose a danger to rabbits and other pets⟩
***syn*** predaceous (*or* predacious), rapacious
***rel*** carnivorous; aggressive, deadly, ferocious, fierce, savage, violent; untamed, wild
***near ant*** herbivorous, vegetarian; gentle, submissive, tame
**predecessor** *n* something belonging to an earlier time from which something else was later developed — see ANCESTOR 2
**predestine** *vb* to determine the fate of in advance — see DESTINE
**predetermine** *vb* to determine the fate of in advance — see DESTINE
**predicament** *n* a difficult, puzzling, or embarrassing situation from which there is no easy escape ⟨if you had told the truth in the first place, we wouldn't be in this *predicament*⟩
***syn*** corner, fix, hole, jam, pickle, spot
***rel*** difficulty, dilemma, hot water, pinch, plight, quagmire, quandary, scrape, trouble; deadlock, halt, impasse, stalemate, standstill; clutch, crisis, crossroad, emergency, exigency, juncture, strait
**predicate** *vb* to find a basis — see BASE
**predict** *vb* to tell of or describe beforehand — see FORETELL
**predicting** *n* a declaration that something will happen in the future — see PREDICTION
**prediction** *n* a declaration that something will happen in the future ⟨we were all

amazed when the fortune-teller's *predictions* turned out to be true⟩
***syn*** auguring, cast, forecast, forecasting, foretelling, predicting, presaging, prognosis, prognosticating, prognostication, prophecy, soothsaying
***rel*** augury, omen, portent, sign; anticipation, foreknowledge; foresight; conjecture, guess, surmise

**predictive** *adj* being a sign of a later course of events — see PROPHETIC

**predilection** *n* a habitual attraction to some activity or thing — see INCLINATION 1

**predisposition** *n* a habitual attraction to some activity or thing — see INCLINATION 1

**predominance** *n* controlling power or influence over others — see SUPREMACY 1

**predominant** *adj* coming before all others in importance — see FOREMOST 1

**predominantly** *adv* for the most part — see CHIEFLY

**preeminence** *n* **1** exceptionally high quality — see EXCELLENCE 1
**2** controlling power or influence over others — see SUPREMACY 1
**3** the fact or state of being above others in rank or importance — see EMINENCE 1

**preeminent** *adj* **1** coming before all others in importance — see FOREMOST 1
**2** highest in rank or authority — see HEAD
**3** standing above others in rank, importance, or achievement — see EMINENT

**preempt** *vb* to take or make use of without authority or right — see APPROPRIATE 1

**preface** *n* a short section (as of a book) that leads to or explains the main part — see INTRODUCTION

**prefer** *vb* **1** to show partiality toward ⟨I generally *prefer* chocolate ice cream over vanilla⟩
***syn*** favor, lean (toward), like
***rel*** adore, cotton (to), delight (in), dig, enjoy, fancy, groove (on), relish, revel (in); choose, cull, handpick, name, pick, select, single (out), take; covet, crave, desire, want, wish (for); bias, prejudice; incline (towards), tend (to); admire, appreciate, cherish, prize, treasure, value
***phrases*** be partial to
***near ant*** disfavor, dislike; abhor, abominate, detest, hate, loathe; decline, refuse, reject, turn down; discard, jettison, throw away, throw out
**2** to decide to accept (someone or something) from a group of possibilities — see CHOOSE 1

**preferably** *adv* by choice or preference — see RATHER 1

**preference** *n* **1** a person or thing that is preferred over others — see FAVORITE
**2** positive regard for something — see LIKING
**3** the power, right, or opportunity to choose — see CHOICE 1

**preferment** *n* a raising or a state of being raised to a higher rank or position — see ADVANCEMENT 1

**preferred** *adj* singled out from a number or group as more to one's liking — see SELECT 1

**prefigure** *vb* to give a slight indication of beforehand — see FORESHADOW

**prefiguring** *n* something believed to be a sign or warning of a future event — see OMEN

**pregnancy** *n* the state of containing unborn young within the body ⟨an elephant's *pregnancy* can last almost a year⟩
***syn*** gestation
***rel*** conception; begetting, breeding, generation, siring, spawning
***near ant*** barrenness, infertility

**pregnant** *adj* **1** containing unborn young within the body ⟨we only realized that our cat had been *pregnant* when she unexpectedly delivered three kittens⟩
***syn*** expectant, gravid
***rel*** childbearing; brooding; conceiving, impregnated
***phrases*** with child, with young
***near ant*** barren, infertile; aborting, miscarrying; delivered
***ant*** nonpregnant
**2** clearly conveying a special meaning (as one's mood) — see EXPRESSIVE

**prejudgment** *n* an attitude, belief, or impression formed in advance of actual experience of something — see PREPOSSESSION 1

**prejudice** *n* **1** an attitude that always favors one way of feeling or acting especially without considering any other possibilities — see BIAS
**2** hatred of or discrimination against a person or persons based on their race — see RACISM 2

**prejudice** *vb* to cause to have often negative opinions formed without sufficient knowledge ⟨all the bad stories I had heard about that teacher *prejudiced* me against him even before the first class⟩
***syn*** bias
***rel*** dispose, incline, predispose; influence, prepossess; convince, persuade, suggest

**prejudiced** *adj* **1** inclined to favor one side over another — see PARTIAL 1
**2** unwilling to grant other people social rights or to accept other viewpoints — see INTOLERANT 2

**prejudicial** *adj* **1** causing or capable of causing harm — see HARMFUL
**2** opposed to one's interests — see ADVERSE 1

**preliminary** *adj* coming before the main part or item usually to introduce or prepare for what follows ⟨we need to do some *preliminary* research in order to properly focus the experiment⟩
***syn*** introductory, preparatory
***rel*** introducing, prefacing, preparing, readying; premonitory, warning; basic, fundamental; ahead, early, former, preceding, previous, prior

*near ant* after, behind, following, subsequent

**prelude** *n* a short section (as of a book) that leads to or explains the main part — see INTRODUCTION

**premature** *adj* occurring before the usual or expected time — see EARLY 2

**prematurely** *adv* before the usual or expected time — see EARLY

**premier** *adj* **1** coming before all others in time or order — see FIRST 1
**2** highest in rank or authority — see HEAD
**3** coming before all others in importance — see FOREMOST 1

**premise** *n* **1** something taken as being true or factual and used as a starting point for a course of action or reasoning — see ASSUMPTION
**2 premises** *pl* the area around and belonging to a building — see GROUND 1

**premise** *vb* to take as true or as a fact without actual proof — see ASSUME 2

**premium** *adj* commanding a large price — see COSTLY

**premium** *n* something given in recognition of achievement — see AWARD

**premonition** *n* a feeling that something bad will happen ⟨she had a *premonition* that her cat would somehow get hurt that day⟩
*syn* foreboding, presage, presentiment
*rel* anticipation, foreknowledge; insight, intuition; augury, omen, portent, sign; impression, suspicion; anxiety, apprehension, care, concern, disquiet, doubt, dread, fear, misgiving, unease, worry; foresight

**preoccupation** *n* something about which one is constantly thinking or concerned — see FIXATION

**preoccupied** *adj* lost in thought and unaware of one's surroundings or actions — see ABSENTMINDED 1

**preparatory** *adj* coming before the main part or item usually to introduce or prepare for what follows — see PRELIMINARY

**prepare** *vb* **1** to make ready in advance ⟨I think I *prepared* myself well for this test⟩ ⟨we *prepared* the classroom for the important visitors by getting rid of some unsightly clutter⟩
*syn* fit, fix, lay, ready
*rel* brace, fortify, steel; batten, gather, gear (up), mount, train; boot (up), prime; arrange, set, spread; arm, equip, furnish, outfit, provide, supply; incline, predispose; draft, draw (up), frame; warm (up)
**2** to make competent (as by training, skill, or ability) for a particular office or function — see QUALIFY 2
**3** to put (something) into proper and usually carefully worked out written form — see COMPOSE 1

**prepared** *adj* being in a state of fitness for some experience or action — see READY 1

**prepossession** *n* **1** an attitude, belief, or impression formed in advance of actual experience of something ⟨the foreign tourists' *prepossessions* about life in the U.S. had been formed by many hours of American TV shows⟩
*syn* preconception, prejudgment
*rel* bias, prejudice; conjecture, hypothesis, imagining, predetermination, presumption, presupposition, speculation, supposition, theorizing, theory; concept, thought
**2** something about which one is constantly thinking or concerned — see FIXATION

**preposterous** *adj* **1** conceived or made without regard for reason or reality — see FANTASTIC 1
**2** showing or marked by a lack of good sense or judgment — see FOOLISH 1
**3** so foolish or pointless as to be worthy of scornful laughter — see RIDICULOUS 1

**preposterousness** *n* lack of good sense or judgment — see FOOLISHNESS 1

**prerogative** *n* something to which one has a just claim — see RIGHT 1

**presage** *n* **1** a feeling that something bad will happen — see PREMONITION
**2** something believed to be a sign or warning of a future event — see OMEN

**presage** *vb* to tell of or describe beforehand — see FORETELL

**presaging** *n* a declaration that something will happen in the future — see PREDICTION

**prescience** *n* **1** the special ability to see or know about events before they actually occur — see FORESIGHT 1
**2** concern or preparation for the future — see FORESIGHT 2

**prescient** *adj* having or showing awareness of and preparation for the future — see FORESIGHTED

**prescribe** *vb* to give the rules about (something) clearly and exactly ⟨in chess, you can move the various pieces only in certain *prescribed* ways⟩
*syn* define, lay down, specify
*rel* decree, dictate, ordain; assign, direct, fix, set, settle; arrange, order; choose, select; adjure, bid, charge, command, enjoin, instruct, tell; conduct, control, lead, manage; coerce, constrain, force; oblige, require

**presence** *n* **1** a position within view ⟨men should watch their language when in the *presence* of ladies⟩
*syn* sight
*rel* nearness, proximity
**2** the outward form of someone or something especially as indicative of a quality — see APPEARANCE 1

**present** *adj* **1** existing or in progress right now ⟨I am very busy at the *present* moment⟩
*syn* current, extant, ongoing, present-day
*rel* contemporary, mod, modern, new, newfangled, new-fashioned, now, recent, red-hot, space-age, ultramodern, up-to-date; being, breathing, existing, living
*near ant* done, ended, finished, over; ancient, antediluvian, antiquated, antique, archaic, dated, fusty, musty, noncontem-

porary, obsolete, old, oldfangled, old-fashioned, old-time, out-of-date, outworn, passé; bygone, erstwhile, formerly
***ant*** ago, past; future
**2** being within the confines of a specified place ⟨all of you are required to be *present* for every class⟩
***syn*** attending
***rel*** accompanying, observing, participating; available; abounding; latent; breathing, existing, existent, extant, live
***phrases*** in attendance, on hand
***near ant*** departed, gone, retired; nonexistent; AWOL, truant; dead, departed, lost, vanished; delayed, late, overdue, tardy
***ant*** absent, away, missing, out

**present** *n* **1** the time currently existing or in progress ⟨I cannot talk to you at *present*, but perhaps in a few minutes⟩
***syn*** moment, now, today
***rel*** phase, stage, state; tonight, tomorrow
***near ant*** yesterday, yesteryear
***ant*** past; future
**2** something given to someone without expectation of a return — see GIFT 1

**present** *vb* **1** to bring before the public in performance or exhibition ⟨we will *present* a performance of *Our Town* this week⟩
***syn*** carry, give, mount, offer, stage
***rel*** display, exhibit, show; preview; act, impersonate, perform, play, portray; depict, dramatize, enact, render, represent; extend, proffer, tender
**2** to make (one person) known (to another) socially — see INTRODUCE 1
**3** to make a present of — see GIVE 1

**presentation** *n* something given to someone without expectation of a return — see GIFT 1

**present–day** *adj* **1** being or involving the latest methods, concepts, information, or styles — see MODERN
**2** existing or in progress right now — see PRESENT 1

**presentiment** *n* a feeling that something bad will happen — see PREMONITION

**presently** *adv* **1** at or within a short time — see SHORTLY 2
**2** at the present time — see NOW 1

**preservation** *n* **1** the act or activity of keeping something in an existing and usually satisfactory condition — see MAINTENANCE
**2** the careful maintaining and protection of something valuable especially in its natural or original state — see CONSERVATION 1

**preserve** *vb* to keep in good condition — see MAINTAIN 1

**preserving** *n* the act or activity of keeping something in an existing and usually satisfactory condition — see MAINTENANCE

**president** *n* a person in charge of a meeting — see CHAIR 1

**preside** (over) *vb* to exercise authority or power over — see GOVERN 1

**presiding** *adj* highest in rank or authority — see HEAD

**press** *n* a great number of persons or things gathered together — see CROWD 1

**press** *vb* **1** to push steadily against with some force ⟨an old doorbell that requires you to *press* the button hard⟩
***syn*** bear (down on), depress, shove, weigh (on *or* upon)
***rel*** compress, squash, squeeze; compel, force, pressure; lean (on *or* against), muscle; drive, propel, thrust; compact, constrict, contract, crush, scrunch, wring; cram, jam, jam-pack, pack, stuff, wedge
**2** to apply external pressure on so as to force out the juice or contents of ⟨my family will only drink juice from freshly *pressed* oranges⟩
***syn*** crush, express, mash, squeeze
***rel*** pulp, puree; extract, extrude
**3** to gather into a closely packed group ⟨everyone *pressed* around me to see the pictures⟩
***syn*** bunch, cluster, crowd, huddle
***rel*** assemble, collect, congregate, flock, gather, herd, swarm, throng; encircle, mob, surround; embrace, hug
**4** to force one's way ⟨we continued to *press* deeper and deeper into the tangled rain forest⟩
***syn*** bulldoze, elbow, muscle, push
***rel*** jostle; ram, shove, thrust
**5** to cause (a person) to give in to pressure — see FORCE
**6** to try to persuade (someone) through earnest appeals to follow a course of action — see URGE

**press** (for) *vb* to ask for (something) earnestly or with authority — see DEMAND 1

**pressing** *adj* needing immediate attention — see ACUTE 2

**pressure** *n* **1** the burden on one's emotional or mental well-being created by demands on one's time — see STRESS 1
**2** the use of power to impose one's will on another — see FORCE 2

**pressure** *vb* to cause (a person) to give in to pressure — see FORCE

**prestidigitator** *n* one who practices tricks and illusions for entertainment — see MAGICIAN 2

**prestigious** *adj* **1** having a good reputation especially in a field of knowledge — see RESPECTABLE 1
**2** standing above others in rank, importance, or achievement — see EMINENT

**presto** *adv* with great speed — see FAST 1

**presumably** *adv* **1** to all outward appearances — see APPARENTLY
**2** without much doubt — see PROBABLY

**presume** *vb* **1** to form an opinion from little or no evidence — see GUESS 1
**2** to take as true or as a fact without actual proof — see ASSUME 2

**presumed** *adj* appearing to be true on the basis of evidence that may or may not be confirmed — see APPARENT 1

**presuming** *adj* showing a lack of proper social reserve or modesty — see PRESUMPTUOUS 1

**presumption** *n* **1** shameless boldness — see EFFRONTERY
**2** something taken as being true or factual and used as a starting point for a course of action or reasoning — see ASSUMPTION

**presumptuous** *adj* **1** showing a lack of proper social reserve or modesty ⟨it's a little *presumptuous* of you to assume that I'm your new best friend just because I invited you along⟩
***syn*** bold, familiar, forward, free, immodest, overfamiliar, presuming
***rel*** arrogant, complacent, conceited, egoistic, egotistic (*or* egotistical), important, overweening, pompous, prideful, proud, self-assertive, self-conceited, self-important, self-satisfied, smug, uppity, vain, vainglorious; cavalier, disdainful, haughty, lordly, pretentious, snobbish, stuck-up, supercilious, superior; audacious, brash, brassy, brazen, fresh, impertinent, impudent, pert, saucy; confident, self-assured, self-confident, sure; boastful, braggart, bragging; domineering, high-handed, imperious; self-centered, selfish
***near ant*** humble, meek, unassertive; bashful, retiring, shy; diffident, self-doubting
***ant*** modest, unassuming
**2** having a feeling of superiority that shows itself in an overbearing attitude — see ARROGANT
**3** thrusting oneself where one is not welcome or invited — see INTRUSIVE

**presumptuousness** *n* **1** an exaggerated sense of one's importance that shows itself in the making of excessive or unjustified claims — see ARROGANCE
**2** shameless boldness — see EFFRONTERY

**presuppose** *vb* to take as true or as a fact without actual proof — see ASSUME 2

**presupposition** *n* something taken as being true or factual and used as a starting point for a course of action or reasoning — see ASSUMPTION

**pretend** *adj* not real and existing only in the imagination — see IMAGINARY

**pretend** *vb* **1** to take on a false or deceptive appearance ⟨I *pretended* that I was scared of the vacuum cleaner⟩
***syn*** dissemble, let on
***rel*** act, impersonate, masquerade, play, pose; affect, assume, counterfeit, fake, feign, profess, put on, simulate; camouflage, conceal, disguise, mask; bluff, feint
***phrases*** make a pretense, make a show, make believe, put on an act, put up a front
**2** to present a false appearance of — see FEIGN

**pretended** *adj* lacking in natural or spontaneous quality — see ARTIFICIAL 1

**pretender** *n* one who makes false claims of identity or expertise — see IMPOSTOR

**pretense** *or* **pretence** *n* **1** the quality or state of appearing or trying to appear more important or more valuable than is the case ⟨she seemed to be a very down-to-earth woman who was completely free of *pretense*⟩
***syn*** affectation, affectedness, grandiosity, pretension, pretentiousness
***rel*** arrogance, complacency, conceit, egotism, pride, self-assertion, self-conceit, self-importance, self-satisfaction, smugness, vainglorious ness, vainglory, vainness, vanity; disdain, haughtiness, lordliness, snobbery, snobbishness, superciliousness, superiority; confidence, presumption, self-assurance, self-confidence, sureness; boastfulness, braggadocio; aggressiveness, assertiveness, audaciousness, boldness, brassiness, cheekiness, cockiness, forwardness, impudence, insolence, rudeness; grandiloquence; flashiness, gaudiness, ostentation, show, showiness
***near ant*** demureness, humbleness, humility, meekness, modesty; bashfulness, diffidence, shyness, timidity; naturalness, sincerity
**2** a display of emotion or behavior that is insincere or intended to deceive — see MASQUERADE
**3** an entitlement to something — see CLAIM 1
**4** an exaggerated sense of one's importance that shows itself in the making of excessive or unjustified claims — see ARROGANCE

**pretension** *n* **1** an entitlement to something — see CLAIM 1
**2** an exaggerated sense of one's importance that shows itself in the making of excessive or unjustified claims — see ARROGANCE
**3** the quality or state of appearing or trying to appear more important or more valuable than is the case — see PRETENSE 1
**4** something that one hopes or intends to accomplish — see GOAL

**pretentious** *adj* **1** self-consciously trying to present an appearance of grandeur or importance ⟨the *pretentious* hosts served caviar at their party, even though they themselves dislike it⟩
***syn*** affected, grandiose, highfalutin, ostentatious, pompous
***rel*** grandiloquent, high-sounding, sententious; arrogant, complacent, conceited, egoistic, egotistic (*or* egotistical), important, overweening, prideful, proud, self-assertive, self-conceited, self-important, self-satisfied, smug, uppity, vain, vainglorious; cavalier, disdainful, haughty, lordly, snobbish, snobby, stuck-up, supercilious, superior; confident, self-assured, self-confident, sure; boastful, braggart, bragging; aggressive, assertive, audacious, bold, brassy, cheeky, cocky, forward, impudent, insolent, rude; flashy, flaunting, gaudy, showy
***near ant*** demure, homely, humble, lowly, meek, retiring, unassertive, unassuming; bashful, diffident, mousy (*or* mousey), overmodest, passive, quiet, reserved, shy, timid

*ant* modest, unpretentious

**2** having a feeling of superiority that shows itself in an overbearing attitude — see ARROGANT

**pretentiousness** *n* **1** an exaggerated sense of one's importance that shows itself in the making of excessive or unjustified claims — see ARROGANCE

**2** excessive or unnecessary display — see OSTENTATION

**3** the quality or state of appearing or trying to appear more important or more valuable than is the case — see PRETENSE 1

**preternatural** *adj* of, relating to, or being part of a reality beyond the observable physical universe — see SUPERNATURAL 1

**prettiness** *n* the qualities in a person or thing that as a whole give pleasure to the senses — see BEAUTY 1

**pretty** *adj* very pleasing to look at — see BEAUTIFUL

**pretty** *adv* to some degree or extent — see FAIRLY

**prevail** *vb* **1** to achieve victory (as in a contest) — see WIN 1

**2** to continue to operate or to meet one's needs — see HOLD OUT

**prevail** (on *or* upon) *vb* to cause (someone) to agree with a belief or course of action by using arguments or earnest requests — see PERSUADE

**prevail** (over) *vb* to achieve a victory over — see BEAT 2

**prevailing** *adj* **1** accepted, used, or practiced by most people — see CURRENT 1

**2** held by or applicable to a majority of the people — see GENERAL 3

**prevalence** *n* the fact or state of happening often — see FREQUENCY

**prevalent** *adj* accepted, used, or practiced by most people — see CURRENT 1

**prevaricate** *vb* to make a statement one knows to be untrue — see LIE 1

**prevarication** *n* a statement known by its maker to be untrue and made in order to deceive — see LIE

**prevaricator** *n* a person who tells lies — see LIAR

**prevent** *vb* to keep from happening by taking action in advance ⟨a lot of problems would have been *prevented* if we'd just prepared better⟩

*syn* avert, forestall, help, obviate, preclude

*rel* anticipate, provide; negate, neutralize, nullify; avoid, save; baffle, balk, checkmate, deter, foil, frustrate, thwart; bar, block, hamper, hinder, impede, interfere (with), retard, stall; deflect, fend (off), head (off), stave off, stop, ward (off); avoid, circumvent, dodge, elude, escape, evade; forbid, inhibit, prohibit; arrest, check, halt, stop; counteract, offset

*near ant* abet, aid, assist; ease, facilitate, smooth; advance, cultivate, encourage, forward, foster, further, nurture, promote; allow, leave, let, permit

**preventative** *adj* concerned with or serving to keep something from happening — see PREVENTIVE

**prevention** *n* the act or practice of keeping something from happening ⟨good crowd control is crucial to the *prevention* of riots⟩

*syn* averting, forestallment, obviating, precluding

*rel* avoidance, circumvention; negation, neutralization, nullification; baffling, balking, checkmate, debarment, determent, deterrence, foiling, frustration, thwarting; bar, block, hindrance, interference; interdiction, prohibition

*near ant* aid, assistance; facilitation; advancement, cultivation, encouragement, nurture, promotion

**preventive** *adj* concerned with or serving to keep something from happening ⟨if you start taking this *preventive* medicine now, you may not get sick after all⟩

*syn* precautionary, preventative

*rel* deterrent, deterring; negating, neutralizing, nullifying; baffling, balking, foiling, frustrating, thwarting; blocking, hampering, hindering, impeding, retardant, stalling

*near ant* abetting, aiding, assisting; easing, facilitating, smoothing; encouraging, forwarding, fostering, furthering, nurturing, promoting

**previous** *adj* going before another in time or order ⟨the new instructor should consult with the *previous* teacher about the lesson plans⟩ ⟨the *previous* math problem also included a reference to store discounts⟩

*syn* antecedent, anterior, foregoing, precedent, preceding, prior

*rel* advance, early, premature; earliest, first, inaugural, initial, maiden, original, pioneer; preexisting; introductory, preliminary; erstwhile, former, whilom

*near ant* advanced, late; final, last, terminal, ultimate

*ant* after, ensuing, following, subsequent, succeeding

**previously** *adv* so as to precede something in order of time — see AHEAD 1

**previous to** *prep* earlier than — see BEFORE 1

**prey** *n* an animal that is hunted or killed ⟨rabbits are common *prey* for owls and hawks⟩

*syn* chase, quarry

*rel* game; kill, victim; creature, critter, beast, brute; target

*near ant* carnivore; chaser, hunter, pursuer; killer, murderer

*ant* predator

**prey** (on *or* upon) *vb* to seize and eat (something) as prey ⟨a fox has been *preying on* the chickens⟩

*syn* feed (on, upon, *or* off)

---

*syn* synonym(s) *rel* related words
*ant* antonym(s) *near ant* near antonym(s)

*rel* chase, hunt, pursue; destroy, dispatch, do in, fell, kill, slay

**price** *n* **1** the amount of money that is demanded as payment for something ⟨I really wanted to buy that shirt, but the *price* was more money than I had⟩
*syn* charge, cost, fee, figure
*rel* list price, market value, rate, tariff, unit price; carrying charge, overcharge, surcharge; deduction, discount, markdown, reduction, sale; deposit; down payment; account, bill, check, invoice, tab
**2** the loss or penalty involved in achieving a goal ⟨I finished the essay, but the *price* was losing a night's sleep⟩
*syn* cost
*rel* expense, toll; forfeit, penalty, sacrifice
**3** something offered or given in return for a service performed — see REWARD

**prick** *n* **1** a mark or small hole made by a pointed instrument ⟨the immunization shot left a *prick* on my arm that turned into a bruise⟩
*syn* perforation, pinhole, pinprick, punch, puncture, stab
*rel* gouge, groove, hollow; break, cut, gash, notch, rupture, slash, slit
**2** a sharp unpleasant sensation usually felt in some specific part of the body — see PAIN 1

**prickly** *adj* likely to cause a scratch — see SCRATCHY 1

**pride** *n* **1** a reasonable or justifiable sense of one's worth or importance ⟨finishing that survival course gave me a real sense of *pride* and confidence in my abilities⟩
*syn* ego, pridefulness, self-esteem, self-regard, self-respect
*rel* confidence, self-assurance, self-confidence; dignity, face, honor, prestige
*near ant* disgrace, humiliation, shame; demureness, humbleness, humility, modesty; diffidence, meekness, shyness, timidity, timidness
**2** an asset that brings praise or renown — see GLORY 2
**3** an often unjustified feeling of being pleased with oneself or with one's situation or achievements — see COMPLACENCE

**pride** *vb* to think highly of (oneself) ⟨he *prides* himself on the quality of his writing⟩
*syn* flatter, plume
*rel* boast, brag, vaunt; congratulate, felicitate

**prideful** *adj* **1** having or displaying feelings of scorn for what is regarded as beneath oneself — see PROUD 1
**2** having too high an opinion of oneself — see CONCEITED

**pridefulness** *n* **1** a reasonable or justifiable sense of one's worth or importance — see PRIDE 1
**2** an often unjustified feeling of being pleased with oneself or with one's situation or achievements — see COMPLACENCE

**priest** *n* a person specially trained and authorized to conduct religious services in a Christian church — see CLERGYMAN

**priestly** *adj* of, relating to, or characteristic of the clergy — see CLERICAL

**prim** *adj* given to or marked by very conservative standards regarding personal behavior or morals — see STRAITLACED

**primal** *adj* relating to or occurring near the beginning of a process, series, or time period — see EARLY 1

**primarily** *adv* **1** in the beginning — see ORIGINALLY
**2** for the most part — see CHIEFLY

**primary** *adj* **1** coming before all others in importance — see FOREMOST 1
**2** done or working without something else coming in between — see DIRECT 1
**3** highest in rank or authority — see HEAD

**prime** *adj* **1** highest in rank or authority — see HEAD
**2** of the very best kind — see EXCELLENT

**prime** *n* **1** a state or time of great activity, thriving, or achievement — see BLOOM 1
**2** individuals carefully selected as being the best of a class — see ELITE

**primer** *n* a book used for instruction in a subject — see TEXTBOOK

**primeval** *adj* relating to or occurring near the beginning of a process, series, or time period — see EARLY 1

**primitive** *adj* **1** belonging to or characteristic of an early level of skill or development ⟨*primitive* wooden tools were used before the Iron Age⟩
*syn* crude, low, rude, rudimentary
*rel* basic, simple, uncomplicated; homely, homespun, unsophisticated; early, primeval, primordial; backward, underdeveloped, undeveloped; aged, ancient, antediluvian, antiquated, antique, dated, fusty, hoary, musty, obsolete, old, oldfangled, old-fashioned, old-time, out-of-date, outworn, passé, past
*near ant* complex, complicated, intricate, involved, sophisticated; full-blown, full-grown, grown, mature, matured, perfected, ripe, ripened; civilized, cultivated, enlightened, refined; contemporary, current, latest, mod, modern, new, newfangled, new-fashioned, novel, now, present-day, space-age, ultramodern, up-to-date
*ant* advanced, developed, evolved, higher
**2** relating to or occurring near the beginning of a process, series, or time period — see EARLY 1

**primordial** *adj* relating to or occurring near the beginning of a process, series, or time period — see EARLY 1

**prince** *n* a person of rank, power, or influence in a particular field — see MAGNATE

**princely** *adj* fit for or worthy of a royal ruler — see MONARCHICAL

**principal** *adj* **1** coming before all others in importance — see FOREMOST 1
**2** highest in rank or authority — see HEAD

**principal** *n* the person who has the most important role in a play, movie, or TV show — see STAR 2

**principally** *adv* for the most part — see CHIEFLY

**principled** *adj* 1 following the accepted rules of moral conduct — see HONORABLE 1
2 guided by or in accordance with one's sense of right and wrong — see CONSCIENTIOUS 1

**principles** *n pl* 1 general or basic truths on which other truths or theories can be based ⟨if you don't learn the *principles* of algebra now, you won't understand much later on⟩
*syn* basics, elements, essentials, fundamentals, rudiments
*rel* basis, foundation, groundwork; nitty-gritty; belief, canon, doctrine, dogma, faith, philosophy; axiom, law, precept, tenet; rule, standard; theorem
*near ant* details, trivia
2 the code of good conduct for an individual or group — see ETHICS

**print** *n* 1 a perceptible trace left by pressure ⟨one telltale sign that I had been napping was the *print* left by the chenille bedspread on my cheek⟩
*syn* impress, impression, imprint, stamp
*rel* dent, hollow, indentation; mark, sign
2 a picture created from an image recorded on a light-sensitive surface by a camera — see PHOTOGRAPH

**print** *vb* to produce and release for distribution in printed form — see PUBLISH 1

**prior** *adj* going before another in time or order — see PREVIOUS

**priority** *n* the right to one's attention before other things considered less important ⟨the principal has decided to give your request *priority*, so you'll have a meeting early tomorrow morning⟩
*syn* precedence, right-of-way
*rel* preference; urgency; ascendancy, preeminence, primacy, supremacy; transcendence; order, progression, sequence, succession

**prior to** *prep* earlier than — see BEFORE 1

**priory** *n* a residence for men under religious vows — see MONASTERY

**prison** *n* a place of confinement for persons held in lawful custody — see JAIL

**prisoner** *n* one that has been taken and held in confinement — see CAPTIVE

**pristine** *adj* being in an original and unused or unspoiled state — see FRESH 1

**private** *adj* 1 not known or meant to be known by the general populace ⟨that he is planning to retire is *private* information until he makes a public announcement⟩
*syn* confidential, hushed, inside, intimate, nonpublic, privy, secret
*rel* classified, top secret; unadvertised, unannounced, undisclosed, unmentioned; clandestine, collusive, conspiratorial, covert; surreptitious, undercover, underhand, underhanded; personal; closeted, concealed, hidden; repressed, silenced, stifled, suppressed
*near ant* well-known; advertised, aired, announced, blazed, broadcast, declared, disclosed, divulged, enunciated, heralded, proclaimed, professed, promulgated, publicized, published, reported, spotlighted; general, popular, prevailing, vulgar; prevalent, rife, widespread; communal, shared
*ant* common, open, public
2 undertaken or done so as to escape being observed or known by others — see SECRET 1
3 of, relating to, or belonging to a single person — see INDIVIDUAL 1

**privation** *n* the state of being robbed of something normally enjoyed ⟨the constant *privation* of sleep was starting to affect my schoolwork⟩
*syn* deprivation, loss
*rel* lack, need, want; dispossession; denial, forfeit, forfeiture, penalty, sacrifice; bereavement
*near ant* ownership, possession; accumulation, acquiring, gain

**privilege** *n* something granted as a special favor ⟨you will have the *privilege* of leading the line today⟩
*syn* appanage, boon, concession, honor
*rel* courtesy; claim, entitlement, right; birthright; perquisite, prerogative; charter, grant, patent; exemption, immunity, waiver
*near ant* duty, obligation, responsibility

**privy** *adj* 1 not known or meant to be known by the general populace — see PRIVATE 1
2 undertaken or done so as to escape being observed or known by others — see SECRET 1
3 of, relating to, or belonging to a single person — see INDIVIDUAL 1

**prize** *n* 1 someone or something unusually desirable ⟨in her parents' view, her current boyfriend is certainly no *prize*⟩
*syn* catch, gem, jewel, pearl, plum, treasure
*rel* find, godsend, goody, valuable, windfall; booty, loot, spoil; glory, pride; jackpot, treasure trove
*near ant* lemon, loser
2 something given in recognition of achievement — see AWARD

**[1]prize** *vb* 1 to draw out by force or with effort — see EXTRACT
2 to raise, move, or pull apart with or as if with a lever — see [1]PRY 1

**[2]prize** *vb* to hold dear — see LOVE 1

**prizefighter** *n* one that engages in the sport of fighting with the fists — see BOXER

**probability** *n* 1 the quality or state of being likely to occur ⟨the plot of the movie thriller was exciting and surprising but woefully lacking in *probability*⟩
*syn* likelihood, likeliness

---

*syn* synonym(s) *rel* related words
*ant* antonym(s) *near ant* near antonym(s)

*rel* credibility, plausibility; liability; feasibility, feasibleness, possibility, potentiality, reasonability, viability
*near ant* doubtfulness, dubiousness; impracticability, impracticality; implausibility, incredibility
*ant* improbability, unlikelihood, unlikeliness
**2** a measure of how often an event will occur instead of another ⟨the *probability* of flipping a coin and getting heads fifty times in a row is not good⟩
*syn* chance, odds, percentage
*rel* outlook, prospect; possibility, potential, potentiality

**probable** *adj* **1** worthy of being accepted as true or reasonable — see BELIEVABLE
**2** having a high chance of occurring — see LIKELY 1

**probably** *adv* without much doubt ⟨we would *probably* win that bet⟩
*syn* doubtless, likely, presumably
*rel* mayhap, perchance, perhaps, possibly; conceivably, imaginably, plausibly, practically, reasonably; potentially; assuredly, certainly, clearly, conclusively, decisively, definitely, definitively, indubitably, positively, surely
*near ant* implausibly, inconceivably, incredibly, unbelievably
*ant* improbably

**probe** *n* a systematic search for the truth or facts about something — see INQUIRY 1

**probe** *vb* **1** to search through or into — see EXPLORE 1
**2** to go into or range over for purposes of discovery — see EXPLORE 2

**probing** *n* a systematic search for the truth or facts about something — see INQUIRY 1

**probity** *n* **1** conduct that conforms to an accepted standard of right and wrong — see MORALITY 1
**2** devotion to telling the truth — see HONESTY 1
**3** faithfulness to high moral standards — see HONOR 1

**problem** *n* **1** something that requires thought and skill for resolution ⟨the *problem* of world hunger⟩
*syn* case, knot, matter, trouble
*rel* issue, question; challenge; corner, fix, hole, hot water, jam, pickle, predicament, situation; glitch, hitch, snag; conundrum, enigma, mystery, puzzle, puzzlement, riddle; brainteaser, perplexer, poser, stumper
*ant* answer, solution
**2** an interrogative expression often used to test knowledge — see QUESTION 1
**3** something that is a source of irritation — see ANNOYANCE 3

**problematic** *also* **problematical** *adj* **1** requiring exceptional skill or caution in performance or handling — see TRICKY
**2** giving good reason for being doubted, questioned, or challenged — see DOUBTFUL 2

**procedure** *n* **1** a usually fixed or ordered series of actions or events leading to a result — see PROCESS 1
**2** a way of acting or proceeding — see COURSE 1

**proceed** *vb* to move forward along a course — see GO 1

**proceed (along)** *vb* to make one's way through, across, or over — see TRAVERSE

**proceeding** *adj* being in progress or development — see ONGOING 1

**proceeding** *n* **1** a court case for enforcing a right or claim — see LAWSUIT
**2** a usually fixed or ordered series of actions or events leading to a result — see PROCESS 1

**proceeds** *n pl* **1** an increase usually measured in money that comes from labor, business, or property — see INCOME
**2** the amount of money left when expenses are subtracted from the total amount received — see PROFIT 1

**process** *n* **1** a usually fixed or ordered series of actions or events leading to a result ⟨the *process* by which the elastic fibers spun by silkworms is turned into soft, lustrous cloth⟩
*syn* course, operation, procedure, proceeding
*rel* fashion, manner, method, mode, style, system, technique, way; approach, blueprint, design, game plan, layout, plan, plot, program, scheme, strategy; accomplishment, achievement, attainment, enterprise, performance, undertaking, work; activity, functioning, movement
**2** forward movement in time or place — see ADVANCE 1

**procession** *n* **1** a body of individuals moving along in an orderly and often ceremonial way — see CORTEGE 2
**2** forward movement in time or place — see ADVANCE 1

**proclaim** *vb* to make known openly or publicly — see ANNOUNCE

**proclivity** *n* a habitual attraction to some activity or thing — see INCLINATION 1

**procreate** *vb* to bring forth offspring ⟨in life science class we learned how animals *procreate*⟩
*syn* breed, multiply, propagate, reproduce
*rel* bear, beget, engender, generate, get, mother, parent, produce, sire; hatch, spawn

**procurable** *adj* possible to get — see AVAILABLE 1

**procurator** *n* a person who acts or does business for another — see AGENT 2

**procure** *vb* to receive as return for effort — see EARN 1

**prod** *vb* **1** to urge or push forward with or as if with a pointed object ⟨my sister keeps *prodding* me with her pencil to move along faster⟩
*syn* goad, spur
*rel* chuck, jab, jog, nudge, poke; bore, drill, pierce, prick, punch, puncture, stab, stick; drive, propel

2 to try to persuade (someone) through earnest appeals to follow a course of action — see URGE

**prodigal** *adj* given to spending money freely or foolishly ⟨the *prodigal* child always spent her allowance the minute she got it⟩
*syn* extravagant, profligate, spendthrift, squandering, thriftless, unthrifty, wasteful
*rel* improvident, myopic, shortsighted; bountiful, generous, lavish, liberal, openhanded, openhearted, philanthropic; careless, heedless, imprudent, incautious, injudicious, unwise; indulgent, reckless, self-indulgent, splurging, wanton
*near ant* cheap, close, mean, miserly, niggardly, parsimonious, penurious, pinching, spare, sparing, stingy, tight, tightfisted; careful, judicious, prudent, sensible, wise; farsighted, forehanded, foresighted, forethoughtful, provident
*ant* conserving, economical, economizing, frugal, scrimping, skimping, thrifty

**prodigal** *n* someone who carelessly spends money ⟨the million-dollar lottery winner was such a *prodigal* that there was no money left after a few years⟩
*syn* profligate, spender, spendthrift, squanderer, waster, wastrel
*near ant* miser, skinflint, tightwad; conserver, saver
*ant* economizer

**prodigality** *n* 1 an instance of spending money or resources without care or restraint — see WASTE 1
2 the quality or fact of being free or wasteful in the expenditure of money — see EXTRAVAGANCE 1

**prodigious** *adj* 1 causing wonder or astonishment — see MARVELOUS 1
2 unusually large — see HUGE

**prodigy** *n* something extraordinary or surprising — see WONDER 1

**produce** *n* something produced by physical or intellectual effort — see PRODUCT 1

**produce** *vb* 1 to be the cause of (a situation, action, or state of mind) — see EFFECT
2 to bring forth from the womb — see BEAR 1
3 to bring into being by combining, shaping, or transforming materials — see MAKE 1

**product** *n* 1 something produced by physical or intellectual effort ⟨that book is the *product* of years of work⟩ ⟨a rebuilt car which is the *product* of several people's labor⟩
*syn* affair, fruit, handiwork, output, produce, production, thing, work, yield
*rel* article, commodity, object; goods, line, merchandise, wares; handcraft, handicraft; aftereffect, aftermath, conclusion, consequence, development, effect, issue, outcome, result, upshot; by-product, derivative, offshoot, outgrowth, residual, side effect, spin-off
2 a condition or occurrence traceable to a cause — see EFFECT 1

**production** *n* something produced by physical or intellectual effort — see PRODUCT 1

**productive** *adj* 1 having a role in deciding something's final form — see FORMATIVE
2 producing abundantly — see FERTILE
3 producing or capable of producing a desired result — see EFFECTIVE 1

**productiveness** *n* the power to produce a desired result — see EFFICACY

**profane** *adj* 1 not involving religion or religious matters ⟨it was hard to juggle the requirements of church and our more *profane* duties⟩
*syn* secular, temporal
*rel* atheistic, godless, irreligious, pagan; lay, nonclerical; nondenominational; nonsectarian; earthly, mundane, terrestrial, worldly; material, physical, substantial; bodily, carnal, corporal, fleshly; blasphemous, impious, irreverent, sacrilegious; unconsecrated, unhallowed, unsanctified
*near ant* divine, spiritual; consecrated, hallowed, holy, sanctified; churchly, devout, godly, pious, prayerful, reverent, worshipful; ethereal, insubstantial, metaphysical, unsubstantial; bodiless, immaterial, incorporeal, nonphysical
*ant* religious, sacred
2 not showing proper reverence for the holy or sacred — see IRREVERENT

**profane** *vb* 1 to lower in character or dignity — see DEBASE 1
2 to put to a bad or improper use — see MISAPPLY
3 to treat (a sacred place or object) shamefully or with great disrespect — see DESECRATE

**profess** *vb* 1 to present a false appearance of — see FEIGN
2 to state clearly and strongly — see ASSERT 1
3 to state as a fact usually forcefully — see CLAIM 1

**profession** *n* 1 a solemn and often public declaration of the truth or existence of something — see PROTESTATION
2 the activity by which one regularly makes a living — see OCCUPATION

**proffer** *n* something which is presented for consideration — see PROPOSAL

**proffer** *vb* 1 to put before another for acceptance or consideration — see OFFER 1
2 to set before the mind for consideration — see PROPOSE 1

**proficiency** *n* 1 a highly developed skill in or knowledge of something — see COMMAND 2
2 knowledge gained by actually doing or living through something — see EXPERIENCE 1

**proficient** *adj* having or showing exceptional knowledge, experience, or skill in a field of endeavor ⟨she is quite *proficient* at computer repair⟩ ⟨a *proficient* rendition of a difficult piano piece⟩
*syn* accomplished, ace, adept, consummate, crack, crackerjack, experienced,

*syn* synonym(s) *rel* related words
*ant* antonym(s) *near ant* near antonym(s)

expert, good, great, master, masterful, masterly, practiced (*or* practised), skilled, skillful, versed, veteran, virtuoso
***rel*** adroit, clever, deft, dexterous (*also* dextrous), handy; gifted, talented; experienced, polished, refined; effective, effectual, efficient, workmanlike; able, capable, competent, fit, qualified; educated, knowledgeable, schooled, taught, trained, tutored; all-around (*also* all-round), well-rounded; long-term, old
***near ant*** incapable, incompetent, inept, unable, unfit, unqualified; artless, crude, rude; ineffective, ineffectual, inefficient; ungifted, untalented; ignorant, unschooled, untaught, untrained, untutored; beginning, green, inexperienced, new, raw, untested, untried; rough, unpolished
***ant*** amateur, amateurish, inexperienced, inexpert, unexperienced, unpracticed, unprofessional, unseasoned, unskilled, unskillful

**proficiently** *adv* in a skillful or expert manner — see WELL 3

**profit** *n* **1** the amount of money left when expenses are subtracted from the total amount received ⟨after we deducted the cost of sugar, lemons, and paper cups, the *profit* from a day of lemonade sales was about $20⟩
***syn*** earnings, gain, lucre, net, payoff, proceeds, return
***rel*** killing, windfall; gross; compensation, emolument, income, pay, payment, remittal, requital, salary, wages; interest, return, yield; (the) black; royalty
***near ant*** cost, expenditure, expense, loss, outgo, outlay
**2** an increase usually measured in money that comes from labor, business, or property — see INCOME

**profit** *vb* to provide with something useful or desirable — see BENEFIT

**profitable** *adj* **1** yielding a profit ⟨selling lemonade turned out to be a *profitable* venture⟩
***syn*** fat, gainful, lucrative, paying, remunerative
***rel*** advantageous, beneficial, rewarding, useful, worthwhile
***ant*** unprofitable
**2** conferring benefits; promoting or contributing to personal or social well-being — see BENEFICIAL

**profligate** *adj* given to spending money freely or foolishly — see PRODIGAL

**profligate** *n* **1** someone who carelessly spends money — see PRODIGAL
**2** a person who has sunk below the normal moral standard — see DEGENERATE

**profound** *adj* **1** difficult for one of ordinary knowledge or intelligence to understand ⟨a *profound* observation about good and evil that few listeners fully grasped⟩
***syn*** abstruse, deep, esoteric, recondite
***rel*** erudite, learned, scholarly; academic, pedantic; complex, complicated, hard; darkling, enigmatic (*also* enigmatical), inscrutable, mysterious, mystic, uncanny; impenetrable, incomprehensible, unfathomable, unintelligible; ambiguous, cryptic; unanswerable, unknowable; baffling, bewildering, confounding, confusing, mystifying, perplexing, puzzling
***near ant*** easy, facile, simple, straightforward; comprehensible, fathomable, intelligible, understandable; clear, obvious, plain
***ant*** shallow
**2** extreme in degree, power, or effect — see INTENSE
**3** having no exceptions or restrictions — see ABSOLUTE 2

**profoundness** *n* the quality of being great in extent (as of insight) — see DEPTH 2

**profundity** *n* the quality of being great in extent (as of insight) — see DEPTH 2

**profuse** *adj* pouring forth in great amounts ⟨we received *profuse* thanks for our efforts⟩ ⟨a *profuse* rush of water from the collapsing dike⟩
***syn*** copious, galore, gushing, lavish, riotous
***rel*** abounding, abundant, ample, bounteous, bountiful, liberal, plenteous, plentiful; extravagant, luxuriant; fat, fecund, fertile; free, liberal, munificent, openhanded, unsparing, unstinting; excessive, immoderate; adequate, complete, enough, sufficient
***near ant*** meager, niggardly, poor, scant, scanty, spare, sparse, stingy; deficient, inadequate, incomplete, insufficient, lacking, unsatisfactory, wanting; bare, mere, minimal; slight, small
***ant*** dribbling, trickling

**profusion** *n* a considerable amount — see LOT 2

**progeny** *n* the descendants of a person, animal, or plant — see OFFSPRING

**prognosis** *n* a declaration that something will happen in the future — see PREDICTION

**prognosticate** *vb* to tell of or describe beforehand — see FORETELL

**prognosticating** *n* a declaration that something will happen in the future — see PREDICTION

**prognostication** *n* a declaration that something will happen in the future — see PREDICTION

**prognosticator** *n* one who predicts future events or developments — see PROPHET

**program** *n* **1** a listing of things to be presented or considered (as at a concert or play) ⟨the *program* will tell us the scheduled order of musical numbers⟩
***syn*** agenda, calendar, docket, schedule, timetable
***rel*** card, exercises; arrangement, order, organization
**2** a method worked out in advance for achieving some objective — see PLAN 1
**3** a way of acting or proceeding — see COURSE 1

**progress** *n* **1** forward movement in time or place — see ADVANCE 1

2 the act or process of going from the simple or basic to the complex or advanced — see DEVELOPMENT 1

**progress** *vb* 1 to become mature — see MATURE
2 to move forward along a course — see GO 1

**progression** *n* 1 a series of things linked together — see CHAIN 1
2 forward movement in time or place — see ADVANCE 1
3 the act or process of going from the simple or basic to the complex or advanced — see DEVELOPMENT 1

**progressive** *adj* 1 being far along in development — see ADVANCED 1
2 not bound by traditional ways or beliefs — see LIBERAL 1

**prohibit** *vb* to order not to do or use or to be done or used — see FORBID

**prohibited** *adj* that may not be permitted — see IMPERMISSIBLE

**prohibiting** *n* the act of ordering that something not be done or used — see PROHIBITION 1

**prohibition** *n* 1 the act of ordering that something not be done or used ⟨the principal's *prohibition* against the use of cell phones in the school building met with unanimous approval by the teachers⟩
*syn* banning, barring, enjoining, forbidding, interdicting, interdiction, outlawing, prohibiting, proscribing, proscription
*rel* bidding, charging, decreeing, dictation, direction, instruction; deterrence, discouragement, dissuading; repression, suppression; coercion, compulsion, constraint, force
*near ant* allowance, permission, sufferance, toleration; approval, endorsement; encouragement, promotion, support; compliance, obedience
2 an order that something not be done or used ⟨the school issued a *prohibition* against wearing clothing with obscene and provocative slogans⟩
*syn* ban, embargo, interdict, interdiction, proscription, veto
*rel* taboo (*also* tabu); injunction; constraint, inhibition, limitation, restraint, restriction; deterrent, discouragement; repression, suppression; prevention; denial, disallowance, negation, refusal, rejection; objection, protest
*near ant* sufferance, tolerance, toleration; allowance, allowing, authorization, consent, granting, leave, letting, license (*or* licence), licensing, permission, permitting, sanctioning; approval, endorsement; enabling, encouragement, facilitation, promotion, support; compliance, obedience; accession, acquiescence, agreement, assent
*ant* prescription

**project** *n* a method worked out in advance for achieving some objective — see PLAN 1

**project** *vb* 1 to extend outward beyond a usual point — see BULGE
2 to work out the details of (something) in advance — see PLAN 1

**projection** *n* a part that sticks out from the general mass of something — see BULGE

**proletarian** *adj* belonging to the class of people of low social or economic rank — see IGNOBLE 1

**proletariat** *n* people looked down upon as ignorant and of the lowest class — see RABBLE

**proliferate** *vb* to become greater in extent, volume, amount, or number — see INCREASE 2

**proliferation** *n* 1 something added (as by growth) — see INCREASE 1
2 the act or process of becoming greater in number — see MULTIPLICATION

**prolific** *adj* producing abundantly — see FERTILE

**prolix** *adj* using or containing more words than necessary to express an idea — see WORDY

**prolixity** *n* the use of too many words to express an idea — see VERBIAGE

**prologue** *n* a short section (as of a book) that leads to or explains the main part — see INTRODUCTION

**prolong** *vb* to make longer — see EXTEND 1

**prolongation** *n* the act of making longer — see EXTENSION 1

**prolonging** *n* the act of making longer — see EXTENSION 1

**prom** *n* a social gathering for dancing — see DANCE

**prominence** *n* an area of high ground — see HEIGHT 4

**prominent** *adj* 1 likely to attract attention — see NOTICEABLE
2 widely known — see FAMOUS

**promiscuous** *adj* consisting of many things of different sorts — see MISCELLANEOUS

**promise** *n* a person's solemn declaration that he or she will do or not do something ⟨he gave a *promise* that he would arrive on time⟩
*syn* oath, pledge, troth, vow, word
*rel* appointment, arrangement, commitment, engagement; compact, contract, covenant; assurance, guarantee, guaranty; bail, bond, deposit, gage, pawn, security, token, warranty

**promise** *vb* 1 to make a solemn declaration of intent ⟨I *promised* not to fight with my sister⟩
*syn* covenant, pledge, swear, vow
*rel* affiance, betroth, plight, troth; accede, agree, assent, consent; contract, engage, guarantee, undertake; affirm, assert, aver, avouch, avow, declare, insist, warrant
*phrases* give one's word
2 to show signs of a favorable or successful outcome — see BODE

**promising** *adj* 1 having qualities which inspire hope — see HOPEFUL 1

2 pointing toward a happy outcome — see FAVORABLE 2

**promontory** *n* 1 an area of high ground jutting out into a body of water beyond the line of the coast — see HEADLAND 1
2 an area of land that juts out into a body of water — see [2]CAPE

**promote** *vb* 1 to move higher in rank or position ⟨the Navy *promoted* her to captain for her record of outstanding performance⟩
*syn* advance, elevate, raise, upgrade
*rel* forward, further; aggrandize, boost, heighten, improve, lift, uplift; commission, ennoble, knight; acclaim, applaud, celebrate, cite, commend, compliment, congratulate, decorate; eulogize, extol (*also* extoll), glorify, hail, honor, laud, praise, salute
*near ant* depose, dethrone, dismiss, expel, impeach, oust, overthrow, remove, unmake, unseat; demean, disgrace, dishonor, humble, humiliate, mortify, shame, take down; censure, condemn, damn, denounce, reprobate
*ant* abase, degrade, demote, downgrade, lower, reduce
2 to help the growth or development of — see FOSTER 1
3 to look after or assist the growth of by labor and care — see GROW 1
4 to provide publicity for — see PUBLICIZE 1

**promoter** *n* a person who actively supports or favors a cause — see EXPONENT

**promotion** *n* a raising or a state of being raised to a higher rank or position — see ADVANCEMENT 1

**prompt** *adj* 1 done, carried out, or given without delay ⟨*prompt* treatment of snakebites is always advisable⟩
*syn* immediate, punctual, timely
*rel* apt, quick, ready, willing; opportune, seasonable; early
*near ant* delinquent, latish, overdue; behind, behindhand, delayed, detained; dilatory, laggard, slow
*ant* belated, late, tardy
2 having or showing the ability to respond without delay or hesitation — see QUICK 1

**prompt** *vb* 1 to be the cause of (a situation, action, or state of mind) — see EFFECT
2 to try to persuade (someone) through earnest appeals to follow a course of action — see URGE

**promptitude** *n* the quality or habit of arriving on time ⟨the teacher's *promptitude* was such that you could set your watch by his morning arrival⟩
*syn* promptness, punctuality, timeliness
*rel* aptness, quickness, readiness, willingness; earliness
*near ant* belatedness, lateness; slowness
*ant* tardiness

**promptly** *adv* without delay — see IMMEDIATELY

**promptness** *n* the quality or habit of arriving on time — see PROMPTITUDE

**promulgate** *vb* to make known openly or publicly — see ANNOUNCE

**prone** *adj* 1 having a tendency to be or act in a certain way ⟨he was *prone* to emotional outbursts under stress⟩
*syn* apt, given, inclined, tending
*rel* choosing, preferring; disposed, likely, predisposed, willing
*near ant* averse, disinclined, indisposed, loath (*or* loth), unwilling
2 lying with the face downwards ⟨stretched out *prone* on the bed for a backrub⟩
*syn* prostrate
*rel* flat, recumbent; reclining, reposing; horizontal
*near ant* erect, raised, standing, upright, upstanding, vertical
*ant* supine

**proneness** *n* an established pattern of behavior — see TENDENCY 1

**pronounced** *adj* 1 likely to attract attention — see NOTICEABLE
2 very noticeable especially for being incorrect or bad — see EGREGIOUS

**pronto** *adv* 1 with great speed — see FAST 1
2 without delay — see IMMEDIATELY

**proof** *n* something presented in support of the truth or accuracy of a claim ⟨she presented *proof* that she had not cheated⟩
*syn* attestation, confirmation, corroboration, documentation, evidence, substantiation, testament, testimony, validation, witness
*rel* (the) goods; certificate, document, exhibit; demonstration, illustration; authentication, identification, manifestation, verification
*near ant* rebuttal, refutation; accusation, allegation, charge; assumption, conjecture, guess, presumption, surmise, suspicion
*ant* disproof

**prop** (up) *vb* 1 to hold up or serve as a foundation for — see SUPPORT 3
2 to provide (someone) with what is useful or necessary to achieve an end — see HELP 1

**propagate** *vb* 1 to bring forth offspring — see PROCREATE
2 to cause to be known over a considerable area or by many people — see SPREAD 1

**propel** *vb* 1 to apply force to (someone or something) so that it moves in front of one — see PUSH 1
2 to cause to function — see ACTIVATE
3 to set or keep in motion — see MOVE 2

**propensity** *n* 1 an established pattern of behavior — see TENDENCY 1
2 a habitual attraction to some activity or thing — see INCLINATION 1

**proper** *adj* 1 following the established traditions of refined society and good taste ⟨the formal ball called for *proper* attire—tuxedos and full-length gowns only⟩
*syn* correct, decent, decorous, genteel, nice, polite, respectable, seemly

*rel* acceptable, adequate, satisfactory, tolerable; dress, dressy, formal; dignified, elegant, gracious; priggish, prim, stuffy; apt, material, relevant; compatible, congenial, harmonious; allowed, authorized, kosher, permitted
*near ant* intolerable, unacceptable, unsatisfactory; casual, grungy, informal; seedy, shabby, tacky; banned, barred, disallowed; forbidden, interdicted, outlawed, prohibited, proscribed; awkward, gauche, ungraceful
*ant* improper, incorrect, indecent, indecorous, unbecoming, unseemly
**2** being in agreement with the truth or a fact or a standard — see CORRECT 1
**3** marked by or showing careful attention to set forms and details — see CEREMONIOUS 1
**4** meeting the requirements of a purpose or situation — see FIT 1
**5** serving to identify as belonging to an individual or group — see CHARACTERISTIC 1

**properly** *adv* in a manner suitable for the occasion or purpose ⟨the scouts were *properly* dressed for a week of camping⟩
*syn* appropriately, congruously, correctly, fittingly, happily, meetly, rightly, suitably
*rel* well; acceptably, adequately, passably, satisfactorily, tolerably; decently, decorously
*near ant* unacceptably, unsatisfactorily; inopportunely, unfortunately, unseasonably; inaptly, irrelevantly; awkwardly, ungracefully
*ant* improperly, inappropriately, incongruously, incorrectly, unsuitably, wrongly

**property** *n* **1** a small piece of land that is developed or available for development — see LOT 1
**2** something that sets apart an individual from others of the same kind — see CHARACTERISTIC

**prophecy** *n* a declaration that something will happen in the future — see PREDICTION

**prophesier** *n* one who predicts future events or developments — see PROPHET

**prophesy** *vb* to tell of or describe beforehand — see FORETELL

**prophet** *n* one who predicts future events or developments ⟨a *prophet* who swore he could see wars before they happened⟩
*syn* augur, diviner, forecaster, foreseer, foreteller, fortune-teller, futurist, prognosticator, prophesier, seer, soothsayer
*rel* prophetess; mystic, oracle; astrologer

**prophetic** *or* **prophetical** *adj* being a sign of a later course of events ⟨the breaking of the cereal bowl was a *prophetic* start to a day filled with accidents and foul-ups⟩
*syn* predictive
*rel* baleful, dire, foreboding, menacing, portentous, sinister, threatening; inauspicious, unpromising; oracular; revelatory, telling
*near ant* auspicious, promising, propitious, rosy

**propitiate** *vb* to lessen the anger or agitation of — see PACIFY

**propitiatory** *adj* tending to lessen or avoid conflict or hostility — see PACIFIC 1

**propitious** *adj* **1** having qualities which inspire hope — see HOPEFUL 1
**2** pointing toward a happy outcome — see FAVORABLE 2

**proponent** *n* a person who actively supports or favors a cause — see EXPONENT

**proportion** *n* **1** a balanced, pleasing, or suitable arrangement of parts — see HARMONY 1
**2** something belonging to, due to, or contributed by an individual member of a group — see SHARE 1
**3** the relationship in quantity, amount, or size between two or more things — see RATIO
**4** the total amount of measurable space or surface occupied by something — see [1]SIZE

**proportional** *adj* corresponding in size, amount, extent, or degree ⟨each child receives an allowance *proportional* to his or her age and needs⟩
*syn* commensurate, proportionate
*rel* balanced, symmetrical; correlative, reciprocal; contingent, dependent, relative; akin, comparable, similar
*phrases* in proportion
*near ant* asymmetrical (*or* asymmetric), distorted, irregular, lopsided, nonsymmetrical, twisted, unsymmetrical; unbalanced
*ant* disproportionate

**proportionate** *adj* corresponding in size, amount, extent, or degree — see PROPORTIONAL

**proposal** *n* something which is presented for consideration ⟨the city council is accepting *proposals* for ways to use that land⟩
*syn* offer, proffer, proposition, suggestion
*rel* feeler, overture; motion; advancement, nomination, recommendation; presentation, submission, tender; arrangement, game, ground plan, layout, line, plan, plot, project, strategy, system; conception, idea, notion, thought

**propose** *vb* **1** to set before the mind for consideration ⟨he *proposed* that we go for a walk this afternoon⟩
*syn* advance, offer, pose, proffer, propound, suggest, vote
*rel* move; nominate, recommend; present, submit, tender; file, lay, lodge; arrange, calculate, chart, contrive, cover, frame, map, plan, plot, shape
*phrases* put forward
**2** to have in mind as a purpose or goal — see INTEND

**proposition** *n* **1** an idea that is the starting point for making a case or conducting an investigation — see THEORY

2 something which is presented for consideration — see PROPOSAL

**propound** *vb* to set before the mind for consideration — see PROPOSE 1

**proprieties** *n pl* personal conduct or behavior as evaluated by an accepted standard of appropriateness for a social or professional setting — see MANNER 1

**proprietor** *n* one who has a legal or rightful claim to ownership ⟨I am the sole *proprietor* of my car⟩
*syn* holder, owner, possessor
*rel* homeowner, landowner
*near ant* squatter; lessee, renter, tenant

**propriety** *n* socially acceptable behavior — see DECENCY 1

**prorate** *vb* to give out (something) in appropriate amounts or to appropriate individuals — see ADMINISTER 1

**prosaic** *adj* 1 being of the type that is encountered in the normal course of events — see ORDINARY 1
2 having to do with the practical details of regular life — see MUNDANE 1

**proscribe** *vb* to order not to do or use or to be done or used — see FORBID

**proscribed** *adj* that may not be permitted — see IMPERMISSIBLE

**proscribing** *n* the act of ordering that something not be done or used — see PROHIBITION 1

**proscription** *n* 1 the act of ordering that something not be done or used — see PROHIBITION 1
2 an order that something not be done or used — see PROHIBITION 2

**proselyte** *n* a person who has recently been persuaded to join a religious sect — see CONVERT 1

**proselytize** *vb* to persuade to change to one's religious faith — see CONVERT 1

**prospect** *n* 1 all that can be seen from a certain point — see VIEW 1
2 one who seeks an office, honor, position, or award — see CANDIDATE

**prospect** *vb* to go into or range over for purposes of discovery — see EXPLORE 2

**prosper** *vb* 1 to grow vigorously — see THRIVE 1
2 to reach a desired level of accomplishment — see SUCCEED 2

**prospering** *adj* marked by vigorous growth and well-being especially economically — see PROSPEROUS 1

**prosperous** *adj* 1 marked by vigorous growth and well-being especially economically ⟨a *prosperous* business that will soon be expanding⟩
*syn* booming, flourishing, golden, palmy, prospering, roaring, successful, thriving
*rel* affluent, moneyed (*or* monied), opulent, rich, substantial, wealthy, well-heeled, well-off, well-to-do; comfortable
*near ant* declining, dying, failing, floundering, languishing, struggling; bankrupt, bankrupted, insolvent
*ant* unsuccessful
2 having attained a desired end or state of good fortune — see SUCCESSFUL 1
3 growing thickly and vigorously — see RANK 1

**prostitute** *n* a woman who engages in sexual activities for money ⟨the town was horrified to discover that she had once been a *prostitute*⟩
*syn* harlot, whore
*rel* coquette, flirt, libertine, siren, tempter, temptress, wench

**prostitute** *vb* 1 to lower in character or dignity — see DEBASE 1
2 to put to a bad or improper use — see MISAPPLY

**prostitution** *n* the practice of engaging in sexual activities for money ⟨*prostitution* is illegal in most states⟩
*syn* harlotry

**prostrate** *adj* 1 depleted in strength, energy, or freshness — see WEARY 1
2 lacking bodily strength — see WEAK 1
3 lying with the face downwards — see PRONE 2

**prostrate** *vb* 1 to diminish the physical strength of — see WEAKEN 1
2 to render powerless, ineffective, or unable to move — see PARALYZE
3 to subject to incapacitating emotional or mental stress — see OVERWHELM 1

**prostrated** *adj* lacking bodily strength — see WEAK 1

**prostration** *n* a complete depletion of energy or strength — see FATIGUE

**protean** *adj* able to do many different kinds of things — see VERSATILE

**protect** *vb* to drive danger or attack away from — see DEFEND 1

**protection** *n* 1 means or method of defending — see DEFENSE 1
2 someone that protects — see PROTECTOR
3 the state of not being exposed to danger — see SAFETY 1

**protective** *adj* intended to resist or prevent attack or aggression — see DEFENSIVE

**protector** *n* someone that protects ⟨a bigger girl served as her *protector* against bullies at school⟩
*syn* custodian, defender, guard, protection
*rel* bodyguard, champion; keeper, lookout, sentinel, sentry, warden, warder, watch, watchdog, watchman; conserver, keeper, preserver, saver

**protest** *n* a feeling or declaration of disapproval or dissent — see OBJECTION

**protest** *vb* 1 to state as a fact usually forcefully — see CLAIM 1
2 to present an opposing opinion or argument — see OBJECT

**protestation** *n* a solemn and often public declaration of the truth or existence of something ⟨the governor went on television to make a passionate *protestation* of his innocence in the bribery scandal⟩
*syn* affirmation, assertion, avouchment, avowal, claim, declaration, insistence, profession
*rel* announcement, declaration, proclamation, pronouncement; argument,

justification, rationalization, reason; confirmation, vindication
*near ant* disclaimer; challenge, dispute, question; confutation, disproof, rebuttal, refutation; contradiction, denial, negation
*ant* disavowal

**prototype** *n* something from which copies are made — see ORIGINAL

**protract** *vb* to make longer — see EXTEND 1

**protrude** *vb* to extend outward beyond a usual point — see BULGE

**protrusion** *n* a part that sticks out from the general mass of something — see BULGE

**protuberance** *n* a part that sticks out from the general mass of something — see BULGE

**proud** *adj* **1** having or displaying feelings of scorn for what is regarded as beneath oneself ⟨the unemployed woman was too *proud* to take a job as a maid⟩
*syn* disdainful, haughty, highfalutin, lofty, lordly, prideful, superior
*rel* complacent, conceited, egoistic, egotistic (*or* egotistical), important, self-assertive, self-conceited, self-important, self-satisfied, smug, uppity, vain, vainglorious; arrogant, pretentious, snobbish, stuck-up, supercilious; cavalier, overbearing, overweening, peremptory, swaggering; high-sounding, pompous; condescending, patronizing; cocky, overconfident, presumptuous; bloated, boastful, bombastic; audacious, bold, brash, brassy, cheeky, cocksure, forward, impertinent, impudent, saucy; confident, presuming, self-assured, self-confident, sure; domineering, high-handed, imperious; self-centered, selfish; dominating, magisterial, masterful
*near ant* demure, homely, meek, unassuming, unpretentious; bashful, retiring, shy, timid; diffident, self-doubting; acquiescent, compliant, deferential, resigned, submissive, unassertive, yielding; apologetic, cowering, cringing, shrinking; passive, quiet, reserved, subdued, unobtrusive
*ant* humble, lowly, modest
**2** having too high an opinion of oneself — see CONCEITED
**3** large and impressive in size, grandeur, extent, or conception — see GRAND 1

**provable** *adj* capable of being proven as true or real — see VERIFIABLE

**prove** *vb* **1** to show the existence or truth of by evidence ⟨the prosecutor used DNA evidence to *prove* the defendant's guilt⟩
*syn* demonstrate, document, establish, substantiate, validate
*rel* back (up), buttress, corroborate; evidence, evince, record, support, witness; adduce, attest, authenticate, certify, identify; confirm, sustain, verify; clinch, nail, settle; depose, testify
*near ant* challenge, dispute, object; allege, assume, conjecture, guess, presume, surmise, suspect
*ant* disprove, rebut, refute
**2** to come to be — see COME OUT 1
**3** to gain full recognition or acceptance of — see ESTABLISH 1

**provender** *n* substances intended to be eaten — see FOOD

**proverb** *n* an often stated observation regarding something from common experience — see SAYING

**provide** *vb* to put (something) into the possession of someone for use or consumption — see FURNISH 2

**provide** (for) *vb* to pay the living expenses of — see SUPPORT 2

**providence** *n* **1** careful management of material resources — see ECONOMY
**2** concern or preparation for the future — see FORESIGHT 2
**3** *cap* the being worshipped as the creator and ruler of the universe — see DEITY 2

**provident** *adj* **1** careful in the management of money or resources — see FRUGAL
**2** having or showing awareness of and preparation for the future — see FORESIGHTED

**providential** *adj* coming or happening by good luck especially unexpectedly — see FORTUNATE 1

**province** *n* a region of activity, knowledge, or influence — see FIELD 2

**provincial** *adj* not broad or open in views or opinions — see NARROW 2

**provincial** *n* an awkward or simple person especially from a small town or the country — see HICK

**provision** *n* **1** something upon which the carrying out of an agreement or offer depends — see CONDITION 2
**2 provisions** *pl* substances intended to be eaten — see FOOD

**provision** *vb* to provide food or meals for — see FEED 1

**provisional** *adj* intended to last, continue, or serve for a limited time — see TEMPORARY 1

**proviso** *n* something upon which the carrying out of an agreement or offer depends — see CONDITION 2

**provocation** *n* **1** something that arouses a strong response from another ⟨Dad only gets angry from the greatest of *provocations*⟩
*syn* excitement, incitement, instigation, stimulant, stimulation, stimulus
*rel* encouragement, goad, incentive, inducement, jog, prod, spur; induction, inspiration, motivation; aggravation, annoyance, bother, exasperation, frustration, hassle, headache, irritant, nuisance, peeve, pest
*near ant* subduing
**2** something that arouses action or activity — see IMPULSE

---

*syn* synonym(s) *rel* related words
*ant* antonym(s) *near ant* near antonym(s)

**provocative** *adj* serving or likely to arouse a strong reaction ⟨a *provocative* editorial that sparked a heated discussion⟩
***syn*** exciting, inciting, instigating, piquing, provoking, stimulating
***rel*** explosive, fiery, incendiary, inflammatory, triggering; inducing, inspirational, inspiring, motivating; jeering, taunting, teasing; activating, energizing, galvanizing, quickening, vitalizing; angering, enraging, maddening, upsetting; aggravating, annoying, bothersome, exasperating, galling, irksome, irritating, pesky, vexatious, vexing
***near ant*** subduing

**provoke** *vb* **1** to rouse to strong feeling or action ⟨his teasing finally *provoked* her to anger⟩ ⟨a strong chilling breeze *provoked* the picnickers to move inside⟩
***syn*** arouse, encourage, excite, fire (up), incite, instigate, move, pique, stimulate, stir
***rel*** fan, inflame, kindle, trigger; activate, energize, galvanize, induce, inspire, motivate, quicken, vitalize; abet, ferment, foment, raise, whip (up); anger, enrage, madden, upset; jeer, taunt, tease; aggravate, annoy, bother, exasperate, gall, get, irritate, vex
***near ant*** calm, soothe, subdue, tranquilize (*also* tranquillize)
**2** to cause or encourage the development of — see INCITE 1

**provoking** *adj* serving or likely to arouse a strong reaction — see PROVOCATIVE

**proximity** *n* the state or condition of being near ⟨the *proximity* of the curtains to the fireplace was a cause of concern to the safety inspector⟩
***syn*** closeness, contiguity, immediacy, nearness
***rel*** abutment, juxtaposition
***ant*** distance, remoteness

**proxy** *n* a person who acts or does business for another — see AGENT 2

**prude** *n* a person who is greatly concerned with seemly behavior and morality especially regarding sexual matters ⟨it's not true that only a *prude* would object to being pressured for physical intimacy⟩
***syn*** moralist, puritan
***rel*** goody-goody; fuddy-duddy, old maid, prig, spoilsport
***near ant*** libertarian, libertine

**prudence** *n* the ability to make intelligent decisions especially in everyday matters — see COMMON SENSE

**prudent** *adj* **1** having or showing good judgment and restraint especially in conduct or speech — see DISCREET
**2** suitable for bringing about a desired result under the circumstances — see EXPEDIENT

**prudery** *n* a tendency to care a great deal about seemly behavior and morals especially in sexual matters ⟨such *prudery* regarding artistic depictions of the nude has no place on a college campus⟩
***syn*** prudishness, puritanism
***rel*** priggishness, primness; morality, virtue
***near ant*** libertarianism

**prudish** *adj* given to or marked by very conservative standards regarding personal behavior or morals — see STRAITLACED

**prudishness** *n* a tendency to care a great deal about seemly behavior and morals especially in sexual matters — see PRUDERY

**prune** *vb* to make (as hair) shorter with or as if with the use of shears — see CLIP

[1]**pry** *vb* **1** to raise, move, or pull apart with or as if with a lever ⟨it took some effort to *pry* up the trap door⟩
***syn*** jimmy, lever, prize
***rel*** elevate, hoist, lift, uplift; break, break up, detach, disengage, disjoin, divide, part, pull, separate; shift
***near ant*** connect, join
**2** to draw out by force or with effort — see EXTRACT

[2]**pry** *vb* to interest oneself in what is not one's concern — see INTERFERE

**prying** *adj* **1** interested in what is not one's own business — see CURIOUS 1
**2** thrusting oneself where one is not welcome or invited — see INTRUSIVE

**psalm** *n* a religious song — see HYMN

**psalmody** *n* a book of hymns — see HYMNAL

**pseudo** *adj* lacking in natural or spontaneous quality — see ARTIFICIAL 1

**pseudonym** *n* a fictitious or assumed name ⟨the most notorious serial killer of the 19th century remains known only by the *pseudonym* of Jack the Ripper⟩
***syn*** alias
***rel*** nom de plume, pen name; appellation, designation; misnomer; epithet, nickname, sobriquet (*also* soubriquet)

**pshaw** *interj* how surprising, doubtful, or unbelievable — see NO

**psyche** *n* an immaterial force within a human being thought to give the body life, energy, and power — see SOUL 1

**psychological** *also* **psychologic** *adj* of or relating to the mind — see MENTAL 1

**psychopath** *n* a person judged to be legally or medically insane — see LUNATIC 1

**psychotic** *n* a person judged to be legally or medically insane — see LUNATIC 1

**pub** *n* a place of business where alcoholic beverages are sold to be consumed on the premises — see BARROOM

**public** *adj* **1** not known by only a select few ⟨it was *public* knowledge that they were expecting a baby⟩
***syn*** open
***rel*** general, popular; unclassified, well-known; advertised, aired, announced, broadcast, declared, disclosed, divulged, heralded, posted, proclaimed, promulgated, publicized, published, spotlighted; current, prevalent, rife, widespread; communal, shared; reported, reputed, rumored

***near ant*** classified; unadvertised, unannounced, undisclosed; clandestine, collusive, conspiratorial, covert; surreptitious, undercover, underhand, underhanded; intimate, personal; concealed, repressed, reserved, silenced, stifled, suppressed, withheld; recanted, retracted, revoked
***ant*** confidential, private, privy, secret
**2** freely available for use or participation by all — see OPEN 2
**3** of or relating to a nation — see NATIONAL
**4** held by or applicable to a majority of the people — see GENERAL 3
**5** used or done by a number of people as a group — see COLLECTIVE

**public** *n* human beings in general — see PEOPLE 1

**public house** *n* **1** a place that provides rooms and usually a public dining room for overnight guests — see HOTEL
**2** *chiefly British* a place of business where alcoholic beverages are sold to be consumed on the premises — see BARROOM

**publicity** *n* newsworthy information released to the media that is designed to gain public attention or support for a person, business, or cause ⟨an endless flow of *publicity* for our charity event resulted in a great turnout⟩
***syn*** ballyhoo
***rel*** ad, advertisement, commercial, message, plug, promotion, spot, word; banner, bill, billboard, placard, poster, sign; advertising, marketing, propaganda; pronouncement, publication, release; broadcast, bulletin, dispatch, newscast, report, story; testimonial, write-up

**publicize** *vb* **1** to provide publicity for ⟨the movie studios widely *publicized* their summer blockbusters⟩
***syn*** ballyhoo, plug, promote, tout
***rel*** advertise; push; acclaim, hail, laud, praise; recommend, review; announce, broadcast, publish
**2** to make known openly or publicly — see ANNOUNCE

**public servant** *n* **1** a person who holds a public office — see OFFICIAL
**2** a worker in a government agency — see BUREAUCRAT

**publish** *vb* **1** to produce and release for distribution in printed form ⟨our local animal shelter *publishes* a newsletter⟩
***syn*** get out, issue, print
***rel*** serialize; contribute, edit, syndicate; manufacture, produce; distribute, market
***near ant*** censor, suppress
**2** to make known openly or publicly — see ANNOUNCE

**puck** *n* an imaginary being usually having a small human form and magical powers — see FAIRY

**puddle** *n* a small often deep body of water — see [1]POOL

**pudginess** *n* the condition of having an excess of body fat — see CORPULENCE

**pudgy** *adj* having an excess of body fat — see FAT 1

**puerile** *adj* **1** having or showing the annoying qualities (as silliness) associated with children — see CHILDISH
**2** lacking in adult experience or maturity — see CALLOW
**3** lacking in seriousness or maturity — see GIDDY 1

**puff** *n* a slight or gentle movement of air — see BREEZE 1

**puff** *vb* to breathe hard, quickly, or with difficulty — see GASP

**pugilist** *n* one that engages in the sport of fighting with the fists — see BOXER

**pugnacious** *adj* feeling or displaying eagerness to fight — see BELLIGERENT

**pugnacity** *n* an inclination to fight or quarrel — see BELLIGERENCE

**puissance** *n* the ability to exert effort for the accomplishment of a task — see POWER 2

**puissant** *adj* having great power or influence — see IMPORTANT 2

**pule** *vb* to utter feeble plaintive cries — see WHIMPER

**pull** *n* **1** the act or an instance of applying force on something so that it moves in the direction of the force ⟨I gave the door such a *pull* that when it suddenly opened, I nearly fell backwards⟩
***syn*** draw, haul, jerk, pluck, tug, wrench, yank
***rel*** drag, tow; hitch, jerk, twitch; grab, snatch
***near ant*** heave, shove, thrust
***ant*** push
**2** the power to direct the thinking or behavior of others usually indirectly — see INFLUENCE 1

**pull** *vb* **1** to cause to follow by applying steady force on ⟨a team of horses *pulling* a heavy wagon⟩
***syn*** drag, draw, hale, haul, lug, tow, tug
***rel*** attract; jerk, yank; carry, convey, ferry, move, transport
***near ant*** shove, thrust
***ant*** drive, propel, push
**2** to draw out by force or with effort — see EXTRACT
**3** to injure by overuse, misuse, or pressure — see STRAIN 1

**pull** (out) *vb* to leave a place often for another — see GO 2

**pulp** *vb* to cause to become a pulpy mass — see CRUSH 1

**pulpiness** *n* the quality or state of being full of juice — see SUCCULENCE

**pulpy** *adj* **1** full of juice — see JUICY
**2** giving easily to the touch — see SOFT 3

**pulsate** *vb* to expand and contract in a rhythmic manner ⟨the heart muscle *pulsates* regularly to pump blood⟩
***syn*** beat, palpitate, pit-a-pat, pitter-patter, pulse, throb
***rel*** fluctuate, oscillate, vibrate; quiver, tremble

**pulsation** *n* a rhythmic expanding and contracting ⟨you should press against the

artery in your wrist and count the *pulsations* to calculate your heart rate〉
***syn*** beat, palpitation, pulse, throb
***rel*** fluctuation, oscillation, vibration; quiver, tremble, tremor

**pulse** *n* a rhythmic expanding and contracting — see PULSATION

**pulse** *vb* to expand and contract in a rhythmic manner — see PULSATE

**pulverize** *vb* **1** to bring to a complete end the physical soundness, existence, or usefulness of — see DESTROY 1
**2** to reduce to fine particles — see POWDER

**puma** *n* a large tawny cat of the wild — see COUGAR

**pummel** *vb* to strike repeatedly — see BEAT 1

**pump** *vb* **1** to make short up-and-down movements — see NOD
**2** to put a series of questions to — see EXAMINE 1
**3** to remove (liquid) gradually or completely — see DRAIN 1

[1]**punch** *n* **1** the quality of an utterance that provokes interest and produces an effect 〈the real *punch* of the speech came in its closing lines〉
***syn*** cogency, effectiveness, force, forcefulness, impact, point
***rel*** payoff; importance, significance; appeal, attraction, charm, fascination
**2** active strength of body or mind — see VIGOR 1
**3** a hard strike with a part of the body or an instrument — see [1]BLOW

[2]**punch** *n* a mark or small hole made by a pointed instrument — see PRICK 1

**punch** *vb* **1** to deliver a blow to (someone or something) usually in a strong vigorous manner — see HIT 1
**2** to make a hole or series of holes in — see PERFORATE
**3** to urge, push, or force onward — see DRIVE 1

**puncheon** *n* an enclosed wooden vessel for holding beverages — see CASK

**punctual** *adj* done, carried out or given without delay — see PROMPT 1

**punctuality** *n* the quality or habit of arriving on time — see PROMPTITUDE

**puncture** *n* a mark or small hole made by a pointed instrument — see PRICK 1

**puncture** *vb* **1** to make a hole or series of holes in — see PERFORATE
**2** to penetrate or hold (something) with a pointed object — see IMPALE

**pungency** *n* **1** a harsh or sharp quality — see EDGE 1
**2** the quality or state of being stimulating to the mind or senses — see PIQUANCY

**pungent** *adj* **1** having a powerfully stimulating odor or flavor — see SHARP 3
**2** marked by the use of wit that is intended to cause hurt feelings — see SARCASTIC
**3** sharp and pleasantly stimulating to the mind or senses — see PIQUANT

**puniness** *n* the quality or state of being little in size — see SMALLNESS

**punish** *vb* to inflict a penalty on for a fault or crime 〈the child was *punished* for breaking dishes on purpose〉 〈if caught, the thief will be severely *punished*〉
***syn*** castigate, chasten, chastise, correct, discipline, penalize
***rel*** assess, charge, dock, fine, impose, levy, mulct; convict, sentence; condemn, damn, denounce; criticize, reprove; wreak
***near ant*** forfeit; get off, ransom, release; commute, reprieve; absolve, acquit, exculpate, exonerate, vindicate
***ant*** excuse, pardon, spare

**punisher** *n* one who inflicts punishment in return for an injury or offense — see NEMESIS 1

**punishment** *n* suffering, loss, or hardship imposed in response to a crime or offense 〈the child's *punishment* was confiscation of his toys for a day〉
***syn*** castigation, chastisement, correction, desert, discipline, nemesis, penalty, wrath
***rel*** reprisal, retaliation, retribution, revenge, vengeance; assessment, charge, fine, mulct; example, sentence; confinement, imprisonment, incarceration; condemnation, damnation, denouncement; criticism, reproof
***near ant*** amnesty, indemnity, pardon, parole; acquittal, exculpation, exoneration, vindication; exemption, immunity, impunity; release; commutation, reprieve; absolution, forgiveness, remission, remitment; condonation, disregard, overlooking

**punitive** *adj* inflicting, involving, or serving as punishment 〈any misbehavior was immediately met with a *punitive* response〉 〈the company had to pay a million dollars in *punitive* damages〉
***syn*** castigating, chastening, chastising, correcting, correctional, corrective, disciplinary, disciplining, penal, penalizing
***rel*** retaliatory, retributive, retributory, revengeful; vengeful, wrathful
***near ant*** compensatory; acquitting, exculpating, exculpatory, exonerating, vindicating; absolving, condoning, pardoning, remitting; commuting, reprieving

**punk** *adj* **1** falling short of a standard — see BAD 1
**2** extremely unsatisfactory — see WRETCHED 1
**3** temporarily suffering from a disorder of the body — see SICK 1

**punk** *n* a violent, brutal person who is often a member of an organized gang — see HOODLUM

**puny** *adj* of a size that is less than average — see SMALL 1

**pupil** *n* **1** one who attends a school — see STUDENT
**2** one who follows the opinions or teachings of another — see FOLLOWER

**puppet** *n* **1** a small figure often of a human being used especially as a child's plaything — see DOLL 1
**2** one that is or can be used to further the purposes of another — see PAWN 1

**purchasable** *adj* open to improper influence and especially bribery — see VENAL
**purchase** *vb* to get possession of (something) by giving money in exchange for — see BUY
**pure** *adj* **1** free from added matter ⟨I'm allergic to any jewelry that isn't *pure* silver⟩ ⟨the solution must be kept *pure* for the experiment to work⟩
*syn* absolute, fine, neat, plain, purified, refined, straight, unadulterated, unalloyed, undiluted, unmixed
*rel* clarified, filtered, refined; clean, uncontaminated, uncorrupted, undefiled, unpolluted, untainted; rendered, tried; concentrated, full-bodied, strong; uncombined
*near ant* befouled, besmirched, contaminated, corrupted, debased, defiled, fouled, polluted, soiled, spoiled, sullied, tainted; amalgamated, blended, coalesced, combined, commingled, compounded, incorporated, intermingled, intermixed, merged, mingled; conjoined, fused, joined, linked, united; cheapened, doctored, watered (down)
*ant* adulterated, alloyed, diluted, impure, mixed
**2** free from any trace of the coarse or indecent — see CHASTE
**3** free from sin — see INNOCENT 1
**4** having no exceptions or restrictions — see ABSOLUTE 2
**purebred** *adj* of unmixed ancestry ⟨that horse is a *purebred* Arabian⟩
*syn* full-blooded, pedigreed, thoroughbred
*rel* inbred
*near ant* crossbred, crossed, hybridized, interbred, outcrossed
*ant* hybrid, mixed, mongrel
**purely** *adv* with purity of thought and deed ⟨the devout girl vowed to live her life *purely* and in the service of God⟩
*syn* chastely, innocently; morally, righteously; modestly, virtuously
*rel* decently, decorously, properly; priggishly, primly, prudishly
*near ant* indecently, obscenely, vulgarly; lasciviously, lewdly, lustfully
*ant* evilly, immorally, impurely, sinfully, wickedly
**purge** *vb* to free from moral guilt or blemish especially ceremonially — see PURIFY 1
**purification** *n* the act or fact of freeing from sin or moral guilt ⟨some people must undergo a ritual *purification* after certain activities⟩
*syn* cleansing, sanctification
*rel* rebirth, regeneration, restoration; grace, redemption, salvation; absolution, forgiveness, remission; acquittal, clearance, clearing, exoneration, vindication; atonement, expiation
*near ant* blasphemy, defilement, desecration, profanation, violation; corruption, debasement, perversion; contamination, pollution, sullying, tarnishing
**purified** *adj* free from added matter — see PURE 1
**purify** *vb* **1** to free from moral guilt or blemish especially ceremonially ⟨Catholics go to confession to be *purified*⟩
*syn* cleanse, purge, sanctify
*rel* amend, improve, refine; heal, regenerate, restore; elevate, ennoble, uplift; absolve, acquit, clear, exonerate, vindicate
*near ant* corrupt, debase, debauch, defile, degrade, demean, deprave, pervert, stain, warp; poison, profane, prostitute; sully, tarnish
**2** to remove usually visible impurities from — see CLARIFY 1
**puritan** *n* a person who is greatly concerned with seemly behavior and morality especially regarding sexual matters — see PRUDE
**puritanical** *adj* given to or marked by very conservative standards regarding personal behavior or morals — see STRAITLACED
**puritanism** *n* a tendency to care a great deal about seemly behavior and morals especially in sexual matters — see PRUDERY
**purity** *n* the quality or state of being morally pure — see CHASTITY
**purlieus** *n pl* the area around a city — see ENVIRONS 1
**purloin** *vb* to take (something) without right and with an intent to keep — see STEAL 1
**purloiner** *n* one who steals — see THIEF
**purport** *n* the idea that is conveyed or intended to be conveyed to the mind by language, symbol, or action — see MEANING 1
**purpose** *n* **1** something that one hopes or intends to accomplish — see GOAL
**2** the action for which a person or thing is specially fitted or used or for which a thing exists — see ROLE
**purposeful** *adj* **1** fully committed to achieving a goal — see DETERMINED 1
**2** made, given, or done with full awareness of what one is doing — see INTENTIONAL
**purposefully** *adv* with full awareness of what one is doing — see INTENTIONALLY
**purposefulness** *n* firm or unwavering adherence to one's purpose — see DETERMINATION 1
**purposely** *adv* with full awareness of what one is doing — see INTENTIONALLY
**purr** *n* a monotonous sound like that of an insect in motion — see HUM
**purse** *n* a container for carrying money and small personal items ⟨I left my *purse* at home, so I can't buy anything after all⟩
*syn* bag, handbag, pocketbook
*rel* billfold, wallet; compact, vanity; poke, pouch, sack; backpack, haversack, knapsack, rucksack
**pursue** *vb* **1** to go after or on the track of — see FOLLOW 2
**2** to go in search of — see SEEK 1

*syn* synonym(s) *rel* related words
*ant* antonym(s) *near ant* near antonym(s)

**pursuing** *n* the act of going after or in the tracks of another — see PURSUIT

**pursuit** *n* the act of going after or in the tracks of another ⟨the constant *pursuit* of the rock band by a horde of screaming fans as they roamed about the city⟩
*syn* chase, chasing, dogging, following, hounding, pursuing, shadowing, tagging, tailing, tracing, tracking, trailing
*rel* tagging along; path, track, trail; search, seeking

**push** *vb* **1** to apply force to (someone or something) so that it moves in front of one ⟨I had to *push* my damaged bike all the way home⟩
*syn* drive, propel, shove, thrust
*rel* impel, move; bear (down), compress, depress, jam, pressure, squash, squeeze, weigh (upon); bulldoze, compel, force, lean (on *or* against), muscle, ram
**2** to force one's way — see PRESS 4

**pushover** *n* something that is easy to do — see CINCH

**pusillanimous** *adj* having or showing a shameful lack of courage — see COWARDLY

[1]**puss** *n slang* the front part of the head — see FACE 1

[2]**puss** *n* a small domestic animal known for catching mice — see CAT 1

**pussy** *n* a small domestic animal known for catching mice — see CAT 1

**pussyfoot** *vb* **1** to avoid giving a definite answer or position — see EQUIVOCATE
**2** to move about in a sly or secret manner — see SNEAK 1

**put** *vb* **1** to arrange something in a certain spot or position — see PLACE 1
**2** to convey in appropriate or telling terms — see PHRASE
**3** to decide the size, amount, number, or distance of (something) without actual measurement — see ESTIMATE 2
**4** to establish or apply as a charge or penalty — see IMPOSE

**put by** *vb* to put (something of future use or value) in a safe or secret place — see HOARD

**put–down** *n* **1** an act or expression showing scorn and usually intended to hurt another's feelings — see INSULT
**2** the act of making a person or a thing seem little or unimportant — see DEPRECIATION

**put down** *vb* **1** to express scornfully one's low opinion of — see DECRY 1
**2** to make a written note of — see RECORD 1
**3** to put (someone or something) on a list — see [1]LIST 2
**4** to put a stop to (something) by the use of force — see QUELL 1

**put in** *vb* to put or set into the ground to grow — see PLANT

**put off** *vb* **1** to assign to a later time — see POSTPONE
**2** to rid oneself of (a garment) — see REMOVE 1

**put–on** *adj* lacking in natural or spontaneous quality — see ARTIFICIAL 1

**put–on** *n* a display of emotion or behavior that is insincere or intended to deceive — see MASQUERADE

**put on** *vb* **1** to place on one's person ⟨I *put on* a coat and shoes to go outside⟩
*syn* don, slip (on *or* into), throw (on)
*rel* apparel, array, attire, bedeck, bedizen, bundle up, caparison, clothe, doll up, dress, garb, rig, robe, suit, trick, uniform; overdress
*near ant* disrobe, strip, undress
*ant* doff, remove, take off
**2** to describe or express in too strong terms — see OVERSTATE
**3** to present a false appearance of — see FEIGN

**put out** *vb* **1** to bring to bear especially forcefully or effectively — see EXERT
**2** to cause to cease burning — see EXTINGUISH 1
**3** to disturb the peace of mind of (someone) especially by repeated disagreeable acts — see IRRITATE 1

**putrefaction** *n* the process by which dead organic matter separates into simpler substances — see CORRUPTION 1

**putrefied** *adj* having undergone organic breakdown — see ROTTEN 1

**putrefy** *vb* to go through decomposition — see DECAY 1

**putrid** *adj* having undergone organic breakdown — see ROTTEN 1

**putter** (around) *vb* to spend time in aimless activity — see FIDDLE (AROUND)

**putterer** *n* a person who regularly or occasionally engages in an activity without being or becoming an expert at it — see AMATEUR

**put up** *vb* **1** to fix in an upright position — see ERECT 1
**2** to form by putting together parts or materials — see BUILD
**3** to offer for sale to the public — see MARKET
**4** to provide with living quarters or shelter — see HOUSE 1

**puzzle** *n* something hard to understand or explain — see MYSTERY

**puzzle** *vb* to throw into a state of mental uncertainty — see CONFUSE 1

**puzzle** (out) *vb* to find an answer for through reasoning — see SOLVE

**puzzlement** *n* **1** a state of mental uncertainty — see CONFUSION 1
**2** something hard to understand or explain — see MYSTERY

**pygmy** *adj* of a size that is less than average — see SMALL 1

**pygmy** *n* a living thing much smaller than others of its kind — see DWARF 1

# Q

**quack** *n* one who makes false claims of identity or expertise — see IMPOSTOR

**quadrangle** *n* an open space wholly or partly enclosed (as by buildings or walls) — see COURT 2

**quaff** *n* the portion of a serving of a beverage that is swallowed at one time — see DRINK 2

**quaff** *vb* to swallow in liquid form — see DRINK 1

**quail** *vb* **1** to draw back in fear, pain, or disgust — see FLINCH
**2** to draw back or crouch down in fearful submission — see COWER

**quaint** *adj* **1** different from the ordinary in a way that causes curiosity or suspicion — see ODD 2
**2** pleasantly reminiscent of an earlier time — see OLD-FASHIONED 1

**quake** *n* a shaking of the earth — see EARTHQUAKE

**quake** *vb* to make a series of small irregular or violent movements — see SHAKE 1

**quaking** *adj* marked by or given to small uncontrollable bodily movements — see SHAKY 1

**qualification** *n* **1** a skill, an ability, or knowledge that makes a person able to do a particular job ⟨the fashion firm was looking for an applicant who could list superior sewing skills among his or her *qualifications*⟩
***syn*** capability, credentials, stuff
***rel*** command, expertise, mastery, proficiency; ability, capacity, competence, competency, facility, faculty; flair, genius, gift, talent; forte, specialty; fitness, suitability, suitableness; makings, potentiality
**2** something upon which the carrying out of an agreement or offer depends — see CONDITION 2

**qualified** *adj* having the required skills for an acceptable level of performance — see COMPETENT

**qualify** *vb* **1** to limit the meaning of (as a noun) ⟨*qualifying* the noun "adventure" in the title of your story with a descriptive adjective would make it more attention-grabbing⟩
***syn*** modify, restrict
***rel*** alter, distort, twist; narrow; compare, conjugate, decline, inflect
***near ant*** broaden, expand, widen
**2** to make competent (as by training, skill, or ability) for a particular office or function ⟨raising five children has *qualified* her to be an advice columnist on parenting⟩
***syn*** equip, fit, prepare, ready, season
***rel*** accustom, adapt, adjust, condition, groom, habituate, shape, tailor, train; authorize, entitle; empower, enable
**3** to give a right to — see ENTITLE 1
**4** to give official or legal power to — see AUTHORIZE 1

**quality** *n* **1** degree of excellence ⟨we expect a high *quality* of service in such a fancy restaurant⟩
***syn*** caliber (*or* calibre), class, grade, rate
***rel*** hallmark, standard; mark; footing, place, position, rank, standing, stature, status
**2** high position within society — see RANK 2
**3** something that sets apart an individual from others of the same kind — see CHARACTERISTIC

**qualm** *n* an uneasy feeling about the rightness of what one is doing or going to do ⟨she had no *qualms* about selling her old term papers to other students, even though it was against the academic honor code⟩
***syn*** compunction, misgiving, scruple
***rel*** conscience; distrust, doubt, mistrust, suspicion, uncertainty; qualmishness, unease, uneasiness; reluctance, unwillingness; demur, objection, protest; guilt, regret, remorse, self-reproach, shame; contrition, penitence, repentance
***near ant*** aplomb, assurance, certainty, certitude, confidence, conviction, self-assurance, self-confidence, sureness

**qualmish** *adj* affected with nausea — see NAUSEOUS

**qualmishness** *n* **1** a disturbed condition of the stomach in which one feels like vomiting — see NAUSEA 1
**2** the tendency to be or state of being squeamish — see DELICACY 3

**quandary** *n* a situation in which one has to choose between two or more equally unsatisfactory choices — see DILEMMA

**quantity** *n* **1** a considerable amount — see LOT 2
**2** a given or particular mass or aggregate of matter — see AMOUNT

**quarrel** *n* an often noisy or angry expression of differing opinions — see ARGUMENT 1

**quarrel** *vb* to express different opinions about something often angrily — see ARGUE 2

**quarreler** *or* **quarreller** *n* a person who takes part in a dispute — see DISPUTANT

**quarrelsome** *adj* **1** feeling or displaying eagerness to fight — see BELLIGERENT
**2** given to arguing — see ARGUMENTATIVE 1

---

***syn*** synonym(s) ***rel*** related words
***ant*** antonym(s) ***near ant*** near antonym(s)

**quarry** *n* an animal that is hunted or killed — see PREY

**quarter** *n* **1** an area (as of a city) set apart for some purpose or having some special feature — see DISTRICT
**2** kind, gentle, or compassionate treatment especially towards someone who is undeserving of it — see MERCY 1
**3** the place where someone is assigned to stand or remain — see STATION 1
**4 quarters** *pl* the place where one lives — see HOME 1

**quarter** *vb* to provide with living quarters or shelter — see HOUSE 1

[1]**quash** *vb* to put a stop to (something) by the use of force — see QUELL 1

[2]**quash** *vb* to put an end to by formal action — see ABOLISH

**quaver** *vb* to sing with the alternation of two musical tones — see WARBLE

**quavery** *adj* marked by or given to small uncontrollable bodily movements — see SHAKY 1

**quay** *n* a structure used by boats and ships for taking on or landing cargo and passengers — see DOCK

**queasiness** *n* **1** a disturbed condition of the stomach in which one feels like vomiting — see NAUSEA 1
**2** the tendency to be or state of being squeamish — see DELICACY 3

**queasy** *also* **queazy** *adj* affected with nausea — see NAUSEOUS

**queenly** *adj* fit for or worthy of a royal ruler — see MONARCHICAL

**queer** *adj* **1** affected with nausea — see NAUSEOUS
**2** different from the ordinary in a way that causes curiosity or suspicion — see ODD 2
**3** noticeably different from what is generally found or experienced — see UNUSUAL 1

**queerish** *adj* **1** affected with nausea — see NAUSEOUS
**2** different from the ordinary in a way that causes curiosity or suspicion — see ODD 2

**queerness** *n* a disturbed condition of the stomach in which one feels like vomiting — see NAUSEA 1

**quell** *vb* **1** to put a stop to (something) by the use of force ⟨the National Guard was called in to help *quell* the late-night disturbances downtown⟩
***syn*** clamp down (on), crack down (on), crush, put down, quash, repress, silence, snuff (out), squash, squelch, subdue, suppress
***rel*** douse, extinguish, put out, quench; smother, stifle, strangle; annihilate, destroy, smash; exterminate, obliterate, wipe out; conquer, overcome, overwhelm, subjugate, vanquish
***near ant*** abet, aid, assist, help, support; incite, instigate, provoke, stir; advance, encourage, foster, further, promote
**2** to stop the noise or speech of — see SILENCE 1

**quench** *vb* **1** to cause to cease burning — see EXTINGUISH 1
**2** to put a complete end to (a physical need or desire) — see SATISFY 1

**quencher** *n* a liquid suitable for drinking — see DRINK 1

**querulous** *adj* given to complaining a lot — see FUSSY 1

**query** *n* an act or instance of asking for information — see QUESTION 2

**query** *vb* **1** to demand proof of the truth or rightness of — see CHALLENGE 1
**2** to put a question or questions to — see ASK 1
**3** to put a series of questions to — see EXAMINE 1

**quest** *n* an act or process of looking carefully or thoroughly for someone or something — see SEARCH

**quest** *vb* **1** to ask for (something) earnestly or with authority — see DEMAND 1
**2** to go in search of — see SEEK 1
**3** to make a request for — see ASK (FOR) 1

**question** *n* **1** an interrogative expression often used to test knowledge ⟨because I have missed so many classes, I had a hard time answering every *question* on today's surprise quiz⟩
***syn*** problem
***rel*** brainteaser, conundrum, poser, puzzle, quiz, riddle, stickler, stumper
***near ant*** answer, response, solution
**2** an act or instance of asking for information ⟨after reading the brief statement to the reporters, the lawyer ended the press conference by saying, "No more *questions*, please"⟩ ⟨the dozens of *questions* researched by the reference librarians⟩
***syn*** call, inquiry, request, query
***rel*** questionnaire, survey; inquisition, interrogating, interrogation, questioning
**3** a feeling or declaration of disapproval or dissent — see OBJECTION
**4** a major object of interest or concern (as in a discussion or artistic composition) — see MATTER 1

**question** *vb* **1** to demand proof of the truth or rightness of — see CHALLENGE 1
**2** to give serious and careful thought to — see PONDER
**3** to have no trust or confidence in — see DISTRUST
**4** to put a question or questions to — see ASK 1
**5** to put a series of questions to — see EXAMINE 1

**questionable** *adj* **1** giving good reason for being doubted, questioned, or challenged — see DOUBTFUL 2
**2** not likely to be true or to occur — see IMPROBABLE
**3** open to question or dispute — see DEBATABLE 1

**questioner** *n* a person who is always ready to doubt or question the truth or existence of something — see SKEPTIC

**questioning** *adj* inclined to doubt or question claims — see SKEPTICAL 1

**queue** *n* a series of persons or things arranged one behind another — see LINE 1

**quibble** *vb* to make often peevish criticisms or objections about matters that are minor, unimportant, or irrelevant ⟨he spent the entire evening *quibbling* about the historical inaccuracies in the television series on World War II⟩
***syn*** carp, cavil, fuss, nitpick
***rel*** criticize, fault; beef, bellyache, complain, crab, croak, gripe, grouse, growl, grumble, moan, squawk, wail, whine, yammer; murmur, mutter
***phrases*** split hairs
***near ant*** applaud, commend, compliment, praise, recommend; approve, back, endorse (*also* indorse), support

**quick** *adj* **1** having or showing the ability to respond without delay or hesitation ⟨she was a *quick* wit, always ready with a pun or joke when the moment called for one⟩
***syn*** alacritous, alert, expeditious, prompt, ready, willing
***rel*** receptive, responsive; immediate, instant, instantaneous, summary; fast, hit-and-run, rapid, speedy, swift; eager, keen, sharp; apt, clever, smart
***near ant*** unresponsive; dull, indolent, laggard, lazy, logy, slothful, slow, sluggish, tardy; dormant, idle, inactive, inert
**2** having or showing quickness of mind — see INTELLIGENT 1
**3** moving, proceeding, or acting with great speed — see FAST 1

**quick** *adv* with great speed — see FAST 1

**quick** *n* the seat of one's deepest thoughts and emotions — see CORE 1

**quicken** *vb* **1** to cause to move or proceed fast or faster — see HURRY 1
**2** to give life, vigor, or spirit to — see ANIMATE

**quickly** *adv* with great speed — see FAST 1

**quickness** *n* a high rate of movement or performance — see SPEED

**quick–tempered** *adj* easily irritated or annoyed — see IRRITABLE

**quick–witted** *adj* having or showing quickness of mind — see INTELLIGENT 1

**quiescence** *n* **1** a state of temporary inactivity — see ABEYANCE
**2** lack of action or activity — see INACTION

**quiescent** *adj* slow to move or act — see INACTIVE 1

**quiet** *adj* **1** free from disturbing noise or uproar ⟨left the din of the rock concert and went to a *quiet* restaurant where we could hear one another talk⟩
***syn*** calm, hushed, peaceful, restful, serene, still, stilly, tranquil
***rel*** noiseless, silent, soundless; speechless, wordless; dead, motionless, quiescent; muffled, muted, quieted
***near ant*** crazy, tempestuous, wild
***ant*** boisterous, clamorous, clattery, deafening, loud, noisy, raucous, rip-roaring, roistering, romping, rowdy, tumultuous, uproarious, woolly (*also* wooly)
**2** not excessively showy ⟨she decided to wear a *quiet* business suit to the interview instead of her blue satin party dress⟩
***syn*** conservative, muted, restrained, subdued, toned-down, understated, unpretentious
***rel*** appropriate, fit, fitting, proper, suitable; modest, plain, simple, unadorned; inconspicuous, unobtrusive; tasteful; drab, mousy (*or* mousey); practical, sensible
***near ant*** meretricious; graceless, inelegant, tacky, tasteless, vulgar; baroque, fancy, frilly, gilded, ornate, rococo; overdecorated, overdone, overwrought
***ant*** flamboyant, flashy, garish, gaudy, glitzy, loud, ostentatious, splashy, swank (*or* swanky), tawdry
**3** free from storms or physical disturbance — see CALM 1
**4** hidden from view — see SECLUDED
**5** mostly or entirely without sound — see SILENT 3
**6** not loud in pitch or volume — see SOFT 1

**quiet** *n* **1** a state of freedom from storm or disturbance — see CALM
**2** the near or complete absence of sound — see SILENCE 2

**quiet** *adv* without motion — see STILL 1

**quiet** *vb* **1** to become still and orderly ⟨told his rowdy class to *quiet* down during the lesson⟩
***syn*** calm (down), cool, hush, settle (down)
***rel*** relax, tranquilize (*also* tranquillize), unwind
***near ant*** agitate, discompose, disrupt, disturb, provoke, rile, ruffle, stir; annoy, irritate
***ant*** act up, carry on, cut up
**2** to free from distress or disturbance — see CALM 1

**quiet** (down) *vb* to stop talking — see SHUT UP

**quieted** *adj* mostly or entirely without sound — see SILENT 3

**quieting** *adj* tending to calm the emotions and relieve stress — see SOOTHING 1

**quietly** *adv* without motion — see STILL 1

**quietness** *n* **1** a state of freedom from storm or disturbance — see CALM
**2** the near or complete absence of sound — see SILENCE 2

**quietude** *n* **1** a state of freedom from storm or disturbance — see CALM
**2** the near or complete absence of sound — see SILENCE 2

**quietus** *n* **1** a freeing from an obligation or responsibility — see RELEASE 1
**2** the permanent stopping of all the vital bodily activities — see DEATH 1

**quintessence** *n* **1** the most perfect type or example ⟨the Parthenon in Greece was considered the *quintessence* of the perfectly proportioned building⟩
***syn*** beau ideal, classic, epitome, exemplar, ideal, perfection

---

***syn*** synonym(s) ***rel*** related words
***ant*** antonym(s) ***near ant*** near antonym(s)

*rel* archetype, model, prototype; paradigm, standard; nonpareil, paragon; embodiment, incarnation, personification; acme, height, last word, ultimate, zenith
**2** the quality or qualities that make a thing what it is — see ESSENCE

**quintessential** *adj* constituting, serving as, or worthy of being a pattern to be imitated — see MODEL

**quip** *n* something said or done to cause laughter — see JOKE 1

**quip** *vb* to make jokes — see JOKE

**quirk** *n* an odd or peculiar habit — see IDIOSYNCRASY

**quirky** *adj* different from the ordinary in a way that causes curiosity or suspicion — see ODD 2

**quisling** *n* one who betrays a trust or an allegiance — see TRAITOR

**quit** *adj* no longer burdened with something unpleasant or painful — see FREE 2

**quit** *vb* **1** to give up (a job or office) ⟨decided to *quit* his job at the fast-food restaurant⟩
*syn* leave, resign (from), retire (from), step down (from)
*rel* abandon, vacate; drop out (of), throw up
*phrases* give notice
*near ant* hire (out *or* on)
*ant* stay (at)
**2** to stop doing (something) permanently ⟨told her it was high time she *quit* smoking⟩
*syn* discontinue, drop, give up, knock off, lay off (of)
*rel* break off, break up, close, conclude, end, expire, finish; pause, taper off; throw up; cease, desist, leave off
*phrases* have done (with)
*near ant* go, run on; hang on, hold on, persevere, persist; follow through, see out; resume; preserve, stay
*ant* carry on, continue, keep, keep up, maintain
**3** to bring (as an action or operation) to an immediate end — see STOP 1
**4** to cause to remain behind — see LEAVE 1
**5** to cease resistance (as to another's arguments, demands, or control) — see YIELD 3
**6** to come to an end — see CEASE 1
**7** to give what is owed for — see PAY 2
**8** to leave a place often for another — see GO 2
**9** to manage the actions of (oneself) in a particular way — see BEHAVE

**quite** *adv* **1** to a full extent or degree — see FULLY 1
**2** to some degree or extent — see FAIRLY

**quittance** *n* **1** a freeing from an obligation or responsibility — see RELEASE 1
**2** payment to another for a loss or injury — see COMPENSATION 1

**quitting** *n* the act of leaving a place — see DEPARTURE

**quiver** *n* an instance of shaking involuntarily with fear or cold — see SHIVER 1

**quiver** *vb* to make a series of small irregular or violent movements — see SHAKE 1

**quivering** *n* a series of slight movements by a body back and forth or from side to side — see VIBRATION

**quiz** *vb* **1** to put a question or questions to — see ASK 1
**2** to put a series of questions to — see EXAMINE 1

**quiz** *n* **1** a person who causes repeated emotional pain, distress, or annoyance to another — see TORMENTOR
**2** a set of questions or problems designed to assess knowledge, skills, or intelligence — see EXAMINATION 1

**quizzer** *n* a person who causes repeated emotional pain, distress, or annoyance to another — see TORMENTOR

**quizzical** *adj* marked by or expressive of mild or good-natured teasing ⟨my puns are usually greeted with loud *quizzical* groans by my so-called friends⟩
*syn* bantering, chaffing, fooling, funning, jesting, joking, joshing, kidding, rallying, razzing, ribbing
*rel* bandying, quipping; deriding, derisive, derisory, jeering, mocking, ridiculing, taunting; contemptuous, sarcastic, scornful

**quota** *n* something belonging to, due to, or contributed by an individual member of a group — see SHARE 1

**quotation** *n* a passage referred to, repeated, or offered as an example ⟨the beautiful autumn day brought to mind this *quotation* from Thoreau: "So live in each season as it passes; breathe the air, drink the drink, taste the fruit, and resign yourself to the influences of each"⟩
*syn* citation, quote
*rel* allusion, reference; excerpt, extract; line, part, section

**quote** *n* a passage referred to, repeated, or offered as an example — see QUOTATION

**quote** *vb* **1** to give as an example ⟨I could *quote* to you a hundred instances in the past when you've lied to me⟩
*syn* adduce, cite, instance, mention
*rel* exemplify, represent; illustrate, refer (to); document, substantiate
**2** to make reference to or speak about briefly but specifically — see MENTION 1
**3** to say after another — see REPEAT 3

# R

**rabble** *n* people looked down upon as ignorant and of the lowest class ⟨the crown prince was reminded that even the *rabble* of the realm deserved his attention and compassion⟩
***syn*** proletariat, riffraff, scum, trash
***rel*** dregs; herd, masses, mob, people, populace, public, rank and file; bourgeoisie, middle class, working class
***near ant*** elect, establishment; gentlefolk, nobility
***ant*** aristocracy, elite, gentry, society, upper class, upper crust

**rabble–rouser** *n* a person who stirs up public feelings especially of discontent — see AGITATOR

**rabid** *adj* **1** being very far from the center of public opinion — see EXTREME 2
**2** feeling or showing anger — see ANGRY
**3** marked by bursts of destructive force or intense activity — see VIOLENT 1
**4** marked by great and often stressful excitement or activity — see FURIOUS 1

**race** *n* a group of persons who come from the same ancestor — see FAMILY 1

**race** *vb* **1** to engage in a contest — see COMPETE
**2** to proceed or move quickly — see HURRY 2

**raceway** *n* an open man-made passageway for water — see CHANNEL 1

**racial** *adj* of, relating to, or reflecting the traits exhibited by a group of people with a common ancestry and culture ⟨humanitarian aid workers are often given special training to help them understand the *racial* differences between them and the people they will be serving⟩
***syn*** ethnic, tribal
***rel*** familial; folk; kin, kindred; cultural, multicultural, national

**racialism** *n* **1** the belief that certain races of people are by birth and nature superior to others — see RACISM 1
**2** hatred of or discrimination against a person or persons based on their race — see RACISM 2

**racialist** *n* a person who believes that one race should control all others — see SUPREMACIST

**racism** *n* **1** the belief that certain races of people are by birth and nature superior to others ⟨Hitler's declaration of his belief in a "master race" was the first indication of the inherent *racism* of the Nazi movement⟩
***syn*** racialism
***rel*** apartheid, segregation; eugenics
***near ant*** desegregation, integration
**2** hatred of or discrimination against a person or persons based on their race ⟨the 1963 bombing of the Sixteenth Street Baptist Church in Birmingham, Alabama, was one of the most notorious incidents of *racism* that occurred during the civil rights movement of the 1960s⟩
***syn*** prejudice, racialism
***rel*** apartheid, jim crow, segregation; bigotry, intolerance, narrow-mindedness, narrowness

**racist** *n* a person who believes that one race should control all others — see SUPREMACIST

**rack** *vb* **1** to cause persistent suffering to — see AFFLICT
**2** to injure by overuse, misuse, or pressure — see STRAIN 1

**racket** *n* **1** a scheme in which the victim is cheated out of his money after first gaining his trust — see CONFIDENCE GAME
**2** loud, confused, and usually unharmonious sound — see NOISE 1

**racketeer** *n* a person who gets money from another by using force or threats ⟨the *racketeer* threatened to have his thugs vandalize the shop if the shopkeeper didn't pay him a monthly bribe⟩
***syn*** blackmailer, extortioner, extortionist
***rel*** crook, gangster, hoodlum, mafioso, mobster; bully, ruffian, thug; cheat, cheater, chiseler, confidence man, defrauder, double-dealer, gouger, gyp, hustler, profiteer, shark, sharper, swindler

**racking** *adj* intensely or unbearably painful — see EXCRUCIATING 1

**rack up** *vb* to gain (as points or runs in a game) as credit towards one's total number of points — see SCORE 2

**racy** *adj* **1** having much high-spirited energy and movement — see LIVELY 1
**2** hinting at or intended to call to mind matters regarded as indecent — see SUGGESTIVE 1

**radiance** *n* **1** the quality or state of having or giving off light — see BRILLIANCE 1
**2** the steady giving off of the form of radiation that makes vision possible — see LIGHT 1

**radiant** *adj* **1** having or being an outward sign of good feelings (as of love, confidence, or happiness) ⟨left the interview with a *radiant* smile on her face, confident she had gotten the job⟩ ⟨a *radiant* bride⟩
***syn*** aglow, beaming, glowing, sunny
***rel*** brilliant, dazzling, effulgent, gleaming, luminous, refulgent, shining, starry; blithe, blithesome, bright, cheerful, cheery, chipper, gay, gladsome, lightsome, merry, mirthful, optimistic, up-

---

***syn*** synonym(s) ***rel*** related words
***ant*** antonym(s) ***near ant*** near antonym(s)

beat; jocund, jovial, laughing, smiling; blooming, rosy
*near ant* flat, listless, stoic (*or* stoical), unemotional; dark, darkening, depressing, dismal, gloomy, glum, gray (*also* grey), melancholy, sullen; frowning, glaring, glowering, lowering (*also* louring), scowling
**2** giving off or reflecting much light — see BRIGHT 1

**radiate** *vb* **1** to extend outwards from or as if from a central point ⟨the heat *radiating* from the fire⟩ ⟨the spokes of a bicycle wheel *radiate* from the hub towards the rim⟩
*syn* branch, diverge, fan (out)
*rel* diffuse, dispel, disperse, dissipate; fork, stem; divide, separate, split; scatter, splay, spread; arise, derive, emanate, flow, issue, proceed, spring
*near ant* approach, close in (on), near; center (on), centralize
*ant* concentrate, converge, focus, funnel, meet
**2** to emit rays of light — see SHINE 1

**radical** *adj* **1** being very far from the center of public opinion — see EXTREME 2
**2** not bound by traditional ways or beliefs — see LIBERAL 1

**radical** *n* a person who favors rapid and sweeping changes especially in laws and methods of government ⟨*radicals* staged large, violent protests in the hopes of toppling the government⟩
*syn* extremist, revolutionary, revolutionist
*rel* leftist, red; progressive, reformer; anarchist, subversive; agitator, insurgent, insurrectionist, rebel; secessionist, separatist
*near ant* conservative, reactionary, rightist, Tory
*ant* moderate

**raffish** *adj* lacking in refinement or good taste — see COARSE 2

**raffishness** *n* the quality or state of lacking refinement or good taste — see VULGARITY 1

**raft** *n* a considerable amount — see LOT 2

**rage** *n* **1** a state of wildly excited activity or emotion — see FRENZY
**2** an intense emotional state of displeasure with someone or something — see ANGER
**3** a practice or interest that is very popular for a short time — see FAD

**rage** *vb* **1** to express one's anger usually violently ⟨the bad call prompted the coach to *rage* about the refereeing, even throwing his clipboard at one referee⟩
*syn* bristle, fume, storm
*rel* blow up, flare (up), flip; bluster, carry on, fulminate, rampage, rant, rave, take on; burn, foam, seethe, smolder, steam; chafe, fret, stew
*near ant* allay, appease, pacify, soothe; check, collect, compose, contain, curb, hold in, rein, repress, restrain, smother, subdue, suppress; moderate, tone (down), temper; ease, let up, relax; calm, cool, hush, quell, quiet, settle, still
**2** to be excited or emotionally stirred up with anger — see BOIL 1

**ragged** *adj* **1** having an uneven edge or outline ⟨the Rocky Mountains cut an angular, *ragged* profile against the sky, in contrast to the rounded silhouette of the rolling, green Adirondack Mountains⟩
*syn* broken, craggy, jagged, scraggly, scraggy
*rel* saw-toothed, serrate, serrated; harsh, rough, rugged; irregular, nonuniform
*near ant* regular, uniform; flat, level, plane
*ant* clean, even, smooth, unbroken
**2** worn or torn into or as if into rags ⟨finally convinced her to throw away her favorite pair of jeans, *ragged* from decades of yard work⟩
*syn* frayed, raggedy, ratty, seedy, shabby, tattered, threadbare, worn-out
*rel* dowdy, scruffy; dingy, faded; shredded; holey, patchy
**3** not having a level or smooth surface — see UNEVEN 1
**4** wearing torn or worn out clothes — see TATTERED 1

**raggedy** *adj* **1** wearing torn or worn out clothes — see TATTERED 1
**2** worn or torn into or as if into rags — see RAGGED 2

**rags** *n pl* covering for the human body — see CLOTHING

**ragtag** *adj* wearing torn or worn out clothes — see TATTERED 1

**raid** *n* **1** a sudden attack on and entrance into hostile territory ⟨repeated Viking *raids* wore down the defenses of the seaside village⟩
*syn* descent, foray, incursion, inroad, invasion, irruption
*rel* pillage, plunder; aggression, assault, offense (*or* offence), offensive, onset, onslaught, siege, storm, strike; charge, sally, sortie; ambuscade, ambush, surprise; air raid, blitz, blitzkrieg, bombardment
**2** the act or action of setting upon with force or violence — see ATTACK 1

**raid** *vb* **1** to enter for conquest or plunder — see INVADE
**2** to take sudden, violent action against — see ATTACK 1

**raider** *n* one that starts armed conflict against another especially without reasonable cause — see AGGRESSOR

**rail** *n* **1** a protective barrier consisting of a horizontal bar and its supports — see RAILING
**2** a roadway overlaid with parallel steel rails over which trains travel — see RAILROAD

**rail** (at *or* against) *vb* to criticize (someone) severely or angrily especially for personal failings — see SCOLD

**railer** *n* a person given to harsh judgments and to finding faults — see CRITIC 1

**railing** *n* a protective barrier consisting of a horizontal bar and its supports ⟨had to

put a *railing* on the balcony when the baby started walking⟩
*syn* balustrade, banister, guardrail, rail
*rel* handrail; taffrail; bar; fender

**raillery** *n* good-natured teasing or exchanging of clever remarks — see BANTER

**railroad** *n* a roadway overlaid with parallel steel rails over which trains travel ⟨Grandpa used to walk along the main *railroad* in town to get to school⟩
*syn* rail, railway, road
*rel* el, elevated, elevated railroad; monorail

**railway** *n* a roadway overlaid with parallel steel rails over which trains travel — see RAILROAD

**raiment** *n* covering for the human body — see CLOTHING

**rain** *n* **1** a steady falling of water from the sky in significant quantity ⟨Mom yelled at us to come in out of the *rain* before we caught cold⟩
*syn* cloudburst, deluge, downpour, rainfall, rainstorm, storm, wet
*rel* precipitation, shower; thunderstorm
*near ant* drizzle, mist, sprinkle
**2** a heavy fall of objects ⟨the Norman invaders fled when the castle's defenders threw a *rain* of stones down upon them⟩
*syn* hail, shower, storm
*rel* barrage, broadside, cannonade, fusillade, salvo, volley; flood, gush, rush, spate, torrent; eruption, outbreak, outburst

**rain** *vb* **1** to fall as water in a continuous stream of drops from the clouds ⟨it started *raining* this morning and hasn't let up since⟩
*syn* pour, precipitate, storm
*rel* shower; hail, squall; deluge, flood
*phrases* rain cats and dogs
*near ant* drizzle, mist, spit, sprinkle
**2** to give readily and in large quantities ⟨she *rained* praise upon her graduating students⟩ ⟨the squadron *rained* bombs on the enemy's fortifications⟩
*syn* heap, lavish, pour, shower
*rel* gush, stream; flood, inundate, overflow; bombard, hail
*near ant* hold back, keep, reserve, retain, withhold

**raincoat** *n* a coat made of water-resistant material ⟨grabbed my umbrella and *raincoat* before going out in the thunderstorm⟩
*syn* mackintosh (*or* macintosh) [*chiefly British*], oilskin, slicker, waterproof [*chiefly British*]
*rel* rainwear; poncho, sou'wester, trench coat

**rainfall** *n* a steady falling of water from the sky in significant quantity — see RAIN 1

**rainstorm** *n* a steady falling of water from the sky in significant quantity — see RAIN 1

**rainy** *adj* marked by or abounding with rain ⟨found that the cold, *rainy* weather made his joints swell and ache⟩
*syn* pouring, precipitating, stormy, wet
*rel* drizzling, drizzly, misty, spitting, sprinkling
*near ant* dry

**raise** *n* something added (as by growth) — see INCREASE 1

**raise** *vb* **1** to move from a lower to a higher place or position ⟨asked the students to *raise* their hands if they knew the answer⟩
*syn* boost, crane, elevate, heave, heft, heighten, hike, hoist, jack (up), lift, perk (up), pick up, up, uphold, uplift, upraise
*rel* ascend, mount, rise; rear, upend
*near ant* descend, fall, pitch, plunge, slip; bear, depress, press, push; sink, submerge
*ant* drop, lower
**2** to bring to maturity through care and education — see BRING UP 1
**3** to cause or encourage the development of — see INCITE 1
**4** to draw out (something hidden, latent, or reserved) — see EDUCE
**5** to fix in an upright position — see ERECT 1
**6** to form by putting together parts or materials — see BUILD
**7** to look after or assist the growth of by labor and care — see GROW 1
**8** to make greater in size, amount, or number — see INCREASE 1
**9** to move higher in rank or position — see PROMOTE 1
**10** to present or bring forward for discussion — see INTRODUCE 2

**raised** *adj* **1** being at a higher level than average — see HIGH 2
**2** being positioned above a surface — see ELEVATED 1
**3** rising straight up — see ERECT

**rake** *vb* to look through (as a place) carefully or thoroughly in an effort to find or discover something — see SEARCH 1

**rakishly** *adv* in a bright and showy way — see GAILY 3

**rally** *n* **1** an act of gathering forces together to renew or attempt an effort ⟨in a last-minute *rally* the Confederates at Bull Run were able to turn a near defeat into an upset victory⟩
*syn* marshaling (*or* marshalling), mobilization, rallying
*rel* call-up, summons; convening, muster, mustering
**2** a mass meeting for the purpose of displaying or arousing support for a cause or person ⟨a huge *rally* for the candidate on the eve of the election⟩
*syn* demonstration
*rel* assembly, convention, gathering; march; protest, sit-down, sit-down strike, sit-in, strike
**3** the process or period of gradually regaining one's health and strength — see CONVALESCENCE

[1]**rally** *vb* **1** to assemble and make ready for action — see MOBILIZE

---

*syn* synonym(s) *rel* related words
*ant* antonym(s) *near ant* near antonym(s)

2 to become healthy and strong again after illness or weakness — see CONVALESCE
3 to regain a former or normal state — see RECOVER 2

**²rally** *vb* to make fun of in a good-natured way — see TEASE 1

**rallying** *n* an act of gathering forces together to renew or attempt an effort — see RALLY 1

**rallying** *adj* marked by or expressive of mild or good-natured teasing — see QUIZZICAL

**ram** *vb* **1** to come into usually forceful contact with something — see HIT 2
2 to fit (something) into a tight space — see CROWD 1

**ramble** *n* a relaxed journey on foot for exercise or pleasure — see WALK

**ramble** *vb* **1** to talk at length without sticking to a topic or getting to a point ⟨the teenagers sat around the pizza parlor, *rambling* on about dating, homework, movies, and the local football team⟩
*syn* maunder, rattle, run on
*rel* deviate, digress, stray, wander; sidetrack; blab, chatter, gab, gabble, jabber, patter, prate, prattle
2 to move about from place to place aimlessly — see WANDER

**rambler** *n* a person who roams about without a fixed route or destination — see NOMAD

**rambling** *adj* **1** passing from one topic to another — see DISCURSIVE
2 using or containing more words than necessary to express an idea — see WORDY

**rambunctious** *adj* being rough or noisy in a high-spirited way — see BOISTEROUS

**ramify** *vb* to set or force apart — see SEPARATE 1

**rampage** *n* a state of wildly excited activity or emotion — see FRENZY

**rampant** *adj* **1** showing no signs of being under control ⟨the mayor promised to put a stop to the *rampant* crime that plagued the city⟩
*syn* intemperate, unbridled, unchecked, uncontrolled, uncurbed, ungoverned, unhampered, unhindered, unrestrained
*rel* uncontrollable, ungovernable; immoderate; riotous, uninhibited, wild
*near ant* moderate, tempered
*ant* checked, controlled, curbed, hampered, hindered, restrained, temperate
2 growing thickly and vigorously — see RANK 1

**ramrod** *adj* given to exacting standards of discipline and self-restraint — see SEVERE 1

**ranch** *n* a piece of land and its buildings used to grow crops or raise livestock — see FARM

**rancor** *n* a deep-seated ill will — see ENMITY

**rancorous** *adj* having or showing deep-seated resentment — see BITTER 1

**random** *adj* lacking a definite plan, purpose, or pattern ⟨since we were new in town, our choice of a vet for our dog was entirely *random*⟩
*syn* aimless, arbitrary, desultory, erratic, haphazard, hit-or-miss, scattered, slapdash, stray
*rel* accidental, casual, chance, fluky, fortuitous, inadvertent, incidental, lucky, unconsidered, unintended, unintentional, unplanned, unpremeditated; irregular, sporadic, spot; objectless, purposeless; indiscriminate, unsystematic; unaimed, undirected
*near ant* established, fixed, regular, set, stable, steady; constant, continuous, even; arranged, managed, orchestrated, ordered, planned; aware, conscious, deliberate, purposeful, thoughtful
*ant* methodical, nonrandom, orderly, systematic

**randomly** *adv* without definite aim, direction, rule, or method — see HIT OR MISS

**range** *n* **1** open land over which livestock may roam and feed ⟨knew exactly how many head of cattle were turned out on the *range* that morning to graze⟩
*syn* lea, pasturage, pasture
*rel* ranch, station; feedlot, stockyard, yard; grassland, pampas, prairie, savanna (*also* savannah), steppe
2 an area over which activity, capacity, or influence extends ⟨didn't know she had such a wide *range* of knowledge until I talked to her⟩
*syn* amplitude, breadth, compass, dimension(s), extent, reach, realm, scope, sweep, width
*rel* gamut, spectrum, spread; domain, field, sphere; horizon, panorama
3 the distance or extent between possible extremes ⟨an actor who can go through the full *range* of emotion, from joy to sorrow, in mere minutes⟩
*syn* gamut, scale, spectrum, spread, stretch
*rel* measure, pitch, scale; amplitude, compass, dimension(s), extent, reach, realm, scope, sweep, width
4 a relaxed journey on foot for exercise or pleasure — see WALK
5 a series of persons or things arranged one behind another — see LINE 1
6 an appliance that prepares food for consumption by heating it — see COOKER 1
7 the place where a plant or animal is usually or naturally found — see HOME 2

**range** *vb* **1** to arrange or assign according to type — see CLASSIFY 1
2 to move about from place to place aimlessly — see WANDER
3 to occur within a continuous range of variation — see RUN 4
4 to put into a particular arrangement — see ORDER 1

**ranging** *adj* traveling from place to place — see ITINERANT

**rangy** *adj* being tall, thin and usually loose-jointed — see LANKY

**rank** *adj* **1** growing thickly and vigorously ⟨covered with trumpet vines so *rank* you couldn't see the trellis beneath them⟩
*syn* lush, luxuriant, prosperous, rampant, weedy
*rel* lavish, profuse; overgrown, overrun; close, dense, thick
*near ant* dormant; blighted, stunted
*ant* sparse
**2** having an unpleasant smell — see MALODOROUS
**3** very noticeable especially for being incorrect or bad — see EGREGIOUS

**rank** *n* **1** the placement of someone or something in relation to others in a vertical arrangement ⟨attained the highest *rank* in Boy Scouting⟩
*syn* degree, footing, level, place, position, ranking, situation, standing, station, status
*rel* condition, echelon, estate, order, walk; capacity, function; rating
**2** high position within society ⟨was born a woman of *rank* who socialized only with other members of the elite⟩
*syn* class, dignity, quality, standing
*rel* gentility, gentleness, nobility, nobleness; grandness, highness, loftiness; distinction, precedence, preeminence, primacy; caste, position, station, status; preferment
*near ant* debasement, degradation; subordinateness, subordination; baseness, commonness, inferiority, lowliness, lowness
**3** a series of people or things arranged side by side — see ROW 1
**4** *usually* **ranks** *pl* one of the units into which a whole is divided on the basis of a common characteristic — see CLASS 2

**rank** *vb* **1** to take or have a certain position within a group arranged in vertical classes ⟨my favorite pitcher *ranks* first in the league for number of consecutive outs⟩
*syn* be, grade, place, rate
*rel* seed; count; class, classify, set, sort; install, instate
**2** to arrange or assign according to type — see CLASSIFY 1

**rank and file** *n* the body of the community as contrasted with the elite — see MASS 1

**ranking** *n* **1** a scheme of rank or order — see ³SCALE 1
**2** the placement of someone or something in relation to others in a vertical arrangement — see RANK 1

**rankle** *vb* to make angry — see ANGER

**rankling** *adj* causing annoyance — see ANNOYING

**ransack** *vb* **1** to search through with the intent of committing robbery ⟨it was clear that the thieves who had *ransacked* the museum were professionals—they bypassed most of the exhibits and went straight for the vaults⟩
*syn* despoil, loot, maraud, pillage, plunder, sack, strip
*rel* burglarize; comb, hunt, rake, rifle, rummage; harry, raid; ravish
**2** to look through (as a place) carefully or thoroughly in an effort to find or discover something — see SEARCH 1

**ransom** *vb* to free from captivity or punishment by paying a price ⟨the prince emptied the treasury to *ransom* his son from the kidnappers⟩
*syn* redeem
*rel* bail; deliver, rescue, save; emancipate, liberate; recover, regain, retrieve; release; buy; salvage

**rant** *n* **1** a long angry speech or scolding — see TIRADE
**2** boastful speech or writing — see BOMBAST 1

**rant** *vb* to talk loudly and wildly ⟨when the salesclerk gave him incorrect change, he began *ranting* about the sorry state of math education today⟩
*syn* bluster, fulminate, rave, spout
*rel* sound off, speak out, speak up; blare, blurt out, bolt; declaim, harangue, mouth, orate, pontificate; carry on, rage, storm, take on
*near ant* grunt, murmur, mutter, slur; breathe, whisper

**¹rap** *n* **1** a formal claim of criminal wrongdoing against a person — see CHARGE 1
**2** a hard strike with a part of the body or an instrument — see ¹BLOW
**3** responsibility for wrongdoing or failure — see BLAME 1

**²rap** *n* friendly, informal conversation or an instance of this — see CHAT

**³rap** *n* the smallest amount or part imaginable — see JOT

**¹rap** *vb* to deliver a blow to (someone or something) usually in a strong vigorous manner — see HIT 1
**2** to strike or cause to strike lightly and usually rhythmically — see ¹TAP

**²rap** *vb* to engage in casual or rambling conversation — see CHAT

**rapacious** *adj* **1** having a huge appetite — see VORACIOUS 1
**2** living by killing and eating other animals — see PREDATORY
**3** having or marked by an eager and often selfish desire especially for material possessions — see GREEDY 1

**rapaciousness** *n* an intense selfish desire for wealth or possessions — see GREED

**rapacity** *n* an intense selfish desire for wealth or possessions — see GREED

**rapid** *adj* moving, proceeding, or acting with great speed — see FAST 1

**rapid–fire** *adj* moving, proceeding, or acting with great speed — see FAST 1

**rapidity** *n* a high rate of movement or performance — see SPEED

**rapidly** *adv* with great speed — see FAST 1

**rapidness** *n* a high rate of movement or performance — see SPEED

**rapport** *n* a friendly relationship marked by ready communication and mutual understanding ⟨his good *rapport* with his

---

*syn* synonym(s) *rel* related words
*ant* antonym(s) *near ant* near antonym(s)

students was one of the reasons why the school board named him Teacher of the Year⟩
*syn* communion, fellowship, rapprochement
*rel* accord, agreement, concord, harmony; oneness, solidarity, togetherness, unity; affinity, empathy, sympathy, understanding; amity, chummines, companionship, friendship; reciprocity, symbiosis
*near ant* alienation, disaffection, estrangement; coldness, cold shoulder, distance, iciness; animosity, antagonism, enmity, hostility, rancor, spite

**rapprochement** *n* a friendly relationship marked by ready communication and mutual understanding — see RAPPORT

**rapscallion** *n* **1** a mean, evil, or unprincipled person — see VILLAIN
**2** an appealingly mischievous person — see SCAMP 1

**rapt** *adj* having the mind fixed on something — see ATTENTIVE

**rapture** *n* a state of overwhelming usually pleasurable emotion — see ECSTASY

**rapturous** *adj* experiencing or marked by overwhelming usually pleasurable emotion — see ECSTATIC

**rare** *adj* **1** being out of the ordinary — see EXCEPTIONAL
**2** having qualities that appeal to a refined taste — see CHOICE
**3** not often occurring or repeated — see INFREQUENT
**4** noticeably different from what is generally found or experienced — see UNUSUAL 1

**rarely** *adv* not often — see SELDOM

**raring** *adj* showing urgent desire or interest — see EAGER

**rarity** *n* something strange or unusual that is an object of interest — see CURIOSITY 2

**rascal** *n* **1** a mean, evil, or unprincipled person — see VILLAIN
**2** an appealingly mischievous person — see SCAMP 1

**rascality** *n* playful, reckless behavior that is not intended to cause serious harm — see MISCHIEF 1

**rascally** *adj* tending to or exhibiting reckless playfulness — see MISCHIEVOUS 1

**rash** *adj* acting or done with excessive or careless speed — see HASTY 1

**rashly** *adv* with excessive or careless speed — see HASTILY 1

**rasp** *n* a harsh grating sound ⟨the rusted lock opened with a *rasp*⟩
*syn* creak, grind, scrape, scratch
*rel* clash, jangle, jar; croak; blast, bleat, bray, screech

**rasp** *vb* **1** to make smooth by friction — see GRIND 1
**2** to pass roughly and noisily over or against a surface — see SCRAPE 1
**3** to disturb the peace of mind of (someone) especially by repeated disagreeable acts — see IRRITATE 1

**raspberry** *n* a vocal sound made to express scorn or disapproval — see CATCALL

**rasping** *adj* harsh and dry in sound — see HOARSE

**raspy** *adj* harsh and dry in sound — see HOARSE

**rat** (on) *vb* to leave (a cause or party) often in order to take up another — see DEFECT

**rate** *n* **1** degree of excellence — see QUALITY 1
**2** the relationship in quantity, amount, or size between two or more things — see RATIO

[1]**rate** *vb* **1** to be or make worthy of (as a reward or punishment) — see EARN 2
**2** to make an approximate or tentative judgment regarding — see ESTIMATE 1
**3** to take or have a certain position within a group arranged in vertical classes — see RANK 1
**4** to think of in a particular way — see CONSIDER 1

[2]**rate** *vb* to criticize (someone) severely or angrily especially for personal failings — see SCOLD

**rather** *adv* **1** by choice or preference ⟨I would *rather* go to the movies than stay at home⟩
*syn* first, preferably, readily, soon, willingly
*rel* alternately, alternatively, either, instead; electively, optionally; desirably, gladly, wishfully; voluntarily
*near ant* reluctantly; forcibly, willy-nilly
*ant* involuntarily, unwillingly
**2** as a substitute — see INSTEAD
**3** to some degree or extent — see FAIRLY

**ratify** *vb* to give official acceptance of something as satisfactory — see APPROVE

**ratio** *n* the relationship in quantity, amount, or size between two or more things ⟨the *ratio* of students to teachers in my school is nine to one⟩
*syn* proportion, rate
*rel* average; frequency; correspondence; percentage
*near ant* disproportion

**ration** *vb* to give as a share or portion — see ALLOT

**rational** *adj* **1** having the ability to reason ⟨human beings are *rational* creatures⟩
*syn* intelligent, reasonable, reasoning, thinking
*rel* analytic (*or* analytical), logical; brainy, cerebral, highbrow, intellectual; cognitive, mental; practical, sane, sensible
*near ant* brainless, mindless, stupid; illogical
*ant* irrational, nonrational, unintelligent, unreasonable, unreasoning, unthinking
**2** according to the rules of logic — see LOGICAL 1
**3** based on sound reasoning or information — see GOOD 1

**rationale** *n* a statement given to explain a belief or act — see REASON 1

**rationalize** *vb* to give the reason for or cause of — see EXPLAIN 2

**rattle** *vb* **1** to make a series of short sharp noises ⟨the children tromped through the

kitchen, making the plates on the shelf *rattle*〉
***syn*** clack, clatter
***rel*** chink, chirp, clank, click, clink; clang, clash, crash; spatter, sputter
**2** to engage in casual or rambling conversation — see CHAT
**3** to talk at length without sticking to a topic or getting to a point — see RAMBLE 1
**4** to throw into a state of self-conscious distress — see EMBARRASS 1

**rattling** *adj* moving, proceeding, or acting with great speed — see FAST 1

**rattling** *adv* to a great degree — see VERY 1

**ratty** *adj* **1** showing signs of advanced wear and tear and neglect — see SHABBY 1
**2** worn or torn into or as if into rags — see RAGGED 2

**raucous** *adj* being rough or noisy in a high-spirited way — see BOISTEROUS

**ravage** *vb* to bring destruction to (something) through violent action 〈Hurricane Andrew *ravaged* Louisiana and Florida in 1992, causing $19 billion in damage〉
***syn*** destroy, devastate, ruin, scourge
***rel*** despoil, foray, harry, loot, maraud, pillage, plunder, sack, strip; annihilate, desolate, extirpate, obliterate, smash, waste, wipe out, wreck; decimate, mow; demolish, raze; crush, overpower, overrun, overthrow, overwhelm
***near ant*** recondition, recover, redeem, rehabilitate, restore

**rave** *vb* to make an exaggerated display of affection or enthusiasm — see GUSH 2
**2** to talk loudly and wildly — see RANT

**rave** *n, often* **raves** *pl* enthusiastic and usually public expression of approval — see APPLAUSE

**ravel** (out) *vb* to separate the various strands of — see UNRAVEL 1

**raven** *adj* having the color of soot or coal — see BLACK 1

**ravenous** *adj* having a huge appetite — see VORACIOUS 1

**ravine** *n* a narrow opening between hillsides or mountains that can be used for passage — see CANYON

**ravish** *vb* to fill with overwhelming emotion (as wonder or delight) — see ENTRANCE

**ravishing** *adj* very pleasing to look at — see BEAUTIFUL

**raw** *adj* **1** not cooked 〈you should wash your hands after handling *raw* chicken〉
***syn*** uncooked
***rel*** unbaked, unheated; rare; underdone
***near ant*** well-done; overdone; baked, boiled, braised, broiled, fried, grilled, heated, roasted, sautéed
***ant*** cooked
**2** being such as found in nature and not altered by processing or refining — see CRUDE 1
**3** lacking in adult experience or maturity — see CALLOW
**4** marked by wet and windy conditions — see FOUL 1
**5** uncomfortably cool — see CHILLY 1
**6** causing intense discomfort to one's skin — see CUTTING 1

**raw deal** *n* unfair or inadequate treatment of someone or something or an instance of this — see DISSERVICE

**rawhide** *vb* to strike repeatedly with something long and thin or flexible — see WHIP 1

**raw material** *n* the basic elements from which something can be developed — see MAKING

**rawness** *n* an uncomfortable degree of coolness — see CHILL

**ray** *n* **1** a narrow sharply defined line of light radiating from an object — see SHAFT 1
**2** a very small amount — see PARTICLE 1

**raze** *vb* **1** to bring to a complete end the physical soundness, existence, or usefulness of — see DESTROY 1
**2** to destroy (as a building) completely by knocking down or breaking to pieces — see DEMOLISH 1

**razz** *vb* to make fun of in a good-natured way — see TEASE 1

**razzing** *adj* marked by or expressive of mild or good-natured teasing — see QUIZZICAL

**reach** *n* **1** a wide space or area — see EXPANSE
**2** an area over which activity, capacity, or influence extends — see RANGE 2

**reach** *vb* **1** to shift possession of (something) from one person to another — see PASS 1
**2** to transmit information or requests to — see CONTACT

**reachable** *adj* situated within easy reach — see CONVENIENT

**reacquire** *vb* to get again in one's possession — see RECOVER 1

**react** *vb* to act or behave in response (as to a stimulus or influence) 〈it was my first touchdown, and I didn't know how to *react* to the cheers of the crowd〉
***syn*** reply, respond
***rel*** answer, return; retaliate; construe, interpret, read, take, understand
***near ant*** act, behave; affect, cause, draw, effect

**reaction** *n* action or behavior that is done in return to other action or behavior 〈we were startled by her extreme *reaction* to the bad grade〉
***syn*** reply, response, take
***rel*** answer, return; backlash; rebound; revulsion, rise; jerk, start, twitch
***near ant*** action, behavior; cause, effect

**reactionary** *adj* tending to favor established ideas, conditions, or institutions — see CONSERVATIVE

**reactionary** *n* **1** a person whose political beliefs are centered on tradition and keeping things the way they are — see CONSERVATIVE 1
**2** a person with old-fashioned ideas — see FOGY

**read** *vb* to go over and mentally take in the content of ⟨he always *reads* the newspaper in the morning as he eats breakfast⟩
*syn* peruse, pore (over)
*rel* browse, dip (into), leaf (through), scan, skim, thumb (through); slog (through), wade (through); reread; proofread; decipher; review, study; apprehend, comprehend, get, grasp, make, make out, perceive, see, understand

**readdress** *vb* to consider again especially with the possibility of change or reversal — see RECONSIDER

**readily** *adv* **1** by choice or preference — see RATHER 1
**2** without difficulty — see EASILY

**reading** *n* something assigned to be read or studied — see LESSON

**ready** *adj* **1** being in a state of fitness for some experience or action ⟨after studying for a whole month, she felt *ready* for the final exam⟩
*syn* fit, go, prepared, set
*rel* conditioned, primed; braced, fortified, steeled; qualified, trained
*near ant* unqualified, untrained
*ant* half-cocked, unprepared, unready
**2** having a desire or inclination (as for a specified course of action) — see WILLING 1
**3** having or showing the ability to respond without delay or hesitation — see QUICK 1
**4** involving minimal difficulty or effort — see EASY 1

**ready** *vb* **1** to make competent (as by training, skill, or ability) for a particular office or function — see QUALIFY 2
**2** to make ready in advance — see PREPARE 1
**3** to prepare (oneself) mentally or emotionally — see FORTIFY 1

**ready–made** *adj* made beforehand in large numbers ⟨the store was full of inexpensive *ready-made* clothing⟩
*syn* mass-produced, store
*rel* ready-to-wear; commercial; prefabricated
*near ant* handcrafted, handmade, homemade; tailored, tailor-made
*ant* custom, custom-made

**real** *adj* **1** being exactly as appears or as claimed — see AUTHENTIC 1
**2** existing in fact and not merely as a possibility — see ACTUAL
**3** free from any intent to deceive or impress others — see GUILELESS

**real** *adv* to a great degree — see VERY 1

**realistic** *adj* **1** willing to see things as they really are and deal with them sensibly ⟨our guidance counselor encouraged us to be more *realistic* in our job choices, so we reluctantly gave up the idea of becoming professional snake charmers⟩
*syn* down-to-earth, earthy, hardheaded, matter-of-fact, practical, pragmatic (*also* pragmatical)
*rel* philistine, utilitarian; logical, no-nonsense, rational, reasonable, sane, sensible, sound; hard-boiled, unromantic, unsentimental; cynical, disillusioned
*near ant* fanciful, fantastic, imaginative; romantic, sentimental; illogical, insane, irrational, unreasonable; theoretical (*also* theoretic)
*ant* idealistic, impractical, unrealistic, utopian, visionary
**2** closely resembling the object imitated — see NATURAL 2

**reality** *n* **1** something that actually exists — see FACT 2
**2** the fact of being or of being real — see EXISTENCE
**3** the quality of being actual — see FACT 1

**realizable** *adj* capable of being done or carried out — see POSSIBLE 1

**realization** *n* the state of being actual or complete — see FRUITION

**realize** *vb* **1** to come to an awareness — see DISCOVER 1
**2** to receive as return for effort — see EARN 1

**really** *adv* **1** in actual fact — see VERY 2
**2** to tell the truth — see ACTUALLY 1
**3** without any question — see INDEED 1

**realm** *n* **1** a region of activity, knowledge, or influence — see FIELD 2
**2** an area over which activity, capacity, or influence extends — see RANGE 2

**reams** *n pl* a considerable amount — see LOT 2

**reanalyze** *vb* to consider again especially with the possibility of change or reversal — see RECONSIDER

**reanimate** *vb* to bring back to life, practice, or activity — see REVIVE 1

**reanimated** *adj* made or become fresh in spirits or vigor — see NEW 4

**reanimation** *n* the act or an instance of bringing something back to life, public attention, or vigorous activity — see REVIVAL

**reap** *vb* to catch or collect (a crop or natural resource) for human use — see HARVEST

**reappraisal** *n* a usually critical look at a past event — see REVIEW 1

**rear** *adj* being at or in the part of something opposite the front part — see BACK

**rear** *n* the part of the body upon which someone sits — see BUTTOCKS

**rear** *vb* **1** to bring to maturity through care and education — see BRING UP 1
**2** to fix in an upright position — see ERECT 1
**3** to form by putting together parts or materials — see BUILD
**4** to look after or assist the growth of by labor and care — see GROW 1

**rearmost** *adj* following all others of the same kind in order or time — see LAST

**rearward** *adj* **1** being at or in the part of something opposite the front part — see BACK
**2** directed, turned, or done toward the back — see BACKWARD

**reason** *n* **1** a statement given to explain a belief or act ⟨gave a good *reason* for her seemingly suspicious behavior⟩

*syn* argument, case, explanation, rationale
*rel* alibi, defense, excuse, justification; appeal, plea; guise, pretense (*or* pretence), pretext, rationalization
**2** something (as a belief) that serves as the basis for another thing ⟨a firm belief that we are here on earth to help others is the *reason* for her tireless volunteer work⟩
*syn* grounds, motive, wherefore, why
*rel* antecedent, cause, occasion
**3** an explanation that frees one from fault or blame — see EXCUSE
**4** someone or something responsible for a result — see CAUSE 1
**5** the ability to learn and understand or to deal with problems — see INTELLIGENCE 1
**6** the normal or healthy condition of the mental abilities — see MIND 2
**7** the thought processes that have been established as leading to valid solutions to problems — see LOGIC

**reason** *vb* **1** to form an opinion through reasoning and information — see INFER 1
**2** to state (something) as a reason in support of or against something under consideration — see ARGUE 1

**reasonable** *adj* **1** according to the rules of logic — see LOGICAL 1
**2** based on sound reasoning or information — see GOOD 1
**3** costing little — see CHEAP 1
**4** having the ability to reason — see RATIONAL 1

**reasonably** *adv* with good reason or courtesy — see WELL 4

**reasoned** *adj* **1** based on sound reasoning or information — see GOOD 1
**2** being or provable by reasoning in which the conclusion follows necessarily from given information — see DEDUCTIVE
**3** decided on as a result of careful thought — see DELIBERATE 1

**reasoning** *adj* having the ability to reason — see RATIONAL 1

**reasoning** *n* the thought processes that have been established as leading to valid solutions to problems — see LOGIC

**reassure** *vb* to ease the grief or distress of — see COMFORT 1

**reata** *n* a rope or long leather thong with a noose used especially for catching livestock — see LASSO

**rebel** *n* a person who rises up against authority ⟨the *rebel* would not submit peacefully, even after he was captured⟩
*syn* insurgent, insurrectionary, insurrectionist, mutineer, red, revolter, revolutionary, revolutionist, revolutionizer
*rel* challenger, defier, resister; anarchist; extremist, malcontent, radical
*near ant* loyalist, supporter; counterrevolutionary, counterrevolutionist

**rebel** *vb* to rise up against established authority ⟨the colonists *rebelled* when the unfair tax was imposed⟩
*syn* mutiny, revolt
*rel* defy, disobey; revolutionize
*near ant* obey, submit; attend, serve

**rebel** (against) *vb* to go against the commands, prohibitions, or rules of — see DISOBEY

**rebellion** *n* open fighting against authority (as one's own government) ⟨the *rebellion* would have failed if not for the aid sent by other countries⟩
*syn* insurgency, insurrection, mutiny, revolt, revolution, uprising
*rel* coup, coup d'état, overthrow; sedition, treachery, treason; sabotage, subversion
*near ant* counterrevolution

**rebellious** *adj* **1** taking part in a rebellion ⟨the *rebellious* troops fought a pitched battle with divisions still loyal to the government⟩
*syn* insurgent, insurrectionary, mutinous, revolutionary
*rel* seditious, traitorous, treacherous, treasonous
*near ant* loyal; obedient
**2** given to resisting authority or another's control — see DISOBEDIENT

**rebelliousness** *n* refusal to obey — see DISOBEDIENCE

**rebirth** *n* the act or an instance of bringing something back to life, public attention, or vigorous activity — see REVIVAL

**rebound** *vb* **1** to regain a former or normal state — see RECOVER 2
**2** to strike and fly off at an angle — see GLANCE 1

**rebuff** *n* treatment that is deliberately unfriendly — see COLD SHOULDER

**rebuke** *n* an often public or formal expression of disapproval — see CENSURE

**rebuke** *vb* **1** to criticize (someone) usually gently so as to correct a fault ⟨*rebuked* the toddler for his habit of telling fibs⟩
*syn* admonish, chide, reprimand, reproach, reprove
*rel* berate, castigate, chew out, dress down, flay, jaw, keelhaul, lambaste (*or* lambast), lecture, rail (at *or* against), scold, score, upbraid; abuse, assail, attack, bad-mouth, blame, blast, censure, condemn, criticize, crucify, denounce, dis [*slang*], excoriate, fault, knock, lash, pan, reprehend, slam; belittle, disparage, mock, put down; ridicule, scoff, scorn
*near ant* approve, endorse (*also* indorse), sanction; extol (*also* extoll), laud, praise
**2** to criticize (someone) severely or angrily especially for personal failings — see SCOLD
**3** to express public or formal disapproval of — see CENSURE 1

**rebut** *vb* to prove to be false — see DISPROVE

**recalcitrance** *n* refusal to obey — see DISOBEDIENCE

**recalcitrant** *adj* **1** given to resisting authority or another's control — see DISOBEDIENT

---

*syn* synonym(s) *rel* related words
*ant* antonym(s) *near ant* near antonym(s)

**2** given to resisting control or discipline by others — see UNCONTROLLABLE

**recall** *n* **1** a particular act or instance of recalling or the thing remembered — see MEMORY 2
**2** the act of putting an end to something planned or previously agreed to — see CANCELLATION

**recall** *vb* **1** to bring back to mind — see REMEMBER
**2** to put an end to (something planned or previously agreed to) — see CANCEL 1

**recant** *vb* to solemnly or formally reject or go back on (as something formerly adhered to) — see ABJURE

**recap** *n* a short statement of the main points — see SUMMARY

**recap** *vb* to make into a short statement of the main points (as of a report) — see SUMMARIZE

**recapitulate** *vb* to make into a short statement of the main points (as of a report) — see SUMMARIZE

**recapitulation** *n* a short statement of the main points — see SUMMARY

**recapture** *vb* to get again in one's possession — see RECOVER 1

**recast** *vb* to make different in some way — see CHANGE 1

**recede** *vb* **1** to grow less in scope or intensity especially gradually — see DECREASE 2
**2** to move back or away (as from something difficult, dangerous, or disagreeable) — see RETREAT 1

**recently** *adv* not long ago — see NEWLY

**receptacle** *n* something into which a liquid or smaller objects can be put for storage or transportation — see CONTAINER

**reception** *n* a social gathering — see PARTY 1

**receptive** *adj* willing to consider new or different ideas — see OPEN-MINDED 1

**recess** *n* **1** a hollowed-out space in a wall — see NICHE 1
**2** a period during which the usual routine of school or work is suspended — see VACATION
**3** a momentary halt in an activity — see PAUSE
**4** a sunken area forming a separate space — see HOLE 2

**recess** *vb* to bring to a formal close for a period of time — see ADJOURN

**recessed** *adj* curved inward — see HOLLOW

**recession** *n* **1** a period of decreased economic activity — see DEPRESSION 1
**2** an act of moving away especially from something difficult, dangerous, or disagreeable — see RETREAT 1

**reciprocal** *adj* related to each other in such a way that one completes the other — see COMPLEMENTARY

**recite** *vb* **1** to give an oral or written account of in some detail — see TELL 1
**2** to give from memory — see REPEAT 2

**reckless** *adj* **1** having or showing a lack of concern for the consequences of one's actions ⟨the *reckless* skiers were making everyone nervous by schussing down the mountainside at lightning speed⟩
***syn*** daredevil, devil-may-care, foolhardy, irresponsible
***rel*** adventurous, bold, daring, venturesome; hasty, headlong, hotheaded, impetuous, precipitate, rash, wild; nonchalant, unconcerned, unworried; careless, heedless, inattentive, incautious, unheeding; inconsiderate, thoughtless, unthinking
***near ant*** careful, cautious, circumspect, heedful; overcareful, overcautious, timid
***ant*** responsible
**2** foolishly adventurous or bold — see FOOLHARDY 1

**reckon** *vb* **1** to decide the size, amount, number, or distance of (something) without actual measurement — see ESTIMATE 2
**2** *chiefly dialect* to have as an opinion — see BELIEVE 2
**3** to determine (a value) by doing the necessary mathematical operations — see CALCULATE 1
**4** to place reliance or trust — see DEPEND 2
**5** to think of in a particular way — see CONSIDER 1

**reckoning** *n* **1** the act of placing a value on the nature, character, or quality of something — see ESTIMATE 1
**2** the act or process of performing mathematical operations to find a value — see CALCULATION

**reclaim** *vb* **1** to get again in one's possession — see RECOVER 1
**2** to make better in behavior or character — see REFORM 1
**3** to obtain (a raw material) by separating it from a by-product or waste product — see RECYCLE

**reclamation** *n* the act or process of getting something back — see RECOVERY 1

**recluse** *n* a person who lives away from others ⟨he was sick of cities and crowds, so he decided to go live by himself in the woods as a *recluse*⟩
***syn*** anchorite, hermit, solitary
***rel*** homebody, shut-in; monk
***near ant*** socialite

**recognize** *vb* to show appreciation, respect, or affection for (someone) with a public celebration — see HONOR

**recoil** *vb* to draw back in fear, pain, or disgust — see FLINCH

**recollect** *vb* to bring back to mind — see REMEMBER

**re–collect** *vb* **1** to gain emotional or mental control of — see COLLECT 1
**2** to get again in one's possession — see RECOVER 1

**recollection** *n* **1** a particular act or instance of recalling or the thing remembered — see MEMORY 2
**2** the power or process of recalling what has been previously learned or experienced — see MEMORY 1

**recommend** *vb* to put forward as one's choice for a wise or proper course of action — see ADVISE 2

**recompense** *n* **1** payment to another for a loss or injury — see COMPENSATION 1
**2** something (as money) that is given or received in return for goods or services — see PAYMENT 2

**recompense** *vb* **1** to give (someone) the sum of money owed for goods or services received — see PAY 1
**2** to give what is owed for — see PAY 2
**3** to provide (someone) with a just payment for loss or injury — see COMPENSATE 1

**reconceive** *vb* to consider again especially with the possibility of change or reversal — see RECONSIDER

**reconcile** *vb* to bring to a state free of conflicts, inconsistencies, or differences — see HARMONIZE 2

**recondite** *adj* difficult for one of ordinary knowledge or intelligence to understand — see PROFOUND 1

**recondition** *vb* to put into good shape or working order again — see MEND 1

**reconsider** *vb* to consider again especially with the possibility of change or reversal ⟨the new information forced the general to *reconsider* his plan of attack⟩
***syn*** readdress, reanalyze, reconceive, reevaluate, reexamine, rethink, review, reweigh
***rel*** reappraise, reassess; amend, correct, emend, rectify, reform, remedy, revise
***phrases*** change one's mind (about), go over, think better of, view in a new light
***near ant*** assert, defend, maintain, uphold

**reconsideration** *n* a usually critical look at a past event — see REVIEW 1

**record** *n* **1** a relating of events usually in the order in which they happened — see ACCOUNT 1
**2** an account of important events in the order in which they happened — see HISTORY 1

**record** *vb* **1** to make a written note of ⟨the reporter *recorded* the events of the evening in her notebook for later reference⟩
***syn*** jot (down), log, mark, note, put down, register, set down
***rel*** chronicle; chalk (up), score; rerecord
**2** to put (someone or something) on a list — see [1]LIST 2

**recount** *vb* to give an oral or written account of in some detail — see TELL 1

**recoup** *vb* **1** to get again in one's possession — see RECOVER 1
**2** to provide (someone) with a just payment for loss or injury — see COMPENSATE 1

**recoupment** *n* **1** payment to another for a loss or injury — see COMPENSATION 1
**2** the act or process of getting something back — see RECOVERY 1

**recourse** *n* something that one uses to accomplish an end especially when the usual means is not available — see RESOURCE 1

**recover** *vb* **1** to get again in one's possession ⟨after fishing around in the garbage for ten minutes, I was able to *recover* my lost keys⟩
***syn*** reacquire, recapture, reclaim, recollect, recoup, regain, repossess, retake, retrieve
***rel*** recruit, replenish; redeem, repurchase; rescue
***phrases*** get back
***near ant*** lose, mislay, misplace
**2** to regain a former or normal state ⟨after a disastrous first half, the team was able to *recover* toward the end of the game and manage a win⟩
***syn*** rally, rebound, snap back
***rel*** reanimate, revitalize, revive
***phrases*** make a comeback
***near ant*** decline, fail, worsen
**3** to become healthy and strong again after illness or weakness — see CONVALESCE
**4** to obtain (a raw material) by separating it from a by-product or waste product — see RECYCLE

**recovery** *n* **1** the act or process of getting something back ⟨the *recovery* of the sunken boat took over a week⟩
***syn*** reclamation, recoupment, repossession, retrieval
***rel*** recruitment, replenishment; redemption, rescue
***near ant*** loss, misplacement
**2** the process or period of gradually regaining one's health and strength — see CONVALESCENCE

**recreant** *adj* **1** having or showing a shameful lack of courage — see COWARDLY
**2** not true in one's allegiance to someone or something — see FAITHLESS

**recreant** *n* **1** a person who abandons a cause or organization usually without right — see RENEGADE
**2** a person who shows a shameful lack of courage in the face of danger — see COWARD
**3** one who betrays a trust or an allegiance — see TRAITOR

**recreate** *vb* **1** to bring back to a former condition or vigor — see RENEW 1
**2** to engage in activity for amusement — see PLAY 1

**recreated** *adj* made or become fresh in spirits or vigor — see NEW 4

**recreation** *n* **1** activity engaged in to amuse oneself — see PLAY 1
**2** someone or something that provides amusement or enjoyment — see FUN 1
**3** the act or activity of providing pleasure or amusement especially for the public — see ENTERTAINMENT 1

**recruit** *n* a person who is just starting out in a field of activity — see BEGINNER

**rectifiable** *adj* capable of being corrected — see REMEDIABLE

---

***syn*** synonym(s) ***rel*** related words
***ant*** antonym(s) ***near ant*** near antonym(s)

**rectify** *vb* to remove errors, defects, deficiencies, or deviations from — see CORRECT 1

**rectifying** *adj* serving to raise or adjust something to some standard or proper condition — see CORRECTIVE 1

**rectitude** *n* **1** conduct that conforms to an accepted standard of right and wrong — see MORALITY 1
**2** faithfulness to high moral standards — see HONOR 1

**recuperate** *vb* to become healthy and strong again after illness or weakness — see CONVALESCE

**recuperation** *n* the process or period of gradually regaining one's health and strength — see CONVALESCENCE

**recurrent** *adj* occurring or appearing at intervals — see INTERMITTENT 1

**recurring** *adj* occurring or appearing at intervals — see INTERMITTENT 1

**recycle** *vb* to obtain (a raw material) by separating it from a by-product or waste product ⟨*recycling* the aluminum from pop cans is environmentally sound⟩
***syn*** reclaim, recover
***rel*** reuse; process

**red** *n* a person who rises up against authority — see REBEL

**red–blooded** *adj* having active strength of body or mind — see VIGOROUS 1

**redden** *vb* to develop a rosy facial color (as from excitement or embarrassment) — see BLUSH

**redeem** *vb* **1** to do what is required by the terms of — see FULFILL 1
**2** to free from captivity or punishment by paying a price — see RANSOM
**3** to free from the penalties or consequences of sin — see SAVE 1
**4** to make better in behavior or character — see REFORM 1

**redeemer** *n* one that saves from danger or destruction — see SAVIOR

**red–hot** *adj* **1** being or involving the latest methods, concepts, information, or styles — see MODERN
**2** having a notably high temperature — see HOT 1
**3** having or expressing great depth of feeling — see FERVENT

**redo** *vb* **1** to make different in some way — see CHANGE 1
**2** to make or do again — see REPEAT 4

**redoing** *n* the act, process, or result of making different — see CHANGE

**redolence** *n* **1** a sweet or pleasant smell — see FRAGRANCE
**2** the quality of a thing that makes it perceptible to the sense organs in the nose — see SMELL

**redolent** *adj* having a pleasant smell — see FRAGRANT

**redouble** *vb* **1** to make markedly greater in measure or degree — see INTENSIFY
**2** to make twice as great or as many — see DOUBLE 1

**redoubtable** *adj* causing fear — see FEARFUL 1

**redraft** *vb* to prepare for publication by correcting, rewriting, or updating — see EDIT

**redress** *n* payment to another for a loss or injury — see COMPENSATION 1

**reduce** *vb* **1** to bring to a lower grade or rank — see DEMOTE
**2** to make smaller in amount, volume, or extent — see DECREASE 1

**reduction** *n* **1** something that is or may be subtracted — see DEDUCTION 1
**2** the amount by which something is lessened — see DECREASE

**redundancy** *n* the use of too many words to express an idea — see VERBIAGE

**reduplicate** *vb* **1** to make an exact likeness of — see COPY 1
**2** to make or do again — see REPEAT 4

**reduplication** *n* **1** something that is made to look exactly like something else — see COPY
**2** the act of saying or doing over again — see REPEAT

**reecho** *vb* to continue or be repeated in a series of reflected sound waves — see REVERBERATE

**reek** *n* **1** a strong unpleasant smell — see STINK
**2** an atmospheric condition in which suspended particles in the air rob it of its transparency — see HAZE 1

**reek** *vb* to give off an extremely unpleasant smell — see STINK

**reeking** *adj* having an unpleasant smell — see MALODOROUS

**reeky** *adj* having an unpleasant smell — see MALODOROUS

**reel** *n* a rapid turning about on an axis or central point — see SPIN 1

**reel** *vb* **1** to be in a confused state as if from being twirled around — see SPIN 2
**2** to move forward while swaying from side to side — see STAGGER 1

**reeling** *adj* having a feeling of being whirled about and in danger of falling down — see DIZZY 1

**reenergized** *adj* made or become fresh in spirits or vigor — see NEW 4

**reevaluate** *vb* to consider again especially with the possibility of change or reversal — see RECONSIDER

**reexamination** *n* a usually critical look at a past event — see REVIEW 1

**reexamine** *vb* to consider again especially with the possibility of change or reversal — see RECONSIDER

**refashion** *vb* to make different in some way — see CHANGE 1

**refashioning** *n* the act, process, or result of making different — see CHANGE

**refer** *vb* to have a relation or connection — see APPLY 1

**refer (to)** *vb* **1** to make reference to or speak about briefly but specifically — see MENTION 1
**2** to use or seek out as a source of aid, relief, or advantage — see RESORT (TO) 1

**referee** *vb* to give an opinion about (something at issue or in dispute) — see JUDGE 1

**reference** *n* relation to or concern with something specified — see RESPECT 1
**refine** *vb* to make better — see IMPROVE
**refined** *adj* **1** being far along in development — see ADVANCED 1
**2** free from added matter — see PURE 1
**3** having or showing a taste for the fine arts and gracious living — see CULTIVATED
**4** having or showing elegance — see ELEGANT 1
**5** made or done with extreme care and accuracy — see FINE 2
**6** satisfying or pleasing because of fineness or mildness — see DELICATE 1
**refinement** *n* **1** an instance of notable progress in the development of knowledge, technology, or skill — see ADVANCE 2
**2** a high level of taste and enlightenment as a result of extensive intellectual training and exposure to the arts — see CULTURE 1
**3** dignified or restrained beauty of form, appearance, or style — see ELEGANCE
**reflect** *vb* to reproduce or show (an exact likeness) as a mirror would ⟨her face was *reflected* in the waters of the still pond⟩
***syn*** image, mirror
***rel*** copy, duplicate, imitate, reduplicate, repeat, replicate, reproduce
**reflection** *n* **1** a briefly expressed opinion — see REMARK
**2** a cause of shame — see DISGRACE 2
**reflective** *adj* given to or marked by long, quiet thinking — see CONTEMPLATIVE
**reform** *vb* **1** to make better in behavior or character ⟨a *reformed* criminal who is now a productive member of society⟩
***syn*** reclaim, redeem, rehabilitate
***rel*** amend, improve; cleanse, purify, restore
***near ant*** abase, corrupt, debauch, degrade, demean, demoralize, deprave, pervert, poison, profane, prostitute, subvert, warp
**2** to remove errors, defects, deficiencies, or deviations from — see CORRECT 1
**reformative** *adj* serving to raise or adjust something to some standard or proper condition — see CORRECTIVE 1
**reformatory** *adj* serving to raise or adjust something to some standard or proper condition — see CORRECTIVE 1
**refractoriness** *n* refusal to obey — see DISOBEDIENCE
**refractory** *adj* **1** given to resisting authority or another's control — see DISOBEDIENT
**2** given to resisting control or discipline by others — see UNCONTROLLABLE
**refrain** *n* a part of a song or hymn that is repeated every so often — see CHORUS 2
**refrain** (from) *vb* to resist the temptation of — see FORBEAR
**refresh** *vb* to bring back to a former condition or vigor — see RENEW 1
**refreshed** *adj* made or become fresh in spirits or vigor — see NEW 4
**refreshen** *vb* to bring back to a former condition or vigor — see RENEW 1
**refreshing** *adj* having a renewing effect on the state of the body or mind — see TONIC
**refrigerate** *vb* to cause to lose heat — see COOL 1
**refuge** *n* something (as a building) that offers cover from the weather or protection from danger — see SHELTER
**refugee** *n* a person forced to emigrate for political reasons — see ÉMIGRÉ 1
**refulgence** *n* the quality or state of having or giving off light — see BRILLIANCE 1
**refulgent** *adj* giving off or reflecting much light — see BRIGHT 1
**refund** *vb* to make a return payment to — see REPAY
**refusal** *n* an unwillingness to grant something asked for — see DENIAL 1
**refuse** *n* discarded or useless material — see GARBAGE
**refuse** *vb* **1** to be unwilling to grant — see DENY 2
**2** to show unwillingness to accept, do, engage in, or agree to — see DECLINE 1
**refute** *vb* to prove to be false — see DISPROVE
**regain** *vb* to get again in one's possession — see RECOVER 1
**regal** *adj* **1** fit for or worthy of a royal ruler — see MONARCHICAL
**2** large and impressive in size, grandeur, extent, or conception — see GRAND 1
**regale** *vb* **1** to cause (someone) to pass the time agreeably occupied — see AMUSE
**2** to entertain with a fancy meal — see FEAST
**regalia** *n* dressy clothing — see FINERY
**regard** *n* **1** a feeling of great approval and liking — see ADMIRATION 1
**2** an instance of looking especially briefly — see LOOK 2
**3** relation to or concern with something specified — see RESPECT 1
**4 regards** *pl* best wishes — see COMPLIMENT
**regard** *vb* **1** to make note of (something) through the use of one's eyes — see SEE 1
**2** to take notice of and be guided by — see HEED 1
**3** to think of in a particular way — see CONSIDER 1
**4** to think very highly or favorably of — see ADMIRE
**regardful** *adj* marked by or showing proper regard for another's higher status — see RESPECTFUL
**regarding** *prep* having to do with — see ABOUT 1
**regardless** *adv* in spite of everything ⟨the weather looked bad, but they were resolved to go on with their picnic *regardless*⟩
***syn*** anyhow, anyway
***rel*** nevertheless
***phrases*** in any case, no matter

**regenerate** *vb* **1** to bring back to a former condition or vigor — see RENEW 1
**2** to bring back to life, practice, or activity — see REVIVE 1
**regenerated** *adj* made or become fresh in spirits or vigor — see NEW 4
**regeneration** *n* the act or an instance of bringing something back to life, public attention, or vigorous activity — see REVIVAL
**regime** *also* **régime** *n* lawful control over the affairs of a political unit (as a nation) — see RULE 2
**regimen** *n* lawful control over the affairs of a political unit (as a nation) — see RULE 2
**region** *n* **1** a part or portion having no fixed boundaries ⟨if you look in the upper left *region* of the sky, you can see the constellation Orion⟩
*syn* area, demesne, field, zone
*rel* section; locale, locality, location, locus, place, point, position, site, spot
**2** a broad geographical area ⟨corn is mostly grown in the central *regions* of the country⟩
*syn* belt, land, part(s), tract, zone
*rel* district, territory
[1]**register** *n* a person whose job is to keep records — see CLERK 1
[2]**register** *n* a record of a series of items (as names or titles) usually arranged according to some system — see [1]LIST
**register** *vb* **1** to enter in a list or roll — see ENROLL 1
**2** to make a written note of — see RECORD 1
**3** to put (someone or something) on a list — see [1]LIST 2
**registrar** *n* a person whose job is to keep records — see CLERK 1
**registration** *n* the number of individuals registered ⟨there was a large *registration* for the popular swim classes at the community center⟩
*syn* enrollment, registry
*rel* class
**registry** *n* **1** a record of a series of items (as names or titles) usually arranged according to some system — see [1]LIST
**2** the number of individuals registered — see REGISTRATION
**regress** *vb* to go back to a previous and usually lower state or level ⟨in extreme circumstances, people sometimes *regress* to the behavior they exhibited in childhood⟩
*syn* retrogress, revert
*rel* backslide, lapse, relapse; return
*near ant* grow, mature, ripen
*ant* advance, develop, evolve, progress
**regression** *n* the act or an instance of going back to an earlier and lower level especially of intelligence or behavior ⟨the *regression* to really childish behavior that boys often undergo when put in large groups⟩
*syn* retrogression, reversion
*rel* backslide, lapse, relapse; return; nondevelopment
*near ant* growth, maturation, ripening
*ant* advancement, development, evolution, progression
**regret** *n* a feeling of responsibility for wrongdoing — see GUILT 1
**regret** *vb* to feel sorry or dissatisfied about ⟨we *regret* any inconvenience that we may have caused you⟩
*syn* bemoan, deplore, lament, repent, rue
*rel* bewail, grieve (for), mourn, sorrow (for)
**regretful** *adj* **1** expressing or suggesting mourning — see MOURNFUL 1
**2** feeling sorrow for a wrong that one has done — see CONTRITE 1
**regretfully** *adv* with feelings of bitterness or grief — see HARD 2
**regrettable** *adj* of a kind to cause great distress ⟨the explorers forged ahead despite the *regrettable* loss of some of their companions⟩
*syn* deplorable, distressful, distressing, grievous, heartbreaking, heartrending, lamentable, unfortunate, woeful
*rel* affecting, moving, poignant, touching; awful, dire, dreadful, fearful, terrible; horrible, horrifying, intolerable, overwhelming, shocking, sickening, unbearable; miserable, pitiful, wretched; calamitous, disastrous
*near ant* gratifying, pleasing, rewarding, satisfying; comforting, encouraging, heartening; cheering, heartwarming, inspiring; fortunate, happy, lucky
**regular** *adj* **1** appearing or occurring repeatedly from time to time ⟨what with one or another of our pets having problems, we've been *regular* visitors at the animal hospital⟩
*syn* constant, frequent, habitual, periodic, repeated, steady
*rel* chronic, confirmed, inveterate; expected, usual
*near ant* unexpected, unusual
*ant* inconstant, infrequent, irregular
**2** following a set method, arrangement, or pattern — see METHODICAL
**3** following or agreeing with established form, custom, or rules — see FORMAL 1
**4** having no exceptions or restrictions — see ABSOLUTE 2
**5** having or showing the qualities associated with the members of a particular group or kind — see TYPICAL 1
**regular** *n* a person engaged in military service — see SOLDIER
**regularize** *vb* to make agree with a single established standard or model — see STANDARDIZE
**regulate** *vb* **1** to keep from exceeding a desirable degree or level (as of expression) — see CONTROL 1
**2** to look after and make decisions about — see CONDUCT 1
**regulation** *n* **1** a statement spelling out the proper procedure or conduct for an activity — see RULE 1
**2** the act or activity of looking after and making decisions about something — see CONDUCT 1

3 the duty or function of watching or guarding for the sake of proper direction or control — see SUPERVISION 1

**regulator** *n* a mechanism for adjusting the operation of a device, machine, or system — see CONTROL 1

**rehabilitate** *vb* 1 to make better in behavior or character — see REFORM 1
2 to restore to a healthy condition — see HEAL 1

**rehabilitation** *n* the process or period of gradually regaining one's health and strength — see CONVALESCENCE

**rehearsal** *n* a private performance or session in preparation for a public appearance ⟨we made a few mistakes in *rehearsal*, but we were pretty sure that we'd be okay on opening night⟩
*syn* dry run, practice (*also* practise), trial
*rel* dress rehearsal; preview; drill, exercise

**rehearse** *vb* 1 to do over and over so as to become skilled — see PRACTICE
2 to give an oral or written account of in some detail — see TELL 1
3 to say or state again — see REPEAT 1
4 to specify one after another — see ENUMERATE 1

**reimburse** *vb* to make a return payment to — see REPAY

**rein** *n* the place of leadership or command — see HEAD 2

**rein** (in) *vb* to keep from exceeding a desirable degree or level (as of expression) — see CONTROL 1

**reiterate** *vb* 1 to make or do again — see REPEAT 4
2 to say or state again — see REPEAT 1

**reiteration** *n* the act of saying or doing over again — see REPEAT

**reiterative** *adj* marked by repetition — see REPETITIVE

**reject** *n* 1 one who is cast out or rejected by society — see OUTCAST
2 something separated from a group or lot for not being as good as the others — see CULL

**reject** *vb* 1 to be unwilling to grant — see DENY 2
2 to declare not to be true — see DENY 1
3 to get rid of as useless or unwanted — see DISCARD
4 to show unwillingness to accept, do, engage in, or agree to — see DECLINE 1

**rejected** *adj* left unoccupied or unused — see ABANDONED

**rejection** *n* 1 a refusal to confirm the truth of a statement — see DENIAL 2
2 an unwillingness to grant something asked for — see DENIAL 1
3 something separated from a group or lot for not being as good as the others — see CULL

**rejoice** *vb* 1 to feel or express joy or triumph — see EXULT
2 to give satisfaction to — see PLEASE

**rejoicing** *adj* having or expressing feelings of joy or triumph — see EXULTANT

**rejoin** *vb* to speak or write in reaction to a question or to another reaction — see ANSWER 1

**rejoinder** *n* something spoken or written in reaction especially to a question — see ANSWER 1

**rejuvenate** *vb* 1 to bring back to a former condition or vigor — see RENEW 1
2 to bring back to life, practice, or activity — see REVIVE 1

**rejuvenation** *n* the act or an instance of bringing something back to life, public attention, or vigorous activity — see REVIVAL

**rekindle** *vb* to bring back to life, practice, or activity — see REVIVE 1

**relate** *vb* 1 to form a close personal relationship — see COMMUNE
2 to give an oral or written account of in some detail — see TELL 1
3 to have a relation or connection — see APPLY 1
4 to think of (something) in combination — see ASSOCIATE 2

**related** *adj* having a close connection like that between family members ⟨the *related* fields of anthropology and archaeology⟩
*syn* affiliated, akin, allied, kindred
*rel* associated, connected; alike, analogous, comparable, correspondent, corresponding, like, matching, parallel, resembling, similar, such, suchlike; identical, same; germane, pertinent, relevant
*near ant* different, disparate, dissimilar, distinct, distinctive, distinguishable, diverse, other, unalike, unlike
*ant* unrelated

**relation** *n* 1 **relations** *pl* doings between individuals or groups ⟨*relations* between the rival newspapers remained friendly despite their competition for the same stories⟩
*syn* dealings, interaction, intercourse
*rel* interrelationship
2 a person connected with another by blood or marriage — see RELATIVE
3 the fact or state of having something in common — see CONNECTION 1
4 the state of having shared interests or efforts (as in social or business matters) — see ASSOCIATION 1

**relationship** *n* 1 the fact or state of having something in common — see CONNECTION 1
2 the state of having shared interests or efforts (as in social or business matters) — see ASSOCIATION 1

**relative** *adj* 1 being such only when compared to something else — see COMPARATIVE
2 having to do with the matter at hand — see PERTINENT

**relative** *n* a person connected with another by blood or marriage ⟨it's always fun to see all your *relatives* at a big family gathering⟩
*syn* kin, kinsman, relation

---

*syn* synonym(s) *rel* related words
*ant* antonym(s) *near ant* near antonym(s)

*rel* in-law; kinswoman; blood, clan, family, folk, house, kindred, kinfolk, kinsfolk, line, lineage, people, race, stock, tribe

**relatively** *adv* to some degree or extent — see FAIRLY

**relax** *vb* **1** to get rid of nervous tension or anxiety ⟨she took deep breaths to *relax* before going on stage⟩
*syn* unwind
*rel* loosen (up), unbend; repose, rest; alleviate, comfort, ease, relieve; calm, compose, cool, quiet, settle
*ant* tense (up)
**2** to make less taut — see SLACKEN
**3** to refrain from labor or exertion — see REST 1

**relaxation** *n* **1** activity engaged in to amuse oneself — see PLAY 1
**2** freedom from activity or labor — see [1]REST 1

**relaxed** *adj* **1** enjoying physical comfort — see COMFORTABLE 2
**2** not bound by rigid standards — see EASYGOING 2
**3** not tightly fastened, tied, or stretched — see LOOSE 1

**relaxing** *adj* tending to calm the emotions and relieve stress — see SOOTHING 1

**release** *n* **1** a freeing from an obligation or responsibility ⟨after they declared bankruptcy, the bank agreed to a *release* from their debt⟩
*syn* delivery, discharge, quietus, quittance
*rel* exemption, immunity, waiver
**2** a document containing a declaration of an intentional giving up of a right, claim, or privilege — see WAIVER
**3** a published statement informing the public of a matter of general interest — see ANNOUNCEMENT

**release** *vb* **1** to set free (from a state of being held in check) ⟨he *released* his anger with a great yell of frustration⟩
*syn* loose, loosen, uncork, unleash, unlock, unloose, unloosen
*rel* discharge, emancipate, enfranchise, free, liberate, manumit, spring, unbind, uncage, unchain, unfetter; air, express, vent
*near ant* manacle, shackle, trammel; bind, confine, enchain, fetter
*ant* bridle, check, constrain, contain, control, curb, govern, hold in, inhibit, regulate, rein (in), restrain, tame
**2** to find emotional release for — see TAKE OUT 1
**3** to set free (as from slavery or confinement) — see FREE 1
**4** to set free from entanglement or difficulty — see EXTRICATE
**5** to throw or give off — see EMIT 1

**relent** *vb* to grow less in scope or intensity especially gradually — see DECREASE 2

**relentless** *adj* showing no signs of slackening or yielding in one's purpose — see UNYIELDING 1

**relevance** *n* the fact or state of being pertinent — see PERTINENCE

**relevancy** *n* the fact or state of being pertinent — see PERTINENCE

**relevant** *adj* having to do with the matter at hand — see PERTINENT

**reliability** *n* worthiness as the recipient of another's trust or confidence ⟨we never had to question the *reliability* of the park rangers in an emergency⟩
*syn* dependability, reliableness, solidity, solidness, sureness, trustworthiness
*rel* infallibility
*near ant* doubtfulness, dubiousness

**reliable** *adj* worthy of one's trust — see DEPENDABLE

**reliableness** *n* worthiness as the recipient of another's trust or confidence — see RELIABILITY

**reliance** *n* **1** something or someone to which one looks for support — see DEPENDENCE 2
**2** the quality or state of needing something or someone — see DEPENDENCE 1

**relic** *n* **1** a tiny often physical indication of something lost or vanished — see VESTIGE
**2** something belonging to or surviving from an earlier period — see ANTIQUE

**relief** *n* **1** a feeling of ease from grief or trouble — see COMFORT 1
**2** a person or thing that takes the place of another — see SUBSTITUTE
**3** reduction of or freedom from pain — see EASE 1

**relieve** *vb* **1** to make more bearable or less severe — see HELP 2
**2** to set (a person or thing) free of something that encumbers — see RID

**religion** *n* **1** a body of beliefs and practices regarding the supernatural and the worship of one or more deities ⟨the Jewish *religion* has followers in many parts of the globe⟩
*syn* credo, creed, cult, faith, persuasion
*rel* church, communion, denomination, sect; belief, doctrine, dogma, theology; monotheism, polytheism, theism
*near ant* agnosticism, atheism, secularism
**2** belief and trust in and loyalty to God — see FAITH 1

**religious** *adj* **1** of, relating to, or used in the practice or worship services of a religion ⟨J.S. Bach wrote some of the most beautiful *religious* music in the world⟩
*syn* devotional, sacred, spiritual
*rel* blessed, consecrated, hallowed, holy, sacrosanct, sanctified; liturgical, ritual, sacramental
*near ant* earthly, mundane, worldly; irreligious, semireligious
*ant* nonreligious, profane, secular
**2** showing a devotion to God and to a life of virtue — see HOLY 1

**relinquish** *vb* **1** to give (something) over to the control or possession of another usually under duress — see SURRENDER 1
**2** to give up (as a position of authority) formally — see ABDICATE

**relinquishment** *n* the usually forced yielding of one's person or possessions to the control of another — see SURRENDER

**relish** *n* **1** positive regard for something — see LIKING
**2** the feeling experienced when one's wishes are met — see PLEASURE 1

**relish** *vb* to take pleasure in — see ENJOY 1

**reluctance** *n* a lack of willingness or desire to do or accept something ⟨the mice showed an odd *reluctance* to eat the cheese we had put out for them⟩
***syn*** disinclination, hesitance, hesitancy, unwillingness
***rel*** faltering, hesitation, indecision, irresolution, shilly-shallying, staggering, vacillation, wavering, wobbling; distrust, distrustfulness, doubt, incertitude, misgiving, mistrust, mistrustfulness, skepticism, suspicion, uncertainty
***near ant*** certainty, certitude, sureness, surety
***ant*** inclination, willingness

**reluctant** *adj* having doubts about the wisdom of doing something — see HESITANT

**rely** *vb* to place reliance or trust — see DEPEND 2

**remain** *vb* to continue to be in a place for a significant amount of time — see STAY 1

**remainder** *n* **1** a remaining group or portion ⟨the *remainder* of the pills were saved in case they were needed later⟩
***syn*** balance, leavings, leftovers, odds and ends, remains, remnant, residue, rest
***rel*** fragment, scrap; oddment, scraping(s), stub, stump; excess, surplus
***near ant*** bulk, most
**2** an unused or unwanted piece or item typically of small size or value — see [1]SCRAP 1

**remains** *n pl* **1** the portion or bits of something left over or behind after it has been destroyed ⟨the *remains* of the house ripped apart by the tornado littered the block for weeks afterward⟩
***syn*** ashes, debris, residue, rubble, ruins, wreck, wreckage
***rel*** detritus, flotsam, jetsam; garbage, refuse, trash
**2** a dead body — see CORPSE
**3** a remaining group or portion — see REMAINDER 1

**remake** *vb* **1** to make different in some way — see CHANGE 1
**2** to make or do again — see REPEAT 4

**remaking** *n* the act, process, or result of making different — see CHANGE

**remark** *n* a briefly expressed opinion ⟨the speaker made some short *remarks* about the new museum before officially opening the doors to visitors⟩
***syn*** comment, note, observation, reflection
***rel*** analysis, commentary, exposition; annotation; belief, conviction, eye, feeling, judgment (*or* judgement), mind, notion, opinion, persuasion, sentiment, verdict, view

**remark** *vb* **1** to make a statement of one's opinion ⟨he *remarked* on the attractiveness of the background music in the restaurant⟩
***syn*** comment, note, observe, opine
***rel*** articulate, express, say, speak, state, talk, tell, utter, verbalize, vocalize
**2** to make note of (something) through the use of one's eyes — see SEE 1

**remarkable** *adj* **1** different from the ordinary in a way that causes curiosity or suspicion — see ODD 2
**2** likely to attract attention — see NOTICEABLE

**remediable** *adj* capable of being corrected ⟨the problems with the local transportation system were severe but still *remediable*⟩
***syn*** correctable, fixable, rectifiable, repairable, reparable
***rel*** amendable, improvable, resolvable; redeemable
***near ant*** irredeemable, irretrievable, unrecoverable
***ant*** incorrigible, irremediable, irreparable

**remedial** *adj* serving to raise or adjust something to some standard or proper condition — see CORRECTIVE 1

**remedy** *n* **1** a substance or preparation used to treat disease — see MEDICINE
**2** something that corrects or counteracts something undesirable — see CURE 1

**remedy** *vb* **1** to bring about recovery from — see CURE 1
**2** to remove errors, defects, deficiencies, or deviations from — see CORRECT 1

**remedying** *adj* serving to raise or adjust something to some standard or proper condition — see CORRECTIVE 1

**remember** *vb* to bring back to mind ⟨I *remember* the fun we had last summer very clearly, but I can't *remember* anything I learned in school yesterday⟩
***syn*** hark back (to), mind [*chiefly dialect*], recall, recollect, reminisce (about), think (of)
***rel*** recapture, recur; educe, elicit, evoke, extract, remind; relive
***phrases*** look back (on *or* upon)
***near ant*** disregard, ignore, neglect, overlook; lose, miss; blank (out)
***ant*** forget, unlearn

**remembrance** *n* **1** a particular act or instance of recalling or the thing remembered — see MEMORY 2
**2** something that serves to keep alive the memory of a person or event — see MEMORIAL
**3** the power or process of recalling what has been previously learned or experienced — see MEMORY 1

**reminder** *n* something that serves to keep alive the memory of a person or event — see MEMORIAL

**reminisce** (about) *vb* to bring back to mind — see REMEMBER

**reminiscence** *n* **1** a particular act or instance of recalling or the thing remembered — see MEMORY 2

***syn*** synonym(s) ***rel*** related words
***ant*** antonym(s) ***near ant*** near antonym(s)

2 the power or process of recalling what has been previously learned or experienced — see MEMORY 1

**reminiscent** *adj* provoking a memory or mental association — see SUGGESTIVE 2

**remiss** *adj* failing to give proper care and attention — see NEGLIGENT

**remission** *n* release from the guilt or penalty of an offense — see PARDON

**remissness** *n* failure to take the care that a cautious person usually takes — see NEGLIGENCE 1

**remit** *vb* 1 to grow less in scope or intensity especially gradually — see DECREASE 2
2 to overlook or dismiss as of little importance — see EXCUSE 1

**remitment** *n* the act of offering money in exchange for goods or services — see PAYMENT 1

**remittable** *adj* worthy of forgiveness — see VENIAL

**remittal** *n* release from the guilt or penalty of an offense — see PARDON

**remittance** *n* 1 something (as money) that is given or received in return for goods or services — see PAYMENT 2
2 the act of offering money in exchange for goods or services — see PAYMENT 1

**remnant** *n* 1 a remaining group or portion — see REMAINDER 1
2 an unused or unwanted piece or item typically of small size or value — see [1]SCRAP 1

**remodel** *vb* to make different in some way — see CHANGE 1

**remodeling** *n* the act, process or result of making different — see CHANGE

**remonstrance** *n* a feeling or declaration of disapproval or dissent — see OBJECTION

**remonstrate** (with) *vb* to present an opposing opinion or argument — see OBJECT

**remorse** *n* a feeling of responsibility for wrongdoing — see GUILT 1

**remorseful** *adj* 1 feeling sorrow for a wrong that one has done — see CONTRITE 1
2 suffering from or expressive of a feeling of responsibility for wrongdoing — see GUILTY 2

**remorsefulness** *n* a feeling of responsibility for wrongdoing — see GUILT 1

**remorseless** *adj* not sorry for having done wrong ⟨the *remorseless* killer was sentenced to life in prison without chance of parole⟩
*syn* impenitent, unrepentant
*rel* compassionless, cruel, merciless, pitiless, ruthless, unmerciful; shameless, unashamed
*near ant* ashamed, hangdog, shamed, shamefaced
*ant* contrite, guilty, penitent, regretful, remorseful, repentant, sorry

**remote** *adj* 1 small in degree ⟨there's a *remote* chance that it'll rain today, so I brought an umbrella⟩
*syn* negligible, off, outside, slight, slim, small
*near ant* great, large; distinct, significant
*ant* good
2 having or showing a lack of friendliness or interest in others — see COOL 1
3 hidden from view — see SECLUDED
4 not close in time or space — see DISTANT 1

**remotest** *adj* most distant from a center — see EXTREME 1

**removal** *n* the getting rid of whatever is unwanted or useless — see DISPOSAL 1

**remove** *n* the space or amount of space between two points, lines, surfaces, or objects — see DISTANCE

**remove** *vb* 1 to rid oneself of (a garment) ⟨I *removed* my coat as soon as I got inside⟩
*syn* doff, peel (off), put off, take off
*rel* husk, shed
*near ant* wear
*ant* don, put on, slip (into)
2 to take away from a place or position ⟨he carefully *removed* the old manuscript from the shelf⟩
*syn* clear, draw, withdraw
*rel* demount, dislodge; abstract, cut, extract, pull; move, shift, transfer
*near ant* mount
*ant* place, put
3 to change the place or position of — see MOVE 1
4 to let go from office, service, or employment — see DISMISS 1

**removed** *adj* not close in time or space — see DISTANT 1

**remunerate** *vb* 1 to give (someone) the sum of money owed for goods or services received — see PAY 1
2 to provide (someone) with a just payment for loss or injury — see COMPENSATE 1

**remuneration** *n* 1 the act of offering money in exchange for goods or services — see PAYMENT 1
2 payment to another for a loss or injury — see COMPENSATION 1
3 something (as money) that is given or received in return for goods or services — see PAYMENT 2

**remunerative** *adj* yielding a profit — see PROFITABLE 1

**rend** *vb* to cause (something) to separate into jagged pieces by violently pulling at it — see TEAR 1

**render** *vb* to give (something) over to the control or possession of another usually under duress — see SURRENDER 1

**rendezvous** *vb* to come together into one body or place — see ASSEMBLE 1

**rendezvous** *n* 1 a place for spending time or for socializing — see HANGOUT
2 an agreement to be present at a specified time and place — see ENGAGEMENT 2

**renegade** *n* a person who abandons a cause or organization usually without right ⟨a band of *renegades* who had deserted their infantry units and were making their way to Mexico⟩
*syn* defector, deserter, recreant

*rel* betrayer, double-crosser, quisling, traitor, turncoat; chicken, coward, craven, dastard, poltroon; defier, insurgent, insurrectionary, insurrectionist, mutineer, rebel, red, revolter, revolutionary, revolutionist, revolutionizer
*near ant* adherent, disciple, follower, zealot
*ant* loyalist

**renege** *vb* to break a promise or agreement ⟨Dad promised to take me out for ice cream on the weekend, only to *renege* on Saturday morning⟩
*syn* back down, back off, cop out
*rel* chicken (out); disavow, recall, recant, retract, take back, withdraw
*phrases* go back on
*near ant* follow through; fulfill (*or* fulfil), honor

**renew** *vb* **1** to bring back to a former condition or vigor ⟨the trip to New York *renewed* our enthusiasm for travel⟩
*syn* freshen, recreate, refresh, refreshen, regenerate, rejuvenate, restore, revitalize, revive
*rel* make over, refurbish, rehabilitate, remake, remodel, renovate; refill, replenish, resupply
**2** to begin again or return to after an interruption — see RESUME
**3** to bring back to life, practice, or activity — see REVIVE 1

**renewal** *n* the act or an instance of bringing something back to life, public attention, or vigorous activity — see REVIVAL

**renewed** *adj* made or become fresh in spirits or vigor — see NEW 4

**renounce** *vb* **1** to give up (as a position of authority) formally — see ABDICATE
**2** to solemnly or formally reject or go back on (as something formerly adhered to) — see ABJURE

**renouncement** *n* the act or practice of giving up or rejecting something once enjoyed or desired — see RENUNCIATION

**renovate** *vb* to put into good shape or working order again — see MEND 1

**renown** *n* the fact or state of being known to the public — see FAME

**renowned** *adj* widely known — see FAMOUS

**rent** *n* **1** a long deep cut — see GASH
**2** an open space in a barrier (as a wall or hedge) — see GAP 1

**rent** *vb* **1** to give the possession and use of (something) in return for periodic payment ⟨we *rented* the apartment to a college student for $500 a month⟩
*syn* lease, let [*chiefly British*]
*rel* charter, hire; lodge; sublease, sublet
**2** to take or get the temporary use of (something) for a set sum — see HIRE 1

**renter** *n* **1** one who rents a room or apartment in another's house — see TENANT
**2** the owner of land or housing that is rented to another — see LANDLORD

**renunciation** *n* the act or practice of giving up or rejecting something once enjoyed or desired ⟨his *renunciation* of his smoking habit pleased his whole family⟩
*syn* abnegation, renouncement, repudiation, self-denial
*rel* denial, refusal; relinquishment, resignation, surrender
*near ant* acceptance; adoption, embrace, espousal
*ant* indulgence, self-indulgence

**reopen** *vb* to begin again or return to after an interruption — see RESUME

**repair** *n* a state of being or fitness — see CONDITION 1

**repair** *vb* to put into good shape or working order again — see MEND 1

**repairable** *adj* capable of being corrected — see REMEDIABLE

**reparable** *adj* capable of being corrected — see REMEDIABLE

**reparation** *n* payment to another for a loss or injury — see COMPENSATION 1

**repartee** *n* **1** a quick witty response — see RETORT 1
**2** good-natured teasing or exchanging of clever remarks — see BANTER

**repast** *n* food eaten or prepared for eating at one time — see MEAL

**repay** *vb* to make a return payment to ⟨I *repaid* my friend the twenty dollars he had lent me⟩
*syn* refund, reimburse
*rel* quit, satisfy, settle
*phrases* pay back

**repeal** *n* the act of putting an end to something planned or previously agreed to — see CANCELLATION

**repeal** *vb* **1** to put an end to (something planned or previously agreed to) — see CANCEL 1
**2** to put an end to by formal action — see ABOLISH

**repeat** *n* the act of saying or doing over again ⟨the news story will be broadcast on the six o'clock show, with a *repeat* on the 11 o'clock newscast⟩
*syn* duplication, reduplication, reiteration, repetition, replication
*rel* rerun

**repeat** *vb* **1** to say or state again ⟨I *repeated* the address over and over until I had it memorized⟩
*syn* din, rehearse, reiterate
*rel* echo, parrot; mouth
**2** to give from memory ⟨*repeated* correctly all the verses she had memorized⟩
*syn* recite, say
*rel* declaim, mouth, orate, speak
*near ant* read
**3** to say after another ⟨now *repeat* the oath after me⟩
*syn* echo, parrot, quote
*rel* mouth; copy, imitate, mimic
**4** to make or do again ⟨try not to *repeat* your mistakes⟩
*syn* duplicate, redo, reduplicate, reiterate, remake, replicate
*rel* renew

**repeated** *adj* appearing or occurring repeatedly from time to time — see REGULAR 1

**repeatedly** *adv* many times — see OFTEN

**repel** *vb* **1** to drive back ⟨the defenders *repelled* the attacking army after several hours of fierce fighting⟩
*syn* fend (off), repulse, stave off
*rel* hold off, resist, withstand; deflect, ward (off); rebuff, snub, spurn
*near ant* welcome
**2** to cause to feel disgust — see DISGUST
**3** to refuse to give in to — see RESIST

**repelled** *adj* filled with disgust — see SICK 2

**repellent** *also* **repellant** *adj* causing intense displeasure, disgust, or resentment — see OFFENSIVE 1

**repent** *vb* to feel sorry or dissatisfied about — see REGRET

**repentance** *n* a feeling of responsibility for wrongdoing — see GUILT 1

**repentant** *adj* **1** feeling sorrow for a wrong that one has done — see CONTRITE 1
**2** suffering from or expressive of a feeling of responsibility for wrongdoing — see GUILTY 2

**repercussion** *n* the power to bring about a result on another — see EFFECT 2

**repetition** *n* the act of saying or doing over again — see REPEAT

**repetitious** *adj* marked by repetition — see REPETITIVE

**repetitive** *adj* marked by repetition ⟨the *repetitive* lyrics of so many rock songs⟩
*syn* reiterative, repetitious

**rephrase** *vb* to express something (as a text or statement) in different words — see PARAPHRASE

**rephrasing** *n* an instance of expressing something in different words — see PARAPHRASE

**repine** *vb* to express dissatisfaction, pain, or resentment usually tiresomely — see COMPLAIN

**repine** (for) *vb* to have an earnest wish to own or enjoy — see DESIRE

**replace** *vb* **1** to take the place of ⟨the old street lights were *replaced* with more energy-efficient models⟩
*syn* displace, substitute, supersede, supplant
*rel* preempt, usurp
**2** to bring, send, or put back to a former or proper place — see RETURN 1

**replacement** *n* a person or thing that takes the place of another — see SUBSTITUTE

**replete** *adj* possessing or covered with great numbers or amounts of something specified — see RIFE

**replica** *n* **1** something or someone that strongly resembles another — see IMAGE 1
**2** something that is made to look exactly like something else — see COPY

**replicate** *vb* **1** to make an exact likeness of — see COPY 1
**2** to make or do again — see REPEAT 4

**replication** *n* **1** something that is made to look exactly like something else — see COPY
**2** the act of saying or doing over again — see REPEAT

**reply** *n* **1** action or behavior that is done in return to other action or behavior — see REACTION
**2** something spoken or written in reaction especially to a question — see ANSWER 1

**reply** *vb* **1** to act or behave in response (as to a stimulus or influence) — see REACT
**2** to speak or write in reaction to a question or to another reaction — see ANSWER 1

**report** *n* **1** a loud explosive sound — see CLAP 1
**2** a relating of events usually in the order in which they happened — see ACCOUNT 1
**3** overall quality as seen or judged by people in general — see REPUTATION

**report** *vb* to give an oral or written account of in some detail — see TELL 1

**reporter** *n* a person employed by a newspaper, magazine, or radio or television station to gather, write, or report news ⟨the *reporter* was careful to ask as many questions as possible without annoying anyone⟩
*syn* correspondent, journalist
*rel* announcer, broadcaster, newscaster, newsman, newspaperman; anchor, anchorman, anchorperson, anchorwoman, legman; columnist, commentator, copyreader, editor, sportswriter, staffer

**repose** *n* **1** a natural periodic loss of consciousness during which the body restores itself — see SLEEP 1
**2** a state of freedom from storm or disturbance — see CALM
**3** freedom from activity or labor — see [1]REST 1

**repose** *vb* to refrain from labor or exertion — see REST 1

**repository** *n* a building for storing goods — see STOREHOUSE

**repossess** *vb* to get again in one's possession — see RECOVER 1

**repossession** *n* the act or process of getting something back — see RECOVERY 1

**reprehend** *vb* **1** to declare to be morally wrong or evil — see CONDEMN 1
**2** to express one's unfavorable opinion of the worth or quality of — see CRITICIZE

**reprehensible** *adj* **1** deserving reproach or blame — see BLAMEWORTHY
**2** provoking or likely to provoke protest — see OBJECTIONABLE

**represent** *vb* **1** to point out the chief quality or qualities of an individual or group — see CHARACTERIZE 1
**2** to present a picture of — see PICTURE 1
**3** to serve as a material counterpart of — see SYMBOLIZE 1

**representative** *n* **1** a person who acts or does business for another — see AGENT 2
**2** a person sent on a mission to represent another — see AMBASSADOR

3 one of a group or collection that shows what the whole is like — see EXAMPLE

**representative** *adj* 1 having or showing the qualities associated with the members of a particular group or kind — see TYPICAL 1
2 having the function or meaning of a symbol — see SYMBOLIC

**repress** *vb* 1 to put a stop to (something) by the use of force — see QUELL 1
2 to refrain from openly showing or uttering — see SUPPRESS 2

**repression** *n* the checking of one's true feelings and impulses when dealing with others — see CONSTRAINT 1

**reprimand** *n* an often public or formal expression of disapproval — see CENSURE

**reprimand** *vb* 1 to criticize (someone) severely or angrily especially for personal failings — see SCOLD
2 to criticize (someone) usually gently so as to correct a fault — see REBUKE 1
3 to express public or formal disapproval of — see CENSURE 1

**reprisal** *n* the act or an instance of paying back an injury with an injury — see REVENGE

**reproach** *n* 1 a cause of shame — see DISGRACE 2
2 an often public or formal expression of disapproval — see CENSURE
3 the state of having lost the esteem of others — see DISGRACE 1

**reproach** *vb* 1 to criticize (someone) severely or angrily especially for personal failings — see SCOLD
2 to criticize (someone) usually gently so as to correct a fault — see REBUKE 1
3 to express public or formal disapproval of — see CENSURE 1

**reproachable** *adj* deserving reproach or blame — see BLAMEWORTHY

**reprobate** *adj* having or showing lowered moral character or standards — see CORRUPT

**reprobate** *n* a mean, evil, or unprincipled person — see VILLAIN

**reprobate** *vb* to declare to be morally wrong or evil — see CONDEMN 1

**reproduce** *vb* 1 to bring forth offspring — see PROCREATE
2 to make an exact likeness of — see COPY 1

**reproduction** *n* something that is made to look exactly like something else — see COPY

**reproof** *n* an often public or formal expression of disapproval — see CENSURE

**reprove** *vb* 1 to criticize (someone) usually gently so as to correct a fault — see REBUKE 1
2 to express public or formal disapproval of — see CENSURE 1
3 to hold an unfavorable opinion of — see DISAPPROVE

**republic** *n* government in which the supreme power is held by the people and used by them directly or indirectly through representation — see DEMOCRACY

**republican** *adj* of, relating to, or favoring political democracy — see DEMOCRATIC

**repudiate** *vb* 1 to declare not to be true — see DENY 1
2 to refuse to acknowledge as one's own or as one's responsibility — see DISCLAIM 1
3 to show unwillingness to accept, do, engage in, or agree to — see DECLINE 1

**repudiation** *n* 1 a refusal to confirm the truth of a statement — see DENIAL 2
2 the act or practice of giving up or rejecting something once enjoyed or desired — see RENUNCIATION

**repugnance** *n* a dislike so strong as to cause stomach upset or queasiness — see DISGUST

**repugnant** *adj* causing intense displeasure, disgust, or resentment — see OFFENSIVE 1

**repulse** *n* treatment that is deliberately unfriendly — see COLD SHOULDER

**repulse** *vb* 1 to cause to feel disgust — see DISGUST
2 to drive back — see REPEL 1

**repulsed** *adj* filled with disgust — see SICK 2

**repulsion** *n* a dislike so strong as to cause stomach upset or queasiness — see DISGUST

**repulsive** *adj* causing intense displeasure, disgust, or resentment — see OFFENSIVE 1

**repulsiveness** *n* the quality of inspiring intense dread or dismay — see HORROR 1

**reputable** *adj* having a good reputation especially in a field of knowledge — see RESPECTABLE 1

**reputation** *n* overall quality as seen or judged by people in general ⟨the college's athletic department has a good *reputation*, but the school's science facilities are a bit lacking⟩
***syn*** character, mark, name, note, report, repute
***rel*** credit, honor; celebrity, fame, notoriety, renown
***near ant*** infamy

**repute** *n* overall quality as seen or judged by people in general — see REPUTATION

**reputed** *adj* 1 appearing to be true on the basis of evidence that may or may not be confirmed — see APPARENT 1
2 having a good reputation especially in a field of knowledge — see RESPECTABLE 1

**request** *n* an act or instance of asking for information — see QUESTION 2

**request** *vb* 1 to give a request or demand for — see ORDER 2
2 to make a request for — see ASK (FOR) 1
3 to make a request of — see ASK 2

**requiem** *n* a composition expressing one's grief over a loss — see LAMENT 2

**require** *vb* to have as a requirement — see NEED 1

---

***syn*** synonym(s) ***rel*** related words
***ant*** antonym(s) ***near ant*** near antonym(s)

**required** *adj* **1** forcing one's compliance or participation by or as if by law — see MANDATORY
**2** impossible to do without — see ESSENTIAL 1
**requirement** *n* something necessary, indispensable, or unavoidable — see ESSENTIAL 1
**requisite** *adj* impossible to do without — see ESSENTIAL 1
**requisite** *n* something necessary, indispensable, or unavoidable — see ESSENTIAL 1
**requisition** *n* something that someone insists upon having — see DEMAND 1
**requisition** *vb* to give a request or demand for — see ORDER 2
**requital** *n* **1** payment to another for a loss or injury — see COMPENSATION 1
**2** something (as money) that is given or received in return for goods or services — see PAYMENT 2
**3** the act or an instance of paying back an injury with an injury — see REVENGE
**requite** *vb* **1** to provide (someone) with a just payment for loss or injury — see COMPENSATE 1
**2** to punish in kind the wrongdoer responsible for — see AVENGE
**rescind** *vb* **1** to put an end to (something planned or previously agreed to) — see CANCEL 1
**2** to put an end to by formal action — see ABOLISH
**rescission** *n* the act of putting an end to something planned or previously agreed to — see CANCELLATION
**rescue** *vb* to remove from danger or harm — see SAVE 2
**rescuer** *n* one that saves from danger or destruction — see SAVIOR
**research** *n* a systematic search for the truth or facts about something — see INQUIRY 1
**research** *vb* to search through or into — see EXPLORE 1
**resemblance** *n* **1** a point which two or more things share in common — see SIMILARITY 2
**2** the quality or state of having many qualities in common — see SIMILARITY 1
**resembling** *adj* having qualities in common — see ALIKE
**resentful** *adj* **1** having or showing deep-seated resentment — see BITTER 1
**2** having or showing mean resentment of another's possessions or advantages — see ENVIOUS
**resentfully** *adv* with feelings of bitterness or grief — see HARD 2
**resentment** *n* **1** a lingering ill will towards a person for a real or imagined wrong — see GRUDGE 1
**2** a painful awareness of another's possessions or advantages and a desire to have them too — see ENVY
**3** the feeling of being offended or resentful after a slight or indignity — see PIQUE
**reservation** *n* something upon which the carrying out of an agreement or offer depends — see CONDITION 2
**reserve** *n* **1** the checking of one's true feelings and impulses when dealing with others — see CONSTRAINT 1
**2** a collection of things kept available for future use or need — see STORE
**3** a person or thing that takes the place of another — see SUBSTITUTE
**4** an interchangeable part or piece of equipment that is kept on hand for replacement of an original — see SPARE
**reserve** *vb* **1** to arrange to have something (as a hotel room) held for one's future use ⟨we made sure to *reserve* a kennel for our dog several months before the start of the family vacation⟩
***syn*** bespeak, book
***rel*** earmark; contract, engage, retain
**2** to continue to have in one's possession or power — see KEEP 2
**3** to keep or intend for a special purpose — see DEVOTE 1
**reserved** *adj* tending not to speak frequently (as by habit or inclination) — see SILENT 2
**reside** *vb* to have a home — see LIVE 1
**residence** *n* the place where one lives — see HOME 1
**resident** *n* one who lives permanently in a place — see INHABITANT
**resider** *n* one who lives permanently in a place — see INHABITANT
**residue** *n* **1** the portion or bits of something left over or behind after it has been destroyed — see REMAINS 1
**2** a remaining group or portion — see REMAINDER 1
**resign** *vb* to give up (as a position of authority) formally — see ABDICATE
**resign** (from) *vb* to give up (a job or office) — see QUIT 1
**resigned** *adj* receiving or enduring without offering resistance — see PASSIVE
**resilient** *adj* able to revert to original size and shape after being stretched, squeezed, or twisted — see ELASTIC 1
**resist** *vb* to refuse to give in to ⟨it is important to *resist* the temptation to run away from your problems⟩
***syn*** buck, defy, fight, oppose, repel, withstand
***rel*** battle, combat, contend (with), counter; contest, dispute; baffle, balk, foil, frustrate, thwart; check, counter, hinder, obstruct, stem
***ant*** bow (to), capitulate (to), give in (to), submit (to), succumb (to), surrender (to), yield (to)
**resistance** *n* **1** the inclination to resist ⟨there was much *resistance* to the idea of removing our baseball caps while eating⟩
***syn*** defiance, opposition
***rel*** demur, objection, protest, remonstrance; compunction, misgiving, reservation; disobedience, noncompliance
***near ant*** compliance, obedience; acceptance, approval
***ant*** acquiescence
**2** a secret organization in a conquered country fighting against enemy forces ⟨soldiers from the *resistance* were cap-

tured after a short battle outside the foreign ministry⟩
*syn* underground
*rel* cabal, conspiracy

**resolute** *adj* fully committed to achieving a goal — see DETERMINED 1

**resoluteness** *n* firm or unwavering adherence to one's purpose — see DETERMINATION 1

**resolution** *n* **1** a position arrived at after consideration — see DECISION 1
**2** firm or unwavering adherence to one's purpose — see DETERMINATION 1

**resolvable** *adj* capable of having the reason for or cause of determined — see SOLVABLE

**resolve** *n* firm or unwavering adherence to one's purpose — see DETERMINATION 1

**resolve** *vb* **1** to come to a judgment after discussion or consideration — see DECIDE 1
**2** to find an answer for through reasoning — see SOLVE
**3** to set or force apart — see SEPARATE 1

**resolved** *adj* fully committed to achieving a goal — see DETERMINED 1

**resonant** *adj* marked by conspicuously full and rich sounds or tones ⟨the orator's *resonant* voice filled the hall⟩
*syn* golden, resounding, reverberant, reverberating, ringing, round, sonorous, vibrant
*rel* deep, full, mellifluous, mellow, rich; loud, powerful, stentorian, thundering, thunderous
*near ant* cavernous, hollow; faint, low, murmurous, muted, smothered, soft, weak; thin, tinny

**resonate** *vb* to continue or be repeated in a series of reflected sound waves — see REVERBERATE

**resort** (to) *vb* **1** to use or seek out as a source of aid, relief, or advantage ⟨we were so desperate for better grades on our homework that we were forced to *resort to* spending all our evenings at the library⟩
*syn* go (to), refer (to), turn (to)
*rel* employ, use, utilize; depend (on), rely (on)
*phrases* fall back on
**2** to go to or spend time in often — see FREQUENT

**resort** *n* **1** a place for spending time or for socializing — see HANGOUT
**2** something that one uses to accomplish an end especially when the usual means is not available — see RESOURCE 1

**resound** *vb* to continue or be repeated in a series of reflected sound waves — see REVERBERATE

**resounding** *adj* **1** full of or characterized by the presence of noise — see NOISY 2
**2** marked by a high volume of sound — see LOUD 1
**3** marked by conspicuously full and rich sounds or tones — see RESONANT
**4** marked by or uttered with forcefulness — see EMPHATIC 1

**resource** *n* **1** something that one uses to accomplish an end especially when the usual means is not available ⟨we used every possible *resource* to raise the funds needed to save our town's oldest house⟩
*syn* expedient, recourse, resort
*rel* hope, opportunity, possibility, relief; makeshift, replacement, stopgap, substitute
**2 resources** *pl* available money — see FUND 2

**respect** *n* **1** relation to or concern with something specified ⟨with *respect* to your application⟩
*syn* reference, regard
**2** a feeling of great approval and liking — see ADMIRATION 1
**3 respects** *pl* best wishes — see COMPLIMENT

**respect** *vb* to think very highly or favorably of — see ADMIRE

**respectable** *adj* **1** having a good reputation especially in a field of knowledge ⟨no *respectable* dietician would advise people to eat just one kind of food⟩
*syn* esteemed, name, prestigious, reputable, reputed, respected
*rel* honorable, worthy; creditable, good, praiseworthy; celebrated, distinguished, famed, famous, honored, illustrious, notable, prominent, renowned, well-known
*ant* disreputable, loose
**2** following the accepted rules of moral conduct — see HONORABLE 1
**3** following the established traditions of refined society and good taste — see PROPER 1
**4** of a level of quality that meets one's needs or standards — see ADEQUATE
**5** sufficiently large in size, amount, or number to merit attention — see CONSIDERABLE 1

**respected** *adj* having a good reputation especially in a field of knowledge — see RESPECTABLE 1

**respectful** *adj* marked by or showing proper regard for another's higher status ⟨the children were remarkably *respectful* while in the President's office⟩
*syn* deferential, dutiful, regardful
*rel* reverent, reverential, venerating, worshipful; fawning, groveling (*or* grovelling), obsequious, servile, subservient, sycophantic, toadying; civil, courteous, gracious, polite
*near ant* abusive, insulting, offensive; contemptuous, impudent, irreverent; discourteous, insolent, rude, uncivil
*ant* disrespectful

**respecting** *prep* having to do with — see ABOUT 1

**respective** *adj* not the same or shared — see SEPARATE 1

**respire** *vb* to inhale and exhale air — see BREATHE 1

**resplendence** *n* impressiveness of beauty on a large scale — see MAGNIFICENCE

---

*syn* synonym(s) *rel* related words
*ant* antonym(s) *near ant* near antonym(s)

**respond** *vb* **1** to act or behave in response (as to a stimulus or influence) — see REACT
**2** to speak or write in reaction to a question or to another reaction — see ANSWER 1

**response** *n* **1** action or behavior that is done in return to other action or behavior — see REACTION
**2** something spoken or written in reaction especially to a question — see ANSWER 1

**responsibility** *n* **1** the state of being held as the cause of something that needs to be set right ⟨*responsibility* for the accident lies with the driver who was speeding⟩
***syn*** blame, fault, liability
***rel*** accountability
**2** something one must do because of prior agreement — see OBLIGATION

**responsible** *adj* **1** being the one who must meet an obligation or suffer the consequences for failing to do so ⟨each student is *responsible* for getting his or her own homework done on time⟩
***syn*** accountable, answerable, liable
***rel*** beholden, indebted, obligated, obliged
***near ant*** exempt, immune
***ant*** irresponsible, unaccountable
**2** worthy of one's trust — see DEPENDABLE

[1]**rest** *n* **1** freedom from activity or labor ⟨I'm looking forward to enjoying some *rest* at the end of the school term⟩
***syn*** ease, leisure, relaxation, repose
***rel*** catnapping, dozing, napping, resting, sleep, slumber, slumbering, snoozing; quiet, silence, stillness; calm, peace, peacefulness, placidity, restfulness, serenity, tranquillity (*or* tranquility)
***near ant*** pressure, strain, stress, tension
***ant*** exertion, labor, toil, work
**2** a natural periodic loss of consciousness during which the body restores itself — see SLEEP 1

[2]**rest** *n* a remaining group or portion — see REMAINDER 1

**rest** *vb* **1** to refrain from labor or exertion ⟨a beach resort that caters to gung ho exercisers and athletes as well as vacationers who just want to *rest*⟩
***syn*** bask, loll, lounge, relax, repose
***rel*** bum, goldbrick, idle, loaf, slack (off)
***near ant*** drudge, grub, hump, hustle, labor, moil, peg (away), plod, plow, plug, slave, slog, strain, strive, struggle, sweat, toil, travail, work; exercise, work out
**2** be in a state of sleep — see SLEEP 1
**3** to find a basis — see BASE

**restart** *vb* to begin again or return to after an interruption — see RESUME

**restate** *vb* to express something (as a text or statement) in different words — see PARAPHRASE

**restatement** *n* an instance of expressing something in different words — see PARAPHRASE

**restating** *n* an instance of expressing something in different words — see PARAPHRASE

**restaurant** *n* a public establishment where meals are served to paying customers for consumption on the premises ⟨when we get sick of cooking dinner at home, we like to go out to eat at a nice *restaurant*⟩
***syn*** café (*also* cafe), diner, grill
***rel*** cafeteria, coffeehouse, garden, luncheonette, lunchroom, snack bar, tearoom; bar, barroom, inn, tavern

**restful** *adj* free from disturbing noise or uproar — see QUIET 1

**restfulness** *n* a state of freedom from storm or disturbance — see CALM

**resting** *adj* being in a state of suspended consciousness — see ASLEEP 1

**resting** *n* a natural periodic loss of consciousness during which the body restores itself — see SLEEP 1

**restitution** *n* payment to another for a loss or injury — see COMPENSATION 1

**restive** *adj* **1** given to resisting authority or another's control — see DISOBEDIENT
**2** lacking or denying rest — see RESTLESS 1

**restiveness** *n* **1** a disturbed or uneasy state — see UNREST
**2** a state of nervousness marked by sudden jerky movements — see JUMPINESS

**restless** *adj* **1** lacking or denying rest ⟨the worried mother spent a *restless* night, tossing and turning in bed for hours⟩
***syn*** restive, uneasy, unquiet, unrestful
***rel*** agitated, distressed, disturbed, perturbed, troubled, unsettled; aflutter, anxious, dithery, edgy, fidgety, het up, hung up, jittery, jumpy, nervous, nervy, tense, upset, uptight, worried
***near ant*** calm, easy, peaceful, quiet, relaxing, tranquil
***ant*** restful
**2** marked by or causing agitation or uncomfortable feelings — see NERVOUS 2

**restlessness** *n* **1** a disturbed or uneasy state — see UNREST
**2** the state of being bored — see BOREDOM

**restorative** *adj* **1** good for the health — see HEALTHFUL
**2** having a renewing effect on the state of the body or mind — see TONIC

**restore** *vb* **1** to bring back to a former condition or vigor — see RENEW 1
**2** to bring, send, or put back to a former or proper place — see RETURN 1

**restrain** *vb* **1** to keep from exceeding a desirable degree or level (as of expression) — see CONTROL 1
**2** to take or keep under one's control by authority of law — see ARREST 1

**restrained** *adj* not excessively showy — see QUIET 2

**restraint** *n* **1** the checking of one's true feelings and impulses when dealing with others — see CONSTRAINT 1
**2** something that limits one's freedom of action or choice — see RESTRICTION 1

3 the power to control one's actions, impulses, or emotions — see WILL 1

**restrict** *vb* 1 to set bounds or an upper limit for — see LIMIT 1
2 to limit the meaning of (as a noun) — see QUALIFY 1

**restricted** *adj* having distinct or certain limits — see LIMITED 1

**restriction** *n* 1 something that limits one's freedom of action or choice ⟨my parents placed several *restrictions* on the party we were planning⟩
*syn* check, condition, constraint, curb, fetter, limitation, restraint
*rel* exception, proviso, qualification, reservation, stipulation, strings
*near ant* freedom, latitude
2 the act or practice of keeping something (as an activity) within certain boundaries ⟨the *restriction* of surfing to the southern end of the beach rankled some surfers⟩
*syn* confinement, limitation
*rel* constraint, restraint; isolation, segregation

**rest room** *n* a room furnished with a fixture for flushing body waste — see TOILET

**result** *n* 1 a condition or occurrence traceable to a cause — see EFFECT 1
2 something attained by mental effort and especially by computation — see ANSWER 2

**result** (in) *vb* to be the cause of (a situation, action, or state of mind) — see EFFECT

**resultant** *adj* coming as a result ⟨frequent trips to the ice cream parlor and the *resultant* gain in weight were starting to affect my tennis game⟩
*syn* attendant, consequent, consequential, due (to)
*rel* accompanying, coincident, concomitant
*near ant* causal

**resultant** *n* a condition or occurrence traceable to a cause — see EFFECT 1

**resume** *vb* to begin again or return to after an interruption ⟨we *resumed* the game as soon as the rain had passed⟩
*syn* continue, renew, reopen, restart
*rel* resuscitate, revive
*near ant* complete, conclude, consummate, end, finalize, finish; belay, break, can, cease, check, cut, desist, discontinue, drop, halt, knock off, leave off, quit, scuttle, shut off, stay, stop, terminate

**résumé** *or* **resume** *also* **resumé** *n* a short statement of the main points — see SUMMARY

**resurgence** *n* the act or an instance of bringing something back to life, public attention, or vigorous activity — see REVIVAL

**resurrect** *vb* to bring back to life, practice, or activity — see REVIVE 1

**resurrection** *n* the act or an instance of bringing something back to life, public attention, or vigorous activity — see REVIVAL

**resuscitate** *vb* to bring back to life, practice, or activity — see REVIVE 1

**resuscitated** *adj* made or become fresh in spirits or vigor — see NEW 4

**resuscitation** *n* the act or an instance of bringing something back to life, public attention, or vigorous activity — see REVIVAL

**retail** *vb* to offer for sale to the public — see MARKET

**retain** *vb* 1 to continue to have in one's possession or power — see KEEP 2
2 to keep, control, or experience as one's own — see HAVE 1
3 to provide with a paying job — see EMPLOY 1

**retainer** *n* a person hired to perform household or personal services — see SERVANT

**retake** *vb* to get again in one's possession — see RECOVER 1

**retaliate** *vb* to punish in kind the wrongdoer responsible for — see AVENGE

**retaliation** *n* the act or an instance of paying back an injury with an injury — see REVENGE

**retard** *vb* to cause to move or proceed at a less rapid pace — see SLOW 1

**retardation** *n* a usually gradual decrease in the pace or level of activity of something — see SLOWDOWN

**retarding** *n* a usually gradual decrease in the pace or level of activity of something — see SLOWDOWN

**retch** *vb* to discharge the contents of the stomach through the mouth — see VOMIT

**rethink** *vb* to consider again especially with the possibility of change or reversal — see RECONSIDER

**reticent** *adj* 1 given to keeping one's activities hidden from public observation or knowledge — see SECRETIVE
2 tending not to speak frequently (as by habit or inclination) — see SILENT 2

**retinue** *n* a body of employees or servants who accompany and wait on a person — see CORTEGE 1

**retire** *vb* 1 to go to one's bed in order to sleep — see BED
2 to let go from office, service, or employment — see DISMISS 1
3 to move back or away (as from something difficult, dangerous, or disagreeable) — see RETREAT 1

**retire** (from) *vb* to give up (a job or office) — see QUIT 1

**retired** *adj* hidden from view — see SECLUDED

**retirement** *n* an act of moving away especially from something difficult, dangerous, or disagreeable — see RETREAT 1

**retiring** *adj* 1 not comfortable around people — see SHY 2
2 not having or showing any feelings of superiority, self-assertiveness, or showiness — see HUMBLE 1

---

*syn* synonym(s) *rel* related words
*ant* antonym(s) *near ant* near antonym(s)

**retiringness** *n* the absence of any feelings of being better than others — see HUMILITY

**retort** *n* **1** a quick witty response ⟨the clever boy responded to the bully's threat with a rude *retort*⟩
*syn* comeback, repartee, riposte
*rel* back talk; crack, quip, sally, wisecrack, witticism; cut, insult, put-down
**2** something spoken or written in reaction especially to a question — see ANSWER 1

**retort** *vb* to speak or write in reaction to a question or to another reaction — see ANSWER 1

**retract** *vb* to solemnly or formally reject or go back on (as something formerly adhered to) — see ABJURE

**retreat** *n* **1** an act of moving away especially from something difficult, dangerous, or disagreeable ⟨we made a strategic *retreat* when we realized that we were outnumbered⟩
*syn* recession, retirement, revulsion, withdrawal
*rel* flinch, recoil, shrinking
*ant* advancement
**2** something (as a building) that offers cover from the weather or protection from danger — see SHELTER

**retreat** *vb* **1** to move back or away (as from something difficult, dangerous, or disagreeable) ⟨we *retreated* to the safety of the cellar at the first sign of the tornado⟩
*syn* back (away), fall back, recede, retire, withdraw
*rel* flinch, recoil, shrink; chicken (out); back down, backtrack; abandon, depart, evacuate, go, leave, quit, vacate
*phrases* give way, lose ground
*near ant* beard, brave, brazen, breast, confront, dare, defy, face, outbrave
*ant* advance
**2** to hasten away from something dangerous or frightening — see RUN 2

**retribution** *n* the act or an instance of paying back an injury with an injury — see REVENGE

**retrieval** *n* the act or process of getting something back — see RECOVERY 1

**retrieve** *vb* to get again in one's possession — see RECOVER 1

**retrograde** *adj* directed, turned, or done toward the back — see BACKWARD

**retrogress** *vb* to go back to a previous and usually lower state or level — see REGRESS

**retrogression** *n* the act or an instance of going back to an earlier and lower level especially of intelligence or behavior — see REGRESSION

**retrospect** *n* a usually critical look at a past event — see REVIEW 1

**retrospection** *n* a usually critical look at a past event — see REVIEW 1

**return** *n* **1** something spoken or written in reaction especially to a question — see ANSWER 1
**2** an increase usually measured in money that comes from labor, business, or property — see INCOME
**3** the amount of money left when expenses are subtracted from the total amount received — see PROFIT 1

**return** *vb* **1** to bring, send, or put back to a former or proper place ⟨when I'm done reading a book, I always *return* it to the very shelf I got it from⟩
*syn* replace, restore
*near ant* remove, take
**2** to produce as revenue — see YIELD 2
**3** to speak or write in reaction to a question or to another reaction — see ANSWER 1

**revamp** *vb* **1** to make different in some way — see CHANGE 1
**2** to prepare for publication by correcting, rewriting, or updating — see EDIT
**3** to put into good shape or working order again — see MEND 1

**revamping** *n* the act, process, or result of making different — see CHANGE

**reveal** *vb* **1** to make known (as information previously kept secret) ⟨at the end of the book, the detective *reveals* the identity of the mysterious stranger⟩
*syn* bare, disclose, discover, divulge, expose, spill, tell, unbosom, uncloak, uncover, unmask, unveil
*rel* debunk, show up; unclothe, undrape; advertise, announce, blaze, broadcast, declare, placard, post, proclaim, promulgate, publicize, publish, sound; betray, blab, give away, leak, let on; inform, squeal, talk; communicate, impart, relate; acknowledge, admit, avow, concede, confess, own; disinter, unearth
*phrases* spill the beans (about)
*near ant* camouflage, disguise; gild, gloss (over), varnish, whitewash; becloud, bedim, befog, cloud, darken, eclipse, obscure, overcast, overshadow, shade
*ant* cloak, conceal, cover (up), enshroud, hide, mask, shroud, veil
**2** to make known (something abstract) through outward signs — see SHOW 2

**revealing** *adj* clearly conveying a special meaning (as one's mood) — see EXPRESSIVE

**revel** *n* a time or instance of carefree fun — see FLING 1

**revel** (in) *vb* to take pleasure in — see ENJOY 1

**revelation** *n* the act or an instance of making known something previously unknown or concealed ⟨the *revelation* of the movie star's secret marriage by the tabloids⟩ ⟨a new biography of the former president that contains several shocking *revelations*⟩
*syn* disclosure, divulgence, exposure
*rel* bombshell, surprise; acknowledgment (*also* acknowledgement), admission, avowal, concession, confession
*near ant* concealment, cover-up

**reveler** *or* **reveller** *n* one who engages in merrymaking especially in honor of a special occasion — see CELEBRANT

**reveling** *n* joyful or festive activity — see MERRYMAKING
**revelry** *n* joyful or festive activity — see MERRYMAKING
**revenge** *n* the act or an instance of paying back an injury with an injury ⟨my *revenge* on the bully who stole my lunch money was the talk of the whole school⟩
***syn*** reprisal, requital, retaliation, retribution, vengeance
***rel*** counter, counterattack, counteroffensive; castigation, chastisement, correction; desert(s), discipline, nemesis, penalty, punishment, wrath; amends, compensation, indemnification, indemnity, quittance, recompense, recoupment, redress, remuneration, reparation(s), restitution
***near ant*** clemency, grace, leniency, lenity, mercy; forgiveness, pardon, remission
**revenge** *vb* to punish in kind the wrongdoer responsible for — see AVENGE
**revengeful** *adj* likely to seek revenge — see VINDICTIVE
**revenue** *n* an increase usually measured in money that comes from labor, business, or property — see INCOME
**reverberant** *adj* marked by conspicuously full and rich sounds or tones — see RESONANT
**reverberate** *vb* to continue or be repeated in a series of reflected sound waves ⟨a room with nothing but hard surfaces will cause the music from your audio system to *reverberate*⟩
***syn*** echo, reecho, resonate, resound, sound
***near ant*** damp, dampen, deaden, dull, quiet
**reverberating** *adj* marked by conspicuously full and rich sounds or tones — see RESONANT
**revere** *vb* to offer honor or respect to (someone) as a divine power — see WORSHIP 1
**revered** *adj* deserving honor and respect especially by reason of age — see VENERABLE 1
**reverence** *vb* to offer honor or respect to (someone) as a divine power — see WORSHIP 1
**reverend** *adj* deserving honor and respect especially by reason of age — see VENERABLE 1
**reverend** *n* a person specially trained and authorized to conduct religious services in a Christian church — see CLERGYMAN
**reverie** *also* **revery** *n* the state of being lost in thought ⟨unfortunately, I was deep in *reverie* when the teacher called my name⟩
***syn*** daydreaming, study, trance, woolgathering
***rel*** contemplation, meditation, musing; absentmindedness, absorption, abstraction, preoccupation; chimera, conceit, daydream, delusion, dream, fancy, fantasy (*also* phantasy), figment, hallucination, illusion, phantasm, pipe dream, unreality, vision
**reversal** *n* a change in status for the worse usually temporarily — see REVERSE 1
**reverse** *n* **1** a change in status for the worse usually temporarily ⟨the loss of my paper route was just the first of my financial *reverses* since the start of the new year⟩
***syn*** lapse, reversal, setback
***rel*** disappointment, frustration, letdown; comedown, decline, descent, down, downfall, fall; turnabout, turnaround; recession, regression, retrogression, reversion; relapse; breakdown, collapse, crash, meltdown, ruin, undoing
***near ant*** status quo
**2** something that is as different as possible from something else — see OPPOSITE
**reverse** *vb* **1** to change (as an opinion) to the contrary ⟨the principal refused to *reverse* his decision regarding the use of cellular phones⟩
***syn*** switch
***rel*** abrogate, overturn, repeal, rescind, revoke, strike (down); countermand, about-face, backtrack, revert
***near ant*** maintain, support, uphold
**2** to change the position of (an object) so that the opposite side or end is showing ⟨when one side of the cleaning cloth gets dirty, just *reverse* it⟩ ⟨you can *reverse* the jacket for a whole new look⟩
***syn*** flip, invert, turn (over)
***rel*** transpose; exchange, interchange, shift, switch; overturn, upset
**reversion** *n* the act or an instance of going back to an earlier and lower level especially of intelligence or behavior — see REGRESSION
**revert** *vb* to go back to a previous and usually lower state or level — see REGRESS
**review** *n* **1** a usually critical look at a past event ⟨a *review* of yesterday's football game gave us a lot of good ideas on how to improve for the next one⟩
***syn*** reappraisal, reconsideration, reexamination, retrospect, retrospection
***rel*** recap, recapitulation, rehash
***near ant*** preview
**2** a close look at or over someone or something in order to judge condition — see INSPECTION
**3** a publication that appears at regular intervals — see JOURNAL
**4** an essay evaluating or analyzing something — see CRITICISM
**review** *vb* **1** to consider again especially with the possibility of change or reversal — see RECONSIDER
**2** to look over closely (as for judging quality or condition) — see INSPECT
**reviewer** *n* a person who makes or expresses a judgment on the quality of offerings in some field of endeavor — see CRITIC 2
**revise** *n* the act, process, or result of making different — see CHANGE
**revise** *vb* **1** to make different in some way — see CHANGE 1

2 to prepare for publication by correcting, rewriting, or updating — see EDIT

**revision** *n* the act, process, or result of making different — see CHANGE

**revitalization** *n* the act or an instance of bringing something back to life, public attention, or vigorous activity — see REVIVAL

**revitalize** *vb* 1 to bring back to a former condition or vigor — see RENEW 1
2 to bring back to life, practice, or activity — see REVIVE 1

**revival** *n* the act or an instance of bringing something back to life, public attention, or vigorous activity ⟨there was a *revival* of interest in the author's classic horror stories after a film version of his best-known story was released⟩
*syn* reanimation, rebirth, regeneration, rejuvenation, renewal, resurgence, resurrection, resuscitation, revitalization
*rel* renaissance, renascence; reactivation; rally, recovery, recuperation
*near ant* death, expiration, extinction

**revive** *vb* 1 to bring back to life, practice, or activity ⟨an effort to *revive* the once-common custom of celebrating May 1 as a springtime festival of games and dances⟩
*syn* reanimate, regenerate, rejuvenate, rekindle, renew, resurrect, resuscitate, revitalize
*rel* reactivate, restart
*near ant* extinguish, quench, suppress
2 to bring back to a former condition or vigor — see RENEW 1
3 to gain consciousness again — see COME TO

**revived** *adj* made or become fresh in spirits or vigor — see NEW 4

**reviving** *adj* having a renewing effect on the state of the body or mind — see TONIC

**revocation** *n* the act of putting an end to something planned or previously agreed to — see CANCELLATION

**revoke** *vb* to put an end to (something planned or previously agreed to) — see CANCEL 1

**revolt** *n* open fighting against authority (as one's own government) — see REBELLION

**revolt** *vb* 1 to cause to feel disgust — see DISGUST
2 to rise up against established authority — see REBEL

**revolted** *adj* filled with disgust — see SICK 2

**revolter** *n* a person who rises up against authority — see REBEL

**revolting** *adj* causing intense displeasure, disgust, or resentment — see OFFENSIVE 1

**revolution** *n* 1 a rapid turning about on an axis or central point — see SPIN 1
2 open fighting against authority (as one's own government) — see REBELLION

**revolutionary** *adj* 1 being very far from the center of public opinion — see EXTREME 2
2 taking part in a rebellion — see REBELLIOUS 1

**revolutionary** *n* 1 a person who favors rapid and sweeping changes especially in laws and methods of government — see RADICAL
2 a person who rises up against authority — see REBEL

**revolutionist** *adj* being very far from the center of public opinion — see EXTREME 2

**revolutionist** *n* 1 a person who favors rapid and sweeping changes especially in laws and methods of government — see RADICAL
2 a person who rises up against authority — see REBEL

**revolutionizer** *n* a person who rises up against authority — see REBEL

**revolve** *vb* 1 to move (something) in a curved or circular path on or as if on an axis — see TURN 1
2 to move in circles around an axis or center — see SPIN 1

**revulsion** *n* 1 a dislike so strong as to cause stomach upset or queasiness — see DISGUST
2 an act of moving away especially from something difficult, dangerous, or disagreeable — see RETREAT 1

**reward** *n* something offered or given in return for a service performed ⟨there was a *reward* of twenty dollars for the return of her missing cat⟩
*syn* bounty, price
*rel* bonus, lagniappe, premium; bonanza, jackpot, treasure trove; award, decoration, distinction, honor, plume, premium, prize; gratuity, tip; desert(s), wages

**reward** *vb* to give something as a token of gratitude or admiration for a service or achievement ⟨the firefighters were *rewarded* by the city for their heroic actions with vacations⟩
*syn* award
*rel* cite, decorate, honor, remember; compensate, pay, recompense, requite; reimburse, repay; acclaim, applaud, commend, compliment, hail, praise, salute

**rewarding** *adj* making one feel good inside — see HEARTWARMING

**reweigh** *vb* to consider again especially with the possibility of change or reversal — see RECONSIDER

**reword** *vb* to express something (as a text or statement) in different words — see PARAPHRASE

**rewording** *n* an instance of expressing something in different words — see PARAPHRASE

**rework** *vb* 1 to make different in some way — see CHANGE 1
2 to prepare for publication by correcting, rewriting, or updating — see EDIT

**reworking** *n* the act, process, or result of making different — see CHANGE

**rhapsodic** *also* **rhapsodical** *adj* experiencing or marked by overwhelming usually pleasurable emotion — see ECSTATIC

**rhapsodically** *adv* in an enthusiastic manner — see SKY-HIGH
**rhapsodize** *vb* to make an exaggerated display of affection or enthusiasm — see GUSH 2
**rhapsody** *n* a state of overwhelming usually pleasurable emotion — see ECSTASY
**rhetoric** *n* **1** language that is impressive-sounding but not meaningful or sincere ⟨the mayor's promise to fight drugs was just *rhetoric*, since there was no money in the city budget for a drug program⟩
***syn*** bombast, gas, grandiloquence, hot air, oratory, wind
***rel*** claptrap, drivel, gibberish, hogwash, humbug, jabberwocky, jazz, moonshine, nonsense; affectedness, floweriness, grandiosity, loftiness, pomposity, pretension, pretentiousness; verboseness, verbosity, windiness, wordiness
**2** the art or power of speaking or writing in a forceful and convincing way — see ELOQUENCE
**rhetorical** *adj* marked by the use of impressive-sounding but mostly meaningless words and phrases ⟨an essay on civic duty that was mostly *rhetorical*, full of flowery quotations but providing nothing helpful⟩
***syn*** bombastic, gaseous, gassy, grandiloquent, oratorical, windy
***rel*** elevated, florid, flowery, grandiose, highfalutin, high-flown, high-sounding, inflated, lofty, pompous, pretentious, stilted; overdone, verbose, wordy
***near ant*** eloquent, well-spoken; bald, direct, matter-of-fact, plain, plainspoken, simple, stark, straightforward, unadorned, unaffected, unpretentious
**rhythm** *n* the recurrent pattern formed by a series of sounds having a regular rise and fall in intensity ⟨the steady *rhythm* of the rain falling on the roof⟩
***syn*** beat, cadence, measure, meter
***rel*** accent, accentuation, emphasis, stress; drum, throb; lilt, movement, sway; hexameter, pentameter, tetrameter, trimeter
**rhythmic** *or* **rhythmical** *adj* marked by or occurring with a noticeable regularity in the rise and fall of sound ⟨lulled to sleep by the *rhythmic* sound of her mother's voice reading the Bible⟩
***syn*** cadenced, measured, metric, metrical
***rel*** even, regular, steady, uniform; lilting, musical, swaying
***ant*** unmeasured, unrhythmic
**riata** *n* a rope or long leather thong with a noose used especially for catching livestock — see LASSO
**rib** *vb* to make fun of in a good-natured way — see TEASE 1
**ribald** *adj* **1** depicting or referring to sexual matters in a way that is unacceptable in polite society — see OBSCENE 1
**2** hinting at or intended to call to mind matters regarded as indecent — see SUGGESTIVE 1

***syn*** synonym(s) ***rel*** related words
***ant*** antonym(s) ***near ant*** near antonym(s)

**ribaldry** *n* the quality or state of being obscene — see OBSCENITY 1
**ribbing** *adj* marked by or expressive of mild or good-natured teasing — see QUIZZICAL
**ribbon** *n* a long narrow piece of material — see STRIP
**rich** *adj* **1** having goods, property, or money in abundance ⟨Tanya's dad works as chauffeur for the *richest* man in town, a big oil baron⟩
***syn*** affluent, flush, loaded, moneyed (*or* monied), opulent, wealthy, well-heeled, well-off, well-to-do
***rel*** comfortable, propertied, prosperous, successful; flourishing, prospering, thriving; advantaged, blessed, privileged
***near ant*** deprived, disadvantaged, underprivileged; bankrupt, bankrupted, beggared, broke, indebted, insolvent, pauperized, ruined, stone-broke; depressed, pinched, reduced, straitened; low, short
***ant*** destitute, impecunious, impoverished, indigent, needy, penniless, penurious, poor, poverty-stricken
**2** containing much seasoning, fat, or sugar ⟨stay away from *rich* foods before you sing tonight⟩
***syn*** heavy
***rel*** buttery, fat, fatty, greasy, oily; caloric, calorific, fattening; cloying, filling, overfilling, satiating, sating; spicy, sugary; creamy, sauced
***near ant*** natural, plain, simple; unseasoned; diet, nonfattening, slimming; nonfat
***ant*** light
**3** having an abundance of some characteristic quality (as flavor) — see FULL-BODIED
**4** producing abundantly — see FERTILE
**riches** *n* the total of one's money and property — see WEALTH 1
**richly** *adv* in a luxurious manner — see HIGH
**richness** *n* the amusing quality or element in something — see HUMOR 1
**rick** *n* a quantity of things thrown or stacked on one another — see [1]PILE 1
**ricochet** *vb* to strike and fly off at an angle — see GLANCE 1
**rid** *vb* to set (a person or thing) free of something that encumbers ⟨worked two jobs to *rid* himself of debt⟩
***syn*** clear, disburden, disencumber, free, relieve, unburden
***rel*** discharge, emancipate, enfranchise, liberate, loose, loosen, manumit, release, spring, unbind, uncage, unchain, unfetter; bail (out), deliver, redeem, rescue; disengage, disentangle, extricate
***near ant*** bog (down), fetter, restrain, shackle, subject, weigh (down), weight (down)
***ant*** burden, encumber, saddle
**riddance** *n* the getting rid of whatever is unwanted or useless — see DISPOSAL 1
**riddle** *n* something hard to understand or explain — see MYSTERY

**riddle** *vb* to find an answer for through reasoning — see SOLVE

**ride** *n* a means of getting to a destination in a vehicle driven by another ⟨Laurie sometimes gets a *ride* to school from her neighbor⟩
*syn* lift, transportation
*rel* drive, spin, turn; joyride; conveyance, passage, transit, transport

**ride** *vb* **1** to attack repeatedly with mean put-downs or insults — see TEASE 2
**2** to make fun of in a good-natured way — see TEASE 1
**3** to rest or move along the surface of a liquid or in the air — see FLOAT

**ride** (out) *vb* to come safely through — see SURVIVE 1

**ridge** *n* the line formed when two sloping surfaces come together along their topmost edge ⟨pigeons roosting along the *ridge* of the roof⟩
*syn* crest
*rel* divide; backbone, chine, ridgepole, spine; eminence, peak, prominence, promontory, rise

**ridicule** *n* the making of unkind jokes as a way of showing one's scorn for someone or something ⟨the early efforts by the suffragists to obtain voting rights for women were met with *ridicule*⟩
*syn* derision, mockery
*rel* contempt, disdain, scorn; belittlement, deprecation, disparagement; insult, put-down; laughter, snickering; burlesque, caricature, mimicry, satire
*near ant* applause, approval, commendation, praise

**ridicule** *vb* to make (someone or something) the object of unkind laughter ⟨the term "big bang theory" was originally coined to *ridicule* the belief that the universe was created by a giant explosion⟩
*syn* deride, gibe (*or* jibe), jeer, laugh (at), mock, scout
*rel* scoff (at), scorn, sneer (at); badmouth, belittle, decry, disparage, poohpooh (*also* pooh), put down, chaff, jive, josh, kid, quiz, rally, razz, rib, ride, tease; bait, bug, harass, harry, hassle, heckle, needle, pester, target, taunt, torment; ape, burlesque, caricature, imitate, lampoon, mimic, parody, parrot, satirize, take off (on), travesty
*phrases* make fun of, poke fun at
*near ant* applaud, approve, commend, endorse (*also* indorse), sanction

**ridiculer** *n* a person who causes repeated emotional pain, distress, or annoyance to another — see TORMENTOR

**ridiculous** *adj* **1** so foolish or pointless as to be worthy of scornful laughter ⟨a movie thriller with such a *ridiculous* plot that it gets only guffaws from audiences⟩
*syn* absurd, comical, derisive, derisory, farcical, laughable, ludicrous, preposterous, risible, silly
*rel* asinine, brainless, dumb, fatuous, foolish, half-witted, harebrained, idiotic, imbecilic, inane, jerky, moronic, nonsensical, simpleminded, stupid, unwise, weak-minded, witless; balmy, cockeyed, crazy, cuckoo, daffy, daft, dotty, insane, kooky, loony (*also* looney), lunatic, mad, nutty, screwball, senseless, wacky; fantastic, far-fetched, inconceivable, incredible, unbelievable, unreal, unreasonable
*near ant* earnest, serious, solemn; believable, conceivable, credible, logical, rational, realistic, reasonable, sensible
**2** causing or intended to cause laughter — see FUNNY 1

**rife** *adj* possessing or covered with great numbers or amounts of something specified ⟨our school is *rife* with rumors about the incoming principal⟩
*syn* abounding, flush, fraught, replete, swarming, teeming, thick, thronging
*rel* brimming, bulging, bursting, chockfull (*or* chockful), crammed, crowded, fat, filled, full, jammed, jam-packed, loaded, packed, saturated, stuffed; clogged, congested, overcrowded, overfilled, overflowing, overfull, overloaded, overstuffed, surfeited; alive, animated, astir, bustling, busy, buzzing, humming, lively
*near ant* bare, barren, blank, devoid, empty, stark, vacant, void; depleted, drained, exhausted; deficient, incomplete, insufficient, short

**riffraff** *n* **1** discarded or useless material — see GARBAGE
**2** people looked down upon as ignorant and of the lowest class — see RABBLE

**rifle** *vb* to look through (as a place) carefully or thoroughly in an effort to find or discover something — see SEARCH 1

**rift** *n* **1** an irregular usually narrow break in a surface created by pressure — see CRACK 1
**2** an open space in a barrier (as a wall or hedge) — see GAP 1

**rig** *n* a horse-drawn wheeled vehicle for carrying passengers — see CARRIAGE 1

**rig** *vb* to provide (someone) with what is needed for a task or activity — see FURNISH 1

**rig** (out) *vb* to outfit with clothes and especially fine or special clothes — see CLOTHE 1

**right** *adj* **1** following an original exactly — see FAITHFUL 2
**2** being exactly as appears or as claimed — see AUTHENTIC 1
**3** being in agreement with the truth or a fact or a standard — see CORRECT 1
**4** being what is called for by accepted standards of right and wrong — see JUST 1
**5** conforming to a high standard of morality or virtue — see GOOD 2
**6** free from irregularities (as curves, bends, or angles) in course — see STRAIGHT 1
**7** having full use of one's mind and control over one's actions — see SANE
**8** meeting the requirements of a purpose or situation — see FIT 1

**right** *adv* **1** as stated or indicated without the slightest difference — see EXACTLY 1

2 in a direct line or course — see DIRECTLY 1
3 to a great degree — see VERY 1

**right** *n* 1 something to which one has a just claim ⟨everyone has the *right* to life, liberty, and the pursuit of happiness⟩
*syn* appanage, birthright, prerogative
*rel* due, entitlement, perquisite, privilege
2 an entitlement to something — see CLAIM 1
3 the act or practice of giving to others what is their due — see JUSTICE 1

**right away** *adv* without delay — see IMMEDIATELY

**righteous** *adj* 1 conforming to a high standard of morality or virtue — see GOOD 2
2 following the accepted rules of moral conduct — see HONORABLE 1

**righteously** *adv* with purity of thought and deed — see PURELY

**righteousness** *n* 1 conduct that conforms to an accepted standard of right and wrong — see MORALITY 1
2 faithfulness to high moral standards — see HONOR 1

**rightful** *adj* being what is called for by accepted standards of right and wrong — see JUST 1

**rightist** *n* a person whose political beliefs are centered on tradition and keeping things the way they are — see CONSERVATIVE

**rightly** *adv* in a manner suitable for the occasion or purpose — see PROPERLY

**right–minded** *adj* conforming to a high standard of morality or virtue — see GOOD 2

**rightness** *n* the quality or state of being especially suitable or fitting — see APPROPRIATENESS

**right now** *adv* 1 at the present time — see NOW 1
2 without delay — see IMMEDIATELY

**right–of–way** *n* the right to one's attention before other things considered less important — see PRIORITY

**rigid** *adj* 1 not allowing for any exceptions or loosening of standards ⟨*rigid* enforcement of drug laws⟩
*syn* exacting, inflexible, rigorous, strict, stringent, uncompromising
*rel* close, conscientious, scrupulous, undeviating; adamant, adamantine, determined, dogged, firm, relentless, resolved, single-minded, steadfast, stubborn, tenacious, unbending, unflinching; immovable, implacable, unrelenting, unyielding; austere, demanding, flinty, grim, hard, hardened, hardhearted, harsh, ironbound, severe, stern, tough
*near ant* acquiescent, compliant, compromising, pliable, pliant, relenting, yielding; easy, easygoing, gentle, indulgent, kindly, lenient, merciful, mild, pampering, soft, spoiling, tolerant
*ant* flexible, lax, loose, relaxed
2 given to exacting standards of discipline and self-restraint — see SEVERE 1
3 having a consistency that does not easily yield to pressure — see FIRM 2
4 incapable of or highly resistant to bending — see STIFF 1
5 sticking to an opinion, purpose, or course of action in spite of reason, arguments, or persuasion — see OBSTINATE
6 stretched with little or no give — see TAUT

**rigidity** *n* the quality or state of being demanding or unyielding (as in discipline or criticism) — see SEVERITY

**rigidly** *adv* without any relaxation of standards or precision — see STRICTLY

**rigidness** *n* the quality or state of being demanding or unyielding (as in discipline or criticism) — see SEVERITY

**rigmarole** *n* unintelligible or meaningless talk — see GIBBERISH

**rigor** *n* something that is a cause for suffering or special effort especially in the attainment of a goal — see DIFFICULTY 1

**rigorous** *adj* 1 given to exacting standards of discipline and self-restraint — see SEVERE 1
2 meeting the highest standard of accuracy — see PRECISE 1
3 not allowing for any exceptions or loosening of standards — see RIGID 1

**rigorously** *adv* without any relaxation of standards or precision — see STRICTLY

**rigorousness** *n* 1 the quality or state of being demanding or unyielding (as in discipline or criticism) — see SEVERITY
2 the quality or state of being very accurate — see PRECISION

**rile** *vb* to disturb the peace of mind of (someone) especially by repeated disagreeable acts — see IRRITATE 1

**rile** *vb* to make angry — see ANGER

**riled** *adj* feeling or showing anger — see ANGRY

**riling** *adj* causing annoyance — see ANNOYING

**rill** *n* a natural body of running water smaller than a river — see CREEK 1

**rim** *n* the line or relatively narrow space that marks the outer limit of something — see BORDER 1

**rim** *vb* to serve as a border for — see BORDER

**rime** *n* a covering of tiny ice crystals on a cold surface — see FROST

**rime** *vb* to cover with a hardened layer — see ENCRUST

**ring** *n* 1 a group involved in secret or criminal activities ⟨a *ring* of counterfeiters passing phony $20 bills⟩
*syn* cabal, conspiracy, gang, Mafia, mob, syndicate
*rel* circle, clan, clique, coterie, crowd; junta, oligarchy
2 a circular strip ⟨a metal *ring* encircled the barrel⟩
*syn* band, circle, eye, hoop, loop, round
*rel* belt, cincture, collar, girdle; wreath; coil, spiral

---

*syn* synonym(s) *rel* related words
*ant* antonym(s) *near ant* near antonym(s)

3 a communication by telephone — see CALL 3
4 a group of people sharing a common interest and relating together socially — see GANG 2
5 something with a perfectly round circumference — see CIRCLE 1

**ring** *vb* 1 to make the clear sound heard when metal vibrates ⟨I didn't hear the doorbell *ring*⟩
*syn* chime, knell, peal, toll
*rel* clang, clank, ding, jangle, jingle, ping, tinkle; resound, reverberate
2 to form a circle around — see SURROUND
3 to pass completely around — see ENCIRCLE 1

**ring** (up) *vb, chiefly British* to make a telephone call to — see CALL 2

**ringer** *n* something or someone that strongly resembles another — see IMAGE 1

**ringing** *adj* 1 marked by a high volume of sound — see LOUD 1
2 marked by conspicuously full and rich sounds or tones — see RESONANT

**ringlet** *n* a length of hair that forms a loop or series of loops — see CURL

**rinse** *vb* to pour liquid over or through in order to cleanse — see FLUSH 1

**riot** *n* someone or something that is very funny — see SCREAM

**riotous** *adj* 1 causing or intended to cause laughter — see FUNNY 1
2 pouring forth in great amounts — see PROFUSE

**rip** *n* a long deep cut — see GASH

**rip** *vb* 1 to cause (something) to separate into jagged pieces by violently pulling at it — see TEAR 1
2 to penetrate with a sharp edge (as a knife) — see CUT 1
3 to proceed or move quickly — see HURRY 2
4 to separate or remove by forceful pulling — see TEAR 2

**ripe** *adj* fully grown or developed — see MATURE 1

**ripen** *vb* to become mature — see MATURE

**ripened** *adj* fully grown or developed — see MATURE 1

**ripening** *n* the process of becoming mature — see MATURATION

**rip–off** *n* an instance of theft — see THEFT 2

**rip off** *vb* 1 to remove valuables from (a place) unlawfully — see ROB
2 to take (something) without right and with an intent to keep — see STEAL 1

**riposte** *n* a quick witty response — see RETORT 1

**ripple** *vb* to flow in a broken irregular stream — see GURGLE

**rip–roaring** *adj* causing great emotional or mental stimulation — see EXCITING 1

**rise** *n* 1 a raising or a state of being raised to a higher rank or position — see ADVANCEMENT 1
2 an area of high ground — see HEIGHT 4
3 an upward slope — see ASCENT 2
4 something added (as by growth) — see INCREASE 1
5 the act or an instance of rising or climbing up — see ASCENT 1

**rise** *vb* 1 to become greater in extent, volume, amount, or number — see INCREASE 2
2 to leave one's bed — see ARISE 1
3 to move or extend upward — see ASCEND

**risible** *adj* 1 causing or intended to cause laughter — see FUNNY 1
2 so foolish or pointless as to be worthy of scornful laughter — see RIDICULOUS 1

**rising** *n* the act or an instance of rising or climbing up — see ASCENT 1

**risk** *n* 1 something that may cause injury or harm — see DANGER 2
2 the state of not being protected from injury, harm, or evil — see DANGER 1

**risk** *vb* 1 to take a chance on ⟨Colette didn't want to *risk* running out of film on her trip, so she brought along a dozen rolls⟩
*syn* chance, gamble (on), hazard, venture
*rel* brave, challenge, dare, defy, face; compromise, endanger, imperil, jeopardize, menace; expose, subject; bet (on), wager
2 to place in danger — see ENDANGER

**risky** *adj* involving potential loss or injury — see DANGEROUS

**rite** *n* an oft-repeated action or series of actions performed in accordance with tradition or a set of rules ⟨the annual summer *rite* of loading up the car for the big family vacation⟩
*syn* ceremonial, ceremony, form, formality, observance, ritual, solemnity
*rel* amenities, civility, decorum, etiquette, graces, proprieties; convention, custom, habit, manners, mores, practice (*also* practise), standard, tradition, way; celebration, service

**ritual** *n* an oft-repeated action or series of actions performed in accordance with tradition or a set of rules — see RITE

**rival** *n* 1 one that is equal to another in status, achievement, or value — see EQUAL
2 one that takes a position opposite another in a competition or conflict — see OPPONENT 1
3 one who strives for the same thing as another — see COMPETITOR

**rivalry** *n* an earnest effort for superiority or victory over another — see CONTEST 1

**rive** *vb* to cause (something) to separate into jagged pieces by violently pulling at it — see TEAR 1

**rivet** *vb* to fix (as one's attention) steadily toward a central objective — see CONCENTRATE 2

**riveting** *adj* holding the attention or provoking interest — see INTERESTING

**rivulet** *n* a natural body of running water smaller than a river — see CREEK 1

**road** *n* 1 a passage cleared for public vehicular travel — see WAY 1
2 a roadway overlaid with parallel steel rails over which trains travel — see RAILROAD

**roadhouse** *n* a bar or restaurant offering special nighttime entertainment (as music, dancing, or comedy acts) — see NIGHTCLUB

**roadway** *n* a passage cleared for public vehicular travel — see WAY 1

**roam** *vb* to move about from place to place aimlessly — see WANDER

**roamer** *n* a person who roams about without a fixed route or destination — see NOMAD

**roaming** *adj* traveling from place to place — see ITINERANT

**roar** *n* **1** a violent shouting — see CLAMOR 1
**2** loud, confused, and usually unharmonious sound — see NOISE 1

**roar** *vb* to make a long loud deep noise or cry ⟨its engine *roared* as the car sped away⟩
***syn*** bellow, boom, growl, thunder
***rel*** grumble, roll, rumble; blare, blast, peal, scream, screech, shriek, squall; cry, holler, hoot, shout, whoop, yell; caterwaul, howl, wail, yowl
***near ant*** mumble, murmur, mutter, whisper; squeak, whimper

**roaring** *adj* **1** marked by a high volume of sound — see LOUD 1
**2** marked by vigorous growth and well-being especially economically — see PROSPEROUS 1

**roast** *vb* to make fun of in a good-natured way — see TEASE 1

**roasting** *adj* having a notably high temperature — see HOT 1

**rob** *vb* to remove valuables from (a place) unlawfully ⟨in jail for *robbing* a bank⟩
***syn*** burglarize, rip off, steal (from)
***rel*** despoil, loot, pillage, plunder, sack, spoil, strip; bleed, break in, cheat, chisel, cozen, defraud, exploit, fleece, gyp, mulct, rook, squeeze, stick, swindle; hold up, mug, stick up

**robber** *n* one who steals — see THIEF

**robbery** *n* the unlawful taking and carrying away of property without the consent of its owner — see THEFT 1

**robe** *vb* to outfit with clothes and especially fine or special clothes — see CLOTHE 1

**robotic** *adj* designed to replace or decrease human labor and especially physical labor — see LABORSAVING

**robust** *adj* **1** enjoying health and vigor — see HEALTHY 1
**2** having active strength of body or mind — see VIGOROUS 1
**3** having an abundance of some characteristic quality (as flavor) — see FULL-BODIED
**4** not showing weakness or uncertainty — see FIRM 1

**robustness** *n* **1** the condition of being sound in body — see HEALTH
**2** the quality or state of having abundant or intense activity — see VITALITY 1

***syn*** synonym(s) ***rel*** related words
***ant*** antonym(s) ***near ant*** near antonym(s)

**rock** *vb* **1** to make a series of unsteady side-to-side motions ⟨the boat was *rocking* so much that Rosa felt seasick⟩
***syn*** careen, lurch, pitch, roll, seesaw, sway, toss, wobble
***rel*** blunder, dodder, falter, flounder, halt, hitch, hobble, jerk, reel, stagger, stumble, teeter, toddle, totter, tumble, waddle, weave; oscillate, undulate, wag, waggle
**2** to swing unsteadily back and forth or from side to side — see TEETER 1

**rock bottom** *n* the lowest part, place, or point — see BOTTOM 3

**rocket** *vb* **1** to proceed or move quickly — see HURRY 2
**2** to rise abruptly and rapidly — see SKYROCKET

**rod** *n* **1** a heavy rigid stick used as a weapon or for punishment — see CLUB 1
**2** a straight piece (as of wood or metal) that is longer than it is wide — see BAR 1

**rogue** *n* **1** a mean, evil, or unprincipled person — see VILLAIN
**2** an appealingly mischievous person — see SCAMP 1

**roguish** *adj* tending to or exhibiting reckless playfulness — see MISCHIEVOUS 1

**roguishness** *n* playful, reckless behavior that is not intended to cause serious harm — see MISCHIEF 1

**roil** *vb* **1** to be in a state of violent rolling motion — see SEETHE 1
**2** to make angry — see ANGER

**roiled** *adj* **1** feeling or showing anger — see ANGRY
**2** having visible particles in liquid suspension — see CLOUDY 1

**roisterer** *n* one who engages in merrymaking especially in honor of a special occasion — see CELEBRANT

**role** *also* **rôle** *n* the action for which a person or thing is specially fitted or used or for which a thing exists ⟨in science class we're studying the *role* of sunlight in the body's production of vitamin D⟩
***syn*** capacity, function, job, part, place, position, purpose, task, work
***rel*** affair, business, concern, involvement, participation; niche, office, post, situation; calling, occupation, pursuit, vocation; activity, assignment, charge, commission, duty, mission, responsibility, service, use

**roll** *n* **1** a rapid turning about on an axis or central point — see SPIN 1
**2** a record of a series of items (as names or titles) usually arranged according to some system — see [1]LIST

**roll** *vb* **1** to form into a round compact mass — see WAD
**2** to make a low heavy rolling sound — see RUMBLE
**3** to make a series of unsteady side-to-side motions — see ROCK 1
**4** to move (something) in a curved or circular path on or as if on an axis — see TURN 1
**5** to move in a stream — see FLOW 1
**6** to move in circles around an axis or center — see SPIN 1

7 to move or proceed smoothly and readily — see FLOW 2

**rollick** *n* a time or instance of carefree fun — see FLING 1

**rollick** *vb* 1 to engage in activity for amusement — see PLAY 1
2 to play and run about happily — see FROLIC 1

**rollicking** *adj* given to good-natured joking or teasing — see PLAYFUL

**rollicking** *n* activity engaged in to amuse oneself — see PLAY 1

**roly–poly** *adj* having an excess of body fat — see FAT 1

**romance** *n* a brief romantic relationship — see AFFAIR 1

**romantic** *adj* excitingly or mysteriously unusual — see EXOTIC

**romantic** *n* one whose conduct is guided more by the image of perfection than by the real world — see IDEALIST

**romanticist** *n* one whose conduct is guided more by the image of perfection than by the real world — see IDEALIST

**romanticize** *vb* to represent or think of as better than reality — see IDEALIZE

**romp** *n* a time or instance of carefree fun — see FLING 1

**romp** *vb* to play and run about happily — see FROLIC 1

**roof** *n* 1 a raised covering over something for decoration or protection — see CANOPY
2 the place where one lives — see HOME 1

**roof** *vb* to provide with living quarters or shelter — see HOUSE 1

**rook** *vb* to rob by the use of trickery or threats — see FLEECE

**rookie** *n* a person who is just starting out in a field of activity — see BEGINNER

**room** *n* 1 an extent or area available for or used up by some activity or thing ⟨need more *room* to do a cartwheel⟩ ⟨made *room* for him on the bench⟩
*syn* elbowroom, place, space, way
*rel* capacity, range, scope; clearance, freedom, latitude, leeway, play
2 an area within a building that has been set apart from surrounding space by a wall ⟨finally had a *room* to himself when his brother went off to college⟩
*syn* apartment, cell, chamber, closet
*rel* accommodation, berth, booth, cabin, compartment, cubicle
3 a favorable combination of circumstances, time, and place — see OPPORTUNITY

**roomer** *n* one who rents a room or apartment in another's house — see TENANT

**roomy** *adj* more than adequate or average in capacity — see SPACIOUS

**roost** *vb* 1 to come to rest after descending from the air — see ALIGHT
2 to establish or place comfortably or snugly — see ENSCONCE 1

**root** *vb* to set solidly in or as if in surrounding matter — see ENTRENCH

**root** (out) *vb* 1 to destroy all traces of — see ANNIHILATE 1
2 to draw out by force or with effort — see EXTRACT

**rooted** *adj* firmly established over time — see INVETERATE 1

**rope** *n* a length of braided, flexible material that is used for tying or connecting things — see CORD

**ropy** *adj* being of a consistency that resists flow — see THICK 2

**roquelaure** *n* a sleeveless garment worn so as to hang over the shoulders, arms, and back — see [1]CAPE

**rose–colored** *adj* having qualities which inspire hope — see HOPEFUL 1

**roster** *n* a record of a series of items (as names or titles) usually arranged according to some system — see [1]LIST

**rostrum** *n* a level usually raised surface — see PLATFORM

**rosy** *adj* 1 having a healthy reddish skin tone — see RUDDY
2 having qualities which inspire hope — see HOPEFUL 1

**rot** *n* 1 language, behavior, or ideas that are absurd and contrary to good sense — see NONSENSE 1
2 the process by which dead organic matter separates into simpler substances — see CORRUPTION 1
3 unintelligible or meaningless talk — see GIBBERISH

**rot** *vb* 1 to become worse or of less value — see DETERIORATE
2 to go through decomposition — see DECAY 1

**rotate** *vb* 1 to move (something) in a curved or circular path on or as if on an axis — see TURN 1
2 to move in circles around an axis or center — see SPIN 1

**rotation** *n* a rapid turning about on an axis or central point — see SPIN 1

**rote** *n* 1 an established and often automatic or monotonous series of actions followed when engaging in some activity — see ROUTINE 1
2 the body of knowledge that has been retained in one's mind or the use of it — see HEART 2

**rotten** *adj* 1 having undergone organic breakdown ⟨*rotten*, smelly meat that should have been refrigerated⟩
*syn* addled, bad, corrupted, decayed, decomposed, putrefied, putrid, spoiled
*rel* curdled, fermented, rancid, sour, soured, turned; contaminated, defiled, fouled, polluted, tainted; corroded, crumbled, degenerated, deteriorated, disintegrated; decaying, decomposing, moldering, moldy, putrefying, rotting
*near ant* fresh, good, preserved; pristine, uncontaminated, undefiled, unpolluted, unspoiled, untainted, untouched
2 falling short of a standard — see BAD 1
3 not conforming to a high moral standard; morally unacceptable — see BAD 2
4 not giving pleasure to the mind or senses — see UNPLEASANT

5 extremely unsatisfactory — see WRETCHED 1
6 of low quality — see CHEAP 2

**rotund** *adj* having an excess of body fat — see FAT 1

**rotundity** *n* the condition of having an excess of body fat — see CORPULENCE

**rough** *adj* 1 covered with or as if with hair — see HAIRY 1
2 marked by bursts of destructive force or intense activity — see VIOLENT 1
3 marked by wet and windy conditions — see FOUL 1
4 not having a level or smooth surface — see UNEVEN 1
5 requiring considerable physical or mental effort — see HARD 2
6 difficult to endure — see HARSH 1
7 harsh and threatening in manner or appearance — see GRIM 1
8 hastily or roughly constructed — see RUDE 1
9 lacking in refinement or good taste — see COARSE 2
10 made of or resembling hair — see HAIRY 2
11 marked by a series of sharp quick motions — see JERKY 1

**rough** (up) *vb* to abuse physically — see MANHANDLE 1

**roughened** *adj* not having a level or smooth surface — see UNEVEN 1

**roughhewn** *adj* 1 hastily or roughly constructed — see RUDE 1
2 lacking in refinement or good taste — see COARSE 2
3 lacking social grace and assurance — see AWKWARD 1

**roughhouse** *n* wildly playful or mischievous behavior — see HORSEPLAY

**roughhousing** *n* wildly playful or mischievous behavior — see HORSEPLAY

**roughly** *adv* in a manner so as to cause loss or suffering — see HARDLY 1

**roughneck** *n* a violent, brutal person who is often a member of an organized gang — see HOODLUM

**roughness** *n* 1 a harsh or sharp quality — see EDGE 1
2 the quality or state of lacking refinement or good taste — see VULGARITY 1

**round** *adj* 1 having every part of the surface the same distance from the center ⟨*round* golf balls⟩ ⟨the earth is not perfectly *round*⟩
*syn* global, spherical
*rel* annular, circular, disklike (*or* disclike), ringlike; curved, looped, spiral; balled, rotund, rounded, roundish; elliptic (*or* elliptical), oval, ovate, ovoid
2 having an excess of body fat — see FAT 1
3 marked by conspicuously full and rich sounds or tones — see RESONANT
4 being neither more nor less than a certain amount, number, or extent — see EVEN 1

**round** *adv* 1 from beginning to end — see THROUGH 1
2 on all sides or in every direction — see AROUND 1
3 toward the opposite direction — see AROUND 2

**round** *n* 1 a circular strip — see RING 2
2 a series of events or actions that repeat themselves regularly and in the same order — see CYCLE 1
3 something with a perfectly round circumference — see CIRCLE 1

**round** *prep* in random positions within the boundaries of — see AROUND 2

**round** *vb* 1 to form into a round compact mass — see WAD
2 to pass completely around — see ENCIRCLE 1
3 to turn away from a straight line or course — see CURVE 1

**round** (off *or* out) *vb* 1 to bring (an event) to a natural or appropriate stopping point — see CLOSE 3
2 to serve as a completing element to — see COMPLEMENT

**roundabout** *adj* not straightforward or direct — see INDIRECT

**roundly** *adv* with attention to all aspects or details — see THOROUGHLY 1

**roundtable** *n* 1 a coming together of a number of persons for a specified purpose — see MEETING 1
2 a meeting featuring a group discussion — see FORUM

**roundup** *n* a short statement of the main points — see SUMMARY

**round up** *vb* to bring together in one body or place — see GATHER 1

**rouse** *vb* 1 to cause to stop sleeping — see WAKE 1
2 to cease to be asleep — see WAKE 2

**rousing** *adj* causing great emotional or mental stimulation — see EXCITING 1

**rout** *n* failure to win a contest — see DEFEAT 1

**rout** *vb* 1 to achieve a victory over — see BEAT 2
2 to defeat by a large margin — see WHIP 2
3 to drive or force out — see EJECT 1

**route** *n* 1 a passage cleared for public vehicular travel — see WAY 1
2 an established course for traveling from one place to another — see PASSAGE 1
3 the direction along which something or someone moves — see PATH 1

**route** *vb* to point out the way for (someone) especially from a position in front — see LEAD 1

**routine** *adj* 1 being of the type that is encountered in the normal course of events — see ORDINARY 1
2 following or agreeing with established form, custom, or rules — see FORMAL 1
3 often observed or encountered — see COMMON 1

**routine** *n* 1 an established and often automatic or monotonous series of actions followed when engaging in some activity ⟨part of my morning *routine* is drinking a

---

*syn* synonym(s) *rel* related words
*ant* antonym(s) *near ant* near antonym(s)

cup of hot chocolate while waiting for the bus〉
*syn* groove, pattern, rote, rut, treadmill
*rel* custom, fashion, habit, practice (*also* practise), trick, wont; approach, manner, method, procedure, strategy, style, tack, way; design, plan, program, scheme; convention, policy, tradition
**2** something done over and over in order to develop skill — see EXERCISE 2

**rove** *vb* to move about from place to place aimlessly — see WANDER

**rover** *n* **1** a person who roams about without a fixed route or destination — see NOMAD
**2** someone who engages in robbery of ships at sea — see PIRATE

**roving** *adj* traveling from place to place — see ITINERANT

**row** *n* **1** a series of people or things arranged side by side 〈stood in a *row* to have their picture taken〉 〈three *rows* of eight jelly beans equals 24 jelly beans〉
*syn* bank, rank
*rel* chain, column, cue, file, line, procession, queue, string, train; echelon, tier; array, sequence
**2** a passage cleared for public vehicular travel — see WAY 1
**3** a rough and often noisy fight usually involving several people — see BRAWL 1
**4** a state of noisy, confused activity — see COMMOTION
**5** an often noisy or angry expression of differing opinions — see ARGUMENT 1

[1]**row** *vb* to move a boat by means of oars 〈*rowed* around the lake〉
*syn* oar, paddle, scull
*rel* canoe; pole, punt

[2]**row** *vb* to express different opinions about something often angrily — see ARGUE 2

**rowdy** *adj* being rough or noisy in a high-spirited way — see BOISTEROUS

**rowdy** *n* a violent, brutal person who is often a member of an organized gang — see HOODLUM

**rower** *n* a person who drives a boat forward by means of oars — see OARSMAN

**royal** *adj* **1** fit for or worthy of a royal ruler — see MONARCHICAL
**2** large and impressive in size, grandeur, extent, or conception — see GRAND 1

**rub** *vb* **1** to damage or diminish by continued friction — see ABRADE 1
**2** to make smooth by friction — see GRIND 1
**3** to make smooth or glossy usually by repeatedly applying surface pressure — see POLISH

**rubbed** *adj* having a shiny surface or finish — see GLOSSY

**rubberlike** *adj* able to revert to original size and shape after being stretched, squeezed, or twisted — see ELASTIC 1

**rubberneck** *vb* to look long and hard in wonder or surprise — see GAPE

**rubbery** *adj* able to revert to original size and shape after being stretched, squeezed, or twisted — see ELASTIC 1

**rubbish** *n* discarded or useless material — see GARBAGE

**rubbishy** *adj* of low quality — see CHEAP 2

**rubble** *n* the portion or bits of something left over or behind after it has been destroyed — see REMAINS 1

**rubicund** *adj* having a healthy reddish skin tone — see RUDDY

**rub out** *vb* to destroy all traces of — see ANNIHILATE 1

**rubric** *n* a word or series of words often in larger letters placed at the beginning of a passage or at the top of a page in order to introduce or categorize — see HEADING

**rucksack** *n* a soft-sided case designed for carrying belongings especially on the back — see PACK 1

**ruckus** *n* **1** a rough and often noisy fight usually involving several people — see BRAWL 1
**2** a state of noisy, confused activity — see COMMOTION

**ruction** *n* **1** a rough and often noisy fight usually involving several people — see BRAWL 1
**2** a state of noisy, confused activity — see COMMOTION

**ruddy** *adj* having a healthy reddish skin tone 〈his *ruddy* complexion runs in the family〉
*syn* blooming, florid, flush, glowing, rosy, rubicund, sanguine
*rel* bronzed, brown, suntanned, tanned; flushed, pink, pinkish, warm; cherubic
*near ant* ashen, ashy, pale, pallid, pasty, sallow, wan, waxen, waxy; blanched, white, whitened; anemic, peaked, sick, sickly; bloodless, cadaverous, deathlike

**rude** *adj* **1** hastily or roughly constructed 〈a *rude* shelter built from unfinished logs by some forgotten pioneer〉
*syn* artless, clumsy, crude, rough, roughhewn, unrefined
*rel* defective, faulty, flawed, imperfect; imprecise, inexact; inartistic, undressed, unfinished, unpolished, unworked; amateur, amateurish, inexpert, unprofessional, unskilled, unskillful; primitive, rudimentary
*near ant* faultless, finished, meticulous, perfected, polished, well-done; adept, adroit, dexterous (*also* dextrous), expert, masterful, masterly, neat, practiced (*or* practised), skillful, workmanlike; artful, artistic, sophisticated; exact, precise
*ant* refined
**2** belonging to or characteristic of an early level of skill or development — see PRIMITIVE 1
**3** lacking in refinement or good taste — see COARSE 2
**4** not civilized — see SAVAGE 1
**5** showing a lack of manners or consideration for others — see IMPOLITE

**rudeness** *n* **1** rude behavior — see DISCOURTESY
**2** the quality or state of lacking refinement or good taste — see VULGARITY 1

**rudimentary** *adj* **1** belonging to or characteristic of an early level of skill or development — see PRIMITIVE 1
**2** of or relating to the simplest facts or theories of a subject — see ELEMENTARY

**rudiments** *n pl* general or basic truths on which other truths or theories can be based — see PRINCIPLES 1

**rue** *n* a feeling of responsibility for wrongdoing — see GUILT 1

**rue** *vb* to feel sorry or dissatisfied about — see REGRET

**rueful** *adj* **1** expressing or suggesting mourning — see MOURNFUL 1
**2** feeling sorrow for a wrong that one has done — see CONTRITE 1
**3** deserving of one's pity — see PATHETIC 1

**ruefully** *adv* with feelings of bitterness or grief — see HARD 2

**ruffian** *n* a violent, brutal person who is often a member of an organized gang — see HOODLUM

**ruffle** *n* a strip of fabric gathered or pleated on one edge and used as trimming ⟨likes lace curtains without *ruffles* and chintz curtains with *ruffles*⟩
***syn*** flounce, frill, furbelow
***rel*** border, edging, fringe, trim; pleat, ruff; bunting, skirting

**rugged** *adj* **1** able to withstand hardship, strain, or exposure — see HARDY 1
**2** difficult to endure — see HARSH 1
**3** harsh and threatening in manner or appearance — see GRIM 1
**4** having muscles capable of exerting great physical force — see STRONG 1
**5** not having a level or smooth surface — see UNEVEN 1

**ruin** *n* **1** the state or fact of being rendered nonexistent, physically unsound, or useless — see DESTRUCTION
**2 ruins** *pl* the portion or bits of something left over or behind after it has been destroyed — see REMAINS 1

**ruin** *vb* **1** to cause to lose one's fortune and become unable to pay one's debts ⟨*ruined* by the Great Chicago Fire of 1871, the industrialist was forced to sell his mansion and start all over again⟩
***syn*** bankrupt, bust
***rel*** beggar, impoverish, pauperize; break, reduce, straiten; clean (out), wipe out
***near ant*** enrich, richen
**2** to bring destruction to (something) through violent action — see RAVAGE
**3** to bring to a complete end the physical soundness, existence, or usefulness of — see DESTROY 1

**ruination** *n* the state or fact of being rendered nonexistent, physically unsound, or useless — see DESTRUCTION

**ruinous** *adj* **1** bringing about ruin or misfortune — see FATAL 1
**2** causing or tending to cause destruction — see DESTRUCTIVE 1

***syn*** synonym(s) ***rel*** related words
***ant*** antonym(s) ***near ant*** near antonym(s)

**rule** *n* **1** a statement spelling out the proper procedure or conduct for an activity ⟨read the *rules* that are posted before you use the pool⟩
***syn*** bylaw, ground rule, regulation
***rel*** code, constitution, decalogue; act, law, ordinance, statute; command, decree, dictate, directive, edict, fiat, order; axiom, fundamental, maxim, precept; moral, principle, value; prohibition, restriction; convention, custom, habit, manners, mores, practice (*also* practise), tradition, way; blueprint, canon, formula, guide, guideline, recipe, standard
**2** lawful control over the affairs of a political unit (as a nation) ⟨the years during which Russia was under Communist *rule*⟩
***syn*** administration, authority, governance, government, jurisdiction, regime (*also* régime), regimen
***rel*** reign; dominion, power, sovereignty, supremacy, sway; command, leadership; direction, management, regulation, superintendence, supervision; dictatorship, domination, mastery, oppression, subjugation, tyranny

**rule** *vb* to exercise authority or power over — see GOVERN

**rule** (on) *vb* to give an opinion about (something at issue or in dispute) — see JUDGE 1

**rule out** *vb* to prevent the participation or inclusion of — see EXCLUDE

**ruler** *n* one who rules over a people with a sole, supreme, and usually hereditary authority — see MONARCH

**ruling** *n* **1** a decision made by a court or tribunal regarding a case it has heard — see SENTENCE
**2** an order publicly issued by an authority — see EDICT 1

**rumble** *vb* to make a low heavy rolling sound ⟨when thunder *rumbled* in the distant sky, we wisely began packing up our stuff⟩
***syn*** growl, grumble, lumber, roll
***rel*** boom, drum, thunder

**ruminant** *adj* given to or marked by long, quiet thinking — see CONTEMPLATIVE

**ruminate** *vb* to give serious and careful thought to — see PONDER

**rummage** *n* an unorganized collection or mixture of various things — see MISCELLANY 1

**rummage** *vb* to look through (as a place) carefully or thoroughly in an effort to find or discover something — see SEARCH 1

**rumor** *vb* to make (as a piece of information) the subject of common talk without any authority or confirmation of accuracy ⟨for years people have been *rumoring* the principal's imminent retirement⟩
***syn*** bruit (about), circulate, noise (about), whisper
***rel*** bandy (about), blab, gossip; disclose, divulge, report, reveal, tell; hint, imply, insinuate, intimate, let on, suggest; broadcast, promulgate, propagate, spread

**rump** *n* the part of the body upon which someone sits — see BUTTOCKS

**rumple** *vb* **1** to create (as by crushing) an irregular mass of creases in — see CRUMPLE 1
**2** to develop creases or folds — see WRINKLE 1
**3** to undo the proper order or arrangement of — see DISORDER

**rumpled** *adj* lacking in order neatness, and often cleanliness — see MESSY

**rumpus** *n* a state of noisy, confused activity — see COMMOTION

**run** *n* **1** a prevailing or general movement or inclination — see TREND 1
**2** *chiefly Midland* a natural body of running water smaller than a river — see CREEK 1
**3** the period during which something exists, lasts, or is in progress — see DURATION 1
**4** the right to act or move freely — see FREEDOM 2

**run** *vb* **1** to go at a pace faster than a walk ⟨*ran* all the way to the bus stop, but still missed the bus⟩
*syn* dash, gallop, jog, scamper, sprint, trip, trot
*rel* bound, canter, leap, lope, skip, spring; foot (it), hoof (it), hotfoot (it), leg (it); nip, race, scuttle, step (along)
*near ant* amble, lumber, plod, saunter, shamble, shuffle, stroll; crawl, creep, poke; plod, trudge; hobble, limp
**2** to hasten away from something dangerous or frightening ⟨rather than *run* from a black bear, it's better to hold your ground and make lots of noise⟩
*syn* bolt, break, flee, fly, retreat, run away, run off
*rel* abscond, clear out, decamp, elope, escape, light out, retreat, scat, scram, skip (out)
*phrases* beat it, turn tail
*near ant* beard, brave, confront, dare, defy, face
**3** to be positioned along a certain course or in a certain direction ⟨the road *runs* along the river for a while⟩
*syn* extend, go, head, lead, lie
*rel* cross, cut, pass; follow, span, traverse
**4** to occur within a continuous range of variation ⟨the electric bill *runs* between 30 and 50 dollars a month⟩
*syn* go, range, vary
*rel* alternate, move, shift; change, mutate; extend, reach, stretch, sweep
**5** to move in a stream — see FLOW 1
**6** to proceed or move quickly — see HURRY 2
**7** to show a liking or proneness (for something) — see LEAN 2
**8** to urge, push, or force onward — see DRIVE 1
**9** to control the mechanical operation of — see OPERATE 1
**10** to eventually have as a state or quality — see BECOME
**11** to go from a solid to a liquid state — see LIQUEFY
**12** to look after and make decisions about — see CONDUCT 1
**13** to cause to function — see ACTIVATE

**run away** *vb* **1** to get free from a dangerous or confining situation — see ESCAPE 1
**2** to hasten away from something dangerous or frightening — see RUN 2

**run–down** *adj* **1** showing signs of advanced wear and tear and neglect — see SHABBY 1
**2** temporarily suffering from a disorder of the body — see SICK 1

**run down** *vb* to come upon after searching, study, or effort — see FIND 1

**run–in** *n* a brief clash between enemies or rivals — see ENCOUNTER

**runner** *n* one that carries a message or does an errand — see MESSENGER

**running** *adj* being in effective operation — see ACTIVE 1

**running** *n* the act or activity of looking after and making decisions about something — see CONDUCT 1

**runny** *adj* having an overly soft liquid consistency ⟨*runny* scrambled eggs⟩
*syn* soupy, watery
*rel* flowing, fluid, liquefied; dilute, diluted, thin, thinned, watered (down), weak; slushy, soggy, wet
*near ant* syrupy, viscid, viscous; creamy, heavy, thick, thickened, thickish; gelatinous, gluey, glutinous, gooey, gummy, sticky

**run off** *vb* **1** to drive or force out — see EJECT 1
**2** to get free from a dangerous or confining situation — see ESCAPE 1
**3** to hasten away from something dangerous or frightening — see RUN 2

**run–of–the–mill** *adj* **1** being of the type that is encountered in the normal course of events — see ORDINARY 1
**2** of average to below average quality — see MEDIOCRE 1

**run on** *vb* **1** to engage in casual or rambling conversation — see CHAT
**2** to remain indefinitely in existence or in the same state — see CONTINUE 1
**3** to talk at length without sticking to a topic or getting to a point — see RAMBLE 1

**run over** *vb* to flow over the brim or top of — see OVERFLOW 1

**runt** *n* a living thing much smaller than others of its kind — see DWARF 1

**run through** *vb* to use up carelessly — see WASTE 1

**rural** *adj* of, relating to, associated with, or typical of open areas with few buildings or people ⟨grew up in a *rural* community where more than half the people were farmers⟩ ⟨a painter noted for his *rural* landscapes⟩
*syn* bucolic, country, pastoral, rustic
*rel* countrified (*also* countryfied), provincial; agrarian, agricultural

*near ant* citified, urbanized; metropolitan, municipal; nonagricultural, nonfarm
*ant* urban

**rush** *n* **1** excited and often showy or disorderly speed — see HURRY 1
**2** the act or action of setting upon with force or violence — see ATTACK 1

**rush** *vb* **1** to cause to move or proceed fast or faster — see HURRY 1
**2** to flow out in great quantities or with force — see GUSH 1
**3** to proceed or move quickly — see HURRY 2
**4** to take sudden, violent action against — see ATTACK 1

**rushed** *adj* acting or done with excessive or careless speed — see HASTY 1

**rustic** *adj* of, relating to, associated with, or typical of open areas with few buildings or people — see RURAL

**rustic** *n* an awkward or simple person especially from a small town or the country — see HICK

**rustle** *vb* to proceed or move quickly — see HURRY 2

**rustler** *n* an ambitious person who eagerly goes after what is desired — see GO-GETTER

**rut** *n* an established and often automatic or monotonous series of actions followed when engaging in some activity — see ROUTINE 1

**ruthless** *adj* having or showing a lack of sympathy or tender feelings — see HARD 1

# S

**sable** *adj* having the color of soot or coal — see BLACK 1

**saccharine** *adj* appealing to the emotions in an obvious and tiresome way — see CORNY

**sacerdotal** *adj* of, relating to, or characteristic of the clergy — see CLERICAL

**sack** *n* **1** a container made of a flexible material (as paper or plastic) — see BAG 1
**2** a place set aside for sleeping — see BED 1

**sack** *vb* **1** to let go from office, service, or employment — see DISMISS 1
**2** to search through with the intent of committing robbery — see RANSACK 1

**sacred** *adj* **1** not to be violated, criticized, or tampered with ⟨we took a *sacred* oath not to let anyone find our hideout⟩
*syn* holy, inviolable, sacrosanct, unassailable, untouchable
*rel* inviolate, pure; privileged, protected, shielded; exempt, immune
*near ant* blasphemous, irreverent, profane
**2** of, relating to, or being God — see HOLY 3
**3** of, relating to, or used in the practice or worship services of a religion — see RELIGIOUS 1
**4** set apart or worthy of veneration by association with God — see HOLY 2

**sacrifice** *n* something offered to a god ⟨the herders selected their best lamb as a *sacrifice* in order to receive blessings from their god⟩
*syn* immolation, offering, victim
*rel* holocaust; contribution, donation

**sacrifice** *vb* to give up as an offering to a god ⟨in the Old Testament Abraham was willing to *sacrifice* even his son to God⟩
*syn* immolate, offer
*rel* consecrate, dedicate, devote; give, surrender, yield

**sacrilege** *n* an act of great disrespect shown to God or to sacred ideas, people, or things — see BLASPHEMY

**sacrilegious** *adj* not showing proper reverence for the holy or sacred — see IRREVERENT

**sacristy** *n* a room in a church building for sacred furnishings (as vestments) ⟨our choir robes were stored in the *sacristy*⟩
*syn* vestry
*rel* cloakroom

**sacrosanct** *adj* **1** not to be violated, criticized, or tampered with — see SACRED 1
**2** set apart or worthy of veneration by association with God — see HOLY 2

**sad** *adj* **1** feeling unhappiness ⟨movies in which the hero dies always make us feel *sad*⟩
*syn* bad, blue, brokenhearted, crestfallen, dejected, depressed, despondent, disconsolate, doleful, down, downcast, downhearted, droopy, forlorn, gloomy, glum, heartbroken, heartsick, heartsore, inconsolable, joyless, low, low-spirited, melancholy, miserable, mournful, saddened, sorrowful, sorry, unhappy, woebegone, woeful, wretched
*rel* aggrieved, distressed, troubled; despairing, hopeless; disappointed, discouraged, disheartened, dispirited; suicidal; dolorous, lugubrious, plaintive, tearful; regretful, rueful; grieving, wailing, weeping; black, bleak, cheerless, comfortless, dark, darkening, depressing, desolate, dismal, drear, dreary, funereal, gray (*also*

grey), morbid, morose, murky, saturnine, somber (*or* sombre), sullen
***near ant*** ecstatic, elated, enraptured, entranced, euphoric, exhilarated, exuberant, exultant; blithe, blithesome, gay, jocund, jolly, jovial, lightsome, merry, mirthful; excited, thrilled; hopeful, optimistic; encouraged, heartened; animated, jaunty, lively, perky, sprightly, vivacious; content, gratified, pleased, satisfied; beaming, grinning, laughing, smiling; boon, carefree, careless, cavalier, devil-may-care, easygoing, happy-go-lucky, insouciant, lighthearted, unconcerned
***ant*** blissful, buoyant, buoyed, cheerful, cheery, chipper, delighted, glad, gladdened, gladsome, gleeful, happy, joyful, joyous, jubilant, sunny, upbeat
**2** causing unhappiness ⟨the *sad* news about our uncle's death made my father cry⟩
***syn*** depressing, dismal, drear, dreary, heartbreaking, heartrending, melancholy, pathetic, saddening, sorry, tearful, teary
***rel*** discomforting, discomposing, disquieting, distressing, disturbing, perturbing; affecting, moving, poignant, touching; discouraging, disheartening, dispiriting
***near ant*** heartening, heartwarming, inspiring, stimulating, stirring; uplifting; agreeable, pleasant, pleasurable; exhilarating, thrilling
***ant*** cheering, cheery, glad, happy

**sadden** *vb* to make sad — see DEPRESS 1
**saddened** *adj* feeling unhappiness — see SAD 1
**saddening** *adj* causing unhappiness — see SAD 2
**saddle** *vb* to place a weight or burden on — see LOAD 1
**sadism** *n* the willful infliction of pain and suffering on others — see CRUELTY
**sadistic** *adj* having or showing the desire to inflict severe pain and suffering on others — see CRUEL 1
**sadly** *adv* with feelings of bitterness or grief — see HARD 2
**sadness** *n* a state or spell of low spirits ⟨she was filled with *sadness* at the thought of having to leave her family⟩
***syn*** blues, dejection, depression, desolation, despondency, disconsolateness, dispiritedness, doldrums, downheartedness, dreariness, dumps, forlornness, gloom, gloominess, heartsickness, joylessness, melancholy, mopes, oppression, unhappiness
***rel*** melancholia, self-pity; anguish, dolor, grief, sorrow; dolefulness, mournfulness, somberness, sorrowfulness, woefulness; agony, distress, pain; misery, woe, wretchedness; discouragement, disheartenment; moodiness; despair, desperation, hopelessness; boredom, ennui, tedium
***near ant*** gaiety (*also* gayety), gayness, glee, gleefulness, humor, jollity, joviality, lightheartedness, merriment, mirth, mirthfulness; cheer, cheerfulness, hopefulness, optimism, sunniness; content, contentedness, contentment, satisfaction; delight, gratification
***ant*** bliss, blissfulness, ecstasy, elatedness, elation, euphoria, exhilaration, exuberance, exultation, felicity, gladness, gladsomeness, happiness, heaven, intoxication, joy, joyfulness, joyousness, jubilation, rapture, rapturousness

**safe** *adj* **1** not exposed to the threat of loss or injury ⟨the minute the rain started, we ran to a place where we were *safe* from getting wet⟩
***syn*** all right, alright, secure
***rel*** hale, healthy, intact, sound, well, whole; scatheless, unharmed, unhurt, uninjured, unscathed
***near ant*** damaged, harmed, hurt, injured, scathed, wounded
***ant*** endangered, imperiled, insecure, liable, threatened, unsafe, vulnerable
**2** providing safety ⟨we tried to find a *safe* place to hide the candy⟩
***syn*** secure, snug
***rel*** guarding, protecting, safeguarding, sheltering, shielding; defended, guarded, protected, sheltered, shielded; impregnable, inviolable, invulnerable, unassailable, unconquerable
***near ant*** undefended, unguarded, unprotected, vulnerable
***ant*** dangerous, hazardous, insecure, risky, unsafe
**3** having or showing a close attentiveness to avoiding danger or trouble — see CAREFUL 1
**4** not causing injury or hurt — see HARMLESS
**5** worthy of one's trust — see DEPENDABLE

**safe** *n* a specially reinforced container to keep valuables safe ⟨the hotel recommended that we keep all our valuables in its *safe* during our stay⟩
***syn*** coffer, safe-deposit box, strongbox
***rel*** vault; locker, storeroom, treasury; footlocker, trunk

**safe–deposit box** *n* a specially reinforced container to keep valuables safe — see SAFE
**safeguard** *n* means or method of defending — see DEFENSE 1
**safeguard** *vb* to drive danger or attack away from — see DEFEND 1
**safekeeping** *n* responsibility for the safety and well-being of someone or something — see CUSTODY
**safeness** *n* the state of not being exposed to danger — see SAFETY 1
**safety** *n* **1** the state of not being exposed to danger ⟨we were lucky to make it to *safety* just as the lions broke loose from their cage at the zoo⟩
***syn*** protection, safeness, security
***rel*** aegis, defense, guardianship, ward; guard, safeguard, screen, shield; asylum, harbor, haven, refuge, retreat, shelter; inviolability, invulnerability
***near ant*** hazard, risk, threat; instability, precariousness

*ant* danger, distress, endangerment, imperilment, jeopardy, peril, trouble
**2** a protective device (as on a weapon) to prevent accidental operation ⟨the gun couldn't be fired as long as the *safety* was on⟩
*syn* guard
*rel* lock

**sag** *n* the extent to which something hangs or dips below a straight line ⟨if there's too much *sag* in the rod, the curtains will drag on the floor⟩
*syn* droop, slack, slackness
*rel* laxity, laxness, looseness
*near ant* tautness, tenseness, tension, tightness

**sag** *vb* **1** to be limp from lack of water or vigor — see DROOP 1
**2** to decline gradually from a standard level — see SLIP 1
**3** to lose bodily strength or vigor — see WEAKEN 2

**sagacious** *adj* having or showing deep understanding and intelligent application of knowledge — see WISE 1

**sagaciousness** *n* the ability to understand inner qualities or relationships — see WISDOM 1

**sagacity** *n* the ability to understand inner qualities or relationships — see WISDOM 1

**sage** *adj* having or showing deep understanding and intelligent application of knowledge — see WISE 1

**sage** *n* a person of deep wisdom or learning ⟨the young prince visited the *sage* to learn the meaning of life⟩
*syn* savant, scholar
*rel* brain, egghead, genius, highbrow, intellectual, thinker; guru, mahatma; rabbi; master, mentor, teacher
*near ant* blockhead, dodo, dolt, donkey, dope, dumbbell, dummy, dunce, fathead, fool, goon, half-wit, idiot, ignoramus, imbecile, jackass, knothead, know-nothing, moron, nincompoop, ninny, nitwit, numskull (*or* numbskull), pinhead, simpleton, stock, turkey

**sageness** *n* the ability to understand inner qualities or relationships — see WISDOM 1

**sagging** *adj* bending downward or forward — see NODDING

**sail** *n* a journey over water in a vessel ⟨we went for a brief *sail* on the bay to relax⟩
*syn* crossing, cruise, passage, voyage

**sail** *vb* **1** to travel on water in a vessel ⟨I can't *sail* when there's any breeze at all because I get seasick easily⟩
*syn* boat, cruise, navigate, voyage
*rel* yacht; coast; log
*phrases* make sail
**2** to move or proceed smoothly and readily — see FLOW 2
**3** to rest or move along the surface of a liquid or in the air — see FLOAT

**sailboat** *n* a boat equipped with one or more sails ⟨we were stuck in the *sailboat* for an hour until the wind came up and we could move again⟩
*syn* bark, dinghy, windjammer
*rel* brigantine, caravel, catboat, clipper, corvette, cutter, frigate, galleon, galley, junk, ketch, lugger, outrigger, pinnace, schooner, shallop, ship, sloop, square-rigger, xebec, yacht, yawl; bottom, craft, vessel

**sailor** *n* one who operates or navigates a seagoing vessel ⟨the *sailors* were glad to be arriving in port after their long voyage⟩
*syn* gob, jack, jack-tar, mariner, navigator, salt, sea dog, seafarer, seaman, swab, tar
*rel* crewman, deckhand

**saint** *vb* to declare to be a saint and worthy of public respect ⟨Brigid of Sweden was *sainted* in October of 1391⟩
*syn* canonize
*rel* deify, worship; consecrate, hallow, sanctify; beatify, venerate

**sainted** *adj* showing a devotion to God and to a life of virtue — see HOLY 1

**sainthood** *n* the quality or state of being spiritually pure or virtuous — see HOLINESS

**saintliness** *n* the quality or state of being spiritually pure or virtuous — see HOLINESS

**saintly** *adj* showing a devotion to God and to a life of virtue — see HOLY 1

**saintship** *n* the quality or state of being spiritually pure or virtuous — see HOLINESS

**salable** *or* **saleable** *adj* **1** fit or likely to be sold especially on a large scale — see COMMERCIAL
**2** fit to be offered for sale — see MARKETABLE 1

**salary** *n* the money paid regularly to a person for labor or services — see WAGE

**sale** *n* the transfer of ownership of something from one person to another for a price ⟨my neighbor tried to make a *sale*, but no one was interested in buying his old car⟩
*syn* deal, trade, transaction
*rel* auction; haggle, negotiation; bargain, buy; purchase; clearance; fair; garage sale, rummage sale, yard sale

**salesclerk** *n* a person employed to sell goods or services especially in a store — see SALESPERSON

**salesman** *n* a person employed to sell goods or services especially in a store — see SALESPERSON

**salesperson** *n* a person employed to sell goods or services especially in a store ⟨we asked a *salesperson* to see if they had any shoes in the stockroom in our size⟩
*syn* clerk, salesclerk, salesman
*rel* salespeople; saleswoman

**saline** *adj* of, relating to, or containing salt — see SALTY 1

**salinity** *n* the quality or state of being salty — see SALTINESS

**saliva** *n* the fluid that is secreted into the mouth by certain glands ⟨our mouths

*syn* synonym(s) *rel* related words
*ant* antonym(s) *near ant* near antonym(s)

filled with *saliva* when we smelled the delicious dinner〉
*syn* slobber, spit, spittle
*rel* foam, froth; expectoration, sputum

**salivate** *vb* to let saliva or some other substance flow from the mouth — see DROOL

**sallow** *adj* lacking the warm skin color indicative of or associated with good health — see SICKLY 2

**sally** *n* **1** a short trip for pleasure — see EXCURSION 1
**2** something said or done to cause laughter — see JOKE 1

**sally** (forth) *vb* to leave a place often for another — see GO 2

**salon** *n* **1** a building or part of a building in which objects of interest are displayed — see MUSEUM
**2** a building, room, or suite of rooms occupied by a service business — see PLACE 2

**saloon** *n* a place of business where alcoholic beverages are sold to be consumed on the premises — see BARROOM

**salt** *adj* of, relating to, or containing salt — see SALTY 1

**salt** *n* one who operates or navigates a seagoing vessel — see SAILOR

**salt away** *vb* to put (something of future use or value) in a safe or secret place — see HOARD

**saltiness** *n* the quality or state of being salty 〈the *saltiness* of the pretzels went well with the soda pop we were drinking〉
*syn* brininess, salinity, saltness
*near ant* purity; sweetness

**saltness** *n* the quality or state of being salty — see SALTINESS

**salty** *adj* **1** of, relating to, or containing salt 〈*salty* sea water is safe to swim in, but you really shouldn't swallow it〉
*syn* briny, saline, salt
*rel* brackish
*near ant* sweet; clear, pure
**2** hinting at or intended to call to mind matters regarded as indecent — see SUGGESTIVE 1

**salubrious** *adj* good for the health — see HEALTHFUL

**salutary** *adj* **1** conferring benefits; promoting or contributing to personal or social well-being — see BENEFICIAL
**2** good for the health — see HEALTHFUL

**salutation** *n* **1** a formal expression of praise — see ENCOMIUM
**2** an expression of goodwill upon meeting — see HELLO

**salute** *n* an expression of goodwill upon meeting — see HELLO

**salute** *vb* to declare enthusiastic approval of — see ACCLAIM

**salvation** *n* the saving from danger or evil 〈we spent the night in the jungle praying for *salvation* from the dangerous animals〉
*syn* deliverance
*rel* ransom, recovery, redemption, rescue; extrication; defense, protection, safeguarding; conservation, preservation

**salvo** *n* a rapid or overwhelming outpouring of many things at once — see BARRAGE

**same** *adj* **1** resembling another in every respect 〈I bought the *same* shirt at the mall for five dollars less〉
*syn* coequal, duplicate, equal, even, identical, indistinguishable
*rel* akin, alike, analogous, comparable, correspondent, corresponding, equivalent, like, matching, parallel, similar, such, suchlike, tantamount
*near ant* disparate, diverse, varied, various; distinct, distinctive
*ant* different, dissimilar, distinguishable, other, unalike, unlike
**2** being one and not another 〈that's the *same* guy I saw down at the beach yesterday〉
*syn* identical, selfsame, very
*near ant* disparate, dissimilar, distinct, distinctive, distinguishable, diverse, unalike, unlike, varied, various
*ant* another, different, other

**sameness** *n* **1** a tedious lack of variety — see MONOTONY
**2** the state of being exactly alike — see IDENTITY 1
**3** the state or fact of being exactly the same in number, amount, status, or quality — see EQUIVALENCE

**sample** *n* **1** a number of things selected from a group to stand for the whole 〈based on a *sample* of the menu items, we decided that this was the best restaurant in town〉
*syn* cross section
*rel* case, example, exemplar, illustration, instance, representative, specimen; selection
**2** one of a group or collection that shows what the whole is like — see EXAMPLE

**sample** *vb* to put (something) to a test — see TRY (OUT) 1

**sanctification** *n* **1** the act of making something holy through religious ritual — see CONSECRATION
**2** the act or fact of freeing from sin or moral guilt — see PURIFICATION

**sanctified** *adj* set apart or worthy of veneration by association with God — see HOLY 2

**sanctify** *vb* **1** to free from moral guilt or blemish especially ceremonially — see PURIFY 1
**2** to make holy through prayers or ritual — see BLESS 1

**sanctimoniousness** *n* the pretending of having virtues, principles, or beliefs that one in fact does not have — see HYPOCRISY

**sanction** *n* the approval by someone in authority for the doing of something — see PERMISSION

**sanction** *vb* to give official acceptance of something as satisfactory — see APPROVE

**sanctioned** *adj* ordered or allowed by those in authority — see OFFICIAL

**sanctity** *n* the quality or state of being spiritually pure or virtuous — see HOLINESS

**sanctuary** *n* **1** a place that is considered sacred (as within a religion) — see SHRINE
**2** something (as a building) that offers cover from the weather or protection from danger — see SHELTER

**sanctum** *n* **1** a place that is considered sacred (as within a religion) — see SHRINE
**2** something (as a building) that offers cover from the weather or protection from danger — see SHELTER

**sand** *vb* to make smooth by friction — see GRIND 1

**sandwich** *vb* to fit (something) into a tight space — see CROWD 1

**sandy** *adj* of a pale yellow or yellowish brown color — see BLOND

**sane** *adj* having full use of one's mind and control over one's actions ⟨the court ruled that the woman was indeed *sane* when she made out her will⟩
***syn*** balanced, clearheaded, lucid, normal, right, stable
***rel*** clear, logical, rational, reasonable; judicious, levelheaded, sensible, wise; healthy, sound
***near ant*** balmy, bananas, batty, crackbrained, cracked, cuckoo, daffy, daft, dotty, loco [*slang*], loony (*also* looney), moonstruck, nuts, nutty, off, screwy, wacky; aberrant, disordered; delusional, neurotic, paranoid, psychotic, schizophrenic; eccentric, odd, queer, strange; foolish, senseless, witless; irrational, unreasonable; berserk, delirious; depressed, despondent; distraught, frantic, frenzied, hysterical
***ant*** crazed, crazy, demented, deranged, insane, lunatic, mad, maniacal (*also* maniac), mental, unbalanced, unsound

**saneness** *n* the normal or healthy condition of the mental abilities — see MIND 2

**sanguinary** *adj* eager for or marked by the shedding of blood, extreme violence, or killing — see BLOODTHIRSTY

**sanguine** *adj* **1** eager for or marked by the shedding of blood, extreme violence, or killing — see BLOODTHIRSTY
**2** having a healthy reddish skin tone — see RUDDY
**3** having or showing a mind free from doubt — see CERTAIN 2

**sanguinity** *n* an inclination to believe in the most favorable outcome — see OPTIMISM

**sanitary** *adj* free from filth, infection, or dangers to health ⟨the nurse made sure that everything in the room was *sanitary* so that the baby wouldn't get sick⟩
***syn*** aseptic, germfree, hygienic, sterile
***rel*** antibacterial, antibiotic, antiseptic, germicidal; clean, immaculate, spick-and-span (*or* spic-and-span), spotless, stainless, unsoiled, unsullied; beneficial, healthful, healthy, restorative, salubrious, salutary, wholesome
***near ant*** pathogenic; bedraggled, besmirched, dingy, dirty, draggled, dusty, filthy, foul, grimy, grubby, grungy, mucky, muddy, nasty, soiled, sordid, stained, sullied, unclean, uncleanly; insalubrious, noxious, unhealthful, unhealthy, unwholesome
***ant*** insanitary, unhygienic, unsanitary

**sanitary landfill** *n* a place where discarded materials (as trash) are dumped — see DUMP 1

**sanity** *n* the normal or healthy condition of the mental abilities — see MIND 2

**sans** *prep* not having — see WITHOUT 1

**sap** *n* **1** active strength of body or mind — see VIGOR 1
**2** one who is easily deceived or cheated — see DUPE

**sap** *vb* to diminish the physical strength of — see WEAKEN 1

**sapience** *n* the ability to understand inner qualities or relationships — see WISDOM 1

**sapient** *adj* having or showing deep understanding and intelligent application of knowledge — see WISE 1

**sapped** *adj* lacking bodily strength — see WEAK 1

**sappiness** *n* the state or quality of having an excess of tender feelings (as of love, nostalgia, or compassion) — see SENTIMENTALITY

**sappy** *adj* **1** appealing to the emotions in an obvious and tiresome way — see CORNY
**2** showing or marked by a lack of good sense or judgment — see FOOLISH 1

**sarcasm** *n* an act or expression showing scorn and usually intended to hurt another's feelings — see INSULT

**sarcastic** *adj* marked by the use of wit that is intended to cause hurt feelings ⟨her *sarcastic* comments that my singing reminded her of the time her dog was sick⟩
***syn*** acrid, biting, caustic, cutting, mordant, pungent, sardonic, satiric (*or* satirical), scalding, scathing, sharp, smart-alecky (*or* smart-aleck), tart
***rel*** acid, acidic, cross, sour; incisive, trenchant; cynical, dry, ironic, wry; facetious, flippant, tongue-in-cheek; acrimonious, bitter, resentful; harsh, rough, severe, stringent; concise, crisp, curt, pithy, succinct, terse; backhanded, insincere
***near ant*** amusing, droll, merry, playful, sportive, waggish; gentle, mild; bland; good-humored, good-natured; diplomatic, polite, smooth, suave, urbane; affable, cordial, genial, gracious

**sardonic** *adj* marked by the use of wit that is intended to cause hurt feelings — see SARCASTIC

**sash** *n* a strip of flexible material (as leather) worn around the waist — see [2]BELT

**sass** *n* disrespectful or argumentative talk given in response to a command or request — see BACK TALK
**sassy** *adj* displaying or marked by rude boldness — see NERVY 1
**Satan** *n* the supreme personification of evil often represented as the ruler of Hell — see DEVIL 1
**satanic** *adj* of, relating to, or worthy of an evil spirit — see FIENDISH
**sate** *vb* 1 to fill with food to capacity — see GORGE 1
2 to put a complete end to (a physical need or desire) — see SATISFY 1
**sated** *adj* having one's appetite completely satisfied — see FULL 3
**satiate** *adj* having one's appetite completely satisfied — see FULL 3
**satiate** *vb* to put a complete end to (a physical need or desire) — see SATISFY 1
**satiated** *adj* having one's appetite completely satisfied — see FULL 3
**satin** *adj* 1 having a shiny surface or finish — see GLOSSY
2 smooth or delicate in appearance or feel — see SOFT 2
**satiny** *adj* 1 having a shiny surface or finish — see GLOSSY
2 smooth or delicate in appearance or feel — see SOFT 2
**satire** *n* a creative work that uses sharp humor to point up the foolishness of a person, institution, or human nature in general ⟨a *satire* about the music industry in which a handsome but untalented youth is turned into a rock star⟩
*syn* lampoon
*rel* burlesque, caricature, parody, spoof, takeoff; comedy, farce, sketch, slapstick, squib; derision, ridicule; mockery, travesty
**satiric** *or* **satirical** *adj* marked by the use of wit that is intended to cause hurt feelings — see SARCASTIC
**satisfaction** *n* 1 the feeling experienced when one's wishes are met — see PLEASURE 1
2 payment to another for a loss or injury — see COMPENSATION 1
**satisfactorily** *adv* 1 in a satisfactory way — see WELL 1
2 in or to a degree or quantity that meets one's requirements or satisfaction — see ENOUGH 1
**satisfactoriness** *n* the quality or state of meeting one's needs adequately — see SUFFICIENCY
**satisfactory** *adj* 1 being to one's liking ⟨we found the meal most *satisfactory*⟩
*syn* agreeable, all right, alright, copacetic (*also* copasetic *or* copesetic), fine, good, OK (*or* okay), palatable
*rel* delectable, delicious, delightful, dreamy, felicitous, gratifying, nice, pleasant, pleasing, scrumptious, welcome; acceptable, adequate, decent, passable, tolerable
*ant* disagreeable, unsatisfactory
2 of a level of quality that meets one's needs or standards — see ADEQUATE
**satisfied** *adj* 1 experiencing pleasure, satisfaction, or delight — see GLAD 1
2 feeling that one's needs or desires have been met — see CONTENT
**satisfy** *vb* 1 to put a complete end to (a physical need or desire) ⟨they *satisfied* their hunger after the game with a big pasta dinner⟩
*syn* assuage, quench, sate, satiate
*rel* cater (to), gratify, indulge; alleviate, lighten, relieve
*near ant* arouse, excite, pique, stimulate; tantalize, tease
2 to cause (someone) to agree with a belief or course of action by using arguments or earnest requests — see PERSUADE
3 to do what is required by the terms of — see FULFILL 1
4 to give satisfaction to — see PLEASE
**satisfying** *adj* 1 giving pleasure or contentment to the mind or senses — see PLEASANT
2 having the power to persuade — see COGENT
3 making one feel good inside — see HEARTWARMING
**satisfyingly** *adv* in a pleasing way — see WELL 5
**saturate** *vb* to wet thoroughly with liquid — see SOAK 1
**saturated** *adj* containing, covered with, or thoroughly penetrated by water — see WET
**saturnine** *adj* causing or marked by an atmosphere lacking in cheer — see GLOOMY 1
**sauce** *n* 1 a savory fluid food used as a topping or accompaniment to a main dish ⟨the chef poured *sauce* over the meat just before he served it⟩
*syn* dressing, gravy
*rel* condiment, relish, seasoning; fixing(s), garnish, topping; dip, marinade
2 disrespectful or argumentative talk given in response to a command or request — see BACK TALK
3 shameless boldness — see EFFRONTERY
**sauciness** *n* shameless boldness — see EFFRONTERY
**saucy** *adj* displaying or marked by rude boldness — see NERVY 1
**saunter** *n* a relaxed journey on foot for exercise or pleasure — see WALK
**sausage** *n* a rod-shaped portion of seasoned ground meat in a casing ⟨a couple of *sausages* and eggs make a good breakfast⟩
*syn* link
*rel* bologna, frankfurter, hot dog, knockwurst, liverwurst, pepperoni, salami, wiener
**savage** *adj* 1 not civilized ⟨Tarzan is usually portrayed as a noble but *savage* warrior of the jungle⟩
*syn* barbarous, heathen, heathenish, Neanderthal, rude, uncivil, uncivilized, uncultivated, wild
*rel* coarse, crude, primitive, rough; uncouth, uncultured

***near ant*** cultured, enlightened, humane, sophisticated; genteel, polite, refined, urbane, well-bred
***ant*** civilized
**2** having or showing the desire to inflict severe pain and suffering on others — see CRUEL 1
**3** living outdoors without taming or domestication by humans — see WILD 1
**4** violently unfriendly or aggressive in disposition — see FIERCE 1

**savage** *n* **1** a mean, evil, or unprincipled person — see VILLAIN 1
**2** an uncivilized person — see HEATHEN 2

**savageness** *n* the willful infliction of pain and suffering on others — see CRUELTY

**savagery** *n* the willful infliction of pain and suffering on others — see CRUELTY

**savanna** *also* **savannah** *n* a broad area of level or rolling treeless country — see PLAIN

**savant** *n* a person of deep wisdom or learning — see SAGE

**save** *prep* not including — see EXCEPT

**save** *vb* **1** to free from the penalties or consequences of sin ⟨the Christian belief that Jesus lived and died to *save* humanity⟩
***syn*** deliver, redeem
***rel*** reclaim, reform; forgive, pardon, remit; bless, hallow; consecrate, purify, sanctify
**2** to remove from danger or harm ⟨the fire fighter *saved* my brother from the burning building⟩
***syn*** bail out, deliver, rescue
***rel*** salvage; emancipate, free, liberate, manumit, release; disentangle, extricate; recover
***ant*** compromise, endanger, imperil, jeopardize
**3** to avoid unnecessary waste or expense — see ECONOMIZE
**4** to keep in good condition — see MAINTAIN 1
**5** to keep or intend for a special purpose — see DEVOTE 1

**saver** *n* one that saves from danger or destruction — see SAVIOR

**saving** *conj* if it were not for the fact that — see EXCEPT

**saving** *prep* not including — see EXCEPT

**savior** *or* **saviour** *n* one that saves from danger or destruction ⟨the policeman proved to be our *savior*, arriving on the scene just as we were about to be mugged⟩
***syn*** deliverer, redeemer, rescuer, saver
***rel*** custodian, defender, guard, guardian, keeper, lookout, protector, sentinel, sentry, warden, warder, watch, watchman

**savor** *n* **1** the property of a substance that can be identified by the sense of taste — see TASTE 1
**2** the quality of being delicious — see DELICIOUSNESS

**savor** *vb* to make more pleasant to the taste by adding something intensely flavored — see SEASON 1

**savoriness** *n* the quality of being delicious — see DELICIOUSNESS

**savorless** *adj* lacking in taste or flavor — see INSIPID 1

**savory** *adj* **1** having a pleasant smell — see FRAGRANT
**2** very pleasing to the sense of taste — see DELICIOUS 1

**savvy** *n* knowledge gained by actually doing or living through something — see EXPERIENCE 1

**saw** *n* an often stated observation regarding something from common experience — see SAYING

**saw-toothed** *adj* notched or toothed along the edge — see SERRATED

**say** *vb* **1** to express (a thought or emotion) in words ⟨why don't you just *say* what's on your mind?⟩
***syn*** articulate, speak, state, talk, tell, utter, verbalize, vocalize
***rel*** air, discuss, express, give, look, sound, state, vent, ventilate, voice; advertise, announce, blaze, broadcast, declare, enunciate, proclaim, publicize, publish; affirm, allege, assert, aver, avouch, avow; breathe, drawl, gasp, mouth, murmur, shout, splutter, spout, whisper; couch, formulate, phrase, put, word; comment, remark
***phrases*** put into words
***near ant*** stifle, suppress
**2** to convey in appropriate or telling terms — see PHRASE
**3** to give from memory — see REPEAT 2

**say** *n* the right to express a wish, choice, or opinion — see VOICE 1

**saying** *n* an often stated observation regarding something from common experience ⟨there's an old *saying* that you should let sleeping dogs lie⟩
***syn*** adage, aphorism, byword, epigram, maxim, proverb, saw
***rel*** cliché, commonplace, platitude; expression, felicity; axiom, motto, precept, truism, truth; observation, reflection, remark

**scabby** *adj* arousing or deserving of one's loathing and disgust — see CONTEMPTIBLE 1

**scads** *n pl* a considerable amount — see LOT 2

**scalawag** *or* **scallywag** *n* a mean, evil, or unprincipled person — see VILLAIN

**scalding** *adj* **1** having a notably high temperature — see HOT 1
**2** marked by the use of wit that is intended to cause hurt feelings — see SARCASTIC

**[1]scale** *n* a device for measuring weight ⟨I hate getting on the bathroom *scale*⟩
***syn*** balance
***rel*** gravimeter

**[2]scale** *n* a small thin piece of material that resembles an animal scale ⟨*scales* of mica were embedded in the granite⟩
***syn*** lamella, lamina, plate
***rel*** chip, flake, sliver, splinter

---

***syn*** synonym(s) ***rel*** related words
***ant*** antonym(s) ***near ant*** near antonym(s)

[3]**scale** *n* **1** a scheme of rank or order ⟨a student who scored very highly on a standard intelligence *scale*⟩
***syn*** graduation, ladder, ordering, ranking
***rel*** arrangement, array, disposal, disposition, distribution, order, sequence, series
**2** the distance or extent between possible extremes — see RANGE 3

**scale** *vb* to find out the size, extent, or amount of — see MEASURE

**scaly** *adj* composed of or covered with scales ⟨the snake's *scaly* skin was dry to the touch⟩
***syn*** squamous
***rel*** scalelike
***near ant*** smooth
***ant*** scaleless

**scamp** *n* **1** an appealingly mischievous person ⟨those little *scamps* are always getting into trouble, but no one has the heart to punish them⟩
***syn*** devil, hellion, imp, mischief, monkey, rapscallion, rascal, rogue, urchin
***rel*** cutup, madcap, skylarker; ragamuffin; brat, disrupter, nuisance; juvenile delinquent; gamin, gamine
***near ant*** beast, boor, cad, churl, clown, creep, cretin, cur, heel, joker, louse, lout, skunk, snake, stinker; knave, scalawag (*or* scallywag), scoundrel, villain
**2** a mean, evil, or unprincipled person — see VILLAIN

**scamper** *vb* to go at a pace faster than a walk — see RUN 1

**scan** *n* a close look at or over someone or something in order to judge condition — see INSPECTION

**scan** *vb* to look over closely (as for judging quality or condition) — see INSPECT

**scandal** *n* a cause of shame — see DISGRACE 2

**scandalous** *adj* **1** causing intense displeasure, disgust, or resentment — see OFFENSIVE 1
**2** causing or intended to cause unjust injury to a person's good name — see LIBELOUS

**scant** *adj* less plentiful than what is normal, necessary, or desirable — see MEAGER

**scant** *vb* to use or give out in stingy amounts — see SPARE

**scantiness** *n* a falling short of an essential or desirable amount or number — see DEFICIENCY

**scanty** *adj* less plentiful than what is normal, necessary, or desirable — see MEAGER

**scapegoat** *n* a person or thing taking the blame for others ⟨companies often use the economy as a *scapegoat* to avoid taking responsibility for dropping sales⟩
***syn*** fall guy, goat, whipping boy
***rel*** victim; butt, dupe, fool, laughingstock, mockery, monkey; excuse

**scar** *n* something that spoils the appearance or completeness of a thing — see BLEMISH

**scarce** *adj* **1** less plentiful than what is normal, necessary, or desirable — see MEAGER
**2** not coming up to a usual standard or meeting a particular need — see SHORT 3

**scarcely** *adv* **1** by a very small margin — see JUST 2
**2** certainly not — see HARDLY 2

**scarceness** *n* a falling short of an essential or desirable amount or number — see DEFICIENCY

**scarcity** *n* a falling short of an essential or desirable amount or number — see DEFICIENCY

**scare** *vb* to strike with fear — see FRIGHTEN

**scared** *adj* filled with fear or dread — see AFRAID 1

**scare up** *vb* to come upon after searching, study, or effort — see FIND 1

**scarp** *n* a steep wall of rock, earth, or ice — see CLIFF

**scary** *adj* **1** causing fear — see FEARFUL 1
**2** easily frightened — see SHY 1

**scathe** *vb* to criticize harshly and usually publicly — see ATTACK 2

**scathing** *adj* marked by the use of wit that is intended to cause hurt feelings — see SARCASTIC

**scatter** *vb* **1** to cause (members of a group) to move widely apart ⟨the noise of the backfiring car *scattered* the pigeons⟩
***syn*** clear out, disband, dispel, disperse, dissipate
***rel*** break up, isolate, part, segregate, separate, split up; diffuse, disseminate, diverge, spread
***near ant*** agglutinate, conglomerate; unify, unite
***ant*** assemble, cluster, collect, concentrate, congregate, gather
**2** to cover by or as if by scattering something over or on ⟨the hillside was *scattered* with wildflowers⟩
***syn*** bestrew, dot, pepper, sow, spray, sprinkle, strew
***rel*** blanket, dust; stud; dapple, fleck, speckle, spot, stipple

**scatterbrained** *adj* lacking in seriousness or maturity — see GIDDY 1

**scattered** *adj* lacking a definite plan, purpose, or pattern — see RANDOM

**scattering** *n* **1** an act or process in which something scatters or is scattered ⟨the *scattering* of the protesters suddenly turned violent and chaotic⟩
***syn*** disbandment, dispersal, dispersion, dissipation
***near ant*** assembly, collection, concentration, gathering
**2** a small number — see FEW

**scenario** *n* the written form of a story prepared for film production — see SCREENPLAY

**scene** *n* **1** the place and time in which the action for a portion of a dramatic work (as a movie) is set ⟨the first *scene* was the kitchen of a fancy restaurant during dinner⟩
***syn*** background, setting

*rel* backdrop, scenery, set; tableau
**2** an outburst or display of excited anger — see TANTRUM
**3** position with regard to conditions and circumstances — see SITUATION 1
**4** the array of painted backgrounds and furnishings used for a scene in a stage production — see SCENERY

**scenery** *n* the array of painted backgrounds and furnishings used for a scene in a stage production ⟨the *scenery* in the high school production was all handmade⟩
*syn* scene, set
*rel* backdrop, drop; background, setting; prop, property

**scent** *n* **1** a sweet or pleasant smell — see FRAGRANCE
**2** the quality of a thing that makes it perceptible to the sense organs in the nose — see SMELL 1

**scent** *vb* **1** to fill or infuse with a pleasant odor or odor-releasing substance ⟨fancy bars of soap *scented* with lavender⟩
*syn* perfume
*near ant* deodorize
**2** to become aware of by means of the sense organs in the nose — see SMELL
**3** to have a vague awareness of — see FEEL 1

**scented** *adj* having a pleasant smell — see FRAGRANT

**schedule** *n* **1** a listing of things to be presented or considered (as at a concert or play) — see PROGRAM 1
**2** a record of a series of items (as names or titles) usually arranged according to some system — see [1]LIST

**schedule** *vb* to put (someone or something) on a list — see [1]LIST 2

**scheduled** *adj* being in accordance with the prescribed, normal, or logical course of events — see DUE 2

**schematize** *vb* to work out the details of (something) in advance — see PLAN 1

**scheme** *n* **1** a clever often underhanded means to achieve an end — see TRICK 1
**2** a secret plan for accomplishing evil or unlawful ends — see PLOT 1
**3** a method worked out in advance for achieving some objective — see PLAN 1

**scheme** *vb* to engage in a secret plan to accomplish evil or unlawful ends — see PLOT

**scheme** (out) *vb* to work out the details of (something) in advance — see PLAN 1

**schism** *n* **1** a lack of agreement or harmony — see DISCORD
**2** the act or process of a whole separating into two or more parts or pieces — see SEPARATION 1

**schmaltz** *also* **schmalz** *n* something (as a work of literature or music) that is too sentimental — see CORN

**schmaltzy** *adj* appealing to the emotions in an obvious and tiresome way — see CORNY

**scholar** *n* **1** a person of deep wisdom or learning — see SAGE
**2** a person with a high level of knowledge or skill in a field — see EXPERT
**3** one who attends a school — see STUDENT

**scholarly** *adj* **1** having or displaying advanced knowledge or education — see EDUCATED
**2** of or relating to schooling or learning especially at an advanced level — see ACADEMIC

**scholarship** *n* the understanding and information gained from being educated — see EDUCATION 2

**scholastic** *adj* of or relating to schooling or learning especially at an advanced level — see ACADEMIC

**school** *n* a place or establishment for teaching and learning ⟨one of the first *schools* in the country to admit girls as students⟩
*syn* academy, seminary
*rel* elementary school, grammar school, high school, junior high school, middle school, preparatory school, public school, secondary school, trade school; Sunday school, yeshiva (*also* yeshivah)

**school** *vb* to cause to acquire knowledge or skill in some field — see TEACH

**schooling** *n* the act or process of imparting knowledge or skills to another — see EDUCATION 1

**schoolteacher** *n* a person whose occupation is to give formal instruction in a school — see TEACHER

**science** *n* **1** a body of facts learned by study or experience — see KNOWLEDGE 1
**2** the understanding and information gained from being educated — see EDUCATION 2

**scintillate** *vb* **1** to give off sparks — see SPARK 1
**2** to shoot forth bursts of light — see FLASH 1

**scoffer** *n* a person who causes repeated emotional pain, distress, or annoyance to another — see TORMENTOR

**scold** *n* a person given to harsh judgments and to finding faults — see CRITIC 1

**scold** *vb* to criticize (someone) severely or angrily especially for personal failings ⟨he *scolded* the kids for not cleaning up the mess they had made in the kitchen⟩
*syn* berate, castigate, chew out, dress down, flay, jaw, keelhaul, lambaste (*or* lambast), lecture, rail (at *or* against), rate, rebuke, reprimand, reproach, score, upbraid
*rel* admonish, chide, remonstrate (with), reprove; abuse, assail, attack, bad-mouth, blame, blast, censure, condemn, criticize, crucify, denounce, dis [*slang*], excoriate, fault, knock, lash, pan, reprehend, slam; belittle, disparage, mock, put down; ridicule, scoff, scorn
*phrases* read the riot act (to), take to task
*near ant* approve, endorse (*also* indorse), sanction; extol (*also* extoll), laud, praise

---

*syn* synonym(s) *rel* related words
*ant* antonym(s) *near ant* near antonym(s)

**scoop** *n* **1** a utensil with a bowl and a handle that is used especially in cooking and serving food — see SPOON
**2** information not generally available to the public — see DOPE 1
**scoop** *vb* to lift out with something that holds liquid — see DIP 2
**scoot** *vb* to proceed or move quickly — see HURRY 2
**scope** *n* an area over which activity, capacity, or influence extends — see RANGE 2
**scorch** *vb* to burn on the surface ⟨the picnickers kept *scorching* their marshmallows, deliberately sticking their skewers into the licking flames of the campfire⟩
***syn*** char, sear, singe
***rel*** fire, ignite, inflame, kindle, light; bake, cremate, incinerate; scald, scathe
**scorching** *adj* having a notably high temperature — see HOT 1
**score** *n* a lingering ill will towards a person for a real or imagined wrong — see GRUDGE 1
**score** *vb* **1** to mark with or as if with a line or groove ⟨the glassblower *scored* the glass rod first so that it would break cleanly⟩
***syn*** groove, scribe, seam
***rel*** abrade, file, graze, rasp, scarify, scratch
**2** to gain (as points or runs in a game) as credit towards one's total number of points ⟨he *scored* the winning goal in the final minute of play⟩
***syn*** rack up, tally
***rel*** triumph, win; best, defeat
***near ant*** lose
**3** to obtain (as a goal) through effort — see ACHIEVE 1
**4** to criticize (someone) severely or angrily especially for personal failings — see SCOLD
**scorn** *n* open dislike for someone or something considered unworthy of one's concern or respect — see CONTEMPT
**scorn** *vb* **1** to show contempt for ⟨*scorned* the religious traditions of their ancestors⟩
***syn*** disdain, high-hat, slight, sniff (at), snub
***rel*** scout; abhor, despise, detest, hate, loathe; disapprove (of), discountenance, disfavor, frown (on *or* upon)
***phrases*** look down on, sneeze at
***near ant*** cherish, prize, treasure, value; admire, esteem; revere, venerate, worship; accept, appreciate, approve (of), care (for), countenance, favor, OK (*or* okay), subscribe (to)
***ant*** honor, respect
**2** to ignore in a disrespectful manner ⟨she *scorned* the suggestions of her classmates for the parade float⟩
***syn*** despise, disregard, flout
***rel*** dismiss, forget, ignore, neglect, overlook, overpass, pass over, slight, slur (over)
***near ant*** accept, approve; use
**scorner** *n* a person who causes repeated emotional pain, distress, or annoyance to another — see TORMENTOR
**scornful** *adj* **1** feeling or showing open dislike for someone or something regarded as undeserving of respect or concern — see CONTEMPTUOUS 1
**2** intended to make a person or thing seem of little importance or value — see DEROGATORY
**Scot** *n* a person born or living in Scotland ⟨my grandfather was a *Scot*, but my grandmother was Welsh⟩
***syn*** Scotchman, Scotsman, Scottie
**Scotch** *adj* of, relating to, or characteristic of the people of Scotland — see SCOTTISH
**Scotchman** *n* a person born or living in Scotland — see SCOT
**Scots** *adj* of, relating to, or characteristic of the people of Scotland — see SCOTTISH
**Scotsman** *n* a person born or living in Scotland — see SCOT
**Scottie** *n* a person born or living in Scotland — see SCOT
**Scottish** *adj* of, relating to, or characteristic of the people of Scotland ⟨golf was originally a *Scottish* game⟩
***syn*** Scotch, Scots
**scoundrel** *n* a mean, evil, or unprincipled person — see VILLAIN
**scour** *vb* to look through (as a place) carefully or thoroughly in an effort to find or discover something — see SEARCH 1
**scourge** *n* **1** a long thin or flexible tool for striking — see WHIP
**2** one who inflicts punishment in return for an injury or offense — see NEMESIS 1
**scourge** *vb* **1** to bring destruction to (something) through violent action — see RAVAGE
**2** to strike repeatedly with something long and thin or flexible — see WHIP 1
**scout** *n* a member of the human race — see HUMAN
**scout** *vb* to make (someone or something) the object of unkind laughter — see RIDICULE
**scout** (up) *vb* to come upon after searching, study, or effort — see FIND 1
**scowl** *n* a twisting of the facial features in disgust or disapproval — see GRIMACE
**scowl** *vb* to look with anger or disapproval — see FROWN
**scrabble** *n* a forceful effort to reach a goal or objective — see STRUGGLE 1
**scraggly** *adj* having an uneven edge or outline — see RAGGED 1
**scraggy** *adj* **1** having an uneven edge or outline — see RAGGED 1
**2** not having a level or smooth surface — see UNEVEN 1
**scramble** *n* an unorganized collection or mixture of various things — see MISCELLANY 1
**scramble** *vb* **1** to move (as up or over something) often with the help of the hands in holding or pulling — see CLIMB 1
**2** to undo the proper order or arrangement of — see DISORDER

**[1]scrap** *n* **1** an unused or unwanted piece or item typically of small size or value ⟨only a *scrap* of silk was left on the sewing table after they had finished the project⟩
*syn* end, fag end, leftover, oddment, remainder, remnant, stub
*rel* leavings, odds and ends, remains, residual, residue, scraping(s), stump; balance, rest; chip, flake, fragment, piece, sliver, splinter; ribbon(s), shred, tatter
*near ant* whole
**2** a broken or irregular part of something that often remains incomplete — see FRAGMENT
**3** a physical dispute between opposing individuals or groups — see FIGHT 1
**4** a very small piece — see BIT 1
**5** discarded or useless material — see GARBAGE

**[2]scrap** *n* an often noisy or angry expression of differing opinions — see ARGUMENT 1

**[1]scrap** *vb* to express different opinions about something often angrily — see ARGUE 2

**[2]scrap** *vb* to get rid of as useless or unwanted — see DISCARD

**scrape** *n* **1** a brief clash between enemies or rivals — see ENCOUNTER
**2** a harsh grating sound — see RASP

**scrape** *vb* **1** to pass roughly and noisily over or against a surface ⟨the rusty old gate *scraped* whenever anyone managed to open it⟩
*syn* grate, grind, rasp, scratch
*rel* rub; groan, whine
*near ant* glide, skate, slide
**2** to damage by rubbing against a sharp or rough surface ⟨she *scraped* her knee when she fell down⟩
*syn* abrade, graze, scratch, scuff
*rel* bark, skin; chafe, fret, gall; claw, cut, lacerate; bruise, contuse
*near ant* polish, smooth, soften, wax
**3** to get with great difficulty — see EKE OUT
**4** to press or strike against or together so as to make a scraping sound — see GRIND 2

**scrape** (together) *vb* to bring together in one body or place — see GATHER 1

**scrappiness** *n* an inclination to fight or quarrel — see BELLIGERENCE

**scrapping** *n* the getting rid of whatever is unwanted or useless — see DISPOSAL 1

**scrappy** *adj* **1** feeling or displaying eagerness to fight — see BELLIGERENT
**2** given to arguing — see ARGUMENTATIVE 1

**scratch** *n* a harsh grating sound — see RASP

**scratch** *vb* **1** to damage by rubbing against a sharp or rough surface — see SCRAPE 2
**2** to pass roughly and noisily over or against a surface — see SCRAPE 1
**3** to write or draw hastily or carelessly — see SCRIBBLE

**scratch** (out) *vb* **1** to compose and set down on paper the words of — see WRITE 1
**2** to show (something written) to be no longer valid by drawing a cross over or a line through it — see X (OUT)

**scratchy** *adj* **1** likely to cause a scratch ⟨*scratchy* shrubbery that's intended to keep kids and pets off the old man's property⟩
*syn* brambly, prickly, thistly, thorny
*rel* burred; coarse, jagged, rough; irritating, itchy, stinging
*near ant* polished, smooth, soft, soothing; gentle
**2** harsh and dry in sound — see HOARSE

**scrawl** *vb* to write or draw hastily or carelessly — see SCRIBBLE

**scream** *n* someone or something that is very funny ⟨that new comedy is a *scream*⟩
*syn* laugh, riot
*rel* howler; crack, gag, jest, joke, pleasantry, quip, sally, waggery, wisecrack, witticism; caution, sight
*near ant* bummer, downer

**scream** *vb* to cry out loudly and emotionally ⟨we *screamed* when the roller coaster began its thirty foot plunge⟩
*syn* howl, screech, shriek, shrill, squall, squeal, yelp, yell
*rel* bay, caterwaul, keen, squawk, wail, yawp (*or* yaup), yowl; bawl, call, cry, holler, shout, vociferate
*near ant* murmur, mutter, whisper

**screaming** *adj* **1** arousing a strong and usually superficial interest or emotional reaction — see SENSATIONAL 1
**2** causing or intended to cause laughter — see FUNNY 1

**screech** *vb* to cry out loudly and emotionally — see SCREAM

**screeching** *adj* having a high musical pitch or range — see SHRILL

**screen** *n* **1** the art or business of making a movie — see MOVIE 2
**2** means or method of defending — see DEFENSE 1

**screen** *vb* **1** to drive danger or attack away from — see DEFEND 1
**2** to keep secret or shut off from view — see [1]HIDE 2
**3** to pass through a filter — see STRAIN 2
**4** to place a protective layer over — see COVER 3

**screenplay** *n* the written form of a story prepared for film production ⟨each actor was given a copy of the *screenplay* to study⟩
*syn* scenario, script
*rel* story, text

**screw** *vb* to twist (something) out of a natural or normal shape or condition — see CONTORT

**screwball** *adj* showing or marked by a lack of good sense or judgment — see FOOLISH 1

**screwball** *n* a person of odd or whimsical habits — see ECCENTRIC

**screwing** *n* the twisting of something out of its natural or normal shape or condition — see CONTORTION
**screwlike** *adj* turning around an axis like the thread of a screw — see SPIRAL
**screwy** *adj* **1** different from the ordinary in a way that causes curiosity or suspicion — see ODD 2
**2** having or showing a very abnormal or sick state of mind — see INSANE 1
**scribble** *vb* to write or draw hastily or carelessly ⟨she *scribbled* a quick note on the pad by the door before leaving⟩
***syn*** scratch, scrawl
***rel*** doodle; jot (down); ink, inscribe, letter, pen, pencil, print, write
**scribe** *n* a person whose job is to keep records — see CLERK 1
**scribe** *vb* to mark with or as if with a line or groove — see SCORE 1
**scrimmage** *n* a physical dispute between opposing individuals or groups — see FIGHT 1
**scrimmage** (with) *vb* to oppose (someone) in physical conflict — see FIGHT 1
**scrimp** *vb* to avoid unnecessary waste or expense — see ECONOMIZE
**scrimping** *adj* careful in the management of money or resources — see FRUGAL
**scrimping** *n* careful management of material resources — see ECONOMY
**script** *n* **1** the form or style of a particular person's writing — see HANDWRITING 1
**2** the written form of a story prepared for film production — see SCREENPLAY
**3** writing done by hand — see HANDWRITING 2
**Scripture** *n* a book made up of the writings accepted by Christians as coming from God — see BIBLE
**scrooge** *n* a mean grasping person who is usually stingy with money — see MISER
**scrounge** *vb* to get with great difficulty — see EKE OUT
**scrub** *n* a living thing much smaller than others of its kind — see DWARF 1
**scruffy** *adj* showing signs of advanced wear and tear and neglect — see SHABBY 1
**scrumptious** *adj* very pleasing to the sense of taste — see DELICIOUS 1
**scrunch** *vb* **1** to create (as by crushing) an irregular mass of creases in — see CRUMPLE 1
**2** to lie low with the limbs close to the body — see CROUCH
**3** to press or strike against or together so as to make a scraping sound — see GRIND 2
**scruple** *n* **1** a very small amount — see PARTICLE 1
**2** a very small piece — see BIT 1
**3** an uneasy feeling about the rightness of what one is doing or going to do — see QUALM
**scrupulous** *adj* guided by or in accordance with one's sense of right and wrong — see CONSCIENTIOUS 1
**scrupulousness** *n* strict attentiveness to what one is doing — see CARE 1
**scrutinize** *vb* to look over closely (as for judging quality or condition) — see INSPECT
**scrutiny** *n* a close look at or over someone or something in order to judge condition — see INSPECTION
**scuff** *vb* **1** to damage by rubbing against a sharp or rough surface — see SCRAPE 2
**2** to move heavily or clumsily — see LUMBER 1
**scuffle** *n* a physical dispute between opposing individuals or groups — see FIGHT 1
**scuffle** *vb* **1** to move heavily or clumsily — see LUMBER 1
**2** to seize and attempt to unbalance one another for the purpose of achieving physical mastery — see WRESTLE
**scull** *vb* to move a boat by means of oars — see [1]ROW
**sculler** *n* a person who drives a boat forward by means of oars — see OARSMAN
**sculpt** *vb* to create a three-dimensional representation of (something) using solid material ⟨I *sculpted* a figure of a giraffe out of clay in art class today⟩
***syn*** carve, sculpture
***rel*** chisel, engrave, etch, grave, incise, inscribe; cast, form, model, mold, shape
**sculpture** *vb* to create a three-dimensional representation of (something) using solid material — see SCULPT
**scum** *n* people looked down upon as ignorant and of the lowest class — see RABBLE
**scummy** *adj* arousing or deserving of one's loathing and disgust — see CONTEMPTIBLE 1
**scurry** *vb* to proceed or move quickly — see HURRY 2
**scurvy** *adj* arousing or deserving of one's loathing and disgust — see CONTEMPTIBLE 1
**scuttle** *vb* to proceed or move quickly — see HURRY 2
**sea** *n* the whole body of salt water that covers nearly three-fourths of the earth — see OCEAN
**sea devil** *n* any of several extremely large rays — see DEVILFISH
**sea dog** *n* one who operates or navigates a seagoing vessel — see SAILOR
**seafarer** *n* one who operates or navigates a seagoing vessel — see SAILOR
**seam** *vb* to mark with or as if with a line or groove — see SCORE 1
**seaman** *n* one who operates or navigates a seagoing vessel — see SAILOR
**sear** *vb* **1** to burn on the surface — see SCORCH
**2** to make dry — see DRY 1
**search** *n* an act or process of looking carefully or thoroughly for someone or something ⟨the *search* for the lost puppy took hours⟩
***syn*** hunt, quest
***rel*** chase, pursuit; reconnaissance, scout; canvas, survey; exploration, probe; forage

**search** *vb* **1** to look through (as a place) carefully or thoroughly in an effort to find or discover something ⟨we *searched* the closet for half an hour until we found the missing shoe⟩
*syn* comb, dig (through), dredge, hunt (through), rake, ransack, rifle, rummage, scour
*rel* audit, check (out), examine, inspect, investigate, review, scan, scrutinize, survey; ascertain, descry, detect, determine, discover, ferret (out), find, find out, get, hit (on *or* upon), learn, locate, run down, scare up, track (down); explore, probe, prospect, skirmish, snoop; browse, glance (over), look over; peruse, study
*near ant* hide; abandon, lose; ignore, neglect
**2** to go into or range over for purposes of discovery — see EXPLORE 2
**search** (for *or* out) *vb* to go in search of — see SEEK 1
**searing** *adj* having a notably high temperature — see HOT 1
**season** *vb* **1** to make more pleasant to the taste by adding something intensely flavored ⟨the chef *seasoned* the vegetables as soon as they came out of the oven⟩
*syn* flavor, savor, spice
*rel* enhance, enrich, sauce; salt, pepper
**2** to bring to a proper or desired state of fitness — see CONDITION 1
**3** to make able to withstand physical hardship, strain, or exposure — see HARDEN 2
**4** to make competent (as by training, skill, or ability) for a particular office or function — see QUALIFY 2
**seasonable** *adj* especially suitable for a certain time — see TIMELY 1
**seasoning** *n* **1** something (as a spice or herb) that adds an agreeable or interesting taste to food ⟨the stew was too bland before they added the *seasoning*⟩
*syn* flavor, flavoring, spice
*rel* sauce
**2** something used to enhance the flavor of cooked or prepared food — see CONDIMENT
**seat** *n* **1** a place from which authority is exercised ⟨all applications had to be submitted at the county *seat* for proper processing⟩
*syn* command, headquarters
*rel* center, home; capital
**2** the part of the body upon which someone sits — see BUTTOCKS
**3** a thing or place that is of greatest importance to an activity or interest — see CENTER 1
**seat** *vb* to cause to sit down ⟨the usher *seated* them in the third row⟩
*syn* set down, sit
*rel* ensconce, settle; lay, lie, rest; place, put; recline, repose
**seclude** *vb* to set or keep apart from others — see ISOLATE

---

*syn* synonym(s) *rel* related words
*ant* antonym(s) *near ant* near antonym(s)

**secluded** *adj* hidden from view ⟨we stayed in a *secluded* resort, far away from the regular tourist crowds⟩
*syn* cloistered, covert, isolated, quiet, remote, retired, secret, sheltered
*rel* lonely, reclusive, solitary; private
*near ant* obvious, visible; exposed
**secludedness** *n* the state of being alone or kept apart from others — see ISOLATION
**seclusion** *n* the state of being alone or kept apart from others — see ISOLATION
**second** *n* a very small space of time — see INSTANT
**secondary** *adj* **1** taken or created from something original or basic ⟨history textbooks are *secondary* sources for historical information and do not represent original research⟩
*syn* derivative, secondhand
*rel* unoriginal; consequent, resultant
*near ant* fundamental, nonderivative; first, primary
*ant* basic, original
**2** of little or less value or merit — see INFERIOR 2
**second–class** *adj* of little or less value or merit — see INFERIOR 2
**secondhand** *adj* taken or created from something original or basic — see SECONDARY 1
**second–rate** *adj* **1** of average to below average quality — see MEDIOCRE 1
**2** of little or less value or merit — see INFERIOR 2
**3** of low quality — see CHEAP 2
**secrecy** *n* the practice or habit of keeping secrets or keeping one's affairs secret ⟨in picking helpers for a surprise party, you'd very much want to choose people known for their *secrecy*⟩
*syn* closeness, secretiveness
*rel* discreetness, discretion, prudence; circumspection, wariness; reserve, reticence, silence, taciturnity; furtiveness, shiftiness, slyness, sneakiness, underhandedness; concealment, stealth, subterfuge
*near ant* candor, frankness, honesty, openness; imprudence, indiscretion
**secret** *adj* **1** undertaken or done so as to escape being observed or known by others ⟨a *secret* operation to rescue captive soldiers behind enemy lines⟩
*syn* clandestine, covert, furtive, hugger-mugger, private, privy, sneak, sneaking, sneaky, stealthy, surreptitious, undercover, underground, underhand, underhanded
*rel* classified, confidential, restricted, top secret, undisclosed; concealed, hidden, secreted, subterranean, unadvertised, unexposed
*near ant* acknowledged, avowed; aboveboard, straightforward, unconcealed, undisguised; unclassified, unrestricted; clear, evident, manifest, obvious, patent, plain
*ant* open, overt, public

2 working on missions in which one's objectives, activities, or true identity are not publicly revealed ⟨*secret* agents whose wartime exploits were known only by top government officials⟩
***syn*** undercover
***rel*** covert, private, secretive, subterranean
***near ant*** overt
3 hidden from view — see SECLUDED
4 not known or meant to be known by the general populace — see PRIVATE 1

**secret** *n* 1 information shared only with another or with a select few ⟨they're best friends and are constantly sharing *secrets*⟩
***syn*** confidence
***rel*** dope, lowdown
***near ant*** open secret
2 something hard to understand or explain — see MYSTERY

**secrete** *vb* to put into a hiding place — see [1]HIDE 1

**secretion** *n* the placing of something out of sight — see CONCEALMENT 1

**secretive** *adj* given to keeping one's activities hidden from public observation or knowledge ⟨the intelligence agency remained *secretive* despite the media's demands for more openness in government⟩
***syn*** close, closemouthed, dark, reticent, uncommunicative
***rel*** quiet, reserved, silent, taciturn, tight-lipped; discreet, prudent; clandestine, covert, furtive, hugger-mugger, secret, sneak, sneaky, stealthy, surreptitious, undercover, underhand, underhanded
***near ant*** candid, frank, honest; blunt, outspoken, tactless
***ant*** communicative, open

**secretiveness** *n* the practice or habit of keeping secrets or keeping one's affairs secret — see SECRECY

**sect** *n* a group of people acting together within a larger group — see FACTION

**sectarian** *adj* not broad or open in views or opinions — see NARROW 2

**section** *n* 1 an area (as of a city) set apart for some purpose or having some special feature — see DISTRICT
2 one of the pieces from which something is designed to be assembled — see PART 1

**secular** *adj* not involving religion or religious matters — see PROFANE 1

**secure** *adj* 1 firmly positioned in place and difficult to dislodge — see TIGHT 2
2 having or showing great faith in oneself or one's abilities — see CONFIDENT 1
3 not exposed to the threat of loss or injury — see SAFE 1
4 providing safety — see SAFE 2

**secure** *vb* 1 to drive danger or attack away from — see DEFEND 1
2 to make sure, certain, or safe — see ENSURE
3 to put securely in place or in a desired position — see FASTEN 2
4 to receive as return for effort — see EARN 1

**security** *n* 1 means or method of defending — see DEFENSE 1
2 something given or held to assure that the giver will keep a promise — see PLEDGE 1
3 the state of not being exposed to danger — see SAFETY 1

**sedate** *adj* not joking or playful in mood or manner — see SERIOUS 1

**sedative** *adj* tending to calm the emotions and relieve stress — see SOOTHING 1

**sediment** *n* matter that settles to the bottom of a body of liquid — see DEPOSIT 1

**sediment** *vb* to cause to come to rest at the bottom (as of a liquid) — see SETTLE 1

**seduce** *vb* to lead away from a usual or proper course by offering some pleasure or advantage — see LURE

**seducer** *n* one that tries to get a person to give in to a desire — see TEMPTER

**seduction** *n* the act or pressure of giving in to a desire especially when ill-advised — see TEMPTATION 1

**seductive** *adj* having an often mysterious or magical power to attract — see FASCINATING 1

**seductiveness** *n* the power of irresistible attraction — see CHARM 2

**seductress** *n* a woman whom men find irresistibly attractive — see SIREN

**sedulous** *adj* involved in often constant activity — see BUSY 1

**sedulously** *adv* with great effort or determination — see HARD 1

**see** *vb* 1 to make note of (something) through the use of one's eyes ⟨out of the corner of my eye I *saw* the deer run into the woods⟩
***syn*** behold, descry, discern, distinguish, espy, eye, look (at), note, notice, observe, perceive, regard, remark, sight, spy, view, witness
***rel*** identify, make out, pick out; attend (to), consider, heed, mark, mind; study, watch; examine, inspect, scan, scrutinize, survey; glance (at), glimpse, peer (at)
***phrases*** get a load of [*slang*], lay eyes on, set eyes on
***near ant*** disregard, ignore, neglect, overpass, pass over; miss, overlook
2 to come to a knowledge of (something) by living through it — see EXPERIENCE
3 to come to an awareness — see DISCOVER 1
4 to have a vague awareness of — see FEEL 1
5 to make a social call upon — see VISIT 1
6 to recognize the meaning of — see COMPREHEND 1

**seeable** *adj* capable of being seen — see VISIBLE

**seed** *n* the descendants of a person, animal, or plant — see OFFSPRING

**seed** *vb* to put or set into the ground to grow — see PLANT

**seediness** *n* the state of being unattended to or not cared for — see NEGLECT 1

**seedy** *adj* 1 showing signs of advanced wear and tear and neglect — see SHABBY 1

2 worn or torn into or as if into rags — see RAGGED 2

**seeing** *conj* for the reason that — see SINCE

**seek** *vb* 1 to go in search of ⟨the knights of the Round Table fervently *sought* the Holy Grail⟩
*syn* cast about (for), cast around (for), forage (for), hunt, look up, pursue, quest, search (for *or* out)
*rel* ferret (out), root (out)
*phrases* look for
*near ant* hide, lose; ignore, neglect
2 to make a request for — see ASK (FOR) 1
3 to make an effort to do — see ATTEMPT

**seeker** *n* one who seeks an office, honor, position, or award — see CANDIDATE

**seem** *vb* to give the impression of being ⟨I tried to cheer them up because they *seemed* depressed⟩
*syn* act, appear, look, make, sound
*rel* dissemble, pretend; resemble, suggest; hint, imply, insinuate

**seeming** *adj* appearing to be true on the basis of evidence that may or may not be confirmed — see APPARENT 1

**seemingly** *adv* to all outward appearances — see APPARENTLY

**seemliness** *n* the quality or state of being especially suitable or fitting — see APPROPRIATENESS

**seemly** *adj* following the established traditions of refined society and good taste — see PROPER 1

**seep** *vb* to flow forth slowly through small openings — see EXUDE

**seer** *n* one who predicts future events or developments — see PROPHET

**seesaw** *vb* 1 to make a series of unsteady side-to-side motions — see ROCK 1
2 to make short up-and-down movements — see NOD

**seethe** *vb* 1 to be in a state of violent rolling motion ⟨the water *seethed* with schools of feeding piranha⟩
*syn* boil, churn, roil
*rel* reel, spin, swirl, whirl; agitate, stir
*near ant* abate, calm, subside
2 to be excited or emotionally stirred up with anger — see BOIL 1

**segment** *n* one of the pieces from which something is designed to be assembled — see PART 1

**segregate** *vb* to set or keep apart from others — see ISOLATE

**segregation** *n* the state of being alone or kept apart from others — see ISOLATION

**seize** *vb* 1 to recognize the meaning of — see COMPREHEND 1
2 to take or keep under one's control by authority of law — see ARREST 1
3 to take physical control or possession of (something) suddenly or forcibly — see CATCH 1

**seizure** *n* a sudden experiencing of a physical or mental disorder — see ATTACK 2

**seldom** *adv* not often ⟨we *seldom* go to the theater downtown because its prices are so high⟩
*syn* infrequently, little, rarely
*rel* ne'er, never
*phrases* hardly ever
*near ant* generally, usually; always, constantly, continuously, endlessly, eternally, ever, everlastingly, evermore, forever, invariably; recurrently, repeatedly
*ant* frequently, often

**select** *adj* 1 singled out from a number or group as more to one's liking ⟨they use only *select* beans to make their coffee⟩
*syn* chosen, elect, favored, picked, preferred, selected
*rel* fashionable; exclusive; culled, screened, weeded (out), winnowed (out)
*near ant* average, common, commonplace, ordinary, run-of-the-mill
2 having qualities that appeal to a refined taste — see CHOICE

**select** *vb* to decide to accept (someone or something) from a group of possibilities — see CHOOSE 1

**selected** *adj* singled out from a number or group as more to one's liking — see SELECT 1

**selecting** *n* the act or process of selecting — see SELECTION 1

**selection** *n* 1 the act or process of selecting ⟨his *selection* of a running mate was a long, tedious affair⟩
*syn* choice, choosing, election, picking, selecting
*rel* option; appointment, assignment, designation, naming, nomination
2 a person or thing that is chosen — see CHOICE 2

**selective** *adj* tending to select carefully ⟨we were highly *selective* about the music we listened to while trying out loudspeakers⟩
*syn* choosy (*or* choosey), particular, picky
*rel* fastidious, finicky, fussy; discerning, discriminating, judicious
*near ant* indiscriminate
*ant* nonselective

**selector** *n* someone with the right or responsibility for making a selection ⟨the librarians who are the *selectors* of the annual award for best children's book⟩
*syn* chooser, namer, picker
*rel* elector, voter

**self–acting** *adj* designed to replace or decrease human labor and especially physical labor — see LABORSAVING

**self–admiration** *n* an often unjustified feeling of being pleased with oneself or with one's situation or achievements — see COMPLACENCE

**self–assertive** *adj* having or showing a bold forcefulness in the pursuit of a goal — see AGGRESSIVE 1

**self–assurance** *n* great faith in oneself or one's abilities — see CONFIDENCE 1

**self–assured** *adj* having or showing great faith in oneself or one's abilities — see CONFIDENT 1

**self–centered** *adj* overly concerned with one's own desires, needs, or interests — see EGOCENTRIC
**self–centeredness** *n* excessive interest in oneself — see EGOISM
**self–conceit** *n* an often unjustified feeling of being pleased with oneself or with one's situation or achievements — see COMPLACENCE
**self–conceited** *adj* having too high an opinion of oneself — see CONCEITED
**self–confidence** *n* great faith in oneself or one's abilities — see CONFIDENCE 1
**self–confident** *adj* having or showing great faith in oneself or one's abilities — see CONFIDENT 1
**self–containment** *n* the power to control one's actions, impulses, or emotions — see WILL 1
**self–control** *n* **1** the power to control one's actions, impulses, or emotions — see WILL 1
**2** the checking of one's true feelings and impulses when dealing with others — see CONSTRAINT 1
**self–denial** *n* the act or practice of giving up or rejecting something once enjoyed or desired — see RENUNCIATION
**self–destruction** *n* the act of deliberately killing oneself — see SUICIDE
**self–determination** *n* the act or power of making one's own choices or decisions — see FREE WILL
**self–discipline** *n* the power to control one's actions, impulses, or emotions — see WILL 1
**self–esteem** *n* **1** a reasonable or justifiable sense of one's worth or importance — see PRIDE 1
**2** an often unjustified feeling of being pleased with oneself or with one's situation or achievements — see COMPLACENCE
**3** great faith in oneself or one's abilities — see CONFIDENCE 1
**self–governing** *adj* **1** not being under the rule or control of another — see FREE 1
**2** of, relating to, or favoring political democracy — see DEMOCRATIC
**self–government** *n* **1** government in which the supreme power is held by the people and used by them directly or indirectly through representation — see DEMOCRACY
**2** the power to control one's actions, impulses, or emotions — see WILL 1
**3** the state of being free from the control or power of another — see FREEDOM 1
**selfhood** *n* the set of qualities that make a person different from other people — see INDIVIDUALITY
**self–identity** *n* the set of qualities that make a person different from other people — see INDIVIDUALITY
**self–importance** *n* **1** an exaggerated sense of one's importance that shows itself in the making of excessive or unjustified claims — see ARROGANCE
**2** an often unjustified feeling of being pleased with oneself or with one's situation or achievements — see COMPLACENCE
**self–important** *adj* having too high an opinion of oneself — see CONCEITED
**self–interest** *n* excessive interest in oneself — see EGOISM
**selfish** *adj* overly concerned with one's own desires, needs, or interests — see EGOCENTRIC
**selfishness** *n* excessive interest in oneself — see EGOISM
**self–possessed** *adj* free from emotional or mental agitation — see CALM 2
**self–possession** *n* **1** evenness of emotions or temper — see EQUANIMITY
**2** the power to control one's actions, impulses, or emotions — see WILL 1
**self–protective** *adj* intended to resist or prevent attack or aggression — see DEFENSIVE
**self–regard** *n* **1** excessive interest in oneself — see EGOISM
**2** a reasonable or justifiable sense of one's worth or importance — see PRIDE 1
**self–reliance** *n* the ability to care for one's self — see SELF-SUFFICIENCY
**self–reliant** *adj* able to take care of oneself without outside help — see SELF-SUFFICIENT
**self–reproach** *n* a feeling of responsibility for wrongdoing — see GUILT 1
**self–respect** *n* a reasonable or justifiable sense of one's worth or importance — see PRIDE 1
**self–restraint** *n* **1** the power to control one's actions, impulses, or emotions — see WILL 1
**2** the checking of one's true feelings and impulses when dealing with others — see CONSTRAINT 1
**self–rule** *n* government in which the supreme power is held by the people and used by them directly or indirectly through representation — see DEMOCRACY
**self–ruling** *adj* of, relating to, or favoring political democracy — see DEMOCRATIC
**selfsame** *adj* being one and not another — see SAME 2
**self–satisfaction** *n* an often unjustified feeling of being pleased with oneself or with one's situation or achievements — see COMPLACENCE
**self–satisfied** *adj* having too high an opinion of oneself — see CONCEITED
**self–seeker** *n* one who does things only for his own benefit and with little regard for right and wrong ⟨he was accused of being a *self-seeker*, of being nice only to people who could do him favors⟩
***syn*** opportunist, temporizer
***rel*** egoist, egotist; conniver, machinator, plotter, schemer
**self–seeking** *adj* **1** having a strong desire for personal advancement — see AMBITIOUS 1
**2** overly concerned with one's own desires, needs, or interests — see EGOCENTRIC

**self–starter** *n* an ambitious person who eagerly goes after what is desired — see GO-GETTER

**self–sufficiency** *n* the ability to care for one's self ⟨*self-sufficiency* is a goal that all teenagers should work towards⟩
***syn*** independence, self-reliance, self-support
***rel*** autonomy, self-determination; potency, power, resilience, strength
***near ant*** helplessness, impotence, inadequacy, weakness
***ant*** dependence, reliance

**self–sufficient** *adj* able to take care of oneself without outside help ⟨the college student worked nights so that he would be *self-sufficient*⟩
***syn*** independent, self-reliant, self-supporting
***rel*** potent, powerful, resilient, strong
***near ant*** helpless, inadequate, insufficient; impotent, weak
***ant*** dependent, reliant

**self–support** *n* the ability to care for one's self — see SELF-SUFFICIENCY

**self–supporting** *adj* able to take care of oneself without outside help — see SELF-SUFFICIENT

**self–will** *n* a steadfast adherence to an opinion, purpose, or course of action — see OBSTINACY

**self–willed** *adj* sticking to an opinion, purpose, or course of action in spite of reason, arguments, or persuasion — see OBSTINATE

**sell** *vb* to offer for sale to the public — see MARKET

**sell** (for) *vb* to have a price of — see COST

**sell** (out) *vb* to be unfaithful or disloyal to — see BETRAY 1

**seller** *n* the person in a business deal who hands over an item in exchange for money — see VENDOR

**sellout** *n* the act or fact of violating the trust or confidence of another — see BETRAYAL

**semblance** *n* **1** a display of emotion or behavior that is insincere or intended to deceive — see MASQUERADE
**2** outward and often deceptive indication — see APPEARANCE 2

**semidarkness** *n* a time or place of little or no light — see DARK 1

**seminar** *n* **1** a coming together of a number of persons for a specified purpose — see MEETING 1
**2** a meeting featuring a group discussion — see FORUM

**seminary** *n* a place or establishment for teaching and learning — see SCHOOL

**send** *vb* to cause to go or be taken from one place to another ⟨they promised to *send* the package in the morning⟩
***syn*** consign, pack (off), ship, transfer, transmit, transport
***rel*** convey, deliver, hand over; advance, drop, launch, remit; address, forward; bestow, contribute, donate, give, present
***near ant*** acquire, draw, earn, gain, garner, get, obtain, procure, secure
***ant*** accept, receive

**senior** *adj* being of advanced years and especially past middle age — see ELDERLY

**senior** *n* **1** one who is older than another ⟨since the man next door is my *senior* by a number of years, I always address him as "Mr. Barton"⟩
***syn*** elder
***rel*** ancestor, forerunner, predecessor
***near ant*** contemporary, peer; descendant (*or* descendent), successor
***ant*** junior
**2** one who is above another in rank, station, or office — see SUPERIOR
**3** the senior member of a group — see DEAN

**senior citizen** *n* a person of advanced years ⟨more and more *senior citizens* are living active, rewarding lives⟩
***syn*** ancient, elder, golden-ager, oldster, old-timer
***rel*** senior; graybeard, patriarch; beldam (*or* beldame), grandam (*or* grandame); adult, grown-up
***near ant*** adolescent, minor; child, cub, juvenile, kid
***ant*** youngster, youth

**sensation** *n* **1** an indefinite physical response to a stimulus ⟨we felt just the barest *sensation* of warmth when we leaned against the radiator⟩
***syn*** feel, feeling, sense
***rel*** impression, perception; hint, suggestion
**2** a practice or interest that is very popular for a short time — see FAD
**3** something extraordinary or surprising — see WONDER 1

**sensational** *adj* **1** arousing a strong and usually superficial interest or emotional reaction ⟨the *sensational* news story caused a stir, but after a few days everyone forgot about it⟩
***syn*** lurid, screaming
***rel*** colorful, juicy, racy; dramatic, histrionic, melodramatic, theatrical; coarse, vulgar
***near ant*** innocuous, inoffensive; dignified, formal, proper, restrained
**2** of or relating to physical sensation or the senses — see SENSORY
**3** of the very best kind — see EXCELLENT

**sense** *n* **1** an indefinite physical response to a stimulus — see SENSATION 1
**2** the ability to learn and understand or to deal with problems — see INTELLIGENCE 1
**3** the ability to make intelligent decisions especially in everyday matters — see COMMON SENSE
**4** the idea that is conveyed or intended to be conveyed to the mind by language, symbol, or action — see MEANING 1

5 the thought processes that have been established as leading to valid solutions to problems — see LOGIC

**sense** *vb* to have a vague awareness of — see FEEL 1

**senseless** *adj* 1 having lost consciousness — see UNCONSCIOUS 1
2 having no meaning — see MEANINGLESS
3 not having or showing an ability to absorb ideas readily — see STUPID 1
4 showing or marked by a lack of good sense or judgment — see FOOLISH 1

**senselessness** *n* 1 lack of good sense or judgment — see FOOLISHNESS 1
2 language, behavior, or ideas that are absurd and contrary to good sense — see NONSENSE 1
3 the quality or state of lacking intelligence or quickness of mind — see STUPIDITY 1

**sensibilities** *n* general emotional condition — see FEELING 2

**sensible** *adj* 1 able to be perceived by a sense or by the mind — see PERCEPTIBLE
2 according to the rules of logic — see LOGICAL 1
3 based on sound reasoning or information — see GOOD 1
4 having specified facts or feelings actively impressed on the mind — see CONSCIOUS

**sensibleness** *n* the ability to make intelligent decisions especially in everyday matters — see COMMON SENSE

**sensitive** *adj* 1 able to sense slight impressions or differences — see ACUTE 1
2 being in a situation where one is likely to meet with harm — see LIABLE 1
3 easily injured without careful handling — see TENDER 1
4 of or relating to physical sensation or the senses — see SENSORY

**sensor** *n* a device that detects some physical quantity and responds usually with a transmitted signal ⟨the thief accidentally triggered the motion *sensor*, which alerted the police⟩
*syn* detector
*rel* eye; electric eye, photoelectric cell; alarm, trigger

**sensory** *adj* of or relating to physical sensation or the senses ⟨trying to listen to music while watching the TV and eating dinner caused a sort of *sensory* overload⟩
*syn* sensational, sensitive, sensuous
*rel* afferent, receptive; sensual
*near ant* extrasensory, intuitional

**sensual** *adj* pleasing to the physical senses ⟨the *sensual* feel of a velvet shirt against the skin⟩
*syn* carnal, fleshly, luscious, sensuous, voluptuous
*rel* bodily, corporeal; agreeable, delectable, delicious, delightful, dreamy, gratifying, palatable, pleasant, pleasing, pleasurable, scrumptious; epicurean, luxurious, self-indulgent
*near ant* harsh, painful, uncomfortable

**sensuous** *adj* 1 of or relating to physical sensation or the senses — see SENSORY
2 pleasing to the physical senses — see SENSUAL

**sentence** *n* a decision made by a court or tribunal regarding a case it has heard ⟨the court-martial pronounced a *sentence* of not guilty on all counts of cowardice⟩
*syn* doom, finding, holding, judgment (*or* judgement), ruling
*rel* verdict; injunction; decree, edict, order; declaration, deliverance, dictum, pronouncement; conclusion, decision, determination, opinion, resolution; discipline, penalty, punishment

**sentence** *vb* to impose a judicial punishment on ⟨the judge *sentenced* him to a fine of fifty dollars and time served⟩
*syn* condemn, damn, doom
*rel* adjudge, judge; castigate, chasten, chastise, correct, discipline, penalize, punish; conclude, decide, determine, find, opine, resolve

**sentient** *adj* having specified facts or feelings actively impressed on the mind — see CONSCIOUS

**sentiment** *n* 1 a subjective response to a person, thing, or situation — see FEELING 1
2 an idea that is believed to be true or valid without positive knowledge — see OPINION 1

**sentimental** *adj* appealing to the emotions in an obvious and tiresome way — see CORNY

**sentimentalism** *n* the state or quality of having an excess of tender feelings (as of love, nostalgia, or compassion) — see SENTIMENTALITY

**sentimentality** *n* the state or quality of having an excess of tender feelings (as of love, nostalgia, or compassion) ⟨the *sentimentality* of the story of star-crossed lovers only made it even more popular with moviegoers⟩
*syn* mawkishness, mush, sappiness, sentimentalism, sloppiness
*rel* emotion; sentiment; corn, schmaltz (*also* schmalz)
*near ant* cynicism, hardheadedness, hardheartedness

**sentinel** *n* a person or group that watches over someone or something — see GUARD 1

**sentry** *n* a person or group that watches over someone or something — see GUARD 1

**separable** *adj* capable of being split into two or more parts or pieces ⟨the outdated belief that the atom is the smallest particle of matter and is not *separable*⟩
*syn* divisible
*rel* detachable
*near ant* combinable, joinable
*ant* indivisible, inseparable

**separate** *adj* 1 not the same or shared ⟨we stayed in *separate* apartments on our vacation⟩
*syn* different, individual, respective

*rel* disparate, dissimilar, distinct, distinctive, distinguishable, diverse, unalike, varied
*near ant* identical, selfsame, very
*ant* same
**2** not physically attached to another unit ⟨the housing development has 200 *separate* homes, each with its own enclosed yard⟩
*syn* detached, disconnected, discrete, freestanding, single, unattached, unconnected
*rel* independent, self-contained; individual, private
*ant* attached, connected, joined
**3** not being under the rule or control of another — see FREE 1
**4** of, relating to, or belonging to a single person — see INDIVIDUAL 1

**separate** *vb* **1** to set or force apart ⟨we tried to *separate* the gluey pages, but they were stuck tight⟩
*syn* break up, disconnect, disjoin, disjoint, dissever, dissociate, disunite, divide, divorce, part, ramify, resolve, sever, split, sunder, uncouple, unlink, unyoke
*rel* decompose, disassemble, dissolve; bisect, fractionate, halve, quarter, segment, subdivide; break, rend, rip, rupture, tear; cut off, insulate, isolate, seclude, segregate, sequester; detach, disengage, disentangle, untie
*near ant* assemble, associate, blend, combine, mingle, mix; connect, couple; unify; accumulate, agglutinate, attach, bind, cement, close, fasten, fuse, stick, weld
*ant* join, link, unify, unite
**2** to go or move in different directions from a central point ⟨the searchers *separated* in order to cover more ground⟩
*syn* branch (out), diverge, divide, fork
*rel* bestrew, broadcast, clear out, disband, dispel, disperse, dissipate, distribute, scatter, sow; distance, recede, retreat
*near ant* assemble, gather, meet
*ant* converge, join
**3** to arrange or assign according to type — see CLASSIFY 1
**4** to set or keep apart from others — see ISOLATE
**5** to understand or point out the difference — see DISTINGUISH 1

**separateness** *n* the state of being alone or kept apart from others — see ISOLATION

**separation** *n* **1** the act or process of a whole separating into two or more parts or pieces ⟨the *separation* of Czechoslovakia into the Czech Republic and Slovakia⟩
*syn* breakup, dissolution, disunion, division, fractionation, partition, schism, split
*rel* breach, rupture; decomposition, disassembly, segmentation, subdivision; dispersal, scattering; administration, apportionment, distribution; isolation, seclusion, segregation, sequestration
*near ant* assemblage, association; attachment, connection, link, linkage, linkup; combination, fusion
*ant* unification, union
**2** the state of being kept distinct ⟨the *separation* of church and state is an important concept in the United States⟩
*syn* demarcation, discreteness, discrimination, distinction
*rel* differentiation
*near ant* blurring, confusion
**3** a movement in different directions away from a common point — see DIVERGENCE
**4** an open space in a barrier (as a wall or hedge) — see GAP 1
**5** the act or process of two or more persons going off in different directions — see PARTING 1

**sepulcher** *or* **sepulchre** *n* a final resting place for a dead person — see GRAVE

**sepulchral** *adj* causing or marked by an atmosphere lacking in cheer — see GLOOMY 1

**sepulture** *n* **1** a final resting place for a dead person — see GRAVE
**2** the act or ceremony of putting a dead body in its final resting place — see BURIAL

**sequel** *n* a condition or occurrence traceable to a cause — see EFFECT 1

**sequence** *n* **1** a condition or occurrence traceable to a cause — see EFFECT 1
**2** a series of things linked together — see CHAIN 1
**3** the way objects in space or events in time are arranged or follow one another — see ORDER 1

**sequential** *adj* following one after another without others coming in between — see CONSECUTIVE

**sequester** *vb* **1** to set or keep apart from others — see ISOLATE
**2** to take ownership or control of (something) by right of one's authority — see CONFISCATE

**sequestration** *n* the state of being alone or kept apart from others — see ISOLATION

**sere** *adj* marked by little or no precipitation or humidity — see DRY 1

**serene** *adj* **1** free from disturbing noise or uproar — see QUIET 1
**2** free from emotional or mental agitation — see CALM 2
**3** free from storms or physical disturbance — see CALM 1

**sereneness** *n* a state of freedom from storm or disturbance — see CALM

**serenity** *n* **1** a state of freedom from storm or disturbance — see CALM
**2** evenness of emotions or temper — see EQUANIMITY

**serial** *adj* appearing in parts or numbers that follow regularly ⟨"Uncle Tom's Cabin" first appeared as a *serial* novel from 1851 to 1852⟩
*syn* episodic, periodic, periodical
*rel* sequential; recurrent, regular

**serious** *adj* **1** not joking or playful in mood or manner ⟨our parents were quite *serious* when they told us not to stay out too late⟩
***syn*** earnest, grave, humorless, no-nonsense, sedate, severe, sober, solemn, staid, uncomic, unfunny, unsmiling, weighty
***rel*** harsh, stern, strict; dignified, distinguished, elevated, serious-minded
***near ant*** antic, comic, comical, droll, farcical, funny, hilarious, hysterical, laughable, light, light-headed, ludicrous, ridiculous, risible, riotous screaming, side-splitting, uproarious; featherbrained, flighty, frivolous, goofy, harebrained, lighthearted, puerile, scatterbrained; absurd, asinine, balmy, brainless, cockeyed, crazy, cuckoo, daffy, daft, dotty, fatuous, foolish, half-witted, insane, jerky, kooky, loony (*also* looney), lunatic, mad, nonsensical, nutty, preposterous, sappy, screwball, senseless, silly, unwise, wacky, weak-minded, witless, zany
***ant*** facetious, flip, flippant, humorous, jesting, jocular, joking, playful
**2** having a matter of importance as its topic ⟨a very *serious* film that dealt with the aftermath of the Gulf War⟩
***syn*** grave, heavy, weighty
***rel*** big, consequential, eventful, important, major, material, meaningful, momentous, significant, substantial
***near ant*** insignificant, little, minor, slight, small, trivial, unimportant
***ant*** light
**3** involving potential loss or injury — see DANGEROUS

**seriousness** *n* a mental state free of jesting or trifling — see EARNESTNESS

**sermon** *n* a public speech usually by a member of the clergy for the purpose of giving moral guidance or uplift ⟨a *sermon* whose message was that we should love our neighbors as much as we love ourselves⟩
***syn*** homily
***rel*** lecture, speech; lesson

**serpent** *n* a limbless reptile with a long body — see SNAKE 1

**serpentine** *adj* marked by a long series of irregular curves — see CROOKED 1

**serrate** *adj* notched or toothed along the edge — see SERRATED

**serrated** *adj* notched or toothed along the edge ⟨you should use a *serrated* knife when cutting bread, so you don't squash the loaf⟩
***syn*** saw-toothed, serrate
***rel*** wavy
***near ant*** flat, smooth

**serried** *adj* having little space between items or parts — see CLOSE 1

**servant** *n* a person hired to perform household or personal services ⟨the wealthy family had *servants* to clean and cook for them⟩
***syn*** domestic, flunky (*also* flunkey), lackey, menial, retainer, steward
***rel*** butler, footman, groom, houseboy, man, majordomo, manservant, servitor, valet; handmaiden (*also* handmaid), housekeeper, housemaid, lady-in-waiting, maid, maidservant, wench, woman; attendant, follower
***near ant*** boss, captain, chief, foreman, head, headman, helmsman, kingpin, leader, taskmaster
***ant*** master

**serve** *vb* **1** to be a servant for ⟨he *served* his master faithfully for twenty years⟩
***syn*** slave (for), work (for)
***phrases*** wait on, wait upon
**2** to be enough ⟨they made the pasta *serve* for eight guests⟩
***syn*** do, suffice
***rel*** answer, suit; assuage, content, quench, sate, satiate, satisfy
**3** to be fitting or proper — see DO 1
**4** to behave toward in a stated way — see TREAT 1
**5** to have a certain purpose — see FUNCTION
**6** to provide with something useful or desirable — see BENEFIT

**server** *n* a person who serves food or drink ⟨we had barely finished ordering when the *server* brought our salads⟩
***syn*** waiter
***rel*** waitress; bartender; steward, stewardess

**service** *adj* of or relating to the armed services — see MILITARY 1

**service** *n* **1** an act of kind assistance — see FAVOR 1
**2** the capacity for being useful for some purpose — see USE 2
**3** the combined army, air force, and navy of a nation — see ARMED FORCES

**serviceability** *n* the capacity for being useful for some purpose — see USE 2

**serviceable** *adj* **1** capable of being put to use or account — see PRACTICAL 1
**2** capable of or suitable for being used for a particular purpose — see USABLE 1

**serviceableness** *n* the capacity for being useful for some purpose — see USE 2

**serviceman** *n* a person engaged in military service — see SOLDIER

**servility** *n* the state of being a slave — see SLAVERY 1

**servitude** *n* the state of being a slave — see SLAVERY 1

**set** *adj* **1** being in a state of fitness for some experience or action — see READY 1
**2** firmly positioned in place and difficult to dislodge — see TIGHT 2
**3** fully committed to achieving a goal — see DETERMINED 1
**4** having been established and usually not subject to change — see FIXED 1
**5** of a particular or exact sort — see EXPRESS 1

**set** *n* **1** a group of people acting together within a larger group — see FACTION
**2** a group of people sharing a common interest and relating together socially — see GANG 2
**3** a number of things considered as a unit — see GROUP 1

4 one of the units into which a whole is divided on the basis of a common characteristic — see CLASS 2
5 the array of painted backgrounds and furnishings used for a scene in a stage production — see SCENERY

**set** *vb* 1 to cover and warm eggs to hatch them ⟨the hen *set* for days⟩
*syn* brood, hatch, incubate, sit
*rel* lay, spawn; pip
2 to decide upon (the time or date for an event) usually from a position of authority — see APPOINT 1
3 to make an approximate or tentative judgment regarding — see ESTIMATE 1
4 *chiefly dialect* to rest on the buttocks or haunches — see SIT 1
5 to point or turn (something) toward a target or goal — see AIM 1
6 to come to an agreement or decision concerning the details of — see ARRANGE 1
7 to put securely in place or in a desired position — see FASTEN 2
8 to turn from a liquid into a substance resembling jelly — see COAGULATE
9 to arrange something in a certain spot or position — see PLACE 1
10 to become physically firm or solid — see HARDEN 1

**setback** *n* a change in status for the worse usually temporarily — see REVERSE 1

**set down** *vb* 1 to cause to sit down — see SEAT
2 to make a written note of — see RECORD 1

**set in** *vb* to come into existence — see BEGIN 2

**set off** *vb* to cause to function — see ACTIVATE

**settee** *n* a long upholstered piece of furniture designed for several sitters — see COUCH

**setting** *n* 1 the circumstances, conditions, or objects by which one is surrounded — see ENVIRONMENT
2 the place and time in which the action for a portion of a dramatic work (as a movie) is set — see SCENE 1

**settle** *vb* 1 to cause to come to rest at the bottom (as of a liquid) ⟨the light rain will *settle* the dust in the air⟩ ⟨careful handling will *settle* the lees in the bottom of the wine bottle⟩
*syn* lay, sediment
*rel* filter, screen, sieve, sift, strain; resettle
*near ant* disturb, mix, stir
*ant* raise
2 to give an opinion about (something at issue or in dispute) — see JUDGE 1
3 to come to an agreement or decision concerning the details of — see ARRANGE 1
4 to come to rest after descending from the air — see ALIGHT
5 to establish or place comfortably or snugly — see ENSCONCE 1
6 to free from distress or disturbance — see CALM 1
7 to gain emotional or mental control of — see COLLECT 1
8 to give what is owed for — see PAY 2
9 to make final, definite, or beyond dispute — see CLINCH
10 to stop the noise or speech of — see SILENCE 1

**settle** (down) *vb* to become still and orderly — see QUIET 1

**settled** *adj* 1 firmly established over time — see INVETERATE 1
2 having been established and usually not subject to change — see FIXED 1

**settlement** *n* an arrangement about action to be taken — see AGREEMENT 2

**settler** *n* 1 a person who settles in a new region — see FRONTIERSMAN
2 one that leaves one place to settle in another — see EMIGRANT

**setup** *n* 1 the way in which something is sized, arranged, or organized — see FORMAT 1
2 the way objects in space or events in time are arranged or follow one another — see ORDER 1

**set up** *vb* 1 to arrange something in a certain spot or position — see PLACE 1
2 to be responsible for the creation and early operation or use of — see FOUND
3 to fix in an upright position — see ERECT 1
4 to form by putting together parts or materials — see BUILD

**seven seas** *n pl* the whole body of salt water that covers nearly three-fourths of the earth — see OCEAN

**sever** *vb* to set or force apart — see SEPARATE 1

**severe** *adj* 1 given to exacting standards of discipline and self-restraint ⟨a *severe*, uncompromising teacher who locked the classroom door precisely when the bell rang and let no one in afterward⟩
*syn* austere, authoritarian, flinty, hard, harsh, heavy-handed, ramrod, rigid, rigorous, stern, strict
*rel* demanding, exacting; uncharitable, unforgiving; adamant, adamantine, hardened, hardhearted, immovable, implacable, inflexible, ossified, unbending, uncompromising, unyielding; dour, gruff; ascetic, monastic; browbeating, bullying; determined, firm, resolved, single-minded, steadfast, unflinching; dogged, intractable, obstinate, relentless
*near ant* easy, easygoing, laid-back, undemanding; charitable, kind, merciful, patient, soft, softhearted; accepting, compromising, yielding; responsive, willing; acquiescent, agreeable, amenable, compliant, flexible, pliable, pliant
*ant* forbearing, indulgent, lax, lenient, tolerant
2 harsh and threatening in manner or appearance — see GRIM 1
3 not joking or playful in mood or manner — see SERIOUS 1
4 difficult to endure — see HARSH 1

*syn* synonym(s) *rel* related words
*ant* antonym(s) *near ant* near antonym(s)

5 requiring considerable physical or mental effort — see HARD 2

**severely** *adv* in a manner so as to cause loss or suffering — see HARDLY 1

**severity** *n* the quality or state of being demanding or unyielding (as in discipline or criticism) ⟨Jane's parents were legendary for the *severity* of their discipline—she never got away with so much as a white lie⟩
*syn* hardness, harshness, inflexibility, rigidity, rigidness, rigorousness, sternness, strictness
*rel* hardheartedness, implacability, obduracy; dourness, gruffness; asceticism, austerity, monasticism; determination, firmness, resolve, steadfastness; obstinacy, stubbornness
*near ant* forbearance, indulgence, kindness, lenience, patience, softness, tenderness, tolerance; responsiveness, willingness; compliance, pliability
*ant* flexibility, gentleness, laxness, mildness

**sew** *vb* to close up with a series of interlacing stitches ⟨luckily, Mom was able to *sew* the tear in my pants so skillfully that they looked as good as new⟩
*syn* darn, stitch
*rel* mend, patch, repair; baste, ease, fell, finish, overcast; crochet, knit, quilt

**sew up** *vb* to have complete control over — see MONOPOLIZE

**sex** *n* sexual union involving penetration of the vagina by the penis — see SEXUAL INTERCOURSE

**sexual intercourse** *n* sexual union involving penetration of the vagina by the penis ⟨many people believe that it's best to wait to experience *sexual intercourse* until you're mature enough to handle it⟩
*syn* coitus, copulating, copulation, intercourse, mating, sex, sexual relations
*rel* fornication; safe sex; sexuality
*phrases* making love

**sexual relations** *n pl* sexual union involving penetration of the vagina by the penis — see SEXUAL INTERCOURSE

**sexy** *adj* of, relating to, or expressing sexual attraction — see EROTIC

**shabby** *adj* 1 showing signs of advanced wear and tear and neglect ⟨*shabby* wallpaper that was peeling from the walls⟩
*syn* dilapidated, dog-eared, grungy, mangy, mean, miserable moth-eaten, neglected, ratty, run-down, scruffy, seedy, tacky, threadbare
*rel* abandoned, desolate, forlorn; broken-down, decrepit, worn-out; bedraggled, dingy, ragged, tattered; decaying, deteriorated, deteriorating, ramshackle; broken, damaged, destroyed, harmed, hurt, impaired, injured, ruined, wrecked
*phrases* gone to seed
*near ant* brand-new, fresh, new; cared-for, kept-up, maintained; mended, patched, rebuilt, reconstructed; smart, spiffy, spruce
2 worn or torn into or as if into rags — see RAGGED 2

**shack** *n* a small, simply constructed, and often temporary dwelling ⟨a farmer's *shack* cut in the fields that's used for lambing and as a shelter from storms⟩
*syn* cabin, camp, hovel, hut, hutch, shanty
*rel* lean-to, shed; cot, cottage, lodge; cabana; bungalow, chalet; hogan, wickiup, wigwam

**shackle** *n* 1 something that physically prevents free movement — see BOND 1
2 **shackles** *pl* something that makes movement or progress more difficult — see ENCUMBRANCE

**shackle** *vb* 1 to confine or restrain with or as if with chains — see BIND 1
2 to create difficulty for the work or activity of — see HAMPER

**shade** *n* 1 partial darkness due to the obstruction of light rays ⟨it was hard to see in the *shade* after being in the brilliant sunlight⟩ ⟨the trees cast *shade*⟩
*syn* penumbra, shadiness, shadow, umbra
*rel* blackness, dimness, duskiness, gloominess, murkiness, obscurity, somberness; cloudiness, dullness (*also* dulness)
*near ant* brightness, brilliance, effulgence, illumination, incandescence, light, lightness, lucidity, lucidness, luminosity, radiance
2 a time or place of little or no light — see DARK 1
3 a property that becomes apparent when light falls on an object and by which things that are identical in form can be distinguished — see COLOR 1
4 a very small amount — see PARTICLE 1
5 the soul of a dead person thought of especially as appearing to living people — see GHOST

**shade** *vb* to shelter (something) from light and heat ⟨the trees *shaded* us quite nicely from the noonday sun⟩
*syn* shadow
*rel* cloud, darken, dim, dull; canopy, cover, protect, screen
*near ant* illuminate, light, lighten; expose

**shaded** *adj* protected from the sun's rays — see SHADY 1

**shadiness** *n* partial darkness due to the obstruction of light rays — see SHADE 1

**shadow** *n* 1 a person whose business is solving crimes and catching criminals or gathering information that is not easy to get — see DETECTIVE
2 partial darkness due to the obstruction of light rays — see SHADE 1
3 **shadows** *pl* a time or place of little or no light — see DARK 1
4 a tiny often physical indication of something lost or vanished — see VESTIGE
5 a very small amount — see PARTICLE 1
6 the soul of a dead person thought of especially as appearing to living people — see GHOST

**shadow** *vb* 1 to go after or on the track of — see FOLLOW 2
2 to make dark, dim, or indistinct — see CLOUD 1

3 to shelter (something) from light and heat — see SHADE

**shadowed** *adj* protected from the sun's rays — see SHADY 1

**shadowing** *n* the act of going after or in the tracks of another — see PURSUIT

**shadowy** *adj* **1** not seen or understood clearly — see FAINT 1
**2** protected from the sun's rays — see SHADY 1

**shady** *adj* **1** protected from the sun's rays ⟨a lovely *shady* spot in the park that was pleasantly cool⟩
*syn* shaded, shadowed, shadowy
*rel* canopied, covered, sheltered; cloudy; dark, darkened, darkish, darkling, darksome, dim, dimmed, dusky, gloomy, moonless, murky, obscure, obscured, pitch-black, pitch-dark, somber (*or* sombre), sunless
*near ant* bedazzling, bright, brightened, brilliant, dazzling, effulgent, illuminated, illumined, incandescent, light, lighted (*or* lit), lucent, lucid, luminous; beaming, lambent, radiant, shining; lustrous
*ant* sunny
**2** given to or marked by cheating and deception — see DISHONEST 2
**3** giving good reason for being doubted, questioned, or challenged — see DOUBTFUL 2
**4** given to acting in secret and to concealing one's intentions — see SNEAKY 1

**shaft** *n* **1** a narrow sharply defined line of light radiating from an object ⟨*shafts* of late-afternoon sunlight pierced the blinds and streaked the floor⟩
*syn* beam, ray
*rel* moonbeam, sunbeam; laser, spotlight
**2** a weapon with a long straight handle and sharp head or blade — see SPEAR

**shaggy** *adj* **1** covered with or as if with hair — see HAIRY 1
**2** made of or resembling hair — see HAIRY 2

**shake** *vb* **1** to make a series of small irregular or violent movements ⟨the bus rattled and *shook* as it barreled down a rutted road⟩
*syn* agitate, convulse, joggle, jolt, jounce, quake, quiver, shudder, vibrate, wobble
*rel* rock, sway; quaver, shiver, tremble; dodder, waver; flicker, fluctuate, flutter, oscillate, wave; beat, palpitate, pit-a-pat, pitter-patter, pulsate, pulse, throb
**2** to get or keep away from (as a responsibility) through cleverness or trickery — see ESCAPE 2

**shake** *n* **1** a very small space of time — see INSTANT
**2 shakes** *pl* a sense of panic or extreme nervousness — see JITTERS

**shake up** *vb* to cause an often unpleasant surprise for — see SHOCK 1

**shakiness** *n* the quality or state of not being firmly fixed in position — see INSTABILITY

**shaking** *adj* marked by or given to small uncontrollable bodily movements — see SHAKY 1

**shaking** *n* **1** a series of slight movements by a body back and forth or from side to side — see VIBRATION
**2** the act or a means of getting or keeping away from something undesirable — see ESCAPE 2

**shaky** *adj* **1** marked by or given to small uncontrollable bodily movements ⟨the old man's hands were so *shaky* that I was afraid he'd drop the glass⟩
*syn* quaking, quavery, shaking, shuddering, shuddery, tottery, trembling, tremulous, wobbling, wobbly
*rel* shivering, shivery
*near ant* controlled, firm, settled, stable, steady
**2** giving good reason for being doubted, questioned, or challenged — see DOUBTFUL 2

**shall** *vb* to be under necessity or obligation to — see NEED 2

**shallow** *adj* **1** lacking significant physical depth ⟨the dog quickly dug a *shallow* hole that was barely deep enough to accommodate his bone⟩
*syn* depthless, shoal
*rel* skin-deep, superficial, surface; fathomable, measurable; finite, limited, measured, restricted; even, flat, flush, horizontal, level, plane, smooth
*near ant* abysmal, abyssal, bottomless, boundless, endless, immeasurable, inestimable, infinite, limitless, measureless, unfathomable, unlimited, vast; navigable
*ant* deep
**2** having or showing a lack of depth of understanding or character — see SUPERFICIAL 2

**shallow** *n, usually* **shallows** *pl* a place where a body of water (as a sea or river) is shallow — see SHOAL

**sham** *adj* **1** being such in appearance only and made with or manufactured from usually cheaper materials — see IMITATION
**2** being such in appearance only and made or manufactured with the intention of committing fraud — see COUNTERFEIT
**3** lacking in natural or spontaneous quality — see ARTIFICIAL 1

**sham** *n* **1** a poor, insincere, or insulting imitation of something — see MOCKERY 1
**2** an imitation that is passed off as genuine — see FAKE 1

**sham** *vb* to present a false appearance of — see FEIGN

**shamble** *vb* to move heavily or clumsily — see LUMBER 1

**shambles** *n pl* **1** a dirty or messy place — see PIGPEN
**2** a state in which everything is out of order — see CHAOS

**shame** *n* **1** a feeling of responsibility for wrongdoing — see GUILT 1
**2** a regrettable or blameworthy act — see CRIME 2

---

*syn* synonym(s) *rel* related words
*ant* antonym(s) *near ant* near antonym(s)

3 the state of having lost the esteem of others — see DISGRACE 1

**shame** *vb* to reduce to a lower standing in one's own eyes or in others' eyes — see HUMBLE

**shamed** *adj* suffering from or expressive of a feeling of responsibility for wrongdoing — see GUILTY 2

**shamefaced** *adj* suffering from or expressive of a feeling of responsibility for wrongdoing — see GUILTY 2

**shameful** *adj* not respectable — see DISREPUTABLE

**shanty** *n* a small, simply constructed, and often temporary dwelling — see SHACK

**shape** *n* 1 a state of being or fitness — see CONDITION 1
2 the outward appearance of something as distinguished from its substance — see FORM 1
3 the type of body that a person has — see PHYSIQUE

**shape** *vb* to change (something) so as to make it suitable for a new use or situation — see ADAPT

**shape** (up) *vb* to take on a definite form — see FORM 1

**shapeless** *adj* 1 badly or imperfectly formed — see MALFORMED
2 having no definite or recognizable form — see FORMLESS

**share** *n* 1 something belonging to, due to, or contributed by an individual member of a group ⟨my *share* of the lottery winnings is over a million dollars⟩ ⟨Sue's *share* of the bill comes to $13.44⟩
*syn* allotment, allowance, cut, part, portion, proportion, quota
*rel* lot, ration; commission, percentage; member, partition, section, segment
*near ant* aggregate, composite, compound, sum, total, totality; whole
2 a legal right to participation in the advantages, profits, and responsibility of something — see INTEREST 1

**share** *vb* to take a share or part — see PARTAKE

**shared** *adj* used or done by a number of people as a group — see COLLECTIVE

**sharer** *n* one who takes part in something — see PARTICIPANT

**shark** *n* 1 a dishonest person who uses clever means to cheat others out of something of value — see TRICKSTER 1
2 a person with a high level of knowledge or skill in a field — see EXPERT

**sharp** *adj* 1 having an edge thin enough to cut or pierce something ⟨be careful, as that knife is *sharp* enough to slice off a finger⟩
*syn* cutting, edged, edgy, ground, honed, keen, sharpened, stropped, trenchant, whetted
*rel* clawlike; jabbing, jagged, lacerating, piercing, scratching, stabbing
*near ant* rounded, seamless, smooth; soft; even, flat, level, slick
*ant* blunt, blunted, dull, culled, obtuse
2 causing intense mental or physical distress ⟨sudden *sharp* pains in your right lower belly can be a sign of appendicitis⟩
*syn* acute, agonizing, biting, excruciating, smart, smarting
*rel* bitter, cutting, keen, penetrating, piercing, raw, stinging; afflicting, distressing, disturbing, upsetting; cruel, grievous, harsh, heartrending, hurtful, lacerating, painful, paralyzing, severe, tormenting, torturous; insufferable, insupportable, intolerable, unacceptable, unbearable, unsupportable; appalling, awful, bad, dire, dreadful, ghastly, horrible, miserable, nasty, rotten, terrible, vile, wretched
*near ant* painless; acceptable, bearable, endurable, supportable, sustainable, tolerable; livable (*also* liveable), sufferable
*ant* dull
3 having a powerfully stimulating odor or flavor ⟨the cheese is so *sharp* that its rank aroma can practically clear a room⟩
*syn* nippy, pungent, strong
*rel* acid, acidic; acrid, bitter, harsh; piquant, spicy, tart, zesty; putrid, rancid, rank; acute, keen; animating, energizing, exciting, galvanizing, invigorating, provocative; appetizing, delectable, delicious, palatable, toothsome; flavorful, savory, tasty
*near ant* aged, mellow; gentle, soft; flat, flavorless, insipid; savorless, tasteless; dilute, thin, watery, weak
*ant* bland, mild, smooth
4 tapering to a thin tip — see POINTED 1
5 being in the latest or current fashion — see STYLISH
6 being strikingly neat and trim in style or appearance — see SMART 1
7 causing intense discomfort to one's skin — see CUTTING 1
8 given to or marked by cheating and deception — see DISHONEST 2
9 having or showing a practical cleverness or judgment — see SHREWD
10 having or showing quickness of mind — see INTELLIGENT 1
11 marked by the use of wit that is intended to cause hurt feelings — see SARCASTIC
12 able to sense slight impressions or differences — see ACUTE 1
13 uncomfortably cool — see CHILLY 1

**sharp** *adv* as stated or indicated without the slightest difference — see EXACTLY 1

**sharpen** *vb* to make sharp or sharper ⟨you need to *sharpen* your penknife's blade frequently in order to be able to whittle properly⟩
*syn* edge, grind, hone, strop, whet
*rel* file
*near ant* buff, burnish, gloss, polish, round, smooth
*ant* blunt, dull

**sharpened** *adj* having an edge thin enough to cut or pierce something — see SHARP 1

**sharper** *n* a dishonest person who uses clever means to cheat others out of something of value — see TRICKSTER 1

**sharp–eyed** *adj* having unusually keen vision ⟨a very *sharp-eyed* child found the last Easter egg, which was hidden in the flower arrangement⟩
***syn*** clear-sighted, lynx-eyed
***rel*** sighted; alert, attentive, aware, observant, observing, vigilant, watchful
***near ant*** blind, eyeless, sightless, stoneblind, unseeing; astigmatic, myopic, nearsighted, shortsighted; unobservant, unobserving; purblind

**sharply** *adv* in a strikingly neat and trim manner — see SMARTLY

**sharpness** *n* **1** a harsh or sharp quality — see EDGE 1
**2** an uncomfortable degree of coolness — see CHILL

**sharpshooter** *n* a person skilled in shooting at a target — see MARKSMAN

**sharp–witted** *adj* **1** having or showing a practical cleverness or judgment — see SHREWD
**2** having or showing quickness of mind — see INTELLIGENT 1

**shatter** *vb* **1** to bring to a complete end the physical soundness, existence, or usefulness of — see DESTROY 1
**2** to cause to break open or into pieces by or as if by an explosive — see BLAST 1
**3** to cause to break with violence and much noise — see SMASH 1

**shave** *vb* **1** to make (as hair) shorter with or as if with the use of shears — see CLIP
**2** to pass lightly across or touch gently especially in passing — see BRUSH

**shaver** *n* a male person who has not yet reached adulthood — see BOY

**shear** *vb* to make (as hair) shorter with or as if with the use of shears — see CLIP

**sheath** *n* something that encloses another thing especially to protect it — see [1]CASE 1

**sheathe** *vb* to cover with something that protects ⟨sometimes shipbuilders *sheathe* a ship's bottom with copper for extra protection from barnacles and other threats⟩
***syn*** face
***rel*** apparel, array, clothe, dress, garb, robe; side, skin; embosom, embower, embrace, encase, enclose (*also* inclose), encompass, enshroud, envelop, enwrap, invest, lap, mantle, shroud, surround, swathe, veil, wrap; blanket, overlay, overspread
***near ant*** bare, denude, expose, strip

**shed** *vb* **1** to cast (a natural bodily covering or appendage) aside ⟨a snake's skin doesn't grow as the snake does, so every so often the snake will *shed* its old skin⟩
***syn*** exfoliate, molt, slough (*also* sluff)
***rel*** flake, peel, scale; discard
**2** to get rid of as useless or unwanted — see DISCARD

**sheen** *n* brightness created by light reflected from a surface — see SHINE 1

**sheep** *n* an innocent or gentle person — see LAMB

***syn*** synonym(s) ***rel*** related words
***ant*** antonym(s) ***near ant*** near antonym(s)

**sheepish** *adj* not comfortable around people — see SHY 2

**sheepishly** *adv* in manner showing no signs of pride or self-assertion — see LOWLY

**sheer** *adj* **1** very thin and easy to see through ⟨we had to get window shades because passersby could see right through our *sheer* curtains⟩
***syn*** filmy, gauzy, gossamer, gossamery, transparent
***rel*** clear, limpid, liquid, lucent, pellucid; lucid, translucent; dainty, delicate, flimsy, fragile, frail; colorless, uncolored
***near ant*** opaque; cloudy, foggy, hazy, misty, murky, smoky (*also* smokey); drab, dull, lackluster, lusterless
**2** having no exceptions or restrictions — see ABSOLUTE 2
**3** having an incline approaching the perpendicular — see STEEP 1

**sheer** *vb* **1** to change one's course or direction — see TURN 3
**2** to depart abruptly from a straight line or course — see SWERVE 1

**sheet** *vb* to form a layer over — see COVER 2

**shell** *n* **1** something that encloses another thing especially to protect it — see [1]CASE 1
**2** the arrangement of parts that gives something its basic form — see FRAME 1

**shell** *vb* **1** to remove the natural covering of — see PEEL
**2** to use bombs or artillery against — see BOMBARD

**shellacking** *n* failure to win a contest — see DEFEAT 1

**shell–shocked** *adj* suffering from high levels of physical and especially psychological stress — see STRESSED-OUT

**shelter** *n* something (as a building) that offers cover from the weather or protection from danger ⟨the sudden fierce storm forced us to run to the nearest *shelter*⟩
***syn*** asylum, harbor, harborage, haven, refuge, retreat, sanctuary, sanctum
***rel*** anchorage, mooring, port; cover, screen; abode, diggings, domicile, dwelling, habitation, house, housing, lodging, lodgment (*or* lodgement), pad, place, quarters, residence, rest, roof; den, lair, hermitage, hideaway, hideout; fastness, fort, fortress, palisade, stronghold; lean-to, shed, windbreak

**shelter** *vb* **1** to be or provide a shelter for ⟨the abandoned barn *shelters* a colony of stray cats⟩
***syn*** harbor
***rel*** cover, defend, protect, safeguard, screen, shield, ward; domicile, house, place; shade, shadow
***near ant*** expose
**2** to provide with living quarters or shelter — see HOUSE 1

**sheltered** *adj* hidden from view — see SECLUDED

**shelve** *vb* to assign to a later time — see POSTPONE

**shenanigans** *n pl* **1** playful, reckless behavior that is not intended to cause serious harm — see MISCHIEF 1
**2** wildly playful or mischievous behavior — see HORSEPLAY
**shepherd** *vb* to give advice and instruction to (someone) regarding the course or process to be followed — see GUIDE 1
**shibboleth** *n* **1** an attention-getting word or phrase used to publicize something (as a campaign or product) — see SLOGAN
**2** an idea or expression that has been used by many people — see COMMONPLACE
**shield** *n* means or method of defending — see DEFENSE 1
**shield** *vb* **1** to drive danger or attack away from — see DEFEND 1
**2** to place a protective layer over — see COVER 3
**shift** *n* **1** an action planned or taken to achieve a desired result — see MEASURE 1
**2** the act or an instance of changing position — see MOVEMENT 1
**shift** *vb* **1** to change the place or position of — see MOVE 1
**2** to change one's position — see MOVE 3
**3** to pass from one form, state, or level to another — see CHANGE 2
**4** to give up (something) and take something else in return — see CHANGE 3
**5** to meet one's day-to-day needs — see GET ALONG 1
**shifting** *n* the act or an instance of changing position — see MOVEMENT 1
**shiftless** *adj* not easily aroused to action or work — see LAZY
**shiftlessness** *n* an inclination not to do work or engage in activities — see LAZINESS
**shifty** *adj* **1** given to acting in secret and to concealing one's intentions — see SNEAKY 1
**2** given to or marked by cheating and deception — see DISHONEST 2
**shillelagh** *n* a heavy rigid stick used as a weapon or for punishment — see CLUB 1
**shilly–shally** *vb* to show uncertainty about the right course of action — see HESITATE
**shilly–shallying** *n* the act or an instance of pausing because of uncertainty about the right course of action — see HESITATION
**shimmer** *vb* to shoot forth bursts of light — see FLASH 1
**shindig** *n* a social gathering — see PARTY 1
**shindy** *n* a state of noisy, confused activity — see COMMOTION
**shine** *n* **1** brightness created by light reflected from a surface ⟨the troop inspector insisted on nothing less than a dazzling *shine* from every pair of shoes in the line of review⟩
*syn* gloss, luster (*or* lustre), polish, sheen
*rel* glare, gleam, glimmer, glint, glisten, glow, shimmer; flicker, sparkle, twinkle; illumination, irradiation; iridescence, luminescence; brightness, brilliance, luminosity, radiance; finish, glaze
*near ant* dimness, dinginess, dirtiness, drabness, dullness (*also* dulness), flatness; grayness, paleness; cloudiness, gloom, murkiness, obscurity, somberness
**2** the steady giving off of the form of radiation that makes vision possible — see LIGHT 1
**3** positive regard for something — see LIKING
**shine** *vb* **1** to emit rays of light ⟨the sun appears to *shine* particularly brightly in summer because that is when it's closest to the Earth⟩
*syn* beam, radiate
*rel* blaze, burn, fire, flame, gleam, glimmer, glint, glisten, glitter, glow, shimmer; blink, flare, flash, flicker, scintillate, sparkle, twinkle, wink; beat (down), glare; brighten, illuminate, illumine, irradiate, light, lighten; bedazzle, blind, daze, dazzle
*near ant* blacken, darken; lower (*also* lour)
**2** to make smooth or glossy usually by repeatedly applying surface pressure — see POLISH
**shining** *adj* giving off or reflecting much light — see BRIGHT 1
**shiny** *adj* giving off or reflecting much light — see BRIGHT 1
**ship** *n* a large craft for travel by water ⟨we chose to spend our vacation on a cruise *ship* traveling through the Caribbean⟩
*syn* boat, vessel
*rel* argosy, containership, corvette, cruiser, cutter, destroyer, ferryboat, flagship, freighter, icebreaker, ironclad, lightship, liner, man-of-war, merchantman, merchant ship, packet, steamer, supertanker, tanker, trader, tramp, transport, warship
**ship** *vb* to cause to go or be taken from one place to another — see SEND
**shippable** *adj* capable of being taken from one place to another by public carrier ⟨only boxes of five pounds and under are *shippable* by the postal service⟩
*syn* transferable, transmittable, transportable
*rel* addressable
*ant* nontransferable, receivable
**shipshape** *adj* being clean and in good order — see NEAT 1
**shipwreck** *n* the destruction or loss of a ship ⟨the *shipwreck* of much of the Spanish Armada ended Spain's plans for invading England⟩
*syn* shipwrecking, wreck, wreckage, wrecking
*rel* beaching, grounding, stranding; foundering, sinking
*near ant* salvage, salvaging
**shipwreck** *vb* to cause irreparable damage to (a ship) by running aground or sinking ⟨the helmsman fell asleep at the wheel and *shipwrecked* his yacht on the rocks⟩
*syn* strand, wreck
*rel* beach, founder, sink
*near ant* salvage

**shipwrecking** *n* the destruction or loss of a ship — see SHIPWRECK

**shirk** *vb* **1** to get or keep away from (as a responsibility) through cleverness or trickery — see ESCAPE 2
**2** to leave undone or unattended to especially through carelessness — see NEGLECT 2

**shirker** *n* one who deliberately avoids work or duty — see SLACKER

**shirty** *adj, chiefly British* feeling or showing anger — see ANGRY

**shiver** *n* **1** an instance of shaking involuntarily with fear or cold ⟨Joe experienced a sudden *shiver* when confronted with the sight of the dark basement⟩
*syn* quiver, shudder, tremble
*rel* agitation, convulsing, jolt, quake, shake, tremor, vibration, wobble; fluctuation, flutter, oscillation, wave; beat, palpitation, pulsation, pulse, throb
**2 shivers** *pl* a sense of panic or extreme nervousness — see JITTERS

**shivery** *adj* having a low or subnormal temperature — see COLD 1

**shoal** *adj* lacking significant physical depth — see SHALLOW 1

**shoal** *n* a place where a body of water (as a sea or river) is shallow ⟨the *shoals* off Nantucket Island are famous as the final resting places of many ill-fated ships⟩
*syn* ford, shallows
*rel* bank, bar, sandbank, sandbar
*near ant* trench; abyss, deep, depth

**shock** *n* **1** a forceful coming together of two things — see IMPACT 1
**2** the state of being strongly impressed by something unexpected or unusual — see SURPRISE 2

**shock** *vb* **1** to cause an often unpleasant surprise for ⟨Mom was *shocked* by the terrible news that her cousin had died in an accident⟩ ⟨Jack was *shocked* to find out that his grades were much lower than he realized⟩
*syn* appall, bowl (over), floor, jolt, shake up
*rel* affright, alarm, dismay, frighten, horrify, panic, scare, spook, startle, terrify, terrorize; disgust, nauseate, repel, revolt, sicken, turn off; displease, offend, outrage, scandalize; amaze, astound, awe; chill, daunt, demoralize, dispirit, unman, unnerve; discompose, disconcert, disquiet, disturb, perturb, unsettle, upset; crush, overpower, overwhelm
*phrases* knock for a loop
*near ant* cushion; delight, gratify, please, rejoice, tickle; charm, entice, tempt; cheer, comfort, console, solace, soothe; reassure
**2** to make a strong impression on (someone) with something unexpected — see SURPRISE 1
**3** to strike with fear — see FRIGHTEN

**shocked** *adj* **1** affected with sudden and great wonder or surprise — see THUNDERSTRUCK
**2** filled with disgust — see SICK 2

**shocking** *adj* **1** causing a strong emotional reaction because unexpected — see SURPRISING 1
**2** causing fear — see FEARFUL 1
**3** causing intense displeasure, disgust, or resentment — see OFFENSIVE 1
**4** extremely disturbing or repellent — see HORRIBLE 1

**shoddy** *adj* of low quality — see CHEAP 2

**shoes** *n pl* a way of looking at or thinking about something — see POINT OF VIEW

**shoestring** *n* a very small sum of money — see MITE 1

**shoot** *n* a branch of a main stem especially of a plant — see OFFSHOOT 1

**shoot** *vb* **1** to cause (a projectile) to be driven forward with force ⟨BB guns *shoot* small round metal pellets⟩
*syn* blast, discharge, fire, loose
*rel* launch, project; blaze (at), snipe (at); cast, catapult, fling, heave, hurl, pelt, pitch, sling, throw, toss
**2** to cause a weapon to release a missile with great force ⟨soldiers train extensively to learn to *shoot* accurately and quickly⟩
*syn* blast, discharge, fire
*rel* blaze, pepper, snipe
**3** to strike with a missile from a gun ⟨hunters can *shoot* deer only during the legally specified open season⟩
*syn* drill, gun, plug, pop
*rel* blaze, pepper; blast (at), fire (at); pick off; overshoot; snipe (at); croak [*slang*], destroy, dispatch, do in, fell, kill, slay; annihilate, blot out, butcher, decimate, massacre, slaughter, wipe out
**4** to proceed or move quickly — see HURRY 2
**5** to take a photograph of — see PHOTOGRAPH
**6** to throw or give off — see EMIT 1

**shoot** (up) *vb* to rise abruptly and rapidly — see SKYROCKET

**shooter** *n* **1** a person skilled in shooting at a target — see MARKSMAN
**2** one who takes photographs — see PHOTOGRAPHER

**shop** *n* **1** *also* **shoppe** an establishment where goods are sold to consumers ⟨the only *shop* which carries that game is halfway across the state⟩
*syn* bazaar, emporium, store
*rel* market, marketplace, outlet, showroom; boutique, department store, dime store, five-and-ten, thrift shop, variety store
**2** a building or set of buildings for the manufacturing of goods — see FACTORY

[1]**shore** *n* something that holds up or serves as a foundation for something else — see SUPPORT 1

[2]**shore** *n* the usually sandy or gravelly land bordering a body of water — see BEACH

**shore** (up) *vb* to hold up or serve as a foundation for — see SUPPORT 3

---

*syn* synonym(s) *rel* related words
*ant* antonym(s) *near ant* near antonym(s)

**short** *adj* **1** having relatively little height ⟨a lot of boys are *shorter* than the girls in middle school, but they quickly catch up by high school⟩
*syn* little, low, low-lying
*rel* dwarf, dwarfish; petite, slight; diminutive, little, pint-size (*or* pint-sized), small, smallish; bantam, bitty, dinky, miniature, minimized, minute, puny, teeny, teeny-weeny, tiny, undersized, wee; dumpy, flat, scrubby, squat, squatty, stubby, stumpy, stunted
*near ant* elevated, lifted, raised, uplifted, upswept; high-rise, statuesque; gangling, gangly, lanky, rangy
*ant* high, lofty, tall, towering
**2** not lasting for a considerable time ⟨fortunately for those of us in the hot sun, the graduation speech was *short* and to the point⟩
*syn* brief, condensed, little
*rel* abbreviated, abridged, curtailed, cutback, shortened; compact, condensed; abrupt, sudden; ephemeral, fleeting, momentary, short-lived, transient, transitory; impermanent; compendious, concise, crisp, epigrammatic, laconic, pithy, succinct, summary, terse; short-range, short-term
*near ant* endless, everlasting, interminable, persistent, unending; longish, overlong, prolonged, protracted; permanent; enlarged, expanded, supplemented; long-range, long-term
*ant* extended, great, lengthy, long, long-lived, marathon
**3** not coming up to a usual standard or meeting a particular need ⟨regrettably, the art supplies are *short* this year, so you'll have to share⟩
*syn* deficient, inadequate, insufficient, lacking, scarce, shy, wanting
*rel* hand-to-mouth, light, meager, niggardly, poor, scant, scarcity, skimpy, slender, slim, spare, sparse, stingy; bare, mere, minimum; slight, small
*near ant* abundant, ample, bounteous, bountiful, copious, generous, liberal, plenteous, plentiful; enlarged, expanded, supplemented; abounding, overflowing, teeming; lavish, luxuriant, rich; big, considerable, hefty, jumbo, large, largish, oversize (*or* oversized), sizable (*or* sizeable), substantial, super
*ant* adequate, enough, sufficient
**4** having a texture that readily breaks into little pieces under pressure — see CRISP 1

**short** *adv* with great suddenness ⟨the bicyclist ahead of me unexpectedly pulled up *short* and I plowed into him⟩
*syn* abruptly, suddenly
*rel* quickly; surprisingly, unexpectedly
*near ant* gradually, slowly; hesitantly

**shortage** *n* a falling short of an essential or desirable amount or number — see DEFICIENCY

**shortchange** *vb* to rob by the use of trickery or threats — see FLEECE

**shortcoming** *n* a defect in character — see FAULT 1

**shorten** *vb* to make less in extent or duration ⟨we decided to *shorten* the distance we had to walk home by cutting across the neighbor's lawn⟩ ⟨if Grandma has to go shopping today, you'll need to *shorten* your visit⟩
*syn* abbreviate, abridge, curtail, cut back
*rel* digest, summarize; abate, compress, constrict, contract, cut, cut down, pare, prune, trim; decrease, de-escalate, deflate, diminish, dock, dwindle, lessen, lower, moderate, modify, reduce, retrench, shrink, slash, taper
*near ant* enlarge, expand, supplement; add, aggrandize, amplify, augment, balloon, boost, dilate, escalate, heighten, increase, maximize, raise; blow up, distend, inflate, swell
*ant* elongate, extend, lengthen, prolong, protract

**short-lived** *adj* lasting only for a short time — see MOMENTARY

**shortly** *adv* **1** in a few words ⟨the sudden closing of the restaurant was announced only with a *shortly* worded sign: "Out of Business"⟩
*syn* briefly, compactly, concisely, crisply, laconically, pithily, succinctly, summarily, tersely
*rel* aphoristically; exactly, precisely; abruptly, bluntly, brusquely, curtly
*phrases* in a nutshell
*near ant* redundantly, repetitiously
*ant* diffusely, long-windedly, verbosely, wordily
**2** at or within a short time ⟨the test will begin *shortly*, so don't go too far away to find a bathroom⟩
*syn* anon, momentarily, presently, soon
*rel* directly, forthwith, immediately, instantly, now, promptly, pronto, right away, right now, straightaway
*phrases* by and by

**shortness** *n* the condition of being short — see BREVITY 1

**shortsighted** *adj* **1** able to see near things more clearly than distant ones — see NEARSIGHTED
**2** not thinking about and providing for the future — see IMPROVIDENT

**short story** *n* a work with imaginary characters and events that is shorter and usually less complex than a novel — see STORY 1

**short-tempered** *adj* easily irritated or annoyed — see IRRITABLE

**short-term** *adj* intended to last, continue, or serve for a limited time — see TEMPORARY 1

**shot** *n* **1** a directed propelling of a missile by a firearm or artillery piece ⟨cannon operators often had to use several *shots* to figure out the range of their targets⟩
*syn* blasting, discharge, firing
*rel* potshot; barrage, bombardment, broadside, burst, cannonade, fusillade, hail, salvo, storm, volley

**2** an effort to do or accomplish something — see ATTEMPT
**3** a picture created from an image recorded on a light-sensitive surface by a camera — see PHOTOGRAPH
**4** a person skilled in shooting at a target — see MARKSMAN
**5** the portion of a serving of a beverage that is swallowed at one time — see DRINK 2

**should** *vb* to be under necessity or obligation to — see NEED 2

**shoulder** *vb* to take to or upon oneself — see ASSUME 1

**shout** *n* a loud vocal expression of strong emotion ⟨Jason gave a sudden *shout* of surprise when the shower abruptly turned ice-cold⟩
***syn*** cry, holler, hoot, howl, yell, yowl, whoop
***rel*** scream, screech, shriek, squall, squeak, squeal, yelp; bellow, clamor, roar; caterwaul, wail
***near ant*** mumble, murmur, mutter; gasp, whimper, whisper

**shout** *vb* to speak so as to be heard at a distance — see CALL 1

**shove** *vb* **1** to apply force to (someone or something) so that it moves in front of one — see PUSH 1
**2** to push steadily against with some force — see PRESS 1

**shove** (off) *vb* to leave a place often for another — see GO 2

**shovel** *vb* to hollow out or form (something) by removing earth — see DIG 1

**show** *n* **1** an outward and often exaggerated indication of something abstract (as a feeling) for effect ⟨the children made a *show* of disgust when confronted with asparagus⟩
***syn*** demonstration, display, exhibition, flaunting
***rel*** act, pretense (*or* pretence), simulation; affectation, pose, sham; betrayal, disclosure
**2** a display of emotion or behavior that is insincere or intended to deceive — see MASQUERADE
**3** outward and often deceptive indication — see APPEARANCE 2
**4** a public showing of objects of interest — see EXHIBITION 1

**show** *vb* **1** to present so as to invite notice or attention ⟨Julie made sure she *showed* the test paper with a big A on it to everyone in her family⟩
***syn*** display, disport, exhibit, expose, flash, flaunt, parade, show off, sport, strut, unveil
***rel*** brandish, flourish; advertise, air, broadcast, proclaim, publicize; divulge, talk (about), tell (of); bare, discover, reveal, uncloak, uncover
***near ant*** camouflage, disguise, mask; conceal, cover, curtain, enshroud, hide, obscure, occult, shroud, veil
**2** to make known (something abstract) through outward signs ⟨John's expressive face *shows* his every thought and emotion clearly⟩
***syn*** bespeak, betray, demonstrate, display, expose, evince, give away, manifest, reveal
***rel*** bare, disclose, unbosom, uncloak, uncover; advertise, air, broadcast, proclaim, publicize
***near ant*** belie, misrepresent; distort, falsify, garble, twist; camouflage, disguise; gild, gloss (over), varnish, whitewash; conceal, counterfeit, cover, hide, mask, obscure, veil
**3** to gain full recognition or acceptance of — see ESTABLISH 1
**4** to give advice and instruction to (someone) regarding the course or process to be followed — see GUIDE 1
**5** to point out the way for (someone) especially from a position in front — see LEAD 1

**shower** *n* **1** a heavy fall of objects — see RAIN 2
**2** a rapid or overwhelming outpouring of many things at once — see BARRAGE

**shower** *vb* to give readily and in large quantities — see RAIN 2

**showiness** *n* excessive or unnecessary display — see OSTENTATION

**show off** *vb* **1** to engage in attention-getting playful or boisterous behavior — see CUT UP
**2** to present so as to invite notice or attention — see SHOW 1

**show up** *vb* **1** to come into view — see APPEAR 1
**2** to get to a destination — see COME 2
**3** to reveal the true nature of — see EXPOSE 1

**showy** *adj* likely to attract attention — see NOTICEABLE

**shred** *n* a very small amount — see PARTICLE 1

**shred** *vb* to cause (something) to separate into jagged pieces by violently pulling at it — see TEAR 1

**shrew** *n* a bad-tempered scolding woman ⟨Rip Van Winkle went off into mountains to escape his wife, a *shrew* who made his life miserable⟩
***syn*** fury, harpy, termagant, virago
***rel*** carper, castigator, censurer, caviler (*or* caviller), critic, faultfinder, nitpicker, railer, scold; belittler, derider, detractor; pettifogger, quibbler

**shrewd** *adj* having or showing a practical cleverness or judgment ⟨a *shrewd* used car dealer who knew how to make the best possible deal⟩ ⟨*shrewd* investments that paid off big⟩
***syn*** astute, canny, clear-sighted, hard-headed, knowing, sharp, sharp-witted, smart
***rel*** artful, cagey (*also* cagy), crafty, cunning, devious, foxy, guileful, slick, sly, subtle, wily; discerning, insightful, perceptive, perspicacious, sagacious, sage, sapient, wise; experienced, veteran; dis-

criminating, discriminative; agile, alert, brainy, bright, brilliant, clever, intelligent, keen, quick, quick-witted; apt, ingenious, resourceful; informed, knowledgeable, well-read
*near ant* artless, guileless, ingenuous, innocent, naive (*or* naïve); exploitable, gullible; undiscerning, unperceptive, unwise; dense, dull, obtuse; brainless, dumb, feebleminded, simple, slow, stupid, unintelligent, weak-minded; foolish, idiotic, imbecilic, moronic, silly, simple, thoughtless, witless; ignorant, uninformed
*ant* unknowing

**shriek** *vb* to cry out loudly and emotionally — see SCREAM

**shrieking** *adj* having a high musical pitch or range — see SHRILL

**shrill** *adj* having a high musical pitch or range ⟨the *shrill* sound of a policeman's whistle⟩
*syn* acute, high-pitched, piping, screeching, shrieking, squeaking, squeaky, treble, whistling
*rel* peeping, thin, tinny; piercing, earsplitting, piercing, penetrating, strident; squealing, whining, yelping
*near ant* gruff
*ant* bass, deep, low, throaty

**shrill** *vb* to cry out loudly and emotionally — see SCREAM

**shrimp** *n* **1** a living thing much smaller than others of its kind — see DWARF 1
**2** a person of no importance or influence — see NOBODY

**shrine** *n* a place that is considered sacred (as within a religion) ⟨for centuries pilgrims have traveled to the *shrine* of Saint Thomas à Becket in Canterbury, England⟩
*syn* sanctuary, sanctum
*rel* reliquary

**shrink** *vb* **1** to become smaller in size or volume through the drawing together of particles of matter — see CONTRACT 2
**2** to draw back in fear, pain, or disgust — see FLINCH
**3** to grow less in scope or intensity especially gradually — see DECREASE 2

**shrinkage** *n* the amount by which something is lessened — see DECREASE

**shroud** *n* something that covers or conceals like a piece of cloth — see CLOAK 1

**shroud** *vb* **1** to keep secret or shut off from view — see [1]HIDE 2
**2** to make dark, dim, or indistinct — see CLOUD 1
**3** to surround or cover closely — see ENFOLD 1

**shrug off** *vb* to overlook or dismiss as of little importance — see EXCUSE 1

**shuck** *vb* to remove the natural covering of — see PEEL

**shuck** (off) *vb* to get rid of as useless or unwanted — see DISCARD

**shudder** *n* an instance of shaking involuntarily with fear or cold — see SHIVER 1

**shudder** *vb* to make a series of small irregular or violent movements — see SHAKE 1

**shuddering** *adj* marked by or given to small uncontrollable bodily movements — see SHAKY 1

**shuddering** *n* a series of slight movements by a body back and forth or from side to side — see VIBRATION

**shuddery** *adj* marked by or given to small uncontrollable bodily movements — see SHAKY 1

**shuffle** *n* an unorganized collection or mixture of various things — see MISCELLANY 1

**shuffle** *vb* **1** to move heavily or clumsily — see LUMBER 1
**2** to undo the proper order or arrangement of — see DISORDER

**shun** *vb* to get or keep away from (as a responsibility) through cleverness or trickery — see ESCAPE 2

**shunning** *n* the act or a means of getting or keeping away from something undesirable — see ESCAPE 2

**shush** *vb* to stop the noise or speech of — see SILENCE 1

**shut** *vb* **1** to position (something) so as to prevent passage through an opening — see CLOSE 1
**2** to stop the operations of — see CLOSE 2

**shutdown** *n* the stopping of a process or activity — see END 1

**shutoff** *n* the stopping of a process or activity — see END 1

**shut off** *vb* to bring (as an action or operation) to an immediate end — see STOP 1

**shutterbug** *n* one who takes photographs — see PHOTOGRAPHER

**shut up** *vb* to stop talking ⟨it's not polite to tell your classmates to *shut up*, even if you disagree with them⟩
*syn* clam up, hush, quiet (down)
*rel* calm (down), cool (down), settle (down); haw, hem
*ant* speak, talk

**shy** *adj* **1** easily frightened ⟨a *shy* cat who hid under the bed every time she heard any loud noise⟩
*syn* fainthearted, fearful, mousy (*or* mousey), scary, skittish, timid, timorous
*rel* chicken, chickenhearted, cowardly, craven, dastardly, lily-livered, jittery, jumpy, pusillanimous, spineless, unheroic, yellow; anxious, apprehensive, nervous; afraid, alarmed, horrified, panicked, panicky, scared, shocked, spooked, startled, terrified, terrorized
*near ant* brave, courageous, dauntless, doughty, fearless, gallant, greathearted, heroic, intrepid, lionhearted, stalwart, stout, stouthearted, valiant, valorous; assured, confident, self-assured, self-confident; determined, firm, game, plucky, resolute, unflinching, unswerving; mettlesome, spirited, spunky
*ant* adventuresome, adventurous, audacious, bold, daring, dashing, gutsy, hardy, venturous, venturesome
**2** not comfortable around people ⟨a *shy* person who finds talking to anyone but a close friend to be an awkward and unpleasant experience⟩

*syn* bashful, coy, demure, diffident, introverted, modest, retiring, sheepish
*rel* antisocial, unsociable, unsocial; awkward, embarrassed, self-conscious, unadventurous, unassertive, unenterprising; inhibited, reserved, uneasy, uptight
*near ant* convivial, sociable, social; bold, dashing, forceful; brash, forward, uninhibited, unreserved
*ant* extroverted (*also* extraverted), immodest, outgoing
**3** not coming up to a usual standard or meeting a particular need — see SHORT 3

**sick** *adj* **1** temporarily suffering from a disorder of the body ⟨Jessie was *sick* with a cold on Monday and had to stay home from school⟩
*syn* ailing, bad, down, ill, indisposed, peaked, poorly, punk, run-down, sickened, unhealthy, unsound, unwell
*rel* nauseated, nauseous, qualmish, queasy (*also* queazy), sickish, squeamish; airsick, carsick, seasick, dizzy, lighthearted, woozy; achy, feverish; diseased, disordered; feeble, frail, infirm, sickly, weak, weakly; afflicted, troubled; challenged, crippled, debilitated, disabled, incapacitated, lame
*phrases* out of sorts, under the weather
*near ant* cured; better, convalescing, improved, mending, recovering, recuperating, rehabilitated; hardy, hearty, lusty, robust, rugged, stalwart, strong, tough; blooming, bouncing, flourishing, flush, thriving
*ant* chipper, hale, healthful, healthy, sound, well, whole, wholesome
**2** filled with disgust ⟨it makes me *sick* to think of someone hurting a helpless animal⟩
*syn* disgusted, nauseated, repelled, repulsed, revolted, shocked, sickened, squeamish
*rel* angry, displeased, mad, upset
*near ant* delighted, pleased, thrilled; beguiled, bewitched, captivated, charmed, enchanted, enthralled, fascinated, mesmerized
**3** affected with nausea — see NAUSEOUS
**4** having one's patience, interest, or pleasure exhausted — see WEARY 2

**sicken** *vb* to cause to feel disgust — see DISGUST

**sicken** (with) *vb* to become affected with (a disease or disorder) — see CONTRACT 1

**sickened** *adj* **1** temporarily suffering from a disorder of the body — see SICK 1
**2** filled with disgust — see SICK 2

**sickening** *adj* causing intense displeasure, disgust, or resentment — see OFFENSIVE 1

**sickish** *adj* affected with nausea — see NAUSEOUS

**sickly** *adj* chronically or repeatedly suffering from poor health ⟨a *sickly* foal that seemed to catch everything that the other horses had⟩
*syn* ailing, invalid, weakly
*rel* bedridden; delicate, fragile, frail; dying, fading, incurable, moribund; challenged, crippled, debilitated, incapacitated, lame; decrepit, enfeebled, feeble, infirm, weak, weakened, worn-out
*near ant* able-bodied, nondisabled, nonhandicapped
*ant* healthy, well

**sickness** *n* **1** the condition of not being in good health ⟨Jamie pleaded *sickness* and tried to stay home from school every single time there was a spelling test scheduled⟩
*syn* illness, indisposition, unhealthiness, unsoundness
*rel* malaise; ailment, condition, disease, disorder, malady, trouble, upset; debility, decrepitude, feebleness, frailness, infirmity, lameness
*near ant* fettle, fitness, shape; hardiness, heartiness, lustiness, robustness, ruggedness, stamina, strength, toughness, vigor, vigorousness, vitality; bloom, flush, flushness; weal, welfare, well-being
*ant* health, healthiness, soundness, wellness, wholeness, wholesomeness
**2** an abnormal state that disrupts a plant or animal's normal bodily functioning — see DISEASE 1
**3** a disturbed condition of the stomach in which one feels like vomiting — see NAUSEA 1

**side** *adj* of, relating to, or located on one side ⟨please bring all deliveries to the *side* door⟩
*syn* lateral
*rel* left, right; one-sided

**side** *n* **1** a place, space, or direction away from or beyond a central point or line ⟨will everyone who wants to sign up for volleyball please stand off to this *side* of the gym?⟩
*syn* flank, hand
*rel* direction, face, outside, underpart, underside; lee, leeward, windward; left, right
**2** a certain way in which something appears or may be regarded — see ASPECT 1
**3** a group of people acting together within a larger group — see FACTION

**sideboard** *n* a storage case typically having doors and shelves — see CABINET

**sidekick** *n* a person who helps a more skilled person — see HELPER

**side-splitting** *adj* causing or intended to cause laughter — see FUNNY 1

**sidestep** *vb* **1** to avoid having to comply with (something) especially through cleverness — see CIRCUMVENT 1
**2** to move suddenly aside or to and fro — see DODGE 1

**sideways** *adv* with one side faced forward ⟨I had to walk *sideways* to get between the two towering piles of boxes⟩
*syn* broadside, edgewise, sidewise
*rel* aslant, obliquely, indirectly; laterally, sideward (*or* sidewards)
*near ant* dead, direct, right, straight

---

*syn* synonym(s) *rel* related words
*ant* antonym(s) *near ant* near antonym(s)

**sidewise** *adv* with one side faced forward — see SIDEWAYS

**siege** *n* **1** a sudden experiencing of a physical or mental disorder — see ATTACK 2
**2** the cutting off of an area by military means to stop the flow of people or supplies — see BLOCKADE

**siesta** *n* a short sleep — see ¹NAP

**sigh** *vb* to take in and let out a deep audible breath or to make a similar sound ⟨Mom always used to *sigh* loudly whenever she found a mess on the floor⟩ ⟨a breeze *sighed* through the leaves⟩
***syn*** sough
***rel*** gasp, huff, pant, puff, wheeze; breathe, respire; exhale, expire, inhale, inspire; yawn

**sigh** (for) *vb* to have an earnest wish to own or enjoy — see DESIRE

**sight** *n* **1** a position within view — see PRESENCE 1
**2** an instance of looking especially briefly — see LOOK 2
**3** something unpleasant to look at — see EYESORE
**4** the ability to see — see EYESIGHT

**sight** *vb* to make note of (something) through the use of one's eyes — see SEE 1

**sightless** *adj* lacking the power of sight — see BLIND

**sightly** *adj* very pleasing to look at — see BEAUTIFUL

**sightseer** *n* a person who travels for pleasure — see TOURIST

**sign** *n* **1** a movement of the body or limbs that expresses or emphasizes an idea or feeling — see GESTURE 1
**2** a written or printed mark that is meant to convey information to the reader — see CHARACTER 1

**sign** *vb* to write one's name on (as a document) ⟨you'll have to *sign* the contract for it to be legal⟩
***syn*** autograph
***rel*** countersign, endorse (*also* indorse), register, sign on; author, pen, pencil (in), scratch (out), scrawl, scribble, write

**signal** *adj* standing above others in rank, importance, or achievement — see EMINENT

**signal** *n* **1** an object intended to give public notice or warning ⟨stop signs are *signals* for vehicles to come to a full stop— not suggestions for slowing down, as some drivers seem to think⟩
***syn*** flag, tocsin
**2** a movement of the body or limbs that expresses or emphasizes an idea or feeling — see GESTURE 1

**signal** *vb* to direct or notify by a movement or gesture — see MOTION

**significance** *n* **1** the idea that is conveyed or intended to be conveyed to the mind by language, symbol, or action — see MEANING 1
**2** the quality or state of being important — see IMPORTANCE

**significant** *adj* **1** clearly conveying a special meaning (as one's mood) — see EXPRESSIVE
**2** indicating something — see INDICATIVE
**3** having great meaning or lasting effect — see IMPORTANT 1
**4** having great power or influence — see IMPORTANT 2
**5** sufficiently large in size, amount, or number to merit attention — see CONSIDERABLE 1

**signification** *n* the idea that is conveyed or intended to be conveyed to the mind by language, symbol, or action — see MEANING 1

**signify** *vb* **1** to be of importance — see MATTER
**2** to communicate or convey (as an idea) to the mind — see MEAN 1

**signifying** *adj* indicating something — see INDICATIVE

**sign on** (for) *vb* to become a member of — see ENTER 2

**sign up** (for) *vb* to become a member of — see ENTER 2

**silence** *n* **1** incapacity for or restraint from speaking ⟨the teacher expects complete *silence* from everyone during all tests⟩
***syn*** dumbness, muteness, speechlessness, stillness
***rel*** inarticulateness, voicelessness; reserve, reticence, reticency, taciturnity
***near ant*** communication, speaking, talking; eloquence, fluency, volubility; chattiness, garrulousness, loquaciousness, loquacity, talkativeness; verboseness, verbosity, wordiness, wordiness
**2** the near or complete absence of sound ⟨the *silence* of the garden was refreshing after the din of the party inside⟩
***syn*** hush, quiet, quietness, quietude, still, stillness
***rel*** calm, lull, peacefulness, tranquillity (*or* tranquility)
***near ant*** din, clamor, hubbub, racket, tumult, uproar
***ant*** noise, sound

**silence** *vb* **1** to stop the noise or speech of ⟨the instructor quickly *silenced* anyone who tried to interrupt⟩ ⟨we need to have a repairman come and *silence* that door alarm⟩
***syn*** hush, mute, quell, settle, shush, still
***near ant*** agitate, stir
**2** to put a stop to (something) by the use of force — see QUELL 1

**silent** *adj* **1** deliberately refraining from speech ⟨the *silent* child had to be prompted to say hello⟩
***syn*** dumb, mum, mute, speechless, uncommunicative
***rel*** inarticulate, tongue-tied; nonvocal, voiceless
***near ant*** articulate, eloquent, fluent, voluble; gabby, garrulous, loquacious, talkative, talky; outspoken, unreserved, vocal
***ant*** communicative, speaking, talking
**2** tending not to speak frequently (as by habit or inclination) ⟨a naturally *silent* boy, he was often overshadowed by his louder siblings⟩

*syn* closemouthed, laconic, reserved, reticent, taciturn, tight-lipped, uncommunicative
*rel* inhibited, introverted, restrained; sedate, self-contained, sober, staid
*near ant* free-spoken, outspoken, vocal; blabby, gossipy, talebearing; long-winded, verbose, windy, wordy
*ant* chatty, communicative, conversational, gabby, garrulous, loquacious, talkative, talky, unreserved
**3** mostly or entirely without sound ⟨the room was so *silent* that you could have heard a pin drop⟩
*syn* hushed, muted, noiseless, quiet, quieted, soundless, still
*rel* peaceful, tranquil
*ant* noisy, unquiet

**silhouette** *n* a line that traces the outer limits of an object or surface — see OUTLINE 1

**silhouette** *vb* to draw or make apparent the outline of — see OUTLINE 1

**silken** *adj* smooth or delicate in appearance or feel — see SOFT 2

**silky** *adj* smooth or delicate in appearance or feel — see SOFT 2

**silliness** *n* **1** lack of good sense or judgment — see FOOLISHNESS 1
**2** language, behavior, or ideas that are absurd and contrary to good sense — see NONSENSE 1

**silly** *adj* **1** lacking in seriousness or maturity — see GIDDY 1
**2** showing or marked by a lack of good sense or judgment — see FOOLISH 1
**3** so foolish or pointless as to be worthy of scornful laughter — see RIDICULOUS 1

**silver** *adj* of the color gray — see GRAY 1

**silver** *n* eating and serving utensils — see TABLEWARE 1

**silverware** *n* eating and serving utensils — see TABLEWARE 1

**silvery** *adj* of the color gray — see GRAY 1

**similar** *adj* having qualities in common — see ALIKE

**similarity** *n* **1** the quality or state of having many qualities in common ⟨the *similarity* between the two essays is too great to be coincidental — one student virtually copied the other⟩
*syn* alikeness, community, correspondence, likeness, parallelism, resemblance, similitude
*rel* analogousness; equivalence, equivalency, parity; identicalness, identity, sameness; correlation, relationship; exchangeability, interchangeability; accordance, agreement, compatibility, conformity, congruity
*near ant* inequality; conflict, disagreement, discrepancy, disparity, variance; incompatibility, incongruity, incongruousness
*ant* dissimilarity, unlikeness
**2** a point which two or more things share in common ⟨the only *similarity* between this project and the last one is that both will involve some lab work⟩
*syn* correspondence, parallel, resemblance, similitude
*rel* counterpart, equal, equivalent
*near ant* difference, discrepancy; deviance, divergence; change, modification, variation
*ant* dissimilarity

**similarly** *adv* in like manner — see ALSO 1

**similitude** *n* **1** the quality or state of having many qualities in common — see SIMILARITY 1
**2** a point which two or more things share in common — see SIMILARITY 2

**simmer** *vb* to cook in a liquid heated to the point that it gives off steam — see BOIL 2

**simple** *adj* **1** free from all additions or embellishment — see PLAIN 1
**2** free from any intent to deceive or impress others — see GUILELESS
**3** having no exceptions or restrictions — see ABSOLUTE 2
**4** involving minimal difficulty or effort — see EASY 1
**5** lacking in worldly wisdom or informed judgment — see NAIVE 1
**6** lacking in education or the knowledge gained from books — see IGNORANT 1
**7** not having or showing an ability to absorb ideas readily — see STUPID 1

**simpleminded** *adj* **1** lacking in worldly wisdom or informed judgment — see NAIVE 1
**2** showing or marked by a lack of good sense or judgment — see FOOLISH 1

**simpleness** *n* **1** the quality or state of being simple and sincere — see NAÏVETÉ 1
**2** the quality or state of lacking intelligence or quickness of mind — see STUPIDITY 1

**simpleton** *n* **1** a person who lacks good sense or judgment — see FOOL 1
**2** a stupid person — see IDIOT

**simplicity** *n* **1** the quality or state of having a form or structure of few parts or elements ⟨the *simplicity* of this machine should enable everyone to learn how to use it⟩
*syn* plainness, unsophistication
*rel* homogeneity, unity
*ant* complexity, complication, elaborateness, intricacy, sophistication
**2** clearness of expression ⟨the *simplicity* of this poem is beautiful⟩
*syn* clarity, explicitness, lucidity, lucidness, perspicuity, perspicuousness
*rel* incisiveness, directness, forthrightness, openness, straightforwardness
*near ant* ambiguity, equivocalness; incomprehensibility, unintelligibility; circuitousness, deviousness, indirectness, indistinctness; dimness, disjointedness, incoherence; faintness, fuzziness, muddiness, nebulousness, vagueness
*ant* obscurity
**3** lack of good sense or judgment — see FOOLISHNESS 1

---

*syn* synonym(s) *rel* related words
*ant* antonym(s) *near ant* near antonym(s)

4 the quality or state of being simple and sincere — see NAÏVETÉ 1

**simplify** *vb* to make less complex ⟨you need to *simplify* this process somewhat or you'll never finish it today⟩
*syn* streamline
*rel* oversimplify; prune, strip (down), trim; purify, refine
*near ant* elaborate
*ant* complicate, perplex, sophisticate

**simply** *adv* 1 for nothing other than — see SOLELY 1
2 nothing more than — see JUST 3

**simulate** *vb* to present a false appearance of — see FEIGN

**simulated** *adj* 1 being such in appearance only and made with or manufactured from usually cheaper materials — see IMITATION
2 lacking in natural or spontaneous quality — see ARTIFICIAL 1

**simultaneous** *adj* existing or occurring at the same period of time — see CONTEMPORARY 1

**simultaneously** *adv* at one and the same time — see TOGETHER 1

**sin** *n* 1 a breaking of a moral or legal code — see OFFENSE 1
2 that which is morally unacceptable — see EVIL
3 immoral conduct or practices harmful or offensive to society — see VICE 1
4 a regrettable or blameworthy act — see CRIME 2

**sin** *vb* to commit an offense — see OFFEND 1

**since** *conj* for the reason that ⟨*since* I've done all my chores today, I should be allowed to go out and play⟩
*syn* as, because, for, inasmuch as, now, seeing, whereas
*phrases* as long as (*or* so long as), in view (*or* light) of the fact

**sincere** *adj* free from any intent to deceive or impress others — see GUILELESS

**sincerely** *adv* without any attempt to impress by deception or exaggeration — see NATURALLY 3

**sinew** *n* the ability to exert effort for the accomplishment of a task — see POWER 2

**sinewy** *adj* 1 having muscles capable of exerting great physical force — see STRONG 1
2 marked by a well-developed musculature — see MUSCULAR 1

**sinful** *adj* not conforming to a high moral standard; morally unacceptable — see BAD 2

**sinfulness** *n* the state or quality of being utterly evil — see ENORMITY 1

**sing** *vb* 1 to produce musical sounds with the voice ⟨it's relatively rare to find actors who can also *sing* well⟩
*syn* carol, chant, descant, vocalize
*rel* belt, croon, harmonize, hum, lilt, quaver, scat, sharp, slur, trill, troll, warble, yodel; serenade
2 to utter in musical or drawn out tones — see CHANT 1
3 to utter one's distinctive animal sound — see CRY 2

**singe** *vb* to burn on the surface — see SCORCH

**singer** *n* one who sings ⟨a famous opera *singer* will be performing tomorrow⟩
*syn* caroler (*or* caroller), songster, vocalist, vocalizer, voice
*rel* harmonizer, hummer, warbler, yodeler; serenader; cantor, chorist; songstress

**single** *adj* 1 not married ⟨there was such a shortage of *single* men in the neighborhood that he had his pick of girlfriends⟩
*syn* unattached, unmarried, unwed
*rel* fancy-free, footloose; marriageable, unmated, unpaired; divorced, separated
*near ant* mated, paired; affianced, betrothed, committed, engaged, pledged, promised; remarried
*ant* attached, espoused, married, wed
2 belonging only to the one person, unit, or group named — see SOLE 1
3 not physically attached to another unit — see SEPARATE 2

**single** (out) *vb* 1 to decide to accept (someone or something) from a group of possibilities — see CHOOSE 1
2 to find out or establish the identity of — see IDENTIFY 1

**single-handedly** *adv* without aid or support — see ALONE 1

**singly** *adv* without aid or support — see ALONE 1

**singular** *adj* 1 being out of the ordinary — see EXCEPTIONAL
2 noticeably different from what is generally found or experienced — see UNUSUAL 1
3 of, relating to, or belonging to a single person — see INDIVIDUAL 1
4 being the one or ones of a class with no other members — see ONLY 2

**singularity** *n* an odd or peculiar habit — see IDIOSYNCRASY

**sinister** *adj* being or showing a sign of evil or calamity to come — see OMINOUS

**sink** *vb* 1 to become worse or of less value — see DETERIORATE
2 to go to a lower level — see DROP 2

**sinner** *n* a person who commits moral wrongs — see EVILDOER 1

**sinuous** *adj* marked by a long series of irregular curves — see CROOKED 1

**sip** *n* the portion of a serving of a beverage that is swallowed at one time — see DRINK 2

**sip** *vb* to swallow in liquid form — see DRINK 1

**siphon** *vb* 1 to remove (liquid) gradually or completely — see DRAIN 1
2 to cause to move to a central point or along a restricted pathway — see CHANNEL

**sire** *vb* to become the father of — see FATHER

**siren** *n* a woman whom men find irresistibly attractive ⟨one of history's most famous *sirens*, Cleopatra charmed both Julius Caesar and Mark Antony⟩

*syn* enchantress, seductress, temptress
*rel* charmer, seducer

**sissy** *adj* having or displaying qualities more suitable for women than for men — see EFFEMINATE

**sissy** *n* a person who shows a shameful lack of courage in the face of danger — see COWARD

**sit** *vb* **1** to rest on the buttocks or haunches ⟨everybody needs to *sit* down, or no one will be able to see the movie⟩
*syn* set [*chiefly dialect*]
*rel* perch; lounge, slouch, sprawl, squat, straddle
*near ant* arise, get up, rise, stand
**2** to cause to sit down — see SEAT
**3** to cover and warm eggs to hatch them — see SET 1
**4** to occupy a place or location — see STAND 1

**site** *n* the area or space occupied by or intended for something — see PLACE 1

**sitter** *n* a girl or woman employed to care for a young child or children — see NURSE

**sitting duck** *n* a person or thing that is the object of abuse, criticism, or ridicule — see TARGET 1

**situate** *vb* to arrange something in a certain spot or position — see PLACE 1

**situation** *n* **1** position with regard to conditions and circumstances ⟨the school's *situation* is improving with additional financial help⟩
*syn* footing, picture, posture, scene, status
*rel* rank, standing; place, spot, state; score, status quo
**2** an assignment at which one regularly works for pay — see JOB 1
**3** the placement of someone or something in relation to others in a vertical arrangement — see RANK 1

**sixth sense** *n* the power of seeing or knowing about things that are not present to the senses — see CLAIRVOYANCE

**sizable** *or* **sizeable** *adj* **1** of a size greater than average of its kind — see LARGE
**2** sufficiently large in size, amount, or number to merit attention — see CONSIDERABLE 1

**sizably** *adv* to a large extent or degree — see GREATLY 2

**size** *n* the total amount of measurable space or surface occupied by something ⟨we worried that the immense *size* of the sofa would make getting it through the doorway impossible⟩
*syn* dimension, extent, magnitude, measure, measurement, proportion
*rel* area; capaciousness, commodiousness, roominess, spaciousness; ampleness, amplitude, bigness, bulk, bulkiness, enormousness, grandness, greatness, grossness, heftiness, hugeness, immenseness, immensity, largeness, mass, massiveness, monstrousness, stupendousness, tremendousness, vastness, volume, voluminousness

**size** *n* a substance used to stick things together — see GLUE

**sizzle** *n* a sound similar to the speech sound \s\ stretched out — see HISS 1

**sizzle** *vb* to make a sound like that of stretching out the speech sound \s\ — see HISS

**skeletal** *adj* suffering extreme weight loss as a result of hunger or disease — see EMACIATED

**skeleton** *n* the arrangement of parts that gives something its basic form — see FRAME 1

**skeptic** *n* a person who is always ready to doubt or question the truth or existence of something ⟨the demand by *skeptics* that believers in Bigfoot produce some hard evidence of that hairy humanoid⟩
*syn* disbeliever, doubter, questioner, unbeliever
*rel* cynic, misanthrope, pessimist; derider, ridiculer, scoffer
*near ant* chump, dupe, gull, pigeon, sucker

**skeptical** *adj* **1** inclined to doubt or question claims ⟨it's good to be *skeptical* about what you see on TV⟩
*syn* disbelieving, distrustful, doubting, incredulous, leery, mistrustful, questioning, suspecting, suspicious, unbelieving
*rel* paranoid; critical, puzzled, quizzical; careful, cautious, guarded, leery, wary, watchful; cynical, experienced, knowing, sophisticated, worldly, worldly-wise; curious, inquiring, inquisitive, nosy (*or* nosey), snoopy; uncertain, unconvinced, undecided, undetermined, unsettled, unsure; hesitant
*near ant* green, ingenuous, innocent, naive (*or* naïve), simple, simpleminded, unknowing, unsophisticated, unworldly, wide-eyed; certain, confident, positive, sure; callow, inexperienced, raw; childlike, idealistic, impractical; beguiled, deceived, duped, gulled, tricked; careless, heedless, unsuspecting, unsuspicious, unwary
*ant* credulous, gullible, trustful, trusting, uncritical, unquestioning
**2** not feeling sure about the truth, wisdom, or trustworthiness of someone or something — see DOUBTFUL 1

**skeptically** *adv* with distrust — see ASKANCE

**skepticism** *n* a feeling or attitude that one does not know the truth, truthfulness, or trustworthiness of someone or something — see DOUBT

**sketch** *n* **1** a picture using lines to represent the chief features of an object or scene — see DRAWING
**2** a vivid representation in words of someone or something — see DESCRIPTION 1

**sketch** *vb* **1** to draw or make apparent the outline of — see OUTLINE 1
**2** to give a representation or account of in words — see DESCRIBE 1

**skewed** *adj* inclined or twisted to one side — see AWRY

**skewer** *vb* to penetrate or hold (something) with a pointed object — see IMPALE

**skill** *n* **1** subtle or imaginative ability in inventing, devising, or executing something ⟨with unbelievable *skill*, the expert in origami transformed a few sheets of paper into a menagerie of exotic animals⟩
***syn*** adeptness, adroitness, art, artfulness, artifice, artistry, cleverness, craft, cunning, deftness, masterfulness, skillfulness
***rel*** dexterity, ease, finesse, handiness; experience, expertise, expertness, know-how, proficiency; creativity, ingenuity, inventiveness, knowledge, learning; aptitude, bent, flair, gift, knack, talent
***near ant*** amateurishness, awkwardness, clumsiness, crudeness, rudeness; inability, inadequacy, incapability, incapacity, incompetence, ineffectiveness, ineffectualness, inefficiency
***ant*** artlessness, ineptitude, ineptness, maladroitness
**2 skills** *pl* knowledge gained by actually doing or living through something — see EXPERIENCE 1

**skilled** *adj* having or showing exceptional knowledge, experience, or skill in a field of endeavor — see PROFICIENT

**skillful** *adj* **1** accomplished with trained ability ⟨the ice skater performed a *skillful* and graceful series of jumps⟩
***syn*** adroit, artful, delicate, dexterous (*also* dextrous), expert, masterful, masterly, practiced (*or* practised), virtuoso, workmanlike
***rel*** facile, smooth; artistic, creative, fancy, ingenious, neat; adept, clever, cunning; able, adequate, capable, competent
***near ant*** awkward, clumsy, crude; ineffective, ineffectual; incompetent, inept
***ant*** amateur, amateurish, artless, rude, unprofessional, unskillful
**2** having or showing exceptional knowledge, experience, or skill in a field of endeavor — see PROFICIENT

**skillfully** *adv* in a skillful or expert manner — see WELL 3

**skillfulness** *n* subtle or imaginative ability in inventing, devising, or executing something — see SKILL 1

**skim** *vb* **1** to move or proceed smoothly and readily — see FLOW 2
**2** to pass lightly across or touch gently especially in passing — see BRUSH
**3** to strike and fly off at an angle — see GLANCE 1
**4** to take a quick or hasty look — see GLANCE 2

**skimp** *vb* to avoid unnecessary waste or expense — see ECONOMIZE

**skimp** (on) *vb* to use or give out in stingy amounts — see SPARE

**skimping** *n* careful management of material resources — see ECONOMY

**skimpy** *adj* less plentiful than what is normal, necessary, or desirable — see MEAGER

**skin** *n* **1** an outer part or layer — see EXTERIOR
**2** the outer covering of an animal removed for its commercial value — see HIDE 1
**3** the hairless natural covering of an animal prepared for use — see LEATHER 1

**skin** *vb* **1** to remove the natural covering of — see PEEL
**2** to rob by the use of trickery or threats — see FLEECE

**skin-deep** *adj* **1** lying on or affecting only the outer layer of something — see SUPERFICIAL 1
**2** having or showing a lack of depth of understanding or character — see SUPERFICIAL 2

**skinflint** *n* a mean grasping person who is usually stingy with money — see MISER

**skinny** *adj* **1** being of less than usual width — see NARROW 1
**2** having a noticeably small amount of body fat — see THIN 1

**skip** *vb* **1** to move with a light bouncing step ⟨children *skipping* across the playground⟩
***syn*** bound, hop, lope, trip
***rel*** caper, frisk, gambol, romp; skim, skitter; jump, leap, vault
***near ant*** lumber, plod, trudge
**2** to fail to attend — see CUT 2
**3** to strike and fly off at an angle — see GLANCE 1

**skipper** *n* a person in overall command of a ship — see CAPTAIN 1

**skirmish** *n* **1** a brief clash between enemies or rivals — see ENCOUNTER
**2** a physical dispute between opposing individuals or groups — see FIGHT

**skirmish** (with) *vb* to oppose (someone) in physical conflict — see FIGHT 1

**skirt** *n* the line or relatively narrow space that marks the outer limit of something — see BORDER 1

**skirt** *vb* **1** to avoid by going around — see DETOUR 1
**2** to avoid having to comply with (something) especially through cleverness — see CIRCUMVENT 1
**3** to be adjacent to — see ADJOIN 1
**4** to serve as a border for — see BORDER

**skirting** *adj* having a border in common — see ADJACENT

**skittish** *adj* **1** easily excited by nature — see EXCITABLE
**2** easily frightened — see SHY 1

**skittishness** *n* a state of nervousness marked by sudden jerky movements — see JUMPINESS

**skulk** *vb* to move about in a sly or secret manner — see SNEAK 1

**skulker** *n* someone who acts in a sly and secret manner — see SNEAK

**skull** *n* the case of bone that encloses the brain and supports the jaws of vertebrates ⟨anthropologists just found the *skull* of a prehistoric man in the desert⟩
***syn*** cranium
***rel*** braincase; death's-head; head, noddle, noggin, pate, poll; crown, scalp

**skunk** *n* a person whose behavior is offensive to others — see JERK 1

**skunk** *vb* **1** to defeat by a large margin — see WHIP 2

**2** to achieve a victory over — see BEAT 2

**sky** *n* the expanse of air surrounding the earth ⟨the *sky* usually looks deep blue on a bright clear day⟩

***syn*** blue, firmament, heaven(s), high

***rel*** horizon, skyline

**sky–high** *adv* in an enthusiastic manner ⟨some reviewers had praised the movie *sky-high*, but we thought that it was just a so-so comedy⟩

***syn*** enthusiastically, exuberantly, madly, rhapsodically

***rel*** avidly, eagerly, excitedly, impatiently, keenly; fanatically, rabidly, zealously

***near ant*** aloofly, disinterestedly, impassively, incuriously; hesitantly, reluctantly, unwillingly

***ant*** apathetically, indifferently, lukewarmly, perfunctorily

**skylark** *vb* to engage in attention-getting playful or boisterous behavior — see CUT UP

**skylarking** *n* wildly playful or mischievous behavior — see HORSEPLAY

**skyrocket** *vb* to rise abruptly and rapidly ⟨the price of candy bars in the vending machine has *skyrocketed* over the past few months⟩

***syn*** rocket, shoot (up), soar, zoom

***rel*** accumulate, appreciate, balloon, build (up), burgeon, enlarge, escalate, expand, increase, mount, multiply, mushroom, proliferate, snowball, swell, wax; crest, peak, surge; heighten, intensify

***near ant*** collapse, fall; contract, decrease, diminish, drop, lessen, wane

***ant*** nose-dive, plummet, plunge, slump, tumble

**skyward** *adv* to or in a higher place — see ABOVE

**slack** *adj* **1** failing to give proper care and attention — see NEGLIGENT

**2** not bound by rigid standards — see EASYGOING 2

**3** not tightly fastened, tied, or stretched — see LOOSE 1

**slack** *n* **1** the extent to which something hangs or dips below a straight line — see SAG

**2 slacks** *pl* an outer garment covering each leg separately from waist to ankle — see PANTS

**slack** *vb* to make less taut — see SLACKEN

**slacken** *vb* to make less taut ⟨you'll need to *slacken* the rope a bit to get it free of that post⟩

***syn*** ease, loosen, relax, slack

***rel*** detach, free, unbind, undo, unfasten, untie

***near ant*** attach, bind, fasten, tie; constrain, restrain

***ant*** strain, stretch, tense, tighten

***syn*** synonym(s) ***rel*** related words
***ant*** antonym(s) ***near ant*** near antonym(s)

**slackened** *adj* not tightly fastened, tied, or stretched — see LOOSE 1

**slacker** *n* one who deliberately avoids work or duty ⟨there will be no *slackers* tolerated in this group—anyone who doesn't do their share will get booted out⟩

***syn*** goldbrick, shirker

***rel*** malingerer; dropout, quitter; drone, idler, lazybones, loafer, slouch, slug, sluggard; dallier, lingerer, loiterer, lounger, saunterer; dawdler, laggard, putterer, slowpoke

***near ant*** live wire, powerhouse; doer, go-getter, hummer, hustler, rustler, self-starter

**slackness** *n* **1** failure to take the care that a cautious person usually takes — see NEGLIGENCE 1

**2** the extent to which something hangs or dips below a straight line — see SAG

**slam** *n* **1** a hard strike with a part of the body or an instrument — see BLOW 1

**2** a loud explosive sound — see CLAP 1

**slam** *vb* **1** to shove into a closed position with force and noise ⟨the sulky child ran into her room and *slammed* the door loudly⟩

***syn*** bang

***rel*** close, shut, stop; bar, batten (down), bolt, chain, fasten, latch, lock, seal, secure

***near ant*** open; unbar, unbolt, unfasten, unlatch, unlock, unseal

**2** to deliver a blow to (someone or something) usually in a strong vigorous manner — see HIT 1

**3** to come into usually forceful contact with something — see HIT 2

**4** to criticize harshly and usually publicly — see ATTACK 2

**slander** *n* the making of false statements that damage another's reputation ⟨unhappy that she hadn't won, the girl resorted to *slander* and claimed that the winner's science project had actually been done by his father⟩

***syn*** aspersing, blackening, defamation, defaming, libel, libeling, maligning, smearing, traducing, vilification, vilifying

***rel*** aspersion, innuendo, smear; backbiting, detraction; abuse, invective, vituperation; attack, criticism, censure, denunciation; contempt, disdain, scorn; belittlement, disparagement; cattiness, despite, hatefulness, malevolence, malice, maliciousness, malignancy, malignity, meanness, nastiness, spite, spitefulness, spleen, venom, viciousness

***near ant*** acclaim, accolade, applause, commendation, praise; esteem, honor, respect; adulation, flattery; adoration, reverence, veneration, worship

**slander** *vb* to make untrue and harmful statements about ⟨for some reason, that newspaper seems determined to *slander* one particular celebrity⟩

***syn*** asperse, blacken, defame, libel, malign, smear, traduce, vilify

*rel* belittle, detract, disparage; discredit, disgrace, dishonor, shame; abase, debase, degrade, humble, humiliate; disdain, scorn
*near ant* exalt, glorify, honor; acclaim, applaud, commend, praise; esteem, respect; admire, regard; adore, revere, venerate, worship

**slanderous** *adj* causing or intended to cause unjust injury to a person's good name — see LIBELOUS

**slang** *n* the special terms or expressions of a particular group or field — see TERMINOLOGY

**slant** *n* **1** the degree to which something rises up from a position level with the horizon ⟨the road has just enough of a *slant* to make bicycling up it a little strenuous⟩
*syn* cant, diagonal, grade, gradient, inclination, incline, lean, pitch, slope, tilt, upgrade
*rel* ascent, bank, climb, rise
*near ant* declension, declination, decline, declivity, descent, dip, downgrade, fall, receding
**2** a way of looking at or thinking about something — see POINT OF VIEW

**slant** *vb* to set or cause to be at an angle — see LEAN 1

**slanted** *adj* **1** inclined or twisted to one side — see AWRY
**2** running in a slanting direction — see DIAGONAL

**slanting** *adj* inclined or twisted to one side — see AWRY

**slantways** *adv* so as to slant — see SLANTWISE

**slantwise** *adj* **1** inclined or twisted to one side — see AWRY
**2** running in a slanting direction — see DIAGONAL

**slantwise** *adv* so as to slant ⟨be careful not to lay the first boards *slantwise*, or the whole bookcase won't be straight⟩
*syn* slantways
*rel* down, downward (*or* downwards), up, upward (*or* upwards)

**slap** *n* a hard strike with a part of the body or an instrument — see [1]BLOW

**slap** *vb* to deliver a blow to (someone or something) usually in a strong vigorous manner — see HIT 1

**slapdash** *adj* lacking a definite plan, purpose, or pattern — see RANDOM

**slapjack** *n* a flat cake made from thin batter and cooked on both sides (as on a griddle) — see PANCAKE

**slapstick** *n* humorous entertainment — see COMEDY

**slash** *n* a long deep cut — see GASH

**slash** *vb* **1** to penetrate with a sharp edge (as a knife) — see CUT 1
**2** to strike repeatedly with something long and thin or flexible — see WHIP 1

**slate** *adj* of the color gray — see GRAY 1

**slate** *vb* to put (someone or something) on a list — see [1]LIST 2

**slated** *adj* being in accordance with the prescribed, normal, or logical course of events — see DUE 2

**slaty** *adj* of the color gray — see GRAY 1

**slaughter** *n* the killing of a large number of people — see MASSACRE

**slaughter** *vb* to kill on a large scale — see MASSACRE

**slave** *n* **1** a person who is considered the property of another person ⟨many American *slaves* reached freedom in the North through the network known as the Underground Railroad⟩
*syn* bondman, bondsman, chattel, thrall
*rel* helot, serf; attendant, domestic, drudge, lackey, menial, servant
*near ant* freedman; enslaver, slave driver, slaveholder, slaver; master, taskmaster
*ant* freeman
**2** a person who does very hard or dull work ⟨unappreciated office *slaves* who perform the necessary but tedious task of filing paperwork⟩
*syn* drudge, drudger, fag, grubber, laborer, peon, plugger, slogger, toiler, worker
*rel* workhorse; coolie, serf
*near ant* goldbrick, shirker; drone, idler, lazybones, loafer, slouch, slug, sluggard

**slave** *vb* to devote serious and sustained effort — see LABOR

**slave** (for) *vb* to be a servant for — see SERVE 1

**slave driver** *n* a boss who assigns much work — see TASKMASTER 1

**slaver** *vb* to let saliva or some other substance flow from the mouth — see DROOL

**slavery** *n* **1** the state of being a slave ⟨a child born into *slavery* was considered simply another addition to the master's wealth and property⟩
*syn* bondage, enslavement, servility, servitude, thrall, thralldom (*or* thraldom), yoke
*rel* peonage, serfdom; dependence, subjection, subjugation; captivity, enchainment, imprisonment, incarceration
*near ant* emancipation, enfranchisement, liberation, manumission; autonomy, independence, self-government, sovereignty
*ant* freedom, liberty
**2** very hard or unpleasant work — see TOIL

**slavish** *adj* using or marked by the use of something else as a basis or model — see IMITATIVE

**slavishly** *adv* with great effort or determination — see HARD 1

**slay** *vb* **1** to deprive of life — see KILL 1
**2** to put to death deliberately — see MURDER 1

**slaying** *n* the intentional and unlawful taking of another person's life — see HOMICIDE

**sleazy** *adj* of low quality — see CHEAP 2

**sleek** *adj* having a shiny surface or finish — see GLOSSY

**sleep** *n* **1** a natural periodic loss of consciousness during which the body re-

stores itself ⟨eight hours of *sleep* or more are necessary for children and teenagers to function⟩
*syn* catnapping, dozing, napping, repose, rest, resting, slumber, slumbering, snoozing
*rel* catnap, doze, drowse, forty winks, nap, siesta, snooze, wink; oversleeping; dreaming, rapid eye movement
*near ant* insomnia, sleeplessness
*ant* consciousness, wakefulness
**2** the state of being dead — see DEATH 2

**sleep** *vb* **1** be in a state of sleep ⟨the baby *slept* for the entire length of the car trip⟩
*syn* catnap, doze, nap, rest, slumber, snooze
*rel* drowse (off), nod (off); oversleep; dream, hibernate
*near ant* arise, arouse, awake, rise
**2** to engage in sexual intercourse — see COPULATE

**sleeper** *n* one who sleeps ⟨Joe is a restless *sleeper* who always wakes up with the covers kicked off⟩
*syn* dozer, slumberer
*rel* nodder
*near ant* insomniac; riser, waker

**sleepiness** *n* the quality or state of desiring or needing sleep ⟨Sarah suffered such *sleepiness* in class that there were days when she could hardly keep her eyes open⟩
*syn* drowsiness, somnolence
*rel* lassitude, lethargy, sluggishness, torpor; dozing, resting, sleeping, slumbering; oversleeping
*near ant* awareness, consciousness
*ant* insomnia, sleeplessness, wakefulness

**sleeping** *adj* being in a state of suspended consciousness — see ASLEEP 1

**sleepless** *adj* not sleeping or able to sleep — see WAKEFUL

**sleepy** *adj* **1** desiring or needing sleep ⟨the *sleepy* children were carried up to bed⟩
*syn* drowsy, slumberous (*or* slumbrous), somnolent
*rel* asleep, dormant, dozing, resting, sleeping, slumbering; nodding, yawning
*near ant* restive, restless, sleepless
*ant* alert, awake, conscious, wakeful, wide-awake
**2** slow to move or act — see INACTIVE 1

**sleight** *n* **1** a clever often underhanded means to achieve an end — see TRICK 1
**2** mental skill or quickness — see DEXTERITY 1
**3** ease and grace in physical activity — see DEXTERITY 2

**slender** *adj* **1** being of less than usual width — see NARROW 1
**2** having a noticeably small amount of body fat — see THIN 1
**3** less plentiful than what is normal, necessary, or desirable — see MEAGER

**sleuth** *n* a person whose business is solving crimes and catching criminals or gathering information that is not easy to get — see DETECTIVE

**slice** *n* a piece that has been separated from the whole by cutting — see CUT 1

**slice** *vb* **1** to cut into long slender pieces — see SLIVER
**2** to penetrate with a sharp edge (as a knife) — see CUT 1

**slick** *adj* **1** having or being a surface so smooth as to make sliding or falling likely ⟨roads are often *slick* during the first hour of a rainstorm⟩
*syn* greased, greasy, lubricated, oiled, slicked, slippery, slithery
*rel* brushed, buffed, burnished, glossed, ground, polished, rubbed, shined; coated, glazed, waxed; soapy, waxy; rasped, sandblasted, sanded, sandpapered, scoured, scraped, scrubbed
*near ant* coarsened, rough, roughened, scuffed, uneven
**2** clever at attaining one's ends by indirect and often deceptive means — see ARTFUL 1

**slick** *vb* to coat (something) with a slippery substance in order to reduce friction — see LUBRICATE

**slicked** *adj* having or being a surface so smooth as to make sliding or falling likely — see SLICK 1

**slicker** *n* a coat made of water-resistant material — see RAINCOAT

**slickness** *n* skill in achieving one's ends through indirect, subtle, or underhanded means — see CUNNING 1

**slide** *vb* **1** to move about in a sly or secret manner — see SNEAK 1
**2** to move or proceed smoothly and readily — see FLOW 2

**slight** *adj* **1** lacking bodily strength — see WEAK 1
**2** lacking importance — see UNIMPORTANT
**3** of a size that is less than average — see SMALL 1
**4** so small or unimportant as to warrant little or no attention — see NEGLIGIBLE 1
**5** small in degree — see REMOTE 1

**slight** *n* an act or expression showing scorn and usually intended to hurt another's feelings — see INSULT

**slight** *vb* **1** to cause hurt feelings or deep resentment in — see INSULT
**2** to deliberately ignore or treat rudely — see SNUB 1
**3** to show contempt for — see SCORN 1
**4** to fail to give proper attention to — see NEGLECT 1

**slightest** *adj* being the least in amount, number, or size possible — see MINIMAL

**slighting** *adj* intended to make a person or thing seem of little importance or value — see DEROGATORY

**slightly** *adv* **1** by a very small margin — see JUST 2
**2** in a very small quantity or degree — see LITTLE 1

**slightness** *n* **1** the quality or state of being little in size — see SMALLNESS

2 the state or quality of having little weight — see [1]LIGHTNESS 1

**slim** *adj* **1** being of less than usual width — see NARROW 1
**2** having a noticeably small amount of body fat — see THIN 1
**3** less plentiful than what is normal, necessary, or desirable — see MEAGER
**4** small in degree — see REMOTE 1

**slime** *n* soft wet earth — see MUD

**slimy** *adj* full of or covered with soft wet earth — see MUDDY 1

[1]**sling** *vb* to place on an elevated point without support from below — see HANG 1

[2]**sling** *vb* to send through the air especially with a quick forward motion of the arm — see THROW

**slink** *vb* to move about in a sly or secret manner — see SNEAK 1

[1]**slip** *n* a long narrow piece of material — see STRIP

[2]**slip** *n* **1** an unintentional departure from truth or accuracy — see ERROR 1
**2** the act of going down from an upright position suddenly and involuntarily — see FALL 1
**3** the act or an instance of getting free from danger or confinement — see ESCAPE 1

**slip** *vb* **1** to decline gradually from a standard level ⟨Susie's grades *slipped* somewhat after she joined five after-school activities⟩
***syn*** sag
***rel*** drop, fall, slump; flag, sink, slacken, slow (down), weaken; abate, contract, decrease, de-escalate, die (down), diminish, dwindle, ebb, lessen, let up, lower, moderate, recede, relent, shrink, subside, taper, taper off, wane
***near ant*** rocket, shoot (up), soar; balloon, burgeon, enlarge, escalate, expand, increase, mount, multiply, mushroom, proliferate, snowball, swell, wax; crest, peak, surge
**2** to go down from an upright position suddenly and involuntarily — see FALL 1
**3** to introduce in a gradual, secret, or clever way — see INSINUATE
**4** to move about in a sly or secret manner — see SNEAK 1
**5** to move or proceed smoothly and readily — see FLOW 2

**slip** (on *or* into) *vb* to place on one's person — see PUT ON 1

**slippery** *adj* **1** given to acting in secret and to concealing one's intentions — see SNEAKY 1
**2** hard to find, capture, or isolate — see ELUSIVE
**3** having or being a surface so smooth as to make sliding or falling likely — see SLICK 1

**slipup** *n* an unintentional departure from truth or accuracy — see ERROR 1

**slit** *n* a long deep cut — see GASH

**slit** *vb* to penetrate with a sharp edge (as a knife) — see CUT 1

**slither** *vb* to move slowly with the body close to the ground — see CRAWL 1

**slithery** *adj* having or being a surface so smooth as to make sliding or falling likely — see SLICK 1

**sliver** *n* a small flat piece separated from a whole — see CHIP 1

**sliver** *vb* to cut into long slender pieces ⟨carefully *slivered* the rattan stems into strips for basketry⟩
***syn*** slice, splinter
***rel*** chip, chop, dice, hash, mince; saw, scissor; cleave, rive, split; gash, incise, rip, slash, slit

**slob** *n* **1** a dirty or sloppy person ⟨only a *slob* would let his bedroom get so messy that his own mother couldn't remember what the floor looked like⟩
***syn*** sloven
***rel*** slattern, slut
***near ant*** cleaner
***ant*** old maid
**2** a person whose behavior is offensive to others — see JERK 1

**slobber** *n* the fluid that is secreted into the mouth by certain glands — see SALIVA

**slobber** *vb* **1** to let saliva or some other substance flow from the mouth — see DROOL
**2** to make an exaggerated display of affection or enthusiasm — see GUSH 2

**slog** *vb* **1** to deliver a blow to (someone or something) usually in a strong vigorous manner — see HIT 1
**2** to devote serious and sustained effort — see LABOR

**slogan** *n* an attention-getting word or phrase used to publicize something (as a campaign or product) ⟨within days, virtually everyone was familiar with the newest advertising *slogan* for that brand of soda⟩
***syn*** cry, shibboleth, watchword
***rel*** tag line; expression, idiom; cliché; maxim, motto

**slogger** *n* a person who does very hard or dull work — see SLAVE 2

**slop** *n* **1** soft wet earth — see MUD
**2 slops** *pl* solid matter discharged from an animal's alimentary canal — see DROPPING 1

**slope** *n* the degree to which something rises up from a position level with the horizon — see SLANT

**slope** *vb* to set or cause to be at an angle — see LEAN 1

**sloped** *adj* running in a slanting direction — see DIAGONAL

**sloping** *adj* running in a slanting direction — see DIAGONAL

**sloppily** *adv* in a careless or unfashionable manner ⟨everyone dressed *sloppily* for the task of cleaning out the garage⟩
***syn*** dowdily, slovenly, unstylishly
***rel*** slatternly; chaotically, messily, untidily; shabbily, sleazily; dingily, dirtily, filthily, foully, grubbily, nastily
***near ant*** neatly, orderly, tidily; fashionably, modishly; carefully, fastidiously, fussily, meticulously; cleanly, immaculately, spotlessly
***ant*** nattily, sharply, smartly, sprucely

**sloppiness** *n* the state or quality of having an excess of tender feelings (as of love, nostalgia, or compassion) — see SENTIMENTALITY

**sloppy** *adj* **1** lacking neatness in dress or person ⟨a *sloppy* child who always seems to have spilled something on his clothes⟩
*syn* dowdy, frowsy (*or* frowzy), slovenly, unkempt, untidy
*rel* slatternly, sluttish; chaotic, cluttered, confused, disarranged, disheveled (*or* dishevelled), disordered, messed, messy, muddled, mussed, mussy, rumpled, uncombed, wrinkled; shabby, sleazy; besmirched, blackened, dingy, dirty, filthy, foul, grimy, grubby, grungy, mucky, nasty, soiled, spotted, squalid, stained, sullied, unclean, uncleanly
*near ant* chic, fashionable, modish, stylish; combed, groomed; neat, ordered, orderly, tidy; careful, fastidious, fussy, meticulous; clean, cleaned, cleanly, immaculate, sparkling, spotless, stainless, unsoiled, unsullied
*ant* dapper, dashing, dolled up, sharp, smart, spruce
**2** lacking in order, neatness, and often cleanliness — see MESSY
**3** appealing to the emotions in an obvious and tiresome way — see CORNY

**slosh** *vb* to move with a splashing motion ⟨the baby gurgled contentedly as the water *sloshed* gently around him in the bathtub⟩
*syn* lap, plash, splash, swash
*rel* babble, bubble, gurgle, ripple

**sloth** *n* an inclination not to do work or engage in activities — see LAZINESS

**slothful** *adj* not easily aroused to action or work — see LAZY

**slouch** *n* a lazy person — see LAZYBONES

**slough** *also* **slue** *n* spongy land saturated or partially covered with water — see SWAMP

**slough** *also* **sluff** *vb* **1** to cast (a natural bodily covering or appendage) aside — see SHED 1
**2** to get rid of as useless or unwanted — see DISCARD

**sloven** *n* a dirty or sloppy person — see SLOB 1

**slovenly** *adj* lacking neatness in dress or person — see SLOPPY 1

**slovenly** *adv* in a careless or unfashionable manner — see SLOPPILY

**slow** *adj* **1** moving or proceeding at less than the normal, desirable, or required speed ⟨because of the holiday, traffic to the beach was particularly *slow*⟩ ⟨*slow* readers⟩
*syn* crawling, creeping, dallying, dawdling, dilatory, dillydallying, dragging, laggard, lagging, languid, leisurely, poking, poky (*or* pokey), sluggish, tardy, unhurried
*rel* deliberate, measured; inactive, inert, lethargic, loafing, lounging; lingering, loitering, tarrying; ambling, inching, plodding, shuffling, strolling; decelerating, slowing; filibustering, procrastinating, stalling
*near ant* expeditious, prompt, ready; accelerated, hastened, quickened; hurried, rushed
*ant* barreling, bolting, breakneck, breathless, brisk, careering, dizzy, fast, fleet, flying, hasty, hurrying, lightning, quick, racing, rapid, rocketing, running, rushing, scooting, scudding, scurrying, snappy, speeding; speedy, swift, whirling, whirlwind, whisking, zipping
**2** not having or showing an ability to absorb ideas readily — see STUPID 1

**slow** *adv* at a pace that is less than usual, desirable, or expected ⟨you need to go *slow* with this experiment, or you'll make mistakes⟩
*syn* laggardly, leisurely, slowly, sluggishly, tardily
*rel* carefully, cautiously, deliberately, purposefully; ploddingly
*near ant* immediately, posthaste, presto, promptly, pronto, readily, soon; impetuously, impulsively, rashly, recklessly; abruptly, suddenly
*ant* apace, briskly, fast, fleetly, full tilt, hastily, quick, quickly, rapidly, snappily, speedily, swift, swiftly

**slow** *vb* to cause to move or proceed at a less rapid pace ⟨if you don't *slow* your delivery down a bit, your speech will be over too soon⟩
*syn* brake, decelerate, retard
*rel* halt, stop; encumber, hamper, handicap, hinder, hobble, hold back, hold up, impede, inhibit, obstruct, tie up; arrest, check, constrain, curb, rein, restrain; baffle, foil, frustrate, sabotage, thwart
*near ant* drive, encourage, goad, propel, push, spur, stir, urge; advance, aid, dispatch, ease, expedite, facilitate, forward, further, help
*ant* accelerate, hasten, hurry, quicken, rush, speed (up), step up

**slowdown** *n* a usually gradual decrease in the pace or level of activity of something ⟨disease experts are encouraged by the recent *slowdown* in the spread of the virus⟩
*syn* braking, deceleration, letup, retardation, retarding
*rel* decline, drop, slump; ebb, remission, retreat, wane; flagging, weakening; arrest, check, halt, stoppage; collapse, crash, fall, plunge
*ant* acceleration, hastening, quickening

**slowly** *adv* at a pace that is less than usual, desirable, or expected — see SLOW

**slowness** *n* the quality or state of lacking intelligence or quickness of mind — see STUPIDITY 1

**slowpoke** *n* someone who moves slowly or more slowly than others ⟨quit being such a *slowpoke* this morning, or you'll be late⟩

*syn* crawler, creeper, dallier, dawdler, dragger, laggard, lagger, lingerer, loiterer, snail, stick-in-the-mud, straggler
*rel* latecomer; drone, idler, lazybones, loafer, lounger, slouch, slug, sluggard; delayer, procrastinator
*near ant* go-getter, hustler, scrambler; hurrier, rusher, speeder
*ant* speedster

**sludge** *n* soft wet earth — see MUD

**sludgy** *adj* full of or covered with soft wet earth — see MUDDY 1

**[1]slug** *n* a hard strike with a part of the body or an instrument — see [1]BLOW

**[2]slug** *n* **1** a lazy person — see LAZYBONES
**2** the portion of a serving of a beverage that is swallowed at one time — see DRINK 2

**slug** *vb* to deliver a blow to (someone or something) usually in a strong vigorous manner — see HIT 1

**sluggard** *n* a lazy person — see LAZYBONES

**sluggish** *adj* **1** moving or proceeding at less than the normal, desirable, or required speed — see SLOW 1
**2** slow to move or act — see INACTIVE 1

**sluggishly** *adv* at a pace that is less than usual, desirable, or expected — see SLOW

**sluice** *vb* to pour liquid over or through in order to cleanse — see FLUSH 1

**slumber** *n* a natural periodic loss of consciousness during which the body restores itself — see SLEEP 1

**slumber** *vb* **1** be in a state of sleep — see SLEEP 1
**2** to sleep lightly or briefly — see NAP 1

**slumberer** *n* one who sleeps — see SLEEPER

**slumbering** *adj* being in a state of suspended consciousness — see ASLEEP 1

**slumbering** *n* a natural periodic loss of consciousness during which the body restores itself — see SLEEP 1

**slumberous** *or* **slumbrous** *adj* **1** desiring or needing sleep — see SLEEPY 1
**2** tending to cause sleep — see HYPNOTIC

**slump** *n* a period of decreased economic activity — see DEPRESSION 1

**slur** *n* an act or expression showing scorn and usually intended to hurt another's feelings — see INSULT

**slur** (over) *vb* to fail to give proper attention to — see NEGLECT 1

**slurp** *vb* to swallow in liquid form — see DRINK 1

**slush** *n* **1** language, behavior, or ideas that are absurd and contrary to good sense — see NONSENSE 1
**2** soft wet earth — see MUD

**slushy** *adj* full of or covered with soft wet earth — see MUDDY 1

**sly** *adj* **1** clever at attaining one's ends by indirect and often deceptive means — see ARTFUL 1
**2** given to acting in secret and to concealing one's intentions — see SNEAKY 1
**3** tending to or exhibiting reckless playfulness — see MISCHIEVOUS 1

**slyness** *n* skill in achieving one's ends through indirect, subtle, or underhanded means — see CUNNING 1

**smack** *n* a hard strike with a part of the body or an instrument — see [1]BLOW

**smack** *vb* to deliver a blow to (someone or something) usually in a strong vigorous manner — see HIT 1

**smack–dab** *adv* as stated or indicated without the slightest difference — see EXACTLY 1

**small** *adj* **1** of a size that is less than average ⟨a *small* cat who never weighed more than five pounds⟩
*syn* bantam, diminutive, dinky, dwarf, dwarfish, fine, little, pint-size (*or* pint-sized), pocket, pocket-size (*also* pocket-sized), puny, pygmy, slight, smallish, undersized
*rel* petite; scrubby, stunted; bitty, inappreciable, infinitesimal, micro, microscopic (*also* microscopical), midget, miniature, miniaturized, minute, teeny, teeny-weeny, tiny, wee; underweight; meager (*or* meagre), niggardly, poor, scant, scanty, scarce, skimpy, slender, slim, spare, sparse, stingy; deficient, inadequate, insufficient, lacking, wanting
*near ant* bulky, hefty, hulking, massive, voluminous; cavernous, colossal, elephantine, enormous, giant, gigantic, gross, Herculean, heroic, huge, immense, jumbo, mammoth, monolithic, monstrous, monumental, prodigious, staggering, stupendous, tremendous, vast; abundant, ample, appreciable, bountiful, copious, generous, healthy, liberal, plenteous, plentiful; fat, thick; broad, wide; boundless, cosmic, immeasurable, infinite; adequate, enough, sufficient
*ant* big, bumper, considerable, goodly, good-sized, grand, great, handsome, king-size (*or* king-sized), large, largish, outsize (*also* outsized), oversize (*or* oversized), sizable (*or* sizeable), substantial, super, whacking, whopping
**2** small in degree — see REMOTE 1
**3** lacking importance — see UNIMPORTANT
**4** not broad or open in views or opinions — see NARROW 2

**small arm** *n* a portable weapon from which a shot is discharged by gunpowder — see GUN 1

**smaller** *adj* having not so great importance or rank as another — see LESSER

**small–fry** *adj* lacking importance — see UNIMPORTANT

**smallish** *adj* of a size that is less than average — see SMALL 1

**small–minded** *adj* **1** unwilling to grant other people social rights or to accept other viewpoints — see INTOLERANT 2
**2** not broad or open in views or opinions — see NARROW 2

**smallness** *n* the quality or state of being little in size ⟨my grandmother was surprised by the *smallness* of the latest electronic devices⟩

*syn* diminutiveness, fineness, littleness, puniness, slightness
*rel* minuteness, tininess; meagerness, poorness, scantiness, scarceness, scarcity, skimpiness, slenderness, slimness, spareness, sparseness, stinginess; deficiency, inadequacy
*near ant* enormity, enormousness, grossness, hugeness, immenseness, immensity, stupendousness; extensiveness, vastness; excessiveness, extravagance, extremeness, immoderacy; abundance, ampleness, bountifulness, copiousness, healthiness, liberality; adequacy, sufficiency; heaviness, heftiness, weightiness; bulkiness, massiveness, voluminousness
*ant* bigness, grandness, greatness, largeness, magnitude

**small talk** *n* friendly, informal conversation or an instance of this — see CHAT

**smart** *adj* **1** being strikingly neat and trim in style or appearance ⟨dressed in their *smart* new uniforms, the cadets proudly paraded around the grounds of the military school⟩
*syn* dapper, natty, sharp, spruce
*rel* dressy, elegant, formal; neat, orderly, tidy; fashionable, modish, stylish; careful, fastidious, fussy, meticulous; clean, immaculate, spotless
*near ant* messy, untidy; shabby, sleazy; dingy, dirty, filthy, foul, grimy, grubby, nasty; dowdy, inelegant, unfashionable, unstylish
*ant* sloppy, slovenly
**2** being in the latest or current fashion — see STYLISH
**3** causing intense mental or physical distress — see SHARP 2
**4** given to or marked by mature intelligent humor — see WITTY
**5** making light of something usually regarded as serious or sacred — see FLIPPANT
**6** having or showing a practical cleverness or judgment — see SHREWD
**7** having or showing quickness of mind — see INTELLIGENT 1
**8** having a wide and refined knowledge of the world especially from personal experience — see WORLDLY-WISE

**smart** *n* a sharp unpleasant sensation usually felt in some specific part of the body — see PAIN 1

**smart** *vb* to feel or cause physical pain — see HURT 1

**smart aleck** *n* a person who likes to show off in a clever but annoying way ⟨some *smart aleck* in the audience kept shouting clever insults at the speaker⟩
*syn* smarty (*or* smartie), wiseacre, wise guy
*rel* know-it-all; wisecracker; hotshot, show-off

**smart–alecky** *or* **smart–aleck** *adj* **1** making light of something usually regarded as serious or sacred — see FLIPPANT
**2** marked by the use of wit that is intended to cause hurt feelings — see SARCASTIC

**smarting** *adj* **1** causing intense discomfort to one's skin — see CUTTING 1
**2** causing intense mental or physical distress — see SHARP 2

**smartly** *adv* in a strikingly neat and trim manner ⟨the *smartly* dressed scouts marched at the head of the Memorial Day parade⟩
*syn* dashingly, nattily, sharply, sprucely
*rel* neatly, orderly, tidily, trimly; elegantly, fashionably, modishly, stylishly, swankily; carefully, fastidiously, fussily, meticulously; cleanly, immaculately, spotlessly
*near ant* dowdily, inelegantly, unstylishly; slatternly; messily, untidily; shabbily, sleazily; dingily, dirtily, filthily, foully, grubbily, nastily
*ant* sloppily, slovenly

**smarty** *or* **smartie** *n* a person who likes to show off in a clever but annoying way — see SMART ALECK

**smash** *n* **1** a forceful coming together of two things — see IMPACT 1
**2** the violent coming together of two bodies into destructive contact — see CRASH 1
**3** a hard strike with a part of the body or an instrument — see [1]BLOW
**4** a loud explosive sound — see CLAP 1
**5** a person or thing that is successful — see HIT 1

**smash** *vb* **1** to cause to break with violence and much noise ⟨deliberately *smashed* a glass against the brick fireplace⟩
*syn* crash, shatter
*rel* bust, fracture, fragment; bash, demolish, destroy, pulverize, ruin, wreck; shiver, splinter, split; crack, crunch, crush, snap
**2** to cause to break open or into pieces by or as if by an explosive — see BLAST 1
**3** to bring to a complete end the physical soundness, existence, or usefulness of — see DESTROY 1
**4** to come into usually forceful contact with something — see HIT 2

**smashup** *n* the violent coming together of two bodies into destructive contact — see CRASH 1

**smattering** *n* a small number — see FEW

**smear** *vb* **1** to rub an oily or sticky substance over ⟨the toddler gleefully *smeared* her hair and face with maple syrup⟩
*syn* anoint, bedaub, besmear, daub
*rel* coat, paint, plaster; grease, oil; gum, lard, pitch, tar; begrime, besmirch, blacken, dirty, foul, grime, mire, muddy, smirch, smudge, soil, stain, sully
**2** to make untrue and harmful statements about — see SLANDER

**smearing** *n* the making of false statements that damage another's reputation — see SLANDER

**smell** *n* the quality of a thing that makes it perceptible to the sense organs in the

nose ⟨the *smell* of vanilla is supposed to be very soothing⟩
*syn* odor, redolence, scent, sniff
*rel* whiff; aroma, bouquet, fragrance, perfume; ambrosia, lusciousness, savor, savoriness, spice, tang; acridness, fetidness, foulness, noisomeness, rancidity, rankness, stench, stink; incense, musk
**smell** *vb* **1** to become aware of by means of the sense organs in the nose ⟨we *smelled* the aroma of freshly baked cookies as soon as we walked in the house⟩
*syn* nose, scent, sniff, whiff
*rel* breathe, drink (in), inhale
**2** to have a vague awareness of — see FEEL 1
**smelly** *adj* having an unpleasant smell — see MALODOROUS
**smidgen** *also* **smidgeon** *or* **smidgin** *n* a very small amount — see PARTICLE 1
**smile** *vb* **1** to express an emotion (as amusement) by curving the lips upward ⟨he *smiled* in pleasure when he saw the giant sign welcoming him home⟩
*syn* beam, grin
*rel* laugh, simper; smirk, sneer
*near ant* grimace; frown, glare, glower, scowl
**2** to express scornful amusement by means of facial contortions — see SNEER
**smirch** *n* a mark of guilt or disgrace — see STAIN 1
**smirch** *vb* **1** to make dirty — see DIRTY
**2** to reduce to a lower standing in one's own eyes or in others' eyes — see HUMBLE
**smite** *vb* to deliver a blow to (someone or something) usually in a strong vigorous manner — see HIT 1
**smog** *n* an atmospheric condition in which suspended particles in the air rob it of its transparency — see HAZE 1
**smoggy** *adj* filled with or dimmed by fine particles (as of dust or water) in suspension — see HAZY 1
**smooch** *vb* to touch one another with the lips as a sign of love — see KISS 1
**smooth** *adj* **1** having or showing very polished and worldly manners — see SUAVE
**2** involving minimal difficulty or effort — see EASY 1
**3** having a surface without bends, breaks, or irregularities — see LEVEL
**smooth** *vb* **1** to free from obstruction or difficulty — see EASE 1
**2** to make free from breaks, curves, or bumps — see EVEN 1
**3** to make smooth or glossy usually by repeatedly applying surface pressure — see POLISH
**smoothly** *adv* without difficulty — see EASILY
**smother** *vb* **1** to be or cause to be killed by lack of breathable air ⟨you should never play inside discarded appliances because you could become trapped and *smother*⟩
*syn* choke, stifle, strangle, suffocate
*rel* garrote (*or* garotte), throttle; asphyxiate; drown
*near ant* breathe, exhale, expire, inhale, inspire
**2** to refrain from openly showing or uttering — see SUPPRESS 2
**smudge** *vb* to make dirty — see DIRTY
**smug** *adj* having too high an opinion of oneself — see CONCEITED
**smugness** *n* an often unjustified feeling of being pleased with oneself or with one's situation or achievements — see COMPLACENCE
**smut** *n* foul matter that mars the purity or cleanliness of something — see FILTH 1
**smuttiness** *n* the quality or state of being obscene — see OBSCENITY 1
**smutty** *adj* **1** depicting or referring to sexual matters in a way that is unacceptable in polite society — see OBSCENE 1
**2** not clean — see DIRTY 1
**snag** *n* a danger or difficulty that is hidden or not easily recognized — see PITFALL 1
**snail** *n* someone who moves slowly or more slowly than others — see SLOWPOKE
**snake** *n* **1** a limbless reptile with a long body ⟨*snakes* are cold-blooded, so they regulate their body temperature by alternately basking in sunlight and seeking shade⟩
*syn* serpent, viper
*rel* adder, anaconda, asp, blacksnake, boa, bull snake, bushmaster, cobra, constrictor, copperhead, coral snake, cottonmouth, mocca-sin, diamondback rattlesnake, fer-de-lance, garter snake, glass snake, gopher snake, green snake, hognose snake, indigo snake, king cobra, king snake, krait, mamba, milk snake, pit viper, puff adder, python, racer, rat snake, rattlesnake, sea serpent, sidewinder, water moccasin, water snake
**2** a person whose behavior is offensive to others — see JERK 1
**snake** *vb* **1** to move about in a sly or secret manner — see SNEAK 1
**2** to move slowly with the body close to the ground — see CRAWL 1
**snap** *adj* **1** involving minimal difficulty or effort — see EASY 1
**2** made or done without previous thought or preparation — see EXTEMPORANEOUS
**snap** *n* **1** a loud explosive sound — see CLAP 1
**2** a picture created from an image recorded on a light-sensitive surface by a camera — see PHOTOGRAPH
**3** active strength of body or mind — see VIGOR 1
**4** a weather condition marked by low temperatures — see COLD
**5** a very small amount — see PARTICLE 1
**6** something that is easy to do — see CINCH
**snap** *vb* **1** to speak sharply or irritably ⟨the shopkeeper finally *snapped* at one customer who couldn't seem to make up his mind⟩
*syn* bark, snarl
*rel* shout, yell; blow up, explode

2 to break suddenly with an explosive sound — see CRACK 1
3 to take a photograph of — see PHOTOGRAPH

**snap** (up) *vb* to take physical control or posses-sion of (something) suddenly or forcibly — see CATCH 1

**snapback** *n* the process or period of gradually regaining one's health and strength — see CONVALESCENCE

**snap back** *vb* 1 to become healthy and strong again after illness or weakness — see CONVALESCE
2 to regain a former or normal state — see RECOVER 2

**snappily** *adv* with great speed — see FAST 1

**snappish** *adj* easily irritated or annoyed — see IRRITABLE

**snappy** *adj* 1 being in the latest or current fashion — see STYLISH
2 easily irritated or annoyed — see IRRITABLE
3 having a low or subnormal temperature — see COLD 1
4 having much high-spirited energy and movement — see LIVELY 1
5 moving, proceeding, or acting with great speed — see FAST 1

**snapshot** *n* a picture created from an image recorded on a light-sensitive surface by a camera — see PHOTOGRAPH

**snare** *n* 1 a device or scheme for capturing another by surprise — see TRAP 1
2 something that catches and holds — see WEB 1

**snare** *vb* 1 to catch or hold as if in a net — see ENTANGLE 2
2 to take physical control or possession of (something) suddenly or forcibly — see CATCH 1

[1]**snarl** *vb* to speak sharply or irritably — see SNAP 1

[2]**snarl** *vb* to twist together into a usually confused mass — see ENTANGLE 1

**snatch** *vb* to take physical control or possession of (something) suddenly or forcibly — see CATCH 1

**snatching** *n* an instance of theft — see THEFT 2

**snazzy** *adj* attractively eye-catching in style — see JAZZY 1

**sneak** *adj* undertaken or done so as to escape being observed or known by others — see SECRET 1

**sneak** *n* someone who acts in a sly and secret manner ⟨"Why, you little *sneak*," Mom exclaimed, "you made my birthday present right under my nose!"⟩
*syn* lurker, skulker
*rel* skunk, snake; sharper, slicker, swindler; stalker

**sneak** *vb* 1 to move about in a sly or secret manner ⟨the little kids *sneak* around upstairs when they're supposed to be in bed⟩
*syn* lurk, mouse, pussyfoot, skulk, slide, slink, slip, snake, steal
*rel* crawl, creep, edge, inch, worm; pad, tiptoe
2 to introduce in a gradual, secret, or clever way — see INSINUATE

**sneakiness** *n* skill in achieving one's ends through indirect, subtle, or underhanded means — see CUNNING 1

**sneaking** *adj* 1 given to acting in secret and to concealing one's intentions — see SNEAKY 1
2 undertaken or done so as to escape being observed or known by others — see SECRET 1

**sneaky** *adj* 1 given to acting in secret and to concealing one's intentions ⟨the *sneaky* little girl was clearly up to something⟩
*syn* furtive, shady, shifty, slippery, sly, sneaking, stealthy
*rel* devious, guileful; close, close-mouthed, reticent, secretive; clandestine, covert, dark; deceitful, deceiving, deceptive, tricky, underhand, underhanded; crooked, dishonest, double-dealing, two-faced; lying, mendacious, untrustworthy, untruthful; insidious, perfidious, treacherous
*near ant* aboveboard, forthright, straightforward; candid, frank, open, plain; honest, trustworthy, truthful
2 undertaken or done so as to escape being observed or known by others — see SECRET 1

**sneer** *vb* to express scornful amusement by means of facial contortions ⟨the most popular girl in school *sneered* every time she saw the "nerds"⟩
*syn* laugh, smile, snicker, snigger
*rel* sniff, snort; catcall, hoot, insult, jeer, mock, ridicule; decry, despise, disdain; scorn

**snicker** *n* an explosive sound that is a sign of amusement — see LAUGH 1

**snicker** *vb* to express scornful amusement by means of facial contortions — see SNEER

**snide** *adj* not following or in accordance with standards of honor and decency — see IGNOBLE 2

**sniff** *n* the quality of a thing that makes it perceptible to the sense organs in the nose — see SMELL

**sniff** *vb* to become aware of by means of the sense organs in the nose — see SMELL 1

**sniff** (at) *vb* to show contempt for — see SCORN 1

**snigger** *n* an explosive sound that is a sign of amusement — see LAUGH 1

**snigger** *vb* to express scornful amusement by means of facial contortions — see SNEER

**snip** *vb* to make (as hair) shorter with or as if with the use of shears — see CLIP

**snippet** *n* a very small piece — see BIT 1

**snippy** *adj* 1 being or characterized by direct, brief, and potentially rude speech or manner — see BLUNT 1

*syn* synonym(s) *rel* related words
*ant* antonym(s) *near ant* near antonym(s)

2 easily irritated or annoyed — see IRRITABLE

[1]**snitch** *vb* to give information (as to the authorities) about another's improper or unlawful activities — see SQUEAL 1

[2]**snitch** *vb* to take (something) without right and with an intent to keep — see STEAL 1

**snitcher** *n* a person who provides secret information about another's wrongdoing — see INFORMER

**snoop** *vb* to interest oneself in what is not one's concern — see INTERFERE

**snoopy** *adj* 1 interested in what is not one's own business — see CURIOUS 1
2 thrusting oneself where one is not welcome or invited — see INTRUSIVE

**snooze** *n* a short sleep — see NAP

**snooze** *vb* 1 be in a state of sleep — see SLEEP 1
2 to sleep lightly or briefly — see [1]NAP 1

**snoozing** *n* a natural periodic loss of consciousness during which the body restores itself — see SLEEP 1

**snort** *n* 1 a vocal sound made to express scorn or disapproval — see CATCALL
2 the portion of a serving of a beverage that is swallowed at one time — see DRINK 2

**snow** *vb* to cause to believe what is untrue — see DECEIVE

**snowball** *vb* to become greater in extent, volume, amount, or number — see INCREASE 2

**snow under** *vb* 1 to defeat by a large margin — see WHIP 2
2 to subject to incapacitating emotional or mental stress — see OVERWHELM 1

**snub** *n* treatment that is deliberately unfriendly — see COLD SHOULDER

**snub** *vb* 1 to deliberately ignore or treat rudely ⟨the snob in town always *snubbed* anyone she thought was beneath her⟩
*syn* cold-shoulder, cut, slight
*rel* ostracize; brush (aside *or* off), disdain, rebuff, reject, repulse; disregard, forget, neglect, overlook, overpass, pass over, shrug off
2 to show contempt for — see SCORN 1

**snuff** (out) *vb* 1 to cause to cease burning — see EXTINGUISH 1
2 to destroy all traces of — see ANNIHILATE 1
3 to put a stop to (something) by the use of force — see QUELL 1

**snug** *adj* 1 being clean and in good order — see NEAT 1
2 providing physical comfort — see COMFORTABLE 1
3 enjoying physical comfort — see COMFORTABLE 2
4 firmly positioned in place and difficult to dislodge — see TIGHT 2
5 providing safety — see SAFE 2

**snug** *vb* to sit or recline comfortably or cozily — see SNUGGLE 1

**snuggle** *vb* 1 to sit or recline comfortably or cozily ⟨it's particularly nice to *snuggle* next to the fire on a snowy day⟩
*syn* cuddle, curl up, nestle, snug
*rel* huddle
2 to lie close — see NUZZLE

**so** *adj* being in agreement with the truth or a fact or a standard — see CORRECT 1

**so** *adv* 1 for this or that reason — see THEREFORE
2 in like manner — see ALSO 1
3 to a great degree — see VERY 1

**soak** *n* a person who makes a habit of getting drunk — see DRUNK 1

**soak** *vb* 1 to wet thoroughly with liquid ⟨we ran for home as soon as the rain started, but our clothes still ended up *soaked*⟩
*syn* drench, drown, impregnate, saturate, sop, souse, steep
*rel* marinate; presoak; dip, immerse, inundate, submerge; bathe, douse, wash, water, wet; infiltrate, penetrate, permeate
*near ant* dehydrate, dry; drain, empty, void
*ant* wring (out)
2 to charge (someone) too much for goods or services — see OVERCHARGE 1
3 to make wet — see WET

**soak** (up) *vb* to take in (something liquid) through small openings — see ABSORB 1

**soaked** *adj* containing, covered with, or thoroughly penetrated by water — see WET

**soaking** *adj* containing, covered with, or thoroughly penetrated by water — see WET

**soap** *n* a substance used for cleaning — see CLEANER

**soar** *n* the act or an instance of rising or climbing up — see ASCENT 1

**soar** *vb* 1 to move or extend upward — see ASCEND
2 to move through the air with or as if with outstretched wings — see FLY 1
3 to rise abruptly and rapidly — see SKYROCKET

**sob** *vb* to shed tears often while making meaningless sounds as a sign of pain or distress — see CRY 1

**sober** *adj* 1 not having one's mind affected by alcohol ⟨it's important to stay *sober* if you're going to be driving a car⟩
*syn* clearheaded, straight
*rel* abstemious, abstinent, dry, temperate
*near ant* alcoholic
*ant* befuddled, dissipated, drunk, drunken, high, inebriate, inebriated, intoxicated, loaded [*slang*], soused, tipsy
2 based on sound reasoning or information — see GOOD 1
3 not joking or playful in mood or manner — see SERIOUS 1

**soberness** *n* a mental state free of jesting or trifling — see EARNESTNESS

**sobriety** *n* a mental state free of jesting or trifling — see EARNESTNESS

**sobriquet** *also* **scubriquet** *n* a descriptive or familiar name given instead of or in addition to the one belonging to an individual — see NICKNAME

**sociability** *n* the quality or state of being social ⟨her *sociability* was called into question when she said she hated parties⟩

*syn* conviviality, gregariousness
*rel* amiability, friendliness, neighborliness; camaraderie, companionship, fellowship; boldness, brashness, extroversion (*or* extraversion), forwardness, immodesty
*near ant* bashfulness, coyness, diffidence, shyness, timidity, timidness; introversion; modesty

**sociable** *adj* **1** likely to seek or enjoy the company of others — see CONVIVIAL
**2** showing a natural kindness and courtesy especially in social situations — see GRACIOUS 1

**social** *adj* likely to seek or enjoy the company of others — see CONVIVIAL

**socialize** *vb* to take part in social activities ⟨he likes to *socialize* with his coworkers after work ends⟩
*syn* associate, fraternize, hobnob, mingle, mix
*phrases* rub elbows, rub shoulders
*near ant* avoid, eschew, shun; slight, snub

**society** *n* **1** a group of persons formally joined together for some common interest — see ASSOCIATION 2
**2** human beings in general — see PEOPLE 1
**3** the feeling of closeness and friendship that exists between companions — see COMPANIONSHIP
**4** the way people live at a particular time and place — see CIVILIZATION 1

**sock** *n* **1** a close-fitting covering for the foot and leg — see STOCKING
**2** a hard strike with a part of the body or an instrument — see [1]BLOW

**sock** *vb* to deliver a blow to (someone or something) usually in a strong vigorous manner — see HIT 1

**sod** *n* the land of one's birth, residence, or citizenship — see COUNTRY 1

**sodality** *n* a group of persons formally joined together for some common interest — see ASSOCIATION 2

**sodden** *adj* containing, covered with, or thoroughly penetrated by water — see WET

**sofa** *n* a long upholstered piece of furniture designed for several sitters — see COUCH

**soft** *adj* **1** not loud in pitch or volume ⟨*soft* music played in the background while we ate⟩
*syn* dull, low, quiet
*rel* dead, silent, still; dreamy, peaceful, restful, soothing, tranquil; muffled, muted, softened, toned (down)
*near ant* brazen, dinning, discordant, noisy, obstreperous, raucous, rip-roaring, vociferous; grating, harsh, shrill, strident
*ant* blaring, blasting, booming, clamorous, clangorous, deafening, earsplitting, loud, piercing, resounding, ringing, roaring, sonorous, stentorian, thunderous
**2** smooth or delicate in appearance or feel ⟨I like this sweater the best because it is so *soft* and comfortable⟩
*syn* cottony, downy, satin, satiny, silken, silky, velvety
*rel* creamy; delicate, fine, slick, smooth
*near ant* bumpy, lumpy, pebbly; broken, jagged, ragged, rugged; grainy, granular, gritty
*ant* coarse, harsh, rough, scratchy
**3** giving easily to the touch ⟨*soft* mattresses make it very easy to fall asleep, but they have a tendency to get lumpy⟩
*syn* flabby, mushy, pulpy, spongy, squashy, squishy
*rel* unhardened; doughy, fleshy; droopy, flaccid, floppy, lank, limp, slack, yielding; compressible, malleable, pliable, pliant, workable
*near ant* inflexible, resilient, rigid, stiff, tense; resistant, sound, strong, sturdy, tough, unyielding; hardened, indurated, tempered
*ant* firm, hard, solid
**4** involving minimal difficulty or effort — see EASY 1
**5** lacking bodily strength — see WEAK 1
**6** lacking strength of will or character — see WEAK 2
**7** not harsh or stern especially in manner, nature, or effect — see GENTLE 1
**8** providing physical comfort — see COMFORTABLE 1

**soften** *vb* **1** to diminish the physical strength of — see WEAKEN 1
**2** to lessen the shock of — see CUSHION

**softened** *adj* lacking bodily strength — see WEAK 1

**softhearted** *adj* having or marked by sympathy and consideration for others — see HUMANE 1

**softheartedness** *n* the capacity for feeling for another's unhappiness or misfortune — see HEART 1

**softness** *n* the quality or state of lacking strength of will or character — see WEAKNESS 2

**soft–soap** *vb* **1** to get (someone) to do something by gentle urging, special attention, or flattery — see COAX
**2** to praise too much — see FLATTER 1

**soft soap** *n* excessive praise — see FLATTERY

**softy** *or* **softie** *n* a person lacking in physical strength — see WEAKLING 1

**soggy** *adj* containing, covered with, or thoroughly penetrated by water — see WET

**soil** *n* **1** foul matter that mars the purity or cleanliness of something — see FILTH 1
**2** the loose surface material in which plants naturally grow — see DIRT 1
**3** the solid part of our planet's surface as distinguished from the sea and air — see EARTH 2

**soil** *vb* to make dirty — see DIRTY

**soiled** *adj* not clean — see DIRTY 1

**sojourn** *n* a temporary residing as another's guest — see VISIT 1

*syn* synonym(s) *rel* related words
*ant* antonym(s) *near ant* near antonym(s)

**sojourn** *vb* to reside as a temporary guest — see VISIT 2
**solace** *n* 1 a feeling of ease from grief or trouble — see COMFORT 1
2 the giving of hope and strength in times of grief, distress, or suffering — see CONSOLATION 1
**solace** *vb* to ease the grief or distress of — see COMFORT 1
**solacing** *n* the giving of hope and strength in times of grief, distress, or suffering — see CONSOLATION 1
**solar plexus** *n* the part of the body between the chest and the pelvis — see STOMACH
**soldier** *n* a person engaged in military service ⟨one of the goals of war is to keep as many *soldiers* as possible from being killed⟩
*syn* fighter, legionary, legionnaire, man-at-arms, regular, serviceman, warrior
*rel* servicewoman; cavalier, cuirassier, dragoon, trooper; dogface, doughboy, footman, foot soldier, infantryman; commando, marine, ranger; artilleryman, musketeer, rifleman; archer, lancer, spearman; Confederate, Continental, Federal, GI, guardsman, Rough Rider; guerilla, irregular, partisan; combatant, noncombatant; mercenary, soldier of fortune; veteran, war-horse; conscript, draftee, recruit; reservist
*ant* civilian
**soldierly** *adj* of, relating to, or suitable for war or a warrior — see MARTIAL 1
**sole** *adj* 1 belonging only to the one person, unit, or group named ⟨the landowner has *sole* rights to the property, so he can do whatever he wants to with it⟩
*syn* exclusive, single, unshared
*rel* proprietary
*near ant* joint, mutual, shared
*ant* nonexclusive
2 being the one or ones of a class with no other members — see ONLY 2
**solecism** *n* a socially improper or unsuitable act or remark — see IMPROPRIETY 2
**solely** *adv* 1 for nothing other than ⟨I fight *solely* for my country, not for money!⟩
*syn* alone, exclusively, just, only, simply
*rel* mainly, mostly, primarily
*near ant* additionally, also, likewise
2 without aid or support — see ALONE 1
**solemn** *adj* 1 having or showing a serious and reserved manner — see DIGNIFIED
2 not joking or playful in mood or manner — see SERIOUS 1
**solemnity** *n* 1 a mental state free of jesting or trifling — see EARNESTNESS
2 an oft-repeated action or series of actions performed in accordance with tradition or a set of rules — see RITE
**solicit** *vb* 1 to go around and approach (people) with a request for opinions or information — see CANVASS
2 to make a request for — see ASK (FOR) 1
3 to make a request of — see ASK 2
4 to make a request to (someone) in an earnest or urgent manner — see BEG
**solicitation** *n* an earnest request — see PLEA 1
**soliciting** *adj* asking humbly — see SUPPLIANT
**solicitor** *n* 1 one that tries to get a person to give in to a desire — see TEMPTER
2 one who asks earnestly for a favor or gift — see SUPPLICANT
**solicitous** *adj* 1 given to or made with heedful anticipation of the needs and happiness of others — see THOUGHTFUL 1
2 showing urgent desire or interest — see EAGER
**solicitude** *n* an uneasy state of mind usually over the possibility of an anticipated misfortune or trouble — see ANXIETY 1
**solid** *adj* 1 based on sound reasoning or information — see GOOD 1
2 having a consistency that does not easily yield to pressure — see FIRM 2
3 having or consisting of a single color — see MONOCHROMATIC
4 not showing weakness or uncertainty — see FIRM 1
5 worthy of one's trust — see DEPENDABLE
**solidify** *vb* 1 to become physically firm or solid — see HARDEN 1
2 to take on a definite form — see FORM 1
**solidity** *n* worthiness as the recipient of another's trust or confidence — see RELIABILITY
**solidness** *n* worthiness as the recipient of another's trust or confidence — see RELIABILITY
**solitariness** *n* the state of being alone or kept apart from others — see ISOLATION
**solitary** *adj* 1 being the one or ones of a class with no other members — see ONLY 2
2 not being in the company of others — see ALONE 1
**solitary** *n* a person who lives away from others — see RECLUSE
**solitude** *n* the state of being alone or kept apart from others — see ISOLATION
**solo** *adj* not being in the company of others — see ALONE 1
**solon** *n* a member of an organized body of persons having the authority to make laws — see LEGISLATOR
**soluble** *adj* capable of having the reason for or cause of determined — see SOLVABLE
**solution** *n* something attained by mental effort and especially by computation — see ANSWER 2
**solvable** *adj* capable of having the reason for or cause of determined ⟨I'm sure that the mystery of what happened to the missing pizza is *solvable*⟩
*syn* answerable, explainable, explicable, resolvable, soluble
*rel* analyzable, decipherable; feasible, workable
*near ant* impossible
*ant* inexplicable, insoluble, unexplainable, unsolvable

**solve** *vb* to find an answer for through reasoning ⟨it took me half an hour to *solve* the logic puzzle⟩
***syn*** answer, break, crack, dope (out), figure out, puzzle (out), resolve, riddle, unravel, work, work out
***rel*** clear (up), iron out, straighten (out), unscramble, untangle, untie; divine, guess; decipher, decode
**somatic** *adj* of or relating to the human body — see PHYSICAL 1
**somber** *or* **sombre** *adj* **1** being without light or without much light — see DARK 1
**2** causing or marked by an atmosphere lacking in cheer — see GLOOMY 1
**some** *adj* known but not named — see CERTAIN 1
**some** *adv* very close to but not completely — see ALMOST
**somebody** *n* a person who is widely known and usually much talked about — see CELEBRITY 1
**someday** *adv* at a later time — see YET 1
**something** *adv* **1** to a great degree — see VERY 1
**2** to some degree or extent — see FAIRLY
**something** *n* one that has a real and independent existence — see ENTITY
**sometime** *adj* having been such at some previous time — see FORMER
**sometime** *adv* at a later time — see YET 1
**sometimes** *adv* on some occasions ⟨*sometimes* I like to go skiing, and *sometimes* I prefer to stay inside where it's warm⟩
***syn*** now, occasionally
***rel*** intermittently, periodically; infrequently, rarely, seldom; irregularly, sporadically
***phrases*** at times, from time to time, now and then, once in a while
***near ant*** frequently, often, oftentimes (*or* ofttimes); commonly, ordinarily, regularly, usually; always, constantly, invariably; continually, continuously, incessantly, perpetually, unceasingly, uninterruptedly; endlessly, ever, interminably
**somewhat** *adv* to some degree or extent — see FAIRLY
**somnolence** *n* the quality or state of desiring or needing sleep — see SLEEPINESS
**somnolent** *adj* desiring or needing sleep — see SLEEPY 1
**song** *n* **1** a short musical composition for the human voice often with instrumental accompaniment ⟨she sang a short *song* for the talent show⟩
***syn*** ballad, ditty, jingle, lay, lyric, vocal
***rel*** anthem, canticle, carol, chorale, hymn, noel, psalm, spiritual; dirge, lament, requiem, threnody; hallelujah, paean; aria, barcarole (*or* barcarolle), blues, cantata, chantey (*or* chanty), chorus, croon, descant, glee, lullaby, madrigal, motet, part-song, pop, rocker, round, roundelay, serenade, troll

***syn*** synonym(s) ***rel*** related words
***ant*** antonym(s) ***near ant*** near antonym(s)

**2** a composition using rhythm and often rhyme to create a lyrical effect — see POEM
**3** a rhythmic series of musical tones arranged to give a pleasing effect — see MELODY
**4** a very small sum of money — see MITE 1
**5** writing that uses rhythm, vivid language, and often rhyme to provoke an emotional response — see POETRY 1
**songster** *n* one who sings — see SINGER
**songwriter** *n* a person who writes musical compositions — see COMPOSER
**sonny** *n* a male person who has not yet reached adulthood — see BOY
**sonorous** *adj* **1** marked by a high volume of sound — see LOUD 1
**2** marked by conspicuously full and rich sounds or tones — see RESONANT
**soon** *adv* **1** at or within a short time — see SHORTLY 2
**2** by choice or preference — see RATHER 1
**3** with great speed — see FAST 1
**soothe** *vb* **1** to ease the grief or distress of — see COMFORT 1
**2** to free from distress or disturbance — see CALM 1
**3** to make more bearable or less severe — see HELP 2
**soothing** *adj* **1** tending to calm the emotions and relieve stress ⟨the *soothing* music eventually put the entire yoga class in the proper mood⟩
***syn*** calming, comforting, dreamy, lulling, narcotic, pacifying, quieting, relaxing, sedative, tranquilizing (*also* tranquillizing)
***rel*** hypnotic, opiate; anesthetic, deadening, depressant, numbing
***near ant*** energizing, invigorating, stimulant, stimulating; aggravating, annoying, bothersome, exasperating, galling, grating, irksome, irritating, troublesome, vexing
**2** not harsh or stern especially in manner, nature, or effect — see GENTLE 1
**soothsayer** *n* one who predicts future events or developments — see PROPHET
**soothsaying** *n* a declaration that something will happen in the future — see PREDICTION
**sop** *n* something given or promised in order to improperly influence a person's conduct or decision — see BRIBE
**sop** *vb* to wet thoroughly with liquid — see SOAK 1
**sophisticate** *n* a person with the outlook, experience, and manners thought to be typical of big city dwellers — see COSMOPOLITAN
**sophisticate** *vb* to make complex or difficult — see COMPLICATE
**sophisticated** *adj* **1** having a wide and refined knowledge of the world especially from personal experience — see WORLDLY-WISE
**2** having many parts or aspects that are usually interrelated — see COMPLEX 1

**3** having or showing very polished and worldly manners — see SUAVE
**4** made or done with great care or with much detail — see ELABORATE 1

**sophistication** *n* the state or quality of having many interrelated parts or aspects — see COMPLEXITY 1

**soppy** *adj* containing, covered with, or thoroughly penetrated by water — see WET

**sorcerer** *n* a person skilled in using supernatural forces — see MAGICIAN 1

**sorceress** *n* a woman believed to have often harmful supernatural powers — see WITCH 1

**sorcery** *n* the power to control natural forces through supernatural means — see MAGIC 1

**sordid** *adj* **1** not clean — see DIRTY 1
**2** not following or in accordance with standards of honor and decency — see IGNOBLE 2

**sore** *adj* **1** causing or feeling bodily pain — see PAINFUL 1
**2** feeling or showing anger — see ANGRY
**3** having or showing deep-seated resentment — see BITTER 1

**sorely** *adv* with feelings of bitterness or grief — see HARD 2

**sorriness** *n* deep sadness especially for the loss of someone or something loved — see SORROW

**sorrow** *n* deep sadness especially for the loss of someone or something loved ⟨he felt great *sorrow* at the loss of his beloved pet⟩
*syn* affliction, anguish, dolefulness, dolor, grief, heartache, heartbreak, sorriness, woe
*rel* agony, distress, pain, suffering, torment; blues, dejection depression, desolateness, desolation, despondency, disconsolateness, dispiritedness, distress, doldrums, downheartedness, dreariness, dumps, forlornness, gloom, gloominess, heartsickness, joylessness, melancholy, miserableness, misery, mopes, oppression, sadness, unhappiness, wretchedness; regret, remorse, rue
*near ant* gaiety (*also* gayety), gayness, humor, jollity, joviality, lightheartedness, merriment, merrymaking, mirth, mirthfulness; hopefulness, optimism; enjoyment; content, contentedness
*ant* blessedness, bliss, blissfulness, cheer, cheerfulness, cheeriness, delight, ecstasy, elatedness, elation, euphoria, exhilaration, exuberance, exultation, gladness, gladsomeness, glee, gleefulness, happiness, joy, joyfulness, joyousness, jubilation, pleasure, rapture, rapturousness

**sorrow** *vb* to feel deep sadness or mental pain — see GRIEVE

**sorrowful** *adj* **1** expressing or suggesting mourning — see MOURNFUL 1
**2** feeling unhappiness — see SAD 1

**sorrowfully** *adv* with feelings of bitterness or grief — see HARD 2

**sorry** *adj* **1** arousing or deserving of one's loathing and disgust — see CONTEMPTIBLE 1
**2** causing unhappiness — see SAD 2
**3** deserving pitying scorn (as for inadequacy) — see PITIFUL 1
**4** feeling sorrow for a wrong that one has done — see CONTRITE 1
**5** feeling unhappiness — see SAD 1
**6** expressing or suggesting mourning — see MOURNING 1
**7** deserving of one's pity — see PATHETIC 1

**sort** *n* **1** a number of persons or things that are grouped together because they have something in common ⟨I prefer jackets with zippers to the *sort* that close with buttons⟩
*syn* breed, class, description, feather, ilk, kind, like, manner, nature, order, type
*rel* model; sample, specimen; bracket, category, division, family, grade, group, lot, persuasion, rank(s), set
**2** a member of the human race — see HUMAN

**sort** *vb* to arrange or assign according to type — see CLASSIFY 1

**sort of** *adv* to some degree or extent — see FAIRLY

**so–so** *adj* of average to below average quality — see MEDIOCRE 1

**so–so** *adv* in a satisfactory way — see WELL 1

**sot** *n* a person who makes a habit of getting drunk — see DRUNK 1

**sough** *vb* to take in and let out a deep audible breath or to make a similar sound — see SIGH

**soul** *n* **1** an immaterial force within a human being thought to give the body life, energy, and power ⟨many religions teach that the *soul* is immortal⟩
*syn* psyche, spirit
*rel* life, vitality
*near ant* body, flesh
**2** a member of the human race — see HUMAN
**3** the quality or qualities that make a thing what it is — see ESSENCE
**4** the seat of one's deepest thoughts and emotions — see CORE 1

**soulless** *adj* having or showing a lack of sympathy or tender feelings — see HARD 1

**sound** *adj* **1** according to the rules of logic — see LOGICAL 1
**2** enjoying health and vigor — see HEALTHY 1
**3** marked by the ability to withstand stress without structural damage or distortion — see STABLE 1

**sound** *n* **1** a narrow body of water between two land masses — see CHANNEL 2
**2** range of hearing — see EARSHOT

[1]**sound** *vb* **1** to continue or be repeated in a series of reflected sound waves — see REVERBERATE
**2** to give the impression of being — see SEEM

**3** to make known (as an idea, emotion, or opinion) — see EXPRESS 1
**4** to make known openly or publicly — see ANNOUNCE

**[2]sound** *vb* **1** to measure the depth of (as a body of water) typically with a weighted line ⟨the pilot *sounded* the river to make sure we weren't in any danger of running aground⟩
***syn*** fathom, plumb
***rel*** gauge (*also* gage), measure, scale
**2** to cast oneself head first into deep water — see DIVE

**soundless** *adj* mostly or entirely without sound — see SILENT 3

**soundness** *n* **1** the ability to withstand force or stress without being distorted, dislodged, or damaged — see STABILITY 1
**2** the condition of being sound in body — see HEALTH

**sound off** *vb* to voice one's opinions freely with force — see SPEAK UP

**soup** *n* an atmospheric condition in which suspended particles in the air rob it of its transparency — see HAZE 1

**soupy** *adj* **1** filled with or dimmed by fine particles (as of dust or water) in suspension — see HAZY 1
**2** having an overly soft liquid consistency — see RUNNY

**sour** *adj* **1** causing or characterized by the one of the four basic taste sensations that is produced chiefly by acids ⟨the *sour* candy made our mouths all wrinkly inside⟩
***syn*** acid, acidic, tart, vinegary
***rel*** dry, soured, unsweetened; pungent, sharp, tangy; astringent, puckery; acetic; hyperacid
***near ant*** sweet; bland, smooth
**2** not giving pleasure to the mind or senses — see UNPLEASANT

**sour** *vb* to cause to change from friendly or loving to unfriendly or uncaring — see ESTRANGE

**source** *n* the beginning part of a stream — see HEADWATER

**souring** *n* the loss of friendship or affection — see ESTRANGEMENT

**souse** *n* a person who makes a habit of getting drunk — see DRUNK 1

**souse** *vb* **1** to make wet — see WET
**2** to sink or push (something) briefly into or as if into a liquid — see DIP 1
**3** to wet thoroughly with liquid — see SOAK 1

**soused** *adj* **1** being under the influence of alcohol — see DRUNK
**2** containing, covered with, or thoroughly penetrated by water — see WET

**souvenir** *n* something that serves to keep alive the memory of a person or event — see MEMORIAL

**sovereign** *adj* **1** coming before all others in importance — see FOREMOST 1
**2** not being under the rule or control of another — see FREE 1

**sovereign** *n* one who rules over a people with a sole, supreme, and usually hereditary authority — see MONARCH

**sovereignty** *n* **1** the state of being free from the control or power of another — see FREEDOM 1
**2** a body of people composed of one or more nationalities usually with its own territory and government — see NATION

**sow** *vb* **1** to cover by or as if by scattering something over or on — see SCATTER 2
**2** to put or set into the ground to grow — see PLANT

**spa** *n* a building or room used for sports activities and exercising — see GYM

**space** *n* **1** an extent or area available for or used up by some activity or thing — see ROOM 1
**2** an indefinite but usually short period of time — see WHILE 1

**space–age** *adj* being or involving the latest methods, concepts, information, or styles — see MODERN

**spacing** *n* the space or amount of space between two points, lines, surfaces, or objects — see DISTANCE

**spacious** *adj* more than adequate or average in capacity ⟨almost all of the guests were able to fit into the *spacious* living room⟩
***syn*** ample, capacious, commodious, roomy
***rel*** broad, wide; big, bulky, considerable, generous, goodly, good-sized, grand, great, handsome, hefty, hulking, king-size (*or* king-sized), large, largish, outsize (*also* outsized), oversize (*or* oversized), sizable (*or* sizeable), substantial, super, voluminous; enormous, immense, vast; expansive, extended, extensive; boundless, limitless, unbounded
***near ant*** confined, cramped, limited, narrow, restricted; small, snug, tight, tiny

**span** *vb* to find out the size, extent, or amount of — see MEASURE

**spank** *n* a hard strike with a part of the body or an instrument — see [1]BLOW

**spanking** *adj* having much high-spirited energy and movement — see LIVELY 1

**spare** *adj* **1** being over what is needed ⟨I had some *spare* time to kill, so I cleaned up my room a bit⟩
***syn*** excess, extra, superfluous, supernumerary, surplus
***rel*** accessory, additional, supplemental, supplementary; dispensable, extraneous, gratuitous, needless, nonessential, unessential, unnecessary, unneeded, unwanted
***near ant*** inadequate, insufficient, meager, scant, scanty, scarce, short, sparse
**2** giving or sharing as little as possible — see STINGY 1
**3** having a noticeably small amount of body fat — see THIN 1
**4** less plentiful than what is normal, necessary, or desirable — see MEAGER

**spare** *n* an interchangeable part or piece of equipment that is kept on hand for replacement of an original ⟨first we took

---

***syn*** synonym(s) ***rel*** related words
***ant*** antonym(s) ***near ant*** near antonym(s)

the burnt light bulb out, and then we replaced it with the *spare*〉
*syn* extra, reserve
*rel* backup, substitute; stock; copy, double, duplicate, replacement
*near ant* archetype, original

**spare** *vb* to use or give out in stingy amounts 〈I'll have a banana split and don't *spare* the whipped cream〉
*syn* scant, skimp (on), stint (on)
*rel* dole (out), mete (out), portion (out), ration (out); pinch, shortchange
*near ant* lavish, rain

**sparing** *adj* **1** careful in the management of money or resources — see FRUGAL
**2** giving or sharing as little as possible — see STINGY 1

**spark** *n* a very small amount — see PARTICLE 1

**spark** *vb* **1** to give off sparks 〈the broken radio *sparked* and smoked the instant it was plugged in〉
*syn* scintillate, sparkle
*rel* flash; burn
**2** to cause to function — see ACTIVATE

**sparkle** *vb* **1** to give off sparks — see SPARK 1
**2** to shoot forth bursts of light — see FLASH 1

**sparky** *adj* having much high-spirited energy and movement — see LIVELY 1

**sparse** *adj* less plentiful than what is normal, necessary, or desirable — see MEAGER

**spasm** *n* **1** a painful sudden tightening of a muscle — see CRAMP
**2** a sudden intense expression of strong feeling — see OUTBURST 1

**spasmodic** *adj* lacking in steadiness or regularity of occurrence — see FITFUL

**spat** *n* an often noisy or angry expression of differing opinions — see ARGUMENT 1

**spat** *vb* to express different opinions about something often angrily — see ARGUE 2

**spate** *n* a great flow of water or of something that overwhelms — see FLOOD

**spatter** *vb* **1** to cause (something liquid or mushy) to move along in sheets — see SPLASH 1
**2** to wet or soil by striking with something liquid or mushy — see SPLASH 2

**spawn** *n* the descendants of a person, animal, or plant — see OFFSPRING

**spawn** *vb* to be the cause of (a situation, action, or state of mind) — see EFFECT

**speak** *vb* **1** to express (a thought or emotion) in words — see SAY 1
**2** to give a formal often extended talk on a subject — see TALK 1

**speak** (to *or* with) *vb* to communicate with by means of spoken words — see TALK 1

**speaker** *n* **1** a person in charge of a meeting — see CHAIR 1
**2** a person who speaks for another or for a group — see SPOKESPERSON

**speak out** *vb* to voice one's opinions freely with force — see SPEAK UP

**speak up** *vb* to voice one's opinions freely with force 〈she's never been afraid to *speak up* in class〉
*syn* sound off, speak out, spout (off)
*rel* bawl, call, cry, holler, shout, sing (out), vociferate, yell; articulate, enunciate
*phrases* speak one's mind
*near ant* hush, suppress; quiet

**spear** *n* a weapon with a long straight handle and sharp head or blade 〈the Roman gladiator thrust his *spear* triumphantly into the lion's side〉
*syn* javelin, lance, pike, pikestaff, shaft
*rel* dart, spike; gaff, halberd, harpoon, trident

**spear** *vb* to penetrate or hold (something) with a pointed object — see IMPALE

**spearhead** *vb* to serve as leader of — see LEAD 2

**special** *adj* **1** being the one or ones of a class with no other members — see ONLY 2
**2** granted special treatment or attention — see DARLING 1
**3** of a particular or exact sort — see EXPRESS 1

**speciality** *n* something for which a person shows a special talent — see FORTE

**specialized** *adj* used by or intended for experts in a particular field of knowledge — see TECHNICAL

**specialty** *n* **1** a region of activity, knowledge, or influence — see FIELD 2
**2** something for which a person shows a special talent — see FORTE

**species** *n* one of the units into which a whole is divided on the basis of a common characteristic — see CLASS 2

**specific** *adj* **1** of a particular or exact sort — see EXPRESS 1
**2** so clearly expressed as to leave no doubt about the meaning — see EXPLICIT

**specific** *n* a substance or preparation used to treat disease — see MEDICINE

**specificity** *n* careful thoroughness of detail — see PARTICULARITY 1

**specify** *vb* **1** to give the rules about (something) clearly and exactly — see PRESCRIBE
**2** to make reference to or speak about briefly but specifically — see MENTION 1

**specimen** *n* **1** a member of the human race — see HUMAN
**2** one of a group or collection that shows what the whole is like — see EXAMPLE

**specious** *adj* tending or having power to deceive — see DECEPTIVE 1

**speck** *n* **1** a small area that is different (as in color) from the main part — see SPOT 1
**2** a very small amount — see PARTICLE 1
**3** a very small piece — see BIT 1

**speck** *vb* to mark with small spots especially unevenly — see SPOT

**speckle** *n* a small area that is different (as in color) from the main part — see SPOT 1

**speckle** *vb* to mark with small spots especially unevenly — see SPOT

**speckled** *adj* marked with spots — see SPOTTED 1

**specs** *n pl* a pair of lenses set in a frame that is held in place with ear supports and which are usually worn to correct vision — see GLASSES 1

**spectacles** *n pl* a pair of lenses set in a frame that is held in place with ear supports and which are usually worn to correct vision — see GLASSES 1

**specter** *or* **spectre** *n* the soul of a dead person thought of especially as appearing to living people — see GHOST

**spectrum** *n* the distance or extent between possible extremes — see RANGE 3

**speculate** *vb* to form an opinion from little or no evidence — see GUESS 1

**speculation** *n* a risky undertaking — see GAMBLE

**speculative** *adj* existing only as an assumption or speculation — see THEORETICAL 1

**speech** *n* **1** a usually formal discourse delivered to an audience ⟨the guest of honor gave a short *speech* in appreciation of the award⟩
*syn* address, declamation, harangue, oration, talk
*rel* diatribe, rant, tirade; eulogy, panegyric, tribute; keynote address, lecture; homily, sermon; monologue, soliloquy; pitch, presentation, spiel
**2** the stock of words, pronunciation, and grammar used by a people as their basic means of communication — see LANGUAGE 1

**speechless** *adj* **1** deliberately refraining from speech — see SILENT 1
**2** unable to speak — see MUTE 1

**speechlessness** *n* incapacity for or restraint from speaking — see SILENCE 1

**speed** *n* a high rate of movement or performance ⟨we did our homework with as much *speed* as possible so we could go to the movies⟩
*syn* celerity, fastness, fleetness, haste, hurry, quickness, rapidity, rapidness, speediness, swiftness, velocity
*rel* clip, pace, rate, tempo; drive, hustle; acceleration, rush; dispatch, expedition, expeditiousness, promptness
*near ant* languidness, languor, leisureliness, lethargy, torpor; reluctance; deliberateness, deliberation
*ant* slowness, sluggishness

**speed** *vb* to proceed or move quickly — see HURRY 2

**speed** (up) *vb* to cause to move or proceed fast or faster — see HURRY 1

**speedboat** *n* a boat equipped with a motor — see MOTORBOAT

**speedily** *adv* with great speed — see FAST 1

**speediness** *n* a high rate of movement or performance — see SPEED

**speedy** *adj* moving, proceeding, or acting with great speed — see FAST 1

**spell** *n* **1** a spoken word or set of words believed to have magic power ⟨the witch cast a *spell* that turned the prince into a toad⟩
*syn* bewitchment, charm, conjuration, enchantment, incantation
*rel* curse, hex, jinx; black magic, conjuring, magic, mojo, necromancy, sorcery, voodooism, witchcraft, witchery, wizardry
**2** a sudden experiencing of a physical or mental disorder — see ATTACK 2
**3** an indefinite but usually short period of time — see WHILE 1

**spell** *vb* **1** to cast a spell on — see BEWITCH 1
**2** to communicate or convey (as an idea) to the mind — see MEAN 1

**spellbind** *vb* to hold the attention of as if by a spell — see ENTHRALL 1

**spellbound** *adj* being or appearing to be under a magic spell — see ENCHANTED

**spell out** *vb* to make plain or understandable — see EXPLAIN 1

**spend** *vb* **1** to hand over or use up in payment ⟨I always end up *spending* too much money at the mall⟩
*syn* disburse, expend, give, lay out, pay
*rel* lavish, rain; blow; squander, waste
*near ant* cache, hoard, save; acquire, earn, make
**2** to make complete use of — see DEPLETE
**3** to use up carelessly — see WASTE 1

**spender** *n* someone who carelessly spends money — see PRODIGAL

**spendthrift** *adj* given to spending money freely or foolishly — see PRODIGAL

**spendthrift** *n* someone who carelessly spends money — see PRODIGAL

**spent** *adj* depleted in strength, energy, or freshness — see WEARY 1

**spew** *vb* **1** to flow out in great quantities or with force — see GUSH 1
**2** to throw out or off (something from within) often violently — see ERUPT 1

**sphere** *n* **1** a more or less round body or mass — see [1]BALL 1
**2** a region of activity, knowledge, or influence — see FIELD 2

**spherical** *adj* having every part of the surface the same distance from the center — see ROUND 1

**spice** *n* **1** a sweet or pleasant smell — see FRAGRANCE
**2** something (as a spice or herb) that adds an agreeable or interesting taste to food — see SEASONING 1

**spice** *vb* to make more pleasant to the taste by adding something intensely flavored — see SEASON 1

**spick–and–span** *or* **spic–and–span** *adj* **1** free from dirt or stain — see CLEAN 1
**2** recently made and never used before — see NEW 3

**spicy** *adj* hinting at or intended to call to mind matters regarded as indecent — see SUGGESTIVE 1

**spigot** *n* a fixture for controlling the flow of a liquid — see FAUCET

**spike** *vb* to penetrate or hold (something) with a pointed object — see IMPALE

---

*syn* synonym(s) *rel* related words
*ant* antonym(s) *near ant* near antonym(s)

**spill** *n* the act of going down from an upright position suddenly and involuntarily — see FALL 1

**spill** *vb* to make known (as information previously kept secret) — see REVEAL 1

**spin** *n* **1** a rapid turning about on an axis or central point ⟨the ice skater moved into a tight *spin* at the end of her routine⟩
*syn* gyration, pirouette, reel, revolution, roll, rotation, twirl, wheel, whirl
*rel* circuit, circulation; coil, curl, curve, spiral, twist; circle, orbit; eddy, swirl
**2** a state of mental confusion — see HAZE 2

**spin** *vb* **1** to move in circles around an axis or center ⟨after *spinning* around three times blindfolded, I tried to pin the tail on the donkey and almost fell over⟩
*syn* gyrate, pirouette, revolve, roll, rotate, turn, twirl, wheel, whirl
*rel* coil, curl, curve, round, spiral, twine, twist, wind; circle, orbit
**2** to be in a confused state as if from being twirled around ⟨my head *spun* as I contemplated all the possible problems this could cause⟩
*syn* reel, swim, whirl
*near ant* calm, collect; settle, steady
**3** to move (something) in a curved or circular path on or as if on an axis — see TURN 1

**spinal column** *n* a column of bones supporting the trunk of a vertebrate animal — see SPINE

**spindling** *adj* being tall, thin and usually loose-jointed — see LANKY

**spindly** *adj* being tall, thin and usually loose-jointed — see LANKY

**spine** *n* a column of bones supporting the trunk of a vertebrate animal ⟨he hurt his *spine* in the accident, but the doctor says he'll be walking again in no time⟩
*syn* backbone, chine, spinal column, vertebral column
*rel* back, spinal cord; vertebra

**spineless** *adj* **1** lacking strength of will or character — see WEAK 2
**2** having or showing a shameful lack of courage — see COWARDLY

**spinelessness** *n* **1** the quality or state of lacking strength of will or character — see WEAKNESS 2
**2** a shameful lack of courage in the face of danger — see COWARDICE

**spin–off** *n* something that naturally develops or is developed from something else — see DERIVATIVE

**spiny** *adj* requiring exceptional skill or caution in performance or handling — see TRICKY

**spiral** *adj* turning around an axis like the thread of a screw ⟨a *spiral* staircase takes visitors up into the Statue of Liberty⟩
*syn* coiling, corkscrew, helical, screwlike, winding
*rel* curving, curling, twisting
*near ant* lineal, linear; straight

**spiral** *vb* to follow a circular or spiral course — see WIND

**spirit** *n* **1** an immaterial force within a human being thought to give the body life, energy, and power — see SOUL 1
**2** a state of mind dominated by a particular emotion — see MOOD 1
**3** the soul of a dead person thought of especially as appearing to living people — see GHOST
**4 spirits** *pl* a fermented or distilled beverage that can make a person drunk — see ALCOHOL

**spirited** *adj* **1** marked by a lively display of strong feeling ⟨the town meeting featured a *spirited* debate about the proposed ban on skateboarding in the plaza downtown⟩
*syn* fiery, gingery, high-spirited, mettlesome, peppery, spunky
*rel* animate, animated, bouncing, bouncy, brisk, energetic, frisky, jaunty, jazzy, peppy, perky, pert, racy, snappy, spanking, sparky, sprightly, springy, vital, vivacious, zippy; ardent, fervent, impassioned, passionate
*near ant* boring, dull, lifeless
*ant* spiritless
**2** having much high-spirited energy and movement — see LIVELY 1

**spiritless** *adj* lacking bodily energy or motivation — see LISTLESS

**spiritual** *adj* **1** not composed of matter — see IMMATERIAL 1
**2** of, relating to, or used in the practice or worship services of a religion — see RELIGIOUS 1

**spiritual** *n* a religious song — see HYMN

**[1]spit** *n* an area of land that juts out into a body of water — see [2]CAPE

**[2]spit** *n* **1** something or someone that strongly resembles another — see IMAGE 1
**2** the fluid that is secreted into the mouth by certain glands — see SALIVA

**spite** *n* the desire to cause pain for the satisfaction of doing harm — see MALICE

**spiteful** *adj* having or showing a desire to cause someone pain or suffering for the sheer enjoyment of it — see HATEFUL

**spitefully** *adv* in a mean or spiteful manner — see NASTILY

**spitefulness** *n* the desire to cause pain for the satisfaction of doing harm — see MALICE

**spittle** *n* the fluid that is secreted into the mouth by certain glands — see SALIVA

**spit up** *vb* to discharge the contents of the stomach through the mouth — see VOMIT

**splash** *vb* **1** to cause (something liquid or mushy) to move along in sheets ⟨I always *splash* water at my sister when we go to the pool⟩
*syn* spatter
*rel* dabble, lap, plash, wash
**2** to wet or soil by striking with something liquid or mushy ⟨the bus *splashed* us as it passed⟩
*syn* bespatter, dash, plash, spatter, splatter
*rel* drench, drown, impregnate, saturate, soak, sop, souse, steep; bathe, douse, wash, water, wet; throw; spray; slop, sprinkle; squirt

**3** to flow along or against — see WASH 1
**4** to flow in a broken irregular stream — see GURGLE
**5** to move with a splashing motion — see SLOSH

**splashy** *adj* **1** likely to attract attention — see NOTICEABLE
**2** attractively eye-catching in style — see JAZZY 1
**3** excessively showy — see GAUDY

**splatter** *vb* to wet or soil by striking with something liquid or mushy — see SPLASH 2

**spleen** *n* **1** an intense emotional state of displeasure with someone or something — see ANGER
**2** the desire to cause pain for the satisfaction of doing harm — see MALICE

**splendid** *adj* **1** large and impressive in size, grandeur, extent, or conception — see GRAND 1
**2** of the very best kind — see EXCELLENT

**splendidly** *adv* in a pleasing way — see WELL 5

**splendor** *n* **1** impressiveness of beauty on a large scale — see MAGNIFICENCE
**2** the quality or state of having or giving off light — see BRILLIANCE 1

**splenetic** *adj* having or showing a habitually bad temper — see ILL-TEMPERED

**splint** *n* a small flat piece separated from a whole — see CHIP 1

**splinter** *n* a small flat piece separated from a whole — see CHIP 1

**splinter** *vb* to cut into long slender pieces — see SLIVER

**split** *adj* disagreeing with each other — see DIVIDED

**split** *n* **1** an irregular usually narrow break in a surface created by pressure — see CRACK 1
**2** the act or process of a whole separating into two or more parts or pieces — see SEPARATION 1

**split** *vb* to set or force apart — see SEPARATE 1

**split second** *n* a very small space of time — see INSTANT

**splotch** *n* a small area that is different (as in color) from the main part — see SPOT 1

**splotch** *vb* to mark with small spots especially unevenly — see SPOT

**splotched** *adj* having blotches of two or more colors — see PIED

**splotchy** *adj* marked with spots — see SPOTTED 1

**spoil** *n* valuables stolen or taken by force — see LOOT

**spoil** *vb* **1** to affect slightly with something morally bad or undesirable — see TAINT 1
**2** to go through decomposition — see DECAY 1
**3** to reduce the soundness, effectiveness, or perfection of — see DAMAGE 1
**4** to treat with great or excessive care — see BABY

---

***syn*** synonym(s) ***rel*** related words
***ant*** antonym(s) ***near ant*** near antonym(s)

**spoilage** *n* the process by which dead organic matter separates into simpler substances — see CORRUPTION 1

**spoiled** *adj* having undergone organic breakdown — see ROTTEN 1

**spoilsport** *n* a person who spoils the pleasure of others — see KILLJOY

**spoken** *adj* made or carried on through speaking rather than in writing — see VERBAL 2

**spokesman** *n* a person who speaks for another or for a group — see SPOKESPERSON

**spokesperson** *n* a person who speaks for another or for a group ⟨the *spokesperson* for the protesting students presented their demands to the principal⟩
***syn*** mouthpiece, speaker, spokesman
***rel*** spokeswoman; sayer, talker; agent, delegate, deputy, representative

**sponge** *n* a person who is supported or seeks support from another without making an adequate return — see LEECH

**sponge** *vb* to take in (something liquid) through small openings — see ABSORB 1

**sponger** *n* a person who is supported or seeks support from another without making an adequate return — see LEECH

**spongy** *adj* giving easily to the touch — see SOFT 3

**sponsor** *n* a person who takes the responsibility for some other person or thing ⟨you need a *sponsor* to recommend you in order to get into the exclusive country club⟩
***syn*** backer, guarantor, patron, surety
***rel*** chaperone (*or* chaperon); advocate, champion, supporter; benefactor; coach, mentor, teacher

**spontaneity** *n* carefree freedom from constraint — see ABANDON

**spontaneous** *adj* done instantly and without conscious thought or decision — see AUTOMATIC 1

**spoof** *n* a work that imitates and exaggerates another work for comic effect — see PARODY 1

**spook** *n* **1** a person who tries secretly to obtain information for one country in the territory of another usually unfriendly country — see SPY
**2** the soul of a dead person thought of especially as appearing to living people — see GHOST

**spook** *vb* to strike with fear — see FRIGHTEN

**spooked** *adj* filled with fear or dread — see AFRAID 1

**spooky** *adj* **1** easily excited by nature — see EXCITABLE
**2** fearfully and mysteriously strange or fantastic — see EERIE

**spoon** *n* a utensil with a bowl and a handle that is used especially in cooking and serving food ⟨it's easier to eat soup with a *spoon* than with a fork⟩
***syn*** dipper, ladle, scoop
***rel*** skimmer

**spoon** *vb* to lift out with something that holds liquid — see DIP 2

**sporadic** *adj* **1** lacking in steadiness or regularity of occurrence — see FITFUL
**2** not often occurring or repeated — see INFREQUENT
**sport** *n* **1** activity engaged in to amuse oneself — see PLAY 1
**2** an attitude or manner not to be taken seriously — see FUN 2
**sport** *vb* **1** to engage in activity for amusement — see PLAY 1
**2** to play and run about happily — see FROLIC 1
**3** to present so as to invite notice or attention — see SHOW 1
**sportive** *adj* given to good-natured joking or teasing — see PLAYFUL
**sportiveness** *n* a natural disposition for playful behavior — see PLAYFULNESS
**sportsmanlike** *adj* following or according to the rules — see FAIR 3
**sportsmanly** *adj* following or according to the rules — see FAIR 3
**spot** *n* **1** a small area that is different (as in color) from the main part ⟨in summer the white coat of the snow leopard is studded with brownish black *spots*⟩
***syn*** blotch, dapple, dot, eyespot, fleck, mottle, patch, point, speck, speckle, splotch
***rel*** birthmark, freckle, mole; blot, mark, smear, smudge, stain; spatter, splash
**2** a difficult, puzzling, or embarrassing situation from which there is no easy escape — see PREDICAMENT
**3** a mark of guilt or disgrace — see STAIN 1
**4** a very small amount — see PARTICLE 1
**5** the area or space occupied by or intended for something — see PLACE 1
**spot** *vb* to mark with small spots especially unevenly ⟨to give the effect of sunlight on water, the artist *spotted* the lake in his painting with flecks of gold paint⟩
***syn*** blotch, dapple, dot, fleck, freckle, marble, mottle, pepper, speck, speckle, splotch, sprinkle, stipple
***rel*** blot, dye, stain; streak, stripe; intersperse, stud; bespatter, spatter
**spotless** *adj* free from dirt or stain — see CLEAN 1
**spotted** *adj* **1** marked with spots ⟨the *spotted* tablecloth clashed with the stripes on the wallpaper⟩
***syn*** dappled (*also* dapple), dotted, flecked, freckled, mottled, speckled, splotchy, spotty, stippled, variegated
***rel*** spangled; marbled, moiré (*or* moire), veined; motley, multicolored; piebald, roan
***near ant*** solid
**2** having blotches of two or more colors — see PIED
**spotting** *n* the act or process of sighting or learning the existence of something for the first time — see DISCOVERY 1
**spotty** *adj* **1** lacking in steadiness or regularity of occurrence — see FITFUL
**2** marked with spots — see SPOTTED 1
**spouse** *n* the person to whom another is married ⟨employees and their *spouses* are covered by the health plan⟩
***syn*** consort, mate, partner
***rel*** husband, man, old man; lady, wife
***near ant*** single; bachelor; maid, maiden, spinster
**spout** *n* a pipe or channel for carrying off water from a roof — see GUTTER 1
**spout** *vb* **1** to flow out in great quantities or with force — see GUSH 1
**2** to talk loudly and wildly — see RANT
**3** to throw out or off (something from within) often violently — see ERUPT 1
**spout** (off) *vb* to voice one's opinions freely with force — see SPEAK UP
**spray** *vb* to cover by or as if by scattering something over or on — see SCATTER 2
**spread** *n* **1** a decorative cloth used as a top covering for a bed — see COUNTERPANE
**2** a large fancy meal often accompanied by ceremony or entertainment — see FEAST
**3** a wide space or area — see EXPANSE
**4** the distance or extent between possible extremes — see RANGE 3
**5** the space or amount of space between two points, lines, surfaces, or objects — see DISTANCE
**spread** *vb* **1** to cause to be known over a considerable area or by many people ⟨*spread* the news!⟩
***syn*** broadcast, circulate, disseminate, propagate
***rel*** radiate, sprawl; diffuse, dispense, disperse, dissipate, scatter, sow; communicate, pass (on), transmit
***near ant*** conceal, hide, hold (in), secrete; contain, limit, restrict
**2** to put a layer of on a surface ⟨we *spread* the fertilizer over the lawn evenly until it was fully covered⟩
***syn*** apply, lay
***rel*** dab, daub, plaster, smear; blanket, carpet, coat, cover, layer, overlay, overlie, overspread, sheet, surface
***near ant*** peel, strip, uncover
**3** to become known — see GET OUT 1
**4** to cause (something) to pass from one to another — see COMMUNICATE 1
**spread** (out) *vb* to arrange the parts of (something) over a wider area — see OPEN 3
**spreading** *adj* exciting a similar feeling or reaction in others — see CONTAGIOUS 2
**spree** *n* a time or instance of carefree fun — see FLING 1
**sprightliness** *n* the quality or state of having abundant or intense activity — see VITALITY 1
**sprightly** *adv* in a quick and spirited manner — see GAILY 2
**sprightly** *adj* having much high-spirited energy and movement — see LIVELY 1
**spring** *n* an act of leaping into the air — see JUMP 1
**spring** *vb* **1** to come into existence — see BEGIN 2
**2** to propel oneself upward or forward into the air — see JUMP 1

3 to set free (as from slavery or confinement) — see FREE 1

**spring** (for) *vb* to give what is owed for — see PAY 2

**spring** (up) *vb* to come to one's attention especially gradually or unexpectedly — see ARISE 2

**springy** *adj* 1 able to revert to original size and shape after being stretched, squeezed, or twisted — see ELASTIC 1
2 having much high-spirited energy and movement — see LIVELY 1

**sprinkle** *n* 1 a light or fine rain — see DRIZZLE
2 a small number — see FEW

**sprinkle** *vb* 1 to cover by or as if by scattering something over or on — see SCATTER 2
2 to mark with small spots especially unevenly — see SPOT

**sprinkling** *n* 1 a small number — see FEW
2 a very small amount — see PARTICLE 1

**sprint** *vb* to go at a pace faster than a walk — see RUN 1

**sprite** *n* an imaginary being usually having a small human form and magical powers — see FAIRY

**spruce** *adj* being strikingly neat and trim in style or appearance — see SMART 1

**sprucely** *adv* in a strikingly neat and trim manner — see SMARTLY

**spry** *adj* moving easily — see GRACEFUL 1

**spryness** *n* ease and grace in physical activity — see DEXTERITY 2

**spume** *n* a light mass of fine bubbles formed in or on a liquid — see FOAM

**spunk** *n* the strength of mind that enables a person to endure pain or hardship — see FORTITUDE

**spunky** *adj* marked by a lively display of strong feeling — see SPIRITED 1

**spur** *n* something that arouses action or activity — see IMPULSE

**spur** *vb* to urge or push forward with or as if with a pointed object — see PROD 1

**spurious** *adj* 1 being such in appearance only and made or manufactured with the intention of committing fraud — see COUNTERFEIT
2 lacking in natural or spontaneous quality — see ARTIFICIAL 1

**spurn** *vb* to show unwillingness to accept, do, engage in, or agree to — see DECLINE 1

**spur–of–the–moment** *adj* made or done without previous thought or preparation — see EXTEMPORANEOUS

**spurt** *n* a sudden and usually temporary growth of activity — see OUTBREAK

**spurt** *vb* 1 to flow out in great quantities or with force — see GUSH 1
2 to throw out or off (something from within) often violently — see ERUPT 1

**sputter** *vb* to speak rapidly, inarticulately, and usually unintelligibly — see BABBLE 1

---

*syn* synonym(s) *rel* related words
*ant* antonym(s) *near ant* near antonym(s)

**spy** *n* a person who tries secretly to obtain information for one country in the territory of another usually unfriendly country ⟨the government *spy* risked his life every day to get vital information back to his country⟩
*syn* operative, spook
*rel* counterspy, shadow
*phrases* secret agent, undercover agent

**spy** *vb* to make note of (something) through the use of one's eyes — see SEE 1

**spying** *n* the secret gathering of information on others — see ESPIONAGE

**squabble** *n* an often noisy or angry expression of differing opinions — see ARGUMENT 1

**squabble** *vb* to express different opinions about something often angrily — see ARGUE 2

**squabbler** *n* a person who takes part in a dispute — see DISPUTANT

**squad** *n* a group of people working together on a task — see GANG 1

**squalidness** *n* the state or quality of being dirty — see DIRTINESS 1

**squall** *n* 1 a disturbance of the atmosphere accompanied by wind and often by precipitation (as rain or snow) — see STORM 1
2 a state of noisy, confused activity — see COMMOTION

**squall** *vb* to cry out loudly and emotionally — see SCREAM

**squally** *adj* marked by wet and windy conditions — see FOUL 1

**squamous** *adj* composed of or covered with scales — see SCALY

**squander** *vb* to use up carelessly — see WASTE 1

**squanderer** *n* someone who carelessly spends money — see PRODIGAL

**squandering** *adj* given to spending money freely or foolishly — see PRODIGAL

**square** *adj* marked by justice, honesty, and freedom from bias — see FAIR 2

**square** *vb* 1 to be in agreement on every point — see CHECK 1
2 to influence someone with a bribe — see BRIBE

**squarely** *adv* as stated or indicated without the slightest difference — see EXACTLY 1

**squash** *vb* 1 to cause to become a pulpy mass — see CRUSH 1
2 to put a stop to (something) by the use of force — see QUELL 1

**squashy** *adj* giving easily to the touch — see SOFT 3

**squat** *adj* being compact and broad in build and often short in stature — see STOCKY

**squat** *vb* to lie low with the limbs close to the body — see CROUCH

**squatty** *adj* being compact and broad in build and often short in stature — see STOCKY

**squawk** *n* an expression of dissatisfaction, pain, or resentment — see COMPLAINT 1

**squawk** *vb* to express dissatisfaction, pain, or resentment usually tiresomely — see COMPLAIN

**squeak** *vb* to make a short shrill noise ⟨a loose board that *squeaked* every time we walked on the floor⟩
*syn* creak
*rel* cheep, peep; scream, screech, shriek, shrill, sing, squeal, yelp, yip

**squeaking** *adj* having a high musical pitch or range — see SHRILL

**squeaky** *adj* having a high musical pitch or range — see SHRILL

**squeal** *vb* **1** to give information (as to the authorities) about another's improper or unlawful activities ⟨as soon as the stool pigeon got to the police station, he *squealed* to the police about the whole smuggling operation⟩
*syn* inform, snitch, talk, tell
*rel* betray, give away, rat (on), turn in; blab, tattle; tip (off)
**2** to cry out loudly and emotionally — see SCREAM

**squealer** *n* a person who provides secret information about another's wrongdoing — see INFORMER

**squeamish** *adj* **1** affected with nausea — see NAUSEOUS
**2** filled with disgust — see SICK 2

**squeamishness** *n* **1** a disturbed condition of the stomach in which one feels like vomiting — see NAUSEA 1
**2** the tendency to be or state of being squeamish — see DELICACY 3

**squeeze** *vb* **1** to apply external pressure on so as to force out the juice or contents of — see PRESS 2
**2** to fit (something) into a tight space — see CROWD 1
**3** to get with great difficulty — see EKE OUT
**4** to reduce in size or volume by or as if by pressing parts or members together — see COMPRESS 1
**5** to rob by the use of trickery or threats — see FLEECE

**squeezing** *n* the act or process of reducing the size or volume of something by or as if by pressing — see COMPRESSION

**squelch** *vb* to put a stop to (something) by the use of force — see QUELL 1

**squinch** *vb* **1** to lie low with the limbs close to the body — see CROUCH
**2** to twist (something) out of a natural or normal shape or condition — see CONTORT

**squinching** *n* the twisting of something out of its natural or normal shape or condition — see CONTORTION

**squire** *vb* to go along with in order to provide assistance, protection, or companionship — see ACCOMPANY

**squirm** *vb* to make jerky or restless movements — see FIDGET

**squirrel** (away) *vb* to put (something of future use or value) in a safe or secret place — see HOARD

**squirt** *vb* to flow out in great quantities or with force — see GUSH 1

**squishy** *adj* giving easily to the touch — see SOFT 3

**stab** *n* **1** a mark or small hole made by a pointed instrument — see PRICK 1
**2** an effort to do or accomplish something — see ATTEMPT

**stab** *vb* to penetrate or hold (something) with a pointed object — see IMPALE

**stability** *n* **1** the ability to withstand force or stress without being distorted, dislodged, or damaged ⟨the bridge was designed with such great *stability* that it supposedly will not collapse even under the harshest weather conditions⟩
*syn* firmness, soundness, steadiness, strength, sturdiness
*rel* dependability, durability, reliability; solidity, solidness; cohesion, toughness
*near ant* insecurity, weakness
*ant* instability, unsoundness, unsteadiness
**2** the state of continuing without change — see CONSTANCY 1

**stable** *adj* **1** marked by the ability to withstand stress without structural damage or distortion ⟨the tower was *stable* enough to withstand the strongest winds without collapsing⟩
*syn* fast, firm, sound, stalwart, strong, sturdy
*rel* dependable, durable, reliable; solid; cohesive, tough
*near ant* insecure, weak
*ant* unsound, unstable, unsteady
**2** having been established and usually not subject to change — see FIXED 1
**3** having full use of one's mind and control over one's actions — see SANE
**4** not undergoing a change in condition — see CONSTANT 1

**stack** *n* **1** a considerable amount — see LOT 2
**2** a quantity of things thrown or stacked on one another — see [1]PILE 1

**stack** *vb* to lay or throw on top of one another — see PILE

**stack up** (against *or* with) *vb* to come near or nearer to in character or quality — see APPROXIMATE

**stadium** *n* a large usually roofless building for sporting events with tiers of seats for spectators ⟨the football game will be held at the new *stadium*, which seats 100,000 people⟩
*syn* bowl, circus, coliseum, colosseum
*rel* gym, gymnasium; spa; arena, hippodrome

**staff** *n* **1** a body of persons at work or available for work — see FORCE 1
**2** a heavy rigid stick used as a weapon or for punishment — see CLUB 1

**stage** *n* **1** a level usually raised surface — see PLATFORM
**2** a portion of a trip — see LEG 2
**3** an individual part of a process, series, or ranking — see DEGREE 1
**4** the public performance of plays — see DRAMA 1

**stage** *vb* to bring before the public in performance or exhibition — see PRESENT 1

**stagger** *vb* **1** to move forward while swaying from side to side ⟨I was so tired last night that I just *staggered* upstairs to bed without eating dinner⟩
*syn* careen, dodder, lurch, reel, teeter, totter, waddle
*rel* rock, sway, weave, wobble; clump, flounder, lumber, lump, pound, scuff, scuffle, shamble, shuffle, stamp, stomp, stumble, tramp, tromp
**2** to show uncertainty about the right course of action — see HESITATE
**staggering** *adj* causing wonder or astonishment — see MARVELOUS 1
**staid** *adj* **1** not joking or playful in mood or manner — see SERIOUS 1
**2** having or showing a serious and reserved manner — see DIGNIFIED
**stain** *n* **1** a mark of guilt or disgrace ⟨the *stain* of this cowardly act would haunt him for the rest of his career⟩
*syn* blot, brand, smirch, spot, stigma, taint
*rel* discredit, disgrace, dishonor, disrepute, guilt, ignominy, infamy, odium, opprobrium, reproach, shame
*near ant* award, credit, honor
**2** a substance used to color other materials — see PIGMENT
**stain** *vb* **1** to affect slightly with something morally bad or undesirable — see TAINT 1
**2** to give color or a different color to — see COLOR 1
**3** to make dirty — see DIRTY
**stained** *adj* not clean — see DIRTY 1
**stainless** *adj* free from dirt or stain — see CLEAN 1
**stake** *n* **1** a legal right to participation in the advantages, profits, and responsibility of something — see INTEREST 1
**2** the money or thing risked on the outcome of an uncertain event — see BET
**stake** *vb* **1** to provide money for — see FINANCE 1
**2** to risk (something) on the outcome of an uncertain event — see BET
**stale** *adj* used or heard so often as to be dull ⟨viewers were bored by the *stale* story lines of the new crop of sitcoms⟩
*syn* banal, commonplace, hackney, hackneyed, moth-eaten, musty, stereotyped, threadbare, tired, trite
*rel* canned, unimaginative, uninspired, unoriginal; normal, ordinary, rote, routine, standard, stock, typical, usual; boring, drab, dreary, dry, dull, flat, heavy, humdrum, jading, leaden, monotonous, pedestrian, ponderous, prosaic, tame, tedious, tiresome, tiring, unanimated, undramatic, uninteresting, vapid, wearisome, weary, wearying; corny, maudlin, mawkish, mushy, saccharine, sappy, schmaltzy, sentimental, sloppy, sugar-coated, sugary
*near ant* animating, energizing, enlivening, exciting, galvanizing, invigorating, stimulating; absorbing, engaging, engrossing, gripping, interesting, intriguing, involving; atypical, extraordinary, uncommon, unusual
*ant* fresh, new, original
**stalemate** *n* **1** a point in a struggle where neither side is capable of winning or willing to give in — see IMPASSE
**2** a situation in which neither participant in a contest, competition, or struggle comes out ahead of the other — see TIE 1
**stalk** *vb* **1** to seek out (game) for food or sport — see HUNT 1
**2** to walk with exaggerated arm and leg movements — see STRUT 1
**stall** *vb* **1** to bring (something) to a standstill — see [1]HALT 1
**2** to stop functioning — see FAIL 1
**stalwart** *adj* **1** feeling or displaying no fear by temperament — see BRAVE
**2** having muscles capable of exerting great physical force — see STRONG 1
**3** marked by the ability to withstand stress without structural damage or distortion — see STABLE 1
**stamp** *n* a perceptible trace left by pressure — see PRINT 1
**stamp** *vb* **1** to move heavily or clumsily — see LUMBER 1
**2** to tread on heavily so as to crush or injure — see TRAMPLE
**stamp** (out) *vb* to destroy all traces of — see ANNIHILATE 1
**stance** *n* a general way of holding the body — see POSTURE 1
**stanchion** *n* an upright shaft that supports an overhead structure — see PILLAR 1
**stand** *n* a level usually raised surface — see PLATFORM
**stand** *vb* **1** to occupy a place or location ⟨the monument *stands* in the middle of the town plaza⟩
*syn* be, lie, sit
*rel* command, overlook; remain, rest, stay; await, wait; post, station
**2** to put up with (something painful or difficult) — see BEAR 2
**3** to give what is owed for — see PAY 2
**standard** *adj* **1** accepted, used, or practiced by most people — see CURRENT 1
**2** being of the type that is encountered in the normal course of events — see ORDINARY 1
**3** having or showing the qualities associated with the members of a particular group or kind — see TYPICAL 1
**standard** *n* **1** something set up as an example against which others of the same type are compared ⟨the animation in that movie set the *standard* against which all later animated cartoons were judged⟩
*syn* benchmark, criterion, grade, mark, measure, par, touchstone, yardstick
*rel* rule; case, example, instance; acme, apex, meridian, peak, pinnacle, summit, zenith
*near ant* aberration, abnormality, deviation
**2** a piece of cloth with a special design that is used as an emblem or for signaling — see FLAG 1

*syn* synonym(s) *rel* related words
*ant* antonym(s) *near ant* near antonym(s)

3 what is typical of a group, class, or series — see AVERAGE
4 **standards** *pl* the code of good conduct for an individual or group — see ETHICS
**standardize** *vb* to make agree with a single established standard or model ⟨the plan is to *standardize* the test for reading comprehension so that we can see how students across the state compare⟩
*syn* formalize, homogenize, normalize, regularize
*rel* codify, organize, systematize; average, equalize, even; accredit, certify; control, govern, regulate; coordinate, harmonize, integrate, reconcile, synthesize
*near ant* customize, individualize, tailor
**standby** *n* something or someone to which one looks for support — see DEPENDENCE 2
**stand-in** *n* a person or thing that takes the place of another — see SUBSTITUTE
**stand in** *vb* to serve as a replacement usually for a time only — see COVER 1
**standing** *adj* 1 fixed in a place or position — see STATIONARY 1
2 rising straight up — see ERECT
**standing** *n* 1 high position within society — see RANK 2
2 the period during which something exists, lasts, or is in progress — see DURATION 1
3 the placement of someone or something in relation to others in a vertical arrangement — see RANK 1
**standoff** *n* a situation in which neither participant in a contest, competition, or struggle comes out ahead of the other — see TIE 1
**standoffish** *adj* having or showing a lack of friendliness or interest in others — see COOL 1
**standout** *n* a person who is widely known and usually much talked about — see CELEBRITY 1
**stand out** *vb* to extend outward beyond a usual point — see BULGE
**standpoint** *n* a way of looking at or thinking about something — see POINT OF VIEW
**standstill** *n* a point in a struggle where neither side is capable of winning or willing to give in — see IMPASSE
**staple** *n* the main or greater part of something as distinguished from its appendages — see BODY 1
**star** *adj* 1 of or relating to the stars — see STELLAR 1
2 standing above others in rank, importance, or achievement — see EMINENT
3 widely known — see FAMOUS
**star** *n* 1 a ball-shaped gaseous celestial body that shines by its own light ⟨it's difficult to see the *stars* at night in the middle of the city because of all the streetlights⟩
*syn* luminary sun
*rel* constellation; dwarf, fixed star, giant star, lodestar (*also* loadstar), neutron star, nova, red giant, supernova, variable star, white dwarf
2 the person who has the most important role in a play, movie, or TV show ⟨when the *star* of the school play came down with the flu on opening night, her understudy got to go on⟩
*syn* lead, principal
*rel* leading lady, leading man; superstar; ingenue (*or* ingénue), starlet
*near ant* extra, supernumerary
3 a person who is widely known and usually much talked about — see CELEBRITY 1
**starch** *n* active strength of body or mind — see VIGOR 1
**starchy** *adj* marked by or showing careful attention to set forms and details — see CEREMONIOUS 1
**star-crossed** *adj* having, prone to, or marked by bad luck — see UNLUCKY
**stare** *vb* to look long and hard in wonder or surprise — see GAPE
**stark** *adj* 1 harsh and threatening in manner or appearance — see GRIM 1
2 having no exceptions or restrictions — see ABSOLUTE 2
3 lacking contents that could or should be present — see EMPTY 1
4 producing inferior or only a small amount of vegetation — see BARREN 1
**starry** *adj* of or relating to the stars — see STELLAR 1
**start** *n* the point at which something begins — see BEGINNING
**start** *vb* 1 to move suddenly and sharply (as in surprise) ⟨I *started* from my chair when I heard the sudden scream⟩
*syn* bolt, jump, startle
*rel* jerk, twitch; flinch, recoil; bound, leap, spring; react, respond
2 to be responsible for the creation and early operation or use of — see FOUND
3 to cause to function — see ACTIVATE
4 to come into existence — see BEGIN 2
5 to extend outward beyond a usual point — see BULGE
6 to take the first step in (a process or course of action) — see BEGIN 1
**startle** *vb* 1 to make a strong impression on (someone) with something unexpected — see SURPRISE 1
2 to move suddenly and sharply (as in surprise) — see START 1
3 to strike with fear — see FRIGHTEN
**startling** *adj* causing a strong emotional reaction because unexpected — see SURPRISING 1
**starved** *adj* feeling a desire or need for food — see HUNGRY 1
**starving** *adj* feeling a desire or need for food — see HUNGRY 1
**stash** *n* a supply stored up and often hidden away — see HOARD 1
**stash** *vb* to put (something of future use or value) in a safe or secret place — see HOARD
**stashing** *n* the placing of something out of sight — see CONCEALMENT 1
**state** *adj* of or relating to a nation — see NATIONAL

**state** *n* a body of people composed of one or more nationalities usually with its own territory and government — see NATION
**state** *vb* **1** to convey in appropriate or telling terms — see PHRASE
**2** to express (a thought or emotion) in words — see SAY 1
**3** to make known (as an idea, emotion, or opinion) — see EXPRESS 1
**state house** *n* the building in which a state legislature meets — see CAPITOL
**stateliness** *n* **1** a dignified bearing or appearance befitting royalty — see MAJESTY 1
**2** dignified or restrained beauty of form, appearance, or style — see ELEGANCE
**3** impressiveness of beauty on a large scale — see MAGNIFICENCE
**stately** *adj* **1** having or showing a serious and reserved manner — see DIGNIFIED
**2** having or showing elegance — see ELEGANT 1
**3** large and impressive in size, grandeur, extent, or conception — see GRAND 1
**4** very dignified in form, tone, or style — see ELEVATED 2
**statement** *n* **1** a record of goods sold or services performed together with the costs due — see [1]BILL 1
**2** an act, process, or means of putting something into words — see EXPRESSION 1
**3** something that is said — see WORD 2
**static** *adj* fixed in a place or position — see STATIONARY 1
**station** *n* **1** the place where someone is assigned to stand or remain ⟨the soldiers remained at their *station* even though a huge enemy force was approaching⟩
***syn*** position, post, quarter
***rel*** assignment, detail
**2** a regular stopping place ⟨the historic house was once a *station* on the Underground Railroad, the network that helped slaves reach freedom in the North⟩
***syn*** stop, way station
***rel*** depot, terminal; layover, stopover
**3** the placement of someone or something in relation to others in a vertical arrangement — see RANK 1
**station** *vb* to assign to a place or position — see [2]POST
**stationary** *adj* **1** fixed in a place or position ⟨a *stationary* bicycle is good for exercise, but you won't enjoy the scenery very much⟩
***syn*** immobile, nonmoving, standing, static
***rel*** immovable, irremovable, nonmotile, unmovable; frozen, motionless, stagnant, still, unbudging
***near ant*** motile
***ant*** mobile, movable (*or* moveable), moving, nonstationary
**2** not undergoing a change in condition — see CONSTANT 1
**statuette** *n* a small statue — see FIGURINE

***syn*** synonym(s) ***rel*** related words
***ant*** antonym(s) ***near ant*** near antonym(s)

**stature** *n* the distance of something or someone from bottom to top — see HEIGHT 3
**status** *n* **1** position with regard to conditions and circumstances — see SITUATION 1
**2** the placement of someone or something in relation to others in a vertical arrangement — see RANK 1
**status quo** *n* the state or fact of being the way things usually are — see NORMALITY
**statute** *n* a rule of conduct or action laid down by a governing authority and especially a legislator — see LAW 1
**staunch** *or* **stanch** *adj* firm in one's allegiance to someone or something — see FAITHFUL 1
**stave off** *vb* to drive back — see REPEL 1
[1]**stay** *n* a temporary residing as another's guest — see VISIT 1
[2]**stay** *n* something that holds up or serves as a foundation for something else — see SUPPORT 1
**stay** *vb* **1** to continue to be in a place for a significant amount of time ⟨let's *stay* inside this pavilion until it stops raining⟩
***syn*** abide, dwell, hang around, remain, stick around, tarry
***rel*** await, hang on, hold on, wait; dally, linger, loiter; keep
***ant*** go, leave, quit
**2** to bring (something) to a standstill — see [1]HALT 1
**3** to hold up or serve as a foundation for — see SUPPORT 3
**4** to remain in place in readiness or expectation of something — see WAIT
**5** to reside as a temporary guest — see VISIT 2
**steadfast** *adj* firm in one's allegiance to someone or something — see FAITHFUL 1
**steadfastness** *n* adherence to something to which one is bound by a pledge or duty — see FIDELITY
**steadiness** *n* **1** the ability to withstand force or stress without being distorted, dislodged, or damaged — see STABILITY 1
**2** the state of continuing without change — see CONSTANCY 1
**steady** *adj* **1** firm in one's allegiance to someone or something — see FAITHFUL 1
**2** appearing or occurring repeatedly from time to time — see REGULAR 1
**3** not undergoing a change in condition — see CONSTANT 1
**4** not varying — see UNIFORM
**5** worthy of one's trust — see DEPENDABLE
**steal** *n* something bought or offered for sale at a desirable price — see BARGAIN 1
**steal** *vb* **1** to take (something) without right and with an intent to keep ⟨the guy who tried to *steal* my car was sentenced to a year in jail⟩
***syn*** appropriate, filch, hook, misappropriate, nip, pilfer, pinch, pocket, purloin, rip off, snitch, swipe, thieve
***rel*** burglarize, fleece, rob; loot, pillage, plunder, sack; hijack (*or* highjack); pick, rifle; poach, rustle, shoplift; collar, grab,

grasp, nail, seize, snatch, take; mooch, sponge; abduct, kidnap, shanghai, spirit
*phrases* make away with, run off with, walk off with
*near ant* buy, purchase; bestow, contribute, donate, give, present
**2** to move about in a sly or secret manner — see SNEAK 1

**steal** (from) *vb* to remove valuables from (a place) unlawfully — see ROB

**stealer** *n* one who steals — see THIEF

**stealing** *n* the unlawful taking and carrying away of property without the consent of its owner — see THEFT 1

**stealthy** *adj* **1** given to acting in secret and to concealing one's intentions — see SNEAKY 1
**2** undertaken or done so as to escape being observed or known by others — see SECRET 1

**steam** *vb* to be excited or emotionally stirred up with anger — see BOIL 1

**steaming** *adj* feeling or showing anger — see ANGRY

**steed** *n* a large hoofed domestic animal that is used for carrying or drawing loads and for riding — see HORSE

**steel** *n* a hand weapon with a length of metal sharpened on one or both sides and usually tapered to a sharp point — see SWORD

**steel** *vb* **1** to fill with courage or strength of purpose — see ENCOURAGE 1
**2** to make able to withstand physical hardship, strain, or exposure — see HARDEN 2
**3** to prepare (oneself) mentally or emotionally — see FORTIFY 1

**steely** *adj* **1** harsh and threatening in manner or appearance — see GRIM 1
**2** of the color gray — see GRAY 1

**steep** *adj* **1** having an incline approaching the perpendicular ⟨a very *steep* rock face that was nearly impossible to climb⟩
*syn* abrupt, bold, precipitous, sheer
*rel* perpendicular, plumb, straight, vertical; craggy, hilly, mountainous, scarped; angled, canted, cocked, heeled, inclined, listed, slanted, sloped, tilted, tipped
*near ant* gentle, gradual, moderate; even, flat, flush, horizontal, level, plane, smooth, unruffled, unwrinkled
*ant* easy
**2** going beyond a normal or acceptable limit in degree or amount — see EXCESSIVE

**steep** *vb* **1** to cause (as a person) to become filled or saturated with a certain quality or principle — see INFUSE
**2** to wet thoroughly with liquid — see SOAK 1

**steer** *vb* to point out the way for (someone) especially from a position in front — see LEAD 1

**stellar** *adj* **1** of or relating to the stars ⟨humankind's dream of *stellar* navigation is hampered by the vast distances between the stars, even in our own galaxy⟩
*syn* astral, star, starry
*rel* celestial, empyrean, heavenly; astronomical (*also* astronomic), astrophysical; astronautic (*or* astronautical); starlike, star-spangled
**2** of the very best kind — see EXCELLENT

**stench** *n* a strong unpleasant smell — see STINK

**stentorian** *adj* marked by a high volume of sound — see LOUD 1

**step** *n* **1** an action planned or taken to achieve a desired result — see MEASURE 1
**2** an individual part of a process, series, or ranking — see DEGREE 1
**3** the mark or impression made by a foot — see FOOTPRINT
**4 steps** *pl* the direction along which something or someone moves — see PATH 1

**step** *vb* **1** to go on foot — see WALK
**2** to perform a series of usually rhythmic bodily movements to music — see DANCE 1

**step** (along) *vb* to proceed or move quickly — see HURRY 2

**step–by–step** *adj* proceeding or changing by steps or degrees — see GRADUAL

**step down** (from) *vb* **1** to give up (a job or office) — see QUIT 1
**2** to give up (as a position of authority) formally — see ABDICATE

**steppe** *n* a broad area of level or rolling treeless country — see PLAIN

**step up** *vb* to make markedly greater in measure or degree — see INTENSIFY

**stereotype** *n* an idea or statement about all of the members of a group or all the instances of a situation — see GENERALIZATION

**stereotyped** *adj* used or heard so often as to be dull — see STALE

**sterile** *adj* **1** not able to produce fruit or offspring ⟨*sterile* couples sometimes choose to adopt needy children⟩ ⟨the apple tree turned out to be *sterile*, never yielding a crop of apples⟩
*syn* barren, impotent, infertile, unfruitful
*rel* altered, desexed, neutered, sterilized; castrated, emasculated, gelded; spayed; fruitless, unproductive
*near ant* fecund, luxuriant, productive, prolific; enriched, fertilized, rich; impregnated, pregnant; potent; bearing, producing, yielding; blooming, bursting, flourishing, swarming, teeming
*ant* fat, fertile, fruitful
**2** free from filth, infection, or dangers to health — see SANITARY

**sterling** *adj* of the very best kind — see EXCELLENT

**stern** *adj* **1** given to exacting standards of discipline and self-restraint — see SEVERE 1
**2** harsh and threatening in manner or appearance — see GRIM 1

**sternly** *adv* in a manner so as to cause loss or suffering — see HARDLY 1

**sternness** *n* the quality or state of being demanding or unyielding (as in discipline or criticism) — see SEVERITY

**stevedore** *n* one who loads and unloads ships at a port — see DOCKWORKER

**stew** *n* **1** a state of nervous or irritated concern — see FRET
**2** a state of noisy, confused activity — see COMMOTION

**stew** *vb* **1** to cook in a liquid heated to the point that it gives off steam — see BOIL 2
**2** to experience concern or anxiety — see WORRY 1

**steward** *n* a person hired to perform household or personal services — see SERVANT

**stick** *vb* **1** to hold to something firmly as if by adhesion ⟨those magnets are strong enough to *stick* well to the refrigerator⟩
***syn*** adhere, cleave, cling, hew
***rel*** bind, cohere, fasten, fuse, glue, unite
***near ant*** loosen; drop, fall
**2** to arrange something in a certain spot or position — see PLACE 1
**3** to penetrate or hold (something) with a pointed object — see IMPALE
**4** to rob by the use of trickery or threats — see FLEECE

**stick** (to *or* with) *vb* to give steadfast support to — see ADHERE

**stick around** *vb* to continue to be in a place for a significant amount of time — see STAY 1

**stick–in–the–mud** *n* **1** a person with old-fashioned ideas — see FOGY
**2** someone who moves slowly or more slowly than others — see SLOWPOKE

**stick out** *vb* **1** to extend outward beyond a usual point — see BULGE
**2** to put up with (something painful or difficult) — see BEAR 2

**sticks** *n pl* the open rural area outside of big towns and cities — see COUNTRY 2

**sticky** *adj* **1** being of such a thick consistency as to readily cling to objects upon contact ⟨the *sticky* maple syrup was a mess to clean up⟩
***syn*** adhesive, adhesive, gluey, glutinous, gooey, gummy, viscid, viscous
***rel*** ropy, tacky; adherent, tenacious
***ant*** nonadhesive, nonviscous
**2** containing or characterized by an uncomfortable amount of moisture — see HUMID

**stiff** *adj* **1** incapable of or highly resistant to bending ⟨use a *stiff* piece of paper for the project⟩
***syn*** inflexible, rigid, stiffened, unyielding
***rel*** inelastic; firm, hard, solid, sound, strong; brittle, crisp; compact, dense, substantial; arthritic, rheumatic; nonelastic, nonmalleable
***near ant*** elastic, resilient, springy, stretchy, workable; malleable; droopy, flabby, flaccid, mushy, semisoft, soft, squashy, squishy; lank, limber, limp, lissome (*also* lissom), lithe, willowy
***ant*** flexible, floppy, pliable, pliant, supple, yielding
**2** difficult to endure — see HARSH 1
**3** going beyond a normal or acceptable limit in degree or amount — see EXCESSIVE
**4** having a consistency that does not easily yield to pressure — see FIRM 2
**5** lacking social grace and assurance — see AWKWARD 1
**6** requiring considerable physical or mental effort — see HARD 2

**stiffened** *adj* incapable of or highly resistant to bending — see STIFF 1

**stiffly** *adv* **1** in a manner so as to cause loss or suffering — see HARDLY 1
**2** in a vigorous and forceful manner — see HARD 3

**stifle** *vb* **1** to be or cause to be killed by lack of breathable air — see SMOTHER 1
**2** to refrain from openly showing or uttering — see SUPPRESS 2

**stifling** *adj* lacking fresh air — see STUFFY 1

**stigma** *n* a mark of guilt or disgrace — see STAIN 1

**still** *adj* **1** free from disturbing noise or uproar — see QUIET 1
**2** free from storms or physical disturbance — see CALM 1
**3** mostly or entirely without sound — see SILENT 3

**still** *adv* **1** without motion ⟨now, you have to sit very *still* while the hairdresser cuts your hair⟩
***syn*** motionlessly, quiet, quietly
***rel*** immovably; inactively
***near ant*** movably
**2** in spite of that — see HOWEVER

**still** *n* **1** a state of freedom from storm or disturbance — see CALM
**2** the near or complete absence of sound — see SILENCE 2

**still** *vb* **1** to bring (something) to a standstill — see [1]HALT 1
**2** to free from distress or disturbance — see CALM 1
**3** to stop the noise or speech of — see SILENCE 1

**stillness** *n* **1** a state of freedom from storm or disturbance — see CALM
**2** incapacity for or restraint from speaking — see SILENCE 1
**3** the near or complete absence of sound — see SILENCE 2

**stilly** *adj* **1** free from disturbing noise or uproar — see QUIET 1
**2** free from storms or physical disturbance — see CALM 1

**stilted** *adj* lacking social grace and assurance — see AWKWARD 1

**stimulant** *n* **1** something that arouses a strong response from another — see PROVOCATION 1
**2** something that arouses action or activity — see IMPULSE

**stimulate** *vb* **1** to give life, vigor, or spirit to — see ANIMATE
**2** to rouse to strong feeling or action — see PROVOKE 1

**stimulating** *adj* **1** causing great emotional or mental stimulation — see EXCITING 1

---

***syn*** synonym(s) ***rel*** related words
***ant*** antonym(s) ***near ant*** near antonym(s)

2 having a renewing effect on the state of the body or mind — see TONIC
3 serving or likely to arouse a strong reaction — see PROVOCATIVE

**stimulation** *n* something that arouses a strong response from another — see PROVOCATION 1

**stimulative** *adj* having a renewing effect on the state of the body or mind — see TONIC

**stimulus** *n* 1 something that arouses a strong response from another — see PROVOCATION 1
2 something that arouses action or activity — see IMPULSE

**sting** *n* a sharp unpleasant sensation usually felt in some specific part of the body — see PAIN 1

**sting** *vb* 1 to charge (someone) too much for goods or services — see OVERCHARGE 1
2 to rob by the use of trickery or threats — see FLEECE

**stinginess** *n* the quality of being overly sparing with money — see PARSIMONY

**stinging** *adj* causing intense discomfort to one's skin — see CUTTING 1

**stingy** *adj* 1 giving or sharing as little as possible ⟨until his redemption, Ebenezer Scrooge is the classic example of a very *stingy*, heartless miser⟩
*syn* cheap, close, closefisted, mean, niggard, niggardly, parsimonious, penurious, pinching, spare, sparing, stinting, tight, tightfisted, uncharitable
*rel* careful, chary, conserving, economical, economizing, frugal, saving, scrimping, skimping, thrifty; acquisitive, avaricious, avid, coveting, covetous, desirous, grasping, greedy, hoggish, itchy, mercenary, rapacious, selfish, shabby, small, sordid; begrudging, envious, grudging, resentful; inhospitable
*near ant* altruistic, selfless, unselfish; extravagant, free, handsome, lavish, profuse; beneficent, benevolent, hospitable, humanitarian, philanthropic; compassionate, good-hearted, greathearted, kindly, magnanimous, openhearted; thriftless, unthrifty; dissipating, frittering, prodigal, profligate, spendthrift, splurging, squandering, wasteful, wasting
*ant* bounteous, bountiful, charitable, freehanded, generous, liberal, munificent, openhanded, unsparing, unstinting
2 less plentiful than what is normal, necessary, or desirable — see MEAGER

**stink** *n* a strong unpleasant smell ⟨the *stink* of burned plastic lingered in the kitchen for days after we accidentally melted a spatula on the stove⟩
*syn* reek, stench
*rel* acridness, fetidness, foulness, fustiness, malodorousness, mustiness, rancidity, rankness, staleness; badness, vileness; dirt, dirtiness, filth, filthiness, nastiness; odor, redolence, scent, sniff
*near ant* floweriness, lusciousness, savoriness, spiciness, sweetness; bouquet; ambrosia
*ant* aroma, fragrance, perfume

**stink** *vb* to give off an extremely unpleasant smell ⟨the dog *stinks* because she tangled with a skunk again⟩
*syn* reek
*rel* exhale, savor, smell; decay, decompose, rot, spoil; disgust, offend, repulse, revolt

**stinker** *n* a person whose behavior is offensive to others — see JERK 1

**stinking** *adj* having an unpleasant smell — see MALODOROUS

**stinky** *adj* having an unpleasant smell — see MALODOROUS

**stint** *n* 1 a fixed period of time during which a person holds a job or position — see TERM 1
2 a piece of work that needs to be done regularly — see CHORE 1

**stint** (on) *vb* to use or give out in stingy amounts — see SPARE

**stinting** *adj* giving or sharing as little as possible — see STINGY 1

**stipend** *n* the money paid regularly to a person for labor or services — see WAGE

**stipple** *vb* to mark with small spots especially unevenly — see SPOT

**stippled** *adj* marked with spots — see SPOTTED 1

**stipulate** (for) *vb* to ask for (something) earnestly or with authority — see DEMAND 1

**stipulation** *n* something upon which the carrying out of an agreement or offer depends — see CONDITION 2

**stir** *n* 1 a state of noisy, confused activity — see COMMOTION
2 the act or an instance of changing position — see MOVEMENT 1

**stir** *vb* 1 to cause (as a liquid) to move about in a circle especially repeatedly ⟨the recipe says to *stir* the mixture carefully until it's properly blended⟩
*syn* agitate, churn, swirl, whirl
*rel* beat, paddle, whip, whisk; reel, shake, wheel
2 to change one's position — see MOVE 3
3 to rouse to strong feeling or action — see PROVOKE 1

**stir** (up) *vb* to cause or encourage the development of — see INCITE 1

**stirring** *adj* 1 causing great emotional or mental stimulation — see EXCITING 1
2 having the power to affect the feelings or sympathies — see MOVING

**stirring** *n* the act or an instance of changing position — see MOVEMENT 1

**stitch** *n* a sharp unpleasant sensation usually felt in some specific part of the body — see PAIN 1

**stitch** *vb* to close up with a series of interlacing stitches — see SEW

**stock** *adj* accepted, used, or practiced by most people — see CURRENT 1

**stock** *n* 1 a group of persons who come from the same ancestor — see FAMILY 1
2 a stupid person — see IDIOT

**3** firm belief in the integrity, ability, effectiveness, or genuineness of someone or something — see TRUST 1
**4** the line of ancestors from whom a person is descended — see ANCESTRY

**stockade** *n* a place of confinement for persons held in lawful custody — see JAIL

**stocking** *n* a close-fitting covering for the foot and leg ⟨be sure to wear your thick wool *stockings* if it's cold today⟩
*syn* hose, sock
*rel* hosiery; anklet, bobby socks, bootee

**stockpile** *n* a supply stored up and often hidden away — see HOARD 1

**stockpile** *vb* to put (something of future use or value) in a safe or secret place — see HOARD

**stocky** *adj* being compact and broad in build and often short in stature ⟨he was a tough, *stocky* little boy, muscular and solid⟩
*syn* chunky, dumpy, heavyset, squat, squatty, stout, stubby, stumpy, thickset
*rel* beefy, brawny, bulky, burly, husky, sturdy, thick, thickish, weighty; chubby, corpulent, fat, fleshy, full, gross, heavy, obese, overweight, plump, portly, pudgy, roly-poly, rotund, round, tubby; paunchy, potbellied; flabby, soft
*near ant* delicate, fragile, frail, puny; lean, skinny, slender, slim, spare, thin; angular, bony, gaunt, lank, lanky, rawboned, sinewy; scraggy, scrawny, slight; anorexic, cadaverous, emaciated, haggard, skeletal, wasted; spindly, twiggy, waspish, weedy, willowy, wiry

**stodgy** *adj* causing weariness, restlessness, or lack of interest — see BORING

**stoic** *or* **stoical** *adj* **1** accepting pains or hardships calmly or without complaint — see PATIENT 1
**2** not feeling or showing emotion — see IMPASSIVE 1

**stolid** *adj* **1** not expressing any emotion — see BLANK 1
**2** not feeling or showing emotion — see IMPASSIVE 1

**stomach** *n* the part of the body between the chest and the pelvis ⟨please don't lean on my *stomach* —I just had a big meal⟩
*syn* abdomen, belly, breadbasket [*slang*], gut, solar plexus, tummy
*rel* middle, midriff, waist; paunch, potbelly; thorax

**stomach** *vb* to put up with (something painful or difficult) — see BEAR 2

**stomachache** *n* abdominal pain especially when focused in the digestive organs ⟨you can stay home from school tomorrow if you still have a *stomachache*⟩
*syn* bellyache
*rel* colic, cramps

**stomp** *vb* **1** to move heavily or clumsily — see LUMBER 1
**2** to tread on heavily so as to crush or injure — see TRAMPLE

---

*syn* synonym(s) *rel* related words
*ant* antonym(s) *near ant* near antonym(s)

**stone blind** *adj* lacking the power of sight — see BLIND

**stone–broke** *adj* lacking money or material possessions — see POOR 1

**stoneware** *n* articles made of baked clay — see CROCKERY

**stony** *also* **stoney** *adj* having or showing a lack of sympathy or tender feelings — see HARD 1

**stool pigeon** *n* a person who provides secret information about another's wrongdoing — see INFORMER

**stoop** *vb* to descend to a level that is beneath one's dignity — see CONDESCEND 1

**stooping** *adj* bending downward or forward — see NODDING

**stop** *n* **1** a brief halt in a journey ⟨our guide called for a *stop* at the trail hut to eat and rest a bit⟩
*syn* layover, stopover
*rel* break, pause, rest
**2** a regular stopping place — see STATION 2
**3** something that makes movement or progress more difficult — see ENCUMBRANCE
**4** the stopping of a process or activity — see END 1

**stop** *vb* **1** to bring (as an action or operation) to an immediate end ⟨please *stop* that running in the library⟩
*syn* break, break off, can, cease, cut (out), desist (from), discontinue, drop, end, halt, knock off, lay off, leave off, quit, shut off
*rel* complete, conclude, finish; close (down); deactivate; block, blockade, dam, delay, detain, hinder, hold, hold back, impede, obstruct, stem; call, suspend; arrest, brake, check, clamp down, rein (in), squash, squelch, stamp, stanch (*also* staunch), stunt, suppress, turn back; pause, stay, suspend; abolish, abort, annul, demolish, destroy, dissolve, kill, ruin, scuttle, snuff
*phrases* have done with, put the kibosh on
*near ant* carry on, continue, follow through, keep up, run on; advance, proceed, progress; actuate, drive, impel, propel, stir
**2** to bring (something) to a standstill — see [1]HALT 1
**3** to close up so that no empty spaces remain — see FILL 2
**4** to come to an end — see CEASE 1

**stop** (by *or* in) *vb* to make a brief visit — see CALL 3

**stop** (up) *vb* to prevent passage through — see CLOG 1

**stopcock** *n* a fixture for controlling the flow of a liquid — see FAUCET

**stopgap** *n* a temporary replacement — see MAKESHIFT

**stopover** *n* a brief halt in a journey — see STOP 1

**stoppage** *n* the stopping of a process or activity — see END 1

**storage** *n* a building for storing goods — see STOREHOUSE

**store** *adj* made beforehand in large numbers — see READY-MADE

**store** *n* **1** a collection of things kept available for future use or need ⟨Dad has a *store* of funny stories for when conversation lags at company parties⟩
*syn* cache, deposit, hoard, reserve
*rel* budget, fund, nest egg, pool, reservoir, stock, stockpile, supply; accumulation, assemblage, collection, gathering
**2** a supply stored up and often hidden away — see HOARD 1
**3** an establishment where goods are sold to consumers — see SHOP 1

**store** *vb* **1** to place somewhere for safekeeping or ready availability ⟨we decided to *store* the lawn mower in the shed instead of the garage⟩
*syn* keep, stow
*rel* garage, house; file, pack, shelve
**2** to put (something of future use or value) in a safe or secret place — see HOARD

**storehouse** *n* a building for storing goods ⟨the company has a large *storehouse* filled with lumber for manufacturing its line of furniture⟩
*syn* depository, depot, magazine, repository, storage, stowage, warehouse
*rel* cache, stockroom, storeroom; bank, bin, container, locker, safe-deposit box, strongbox; arsenal, dump

**storm** *n* **1** a disturbance of the atmosphere accompanied by wind and often by precipitation (as rain or snow) ⟨a winter *storm* bringing about six inches of snow⟩
*syn* squall, tempest
*rel* blizzard, hail storm, ice storm, northeaster, norther, rainstorm, sandstorm, snowstorm, southeaster, southwester, thunderstorm, windstorm; cyclone, hurricane, typhoon
**2** a heavy fall of objects — see RAIN 2
**3** a rapid or overwhelming outpouring of many things at once — see BARRAGE
**4** a state of noisy, confused activity — see COMMOTION
**5** a steady falling of water from the sky in significant quantity — see RAIN 1
**6** a sudden intense expression of strong feeling — see OUTBURST 1
**7** a violent disturbance (as of the political or social order) — see CONVULSION

**storm** *vb* **1** to express one's anger usually violently — see RAGE 1
**2** to fall as water in a continuous stream of drops from the clouds — see RAIN 1
**3** to take sudden, violent action against — see ATTACK 1

**stormy** *adj* **1** marked by bursts of destructive force or intense activity — see VIOLENT 1
**2** marked by or abounding with rain — see RAINY
**3** marked by sudden or violent disturbance — see CONVULSIVE
**4** marked by turmoil or disturbance especially of natural elements — see WILD 3
**5** marked by wet and windy conditions — see FOUL 1

**story** *n* **1** a work with imaginary characters and events that is shorter and usually less complex than a novel ⟨if you go right to bed, Daddy will read a *story* to you⟩
*syn* narrative, novelette, novella, short story, tale, yarn
*rel* exemplum, fable, parable; anecdote, joke; fairy tale, folktale, legend, myth, romance; account, annals, chronicle, history, record, report
**2** a brief account of something interesting that happened especially to one personally ⟨Grandpa is always telling *stories* about what it was like growing up on a farm⟩
*syn* anecdote, tale, yarn
*rel* episode, event, happening, incident, occurrence; recital, recitation
**3** a report of recent events or facts not previously known — see NEWS
**4** a relating of events usually in the order in which they happened — see ACCOUNT 1
**5** a rumor or report of a personal or sensational nature — see TALE 1
**6** a statement known by its maker to be untrue and made in order to deceive — see LIE

**storyteller** *n* a person who tells lies — see LIAR

**stout** *adj* **1** able to withstand hardship, strain, or exposure — see HARDY 1
**2** being compact and broad in build and often short in stature — see STOCKY
**3** feeling or displaying no fear by temperament — see BRAVE
**4** having muscles capable of exerting great physical force — see STRONG 1
**5** not showing weakness or uncertainty — see FIRM 1

**stouthearted** *adj* feeling or displaying no fear by temperament — see BRAVE

**stoutly** *adv* in a vigorous and forceful manner — see HARD 3

**stoutness** *n* strength of mind to carry on in spite of danger — see COURAGE

**stow** *vb* **1** to place somewhere for safekeeping or ready availability — see STORE 1
**2** to put (something of future use or value) in a safe or secret place — see HOARD

**stowage** *n* a building for storing goods — see STOREHOUSE

**straggler** *n* someone who moves slowly or more slowly than others — see SLOWPOKE

**straight** *adj* **1** free from irregularities (as curves, bends, or angles) in course ⟨in the wide, open spaces of the West some rural roads are incredibly *straight*⟩
*syn* linear, right, straightaway, straightforward
*rel* unbent, uncurled, untwisted; direct, undeviating, unswerving
*near ant* bowed, rounded; entwined, kinked, swirled, turned, turning, twined, twining, twisted, twisting, veering, warped; bending, coiled, coiling, corkscrew, curled, curling, curved, curving, looped, looping, spiral, spiraling (*or* spi-

ralling), winding; meandering, weaving; devious, serpentine, sinuous, zigzag, zigzagging
*ant* crooked
**2** conforming to a high standard of morality or virtue — see GOOD 2
**3** free from added matter — see PURE 1
**4** free in expressing one's true feelings and opinions — see FRANK
**5** going straight to the point clearly and firmly — see STRAIGHTFORWARD 1
**6** not having one's mind affected by alcohol — see SOBER 1

**straight** *adv* **1** in a direct line or course — see DIRECTLY 1
**2** in an honest and direct manner — see STRAIGHTFORWARD

**straightaway** *adj* **1** done or occurring without any noticeable lapse in time — see INSTANTANEOUS
**2** free from irregularities (as curves, bends, or angles) in course — see STRAIGHT 1

**straightaway** *adv* without delay — see IMMEDIATELY

**straighten** *vb* to cause to follow a line that is without bends or curls ⟨*straighten* that extension cord—it should be just long enough to reach the wall outlet⟩
*syn* unbend, uncurl
*rel* uncoil, unwind; disentangle, untangle, untwine, untwist
*near ant* arc, bend, bow, hook, round; entwine, kink, swirl, turn, twine, twist; coil, loop, spiral, wind
*ant* bend, crook, curl, curve

**straightforward** *also* **straightforwards** *adv* in an honest and direct manner ⟨she finally told him *straightforward* that she wasn't interested in a date⟩
*syn* directly, forthrightly, foursquare, plain, plainly, straight, straightforwardly
*rel* candidly, frankly, honestly, openheartedly, openly, unguardedly, unreservedly; artlessly, earnestly, sincerely; abruptly, bluntly, brusquely, curtly, gruffly, sharply; impolitely, inconsiderately, rudely, tactlessly; truthfully, veraciously
*near ant* long-windedly, verbosely, wordily; civilly, courteously, diplomatically, politely, tactfully; deceitfully, mendaciously, untruthfully; erroneously, fallaciously, falsely, hypocritically, insincerely; ambiguously, circuitously, equivocally, evasively, indirectly

**straightforward** *adj* **1** going straight to the point clearly and firmly ⟨a *straightforward* account of the football game with no digressions or personal comments⟩
*syn* direct, forthright, foursquare, plain, straight
*rel* aboveboard, candid, frank, free-spoken, honest, open, openhearted, outspoken, plainspoken, unguarded, unreserved; artless, earnest, sincere; uninhibited, unrestrained; abrupt, bluff, blunt, brusque, curt, gruff, sharp; impolite, inconsiderate, rude, tactless, undiplomatic; true, truthful, veracious
*near ant* circumlocutory, long-winded, prolix, verbose, wordy; inhibited, reserved, restrained; civil, courteous, polite, tactful; deceitful, lying, mendacious, untruthful; erroneous, fallacious, false; ambiguous, equivocal, evasive, misleading; double-dealing, hypocritical, two-faced
*ant* circuitous, indirect, roundabout
**2** free from irregularities (as curves, bends, or angles) in course — see STRAIGHT 1
**3** free in expressing one's true feelings and opinions — see FRANK

**straightforwardly** *adv* in an honest and direct manner — see STRAIGHTFORWARD

**straightforwardness** *n* the free expression of one's true feelings and opinions — see CANDOR

**straightway** *adv* without delay — see IMMEDIATELY

[1]**strain** *n* **1** the line of ancestors from whom a person is descended — see ANCESTRY
**2** a rhythmic series of musical tones arranged to give a pleasing effect — see MELODY
**3** a very small amount — see PARTICLE 1

[2]**strain** *n* the burden on one's emotional or mental well-being created by demands on one's time — see STRESS 1

**strain** *vb* **1** to injure by overuse, misuse, or pressure ⟨in order to lift something heavy, squat down and lift with your legs, or you'll *strain* your back⟩
*syn* pull, rack, stretch, wrench
*rel* fray, tax, weaken; damage, harm, hurt, impair, wound; batter, bruise, tear; cripple, lame, mangle, mutilate
**2** to pass through a filter ⟨better *strain* that coffee carefully to get all the grounds out⟩
*syn* filter, screen
*rel* percolate; refilter
**3** to devote serious and sustained effort — see LABOR
**4** to flow forth slowly through small openings — see EXUDE
**5** to subject (a personal quality or faculty) to often excessive stress — see TRY (OUT) 2

**strained** *adj* lacking in natural or spontaneous quality — see ARTIFICIAL 1

**strait** *n* **1** a narrow body of water between two land masses — see CHANNEL 2
**2** *often* **straits** *pl* a state of great suffering of body or mind — see DISTRESS 1

**straitlaced** *or* **straightlaced** *adj* given to or marked by very conservative standards regarding personal behavior or morals ⟨a very *straitlaced* old lady who believed women shouldn't even show a bare ankle in public⟩
*syn* prim, prudish, puritanical
*rel* priggish, staid, stuffy; genteel, proper, refined; decent, honest, moral, right, righteous, upright, virtuous
*near ant* liberated, permissive; bad, immoral, improper, indecent, lax, loose,

---

*syn* synonym(s) *rel* related words
*ant* antonym(s) *near ant* near antonym(s)

wicked; debauched, degenerate, degraded, depraved, perverted

**strand** *n* the usually sandy or gravelly land bordering a body of water — see BEACH

**strand** *vb* to cause irreparable damage to (a ship) by running aground or sinking — see SHIPWRECK

**stranded** *adj* resting on the shore or bottom of a body of water — see AGROUND

**strange** *adj* **1** different from the ordinary in a way that causes curiosity or suspicion — see ODD 2
**2** excitingly or mysteriously unusual — see EXOTIC
**3** not known or experienced before — see NEW 2
**4** noticeably different from what is generally found or experienced — see UNUSUAL 1

**stranger** *n* a person who is not native to or known to a community ⟨the people of the island are quick to make *strangers* feel at home⟩
***syn*** foreigner, nonnative, outlander, outsider
***rel*** alien; outcast, pariah; drifter, transient, wanderer
***near ant*** buddy, chum, comrade, confidant, crony, familiar, friend, intimate, pal; acquaintance, associate, cohort, colleague, companion fellow, hearty, hobnobber, mate, partner, peer; adversary, antagonist, enemy, foe, opponent, rival; archenemy, nemesis; citizen, inhabitant, resident
***ant*** native

**strangle** *vb* **1** to be or cause to be killed by lack of breathable air — see SMOTHER 1
**2** to keep (someone) from breathing by exerting pressure on the windpipe — see CHOKE 1
**3** to refrain from openly showing or uttering — see SUPPRESS 2

**stratagem** *n* a clever often underhanded means to achieve an end — see TRICK 1

**strategy** *n* **1** a method worked out in advance for achieving some objective — see PLAN 1
**2** the means or procedure for doing something — see METHOD

**stratum** *n* one of the segments of society into which people are grouped — see CLASS 1

**straw** *adj* of a pale yellow or yellowish brown color — see BLOND

**stray** *adj* lacking a definite plan, purpose, or pattern — see RANDOM

**streak** *n* **1** a line or long narrow section differing in color from the background — see STRIPE
**2** a very small amount — see PARTICLE 1

**streak** *vb* to make stripes on — see STRIPE

**streaked** *adj* having stripes — see STRIPED

**stream** *vb* **1** to cause to flow in a stream — see POUR 1
**2** to move in a stream — see FLOW 1
**3** to move or proceed smoothly and readily — see FLOW 2

**streamer** *n* a piece of cloth with a special design that is used as an emblem or for signaling — see FLAG 1

**streamlet** *n* a natural body of running water smaller than a river — see CREEK 1

**streamline** *vb* to make less complex — see SIMPLIFY

**street** *n* a passage cleared for public vehicular travel — see WAY 1

**strength** *n* **1** the ability to exert effort for the accomplishment of a task — see POWER 2
**2** the ability to withstand force or stress without being distorted, dislodged, or damaged — see STABILITY 1

**strengthen** *vb* **1** to increase the ability of (as a muscle) to exert physical force ⟨lifting weights every day will eventually *strengthen* your muscles⟩ ⟨the Army makes new recruits run for miles in order to *strengthen* them⟩
***syn*** beef (up), fortify, harden, toughen
***rel*** anneal, temper; firm (up), tone (up); energize, invigorate, vitalize; restrengthen
***near ant*** cripple, incapacitate, paralyze; damage, harm, hurt, impair, injure; break down, wear out; sap, undermine
***ant*** debilitate, enervate, enfeeble, weaken
**2** to make able to withstand physical hardship, strain, or exposure — see HARDEN 2
**3** to make markedly greater in measure or degree — see INTENSIFY
**4** to prepare (oneself) mentally or emotionally — see FORTIFY 1

**strenuous** *adj* **1** marked by or uttered with forcefulness — see EMPHATIC 1
**2** requiring considerable physical or mental effort — see HARD 2

**strenuously** *adv* **1** in a vigorous and forceful manner — see HARD 3
**2** with great effort or determination — see HARD 1

**stress** *n* **1** the burden on one's emotional or mental well-being created by demands on one's time ⟨with a full-time job and her college courses, the young woman is under a lot of *stress* right now⟩
***syn*** pressure, strain, tension
***rel*** load, weight; anxiety, concern, uneasiness, worry; aggravation, anger, annoyance, exasperation, irritation, persecution, trouble
***near ant*** comfort, consolation
**2** a special notice or importance given to something — see EMPHASIS 1

**stress** *vb* to indicate the importance of by giving prominent display — see EMPHASIZE

**stressed-out** *adj* suffering from high levels of physical and especially psychological stress ⟨I'm becoming *stressed-out* from trying to keep up with the demands of my school work and the grueling workouts for the football team⟩
***syn*** shell-shocked
***rel*** burned-out (*or* burnt-out), exhausted, tired, worn-out; undone, unmanned, unnerved, unstrung; edgy, nervous, tense, uneasy; agitated, disturbed, perturbed,

troubled, upset; aggravated, angry, annoyed, exasperated, irritated
*near ant* relaxed, rested

**stretch** *adj* able to revert to original size and shape after being stretched, squeezed, or twisted — see ELASTIC 1

**stretch** *n* **1** a wide space or area — see EXPANSE
**2** an indefinite but usually short period of time — see WHILE 1
**3** the distance or extent between possible extremes — see RANGE 3
**4** the space or amount of space between two points, lines, surfaces, or objects — see DISTANCE

**stretch** *vb* **1** to add to the interest of by including made-up details — see EMBROIDER
**2** to injure by overuse, misuse, or pressure — see STRAIN 1
**3** to make longer — see EXTEND 1
**4** to subject (a personal quality or faculty) to often excessive stress — see TRY (OUT) 2

**stretch** (out) *vb* to arrange the parts of (something) over a wider area — see OPEN 3

**stretchable** *adj* able to revert to original size and shape after being stretched, squeezed, or twisted — see ELASTIC 1

**stretching** *n* **1** the act of making longer — see EXTENSION 1
**2** the representation of something in terms that go beyond the facts — see EXAGGERATION

**strew** *vb* to cover by or as if by scattering something over or on — see SCATTER 2

**strict** *adj* **1** following an original exactly — see FAITHFUL 2
**2** given to exacting standards of discipline and self-restraint — see SEVERE 1
**3** not allowing for any exceptions or loosening of standards — see RIGID 1

**strictly** *adv* without any relaxation of standards or precision ⟨*strictly* speaking, Columbus did not discover America—the people living there had long known about it⟩ ⟨the rules must be *strictly* obeyed⟩
*syn* exactly, precisely, rigidly, rigorously
*rel* carefully, conscientiously, meticulously, scrupulously
*ant* imprecisely, inexactly, loosely

**strictness** *n* the quality or state of being demanding or unyielding (as in discipline or criticism) — see SEVERITY

**stricture** *n* an often public or formal expression of disapproval — see CENSURE

**stride** *vb* to move along with a steady regular step especially in a group — see MARCH 1

**strife** *n* a lack of agreement or harmony — see DISCORD

**strike** *n* **1** a work stoppage by a body of workers intended to force an employer to meet their demands ⟨the nurses will go on *strike* tomorrow unless they're finally given a pay raise⟩
*syn* walkout
*rel* shutdown, shutoff, sit-down, slowdown; lockout
**2** the act or action of setting upon with force or violence — see ATTACK 1
**3** a feature of someone or something that creates difficulty for achieving success — see DISADVANTAGE
**4** a forceful coming together of two things — see IMPACT 1

**strike** *vb* **1** to refuse to work in order to force an employer to meet demands ⟨the union is calling for its members to *strike* until the mining company agrees to meet safety standards⟩
*syn* walk out
*rel* knock off, lay off; leave, quit, resign; decamp, depart, exit, go, leave, light out, part
**2** to act upon (a person or a person's feelings) so as to cause a response — see [1]AFFECT 1
**3** to come into the mind of — see OCCUR (TO)
**4** to come into usually forceful contact with something — see HIT 2
**5** to deliver a blow to (someone or something) usually in a strong vigorous manner — see HIT 1
**6** to take apart — see DISASSEMBLE
**7** to take sudden, violent action against — see ATTACK 1

**strike** (into) *vb* to take the first step in (a process or course of action) — see BEGIN 1

**strike** (out) *vb* to show (something written) to be no longer valid by drawing a cross over or a line through it — see X (OUT)

**striking** *adj* **1** likely to attract attention — see NOTICEABLE
**2** very noticeable especially for being incorrect or bad — see EGREGIOUS

**string** *n* **1** a length of braided, flexible material that is used for tying or connecting things — see CORD 1
**2** a series of persons or things arranged one behind another — see LINE 1
**3** a series of things linked together — see CHAIN 1

**string** *vb* to put together into a series by means of or as if by means of a thread — see THREAD 2

**string along** *vb* to cause to believe what is untrue — see DECEIVE

**stringent** *adj* not allowing for any exceptions or loosening of standards — see RIGID 1

**stringy** *adj* resembling or having the texture of a mass of strings ⟨*stringy* hair that clearly needed a good washing⟩
*syn* fibrous
*rel* knotty, ropy, thready; sinewy, wiry

**strip** *n* a long narrow piece of material ⟨now tear the paper into *strips* and fold them up carefully⟩
*syn* list, ribbon, slip
*rel* band, bandage, belt, binding, strap, swath, tape

**strip** *vb* **1** to remove clothing from — see UNDRESS

---

*syn* synonym(s) *rel* related words
*ant* antonym(s) *near ant* near antonym(s)

2 to search through with the intent of committing robbery — see RANSACK 1

**stripe** *n* a line or long narrow section differing in color from the background ⟨the United States flag has seven red *stripes*⟩
*syn* band, bar, streak
*rel* blaze, crossbar, pinstripe

**stripe** *vb* to make stripes on ⟨the children carefully *striped* the paper with red and blue paint⟩
*syn* band, bar, streak
*rel* blaze

**striped** *adj* having stripes ⟨the zebra is a black-and-white *striped* animal⟩
*syn* barred, streaked
*rel* corded, tabby

**stripling** *n* a male person who has not yet reached adulthood — see BOY

**stripped** *adj* 1 lacking a usual or natural covering — see NAKED 2
2 lacking or shed of clothing — see NAKED 1

**strive** *vb* 1 to devote serious and sustained effort — see LABOR
2 to make an effort to do — see ATTEMPT

**stroke** *n* a hard strike with a part of the body or an instrument — see [1]BLOW

**stroke** *vb* to touch or handle in a tender or loving manner — see FONDLE

**stroke** (out) *vb* to slow (something written) to be no longer valid by drawing a cross over or a line through it — see X (OUT)

**stroll** *n* a relaxed journey on foot for exercise or pleasure — see WALK

**stroller** *n* a person who roams about without a fixed route or destination — see NOMAD

**strong** *adj* 1 having muscles capable of exerting great physical force ⟨I need some *strong* people to help me move furniture⟩
*syn* brawny, muscular, rugged, sinewy, stalwart, stout
*rel* forceful, mighty, potent, powerful, puissant; able-bodied, athletic, fit, trim; beefy, burly, husky, strapping; masculine, virile; hard, inured, strengthened, sturdy, tough, toughened; energetic, energized, invigorated, lusty, red-blooded, robust, vigorous, vitalized; hale, healthy, hearty, sound
*near ant* challenged, disabled, incapacitated, paralyzed; impotent, powerless; puny, slight, small, unfit, unhealthy
*ant* delicate, feeble, frail, weak, wimpy
2 able to withstand hardship, strain, or exposure — see HARDY 1
3 having a powerfully stimulating odor or flavor — see SHARP 3
4 having an abundance of some characteristic quality (as flavor) — see FULL-BODIED
5 having an unpleasant smell — see MALODOROUS
6 having great power or influence — see IMPORTANT 2
7 having the power to persuade — see COGENT
8 marked by the ability to withstand stress without structural damage or distortion — see STABLE 1
9 not showing weakness or uncertainty — see FIRM 1

**strongbox** *n* a specially reinforced container to keep valuables safe — see SAFE

**stronghold** *n* a structure or place from which one can resist attack — see FORT

**strongly** *adv* in a vigorous and forceful manner — see HARD 3

**strop** *vb* to make sharp or sharper — see SHARPEN

**stropped** *adj* having an edge thin enough to cut or pierce something — see SHARP 1

**structure** *n* 1 something built as a dwelling, shelter, or place for human activity — see BUILDING
2 something put together by arranging or connecting an array of parts — see CONSTRUCTION 1
3 the arrangement of parts that gives something its basic form — see FRAME 1

**struggle** *n* 1 a forceful effort to reach a goal or objective ⟨a physically challenged child's determined *struggle* to make straight A's in school⟩
*syn* battle, fight, fray, scrabble
*rel* effort, exertion, labor, pains, trouble, work; drudgery, grind, sweat, toil, travail; combat, conflict, contest, strife, tussle, war, warfare; attempt, endeavor, essay, try
2 a physical dispute between opposing individuals or groups — see FIGHT 1
3 an earnest effort for superiority or victory over another — see CONTEST 1

**struggle** *vb* to devote serious and sustained effort — see LABOR

**strut** *vb* 1 to walk with exaggerated arm and leg movements ⟨the toy soldiers in the Christmas pageant *strutted* stiffly across the stage⟩
*syn* prance, stalk, swagger
*rel* flounce, mince, traipse; pussyfoot, tiptoe; parade, promenade; pad, step, tread; pace, stride; lumber, lurch, pound, shamble, shuffle, stagger
2 to present so as to invite notice or attention — see SHOW 1

**stub** *n* an unused or unwanted piece or item typically of small size or value — see [1]SCRAP 1

**stubborn** *adj* sticking to an opinion, purpose, or course of action in spite of reason, arguments, or persuasion — see OBSTINATE

**stubbornness** *n* a steadfast adherence to an opinion, purpose, or course of action — see OBSTINACY

**stubby** *adj* being compact and broad in build and often short in stature — see STOCKY

**stuck** *adj* firmly positioned in place and difficult to dislodge — see TIGHT 2

**stuck-up** *adj* having too high an opinion of oneself — see CONCEITED

**student** *n* one who attends a school ⟨a straight-A *student* at the local high school⟩

*syn* pupil, scholar
*rel* schoolboy, schoolchild, schoolgirl; schoolfellow, schoolmate; collegian, postgraduate, undergraduate; freshman, junior, senior, sophomore; underclassman, upperclassman

**studied** *adj* decided on as a result of careful thought — see DELIBERATE 1

**study** *n* **1** a systematic search for the truth or facts about something — see INQUIRY 1
**2** the state of being lost in thought — see REVERIE

**study** *vb* **1** to use the mind to acquire knowledge ⟨you'll have to *study* hard and learn all about the Revolutionary War in order to pass the history test⟩
*syn* bone (up)
*rel* cram; analyze, deduce, find out; learn, read; research, restudy
*phrases* go over, go through
**2** to commit to memory — see MEMORIZE
**3** to give serious and careful thought to — see PONDER

**stuff** *n* **1** a skill, an ability, or knowledge that makes a person able to do a particular job — see QUALIFICATION 1
**2** the basic elements from which something can be developed — see MAKING
**3** the quality or qualities that make a thing what it is — see ESSENCE

**stuff** *vb* **1** to close up so that no empty spaces remain — see FILL 2
**2** to fill with food to capacity — see GORGE 1
**3** to fit (something) into a tight space — see CROWD 1
**4** to prevent passage through — see CLOG 1
**5** to put into (something) as much as can be held or contained — see FILL 1

**stuffed** *adj* **1** containing or seeming to contain the greatest quantity or number possible — see FULL 1
**2** having one's appetite completely satisfied — see FULL 3

**stuffer** *n* one who eats greedily or too much — see GLUTTON

**stuffing** *n* soft material that is used to fill the hollow parts of something — see FILLING

**stuffy** *adj* **1** lacking fresh air ⟨the house was so *stuffy* after being closed up for a month⟩
*syn* breathless, close, stifling, suffocating
*rel* airless, unventilated; heavy, oppressive, thick
*near ant* bracing, brisk, invigorating, refreshed, sweet; ventilated
*ant* airy, breezy
**2** causing weariness, restlessness, or lack of interest — see BORING

**stumble** *n* **1** an unintentional departure from truth or accuracy — see ERROR 1
**2** the act of going down from an upright position suddenly and involuntarily — see FALL 1

**stumble** *vb* **1** to go down from an upright position suddenly and involuntarily — see FALL 1
**2** to make progress in a clumsy, struggling manner — see FLOUNDER 1
**3** to move heavily or clumsily — see LUMBER 1

**stumble** (on *or* onto) *vb* to come upon unexpectedly or by chance — see HAPPEN (ON *OR* UPON)

**stumble** (upon) *vb* to come upon face-to-face or as if face-to-face — see MEET 1

**stumbling block** *n* something that makes progress or movement more difficult — see ENCUMBRANCE

**stump** *vb* **1** to move heavily or clumsily — see LUMBER 1
**2** to invite (someone) to take part in a contest or to perform a feat — see CHALLENGE 2

**stumpy** *adj* being compact and broad in build and often short in stature — see STOCKY

**stun** *vb* **1** to make senseless or dizzy by a blow ⟨a powerful uppercut to the jaw *stunned* the boxer and sent him crashing to the canvas⟩
*syn* daze
*rel* deaden, knock out, paralyze; benumb, numb, stupefy; bowl (over), knock (down)
*phrases* knock for a loop
**2** to make a strong impression on (someone) with something unexpected — see SURPRISE 1

**stunned** *adj* **1** affected with sudden and great wonder or surprise — see THUNDERSTRUCK
**2** suffering from mental confusion — see DIZZY 2

**stunner** *n* **1** a lovely woman — see BEAUTY 2
**2** something that makes a strong impression because it is so unexpected — see SURPRISE 1

**stunning** *adj* **1** causing a strong emotional reaction because unexpected — see SURPRISING 1
**2** causing wonder or astonishment — see MARVELOUS 1
**3** very pleasing to look at — see BEAUTIFUL

**stunt** *n* an act of notable skill, strength, or cleverness — see FEAT 1

**stunt** *vb* to hold back the normal growth of ⟨unfortunately, an unusually dry summer seems to have permanently *stunted* the tree⟩
*syn* dwarf, suppress
*rel* arrest, catch, check, halt, hold up, stall, stay, still, stop; balk, block, hold back, impede, obstruct, stem
*near ant* advance, boost, encourage, forward, promote

**stupefied** *adj* **1** affected with sudden and great wonder or surprise — see THUNDERSTRUCK

2 suffering from mental confusion — see DIZZY 2

**stupefy** *vb* to make a strong impression on (someone) with something unexpected — see SURPRISE 1

**stupefying** *adj* causing a strong emotional reaction because unexpected — see SURPRISING 1

**stupendous** *adj* causing wonder or astonishment — see MARVELOUS 1

**stupendously** *adv* to a large extent or degree — see GREATLY 2

**stupendousness** *n* impressiveness of beauty on a large scale — see MAGNIFICENCE

**stupid** *adj* 1 not having or showing an ability to absorb ideas readily ⟨it's not nice to constantly call your brother *stupid* and ugly⟩ ⟨don't ask *stupid* questions⟩
*syn* brainless, dense, doltish, dopey, dorky [*slang*], dull, dumb, fatuous, half-witted, mindless, oafish, obtuse, senseless, simple, slow, thick, thickheaded, unintelligent, vacuous, weak-minded, witless
*rel* feebleminded, retarded, simpleminded; foolish, idiotic, imbecile, imbecilic, moronic; ignorant, illiterate, lowbrow, uneducated, uninformed, untaught, unthinking; absurd, asinine, balmy, cockeyed, crazy, cuckoo, daffy, daft, dotty, harebrained, insane, kooky, loony (*also* looney), lunatic, mad, nonsensical, nutty, preposterous, sappy, screwball, silly, unwise, wacky, zany; fallacious, illogical, invalid, irrational, unreasonable
*near ant* ingenious, resourceful; acute, astute, discerning, insightful, keen, knowing, perceptive, perspicacious, sagacious, sage, sapient, savvy, wise; cerebral, erudite, highbrow, intellectual, knowledgeable, learned, literate, scholarly, thinking, well-read; educated, informed, schooled, skilled, trained; crafty, cunning, foxy, shrewd, wily; judicious, prudent, sane, sensible, sound; logical, rational, reasonable, valid
*ant* apt, brainy, bright, brilliant, clever, intelligent, keen, nimble, quick, quick-witted, sharp, sharp-witted, smart
2 causing weariness, restlessness, or lack of interest — see BORING
3 showing or marked by a lack of good sense or judgment — see FOOLISH 1

**stupidity** *n* 1 the quality or state of lacking intelligence or quickness of mind ⟨the *stupidity* of the dialogue between the two romantic leads had movie audiences giggling uncontrollably⟩
*syn* brainlessness, denseness, density, doltishness, dopiness, dullness (*also* dulness), dumbness, fatuity, foolishness, mindlessness, oafishness, obtuseness, senselessness, simpleness, slowness, stupidness, vacuity, witlessness
*rel* absurdity, asininity, balminess, craziness, daftness, folly, idiocy, inanity, insanity, lunacy, madness, nonsensicalness, nuttiness, preposterousness, silliness, simplicity, wackiness, zaniness; fallacy, irrationality, unreasonableness
*near ant* acumen, alertness, astuteness, discernment, insight, judgment (*or* judgement), perception, perspicacity; sagacity, sageness, sapience, wisdom, wit; logicalness, rationality, reasonableness, soundness, validity
*ant* braininess, brightness, brilliance, cleverness, intelligence, keenness, quickness, quick-wittedness, sharpness, smartness
2 a foolish act or idea — see FOLLY 1
3 language, behavior, or ideas that are absurd and contrary to good sense — see NONSENSE 1

**stupidness** *n* the quality or state of lacking intelligence or quickness of mind — see STUPIDITY 1

**sturdily** *adv* in a vigorous and forceful manner — see HARD 3

**sturdiness** *n* the ability to withstand force or stress without being distorted, dislodged, or damaged — see STABILITY 1

**sturdy** *adj* 1 able to withstand hardship, strain, or exposure — see HARDY 1
2 marked by the ability to withstand stress without structural damage or distortion — see STABLE 1
3 not showing weakness or uncertainty — see FIRM 1

**style** *n* 1 a distinctive way of putting ideas into words ⟨I correctly identified the quotation because I recognized Mark Twain's inimitable *style*⟩
*syn* fashion, locution, manner, mode, phraseology, tone, vein
*rel* delivery, elocution; archaism, colloquialism, regionalism; acceptation, connotation, denotation, idiom
2 the means or procedure for doing something — see METHOD
3 a practice or interest that is very popular for a short time — see FAD

**style** *vb* to give a name to — see NAME 1

**styleless** *adj* marked by an obvious lack of style or good taste — see TACKY 1

**stylish** *adj* being in the latest or current fashion ⟨a pretty, *stylish* dress⟩
*syn* à la mode (*also* a la mode), chic, fashionable, in, modish, sharp, smart, snappy
*rel* dapper, dashing, natty, rakish, spiffy, spruce; posh, ritzy, swank (*or* swanky); elegant, graceful, handsome, majestic, refined, sophisticated, stately, tasteful, understated; dandyish, dudish, foppish; classic, exquisite, quiet, restrained, simple; affected, grandiose, pretentious
*near ant* tacky, unattractive, unbecoming; graceless, inelegant, tasteless, unhandsome; frowsy (*or* frowzy), sloppy, slovenly, unkempt, untidy; disheveled (*or* dishevelled), messy, mussy, rumpled, wrinkled; shabby, sleazy
*ant* dowdy, outmoded, styleless, unfashionable, unstylish

**suasion** *n* the act of reasoning or pleading with someone to accept a belief or course of action — see PERSUASION 1

**suave** *adj* having or showing very polished and worldly manners ⟨the *suave* gentleman was a great favorite of the elegant

ladies who attended parties at the embassy〉
*syn* debonair, smooth, sophisticated, urbane
*rel* glib, slick, unctuous; civilized, cultivated, cultured, graceful, poised, polished, refined; cosmopolitan, smart, worldly-wise; experienced, knowing, practiced (*or* practised), schooled, seasoned; amiable, appealing, attractive; assured, calm, collected, composed, confident, cool, placid, secure, self-assured, self-confident, self-possessed, serene, tranquil, undisturbed, unperturbed
*near ant* awkward, clumsy, gauche, graceless, stiff, stilted, uncomfortable, uneasy, ungraceful, wooden; callow, green, inexperienced, raw; parochial, provincial, roughhewn, rustic; inelegant, philistine, uncivilized, uncultured, unrefined; unsophisticated, unworldly; gawky, lubberly, stodgy, ungainly; diffident, insecure
*ant* boorish, churlish, clownish, loutish, uncouth

[1]**sub** *n* a large sandwich on a long split roll — see SUBMARINE

[2]**sub** *n* a person or thing that takes the place of another — see SUBSTITUTE

**sub** *vb* to serve as a replacement usually for a time only — see COVER 1

**subdue** *vb* **1** to achieve a victory over — see BEAT 2
**2** to bring under one's control by force of arms — see CONQUER 1
**3** to put a stop to (something) by the use of force — see QUELL 1

**subdued** *adj* not excessively showy — see QUIET 2

**subduer** *n* one that defeats an enemy or opponent — see VICTOR 1

**subduing** *n* the act or process of bringing someone or something under one's control — see CONQUEST

**subject** *n* **1** a major object of interest or concern (as in a discussion or artistic composition) — see MATTER 1
**2** a person who owes allegiance to a government and is protected by it — see CITIZEN 1

**subject** *vb* to bring under one's control by force of arms — see CONQUER 1

**subject** (to) *adj* **1** determined by something else — see DEPENDENT 2
**2** being in a situation where one is likely to meet with harm — see LIABLE 1

**subjecting** *n* the act or process of bringing someone or something under one's control — see CONQUEST

**subjection** *n* the act or process of bringing someone or something under one's control — see CONQUEST

**subjugate** *vb* to bring under one's control by force of arms — see CONQUER 1

**subjugating** *n* the act or process of bringing someone or something under one's control — see CONQUEST

**subjugation** *n* the act or process of bringing someone or something under one's control — see CONQUEST

**sublime** *adj* **1** causing wonder or astonishment — see MARVELOUS 1
**2** having, characterized by, or arising from a dignified and generous nature — see NOBLE 2

**sublimeness** *n* impressiveness of beauty on a large scale — see MAGNIFICENCE

**submarine** *adj* living, lying, or occurring below the surface of the water — see UNDERWATER

**submarine** *n* a large sandwich on a long split roll 〈always orders a roast beef *submarine* with the works〉
*syn* grinder, hero, hoagie, Italian sandwich, po'boy (*also* poor boy), sub

**submerge** *vb* **1** to cover or become filled with a flood — see FLOOD
**2** to sink or push (something) briefly into or as if into a liquid — see DIP 1

**submerged** *adj* living, lying, or occurring below the surface of the water — see UNDERWATER

**submerse** *vb* **1** to cover or become filled with a flood — see FLOOD
**2** to sink or push (something) briefly into or as if into a liquid — see DIP 1

**submission** *n* **1** a bending to the authority or control of another — see OBEDIENCE 1
**2** the usually forced yielding of one's person or possessions to the control of another — see SURRENDER

**submissive** *adj* readily giving in to the command or authority of another — see OBEDIENT

**submissively** *adv* in manner showing no signs of pride or self-assertion — see LOWLY

**submissiveness** *n* a readiness or willingness to yield to the wishes of others — see COMPLIANCE 1

**submit** *vb* **1** to cease resistance (as to another's arguments, demands, or control) — see YIELD 3
**2** to give up and cease resistance (as to a liking, temptation, or habit) — see YIELD 1
**3** to yield to the control or power of enemy forces — see FALL 2

**submitting** *n* the usually forced yielding of one's person or possessions to the control of another — see SURRENDER

**subordinate** *adj* having not so great importance or rank as another — see LESSER

**subordinate** *n* one who is of lower rank and typically under the authority of another — see UNDERLING

**subordination** *n* a bending to the authority or control of another — see OBEDIENCE 1

**subpoena** *n* a written notice ordering a person to appear in court — see SUMMONS

**subscribe** (to) *vb* to have a favorable opinion of — see APPROVE (OF)

---

*syn* synonym(s) *rel* related words
*ant* antonym(s) *near ant* near antonym(s)

**subsequent** *adj* being, occurring, or carried out at a time after something else ⟨I'll do the first problem as an example, but all *subsequent* efforts must be done on your own⟩
***syn*** after, ensuing, later, posterior
***rel*** behind, belated, delayed, late, slow; eventual, last, ultimate; following
***near ant*** advance, early, premature
***ant*** antecedent, anterior, fore, precedent, preceding, previous, prior
**subsequently** *adv* following in time or place — see AFTER
**subside** *vb* to grow less in scope or intensity especially gradually — see DECREASE 2
**subsidize** *vb* **1** to furnish (as an institution) with a regular source of income — see ENDOW 2
**2** to provide money for — see FINANCE 1
**subsidy** *n* a sum of money allotted for a specific use by official or formal action — see APPROPRIATION
**subsist** *vb* to have life — see BE 1
**subsistence** *n* **1** the fact of being or of being real — see EXISTENCE
**2** uninterrupted or lasting existence — see CONTINUATION
**substance** *n* **1** the basic elements from which something can be developed — see MAKING
**2** the quality or qualities that make a thing what it is — see ESSENCE
**3** the total of one's money and property — see WEALTH 1
**4** one that has a real and independent existence — see ENTITY
**substance abuser** *n* a person who regularly uses drugs especially illegally — see DOPER
**substandard** *adj* falling short of a standard — see BAD 1
**substantial** *adj* **1** having great meaning or lasting effect — see IMPORTANT 1
**2** of a size greater than average of its kind — see LARGE
**3** relating to or composed of matter — see MATERIAL 1
**4** sufficiently large in size, amount, or number to merit attention — see CONSIDERABLE 1
**substantiality** *n* the quality or state of being large in size — see LARGENESS
**substantially** *adv* for the most part — see CHIEFLY
**substantiate** *vb* **1** to gain full recognition or acceptance of — see ESTABLISH 1
**2** to give evidence or testimony to the truth or factualness of — see CONFIRM
**3** to represent in visible form — see EMBODY 2
**4** to show the existence or truth of by evidence — see PROVE 1
**substantiating** *adj* serving to give support to the truth or factualness of something — see CORROBORATIVE
**substantiation** *n* something presented in support of the truth or accuracy of a claim — see PROOF
**substitute** *adj* **1** being such in appearance only and made with or manufactured from usually cheaper materials — see IMITATION
**2** taking the place of one that came before — see NEW 1
**substitute** *n* a person or thing that takes the place of another ⟨you'll be getting a *substitute* until your regular teacher is feeling better⟩ ⟨if you like, you can use nuts as a *substitute* for coconut in that recipe⟩
***syn*** backup, pinch hitter, relief, replacement, reserve, stand-in, sub
***rel*** alternate, understudy; apology, makeshift, stopgap; agent, attorney, commissary, delegate, deputy, envoy, factor, procurator, proxy, representative, surrogate; assistant, second
**substitute** *vb* **1** to give up (something) and take something else in return — see CHANGE 3
**2** to serve as a replacement usually for a time only — see COVER 1
**3** to take the place of — see REPLACE 1
**subterfuge** *n* the use of clever underhanded actions to achieve an end — see TRICKERY
**subtle** *adj* **1** clever at attaining one's ends by indirect and often deceptive means — see ARTFUL 1
**2** made or done with extreme care and accuracy — see FINE 2
**3** satisfying or pleasing because of fineness or mildness — see DELICATE 1
**subtleness** *n* skill in achieving one's ends through indirect, subtle, or underhanded means — see CUNNING 1
**subtlety** *n* skill in achieving one's ends through indirect, subtle, or underhanded means — see CUNNING 1
**subtract** *vb* to take away (an amount or number) from a total ⟨if you *subtract* 10 from 23, you get 13⟩ ⟨you can *subtract* the time you spent daydreaming from your total homework time⟩
***syn*** deduct, take off
***rel*** decrease, diminish, discount, downsize, lessen, lower, reduce; abbreviate, abridge, clip, crop, curtail, cut, cut back, cut down, dock, pare, prune, retrench, shorten, slash, trim, truncate, whittle
***near ant*** adjoin, annex, append, tack (on); add (to), complement, supplement; enhance, heighten, intensify; aggrandize, amplify, augment, boost, enlarge, escalate, expand, increase, raise
***ant*** add
**subtraction** *n* the act or an instance of taking away from a total ⟨the dog was responsible for the unexplained *subtraction* in the number of potato chips on my sister's plate⟩
***syn*** deduction
***rel*** discount; abatement, decline, decrement, diminishment, diminution, drop, fall, loss, reduction, shrinkage; curtailment, cut, cutback
***near ant*** boost, enlargement, gain, increase, increment, raise, rise; accretion,

accrual, accumulation, addendum, appendix, supplement
*ant* addition

**suburbia** *n* the area around a city — see ENVIRONS 1

**subvert** *vb* to lower in character or dignity — see DEBASE 1

**succeed** *vb* **1** to turn out as planned or desired ⟨the advertising campaign that finally *succeeded* used humor to sell the product⟩
*syn* click, deliver, go over, pan out, work out
*rel* catch on; flourish, prosper, thrive
*phrases* catch fire
*near ant* languish; flounder, struggle; decline, slip, slump, wane
*ant* collapse, fail, flop, flunk, fold, wash out
**2** to reach a desired level of accomplishment ⟨if you want to *succeed* in show business, you have to feel comfortable in front of an audience⟩
*syn* flourish, prosper, thrive
*rel* prevail, triumph, win
*phrases* get ahead, make good, make it
*near ant* flounder, struggle
*ant* fail
**3** to come after in time — see FOLLOW 1

**succeeding** *adj* **1** being the one that comes immediately after another — see NEXT
**2** following one after another without others coming in between — see CONSECUTIVE

**success** *n* **1** a person or thing that is successful — see HIT 1
**2** a successful result brought about by hard work — see ACCOMPLISHMENT 1

**successful** *adj* **1** having attained a desired end or state of good fortune ⟨the family runs several *successful* restaurants⟩
*syn* flourishing, going, palmy, prosperous, thriving, triumphant
*rel* coming, promising; booming, growing, roaring, robust
*near ant* futureless, hopeless, inauspicious, no-good; collapsing, failing, flopping, flunking, folding, washing-out; declining, slipping, slumping, waning; bankrupt, destroyed, ruined, wrecked
*ant* failed, unsuccessful
**2** marked by vigorous growth and well-being especially economically — see PROSPEROUS 1

**successional** *adj* following one after another without others coming in between — see CONSECUTIVE

**successive** *adj* following one after another without others coming in between — see CONSECUTIVE

**succinct** *adj* marked by the use of few words to convey much information or meaning — see CONCISE

**succinctly** *adv* in a few words — see SHORTLY 1

**succinctness** *n* the quality or state of being marked by or using only few words to convey much meaning ⟨Caesar's observation, "I came, I saw, I conquered," is famous for its *succinctness*⟩
*syn* brevity, briefness, compactness, conciseness, crispness, pithiness, terseness
*rel* abruptness, bluntness, brusqueness, curtness, shortness
*near ant* redundancy, repetitiousness
*ant* diffuseness, long-windedness, prolixity, verbosity, wordiness

**succulence** *n* the quality or state of being full of juice ⟨the *succulence* of the apple was such that the first bite sent juice running down my chin⟩
*syn* fleshiness, juiciness, pulpiness
*rel* sap, sappiness

**succulent** *adj* full of juice — see JUICY

**succumb** *vb* **1** to cease resistance (as to another's arguments, demands, or control) — see YIELD 3
**2** to give up and cease resistance (as to a liking, temptation, or habit) — see YIELD 1
**3** to stop living — see DIE 1
**4** to yield to the control or power of enemy forces — see FALL 2

**such** *adj* having qualities in common — see ALIKE

**suchlike** *adj* having qualities in common — see ALIKE

**suck** (up) *vb* to take in (something liquid) through small openings — see ABSORB 1

**sucker** *n* one who is easily deceived or cheated — see DUPE

**suddenly** *adv* **1** with great suddenness — see SHORT
**2** without warning — see UNAWARES

**suds** *n* a light mass of fine bubbles formed in or on a liquid — see FOAM

**sudsy** *adj* covered with, consisting of, or resembling foam — see FOAMY

**sue** (for) *vb* to make a request for — see ASK (FOR) 1

**suer** *n* the person in a legal proceeding who makes a charge of wrongdoing against another — see COMPLAINANT

**suffer** *vb* **1** to give permission to — see ALLOW 2
**2** to come to a knowledge of (something) by living through it — see EXPERIENCE
**3** to feel deep sadness or mental pain — see GRIEVE
**4** to give permission for or to approve of — see ALLOW 1

**sufferable** *adj* capable of being endured — see BEARABLE

**sufferance** *n* **1** the approval by someone in authority for the doing of something — see PERMISSION
**2** the capacity to endure what is difficult or disagreeable without complaining — see PATIENCE

**suffice** *vb* to be enough — see SERVE 2

**sufficiency** *n* the quality or state of meeting one's needs adequately ⟨the *sufficiency* of the portions is such that you will leave the restaurant with a full stomach but without doggie bags⟩

---

*syn* synonym(s) *rel* related words
*ant* antonym(s) *near ant* near antonym(s)

***syn*** acceptability, adequacy, satisfactoriness
***rel*** appropriateness, correctness, fitness, goodness, propernes-, rightness, seemliness, suitability, suitableness; bountifulness, copiousness, excess, overabundance, oversupply, surfeit, surplus; abundance, amplitude, plenitude, plenty
***near ant*** lack, want; dearth, shortage; meagerness, paucity, poorness, poverty, rareness, rarity, scantiness, scarceness, scarcity, skimpiness; necessity, need, privation
***ant*** inadequacy, insufficiency

**sufficiently** *adv* in or to a degree or quantity that meets one's requirements or satisfaction — see ENOUGH 1

**suffocate** *vb* to be or cause to be killed by lack of breathable air — see SMOTHER 1

**suffocating** *adj* lacking fresh air — see STUFFY 1

**suffrage** *n* the right to formally express one's position or will in an election — see VOTE 1

**suffuse** *vb* **1** to cause (as a person) to become filled or saturated with a certain quality or principle — see INFUSE
**2** to spread throughout — see PERMEATE

**sugarcoated** *adj* appealing to the emotions in an obvious and tiresome way — see CORNY

**sugary** *adj* appealing to the emotions in an obvious and tiresome way — see CORNY

**suggest** *vb* **1** to convey an idea indirectly — see HINT
**2** to put forward as one's choice for a wise or proper course of action — see ADVISE 2
**3** to set before the mind for consideration — see PROPOSE 1

**suggestion** *n* **1** a slight or indirect pointing to something (as a solution or explanation) — see HINT 1
**2** something which is presented for consideration — see PROPOSAL

**suggestive** *adj* **1** hinting at or intended to call to mind matters regarded as indecent ⟨making *suggestive* remarks to one's classmates will not be tolerated⟩
***syn*** bawdy, lewd, racy, ribald, salty, spicy
***rel*** leering; coarse, crude, earthy, foul, gross; dirty, filthy, lascivious, nasty, obscene, pornographic, smutty, unprintable, vulgar; indecorous, unbecoming; naughty, wicked; exceptionable, objectionable, unacceptable, undesirable, unwanted, unwelcome
***near ant*** clean, decent; innocuous, inoffensive; priggish, prim, prudish, puritanical, straitlaced (*or* straightlaced), Victorian; correct, decorous, genteel, polite, proper, seemly; acceptable, agreeable, desirable, pleasant, pleasing, welcome; appropriate, becoming, fit, meet, suitable; immaculate, pure, spotless
**2** provoking a memory or mental association ⟨a haunting and *suggestive* song about a long-lost love⟩
***syn*** evocative, reminiscent
***rel*** eloquent, expressive, meaningful, significant; affecting, emotional, moving, poignant, stirring, touching; exciting, provocative, provoking, rousing, stimulating
**3** clearly conveying a special meaning (as one's mood) — see EXPRESSIVE

**suicide** *n* the act of deliberately killing oneself ⟨teenagers are more prone to *suicide* because they mistakenly believe their troubles are insurmountable⟩
***syn*** self-destruction
***rel*** martyrdom; foul play, homicide, murder, slaying; killing, manslaughter; assassination, execution; euthanasia, mercy killing

**suit** *n* **1** a court case for enforcing a right or claim — see LAWSUIT
**2** an earnest request — see PLEA 1

**suit** *vb* **1** to be fitting or proper — see DO 1
**2** to give satisfaction to — see PLEASE
**3** to outfit with clothes and especially fine or special clothes — see CLOTHE 1

**suitability** *n* the quality or state of being especially suitable or fitting — see APPROPRIATENESS

**suitable** *adj* **1** having the required skills for an acceptable level of performance — see COMPETENT
**2** meeting the requirements of a purpose or situation — see FIT 1

**suitableness** *n* the quality or state of being especially suitable or fitting — see APPROPRIATENESS

**suitably** *adv* in a manner suitable for the occasion or purpose — see PROPERLY

**suitcase** *n* a bag carried by hand and designed to hold a traveler's clothing and personal articles — see TRAVELING BAG

**suite** *n* **1** a body of employees or servants who accompany and wait on a person — see CORTEGE 1
**2** a number of things considered as a unit — see GROUP 1
**3** a room or set of rooms in a private house or a block used as a separate dwelling place — see APARTMENT 1

**suitor** *n* **1** a man who courts a woman usually with the goal of marrying her ⟨my sister finally married her *suitor* of six years on Sunday⟩
***syn*** gallant, swain, wooer
***rel*** beau, boyfriend, fellow, man; admirer, crush, steady; beloved, darling, dear, favorite, flame, honey, love, lover, sweet, sweetheart, valentine; date, escort; fiancé, intended
**2** one who asks earnestly for a favor or gift — see SUPPLICANT

**sulk** *n* a state of resentful silence or irritability ⟨a child sitting in a *sulk* over a minor disagreement⟩
***syn*** pet, pouts, sulkiness, sullenness
***rel*** blues, dumps, mopes; surliness; biliousness, crankiness, crossness, crotchetiness, grouchiness, grumpiness, irascibility, irritability, peevishness, perverseness, perversity, pettishness, petulance, testiness, waspishness; cantankerousness, disagreeableness, orneriness

*near ant* sociability; cheerfulness, gaiety (*also* gayety), gladsomeness, good-humoredness, high-spiritedness, lightheartedness, perkiness

**sulk** *vb* to silently go about in a bad mood ⟨the toddler *sulked* all day whenever he didn't get his way⟩
*syn* mope, pout
*rel* brood, dwell (on), mull (over), muse (over), ponder; frown, glower, lower (*also* lour), scowl; carry on, take on

**sulkiness** *n* a state of resentful silence or irritability — see SULK

**sulky** *adj* given to or displaying a resentful silence and often irritability ⟨our teenage daughter turns *sulky* if we refuse to let her borrow the car⟩
*syn* glum, pouting, sullen, surly
*rel* dour, gloomy, morose; choleric, crabby, cranky, cross, crotchety, grouchy, grumpy, irascible, irritable, peevish, perverse, pettish, petulant, quick-tempered, short-tempered, snappy, snippy, testy, waspish; brooding, moping; bearish, bilious, cantankerous, disagreeable, dyspeptic, ill-humored, ill-natured, ill-tempered, ornery; sensitive, temperamental, thin-skinned, touchy
*near ant* sociable; cheerful, cheery, gladsome, good-humored, good-natured, perky

**sullen** *adj* **1** causing or marked by an atmosphere lacking in cheer — see GLOOMY 1
**2** given to or displaying a resentful silence and often irritability — see SULKY

**sullenness** *n* a state of resentful silence or irritability — see SULK

**sullied** *adj* not clean — see DIRTY 1

**sully** *vb* to make dirty — see DIRTY

**sultry** *adj* **1** containing or characterized by an uncomfortable amount of moisture — see HUMID
**2** having a notably high temperature — see HOT 1

**sum** *n* **1** a complete amount of something — see WHOLE
**2** a short statement of the main points — see SUMMARY

**sum** *vb* to combine (numbers) into a single sum — see ADD 2

**sum** (to *or* into) *vb* to have a total of — see AMOUNT (TO) 1

**summarily** *adv* in a few words — see SHORTLY 1

**summarization** *n* a short statement of the main points — see SUMMARY

**summarize** *vb* to make into a short statement of the main points (as of a report) ⟨the closing minute of the newscast *summarizes* the main story of the day⟩
*syn* abstract, digest, encapsulate, epitomize, outline, recap, recapitulate, sum up, wrap up
*rel* abridge, condense, curtail, shorten; downsize, shrink; concentrate, consolidate; simplify, streamline
*near ant* amplify, elaborate (on *or* upon), enlarge (on *or* upon), expand

**summary** *adj* marked by the use of few words to convey much information or meaning — see CONCISE

**summary** *n* a short statement of the main points ⟨many book reports choose to begin with a *summary* of the book⟩
*syn* abstract, digest, encapsulation, epitome, outline, précis, recap, recapitulation, résumé (*or* resume *also* resumé), roundup, sum, summarization, synopsis
*rel* abbreviation, abridgment (*or* abridgement), condensation, curtailment, shortening; brief; rundown; simplification, streamlining
*near ant* amplification, enlargement, expansion

**summation** *n* a complete amount of something — see WHOLE

**summit** *n* the highest part or point — see HEIGHT 1

**summon** *vb* **1** to demand or request the presence or service of ⟨without explanation, the principal *summoned* me to his office⟩
*syn* call, hail
*rel* cite, subpoena; assemble, convene, convoke, muster; ask, bid, invite; command, order, request, requisition; beckon, demand, invoke
*phrases* send for
*near ant* dismiss, send (away), turn away
**2** to call into being through the use of one's inner resources or powers ⟨managed to *summon* a bright smile despite the gloomy day⟩
*syn* conjure (up), gather (up)
*rel* educe, elicit, evoke, raise
**3** to bring together in assembly by or as if by command — see CONVOKE

**summons** *n* a written notice ordering a person to appear in court ⟨if you ignore a court *summons*, you will be fined⟩
*syn* subpoena
*rel* warrant, writ

**sumptuous** *adj* showing obvious signs of wealth and comfort — see LUXURIOUS

**sumptuously** *adv* in a luxurious manner — see HIGH

**sum up** *vb* to make into a short statement of the main points (as of a report) — see SUMMARIZE

**sun** *n* **1** the light given off by the star around which the planet Earth revolves ⟨be sure to wear sunscreen if you plan to spend more than a few minutes in the *sun*⟩
*syn* sunlight, sunshine
*rel* sunburst; daylight
*near ant* cloudiness; penumbra, shade, shadiness, shadow, umbra
**2** a ball-shaped gaseous celestial body that shines by its own light — see STAR 1

**sunder** *vb* to set or force apart — see SEPARATE 1

**sundown** *n* the time from when the sun begins to set to the onset of total darkness — see DUSK 1

**sundowner** *n, Australian* a homeless wanderer who may beg or steal for a living — see TRAMP

**sundries** *n pl* small useful items — see NOTION 1

**sunken** *adj* **1** curved inward — see HOLLOW
**2** living, lying, or occurring below the surface of the water — see UNDERWATER

**sunlight** *n* the light given off by the star around which the planet Earth revolves — see SUN 1

**sunny** *adj* **1** having or being an outward sign of good feeling (as of love, confidence, or happiness) — see RADIANT 1
**2** having or showing a good mood or disposition — see CHEERFUL 1
**3** indicative of or marked by high spirits or good humor — see MERRY
**4** not stormy or cloudy — see FAIR 1

**sunrise** *n* the first appearance of light in the morning or the time of its appearance — see DAWN 1

**sunset** *n* the time from when the sun begins to set to the onset of total darkness — see DUSK 1

**sunshine** *n* the light given off by the star around which the planet Earth revolves — see SUN 1

**sunshiny** *adj* not stormy or cloudy — see FAIR 1

**sunup** *n* the first appearance of light in the morning or the time of its appearance — see DAWN 1

**sup** *n* the portion of a serving of a beverage that is swallowed at one time — see DRINK 2

**sup** *vb* to swallow in liquid form — see DRINK 1

**super** *adj* unusually large — see HUGE

**super** *adv* to a great degree — see VERY 1

**superabundance** *n* **1** an amount or supply more than sufficient to meet one's needs — see PLENTY 1
**2** the state or an instance of going beyond what is usual, proper, or needed — see EXCESS

**superb** *adj* of the very best kind — see EXCELLENT

**superbness** *n* **1** exceptionally high quality — see EXCELLENCE 1
**2** impressiveness of beauty on a large scale — see MAGNIFICENCE

**supercilious** *adj* having a feeling of superiority that shows itself in an overbearing attitude — see ARROGANT

**superciliousness** *n* an exaggerated sense of one's importance that shows itself in the making of excessive or unjustified claims — see ARROGANCE

**superficial** *adj* **1** lying on or affecting only the outer layer of something ⟨a *superficial* scratch that barely even broke the skin⟩
***syn*** skin-deep, surface
***rel*** depthless, shallow, shoal; two-dimensional
***near ant*** deep, deep-rooted, deep-seated, subcutaneous, subterranean
**2** having or showing a lack of depth of understanding or character ⟨a *superficial* analysis of how movie and video violence affects young people⟩
***syn*** facile, one-dimensional, shallow, skin-deep
***rel*** cursory, hasty, sketchy; aimless, desultory, haphazard, hit-or-miss, random; limited, narrow, restricted
***near ant*** discerning, penetrating; definitive, hard; broad, complete, comprehensive, exhaustive, extensive, far-reaching, wide; general, global, inclusive; detailed, in-depth; critical
***ant*** deep, profound

**superfluity** *n* **1** something adding to pleasure or comfort but not absolutely necessary — see LUXURY 1
**2** the state or an instance of going beyond what is usual, proper, or needed — see EXCESS

**superfluous** *adj* being over what is needed — see SPARE 1

**superheated** *adj* having a notably high temperature — see HOT 1

**superhuman** *adj* **1** being so extraordinary or abnormal as to suggest powers which violate the laws of nature — see SUPERNATURAL 2
**2** of, relating to, or being part of a reality beyond the observable physical universe — see SUPERNATURAL 1

**superintend** *vb* **1** to be in charge of — see BOSS 1
**2** to look after and make decisions about — see CONDUCT 1
**3** to take charge of especially on behalf of another — see ²TEND 1

**superintendence** *n* **1** the act or activity of looking after and making decisions about something — see CONDUCT 1
**2** the duty or function of watching or guarding for the sake of proper direction or control — see SUPERVISION 1

**superintendency** *n* the duty or function of watching or guarding for the sake of proper direction or control — see SUPERVISION 1

**superintendent** *n* a person who manages or directs — see EXECUTIVE

**superior** *adj* **1** having a feeling of superiority that shows itself in an overbearing attitude — see ARROGANT
**2** having or displaying feelings of scorn for what is regarded as beneath oneself — see PROUD 1
**3** of the very best kind — see EXCELLENT
**4** standing above others in rank, importance, or achievement — see EMINENT

**superior** *n* one who is above another in rank, station, or office ⟨if a customer is rude to you, report it to your *superior* and they'll handle it⟩
***syn*** better, elder, senior
***rel*** boss, chief, head, leader, master
***near ant*** assistant, deputy
***ant*** inferior, subordinate, underling

**superiority** *n* **1** an exaggerated sense of one's importance that shows itself in the

making of excessive or unjustified claims — see ARROGANCE
**2** exceptionally high quality — see EXCELLENCE 1
**3** the fact or state of being above others in rank or importance — see EMINENCE 1

**superlative** *adj* of the very best kind — see EXCELLENT

**supernal** *adj* **1** of the very best kind — see EXCELLENT
**2** of, relating to, or suggesting heaven — see CELESTIAL

**supernatural** *adj* **1** of, relating to, or being part of a reality beyond the observable physical universe ⟨Susie believes in ghosts, guardian angels, and other *supernatural* beings⟩
***syn*** metaphysical, preternatural, superhuman, unearthly
***rel*** occult; extrasensory; celestial, divine, heavenly
***ant*** natural
**2** being so extraordinary or abnormal as to suggest powers which violate the laws of nature ⟨he seems to read books with *supernatural* speed⟩
***syn*** magical, miraculous, phenomenal, superhuman, uncanny, unearthly
***rel*** bizarre, curious, far-out, funny, kinky, outlandish, out-of-the-way, outrageous, outré, peculiar, quaint, queer, queerish, quirky, remarkable, screwy, strange, wacky, way-out, weird, wild; baffling, bewildering, confounding, mystifying, perplexing, puzzling, shocking; aberrant, abnormal, atypical, extraordinary, fantastic, flaky, freak, freakish, idiosyncratic, rare, singular, uncommon, unique, unusual, unwonted; unconventional, uncustomary, unorthodox; conspicuous, notable, noticeable, outstanding, prominent, salient, striking
***near ant*** average, commonplace, everyday, garden, ordinary, prosaic, routine, run-of-the-mill, typical, unexceptional, unremarkable, usual, workaday; expected, familiar, predictable; common, customary, frequent, habitual, regular, wonted
**3** of, relating to, or being God — see HOLY 3

**supernumerary** *adj* being over what is needed — see SPARE 1

**supersede** *vb* to take the place of — see REPLACE 1

**superstar** *n* a person who is widely known and usually much talked about — see CELEBRITY 1

**supervene** *vb* to come after in time — see FOLLOW 1

**supervise** *vb* **1** to be in charge of — see BOSS 1
**2** to look after and make decisions about — see CONDUCT 1
**3** to take charge of especially on behalf of another — see ²TEND 1

**supervision** *n* **1** the duty or function of watching or guarding for the sake of proper direction or control ⟨our French teacher has *supervision* of all activities of the French Club⟩
***syn*** care, charge, guidance, headship, oversight, regulation, superintendence, superintendency
***rel*** monitoring, observing; administration, control, direction, management, running; leadership, piloting, shepherding, steering; government, reign, rule; aegis, guardianship, protection, tutelage
**2** the act or activity of looking after and making decisions about something — see CONDUCT 1

**supervisor** *n* a person who manages or directs — see EXECUTIVE

**supervisory** *adj* suited for or relating to the directing of things — see EXECUTIVE

**supplant** *vb* to take the place of — see REPLACE 1

**supple** *adj* **1** able to bend easily without breaking — see WILLOWY
**2** able to revert to original size and shape after being stretched, squeezed, or twisted — see ELASTIC 1

**supplement** *n* **1** something added (as by growth) — see INCREASE 1
**2** something that serves to complete or make up for a deficiency in something else — see COMPLEMENT 1

**supplemental** *adj* available to supply something extra when needed — see AUXILIARY

**supplementary** *adj* **1** available to supply something extra when needed — see AUXILIARY
**2** related to each other in such a way that one completes the other — see COMPLEMENTARY

**suppliant** *adj* asking humbly ⟨the *suppliant* student pleaded for a second chance⟩
***syn*** beseeching, entreating, imploring, pleading, prayerful, soliciting, supplicant, supplicating
***rel*** importunate, insistent, persistent

**suppliant** *n* one who asks earnestly for a favor or gift — see SUPPLICANT

**supplicant** *adj* asking humbly — see SUPPLIANT

**supplicant** *n* one who asks earnestly for a favor or gift ⟨the new governor soon had to deal with a long line of *supplicants* asking for jobs and other political favors⟩
***syn*** petitioner, pleader, solicitor, suitor, suppliant
***rel*** beggar, mendicant, panhandler; asker, requester, suer

**supplicate** *vb* to make a request to (someone) in an earnest or urgent manner — see BEG

**supplicating** *adj* asking humbly — see SUPPLIANT

**supplication** *n* an earnest request — see PLEA 1

**supply** *n* the number of individuals or amount of something available at any given time ⟨the *supply* of grown-ups will-

***syn*** synonym(s) ***rel*** related words
***ant*** antonym(s) ***near ant*** near antonym(s)

ing to coach soccer seems to be shrinking〉
*syn* budget, fund, pool
*rel* reserve, reservoir, resource; cache, hoard, stockpile; refill, renewal, replacement; kitty, nest egg, pot, purse; source, well, wellspring

**supply** *vb* **1** to provide (someone) with what is needed for a task or activity — see FURNISH 1
**2** to put (something) into the possession of someone for use or consumption — see FURNISH 2

**support** *n* **1** something that holds up or serves as a foundation for something else 〈if you don't add a couple more *supports* to that tower of blocks, it's going to fall down〉
*syn* brace, bulwark, buttress, mount, mounting, shore, stay, underpinning
*rel* column, pedestal, pilaster, pillar; arch, bracket, cantilever, crutch, mainstay, peg, post, stake, stanchion, stand, stilt, truss; base, foundation, frame
**2** an act or instance of helping — see HELP 1
**3** something or someone to which one looks for support — see DEPENDENCE 2

**support** *vb* **1** to promote the interests or cause of 〈my parents *support* the local schools both by volunteering and by fiercely opposing funding cuts at town meetings〉
*syn* advocate, back, champion, endorse (*also* indorse), patronize
*rel* adopt, embrace, espouse; abet, aid, assist, prop (up), second; bolster, boost, buttress, reinforce; bail out, deliver, rescue, save
*phrases* stand up for
*near ant* baffle, foil, frustrate, interfere, oppose, sabotage, thwart; desert, disappoint, fail, let down
**2** to pay the living expenses of 〈a young widow *supporting* a sick mother as well as two small children on a teacher's salary〉
*syn* maintain, provide (for)
*rel* finance, fund, stake
*phrases* foot the bills for, take care of
**3** to hold up or serve as a foundation for 〈pillars *supporting* the bridge〉
*syn* bear, bolster, brace, buttress, carry, prop (up), shore (up), stay, underpin, uphold
*rel* steady, truss, underlie
**4** to continue to declare to be true or proper despite opposition or objections — see MAINTAIN 2
**5** to give evidence or testimony to the truth or factualness of — see CONFIRM
**6** to provide (someone) with what is useful or necessary to achieve an end — see HELP 1
**7** to put up with (something painful or difficult) — see BEAR 2

**supportable** *adj* **1** capable of being defended with good reasoning against verbal attack — see TENABLE 1
**2** capable of being endured — see BEARABLE
**3** capable of being proven as true or real — see VERIFIABLE

**supporter** *n* **1** a person who actively supports or favors a cause — see EXPONENT
**2** someone associated with another to give assistance or moral support — see ALLY

**supporting** *adj* serving to give support to the truth or factualness of something — see CORROBORATIVE

**supportive** *adj* serving to give support to the truth or factualness of something — see CORROBORATIVE

**suppose** *vb* **1** to decide the size, amount, number, or distance of (something) without actual measurement — see ESTIMATE 2
**2** to form an opinion from little or no evidence — see GUESS 1
**3** to have as an opinion — see BELIEVE 2
**4** to take as true or as a fact without actual proof — see ASSUME 2

**supposed** *adj* appearing to be true on the basis of evidence that may or may not be confirmed — see APPARENT 1

**supposedly** *adv* to all outward appearances — see APPARENTLY

**supposition** *n* **1** an idea that is the starting point for making a case or conducting an investigation — see THEORY
**2** an opinion or judgment based on little or no evidence — see CONJECTURE
**3** something taken as being true or factual and used as a starting point for a course of action or reasoning — see ASSUMPTION

**suppositional** *adj* existing only as an assumption or speculation — see THEORETICAL 1

**suppress** *vb* **1** to keep from being publicly known 〈the government tried to *suppress* the truth about that incident〉
*syn* cover (up), hush (up)
*rel* censor, silence; repress, smother, squash, squelch, stifle
*phrases* keep a lid on
*near ant* debunk, expose, reveal, show up, uncloak, uncover, unmask; disclose, divulge, tell, unveil; broadcast, circulate, publish, spread; describe, narrate, recite, recount, rehearse, relate, report
**2** to refrain from openly showing or uttering 〈he managed to *suppress* a scream at the sight of the dead body〉 〈*suppressed* her anger〉
*syn* choke (back), pocket, repress, smother, stifle, strangle, swallow
*rel* control, govern, handle, manage; bridle, check, curb, hold back, quell; bottle up, contain, hold in; muffle, squelch
*near ant* loose, release, take out, unleash, vent
**3** to hold back the normal growth of — see STUNT
**4** to put a stop to (something) by the use of force — see QUELL 1

**suppression** *n* the checking of one's true feelings and impulses when dealing with others — see CONSTRAINT 1

**supremacist** *n* a person who believes that one race should control all others ⟨white *supremacists* were arrested for painting racial slurs on a church⟩
***syn*** racialist, racist
***rel*** segregationist; bigot

**supremacy** *n* **1** controlling power or influence over others ⟨the Roman empire had *supremacy* over the entire Mediterranean world⟩
***syn*** ascendancy, dominance, dominion, predominance, preeminence
***rel*** primacy, superiority; lordship, scepter, sovereignty; arm, authority, clutch, command, control, grip, hold, mastery, sway; take-over; direction, jurisdiction, management; clout, pull, weight; eminence, importance, moment; prerogative, privilege, right
***near ant*** helplessness, weakness; impotence, powerlessness
**2** exceptionally high quality — see EXCELLENCE 1

**supreme** *adj* **1** highest in rank or authority — see HEAD
**2** coming before all others in importance — see FOREMOST 1
**3** of the greatest or highest degree or quantity — see ULTIMATE 1

**Supreme Being** *n* the being worshipped as the creator and ruler of the universe — see DEITY 2

**surcease** *n* the stopping of a process or activity — see END 1

**surcharge** *vb* to charge (someone) too much for goods or services — see OVERCHARGE 1

**surcoat** *n* a warm outdoor coat — see OVERCOAT

**sure** *adj* **1** having or showing a mind free from doubt — see CERTAIN 2
**2** impossible to avoid or evade — see INEVITABLE
**3** not likely to fail — see INFALLIBLE 2
**4** worthy of one's trust — see DEPENDABLE

**surely** *adv* without any question — see INDEED 1

**sureness** *n* **1** a state of mind in which one is free from doubt — see CONFIDENCE 2
**2** worthiness as the recipient of another's trust or confidence — see RELIABILITY

**surety** *n* **1** a formal agreement to fulfill an obligation — see GUARANTEE 1
**2** a person who takes the responsibility for some other person or thing — see SPONSOR

**surf** *n* a light mass of fine bubbles formed in or on a liquid — see FOAM

**surface** *adj* lying on or affecting only the outer layer of something — see SUPERFICIAL 1

**surface** *n* an outer part or layer — see EXTERIOR

**surface** *vb* **1** to come to one's attention especially gradually or unexpectedly — see ARISE 2
**2** to penetrate the surface (as of water) from below — see BROACH 1

**surfeit** *n* the state or an instance of going beyond what is usual, proper, or needed — see EXCESS

**surfeit** *vb* to fill with food to capacity — see GORGE 1

**surfeited** *adj* having one's appetite completely satisfied — see FULL 3

**surge** *n* a moving ridge on the surface of water — see WAVE

**surly** *adj* **1** given to or displaying a resentful silence and often irritability — see SULKY
**2** having or showing a habitually bad temper — see ILL-TEMPERED

**surmise** *n* an opinion or judgment based on little or no evidence — see CONJECTURE

**surmise** *vb* to form an opinion from little or no evidence — see GUESS 1

**surmount** *vb* to achieve a victory over — see BEAT 2

**surpass** *vb* **1** to be greater, better, or stronger than ⟨she always tried to *surpass* her older brother at anything he did⟩
***syn*** beat, better, eclipse, excel, outdistance, outdo, outshine, outstrip, overtop, top, transcend
***rel*** exceed, outpace, outrun, overpass; best, clobber, conquer, crush, defeat, drub, lick, master, overcome, overmatch, prevail (over), rout, skunk, subdue, surmount, thrash, trim, triumph (over), trounce, wallop, whip, win (against), worst; outweigh, overbear, overshadow
***phrases*** go one better
***near ant*** lose (to)
**2** to go beyond the limit of — see EXCEED

**surplus** *adj* being over what is needed — see SPARE 1

**surplus** *n* the state or an instance of going beyond what is usual, proper, or needed — see EXCESS

**surprise** *also* **surprize** *vb* **1** to make a strong impression on (someone) with something unexpected ⟨I was very *surprised* when my parents offered to pay for guitar lessons⟩
***syn*** amaze, astonish, astound, bowl (over), dumbfound (*also* dumfound), flabbergast, floor, shock, startle, stun, stupefy
***rel*** befuddle, bewilder, confound, confuse, discomfit, disconcert, dismay, muddle, nonplus, perplex
***phrases*** knock for a loop, take aback, take by surprise
**2** to lie in wait for and attack by surprise — see AMBUSH

**surprise** *n* **1** something that makes a strong impression because it is so unexpected ⟨the birthday party was such a complete *surprise* that Jane was speechless for a moment⟩
***syn*** bolt, bombshell, jar, jolt, stunner
***rel*** shock, thunderclap; revelation, shocker

---

***syn*** synonym(s) ***rel*** related words
***ant*** antonym(s) ***near ant*** near antonym(s)

2 the state of being strongly impressed by something unexpected or unusual ⟨Danny stared in utter *surprise* at the deer in his living room⟩
*syn* amazement, astonishment, shock
*rel* awe, wonder, wonderment; startle; bewilderment, confusion, discomfiture, dismay
3 a scheme in which hidden persons wait to attack by surprise — see AMBUSH 1

**surprising** *adj* 1 causing a strong emotional reaction because unexpected ⟨the *surprising* news that they were going to have a baby had them rushing to buy nursery furniture⟩
*syn* amazing, astonishing, astounding, dumbfounding (*or* dumfounding), eye-opening, flabbergasting, shocking, startling, stunning, stupefying
*rel* unannounced, unanticipated, unexpected, unforeseen; awesome, awful, breathtaking, fabulous, marvelous (*or* marvellous), miraculous, portentous, prodigious, staggering, stupendous, sublime, wonderful, wondrous; extraordinary, phenomenal, rare, sensational, spectacular; befuddling, bewildering, confounding, confusing, discomfiting, disconcerting, dismaying, muddling, nonplussing, perplexing; incomprehensible, inconceivable, incredible, unbelievable, unimaginable, unthinkable; singular, uncommon, unique, unusual, unwonted; conspicuous, notable, noticeable, outstanding, remarkable; impressive, striking
*near ant* common, customary, mundane, normal, ordinary, typical, unexceptional, unremarkable, usual
2 causing wonder or astonishment — see MARVELOUS 1

**surrender** *n* the usually forced yielding of one's person or possessions to the control of another ⟨the police demanded the *surrender* of all hostages as a condition for allowing the hijackers safe passage out of the country⟩
*syn* capitulating, capitulation, relinquishment, submission, submitting
*rel* acceptance, acquiescence, concession; compromise; appeasement, conciliation; capture, fall
*near ant* resistance

**surrender** *vb* 1 to give (something) over to the control or possession of another usually under duress ⟨Annie *surrendered* the doll to her mother after a brief struggle⟩ ⟨the commander *surrendered* the garrison without having fired a single shot⟩
*syn* cede, deliver, give up, hand over, relinquish, render, turn over, yield
*rel* commit, consign, entrust; waive; renounce, resign; abandon, desert, discard, forsake, shed
*near ant* keep, retain, withhold
2 to cease resistance (as to another's arguments, demands, or control) — see YIELD 3
3 to give up (as a position of authority) formally — see ABDICATE
4 to give up and cease resistance (as to a liking, temptation, or habit) — see YIELD 1
5 to yield to the control or power of enemy forces — see FALL 2

**surreptitious** *adj* undertaken or done so as to escape being observed or known by others — see SECRET 1

**surround** *vb* to form a circle around ⟨she was *surrounded* by cheering fans within moments of scoring the winning goal⟩
*syn* circle, encircle, enclose (*also* inclose), encompass, ring
*rel* fence (in), hem (in), wall; besiege, entrench (*also* intrench), invest

**surroundings** *n pl* the circumstances, conditions, or objects by which one is surrounded — see ENVIRONMENT

**surveillance** *n* the act or state of being constantly attentive and responsive to signs of opportunity, activity, or danger — see VIGILANCE

**survey** *n* a close look at or over someone or something in order to judge condition — see INSPECTION

**survey** *vb* 1 to go around and approach (people) with a request for opinions or information — see CANVASS
2 to look over closely (as for judging quality or condition) — see INSPECT

**survive** *vb* 1 to come safely through ⟨the cat miraculously *survived* a two-story fall⟩
*syn* ride (out), weather
*rel* outlast, outlive; pull through; abide, continue, endure, hang on, last, lead, persist; be, breathe, exist, live, subsist; flourish, prosper, thrive
*near ant* croak [*slang*], decease, depart, die, expire, pass (on), pass away, perish, succumb; disappear, evaporate, fade, vanish; cease, end, stop
2 to continue to operate or to meet one's needs — see HOLD OUT

**susceptibility** *n* the quality or state of having little resistance to some outside agent ⟨Carol's unfortunate *susceptibility* to viruses meant she was nearly always sick⟩ ⟨Stephen had a well-known *susceptibility* to anyone with a pathetic story⟩
*syn* defenselessness, vulnerability, weakness
*rel* helplessness, powerlessness; passiveness, passivity; feebleness, frailness; exposure, liability, openness, sensitivity; receptiveness, receptivity; easiness, gullibility, naïveté (*also* naivete); credulity, credulousness
*near ant* immunity; impenetrability, indomitability, indomitableness, invincibility
*ant* invulnerability

**susceptible** *adj* 1 being in a situation where one is likely to meet with harm — see LIABLE 1
2 lacking protection from danger or resistance against attack — see HELPLESS 1
3 readily taken advantage of — see EASY 2

**suspect** *adj* giving good reason for being doubted, questioned, or challenged — see DOUBTFUL 2

**suspect** *vb* **1** to form an opinion from little or no evidence — see GUESS 1
**2** to have no trust or confidence in — see DISTRUST

**suspecting** *adj* inclined to doubt or question claims — see SKEPTICAL 1

**suspend** *vb* **1** to bring to a formal close for a period of time — see ADJOURN
**2** to place on an elevated point without support from below — see HANG 1

**suspense** *n* a state of temporary inactivity — see ABEYANCE

**suspension** *n* a state of temporary inactivity — see ABEYANCE

**suspicion** *vb, chiefly dialect* to form an opinion from little or no evidence — see GUESS 1

**suspicion** *n* **1** a feeling or attitude that one does not know the truth, truthfulness, or trustworthiness of someone or something — see DOUBT
**2** a very small amount — see PARTICLE 1

**suspicious** *adj* **1** giving good reason for being doubted, questioned, or challenged — see DOUBTFUL 2
**2** inclined to doubt or question claims — see SKEPTICAL 1
**3** not feeling sure about the truth, wisdom, or trustworthiness of someone or something — see DOUBTFUL 1

**suspiciously** *adv* with distrust — see ASKANCE

**sustain** *vb* **1** to supply with nourishment ⟨a granola bar will *sustain* you long enough to last until lunch⟩
***syn*** nourish, nurture
***rel*** sate, satiate, satisfy; cloy, fill, surfeit; fortify, strengthen; feed; board, cater, provision
**2** to come to a knowledge of (something) by living through it — see EXPERIENCE
**3** to put up with (something painful or difficult) — see BEAR 2

**sustainable** *adj* **1** capable of being defended with good reasoning against verbal attack — see TENABLE 1
**2** capable of being proven as true or real — see VERIFIABLE
**3** capable of being endured — see BEARABLE

**swab** *n* one who operates or navigates a seagoing vessel — see SAILOR

**swag** *n* valuables stolen or taken by force — see LOOT

**swagger** *vb* **1** to praise or express pride in one's own possessions, qualities, or accomplishments often to excess — see BOAST
**2** to walk with exaggerated arm and leg movements — see STRUT 1

**swain** *n* **1** a male romantic companion — see BOYFRIEND
**2** a man who courts a woman usually with the goal of marrying her — see SUITOR 1

**swallow** *n* the portion of a serving of a beverage that is swallowed at one time — see DRINK 2

**swallow** *vb* **1** to take into the stomach through the mouth and throat ⟨try not to *swallow* the toothpaste, because it's not good for you⟩
***syn*** down, ingest
***rel*** drink, imbibe, sip; bolt, devour, gobble (up *or* down), gulp; consume, eat, mouth (down); gorge, scarf, scoff, wolf; chew, gnaw (at *or* on), lap, lick, nibble (on); dispatch, polish off
**2** to refrain from openly showing or uttering — see SUPPRESS 2
**3** to regard as right or true — see BELIEVE 1

**swamp** *n* spongy land saturated or partially covered with water ⟨be careful in the *swamp*, because alligators sometimes lurk there⟩
***syn*** bog, fen, marsh, marshland, mire, morass, muskeg, slough (*also* slue), swampland
***rel*** quagmire; muck, mud, ooze, slime, slop, sludge, slush

**swamp** *vb* **1** to cover or become filled with a flood — see FLOOD
**2** to subject to incapacitating emotional or mental stress — see OVERWHELM 1

**swampland** *n* spongy land saturated or partially covered with water — see SWAMP

**swank** *or* **swanky** *adj* excessively showy — see GAUDY

**swank** *n* excessive or unnecessary display — see OSTENTATION

**swankily** *adv* in a bright and showy way — see GAILY 3

**swap** *n* a giving or taking of one thing of value in return for another — see EXCHANGE 1

**swap** *vb* to give up (something) and take something else in return — see CHANGE 3

**swarm** *n* a great number of persons or things gathered together — see CROWD 1

**swarm** *vb* to move upon or fill (something) in great numbers — see CROWD 2

**swarming** *adj* possessing or covered with great numbers or amounts of something specified — see RIFE

**swash** *vb* to move with a splashing motion — see SLOSH

**swat** *n* a hard strike with a part of the body or an instrument — see [1]BLOW

**swat** *vb* to deliver a blow to (someone or something) usually in a strong vigorous manner — see HIT 1

**swathe** *vb* to surround or cover closely — see ENFOLD 1

**sway** *n* **1** the power to bring about a result on another — see EFFECT 2
**2** the power to direct the thinking or behavior of others usually indirectly — see INFLUENCE 1
**3** the right or means to command or control others — see POWER 1

**sway** *vb* **1** to act upon (a person or a person's feelings) so as to cause a response — see [1]AFFECT 1
**2** to make a series of unsteady side-to-side motions — see ROCK 1
**swear** *vb* **1** to use offensive or indecent language ⟨you're not allowed to *swear* in this house⟩
*syn* blaspheme, curse, cuss
*rel* confound, damn, execrate, imprecate; fulminate, rail, rant
**2** to make a solemn declaration of intent — see PROMISE 1
**3** to make a solemn declaration under oath for the purpose of establishing a fact — see TESTIFY
**swearword** *n* a disrespectful or indecent word or expression ⟨this is a list of *swearwords* that will not be permitted in my classroom⟩
*syn* curse, cuss, expletive, obscenity, vulgarism
*rel* profanity; execration, imprecation, malediction; epithet, name; oath
**sweat** *n* **1** the active use of energy in producing a result — see EFFORT
**2** very hard or unpleasant work — see TOIL
**sweat** *vb* **1** to devote serious and sustained effort — see LABOR
**2** to experience concern or anxiety — see WORRY 1
**3** to work hard and long — see TOIL
**4** to flow forth slowly through small openings — see EXUDE
**sweep** *n* an area over which activity, capacity, or influence extends — see RANGE 2
**sweep** *vb* **1** to move or proceed smoothly and readily — see FLOW 2
**2** to turn away from a straight line or course — see CURVE 1
**sweepstakes** *n pl* a competitive encounter between individuals or groups carried on for amusement, exercise, or in pursuit of a prize — see GAME 1
**sweet** *adj* **1** granted special treatment or attention — see DARLING 1
**2** having a pleasant smell — see FRAGRANT
**3** having an easygoing and pleasing manner especially in social situations — see AMIABLE
**4** having qualities that tend to make one loved — see LOVABLE
**sweet** *n* **1** a food having a high sugar content ⟨remember to brush your teeth after eating *sweets*⟩
*syn* confection, sweetmeat
*rel* confectionery; candy, dessert, pastry
**2** a person with whom one is in love — see SWEETHEART
**sweetheart** *n* a person with whom one is in love ⟨I married my high-school *sweetheart* as soon as we both finished college⟩
*syn* beloved, darling, dear, flame, honey, love, sweet
*rel* beau, boyfriend, fellow, lover, man, swain; gal, girl, girlfriend, ladylove, mistress; date, escort; gallant, suitor, wooer; groom, husband; fiancé, intended; admirer, crush, steady
**sweetmeat** *n* a food having a high sugar content — see SWEET 1
**sweetness** *n* the state or quality of having a pleasant or agreeable manner in socializing with others — see AMIABILITY 1
**swell** *adj* of the very best kind — see EXCELLENT
**swell** *n* a moving ridge on the surface of water — see WAVE
**swell** *vb* **1** to become greater in extent, volume, amount, or number — see INCREASE 2
**2** to make greater in size, amount, or number — see INCREASE 1
**swelling** *n* a small rounded mass of swollen tissue — see BUMP 1
**sweltering** *adj* having a notably high temperature — see HOT 1
**swerve** *vb* **1** to depart abruptly from a straight line or course ⟨the car *swerved* sharply to avoid the squirrel in the road⟩
*syn* sheer, veer, yaw
*rel* skew, slew (*also* slue); arc, arch, bend, bow, crook, curve, hook, round, sweep, wheel; circle, coil, curl, loop, spiral; turn, twist, wind; deviate, stray, wander, waver
*ant* straighten
**2** to turn away from a straight line or course — see CURVE 1
**3** to cause to turn away from a straight line — see BEND 1
**swift** *adj* moving, proceeding, or acting with great speed — see FAST 1
**swift** *adv* with great speed — see FAST 1
**swiftly** *adv* with great speed — see FAST 1
**swiftness** *n* a high rate of movement or performance — see SPEED
**swig** *n* the portion of a serving of a beverage that is swallowed at one time — see DRINK 2
**swig** *vb* to swallow in liquid form — see DRINK 1
**swill** *n* the portion of a serving of a beverage that is swallowed at one time — see DRINK 2
**swill** *vb* **1** to eat greedily or to excess — see GORGE 2
**2** to swallow in liquid form — see DRINK 1
**swiller** *n* one who eats greedily or too much — see GLUTTON
**swim** *vb* to be in a confused state as if from being twirled around — see SPIN 2
**swimmingly** *adv* in a pleasing way — see WELL 5
**swindle** *n* a scheme in which the victim is cheated out of his money after first gaining his trust — see CONFIDENCE GAME
**swindle** *vb* to rob by the use of trickery or threats — see FLEECE
**swindler** *n* a dishonest person who uses clever means to cheat others out of something of value — see TRICKSTER 1
**swing** *vb* **1** to change one's course or direction — see TURN 3
**2** to change the course or direction of (something) — see TURN 2

**3** to deal with (something) usually skillfully or efficiently — see HANDLE 1
**4** to move (something) in a curved or circular path on or as if on an axis — see TURN 1
**5** to place on an elevated point without support from below — see HANG 1

**swipe** *n* a hard strike with a part of the body or an instrument — see [1]BLOW

**swipe** *vb* **1** to come into usually forceful contact with something — see HIT 2
**2** to deliver a blow to (someone or something) usually in a strong vigorous manner — see HIT 1
**3** to take (something) without right and with an intent to keep — see STEAL 1

**swiping** *n* an instance of theft — see THEFT 2

**swirl** *vb* **1** to cause (as a liquid) to move about in a circle especially repeatedly — see STIR 1
**2** to move (something) in a curved or circular path on or as if on an axis — see TURN 1

**swish** *n* a sound similar to the speech sound \s\ stretched out — see HISS 1

**swish** *vb* to make a sound like that of stretching out the speech sound \s\ — see HISS

**switch** *n* **1** a long thin or flexible tool for striking — see WHIP
**2** a quick jerky movement from side to side or up and down — see WAG 1

**switch** *vb* **1** to give up (something) and take something else in return — see CHANGE 3
**2** to move from side to side or up and down with quick jerky motions — see WAG
**3** to strike repeatedly with something long and thin or flexible — see WHIP 1
**4** to change (as an opinion) to the contrary — see REVERSE 1

**swoon** *n* a temporary or permanent state of unconsciousness — see FAINT

**swoon** *vb* to lose consciousness — see FAINT

**sword** *n* a hand weapon with a length of metal sharpened on one or both sides and usually tapered to a sharp point ⟨once upon a time dueling with *swords* was the gentlemanly way to settle a point of honor⟩
***syn*** blade, steel
***rel*** broadsword, cutlass, rapier, saber (*or* sabre), scimitar

**sycophant** *n* a person who flatters another in order to get ahead ⟨my teacher isn't fooled by the class *sycophants*, who are always telling her what a wonderful teacher she is⟩
***syn*** fawner, flunky (*also* flunkey), toady
***rel*** yes-man; hanger-on, leech, parasite, sponge, sponger; henchman, lackey, minion, satellite, slave, stooge; admirer, cultist, devotee, enthusiast, fan, groveler (*or* groveller), idolater (*or* idolator), worshipper (*or* worshiper), zealot; adherent, convert, disciple, follower, partisan, pupil, votary

**symbol** *n* **1** a device, design, or figure used as an identifying mark — see EMBLEM
**2** a written or printed mark that is meant to convey information to the reader — see CHARACTER 1

**symbolic** *also* **symbolical** *adj* having the function or meaning of a symbol ⟨the teddy bear in the story was intended to be *symbolic* of a mother's love⟩
***syn*** emblematic (*also* emblematical), representative
***rel*** figurative, metaphorical; allegorical
***ant*** nonsymbolic

**symbolize** *vb* to serve as a material counterpart of ⟨the flag *symbolizes* our country⟩
***syn*** represent
***rel*** embody, epitomize, incarnate, manifest, materialize, personalize, personify; exemplify, illustrate
***phrases*** stand for

**symmetry** *n* a balanced, pleasing, or suitable arrangement of parts — see HARMONY 1

**sympathetic** *adj* **1** having or showing the capacity for sharing the feelings of another ⟨a *sympathetic* smile⟩ ⟨Jane was always a *sympathetic* listener⟩
***syn*** compassionate, humane, understanding
***rel*** gentle, sensitive, softhearted, tender, tenderhearted, warm, warmhearted; benevolent, benignant, charitable, kind; clement, lenient, merciful; cordial, friendly, good-natured, good-tempered, gracious; affectionate, loving
***near ant*** inconsiderate, insensitive, thoughtless, unthinking; uncaring, unloving; merciless, pitiless, ruthless; grim, hard-bitten, hard-boiled, harsh, oppressive, rough, severe, stern, tough, ungentle; abusive, acrimonious, disagreeable, hateful, ill-natured, ill-tempered, malevolent, malicious, mean, rancorous, spiteful, surly, virulent
***ant*** callous, cold-blooded, hardhearted, heartless, inhuman, inhumane, unfeeling, unsympathetic
**2** having or marked by sympathy and consideration for others — see HUMANE 1

**sympathize** (with) *vb* to have sympathy for — see PITY

**sympathizer** *n* someone associated with another to give assistance or moral support — see ALLY

**sympathy** *n* **1** sorrow or the capacity to feel sorrow for another's suffering or misfortune ⟨although I'd never lost a relative, I felt great *sympathy* for the classmate whose grandfather died⟩
***syn*** commiseration, compassion, feeling
***rel*** condolence, regret; humanity, kindheartedness, kindliness, kindness, mercy, pity, softheartedness; affinity, empathy, rapport, sensitivity; altruism, benevolence, benignity, charity, generosity, goodwill, humanitarianism, philanthropy

---

***syn*** synonym(s) ***rel*** related words
***ant*** antonym(s) ***near ant*** near antonym(s)

***near ant*** indifference, insensitivity, unconcern; cruelty, harshness; animosity, antipathy, dislike, hatred, hostility
***ant*** callousness, hardheartedness, heartlessness
**2** the capacity for feeling for another's unhappiness or misfortune — see HEART 1

**symphonic** *adj* having a pleasing mixture of notes — see HARMONIOUS 1

**symphony** *n* **1** a balanced, pleasing, or suitable arrangement of parts — see HARMONY 1
**2** a usually large group of musicians playing together — see ²BAND 1

**symphony orchestra** *n* a usually large group of musicians playing together — see ²BAND 1

**symposium** *n* a meeting featuring a group discussion — see FORUM

**symptomatic** *adj* serving to identify as belonging to an individual or group — see CHARACTERISTIC 1

**synchronous** *adj* existing or occurring at the same period of time — see CONTEMPORARY 1

**syndicate** *n* **1** a group involved in secret or criminal activities — see RING 1
**2** a number of businesses or enterprises united for commercial advantage — see CARTEL

**synopsis** *n* a short statement of the main points — see SUMMARY

**synthetic** *adj* being such in appearance only and made with or manufactured from usually cheaper materials — see IMITATION

**syringe** *n* a slender hollow instrument by which material is put into or taken from the body through the skin — see NEEDLE 1

**syrupy** *adj* being of a consistency that resists flow — see THICK 2

**system** *n* **1** something made up of many interdependent or related parts ⟨the national highway *system* allows travel from one end of the country to the other⟩ ⟨the democratic *system* of checks and balances in government⟩
***syn*** complex, network
***rel*** interlacement, Internet, net, web; aggregate, conglomerate, totality, whole
**2** a method worked out in advance for achieving some objective — see PLAN 1
**3** the means or procedure for doing something — see METHOD

**systematic** *adj* following a set method, arrangement, or pattern — see METHODICAL

**systematize** *vb* to put into a particular arrangement — see ORDER 1

**systematized** *adj* following a set method, arrangement, or pattern — see METHODICAL

# T

**tab** *n* **1** a record of goods sold or services performed together with the costs due — see ¹BILL 1
**2** the amount owed at a bar or restaurant or the slip of paper stating the amount — see CHECK 1

**tabernacle** *n* a building for public worship and especially Christian worship — see CHURCH 1

**table** *n* **1** a leg-mounted piece of furniture with a broad flat top designed for the serving of food ⟨we sat at the kitchen *table*, playing cards for hours on end⟩
***syn*** board
***rel*** coffee table, refectory table; bar, counter; buffet, sideboard
**2** food eaten or prepared for eating at one time — see MEAL
**3** a broad flat area of elevated land — see PLATEAU
**4** a record of a series of items (as names or titles) usually arranged according to some system — see ¹LIST
**5** substances intended to be eaten — see FOOD

**tableland** *n* a broad flat area of elevated land — see PLATEAU

**tablet** *n* **1** a number of sheets of writing paper glued together at one edge — see PAD 1
**2** a small mass containing medicine to be taken orally — see PILL

**table talk** *n* friendly, informal conversation or an instance of this — see CHAT

**tableware** *n* **1** eating and serving utensils ⟨we ran short of *tableware*, so Emily went next door and borrowed some forks and knives⟩
***syn*** flatware, silver, silverware
***rel*** place setting, setting; silver plate; cutlery; chopstick, fork, knife, spoon, tablespoon, teaspoon
**2** dishes used for eating or serving food or drink ⟨Betty would take out her good *tableware* only on special occasions, as when the mayor came to dinner⟩
***syn*** dinnerware
***rel*** setting; china, chinaware, crockery, earthenware, porcelain, pottery, stoneware, ware; crystal, glassware; plate, saucer; cup, glass, goblet, mug, teacup; bowl, casserole, charger, platter, tureen

**taboo** *also* **tabu** *adj* that may not be permitted — see IMPERMISSIBLE

**tacit** *adj* understood although not put into words — see IMPLICIT

**taciturn** *adj* tending not to speak frequently (as by habit or inclination) — see SILENT 2

**tack** *n* the means or procedure for doing something — see METHOD

**tack** (on) *vb* to join (something) to a mass, quantity, or number so as to bring about an overall increase — see ADD 1

**tackle** *n* items needed for the performance of a task or activity — see EQUIPMENT

**tackle** *vb* to start work on energetically — see ATTACK 3

**tacky** *adj* **1** marked by an obvious lack of style or good taste ⟨it was *tacky* to wear sneakers, but Tracey's dress shoes hurt her feet⟩ ⟨*tacky* plastic flowers⟩
***syn*** cheesy, dowdy, inelegant, styleless, tasteless, trashy, unfashionable, unstylish
***rel*** inappropriate, incorrect, unbecoming, unseemly, unsuitable, wrong; outmoded, out-of-date, passé; coarse, crude, unrefined, vulgar; cheap, common, inferior, junky, lousy, low-grade, second-rate, shoddy, sleazy, tawdry; gaudy, loud, ostentatious, overdone, showy, splashy
***near ant*** appropriate, becoming, correct, fitting, proper, right, seemly, suitable; genteel, handsome, neat, quiet, refined, understated; contemporary, modern, up-to-date
***ant*** elegant, fashionable, modish, ritzy, smart, stylish, tasteful
**2** showing signs of advanced wear and tear and neglect — see SHABBY 1

**tact** *n* the ability to deal with others in touchy situations without offending them ⟨with supreme *tact*, Isabel suggested to her neighbor that her flower garden was probably not the best place for his dog to use as a bathroom⟩
***syn*** diplomacy, tactfulness
***rel*** considerateness, consideration, courtesy, delicacy, graciousness, thoughtfulness; civility, etiquette, mannerliness, manners, politeness; charm, gallantry, gentility, grace, gracefulness, suaveness, suavity; adroitness, deftness, dexterity, finesse; deference, regard, respect
***near ant*** discourteousness, discourtesy, inconsiderateness, inconsideration, indelicacy, thoughtlessness, ungraciousness, unthoughtfulness; impoliteness, incivility; boorishness, brashness, brassiness, loutishness; awkwardness, gauchness, gracelessness, maladroitness; disregard, disrespect, impertinence, impudence, insolence, rudeness
***ant*** tactlessness

**tactful** *adj* having or showing tact ⟨Allie tried to be *tactful* when asked to comment on the short story that a classmate had written⟩
***syn*** diplomatic
***rel*** considerate, courteous, delicate, gracious, thoughtful; civil, mannerly, polite; charming, gallant, genteel, suave; deferential, regardful, respectful
***near ant*** discourteous, inconsiderate, indelicate, thoughtless, ungracious, unthoughtful; ill-bred, ill-mannered, impolite, uncivil, unmannerly; boorish, brash, brassy, loutish; disregardful, disrespectful, impertinent, impudent, insolent, rude
***ant*** tactless, undiplomatic

**tactfulness** *n* the ability to deal with others in touchy situations without offending them — see TACT

**tactical** *adj* suitable for bringing about a desired result under the circumstances — see EXPEDIENT

**tactics** *n pl* the means or procedure for doing something — see METHOD

**tactless** *adj* showing poor judgment especially in personal relationships or social situations — see INDISCREET

**tad** *n* a male person who has not yet reached adulthood — see BOY

**tag** *n* a slip (as of paper or cloth) that is attached to something to identify or describe it — see LABEL

**tag** *vb* **1** to attach an identifying slip to — see LABEL 1
**2** to go after or on the track of — see FOLLOW 2

**tagging** *n* the act of going after or in the tracks of another — see PURSUIT

**tail** *n* a person whose business is solving crimes and catching criminals or gathering information that is not easy to get — see DETECTIVE

**tail** *vb* to go after or on the track of — see FOLLOW 2

**tailing** *n* the act of going after or in the tracks of another — see PURSUIT

**tailored** *adj* made or fitted to the needs or preferences of a specific customer — see CUSTOM-MADE

**tailor–made** *adj* made or fitted to the needs or preferences of a specific customer — see CUSTOM-MADE

**taint** *n* a mark of guilt or disgrace — see STAIN 1

**taint** *vb* **1** to affect slightly with something morally bad or undesirable ⟨criticism of her sister's singing that was *tainted* by envy⟩ ⟨a tendency toward conceitedness *taints* that athlete's status as a role model⟩
***syn*** blemish, mar, poison, spoil, stain, tarnish, touch, vitiate
***rel*** besmear, besmirch, blacken, cloud, dirty, discolor, smear, smirch, smudge, smut, soil, sully, tar; color, distort, twist; damage, deface, flaw, harm, hurt, impair; destroy, ruin, wreck
***near ant*** cleanse, purify; elevate, ennoble, uplift
**2** to make unfit for use by the addition of something harmful or undesirable — see CONTAMINATE

**tainted** *adj* containing foreign or lower-grade substances — see IMPURE

**take** *n* **1** action or behavior that is done in return to other action or behavior — see REACTION
**2** the total amount collected or obtained especially at one time — see HAUL 1

---

***syn*** synonym(s) ***rel*** related words
***ant*** antonym(s) ***near ant*** near antonym(s)

**take** *vb* **1** to reach for and take hold of by embracing with the fingers or arms ⟨*take* my hand, or we'll get separated in this crowd⟩
***syn*** clasp, grasp, grip, hold
***rel*** clench, cling (to), clutch, hang on (to), hold on (to); catch, nab, seize, snatch
***phrases*** lay hold of
***near ant*** discharge, drop, free, liberate, release; give, hand, relinquish, unhand
**2** to agree to receive whether willingly or reluctantly ⟨will you *take* that call?⟩ ⟨*took* a cut in pay⟩
***syn*** accept, have
***rel*** accede (to), assent (to), concede (to), consent (to), OK (*or* okay); acquiesce (to), bow (to), capitulate (to), give in (to), submit (to), succumb (to), surrender (to), yield (to); bear, endure, shoulder, tolerate, swallow; adopt, embrace, welcome
***near ant*** dissent (to), object (to), oppose, protest; hold off, resist, withstand
***ant*** decline, refuse, reject, spurn, turn down
**3** to become affected with (a disease or disorder) — see CONTRACT 1
**4** to decide to accept (someone or something) from a group of possibilities — see CHOOSE 1
**5** to get possession of (something) by giving money in exchange for — see BUY
**6** to have as a requirement — see NEED 1
**7** to make or have room for — see ACCOMMODATE 1
**8** to produce a desired effect — see ACT 2
**9** to put up with (something painful or difficult) — see BEAR 2

**take** (for) *vb* to think of in a particular way — see CONSIDER

**take back** *vb* to solemnly or formally reject or go back on (as something formerly adhered to) — see ABJURE

**take down** *vb* **1** to reduce to a lower standing in one's own eyes or in others' eyes — see HUMBLE
**2** to take apart — see DISASSEMBLE

**take in** *vb* **1** to cause to believe what is untrue — see DECEIVE
**2** to have as part of a whole — see INCLUDE
**3** to provide with living quarters or shelter — see HOUSE 1

**takeoff** *n* **1** a rising from a surface at the start of a flight (as of a rocket) — see LIFT-OFF
**2** a work that imitates and exaggerates another work for comic effect — see PARODY 1

**take off** *vb* **1** to leave a place often for another — see GO 2
**2** to rid oneself of (a garment) — see REMOVE 1
**3** to take away (an amount or number) from a total — see SUBTRACT

**take off** (on) *vb* to copy or exaggerate (someone or something) in order to make fun of — see MIMIC 1

**take on** *vb* **1** to enter into contest or conflict with — see ENGAGE 2
**2** to provide with a paying job — see EMPLOY 1

**take out** *vb* **1** to find emotional release for ⟨*took out* his frustrations by splitting a cord of firewood⟩
***syn*** loose, release, unleash, vent
***phrases*** give way (to)
***near ant*** control, govern, handle, manage; bridle, check, contain, curb, hold back, hold in, quell, restrain, smother; allay, lull, quiet, soothe, still; choke, inhibit, muffle, pocket, repress, stifle, strangle, swallow
***ant*** bottle (up), repress, suppress
**2** to go on a social engagement with — see DATE 1

**take over** *vb* **1** to serve as a replacement usually for a time only — see COVER 1
**2** to take to or upon oneself — see ASSUME 1

**take up** *vb* to take for one's own use (something originated by another) — see ADOPT

**taking** *adj* very pleasing to look at — see BEAUTIFUL

**tale** *n* **1** a rumor or report of a personal or sensational nature ⟨don't believe the *tales* you hear about our neighbor's kid⟩
***syn*** story, whisper
***rel*** dirt, gossip, scuttlebutt, talebearing, talk, tattle; defamation, libel, slander; hearsay; fabrication, fairy tale, falsehood, falsity, fib, lie
**2** a brief account of something interesting that happened especially to one personally — see STORY 2
**3** a statement known by its maker to be untrue and made in order to deceive — see LIE
**4** a work with imaginary characters and events that is shorter and usually less complex than a novel — see STORY 1

**talebearer** *n* a person who provides secret information about another's wrongdoing — see INFORMER

**talent** *n* a special and usually inborn ability ⟨Liza's musical *talent* was already apparent by the time she was five⟩ ⟨Jim's *talent* for coming up with really funny answers⟩
***syn*** aptitude, endowment, faculty, flair, genius, gift, knack
***rel*** bent, inclination, leaning, partiality, penchant, predilection, predisposition, proclivity, propensity, turn; ear, eye, head, mind, nose; feel, hang, instinct, touch, way; capability, competence, facility, proficiency, skill; capacity, power, potential
***near ant*** disability, handicap, inability, incapacity; shortcoming, weakness

**talisman** *n* something worn or kept to bring good luck or keep away evil — see CHARM 1

**talk** *n* **1** a usually formal discourse delivered to an audience — see SPEECH 1
**2** an exchange of views for the purpose of exploring a subject or deciding an issue — see DISCUSSION 1

**3** friendly, informal conversation or an instance of this — see CHAT

**talk** *vb* **1** to give a formal often extended talk on a subject ⟨detective Connolly often *talks* at school assemblies about safety⟩
*syn* declaim, descant, discourse, expatiate, harangue, lecture, orate, speak
*rel* recite, soliloquize; mouth, spout; filibuster; stump; eulogize
*phrases* hold forth, take the floor
**2** to engage in casual or rambling conversation — see CHAT
**3** to express (a thought or emotion) in words — see SAY 1
**4** to give information (as to the authorities) about another's improper or unlawful activities — see SQUEAL 1
**5** to relate sometimes questionable or secret information of a personal nature — see GOSSIP

**talk** (into) *vb* to cause (someone) to agree with a belief or course of action by using arguments or earnest request — see PERSUADE 1

**talk** (to) *vb* to communicate with by means of spoken words ⟨Patty had never *talked to* a real live cowboy before⟩
*syn* chat (with), converse (with), speak (to *or* with)
*rel* accost, address, greet, hail, herald; inform, notify, tell
*phrases* engage in conversation

**talkative** *adj* fond of talking or conversation ⟨a *talkative* outgoing tour guide showed our school group around the city⟩
*syn* chatty, conversational, gabby, garrulous, loquacious, talky
*rel* communicative, expansive; demonstrative, effusive, gushing; outspoken, unreserved, vocal; articulate, fluent, glib, voluble; blabby, gossipy, talebearing; long-winded, prolix, verbose, windy, wordy; extroverted (*also* extraverted), gregarious, outgoing, sociable
*near ant* quiet, shy; mum, mute, silent, speechless, tongue-tied, wordless; evasive, nonvocal, secretive, self-contained, uncommunicative; aloof, introverted, unsociable, withdrawn
*ant* closemouthed, laconic, reserved, reticent, taciturn, tight-lipped

**talker** *n* a person who talks constantly — see CHATTERBOX

**talk over** *vb* to talk about (an issue) usually from various points of view and for the purpose of arriving at a decision or opinion — see DISCUSS

**talky** *adj* fond of talking or conversation — see TALKATIVE

**tall** *adj* **1** extending to a great distance upward — see HIGH 1
**2** requiring considerable physical or mental effort — see HARD 2

**tally** *n* a total number obtained or recorded by noting each thing as it was being added — see COUNT 1

**tally** *vb* **1** to be in agreement on every point — see CHECK 1
**2** to gain (as points or runs in a game) as credit towards one's total number of points — see SCORE 2

**tame** *adj* **1** changed from the wild state so as to become useful and obedient to humans ⟨every evening, a Canada goose is at the food trough with our *tame* geese⟩
*syn* domestic, domesticated, tamed
*rel* broken, housebroken, trained; docile, gentle
*near ant* unbroken, untrained
*ant* feral, nondomesticated, undomesticated, untamed, wild
**2** causing weariness, restlessness, or lack of interest — see BORING

**tame** *vb* to keep from exceeding a desirable degree or level (as of expression) — see CONTROL 1

**tamed** *adj* changed from the wild state so as to become useful and obedient to humans — see TAME 1

**tamper** (with) *vb* to handle thoughtlessly, ignorantly, or mischievously ⟨someone has *tampered with* my computer files⟩
*syn* fiddle (with), fool (with), mess (with), monkey (with), play (with), tinker (with)
*rel* alter, doctor, manhandle, manipulate, misuse; butt in, interfere, intrude, meddle

**tan** *vb* to strike repeatedly with something long and thin or flexible — see WHIP 1

**tangent** *n* a departure from the subject under consideration ⟨in the middle of her description of her dog's symptoms, she went off on a *tangent* about its cute behavior⟩
*syn* digression, excursion
*rel* aside, parenthesis; rambling; circuitousness, circularity, circumlocution

**tangible** *adj* capable of being perceived by the sense of touch ⟨a firm belief in the existence of the soul, even though it is not at all *tangible*⟩
*syn* palpable, touchable
*rel* tactile; corporeal, physical; actual, concrete, embodied, existent, material, real, substantial; discernible, observable, perceptible, sensible
*near ant* bodiless, immaterial, incorporeal, insubstantial, nonmaterial, nonphysical, unsubstantial; abstract, ethereal, spiritual, unreal
*ant* impalpable, intangible

**tangle** *vb* **1** to catch or hold as if in a net — see ENTANGLE 2
**2** to twist together into a usually confused mass — see ENTANGLE 1

**tantrum** *n* an outburst or display of excited anger ⟨had a *tantrum* when he found his little sister using his model paints⟩
*syn* blowup, explosion, fireworks, fit, huff, scene
*rel* eruption, flare-up, outburst, storm, uproar; agitation, delirium, distraction, frenzy, furor, furore, fury, hysteria, rage,

rampage, uproar; convulsion(s), paroxysm, seizure, spasm, upheaval; reaction, rise; dander, temper; pet, pouts, sulk(s)

**tap** *n* a fixture for controlling the flow of a liquid — see FAUCET

[1]**tap** *vb* to strike or cause to strike lightly and usually rhythmically ⟨*tapped* her foot in time to the music⟩ ⟨kept *tapping* the desk with his pencil⟩
*syn* beat, drum, rap, thrum
*rel* bang, hammer, hit, knock, pound, thud, thump, thwack, whack; chink, clatter, clink, ping; pat, chuck, clap, flick, tip

[2]**tap** *vb* to remove (liquid) gradually or completely — see DRAIN 1

**taper** *vb* to grow less in scope or intensity especially gradually — see DECREASE 2

**taper off** *vb* to grow less in scope or intensity especially gradually — see DECREASE 2

**tar** *n* one who operates or navigates a seagoing vessel — see SAILOR

**tardily** *adv* at a pace that is less than usual, desirable, or expected — see SLOW

**tardiness** *n* the quality or state of being late — see LATENESS

**tardy** *adj* 1 moving or proceeding at less than the normal, desirable, or required speed — see SLOW 1
2 not arriving, occurring, or settled at the due, usual, or proper time — see LATE 1

**target** *n* 1 a person or thing that is the object of abuse, criticism, or ridicule ⟨Cinderella became the *target* of her stepsisters' envy⟩
*syn* butt, mark, sitting duck, victim
*rel* laughingstock, mockery; fall guy, goat, scapegoat, whipping boy
*near ant* gossip, gossiper, talebearer, tattler, tattletale, troublemaker; defamer, libeler (*or* libeller), traducer; baiter, heckler, needler, rubber, taunter, teaser, tormentor; derider, insulter, mocker, ridiculer, scoffer, scorner; caricaturist, lampooner, parodist, satirist
2 a person or thing that is made fun of — see LAUGHINGSTOCK
3 something that one hopes or intends to accomplish — see GOAL

**tarnish** *vb* to affect slightly with something morally bad or undesirable — see TAINT 1

**tarry** *vb* 1 to continue to be in a place for a significant amount of time — see STAY 1
2 to move or act slowly — see DELAY 1
3 to reside as a temporary guest — see VISIT 2

**tart** *adj* 1 causing or characterized by the one of the four basic taste sensations that is produced chiefly by acids — see SOUR 1
2 marked by the use of wit that is intended to cause hurt feelings — see SARCASTIC

**tartness** *n* 1 a harsh or sharp quality — see EDGE 1
2 biting sharpness of feeling or expression — see ACRIMONY 1

**task** *n* 1 a piece of work that needs to be done regularly — see CHORE 1
2 the action for which a person or thing is specially fitted or used or for which a thing exists — see ROLE

**taskmaster** *n* 1 a boss who assigns much work ⟨pitiless *taskmaster* that he was, Ebenezer Scrooge only reluctantly let his ill-paid clerk have Christmas day off⟩
*syn* slave driver
*rel* enslaver; authoritarian, disciplinarian, discipliner, martinet, stickler; despot, dictator, oppressor, tyrant; dominator, overlord
2 the person (as an employer or supervisor) who tells people and especially workers what to do — see BOSS

**taste** *n* 1 the property of a substance that can be identified by the sense of taste ⟨Nora can't stand the *taste* of cherry-flavored cough syrup⟩
*syn* flavor, savor
*rel* relish, smack, tang; savoriness, tastiness; aftertaste
2 a small piece or quantity of food — see MORSEL 1
3 positive regard for something — see LIKING

**taste** *vb* 1 to come to a knowledge of (something) by living through it — see EXPERIENCE
2 to have a vague awareness of — see FEEL 1

**tasteful** *adj* having or showing elegance — see ELEGANT 1

**tasteless** *adj* 1 lacking in refinement or good taste — see COARSE 2
2 lacking in taste or flavor — see INSIPID 1
3 marked by an obvious lack of style or good taste — see TACKY 1

**tastelessness** *n* the quality or state of lacking refinement or good taste — see VULGARITY 1

**tastiness** *n* the quality of being delicious — see DELICIOUSNESS

**tasty** *adj* very pleasing to the sense of taste — see DELICIOUS 1

**tatter** *vb* to cause (something) to separate into jagged pieces by violently pulling at it — see TEAR 1

**tattered** *adj* 1 wearing torn or worn out clothes ⟨arrived at the refugee camp *tattered* and exhausted⟩
*syn* ragged, raggedy, ragtag
*rel* bedraggled, scruffy, shabby, threadbare
*near ant* decked (out), dolled up, dressed up; spiffy
2 worn or torn into or as if into rags — see RAGGED 2

**tattle** *vb* to relate sometimes questionable or secret information of a personal nature — see GOSSIP

**tattler** *n* a person who provides secret information about another's wrongdoing — see INFORMER

**tattletale** *n* a person who provides secret information about another's wrongdoing — see INFORMER

**taunt** *vb* to attack repeatedly with mean put-downs or insults — see TEASE 2

**taunter** *n* a person who causes repeated emotional pain, distress, or annoyance to another — see TORMENTOR

**taut** *adj* stretched with little or no give ⟨a *taut* clothesline⟩
***syn*** drawn, rigid, tense, tight
***rel*** firm, inflexible, stiff, tightened, unrelaxed, unyielding
***near ant*** drooping, droopy, flaccid, floppy, hanging, lank, limp, loosened, relaxed, slackened, yielding
***ant*** lax, loose, slack

**tavern** *n* **1** a place of business where alcoholic beverages are sold to be consumed on the premises — see BARROOM
**2** a place that provides rooms and usually a public dining room for overnight guests — see HOTEL

**tawdry** *adj* excessively showy — see GAUDY

**tawny** *adj* of a pale yellow or yellowish brown color — see BLOND

**tax** *n* a charge usually of money collected by the government from people or businesses for public use ⟨the state sales *tax* boosted the final cost of my new computer⟩
***syn*** assessment, duty, imposition, impost, levy
***rel*** custom(s), excise, income tax, poll tax, sales tax, tariff, toll, tribute, withholding tax; surcharge, surtax; revenue

**tax** *vb* to subject (a personal quality or faculty) to often excessive stress — see TRY (OUT) 2

**taxi** *n* an automobile that carries passengers for a fare usually determined by the distance traveled — see TAXI

**taxicab** *n* an automobile that carries passengers for a fare usually determined by the distance traveled ⟨took a *taxicab* to the airport⟩
***syn*** cab, hack, taxi
***rel*** hackney; limousine; rickshaw (*also* ricksha)

**taxing** *adj* requiring much time, effort, or careful attention — see DEMANDING 1

**teach** *vb* to cause to acquire knowledge or skill in some field ⟨*taught* us about the basics of organic gardening⟩
***syn*** educate, indoctrinate, instruct, school, train, tutor
***rel*** coach, mentor, drill, fit, ground, prepare, prime, qualify; direct, guide, lead, rear; catechize, lecture, moralize, preach; implant, inculcate, instill (*also* instil); homeschool; edify, enlighten; brief, familiarize, impart (to), inform, verse; initiate, introduce, show; reeducate, retrain

**teacher** *n* a person whose occupation is to give formal instruction in a school ⟨a young man who ardently wants to become a *teacher* and teach first grade⟩
***syn*** educator, instructor, pedagogue, preceptor, schoolteacher
***rel*** headmaster, master, schoolmaster; headmistress, schoolmarm (*or* schoolma'am), schoolmistress; coach, guide, guru, trainer; mentor, tutor; drillmaster; dean, don, professor; pedant; governess, homeschooler; catechist, lecturer, moralizer, preacher

**teaching** *n* the act or process of imparting knowledge or skills to another — see EDUCATION 1

**team** *n* a group of people working together on a task — see GANG 1

**team** (up) *vb* to participate or assist in a joint effort to accomplish an end — see COOPERATE 1

**teamwork** *n* the work and activity of a number of persons who individually contribute toward the efficiency of the whole ⟨it takes *teamwork* to pull off a successful fund-raiser⟩
***syn*** collaboration, cooperation, coordination
***rel*** fellowship, partnership; community, mutualism, symbiosis; synergism; communion, oneness, solidarity, togetherness, unity

**tear** *n* a long deep cut — see GASH

**tear** *vb* **1** to cause (something) to separate into jagged pieces by violently pulling at it ⟨angrily *tore* the letter to shreds⟩
***syn*** rend, rip, rive, shred, tatter
***rel*** break, cleave, rupture, split; cut, gash, incise, lacerate, slash; butcher, dismember, dissect, hack, mangle
**2** to separate or remove by forceful pulling ⟨*tore* the book from his hand⟩
***syn*** rip, wrench, wrest, yank
***rel*** grab, nab, seize, snap (up), snatch; lop (off), nip, jerk; amputate, cut (off), dissever, sever; force, pry
***near ant*** reattach
**3** to proceed or move quickly — see HURRY 2

**tear** (out) *vb* to draw out by force or with effort — see EXTRACT

**tear down** *vb* **1** to bring to a complete end the physical soundness, existence, or usefulness of — see DESTROY 1
**2** to destroy (as a building) completely by knocking down or breaking to pieces — see DEMOLISH 1

**tearful** *adj* **1** given to expressing strong emotion (as sorrow) by readily shedding tears ⟨a *tearful* woman who can be counted on to cry at every wedding, anniversary, and funeral⟩
***syn*** lachrymose, teary
***rel*** emotional; maudlin, mawkish, sentimental; bawling, blubbering, crying, keening, sniffling, sniveling, sobbing, wailing, weeping, whimpering; bemoaning, bewailing; doleful, dolorous, grieving, mournful, plaintive; funereal, gloomy, lugubrious; brokenhearted, sad, sorrowful, woeful
***near ant*** grinning, laughing, smiling; blithe, blithesome, cheerful, cheery, gay, happy, lighthearted, lightsome, merry, mirthful, sunny
**2** causing unhappiness — see SAD 2

**teary** *adj* **1** causing unhappiness — see SAD 2

2 given to expressing strong emotion (as sorrow) by readily shedding tears — see TEARFUL 1

**tease** *n* 1 a person who causes repeated emotional pain, distress, or annoyance to another — see TORMENTOR
2 one who is obnoxiously annoying — see NUISANCE 1

**tease** *vb* 1 to make fun of in a good-natured way ⟨Hilary liked to *tease* her twin brother about his girlfriend⟩
*syn* chaff, jive, josh, kid, rally, razz, rib, ride, roast
*rel* banter, joke; fool, fun, string along; jest, quip, wisecrack
2 to attack repeatedly with mean put-downs or insults ⟨some of the boys *teased* Michael because his parents were hog farmers⟩
*syn* bait, bug, hassle, heckle, needle, ride, taunt
*rel* haze; gibe (*or* jibe), mock, ridicule; annoy, bother, chafe, fret, nag, nettle, irritate, gall, get, gnaw (at), pester, trouble, vex; aggravate, exasperate, goad, test, try; aggrieve, agitate, bedevil, beleaguer, discomfort, disturb, perturb; badger, dog, hound; browbeat, bully, hector; harass, harry, persecute, plague, terrorize, torment, torture
*phrases* pick on

**teaser** *n* 1 a person who causes repeated emotional pain, distress, or annoyance to another — see TORMENTOR
2 one who is obnoxiously annoying — see NUISANCE 1

**teasing** *n* the act of making unwelcome intrusions upon another — see ANNOYANCE 1

**technical** *adj* used by or intended for experts in a particular field of knowledge ⟨although the owner's manual for the receiver was supposedly written for the average consumer, it's filled with *technical* language⟩
*syn* specialized
*rel* esoteric, especial, exclusive, limited, narrow, peculiar, restricted, special, specific, unique; authoritative, expert, professional, specialist (*or* specialistic)
*near ant* common, generalized, generic, nonexclusive, nonspecific, ordinary, universal; inexpert, lay, nonprofessional, unprofessional
*ant* general, nonspecialized, nontechnical

**technique** *n* the means or procedure for doing something — see METHOD

**tedious** *adj* causing weariness, restlessness, or lack of interest — see BORING

**tedium** *n* the state of being bored — see BOREDOM

**teeming** *adj* possessing or covered with great numbers or amounts of something specified — see LIFE

**teeny** *adj* very small in size — see TINY

**teeny–weeny** *adj* very small in size — see TINY

**teeter** *vb* 1 to swing unsteadily back and forth or from side to side ⟨*teetered* at the edge of the pool⟩
*syn* falter, rock, totter, waver, wobble
*rel* flounder, lurch, stumble, toddle; quaver, tremble; careen, reel, stagger, weave
2 to move forward while swaying from side to side — see STAGGER 1
3 to show uncertainty about the right course of action — see HESITATE

**telephone** *vb* to make a telephone call to — see CALL 2

**tell** *vb* 1 to give an oral or written account of in some detail ⟨*told* the story of how they had met⟩
*syn* describe, narrate, recite, recount, rehearse, relate, report
*rel* deliver, give, state, utter, voice; detail, enumerate, itemize, particularize; disclose, divulge, reveal; delineate, depict, express, render, sketch
2 to express (a thought or emotion) in words — see SAY 1
3 to find the sum of (a collection of things) by noting each one as it is being added — see COUNT 1
4 to give information (as to the authorities) about another's improper or unlawful activities — see SQUEAL 1
5 to give information to — see ENLIGHTEN 1
6 to issue orders to (someone) by right of authority — see COMMAND 1
7 to make known (as information previously kept secret) — see REVEAL 1

**tell** (on) *vb* to act upon (a person or a person's feelings) so as to cause a response — see [1]AFFECT 1

**telling** *adj* having the power to persuade — see COGENT

**telltale** *adj* indicating something — see INDICATIVE

**telltale** *n* a person who provides secret information about another's wrongdoing — see INFORMER

**temerity** *n* shameless boldness — see EFFRONTERY

**temperance** *n* an avoidance of extremes in one's actions, beliefs, or habits ⟨Mr. Grindell attributes his ripe old age to *temperance* in all things, especially eating and drinking⟩
*syn* moderateness, moderation, temperateness
*rel* constraint, control, discipline, restraint, self-control, self-discipline; asceticism, austerity, frugality, mortification, sacrifice, self-denial, self-deprivation; abnegation, abstention, avoidance, eschewal, forbearance; modesty, rationality, reasonableness; abstinence, soberness, sobriety
*near ant* excess, superfluity; extremeness, extremity; unconstraint, unrestraint; extremism, radicalness; irrationality, unreasonableness
*ant* excessiveness, immoderacy, intemperance, intemperateness

**temper** *n* 1 a special quality or impression associated with something — see AURA
2 a state of mind dominated by a particular emotion — see MOOD 1

3 one's characteristic attitude or mood — see DISPOSITION 1

**temperament** *n* one's characteristic attitude or mood — see DISPOSITION 1

**temperamental** *adj* 1 frequently influenced by moods and especially bad moods — see MOODY

2 likely to change frequently, suddenly, or unexpectedly — see FICKLE 1

**temperate** *adj* 1 avoiding extremes in behavior or expression — see MODERATE 1

2 marked by temperatures that are neither too high nor too low — see CLEMENT

**temperateness** *n* an avoidance of extremes in one's actions, beliefs, or habits — see TEMPERANCE

**tempest** *n* 1 a disturbance of the atmosphere accompanied by wind and often by precipitation (as rain or snow) — see STORM 1

2 a violent disturbance (as of the political or social order) — see CONVULSION

**tempestuous** *adj* 1 marked by bursts of destructive force or intense activity — see VIOLENT 1

2 marked by sudden or violent disturbance — see CONVULSIVE

3 marked by turmoil or disturbance especially of natural elements — see WILD 3

4 marked by wet and windy conditions — see FOUL 1

**temple** *n* a building for public worship and especially Christian worship — see CHURCH 1

**temporal** *adj* 1 having to do with life on earth especially as opposed to that in heaven — see EARTHLY

2 not involving religion or religious matters — see PROFANE 1

**temporary** *adj* 1 intended to last, continue, or serve for a limited time ⟨summer workers look for *temporary* accommodations in private homes⟩ ⟨a *temporary* cook until a permanent replacement can be found⟩

***syn*** impermanent, interim, provisional, short-term

***rel*** acting; alternate, proxy, substitute; expedient, improvised, makeshift; intermediary, intermediate, transitional; ephemeral, short-lived, transitory; conditional, contingent, limited, qualified, short-range, tentative; replaceable, terminable

***near ant*** final, fixed, set, settled; unconditional, unlimited, unqualified; extended, lasting, long-range, standing; dateless, endless, enduring, eternal, everlasting, perpetual, timeless, unending

***ant*** long-term, permanent

2 lasting only for a short time — see MOMENTARY

**temporizer** *n* one who does things only for his own benefit and with little regard for right and wrong — see SELF-SEEKER

**tempt** *vb* to lead away from a usual or proper course by offering some pleasure or advantage — see LURE

**temptation** *n* 1 the act or pressure of giving in to a desire especially when ill-advised ⟨resisted the *temptation* to go sailing and did his chores instead⟩

***syn*** allurement, enticement, lure, seduction

***rel*** appeal, attraction; beckoning, invitation; inducement, influence, persuasion, power, sway

2 something that persuades one to perform an action for pleasure or gain — see LURE 1

**tempter** *n* one that tries to get a person to give in to a desire ⟨there is no greater *tempter* to put off studying than my dog when he wants to play⟩

***syn*** baiter, seducer, solicitor

***rel*** enchantress, siren, temptress; briber, inducer, persuader; corrupter (*or* corruptor), debaucher, undoer

**temptress** *n* a woman whom men find irresistibly attractive — see SIREN

**tenable** *adj* 1 capable of being defended against physical attack ⟨the soldiers' encampment on the open plain was not *tenable*, so they retreated to higher ground⟩

***syn*** defensible

***rel*** defended, guarded, protected, safeguarded, secure, secured, shielded; impregnable, indomitable, invincible, inviolable, invulnerable, unassailable, unbeatable, unconquerable, untouchable

***near ant*** assailable, exposed, insecure, liable, open, susceptible, undefended, unguarded, unprotected, unsecured, unshielded; defenseless, helpless, powerless, vulnerable, weak

***ant*** indefensible, untenable

2 capable of being defended with good reasoning against verbal attack ⟨the *tenable* theory that a giant meteor strike set off a chain of events resulting in the demise of the dinosaurs⟩

***syn*** defendable, defensible, justifiable, maintainable, supportable, sustainable

***rel*** rational, reasonable, sensible; acceptable, admissible, allowable, exceptionable, legitimate, passable, unobjectionable, viable, warrantable; confirmable, provable, verifiable; explainable, explicable

***near ant*** absurd, irrational, ridiculous; extreme, outrageous, unreasonable; groundless, objectionable, unacceptable, unfounded; inexplicable, unexplainable

***ant*** indefensible, insupportable, unjustifiable, untenable

**tenacious** *adj* continuing despite difficulties, opposition, or discouragement — see PERSISTENT

**tenaciousness** *n* a steadfast adherence to an opinion, purpose, or course of action — see OBSTINACY

**tenacity** *n* a steadfast adherence to an opinion, purpose, or course of action — see OBSTINACY

---

***syn*** synonym(s) ***rel*** related words
***ant*** antonym(s) ***near ant*** near antonym(s)

**tenant** *n* one who rents a room or apartment in another's house ⟨the laundry in the basement is for *tenants* only⟩
*syn* boarder, lodger, renter, roomer
*rel* roommate; guest, visitor; occupant, resident, resider
*near ant* landholder, landowner, proprietor; landlady; slumlord; host, innkeeper
*ant* landlord

[1]**tend** *vb* to show a liking or proneness (for something) — see LEAN 2

[2]**tend** *vb* **1** to take charge of especially on behalf of another ⟨*tend* the store while I run an errand⟩
*syn* attend, care (for), mind, oversee, superintend, supervise
*rel* direct, manage; guard, patrol, protect, safeguard; baby, baby-sit, chaperone (*or* chaperon), mother, shepherd
*phrases* look after, see to
*near ant* abandon, disregard, forget, ignore, neglect
**2** to look after or assist the growth of by labor and care — see GROW 1
**3** to work by plowing, sowing, and raising crops on — see FARM

**tendency** *n* **1** an established pattern of behavior ⟨a *tendency* to drop things⟩ ⟨a *tendency* to make snap judgements⟩
*syn* aptness, proneness, propensity, way
*rel* bent, disposition, inclination, leaning, penchant, predilection, predisposition, proclivity; custom, habit, pattern, practice (*also* practise), routine, wont; oddity, peculiarity, quirk, singularity, trick
*near ant* averseness, disinclination, indisposition
**2** a prevailing or general movement or inclination — see TREND 1
**3** a habitual attraction to some activity or thing — see INCLINATION 1

**tender** *adj* **1** easily injured without careful handling ⟨a *tender* wound⟩ ⟨*tender* plants that cannot take the cold⟩ ⟨*tender* pride that got bruised when his girlfriend dumped him⟩
*syn* delicate, fragile, frail, sensitive
*rel* breakable, brittle; flimsy, puny, soft, weak; nonhardy, perishable, resistless, susceptible, unresistant, vulnerable, yielding
*near ant* durable, firm, flinty, hard, hardy, resistant, robust, rugged, solid, sound, stiff, stout, strong, sturdy, substantial; nonbreakable, unbreakable; hardened, inured, strengthened, tempered, toughened
*ant* tough
**2** feeling or showing love — see LOVING
**3** having or marked by sympathy and consideration for others — see HUMANE 1
**4** lacking bodily strength — see WEAK 1
**5** not harsh or stern especially in manner, nature, or effect — see GENTLE 1

**tender** *n* something (as pieces of stamped metal or printed paper) customarily and legally used as a medium of exchange, a measure of value, or a means of payment — see MONEY

**tender** *vb* to put before another for acceptance or consideration — see OFFER 1

**tenderfoot** *n* a person who is just starting out in a field of activity — see BEGINNER

**tenderhearted** *adj* **1** feeling or showing love — see LOVING
**2** having or marked by sympathy and consideration for others — see HUMANE 1

**tending** *adj* having a tendency to be or act in a certain way — see PRONE 1

**tenement** *n* a room or set of rooms in a private house or a block used as a separate dwelling place — see APARTMENT 1

**tense** *adj* **1** feeling or showing uncomfortable feelings of uncertainty — see NERVOUS 1
**2** marked by or causing agitation or uncomfortable feelings — see NERVOUS 2
**3** stretched with little or no give — see TAUT

**tension** *n* the burden on one's emotional or mental well-being created by demands on one's time — see STRESS 1

**tent** *n* a raised covering over something for decoration or protection — see CANOPY

**tentative** *adj* determined by something else — see DEPENDENT 2

**tenure** *n* a fixed period of time during which a person holds a job or position — see TERM 1

**tepid** *adj* **1** showing little or no interest or enthusiasm ⟨the proposed table tennis club met with only a *tepid* response⟩
*syn* halfhearted, lukewarm, uneager, unenthusiastic
*rel* apathetic, disinterested, dispassionate, indifferent, neutral, uncaring, uninterested; lackadaisical, languid, listless, perfunctory, undemonstrative, unemotional, unresponsive; unfeeling, unsympathetic; chill, chilly, cold, cool, frigid, frosty, glacial, icy, unfriendly, wintry
*near ant* agog, ardent, avid, exuberant, gung ho, impassioned, raring; engaged, engrossed, interested; ready, willing; cordial, friendly, genial, warmhearted
*ant* eager, enthusiastic, hearty, keen, passionate, warm, wholehearted
**2** having or giving off heat to a moderate degree — see WARM 1

**term** *n* **1** a fixed period of time during which a person holds a job or position ⟨elected for a two-year *term* as mayor⟩
*syn* hitch, stint, tenure, tour
*rel* shift, watch; go, turn; duration, standing, time; cycle, span, spell, stretch; life, life span, lifetime
**2** a pronounceable series of letters having a distinct meaning especially in a particular field — see WORD 1

**term** *vb* to give a name to — see NAME 1

**termagant** *n* a bad-tempered scolding woman — see SHREW

**terminal** *adj* following all others of the same kind in order or time — see LAST

**terminate** *vb* **1** to bring (an event) to a natural or appropriate stopping point — see CLOSE 3
**2** to come to an end — see CEASE 1
**3** to mark the limits of — see LIMIT 2

**terminated** *adj* brought or having come to an end — see COMPLETE 2
**terminating** *adj* following all others of the same kind in order or time — see LAST
**termination** *n* **1** a real or imaginary point beyond which a person or thing cannot go — see LIMIT
**2** the act of ceasing to exist — see DEATH 3
**3** the stopping of a process or activity — see END 1
**terminology** *n* the special terms or expressions of a particular group or field ⟨the *terminology* favored by sportscasters⟩ ⟨medical *terminology* that can be hard for the patient to understand⟩
***syn*** argot, cant, dialect, jargon, language, lingo, patois, patter, slang, vocabulary
***rel*** colloquialism, idiom, localism, parlance, pidgin, provincialism, regionalism, speech, vernacular; journalese
**terrestrial** *adj* having to do with life on earth especially as opposed to that in heaven — see EARTHLY
**terrible** *adj* **1** causing fear — see FEARFUL 1
**2** extreme in degree, power, or effect — see INTENSE
**3** extremely disturbing or repellent — see HORRIBLE 1
**4** extremely unsatisfactory — see WRETCHED 1
**5** of low quality — see CHEAP 2
**terribly** *adv* to a great degree — see VERY 1
**terrific** *adj* of the very best kind — see EXCELLENT
**terrified** *adj* filled with fear or dread — see AFRAID 1
**terrify** *vb* to strike with fear — see FRIGHTEN
**terrifying** *adj* causing fear — see FEARFUL 1
**territory** *n* the place where a plant or animal is usually or naturally found — see HOME 2
**terror** *n* the emotion experienced in the presence or threat of danger — see FEAR
**terrorize** *vb* to strike with fear — see FRIGHTEN
**terrorized** *adj* filled with fear or dread — see AFRAID 1
**terse** *adj* marked by the use of few words to convey much information or meaning — see CONCISE
**tersely** *adv* in a few words — see SHORTLY 1
**terseness** *n* the quality or state of being marked by or using only few words to convey much meaning — see SUCCINCTNESS
**test** *n* **1** a procedure or operation carried out to resolve an uncertainty — see EXPERIMENT
**2** a set of questions or problems designed to assess knowledge, skills, or intelligence — see EXAMINATION 1

***syn*** synonym(s) ***rel*** related words
***ant*** antonym(s) ***near ant*** near antonym(s)

**test** *vb* **1** to put (something) to a test — see TRY (OUT) 1
**2** to subject (a personal quality or faculty) to often excessive stress — see TRY (OUT) 2
**testament** *n* something presented in support of the truth or accuracy of a claim — see PROOF
**testify** *vb* to make a solemn declaration under oath for the purpose of establishing a fact ⟨Mrs. Pattle was called to *testify* against the man whom she saw stealing her neighbor's car⟩
***syn*** attest, depose, swear, witness
***rel*** vouch; vow, promise
***phrases*** bear witness
**testify** (to) *vb* to declare (something) to be true or genuine — see CERTIFY 1
**testimony** *n* something presented in support of the truth or accuracy of a claim — see PROOF
**testiness** *n* readiness to show annoyance or impatience — see PETULANCE
**testy** *adj* easily irritated or annoyed — see IRRITABLE
**tête–à–tête** *adv* in person and usually privately ⟨met *tête-à-tête* with the student's parents to discuss his disciplinary problems in class⟩
***syn*** face-to-face, personally
***rel*** familiarly, intimately; confidentially, secretly; directly, immediately
***phrases*** in private
***near ant*** distantly, indirectly; openly, publicly
**tête–à–tête** *n* friendly, informal conversation or an instance of this — see CHAT
**text** *n* a book used for instruction in a subject — see TEXTBOOK
**textbook** *n* a book used for instruction in a subject ⟨new, up-to-date middle school science *textbooks*⟩
***syn*** handbook, manual, primer, text
***rel*** schoolbook; grammar, reader, speller; tract, treatise; dictionary, lexicon, vocabulary, wordbook; encyclopedia, reference; bible, guide, guidebook
**textile** *n* a woven or knitted material (as of cotton or nylon) — see CLOTH
**thankful** *adj* feeling or expressing gratitude — see GRATEFUL 1
**thankfulness** *n* acknowledgment of having received something good from another — see THANKS
**thankless** *adj* not showing gratitude ⟨a *thankless* guest who complained that my home cooking was not to her liking⟩
***syn*** unappreciative, ungrateful
***rel*** rude, thoughtless, ungracious
***near ant*** beholden, indebted; gratified, pleased; courteous, gracious, thoughtful
***ant*** appreciative, grateful, obliged, thankful
**2** not likely to be appreciated by those who benefit ⟨the *thankless* job of cleaning up after a party⟩
***syn*** unappreciated
***rel*** uncredited, underrated, undervalued, unnoticed, unrecognized, unrewarded, unsung, unvalued

*near ant* credited, esteemed, honored, prized, recognized, regarded, rewarded, valued; creditable, meritorious, praiseworthy
*ant* appreciated, thanked

**thanks** *n pl* acknowledgment of having received something good from another ⟨to express our *thanks* we'd like to present you with this plaque⟩
*syn* appreciation, appreciativeness, gratefulness, gratitude, thankfulness
*rel* thanksgiving; gratification, indebtedness, satisfaction; acknowledgment (*also* acknowledgement), recognition, tribute
*ant* ingratitude, thanklessness, ungratefulness

**thaw** *vb* to go from a solid to a liquid state — see LIQUEFY

**thawed** *adj* freed from a frozen state by exposure to warmth ⟨recommends cooking *thawed* fish within 24 hours⟩
*syn* defrosted, unfrozen
*rel* liquefied, melted, molten; deiced; heated, warmed
*near ant* chilled, iced, refrigerated; quick-frozen, refrozen, supercooled; congealed, glaciated, semisolid; frostbitten, frosty, icy
*ant* frozen, unthawed

**theater** *or* **theatre** *n* **1** a building or part of a building where movies are shown ⟨there's still one *theater* in town that shows movies for two dollars⟩
*syn* cinema, playhouse
*rel* nickelodeon; multiplex; drive-in
**2** the public performance of plays — see DRAMA 1
**3** a large room or building for enclosed public gatherings — see HALL 3

**theatrical** *adj* **1** given to or marked by attention-getting behavior suggestive of stage acting ⟨after stepping out of their hired limousine, the prom couple made a *theatrical* entrance in their evening clothes⟩
*syn* dramatic, histrionic, melodramatic
*rel* overacted, overdone, sensational, staged; conspicuous, elaborate, flamboyant, grandiose, ostentatious, showy; affected, artificial, exaggerated, formal, mannered, pretentious, self-conscious, studied, unnatural
*near ant* nondramatic, nontheatrical, unaffected, underplayed, unpretentious; muted, restrained, subdued, toned (down); conservative, discreet, inconspicuous; modest, quiet, plain, simple
*ant* undramatic, untheatrical
**2** having the general quality or effect of a stage performance — see DRAMATIC 1

**theatricals** *n pl* the public performance of plays — see DRAMA 1

**theft** *n* **1** the unlawful taking and carrying away of property without the consent of its owner ⟨*theft* has never been a big problem at our school⟩
*syn* larceny, robbery, stealing, thievery
*rel* burglary, housebreaking; embezzlement, embezzling, graft, misappropriation; filching, pilfering, purloining, shoplifting; abduction, hijacking, kidnapping, shanghaiing; despoilment, despoliation, looting, pillage, plundering, rapine; poaching, rustling, smuggling; banditry, piracy
**2** an instance of theft ⟨the police found the stolen car an hour after the *theft* was reported⟩
*syn* grab, pinch, rip-off, snatching, swiping
*rel* burglary, holdup, mugging, stickup; confidence game, con game

**theme** *n* **1** a major object of interest or concern (as in a discussion or artistic composition) — see MATTER 1
**2** a short piece of writing done as a school exercise — see COMPOSITION 2
**3** a short piece of writing typically expressing a point of view — see ESSAY 1

**then** *adv* in addition to what has been said — see MORE 1

**theoretical** *also* **theoretic** *adj* **1** existing only as an assumption or speculation ⟨the merits of the new testing procedures are purely *theoretical*, since no one has ever used them before⟩
*syn* conjectural, hypothetical, speculative, suppositional
*rel* alleged, assumed, presumed, presupposed, proposed, supposed, unproved, unproven, untested; academic, debatable, moot; abstract, conceptual, intellectual; nonclinical, nonpractical; nonempirical
*near ant* clinical, practical; concrete, defined, definite, distinct; attested, authenticated, confirmed, demonstrated, established, proven, substantiated, tested, time-tested, validated, verified; empirical (*also* empiric), observational
*ant* actual, factual, real
**2** dealing with or expressing a quality or idea — see ABSTRACT 1

**theory** *n* an idea that is the starting point for making a case or conducting an investigation ⟨set out to prove her *theory* that people can't really taste any difference between colas, so they buy according to the product's image⟩
*syn* hypothesis, proposition, supposition
*rel* assumption, concession, premise, presumption, presupposition; generalization, guess, guesswork, inference, speculation, surmise; proffer, proposal, suggestion; feeling, hunch, impression, inkling, notion, suspicion; abstraction, concept, conception
*near ant* assurance, certainty, fact, knowledge

**thereafter** *adv* following in time or place — see AFTER

**therefore** *adv* for this or that reason ⟨it's snowing hard; *therefore* I think we should stay home⟩
*syn* accordingly, consequently, ergo, hence, so, thereupon, thus, wherefore

**theretofore** *adv* up to this or that time — see HITHERTO

**thereupon** *adv* for this or that reason — see THEREFORE

**thesis** *n* an idea or opinion that is put forth in a discussion or debate — see CONTENTION

**thick** *adj* **1** having or being of relatively great depth or extent from one surface to its opposite ⟨a *thick* board was laid across the pit⟩
*syn* chunky, fat
*rel* bulky, dense, hefty, thickish; broad, deep, wide
*near ant* narrow, shallow
*ant* skinny, slender, slim, thin
**2** being of a consistency that resists flow ⟨*thick* maple syrup for pancakes⟩
*syn* ropy, syrupy, viscid, viscous
*rel* creamy, heavy, slushy, thickened, thickish, turbid, undiluted; gluey, glutinous, sticky; gelatinous, gooey, gummy, jellylike; concentrated, condensed
*near ant* flowing, fluid; dilute, diluted, liquid, watered (down), weak
*ant* runny, soupy, thin, watery
**3** closely acquainted — see FAMILIAR 1
**4** having a greater than usual measure across — see WIDE 1
**5** having little space between items or parts — see CLOSE 1
**6** not having or showing an ability to absorb ideas readily — see STUPID 1
**7** possessing or covered with great numbers or amounts of something specified — see RIFE

**thick** *n* the most intense or characteristic phase of something ⟨in the *thick* of winter many Northerners are dreaming of tropical islands⟩
*syn* deep, depth, height, middle, midst
*rel* center, heart

**thicket** *n* a thick patch of shrubbery, small trees, or underbrush ⟨flushed a pheasant from a *thicket* of willows⟩
*syn* brake, brushwood, chaparral, coppice, copse, covert
*rel* canebrake; brush, bush, scrub, scrubland; bramble, jungle, tangle; grove, hedge, stand, woodlot; forest, greenwood, wildwood, wood, woodland

**thickheaded** *adj* not having or showing an ability to absorb ideas readily — see STUPID 1

**thickness** *n* the degree to which a fluid can resist flowing — see CONSISTENCY

**thickset** *adj* being compact and broad in build and often short in stature — see STOCKY

**thief** *n* one who steals ⟨sentenced the *thief* who stole Mrs. Stuckey's rosebushes to 30 hours of community service in the municipal rose garden⟩
*syn* pincher, purloiner, robber, stealer
*rel* burglar, housebreaker; embezzler, grafter; kleptomaniac; pickpocket, pilferer, rifler, shoplifter; abductor, hijacker, kidnapper, skyjacker; despoiler, looter, plunderer, ransacker, ravisher; poacher, rustler, smuggler; bandit, highwayman, pirate; grabber, mugger

**thieve** *vb* to take (something) without right and with an intent to keep — see STEAL 1

**thievery** *n* the unlawful taking and carrying away of property without the consent of its owner — see THEFT 1

**thin** *adj* **1** having a noticeably small amount of body fat ⟨after her bout with pneumonia, she looked *thinner*⟩
*syn* lean, skinny, slender, slim, spare
*rel* angular, bony, rawboned, scraggy, scrawny, sinewy; lank, lanky, rangy, reedy, spindling, spindly, twiggy, waspish, weedy, willowy, wiry; anorexic, cadaverous, emaciated, gaunt, haggard, pinched, skeletal, wasted, wizened; puny, meager (*or* meagre), slight
*near ant* beefy, bulky, chunky, fleshy, heavy, heavyset, stocky, stout, thick, thickset, weighty; brawny, burly, husky; dumpy, pudgy, roly-poly, squat, stubby; paunchy, potbellied; flabby, soft; buxom; fleshed-out, full, round
*ant* chubby, corpulent, fat, gross, obese, overweight, plump, portly, rotund, tubby
**2** being of less than usual width — see NARROW 1
**3** not containing very much of some important element — see WEAK 3

**thin** *vb* to alter (something) for the worse with the addition of foreign or lower-grade substances — see ADULTERATE

**thing** *n* **1** a member of the human race — see HUMAN
**2** one that has a real and independent existence — see ENTITY
**3** something done by someone — see ACTION 1
**4** something material that can be perceived by the senses — see OBJECT 1
**5** something produced by physical or intellectual effort — see PRODUCT 1
**6** something that happens — see EVENT 1
**7** something that one hopes or intends to accomplish — see GOAL
**8** something to be dealt with — see MATTER 2
**9 things** *pl* transportable items that one owns — see POSSESSION 2

**think** *vb* to have as an opinion — see BELIEVE 2

**think** (about *or* over) *vb* to give serious and careful thought to — see PONDER

**think** (of) *vb* to bring back to mind — see REMEMBER

**think** (up) *vb* to create or think of by clever use of the imagination — see INVENT

**thinker** *n* a very smart person — see GENIUS 1

**thinking** *adj* having the ability to reason — see RATIONAL 1

**thinned** *adj* **1** containing foreign or lower-grade substances — see IMPURE
**2** not containing very much of some important element — see WEAK 3

**thirst** *n* **1** a strong wish for something — see DESIRE
**2** urgent desire or interest — see EAGERNESS

**thirst** (for) *vb* to have an earnest wish to own or enjoy — see DESIRE
**thirsty** *adj* **1** marked by little or no precipitation or humidity — see DRY 1
**2** showing urgent desire or interest — see EAGER
**this** *adj* being the less far of two — see NEAR 1
**thistly** *adj* likely to cause a scratch — see SCRATCHY 1
**thorn** *n* something that is a source of irritation — see ANNOYANCE 3
**thorny** *adj* **1** likely to cause a scratch — see SCRATCHY 1
**2** requiring exceptional skill or caution in performance or handling — see TRICKY
**thorough** *adj* **1** having no exceptions or restrictions — see ABSOLUTE 2
**2** including many small descriptive features — see DETAILED 1
**3** trying all possibilities — see EXHAUSTIVE
**thoroughbred** *adj* of unmixed ancestry — see PUREBRED
**thoroughfare** *n* a passage cleared for public vehicular travel — see WAY 1
**thoroughgoing** *adj* **1** having no exceptions or restrictions — see ABSOLUTE 2
**2** trying all possibilities — see EXHAUSTIVE
**thoroughly** *adv* **1** with attention to all aspects or details ⟨they searched the grounds *thoroughly* for any sign of the intruder⟩
***syn*** completely, comprehensively, detailedly, exhaustively, fully, minutely, roundly, totally
***rel*** all-out, full blast, intensively; broadly, extensively, generally, globally, widely; conclusively, consummately, definitely, perfectly
***phrases*** in detail
***near ant*** aimlessly, desultorily, haphazardly, hit-or-miss, randomly; cursorily, imperfectly, inadequately, narrowly, shallowly, sketchily, summarily, superficially; indeterminately, nebulously, vaguely
**2** to a full extent or degree — see FULLY 1
**though** *conj* in spite of the fact that — see ALTHOUGH
**though** *adv* in spite of that — see HOWEVER
**thought** *n* **1** a careful weighing of the reasons for or against something — see CONSIDERATION 1
**2** something imagined or pictured in the mind — see IDEA
**thoughtful** *adj* **1** given to or made with heedful anticipation of the needs and happiness of others ⟨a *thoughtful* offer to watch the neighbors' children on moving day⟩ ⟨a *thoughtful* aunt who never forgets the birthday of a niece or nephew⟩
***syn*** attentive, considerate, kind, solicitous
***rel*** brotherly, good, good-hearted, helpful, hospitable, kindhearted, kindly, neighborly, nice; caring, compassionate, sympathetic, tender; chivalrous, courteous, courtly, gallant, gracious, polite; diplomatic, tactful; deferential, dutiful, obliging, regardful, respectful; altruistic, beneficent, benevolent, benignant, humane, selfless, unselfish; charitable, generous, magnanimous
***near ant*** inattentive, uncaring, unheeding; inhospitable, unkind, unkindly, unneighborly; ill-bred, ill-mannered, impolite, rude, uncivil, uncourteous, unmannerly; unhelpful, unobliging; malevolent, malicious, mean, spiteful
***ant*** heedless, inconsiderate, thoughtless, unthinking
**2** decided on as a result of careful thought — see DELIBERATE 1
**3** given to or marked by long, quiet thinking — see CONTEMPLATIVE
**thoughtfully** *adv* with good reason or courtesy — see WELL 4
**thoughtless** *adj* showing a lack of manners or consideration for others — see IMPOLITE
**thrall** *n* **1** a person who is considered the property of another person — see SLAVE 1
**2** the state of being a slave — see SLAVERY 1
**thralldom** *cr* **thraldom** *n* the state of being a slave — see SLAVERY 1
**thrash** *vb* **1** to achieve a victory over — see BEAT 2
**2** to defeat by a large margin — see WHIP 2
**3** to strike repeatedly with something long and thin or flexible — see WHIP 1
**4** to strike repeatedly — see BEAT 1
**thread** *vb* **1** to scatter or set here and there among other things ⟨this history book *threads* excerpts from the diaries of pioneer women into its account of the settlement of the West⟩
***syn*** interlace, intersperse, interweave, lace, weave, wreathe
***rel*** insert, intermingle, mingle, mix; alternate, juxtapose; amalgamate, assimilate, blend, combine, commingle, embody, fuse, incorporate, integrate, merge
**2** to put together into a series by means of or as if by means of a thread ⟨the reporter *threaded* his newspaper articles about the basketball team into a book that was essentially a chronicle of their championship season⟩
***syn*** concatenate, string
***rel*** chain, connect, join, link, unite; interlace, intersperse, intertwine, interweave, lace, weave, wreathe
**threadbare** *adj* **1** showing signs of advanced wear and tear and neglect — see SHABBY 1
**2** used or heard so often as to be dull — see STALE
**3** worn or torn into or as if into rags — see RAGGED 2
**threat** *n* something that may cause injury or harm — see DANGER 2
**threaten** *vb* to remain poised to inflict harm, danger, or distress on ⟨unless the home fans' unacceptable behavior and

name-calling stops, the possibility of expulsion from the league *threatens* the school's basketball team〉
***syn*** hang (over), hover (over), impend (over), menace, overhang
***rel*** endanger, hazard, imperil, jeopardize

**threatening** *adj* **1** giving signs of immediate occurrence — see IMMINENT 1
**2** being or showing a sign of evil or calamity to come — see OMINOUS
**3** involving potential loss or injury — see DANGEROUS

**threefold** *adj* having three units or parts — see TRIPLE

**threesome** *n* a group of three 〈the *threesome* from Crystal Falls—Jocelyn, Katie, and Lynn—missed their plane and joined up with the rest of the group the next day〉
***syn*** triad, trinity, trio, triple, triplet, triumvirate
***rel*** trilogy; triplicate; triplex

**threnody** *n* a composition expressing one's grief over a loss — see LAMENT 2

**threshold** *n* the point at which something begins — see BEGINNING

**thrift** *n* careful management of material resources — see ECONOMY

**thriftless** *adj* given to spending money freely or foolishly — see PRODIGAL

**thrifty** *adj* careful in the management of money or resources — see FRUGAL

**thrill** *n* a pleasurably intense stimulation of the feelings 〈everyone gets a real *thrill* out of the Independence Day fireworks〉
***syn*** bang, exhilaration, kick, titillation
***rel*** arousal, electrification, intoxication, stimulation; jolt, shock, surprise; delectation, delight, enjoyment, joy, lift, pleasure; amusement, diversion, entertainment, fun, treat

**thrill** *vb* to cause a pleasurable stimulation of the feelings 〈was *thrilled* by the news of Betsy's promotion〉
***syn*** electrify, excite, exhilarate, galvanize, intoxicate, titillate, turn on
***rel*** arouse, incite, inspire, provoke, stimulate; bewitch, captivate, charm, delight, enchant, enthrall (*or* enthral), hypnotize, mesmerize, rivet, spellbind; interest, intrigue, tantalize
***near ant*** bore, jade, pall, tire, weary; deject, demoralize, discourage, dishearten, dispirit

**thrilling** *adj* causing great emotional or mental stimulation — see EXCITING 1

**thrive** *vb* **1** to grow vigorously 〈these plants *thrive* with relatively little sunlight〉
***syn*** burgeon, flourish, prosper
***rel*** luxuriate, overgrow, proliferate, shoot up; germinate, root, sprout; bloom, flower, fruit, produce, propagate, regenerate, seed
**2** to reach a desired level of accomplishment — see SUCCEED 2

***syn*** synonym(s) ***rel*** related words
***ant*** antonym(s) ***near ant*** near antonym(s)

**thriving** *adj* **1** having attained a desired end or state of good fortune — see SUCCESSFUL 1
**2** marked by much life, movement, or activity — see ALIVE 2
**3** marked by vigorous growth and well-being especially economically — see PROSPEROUS 1

**throaty** *adj* **1** harsh and dry in sound — see HOARSE
**2** having a low musical pitch or range — see DEEP 2

**throb** *n* a rhythmic expanding and contracting — see PULSATION

**throb** *vb* to expand and contract in a rhythmic manner — see PULSATE

**throe** *n* a sharp unpleasant sensation usually felt in some specific part of the body — see PAIN 1

**throng** *n* a great number of persons or things gathered together — see CROWD 1

**throng** *vb* to move upon or fill (something) in great numbers — see CROWD 2

**thronging** *adj* possessing or covered with great numbers or amounts of something specified — see RIFE

**throttle** *vb* to keep (someone) from breathing by exerting pressure on the windpipe — see CHOKE 1

**through** *adv* **1** from beginning to end 〈read the letter *through* twice〉 〈never once missed class the whole year *through*〉
***syn*** around, over, round, throughout
**2** from one side to the other of an intervening space — see OVER 1

**through** *prep* **1** in or into the middle of — see AMONG
**2** in random positions within the boundaries of — see AROUND 2
**3** in the course of — see DURING
**4** to the opposite side of — see ACROSS
**5** along the way of — see BY 1
**6** as the result of — see BECAUSE OF
**7** using the means or agency of — see BY 2

**through** *adj* brought or having come to an end — see COMPLETE 2

**throughout** *prep* **1** in random positions within the boundaries of — see AROUND 2
**2** in the course of — see DURING

**throughout** *adv* **1** from beginning to end — see THROUGH 1
**2** in every place or in all places — see EVERYWHERE

**throw** *vb* to send through the air especially with a quick forward motion of the arm 〈*threw* a life preserver to the drowning man〉
***syn*** cast, catapult, chuck, dash, fire, fling, heave, hurl, hurtle, launch, lob, loft, peg, pelt, pitch, sling, toss
***rel*** bowl, flip, hook, pass, roll, shoot; buck, eject, impel, precipitate, project, propel, rifle, thrust

**throw** (on) *vb* to place on one's person — see PUT ON 1

**throw away** *vb* **1** to get rid of as useless or unwanted — see DISCARD
**2** to use up carelessly — see WASTE 1

**throwing away** *n* the getting rid of whatever is unwanted or useless — see DISPOSAL 1

**throw out** *vb* **1** to drive or force out — see EJECT 1
**2** to get rid of as useless or unwanted — see DISCARD

**throw up** *vb* **1** to discharge the contents of the stomach through the mouth — see VOMIT
**2** to make or assemble roughly or hastily — see COBBLE (TOGETHER)

**thrum** *n* a monotonous sound like that of an insect in motion — see HUM

**thrum** *vb* to strike or cause to strike lightly and usually rhythmically — see [1]TAP

**thrust** *vb* to apply force to (someone or something) so that it moves in front of one — see PUSH 1

**thud** *n* a hard strike with a part of the body or an instrument — see [1]BLOW

**thud** *vb* to come into usually forceful contact with something — see HIT 2

**thug** *n* a violent, brutal person who is often a member of an organized gang — see HOODLUM

**thumb** *vb* to travel by securing free rides — see HITCHHIKE

**thump** *n* a hard strike with a part of the body or an instrument — see [1]BLOW

**thump** *vb* **1** to deliver a blow to (someone or something) usually in a strong vigorous manner — see HIT 1
**2** to strike repeatedly — see BEAT 1

**thunder** *vb* to make a long loud deep noise or cry — see ROAR

**thunderous** *adj* marked by a high volume of sound — see LOUD 1

**thunderstruck** *adj* affected with sudden and great wonder or surprise ⟨Colin was *thunderstruck* when his parents told him he was adopted⟩
***syn*** amazed, astonished, astounded, awestruck, bowled over, dumbfounded (*or* dumfounded), flabbergasted, shocked, stunned, stupefied
***rel*** startled, surprised; aghast, appalled, dismayed, horrified; bewildered, confused, dazed, overwhelmed; agape, awed, awesome, open-mouthed, wide-eyed, widemouthed
***near ant*** casual, nonchalant, unruffled
***ant*** unawed

**thus** *adv* for this or that reason — see THEREFORE

**thus far** *adv* up to this or that time — see HITHERTO

**thwack** *n* **1** a hard strike with a part of the body or an instrument — see [1]BLOW
**2** a loud explosive sound — see CLAP 1

**thwack** *vb* to deliver a blow to (someone or something) usually in a strong vigorous manner — see HIT 1

**thwart** *vb* to prevent from achieving a goal — see FRUSTRATE

**tick (off)** *vb* to specify one after another — see ENUMERATE 1

**ticket** *n* **1** a small sheet of plastic, paper, or paperboard showing that the bearer has a claim to something (as admittance) ⟨only people with *tickets* will be allowed past the front gates⟩
***syn*** check, coupon, pass
***rel*** certificate, note, token, voucher
**2** a slip (as of paper or cloth) that is attached to something to identify or describe it — see LABEL

**ticket** *vb* to attach an identifying slip to — see LABEL 1

**tickled** *adj* experiencing pleasure, satisfaction, or delight — see GLAD 1

**ticklish** *adj* requiring exceptional skill or caution in performance or handling — see TRICKY

**tidbit** *also* **titbit** *n* **1** something that is pleasing to eat because it is rare or a luxury — see DELICACY 1
**2** a small piece or quantity of food — see MORSEL 1

**tide** *n* a prevailing or general movement or inclination — see TREND 1

**tidied** *adj* being clean and in good order — see NEAT 1

**tidings** *n pl* a report of recent events or facts not previously known — see NEWS

**tidy** *adj* **1** being clean and in good order — see NEAT 1
**2** of a size greater than average of its kind — see LARGE
**3** sufficiently large in size, amount, or number to merit attention — see CONSIDERABLE 1

**tie** *n* **1** a situation in which neither participant in a contest, competition, or struggle comes out ahead of the other ⟨the competition for first place in the dessert division ended in a *tie* between the chocolate pecan pie and the walnut fudge tart⟩
***syn*** dead heat, draw, stalemate, standoff
***rel*** deadlock, impasse; photo finish; toss-up
**2** a uniting or binding force or influence — see BOND 2

**tie** *vb* **1** to gather into a tight mass by means of a line or cord ⟨*tied* the newspapers into a bundle⟩
***syn*** band, bind, gird, truss
***rel*** cinch, cord, rope, strap, thread, wire; lash, leash, tether; interlace, intertwine, interweave, lace; entangle, knot, snarl, tangle, twist; coil, wind
***near ant*** undo, unfasten, unlace, unlash, unloose, unloosen, unthread; unleash, untether; disentangle, uncoil, untangle, untwine, untwist, unwind
***ant*** unbind, untie
**2** to produce something equal to (as in quality or value) — see EQUAL 1

**tie–up** *n* the state of having shared interests or efforts (as in social or business matters) — see ASSOCIATION 1

**tie up** *vb* to create difficulty for the work or activity of — see HAMPER

**tiff** *n* an often noisy or angry expression of differing opinions — see ARGUMENT 1

**tight** *adj* **1** not allowing penetration (as by gas, liquid, or light) ⟨a *tight* hull that was no match for an iceberg⟩

*syn* impenetrable, impermeable, impervious
*rel* close, compact, dense, snug, thick; airtight, hermetic, watertight; lightproof, soundproof, waterproof
*near ant* absorbent, leaky, porous, unsealed
*ant* penetrable, permeable
**2** firmly positioned in place and difficult to dislodge ⟨a *tight* screw that won't come loose⟩ ⟨a jar with a *tight* lid⟩
*syn* fast, firm, frozen, jammed, lodged, secure, set, snug, stuck, wedged
*rel* bonded, cemented, glued; anchored, clamped; embedded, entrenched (*also* intrenched), implanted; attached, bound, fastened, secured; immovable, unyielding
*near ant* detached, dislodged, freed, loosened, unattached, unbound, undone, unfastened, unsecured; movable (*or* moveable), yielding
*ant* insecure, loose
**3** giving or sharing as little as possible — see STINGY 1
**4** having little space between items or parts — see CLOSE 1
**5** showing little difference in the standing of the competitors — see CLOSE 3
**6** stretched with little or no give — see TAUT

**tightfisted** *adj* giving or sharing as little as possible — see STINGY 1

**tight–lipped** *adj* tending not to speak frequently (as by habit or inclination) — see SILENT 2

**tightness** *n* the quality of being overly sparing with money — see PARSIMONY

**tightwad** *n* a mean grasping person who is usually stingy with money — see MISER

**till** *vb* to work by plowing, sowing, and raising crops on — see FARM

**tiller** *n* a person who cultivates the land and grows crops on it — see FARMER

**tilt** *n* the act of positioning or an instance of being positioned at an angle ⟨indicated her approval with a slight forward *tilt* of her head⟩
*syn* angling, bend, cock, inclination, list, tip
*rel* turn, twist, veer; bow, dip, nod

**tilt** *vb* to set or cause to be at an angle — see LEAN 1

**tilted** *adj* **1** inclined or twisted to one side — see AWRY
**2** running in a slanting direction — see DIAGONAL

**tilting** *adj* running in a slanting direction — see DIAGONAL

**timber** *n* **1** a dense growth of trees and shrubs covering a large area — see FOREST
**2** tree logs as prepared for human use — see WOOD

**timberland** *n* a dense growth of trees and shrubs covering a large area — see FOREST

**time** *n* **1** a particular point at which an event takes place — see OCCASION 1
**2** an exciting or noteworthy event that one experiences firsthand — see ADVENTURE
**3** an extent of time associated with a particular person or thing — see AGE 1
**4** the period during which something exists, lasts, or is in progress — see DURATION 1

**timeliness** *n* the quality or habit of arriving on time — see PROMPTITUDE

**timely** *adj* **1** especially suitable for a certain time ⟨a *timely* invitation to lunch that came just as I was starting to feel hungry⟩
*syn* opportune, seasonable
*rel* appropriate, apt, fit, fitting, meet, pat, proper, relevant, suitable; fortunate, lucky, propitious; anticipated, expected; prompt, punctual, undelayed
*near ant* improper, inappropriate, irrelevant, unfit, unsuitable; unfortunate, unlucky; behind, behindhand, belated, delayed, delinquent, late, latish, overdue, postponed, slow, tardy; anticipatory, early, precocious, premature; abrupt, sudden, unanticipated, unexpected
*ant* inopportune, unseasonable, untimely
**2** done, carried out, or given without delay — see PROMPT 1

**timepiece** *n* a device to measure time ⟨the only *timepiece* she used at the cabin was a garden sundial⟩
*syn* chronometer, clock, timer
*rel* alarm clock, atomic clock, cuckoo clock, grandfather clock, time clock; hourglass, sandglass, sundial, water clock; chronograph, stopwatch, watch

**timer** *n* a device to measure time — see TIMEPIECE

**timetable** *n* a listing of things to be presented or considered (as at a concert or play) — see PROGRAM 1

**timid** *adj* easily frightened — see SHY 1

**timidity** *n* lack of willingness to assert oneself and take risks ⟨none of the scouts showed the least *timidity* about rappeling down the cliff⟩
*syn* faintheartedness, timidness, timorousness
*rel* bashfulness, constraint, embarrassment, inhibition, restraint, shyness, skittishness; hesitation, indecision, indecisiveness, irresoluteness, irresolution; alarm, anxiety, apprehension, concern, discomposure, dismay, fear, panic, upset, worry; cowardice, cowardliness, cravenness, spinelessness, yellowness
*near ant* assurance, confidence, self-assurance, self-confidence; composure, coolness, insouciance, nonchalance, unconcern; backbone, decisiveness, determination, fiber, firmness, fortitude, gameness, grit, gumption, mettle, resoluteness, resolution, spunk; bravery, courage, courageousness, daring, dauntlessness, doughtiness, fearlessness, intrepidity, intrepidness
*ant* audaciousness, audacity, boldness, guts, nerve

**timidness** *n* lack of willingness to assert oneself and take risks — see TIMIDITY

**timorous** *adj* easily frightened — see SHY 1

**timorousness** *n* lack of willingness to assert oneself and take risks — see TIMIDITY

**tincture** *n* a substance used to color other materials — see PIGMENT

**tinge** *n* a property that becomes apparent when light falls or an object and by which things that are identical in form can be distinguished — see COLOR 1

**tinge** *vb* to give color or a different color to — see COLOR 1

**tingle** *n* a sharp unpleasant sensation usually felt in some specific part of the body — see PAIN 1

**tinker** (with) *vb* to handle thoughtlessly, ignorantly, or mischievously — see TAMPER

**tinkle** *n* a series of short high ringing sounds ⟨Mrs. Mouse ignored the warning *tinkle* of the cat's bell, and now her children are orphans⟩
***syn*** chime(s), jingle, tintinnabulation
***rel*** clatter, jangle, rattle; chink, clang, clank, clink, dingdong, ping, ring, toll; chirr, ripple, trill, warble

**tinkle** *vb* to make a repeated sharp light ringing sound — see JINGLE

**tint** *vb* to give color or a different color to — see COLOR 1

**tint** *n* a property that becomes apparent when light falls on an object and by which things that are identical in form can be distinguished — see COLOR 1

**tintinnabulation** *n* a series of short high ringing sounds — see TINKLE

**tiny** *adj* very small in size ⟨the forest ranger showed us how every square foot of forest is alive with *tiny* creatures⟩
***syn*** atomic, bitty, infinitesimal, microminiature, microscopic (*also* microscopical), miniature, minute, teeny, teeny-weeny, wee
***rel*** diminutive, dwarf, little, midget, model, petite, pocket, pocket-size (*also* pocket-sized), pygmy, small, smallish, dinky, dwarfish, insignificant, pint-size (*or* pint-sized), puny, scrubby, undersized
***near ant*** big, bulky, bumper, considerable, extensive, good, goodly, good-sized, grand, great, gross, handsome, hefty, hulking, jumbo, king-size (*or* king-sized), large, largish, major, outsize (*also* outsized), oversize (*or* oversized), sizable (*or* sizeable), substantial, super, whacking, whopping; formicable, grandiose, imposing, lofty, majestic, monolithic, staggering, stupendous, towering; boundless, cavernous, immeasurable, infinite, vast, vasty, voluminous
***ant*** astronomical (*also* astronomic), colossal, cosmic, elephantine, enormous, giant, gigantic, herculean, heroic, huge, immense, mammoth, massive, monster, monstrous, monumental, mountainous, prodigious, titanic, tremendous

**tip** *n* **1** a piece of advice or useful information especially from an expert ⟨got some *tips* from a horticulturist on how to get my violets to bloom⟩
***syn*** hint, lead, pointer
***rel*** advice, advisement, assistance, counsel, guidance, recommendation, suggestion; caution, cautioning, sign, signal, telltale, tip-off, warning; brief, direction, feedback, instruction, observation; prompt, reminder, urging; answer, clue, solution
**2** information not generally available to the public — see DOPE 1

[2]**tip** *n* **1** a small sum of money given for a service over and above what is due ⟨gave our waiter an extra large *tip* for such fantastic service⟩
***syn*** gratuity, perquisite
***rel*** donation, gift, lagniappe, largess (*or* largesse), present; bonus, favor, reward; contribution, offering
**2** something given in addition to what is ordinarily expected or owed — see BONUS

[3]**tip** *n* the act of positioning or an instance of being positioned at an angle — see TILT

[4]**tip** *n* the last and usually sharp or tapering part of something long and narrow — see POINT 2

**tip** *vb* to set or cause to be at an angle — see LEAN 1

**tipped** *adj* tapering to a thin tip — see POINTED 1

**tipping** *adj* inclined or twisted to one side — see AWRY

**tippler** *n* a person who makes a habit of getting drunk — see DRUNK 1

**tipsy** *adj* being under the influence of alcohol — see DRUNK

**tip–top** *adj* of the very best kind — see EXCELLENT

**tip–top** *n* the highest part or point — see HEIGHT 1

**tirade** *n* a long angry speech or scolding ⟨after the inspection by the health department, Jay had to listen to his boss's *tirade* about keeping the restaurant's kitchen cleaner⟩
***syn*** diatribe, harangue, rant
***rel*** assault, attack, invective, lambasting, lashing, tongue-lashing, vituperation; berating, chewing out, rebuke, reprimand, reproach, reproof; abuse, castigation, censure, condemnation, criticism, denunciation; belittlement, deprecation, depreciation, disparagement, dissing; excoriation, execration, revilement; admonishment, admonition, lecture, sermon
***near ant*** encomium, eulogy, panegyric, rhapsody, tribute; acclaim, acclamation, accolade, citation, homage, honor, praise; approval, blessing, commendation, endorsement, sanction; ovation, plaudit, rave

**tire** *vb* **1** to diminish the physical strength of — see WEAKEN 1

2 to make weary and restless by being dull or monotonous — see [2]BORE
3 to use up all the physical energy of — see EXHAUST 1

**tired** *adj* 1 depleted in strength, energy, or freshness — see WEARY 1
2 having one's patience, interest, or pleasure exhausted — see WEARY 2
3 used or heard so often as to be dull — see STALE

**tiredness** *n* 1 a complete depletion of energy or strength — see FATIGUE
2 the state of being bored — see BOREDOM

**tireless** *adj* showing no signs of weariness even after long hard effort ⟨a *tireless* advocate for human rights⟩
***syn*** indefatigable, inexhaustible, unflagging, untiring, unwearying, weariless
***rel*** assiduous, conscientious, diligent, meticulous, painstaking, sedulous; determined, dogged, patient, persevering, persistent, pertinacious, plodding, relentless, steadfast, steady, stubborn, tenacious, unabating, unfailing, unfaltering, unflinching, unrelenting, unremitting, unwavering; active, busy, dynamic, energetic, feverish, spirited, vigorous; hard, industrious, intense, laborious, slavish, strenuous
***near ant*** indolent, lackadaisical, laggard, lazy, listless, shiftless, slothful, sluggish; apathetic, casual, desultory, languid, spiritless; beat, broken, burned-out (*or* burnt-out), done in, drained, enervated, jaded, overtaxed, overworked, played out, sapped, spent, tuckered (out), wearied, worn-out

**tirelessly** *adv* with great effort or determination — see HARD 1

**tiresome** *adj* causing weariness, restlessness, or lack of interest — see BORING

**tiring** *adj* causing weariness, restlessness, or lack of interest — see BORING

**titan** *n* something that is unusually large and powerful — see GIANT

**titanic** *adj* unusually large — see HUGE

**titillate** *vb* to cause a pleasurable stimulation of the feelings — see THRILL

**titillation** *n* a pleasurably intense stimulation of the feelings — see THRILL

**title** *n* 1 a word or combination of words by which a person or thing is regularly known — see NAME 1
2 a word or series of words often in larger letters placed at the beginning of a passage or at the top of a page in order to introduce or categorize — see HEADING
3 the position occupied by the one who comes in first in a competition — see CROWN 2

**title** *vb* to give a name to — see NAME 1

**titter** *n* an explosive sound that is a sign of amusement — see LAUGH 1

**tittle** *n* 1 a very small piece — see BIT 1
2 the smallest amount or part imaginable — see JOT

**titular** *adj* being something in name or form only — see NOMINAL 1

**tizzy** *n* a state of nervous or irritated concern — see FRET

**to** *prep* earlier than — see BEFORE 1

**toady** *n* a person who flatters another in order to get ahead — see SYCOPHANT

**toady** *vb* to use flattery or the doing of favors in order to win approval especially from a superior — see FAWN

**toast** *vb* to cause to have or give off heat to a moderate degree — see WARM 1

**toasty** *adj* having or giving off heat to a moderate degree — see WARM 1

**tocsin** *n* 1 an object intended to give public notice or warning — see SIGNAL 1
2 something that tells of approaching danger or risk — see WARNING 2

**today** *adv* at the present time — see NOW 1

**today** *n* the time currently existing or in progress — see PRESENT 1

**to–do** *n* a state of noisy, confused activity — see COMMOTION

**together** *adv* 1 at one and the same time ⟨the two packages, although sent on different days, arrived *together*⟩
***syn*** coincidentally, coincidently, concurrently, contemporaneously, simultaneously
***rel*** close, immediately, narrowly, near
***phrases*** at once
***near ant*** apart, independently, individually, singly; consecutively, successively
***ant*** separately
2 in or by combined action or effort ⟨working *together*, we can get this project done on time⟩
***syn*** conjointly, jointly
***rel*** collectively, mutually, reciprocally, unanimously, unitedly; cooperatively, symbiotically
***phrases*** in concert
***ant*** apart, independently, individually, separately, severally, singly, unilaterally

**togs** *n pl* 1 clothing chosen as appropriate for a specific situation — see OUTFIT 1
2 covering for the human body — see CLOTHING

**toil** *n* very hard or unpleasant work ⟨after years of *toil* in a sweatshop, Kim was finally able to start her own dressmaking business⟩
***syn*** drudgery, grind, labor, slavery, sweat, travail
***rel*** effort, exertion, pains, struggle, trouble; chore, duty, job, obligation, responsibility; routine, tedium, treadmill
***near ant*** ease, leisure, relaxation, repose, rest; amusement, diversion, entertainment, recreation, sport; idleness, inactivity, inertia, inertness
***ant*** fun, play

**toil** *vb* to devote serious and sustained effort — see LABOR

**toiler** *n* a person who does very hard or dull work — see SLAVE 2

**toilet** *n* a room furnished with a fixture for flushing body waste ⟨we were directed to the *toilets* in the church basement⟩

---

***syn*** synonym(s) ***rel*** related words
***ant*** antonym(s) ***near ant*** near antonym(s)

*syn* bath, bathroom, latrine, lavatory, rest room, washroom, water closet
*rel* commode; outhouse, privy

**toilsome** *adj* **1** requiring considerable physical or mental effort — see HARD 2
**2** requiring much time, effort, or careful attention — see DEMANDING 1

**token** *n* something that serves to keep alive the memory of a person or event — see MEMORIAL

**tolerable** *adj* **1** capable of being endured — see BEARABLE
**2** of a level of quality that meets one's needs or standards — see ADEQUATE

**tolerably** *adv* in a satisfactory way — see WELL 1

**tolerance** *n* the capacity to endure what is difficult or disagreeable without complaining — see PATIENCE

**tolerant** *adj* **1** accepting pains or hardships calmly or without complaint — see PATIENT 1
**2** receiving or enduring without offering resistance — see PASSIVE

**tolerate** *vb* to put up with (something painful or difficult) — see BEAR 2

**tolerating** *adj* receiving or enduring without offering resistance — see PASSIVE

**toll** *vb* to make the clear sound heard when metal vibrates — see RING 1

**tomb** *n* a final resting place for a dead person — see GRAVE

**tomboyish** *adj* having qualities or traits that are traditionally considered inappropriate for a girl or woman — see UNFEMININE

**tombstone** *n* a shaped stone laid over or erected near a grave and usually bearing an inscription to identify and preserve the memory of the deceased ⟨the many *tombstones* marking the graves of children in the old cemetery reveal the harshness of pioneer life⟩
*syn* gravestone, headstone, monument
*rel* cross, marker, plaque, stone, table, tablet; monolith, obelisk, pillar; memorial, shrine

**tome** *n* a set of printed sheets of paper bound together between covers and forming a work of fiction or nonfiction — see BOOK 1

**tomfoolery** *n* wildly playful or mischievous behavior — see HORSEPLAY

**tone** *n* **1** a distinctive way of putting ideas into words — see STYLE 1
**2** a property that becomes apparent when light falls on an object and by which things that are identical in form can be distinguished — see COLOR 1
**3** the set of qualities that makes a person, a group of people, or a thing different from others — see NATURE 1

**toned-down** *adj* not excessively showy — see QUIET 2

**tongue** *n* the stock of words, pronunciation, and grammar used by a people as their basic means of communication — see LANGUAGE

**tonic** *adj* having a renewing effect on the state of the body or mind ⟨breathe in clear *tonic* mountain air⟩ ⟨never underestimate the *tonic* power of humor on a sick person⟩
*syn* bracing, invigorating, refreshing, restorative, reviving, stimulating, stimulative, vitalizing
*rel* conditioning, strengthening; animating, exhilarating, exhilarative, quickening, sharp; corrective, curative, curing, medicinal, rectifying, reformative, reformatory, remedial, remedying, reparative, therapeutic; beneficial, healthful, healthy, helpful, salubrious, salutary, wholesome
*near ant* deadening, debilitating, enervating, enfeebling, exhausting, numbing, sapping, weakening

**too** *adv* **1** beyond a normal or acceptable limit ⟨Ryan thought the test was *too* hard, but, on the other hand, he hadn't studied for it⟩
*syn* devilishly, excessively, exorbitantly, inordinately, monstrously, overly, overmuch, unacceptably, unduly
*rel* extravagantly, immoderately, intemperately; extortionately, inexcusably, intolerably, unbearably, unconscionably, unreasonably; improperly, inappropriately; abnormally, extraordinarily, freakishly, singularly, uncommonly, uncustomarily, unusually; astronomically, considerably, eminently, especially, exceedingly, exceptionally, extensively, extra, extremely, incredibly, remarkably, significantly, substantially, super, very, whacking
*phrases* to a fault
*near ant* acceptably, moderately, modestly, reasonably, temperately; barely, hardly, just, marginally, minimally, scarcely
*ant* deficiently, inadequately, insufficiently
**2** in addition to what has been said — see MORE 1
**3** to a great degree — see VERY 1

**tool** *n* **1** an article intended for use in work — see IMPLEMENT
**2** one that is or can be used to further the purposes of another — see PAWN 1
**3** one who is easily deceived or cheated — see DUPE

**tooth and nail** *adv* with all power or resources being used — see FULL BLAST

**toothsome** *adj* very pleasing to the sense of taste — see DELICIOUS 1

**top** *adj* **1** being at a point or level higher than all others ⟨an office in the *top* story of the building⟩ ⟨the *top* student in our graduating class⟩
*syn* highest, loftiest, topmost, upmost, uppermost
*rel* higher, loftier, upper; maximized, maximum, peaked, utmost; chief, first, foremost, head, leading, predominant, preeminent, premier, principal; dominant, dominating, eminent, prominent, towering; elevated, escalated, heightened, jacked (up), lifted, raised, uplifted, upraised

*near ant* below, lower, under; low, lowered, low-lying, sunken
*ant* lowermost, lowest, nethermost, undermost
**2** of the greatest or highest degree or quantity — see ULTIMATE 1
**3** of the highest degree — see FULL 2
**4** of the very best kind — see EXCELLENT

**top** *n* **1** a piece placed over an open container to hold in, protect, or conceal its contents — see COVER 1
**2** the highest part or point — see HEIGHT 1

**top** *vb* to be greater, better, or stronger than — see SURPASS 1

**topcoat** *n* a warm outdoor coat — see OVERCOAT

**topic** *n* a major object of interest or concern (as in a discussion or artistic composition) — see MATTER 1

**topmost** *adj* **1** being at a point or level higher than all others — see TOP 1
**2** of the highest degree — see FULL 2

**top–notch** *adj* of the very best kind — see EXCELLENT

**topper** *n* something (as a fact or argument) that is decisive or overwhelming — see CLINCHER

**topple** *vb* to go down from an upright position suddenly and involuntarily — see FALL 1

**topsy–turvy** *adj* lacking in order, neatness, and often cleanliness — see MESSY

**torment** *n* **1** a situation or state that causes great suffering and unhappiness — see HELL 2
**2** a state of great suffering of body or mind — see DISTRESS 1

**torment** *vb* to cause persistent suffering to — see AFFLICT

**tormenting** *adj* **1** hard to accept or bear especially emotionally — see BITTER 2
**2** intensely or unbearably painful — see EXCRUCIATING 1

**tormentor** *n* a person who causes repeated emotional pain, distress, or annoyance to another ⟨Phillip was relieved when his *tormentor* moved away, and he no longer had to take pains to avoid the bully⟩
*syn* baiter, heckler, mocker, needler, oppressor, persecutor, quiz, quizzer, ridiculer, scoffer, scorner, taunter, tease, teaser, torturer
*rel* belittler, derider, detractor, insulter; smart aleck, smarty (*or* smartie), wiseacre, wiseguy; lampooner, satirist; accuser, blamer, troublemaker; assailant, attacker, molester; bother, disturber, pest
*near ant* defender, deliverer, protector, rescuer, saviour; comforter, consoler, solace, soother, succorer

**torpid** *adj* **1** lacking bodily strength — see WEAK 1
**2** slow to move or act — see INACTIVE 1

**torrent** *n* a great flow of water or of something that overwhelms — see FLOOD

**torrid** *adj* having a notably high temperature — see HOT 1

**tortuous** *adj* marked by a long series of irregular curves — see CROOKED 1

**torture** *n* **1** a situation or state that causes great suffering and unhappiness — see HELL 2
**2** a state of great suffering of body or mind — see DISTRESS 1

**torture** *vb* to cause persistent suffering to — see AFFLICT

**torturer** *n* a person who causes repeated emotional pain, distress, or annoyance to another — see TORMENTOR

**torturing** *adj* intensely or unbearably painful — see EXCRUCIATING 1

**torturous** *adj* intensely or unbearably painful — see EXCRUCIATING 1

**toss** *vb* **1** to make a series of unsteady side-to-side motions — see ROCK 1
**2** to make jerky or restless movements — see FIDGET
**3** to send through the air especially with a quick forward motion of the arm — see THROW

**toss** (down *or* off) *vb* to swallow in liquid form — see DRINK 1

**total** *adj* **1** having no exceptions or restrictions — see ABSOLUTE 2
**2** not lacking any part or member that properly belongs to it — see COMPLETE 1
**3** trying all possibilities — see EXHAUSTIVE

**total** *n* a complete amount of something — see WHOLE

**total** *vb* **1** to have a total of — see AMOUNT (TO) 1
**2** to combine (numbers) into a single sum — see ADD 2

**totalitarianism** *n* a system of government in which the ruler has unlimited power — see DESPOTISM

**totality** *n* a complete amount of something — see WHOLE

**totally** *adv* **1** to a full extent or degree — see FULLY 1
**2** with attention to all aspects or details — see THOROUGHLY 1

**tote** *vb* to support and take from one place to another — see CARRY 1

**totter** *vb* **1** to move forward while swaying from side to side — see STAGGER 1
**2** to swing unsteadily back and forth or from side to side — see TEETER 1

**tottery** *adj* marked by or given to small uncontrollable bodily movements — see SHAKY 1

**touch** *n* a very small amount — see PARTICLE 1

**touch** *vb* **1** to come into bodily contact with (something) so as to perceive a slight pressure on the skin ⟨be careful not to *touch* this pan—it's still hot⟩
*syn* feel
*rel* caress, embrace, finger, fondle, hug, paw, rub, stroke; brush, graze; clasp, clench, cling (to), clutch, grasp, grip, handle, hold, palm; chuck, clap, dab, flick, pat, tag, tap, tip; hit, knock, pound, rap, whack

2 to act upon (a person or a person's feelings) so as to cause a response — see [1]AFFECT 1
3 to affect slightly with something morally bad or undesirable — see TAINT 1
4 to be adjacent to — see ADJOIN 1
5 to be the business or affair of — see CONCERN 2

**touch** (on *or* upon) *vb* to make reference to or speak about briefly but specifically — see MENTION 1

**touchable** *adj* capable of being perceived by the sense of touch — see TANGIBLE

**touch down** *vb* to come to rest after descending from the air — see ALIGHT

**touching** *adj* 1 having a border in common — see ADJACENT
2 having the power to affect the feelings or sympathies — see MOVING

**touch off** *vb* to cause to function — see ACTIVATE

**touchstone** *n* something set up as an example against which others of the same type are compared — see STANDARD 1

**touchy** *adj* requiring exceptional skill or caution in performance or handling — see TRICKY

**tough** *adj* 1 not easily chewed ⟨her steak was so *tough* that she suggested the waiter use it as a hockey puck⟩
*syn* chewy, leathery
*rel* fibrous, gristly sinewy, stringy; brittle, crunchy, hard
*near ant* mushy, soft
*ant* tender
2 able to withstand hardship, strain, or exposure — see HARDY 1
3 difficult to endure — see HARSH 1
4 requiring considerable physical or mental effort — see HARD 2
5 requiring exceptional skill or caution in performance or handling — see TRICKY

**tough** *n* a violent, brutal person who is often a member of an organized gang — see HOODLUM

**toughen** *vb* 1 to increase the ability of (as a muscle) to exert physical force — see STRENGTHEN 1
2 to make able to withstand physical hardship, strain, or exposure — see HARDEN 2

**toughened** *adj* able to withstand hardship, strain, or exposure — see HARDY 1

**toughie** *n* a violent, brutal person who is often a member of an organized gang — see HOODLUM

**tour** *n* a fixed period of time during which a person holds a job or position — see TERM 1

**tour** *vb* to take a trip especially of some distance — see TRAVEL 1

**tourist** *n* a person who travels for pleasure ⟨*tourists* from all over like to take pictures of the alligators in the bayou⟩
*syn* excursionist, sightseer, traveler (*or* traveller), tripper [*chiefly British*]
*rel* holidayer, vacationer, vacationist; guest, visitor; transient; journeyer, pilgrim, wayfarer

**tournament** *n* a competitive encounter between individuals or groups carried on for amusement, exercise, or in pursuit of a prize — see GAME 1

**tourney** *n* a competitive encounter between individuals or groups carried on for amusement, exercise, or in pursuit of a prize — see GAME 1

**tousle** *vb* to undo the proper order or arrangement of — see DISORDER

**tousled** *adj* lacking in order, neatness, and often cleanliness — see MESSY

**tout** *vb* 1 to praise or publicize lavishly and often excessively ⟨a new cleaning agent *touted* as the only product a homeowner needs for all his or her cleaning chores⟩
*syn* ballyhoo, crack up, glorify, trumpet
*rel* advance, advertise, announce, boost, herald, offer, plug, promote, publicize; assert, aver, claim, declare, lay down, make out, proclaim, pronounce
2 to declare enthusiastic approval of — see ACCLAIM
3 to provide publicity for — see PUBLICIZE 1

**tow** *vb* to cause to follow by applying steady force on — see PULL 1

**toward** *or* **towards** *prep* having to do with — see ABOUT 1

**tower** *n* a large, magnificent, or massive building — see EDIFICE 1

**towering** *adj* 1 extending to a great distance upward — see HIGH 1
2 going beyond a normal or acceptable limit in degree or amount — see EXCESSIVE
3 very dignified in form, tone, or style — see ELEVATED 2

**town** *n* a thickly settled, highly populated area — see CITY

**townie** *n* a person who lives in a town on a permanent basis — see BURGHER

**toxic** *adj* containing or contaminated with a substance capable of injuring or killing a living thing — see POISONOUS

**toxin** *n* a substance that by chemical action can kill or injure a living thing — see POISON

**trace** *n* 1 a mark or series of marks left on a surface by something that has passed along it — see TRACK 1
2 a passage cleared for public vehicular travel — see WAY 1
3 a rough course or way formed by or as if by repeated footsteps — see TRAIL 1
4 a tiny often physical indication of something lost or vanished — see VESTIGE
5 a very small amount — see PARTICLE 1

**trace** *vb* 1 to draw or make apparent the outline of — see OUTLINE 1
2 to go after or on the track of — see FOLLOW 2

**tracing** *n* the act of going after or in the tracks of another — see PURSUIT

**track** *n* 1 a mark or series of marks left on a surface by something that has passed along it ⟨a muddy *track* across the kitchen floor⟩
*syn* imprint, trace, trail

*rel* footprint, footstep, path, print, step, tread; artifact, evidence, leavings, mark, relic, remainder, remain(s), reminder, remnant, residual, residue, sign, spoor, telltale, token, vestige; clue, cue, hint, indication, inkling, intimation, suggestion; scent, shadow, whiff
**2** a rough course or way formed by or as if by repeated footsteps — see TRAIL 1
**3** the direction along which something or someone moves — see PATH 1

**track** *vb* to go after or on the track of — see FOLLOW 2

**track** (down) *vb* to come upon after searching, study, or effort — see FIND 1

**tracking** *n* the act of going after or in the tracks of another — see PURSUIT

**tract** *n* **1** a broad geographical area — see REGION 2
**2** a small area of usually open land — see FIELD 1
**3** a small piece of land that is developed or available for development — see LOT 1

**tractable** *adj* readily giving in to the command or authority of another — see OBEDIENT

**trade** *n* **1** a giving or taking of one thing of value in return for another — see EXCHANGE 1
**2** an occupation requiring skillful use of the hands — see CRAFT 1
**3** the activity by which one regularly makes a living — see OCCUPATION
**4** the buying and selling of goods especially on a large scale and between different places — see COMMERCE
**5** the transfer of ownership of something from one person to another for a price — see SALE

**trade** *vb* **1** to carry on the business of buying and selling goods or other property ⟨the U.S. agreed to *trade* with China⟩
*syn* deal, traffic
*rel* bargain, barter, horse-trade, negotiate, transact; auction, exchange, merchandise, rebuy, resell, swap; buy, purchase; distribute, market, peddle, retail, sell, supply, vend, wholesale; bootleg, fence, smuggle; corner, monopolize, undersell; invest, speculate
*near ant* boycott
**2** to give up (something) and take something else in return — see CHANGE 3

**trademark** *n* **1** a device (as a word) identifying the maker of a piece of merchandise and legally reserved for the exclusive use of that person or company ⟨*Kleenex* is a *trademark* for a cleansing tissue⟩
*syn* brand
*rel* hallmark, imprint, label, logo, mark, name, service mark, stamp; copyright, patent
**2** a device, design, or figure used as an identifying mark — see EMBLEM

**trader** *n* a buyer and seller of goods for profit — see MERCHANT

**tradesman** *n* **1** a buyer and seller of goods for profit — see MERCHANT
**2** a person whose occupation requires skill with the hands — see ARTISAN

**tradition** *n* **1** an inherited or established way of thinking, feeling, or doing ⟨the town *tradition* of having the oldest resident ride at the head of the parade⟩
*syn* convention, custom
*rel* ethic, form, mode, mores, norm, values; birthright, inheritance, legacy; folklore, lore, superstition; culture, heritage, lifestyle
**2** the body of customs, beliefs, stories, and sayings associated with a people, thing, or place — see FOLKLORE

**traditional** *adj* **1** based on customs usually handed down from a previous generation ⟨Ruben had a *traditional* Passover meal at his grandparents' house⟩
*syn* classical, conventional, customary
*rel* authentic, established, fixed, historical; common, habitual, orthodox, usual; ancestral, historic, old-time, old-world; aged, age-old, ancient, hoary, old, venerable; ageless, dateless, immemorial, timeless
*near ant* contemporary, current, modern, modernized, new, present-day, updated, up-to-date; futuristic, hot, latest, mod, modernistic, newfangled, new-fashioned, red-hot, space-age, ultramodern; nonconformist, nonorthodox, original, progressive, revolutionary, unorthodox, unusual
*ant* nontraditional, unconventional, uncustomary
**2** tending to favor established ideas, conditions, or institutions — see CONSERVATIVE 1

**traduce** *vb* to make untrue and harmful statements about — see SLANDER

**traducing** *n* the making of false statements that damage another's reputation — see SLANDER

**traffic** *n* the buying and selling of goods especially on a large scale and between different places — see COMMERCE

**traffic** *vb* to carry on the business of buying and selling goods or other property — see TRADE 1

**trafficker** *n* a buyer and seller of goods for profit — see MERCHANT

**tragedy** *n* a sudden violent event that brings about great loss or destruction — see DISASTER

**trail** *n* **1** a rough course or way formed by or as if by repeated footsteps ⟨took a *trail* through the woods to get to the main road⟩
*syn* footpath, path, pathway, trace, track
*rel* bridle path; towpath; bypath, byroad, byway, passageway, walkway; detour, shortcut; course, passage, road, route, run, runway, way
**2** a mark or series of marks left on a surface by something that has passed along it — see TRACK 1

**trail** *vb* to go after or on the track of — see FOLLOW 2

---

*syn* synonym(s) *rel* related words
*ant* antonym(s) *near ant* near antonym(s)

**trailer** *n* a motor vehicle that is specially equipped for living while traveling — see CAMPER

**trailing** *n* the act of going after or in the tracks of another — see PURSUIT

**train** *n* **1** a body of employees or servants who accompany and wait on a person — see CORTEGE 1
**2** a group of vehicles traveling together or under one management — see FLEET
**3** a series of persons or things arranged one behind another — see LINE 1
**4** a series of things linked together — see CHAIN 1

**train** *vb* **1** to bring to a proper or desired state of fitness — see CONDITION 1
**2** to cause to acquire knowledge or skill in some field — see TEACH
**3** to fix (as one's attention) steadily toward a central objective — see CONCENTRATE 2
**4** to point or turn (something) toward a target or goal — see AIM 1

**trainer** *n* a person who trains performers or athletes — see COACH

**training** *n* **1** something done over and over in order to develop skill — see EXERCISE 2
**2** the act or process of imparting knowledge or skills to another — see EDUCATION 1

**traipse** *vb* **1** to go on foot — see WALK
**2** to move about from place to place aimlessly — see WANDER

**trait** *n* something that sets apart an individual from others of the same kind — see CHARACTERISTIC

**traitor** *n* one who betrays a trust or an allegiance ⟨accused by her family of being a *traitor* when she sold their traditionally animal-friendly business to a competitor known to use animals for testing its products⟩
***syn*** apostate, betrayer, double-crosser, quisling, recreant, turncoat
***rel*** collaborationist, collaborator, subversive; conspirator, intriguer, plotter, schemer; defector, deserter, renegade; blabbermouth, gossip, gossiper, informant, informer, rat, snitcher, talebearer, talker, tattler, tattletale

**traitorous** *adj* not true in one's allegiance to someone or something — see FAITHLESS

**trammel** *n* something that makes movement or progress more difficult — see ENCUMBRANCE

**trammel** *vb* **1** to confine or restrain with or as if with chains — see BIND 1
**2** to create difficulty for the work or activity of — see HAMPER

**tramp** *n* a homeless wanderer who may beg or steal for a living ⟨the police encouraged the *tramps* who were sleeping in the park to spend the bitterly cold night in the homeless shelter⟩
***syn*** bum, hobo, sundowner [*Australian*], vagabond, vagrant
***rel*** drifter, roamer, transient; beggar, derelict; dodger, malingerer, shirker, slacker; gamine, ragamuffin, urchin, waif

**tramp** *vb* **1** to move heavily or clumsily — see LUMBER 1
**2** to tread on heavily so as to crush or injure — see TRAMPLE

**trample** *vb* to tread on heavily so as to crush or injure ⟨Isabel looked out her window and beheld the neighbor's Labrador retriever *trampling* her begonias⟩
***syn*** stamp, stomp, tramp, tromp
***rel*** override, run down, run over, step (on); mash, smash, squash; boot, kick

**trance** *n* the state of being lost in thought — see REVERIE

**tranquil** *adj* **1** free from disturbing noise or uproar — see QUIET 1
**2** free from emotional or mental agitation — see CALM 2
**3** free from storms or physical disturbance — see CALM 1

**tranquilize** *also* **tranquillize** *vb* to free from distress or disturbance — see CALM 1

**tranquilizing** *also* **tranquillizing** *adj* tending to calm the emotions and relieve stress — see SOOTHING 1

**tranquillity** *or* **tranquility** *n* **1** a state of freedom from storm or disturbance — see CALM
**2** evenness of emotions or temper — see EQUANIMITY

**transaction** *n* the transfer of ownership of something from one person to another for a price — see SALE

**transcend** *vb* to be greater, better, or stronger than — see SURPASS 1

**transfer** *vb* **1** to give over the legal possession or ownership of ⟨Claire's grandfather agreed to *transfer* certain stocks to her when she turned 18⟩
***syn*** alienate, assign, cede, deed, make over
***rel*** bequeath, hand down, leave, pass down, will; bestow, confer, contribute, deliver, donate, grant, hand over, move, pass, present, release, relinquish, surrender, turn in, turn over, transmit, vest, yield; consign, entrust, trust; lease, lend, loan, rent
**2** to cause (something) to pass from one to another — see COMMUNICATE 1
**3** to cause to go or be taken from one place to another — see SEND
**4** to change the place or position of — see MOVE 1
**5** to put (something) into the possession or safekeeping of another — see GIVE 2
**6** to shift possession of (something) from one person to another — see PASS 1

**transferable** *adj* capable of being taken from one place to another by public carrier — see SHIPPABLE

**transfiguration** *n* a change in form, appearance, or use — see CONVERSION

**transfigure** *vb* to change in form, appearance, or use — see CONVERT 2

**transfix** *vb* to penetrate or hold (something) with a pointed object — see IMPALE

**transform** *vb* to change in form, appearance, or use — see CONVERT 2

**transformation** *n* a change in form, appearance, or use — see CONVERSION

**transfuse** *vb* **1** to cause (something) to pass from one to another — see COMMUNICATE 1
**2** to spread throughout — see PERMEATE

**transgress** *vb* **1** to commit an offense — see OFFEND 1
**2** to fail to keep — see VIOLATE 1

**transgression** *n* **1** a breaking of a moral or legal code — see OFFENSE 1
**2** a failure to uphold the requirements of law, duty, or obligation — see BREACH 1

**transient** *adj* lasting only for a short time — see MOMENTARY

**transitory** *adj* lasting only for a short time — see MOMENTARY

**translate** *vb* to express something (as a text or statement) in different words — see PARAPHRASE

**translating** *n* an instance of expressing something in different words — see PARAPHRASE

**translation** *n* an instance of expressing something in different words — see PARAPHRASE

**transmit** *vb* **1** to cause (something) to pass from one to another — see COMMUNICATE 1
**2** to cause to go or be taken from one place to another — see SEND
**3** to put (something) into the possession or safekeeping of another — see GIVE 2

**transmittable** *adj* **1** capable of being passed by physical contact from one person to another — see CONTAGIOUS 1
**2** capable of being taken from one place to another by public carrier — see SHIPPABLE

**transparency** *n* the state or quality of being easily seen through — see CLARITY 1

**transparent** *adj* **1** easily seen through — see CLEAR 1
**2** not subject to misinterpretation or more than one interpretation — see CLEAR 2
**3** very thin and easy to see through — see SHEER 1

**transpire** *vb* to take place — see HAPPEN

**transport** *n* **1** a state of overwhelming usually pleasurable emotion — see ECSTASY
**2** something used to carry goods or passengers — see CONVEYANCE

**transport** *vb* **1** to cause to go or be taken from one place to another — see SEND
**2** to fill with great joy — see ELATE
**3** to fill with overwhelming emotion (as wonder or delight) — see ENTRANCE
**4** to force to leave a country — see BANISH 1
**5** to support and take from one place to another — see CARRY 1

**transportable** *adj* capable of being taken from one place to another by public carrier — see SHIPPABLE

**transportation** *n* **1** a means of getting to a destination in a vehicle driven by another — see RIDE
**2** something used to carry goods or passengers — see CONVEYANCE

**transpose** *vb* to change the place or position of — see MOVE 1

**transversely** *adv* in a line or direction running from corner to corner — see CROSSWISE

**trap** *n* **1** a device or scheme for capturing another by surprise ⟨undercover agents devised a *trap* to catch the counterfeiters⟩ ⟨a bear *trap*⟩
***syn*** ambush, net, snare, web
***rel*** entanglement, entrapment; booby trap, catch, hazard, pitfall, snag; deception, ploy, ruse, subterfuge, trick
**2** a scheme in which hidden persons wait to attack by surprise — see AMBUSH 1

**trap** *vb* **1** to catch or hold as if in a net — see ENTANGLE 2
**2** to take physical control or possession of (something) suddenly or forcibly — see CATCH 1

**trash** *n* **1** discarded or useless material — see GARBAGE
**2** language, behavior, or ideas that are absurd and contrary to good sense — see NONSENSE 1
**3** people looked down upon as ignorant and of the lowest class — see RABBLE

**trashy** *adj* **1** marked by an obvious lack of style or good taste — see TACKY 1
**2** of low quality — see CHEAP 2

**travail** *n* very hard or unpleasant work — see TOIL

**travail** *vb* to devote serious and sustained effort — see LABOR

**travel** *vb* **1** to take a trip especially of some distance ⟨loves to *travel* and has been to 34 countries⟩
***syn*** journey, peregrinate, pilgrimage, tour, trek, voyage
***rel*** gallivant (*also* galavant), hop, jaunt, knock (about), ramble, roam, rove, traipse, wander; cruise, drive, fly, jet, motor, navigate, sail
**2** to make one's way through, across, or over — see TRAVERSE

**travel** *n, often* **travels** *pl* a going from one place to another usually of some distance — see JOURNEY

**traveler** *or* **traveller** *n* a person who travels for pleasure — see TOURIST

**traveling bag** *n* a bag carried by hand and designed to hold a traveler's clothing and personal articles ⟨*traveling bags* made of lightweight but tough fabrics⟩
***syn*** carryall, grip, handbag, portmanteau, suitcase
***rel*** carpetbag, duffel bag, kit; backpack, haversack, knapsack, rucksack; attaché case, valise; baggage, bags, luggage

---

***syn*** synonym(s) ***rel*** related words
***ant*** antonym(s) ***near ant*** near antonym(s)

**traverse** *vb* to make one's way through, across, or over ⟨Julie watched the spider *traverse* the entire wall from floor to ceiling⟩
***syn*** cover, crisscross, cross, cut (across), follow, go, pass (over), proceed (along), travel
***rel*** hike, tread, walk; ride

**travesty** *n* a poor, insincere, or insulting imitation of something — see MOCKERY 1

**travesty** *vb* to copy or exaggerate (someone or something) in order to make fun of — see MIMIC 1

**treacherous** *adj* not true in one's allegiance to someone or something — see FAITHLESS

**treachery** *n* the act or fact of violating the trust or confidence of another — see BETRAYAL

**tread** *vb* to go on foot — see WALK

**treadmill** *n* an established and often automatic or monotonous series of actions followed when engaging in some activity — see ROUTINE 1

**treason** *n* the act or fact of violating the trust or confidence of another — see BETRAYAL

**treasure** *n* **1** an asset that brings praise or renown — see GLORY 2
**2** someone or something unusually desirable — see PRIZE 1

**treasure** *vb* to hold dear — see LOVE 1

**treat** *n* **1** a source of great satisfaction — see DELIGHT 1
**2** something that is pleasing to eat because it is rare or a luxury — see DELICACY 1

**treat** *vb* **1** to behave toward in a stated way ⟨she tries to *treat* all of her students fairly and equally, regardless of her personal feelings toward them⟩
***syn*** act (toward), be (to), deal (with), handle, serve, use
***rel*** consider, regard, react (to), respond (to)
**2** to deal with (something) usually skillfully or efficiently — see HANDLE 1
**3** to exchange viewpoints or seek advice for the purpose of finding a solution to a problem — see CONFER 2
**4** to give medical treatment to — see DOCTOR 1

**treat** (of) *vb* to have (something) as a subject matter — see CONCERN 1

**treaty** *n* a formal agreement between two or more nations or peoples ⟨in accordance with a *treaty* between the United States and the tribes of the Pacific Northwest, commercial fishing of certain kinds of salmon is limited to Native Americans⟩
***syn*** accord, alliance, compact, convention, covenant, pact
***rel*** bargain, charter, contract, deal, settlement, understanding

**treble** *adj* **1** having a high musical pitch or range — see SHRILL
**2** having three units or parts — see TRIPLE

**trek** *n* a going from one place to another usually of some distance — see JOURNEY

**trek** *vb* to take a trip especially of some distance — see TRAVEL 1

**tremble** *n* an instance of shaking involuntarily with fear or cold — see SHIVER 1

**trembling** *adj* marked by or given to small uncontrollable bodily movements — see SHAKY 1

**trembling** *n* a series of slight movements by a body back and forth or from side to side — see VIBRATION

**tremendous** *adj* unusually large — see HUGE

**tremendously** *adv* to a large extent or degree — see GREATLY 2

**tremor** *n* a shaking of the earth — see EARTHQUAKE

**tremulous** *adj* marked by or given to small uncontrollable bodily movements — see SHAKY 1

**trench** *n* a long narrow channel dug in the earth — see DITCH

**trenchant** *adj* having an edge thin enough to cut or pierce something — see SHARP 1

**trend** *n* **1** a prevailing or general movement or inclination ⟨according to the survey, there's a growing *trend* for companies to run their own day-care centers for the benefit of employees⟩
***syn*** current, drift, leaning, run, tendency, tide, wind
***rel*** curve, shift, swing, turn; custom, habit, propensity, tenor, way
**2** a practice or interest that is very popular for a short time — see FAD

**trend** *vb* to show a liking or proneness (for something) — see LEAN 2

**trepidation** *n* the emotion experienced in the presence or threat of danger — see FEAR

**trespass** *n* **1** a breaking of a moral or legal code — see OFFENSE 1
**2** a failure to uphold the requirements of law, duty, or obligation — see BREACH 1

**trespass** *vb* to commit an offense — see OFFEND 1

**triad** *n* a group of three — see THREESOME

**triadic** *adj* having three units or parts — see TRIPLE

**trial** *adj* made or done as an experiment — see EXPERIMENTAL 1

**trial** *n* **1** a test of faith, patience, or strength ⟨Nancy found living with her cousin a real *trial* and couldn't wait for the summer to end⟩
***syn*** cross, crucible, gauntlet (*also* gantlet), ordeal
***rel*** adversity, affliction, asperity, misfortune, mishap, privation, tragedy, tribulation, trouble, vicissitude, woe; challenge, complication, difficulty, grief, hardship, rigor; annoyance, discomfort, inconvenience, nuisance
**2** a private performance or session in preparation for a public appearance — see REHEARSAL
**3** a procedure or operation carried out to resolve an uncertainty — see EXPERIMENT
**4** an effort to do or accomplish something — see ATTEMPT

**tribal** *adj* of, relating to, or reflecting the traits exhibited by a group of people with a common ancestry and culture — see RACIAL

**tribe** *n* a group of persons who come from the same ancestor — see FAMILY 1

**tribulation** *n* a state of great suffering of body or mind — see DISTRESS 1

**tribunal** *n* an assembly of persons for the administration of justice — see COURT 3

**tribute** *n* a formal expression of praise — see ENCOMIUM

**trice** *n* a very small space of time — see INSTANT

**trick** *n* **1** a clever often underhanded means to achieve an end ⟨used every *trick* in the book to get out of appearing in the fashion show featuring clothes for teens⟩
*syn* artifice, device, dodge, gimmick, jig, ploy, scheme, sleight, stratagem, wile
*rel* bluff, deception, feint; fraud, hoax, swindle
**2** a playful or mischievous act intended as a joke — see PRANK
**3** a usual manner of behaving or doing — see HABIT
**4** an act of notable skill, strength, or cleverness — see FEAT 1
**5** an odd or peculiar habit — see IDIOSYNCRASY

**trick** *vb* to cause to believe what is untrue — see DECEIVE

**trickery** *n* the use of clever underhanded actions to achieve an end ⟨Delia resorted to *trickery*—even loading up the fishing equipment—to induce her dog into the car for his vet appointment⟩
*syn* artifice, chicanery, hanky-panky, jugglery, legerdemain, subterfuge, wile
*rel* artfulness, caginess, craftiness, cunning, deviousness, foxiness, shadiness, sharpness, shiftiness, slickness, slipperiness, slyness, sneakiness, treachery, underhandedness, wiliness; deceit, deceitfulness, deception, deceptiveness, dishonesty, dissimulation, double-dealing, duplicity, guile, hypocrisy, insincerity; fakery, humbuggery, imposture, quackery; design, plotting, scheming, secrecy, stealth

**trickle** *vb* **1** to fall or let fall in or as if in drops — see DRIP
**2** to flow in a broken irregular stream — see GURGLE

**trickster** *n* **1** a dishonest person who uses clever means to cheat others out of something of value ⟨a heartless *trickster* swindled the elderly woman out of her life savings⟩
*syn* cheat, cheater, confidence man, cozener, defrauder, dodger, hoaxer, shark, sharper, swindler
*rel* double-crosser, double-dealer; bluffer, charlatan, fake, faker, humbug, imposter, mountebank, pretender, quack; adventurer, fox, knave, prankster, rascal, rogue; slicker, smoothy (*or* smoothie); plotter, schemer, sneak
**2** one who practices tricks and illusions for entertainment — see MAGICIAN 2

**tricky** *adj* requiring exceptional skill or caution in performance or handling ⟨a *tricky* musical passage for the woodwind section⟩
*syn* catchy, delicate, difficult, knotty, problematic (*also* problematical), spiny, thorny, ticklish, touchy, tough
*rel* abstract, abstruse, complex, complicated, hard, intricate, involved, recondite; stubborn, troublesome, vexatious, vexing; burdensome, demanding, discommoding, exacting, importunate, inconvenient, onerous, oppressive, painful
*near ant* easy, manageable, painless, straightforward, uncomplicated, undemanding, untroublesome

**tried** *adj* worthy of one's trust — see DEPENDABLE

**tried–and–true** *adj* worthy of one's trust — see DEPENDABLE

**trifle** *n* something of little importance ⟨let us not speak of *trifles* when our nation may be going to war⟩
*syn* child's play, frippery, nothing, triviality
*rel* naught, nothingness, smoke, zero; molehill, peanuts, pittance, song, straw, two bits; nonsense, trivia

**trifle** *vb* **1** to show a liking for someone of the opposite sex just for fun — see FLIRT
**2** to spend time in aimless activity — see FIDDLE (AROUND)

**trifling** *adj* **1** lacking importance — see UNIMPORTANT
**2** so small or unimportant as to warrant little or no attention — see NEGLIGIBLE 1

**trigger** *vb* to cause to function — see ACTIVATE

**trill** *vb* to sing with the alternation of two musical tones — see WARBLE

**trim** *adj* being clean and in good order — see NEAT 1

**trim** *n* **1** a state of being or fitness — see CONDITION 1
**2** something that decorates or beautifies — see DECORATION 1

**trim** *vb* **1** to achieve a victory over — see BEAT 2
**2** to defeat by a large margin — see WHIP 2
**3** to make (as hair) shorter with or as if with the use of shears — see CLIP
**4** to make more attractive by adding something that is beautiful or becoming — see DECORATE

**trimmer** *n* one that defeats an enemy or opponent — see VICTOR 1

**trimming** *n* failure to win a contest — see DEFEAT 1

**trinity** *n* a group of three — see THREESOME

**trinket** *n* a small object displayed for its attractiveness or interest — see KNICKKNACK

**trio** *n* a group of three — see THREESOME

**trip** *n* a going from one place to another usually of some distance — see JOURNEY
**trip** *vb* **1** to go at a pace faster than a walk — see RUN 1
**2** to go down from an upright position suddenly and involuntarily — see FALL 1
**3** to move with a light bouncing step — see SKIP 1
**tripartite** *adj* having three units or parts — see TRIPLE
**triple** *adj* having three units or parts ⟨a *triple* scoop of chocolate ice cream⟩
***syn*** threefold, treble, triadic, tripartite, triplex
***rel*** triplicate
**triple** *n* a group of three — see THREESOME
**triplet** *n* a group of three — see THREESOME
**triplex** *adj* having three units or parts — see TRIPLE
**tripper** *n, chiefly British* a person who travels for pleasure — see TOURIST
**trippingly** *adv* in a quick and spirited manner — see GAILY 2
**trite** *adj* used or heard so often as to be dull — see STALE
**triumph** *n* **1** a successful result brought about by hard work — see ACCOMPLISHMENT 1
**2** an instance of defeating an enemy or opponent — see VICTORY
**triumph** *vb* **1** to achieve victory (as in a contest) — see WIN 1
**2** to feel or express joy or triumph — see EXULT
**triumph** (over) *vb* to achieve a victory over — see BEAT 2
**triumphant** *adj* **1** having attained a desired end or state of good fortune — see SUCCESSFUL 1
**2** having or expressing feelings of joy or triumph — see EXULTANT
**triumvirate** *n* a group of three — see THREESOME
**trivial** *adj* **1** lacking importance — see UNIMPORTANT
**2** so small or unimportant as to warrant little or no attention — see NEGLIGIBLE 1
**triviality** *n* something of little importance — see TRIFLE
**troll** *n* an imaginary being usually having a small human form and magical powers — see FAIRY
**tromp** *vb* **1** to move heavily or clumsily — see LUMBER 1
**2** to tread on heavily so as to crush or injure — see TRAMPLE
**troop** *n* **1** an organized group of stage performers — see COMPANY 1
**2 troops** *pl* the combined army, air force, and navy of a nation — see ARMED FORCES
**tropical** *adj* being near the equator — see LOW 1
**trot** *vb* **1** to go at a pace faster than a walk — see RUN 1
**2** to proceed or move quickly — see HURRY 2
**troth** *n* **1** a person's solemn declaration that he or she will do or not do something — see PROMISE
**2** the act or state of being engaged to be married — see ENGAGEMENT 1
**troth** *vb* to obligate by prior agreement — see PLEDGE 1
**trouble** *n* **1** an abnormal state that disrupts a plant's or animal's normal bodily functioning — see DISEASE
**2** something that may cause injury or harm — see DANGER 2
**3** something that requires thought and skill for resolution — see PROBLEM 1
**4** the active use of energy in producing a result — see EFFORT
**5** the state of not being protected from injury, harm, or evil — see DANGER 1
**trouble** *vb* **1** to experience concern or anxiety — see WORRY 1
**2** to cause discomfort to or trouble for — see INCONVENIENCE
**troubled** *adj* feeling or showing uncomfortable feelings of uncertainty — see NERVOUS 1
**troublesome** *adj* causing worry or anxiety ⟨the *troublesome* news that there will be more cuts in the school budget⟩
***syn*** discomforting, discomposing, disquieting, distressing, disturbing, perturbing, troubling, troublous, unsettling, upsetting, worrisome
***rel*** daunting, demoralizing, discomfiting, disconcerting, discouraging, disheartening, dismaying, dispiriting
***near ant*** calming, quieting, settling, soothing
***ant*** reassuring, untroublesome
**troubling** *adj* causing worry or anxiety — see TROUBLESOME
**troublous** *adj* causing worry or anxiety — see TROUBLESOME
**trough** *n* **1** a long hollow cylinder for carrying a substance (as a liquid or gas) — see PIPE 1
**2** a long narrow channel dug in the earth — see DITCH
**3** a pipe or channel for carrying off water from a roof — see GUTTER 1
**trounce** *vb* **1** to achieve a victory over — see BEAT 2
**2** to defeat by a large margin — see WHIP 2
**trouncing** *n* failure to win a contest — see DEFEAT 1
**troupe** *n* an organized group of stage performers — see COMPANY 1
**trouper** *n* one who acts professionally (as in a play, movie, or television show) — see ACTOR
**trousers** *n pl* an outer garment covering each leg separately from waist to ankle — see PANTS
**truce** *n* a temporary stopping of fighting ⟨both sides agreed to a 24-hour *truce* beginning at midnight on Christmas Eve⟩
***syn*** armistice, cease-fire
***rel*** accord, reconciliation; peace, peacetime

**truck** *n* a giving or taking of one thing of value in return for another — see EXCHANGE 1

**truculence** *n* an inclination to fight or quarrel — see BELLIGERENCE

**truculent** *adj* feeling or displaying eagerness to fight — see BELLIGERENT

**trudge** *vb* to make progress in a clumsy, struggling manner — see FLOUNDER 1

**true** *adj* **1** being exactly as appears or as claimed — see AUTHENTIC 1
**2** being in agreement with the truth or a fact or a standard — see CORRECT 1
**3** existing in fact and not merely as a possibility — see ACTUAL
**4** firm in one's allegiance to someone or something — see FAITHFUL 1
**5** following an original exactly — see FAITHFUL 2
**6** free from any intent to deceive or impress others — see GUILELESS
**7** restricted to or based on fact — see FACTUAL 1
**8** worthy of one's trust — see DEPENDABLE

**true–blue** *adj* firm in one's allegiance to someone or something — see FAITHFUL 1

**truism** *n* an idea or expression that has been used by many people — see COMMONPLACE

**truly** *adv* **1** not merely this but also — see EVEN
**2** to tell the truth — see ACTUALLY 1
**3** without any question — see INDEED 1

**trumpery** *adj* of low quality — see CHEAP 2

**trumpet** *vb* to praise or publicize lavishly and often excessively — see TOUT 1

**truncheon** *n* a heavy rigid stick used as a weapon or for punishment — see CLUB 1

**trunk** *n* a covered rectangular container for storing or transporting things — see CHEST

**truss** *vb* to gather into a tight mass by means of a line or cord — see TIE 1

**trust** *n* **1** firm belief in the integrity, ability, effectiveness, or genuineness of someone or something ⟨a relationship of mutual *trust* between lawyer and client⟩
***syn*** confidence, credence, faith, stock
***rel*** acceptance, assurance, assuredness, certainty, certitude, conviction, positiveness, sureness; credit, dependence, hope, reliance
***near ant*** disbelief, incredulity, unbelief; doubt, dubiousness, incertitude, nonconfidence, skepticism, suspicion, uncertainty
***ant*** distrust, mistrust
**2** a number of businesses or enterprises united for commercial advantage — see CARTEL
**3** responsibility for the safety and well-being of someone or something — see CUSTODY
**4** the right to take possession of goods before paying for them — see CREDIT 1

**trust** *vb* **1** to give a task, duty, or responsibility to — see ENTRUST 1
**2** to put (something) into the possession or safekeeping of another — see GIVE 2
**3** to regard as right or true — see BELIEVE 1

**trustful** *adj* having or showing trust in another — see TRUSTING 1

**trusting** *adj* **1** having or showing trust in another ⟨Delia couldn't look into her dog's *trusting* eyes as she drove him to the vet⟩
***syn*** confiding, trustful
***rel*** artless, childlike, credulous, guileless, gullible, innocent, naive (*also* naïve), simple, unsophisticated; dependent, hopeful, reliant; accepting, believing, certain, confident, convinced, overconfident, secure, sure, unquestioning, unsuspecting, unsuspicious, unwary
***near ant*** disbelieving, incredulous, unbelieving, unconvinced, unpersuaded; hesitant, leery, oversuspicious, skeptical, suspicious, uncertain, unsure, wary
***ant*** distrustful, doubtful, doubting, mistrustful
**2** readily taken advantage of — see EASY 2

**trustworthiness** *n* worthiness as the recipient of another's trust or confidence — see RELIABILITY

**trustworthy** *adj* worthy of one's trust — see DEPENDABLE

**trusty** *adj* worthy of one's trust — see DEPENDABLE

**truth** *n* agreement with fact or reality ⟨there is no *truth* to her accusation that Emory cheated on the test⟩
***syn*** factuality, verity
***rel*** accuracy, actuality, authenticity, correctness; credibility, honesty, trustworthiness, truthfulness, veracity; dependability, reliability
***near ant*** erroneousness, fallaciousness, fallacy; falsehood, fiction, inaccuracy, incorrectness; deceit, dishonesty, mendacity, untruthfulness
***ant*** falseness, falsity, untruth

**truthful** *adj* being in the habit of telling the truth ⟨a *truthful* youngster who wouldn't just make up a story like that⟩
***syn*** honest, veracious
***rel*** candid, frank, open, plainspoken; believable, credible, veritable, true; conscientious, moral, principled, scrupulous; dependable, reliable, trustworthy, trusty
***near ant*** fallacious, false, untrue; unbelievable, undependable, unreliable, untrustworthy; bluffing, dissembling, dissimulating, duplicitous, equivocating, hypocritical, insincere, posing, pretending; artful, deceitful, deceptive, devious, slick, slippery, sly, sneaky, treacherous, tricky, underhanded, wily
***ant*** dishonest, fibbing, lying, mendacious, prevaricating, untruthful

**truthfully** *adv* to tell the truth — see ACTUALLY 1

**truthfulness** *n* devotion to telling the truth — see HONESTY 1

---

***syn*** synonym(s) ***rel*** related words
***ant*** antonym(s) ***near ant*** near antonym(s)

**try** *n* an effort to do or accomplish something — see ATTEMPT

**try** *vb* to make an effort to do — see ATTEMPT

**try** (out) *vb* **1** to put (something) to a test ⟨want to *try out* my new skateboard?⟩ ⟨*tried* his skill at archery⟩
*syn* sample, test
*rel* check out, examine, experiment (with), explore, feel (out), research
**2** to subject (a personal quality or faculty) to often excessive stress ⟨you're *trying* my patience⟩
*syn* strain, stretch, tax, test
*rel* demand, exact, importune, press, pressure, push; aggravate, agitate, exasperate, get (to), gnaw (at), grate, harass, harry, hassle, irk, irritate, pain, pester

**trying** *adj* difficult to endure — see HARSH 1

**tryst** *n* an agreement to be present at a specified time and place — see ENGAGEMENT 2

**tubby** *adj* having an excess of body fat — see FAT 1

**tube** *n* a long hollow cylinder for carrying a substance (as a liquid or gas) — see PIPE 1

**tucker** (out) *vb* to use up all the physical energy of — see EXHAUST 1

**tuckered** (out) *adj* depleted in strength, energy, or freshness — see WEARY 1

**tug** *n* the act or an instance of applying force on something so that it moves in the direction of the force — see PULL 1

**tug** *vb* to cause to follow by applying steady force on — see PULL 1

**tug–of–war** *n* an earnest effort for superiority or victory over another — see CONTEST 1

**tumble** *n* **1** an unorganized collection or mixture of various things — see MISCELLANY 1
**2** the act of going down from an upright position suddenly and involuntarily — see FALL 1

**tumble** *vb* **1** to go down from an upright position suddenly and involuntarily — see FALL 1
**2** to go to a lower level — see DROP 2
**3** to undo the proper order or arrangement of — see DISORDER

**tumble** (to) *vb* to recognize the meaning of — see COMPREHEND 1

**tumbled** *adj* lacking in order, neatness, and often cleanliness — see MESSY

**tummy** *n* the part of the body between the chest and the pelvis — see STOMACH

**tumor** *n* an abnormal mass of tissue — see GROWTH 1

**tumult** *n* **1** a state of noisy, confused activity — see COMMOTION
**2** a violent disturbance (as of the political or social order) — see CONVULSION
**3** a violent shouting — see CLAMOR 1

**tumultuous** *adj* **1** marked by sudden or violent disturbance — see CONVULSIVE
**2** marked by turmoil or disturbance especially of natural elements — see WILD 3

**tundra** *n* a broad area of level or rolling treeless country — see PLAIN

**tune** *n* **1** a rhythmic series of musical tones arranged to give a pleasing effect — see MELODY
**2** a state of consistency — see CONFORMITY 1

**tuneful** *adj* having a pleasing mixture of notes — see HARMONIOUS 1

**turbid** *adj* having visible particles in liquid suspension — see CLOUDY 1

**turbulent** *adj* **1** marked by bursts of destructive force or intense activity — see VIOLENT 1
**2** marked by turmoil or disturbance especially of natural elements — see WILD 3
**3** marked by wet and windy conditions — see FOUL 1

**turkey** *n* **1** a person who lacks good sense or judgment — see FOOL 1
**2** a stupid person — see IDIOT
**3** something that has failed — see FAILURE 3

**turmoil** *n* **1** a disturbed or uneasy state — see UNREST
**2** a state of noisy, confused activity — see COMMOTION

**turn** *n* **1** a relaxed journey on foot for exercise or pleasure — see WALK
**2** an act of kind assistance — see FAVOR 1
**3** a habitual attraction to some activity or thing — see INCLINATION 1
**4** something that curves or is curved — see BEND 1

**turn** *vb* **1** to move (something) in a curved or circular path on or as if on an axis ⟨*turned* the doorknob as quietly as possible⟩
*syn* pivot, revolve, roll, rotate, spin, swing, swirl, twirl, twist, wheel, whirl
*rel* screw, unscrew; twiddle; crank, reel, wind; circulate
**2** to change the course or direction of (something) ⟨the dog *turned* the stampeding flock of sheep around⟩ ⟨he *turned* his cart uphill⟩
*syn* deflect, divert, swing, veer, wheel, whip
*rel* avert, move, rechannel, shift, shunt, sidetrack, switch, transfer; swivel, twist, whirl, zigzag; bend, curve, sway; reverse, turn back
**3** to change one's course or direction ⟨we *turned* left at the light⟩ ⟨the storm unexpectedly *turned* south and missed our area⟩
*syn* detour, deviate, sheer, swing, turn off, veer
*rel* tack, zigzag; double (back), turn back
**4** to eventually have as a state or quality — see BECOME
**5** to move in circles around an axis or center — see SPIN 1

**turn** (over) *vb* to change the position of (an object) so that the opposite side or end is showing — see REVERSE 2

**turn** (to) *vb* to use or seek out as a source of aid, relief, or advantage — see RESORT (TO) 1

**turncoat** *n* one who betrays a trust or an allegiance — see TRAITOR

**turn down** *vb* to show unwillingness to accept, do, engage in, or agree to — see DECLINE 1

**turn in** *vb* to go to one's bed in order to sleep — see BED

**turning point** *n* a point in a chain of events at which an important change (as in one's fortunes) occurs ⟨the *turning point* came when Victor finally admitted he was a werewolf⟩
*syn* climax, landmark, milestone
*rel* break, clincher, highlight; conversion, metamorphosis, transfiguration, transformation, turnabout, turnaround; clutch, crisis, crossroad(s), crunch, emergency, exigency, head, juncture, zero hour

**turn off** *vb* **1** to cause to feel disgust — see DISGUST
**2** to change one's course or direction — see TURN 3

**turn–on** *n* something that persuades one to perform an action for pleasure or gain — see LURE 1

**turn on** *vb* **1** to cause a pleasurable stimulation of the feelings — see THRILL
**2** to cause to function — see ACTIVATE

**turn out** *vb* to come to be — see COME OUT 1

**turn over** *vb* **1** to give (something) over to the control or possession of another usually under duress — see SURRENDER 1
**2** to put (something) into the possession or safekeeping of another — see GIVE 2

**turnpike** *n* a passage cleared for public vehicular travel — see WAY 1

**turn up** *vb* **1** to come into view — see APPEAR 1
**2** to get to a destination — see COME 2

**tussle** *n* a physical dispute between opposing individuals or groups — see FIGHT 1

**tussle** *vb* to seize and attempt to unbalance one another for the purpose of achieving physical mastery — see WRESTLE

**tutelage** *n* the act or process of imparting knowledge or skills to another — see EDUCATION 1

**tutor** *vb* **1** to cause to acquire knowledge or skill in some field — see TEACH
**2** to give advice and instruction to (someone) regarding the course or process to be followed — see GUIDE 1

**tutoring** *n* the act or process of imparting knowledge or skills to another — see EDUCATION 1

**twain** *n* two things of the same or similar kind that match or are considered together — see PAIR

**tweet** *vb* to make a short sharp sound like a small bird — see CHIRP

**twerp** *n* a person of no importance or influence — see NOBODY

**twice** *adv* to two times the amount or degree — see DOUBLY

**twilight** *n* **1** a time or place of little or no light — see DARK 1
**2** the time from when the sun begins to set to the onset of total darkness — see DUSK 1

**twin** *adj* consisting of two members or parts that are usually joined — see DOUBLE 1

**twin** *n* either of a pair matched in one or more qualities — see MATE 1

**twine** *vb* to follow a circular or spiral course — see WIND

**twinge** *n* a sharp unpleasant sensation usually felt in some specific part of the body — see PAIN 1

**twinkle** *n* a very small space of time — see INSTANT

**twinkle** *vb* **1** to shine with light at regular intervals — see BLINK 1
**2** to shoot forth bursts of light — see FLASH 1

**twinkling** *n* a very small space of time — see INSTANT

**twirl** *n* a rapid turning about on an axis or central point — see SPIN 1

**twirl** *vb* **1** to move (something) in a curved or circular path on or as if on an axis — see TURN 1
**2** to move in circles around an axis or center — see SPIN 1

**twist** *n* a forceful rotating or pulling motion for the purpose of dislodging something — see WRENCH 1

**twist** *vb* **1** to change so much as to create a wrong impression or alter the meaning of — see GARBLE
**2** to follow a circular or spiral course — see WIND
**3** to move (something) in a curved or circular path on or as if on an axis — see TURN 1
**4** to move by or as if by a forceful rotation — see WRENCH 1

**twisted** *adj* marked by a long series of irregular curves — see CROOKED 1

**twisting** *adj* marked by a long series of irregular curves — see CROOKED 1

**twisting** *n* a forceful rotating or pulling motion for the purpose of dislodging something — see WRENCH 1

**twitch** *vb* **1** to make jerky or restless movements — see FIDGET
**2** to move or cause to move with a sharp quick motion — see JERK 1

**twitching** *n* a series of slight movements by a body back and forth or from side to side — see VIBRATION

**twitter** *n* a state of nervous or irritated concern — see FRET

**twitter** *vb* **1** to engage in casual or rambling conversation — see CHAT
**2** to make a short sharp sound like a small bird — see CHIRP

**two–faced** *adj* not being or expressing what one appears to be or express — see INSINCERE

**twofold** *adj* being twice as great or as many — see DOUBLE 2

---

*syn* synonym(s) *rel* related words
*ant* antonym(s) *near ant* near antonym(s)

**twosome** *n* two things of the same or similar kind that match or are considered together — see PAIR

**tycoon** *n* a person of rank, power, or influence in a particular field — see MAGNATE

**type** *n* **1** a number of persons or things that are grouped together because they have something in common — see SORT 1
**2** one of the units into which a whole is divided on the basis of a common characteristic — see CLASS 2

**typical** *adj* **1** having or showing the qualities associated with the members of a particular group or kind ⟨*typical* behavior for a two-year-old⟩
***syn*** archetypal, average, characteristic, normal, regular, representative, standard
***rel*** common, conventional, customary, ordinary, usual, worted; expected, familiar, habitual, predictable, routine, unexceptional, unremarkable; predominant, preponderant
***near ant*** uncommon, unconventional, uncustomary, unusual, unwonted; distinctive, especial, exceptional, extraordinary, infrequent, noteworthy, rare, remarkable, singular, special, unexpected, unfamiliar, unique, unpredictable; eccentric, idiosyncratic, nonconformist, peculiar, unknown, unorthodox; curious, funny, odd, queer, strange; bizarre, fantastic, far-out, freak, freakish, out-of-the-way, outrageous, outré, unnatural, weird, wild
***ant*** aberrant, abnormal, anomalous, atypical, deviant, irregular, nonrepresentative, nontypical
**2** serving to identify as belonging to an individual or group — see CHARACTERISTIC 1

**typically** *adv* according to the usual course of things — see NATURALLY 2

**tyrannical** *also* **tyrannic** *adj* **1** exercising power or authority without interference by others — see ABSOLUTE 1
**2** fond of ordering people around — see BOSSY

**tyrannous** *adj* **1** exercising power or authority without interference by others — see ABSOLUTE 1
**2** fond of ordering people around — see BOSSY

**tyranny** *n* a system of government in which the ruler has unlimited power — see DESPOTISM

**tyrant** *n* a person who uses power or authority in a cruel, unjust, or harmful way — see DESPOT

**tyro** *n* a person who is just starting out in a field of activity — see BEGINNER

# U

**ubiquitous** *adj* **1** often observed or encountered — see COMMON 1
**2** present in all places and at all times — see OMNIPRESENT

**ugly** *adj* **1** unpleasant to look at ⟨her first attempt at painting was pretty *ugly* —a portrait of her sister that was not at all flattering⟩
***syn*** grotesque, hideous, homely, ill-favored, unappealing, unattractive, unbeautiful, unhandsome, unlovely, unpleasing, unpretty, unsightly, vile
***rel*** disgusting, repugnant, repulsive, revolting; unimposing, unprepossessing, unimpressive; plain, unaesthetic, unbecoming, unshapely
***near ant*** becoming, bonny [*chiefly British*], cute, shapely; imposing, impressive, prepossessing
***ant*** attractive, beauteous, beautiful, comely, cute, fair, gorgeous, handsome, lovely, pretty, stunning, taking
**2** causing intense displeasure, disgust, or resentment — see OFFENSIVE 1

**ultimate** *adj* **1** of the greatest or highest degree or quantity ⟨the *ultimate* speed yet attained by a land-based vehicle⟩
***syn*** consummate, maximum, most, nth, paramount, supreme, top, utmost, uttermost
***rel*** unequaled (*or* unequalled), unmatched, unparalleled, unrivaled (*or* unrivalled), unsurpassed; topmost, upmost, uppermost
***near ant*** littlest, smallest; lowest
***ant*** least, minimal, minimum
**2** following all others of the same kind in order or time — see LAST
**3** most distant from a center — see EXTREME 1

**ultimately** *adv* at a later time — see YET 1

**ultimatum** *n* something that someone insists upon having — see DEMAND 1

**ultra** *adj* being very far from the center of public opinion — see EXTREME 2

**ultramodern** *adj* being or involving the latest methods, concepts, information, or styles — see MODERN

**ultramodernist** *n* a person with very modern ideas — see MODERN

**umbra** *n* **1** a time or place of little or no light — see DARK 1
**2** partial darkness due to the obstruction of light rays — see SHADE 1

**umbrage** *n* the feeling of being offended or resentful after a slight or indignity — see PIQUE

**umpire** *vb* to give an opinion about (something at issue or in dispute) — see JUDGE 1

**unabashed** *adj* not embarrassed or ashamed ⟨*unabashed* by their booing and hissing, he continued with his performance⟩
*syn* unashamed, unblushing, unembarrassed
*rel* prideful, proud; bold, brassy, brazen, impudent, insolent, saucy, shameless; unapologetic, undaunted, undeterred, undismayed; unblinking, unflinching, unshrinking
*near ant* discomfited, disconcerted, nonplussed (*also* nonplused)
*ant* abashed, ashamed, embarrassed, shamefaced, sheepish
**unacceptable** *adj* falling short of a standard — see BAD 1
**unacceptably** *adv* **1** beyond a normal or acceptable limit — see TOO 1
**2** in an unsatisfactory way — see BADLY
**unacclimated** *adj* not having acquired a habit or tolerance — see UNUSED 1
**unaccompanied** *adj* not being in the company of others — see ALONE 1
**unaccountable** *adj* impossible to explain — see INEXPLICABLE
**unaccustomed** *adj* **1** not having acquired a habit or tolerance — see UNUSED 1
**2** not known or experienced before — see NEW 2
**3** noticeably different from what is generally found or experienced — see UNUSUAL 1
**unachievable** *adj* incapable of being solved or accomplished — see IMPOSSIBLE
**unacquainted** *adj* not informed about or aware of something — see IGNORANT 2
**unadapted** *adj* not having acquired a habit or tolerance — see UNUSED 1
**unadjusted** *adj* not having acquired a habit or tolerance — see UNUSED 1
**unadorned** *adj* free from all additions or embellishment — see PLAIN 1
**unadulterated** *adj* **1** free from added matter — see PURE 1
**2** having no exceptions or restrictions — see ABSOLUTE 2
**unadvisable** *adj* showing poor judgment especially in personal relationships or social situations — see INDISCREET
**unaesthetic** *adj* disagreeable to one's aesthetic or artistic sense — see HARSH 2
**unaffected** *adj* free from any intent to deceive or impress others — see GUILELESS
**unaffectedly** *adv* without any attempt to impress by deception or exaggeration — see NATURALLY 3
**unaided** *adv* without aid or support — see ALONE 1
**unalike** *adj* being not of the same kind — see DIFFERENT 1
**unallied** *adj* not favoring or joined to either side in a quarrel, contest, or war — see NEUTRAL
**unalloyed** *adj* **1** free from added matter — see PURE 1
**2** having no exceptions or restrictions — see ABSOLUTE 2
**unalterable** *adj* not capable of changing or being changed — see INFLEXIBLE 1
**unambiguous** *adj* **1** not subject to misinterpretation or more than one interpretation — see CLEAR 2
**2** so clearly expressed as to leave no doubt about the meaning — see EXPLICIT
**unanimated** *adj* causing weariness, restlessness, or lack of interest — see BORING
**unanimity** *n* the act or fact of being of one opinion about something — see AGREEMENT 1
**unanimous** *adj* having or marked by agreement in feeling or action — see HARMONIOUS 3
**unanswerable** *adj* not capable of being challenged or proved wrong — see IREFUTABLE
**unanticipated** *adj* not expected — see UNEXPECTED
**unappealing** *adj* unpleasant to look at — see UGLY 1
**unappeasable** *adj* showing no signs of slackening or yielding in one's purpose — see UNYIELDING 1
**unappetizing** *adj* disagreeable or disgusting to the sense of taste — see DISTASTEFUL 1
**unappreciated** *adj* not likely to be appreciated by those who benefit — see THANKLESS 2
**unappreciative** *adj* not showing gratitude — see THANKLESS 1
**unapproachable** *adj* hard or impossible to get to or get at — see INACCESSIBLE
**unapt** *adj* **1** not appropriate for a particular occasion or situation — see INAPPROPRIATE
**2** not likely to be true or to occur — see IMPROBABLE
**unashamed** *adj* not embarrassed or ashamed — see UNABASHED
**unasked** *adj* not searched or asked for — see UNSOUGHT
**unassailable** *adj* not to be violated, criticized, or tampered with — see SACRED 1
**unassisted** *adv* without aid or support — see ALONE 1
**unassuming** *adj* not having or showing any feelings of superiority, self-assertiveness, or showiness — see HUMBLE 1
**unattached** *adj* **1** not married — see SINGLE 1
**2** not physically attached to another unit — see SEPARATE 2
**unattainable** *adj* **1** hard or impossible to get to or get at — see INACCESSIBLE
**2** incapable of being solved or accomplished — see IMPOSSIBLE
**unattractive** *adj* unpleasant to look at — see UGLY 1
**unauthentic** *adj* being such in appearance only and made or manufactured with the intention of committing fraud — see COUNTERFEIT
**unavailable** *adj* hard or impossible to get to or get at — see INACCESSIBLE

*syn* synonym(s) *rel* related words
*ant* antonym(s) *near ant* near antonym(s)

**unavailing** *adj* producing no results — see FUTILE
**unavoidable** *adj* impossible to avoid or evade — see INEVITABLE
**unavoidably** *adv* because of necessity — see NEEDS
**unaware** *adj* not informed about or aware of something — see IGNORANT 2
**unaware** *adv* without warning — see UNAWARES
**unawareness** *n* the state of being unaware or uninformed — see IGNORANCE 1
**unawares** *adv* without warning ⟨the thunderstorm caught us *unawares*, and we scrambled to get off the ridge as lightning started to flash⟩
*syn* aback, suddenly, unaware, unexpectedly
*rel* abruptly, short
*phrases* all of a sudden
*near ant* slowly; obviously
**unbalance** *vb* to cause to go insane or as if insane — see CRAZE
**unbalanced** *adj* **1** having or showing a very abnormal or sick state of mind — see INSANE 1
**2** not being in or able to maintain a state of balance — see UNSTABLE 1
**unbaptized** *adj* not named or identified by a name — see NAMELESS 1
**unbearable** *adj* more than can be put up with ⟨this heat is *unbearable* —when are we going to get air-conditioning?⟩
*syn* insufferable, insupportable, intolerable, unendurable, unsupportable
*rel* unacceptable; crushing, overwhelming; comfortless, harsh, painful, uncomfortable
*near ant* acceptable; adequate
*ant* endurable, sufferable, supportable, tolerable
**unbeatable** *adj* incapable of being defeated, overcome, or subdued — see INVINCIBLE
**unbeautiful** *adj* unpleasant to look at — see UGLY 1
**unbecoming** *adj* not appropriate for a particular occasion or situation — see INAPPROPRIATE
**unbeknownst** *also* **unbeknown** *adj* happening or existing without one's knowledge — see UNKNOWN 1
**unbelief** *n* refusal to accept as true — see DISBELIEF
**unbelievable** *adj* too extraordinary or improbable to believe — see INCREDIBLE
**unbeliever** *n* a person who is always ready to doubt or question the truth or existence of something — see SKEPTIC
**unbelieving** *adj* inclined to doubt or question claims — see SKEPTICAL
**unbend** *vb* to cause to follow a line that is without bends or curls — see STRAIGHTEN
**unbending** *adj* sticking to an opinion, purpose, or course of action in spite of reason, arguments, or persuasion — see OBSTINATE
**unbiased** *adj* marked by justice, honesty, and freedom from bias — see FAIR 2
**unbidden** *also* **unbid** *adj* not searched or asked for — see UNSOUGHT
**unbind** *vb* **1** to disengage the knotted parts of — see UNTIE
**2** to set free (as from slavery or confinement) — see FREE 1
**unblemished** *adj* being entirely without fault or flaw — see PERFECT 1
**unblock** *vb* to rid the surface of (as an area) from things in the way — see CLEAR 1
**unblushing** *adj* not embarrassed or ashamed — see UNABASHED
**unborn** *adj* of a time after the present — see FUTURE
**unbosom** *vb* to make known (as information previously kept secret) — see REVEAL 1
**unbound** *adj* not bound, confined, or detained by force — see FREE 3
**unbounded** *adj* being or seeming to be without limits — see INFINITE
**unbraid** *vb* to separate the various strands of — see UNRAVEL 1
**unbridled** *adj* showing no signs of being under control — see RAMPANT 1
**unbroken** *adj* **1** going on and on without any interruptions — see CONTINUOUS
**2** living outdoors without taming or domestication by humans — see WILD 1
**unbudging** *adj* incapable of moving or being moved — see IMMOVABLE 1
**unburden** *vb* **1** to empty or rid of cargo — see UNLOAD 1
**2** to set (a person or thing) free of something that encumbers — see RID
**unburdened** *adj* no longer burdened with something unpleasant or painful — see FREE 2
**uncage** *vb* to set free (as from slavery or confinement) — see FREE 1
**uncalled–for** *adj* **1** not needed by the circumstances or to accomplish an end — see UNNECESSARY
**2** showing a lack of manners or consideration for others — see IMPOLITE
**uncanny** *adj* **1** being beyond one's powers to know, understand, or explain — see MYSTERIOUS 1
**2** being so extraordinary or abnormal as to suggest powers which violate the laws of nature — see SUPERNATURAL 2
**3** fearfully and mysteriously strange or fantastic — see EERIE
**uncataloged** *adj* not appearing on a list — see UNLISTED
**unceasing** *adj* going on and on without any interruptions — see CONTINUOUS
**uncelebrated** *adj* not widely known — see OBSCURE 2
**unceremonious** *adj* not rigidly following established form, custom, or rules — see INFORMAL 1
**uncertain** *adj* **1** likely to change frequently, suddenly, or unexpectedly — see FICKLE 1
**2** not feeling sure about the truth, wisdom, or trustworthiness of someone or something — see DOUBTFUL 1

**uncertainty** *n* a feeling or attitude that one does not know the truth, truthfulness, or trustworthiness of someone or something — see DOUBT
**unchain** *vb* to set free (as from slavery or confinement) — see FREE 1
**unchangeable** *adj* not capable of changing or being changed — see INFLEXIBLE 1
**unchangeableness** *n* the state of continuing without change — see CONSTANCY 1
**unchanging** *adj* **1** not undergoing a change in condition — see CONSTANT 1
**2** not varying — see UNIFORM
**uncharitable** *adj* **1** giving or sharing as little as possible — see STINGY 1
**2** having or showing a lack of sympathy or tender feelings — see HARD 1
**unchecked** *adj* showing no signs of being under control — see RAMPANT 1
**unchristened** *adj* not named or identified by a name — see NAMELESS 1
**uncivil** *adj* **1** not civilized — see SAVAGE 1
**2** showing a lack of manners or consideration for others — see IMPOLITE
**uncivilized** *adj* not civilized — see SAVAGE
**unclad** *adj* lacking or shed of clothing — see NAKED 1
**unclean** *adj* not clean — see DIRTY 1
**uncleanliness** *n* the state or quality of being dirty — see DIRTINESS 1
**uncleanly** *adj* not clean — see DIRTY 1
**uncleanness** *n* the state or quality of being dirty — see DIRTINESS 1
**unclear** *adj* **1** not clearly expressed — see VAGUE 1
**2** not seen or understood clearly — see FAINT 1
**uncloak** *vb* **1** to make known (as information previously kept secret) — see REVEAL 1
**2** to reveal the true nature of — see EXPOSE 1
**unclog** *vb* **1** to arrange clear passage of (something) by removing obstructions — see OPEN 2
**2** to free from obstruction or difficulty — see EASE 1
**unclogged** *adj* allowing passage without obstruction — see OPEN 1
**unclose** *vb* to change from a closed to an open position — see OPEN 1
**unclosed** *adj* allowing passage without obstruction — see OPEN 1
**unclothe** *vb* to remove clothing from — see UNDRESS
**unclothed** *adj* lacking or shed of clothing — see NAKED 1
**unclouded** *adj* not stormy or cloudy — see FAIR 1
**uncluttered** *adj* being clean and in good order — see NEAT 1
**uncolored** *adj* lacking an addition of color — see COLORLESS
**uncomfortable** *adj* **1** causing discomfort ⟨unfortunately, dressing up for the dance meant wearing an *uncomfortable* shirt⟩
*syn* comfortless, discomforting, harsh
*rel* aching, hurting, nasty, painful, sore; distressing, disturbing, upsetting; awkward, cumbersome, inconvenient, ungainly; uneasy
*near ant* easy, soothing; cozy, snug
*ant* comfortable
**2** causing embarrassment — see AWKWARD 3
**3** lacking social grace and assurance — see AWKWARD 1
**uncomic** *adj* not joking or playful in mood or manner — see SERIOUS 1
**uncommon** *adj* **1** being out of the ordinary — see EXCEPTIONAL
**2** noticeably different from what is generally found or experienced — see UNUSUAL 1
**uncommunicative** *adj* **1** deliberately refraining from speech — see SILENT 1
**2** given to keeping one's activities hidden from public observation or knowledge — see SECRETIVE
**3** tending not to speak frequently (as by habit or inclination) — see SILENT 2
**uncomplaining** *adj* accepting pains or hardships calmly or without complaint — see PATIENT 1
**uncomplimentary** *adj* intended to make a person or thing seem of little importance or value — see DEROGATORY
**uncompromising** *adj* **1** not allowing for any exceptions or loosening of standards — see RIGID 1
**2** sticking to an opinion, purpose, or course of action in spite of reason, arguments, or persuasion — see OBSTINATE
**unconcern** *n* lack of interest or concern — see INDIFFERENCE
**unconcerned** *adj* **1** having or showing a lack of concern or seriousness — see CAREFREE
**2** having or showing a lack of interest or concern — see INDIFFERENT 1
**unconditional** *adj* having no exceptions or restrictions — see ABSOLUTE 2
**unconfined** *adj* not bound, confined, or detained by force — see FREE 3
**uncongenial** *adj* not giving pleasure to the mind or senses — see UNPLEASANT
**unconnected** *adj* **1** not clearly or logically connected — see INCOHERENT 1
**2** not physically attached to another unit — see SEPARATE 2
**unconquerable** *adj* incapable of being defeated, overcome, or subdued — see INVINCIBLE
**unconscionable** *adj* **1** going beyond a normal or acceptable limit in degree or amount — see EXCESSIVE
**2** not guided by or showing a concern for what is right — see UNPRINCIPLED
**unconscious** *adj* **1** having lost consciousness ⟨the guard was knocked *unconscious* by a blow to the head⟩
*syn* cold, insensible, senseless
*rel* semiconscious; anesthetized
*near ant* alert, awake, aware, up
*ant* conscious

*syn* synonym(s) *rel* related words
*ant* antonym(s) *near ant* near antonym(s)

2 not informed about or aware of something — see IGNORANT 2

**unconsidered** *adj* made or done without previous thought or preparation — see EXTEMPORANEOUS

**unconsolidated** *adj* consisting of particles that do not stick together — see LOOSE 2

**uncontrollable** *adj* given to resisting control or discipline by others ⟨the *uncontrollable* child kept throwing tantrums in public and creating scenes⟩
*syn* froward, headstrong, intractable, recalcitrant, refractory, ungovernable, unmanageable, unruly, untoward, wayward, willful (*or* wilful)
*rel* contrary, incorrigible, obstinate, perverse, self-willed, stubborn; undisciplined, unpunished; uncontrolled, ungoverned, wild; boisterous, rambunctious, rowdy; disobedient, insubordinate, rebellious; misbehaving, naughty
*phrases* out of hand
*near ant* docile, obedient, well-behaved; compliant, submissive, yielding
*ant* controllable, governable, tractable

**uncontrolled** *adj* showing no signs of being under control — see RAMPANT 1

**unconventional** *adj* 1 deviating from commonly accepted beliefs or practices — see HERETICAL
2 not bound by traditional ways or beliefs — see LIBERAL 1
3 not rigidly following established form, custom, or rules — see INFORMAL 1

**unconvinced** *adj* not feeling sure about the truth, wisdom, or trustworthiness of someone or something — see DOUBTFUL 1

**unconvincing** *adj* too extraordinary or improbable to believe — see INCREDIBLE

**uncooked** *adj* not cooked — see RAW 1

**uncordial** *adj* lacking in friendliness or warmth of feeling — see COLD 2

**uncork** *vb* to set free (from a state of being held in check) — see RELEASE 1

**uncountable** *adj* too many to be counted — see COUNTLESS

**uncounted** *adj* too many to be counted — see COUNTLESS

**uncouple** *vb* to set or force apart — see SEPARATE 1

**uncouth** *adj* 1 having or showing crudely insensitive or impolite manners — see CLOWNISH
2 lacking in refinement or good taste — see COARSE 2

**uncover** *vb* 1 to make known (as information previously kept secret) — see REVEAL 1
2 to reveal the true nature of — see EXPOSE 1

**uncovered** *adj* lacking a usual or natural covering — see NAKED 2

**uncritical** *adj* lacking in worldly wisdom or informed judgment — see NAIVE 1

**uncrown** *vb* to remove from a position of prominence or power (as a throne) — see DEPOSE 1

**unctuous** *adj* 1 not being or expressing what one appears to be or express — see INSINCERE
2 overly or insincerely flattering — see FULSOME

**uncultivated** *adj* 1 existing without human habitation or cultivation — see WILD 2
2 lacking in refinement or good taste — see COARSE 2
3 not civilized — see SAVAGE 1

**uncultured** *adj* lacking in refinement or good taste — see COARSE 2

**uncurbed** *adj* showing no signs of being under control — see RAMPANT 1

**uncurious** *adj* having or showing a lack of interest or concern — see INDIFFERENT 1

**uncurl** *vb* to cause to follow a line that is without bends or curls — see STRAIGHTEN

**uncustomary** *adj* 1 being out of the ordinary — see EXCEPTIONAL
2 noticeably different from what is generally found or experienced — see UNUSUAL 1

**undaunted** *adj* feeling or displaying no fear by temperament — see BRAVE

**undeceive** *vb* to free from mistaken beliefs or foolish hopes — see DISILLUSION

**undecided** *adj* 1 not yet settled or decided — see PENDING 1
2 not feeling sure about the truth, wisdom, or trustworthiness of someone or something — see DOUBTFUL 1

**undecorated** *adj* free from all additions or embellishment — see PLAIN 1

**undefended** *adj* lacking protection from danger or resistance against attack — see HELPLESS 1

**undefined** *adj* not seen or understood clearly — see FAINT 1

**undemonstrative** *adj* not feeling or showing emotion — see IMPASSIVE 1

**undeniable** *adj* not capable of being challenged or proved wrong — see IREFUTABLE

**undeniably** *adv* without any question — see INDEED 1

**under** *adj* having not so great importance or rank as another — see LESSER

**under** *adv* in or to a lower place — see BELOW 1

**under** *prep* in a lower position than — see BELOW

**underbelly** *n* the side or part facing downward from something — see BOTTOM 1

**underbody** *n* the side or part facing downward from something — see BOTTOM 1

**underclothes** *n pl* clothing intended to be worn underneath other clothing — see UNDERWEAR

**underclothing** *n* clothing intended to be worn underneath other clothing — see UNDERWEAR

**undercover** *adj* 1 undertaken or done so as to escape being observed or known by others — see SECRET 1
2 working on missions in which one's objectives, activities, or true identity are not publicly revealed — see SECRET 2

**undergarments** *n pl* clothing intended to be worn underneath other clothing — see UNDERWEAR

**undergo** *vb* to come to a knowledge of (something) by living through it — see EXPERIENCE

**underground** *adj* undertaken or done so as to escape being observed or known by others — see SECRET 1

**underground** *n* a secret organization in a conquered country fighting against enemy forces — see RESISTANCE 2

**underhand** *adj* **1** given to or marked by cheating and deception — see DISHONEST 2
**2** undertaken or done so as to escape being observed or known by others — see SECRET 1

**underhanded** *adj* **1** given to or marked by cheating and deception — see DISHONEST 2
**2** undertaken or done so as to escape being observed or known by others — see SECRET 1

**underline** *vb* to indicate the importance of by giving prominent display — see EMPHASIZE

**underling** *n* one who is of lower rank and typically under the authority of another ⟨he instructed his *underlings* to carry out the order immediately⟩
***syn*** inferior, junior, subordinate
***rel*** attendant, follower, retainer; domestic, menial, steward; flunky (*also* flunkey), henchman, lackey, minion; adjutant, aid, aide, assistant, coadjutor, deputy, second; helpmate, helpmeet, mate, sidekick
***near ant*** boss, captain, chief, foreman, head, headman, helmsman, kingpin, leader, master, taskmaster
***ant*** senior, superior

**underlying** *adj* of or relating to the simplest facts or theories of a subject — see ELEMENTARY

**underneath** *adv* in or to a lower place — see BELOW 1

**underpin** *vb* to hold up or serve as a foundation for — see SUPPORT 3

**underpinning** *n* **1** an immaterial thing upon which something else rests — see BASE 1
**2** something that holds up or serves as a foundation for something else — see SUPPORT 1

**underprivileged** *adj* kept from having the necessities of life or a healthful environment — see DEPRIVED

**underscore** *vb* to indicate the importance of by giving prominent display — see EMPHASIZE

**underside** *n* the side or part facing downward from something — see BOTTOM 1

**undersized** *adj* of a size that is less than average — see SMALL 1

**understand** *vb* **1** to form an opinion through reasoning and information — see INFER 1
**2** to have a practical understanding of — see KNOW 1
**3** to recognize the meaning of — see COMPREHEND 1

**understanding** *adj* having or showing the capacity for sharing the feelings of another — see SYMPATHETIC 1

**understanding** *n* **1** an arrangement about action to be taken — see AGREEMENT 2
**2** the knowledge gained from the process of coming to know or understand something — see COMPREHENSION

**understated** *adj* not excessively showy — see QUIET 2

**undersurface** *n* the side or part facing downward from something — see BOTTOM 1

**undertake** *vb* to take to or upon oneself — see ASSUME 1

**undertaker** *n* a person who manages funerals and prepares the dead for burial or cremation — see FUNERAL DIRECTOR

**underwater** *adj* living, lying, or occurring below the surface of the water ⟨*underwater* plants don't require as much light to grow as surface plants⟩ ⟨*underwater* exploring takes a long time because you can't move quickly⟩
***syn*** aquatic, submarine, submerged, sunken
***rel*** oceanic; abysmal, abyssal, deep, deep-sea, deepwater

**under way** *adj* being in progress or development — see ONGOING 1

**underwear** *n* clothing intended to be worn underneath other clothing ⟨*underwear* has got to be the most boring thing that one could ever receive as a birthday present!⟩
***syn*** underclothes, underclothing, undergarments, undies
***rel*** lingerie; pantie (*or* panty), slip, underskirt; briefs, drawers, long johns, pants, shorts, underdrawers, underpants, undershirt, union suit; nightdress, nightgown, nightshirt, pajamas, pj's
***near ant*** outerwear

**underweight** *adj* having little weight — see [1]LIGHT 1

**underwrite** *vb* to provide money for — see FINANCE 1

**undesired** *adj* not searched or asked for — see UNSOUGHT

**undetermined** *adj* **1** not seen or understood clearly — see FAINT 1
**2** not yet settled or decided — see PENDING 1

**undeviating** *adj* not varying — see UNIFORM

**undies** *n pl* clothing intended to be worn underneath other clothing — see UNDERWEAR

**undiluted** *adj* free from added matter — see PURE 1

**undisturbed** *adj* free from emotional or mental agitation — see CALM 2

**undivided** *adj* not divided or scattered among several areas of interest or concern — see WHOLE 1

**undo** *vb* **1** to deprive of courage or confidence — see UNNERVE 1

**2** to disengage the knotted parts of — see UNTIE

**3** to trouble the mind of; to make uneasy — see DISTURB 1

**undomesticated** *adj* living outdoors without taming or domestication by humans — see WILD 1

**undoubtedly** *adv* without any question — see INDEED 1

**undress** *vb* to remove clothing from ⟨Mom *undressed* the mud-covered little toddler and plopped her in the bath⟩

***syn*** disrobe, strip, unclothe

***rel*** bare, denude, divest, expose, uncover, undrape, unveil; bark, flay, peel, skin

***near ant*** apparel, array, attire, caparison, clothe, costume, cover, deck, dress, feather, garb, garment, invest, rig (out), vest; cloak, mantle; drape, swaddle, swathe; accoutre (*or* accouter), equip, furnish, outfit

***ant*** dress, gown, robe

**undressed** *adj* **1** being such as found in nature and not altered by processing or refining — see CRUDE 1

**2** lacking or shed of clothing — see NAKED 1

**undue** *adj* going beyond a normal or acceptable limit in degree or amount — see EXCESSIVE

**unduly** *adv* beyond a normal or acceptable limit — see TOO 1

**undyed** *adj* lacking an addition of color — see COLORLESS

**undying** *adj* lasting forever — see EVERLASTING

**uneager** *adj* showing little or no interest or enthusiasm — see TEPID 1

**unearth** *vb* to remove from place of burial — see EXHUME

**unearthing** *n* the act or process of sighting or learning the existence of something for the first time — see DISCOVERY 1

**unearthly** *adj* **1** being so extraordinary or abnormal as to suggest powers which violate the laws of nature — see SUPERNATURAL 2

**2** fearfully and mysteriously strange or fantastic — see EERIE

**3** of, relating to, or being part of a reality beyond the observable physical universe — see SUPERNATURAL 1

**uneasiness** *n* **1** a disturbed or uneasy state — see UNREST

**2** an uneasy state of mind usually over the possibility of an anticipated misfortune or trouble — see ANXIETY 1

**uneasy** *adj* **1** feeling or showing uncomfortable feelings of uncertainty — see NERVOUS 1

**2** lacking or denying rest — see RESTLESS 1

**3** lacking social grace and assurance — see AWKWARD

**uneducated** *adj* lacking in education or the knowledge gained from books — see IGNORANT 1

**unembarrassed** *adj* not embarrassed or ashamed — see UNABASHED

**unemotional** *adj* not feeling or showing emotion — see IMPASSIVE 1

**unending** *adj* lasting forever — see EVERLASTING

**unencurable** *adj* more than can be put up with — see UNBEARABLE

**unenjoyable** *adj* not giving pleasure to the mind or senses — see UNPLEASANT

**unenthusiastic** *adj* showing little or no interest or enthusiasm — see TEPID 1

**unequal** *adj* not staying constant — see UNEVEN 2

**unequaled** *or* **unequalled** *adj* having no equal or rival for excellence or desirability — see ONLY 1

**unequivocal** *adj* **1** having no exceptions or restrictions — see ABSOLUTE 2

**2** not subject to misinterpretation or more than one interpretation — see CLEAR 2

**3** so clearly expressed as to leave no doubt about the meaning — see EXPLICIT

**unerring** *adj* not being or likely to be wrong — see INFALLIBLE 1

**unessential** *adj* not needed by the circumstances or to accomplish an end — see UNNECESSARY

**unethical** *adj* **1** not conforming to a high moral standard; morally unacceptable — see BAD 2

**2** not guided by or showing a concern for what is right — see UNPRINCIPLED

**uneven** *adj* **1** not having a level or smooth surface ⟨we had to plane and sand down the *uneven* wooden board before we could paint it⟩

***syn*** broken, bumpy, coarse, irregular, jagged, lumpy, pebbly, ragged, rough, roughened, rugged, scraggy

***rel*** lopsided, unbalanced; inexact, irregular, unaligned; rutted, rutty, undulating, wavy; burred, harsh, nubbly, nubby, scraggly, scratchy; nonuniform

***near ant*** exact, uniform; aligned, regular, true; horizontal, tabular; plumb, straight, vertical; flush

***ant*** even, flat, level, plane, smooth

**2** not staying constant ⟨the level of attendance at the ball park has been very *uneven* this season⟩

***syn*** changing, erratic, fluctuating, irregular, unequal, unstable, unsteady, varying

***rel*** capricious, changeable, changeful, choppy, fickle, fluid, inconsistent, inconstant, mercurial, mutable, uncertain, unsettled, variable, volatile

***ant*** changeless, constant, stable, steady, unchanging, unvarying

**3** inclined or twisted to one side — see AWRY

**unexampled** *adj* having no equal or rival for excellence or desirability — see ONLY 1

**unexceptional** *adj* being of the type that is encountered in the normal course of events — see ORDINARY 1
**unexpected** *adj* not expected ⟨the pop quiz was *unexpected*, but fortunately I was prepared⟩
***syn*** unanticipated, unforeseen, unlooked-for
***rel*** unintended, unplanned; improbable, unlikely; startling, surprising
***near ant*** predicted, prophesied
***ant*** anticipated, expected, foreseen
**unexpectedly** *adv* without warning — see UNAWARES
**unexplainable** *adj* impossible to explain — see INEXPLICABLE
**unexpressed** *adj* understood although not put into words — see IMPLICIT
**unfailing** *adj* **1** not being or likely to be wrong — see INFALLIBLE 1
**2** not likely to fail — see INFALLIBLE 2
**unfailingly** *adv* on every relevant occasion — see ALWAYS 1
**unfair** *adj* not being in accordance with the rules or standards of what is fair in sport — see FOUL 2
**unfairness** *n* the state of being unfair or unjust — see INJUSTICE 1
**unfaithful** *adj* not true in one's allegiance to someone or something — see FAITHLESS
**unfaithfulness** *n* **1** lack of faithfulness especially to one's husband or wife — see INFIDELITY 1
**2** the act or fact of violating the trust or confidence of another — see BETRAYAL
**unfamiliar** *adj* not known or experienced before — see NEW 2
**unfamiliarity** *n* the state of being unaware or uninformed — see IGNORANCE 1
**unfashionable** *adj* marked by an obvious lack of style or good taste — see TACKY 1
**unfasten** *vb* to disengage the knotted parts of — see UNTIE
**unfathomable** *adj* **1** being or seeming to be without limits — see INFINITE
**2** impossible to understand — see INCOMPREHENSIBLE
**unfavorable** *adj* opposed to one's interests — see ADVERSE 1
**unfeeling** *adj* **1** having or showing a lack of sympathy or tender feelings — see HARD 1
**2** lacking in sensation or feeling — see NUMB
**unfeignedly** *adv* without any attempt to impress by deception or exaggeration — see NATURALLY 3
**unfeminine** *adj* having qualities or traits that are traditionally considered inappropriate for a girl or woman ⟨in bygone days pants were considered *unfeminine*, and even women bicycling were expected to wear skirts⟩
***syn*** hoydenish, manlike, mannish, tomboyish, unladylike, unwomanly
***rel*** gentlemanly, male, manly, masculine
***near ant*** effeminate, girlish, sissy, unmanly, unmasculine, womanish, womanlike; distaff, petticoat
***ant*** female, feminine, ladylike, womanly
**unfetter** *vb* to set free (as from slavery or confinement) — see FREE 1
**unfit** *adj* **1** lacking qualities (as knowledge, skill, or ability) required to do a job — see INCOMPETENT
**2** not appropriate for a particular occasion or situation — see INAPPROPRIATE
**unfitness** *n* **1** the quality or state of being unsuitable or unfitting — see INAPPROPRIATENESS 1
**2** the quality or state of not being socially proper — see IMPROPRIETY 1
**unflagging** *adj* showing no signs of weariness even after long hard effort — see TIRELESS
**unflappable** *adj* not easily panicked or upset ⟨the *unflappable* teacher never even blinked when the wall map came crashing down⟩
***syn*** imperturbable, nerveless, unshakable
***rel*** calm, collected, composed, cool, coolheaded, nonchalant, placid, self-possessed, serene, tranquil, undisturbed, unperturbed, unruffled, unshaken, untroubled, unworried
***near ant*** panicky; aflutter, anxious, dithery, edgy, het up, hung up, jittery, jumpy, nervous, nervy, perturbed, shaky, tense, troubled, uneasy, upset, uptight, worried
***ant*** perturbable, shakable
**unfledged** *adj* lacking in adult experience or maturity — see CALLOW
**unflinching** *adj* showing no signs of slackening or yielding in one's purpose — see UNYIELDING 1
**unfold** *vb* **1** to arrange the parts of (something) over a wider area — see OPEN 3
**2** to gradually become clearer or more detailed — see DEVELOP 1
**3** to produce flowers — see BLOOM
**unforced** *adj* done, made, or given with one's own free will — see VOLUNTARY 1
**unforeseen** *adj* not expected — see UNEXPECTED
**unforgivable** *adj* too bad to be excused or justified — see INEXCUSABLE
**unformed** *adj* having no definite or recognizable form — see FORMLESS
**unfortunate** *adj* **1** bringing about ruin or misfortune — see FATAL 1
**2** having, prone to, or marked by bad luck — see UNLUCKY
**3** of a kind to cause great distress — see REGRETTABLE
**unfounded** *adj* having no basis in reason or fact — see GROUNDLESS
**unfriendly** *adj* **1** lacking in friendliness or warmth of feeling — see COLD 2
**2** marked by opposition or ill will — see HOSTILE 1
**3** opposed to one's interests — see ADVERSE 1
**unfrozen** *adj* freed from a frozen state by exposure to warmth — see THAWED
**unfruitful** *adj* not able to produce fruit or offspring — see STERILE 1

**unfunny** *adj* not joking or playful in mood or manner — see SERIOUS 1

**ungainly** *adj* **1** difficult to use or operate especially because of size, weight, or design — see CUMBERSOME
**2** lacking in physical ease and grace in movement or in the use of the hands — see CLUMSY 1

**ungentle** *adj* harsh and threatening in manner or appearance — see GRIM 1

**ungodly** *adj* falling short of a standard — see BAD 1

**ungovernable** *adj* **1** given to resisting authority or another's control — see DISOBEDIENT
**2** given to resisting control or discipline by others — see UNCONTROLLABLE

**ungoverned** *adj* showing no signs of being under control — see RAMPANT 1

**ungraceful** *adj* lacking social grace and assurance — see AWKWARD 1

**ungracious** *adj* showing a lack of manners or consideration for others — see IMPOLITE

**ungraciousness** *n* rude behavior — see DISCOURTESY

**ungrateful** *adj* not showing gratitude — see THANKLESS 1

**ungrounded** *adj* **1** having no basis in reason or fact — see GROUNDLESS
**2** not informed about or aware of something — see IGNORANT 2

**unguarded** *adj* **1** free in expressing one's true feelings and opinions — see FRANK
**2** lacking protection from danger or resistance against attack — see HELPLESS 1
**3** not paying or showing close attention especially for the purpose of avoiding trouble — see CARELESS 1

**unhampered** *adj* showing no signs of being under control — see RAMPANT 1

**unhandsome** *adj* unpleasant to look at — see UGLY 1

**unhandy** *adj* **1** difficult to use or operate especially because of size, weight, or design — see CUMBERSOME
**2** lacking in physical ease and grace in movement or in the use of the hands — see CLUMSY 1

**unhappily** *adv* with feelings of bitterness or grief — see HARD 2

**unhappiness** *n* a state or spell of low spirits — see SADNESS

**unhappy** *adj* **1** feeling unhappiness — see SAD 1
**2** having, prone to, or marked by bad luck — see UNLUCKY
**3** not appropriate for a particular occasion or situation — see INAPPROPRIATE

**unhealthful** *adj* bad for the well-being of the body — see UNHEALTHY 1

**unhealthiness** *n* the condition of not being in good health — see SICKNESS 1

**unhealthy** *adj* **1** bad for the well-being of the body ⟨we knew that the junk food at the carnival was *unhealthy*, but it tasted so good!⟩
***syn*** noisome, noxious, unhealthful, unwholesome
***rel*** insanitary, unhygienic, unsanitary; nonnutritious; poisonous, toxic; fatal, lethal, mortal
***near ant*** hygienic, sanitary; nutritious
***ant*** healthful, healthy
**2** involving potential loss or injury — see DANGEROUS
**3** temporarily suffering from a disorder of the body — see SICK 1

**unheard–of** *adj* not known or experienced before — see NEW 2

**unheroic** *adj* having or showing a shameful lack of courage — see COWARDLY

**unhindered** *adj* showing no signs of being under control — see RAMPANT 1

**unhinge** *vb* **1** to cause to go insane or as if insane — see CRAZE
**2** to trouble the mind of; to make uneasy — see DISTURB 1

**unhurried** *adj* moving or proceeding at less than the normal, desirable, or required speed — see SLOW 1

**unidentified** *adj* **1** known but not named — see CERTAIN 1
**2** not named or identified by a name — see NAMELESS 1

**unification** *n* the act or an instance of joining two or more things into one — see UNION 1

**uniform** *adj* not varying ⟨with flat-screen TVs, picture sharpness is *uniform* over the entire screen, even in the corners⟩
***syn*** invariant, steady, unchanging, undeviating, unvarying, unwavering
***rel*** immutable, invariable, unalterable, unchangeable
***ant*** changing, deviating, varying

**uniform** *n* the distinctive clothing worn by members of a particular group ⟨the band *uniform* was brown with red and white stripes⟩
***syn*** livery, outfit
***rel*** fatigues, full dress, regimentals; costume, finery, regalia

**unify** *vb* **1** to bring (something) to a central point or under a single control — see CENTRALIZE
**2** to come together to form a single unit — see UNITE 1

**unimaginable** *adj* too extraordinary or improbable to believe — see INCREDIBLE

**unimportant** *adj* lacking importance ⟨we figured that the details were *unimportant* as long as we got the basic design correct⟩
***syn*** frivolous, inconsequential, inconsiderable, insignificant, little, minor, minute, negligible, slight, small, small-fry, trifling, trivial
***rel*** jerkwater, one-horse; paltry, petty, worthless; anonymous, nameless, obscure, uncelebrated, unknown
***near ant*** decisive, fatal, fateful; distinctive, exceptional, impressive, outstanding, prominent, remarkable; valuable, worthwhile, worthy; distinguished, eminent, great, illustrious, preeminent, prestigious; famous, notorious, renowned; all-important, basic, essential, fundamental

*ant* big, consequential, eventful, important, major, material, meaningful, momentous, significant, substantial, weighty

**uninflammable** *adj* incapable of being burned — see INCOMBUSTIBLE

**uninformed** *adj* not informed about or aware of something — see IGNORANT 2

**uninhibited** *adj* showing feeling freely — see DEMONSTRATIVE

**uninstructed** *adj* lacking in education or the knowledge gained from books — see IGNORANT 1

**unintelligent** *adj* not having or showing an ability to absorb ideas readily — see STUPID 1

**unintelligible** *adj* impossible to understand — see INCOMPREHENSIBLE

**unintended** *adj* **1** happening by chance — see ACCIDENTAL
**2** not made or done willingly or by choice — see INVOLUNTARY 1

**unintentional** *adj* **1** happening by chance — see ACCIDENTAL
**2** not made or done willingly or by choice — see INVOLUNTARY 1

**uninterested** *adj* having or showing a lack of interest or concern — see INDIFFERENT 1

**uninteresting** *adj* causing weariness, restlessness, or lack of interest — see BORING

**uninterrupted** *adj* going on and on without any interruptions — see CONTINUOUS

**uninvited** *adj* not searched or asked for — see UNSOUGHT

**union** *n* **1** the act or an instance of joining two or more things into one ⟨the *union* of East Germany and West Germany that became possible after the fall of communism⟩
*syn* combination, combining, connecting, connection, consolidation, coupling, junction, linking, merging, unification
*rel* amalgamation, blend, commingling, compounding, fusion, intermingling, intermixture, mingling, mix, mixture; reunification, reunion
*near ant* detachment, divorcement, separation, severance
*ant* breakup, disconnection, dissolution, disunion, division, parting, partition, schism, split
**2** an association of persons, parties, or states for mutual assistance and protection — see CONFEDERACY
**3** the state of having shared interests or efforts (as in social or business matters) — see ASSOCIATION 1

**unique** *adj* **1** of, relating to, or belonging to a single person — see INDIVIDUAL 1
**2** being out of the ordinary — see EXCEPTIONAL
**3** being the one or ones of a class with no other members — see ONLY 2
**4** noticeably different from what is generally found or experienced — see UNUSUAL 1

**unison** *n* the act or fact of being of one opinion about something — see AGREEMENT 1

**unite** *vb* **1** to come together to form a single unit ⟨using the microscope, we watched the water droplets *unite* into a single pool⟩
*syn* associate, coalesce, combine, conjoin, conjugate, connect, couple, fuse, join, link (up), marry, unify
*rel* mate, yoke; ally, confederate, league; chain, compound, hitch, hook; congregate, gather, meet; recombine, rejoin, reunify, reunite
*near ant* detach, disconnect, disjoin, disjoint, dissociate, disunite, divide, divorce, fractionate, isolate, resolve, uncouple, unyoke; disband, disperse, scatter
*ant* break up, dissever, part, section, separate, sever, split, sunder, unlink
**2** to bring (something) to a central point or under a single control — see CENTRALIZE
**3** to form or enter into an association that furthers the interests of its members — see ALLY

**united** *adj* **1** having or marked by agreement in feeling or action — see HARMONIOUS 3
**2** used or done by a number of people as a group — see COLLECTIVE

**unity** *n* a balanced, pleasing, or suitable arrangement of parts — see HARMONY 1

**universal** *adj* **1** able to do many different kinds of things — see VERSATILE
**2** belonging or relating to the whole — see GENERAL 1
**3** covering everything or all important points — see ENCYCLOPEDIC
**4** present in all places and at all times — see OMNIPRESENT

**universe** *n* the whole body of things observed or assumed ⟨the theory that the *universe* is constantly expanding⟩
*syn* cosmos, creation, macrocosm, nature, world
*rel* existence, reality
*near ant* nothingness, void

**unjustifiable** *adj* too bad to be excused or justified — see INEXCUSABLE

**unjustness** *n* the state of being unfair or unjust — see INJUSTICE 1

**unkempt** *adj* **1** lacking in order, neatness, and often cleanliness — see MESSY
**2** lacking neatness in dress or person — see SLOPPY 1

**unknowing** *adj* **1** lacking in worldly wisdom or informed judgment — see NAIVE 1
**2** not informed about or aware of something — see IGNORANT 2

**unknown** *adj* **1** happening or existing without one's knowledge ⟨*unknown* to me was the fact that while I was out, my family was hurriedly preparing a surprise birthday party⟩
*syn* unbeknownst (*also* unbeknown)
*rel* unperceived, unrecognized, unsuspected; unaware, unconscious, unmind-

---

*syn* synonym(s) *rel* related words
*ant* antonym(s) *near ant* near antonym(s)

ful; unknowing, unsuspecting, unwitting; ignorant, unacquainted, unfamiliar
**2** not known or experienced before — see NEW 2
**3** not widely known — see OBSCURE 2

**unlade** *vb* to empty or rid of cargo — see UNLOAD 1

**unladylike** *adj* having qualities or traits that are traditionally considered inappropriate for a girl or woman — see UNFEMININE

**unlash** *vb* to disengage the knotted parts of — see UNTIE

**unlawful** *adj* contrary to or forbidden by law — see ILLEGAL 1

**unlearn** *vb* to be unable to recall or think of — see FORGET 1

**unlearned** *adj* lacking in education or the knowledge gained from books — see IGNORANT 1

**unleash** *vb* **1** to set free (from a state of being held in check) — see RELEASE 1
**2** to find emotional release for — see TAKE OUT 1

**unlettered** *adj* lacking in education or the knowledge gained from books — see IGNORANT 1

**unlike** *adj* being not of the same kind — see DIFFERENT 1

**unlikely** *adj* not likely to be true or to occur — see IMPROBABLE

**unlikeness** *n* the quality or state of being different — see DIFFERENCE 1

**unlimited** *adj* **1** being or seeming to be without limits — see INFINITE
**2** not limited or specialized in application or purpose — see GENERAL 4

**unlink** *vb* to set or force apart — see SEPARATE 1

**unlisted** *adj* not appearing on a list ⟨she kept her phone number *unlisted* so as to reduce the number of unwanted calls⟩
***syn*** uncataloged, unrecorded, unregistered
***rel*** unwritten; unidentified, unspecified; undisclosed, unknown, unrevealed
***ant*** cataloged (*or* catalogued), listed, recorded, registered

**unliterary** *adj* used in or suitable for speech and not formal writing — see COLLOQUIAL 1

**unload** *vb* **1** to empty or rid of cargo ⟨the dockworkers *unloaded* the ship⟩
***syn*** disburden, discharge, disencumber, unburden, unlade, unpack
***rel*** free, lighten, relieve; clear, empty, evacuate, vacate, void
***near ant*** charge, cram, fill, heap, jam, jam-pack, stuff
***ant*** load, pack
**2** to get rid of as useless or unwanted — see DISCARD

**unlock** *vb* to set free (from a state of being held in check) — see RELEASE 1

**unlooked-for** *adj* not expected — see UNEXPECTED

**unloose** *vb* to set free (from a state of being held in check) — see RELEASE 1

**unloosen** *vb* to set free (from a state of being held in check) — see RELEASE 1

**unlovely** *adj* **1** not giving pleasure to the mind or senses — see UNPLEASANT
**2** unpleasant to look at — see UGLY 1

**unlucky** *adj* having, prone to, or marked by bad luck ⟨the *unlucky* campers had rain all week⟩ ⟨I'm so *unlucky* I don't bother to play the lottery⟩ ⟨an *unlucky* throw of the dice⟩
***syn*** hapless, ill-fated, ill-starred, luckless, star-crossed, unfortunate, unhappy
***rel*** adverse, ill, inauspicious, unfavorable, unpromising, untoward; calamitous, catastrophic, disastrous; damned, doomed, tragic
***near ant*** blessed, favored, gifted, privileged; auspicious, fair, favorable, golden, promising, propitious
***ant*** fortunate, happy, lucky

**unmake** *vb* to remove from a position of prominence or power (as a throne) — see DEPOSE 1

**unman** *vb* **1** to deprive of courage or confidence — see UNNERVE 1
**2** to lessen the courage or confidence of — see DISCOURAGE 1

**unmanageable** *adj* given to resisting control or discipline by others — see UNCONTROLLABLE

**unmanly** *adj* having or displaying qualities more suitable for women than for men — see EFFEMINATE

**unmannerly** *adj* showing a lack of manners or consideration for others — see IMPOLITE

**unmarried** *adj* not married — see SINGLE 1

**unmask** *vb* **1** to make known (as information previously kept secret) — see REVEAL 1
**2** to reveal the true nature of — see EXPOSE 1

**unmatched** *adj* **1** being one of a pair or set without a corresponding mate — see ODD 1
**2** having no equal or rival for excellence or desirability — see ONLY 1

**unmelodious** *adj* marked by or producing a harsh combination of sounds — see DISSONANT

**unmerciful** *adj* having or showing a lack of sympathy or tender feelings — see HARD 1

**unmindful** *adj* not informed about or aware of something — see IGNORANT 2

**unmistakable** *adj* not subject to misinterpretation or more than one interpretation — see CLEAR 2

**unmitigated** *adj* having no exceptions or restrictions — see ABSOLUTE 2

**unmixed** *adj* free from added matter — see PURE 1

**unmoral** *adj* not guided by or showing a concern for what is right — see UNPRINCIPLED

**unmovable** *adj* incapable of moving or being moved — see IMMOVABLE 1

**unmusical** *adj* marked by or producing a harsh combination of sounds — see DISSONANT

**unnamed** *adj* **1** known but not named — see CERTAIN 1
**2** not named or identified by a name — see NAMELESS 1
**unnatural** *adj* **1** departing from some accepted standard of what is normal — see DEVIANT
**2** lacking in natural or spontaneous quality — see ARTIFICIAL 1
**unnecessary** *adj* not needed by the circumstances or to accomplish an end ⟨a hair dryer was an *unnecessary* item on a trip to the desert⟩
***syn*** dispensable, gratuitous, needless, nonessential, uncalled-for, unessential, unwarranted
***rel*** discretionary, elective, optional; extra, extraneous, irrelevant, redundant, superfluous
***near ant*** all-important, crucial, important, vital; imperative, pressing, urgent
***ant*** essential, indispensable, necessary, needed, needful, required
**unnerve** *vb* **1** to deprive of courage or confidence ⟨the riding accident so *unnerved* me that for a while I was afraid to get back on a horse⟩
***syn*** demoralize, emasculate, undo, unman, unstring
***rel*** debilitate, enervate, enfeeble, weaken; prostrate, sap, soften, tire, waste; frighten, scare, terrify, terrorize; daunt, discourage, dishearten, dismay, dispirit; craze, derange, madden, unbalance, unhinge; discompose, disquiet, disturb, faze, perturb, unsettle, upset
***near ant*** fortify, strengthen; embolden, encourage, hearten
***ant*** nerve
**2** to lessen the courage or confidence of — see DISCOURAGE 1
**unnerving** *adj* marked by or causing agitation or uncomfortable feelings — see NERVOUS 2
**unnoted** *adj* not widely known — see OBSCURE 2
**unnoticeable** *adj* not readily seen or noticed — see UNOBTRUSIVE
**unnumbered** *adj* too many to be counted — see COUNTLESS
**unobstructed** *adj* allowing passage without obstruction — see OPEN 1
**unobtainable** *adj* hard or impossible to get to or get at — see INACCESSIBLE
**unobtrusive** *adj* not readily seen or noticed ⟨the notice that an 18% tip would be automatically added was so *unobtrusive* we almost didn't see it at the bottom of the menu⟩
***syn*** inconspicuous, unnoticeable
***rel*** unnoticed; impalpable, imperceptible, inappreciable, indistinguishable, insensible; faint, indistinct, obscure; concealed, hidden
***near ant*** arresting, eye-catching, showy, striking; apparent, blatant, clear, distinct, evident, manifest, obvious, plain, unmistakable
***ant*** conspicuous, noticeable
**unoriginal** *adj* using or marked by the use of something else as a basis or model — see IMITATIVE
**unorthodox** *adj* **1** deviating from commonly accepted beliefs or practices — see HERETICAL
**2** not bound by traditional ways or beliefs — see LIBERAL 1
**3** not rigidly following established form, custom, or rules — see INFORMAL 1
**unpack** *vb* to empty or rid of cargo — see UNLOAD 1
**unpaid** *adj* not yet paid — see OUTSTANDING 1
**unpainted** *adj* lacking an addition of color — see COLORLESS
**unpaired** *adj* being one of a pair or set without a corresponding mate — see ODD 1
**unpalatable** *adj* disagreeable or disgusting to the sense of taste — see DISTASTEFUL 1
**unparalleled** *adj* having no equal or rival for excellence or desirability — see ONLY 1
**unpardonable** *adj* too bad to be excused or justified — see INEXCUSABLE
**unperturbed** *adj* free from emotional or mental agitation — see CALM 2
**unplanned** *adj* **1** happening by chance — see ACCIDENTAL
**2** made or done without previous thought or preparation — see EXTEMPORANEOUS
**unpleasant** *adj* not giving pleasure to the mind or senses ⟨the burnt pot roast had a very *unpleasant* odor⟩
***syn*** bad, disagreeable, displeasing, distasteful, nasty, rotten, sour, uncongenial, unlovely, unpleasing, unsatisfying, unwelcome
***rel*** abhorrent, abominable, appalling, awful, beastly, disgusting, dreadful, foul, hideous, horrendous, horrible, horrid, invidious, loathsome, nauseating, noisome, obnoxious, obscene, odious, repellent (*also* repellant), repugnant, repulsive, revolting, scandalous, shocking, sickening, ugly, villainous; annoying, galling, irritating, vexing
***near ant*** delectable, delicious, delightful, dreamy, felicitous; affable, amiable, friendly, genial, good-natured, good-tempered, gracious, sweet, well-disposed
***ant*** agreeable, congenial, good, grateful, gratifying, nice, palatable, pleasant, pleasing, pleasurable, satisfying, welcome
**unpleasing** *adj* **1** not giving pleasure to the mind or senses — see UNPLEASANT
**2** unpleasant to look at — see UGLY 1
**unpolished** *adj* lacking in refinement or good taste — see COARSE 2
**unprecedented** *adj* not known or experienced before — see NEW 2
**unpredictable** *adj* likely to change frequently, suddenly, or unexpectedly — see FICKLE 1
**unprejudiced** *adj* marked by justice, honesty, and freedom from bias — see FAIR 2

**unpremeditated** *adj* **1** happening by chance — see ACCIDENTAL
**2** made or done without previous thought or preparation — see EXTEMPORANEOUS
**unprepared** *adj* made or done without previous thought or preparation — see EXTEMPORANEOUS
**unpretending** *adj* free from any intent to deceive or impress others — see GUILELESS
**unpretentious** *adj* **1** free from any intent to deceive or impress others — see GUILELESS
**2** not excessively showy — see QUIET 2
**3** not having or showing any feelings of superiority, self-assertiveness, or showiness — see HUMBLE 1
**unpretentiously** *adv* without any attempt to impress by deception or exaggeration — see NATURALLY 3
**unpretty** *adj* unpleasant to look at — see UGLY 1
**unprincipled** *adj* not guided by or showing a concern for what is right ⟨the *unprincipled* businessman made a lot of money—and didn't care how he made it⟩
***syn*** cutthroat, immoral, Machiavellian, unconscionable, unethical, unmoral, unscrupulous
***rel*** calculating, intriguing, opportunistic, scheming; merciless, pitiless, remorseless, ruthless; crooked, deceitful, dishonest; corrupt, debased, debauched, decadent, degenerate, degraded, demoralized, depraved, dissipated
***near ant*** good, just, noble, righteous, virtuous
***ant*** ethical, moral, principled, scrupulous
**unprintable** *adj* depicting or referring to sexual matters in a way that is unacceptable in polite society — see OBSCENE 1
**unprocessed** *adj* being such as found in nature and not altered by processing or refining — see CRUDE 1
**unproductive** *adj* **1** producing inferior or only a small amount of vegetation — see BARREN 1
**2** producing no results — see FUTILE
**unprofessional** *adj* lacking or showing a lack of expert skill — see AMATEURISH
**unprofitable** *adj* producing no results — see FUTILE
**unprogressive** *adj* tending to favor established ideas, conditions, or institutions — see CONSERVATIVE 1
**unprotected** *adj* lacking protection from danger or resistance against attack — see HELPLESS 1
**unqualified** *adj* **1** having no exceptions or restrictions — see ABSOLUTE 2
**2** lacking qualities (as knowledge, skill, or ability) required to do a job — see INCOMPETENT
**3** not limited or specialized in application or purpose — see GENERAL 4
**unquestionable** *adj* not capable of being challenged or proved wrong — see IRREFUTABLE
**unquestionably** *adv* without any question — see INDEED 1
**unquiet** *adj* **1** feeling or showing uncomfortable feelings of uncertainty — see NERVOUS 1
**2** lacking or denying rest — see RESTLESS 1
**unravel** *vb* **1** to separate the various strands of ⟨it took us forever to *unravel* the jumbled mass of Christmas tree lights⟩
***syn*** disentangle, ravel (out), unbraid, unsnarl, untangle, untwine, untwist
***rel*** smooth, straighten (out); undo, unlace, unstring, unthread, untie, unwind
***near ant*** braid, knot, lace, tie, wind
***ant*** entangle, snarl, tangle
**2** to find an answer for through reasoning — see SOLVE
**unreachable** *adj* hard or impossible to get to or get at — see INACCESSIBLE
**unread** *adj* lacking in education or the knowledge gained from books — see IGNORANT 1
**unreal** *adj* **1** conceived or made without regard for reason or reality — see FANTASTIC 1
**2** not real and existing only in the imagination — see IMAGINARY
**unreality** *n* a conception or image created by the imagination and having no objective reality — see FANTASY 1
**unreasonable** *adj* **1** having no basis in reason or fact — see GROUNDLESS
**2** not using or following good reasoning — see ILLOGICAL
**unreasoning** *adj* not using or following good reasoning — see ILLOGICAL
**unrecorded** *adj* not appearing on a list — see UNLISTED
**unrecoverable** *adj* **1** not capable of being cured or reformed — see HOPELESS 1
**2** not capable of being repaired, regained, or undone — see IRREPARABLE
**unredeemable** *adj* **1** not capable of being cured or reformed — see HOPELESS 1
**2** not capable of being repaired, regained, or undone — see IRREPARABLE
**unrefined** *adj* **1** being such as found in nature and not altered by processing or refining — see CRUDE 1
**2** hastily or roughly constructed — see RUDE 1
**3** lacking in refinement or good taste — see COARSE 2
**unregistered** *adj* not appearing on a list — see UNLISTED
**unrehearsed** *adj* made or done without previous thought or preparation — see EXTEMPORANEOUS
**unrelenting** *adj* **1** sticking to an opinion, purpose, or course of action in spite of reason, arguments, or persuasion — see OBSTINATE
**2** showing no signs of slackening or yielding in one's purpose — see UNYIELDING 1
**unremarkable** *adj* being of the type that is encountered in the normal course of events — see ORDINARY 1
**unremitting** *adj* going on and on without any interruptions — see CONTINUOUS

**unrepentant** *adj* not sorry for having done wrong — see REMORSELESS
**unreserved** *adj* **1** free in expressing one's true feelings and opinions — see FRANK
**2** showing feeling freely — see DEMONSTRATIVE
**unresistant** *adj* **1** lacking protection from danger or resistance against attack — see HELPLESS 1
**2** receiving or enduring without offering resistance — see PASSIVE
**unresisting** *adj* receiving or enduring without offering resistance — see PASSIVE
**unresolved** *adj* not yet settled or decided — see PENDING 1
**unrest** *n* a disturbed or uneasy state ⟨*unrest* gripped the city as the people nervously awaited the expected bombardment⟩ ⟨his stomach *unrest* was just a sign of stage fright⟩
***syn*** disquiet, ferment, restiveness, restlessness, turmoil, uneasiness
***rel*** fidgets; agitation, commotion, confusion, tumult, turbulence, upheaval; anarchy, chaos, disorder
***near ant*** order, orderliness
***ant*** calm, ease, peace, quiet
**unrestful** *adj* lacking or denying rest — see RESTLESS 1
**unrestrained** *adj* **1** not bound by rigid standards — see EASYGOING 2
**2** not bound, confined, or detained by force — see FREE 3
**3** showing feeling freely — see DEMONSTRATIVE
**4** showing no signs of being under control — see RAMPANT 1
**unrestraint** *n* carefree freedom from constraint — see ABANDON
**unrestricted** *adj* **1** freely available for use or participation by all — see OPEN 2
**2** not bound by rigid standards — see EASYGOING 2
**3** not limited or specialized in application or purpose — see GENERAL 4
**unrighteous** *adj* not conforming to a high moral standard; morally unacceptable — see BAD 2
**unripe** *adj* lacking in adult experience or maturity — see CALLOW
**unripened** *adj* lacking in adult experience or maturity — see CALLOW
**unrivaled** *or* **unrivalled** *adj* having no equal or rival for excellence or desirability — see ONLY 1
**unruliness** *n* refusal to obey — see DISOBEDIENCE
**unruly** *adj* **1** given to resisting authority or another's control — see DISOBEDIENT
**2** given to resisting control or discipline by others — see UNCONTROLLABLE
**3** not restrained by or under the control of legal authority — see LAWLESS
**unsafe** *adj* **1** involving potential loss or injury — see DANGEROUS
**2** not paying or showing close attention especially for the purpose of avoiding trouble — see CARELESS 1
**unsatisfactorily** *adv* in an unsatisfactory way — see BADLY
**unsatisfactory** *adj* falling short of a standard — see BAD 1
**unsatisfying** *adj* not giving pleasure to the mind or senses — see UNPLEASANT
**unsavory** *adj* **1** disagreeable or disgusting to the sense of taste — see DISTASTEFUL 1
**2** not conforming to a high moral standard; morally unacceptable — see BAD 2
**unsay** *vb* to solemnly or formally reject or go back on (as something formerly adhered to) — see ABJURE
**unschooled** *adj* lacking in education or the knowledge gained from books — see IGNORANT 1
**unscrupulous** *adj* not guided by or showing a concern for what is right — see UNPRINCIPLED
**unseasonable** *adj* occurring before the usual or expected time — see EARLY 2
**unseasonably** *adv* before the usual or expected time — see EARLY
**unseat** *vb* to remove from a position of prominence or power (as a throne) — see DEPOSE 1
**unsecured** *adj* not tightly fastened, tied, or stretched — see LOOSE 1
**unseemly** *adj* not appropriate for a particular occasion or situation — see INAPPROPRIATE
**unselfish** *adj* giving or sharing in abundance and without hesitation — see GENEROUS 1
**unselfishness** *n* the quality or state of being generous — see LIBERALITY
**unsettle** *vb* to trouble the mind of; to make uneasy — see DISTURB 1
**unsettled** *adj* **1** likely to change frequently, suddenly, or unexpectedly — see FICKLE 1
**2** not yet paid — see OUTSTANDING 1
**3** not yet settled or decided — see PENDING 1
**4** not feeling sure about the truth, wisdom, or trustworthiness of someone or something — see DOUBTFUL 1
**unsettling** *adj* **1** causing worry or anxiety — see TROUBLESOME
**2** marked by or causing agitation or uncomfortable feelings — see NERVOUS 2
**unshakable** *adj* not easily panicked or upset — see UNFLAPPABLE
**unshaken** *adj* free from emotional or mental agitation — see CALM 2
**unshaped** *adj* having no definite or recognizable form — see FORMLESS
**unshared** *adj* belonging only to the one person, unit, or group named — see SOLE 1
**unshielded** *adj* lacking protection from danger or resistance against attack — see HELPLESS 1
**unshorn** *adj* covered with or as if with hair — see HAIRY 1
**unsightly** *adj* unpleasant to look at — see UGLY 1

**unskilled** *adj* **1** lacking or showing a lack of expert skill — see AMATEURISH
**2** lacking qualities (as knowledge, skill, or ability) required to do a job — see INCOMPETENT

**unskillful** *adj* **1** lacking qualities (as knowledge, skill, or ability) required to do a job — see INCOMPETENT
**2** lacking or showing a lack of expert skill — see AMATEURISH

**unsmiling** *adj* not joking or playful in mood or manner — see SERIOUS 1

**unsnarl** *vb* to separate the various strands of — see UNRAVEL 1

**unsociable** *adj* having or showing a lack of friendliness or interest in others — see COOL 1

**unsoiled** *adj* free from dirt or stain — see CLEAN 1

**unsolicited** *adj* not searched or asked for — see UNSOUGHT

**unsolvable** *adj* incapable of being solved or accomplished — see IMPOSSIBLE

**unsophisticated** *adj* lacking in worldly wisdom or informed judgment — see NAIVE 1

**unsophistication** *n* **1** the quality or state of being simple and sincere — see NAÏVETÉ 1
**2** the quality or state of having a form or structure of few parts or elements — see SIMPLICITY 1

**unsought** *adj* not searched or asked for ⟨the meddling neighbor insisted on giving us *unsought* advice⟩
*syn* unasked, uninvited (*also* unbid), undesired, uninvited, unsolicited, unwanted, unwelcome
*rel* objectionable, offensive, unacceptable, undesirable; uncalled-for, unnecessary
*near ant* necessary, needed, required
*ant* desired, solicited, wanted, welcome

**unsound** *adj* **1** having or showing a very abnormal or sick state of mind — see INSANE 1
**2** not being in agreement with what is true — see FALSE 1
**3** not using or following good reasoning — see ILLOGICAL
**4** temporarily suffering from a disorder of the body — see SICK 1

**unsoundness** *n* the condition of not being in good health — see SICKNESS 1

**unsparing** *adj* **1** giving or sharing in abundance and without hesitation — see GENEROUS 1
**2** having or showing a lack of sympathy or tender feelings — see HARD 1

**unspeakable** *adj* beyond the power to describe — see INDESCRIBABLE

**unspecialized** *adj* not limited or specialized in application or purpose — see GENERAL 4

**unspecified** *adj* known but not named — see CERTAIN 1

**unspoken** *adj* understood although not put into words — see IMPLICIT

**unsportsmanlike** *adj* not being in accordance with the rules or standards of what is fair in sport — see FOUL 2

**unstable** *adj* **1** not being in or able to maintain a state of balance ⟨when we put the books down on the *unstable* desk, the whole stack went crashing to the floor⟩
*syn* unbalanced, unsteady
*rel* rickety, shaky, tottery, wobbly; cockeyed, lopsided, uneven
*near ant* even, level, straight; sound, sturdy, substantial
*ant* balanced, stable, steady
**2** likely to change frequently, suddenly, or unexpectedly — see FICKLE 1
**3** not staying constant — see UNEVEN 2

**unstained** *adj* lacking an addition of color — see COLORLESS

**unsteadiness** *n* the quality or state of not being firmly fixed in position — see INSTABILITY

**unsteady** *adj* **1** lacking in steadiness or regularity of occurrence — see FITFUL
**2** likely to change frequently, suddenly, or unexpectedly — see FICKLE 1
**3** not being in or able to maintain a state of balance — see UNSTABLE 1
**4** not staying constant — see UNEVEN 2

**unstop** *vb* to arrange clear passage of (something) by removing obstructions — see OPEN 2

**unstopped** *adj* allowing passage without obstruction — see OPEN 1

**unstring** *vb* **1** to cause to go insane or as if insane — see CRAZE
**2** to deprive of courage or confidence — see UNNERVE 1

**unstructured** *adj* having no definite or recognizable form — see FORMLESS

**unstylish** *adj* marked by an obvious lack of style or good taste — see TACKY 1

**unstylishly** *adv* in a careless or unfashionable manner — see SLOPPILY

**unsubstantial** *adj* **1** not composed of matter — see IMMATERIAL 1
**2** being of a material lacking in sturdiness or substance — see FLIMSY 1
**3** lacking bodily strength — see WEAK 1

**unsubstantiated** *adj* having no basis in reason or fact — see GROUNDLESS

**unsuccessful** *adj* producing no results — see FUTILE

**unsuitable** *adj* not appropriate for a particular occasion or situation — see INAPPROPRIATE

**unsuitably** *adv* in a mistaken or inappropriate way — see WRONGLY

**unsullied** *adj* free from dirt or stain — see CLEAN 1

**unsung** *adj* not widely known — see OBSCURE 2

**unsupportable** *adj* more than can be put up with — see UNBEARABLE

**unsupported** *adj* having no basis in reason or fact — see GROUNDLESS

**unsure** *adj* not feeling sure about the truth, wisdom, or trustworthiness of someone or something — see DOUBTFUL 1

**unsurpassable** *adj* having no equal or rival for excellence or desirability — see ONLY 1
**unsurpassed** *adj* **1** having no equal or rival for excellence or desirability — see ONLY 1
**2** of the very best kind — see EXCELLENT
**unsuspecting** *adj* lacking in worldly wisdom or informed judgment — see NAIVE 1
**unsuspicious** *adj* lacking in worldly wisdom or informed judgment — see NAIVE 1
**unsympathetic** *adj* **1** having or showing a lack of sympathy or tender feelings — see HARD 1
**2** lacking in friendliness or warmth of feeling — see COLD 2
**3** marked by opposition or ill will — see HOSTILE 1
**4** opposed to one's interests — see ADVERSE 1
**untamed** *adj* **1** existing without human habitation or cultivation — see WILD 2
**2** living outdoors without taming or domestication by humans — see WILD 1
**untangle** *vb* **1** to separate the various strands of — see UNRAVEL 1
**2** to set free from entanglement or difficulty — see EXTRICATE
**untaught** *adj* lacking in education or the knowledge gained from books — see IGNORANT 1
**unthinkable** *adj* too extraordinary or improbable to believe — see INCREDIBLE
**unthrifty** *adj* given to spending money freely or foolishly — see PRODIGAL
**unthrone** *vb* to remove from a position of prominence or power (as a throne) — see DEPOSE 1
**untidy** *adj* **1** lacking in order, neatness, and often cleanliness — see MESSY
**2** lacking neatness in dress or person — see SLOPPY 1
**untie** *vb* to disengage the knotted parts of ⟨she always made sure to *untie* her shoelaces before removing her shoes⟩
***syn*** unbind, undo, unfasten, unlash
***rel*** unbraid, unlace; disentangle, ravel, unbraid, unravel, unsnarl, untangle, unwind; loose, loosen
***near ant*** braid, interlace, interweave, lace, wind; entangle, snarl, tangle
***ant*** bind, fasten, knot, lash, tie
**untimely** *adj* occurring before the usual or expected time — see EARLY 2
**untiring** *adj* showing no signs of weariness even after long hard effort — see TIRELESS
**untitled** *adj* not named or identified by a name — see NAMELESS 1
**untold** *adj* too many to be counted — see COUNTLESS
**untouchable** *adj* **1** hard or impossible to get to or get at — see INACCESSIBLE
**2** not to be violated, criticized, or tampered with — see SACRED 1
**untoward** *adj* **1** given to resisting authority or another's control — see DISOBEDIENT
**2** given to resisting control or discipline by others — see UNCONTROLLABLE
**untreated** *adj* being such as found in nature and not altered by processing or refining — see CRUDE 1
**untroubled** *adj* **1** free from emotional or mental agitation — see CALM 2
**2** free from storms or physical disturbance — see CALM 1
**untrue** *adj* **1** not being in agreement with what is true — see FALSE 1
**2** not true in one's allegiance to someone or something — see FAITHLESS
**untruth** *n* **1** a false idea or belief — see FALLACY 1
**2** a statement known by its maker to be untrue and made in order to deceive — see LIE
**3** the quality or state of being false — see FALLACY 2
**untruthful** *adj* **1** not being in agreement with what is true — see FALSE 1
**2** telling or containing lies — see DISHONEST 1
**untruthfulness** *n* the tendency to tell lies — see DISHONESTY 1
**untutored** *adj* lacking in education or the knowledge gained from books — see IGNORANT 1
**untwine** *vb* to separate the various strands of — see UNRAVEL 1
**untwist** *vb* to separate the various strands of — see UNRAVEL 1
**unusable** *adj* not capable of being put to use or account — see IMPRACTICAL
**unused** *adj* **1** not having acquired a habit or tolerance ⟨while in Mexico we tried to stay out of the sun because we were simply *unused* to the tropical heat⟩
***syn*** unacclimated, unaccustomed, unadapted, unadjusted
***rel*** unhardened, unseasoned
***near ant*** unaffected, uninfluenced
***ant*** acclimated, accustomed, adapted, adjusted, habituated, used
**2** recently made and never used before — see NEW 3
**unusual** *adj* **1** noticeably different from what is generally found or experienced ⟨finding some *unusual* shells by the high-tide mark, we brought them home for our collection⟩
***syn*** curious, extraordinary, funny, odd, offbeat, peculiar, queer, rare, singular, strange, unaccustomed, uncommon, uncustomary, unique, weird
***rel*** bizarre, eccentric, far-out, outlandish, outré, way-out; aberrant, abnormal, atypical, exceptional, irregular; newsworthy, notable, noteworthy, noticeable, particular, remarkable, special
***near ant*** unexceptional; expected, predictable; familiar, normal, regular, typical
***ant*** common, ordinary, usual
**2** being out of the ordinary — see EXCEPTIONAL

**unutterable** *adj* beyond the power to describe — see INDESCRIBABLE
**unvarnished** *adj* free from all additions or embellishment — see PLAIN 1
**unvarying** *adj* **1** not undergoing a change in condition — see CONSTANT 1
**2** not varying — see UNIFORM
**unveil** *vb* **1** to make known (as information previously kept secret) — see REVEAL 1
**2** to present so as to invite notice or attention — see SHOW 1
**unvoiced** *adj* understood although not put into words — see IMPLICIT
**unwanted** *adj* not searched or asked for — see UNSOUGHT
**unwarrantable** *adj* too bad to be excused or justified — see INEXCUSABLE
**unwarranted** *adj* **1** not needed by the circumstances or to accomplish an end — see UNNECESSARY
**2** having no basis in reason or fact — see GROUNDLESS
**unwary** *adj* **1** lacking in worldly wisdom or informed judgment — see NAIVE 1
**2** not paying or showing close attention especially for the purpose of avoiding trouble — see CARELESS 1
**unwavering** *adj* not varying — see UNIFORM
**unwearying** *adj* showing no signs of weariness even after long hard effort — see TIRELESS
**unwed** *adj* not married — see SINGLE 1
**unwelcome** *adj* **1** not giving pleasure to the mind or senses — see UNPLEASANT
**2** not searched or asked for — see UNSOUGHT
**unwell** *adj* temporarily suffering from a disorder of the body — see SICK 1
**unwholesome** *adj* bad for the well-being of the body — see UNHEALTHY 1
**unwieldy** *adj* difficult to use or operate especially because of size, weight, or design — see CUMBERSOME
**unwilling** *adj* not made or done willingly or by choice — see INVOLUNTARY 1
**unwillingness** *n* a lack of willingness or desire to do or accept something — see RELUCTANCE
**unwind** *vb* to get rid of nervous tension or anxiety — see RELAX 1
**unwise** *adj* **1** showing or marked by a lack of good sense or judgment — see FOOLISH 1
**2** showing poor judgment especially in personal relationships or social situations — see INDISCREET
**unwitting** *adj* **1** happening by chance — see ACCIDENTAL
**2** not informed about or aware of something — see IGNORANT 2
**unwomanly** *adj* having qualities or traits that are traditionally considered inappropriate for a girl or woman — see UNFEMININE
**unwonted** *adj* being out of the ordinary — see EXCEPTIONAL
**unworkable** *adj* not capable of being put to use or account — see IMPRACTICAL
**unworldliness** *n* the quality or state of being simple and sincere — see NAÏVETÉ 1
**unworldly** *adj* lacking in worldly wisdom or informed judgment — see NAIVE 1
**unworried** *adj* free from emotional or mental agitation — see CALM 2
**unwritten** *adj* made or carried on through speaking rather than in writing — see VERBAL 2
**unyielding** *adj* **1** showing no signs of slackening or yielding in one's purpose ⟨the pioneers faced the challenge of settling the frontier with *unyielding* courage⟩
***syn*** determined, dogged, grim, implacable, relentless, unappeasable, unflinching, unrelenting
***rel*** hardheaded, headstrong, mulish, obdurate, opinionated, peevish, pertinacious, perverse, pigheaded, self-willed, stubborn, uncooperative, willful (*or* wilful); merciless, ruthless, unforgiving
***near ant*** slackening, softening, yielding; impotent, invertebrate, slack, spineless, weak
**2** having a consistency that does not easily yield to pressure — see FIRM 2
**3** incapable of or highly resistant to bending — see STIFF 1
**4** sticking to an opinion, purpose, or course of action in spite of reason, arguments, or persuasion — see OBSTINATE
**unyoke** *vb* to set or force apart — see SEPARATE 1
**up** *adj* **1** being at a higher level than average — see HIGH 2
**2** brought or having come to an end — see COMPLETE 2
**3** having information especially as a result of study or experience — see FAMILIAR 2
**up** *vb* **1** to make greater in size, amount, or number — see INCREASE 1
**2** to move from a lower to a higher place or position — see RAISE 1
**3** to move or extend upward — see ASCEND
**upbeat** *adj* **1** having or showing a good mood or disposition — see CHEERFUL 1
**2** having qualities which inspire hope — see HOPEFUL 1
**upbraid** *vb* to criticize (someone) severely or angrily especially for personal failings — see SCOLD
**upcoming** *adj* being soon to appear or take place — see FORTHCOMING
**up–country** *n* a rural region that forms the edge of the settled or developed part of a country — see FRONTIER 2
**upend** *vb* to fix in an upright position — see ERECT 1
**upgrade** *n* **1** an upward slope — see ASCENT 2
**2** a raising or a state of being raised to a higher rank or position — see ADVANCEMENT 1
**3** the degree to which something rises up from a position level with the horizon — see SLANT

**upgrade** *vb* to move higher in rank or position — see PROMOTE 1
**upheaval** *n* a violent disturbance (as of the political or social order) — see CONVULSION
**uphold** *vb* **1** to continue to declare to be true or proper despite opposition or objections — see MAINTAIN 2
**2** to hold up or serve as a foundation for — see SUPPORT 3
**3** to move from a lower to a higher place or position — see RAISE 1
**upkeep** *n* the act or activity of keeping something in an existing and usually satisfactory condition — see MAINTENANCE
**upland** *n* an area of high ground — see HEIGHT 4
**uplift** *vb* to move from a lower to a higher place or position — see RAISE 1
**uplifted** *adj* being positioned above a surface — see ELEVATED 1
**upmost** *adj* being at a point or level higher than all others — see TOP 1
**upon** *prep* in or into contact with — see AGAINST
**upper–class** *adj* of high birth, rank, or station — see NOBLE 1
**upper class** *n* the highest class in a society — see ARISTROCRACY
**upper crust** *n* **1** individuals carefully selected as being the best of a class — see ELITE
**2** the highest class in a society — see ARISTROCRACY
**upper hand** *n* the more favorable condition or position in a competition — see ADVANTAGE 1
**uppermost** *adj* being at a point or level higher than all others — see TOP 1
**uppish** *adj* having a feeling of superiority that shows itself in an overbearing attitude — see ARROGANT
**uppity** *adj* having a feeling of superiority that shows itself in an overbearing attitude — see ARROGANT
**upraise** *vb* **1** to move from a lower to a higher place or position — see RAISE 1
**2** to fix in an upright position — see ERECT 1
**upraised** *adj* being positioned above a surface — see ELEVATED 1
**upright** *adj* **1** conforming to a high standard of morality or virtue — see GOOD 2
**2** following the accepted rules of moral conduct — see HONORABLE 1
**3** rising straight up — see ERECT
**uprightness** *n* **1** conduct that conforms to an accepted standard of right and wrong — see MORALITY 1
**2** faithfulness to high moral standards — see HONOR 1
**uprise** *vb* **1** to leave one's bed — see ARISE 1
**2** to move or extend upward — see ASCEND

---

***syn*** synonym(s) ***rel*** related words
***ant*** antonym(s) ***near ant*** near antonym(s)

**uprising** *n* open fighting against authority (as one's own government) — see REBELLION
**uproar** *n* **1** a state of noisy, confused activity — see COMMOTION
**2** a state of wildly excited activity or emotion — see FRENZY
**3** a violent disturbance (as of the political or social order) — see CONVULSION
**4** a violent shouting — see CLAMOR 1
**uproarious** *adj* causing or intended to cause laughter — see FUNNY 1
**uproot** *vb* to draw out by force or with effort — see EXTRACT
**upset** *adj* feeling or showing uncomfortable feelings of uncertainty — see NERVOUS 1
**upset** *n* an act or instance of the order of things being disturbed ⟨the move to a new town is just the latest in a series of *upsets* for my family over the last year⟩
***syn*** derangement, dislocation, disruption, disturbance
***rel*** convulsion, revolution, upheaval
**upset** *vb* **1** to trouble the mind of; to make uneasy — see DISTURB 1
**2** to turn on one's side or upside down — see CAPSIZE
**3** to undo the proper order or arrangement of — see DISORDER
**upsetting** *adj* causing worry or anxiety — see TROUBLESOME
**upshot** *n* a condition or occurrence traceable to a cause — see EFFECT 1
**upside–down** *adj* lacking in order, neatness, and often cleanliness — see MESSY
**upstanding** *adj* **1** following the accepted rules of moral conduct — see HONORABLE 1
**2** rising straight up — see ERECT
**upsweep** *vb* to move or extend upward — see ASCEND
**uptight** *adj* feeling or showing uncomfortable feelings of uncertainty — see NERVOUS 1
**up–to–date** *adj* **1** being or involving the latest methods, concepts, information, or styles — see MODERN
**2** having information especially as a result of study or experience — see FAMILIAR 2
**upturn** *vb* to move or extend upward — see ASCEND
**urbane** *adj* having or showing very polished and worldly manners — see SUAVE
**urbanize** *vb* to accustom to the ways of the city — see CITIFY
**urchin** *n* an appealingly mischievous person — see SCAMP 1
**urge** *n* a strong wish for something — see DESIRE
**urge** *vb* to try to persuade (someone) through earnest appeals to follow a course of action ⟨our teacher *urged* us to do a good job on the assignment⟩
***syn*** egg (on), encourage, exhort, goad, press, prod, prompt
***rel*** drive, propel, spur, stimulate; hurry, hustle, push, rush; beseech, implore, importune; blandish, cajole, coax, soft-soap,

wheedle; high-pressure, nag, needle, pressure; foment, incite, instigate, provoke, stir (up)
*near ant* deter, discourage, dissuade; brake, check, constrain, curb, hold back, inhibit, restrain
**urgent** *adj* needing immediate attention — see ACUTE 2
**usable** *adj* 1 capable of or suitable for being used for a particular purpose ⟨although the spade was *usable* as a snow shovel, it didn't do a very good job⟩
*syn* available, employable, exploitable, fit, functional, operable, practicable, serviceable, useful
*rel* applicable, relevant; doable, feasible; reusable
*near ant* outdated, outmoded
*ant* impracticable, inoperable, nonfunctional, unavailable, unemployable, unusable
2 capable of being put to use or account — see PRACTICAL 1
**usage** *n* the act or practice of employing something for a particular purpose — see USE 1
**use** *n* 1 the act or practice of employing something for a particular purpose ⟨the *use* of boom boxes was strictly prohibited in the park⟩
*syn* application, employment, exercise, operation, play, usage
*rel* exertion; reuse
*near ant* disuse
2 the capacity for being useful for some purpose ⟨the broken grill wasn't going to be of much *use* in cooking the hamburgers⟩
*syn* account, avail, service, serviceability, serviceableness, usefulness, utility
*rel* advantage, benefit, gain; aid, assistance, help; applicability, appropriateness, fitness, relevance; profit, value, worth
*near ant* inapplicability, inappropriateness
*ant* uselessness, worthlessness
3 positive regard for something — see LIKING
**use** *vb* 1 to put into action or service ⟨I think I'm going to need to *use* the large hammer for this project⟩
*syn* apply, employ, exercise, exploit, harness, operate, utilize
*rel* handle, manipulate, wield; direct, run, work; recycle, reuse
*phrases* draw on (*or* upon), make use of
*near ant* ignore, neglect; misapply, misuse
2 to behave toward in a stated way — see TREAT 1
3 to take unfair advantage of — see EXPLOIT 1
**used** *adj* being in the habit or custom — see ACCUSTOMED
**useful** *adj* 1 capable of being put to use or account — see PRACTICAL 1
2 capable of or suitable for being used for a particular purpose — see USABLE 1
**usefulness** *n* the capacity for being useful for some purpose — see USE 2
**useless** *adj* 1 not capable of being put to use or account — see IMPRACTICAL
2 producing no results — see FUTILE
**user** *n* a person who regularly uses drugs especially illegally — see DOPER
**use up** *vb* to make complete use of — see DEPLETE
**usher** *vb* to point out the way for (someone) especially from a position in front — see LEAD 1
**usual** *adj* 1 accepted, used, or practiced by most people — see CURRENT 1
2 being of the type that is encountered in the normal course of events — see ORDINARY 1
3 often observed or encountered — see COMMON 1
**usually** *adv* according to the usual course of things — see NATURALLY 2
**usurp** *vb* to take or make use of without authority or right — see APPROPRIATE 1
**utensil** *n* an article intended for use in work — see IMPLEMENT
**utility** *n* the capacity for being useful for some purpose — see USE 2
**utilize** *vb* to put into action or service — see USE 1
**utmost** *adj* 1 most distant from a center — see EXTREME 1
2 of the greatest or highest degree or quantity — see ULTIMATE 1
3 of the highest degree — see FULL 2
**utopia** *n* a place or state of great happiness — see PARADISE 1
**utopian** *n* one whose conduct is guided more by the image of perfection than by the real world — see IDEALIST
**utter** *adj* having no exceptions or restrictions — see ABSOLUTE 2
**utter** *vb* 1 to send forth using the vocal chords ⟨she tried not to *utter* a sound as the doctor gave her a flu shot⟩
*syn* emit
*rel* blurt (out), ejaculate, exclaim; gasp, groan, heave, hoot, moan, pant, quaver, snarl, sob, sputter, squawk, squeak, squeal, stammer, stutter, whimper, yowl; mouth, whisper
2 to express (a thought or emotion) in words — see SAY 1
**utterance** *n* 1 an act, process, or means of putting something into words — see EXPRESSION 1
2 something that is said — see WORD 2
**uttered** *adj* created by the body's organs of sound — see VOCAL
**utterly** *adv* 1 to a full extent or degree — see FULLY 1
2 to a large extent or degree — see GREATLY 2
**uttermost** *adj* of the greatest or highest degree or quantity — see ULTIMATE 1

# V

**vacancy** *n* **1** empty space ⟨the vast *vacancy* that exists between our solar system and the nearest star having its own orbiting planets⟩
***syn*** blank, blankness, emptiness, vacuity, void
***rel*** nothingness; vacuum; bareness, barrenness, bleakness, desolateness, hollowness
***near ant*** fullness, repleteness
**2** the quality or state of being empty ⟨the *vacancy* of the cavernous gymnasium was eerily apparent to me as I shot baskets alone⟩
***syn*** bareness, emptiness, vacuity
***rel*** hollowness; blankness, vacuum, void; barrenness, bleakness, desolateness; availability, clearness, openness; depletion, dryness, exhaustion
***near ant*** completeness; abundance, fatness, repleteness
***ant*** fullness

**vacant** *adj* **1** lacking contents that could or should be present — see EMPTY 1
**2** not being in a state of use, activity, or employment — see INACTIVE 2
**3** not expressing any emotion — see BLANK 1

**vacate** *vb* to remove the contents of — see EMPTY

**vacated** *adj* left unoccupied or unused — see ABANDONED

**vacation** *n* a period during which the usual routine of school or work is suspended ⟨we take a *vacation* at the beach for a week every year⟩
***syn*** break, holiday [*chiefly British*], leave, recess
***rel*** furlough, liberty; breather, relaxation, respite, rest; interim, intermission, interval; feast, holy day, legal holiday; honeymoon; idling, loafing, lounging, slacking off
***near ant*** routine, work

**vacation** *vb* to take or spend a vacation ⟨Sue is hoping to *vacation* in Spain this summer⟩
***syn*** holiday
***rel*** escape, get away; break, ease up, let up, relax, rest; bum, goldbrick, idle, loaf, lounge, slack off
***near ant*** drudge, endeavor, grub, hump, hustle, labor, moil, peg (away), plod, plow, plug, slave, slog, strain, strive, struggle, sweat, toil, travail, work

**vacillate** *vb* to show uncertainty about the right course of action — see HESITATE

***syn*** synonym(s) ***rel*** related words
***ant*** antonym(s) ***near ant*** near antonym(s)

**vacillation** *n* the act or an instance of pausing because of uncertainty about the right course of action — see HESITATION

**vacuity** *n* **1** empty space — see VACANCY 1
**2** the quality or state of being empty — see VACANCY 2
**3** the quality or state of lacking intelligence or quickness of mind — see STUPIDITY 1

**vacuous** *adj* not having or showing an ability to absorb ideas readily — see STUPID 1

**vagabond** *adj* traveling from place to place — see ITINERANT

**vagabond** *n* **1** a homeless wanderer who may beg or steal for a living — see TRAMP
**2** a person who roams about without a fixed route or destination — see NOMAD

**vagary** *n* a sudden impulsive and apparently unmotivated idea or action — see WHIM

**vagrant** *adj* traveling from place to place — see ITINERANT

**vagrant** *n* a homeless wanderer who may beg or steal for a living — see TRAMP

**vague** *adj* **1** not clearly expressed ⟨Johnny gave as *vague* a reply to the test question as he could, hoping for partial credit⟩
***syn*** fuzzy, indefinite, unclear
***rel*** ambiguous, cryptic, dark, enigmatic (*also* enigmatical), equivocal, murky, nebulous, obscure, unintelligible; bleary, dim, faint, foggy, hazy, indeterminate, indistinguishable, uncertain, undefinable, undefined, undetermined; inexplicable, inscrutable, mysterious; baffling, bewildering, confounding, confusing, mystifying, perplexing, puzzling, unfathomable
***near ant*** candid, direct, forthright, foursquare, frank, honest, open, openhearted, outspoken, plainspoken, straight, straightforward, unguarded; obvious, plain, unambiguous, understandable, unequivocal; comprehensible, fathomable, intelligible; defined, distinct; blatant, patent, unmistakable
***ant*** clear, definite, explicit, specific
**2** not seen or understood clearly — see FAINT 1

**vain** *adj* **1** having too high an opinion of oneself — see CONCEITED
**2** producing no results — see FUTILE

**vainglorious** *adj* having too high an opinion of oneself — see CONCEITED

**vainglorious**ness *n* an often unjustified feeling of being pleased with oneself or with one's situation or achievements — see COMPLACENCE

**vainglory** *n* an often unjustified feeling of being pleased with oneself or with one's situation or achievements — see COMPLACENCE

**vainness** *n* an often unjustified feeling of being pleased with oneself or with one's situation or achievements — see COMPLACENCE

**vale** *n* an area of lowland between hills or mountains — see VALLEY

**valedictory** *adj* given, taken, or performed at parting — see PARTING

**valiant** *adj* feeling or displaying no fear by temperament — see BRAVE

**valid** *adj* **1** according to the rules of logic — see LOGICAL 1
**2** based on sound reasoning or information — see GOOD 1

**validate** *vb* **1** to give evidence or testimony to the truth or factualness of — see CONFIRM
**2** to show the existence or truth of by evidence — see PROVE 1

**validation** *n* something presented in support of the truth or accuracy of a claim — see PROOF

**valley** *n* an area of lowland between hills or mountains ⟨the *valley* will be the first to flood if the river rises⟩
***syn*** dale, hollow, vale
***rel*** canyon, dell, depression, dingle, glen, ravine, rift valley, basin, bowl
***near ant*** alp, mount, peak; mountain range; mountaintop, pinnacle, precipice, summit

**valor** *n* strength of mind to carry on in spite of danger — see COURAGE

**valorous** *adj* feeling or displaying no fear by temperament — see BRAVE

**valuable** *adj* commanding a large price — see COSTLY

**valuation** *n* **1** the act of placing a value on the nature, character, or quality of something — see ESTIMATE 1
**2** the amount of money for which something will find a buyer — see VALUE 1
**3** the relative usefulness or importance of something as judged by specific qualities — see WORTH 1

**value** *n* **1** the amount of money for which something will find a buyer ⟨the real *value* of that house is close to a million dollars⟩
***syn*** market value, valuation, worth
***rel*** charge, cost, fee, figure, price; appraisal, assessment, estimate, estimation, evaluation; face value, list price, unit price
**2** a quality that gives something special worth — see EXCELLENCE 2
**3** the relative usefulness or importance of something as judged by specific qualities — see WORTH 1

**value** *vb* **1** to hold dear — see LOVE 1
**2** to make an approximate or tentative judgment regarding — see ESTIMATE 1

**valueless** *adj* having no usefulness — see WORTHLESS

**valve** *n* a fixture for controlling the flow of a liquid — see FAUCET

**vandal** *n* a person who damages or destroys property on purpose ⟨a group of *vandals* broke into school and painted graffiti on the walls⟩
***syn*** defacer
***rel*** demolisher, desecrater (*or* desecrator), despoiler, destroyer, dynamiter, ravager, ruiner, saboteur, wrecker; looter, pillager, plunderer, spoiler
***near ant*** conserver, preserver, protector, saver

**vandalism** *n* deliberate damaging or destroying of another's property ⟨anyone guilty of *vandalism* to school property will be expelled⟩
***syn*** defacement
***rel*** demolishing, demolishment, desecrating, desecration, despoiling, despoilment, destruction, ravaging, ruin, ruination, wrecking; sabotage; looting, pillaging, plunder, plundering, sacking
***near ant*** conservation, preservation, protection, saving

**vandalize** *vb* to deliberately cause the damage or destruction of another's property ⟨he decided to *vandalize* the store because the owner had kicked him out⟩
***syn*** deface
***rel*** desecrate, violate; break, damage, despoil, harm, hurt, impair, mar, shatter, spoil; demolish, destroy, devastate, ravage, raze, ruin, scourge, smash, tear down, waste, wipe out, wreck; sabotage; loot, pillage, plunder, sack
***near ant*** conserve, preserve, protect, save; build, rebuild

**vanguard** *n* the leading or most important part of a movement — see FOREFRONT

**vanish** *vb* to cease to be visible — see DISAPPEAR

**vanished** *adj* no longer existing — see EXTINCT

**vanity** *n* an often unjustified feeling of being pleased with oneself or with one's situation or achievements — see COMPLACENCE

**vanquish** *vb* to bring under one's control by force of arms — see CONQUER 1

**vanquisher** *n* one that defeats an enemy or opponent — see VICTOR 1

**vanquishing** *n* the act or process of bringing someone or something under one's control — see CONQUEST

**vantage** *n* the more favorable condition or position in a competition — see ADVANTAGE 1

**variable** *adj* **1** capable of being readily changed — see FLEXIBLE 1
**2** likely to change frequently, suddenly, or unexpectedly — see FICKLE 1

**variance** *n* a lack of agreement or harmony — see DISCORD

**variation** *n* the act, process, or result of making different — see CHANGE

**varicolored** *adj* marked by a variety of usually vivid colors — see COLORFUL

**varied** *adj* consisting of many things of different sorts — see MISCELLANEOUS

**variegated** *adj* **1** marked by a variety of usually vivid colors — see COLORFUL
**2** marked with spots — see SPOTTED 1

**variety** *n* **1** the quality or state of being composed of many different elements or

types ⟨the sheer *variety* of the city's ethnic restaurants was dazzling⟩
***syn*** assortment, diverseness, diversity, miscellaneousness, variousness
***rel*** heterogeneousness; disparateness, disparity, dissimilarity, distinction, distinctiveness, distinctness, unlikeness
***near ant*** homogeneity, likeness, sameness, similarity; fewness, paucity
**2** an unorganized collection or mixture of various things — see MISCELLANY 1

**variousness** *n* the quality or state of being composed of many different elements or types — see VARIETY 1

**varlet** *n* a mean, evil, or unprincipled person — see VILLAIN

**vary** *vb* **1** to be unlike; to not be the same — see DIFFER 1
**2** to make different in some way — see CHANGE 1
**3** to occur within a continuous range of variation — see RUN 4
**4** to pass from one form, state, or level to another — see CHANGE 2

**varying** *adj* not staying constant — see UNEVEN 2

**vast** *adj* unusually large — see HUGE

**vastly** *adv* to a large extent or degree — see GREATLY 2

**vastness** *n* the quality or state of being very large — see IMMENSITY

**vasty** *adj* unusually large — see HUGE

[1]**vault** *n* an underground burial chamber — see CRYPT

[2]**vault** *n* an act of leaping into the air — see JUMP 1

**vault** *vb* to propel oneself upward or forward into the air — see JUMP 1

**veer** *vb* **1** to change one's course or direction — see TURN 3
**2** to change the course or direction of (something) — see TURN 2
**3** to depart abruptly from a straight line or course — see SWERVE 1

**vegetation** *n* green leaves or plants — see GREENERY 1

**vehemence** *n* **1** the quality or state of being forceful (as in expression) ⟨the *vehemence* in her voice when she said that she never gossiped surprised me⟩
***syn*** aggressiveness, assertiveness, emphasis, fierceness, forcefulness, intensity, vigorousness
***rel*** potency, power, strength; eloquence; fervency, insistence, passion, warmth; absoluteness, clearness, incisiveness, plainness
***near ant*** ambiguity, equivocation
***ant*** feebleness, mildness, weakness
**2** depth of feeling — see ARDOR 1

**vehement** *adj* **1** marked by or uttered with forcefulness — see EMPHATIC 1
**2** extreme in degree, power, or effect — see INTENSE
**3** having or expressing great depth of feeling — see FERVENT

***syn*** synonym(s) ***rel*** related words
***ant*** antonym(s) ***near ant*** near antonym(s)

**vehicle** *n* **1** something used to achieve an end — see AGENT 1
**2** something used to carry goods or passengers — see CONVEYANCE

**veil** *n* something that covers or conceals like a piece of cloth — see CLOAK 1

**veil** *vb* **1** to keep secret or shut off from view — see [1]HIDE 2
**2** to surround or cover closely — see ENFOLD 1

**vein** *n* a distinctive way of putting ideas into words — see STYLE 1

**veld** *or* **veldt** *n* a broad area of level or rolling treeless country — see PLAIN

**velocity** *n* a high rate of movement or performance — see SPEED

**velvety** *adj* smooth or delicate in appearance or feel — see SOFT 2

**venal** *adj* open to improper influence and especially bribery ⟨that judge is known for being *venal* and easily bought⟩
***syn*** bribable, corruptible, purchasable
***rel*** hack, mercenary; crooked, cutthroat, dishonest, unethical, unprincipled, unscrupulous; corrupt, debased, debauched, degenerate, degraded, demoralized, depraved, dissipated, dissolute, perverse, perverted, warped; bad, evil, immoral, iniquitous, nefarious, sinful, vicious, wicked
***near ant*** ethical, honest, principled; good, moral, righteous, virtuous
***ant*** incorruptible, uncorruptible

**vend** *vb* to offer for sale to the public — see MARKET

**vendor** *also* **vender** *n* the person in a business deal who hands over an item in exchange for money ⟨we're thinking of making a deal with that other software *vendor*⟩
***syn*** dealer, merchandiser, seller
***rel*** auctioneer, concessionaire; blackmarketer, bootlegger, fence, fencer, hustler, smuggler, trader; distributor, retailer; sacrificer; wholesaler; hawker, huckster, peddler (*also* pedlar); salesclerk, salesman, salesperson, saleswoman; exporter, handler; bargainer, haggler, horse trader, palterer
***near ant*** consumer, end user, user
***ant*** buyer, purchaser

**veneer** *n* an outer part or layer — see EXTERIOR

**venerable** *adj* **1** deserving honor and respect especially by reason of age ⟨the *venerable* old man was a cherished source of advice and wisdom for the villagers⟩
***syn*** hallowed, revered, reverend, venerated
***rel*** honorable, reputable, respectable; honored, respected, reverenced; admirable, estimable, redoubtable; good, moral, righteous
***near ant*** bad, discreditable, disgraceful, dishonorable, disreputable, ignominious, infamous, loose, notorious, shameful; immoral, seamy, shady, sordid, unsavory, vile, wicked; base, contemptible, despicable, detestable, dirty, low, mean, wretched

2 dating or surviving from the distant past — see ANCIENT 1

**venerate** *vb* to offer honor or respect to (someone) as a divine power — see WORSHIP 1

**venerated** *adj* deserving honor and respect especially by reason of age — see VENERABLE 1

**vengeance** *n* the act or an instance of paying back an injury with an injury — see REVENGE

**vengeful** *adj* likely to seek revenge — see VINDICTIVE

**venial** *adj* worthy of forgiveness ⟨stealing pencils is a *venial* offense⟩
*syn* excusable, forgivable, pardonable, remittable
*rel* justifiable, redeemable; allowable; insignificant, minor, trifling, trivial; harmless, tolerable
*near ant* abominable, criminal, damning, evil, heinous; sinful, vile, wicked
*ant* inexcusable, mortal, unforgivable, unpardonable

**venom** *n* 1 a substance that by chemical action can kill or injure a living thing — see POISON
2 the desire to cause pain for the satisfaction of doing harm — see MALICE

**venomous** *adj* containing or contaminated with a substance capable of injuring or killing a living thing — see POISONOUS

**vent** *vb* 1 to find emotional release for — see TAKE OUT 1
2 to make known (as an idea, emotion, or opinion) — see EXPRESS 1
3 to throw or give off — see EMIT 1

**ventilate** *vb* to make known (as an idea, emotion, or opinion) — see EXPRESS 1

**venture** *n* a risky undertaking — see GAMBLE

**venture** *vb* 1 to place in danger — see ENDANGER
2 to take a chance on — see RISK 1

**venturesome** *adj* 1 inclined or willing to take risks — see BOLD 1
2 involving potential loss or injury — see DANGEROUS

**venturous** *adj* inclined or willing to take risks — see BOLD 1

**veracious** *adj* 1 being in the habit of telling the truth — see TRUTHFUL
2 following an original exactly — see FAITHFUL 2

**veracity** *n* 1 devotion to telling the truth — see HONESTY 1
2 the quality or state of being very accurate — see PRECISION

**verbal** *adj* 1 of or relating to words or language ⟨the child didn't yet have the *verbal* skills needed to tell the doctor about the pain he was experiencing⟩
*syn* lexical, linguistic
*rel* communicative, conversational
2 made or carried on through speaking rather than in writing ⟨a *verbal* agreement carries less force than a written contract⟩
*syn* oral, spoken, unwritten
*rel* implicit, informal; articulated, verbalized; given, pronounced, said, sounded, stated, told, voiced
*near ant* explicit, formal
*ant* written

**verbalize** *vb* to express (a thought or emotion) in words — see SAY 1

**verbatim** *adv* in the same words ⟨you can't just copy the encyclopedia article *verbatim* for your report—that's plagiarism⟩
*syn* directly, exactly
*rel* accurately, precisely; identically; literally
*phrases* word for word
*near ant* basically, essentially; carelessly, freely, imprecisely, inaccurately, loosely
*ant* inexactly

**verbiage** *n* the use of too many words to express an idea ⟨teachers loathe the *verbiage* that students resort to in order to pad a paper⟩
*syn* circumlocution, diffuseness, longwindedness, prolixity, redundancy, verboseness, verbosity, windiness, wordiness
*rel* circuitousness, circularity; tautology; reiteration, repetition, repetitiousness; embellishment, embroidering, exaggeration, hyperbole
*near ant* brevity, briefness, compactness, conciseness, crispness, pithiness, succinctness, terseness

**verbose** *adj* using or containing more words than necessary to express an idea — see WORDY

**verboseness** *n* the use of too many words to express an idea — see VERBIAGE

**verbosity** *n* the use of too many words to express an idea — see VERBIAGE

**verdant** *adj* covered with a thick, healthy natural growth — see LUSH 1

**verdict** *n* 1 a position arrived at after consideration — see DECISION 1
2 an idea that is believed to be true or valid without positive knowledge — see OPINION 1

**verdure** *n* green leaves or plants — see GREENERY 1

**verge** (on)*vb* 1 to be adjacent to — see ADJOIN 1
2 to come very close to being — see BORDER (ON)

**verge** *n* the line or relatively narrow space that marks the outer limit of something — see BORDER 1

**verging** *adj* having a border in common — see ADJACENT

**verifiable** *adj* capable of being proven as true or real ⟨we're not sure whether that's a *verifiable* hypothesis⟩ ⟨you need a *verifiable* note from your doctor to be excused from gym class⟩
*syn* confirmable, demonstrable, provable, supportable, sustainable
*rel* certifiable, documentable, warrantable; excusable, justifiable; alleged, assumed, conjectured, guessed, presumed, surmised, suspected
*near ant* debatable, disputable, refutable
*ant* insupportable, unsupportable

**verify** *vb* to give evidence or testimony to the truth or factualness of — see CONFIRM
**verifying** *adj* serving to give support to the truth or factualness of something — see CORROBORATIVE
**verily** *adv* **1** to tell the truth — see ACTUALLY 1
**2** not merely this but also — see EVEN
**veritably** *adv* in actual fact — see VERY 2
**verity** *n* **1** agreement with fact or reality — see TRUTH
**2** devotion to telling the truth — see HONESTY 1
**vernacular** *adj* used in or suitable for speech and not formal writing — see COLLOQUIAL 1
**versatile** *adj* able to do many different kinds of things ⟨a *versatile* baseball player can play any position⟩ ⟨this tool is *versatile* enough to serve as a wrench or pliers⟩
***syn*** adaptable, all-around (*also* all-round), protean, universal
***rel*** multipurpose; well-rounded; able, ace, adept, experienced, expert, masterful, skilled, skillful; adjustable, alterable, changeable, elastic, flexible, fluid, malleable, modifiable, variable
***near ant*** limited; amateur, inexperienced
**verse** *n* **1** a composition using rhythm and often rhyme to create a lyrical effect — see POEM
**2** writing that uses rhythm, vivid language, and often rhyme to provoke an emotional response — see POETRY 1
**versed** *adj* **1** having information especially as a result of study or experience — see FAMILIAR 2
**2** having or showing exceptional knowledge, experience, or skill in a field of endeavor — see PROFICIENT
**versifier** *n* a person who writes poetry — see POET
**vertebral column** *n* a column of bones supporting the trunk of a vertebrate animal — see SPINE
**vertical** *adj* rising straight up — see ERECT
**verve** *adj* active strength of body or mind — see VIGOR 1
**very** *adj* **1** being one and not another — see SAME 2
**2** being this and no more — see MERE
**3** existing in fact and not merely as a possibility — see ACTUAL
**very** *adv* **1** to a great degree ⟨that was a *very* brave thing to do⟩
***syn*** awful, awfully, beastly, deadly, especially, exceedingly (*also* exceeding), extra, extremely, far, frightfully, full, greatly, heavily, highly, hugely, jolly, mightily, mighty, mortally, most, much, particularly, rattling, real, right, so, something, super, terribly, too, whacking
***rel*** completely, entirely, purely, thoroughly, totally, utterly; eminently, exceptionally; considerably, extensively, significantly, substantially; appreciably, discernibly, noticeably, palpably; abundantly, plentifully; astronomically, grandly, monstrously, monumentally
***phrases*** by far, far and away, good and, in particular
***near ant*** meagerly, scantily; barely, hardly, just, marginally, minimally, scarcely
***ant*** little, negligibly, nominally, slightly
**2** in actual fact ⟨the *very* same thing happened to me⟩
***syn*** actually, authentically, genuinely, really, veritably
***rel*** accurately, exactly, just, precisely, right, sharp, smack-dab, squarely; almost, nearly, practically; literally, truly
***phrases*** in truth
***near ant*** apparently, ostensibly, outwardly, seemingly
***ant*** professedly, supposedly
**vessel** *n* **1** a large craft for travel by water — see SHIP
**2** a small buoyant structure for travel on water — see BOAT 1
**3** a usually circular utensil for holding something (as food) — see DISH
**4** something into which a liquid or smaller objects can be put for storage or transportation — see CONTAINER
**vest** *vb* to put (something) into the possession or safekeeping of another — see GIVE 2
**vestibule** *n* the entrance room of a building — see HALL 1
**vestige** *n* a tiny often physical indication of something lost or vanished ⟨a few strange words carved on a tree were the only *vestige* of the lost colony of Roanoke⟩
***syn*** relic, shadow, trace
***rel*** memento, remembrance, reminder; artifact; afterimage, aftertaste; balance, oddment, remainder, remnant, scrap, scraping(s); leavings, remains, residual, residue, rest
**vestry** *n* a room in a church building for sacred furnishings (as vestments) — see SACRISTY
**vet** *n* a person with long experience in a specified area — see VETERAN
**veteran** *adj* having or showing exceptional knowledge, experience, or skill in a field of endeavor — see PROFICIENT
**veteran** *n* a person with long experience in a specified area ⟨as a *veteran* of politics, she is often consulted by eager young hopefuls⟩
***syn*** old hand, old-timer, vet
***rel*** war-horse; expert, master, pro, professional
***near ant*** apprentice, cub; boot, novitiate; amateur, dilettante; learner, student, trainee; candidate, entrant, probationer
***ant*** beginner, colt, fledgling, freshman, greenhorn, neophyte, newcomer, novice, recruit, rookie, tenderfoot, tyro
**veto** *n* an order that something not be done or used — see PROHIBITION 2
**veto** *vb* to reject by or as if by a vote — see NEGATIVE 1

**vex** *vb* to disturb the peace of mind of (someone) especially by repeated disagreeable acts — see IRRITATE 1

**vexation** *n* 1 the act of making unwelcome intrusions upon another — see ANNOYANCE 1
2 the feeling of impatience or anger caused by another's repeated disagreeable acts — see ANNOYANCE 2

**vexatious** *adj* causing annoyance — see ANNOYING

**vexing** *adj* causing annoyance — see ANNOYING

**via** *prep* along the way of — see BY 1

**viable** *adj* capable of being done or carried out — see POSSIBLE 1

**viands** *n pl* substances intended to be eaten — see FOOD

**vibrancy** *n* the quality or state of having abundant or intense activity — see VITALITY 1

**vibrant** *adj* 1 marked by much life, movement, or activity — see ALIVE 2
2 marked by conspicuously full and rich sounds or tones — see RESONANT

**vibrate** *vb* to make a series of small irregular or violent movements — see SHAKE 1

**vibration** *n* a series of slight movements by a body back and forth or from side to side ⟨the *vibration* of the floor caused by thundering feet in the hallway⟩
*syn* jiggling, oscillation, quivering, shaking, shuddering, trembling, twitching
*rel* jiggle, palpitation, shake, shudder, tremor, twitch

**vice** *n* 1 immoral conduct or practices harmful or offensive to society ⟨that section of the city is legendary for crime and *vice*⟩
*syn* corruption, debauchery, depravity, immorality, iniquity, licentiousness, sin
*rel* bad, badness, blackness, evil, evildoing, ill, wickedness, wrong, villainy; atrociousness, evilness, heinousness, nefariousness, sinfulness, unscrupulousness, viciousness, vileness; devilry (*or* deviltry), fiendishness; corruptness, debasement, degeneracy degeneration, depravedness, dissolution; indecency, lasciviousness, lewdness, looseness, perversion; abomination, anathema, taboo (*also* tabu); criminality, reprehensibleness; baseness, despicableness, dirtiness, lowness, meanness; lousiness, miserableness, wretchedness
*near ant* good, right; honesty, honor, integrity, legitimacy, probity, rectitude, scrupulousness, uprightness; goodness, righteousness, virtuousness; blamelessness; chastity, innocence, perfection, pureness, purity, spotlessness; cleanness, correctness, decency, decorousness, propriety, rightness, seemliness
*ant* morality, virtue
2 a defect in character — see FAULT 1

**vicious** *adj* 1 extreme in degree, power, or effect — see INTENSE
2 having or showing the desire to inflict severe pain and suffering on others — see CRUEL 1
3 not conforming to a high moral standard; morally unacceptable — see BAD 2
4 violently unfriendly or aggressive in disposition — see FIERCE 1

**viciously** *adv* in a mean or spiteful manner — see NASTILY

**viciousness** *n* 1 the desire to cause pain for the satisfaction of doing harm — see MALICE
2 the willful infliction of pain and suffering on others — see CRUELTY

**victim** *n* 1 a person or thing harmed, lost, or destroyed — see CASUALTY 1
2 a person or thing that is the object of abuse, criticism, or ridicule — see TARGET 1
3 something offered to a god — see SACRIFICE

**victimize** *vb* to rob by the use of trickery or threats — see FLEECE

**victor** *n* 1 one that defeats an enemy or opponent ⟨the computer is usually the *victor* in a chess match against a human opponent⟩
*syn* beater, conqueror, master, subduer, trimmer, vanquisher, whipper, winner
*rel* champion, finalist; ruler, subjugator
*near ant* pushover, quitter; failure, flop, washout
*ant* loser
2 the person who comes in first in a competition — see CHAMPION 1

**victory** *n* an instance of defeating an enemy or opponent ⟨with great effort, our team managed an upset *victory* in the final moments⟩
*syn* triumph, win
*rel* conquest, mastery, subjugation, vanquishing; landslide, shutout, sweep; success; takeover
*near ant* upset; collapse, debacle (*also* débâcle), failure, fizzle, flop, folding, nonsuccess, washout; decline, slip, slump, wane; lurch, setback
*ant* beating, defeat, licking, loss, overthrow, rout, shellacking, trimming, whipping

**victuals** *n pl* substances intended to be eaten — see FOOD

**vie** *vb* to engage in a contest — see COMPETE

**view** *n* 1 all that can be seen from a certain point ⟨the *view* of the mountains from the inn's porch is spectacular⟩
*syn* lookout, outlook, panorama, prospect, vista
*rel* landscape, scene, scenery; ken, sight
2 an idea that is believed to be true or valid without positive knowledge — see OPINION 1
3 an instance of looking especially briefly — see LOOK 2

**view** *vb* to make note of (something) through the use of one's eyes — see SEE 1

**viewpoint** *n* a way of looking at or thinking about something — see POINT OF VIEW

**vigilance** *n* the act or state of being constantly attentive and responsive to signs

of opportunity, activity, or danger ⟨eternal *vigilance* is the price of freedom⟩
***syn*** alertness, attentiveness, lookout, surveillance, watch, watchfulness
***rel*** aliveness, awareness, consciousness, sensitivity; heedfulness, observance, observation; sleeplessness, wakefulness; care, carefulness, caution, chariness, wariness; preparation, readiness
***near ant*** absentmindedness, absorption, abstraction, daydreaming, daze, distraction; engrossment, obliviousness, preoccupation; unawareness, unconsciousness; carelessness, heedlessness, inattention, inattentiveness; unwariness

**vigilant** *adj* paying close attention usually for the purpose of anticipating approaching danger or opportunity — see ALERT 1

**vigilante** *n* one who inflicts punishment in return for an injury or offense — see NEMESIS 1

**vigor** *n* **1** active strength of body or mind ⟨she was picked for the soccer team because of her *vigor* and enthusiasm⟩
***syn*** bounce, dash, drive, energy, esprit, ginger, go, hardihood, life, pep, punch, sap, snap, starch, verve, vim, vitality, zing, zip
***rel*** animation, briskness, jauntiness, liveliness, spiritedness, sprightliness, vivaciousness, vivacity; ardor, fervor, fire, passion, zeal; main, might, muscle, potency, power, puissance, strength; brawniness, fitness, hardiness, huskiness, virility; haleness, health, healthiness, soundness, wellness
***near ant*** indolence, laziness; debilitation, debility, delicacy, delicateness, disablement, enfeeblement, faintness, feebleness, frailness, frailty, impotence, infirmity, powerlessness, puniness, slightness, softness, tenderness, weakness; enervation, exhaustion, prostration
***ant*** lethargy, listlessness, sluggishness
**2** the ability to exert effort for the accomplishment of a task — see POWER 2

**vigorous** *adj* **1** having active strength of body or mind ⟨he remains healthy and *vigorous* despite being over eighty years old⟩
***syn*** dynamic, energetic, flush, gingery, lusty, peppy, red-blooded, robust, vital
***rel*** animated, lively, spirited, sprightly, vivacious; energized, enlivened, invigorated, vitalized; firm, fortified, mettlesome, mighty, powerful, puissant, strong; refreshed, rejuvenated, revitalized; able-bodied, beefy, brawny, fit, fortified, hardy, husky, rugged, stalwart, stout, strapping, sturdy, tough; hale, healthy, sound; capable, competent
***near ant*** delicate, effete, enervated, faint, feeble, frail, infirm, weak, weakened; impotent, powerless, prostrate, prostrated, sapped, tired; indolent, lackadaisical, languid, lazy; invertebrate, nerveless, soft, spineless, wimpy; ill, unhealthy, unsound, unwell; broken-down, debilitated, decrepit, disabled, wasted, worn-out
***ant*** lethargic, listless, sluggish, torpid
**2** able to withstand hardship, strain, or exposure — see HARDY 1
**3** marked by or uttered with forcefulness — see EMPHATIC 1
**4** not showing weakness or uncertainty — see FIRM 1

**vigorously** *adv* in a vigorous and forceful manner — see HARD 3

**vigorousness** *n* the quality or state of being forceful (as in expression) — see VEHEMENCE 1

**vile** *adj* **1** not conforming to a high moral standard; morally unacceptable — see BAD 2
**2** not following or in accordance with standards of honor and decency — see IGNOBLE 2
**3** unpleasant to look at — see UGLY 1

**vileness** *n* the state or quality of being utterly evil — see ENORMITY 1

**vilification** *n* the making of false statements that damage another's reputation — see SLANDER

**vilify** *vb* to make untrue and harmful statements about — see SLANDER

**vilifying** *n* the making of false statements that damage another's reputation — see SLANDER

**villa** *n* a large impressive residence — see MANSION

**villager** *n* a person who lives in a town on a permanent basis — see BURGHER

**villain** *n* a mean, evil, or unprincipled person ⟨only a heartless *villain* would kidnap a baby for ransom⟩
***syn*** beast, brute, devil, evildoer, fiend, heavy, knave, miscreant, monster, no-good, rapscallion, rascal, reprobate, rogue, savage, scalawag (*or* scallywag), scamp, scoundrel, varlet, wretch
***rel*** blackguard; criminal, crook, culprit, felon, lawbreaker, malefactor, offender, transgressor; perpetrator, sinner, trespasser, wrongdoer; cad, heel; bravo, desperado, outlaw; convict, jailbird; assassin, cutthroat, gangster, gunman, hoodlum, racketeer, ruffian, thug; ne'er-do-well, trash
***near ant*** angel, saint; hero

**villainous** *adj* not conforming to a high moral standard; morally unacceptable — see BAD 2

**villainously** *adv* in a mean or spiteful manner — see NASTILY

**villainy** *n* that which is morally unacceptable — see EVIL

**vim** *n* active strength of body or mind — see VIGOR 1

**vindicate** *vb* **1** to free from a charge of wrongdoing — see EXCULPATE
**2** to give evidence or testimony to the truth or factualness of — see CONFIRM

**vindicating** *adj* serving to give support to the truth or factualness of something — see CORROBORATIVE

---

***syn*** synonym(s) ***rel*** related words
***ant*** antonym(s) ***near ant*** near antonym(s)

**vindictive** *adj* likely to seek revenge ⟨be careful not to annoy the *vindictive* old woman who lives down the street⟩
***syn*** revengeful, vengeful
***rel*** avenging; resentful, uncharitable, unforgiving; catty, cruel, despiteful, hateful, malevolent, malicious, malign, malignant, mean, nasty, sadistic, spiteful, vicious, virulent; grim, implacable, merciless, relentless, unrelenting; baleful, baneful, evil; harsh, hostile, inimical
***near ant*** charitable, forgiving, merciful, relenting; benevolent, benign, benignant, loving; brotherly, compassionate, good, good-hearted, kind, kindhearted, kindly, sympathetic, warm, warmhearted; altruistic, humane, humanitarian, philanthropic; sweet, tender, tenderhearted; high-minded, magnanimous, noble

**vinegary** *adj* causing or characterized by the one of the four basic taste sensations that is produced chiefly by acids — see SOUR 1

**violate** *vb* **1** to fail to keep ⟨you *violated* the school rule against swearing at sporting events⟩
***syn*** breach, break, infringe, transgress
***rel*** disobey, rebel; brush off, disregard, ignore, overlook, overpass, pass over, tune out, wink (at); dismiss, pooh-pooh (*also* pooh), scorn, shrug off; defy, resist, withstand
***near ant*** defer (to), serve, submit (to), surrender (to), yield (to); attend, hear, heed, listen (to), mark, note, notice, regard, watch
***ant*** comply (with), conform (to), follow, mind, obey, observe
**2** to treat (a sacred place or object) shamefully or with great disrespect — see DESECRATE

**violation** *n* **1** a breaking of a moral or legal code — see OFFENSE 1
**2** a failure to uphold the requirements of law, duty, or obligation — see BREACH 1

**violence** *n* the use of brute strength to cause harm to a person or property ⟨the police believe that the woman died of natural causes rather than as a result of *violence*⟩
***syn*** force, foul play
***rel*** coercion, compulsion, constraint, duress, pressure; damage, detriment, harm, hurt, impairment, injury; crippling, maiming, mayhem, mutilation; assault, attack, bashing, battering, battery, batting, beating, beating, bludgeoning, buffeting, clubbing, drubbing, flogging, hammering, lacing, licking, mauling, pelting, pommeling, pounding, pummeling, thrashing, thumping, walloping, whaling, whipping; onslaught, outbreak, outrage, paroxysm, rampage, revolt, riot, shock, terror, threat, turbulence, upheaval, uproar; browbeating, bulldozing, bullying
***near ant*** pacifism
***ant*** nonviolence

**violent** *adj* **1** marked by bursts of destructive force or intense activity ⟨a *violent* fight that left several people badly hurt⟩
***syn*** explosive, ferocious, fierce, furious, hot, rabid, rough, stormy, tempestuous, turbulent, volcanic
***rel*** brutal, savage, vicious; antagonistic, hostile; aggressive, assertive, bellicose, belligerent, combative, contentious, gladiatorial, quarrelsome; frantic, frenzied, mad; destructive, ruinous
***near ant*** calm, pacific, serene, tranquil; nonbelligerent, unaggressive, unassertive
***ant*** nonviolent, peaceable, peaceful
**2** extreme in degree, power, or effect — see INTENSE
**3** marked by great and often stressful excitement or activity — see FURIOUS 1

**VIP** *n* a person who is widely known and usually much talked about — see CELEBRITY 1

**viper** *n* a limbless reptile with a long body — see SNAKE 1

**virago** *n* a bad-tempered scolding woman — see SHREW

**virgin** *adj* **1** never having had sexual relations ⟨*virgin* boys are sometimes unfairly teased⟩
***syn*** maiden, virginal
***rel*** chaste, modest, pure; innocent, untouched; abstinent, celibate; unmarried, unwed
**2** being in an original and unused or unspoiled state — see FRESH 1

**virginal** *adj* never having had sexual relations — see VIRGIN 1

**virile** *adj* considered characteristic of or appropriate for men — see MASCULINE

**virility** *n* the set of qualities considered appropriate for or characteristic of men ⟨many cultures value *virility* as a sign of power⟩
***syn*** manhood, manliness, masculinity
***rel*** maleness; boyishness, mannishness, tomboyishness
***near ant*** girlishness; femaleness; girlhood, maidenhood
***ant*** femininity

**virtually** *adv* very close to but not completely — see ALMOST

**virtue** *n* **1** a quality that gives something special worth — see EXCELLENCE 2
**2** conduct that conforms to an accepted standard of right and wrong — see MORALITY 1

**virtuoso** *adj* **1** accomplished with trained ability — see SKILLFUL
**2** having or showing exceptional knowledge, experience, or skill in a field of endeavor — see PROFICIENT

**virtuoso** *n* a person with a high level of knowledge or skill in a field — see EXPERT

**virtuous** *adj* conforming to a high standard of morality or virtue — see GOOD 2

**virtuously** *adv* with purity of thought and deed — see PURELY

**virtuousness** *n* conduct that conforms to an accepted standard of right and wrong — see MORALITY 1

**virulence** *n* biting sharpness of feeling or expression — see ACRIMONY 1

**virulent** *adj* having or showing a desire to cause someone pain or suffering for the sheer enjoyment of it — see HATEFUL
**virulently** *adv* in a mean or spiteful manner — see NASTILY
**visage** *n* **1** facial appearance regarded as an indication of mood or feeling — see LOOK 1
**2** the front part of the head — see FACE 1
**viscera** *n pl* the internal organs of the body — see GUT 1
**viscid** *adj* **1** being of a consistency that resists flow — see THICK 2
**2** being of such a thick consistency as to readily cling to objects upon contact — see STICKY 1
**viscosity** *n* the degree to which a fluid can resist flowing — see CONSISTENCY
**viscous** *adj* **1** being of a consistency that resists flow — see THICK 2
**2** being of such a thick consistency as to readily cling to objects upon contact — see STICKY 1
**visible** *adj* capable of being seen ⟨the *visible* light spectrum runs from red to violet⟩
***syn*** apparent, observable, seeable, visual
***rel*** external, outer, outward; detectable, discernible, noticeable, perceptible; clear, conspicuous, evident, eye-catching, manifest, obvious, plain, prominent, striking
***near ant*** disappeared, dissolved, evanesced, evaporated, melted, vanished; imperceptible, inconspicuous, indistinct, unnoticeable; faint, insignificant, slight, vague; buried, concealed, covert, disguised, hidden, latent, obscure, shrouded
***ant*** invisible, unseeable
**vision** *n* **1** a conception or image created by the imagination and having no objective reality — see FANTASY 1
**2** a series of often striking pictures created by the imagination during sleep — see DREAM 1
**3** the ability to see — see EYESIGHT
**4** the soul of a dead person thought of especially as appearing to living people — see GHOST
**vision** *vb* to form a mental picture of — see IMAGINE 1
**visionary** *n* one whose conduct is guided more by the image of perfection than by the real world — see IDEALIST
**visit** *n* **1** a temporary residing as another's guest ⟨my aunt always looks forward to her week-long annual *visit* with her mother⟩
***syn*** sojourn, stay
***rel*** field trip; layover, stopover
**2** a coming to see another briefly for social or business reasons — see CALL 2
**visit** *vb* **1** to make a social call upon ⟨the club ladies make a point of *visiting* everyone who moves into the neighborhood⟩
***syn*** call (on *or* upon), see
***rel*** look up, seek (out); frequent, hang out (at), haunt
***phrases*** drop in on
***near ant*** brush (off), cold-shoulder, ignore, snub
**2** to reside as a temporary guest ⟨Johnny loves it when his friend Susie comes to *visit* for a month every summer⟩
***syn*** sojourn, stay, tarry
***rel*** frequent, hang out (at), haunt; inhabit, occupy
***near ant*** abide, dwell, live, reside
**3** to engage in casual or rambling conversation — see CHAT
**4** to go to or spend time in often — see FREQUENT
**5** to make a brief visit — see CALL 3
**visitant** *n* a person who visits another — see GUEST
**visitation** *n* a coming to see another briefly for social or business reasons — see CALL 2
**visitor** *n* a person who visits another — see GUEST 1
**visor** *also* **vizor** *n* the projecting front part of a hat or cap ⟨the *visor* of her baseball cap shades her eyes nicely⟩
***syn*** bill, brim, peak
***rel*** shade
**vista** *n* all that can be seen from a certain point — see VIEW 1
**visual** *adj* **1** of, relating to, or used in vision ⟨the eyes are the primary *visual* organs in humans⟩
***syn*** ocular, optic, optical
***rel*** seeing, sighted; focusing
***ant*** nonvisual
**2** capable of being seen — see VISIBLE
**3** consisting of or relating to pictures — see PICTORIAL 1
**visualize** *vb* to form a mental picture of — see IMAGINE 1
**vital** *adj* **1** having active strength of body or mind — see VIGOROUS 1
**2** having much high-spirited energy and movement — see LIVELY 1
**3** impossible to do without — see ESSENTIAL 1
**4** likely to cause or capable of causing death — see DEADLY
**5** of the greatest possible importance — see CRUCIAL
**vitality** *n* **1** the quality or state of having abundant or intense activity ⟨a city known for the *vitality* of its entertainment and sports scenes⟩
***syn*** animation, briskness, exuberance, jazziness, liveliness, lustiness, peppiness, robustness, sprightliness, vibrancy
***rel*** buoyancy, jauntiness, springiness; brightness, cheer, cheerfulness, effervescence, vivacity, vivaciousness; eagerness, enthusiasm, keenness, spiritedness; friskiness, impishness, pertness, playfulness
***near ant*** indolence, laziness; languor, lethargy, limpness, listlessness, sleepiness, sluggishness, torpor, weariness; apathy, impassivity; dullness (*or* dulness), tediousness, tedium
***ant*** inactivity, lifelessness
**2** active strength of body or mind — see VIGOR 1

---

***syn*** synonym(s) ***rel*** related words
***ant*** antonym(s) ***near ant*** near antonym(s)

**vitalize** *vb* to give life, vigor, or spirit to — see ANIMATE
**vitalizing** *adj* having a renewing effect on the state of the body or mind — see TONIC
**vitals** *n pl* the internal organs of the body — see GUT 1
**vitiate** *vb* **1** to affect slightly with something morally bad or undesirable — see TAINT 1
**2** to reduce the soundness, effectiveness, or perfection of — see DAMAGE 1
**vitriol** *n* **1** biting sharpness of feeling or expression — see ACRIMONY 1
**2** harsh insulting language — see ABUSE 1
**vittles** *n pl* substances intended to be eaten — see FOOD
**vituperate** *vb* to criticize harshly and usually publicly — see ATTACK 2
**vituperation** *n* harsh insulting language — see ABUSE 1
**vivacious** *adj* **1** having much high-spirited energy and movement — see LIVELY 1
**2** joyously unrestrained — see EXUBERANT
**vivid** *adj* producing a mental picture through clear and impressive description — see GRAPHIC 1
**vivify** *vb* to give life, vigor, or spirit to — see ANIMATE
**vizard** *n* a cover or partial cover for the face used to disguise oneself — see MASK 1
**vocabulary** *n* **1** the special terms or expressions of a particular group or field — see TERMINOLOGY
**2** the stock of words, pronunciation, and grammar used by a people as their basic means of communication — see LANGUAGE 1
**vocal** *adj* created by the body's organs of sound ⟨our cat is given to making strange *vocal* noises in the dead of night⟩
***syn*** oral, uttered, voiced
***rel*** articulate, articulated, spoken; breathed, drawled, gasped, mouthed, mumbled, murmured, muttered, shouted, spluttered, sputtered, whispered
***near ant*** inarticulate; mute, quiet, silent; unexpressed, unspoken, unuttered, unvoiced
***ant*** nonvocal
**vocal** *n* a short musical composition for the human voice often with instrumental accompaniment — see SONG 1
**vocalist** *n* one who sings — see SINGER
**vocalize** *vb* **1** to express (a thought or emotion) in words — see SAY 1
**2** to produce musical sounds with the voice — see SING 1
**vocalizer** *n* one who sings — see SINGER
**vocation** *n* the activity by which one regularly makes a living — see OCCUPATION
**vociferate** *vb* to speak so as to be heard at a distance — see CALL 1
**vociferous** *adj* engaging in or marked by loud and insistent cries especially of protest ⟨*vociferous* opponents of the bill protested angrily outside the chambers of the legislature⟩
***syn*** blatant, clamorous, obstreperous
***rel*** clangorous, dinning, discordant, noisy; loudmouthed, outspoken, vocal; boisterous, rowdy, uproarious; cacophonous, dissonant, shrill, strident; blaring, booming, brassy, brazen
***near ant*** noiseless, quiet, silent, soundless, still; calm, hushed, subdued
**vogue** *adj* enjoying widespread favor or approval — see POPULAR 1
**vogue** *n* **1** a practice or interest that is very popular for a short time — see FAD
**2** the state of enjoying widespread approval — see POPULARITY
**voice** *n* **1** the right to express a wish, choice, or opinion ⟨everyone will have a *voice* in the decision of where to go for our field trip⟩
***syn*** say, vote
***rel*** part, role, share; enfranchisement, franchise, suffrage; judgment (*or* judgement), say-so; belief, conviction, opinion, sentiment, view
**2** an act, process, or means of putting something into words — see EXPRESSION 1
**3** one who sings — see SINGER
**voice** *vb* to make known (as an idea, emotion, or opinion) — see EXPRESS 1
**voiced** *adj* created by the body's organs of sound — see VOCAL
**voiceless** *adj* unable to speak — see MUTE 1
**void** *vb* to put an end to by formal action — see ABOLISH
**void** *adj* **1** having no legal or binding force — see NULL 1
**2** lacking contents that could or should be present — see EMPTY 1
**3** utterly lacking in something needed, wanted, or expected — see DEVOID 1
**void** *n* empty space — see VACANCY 1
**void** *vb* to remove the contents of — see EMPTY
**volatile** *adj* likely to change frequently, suddenly, or unexpectedly — see FICKLE 1
**volcanic** *adj* marked by bursts of destructive force or intense activity — see VIOLENT 1
**volition** *n* the act or power of making one's own choices or decisions — see FREE WILL
**volley** *n* a rapid or overwhelming outpouring of many things at once — see BARRAGE
**volume** *n* **1** a considerable amount — see LOT 2
**2** a given or particular mass or aggregate of matter — see AMOUNT
**3** a set of printed sheets of paper bound together between covers and forming a work of fiction or nonfiction — see BOOK 1
**voluminous** *adj* of a size greater than average of its kind — see LARGE
**voluminousness** *n* the quality or state of being large in size — see LARGENESS

**voluntarily** *adv* of one's own free will ⟨you took part in this *voluntarily*, so you have no cause to complain⟩
***syn*** freely, willingly
***rel*** consciously, knowingly, wittingly
***phrases*** of one's own accord
***near ant*** unconsciously, unknowingly, unwittingly
***ant*** involuntarily, unwillingly

**voluntary** *adj* **1** done, made, or given with one's own free will ⟨a *voluntary* contribution to the school's fund-raising drive⟩
***syn*** freewill, unforced, volunteer, willing
***rel*** discretionary, elective, nonobligatory, optional; impulsive, instinctive, spontaneous, unforced, unpremeditated; conscious, deliberate, intentional, knowing, willful (*or* wilful)
***near ant*** compulsory, mandatory, necessary, nonelective, obligatory, ordered, required
***ant*** coerced, forced, involuntary
**2** subject to one's freedom of choice — see OPTIONAL

**volunteer** *adj* done, made, or given with one's own free will — see VOLUNTARY 1

**voluptuous** *adj* pleasing to the physical senses — see SENSUAL

**vomit** *vb* to discharge the contents of the stomach through the mouth ⟨the children with the flu *vomited* every time they tried to eat something⟩
***syn*** gag, heave, retch, spit up, throw up
***rel*** disgorge, regurgitate; eject, expel, spew

**voodoo** *n* a person skilled in using supernatural forces — see MAGICIAN 1

**voodooism** *n* the power to control natural forces through supernatural means — see MAGIC 1

**voracious** *adj* **1** having a huge appetite ⟨it seemed like the *voracious* kitten was eating her weight in food every day⟩
***syn*** gluttonous, greedy, hoggish, piggish, rapacious, ravenous
***rel*** hearty, wolfish; devouring, gobbling, gorging, gormandizing, insatiable, unquenchable; empty, famished, hungry, starved, starving; malnourished, underfed, undernourished
***near ant*** full, content, sated, satisfied
**2** showing urgent desire or interest — see EAGER

**vortex** *n* water moving rapidly in a circle with a hollow in the center — see WHIRLPOOL

**votary** *n* one who follows the opinions or teachings of another — see FOLLOWER

**vote** *n* **1** the right to formally express one's position or will in an election ⟨in the United States, women were granted the *vote* by the Nineteenth Amendment in 1920⟩
***syn*** enfranchisement, franchise, suffrage
***rel*** say, voice
***ant*** disenfranchisement
**2** a piece of paper indicating a person's preferences in an election — see BALLOT
**3** the right to express a wish, choice, or opinion — see VOICE 1

**vote** *vb* to set before the mind for consideration — see PROPOSE 1

**vouch** (for) *vb* to declare (something) to be true or genuine — see CERTIFY 1

**vow** *n* a person's solemn declaration that he or she will do or not do something — see PROMISE

**vow** *vb* to make a solemn declaration of intent — see PROMISE 1

**voyage** *n* a journey over water in a vessel — see SAIL

**voyage** *vb* **1** to take a trip especially of some distance — see TRAVEL 1
**2** to travel on water in a vessel — see SAIL 1

**vulgar** *adj* **1** belonging to the class of people of low social or economic rank — see IGNOBLE 1
**2** depicting or referring to sexual matters in a way that is unacceptable in polite society — see OBSCENE 1
**3** held by or applicable to a majority of the people — see GENERAL 3
**4** lacking in refinement or good taste — see COARSE 2
**5** used in or suitable for speech and not formal writing — see COLLOQUIAL 1

**vulgarism** *n* a disrespectful or indecent word or expression — see SWEARWORD

**vulgarity** *n* **1** the quality or state of lacking refinement or good taste ⟨our cousins' general *vulgarity* and poor manners irritate my mother⟩
***syn*** coarseness, commonness, crassness, crudeness, grossness, indelicacy, indelicateness, lowness, raffishness, roughness, rudeness, tastelessness
***rel*** boorishness, churlishness, clownishness, loutishness; insensitivity, thoughtlessness; gracelessness, tackiness
***near ant*** courtliness; elegance, grace, graciousness; consideration, sensitivity, thoughtfulness
***ant*** cultivation, gentility, polish, refinement, tastefulness
**2** the quality or state of being obscene — see OBSCENITY 1

**vulnerability** *n* **1** the quality or state of having little resistance to some outside agent — see SUSCEPTIBILITY
**2** the state of being left without shelter or protection against something harmful — see EXPOSURE 1

**vulnerable** *adj* **1** being in a situation where one is likely to meet with harm — see LIABLE 1
**2** lacking protection from danger or resistance against attack — see HELPLESS 1

# W

**wackiness** *n* lack of good sense or judgment — see FOOLISHNESS 1

**wacky** *adj* 1 different from the ordinary in a way that causes curiosity or suspicion — see ODD 2
2 having or showing a very abnormal or sick state of mind — see INSANE 1
3 showing or marked by a lack of good sense or judgment — see FOOLISH 1

**wad** *n* 1 a considerable amount — see LOT 2
2 a small uneven mass — see LUMP 1
3 a very large amount of money — see FORTUNE 2

**wad** *vb* to form into a round compact mass ⟨she *wadded* up the paper and threw it in the wastebasket⟩
***syn*** agglomerate, ball, roll, round
***rel*** clump, lump; bead
***near ant*** open, spread, unfold
***ant*** unroll

**waddle** *vb* to move forward while swaying from side to side — see STAGGER 1

**wade** (into) *vb* to start work on energetically — see ATTACK 3

**waft** *n* a slight or gentle movement of air — see BREEZE 1

**waft** *vb* to rest or move along the surface of a liquid or in the air — see FLOAT

**wag** *n* 1 a quick jerky movement from side to side or up and down ⟨the dog gave its tail a single *wag* before it flopped back down⟩
***syn*** switch, waggle
***rel*** oscillation, swing; flap, flutter, wave; jerk, shake, twitch, wiggle
2 a person (as a writer) noted for or specializing in humor — see HUMORIST

**wag** *vb* to move from side to side or up and down with quick jerky motions ⟨the cat's tail *wagged* back and forth in annoyance⟩
***syn*** switch, waggle
***rel*** oscillate, swing; beat, flail, flap, flop, whip; flick, flicker, flutter, wave; jerk, shake, twitch, wiggle

**wage** *n, often* **wages** *pl* the money paid regularly to a person for labor or services ⟨the *wage* you earn is more than enough to support us comfortably⟩
***syn*** emolument, hire, pay, payment, salary, stipend
***rel*** minimum wage, take-home pay; compensation, recompense, remittance, remuneration, requital, return; check, commission, paycheck; recoupment, redress, reparation, restitution; reimbursement, repayment; profit, takings, yield

**wager** *n* the money or thing risked on the outcome of an uncertain event — see BET

**wager** *vb* to risk (something) on the outcome of an uncertain event — see BET

**wagerer** *n* one that bets (as on the outcome of a contest or sports event) — see BETTOR

**waggery** *n* 1 playful, reckless behavior that is not intended to cause serious harm — see MISCHIEF 1
2 something said or done to cause laughter — see JOKE 1

**waggish** *adj* tending to or exhibiting reckless playfulness — see MISCHIEVOUS 1

**waggle** *n* a quick jerky movement from side to side or up and down — see WAG 1

**waggle** *vb* to move from side to side or up and down with quick jerky motions — see WAG

**wagon** *n* a wheeled usually horse-drawn vehicle used for hauling — see CART

**wail** *n* 1 a crying out in grief — see LAMENT 1
2 a long low sound indicating pain or grief — see MOAN 1

**wail** *vb* 1 to express dissatisfaction, pain, or resentment usually tiresomely — see COMPLAIN
2 to make a long loud mournful sound — see HOWL 1
3 to utter a moan — see MOAN 1

**wail** (for) *vb* to feel or express sorrow for — see LAMENT 1

**wailing** *adj* expressing or suggesting mourning — see MOURNFUL 1

**wain** *n* a wheeled usually horse-drawn vehicle used for hauling — see CART

**waist** *n* the middle region of the human body — see MIDRIFF

**waistline** *n* the middle region of the human body — see MIDRIFF

**wait** *n* an instance or period of being prevented from going about one's business — see DELAY

**wait** *vb* to remain in place in readiness or expectation of something ⟨hurry up, as your sisters are already at the door *waiting* for you⟩
***syn*** await, bide, hold on, stay
***rel*** hang around, linger, stick around; anticipate, expect
***phrases*** bide one's time

**waiter** *n* a person who serves food or drink — see SERVER

**waiver** *n* a document containing a declaration of an intentional giving up of a right, claim, or privilege ⟨before the hospital will treat you, you have to sign a *waiver* in which you give up your right to sue⟩
***syn*** release
***rel*** dispensation, exemption; abdication, relinquishment, renouncement; renunciation, surrender

**wake** *vb* 1 to cause to stop sleeping ⟨my banging around in the kitchen *woke* the cat⟩

*syn* arouse, awake, awaken, rouse, waken
*rel* raise, revive; reawake, reawaken; agitate, disturb, excite, provoke, stimulate, stir
*near ant* hypnotize, mesmerize; lay (down)
*ant* lull
**2** to cease to be asleep ⟨I *woke* with a start when the door slammed⟩
*syn* arouse, awake, awaken, rouse, waken
*rel* arise, get up, rise, uprise; watch; revive; reawake, reawaken; shift, stir
*near ant* catnap, doze, drop (off), nap, nod, sleep, slumber, snooze; bed (down), couch, retire, turn in; oversleep

**wakeful** *adj* not sleeping or able to sleep ⟨the mother remained *wakeful* until her child returned home⟩
*syn* awake, sleepless, wide-awake
*rel* aroused, awakened, roused, wakened; aware, conscious; revived; reawakened
*near ant* drowsy, nodding, sleepy, slumberous, somnolent; dreaming; hypnotized, mesmerized
*ant* asleep, dormant, dozing, napping, resting, sleeping, slumbering

**waken** *vb* **1** to cause to stop sleeping — see WAKE 1
**2** to cease to be asleep — see WAKE 2

**walk** *n* a relaxed journey on foot for exercise or pleasure ⟨we went for a long *walk* outside because it was such a nice night⟩
*syn* constitutional, perambulation, ramble, range, saunter, stroll, turn
*rel* parade, promenade; expedition, hike, march, peregrination, tramp, travel, trek, trip; excursion, jaunt, junket, outing, sally, spin, tour; pilgrimage, progress, safari

**walk** *vb* to go on foot ⟨I *walked* slowly to school⟩
*syn* foot (it), hoof (it), leg (it), pad, step, traipse, tread
*rel* parade, promenade; march, pace, stride; hike, peregrinate, trek; amble, perambulate, ramble, saunter, stroll, wander; clump, stomp, stump, tramp, tromp; plod, trudge; hobble, limp; mince, prance, pussyfoot, tiptoe; stalk, strut, swagger; lumber, lurch, pound, shamble, shuffle, stagger; nip, trip, trot

**walking out** *n* the act of leaving a place — see DEPARTURE

**walkout** *n* a work stoppage by a body of workers intended to force an employer to meet their demands — see STRIKE 1

**walk out** *vb* **1** to leave a place often for another — see GO 2
**2** to refuse to work in order to force an employer to meet demands — see STRIKE 1

**wall** *n* **1** a physical object that blocks the way — see BARRIER
**2** means or method of defending — see DEFENSE 1

**wall** (in) *vb* to close or shut in by or as if by barriers — see ENCLOSE 1

**wallop** *n* **1** a forceful coming together of two things — see IMPACT 1
**2** a hard strike with a part of the body or an instrument — see [1]BLOW

**wallop** *vb* **1** to strike repeatedly — see BEAT 1
**2** to achieve a victory over — see BEAT 2
**3** to defeat by a large margin — see WHIP 2
**4** to deliver a blow to (someone or something) usually in a strong vigorous manner — see HIT 1

**wampum** *n slang* something (as pieces of stamped metal or printed paper) customarily and legally used as a medium of exchange, a measure of value, or a means of payment — see MONEY

**wan** *adj* lacking a healthy skin color — see PALE 2

**wander** *vb* to move about from place to place aimlessly ⟨we just went outside and *wandered* around until it was time to go⟩
*syn* gad (about), gallivant (*also* galavant), knock (about), maunder, meander, mooch, mope, ramble, range, roam, rove, traipse
*rel* amble, saunter, stroll; bum, hobo; straggle, stray; prowl, tramp, travel

**wanderer** *n* a person who roams about without a fixed route or destination — see NOMAD

**wandering** *adj* traveling from place to place — see ITINERANT

**wane** *vb* to grow less in scope or intensity especially gradually — see DECREASE 2

**wangle** *vb* to plan out usually with subtle skill or care — see ENGINEER

**want** *n* **1** the fact or state of being absent — see LACK 1
**2** a falling short of an essential or desirable amount or number — see DEFICIENCY
**3** a state of being without something necessary, desirable, or useful — see NEED 1
**4** the state of lacking sufficient money or material possessions — see POVERTY 1

**want** *vb* **1** to have an earnest wish to own or enjoy — see DESIRE
**2** to have as a requirement — see NEED 1
**3** to see fit — see CHOOSE 2
**4** to wish to have — see LIKE 1

**wanting** *adj* **1** falling short of a standard — see BAD 1
**2** not coming up to a usual standard or meeting a particular need — see SHORT 3
**3** not present or in evidence — see ABSENT 2

**wanting** *prep* not having — see WITHOUT 1

**wanton** *adj* **1** depicting or referring to sexual matters in a way that is unacceptable in polite society — see OBSCENE 1
**2** having a strong sexual desire — see LUSTFUL
**3** having or showing the desire to inflict severe pain and suffering on others — see CRUEL 1

**wantonness** *n* the willful infliction of pain and suffering on others — see CRUELTY

---

*syn* synonym(s) *rel* related words
*ant* antonym(s) *near ant* near antonym(s)

**war** *n* **1** a state of armed violent struggle between states, nations, or groups ⟨the United States declared *war* on Japan after the bombing of Pearl Harbor⟩
*syn* conflict, hostilities, hot war
*rel* civil war, cold war, holy war, limited war, world war; action, battle, engagement; combat, fighting, warfare; belligerency; wartime
*near ant* demilitarization, demobilization, disarmament; pacification; cease-fire, truce; calm, peacefulness, tranquility
*ant* peace
**2** a lack of agreement or harmony — see DISCORD

**war** (against) *vb* to oppose (someone) in physical conflict — see FIGHT 1

**warble** *n* a rhythmic series of musical tones arranged to give a pleasing effect — see MELODY

**warble** *vb* to sing with the alternation of two musical tones ⟨the skylark *warbled* prettily outside our window⟩
*syn* quaver, trill
*rel* slur; yodel; belt, carol, chant, chorus, croon, descant, harmonize, troll, vocalize; lilt, scat

**ward** *n* **1** means or method of defending — see DEFENSE 1
**2** responsibility for the safety and well-being of someone or something — see CUSTODY

**ward** *vb* to drive danger or attack away from — see DEFEND 1

**warden** *n* **1** a person or group that watches over someone or something — see GUARD 1
**2** a person who takes care of a property sometimes for an absent owner — see CUSTODIAN 1

**warder** *n* a person or group that watches over someone or something — see GUARD 1

**warehouse** *n* a building for storing goods — see STOREHOUSE

**wares** *n pl* products that are bought and sold in business — see MERCHANDISE

**warfare** *n* **1** a lack of agreement or harmony — see DISCORD
**2** an earnest effort for superiority or victory over another — see CONTEST 1

**wariness** *n* a close attentiveness to avoiding danger — see CAUTION 1

**warlike** *adj* feeling or displaying eagerness to fight — see BELLIGERENT

**warm** *adj* **1** having or giving off heat to a moderate degree ⟨the pan was still *warm*, but no longer too hot to touch⟩
*syn* heated, lukewarm, tepid, toasty, warmed
*rel* thawed; broiling, burning, fiery, hot, piping hot, red-hot, roasting, scalding, scorching, searing, sultry, sweltering, torrid; overheated, roasted, superheated, sweltering; blazing, glowing, molten, sizzling; reheated
*near ant* arctic, bitter, bleak, chill, chilly, cold, freezing, frigid, frosty, glacial, ice-cold, iced, icy, nippy, polar, raw, sharp, snappy, snowy, subfreezing, subzero, wintry; unthawed; frosted; benumbed, nipped, numb
*ant* chilled, cool, cooled, refrigerated, unheated
**2** having or expressing great depth of feeling — see FERVENT
**3** having or showing kindly feeling and sincere interest — see FRIENDLY 1
**4** showing or expressing acceptance or approval — see POSITIVE

**warm** *vb* **1** to cause to have or give off heat to a moderate degree ⟨you'll need to *warm* the food in the microwave⟩
*syn* heat, toast
*rel* overheat, superheat; reheat; burn, char, fire, scald, scorch, sear
*near ant* freeze, frost, ice
*ant* chill, cool, refrigerate
**2** to give satisfaction to — see PLEASE

**warm-blooded** *adj* having or expressing great depth of feeling — see FERVENT

**warmed** *adj* having or giving off heat to a moderate degree — see WARM 1

**warmhearted** *adj* **1** having or marked by sympathy and consideration for others — see HUMANE 1
**2** having or showing kindly feeling and sincere interest — see FRIENDLY 1

**warmness** *n* the quality or state of being moderate in temperature — see WARMTH 1

**warmonger** *n* one who urges or attempts to cause a war ⟨fortunately, the *warmongers* met with overwhelming opposition⟩
*syn* hawk, jingo, militarist
*rel* agitator, firebrand, fomenter, instigator, rabble-rouser; belligerent, combatant, militant; chauvinist
*near ant* peacemaker
*ant* dove, pacifist

**warmth** *n* **1** the quality or state of being moderate in temperature ⟨the cozy *warmth* of the inn's parlor was a welcome relief from the wintry weather outside⟩
*syn* lukewarmness, warmness
*rel* glow, radiance; heat, hotness, sultriness, stuffiness
*near ant* bitterness, bleakness, cold, coldness, frigidity, frostiness, iciness, rawness, sharpness; frost
*ant* chill, chilliness, coolness
**2** depth of feeling — see ARDOR 1

**warn** *vb* to give notice to beforehand especially of danger or risk ⟨Dad *warned* us that if we continued playing so rough, someone was sure to get hurt⟩
*syn* alert, caution, forewarn
*rel* augur, forecast, foretell, predict, presage, prognosticate, prophesy; advise, apprise, inform, notify; admonish; bode, forebode, portend
*near ant* imperil, risk

**warning** *adj* serving as or offering a warning — see CAUTIONARY

**warning** *n* **1** the act or an instance of telling beforehand of danger or risk ⟨she delivered a strict *warning* that anyone who was caught cheating would get expelled⟩

*syn* admonition, alarm, alert, caution, forewarning, notice
*rel* auguring, augury, forecasting, foretelling, predicting, prediction, presaging, prognosticating, prophecy, prophesying; apprising, informing, notification, notifying; advice, counsel, guidance, recommendation, suggestion; announcement, declaration
**2** something that tells of approaching danger or risk ⟨the ominously darkening sky was a *warning* that a tornado was approaching⟩
*syn* caution, tocsin
*rel* omen, portent; notification; buoy, knell, sign, signal; foretaste, foretoken; announcement, declaration

**warp** *vb* **1** to change so much as to create a wrong impression or alter the meaning of — see GARBLE
**2** to lower in character or dignity — see DEBASE 1
**3** to twist (something) out of a natural or normal shape or condition — see CONTORT

**warped** *adj* having or showing lowered moral character or standards — see CORRUPT

**warping** *n* the twisting of something out of its natural or normal shape or condition — see CONTORTION

**warrant** *vb* **1** to assume responsibility for the satisfactory quality or performance of ⟨the computer company unconditionally *warrants* all of its products for one full year⟩
*syn* guarantee
*rel* attest, authenticate, avouch, certify, testify (to), vouch (for), witness; assure, bond, contract, covenant; pledge, plight, swear, vow; adhere, assert, declare, insist; insure
**2** to give official acceptance of something as satisfactory — see APPROVE
**3** to have as a requirement — see NEED 1
**4** to state as a fact usually forcefully — see CLAIM 1

**warranted** *adj* being what is called for by accepted standards of right and wrong — see JUST 1

**warranty** *n* a formal agreement to fulfill an obligation — see GUARANTEE 1

**warrior** *n* a person engaged in military service — see SOLDIER

**wary** *adj* having or showing a close attentiveness to avoiding danger or trouble — see CAREFUL 1

**wash** *vb* **1** to flow along or against ⟨crystal-clear waters gently *wash* the island's unspoiled beaches⟩
*syn* lap, lave, splash
*rel* gurgle, ripple, slosh
**2** to flow in a broken irregular stream — see GURGLE
**3** to make wet — see WET
**4** to pour liquid over or through in order to cleanse — see FLUSH 1

**washed** *adj* containing, covered with, or thoroughly penetrated by water — see WET

**washed–out** *adj* lacking intensity of color — see PALE 1

**washed–up** *adj* having lost forcefulness, courage, or spirit — see EFFETE 1

**washout** *n* something that has failed — see FAILURE 3

**wash out** *vb* **1** to be unsuccessful — see FAIL 2
**2** to make white or whiter by removing color — see WHITEN
**3** to use up all the physical energy of — see EXHAUST 1

**washroom** *n* a room furnished with a fixture for flushing body waste — see TOILET

**waspish** *adj* easily irritated or annoyed — see IRRITABLE

**waspishness** *n* readiness to show annoyance or impatience — see PETULANCE

**wassail** *n* a bout of drinking — see CAROUSE

**wastage** *n* the state or fact of being rendered nonexistent, physically unsound, or useless — see DESTRUCTION

**waste** *adj* producing inferior or only a small amount of vegetation — see BARREN 1

**waste** *n* **1** an instance of spending money or resources without care or restraint ⟨it seems like a *waste* to spend my entire paycheck on a bigger TV⟩
*syn* extravagance, prodigality
*rel* indulgence, luxury, splurge; loss, wastage; generosity, liberality, openhandedness, profligacy; improvidence, shortsightedness; overindulgence, self-indulgence; excess, immoderacy, overkill; carelessness, heedlessness, imprudence, incautiousness; recklessness
*near ant* necessity; economizing, economy, frugality, saving, scrimping, skimping; austerity, moderation, restraint, temperance, temperateness
**2** discarded or useless material — see GARBAGE
**3** land that is uninhabited or not fit for crops — see WASTELAND
**4** solid matter discharged from an animal's alimentary canal — see DROPPING 1

**waste** *vb* **1** to use up carelessly ⟨he *wasted* most of his allowance by buying comic books⟩
*syn* blow, dissipate, fritter (away), lavish, misspend, run through, spend, squander, throw away
*rel* splurge; consume, deplete, exhaust, impoverish; indulge, overindulge; disburse, expend, lay out
*near ant* economize, scrimp, skimp; preserve, protect, save; hoard, lay up
*ant* conserve
**2** to bring to a complete end the physical soundness, existence, or usefulness of — see DESTROY 1
**3** to diminish the physical strength of — see WEAKEN 1

**waste** (away) *vb* to lose bodily strength or vigor — see WEAKEN 2

**wasted** *adj* **1** lacking bodily strength — see WEAK 1
**2** suffering extreme weight loss as a result of hunger or disease — see EMACIATED

**wasteful** *adj* given to spending money freely or foolishly — see PRODIGAL

**wastefulness** *n* the quality or fact of being free or wasteful in the expenditure of money — see EXTRAVAGANCE 1

**wasteland** *n* land that is uninhabited or not fit for crops ⟨with proper irrigation and fertilizer, they turned the desert *wasteland* into a fertile plain⟩
*syn* barren, desert, desolation, waste
*rel* badland; bush, brush; dust bowl; hinterland, upland; open, open air, outdoors, out-of-doors; nature, wild, wilderness

**waster** *n* someone who carelessly spends money — see PRODIGAL

**wastrel** *n* someone who carelessly spends money — see PRODIGAL

**watch** *n* **1** a person or group that watches over someone or something — see GUARD 1
**2** the act or state of being constantly attentive and responsive to signs of activity, opportunity, or danger — see VIGILANCE

**watch** *vb* **1** to keep one's eyes on ⟨I turned my head to continue *watching* the bird as it flew away⟩
*syn* eye, observe
*rel* behold, look, regard, see, view; gape, gawk, gaze, glare, goggle, peer, rubber-neck, stare; guard, wake, ward; monitor, read; spy; glance, glimpse, peek, peep
*near ant* blink, wink
**2** to take notice of and be guided by — see HEED 1
**3** to pay continued close attention to (something) for a particular purpose — see MONITOR
**4** to have an interest or concern for — see CARE

**watch** (for) *vb* to believe in the future occurrence of (something) — see EXPECT

**watchful** *adj* paying close attention usually for the purpose of anticipating approaching danger or opportunity — see ALERT 1

**watchfulness** *n* the act or state of being constantly attentive and responsive to signs of opportunity, activity, or danger — see VIGILANCE

**watchman** *n* **1** a person or group that watches over someone or something — see GUARD 1
**2** a person who takes care of a property sometimes for an absent owner — see CUSTODIAN 1

**watch out** (for) *vb* to be cautious of or on guard against — see BEWARE (OF)

**watchword** *n* **1** a word or phrase that must be spoken by a person in order to pass a guard — see PASSWORD
**2** an attention-getting word or phrase used to publicize something (as a campaign or product) — see SLOGAN

**water** *vb* to make wet — see WET

**water** (down) *vb* to alter (something) for the worse with the addition of foreign or lower-grade substances — see ADULTERATE

**water closet** *n* a room furnished with a fixture for flushing body waste — see TOILET

**watercourse** *n* an open man-made passageway for water — see CHANNEL 1

**watercraft** *n* a small buoyant structure for travel on water — see BOAT 1

**watered** *adj* containing, covered with, or thoroughly penetrated by water — see WET

**waterfall** *n* a fall of water usually from a great height ⟨I used to like to throw sticks in the stream and watch them go over the *waterfall*⟩
*syn* cascade, cataract, fall(s)
*rel* rapid(s), white water; eddy, riffle; undertow, vortex, whirlpool

**waterless** *adj* marked by little or no precipitation or humidity — see DRY 1

**waterlogged** *adj* containing, covered with, or thoroughly penetrated by water — see WET

**waterproof** *n chiefly British* a coat made of water-resistant material — see RAINCOAT

**waterproof** *adj* made of or treated with material that does not allow water to penetrate ⟨luckily, my backpack is *waterproof*, so my notes didn't get wet⟩
*syn* waterproofed, watertight
*rel* rainproof; water-repellent, water-resistant; nonabsorbent, nonporous
*near ant* absorbent, porous

**waterproofed** *adj* made of or treated with material that does not allow water to penetrate — see WATERPROOF

**waterspout** *n* a pipe or channel for carrying off water from a roof — see GUTTER 1

**watertight** *adj* made of or treated with material that does not allow water to penetrate — see WATERPROOF

**waterway** *n* an open man-made passageway for water — see CHANNEL 1

**watery** *adj* **1** containing, covered with, or thoroughly penetrated by water — see WET
**2** having an overly soft liquid consistency — see RUNNY
**3** not containing very much of some important element — see WEAK 3

**wave** *n* a moving ridge on the surface of water ⟨the toddler was almost knocked down by the *waves* created by the speedboat⟩
*syn* billow, surge, swell
*rel* sea(s); breaker, whitecap; curl; comber, roller; eddy, riffle, ripple, wavelet; tidal wave, tsunami; undertow, vortex, whirlpool

**wave** *vb* to direct or notify by a movement or gesture — see MOTION

**waver** *vb* **1** to show uncertainty about the right course of action — see HESITATE
**2** to swing unsteadily back and forth or from side to side — see TEETER 1

**wavering** *n* the act or an instance of pausing because of uncertainty about the right course of action — see HESITATION

**wax** *vb* **1** to become greater in extent, volume, amount, or number — see INCREASE 2

**2** to coat (something) with a slippery substance in order to reduce friction — see LUBRICATE

**3** to eventually have as a state or quality — see BECOME

**way** *n* **1** a passage cleared for public vehicular travel ⟨the town honored the local sports hero by naming after him a short *way* connecting two shopping centers⟩

***syn*** artery, avenue, boulevard, drag, drive, expressway, freeway, highroad, highway, pass, passageway, pike, road, roadway, route, row, street, thoroughfare, trace, turnpike

***rel*** causeway; alley, alleyway, bystreet, byway, catwalk, court, lane, place; approach, concourse, path, walkway; access; dead end; aisle, corridor, course, line; track, trail; channel; corduroy, tarmac; crossroad; bypass, overpass, underpass; cloverleaf, rotary

**2** a usual manner of behaving or doing — see HABIT

**3** an established course for traveling from one place to another — see PASSAGE 1

**4** an established pattern of behavior — see TENDENCY 1

**5** an extent or area available for or used up by some activity or thing — see ROOM 1

**6** the direction along which something or someone moves — see PATH 1

**7** the means or procedure for doing something — see METHOD

**8** the opening through which one can enter or leave a structure — see DOOR 2

**9** the power, right, or opportunity to choose — see CHOICE 1

**10** the space or amount of space between two points, lines, surfaces, or objects — see DISTANCE

**wayfarer** *n* a person who roams about without a fixed route or destination — see NOMAD

**wayfaring** *adj* traveling from place to place — see ITINERANT

**waylay** *vb* to lie in wait for and attack by surprise — see AMBUSH

**way–out** *adj* different from the ordinary in a way that causes curiosity or suspicion — see ODD 2

**way station** *n* a regular stopping place — see STATION 2

**wayward** *adj* **1** given to resisting authority or another's control — see DISOBEDIENT

**2** given to resisting control or discipline by others — see UNCONTROLLABLE

**weak** *adj* **1** lacking bodily strength ⟨the little boy was simply too *weak* to lift the box⟩

***syn*** debilitated, delicate, effete, enervated, enfeebled, faint, feeble, frail, infirm, languid, low, prostrate, prostrated, sapped, slight, soft, softened, tender, torpid, unsubstantial, wasted, weakened, wimpy

***rel*** challenged, disabled, incapacitated; paralyzed; broken-down, decrepit, worn out; impotent, powerless, puny; breakable, flimsy, fragile; dizzy, groggy, rocky, unsteady, woozy; exhausted, tired, weary; damaged, harmed, hurt, impaired, injured; resistless, susceptible, unresistant, vulnerable, yielding

***near ant*** able-bodied, athletic, beefy, brawny, fit, husky, muscular, sinewy, strapping, virile; hard, hardy, lusty, robust, sturdy, tough; fortified, hardened, inured, strengthened, toughened; energetic, energized, invigorated, vigorous, vitalized; hale, healthy, sound; capable, competent; convalescing, recovering, recuperating

***ant*** mighty, powerful, rugged, stalwart, stout, strong

**2** lacking strength of will or character ⟨the opinion that overweight people are just *weak* individuals who easily give in to temptation⟩

***syn*** characterless, effete, frail, invertebrate, nerveless, soft, spineless, weakened, wimpy, wishy-washy

***rel*** forceless, ineffective, ineffectual; impotent, powerless; emasculated, unnerved; pliable, submissive; corrupt, unprincipled, unscrupulous, villainous; cowardly, craven, lily-livered

***near ant*** ethical, good, moral, principled, right, righteous, upright, virtuous; determined, mettlesome, resolute; courageous, stalwart, stouthearted

***ant*** backboned, firm, strong, tough

**3** not containing very much of some important element ⟨the coffee came out too *weak* because I didn't put enough ground beans in⟩

***syn*** dilute, diluted, thin, thinned, watery, weakened

***rel*** adulterated, watered (down)

***near ant*** enriched, fortified; concentrated, condensed, evaporated

***ant*** full-bodied, rich, strong

**4** not using or following good reasoning — see ILLOGICAL

**5** unable to act or achieve one's purpose — see POWERLESS

**weaken** *vb* **1** to diminish the physical strength of ⟨several days of hardship in the desert had *weakened* them⟩

***syn*** debilitate, enervate, enfeeble, prostrate, sap, soften, tire, waste

***rel*** cripple, disable, incapacitate; deplete, depress, exhaust, impoverish, unman, wash out; damage, harm, hurt, impair, injure; break down, wear out; paralyze

***near ant*** energize, invigorate, vitalize; harden, season, toughen

***ant*** beef (up), fortify, recruit, strengthen

---

***syn*** synonym(s) ***rel*** related words
***ant*** antonym(s) ***near ant*** near antonym(s)

2 to lose bodily strength or vigor ⟨the bodybuilder *weakened* once she eased off on her workouts⟩
*syn* decay, droop, fail, flag, go, lag, languish, sag, waste (away), wilt
*rel* break down, wear out; yield
*near ant* convalesce, recover, recuperate; gain
2 to alter (something) for the worse with the addition of foreign or lower-grade substances — see ADULTERATE

**weakened** *adj* 1 containing foreign or lower-grade substances — see IMPURE
2 lacking bodily strength — see WEAK 1
3 lacking strength of will or character — see WEAK 2
4 not containing very much of some important element — see WEAK 3

**weakening** *n* a gradual sinking and wasting away of mind or body — see DECLINE 1

**weakling** *n* 1 a person lacking in physical strength ⟨he was a *weakling* until high school, when he started working out to put on muscle⟩
*syn* softy (*or* softie), wimp
*rel* pushover, sissy
*ant* powerhouse
2 a person without strength of character ⟨only a *weakling* would be willing to lie to save himself from punishment⟩
*syn* mollycoddle, wimp
*rel* coward, mouse
*ant* stalwart

**weakly** *adj* chronically or repeatedly suffering from poor health — see SICKLY 1

**weak-minded** *adj* 1 not having or showing an ability to absorb ideas readily — see STUPID 1
2 showing or marked by a lack of good sense or judgment — see FOOLISH 1

**weakness** *n* 1 the quality or state of lacking physical strength or vigor ⟨the flu left me with such *weakness* that I could hardly stand⟩
*syn* debilitation, debility, delicacy, delicateness, enfeeblement, faintness, feebleness, frailness, frailty, infirmity, languor, lowness
*rel* decay, decrepitude; breakdown, collapse, exhaustion, nervous breakdown, prostration; defenselessness, helplessness; softness, tenderness; disablement, incapacitation; damage, harm, hurt, impairment, injury
*near ant* energy, vitality; brawniness, fitness, huskiness, virility; hardness, ruggedness, stoutness, sturdiness, toughness; haleness, health, healthiness, soundness
*ant* hardihood, hardiness, robustness, strength, vigor
2 the quality or state of lacking strength of will or character ⟨in a moment of *weakness* he shoplifted the comic book⟩
*syn* frailness, frailty, softness, spinelessness
*rel* collapse; failing, flaw, foibles, peccadillo; evil, immorality, wickedness; corruption, corruptness
*near ant* discipline, self-discipline; goodness, morality, rightness, righteousness, uprightness, virtuousness
*ant* backbone, firmness, fortitude, mettle, resoluteness, strength
3 a defect in character — see FAULT 1
4 the quality or state of having little resistance to some outside agent — see SUSCEPTIBILITY

**weal** *n* the state of doing well especially in relation to one's happiness or success — see WELFARE

**wealth** *n* 1 the total of one's money and property ⟨her *wealth* increased to the point where she could afford several luxurious homes⟩
*syn* assets, capital, fortune, means, opulence, riches, substance, wherewithal
*rel* belongings, chattels, effects, holdings, paraphernalia, possessions, things; finances, money; king's ransom, mint, wad; abundance, affluence, prosperity, success; treasure, valuables; accession, acquisition, personalty, property; nest egg, reserve, resources, savings, treasury; collateral; heap, pile, pot; bonanza, mine, treasure trove
*near ant* debts, liabilities; indebtedness
2 a considerable amount — see LOT 2
3 an amount or supply more than sufficient to meet one's needs — see PLENTY 1

**wealthy** *adj* having goods, property, or money in abundance — see RICH 1

**wear** *n* 1 the result of long and hard use ⟨after several years, the carpet was finally showing *wear*⟩
*syn* wear and tear
*rel* abrasion, corrosion, erosion, erasure; decomposition, disintegration
*near ant* fixing, mending, patching, rebuilding, reconditioning, reconstruction, renovation, repair, revamping
2 covering for the human body — see CLOTHING

**wear** *vb* 1 to use up all the physical energy of — see EXHAUST 1
2 to damage or diminish by continued friction — see ABRADE 1

**wear and tear** *n* the result of long and hard use — see WEAR 1

**wearied** *adj* 1 depleted in strength, energy, or freshness — see WEARY 1
2 having one's patience, interest, or pleasure exhausted — see WEARY 2

**weariless** *adj* showing no signs of weariness even after long hard effort — see TIRELESS

**weariness** *n* 1 a complete depletion of energy or strength — see FATIGUE
2 the state of being bored — see BOREDOM

**wearisome** *adj* causing weariness, restlessness, or lack of interest — see BORING

**wear out** *vb* to use up all the physical energy of — see EXHAUST 1

**weary** *adj* 1 depleted in strength, energy, or freshness ⟨I am just too *weary* to do any more work tonight⟩
*syn* beat, burned-out (*or* burnt-out), bushed, dead, done in, drained, effete, ex-

hausted, fatigued, jaded, limp, logy, played out, prostrate, spent, tired, tuckered (out), wearied, worn, worn-out
***rel*** overtaxed, overworked; run-down; debilitated, enervated, enfeebled, sapped, weakened
***phrases*** worn to a frazzle
***near ant*** refreshed, rejuvenated, relaxed, rested, revitalized; active, energetic, invigorated, strengthened, strong, tireless, vitalized
***ant*** untired
**2** having one's patience, interest, or pleasure exhausted ⟨I am totally *weary* of this constant bickering⟩
***syn*** bored, fed up, jaded, sick, tired, wearied
***rel*** apathetic, disinterested, uninterested; glutted, sated, satiated, surfeited; dejected, demoralized, discouraged, disheartened, dispirited; beat, burned-out (*or* burnt-out), bushed, done in, drained, enervated, exhausted, fatigued, limp, played out, tuckered, worn-out; annoyed, frustrated, irritated; disgusted, nauseated, repulsed
***near ant*** animated, energized, enlivened, excited, galvanized, invigorated, stimulated, vitalized; amused, entertained; beguiled, bewitched, captivated, charmed, enchanted, enthralled, fascinated, hypnotized, mesmerized; delighted, pleased, thrilled
***ant*** absorbed, engaged, engrossed, gripped, interested, intrigued
**3** causing weariness, restlessness, or lack of interest — see BORING

**weary** *vb* **1** to make weary and restless by being dull or monotonous — see ²BORE
**2** to use up all the physical energy of — see EXHAUST 1

**wearying** *adj* causing weariness, restlessness, or lack of interest — see BORING

**weather** *vb* to come safely through — see SURVIVE 1

**weave** *vb* to scatter or set here and there among other things — see THREAD 1

**web** *n* **1** something that catches and holds ⟨he was caught in the *web* of branches⟩ ⟨she was trapped by her own *web* of lies⟩
***syn*** entanglement, net, snare
***rel*** mesh, trap; knot, snarl, tangle; labyrinth, maze; cobweb, spiderweb
**2** a device or scheme for capturing another by surprise — see TRAP 1

**wed** *vb* **1** to give in marriage — see MARRY 2
**2** to perform the ceremony of marriage for — see MARRY 1
**3** to take a spouse — see MARRY 4
**4** to take as a spouse — see MARRY 3

**wedded** *adj* of or relating to marriage — see MARITAL

**wedding** *n* a ceremony in which two people are united in matrimony ⟨they chose to have the *wedding* outdoors in the spring⟩
***syn*** bridal, espousal, marriage, nuptial(s)
***rel*** match, matrimony, wedlock; reception; engagement, hand, pledge, promise, proposal, troth

**wedge** *vb* to fit (something) into a tight space — see CROWD 1

**wedged** *adj* firmly positioned in place and difficult to dislodge — see TIGHT 2

**wedlock** *n* a union representing a special kind of social and legal partnership between two people — see MARRIAGE 1

**wee** *adj* very small in size — see TINY

**weedy** *adj* growing thickly and vigorously — see RANK 1

**weep** *vb* **1** to flow forth slowly through small openings — see EXUDE
**2** to shed tears often while making meaningless sounds as a sign of pain or distress — see CRY 1

**weeping** *adj* expressing or suggesting mourning — see MOURNFUL 1

**weigh** *vb* **1** to be of importance — see MATTER
**2** to give serious and careful thought to — see PONDER

**weigh** (on *or* upon) *vb* to push steadily against with some force — see PRESS 1

**weighed** *adj* decided on as a result of careful thought — see DELIBERATE 1

**weight** *n* **1** the amount that something weighs ⟨I'm not allowed to lift anything with a *weight* of over ten pounds⟩
***syn*** heaviness, heft
***rel*** mass; tonnage; deadweight; heftiness, massiveness, ponderousness, weightiness; solidity, solidness, substantiality; burdensomeness, cumbersomeness
**2** the quality or state of being important — see IMPORTANCE
**3** a mass or quantity of something taken up and carried, conveyed, or transported — see LOAD 1
**4** a special notice or importance given to something — see EMPHASIS 1
**5** the main or greater part of something as distinguished from its appendages — see BODY 1
**6** the power to direct the thinking or behavior of others usually indirectly — see INFLUENCE 1

**weight** *vb* to place a weight or burden on — see LOAD 1

**weightiness** *n* **1** the state or quality of being heavy ⟨the *weightiness* of the bookcase made it difficult to move⟩
***syn*** avoirdupois, heaviness, heftiness, massiveness, ponderousness
***rel*** overweight; solidity, solidness, substantiality; bulk, bulkiness, hugeness; burdensomeness, cumbersomeness
***near ant*** airiness, delicacy, etherealness; flimsiness, fluffiness, insubstantiality, slightness
***ant*** lightness, weightlessness
**2** the quality or state of being important — see IMPORTANCE

**weightless** *adj* having little weight — see ¹LIGHT 1

**weightlessness** *n* the state or quality of having little weight — see ¹LIGHTNESS 1

---

***syn*** synonym(s) ***rel*** related words
***ant*** antonym(s) ***near ant*** near antonym(s)

**weighty** *adj* **1** having a matter of importance as its topic — see SERIOUS 2
**2** having great meaning or lasting effect — see IMPORTANT 1
**3** having great weight — see HEAVY 1
**4** not joking or playful in mood or manner — see SERIOUS 1
**5** having power over the minds or behavior of others — see INFLUENTIAL 1
**weird** *adj* **1** different from the ordinary in a way that causes curiosity or suspicion — see ODD 2
**2** fearfully and mysteriously strange or fantastic — see EERIE
**3** having seemingly supernatural qualities or powers — see MYSTIC 1
**4** noticeably different from what is generally found or experienced — see UNUSUAL 1
**weirdo** *n* a person of odd or whimsical habits — see ECCENTRIC
**welcome** *adj* giving pleasure or contentment to the mind or senses — see PLEASANT
**welcome** *n* an expression of goodwill upon meeting — see HELLO
**welcome** *vb* receive or accept gladly or readily ⟨the eager recruits *welcomed* every new project with which they were presented⟩
***syn*** embrace
***rel*** adopt, espouse, take up; greet, hail; enjoy, like, prefer; choose, cull, decide (on), elect, handpick, name, opt (for), pick, select, single (out), take
***near ant*** decline, refuse, reject, turn down
**welfare** *n* the state of doing well especially in relation to one's happiness or success ⟨the social worker was pleased at the improvement in the child's *welfare*⟩
***syn*** good, interest, weal, well-being
***rel*** prosperity, success, successfulness; fitness, health, healthiness, robustness, soundness, wellness, wholeness, wholesomeness; bliss, felicity, happiness, joy; advantage, benefit, gain, sake; content, contentedness, gratification, satisfaction
***near ant*** unhealthiness, unsoundness; misery, sadness, unhappiness, wretchedness
**well** *adv* **1** in a satisfactory way ⟨our current system for dividing household chores works *well*, so let's keep it⟩
***syn*** acceptably, adequately, all right, fine, good, nicely, OK (*or* okay), passably, satisfactorily, so-so, tolerably
***rel*** appropriately, congruously, correctly, decently, decorously, felicitously, fittingly, meetly, rightly, seemly, suitably
***near ant*** unbearably; inappropriately, incorrectly, indecently, unsuitably
***ant*** bad, badly, inadequately, intolerably, poorly, unacceptably, unsatisfactorily
**2** in a generous manner ⟨the warm and gracious couple always treat overnight guests *well*⟩
***syn*** bountifully, generously, handsomely, liberally, munificently
***rel*** considerately, courteously, hospitably, kindly, nicely, reasonably, thoughtfully; affably, amiably, cheerfully, cheerily, genially, good-naturedly, graciously
***near ant*** contemptuously, disdainfully, rudely, scornfully; obnoxiously, provocatively; coldly, coolly, frigidly, hostilely; angrily, belligerently
***ant*** stingily
**3** in a skillful or expert manner ⟨she plays the piano very *well*⟩
***syn*** ably, adeptly, capably, competently, expertly, masterfully, proficiently, skillfully
***rel*** aptly; adroitly, deftly, dexterously
***near ant*** inaptly
***ant*** incapably, incompetently, inefficiently, ineptly, inexpertly, poorly, unskillfully
**4** with good reason or courtesy ⟨we cannot *well* get out of going to your cousin's wedding⟩
***syn*** considerately, courteously, kindly, nicely, reasonably, thoughtfully
***rel*** pleasantly; excusably, justifiably
***near ant*** contemptuously, disdainfully, rudely, scornfully
**5** in a pleasing way ⟨the day went *well*, despite the rough beginning⟩
***syn*** agreeably, delectably, deliciously, delightfully, dreamily, favorably, felicitously, gloriously, nicely, pleasantly, pleasingly, satisfyingly, splendidly, swimmingly
***rel*** finely, grandly; advantageously, helpfully; fortunately, happily, luckily; prosperously, successfully
***ant*** badly
**6** to a full extent or degree — see FULLY 1
**well** *adj* enjoying health and vigor — see HEALTHY 1
**well** *interj* how surprising, doubtful, or unbelievable — see NO
**well–being** *n* the state of doing well especially in relation to one's happiness or success — see WELFARE
**wellborn** *adj* of high birth, rank, or station — see NOBLE 1
**well–bred** *adj* showing consideration, courtesy, and good manners — see POLITE 1
**well–disposed** *adj* having an easygoing and pleasing manner especially in social situations — see AMIABLE
**well–founded** *adj* based on sound reasoning or information — see GOOD 1
**well–heeled** *adj* having goods, property, or money in abundance — see RICH 1
**well–known** *adj* widely known — see FAMOUS
**wellness** *n* the condition of being sound in body — see HEALTH
**well–nigh** *adv* very close to but not completely — see ALMOST
**well–off** *adj* having goods, property, or money in abundance — see RICH 1
**well–read** *adj* having or displaying advanced knowledge or education — see EDUCATED
**well–spoken** *adj* able to express oneself clearly and well — see ARTICULATE
**well–to–do** *adj* having goods, property, or money in abundance — see RICH 1

**welter** *n* **1** a state of noisy, confused activity — see COMMOTION
**2** an unorganized collection or mixture of various things — see MISCELLANY 1
**wet** *adj* containing, covered with, or thoroughly penetrated by water ⟨I left the car windows open while it rained, and the seats got all *wet*⟩
*syn* awash, bathed, doused, drenched, dripping, saturated, soaked, soaking, sodden, soggy, soppy, soused, washed, watered, waterlogged, watery
*rel* deluged, drowned, flooded, inundated, overflowed; submerged, swamped; hydrated; dipped, dunked, splashed; aqueous; steeped; flushed, irrigated, laved, rinsed, sluiced; clammy, damp, dank, humid, moist
*near ant* waterproof, water-resistant, water-repellent, watertight; baked, dehydrated, freeze-dried; droughty, parched, sere, sunbaked, thirsty; wrung
*ant* arid, dry, unwatered, waterless
**2** marked by or abounding with rain — see RAINY
**wet** *n* a steady falling of water from the sky in significant quantity — see RAIN 1
**wet** *vb* to make wet ⟨you need to *wet* your hair thoroughly first⟩
*syn* bathe, douse, drench, soak, souse, wash, water
*rel* damp, dampen, humidify, hydrate, moisten; deluge, drown, flood, inundate, overflow; submerge, swamp; splash; impregnate, saturate, steep; flush, irrigate, lave, rinse, sluice; dip, dunk
*near ant* bake, dehydrate, evaporate, freeze-dry, parch; wring; dehumidify
*ant* dry
**whack** *n* **1** an effort to do or accomplish something — see ATTEMPT
**2** a hard strike with a part of the body or an instrument — see [1]BLOW
**3** a loud explosive sound — see CLAP 1
**whack** *vb* to deliver a blow to (someone or something) usually in a strong vigorous manner — see HIT 1
**whacking** *adj* unusually large — see HUGE
**whacking** *adv* to a great degree — see VERY 1
**whale** *n* something that is unusually large and powerful — see GIANT
**whale** *vb* **1** to deliver a blow to (someone or something) usually in a strong vigorous manner — see HIT 1
**2** to strike repeatedly with something long and thin or flexible — see WHIP 1
**3** to strike repeatedly — see BEAT 1
**wharf** *n* a structure used by boats and ships for taking on or landing cargo and passengers — see DOCK
**what** *interj* how surprising, doubtful, or unbelievable — see NO
**wheedle** *vb* to get (someone) to do something by gentle urging, special attention, or flattery — see COAX

*syn* synonym(s) *rel* related words
*ant* antonym(s) *near ant* near antonym(s)

**wheel** *n* a rapid turning about on an axis or central point — see SPIN 1
**wheel** *vb* **1** to change the course or direction of (something) — see TURN 2
**2** to move (something) in a curved or circular path on or as if on an axis — see TURN 1
**3** to move in circles around an axis or center — see SPIN 1
**4** to turn away from a straight line or course — see CURVE 1
**wheeze** *vb* to breathe hard, quickly, or with difficulty — see GASP
**whelm** *vb* to subject to incapacitating emotional or mental stress — see OVERWHELM 1
**when** *conj* in spite of the fact that — see ALTHOUGH
**where** *adv* at, in, or to what place ⟨*where* will you be tonight?⟩
*syn* whereabouts (*also* whereabout), whither
*rel* wherever
**whereabouts** *also* **whereabout** *adv* at, in, or to what place — see WHERE
**whereas** *conj* for the reason that — see SINCE
**wherefore** *adv* for this or that reason — see THEREFORE
**wherefore** *n* something (as a belief) that serves as the basis for another thing — see REASON 2
**wherewithal** *n* **1** available money — see FUND 2
**2** the total of one's money and property — see WEALTH 1
**whet** *vb* to make sharp or sharper — see SHARPEN
**whetted** *adj* having an edge thin enough to cut or pierce something — see SHARP 1
**whiff** *vb* to become aware of by means of the sense organs in the nose — see SMELL 1
**while** *conj* in spite of the fact that — see ALTHOUGH
**while** *n* **1** an indefinite but usually short period of time ⟨we stayed at school for a *while* longer⟩
*syn* bit, space, spell, stretch
*rel* lapse; season, span; day, epoch, era; flash, instant, jiffy, minute, moment, second, shake, spurt, trice, twinkle, twinkling, wink; aeon (*or* eon), age, eternity; interim, interlude, intermission, interval
**2** the active use of energy in producing a result — see EFFORT
**whilom** *adj* having been such at some previous time — see FORMER
**whilst** *conj chiefly British* in spite of the fact that — see ALTHOUGH
**whim** *n* a sudden impulsive and apparently unmotivated idea or action ⟨on a *whim*, we stopped at the roadside stand to get ice cream⟩
*syn* caprice, fancy, freak, notion, vagary, whimsy (*also* whimsey)
*rel* capriciousness, freakishness, whimsicality; conceit; concept, conception, image, impression, picture, thought; brainstorm, inspiration

**whimper** *vb* to utter feeble plaintive cries ⟨the dog *whimpered* to be let in⟩
*syn* mewl, pule
*rel* fuss, snivel, snuffle, whine; bawl, cry, weep; peep, squeak; yelp; mumble, murmur, mutter
*near ant* scream, screech, shriek, squeal; howl, squall, wail, yowl; call, caterwaul, squawk; bellow, roar

**whimsical** *adj* prone to sudden illogical changes of mind, ideas, or actions ⟨it's hard to make plans with my *whimsical* best friend⟩
*syn* capricious, freakish, impulsive
*rel* mercurial, moody, temperamental, volatile; eccentric, flaky, quirky; arbitrary, erratic, fickle, inconstant, irregular, willful (*or* wilful); impractical, quixotic, romantic
*near ant* equable; levelheaded, logical, practical, reasonable, sensible; fast, fixed, hard-and-fast, immutable, inflexible, invariable, unalterable, unchangeable; changeless, constant, established, set, settled, stable, steadfast, steady, unchanging, unvarying

**whimsicality** *n* an inclination to sudden illogical changes of mind, ideas, or actions ⟨her *whimsicality* made her unpredictable⟩
*syn* capriciousness, freakishness, impulsiveness
*rel* moodiness, volatility; eccentricity, flakiness; changeability, unpredictability; arbitrariness, fickleness, inconstancy, irregularity, willfulness; changeability, flexibility, mutability, variability
*near ant* levelheadedness, practicality, reasonableness; fastness, fixedness, immutability, inflexibility, invariability; changelessness, constancy, stability, steadfastness, steadiness

**whimsy** *also* **whimsey** *n* a sudden impulsive and apparently unmotivated idea or action — see WHIM

**whine** *vb* to express dissatisfaction, pain, or resentment usually tiresomely — see COMPLAIN

**whiner** *n* **1** a person who makes frequent complaints usually about little things — see CRYBABY
**2** an irritable and complaining person — see GROUCH

**whinny** *vb* to make the cry typical of a horse — see NEIGH

**whip** *n* a long thin or flexible tool for striking ⟨please do not use your belt as a *whip*⟩
*syn* flogger, lash, scourge, switch
*rel* blacksnake, cat-o'-nine-tails, cowhide, crop, knout, quirt, rawhide, strap; cane, club, cudgel, flail; stripe

**whip** *vb* **1** to strike repeatedly with something long and thin or flexible ⟨*whipped* the animal when it did not move fast enough to please him⟩
*syn* birch, cowhide, flagellate, flail, flog, hide, horsewhip, lash, rawhide, scourge, slash, switch, tan, thrash, whale
*rel* cane, club, cudgel; stripe; bang, bop, box, bust, clap, clip, clobber, clout, crack, cuff, hit, knock, lam, paste, punch, slap, slug, smack, smite, sock, spank, swat, swipe, thwack, wallop, whack; bash, batter, belt, bludgeon, buffet, bung, drub, hammer, lace, lambaste (*or* lambast), lick, mangle, maul, pelt, pound, pummel, rough, thump
**2** to defeat by a large margin ⟨we *whipped* them 13-0 in the last game⟩
*syn* clobber, drub, rout, skunk, snow under, thrash, trim, trounce, wallop
*rel* beat, best, conquer, hurdle, lick, master, overbear, overcome, overmatch, prevail (over), subdue, surmount, throw, triumph (over), win (against), worst; crush, overpower, overthrow, subjugate, vanquish; exceed, outdo, surpass
**3** to achieve a victory over — see BEAT 2
**4** to change the course or direction of (something) — see TURN 2
**5** to move or cause to move with a striking motion — see FLAP
**6** to strike repeatedly — see BEAT 1

**whip (up)** *vb* to cause or encourage the development of — see INCITE 1

**whipper** *n* one that defeats an enemy or opponent — see VICTOR 1

**whippersnapper** *n* a person of no importance or influence — see NOBODY

**whipping** *n* failure to win a contest — see DEFEAT 1

**whipping boy** *n* a person or thing taking the blame for others — see SCAPEGOAT

**whir** *also* **whirr** *vb* to fly, turn, or move rapidly with a fluttering or vibratory sound ⟨the hummingbird *whirred* as it hovered over a flower⟩ ⟨our tires *whirred* as we traveled over the rough road⟩
*syn* buzz, drone, hum, whish, whiz (*or* whizz), zip, zoom
*rel* thrum; hiss, murmur, purr, rustle, sigh, whisper

**whir** *n* a monotonous sound like that of an insect in motion — see HUM

**whirl** *n* **1** a rapid turning about on an axis or central point — see SPIN 1
**2** a state of mental uncertainty — see CONFUSION 1
**3** a state of noisy, confused activity — see COMMOTION

**whirl** *vb* **1** to cause (as a liquid) to move about in a circle especially repeatedly — see STIR 1
**2** to move (something) in a curved or circular path on or as if on an axis — see TURN 1
**3** to move in circles around an axis or center — see SPIN 1
**4** to proceed or move quickly — see HURRY 2
**5** to be in a confused state as if from being twirled around — see SPIN 2

**whirling** *adj* having a feeling of being whirled about and in danger of falling down — see DIZZY 1

**whirlpool** *n* water moving rapidly in a circle with a hollow in the center ⟨in *The Odyssey*, Ulysses is trapped between the

six-headed monster Scylla and Charybdis, a deadly *whirlpool* that threatens to suck his ship down〉
***syn*** maelstrom, vortex
***rel*** eddy, swirl, whirl

**whirlwind** *adj* moving, proceeding, or acting with great speed — see FAST 1

**whish** *n* a sound similar to the speech sound \s\ stretched out — see HISS 1

**whish** *vb* **1** to fly, turn, or move rapidly with a fluttering or vibratory sound — see WHIRR
**2** to make a sound like that of stretching out the speech sound \s\ — see HISS

**whisk** *vb* **1** to cause to move or proceed fast or faster — see HURRY 1
**2** to move or proceed smoothly and readily — see FLOW 2
**3** to proceed or move quickly — see HURRY 2

**whisper** *n* a rumor or report of a personal or sensational nature — see TALE 1

**whisper** *vb* to make (as a piece of information) the subject of common talk without any authority or confirmation of accuracy — see RUMOR

**whistling** *adj* having a high musical pitch or range — see SHRILL

**whit** *n* the smallest amount or part imaginable — see JOT

**white** *adj* **1** lacking an addition of color — see COLORLESS
**2** not causing injury or hurt — see HARMLESS

**whiten** *vb* to make white or whiter by removing color 〈years of sunlight had almost completely *whitened* the flag〉
***syn*** blanch, bleach, blench, decolorize, dull, fade, pale, wash out
***rel*** brighten, lighten; dim, matte (*also* mat *or* matt); whitewash; frost, silver
***near ant*** blacken; blotch, discolor, mottle, shade, splotch, spot, tarnish; color, dye, paint, stain, tinge, tint; burnish, polish, shine
***ant*** darken, deepen

**whitewash** *vb* to make (something) seem less bad by offering excuses — see PALLIATE 1

**whither** *adv* at, in, or to what place — see WHERE

[1]**whiz** *or* **whizz** *n* **1** a sound similar to the speech sound \s\ stretched out — see HISS 1
**2** a monotonous sound like that of an insect in motion — see HUM

[2]**whiz** *n* **1** a person with a high level of knowledge or skill in a field — see EXPERT
**2** a very smart person — see GENIUS 1

**whiz** *or* **whizz** *vb* **1** to make a sound like that of stretching out the speech sound \s\ — see HISS
**2** to fly, turn, or move rapidly with a fluttering or vibratory sound — see WHIRR

**whole** *adj* **1** not divided or scattered among several areas of interest or concern 〈you'll need to put your *whole* effort into this project〉
***syn*** all, concentrated, entire, exclusive, focused (*also* focussed), undivided
***rel*** absolute, complete, full, thorough, total; comprehensive, intact, integral, perfect
***near ant*** deficient, fragmental, fragmentary, incomplete, partial
***ant*** diffuse, divided, scattered
**2** enjoying health and vigor — see HEALTHY 1
**3** not lacking any part or member that properly belongs to it — see COMPLETE 1

**whole** *n* a complete amount of something 〈the landlord eventually refunded the *whole* of our deposit〉
***syn*** aggregate, full, sum, summation, total, totality
***rel*** gross; completeness, comprehensiveness, entirety; bulk, lion's share, mass
***phrases*** the whole kit and kaboodle, the whole shebang
***near ant*** net

**wholehearted** *adj* characterized by unqualified enthusiasm — see HEARTY 1

**wholeness** *n* the condition of being sound in body — see HEALTH

**whole number** *n* a character used to represent a mathematical value — see NUMBER

**wholesome** *adj* **1** enjoying health and vigor — see HEALTHY 1
**2** good for the health — see HEALTHFUL

**wholesomeness** *n* the condition of being sound in body — see HEALTH

**wholly** *adv* to a full extent or degree — see FULLY 1

**whoop** *n* a loud vocal expression of strong emotion — see SHOUT

**whopper** *n* **1** a statement known by its maker to be untrue and made in order to deceive — see LIE
**2** something that is unusually large and powerful — see GIANT

**whopping** *adj* unusually large — see HUGE

**whore** *n* a woman who engages in sexual activities for money — see PROSTITUTE

**why** *interj* how surprising, doubtful, or unbelievable — see NO

**why** *n* something (as a belief) that serves as the basis for another thing — see REASON 2

**wicked** *adj* **1** not conforming to a high moral standard; morally unacceptable — see BAD 2
**2** tending to or exhibiting reckless playfulness — see MISCHIEVOUS 1

**wickedly** *adv* in a mean or spiteful manner — see NASTILY

**wickedness** *n* **1** playful, reckless behavior that is not intended to cause serious harm — see MISCHIEF 1
**2** the state or quality of being utterly evil — see ENORMITY 1

**wide** *adj* **1** having a greater than usual measure across 〈the river was so *wide* that it was impossible to cross it in less than a day〉

*syn* broad, fat, thick
*rel* expansive, extensive; commodious, roomy, spacious
*near ant* fine, hairlike; elongated; needlelike; close, compressed, condensed, constricted, contracted, squeezed, tight, tightened
*ant* narrow, skinny, slender, slim, thin
2 having considerable extent — see EXTENSIVE

**wide–awake** *adj* 1 not sleeping or able to sleep — see WAKEFUL
2 paying close attention usually for the purpose of anticipating approaching danger or opportunity — see ALERT 1

**wide–eyed** *adj* lacking in worldly wisdom or informed judgment — see NAIVE 1

**widespread** *adj* having considerable extent — see EXTENSIVE

**width** *n* an area over which activity, capacity, or influence extends — see RANGE 2

**wield** *vb* to bring to bear especially forcefully or effectively — see EXERT

**wife** *n* the female partner in a marriage ⟨a husband and *wife* who treat each other as equals in their marriage⟩
*syn* helpmate, helpmeet, lady
*rel* bride; consort, mate, partner, spouse; dowager, matron; homemaker, housewife

**wiggle** *vb* to make jerky or restless movements — see FIDGET

**wight** *n* a member of the human race — see HUMAN

**wild** *adj* 1 living outdoors without taming or domestication by humans ⟨*wild* animals can be shy or aggressive when confronted by humans⟩
*syn* feral, savage, unbroken, undomesticated, untamed
*rel* uncontrolled, unsubdued; bestial, brutal, brute; barbarous, uncivilized
*near ant* controlled, subdued; housebroken, trained; civilized, socialized
*ant* broken, busted, domestic, domesticated, tame, tamed
2 existing without human habitation or cultivation ⟨that land has been completely *wild* since the owners abandoned it⟩
*syn* natural, uncultivated, untamed
*rel* native; uninhabited; overgrown, untended; waste; undeveloped
*near ant* inhabited; developed
*ant* cultivated, tamed
3 marked by turmoil or disturbance especially of natural elements ⟨a *wild* night, full of wind and rain⟩
*syn* stormy, tempestuous, tumultuous, turbulent
*rel* blustery, rough, violent; brutal, harsh, severe; unsettled
*near ant* calm, halcyon, peaceful, placid, quiet, serene, tranquil
4 conceived or made without regard for reason or reality — see FANTASTIC 1
5 different from the ordinary in a way that causes curiosity or suspicion — see ODD 2
6 marked by great and often stressful excitement or activity — see FURIOUS 1
7 not civilized — see SAVAGE 1

**wild** *adv* in a confused and reckless manner — see HELTER-SKELTER 1

**wild** *n* that part of the physical world that is removed from human habitation — see NATURE 2

**wilderness** *n* that part of the physical world that is removed from human habitation — see NATURE 2

**wildly** *adv* in a confused and reckless manner — see HELTER-SKELTER 1

**wile** *n* 1 a clever often underhanded means to achieve an end — see TRICK 1
2 the use of clever underhanded actions to achieve an end — see TRICKERY

**wile** *vb* to attract or delight as if by magic — see CHARM 1

**wiliness** *n* 1 skill in achieving one's ends through indirect, subtle, or underhanded means — see CUNNING 1
2 the inclination or practice of misleading others through lies or trickery — see DECEIT

**will** *n* 1 the power to control one's actions, impulses, or emotions ⟨she kept her face still by sheer force of *will*⟩
*syn* restraint, self-containment, self-control, self-discipline, self-government, self-possession, self-restraint, willpower
*rel* self-denial; moderation, temperance; determination, nerve; command, control, discipline, mastery; aplomb, assurance, composure, confidence, coolness, equanimity, poise, self-confidence; discretion
*near ant* gratification, indulgence, self-indulgence; immoderacy, intemperance, overindulgence; demerit, failing, fault, feebleness, foible, frailty, shortcoming, vice, weakness
2 the act or power of making one's own choices or decisions — see FREE WILL

**will** *vb* 1 to give by means of a will — see LEAVE 2
2 to see fit — see CHOOSE 2

**willful** *or* **wilful** *adj* 1 given to resisting authority or another's control — see DISOBEDIENT
2 given to resisting control or discipline by others — see UNCONTROLLABLE
3 having or showing a tendency to force one's will on others without any regard to fairness or necessity — see ARBITRARY 1
4 made, given, or done with full awareness of what one is doing — see INTENTIONAL
5 sticking to an opinion, purpose, or course of action in spite of reason, arguments, or persuasion — see OBSTINATE

**willfully** *adv* with full awareness of what one is doing — see INTENTIONALLY

**willfulness** *n* 1 a steadfast adherence to an opinion, purpose, or course of action — see OBSTINACY
2 refusal to obey — see DISOBEDIENCE

**willies** *n pl* a sense of panic or extreme nervousness — see JITTERS

**willing** *adj* 1 having a desire or inclination (as for a specified course of action) ⟨I'm a little confused, but perfectly *willing* to do as you ask⟩

*syn* amenable, disposed, game, glad, inclined, ready
*rel* predisposed; agreeable, compliant, obedient, submissive; favorable, receptive; prepared, prompt, quick, responsive, swift
*near ant* averse, loath, reluctant
*ant* disinclined, unwilling
**2** having or showing the ability to respond without delay or hesitation — see QUICK 1
**3** done, made, or given with one's own free will — see VOLUNTARY 1

**willingly** *adv* **1** by choice or preference — see RATHER 1
**2** of one's own free will — see VOLUNTARILY

**willingness** *n* cheerful readiness to do something — see ALACRITY

**williwaw** *n* a sudden brief rush of wind — see GUST 1

**willowy** *adj* able to bend easily without breaking ⟨the rattan's stems are split into *willowy* staves that are woven together to produce exquisite baskets⟩
*syn* flexible, limber, lissome (*also* lissom), lithe, pliable, pliant, supple
*rel* adaptable, ductile, elastic, fluid, malleable, modifiable, plastic, variable, yielding; flaccid, floppy
*near ant* inelastic, nonmalleable, unyielding; breakable, brittle, fragile
*ant* inflexible, rigid, stiff

**willpower** *n* the power to control one's actions, impulses, or emotions — see WILL 1

**wilt** *vb* **1** to be limp from lack of water or vigor — see DROOP 1
**2** to lose bodily strength or vigor — see WEAKEN 2
**3** to lose liveliness, force, or freshness — see WITHER

**wily** *adj* clever at attaining one's ends by indirect and often deceptive means — see ARTFUL 1

**wimp** *n* **1** a person lacking in physical strength — see WEAKLING 1
**2** a person without strength of character — see WEAKLING 2

**wimpy** *adj* **1** lacking bodily strength — see WEAK 1
**2** lacking strength of will or character — see WEAK 2

**win** *n* an instance of defeating an enemy or opponent — see VICTORY

**win** *vb* **1** to achieve victory (as in a contest) ⟨the kind of person who always has to *win* —even if the game is just for fun⟩
*syn* conquer, prevail, triumph
*rel* overcome, sweep; squeak, squeeze; contend, vie; succeed
*phrases* carry the day
*near ant* collapse, fail, flop, fold, wash out; flounder, struggle; decline, slip, slump, wane
*ant* lose
**2** to receive as return for effort — see EARN 1
**3** to obtain (as a goal) through effort — see ACHIEVE 1

**win** (against) *vb* to achieve a victory over — see BEAT 2

**win** (over) *vb* to cause (someone) to agree with a belief or course of action by using arguments or earnest requests — see PERSUADE

**wince** *vb* to draw back in fear, pain, or disgust — see FLINCH

[1]**wind** *n* **1** noticeable movement of air in a particular direction ⟨there's a *wind* coming from underneath the front door⟩
*syn* current, draft
*rel* blast, blow, flurry, gale, gust, head wind, squall, tail wind, tempest, tornado, windstorm; breath, breeze, puff, waft, zephyr
**2** a prevailing or general movement or inclination — see TREND 1
**3** language that is impressive-sounding but not meaningful or sincere — see RHETORIC 1

[2]**wind** *n* something that curves or is curved — see BEND 1

**wind** *vb* to follow a circular or spiral course ⟨flowering vines *wind* around the porch's graceful columns⟩
*syn* coil, curl, entwine, spiral, twine, twist
*rel* arc, arch, bend, crook, curve, hook, sweep, swerve, turn, veer, wheel; swirl, whirl; circle, encircle, loop, interlace, intertwine, lace; bow, bulge; meander, weave, zigzag
*near ant* straighten

**windfall** *n* something that provides happiness or does good for a person or thing — see BLESSING 2

**windiness** *n* the use of too many words to express an idea — see VERBIAGE

**winding** *adj* **1** marked by a long series of irregular curves — see CROOKED 1
**2** turning around an axis like the thread of a screw — see SPIRAL

**windjammer** *n* a boat equipped with one or more sails — see SAILBOAT

**windup** *n* the last part of a process or action — see FINALE

**wind up** *vb* **1** to bring (an event) to a natural or appropriate stopping point — see CLOSE 3
**2** to come to an end — see CEASE 1

**windy** *adj* **1** marked by strong wind or more wind than usual ⟨one particularly *windy* day should shake the last of the autumn leaves from the trees⟩
*syn* blowy, blustery, breezy, gusty
*rel* drafty; stormy, tempestuous
*near ant* breathless, calm, motionless, still
**2** marked by the use of impressive-sounding but mostly meaningless words and phrases — see RHETORICAL
**3** using or containing more words than necessary to express an idea — see WORDY

**wing** *n* a group of people acting together within a larger group — see FACTION

---

*syn* synonym(s) *rel* related words
*ant* antonym(s) *near ant* near antonym(s)

**wing** *vb* to move through the air with or as if with outstretched wings — see FLY 1

**wink** *n* 1 a short sleep — see [1]NAP
2 a very small space of time — see INSTANT

**wink** *vb* 1 to rapidly open and close one's eyes ⟨she *winked* several times to get the dust and grit out of her eyes⟩
***syn*** blink
***rel*** bat, flutter; squint
2 to shine with light at regular intervals — see BLINK 1
3 to shoot forth bursts of light — see FLASH 1
4 to secretly sympathize with or pretend ignorance of something improper or unlawful — see CONNIVE

**wink** (at) *vb* to overlook or dismiss as of little importance — see EXCUSE 1

**winner** *n* 1 a person or thing that is successful — see HIT 1
2 one that defeats an enemy or opponent — see VICTOR 1
3 the person who comes in first in a competition — see CHAMPION 1

**winning** *adj* 1 having qualities that tend to make one loved — see LOVABLE
2 likely to win one's affection — see INGRATIATING

**winsome** *adj* likely to win one's affection — see INGRATIATING

**wintry** *adj* 1 having a low or subnormal temperature — see COLD 1
2 lacking in friendliness or warmth of feeling — see COLD 2

**wipe out** *vb* to destroy all traces of — see ANNIHILATE 1

**wire** *n* a length of braided, flexible material that is used for tying or connecting things — see CORD

**wisdom** *n* 1 the ability to understand inner qualities or relationships ⟨with age and experience comes *wisdom* —hopefully⟩ ⟨neither book learning nor simple intelligence should be confused with *wisdom*⟩
***syn*** discernment, insight, perception, perceptiveness, sagaciousness, sagacity, sageness, sapience
***rel*** acuity, acumen, astuteness, penetration, perspicacity, sensitivity, understanding; appreciation, apprehension, comprehension, grasp; braininess, brain(s), brightness, brilliance, canniness, cleverness, gray matter, intellect, intelligence, judgment (*or* judgement), mentality, power, reason, sense, smartness, wit; discrimination, judiciousness, prudence, sanity; logic, rationality
***near ant*** density dullness (*or* dulness), obtuseness; brainlessness, folly, foolishness, idiocy, imbecility, mindlessness, silliness, simpleness, stupidity, witlessness; illogic, irrationality, unreasonableness, unsoundness; craziness, insanity, lunacy, madness; preposterousness, senselessness, silliness, zaniness
2 a body of facts learned by study or experience — see KNOWLEDGE 1
3 the ability to make intelligent decisions especially in everyday matters — see COMMON SENSE

**wise** *adj* 1 having or showing deep understanding and intelligent application of knowledge ⟨a respected and *wise* old judge famous for her sensible rulings⟩
***syn*** discerning, insightful, perceptive, sagacious, sage, sapient
***rel*** acute, perspicacious; experienced; discriminating, discriminative; brainy, brilliant, bright, clever, intelligent, keen, nimble, quick, quick-witted, smart; cerebral, erudite, knowledgeable, learned, literate, scholarly; astute, sharp, shrewd; contemplative, reflective, thoughtful
***near ant*** dense, dull, obtuse; brainless, dumb, feebleminded, foolish, idiotic, imbecilic, moronic, silly, simple, slow, stupid, thoughtless, unintelligent, witless; undiscriminating
***ant*** undiscerning, unperceptive, unwise
2 having inside information ⟨they fooled everyone else, but I'd heard them talking and was *wise* to their true intentions⟩
***syn*** hip, knowing
***rel*** alerted, aware, clued, forewarned, informed, prepared, ready, warned; observant, observing, sharp, sharp-eyed; alert, attentive, open-eyed, vigilant, watchful
***phrases*** in the know
***near ant*** oblivious, unaware, unconscious, uninformed, unperceiving, unseeing, unwitting; heedless, unmindful, unobservant, unobserving; unprepared, unready, unwary
***ant*** unknowing
3 suitable for bringing about a desired result under the circumstances — see EXPEDIENT

**wise** (up) *vb* to give information to — see ENLIGHTEN 1

**wiseacre** *n* a person who likes to show off in a clever but annoying way — see SMART ALECK

**wisecrack** *n* something said or done to cause laughter — see JOKE 1

**wisecrack** *vb* to make jokes — see JOKE

**wise guy** *n* a person who likes to show off in a clever but annoying way — see SMART ALECK

**wish** *vb* to see fit — see CHOOSE 2

**wish** (for) *vb* to have an earnest wish to own or enjoy — see DESIRE

**wishy–washy** *adj* 1 lacking in qualities that make for spirit and character ⟨this story is too *wishy-washy*; you need to add some verve to it⟩
***syn*** banal, flat, insipid
***rel*** unentertaining, unexciting, uninspiring, unrewarding, unsatisfying; bland, boring, drab, dreary, dry, dull, heavy, humdrum, jading, leaden, monotonous, pedestrian, ponderous, tedious, tiresome, tiring, uninteresting, wearisome, weary, wearying; inane; innocuous, inoffensive; mild, soft, subdued, tame, weak; common, commonplace, ordinary, stale, unexceptional

***near ant*** piquant, poignant, pungent, racy, spicy; meaty, substantial; entertaining, exciting, galvanizing, inspiring, invigorating, thrilling
**2** lacking strength of will or character — see WEAK 2

**wit** *n* **1** a person (as a writer) noted for or specializing in humor — see HUMORIST
**2** the ability to make intelligent decisions especially in everyday matters — see COMMON SENSE
**3** the normal or healthy condition of the mental abilities — see MIND 2

**witch** *n* **1** a woman believed to have often harmful supernatural powers ⟨in the old days women were sometimes accused of being *witches* and using evil magic to make the crops fail or an animal die suddenly⟩
***syn*** enchantress, hag, hex, sorceress
***rel*** charmer, conjuror (*or* conjurer), enchanter, necromancer, voodoo; magician, sorcerer, warlock, wizard
**2** a mean or ugly old woman — see CRONE
**3** a person skilled in using supernatural forces — see MAGICIAN 1

**witchcraft** *n* the power to control natural forces through supernatural means — see MAGIC 1

**witchery** *n* **1** the power of irresistible attraction — see CHARM 2
**2** the power to control natural forces through supernatural means — see MAGIC 1

**with** *prep* **1** as the result of — see BECAUSE OF
**2** using the means or agency of — see BY 2
**3** without being prevented by — see DESPITE

**withal** *adv* **1** in addition to what has been said — see MORE 1
**2** in spite of that — see HOWEVER

**withdraw** *vb* **1** to move back or away (as from something difficult, dangerous, or disagreeable) — see RETREAT 1
**2** to solemnly or formally reject or go back on (as something formerly adhered to) — see ABJURE
**3** to take away from a place or position — see REMOVE 2

**withdrawal** *n* an act of moving away especially from something difficult, dangerous, or disagreeable — see RETREAT 1

**wither** *vb* to lose liveliness, force, or freshness ⟨shortly after the moon landing, interest in the space program *withered*⟩ ⟨the old man seemed to *wither* suddenly when he turned eighty⟩
***syn*** dry, wilt
***rel*** mummify, shrivel, wizen; decline, fade, wane; decrease, diminish, lessen
***near ant*** freshen, revive; flourish, prosper, thrive; develop, grow, increase, wax; crest, peak, surge

**withhold** *vb* **1** to be unwilling to grant — see DENY 2
**2** to continue to have in one's possession or power — see KEEP 2

**within** *n* an interior or internal part — see INSIDE 1

**without** *prep* **1** not having ⟨spent two days *without* food⟩
***syn*** minus, sans, wanting
**2** out of the reach or sphere of — see BEYOND 2

**withstand** *vb* to refuse to give in to — see RESIST

**witless** *adj* **1** not having or showing an ability to absorb ideas readily — see STUPID 1
**2** showing or marked by a lack of good sense or judgment — see FOOLISH 1

**witlessness** *n* **1** lack of good sense or judgment — see FOOLISHNESS 1
**2** the quality or state of lacking intelligence or quickness of mind — see STUPIDITY 1

**witness** *n* something presented in support of the truth or accuracy of a claim — see PROOF

**witness** *vb* **1** to declare (something) to be true or genuine — see CERTIFY 1
**2** to make note of (something) through the use of one's eyes — see SEE 1
**3** to make a solemn declaration under oath for the purpose of establishing a fact — see TESTIFY

**witticism** *n* something said or done to cause laughter — see JOKE 1

**wittingly** *adv* with full awareness of what one is doing — see INTENTIONALLY

**witty** *adj* given to or marked by mature intelligent humor ⟨Susan is popular because she is so *witty* and fun-loving⟩ ⟨he's well-known for his *witty* retorts⟩
***syn*** clever, facetious, humorous, jocular, smart
***rel*** cerebral, highbrow, intellectual; bantering, frivolous, jesting, joking, joshing, teasing; antic, comic, comical, droll, farcical, funny, hysterical, laughable, ludicrous, ridiculous, riotous, risible, rollicking, screaming, side-splitting, uproarious; amusing, diverting, entertaining; mischievous, playful, prankish; jocose, jocund, jolly, jovial, laughing, merry, mirthful, sunny; scintillating, sparkling; flip, flippant, pert, smart-alecky (*or* smart-aleck); whimsical
***near ant*** brainless, lowbrow, stupid, witless; corny, hackneyed, lame; humorless, uncomic, unfunny; earnest, grave, serious, sober, solemn, somber (*or* sombre); doleful, dolorous, lachrymose, plaintive, sorry, tearful, woeful

**wizard** *n* **1** a person skilled in using supernatural forces — see MAGICIAN 1
**2** a person with a high level of knowledge or skill in a field — see EXPERT
**3** a very smart person — see GENIUS 1

**wizardry** *n* the power to control natural forces through supernatural means — see MAGIC 1

---

***syn*** synonym(s) ***rel*** related words
***ant*** antonym(s) ***near ant*** near antonym(s)

**wobble** *vb* **1** to make a series of small irregular or violent movements — see SHAKE 1
**2** to make a series of unsteady side-to-side motions — see ROCK 1
**3** to show uncertainty about the right course of action — see HESITATE
**4** to swing unsteadily back and forth or from side to side — see TEETER 1

**wobbling** *adj* marked by or given to small uncontrollable bodily movements — see SHAKY 1

**wobbling** *n* the act or an instance of pausing because of uncertainty about the right course of action — see HESITATION

**wobbly** *adj* marked by or given to small uncontrollable bodily movements — see SHAKY 1

**woe** *n* **1** a state of great suffering of body or mind — see DISTRESS 1
**2** deep sadness especially for the loss of someone or something loved — see SORROW

**woebegone** *adj* feeling unhappiness — see SAD 1

**woeful** *adj* **1** expressing or suggesting mourning — see MOURNFUL 1
**2** feeling unhappiness — see SAD 1
**3** of a kind to cause great distress — see REGRETTABLE

**woefully** *adv* with feelings of bitterness or grief — see HARD 2

**woman** *n* an adult female human being ⟨for a while, the toddler called every *woman* "mama"⟩
***syn*** female, lady
***rel*** dame, gentlewoman; madam, madame, senora (*or* señora); beauty, belle, chick [*slang*], damsel, doll, gal, girl, ingenue (*or* ingénue), lass, lassie, mademoiselle, maid, maiden, miss, senorita (*or* señorita)

**womanish** *adj* **1** having or displaying qualities more suitable for women than for men — see EFFEMINATE
**2** of, relating to, or marked by qualities traditionally associated with women — see FEMININE 1

**womanlike** *adj* **1** having or displaying qualities more suitable for women than for men — see EFFEMINATE
**2** of, relating to, or marked by qualities traditionally associated with women — see FEMININE 1

**womanly** *adj* **1** having or displaying qualities more suitable for women than for men — see EFFEMINATE
**2** of, relating to, or marked by qualities traditionally associated with women — see FEMININE 1

**wonder** *n* **1** something extraordinary or surprising ⟨the cunningly crafted miniature of our house is a *wonder*, perfect in every detail⟩
***syn*** caution, flash, marvel, miracle, phenomenon, portent, prodigy, sensation
***rel*** curiosity, sight, spectacle; apparition, appearance
**2** the rapt attention and deep emotion caused by the sight of something extraordinary ⟨when we first saw the pyramids of Egypt, we gazed with openmouthed *wonder*⟩
***syn*** admiration, amazement, astonishment, awe, wonderment
***rel*** dread; fear; respect, reverence, veneration; curiosity, interest; shock, surprise; disbelief, incomprehension, incredulity; beguilement, bewitchment, captivation, enchantment, fascination; animation, enlightenment, enlivenment, excitement, invigoration, stimulation; absorption, engagement, engrossment, enthrallment, immersion, involvement
***near ant*** apathy, disinterest, incuriosity, indifference, unconcern; boredom, doldrums, ennui, listlessness, restlessness, tedium, tiredness, weariness; cheerlessness, dispiritedness, joylessness, melancholy

**wonderful** *adj* **1** causing wonder or astonishment — see MARVELOUS 1
**2** of the very best kind — see EXCELLENT

**wondering** *adj* filled with amazement or wonder — see OPENMOUTHED

**wonderment** *n* the rapt attention and deep emotion caused by the sight of something extraordinary — see WONDER 2

**wondrous** *adj* causing wonder or astonishment — see MARVELOUS 1

**wont** *adj* being in the habit or custom — see ACCUSTOMED

**wont** *n* a usual manner of behaving or doing — see HABIT

**woo** *vb* to act so as to make (something) more likely — see COURT 1

**wood** *n* tree logs as prepared for human use ⟨a huge load of *wood* outside the furniture maker's factory⟩
***syn*** lumber, timber
***rel*** beam, brace, pile, post, ridgepole, sill, splint, stake, stave, stick; bar, billet, block; cordwood, firewood

**wood** *n, often* **woods** *pl* a dense growth of trees and shrubs covering a large area — see FOREST

**wooden** *adj* lacking social grace and assurance — see AWKWARD 1

**woodland** *n* a dense growth of trees and shrubs covering a large area — see FOREST

**wooer** *n* a man who courts a woman usually with the goal of marrying her — see SUITOR 1

**wool** *n* the hairy covering of a mammal especially when fine, soft, and thick — see FUR 1

**woolgathering** *n* the state of being lost in thought — see REVERIE

**woolly** *also* **wooly** *adj* **1** made of or resembling hair — see HAIRY 2
**2** covered with or as if with hair — see HAIRY 1

**word** *n* **1** a pronounceable series of letters having a distinct meaning especially in a particular field ⟨my doctor used all of these medical *words* that I didn't understand⟩
***syn*** expression, term
***rel*** linguistic form, monosyllable, morpheme; collocation, idiom, locution,

phrase; archaism, coinage, colloquialism, euphemism, loan word, modernism, neologism
**2** something that is said ⟨people who believe that the Bible is the literal *word* of God⟩
***syn*** statement, utterance
***rel*** communication, message; announcement, declamation, declaration, manifesto, proclamation, pronouncement
**3** a report of recent events or facts not previously known — see NEWS
**4** a person's solemn declaration that he or she will do or not do something — see PROMISE
**5** a statement of what to do that must be obeyed by those concerned — see COMMAND 1

**word** *vb* to convey in appropriate or telling terms — see PHRASE

**wordbook** *n* a reference book giving information about the meanings, pronunciations, uses, and origins of words listed in alphabetical order — see DICTIONARY

**wordiness** *n* the use of too many words to express an idea — see VERBIAGE

**wording** *n* the way in which something is put into words ⟨it's important to get the *wording* of this law precisely correct⟩
***syn*** diction, language, phraseology, phrasing
***rel*** expression, formulation, locution; enunciation, phrase, speech, style, utterance, voice

**wordless** *adj* understood although not put into words — see IMPLICIT

**wordy** *adj* using or containing more words than necessary to express an idea ⟨your paper is two pages too long—it doesn't need to be so *wordy*⟩
***syn*** circuitous, circumlocutory, diffuse, long-winded, prolix, rambling, verbose, windy
***rel*** chatty, communicative, conversational, gabby, garrulous, loquacious, talkative, talky, voluble; redundant, repetitious, tautological; embellished, embroidered, exaggerated; bombastic, grandiloquent, highfalutin
***near ant*** brief, short; aphoristic, epigrammatic, sententious; compendious, summary; abbreviated, abridged, condensed, shortened; abrupt, blunt, brusque, curt, laconic, snippy
***ant*** compact, concise, crisp, pithy, succinct, terse

**work** *n* **1** a literary, musical, or artistic production — see COMPOSITION 1
**2** something produced by physical or intellectual effort — see PRODUCT 1
**3** the action for which a person or thing is specially fitted or used or for which a thing exists — see ROLE
**4** the active use of energy in producing a result — see EFFORT
**5** the activity by which one regularly makes a living — see OCCUPATION
**6 works** *pl* a building or set of buildings for the manufacturing of goods — see FACTORY

**work** *vb* **1** to be the cause of (a situation, action, or state of mind) — see EFFECT
**2** to find an answer for through reasoning — see SOLVE
**3** to have a certain purpose — see FUNCTION
**4** to produce a desired effect — see ACT 2
**5** to set or keep in motion — see MOVE 2
**6** to control the mechanical operation of — see OPERATE 1
**7** to devote serious and sustained effort — see LABOR

**work** (for) *vb* to be a servant for — see SERVE 1

**work** (in) *vb* to introduce in a gradual, secret, or clever way — see INSINUATE

**workable** *adj* **1** capable of being done or carried out — see POSSIBLE 1
**2** capable of being put to use or account — see PRACTICAL 1

**workaday** *adj* **1** being of the type that is encountered in the normal course of events — see ORDINARY 1
**2** having to do with the practical details of regular life — see MUNDANE 1
**3** not designed for special occasions — see CASUAL 1

**worker** *n* **1** a person who does very hard or dull work — see SLAVE 2
**2** one who works for another for wages or a salary — see EMPLOYEE

**working** *adj* **1** being in effective operation — see ACTIVE 1
**2** capable of being put to use or account — see PRACTICAL 1
**3** involved in often constant activity — see BUSY 1

**workmanlike** *adj* accomplished with trained ability — see SKILLFUL 1

**workout** *n* something done over and over in order to develop skill — see EXERCISE 2

**work out** *vb* **1** to find an answer for through reasoning — see SOLVE
**2** to produce or bring about especially by long or repeated effort — see HAMMER (OUT)
**3** to turn out as planned or desired — see SUCCEED 1
**4** to determine (a value) by doing the necessary mathematical operations — see CALCULATE 1

**workshop** *n* a building or set of buildings for the manufacturing of goods — see FACTORY

**world** *n* **1** human beings in general — see PEOPLE 1
**2** the celestial body on which we live — see EARTH 1
**3** the whole body of things observed or assumed — see UNIVERSE

**worldly** *adj* **1** having a wide and refined knowledge of the world especially from personal experience — see WORLDLY-WISE

2 having to do with life on earth especially as opposed to that in heaven — see EARTHLY

**worldly–wise** *adj* having a wide and refined knowledge of the world especially from personal experience ⟨having followed their father on his military assignments all over the world, the Johnson kids have become very *worldly-wise*⟩
*syn* cosmopolitan, smart, sophisticated, worldly
*rel* suave, urbane; civilized, cultivated, cultured, polished, refined; experienced, knowing, practiced, schooled, seasoned; bored, cynical, jaded, skeptical; down-to-earth, pragmatic (*also* pragmatical), realistic, sober
*near ant* callow, green, inexperienced, raw; parochial, provincial, rustic; philistine, uncivilized, uncultured, unrefined; childlike, simple, simpleminded; idealistic, impractical; uncritical, unknowing
*ant* ingenuous, innocent, naive (*or* naïve), unsophisticated, unworldly, wide-eyed

**worm** *vb* 1 to advance gradually beyond the usual or desirable limits — see ENCROACH
2 to introduce in a gradual, secret, or clever way — see INSINUATE
3 to move slowly with the body close to the ground — see CRAWL 1

**worn** *adj* depleted in strength, energy, or freshness — see WEARY 1

**worn–out** *adj* 1 depleted in strength, energy, or freshness — see WEARY 1
2 worn or torn into or as if into rags — see RAGGED 2

**worried** *adj* feeling or showing uncomfortable feelings of uncertainty — see NERVOUS 1

**worrisome** *adj* 1 causing worry or anxiety — see TROUBLESOME
2 marked by or causing agitation or uncomfortable feelings — see NERVOUS 2

**worry** *n* an uneasy state of mind usually over the possibility of an anticipated misfortune or trouble — see ANXIETY 1

**worry** *vb* 1 to experience concern or anxiety ⟨they *worried* for days about the upcoming exam⟩
*syn* bother, fear, fret, stew, sweat, trouble
*rel* agonize; long, pine, yearn; chafe; despair
*phrases* care a hang, give a hang
*near ant* accept; abide, bear, endure, stick out, stomach, sustain, take, tolerate
2 to trouble the mind of; to make uneasy — see DISTURB 1

**worsen** *vb* to become worse or of less value — see DETERIORATE

**worship** *n* excessive admiration of or devotion to a person ⟨his *worship* of his big brother meant that he'd go to any extreme for his idol⟩
*syn* adulation, deification, idolatry, idolization, worshipping (*also* worshiping)
*rel* adoration, deference, glorification, reverence, veneration; idealization, romanticization; affection, fancy, favor, fondness, like, liking, love; appreciation, esteem, regard, respect; approval
*near ant* condemnation, disapproval, disfavor, dislike, dismissal, disregard, hatred, loathing, scorn

**worship** *vb* 1 to offer honor or respect to (someone) as a divine power ⟨the ancient Greeks *worshipped* many different gods⟩
*syn* adore, deify, glorify, revere, reverence, venerate
*rel* admire, honor, love, regard, respect; dignify, exalt, magnify; extol (*also* extoll), laud, praise; delight, gratify, please, satisfy
*near ant* blaspheme, desecrate, profane, violate; affront, dishonor, disrespect, insult, offend, outrage, pique, ridicule, scorn, slight; displease; defame, disparage, libel, malign, slander, slur, smear
2 to feel passion, devotion, or tenderness for — see LOVE 2
3 to love or admire too much — see IDOLIZE

**worshipful** *adj* reflecting great admiration or devotion ⟨a movie fan's *worshipful* stare upon finally meeting her idol⟩ ⟨a teacher surrounded by *worshipful* little children⟩
*syn* adoring, adulatory, deifying, idolizing, worshipping (*also* worshiping)
*rel* glorifying, reverential, venerating; affectionate, fond, loving; appreciative, deferential, respectful; approving
*near ant* condemning, contemptuous, disapproving, hateful, loathing, scornful

**worshipping** *also* **worshiping** *n* excessive admiration of or devotion to a person — see WORSHIP

**worshipping** *also* **worshiping** *adj* reflecting great admiration or devotion — see WORSHIPFUL

**worst** *vb* to achieve a victory over — see BEAT 2

**worth** *n* 1 the relative usefulness or importance of something as judged by specific qualities ⟨money alone cannot determine the true *worth* of some things⟩
*syn* account, merit, valuation, value
*rel* assessment, estimation, evaluation; excellence, greatness, perfection; consequence, importance, significance, weight; desirability
*near ant* emptiness, worthlessness; baseness, cheapness, inferiority, meanness, paltriness, pettiness, poorness; deficiency, inadequacy, insufficiency, unacceptability
2 the amount of money for which something will find a buyer — see VALUE 1

**worthless** *adj* having no usefulness ⟨that expensive toy is *worthless* now that it's broken⟩
*syn* chaffy, empty, no-good, junky, null, valueless
*rel* base, cheap, inferior, lousy, low-grade, second-rate; bad, defective, flawed, imperfect, substandard, unsatisfactory; deficient, inadequate, insufficient, unacceptable
*near ant* invaluable, precious, priceless; cherished, esteemed, prized, treasured;

choice, exceptional, fancy, high-grade, special
***ant*** useful, valuable, worthy

**worthy** *adj* having sufficient worth or merit to receive one's honor, esteem, or reward ⟨made charitable contributions to the American Red Cross and other *worthy* causes⟩ ⟨a *worthy* opponent in a tennis match⟩
***syn*** deserving, good, meritorious
***rel*** admirable, commendable, creditable, laudable, praiseworthy; invaluable, priceless; cherished, prized, treasured; choice, excellent, exceptional, fancy, high-grade, primary, prime, special
***near ant*** base, cheap, inferior, second-rate, substandard; bad, defective, flawed, imperfect; deficient, inadequate, insufficient, unacceptable, unsatisfactory
***ant*** no-good, undeserving, valueless, worthless

**wound** *vb* **1** to cause bodily damage to — see INJURE 1
**2** to cause hurt feelings or deep resentment in — see INSULT

**wraith** *n* the soul of a dead person thought of especially as appearing to living people — see GHOST

**wrangle** *n* an often noisy or angry expression of differing opinions — see ARGUMENT 1

**wrangle** *vb* to express different opinions about something often angrily — see ARGUE 2

**wrangler** *n* a person who takes part in a dispute — see DISPUTANT

**wrap** *vb* **1** to encircle or bind with or as if with a belt — see GIRD 1
**2** to surround or cover closely — see ENFOLD 1

**wrap up** *vb* **1** to bring (an event) to a natural or appropriate stopping point — see CLOSE 3
**2** to make into a short statement of the main points (as of a report) — see SUMMARIZE 1

**wrath** *n* **1** an intense emotional state of displeasure with someone or something — see ANGER
**2** suffering, loss, or hardship imposed in response to a crime or offense — see PUNISHMENT

**wrathful** *adj* feeling or showing anger — see ANGRY

**wrathfulness** *n* an intense emotional state of displeasure with someone or something — see ANGER

**wreathe** *vb* to scatter or set here and there among other things — see THREAD 1

**wreck** *n* **1** the portion or bits of something left over or behind after it has been destroyed — see REMAINS 1
**2** the destruction or loss of a ship — see SHIPWRECK
**3** the violent coming together of two bodies into destructive contact — see CRASH 1

**wreck** *vb* **1** to cause irreparable damage to (a ship) by running aground or sinking — see SHIPWRECK
**2** to bring to a complete end the physical soundness, existence, or usefulness of — see DESTROY 1

**wreckage** *n* **1** the state or fact of being rendered nonexistent, physically unsound, or useless — see DESTRUCTION
**2** the portion or bits of something left over or behind after it has been destroyed — see REMAINS 1
**3** the destruction or loss of a ship — see SHIPWRECK

**wrecking** *n* the destruction or loss of a ship — see SHIPWRECK

**wrench** *n* **1** a forceful rotating or pulling motion for the purpose of dislodging something ⟨a sharp *wrench* only served to lodge the bent nail more securely into the wood⟩
***syn*** twist, twisting, wrenching, wresting, wringing
***rel*** draft, draw, extraction, pull, tug, yank; dislocation, displacement
**2** the act or an instance of applying force on something so that it moves in the direction of the force — see PULL 1

**wrench** *vb* **1** to move by or as if by a forceful rotation ⟨with one last sharp yank, he *wrenched* the cap off the medicine bottle⟩
***syn*** twist, wrest, wring
***rel*** draw, dredge (up), extract, jerk, lug, pluck, pull, tug, tweak, yank; jimmy, lever, pry; budge, dislocate, displace, disturb, remove; shift, transfer, transpose
**2** to injure by overuse, misuse, or pressure — see STRAIN 1
**3** to separate or remove by forceful pulling — see TEAR 2

**wrenching** *n* a forceful rotating or pulling motion for the purpose of dislodging something — see WRENCH 1

**wrest** *vb* **1** to draw out by force or with effort — see EXTRACT 1
**2** to get (as money) by the use of force or threats — see EXTORT
**3** to get with great difficulty — see EKE OUT
**4** to move by or as if by a forceful rotation — see WRENCH 1
**5** to separate or remove by forceful pulling — see TEAR 2

**wresting** *n* a forceful rotating or pulling motion for the purpose of dislodging something — see WRENCH 1

**wrestle** *vb* to seize and attempt to unbalance one another for the purpose of achieving physical mastery ⟨the sisters *wrestled* on the floor over the last cookie⟩
***syn*** grapple, scuffle, tussle
***rel*** battle, clash (with), combat, contend, fight, war (against); duel, bash, batter, beat, buffet, hit, punch, slug, strike; box, spar; brawl, skirmish

**wretch** *n* a mean, evil, or unprincipled person — see VILLAIN

**wretched** *adj* **1** extremely unsatisfactory ⟨this paper is simply *wretched*—you'll have to rewrite it⟩

*syn* atrocious, awful, execrable, lousy, punk, rotten, terrible
*rel* bad, deficient, inferior, off, poor, substandard, unsatisfactory, wanting; contemptible, miserable, shameful; defective, faulty, flawed; low-grade, mediocre, reprehensible, second-rate; bum, useless, valueless, worthless; inadequate, insufficient, lacking; abominable, odious, vile
*near ant* choice, excellent, exceptional, first-class, first-rate, premium, prime, superior; adequate, sufficient; acceptable, satisfactory
*ant* great, marvelous (*or* marvellous), wonderful
**2** arousing or deserving of one's loathing and disgust — see CONTEMPTIBLE 1
**3** causing or marked by an atmosphere lacking in cheer — see GLOOMY 1
**4** falling short of a standard — see BAD 1
**5** feeling unhappiness — see SAD 1
**6** not following or in accordance with standards of honor and decency — see IGNOBLE 2
**7** of low quality — see CHEAP 2
**8** deserving of one's pity — see PATHETIC 1

**wretchedly** *adv* with feelings of bitterness or grief — see HARD 2

**wriggle** *vb* **1** to make jerky or restless movements — see FIDGET
**2** to move slowly with the body close to the ground — see CRAWL 1

**wring** *vb* **1** to get (as money) by the use of force or threats — see EXTORT
**2** to get with great difficulty — see EKE OUT
**3** to move by or as if by a forceful rotation — see WRENCH 1

**wringing** *n* a forceful rotating or pulling motion for the purpose of dislodging something — see WRENCH 1

**wrinkle** *n* **1** a small fold in a soft and otherwise smooth surface ⟨the old woman's face creased into *wrinkles* as she smiled⟩ ⟨the curtains cascaded onto the floor in ripples and *wrinkles*⟩
*syn* crease, crimp, crinkle, furrow
*rel* corrugation, layer, loop, plait, pleat, ply, pucker, seam, tuck; crow's-foot
**2** something (as a device) created for the first time through the use of the imagination — see INVENTION 1

**wrinkle** *vb* **1** to develop creases or folds ⟨if you don't fold clothes promptly after drying, they'll *wrinkle*⟩
*syn* crease, crinkle, furrow, rumple
*rel* collapse, crumple, double, fold
**2** to create (as by crushing) an irregular mass of creases in — see CRUMPLE 1

**write** *vb* **1** to compose and set down on paper the words of ⟨*write* a theme in which you name your choice for the most important person in human history⟩
*syn* author, pen, pencil (in), scratch (out)
*rel* cast, compose, craft, draft, draw (up), formulate, frame, prepare; recast, redraft, revise, rewrite; letter, print, type, typewrite; record, take down, transcribe; autograph, register, sign; couch, express, phrase, put, word
**2** to engage in an exchange of written messages — see CORRESPOND 1

**writer** *n* a person who creates a written work — see AUTHOR 1

**write off** *vb* **1** to express scornfully one's low opinion of — see DECRY 1
**2** to lower the price or value of — see DEPRECIATE 1

**writhe** *vb* to make jerky or restless movements — see FIDGET

**wrong** *adj* **1** falling short of a standard — see BAD 1
**2** having an opinion that does not agree with truth or the facts — see INCORRECT 1
**3** not appropriate for a particular occasion or situation — see INAPPROPRIATE
**4** not being in agreement with what is true — see FALSE 1
**5** not conforming to a high moral standard; morally unacceptable — see BAD 2

**wrong** *adv* off the desired or intended path or course ⟨all of our carefully laid plans went *wrong*⟩
*syn* afield, amiss, astray, awry
*rel* badly; faultily, improperly, inappropriately, incorrectly, mistakenly, wrongly; inadequately, insufficiently
*near ant* perfectly; auspiciously, favorably, promisingly; correctly, properly, rightly; appropriately, fittingly, suitably
*ant* aright, right, well

**wrong** *n* **1** that which is morally unacceptable — see EVIL
**2** unfair or inadequate treatment of someone or something or an instance of this — see DISSERVICE

**wrongdoer** *n* a person who commits moral wrongs — see EVILDOER 1

**wrongdoing** *n* **1** a breaking of a moral or legal code — see OFFENSE 1
**2** improper or illegal behavior — see MISCONDUCT

**wrongful** *adj* contrary to or forbidden by law — see ILLEGAL 1

**wrongly** *adv* in a mistaken or inappropriate way ⟨you have *wrongly* interpreted this passage in the Bible⟩
*syn* amiss, erroneously, faultily, improperly, inaccurately, inappropriately, inaptly, incorrectly, mistakenly, unsuitably
*rel* fallibly, imperfectly; extraneously, irrelevantly, meaninglessly, pointlessly, senselessly; inadequately, insufficiently; undesirably, unsatisfactorily; foolishly, unwisely
*near ant* infallibly, perfectly; meaningfully, pertinently, relevantly, sensibly; acceptably, adequately, satisfactorily, sufficiently; prudently, sagely, wisely
*ant* appropriately, aptly, correctly, fittingly, properly, right, rightly, suitably

**wrongness** *n* the quality or state of being unsuitable or unfitting — see INAPPROPRIATENESS 1

**wroth** *adj* feeling or showing anger — see ANGRY

# X

**X** (out) *vb* to show (something written) to be no longer valid by drawing a cross over or a line through it ⟨*x out* the names of the people who have already left⟩
***syn*** cancel, cross (out), delete, kill, scratch (out), strike (out), stroke (out)
***rel*** blot out, efface, erase, expunge, obliterate, rub out, wipe out; cut, excise, remove

# Y

**yammer** *vb* to express dissatisfaction, pain, or resentment usually tiresomely — see COMPLAIN
**yank** *n* the act or an instance of applying force on something so that it moves in the direction of the force — see PULL 1
**yank** *vb* **1** to move or cause to move with a sharp quick motion — see JERK 1
**2** to draw out by force or with effort — see EXTRACT
**3** to separate or remove by forceful pulling — see TEAR 2
**yard** *n* **1** an open space wholly or partly enclosed (as by buildings or walls) — see COURT 2
**2** the area around and belonging to a building — see GROUND 1
**yardstick** *n* something set up as an example against which others of the same type are compared — see STANDARD 1
**yarn** *n* **1** a brief account of something interesting that happened especially to one personally — see STORY 2
**2** a work with imaginary characters and events that is shorter and usually less complex than a novel — see STORY 1
**yaw** *vb* to depart abruptly from a straight line or course — see SWERVE 1
**yea** *adv* **1** not merely this but also — see EVEN
**2** used to express agreement — see YES
**yeah** *adv* used to express agreement — see YES
**yearn** (for) *vb* to have an earnest wish to own or enjoy — see DESIRE
**yearning** *n* a strong wish for something — see DESIRE
**yeast** *n* something that arouses action or activity — see IMPULSE
**yell** *n* a loud vocal expression of strong emotion — see SHOUT
**yell** *vb* **1** to cry out loudly and emotionally — see SCREAM
**2** to speak so as to be heard at a distance — see CALL 1

***syn*** synonym(s) ***rel*** related words
***ant*** antonym(s) ***near ant*** near antonym(s)

**yellow** *adj* having or showing a shameful lack of courage — see COWARDLY
**yellowness** *n* a shameful lack of courage in the face of danger — see COWARDICE
**yelp** *vb* to cry out loudly and emotionally — see SCREAM
**yen** *n* a strong wish for something — see DESIRE
**yes** *adv* used to express agreement ⟨*yes*, I'll be ready for the test tomorrow⟩
***syn*** all right, alright, aye (*also* ay), OK (*or* okay), yea, yeah
***rel*** certainly, indeed, indisputably, undoubtedly, unquestionably
***ant*** nay, no, no way
**yesterday** *n* the events or experience of former times — see PAST
**yesteryear** *n* the events or experience of former times — see PAST
**yet** *adv* **1** at a later time ⟨we may *yet* figure it out⟩
***syn*** eventually, finally, someday, sometime, ultimately
***phrases*** at last, at length, at long last
***near ant*** ne'er, never, nevermore
**2** in addition to what has been said — see MORE 1
**3** in spite of that — see HOWEVER
**4** up to this or that time — see HITHERTO
**yet** *conj* if it were not for the fact that — see EXCEPT
**yield** *n* **1** an increase usually measured in money that comes from labor, business, or property — see INCOME
**2** something produced by physical or intellectual effort — see PRODUCT 1
**3** the total amount collected or obtained especially at one time — see HAUL 1
**yield** *vb* **1** to give up and cease resistance (as to a liking, temptation, or habit) ⟨I finally *yielded* to temptation and had a bowl of ice cream⟩
***syn*** bow, give in, submit, succumb, surrender
***rel*** gratify, indulge, wallow; acquiesce (to), concede (to)

***near ant*** battle, breast, combat, confront, counter, defy, face, meet, object, oppose, repel; thwart, withstand
***ant*** hold off, resist
**2** to produce as revenue ⟨I expect that stock to *yield* at least 14% profit this year⟩
***syn*** give, pay, return
***rel*** bring in, produce, afford, furnish, provide, supply
**3** to cease resistance (as to another's arguments, demands, or control) ⟨after insisting that her answer was not incorrect, Mary *yielded* when her teacher threatened her with detention⟩
***syn*** bow, budge, capitulate, concede, give in, knuckle under, quit, submit, succumb, surrender
***rel*** acquiesce
***near ant*** contend, fight
***ant*** resist
**4** to be the cause of (a situation, action, or state of mind) — see EFFECT
**5** to fall down or in as a result of physical pressure — see COLLAPSE 1
**6** to give (something) over to the control or possession of another usually under duress — see SURRENDER 1

**yielding** *adj* **1** receiving or enduring without offering resistance — see PASSIVE
**2** not stiff in structure — see LIMP 1

**yoke** *n* the state of being a slave — see SLAVERY 1

**yoke** *vb* to put or bring together so as to form a new and longer whole — see CONNECT 1

**yokel** *n* an awkward or simple person especially from a small town or the country — see HICK

**yon** *adv* at or to a greater distance or more advanced point — see FARTHER

**yonder** *adv* at or to a greater distance or more advanced point — see FARTHER

**yore** *n* the events or experience of former times — see PAST

**young** *adj* being in the early stage of life, growth, or development ⟨a *young* cat requires more food than an older one⟩ ⟨a *young* tree that will eventually reach 50 feet tall⟩
***syn*** adolescent, immature, juvenile, youngish, youthful
***rel*** minor, underage; embryonic; callow, green, inexperienced, puerile, raw; babyish, childish, childlike, infantile; undeveloped, unfinished, unfledged, unformed, unripe, unripened; blooming, blossoming, burgeoning, flourishing, flowering
***near ant*** aged, aging, elderly, old; full-blown, full-fledged; golden, mellow, ripe, ripened
***ant*** adult, full-grown, mature, matured

**youngish** *adj* being in the early stage of life, growth, or development — see YOUNG

**youngster** *n* a young person who is between infancy and adulthood — see CHILD 1

**youth** *n* **1** a male person who has not yet reached adulthood — see BOY
**2** a young person who is between infancy and adulthood — see CHILD 1
**3** the state or time of being a child — see CHILDHOOD

**youthful** *adj* being in the early stage of life, growth, or development — see YOUNG

**yowl** *n* a loud vocal expression of strong emotion — see SHOUT

**yowl** *vb* to make a long loud mournful sound — see HOWL 1

**yo–yo** *n* a person who lacks good sense or judgment — see FOOL 1

**yuletide** *n* the season celebrating Christmas ⟨these days, as far as the stores are concerned, *yuletide* starts in September⟩
***syn*** Christmastime, Noel
***rel*** Advent; Christmas, nativity, Xmas, yule

**yummy** *adj* very pleasing to the sense of taste — see DELICIOUS 1

# Z

**zaniness** *n* lack of good sense or judgment — see FOOLISHNESS 1

**zany** *adj* showing or marked by a lack of good sense or judgment — see FOOLISH 1

**zany** *n* a comically dressed performer (as at a circus) who entertains with playful tricks and ridiculous behavior — see CLOWN 1

**zap** *vb* to deliver a blow to (someone or something) usually in a strong vigorous manner — see HIT 1

**zealot** *n* one who is intensely or excessively devoted to a cause ⟨some people called John a *zealot* because he was always crusading for human rights⟩
***syn*** crusader, fanatic, militant, partisan
***rel*** activist; dreamer, visionary; cultist, disciple, follower, idolizer, votary; addict, aficionado, buff, bug, devotee, enthusiast, fan, fancier, fiend, freak, lover, maniac, nut; backer, patron, promoter, supporter; booster, rooter, well-wisher; faddist
***near ant*** dabbler, dilettante

**zenith** *n* the highest part or point — see HEIGHT 1

**zephyr** *n* a slight or gentle movement of air — see BREEZE 1

**zero** *n* **1** the numerical symbol 0 or the absence of number or quantity represented by it ⟨anything multiplied by *zero* comes out to zero⟩

*syn* aught, cipher, goose egg, naught (*also* nought), nil, nothing, oh, zilch, zip
*rel* blank, void
**2** a person of no importance or influence — see NOBODY

**zero hour** *n* a time or state of affairs requiring prompt or decisive action — see EMERGENCY

**zest** *n* the quality or state of being stimulating to the mind or senses — see PIQUANCY

**zesty** *adj* sharp and pleasantly stimulating to the mind or senses — see PIQUANT

**zigzag** *vb* to move suddenly aside or to and fro — see DODGE 1

**zilch** *n* **1** a person of no importance or influence — see NOBODY
**2** the numerical symbol 0 or the absence of number or quantity represented by it — see ZERO 1

**zing** *n* active strength of body or mind — see VIGOR 1

**zip** *n* **1** active strength of body or mind — see VIGOR 1
**2** the numerical symbol 0 or the absence of number or quantity represented by it — see ZERO 1

**zip** *vb* **1** to fly, turn, or move rapidly with a fluttering or vibratory sound — see WHIRR
**2** to make an irregular series of quick, sudden movements — see FLIT
**3** to proceed or move quickly — see HURRY 2

**zippy** *adj* having much high-spirited energy and movement — see LIVELY 1

**zone** *n* **1** a broad geographical area — see REGION 2
**2** a part or portion having no fixed boundaries — see REGION 1

**zoom** *n* a monotonous sound like that of an insect in motion — see HUM

**zoom** *vb* **1** to fly, turn, or move rapidly with a fluttering or vibratory sound — see WHIRR
**2** to proceed or move quickly — see HURRY 2
**3** to rise abruptly and rapidly — see SKYROCKET